The COMPACT
Bedford
Introduction to
Drama

The COMPACT
Bedford
Introduction to
Drama

SEVENTH EDITION

Lee A. Jacobus
University of Connecticut

BEDFORD / ST. MARTIN'S
Boston ◆ New York

For Bedford/St. Martin's

Senior Developmental Editor: Caroline Thompson
Production Supervisor: Samuel Jones
Senior Marketing Manager: Stacey Propps
Editorial Assistant: Regina Tavani
Project Management: Lifland et al., Bookmakers
Photo Research Manager: Martha Friedman
Permissions Manager: Kalina K. Ingham
Senior Art Director: Anna Palchik
Text Design: Claire Seng-Niemoeller
Cover Design: Donna Lee Dennison
Cover Photo: Dion Johnstone as Caliban in *The Tempest*, Stratford Shakespeare Festival 2010. Courtesy the Stratford Shakespeare Festival Archives. Photography by David Hou.
Composition: S4Carlisle Publishing Services
Printing and Binding: Quad/Graphics

President, Bedford/St. Martin's: Denise B. Wydra
Presidents, Macmillan Higher Education: Joan E. Feinberg and Tom Scotty
Editor in Chief: Karen S. Henry
Director of Marketing: Karen R. Soeltz
Production Director: Susan W. Brown
Associate Production Director: Elise S. Kaiser
Manager, Publishing Services: Andrea Cava

Library of Congress Control Number: 2012942371

Manufactured in the United States of America.

7   6   5   4   3   2
f   e   d   c   b   a

For information, write: Bedford/St. Martin's, 75 Arlington Street, Boston, MA 02116 (617-399-4000)

ISBN 978-1-4576-0633-5

Acknowledgments

Preface for Instructors

The Compact Bedford Introduction to Drama, Seventh Edition, owes its existence to the continual demand for a briefer (and less expensive) collection of plays than the longer edition provides—but with the historical and critical material that is essential for a full understanding of different ages of drama. Instructors in many theater and literature programs convinced us that, although a shorter version of *The Bedford Introduction to Drama* should be concise, it should not ignore the problems of performance, issues concerning drama criticism, and the needs of instructors who want their students to write intelligently about drama.

As a result of this demand, *The Compact Bedford Introduction to Drama* has all the features of the longer edition, but with only twenty-eight plays. Nonetheless, it affords the most comprehensive collection available in a compact drama anthology. The book also offers a full array of background material about the plays and playwrights, encouraging students to think critically about all aspects of a play as a work of literature and performance.

Even when it appears most timeless, all drama, like all literature, is a product not only of language and style but also of its era, including a complex range of political, social, and ethnic influences. *The Compact Bedford Introduction to Drama* offers a succinct but thorough history of Western drama, complemented by coverage of Asian drama. A general introduction gives an overview of the great ages of drama, the major genres and elements, and the cultural value of drama. Throughout the book, introductions to significant periods of drama, the playwrights, and the plays focus on the cultural contexts of the works and on their stage history. The timeline following the introduction to each dramatic period presents important developments in theater history in their appropriate cultural contexts.

Accompanying all the plays are thorough biographical and critical introductions; brief performance histories; commentaries by playwrights, directors, actors, reviewers, and critics; and photographs of landmark productions. These play-specific materials are complemented by two casebooks—one on *The Tempest* and one on *Death of a Salesman*—that present a focused study of important cultural and historical contexts.

A number of features emphasize plays in performance. Richly illustrated sections on staging and theater design in each historical introduction include detailed diagrams of period theaters, along with a discussion of the major technical innovations in staging. An illustrated section on "The Actor" in each historical introduction explores the development of acting styles, methods, and techniques in every major period of drama. A marginal quotation, often an appreciative comment by an actor, director, or other playwright, accompanies each biographical introduction, illuminating a particular playwright or work. More than 130 photographs and stage diagrams throughout the book help students visualize the plays in performance.

The Compact Bedford Introduction to Drama is also a complete resource for the beginning student. In the general introduction, a discussion of the elements of drama defines important terms and concepts and demonstrates these concepts in action, drawing its examples from Lady Isabella Augusta Gregory's one-act play *The Rising of the Moon.*

"Writing about Drama" at the end of the book offers students possible approaches for commenting on dramatic literature and points the way for developing ideas that can result in probing critical essays. From prewriting to outlining and drafting, the process of writing about drama is illustrated by reference to *The Rising of the Moon,* and a sample essay on the play provides one model of drama criticism for students. Especially useful for assignments involving attendance at theater productions, the section "Writing a Review" analyzes professional reviews and offers suggestions for students who are writing reviews.

The "Glossary of Dramatic Terms" clearly and concisely defines concepts and terms. When these terms are first introduced and defined in the text, they appear in boldface.

New to This Edition

New Plays

Ten plays are new to the seventh edition including several exciting twentieth-century and contemporary works. The selection of new contemporary plays is informed by research into the most frequently produced plays of recent seasons, increasing the likelihood that students will have opportunities to see performances of the plays they read. Among the new contemporary works are Caryl Churchill's *Cloud Nine,* Suzan-Lori Parks's *Topdog/Underdog,* Sarah Ruhl's *Eurydice,* John Patrick Shanley's *Doubt,* and Lynn Nottage's *Ruined.* In response to requests from reviewers, the seventh edition brings back some favorites from previous editions, including Susan Glaspell's *Trifles,* Tennessee Williams's *Cat on a Hot Tin Roof,* and Samuel Beckett's *Endgame.*

Expanded Coverage of Shakespeare

The Compact Bedford Introduction to Drama has always included two plays by Shakespeare to offer students a unique opportunity to study and write in depth about a significant figure in the development of drama. The seventh edition now includes *Hamlet* and *The Tempest,* accompanied by a new critical casebook designed to help students understand Shakespeare's cultural influence and develop their own critical approach to *The Tempest.* In the casebook, excerpts from William Strachey's *True Repertory of the Wreck* and Montaigne's *Of the Cannibals* provide context, and writings by Samuel Taylor Coleridge, Robert Browning, E. K. Chambers, Aimé Césaire, Ania Loomba, and Marjorie Garber offer a range of critical approaches and responses to the play.

New Design and Web Site

The seventh edition is designed to be not only visually striking but more readable and teachable than ever. The new design highlights the rich contextual features of the book, including historical introductions, timelines, casebooks, and commentaries, while increasing the readability of the plays. As in previous editions, plenty of space is devoted to performance photographs and illustrations. Photographs are integrated into the texts of the plays in the very scenes that they depict to help students visualize the performance.

New marginal notes throughout the book refer students to free and open resources on the book's fully updated and redesigned companion Web site, **bedfordstmartins.com/jacobus**. The site offers extensive materials to help students succeed in the course, including discussion questions and assignments for every play, links to additional resources on each of the playwrights and casebooks, in-depth drama tutorials, and annotated links to drama organizations, theaters, and other drama resources. A stylistic casebook on American melodrama and the full text of Anna Cora Mowatt's *Fashion* are available for download for the convenience of instructors who wish to cover the topic of melodrama in depth. The full text of Aphra Behn's *The Rover* (from the full anthology) and an additional cultural casebook (from the fourth edition) focusing on the Abbey Theatre and the Irish Literary Renaissance are also available for download.

Instructor Resources and DVD/VHS Library

Resources for instructors include a selected bibliography for each major dramatic period and its playwrights, a list of suggested audiovisual resources, and additional assignment ideas. These resources can be downloaded from **bedfordstmartins.com/jacobus** or **bedfordstmartins.com/jacobus/catalog**.

A selection of DVDs and videotapes of plays included in the book is available for qualified adopters. Contact your Bedford/St. Martin's sales representative for more information.

Full Edition

The Bedford Introduction to Drama, Seventh Edition, contains fifty-four plays, forty commentaries, and four casebooks. For more information and a complete table of contents, visit **bedfordstmartins.com/jacobus/catalog**. To order the full edition, use ISBN 978-1-4576-0632-8.

Acknowledgments

I am grateful to the following reviewers who offered suggestions and advice for the seventh edition: David Adamson, University of North Carolina; Terri Bourus, Indiana University-Purdue University Indianapolis; Marnie Brennan, Harrisburg Area Community College; Eileen Curley, Marist College; Keri De Deo, Sheridan College; Joseph Fahey, Ohio State University; Christine Frezza, Southern Utah University; L. Douglas Grissom, University of Virginia; Adam Heffernan, Baldwin-Wallace College; Lori Horvik, North Dakota State University; Geri Jacobs, Jackson Community College; Melissa J. Jones, Michigan University; Aaron Kitch, Bowdoin College; Scott Richard Klein, Cameron University; Jay Morong, University of North Carolina at Charlotte; Harry B. Parker, Texas Christian University; Stephen Rowe, Queens College of City University of New York; Jonathan Shultz, Austin Community College; David S. Thompson, Agnes Scott College; Michele Turner, Louisiana State University; Cigdem Usekes, Western Connecticut State University; Kathryn H. Williams, University of North Carolina at Chapel Hill; James F. Wilson, LaGuardia

Community College; and Nan Withers-Wilson, Loyola University Chicago. Tammy Veach of Eastern Illinois University assisted in updating and creating new resources for the companion Web site.

I am especially grateful to the people who worked behind the scenes at Bedford/St. Martin's to produce this book. I thank editorial assistant Regina Tavani for coordinating reviews, managing tasks large and small to prepare the manuscript for production, and overseeing the development of content for the Web site. Project manager Sally Lifland managed the production of this complex project with aplomb and kept the book on schedule. Art director Donna Dennison designed the stunning cover.

As always, I owe an immense debt of gratitude to the imaginative and intelligent guidance of Denise Wydra, president of Bedford/St. Martin's; Joan Feinberg, president of Macmillan Higher Education; and their predecessor, Charles Christensen. They have been friends of this book from the beginning and have helped give it special meaning. Karen Henry, my editor and muse for the first three editions of this book, is a passionate fan of theater and the values for which this book stands. Even now she remains close to this project. Mika De Roo, my editor for the fifth edition, was enthusiastic and helpful from the first. Maura Shea, my editor for the fourth edition, and again happily for the sixth edition, sets a standard that few can match. Her taste, judgment, and editorial eye helped make this book what it is. She is my vision of the ideal editor, both talented and skilled, and aiming unerringly to help make this the best book it can be. Carrie Thompson, editor for the current edition, was remarkable in her devotion to this project. She read all the plays we considered and made shrewd and splendid suggestions that I happily followed. Having an editor passionate about drama, as Carrie is, supporting a project as huge and challenging as this is, has made the entire experience a great pleasure. She raised the bar on this edition. Great editors like Carrie are a national treasure.

Lee A. Jacobus
University of Connecticut, Storrs

Contents

Renaissance Drama 146

Late-Seventeenth- and Eighteenth-Century Drama 300

Nineteenth-Century Drama Through the Turn of the Twentieth Century   361

Drama in the Early- and Mid-Twentieth Century   494

Writing about Drama   1073

The COMPACT
Bedford
Introduction to
Drama

Introduction: Thinking about Drama

The word *drama* comes from an early Greek word, *dran*, meaning "to do something." Drama implies doing something of considerable importance. In modern terms, a dramatic action is the plot or storyline of a play. The ingredients of any drama are the plot; the characters, represented on stage by actors; their actions, described by gestures and movement; thought—the ideas in the play—revealed in dialogue and behavior; spectacle, represented by scenery, music, costume, and lighting; and, finally, audiences who respond to the entire mixture.

When we are in the theater, we see the actors, hear the lines, are aware of the setting, and sense the theatrical community of which we are a part. Even when reading a play, we should imagine actors speaking lines and visualize a setting in which those lines are spoken. Drama is an experience in which we participate on many levels simultaneously. On one level, we may believe that what we see is really happening; on another level, we know it is only make-believe. On one level we may be amused, but on another level we realize that serious statements about human nature are being made. Drama both entertains and instructs.

What Is Drama?

When Aristotle wrote about drama in the *Poetics,* a work providing one of the earliest and most influential theories of drama, he began by explaining drama as the imitation of an action (**mimesis**). Those analyzing his work have interpreted this statement in several ways. One interpretation is that drama imitates life. On the surface, this observation may seem simple, even obvious. But on reflection, we begin to find complex significance in his comment. The drama of the Greeks, for example, with its intense mythic structure, its formidable speeches, and its profound actions, often seems larger than life or other than life. Yet we recognize characters saying words that we ourselves are capable of saying, doing things that we ourselves might do. The great Greek tragedies are certainly lifelike and certainly offer literary mirrors in which we can examine human nature. And the same is true of Greek comedies.

The relationship between drama and life has always been subtle and complex. In some plays, such as Luigi Pirandello's *Six Characters in Search of an Author,* it is one of the central issues. We begin our reading or viewing of most

1

plays knowing that the dramatic experience is not absolutely real in the sense that, for example, the actor playing Hamlet does not truly die or truly see a ghost or truly frighten his mother. The play imitates those imagined actions, but when done properly it is realistic enough to make us fear, if only for a moment, that they could be real.

We see significance in the actions Hamlet imitates; his actions help us live our own lives more deeply, more intensely, because they give us insight into the possibilities of life. In an important sense, we share the experience of a character such as Hamlet when, for example, he soliloquizes over the question of whether it is better to die than to live in a world filled with sin and crime. We are all restricted to living this life as ourselves; drama is one art form that helps us realize the potential of life, for both the good and the bad.

Drama and Ritual

Such imaginative participation is only a part of what we derive from drama. In its origins, drama seems to have evolved from ancient Egyptian and Greek rituals, ceremonies that were performed the same way again and again and were thought to have a propitious effect on the relationship between the people and their gods.

In ancient Egypt, some religious rituals evolved into repeated passion plays, such as those celebrating Isis and Osiris at the festivals of Heb-Seb at Sakkara some three thousand years ago. Greek drama was first performed during yearly religious celebrations dedicated to the god Dionysus. The early Greek playwrights, such as Sophocles in *Oedipus Rex* and *Antigone,* emphasized the interaction between the will of the gods and the will of human beings, often pitting the truths of men and women against the truths of the gods. The interpretation of the myths by the Greek playwrights over a two-hundred-year period helped the Greek people participate in the myths, understand them, and relate them to their daily lives.

In the thirteenth and fourteenth centuries, drama thrived in Japan, reaching a pinnacle in the Nō drama of Zeami Motokiyo and his father, Kan'ami. Japanese Nō drama combines music and movement in intricate patterns of ritualistic formality. Nō developed in a Buddhist environment and expressed the deep religious values associated with Buddhism. Although it began as a provincial form, the beauty of Nō—its deep meditative pauses and extraordinary dancelike movement—quickly made it the major style of drama in medieval Japan.

The rebirth of Western drama in the Middle Ages—after the fall of Rome and the loss of classical artistic traditions—took place first in monasteries, then later in and about the cathedrals of Europe. It evolved from medieval religious ceremonies that helped the faithful understand more about their own moral predicament. *Everyman,* a late play in the medieval theater (it was written about 1500), concerns itself with the central issue of reward and punishment for the immortal soul after this life.

Drama: The Illusion of Reality

From the beginning, drama has had the capacity to hold up an illusion of reality like the reflection in a mirror: we take the reality for granted while recognizing that it is nonetheless illusory. As we have seen, Aristotle described drama, or **dramatic illusion,** as an imitation of an action. But unlike the reflection in a mirror, the action of most drama is drawn not from our actual experience of life but from our potential or imagined experience. In the great Greek dramas, the illusion includes the narratives of ancient myths that were thought to offer profound illumination.

Different ages have had different approaches to representing reality onstage. Greek actors spoke in verse and wore masks. Except in the case of some comedies and **satyr plays**, the staging consisted of very little setting and no special costumes. Medieval drama was sometimes acted on pageant wagons and carts, but the special machinery developed to suggest hellfire and the presence of devils was said to be so realistic as to be frightening. Audiences of the Elizabethan age (named for Elizabeth I, who ruled England from 1558 to 1603) were accustomed to actors who spoke directly to the crowds at their feet near the apron of the stage. All Elizabethan plays were done in essentially contemporary clothing, often with no more scenery than a suggestion in the spoken descriptions of the players. The actors recited their lines in verse, except when the author had a particular reason to use prose—for example, to imply that the speaker was of low social station. Yet Elizabethans reported that their theater was much like life itself.

In Shakespeare's *A Midsummer Night's Dream,* fairies, enchantments, an ass's head on the shoulders of a man all are presented as illusions, and we accept them. They inform the audience—in Shakespeare's day and in modern times—not by showing us ourselves in a mirror but by demonstrating that even fantastic realities have significance for us.

Certainly *A Midsummer Night's Dream* gives us insight into the profound range of human emotions. We learn about the pains of rejection when we see Helena longing for Demetrius, who in turn longs for Hermia. We learn about jealousy and possessiveness when we see Oberon cast a spell on his wife, Titania, over a dispute concerning a changeling. And we learn, too, about the worldly ambitions of the "rude mechanicals" who themselves put on a play whose reality they fear might frighten their audience. They solve the problem by reminding their audience that it is only a play and that they need not fear that reality will spoil their pleasure.

In modern drama, the dramatic illusion of reality includes not just the shape of an action, the events, and the characters but also the details of everyday life. When the action changes locale, the setting changes as well. Some contemporary playwrights make an effort to re-create a reality close to the one we live in. Some modern plays, such as August Wilson's *Fences,* make a precise representation of reality a primary purpose, shaping the tone of the language to reflect the way modern people speak, re-creating contemporary reality in the setting, language, and other elements of the drama.

But describing a play as an illusion of reality in no way means that it represents the precise reality that we take for granted in our everyday experience. Rather, drama ranges widely and explores multiple realities, some of which may seem very close to our own and some of which may seem improbably removed from our everyday experience.

Seeing a Play Onstage

For an audience, drama is one of the most powerful artistic experiences. When we speak about participating in drama, we mean that as a member of the audience we become a part of the action that unfolds. This is a mysterious phenomenon.

When we see a play today, we are usually seated in a darkened theater looking at a lighted stage. In ages past, this contrast was not the norm. Greek plays took place outdoors during the morning and the afternoon; most Elizabethan plays were staged outdoors in the afternoon; in the Renaissance, some plays began to be staged indoors with ingenious systems of lighting that involved candles and reflectors. In the early nineteenth century, most theaters used gaslight onstage; electricity took over in the later part of the century, and its use has grown increasingly complex. In most large theaters today, computerized lighting boards have replaced Renaissance candles.

Sitting in the darkness has made the experience of seeing Greek and Elizabethan plays much different for us than it was for the original audiences. We do not worry about being seen by the "right people" or about studying the quality of the audience, as people did during the Restoration in the late seventeenth century. The darkness isolates us from all except those who sit adjacent to us. Yet we instantly respond when others in the audience laugh, when they gasp, when they shift restlessly. We recognize in those moments that we are part of a larger community drawn together by theater and that we are all involved in the dramatic experience.

Theaters and Their Effect

Different kinds of theaters make differing demands on actors and audiences. Despite its huge size, the open **arena** style theater of the early Greeks brought the audience into a special kind of intimacy with the actors. The players came very close to the first rows of seats, and the acoustics sometimes permitted even a whisper onstage to be audible in the far seats. The Greek theater also imparted a sense of formality to the occasion of drama. For one thing, its symmetry and circularity were accompanied by a relatively rigid seating plan. Public officials and nobility sat in special seats. Then each section of the theater was given over to specific families, and the less desirable edges of the seating area were devoted to travelers and strangers to the town. One knew one's place in the Greek theater. Its regularity gave the community a sense of order.

Medieval theater also gave its audiences a sense of community, both when it used playing areas called *mansions* inside and outside the churches and when it used wagons wheeled about in processions in the streets or outside the city walls. That the medieval theater repeated the same cycles of plays again and again for about two hundred years, to the delight of many European communities, tells us something about the stability of those communities. Their drama was integrated with their religion, and both helped them express their sense of belonging to the church and the community.

In some medieval performances, the actors came into the audience, breaking the sense of distance or the illusion of separation. It is difficult for us to know how much participation and involvement in the action the medieval audience felt. Modern audiences have responded very well to productions of medieval plays such as *The Second Shepherds' Pageant, Noah's Flood,* and *Everyman,* and we have every reason to think that medieval audiences enjoyed their dramas immensely. The guilds that performed them took pride in making their plays as exciting and involving as possible.

The Elizabethan playhouse was a wooden structure providing an enclosed space, approximately seventy-two feet in diameter, around a courtyard open to the sky. A covered stage thrust into the courtyard. As in the Greek theater, the audience was arranged somewhat by social station. Around the stage, which was about five feet off the ground, stood the groundlings, those who paid the least for their entrance. Then in covered galleries in the building itself sat patrons who paid extra for a seat. The effect of the enclosed structure was of a small, contained world. Actors were in the habit of speaking directly to members of the audience, and the audience rarely kept a polite silence. It was a busy, humming theater that generated intimacy and involvement between actors and audience.

The proscenium stage of the nineteenth and twentieth centuries distanced the audience from the play, providing a clear frame (the **proscenium**) behind which the performers acted out their scenes. This detachment was especially effective for plays that demanded a high degree of realism because the effect of the proscenium is to make the audience feel that it is witnessing the action as a silent observer, looking in as if through an imaginary fourth wall on a living room or other intimate space in which the action takes place. The proscenium arch gives the illusion that the actors are in a world of their own, unaware of the audience's presence.

In the twentieth century, some of the virtues of the Greek arena theater, or **theater in the round**, were rediscovered. In an effort to close the distance between audience and players, Antonin Artaud, the French actor and director, developed in the 1920s and 1930s a concept called the *theater of cruelty*. Using theater in the round, Artaud robbed the audience of the comfort of watching a distant stage and pressed his actors into the space of the viewers. His purpose was to force theatergoers to deal with the primary issues of the drama by stripping them of the security of darkness and anonymity. Theaters in the Soviet Union and Britain developed similar spaces in the 1930s and 1940s, and since the 1950s the Arena Theater in Washington, D.C., and the Circle in the Square in New York City have continued the tradition.

The thrust stage, a modern revision of Shakespeare's Globe Theatre stage, was designed in 1948 by Sir Tyrone Guthrie for the Assembly Hall in Edinburgh, Scotland. He further refined it in the Festival Theatre in Stratford, Ontario (1957), and in his famous Tyrone Guthrie Theater (1963) in Minneapolis. The audience sits on three sides of a stage that thrusts out from a flat area incorporating balconies, doors, and sometimes stairs. The thrust stage often intensifies the intimacy of the dramatic experience.

Twenty-first-century theater is eclectic. It uses thrust, arena, proscenium, and every other kind of stage already described. Some contemporary site-specific theater also converts nontheatrical space, such as warehouses or city streets, into space for performance.

Reading a Play

Reading a play is a different experience from seeing it enacted. For one thing, readers do not have the benefit of the interpretations made by a director, actors, and scene designers in presenting a performance. These interpretations are all critical judgments based on a director's ideas of how the play should be presented and on actors' insights into the meaning of the play.

A reading of a play produces an interpretation that remains in our heads and is not translated to the stage. The dramatic effect of the staging is lost to us unless we make a genuine effort to visualize it and to understand its contribution to the dramatic experience. For a fuller experience of the drama when reading plays, one should keep in mind the historical period and the conventions of staging that are appropriate to the period and that are specified by the playwright.

Some plays were prepared by their authors for reading as well as for staging, as evident in plays whose stage directions supply information that would be unavailable to an audience, such as the color of the characters' eyes, characters' secret motives, and other such details. Occasionally, stage directions, such as those of Bernard Shaw and Tennessee Williams, are written in a poetic prose that can be appreciated only by a reader.

It is not a certainty that seeing a play will produce an experience more "true" to the play's meaning than reading it. Every act of reading silently or speaking the lines aloud is an act of interpretation. No one can say which is the best interpretation. Each has its own merits, and the ideal is probably to read *and* see any play.

For links to theaters, drama organizations, and reviews, click on *Drama Links* at bedfordstmartins.com/jacobus.

The Great Ages of Drama

Certain historical periods have produced great plays and great playwrights, although why some periods generate more dramatic activity than others is still a matter of conjecture by scholars examining the social, historical, and religious conditions of the times. Each of the great ages of drama has affected the way plays have been written, acted, and staged in successive ages. In every age, drama borrows important elements from each earlier period.

Egyptian Drama

Although scholars disagree in their interpretations of archaeological evidence, it is quite likely that ancient Egyptian drama was highly developed. One of the key artifacts supporting this assertion is an incised stone stela (c. 1868 BCE) describing the roles that an official named Ikhernofret played in a celebration that included characters and dramatic action. The Abydos Passion Play, as some modern scholars call this event, was performed annually from approximately 2500 to 500 BCE. It is the story of Osiris (the equivalent of the Greek Dionysus), who was murdered in an act of trickery by his jealous brother Seth. Osiris was dismembered (as was Dionysus in Greek myth) and his parts scattered over the land. Isis, both wife and sister of Osiris, gathered most of the parts of Osiris in order to make possible his resurrection. The celebration seems to have been timed to reflect a pattern of agricultural renewal that the rebirth myth of Osiris satisfies. In his account of his role in the event, as recorded on the stela, Ikhernofret says,

> I did everything that His Person commanded, putting into effect my lord's command for his father, Osiris-Khentyamentiu, Lord of Abydos, great of power, who is in the Thinite nome. I acted as beloved son of Osiris-Khentyamentiu. I embellished his great barque of eternity; I made for it a shrine which displays the beauties of Khentyamentiu, in gold, silver, lapis-lazuli, bronze, sesnedjem-wood and cedar[?]. I fashioned the gods in his train. I made their shrines anew. I caused the temple priesthood to do their duties, I caused them to know the custom of every day, the festival of the Head-of-the-Year. I controlled work on the neshmet-barque; I fashioned the shrine and adorned the breast of the Lord of Abydos with lapis-lazuli and turquoise, electrum and every precious stone, as an adornment of the divine limbs. I changed the clothes of the god at his appearance, in the office of Master of Secrets and in my job as sem-priest. I was clean of arm in adoring the god, a sem clean of fingers.
>
> I organized the going forth of Wepwawet when he proceeded to avenge his father; I drove away the rebels from the neshmet-barque; I overthrew the enemies of Osiris; I celebrated the great going forth. I followed the god at his going, and

caused the ship to sail, Thoth steering the sailing. I equipped the barque with a chapel and affixed (Osiris's) beautiful adornments when he proceeded to the district of Peqer. I cleared the ways of the god to his tomb before Peqer. I avenged Wennefer that day of the great fight; I overthrew all his enemies upon the sandbanks of Nedyt; I caused him to proceed into the great barque. It raised up his beauties, I making glad the people/tomb owners of the Eastern Desert, creating joy amongst the people/tomb owners of the Western Desert; they saw the beauties of the neshmet-barque when it touched land at Abydos, when it brought Osiris-Khentyamentiu to his palace; I followed the god to his house, I carried out his purification and extended his seat and solved the problems of his residence [. . . and amongst] his entourage.[1]

Parts of the celebration were public in the outdoors, but parts were also played within the walls of the temple by priests. Little if anything is known about the mysteries they performed, but Herodotus (c. 484–c. 430 BCE), who claimed to have traveled in Egypt, reported seeing public participation in mock battles associated with the celebration.

Another festival, called the Heb-Seb, performed at the pyramid complex of Sakkara in the thirtieth year of a pharaoh's reign (and then every third year following), involved dance, music, and pageantry that closely resembled dramatic action. The purpose of the festival was to celebrate the longevity of the pharaoh and the resultant wellness of the land. The associated "Pyramid Texts" from Sakkara (c. 3000 BCE) also treat the resurrection of Osiris and may imply the existence of an early form of the celebration of Heb-Seb. All these festivals, supplemented by those from Busiris and Memphis in Egypt, suggest that although the Greeks believed they had invented drama, it is much more likely that the Egyptians had done so.

Greek Drama

The Greeks of the fifth century BCE are credited with the first masterful dramatic age, which lasted from the birth of Aeschylus (c. 525 BCE) to the death of Aristophanes (c. 385 BCE). Their theaters were supported by public funds, and the playwrights competed for prizes during the great festivals of Dionysus. Sometimes as many as ten to fifteen thousand people sat in the theaters and watched with a sense of delight and awe as the actors played out their tales.

Theater was extremely important to the Greeks as a way of interpreting their relationships with their gods and of reinforcing their sense of community. The fifth-century-BCE audience, mostly wealthy citizens, came early in the morning and spent the entire day in the theater. Drama for the Greeks was not mere escapism or entertainment, not a frill or a luxury. Connected as it was with religious festivals, it was a cultural necessity.

Sophocles' plays *Oedipus Rex* and *Antigone* are examples of the powerful tragedies that have transfixed audiences for centuries. Euripides, slightly younger than Sophocles, was also a prize-winning tragedian. His *Trojan Women, Alcestis, Medea, The Bacchae,* and *Elektra* [*Electra*] are still performed and still exert an influence on today's drama. The same is true of Aeschylus, who was slightly older than both and whose *Agamemnon, The Libation Bearers, The Eumenides* (known collectively as the *Oresteia*), and *Prometheus Bound* have all been among the most lasting of plays.

[1]From http://www.touregypt.net/passionplay.htm; also in Henry Breasted's *Ancient Records of Egypt*, part 2 (1906–07).

In addition to such great tragedians, the Greeks also produced the important comedians Aristophanes and Menander (late fourth century BCE), whose work has been plundered for plays as diverse as a Shakespeare comedy and a Broadway musical. Aristophanes' *Lysistrata,* in which the Athenian and Spartan women agree to withhold sex from their husbands until the men promise to stop making war, is a sometimes crude social comedy. Menander produced a more refined type of comedy that made the culture laugh at itself. Both styles of comedy are staples of popular entertainment even today. Menander's comedies were the basis of later social comedy in which society's ways of behavior are criticized. Such social comedy is exemplified in William Congreve's eighteenth-century *The Way of the World* and Molière's *Tartuffe.*

Roman Drama

The Romans became aware of Greek drama in the third century BCE and began to import Greek actors and playwrights. Because of many social and cultural differences between the societies, however, drama never took a central role in the life of the average Roman. Seneca, who is now viewed as Rome's most important tragedian, almost certainly wrote his plays to be read rather than to be seen onstage.

Roman comedy produced two great playwrights, Plautus and Terence, who helped develop the **stock** (or type) **character,** such as the skinflint or the prude. Plautus was the great Roman comedian in the tradition of Menander. Plautus's best-known plays are *The Braggart Warrior* and *The Twin Menaechmi;* during the Renaissance, when all European schoolchildren read Latin, his works were favorites.

Terence's work was praised during the Middle Ages and the Renaissance as being smoother, more elegant, and more polished and refined than Plautus's. In his own age, Terence was less admired by the general populace but more admired by connoisseurs of drama. His best-known plays—*The Woman of Andros, Phormio,* and *The Brothers*—are rarely performed today.

Drama took its place beside many other forms of entertainment in Roman culture—sports events, gladiator battles to the death, chariot races, the slaughter of wild beasts, and sacrifices of Christians and others to animals. The Roman public, when it did attend plays, enjoyed farces and relatively coarse humor. The audiences for Plautus and Terence, aristocratic in taste, may not have represented the cross-section of the community that was typical of Greek audiences.

Medieval Drama

After the fall of Rome and the spread of the Goths and Visigoths across southern Europe in the fifth century CE, Europe experienced a total breakdown of the strong central government Rome had provided. When Rome fell, Greek and Roman culture virtually disappeared. The great classical texts went largely unread until the end of the medieval period in the fourteenth and fifteenth centuries; however, expressions of culture, including art forms such as drama, did not entirely disappear. During the medieval period, the power and influence of the Church grew extensively, and it tried to fill the gap left by the demise of the Roman empire. The Church became a focus of both religious and secular activity for people all over Europe.

After almost five centuries of relative inactivity, European drama was reborn in religious ceremonies in monasteries. It moved inside churches, then out of doors by the twelfth century, perhaps because its own demands outgrew its circumstances. Drama had become more than an adjunct to the religious ceremonies that had spawned it.

One reason the medieval European communities regarded their drama so highly is that it expressed many of their concerns and values. The age was highly religious; in addition, the people who produced the plays were members of guilds whose personal pride was represented in their work. Their plays came to be called **mystery plays** because the trade that each guild represented was a special skill—a mystery to the average person. Of course, the pun on religious mystery was understood by most audiences.

Many of these plays told stories drawn from the Bible. The tales of Noah's Ark, Abraham and Isaac, and Samson and Delilah all had dramatic potential, and the mystery plays capitalized on that potential, as did plays on the life and crucifixion of Christ. Among mystery plays, *The Second Shepherds' Pageant* and *Abraham and Isaac* are still performed regularly.

Most mystery plays were gathered into groups of plays called **cycles,** dramatizing incidents from the Bible, among other sources. They were usually performed outdoors, at times on movable wagons that doubled as stages. Either the audience moved from wagon to wagon to see each play in a cycle or the wagons moved among the audience.

In the fifteenth and sixteenth centuries, a form of play developed that was not associated with cycles or with the guilds. These were the **morality plays,** and their purpose was to touch on larger contemporary issues that had a moral overtone. *Everyman,* the best known of the morality plays, was performed in many nations in various languages.

Renaissance Drama

The revival of learning in the Renaissance, beginning in Italy in the fourteenth century, had considerable effect on drama because classical Greek and Roman plays were discovered and studied. In the academies in Italy, some experiments in re-creating Greek and Roman plays introduced music into drama. New theaters, such as Teatro Olympico in Vicenza (1579), were built to produce these plays; they allow us to see how the Renaissance reconceived the classical stage. Some of these experiments developed into modern opera. The late medieval traditions of the Italian theater's **commedia dell'arte**, a stylized improvisational slapstick comedy performed by actors' guilds, began to move beyond Italy into other European nations. The commedia's stock characters, Harlequins and Pulcinellas, began to appear in many countries in Europe.

Elizabethan drama and Jacobean drama (named for King James I, who succeeded Elizabeth and reigned from 1603 to 1625) developed most fully during the fifty years from approximately 1590 to 1640. Audiences poured into the playhouses eager for plays about history and for the great tragedies of Christopher Marlowe, such as *Doctor Faustus,* and of Shakespeare, including *Macbeth, Hamlet, Othello, Julius Caesar,* and *King Lear.* But there were others as well: Middleton and Rowley's *The Changeling,* Cyril Tourneur's *Revenger's Tragedy,* John Webster's *The White Devil* and his sensational *The Duchess of Malfi.*

The great comedies of the age came mostly from the pen of William Shakespeare: *A Midsummer Night's Dream, The Comedy of Errors, As You Like It, Much Ado about Nothing, The Taming of the Shrew,* and *Twelfth Night.* Many of these plays derived from Italian originals, usually novellas or popular poems and sometimes comedies. But Shakespeare, of course, elevated and vastly improved everything he borrowed.

Ben Jonson, a playwright who was significantly influenced by the classical writers, was also well represented on the Elizabethan stage, with *Volpone,*

The Alchemist, Every Man in His Humour, Bartholomew Fair, and other durable comedies. Jonson is also important for his contributions to the **masque,** an aristocratic entertainment that featured music, dance, and fantastic costuming. His *Masque of Blackness* was performed in the royal court with the queen as a performer.

The Elizabethan stage sometimes grew bloody, with playwrights and audiences showing a passion for tragedies that, like *Hamlet,* centered on revenge and often ended with most of the characters meeting a premature death. Elizabethan plays also show considerable variety, with many plays detailing the history of English kings and, therefore, the history of England. It was a theater of powerful effect, and contemporary diaries indicate that the audiences delighted in it.

Throughout the Renaissance, women were not allowed on stage; men and boys played the female roles. Theaters in Shakespeare's day were built outside city limits in seamy neighborhoods near brothels and bear-baiting pits, where chained bears were set upon by large dogs for the crowd's amusement. Happily, the theaters' business was good; the plays were constructed of remarkable language that seems to have fascinated all social classes, since all flocked to the theater by the thousands.

Theaters also flourished in Spain in this period, producing Lope de Vega (1562–1635), who may have written as many as seventeen hundred plays. Vega's immediate successor, Pedro Calderón de la Barca (1600–1681), is sometimes considered to be more polished in style, but also more stiffly aristocratic in appeal. He wrote fewer plays than Vega, but still produced an amazing body of work. He is said to have written at least 111 dramas and seventy or eighty *auto sacramentales,* the Spanish equivalent of religious morality plays, designed for special religious ceremonies. Calderón is best known for *La vida es sueño (Life Is a Dream),* which is still performed today.

Late-Seventeenth- and Eighteenth-Century Drama

After the Puritan reign in England from 1642 (when the theaters were closed) to 1660, during which dramatic productions were almost nonexistent, the theater was suddenly revived. In 1660, Prince Charles, having been sent to France by his father during the English Civil War, was invited back to be king, thus beginning what was known in England as the Restoration. It was a gay, exciting period, in stark contrast to the gray Puritan era. During the Restoration, new indoor theaters modeled on those in France were built, and a new generation of actors and actresses (women took part in plays for the first time in England) came forth to participate in the dramatic revival.

Since the mid-seventeenth century, French writers, interpreting Aristotle's description of Greek drama, had leaned toward development of a classical theater, which was supposed to observe the "unities" of time, place, and action: a play had one plot and one setting and covered the action of one day. In 1637, Pierre Corneille wrote *Le Cid,* using relatively modern Spanish history as his theme and following certain classical techniques. Jean-Baptiste Racine was Corneille's successor, and his plays became even more classical by focusing on classical topics. His work includes *Andromache, Britannicus,* and, possibly his best play, *Phaedra.* Racine retired from the stage at the end of the seventeenth century, but he left a powerful legacy of classicism that reached well into the eighteenth century.

Molière, an actor and producer, was the best comedian of seventeenth-century France. *Tartuffe, The Misanthrope,* and several of his other plays are still produced regularly. Molière was classical in his way, borrowing ancient comedy's technique of using type, or stock, characters in his social satires.

Among the important English playwrights of the new generation were Aphra Behn, the first female professional writer, whose play *The Rover* was one of the most popular plays of the late seventeenth century, and William Congreve, whose best-known play, *The Way of the World,* is still often produced. The latter is a lively comedy that aimed to chasten as well as entertain Congreve's audiences.

The eighteenth century saw the tradition of social comedy continued in Richard Brinsley Sheridan's *School for Scandal* and Oliver Goldsmith's *She Stoops to Conquer.* The drama of this period focuses on social manners, and much of it is **satire**—that is, drama that offers mild criticism of society and holds society up to comic ridicule. But underlying that ridicule is the relatively noble motive of reforming society. We can see some of that motive at work in the plays of Molière and Goldsmith. We see it even more in John Gay's *The Beggar's Opera,* the most popular drama of the eighteenth century.

During much of the eighteenth century, theater in France centered on the court and was controlled by a small coterie of snobbish people. The situation in England was not quite the same, although the audiences were snobbish and socially conscious. They went to the theater to be seen, and they often went in claques—groups of like-minded patrons who applauded or booed together to express their views. Theater was important, but attendance at it was like a material possession, something to be displayed for others to admire.

A wide variety of drama was extant in Japan in the late sixteenth and early seventeenth centuries. Kabuki theater, the most remarkable form of popular Japanese drama and a lasting form still seen today in theaters around the world, evolved in this period. Kabuki is performed with music, and the resulting intensity would have surprised Western playwrights and audiences of that time. The emphasis shifted from the personality of the player to the situations and circumstances portrayed in the drama. Chikamatsu Monzaemon developed the form and was the most inventive of the Kabuki playwrights. His play *The Love Suicides at Sonezaki* was based on a genuine love suicide (*shinjū* in Japanese) and created a craze for love suicide plays that resulted in an edict in 1722 that banned them entirely. Some modern writers claim that the quality of his drama was not equaled in Japan for more than two hundred years.

Drama from the Nineteenth Century through the Turn of the Twentieth Century

English playwrights alone produced more than thirty thousand plays during the nineteenth century. Most of the plays were sentimental, melodramatic, and dominated by a few very powerful actors, stars who often overwhelmed the works written for them. The audiences were quite different from those of the seventeenth and eighteenth centuries. The upwardly mobile urban middle classes and the moneyed factory and mill owners who had benefited economically from the industrial revolution demanded a drama that would entertain them.

The audiences were generally not well educated, nor were they interested in plays that were intellectually demanding. Instead, they wanted escapist and sentimental entertainment that was easy to respond to and did not challenge their basic values. Revivals of old plays and adaptations of Shakespeare were also common in the age, with great stars like Edmund Kean, Sir Henry Irving, Edwin Forrest, Edwin Booth, and William Macready using the plays as platforms for overwhelming, and sometimes overbearing, performances. Thrillers were especially popular, as were historical plays and melodramatic plays featuring a helpless heroine.

As an antidote to such a diet, the new Realist movement in literature, exemplified by the achievements of French novelists Émile Zola and Gustave Flaubert, finally reached the stage in the 1870s and 1880s in plays by August Strindberg and Henrik Ibsen. Revolutionizing Western drama, these Scandinavians forced their audiences to confront more important issues and deeper psychological concerns than those facing earlier audiences.

Strindberg's *Miss Julie,* a psychological study, challenged social complacency based on class and social differences. Ibsen's *A Doll House* struck a blow for feminism, but it did not amuse all audiences. Some were horrified at the thought that Nora Helmer was to be taken as seriously as her husband. Such a view was heretical, but it was also thrilling for a newly awakened European conscience. Those intellectuals and writers who responded positively to Ibsen, including Bernard Shaw, acted as the new conscience and began a move that soon transformed drama. Feminism is also a theme, but perhaps less directly, of Ibsen's *Hedda Gabler,* the story of a woman whose frustration at being cast in an inferior role contributes to a destructive — and ultimately self-destructive — impulse. Both plays are acted in a physical setting that seems to be as ordinary as a nineteenth-century sitting room, with characters as small — and yet as large — as the people who watched them.

The Russian Anton Chekhov's plays *Three Sisters, Uncle Vanya,* and *The Cherry Orchard,* written at the turn of the twentieth century, are realistic as well, but they are also patient examinations of character, rather than primarily problem plays like Ibsen's *Ghosts* and *The Master Builder.* Chekhov was aware of social change in Russia, especially the changes that revealed a hitherto repressed class of peasants evolving into landowners and merchants. *The Cherry Orchard* is suffused with an overpowering sense of inevitability through which Chekhov depicts the conflict between the necessity for change and a nostalgia for the past. The comedies of Oscar Wilde, such as *Lady Windermere's Fan* and *The Importance of Being Earnest,* poke fun at the foibles of the upper classes. Amusing as these plays are, their satirical quality constitutes social criticism.

These plays introduced a modern realism of a kind that was rare in earlier drama. Melodrama of the nineteenth century was especially satisfying to mass audiences because the good characters were very good, the bad characters were very bad, and justice was meted out at the end. But it is difficult in Chekhov to be sure who the heroes and villains are. Nothing is as clear-cut in these plays as it is in popular melodramas. Instead, Chekhov's plays are as complicated as life itself. Such difficulties of distinction have become the norm of the most important of contemporary drama.

Drama in the Early and Mid-Twentieth Century

The drama of the early twentieth century nurtured the seeds of late-nineteenth-century realism into bloom, but sometimes this drama experimented with audience expectations. Eugene O'Neill's *Desire under the Elms* is a tragedy that features the ordinary citizen rather than the noble. This play focuses on New

England farmers as tragic characters. Arthur Miller's *Death of a Salesman* invokes a sense of dreadful inevitability within the world of the commercial salesman, the ordinary man. As in many other twentieth-century tragedies, the point is that the life of the ordinary man can be as tragic as that of Oedipus.

Luigi Pirandello experiments with reality in *Six Characters in Search of an Author,* a play that has a distinctly absurd quality, since it expects us to accept the notion that the characters on the stage are waiting for an author to put them into a play. Pirandello plays with our sense of illusion and of expectation and realism to such an extent that he forces us to reexamine our concepts of reality.

Bertolt Brecht's *Mother Courage,* an example of what the playwright called **epic drama**, explores war from a complex series of viewpoints. On the one hand, Courage is a powerful figure who has been seen as a model of endurance, but Brecht also wanted his audience to see that Courage brings on much of her own suffering by trying to profit from war. The sole act of self-sacrifice in the play comes at the end, when Kattrin beats her drum to warn villagers of the approach of a destroying army. Brecht produced the play early in World War II as a protest. Playwrights around the world responded to events such as World War I, the Communist revolution, and the Great Depression by writing plays that no longer permitted audiences to sit comfortably and securely in darkened theaters. Brecht and other playwrights instead came out to get their audiences, to make them feel and think, to make them realize their true condition.

Samuel Beckett's dramatic career began with *Waiting for Godot,* which audiences interpreted as an examination of humans' eternal vigilance for the revelation of God or of some transcendent meaning in their lives. In the play, Godot never comes, yet the characters do not give up hope. *Endgame*'s characters seem to be awaiting the end of the world: in the 1950s, the shadow of nuclear extinction cast by the cold war dominated most people's imagination.

Tennessee Williams relied on personal experience in writing *Cat on a Hot Tin Roof,* which portrays themes of homosexuality and marital sexual tension—themes that were not discussed in contemporary American theater except in veiled mythic terms, in the manner, for example, of O'Neill's *Desire under the Elms.*

Nigerian playwright Wole Soyinka, who won the Nobel Prize for literature in 1986, portrays the complex intersection of a person's past and the present in his play *The Strong Breed,* set in an African village reminiscent of the Greek *polis.* He experiments with Greek tragic forms in *The Bacchae of Euripides,* which is also set in Africa. Soyinka's insights into the nature of culture and drama provide us with a new way of reflecting on drama's power in our lives.

Modern dramatists from the turn of the twentieth century to the Korean War explored in many different directions and developed new approaches to themes of dramatic illusion as well as to questions concerning the relationship of an audience to the stage and the players.

Contemporary Drama

The twenty-first-century stage is vibrant. The great commercial theaters of England and the United States are sometimes hampered by high production costs, but regional theaters everywhere are producing fine drama. The National Theatre in London has made inexpensive seats available for most of its plays, and other theaters are doing the same. In Latin America, Germany, Japan,

China, France, and elsewhere, the theater is active and exciting. Poland's experiments in drama, led by Jerzy Grotowski's "Poor Theater," inspired experimentation that has spread throughout the world of drama. Russia, too, has produced a number of plays that have achieved worldwide currency.

The hallmark of many of these plays has been experimentalism. Caryl Churchill's *Top Girls* features characters who claim to be Pope Joan, Patient Griselda, and Lady Nijo, as well as being "themselves"—all this in the milieu of a feminist employment agency. Her newer play, *Far Away,* is a portrait of an apocalyptic world as viewed by a girl.

Sam Shepard, well known as an actor, was for many years among the most experimental playwrights living in New York's Greenwich Village. His *True West* begins as a relatively straightforward play about Austin and Lee, two brothers, but quickly reveals the drama that lies beneath the surface. Lee has arrived to steal his mother's television set but ends by stealing something of his brother's personality. *Buried Child* examines some frightening secrets in a dysfunctional family.

Suzan-Lori Parks has made a career of writing experimental plays, from the Brechtian *The Death of the Last Black Man in the Whole Entire World,* which structures itself in "panels" (brief, intense scenes that connect imaginatively), to *365 Days/365 Plays,* for which she wrote a play a day for a year. Tony Kushner employs similar techniques in *Angels in America.* Its brilliantly staged scenes are filled with emotional intensity, and the audience is carried on waves of imaginative speculation on America's history as well as on America's present. Moisés Kaufman and the members of the Tectonic Theater Project used highly inventive means to produce *The Laramie Project,* a play built around the murder of a young gay man, Matthew Shepherd, in Wyoming. It was a shocking crime both to the nation at large and to the local community in Laramie. The members of the project conducted many interviews with people in Laramie over a period of more than a year, and the resultant drama, largely developed from the interviews, revealed a range of surprising responses and surprising emotions. Experimentation is probably at the heart of the work of many playwrights, although it still does not please mainstream audiences to the same degree that traditional drama does.

Not all modern theater is experimental, however. August Wilson's *Fences* shows us the pain of life at the lower end of the economic ladder in a form that is recognizably realistic and plausible. The play is set in the 1950s and focuses on Troy Maxson, a black man, and his relationship with his son and his wife. Tenement life is one subject of the play, but the most important subject is the courage it takes to keep going after tasting defeat. The entire drama develops within the bounds of conventional nineteenth-century realism.

The most celebrated of contemporary playwrights seem to mix experimental and conventional dramatic techniques. Tom Stoppard, whose work is cerebral and witty, as in his pastiche of *Hamlet* called *Rosencrantz and Guildenstern Are Dead,* continues to delve into literature for much of his work. *The Invention of Love* treats the hopeless love of the Oxford classical scholar and poet A. E. Housman for a young athlete, Moses Jackson. The play begins with Housman crossing the river Styx into the underworld. Throughout, the older Housman watches himself as a young man and offers his sentiments. *Arcadia,* unlike some of Stoppard's early works, is a deeply emotional play about a thirteen-year-old girl, Lady Thomasina Coverly, gifted mathematically in an age in which such fields of study were reserved for men. The play takes place in one country house in Derbyshire, England, in both 1809 and 1989, contrasting several modes of thought and feeling—classical, romantic, and modern.

Paula Vogel's plays frequently interrupt the dramatic action with asides, but they are also imaginatively structured so that time feels fluid and the action moves in emotionally significant sweeps. *The Baltimore Waltz,* derived from Vogel's experience of watching her brother die of AIDS, brings humor to a tragic situation. Similarly, *How I Learned to Drive,* which sensitively treats the subject of sexual molestation in families, also has comic moments.

Recent Irish playwrights have provided us with a range of powerful plays that invoke horror, joy, and the supernatural. *Faith Healer, Translations, Dancing at Lughnasa,* and *Molly Sweeney* are only some of Brian Friel's celebrated plays. Friel has experimented with using both a single character and a full cast and has used many unusual techniques. For example, in *Translations,* English- and Irish-speaking characters are unable to communicate with one another, although in reality the actors all speak English for the audience. Conor McPherson's *Shining City* includes a bit of supernatural mystery typical of his work; *The Weir* incorporates a ghost story, and *The Seafarer* contains echoes of Irish myth and an appearance by the Devil. Martin McDonagh has had multiple plays running on Broadway and London's West End at the same time. *The Beauty Queen of Leenane, The Lonesome West, The Lieutenant of Inishmore,* and *The Pillowman* have all been nominated for Tony Awards.

Among other contemporary successes that have been produced internationally and in regional theaters are Sarah Ruhl's plays, which have stimulated audiences with their adventurous productions. *The Clean House* features a Brazilian housekeeper who searches for the perfect joke, which she eventually tells in Portuguese. *Eurydice* is a moving interpretation of the Greek myth of Orpheus and Eurydice, written as a hymn to Ruhl's father, who had died of cancer. *In the Next Room or the Vibrator Play,* a Tony Award nominee in 2010, examines late-nineteenth-century treatments of hysteria. Ruhl's satire is based on the assumption by some early psychologists that the vast majority of women's problems could be cured with the vibrator.

Other writers who have made an impact on contemporary theater include John Patrick Shanley, whose *Doubt* won the Pulitzer Prize for drama and the Tony Award for best play in 2005; Yasmina Reza, a French playwright whose plays *Art* and *God of Carnage* won Tony Awards in 1998 and 2009; Tracy Letts, whose *August: Osage County,* a portrait of a highly volatile family, won the Pulitzer Prize and the Tony Award for best play in 2008; and Lynn Nottage, who followed her plays *Poof!, Crumbs from the Table of Joy,* and *Intimate Apparel* with *Ruined,* a tale set in modern Africa that won the Pulitzer Prize in 2009. The theater of the twenty-first century continues with extraordinary energy to explore issues of social, historical, and psychological importance, using a wide range of techniques to which audiences respond positively.

Genres of Drama

Drama since the great age of the Greeks has taken several different forms. As we have seen, tragedies were one genre that pleased Greek audiences, and comedies pleased the Romans. In later ages, a blend of the comic and the tragic produced a hybrid genre: tragicomedy. In our time, unless a play is modeled on the Greek or Shakespearean tragedies, as is O'Neill's *Desire under the Elms*, it is usually considered tragicomic rather than tragic. Our age still enjoys the kind of comedy that people laugh at, although most plays that are strictly comedy are frothy, temporarily entertaining, and not lasting.

Tragedy

Tragedy demands a specific worldview. Aristotle, in his *Poetics*, points out that the tragic hero or heroine should be noble of birth, perhaps a king like Oedipus or a princess like Antigone. This has often been interpreted to mean that the tragic hero or heroine should be more magnanimous, more daring, and larger in spirit than the average person.

Modern tragedies have rediscovered tragic principles, and while O'Neill and Miller rely on Aristotle's precepts, they have shown that in a modern society shorn of the distinctions between noble and peasant, it is possible for audiences to see the greatness in all classes. This insight has given us a new way of orienting ourselves to the concept of fate; to **hamartia**, the wrong act that leads a person to a tragic end; and to the hero's or heroine's relationship to the social order.

Aristotle suggested that plot was the heart and soul of tragedy and that character came second. But most older tragedies take the name of the tragic hero or heroine as their title; this signifies the importance that dramatists invested in their tragic characters. Yet they also heeded Aristotle's stipulation that tragic action should have one plot rather than the double or triple plots that often characterize comedies. (Shakespeare was soundly criticized in the eighteenth century for breaking this rule in his tragedies.) And older tragedies paid attention to the concept of **peripeteia**, which specifies that the progress of the tragic characters sometimes leads them to a reversal: they get what they want, but what they want turns out to be destructive. Aristotle especially valued a plot in which the reversal takes place simultaneously with the recognition of the truth, or the shift from ignorance to awareness, as it does in Sophocles' *Oedipus Rex*.

Playwrights in the seventeenth and eighteenth centuries in France were especially interested in following classical precepts. They were certain that Greek tragedy and Roman comedy were the epitome of excellence in drama. They interpreted Aristotle's discussion of dramatic integrity as a set of rules governing dramatic form. These became known as drama's **three unities**, specifying one plot, a single action that takes place in one day, and a single setting. The neoclassical reinterpretation of the unities was probably much stricter than Aristotle intended.

Comedy

Two kinds of comedy developed among the ancient Greeks: **Old Comedy**, which resembles **farce** (light drama characterized by broad satirical comedy and an improbable plot) and often pokes fun at individuals with social and political power, and **New Comedy**, which is a more refined commentary on the condition of society.

Old Comedy survives in the masterful works of Aristophanes, such as *Lysistrata*, while New Comedy hearkens back to the lost plays of Menander and resurfaces in plays such as Molière's *Tartuffe*. Molière uses humor but mixes it with a serious level of social commentary. Modern **comedy of manners** studies and sometimes ridicules modern society, as in Oscar Wilde's *The Importance of Being Earnest*.

Comedy is not always funny. Chekhov thought *The Cherry Orchard* was a comedy, whereas his producer, the great Constantin Stanislavski, who trained actors to interpret Chekhov's lines and who acted in other Chekhov plays, thought it was a tragedy. The argument may have centered on the ultimate effect of the play on its audiences, but it may also have centered on the question of laughter. There are laughs in *The Cherry Orchard*, but they usually come at the expense of a character or a social group. This is true, as well, of Samuel Beckett's *Waiting for Godot* and *Krapp's Last Tape*. We may laugh, but we know that the play is at heart very serious.

Tragicomedy

Since the early seventeenth century, serious plays have been called **tragicomedies** when they do not adhere strictly to the structure of tragedy, which emphasizes the nobility of the hero or heroine, fate, the wrong action of the hero or heroine, and a resolution that includes death, exile, or a similar end. Many serious plays have these qualities, but they also have some of the qualities of comedy: a commentary on society, raucous behavior that draws laughs, and a relatively happy ending. Yet their darkness is such that we can hardly feel comfortable regarding them as comedies.

Plays such as Sam Shepard's *Buried Child* and Lorraine Hansberry's *A Raisin in the Sun* can be considered tragicomedy. Indeed, the modern temperament has especially relied on the mixture of comic and tragic elements for its most serious plays. Eugene O'Neill, Tennessee Williams, Harold Pinter, Caryl Churchill, Yasmina Reza, Sarah Ruhl, and Tracy Letts have all been masters of tragicomedy.

In contemporary drama, tragicomedy takes several forms. One is the play whose seriousness is relieved by comic moments; another is the play whose comic structure absorbs a tragic moment and continues to express affirmation. Yet another is the dark comedy whose sardonic humor leaves us wondering how we can laugh at something that is ultimately frightening. This is the case with some absurdist comedies, which insist that there is no meaning in events other than the meaning we invent for ourselves. Pinter's *The Homecoming* and Beckett's *Endgame* are such plays. They are funny yet sardonic, and when we laugh we do so uneasily.

Other genres of drama exist, although they are generally versions of tragedy, comedy, and tragicomedy. Improvisational theater, in which actors use no scripts and may switch roles at any moment, defies generic description. Musical comedies and operas are dramatic entertainments that have established their own genres related in some ways to the standard genres of drama.

Genre distinctions are useful primarily because they establish expectations in the minds of audiences with theatrical experience. Tragedies and comedies make different demands on an audience. According to Marsha Norman's explanation of the "rules" of drama, you have to know in a play just what is at stake. Understanding the principles that have developed over the centuries to create the genres of drama helps us know what is at stake.

Elements of Drama

All plays share some basic elements with which playwrights and producers work: plots, characters, settings, dialogue, movement, and themes. In addition, many modern plays pay close attention to lighting, costuming, music, and props. When we respond to a play, we observe the elements of drama in action together, and the total experience is rich, complex, and subtle. Occasionally, we respond primarily to an individual element—the theme or characterization, for instance—but that is rare. Our awareness of the elements of drama is most useful when we are thinking analytically about a play and the way it affects us.

For the sake of discussion, we will consider the way the basic elements of drama function in Lady Gregory's one-act play *The Rising of the Moon* (which follows this section). It has all the elements we expect from drama, and it is both a brief and a very successful play.

Plot

Plot is a term for the action of a drama. Plot implies that the **action** has a shape and form that will ultimately prove satisfying to the audience. Generally, a carefully plotted play begins with **exposition**, an explanation of what happened before the play began and of how the characters arrived at their present situation. The play continues, using **suspense** to build tension in the audience and in the characters and to develop further the pattern of **rising action**. The audience wonders what is going to happen, sees the characters set in motion, and then watches as certain questions implied by the drama are answered one by one. The action achieves its greatest tension as it moves to a point of **climax**, when a revelation is experienced, usually by the chief characters. Once the climax has been reached, the plot continues, sometimes very briefly, in a pattern of **falling action** as the drama reaches its conclusion and the characters understand their circumstances and themselves better than they did at the beginning of the play.

The function of plot is to give action a form that helps us understand elements of the drama in relation to one another. Plays can have several interrelated plots or only one. Lady Gregory's *The Rising of the Moon* has one very simple plot: a police sergeant is sent out with two policemen to make sure a political rebel does not escape from the area. The effect of the single plot is that the entire play focuses intensely on the interaction between the rebel, disguised as a ballad singer, and the sergeant. The sergeant meets the rebel, listens to him sing ballads, and then recognizes in him certain qualities they share. The audience wonders whether a reward of one hundred pounds will encourage the sergeant to arrest the ballad singer or, instead, the ballad singer's sense that his cause is just will persuade the sergeant to let him go. The climax of the action occurs when the sergeant's two policemen return and, as the ballad singer hides behind a barrel, ask whether the sergeant has seen any signs of the rebel. Not until that moment does the audience know for sure what the sergeant will do. When he gives his answer, the falling action begins.

Plots depend on **conflict** between characters, and in *The Rising of the Moon* the conflict is very deep. It is built into the characters themselves, but it is also part of the institution of law that the sergeant serves and the ongoing struggle for justice that the ballad singer serves. This conflict, still evident today, was a very significant national issue in Ireland when the play was first produced in Dublin in 1907.

Lady Gregory works subtly with the conflict between the sergeant and the ballad singer, showing that although they are on completely opposite sides of the law—and of the important political issues—they are more alike than they are different. The ballad singer begins to sing the "Granuaile," a revolutionary

For a tutorial on the elements of drama, click on *VirtualLit Drama Tutorials* at **bedfordstmartins.com/jacobus**.

song about England's unlawful dominance over Ireland through seven centuries; when he leaves out a line, the sergeant supplies it. In that action the sergeant reveals that even though he is paid by the English to keep law and order, his roots lie with the Irish people. By his knowledge of the revolutionary songs he reveals his sympathies.

Characterization   Lady Gregory has effectively joined **character** and conflict in *The Rising of the Moon:* as the conflict is revealed, the characters of the sergeant and the ballad singer are also revealed. At first the sergeant seems eager to get the reward, and he acts bossy with Policeman X and Policeman B. And when he first meets the ballad singer, he seems demanding and policemanlike. It is only when he begins to sense who the ballad singer really is that he changes and reveals a deep, sympathetic streak.

Lady Gregory, in a note to the play, said that in Ireland when the play was first produced, those who wanted Ireland to become part of England were incensed to see a policeman portrayed so as to show his sympathies with rebels. Those who wished Ireland to become a separate nation from England were equally shocked to see a policeman portrayed so sympathetically.

The sergeant and the ballad singer are both major characters in the play, but it is not clear that either is the villain or the hero. When the play begins, the sergeant seems to be the hero because he represents the law, and the ballad singer appears to be the villain because he has escaped from prison. But as the action develops, those characterizations change. What replaces them is an awareness of the complications that underlie the relationship between the law and the lawbreaker in some circumstances. This is part of the point of Lady Gregory's play.

Lady Gregory has given a very detailed portrait of both main characters, although in a one-act play she does not have enough space to be absolutely thorough in developing them. Yet we get an understanding of the personal ambitions of each character, and we understand both their relationship to Ireland and their particular allegiances as individuals. They speak with each other in enough detail to show that they understand each other, and when the ballad singer hides behind the barrel at the approach of the other two policemen, he indicates that he trusts the sergeant not to reveal him.

Policeman X and Policeman B are only sketched in. Yet their presence is important. It is with them that the sergeant reveals his official personality, and it is their presence at the end that represents the most important threat to the security of the ballad singer. We know, though, little or nothing about them personally. They are functionaries, a little like Rosencrantz and Guildenstern in *Hamlet,* but without the differentiating characterizations that Shakespeare was able to give minor players in his full-length play.

The plays collected in this book have some of the most remarkable characters ever created in literature. Tragedy usually demands complex characters, such as Oedipus, Antigone, Medea, Hamlet, and Willy Loman. We come to know them through their own words, through their interaction with other characters, through their expression of feelings, through their decisions, and through their presence onstage depicted in movement and gesture.

Tragicomedies offer individualized and complex characters, such as Madame Ranevskaya in *The Cherry Orchard,* Miss Julie in Strindberg's play by that name, and Nora Helmer in *A Doll House.* But just as effective in certain kinds of drama are characters drawn as types, such as Alceste, the misanthrope in Molière's play, and Everyman in medieval drama.

In many plays we see that the entire shape of the action derives from the characters, from their strengths and weaknesses. In such plays we do not feel that the action lies outside the characters and that they must live through an arbitrary sequence of events. Instead we believe that they create their own opportunities and problems.

Setting

The **setting** of a play includes many things. First, this term refers to the time and place in which the action occurs. Second, it refers to the scenery, the physical elements that appear onstage to vivify the author's stage directions. In Lady Gregory's play, we have a dock with barrels to suggest the locale, and darkness suggests night. These are important details that influence the emotional reaction of the audience.

Some plays make use of very elaborate settings; for example, August Wilson's *Fences* is produced with a detailed tenement backyard onstage. Others make use of simple settings, such as the empty stage of Pirandello's *Six Characters in Search of an Author.*

Lady Gregory's setting derives from her inspiration for the play. She visited the quays—places where boats dock and leave with goods—as a young girl and imagined how someone might escape from the nearby prison and make his getaway "under a load of kelp" in one of the ships. The quay represents the meeting of the land and water, and it represents the getaway, the possibility of freedom. The barrel is a symbol of trade, and the sergeant and the ballad singer sit on its top and trade the words of a revolutionary song with each other.

The title of the play refers to another element of the setting: the moonlight. The night protects the ballad singer, and it permits the sergeant to bend his sworn principles a bit. The rising of the moon, as a rebel song suggests, signifies a change in society, the time when "the small shall rise up and the big shall fall down." Lady Gregory uses these elements in the play in a very effective way, interrelating them so that their significance becomes increasingly apparent as the play progresses.

Dialogue

Plays depend for their unfolding on dialogue. The **dialogue** is the verbal exchanges between the characters. Since there is no description or commentary on the action, as there is in most novels, the dialogue must tell the whole story. Fine playwrights have developed ways of revealing character, advancing action, and introducing themes by a highly efficient use of dialogue.

Dialogue is spoken by one character to another, who then responds. But sometimes, as in Shakespeare's *Hamlet,* a character delivers a **soliloquy,** in which he or she speaks onstage to him- or herself. Ordinarily, such speeches take on importance because they are thought to be especially true. Characters, when they speak to each other, may well wish to deceive, but generally, when they speak to themselves, they have no reason to say anything but the truth.

In *The Rising of the Moon,* Lady Gregory has written an unusual form of dialogue that reveals a regional way of speaking. Lady Gregory was Anglo-Irish, but she lived in the west of Ireland and was familiar with the speech patterns that the characters in this play would have used. She has been recognized for her ability to re-create the speech of the rural Irish, and passages such as the following are meant to reveal the peculiarities of the rhythms and syntax of English as it was spoken in Ireland at the turn of the century:

> SERGEANT: Is he as bad as that?
> MAN: He is then.
> SERGEANT: Do you tell me so?

Lady Gregory makes a considerable effort to create dialogue that is rich in local color as well as in spirit. John Millington Synge, another Irish playwright, whose dialogue in *Riders to the Sea* is also an effort to re-create the sounds and rhythms of rural Irish speech, once said, "In a good play every speech should be as fully flavored as a nut or apple, and such speeches cannot be written by anyone who works among people who have shut their lips on poetry." Lady Gregory, who produced Synge's plays at the Abbey Theatre in Dublin, would certainly agree, as her dialogue in *The Rising of the Moon* amply shows.

Music

Lady Gregory introduces another dramatic element: music. In *The Rising of the Moon*, the music is integral to the plot because it allows the ballad singer, by omitting a line of a rebel song, gradually to expose the sergeant's sympathies with the rebel cause. The sergeant is at first mindful of his duty and insists that the balladeer stop, but eventually he is captivated by the music. As the ballad singer continues, he sings a song containing the title of the play, and the audience or reader realizes that the title exposes the play's rebel sympathies.

Incidental music is present in a great many of Shakespeare's plays. His songs are often cited for their particular excellence. Ophelia's song in act IV of *Hamlet* is deeply touching as a revelation of her mental disturbance. The song moves Laertes, who says, "Do you see this, O God?," and the audience, too, is moved. In the last act of *A Midsummer Night's Dream*, Shakespeare includes both music and dance to intensify the celebration of young lovers. The most frequently produced play of the eighteenth century, John Gay's *The Beggar's Opera*, used sixty-nine popular ballad tunes to punctuate the action. The *melo* in *melodrama* signals music, and nineteenth-century melodramas often began and ended with musical interludes.

Movement

We as readers or witnesses are energized by the movement of the characters in a play. As we read, stage directions inform us where the characters are, when they move, how they move, and perhaps even what the significance of their movement is. In modern plays, the author may give many directions for the action; in earlier plays, stage directions are few and often supplemented by those of a modern editor. In performance, the movements that you see may well have been invented by the director, although the text of a play often requires certain actions, as in the ghost scene and the final dueling scene in *Hamlet*. In some kinds of drama, such as musical comedy and Greek drama, part of the action may be danced.

Lady Gregory moves the ballad singer and the sergeant in telling ways. They move physically closer to each other as they become closer in their thinking. Their movement seems to pivot around the barrel, and in one of the most charming moments of the play, their eyes meet when the ballad singer sits on the barrel and comments on the way the sergeant is pacing back and forth. They then both sit on the barrel, facing in opposite directions, and share a pipe between them, almost as a peace offering.

Theme

The **theme** of a play is its message, its central concerns—in short, what the play is about. It is by no means a simple thing to decide what the theme of a play is, and many plays contain several themes rather than a single one. Often, the search for a theme tempts us to oversimplify, reducing a complex play to a relatively simple catchphrase.

Sophocles' *Antigone* focuses on the conflict between human law and the law of the gods when following both sets of laws seems to be impossible. Antigone wishes to honor the gods by burying her brother, but the law of Kreon decrees that he shall have no burial, since he is technically a traitor to the state. Similar themes are present in other Greek plays. *Hamlet* has many themes. On a very elementary level, the main theme of *Hamlet* is revenge. This is played out in the obligation of a son to avenge the murder of a father, even when the murderer is a kinsman. Another theme centers on corruption in the state of Denmark.

Lady Gregory's play has revolution as one theme. The rising of the moon is a sign for "the rising," or revolution, of the people against their English oppressors. The sergeant is an especially English emblem of oppression because the police were established by an Englishman, Robert Peele. At one point, the balladeer suggests the song "The Peeler and the Goat," but rejects it because in slang a "peeler" is a policeman.

Another important theme in *The Rising of the Moon* is that of unity among the Irish people. The sergeant seems to be at an opposite pole from the ballad singer when the play opens. He is posting signs announcing a reward that he could well use, since he is a family man. But as the play proceeds, the sergeant moves closer in thought to the Irish people, represented by the rebel, the ballad singer.

If concerned that readers and viewers will miss their thematic intentions, playwrights sometimes reveal these in one or two speeches. Usually, a careful reader or viewer has already divined the theme, and the speeches are intrusive. But Lady Gregory is able to introduce thematic material in certain moments of dialogue, as in this comment by the sergeant, revealing that the police are necessary to prevent a revolution:

> SERGEANT: Well, we have to do our duty in the force. Haven't we the whole coun-
> try depending on us to keep law and order? It's those that are down would be
> up and those that are up would be down, if it wasn't for us.

For the most part, the thematic material in *The Rising of the Moon* is spread evenly throughout, as is the case in most good plays.

In every play, the elements of drama will work differently, sometimes giving us the feeling that character is dominant over theme, or plot over character, or setting over both. Ordinarily, critics believe that character, plot, and theme are the most important elements of drama, while setting, dialogue, music, and movement come next. But in the best of dramas each has its importance and each balances the others. The plays in this collection strive for that harmony and achieve it memorably.

Lady Gregory

Isabella Augusta Persse (1852–1932) was born in the west of Ireland. Her family was known as "ascendancy stock"—that is, they were educated, wealthy, and Protestant, living in a land that was largely uneducated, poverty-ridden, and Roman Catholic. A gulf existed between the rich ascendancy families, who lived in great houses with considerable style, partaking in lavish hunts and balls, and the impoverished Irish, who lived in one-room straw-roofed homes and worked the soil with primitive tools.

Lady Gregory took a strong interest in the Irish language, stimulated in part by a nurse who often spoke the language to her when she was a child. Her nurse was an important source of Irish folklore and a contact with the people who lived in the modest cottages around her family estate. It was extraordinary for any wealthy Protestant to pay attention to the language or the life of the poor laborers of the west of Ireland. Yet these are the people who figure most prominently in the plays that Lady Gregory wrote in later life.

Isabella Persse met Sir William Gregory when she was on a family trip to Nice and Rome. They were actually neighbors in Ireland but only slightly acquainted. He was also of Irish ascendancy stock and had been governor of Ceylon. They were married a year after they met, when she was twenty-eight and he was sixty-three. Their marriage was apparently quite successful, and in 1881 their son, Robert Gregory, was born. They used the family home, Coole Park, as a retreat for short periods, but most of their time was spent traveling and living in London, where Sir William was a trustee of the National Gallery of Art. W. B. Yeats, Bernard Shaw, and numerous other important literary figures spent time in Coole Park and its beautiful great house in the early part of the twentieth century.

Lady Gregory led a relatively conventional life until Sir William Gregory died in 1892. According to the laws of that time, the estate passed to her son, so she anticipated a life of relatively modest circumstances. In the process of finishing Sir William's memoirs, she found herself to be a gifted writer. She used some of her spare time to learn Irish well enough to talk with the old cottagers in the hills, where she went to gather folklore and old songs. Although W. B. Yeats and others had collected volumes of Irish stories and poems, they did not know Irish well enough to authenticate what they heard. Lady Gregory published her Kiltartan tales (she had dubbed her neighborhood Kiltartan) as a way of preserving the rapidly disappearing myths and stories that were still told around the hearth as a matter of course in rural Ireland.

She was already an accomplished writer when she met W. B. Yeats in 1894. Their meeting was of immense importance for the history of drama, since they decided to marshal their complementary talents and abilities to create an Irish theater. Their discussions included certain Irish neighbors, among them Edward Martyn, a Catholic whose early plays had been very successful. They also talked with Dr. Douglas Hyde, a mythographer and linguist and the first president of modern Ireland. Another neighbor who took part, the flamboyant George Moore, was a well-established novelist and playwright.

The group's first plays—Yeats's *The Countess Cathleen* and Martyn's *The Heather Field*—were performed on May 8 and 9, 1899, under the auspices of the newly formed Irish Literary Theatre in Dublin at the Ancient Concert

Rooms. Dedicated to producing plays by Irish playwrights on Irish themes, the Irish Literary Theatre became an immediate success. The greatest problem the founders faced was finding more plays. Lady Gregory tried her own hand and became, at age fifty, a playwright.

Her ear for people's speech was unusually good—good enough that she was able to give the great poet Yeats lessons in dialogue and to help him prepare his own plays for the stage. She collaborated with Yeats on *The Pot of Broth* in 1902, the year she wrote her first plays, *The Jackdaw* and *A Losing Game*. Her first produced play, *Twenty-Five*, was put on in 1903. By 1904, the group had rented the historic Abbey Theatre. Some of her plays were quite popular and were successful even in later revivals: *Spreading the News* (1904); *Kincora* and *The White Cockade* (1905); and *Hyacinth Halvey, The Doctor in Spite of Himself, The Gaol Gate,* and *The Canavans* (all 1906). The next year, there were troubles at the Abbey over John Millington Synge's *Playboy of the Western World.* The middle-class audience resented the portrait of Irish peasants as people who would celebrate a self-confessed father-killer, even though he had not actually done the "gallous deed." Lady Gregory faced down rioting audience members who were protesting what she was convinced was excellent drama.

In 1918, her son, a World War I pilot, was shot down over Italy. The years that followed were to some extent years of struggle. Lady Gregory managed the Abbey Theatre, directed its affairs, and developed new playwrights, among them Sean O'Casey. During the Irish Civil War (1920–1922), she was physically threatened, and eventually her family home, Roxborough, was burned. In 1926, after discovering that she had cancer, she made arrangements to sell Coole Park to the government with the agreement that she could remain there for life. She died in 1932, the writer of a large number of satisfying plays and the prime mover in developing one of the twentieth century's most important literary theaters.

The Rising of the Moon

One of Lady Gregory's shortest but most popular plays, *The Rising of the Moon* is openly political in its themes. Lady Gregory had been writing plays only a short time, and she was directing the Abbey Theatre Company when it produced this play in 1907. Her interest in Irish politics developed, she said, when she was going through the papers of a distant relative of her husband. That man had been in the Castle, the offices of the English authorities given the task of ruling Ireland from Dublin. She said that the underhanded dealings revealed in those papers persuaded her that Ireland would need to be a nation apart from England if justice were ever to be done.

In 1907, the question of union with England or separation and nationhood was on everyone's lips. Ireland was calm, and people in Dublin were relatively prosperous and by no means readying for a fight or a revolution. Yet there had been a tradition of risings against the English dating back to the Elizabethan age and earlier. In 1907, the average Irish person believed that revolution was a thing of the past; actually, it was less than ten years in the future. Certain organizations, notably the widespread Gaelic League and the less-known Sinn Féin (We Ourselves), had been developing to promote Irish lore, language, and culture. English was the dominant language in Ireland, since it was the language of commerce, but its use tended to obliterate the Irish culture. Lady Gregory's work with the Abbey Theatre, which was making one of the age's most important contributions to Irish culture, thus coincided with growing interest throughout Ireland in rediscovering its literary past.

The title *The Rising of the Moon* comes from a popular old rebel song that pointed to the rising of the moon as the signal for the rising of peoples against oppression. The main characters of the play represent the two opposing forces in Ireland: freedom and independence, personified by the ballad singer ("a Ragged Man"), and law and order, represented by the sergeant. The ballad singer is aligned with those who want to change the social structure of Ireland so that the people now on the bottom will be on top. The sergeant's job is to preserve the status quo and avoid such a turning of the tables.

In an important way, the sergeant and the ballad singer represent the two alternatives that face the modern Irish—now as in the past. One alternative is to accept the power of the English and be in their pay, like the sergeant; such a person would be well fed and capable of supporting a family. The other alternative is to follow the revolutionary path of the ballad singer and risk prison, scorn, and impoverishment. The ballad singer is a ragged man because he has been totally reduced in circumstances by his political choices.

For Lady Gregory, this play was a serious political statement. She and W. B. Yeats—both aristocratic Protestant Irish—were sympathetic to Irish revolutionary causes. They each wrote plays that struck a revolutionary note during this period. Neither truly expected a revolution; when the Easter Uprising of 1916 was put down with considerable loss of life, Yeats lamented that his plays may have sent some young men to their deaths.

The success of *The Rising of the Moon* lies in Lady Gregory's exceptional ear for dialogue. She captures the way people speak, and she also manages to draw the characters of the sergeant and the ballad singer so as to gain our sympathies for both. In a remarkably economic fashion, she dramatizes the problem of politics in Ireland, characterizing the two polarities and revealing some of the complexities that face anyone who tries to understand them.

For discussion questions and assignments on *The Rising of the Moon*, visit bedfordstmartins.com/jacobus.

LADY GREGORY (1852–1932)

The Rising of the Moon   1907

Persons

SERGEANT	POLICEMAN B
POLICEMAN X	A RAGGED MAN

Scene: *Side of a quay in a seaport town. Some posts and chains. A large barrel. Enter three policemen. Moonlight.*

(Sergeant, who is older than the others, crosses the stage to right and looks down steps. The others put down a pastepot and unroll a bundle of placards.)

POLICEMAN B: I think this would be a good place to put up a notice. (*He points to barrel.*)

POLICEMAN X: Better ask him. (*Calls to Sergeant.*) Will this be a good place for a placard?

(*No answer.*)

POLICEMAN B: Will we put up a notice here on the barrel?

(*No answer.*)

SERGEANT: There's a flight of steps here that leads to the water. This is a place that should be minded well. If he got down here, his friends might have a boat to meet him; they might send it in here from outside.

POLICEMAN B: Would the barrel be a good place to put a notice up?

SERGEANT: It might; you can put it there.

(*They paste the notice up.*)

SERGEANT (*reading it*): Dark hair—dark eyes, smooth face, height five feet five—there's not much to take hold of in that—It's a pity I had no chance of seeing him before he broke out of jail. They say he's a wonder, that it's he makes all the plans for the whole organization. There isn't another man in Ireland would have broken jail the way he did. He must have some friends among the jailers.

POLICEMAN B: A hundred pounds is little enough for the Government to offer for him. You may be sure any man in the force that takes him will get promotion.

SERGEANT: I'll mind this place myself. I wouldn't wonder at all if he came this way. He might come slipping along there (*points to side of quay*), and his friends might be waiting for him there (*points down steps*), and once he got away it's little chance we'd have of finding him; it's maybe under a load of kelp he'd be in a fishing boat, and not one to help a married man that wants it to the reward.

POLICEMAN X: And if we get him itself, nothing but abuse on our heads for it from the people, and maybe from our own relations.

SERGEANT: Well, we have to do our duty in the force. Haven't we the whole country depending on us to keep law and order? It's those that are down would be up and those that are up would be down, if it wasn't for us. Well, hurry on, you have plenty of other places to placard yet, and come back here then to me. You can take the lantern. Don't be too long now. It's very lonesome here with nothing but the moon.

POLICEMAN B: It's a pity we can't stop with you. The Government should have brought more police into the town, with *him* in jail, and at assize° time too. Well, good luck to your watch.

(*They go out.*)

SERGEANT (*walks up and down once or twice and looks at placard*): A hundred pounds and promotion sure. There must be a great deal of spending in a hundred pounds. It's a pity some honest man not to be better of that.

(*A Ragged Man appears at left and tries to slip past. Sergeant suddenly turns.*)

SERGEANT: Where are you going?

assize: Judicial inquest.

MAN: I'm a poor ballad-singer, your honor. I thought to sell some of these (*holds out bundle of ballads*) to the sailors.

(*He goes on.*)

SERGEANT: Stop! Didn't I tell you to stop? You can't go on there.

MAN: Oh, very well. It's a hard thing to be poor. All the world's against the poor!

SERGEANT: Who are you?

MAN: You'd be as wise as myself if I told you, but I don't mind. I'm one Jimmy Walsh, a ballad-singer.

SERGEANT: Jimmy Walsh? I don't know that name.

MAN: Ah, sure, they know it well enough in Ennis. Were you ever in Ennis, sergeant?

SERGEANT: What brought you here?

MAN: Sure, it's to the assizes I came, thinking I might make a few shillings here or there. It's in the one train with the judges I came.

SERGEANT: Well, if you came so far, you may as well go farther, for you'll walk out of this.

MAN: I will, I will; I'll just go on where I was going.

(*Goes toward steps.*)

SERGEANT: Come back from those steps; no one has leave to pass down them tonight.

MAN: I'll just sit on the top of the steps till I see will some sailor buy a ballad off me that would give me my supper. They do be late going back to the ship. It's often I saw them in Cork carried down the quay in a handcart.

SERGEANT: Move on, I tell you. I won't have anyone lingering about the quay tonight.

MAN: Well, I'll go. It's the poor have the hard life! Maybe yourself might like one, sergeant. Here's a good sheet now. (*Turns one over.*) "Content and a pipe"— that's not much. "The Peeler and the goat"—you wouldn't like that. "Johnny Hart"—that's a lovely song.

SERGEANT: Move on.

MAN: Ah, wait till you hear it. (*Sings.*)

There was a rich farmer's daughter lived near the town of Ross;
She courted a Highland soldier, his name was Johnny Hart;
Says the mother to her daughter, "I'll go distracted mad
If you marry that Highland soldier dressed up in Highland plaid."

SERGEANT: Stop that noise.

(*Man wraps up his ballads and shuffles toward the steps.*)

SERGEANT: Where are you going?

MAN: Sure you told me to be going, and I am going.

SERGEANT: Don't be a fool. I didn't tell you to go that way; I told you to go back to the town.

MAN: Back to the town, is it?

SERGEANT (*taking him by the shoulder and shoving him before him*): Here, I'll show you the way. Be off with you. What are you stopping for?

MAN (*who has been keeping his eye on the notice, points to it*): I think I know what you're waiting for, sergeant.

SERGEANT: What's that to you?

MAN: And I know well the man you're waiting for—I know him well—I'll be going.

(*He shuffles on.*)

SERGEANT: You know him? Come back here. What sort is he?

MAN: Come back is it, sergeant? Do you want to have me killed?

SERGEANT: Why do you say that?

MAN: Never mind. I'm going. I wouldn't be in your shoes if the reward was ten times as much. (*Goes on off stage to left.*) Not if it was ten times as much.

SERGEANT (*rushing after him*): Come back here, come back. (*Drags him back.*) What sort is he? Where did you see him?

MAN: I saw him in my own place, in the County Clare. I tell you you wouldn't like to be looking at him. You'd be afraid to be in the one place with him. There isn't a weapon he doesn't know the use of, and as to strength, his muscles are as hard as that board (*slaps barrel*).

SERGEANT: Is he as bad as that?

MAN: He is then.

SERGEANT: Do you tell me so?

MAN: There was a poor man in our place, a sergeant from Ballyvaughan.—It was with a lump of stone he did it.

SERGEANT: I never heard of that.

MAN: And you wouldn't, sergeant. It's not everything that happens gets into the papers. And there was a policeman in plain clothes, too. . . . It is in Limerick he was. . . . It was after the time of the attack on the police barrack at Kilmallock. . . . Moonlight . . . just like this . . . waterside. . . . Nothing was known for certain.

SERGEANT: Do you say so? It's a terrible county to belong to.

MAN: That's so, indeed! You might be standing there, looking out that way, thinking you saw him coming up this side of the quay (*points*), and he might be coming up this other side (*points*), and he'd be on you before you knew where you were.

SERGEANT: It's a whole troop of police they ought to put here to stop a man like that.

MAN: But if you'd like me to stop with you, I could be looking down this side. I could be sitting up here on this barrel.

SERGEANT: And you know him well, too?

MAN: I'd know him a mile off, sergeant.

SERGEANT: But you wouldn't want to share the reward?

MAN: Is it a poor man like me, that has to be going the roads and singing in fairs, to have the name on him that he took a reward? But you don't want me. I'll be safer in the town.

SERGEANT: Well, you can stop.

MAN (*getting up on barrel*): All right, sergeant. I wonder, now, you're not tired out, sergeant, walking up and down the way you are.

SERGEANT: If I'm tired I'm used to it.

MAN: You might have hard work before you tonight yet. Take it easy while you can. There's plenty of room up here on the barrel, and you see farther when you're higher up.

SERGEANT: Maybe so. (*Gets up beside him on barrel, facing right. They sit back to back, looking different ways.*) You made me feel a bit queer with the way you talked.

MAN: Give me a match, sergeant (*he gives it and man lights pipe*); take a draw yourself? It'll quiet you. Wait now till I give you a light, but you needn't turn round. Don't take your eye off the quay for the life of you.

SERGEANT: Never fear, I won't. (*Lights pipe. They both smoke.*) Indeed it's a hard thing to be in the force, out at night and no thanks for it, for all the danger we're in. And it's little we get but abuse from the people, and no choice but to obey our orders, and never asked when a man is sent into danger, if you are a married man with a family.

MAN (*sings*): As through the hills I walked to view the hills and shamrock plain,
I stood awhile where nature smiles to view the rocks and streams,
On a matron fair I fixed my eyes beneath a fertile vale,
And she sang her song it was on the wrong of poor old Granuaile.

SERGEANT: Stop that; that's no song to be singing in these times.

MAN: Ah, sergeant, I was only singing to keep my heart up. It sinks when I think of him. To think of us two sitting here, and he creeping up the quay, maybe, to get to us.

SERGEANT: Are you keeping a good lookout?

MAN: I am; and for no reward too. Amn't I the foolish man? But when I saw a man in trouble, I never could help trying to get him out of it. What's that? Did something hit me?

(*Rubs his heart.*)

SERGEANT (*patting him on the shoulder*): You will get your reward in heaven.

MAN: I know that, I know that, sergeant, but life is precious.

SERGEANT: Well, you can sing if it gives you more courage.

MAN (*sings*): Her head was bare, her hands and feet with iron bands were bound,
Her pensive strain and plaintive wail mingles with the evening gale,
And the song she sang with mournful air, I am old Granuaile.
Her lips so sweet that monarchs kissed . . .

SERGEANT: That's not it. . . . "Her gown she wore was stained with gore." . . . That's it—you missed that.

MAN: You're right, sergeant, so it is; I missed it. (*Repeats line.*) But to think of a man like you knowing a song like that.

SERGEANT: There's many a thing a man might know and might not have any wish for.

MAN: Now, I daresay, sergeant, in your youth, you used to be sitting up on a wall, the way you are sitting up on this barrel now, and the other lads beside you, and you singing "Granuaile"? . . .

SERGEANT: I did then.

MAN: And the "Shan Van Vocht"? . . .

SERGEANT: I did then.

MAN: And the "Green on the Cape"?

SERGEANT: That was one of them.

MAN: And maybe the man you are watching for tonight used to be sitting on the wall, when he was young, and singing those same songs. . . . It's a queer world. . . .

SERGEANT: Whisht! . . . I think I see something coming. . . . It's only a dog.

MAN: And isn't it a queer world? . . . Maybe it's one of the boys you used to be singing with that time you will be arresting today or tomorrow, and sending into the dock. . . .

SERGEANT: That's true indeed.

MAN: And maybe one night, after you had been singing, if the other boys had told you some plan they had, some plan to free the country, you might have joined with them . . . and maybe it is you might be in trouble now.

SERGEANT: Well, who knows but I might? I had a great spirit in those days.

MAN: It's a queer world, sergeant, and it's little any mother knows when she sees her child creeping on the floor what might happen to it before it has gone through its life, or who will be who in the end.

SERGEANT: That's a queer thought now, and a true thought. Wait now till I think it out. . . . If it wasn't for the sense I have, and for my wife and family, and for me joining the force the time I did, it might be myself now would be after breaking jail and hiding in the dark, and it might be him that's hiding in the dark and that got out of jail would be sitting up here where I am on this barrel. . . . And it might be myself would be creeping up trying to make my escape from himself, and it might be himself would be keeping the law, and myself would be breaking it, and myself would be trying to put a bullet in his head, or to take up a lump of stone the way you said he did . . . no, that myself did. . . . Oh! (*Gasps. After a pause.*) What's that? (*Grasps man's arm.*)

MAN (*jumps off barrel and listens, looking out over water*): It's nothing, sergeant.

SERGEANT: I thought it might be a boat. I had a notion there might be friends of his coming about the quays with a boat.

MAN: Sergeant, I am thinking it was with the people you were, and not with the law you were, when you were a young man.

SERGEANT: Well, if I was foolish then, that time's gone.

MAN: Maybe, sergeant, it comes into your head sometimes, in spite of your belt and your tunic, that it might have been as well for you to have followed Granuaile.

SERGEANT: It's no business of yours what I think.

MAN: Maybe, sergeant, you'll be on the side of the country yet.

SERGEANT (*gets off barrel*): Don't talk to me like that. I have my duties and I know them. (*Looks round.*) That was a boat; I hear the oars.

(*Goes to the steps and looks down.*)

MAN (*sings*): O, then, tell me, Shawn O'Farrell,
  Where the gathering is to be.
In the old spot by the river
  Right well known to you and me!

SERGEANT: Stop that! Stop that, I tell you!

MAN (*sings louder*): One word more, for signal token,
  Whistle up the marching tune,
With your pike upon your shoulder,
  At the Rising of the Moon.

SERGEANT: If you don't stop that, I'll arrest you.

(*A whistle from below answers, repeating the air.*)

SERGEANT: That's a signal. (*Stands between him and steps.*) You must not pass this way. . . . Step farther back. . . . Who are you? You are no ballad-singer.

MAN: You needn't ask who I am; that placard will tell you. (*Points to placard.*)

SERGEANT: You are the man I am looking for.

MAN (*takes off hat and wig. Sergeant seizes them*): I am. There's a hundred pounds on my head. There is a friend of mine below in a boat. He knows a safe place to bring me to.

SERGEANT (*looking still at hat and wig*): It's a pity! It's a pity. You deceived me. You deceived me well.

MAN: I am a friend of Granuaile. There is a hundred pounds on my head.

SERGEANT: It's a pity, it's a pity!

MAN: Will you let me pass, or must I make you let me?

SERGEANT: I am in the force. I will not let you pass.

MAN: I thought to do it with my tongue. (*Puts hand in breast.*) What is that?

VOICE OF POLICEMAN X (*outside*): Here, this is where we left him.

SERGEANT: It's my comrades coming.

MAN: You won't betray me . . . the friend of Granuaile. (*Slips behind barrel.*)

VOICE OF POLICEMAN B: That was the last of the placards.

POLICEMAN X (*as they come in*): If he makes his escape it won't be unknown he'll make it.

(*Sergeant puts hat and wig behind his back.*)

POLICEMAN B: Did anyone come this way?

SERGEANT (*after a pause*): No one.

POLICEMAN B: No one at all?

SERGEANT: No one at all.

POLICEMAN B: We had no orders to go back to the station; we can stop along with you.

SERGEANT: I don't want you. There is nothing for you to do here.

POLICEMAN B: You bade us to come back here and keep watch with you.

SERGEANT: I'd sooner be alone. Would any man come this way and you making all that talk? It is better the place to be quiet.

POLICEMAN B: Well, we'll leave you the lantern anyhow.

(*Hands it to him.*)

SERGEANT: I don't want it. Bring it with you.

POLICEMAN B: You might want it. There are clouds coming up and you have the darkness of the night before you yet. I'll leave it over here on the barrel. (*Goes to barrel.*)

SERGEANT: Bring it with you, I tell you. No more talk.

POLICEMAN B: Well, I thought it might be a comfort to you. I often think when I have it in my hand and can be flashing it about into every dark corner (*doing so*) that it's the same as being beside the fire at home, and the bits of bogwood blazing up now and again.

(*Flashes it about, now on the barrel, now on Sergeant.*)

SERGEANT (*furious*): Be off the two of you, yourselves and your lantern!

(*They go out. Man comes from behind barrel. He and Sergeant stand looking at one another.*)

SERGEANT: What are you waiting for?

MAN: For my hat, of course, and my wig. You wouldn't wish me to get my death of cold?

(*Sergeant gives them.*)

MAN (*going toward steps*): Well, good night, comrade, and thank you. You did me a good turn tonight, and I'm obliged to you. Maybe I'll be able to do as much for you when the small rise up and the big fall down . . . when we all change places at the Rising (*waves his hand and disappears*) of the Moon.

SERGEANT (*turning his back to audience and reading placard*): A hundred pounds reward! A hundred pounds! (*Turns toward audience.*) I wonder, now, am I as great a fool as I think I am?

Greek Drama

Because our historical knowledge of Greek drama is limited to what we can glean from the available contemporary commentaries and from partial archaeological remains—in the form of ruined theaters—we do not know when Greek theater began or what its original impulses were. Our best information points to 534 BCE as the beginning of the formal competitions among playwrights for coveted prizes that continued to be awarded for several centuries. Thespis, credited as the first tragedy writer, seems to have changed the nature of the form by stepping out of the chorus and taking a solo part. But the origin of *tragedy,* the Greek word for which translates to "goat-song" or "song for the sacrificial goat," is obscure. One theory is that tragedy may have developed from the rites of rural cults that sacrificed a she-goat at some Dionysian festivals or from masked animal dances at certain cult celebrations.

One source that may well have influenced the Greeks was the Egyptian civilization of the first millennium BCE. Egyptian culture was fully formed, brilliant, and complex, with numerous religious festivals and a pantheon of gods who resembled, and possibly inspired, those of the Greeks. Although it is not certain that Egypt produced a fully formed dramatic literature, certain major festivals and ceremonies that were performed annually, such as the Abydos Passion Play outlining the death and resurrection of Osiris, seem to have counterparts in Greek rituals and drama. The Abydos Passion Play tells the story of the betrayal and murder of Osiris by his jealous brother Seth, the scattering of his remains, and the efforts of Isis to reclaim and reassemble them to permit his rebirth.

The closest Greek counterpart to Osiris was **Dionysus**, who inspired orgiastic celebrations that found their way into early Greek drama. Dionysus was an agricultural deity, the Greek god of wine and the symbol of life-giving power. In several myths, he, like Osiris, was ritually killed and dismembered and his parts scattered through the land. These myths paralleled the agricultural cycle of death and disintegration during the winter, followed by cultivation and rebirth in the spring, and reinforced the Greeks' understanding of the meaning of birth, life, and death.

The Development of Greek Drama

Drama developed in ancient Greece in close connection with the Dionysia, religious celebrations dedicated to Dionysus. Four Dionysiac celebrations were held each winter in Athens, beginning at the grape harvest and culminating during the first wine tastings: the Rural Dionysia in December, the Lenaia in January, the Anthesteria in February, and the City Dionysia in March. Except for the Anthesteria, the festivals featured drama contests among playwrights, and some of the works performed in those competitions have endured through the centuries. Theories that connect the origins of drama with religion hypothesize that one function of the religious festivals within which the drama competitions took place was the ritual attempt to guarantee fertility and the growth of the crops, on which the society depended.

The **City Dionysia**, the most lavish of the festivals, lasted from five to seven days. It was open to non-Athenians and therefore offered Athenians the opportunity to show off their wealth, their glorious history, and their heroes, who were often honored in parades the day before the plays began. There is some question about what was presented on each day. Two days were probably taken up with dithyrambic contests among the ten tribes of Athens. Generally each tribe presented two choruses—one of men and one of boys—each singing a narrative lyric called a **dithyramb**. Three days were devoted to contests among tragedians, most of whom worked for half the year on three tragedies and a **satyr play**, an erotic piece of comic relief that ended the day's performance. A tragedian's three plays sometimes had related themes or myths, but often they did not. The tragedians wrote the plays; trained and rehearsed the actors; composed music; and created the setting, dances, costumes, and masks. Judges chosen by lottery awarded prizes. First prize went to the tragedian whose four plays were most powerful and most beautifully conceived.

After 486 BCE, when the first comedy competition was held, five and later three comedies were also presented during the festival. The performances were paid for by wealthy Athenians as part of their civic duty. The great Greek plays thus were not commercial enterprises but an important part of civic and religious festivals.

The Greeks and Their Gods

The great achievement of Greek religion was the humanizing of their gods. Apollo, Zeus, Aphrodite, Athena, and Bacchus had recognizable emotions and pleasures. The Greeks built temples to their gods and made offerings at appropriate times to avoid catastrophe and bad luck. But the Greeks had no official religious text, no system of religious belief that they all followed, and few ethical teachings derived from religion. The impression we have today is that Greeks' efforts to define and know the gods were shaped by great artists such as Phidias, who sculpted Zeus at Olympia; Homer, who portrayed the gods in *The Iliad* and *The Odyssey*; and the great Greek playwrights, who sometimes revealed the actions of the gods. Our present knowledge of Greek gods resides in the literary and artistic remains of Greek culture.

Fortunately for us, most Greek drama was associated with important celebrations designed to honor Greek gods. We would not, however, call this drama religious in nature—as we characterize the medieval drama designated to celebrate Christian holidays. What we learn from Greek drama is that the gods can favor individual humans for reasons of their own. And likewise, the gods can choose to punish individual humans. To some extent Greek drama is designed to explain the divine approach to favor and disfavor.

The Greek Stage

At the center of the Greek theater was the **orchestra**, where the chorus sang and danced (*orches* is derived from the Greek for "dancing place"). The audience, sometimes numbering fifteen thousand, sat in rising rows on three sides of the orchestra. The steep sides of a hill formed a natural amphitheater for Greek audiences. Eventually, on the rim of the orchestra, an oblong building called the **skene**, or scene house, developed as a space for the actors and a background for the action. The term **proskenion** was sometimes used to refer to a raised stage added in later times in front of the *skene* where the actors performed. The theater in Epidaurus (Figure 1) was a model for the Greek theater plan (Figure 2).

Greek theaters were widely dispersed from Greece to present-day Turkey, to Sicily, and even to southern France. Wherever the Greeks developed new colonies and city-states, they built theaters. In many of the surviving theaters the acoustics are so fine that a human voice onstage can be heard from any seat in the theater.

Perhaps the most spectacular theatrical device used by the Greek playwrights, the **mekane** ("machine"), was implemented onstage by means of elaborate booms or derricks. Actors were lowered onto the stage to enact the roles of Olympian gods intervening in the affairs of humans. Some commentators, such as Aristotle (384–322 BCE), believed that the *mekane* should be used only if the intercession of deities was in keeping with the character of the play. The last of the great Greek tragedians, Euripides (c. 485–c. 406 BCE), used the device in almost half of his tragedies. In *Medea*, Euripides uses the *mekane* to lift Medea to the roof of the *skene* and into her dragon chariot as a means of resolving the play's conflict. At the end of the play, Medea is beyond

Figure 1. The theater in Epidaurus, Greece, looking east. The best preserved (and now restored) Greek theater, it remains in use today. Built in the fourth century BCE by Polykleitos the Younger and approximately 124 feet in diameter, it seats twelve thousand people and has excellent acoustics.

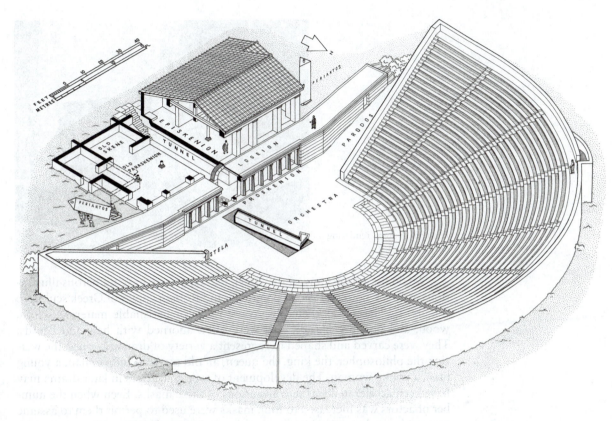

Figure 2. The Hellenistic theater in Eretria, Greece.

her persecutors' reach and is headed for safety in another country. Modern dramatists use a metaphorical version of this device called *deus ex machina* (literally, "the god from the machine") when they rescue characters at the last moment by improbable accidents or strokes of luck. Usually, these are unsatisfying means of solving dramatic problems.

The Greek Actor

According to legend, Thespis (sixth century BCE) was the first actor—the first person to step from the chorus to act in dialogue with it—thus creating the **agon,** or dramatic confrontation. He won the first prize for tragedy in 534 BCE. As the only actor, he took several parts, wearing **masks** to distinguish the different characters. One actor was the norm in tragedies until Aeschylus (c. 525–456 BCE), the first important Greek tragedian whose work survives, introduced a second actor and then Sophocles (c. 496–c. 406 BCE) added a third. Later, comedy used four actors. The chorus and all the actors were male.

Like the actors, the members of the chorus wore masks. At first the masks were simple, but they became more ornate, often decorated with details that established the gender, age, or station of each character. Despite the excellent acoustics in the largest of theaters, the actor had to project his voice for some distance, and certain masks were designed to amplify the voice to reach the most distant rows.

Figure 3. Roman rendering of Greek masks.

We do not possess any of the Greek masks, but we have numerous illustrations in Greek pottery, Roman paintings, and Roman copies of Greek sculpture (Figure 3). The masks themselves were made of perishable materials (cloth, wood, and possibly plaster) and were often adorned with hair and beards. They were carved and shaped to represent a variety of dramatic types: the warrior, the philosopher, the king, the queen, an old man, an old woman, a young man, a young woman. The development of type characters in later drama may have been accelerated by the conventions of these masks. Even when the number of actors was increased to four, masks were used to permit them to assume many roles and create a high level of dramatic complexity.

The demands on Greek actors were considerable. They were expected to be in good physical condition so as to dance with grace. Their voices had to be full and expressive, as well as flexible enough to represent different characters. The audience members sitting close to the actors were often taken by the sincerity or expressiveness of the eyes seen within the mask. Often the authors themselves, such as Thespis and Aeschylus, were among the most prominent actors of their time and were celebrated for their dramatic abilities.

Genres of Greek Drama

Greek drama developed three distinct genres: tragedy, satyr plays, and comedy. The most fully developed and valued genre is tragedy: the story, usually based on Greek myth, of the downfall of a noble figure. The satyr play followed a trilogy of tragedies. A chorus of satyrs, each half man and half goat or beast, enacted scenes from Greek myth in a sometimes crude and farcical fashion. Until the development of comedy, satyr plays provided the emotional relief needed after watching three tragedies. Comedy developed in two subgenres. Old Comedy, associated with Aristophanes, was often coarse and ribald, satirizing the foibles of important politicians and sometimes even important playwrights. New Comedy, associated with Menander, was more refined and avoided criticizing individuals while expressing a broad social criticism.

Tragedy

Greek tragedy focused on a person of noble birth who often had risen to a great height and then fell precipitously. Tragedies showed humans at the mercy of **moira**, their fate, which they only partly understood. One objective of

Greek drama was to have the audience experience a **catharsis,** which Aristotle describes as a purging or purifying of the emotions of pity and fear. According to the Greeks, these are emotions that a person associates with the fall of someone in a high social station, such as a king or queen. A central character, or **protagonist,** of noble birth was therefore an essential element for the playwright striving to evoke catharsis in an audience. Twentieth-century experiments with tragic figures who are ordinary people, such as Arthur Miller's *Death of a Salesman,* as masterful as they are, would not have made sense to the Greeks. For the Greeks, tragedy could befall only the great.

The modern critic Kenneth Burke identified a pattern for Greek tragedies. The tragic figure—for whom the play is usually named—experiences three stages of development: purpose, passion, and perception. The play begins with a purpose, such as finding the source of the plague in *Oedipus Rex.* Then, as the path becomes tangled and events unfold, the tragic figure begins an extensive process of soul-searching and suffers an inner agony—the passion. The perception of the truth involves a fate that the tragic figure would rather not face. It might be death or, as in *Oedipus Rex,* exile. It always involves separation from the human community. For the Greeks, that was the greatest punishment.

According to Aristotle, the tragic hero's perception of the truth is the most intense moment in the drama. He calls it **anagnorisis,** or recognition. Aristotle believed that when this recognition came at the same moment that the tragic figure's fortunes reversed—the **peripeteia**—the tragedy was most fulfilling for the audience. This is the case in *Oedipus Rex.* Aristotle's comments in his *Poetics* on the structure and effect of *Oedipus Rex* remain the most significant critical observations made by a contemporary on Greek theater. (See the excerpt from the *Poetics* that begins on page 67.)

The earliest tragedies seem to have developed from the emotional, intense dithyrambs sung by Athenian choruses. The **chorus** in most tragedies numbered twelve or fifteen men, who usually represented the citizenry in the drama. They dressed simply, and their song was sometimes sung in unison, sometimes delivered by the chorus leader. Originally, there were no actors separate from the chorus.

Eventually the structure of the plays became elaborated into a series of alternations between the characters' dialogue and the choral odes, with each speaking part developing the action or responding to it. Often crucial information furthering the action came from the mouth of a messenger, as in *Oedipus Rex.* The tragedies were structured in three parts: the **prologue** established the conflict; the episodes, or agons, developed the dramatic relationships between characters; and the **exodos** concluded the action. Between these sections the chorus performed different songs: **parodos** while moving onto the stage and **stasima** while standing still. In some plays, the chorus sang choral **odes** called the **strophe** as it moved from right to left. It sang the **antistrophe** while moving back to the right. The actors' episodes consisted of dialogue with each other and with the chorus. The scholar Bernhard Zimmerman has plotted the structure of *Oedipus Rex* in this fashion:

Prologue: Dialogue with Oedipus, the Priests, and Kreon establishing that the plague afflicting Thebes will cease when Laios's murderer is found.

Parodos: The opening hymn of the Chorus appealing to the gods.

First Episode: Oedipus seeks the murderer; Teiresias says it is Oedipus.

First Stasimon: The Chorus supports Oedipus, disbelieving Teiresias.

Second Episode: Oedipus accuses Kreon of being in league with Teiresias and the real murderer. Iokaste pleads for Kreon and tells the oracle of Oedipus's birth and of the death of Laios at the fork of a road. Oedipus sends for the eyewitness of the murder.

Second Stasimon: The Chorus, in a song, grows agitated for Oedipus.

Third Episode: The messenger from Oedipus's "hometown" tells him that his adoptive father has died and is not his real father. Iokaste guesses the truth and Oedipus becomes deeply worried.

Third Stasimon: The Chorus delivers a reassuring, hopeful song.

Fourth Episode: Oedipus, the Shepherd, and the Messenger confront the facts and Oedipus experiences the turning point of the play: he realizes he is the murderer he seeks.

Fourth Stasimon: The Chorus sings of the illusion of human happiness.

Exodos: Iokaste kills herself; Oedipus puts out his eyes; the Chorus and Kreon try to decide the best future action.

As this brief structural outline of *Oedipus Rex* demonstrates, the chorus assumed an important part in the tragedies. In Aeschylus's *Agamemnon*, it represents the elders of the community. In Sophocles' *Oedipus Rex*, it is a group of concerned citizens who give Oedipus advice and make demands on him. In *Antigone*, the chorus consists of men loyal to the state. In Euripides' *Medea*, the chorus is a group of the important women of Corinth.

Satyr Plays

The drama competitions held regularly from 534 BCE consisted usually of the work of three playwrights who each produced three tragedies and one satyr play, a form of comic relief. In a satyr play, the chorus dressed as satyrs, cavorting with a **phallus**, a mock penis, and engaging in riotous, almost slapstick antics. The characters were not psychologically developed, as they were in tragedy; the situations were not socially instructive, as they were in comedy. Rough-hewn and lighthearted, the satyr plays may have been a necessary antidote to the intensity of the tragedies.

Only one satyr play survives, perhaps an indication that the form was not as highly valued as tragedy. In Euripides' *Cyclops*, based on Odysseus's confrontation with the one-eyed giant who dined on a number of his men, Odysseus outwits the giant with the aid of a well-filled wineskin. The powers of Bacchus (Dionysus) are often alluded to, and drunkenness is a prime ingredient. The play is witty, entertaining, and brief. It might well have been the perfect way to end an otherwise serious drama festival.

Comedy

No coherent Greek theories on comedy have come down to us. (Aristotle is said to have written a lost treatise on comedy.) In the *Poetics*, Aristotle points out that comedy shows people from a lower social order than the nobility, who are the main figures in tragedy.

The two greatest Greek comic writers were Aristophanes (c. 448–c. 385 BCE), whose *Lysistrata* appears in this collection, and Menander (c. 342–c. 291 BCE). The first was a master of **Old Comedy** (which lasted from c. 486 to c. 400 BCE), in which individuals—sometimes well known to the audience—could be attacked personally. The humor was often ribald, coarse, and brassy, but according to

Aristotle, it was not vicious. Physical devices onstage, such as the erect phalluses beneath the men's garments in *Lysistrata*, accompanied ribald lines, and Athenian audiences were mightily entertained. Comedy appears to have provided release, but for entirely different emotions from those evoked by tragedy.

The Old Comedy of Aristophanes concentrated on buffoonery and farce. Although we know little about it, a form known as **Middle Comedy** seems to have flourished from approximately 400 to 320 BCE. Our evidence is from statuettes of players that indicate a more realistic portrayal of character and thus a less broad and grotesque form of comedy than in some of the plays of Aristophanes. The **New Comedy** of Menander and others whose work is now lost provided a less ribald humor that centered on the shortcomings of the middle classes. Although Menander enjoyed a great reputation in his own time and was highly regarded by Roman playwrights much later, very little of his work has survived. He is said to have written just over one hundred plays, but only one, *The Grouch*, survives intact. Twenty-three of his plays existed in a manuscript in Constantinople in the sixteenth century, but nothing of that volume seems to have survived. We know a number of titles, such as *The Lady from Andros, The Flatterer,* and *The Suspicious Man.* And we know that the Romans pilfered liberally from his plays. Beyond that we know little.

Menander's New Comedy concentrated on social manners. Instead of attacking individuals, as Aristophanes frequently did, Menander was more likely to attack a vice, such as vanity, or to portray the foibles of a social class. He aimed at his own middle class and established the pattern of parents or guardians struggling, usually over the issue of marriage, against the wishes of their children. The children ordinarily foil their parents' wishes, frequently with the help of an acerbic slave who provides the comedy with most of its humor. This pattern has proved so durable that it is used virtually every day in modern situation comedies on television.

Both Old and New Comedy have influenced theater from the time of the Greeks to the present. The nineteenth-century comedy of Oscar Wilde (in this collection) is an example of New Comedy, and the Marx Brothers' and Three Stooges' movies are examples of Old Comedy.

The Great Age of Greek Drama

The fifth century BCE was not only the great creative age of Athenian theater but also the age of Athenian power in Greek politics. By the beginning of the century, Greece dominated trade in the Mediterranean and therefore in many of the major civilized urban centers of the world. The most important threat to Greek power came from the Persians, living to the east. After the Persians attacked in 490 BCE, Greek city-states such as Athens formed the Delian League to defend themselves, pouring their funds into the treasury at Delos. When the Persians threatened again in 483 BCE, Themistocles (525?–460? BCE), Athenian soldier and statesman, realized he could not win a battle on land. By skillful political moves he managed to create a powerful navy. When the Persians attacked Athens in 480 BCE, Themistocles left a small rear guard to defend the Acropolis, the city's religious fortress. The Persians took the fortress, burned everything, and were lured by a clever ruse to Salamis, where they thought that a puny Athenian navy was making a getaway. Once the Persians set sail for Salamis, Themistocles turned on them and unleashed a powerful fighting force that defeated the Persians once and for all.

In the years immediately following, Athens overstated its role in the Persian defeat and assumed an air of imperial importance. It appropriated the gold in the Delian League treasury, using it to rebuild the Acropolis beginning in 448 BCE. The great Greek general and leader Pericles (495?–429? BCE) chose his friend Phidias to supervise the construction of the Parthenon and the other main buildings that are on the Acropolis even today. The threat of Athenian domination seems to have triggered the Peloponnesian Wars (431–406 BCE), which pitted the Spartan alliance against the Athenian alliance. Athens eventually lost the war and its democratic government.

The events of these years—dominated by interminable wars, threats of a return to tyranny, and cultural instability—are coterminous with the great flourishing of Greek art, drama, and philosophy. The geniuses of Greek drama cluster in the period dating from the birth of Aeschylus (c. 525 BCE) to the death of the philosopher Socrates (399 BCE). Aeschylus wrote *The Persians* (472 BCE); *Seven against Thebes* (467 BCE); and the *Oresteia* (458 BCE), a trilogy centering on Orestes and consisting of *Agamemnon, The Libation Bearers,* and *The Eumenides. The Suppliants* and *Prometheus Bound* are of uncertain dates.

Aeschylus's introduction of a second actor made it possible to intensify the dramatic value of each *agon,* the confrontation between **antagonists**. He is also notable for giving minor characters, such as the watchman who opens *Agamemnon,* both dimension and depth. Aeschylus's *Oresteia,* the only surviving trilogy, tells of the death of Agamemnon and the efforts of his son Orestes to avenge that death.

Sophocles (c. 496–c. 406 BCE) and Euripides (c. 485–406 BCE) learned from Aeschylus and from each other, because they were all sometimes rivals. In addition to *Oedipus Rex* (c. 429 BCE), Sophocles is known today for *Ajax* (c. 442 BCE), *Philoctetes* (c. 409 BCE), *Oedipus at Colonus* (406 BCE), and *Electra* (date uncertain).

Euripides, the last of the great tragedians, may have written as many as ninety-two plays. Of the eighteen that survive, the best known are *Alcestis* (438 BCE), *Medea* (431 BCE), *Electra* (c. 417 BCE), *The Trojan Women* (415 BCE), and *The Bacchae* (produced in 405 BCE). He is especially noteworthy for his portrayal of women and for his experimental approach to theater.

These three tragedians, along with Aristophanes, provide us with insight into the Greek dramatic imagination. They also reveal something of our common humanity, since their achievement—lost though it was for many centuries—shapes our current dramatic practice. The Greeks gave us not only the beginnings of drama but also the basis of drama. We build on it today whenever a play is written and whenever we witness a play.

Timeline Greek Drama

Date	Theater	Political	Social/Cultural
1000–800 BCE			Classic paganism is in full bloom in Greece. Temple of Hera, oldest surviving temple in Olympia, Greece, is built. **9th century:** Age of the Homeric epic; *The Iliad, The Odyssey*
800–700		First Messenian War: Sparta gains power in Greece.	Choral music and dramatic music develop. Hesiod, poet whose *Works and Days* classified the five ages of mankind: Golden (peaceful), Silver (less happy), Bronze (art and warfare), Heroic (Trojan War), and Iron (the present) **776:** First Olympian Festival (predecessor of the modern Olympic games). Only one event is featured: a footrace of approximately 200 meters.
700–600		First written laws of Athens are recorded by Draco.	Sappho of Lesbos, Greek poet Archilochus, Greek lyricist and author of fables Construction of the Acropolis begins in Athens.
600–500	**534:** First contest for best tragedy is held in Athens as part of the annual City Dionysia, a major religious festival. The winning playwright (and actor) is Thespis. **c. 501:** Satyr plays are added to the City Dionysia play competition. Each playwright now has to present a trilogy of tragedies and a satyr play.	**594:** Solon's law allows for the Council of Four Hundred and various reforms pertaining to land ownership and civil liberties. **c. 525–459:** Themistocles, Athenian statesman and naval commander, builds a Greek navy and fortifications. **525–405:** Persians conquer Egypt.	The influence of the oracle at Delphi and its priestess is at its height. The theater of Delphi is built. **c. 582–507:** Pythagoras, philosopher, mathematician, and musical theorist Public libraries in Athens **c. 563–483:** Siddhartha, founder of Buddhism, begins his religious journey in 534. **c. 520–438:** Pindar, Greek musician and poet
500–400	**487–486:** Comedy is introduced as a dramatic form in the City Dionysia. **c. 471:** Aeschylus introduces the second actor in the performance of tragedy at the City Dionysia.	**500–449:** Persian Wars **494:** King Darius of Persia annexes all of Greece. **490:** Athenians defeat the Persians in the Battle of Marathon.	**c. 460–370:** Hippocrates, Greek physician who did much to separate medicine from superstition **485–424:** Herodotus, Greek historian, writes the history of the Persian Wars.

Date	Theater	Political	Social/Cultural
500–400 BCE (continued)	**c. 468:** Sophocles is credited with introducing the third actor in the performance of tragedy at the City Dionysia. **458:** First performance of Aeschylus's trilogy the *Oresteia* at the City Dionysia **458:** *Skene,* or scene house, is introduced in Greek theater. **c. 441:** First performance of Sophocles' *Antigone* at the City Dionysia **c. 430–425:** First Performance of Sophocles' *Oedipus Rex* at the City Dionysia **411:** First performance of Aristophanes' *Lysistrata*	**480:** At the Battle of Thermopylae, the Spartans defeat the Persians. **479:** Xerxes, son of Darius, returns to Persia; the Persian Wars end. **462–429:** Periclean Athens **431:** The Peloponnesian War begins; Athens is defeated in 404. Thucydides records the events in his history *The Peloponnesian War*.	**460–370:** Democritus, Greek philosopher who believed that all living things are composed of atoms **438:** The Parthenon is completed.
400–300	**400–c. 320:** Era of Middle Comedy, which concentrates on more accurately portraying daily life rather than the more fantastic plots of Old Comedy (Aristophanes) **336–300:** Era of New Comedy. Menander and others move further away from Aristophanes; stock characters are common. **335–323:** Aristotle writes *Poetics*.	**395:** The Corinthian War begins. Athens joins with Corinth, Thebes, and Argos to attack Sparta. Athens emerges from the ten-year war as a partially restored power. **332:** Alexander the Great conquers Egypt. **321:** Alexander the Great dies of a fever at age thirty-three. His successors divide the empire into Macedon, Egypt, and the Seleucid empire.	**399:** Socrates is tried and executed for corrupting the youth of Athens. **373:** Plato writes *Republic*. **340–271:** Epicurus, Greek philosopher who believed in pleasure, spontaneity, and freedom of will **320–30:** Hellenistic period of Greek art **307:** The museum and library of Alexandria are begun under Ptolemy Soter.
300–100	**277:** Artists of Dionysus, a performing artists' guild, is formed.		**275–195:** Eratosthenes, Greek scientist, suggests that the earth moves around the sun and makes close estimates of the earth's circumference.
100 BCE–300 CE		**100 BCE–1 CE:** Alexandria is the Mediterranean center of culture and commerce.	
300–400 CE			**346–359:** The Roman emperor Theodosius forbids the celebration of Olympic games in Greece.

Sophocles

Sophocles (c. 496–c. 406 BCE) won more prizes than any other tragedian in the Greek drama competitions, and he never came in lower than second place. His first victory was against the grand old master Aeschylus in 468 BCE. Sophocles' last plays, which he wrote in his eighties, were among his greatest. We have fragments of some ninety plays or poems and seven complete tragedies, and records suggest that his output numbered something over a hundred and twenty plays.

Sophocles lived in interesting times. He would have recalled the first defeat of the Persians in 490 BCE, when the news came via a messenger who had run twenty-six miles from Marathon to Athens. In his adolescence, Athens achieved its astonishing and decisive victory over the Persians at Salamis. His popularity as a tragedian and as a statesman coincided with the development of an imperial attitude in Athens. Athenian society honored the greatness of such men as Aeschylus, Sophocles, Euripides, the historian Herodotus, and all the politicians and artists that Pericles drew to Athens for its rebuilding. It was a golden age shadowed by war.

Sophocles was both sociable and religious, serving as the priest of several religious cults. He was also a man of action, popular enough to be elected as one of Athens's twelve generals; he participated with Pericles in the Samian War (440–439 BCE). His plays—especially *Antigone* (441 BCE), which preceded his election to generalship—often reflect deep political issues. One of his primary themes concerns the relation of the individual to the *polis,* the state itself. Since the Greeks valued the individual and at the same time regarded the *polis* as a sacred bulwark against a return to barbarism, conflicts between the individual and the *polis* were immensely painful.

When Sophocles began writing, he broke with an old tradition. From the time of Thespis (mid-sixth century BCE), each playwright had acted in his own plays. Aeschylus probably did so, but it is on record that Sophocles' voice was not strong enough to permit him to take a part in his plays. He played the lyre well enough to appear onstage, and he participated in a game of ball in one of his plays, but he did not appear as an actor. He also introduced innovations in the structure of his plays by changing the size of the chorus from twelve to fifteen and by adding painted scenery, more props, and a third actor to the two that Aeschylus and other tragedians had used. Sophocles wrote some of his plays with specific actors in mind, much as Shakespeare, Molière, and many other first-rank playwrights have done.

Sophocles was versed in the epics of Homer. Some of his plays derive from the *Iliad* or the *Odyssey,* although Sophocles always adapted the material of others to his own purposes. His nickname was the Attic Bee because he could read their work and always return with a useful idea of his own. The approach he took to the structure of the play, measuring the effect of the rising action of complication and then ensuring that the moment of recognition occurred at the same time the falling action began, was recognized as a supremely elegant skill. Nowhere is this illustrated more definitively than in *Oedipus Rex.*

Bust of Sophocles. The
Capitoline Museum,
Rome.

The plays of Aeschylus, powerful though they are, have a somewhat simpler construction than do Sophocles' more intricately structured plays. The structure of the plays of Euripides, Sophocles' successor, was never as fully worked out; and when Aristotle discussed the nature of tragedy in his *Poetics*, it was to Sophocles that he turned for a model, not to the other two master playwrights of the genre.

Besides the Oedipus plays, Sophocles' other surviving plays are *Philoctetes, Ajax, Trachiniae,* and *Electra.*

Oedipus Rex

Oedipus Rex is one of three plays by Sophocles that treat the fate of Oedipus and his children. The plays were written over a period of thirty years: *Antigone* (first produced in 441 BCE), *Oedipus Rex* (produced approximately fifteen years later, between 430 and 427 BCE), and *Oedipus at Colonus* (produced in 401 BCE, after Sophocles' death). When these plays are produced together today, they are usually performed in the order in which the events took place in Oedipus's and Antigone's lives—*Oedipus Rex, Oedipus at Colonus,* and *Antigone*—almost like the trilogies that Athenian audiences often viewed in the early years of the drama competitions. In fact, the plays were never a unified trilogy, and one of Sophocles' distinctions is that he did not present as trilogies plays that were thematically related, as poets before him had done.

The original narratives of the Oedipus plays were known to Sophocles' audience—with the possible exception of the story of Antigone—and one of the special pleasures for the audience watching the action of *Oedipus Rex* was that they knew the outcome. They watched for the steps, the choices, that led Oedipus to his fate.

Oedipus Rex is the story of a noble man who seeks knowledge that in the end destroys him. His greatness is measured in part by the fact that the gods have prophesied his fate: the gods take interest only in significant men. Before the action of the play begins, Oedipus has set out to discover whether he is truly the son of Polybos and Merope, the people who have reared him. He learns from the oracle of Apollo at Delphi, the most powerful interpreter of the voice and the will of the gods, that he will kill his father and marry his mother. His response is overwhelmingly human: he has seen his *moira,* his fate, and he cannot accept it. His reaction is to do everything he can, including leaving his homeland as quickly as possible, to avoid the possibility of killing Polybos and marrying Merope.

The Greek audience would have known that Oedipus was a descendant of Kadmos, founder of Thebes, who had sown the dragon teeth that produced the Spartoi (the sown men). Legend determined that the rulership of Thebes would be in dispute, with fraternal rivalry resembling that of the Spartoi, who fought and killed each other. This bloody legacy follows Oedipus, but it also reaches into all the plays of the trilogy. For example, in *Antigone* we learn that Antigone's brothers Polyneices and Eteocles killed each other in the shadow of the city walls. Thus, the fate Oedipus attempts to avoid actually dooms most of the characters in the three plays, including his true father, Laios, and his daughter Antigone.

Sophocles develops the drama in terms of **irony**—the disjunction between what seems to be true and what is true. Knowing the outcome of the action, the audience savors the ironic moments from the beginning of the play to the end. Oedipus flees his homeland to avoid fulfilling the prophecy, only to run headlong into the fate foretold by the oracle. He unwittingly returns to his original home, Thebes, and to his parents, murdering Laios, his true father, at a crossroads on the way and marrying Iokaste, his true mother, and becoming king of Thebes. The blind seer Teiresias warns Oedipus not to pursue the truth, but, in human fashion, Oedipus refuses to heed Teiresias's warnings. When the complete truth becomes clear to Oedipus, he physically blinds himself in horror and expiation. Like the blind Teiresias, Oedipus must now look inward for the truth, without the distractions of surface experiences.

The belief that the moral health of the ruler directly affected the security of the *polis* was widespread in Athenian Greece. Indeed, the Athenians regarded their state as fragile—like a human being whose health, physical and moral, could change suddenly. Because the Greeks were concerned for the well-being of their state, the *polis* often figures in the tragedies. The Sophoclean Oedipus plays are usually called "the Theban plays," a nomenclature that reminds us that the story of Oedipus can be read as the story of an individual or as the story of a state.

The underlying conflict in *Oedipus Rex* is political. The political relationship of human beings to the gods, the arbiters of their fate, is dramatized in Oedipus's relationship with the seer Teiresias. If he had his way, Oedipus might disregard Teiresias entirely. But Oedipus cannot command everything, even as ruler. His incomplete knowledge, despite his wisdom, is symptomatic of the limitations of every individual.

The contrast of Oedipus and Kreon, Iokaste's brother, is one of political style. Oedipus is a fully developed character who reveals himself as sympathetic but willful. He acts on his misunderstanding of the prophecy without reconsulting the oracle. He then marries Iokaste and blinds himself, again without reconsulting the oracle. Kreon, who is much less complicated, never acts without consulting the oracle and thoughtfully reflecting on the oracle's message. Oedipus sometimes behaves tyrannically, and he appears eager for power. Kreon takes power only when forced to do so.

The depth of Sophocles' character development was matched only by the work of his contemporary Euripides until the work of Shakespeare almost two thousand years later. Sophocles' drama is one of psychological development. His audiences saw Oedipus as a model for human greatness but also as a model for the human capacity to fall from a great height. The play is about the limits of human knowledge; it is also about the limits and frailty of human happiness.

For discussion questions and assignments on *Oedipus Rex*, visit bedfordstmartins.com/jacobus.

Oedipus Rex in Performance

Oedipus Rex has enjoyed great popularity since its first performance. The Greeks, who originally restricted their plays to one performance, eventually began to revive plays of the masters. *Oedipus* was one of the most popular. In modern times, performance has been almost constant since the seventeenth century. Great dramatists have produced their own adaptations—Corneille (1659), John Dryden (1679), Voltaire (1718), William Butler Yeats (1923), and Jean Cocteau (1931)—proving the durability of the themes and the adaptability of the play. The early American performances (beginning in 1881) were in Greek, but these soon gave way to productions in English. In his *New York Times* review of the October 2000 production in City Center, New York, Ben Brantley said, "Few productions have so hauntingly conveyed the brutal isolation of those who would be king as the National Theatre of Greece's exquisitely staged *Oedipus Rex*, directed by Vassilis Papavassileiou." This production was also presented at the Roman Colosseum, the first theatrical event in that space in 1,500 years. Currently, Greek companies perform the play regularly in the theater of Dionysus in Athens as well as in Epidaurus and elsewhere.

SOPHOCLES (C. 496–C. 406 BCE)

Oedipus Rex   C. 430 BCE

TRANSLATED BY DUDLEY FITTS AND ROBERT FITZGERALD

Characters

OEDIPUS, *King of Thebes, supposed son of Polybos and Merope, King and Queen of Corinth*
IOKASTE, *wife of Oedipus and widow of the late King Laios*
KREON, *brother of Iokaste, a prince of Thebes*
TEIRESIAS, *a blind seer who serves Apollo*
PRIEST
MESSENGER, *from Corinth*
SHEPHERD, *former servant of Laios*
SECOND MESSENGER, *from the palace*
CHORUS OF THEBAN ELDERS
CHORAGOS, *leader of the Chorus*
ANTIGONE *and* ISMENE, *young daughters of Oedipus and Iokaste. They appear in the Exodos but do not speak.*
SUPPLIANTS, GUARDS, SERVANTS

The Scene: Before the palace of Oedipus, King of Thebes. A central door and two lateral doors open onto a platform which runs the length of the facade. On the platform, right and left, are altars; and three steps lead down into the orchestra, or chorus-ground. At the beginning of the action these steps are crowded by suppliants who have brought branches and chaplets of olive leaves and who sit in various attitudes of despair. Oedipus enters.

PROLOGUE°

OEDIPUS: My children, generations of the living
   In the line of Kadmos,° nursed at his ancient hearth:
   Why have you strewn yourselves before these altars
   In supplication, with your boughs and garlands?
5   The breath of incense rises from the city
   With a sound of prayer and lamentation.
                      Children,
   I would not have you speak through messengers,
   And therefore I have come myself to hear you—
   I, Oedipus, who bear the famous name.
   (*To a Priest.*) You, there, since you are eldest in
10   the company,
   Speak for them all, tell me what preys upon you,
   Whether you come in dread, or crave some blessing:

Prologue: Portion of the play explaining the background and current action. **2. Kadmos:** Founder of Thebes.

Tell me, and never doubt that I will help you
In every way I can; I should be heartless
Were I not moved to find you suppliant here. 15
PRIEST: Great Oedipus, O powerful king of Thebes!
   You see how all the ages of our people
   Cling to your altar steps: here are boys
   Who can barely stand alone, and here are priests
   By weight of age, as I am a priest of God, 20
   And young men chosen from those yet unmarried;
   As for the others, all that multitude,
   They wait with olive chaplets in the squares,
   At the two shrines of Pallas,° and where Apollo°
   Speaks in the glowing embers.
                  Your own eyes 25
   Must tell you: Thebes is tossed on a murdering sea
   And can not lift her head from the death surge.
   A rust consumes the buds and fruits of the earth;
   The herds are sick; children die unborn,
   And labor is vain. The god of plague and pyre 30
   Raids like detestable lightning through the city,
   And all the house of Kadmos is laid waste,
   All emptied, and all darkened: Death alone
   Battens upon the misery of Thebes.

You are not one of the immortal gods, we know; 35
   Yet we have come to you to make our prayer
   As to the man surest in mortal ways
   And wisest in the ways of God. You saved us
   From the Sphinx,° that flinty singer, and the tribute
   We paid to her so long; yet you were never 40
   Better informed than we, nor could we teach you:
   A god's touch, it seems, enabled you to help us.

Therefore, O mighty power, we turn to you:
   Find us our safety, find us a remedy,
   Whether by counsel of the gods or of men. 45
   A king of wisdom tested in the past
   Can act in a time of troubles, and act well.
   Noblest of men, restore
   Life to your city! Think how all men call you
   Liberator for your boldness long ago; 50
   Ah, when your years of kingship are remembered,

---

24. Pallas: Pallas Athene, daughter of Zeus and goddess of wisdom. **Apollo:** Son of Zeus and god of the sun, of light and truth. **39. Sphinx:** A winged monster with the body of a lion and the face of a woman, the Sphinx had tormented Thebes with her riddle, killing those who could not solve it. When Oedipus solved the riddle, the Sphinx killed herself.

Let them not say *We rose, but later fell*—
Keep the State from going down in the storm!
Once, years ago, with happy augury,
55   You brought us fortune; be the same again!
No man questions your power to rule the land:
But rule over men, not over a dead city!
Ships are only hulls, high walls are nothing,
When no life moves in the empty passageways.
60   OEDIPUS: Poor children! You may be sure I know
All that you longed for in your coming here.
I know that you are deathly sick; and yet,
Sick as you are, not one is as sick as I.
Each of you suffers in himself alone
65   His anguish, not another's; but my spirit
Groans for the city, for myself, for you.

I was not sleeping, you are not waking me.
No, I have been in tears for a long while
And in my restless thought walked many ways.
70   In all my search I found one remedy,
And I have adopted it: I have sent Kreon,
Son of Menoikeus, brother of the queen,
To Delphi,° Apollo's place of revelation,
To learn there, if he can,
75   What act or pledge of mine may save the city.
I have counted the days, and now, this very day,
I am troubled, for he has overstayed his time.
What is he doing? He has been gone too long.
Yet whenever he comes back, I should do ill
80   Not to take any action the god orders.
PRIEST: It is a timely promise. At this instant
They tell me Kreon is here.
OEDIPUS: O Lord Apollo!
May his news be fair as his face is radiant!
PRIEST: Good news, I gather! he is crowned with bay,
The chaplet is thick with berries.
85   OEDIPUS: We shall soon know;
He is near enough to hear us now.   (*Enter Kreon.*)
          O prince:
Brother: son of Menoikeus:
What answer do you bring us from the god?
KREON: A strong one. I can tell you, great afflictions
90   Will turn out well, if they are taken well.
OEDIPUS: What was the oracle? These vague words
Leave me still hanging between hope and fear.
KREON: Is it your pleasure to hear me with all these
Gathered around us? I am prepared to speak,
But should we not go in?
95   OEDIPUS: Speak to them all,
It is for them I suffer, more than for myself.
KREON: Then I will tell you what I heard at Delphi.
In plain words
The god commands us to expel from the land of
Thebes
100   An old defilement we are sheltering.

---

73. **Delphi:** Site of the oracle, source of religious authority and
prophecy, under the protection of Apollo.

It is a deathly thing, beyond cure;
We must not let it feed upon us longer.
OEDIPUS: What defilement? How shall we rid
ourselves of it?
KREON: By exile or death, blood for blood. It was
Murder that brought the plague-wind on the city.   105
OEDIPUS: Murder of whom? Surely the god has
named him?
KREON: My Lord: Laios once ruled this land,
Before you came to govern us.
OEDIPUS: I know;
I learned of him from others; I never saw him.
KREON: He was murdered; and Apollo commands us
now   110
To take revenge upon whoever killed him.
OEDIPUS: Upon whom? Where are they? Where shall
we find a clue
To solve that crime, after so many years?
KREON: Here in this land, he said. Search reveals
Things that escape an inattentive man.   115
OEDIPUS: Tell me: Was Laios murdered in his house,
Or in the fields, or in some foreign country?
KREON: He said he planned to make a pilgrimage.
He did not come home again.
OEDIPUS: And was there no one,
No witness, no companion, to tell what happened? 120
KREON: They were all killed but one, and he got away
So frightened that he could remember one thing
only.
OEDIPUS: What was that one thing? One may be the
key
To everything, if we resolve to use it.
KREON: He said that a band of highwaymen attacked
them,   125
Outnumbered them, and overwhelmed the king.
OEDIPUS: Strange, that a highwayman should be so
daring—
Unless some faction here bribed him to do it.
KREON: We thought of that. But after Laios' death
New troubles arose and we had no avenger.   130
OEDIPUS: What troubles could prevent your hunting
down the killers?
KREON: The riddling Sphinx's song
Made us deaf to all mysteries but her own.
OEDIPUS: Then once more I must bring what is dark
to light.
It is most fitting that Apollo shows,   135
As you do, this compunction for the dead.
You shall see how I stand by you, as I should,
Avenging this country and the god as well,
And not as though it were for some distant friend,
But for my own sake, to be rid of evil.   140
Whoever killed King Laios might—who knows?—
Lay violent hands even on me—and soon.
I act for the murdered king in my own interest.

Come, then, my children: leave the altar steps,
Lift up your olive boughs!
                              One of you go   145

And summon the people of Kadmos to gather here.
I will do all that I can; you may tell them that.
                                        (*Exit a Page.*)
So, with the help of God,
We shall be saved—or else indeed we are lost.
150 PRIEST: Let us rise, children. It was for this we came,
And now the king has promised it.
Phoibos° has sent us an oracle; may he descend
Himself to save us and drive out the plague.

(*Exeunt*° *Oedipus and Kreon into the palace by the central door. The Priest and the Suppliants disperse right and left. After a short pause the Chorus enters the orchestra.*)

PARODOS° • Strophe° 1

CHORUS: What is God singing in his profound
Delphi of gold and shadow?
What oracle for Thebes, the Sunwhipped city?
Fear unjoints me, the roots of my heart tremble.
5   Now I remember, O Healer, your power, and
wonder:
Will you send doom like a sudden cloud, or
weave it
Like nightfall of the past?
Speak to me, tell me, O
Child of golden Hope, immortal Voice.

Antistrophe° 1

10 Let me pray to Athene, the immortal daughter of Zeus,
And to Artemis° her sister
Who keeps her famous throne in the market ring,
And to Apollo, archer from distant heaven—
O gods, descend! Like three streams leap against
15 The fires of our grief, the fires of darkness;
Be swift to bring us rest!
As in the old time from the brilliant house
Of air you stepped to save us, come again!

Strophe 2

Now our afflictions have no end,
20 Now all our stricken host lies down
And no man fights off death with his mind;
The noble plowland bears no grain,
And groaning mothers can not bear—
See, how our lives like birds take wing,
25 Like sparks that fly when a fire soars,
To the shore of the god of evening.

152. **Phoibos:** Apollo.   153. [S.D.] ***Exeunt:*** Latin for "they go out."   **Parados:** Song or ode chanted by the Chorus on their entry.   **Strophe:** Song sung by the Chorus as they danced from stage right to stage left.   **Antistrophe:** Song sung by the Chorus following the Strophe, as they danced back from stage left to stage right.   **11. Artemis:** The huntress, daughter of Zeus, twin sister of Apollo.

Antistrophe 2

The plague burns on, it is pitiless,
Though pallid children laden with death
Lie unwept in the stony ways,
And old gray women by every path   30
Flock to the strand about the altars
There to strike their breasts and cry
Worship of Phoibos in wailing prayers:
Be kind, God's golden child!

Strophe 3

There are no swords in this attack by fire,   35
No shields, but we are ringed with cries.
Send the besieger plunging from our homes
Into the vast sea-room of the Atlantic
Or into the waves that foam eastward of
Thrace—
For the day ravages what the night spares—   40
Destroy our enemy, lord of the thunder!
Let him be riven by lightning from heaven!

Antistrophe 3

Phoibos Apollo, stretch the sun's bowstring,
That golden cord, until it sing for us,
Flashing arrows in heaven!
                          Artemis, Huntress,   45
Race with flaring lights upon our mountains!
O scarlet god,° O golden-banded brow,
O Theban Bacchos in a storm of Maenads,°

(*Enter Oedipus, center.*)

Whirl upon Death, that all the Undying hate!
Come with blinding torches, come in joy!   50

SCENE 1

OEDIPUS: Is this your prayer? It may be answered.
Come,
Listen to me, act as the crisis demands,
And you shall have relief from all these evils.

Until now I was a stranger to this tale,
As I had been a stranger to the crime.   5
Could I track down the murderer without a
clue?
But now, friends,
As one who became a citizen after the murder,

47. **scarlet god:** Bacchus, god of wine and revelry; also called Dionysus.   48. **Maenads:** Female worshipers of Bacchus (Dionysus).

Douglas Campbell as Oedipus
in a 1957 Tyrone Guthrie
production.

I make this proclamation to all Thebans:
If any man knows by whose hand Laios, son of
10   Labdakos,
Met his death, I direct that man to tell me everything,
No matter what he fears for having so long
        withheld it.
Let it stand as promised that no further trouble
Will come to him, but he may leave the land in
        safety.
Moreover: If anyone knows the murderer to be
15   foreign,
Let him not keep silent: he shall have his reward
        from me.
However, if he does conceal it; if any man
Fearing for his friend or for himself disobeys this
        edict,
Hear what I propose to do:

20   I solemnly forbid the people of this country,
Where power and throne are mine, ever to receive
        that man
Or speak to him, no matter who he is, or let him
Join in sacrifice, lustration,° or in prayer.
I decree that he be driven from every house,
25   Being, as he is, corruption itself to us: the Delphic
Voice of Apollo has pronounced this revelation.
Thus I associate myself with the oracle
And take the side of the murdered king.

As for the criminal, I pray to God—

Whether it be a lurking thief, or one of a number—   30
I pray that that man's life be consumed in evil and
        wretchedness.
And as for me, this curse applies no less
If it should turn out that the culprit is my guest here,
Sharing my hearth.
                You have heard the penalty.
I lay it on you now to attend to this   35
For my sake, for Apollo's, for the sick
Sterile city that heaven has abandoned.
Suppose the oracle had given you no command:
Should this defilement go uncleansed for ever?
You should have found the murderer: your king,   40
A noble king, had been destroyed!
                                    Now I,
Having the power that he held before me,
Having his bed, begetting children there
Upon his wife, as he would have, had he lived—
Their son would have been my children's brother,   45
If Laios had had luck in fatherhood!
(And now his bad fortune has struck him
        down)—
I say I take the son's part, just as though
I were his son, to press the fight for him
And see it won! I'll find the hand that brought   50
Death to Labdakos' and Polydoros' child,
Heir of Kadmos' and Agenor's line.°
And as for those who fail me,
May the gods deny them the fruit of the earth,
Fruit of the womb, and may they rot utterly!   55

23. lustration: Ceremonial purification.

51–52. Labdakos, Polydoros, Kadmos, and Agenor: Father, grandfather, great-grandfather, and great-great-grandfather of Laios.

Let them be wretched as we are wretched, and
   worse!

For you, for loyal Thebans, and for all
Who find my actions right, I pray the favor
Of justice, and of all the immortal gods.

60 CHORAGOS: Since I am under oath, my lord, I swear
I did not do the murder, I can not name
The murderer. Phoibos ordained the search;
Why did he not say who the culprit was?

OEDIPUS: An honest question. But no man in the world
65   Can make the gods do more than the gods will.

CHORAGOS: There is an alternative, I think—

OEDIPUS: Tell me.
Any or all, you must not fail to tell me.

CHORAGOS: A lord clairvoyant to the lord Apollo,
As we all know, is the skilled Teiresias.
One might learn much about this from him,
70   Oedipus.

OEDIPUS: I am not wasting time:
Kreon spoke of this, and I have sent for him—
Twice, in fact; it is strange that he is not here.

CHORAGOS: The other matter—that old report—
   seems useless.

75 OEDIPUS: What was that? I am interested in all reports.

CHORAGOS: The king was said to have been killed by
   highwaymen.

OEDIPUS: I know. But we have no witnesses to that.

CHORAGOS: If the killer can feel a particle of dread,
Your curse will bring him out of hiding!

OEDIPUS: No.
80 The man who dared that act will fear no curse.

(*Enter the blind seer Teiresias, led by a Page.*)

CHORAGOS: But there is one man who may detect the
   criminal.
This is Teiresias, this is the holy prophet
In whom, alone of all men, truth was born.

OEDIPUS: Teiresias: seer: student of mysteries,
85 Of all that's taught and all that no man tells,
Secrets of Heaven and secrets of the earth:
Blind though you are, you know the city lies
Sick with plague; and from this plague, my lord,
We find that you alone can guard or save us.

90 Possibly you did not hear the messengers?
Apollo, when we sent to him,
Sent us back word that this great pestilence
Would lift, but only if we established clearly
The identity of those who murdered Laios.
They must be killed or exiled.

95   Can you use
Birdflight° or any art of divination
To purify yourself, and Thebes, and me
From this contagion? We are in your hands.
There is no fairer duty
100 Than that of helping others in distress.

96. Birdflight: Prophets used the flight of birds to predict the future.

TEIRESIAS: How dreadful knowledge of the truth
   can be
When there's no help in truth! I knew this well,
But did not act on it; else I should not have come.

OEDIPUS: What is troubling you? Why are your eyes
   so cold?

TEIRESIAS: Let me go home. Bear your own fate, and   105
   I'll
Bear mine. It is better so: trust what I say.

OEDIPUS: What you say is ungracious and unhelpful
To your native country. Do not refuse to speak.

TEIRESIAS: When it comes to speech, your own is
   neither temperate   110
Nor opportune. I wish to be more prudent.

OEDIPUS: In God's name, we all beg you—

TEIRESIAS: You are all ignorant.
No; I will never tell you what I know.
Now it is my misery; then, it would be yours.

OEDIPUS: What! You do know something, and will
   not tell us?   115
You would betray us all and wreck the State?

TEIRESIAS: I do not intend to torture myself, or you.
Why persist in asking? You will not persuade me.

OEDIPUS: What a wicked old man you are! You'd try
   a stone's
Patience! Out with it! Have you no feeling at all?   120

TEIRESIAS: You call me unfeeling. If you could only
   see
The nature of your own feelings . . .

OEDIPUS: Why,
Who would not feel as I do? Who could endure
Your arrogance toward the city?

TEIRESIAS: What does it matter?
Whether I speak or not, it is bound to come.

OEDIPUS: Then, if "it" is bound to come, you are   125
   bound to tell me.

TEIRESIAS: No, I will not go on. Rage as you please.

OEDIPUS: Rage? Why not!
                   And I'll tell you what I think:
You planned it, you had it done, you all but
Killed him with your own hands: if you had eyes,   130
I'd say the crime was yours, and yours alone.

TEIRESIAS: So? I charge you, then,
Abide by the proclamation you have made:
From this day forth
Never speak again to these men or to me;   135
You yourself are the pollution of this country.

OEDIPUS: You dare say that! Can you possibly think
   you have
Some way of going free, after such insolence?

TEIRESIAS: I have gone free. It is the truth sustains me.

OEDIPUS: Who taught you shamelessness? It was not
   your craft.

TEIRESIAS: You did. You made me speak. I did not
   want to.   140

OEDIPUS: Speak what? Let me hear it again more
   clearly.

TEIRESIAS: Was it not clear before? Are you tempting me?

OEDIPUS: I did not understand it. Say it again.

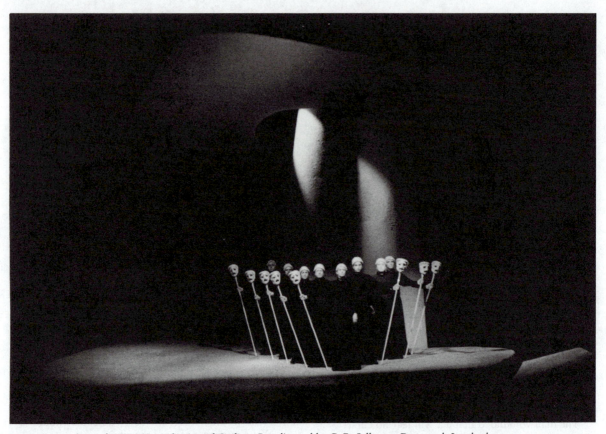

Franz Mertz's design for a 1952 production of *Oedipus Rex* directed by G. R. Sellner at Darmstadt Landestheater.

TEIRESIAS: I say that you are the murderer whom you
    seek.
OEDIPUS: Now twice you have spat out infamy.
145   You'll pay for it!
TEIRESIAS: Would you care for more? Do you wish to
    be really angry?
OEDIPUS: Say what you will. Whatever you say is
    worthless.
TEIRESIAS: I say you live in hideous shame with those
    Most dear to you. You can not see the evil.
150 OEDIPUS: Can you go on babbling like this for ever?
TEIRESIAS: I can, if there is power in truth.
OEDIPUS: There is:
155   But not for you, not for you,
    You sightless, witless, senseless, mad old man!
TEIRESIAS: You are the madman. There is no one here
    Who will not curse you soon, as you curse me.
OEDIPUS: You child of total night! I would not touch
    you;
    Neither would any man who sees the sun.
TEIRESIAS: True: it is not from you my fate will come.
    That lies within Apollo's competence,
    As it is his concern.

OEDIPUS: Tell me, who made 160
    These fine discoveries? Kreon? or someone else?
TEIRESIAS: Kreon is no threat. You weave your own
    doom.
OEDIPUS: Wealth, power, craft of statemanship!
    Kingly position, everywhere admired!
    What savage envy is stored up against these, 165
    If Kreon, whom I trusted, Kreon my friend,
    For this great office which the city once
    Put in my hands unsought—if for this power
    Kreon desires in secret to destroy me!

    He has bought this decrepit fortune-teller, this 170
    Collector of dirty pennies, this prophet fraud—
    Why, he is no more clairvoyant than I am!
                            Tell us:
    Has your mystic mummery ever approached the
    truth?
    When that hellcat the Sphinx was performing here,
    What help were you to these people? 175
    Her magic was not for the first man who came
    along:
    It demanded a real exorcist. Your birds—

What good were they? or the gods, for the matter
    of that?
But I came by,
180 Oedipus, the simple man, who knows nothing—
I thought it out for myself, no birds helped me!
And this is the man you think you can destroy,
That you may be close to Kreon when he's king!
Well, you and your friend Kreon, it seems to me,
185 Will suffer most. If you were not an old man,
You would have paid already for your plot.
CHORAGOS: We can not see that his words or yours
Have been spoken except in anger, Oedipus,
And of anger we have no need. How to accomplish
190 The god's will best: that is what most concerns us.
TEIRESIAS: You are a king. But where argument's
    concerned
I am your man, as much a king as you.
I am not your servant, but Apollo's.
I have no need of Kreon or Kreon's name.

195 Listen to me. You mock my blindness, do you?
But I say that you, with both your eyes, are blind:
You can not see the wretchedness of your life,
Nor in whose house you live, no, nor with whom.
Who are your father and mother? Can you tell me?
200 You do not even know the blind wrongs
That you have done them, on earth and in the
    world below.
But the double lash of your parents' curse will
    whip you
Out of this land some day, with only night
Upon your precious eyes.
205 Your cries then—where will they not be heard?
What fastness of Kithairon° will not echo them?
And that bridal-descant of yours—you'll know it
    then,
The song they sang when you came here to Thebes
And found your misguided berthing.
210 All this, and more, that you can not guess at now,
Will bring you to yourself among your children.

Be angry, then. Curse Kreon. Curse my words.
I tell you, no man that walks upon the earth
Shall be rooted out more horribly than you.
215 OEDIPUS: Am I to bear this from him?—Damnation
Take you! Out of this place! Out of my sight!
TEIRESIAS: I would not have come at all if you had
    not asked me.
OEDIPUS: Could I have told that you'd talk nonsense,
    that
You'd come here to make a fool of yourself, and
    of me?
TEIRESIAS: A fool? Your parents thought me sane
220   enough.

206. Kithairon: The mountain where Oedipus was abandoned
as an infant.

OEDIPUS: My parents again!—Wait: who were my
    parents?
TEIRESIAS: This day will give you a father, and break
    your heart.
OEDIPUS: Your infantile riddles! Your damned
    abracadabra!
TEIRESIAS: You were a great man once at solving
    riddles.
OEDIPUS: Mock me with that if you like; you will
    find it true.   225
TEIRESIAS: It was true enough. It brought about your ruin.
OEDIPUS: But if it saved this town?
TEIRESIAS (*to the Page*): Boy, give me your hand.
OEDIPUS: Yes, boy; lead him away.
                 —While you are here
We can do nothing. Go; leave us in peace.   230
TEIRESIAS: I will go when I have said what I have to say.
How can you hurt me? And I tell you again:
The man you have been looking for all this time,
The damned man, the murderer of Laios,
That man is in Thebes. To your mind he is
    foreign-born,   235
But it will soon be shown that he is a Theban,
A revelation that will fail to please.
                    A blind man,
Who has his eyes now; a penniless man, who is
    rich now;
And he will go tapping the strange earth with
    his staff.
To the children with whom he lives now he will be   240
Brother and father—the very same; to her
Who bore him, son and husband—the very same
Who came to his father's bed, wet with his father's
    blood.
Enough. Go think that over.
If later you find error in what I have said,   245
You may say that I have no skill in prophecy.

(Exit Teiresias, led by his Page.
Oedipus goes into the palace.)

ODE° 1 • Strophe 1

CHORUS: The Delphic stone of prophecies
Remembers ancient regicide
And a still bloody hand.
That killer's hour of flight has come.
He must be stronger than riderless   5
Coursers of untiring wind,
For the son of Zeus° armed with his father's thunder
Leaps in lightning after him;
And the Furies° hold his track, the sad Furies.

Ode: Song sung by the Chorus. **7. son of Zeus:** Apollo.
9. Furies: Spirits called on to avenge crimes, especially against kin.

Antistrophe 1

10 Holy Parnassos'° peak of snow
    Flashes and blinds that secret man,
    That all shall hunt him down:
    Though he may roam the forest shade
    Like a bull gone wild from pasture
15 To rage through glooms of stone.
    Doom comes down on him; flight will not avail him;
    For the world's heart calls him desolate,
    And the immortal voices follow, for ever follow.

Strophe 2

    But now a wilder thing is heard
    From the old man skilled at hearing Fate in the
20   wing-beat of a bird.
    Bewildered as a blown bird, my soul hovers and
        can not find
    Foothold in this debate, or any reason or rest of mind.
    But no man ever brought—none can bring
    Proof of strife between Thebes' royal house,
25 Labdakos' line, and the son of Polybos;°
    And never until now has any man brought word
    Of Laios' dark death staining Oedipus the King.

Antistrophe 2

    Divine Zeus and Apollo hold
    Perfect intelligence alone of all tales ever told;
    And well though this diviner works, he works in
30   his own night;
    No man can judge that rough unknown or trust in
        second sight,
    For wisdom changes hands among the wise.
    Shall I believe my great lord criminal
    At a raging word that a blind old man let fall?
35 I saw him, when the carrion woman° faced him of old,
    Prove his heroic mind. These evil words are lies.

SCENE 2

KREON: Men of Thebes:
    I am told that heavy accusations
    Have been brought against me by King Oedipus.

    I am not the kind of man to bear this tamely.

5   If in these present difficulties
    He holds me accountable for any harm to him
    Through anything I have said or done—why, then,
    I do not value life in this dishonor.
    It is not as though this rumor touched upon
10 Some private indiscretion. The matter is grave.
    The fact is that I am being called disloyal
    To the State, to my fellow citizens, to my friends.

10. **Parnassos:** Mountain sacred to Apollo.   25. **Polybos:** King who adopted Oedipus.   35. **woman:** The Sphinx.

CHORAGOS: He may have spoken in anger, not from
    his mind.
KREON: But did you not hear him say I was the one
    Who seduced the old prophet into lying?   15
CHORAGOS: The thing was said; I do not know how
    seriously.
KREON: But you were watching him! Were his eyes
    steady?
    Did he look like a man in his right mind?
CHORAGOS: I do not know.
    I can not judge the behavior of great men.
    But here is the king himself.

(*Enter Oedipus.*)

OEDIPUS: So you dared come back.   20
    Why? How brazen of you to come to my house,
    You murderer!
                    Do you think I do not know
    That you plotted to kill me, plotted to steal my
        throne?
    Tell me, in God's name: am I coward, a fool,
    That you should dream you could accomplish   25
        this?
    A fool who could not see your slippery game?
    A coward, not to fight back when I saw it?
    You are the fool, Kreon, are you not? hoping
    Without support or friends to get a throne?
    Thrones may be won or bought: you could do
        neither.   30
KREON: Now listen to me. You have talked; let me
    talk, too.
    You can not judge unless you know the facts.
OEDIPUS: You speak well: there is one fact; but I find
    it hard
    To learn from the deadliest enemy I have.
KREON: That above all I must dispute with you.   35
OEDIPUS: That above all I will not hear you deny.
KREON: If you think there is anything good in being
    stubborn
    Against all reason, then I say you are wrong.
OEDIPUS: If you think a man can sin against his own
    kind
    And not be punished for it, I say you are mad.   40
KREON: I agree. But tell me: what have I done to
    you?
OEDIPUS: You advised me to send for that wizard,
    did you not?
KREON: I did. I should do it again.
OEDIPUS: Very well. Now tell me:
    How long has it been since Laios—
KREON: What of Laios?
OEDIPUS: Since he vanished in that onset by the road?   45
KREON: It was long ago, a long time.
OEDIPUS: And this prophet,
    Was he practicing here then?
KREON: He was; and with
    honor, as now.
OEDIPUS: Did he speak of me at that time?
KREON: He never did,
    At least, not when I was present.

Josef Svoboda's stage design for
M. Machacek's 1963 production of
Oedipus Rex in Prague.

OEDIPUS: But . . . the enquiry?
    I suppose you held one?

50 KREON: We did, but we learned nothing.
    OEDIPUS: Why did the prophet not speak against me then?
    KREON: I do not know; and I am the kind of man
      Who holds his tongue when he has no facts to go on.
    OEDIPUS: There's one fact that you know, and you
      could tell it.

55 KREON: What fact is that? If I know it, you shall have it.
    OEDIPUS: If he were not involved with you, he could
      not say
      That it was I who murdered Laios.
    KREON: If he says that, you are the one that knows it!—
      But now it is my turn to question you.

60 OEDIPUS: Put your questions. I am no murderer.
    KREON: First, then: You married my sister?
    OEDIPUS: I married your sister.
    KREON: And you rule the kingdom equally with her?
    OEDIPUS: Everything that she wants she has from me.

KREON: And I am the third, equal to both of you?
OEDIPUS: That is why I call you a bad friend.   65
KREON: No. Reason it out, as I have done.
    Think of this first: would any sane man prefer
    Power, with all a king's anxieties,
    To that same power and the grace of sleep?
    Certainly not I.   70
    I have never longed for the king's power—only his
      rights.
    Would any wise man differ from me in this?
    As matters stand, I have my way in everything
    With your consent, and no responsibilities.
    If I were king, I should be a slave to policy.   75
    How could I desire a scepter more
    Than what is now mine—untroubled influence?
    No, I have not gone mad; I need no honors,
    Except those with the perquisites I have now.
    I am welcome everywhere; every man salutes me,   80
    And those who want your favor seek my ear,

Since I know how to manage what they ask.
Should I exchange this ease for that anxiety?
Besides, no sober mind is treasonable.
85 I hate anarchy
And never would deal with any man who likes it.
Test what I have said. Go to the priestess
At Delphi, ask if I quoted her correctly.
And as for this other thing: if I am found
90 Guilty of treason with Teiresias,
Then sentence me to death. You have my word
It is a sentence I should cast my vote for—
But not without evidence!
                        You do wrong
When you take good men for bad, bad men for good.
95 A true friend thrown aside—why, life itself
Is not more precious!
                    In time you will know this well:
For time, and time alone, will show the just man,
Though scoundrels are discovered in a day.
CHORAGOS: This is well said, and a prudent man
      would ponder it.
100 Judgments too quickly formed are dangerous.
OEDIPUS: But is he not quick in his duplicity?
      And shall I not be quick to parry him?
      Would you have me stand still, hold my peace, and let
      This man win everything, through my inaction?
105 KREON: And you want—what is it, then? To banish me?
OEDIPUS: No, not exile. It is your death I want,
      So that all the world may see what treason means.
KREON: You will persist, then? You will not believe me?
OEDIPUS: How can I believe you?
KREON: Then you are a fool.
OEDIPUS: To save myself?
110 KREON: In justice, think of me.
OEDIPUS: You are evil incarnate.
KREON: But suppose that you are wrong?
OEDIPUS: Still I must rule.
KREON: But not if you rule badly.
OEDIPUS: O city, city!
KREON: It is my city, too!
CHORAGOS: Now, my lords, be still. I see the queen,
115   Iokaste, coming from her palace chambers;
      And it is time she came, for the sake of you both.
      This dreadful quarrel can be resolved through her.

(Enter Iokaste.)

IOKASTE: Poor foolish men, what wicked din is this?
      With Thebes sick to death, is it not shameful
120   That you should take some private quarrel up?
      (To Oedipus.) Come into the house.
                  —And you, Kreon, go now:
      Let us have no more of this tumult over nothing.
KREON: Nothing? No, sister: what your husband
      plans for me
      Is one of two great evils: exile or death.
OEDIPUS: He is right.
125   Why, woman I have caught him squarely
      Plotting against my life.
KREON: No! Let me die
      Accurst if ever I have wished you harm!

IOKASTE: Ah, believe it, Oedipus!
      In the name of the gods, respect this oath of his
      For my sake, for the sake of these people here!   130

Strophe 1

CHORAGOS: Open your mind to her, my lord. Be
      ruled by her, I beg you!
OEDIPUS: What would you have me do?
CHORAGOS: Respect Kreon's word. He has never
      spoken like a fool,
      And now he has sworn an oath.
OEDIPUS: You know what you ask?
CHORAGOS: I do.
OEDIPUS: Speak on, then.
CHORAGOS: A friend so sworn should not be
      baited so,   135
      In blind malice, and without final proof.
OEDIPUS: You are aware, I hope, that what you say
      Means death for me, or exile at the least.

Strophe 2

CHORAGOS: No, I swear by Helios, first in heaven!
      May I die friendless and accurst,   140
      The worst of deaths, if ever I meant that!
      It is the withering fields
          That hurt my sick heart:
      Must we bear all these ills,
      And now your bad blood as well?   145
OEDIPUS: Then let him go. And let me die, if I must,
      Or be driven by him in shame from the land of
          Thebes.
      It is your unhappiness, and not his talk,
      That touches me.
                  As for him—
      Wherever he goes, hatred will follow him.   150
KREON: Ugly in yielding, as you were ugly in rage!
      Natures like yours chiefly torment themselves.
OEDIPUS: Can you not go? Can you not leave me?
KREON: I can.
      You do not know me; but the city knows me,
      And in its eyes I am just, if not in yours.   155

                                        (Exit Kreon.)

Antistrophe 1

CHORAGOS: Lady Iokaste, did you not ask the King
      to go to his chambers?
IOKASTE: First tell me what has happened.
CHORAGOS: There was suspicion without evidence;
      yet it rankled
      As even false charges will.
IOKASTE: On both sides?
CHORAGOS: On both.
IOKASTE: But what was said?   160

CHORAGOS: Oh let it rest, let it be done with!
  Have we not suffered enough?
OEDIPUS: You see to what your decency has brought
    you:
  You have made difficulties where my heart saw
    none.

Antistrophe 2

CHORAGOS: Oedipus, it is not once only I have told
165   you—
  You must know I should count myself unwise
  To the point of madness, should I now forsake
    you—
        You, under whose hand,
           In the storm of another time,
170   Our dear land sailed out free.
  But now stand fast at the helm!
IOKASTE: In God's name, Oedipus, inform your wife
    as well:
  Why are you so set in this hard anger?
OEDIPUS: I will tell you, for none of these men
    deserves
175   My confidence as you do. It is Kreon's work,
  His treachery, his plotting against me.
IOKASTE: Go on, if you can make this clear to me.
OEDIPUS: He charges me with the murder of Laios.
IOKASTE: Has he some knowledge? Or does he speak
    from hearsay?
OEDIPUS: He would not commit himself to such a
180   charge,
  But he has brought in that damnable soothsayer
  To tell his story.
IOKASTE: Set your mind at rest.
  If it is a question of soothsayers, I tell you
  That you will find no man whose craft gives
    knowledge
  Of the unknowable.
185   Here is my proof:
  An oracle was reported to Laios once
  (I will not say from Phoibos himself, but from
  His appointed ministers, at any rate)
  That his doom would be death at the hands of his
    own son—
190   His son, born of his flesh and of mine!

  Now, you remember the story: Laios was killed
  By marauding strangers where three highways
    meet;
  But his child had not been three days in this world
  Before the king had pierced the baby's ankles
195   And left him to die on a lonely mountainside.

  Thus, Apollo never caused that child
  To kill his father, and it was not Laios' fate
  To die at the hands of his son, as he had feared.
  This is what prophets and prophecies are worth!
  Have no dread of them.
200   It is God himself

Who can show us what he wills, in his own way.
OEDIPUS: How strange a shadowy memory crossed
    my mind,
  Just now while you were speaking; it chilled my
    heart.
IOKASTE: What do you mean? What memory do you
    speak of?
OEDIPUS: If I understand you, Laios was killed   205
  At a place where three roads meet.
IOKASTE: So it was said;
  We have no later story.
OEDIPUS: Where did it happen?
IOKASTE: Phokis, it is called: at a place where the
    Theban Way
  Divides into the roads toward Delphi and Daulia.
OEDIPUS: When?
IOKASTE: We had the news not long before you came   210
  And proved the right to your succession here.
OEDIPUS: Ah, what net has God been weaving for me?
IOKASTE: Oedipus! Why does this trouble you?
OEDIPUS: Do not ask me yet.
  First, tell me how Laios looked, and tell me
  How old he was.
IOKASTE: He was tall, his hair just touched   215
  With white; his form was not unlike your own.
OEDIPUS: I think that I myself may be accurst
  By my own ignorant edict.
IOKASTE: You speak strangely.
  It makes me tremble to look at you, my king.
OEDIPUS: I am not sure that the blind man can not see.   220
  But I should know better if you were to tell me—
IOKASTE: Anything—though I dread to hear you ask
    it.
OEDIPUS: Was the king lightly escorted, or did he ride
  With a large company, as a ruler should?
IOKASTE: There were five men with him in all: one
    was a herald;   225
  And a single chariot, which he was driving.
OEDIPUS: Alas, that makes it plain enough!
                But who—
  Who told you how it happened?
IOKASTE: A household servant,
  The only one to escape.
OEDIPUS: And is he still
  A servant of ours?
IOKASTE: No; for when he came back at last   230
  And found you enthroned in the place of the dead
    king,
  He came to me, touched my hand with his, and
    begged
  That I would send him away to the frontier district
  Where only the shepherds go—
  As far away from the city as I could send him.   235
  I granted his prayer; for although the man was a
    slave,
  He had earned more than this favor at my hands.
OEDIPUS: Can he be called back quickly?
IOKASTE: Easily.
  But why?

240 OEDIPUS: I have taken too much upon myself
       Without enquiry; therefore I wish to consult him.
    IOKASTE: Then he shall come.
                               But am I not one also
       To whom you might confide these fears of yours?
    OEDIPUS: That is your right; it will not be denied you,
245   Now least of all; for I have reached a pitch
       Of wild foreboding. Is there anyone
       To whom I should sooner speak?

       Polybos of Corinth is my father.
       My mother is a Dorian: Merope.
250   I grew up chief among the men of Corinth
       Until a strange thing happened—
       Not worth my passion, it may be, but strange.
       At a feast, a drunken man maundering in his cups
       Cries out that I am not my father's son!
255   I contained myself that night, though I felt anger
       And a sinking heart. The next day I visited
       My father and mother, and questioned them. They
             stormed,
       Calling it all the slanderous rant of a fool;
       And this relieved me. Yet the suspicion
260   Remained always aching in my mind;
       I knew there was talk; I could not rest;
       And finally, saying nothing to my parents,
       I went to the shrine at Delphi.

       The god dismissed my question without reply;
       He spoke of other things.
265   Some were clear,
       Full of wretchedness, dreadful, unbearable:
       As, that I should lie with my own mother, breed
       Children from whom all men would turn their
             eyes;
       And that I should be my father's murderer.

270   I heard all this, and fled. And from that day
       Corinth to me was only in the stars
       Descending in that quarter of the sky,
       As I wandered farther and farther on my way
       To a land where I should never see the evil
275   Sung by the oracle. And I came to this country
       Where, so you say, King Laios was killed.

       I will tell you all that happened there, my lady.
       There were three highways
       Coming together at a place I passed;
       And there a herald came towards me, and a
280   chariot
       Drawn by horses, with a man such as you describe
       Seated in it. The groom leading the horses
       Forced me off the road at his lord's command;
       But as this charioteer lurched over towards me
285   I struck him in my rage. The old man saw me
       And brought his double goad down upon my head
       As I came abreast.
                          He was paid back, and more!
       Swinging my club in this right hand I knocked him

       Out of his car, and he rolled on the ground.
                                          I killed him.
       I killed them all.   290
       Now if that stranger and Laios were—kin,
       Where is a man more miserable than I?
       More hated by the gods? Citizen and alien alike
       Must never shelter me or speak to me—
       I must be shunned by all.
                               And I myself   295
       Pronounced this malediction upon myself!

       Think of it: I have touched you with these hands,
       These hands that killed your husband. What
             defilement!

       Am I all evil, then? It must be so,
       Since I must flee from Thebes, yet never again   300
       See my own countrymen, my own country,
       For fear of joining my mother in marriage
       And killing Polybos, my father.
                                  Ah,
       If I was created so, born to this fate,
       Who could deny the savagery of God?   305
       O holy majesty of heavenly powers!
       May I never see that day! Never!
       Rather let me vanish from the race of men
       Than know the abomination destined me!
    CHORAGOS: We too, my lord, have felt dismay at this. 310
       But there is hope: you have yet to hear the shepherd.
    OEDIPUS: Indeed, I fear no other hope is left me.
    IOKASTE: What do you hope from him when he
             comes?
    OEDIPUS: This much:
       If his account of the murder tallies with yours,
       Then I am cleared.
    IOKASTE: What was it that I said   315
       Of such importance?
    OEDIPUS: Why, "marauders," you said.
       Killed the king, according to this man's story,
       If he maintains that still, if there were several,
       Clearly the guilt is not mine: I was alone.
       But if he says one man, singlehanded, did it,   320
       Then the evidence all points to me.
    IOKASTE: You may be sure that he said there were
             several;
       And can he call back that story now? He can not.
       The whole city heard it as plainly as I.
       But suppose he alters some detail of it: 325
       He can not ever show that Laios' death
       Fulfilled the oracle: for Apollo said
       My child was doomed to kill him; and my child—
       Poor baby!—it was my child that died first.

       No. From now on, where oracles are concerned,   330
       I would not waste a second thought on any.
    OEDIPUS: You may be right.
                               But come: let someone go
       For the shepherd at once. This matter must be settled.

IOKASTE: I will send for him.
335   I would not wish to cross you in anything,
        And surely not in this.—Let us go in.

(Exeunt into the palace.)

ODE 2 • Strophe 1

CHORUS: Let me be reverent in the ways of right,
        Lowly the paths I journey on;
        Let all my words and actions keep
        The laws of the pure universe
5   From highest Heaven handed down.
        For Heaven is their bright nurse,
        Those generations of the realms of light;
        Ah, never of mortal kind were they begot,
        Nor are they slaves of memory, lost in sleep:
10   Their Father is greater than Time, and ages not.

Antistrophe 1

        The tyrant is a child of Pride
        Who drinks from his great sickening cup
        Recklessness and vanity,
        Until from his high crest headlong
15   He plummets to the dust of hope.
        That strong man is not strong.
        But let no fair ambition be denied;
        May God protect the wrestler for the State
        In government, in comely policy,
20   Who will fear God, and on his ordinance wait.

Strophe 2

        Haughtiness and the high hand of disdain
        Tempt and outrage God's holy law;
        And any mortal who dares hold
        No immortal Power in awe
25   Will be caught up in a net of pain:
        The price for which his levity is sold.
        Let each man take due earnings, then,
        And keep his hands from holy things,
        And from blasphemy stand apart—
30   Else the crackling blast of heaven
        Blows on his head, and on his desperate heart.
        Though fools will honor impious men,
        In their cities no tragic poet sings.

Antistrophe 2

        Shall we lose faith in Delphi's obscurities,
35   We who have heard the world's core
        Discredited, and the sacred wood
        Of Zeus at Elis praised no more?

        The deeds and the strange prophecies
        Must make a pattern yet to be understood.
        Zeus, if indeed you are lord of all,   40
        Throned in light over night and day,
        Mirror this in your endless mind:
        Our masters call the oracle
        Words on the wind, and the Delphic vision blind!
        Their hearts no longer know Apollo,   45
        And reverence for the gods has died away.

SCENE 3

(Enter Iokaste.)

IOKASTE: Princes of Thebes, it has occurred to me
        To visit the altars of the gods, bearing
        These branches as a suppliant, and this incense.
        Our king is not himself: his noble soul
        Is overwrought with fantasies of dread,   5
        Else he would consider
        The new prophecies in the light of the old.
        He will listen to any voice that speaks disaster,
        And my advice goes for nothing. (*She approaches
            the altar*, *right*.)
                            To you, then, Apollo,
        Lycean lord, since you are nearest, I turn in prayer   10
        Receive these offerings, and grant us deliverance
        From defilement. Our hearts are heavy with fear
        When we see our leader distracted, as helpless
            sailors
        Are terrified by the confusion of their helmsman.

(Enter Messenger.)

MESSENGER: Friends, no doubt you can direct me: 15
        Where shall I find the house of Oedipus,
        Or, better still, where is the king himself?
CHORAGOS: It is this very place, stranger; he is inside.
        This is his wife and mother of his children.
MESSENGER: I wish her happiness in a happy house,   20
        Blest in all the fulfillment of her marriage.
IOKASTE: I wish as much for you: your courtesy
        Deserves a like good fortune. But now, tell me:
        Why have you come? What have you to say to us?
MESSENGER: Good news, my lady, for your house and
            your husband.   25
IOKASTE: What news? Who sent you here?
MESSENGER: I am from Corinth.
        The news I bring ought to mean joy for you,
        Though it may be you will find some grief in it.
IOKASTE: What is it? How can it touch us in both
            ways?
MESSENGER: The word is that the people of the
            Isthmus   30
        Intend to call Oedipus to be their king.
IOKASTE: But old King Polybos—is he not reigning
            still?
MESSENGER: No. Death holds him in his sepulchre.
IOKASTE: What are you saying? Polybos is dead?

MESSENGER: If I am not telling the truth, may I die
35   myself.
IOKASTE (*to a Maidservant*): Go in, go quickly; tell
    this to your master.
    O riddlers of God's will, where are you now!
    This was the man whom Oedipus, long ago,
    Feared so, fled so, in dread of destroying him—
40   But it was another fate by which he died.

(*Enter Oedipus, center.*)

OEDIPUS: Dearest Iokaste, why have you sent for me?
IOKASTE: Listen to what this man says, and then
    tell me
    What has become of the solemn prophecies.
OEDIPUS: Who is this man? What is his news for me?
IOKASTE: He has come from Corinth to announce
45   your father's death!
OEDIPUS: Is it true, stranger? Tell me in your own
    words.
MESSENGER: I can not say it more clearly: the king is
    dead.
OEDIPUS: Was it by treason? Or by an attack of
    illness?
MESSENGER: A little thing brings old men to their
    rest.
OEDIPUS: It was sickness, then?
50   MESSENGER: Yes, and his many years.
OEDIPUS: Ah!
    Why should a man respect the Pythian hearth,° or
    Give heed to the birds that jangle above his head?
    They prophesied that I should kill Polybos,
55   Kill my own father; but he is dead and buried,
    And I am here—I never touched him, never,
    Unless he died of grief for my departure,
    And thus, in a sense, through me. No. Polybos
    Has packed the oracles off with him underground.
    They are empty words.
60   IOKASTE: Had I not told you so?
OEDIPUS: You had; it was my faint heart that
    betrayed me.
IOKASTE: From now on never think of those things
    again.
OEDIPUS: And yet—must I not fear my mother's bed?
IOKASTE: Why should anyone in this world be afraid
65   Since Fate rules us and nothing can be foreseen?
    A man should live only for the present day.

    Have no more fear of sleeping with your mother:
    How many men, in dreams, have lain with their
    mothers!
    No reasonable man is troubled by such things.
70   OEDIPUS: That is true, only—
    If only my mother were not still alive!
    But she is alive. I can not help my dread.
IOKASTE: Yet this news of your father's death is
    wonderful.
OEDIPUS: Wonderful. But I fear the living woman.

52. **Pythian hearth:** Delphi.

MESSENGER: Tell me, who is this woman that you
    fear?   75
OEDIPUS: It is Merope, man; the wife of King
    Polybos.
MESSENGER: Merope? Why should you be afraid of
    her?
OEDIPUS: An oracle of the gods, a dreadful saying.
MESSENGER: Can you tell me about it or are you
    sworn to silence?
OEDIPUS: I can tell you, and I will.   80
    Apollo said through his prophet that I was the
    man
    Who should marry his own mother, shed his
    father's blood
    With his own hands. And so, for all these years
    I have kept clear of Corinth, and no harm has
    come—
    Though it would have been sweet to see my
    parents again.   85
MESSENGER: And is this the fear that drove you out
    of Corinth?
OEDIPUS: Would you have me kill my father?
MESSENGER: As for that
    You must be reassured by the news I gave you.
OEDIPUS: If you could reassure me, I would reward
    you.
MESSENGER: I had that in mind, I will confess: I
    thought   90
    I could count on you when you returned to
    Corinth.
OEDIPUS: No: I will never go near my parents again.
MESSENGER: Ah, son, you still do not know what you
    are doing—
OEDIPUS: What do you mean? In the name of God
    tell me!
MESSENGER: —If these are your reasons for not going
    home.   95
OEDIPUS: I tell you, I fear the oracle may come true.
MESSENGER: And guilt may come upon you through
    your parents?
OEDIPUS: That is the dread that is always in my heart.
MESSENGER: Can you not see that all your fears
    are groundless?
OEDIPUS: Groundless? Am I not my parents' son?   100
MESSENGER: Polybos was not your father.
OEDIPUS: Not my father?
MESSENGER: No more your father than the man
    speaking to you.
OEDIPUS: But you are nothing to me!
MESSENGER: Neither was he.
OEDIPUS: Then why did he call me son?
MESSENGER: I will tell you:
    Long ago he had you from my hands, as a gift.   105
OEDIPUS: Then how could he love me so, if I was not
    his?
MESSENGER: He had no children, and his heart
    turned to you.
OEDIPUS: What of you? Did you buy me? Did you
    find me by chance?

MESSENGER: I came upon you in the woody vales of
　　Kithairon.
OEDIPUS: And what were you doing there?
110　MESSENGER:　　　　　　　　　　　　Tending my flocks.
OEDIPUS: A wandering shepherd?
MESSENGER:　　　　　　　　　　But your savior, son, that day.
OEDIPUS: From what did you save me?
MESSENGER:　　　　　　　　　Your ankles should tell you that.
OEDIPUS: Ah, stranger, why do you speak of that
　　childhood pain?
MESSENGER: I pulled the skewer that pinned your feet
　　together.
OEDIPUS: I have had the mark as long as I can
115　　remember.
MESSENGER: That was why you were given the name°
　　you bear.
OEDIPUS: God! Was it my father or my mother who
　　did it?
　　Tell me!
MESSENGER: I do not know. The man who gave you
　　to me
　　Can tell you better than I.
120　OEDIPUS: It was not you that found me, but another?
MESSENGER: It was another shepherd gave you
　　to me.
OEDIPUS: Who was he? Can you tell me who he was?
MESSENGER: I think he was said to be one of Laios'
　　people.
OEDIPUS: You mean the Laios who was king here
　　years ago?
MESSENGER: Yes; King Laios; and the man was one
125　　of his herdsmen.
OEDIPUS: Is he still alive? Can I see him?
MESSENGER:　　　　　　　　　　　These men here
　　Know best about such things.
OEDIPUS:　　　　　　　　　　Does anyone here
　　Know this shepherd that he is talking about?
　　Have you seen him in the fields, or in the town?
　　If you have, tell me. It is time things were made
130　　plain.
CHORAGOS: I think the man he means is that same
　　shepherd
　　You have already asked to see. Iokaste perhaps
　　Could tell you something.
OEDIPUS:　　　　　　　　　　Do you know anything
　　About him, Lady? Is he the man we have
　　summoned?
　　Is that the man this shepherd means?
135　IOKASTE:　　　　　　　　　　Why think of him?
　　Forget this herdsman. Forget it all.
　　This talk is a waste of time.
OEDIPUS:　　　　　　　　　How can you say that,
　　When the clues to my true birth are in my hands?
IOKASTE: For God's love, let us have no more
　　questioning!
140　　Is your life nothing to you?
　　My own is pain enough for me to bear.

116. name: *Oedipus* literally means "swollen foot."

OEDIPUS: You need not worry. Suppose my mother a
　　slave,
　　And born of slaves: no baseness can touch you.
IOKASTE: Listen to me, I beg you: do not do this thing!
OEDIPUS: I will not listen; the truth must be made
　　known.　　　　　　　　　　　　　　　　　　145
IOKASTE: Everything that I say is for your own good!
OEDIPUS:　　　　　　　　　　　My own good
　　Snaps my patience, then; I want none of it.
IOKASTE: You are fatally wrong! May you never learn
　　who you are!
OEDIPUS: Go, one of you, and bring the shepherd here.
　　Let us leave this woman to brag of her royal name.　150
IOKASTE: Ah, miserable!
　　That is the only word I have for you now.
　　That is the only word I can ever have.

　　　　　　　　　　　　　　(*Exit into the palace.*)

CHORAGOS: Why has she left us, Oedipus? Why has
　　she gone
　　In such a passion of sorrow? I fear this silence:　155
　　Something dreadful may come of it.
OEDIPUS:　　　　　　　　　　　Let it come!
　　However base my birth, I must know about it.
　　The Queen, like a woman, is perhaps ashamed
　　To think of my low origin. But I
　　Am a child of Luck, I can not be dishonored.　160
　　Luck is my mother; the passing months, my
　　brothers,
　　Have seen me rich and poor.
　　　　　　　　　　　　　　　If this is so,
　　How could I wish that I were someone else?
　　How could I not be glad to know my birth?

ODE 3 • Strophe

CHORUS: If ever the coming time were known
　　To my heart's pondering,
　　Kithairon, now by Heaven I see the torches
　　At the festival of the next full moon
　　And see the dance, and hear the choir sing　　5
　　A grace to your gentle shade:
　　Mountain where Oedipus was found,
　　O mountain guard of a noble race!
　　May the god° who heals us lend his aid,
　　And let that glory come to pass　　10
　　For our king's cradling-ground.

Antistrophe

　　Of the nymphs that flower beyond the years,
　　Who bore you,° royal child,

9. god: Apollo.　**13. Who bore you:** The Chorus is asking if
Oedipus is the son of an immortal nymph and a god: Pan,
Apollo, Hermes, or Dionysus.

To Pan° of the hills or the timberline Apollo,
15   Cold in delight where the upland clears,
Or Hermes° for whom Kyllene's° heights are piled?
Or flushed as evening cloud,
Great Dionysos,° roamer of mountains,
He—was it he who found you there,
20   And caught you up in his own proud
Arms from the sweet god-ravisher
Who laughed by the Muses'° fountains?

SCENE 4

OEDIPUS: Sirs: though I do not know the man,
I think I see him coming, this shepherd we want:
He is old, like our friend here, and the men
Bringing him seem to be servants of my house.
5   But you can tell, if you have ever seen him.

(*Enter Shepherd escorted by Servants.*)

CHORAGOS: I know him, he was Laios' man. You can
trust him.
OEDIPUS: Tell me first, you from Corinth: is this the
shepherd
We were discussing?
MESSENGER: This is the very man.
OEDIPUS (*to Shepherd*): Come here. No, look at me.
You must answer
10   Everything I ask.—You belonged to Laios?
SHEPHERD: Yes: born his slave, brought up in his
house.
OEDIPUS: Tell me: what kind of work did you do for
him?
SHEPHERD: I was a shepherd of his, most of my life.
OEDIPUS: Where mainly did you go for pasturage?
SHEPHERD: Sometimes Kithairon, sometimes the hills
15   near-by.
OEDIPUS: Do you remember ever seeing this man out
there?
SHEPHERD: What would he be doing there? This
man?
OEDIPUS: This man standing here. Have you ever
seen him before?
SHEPHERD: No. At least, not to my recollection.
MESSENGER: And that is not strange, my lord. But I'll
20   refresh
His memory: he must remember when we two
Spent three whole seasons together, March to
September,
On Kithairon or thereabouts. He had two flocks;

---

14. **Pan:** God of nature, forests, flocks, and shepherds, depicted
as half man and half goat.   16. **Hermes:** Son of Zeus, messenger
of the gods.   **Kyllene:** Mountain reputed to be the birthplace
of Hermes; also the center of a cult to Hermes.   18. **Dionysos:**
Dionysus, god of wine around whom wild, orgiastic rituals developed; also called Bacchus.   22. **Muses:** Nine sister goddesses
who presided over poetry and music, art and sciences.

I had one. Each autumn I'd drive mine home
And he would go back with his to Laios'
sheepfold.—   25
Is this not true, just as I have described it?
SHEPHERD: True, yes; but it was all so long ago.
MESSENGER: Well, then: do you remember, back in
those days,
That you gave me a baby boy to bring up as my
own?
SHEPHERD: What if I did? What are you trying
to say?   30
MESSENGER: King Oedipus was once that little child.
SHEPHERD: Damn you, hold your tongue!
OEDIPUS: No more of that!
It is your tongue needs watching, not this man's.
SHEPHERD: My king, my master, what is it I have
done wrong?
OEDIPUS: You have not answered his question about
the boy.   35
SHEPHERD: He does not know . . . He is only making
trouble . . .
OEDIPUS: Come, speak plainly, or it will go hard with
you.
SHEPHERD: In God's name, do not torture an old
man!
OEDIPUS: Come here, one of you; bind his arms
behind him.
SHEPHERD: Unhappy king! What more do you wish
to learn?   40
OEDIPUS: Did you give this man the child he speaks
of?
SHEPHERD: I did.
And I would to God I had died that very day.
OEDIPUS: You will die now unless you speak the
truth.
SHEPHERD: Yet if I speak the truth, I am worse than
dead.
OEDIPUS (*to Attendant*): He intends to draw it out,
apparently—   45
SHEPHERD: No! I have told you already that I gave
him the boy.
OEDIPUS: Where did you get him? From your house?
From somewhere else?
SHEPHERD: Not from mine, no. A man gave him
to me.
OEDIPUS: Is that man here? Whose house did he
belong to?
SHEPHERD: For God's love, my king, do not ask me
any more!   50
OEDIPUS: You are a dead man if I have to ask you
again.
SHEPHERD: Then . . . Then the child was from the
palace of Laios.
OEDIPUS: A slave child? or a child of his own line?
SHEPHERD: Ah, I am on the brink of dreadful speech!
OEDIPUS: And I of dreadful hearing. Yet I must hear.   55
SHEPHERD: If you must be told, then . . .
                              They said it was Laios' child;
But it is your wife who can tell you about that.

The Shepherd (Oliver Cliff) tells Oedipus (Kenneth Welsh) the truth about his birth in the Guthrie Theater Company's 1973 production directed by Michael Langham.

OEDIPUS: My wife—Did she give it to you?
SHEPHERD: My lord, she did.
OEDIPUS: Do you know why?
SHEPHERD: I was told to get rid of it.
OEDIPUS: Oh heartless mother!
60 SHEPHERD: But in dread of prophecies . . .
OEDIPUS: Tell me.
SHEPHERD: It was said that the boy would kill his
       own father.
OEDIPUS: Then why did you give him over to this old
       man?
SHEPHERD: I pitied the baby, my king,
       And I thought that this man would take him far away
       To his own country.
65   He saved him—but for what a fate!
       For if you are what this man says you are,
       No man living is more wretched than Oedipus.
OEDIPUS: Ah God!
       It was true!
                 All the prophecies!
                              —Now,
70   O Light, may I look on you for the last time!
       I, Oedipus,
       Oedipus, damned in his birth, in his marriage
           damned,
       Damned in the blood he shed with his own hand!

(*He rushes into the palace.*)

ODE 4 • Strophe 1

CHORUS: Alas for the seed of men.
       What measure shall I give these generations
       That breathe on the void and are void
       And exist and do not exist?
5   Who bears more weight of joy
       Than mass of sunlight shifting in images,
       Or who shall make his thought stay on
       That down time drifts away?
       Your splendor is all fallen.
10   O naked brow of wrath and tears,
       O change of Oedipus!
       I who saw your days call no man blest—
       Your great days like ghosts gone.

Antistrophe 1

       That mind was a strong bow.
15   Deep, how deep you drew it then, hard archer,
       At a dim fearful range,
       And brought dear glory down!
       You overcame the stranger°—
       The virgin with her hooking lion claws—
20   And though death sang, stood like a tower

       To make pale Thebes take heart.
       Fortress against our sorrow!
       True king, giver of laws,
       Majestic Oedipus!
       No prince in Thebes had ever such renown,   25
       No prince won such grace of power.

Strophe 2

       And now of all men ever known
       Most pitiful is this man's story:
       His fortunes are most changed; his state
       Fallen to a low slave's   30
       Ground under bitter fate.
       O Oedipus, most royal one!
       The great door° that expelled you to the light
       Gave at night—ah, gave night to your glory:
       As to the father, to the fathering son.   35
       All understood too late.
       How could that queen whom Laios won,
       The garden that he harrowed at his height,
       Be silent when that act was done?

Antistrophe 2

       But all eyes fail before time's eye,   40
       All actions come to justice there.
       Though never willed, though far down the deep
           past,
       Your bed, your dread sirings,
       Are brought to book at last.
       Child by Laios doomed to die,   45
       Then doomed to lose that fortunate little
           death,
       Would God you never took breath in this air
       That with my wailing lips I take to cry:
       For I weep the world's outcast.
       I was blind, and now I can tell why: 50
       Asleep, for you had given ease of breath
       To Thebes, while the false years went by.

EXODOS°

(*Enter, from the palace, Second Messenger.*)

SECOND MESSENGER: Elders of Thebes, most honored
       in this land,
       What horrors are yours to see and hear, what
           weight
       Of sorrow to be endured, if, true to your birth,
       You venerate the line of Labdakos!
       I think neither Istros nor Phasis, those great
           rivers,   5
       Could purify this place of all the evil

18. **stranger:** The Sphinx.   33. **door:** Iokaste's womb.   **Exodos:** Final scene.

It shelters now, or soon must bring to light—
Evil not done unconsciously, but willed.

The greatest griefs are those we cause ourselves.
10 CHORAGOS: Surely, friend, we have grief enough
        already;
    What new sorrow do you mean?
SECOND MESSENGER: The queen is dead.
CHORAGOS: O miserable queen! But at whose hand?
SECOND MESSENGER: Her own.
    The full horror of what happened you can not
        know,
15 For you did not see it; but I, who did, will tell you
    As clearly as I can how she met her death.

    When she had left us,
    In passionate silence, passing through the court,
    She ran to her apartment in the house,
20 Her hair clutched by the fingers of both hands.
    She closed the doors behind her; then, by that bed
    Where long ago the fatal son was conceived—
    That son who should bring about his father's
        death—
    We heard her call upon Laios, dead so many
        years,
    And heard her wail for the double fruit of her
25   marriage,
    A husband by her husband, children by her child.

    Exactly how she died I do not know:
    For Oedipus burst in moaning and would not
        let us
    Keep vigil to the end: it was by him
    As he stormed about the room that our eyes were
        caught.
    From one to another of us he went, begging a
30   sword,
    Hunting the wife who was not his wife, the
        mother
    Whose womb had carried his own children and
        himself.
    I do not know: it was none of us aided him,
35 But surely one of the gods was in control!
    For with a dreadful cry
    He hurled his weight, as though wrenched out of
        himself,
    At the twin doors: the bolts gave, and he rushed in.
    And there we saw her hanging, her body swaying
    From the cruel cord she had noosed about her
40   neck.
    A great sob broke from him, heartbreaking to hear,
    As he loosed the rope and lowered her to the
        ground.

    I would blot out from my mind what happened
        next!
    For the king ripped from her gown the golden
        brooches

That were her ornament, and raised them, and
    plunged them down
Straight into his own eyeballs, crying, "No more,   45
No more shall you look on the misery about me,
The horrors of my own doing! Too long you have
    known
The faces of those whom I should never have seen,
Too long been blind to those for whom I was
    searching!
From this hour, go in darkness!" And as he spoke,   50
He struck at his eyes—not once, but many times;
And the blood spattered his beard,
Bursting from his ruined sockets like red hail.

So from the unhappiness of two this evil has sprung,
A curse on the man and woman alike. The old   55
Happiness of the house of Labdakos
Was happiness enough: where is it today?
It is all wailing and ruin, disgrace, death—all
The misery of mankind that has a name—
And it is wholly and for ever theirs.   60
CHORAGOS: Is he in agony still? Is there no rest for
    him?
SECOND MESSENGER: He is calling for someone to
    open the doors wide
So that all the children of Kadmos may look upon
His father's murderer, his mother's—no,
I can not say it!
                    And then he will leave Thebes,   65
Self-exiled, in order that the curse
Which he himself pronounced may depart from
    the house.
He is weak, and there is none to lead him,
So terrible is his suffering.
                          But you will see:
Look, the doors are opening; in a moment   70
You will see a thing that would crush a heart of
    stone.

(*The central door is opened; Oedipus, blinded, is led in.*)

CHORAGOS: Dreadful indeed for men to see.
    Never have my own eyes
    Looked on a sight so full of fear.

    Oedipus!   75
    What madness came upon you, what demon
    Leaped on your life with heavier
    Punishment than a mortal man can bear?
    No: I can not even
    Look at you, poor ruined one.   80
    And I would speak, question, ponder,
    If I were able. No.
    You make me shudder.
OEDIPUS: God. God.
    Is there a sorrow greater?   85
    Where shall I find harbor in this world?
    My voice is hurled far on a dark wind.
    What has God done to me?
CHORAGOS: Too terrible to think of, or to see.

A rehearsal for a production of *Oedipus Rex* at the Roman Colosseum in 2000.

Strophe 1

90 OEDIPUS: O cloud of night,
  Never to be turned away: night coming on,
  I can not tell how: night like a shroud!
  My fair winds brought me here.
                        O God. Again
  The pain of the spikes where I had sight,
95 The flooding pain
  Of memory, never to be gouged out.
CHORAGOS: This is not strange.
  You suffer it all twice over, remorse in pain,
  Pain in remorse.

Antistrophe 1

100 OEDIPUS: Ah dear friend
  Are you faithful even yet, you alone?
  Are you still standing near me, will you stay here,
  Patient, to care for the blind?
                        The blind man!
  Yet even blind I know who it is attends me,
105 By the voice's tone—
  Though my new darkness hide the comforter.
CHORAGOS: Oh fearful act!
  What god was it drove you to rake black
  Night across your eyes?

Strophe 2

OEDIPUS: Apollo. Apollo. Dear   110
  Children, the god was Apollo.
  He brought my sick, sick fate upon me.
  But the blinding hand was my own!
  How could I bear to see
  When all my sight was horror everywhere?   115
CHORAGOS: Everywhere; that is true.
OEDIPUS: And now what is left?
  Images? Love? A greeting even,
  Sweet to the senses? Is there anything?
  Ah, no, friends: lead me away.   120
  Lead me away from Thebes.
                        Lead the great wreck
  And hell of Oedipus, whom the gods hate.
CHORAGOS: Your misery, you are not blind to that.
  Would God you had never found it out!

Antistrophe 2

OEDIPUS: Death take the man who unbound   125
  My feet on that hillside
  And delivered me from death to life! What life?
  If only I had died,
  This weight of monstrous doom
  Could not have dragged me and my darlings down.   130

CHORAGOS: I would have wished the same.

OEDIPUS: Oh never to have come here
    With my father's blood upon me! Never
    To have been the man they call his mother's
        husband!
135   Oh accurst! Oh child of evil,
    To have entered that wretched bed—
                    the selfsame one!
    More primal than sin itself, this fell to me.

CHORAGOS: I do not know what words to offer you.
    You were better dead than alive and blind.

OEDIPUS: Do not counsel me any more. This
140   punishment
    That I have laid upon myself is just.
    If I had eyes,
    I do not know how I could bear the sight
    Of my father, when I came to the house of Death,
    Or my mother: for I have sinned against them
145   both
    So vilely that I could not make my peace
    By strangling my own life.
                Or do you think my children,
    Born as they were born, would be sweet to my
        eyes?
    Ah never, never! Nor this town with its high walls,
    Nor the holy images of the gods.
150   For I,
    Thrice miserable!—Oedipus, noblest of all the
        line
    Of Kadmos, have condemned myself to enjoy
    These things no more, by my own malediction
    Expelling that man whom the gods declared
155   To be a defilement in the house of Laios.
    After exposing the rankness of my own guilt,
    How could I look men frankly in the eyes?
    No, I swear it,
    If I could have stifled my hearing at its source,
160   I would have done it and made all this body
    A tight cell of misery, blank to light and sound:
    So I should have been safe in my dark mind
    Beyond external evil.
                Ah Kithairon!
    Why did you shelter me? When I was cast upon
        you,
165   Why did I not die? Then I should never
    Have shown the world my execrable birth.

    Ah Polybos! Corinth, city that I believed
    The ancient seat of my ancestors: how fair
    I seemed, your child! And all the while this evil
    Was cancerous within me!
170   For I am sick
    In my own being, sick in my origin.
    O three roads, dark ravine, woodland and way
    Where three roads met; you, drinking my father's
        blood,
    My own blood, spilled by my own hand: can you
        remember
175   The unspeakable things I did there, and the things

    I went on from there to do?
                O marriage, marriage!
    The act that engendered me, and again the act
    Performed by the son in the same bed—
                    Ah, the net
    Of incest, mingling fathers, brothers, sons,
    With brides, wives, mothers: the last evil   180
    That can be known by men: no tongue can say
    How evil!
            No. For the love of God, conceal me
    Somewhere far from Thebes; or kill me; or hurl me
    Into the sea, away from men's eyes for ever.

    Come, lead me. You need not fear to touch me.   185
    Of all men, I alone can bear this guilt.

(Enter Kreon.)

CHORAGOS: Kreon is here now. As to what you ask,
    He may decide the course to take. He only
    Is left to protect the city in your place.

OEDIPUS: Alas, how can I speak to him? What right
    have I   190
    To beg his courtesy whom I have deeply wronged?

KREON: I have not come to mock you, Oedipus,
    Or to reproach you, either.
    (To Attendants.)   —You, standing there:
    If you have lost all respect for man's dignity,
    At least respect the flame of Lord Helios:°   195
    Do not allow this pollution to show itself
    Openly here, an affront to the earth
    And Heaven's rain and the light of day. No, take
        him
    Into the house as quickly as you can.
    For it is proper   200
    That only the close kindred see his grief.

OEDIPUS: I pray you in God's name, since your
    courtesy
    Ignores my dark expectation, visiting
    With mercy this man of all men most execrable:
    Give me what I ask—for your good, not for mine.   205

KREON: And what is it that you turn to me begging
    for?

OEDIPUS: Drive me out of this country as quickly as
    may be
    To a place where no human voice can ever greet
    me.

KREON: I should have done that before now—only,
    God's will had not been wholly revealed to me.   210

OEDIPUS: But his command is plain: the parricide
    Must be destroyed. I am that evil man.

KREON: That is the sense of it, yes; but as things are,
    We had best discover clearly what is to be done.

OEDIPUS: You would learn more about a man
    like me?   215

KREON: You are ready now to listen to the god.

OEDIPUS: I will listen. But it is to you
    That I must turn for help. I beg you, hear me.

195. Lord Helios: The sun god.

The woman is there—
220 Give her whatever funeral you think proper:
She is your sister.
            —But let me go, Kreon!
Let me purge my father's Thebes of the pollution
Of my living here, and go out to the wild hills,
To Kithairon, that has won such fame with me,
225 The tomb my mother and father appointed for me,
And let me die there, as they willed I should.
And yet I know
Death will not ever come to me through sickness
Or in any natural way: I have been preserved
230 For some unthinkable fate. But let that be.

As for my sons, you need not care for them.
They are men, they will find some way to live.
But my poor daughters, who have shared my table,
Who never before have been parted from their
            father—
235 Take care of them, Kreon; do this for me.

And will you let me touch them with my hands
A last time, and let us weep together?
Be kind, my lord,
Great prince, be kind!
                  Could I but touch them,
240 They would be mine again, as when I had my eyes.

(*Enter Antigone and Ismene, attended.*)

Ah, God!
Is it my dearest children I hear weeping?
Has Kreon pitied me and sent my daughters?
KREON: Yes, Oedipus: I knew that they were dear
            to you
245 In the old days, and know you must love them still.
OEDIPUS: May God bless you for this—and be a
            friendlier
Guardian to you than he has been to me!

Children, where are you?
Come quickly to my hands: they are your
            brother's—
Hands that have brought your father's once clear
250 eyes
To this way of seeing—
                  Ah dearest ones,
I had neither sight nor knowledge then, your father
By the woman who was the source of his own life!
And I weep for you—having no strength to see
            you—,
255 I weep for you when I think of the bitterness
That men will visit upon you all your lives.
What homes, what festivals can you attend
Without being forced to depart again in tears?
And when you come to marriageable age,
260 Where is the man, my daughters, who would dare
Risk the bane that lies on all my children?
Is there any evil wanting? Your father killed
His father; sowed the womb of her who bore him;

Engendered you at the fount of his own existence!
That is what they will say of you.

                              Then, whom   265
Can you ever marry? There are no bridegrooms
      for you,
And your lives must wither away in sterile dreaming.

O Kreon, son of Menoikeus!
You are the only father my daughters have,
Since we, their parents, are both of us gone for ever.   270
They are your own blood: you will not let them
Fall into beggary and loneliness;
You will keep them from the miseries that are mine!
Take pity on them; see, they are only children,
Friendless except for you. Promise me this,   275
Great prince, and give me your hand in token of it.

(*Kreon clasps his right hand.*)

Children:
I could say much, if you could understand me,
But as it is, I have only this prayer for you:
Live where you can, be as happy as you can—   280
Happier, please God, than God has made your
      father.
KREON: Enough. You have wept enough. Now go
      within.
OEDIPUS: I must, but it is hard.
KREON: Time eases all things.
OEDIPUS: You know my mind, then?
KREON: Say what you desire.
OEDIPUS: Send me from Thebes!
KREON: God grant that I may!   285
OEDIPUS: But since God hates me . . .
KREON: No, he will grant your wish.
OEDIPUS: You promise?
KREON: I can not speak beyond my knowledge.
OEDIPUS: Then lead me in.
KREON: Come now, and leave your children.   290
OEDIPUS: No! Do not take them from me!
KREON: Think no longer
That you are in command here, but rather think
How, when you were, you served your own
      destruction.

            (*Exeunt into the house all but
            the Chorus; the Choragos
            chants directly to the audience.*)

CHORAGOS: Men of Thebes: look upon Oedipus.

This is the king who solved the famous riddle   295
And towered up, most powerful of men.
No mortal eyes but looked on him with envy,
Yet in the end ruin swept over him.

Let every man in mankind's frailty
Consider his last day; and let none   300
Presume on his good fortune until he find
Life, at his death, a memory without pain.

COMMENTARIES

Critical comment on the plays of Sophocles has been rich and various and has spanned the centuries. We are especially fortunate to have a commentary from the great age of Greek thought a century after Sophocles himself flourished. In *Oedipus Rex*, Sophocles gave the philosopher Aristotle a perfect drama on which to build a theory of tragedy, and Aristotle's observations have remained the most influential comments made on drama in the West. In some ways they have established the function, limits, and purposes of drama. In the twentieth century, for instance, when Bertolt Brecht tried to create a new theory of the drama, he specifically described his ideas as an alternative to Aristotelian notions.

Although not a critic, Sigmund Freud saw in the Oedipus myth as interpreted by Sophocles a basic psychological phenomenon experienced by all people in their infancy. This "Oedipus complex" is now well established in the history of psychology and in the popular imagination.

The extraordinary range of commentary on the Oedipus story is demonstrated nowhere more amazingly than in Claude Lévi-Strauss's structural reading of the myth, both in Sophocles' version and in other versions. Lévi-Strauss shows that a pattern emerges when certain actions in the play are placed side by side. If he is correct, his theory offers a way to interpret myths and to see why they were valued so highly by the Greeks in their drama.

ARISTOTLE (384–322 BCE)

Poetics: Comedy and Epic and Tragedy   c. 334–323 BCE

TRANSLATED BY GERALD F. ELSE

Aristotle was Plato's most brilliant student and the heir to his teaching mantle. He remained with Plato for twenty years and then began his own school, called the Lyceum. His extant work consists mainly of his lectures, which were recorded by his students and carefully preserved. Called his treatises, they greatly influenced later thought and deal with almost every branch of philosophy, science, and the arts. His *Poetics* remains, more than two thousand years later, a document of immense importance for literary criticism. Although sometimes ambiguous, difficult, and unfinished, it provides insight into the theoretical basis of Greek tragedy and comedy, and it helps us see that the drama was significant enough in intellectual life to warrant an examination by the best Greek minds.

Comedy

Comedy is, as we said it was, an imitation of persons who are inferior; not, however, going all the way to full villainy, but imitating the ugly, of which the ludicrous is one part. The ludicrous, that is, is a failing or a piece of ugliness which causes no pain or destruction; thus, to go on farther, the comic mask° is something ugly and distorted but painless.

Now the stages of development of tragedy, and the men who were responsible for them, have not escaped notice but comedy did escape notice in the beginning because it was not taken seriously. (In fact it was late in its history that the presiding magistrate officially "granted a chorus" to the comic poets; until then they were volunteers.) Thus comedy already possessed certain defining characteristics when the first "comic poets," so-called, appear in the record. Who gave it masks, or prologues, or troupes of actors and all that sort of thing is not known. The composing of plots came originally from Sicily; of the Athenian poets, Crates° was the first to abandon the lampooning mode and compose arguments, that is, plots, of a general nature.

Epic and Tragedy

Well, then, epic poetry followed in the wake of tragedy up to the point of being a (1) good-sized (2) imitation (3) in verse (4) of people who are to be taken seriously; but in its having its verse unmixed with any other and being narrative in character, there they differ. Further, so far as its length is concerned, tragedy tries as hard as it can to exist during a single daylight period, or to vary but little, while the epic is not limited in its time and so differs in that respect. Yet originally they used to do this in tragedies just as much as they did in epic poems.

The constituent elements are partly identical and partly limited to tragedy. Hence anybody who knows about good and bad tragedy knows about epic also; for the elements that the epic possesses appertain to tragedy as well, but those of tragedy are not all found in the epic.

Tragedy and Its Six Constituent Elements

Our discussions of imitative poetry in hexameters,° and of comedy, will come later; at present let us deal with tragedy, recovering from what has been said so far the definition of its essential nature, as it was in development. Tragedy, then, is a process of imitating an action which has serious implications, is complete, and possesses magnitude; by means of language which has been made sensuously attractive, with each of its varieties found separately in the parts; enacted by the persons themselves and not presented through narrative; through a course of pity and fear completing the purification of tragic acts which have those emotional characteristics. By "language made sensuously attractive" I mean language that has rhythm and melody, and by "its varieties found separately" I mean the fact that certain parts of the play are carried on through spoken verses alone and others the other way around, through song.

the comic mask: Actors in Greek drama wore masks behind which they spoke their lines. The masks were made individually for each character.

Crates: Greek actor and playwright (fl. 470 BCE), credited by Aristotle with developing Greek comedy into a fully plotted, credible form. Aristophanes (c. 448–c. 385 BCE), another Greek comic playwright, says that Crates was the first to portray a drunkard onstage.

hexameters: The first known metrical form for classical verse. Each line had six metrical feet, some of which were prescribed in advance. It is the meter used for epic poetry and for poetry designed to teach a lesson. The form has sometimes been used in comparatively modern poetry but rarely with success except in French.

Now first of all, since they perform the imitation through action (by acting it), the adornment of their visual appearance will perforce constitute some part of the making of tragedy; and song-composition and verbal expression also, for those are the media in which they perform the imitation. By "verbal expression" I mean the actual composition of the verses, and by "song-composition" something whose meaning is entirely clear.

Next, since it is an imitation of an action and is enacted by certain people who are performing the action, and since those people must necessarily have certain traits both of character and thought (for it is thanks to these two factors that we speak of people's actions also as having a defined character, and it is in accordance with their actions that all either succeed or fail); and since the imitation of the action is the plot, for by "plot" I mean here the structuring of the events, and by the "characters" that in accordance with which we say that the persons who are acting have a defined moral character, and by "thought" all the passages in which they attempt to prove some thesis or set forth an opinion—it follows of necessity, then, that tragedy as a whole has just six constituent elements, in relation to the essence that makes it a distinct species; and they are plot, characters, verbal expression, thought, visual adornment, and song-composition. For the elements by which they imitate are two (i.e., verbal expression and song-composition), the manner in which they imitate is one (visual adornment), the things they imitate are three (plot, characters, thought), and there is nothing more beyond these. These then are the constituent forms they use.

The Relative Importance of the Six Elements

The greatest of these elements is the structuring of the incidents. For tragedy is an imitation not of men but of a life, an action, and they have moral quality in accordance with their characters but are happy or unhappy in accordance with their actions; hence they are not active in order to imitate their characters, but they include the characters along with the actions for the sake of the latter. Thus the structure of events, the plot, is the goal of tragedy, and the goal is the greatest thing of all.

Again: a tragedy cannot exist without a plot, but it can without characters: thus the tragedies of most of our modern poets are devoid of character, and in general many poets are like that; so also with the relationship between Zeuxis and Polygnotus,° among the painters: Polygnotus is a good portrayer of character, while Zeuxis's painting has no dimension of character at all.

Again: if one strings end to end speeches that are expressive of character and carefully worked in thought and expression, he still will not achieve the result which we said was the aim of tragedy; the job will be done much better by a tragedy that is more deficient in these other respects but has a plot, a structure of events. It is much the same case as with painting: the most beautiful pigments smeared on at random will not give as much pleasure as a black-and-white outline picture. Besides, the most powerful means tragedy has for swaying our feelings, namely the peripeties and recognitions,° are elements of plot.

Zeuxis and Polygnotus: Zeuxis (fl. 420–390 BCE) developed a method of painting in which the figures were rounded and apparently three-dimensional. Thus, he was an illusionistic painter, imitating life in a realistic style. Polygnotus (c. 470–440 BCE) was famous as a painter, and his works were on the Acropolis as well as at Delphi. His draftsmanship was especially praised.

peripeties and recognitions: The turning about of fortune and the recognition, on the part of the tragic hero, of the truth. This is, for Aristotle, a critical moment in the drama, especially if both events happen simultaneously, as they do in *Oedipus Rex*. It is quite possible for these moments to occur at separate times.

Again: an indicative sign is that those who are beginning a poetic career manage to hit the mark in verbal expression and character portrayal sooner than they do in plot construction; and the same is true of practically all the earliest poets.

So plot is the basic principle, the heart and soul, as it were, of tragedy, and the characters come second: [. . .] it is the imitation of an action and imitates the persons primarily for the sake of their action.

Third in rank is thought. This is the ability to state the issues and appropriate points pertaining to a given topic, an ability which springs from the arts of politics and rhetoric; in fact the earlier poets made their characters talk "politically," the present-day poets rhetorically. But "character" is that kind of utterance which clearly reveals the bent of a man's moral choice (hence there is no character in that class of utterances in which there is nothing at all that the speaker is choosing or rejecting), while "thought" is the passages in which they try to prove that something is so or not so, or state some general principle.

Fourth is the verbal expression of the speeches. I mean by this the same thing that was said earlier, that the "verbal expression" is the conveyance of thought through language: a statement which has the same meaning whether one says "verses" or "speeches."

The song-composition of the remaining parts is the greatest of the sensuous attractions, and the visual adornment of the dramatic persons can have a strong emotional effect but is the least artistic element, the least connected with the poetic art; in fact the force of tragedy can be felt even without benefit of public performance and actors, while for the production of the visual effect the property man's art is even more decisive than that of the poets.

General Principles of the Tragic Plot

With these distinctions out of the way, let us next discuss what the structuring of the events should be like, since this is both the basic and the most important element in the tragic art. We have established, then, that tragedy is an imitation of an action which is complete and whole and has some magnitude (for there is also such a thing as a whole that has no magnitude). "Whole" is that which has beginning, middle, and end. "Beginning" is that which does not necessarily follow on something else, but after it something else naturally is or happens; "end," the other way around, is that which naturally follows on something else, either necessarily or for the most part, but nothing else after it; and "middle" that which naturally follows on something else and something else on it. So, then, well constructed plots should neither begin nor end at any chance point but follow the guidelines just laid down.

Furthermore, since the beautiful, whether a living creature or anything that is composed of parts, should not only have these in a fixed order to one another but also possess a definite size which does not depend on chance—for beauty depends on size and order; hence neither can a very tiny creature turn out to be beautiful (since our perception of it grows blurred as it approaches the period of imperceptibility) nor an excessively huge one (for then it cannot all be perceived at once and so its unity and wholeness are lost), if for example there were a creature a thousand miles long—so, just as in the case of living creatures they must have some size, but one that can be taken in a single view, so with plots: they should have length, but such that they are easy to remember. As to a limit of the length, the one is determined by the tragic competitions and the ordinary span of attention. (If they had to compete with a hundred tragedies they would compete by the water clock, as they say used to be done [?].) But the limit fixed by the very nature of the case is: the longer the plot, up to the point of still being perspicuous as a whole, the finer it is so far as size is concerned; or to put it in general terms, the length in which, with things happening in unbroken sequence, a shift takes place either probably or necessarily from bad to good fortune or from good to bad—that is an acceptable norm of length.

But a plot is not unified, as some people think, simply because it has to do with a single person. A large, indeed an indefinite number of things can happen to a given individual, some of which go to constitute no unified event; and in the same way there can be many acts of a given individual from which no single action emerges. Hence it seems clear that those poets are wrong who have composed *Heracleïds*, *Theseïds*, and the like. They think that since Heracles was a single person it follows that the plot will be single too. But Homer, superior as he is in all other respects, appears to have grasped this point well also, thanks either to art or nature, for in composing an *Odyssey* he did not incorporate into it everything that happened to the hero, for example how he was wounded on Mt. Parnassus° or how he feigned madness at the muster, neither of which events, by happening, made it at all necessary or probable that the other should happen. Instead, he composed the *Odyssey*—and the *Iliad* similarly—around a unified action of the kind we have been talking about.

A poetic imitation, then, ought to be unified in the same way as a single imitation in any other mimetic field, by having a single object: since the plot is an imitation of an action, the latter ought to be both unified and complete, and the component events ought to be so firmly compacted that if any one of them is shifted to another place, or removed, the whole is loosened up and dislocated; for an element whose addition or subtraction makes no perceptible extra difference is not really a part of the whole.

From what has been said it is also clear that the poet's job is not to report what has happened but what is likely to happen: that is, what is capable of happening according to the rule of probability or necessity. Thus the difference between the historian and the poet is not in their utterances being in verse or prose (it would be quite possible for Herodotus's work to be translated into verse, and it would not be any the less a history with verse than it is without it); the difference lies in the fact that the historian speaks of what has happened, the poet of the kind of thing that *can* happen. Hence also poetry is a more philosophical and serious business than history; for poetry speaks more of universals, history of particulars. "Universal" in this case is what kind of person is likely to do or say certain kinds of things, according to probability or necessity; that is what poetry aims at, although it gives its persons particular names afterward; while the "particular" is what Alcibiades did or what happened to him.

In the field of comedy this point has been grasped: our comic poets construct their plots on the basis of general probabilities and then assign names to

---

Mt. Parnassus: A mountain in central Greece traditionally sacred to Apollo. In legend, Odysseus was wounded there, but the point Aristotle is making is that the writer of epics need not include every detail of his hero's life in a given work. Homer, in writing the *Odyssey*, was working with a hero, Odysseus, whose story had been legendary long before Homer began writing.

the persons quite arbitrarily, instead of dealing with individuals as the old iambic poets° did. But in tragedy they still cling to the historically given names. The reason is that what is possible is persuasive; so what has not happened we are not yet ready to believe is possible, while what has happened is, we feel, obviously possible: for it would not have happened if it were impossible. Nevertheless, it is a fact that even in our tragedies, in some cases only one or two of the names are traditional, the rest being invented, and in some others none at all. It is so, for example, in Agathon's *Antheus*—the names in it are as fictional as the events—and it gives no less pleasure because of that. Hence the poets ought not to cling at all costs to the traditional plots, around which our tragedies are constructed. And in fact it is absurd to go searching for this kind of authentication, since even the familiar names are familiar to only a few in the audience and yet give the same kind of pleasure to all.

So from these considerations it is evident that the poet should be a maker of his plots more than of his verses, insofar as he is a poet by virtue of his imitations and what he imitates is actions. Hence even if it happens that he puts something that has actually taken place into poetry, he is none the less a poet; for there is nothing to prevent some of the things that have happened from being the kind of things that can happen, and that is the sense in which he is their maker.

Simple and Complex Plots

Among simple plots and actions the episodic are the worst. By "episodic" plot I mean one in which there is no probability or necessity for the order in which the episodes follow one another. Such structures are composed by the bad poets because they are bad poets, but by the good poets because of the actors: in composing contest pieces for them, and stretching out the plot beyond its capacity, they are forced frequently to dislocate the sequence.

Furthermore, since the tragic imitation is not only of a complete action but also of events that are fearful and pathetic,° and these come about best when they come about contrary to one's expectation yet logically, one following from the other; that way they will be more productive of wonder than if they happen merely at random, by chance—because even among chance occurrences the ones people consider most marvelous are those that seem to have come about as if on purpose: for example the way the statue of Mitys at Argos killed the man who had been the cause of Mitys's death, by falling on him while he was attending the festival; it stands to reason, people think, that such things don't happen by chance—so plots of that sort cannot fail to be artistically superior.

Some plots are simple, others are complex; indeed the actions of which the plots are imitations already fall into these two categories. By "simple" action I mean one the development of which being continuous and unified in the manner stated above,

---

old iambic poets: Aristotle may be referring to Archilochus (fl. 650 BCE) and the iambic style he developed. The iamb is a metrical foot of two syllables, a short and a long syllable, and was the most popular metrical style before the time of Aristotle. "Dealing with individuals" implies using figures already known to the audience rather than figures whose names can be arbitrarily assigned because no one knows who they are.

fearful and pathetic: Aristotle said that tragedy should evoke two emotions: terror and pity. The terror results from our realizing that what is happening to the hero might just as easily happen to us; the pity results from our human sympathy with a fellow sufferer. Therefore, the fearful and pathetic represent significant emotions appropriate to our witnessing drama.

the reversal comes without peripety or recognition, and by "complex" action one in which the reversal is continuous but with recognition or peripety or both. And these developments must grow out of the very structure of the plot itself, in such a way that on the basis of what has happened previously this particular outcome follows either by necessity or in accordance with probability; for there is a great difference in whether these events happen because of those or merely after them.

"Peripety" is a shift of what is being undertaken to the opposite in the way previously stated, and that in accordance with probability or necessity as we have just been saying; as for example in the *Oedipus* the man who has come, thinking that he will reassure Oedipus, that is, relieve him of his fear with respect to his mother, by revealing who he once was, brings about the opposite; and in the *Lynceus,* as he (Lynceus) is being led away with every prospect of being executed, and Danaus pursuing him with every prospect of doing the executing, it comes about as a result of the other things that have happened in the play that *he* is executed and Lynceus is saved. And "recognition" is, as indeed the name indicates, a shift from ignorance to awareness, pointing in the direction either of close blood ties or of hostility, of people who have previously been in a clearly marked state of happiness or unhappiness.

The finest recognition is one that happens at the same time as a peripety, as is the case with the one in the *Oedipus*. Naturally, there are also other kinds of recognition: it is possible for one to take place in the prescribed manner in relation to inanimate objects and chance occurrences, and it is possible to recognize whether a person has acted or not acted. But the form that is most integrally a part of the plot, the action, is the one aforesaid; for that kind of recognition combined with peripety will excite either pity or fear (and these are the kinds of action of which tragedy is an imitation according to our definition), because both good and bad fortune will also be most likely to follow that kind of event. Since, further, the recognition is a recognition of persons, some are of one person by the other one only (when it is already known who the "other one" is), but sometimes it is necessary for both persons to go through a recognition, as for example Iphigenia is recognized by her brother° through the sending of the letter, but of him by Iphigenia another recognition is required.

These then are two elements of plot: peripety and recognition; third is the *pathos*. Of these, peripety and recognition have been discussed; a *pathos* is a destructive or painful act, such as deaths on stage, paroxysms of pain, woundings, and all that sort of thing.

SIGMUND FREUD (1856–1939)

The Oedipus Complex 1900–1930°

TRANSLATED BY JAMES STRACHEY

Sigmund Freud was the most celebrated psychiatrist of the twentieth century and the father of psychoanalytic theory. His research into the unconscious changed the way we think about the human mind, and his explorations into the symbolic

---

her brother: Orestes is Iphigenia's brother. Aristotle may be referring to a lost play.
1900–1930: *Interpretation of Dreams* was first published in 1900 and was updated regularly by Freud through eight editions. This passage is taken from the eighth edition, published in 1930.

meaning of dreams have been widely regarded as a breakthrough in connecting the meaning of world myth to personal life.

In his *Interpretation of Dreams* he turned to Sophocles' drama and developed his theories of the Oedipus complex and the Electra complex: the desire to kill one parent and marry the other may be rooted in the deepest natural psychological development of the individual. The following passage provides insight not only into a psychological state that, according to Freud, all humans may share but also into the way in which a man of Freud's temperament read and interpreted a great piece of literature. Like Sophocles himself, Freud believed that the myth underlying *Oedipus Rex* has a meaning and importance for all human beings.

In my experience, which is already extensive, the chief part in the mental lives of all children who later become psychoneurotics is played by their parents. Being in love with the one parent and hating the other are among the essential constituents of the stock of psychical impulses which is formed at that time and which is of such importance in determining the symptoms of the later neurosis. It is not my belief, however, that psychoneurotics differ sharply in this respect from other human beings who remain normal—that they are able, that is, to create something absolutely new and peculiar to themselves. It is far more probable—and this is confirmed by occasional observations on normal children—that they are only distinguished by exhibiting on a magnified scale feelings of love and hatred to their parents which occur less obviously and less intensely in the minds of most children.

This discovery is confirmed by a legend that has come down to us from classical antiquity: a legend whose profound and universal power to move can only be understood if the hypothesis I have put forward in regard to the psychology of children has an equally universal validity. What I have in mind is the legend of King Oedipus and Sophocles' drama which bears his name.

Oedipus, son of Laïus, King of Thebes, and of Jocasta, was exposed [to the elements and left to die] as an infant because an oracle had warned Laïus that the still unborn child would be his father's murderer. The child was rescued and grew up as a prince in an alien court, until, in doubts as to his origin, he too questioned the oracle and was warned to avoid his home since he was destined to murder his father and take his mother in marriage. On the road leading away from what he believed was his home, he met King Laïus and slew him in a sudden quarrel. He came next to Thebes and solved the riddle set him by the Sphinx who barred his way. Out of gratitude the Thebans made him their king and gave him Jocasta's hand in marriage. He reigned long in peace and honor, and she who, unknown to him, was his mother bore him two sons and two daughters. Then at last a plague broke out and the Thebans made inquiry once more of the oracle. It is at this point that Sophocles' tragedy opens. The messengers bring back the reply that the plague will cease when the murderer of Laïus has been driven from the land.

> But he, where is he? Where shall now be read
> The fading record of this ancient guilt?[1]

The action of the play consists in nothing other than the process of revealing, with cunning delays and ever-mounting excitement—a process that can be likened to the work of a psychoanalysis—that Oedipus himself is the murderer of Laïus, but further that he is the son of the murdered man and of Jocasta. Appalled at the

---

[1]Lewis Campbell's translation (1883), lines 108ff [Dudley Fitts and Robert Fitzgerald, *Sophocles: The Oedipus Cycle, an English Version* (Harcourt Brace & Company, 1949), Prologue, lines 112–13].

abomination which he has unwittingly perpetrated, Oedipus blinds himself and forsakes his home. The oracle has been fulfilled.

Oedipus Rex is what is known as a tragedy of destiny. Its tragic effect is said to lie in the contrast between the supreme will of the gods and the vain attempts of mankind to escape the evil that threatens them. The lesson which, it is said, the deeply moved spectator should learn from the tragedy is submission to the divine will and realization of his own impotence. Modern dramatists have accordingly tried to achieve a similar tragic effect by weaving the same contrast into a plot invented by themselves. But the spectators have looked on unmoved while a curse or an oracle was fulfilled in spite of all the efforts of some innocent man: later tragedies of destiny have failed in their effect.

If *Oedipus Rex* moves a modern audience no less than it did the contemporary Greek one, the explanation can only be that its effect does not lie in the contrast between destiny and human will, but is to be looked for in the particular nature of the material on which that contrast is exemplified. There must be something which makes a voice within us ready to recognize the compelling force of destiny in the *Oedipus,* while we can dismiss as merely arbitrary such dispositions as are laid down in [Grillparzer's] *Die Ahnfrau* or other modern tragedies of destiny. And a factor of this kind is in fact involved in the story of King Oedipus. His destiny moves us only because it might have been ours—because the oracle laid the same curse upon us before our birth as upon him. It is the fate of all of us, perhaps, to direct our first sexual impulse toward our mother and our first hatred and our first murderous wish against our father. Our dreams convince us that that is so. King Oedipus, who slew his father Laïus and married his mother Jocasta, merely shows us the fulfillment of our own childhood wishes. But, more fortunate than he, we have meanwhile succeeded, in so far as we have not become psychoneurotics, in detaching our sexual impulses from our mothers and in forgetting our jealousy of our fathers. Here is one in whom these primeval wishes of our childhood have been fulfilled, and we shrink back from him with the whole force of the repression by which those wishes have since that time been held down within us. While the poet, as he unravels the past, brings to light the guilt of Oedipus, he is at the same time compelling us to recognize our own inner minds, in which those same impulses, though suppressed, are still to be found. The contrast with which the closing Chorus leaves us confronted—

> . . . Fix on Oedipus your eyes,
> Who resolved the dark enigma, noblest champion and most wise.
> Like a star his envied fortune mounted beaming far and wide:
> Now he sinks in seas of anguish, whelmed beneath a raging tide . . .[2]

—strikes as a warning at ourselves and our pride, at us who since our childhood have grown so wise and so mighty in our own eyes. Like Oedipus, we live in ignorance of these wishes, repugnant to morality, which have been forced upon us by Nature, and after their revelation we may all of us well seek to close our eyes to the scenes of our childhood.[3]

[2]Lewis Campbell's translation, lines 1524ff [Fitts and Fitzgerald, antistrophe 2, lines 292–96].

[3][*Footnote added by Freud in 1914 edition.*] None of the findings of psychoanalytic research has provoked such embittered denials, such fierce opposition—or such amusing contortions—on the part of critics as this indication of the childhood impulses toward incest which persist in the unconscious. An attempt has even been made recently to make out, in the face of all experience, that the incest should only be taken as "symbolic."—Ferenczi (1912) has proposed an ingenious "overinterpretation" of the Oedipus myth, based on a passage in one of Schopenhauer's letters. [*Added 1919.*] Later studies have shown that the "Oedipus complex," which was touched upon for the first time in the above paragraphs in the *Interpretation of Dreams,* throws a light of undreamt-of importance on the history of the human race and the evolution of religion and morality.

There is an unmistakable indication in the text of Sophocles' tragedy itself that the legend of Oedipus sprang from some primeval dream material which had as its content the distressing disturbance of a child's relation to his parents owing to the first stirrings of sexuality. At a point when Oedipus, though he is not yet enlightened, has begun to feel troubled by his recollection of the oracle, Jocasta consoles him by referring to a dream which many people dream, though, as she thinks, it has no meaning:

> Many a man ere now in dreams hath lain
> With her who bare him. He hath least annoy
> Who with such omens troubleth not his mind.[4]

Today, just as then, many men dream of having sexual relations with their mothers, and speak of the fact with indignation and astonishment. It is clearly the key to the tragedy and the complement to the dream of the dreamer's father being dead. The story of Oedipus is the reaction of the imagination to these two typical dreams. And just as these dreams, when dreamt by adults, are accompanied by feelings of repulsion, so too the legend must include horror and self-punishment. Its further modification originates once again in a misconceived secondary revision of the material, which has sought to exploit it for theological purposes. . . . The attempt to harmonize divine omnipotence with human responsibility must naturally fail in connection with this subject matter just as with any other.

CLAUDE LÉVI-STRAUSS (1908–2009)

From The Structural Study of Myth   1955

Claude Lévi-Strauss was one of a handful of modern anthropologists whose interests span the range of thought, culture, and understanding. His work has been of immense influence on French intellectual life and, by extension, on the intellectual life of modern times. His works include *Triste Tropiques* (translated as *A World on the Wane*), about his own experiences as an anthropologist; *Structural Anthropology*, about the ways in which the study of anthropology implies a study of the structure of thought; and *Mythologies*, a four-volume summation of his thought. The excerpt that follows is structuralist in scope in that it attempts to understand the myth of Oedipus by examining the patterns of repetition in the original narrative. By setting up a grid, Lévi-Strauss begins to sort out the implications of the myth and to seek a meaning that is not necessarily apparent in the chronological order of the narrative. He examines the myth diachronically — across the lines of time — and thereby sees a new range of implications, which he treats as the structural implications of the myth. His reading is complex, suggesting that the Oedipus myth is a vegetation myth explaining the origins of mankind. Lévi-Strauss gives us a new way to interpret the significance of literary myths.

The time has come to give a concrete example of the method we propose. We will use the Oedipus myth which has the advantage of being well known to everybody and for which no preliminary explanation is therefore needed. By doing so,

[4]Lewis Campbell's translation, lines 982ff [Fitts and Fitzgerald, scene 3, lines 67–69].

I am well aware that the Oedipus myth has only reached us under late forms and through literary transfigurations concerned more with esthetic and moral preoccupations than with religious or ritual ones, whatever these may have been. But as will be shown later, this apparently unsatisfactory situation will strengthen our demonstration rather than weaken it.

The myth will be treated as would be an orchestra score perversely presented as a unilinear series and where our task is to reestablish the correct disposition. As if, for instance, we were confronted with a sequence of the type: 1,2,4,7,8,2,3,4,6, 8,1,4,5,7,8,1,2,5,7,3,4,5,6,8 . . . , the assignment being to put all the 1's together, all the 2's, the 3's, etc.; the result is a chart:

1	2		4		7	8
	2	3	4		6	8
1			4 5		7	8
1	2		5		7	
		3 4 5				
					6	8

We will attempt to perform the same kind of operation on the Oedipus myth, trying out several dispositions. [. . .] Let us suppose, for the sake of argument, that the best arrangement is the following (although it might certainly be improved by the help of a specialist in Greek mythology):

Kadmos seeks his sister Europa ravished by Zeus.			
		Kadmos kills the dragon.	
	The Spartoi kill each other.		
			Labdacos (Laios's father) = *lame* (?).
	Oedipus kills his father Laios.		Laios (Oedipus's father) = *left-sided* (?).
		Oedipus kills the Sphinx.	
Oedipus marries his mother Jocasta.			
	Eteocles kills his brother Polyneices.		Oedipus = *swollen-foot* (?).
Antigone buries her brother Polyneices despite prohibition.			

Thus, we find ourselves confronted with four vertical columns each of which includes several relations belonging to the same bundle. Were we to *tell* the myth, we would disregard the columns and read the rows from left to right and from top to bottom. But if we want to *understand* the myth, then we will have to disregard one half of the diachronic° dimension (top to bottom) and read from left to right, column after column, each one being considered as a unit.

All the relations belonging to the same column exhibit one common feature which it is our task to unravel. For instance, all the events grouped in the first column on the left have something to do with blood relations which are overemphasized, i.e., are subject to a more intimate treatment than they should be. Let us say, then, that the first column has as its common feature the *overrating of blood relations*. It is obvious that the second column expresses the same thing, but inverted: *underrating of blood relations*. The third column refers to monsters being slain. As to the fourth, a word of clarification is needed. The remarkable connotation of the surnames in Oedipus's father-line has often been noticed. However, linguists usually disregard it, since to them the only way to define the meaning of a term is to investigate all the contexts in which it appears, and personal names, precisely because they are used as such, are not accompanied by any context. With the method we propose to follow the objection disappears since the myth itself provides its own context. The meaningful fact is no longer to be looked for in the eventual sense of each name, but in the fact that all the names have a common feature: i.e., that they may eventually mean something and that all these hypothetical meanings (which may well remain hypothetical) exhibit a common feature, namely they refer to *difficulties to walk and to behave straight*.

What is then the relationship between the two columns on the right? Column three refers to monsters. The dragon is a chthonian° being which has to be killed in order that mankind be born from the earth; the Sphinx is a monster unwilling to permit men to live. The last unit reproduces the first one which has to do with the *autochthonous*° origin of mankind. Since the monsters are overcome by men, we may thus say that the common feature of the third column is *the denial of the autochthonous origin of man*.

This immediately helps us to understand the meaning of the fourth column. In mythology it is a universal character of men born from the earth that at the moment they emerge from the depth, they either cannot walk or do it clumsily. This is the case of the chthonian beings in the mythology of the Pueblo: Masauwu, who leads the emergence, and the chthonian Shumaikoli are lame ("bleeding-foot," "sore-foot"). The same happens to the Koskimo of the Kwakiutl after they have been swallowed by the chthonian monster, Tsiakish: when they returned to the surface of the earth "they limped forward or tripped sideways." Then the common feature of the fourth column is: *the persistence of the autochthonous origin of man*. It follows that column four is to column three as column one is to column two. The inability to connect two kinds of relationships is overcome (or rather replaced) by the positive statement that contradictory relationships are identical inasmuch as they are both self-contradictory in a similar way. Although this is still a provisional formulation of the structure of mythical thought, it is sufficient at this stage.

---

diachronic: Not ordered linearly in time but through time.
chthonian: From the underworld.
autochthonous: Native, aboriginal; in this case, born of the earth.

Turning back to the Oedipus myth, we may now see what it means. The myth has to do with the inability, for a culture which holds the belief that mankind is autochthonous [. . . ,] to find a satisfactory transition between this theory and the knowledge that human beings are actually born from the union of man and woman. Although the problem obviously cannot be solved, the Oedipus myth provides a kind of logical tool which, to phrase it coarsely, replaces the original problem: born from one or born from two? born from different or born from same? By a correlation of this type, the overrating of blood relations is to the underrating of blood relations as the attempt to escape autochthony is to the impossibility to succeed in it [that escape]. Although experience contradicts theory, social life verifies the cosmology by its similarity of structure. Hence cosmology is true.

Two remarks should be made at this stage.

In order to interpret the myth, we were able to leave aside a point which has until now worried the specialists, namely, that in the earlier (Homeric) versions of the Oedipus myth, some basic elements are lacking, such as Jocasta killing herself and Oedipus piercing his own eyes. These events do not alter the substance of the myth although they can easily be integrated, the first one as a new case of autodestruction (column three) while the second is another case of crippledness (column four). At the same time there is something significant in these additions since the shift from foot to head is to be correlated with the shift from: autochthonous origin negated to: self-destruction.

Thus, our method eliminates a problem which has been so far one of the main obstacles to the progress of mythological studies, namely, the quest for the *true* version, or the *earlier* one. On the contrary, we define the myth as consisting of all its versions; to put it otherwise: a myth remains the same as long as it is felt as such. A striking example is offered by the fact that our interpretation may take into account, and is certainly applicable to, the Freudian use of the Oedipus myth. Although the Freudian problem has ceased to be that of autochthony *versus* bisexual reproduction, it is still the problem of understanding how *one* can be born from *two*: how is it that we do not have only one procreator, but a mother plus a father? Therefore, not only Sophocles, but Freud himself, should be included among the recorded versions of the Oedipus myth on a par with earlier or seemingly more "authentic" versions.

Aristophanes

The best known of the Greek comic playwrights, Aristophanes (c. 448–c. 385 BCE) lived through some of the most difficult times in Athenian history. He watched Athenian democracy fade and decay as factionalism and war took their toll on the strength of the city-state. By the time he died, Athens was caught up in a fierce struggle between supporters of democracy and supporters of oligarchy, government by a small group of leaders.

Aristophanes' plays are democratic in that they appealed to sophisticated and unsophisticated theatergoers alike. Skilled at complex wordplay, he also enjoyed spirited and rowdy comedy. Since his plays were often sharply critical of Athenian policies, his ability to make people laugh was essential to conveying his message. He was a practitioner of what we now call Old Comedy, an irreverent form that ridiculed and insulted prominent people and important institutions. By Aristophanes' time, Old Comedy had become fiercely satirical, especially concerning political matters. Because Aristophanes held strong opinions, he found satire an ideal form for his talents.

Of his more than thirty known plays, only eleven survive. They come from three main periods in his life, beginning, according to legend, when he was a young man, in 427 BCE. *The Acharnians* (425 BCE), from his first period, focuses on the theme of peace. Dicaeopolis (whose name means "honest" or "good citizen") decides to make a separate peace after the Spartans have ravaged the Acharnian vineyards. The Acharnians vow revenge, but Dicaeopolis explains that peace must begin as an individual decision. Aristophanes saw war as a corporate venture; peacemaking was easier for an individual than for a group or a nation.

The Acharnians was followed by *The Peace* in 421 BCE, just before Sparta and Athens signed a treaty, and it seems clearly to have been written in support of the Athenian peace party, whose power had been growing from the time of *The Acharnians* and whose cause had been aided by that play.

His second period was also dominated by the problems of war. Athens's ill-fated expedition to Sicily in violation of the Treaty of Nicias lies thematically beneath the surface of *The Birds* (414 BCE), in which some citizens build Cloud-Cuckoo-Land to come between the world of humans and the world of the gods. *Lysistrata* (411 BCE) is also from this period; its frank antiwar theme is related to the Sicilian wars and to the ultimately devastating Peloponnesian Wars. These were wars fought by Greek city-states in the areas south of Athens, the Peloponnesus. The states had voluntarily contributed money to arm and support Athens against the Persians in 480 BCE—resulting in the Athenian victory at Salamis. The states later became angry when Pericles, the Athenian leader, demanded that they continue giving contributions, much of which he used to fund the rebuilding of the Acropolis and other civic projects in Athens.

The leaders of the other Greek city-states believed that Athens was becoming imperialistic and was overreaching. War broke out between the city-states in 431 BCE and lasted for nearly thirty years. These struggles and the difficulties of conducting a costly, long-distance war in Sicily combined eventually to exhaust the Athenian resources of men and funds. Soundly defeated in 405 BCE,

Athens surrendered to Sparta in 404. Aristophanes lived to see the Spartan ships at rest in the harbors of Athens's chief port, the Piraeus. And he saw, too, the destruction of the walls of the city, leaving it essentially defenseless.

Aristophanes' third and final period, from 393 BCE to his death, includes *The Ecclesiazusae* (c. 392 BCE) (translated as "The Women in Government"), in which women dress as men, find their way into parliament, and pass a new constitution. It is a highly topical play that points to the current situation in Athens and the people's general discontent and anxiety. The last part of *The Plutus,* written five years later, is an allegory about the god of wealth, who is eventually encouraged to make the just wealthy and the unjust poor.

Among the best known of Aristophanes' plays are several whose names refer to the disguises or costumes of the chorus, among them *The Knights*, *The Wasps*, and *The Frogs*. *The Frogs* (405 BCE) is especially interesting for its focus on literary issues. It features a contest in the underworld between Aeschylus, who had been dead more than fifty years, and Euripides, who had just died at a relatively young age. Aristophanes uses the contest to make many enlightening comments about Greek tragedy and the skills of the two authors.

Even in his last period Aristophanes was an innovative force in theater. His last surviving play virtually does away with the chorus as an important character in the action. His later plays resemble modern comedies partly because the chorus does not intrude on the action. His genius helped shape later developments in comedy.

For links to resources about Aristophanes, click on *AuthorLinks* at **bedfordstmartins.com/jacobus.**

Lysistrata

At the time *Lysistrata* was written (411 BCE), Athens had suffered a steady diet of war for more than twenty years. Political groups were actively trying to persuade Athenian leaders to discontinue the policies that had alienated Athens from the other city-states that were once its supporters in the Delian League, the group that had funded Athens's struggle against the Persian threat. Aristophanes opposed the imperialist attitudes that conflicted with the democratic spirit of only a generation earlier.

Lysistrata makes it clear that war was the central business of the nation at that time. No sooner is one campaign ended than another begins. The men encountered by the heroine Lysistrata (whose name means "disband the army") on the Acropolis—men who guard the national security and the national treasury—are old and decrepit. The young men are in the field. As Kalonike tells Lysistrata, her man has been away for five months. Such separations were common, and these women are fed up. Lysistrata has gathered the discontented women together to propose a scheme to bring peace and negotiate a treaty.

The scheme is preposterous, but, as is typical of Old Comedy, its very outrageousness is the source of its strength. In time, the idea begins to seem almost reasonable: Lysistrata asks the women to refuse to engage in sex with their husbands until the men stop making war. The women also seize the Acropolis and hold the treasury hostage. Without the national treasury, there can be no war. And because they are confident of getting the support of the larger community of women in other nations—who suffer as they do—they do not fear the consequences of their acts.

In amusing scenes generated by this situation, Aristophanes pokes fun at both sexes. We hear the gossipy conversation of the women, all of whom arrive late to Lysistrata's meeting. The men are dependent, helpless, and ineffectual, and they cannot resist the takeover. When the truth begins to settle in, the men solicit their wives' attention with enormous erections protruding beneath their gowns, one example of the exaggerated visual humor Aristophanes counted on. The double meanings in the conversations are also a great source of humor.

The wonderful scene 3 between Myrrhine and her husband Kinesias is predicated on the agony of the husband whose wife repeatedly promises sexual favors and then reneges, in order to build his sexual excitement to a fever pitch. It is no wonder that Lysistrata can eventually bring the men to sign any treaties she wants.

This heterosexual hilarity is balanced by a number of homosexual allusions. Kleisthenes, possibly a bisexual Athenian, stands ready to relieve some of the men's sexual discomfort, while Lysistrata admits that if the men do not capitulate, the women will have to satisfy their own needs. Such frankness is typical of Athenian comedy.

Women dominate the action of the play, although we must remember that male actors played women's roles. The women see the stupidity and waste of the war and devise a plan that will end it. Observing that they are the ones who suffer most from the effects of war, the women also note that they pay their taxes in babies. The suffering of women had been a major theme in the tragedies of Euripides, and everyone in Aristophanes' audience would have understood Lysistrata's motivation. The idea that a woman should keep her place is expressed by several characters. And since Athenian audiences would have agreed that women should not meddle in war or government, Aristophanes offered them a fantasy that challenged them on many levels.

Aristophanes praises Lysistrata's ingenuity and her perseverance. When the other women want to give up the plan because of their own sexual needs, she holds firm. She demands that they stand by their resolve. The picture of a strong, independent, intelligent, and capable woman obviously pleased the Athenians because they permitted this play to be performed more than once—an unusual practice. Lysistrata became a recognizable and admirable character in Athenian life.

The following translation of *Lysistrata* has several interesting features. It is composed of scenes, a division not made in the original Greek. Instead of having a chorus of elders, as in *Antigone*, Aristophanes uses two choruses—one of men and one of women—that are truly representative of the people: they are as divided and antagonistic as Sophocles' chorus is united and wise. The **koryphaios** (leader) of the men's chorus speaks alone, often in opposition to the koryphaios of the women's chorus.

The rhyming patterns of some of the songs are approximated in English, and the sense of dialect is maintained in the speech of Lampito, who represents a kind of country bumpkin. She is very muscular from the workouts that she and all other Spartans engaged in; Aristophanes reveals certain Athenian prejudices toward the Spartans in the scene where Lampito is taunted for her physique.

For discussion questions and assignments on *Lysistrata*, visit bedfordstmartins.com/jacobus.

Lysistrata in Performance

Lysistrata has enjoyed and still enjoys numerous productions, on both college and commercial stages. Because it is a bawdy play, it has sometimes run into trouble. In 1932, the New York police shut down a performance and sent out a warrant for the arrest of "Arthur" Aristophanes. In 1959, Dudley Fitts's translation (used here) was performed at the Phoenix Theatre in New York with "women . . . wearing simulated breasts, tipped with sequins, and the ruttish old men stripped down to union suits." Hunter College's 1968 production used rock music, hippie beads, and headbands. Less controversial productions include the first modern version, by Maurice Donnay in Paris (1892), in which Lysistrata takes a general as a lover. The Moscow Art Theater produced a highly acclaimed version in 1923 and brought it to the United States in 1925. That version, modified by Gilbert Seldes (published in book form with illustrations by Picasso), was produced throughout the 1930s. All-black versions of the play have been staged several times since 1938. Since 2001 this play has been produced in many countries, including France in 2006. It was performed in Boston, with Cherry Jones as Lysistrata, in 2002. Theodora Skipitares' well-reviewed version at La Mama in New York in February 2011 experimented with multimedia projections and life-size puppets that helped advance the comedic elements of the play. A surprising Broadway musical version, *Lysistrata Jones*, which opened in December 2011, portrays Lysistrata as a member of a women's basketball team that has not won a game in thirty years. Team members hope to break that streak by withholding sex from their boyfriends. Clearly the essence of Aristophanes' play appeals to modern audiences.

ARISTOPHANES (C. 448–C. 385 BCE)

Lysistrata   411 BCE

TRANSLATED BY DUDLEY FITTS

Persons Represented

LYSISTRATA,
KALONIKE, } *Athenian women*
MYRRHINE,
LAMPITO, *a Spartan woman*
CHORUS
COMMISSIONER
KINESIAS, *husband of Myrrhine*
SPARTAN HERALD
SPARTAN AMBASSADOR
A SENTRY

[BABY SON OF KENESIAS
STRATYLLIS
SPARTANS
ATHENIANS]

Scene: *Athens. First, a public square; later, beneath the walls of the Akropolis;° later, a courtyard within the Akropolis.*

Akropolis: Fortress of Athens, sacred to the goddess Athena.

PROLOGUE°

(*Athens; a public square; early morning; Lysistrata alone.*)

LYSISTRATA: If someone had invited them to a
        festival—
    of Bacchos,° say; or to Pan's° shrine, or to
        Aphrodite's°
    over at Kolias—, you couldn't get through the
        streets,
    what with the drums and the dancing. But now,
    not a woman in sight!
5   Except—oh, yes!

(*Enter Kalonike.*)

    Here's one of my neighbors, at last. Good
        morning, Kalonike.
KALONIKE: Good morning, Lysistrata.
                                        Darling,
    don't frown so! You'll ruin your face!
LYSISTRATA: Never mind my face.
    Kalonike,
    the way we women behave! Really, I don't blame
10   the men
    for what they say about us.
KALONIKE: No; I imagine they're right.
LYSISTRATA: For example: I call a meeting
    to think out a most important matter—and what
        happens?
    The women all stay in bed!
KALONIKE: Oh, they'll be along.
15   It's hard to get away, you know: a husband, a cook,
    a child . . . Home life can be *so* demanding!
LYSISTRATA: What I have in mind is even more
        demanding.
KALONIKE: Tell me: what is it?
LYSISTRATA: It's big.
KALONIKE: Goodness! *How* big?
LYSISTRATA: Big enough for all of us.
KALONIKE: But we're not all here!
LYSISTRATA: We would be, if *that's* what was up!
20   No, Kalonike,
    this is something I've been turning over for nights,
    long sleepless nights.
KALONIKE: It must be getting worn down, then,
    if you've spent so much time on it.
LYSISTRATA: Worn down or not,
    it comes to this: Only we women can save Greece!
KALONIKE: Only we women? Poor Greece!
25 LYSISTRATA: Just the same,

it's up to us. First, we must liquidate
    the Peloponnesians—
KALONIKE: Fun, fun!
LYSISTRATA: —and then the Boiotians.°
KALONIKE: Oh! But not those heavenly eels!
LYSISTRATA: You needn't worry.
    I'm not talking about eels.—But here's the point:
    If we can get the women from those places—   30
    all those Boiotians and Peloponnesians—
    to join us women here, why, we can save all Greece!
KALONIKE: But dearest Lysistrata!
    How can women do a thing so austere, so
    political? We belong at home. Our only armor's   35
    our perfumes, our saffron dresses and
    our pretty little shoes!
LYSISTRATA: Exactly. Those
    transparent dresses, the saffron, the perfume, those
        pretty shoes—
KALONIKE: Oh?
LYSISTRATA: Not a single man would lift
    his spear—
KALONIKE: I'll send my dress to the dyer's tomorrow!
LYSISTRATA: —or grab a shield—
KALONIKE: The sweetest little negligee—   40
LYSISTRATA: —or haul out his sword.
KALONIKE: I know where
    I can buy the dreamiest sandals!
LYSISTRATA: Well, so you see. Now, shouldn't
    the women have come?
KALONIKE: Come? They should have *flown*!
LYSISTRATA: Athenians are always late.
                                But imagine!
    There's no one here from the South Shore, or from
        Salamis.   45
KALONIKE: Things are hard over in Salamis, I swear.
    They have to get going at dawn.
LYSISTRATA: And nobody from Acharnai.
    I thought they'd be here hours ago.
KALONIKE: Well, you'll get
    that awful Theagenes woman: she'll be
    a sheet or so in the wind.
                                But look!   50
    Someone at last! Can you see who they are?

(*Enter Myrrhine and other women.*)

LYSISTRATA: They're from Anagyros.
KALONIKE: They certainly are.
    You'd know them anywhere, by the scent.
MYRRHINE: Sorry to be late, Lysistrata.
                                Oh come,
    don't scowl so. Say something!
LYSISTRATA: My dear Myrrhine,   55
    what is there to say? After all,
    you've been pretty casual about the whole thing.

Prologue: Portion of the play explaining the background and current action.   **2. Bacchos:** Bacchus, god of wine and the object of wild, orgiastic ritual and celebration; also called Dionysus.   **Pan:** God of nature, forests, flocks, and shepherds, depicted as half man and half goat. Pan was considered playful and lecherous.   **Aphrodite:** Goddess of love.

27. Boiotians: Crude-mannered inhabitants of Boiotia, which was noted for its seafood.

MYRRHINE: Couldn't find
my girdle in the dark, that's all.
                                                  But what *is*
"the whole thing"?
KALONIKE: No, we've got to wait
60   for those Boiotians and Peloponnesians.
LYSISTRATA: That's more like it.—But, look!
Here's Lampito!

(*Enter Lampito with women from Sparta.*)

LYSISTRATA: Darling Lampito,
how pretty you are today! What a nice color!
Goodness, you look as though you could strangle a
65   bull!
LAMPITO: Ah think Ah could! It's the work-out
in the gym every day; and, of co'se that dance of ahs
where y' kick yo' own tail.
KALONIKE: What an adorable figure!
LAMPITO: Lawdy, when y' touch me lahk that,
Ah feel lahk a heifer at the altar!
70   LYSISTRATA: And this young lady?
Where is she from?
LAMPITO: Boiotia. Social-Register type.
LYSISTRATA: Ah. "Boiotia of the fertile plain."
KALONIKE: And if you look,
you'll find the fertile plain has just been mowed.
LYSISTRATA: And this lady?
LAMPITO: Hagh, wahd, handsome.
75   She comes from Korinth.
KALONIKE: High and wide's the word for it.
LAMPITO: Which one of you
called this heah meeting, and why?
LYSISTRATA: I did.
LAMPITO: Well, then, tell us:
What's up?
MYRRHINE: Yes, darling, what *is* on your mind, after
                                                      all?
LYSISTRATA: I'll tell you.—But first, one little question.
MYRRHINE: Well?
LYSISTRATA: It's your husbands. Fathers of your
80   children. Doesn't it bother you
that they're always off with the Army? I'll stake my
life,
not one of you has a man in the house this minute!
KALONIKE: Mine's been in Thrace the last five months,
keeping an eye
on that General.
MYRRHINE: Mine's been in Pylos for seven.
LAMPITO: And mahn,
85   whenever he gets a *dis*charge, he goes raht back
with that li'l ole shield of his, and enlists again!
LYSISTRATA: And not the ghost of a lover to be found!
From the very day the war began—
                              those Milesians!
I could skin them alive!
                      —I've not seen so much, even,
90   as one of those leather consolation prizes.—
But there! What's important is: If I've found a way
to end the war, are you with me?

MYRRHINE: I should *say* so!
Even if I have to pawn my best dress and
drink up the proceeds.
KALONIKE: Me, too! Even if they split me
right up the middle, like a flounder.
LAMPITO: Ah'm shorely with you.   95
Ah'd crawl up Taygetos° on mah knees
if that'd bring peace.
LYSISTRATA: All right, then; here it is:
Women! Sisters!
If we really want our men to make peace,
we must be ready to give up—
MYRRHINE: Give up what?   100
Quick, tell us!
LYSISTRATA: But *will* you?
MYRRHINE: We will, even if it kills us.
LYSISTRATA: Then we must give up going to bed with
our men.

(*Long silence.*)

Oh? So now you're sorry? Won't look at me?
Doubtful? Pale? All teary-eyed?
                        But come: be frank with me.
Will you do it, or not? Well? Will you do it?
MYRRHINE: I couldn't. No.   105
Let the war go on.
KALONIKE: Nor I. Let the war go on.
LYSISTRATA: You, you little flounder,
ready to be split up the middle?
KALONIKE: Lysistrata, no!
I'd walk through fire for you—you *know* I
          would!—but don't
ask us to give up *that!* Why, there's nothing like it!   110
LYSISTRATA: And you?
BOIOTIAN: No. I must say *I'd* rather walk
through fire.
LYSISTRATA: What an utterly perverted sex we women
are!
No wonder poets write tragedies about us.
There's only one thing we can think of.
                              But you from Sparta:
if you stand by me, we may win yet! Will you?   115
It means so much!
LAMPITO: Ah sweah, it means *too* much!
By the Two Goddesses,° it does! Asking a girl
to sleep—Heaven knows how long!—in a great
big bed
with nobody there but herself! But Ah'll stay with
you!
Peace comes first!
LYSISTRATA: Spoken like a true Spartan!   120

---

96. **Taygetos:** A mountain range. **117. Two Goddesses:** A woman's oath referring to Demeter, the earth goddess, and her daughter Persephone, who was associated with seasonal cycles of fertility.

KALONIKE: But if—
oh dear!
—if we give up what you tell us to,
will there *be* any peace?

LYSISTRATA: Why, mercy, of course there will!
We'll just sit snug in our very thinnest gowns,
perfumed and powdered from top to bottom, and
those men
125 simply won't stand still! And when we say No,
they'll go out of their minds! And there's your peace.
You can take my word for it.

LAMPITO: Ah seem to remember
that Colonel Menelaos threw his sword away
when he saw Helen's breast° all bare.

KALONIKE: But, goodness me!
What if they just get up and leave us?

130 LYSISTRATA: In that case
we'll have to fall back on ourselves, I suppose.
But they won't.

KALONIKE: I must say that's not much help. But
what if they drag us into the bedroom?

LYSISTRATA: Hang on to the door.

KALONIKE: What if they slap us?

LYSISTRATA: If they do, you'd better give in.
135 But be sulky about it. Do I have to teach you how?
You know there's no fun for men when they have
to force you.
There are millions of ways of getting them to see
reason.
Don't you worry: a man
doesn't like it unless the girl cooperates.

140 KALONIKE: I suppose so. Oh, all right. We'll go along.

LAMPITO: Ah imagine us Spahtans can arrange a
peace. But you
Athenians! Why, you're just war-mongerers!

LYSISTRATA: Leave that to me.
I know how to make them listen.

LAMPITO: Ah don't see how.
After all, they've got their boats; and there's lots
of money
piled up in the Akropolis.

145 LYSISTRATA: The Akropolis? Darling,
we're taking over the Akropolis today!
That's the older women's job. All the rest of us
are going to the Citadel to sacrifice—you
understand me?
And once there, we're in for good!

LAMPITO: Whee! Up the rebels!
Ah can see you're a good strat*ee*gist.

150 LYSISTRATA: Well, then, Lampito,
what we have to do now is take a solemn oath.

LAMPITO: Say it. We'll sweah.

LYSISTRATA: This is it.
—But where's our Inner Guard?
—Look. Guard: you see this shield?

Put it down here. Now bring me the victim's entrails.

KALONIKE: But the oath?

LYSISTRATA: You remember how in Aischylos'
Seven° 155
they killed a sheep and swore on a shield? Well,
then?

KALONIKE: But I don't see how you can swear for
peace on a shield.

LYSISTRATA: What else do you suggest?

KALONIKE: Why not a white horse?
We could swear by that.

LYSISTRATA: And where will you get a white horse?

KALONIKE: I never thought of that. *What* can we do?

LYSISTRATA: I have it! 160
Let's set this big black wine-bowl on the ground
and pour in a gallon or so of Thasian,° and swear
not to add one drop of water.

LAMPITO: Ah lahk *that* oath!

LYSISTRATA: Bring the bowl and the wine-jug.

KALONIKE: Oh, what a simply *huge* one!

LYSISTRATA: Set it down. Girls, place your hands on
the gift-offering. 165
O Goddess of Persuasion! And thou, O Loving-cup:
Look upon this our sacrifice, and
be gracious!

KALONIKE: See the blood spill out. How red and pretty
it is!

LAMPITO: And Ah must say it smells good.

MYRRHINE: Let me swear first! 170

KALONIKE: No, by Aphrodite, we'll match for it!

LYSISTRATA: Lampito: all of you women: come, touch
the bowl,
and repeat after me—remember, this is an oath—:
I WILL HAVE NOTHING TO DO WITH MY
HUSBAND OR MY LOVER

KALONIKE: *I will have nothing to do with my husband
or my lover* 175

LYSISTRATA: THOUGH HE COME TO ME IN
PITIABLE CONDITION

KALONIKE: *Though he come to me in pitiable condition*
(Oh Lysistrata! This is killing me!)

LYSISTRATA: IN MY HOUSE I WILL BE
UNTOUCHABLE

KALONIKE: *In my house I will be untouchable* 180

LYSISTRATA: IN MY THINNEST SAFFRON SILK

KALONIKE: *In my thinnest saffron silk*

LYSISTRATA: AND MAKE HIM LONG FOR ME.

KALONIKE: *And make him long for me.*

LYSISTRATA: I WILL NOT GIVE MYSELF 185

KALONIKE: *I will not give myself*

LYSISTRATA: AND IF HE CONSTRAINS ME

KALONIKE: *And if he constrains me*

LYSISTRATA: I WILL BE COLD AS ICE AND NEVER
MOVE

127–128. **Colonel Menelaos . . . Helen's breast:** Helen, wife of
King Menelaos of Sparta, was abducted by Paris and taken to
Troy. The incident led to the Trojan War.

155. *Seven:* Aeschylus's *Seven against Thebes,* which deals with
the war between the sons of Oedipus for the throne of Thebes.
162. **Thasian:** Wine from Thasos.

190   KALONIKE: *I will be cold as ice and never move*
     LYSISTRATA: I WILL NOT LIFT MY SLIPPERS
         TOWARD THE CEILING
     KALONIKE: *I will not lift my slippers toward the ceiling*
     LYSISTRATA: OR CROUCH ON ALL FOURS LIKE
         THE LIONESS IN THE CARVING
     KALONIKE: *Or crouch on all fours like the lioness in*
        the carving
     LYSISTRATA: AND IF I KEEP THIS OATH LET ME
195   DRINK FROM THIS BOWL
     KALONIKE: *And if I keep this oath let me drink from*
        this bowl
     LYSISTRATA: IF NOT, LET MY OWN BOWL BE
        FILLED WITH WATER.
     KALONIKE: *If not, let my own bowl be filled with*
        water.
     LYSISTRATA: You have all sworn?
     MYRRHINE: We have.
     LYSISTRATA: Then thus
     I sacrifice the victim.

     (*Drinks largely.*)

200   KALONIKE: Save some for us!
     Here's to you, darling, and to you, and to you!

     (*Loud cries offstage.*)

     LAMPITO: What's all *that* whoozy-goozy?
     LYSISTRATA: Just what I told you.
     The older women have taken the Akropolis.
     Now you, Lampito,
     rush back to Sparta. We'll take care of things here.
205   Leave
     these girls here for hostages.
               The rest of you,
     up to the Citadel: and mind you push in the bolts.
     KALONIKE: But the men? Won't they be after us?
     LYSISTRATA: Just you leave
     the men to me. There's not fire enough in the world,
210   or threats either, to make me open these doors
     except on my own terms.
     KALONIKE: I hope not, by Aphrodite!
     After all,
     we've got a reputation for bitchiness to live up to.

                        (*Exeunt.*°)

PARODOS:°
CHORAL EPISODE

(*The hillside just under the Akropolis. Enter Chorus of Old Men with burning torches and braziers; much puffing and coughing.*)

213. [S.D.] ***Exeunt:*** Latin for "they go out." **Parodos:** Song or ode chanted by the Chorus on their entry.

KORYPHAIOS(man):° Forward march, Drakes, old friend:
    never you mind
    that damn big log banging hell down on your back.

Strophe° 1

CHORUS(men): There's this to be said for longevity:
    You see things you thought that you'd never see.
      Look, Strymodoros, who would have thought it?   5
      We've caught it—
                    the New Femininity!
    The wives of our bosom, our board, our bed—
    Now, by the gods, they've gone ahead
    And taken the Citadel (Heaven knows why!),
    Profanèd the sacred statuar-y,   10
                    And barred the doors,
                    The subversive whores!
KORYPHAIOS(m): Shake a leg there, Philurgos, man: the
    Akropolis or bust!
    Put the kindling around here. We'll build one
    almighty big
    bonfire for the whole bunch of bitches, every last one;   15
    and the first we fry will be old Lykon's woman.

Antistrophe° 1

CHORUS(m): They're not going to give me the old
    horse-laugh!
    No, by Demeter, they won't pull this off!
      Think of Kleomenes: even he
      Didn't go free
                 till he brought me his stuff.   20
    A good man he was, all stinking and shaggy,
    Bare as an eel except for the bag he
    Covered his rear with. God, what a mess!
    Never a bath in six years, I'd guess.
                  Pure Sparta, man!   25
                  He also ran.
KORYPHAIOS(m): That was a siege, friends! Seventeen
    ranks strong
    we slept at the Gate. And shall we not do as much
    against these women, whom God and Euripides hate?
    If we don't, I'll turn in my medals from Marathon.   30

Strophe 2

CHORUS(m): Onward and upward! A little push,
    And we're there.

1. **Koryphaios:** Leader of the Chorus; also called Choragos. There are two Choruses and two Koryphaioi, one male and one female. **Strophe:** Song sung by the Chorus as it danced from stage right to stage left. **Antistrophe:** Song sung by the Chorus following the Strophe, as it danced back from stage left to stage right.

Ouch, my shoulders! I could wish
   For a pair
35 Of good strong oxen. Keep your eye
On the fire there, it mustn't die.
   Akh! Akh!
The smoke would make a cadaver cough!

Antistrophe 2

Holy Herakles, a hot spark
40   Bit my eye!
Damn this hellfire, damn this work!
   So say I.
Onward and upward just the same.
(Laches, remember the Goddess: for shame!)
45   Akh! Akh!
The smoke would make a cadaver cough!

KORYPHAIOS(m): At last (and let us give suitable thanks
   to God
for his infinite mercies) I have managed to bring
my personal flame to the common goal. It
   breathes, it lives.
50 Now, gentlemen, let us consider. Shall we insert
the torch, say, into the brazier, and thus extract
a kindling brand? And shall we then, do you think,
push on to the gate like valiant sheep? On the whole
   yes.
But I would have you consider this, too: if they—
55 I refer to the women—should refuse to open,
what then? Do we set the doors afire
and smoke them out? At ease, men. Meditate.
Akh, the smoke! Woof! What we really need
is the loan of a general or two from the Samos
   Command.°
60 At least we've got this lumber off our backs.
That's something. And now let's look to our fire.
O Pot, brave Brazier, touch my torch with flame!
Victory, Goddess, I invoke thy name!
Strike down these paradigms of female pride
65 And we shall hang our trophies up inside.

(Enter Chorus of Old Women on the walls of the
Akropolis, carrying jars of water.)

KORYPHAIOS(woman): Smoke, girls, smoke! There's smoke
   all over the place!
Probably fire, too. Hurry, girls! Fire! Fire!

Strophe 1

CHORUS(women): Nikodike, run!
   Or Kalyke's done
70 To a turn, and poor Kritylla's
Smoked like a ham.
     Damn
These old men! Are we too late?

59. Samos Command: Headquarters of the Athenian military.

I nearly died down at the place
Where we fill our jars:
   Slaves pushing and jostling—   75
   Such a hustling
I never saw in all my days.

Antistrophe 1

But here's water at last.
Haste, sisters, haste!
Slosh it on them, slosh it down,   80
The silly old wrecks!
       Sex
Almighty! What they want's
A hot bath? Good. Send one down.
Athena of Athens town,
   Trito-born!° Helm of Gold!   85
   Cripple the old
Firemen! Help us help them drown!

(The old men capture a woman, Stratyllis.)

STRATYLLIS: Let me go! Let me go!
KORYPHAIOS(w):   You walking corpses,
   have you no shame?
KORYPHAIOS(m):   I wouldn't have believed it!
An army of women in the Akropolis!   90
KORYPHAIOS(w): So we scare you, do we? Grandpa,
   you've seen
only our pickets yet!
KORYPHAIOS(m):   Hey, Phaidrias!
Help me with the necks of these jabbering hens!
KORYPHAIOS(w): Down with your pots, girls! We'll need
   both hands
if these antiques attack us!
KORYPHAIOS(m):   Want your face kicked in?   95
KORYPHAIOS(w): Want your balls chewed off?
KORYPHAIOS(m):   Look out! I've got a stick!
KORYPHAIOS(w): You lay a half-inch of your stick on
   Stratyllis,
and you'll never stick again!
KORYPHAIOS(m): Fall apart!
KORYPHAIOS(w):   I'll spit up your guts!
KORYPHAIOS(m):   Euripides! Master!
How well you knew women!
KORYPHAIOS(w):   Listen to him, Rhodippe,   100
up with the pots!
KORYPHAIOS(m):   Demolition of God,
what good are your pots?
KORYPHAIOS(w):   You refugee from the tomb,
what good is your fire?
KORYPHAIOS(m):   Good enough to make a pyre
to barbecue you!
KORYPHAIOS(w):   We'll squizzle your kindling!
KORYPHAIOS(m): You think so?
KORYPHAIOS(w):   Yah! Just hang around a while!   105
KORYPHAIOS(m): Want a touch of my torch?

85. Trito-born: Athena, goddess of wisdom, was said to have
been born near Lake Tritonis in Libya.

KORYPHAIOS⁽ʷ⁾:   It needs a good soaping.
KORYPHAIOS⁽ᵐ⁾: How about you?
KORYPHAIOS⁽ʷ⁾:   Soap for a senile bridegroom!
KORYPHAIOS⁽ᵐ⁾: Senile? Hold your trap
KORYPHAIOS⁽ʷ⁾:   Just *you* try to hold it!
KORYPHAIOS⁽ᵐ⁾: The yammer of women!
KORYPHAIOS⁽ʷ⁾:   Oh is that so?
110   You're not in the jury room now, you know.
KORYPHAIOS⁽ᵐ⁾: Gentlemen, I beg you, burn off that
        woman's hair!
KORYPHAIOS⁽ʷ⁾: Let it come down!

(*They empty their pots on the men.*)

KORYPHAIOS⁽ᵐ⁾: What a way to drown!
KORYPHAIOS⁽ʷ⁾:   Hot, hey?
KORYPHAIOS⁽ᵐ⁾:   Say, enough!
KORYPHAIOS⁽ʷ⁾: Dandruff
115   needs watering. I'll make you
        nice and fresh.
KORYPHAIOS⁽ᵐ⁾: For God's sake, you,
        hold off!

SCENE 1

(*Enter a Commissioner accompanied by four
constables.*)

COMMISSIONER: These degenerate women! What a
        racket of little drums,
    what a yapping for Adonis° on every house-top!
    It's like the time in the Assembly when I was listening
    to a speech—out of order, as usual—by that fool
5   Demostratos,° all about troops for Sicily,°
    that kind of nonsense—
                    and there was his wife
    trotting around in circles howling
    Alas for Adonis!—
                    and Demostratos insisting
    we must draft every last Zakynthian that can walk—
10 and his wife up there on the roof,
    drunk as an owl, yowling
    Oh weep for Adonis!—
                    and that damned ox Demostratos
    mooing away through the rumpus. That's what we
        get
    for putting up with this wretched woman-business!
KORYPHAIOS⁽ᵐ⁾: Sir, you haven't heard the half of it.
15   They laughed at us!
    Insulted us! They took pitchers of water
    and nearly drowned us! We're still wringing out our
        clothes,
    for all the world like unhousebroken brats.

COMMISSIONER: Serves you right, by Poseidon!
    Whose fault is it if these women-folk of ours   20
    get out of hand? We coddle them,
    we teach them to be wasteful and loose. You'll see a
        husband
    go into a jeweler's. "Look," he'll say,
    "jeweler," he'll say, "you remember that gold choker
    you made for my wife? Well, she went to a dance
        last night   25
    and broke the clasp. Now, I've got to go to Salamis,
    and can't be bothered. Run over to my house tonight,
    will you, and see if you can put it together for her."
    Or another one
    goes to a cobbler—a good strong workman, too,   30
    with an awl that was never meant for child's play.
        "Here,"
    he'll tell him, "one of my wife's shoes is pinching
    her little toe. Could you come up about noon
    and stretch it out for her?"
                    Well, what do you expect?
    Look at me, for example, I'm a Public Officer,   35
    and it's one of my duties to pay off the sailors.
    And where's the money? Up there in the Akropolis!
    And those blasted women slam the door in my face!
    But what are we waiting for?
                    —Look here, constable,
    stop sniffing around for a tavern, and get us   40
    some crowbars. We'll force their gates! As a matter
        of fact,
    I'll do a little forcing myself.

(*Enter Lysistrata, above, with Myrrhine, Kalonike, and
the Boiotian.*)

LYSISTRATA: No need of forcing.
    Here I am, of my own accord. And all this talk
    about locked doors—! We don't need locked doors,
    but just the least bit of common sense.   45
COMMISSIONER: Is that so, ma'am!
                    —Where's my constable?
                    —Constable,
    arrest that woman, and tie her hands behind her.
LYSISTRATA: If he touches me, I swear by Artemis
    there'll be one scamp dropped from the public
        pay-roll tomorrow!
COMMISSIONER: Well, constable? You're not afraid, I
        suppose? Grab her,   50
    two of you, around the middle!
KALONIKE: No, by Pandrosos!°
    Lay a hand on her, and I'll jump on you so hard
    your guts will come out the back door!
COMMISSIONER: That's what *you* think!
    Where's the sergeant?—Here, you: tie up that
        trollop first,
    the one with the pretty talk!

---

2. **Adonis:** Fertility god, loved by Aphrodite. 5. **Demostratos:**
Athenian orator and politician. **Sicily:** Reference to the Sicilian Expedition (415–413 BCE) in which Athens was decisively
defeated.

51. **Pandrosos:** A woman's oath referring to one of the daughters of the founder of Athens.

55 **MYRRHINE:**   By the Moon-Goddess,°
just try! They'll have to scoop you up with a spoon!
COMMISSIONER: Another one!
                              Officer, seize that woman!
                                               I swear
I'll put an end to this riot!
BOIOTIAN: By the Taurian,°
one inch closer, you'll be one screaming bald-head!
COMMISSIONER: Lord, what a mess! And my
60   constables seem ineffective.
But—women get the best of us? By God, no!
                              —Skythians!°
Close ranks and forward march!
LYSISTRATA: "Forward," indeed!
By the Two Goddesses, what's the sense in *that*?
They're up against four companies of women
armed from top to bottom.
65 **COMMISSIONER:**   Forward, my Skythians!
LYSISTRATA: Forward, yourselves, dear comrades!
You grainlettucebeanseedmarket girls!
You garlicandonionbreadbakery girls!
Give it to 'em! Knock 'em down! Scratch 'em!
Tell 'em what you think of 'em!

(*General melee, the Skythians yield.*)

70   —Ah, that's enough!
Sound a retreat: good soldiers don't rob the dead.
COMMISSIONER: A nice day *this* has been for the police!
LYSISTRATA: Well, there you are.—Did you really
        think we women
would be driven like slaves? Maybe now you'll admit
that a woman knows something about spirit.
75 **COMMISSIONER:**   Spirit enough,
especially spirits in bottles! Dear Lord Apollo!
KORYPHAIOS(m): Your Honor, there's no use talking to
        them. Words
mean nothing whatever to wild animals like these.
Think of the sousing they gave us! and the water
80 was not, I believe, of the purest.
KORYPHAIOS(w): You shouldn't have come after us.
        And if you try it again,
you'll be one eye short!—Although, as a matter of
        fact,
what I like best is just to stay at home and read,
like a sweet little bride: never hurting a soul, no,
85 never going out. But if you *must* shake hornets' nests,
look out for the hornets.

Strophe

CHORUS(m): Of all the beasts that God hath wrought
What monster's worse than woman?

Who shall encompass with his thought
Their guile unending? No man.   90

They've seized the Heights, the Rock, the Shrine—
But to what end? I wot not.
Sure there's some clue to their design!
Have you the key? I thought not.
KORYPHAIOS(m): We might question them, I suppose.
        But I warn you, sir,   95
don't believe anything you hear! It would be un-
        Athenian
not to get to the bottom of this plot.
COMMISSIONER: Very well.
My first question is this: Why, so help you God,
did you bar the gates of the Akropolis?
LYSISTRATA: Why?
To keep the money, of course. No money, no war.   100
COMMISSIONER: You think that money's the cause of
        war?
LYSISTRATA: I do.
Money brought about that Peisandros° business
and all the other attacks on the State. Well and good!
They'll not get another cent here!
COMMISSIONER: And what will you do?   105
LYSISTRATA: What a question! From now on, we intend
        to control the Treasury.
COMMISSIONER: Control the Treasury!
LYSISTRATA: Why not? Does that seem strange?
        After all,
we control our household budgets.
COMMISSIONER: But that's different!
LYSISTRATA: "Different"? What do you mean?
COMMISSIONER: I mean simply this: 110
it's the Treasury that pays for National Defense.
LYSISTRATA: Unnecessary. We propose to abolish war.
COMMISSIONER: Good God.—And National
        Security?
LYSISTRATA: Leave that to us.
COMMISSIONER: You?
LYSISTRATA: Us.
COMMISSIONER: We're done for, then!
LYSISTRATA: Never mind.   115
We women will save you in spite of yourselves.
COMMISSIONER: What nonsense!
LYSISTRATA: If you like. But you must accept it, like it
        or not.
COMMISSIONER: Why, this is downright subversion!
LYSISTRATA: Maybe it is.
But we're going to save you, Judge.
COMMISSIONER: I don't *want* to be saved.
LYSISTRATA: Tut. The death-wish. All the more reason.   120
COMMISSIONER: But the idea of women bothering
        themselves about peace and war!
LYSISTRATA: Will you listen to me?

---

55. **Moon-Goddess:** Artemis, goddess of the hunt and of fertility, daughter of Zeus.   58. **Taurian:** Reference to Artemis, who was said to have been worshiped in a cult at Taurica Chersonesos.   61. **Skythians:** Athenian archers.

103. **Peisandros:** A politician who plotted against the Athenian democracy.

COMMISSIONER: Yes. But be brief, or I'll—
LYSISTRATA: This is no time for stupid threats.
COMMISSIONER: By the gods,
I can't stand any more!
AN OLD WOMAN: Can't stand? Well, well.
COMMISSIONER: That's enough out of you, you old
125   buzzard!
     Now, Lysistrata: tell me what you're thinking.
LYSISTRATA: Glad to.
                     Ever since this war began
We women have been watching you men, agreeing
     with you,
keeping our thoughts to ourselves. That doesn't mean
we were happy: we weren't, for we saw how
130   things were going;
but we'd listen to you at dinner
arguing this way and that.
                         —Oh you, and your big
Top Secrets!—
                 And then we'd grin like little patriots
(though goodness knows we didn't feel like
     grinning) and ask you:
"Dear, did the Armistice come up in Assembly
135   today?"
And you'd say, "None of your business! Pipe
     down!" you'd say.
And so we would.
AN OLD WOMAN: *I* wouldn't have, by God!
COMMISSIONER: You'd have taken a beating, then!
                                          —Go on.
LYSISTRATA: Well, we'd be quiet. But then, you know,
     all at once
140 you men would think up something worse than ever.
Even *I* could see it was fatal. And, "Darling,"
     I'd say,
"have you gone completely mad?" And my husband
     would look at me
and say, "Wife, you've got your weaving to attend
     to.
Mind your tongue, if you don't want a slap.
145 'War's a man's affair!'"°
COMMISSIONER: Good words, and well pronounced.
LYSISTRATA: You're a fool if you think so.
                          It was hard enough
to put up with all this banquet-hall strategy.
But then we'd hear you out in the public square:
150 "Nobody left for the draft-quota here in Athens?"
you'd say; and, "No," someone else would say, "not
     a man!"
And so we women decided to rescue Greece.
You might as well listen to us now: you'll have to,
     later.
COMMISSIONER: *You* rescue Greece? Absurd.

LYSISTRATA: You're the absurd one.
COMMISSIONER: You expect me to take orders from a
     woman?
                     I'd die first!   155
LYSISTRATA: Heavens, if that's what's bothering you,
     take my veil,
here, and wrap it around your poor head.
KALONIKE: Yes
and you can have my market-basket, too.
Go home, tighten your girdle, do the washing, mind
your beans! "War's   160
a woman's affair!"
KORYPHAIOS(w):   Ground pitchers! Close ranks!

Antistrophe

CHORUS(w): This is a dance that I know well,
     My knees shall never yield.
Wobble and creak I may, but still
     I'll keep the well-fought field.   165
Valor and grace march on before,
     Love prods us from behind.
Our slogan is EXCELSIOR,
     Our watchword SAVE MANKIND.
KORYPHAIOS(w): Women, remember your grandmothers!
     Remember   170
that little old mother of yours, what a stinger she
     was!
On, on, never slacken. There's a strong wind astern!
LYSISTRATA: O Eros of delight! O Aphrodite! Kyprian!°
If ever desire has drenched our breasts or dreamed
in our thighs, let it work so now on the men of
     Hellas°   175
that they shall tail us through the land, slaves, slaves
to Woman, Breaker of Armies!
COMMISSIONER: And if we do?
LYSISTRATA: Well, for one thing, we shan't have to
     watch you
going to market, a spear in one hand, and heaven
     knows
what in the other.
KALONIKE: Nicely said, by Aphrodite!   180
LYSISTRATA: As things stand now, you're neither men
     nor women.
Armor clanking with kitchen pans and pots—
You sound like a pack of Korybantes!°
COMMISSIONER: A man must do what a man must do.
LYSISTRATA: So I'm told.
But to see a General, complete with Gorgon-shield,   185
     jingling along the dock to buy a couple of herrings!

---

173. Kyprian: Reference to Aphrodite's association with Cyprus
(Kyprus), a place sacred to her and a center for her worship.
175. Hellas: Greece.   **183. Korybantes:** Priestesses of Cybele,
a fertility goddess, who was celebrated in frenzied rituals accompanied by the beating of cymbals.

---

145. 'War's a man's affair!': Quoted from Homer's *Iliad*, VI,
492, Hector's farewell to his wife, Andromache.

KALONIKE: *I saw a Captain the other day*—lovely
fellow he was,
nice curly hair—sitting on his horse; and—can
you believe it?—
he'd just bought some soup, and was pouring it
into his helmet!
190   And there was a soldier from Thrace
swishing his lance like something out of Euripides,
and the poor fruit-store woman got so scared
that she ran away and let him have his figs free!
COMMISSIONER: All this is beside the point.
Will you be so kind
as to tell me how you mean to save Greece?
195   LYSISTRATA: Of course.
Nothing could be simpler.
COMMISSIONER: I assure you, I'm all ears.
LYSISTRATA: Do you know anything about weaving?
Say the yarn gets tangled: we thread it
this way and that through the skein, up and down,
200   until it's free. And it's like that with war.
We'll send our envoys
up and down, this way and that, all over Greece,
until it's finished.
COMMISSIONER: Yarn? Thread? Skein?
Are you out of your mind? I tell you,
war is a serious business.
205   LYSISTRATA: So serious
that I'd like to go on talking about weaving.
COMMISSIONER: All right. Go ahead.
LYSISTRATA: The first thing we have to do
is to wash our yarn, get the dirt out of it.
You see? Isn't there too much dirt here in Athens?
You must wash those men away.
210   Then our spoiled wool—
that's like your job-hunters, out for a life
of no work and big pay. Back to the basket,
citizens or not, allies or not,
or friendly immigrants.
And your colonies?
215   Hanks of wool lost in various places. Pull them
together, weave them into one great whole,
and our voters are clothed for ever.
COMMISSIONER: It would take a woman
to reduce state questions to a matter of carding and
weaving.
LYSISTRATA: You fool! Who were the mothers whose
sons sailed off
to fight for Athens in Sicily?
220   COMMISSIONER: Enough!
I beg you, do not call back those memories.
LYSISTRATA: And then,
instead of the love that every woman needs,
we have only our single beds, where we can
dream
of our husbands off with the Army.
Bad enough for wives!
225   But what about our girls, getting older every day,
and older, and no kisses?
COMMISSIONER: Men get older, too.

LYSISTRATA: Not in the same sense.
A soldier's discharged,
and he may be bald and toothless, yet he'll find
a pretty young thing to go to bed with.
But a woman!
Her beauty is gone with the first gray hair.   230
She can spend her time
consulting the oracles and the fortune-tellers,
but they'll never send her a husband.
COMMISSIONER: Still, if a man can rise to the
occasion—
LYSISTRATA: Rise? Rise, yourself!   235
(*Furiously.*)
Go invest in a coffin!
You've money enough.
I'll bake you
a cake for the Underworld.
And here's your funeral wreath!
(*She pours water upon him.*)
MYRRHINE: And here's another!
(*More water.*)
KALONIKE: And here's
my contribution!
(*More water.*)
LYSISTRATA: What are you waiting for?
All aboard Styx Ferry!
Charon's° calling for you!   240
It's sailing-time: don't disrupt the schedule!
COMMISSIONER: The insolence of women! And
to me!
No, by God, I'll go back to town and show
the rest of the Commission what might happen to
them.   (*Exit Commissioner.*)
LYSISTRATA: Really, I suppose we should have laid
out his corpse   245
on the doorstep, in the usual way.
But never mind.
We'll give him the rites of the dead tomorrow
morning.

(*Exit Lysistrata with Myrrhine and Kalonike.*)

PARABASIS:°
CHORAL EPISODE • Ode° 1

KORYPHAIOS(m): Sons of Liberty, awake! The day of
glory is at hand.

240. **Charon:** The god who ferried the souls of the newly dead
across the river Styx to Hades. **Parabasis:** Section of the
play in which the author presented his own views through the
Koryphaios directly to the audience. The parabasis in *Lysistrata*
is shorter than those in Aristophanes' other works and unusual in that the Koryphaios does not speak directly for the
author. **Ode:** Song sung by the Chorus.

CHORUS(m): I smell tyranny afoot, I smell it rising from
 the land.
 I scent a trace of Hippias,° I sniff upon the breeze
 A dismal Spartan hogo that suggests King
  Kleisthenes.°
5 Strip, strip for action, brothers!
  Our wives, aunts, sisters, mothers
 Have sold us out: the streets are full of godless
  female rages.
 Shall we stand by and let our women confiscate
  our wages?

         [Epirrhema° 1]

KORYPHAIOS(m): Gentlemen, it's a disgrace to Athens, a
 disgrace
 to all that Athens stands for, if we allow these
10 grandmas
 to jabber about spears and shields and making
 friends
 with the Spartans. What's a Spartan? Give me a
 wild wolf
 any day. No. They want the Tyranny back, I
 suppose.
 Are we going to take that? No. Let us look like
15 the innocent serpent, but be the flower under it,
 as the poet sings. And just to begin with,
 I propose to poke a number of teeth
 down the gullet of that harridan over there.

Antode° 1

KORYPHAIOS(w): Oh, is that so? When you get home,
 your own mamma won't know you!
CHORUS(w): Who do you think we are, you senile
20 bravos? Well, I'll show you.
 I bore the sacred vessels in my eighth year,° and at ten
 I was pounding out the barley for Athena Goddess;°
 then
  They made me Little Bear
  At the Brauronian Fair;°
25 I'd held the Holy Basket° by the time I was of age,
 The Blessed Dry Figs had adorned my plump
 decolletage.

        [Antepirrhema° 1]

3. **Hippias:** An Athenian tyrant. **4. Kleisthenes:** A bisexual
Athenian. **Epirrhema:** A part of the parabasis spoken by the
Koryphaios following an ode delivered by his or her half of the
Chorus. **Antode:** Lyric song sung by half of the Chorus in response to the ode sung by the other half. **21. eighth year:** Young
girls between the ages of seven and eleven served in the temple of
Athena in the Akropolis. **22. pounding out the barley for Athena
Goddess:** At age ten a girl could be chosen to grind the sacred grain
of Athena. **24. Brauronian Fair:** A ritual in the cult of Artemis,
who is associated with wild beasts, in which young girls dressed
up as bears and danced for the goddess. **25. Holy Basket:** In one
ritual to Athena, young girls carried baskets of objects sacred to
the goddess. **Antepirrhema:** The speech delivered by the second
Koryphaios after the second half of the Chorus had sung an ode.

KORYPHAIOS(w): A "disgrace to Athens," and I, just at
 the moment
 I'm giving Athens the best advice she ever had?
 Don't I pay taxes to the State? Yes, I pay them
 in baby boys. And what do you contribute, 30
 you impotent horrors? Nothing but waste: all
 our Treasury,° dating back to the Persian Wars,
 gone! rifled! And not a penny out of your pockets!
 Well, then? Can you cough up an answer to that?
 Look out for your own gullet, or you'll get a crack 35
 from this old brogan that'll make your teeth see
 stars!

Ode 2

CHORUS(m): Oh insolence!
 Am I unmanned?
 Incontinence!
 Shall my scarred hand   40
 Strike never a blow
 To curb this flow-
 ing female curse?

 Leipsydrion!°
 Shall I betray
 The laurels won   45
 On that great day?
 Come, shake a leg,
 Shed old age, beg
 The years reverse!   50

         (Epirrhema 2)

KORYPHAIOS(m): Give them an inch, and we're done
 for! We'll have them
 launching boats next and planning naval
 strategy,
 sailing down on us like so many Artemisias.
 Or maybe they have ideas about the cavalry.
 That's fair enough, women are certainly good 55
 in the saddle. Just look at Mikon's paintings,
 all those Amazons wrestling with all those men!
 On the whole, a straitjacket's their best uniform.

Antode 2

CHORUS(w): Tangle with me,
 And you'll get cramps.   60
 Ferocity
 's no use now, Gramps!
 By the Two,
 I'll get through
 To you wrecks yet!   65

32. **Treasury:** Athenian politicians were raiding the funds
that were collected by Athens to finance a war against Persia.
44. **Leipsydrion:** A place where Athenian patriots had hero-
ically fought.

I'll scramble your eggs,
I'll burn your beans,
With my two legs.
You'll see such scenes
70   As never yet
Your two eyes met.
A curse? You bet!

[Antepirrhema 2]

KORYPHAIOS⁽ᵂ⁾: If Lampito stands by me, and that
    delicious Theban girl,
    Ismenia—what good are *you*? You and your
    seven
75   Resolutions! Resolutions? Rationing Boiotian eels
    and making our girls go without them at Hekate's°
    Feast!
    That was statesmanship! And we'll have to put up
    with it
    and all the rest of your decrepit legislation
    until some patriot—God give him strength!—
80   grabs you by the neck and kicks you off the Rock.

SCENE 2

(*Reenter Lysistrata and her lieutenants.*)

KORYPHAIOS⁽ᵂ⁾ (*tragic tone*): Great Queen, fair
    Architect of our emprise,
    Why lookst thou on us with foreboding eyes?
LYSISTRATA: The behavior of these idiotic women!
    There's something about the female temperament
    that I can't bear!
5   KORYPHAIOS⁽ᵂ⁾:   What in the world do you mean?
LYSISTRATA: Exactly what I say.
KORYPHAIOS⁽ᵂ⁾: What dreadful thing has happened?
    Come, tell us: we're all your friends.
LYSISTRATA: It isn't easy
    to say it; yet, God knows, we can't hush it up.
KORYPHAIOS⁽ᵂ⁾: Well, then? Out with it!
10   LYSISTRATA: To put it bluntly,
    we're dying to get laid.
KORYPHAIOS⁽ᵂ⁾:   Almighty God!
LYSISTRATA: Why bring God into it?—No, it's just as
    I say.
    I can't manage them any longer: they've gone
    man-crazy,
    they're all trying to get out.
                    Why, look:
15   one of them was sneaking out the back door
    over there by Pan's cave; another
    was sliding down the walls with rope and tackle;
    another was climbing aboard a sparrow, ready to
    take off
    for the nearest brothel—I dragged *her* back by the
    hair!

76. **Hekate:** Patron of successful wars, object of a Boiotian cult (later associated with sorcery).

They're all finding some reason to leave.
                    Look there!   20
    There goes another one.
                    —Just a minute, you!
    Where are you off to so fast?
FIRST WOMAN: I've got to get home.
    I've a lot of Milesian wool, and the worms are
    spoiling it.
LYSISTRATA: Oh bother you and your worms! Get back
    inside!
FIRST WOMAN: I'll be back right away, I swear I will.   25
    I just want to get it stretched out on my bed.
LYSISTRATA: You'll do no such thing. You'll stay
    right here.
FIRST WOMAN: And my wool?
    You want it ruined?
LYSISTRATA: Yes, for all I care.
SECOND WOMAN: Oh dear! My lovely new flax from
    Amorgos—
    I left it at home, all uncarded!
LYSISTRATA: Another one!   30
    And all she wants is someone to card her flax.
    Get back in there!
SECOND WOMAN: But I swear by the Moon-Goddess
    the minute I get it done, I'll be back!
LYSISTRATA: I say No.
    If you, why not all the other women as well?
THIRD WOMAN: O Lady Eileithyia!° Radiant goddess!
    Thou   35
    intercessor for women in childbirth! Stay, I pray thee,
    oh stay this parturition. Shall I pollute
    a sacred spot?°
LYSISTRATA: And what's the matter with *you*?
THIRD WOMAN: I'm having a baby—any minute now.
LYSISTRATA: But you weren't pregnant yesterday.
THIRD WOMAN: Well, I am today.   40
    Let me go home for a midwife, Lysistrata:
    there's not much time.
LYSISTRATA: I never heard such nonsense.
    What's that bulging under your cloak?
THIRD WOMAN: A little baby boy.
LYSISTRATA: It certainly isn't. But it's something hollow,
    like a basin or—Why, it's the helmet of Athena!   45
    And you said you were having a baby.
THIRD WOMAN: Well, I am! So there!
LYSISTRATA: Then why the helmet?
THIRD WOMAN: I was afraid that my pains
    might begin here in the Akropolis; and I wanted
    to drop my chick into it, just as the dear doves do.
LYSISTRATA: Lies! Evasions!—But at least one thing's
    clear: 50
    you can't leave the place before your purification.°

35. **Eileithyia:** Goddess of childbirth. 37–38. **pollute a sacred spot:** Giving birth on the Akropolis was forbidden because it was sacred ground. 51. **purification:** A ritual cleansing of a woman after childbirth.

THIRD WOMAN: But I can't stay here in the Akropolis!
Last night I dreamed
of the Snake.
FIRST WOMAN: And those horrible owls, the noise they
make!
I can't get a bit of sleep; I'm just about dead.
LYSISTRATA: You useless girls, that's enough: Let's have
55   no more lying.
Of course you want your men. But don't you imagine
that they want you just as much? I'll give you my
word,
their nights must be pretty hard.
                              Just stick it out!
A little patience, that's all, and our battle's won.
60   I have heard an Oracle. Should you like to hear it?
FIRST WOMAN: An Oracle? Yes, tell us!
LYSISTRATA: Here is what it says:
WHEN SWALLOWS SHALL THE HOOPOE
SHUN AND SPURN HIS HOT DESIRE,
ZEUS WILL PERFECT WHAT THEY'VE BEGUN
65   AND SET THE LOWER HIGHER.
FIRST WOMAN: Does that mean we'll be on top?
LYSISTRATA: BUT IF THE SWALLOWS SHALL FALL
OUT
AND TAKE THE HOOPOE'S BAIT,
A CURSE MUST MARK THEIR HOUR OF
DOUBT,
70   INFAMY SEAL THEIR FATE.
THIRD WOMAN: I swear, *that* Oracle's all too clear.
FIRST WOMAN: Oh the dear gods!
LYSISTRATA: Let's not be downhearted, girls. Back to
our places!
The god has spoken. How can we possibly fail him?

(*Exit Lysistrata with the dissident women.*)

CHORAL EPISODE • Strophe

CHORUS(m): I know a little story that I learned way
back in school
Goes like this:
Once upon a time there was a young man—and no
fool—
Named Melanion; and his
One aversion was marriage. He loathed the very
5   thought.
So he ran off to the hills, and in a special grot
Raised a dog, and spent his days
Hunting rabbits. And it says
That he never never never did come home.
10   It might be called a refuge *from* the womb.
All right,
          all right,
                    all right!
We're as bright as young Melanion, and we hate
the very sight
Of you women!
A MAN: How about a kiss, old lady?

A WOMAN: Here's an onion for your eye!   15
A MAN: A kick in the guts, then?
A WOMAN: Try, old bristle-tail, just try!
A MAN: Yet they say Myronides
On hands and knees
Looked just as shaggy fore and aft as I!   20

Antistrophe

CHORUS(w): Well, *I* know a little story, and it's just as
good as yours.
Goes like this:
Once there was a man named Timon—a rough
diamond, of course,
And that whiskery face of his
Looked like murder in the shrubbery. By God, he
was a son   25
Of the Furies, let me tell you! And what did he do
but run
From the world and all its ways,
Cursing mankind! And it says
That his choicest execrations as of then
Were leveled almost wholly at *old* men.   30
All right,
          all right,
                    all right!
But there's one thing about Timon: he could
always stand the sight
of us women.
A WOMAN: How about a crack in the jaw, Pop?
A MAN: I can take it, Ma—no fear!   35
A WOMAN: How about a kick in the face?
A MAN: You'd reveal your old caboose?
A WOMAN: What I'd show,
I'll have you know,
Is an instrument you're too far gone to use.   40

SCENE 3

(*Reenter Lysistrata.*)

LYSISTRATA: Oh, quick, girls, quick! Come here!
A WOMAN: What is it?
LYSISTRATA: A man.
A man simply bulging with love.
                              O Kyprian Queen,°
O Paphian, O Kythereian! Hear us and aid us!
A WOMAN: Where is this enemy?
LYSISTRATA: Over there, by Demeter's shrine.
A WOMAN: Damned if he isn't. But who *is* he?
MYRRHINE: My husband.   5
Kinesias.
LYSISTRATA: Oh then, get busy! Tease him! Undermine
him!

2. **Kyprian Queen:** Aphrodite.

Cherry Jones as Lysistrata in the American Repertory Theater's 2002 production directed by Robert Brustein.

Geraldine James (far left) as Lysistrata in the Old Vic Theatre production in London, 1993.

The Théâtre La Licorne 2006 performance of *Lysistrata*, adapted by Claire Dancoisne.

Wreck him! Give him everything—kissing,
   tickling, nudging,
whatever you generally torture him with—: give
   him everything
except what we swore on the wine we would not
   give.
MYRRHINE: Trust me.
10 LYSISTRATA: I do. But I'll help you get him started.
The rest of you women, stay back.

(*Enter Kinesias.*)

KINESIAS: Oh God! Oh my God!
   I'm stiff from lack of exercise. All I can do to stand
   up.
LYSISTRATA: Halt! Who are you, approaching our lines?
KINESIAS: Me? I.
LYSISTRATA: A man?
KINESIAS: You have eyes, haven't you?
15 LYSISTRATA: Go away.
KINESIAS: Who says so?

LYSISTRATA: Officer of the Day.
KINESIAS: Officer, I beg you,
   by all the gods at once, bring Myrrhine out.
LYSISTRATA: Myrrhine? And who, my good sir, are
   you?
KINESIAS: Kinesias. Last name's Pennison. Her husband.
LYSISTRATA: Oh, of course. I beg your pardon. We're   20
   glad to see you.
   We've heard so much about you. Dearest Myrrhine
   is always talking about Kinesias—never nibbles an
      egg
   or an apple without saying
   "Here's to Kinesias!"
KINESIAS: Do you really mean it?
LYSISTRATA: I do.
   When we're discussing men, she always says   25
   "Well, after all, there's nobody like Kinesias!"
KINESIAS: Good God.—Well, then, please send her
   down here.
LYSISTRATA: And what do *I* get out of it?
KINESIAS: A standing promise.
LYSISTRATA: I'll take it up with her.
                                     (*Exit Lysistrata.*)
KINESIAS: But be quick about it!
   Lord, what's life without a wife? Can't eat. Can't
      sleep.   30
   Every time I go home, the place is so empty, so
   insufferably sad. Love's killing me, Oh,
   hurry!

(*Enter Manes, a slave, with Kinesias's baby; the voice
of Myrrhine is heard offstage.*)

MYRRHINE: But of course I love him! Adore him—
                                             But no,
   he hates love. No. I won't go down.

(*Enter Myrrhine, above.*)

KINESIAS: Myrrhine!
   Darlingest Myrrhinette! Come down quick!   35
MYRRHINE: Certainly not.
KINESIAS: Not? But why, Myrrhine?
MYRRHINE: Why? You don't need me.
KINESIAS: Need you? My God, *look* at me!
MYRRHINE: So long!

(*Turns to go.*)

KINESIAS: Myrrhine, Myrrhine, Myrrhine!
   If not for my sake, for our child!

(*Pinches Baby.*)

                       —All right, you: pipe up!
BABY: Mummie! Mummie! Mummie!
KINESIAS: You hear that?   40
   Pitiful, I call it. Six days now
   with never a bath; no food; enough to break your
      heart!
MYRRHINE: My darlingest child! What a father *you*
   acquired!
KINESIAS: At least come down for his sake.

MYRRHINE: I suppose I must.
45   Oh, this mother business!   (*Exit.*)
KINESIAS: How pretty she is! And younger!
          The harder she treats me, the more bothered I get.

(*Myrrhine enters, below.*)

MYRRHINE: Dearest child,
          you're as sweet as your father's horrid. Give me a kiss.
KINESIAS: Now don't you see how wrong it was to
              get involved
50   in this scheming League of women? It's bad
          for us both.
MYRRHINE: Keep your hands to yourself!
KINESIAS: But our house
          going to rack and ruin?
MYRRHINE: *I don't care.*
KINESIAS: And your knitting
          all torn to pieces by the chickens? Don't you care?
MYRRHINE: Not at all.
55 KINESIAS: And our debt to Aphrodite?
          Oh, *won't* you come back?
MYRRHINE: No.—At least, not until you men
          make a treaty and stop this war.
KINESIAS: Why, I suppose
          that might be arranged.
MYRRHINE: Oh? Well, I suppose
          I might come down then. But meanwhile,
          I've sworn not to.
60 KINESIAS: Don't worry.—Now let's have fun.
MYRRHINE: No! Stop it! I said no!
                              —Although, of course,
          I *do* love you.
KINESIAS: I know you do. Darling Myrrhine:
          come, shall we?
MYRRHINE: Are you out of your mind? In front of the
          child?
KINESIAS: Take him home, Manes.
                        (*Exit Manes with Baby.*)
                              There. He's gone.
                                        Come on!
          There's nothing to stop us now.
65 MYRRHINE: You devil! But where?
KINESIAS: In Pan's cave. What could be snugger than that?
MYRRHINE: But my purification before I go back to
          the Citadel?
KINESIAS: Wash in the Klepsydra.°
MYRRHINE: And my oath?
KINESIAS: Leave the oath to me.
          After all, I'm the man.
MYRRHINE: Well . . . if you say so.
                              I'll go find a bed.
KINESIAS: Oh, bother a bed! The ground's good
70   enough for me.
MYRRHINE: No. You're a bad man, but you deserve
          something better than dirt.   (*Exit Myrrhine.*)
KINESIAS: What a love she is! And how thoughtful!

(*Reenter Myrrhine.*)

MYRRHINE: Here's your bed.
          Now let me get my clothes off.
                                But, good horrors!
          We haven't a mattress.
KINESIAS: Oh, forget the mattress!
MYRRHINE: No.
          Just lying on blankets? Too sordid.
KINESIAS: Give me a kiss.   75
MYRRHINE: Just a second.   (*Exit Myrrhine.*)
KINESIAS: I swear, I'll explode!

(*Reenter Myrrhine.*)

MYRRHINE: Here's your mattress.
          I'll just take my dress off.
                          But look—
          where's our pillow?
KINESIAS: I don't *need* a pillow!
MYRRHINE: Well, *I* do.
                              (*Exit Myrrhine.*)
KINESIAS: I don't suppose even Herakles°
          would stand for this!

(*Reenter Myrrhine.*)

MYRRHINE: There we are. Ups-a-daisy!   80
KINESIAS: So we are. Well, come to bed.
MYRRHINE: But I wonder:
          is everything ready now?
KINESIAS: I can swear to that. Come, darling!
MYRRHINE: Just getting out of my girdle.
                              But remember, now,
          what you promised about the treaty.
KINESIAS: Yes, yes, yes!
MYRRHINE: But no coverlet!
KINESIAS: Damn it, I'll be your coverlet!   85
MYRRHINE: Be right back.   (*Exit Myrrhine.*)
KINESIAS: This girl and her coverlets
          will be the death of me.

(*Reenter Myrrhine.*)

MYRRHINE: Here we are. Up you go!
KINESIAS: Up? I've been up for ages.
MYRRHINE: Some perfume?
KINESIAS: No, by Apollo!
MYRRHINE: Yes, by Aphrodite!
          I don't care whether you want it or not.   90
                              (*Exit Myrrhine.*)
KINESIAS: For love's sake, hurry!

(*Reenter Myrrhine.*)

MYRRHINE: Here, in your hand. Rub it right in.
KINESIAS: Never cared for perfume.
          And this is particularly strong. Still, here goes.
MYRRHINE: What a nitwit I am! I brought you the
          Rhodian bottle.
KINESIAS: Forget it.   95

68. **Klepsydra:** A water clock beneath the walls of the Akropolis. Kinesias's suggestion borders on blasphemy.

79. **Herakles:** Greek hero (Hercules) known for his Twelve Labors.

MYRRHINE: No trouble at all. You just wait here.
(Exit Myrrhine.)
KINESIAS: God damn the man who invented perfume!

(Reenter Myrrhine.)

MYRRHINE: At last! The right bottle!
KINESIAS: I've got the tightest bottle of all,
    and it's right here waiting for you.
    Darling, forget everything else. Do come to bed.
MYRRHINE: Just let me get my shoes off.
100   —And, by the way,
    you'll vote for the treaty?
KINESIAS: I'll think about it.
(Myrrhine runs away.)
    There! That's done it! The damned woman,
    she gets me all bothered, she half kills me,
    and off she runs! What'll I do? Where
    can I get laid?
105   —And you, little prodding pal,
    who's going to take care of *you*? No, you and I
    had better get down to old Foxdog's Nursing Clinic.
CHORUS(m): Alas for the woes of man, alas
    Specifically for you.
110 She's brought you to a pretty pass:
    What are you going to do?
    Split, heart! Sag, flesh! Proud spirit, crack!
    Myrrhine's got you on your back.
KINESIAS: The agony, the protraction!
KORYPHAIOS(m):   Friend,
115 What woman's worth a damn?
    They bitch us all, world without end.
KINESIAS: Yet they're so damned sweet, man!
KORYPHAIOS(m): Calamitous, that's what I say.
    You should have learned that much today.
120 CHORUS(m): O blessed Zeus, roll womankind
    Up into one great ball;
    Blast them aloft on a high wind,
    And once there, let them fall.
    Down, down they'll come, the pretty dears,
125 And split themselves on our thick spears.
(Exit Kinesias.)

SCENE 4

(Enter a Spartan Herald.)

HERALD: Gentlemen, Ah beg you will be so kind
    as to direct me to the Central Committee.
    Ah have a communication.

(Reenter Commissioner.)

COMMISSIONER: Are you a man,
    or a fertility symbol?
HERALD: Ah refuse to answer that question!
5   Ah'm a certified herald from Spahta, and Ah've come
    to talk about an ahmistice.
COMMISSIONER: Then why
    that spear under your cloak?
HERALD: Ah have no speah!

COMMISSIONER: You don't walk naturally, with your tunic
    poked out so. You have a tum or, maybe,
    or a hernia?
HERALD: You lost yo' mahnd, man?
COMMISSIONER: Well,   10
    something's up, I can see that. And I don't like it.
HERALD: Colonel, Ah resent this.
COMMISSIONER: So I see. But what *is* it?
HERALD: A staff
    with a message from Spahta.
COMMISSIONER: Oh, I know about those staffs.
    Well, then, man, speak out: How are things in Sparta?
HERALD: Hahd, Colonel, hahd! We're at a standstill.   15
    Cain't seem to think of anything but women.
COMMISSIONER: How curious! Tell me, do you
    Spartans think
    that maybe Pan's to blame?
HERALD: Pan? No, Lampito and her little naked friends.
    They won't let a man come nigh them.   20
COMMISSIONER: How are you handling it?
HERALD: Losing our mahnds,
    if y' want to know, and walking around hunched over
    lahk men carrying candles in a gale.
    The women have swohn they'll have nothing to do
      with us
    until we get a treaty.
COMMISSIONER: Yes. I know.   25
    It's a general uprising, sir, in all parts of Greece.
    But as for the answer—
              Sir: go back to Sparta
    and have them send us your Armistice Commission.
    I'll arrange things in Athens.
            And I may say
    that my standing is good enough to make them listen.   30
HERALD: A man after mah own haht! Seh, Ah thank
    you.   (Exit Herald.)

CHORAL EPISODE • Strophe

CHORUS(m): Oh these women! Where will you find
    A slavering beast that's more unkind?
      Where's a hotter fire?
    Give me a panther, any day.
    He's not so merciless as they,   5
      And panthers don't conspire.

Antistrophe

CHORUS(w): We may be hard, you silly old ass,
    But who brought you to this stupid pass?
      You're the ones to blame.
    Fighting with us, your oldest friends,   10
    Simply to serve your selfish ends—
      Really, you have no shame!
KORYPHAIOS(m): No, I'm through with women for ever.
KORYPHAIOS(w):   If you say so.
    Still, you might put some clothes on. You look too
      absurd
    standing around naked. Come, get into this cloak.   15

KORYPHAIOS⁽ᵐ⁾: Thank you; you're right. I merely took
  it off
because I was in such a temper.
KORYPHAIOS⁽ʷ⁾:   That's much better.
  Now you resemble a man again.
                                    Why have you been so horrid?
  And look: there's some sort of insect in your eye.
  Shall I take it out?
20 KORYPHAIOS⁽ᵐ⁾:   An insect, is it? So that's
  what's been bothering me. Lord, yes: take it out!
KORYPHAIOS⁽ʷ⁾: You might be more polite.
                                    —But, heavens!
  What an enormous mosquito!
KORYPHAIOS⁽ᵐ⁾:   You've saved my life.
  That mosquito was drilling an artesian well
  in my left eye.
25 KORYPHAIOS⁽ʷ⁾:   Let me wipe
  those tears away.—And now: one little kiss?
KORYPHAIOS⁽ᵐ⁾: No, no kisses.
KORYPHAIOS⁽ʷ⁾: You're so difficult.
KORYPHAIOS⁽ᵐ⁾: You impossible women! How you do
  get around us!
  The poet was right: Can't live with you, or without
30 you.
  But let's be friends.
  And to celebrate, you might join us in an Ode.

Strophe 1

CHORUS⁽ᵐ ᵃⁿᵈ ʷ⁾: Let it never be said
    That my tongue is malicious:
35   Both by word and by deed
  I would set an example that's noble and gracious.
    We've had sorrow and care
    Till we're sick of the tune.
    Is there anyone here
40   Who would like a small loan?
      My purse is crammed,
      As you'll soon find;
  And you needn't pay me back if the Peace gets signed.

Strophe 2

    I've invited to lunch
45   Some Karystian rips°—
    An esurient bunch,
  But I've ordered a menu to water their lips.
    I can still make soup
    And slaughter a pig.
50   You're all coming, I hope?
    But a bath first, I beg!
      Walk right up

45. **Karystian rips:** The Karystians were allies of Athens but were scorned for their primitive ways and loose morals.

As though you owned the place,
And you'll get the front door slammed to in your
  face.

SCENE 5

(*Enter Spartan Ambassador, with entourage.*)

KORYPHAIOS⁽ᵐ⁾: The Commission has arrived from
  Sparta.
              How oddly they're walking!
                      Gentlemen, welcome to Athens!
  How is life in Lakonia?
AMBASSADOR: Need we discuss that?
  Simply use your eyes.
CHORUS⁽ᵐ⁾:   The poor man's right:
                              What a sight!
AMBASSADOR: Words fail me.   5
  But come, gentlemen, call in your Commissioners,
  and let's get down to a Peace.
CHORAGOS⁽ᵐ⁾:   The state we're in! Can't bear
  a stitch below the waist. It's a kind of pelvic
  paralysis.
COMMISSIONER: Won't somebody call Lysistrata?—
                                        Gentlemen,
  we're no better off than you.
AMBASSADOR: So I see.   10
A SPARTAN: Seh, do y'all feel a certain strain early in the
    morning?
AN ATHENIAN: I do, sir. It's worse than a strain.
  A few more days, and there's nothing for us but
    Kleisthenes,
  that broken blossom.
CHORAGOS⁽ᵐ⁾:   But you'd better get dressed again.
  You know these people going around Athens with
    chisels   15
  looking for statues of Hermes.°
ATHENIAN: Sir, you are right.
SPARTAN: He certainly is! Ah'll put mah own clothes
    back on.

(*Enter Athenian Commissioners.*)

COMMISSIONER: Gentlemen from Sparta, welcome.
  This is a sorry business.
SPARTAN (*to one of his own group*): Colonel, we got
    dressed just in time. Ah sweah,
  if they'd seen us the way we were, there'd have been
    a new wah   20
  between the states.
COMMISSIONER: Shall we call the meeting to order?
                                    Now, Lakonians,
  what's your proposal?
AMBASSADOR: We propose to consider peace.

16. **statues of Hermes:** The usual representation of Hermes was with an erect phallus. Statues of Hermes were scattered throughout Athens and were attacked by vandals just before the Sicilian Expedition.

COMMISSIONER: Good. That's on our minds, too.
                                    —Summon Lysistrata.
   We'll never get anywhere without her.
25 AMBASSADOR: Lysistrata?
      Summon Lysis-*any*body! Only, summon!
   KORYPHAIOS(m):   No need to summon:
      here she is, herself.

(Enter Lysistrata.)

COMMISSIONER: Lysistrata! Lion of women!
      This is your hour to be
      hard and yielding, outspoken and shy, austere and
30   gentle. You see here
      the best brains of Hellas (confused, I admit,
      by your devious charming) met as one man
      to turn the future over to you.
   LYSISTRATA: That's fair enough,
      unless you men take it into your heads
35   to turn to each other instead of to us. But I'd know
      soon enough if you did.
                        —Where is Reconciliation?
      Go, some of you: bring her here.

                              (Exeunt two women.)
                              And now, women,
      lead the Spartan delegates to me: not roughly
      or insultingly, as our men handle them, but gently,
40   politely, as ladies should. Take them by the hand,
      or by anything else if they won't give you their hands.

(The Spartans are escorted over.)

      There.—The Athenians next, by any convenient
         handle.

(The Athenians are escorted.)

      Stand there, please.—Now, all of you, listen to me.

*(During the following speech the two women reenter,
carrying an enormous statue of a naked girl; this is
Reconciliation.)*

      I'm only a woman, I know; but I've a mind,
45   and, I think, not a bad one: I owe it to my father
      and to listening to the local politicians.
      So much for that.
                  Now, gentlemen,
      since I have you here, I intend to give you a scolding.
      We are all Greeks.
50   Must I remind you of Thermopylai,° of Olympia,
      of Delphoi? names deep in all our hearts?
      Are they not a common heritage?
                        Yet you men
      go raiding through the country from both sides,
      Greek killing Greek, storming down Greek cities—
55   and all the time the Barbarian across the sea
      is waiting for his chance!
                        —That's my first point.

AN ATHENIAN: Lord! I can hardly contain myself.
LYSISTRATA: As for you Spartans:
      Was it so long ago that Perikleides°
      came here to beg our help? I can see him still,
      his gray face, his sombre gown. And what did he
         want?   60
      An army from Athens. All Messene
      was hot at your heels, and the sea-god splitting your
         land.
      Well, Kimon and his men,
      four thousand strong, marched out and saved all
         Sparta.
      And what thanks do we get? You come back to
         murder us.   65
AN ATHENIAN: They're aggressors, Lysistrata!
A SPARTAN: Ah admit it.
      When Ah look at those laigs, Ah sweah Ah'll
         aggress mahself!
LYSISTRATA: And you, Athenians: do you think you're
      blameless?
      Remember that bad time when we were helpless,
      and an army came from Sparta,   70
      and that was the end of the Thessalian menace,
      the end of Hippias and his allies.
                        And that was Sparta,
      and only Sparta; but for Sparta, we'd be
      cringing slaves today, not free Athenians.

*(From this point, the male responses are less to
Lysistrata than to the statue.)*

A SPARTAN: A well shaped speech.
AN ATHENIAN: Certainly it has its points.   75
LYSISTRATA: Why are we fighting each other? With all
         this history
      of favors given and taken, what stands in the way
      of making peace?
AMBASSADOR: Spahta is ready, ma'am,
      so long as we get that place back.
LYSISTRATA: What place, man?
AMBASSADOR: Ah refer to Pylos.
COMMISSIONER: Not a chance, by God!   80
LYSISTRATA: Give it to them, friend.
COMMISSIONER: But—what shall we have to bargain
         with?
LYSISTRATA: Demand something in exchange.
COMMISSIONER: Good idea.—Well, then:
      Cockeville first, and the Happy Hills, and the
      country between the Legs of Megara.
AMBASSADOR: Mah government objects.   85
LYSISTRATA: Overruled. Why fuss about a pair of legs?

(General assent. The statue is removed.)

AN ATHENIAN: I want to get out of these clothes and
         start my plowing.
A SPARTAN: Ah'll fertilize mahn first, by the Heavenly
         Twins!

---

50. Thermopylai: A narrow pass where, in 480 BCE, an army
of three hundred Spartans held out for three days against a
superior Persian force.

58. Perikleides: Spartan ambassador to Athens who successfully urged Athenians to aid Sparta in quelling a rebellion.

LYSISTRATA: And so you shall,
90   once you've made peace. If you are serious,
      go, both of you, and talk with your allies.
COMMISSIONER: Too much talk already. No, we'll
      stand together.
      We've only one end in view. All that we want
      is our women; and I speak for our allies.
AMBASSADOR: Mah government concurs.
95 AN ATHENIAN: So does Karystos.
LYSISTRATA: Good.—But before you come inside
      to join your wives at supper, you must perform
      the usual lustration. Then we'll open
      our baskets for you, and all that we have is yours.
100   But you must promise upright good behavior
      from this day on. Then each man home with his
      woman!
AN ATHENIAN: Let's get it over with.
A SPARTAN: Lead on. Ah follow.
AN ATHENIAN: Quick as a cat can wink!
                  (*Exeunt all but the Choruses.*)

Antistrophe 1

CHORUS(w): Embroideries and
105   Twinkling ornaments and
      Pretty dresses—I hand
Them all over to you, and with never a qualm.
      They'll be nice for your daughters
      On festival days
110   When the girls bring the Goddess
      The ritual prize.
      Come in, one and all:
      Take what you will.
I've nothing here so tightly corked that you can't
      make it spill.

Antistrophe 2

115   You may search my house
      But you'll not find
      The least thing of use,
Unless your two eyes are keener than mine.
      Your numberless brats
120   Are half starved? and your slaves?
      Courage, grandpa! I've lots
      Of grain left, and big loaves.
      I'll fill your guts,
      I'll go the whole hog;
But if you come too close to me, remember: 'ware
125   the dog!   (*Exeunt Choruses.*)

EXODOS°

(*A Drunken Citizen enters, approaches the gate, and is
halted by a sentry.*)

Exodos: Final scene.

CITIZEN: Open. The. Door.
SENTRY: Now, friend, just shove along!
      —So you want to sit down. If it weren't such an old
      joke,
      I'd tickle your tail with this torch. Just the sort of
      gag
      this audience appreciates.
CITIZEN: I. Stay. Right. Here.
SENTRY: Get away from there, or I'll scalp you!   5
      The gentlemen from Sparta
      are just coming back from dinner.

(*Exit Citizen; the general company reenters; the two
Choruses now represent Spartans and Athenians.*)

A SPARTAN: Ah must say,
      Ah never tasted better grub.
AN ATHENIAN: And those Lakonians!
      They're gentlemen, by the Lord! Just goes to show,
      a drink to the wise is sufficient.
COMMISSIONER: And why not?   10
      A sober man's an ass.
      Men of Athens, mark my words: the only efficient
      Ambassador's a drunk Ambassador. Is that clear?
      Look: we go to Sparta,
      and when we get there we're dead sober. The result?   15
      Everyone cackling at everyone else. They make
      speeches;
      and even if we understand, we get it all wrong
      when we file our reports in Athens. But today—!
      Everybody's happy. Couldn't tell the difference
      between *Drink to Me Only* and   20
      The Star-Spangled Athens.
                        What's a few lies,
      washed down in good strong drink?

(*Reenter the Drunken Citizen.*)

SENTRY: God almighty,
      he's back again!
CITIZEN: I. Resume. My. Place.
A SPARTAN (*to an Athenian*): Ah beg yo', seh,
      take yo' instrument in yo' hand and play for us.   25
      Ah'm told
      yo' understand the intricacies of the floot?
      Ah'd lahk to execute a song and dance
      in honor of Athens,
                  and, of cohse, of Spahta.
CITIZEN: Toot. On. Your. Flute.   30

(*The following song is a solo—an aria—accompanied
by the flute. The Chorus of Spartans begins a slow
dance.*)

A SPARTAN: O Memory,
      Let the Muse speak once more
      In my young voice. Sing glory.
      Sing Artemision's shore,
      Where Athens fluttered the Persians. *Alalai,*°   35

35. *Alalai:* War cry.

Sing glory, that great
Victory! Sing also
Our Leonidas and his men,
Those wild boars, sweat and blood
40 Down in a red drench. Then, then
The barbarians broke, though they had stood
Numberless as the sands before!

O Artemis,
Virgin Goddess, whose darts
45 Flash in our forests: approve
This pact of peace and join our hearts,
From this day on, in love.
Huntress, descend!

LYSISTRATA: All that will come in time.
                                    But now, Lakonians,
50 take home your wives. Athenians, take yours.
Each man be kind to his woman; and you, women
be equally kind. Never again, pray God,
shall we lose our way in such madness.

KORYPHAIOS(Athenian):   And now let's dance our joy.

(*From this point the dance becomes general.*)

CHORUS(Athenian): Dance, you Graces
                                    Artemis, dance
Dance, Phoibos,° Lord of dancing
55   Dance,
In a scurry of Maenads,° Lord Dionysos
                                    Dance, Zeus Thunderer
Dance, Lady Hera°
Queen of the sky
                                    Dance, dance, all you gods

Dance witness everlasting of our pact
Evohi Evohe°   60
Dance for the dearest
                                    the Bringer of Peace
Deathless Aphrodite!

COMMISSIONER: Now let us have another song from
    Sparta.
CHORUS(Spartan): From Taygetos, from Taygetos,
    Lakonian Muse, come down.   65
Sing to the Lord Apollo
    Who rules Amyklai Town.

Sing Athena of the House of Brass!°
Sing Leda's Twins,° that chivalry
    Resplendent on the shore   70
Of our Eurotas; sing the girls
    That dance along before:
Sparkling in dust their gleaming feet,
    Their hair a Bacchant fire,
And Leda's daughter, thyrsos° raised,   75
    Leads their triumphant choir.

CHORUS(S and A): *Evohe!*
                        Evohai!
                                Evohe!
                                        We pass
                        Dancing
                                dancing
                                        to greet
Athena of the House of Brass.

60. *Evohi Evohe:* "Come forth! Come forth!" (an orgiastic cry associated with rituals of Bacchus). **68.** *House of Brass:* Temple to Athena on the Akropolis of Sparta. **69.** *Leda's Twins:* Leda, raped by Zeus, bore quadruplets, two daughters (one of whom was Helen) and two sons. **75. thyrsos:** A staff twined with ivy and carried by Bacchus and his followers.

55. Phoibos: Apollo, god of the sun. **56. Maenads:** Female worshipers of Bacchus (Dionysus). **57. Hera:** Wife of Zeus.

Roman Drama

Indigenous Sources

Roman drama depended heavily on Greek drama, whose myths it often reinterpreted. For centuries plays were performed much as they had been in Greece, although the Romans had less of a taste for tragedy than the Greeks; they preferred comedy. The Roman plays that have come down to us are mostly comic, and those that are tragic seem to have been intended to be read, not performed. Because Roman drama, rather than Greek drama, was known throughout Europe in the Medieval period and the Renaissance, it is of considerable importance. Even through the Elizabethan Age and up to the eighteenth century, Roman drama exerted a greater influence than Greek drama did on the development of modern drama.

Beginning with wood, then moving to stone, the Romans built excellent theaters throughout their realm. Many still exist.

Roman drama has several sources, not all of them well understood. The first and most literary is Greek drama, but among the more curious are the indigenous sources, which are especially difficult to trace. One such source might be the Etruscans, members of an old and obscure civilization in northern Italy that reached its height in the sixth century BCE and that the Romans eventually absorbed. The Etruscans had developed an improvised song and dance that was very entertaining. The town of Atella provided another indigenous comic tradition known as the **Atellan farce**, a very broad and sometimes coarse popular comedy. Such entertainments may have been acted in open spaces or at fairs, probably not on a stage at first.

The Atellan farce is especially interesting for developments in later Roman drama and world drama. The characters in these farces seem to have been **stock characters**, characters who are always recognizable and whose antics are predictable. The most common stock characters in the Atellan farce are Maccus, the clown; Bucco, the stupid, and probably fat, clown; Pappus, the foolish or stubborn old man; and the hunchbacked, wily slave Dossennus. At first these pieces of drama were improvised to a repeatable pattern, often involving a master who tries to get his slave to do his bidding but who somehow ends up being made to look the fool by the cunning slave. When the farces began to develop in Rome, they were written down and played onstage.

The concept of the stock character is associated with the masters of Roman comedy, Plautus and Terence, who often adapted Greek plays and made them their own. The braggart warrior (*miles gloriosus*), a stock character on the Roman stage, reappears in modern plays. The miser has been a mainstay in literature since Roman times and probably is best known today in the form of Scrooge in Dickens's *A Christmas Carol* and *The Miser* of Molière. The parasite was Roman in origin and can be seen today in numerous television situation comedies. Another Roman invention is the use of identical twins for comic effect. Because it permitted a wide range of comic misunderstandings, this device has been used by many playwrights, including Shakespeare in *The Comedy of Errors*. The Roman use of masks made the twins device much easier to employ than it would be in today's productions.

According to legend, in 240 BCE, a slave, Livius Andronicus, presented performances of his Latin translations of a Greek tragedy and a Greek comedy, giving the Romans their first real taste of Greek drama and literature. Livius soon earned his freedom, and his literary career became so firmly established that his translations from the Greek were those read in Rome for more than two hundred years. His translation of the *Odyssey* was the standard text through the time of Cicero (first century BCE).

Roman comedy derived primarily from the New Comedy of Menander, although it could, like Aristophanes' Old Comedy, sometimes be risqué. Comedies were the most well attended and the most performed of Roman dramas. That is not to say that the Romans produced no tragedies. They did, and the influence of Roman tragedy has been as long-lasting as that of Roman comedy. Still, the Roman people preferred to laugh rather than to feel the pity and terror of tragic emotion.

Just as the Greek plays developed in connection with festivals, the Roman plays became associated with games held several times a year. During the games, performances were offered on average every five to eleven days. The Megalesian Games took place in early April, in honor of the Great Mother, the goddess Cybele, whose temple stood on the Palatine Hill. In late April, the Floral Games were held in front of the temple of Flora on the Aventine Hill. The most important were the Roman Games in September and the Plebeian Games in November.

The Greek drama competitions had no counterpart among the Romans, for whom drama was not the primary entertainment during the festivals. Roman playwrights and actors were hired to put on performances to entertain and divert the impatient audiences, who could choose among a variety of spectacles, including gladiator fights, chariot races, and animal baiting. The producer had to please the audience or lose his chance to supply more entertainment.

Roman comedies were sometimes revisions or amalgamations of Greek plays. The themes and characters of Roman tragedies also derived from Greek originals. Figuring often in Roman tragedies was the Trojan War; its characters were reworked into new situations and their agonies reinterpreted.

For costumes the actors wore the Greek tunic (called a **chiton**) and a long white cloak or mantle called the **pallium**. Like the Greeks, the Romans wore a low slipper, called the **sock**, for comedy and shoes with an elevated sole, the **buskin**, for tragedy. For plays that had a totally Roman setting and narrative, the actors wore the Roman toga. Eventually, Roman actors used traditional Greek masks that immediately identified the characters for the audience. (The question of whether the earliest Roman actors wore masks has not been resolved.) The younger Roman characters wore black wigs, older characters wore white wigs, and characters representing slaves wore red wigs.

One of the most intriguing questions concerning Roman plays is the importance of music in the drama. In Greek plays the chorus took most of the responsibility for the music, but in Roman drama actors may have sung their lines, so the Roman plays may have resembled musical comedies. The dialogue in some comedies introduces an interlude of flute playing, indicating that there were times with no actor onstage, no spoken words, and no mimed action, but only a musician to entertain the audience.

The Roman Stage

In the third century BCE, the Romans began building wooden stages that could be taken down quickly and moved as necessary. Eventually, they built stone theaters that followed Greek plans but varied from the Greek model in a number of important respects. They were built on flat ground, rather than on hillsides as were the Greek theaters. The influence of the Romans' early wooden stage was reflected in the permanent buildings in several ways. The Roman stage was elevated, and since there was little or no chorus, the orchestra, in which the chorus moved from place to place, was no longer needed. The **scaena**, or background, against which the action took place, was often three stories tall and was proportionally longer than the Greek *skene* (as in Figure 4). This wide but shallow stage was exploited by the playwrights, who often set their plays on a street with various houses, temples, and other buildings along it.

Figure 4. Roman theater at Sabratha, Libya, with the *frons scaena* still in good shape. This photograph shows how the Romans modified the basic Greek design.

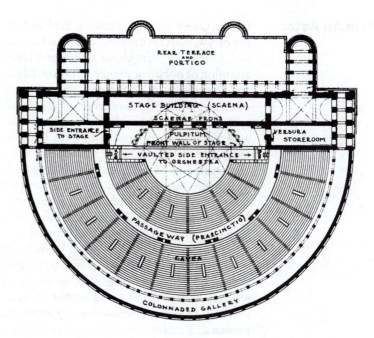

Figure 5. Theater of Marcellus.

The space in front of the *scaena* was known as the **proscaena**, from which the **proscenium arch**, which frames the stage and separates the actors from the audience, developed much later in the Renaissance. The action took place on the *pulpitum*, behind the *proscaena*. The potential for the proscenium arch is evident in the plan of the Theater of Marcellus (Figure 5), where the sections to the left and the right of the stage (*pulpitum*) already indicate a separation from the audience.

As in the plan of the Theater of Marcellus, the *frons scaena* (the front wall, or façade) usually had three doors (some had only two), which were ordinarily established to be doors of separate buildings, sometimes a temple and the homes of chief characters. These doors were active "participants" in the drama; it has been said that the most common line heard in a Roman play is a statement that the door is opening and someone is coming in. The standard Roman play takes great care to justify the entrances and exits of its characters, which may indicate that Roman audiences expected more realism in their comedies than did their Greek counterparts.

The *frons scaena*, the front of the theater, not only was several stories high but also was much more architecturally developed than the *skene* of the Greek theater. The typical Roman architectural devices of multiple arches, columns, and pilasters decorated the *scaena*, giving it a stately appearance. Like the Greek theater, the Roman theater used machinery that permitted actors to be moved through the air and to make entrances from the heavens.

The greatest of the Roman dramatists, Plautus and Terence, would have had their plays produced originally on early wooden stages or on Greek stages. The characteristic Roman theater did not emerge until more than a hundred years after their deaths, in the period of the empire. Seneca could have seen his plays produced in the Roman theater, but they may not ever have been produced in Roman times. His plays may have been closet dramas, designed only to be read.

The Roman Actor

Unlike Greek actors, who were held in high esteem even when they were not the playwrights themselves, actors in Roman times were thought to be undignified. Often they were clever slaves, and rarely were they thought worthy of the attention of nobles or people of power. Many of the theaters in which comedies and tragedies were performed were haphazardly built, uncomfortable wooden structures with rowdy audiences. (Figure 6 shows a scene from a comedy.) Some texts plead with the audience not to hiss after the play; others imply that the audience had to be told what was happening onstage, as though they were incapable of following the action. The stone theaters (the first of which was constructed in 55 BCE) may have served a better audience despite the waning of Roman drama. Roman illustrations of actors show that an altar was often on stage with three actors, all of whom wore masks similar to those worn by Greek actors, which implies that the tradition of masks had been carried on long enough for the Romans to adopt it.

Two great actors are known to us by name. Clodius Aesopus (fl. 55 BCE) was from a good family and rose to be the most noted actor for tragedy. He was so eloquent on stage that he tutored Cicero (106–43 BCE), one of the greatest Roman orators and author of some of the most significant books on rhetoric, the art of persuasion. Quintus Roscius Gallus (c. 126–c. 62 BCE), known as Roscius, was born a slave but, because of his extraordinary skills as a comic actor, rose to freedom and a high rank in Roman society. He too is said to have instructed Cicero, who wrote an oration called *Pro Roscio comoedo* (*For Roscius the Comedian*). The connection between Roman oration and the Roman actor is not accidental. The principles of oration, as laid down by Aristotle in his *Rhetoric* and later developed by Romans such as Quintilian and Cicero, were as useful to the actor as to the politician. Early treatises on acting stress the skills of the orator in the training of the actor.

Figure 6. A Roman bas-relief depicting actors performing a comic scene.

Timeline   Roman Drama

Date	Theater	Political	Social/Cultural
800–600 BCE			**753:** Rome is founded.
600–500			**6th century:** The Circus Maximus is constructed for chariot races and athletic contests. **527–509:** Roman Republic
500–400			**450:** Roman law is codified in the Twelve Tables.
400–300		**390:** Rome is rebuilt after a Gallic invasion.	
300–200	**3rd century:** Atellan farce, lively improvised scenarios based on domestic life, is imported from southern Italy to Rome. **240:** Ludi Romani, a festival in honor of Jupiter, incorporates comedy and tragedy for the first time. The festival, established by the elder Tarquin, Etruscan ruler of Rome, already included chariot races, boxing matches, and other popular entertainments. The plays performed at the festival in 240 are probably translations or imitations of Greek plays. **205–184:** Titus Maccius Plautus writes his plays, including *The Twin Menaechmi*.	**272:** Rome conquers central and southern Italy. **264–241:** First Punic War with Carthage **222:** Rome conquers northern Italy. **218–201:** Second Punic War	**c. 300:** Roman consul Appius Claudius Crassus builds the Appian Way, which stretches from Rome to Capua. **287:** Full equality between plebeians and patricians in Rome
200–100	**160:** Publius Terentius Afer (Terence) writes *The Brothers*. **c. 126–c. 62:** Roscius, a popular Roman actor	**195:** Cato the Elder becomes consul and initiates many reforms in urban development and government representation. **149–146:** The Third Punic War. Rome destroys Carthage and Corinth and conquers Greece. **133:** Tiberius Gracchus, Roman reformer, is murdered at the instigation of the Senate.	**186:** Wild animals are exhibited at the Circus Maximus. Contests between wild animals and humans begin shortly thereafter. **106–43:** Cicero, Roman orator **105:** Gladiatorial contests become part of state festivals.

Timeline   Roman Drama (continued)

Date	Theater	Political	Social/Cultural
100 BCE–1 CE	**1st century:** Theaters are built throughout the Roman empire. **90:** Vitruvius writes *De Architectura*, a treatise on Roman architecture that discusses theatre architecture in Greece and Rome. **55:** The first permanent stone theater is built in Rome. **fl. 55:** Clodius Aesopus, Roman tragedian actor **4 BCE–65 CE:** Seneca. Dates for his plays, including *Medea*, are unknown. Seneca commits suicide after suffering a decline in power and influence.	**69 BCE:** Cleopatra is born. She reigns as queen of Egypt from 51 to 49 and from 48 to her death in 30. **60:** First Triumvirate (Pompey, Crassus, and Julius Caesar) rules Rome. **47:** Herod is appointed King of Judea. **45:** Julius Caesar is declared dictator by Roman Senate. **44:** On the Ides of March Caesar is assassinated. **43–28:** The Second Triumvirate (Antony, Lepidus, and Octavius) rules Rome. **27 BCE–476 CE:** Roman empire **27:** Gaius Octavius, Julius Caesar's grand-nephew, becomes the first emperor of the Roman empire, assuming the name Augustus.	**87–54:** Catullus, Roman poet **70–19:** Virgil (P. Virgilius Maro), poet and author of the *Aeneid* **47:** The library of Ptolemy in Alexandria destroyed by fire; many valuable manuscripts and works of art are lost. **46:** Julius Caesar stages the first *naumachia* (mock sea battle). **43 BCE–17 CE:** Ovid (Publius Ovidius Naso), poet and author of the *Metamorphoses* **22:** Roman pantomime, a predecessor of modern ballet, is introduced by Pylades and Bathyllus. **19:** Horace (65–8 BCE) writes *Ars Poetica*. **4:** Birth of Jesus
1–100		**14:** Augustus dies, and his stepson Tiberius becomes emperor. **37:** Tiberius's grand-nephew Gaius Caesar (Caligula) is named emperor. **41:** Caligula is assassinated by his own guards; his wife and young daughter are also murdered. Caligula's uncle Claudius is named emperor. **54:** Claudius is allegedly poisoned by his wife, Julia Agrippina. Claudius's stepson Nero is named emperor. **68:** Nero commits suicide. **69:** Vespasian is named emperor. He is succeeded by his son Titus.	**c. 30:** Crucifixion of Jesus **64:** Much of Rome is destroyed by fire. Nero blames the fire on Rome's increasing Christian population and initiates the first large-scale persecution of Christians in Rome. **79:** Mount Vesuvius erupts, destroying Pompeii. **80:** The Colosseum is completed.

Date	Theater	Political	Social/Cultural
100–200		**117:** Hadrian becomes emperor.	
		120: Hadrian commissions the building of the Pantheon ("the place of all gods").	
		122–126: Hadrian's Wall is extended across Great Britain.	
	197–202: Tertullian writes *De Spectaculis*, denouncing the theater as anti-Christian.	**138:** Hadrian dies and is succeeded by Antonius Pius and then by Marcus Aurelius.	**c. 130–200:** Galen, Roman physicist and pioneer in anatomy and physiology **164–180:** A devastating plague sweeps the Roman empire.
200–300	**c. 300:** Records of earliest religious plays	Roman citizenship is given to every freeborn subject in the empire. Under Roman rule, Carthage regains prominence as a center of culture and commerce. **220:** Goths invade the Balkan Peninsula and Asia Minor. **257:** Goths invade the Black Sea provinces.	
300–400		**313:** Edict of Milan. Emperor Constantine establishes toleration of Christianity. **331:** Emperor Constantine moves the Roman capital from Rome to Constantinople. **360:** Huns invade Europe.	**354–430:** St. Augustine, author of the influential *City of God* and *Confessions* **c. 360:** Scrolls begin to be replaced by books.
400–500		**401–403:** Visigoths invade Italy.	**c. 400:** In part because of the rise of Christianity, state festivals honoring pagan gods cease in Rome. **404:** Gladiatorial contests are abolished.
		410: Alaric, king of Visigoths, sacks Rome.	**c. 410:** Experiments with alchemy begin. **523:** Wild animal contests are abolished.

Roman Dramatists   The surviving Roman plays come from just three hands: Plautus (254–184 BCE), Terence (c. 190–159 BCE), and Seneca (4 BCE–65 CE). The comedies of Plautus are raucous, broad, and farcical; those of Terence are polished and carefully structured. Seneca wrote tragedies that were well known to Elizabethans such as Marlowe and Shakespeare, and it is clear that the Elizabethan Age found **Senecan tragedy** to be peculiarly suited to its own temperament.

Plautus

All surviving Roman comedy shows the influence of Greek originals. Plautus is among Rome's most famous playwrights and may have been a member of a troupe that performed Atellan comedy. His middle name is Maccius (a form of Maccus, the clown of the farces), possibly alluding to the role he had habitually played. Tradition has it that he was in the theater for a good while before he began writing comedies. His first plays date from 205 BCE, about thirty-five years after Livius introduced Greek drama to the Romans. No one knows how many plays he wrote, and many unauthenticated titles have been assigned to him. About twenty-one plays exist that are thought to be his, the most famous of which are *Amphitryon, The Pot of Gold, The Captives, Curculio, The Braggart Warrior, The Rope,* and *The Twin Menaechmi.*

The last play is probably the best known Roman comedy. It features Menaechmus from Syracuse, who goes to Epidamnus searching for his lost twin. There he meets people who mistake him for his brother: a cook; a prostitute; Sponge, a typical parasite; and even his brother's wife and father-in-law. The comedy exploits all the confusions inherent in mistaken identity.

The Twin Menaechmi

The Twin Menaechmi was the first ancient play to be translated into a modern language and put on the stage (1486 in Italy). It has been adapted by numerous modern playwrights, including Shakespeare in *The Comedy of Errors* and, more recently, Rodgers and Hart in *The Boys from Syracuse* (1938), a musical that ran on Broadway for 235 performances. *Boys* has been revived numerous times and is still a popular summer theater play. The following scene from the beginning of Act III of *The Twin Menaechmi* shows the parasite Sponge mistaking Menaechmus of Syracuse for Sponge's friend Menaechmus of Epidamnus. They have a great go-around over a dress in a typical mixup of the kind that originated with Roman comedies and has been popular in farces and comedies ever since.

PLAUTUS (254–184 BCE)

From The Twin Menaechmi   c. 205–184 BCE

TRANSLATED BY LIONEL CASSON

Act III

SPONGE: I'm over thirty now, and never have I ever in all those years pulled a more damned fool stunt than the one I pulled today: There was this town meeting, and *I* had to dive in and come up right in the middle of it. While I'm standing there with my mouth open, Menaechmus sneaks off on me. I'll bet he's gone to his girlfriend. Perfectly willing to leave me behind, too!

(*Paces up and down a few times, shaking his head bitterly. Then, in a rage.*) Damn, damn, damn the fellow who first figured out town meetings! All they do is keep a busy man away from his business. Why don't people pick a panel of men of leisure for this kind of thing? Hold a roll call at each meeting and whoever doesn't answer gets fined on the spot. There are plenty of persons around who need only one meal a day; they don't have business hours to keep because they don't go after dinner invitations or give them out. They're the ones to fuss with town meetings and town elections. If that's how things were run, I wouldn't have lost my lunch today. He sure wanted me along, didn't he? I'll go in, anyway. There's still hope of leftovers to soothe my soul. (*He is about to go up to the door when it suddenly swings open and Menaechmus of Syracuse appears, standing on the threshold with a garland, a little askew, on his head; he is holding the dress and listening to Lovey who is chattering at him from inside. Sponge quickly backs off into a corner.*) What's this I see? Menaechmus—and he's leaving, garland and all! The table's been cleared! I sure came in time—in time to walk him home. Well, I'll watch what his game is, and then I'll go and have a word with him.

MENAECHMUS OF SYRACUSE (*to Lovey inside*): Take it easy, will you! I'll have it back to you today in plenty of time, altered and trimmed to perfection. (*Slyly.*) Believe me, you'll say it's not your dress; you won't know it any more.

SPONGE (*to the audience*): He's bringing the dress to the dressmaker. The dining's done, the drinks are down—and Sponge spent the lunch hour outside. God damn it I'm not the man I think I am if I don't get even with him for this, but really even. You just watch. I'll give it to him, I will.

MENAECHMUS OF SYRACUSE (*closing the door and walking downstage; to the audience, jubilantly*): Good god, no one ever expected less—and got more blessings from heaven in one day than me. I dined, I wined, I wenched, and (*holding up the dress*) made off with this to which, from this moment on, she hereby forfeits all right, title, and interest.

SPONGE (*straining his ears, to the audience*): I can't make out what he's saying from back here. Is that full-belly talking about me and my right title and interest?

MENAECHMUS OF SYRACUSE (*to the audience*): She said I stole it from my wife and gave it to her. I saw she was mistaking me for someone else, so I promptly played it as if she and I were having a hot and heavy affair and began to yes her; I agreed right down the line to everything she said. Well, to make a long story short, I never had it so good for so little.

SPONGE (*clenching his fists, to the audience*): I'm going up to him. I'm itching to give him the works. (*Leaves his corner and strides belligerently toward Menaechmus.*)

MENAECHMUS OF SYRACUSE (*to the audience*): Someone coming up to me. Wonder who it is?

SPONGE (*roaring*): Well! You featherweight, you filth, you slime, you disgrace to the human race, you double-crossing good-for-nothing! What did I ever do to you that you had to ruin my life? You sure gave me the slip downtown a little while ago! You killed off the day all right—and held the funeral feast without me. Me who was coheir under the will! Where do you come off to do a thing like that!

MENAECHMUS OF SYRACUSE (*too pleased with life to lose his temper*): Mister, will you please tell me what business you and I have that gives you the right to use language like that to a stranger here, someone you never saw in your life? You hand me that talk and I'll hand you something you won't like.

SPONGE (*dancing with rage*): God damn it, you already have! I know god damned well you have!

MENAECHMUS OF SYRACUSE (*amused and curious*): What's your name, mister?

SPONGE (*as before*): Still making jokes, eh? As if you don't know my name!

MENAECHMUS OF SYRACUSE: So help me, so far as I know, I never heard of you or saw you till this minute. But I know one thing for sure: whoever you are, you'd better behave yourself and stop bothering me.

SPONGE (*taken aback for a minute*): Menaechmus! Wake up!

MENAECHMUS OF SYRACUSE (*genially*): Believe me, to the best of my knowledge, I am awake.

SPONGE: You don't know me?

MENAECHMUS OF SYRACUSE (*as before*): If I did, I wouldn't say I didn't.

SPONGE (*incredulously*): You don't know your own parasite?

MENAECHMUS OF SYRACUSE: Mister, it looks to me as if you've got bats in your belfry.

SPONGE (*shaken, but not convinced*): Tell me this: Didn't you steal that dress there from your wife today and give it to Lovey?

MENAECHMUS OF SYRACUSE: Good god, no! I don't have a wife, I never gave anything to any Lovey, and I never stole any dress. Are you in your right mind?

SPONGE (*aside, groaning*): A dead loss, the whole affair. (*To Menaechmus.*) But you came out of your house wearing the dress! I saw you myself!

MENAECHMUS OF SYRACUSE (*exploding*): Damn you! You think everybody's a pervert just because you are? I was wearing this dress? Is that what you're telling me?

SPONGE: I most certainly am.

MENAECHMUS OF SYRACUSE: Now you go straight to the one place fit for you! No — get yourself to the lunatic asylum; you're stark-raving mad.

SPONGE (*venomously*): God damn it, there's one thing nobody in the world is going to stop me from doing: I'm telling the whole story, exactly what happened, to your wife this minute. All these insults are going to boomerang back on your own head. Believe you me, you'll pay for eating that whole lunch yourself. (*Dashes into the house of Menaechmus of Epidamnus.*)

MENAECHMUS OF SYRACUSE (*throwing his arms wide, to the audience*): What's going on here? Must everyone I lay eyes on play games with me this way? Wait—I hear the door.

(*The door of Lovey's house opens, and one of her maids comes out holding a bracelet. She walks over to Menaechmus and, as he looks on blankly, hands it to him.*)

MAID: Menaechmus, Lovey says would you please do her a big favor and drop this at the jeweler's on your way? She wants you to give him an ounce of gold and have him make the whole bracelet over.

MENAECHMUS OF SYRACUSE (*with alacrity*): Tell her I'll not only take care of this but anything else she wants taken care of. Anything at all. (*He takes the piece and examines it absorbedly.*)

MAID (*watching him curiously, in surprise*): Don't you know what bracelet it is?

MENAECHMUS OF SYRACUSE: Frankly no—except that it's gold.

MAID: It's the one you told us you stole from your wife's jewel box when nobody was looking.

MENAECHMUS OF SYRACUSE (*forgetting himself, in high dudgeon*): I never did anything of the kind!

MAID: You mean you don't remember it? Well, if that's the case, you give it right back!

MENAECHMUS OF SYRACUSE (*after a few seconds of highly histrionic deep thought*): Wait a second. No, I *do* remember it. Of course—this is the one I gave her. Oh, and there's something else: Where are the armlets I gave her at the same time?

MAID (*puzzled*): You never gave her any armlets.

MENAECHMUS OF SYRACUSE (*quickly*): Right you are. This was all I gave her.

MAID: Shall I tell her you'll take care of it?

MENAECHMUS OF SYRACUSE: By all means, tell her. I'll take care of it, all right. I'll see she gets it back the same time she gets the dress back.

MAID (*going up to him and stroking his cheek*): Menaechmus dear, will you do me a favor too? Will you have some earrings made for me? Drop earrings, please; ten grams of gold in each. (*Meaningfully.*) It'll make me *so* glad to see you every time you come to the house.

MENAECHMUS OF SYRACUSE: Sure. (*With elaborate carelessness.*) Just give me the gold. I'll pay for the labor myself.

MAID: Please, you pay for the gold too. I'll make it up to you afterward.

MENAECHMUS OF SYRACUSE: No, you pay for the gold. I'll make it up to *you* afterward. Double.

MAID: I don't have the money.

MENAECHMUS OF SYRACUSE (*with a great air of magnanimity*): Well, any time you get it, you just let me have it.

MAID (*turning to go*): I'm going in now. Anything I can do for you?

MENAECHMUS OF SYRACUSE: Yes. Tell her I'll see to both things—(*sotto voce, to the audience*) that they get sold as quickly as possible for whatever they'll bring. (*As the maid starts walking toward the door.*) Has she gone in yet? (*Hearing a slam.*) Ah, she's in, the door's closed. (*Jubilantly.*) The lord loves me! I've had a helping hand from heaven! (*Suddenly looks about warily.*) But why hang around when I have the time and chance to get away from this (*jerking his thumb at Lovey's house*) pimping parlor here? Menaechmus! Get a move on, hit the road, forward march! I'll take off this garland and toss it to the left here (*doing so*). Then, if anyone tries to follow me, he'll think I went that way. Now I'll go and see if I can find my servant. I want to let him know all the blessings from heaven I've had.

(*He races off, stage right. The stage is now empty.*)

Terence

Terence is said to have been a North African slave brought to Rome, whose master realized he was unusually intelligent and gifted. After he was freed, Terence took his place in Roman literary life and produced a body of six plays, all of which still exist: *The Woman of Andros, The Self-Tormentor, The Eunuch, Phormio, The Mother-in-Law,* and *The Brothers.* Terence's plays are notable for carefully including a subplot or secondary action and for avoiding the technique of addressing the audience directly.

The Romans preferred Plautus's broad farcical humor to Terence's more carefully plotted, elegantly styled plays. Terence borrowed liberally from Greek sources, often more than one for each of his plays, to develop unusually complicated plots. A manager or producer worked with him on all his plays, and the musician who worked with him was a slave, Flaccus. Terence's productive life was relatively short. He died on a trip to Greece, apparently worrying over a piece of missing luggage said to have contained new plays.

Terence's situation was unusual: he had two wealthy Roman patrons who were interested in seeing the best Greek comedy brought to the Romans. Consequently, they paid for his productions and gave him more support than the average comic playwright could have expected. In sharp contrast with Plautus's work, which was repetitive in nature, Terence's plays exhibited considerable development of his dramatic skills from the beginning to the end of his work. Terence was more than a translator, but he wrote at a time when Romans were interested in emulating the Greeks, and his fidelity to Greek originals was one of his strongest recommendations.

The Brothers

The ending of *The Brothers*, generally recognized as Terence's masterpiece and certainly the most influential of his plays, has Demea planning a reversal on his brother, Micio. Micio is a good, easygoing bachelor who wishes others well. Demea has been a stern father to one of his sons, Ctesipho, and has tried to steer him in a direction other than the one Ctesipho wants to follow. Demea has entrusted the upbringing of his second son, Aeschinus, to his lenient brother, Micio. Both sons deceive both brothers and end up with the women they want rather than the women the brothers want for them. Meanwhile, Demea gives up and turns the tables on Micio, engineering his brother's marriage to Aeschinus's mother-in-law. In the process of all this, Demea decides to adopt the gentle, easygoing ways of his brother and to forsake his former stern behavior.

This play was adapted in the seventeenth century by Marston, Beaumont and Fletcher, and others. Molière relied on it for his *School for Wives*. At least five plays were adapted from it for the eighteenth-century English stage.

TERENCE (c. 190–159 BCE)

From The Brothers   160 BCE

TRANSLATED BY ROBERT GRAVES

From Act V

MICIO (*to Syrus, within*): My brother ordered it,° say ye! Where is he? . . . Hah, Brother, was it you who ordered this?

DEMEA: Yes, that I did! And in this and all things else I'm ready to do whatever may conduce to the uniting, serving, helping, and the joining together of both families.

My brother ordered it: Demea ordered the breaking down of a wall to allow the two families to communicate. In this way Demea imitates the good-naturedness of his brother, Micio, and traps him into marrying Aeschinus's mother-in-law.

AESCHINUS (*to Micio*): Pray, Sir, let it be so!

MICIO: Well, I've nothing to say against it.

DEMEA: Truth, 'tis no more than we are obliged to do. For first, she's your son's mother-in-law . . .

MICIO: What then?

DEMEA: A very virtuous and modest woman . . .

MICIO: So they say indeed.

DEMEA: Not weighed down by years . . .

MICIO: Not yet.

DEMEA: But past child-bearing: a lonesome woman whom nobody esteems . . .

MICIO (*aside*): What the Devil is he at?

DEMEA: . . . Therefore you ought to marry her; and you Aeschinus, should do what you can to bring this about.

MICIO: Who? I marry?

DEMEA: Yes, you.

MICIO: I, prithee?

DEMEA: Yes, you I say.

MICIO: Pho, you are fooling us, surely?

DEMEA (*to Aeschinus*): If thou hast any life in thee, persuade him to it.

AESCHINUS: Dear Father . . .

MICIO: (*interrupting*): Blockhead! Dost thou take in earnest what he says?

DEMEA: 'Tis in vain to refuse; it can't be avoided.

MICIO: Pho, you are in your dotage!

AESCHINUS: Good Sir, let me win this one favor.

MICIO (*angrily*): Art out of thy wits, let me alone!

DEMEA: Come, come! Hearken for once to what your son says.

MICIO: Haven't ye played the fool enough yet? Shall I at threescore and five marry an old woman who's ready to drop into the grave? This is your wise counsel, is it?

AESCHINUS: Pray, Sir, do; I've promised you shall.

MICIO: You promised, with a mischief! Promise for thyself, thou chit!

DEMEA: Fie, fie! What if he had begged a greater favor from you?

MICIO: As if there were any greater favor than this!

DEMEA: Pray grant his request.

AESCHINUS: Good Sir, be not so hard-hearted.

DEMEA: Pho, promise him for once!

MICIO: Will ye never leave baiting me?

AESCHINUS: Not till I've prevailed, Sir.

MICIO: Truth, this is downright forcing a man.

DEMEA: Come, Micio, be good-natured and consent.

MICIO: Though this be the most damned, foolish, ridiculous whim, and the most averse to my nature that could possibly be, yet since you are so extremely set upon it, I'll humor ye for once.

AESCHINUS: That is excellent, I'm obliged to ye beyond measure.

DEMEA (*aside*): Well, what's next? . . . What shall I say next? This is as I'd have it. . . . What's more to be done?

(*To Micio.*)

Ho! There's Hegio our poor kinsman, and nearest relation; in truth, we ought in conscience to do something for him.

MICIO: What, pray?

DEMEA: There's a small plot of land in the suburbs, which you farm out—pray let's give him that to live on.

MICIO: A small one, say ye?

DEMEA: Though it were a great one, you might yet give it to him. He has been as good as a father to Pamphila; he's a very honest man, our kinsman, and you couldn't bestow it better. Besides, Brother, there's a certain proverb (none of my own, I assure you) which you so well and wisely made use of: "That age has always this ill effect of making us more worldly, as well as wiser." We should do well to avoid this scandal. 'Tis a true proverb, Brother, and ought to be held in mind.

MICIO: What's all this? . . .Well, so let it be, if he has need of it.

AESCHINUS: Brave Father, I vow!

DEMEA: Now you are my true brother, both in body and soul.

MICIO: I'm glad of it.

DEMEA (*aside, laughing*): I've stabbed him with his own weapons, i'fack!

(*Enter Syrus, with a pick-axe upon his shoulders.*)

SYRUS (*to Demea*): The job is done as ye ordered, Sir.

DEMEA: Thou art an honest lad. . . . And upon my conscience I think Syrus deserves his freedom.

MICIO: He, his freedom? For what exploit?

DEMEA: O, for a thousand.

SYRUS: O dear Mr. Demea, you are a rare gentleman, edad you are! You know I've looked after the young gentlemen from their cradles. I taught them, advised them, and instructed them all I possibly could.

DEMEA: Nothing more evident! Nay, more than that, he catered for them, pimped for them, and in the morning took care of a debauchee for them. These are no ordinary accomplishments, I can assure ye.

SYRUS: Your worship's very merry.

DEMEA: Besides, he was prime mover in buying this music-girl. It was he who managed the whole intrigue, and 'tis no more than justice to reward him, as an encouragement to others! In short, Aeschinus desires the same thing.

MICIO (*to Aeschinus*): Do you desire it too?

AESCHINUS: Yes, if you please, Sir.

MICIO: Since 'tis so, come hither, Syrus! Thou art a free man.

(*Syrus kneels down, Micio lays his hand on his head, and after that gives him a cuff on the ear.*)

SYRUS (*rising up*): Generously done! A thousand thanks to ye all, and to you, Mr. Demea.

DEMEA: I'm well satisfied.

AESCHINUS: And I too.

SYRUS: I won't question it, Sir. But I wish heartily my joy were more complete, that my poor spouse Phrygia might be made as free as I am.

DEMEA: Truth, she's a mighty good woman.

SYRUS: And your grandson's first foster-mother, too.

DEMEA: Faith, in good earnest, if for that, she deserves her freedom before any woman in the world.

MICIO: What! For that simple service?

DEMEA: Yes, indeed! In fine, I'll pay for her freedom myself.

SYRUS: God's blessing light upon your worship, and grant all your wishes.

MICIO: Syrus, thou hast made a good day's work of it.

DEMEA: Besides, Brother, it would be a deed of charity to lend him a little money to set up in business that he may face the world without fear. I undertake that he'll soon repay it.

MICIO: Not a penny-piece!

AESCHINUS: He's a very honest fellow, Sir.

SYRUS: Upon my word, I'll repay you the loan. Do but trust me!

AESCHINUS: Pray do, Sir.

MICIO: I'll consider the matter with care.

DEMEA: He shall pay ye, I'll see to that.

SYRUS (*to Demea*): Egad, you're the best man alive.

AESCHINUS: And the pleasantest in the world.

MICIO: What's the meaning of this, Brother? How comes this sudden change of humor? Why this gallant squandering and profusion?

DEMEA: I'll tell ye, Brother. These sons of yours don't reckon you a sweet-natured and pleasant man because you live as you should and do what is just and reasonable, but because you fawn upon them, cocker them up, and give them what they'll spend. Now, son Aeschinus, if you are dissatisfied with my course of life, because I wouldn't indulge you in all things, right or wrong, then I'll not trouble my head with you any further. Be free to squander, buy mistresses, and do what you will! But if you wish me to advise ye, and set ye up, and help ye too in matters of which your youth can give ye but little understanding—matters of which you are over-fond, and don't well consider—see, here I'm ready to stand by you.

AESCHINUS: Dear Sir, we commit ourselves wholly to your charge; for you know what's fitting to be done far better than we . . . But what will ye do for my brother Ctesipho?

DEMEA: Why, let him take the music-girl; and so bid adieu to general wenching.

AESCHINUS: That's very reasonable. (*To the spectators.*) Gentlemen, your favor!

(*Exeunt° all.*)

[s.d.] *Exeunt:* Latin for "they go out."

Seneca

Senecan tragedies were based on either Greek or Roman themes and included murder, other bloodthirsty actions (many of which did not occur on stage but were described), horror of various kinds, ghosts, and long, bombastic speeches. Signs of Senecan influence can be seen in Elizabethan drama, with its taste for many of these devices; plays like *Hamlet* are notable for ending in a pool of blood, with most of the actors lying dead onstage. The theme of revenge was prized by Seneca and, later, by the Elizabethans.

Not a professional theater person, Seneca was wealthy and learned, a philosopher active in the government of Emperor Nero's Rome. His plays, most of which were adapted from Euripides, were probably written only to be read, as was common at the time, or perhaps recited, although there is no record of their having been performed. The Roman people thirsted for mime and farce but had much less taste for serious plays.

Ten plays attributed to Seneca exist, nine of which are surely his and one of which is only possibly his. His most famous are *Mad Hercules, The Phoenician Women, Medea, Phaedra, Agamemnon, Thyestes,* and *The Trojan Women.*

Thyestes

Thyestes, probably adapted from the *Oresteia* of Aeschylus, influenced a number of Elizabethan revenge tragedies, such as Shakespeare's *Hamlet.* The story is gruesome even by modern standards. Thyestes seduces his brother Atreus's wife, and Atreus banishes him. When Thyestes is summoned to Atreus's home, he is suspicious, but he goes, hoping to be able to see his children. The banquet Atreus holds for Thyestes seems to signal reconciliation between the brothers. But when it is over, Atreus brings in the heads of Thyestes' children, revealing that Thyestes has just eaten their bodies in the feast.

The second scene from act V—before Thyestes is told about the meal he has eaten—follows in its entirety. It shows Thyestes wrestling with himself in a passion of uncertainty. Thyestes' soliloquy is a psychological study of the effects of grief, care, uncertainty, and fear. Seneca's plays have many such soliloquies, and their revelations of complex emotional states deeply impressed the age of Shakespeare.

SENECA (4 BCE–65 CE)

From Thyestes

TRANSLATED BY ELLA ISABEL HARRIS

Act V • *Scene II*

(*Thyestes sits alone at the banquet table, half overcome with wine; he tries to sing and be gay, but some premonition of evil weighs upon him.*)

THYESTES (*to himself*): By long grief dulled, put by thy cares, my heart,
Let fear and sorrow fly and bitter need,
Companion of thy timorous banishment,
And shame, hard burden of afflicted souls.
Whence thou has fallen profits more to know
Than whither; great is he who with firm step
Moves on the plain when fallen from the height;
He who, oppressed by sorrows numberless
And driven from his realm, with unbent neck
Carries his burdens, not degenerate
Or conquered, who stands firm beneath the weight
Of all his burdens, he is great indeed.
Now scatter all the clouds of bitter fate,
Put by all signs of thy unhappy days,

In happy fortunes show a happy face,
Forget the old Thyestes. Ah, this vice
Still follows misery: never to trust
In happy days; though better fortunes come,
Those who have borne afflictions find it hard
To joy in better days. What holds me back,
Forbids me celebrate the festal tide?
What cause of grief, arising causelessly,
Bids me to weep? What art thou that forbids
That I should crown my head with festal wreath?
It does forbid, forbid! Upon my head
The roses languish, and my hair that drips
With ointment rises as with sudden fear,
My face is wet with showers of tears that fall
Unwillingly, and groans break off my song.
Grief loves accustomed tears, the wretched feel
That they must weep. I would be glad to make
Most bitter lamentation, and to wail,
And rend this robe with Tyrian purple dyed.
My mind gives warning of some coming grief,
Presages future ills. The storm that smites
When all the sea is calm weighs heavily
Upon the sailor. Fool! What grief, what storm,
Dost thou conceive? Believe thy brother now.
Be what it may, thou fearest now too late,
Or causelessly. I do not wish to be
Unhappy, but vague terror smites my breast.
No cause is evident and yet my eyes
O'erflow with sudden tears. What can it be,
Or grief, or fear? Or has great pleasure tears?

The surviving Roman plays offer enough variety to give us an idea of what the drama achieved. Like so much of Roman culture, Roman drama rested in the shadow of Greek accomplishments. The Romans were responsible for maintaining the Greek texts, allowing us to see a great deal of their work. Although it may be true that much of the Roman drama that was produced no longer exists, what survives shows variety and high quality.

Medieval Drama

The medieval period in Europe (476 CE–1500 CE) began with the collapse of Rome, a calamity of such magnitude that the years between then and the beginning of the Crusades in 1095 have been traditionally, if erroneously, called the Dark Ages. Historians used this term to refer to their lack of knowledge about a time in which no great central powers organized society or established patterns of behavior and standards in the arts.

Drama, or at least records of it, all but disappeared. The major Western institution to profit from the fall of the Roman empire was the Roman Catholic Church, which in the ninth and tenth centuries enjoyed considerable power and influence. Many bishops considered drama a godless activity, a distraction from the piety that the church demanded of its members. During the great age of cathedral building and the great ages of religious painting and religious music—from the seventh century to the thirteenth—drama was reborn in the Church.

The Role of the Church

The Church may well have intended nothing more than the simple dramatization of its message. Or the people may have craved drama, and the Church's response could have been an attempt to answer their needs. In either event, the Church could never have foreseen the outcome of adding a few moments of drama to the liturgy, the church services. **Liturgical drama** began in the tenth century with **tropes**, or embellishments, which were sung during parts of the Mass (the public celebration of the Eucharist). The earliest known example of a trope, called the **Quem Quaeritis** ("Whom seek ye?"), developed at the monastery at Limoges, c. 923–934 CE:

> ANGEL: Whom seek ye in the sepulchre, O ye Christians?
> THREE MARYS: Jesus of Nazareth, who was crucified, O ye Angels.
> ANGEL: He is not here; he is risen as he has foretold.
>   Go, announce that he is risen from the sepulchre.

Some scholars think that in its earliest form this trope was sung by four monks in a dialogue pattern, three monks representing the three Marys at Christ's tomb and the other representing the angel. Tropes like the *Quem*

Quaeritis evolved over the years to include a number of participants as the tropes spread from church to church throughout the Continent. These dramatic interpolations never became dramas separate from the Mass itself, although their success and popularity led to experiments with other dramatic sequences centering on moments in the Mass and in the life of Christ. The actors in these pieces did not think of themselves as specialists or professionals; they were simply monks who belonged to the church. The churchgoers obviously enjoyed the tropes, and more were created to amplify the liturgy.

In the tenth century, Hrosvitha entertained herself and her fellow nuns with imitations of the Roman dramatist Terence. Although her own subject matter was holy in nature, she admired Terence as an amusing comic writer with a polished style. She referred to herself as the "strong voice of Gandersheim," her community in Saxony, and said that she had "not hesitated to imitate in my writings a poet whose works are so widely read, my object being to glorify, within the limits of my poor talent, the laudable chastity of Christian virgins." Her plays are very short moral tales, often illustrating moments in the lives of Christian martyred women. As far as is known, these plays do not seem to have gone beyond the nuns' walls; therefore, they had little effect on the drama developing in the period.

Once dramatic scenes were added that took the action outside of the liturgy, it was not long before dramas were being staged outside the church. The Anglo-Norman drama *Adam,* dating from the twelfth century, has explicit stage directions establishing its setting outside the church. The play is to be staged on the west side of the church with a platform extending from the steps. The characters of Adam, Eve, God (called Figura), and the Devil and his assistants are given costumes and extensive dialogue. The dramatic detail in this play implies a considerable development of plot and action, which, despite its theological matter, is plainly too elaborate to be contained within the service of the Mass.

Once outside the church, drama flourished and soon became independent, although its themes continued to be religious and productions were connected with religious festivals. In 1264, Pope Urban IV added to the religious calendar a new, important feast: Corpus Christi, celebrated beginning on the first Thursday after Trinity Sunday, about two months after Easter. The purpose of the feast was to celebrate the doctrine declaring that the body of Christ was real and present in the Host (consecrated bread or wafer) taken by the faithful in the sacrament of the Eucharist (Communion).

At first, the feast of Corpus Christi was localized in Liège, Belgium. But by decree of Pope Clement V in 1311, it became one of the chief feasts of the church. Among other things, it featured a procession and pageant in which the Host was displayed publicly through the streets of a town. Because of the importance and excitement of this feast, entire communities took part in the celebration.

Miracle Plays

Miracle plays on the subject of miracles performed by saints developed late in the twelfth century both in England and on the Continent. Typically, these plays focused on the Virgin Mary and St. Nicholas, both of whom had strong followings (sometimes described as cults) during the medieval period. Mary is often portrayed as helping those in need or in danger—often at the last minute. Some of those she saved may have seemed to a pious audience to be unsavory sinners, but the point was that the saint saved all who truly wished to be saved.

Although they quickly became public entertainments removed from the church building and were popular as Corpus Christi entertainments throughout the fifteenth century, few miracle plays survive in English because King Henry VIII banned them during his reformation of the Church. As a result, they were not performed or preserved.

The craft guilds—professional organizations of workers involved in the same trade (carpenters, wool merchants, and so on)—soon began competing with each other in producing plays that could be performed during the feast of Corpus Christi. Most of their plays derived from Bible stories and the life of Christ. Religious guilds, such as the Confrèrie of the Passion, produced plays in Paris and elsewhere on the Continent. Because the Bible is silent on many details of Christ's life, some plays invented new material and illuminated dark areas, thereby satisfying the intense curiosity medieval Christians had about events the Bible omitted.

Mystery Plays

The Church did not ignore drama after it left the church buildings. Since plays had religious subject matter and could be used to teach the Bible and to model Christian behavior, they remained of considerable value to the Church.

First performed by the clergy, religious plays dramatized the mystery of Christ's Passion. Later, the Corpus Christi plays were produced by members of craft guilds, and they became known as **craft plays** or **mystery plays**. Beginning in the medieval period, the word *mystery* was used to describe a skill or trade known only to a few who apprenticed and mastered its special techniques; it also referred to religious mysteries.

By the fifteenth century, mystery plays and the feast of Corpus Christi were popular almost everywhere in Europe, and in England certain towns produced exceptionally elaborate cycles with unusually complex and ambitious plays. The **cycles** were groups of from twenty-four to forty-eight plays. Four cycles have been preserved: the Chester, York, Towneley (Wakefield), and N-Town cycles, named for their towns of origin. N-Town plays were a generic version of plays that any town could take and use as its own, although the plays were probably written near Lincoln.

The plays were performed annually, and the texts were carefully preserved. Some of the plays, such as *The Fall of Lucifer*, are very short. Others are longer and more complex and resemble modern plays: *Noah*, from the Wakefield Cycle, which has been produced regularly in recent history; *The Slaughter of Innocents*; and *The Second Shepherds' Pageant*, one of the most entertaining mystery plays.

The producers of the plays often had a sense of appropriateness in their choice of subjects. For example, the Water-Drawers guild sponsored *Noah's Flood*; the Butchers (because they sold "flesh"), *Temptation* and *The Woman Taken in Adultery*; and the Shipwrights, *The Building of the Ark*.

Among the best known mystery plays is the somewhat farcical *The Second Shepherds' Pageant*, which is both funny and serious. It tells of a crafty shepherd named Mak who steals a lamb from his fellow shepherds and takes it home. His wife, Gill, then places it in a cradle and pretends it is her baby. Eventually the shepherds—who suspect Mak from the first—smoke out the fraud and give Mak a blanket-tossing for their trouble. But after they do so, they see a star in the heavens and turn their attention to the birth of baby Jesus, the Lamb of God. They join the Magi and come to pay homage to the Christ Child.

The easy way in which the profane elements of everyday life coexisted with the sacred in medieval times has long interested scholars. The *Second Shepherds' Pageant* virtually breaks into two parts, the first dedicated to the wickedness of Mak and Gill and the horseplay of the shepherds. But once Mak has had his due, the play alters in tone and the sense of devotion to Christian teachings becomes uppermost. The fact that the mystery plays moved away from liturgical Latin to the vernacular (local) language made such a juxtaposition of sacred and profane much more possible.

The dominance of the guilds in producing mystery plays suggests that guilds were enjoying increasing political power and authority. The guilds grew stronger and more influential—probably at the expense of the Church. Some historians have seen this development as crucial to the growing secularization of the Middle Ages.

Morality Plays

Morality plays were never part of any cycle but developed independently as moral tales in the late fourteenth or early fifteenth century on the Continent and in England. They do not illustrate moments in the Bible, nor do they describe the life of Christ or the saints. Instead, they describe the lives of people facing the temptations of the world. The plays are careful to present a warning to the unwary that their souls are always in peril, that the devil is on constant watch, and that people must behave properly if they are to be saved.

One feature of morality plays is their reliance on **allegory**, a favorite medieval device. Allegory is the technique of giving abstract ideas or values a physical representation. In morality plays, abstractions such as goodness became characters in the drama. In modern times, we sometimes use allegory in art, as when we represent justice as a blindfolded woman. Allegorically, justice should act impartially because she does not "see" any distinctions, such as those of rank or privilege, that characterize people standing before a judge.

The use of allegory permitted medieval dramatists to personify abstract values such as sloth, greed, daintiness, vanity, strength, and hope by making them characters and placing them onstage in action. The dramatist specified symbols, clothing, and gestures appropriate to these abstract figures, thus helping the audience recognize the ideas the characters represented. The use of allegory was an extremely durable technique, already established in medieval painting, printed books, and books of emblems, in which, for example, sloth would be shown as a man reclining lazily on a bed or greed would be represented as overwhelmingly fat and vanity as a figure completely absorbed in a mirror.

The central problem in the morality play was the salvation of human beings: an individual's struggle to avoid sin and damnation and achieve salvation in the otherworld. As in *Everyman* (c. 1495), a late-medieval play that is the best known of the morality plays, the subjects were usually abstract battles between certain vices and specific virtues for the possession of the human soul, a theme repeated in the Elizabethan Age in Marlowe's *Doctor Faustus*.

In many ways, the morality play was a dramatized sermon designed to teach a moral lesson. Marked by high seriousness, it was nevertheless entertaining. Using allegory to represent abstract qualities allowed the didactic playwrights to draw clear-cut lines of moral force: Satan was always bad; angels were always good. The allegories were clear, direct, and apparent to all who witnessed the plays.

We do not have much knowledge of the origins of morality plays. Many of them are lost, but some of those that remain are occasionally performed: *The Pride of Life* (the earliest extant morality play), *The Castle of Perseverance, Wisdom, Mankind,* and *Everyman* are the best known. They enjoyed a remarkable popularity in the latter part of the medieval period, all the way up to the early Renaissance.

Japanese Drama

Although Chinese drama and Japanese drama neither influenced nor were influenced by Western drama in the medieval period, from roughly the late twelfth to the beginning of the seventeenth centuries they, like Western drama, were connected to temples, shrines, and religious ceremony. During this period, Japanese Nō drama developed as a highly refined, deliberate, and ritualized form involving ceremonial dance and music as well as a narrative. Centuries later, Nō drama had an influence on Western literature, particularly on writers such as Ezra Pound and playwrights such as W. B. Yeats and Samuel Beckett.

Nō drama developed from a popular form of drama called sarugaku Nō, invented by Kan'ami (1333–1384) in the fourteenth century. The rulers of Japan at that time, shoguns (generals) of the samurai warrior class, enjoyed theater and supported performances of highly sophisticated drama. They preferred sarugaku, or "monkey music"—a form that included gymnastic action, music, dance, and a story line. Kan'ami refined sarugaku into sarugaku Nō, a more deliberate and controlled form that elevated the actor and demanded more skill—the word *Nō* means "skill"—from performers. The refinement Kan'ami brought to the drama was associated with Zen Buddhism, the form of religion favored by the shogun of the period.

Nō drama, which relies on masks, ritual costume, dance, and music, is produced around the world even today. Nō emerged late in the fourteenth century out of Kan'ami's innovations, but it was his son, Zeami Motokiyo (1363–1443), who developed Nō into a serious form marked by the restraint and control associated with Zen Buddhism. The religious influences on Nō drama led to an emphasis on self-control, honorable behavior, and purity of action. Zeami produced a body of drama that can be seen today in the West as well as in the East. *Lady Han (Hanjo)* deals with a realistic situation in which a prostitute falls in love with a traveling captain. Before he leaves, they exchange fans on which a painting of the moon will identify them. Such romances were not uncommon, and the emotions portrayed in Nō drama are derived from living experience.

The Medieval Stage

Relatively little commentary survives about the conventions of medieval staging in Europe, and some of it is contradictory. We know that in the earliest years—after the tropes developed into full-blown religious scenes acted inside

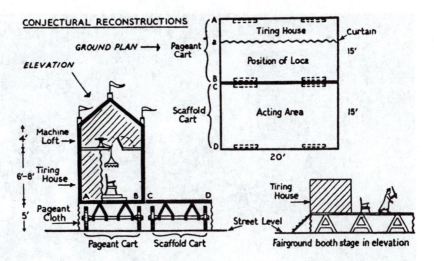

Figure 7. Pageant wagon.

the cathedrals—certain sections of the church were devoted to specific short plays. The later platforms outside the church became known as **mansions**; each mansion represented a building or physical place known to the audience. The audience moved from one mansion to another, seeing play after play, absorbing the dramatic representation of the events, characters, and locale associated with each mansion.

The tradition of moving from mansion to mansion carried over into the performances that took place on wagons with raised stages (Figure 7). Usually, the wagons remained stationary and the audience moved from one to another. During the guild cycles, the pageant carts would move; the performers would give their plays at several locales so that many people could see them (Figure 8).

According to medieval descriptions, drawings, and reconstructions, a **pageant cart** could also be simply a flat surface, drawn on wheels, that had a wagon next to it; these structures touched on their long side. In some cases, a figure could descend from an upper area as if from the clouds, or actors could descend from the pageant cart to the audience's level to enact a descent into an underworld. The stage was, then, a raised platform visible to the audience below.

A curtain concealed a space, usually inside or below the wagon, for changing costumes. The actors used costumes and props, sometimes very elaborate and expensive, in an effort to make the drama more impressive. Indeed, between the thirteenth and the sixteenth centuries, a number of theatrical effects were developed to please a large audience. For instance, in the morality and mystery plays, the devils were often portrayed as frightening, grotesque, and sometimes even comic figures. They became crowd pleasers. A sensational element was developed in some of the plays in the craft cycles, especially those about the lives of the saints and martyrs, in which there were plenty of chances to portray horrifying tortures.

The prop that seems to have pleased audiences the most was a complex machine known as the **mouth of hell** or "Hell mouth," usually a large fish-shaped orifice from which smoke and explosions, fueled by gunpowder, belched

Figure 8. A detail of Denis Van Alsloot's painting *Procession of the Ommeganck at Brussels in 1615* shows horse-drawn pageant wagons on the move, with several plays being performed simultaneously.

constantly. The devils took great delight in stuffing their victims into these maws. According to a contemporary account, one of the machines required seventeen men to operate.

The level of realism achieved by medieval plays was at times startling. In addition to visual realism, medieval plays involved a level of psychological participation on the part of both audience and actor. Sometimes the plays demanded that the actors suffer in accord with the characters they played. Some records attest to characters playing Christ on the cross having to be revived after their hearts stopped, and at least one Judas apparently was hanged just a little too long and had to be resuscitated.

The Medieval Actor

In the early days of liturgical drama, the actors in the tropes were monks, and those in the mystery plays were drawn from the guilds. At first all the actors were male, but records show that eventually women may have taken important roles.

The demands of more sophisticated plays encouraged the development of special skills required for the design and operation of complex stage machines and for the performance of the acrobatics that were expected of certain characters, such as devils. As actors developed facility in delivering lines and as writers found ways to incorporate more challenging elements in their plays, a professionalism no doubt arose, even if actors and writers had few opportunities to earn a living on the stage.

As medieval drama developed in England, France, and Germany, a few plays demanded a large number of actors—sometimes hundreds. The guilds that produced the plays could not always field enough actors from their own numbers and occasionally put out calls for auditions, usually conducted by a committee of the best available actors. Apparently it did not take long for guilds and other producing societies to recognize that some actors were skilled enough to demand recognition and consideration. By the sixteenth century, individual actors were noted for their skills as type characters and sometimes performed the same roles over a period of years. The costuming of actors, as illustrated in contemporary accounts, became extensive and demanding and clearly defined. The devils were attired in red with bizarre masks and performed characteristic wild movements. Military figures wore armor, and noble figures wore rich garments. Essentially, contemporary medieval dress was used in a manner that clarified the character type quickly for the convenience of the audience.

Most of the original early medieval plays were short, but in later years, up through the early sixteenth century, plays became longer. Some took as long as twenty-four hours to produce and involved a great many actors. The early mystery plays were often produced several times during a pageant. When the stage was moved to a new location and a new audience, the actors paraded behind the pageant cart. Because the plays were in the open, the most crucial element of the actor's skill-set was the voice. It was even more important for the medieval actor than for the Greek actor that the voice be commanding and powerful enough to project into the crowd.

By the second half of the sixteenth century, the early Renaissance, groups of wandering actors were producing highly demanding and sophisticated plays, and writers such as Shakespeare were able to join them and make a living. When these professionals secured their own theaters, they had no problems filling them with good drama, with actors, and with an audience.

Dramatic techniques developed in the medieval period were put to good use in the Renaissance theater. For example, the colorful and dramatic devil characters that stalked the mystery plays were transformed into sophisticated villains in Elizabethan drama. The devil Mephistopheles (Mephistophilis) behaves like a smooth Tudor lawyer in Marlowe's *Doctor Faustus;* Iago in *Othello* is suspected of having cloven hooves. Perhaps one important difference is that the Elizabethan devil-villains are truly frightening, since they are so recognizably human in their villainy.

Medieval Drama

Date	Theater	Political	Social/Cultural
400–500		**476:** The fall of Rome and beginning of the Dark Ages **483–565:** Byzantine Emperor Justinian, author of the Code of Civil Laws	**480–524:** Boëthius, Roman scholar, philosopher, and theologian, is executed for treason.
500–600	**500–1000:** Traveling performers proliferate in Europe.		**570–632:** Muhammed, founder of Islam **590–594:** Devastating plague spreads through Europe and kills half the population.
600–700		**614:** Persians take Damascus and Jerusalem.	**636:** Anglo-Saxons are introduced to Christianity. **695:** Jews are persecuted in Spain.
700–800		**768–814:** Charlemagne reigns in France and is crowned Holy Roman Emperor on Christmas Day in 800 by Pope Leo III in Rome. **792:** Beginning of the Viking era in Britain	**c. 710:** Buddhist monasteries in Japan become centers of civilization. **787:** The Council of Nicaea officially rejects iconoclasm.
800–900	**9th century:** Beginnings of liturgical drama	**843:** Treaty of Verdun divides the Holy Roman Empire into German, French, and Italian kingdoms. **850:** Rurik, a Northman, becomes ruler of Kiev, an important Russian trading post. Trade begins with Constantinople, which remains a commercial and cultural center throughout the Dark Ages.	**c. 800–1000:** *Beowulf*, one of the first long poems written in English **855:** Earliest known attempts at polyphonic music **863:** Cyril and Methodius invent a Slavic alphabet called Cyrillic.
900–1000	**c. 900:** Farces make their first appearance since classical times. **925:** Earliest extant Easter trope **965–975:** Compilation of the *Regularis Concordia* (Monastic Agreement) by Ethelwood, bishop of Winchester, England. The *Regularis Concordia* contains the text of the earliest extant playlet in Europe, with directions for its performance. **970:** Plays of Hrosvitha, a German nun and the first known female playwright. The six plays are modeled on the comedies of Terence but deal with serious religious matters.	**c. 970–c. 1020:** Leif Ericson, possibly the first European to venture to North America	**c. 900:** The beginnings of the famous Arabian tales called *A Thousand and One Nights* **975:** Arabic arithmetical notation is brought to Europe by the Arabs. **980–1037:** Avicenna (Ibn Sina), Arab physician and philosopher **990:** Development of systemic musical notation

Date	Theater	Political	Social/Cultural
1000–1100		**1066:** The Normans conquer Britain.	**1054:** The Great Schism separates Eastern and Western Churches in Europe.
		1086: Compilation of the *Domesday Book,* a survey of the British economy, population, and land ownership at that time	**1079–1142:** Peter Abelard, French theologian and philosopher
		1096–1099: First Crusade. Crusaders take Jerusalem from the Arabs.	
1100–1200	**12th century:** Religious plays are first performed outside churches.	**1109–1113:** Anglo-French War	**c. 1125:** Beginnings of French troubadour and trouvère music
		1147–1149: Second Crusade. Crusaders lose Jerusalem to the Arabs.	**1133–1855:** St. Bartholomew's Fair, London, England
		1167–1227: Genghis Khan, founder of Mongol empire	**1167:** Oxford University is founded.
		1189–1193: Third Crusade. Crusaders fail to recapture Jerusalem.	
1200–1300	**13th century:** Beginnings of zaju drama in China	**1202–1204:** Fourth Crusade. Crusaders seize Constantinople.	**c. 1202:** Court jesters appear at European courts.
		1212: Children's Crusade. Thousands of children are sent as crusaders to Jerusalem; most die or are sold as slaves.	**1225:** Guillaume de Lorris writes *Roman de la Rose,* a story of courtly wooing.
		1215: King John of England signs the Magna Carta, guaranteeing habeas corpus, trial by jury, and restrictions on the power of the king.	**1225–1274:** Thomas Aquinas, important Scholastic philosopher
			1254–1324: Marco Polo, Venetian traveler whose accounts of life in China became famous in the West
	1250: *Easter Play of Muri,* beginnings of German drama	**1224–1227:** Anglo-French War	
		1228: Sixth Crusade	**1264:** First celebration of the feast of Corpus Christi
	1276–1277: French poet Adam de la Halle writes *The Play of the Greenwood,* the oldest extant medieval secular drama.		**c. 1282:** Florence emerges as the leading European city of commerce and finance.
		1248: Seventh Crusade	
1300–1400	**14th century:** Beginnings of Nō drama in Japan		**c. 1302:** Dante's *Divine Comedy*
			1304–1374: Petrarch, Italian poet
		1337: Hundred Years War begins.	**1347–1351:** The Black Death kills approximately 75 million people throughout Europe.
	c. 1385–1450: *The Second Shepherds' Pageant,* part of the English Wakefield Cycle		**1360–1400:** *Piers Plowman* and *Sir Gawain and the Green Knight:* achievements of Middle English literature
	1398–1548: Confrèrie de la Passion at Paris performs religious plays.		**1387:** Chaucer's *Canterbury Tales*

Date	Theater	Political	Social/Cultural
1400–1500	**c. 1425:** *The Castle of Perseverance,* English morality play **1429:** Plautus's plays are rediscovered in Italy. **c. 1470:** *Pierre Patheline,* most renowned of medieval French farces **1490:** *Corpus Christi* play of Eger, Bohemia **c. 1495:** *Everyman,* best known English morality play	**1429:** Joan of Arc's troops resist the British siege of Orléans, an important turning point in the Hundred Years War. **1431:** Joan of Arc is captured and burned as a heretic. **1453:** France wins the Hundred Years War and becomes an important continental power. England abandons the Continent to develop its naval forces. **1481:** Spanish Inquisition **1482–1485:** Reign of Richard III. Richard maintains a company of actors at court, which tours surrounding towns when not needed by His Majesty. **1485–1509:** Reign of Henry VII, first of the Tudor rulers. Like Richard III, Henry maintains a company of actors.	**1400–1455:** Fra Angelico, Italian painter **c. 1406–1469:** Fra Lippo Lippi, Italian painter best known for his frescoes **c. 1430:** Modern English develops from Middle English. **c. 1450:** Gutenberg invents movable type. **1485:** Sir Thomas Malory publishes *Le Morte Darthur,* one of the first books printed in England. **1492:** Columbus sets sail across the Atlantic.
1500–1600	**1527:** Henry VIII builds a House of Revels in which to stage court entertainments. **1548:** Production of plays is forbidden in Paris. **1558:** Elizabeth I forbids performance of all religious plays.	**1509–1547:** Reign of Henry VIII **1534:** Henry VIII breaks with the Roman Catholic Church. Drama is used as a political instrument to attack or defend opposing viewpoints. **1558–1603:** Reign of Elizabeth I	**1509:** Pope Clement V resides at Avignon, beginning the Babylonian Captivity, during which Rome is not the papal seat. **1545–1563:** The Council of Trent is convened by the Catholic Church to solidify its control over expressions of Church doctrine. Medieval religious plays are deemed provocative and controversial.

Everyman

The late medieval play *Everyman* may have origins in northern Europe. A Flemish play, *Elckerlijk* ("Everyman"), dates from c. 1495, and the question of whether the English *Everyman* was translated from the Flemish play or whether the latter is a translation of the English *Everyman* has not been settled. Both plays may have had a common origin in an unknown play. The English *Everyman* was produced frequently in the fifteenth and early sixteenth centuries. Its drama was largely theological, its purpose to reform the audience. One indication that entertainment was not the primary goal of this morality play is its lack of the comic moments found in other plays, such as *The Second Shepherds' Pageant.*

The author of the play may have been a priest. This long-standing assumption is based on the fact that the play has much theological content and offers a moral message of the kind one might expect to hear from the pulpit. The theme of the play is fundamental: the inevitability of death. And for that reason, in part, the play continues to have a universal appeal. Modern productions may not give the audience a suitable medieval chill, but the message of the play is still relevant for everyone.

The medieval reliance on allegory is apparent in the naming of the characters in *Everyman:* Death, Kindred, Cousin, Goods, Knowledge, Strength, Beauty, and Everyman himself. Each character does not just stand for a specific quality; he or she *is* that quality. The allegorical way of thinking derived from the medieval faith that everything in the world had a moral meaning. Morality plays depended on this belief and always articulated setting, characters, and circumstances in terms of their moral value. This approach was in keeping with the medieval belief that the soul was always in jeopardy and that life was a test of one's moral condition. When Everyman meets a character, the most important information about his or her moral value is communicated instantly in the character's name, as well as through costumes and props. The character Good Deeds is simply good deeds: there is no need for psychological development because the medieval audience had a full understanding of what good deeds meant and how Good Deeds as a character would behave.

The structure of *Everyman* resembles a journey. Everyman undertakes to see who among all his acquaintances will accompany him on his most important trip: to the grave and the judgment of God Almighty. Seeing life as a journey—or as part of a journey—was especially natural for the medieval mind, which had as models the popular and costly religious pilgrimages to holy shrines and to the Holy Land itself. If life on earth is only part of the journey of the soul, then the morality play helps to put it in clear perspective. This life is not, the play tells us, the most important part of the soul's existence.

For discussion questions and assignments on *Everyman,* visit bedfordstmartins.com/jacobus.

At its core, *Everyman* has a profound commercial metaphor: Everyman is called to square accounts with God. The metaphor of accounting appears early in the play, when Everyman talks about his accounts and reckonings as if they appeared in a book that should go with him to heaven. His life will be examined; if he is found wanting, he will go into the fires of hell. If he has lived profitably from a moral viewpoint, he will enjoy life everlasting. The language of the play is heavily loaded with accounting metaphors that identify it as the product of a society quite unlike that of the Greeks or the Romans.

Such metaphors suggest that *Everyman* directs its message to middle-class merchants for whom accounting was a significant concept.

Like many sermons, *Everyman* imparts a lesson that its auditors were expected to heed. Hence the key points of the play are repeated at the end by the Doctor. For modern audiences, didactic plays are sometimes tedious. For the medieval mind, they represented a delightful way of learning important messages.

Everyman in Performance

Very little is known about early productions of *Everyman*. It was produced in Holland and England for seventy-five years beginning in the mid-fifteenth century. The play disappeared from the stage for centuries, finally resurfacing in 1901 in a production under the auspices of the Elizabethan Stage Society in London, directed by William Poel. Poel designed the costumes and set, directed, and at first played the part of Death; when he got older, he played the part of God. Poel produced *Everyman* many times over the next fifteen years.

The 1901 production was followed by a 1902 revival in New York starring Edith Wynne Matthison and produced by Ben Greet, marking the play's first American performance. Greet continued producing *Everyman* for the next thirty-five years in both England and America.

After seeing Poel's production, Max Reinhardt, the legendary German director, decided to produce *Everyman* in Germany. The Austrian poet and playwright Hugo von Hofmannsthal wrote a new German adaptation, *Jedermann*, for Reinhardt. The adaptation features Everyman as a wealthy burgher, and central to the play is an ornate banquet scene in which Death appears. Hofmannsthal's German adaptation marked a shift in emphasis from the simpler and more personal English *Everyman* to the spectacular *Jedermann* that concentrates on a wealthy man's lustful life and his attempts to get into heaven. *Jedermann* was first produced in Berlin on December 1, 1911. In 1913, Reinhardt produced the play in Salzburg, Austria, at the Salzburg Cathedral square, and except for the years of World War II, Reinhardt's version of *Jedermann* has been performed regularly at the annual Salzburg Festival. The critic Brooks Atkinson found Reinhardt's production "nothing short of miraculous." In a review of Reinhardt's 1927 production, the critic Gilbert Gabriel found *Jedermann* "crammed with splendors for the eye, largesse of bells and uplifting voices for the ear." A reviewer at the 1936 Salzburg Festival production of *Jedermann* wrote that the play "has everything but simplicity."

The popularity of the Reinhardt productions of *Jedermann* paved the way for numerous productions of *Everyman* over the years. In 1936, during the Great Depression in the United States, the WPA (Works Progress Administration) held special Sunday church performances of *Everyman*. Other notable productions include a 1941 *Everyman* in New York, performed by refugee actors from Europe, and a 1955 tour with college casts in New England and California. In 1922, a new English adaptation of the German *Jedermann* by Sir John Martin-Harvey was presented at Stratford-on-Avon. This production toured to London and New York in 1923. In 1936, Sir John's adaptation was performed at the Hollywood Bowl in California with Peggy Wood and Lionel Braham. Long popular with college and community groups, the play continues to be performed around the world.

ANONYMOUS

Everyman   c. 1495

EDITED BY A. C. CAWLEY

Characters

GOD	KNOWLEDGE
MESSENGER	CONFESSION
DEATH	BEAUTY
EVERYMAN	STRENGTH
FELLOWSHIP	DISCRETION
KINDRED	FIVE WITS
COUSIN	ANGEL
GOODS	DOCTOR
GOOD DEEDS	

Here beginneth a treatise how the high Father of Heaven sendeth Death to summon every creature to come and give account of their lives in this world, and is in manner of a moral play.

MESSENGER: I pray you all give your audience,
 And hear this matter with reverence,
 By figure° a moral play:
 The *Summoning of Everyman* called it is,
5 That of our lives and ending shows
 How transitory we be all day.°
 This matter is wondrous precious,
 But the intent of it is more gracious,
 And sweet to bear away.
10 The story saith: Man, in the beginning
 Look well, and take good heed to the ending,
 Be you never so gay!
 Ye think sin in the beginning full sweet,
 Which in the end causeth the soul to weep,
15 When the body lieth in clay.
 Here shall you see how Fellowship and Jollity,
 Both Strength, Pleasure, and Beauty,
 Will fade from thee as flower in May;
 For ye shall hear how our Heaven King
20 Calleth Everyman to a general reckoning:
 Give audience, and hear what he doth say.

           (*Exit.*)

(*God speaketh.*)

GOD: I perceive, here in my majesty,
 How that all creatures be to me unkind,°
 Living without dread in worldly prosperity:
25 Of ghostly sight° the people be so blind,
 Drowned in sin, they know me not for their God;

In worldly riches is all their mind,
They fear not my righteousness, the sharp rod.
My law that I showed, when I for them died,
They forget clean, and shedding of my blood red; 30
I hanged between two, it cannot be denied;
To get them life I suffered to be dead;
I healed their feet, with thorns hurt was my head.
I could do no more than I did, truly;
And now I see the people do clean forsake me: 35
They use the seven deadly sins damnable,
As pride, covetise, wrath, and lechery
Now in the world be made commendable;
And thus they leave of angels the heavenly company.
Every man liveth so after his own pleasure, 40
And yet of their life they be nothing sure:
I see the more that I them forbear
The worse they be from year to year.
All that liveth appaireth° fast;
Therefore I will, in all the haste, 45
Have a reckoning of every man's person;
For, and° I leave the people thus alone
In their life and wicked tempests,
Verily they will become much worse than beasts;
For now one would by envy another up eat; 50
Charity they do all clean forget.
I hoped well that every man
In my glory should make his mansion,
And thereto I had them all elect;
But now I see, like traitors deject,° 55
They thank me not for the pleasure that
 I to them meant,
Nor yet for their being that I them have lent.
I proffered the people great multitude of mercy,
And few there be that asketh it heartily.
They be so cumbered with worldly riches 60
That needs on them I must do justice,
On every man living without fear.
Where art thou, Death, thou mighty messenger?

(*Enter Death.*)

DEATH: Almighty God, I am here at your will,
 Your commandment to fulfill. 65
GOD: Go thou to Everyman,
 And show him, in my name,
 A pilgrimage he must on him take,
 Which he in no wise may escape;

---

3. **By figure:** In form. 6. **all day:** Always. 23. **unkind:** Ungrateful. 25. **ghostly sight:** Spiritual vision.

44. **appaireth:** Degenerates. 47. **and:** If. 55. **deject:** Abject.

70   And that he bring with him a sure reckoning
      Without delay or any tarrying.
                                (God withdraws.)

DEATH: Lord, I will in the world go run overall,
      And cruelly outsearch both great and small;
      Every man will I beset that liveth beastly
75   Out of God's laws, and dreadeth not folly.
      He that loveth riches I will strike with my dart,
      His sight to blind, and from heaven to depart°—
      Except that alms be his good friend—
      In hell for to dwell, world without end.
80   Lo, yonder I see Everyman walking.
      Full little he thinketh on my coming;
      His mind is on fleshly lusts and his treasure,
      And great pain it shall cause him to endure
      Before the Lord, Heaven King.

(Enter Everyman.)

85   Everyman, stand still! Whither art thou going
      Thus gaily? Hast thou thy Maker forget?

EVERYMAN: Why askest thou?
      Wouldest thou wit?°

DEATH: Yea, sir; I will show you:
90   In great haste I am sent to thee
      From God out of his majesty.

EVERYMAN: What, sent to me?

DEATH: Yea, certainly.
      Though thou have forget him here,
95   He thinketh on thee in the heavenly sphere,
      As, ere we depart, thou shalt know.

EVERYMAN: What desireth God of me?

DEATH: That shall I show thee:
      A reckoning he will needs have
100   Without any longer respite.

EVERYMAN: To give a reckoning longer leisure I crave;
      This blind matter troubleth my wit.

DEATH: On thee thou must take a long journey;
      Therefore thy book of count° with thee thou bring,
105   For turn° again thou cannot by no way.
      And look thou be sure of thy reckoning,
      For before God thou shalt answer, and show
      Thy many bad deeds, and good but a few;
      How thou hast spent thy life, and in what wise,
110   Before the chief Lord of paradise.
      Have ado that we were in that way,°
      For, wit thou well, thou shalt make none attorney.°

EVERYMAN: Full unready I am such reckoning to give.
      I know thee not. What messenger art thou?

115 DEATH: I am Death, that no man dreadeth,°
      For every man I rest,° and no man spareth;
      For it is God's commandment
      That all to me should be obedient.

EVERYMAN: O Death, thou comest when I had thee least
      in mind!

In thy power it lieth me to save;
      Yet of my good° will I give thee, if thou will be kind:
      Yea, a thousand pound shalt thou have,
      And defer this matter till another day.   120

DEATH: Everyman, it may not be, by no way.
      I set not by gold, silver, nor riches,   125
      Ne by pope, emperor, king, duke, ne princes;
      For, and I would receive gifts great,
      All the world I might get;
      But my custom is clean contrary.
      I give thee no respite. Come hence, and not tarry.   130

EVERYMAN: Alas, shall I have no longer respite?
      I may say Death giveth no warning!
      To think on thee, it maketh my heart sick,
      For all unready is my book of reckoning.
      But twelve year and I might have abiding,°   135
      My counting-book I would make so clear
      That my reckoning I should not need to fear.
      Wherefore, Death, I pray thee, for God's mercy,
      Spare me till I be provided of remedy.

DEATH: Thee availeth not to cry, weep, and pray;   140
      But haste thee lightly that thou were gone that
          journey,°
      And prove thy friends if thou can;
      For, wit thou well, the tide abideth no man,
      And in the world each living creature
      For Adam's sin must die of nature.°   145

EVERYMAN: Death, if I should this pilgrimage take,
      And my reckoning surely make,
      Show me, for saint charity,°
      Should I not come again shortly?

DEATH: No, Everyman; and thou be once there,   150
      Thou mayst never more come here,
      Trust me verily.

EVERYMAN: O gracious God in the high seat celestial,
      Have mercy on me in this most need!
      Shall I have no company from this vale terrestrial 155
      Of mine acquaintance, that way me to lead?

DEATH: Yea, if any be so hardy
      That would go with thee and bear thee company.
      Hie thee that thou were gone to God's magnificence,
      Thy reckoning to give before his presence.   160
      What, weenest° thou thy life is given thee,
      And thy worldly goods also?

EVERYMAN: I had wend° so, verily.

DEATH: Nay, nay; it was but lent thee;
      For as soon as thou art go,   165
      Another while shall have it, and then go therefro,
      Even as thou has done.
      Everyman, thou art mad! Thou hast thy wits five,
      And here on earth will not amend thy life;
      For suddenly I do come.   170

---

77. **depart:** Separate. **88. wit:** Know. **104. count:** Account.
105. turn: Return. **111. Have ado . . . that way:** Let us see
about making that journey. **112. none attorney:** No one
(your) advocate. **115. no man dreadeth:** Fears no man.
116. rest: Arrest.

121. **good:** Goods. **135. But twelve year . . . abiding:** If I could
stay for just twelve more years. **141. But haste thee . . . that
journey:** But set off quickly on your journey. **145. of nature:**
In the course of nature. **148. for saint charity:** In the name of
holy charity. **161. weenest:** Suppose. **163. wend:** Supposed.

EVERYMAN: O wretched caitiff,° whither shall I flee,
That I might scape this endless sorrow?
Now, gentle Death, spare me till to-morrow,
That I may amend me
175   With good advisement.
DEATH: Nay, thereto I will not consent,
Nor no man will I respite;
But to the heart suddenly I shall smite
Without any advisement.
180   And now out of thy sight I will me hie;
See thou make thee ready shortly,
For thou mayst say this is the day
That no man living may scape away.

                                        (*Exit Death.*)

EVERYMAN: Alas, I may well weep with
        sighs deep!
185   Now have I no manner of company
To help me in my journey, and me to keep;
And also my writing is full unready,
How shall I do now for to excuse me?
I would to God I had never be get!°
190   To my soul a full great profit it had be;
For now I fear pains huge and great.
The time passeth. Lord, help, that all wrought!
For though I mourn it availeth nought.
The day passeth, and is almost ago;°
195   I wot not well what for to do.
To whom were I best my complaint to make?
What and I to Fellowship thereof spake,
And showed him of this sudden chance?
For in him is all mine affiance;°
200   We have in the world so many a day
Be good friends in sport and play.
I see him yonder, certainly.
I trust that he will bear me company;
Therefore to him will I speak to ease my sorrow.
205   Well met, good Fellowship, and good morrow!

(*Fellowship speaketh.*)

FELLOWSHIP: Everyman, good morrow, by this day!
Sir, why lookest thou so piteously?
If any thing be amiss, I pray thee say,
That I may help to remedy.
210   EVERYMAN: Yea, good Fellowship, yea;
I am in great jeopardy.
FELLOWSHIP: My true friend, show to me your mind;
I will not forsake thee to my life's end,
In the way of good company.
215   EVERYMAN: That was well spoken, and lovingly.
FELLOWSHIP: Sir, I must needs know your heaviness;°
I have pity to see you in any distress.
If any have you wronged, ye shall revenged be,
Though I on the ground be slain for thee—
220   Though that I know before that I should die.
EVERYMAN: Verily, Fellowship, gramercy.°

FELLOWSHIP: Tush! by thy thanks I set not a straw.
Show me your grief, and say no more.
EVERYMAN: If I my heart should to you break,°
And then you to turn your mind from me,   225
And would not me comfort when ye hear me speak,
Then should I ten times sorrier be.
FELLOWSHIP: Sir, I say as I will do indeed.
EVERYMAN: Then be you a good friend at need:
I have found you true herebefore.   230
FELLOWSHIP: And so ye shall evermore;
For, in faith, and thou go to hell,
I will not forsake thee by the way.
EVERYMAN: Ye speak like a good friend; I believe
        you well.
I shall deserve° it, and I may.   235
FELLOWSHIP: I speak of no deserving, by this day!
For he that will say, and nothing do,
Is not worthy with good company to go;
Therefore show me the grief of your mind,
As to your friend most loving and kind.   240
EVERYMAN: I shall show you how it is:
Commanded I am to go a journey,
A long way, hard and dangerous,
And give a strait count, without delay,
Before the high Judge, Adonai.°   245
Wherefore, I pray you, bear me company,
As ye have promised, in this journey.
FELLOWSHIP: That is matter indeed.° Promise is duty;
But, and I should take such a voyage on me,
I know it well, it should be to my pain;   250
Also it maketh me afeard, certain.
But let us take counsel here as well as we can,
For your words would fear a strong man.
EVERYMAN: Why, ye said if I had need
Ye would me never forsake, quick ne dead,   255
Though it were to hell, truly.
FELLOWSHIP: So I said, certainly,
But such pleasures be set aside, the sooth to say;
And also, if we took such a journey,
When should we come again?   260
EVERYMAN: Nay, never again, till the day of doom.
FELLOWSHIP: In faith, then will not I come there!
Who hath you these tidings brought?
EVERYMAN: Indeed, Death was with me here.
FELLOWSHIP: Now, by God that all hath bought,°   265
If Death were the messenger,
For no man that is living to-day
I will not go that loath journey—
Not for the father that begat me!
EVERYMAN: Ye promised otherwise, pardie.°   270
FELLOWSHIP: I wot well I said so, truly;
And yet if thou wilt eat, and drink, and make good
        cheer,
Or haunt to women the lusty company,°

---

171. **caitiff:** Captive.   189. **be get:** Been born.   194. **ago:**
Gone.   199. **affiance:** Trust.   216. **heaviness:** Sorrow.   221.
gramercy: Thanks.

224. **break:** Open.   235. **deserve:** Repay.   245. **Adonai:**
Hebrew name for God.   248. **That is matter indeed:** That
is a good reason indeed (for asking me).   265. **bought:**
Redeemed.   270. **pardie:** By God.   273. **haunt to women the
lusty company:** Frequent the lively company of women.

I would not forsake you while the day is clear,°
275   Trust me verily.
EVERYMAN: Yea, thereto ye would be ready!
    To go to mirth, solace, and play,
    Your mind will sooner apply,
    Than to bear me company in my long journey.
280 FELLOWSHIP: Now, in good faith, I will not that way.
    But and thou will murder, or any man kill,
    In that I will help thee with a good will.
EVERYMAN: O, that is a simple advice indeed.
    Gentle fellow, help me in my necessity!
285   We have loved long, and now I need;
    And now, gentle Fellowship, remember me.
FELLOWSHIP: Whether ye have loved me or no,
    By Saint John, I will not with thee go.
EVERYMAN: Yet, I pray thee, take the labor, and do so
    much for me
290   To bring me forward, for saint charity,
    And comfort me till I come without the town.
FELLOWSHIP: Nay, and thou would give me a new gown,
    I will not a foot with thee go;
    But, and thou had tarried, I would not have left thee
    so.
295   And as now God speed thee in thy journey,
    For from thee I will depart as fast as I may.
EVERYMAN: Whither away, Fellowship? Will thou forsake
    me?
FELLOWSHIP: Yea, by my fay!° To God I betake° thee.
EVERYMAN: Farewell, good Fellowship; for thee my heart
    is sore.
300   Adieu for ever! I shall see thee no more.
FELLOWSHIP: In faith, Everyman, farewell now at the
    ending;
    For you I will remember that parting is mourning.

                    (Exit Fellowship.)

EVERYMAN: Alack! shall we thus depart° indeed—
    Ah, Lady, help!—without any more comfort?
305   Lo, Fellowship forsaketh me in my most need.
    For help in this world whither shall I resort?
    Fellowship herebefore with me would merry make,
    And now little sorrow for me doth he take.
    It is said, "In prosperity men friends may find,
310   Which in adversity be full unkind."
    Now whither for succor shall I flee,
    Sith° that Fellowship hath forsaken me?
    To my kinsmen I will, truly,
    Praying them to help me in my necessity;
315   I believe that they will do so,
    For kind will creep where it may not go.°
    I will go say,° for yonder I see them.
    Where be ye now, my friends and kinsmen?

(Enter Kindred and Cousin.)

KINDRED: Here be we now at your commandment.
    Cousin, I pray you show us your intent   320
    In any wise, and do not spare.
COUSIN: Yea, Everyman, and to us declare
    If ye be disposed to go anywhither;
    For, wit you well, we will live and die together.
KINDRED: In wealth and woe we will with you hold,   325
    For over his kin a man may be bold.°
EVERYMAN: Gramercy, my friends and kinsmen kind.
    Now shall I show you the grief of my mind:
    I was commanded by a messenger,
    That is a high king's chief officer;   330
    He bade me go a pilgrimage, to my pain,
    And I know well I shall never come again;
    Also I must give a reckoning strait,
    For I have a great enemy° that hath me in wait,°
    Which intendeth me for to hinder.   335
KINDRED: What account is that which ye must render?
    That would I know.
EVERYMAN: Of all my works I must show
    How I have lived and my days spent;
    Also of ill deeds that I have used   340
    In my time, sith life was me lent;
    And of all virtues that I have refused.
    Therefore, I pray you, go thither with me
    To help to make mine account, for saint charity.
COUSIN: What, to go thither? Is that the matter?   345
    Nay, Everyman, I had liefer fast bread and water°
    All this five year and more.
EVERYMAN: Alas, that ever I was bore!
    For now shall I never be merry,
    If that you forsake me.   350
KINDRED: Ah, sir, what ye be a merry man!
    Take good heart to you, and make no moan.
    But one thing I warn you, by Saint Anne—
    As for me, ye shall go alone.
EVERYMAN: My Cousin, will you not with me go?   355
COUSIN: No, by our Lady! I have the cramp in my toe.
    Trust not to me, for, so God me speed,
    I will deceive you in your most need.
KINDRED: It availeth not us to tice.°
    Ye shall have my maid with all my heart;   360
    She loveth to go to feasts, there to be nice,°
    And to dance, and abroad to start:
    I will give her leave to help you in that journey,
    If that you and she may agree.
EVERYMAN: Now show me the very effect° of your
    mind: 365
    Will you go with me, or abide behind?
KINDRED: Abide behind? Yea, that will I, and I may!
    Therefore farewell till another day.

                    (Exit Kindred.)

---

274. while the day is clear: Until daybreak. **298. fay:** Faith.
betake: Commend. **303. depart:** Part. **312. Sith:** Since.
316. for kind will creep where it may not go: For kinship will
creep where it cannot walk (i.e., blood is thicker than water).
317. say: Essay, try.

326. For over his kin . . . may be bold: For a man may be sure
of his kinsfolk. **334. enemy:** Devil. **hath me in wait:** Has me
under observation. **346. liefer fast bread and water:** Rather
fast on bread and water. **359. tice:** Entice. **361. nice:** Wanton.
365. effect: Tenor.

EVERYMAN: How should I be merry or glad?
370   For fair promises men to me make,
  But when I have most need they me forsake.
  I am deceived; that maketh me sad.
COUSIN: Cousin Everyman, farewell now,
  For verily I will not go with you.
375   Also of mine own an unready reckoning
  I have to account; therefore I make tarrying.
  Now God keep thee, for now I go.
                                 (*Exit Cousin.*)
EVERYMAN: Ah, Jesus, is all come hereto?
  Lo, fair words maketh fools fain;°
380   They promise, and nothing will do, certain.
  My kinsmen promised me faithfully
  For to abide with me steadfastly,
  And now fast away do they flee:
  Even so Fellowship promised me.
385   What friend were best me of to provide?°
  I lose my time here longer to abide.
  Yet in my mind a thing there is:
  All my life I have loved riches;
  If that my Good° now help me might,
390   He would make my heart full light.
  I will speak to him in this distress—
  Where art thou, my Goods and riches?
(*Goods speaks from a corner.*)

GOODS: Who calleth me? Everyman? What! hast thou
    haste?
  I lie here in corners, trussed and piled so high,
395   And in chests I am locked so fast,
  Also sacked in bags. Thou mayst see with thine eye
  I cannot stir; in packs low I lie.
  What would ye have? Lightly° me say.
EVERYMAN: Come hither, Good, in all the haste thou may,
400   For of counsel I must desire thee.
GOODS: Sir, and ye in the world have sorrow or adversity,
  That can I help you to remedy shortly.
EVERYMAN: It is another disease that grieveth me;
  In this world it is not, I tell thee so.
405   I am sent for, another way to go,
  To give a strait count general
  Before the highest Jupiter of all;
  And all my life I have had joy and pleasure in thee,
  Therefore, I pray thee, go with me;
410   For, peradventure, thou mayst before God Almighty
  My reckoning help to clean and purify;
  For it is said ever among
  That money maketh all right that is wrong.
GOODS: Nay, Everyman, I sing another song.
415   I follow no man in such voyages;
  For, and I went with thee,
  Thou shouldst fare much the worse for me;
  For because on me thou did set thy mind,
  Thy reckoning I have made blotted and blind,
420   That thine account thou cannot make truly;

  And that hast thou for the love of me.
EVERYMAN: That would grieve me full sore,
  When I should come to that fearful answer.
  Up, let us go thither together.
GOODS: Nay, not so! I am too brittle, I may not endure; 425
  I will follow no man one foot, be ye sure.
EVERYMAN: Alas, I have thee loved, and had great pleasure
  All my life-days on good and treasure.
GOODS: That is to thy damnation, without leasing,°
  For my love is contrary to the love everlasting; 430
  But if thou had me loved moderately during,
  As to the poor to give part of me,
  Then shouldst thou not in this dolor be,
  Nor in this great sorrow and care.
EVERYMAN: Lo, now was I deceived ere I was ware, 435
  And all I may wite° misspending of time.
GOODS: What, weenest thou that I am thine?
EVERYMAN: I had wend so.
GOODS: Nay, Everyman, I say no.
  As for a while I was lent thee; 440
  A season thou hast had me in prosperity.
  My condition is man's soul to kill;
  If I save one, a thousand I do spill.°
  Weenest thou that I will follow thee?
  Nay, not from this world, verily. 445
EVERYMAN: I had wend otherwise.
GOODS: Therefore to thy soul Good is a thief;
  For when thou art dead, this is my guise—
  Another to deceive in this same wise
  As I have done thee, and all to his soul's reprief.° 450
EVERYMAN: O false Good, cursed may thou be,
  Thou traitor to God, that hast deceived me
  And caught me in thy snare!
GOODS: Marry, thou brought thyself in care,
  Whereof I am glad; 455
  I must needs laugh, I cannot be sad.
EVERYMAN: Ah, Good, thou hast had long my heartly
    love;
  I gave thee that which should be the Lord's
    above.
  But wilt thou not go with me indeed?
  I pray thee truth to say. 460
GOODS: No, so God me speed!
  Therefore farewell, and have good day.
                              (*Exit Goods.*)
EVERYMAN: O, to whom shall I make my moan
  For to go with me in that heavy journey?
  First Fellowship said he would with me gone; 465
  His words were very pleasant and gay,
  But afterward he left me alone.
  Then spake I to my kinsmen, all in despair,
  And also they gave me words fair;
  They lacked no fair speaking, 470
  But all forsook me in the ending.
  Then went I to my Goods, that I loved best,

---

379. fain: Glad.   **385. me of to provide:** To provide myself with.   **389. Good:** Goods.   **398. Lightly:** Quickly.

429. without leasing: Without a lie (i.e., truly).   **436. wite:** Blame.   **443. spill:** Ruin.   **450. reprief:** Shame.

In hope to have comfort, but there had I least;
For my Goods sharply did me tell
475   That he bringeth many into hell.
Then of myself I was ashamed,
And so I am worthy to be blamed;
Thus may I well myself hate.
Of whom shall I now counsel take?
480   I think that I shall never speed
Till that I go to my Good Deed.
But, alas, she is so weak
That she can neither go nor speak;
Yet will I venture on her now.
485   My Good Deeds, where be you?

(*Good Deeds speaks from the ground.*)

GOOD DEEDS: Here I lie, cold in the ground;
Thy sins hath me sore bound,
That I cannot stir.
EVERYMAN: O Good Deeds, I stand in fear!
490   I must you pray of counsel,
For help now should come right well.°
GOOD DEEDS: Everyman, I have understanding
That ye be summoned account to make
Before Messias, of Jerusalem King;
And you do by me,° that journey with you will I
495   take.
EVERYMAN: Therefore I come to you, my moan to make;
I pray you that ye will go with me.
GOOD DEEDS: I would full fain, but I cannot stand,
verily.
EVERYMAN: Why, is there anything on you fall?
500   GOOD DEEDS: Yea, sir, I may thank you of° all;
If ye had perfectly cheered me,
Your book of count full ready had be.
Look, the books of your works and deeds eke!°
Behold how they lie under the feet,
505   To your soul's heaviness.
EVERYMAN: Our Lord Jesus help me!
For one letter here I cannot see.
GOOD DEEDS: There is a blind reckoning in time of
distress.
EVERYMAN: Good Deeds, I pray you help me in this need,
510   Or else I am for ever damned indeed;
Therefore help me to make reckoning
Before the Redeemer of all thing,
That King is, and was, and ever shall.
GOOD DEEDS: Everyman, I am sorry of your fall,
515   And fain would I help you, and I were able.
EVERYMAN: Good Deeds, your counsel I pray you give
me.
GOOD DEEDS: That shall I do verily;
Though that on my feet I may not go,
I have a sister that shall with you also,
520   Called Knowledge, which shall with you abide,
To help you to make that dreadful reckoning.

(*Enter Knowledge.*)

KNOWLEDGE: Everyman, I will go with thee, and be thy
guide,
In thy most need to go by thy side.
EVERYMAN: In good condition I am now in every
thing,
And am wholly content with this good thing,   525
Thanked be God my creator.
GOOD DEEDS: And when she hath brought you there
Where thou shalt heal thee of thy smart,
Then go you with your reckoning and your Good
Deeds together,
For to make you joyful at heart   530
Before the blessed Trinity.
EVERYMAN: My Good Deeds, gramercy!
I am well content, certainly,
With your words sweet.
KNOWLEDGE: Now go we together lovingly   535
To Confession, that cleansing river.
EVERYMAN: For joy I weep; I would we were there!
But, I pray you, give me cognition
Where dwelleth that holy man, Confession.
KNOWLEDGE: In the house of salvation: 540
We shall find him in that place,
That shall us comfort, by God's grace.

(*Knowledge takes Everyman to Confession.*)

Lo, this is Confession. Kneel down and ask mercy,
For he is in good conceit° with God Almighty.
EVERYMAN: O glorious fountain, that all uncleanness
doth clarify,   545
Wash from me the spots of vice unclean,
That on me no sin may be seen.
I come with Knowledge for my redemption,
Redempt with heart° and full contrition;
For I am commanded a pilgrimage to take,   550
And great accounts before God to make.
Now I pray you, Shrift, mother of salvation,
Help my Good Deeds for my piteous exclamation.
CONFESSION: I know your sorrow well, Everyman.
Because with Knowledge ye come to me,   555
I will you comfort as well as I can,
And a precious jewel I will give thee,
Called penance, voider of adversity;
Therewith shall your body chastised be,
With abstinence and perseverance in God's service. 560
Here shall you receive that scourge of me,
Which is penance strong that ye must endure,
To remember thy Savior was scourged for thee
With sharp scourges, and suffered it patiently;
So must thou, ere thou scape that painful
pilgrimage.   565
Knowledge, keep him in this voyage,
And by that time Good Deeds will be with thee.
But in any wise be siker° of mercy,
For your time draweth fast; and° ye will saved be,

---

491. **should come right well:** Would be very welcome.   495. **by me:** As I advise.   500. **of:** For.   503. **eke:** Also.

544. **conceit:** Esteem.   549. **heart:** Heartfelt.   568. **siker:** Sure.   569. **and:** If.

570   Ask God mercy, and he will grant truly.
       When with the scourge of penance man doth him
          bind,
       The oil of forgiveness then shall he find.
       EVERYMAN: Thanked be God for his gracious work!
       For now I will my penance begin;
575   This hath rejoiced and lighted my heart,
       Though the knots be painful and hard within.
       KNOWLEDGE: Everyman, look your penance that ye
          fulfill,
       What pain that ever it to you be;
       And Knowledge shall give you counsel at will
580   How your account ye shall make clearly.
       EVERYMAN: O eternal God, O heavenly figure,
       O way of righteousness, O goodly vision,
       Which descended down in a virgin pure
       Because he would every man redeem,
585   Which Adam forfeited by his disobedience:
       O blessed Godhead, elect and high divine,
       Forgive my grievous offense;
       Here I cry thee mercy in this presence.°
       O ghostly treasure, O ransomer and redeemer,
590   Of all the world hope and conductor,
       Mirror of joy, and founder of mercy,
       Which enlumineth heaven and earth thereby,
       Hear my clamorous complaint, though it late be;
       Receive my prayers, of thy benignity;
595   Though I be a sinner most abominable,
       Yet let my name be written in Moses' table.°
       O Mary, pray to the Maker of all thing,
       Me for to help at my ending;
       And save me from the power of my enemy,
600   For Death assaileth me strongly.
       And, Lady, that I may by mean of thy prayer
       Of your Son's glory to be partner,
       By the means of his passion, I it crave;
       I beseech you help my soul to save.
605   Knowledge, give me the scourge of penance;
       My flesh therewith shall give acquittance:°
       I will now begin, if God give me grace.
       KNOWLEDGE: Everyman, God give you time and space!
       Thus I bequeath you in the hands of our Saviour;
610   Now may you make your reckoning sure.
       EVERYMAN: In the name of the Holy Trinity,
       My body sore punished shall be:
       Take this, body, for the sin of the flesh!

       (*Scourges himself.*)

       Also° thou delightest to go gay and fresh,
615   And in the way of damnation thou did me bring,
       Therefore suffer now strokes and punishing.

Now of penance I will wade the water clear,
To save me from purgatory, that sharp fire.

(*Good Deeds rises from the ground.*)

GOOD DEEDS: I thank God, now I can walk and go,
And am delivered of my sickness and woe.   620
Therefore with Everyman I will go, and not
   spare;
His good works I will help him to declare.
KNOWLEDGE: Now, Everyman, be merry and glad!
Your Good Deeds cometh now; ye may not
   be sad.
Now is your Good Deeds whole and sound,   625
Going upright upon the ground.
EVERYMAN: My heart is light, and shall be evermore;
Now will I smite° faster than I did before.
GOOD DEEDS: Everyman, pilgrim, my special friend,
Blessed be thou without end;   630
For thee is preparate the eternal glory.
Ye have me made whole and sound,
Therefore I will bide by thee in every stound.°
EVERYMAN: Welcome, my Good Deeds; now I hear thy
   voice,
I weep for very sweetness of love.   635
KNOWLEDGE: Be no more sad, but ever rejoice;
God seeth thy living in his throne above.
Put on this garment to thy behoof,°
Which is wet with your tears,
Or else before God you may it miss,   640
When ye to your journey's end come shall.
EVERYMAN: Gentle Knowledge, what do ye it call?
KNOWLEDGE: It is a garment of sorrow:
From pain it will you borrow;°
Contrition it is,   645
That geteth forgiveness;
It pleaseth God passing well.
GOOD DEEDS: Everyman, will you wear it for your
   heal?°
EVERYMAN: Now blessed be Jesu, Mary's Son,
For now have I on true contrition.   650
And let us go now without tarrying;
Good Deeds, have we clear our reckoning?
GOOD DEEDS: Yea, indeed, I have it here.
EVERYMAN: Then I trust we need not fear;
Now, friends, let us not part in twain.   655
KNOWLEDGE: Nay, Everyman, that will we not,
   certain.
GOOD DEEDS: Yet must thou lead with thee
Three persons of great might.
EVERYMAN: Who should they be?
GOOD DEEDS: Discretion and Strength they hight,°   660
And thy Beauty may not abide behind.
KNOWLEDGE: Also ye must call to mind
Your Five Wits as for your counsellors.

---

588. **in this presence:** In the presence of this company.
596. **Moses' table:** Medieval theologians regarded the two
tablets given to Moses on Mount Sinai as symbols of baptism
and penance. Thus Everyman is asking to be numbered among
those who have escaped damnation by doing penance for their
sins. 606. **acquittance:** Satisfaction (as part of the sacrament
of penance). 614. **Also:** As.

628. **smite:** Strike. 633. **stound:** Trial. 638. **behoof:** Advantage. 644. **borrow:** Release. 648. **heal:** Salvation. 660.
hight: Are called.

GOOD DEEDS: You must have them ready at all hours.
665 **EVERYMAN:** How shall I get them hither?
KNOWLEDGE: You must call them all together,
And they will hear you incontinent.°
EVERYMAN: My friends, come hither and be present,
Discretion, Strength, my Five Wits, and Beauty.

(*Enter Beauty, Strength, Discretion, and Five Wits.*)

670 **BEAUTY:** Here at your will we be all ready.
What will ye that we should do?
GOOD DEEDS: That ye would with Everyman go,
And help him in his pilgrimage.
Advise you, will ye with him or not in that voyage?
675 **STRENGTH:** We will bring him all thither,
To his help and comfort, ye may believe me.
DISCRETION: So will we go with him all together.
EVERYMAN: Almighty God, lofed° may thou be!
I give thee laud that I have hither brought
Strength, Discretion, Beauty, and Five Wits. Lack I
680   nought.
And my Good Deeds, with Knowledge clear,
All be in my company at my will here;
I desire no more to my business.
STRENGTH: And I, Strength, will by you stand in
    distress,
685 Though thou would in battle fight on the ground.
FIVE WITS: And though it were through the world
    round,
We will not depart for sweet ne sour.
BEAUTY: No more will I unto death's hour,
Whatsoever thereof befall.
690 **DISCRETION:** Everyman, advise you first of all;
Go with a good advisement and deliberation.
We all give you virtuous monition°
That all shall be well.
EVERYMAN: My friends, harken what I will tell:
695 I pray God reward you in his heavenly sphere.
Now harken, all that be here,
For I will make my testament
Here before you all present:
In alms half my good I will give with my hands twain
700 In the way of charity, with good intent,
And the other half still shall remain
In queth,° to be returned there it ought to be.°
This I do in despite of the fiend of hell,
To go quit out of his peril°
705 Ever after and this day.
KNOWLEDGE: Everyman, harken what I say:
Go to priesthood, I you advise,
And receive of him in any wise°
The holy sacrament and ointment together.
710 Then shortly see ye turn again hither;
We will all abide you here.

667. **incontinent:** Immediately. 678. **lofed:** Praised.
692. **monition:** Forewarning. 702. **queth:** Bequest. **returned
there it ought to be:** This line probably refers to restitution—
that is, the restoration to its proper owner of unlawfully
acquired property. 704. **quit out of his peril:** Free out of his
power. 708. **in any wise:** Without fail.

FIVE WITS: Yea, Everyman, hie you that ye ready were.
There is no emperor, king, duke, ne baron,
That of God hath commission
As hath the least priest in the world being;   715
For of the blessed sacraments pure and benign
He beareth the keys, and thereof hath the cure°
For man's redemption—it is ever sure—
Which God for our soul's medicine
Gave us out of his heart with great pine.°   720
Here in this transitory life, for thee and me,
The blessed sacraments seven there be:
Baptism, confirmation, with priesthood good,
And the sacrament of God's precious flesh and
    blood,
Marriage, the holy extreme unction, and penance; 725
These seven be good to have in remembrance,
Gracious sacraments of high divinity.
EVERYMAN: Fain would I receive that holy body,
And meekly to my ghostly father I will go.
FIVE WITS: Everyman, that is the best that ye can do. 730
God will you to salvation bring,
For priesthood exceedeth all other thing:
To us Holy Scripture they do teach,
And converteth man from sin heaven to reach;
God hath to them more power given   735
Than to any angel that is in heaven.
With five words° he may consecrate,
God's body in flesh and blood to make,
And handleth his Maker between his hands.
The priest bindeth and unbindeth all bands,   740
Both in earth and in heaven.
Thou ministers all the sacraments seven;
Though we kissed thy feet, thou were worthy;
Thou art surgeon that cureth sin deadly:
No remedy we find under God   745
But all only priesthood.°
Everyman, God gave priests that dignity,
And setteth them in his stead among us to be;
Thus be they above angels in degree.

(*Everyman goes to the priest to receive the last sacraments.*)

KNOWLEDGE: If priests be good, it is so, surely.   750
But when Jesus hanged on the cross with
    great smart,
There he gave out of his blessed heart
The same sacrament in great torment:
He sold them not to us, that Lord omnipotent.
Therefore Saint Peter the apostle doth say   755
That Jesu's curse hath all they
Which God their Savior do buy or sell,
Or they for any money do take or tell.°

717. **cure:** Charge. 720. **pine:** Suffering. 737. **five words:**
Hoc est enim Corpus meum ("For this is my body," the words
of the consecration of the body of Christ at Mass). 746.
But all only priesthood: Except only from the priesthood. 755–758. **Therefore Saint Peter . . . do take or tell:**
Reference to the sin of simony, the selling of church offices or
benefits. **tell:** Count out (i.e., sell).

Sinful priests giveth the sinners example bad;
Their children sitteth by other men's fires, I have
760   heard;
And some haunteth women's company
With unclean life, as lusts of lechery:
These be with sin made blind.

FIVE WITS: I trust to God no such may we find;
765   Therefore let us priesthood honor,
And follow their doctrine for our souls' succor.
We be their sheep, and they shepherds be
By whom we all be kept in surety.
Peace, for yonder I see Everyman come,
770   Which hath made true satisfaction.

GOOD DEEDS: Methink it is he indeed.

(*Reenter Everyman.*)

EVERYMAN: Now Jesu be your alder speed!°
I have received the sacrament for my redemption,
And then mine extreme unction:
775   Blessed be all they that counselled me to take it!
And now, friends, let us go without longer
     respite;
I thank God that ye have tarried so long.
Now set each of you on this rood° your hand,
And shortly follow me:
780   I go before there I would be; God be our guide!

STRENGTH: Everyman, we will not from you go
Till ye have done this voyage long.

DISCRETION: I, Discretion, will bide by you also.

KNOWLEDGE: And though this pilgrimage be never so
     strong,°
785   I will never part you fro.

STRENGTH: Everyman, I will be as sure by thee
As ever I did by Judas Maccabee.°

(*Everyman comes to his grave.*)

EVERYMAN: Alas, I am so faint I may not stand;
My limbs under me doth fold.
790   Friends, let us not turn again to this land,
Not for all the world's gold;
For into this cave must I creep
And turn to earth, and there to sleep.

BEAUTY: What, into this grave? Alas!

EVERYMAN: Yea, there shall ye consume, more
795   and less.

BEAUTY: And what, should I smother here?

EVERYMAN: Yea, by my faith, and never more appear.
In this world live no more we shall,
But in heaven before the highest Lord of all.

800   BEAUTY: I cross out all this;° adieu, by Saint John!

---

772. **your alder speed:** The helper of you all. **778. rood:**
Cross. **784. strong:** Grievous. **787. Judas Maccabee:** Judas
Maccabeus, who overcame Syrian domination and won religious freedom for the Jews in 165 BCE, believed that his strength
came not from worldly might but from heaven (1 Maccabees
3:19). **800. I cross out all this:** I cancel all this (i.e., my promise to stay with you).

Scene from the Guthrie Theater production of *Everyman*,
directed by Robert Benedetti.

I take my cap in my lap,° and am gone.

EVERYMAN: What, Beauty, whither will ye?

BEAUTY: Peace, I am deaf; I look not behind me,
Not and thou wouldest give me all the gold in thy
     chest.

(*Exit Beauty.*)

---

801. **I take my cap in my lap:** Doff my cap (so low that it comes)
into my lap.

805 EVERYMAN: Alas, whereto may I trust?
    Beauty goeth fast away from me;
    She promised with me to live and die.
    STRENGTH: Everyman, I will thee also forsake and
        deny;
    Thy game liketh° me not at all.
810 EVERYMAN: Why, then, ye will forsake me all?
    Sweet Strength, tarry a little space.
    STRENGTH: Nay, sir, by the rood of grace!
    I will hie me from thee fast,
    Though thou weep till thy heart to-brast.°
815 EVERYMAN: Ye would ever bide by me, ye said.
    STRENGTH: Yea, I have you far enough conveyed.
    Ye be old enough, I understand,
    Your pilgrimage to take on hand;
    I repent me that I hither came.
820 EVERYMAN: Strength, you to displease I am to blame;
    Yet promise is debt, this ye well wot.
    STRENGTH: In faith, I care not.
    Thou art but a fool to complain;
    You spend your speech and waste your brain.
825 Go thrust thee into the ground!   (Exit Strength.)
    EVERYMAN: I had wend surer I should you have
        found.
    He that trusteth in his Strength
    She him deceiveth at the length.
    Both Strength and Beauty forsaketh me;
830 Yet they promised me fair and lovingly.
    DISCRETION: Everyman, I will after Strength be
        gone;
    As for me, I will leave you alone.
    EVERYMAN: Why, Discretion, will ye forsake me?
    DISCRETION: Yea, in faith, I will go from thee,
835 For when Strength goeth before
    I follow after evermore.
    EVERYMAN: Yet, I pray thee, for the love of the Trinity,
    Look in my grave once piteously.
    DISCRETION: Nay, so nigh will I not come;
840 Farewell, every one!   (Exit Discretion.)
    EVERYMAN: O, all thing faileth, save God alone—
    Beauty, Strength, and Discretion;
    For when Death bloweth his blast,
    They all run from me full fast.
845 FIVE WITS: Everyman, my leave now of thee I take;
    I will follow the other, for here I thee forsake.
    EVERYMAN: Alas, then may I wail and weep,
    For I took you for my best friend.
    FIVE WITS: I will no longer thee keep;
850 Now farewell, and there an end.   (Exit Five Wits.)
    EVERYMAN: O Jesu, help! All hath forsaken me.
    GOOD DEEDS: Nay, Everyman; I will bide with thee.
    I will not forsake thee indeed;
    Thou shalt find me a good friend at need.
    EVERYMAN: Gramercy, Good Deeds! Now may I true
855   friends see.
    They have forsaken me, every one;

I loved them better than my Good Deeds alone.
    Knowledge, will ye forsake me also?
    KNOWLEDGE: Yea, Everyman, when ye to Death shall go;
    But not yet, for no manner of danger.   860
    EVERYMAN: Gramercy, Knowledge, with all my heart.
    KNOWLEDGE: Nay, yet I will not from hence depart
    Till I see where ye shall become.
    EVERYMAN: Methink, alas, that I must be gone
    To make my reckoning and my debts pay,   865
    For I see my time is nigh spent away.
    Take example, all ye that this do hear or see,
    How they that I loved best do forsake me,
    Except my Good Deeds that bideth truly.
    GOOD DEEDS: All earthly things is but vanity: 870
    Beauty, Strength, and Discretion do man forsake,
    Foolish friends, and kinsmen, that fair spake—
    All fleeth save Good Deeds, and that am I.
    EVERYMAN: Have mercy on me, God most mighty;
    And stand by me, thou mother and maid, holy
        Mary.   875
    GOOD DEEDS: Fear not; I will speak for thee.
    EVERYMAN: Here I cry God mercy.
    GOOD DEEDS: Short our end, and minish our pain;
    Let us go and never come again.
    EVERYMAN: Into thy hands, Lord, my soul I
        commend;   880
    Receive it, Lord, that it be not lost.
    As thou me boughtest, so me defend,
    And save me from the fiend's boast,
    That I may appear with that blessed host
    That shall be saved at the day of doom.   885
    In manus tuas, of mights most
    For ever, commendo spiritum meum.°

(He sinks into his grave.)

KNOWLEDGE: Now hath he suffered that we all shall
        endure;
    The Good Deeds shall make all sure.
    Now hath he made ending;   890
    Methinketh that I hear angels sing,
    And make great joy and melody
    Where Everyman's soul received shall be.
    ANGEL: Come, excellent elect spouse, to Jesu!
    Hereabove thou shalt go   895
    Because of thy singular virtue.
    Now the soul is taken the body fro,
    Thy reckoning is crystal-clear.
    Now shalt thou into the heavenly sphere,
    Unto the which all ye shall come   900
    That liveth well before the day of doom.

(Enter Doctor.)

DOCTOR: This moral men may have in mind.
    Ye hearers, take it of worth, old and young,
    And forsake Pride, for he deceiveth you in the end;

809. liketh: Pleases.   814. brast: Break.

886–887. In manus tuas . . . commendo spiritum meum: Into your hands, most mighty One for ever, I commend my spirit.

905 And remember Beauty, Five Wits, Strength, and
        Discretion,
    They all at the last do every man forsake,
    Save his Good Deeds there doth he take.
    But beware, for and they be small
    Before God, he hath no help at all;
910 None excuse may be there for every man.
    Alas, how shall he do then?
    For after death amends may no man make,
    For then mercy and pity doth him forsake.
    If his reckoning be not clear when he doth come,

God will say: "*Ite, maledicti, in ignem eternum.*"°   915
And he that hath his account whole and sound,
High in heaven he shall be crowned;
Unto which place God bring us all thither,
That we may live body and soul together.
Thereto help the Trinity!   920
Amen, say ye, for saint charity.

Thus endeth this moral play of Everyman.

915: "*Ite maledicti, in ignem eternum*": Depart, ye cursed, into everlasting fire.

Renaissance Drama

The period following the Middle Ages in Europe, from about the fourteenth to the seventeenth centuries, is known as the *Renaissance,* a term meaning "rebirth." In this period, a shift away from medieval values and culture was motivated by a revival of classical learning; advances in physics, astronomy, and the biological sciences; exploration of the "New World" of the Americas; and political and economic developments. This shift was not abrupt, however; it was gradual, like a thaw. It began in the south, in Italy, late in the fourteenth century and moved northward through the activities of scholars, travelers, performers, and writers, until it reached England sometime late in the fifteenth century.

The Renaissance built on medieval culture and at the same time developed a secular understanding of the individual in society that eventually transformed this culture, long dominated by the Roman Catholic Church in many spheres—artistic, intellectual, political, as well as spiritual. The transformation was influenced by the work of great writers, scholars, philosophers, and scientists such as Desiderius Erasmus (1466?–1536), Niccolò Machiavelli (1469–1527), Nicolaus Copernicus (1473–1543), Francis Bacon (1561–1626), and Galileo Galilei (1564–1642). In addition, the rise in power of the guilds and the increase in wealth of the successful Italian trading states, which produced large and influential families in cities such as Florence, Venice, Milan, and Genoa, contributed to the erosion of the Church's dominance.

Italian scholars, following classical models, began in the last decades of the fourteenth century to center their studies on human achievements. Such studies, known as the humanities, became the chief concern of the most innovative thinkers of the day. Their interests were well served by the rediscovery of ancient Greek philosophical and scientific texts. Although ancient texts had been preserved in monasteries for centuries, knowledge of them was restricted. A new demand for classical texts, fed by the humanists' focus on ancient models as the source of wisdom and by their return to a liberal arts curriculum established by the Greeks, led to the wide dissemination of the works of Plato, Aristotle, Cicero, and important Greek dramatists during the Renaissance. The achievement of the ancients was an inspiration to Renaissance writers and reaffirmed their conviction that a study of the humanities was the key to transforming the old medieval attitudes into a new, dynamic worldview.

The Italian Theater

Most medieval Italian theater depended on portable stages, but it was clear in the last decades of the fourteenth century that to present the newly rediscovered Roman or Greek plays, something more closely resembling the original Greek theater would be necessary. Fortunately, *The Ten Books of Architecture* (written c. 16–13 BCE) of the great Roman architect Vitruvius was rediscovered in a manuscript in the monastery of St. Gall in Switzerland. It included detailed plans for the Greek-inspired Roman theater.

Using Vitruvius's designs, the Italians began building stages that consisted of raised platforms with a **frons scaena**, the flat front wall used in the Roman theater. The earliest Italian woodcuts show the stages to be relatively simple, with pillars supporting a roof or cover. Curtains stretched between the pillars permitted the actors to enter and exit. Usually, three "doors," with a name over each, indicated the houses of specific characters.

The study of Roman architecture eventually produced, in 1584, one of the wonders of the Renaissance, the Olympic Theatre (Teatro Olimpico) in Vicenza, designed by the great Renaissance architect Andrea Palladio (1508–1580), whose interpretation of Roman architecture was so compelling that it influenced architecture all over the world (Figure 9). The Olympic Theatre, which has been preserved and is still used for performances, has an orchestra, a semicircular seating area, and a multistory frons scaena. It also has several vistas of streets constructed in three-dimensional forced perspective running backward from the frons scaena.

The Olympic Theatre was built with an essentially conservative design that worked well for Roman plays but not for Renaissance plays. It did not inspire new theater designs. In newer theaters, Italian plays had begun to use scenery and painted backdrops that could be changed to suggest a change in location of the action. Carefully painted backdrops were also effective in increasing illusion: one backdrop could immediately locate an action on a city street, and another could help shift the audience imaginatively to a woodland scene. These innovations proved difficult to implement in the Olympic Theatre.

The theory of vanishing-point perspective, developed by the architect Filippo Brunelleschi (1377–1446) and published by Leon Battista Alberti in *On Painting* in 1435, helped revolutionize the design of flat theatrical backdrops. Earlier Renaissance painters had had no way to establish a firm sense of perspective on a flat surface, so all three-dimensional objects appeared flat; all space in a landscape or cityscape seemed shortened and unreal. The use of a single vanishing point—in which lines were lightly drawn from the edges of the canvas (or theatrical backdrop) so that they met in a single point in the center—made it possible to show buildings, trees, and figures in their proper proportion to one another (Figure 10). For the first time, Renaissance painters could achieve lifelike illusions on a flat surface. It was possible to use three-dimensional scenery in the Olympic Theatre—as well as some others—at this time, and the illusion of reality was thus intensified.

The designer Sebastiano Serlio (1475–1554) used the vanishing-point technique, intensified by receding lines of tiles in the floor and on the painted backdrop. Serlio established all-purpose settings for comedy, tragedy, and satire. The rigidity of the backdrops for comedy and tragedy—both used a piazza, a small town square, ringed by stone buildings—restricted their use. But the setting for satire was rustic: trees, bushes, a couple of cottages. Until the nineteenth century, European theaters were equipped with sets of backdrops and wingpieces derived from Serlio's designs.

Figure 9. Designed by Andrea Palladio, the Teatro Olimpico (begun 1579) in Vicenza, Italy, was the first indoor theater of the Renaissance. The scaena's openings produced an illusion of depth.

The most important and long-lasting development of Italian theater design in the mid-sixteenth century was the **proscenium arch**, a "frame" that surrounds the stage, permitting the audience to look in on the scene, whether in a room or in a town square. The arch lent a finished touch to the theater, separating the action from the audience and distancing the actors. The proscenium arch is common in theaters today.

Commedia dell'Arte

Renaissance Italy had two traditions of theater. *Commedia erudita* was learned, almost scholarly, in its interests in Roman staging and Roman plays. **Commedia dell'arte** was less reverent, more slapstick, and generally more popular. It is difficult, however, to say which had more influence on literature over the years. Each made its contribution.

In terms of acting and storytelling, the influence of the commedia dell'arte is almost unparalleled. The term means "comedy performed by professionals." The actors usually had grown up in performing families that made their living touring the countryside, performing at fairs and on feast days. From the early Renaissance through the eighteenth century, the commedia dell'arte entertained all of Europe and influenced comic theater in every nation.

The essence of commedia dell'arte was improvised scripts. A general narrative outline served as a basis, but the speeches were improvised to a degree (with some reliance on set elements and on experience with performing the same role many times). The principal characters were types who soon became familiar all over Europe: Pantalone, the often magisterial but miserly old man, and Arlecchino (Harlequin), the cunning clown. Pulcinella, the Punch of Punch and Judy, and Columbina, the innocent *zanni* (servant characters), began as clowns. They joined a host of other **stock characters** such as pedantic lawyers, a braggart captain, and a serving maid. Certain versions of general characters—such as Arlecchino, who began as a simple *zanno*—became famous and were copied in many countries. When Volpone calls Mosca a "zany" near the end of Ben Jonson's *Volpone,* he reminds his audience that his characters are indebted to the *zanni* in commedia dell'arte. Knowing who the characters were even before the play began was a convenience that Renaissance audiences enjoyed.

Figure 10. Perspective setting designed by Baldassare Peruzzi (1481–1536).

The youthful lovers in the commedia did not require masks, but the old men, the *zanni*, and other characters all had masks that identified them and made them look, to modern eyes, rather grotesque. These masks survive today in the carnival, in Venice, where the commedia began. Stock characters thrive in popular comedies everywhere. Molière and, much later, Bernard Shaw depended on them. One of comedy's greatest sources of energy lies in the delight that audiences have always taken in stock characters. Today hardly a situation comedy on television could survive without them.

The staging of commedia dell'arte was simple. The performances often took place in open air, but sometimes indoors in a more formal theatrical setting. Sometimes performers dispensed with the stage altogether and worked in marketplaces. Their scenarios were farcical crowd pleasers filled with buffoonery. They were based on the **burla** and the **lazzo**. The *burla* was the general plot for any given performance. *Lazzi* were comic routines something like Abbott and Costello's "Who's on First?" skit. Abbott and Costello developed their routine for burlesque, a form of comedy popular in the first half of the twentieth century centering on broad gags, routines, and running jokes. *Lazzi* were carefully planned to seem to be spontaneous interruptions of the action.

Elizabethan Drama

The reign of Queen Elizabeth I (1558–1603) is known as the Elizabethan Age in England—a period of discovery and prosperity as well as a period of great achievement in the arts, especially drama. Sir Francis Drake and Sir Walter Raleigh ventured across the Atlantic Ocean to the "New World," and England secured its economic future by defeating the invasion attempt of the Spanish Armada in 1588. England had become Protestant in the 1530s—one reason Catholic Spain believed it needed to subdue the nation.

Elizabethan England, especially after the defeat of the Armada, produced one of the great ages of drama, rivaling the great age of Greece. During this period, playwrights such as Thomas Kyd (1558–1594), Christopher Marlowe (1564–1593), William Shakespeare (1564–1616), Ben Jonson (1572–1637), John Marston (1576–1634), John Fletcher (1579–1625), John Webster (1580?–1625?), Thomas Middleton (1580?–1627), and John Ford (1586?–c. 1639) drew crowds by the thousands.

That the Elizabethans enjoyed plays with a moral basis is plain from the fact that so much of the great drama of the late sixteenth century and early seventeenth century is moral in character. Still, early Elizabethan plays were less obviously moralistic than the then-popular morality plays. They did not aim specifically to teach a moral lesson, although there are many lessons to be learned from Shakespeare and his contemporaries.

During Shakespeare's youth, wandering players put on a number of plays from **repertory**, their stock of perhaps a dozen current plays they could perform. How many players there were and what their source of plays was we do not know. Much of what we know comes directly from *Hamlet* and the appearance of the players who perform Hamlet's "Mouse-trap." What we learn there tells us that dramatic styles had developed in the English countryside and that theater was thriving.

The Elizabethan Theater

The design of the Elizabethan theater is a matter of some speculation. Many of the plays popular before the theaters were built were performed in a square inn yard, with a balcony above. Audience members looked out their windows or stood in the yard. One location of the earliest English drama is the Inns of Court, essentially a college for law students in London, where students staged plays. The audience there would have been learned, bright, and imaginative. Indeed, the first English tragedy, *Gorboduc,* by Thomas Sackville and Thomas Norton, was played indoors at the Inner Temple, one of the Inns of Court, in 1562, before Marlowe and Shakespeare were born.

The early theaters were often octagonal or circular, like the bear pits in which bears, tied to stakes, were baited by dogs for the amusement of the audience. The stage was raised about five feet from the ground, with levels of seating in several galleries. Approximately half the area over the stage was roofed and contained machinery to lower actors from the "heavens"; it was painted blue with stars to simulate the sky. Some stages were approximately twenty-five by forty feet. Doors or curtained openings at the back of the stage served for entrances and exits, and at the back of the stage was a special room for costume changes. The stage may have contained a section that was normally curtained but that opened to reveal an interior, such as a bedroom. The existence of this feature is, however, in considerable dispute.

Although professional players' groups had long been licensed to perform in France and Italy, until the 1570s professional actors—those who had no other trade—did not enjoy favor in England. Such people could be arrested for vagrancy. The law, however, changed, and actors with royal patronage were permitted to perform. The history of theater changed, too. In 1576, James Burbage (d. 1597) built the first building made specially for plays in England, called simply The Theatre.

Soon there were other theaters: the Swan, the Globe (Figure 11), the Rose, the Fortune, the Hope. The Globe was large enough to accommodate two to three thousand people. Because these theaters were open-air, they could not be used in winter, but all were extraordinarily successful. Shakespeare, who was part owner of the Globe and, later, of the second indoor Blackfriars Theatre, received money from admission fees and from his role as chief playwright. He became rich enough to retire in splendid style to Stratford, his hometown. Few other Elizabethan actors and playwrights had as much of a financial stake in their work as did Shakespeare.

The Elizabethan Actor

In the early 1500s, professional companies roamed the countryside with, usually, four actors and a boy who could play the female roles. They may have been accompanied by musicians. They found work where they could, and sometimes they stirred up controversy and were prevented from performing. Numerous laws enacted to restrict them were rarely enforced. Queen Elizabeth issued a license for a professional company to James Burbage in 1576, the year he built the first theater in England. Burbage's son, Richard Burbage (1567–1619), who was born in Stratford-on-Avon (like Shakespeare, his partner in the theater), became one of the most distinguished actors of the age. He played all the important tragic roles in Shakespeare's plays. By the time the Globe Theatre was built in 1599, their company, The Chamberlain's Men, included some of the

Figure 11. A conjectural reconstruction of the (second) Globe Theatre, 1614–1644.

AA	Main entrances to auditorium		L	Backing painted with clouds. A shutter is here shown
B	Yard for standing spectators			open to allow a god's throne to travel forward.
CC	Entrances to lowest gallery			(c.f. "Cymbeline," Act V sc. IV)
DD	Entrances to staircase leading to upper galleries		M	The throne about to descend to the stage
EE	"Gentlemen's Rooms"		N	Backstage area (or "Tiring-house")
F	The stage		O	Wardrobe and dressing-rooms
G	The stage trap (leading from the "Hell" beneath the		P	Spectator galleries
	stage)		Q	"Fly" gallery in the Heavens
H	Curtained space for "discovery" scenes		R	Playhouse flag (reached from top landing of staircase,
J	Upper stage			and raised to denote performance days)
K	The "Heavens." (This area was probably covered with a			
	stretched canopy that was painted to represent the sky.)			

most acclaimed actors of the day. One of them, Will Kempe (fl. 1600), was the most noted comic actor of the age (Figure 12). He was both a gifted clown and a brilliant dancer. However, as popular as he was with the audience, he left the company suddenly for reasons still unknown and acted elsewhere. His great roles—the Fool in *King Lear,* the first grave digger in *Hamlet,* and Dogberry in *Much Ado About Nothing*—were filled by another actor, Robert Armin (1568–1615), whose reputation grew as large as Kempe's.

Figure 12. William Kempe, a principal comic actor in Shakespeare's earlier plays, is shown dancing next to a musician.

The popularity of actors such as Burbage, Kempe, and Armin indicates how powerful and far-reaching the stage was in Elizabethan England. Despite their successes, actors were still regarded as somewhat disreputable, and stories were told of actors disguised as royalty stopping in a tavern for a drink and fooling the populace, who grew surly at such tricks.

The contemporary styles of acting were probably developed by wandering players throughout the early and mid-sixteenth century—and perhaps even earlier. In *Hamlet,* Shakespeare introduces a group of roaming players and offers us a sample of their high-style formal dialogue, which contrasts sharply with Shakespeare's dialogue. Hamlet critiques and instructs the players, whose style is overdone. In the open-air theaters, this style of acting seems to have evolved into a declamatory mode, in which the actor stands and makes his voice heard throughout the large and sometimes noisy audience. The style Hamlet critiques is probably one that he saw on stages in London. Many of the Elizabethan actors played to the audience as much as they related to each other, a trait that seems to have developed in response to the structure of the stage, with the audience on three sides and with some notables actually sitting on the stage itself. In contrast to many theaters, the Globe Theatre reportedly permitted actors to speak more naturally to one another and thus to render a more realistic performance.

The Elizabethan Audience

The entrance fee to the theaters was a penny, probably the equivalent of five to ten dollars in today's money. For another penny one could take a seat, probably on a bench, in one of the upper galleries. In some theaters, more private spaces were available as well. A great many playgoers were satisfied to stand around the stage and were thus nicknamed "groundlings." Hamlet calls them the "understanding gentlemen of the ground." The more academic playwrights, Marlowe and Jonson, used the term to mean those who would not perfectly understand the significance of the plays.

Shakespeare and other Elizabethan playwrights expected a widely diverse audience—from coarse to extraordinarily polished. Shakespeare had the gift, as did Marlowe and even Jonson in his comedies, to appeal to them all. Shakespeare's plays were given in public playhouses open to everyone. They were also given in university theaters, as in the case of *Macbeth;* in indoor private theaters; and in royal command performances. Shakespeare's universality reveals itself in his appeal to many different kinds of people.

Female Characters on the English Stage

Because the theater was considered morally questionable, women were not allowed to act on English stages. Boys and young men played the parts of young female characters. No Elizabethan commentator makes any complaint about having to put up with a boy playing the part of Juliet or any of Shakespeare's other love interests, such as Desdemona in *Othello,* Ophelia in *Hamlet,* or even Queen Cleopatra. Older women, such as the Nurse in *Romeo and Juliet,* were played by some of the gifted male character actors of the company.

The Masque

The Elizabethan **masque** was a special entertainment for royalty. It was a celebration that included a rudimentary plot, a great deal of singing and dancing, and magnificent costumes and lighting. Masques were usually performed only once, often to celebrate a royal marriage. Masque audiences participated in the dances and were usually delighted by complex machinery that lifted or lowered characters from the skies. The masque was devised in Italy in the 1570s by Count Giovanni Bardi, founder of the Florentine Camerata, a Renaissance group of theatergoers sponsored by Lorenzo de' Medici.

The geniuses of the masque are generally considered to have been Ben Jonson and Inigo Jones. Jones was the architect whose Banqueting Hall at Whitehall in London, which still stands, provided the setting for most of the great masques of the seventeenth century. Jonson and Jones worked together from 1605 to 1631 to produce a remarkable body of masques that today resemble the bones of a dinosaur: what we read on the page suggests in only the vaguest way what the presentation must have been like when the masques were mounted.

Because of the expenses of costuming and staging, most masques were too costly to be produced more than once. The royal treasury was often burdened in Queen Elizabeth's time, and more so after King James took the throne in 1603. Masque costumes were impressive, the scenery astounding, and the effects amazing. In all of this, the words—which are, after all, at the center of Shakespeare's plays as well as other plays of the period—were of least account. As a result of the emphasis on the machinery and designs—the work of Inigo Jones—Jonson abandoned their partnership in a huff, complaining that he could not compete with the scene painters and carpenters.

The value placed on spectacle in the masques tells us something about the taste of the aristocrats, who enjoyed sumptuous foods, clothes, and amusements. Eventually, audiences of the public theaters hungered for spectacle, too. Their appetite was satisfied by masques inserted in the plays of Marston, Webster, and Shakespeare, whose masque in *The Tempest* is a delightful short tribute to the genre. An added device for achieving spectacular effects onstage was huge storm machines installed in the Globe. Some say that one reason Shakespeare wrote *The Tempest* was to take advantage of the new equipment.

Foreign visitors described London theaters as gorgeous places of entertainment far surpassing their own. The quest for more intense spectacle eventually led to disaster in one theater. The Globe actually burned down in 1613 because a cannon in the roof above the stage misfired and brought the house down in real flames.

The royal demand for masques was unaffected by the tragedy of the Globe fire. As Francis Bacon said in his essay "On Masques" (1625), "These things are but toys to come amongst such serious observations. But yet, since princes will have such things, it is better they should be graced with elegancy than daubed with cost. Dancing to song is a thing of great state and pleasure."

Spanish Drama

The Spanish independently developed a corral, or open theatrical space, resembling the Elizabethan inn yard, in which they produced plays. This development may have been an accident of architecture—because of the widespread need for inns and for places to store horses—that permitted the symmetry of growth of the English Elizabethan and the Spanish Golden Age theaters.

The most important playwright of the Spanish theater was Lope de Vega (1562–1635), who is said to have written twelve hundred plays (seven hundred fifty survive). Many of them are relatively brief, and some resemble the scenarios for the commedia dell'arte. A good number, though, are full-length and impressive works, such as *The Sheep Well, The King, The Greatest Alcalde,* and *The Gardener's Dog.* Pedro Calderón de la Barca (1600–1681) became, on Lope de Vega's death, the reigning Spanish playwright. His *Life Is a Dream* is performed regularly throughout the world. Calderón became a priest in 1651 and wrote religious plays that occasionally got him into trouble with the Inquisition, an agency of the Catholic Church that searched out and punished heresy. He was especially imaginative in his use of stage machinery and especially gifted in producing philosophical and poetic dialogue.

Timeline Renaissance Drama

Date	Theater	Political	Social/Cultural
1300–1400	**1377–1446:** Filippo Brunelleschi, an Italian architect, develops vanishing-point perspective, which allows theatrical scenery to be drawn in realistic proportions.		**1348–1353:** Boccaccio's *Decameron* becomes a model for Italian prose. **c. 1386–1466:** Donatello, Italian painter and major innovator in Renaissance sculpture
1400–1500	**1414:** Rediscovery of Vitruvius's *De Architectura* (16–13 BCE). After its publication in 1486, the treatise significantly influences the development of staging practices. **1495:** The Dutch morality play *Elckerlijk* by Peter Dorland van Diest, possibly the prototype for the English *Everyman*	**1494:** The Parliament of Drogheda marks the subservience of Ireland to England.	**1450:** Florence under the Medici family becomes the center of the Renaissance and humanism. **1452–1519:** Leonardo da Vinci, brilliant inventor, architect, musician, and artist **1469–1527:** Niccolò Machiavelli, who writes the political treatise *The Prince* in 1513 and the comedy *Mandragola* between 1513 and 1520 **1473–1543:** Nicolaus Copernicus, founder of modern astronomy **1496:** Henry VII commissions Venetian navigator John Cabot (1450–1498) to discover a new trade route to Asia. **1497:** Cabot reaches the east coast of North America. **1497:** Vasco da Gama (c. 1469–1524) rounds the Cape of Good Hope.
1500–1600	**1508:** Vernacular drama begins in Italy with Ludovico Ariosto's *The Casket*. **1508:** The Hôtel de Bourgogne, a permanent theater building, opens in Paris. **1512:** The word *masque* is first used to denote a poetic drama. **1550–1650:** Golden Age of Spanish drama. The two principal playwrights are Lope de Vega (1562–1635) and Pedro Calderón de la Barca (1600–1681).	**1503:** James IV of Scotland marries Margaret Tudor, daughter of Henry VII. **1517:** Martin Luther protests the sale of indulgences by posting his 95 theses on a church door in Wittenberg, Germany, thus launching the Protestant Reformation in Germany. **1534:** Henry VIII (reigned 1509–1547) breaks with the Roman Catholic Church. **1535:** Henry VIII's Act of Supremacy names him head of the Church of England. Sir Thomas More is executed after refusing to comply with the Act.	**1507:** Pope Julius II announces the sale of indulgences to finance the rebuilding of St. Peter's Basilica in Rome. **1509–1564:** John Calvin, Swiss reformer **c. 1509:** A massive slave trade begins in the New World. **1512:** Copernicus's *Commentariolus* states that the earth and other planets turn around the sun. **1514–1564:** Andreas Vesalius, Dutch physician, founder of modern anatomy **1516–1547:** Henry Howard, Earl of Surrey, English poet **1519:** Hernando Cortés enters Tenochtitlán, capital of Mexico; is received by Montezuma, the Aztec ruler; and assumes control of Mexico in 1521. **1522:** Luther translates the New Testament into German. (He translates the Old Testament in 1534.) **1547–1616:** Miguel de Cervantes, author of the novel *Don Quixote* and many plays

Date	Theater	Political	Social/Cultural
1500–1600 (continued)	**1558–1594:** Playwright Thomas Kyd, author of *The Spanish Tragedy* (c. 1587)	**1547:** Ivan IV (the Terrible) becomes czar of Russia. Moscow is destroyed by fire in the same year.	**c. 1552–1599:** Edmund Spenser, English poet, author of *Faerie Queene*
	1562: The First English tragedy, *Gorboduc,* is performed at the Inns of Court.	**1553–1558:** Reign of Mary I of England. The country returns temporarily to Catholicism.	**1554–1586:** Sir Philip Sidney, poet and soldier, author of *An Apology for Poetry*
	1564–1593: Christopher Marlowe, author of *Doctor Faustus* (c. 1588), *Tamburlaine* (1587), and *Edward the Second* (c. 1592)	**1558–1603:** Reign of Elizabeth I in England. Protestantism becomes the religion of the realm. England emerges as a world power.	**1561–1626:** Francis Bacon, English philosopher and statesman
	1564–1616: William Shakespeare		**1564–1642:** Galileo Galilei, Italian astronomer
	c. 1568: Formation of the Italian commedia dell'arte company I Gelosi	**1570:** Japan opens the port of Nagasaki to trade with the West.	**1571–1630:** Johannes Kepler, German astronomer. His laws accurately describe the revolutions of the planets around the sun.
	1572–1637: Playwright Ben Jonson, author of *Volpone* (1605) and *Bartholomew Fair* (1614)	**1572:** At the Saint Bartholomew's Day Massacre in France, thousands of Protestants are killed.	**1572–1631:** John Donne, English metaphysical poet
	1574: The Earl of Leicester's Men, the first important acting troupe in London, is licensed.		
	1575: *Gammer Gurton's Needle,* early English farce, author unknown		
	1576: James Burbage builds The Theatre for the public performance of plays. Blackfriars, London's first private theater, is also built.		
	1577: John Northbrooke publishes *A Treatise against Dicing, Dancing, Plays, and Interludes,* one of several tracts attacking the growing professional theater.		**1577:** *Chronicles of England, Scotland and Ireland* is published by Raphael Holinshed and provides Shakespeare with information for his historical plays.
	1580–1627: Playwright Thomas Middleton, author of *The Changeling* (with William Rowley, 1622) *and A Chaste Maid in Cheapside* (1630)		**1580:** Sir Francis Drake is the first Englishman to circumnavigate the globe.
	1584: Completion of the Teatro Olimpico in Vicenza, Italy, designed by architect Andrea Palladio (1508–1580)	**1587:** The Catholic Mary Stuart, queen of Scotland, is executed in England.	**1583:** Sir Philip Sidney's *Defence of Poesy* argues for literature's importance in teaching morality and virtue.
	1586?–c. 1639: Playwright John Ford, author of *'Tis Pity She's a Whore* (1633)	**1587–1649:** John Winthrop, first governor of the Massachusetts Bay Colony	
		1588: The English fleet defeats the Spanish Armada.	
		1589: Henry IV, first of the Bourbon line, becomes king of France.	

Date	Theater	Political	Social/Cultural
1500–1600 (continued)	**1593:** London theaters are closed because of a plague, opening again in 1594. **1595–1596:** Shakespeare's comedy *A Midsummer Night's Dream* **1599:** The Globe Theatre is built in London.	**1589:** Russian czar Boris Godunov separates Moscow's church from that in Constantinople. **1595:** The Dutch begin to colonize the East Indies. **1598:** The Edict of Nantes grants French Huguenots freedom of worship. (It is revoked in 1685.)	**1596–1650:** René Descartes, French philosopher, mathematician, and scientist
1600–1700	**1600–1601:** Shakespeare's *Hamlet* **1611–1612:** Shakespeare's *The Tempest* **1613:** Fire destroys the Globe Theatre. **1633:** The Oberammergau Passion play is first performed in Germany. **1642:** The English Parliament closes the theaters.	**1603:** Death of Elizabeth I. James VI of Scotland, son of Mary Stuart, becomes James I of England. **1605:** The Gunpowder Plot, an attempt to blow up the English Parliament and James I, is uncovered. **1618–1648:** The Thirty Years War is initiated by a Protestant revolt in Bohemia against the authority of the Holy Roman emperor. **1625:** Death of James I. His son becomes Charles I of England. **1630:** John Winthrop founds Boston. **1642:** Civil war begins in England. **1643:** Louis XIV becomes king of France at age four. **1649:** Charles I is beheaded in England, beginning the Commonwealth and Protectorate. **1648:** The Treaty of Westphalia ends the Thirty Years War.	**1600:** Dutch opticians invent the telescope. **1602:** The Dutch East India Company is established to trade with the Far East. **1606–1669:** Rembrandt van Rijn, greatest master of the Dutch school of painting **1607:** Jamestown, Virginia, the first permanent settlement across the Atlantic, is founded. **1608–1674:** John Milton, English poet, author of *Paradise Lost* **1611:** The King James Bible is published. **1619:** The first slaves from Africa arrive in Virginia. **1620:** The Pilgrims land at Plymouth Rock, Massachusetts. **1626:** Peter Minuit purchases Manhattan Island from native Indian chiefs. **1632–1704:** John Locke, English philosopher, founder of empiricism

William Shakespeare

Despite the fact that Shakespeare wrote some thirty-seven plays, owned part of his theatrical company, acted in plays, and retired a relatively wealthy man in the city of his birth, there is much we do not know about him. His father was a glovemaker with pretensions to being a gentleman; Shakespeare himself had his coat of arms placed on his home, New Place, purchased in part because it was one of the grandest buildings in Stratford. Church records indicate that he was born in April 1564 and died in April 1616, after having been retired from the stage for two or three years. We know that he married Anne Hathaway in 1582, when he was eighteen and she twenty-six; that he had a daughter Susanna and twins, Judith and Hamnet; and that Hamnet, his only son, died at age eleven. Shakespeare has no direct descendants today.

We know very little about his education. We assume that he went to the local grammar school, since as the son of a burgess he was eligible to attend at no cost. If he did so, he would have received a very strong education based on

This engraving of William Shakespeare by Martin Droeshout appeared in the First Folio Edition, a collection of his plays published in 1623, seven years after his death, by two of his fellow actors.

rhetoric, logic, and classical literature. He would have been exposed to the comedies of Plautus, the tragedies of Seneca, and the poetry of Virgil, Ovid, and a host of other, lesser writers.

A rumor has persisted that he spent some time as a Latin teacher. No evidence exists to suggest that Shakespeare went to a university, although his general learning and knowledge are so extraordinary and broad that generations of scholars have speculated that he may have also gone to the Inns of Court to study law. This cannot be proved, though; thus, some people claim that another person, with considerable university education, must have written his plays. However, no one in the Elizabethan theater had an education of the sort often proposed for Shakespeare. Marlowe and Ben Jonson were the most learned of Elizabethan playwrights, but their work is quite different in character and feeling from that of Shakespeare.

"He was not of an age, but for all time."

–Ben Jonson

One recent theory about Shakespeare's early years suggests that before going to London to work in theater, he belonged to a wandering company of actors much like those who appear in *Hamlet*. It is an ingenious theory and has much to recommend it, including the fact that it would explain how Shakespeare could take the spotlight so quickly as to arouse the anger of more experienced London writers.

Shakespeare did not begin his career writing for the stage but, in the more conventional approach for the age, as a poet. He sought the support of an aristocratic patron, the earl of Southampton. Like many wealthy and polished young courtiers, Southampton felt it a pleasant ornament to sponsor a poet whose works would be dedicated to him. Shakespeare wrote sonnets apparently with Southampton in mind, and, hoping for preferment, the long narrative poems *Venus and Adonis, The Rape of Lucrece,* and *The Phoenix and the Turtle.* However, Southampton eventually decided to become the patron of another poet, John Florio, an Italian who had translated Michel de Montaigne's *Essays.*

Shakespeare's response was to turn to the stage. His first plays were a considerable success: *King Henry VI* in three parts—three full-length plays. Satisfying London's taste for plays that told the history of England's tangled political past, Shakespeare won considerable renown with a lengthy series of plays ranging from *Richard II* through the two parts of *King Henry IV* to *Henry V.* Audiences were delighted; competing playwrights envied his triumphs. Francis Meres's famous book of the period, *Palladis Tamia: Wit's Treasury,* cites Shakespeare as a modern Plautus and Seneca, the best in both comedy and tragedy. Meres says that by 1598 Shakespeare was known for a dozen plays. That his success was firm by this time is demonstrated by his having purchased his large house, New Place, in Stratford in 1597. He could not have done this without financial security.

In the next few years, Shakespeare made a number of interesting purchases of property in Stratford; he also made deals with his own theater company to secure the rights to perform in London. These arrangements produced legal records that give us some of the clearest information we have concerning Shakespeare's activities during this period. His company was called the Lord Chamberlain's Men while Queen Elizabeth was alive but was renamed the King's Men by King James in the spring of 1603, less than two months after Elizabeth died. As the King's Men, Shakespeare's company had considerable

For links to resources about Shakespeare, click on *AuthorLinks* at bedfordstmartins.com/jacobus.

power and success. Its audience sometimes included King James, as for the first performance of *Macbeth*.

Shakespeare was successful as a writer of histories, comedies, and tragedies. He also wrote in another genre, known as romance. These plays share elements with both comedies and tragedies, and they often depend on supernatural or improbable elements. *Cymbeline, The Winter's Tale,* and *The Tempest* are the best known of Shakespeare's romances. They are late works and have a fascinating complexity.

When Shakespeare died on April 23, 1616, he was buried as a gentleman in the church in which he had been baptized in Stratford-upon-Avon. His will left most of his money and possessions to his two daughters, Judith and Susanna.

Hamlet

Hamlet (1600–1601), Shakespeare's boldest, most profound play, is a landmark in the poet's work. It coincides with the new century and the uncertainties of the last years of the old regime, which ended with the death of Queen Elizabeth in 1603. Until the very moment of her death, the succession was in doubt, but at her death she indicated that her cousin James of Scotland would take the throne. The new age was in many ways more complicated, more ambiguous, and more democratic than the old. It was also more dangerous because it was more uncertain.

Hamlet returns to a Denmark and a court that he hardly recognizes, to a mother newly wed to his uncle and in many ways not the woman he remembers, and, finally, to a ghostly father who will not rest until the crimes against him have been avenged. Like Marlowe's Faustus, Hamlet had been a scholar at the University of Wittenberg, where he presumably had studied theology and therefore acquired a special knowledge of the world of the spirits. Perhaps he had studied medicine and law as well. He gives evidence of knowing literature and having a taste for theater, and he is a ready hand with weapons when necessary.

Hamlet is also a melancholic. To the Elizabethan, *melancholic* did not mean depressed, although Hamlet dresses in black and still mourns for his father, even against the wishes of his uncle. The melancholic, rather, was introspective, thoughtful, perhaps world-weary, and possibly a touch sardonic. Above all things, he was an intellectual, a person of wide-ranging knowledge and intelligence, a reliable commentator with a probing mind.

Hamlet's broad intelligence and the penetrating introspection revealed in his soliloquies, such as his famous "To be, or not to be" meditation on suicide, make him a character with more psychological dimension, more "soul," than many people we know in life. In this sense the play is thoroughly modern; it satisfies our modern need to know the interior lives of characters who engage us onstage. Hamlet's range of feeling, his range of felt and expressed emotion, is impressive to any audience.

For a Drama in Depth tutorial on *Hamlet,* click on *VirtualLit Drama Tutorials* at bedfordstmartins.com/jacobus.

Hamlet is a revenge tragedy, a type of play that was especially appealing to the Elizabethans. Thomas Kyd's *The Spanish Tragedy* and John Marston's *Antonio's Revenge* are two examples of successful Elizabethan revenge tragedies. Shakespeare had written an earlier play that could be termed a revenge tragedy, *Titus Andronicus,* in 1594. Below are some characteristic elements of the revenge tragedy.

The revenge of a relative's murder or rape

The revenge of a father by a son, or vice versa

The appearance of a ghost

The hesitancy or delay of the hero

Tricks or devices to achieve revenge

The use of real or pretended insanity

Suicide

Political intrigue in a court

An able, scheming villain who is a ruler above the law

Philosophical soliloquies

Sensational use of horror (murder and gore onstage)

All these elements are present in *Hamlet.* But the play has other important qualities as well. The minor characters are developed in unexpected ways. Ophelia, the innocent, loving woman, becomes a touching figure in her own right. Unable to understand the nature of evil in the Danish court and driven to insanity by Hamlet's rejection of her and by her father's murder, she permits herself to sink to a watery death in a stream. Audiences are moved by her songs, her insane ramblings, and her devotion to her father as well as to Hamlet.

Characters such as Gertrude, Hamlet's mother, reveal a richness of psychology that sometimes startles us. Polonius, Ophelia's father, is virtually a stock character—the old, foolish philosopher—but he takes on special significance when he urges Ophelia to spy for him and when he ultimately dies at the hand of Hamlet. As Hamlet says, it was an unnecessary death for a "wretched, rash, intruding fool." But Polonius's son, Laertes, loved his father, and when Laertes returns grief-stricken, he does not hesitate a moment to get his revenge.

Hamlet's hesitancy is linked with his reputation as a melancholic. Because he thinks things through so deeply, he does not act instantly, as does Laertes. Even when the ghost reveals himself as his father and tells him that he has been murdered and must be avenged, Hamlet fears that the apparition might be a dangerous fakery of the devil to lure him to murder.

But Hamlet shows that he can act swiftly—indeed, rashly. His killing of Polonius is a rash act. He thinks the man behind the tapestry in his mother's bedroom is his uncle, since no other man but her husband has any right to be there. When Hamlet is sent to England with Rosencrantz and Guildenstern, he quickly senses a plot, undoes it, leaps aboard a pirate ship, and negotiates his way home with alacrity. This is not the behavior of a man who cannot act. In the graveyard scene, he acts just as impulsively as Laertes would when he leaps into Ophelia's grave.

Hamlet's talents exhibited in his welcoming of the players in act II show him to be an experienced theatergoer, one with some skills onstage. He is also an expert writer; his additions to *The Murder of Gonzago* convert that imaginary play into a "mousetrap" baited to catch the murderer of his father. In early Renaissance paintings, the mousetrap is a symbol for Jesus Christ, who catches the devil. The allusion would not have been lost on the Elizabethan audience, who would have seen Hamlet's psychological approach as quite reasonable.

Emotions are of great importance to Hamlet. He feels deeply and he watches others to see what their feelings are. He knows that their demeanor may not reveal them as they are, so he must be a careful student of behavior. As he tells his mother, "I know not 'seems.'" What seems is only what is apparent; his procedure is always to penetrate the surfaces of things to know their reality, which is why he uses drama as an instrument to penetrate psychological surfaces.

Hamlet in Performance

Richard Burbage played Hamlet in its original production, which was probably in 1601 but may have been in 1600. He continued playing the part for the rest of his life. *Hamlet* was staged on an English ship off the coast of Africa in 1607. The first American production was in 1759. When one thinks of productions of the play, one thinks of the great actors who played the role. Their names read like a *Who's Who* of acting: David Garrick (1717–1779), Edmund Kean (1789–1833), William Charles Macready (1793–1873), and Sir Henry Irving (1838–1905) were all identified with the role.

In the twentieth century, the two towering Hamlets were John Gielgud and Laurence Olivier, who both acted for the Old Vic Theatre. To interpret the part, Olivier studied psychoanalyst Ernest Jones's essay on Hamlet's Oedipus complex. Jones was a disciple of Freud, who discussed Hamlet in his *Interpretation of Dreams*. Paul Scofield, in Peter Brook's 1955 production, found the part so challenging that he said playing it "feels like trespassing." Since the mid-1950s, Christopher Plummer, Derek Jacobi, and Jonathan Pryce have played the part to acclaim, both on stage and in films. Richard Burton played Hamlet in New York in 1964. Michael Pennington's version for the Royal Shakespeare Company's 1980 production (see photos on p. 194) was well received by both critics and audiences. Pennington believed that the part tested not only one's skill but also one's character. He said, "When things go well you could do three performances a day and still be the last to leave the party, and at other times the part shakes you like a rat."

The number of major productions in the 1980s alone was astonishing: Christopher Walken for the American Shakespeare Festival in Stratford, Connecticut (1982); Roger Rees for the Royal Shakespeare Company in Stratford, England (1984); Kevin Kline for the New York Shakespeare Festival (1986); Ingmar Bergman's acclaimed production in Swedish in Sweden and New York (1988); Daniel Day-Lewis for the National Theatre in London (1989); and Austin Pendleton for the Riverside Shakespeare Company in New York (1989).

Franco Zeffirelli cast Mel Gibson in his 1990 film, which presents a credible Hamlet capable of deep emotional outburst. The setting of the film is lavish, and the interaction between Hamlet and Gertrude has a special psychological valence. *Hamlet* had a banner year in 1995, when Liam Neeson played the

Danish prince in London and New York to considerable acclaim. That production was marked by a careful deemphasis of the great soliloquies. Ralph Fiennes, in the wake of a film success in *Schindler's List*, played Hamlet in Edwardian clothes on Broadway, using madness as "a way of acting out." Keanu Reeves, another film actor, performed the part at the Royal Manitoba Theatre Centre in Winnipeg, Canada. One critic said of Reeves's performance, "His hairstyle changed with his moods." Robert Wilson, known for massive semioperatic productions, played entirely alone, in a production called *Hamlet: A Monologue* that premiered in Houston. In this production, Hamlet, on his deathbed, relives his story in flashbacks; he provides critical speeches of other characters himself. Among his efforts at Shakespeare, Kenneth Branagh took on the title role in a lavish production of *Hamlet* in 1996.

Hamlet has been the dream role not only of great actors but of great actresses as well. Sarah Bernhardt played Hamlet in the late nineteenth century, and Eva Le Gallienne, Siobhan McKenna, and Judith Anderson took on the part in the twentieth century. *Hamlet* has also given rise to numerous spin-offs, the best of which is Tom Stoppard's *Rosencrantz and Guildenstern Are Dead* (1967). Heiner Müller's *Hamlet-machine* (1977) is a respected avant-garde version of the play. Lee Blessing's *Fortinbras* (1991) is an innovative retelling of the play from the point of view of a minor character—except that this character becomes the king. Blessing's success suggests that *Hamlet* is rich enough and inspiring enough to generate numerous further redactions and interpretations. Michael Almereyda's 2000 film version of *Hamlet* starred Ethan Hawke as Hamlet, Sam Shepard as the Ghost, Kyle MacLachlan as Claudius, and Bill Murray as Polonius. It is one of many filmed versions of the play. Today productions of *Hamlet* are being staged in most countries on every continent, from the Globe Theatre in London to the coast of Zealand in Denmark. There is no end in sight for creative interpretations of this great play.

WILLIAM SHAKESPEARE (1564–1616)

Hamlet, Prince of Denmark   c. 1600

[Dramatis Personae

CLAUDIUS, *King of Denmark*
HAMLET, *son to the late King Hamlet, and nephew to the present King*
POLONIUS, *Lord Chamberlain*
HORATIO, *friend to Hamlet*
LAERTES, *son to Polonius*

VOLTIMAND,
CORNELIUS,
ROSENCRANTZ, } *courtiers*
GUILDENSTERN,
OSRIC,
GENTLEMAN,
PRIEST, OR DOCTOR OF DIVINITY

MARCELLUS, } *officers*
BERNARDO,
FRANCISCO, *a solider*
REYNALDO, *servant to Polonius*
PLAYERS
TWO CLOWNS, *grave-diggers*
FORTINBRAS, *Prince of Norway*
CAPTAIN
ENGLISH AMBASSADORS

GERTRUDE, *Queen of Denmark, mother to Hamlet*
OPHELIA, *daughter to Polonius*

LORDS, LADIES, OFFICERS, SOLDIERS, SAILORS, MESSENGERS,
    AND OTHER ATTENDANTS
GHOST *of Hamlet's father*

Scene: Denmark.]

{ACT I • Scene I}°

(*Enter Bernardo and Francisco, two sentinels, [meeting].*)

BERNARDO: Who's there?
FRANCISCO: Nay, answer me.° Stand and unfold yourself.
BERNARDO: Long live the King!
FRANCISCO: Bernardo?
5   BERNARDO: He.
FRANCISCO: You come most carefully upon your hour.
BERNARDO: 'Tis now struck twelve. Get thee to bed,
        Francisco.
FRANCISCO: For this relief much thanks. 'Tis bitter cold,
    And I am sick at heart.
BERNARDO: Have you had quiet guard?
10   FRANCISCO: Not a mouse stirring.
BERNARDO: Well, good night.
    If you do meet Horatio and Marcellus,
    The rivals° of my watch, bid them make haste.

(*Enter Horatio and Marcellus.*)

FRANCISCO: I think I hear them. Stand, ho! Who is there?
HORATIO: Friends to this ground.
15   MARCELLUS: And liegemen to the Dane.°
FRANCISCO: Give you° good night.
MARCELLUS: O, farewell, honest soldier.
    Who hath relieved you?
FRANCISCO: Bernardo hath my place.
    Give you good night.   (*Exit Francisco.*)

Note: The text of *Hamlet* has come down to us in different
versions—such as the first quarto, the second quarto, and the
First Folio. The text used here is largely drawn from the second
quarto. Passages enclosed in square brackets are taken from
one of the other versions, in most cases the First Folio.
I, i. Location: Elsinore castle. A guard platform.   2. me: Francisco
emphasizes that *he* is the sentry currently on watch.   13. rivals:
Partners.   15. liegemen to the Dane: Men sworn to serve the
Danish king.   16. Give you: God give you.

MARCELLUS: Holla, Bernardo!
BERNARDO: Say,
    What, is Horatio there?
HORATIO: A piece of him.
BERNARDO: Welcome, Horatio. Welcome, good
        Marcellus.   20
HORATIO: What, has this thing appear'd again tonight?
BERNARDO: I have seen nothing.
MARCELLUS: Horatio says 'tis but our fantasy,
    And will not let belief take hold of him
    Touching this dreaded sight, twice seen of us.   25
    Therefore I have entreated him along
    With us to watch the minutes of this night,
    That if again this apparition come
    He may approve° our eyes and speak to it.
HORATIO: Tush, tush, 'twill not appear.
BERNARDO: Sit down awhile,   30
    And let us once again assail your ears,
    That are so fortified against our story,
    What we have two nights seen.
HORATIO: Well, sit we down,
    And let us hear Bernardo speak of this.
BERNARDO: Last night of all,   35
    When yond same star that's westward from the pole°
    Had made his° course t' illume that part of heaven
    Where now it burns, Marcellus and myself,
    The bell then beating one—

(*Enter Ghost.*)

MARCELLUS: Peace, break thee off! Look where it
        comes again!   40
BERNARDO: In the same figure, like the King that's dead.
MARCELLUS: Thou art a scholar.° Speak to it, Horatio.
BERNARDO: Looks 'a° not like the King? Mark it, Horatio.
HORATIO: Most like. It harrows me with fear and
        wonder.
BERNARDO: It would be spoke to.
MARCELLUS: Speak to it,° Horatio.   45
HORATIO: What art thou that usurp'st this time of
        night,
    Together with that fair and warlike form
    In which the majesty of buried Denmark°
    Did sometimes° march? By heaven I charge thee
        speak!
MARCELLUS: It is offended.
BERNARDO: See, it stalks away.   50
HORATIO: Stay! Speak, speak. I charge thee, speak.
                                    (*Exit Ghost.*)
MARCELLUS: 'Tis gone, and will not answer.
BERNARDO: How now, Horatio? You tremble and
        look pale.
    Is not this something more than fantasy?
    What think you on 't?   55

29. approve: Corroborate.   36. pole: Polestar.   37. his: Its.
42. scholar: One learned in Latin and able to address spirits.
43. 'a: He.   45. It . . . it: A ghost could not speak until spoken to.   48. buried Denmark: The buried king of Denmark.
49. sometimes: Formerly.

HORATIO: Before my God, I might not this believe
  Without the sensible° and true avouch
  Of mine own eyes.
MARCELLUS: Is it not like the King?
HORATIO: As thou art to thyself.
60 Such was the very armor he had on
  When he the ambitious Norway° combated.
  So frown'd he once when, in an angry parle,°
  He smote the sledded° Polacks° on the ice.
  'Tis strange.
MARCELLUS: Thus twice before, and jump° at this
65   dead hour,
  With martial stalk hath he gone by our watch.
HORATIO: In what particular thought to work I know
      not,
  But, in the gross and scope° of mine opinion,
  This bodes some strange eruption to our state.
MARCELLUS: Good now,° sit down, and tell me, he
70   that knows,
  Why this same strict and most observant watch
  So nightly toils° the subject° of the land,
  And why such daily cast° of brazen cannon,
  And foreign mart° for implements of war,
75 Why such impress° of shipwrights, whose sore task
  Does not divide the Sunday from the week.
  What might be toward,° that this sweaty haste
  Doth make the night joint-laborer with the day?
  Who is 't that can inform me?
HORATIO: That can I,
80 At least, the whisper goes so. Our last king,
  Whose image even but now appear'd to us,
  Was, as you know, by Fortinbras of Norway,
  Thereto prick'd on° by a most emulate° pride,
  Dar'd to the combat; in which our valiant
      Hamlet—
  For so this side of our known world esteem'd
85   him—
  Did slay this Fortinbras; who, by a seal'd compact,
  Well ratified by law and heraldry,
  Did forfeit, with his life, all those his lands
  Which he stood seiz'd° of, to the conqueror;
90 Against the° which a moi'ty competent°
  Was gaged° by our king, which had return'd
  To the inheritance of Fortinbras
  Had he been vanquisher, as, by the same comart°
  And carriage° of the article design'd,

His fell to Hamlet. Now, sir, young Fortinbras,   95
  Of unimproved° mettle hot and full,
  Hath in the skirts° of Norway here and there
  Shark'd up° a list of lawless resolutes°
  For food and diet° to some enterprise
  That hath a stomach° in 't, which is no other—   100
  As it doth well appear unto our state—
  But to recover of us, by strong hand
  And terms compulsatory, those foresaid lands
  So by his father lost. And this, I take it,
  Is the main motive of our preparations,   105
  The source of this our watch, and the chief head°
  Of this post-haste and romage° in the land.
BERNARDO: I think it be no other but e'en so.
  Well may it sort° that this portentous figure
  Comes armed through our watch so like the King   110
  That was and is the question of these wars.
HORATIO: A mote° it is to trouble the mind's eye.
  In the most high and palmy° state of Rome,
  A little ere the mightiest Julius fell,
  The graves stood tenantless and the sheeted° dead   115
  Did squeak and gibber in the Roman streets;
  As° stars with trains of fire and dews of blood,
  Disasters° in the sun; and the moist star°
  Upon whose influence Neptune's° empire stands°
  Was sick almost to doomsday° with eclipse.   120
  And even the like precurse° of fear'd events,
  As harbingers° preceding still° the fates
  And prologue to the omen° coming on,
  Have heaven and earth together demonstrated
  Unto our climatures° and countrymen.   125

(*Enter Ghost.*)

  But soft, behold! Lo where it comes again!
  I'll cross° it, though it blast me. Stay, illusion!
  If thou hast any sound, or use of voice,
  Speak to me!   (*It spreads his arms.*)
  If there be any good thing to be done   130
  That may to thee do ease and grace to me,
  Speak to me!
  If thou art privy to thy country's fate,
  Which, happily,° foreknowing may avoid,

---

57. **sensible:** Confirmed by the senses. 61. **Norway:** King of Norway. 62. **parle:** Parley. 63. **sledded:** Traveling on sleds. **Polacks:** Poles. 65. **jump:** Exactly. 68. **gross and scope:** General view. 70. **Good now:** An expression denoting entreaty or expostulation. 72. **toils:** Causes to toil. **subject:** Subjects. 73. **cast:** Casting. 74. **mart:** Buying and selling. 75. **impress:** Impressment, conscription. 77. **toward:** In preparation. 83. **prick'd on:** Incited. **emulate:** Ambitious. 89. **seiz'd:** Possessed. 90. **Against the:** In return for. **moi'ty competent:** Sufficient portion. 91. **gaged:** Engaged, pledged. 93. **comart:** Joint bargain (?). 94. **carriage:** Import, bearing.

96. **unimproved:** Not turned to account (?) or untested (?). 97. **skirts:** Outlying regions, outskirts. 98. **Shark'd up:** Got together in haphazard fashion. **resolutes:** Desperadoes. 99. **food and diet:** No pay but their keep. 100. **stomach:** Relish of danger. 106. **head:** Source. 107. **romage:** Bustle, commotion. 109. **sort:** Suit. 112. **mote:** Speck of dust. 113. **palmy:** Flourishing. 115. **sheeted:** Shrouded. 117. **As:** This abrupt transition suggests that matter has possibly been omitted between lines 116 and 117. 118. **Disasters:** Unfavorable signs of aspects. **moist star:** Moon, governing tides. 119. **Neptune:** God of the sea. **stands:** Depends. 120. **sick . . . doomsday:** See Matt. 24:29 and Rev. 6:12. 121. **precurse:** Heralding, foreshadowing. 122. **harbingers:** Forerunners. **still:** Continually. 123. **omen:** Calamitous event. 125. **climatures:** Regions. 127. **cross:** Meet, face directly. 134. **happily:** Haply, perchance.

135   O, speak!
      Or if thou hast uphoarded in thy life
      Extorted treasure in the womb of earth,
      For which, they say, you spirits oft walk in death,
                                              (*The cock crows.*)
      Speak of it. Stay, and speak! Stop it, Marcellus.
140   MARCELLUS: Shall I strike at it with my partisan?°
      HORATIO: Do, if it will not stand.   [*They strike at it.*]
      BERNARDO: 'Tis here!
      HORATIO: 'Tis here!
      MARCELLUS: 'Tis gone.   [*Exit Ghost.*]
      We do it wrong, being so majestical,
      To offer it the show of violence;
145   For it is, as the air, invulnerable,
      And our vain blows malicious mockery.
      BERNARDO: It was about to speak when the cock
            crew.
      HORATIO: And then it started like a guilty thing
      Upon a fearful summons. I have heard,
150   The cock, that is the trumpet to the morn,
      Doth with his lofty and shrill-sounding throat
      Awake the god of day, and, at his warning,
      Whether in sea or fire, in earth or air,
      Th' extravagant and erring° spirit hies
155   To his confine; and of the truth herein
      This present object made probation.°
      MARCELLUS: It faded on the crowing of the cock.
      Some say that ever 'gainst° that season comes
      Wherein our Savior's birth is celebrated,
160   The bird of dawning singeth all night long,
      And then, they say, no spirit dare stir abroad;
      The nights are wholesome, then no planets strike,°
      No fairy takes,° nor witch hath power to charm,
      So hallowed and so gracious° is that time.
165   HORATIO: So have I heard and do in part believe it.
      But, look, the morn, in russet mantle clad,
      Walks o'er the dew of yon high eastward hill.
      Break we our watch up, and by my advice
      Let us impart what we have seen tonight
170   Unto young Hamlet; for, upon my life,
      This spirit, dumb to us, will speak to him.
      Do you consent we shall acquaint him with it,
      As needful in our loves, fitting our duty?
      MARCELLUS: Let's do't, I pray, and I this morning know
175   Where we shall find him most conveniently.
                                              (*Exeunt.*)°

{Scene II}°

(*Flourish. Enter Claudius, King of Denmark, Gertrude the Queen, Councilors, Polonius and his son Laertes, Hamlet, cum aliis*° [*including Voltimand and Cornelius*].)

140. partisan: Long-handled spear.   **154. extravagant and erring:** Wandering. (The words have similar meanings.)   **156. probation:** Proof.   **158. 'gainst:** Just before.   **162. strike:** Exert evil influence.   **163. takes:** Bewitches.   **164. gracious:** Full of goodness.   **175.** [S.D.] *Exeunt:* Latin for "they go out." **I, ii. Location:** The castle.   [S.D.] *cum aliis:* With others.

KING: Though yet of Hamlet our dear brother's death
      The memory be green, and that it us befitted
      To bear our hearts in grief and our whole kingdom
      To be contracted in one brow of woe,
      Yet so far hath discretion fought with nature   5
      That we with wisest sorrow think on him,
      Together with remembrance of ourselves.
      Therefore our sometime sister, now our queen,
      Th' imperial jointress° to this warlike state,
      Have we, as 'twere with a defeated joy—   10
      With an auspicious and a dropping eye,
      With mirth in funeral and with dirge in marriage,
      In equal scale weighing delight and dole—
      Taken to wife. Nor have we herein barr'd
      Your better wisdoms, which have freely gone   15
      With this affair along. For all, our thanks.
      Now follows that you know° young Fortinbras,
      Holding a weak supposal° of our worth,
      Or thinking by our late dear brother's death
      Our state to be disjoint and out of frame,   20
      Colleagued with° this dream of his advantage,°
      He hath not fail'd to pester us with message
      Importing° the surrender of those lands
      Lost by his father, with all bands° of law,
      To our most valiant brother. So much for him.   25
      Now for ourself and for this time of meeting.
      Thus much the business is: we have here writ
      To Norway, uncle of young Fortinbras—
      Who, impotent and bed-rid, scarcely hears
      Of this his nephew's purpose—to suppress   30
      His° further gait° herein, in that the levies,
      The lists, and full proportions are all made
      Out of his subject;° and we here dispatch
      You, good Cornelius, and you, Voltimand,
      For bearers of this greeting to old Norway,   35
      Giving to you no further personal power
      To business with the King, more than the scope
      Of these delated° articles allow.   [*Gives a paper.*]
      Farewell, and let your haste commend your duty.
      CORNELIUS, VOLTIMAND: In that, and all things, will
            we show our duty.   40
      KING: We doubt it nothing. Heartily farewell.

                        [*Exit Voltimand and Cornelius.*]

      And now, Laertes, what's the news with you?
      You told us of some suit; what is 't, Laertes?
      You cannot speak of reason to the Dane°
      And lose your voice.° What wouldst thou beg,
            Laertes,   45

9. jointress: Woman possessed of a joint tenancy of an estate. **17. know:** Be informed (that).   **18. weak supposal:** Low estimate.   **21. Colleagued with:** Joined to, allied with.   **dream . . . advantage:** Illusory hope of success.   **23. Importing:** Pertaining to.   **24. bands:** Contracts.   **31. His:** Fortinbras's.   **gait:** Proceeding.   **31–33. in that . . . subject:** Since the levying of troops and supplies is drawn entirely from the King of Norway's own subjects.   **38. delated:** Detailed (variant of *dilated*).   **44. the Dane:** The Danish king.   **45. lose your voice:** Waste your speech.

That shall not be my offer, not thy asking?
The head is not more native° to the heart,
The hand more instrumental° to the mouth,
Than is the throne of Denmark to thy father.
What wouldst thou have, Laertes?

50 LAERTES: My dread lord,
Your leave and favor to return to France,
From whence though willingly I came to Denmark
To show my duty in your coronation,
Yet now I must confess, that duty done,
55 My thoughts and wishes bend again toward France
And bow them to your gracious leave and pardon.°
KING: Have you your father's leave? What says
    Polonius?
POLONIUS: H'ath, my lord, wrung from me my slow
    leave
By laborsome petition, and at last
60 Upon his will I seal'd my hard° consent.
I do beseech you, give him leave to go.
KING: Take thy fair hour, Laertes. Time be thine,
And thy best graces spend it at thy will!
But now, my cousin° Hamlet, and my son—
65 HAMLET: A little more than kin, and less than kind.°
KING: How is it that the clouds still hang on you?
HAMLET: Not so, my lord. I am too much in the sun.°
QUEEN: Good Hamlet, cast thy nighted color off,
And let thine eye look like a friend on Denmark.
70 Do not forever with thy veiled° lids
Seek for thy noble father in the dust.
Thou know'st 'tis common,° all that lives must die,
Passing through nature to eternity.
HAMLET: Ay, madam, it is common.
QUEEN: If it be,
75 Why seems it so particular with thee?
HAMLET: Seems, madam! Nay, it is. I know not "seems."
'Tis not alone my inky cloak, good mother,
Nor customary suits of solemn black,
Nor windy suspiration of forc'd breath,
80 No, nor the fruitful° river in the eye,
Nor the dejected havior of the visage,
Together with all forms, moods, shapes of grief,
That can denote me truly. These indeed seem,
For they are actions that a man might play.
85 But I have that within which passes show;
These but the trappings and the suits of woe.
KING: 'Tis sweet and commendable in your nature,
    Hamlet,
To give these mourning duties to your father.

But you must know your father lost a father,
That father lost, lost his, and the survivor bound   90
In filial obligation for some term
To do obsequious° sorrow. But to persever°
In obstinate condolement° is a course
Of impious stubbornness. 'Tis unmanly grief.
It shows a will most incorrect to heaven,   95
A heart unfortified, a mind impatient,
An understanding simple and unschool'd.
For what we know must be and is as common
As any the most vulgar thing to sense,°
Why should we in our peevish opposition   100
Take it to heart? Fie, 'tis a fault to heaven,
A fault against the dead, a fault to nature,
To reason most absurd, whose common theme
Is death of fathers, and who still hath cried,
From the first corse° till he that died today,   105
"This must be so." We pray you, throw to earth
This unprevailing° woe, and think of us
As of a father; for let the world take note,
You are the most immediate° to our throne,
And with no less nobility of love   110
Than that which dearest father bears his son
Do I impart toward you. For your intent
In going back to school in Wittenberg,°
It is most retrograde° to our desire,
And we beseech you, bend you° to remain   115
Here in the cheer and comfort of our eye,
Our chiefest courtier, cousin, and our son.
QUEEN: Let not thy mother lose her prayers, Hamlet.
I pray thee stay with us, go not to Wittenberg.
HAMLET: I shall in all my best obey you, madam.   120
KING: Why, 'tis a loving and a fair reply.
Be as ourself in Denmark. Madam, come.
This gentle and unforc'd accord of Hamlet
Sits smiling to my heart, in grace whereof
No jocund° health that Denmark drinks today   125
But the great cannon to the clouds shall tell,
And the King's rouse° the heaven shall bruit again,°
Respeaking earthly thunder.° Come away.

                    (*Flourish. Exeunt all but Hamlet.*)

HAMLET: O, that this too too sullied° flesh would melt,
Thaw, and resolve itself into a dew!   130
Or that the Everlasting had not fix'd
His canon° 'gainst self-slaughter! O God, God,
How weary, stale, flat, and unprofitable

---

47. **native:** Closely connected, related. 48. **instrumental:** Serviceable. 56. **leave and pardon:** Permission to depart. 60. **hard:** Reluctant. 64. **cousin:** Any kin not of the immediate family. 65. **A little ... kind:** Closer than an ordinary nephew (since I am stepson), and yet more separated in natural feeling (with pun on *kind,* meaning affectionate and natural, lawful). This line is often read as an aside, but it need not be. 67. **sun:** The sunshine of the King's royal favor (with pun on *son*). 70. **veiled:** Downcast. 72. **common:** Of universal occurrence. (But Hamlet plays on the sense of vulgar in line 74.) 80. **fruitful:** Abundant.

92. **obsequious:** Suited to obsequies or funerals. **persever:** Persevere. 93. **condolement:** Sorrowing. 99. **As ... sense:** As the most ordinary experience. 105. **corse:** Corpse. 107. **unprevailing:** Unavailing. 109. **most immediate:** Next in succession. 113. **Wittenberg:** Famous German university founded in 1502. 114. **retrograde:** Contrary. 115. **bend you:** Incline yourself. 125. **jocund:** Merry. 127. **rouse:** Draft of liquor. **bruit again:** Loudly echo. 128. **thunder:** Of trumpet and kettledrum sounded when the King drinks; see I, iv, 8–12. 129. **sullied:** Defiled. (The early quartos read *sallied,* the Folio *solid.*) 132. **canon:** Law.

Seem to me all the uses of this world!
135   Fie on 't, ah, fie! 'Tis an unweeded garden
That grows to seed. Things rank and gross in
      nature
Possess it merely.° That it should come to this!
But two months dead—nay, not so much, not two.
So excellent a king, that was to° this
140   Hyperion° to a satyr; so loving to my mother
That he might not beteem° the winds of heaven
Visit her face too roughly. Heaven and earth,
Must I remember? Why, she would hang on him
As if increase of appetite had grown
145   By what it fed on, and yet, within a month—
Let me not think on 't. Frailty, thy name is
      woman!—
A little month, or ere those shoes were old
With which she followed my poor father's body,
Like Niobe,° all tears, why she, even she—
150   O God, a beast, that wants discourse of reason,°
Would have mourn'd longer—married with my
      uncle,
My father's brother, but no more like my father
Than I to Hercules. Within a month,
Ere yet the salt of most unrighteous tears
155   Had left the flushing in her galled° eyes,
She married. O, most wicked speed, to post
With such dexterity to incestuous° sheets!
It is not nor it cannot come to good.
But break, my heart, for I must hold my tongue.

(*Enter Horatio, Marcellus, and Bernardo.*)

HORATIO: Hail to your lordship!
160   HAMLET: I am glad to see you well.
Horatio!—or I do forget myself.
HORATIO: The same, my lord, and your poor servant
      ever.
HAMLET: Sir, my good friend; I'll change° that name
      with you.
And what make° you from Wittenberg, Horatio?
165   Marcellus?
MARCELLUS: My good lord.
HAMLET: I am very glad to see you. [*To Bernardo.*]
      Good even, sir.—
But what, in faith, make you from Wittenberg?
HORATIO: A truant disposition, good my lord.
170   HAMLET: I would not hear your enemy say so,
      Nor shall you do my ear that violence

To make it truster of your own report
Against yourself. I know you are no truant.
But what is your affair in Elsinore?
We'll teach you to drink deep ere you depart.   175
HORATIO: My lord, I came to see your father's
      funeral.
HAMLET: I prithee do not mock me, fellow student;
      I think it was to see my mother's wedding.
HORATIO: Indeed, my lord, it followed hard° upon.
HAMLET: Thrift, thrift, Horatio! The funeral bak'd
      meats   180
Did coldly furnish forth the marriage tables.
Would I had met my dearest° foe in heaven
Or° ever I had seen that day, Horatio!
My father!—Methinks I see my father.
HORATIO: Where, my lord?
HAMLET: In my mind's eye, Horatio.   185
HORATIO: I saw him once. 'A° was a goodly king.
HAMLET: 'A was a man, take him for all in all,
      I shall not look upon his like again.
HORATIO: My lord, I think I saw him yesternight.
HAMLET: Saw? Who?   190
HORATIO: My lord, the King your father.
HAMLET: The King my father?
HORATIO: Season your admiration° for a while
With an attent° ear, till I may deliver,
Upon the witness of these gentlemen,
This marvel to you.
HAMLET: For God's love, let me hear!   195
HORATIO: Two nights together had these gentlemen,
Marcellus and Bernardo, on their watch,
In the dead waste and middle of the night,
Been thus encount'red. A figure like your father,
Armed at point° exactly, cap-a-pe,°   200
Appears before them, and with solemn march
Goes slow and stately by them. Thrice he walk'd
By their oppress'd and fear-surprised eyes
Within his truncheon's° length, whilst they, distill'd
Almost to jelly with the act° of fear,   205
Stand dumb and speak not to him. This to me
In dreadful secrecy impart they did,
And I with them the third night kept the watch,
Where, as they had delivered, both in time,
Form of the thing, each word made true and good,   210
The apparition comes. I knew your father;
These hands are not more like.
HAMLET: But where was this?
MARCELLUS: My lord, upon the platform where we
      watch.
HAMLET: Did you not speak to it?
HORATIO: My lord, I did,
But answer made it none. Yet once methought   215
It lifted up it° head and did address

---

137. merely: Completely.   **139. to:** In comparison to.   **140. Hyperion:** Titan sun-god, father of Helios.   **141. beteem:** Allow.   **149. Niobe:** Tantalus's daughter, Queen of Thebes, who boasted that she had more sons and daughters than Leto; for this, Apollo and Artemis, children of Leto, slew her fourteen children. She was turned by Zeus into a stone that continually dropped tears.   **150. wants . . . reason:** Lacks the faculty of reason.   **155. galled:** Irritated, inflamed.   **157. incestuous:** In Shakespeare's day, a marriage like that of Claudius, to his deceased brother's wife, was considered incestuous.   **163. change:** Exchange (i.e., the name of friend).   **164. make:** Do.

179. hard: Close.   **182. dearest:** Direst.   **183. Or:** Ere, before.   **186. 'A:** He.   **192. Season your admiration:** Restrain your astonishment.   **193. attent:** Attentive.   **200. at point:** Completely.   **cap-a-pe:** From head to foot.   **204. truncheon:** Officer's staff.   **205. act:** Action, operation.   **216. it:** Its.

Itself to motion, like as it would speak;
But even then the morning cock crew loud,
And at the sound it shrunk in haste away,
And vanish'd from our sight.

220 HAMLET: 'Tis very strange.
HORATIO: As I do live, my honor'd lord, 'tis true,
   And we did think it writ down in our duty
   To let you know of it.
HAMLET: Indeed, indeed, sirs. But this troubles me.
   Hold you the watch tonight?

225 ALL: We do, my lord.
HAMLET: Arm'd, say you?
ALL: Arm'd, my lord.
HAMLET: From top to toe?
ALL: My lord, from head to foot.
HAMLET: Then saw you not his face?

230 HORATIO: O, yes, my lord. He wore his beaver° up.
HAMLET: What, looked he frowningly?
HORATIO: A countenance more
   In sorrow than in anger.
HAMLET: Pale or red?
HORATIO: Nay, very pale.
HAMLET: And fix'd his eyes upon you?
HORATIO: Most constantly.
HAMLET: I would I had been there.

235 HORATIO: It would have much amaz'd you.
HAMLET: Very like, very like. Stay'd it long?
HORATIO: While one with moderate haste might tell°
   a hundred.
MARCELLUS, BERNARDO: Longer, longer.
HORATIO: Not when I saw 't.
HAMLET: His beard was grizzl'd,—no?

240 HORATIO: It was, as I have seen it in his life,
   A sable silver'd.°
HAMLET: I will watch tonight.
   Perchance 'twill walk again.
HORATIO: I warr'nt it will.
HAMLET: If it assume my noble father's person,
   I'll speak to it, though hell itself should gape

245 And bid me hold my peace. I pray you all,
   If you have hitherto conceal'd this sight,
   Let it be tenable° in your silence still,
   And whatsomever else shall hap tonight,
   Give it an understanding, but no tongue.

250 I will requite your loves. So, fare you well.
   Upon the platform, 'twixt eleven and twelve,
   I'll visit you.
ALL: Our duty to your honor.
HAMLET: Your loves, as mine to you. Farewell.
                          (*Exeunt [all but Hamlet].*)
   My father's spirit in arms! All is not well.
   I doubt° some foul play. Would the night were

255   come!

---

230. **beaver:** Visor on the helmet.   237. **tell:** Count.   241. **sable silver'd:** Black mixed with white.   247. **tenable:** Held tightly.   255. **doubt:** Suspect.

Till then sit still, my soul. Foul deeds will rise,
Though all the earth o'erwhelm them, to men's eyes.
                          (*Exit.*)

{Scene III}°

(*Enter Laertes and Ophelia, his sister.*)

LAERTES: My necessaries are embark'd. Farewell.
   And, sister, as the winds give benefit
   And convoy is assistant,° do not sleep
   But let me hear from you.
OPHELIA: Do you doubt that?
LAERTES: For Hamlet, and the trifling of his favor,   5
   Hold it a fashion and a toy in blood,°
   A violet in the youth of primy° nature,
   Forward,° not permanent, sweet, not lasting,
   The perfume and suppliance° of a minute—
   No more.
OPHELIA: No more but so?
LAERTES: Think it no more.   10
   For nature crescent° does not grow alone
   In thews° and bulk, but, as this temple° waxes,
   The inward service of the mind and soul
   Grows wide withal.° Perhaps he loves you now,
   And now no soil° nor cautel° doth besmirch   15
   The virtue of his will;° but you must fear,
   His greatness weigh'd,° his will is not his own.
   [For he himself is subject to his birth.]
   He may not, as unvalued persons do,
   Carve° for himself; for on his choice depends   20
   The safety and health of this whole state,
   And therefore must his choice be circumscrib'd
   Unto the voice and yielding° of that body
   Whereof he is the head. Then if he says he loves
      you,
   It fits your wisdom so far to believe it   25
   As he in his particular act and place
   May give his saying deed,° which is no further
   Than the main voice of Denmark goes withal.
   Then weigh what loss your honor may sustain
   If with too credent° ear you list° his songs,   30
   Or lose your heart, or your chaste treasure open
   To his unmaster'd importunity.
   Fear it, Ophelia, fear it, my dear sister,
   And keep you in the rear of your affection,
   Out of the shot° and danger of desire.   35

I, iii. Location: Polonius's chambers.   **3. convoy is assistant:** Means of conveyance are available.   **6. toy in blood:** Passing amorous fancy.   **7. primy:** In its prime, springtime.   **8. Forward:** Precocious.   **9. suppliance:** Supply, filler.   **11. crescent:** Growing, waxing.   **12. thews:** Bodily strength.   **temple:** Body.   **14. Grows wide withal:** Grows along with it.   **15. soil:** Blemish.   **cautel:** Deceit.   **16. will:** Desire.   **17. greatness weigh'd:** High position considered.   **20. Carve:** Choose pleasure.   **23. voice and yielding:** Assent, approval.   **27. deed:** Effect.   **30. credent:** Credulous.   **list:** Listen to.   **35. shot:** Range.

The chariest° maid is prodigal enough
If she unmask her beauty to the moon.
Virtue itself scapes not calumnious strokes.
The canker galls° the infants of the spring
40 Too oft before their buttons° be disclos'd,°
And in the morn and liquid dew° of youth
Contagious blastments° are most imminent.
Be wary then; best safety lies in fear.
Youth to itself rebels, though none else near.
45 OPHELIA: I shall the effect of this good lesson keep
As watchman to my heart. But, good my brother,
Do not, as some ungracious pastors do,
Show me the steep and thorny way to heaven,
Whiles, like a puff'd° and reckless libertine,
50 Himself the primrose path of dalliance treads,
And recks° not his own rede.°

(*Enter Polonius.*)

LAERTES: O, fear me not.
I stay too long. But here my father comes.
A double blessing is a double° grace;
Occasion° smiles upon a second leave.
POLONIUS: Yet here, Laertes? Aboard, aboard, for
55   shame!
The wind sits in the shoulder of your sail,
And you are stay'd for. There—my blessing with
    thee!
And these few precepts in thy memory
Look thou character.° Give thy thoughts no tongue
60 Nor any unproportion'd thought his° act.
Be thou familiar,° but by no means vulgar.°
Those friends thou hast, and their adoption tried,°
Grapple them to thy soul with hoops of steel,
But do not dull thy palm with entertainment
65 Of each new-hatch'd, unfledg'd courage.° Beware
Of entrance to a quarrel, but, being in,
Bear't that° th' opposed may beware of thee.
Give every man thy ear, but few thy voice;
Take each man's censure,° but reserve thy judgment.
70 Costly thy habit as thy purse can buy,
But not express'd in fancy; rich, not gaudy,
For the apparel oft proclaims the man,
And they in France of the best rank and station
Are of a most select and generous chief° in that.
75 Neither a borrower nor a lender be,
For loan oft loses both itself and friend,
And borrowing dulleth edge of husbandry.°

This above all: to thine own self be true,
And it must follow, as the night the day,
Thou canst not then be false to any man.   80
Farewell. My blessing season° this in thee!
LAERTES: Most humbly do I take my leave, my lord.
POLONIUS: The time invests° you. Go, your servants
    tend.°
LAERTES: Farewell, Ophelia, and remember well
What I have said to you.   85
OPHELIA: 'Tis in my memory lock'd,
And you yourself shall keep the key of it.
LAERTES: Farewell.   (*Exit Laertes.*)
POLONIUS: What is 't, Ophelia, he hath said to you?
OPHELIA: So please you, something touching the Lord
    Hamlet.   90
POLONIUS: Marry,° well bethought.
'Tis told me he hath very oft of late
Given private time to you, and you yourself
Have of your audience been most free and
    bounteous.
If it be so—as so 'tis put on° me,   95
And that in way of caution—I must tell you
You do not understand yourself so clearly
As it behooves my daughter and your honor.
What is between you? Give me up the truth.
OPHELIA: He hath, my lord, of late made many
    tenders°   100
Of his affection to me.
POLONIUS: Affection? Pooh! You speak like a green
    girl,
Unsifted° in such perilous circumstance.
Do you believe his tenders, as you call them?
OPHELIA: I do not know, my lord, what I should think.   105
POLONIUS: Marry, I will teach you. Think yourself a
    baby
That you have ta'en these tenders° for true pay,
Which are not sterling.° Tender° yourself more
    dearly,
Or—not to crack the wind° of the poor phrase,
Running it thus—you'll tender me a fool.°   110
OPHELIA: My lord, he hath importun'd me with love
In honorable fashion.
POLONIUS: Ay, fashion° you may call it. Go to, go to.
OPHELIA: And hath given countenance° to his speech,
    my lord,
With almost all the holy vows of heaven.   115

---

36. **chariest:** Most scrupulously modest. 39. **canker galls:** Cankerworm destroys. 40. **buttons:** Buds. **disclos'd:** Opened. 41. **liquid dew:** Time when dew is fresh. 42. **blastments:** Blights. 49. **puff'd:** Bloated. 51. **recks:** Heeds. **rede:** Counsel. 53. **double:** I.e., Laertes has already bidden his father goodbye. 54. **Occasion:** Opportunity. 59. **character:** Inscribe. 60. **his:** Its. 61. **familiar:** Sociable. **vulgar:** Common. 62. **tried:** Tested. 65. **courage:** Young man of spirit. 67. **Bear't that:** Manage it so that. 69. **censure:** Opinion, judgment. 74. **generous chief:** Noble eminence (?). 77. **husbandry:** Thrift.

81. **season:** Mature. 83. **invests:** Besieges. **tend:** Attend, wait. 91. **Marry:** By the Virgin Mary (a mild oath). 95. **put on:** Impressed on, told to. 100. **tenders:** Offers. 103. **Unsifted:** Untried. 107. **tenders:** With added meaning here of "promise to pay." 108. **sterling:** Legal currency. **Tender:** Hold. 109. **crack the wind:** Run it until it is broken, winded. 110. **tender me a fool:** (1) Show yourself to me as a fool; (2) show me up as a fool; (3) present me with a grandchild (*fool* was a term of endearment for a child). 113. **fashion:** Mere form, pretense. 114. **countenance:** Credit, support.

POLONIUS: Ay, springes° to catch woodcocks.° I do
    know,
  When the blood burns, how prodigal the soul
  Lends the tongue vows. These blazes, daughter,
  Giving more light than heat, extinct in both
120 Even in their promise, as it is a-making,
  You must not take for fire. From this time
  Be something scanter of your maiden presence.
  Set your entreatments° at a higher rate
  Than a command to parle.° For Lord Hamlet,
125 Believe so much in him° that he is young,
  And with a larger tether may he walk
  Than may be given you. In few,° Ophelia,
  Do not believe his vows, for they are brokers,°
  Not of that dye° which their investments° show,
130 But mere implorators° of unholy suits,
  Breathing° like sanctified and pious bawds,
  The better to beguile. This is for all:
  I would not, in plain terms, from this time forth
  Have you so slander° any moment leisure
135 As to give words or talk with the Lord Hamlet.
  Look to 't, I charge you. Come your ways.
OPHELIA: I shall obey, my lord.   *(Exeunt.)*

{Scene IV}°

(Enter Hamlet, Horatio, and Marcellus.)

HAMLET: The air bites shrewdly; it is very cold.
HORATIO: It is a nipping and an eager air.
HAMLET: What hour now?
HORATIO: I think it lacks of twelve.
MARCELLUS: No, it is struck.
HORATIO: Indeed? I heard it not.
5 It then draws near the season
  Wherein the spirit held his wont to walk.

    *(A flourish of trumpets, and two pieces° go off
    [within].)*

  What does this mean, my lord?
HAMLET: The King doth wake° tonight and takes his
    rouse,°
  Keeps wassail,° and the swagg'ring up-spring° reels;

And as he drains his draughts of Rhenish° down, 10
  The kettle-drum and trumpet thus bray out
  The triumph of his pledge.°
HORATIO: Is it a custom?
HAMLET: Ay, marry, is 't,
  But to my mind, though I am native here
  And to the manner° born, it is a custom 15
  More honor'd in the breach than the observance.°
  This heavy-headed revel east and west°
  Makes us traduc'd and tax'd of° other nations.
  They clepe° us drunkards, and with swinish phrase°
  Soil our addition;° and indeed it takes 20
  From our achievements, though perform'd at
    height,°
  The pith and marrow of our attribute.
  So, oft it chances in particular men,
  That for some vicious mole of nature° in them,
  As in their birth—wherein they are not guilty, 25
  Since nature cannot choose his° origin—
  By the o'ergrowth of some complexion,°
  Oft breaking down the pales° and forts of reason,
  Or by some habit that too much o'er-leavens°
  The form of plausive° manners, that these men, 30
  Carrying, I say, the stamp of one defect,
  Being nature's livery,° or fortune's star,°
  Their virtues else, be they as pure as grace,
  As infinite as man may undergo,
  Shall in the general censure take corruption 35
  From that particular fault. The dram of eale°
  Doth all the noble substance of a doubt°
  To his own scandal.°

(Enter Ghost.)

HORATIO: Look, my lord, it comes!
HAMLET: Angels and ministers of grace defend us!
  Be thou a spirit of health° or goblin damn'd, 40
  Bring with thee airs from heaven or blasts from
    hell,
  Be thy intents wicked or charitable,
  Thou com'st in such a questionable° shape

116. **springes:** Snares. **woodcocks:** Birds easily caught; here used to connote gullibility. 123. **entreatments:** Negotiations for surrender (a military term). 124. **parle:** Discuss terms with the enemy. (Polonius urges his daughter, in the metaphor of military language, not to meet with Hamlet and consider giving in to him merely because he requests an interview.) 125. **so ... him:** This much concerning him. 127. **In few:** Briefly. 128. **brokers:** Go-betweens, procurers. 129. **dye:** Color or sort. **investments:** Clothes (i.e., they are not what they seem). 130. **mere implorators:** Out-and-out solicitors. 131. **Breathing:** Speaking. 134. **slander:** Bring disgrace or reproach upon. **I, iv. Location:** The guard platform. 6. [S.D.] **pieces:** I.e., of ordnance, cannon. 8. **wake:** Stay awake and hold revel. **rouse:** Carouse, drinking bout. 9. **wassail:** Carousal. **up-spring:** Wild German dance.

10. **Rhenish:** Rhine wine. 12. **triumph ... pledge:** His feat in draining the wine in a single draft. 15. **manner:** Custom (of drinking). 16. **More ... observance:** Better neglected than followed. 17. **east and west:** I.e., everywhere. 18. **tax'd of:** Censured by. 19. **clepe:** Call. **with swinish phrase:** By calling us swine. 20. **addition:** Reputation. 21. **at height:** Outstandingly. 24. **mole of nature:** Natural blemish in one's constitution. 26. **his:** Its. 27. **complexion:** Humor (i.e., one of the four humors or fluids thought to determine temperament). 28. **pales:** Palings, fences (as of a fortification). 29. **o'er-leavens:** Induces a change throughout (as yeast works in dough). 30. **plausive:** Pleasing. 32. **nature's livery:** Endowment from nature. **fortune's star:** Mark placed by fortune. 36. **dram of eale:** Small amount of evil (?). 37. **of a doubt:** A famous crux, sometimes emended to *oft about* or *often dout* (i.e., often erase or do out) or to *antidote* (counteract). 38. **To ... scandal:** To the disgrace of the whole enterprise. 40. **of health:** Of spiritual good. 43. **questionable:** Inviting question or conversation.

That I will speak to thee. I'll call thee Hamlet,
45   King, father, royal Dane. O, answer me!
Let me not burst in ignorance, but tell
Why thy canoniz'd° bones, hearsed° in death,
Have burst their cerements;° why the sepulcher
Wherein we saw thee quietly interr'd
50   Hath op'd his ponderous and marble jaws
To cast thee up again. What may this mean,
That thou, dead corse, again in complete steel
Revisits thus the glimpses of the moon,°
Making night hideous, and we fools of nature°
55   So horridly to shake our disposition
With thoughts beyond the reaches of our souls?
Say, why is this? Wherefore? What should we do?
             (*[Ghost] beckons [Hamlet].*)
HORATIO: It beckons you to go away with it,
As if it some impartment° did desire
60   To you alone.
MARCELLUS: Look with what courteous action
It waves you to a more removed ground.
But do not go with it.
HORATIO: No, by no means.
HAMLET: It will not speak. Then I will follow it.
HORATIO: Do not, my lord.
65   HAMLET: Why, what should be the fear?
I do not set my life at a pin's fee,°
And for my soul, what can it do to that,
Being a thing immortal as itself?
It waves me forth again. I'll follow it.
HORATIO: What if it tempt you toward the flood, my
70   Lord
Or to the dreadful summit of the cliff
That beetles o'er° his° base into the sea,
And there assume some other horrible form
Which might deprive your sovereignty of reason,°
75   And draw you into madness? Think of it.
The very place puts toys of desperation,°
Without more motive, into every brain
That looks so many fathoms to the sea
And hears it roar beneath.
HAMLET: It waves me still.
80   Go on, I'll follow thee.
MARCELLUS: You shall not go, my lord.
                          [*They try to stop him.*]
HAMLET: Hold off your hands!
HORATIO: Be rul'd, you shall not go.
HAMLET: My fate cries out,
And makes each petty artery° in this body
As hardy as the Nemean lion's° nerve.°

Still am I call'd. Unhand me, gentlemen.   85
By heaven, I'll make a ghost of him that lets° me!
I say, away! Go on. I'll follow thee.
             (*Exeunt Ghost and Hamlet.*)
HORATIO: He waxes desperate with imagination.
MARCELLUS: Let's follow. 'Tis not fit thus to obey him.
HORATIO: Have after. To what issue° will this come?   90
MARCELLUS: Something is rotten in the state of Denmark.
HORATIO: Heaven will direct it.°
MARCELLUS: Nay, let's follow him. (*Exeunt.*)

{Scene V}°

(*Enter Ghost and Hamlet.*)

HAMLET: Whither wilt thou lead me? Speak. I'll go
        no further.
GHOST: Mark me.
HAMLET: I will.
GHOST: My hour is almost come,
When I to sulph'rous and tormenting flames
Must render up myself.
HAMLET: Alas, poor ghost!
GHOST: Pity me not, but lend thy serious hearing   5
To what I shall unfold.
HAMLET: Speak. I am bound to hear.
GHOST: So art thou to revenge, when thou shalt hear.
HAMLET: What?
GHOST: I am thy father's spirit,   10
Doom'd for a certain term to walk the night,
And for the day confin'd to fast° in fires,
Till the foul crimes° done in my days of nature
Are burnt and purg'd away. But that° I am forbid
To tell the secrets of my prison-house,   15
I could a tale unfold whose lightest word
Would harrow up thy soul, freeze thy young blood,
Make thy two eyes, like stars, start from their
        spheres,°
Thy knotted and combined locks° to part,
And each particular hair to stand an end,°   20
Like quills upon the fearful porpentine.°
But this eternal blazon° must not be
To ears of flesh and blood. List, list, O, list!
If thou didst ever thy dear father love—
HAMLET: O God!   25
GHOST: Revenge his foul and most unnatural murder.
HAMLET: Murder?

---

47. canoniz'd: Buried according to the canons of the church. **hearsed:** Coffined.   **48. cerements:** Grave-clothes. **53. glimpses of the moon:** Earth by night.   **54. fools of nature:** Mere men, limited to natural knowledge.   **59. impartment:** Communication.   **66. fee:** Value.   **72. beetles o'er:** Overhangs threateningly.   **his:** Its. **74. deprive...reason:** Take away the rule of reason over your mind.   **76. toys of desperation:** Fancies of desperate acts (i.e., suicide).   **83. artery:** Sinew.   **84. Nemean lion:** One of the monsters slain by Hercules in his twelve labors.   **nerve:** Sinew.

86. lets: Hinders.   **90. issue:** Outcome.   **92. it:** The outcome. **I, v. Location:** The battlements of the castle.   **12. fast:** Do penance.   **13. crimes:** Sins.   **14. But that:** Were it not that. **18. spheres:** Eye sockets, here compared to the orbits or transparent revolving spheres in which, according to Ptolemaic astronomy, the heavenly bodies were fixed.   **19. knotted...locks:** Hair neatly arranged and confined.   **20. an end:** On end. **21. fearful porpentine:** Frightened porcupine.   **22. eternal blazon:** Revelation of the secrets of eternity.

GHOST: Murder most foul, as in the best it is,
But this most foul, strange, and unnatural.
HAMLET: Haste me to know 't, that I, with wings as
30   swift
As meditation or the thoughts of love,
May sweep to my revenge.
GHOST: I find thee apt;
And duller shouldst thou be than the fat weed
That roots itself in ease on Lethe° wharf,°
35   Wouldst thou not stir in this. Now, Hamlet, hear.
'Tis given out that, sleeping in my orchard,
A serpent stung me. So the whole ear of Denmark
Is by a forged process° of my death
Rankly abus'd.° But know, thou noble youth,
40   The serpent that did sting thy father's life
Now wears his crown.
HAMLET: O my prophetic soul!
My uncle!
GHOST: Ay, that incestuous, that adulterate° beast,
With witchcraft of his wits, with traitorous gifts—
45   O wicked wit and gifts, that have the power
So to seduce!—won to his shameful lust
The will of my most seeming-virtuous queen.
O Hamlet, what a falling-off was there!
From me, whose love was of that dignity
50   That it went hand in hand even with the vow
I made to her in marriage, and to decline
Upon a wretch whose natural gifts were poor
To those of mine!
But virtue, as it never will be moved,
55   Though lewdness court it in a shape of heaven,°
So lust, though to a radiant angel link'd,
Will sate itself in a celestial bed,
And prey on garbage.
But, soft, methinks I scent the morning air.
60   Brief let me be. Sleeping within my orchard,
My custom always of the afternoon,
Upon my secure° hour thy uncle stole,
With juice of cursed hebona° in a vial,
And in the porches of my ears did pour
65   The leprous° distillment, whose effect
Holds such an enmity with blood of man
That swift as quicksilver it courses through
The natural gates and alleys of the body,
And with a sudden vigor it doth posset°
70   And curd, like eager° droppings into milk,
The thin and wholesome blood. So did it mine,
And a most instant tetter° bark'd° about,

Most lazar-like,° with vile and loathsome crust,
All my smooth body.
Thus was I, sleeping, by a brother's hand   75
Of life, of crown, of queen, at once dispatch'd,°
Cut off even in the blossoms of my sin,
Unhous'led,° disappointed,° unanel'd,°
No reck'ning made, but sent to my account
With all my imperfections on my head.   80
O, horrible! O, horrible, most horrible!
If thou hast nature° in thee, bear it not.
Let not the royal bed of Denmark be
A couch for luxury° and damned incest.
But, howsomever thou pursues this act,   85
Taint not thy mind, nor let thy soul contrive
Against thy mother aught. Leave her to heaven
And to those thorns that in her bosom lodge,
To prick and sting her. Fare thee well at once.
The glow-worm shows the matin° to be near,   90
And 'gins to pale his uneffectual fire.°
Adieu, adieu, adieu! Remember me.   [*Exit.*]
HAMLET: O all you host of heaven! O earth! What
    else?
And shall I couple° hell? O fie! Hold, hold, my
    heart,
And you, my sinews, grow not instant old,   95
But bear me stiffly up. Remember thee!
Ay, thou poor ghost, whiles memory holds a seat
In this distracted globe.° Remember thee!
Yea, from the table° of my memory
I'll wipe away all trivial fond° records,   100
All saws° of books, all forms,° all pressures° past
That youth and observation copied there,
And thy commandment all alone shall live
Within the book and volume of my brain,
Unmix'd with baser matter. Yes, by heaven!   105
O most pernicious woman!
O villain, villain, smiling, damned villain!
My tables—meet it is I set it down,
That one may smile, and smile, and be a villain.
At least I am sure it may be so in Denmark.   110
                        [*Writing.*]
So, uncle, there you are. Now to my word;
It is "Adieu, adieu! Remember me."
I have sworn 't.

(*Enter Horatio and Marcellus.*)

HORATIO: My lord, my lord!
MARCELLUS: Lord Hamlet!
HORATIO: Heavens secure him!

---

34. **Lethe:** The river of forgetfulness in Hades. **wharf:** Bank.
38. **forged process:** Falsified account. 39. **abus'd:** Deceived.
43. **adulterate:** Adulterous. 55. **shape of heaven:** Heavenly
form. 62. **secure:** Confident, unsuspicious. 63. **hebona:**
Poison. (The word seems to be a form of *ebony*, though
it is thought perhaps to be related to *henbane*, a poison, or
to *ebenus*, yew.) 65. **leprous:** Causing leprosy-like disfig-
urement. 69. **posset:** Coagulate, curdle. 70. **eager:** Sour,
acid. 72. **tetter:** Eruption of scabs. **bark'd:** Covered with a
rough covering, like bark on a tree.

73. **lazar-like:** Leper-like. 76. **dispatch'd:** Suddenly deprived.
78. **Unhous'led:** Without having received the sacrament (of
Holy Communion). **disappointed:** Unready (spiritually) for
the last journey. **unanel'd:** Without having received extreme
unction. 82. **nature:** The promptings of a son. 84. **luxury:**
Lechery. 90. **matin:** Morning. 91. **uneffectual fire:** Cold
light. 94. **couple:** Add. 98. **globe:** Head. 99. **table:** Writing
tablet. 100. **fond:** Foolish. 101. **saws:** Wise sayings. **forms:**
Images. **pressures:** Impressions stamped.

115 HAMLET: So be it!
MARCELLUS: Illo, ho, ho, my lord!
HAMLET: Hillo, ho, ho,° boy! Come, bird, come.
MARCELLUS: How is 't, my noble lord?
HORATIO: What news, my lord?
HAMLET: O, wonderful!
HORATIO: Good my lord, tell it.
120 HAMLET: No, you will reveal it.
HORATIO: Not I, my lord, by heaven.
MARCELLUS: Nor I, my lord.
HAMLET: How say you, then, would heart of man
    once think it?
    But you'll be secret?
HORATIO, MARCELLUS: Ay, by heaven, my lord.
HAMLET: There's never a villain dwelling in all
    Denmark
125 But he's an arrant° knave.
HORATIO: There needs no ghost, my lord, come from
    the grave
    To tell us this.
HAMLET: Why, right, you are in the right.
    And so, without more circumstance° at all,
    I hold it fit that we shake hands and part,
130 You, as your business and desire shall point you—
    For every man hath business and desire,
    Such as it is—and for my own poor part,
    Look you, I'll go pray.
HORATIO: These are but wild and whirling words, my
    lord.
135 HAMLET: I am sorry they offend you, heartily;
    Yes, faith, heartily.
HORATIO: There's no offense, my lord.
HAMLET: Yes, by Saint Patrick,° but there is, Horatio,
    And much offense too. Touching this vision here,
    It is an honest° ghost, that let me tell you.
140 For your desire to know what is between us,
    O'ermaster 't as you may. And now, good friends
    As you are friends, scholars, and soldiers,
    Give me one poor request.
HORATIO: What is 't, my lord? We will.
HAMLET: Never make known what you have seen
145   tonight.
HORATIO, MARCELLUS: My lord, we will not.
HAMLET: Nay, but swear 't.
HORATIO: In faith,
    My lord, not I.
MARCELLUS: Nor I, my lord, in faith.
HAMLET: Upon my sword.°   [Holds out his sword.]
MARCELLUS: We have sworn, my lord, already.
HAMLET: Indeed, upon my sword, indeed.
                    (Ghost cries under the stage.)

GHOST: Swear.   150
HAMLET: Ha, ha, boy, say'st thou so? Art thou there,
    truepenny?°
    Come on, you hear this fellow in the cellarage.
    Consent to swear.
HORATIO: Propose the oath, my lord.
HAMLET: Never to speak of this that you have seen,
    Swear by my sword.   155
GHOST [beneath]: Swear.
HAMLET: Hic et ubique?° Then we'll shift our ground.
                    [He moves to another spot.]
    Come hither, gentlemen,
    And lay your hands again upon my sword.
    Swear by my sword   160
    Never to speak of this that you have heard.
GHOST [beneath]: Swear by his sword.
HAMLET: Well said, old mole! Canst work i' th' earth
    so fast?
    A worthy pioner!° Once more remove, good friends.
                    [Moves again.]
HORATIO: O day and night, but this is wondrous
    strange!   165
HAMLET: And therefore as a stranger give it welcome.
    There are more things in heaven and earth, Horatio,
    Than are dreamt of in your philosophy.°
    But come;
    Here, as before, never, so help you mercy,   170
    How strange or odd soe'er I bear myself—
    As I perchance hereafter shall think meet
    To put an antic° disposition on—
    That you, at such times seeing me, never shall,
    With arms encumb'red° thus, or this headshake,   175
    Or by pronouncing of some doubtful phrase,
    As "Well, well, we know," or "We could, an if°
    we would,"
    Or "If we list° to speak," or "There be, an if they
    might,"
    Or such ambiguous giving out,° to note°
    That you know aught of me—this do swear,   180
    So grace and mercy at your most need help you.
GHOST [beneath]: Swear.   [They swear.]
HAMLET: Rest, rest, perturbed spirit! So, gentlemen,
    With all my love I do commend me to you;
    And what so poor a man as Hamlet   185
    May do, t' express his love and friending to you,
    God willing, shall not lack. Let us go in together,
    And still° your fingers on your lips, I pray.
    The time is out of joint. O cursed spite,
    That ever I was born to set it right!   190
                    [They wait for him to leave first.]
    Nay, come, let's go together.   (Exeunt.)

---

117. Hillo, ho, ho: A falconer's call to a hawk in air. Hamlet is playing upon Marcellus's *Illo* (i.e., *halloo*). **125. arrant:** Thoroughgoing. **128. circumstance:** Ceremony. **137. Saint Patrick:** The keeper of purgatory and patron saint of all blunders and confusion. **139. honest:** I.e., a real ghost and not an evil spirit. **148. sword:** The hilt in the form of a cross.

151. truepenny: Honest old fellow. **157. Hic et ubique:** Here and everywhere (Latin). **164. pioner:** Pioneer, digger, miner. **168. your philosophy:** This subject called "natural philosophy" or "science" that people talk about. **173. antic:** Fantastic. **175. encumb'red:** Folded or entwined. **177. an if:** If. **178. list:** Were inclined. **179. giving out:** Profession of knowledge. **note:** Give a sign, indicate. **188. still:** Always.

{ACT II • Scene I}°

(*Enter old Polonius, with his man [Reynaldo].*)

POLONIUS: Give him this money and these notes,
    Reynaldo.
REYNALDO: I will, my lord.
POLONIUS: You shall do marvel's° wisely, good
    Reynaldo,
    Before you visit him, to make inquire
    Of his behavior.
5 REYNALDO: My lord, I did intend it.
POLONIUS: Marry, well said, very well said. Look you,
    sir,
    Inquire me first what Danskers° are in Paris,
    And how, and who, what means,° and where they
      keep,°
    What company, at what expense; and finding
10 By this encompassment° and drift° of question
    That they do know my son, come you more nearer
    Than your particular demands will touch it.°
    Take° you, as 'twere, some distant knowledge
      of him,
    As thus, "I know his father and his friends,
15 And in part him." Do you mark this, Reynaldo?
REYNALDO: Ay, very well, my lord.
POLONIUS: "And in part him, but," you may say, "not
    well.
    But, if 't be he I mean, he's very wild,
    Addicted so and so," and there put on° him
20 What forgeries° you please—marry, none so rank
    As may dishonor him, take heed of that,
    But, sir, such wanton,° wild, and usual slips,
    As are companions noted and most known
    To youth and liberty.
REYNALDO: As gaming, my lord.
25 POLONIUS: Ay, or drinking, fencing, swearing,
    Quarreling, drabbing°—you may go so far.
REYNALDO: My lord, that would dishonor him.
POLONIUS: Faith, no, as you may season° it in the
    charge.
    You must not put another scandal on him
30 That he is open to incontinency;°
    That's not my meaning. But breathe his faults so
      quaintly°
    That they may seem the taints of liberty,°
    The flash and outbreak of a fiery mind,

    A savageness in unreclaimed° blood,
    Of general assault.°
REYNALDO: But, my good lord—   35
POLONIUS: Wherefore should you do this?
REYNALDO: Ay, my lord,
    I would know that.
POLONIUS: Marry, sir, here's my drift,
    And, I believe, it is a fetch of wit.°
    You laying these slight sullies on my son,
    As 'twere a thing a little soil'd i' th' working,°   40
    Mark you,
    Your party in converse,° him you would
      sound,°
    Having ever° seen in the prenominate crimes°
    The youth you breathe° of guilty, be assur'd
    He closes with you in this consequence:°   45
    "Good sir," or so, or "friend," or "gentleman,"
    According to the phrase or the addition°
    Of man and country.
REYNALDO: Very good, my lord.
POLONIUS: And then, sir, does 'a this—'a does—
    what was I about to say?
    By the mass, I was about to say something.   50
    Where did I leave?
REYNALDO: At "closes in the consequence."
POLONIUS: At "closes in the consequence," ay, marry.
    He closes thus: "I know the gentleman;
    I saw him yesterday, or th' other day,
    Or then, or then, with such, or such, and, as you say,   55
    There was 'a gaming, there o'ertook in 's rouse,°
    There falling out° at tennis," or perchance,
    "I saw him enter such a house of sale,"
    Videlicet,° a brothel, or so forth. See you now,
    Your bait of falsehood takes this carp° of truth;   60
    And thus do we of wisdom and of reach,°
    With windlasses° and with assays of bias,°
    By indirections find directions° out.
    So by my former lecture and advice
    Shall you my son. You have me, have you not?   65
REYNALDO: My lord, I have.
POLONIUS: God buy ye; fare ye well.
REYNALDO: Good my lord.
POLONIUS: Observe his inclination in yourself.°

II, i. **Location:** Polonius's chambers. **3. marvel's:** Marvelous(ly).
7. Danskers: Danes. **8. what means:** What wealth (they
have). **keep:** Dwell. **10. encompassment:** Roundabout talking. **drift:** Gradual approach or course. **11–12. come . . . it:**
You will find out more this way than by asking pointed questions (particular demands). **13. Take:** Assume, pretend. **19.
put on:** Impute to. **20. forgeries:** Invented tales. **22. wanton:**
Sportive, unrestrained. **26. drabbing:** Whoring. **28. season:**
Temper, soften. **30. incontinency:** Habitual loose behavior. **31. quaintly:** Delicately, ingeniously. **32. taints of liberty:** Faults resulting from freedom.

34. unreclaimed: Untamed. **35. general assault:** Tendency
that assails all unrestrained youth. **38. fetch of wit:** Clever
trick. **40. soil'd i' th' working:** Shopworn. **42. converse:**
Conversation. **sound:** Sound out. **43. Having ever:** If he
has ever. **prenominate crimes:** Before-mentioned offenses.
44. breathe: Speak. **45. closes . . . consequence:** Follows
your lead in some fashion as follows. **47. addition:** Title.
56. o'ertook in 's rouse: Overcome by drink. **57. falling
out:** Quarreling. **59. Videlicet:** Namely. **60. carp:** A fish.
61. reach: Capacity, ability. **62. windlasses:** Circuitous paths
(literally, circuits made to head off the game in hunting).
assays of bias: Attempts through indirection (like the curving
path of the bowling ball, which is biased or weighted to one
side). **63. directions:** The way things really are. **68. in yourself:** In your own person (as well as by asking questions).

REYNALDO: I shall, my lord.
POLONIUS: And let him ply° his music.
70 REYNALDO: Well, my lord.
POLONIUS: Farewell.   (*Exit Reynaldo.*)

(*Enter Ophelia.*)

How now, Ophelia, what's the matter?
OPHELIA: O, my lord, my lord, I have been so affrighted!
POLONIUS: With what, i' th' name of God?
OPHELIA: My lord, as I was sewing in my closet,°
75   Lord Hamlet, with his doublet° all unbrac'd,°
No hat upon his head, his stockings fouled,
Ungart'red, and down-gyved to his ankle,°
Pale as his shirt, his knees knocking each other,
And with a look so piteous in purport
80   As if he had been loosed out of hell
To speak of horrors—he comes before me.
POLONIUS: Mad for thy love?
OPHELIA: My lord, I do not know,
But truly I do fear it.
POLONIUS: What said he?
OPHELIA: He took me by the wrist and held me hard.
85   Then goes he to the length of all his arm,
And, with his other hand thus o'er his brow
He falls to such perusal of my face
As 'a would draw it. Long stay'd he so.
At last, a little shaking of mine arm
90   And thrice his head thus waving up and down,
He rais'd a sigh so piteous and profound
As it did seem to shatter all his bulk°
And end his being. That done, he lets me go,
And, with his head over his shoulder turn'd,
95   He seem'd to find his way without his eyes,
For out o' doors he went without their helps,
And, to the last, bended their light on me.
POLONIUS: Come, go with me. I will go seek the King.
This is the very ecstasy° of love
100   Whose violent property° fordoes° itself
And leads the will to desperate undertakings
As oft as any passion under heaven
That does afflict our natures. I am sorry.
What, have you given him any hard words of late?
105 OPHELIA: No, my good lord, but, as you did command,
I did repel his letters and denied
His access to me.
POLONIUS: That hath made him mad.
I am sorry that with better heed and judgment
I had not quoted° him. I fear'd he did but trifle
And meant to wrack thee; but, beshrew my
110   jealousy!°

By heaven, it is as proper to our age°
To cast beyond° ourselves in our opinions
As it is common for the younger sort
To lack discretion. Come, go we to the King.
This must be known, which, being kept close,°
    might move   115
More grief to hide than hate to utter love.°
Come.

(*Exeunt.*)

{Scene II}°

(*Flourish. Enter King and Queen, Rosencrantz, and Guildenstern [with others].*)

KING: Welcome, dear Rosencrantz and Guildenstern.
Moreover that° we much did long to see you,
The need we have to use you did provoke
Our hasty sending. Something have you heard
Of Hamlet's transformation—so call it,   5
Sith° nor th' exterior nor° the inward man
Resembles that° it was. What it should be,
More than his father's death, that thus hath put him
So much from th' understanding of himself,
I cannot dream of. I entreat you both   10
That, being of so young days° brought up with him,
And sith so neighbor'd to his youth and havior,
That you vouchsafe your rest° here in our court
Some little time, so by your companies
To draw him on to pleasures, and to gather   15
So much as from occasion you may glean,
Whether aught to us unknown afflicts him thus,
That, open'd,° lies within our remedy.
QUEEN: Good gentlemen, he hath much talk'd of you
And sure I am two men there is not living   20
To whom he more adheres. If it will please you
To show us so much gentry° and good will
As to expend your time with us awhile
For the supply and profit° of our hope,
Your visitation shall receive such thanks   25
As fits a king's remembrance.
ROSENCRANTZ: Both your Majesties
Might, by the sovereign power you have of us,
Put your dread pleasures more into command
Than to entreaty.

---

70. **let him ply:** See that he continues to study. 74. **closet:**
Private chamber. 75. **doublet:** Close-fitting jacket. **unbrac'd:**
Unfastened. 77. **down-gyved to his ankle:** Fallen to the ankles
(like gyves or fetters). 92. **bulk:** Body. 99. **ecstasy:** Madness.
100. **property:** Nature. **fordoes:** Destroys. 109. **quoted:** Observed. 110. **beshrew my jealousy:** A plague upon my suspicious nature.

111. **proper . . . age:** Characteristic of us (old) men. 112. **cast
beyond:** Overshoot, miscalculate. 115. **close:** Secret. 115–
116. **might . . . love:** Might cause more grief (to others) by hiding the knowledge of Hamlet's strange behavior to Ophelia than
hatred by telling it. II, ii. **Location:** The castle. 2. **Moreover
that:** Besides the fact that. 6. **Sith:** Since. **nor . . . nor:** Neither . . . nor. 7. **that:** What. 11. **of . . . days:** From such early
youth. 13. **vouchsafe your rest:** Please to stay. 18. **open'd:**
Revealed. 22. **gentry:** Courtesy. 24. **supply and profit:** Aid
and successful outcome.

GUILDENSTERN: But we both obey,
30 And here give up ourselves in the full bent°
    To lay our service freely at your feet,
    To be commanded.
KING: Thanks, Rosencrantz and gentle Guildenstern.
QUEEN: Thanks, Guildenstern and gentle Rosencrantz.
35 And I beseech you instantly to visit
    My too much changed son. Go, some of you,
    And bring these gentlemen where Hamlet is.
GUILDENSTERN: Heavens make our presence and our
        practices
    Pleasant and helpful to him!
QUEEN: Ay, amen!

                        (*Exeunt Rosencrantz
                        and Guildenstern* [*with
                        some Attendants*].)

(*Enter Polonius.*)

POLONIUS: Th' ambassadors from Norway, my good
40   lord,
    Are joyfully return'd.
KING: Thou still° hast been the father of good news.
POLONIUS: Have I, my lord? I assure my good liege
    I hold my duty, as I hold my soul,
45 Both to my God and to my gracious king;
    And I do think, or else this brain of mine
    Hunts not the trail of policy so sure
    As it hath us'd to do, that I have found
    The very cause of Hamlet's lunacy.
50 KING: O, speak of that! That do I long to hear.
POLONIUS: Give first admittance to th' ambassadors.
    My news shall be the fruit° to that great feast.
KING: Thyself do grace to them, and bring them in.
                        (*Exit Polonius.*)
    He tells me, my dear Gertrude, he hath found
55 The head and source of all your son's distemper.
QUEEN: I doubt° it is no other but the main,°
    His father's death, and our o'erhasty marriage.

(*Enter Ambassadors* [*Voltimand and Cornelius, with
Polonius*].)

KING: Well, we shall sift him.—Welcome, my good
        friends!
    Say, Voltimand, what from our brother Norway?
VOLTIMAND: Most fair return of greetings and
60   desires.
    Upon our first,° he sent out to suppress
    His nephew's levies, which to him appear'd
    To be a preparation 'gainst the Polack,
    But, better look'd into, he truly found
65 It was against your Highness. Whereat griev'd
    That so his sickness, age, and impotence
    Was falsely borne in hand,° sends out arrests

On Fortinbras, which he, in brief, obeys,
Receives rebuke from Norway, and in fine°
Makes vow before his uncle never more   70
To give th' assay° of arms against your Majesty.
Whereon old Norway, overcome with joy,
Gives him three score thousand crowns in annual
    fee,
And his commission to employ those soldiers,
So levied as before, against the Polack,   75
With an entreaty, herein further shown,
                        [*Giving a paper.*]
That it might please you to give quiet pass
Through your dominions for this enterprise,
On such regards of safety and allowance°
As therein are set down.
KING: It likes° us well;   80
And at our more consider'd° time we'll read,
Answer, and think upon this business.
Meantime we thank you for your well-took labor.
Go to your rest; at night we'll feast together.
Most welcome home!   (*Exeunt Ambassadors.*)
POLONIUS: This business is well ended. 85
My liege, and madam, to expostulate°
What majesty should be, what duty is,
Why day is day, night night, and time is time,
Were nothing but to waste night, day, and time.
Therefore, since brevity is the soul of wit,°   90
And tediousness the limbs and outward flourishes,
I will be brief. Your noble son is mad.
Mad call I it, for, to define true madness,
What is 't but to be nothing else but mad?
But let that go.
QUEEN: More matter, with less art.   95
POLONIUS: Madam, I swear I use no art at all.
That he is mad, 'tis true; 'tis true 'tis pity,
And pity 'tis 'tis true—a foolish figure,°
But farewell it, for I will use no art.
Mad let us grant him, then, and now remains   100
That we find out the cause of this effect,
Or rather say, the cause of this defect,
For this effect defective comes by cause.°
Thus it remains, and the remainder thus.
Perpend.°   105
I have a daughter—have while she is mine—
Who, in her duty and obedience, mark,
Hath given me this. Now gather, and surmise.
[*Reads the letter.*] "To the celestial and my soul's
    idol,
the most beautified Ophelia"—   110
That's an ill phrase, a vile phrase; "beautified" is a
    vile

---

30. **in . . . bent:** To the utmost degree of our capacity. 42. **still:** Always. 52. **fruit:** Dessert. 56. **doubt:** Fear, suspect. **main:** Chief point, principal concern. 61. **Upon our first:** At our first words on the business. 67. **borne in hand:** Deluded, taken advantage of.

69. **in fine:** In the end. 71. **assay:** Trial. 79. **On . . . allowance:** With such pledges of safety and provisos. 80. **likes:** Pleases. 81. **consider'd:** Suitable for deliberation. 86. **expostulate:** Expound. 90. **wit:** Sound sense or judgment. 98. **figure:** Figure of speech. 103. **For . . . cause:** I.e., for this defective behavior, this madness has a cause. 105. **Perpend:** Consider.

phrase. But you shall hear. Thus: [*Reads.*]
"In her excellent white bosom, these, etc."
QUEEN: Came this from Hamlet to her?
POLONIUS: Good madam, stay awhile; I will be
115   faithful.
                           [*Reads.*]
    "Doubt° thou the stars are fire,
      Doubt that the sun doth move,
    Doubt truth to be a liar,
      But never doubt I love.
120 O dear Ophelia, I am ill at these numbers.° I have
not art to reckon° my groans. But that I love thee
best, O most best, believe it. Adieu.
        Thine evermore, most dear lady, whilst this
             machine° is to him, Hamlet."
125 This in obedience hath my daughter shown me,
And, more above,° hath his solicitings,
As they fell out° by time, by means, and place,
All given to mine ear.
KING: But how hath she
    Receiv'd his love?
POLONIUS: What do you think of me?
130 KING: As of a man faithful and honorable.
POLONIUS: I would fain prove so. But what might you
    think,
When I had seen this hot love on the wing—
As I perceiv'd it, I must tell you that,
Before my daughter told me—what might you,
135 Or my dear Majesty your Queen here, think,
If I had play'd the desk or table-book,°
Or given my heart a winking,° mute and dumb,
Or look'd upon this love with idle sight?°
What might you think? No, I went round° to work,
140 And my young mistress thus I did bespeak:°
"Lord Hamlet is a prince, out of thy star;°
This must not be." And then I prescripts gave her,
That she should lock herself from his resort,
Admit no messengers, receive no tokens.
145 Which done, she took the fruits of my advice;
And he, repelled—a short tale to make—
Fell into a sadness, then into a fast,
Thence to a watch,° thence into a weakness,
Thence to a lightness,° and, by this declension,°
150 Into the madness wherein now he raves,
And all we mourn for.
KING: Do you think this?
QUEEN: It may be, very like.

POLONIUS: Hath there been such a time—I would fain
    know that—
    That I have positively said "'Tis so,"
When it prov'd otherwise?
KING: Not that I know.   155
POLONIUS [*pointing to his head and shoulder*]: Take
    this from this, if this be otherwise.
If circumstances lead me, I will find
Where truth is hid, though it were hid indeed
Within the center.°
KING: How may we try it further?
POLONIUS: You know, sometimes he walks four hours
    together   160
    Here in the lobby.
QUEEN: So he does indeed.
POLONIUS: At such a time I'll loose my daughter to him.
Be you and I behind an arras° then.
Mark the encounter. If he love her not
And be not from his reason fall'n thereon,°   165
Let me be no assistant for a state,
But keep a farm and carters.
KING: We will try it.

(*Enter Hamlet [reading on a book].*)

QUEEN: But look where sadly the poor wretch comes
    reading.
POLONIUS: Away, I do beseech you both, away.
    I'll board° him presently.

        (*Exeunt King and Queen [with Attendants].*)
                O, give me leave.   170
    How does my good Lord Hamlet?
HAMLET: Well, God-a-mercy.°
POLONIUS: Do you know me, my lord?
HAMLET: Excellent well. You are a fishmonger.°
POLONIUS: Not I, my lord.   175
HAMLET: Then I would you were so honest a man.
POLONIUS: Honest, my lord?
HAMLET: Ay, sir. To be honest, as this world goes, is
to be one man pick'd out of ten thousand.
POLONIUS: That's very true, my lord.   180
HAMLET: For if the sun breed maggots in a dead dog, be-
ing a good kissing carrion°—Have you a daughter?
POLONIUS: I have, my lord.
HAMLET: Let her not walk i' th' sun.° Conception° is a
blessing, but as your daughter may conceive, friend,   185
look to 't.

---

116. **Doubt:** Suspect, question.   120. **ill . . . numbers:** Unskilled
at writing verses.   121. **reckon:** (1) Count; (2) number met-
rically, scan.   124. **machine:** Body.   126. **more above:** Moreover.   127. **fell out:** Occurred.   136. **play'd . . . table-book:**
Remained shut up, concealing the information.   137. **winking:** Closing of the eyes.   138. **with idle sight:** Complacently
or uncomprehendingly.   139. **round:** Roundly, plainly.   140.
bespeak: Address.   141. **out of thy star:** Above your sphere,
position.   148. **watch:** State of sleeplessness.   149. **lightness:**
Light-headedness.   **declension:** Decline, deterioration.

159. **center:** Middle point of the earth (which is also the center of the Ptolemaic universe).   163. **arras:** Hanging, tapestry.
165. **thereon:** On that account.   170. **board:** Accost.
172. **God-a-mercy:** Thank you.   174. **fishmonger:** Fish merchant (with connotation of *bawd*, procurer [?]).   182. **good
kissing carrion:** A good piece of flesh for kissing or for the sun
to kiss.   184. **i' th' sun:** With additional implication of the
sunshine of princely favors.   **Conception:** (1) Understanding;
(2) pregnancy.

POLONIUS [*aside*]: How say you by that? Still harping on my daughter. Yet he knew me not at first; 'a said I was a fishmonger. 'A is far gone. And truly in my youth I suff'red much extremity for love, very near this. I'll speak to him again.—What do you read, my lord?

HAMLET: Words, words, words.

POLONIUS: What is the matter,° my lord?

HAMLET: Between who?

POLONIUS: I mean, the matter that you read, my lord.

HAMLET: Slanders, sir, for the satirical rogue says here that old men have gray beards, that their faces are wrinkled, their eyes purging° thick amber and plum-tree gum, and that they have a plentiful lack of wit, together with most weak hams. All which, sir, though I most powerfully and potently believe, yet I hold it not honesty° to have it thus set down, for you your-self, sir, shall grow old as I am, if like a crab you could go backward.

POLONIUS [*aside*]: Though this be madness, yet there is method in 't.—Will you walk out of the air, my lord?

HAMLET: Into my grave.

POLONIUS: Indeed, that's out of the air. [*Aside.*] How pregnant° sometimes his replies are! A happiness° that often madness hits on, which reason and san-ity could not so prosperously° be deliver'd of. I will leave him, [and suddenly contrive the means of meet-ing between him] and my daughter.—My honorable lord, I will most humbly take my leave of you.

HAMLET: You cannot, sir, take from me any thing that I will more willingly part withal—except my life, except my life, except my life.

(*Enter Guildenstern and Rosencrantz.*)

POLONIUS: Fare you well, my lord.

HAMLET: These tedious old fools!°

POLONIUS: You go to seek the Lord Hamlet; there he is.

ROSENCRANTZ [*to Polonius*]: God save you, sir!

[*Exit Polonius.*]

GUILDENSTERN: My honor'd lord!

ROSENCRANTZ: My most dear lord!

HAMLET: My excellent good friends! How dost thou, Guildenstern? Ah, Rosencrantz! Good lads, how do you both?

190
195
200
205
210
215
220
225

---

194. **matter:** Substance (but Hamlet plays on the sense of basis for a dispute).   199. **purging:** Discharging.   203. **hon-esty:** Decency.

210. **pregnant:** Full of meaning.   **happiness:** Felicity of expres-sion.   212. **prosperously:** Successfully.   220. **old fools:** I.e., old men like Polonius.

Hamlet returns to Denmark. Left to right, Voltimand (Jeremy Geidt), Gertrude (Christine Estabrook), Claudius (Mark Metcalf), Hamlet (Mark Rylance), and Laertes (Derek Smith) in the 1991 American Repertory Theater production of *Hamlet,* directed by Ron Daniels.

The dumb-show sequence with Candy Buckley as the Player Queen.

ROSENCRANTZ: As the indifferent° children of the earth.

GUILDENSTERN: Happy in that we are not over-happy.
230   On Fortune's cap we are not the very button.

HAMLET: Nor the soles of her shoe?

ROSENCRANTZ: Neither, my lord.

HAMLET: Then you live about her waist, or in the middle of her favors?

235 GUILDENSTERN: Faith, her privates° we.

HAMLET: In the secret parts of Fortune? O, most true; she is a strumpet.° What news?

ROSENCRANTZ: None, my lord, but the world's grown honest.

240 HAMLET: Then is doomsday near. But your news is not true. [Let me question more in particular. What have you, my good friends, deserv'd at the hands of Fortune that she sends you to prison hither?

GUILDENSTERN: Prison, my lord?

245 HAMLET: Denmark's a prison.

ROSENCRANTZ: Then is the world one.

HAMLET: A goodly one, in which there are many confines,° wards,° and dungeons, Denmark being one o' th' worst.

250 ROSENCRANTZ: We think not so, my lord.

HAMLET: Why then 'tis none to you, for there is nothing either good or bad but thinking makes it so. To me it is a prison.

ROSENCRANTZ: Why then, your ambition makes it one.
255   'Tis too narrow for your mind.

228. indifferent: Ordinary. **235. privates:** Close acquaintances (with sexual pun on *private parts*). **237. strumpet:** Prostitute (a common epithet for indiscriminate Fortune; see line 497, p. 184). **247–248. confines:** Places of confinement. **248. wards:** Cells.

HAMLET: O God, I could be bounded in a nutshell and count myself a king of infinite space, were it not that I have bad dreams.

GUILDENSTERN: Which dreams indeed are ambition, for the very substance of the ambitious° is merely the   260 shadow of a dream.

HAMLET: A dream itself is but a shadow.

ROSENCRANTZ: Truly, and I hold ambition of so airy and light a quality that it is but a shadow's shadow.

HAMLET: Then are our beggars bodies,° and our mon-   265 archs and outstretch'd° heroes the beggars' shadows. Shall we to th' court? For, by my fay,° I cannot reason.

ROSENCRANTZ, GUILDENSTERN: We'll wait upon° you.

HAMLET: No such matter. I will not sort° you with the   270 rest of my servants, for, to speak to you like an honest man, I am most dreadfully attended.°] But, in the beaten way° of friendship, what make° you at Elsinore?

ROSENCRANTZ: To visit you, my lord, no other occasion.   275

HAMLET: Beggar that I am, I am even poor in thanks; but I thank you, and sure, dear friends, my thanks are too dear a halfpenny.° Were you not sent for? Is it your own inclining? Is it a free visitation? Come, come,

260. the very . . . ambitious: That seemingly very substantial thing which the ambitious pursue. **265. bodies:** Solid substances rather than shadows (since beggars are not ambitious). **266. outstretch'd:** (1) Far-reaching in their ambition; (2) elongated as shadows. **267. fay:** Faith. **269. wait upon:** Accompany, attend. **270. sort:** Class, associate. **272. dreadfully attended:** Waited upon in slovenly fashion. **273. beaten way:** Familiar path. **make:** Do. **278. dear a halfpenny:** Expensive at the price of a halfpenny (i.e., of little worth).

280   deal justly with me. Come, come; nay, speak.

GUILDENSTERN: What should we say, my lord?

HAMLET: Why, anything, but to th' purpose. You were
    sent for; and there is a kind of confession in your
    looks which your modesties have not craft enough
285   to color. I know the good King and Queen have sent
    for you.

ROSENCRANTZ: To what end, my lord?

HAMLET: That you must teach me. But let me conjure°
    you, by the rights of our fellowship, by the conso-
290   nancy of our youth,° by the obligation of our ever-
    preserv'd love, and by what more dear a better
    proposer° could charge° you withal, be even° and
    direct with me, whether you were sent for, or no?

ROSENCRANTZ [aside to Guildenstern]: What say you?

295 HAMLET [aside]: Nay then, I have an eye of° you.—If
    you love me, hold not off.

GUILDENSTERN: My lord, we were sent for.

HAMLET: I will tell you why; so shall my anticipation
    prevent your discovery,° and your secrecy to the King
300   and Queen molt no feather.° I have of late—but
    wherefore I know not—lost all my mirth, forgone
    all custom of exercises; and indeed it goes so heavily
    with my disposition that this goodly frame, the earth,
    seems to me a sterile promontory; this most excellent
305   canopy, the air, look you, this brave° o'erhanging fir-
    mament, this majestical roof fretted° with golden fire,
    why, it appeareth nothing to me but a foul and pesti-
    lent congregation of vapors. What a piece of work is
    a man! How noble in reason, how infinite in faculties,
310   in form and moving how express° and admirable, in
    action how like an angel, in apprehension how like
    a god! The beauty of the world, the paragon of ani-
    mals! And yet, to me, what is this quintessence° of
    dust? Man delights not me—no, nor woman neither,
315   though by your smiling you seem to say so.

ROSENCRANTZ: My lord, there was no such stuff in my
    thoughts.

HAMLET: Why did you laugh then, when I said "man
    delights not me"?

320 ROSENCRANTZ: To think, my lord, if you delight not in
    man, what lenten entertainment° the players shall
    receive from you. We coted° them on the way, and
    hither are they coming, to offer you service.

HAMLET: He that plays the king shall be welcome; his
325   Majesty shall have tribute of me. The adventurous

knight shall use his foil and target,° the lover shall
not sigh gratis, the humorous man° shall end his part
in peace, [the clown shall make those laugh whose
lungs are tickle o' th' sere°], and the lady shall say her
mind freely, or the blank verse shall halt° for 't. What 330
players are they?

ROSENCRANTZ: Even those you were wont to take such
delight in, the tragedians of the city.

HAMLET: How chances it they travel? Their residence,°
both in reputation and profit, was better both ways. 335

ROSENCRANTZ: I think their inhibition° comes by the
means of the innovation.°

HAMLET: Do they hold the same estimation they did when
I was in the city? Are they so follow'd?

ROSENCRANTZ: No, indeed, are they not.° 340

[HAMLET: How comes it? Do they grow rusty?

ROSENCRANTZ: Nay, their endeavor keeps in the
wonted° pace. But there is, sir, an aery° of children,
little eyases,° that cry out on the top of question,°
and are most tyrannically° clapp'd for 't. These are 345
now the fashion, and so berattle° the common
stages°—so they call them—that many wearing
rapiers° are afraid of goose-quills° and dare scarce
come thither.

HAMLET: What, are they children? Who maintains 'em? 350
How are they escoted?° Will they pursue the quality°
no longer than they can sing?° Will they not say
afterwards, if they should grow themselves to com-
mon° players—as it is most like, if their means are
no better—their writers do them wrong, to make 355
them exclaim against their own succession?°

ROSENCRANTZ: Faith, there has been much to do° on
both sides, and the nation holds it no sin to tarre°
them to controversy. There was, for a while, no
money bid for argument° unless the poet and the 360
player went to cuffs in the question.°

---

288. **conjure:** Adjure, entreat. 289–290. **consonancy of
our youth:** The fact that we are of the same age. 291–292.
better proposer: More skillful propounded. 292. **charge:**
Urge. **even:** Straight, honest. 295. **of:** On. 299. **prevent
your discovery:** Forestall your disclosure. 300. **molt no
feather:** Not diminish in the least. 305. **brave:** Splendid.
306. **fretted:** Adorned (with fret-work, as in a vaulted ceiling). 310. **express:** Well-framed (?), exact (?). 313. **quintes-
sence:** The fifth essence of ancient philosophy, beyond earth,
water, air, and fire, supposed to be the substance of the heavenly
bodies and to be latent in all things. 321. **lenten entertainment:** Meager reception (appropriate to Lent). 322. **coted:**
Overtook and passed beyond.

326. **foil and target:** Sword and shield. 327. **humorous man:**
Eccentric character, dominated by one trait, or "humor." 329.
tickle o' th' sere: Easy on the trigger, ready to laugh easily. (*Sere* is
part of a gunlock.) 330. **halt:** Limp. 334. **residence:** Remaining
in one place (i.e., in the city). 336. **inhibition:** Formal prohibi-
tion (from acting plays in the city). 337. **innovation:** I.e., the new
fashion in satirical plays performed by boy actors in the "private"
theaters; or, possibly, a political uprising or the strict limitations
set on the theater in London in 1600. 340. **No . . . not:** The following passage (lines 341–367), omitted from the early quartos,
alludes to the so-called War of the Theatres, 1599–1602, the rivalry
between the child companies and the adult actors. 343. **wonted:**
Usual. **aery:** Nest. 344. **eyases:** Young hawks. **cry . . . question:**
Speak shrilly, dominating the controversy (in decrying the public
theaters). 345. **tyrannically:** Outrageous. 346. **berattle:** Berate.
346–347. **common stages:** Public theaters. 347–348. **many wearing rapiers:** Many men of fashion, who were afraid to patron-
ize the common players for fear of being satirized by the poets
who wrote for the children. 348. **goose-quills:** Pens of satirists.
351. **escoted:** Maintained. **quality:** (Acting) profession. 352. **no
longer . . . sing:** Only until their voices change. 353–354. **common:** Regular, adult. 356. **succession:** Future careers. 357. **to do:**
Ado. 358. **tarre:** Set on (as dogs). 360. **argument:** Plot for a
play. 361. **went . . . question:** Came to blows in the play itself.

HAMLET: Is 't possible?

GUILDENSTERN: O, there has been much throwing about of brains.

365 HAMLET: Do the boys carry it away?°

ROSENCRANTZ: Ay, that they do, my lord—Hercules and his load° too.]

HAMLET: It is not very strange, for my uncle is King of Denmark, and those that would make mouths° at
370 him while my father liv'd, give twenty, forty, fifty, a hundred ducats° apiece for his picture in little.° 'Sblood,° there is something in this more than natural, if philosophy could find it out.

(*A flourish [of trumpets within].*)

GUILDENSTERN: There are the players.

375 HAMLET: Gentlemen, you are welcome to Elsinore. Your hands, come then. Th' appurtenance of welcome is fashion and ceremony. Let me comply° with you in this garb,° lest my extent° to the players, which, I tell you, must show fairly outwards,° should more appear
380 like entertainment° than yours. You are welcome. But my uncle-father and aunt-mother are deceiv'd.

GUILDENSTERN: In what, my dear lord?

HAMLET: I am but mad north-north-west.° When the wind is southerly I know a hawk from a handsaw.°

(*Enter Polonius.*)

385 POLONIUS: Well be with you, gentlemen!

HAMLET: Hark you, Guildenstern, and you too; at each ear a hearer. That great baby you see there is not yet out of his swaddling-clouts.°

ROSENCRANTZ: Happily° he is the second time come to
390 them; for they say an old man is twice a child.

HAMLET: I will prophesy he comes to tell me of the players; mark it.—You say right, sir, o' Monday morning, 'twas then indeed.

POLONIUS: My lord, I have news to tell you.

395 HAMLET: My lord, I have news to tell you. When Roscius° was an actor in Rome—

POLONIUS: The actors are come hither, my lord.

HAMLET: Buzz,° buzz!

POLONIUS: Upon my honor—

400 HAMLET: Then came each actor on his ass—

POLONIUS: The best actors in the world, either for tragedy, comedy, history, pastoral, pastoral-comical, historical-pastoral, tragical-historical, tragical-comical-historical-pastoral, scene individable,° or poem unlimited.° Seneca° cannot be too heavy, nor 405 Plautus° too light. For the law of writ and the liberty,° these are the only men.

HAMLET: O Jephthah, judge of Israel,° what a treasure hadst thou!

POLONIUS: What a treasure had he, my lord? 410

HAMLET: Why,
"One fair daughter, and no more,
The which he loved passing° well."

POLONIUS [*aside*]: Still on my daughter.

HAMLET: Am I not i' th' right, old Jephthah? 415

POLONIUS: If you call me Jephthah, my lord, I have a daughter that I love passing well.

HAMLET: Nay, that follows not.

POLONIUS: What follows, then, my lord?

HAMLET: Why, 420
"As by lot, God wot,"°
and then, you know,
"It came to pass, as most like° it was."
The first row° of the pious chanson° will show you more, for look where my abridgement° comes. 425

(*Enter the Players.*)

You are welcome, masters; welcome, all. I am glad to see thee well. Welcome, good friends. O, old friend! Why, thy face is valanc'd° since I saw thee last. Com'st thou to beard° me in Denmark? What, my young lady° and mistress? By 'r lady, your 430 ladyship is nearer to heaven than when I saw you last, by the altitude of a chopine.° Pray God your voice, like a piece of uncurrent° gold, be not crack'd within the ring.° Masters, you are all welcome. We'll e'en to 't like French falconers, fly at anything 435 we see. We'll have a speech straight.° Come, give us a taste of your quality; come, a passionate speech.

---

365. **carry it away:** Win the day. 366–367. **Hercules . . . load:** Thought to be an allusion to the sign of the Globe Theatre, which was Hercules bearing the world on his shoulder. 369. **mouths:** Faces. 371. **ducats:** Gold coins. **in little:** In miniature. 372. **'Sblood:** By His (God's, Christ's) blood. 377. **comply:** Observe the formalities of courtesy. 378. **garb:** Manner. **my extent:** The extent of my showing courtesy. 379. **show fairly outwards:** Look cordial to outward appearances. 380. **entertainment°** A (warm) reception. 383. **north-north-west:** Only partly, at times. 384. **hawk, handsaw:** Mattock (or *hack*) and a carpenter's cutting tool, respectively; also birds, with a play on *hernshaw,* or heron. 388. **swaddling-clouts:** Cloths in which to wrap a newborn baby. 389. **Happily:** Haply, perhaps. 396. **Roscius:** A famous Roman actor who died in 62 BCE. 398. **Buzz:** An interjection used to denote stale news.

404. **scene individable:** A play observing the unity of place. 405. **poem unlimited:** A play disregarding the unities of time and place. **Seneca:** Writer of Latin tragedies. 406. **Plautus:** Writer of Latin comedy. **law . . . liberty:** Dramatic composition both according to rules and without rules (i.e., "classical" and "romantic" dramas). 408. **Jephthah . . . Israel:** Jephthah had to sacrifice his daughter; see Judges 11. Hamlet goes on to quote from a ballad on the theme. 413. **passing:** Surpassingly. 421. **wot:** Knows. 423. **like:** Likely, probable. 424. **row:** Stanza. **chanson:** Ballad, song. 425. **my abridgement:** Something that cuts short my conversation; also, a diversion. 428. **valanc'd:** Fringed (with a beard). 429. **beard:** Confront (with obvious pun). 430. **young lady:** Boy playing women's parts. 432. **chopine:** Thick-soled shoe of Italian fashion. 433. **uncurrent:** Not passable as lawful coinage. 433–434. **crack'd . . . ring:** Changed from adolescent to male voice, no longer suitable for women's roles. (Coins featured rings enclosing the sovereign's head; if the coin was cracked within this ring, it was unfit for currency.) 436. **straight:** At once.

FIRST PLAYER: What speech, my good lord?

HAMLET: I heard thee speak me a speech once, but it
440 was never acted, or, if it was, not above once, for the
play, I remember, pleas'd not the million; 'twas caviary to the general.° But it was—as I receiv'd it, and
others, whose judgments in such matters cried in
the top of° mine—an excellent play, well digested
445 in the scenes, set down with as much modesty as
cunning.° I remember one said there were no sallets°
in the lines to make the matter savory, nor no matter
in the phrase that might indict° the author of affectation, but call'd it an honest method, as wholesome as
450 sweet, and by very much more handsome than fine.°
One speech in 't I chiefly lov'd: 'twas Aeneas' tale to
Dido, and thereabout of it especially when he speaks
of Priam's slaughter.° If it live in your memory, begin
at this line: let me see, let me see—
455 "The rugged Pyrrhus,° like th' Hyrcanian beast"°—
'Tis not so. It begins with Pyrrhus:
"The rugged Pyrrhus, he whose sable° arms,
Black as his purpose, did the night resemble
When he lay couched in the ominous horse,°
Hath now this dread and black complexion
460 smear'd
With heraldry more dismal.° Head to foot
Now is he total gules,° horridly trick'd°
With blood of fathers, mothers, daughters, sons,
Bak'd and impasted° with the parching streets,°
465 That lend a tyrannous and a damned light
To their lord's° murder. Roasted in wrath and fire,
And thus o'er-sized° with coagulate gore,
With eyes like carbuncles, the hellish Pyrrhus
Old grandsire Priam seeks."
470 So proceed you.

POLONIUS: 'Fore God, my lord, well spoken, with good
accent and good discretion.

FIRST PLAYER: "Anon he finds him
Striking too short at Greeks. His antique sword,
Rebellious to his arm, lies where it falls,
475 Repugnant° to command. Unequal match'd,

Pyrrhus at Priam drives, in rage strikes wide,
But with the whiff and wind of his fell° sword
Th' unnerved father falls. [Then senseless Ilium,°]
Seeming to feel this blow, with flaming top
Stoops to his° base, and with a hideous crash   480
Takes prisoner Pyrrhus' ear. For, lo! His sword,
Which was declining on the milky head
Of reverend Priam, seem'd i' th' air to stick.
So as a painted° tyrant Pyrrhus stood,
And, like a neutral to his will and matter,°   485
Did nothing.
But, as we often see, against° some storm,
A silence in the heavens, the rack° stand still,
The bold winds speechless, and the orb below
As hush as death, anon the dreadful thunder   490
Doth rend the region,° so, after Pyrrhus' pause,
Aroused vengeance sets him new a-work,
And never did the Cyclops'° hammers fall
On Mars's armor forg'd for proof eterne°
With less remorse than Pyrrhus' bleeding sword   495
Now falls on Priam.
Out, out, thou strumpet Fortune! All you gods,
In general synod,° take away her power!
Break all the spokes and fellies° from her wheel,
And bowl the round nave° down the hill of
heaven,   500
As low as to the fiends!"

POLONIUS: This is too long.

HAMLET: It shall to the barber's with your beard.—
Prithee say on. He's for a jig° or a tale of bawdry, or
he sleeps. Say on, come to Hecuba.°   505

FIRST PLAYER: "But who, ah woe! had seen the
mobled° queen"—

HAMLET: "The mobled queen?"

POLONIUS: That's good. "Mobled queen" is good.

FIRST PLAYER: "Run barefoot up and down, threat'ning
the flames
With bisson rheum,° a clout° upon that head   510
Where late the diadem stood, and for a robe,
About her lank and all o'er-teemed° loins,
A blanket, in the alarm of fear caught up—
Who this had seen, with tongue in venom steep'd,
'Gainst Fortune's state° would treason have
pronounc'd.°   515
But if the gods themselves did see her then

441–442. **caviary to the general:** Caviar in the multitude (i.e.,
a choice dish too elegant for coarse tastes). 443–444. **cried in
the top of:** Spoke with greater authority than. 446. **cunning:**
Skill. **sallets:** Salad (i.e., spicy improprieties). 448. **indict:**
Convict. 450. **fine:** Elaborately ornamented, showy. 453.
Priam's slaughter: The slaying of the ruler of Troy, when the
Greeks finally took the city. 455. **Pyrrhus:** A Greek hero in
the Trojan War, also known as Neoptolemus, son of Achilles.
Hyrcanian beast: I.e., the tiger. (See Virgil, *Aeneid*, IV, 266;
compare the whole speech with Marlowe's *Dido Queen of
Carthage*, II, i, 214 ff.) 457. **sable:** Black (for reasons
of camouflage during the episode of the Trojan horse).
459. **ominous horse:** Trojan horse, by which the Greeks gained
access to Troy. 461. **dismal:** Ill-omened. 462. **gules:** Red (a
heraldic term). **trick'd:** Adorned, decorated. 464. **impasted:**
Crusted, like a thick paste. **with . . . streets:** By the parching
heat of the streets (because of the fires everywhere). 466. **their
lord's:** Priam's. 467. **o'er-sized:** Covered as with size or glue.
475. **Repugnant:** Disobedient, resistant.

477. **fell:** Cruel. 478. **senseless Ilium:** Insensate Troy. 480.
his: Its. 484. **painted:** Painted in a picture. 485. **like . . . matter:** As though poised indecisively between his intention and
its fulfillment. 487. **against:** Just before. 488. **rack:** Mass of
clouds. 491. **region:** Sky. 493. **Cyclops:** Giant armor makers in the smithy of Vulcan. 494. **proof eterne:** Eternal resistance to assault. 498. **synod:** Assembly. 499. **fellies:** Pieces of
wood forming the rim of a wheel. 500. **nave:** Hub. 504. **jig:**
Comic song and dance often given at the end of a play. 505.
Hecuba: Wife of Priam. 506. **mobled:** Muffled. 510. **bisson rheum:** Blinding tears. **clout:** Cloth. 512. **o'er-teemed:**
Worn out with bearing children. 515. **state:** Rule, managing.
pronounc'd: Proclaimed.

When she saw Pyrrhus make malicious sport
In mincing with his sword her husband's limbs,
The instant burst of clamor that she made,
520 Unless things mortal move them not at all,
Would have made milch° the burning eyes of
     heaven,
And passion in the gods."
POLONIUS: Look whe'er° he has not turn'd his color and
has tears in 's eyes. Prithee, no more.
525 HAMLET: 'Tis well; I'll have thee speak out the rest of
this soon. Good my lord, will you see the players
well bestow'd?° Do you hear, let them be well us'd,
for they are the abstract° and brief chronicles of the
time. After your death you were better have a bad
530 epitaph than their ill report while you live.
POLONIUS: My lord, I will use them according to their
desert.
HAMLET: God's bodkin,° man, much better! Use every
man after his desert, and who shall scape whipping?
535 Use them after your own honor and dignity. The less
they deserve, the more merit is in your bounty. Take
them in.
POLONIUS: Come, sirs.
HAMLET: Follow him, friends. We'll hear a play tomor-
540 row. [*As they start to leave, Hamlet detains the First
Player.*] Dost thou hear me, old friend? Can you play
the Murder of Gonzago?
FIRST PLAYER: Ay, my lord.
HAMLET: We'll ha 't tomorrow night. You could, for
545 need, study a speech of some dozen or sixteen lines,
which I would set down and insert in 't, could you
not?
FIRST PLAYER: Ay, my lord.
HAMLET: Very well. Follow that lord, and look you
550 mock him not.—My good friends, I'll leave you till
night. You are welcome to Elsinore.
                              (*Exeunt Polonius and Players.*)
ROSENCRANTZ: Good my lord!
                    (*Exeunt [Rosencrantz and Guildenstern].*)
HAMLET: Ay, so, God buy you.—Now I am alone.
O, what a rogue and peasant slave am I!
555 Is it not monstrous that this player here,
But in a fiction, in a dream of passion,
Could force his soul so to his own conceit°
That from her working all his visage wann'd,°
Tears in his eyes, distraction in his aspect,
560 A broken voice, and his whole function suiting
With forms to his conceit?° And all for nothing!
For Hecuba!
What's Hecuba to him, or he to Hecuba,

That he should weep for her? What would he do,
Had he the motive and the cue for passion   565
That I have? He would drown the stage with tears
And cleave the general ear with horrid speech,
Make mad the guilty and appall the free,°
Confound the ignorant, and amaze indeed
The very faculties of eyes and ears. Yet I,   570
A dull and muddy-mettled° rascal, peak,°
Like John-a-dreams,° unpregnant of° my cause,
And can say nothing—no, not for a king
Upon whose property° and most dear life
A damn'd defeat was made. Am I a coward?   575
Who calls me villain? Breaks my pate across?
Plucks off my beard, and blows it in my face?
Tweaks me by the nose? Gives me the lie° i' th'
     throat,
As deep as to the lungs? Who does me this?
Ha, 'swounds, I should take it; for it cannot be   580
But I am pigeon-liver'd,° and lack gall
To make oppression bitter, or ere this
I should have fatted all the region kites°
With this slave's offal. Bloody, bawdy villain!
Remorseless, treacherous, lecherous, kindless° villain! 585
[O, vengeance!]
Why, what an ass am I! This is most brave,
That I, the son of a dear father murder'd,
Prompted to my revenge by heaven and hell,
Must, like a whore, unpack my heart with words,   590
And fall a-cursing, like a very drab,°
A stallion!° Fie upon 't, foh! About,° my brains!
Hum, I have heard
That guilty creatures sitting at a play
Have by the very cunning of the scene   595
Been struck so to the soul that presently°
They have proclaim'd their malefactions;
For murder, though it have no tongue, will speak
With most miraculous organ. I'll have these
     Players
Play something like the murder of my father   600
Before mine uncle. I'll observe his looks;
I'll tent° him to the quick. If 'a do blench,°
I know my course. The spirit that I have seen
May be the devil, and the devil hath power
T' assume a pleasing shape; yea, and perhaps   605
Out of my weakness and my melancholy,
As he is very potent with such spirits,°

---

521. **milch:** Milky moist with tears.   523. **whe'er:** Whether.
527. **bestow'd:** Lodged.   528. **abstract:** Summary account.
533. **God's bodkin:** By God's (Christ's) little body, *bodykin*
(not to be confused with *bodkin,* dagger).   557. **conceit:**
Conception.   558. **wann'd:** Grew pale.   560–561. **his whole ...
conceit:** His whole being responded with actions to suit his
thought.

568. **free:** Innocent.   571. **muddy-mettled:** Dull-spirited.
peak: Mope, pine.   572. **John-a-dreams:** Sleepy dreaming
idler.   **unpregnant of:** Not quickened by.   574. **property:** The
crown; perhaps also character, quality.   578. **Gives me the
lie:** Calls me a liar.   581. **pigeon-liver'd:** The pigeon or dove
was popularly supposed to be mild because it secreted no gall.
583. **region kites:** Kites (birds of prey) of the air, from the
vicinity.   585. **kindless:** Unnatural.   591. **drab:** Prostitute.
592. **stallion:** Prostitute (male or female). (Many editors follow
the Folio reading of *scullion.*)   **About:** About it, to work.
596. **presently:** At once.   602. **tent:** Probe.   **blench:** Quail,
flinch.   607. **spirits:** Humors (of melancholy).

Abuses° me to damn me. I'll have grounds
More relative° than this. The play's the thing
610   Wherein I'll catch the conscience of the King.

(*Exit.*)

{ACT III • Scene I}°

(*Enter King, Queen, Polonius, Ophelia, Rosencrantz,
Guildenstern, Lords.*)

KING: And can you, by no drift of conference,°
    Get from him why he puts on this confusion,
    Grating so harshly all his days of quiet
    With turbulent and dangerous lunacy?
ROSENCRANTZ: He does confess he feels himself
5   distracted,
    But from what cause 'a will by no means speak.
GUILDENSTERN: Nor do we find him forward° to be
    sounded,°
    But with a crafty madness keeps aloof
    When we would bring him on to some confession
    Of his true state.
10 QUEEN: Did he receive you well?
ROSENCRANTZ: Most like a gentleman.
GUILDENSTERN: But with much forcing of his
    disposition.°
ROSENCRANTZ: Niggard of question,° but of our
    demands
    Most free in his reply.
QUEEN: Did you assay° him
15   To any pastime?
ROSENCRANTZ: Madam, it so fell out that certain players
    We o'er-raught° on the way. Of these we told him,
    And there did seem in him a kind of joy
    To hear of it. They are here about the court,
20   And, as I think, they have already order
    This night to play before him.
POLONIUS: 'Tis most true,
    And he beseech'd me to entreat your Majesties
    To hear and see the matter.
KING: With all my heart, and it doth much content me
25   To hear him so inclin'd.
    Good gentlemen, give him a further edge,°
    And drive his purpose into these delights.
ROSENCRANTZ: We shall, my lord.
         (*Exeunt Rosencrantz and Guildenstern.*)
KING: Sweet Gertrude, leave us too,
    For we have closely° sent for Hamlet hither,
30   That he, as 'twere by accident, may here

Affront° Ophelia.
Her father and myself, [lawful espials,°]
Will so bestow ourselves that seeing, unseen,
We may of their encounter frankly judge,
And gather by him, as he is behav'd,   35
If 't be th' affliction of his love or no
That thus he suffers for.
QUEEN: I shall obey you.
And for your part, Ophelia, I do wish
That your good beauties be the happy cause
Of Hamlet's wildness. So shall I hope your virtues   40
Will bring him to his wonted way again,
To both your honors.
OPHELIA: Madam, I wish it may.
         [*Exit Queen.*]
POLONIUS: Ophelia, walk you here.—Gracious,° so
    please you,
    We will bestow ourselves. [*To Ophelia.*] Read on
    this book,   [*Gives her a book.*]
    That show of such an exercise° may color°   45
    Your loneliness. We are oft to blame in this—
    'Tis too much prov'd°—that with devotion's visage
    And pious action we do sugar o'er
    The devil himself.
KING [*aside*]: O, 'tis too true!   50
    How smart a lash that speech doth give my
    conscience!
    The harlot's cheek, beautied with plast'ring art,
    Is not more ugly to° the thing° that helps it
    Than is my deed to my most painted word.
    O heavy burden!   55
POLONIUS: I hear him coming. Let's withdraw, my lord.
         [*King and Polonius withdraw.*°]

(*Enter Hamlet.* [*Ophelia pretends to read a book.*])

HAMLET: To be, or not to be, that is the question:
    Whether 'tis nobler in the mind to suffer
    The slings and arrows of outrageous fortune,
    Or to take arms against a sea of troubles,   60
    And by opposing end them. To die, to sleep—
    No more—and by a sleep to say we end
    The heart-ache and the thousand natural shocks
    That flesh is heir to. 'Tis a consummation
    Devoutly to be wish'd. To die, to sleep;   65
    To sleep, perchance to dream. Ay, there's the rub,°
    For in that sleep of death what dreams may come
    When we have shuffled° off this mortal coil,°

---

31. Affront: Confront, meet. **32. espials:** Spies. **43. Gracious:**
Your Grace (i.e., the King). **45. exercise:** Act of devotion. (The
book she reads is a book of devotions, or prayers.) **color:**
Give a plausible appearance to. **47. too much prov'd:** Too
often shown to be true, too often practiced. **53. to:** Compared to. **thing:** I.e., the cosmetic. **56. [s.d.]** *withdraw:*
The King and Polonius may retire behind an arras. The stage
directions specify that they "enter" again near the end of the
scene. **66. rub:** Literally, an obstacle in the game of bowls.
68. shuffled: Sloughed, cast. **coil:** Turmoil.

---

608. Abuses: Deludes. **609. relative:** Closely related, per-
tinent. **III, i. Location:** The castle. **1. drift of conference:**
Direction of conversation. **7. forward:** Willing. **sounded:**
Tested deeply. **12. disposition:** Inclination. **13. question:**
Conversation. **14. assay:** Try to win. **17. o'er-raught:** Over-
took and passed. **26. edge:** Incitement. **29. closely:** Privately.

Must give us pause. There's the respect°
70 That makes calamity of so long life.°
For who would bear the whips and scorns of time,
Th' oppressor's wrong, the proud man's
    contumely,°
The pangs of despis'd° love, the law's delay,
The insolence of office,° and the spurns°
75 That patient merit of th' unworthy takes,
When he himself might his quietus° make
With a bare bodkin?° Who would fardels° bear,
To grunt and sweat under a weary life,
But that the dread of something after death,
80 The undiscover'd country from whose bourn°
No traveler returns, puzzles the will,
And makes us rather bear those ills we have
Than fly to others that we know not of?
Thus conscience does make cowards of us all
85 And thus the native hue° of resolution
Is sicklied o'er with the pale cast° of thought,
And enterprises of great pitch° and moment°
With this regard° their currents° turn awry,
And lose the name of action.—Soft you now,
90 The fair Ophelia. Nymph, in thy orisons°
Be all my sins rememb'red.

OPHELIA: Good my lord,
  How does your honor for this many a day?
HAMLET: I humbly thank you; well, well, well.
OPHELIA: My lord, I have remembrances of yours,
95   That I have longed long to re-deliver.
  I pray you, now receive them.   [*Offers tokens.*]
HAMLET: No, not I, I never gave you aught.
OPHELIA: My honor'd lord, you know right well
      you did,
  And with them words of so sweet breath compos'd
100 As made these things more rich. Their perfume lost,
  Take these again, for to the noble mind
  Rich gifts wax poor when givers prove unkind.
  There, my lord.   [*Gives tokens.*]
HAMLET: Ha, ha! Are you honest?°
105 OPHELIA: My lord?
HAMLET: Are you fair?°
OPHELIA: What means your lordship?
HAMLET: That if you be honest and fair, your honesty°
  should admit no discourse° to your beauty.
110 OPHELIA: Could beauty, my lord, have better commerce°
  than with honesty?

HAMLET: Ay, truly, for the power of beauty will sooner
  transform honesty from what it is to a bawd than the
  force of honesty can translate beauty into his likeness. This was sometime° a paradox,° but now the 115
  time° gives it proof. I did love you once.
OPHELIA: Indeed, my lord, you made me believe so.
HAMLET: You should not have believ'd me, for virtue
  cannot so inoculate° our old stock but we shall relish
  of it.° I lov'd you not.   120
OPHELIA: I was the more deceiv'd.
HAMLET: Get thee to a nunn'ry.° Why wouldst thou be a
  breeder of sinners? I am myself indifferent honest;°
  but yet I could accuse me of such things that it were
  better my mother had not borne me: I am very proud, 125
  revengeful, ambitious, with more offenses at my
  beck° than I have thoughts to put them in, imagination to give them shape, or time to act them in. What
  should such fellows as I do crawling between earth
  and heaven? We are arrant knaves, all; believe none   130
  of us. Go thy ways to a nunn'ry. Where's your father?
OPHELIA: At home, my lord.
HAMLET: Let the doors be shut upon him, that he may
  play the fool nowhere but in 's own house.
  Farewell.   135
OPHELIA: O, help him, you sweet heavens!
HAMLET: If thou dost marry, I'll give thee this plague for
  thy dowry: be thou as chaste as ice, as pure as snow,
  thou shalt not escape calumny. Get thee to a nunn'ry,
  farewell. Or, if thou wilt needs marry, marry a fool, 140
  for wise men know well enough what monsters°
  you° make of them. To a nunn'ry, go, and quickly
  too. Farewell.
OPHELIA: Heavenly powers, restore him!
HAMLET: I have heard of your paintings too, well   145
  enough. God hath given you one face, and you make
  yourselves another. You jig,° and amble, and you lisp,
  you nickname God's creatures, and make your wan-
  tonness your ignorance.° Go to, I'll no more on 't;
  it hath made me mad. I say, we will have no moe   150
  marriage. Those that are married already—all but
  one—shall live. The rest shall keep as they are. To a
  nunn'ry, go.   (*Exit.*)
OPHELIA: O, what a noble mind is here o'erthrown!
  The courtier's, soldier's, scholar's, eye, tongue, sword, 155
  Th' expectancy and rose of the fair state,°

---

69. respect: Consideration. **70. of . . . life:** So long-lived.
72. contumely: Insolent abuse. **73. despis'd:** Rejected.
74. office: Officialdom. **spurns:** Insults. **76. quietus:** Acquittance; here, death. **77. bodkin:** Dagger. **fardels:** Burdens.
80. bourn: Boundary. **85. native hue:** Natural color, complexion. **86. cast:** Shade of color. **87. pitch:** Height (as of a
falcon's flight). **moment:** Importance. **88. regard:** Respect,
consideration. **currents:** Courses. **90. orisons:** Prayers.
104. honest: (1) Truthful; (2) chaste. **106. fair:** (1) Beautiful; (2) just, honorable. **108. your honesty:** Your chastity.
109. discourse: Familiar dealings. **110. commerce:** Dealings.

115. sometime: Formerly. **paradox:** A view opposite to commonly held opinion. **115–116. the time:** The present age.
119. inoculate: Graft, be engrafted to. **119–120. but . . . it:**
That we do not still have about us a taste of the old stock
(i.e., retain our sinfulness). **122. nunn'ry:** (1) Convent;
(2) brothel. **123. indifferent honest:** Reasonably virtuous.
127. beck: Command. **141. monsters:** An allusion to the
horns of a cuckold. **142. you:** You women. **147. jig:** Dance
and sing affectedly and wantonly. **148–149. make . . . ignorance:** Excuse your affection on the grounds of your ignorance.
156. Th' expectancy . . . state: The hope and ornament of the
kingdom made fair (by him).

The glass of fashion and the mold of form,°
Th' observ'd of all observers,° quite, quite down!
And I, of ladies most deject and wretched,
160 That suck'd the honey of his music vows,
Now see that noble and most sovereign reason,
Like sweet bells jangled, out of time and harsh,
That unmatch'd form and feature of blown° youth
Blasted with ecstasy.° O, woe is me,
165 T' have seen what I have seen, see what I see!

(Enter King and Polonius.)

KING: Love? His affections do not that way tend;
Nor what he spake, though it lack'd form a little,
Was not like madness. There's something in his soul,
O'er which his melancholy sits on brood,
170 And I do doubt° the hatch and the disclose°
Will be some danger; which for to prevent,
I have in quick determination
Thus set it down: he shall with speed to England,
For the demand of° our neglected tribute.
175 Haply the seas and countries different
With variable° objects shall expel
This something-settled° matter in his heart,
Whereon his brains still beating puts him thus
From fashion of himself.° What think you on 't?
180 POLONIUS: It shall do well. But yet do I believe
The origin and commencement of his grief
Sprung from neglected love.—How now,
     Ophelia?
You need not tell us what Lord Hamlet said;
We heard it all.—My lord, do as you please,
185 But, if you hold it fit, after the play
Let his queen mother all alone entreat him
To show his grief. Let her be round° with him;
And I'll be plac'd, so please you, in the ear
Of all their conference. If she find him not,
190 To England send him, or confine him where
Your wisdom best shall think.
KING: It shall be so.
Madness in great ones must not unwatch'd go.
                                        (Exeunt.)

{Scene II}°

(Enter Hamlet and three of the Players.)

HAMLET: Speak the speech, I pray you, as I pronounc'd
it to you, trippingly on the tongue. But if you mouth

it, as many of our players° do, I had as lief the town-
crier spoke my lines. Nor do not saw the air too
much with your hand, thus, but use all gently; for in   5
the very torrent, tempest, and, as I may say, whirlwind of your passion, you must acquire and beget
a temperance that may give it smoothness. O, it offends me to the soul to hear a robustious° periwig-
pated° fellow tear a passion to tatters, to very rags, to 10
split the ears of the groundlings,° who for the most
part are capable of° nothing but inexplicable dumb-
shows and noise. I would have such a fellow whipp'd
for o'er-doing Termagant.° It out-herods Herod.°
Pray you, avoid it.   15
FIRST PLAYER: I warrant your honor.
HAMLET: Be not too tame neither, but let your own discretion be your tutor. Suit the action to the word, the
word to the action, with this special observance, that
you o'erstep not the modesty of nature. For anything 20
so o'erdone is from° the purpose of playing, whose
end, both at the first and now, was and is, to hold, as
't were, the mirror up to nature, to show virtue her
feature, scorn her own image, and the very age and
body of the time his° form and pressure.° Now this 25
overdone, or come tardy off,° though it makes the
unskillful laugh, cannot but make the judicious
grieve, the censure of which one° must in your allowance o'erweigh a whole theater of others. O, there
be players that I have seen play, and heard others   30
praise, and that highly, not to speak it profanely,
that, neither having th' accent of Christians nor the
gait of Christian, pagan, nor man, have so strutted
and bellow'd that I have thought some of nature's
journeymen° had made men and not made them   35
well, they imitated humanity so abominably.
FIRST PLAYER: I hope we have reform'd that indifferently°
with us, sir.
HAMLET: O, reform it altogether. And let those that play
your clowns speak no more than is set down for   40
them; for there be of them° that will themselves
laugh, to set on some quantity of barren° spectators
to laugh too, though in the mean time some necessary question of the play be then to be consider'd.

---

157. **The glass . . . form:** The mirror of fashion and the pattern of courtly behavior. 158. **observ'd . . . observers:** The center of attention and honor in the court. 163. **blown:** Blooming. 164. **ecstasy:** Madness. 170. **doubt:** Fear. **disclose:** Disclosure. 174. **For . . . of:** To demand. 176. **variable:** Various. 177. **something-settled:** Somewhat settled. 179. **From . . . himself:** Out of his natural manner. 187. **round:** Blunt. **III, ii. Location:** The castle.

3. **our players:** Indefinite use (i.e., players nowadays). 9. **robustious:** Violent, boisterous. 9–10. **periwig-pated:** Wearing a wig. 11. **groundlings:** Spectators who paid least and stood in the yard of the theater. 12. **capable of:** Susceptible of being influenced by. 14. **Termagant:** A god of the Saracens. (In the St. Nicholas play, one of his worshipers, leaving him in charge of goods, returns to find them stolen, whereupon he beats the god or idol, which howls vociferously.) **Herod:** Herod of Jewry. (In *The Slaughter of the Innocents* and other cycle plays, the part was played with great noise and fury.) 21. **from:** Contrary to. 25. **his:** Its. **pressure:** Stamp, impressed character. 26. **come tardy off:** Inadequately done. 28. **the censure . . . one:** The judgment of even one of whom. 35. **journeymen:** Laborers not yet masters in their trade. 37. **indifferently:** Tolerably. 41. **of them:** Some among them. 42. **barren:** I.e., of wit.

45   That's villainous, and shows a most pitiful ambition
     in the fool that uses it. Go, make you ready.

                                        [*Exeunt Players.*]

(*Enter Polonius, Guildenstern, and Rosencrantz.*)

     How now, my lord? Will the King hear this piece
     of work?
     POLONIUS: And the Queen too, and that presently.°
50   HAMLET: Bid the players make haste.

                                        [*Exit Polonius.*]

     Will you two help to hasten them?
     ROSENCRANTZ: Ay, my lord.   (*Exeunt they two.*)
     HAMLET: What ho, Horatio!

(*Enter Horatio.*)

     HORATIO: Here, sweet lord, at your service.
     HAMLET: Horatio, thou art e'en as just a man
55   As e'er my conversation cop'd withal.°
     HORATIO: O, my dear lord—
     HAMLET: Nay, do not think I flatter;
     For what advancement may I hope from thee
     That no revenue hast but thy good spirits,
     To feed and clothe thee? Why should the poor be
          flatter'd?
60   No, let the candied° tongue lick absurd pomp,
     And crook the pregnant° hinges of the knee
     Where thrift° may follow fawning. Dost thou hear?
     Since my dear soul was mistress of her choice
     And could of men distinguish her election,
65   Sh' hath seal'd thee for herself, for thou hast been
     As one, in suff'ring all, that suffers nothing,
     A man that Fortune's buffets and rewards
     Hast ta'en with equal thanks; and blest are those
     Whose blood° and judgment are so well commeddled°
70   That they are not a pipe for Fortune's finger
     To sound what stop° she please. Give me that man
     That is not passion's slave, and I will wear him
     In my heart's core, ay, in my heart of heart,
     As I do thee.—Something too much of this.—
75   There is a play tonight before the King.
     One scene of it comes near the circumstance
     Which I have told thee of my father's death.
     I prithee, when thou seest that act afoot,
     Even with the very comment of thy soul°
80   Observe my uncle. If his occulted° guilt
     Do not itself unkennel in one speech,
     It is a damned° ghost that we have seen,
     And my imaginations are as foul
     As Vulcan's stithy.° Give him heedful note,

     For I mine eyes will rivet to his face,   85
     And after we will both our judgments join
     In censure of his seeming.°
     HORATIO: Well, my lord.
     If 'a steal aught the whilst this play is playing,
     And scape detecting, I will pay the theft.

([*Flourish.*] *Enter trumpets and kettledrums, King,
Queen, Polonius, Ophelia, [Rosencrantz, Guildenstern,
and other Lords, with Guards carrying torches*].)

     HAMLET: They are coming to the play. I must be idle. Get   90
     you a place.   [*The King, Queen, and courtiers sit.*]
     KING: How fares our cousin Hamlet?
     HAMLET: Excellent, i' faith, of the chameleon's dish:°
     I eat the air, promise-cramm'd. You cannot feed
     capons so.   95
     KING: I have nothing with° this answer, Hamlet. These
     words are not mine.°
     HAMLET: No, nor mine now. [*To Polonius.*] My lord, you
     played once i' th' university, you say?
     POLONIUS: That did I, my lord; and was accounted a   100
     good actor.
     HAMLET: What did you enact?
     POLONIUS: I did enact Julius Caesar. I was killed i' th'
     Capitol; Brutus kill'd me.
     HAMLET: It was a brute part of him to kill so capital a   105
     calf there. Be the players ready?
     ROSENCRANTZ: Ay, my lord; they stay upon your
     patience.
     QUEEN: Come hither, my dear Hamlet, sit by me.
     HAMLET: No, good mother, here's metal more attractive.   110
     POLONIUS [*to the King*]: O, ho, do you mark that?
     HAMLET: Lady, shall I lie in your lap?

                                 [*Lying down at Ophelia's feet.*]

     OPHELIA: No, my lord.
     [HAMLET: I mean, my head upon your lap?
     OPHELIA: Ay, my lord.]   115
     HAMLET: Do you think I meant country° matters?
     OPHELIA: I think nothing, my lord.
     HAMLET: That's a fair thought to lie between maids' legs.
     OPHELIA: What is, my lord?
     HAMLET: Nothing.   120
     OPHELIA: You are merry, my lord.
     HAMLET: Who, I?
     OPHELIA: Ay, my lord.
     HAMLET: O God, your only jig-maker.° What should a
     man do but be merry? For look you how cheerfully   125
     my mother looks, and my father died within 's° two
     hours.

49. presently: At once. **55. my . . . withal:** My contact with
people provided opportunity for encounter with. **60. candied:**
Sugared, flattering. **61. pregnant:** Compliant. **62. thrift:**
Profit. **69. blood:** Passion. **commeddled:** Commingled.
71. stop: Hole in a wind instrument for controlling the
sound. **79. very . . . soul:** Inward and sagacious criticism.
80. occulted: Hidden. **82. damned:** In league with Satan.
84. stithy: Smithy, place of stiths (anvils).

87. censure of his seeming: Judgment of his appearance or behavior. **93. chameleon's dish:** Chameleons were supposed to
feed on air. Hamlet deliberately misinterprets the King's *fares*
as *feeds*. By his phrase *eat the air* he also plays on the idea of
feeding himself with the promise of succession, of being the
heir. **96. have . . . with:** Make nothing of it. **97. are not mine:**
Do not respond to what I asked. **116. country:** With a bawdy
pun. **124. only jig-maker:** Very best composer of jigs (song
and dance). **126. within 's:** Within this.

OPHELIA: Nay, 'tis twice two months, my lord.

HAMLET: So long? Nay then, let the devil wear black for
130   I'll have a suit of sables.° O heavens! Die two months
ago, and not forgotten yet? Then there's hope a great
man's memory may outlive his life half a year. But,
by 'r lady, 'a must build churches, then, or else shall
'a suffer not thinking on,° with the hobby-horse,
135   whose epitaph is "For, O, for, O, the hobby-horse is
forgot."°

(*The trumpets sound. Dumb show follows.*)

(*Enter a King and a Queen [very lovingly]; the Queen
embracing him, and he her. [She kneels and makes show
of protestation unto him.] He takes her up, and declines
his head upon her neck. He lies him down upon a bank
of flowers. She, seeing him asleep, leaves him. Anon
comes in another man, takes off his crown, kisses it,
pours poison in the sleeper's ears, and leaves him. The
Queen returns; finds the King dead, makes passionate
action. The Poisoner, with some three or four, come in
again, seem to condole with her. The dead body is carried away. The Poisoner woos the Queen with gifts; she
seems harsh awhile but in the end accepts love.*)

[*Exeunt.*]

OPHELIA: What means this, my lord?

HAMLET: Marry, this' miching mallecho;° it means
mischief.

140   OPHELIA: Belike° this show imports the argument° of
the play.

(*Enter Prologue.*)

HAMLET: We shall know by this fellow. The players cannot keep counsel;° they'll tell all.

OPHELIA: Will 'a tell us what this show meant?

145   HAMLET: Ay, or any show that you will show him. Be not
you° asham'd to show, he'll not shame to tell you
what it means.

OPHELIA: You are naught, you are naught.° I'll mark the
play.

150   PROLOGUE: For us, and for our tragedy,
Here stooping° to your clemency,
We beg your hearing patiently.   [*Exit.*]

HAMLET: Is this a prologue, or the posy of a ring?°

OPHELIA: 'Tis brief, my lord.

155   HAMLET: As woman's love.

(*Enter [two Players as] King and Queen.*)

PLAYER KING: Full thirty times hath Phoebus' cart°
gone round
Neptune's salt wash° and Tellus'° orbed ground,
And thirty dozen moons with borrowed° sheen
About the world have times twelve thirties been,
Since love our hearts and Hymen° did our hands   160
Unite commutual° in most sacred bands.

PLAYER QUEEN: So many journeys may the sun and
moon
Make us again count o'er ere love be done!
But, woe is me, you are so sick of late,
So far from cheer and from your former state,   165
That I distrust you. Yet, though I distrust,°
Discomfort you, my lord, it nothing° must.
For women's fear and love hold quantity;°
In neither aught, or in extremity.
Now, what my love is, proof° hath made you know,   170
And as my love is siz'd, my fear is so.
Where love is great, the littlest doubts are fear;
Where little fears grow great, great love grows
there.

PLAYER KING: Faith, I must leave thee, love, and
shortly too;
My operant° powers their functions leave to do.°   175
And thou shalt live in this fair world behind,
Honor'd, belov'd; and haply one as kind
For husband shalt thou—

PLAYER QUEEN: O, confound the rest!
Such love must needs be treason in my breast.
In second husband let me be accurst!   180
None wed the second but who kill'd the first.

HAMLET: Wormwood, wormwood.

PLAYER QUEEN: The instances° that second marriage
move°
Are base respects of thrift,° but none of love.
A second time I kill my husband dead,   185
When second husband kisses me in bed.

PLAYER KING: I do believe you think what now you
speak,
But what we do determine oft we break.
Purpose is but the slave to memory,°
Of violent birth, but poor validity,°   190
Which now, like fruit unripe, sticks on the tree,
But fall unshaken when they mellow be.

---

130. **suit of sables:** Garments trimmed with the fur of the sable and hence suited for a wealthy person, not a mourner (with a pun on *sable*, black).   134. **suffer . . . on:** Undergo oblivion.   135–136. **"For . . . forgot":** Verse of a song occurring also in *Love's Labor's Lost*, III, i, 30. The hobby-horse was a character made up to resemble a horse, appearing in the Morris dance and such May-game sports. This song laments the disappearance of such customs under pressure from the Puritans.   138. **this' miching mallecho:** This is sneaking mischief.   140. **Belike:** Probably.   **argument:** Plot.   143. **counsel:** Secret.   145–146. **Be not you:** If you are not.   148. **naught:** Indecent.   151. **stooping:** Bowing.   153. **posy . . . ring:** Brief motto in verse inscribed in a ring.

156. **Phoebus' cart:** The sun god's chariot.   157. **salt wash:** The sea.   **Tellus:** Goddess of the earth, of the *orbed ground*.   158. **borrowed:** Reflected.   160. **Hymen:** God of matrimony.   161. **commutual:** Mutually.   166. **distrust:** Am anxious about.   167. **nothing:** Not at all.   168. **hold quantity:** Keep proportion with one another.   170. **proof:** Experience.   175. **operant:** Active.   **leave to do:** Cease to perform.   183. **instances:** Motives.   **move:** Motivate.   184. **base . . . thrift:** Ignoble considerations of material prosperity.   189. **Purpose . . . memory:** Our good intentions are subject to forgetfulness.   190. **validity:** Strength, durability.

Most necessary 'tis that we forget
To pay ourselves what to ourselves is debt.°
195   What to ourselves in passion we propose,
The passion ending, doth the purpose lose.
The violence of either grief or joy
Their own enactures° with themselves destroy.
Where joy most revels, grief doth most lament;
200   Grief joys, joy grieves, on slender accident.
This world is not for aye,° nor 'tis not strange
That even our loves should with our fortunes
        change;
For 'tis a question left us yet to prove,
Whether love lead fortune, or else fortune love.
205   The great man down, you mark his favorite flies;
The poor advanc'd makes friends of enemies.
And hitherto doth love on fortune tend;
For who not needs° shall never lack a friend,
And who in want° a hollow friend doth try,°
210   Directly seasons him° his enemy.
But, orderly to end where I begun,
Our wills and fates do so contrary run
That our devices still° are overthrown;
Our thoughts are ours, their ends° none of our own.
215   So think thou wilt no second husband wed,
But die thy thoughts when thy first lord is dead.
PLAYER QUEEN: Nor earth to me give food, nor
        heaven light,
Sport and repose lock from me day and night,
To desperation turn my trust and hope,
220   An anchor's cheer° in prison be my scope!°
Each opposite° that blanks° the face of joy
Meet what I would have well and it destroy!
Both here and hence° pursue me lasting strife,
If, once a widow, ever I be wife!
225   HAMLET: If she should break it now!
PLAYER KING: 'Tis deeply sworn. Sweet, leave me here
        awhile;
My spirits grow dull, and fain I would beguile
The tedious day with sleep.   [Sleeps.]
PLAYER QUEEN: Sleep rock thy brain,
230   And never come mischance between us twain!
                                        [Exit.]
HAMLET: Madam, how like you this play?
QUEEN: The lady doth protest too much, methinks.
HAMLET: O, but she'll keep her word.
KING: Have you heard the argument?° Is there no
235   offense in 't?

193–194. **Most . . . debt:** It's inevitable that in time we forget the obligations we have imposed on ourselves. **198. enactures:** Fulfillments. **201. aye:** Ever. **208. who not needs:** He who is not in need (of wealth). **209. who in want:** He who is in need. **try:** Test (his generosity). **210. seasons him:** Ripens him into. **213. devices still:** Intentions continually. **214. ends:** Results. **220. anchor's cheer:** Anchorite's or hermit's fare. **my scope:** The extent of my happiness. **222. opposite:** Adverse thing. **blanks:** Causes to blanch or grow pale. **223. hence:** In the life hereafter. **234. argument:** Plot.

HAMLET: No, no, they do but jest, poison in jest; no
offense i' th' world.
KING: What do you call the play?
HAMLET: "The Mouse-trap." Marry, how? Tropically.°
This play is the image of a murder done in Vienna.   240
Gonzago is the Duke's name; his wife, Baptista. You
shall see anon. 'Tis a knavish piece of work, but what
of that? Your Majesty, and we that have free° souls, it
touches us not. Let the gall'd jade° winch,° our with-
ers° are unwrung.°   245

(Enter Lucianus.)

This is one Lucianus, nephew to the King.
OPHELIA: You are as good as a chorus,° my lord.
HAMLET: I could interpret between you and your love, if
I could see the puppets dallying.°
OPHELIA: You are keen, my lord, you are keen.   250
HAMLET: It would cost you a groaning to take off mine
edge.
OPHELIA: Still better, and worse.°
HAMLET: So° you mistake° your husbands. Begin, mur-
derer, leave thy damnable faces, and begin. Come,   255
the croaking raven doth bellow for revenge.
LUCIANUS: Thoughts black, hands apt, drugs fit, and time
agreeing,
Confederate season,° else no creature seeing,
Thou mixture rank, of midnight weeds collected,   260
With Hecate's ban° thrice blasted, thrice infected,
Thy natural magic and dire property
On wholesome life usurp immediately.
        [Pours the poison into the sleeper's ears.]
HAMLET: 'A poisons him i' th' garden for his estate. His
name's Gonzago. The story is extant, and written in   265
very choice Italian. You shall see anon how the mur-
derer gets the love of Gonzago's wife.
                                    [Claudius rises.]
OPHELIA: The King rises.
[HAMLET: What, frighted with false fire?°]
QUEEN: How fares my lord?   270
POLONIUS: Give o'er the play.

239. Tropically: Figuratively. (The first quarto reading, *trapically,* suggests a pun on *trap* in *Mouse-trap.*) **243. free:** Guiltless. **244. gall'd jade:** Horse whose hide is rubbed by saddle or harness. **winch:** Wince. **244–245. withers:** The part between the horse's shoulder blades. **245. unwrung:** Not rubbed sore. **247. chorus:** In many Elizabethan plays, the forthcoming action was explained by an actor known as the "chorus"; at a puppet show, the actor who spoke the dialogue was known as an "interpreter," as indicated by the lines following. **249. dallying:** With sexual suggestion, continued in *keen* (i.e., sexually aroused), *groaning* (i.e., moaning in pregnancy), and *edge* (i.e., sexual desire or impetuosity). **253. Still . . . worse:** More keen-witted and less decorous. **254. So:** Even thus (in marriage). **mistake:** Mistake, take erringly, falseheartedly. **259. Confederate season:** The time and occasion conspiring (to assist the murderer). **261. Hecate's ban:** The curse of Hecate, the goddess of witchcraft. **269. false fire:** The blank discharge of a gun loaded with powder but not shot.

KING: Give me some light. Away!
POLONIUS: Lights, lights, lights!

(*Exeunt all but Hamlet and Horatio.*)

HAMLET: "Why, let the strucken deer go weep, The hart
275   ungalled° play.
          For some must watch,° while some must sleep;
              Thus runs the world away."°
          Would not this,° sir, and a forest of feathers°—if the
          rest of my fortunes turn Turk with° me—with two
280   Provincial roses° on my raz'd° shoes, get me a fellow-
          ship in a cry of players?°
HORATIO: Half a share.
HAMLET: A whole one, I.
          "For thou dost know, O Damon dear,
285   This realm dismantled° was
          Of Jove himself, and now reigns here
              A very, very—pajock."°
HORATIO: You might have rhym'd.
HAMLET: O good Horatio, I'll take the ghost's word for
290   a thousand pound. Didst perceive?
HORATIO: Very well, my lord.
HAMLET: Upon the talk of pois'ning?
HORATIO: I did very well note him.
HAMLET: Ah, ha! Come, some music! Come, the
295   recorders!°
          "For if the King like not the comedy,
          Why then, belike, he likes it not, perdy"°
          Come, some music!

(*Enter Rosencrantz and Guildenstern.*)

GUILDENSTERN: Good my lord, vouchsafe me a word
300   with you.
HAMLET: Sir, a whole history.
GUILDENSTERN: The King, sir—
HAMLET: Ay, sir, what of him?
GUILDENSTERN: Is in his retirement marvelous dis-
305   temp'red.
HAMLET: With drink, sir?
GUILDENSTERN: No, my lord, with choler.°
HAMLET: Your wisdom should show itself more richer to
          signify this to the doctor, for for me to put him to
310   his purgation would perhaps plunge him into more
          choler.

275. **ungalled:** Unafflicted. 276. **watch:** Remain awake. 274–277. **Why . . . away:** Probably from an old ballad, with allusion to the popular belief that a wounded deer retires to weep and die; cf. *As You Like It,* II, i, 66. 278. **this:** The play. **feathers:** Allusion to the plumes that Elizabethan actors were fond of wearing. 279. **turn Turk with:** Turn renegade against, go back on. 280. **Provincial roses:** Rosettes of ribbon like the roses of a part of France. **raz'd:** With ornamental slashing. 280–281. **fellowship . . . players:** Partnership in a theatrical company. 285. **dismantled:** Stripped, divested. 287. **pajock:** Peacock, a bird with a bad reputation (here substituted for the obvious rhyme-word *ass*). 295. **recorders:** Wind instruments like the flute. 297. **perdy:** A corruption of the French *par dieu,* by God. 307. **choler:** Anger. (But Hamlet takes the word in its more basic humors sense of bilious disorder.)

GUILDENSTERN: Good my lord, put your discourse into
          some frame° and start not so wildly from my affair.
HAMLET: I am tame, sir. Pronounce.
GUILDENSTERN: The Queen, your mother, in most great   315
          affliction of spirit, hath sent me to you.
HAMLET: You are welcome.
GUILDENSTERN: Nay, good my lord, this courtesy is not
          of the right breed. If it shall please you to make me
          a wholesome answer, I will do your mother's com-   320
          mandment; if not, your pardon° and my return shall
          be the end of my business.
HAMLET: Sir, I cannot.
ROSENCRANTZ: What, my lord?
HAMLET: Make you a wholesome answer; my wit's dis-   325
          eas'd. But, sir, such answer as I can make, you shall
          command, or rather, as you say, my mother. There-
          fore no more, but to the matter. My mother, you
          say—
ROSENCRANTZ: Then thus she says: your behavior hath   330
          struck her into amazement and admiration.°
HAMLET: O wonderful son, that can so stonish a mother!
          But is there no sequel at the heels of this mother's
          admiration? Impart.
ROSENCRANTZ: She desires to speak with you in her   335
          closet,° ere you go to bed.
HAMLET: We shall obey, were she ten times our mother.
          Have you any further trade with us?
ROSENCRANTZ: My lord, you once did love me.
HAMLET: And do still, by these pickers and stealers.°   340
ROSENCRANTZ: Good my lord, what is your cause of dis-
          temper? You do surely bar the door upon your own
          liberty, if you deny your griefs to your friend.
HAMLET: Sir, I lack advancement.
ROSENCRANTZ: How can that be, when you have the   345
          voice of the King himself for your succession in
          Denmark?
HAMLET: Ay, sir, but "While the grass grows"°—the
          proverb is something° musty.

(*Enter the Players with recorders.*)

          O, the recorders! Let me see one. [*He takes a recorder.*]   350
          To withdraw° with you: why do you go about to re-
          cover the wind° of me, as if you would drive me into
          a toil?°
GUILDENSTERN: O, my lord, if my duty be too bold, my
          love is too unmannerly.°   355
HAMLET: I do not well understand that. Will you play
          upon this pipe?

313. **frame:** Order. 321. **pardon:** Permission to depart. 331. **admiration:** Wonder. 336. **closet:** Private chamber. 340. **pickers and stealers:** Hands (so called from the catechism, "to keep my hands from picking and stealing"). 348. **While . . . grows:** The rest of the proverb is "the silly horse starves"; Hamlet may not live long enough to succeed to the kingdom. 349. **something:** Somewhat. 351. **withdraw:** Speak privately. 352. **recover the wind:** Get the windward side. 353. **toil:** Snare. 354–355. **if . . . unmannerly:** If I am using an unmannerly boldness, it is my love that occasions it.

GUILDENSTERN: My lord, I cannot.

HAMLET: I pray you.

360 GUILDENSTERN: Believe me, I cannot.

HAMLET: I do beseech you.

GUILDENSTERN: I know no touch of it, my lord.

HAMLET: It is as easy as lying. Govern these ventages°
with your fingers and thumb, give it breath with your
365 mouth, and it will discourse most eloquent music.
Look you, these are the stops.

GUILDENSTERN: But these cannot I command to any
utt'rance of harmony; I have not the skill.

HAMLET: Why, look you now, how unworthy a thing
370 you make of me! You would play upon me, you
would seem to know my stops, you would pluck out
the heart of my mystery, you would sound me from
my lowest note to the top of my compass,° and there
is much music, excellent voice, in this little organ,°
375 yet cannot you make it speak. 'Sblood, do you think
I am easier to be play'd on than a pipe? Call me what
instrument you will, though you can fret° me, you
cannot play upon me.

(Enter Polonius.)

God bless you, sir!

380 POLONIUS: My lord, the Queen would speak with you,
and presently.°

HAMLET: Do you see yonder cloud that's almost in shape
of a camel?

POLONIUS: By th' mass, and 'tis like a camel, indeed.

385 HAMLET: Methinks it is like a weasel.

POLONIUS: It is back'd like a weasel.

HAMLET: Or like a whale?

POLONIUS: Very like a whale.

HAMLET: Then I will come to my mother by and by.°

390 [*Aside.*] They fool me° to the top of my bent.°—I
will come by and by.

POLONIUS: I will say so.   [*Exit.*]

HAMLET: "By and by" is easily said. Leave me, friends.

[*Exeunt all but Hamlet.*]

'Tis now the very witching time° of night,
395 When churchyards yawn and hell itself breathes out
Contagion to this world. Now could I drink hot
blood,
And do such bitter business as the day
Would quake to look on. Soft, now to my mother.
O heart, lose not thy nature! Let not ever
400 The soul of Nero° enter this firm bosom.

Let me be cruel, not unnatural;
I will speak daggers to her, but use none.
My tongue and soul in this be hypocrites:
How in my words somever° she be shent,°
To give them seals° never, my soul, consent!   405

(Exit.)

{Scene III}°

(Enter King, Rosencrantz, and Guildenstern.)

KING: I like him not, nor stands it safe with us
To let his madness range. Therefore prepare you.
I your commission will forthwith dispatch,°
And he to England shall along with you.
The terms° of our estate° may not endure   5
Hazard so near 's as doth hourly grow
Out of his brows.°

GUILDENSTERN: We will ourselves provide.
Most holy and religious fear it is
To keep those many many bodies safe
That live and feed upon your Majesty.   10

ROSENCRANTZ: The single and peculiar° life is bound
With all the strength and armor of the mind
To keep itself from noyance,° but much more
That spirit upon whose weal depends and rests
The lives of many. The cess° of majesty   15
Dies not alone, but like a gulf° doth draw
What's near it with it; or it is a messy wheel
Fix'd on the summit of the highest mount,
To whose huge spokes ten thousand lesser things
Are mortis'd and adjoin'd, which, when it falls,   20
Each small annexment, petty consequence,
Attends° the boist'rous ruin. Never alone
Did the King sigh, but with a general groan.

KING: Arm° you, I pray you, to this speedy voyage,
For we will fetters put about this fear,   25
Which now goes too free-footed.

ROSENCRANTZ: We will haste us.

*(Exeunt Gentlemen [Rosencrantz
and Guildenstern].)*

(Enter Polonius.)

POLONIUS: My lord, he's going to his mother's closet.
Behind the arras° I'll convey myself

---

363. **ventages:** Stops of the recorder.   373. **compass:** Range (of
voice).   374. **organ:** Musical instrument.   377. **fret:** Irritate
(with a quibble, or pun, on *fret* meaning the piece of wood,
gut, or metal that regulates the fingering on an instrument).   381.
presently: At once.   389. **by and by:** Immediately.   390. **fool
me:** Make me play the fool.   **top of my bent:** Limit of my ability or endurance (literally, the extent to which a bow may be
bent).   394. **witching time:** Time when spells are cast and evil is
abroad.   400. **Nero:** Murderer of his mother, Agrippina.

404. **How . . . somever:** However much by my words.   **shent:**
Rebuked.   405. **give them seals:** Confirm them with deeds.
III, iii. Location: The castle.   3. **dispatch:** Prepare, cause to be
drawn up.   5. **terms:** Condition, circumstances.   **our estate:**
My royal position.   7. **brows:** Effronteries, threatening frowns
(?), brain (?).   11. **single and peculiar:** Individual and private.
13. **noyance:** Harm.   15. **cess:** Decease.   16. **gulf:** Whirlpool.
22. **Attends:** Participates in.   24. **Arm:** Prepare.   28. **arras:**
Screen of tapestry placed around the walls of household apart-
ments. (On the Elizabethan stage, the arras was presumably over
a door or discovery space in the tiring-house façade.)

[TOP LEFT] Michael Pennington as Hamlet. [TOP MIDDLE] A scene from the Royal Shakespeare Company's 1980 production. [TOP RIGHT] The grave-digger holds up Yorick's skull as Hamlet and Horatio (Tom Wilkinson) look on. [BOTTOM LEFT] Hamlet, played by Kenneth Branagh, duels Laertes, played by Michael Maloney. Branagh directed this 1996 film. [BOTTOM RIGHT] Carol Royle as Ophelia with Hamlet in the nunnery scene.

To hear the process.° I'll warrant she'll tax him
   home,°
30 And, as you said, and wisely was it said,
'Tis meet that some more audience than a mother,
Since nature makes them partial, should o'erhear
The speech, of vantage.° Fare you well, my liege.
I'll call upon you ere you go to bed,
And tell you what I know.
35 KING: Thanks, dear my lord.
                (*Exit [Polonius].*)
O, my offense is rank, it smells to heaven;
It hath the primal eldest curse° upon 't,
A brother's murder. Pray can I not,
Though inclination be as sharp as will.°
40 My stronger guilt defeats my strong intent,
And, like a man to double business bound,
I stand in pause where I shall first begin,
And both neglect. What if this cursed hand
Were thicker than itself with brother's blood,
45 Is there not rain enough in the sweet heavens
To wash it white as snow? Whereto serves mercy
But to confront the visage of offense?°
And what's in prayer but this twofold force,
To be forestalled° ere we come to fall,
50 Or pardon'd being down? Then I'll look up;
My fault is past. But, O, what form of prayer
Can serve my turn? "Forgive me my foul
   murder"?
That cannot be, since I am still possess'd
Of those effects for which I did the murder,
55 My crown, mine own ambition, and my queen.
May one be pardon'd and retain th' offense?
In the corrupted currents° of this world
Offense's gilded hand° may shove by justice,
And oft 'tis seen the wicked prize° itself
60 Buys out the law. But 'tis not so above.
There is no shuffling,° there the action lies°
In his° true nature, and we ourselves compell'd,
Even to the teeth and forehead° of our faults,
To give in evidence. What then? What rests?°
65 Try what repentance can. What can it not?
Yet what can it, when one cannot repent?
O wretched state! O bosom black as death!
O limed° soul, that, struggling to be free,

Art more engag'd!° Help, angels! Make assay.°
Bow, stubborn knees, and heart with strings of steel, 70
Be soft as sinews of the new-born babe!
All may be well.
                [*He kneels.*]
(*Enter Hamlet [with sword drawn].*)
HAMLET: Now might I do it pat,° now 'a is a-praying;
And now I'll do 't. And so 'a goes to heaven;
And so am I reveng'd. That would be scann'd:° 75
A villain kills my father, and for that,
I, his sole son, do this same villain send
To heaven.
Why, this is hire and salary, not revenge.
'A took my father grossly,° full of bread,° 80
With all his crimes broad blown,° as flush° as
   May;
And how his audit° stands who knows save
   heaven?
But in our circumstance and course° of thought,
'Tis heavy with him. And am I then reveng'd,
To take him in the purging of his soul, 85
When he is fit and season'd for his passage?
No!
Up, sword, and know thou a more horrid hent.°
            [*Puts up his sword.*]
When he is drunk asleep, or in his rage,
Or in th' incestuous pleasure of his bed, 90
At game a-swearing, or about some act
That has no relish of salvation in 't—
Then trip him, that his heels may kick at heaven,
And that his soul may be as damn'd and black
As hell, whereto it goes. My mother stays. 95
This physic° but prolongs thy sickly days.   (*Exit.*)
KING: My words fly up, my thoughts remain below.
Words without thoughts never to heaven go.
                (*Exit.*)

{Scene IV}°

(*Enter [Queen] Gertrude and Polonius.*)

POLONIUS: 'A will come straight. Look you lay° home
   to him.
Tell him his pranks have been too broad° to bear
   with,

29. process: Proceedings. tax him home: Reprove him severely.
33. of vantage: From an advantageous place. 37. primal eldest
curse: The curse of Cain, the first murderer; he killed his
brother Abel. 39. Though ... will: Though my desire is as
strong as my determination. 46–47. Whereto ... offense:
For what function does mercy serve other than to undo the
effects of sin? 49. forestalled: Prevented (from sinning).
57. currents: Courses. 58. gilded hand: Hand offering gold
as a bribe. 59. wicked prize: Prize won by wickedness.
61. shuffling: Escape by trickery. the action lies: The accusation is made manifest, comes up for consideration (a legal
metaphor). 62. his: Its. 63. teeth and forehead: Face to face,
concealing nothing. 64. rests: Remains. 68. limed: Caught
as with birdlime, a sticky substance used to ensnare birds.

69. engag'd: Embedded. assay: Trial. 73. pat: Opportunely.
75. would be scann'd: Needs to be looked into. 80. grossly:
Not spiritually prepared. full of bread: Enjoying his worldly
pleasures. (See Ezek. 16:49.) 81. crimes broad blown: Sins
in full bloom. flush: Lusty. 82. audit: Account. 83. in ...
course: As we see it in our mortal situation. 88. know ...
hent: Await to be grasped by me on a more horrid occasion.
96. physic: Purging (by prayer). III, iv. Location: The queen's
private chamber. 1. lay: Thrust (i.e., reprove him soundly).
2. broad: Unrestrained.

And that your Grace hath screen'd and stood
between
Much heat° and him. I'll sconce° me even here.
5   Pray you, be round° [with him.
HAMLET (*within*): Mother, mother, mother!]
QUEEN: I'll warrant you, fear me not.
Withdraw, I hear him coming.
                    [*Polonius hides behind the arras.*]

(*Enter Hamlet.*)

HAMLET: Now, mother, what's the matter?
10   QUEEN: Hamlet, thou hast thy father° much offended.
HAMLET: Mother, you have my father much offended.
QUEEN: Come, come, you answer with an idle°
tongue.
HAMLET: Go, go, you question with a wicked tongue.
QUEEN: Why, how now, Hamlet?
HAMLET: What's the matter now?
QUEEN: Have you forgot me?
15   HAMLET: No, by the rood,° not so:
You are the Queen, your husband's brother's wife
And—would it were not so!—you are my mother.
QUEEN: Nay, then, I'll set those to you that can speak.
HAMLET: Come, come, and sit you down; you shall
not budge.
20   You go not till I set you up a glass
Where you may see the inmost part of you.
QUEEN: What wilt thou do? Thou wilt not murder me?
Help, ho!
POLONIUS [*behind*]: What, ho! Help!
HAMLET [*drawing*]: How now? A rat? Dead, for a
25   ducat, dead!
                    [*Makes a pass through the arras.*]
POLONIUS [*behind*]: O, I am slain! [*Falls and dies.*]
QUEEN: O me, what hast thou done?
HAMLET: Nay, I know not. Is it the King?
QUEEN: O, what a rash and bloody deed is this!
HAMLET: A bloody deed—almost as bad, good mother,
30   As kill a king, and marry with his brother.
QUEEN: As kill a king!
HAMLET: Ay, lady, it was my word.
          [*Parts the arras and discovers Polonius.*]
Thou wretched, rash, intruding fool, farewell!
I took thee for thy better. Take thy fortune.
Thou find'st to be too busy is some danger.—
35   Leave wringing of your hands. Peace, sit you down,
And let me wring your heart, for so I shall,
If it be made of penetrable stuff,
If damned custom° have not braz'd° it so
That it be proof° and bulwark against sense.°

QUEEN: What have I done, that thou dar'st wag thy
tongue   40
In noise so rude against me?
HAMLET: Such an art
That blurs the grace and blush of modesty,
Calls virtue hypocrite, takes off the rose
From the fair forehead of an innocent love
And sets a blister° there, makes marriage-vows   45
As false as dicers' oaths. O, such a deed
As from the body of contraction° plucks
The very soul, and sweet religion° makes
A rhapsody° of words. Heaven's face does glow
O'er this solidity and compound mass   50
With heated visage, as against the doom,
Is thought-sick at the act.°
QUEEN: Ay me, what act,
That roars so loud and thunders in the index?°
HAMLET: Look here, upon this picture, and on this,
The counterfeit presentment° of two brothers.   55
                    [*Shows her two likenesses.*]
See, what a grace was seated on this brow:
Hyperion's° curls, the front° of Jove himself,
An eye like Mars, to threaten and command,
A station° like the herald Mercury
New-lighted on a heaven-kissing hill—   60
A combination and a form indeed,
Where every god did seem to set his seal,
To give the world assurance of a man.
This was your husband. Look you now, what
follows:
Here is your husband, like a mildew'd ear,°   65
Blasting his wholesome brother. Have you eyes?
Could you on this fair mountain leave to feed,
And batten° on this moor?° Ha, have you eyes?
You cannot call it love, for at your age
The heyday° in the blood is tame, it's humble,   70
And waits upon the judgment, and what judgment
Would step from this to this? Sense,° sure, you
have,
Else could you not have motion, but sure that sense
Is apoplex'd,° for madness would not err,

4. **Much heat:** The king's anger. **sconce:** Ensconce, hide.
5. **round:** Blunt. **10. thy father:** Your stepfather, Claudius.
12. idle: Foolish. **15. rood:** Cross. **38. damned custom:**
Habitual wickedness. **braz'd:** Brazened, hardened. **39. proof:**
Armor. **sense:** Feeling.

45. **sets a blister:** Brands as a harlot. **47. contraction:** The
marriage contract. **48. religion:** Religious vows. **49. rhap-
sody:** Senseless string. **49–52. Heaven's . . . act:** Heaven's face
flushes with anger to look down upon this solid world, this
compound mass, with hot face as though the day of doom
were near, and is thought-sick at the deed (i.e., Gertrude's marriage). **53. index:** Table of contents, prelude, or preface. **55.
counterfeit presentment:** Portrayed representation. **57. Hyperion:** The sun god. **front:** Brow. **59. station:** Manner of
standing. **65. ear:** I.e., of grain. **68. batten:** Gorge. **moor:**
Barren upland. **70. heyday:** State of excitement. **72. Sense:**
Perception through the five senses (the functions of the middle
or sensible soul). **74. apoplex'd:** Paralyzed. (Hamlet goes on
to explain that without such a paralysis of will, mere madness
would not so err, nor would the five senses so enthrall themselves to *ecstasy* or lunacy; even such deranged states of mind
would be able to make the obvious choice between Hamlet
Senior and Claudius.)

75 Nor sense to ecstasy was ne'er so thrall'd
But it reserv'd some quantity of choice
To serve in such a difference. What devil was 't
That thus hath cozen'd° you at hoodman-blind?°
Eyes without feeling, feeling without sight,
80 Ears without hands or eyes, smelling sans° all,
Or but a sickly part of one true sense
Could not so mope.°
O shame, where is thy blush? Rebellious hell,
If thou canst mutine° in a matron's bones,
85 To flaming youth let virtue be as wax,
And melt in her own fire. Proclaim no shame
When the compulsive ardor gives the charge,
Since frost itself as actively doth burn,
And reason panders will.°
90 QUEEN: O Hamlet, speak no more!
Thou turn'st mine eyes into my very soul,
And there I see such black and grained° spots
As will not leave their tinct.°
HAMLET: Nay, but to live
In the rank sweat of an enseamed° bed,
95 Stew'd in corruption, honeying and making love
Over the nasty sty—
QUEEN: O, speak to me no more.
These words, like daggers, enter in my ears.
No more, sweet Hamlet!
HAMLET: A murderer and a villain,
100 A slave that is not twentieth part the tithe°
Of your precedent° lord, a vice° of kings,
A cutpurse of the empire and the rule,
That from a shelf the precious diadem stole,
And put it in his pocket!
105 QUEEN: No more!

(*Enter Ghost* [*in his nightgown*].)

HAMLET: A king of shreds and patches°—
Save me, and hover o'er me with your wings,
You heavenly guards! What would your gracious
figure?
QUEEN: Alas, he's mad!
110 HAMLET: Do you not come your tardy son to chide,
That, laps'd in time and passion,° lets go by
Th' important° acting of your dread command?
O, say!

GHOST: Do not forget. This visitation
Is but to whet thy almost blunted purpose. 115
But, look, amazement° on thy mother sits.
O, step between her and her fighting soul!
Conceit° in weakest bodies strongest works.
Speak to her, Hamlet.
HAMLET: How is it with you, lady?
QUEEN: Alas, how is 't with you, 120
That you do bend your eye on vacancy,
And with th' incorporal° air do hold discourse?
Forth at your eyes your spirits wildly peep,
And, as the sleeping soldiers in th' alarm,
Your bedded° hair, like life in excrements,° 125
Start up and stand an° end. O gentle son,
Upon the heat and flame of thy distemper
Sprinkle cool patience. Whereon do you look?
HAMLET: On him, on him! Look you how pale he
glares!
His form and cause conjoin'd,° preaching to stones, 130
Would make them capable.°—Do not look
upon me,
Lest with this piteous action you convert
My stern effects.° Then what I have to do
Will want true color—tears perchance for blood.°
QUEEN: To whom do you speak this? 135
HAMLET: Do you see nothing there?
QUEEN: Nothing at all, yet all that is I see.
HAMLET: Nor did you nothing hear?
QUEEN: No, nothing but ourselves.
HAMLET: Why, look you there, look how it steals away! 140
My father, in his habit° as he lived!
Look, where he goes, even now, out at the portal!
(*Exit Ghost.*)
QUEEN: This is the very coinage of your brain.
This bodiless creation ecstasy°
Is very cunning in. 145
HAMLET: Ecstasy?
My pulse, as yours, doth temperately keep time,
And makes as healthful music. It is not madness
That I have utter'd. Bring me to the test,
And I the matter will reword, which madness 150
Would gambol° from. Mother, for love of grace,
Lay not that flattering unction° to your soul
That not your trespass but my madness speaks.
It will but skin and film the ulcerous place,
Whiles rank corruption, mining° all within, 155

---

78. **cozen'd:** Cheated. **hoodman-blind:** Blindman's bluff.
80. **sans:** Without. 82. **mope:** Be dazed, act aimlessly.
84. **mutine:** Mutiny. 86–89. **Proclaim . . . will:** Call it no shameful business when the compelling ardor of youth delivers the attack (i.e., commits lechery), since the frost of advanced age burns with as active a fire of lust and reason perverts itself by fomenting lust rather than restraining it. 92. **grained:** Dyed in grain, indelible. 93. **tinct:** Color. 94. **enseamed:** Laden with grease. 100. **tithe:** Tenth part. 101. **precedent:** Former (i.e., the elder Hamlet). **vice:** Buffoon (a reference to the vice of the morality plays). 106. **shreds and patches:** Motley, the traditional costume of the clown or fool. 111. **laps'd . . . passion:** Having allowed time to lapse and passion to cool. 112. **important:** Importunate, urgent.

116. **amazement:** Distraction. 118. **Conceit:** Imagination. 122. **incorporal:** Immaterial. 125. **bedded:** Laid in smooth layers. **excrements:** Outgrowths. 126. **an:** On. 130. **His . . . conjoin'd:** His appearance joined to his cause for speaking. 131. **capable:** Receptive. 132–133. **convert . . . effects:** Divert me from my stern duty. 134. **want . . . blood:** Lack plausibility so that (with a play on the normal sense of *color*) I shall shed tears instead of blood. 141. **habit:** Dress. 144. **ecstasy:** Madness. 151. **gambol:** Skip away. 152. **unction:** Ointment. 155. **mining:** Working under the surface.

Bill Murray as Polonius and
Julia Stiles as Ophelia in
Michael Almereyda's 2000 film
adaptation of *Hamlet,* which
also starred Ethan Hawke as
Hamlet, Sam Shepard as the
Ghost of Hamlet's father, and
Kyle MacLachlan as Claudius.

Infects unseen. Confess yourself to heaven,
Repent what's past, avoid what is to come,
And do not spread the compost° on the weeds
To make them ranker. Forgive me this my virtue;°
160 For in the fatness° of these pursy° times
Virtue itself of vice must pardon beg,
Yea, curb° and woo for leave° to do him good.
QUEEN: O Hamlet, thou hast cleft my heart in twain.
HAMLET: O, throw away the worser part of it,
165 And live the purer wit the other half.
Good night. But go not to my uncle's bed;
Assume a virtue, if you have it not.
That monster, custom, who all sense doth eat,°
Of habits devil,° is angel yet in this,
170 That to the use of actions fair and good
He likewise gives a frock or livery°
That aptly is put on. Refrain tonight,
And that shall lend a kind of easiness
To the next abstinence; the next more easy;
175 For use° almost can change the stamp of nature,
And either° . . . the devil, or throw him out
With wondrous potency. Once more, good night;
And when you are desirous to be bless'd,°

I'll blessing beg of you. For this same lord,
                    [*Pointing to Polonius.*]
I do repent; but heaven hath pleas'd it so   180
To punish me with this, and this with me,
That I must be their scourge and minister.°
I will bestow° him, and will answer well
The death I gave him. So, again, good night.
I must be cruel only to be kind.   185
Thus bad begins and worse remains behind.°
One word more, good lady.
QUEEN: What shall I do?
HAMLET: Not this, by no means, that I bid you do:
Let the bloat° king tempt you again to bed,
Pinch wanton on your cheek, call you his mouse, 190
And let him, for a pair of reechy° kisses,
Or paddling in your neck with his damn'd fingers,
Make yon to ravel all this matter out,
That I essentially am not in madness,
But mad in craft. 'Twere good° you let him know, 195
For who that's but a queen, fair, sober, wise,
Would from a paddock,° from a bat, a gib,°
Such dear concernings° hide? Who would do so?
No, in despite of sense and secrecy,
Unpeg the basket° on the house's top,   200

---

158. **compost:** Manure.   159. **this my virtue:** My virtuous talk
in reproving you.   160. **fatness:** Grossness. **pursy:** Short-
winded, corpulent.   162. **curb:** Bow, bend the knee. **leave:**
Permission.   168. **who . . . eat:** Who consumes all proper or
natural feeling.   169. **Of habits devil:** Devil-like in prompting evil habits.   171. **livery:** An outer appearance, a customary garb (and hence a predisposition easily assumed in time
of stress).   175. **use:** Habit.   176. **And either:** A defective line
usually emended by inserting the word *master* after *either,* following the fourth quarto and early editors.   178. **be bless'd:**
Become blessed (i.e., repentant).

182. **their scourge and minister:** Agent of heavenly retribution.
(By *scourge,* Hamlet also suggests that he himself will eventually suffer punishment in the process of fulfilling heaven's
will.)   183. **bestow:** Stow, dispose of.   186. **behind:** To come.
189. **bloat:** Bloated.   191. **reechy:** Dirty, filthy.   195. **good:**
Said ironically; also the following eight lines.   197. **paddock:**
Toad. **gib:** Tomcat.   198. **dear concernings:** Important affairs.   200. **Unpeg the basket:** Open the cage (i.e., let out the
secret).

Let the birds fly, and, like the famous ape,°
To try conclusions,° in the basket creep
And break your own neck down.
QUEEN: Be thou assur'd, if words be made of breath,
205   And breath of life, I have no life to breathe
What thou hast said to me.
HAMLET: I must to England; you know that?
QUEEN: Alack,
I had forgot. 'Tis so concluded on.
HAMLET: There's letters seal'd, and my two school-
fellows,
210   Whom I will trust as I will adders fang'd,
They bear the mandate; they must sweep my way,°
And marshal me to knavery. Let it work.
For 'tis the sport to have the enginer°
Hoist with° his own petar,° and 't shall go hard
215   But I will delve one yard below their mines,°
And blow them at the moon. O, 'tis most sweet,
When in one line two crafts° directly meet.
This man shall set me packing.°
I'll lug the guts into the neighbor room.
220   Mother, good night indeed. This counselor
Is now most still, most secret, and most grave,
Who was in life a foolish prating knave.
Come, sir, to draw toward an end° with you.
Good night, mother.

(*Exeunt* [*severally, Hamlet dragging in Polonius*].)

{ACT IV • Scene I}°

(*Enter King and Queen, with Rosencrantz and Guildenstern.*)

KING: There's matter in these sighs, these profound
heaves
You must translate; 'tis fit we understand them.
Where is your son?
QUEEN: Bestow this place on us a little while.

[*Exeunt Rosencrantz and Guildenstern.*]

5   Ah, mine own lord, what have I seen tonight!
KING: What, Gertrude? How does Hamlet?
QUEEN: Mad as the sea and wind when both contend
Which is the mightier. In his lawless fit,

Behind the arras hearing something stir,
Whips out his rapier, cries, "A rat, a rat!"   10
And, in this brainish apprehension,° kills
The unseen good old man.
KING: O heavy deed!
It had been so with us, had we been there.
His liberty is full of threats to all—
To you yourself, to us, to everyone.   15
Alas, how shall this bloody deed be answer'd?
It will be laid to us, whose providence°
Should have kept short,° restrain'd, and out of haunt°
This mad young man. But so much was our love
We would not understand what was most fit,   20
But, like the owner of a foul disease,
To keep it from divulging,° let it feed
Even on the pith of life. Where is he gone?
QUEEN: To draw apart the body he hath kill'd,
O'er whom his very madness, like some ore°   25
Among a mineral° of metals base,
Shows itself pure: 'a weeps for what is done.
KING: O Gertrude, come away!
The sun no sooner shall the mountains touch
But we will ship him hence, and this vile deed   30
We must, with all our majesty and skill,
Both countenance and excuse. Ho, Guildenstern!

(*Enter Rosencrantz and Guildenstern.*)

Friends both, go join you with some further aid.
Hamlet in madness hath Polonius slain,
And from his mother's closet hath he dragg'd him.   35
Go seek him out; speak fair, and bring the body
Into the chapel. I pray you, haste in this.

[*Exeunt Rosencrantz and Guildenstern.*]

Come, Gertrude, we'll call up our wisest friends
And let them know both what we mean to do
And what's untimely done°........   40
Whose whisper o'er the world's diameter,°
As level° as the cannon to his blank,°
Transports his pois'ned shot, may miss our name,
And hit the woundless° air. O, come away!
My soul is full of discord and dismay.   (*Exeunt.*)   45

{Scene II}°

(*Enter Hamlet.*)

HAMLET: Safely stow'd.
[ROSENCRANTZ, GUILDENSTERN (*within*): Hamlet! Lord
Hamlet!]

201. **famous ape:** In a story now lost. 202. **conclusions:** Experiments (in which the ape apparently enters a cage from which birds have been released and then tries to fly out of the cage as they have done, falling to his death). 211. **sweep my way:** Go before me. 213. **enginer:** Constructor of military contrivances. 214. **Hoist with:** Blown up by. **petar:** Petard, an explosive used to blow in a door or make a breach. 215. **mines:** Tunnels used in warfare to undermine the enemy's emplacements; Hamlet will countermine by going under their mines. 217. **crafts:** Acts of guile, plots. 218. **set me packing:** Set me to making schemes and set me to lugging (him) and, also, send me off in a hurry. 223. **draw . . . end:** Finish up (with a pun on *draw*, pull). **IV, i. Location:** The castle.

11. **brainish apprehension:** Headstrong conception. 17. **providence:** Foresight. 18. **short:** On a short tether. **out of haunt:** Secluded. 22. **divulging:** Becoming evident. 25. **ore:** Vein of gold. 26. **mineral:** Mine. 40. **And . . . done:** A defective line; conjectures as to the missing words include *so, haply, slander* (Capell and others); *for, haply, slander* (Theobald and others). 41. **diameter:** Extent from side to side. 42. **As level:** With as direct aim. **blank:** White spot in the center of a target. 44. **woundless:** Invulnerable. **IV, ii. Location:** The castle.

HAMLET: But soft, what noise? Who calls on Hamlet?
5   O, here they come.

(*Enter Rosencrantz and Guildenstern.*)

ROSENCRANTZ: What have you done, my lord, with the
dead body?
HAMLET: Compounded it with dust, whereto 'tis kin.
ROSENCRANTZ: Tell us where 'tis, that we may take it
thence
And bear it to the chapel.
10 HAMLET: Do not believe it.
ROSENCRANTZ: Believe what?
HAMLET: That I can keep your counsel and not mine
own. Besides, to be demanded of° a sponge, what
replication° should be made by the son of a king?
15 ROSENCRANTZ: Take you me for a sponge, my lord?
HAMLET: Ay, sir, that soaks up the King's countenance,°
his rewards, his authorities. But such officers do the
King best service in the end. He keeps them, like an
ape an apple, in the corner of his jaw, first mouth'd,
20 to be last swallow'd. When he needs what you have
glean'd, it is but squeezing you, and, sponge, you
shall be dry again.
ROSENCRANTZ: I understand you not, my lord.
HAMLET: I am glad of it. A knavish speech sleeps in° a
25 foolish ear.
ROSENCRANTZ: My lord, you must tell us where the body
is, and go with us to the King.
HAMLET: The body is with the King, but the King is not
with the body.° The King is a thing—
30 GUILDENSTERN: A thing, my lord?
HAMLET: Of nothing.° Bring me to him. [Hide fox, and
all after.°]   (*Exeunt.*)

{Scene III}°

(*Enter King, and two or three.*)

KING: I have sent to seek him, and to find the body.
How dangerous is it that this man goes loose!
Yet must not we put the strong law on him.
He's lov'd of the distracted° multitude,
5   Who like not in their judgment, but their eyes,
And where 'tis so, th' offender's scourge° is weigh'd,°
But never the offense. To bear° all smooth and even,
This sudden sending him away must seem

13. **demanded of:** Questioned by.   14. **replication:** Reply.
16. **countenance:** Favor.   24. **sleeps in:** Has no meaning to.
28–29. **The . . . body:** Perhaps alludes to the legal commonplace of "the king's two bodies," which drew a distinction between the sacred office of kingship and the particular mortal
who possessed it at any given time.   31. **Of nothing:** Of no
account.   31–32. **Hide . . . after:** An old signal cry in the game
of hide-and-seek, suggesting that Hamlet now runs away from
them.   **IV, iii. Location:** The castle.   4. **distracted:** Fickle, unstable.   6. **scourge:** Punishment.   **weigh'd:** Taken into consideration.   7. **bear:** Manage.

Deliberate pause.° Diseases desperate grown
By desperate appliance are reliev'd,   10
Or not at all.

(*Enter Rosencrantz, [Guildenstern,] and all the rest.*)

How now? What hath befall'n?
ROSENCRANTZ: Where the dead body is bestow'd, my
lord,
We cannot get from him.
KING: But where is he?
ROSENCRANTZ: Without, my lord; guarded, to know your
pleasure.
KING: Bring him before us.
ROSENCRANTZ: Ho! Bring in the lord.   15

(*They enter [with Hamlet].*)

KING: Now, Hamlet, where's Polonius?
HAMLET: At supper.
KING: At supper? Where?
HAMLET: Not where he eats, but where 'a is eaten. A
certain convocation of politic worms° are e'en at   20
him. Your worm is your only emperor for diet.° We
fat all creatures else to fat us, and we fat ourselves
for maggots. Your fat king and your lean beggar is
but variable service,° two dishes, but to one table—
that's the end.   25
KING: Alas, alas!
HAMLET: A man may fish with the worm that hath eat°
of a king, and eat of the fish that hath fed of that
worm.
KING: What dost thou mean by this?   30
HAMLET: Nothing but to show you how a king may go a
progress° through the guts of a beggar.
KING: Where is Polonius?
HAMLET: In heaven. Send thither to see. If your messenger find him not there, seek him i' th' other place   35
yourself. But if indeed you find him not within this
month, you shall nose him as you go up the stairs
into the lobby.
KING [*to some Attendants*]: Go seek him there.
HAMLET: 'A will stay till you come.   40

[*Exit Attendants.*]

KING: Hamlet, this deed, for thine especial safety.—
Which we do tender,° as we dearly° grieve
For that which thou hast done—must send thee
hence
[With fiery quickness.] Therefore prepare thyself.
The bark° is ready, and the wind at help,   45
Th' associates tend,° and everything is bent°
For England.

9. **Deliberate pause:** Carefully considered action.   20. **politic
worms:** Crafty worms (suited to a master spy like Polonius).
21. **diet:** Food, eating (with perhaps a punning reference to the
Diet of Worms, a famous convocation held in 1521).   24. **variable service:** Different courses of a single meal.   27. **eat:** Eaten
(pronounced "et").   32. **progress:** Royal journey of state.
42. **tender:** Regard, hold dear.   **dearly:** Intensely.   45. **bark:**
Sailing vessel.   46. **tend:** Wait.   **bent:** In readiness.

HAMLET: For England!

KING: Ay, Hamlet.

50 HAMLET: Good.

KING: So is it, if thou knew'st our purposes.

HAMLET: I see a cherub° that sees them. But, come, for England! Farewell, dear mother.

KING: Thy loving father, Hamlet.

55 HAMLET: My mother. Father and mother is man and wife, man and wife is one flesh, and so, my mother. Come, for England! (*Exit.*)

KING: Follow him at foot;° tempt him with speed aboard.

Delay it not; I'll have him hence tonight.

60 Away! For everything is seal'd and done
That else leans on° th' affair. Pray you, make haste.

[*Exeunt all but the King.*]

And, England,° if my love thou hold'st at aught—
As my great power thereof may give thee sense,
Since yet thy cicatrice° looks raw and red

65 After the Danish sword, and thy free awe°
Pays homage to us—thou mayst not coldly set°
Our sovereign process,° which imports at full,
By letters congruing° to that effect,
The present° death of Hamlet. Do it, England,

70 For like the hectic° in my blood he rages,
And thou must cure me. Till I know 'tis done,
Howe'er my haps,° my joys were ne'er begun.

(*Exit.*)

{Scene IV}°

(*Enter Fortinbras with his Army over the stage.*)

FORTINBRAS: Go, captain, from me greet the Danish king.
Tell him that, by his license,° Fortinbras
Craves the conveyance° of a promis'd march
Over his kingdom. You know the rendezvous.

5 If that his Majesty would aught with us,
We shall express our duty in his eye;°
And let him know so.

CAPTAIN: I will do 't, my lord.

FORTINBRAS: Go softly° on. [*Exeunt all but the Captain.*]

(*Enter Hamlet, Rosencrantz, [Guildenstern,] etc.*)

HAMLET: Good sir, whose powers° are these?

10 CAPTAIN: They are of Norway, sir.

HAMLET: How purposed, sir, I pray you?

CAPTAIN: Against some part of Poland.

HAMLET: Who commands them, sir?

CAPTAIN: The nephew to old Norway, Fortinbras.

HAMLET: Goes it against the main° of Poland, sir, 15
Or for some frontier?

CAPTAIN: Truly to speak, and with no addition,°
We go to gain a little patch of ground
That hath in it no profit but the name.
To pay° five ducats, five, I would not farm it;° 20
Nor will it yield to Norway or the Pole
A ranker° rate, should it be sold in fee.°

HAMLET: Why, then the Polack never will defend it.

CAPTAIN: Yes, it is already garrison'd.

HAMLET: Two thousand souls and twenty thousand ducats 25
Will not debate the question of this straw.°
This is th' imposthume° of much wealth and peace,
That inward breaks, and shows no cause without
Why the man dies. I humbly thank you, sir.

CAPTAIN: God buy you, sir. [*Exit.*]

ROSENCRANTZ: Will 't please you go, my lord? 30

HAMLET: I'll be with you straight. Go a little before.

[*Exit all except Hamlet.*]

How all occasions do inform against° me,
And spur my dull revenge! What is a man,
If his chief good and market of° his time
Be but to sleep and feed? A beast, no more. 35
Sure he that made us with such large discourse,°
Looking before and after, gave us not
That capability and god-like reason
To fust° in us unus'd. Now, whether it be
Bestial oblivion,° or some craven scruple 40
Of thinking too precisely on th' event°—
A thought which, quarter'd, hath but one part wisdom
And ever three parts coward—I do not know
Why yet I live to say "This thing's to do,"
Sith° I have cause and will and strength and means 45
To do 't. Examples gross° as earth exhort me:
Witness this army of such mass and charge°
Led by a delicate and tender prince,
Whose spirit, with divine ambition puff'd
Makes mouths° at the invisible event, 50
Exposing what is mortal and unsure
To all that fortune, death, and danger dare,

---

52. **cherub:** Cherubim are angels of knowledge. 58. **at foot:** Close behind, at heel. 61. **leans on:** Bears upon, is related to. 62. **England:** King of England. 64. **cicatrice:** Scar. 65. **free awe:** Voluntary show of respect. 66. **set:** Esteem. 67. **process:** Command. 68. **congruing:** Agreeing. 69. **present:** Immediate. 70. **hectic:** Persistent fever. 72. **haps:** Fortunes. **IV, iv. Location:** The coast of Denmark. 2. **license:** Permission. 3. **conveyance:** Escort, convoy. 6. **eye:** Presence. 8. **softly:** Slowly. 9. **powers:** Forces.

15. **main:** Main part. 17. **addition:** Exaggeration. 20. **To pay:** I.e., for a yearly rental of. **farm it:** Take a lease of it. 22. **ranker:** Higher. **in fee:** Fee simple, outright. 26. **debate . . . straw:** Settle this trifling matter. 27. **imposthume:** Abscess. 32. **inform against:** Denounce, betray; take shape against. 34. **market of:** Profit of compensation for. 36. **discourse:** Power of reasoning. 39. **fust:** Grow moldy. 40. **oblivion:** Forgetfulness. 41. **event:** Outcome. 45. **Sith:** Since. 46. **gross:** Obvious. 47. **charge:** Expense. 50. **Makes mouths:** Makes scornful faces.

Even for an egg-shell. Rightly to be great
Is not to stir without great argument,
55 But greatly to find quarrel in a straw
When honor's at the stake. How stand I then,
That have a father kill'd, a mother stain'd,
Excitements of° my reason and my blood,
And let all sleep, while, to my shame, I see
60 The imminent death of twenty thousand men,
That, for a fantasy° and trick° of fame,
Go to their graves like beds, fight for a plot°
Whereon the numbers cannot try the cause,°
Which is not tomb enough and continent°
65 To hide the slain? O, from this time forth,
My thoughts be bloody, or be nothing worth!

                                                        (*Exit.*)

{Scene V}°

(*Enter Horatio, [Queen] Gertrude, and a Gentleman.*)

QUEEN: I will not speak with her.
GENTLEMAN: She is importunate, indeed distract.
      Her mood will needs be pitied.
QUEEN: What would she have?
GENTLEMAN: She speaks much of her father, says she
      hears
      There's tricks° i' th' world, and hems, and beats
5   her heart,°
      Spurns enviously at straws,° speaks things in doubt°
      That carry but half sense. Her speech is nothing,
      Yet the unshaped use° of it doth move
      The hearers to collection;° they yawn° at it,
10   And botch° the words up fit to their own thoughts,
      Which, as her winks and nods and gestures yield°
         them,
      Indeed would make one think there might be
         thought,°
      Though nothing sure, yet much unhappily.
HORATIO: 'Twere good she were spoken with, for she may
         strew
15   Dangerous conjectures in ill-breeding° minds.
QUEEN: Let her come in.   [*Exit Gentlemen.*]
      [*Aside.*] To my sick soul, as sin's true nature is,
      Each toy° seems prologue to some great amiss.°

So full of artless jealousy is guilt,
It spills itself in fearing to be spilt.°   20

(*Enter Ophelia [distracted].*)

OPHELIA: Where is the beauteous majesty of Denmark?
QUEEN: How now, Ophelia?
OPHELIA (*she sings*): "How should I your true love
         know
      From another one?
   By his cockle hat° and staff,   25
      And his sandal shoon."°
QUEEN: Alas, sweet lady, what imports this song?
OPHELIA: Say you? Nay, pray you, mark.
   "He is dead and gone, lady,   (*Song.*)
      He is dead and gone;   30
   At his head a grass-green turf,
      At his heels a stone."
      O, ho!
QUEEN: Nay, but Ophelia—
OPHELIA: Pray you mark.   35
   [*Sings.*] "White his shroud as the mountain
         snow"—

(*Enter King.*)

QUEEN: Alas, look here, my lord.
OPHELIA: "Larded° all with flowers   (*Song.*)
   Which bewept to the ground did not go
      With true-love showers."   40
KING: How do you, pretty lady?
OPHELIA: Well, God 'ild° you! They say the owl° was a
   baker's daughter. Lord, we know what we are, but
   know not what we may be. God be at your table!
KING: Conceit° upon her father.   45
OPHELIA: Pray let's have no words of this; but when they
   ask you what it means, say you this:
   "Tomorrow is Saint Valentine's° day.   (*Song.*)
      All in the morning betime,
   And I a maid at your window,   50
      To be your Valentine.
   Then up he rose, and donn'd his clo'es,
      And dupp'd° the chamber-door,
   Let in the maid, that out a maid
      Never departed more."   55
KING: Pretty Ophelia!
OPHELIA: Indeed, la, without an oath, I'll make an end
   on 't:
   [*Sings.*] "By Gis° and by Saint Charity,

---

58. Excitements of: Promptings by. **61. fantasy:** Fanciful caprice. **trick:** Trifle. **62. plot:** I.e., of ground. **63. Whereon . . . cause:** On which there is insufficient room for the soldiers needed to engage in a military contest. **64. continent:** Receptacle, container. **IV, v. Location:** The castle. **5. tricks:** Deceptions. **heart:** Breast. **6. Spurns . . . straws:** Kicks spitefully, takes offense at trifles. **in doubt:** Obscurely. **8. unshaped use:** Distracted manner. **9. collection:** Inference, a guess at some sort of meaning. **yawn:** Wonder, grasp. **10. botch:** Patch. **11. yield:** Deliver, bring forth (her words). **12. thought:** Conjectures. **15. ill-breeding:** Prone to suspect the worst. **18. toy:** Trifle. **amiss:** Calamity.

19–20. So . . . spilt: Guilt is so full of suspicion that it unskillfully betrays itself in fearing betrayal. **25. cockle hat:** Hat with cockleshell stuck in it as a sign that the wearer had been a pilgrim to the shrine of St. James of Compostella in Spain. **26. shoon:** Shoes. **38. Larded:** Decorated. **42. God 'ild:** God yield or reward. **owl:** Refers to a legend about a baker's daughter who was turned into an owl for refusing Jesus bread. **45. Conceit:** Brooding. **48. Valentine's:** This song alludes to the belief that the first girl seen by a man on the morning of this day was his valentine or true love. **53. dupp'd:** Opened. **59. Gis:** Jesus.

Alack, and fie for shame!
60 Young men will do 't, if they come to 't;
    By Cock,° they are to blame.
    Quoth she, 'Before you tumbled me,
        You promised me to wed.'"
    He answers:
65 "'So would I ha' done, by yonder sun,
        An thou hadst not come to my bed.'"
KING: How long hath she been thus?
OPHELIA: I hope all will be well. We must be patient, but
    I cannot choose but weep, to think they would lay
70 him i' th' cold ground. My brother shall know of it;
    and so I thank you for your good counsel. Come, my
    coach! Good night, ladies; good night, sweet ladies;
    good night, good night.

                                                [Exit.]

KING: Follow her close; give her good watch, I pray
        you.   [Exit Horatio.]
75 O, this is the poison of deep grief; it springs
    All from her father's death—and now behold!
    O Gertrude, Gertrude,
    When sorrows come, they come not single spies,°
    But in battalions. First, her father slain;
80 Next, your son gone, and he most violent author
    Of his own just remove; the people muddied,°
    Thick and unwholesome in their thoughts and
        whispers,
    For good Polonius' death; and we have done but
        greenly,°
    In hugger-mugger° to inter him; poor Ophelia
85 Divided from herself and her fair judgment,
    Without the which we are pictures, or mere beasts;
    Last, and as much containing as all these,
    Her brother is in secret come from France,
    Feeds on his wonder, keeps himself in clouds,°
90 And wants° not buzzers° to infect his ear
    With pestilent speeches of his father's death,
    Wherein necessity, of matter beggar'd,°
    Will nothing stick our person to arraign
    In ear and ear.° O my dear Gertrude, this,
95 Like to a murd'ring-piece,° in many places
    Gives me superfluous death.   (A noise within.)
[QUEEN: Alack, what noise is this?]
KING: Attend!
    Where are my Switzers?° Let them guard the door.

(Enter a Messenger.)

    What is the matter?
100 MESSENGER: Save yourself, my lord!

The ocean, overpeering of his list,°
Eats not the flats° with more impiteous° haste
Than young Laertes, in a riotous head,°
O'erbears your officers. The rabble call him lord,
And, as° the world were now but to begin,   105
Antiquity forgot, custom not known,
The ratifiers and props° of every word,°
They cry, "Choose we! Laertes shall be king!"
Caps, hands, and tongues applaud it to the clouds,
"Laertes shall be king, Laertes king!"   110
                                    (A noise within.)
QUEEN: How cheerfully on the false trail they cry!
    O, this is counter,° you false Danish dogs!

(Enter Laertes with others.)

KING: The doors are broke.
LAERTES: Where is this King? Sirs, stand you all without.
ALL: No, let's come in.
LAERTES: I pray you, give me leave.   115
ALL: We will, we will.
                        [They retire without the door.]
LAERTES: I thank you. Keep the door. O thou vile king,
    Give me my father!
QUEEN: Calmly, good Laertes.
                            [She tries to hold him back.]
LAERTES: That drop of blood that's calm proclaims
    me bastard,
    Cries cuckold to my father, brands the harlot   120
    Even here, between the chaste unsmirched brow
    Of my true mother.
KING: What is the cause, Laertes,
    That thy rebellion looks so giant-like?
    Let him go, Gertrude. Do not fear our° person.
    There's such divinity doth hedge a king   125
    That treason can but peep to what it would,°
    Acts little of his will.° Tell me, Laertes,
    Why thou art thus incens'd. Let him go, Gertrude.
    Speak, man.
LAERTES: Where is my father?
KING: Dead.
QUEEN: But not by him.
KING: Let him demand his fill.   130
LAERTES: How came he dead? I'll not be juggled with.
    To hell, allegiance! Vows, to the blackest devil!
    Conscience and grace, to the profoundest pit!
    I dare damnation. To this point I stand,
    That both the worlds I give to negligence,°   135

---

62. **Cock:** A perversion of *God* in oaths. 78. **spies:** Scouts sent in advance of the main force. 81. **muddied:** Stirred up, confused. 83. **greenly:** Imprudently, foolishly. 84. **hugger-mugger:** Secret haste. 89. **in clouds:** I.e., of suspicion and rumor. 90. **wants:** Lacks. **buzzers:** Gossipers, informers. 92. **of matter beggar'd:** Unprovided with facts. 93–94. **Will . . . and ear:** Will not hesitate to accuse my (royal) person in everybody's ears. 95. **murd'ring-piece:** Cannon loaded so as to scatter its shot. 99. **Switzers:** Swiss guards, mercenaries.

101. **overpeering of his list:** Overflowing its shore. 102. **flats:** Flatlands near shore. **impiteous:** Pitiless. 103. **head:** Armed force. 105. **as:** As if. 107. **ratifiers and props:** Refer to *antiquity* and *custom*. **word:** Promise. 112. **counter:** A hunting term meaning to follow the trail in a direction opposite to that which the game has taken. 124. **fear our:** Fear for my. 126. **can . . . would:** Can only glance, as from far off or through a barrier, at what it would intend. 127. **Acts . . . will:** (But) performs little of what it intends. 135. **both . . . negligence:** Both this world and the next are of no consequence to me.

Let come what comes, only I'll be reveng'd
Most throughly° for my father.
KING: Who shall stay you?
LAERTES: My will, not all the world's.°
And for my means, I'll husband them so well,
140 They shall go far with little.
KING: Good Laertes,
If you desire to know the certainty
Of your dear father, is 't writ in your revenge
That, swoopstake,° you will draw both friend and
    foe,
Winner and loser?
145 LAERTES: None but his enemies.
KING: Will you know them then?
LAERTES: To his good friends thus wide I'll ope my arms,
And, like the kind life-rend'ring pelican,°
Repast° them with my blood.
KING: Why, now you speak
Like a good child and a true gentleman.
150 That I am guiltless of your father's death,
And am most sensibly° in grief for it,
It shall as level° to your judgment 'pear
As day does to your eye.
                    (*A noise within:*) "Let her come in."
LAERTES: How now? What noise is that?

(*Enter Ophelia.*)

155 O heat, dry up my brains! Tears seven times salt
Burn out the sense and virtue° of mine eye!
By heaven, thy madness shall be paid with weight°
Till our scale turn the beam.° O rose of May!
Dear maid, kind sister, sweet Ophelia!
160 O heavens, is 't possible a young maid's wits
Should be as mortal as an old man's life?
[Nature is fine in° love, and where 'tis fine,
It sends some precious instance° of itself
After the thing it loves.°]
165 OPHELIA: "They bore him barefac'd on the bier;
                                        (*Song.*)
    [Hey non nonny, nonny, hey nonny,]
And in his grave rain'd many a tear"—
Fare you well, my dove!
LAERTES: Hadst thou thy wits, and didst persuade°
    revenge,
170 It could not move thus.
OPHELIA: You must sing "A-down a-down,
And you call him a-down-a."

O, how the wheel° becomes it! It is the false steward°
that stole his master's daughter.
LAERTES: This nothing's more than matter.°   175
OPHELIA: There's rosemary,° that's for remembrance;
pray you, love, remember. And there is pansies,° that's
for thoughts.
LAERTES: A document° in madness, thoughts and remem-
    brance fitted.   180
OPHELIA: There's fennel° for you, and columbines.°
There's rue° for you, and here's some for me; we may
call it herb of grace o' Sundays. You may wear your
rue with a difference.° There's a daisy.° I would give
you some violets,° but they wither'd all when my   185
father died. They say 'e made a good end—
[*Sings.*] "For bonny sweet Robin is all my joy."
LAERTES: Thought° and affliction, passion, hell itself,
She turns to favor° and to prettiness.
OPHELIA: "And will 'a not come again?   (*Song.*) 190
And will 'a not come again?
    No, no, he is dead,
    Go to thy death-bed,
He never will come again.

"His beard was as white as snow,   195
All flaxen was his poll.°
    He is gone, he is gone,
    And we cast away moan.
God 'a' mercy on his soul!
And of all Christians' souls, I pray God. God buy you. 200
                                              [*Exit.*]
LAERTES: Do you see this, O God?
KING: Laertes, I must commune with your grief,
Or you deny me right. Go but apart,
Make choice of whom your wisest friends you will,
And they shall hear and judge 'twixt you and me.   205
If by direct or by collateral° hand
They find us touch'd,° we will our kingdom give,
Our crown, our life, and all that we call ours,
To you in satisfaction; but if not,
Be you content to lend your patience to us,   210
And we shall jointly labor with your soul
To give it due content.

---

137. **throughly:** Thoroughly. 138. **My will ... world's:** I'll
stop (*stay*) when my will is accomplished, not for anyone
else's. 143. **swoopstake:** Literally, taking all stakes on the
gambling table at once (i.e., indiscriminately); *draw* is also
a gambling term. 147. **pelican:** Refers to the belief that the
female pelican fed its young with its own blood. 148. **Repast:**
Feed. 151. **sensibly:** Feelingly. 152. **level:** Plain. 156. **virtue:** Faculty, power. 157. **paid with weight:** Repaid, avenged
equally or more. 158. **beam:** Crossbar of a balance. 162. **fine
in:** Refined by. 163. **instance:** Token. 164. **After ... loves:**
Into the grave, along with Polonius. 169. **persuade:** Argue
cogently for.

173. **wheel:** Spinning wheel as accompaniment to the song, or
refrain. **false steward:** The story is unknown. 175. **This ...
matter:** This seeming nonsense is more meaningful than
sane utterance. 176. **rosemary:** Used as a symbol of remembrance both at weddings and at funerals. 177. **pansies:** Emblems of love and courtship; perhaps from French *pensées*,
thoughts. 179. **document:** Instruction, lesson. 181. **fennel:**
Emblem of flattery. **columbines:** Emblems of unchastity (?) or
ingratitude (?). 182. **rue:** Emblem of repentance; when mingled
with holy water, it was known as *herb of grace*. 184. **with
a difference:** Suggests that Ophelia and the queen have different causes of sorrow and repentance; perhaps with a play
on *rue* in the sense of ruth, or pity. **daisy:** Emblem of dissem-
bling, faithlessness. 185. **violets:** Emblems of faithfulness.
188. **Thought:** Melancholy. 189. **favor:** Grace. 196. **poll:**
Head. 206. **collateral:** Indirect. 207. **us touch'd:** Me implicated.

LAERTES: Let this be so.
His means of death, his obscure funeral—
No trophy,° sword, nor hatchment° o'er his bones,
215 No noble rite nor formal ostentation°—
Cry to be heard, as 'twere from heaven to earth,
That I must call 't in question.
KING: So you shall;
And where th' offense is, let the great ax fall.
I pray you go with me. *(Exeunt.)*

{Scene VI}°

(Enter Horatio and others.)

HORATIO: What are they that would speak with me?
GENTLEMAN: Seafaring men, sir. They say they have let-
ters for you.
HORATIO: Let them come in. [*Exit Gentleman.*]
5 I do not know from what part of the world
I should be greeted, if not from lord Hamlet.

(Enter Sailors.)

FIRST SAILOR: God bless you sir.
HORATIO: Let him bless thee too.
FIRST SAILOR: 'A shall, sir, an 't please him. There's a letter
10 for you, sir—it came from th' ambassador that was
bound for England—if your name be Horatio, as I
am let to know it is. [*Gives letter.*]
HORATIO [*reads*]: "Horatio, when thou shalt have
overlook'd this, give these fellows some means° to the
15 King; they have letters for him. Ere we were two days
old at sea, a pirate of very warlike appointment° gave
us chase. Finding ourselves too slow of sail, we put
on a compell'd valor, and in the grapple I boarded
them. On the instant they got clear of our ship, so I
20 alone became their prisoner. They have dealt with me
like thieves of mercy,° but they knew what they did:
I am to do a good turn for them. Let the King have
the letters I have sent, and repair thou to me with as
much speed as thou wouldest fly death. I have words
25 to speak in thine ear will make thee dumb; yet are
they much too light for the bore° of the matter. These
good fellows will bring thee where I am. Rosencrantz
and Guildenstern hold their course for England. Of
them I have much to tell thee. Farewell.
30 He that thou knowest thine, Hamlet."
Come, I will give you way for these your letters,
And do 't the speedier that you may direct me
To him from whom you brought them. *(Exeunt.)*

214. **trophy:** Memorial. **hatchment:** Tablet displaying the
armorial bearings of a deceased person. 215. **ostentation:**
Ceremony. **IV, vi. Location:** The castle. 14. **means:** Means
of access. 16. **appointment:** Equipage. 21. **thieves of mercy:**
Merciful thieves. 26. **bore:** Caliber (i.e., importance).

{Scene VII}°

(Enter King and Laertes.)

KING: Now must your conscience my acquittance seal,°
And you must put me in your heart for friend,
Sith you have heard, and with a knowing ear,
That he which hath your noble father slain
Pursued my life.
LAERTES: It well appears. But tell me 5
Why you proceeded not against these feats°
So criminal and so capital° in nature,
As by your safety, greatness, wisdom, all things else,
You mainly° were stirr'd up.
KING: O, for two special reasons,
Which may to you, perhaps, seem much unsinew'd,° 10
But yet to me th' are strong. The Queen his mother
Lives almost by his looks, and for myself—
My virtue or my plague, be it either which—
She's so conjunctive° to my life and soul
That, as the star moves not but in his sphere,° 15
I could not but by her. The other motive,
Why to a public count° I might not go,
Is the great love the general gender° bear him,
Who, dipping all his faults in their affection,
Would, like the spring° that turneth wood to stone, 20
Convert his gyves° to graces, so that my arrows,
Too slightly timber'd° for so loud° a wind,
Would have reverted to my bow again
And not where I had aim'd them.
LAERTES: And so have I a noble father lost, 25
A sister driven into desp'rate terms,°
Whose worth, if praises may go back° again,
Stood challenger on mount° of all the age
For her perfections. But my revenge will come.
KING: Break not your sleeps for that. You must not
think 30
That we are made of stuff so flat and dull
That we can let our beard be shook with danger
And think it pastime. You shortly shall hear more.
I lov'd your father, and we love ourself;
And that, I hope, will teach you to imagine— 35

(Enter a Messenger with letters.)

[How now? What news?]
MESSENGER: [Letters, my lord, from Hamlet:]

IV, vii. Location: The castle. 1. **my acquittance seal:** Confirm
or acknowledge my innocence. 6. **feats:** Acts. 7. **capital:**
Punishable by death. 9. **mainly:** Greatly. 10. **unsinew'd:**
Weak. 14. **conjunctive:** Closely united. 15. **sphere:** The hollow sphere in which, according to Ptolemaic astronomy, the
planets moved. 17. **count:** Account, reckoning. 18. **general
gender:** Common people. 20. **spring:** A spring with such a
concentration of lime that it coats a piece of wood with lime-
stone, in effect gilding it. 21. **gyves:** Fetters (which, gilded
by the people's praise, would look like badges of honor).
22. **slightly timber'd:** Light. **loud:** Strong. 26. **terms:** State,
condition. 27. **go back:** Recall Ophelia's former virtues.
28. **on mount:** On high.

These to your Majesty, this to the Queen.

[*Gives letters.*]

KING: From Hamlet? Who brought them?

MESSENGER: Sailors, my lord, they say; I saw them not.
40   They were given me by Claudio. He receiv'd them
Of him that brought them.

KING: Laertes, you shall hear them.
Leave us.   [*Exit Messenger.*]
[*Reads.*] "High and mighty, you shall know I am set
naked° on your kingdom. Tomorrow shall I beg leave
45   to see your kingly eyes, when I shall, first asking your
pardon° thereunto, recount the occasion of my sudden and more strange return.   Hamlet."
What should this mean? Are all the rest come back?
Or is it some abuse,° and no such thing?

LAERTES: Know you the hand?

50 KING: 'Tis Hamlet's character.° "Naked!"
And in a postscript here, he says "alone."
Can you devise° me?

LAERTES: I am lost in it, my lord. But let him come.
It warms the very sickness in my heart
55   That I shall live and tell him to his teeth,
"Thus didst thou."

KING: If it be so, Laertes—
As how should it be so? How otherwise?°—
Will you be ruled by me?

LAERTES: Ay, my lord,
So° you will not o'errule me to a peace.

60 KING: To thine own peace. If he be now returned,
As checking at° his voyage, and that he means
No more to undertake it, I will work him
To an exploit, now ripe in my device,
Under the which he shall not choose but fall;
65   And for his death no wind of blame shall breathe,
But even his mother shall uncharge the practice°
And call it accident.

LAERTES: My lord, I will be rul'd,
The rather if you could devise it so
That I might be the organ.°

KING: It falls right.
70   You have been talk'd of since your travel much,
And that in Hamlet's hearing, for a quality
Wherein, they say, you shine. Your sum of parts°
Did not together pluck such envy from him
As did that one, and that, in my regard,
75   Of the unworthiest siege.°

LAERTES: What part is that, my lord?

KING: A very riband in the cap of youth,
Yet needful too, for youth no less becomes

The light and careless livery that it wears
Than settled age his sables° and his weeds,°   80
Importing health° and graveness. Two months since
Here was a gentleman of Normandy.
I have seen myself, and serv'd against, the French,
And they can well° on horseback, but this gallant
Had witchcraft in 't; he grew unto his seat,   85
And to such wondrous doing brought his horse
As had he been incorps'd and demi-natured°
With the brave beast. So far he topp'd° my thought
That I, in forgery° of shapes and tricks,
Come short of what he did.

LAERTES: A Norman was 't?   90

KING: A Norman.

LAERTES: Upon my life, Lamord.

KING: The very same.

LAERTES: I know him well. He is the brooch° indeed
And gem of all the nation.

KING: He made confession° of you,   95
And gave you such a masterly report
For art and exercise in your defense,
And for your rapier most especial,
That he cried out, 'twould be a sight indeed,
If one could match you. The scrimers° of their
nation,   100
He swore, had neither motion, guard, nor eye,
If you oppos'd them. Sir, this report of his
Did Hamlet so envenom with his envy
That he could nothing do but wish and beg
Your sudden coming o'er to play° with you.   105
Now, out of this—

LAERTES: What out of this, my lord?

KING: Laertes, was your father dear to you?
Or are you like the painting of a sorrow,
A face without a heart?

LAERTES: Why ask you this?

KING: Not that I think you did not love your father,   110
But that I know love is begun by time,°
And that I see, in passages of proof,°
Time qualifies° the spark and fire of it.
There lives within the very flame of love
A kind of wick or snuff° that will abate it,   115
And nothing is at a like goodness still,°
For goodness, growing to a plurisy,°
Dies in his own too much.° That° we would do,
We should do when we would; for this "would"
changes

---

44. **naked:** Destitute, unarmed, without following. 46. **par-don:** Permission. 49. **abuse:** Deceit. 50. **character:** Hand-writing. 52. **devise:** Explain to. 57. **As . . . otherwise:** How can this (Hamlet's return) be true? Yet how otherwise than true (since we have the evidence of his letter). 59. **So:** Provided that. 61. **checking at:** Turning aside from (like a falcon leaving the quarry to fly at a chance bird). 66. **uncharge the practice:** Acquit the stratagem of being a plot. 69. **organ:** Agent, instrument. 72. **Your . . . parts:** All your other virtues. 75. **unworthiest siege:** Least important rank.

80. **sables:** Rich robes furred with sable. **weeds:** Garments.
81. **Importing health:** Indicating prosperity. 84. **can well:** Are skilled. 87. **incorps'd and demi-natur'd:** Of one body and nearly of one nature (like the centaur). 88. **topp'd:** Surpassed. 89. **forgery:** Invention. 93. **brooch:** Ornament. 95. **confession:** Admission of superiority. 100. **scrimers:** Fencers.
105. **play:** Fence. 111. **begun by time:** Subject to change.
112. **passages of proof:** Actual instances. 113. **qualifies:** Weakens. 115. **snuff:** The charred part of a candlewick.
116. **nothing . . . still:** Nothing remains at a constant level of perfection. 117. **plurisy:** Excess, plethora. 118. **in . . . much:** Of its own excess. **That:** That which.

120 And hath abatements° and delays as many
As there are tongues, are hands, are accidents,°
And then this "should" is like a spendthrift's sigh,°
That hurts by easing.° But, to the quick o' th' ulcer;
Hamlet comes back. What would you undertake
125 To show yourself your father's son in deed
More than in words?
LAERTES: To cut his throat i' th' church!
KING: No place, indeed, should murder sanctuarize;°
Revenge should have no bounds. But, good Laertes,
Will you do this,° keep close within your chamber.
130 Hamlet return'd shall know you are come home.
We'll put on those° shall praise your excellence
And set a double varnish on the fame
The Frenchman gave you, bring you in fine°
    together,
And wager on your heads. He, being remiss,°
135 Most generous,° and free from all contriving,
Will not peruse the foils, so that, with ease,
Or with a little shuffling, you may choose
A sword unbated,° and in a pass of practice°
Requite him for your father.
LAERTES: I will do 't.
140 And for that purpose I'll anoint my sword.
I bought an unction° of a mountebank°
So mortal that, but dip a knife in it,
Where it draws blood no cataplasm° so rare,
Collected from all simples° that have virtue
145 Under the moon, can save the thing from death
That is but scratch'd withal. I'll touch my point
With this contagion, that, if I gall° him slightly,
It may be death.
KING: Let's further think of this,
Weigh what convenience both of time and means
150 May fit us to our shape.° If this should fail,
And that our drift look through our bad
    performance,°
'Twere better not assay'd. Therefore this project
Should have a back or second, that might hold
If this did blast in proof.° Soft, let me see.
155 We'll make a solemn wager on your cunnings—

I ha 't!
When in your motion you are hot and dry—
As° make your bouts more violent to that end—
And that he calls for drink, I'll have prepar'd him
A chalice for the nonce,° whereon but sipping,   160
If he by chance escape your venom'd stuck,°
Our purpose may hold there. [*A cry within.*] But
    stay, what noise?

(*Enter Queen.*)

QUEEN: One woe doth tread upon another's heel,
So fast they follow. Your sister's drowned, Laertes.
LAERTES: Drown'd! O, where?   165
QUEEN: There is a willow grows askant° the brook
That shows his hoar° leaves in the glassy stream;
Therewith fantastic garlands did she make
Of crow-flowers, nettles, daisies, and long purples°
That liberal° shepherds give a grosser name,   170
But our cold° maids do dead men's fingers call them.
There on the pendent boughs her crownet° weeds
Clamb'ring to hang, an envious sliver° broke,
When down her weedy° trophies and herself
Fell in the weeping brook. Her clothes spread wide, 175
And mermaid-like awhile they bore her up,
Which time she chanted snatches of old lauds,°
As one incapable° of her own distress,
Or like a creature native and indued°
Unto that element. But long it could not be   180
Till that her garments, heavy with their drink,
Pull'd the poor wretch from her melodious lay
To muddy death.
LAERTES: Alas, then she is drown'd?
QUEEN: Drown'd, drown'd.
LAERTES: Too much of water hast thou, poor Ophelia, 185
And therefore I forbid my tears. But yet
It is our trick;° nature her custom holds,
Let shame say what it will. [*He weeps.*] When
    these are gone,
The woman will be out.° Adieu, my lord.
I have a speech of fire, that fain would blaze,   190
But that this folly drowns it.   (*Exit.*)
KING: Let's follow, Gertrude.
How much I had to do to calm his rage!
Now fear I this will give it start again;
Therefore let's follow.   (*Exeunt.*)

---

120. **abatements:** Diminutions.   121. **accidents:** Occurrences, incidents.   122. **spendthrift's sigh:** An allusion to the belief that each sigh cost the heart a drop of blood.   123. **hurts by easing:** Costs the heart blood even while it affords emotional relief.   127. **sanctuarize:** Protect from punishment (alludes to the right of sanctuary with which certain religious places were invested).   129. **Will you do this:** If you wish to do this. 131. **put on those:** Instigate those who.   133. **in fine:** Finally. 134. **remiss:** Negligently unsuspicious.   135. **generous:** Noble-minded.   138. **unbated:** Not blunted, having no button.   **pass of practice:** Treacherous thrust.   141. **unction:** Ointment. **mountebank:** Quack doctor.   143. **cataplasm:** Plaster or poultice.   144. **simples:** Herbs.   147. **gall:** Graze, wound. 150. **shape:** Part that we propose to act.   151. **drift . . . performance:** I.e., our intention be disclosed by our bungling. 154. **blast in proof:** Burst in the test (like a cannon).

158. **As:** And you should.   160. **nonce:** Occasion.   161. **stuck:** Thrust (from *stoccado*, a fencing term).   166. **askant:** Aslant. 167. **hoar:** White or gray.   169. **long purples:** Early purple orchids.   170. **liberal:** Free-spoken.   171. **cold:** Chaste.   172. **crownet:** Made into a chaplet or coronet.   173. **envious sliver:** Malicious branch.   174. **weedy:** I.e., of plants.   177. **lauds:** Hymns.   178. **incapable:** Lacking capacity to apprehend.   179. **indued:** Adapted by nature.   187. **It is our trick:** Weeping is our natural way (when sad).   188–189. **When . . . out:** When my tears are all shed, the woman in me will be expended, satisfied.

{ACT V • Scene I}°

(*Enter two Clowns*° [*with spades, etc.*])

FIRST CLOWN: Is she to be buried in Christian burial when she willfully seeks her own salvation?

SECOND CLOWN: I tell thee she is; therefore make her grave straight.° The crowner° hath sat on her, and finds it Christian burial.

FIRST CLOWN: How can that be, unless she drown'd herself in her own defense?

SECOND CLOWN: Why, 'tis found so.

FIRST CLOWN: It must be "se offendendo";° it cannot be else. For here lies the point: if I drown myself wittingly, it argues an act, and an act hath three branches — it is to act, to do, and to perform. Argal,° she drown'd herself wittingly.

SECOND CLOWN: Nay, but hear you, goodman delver —

FIRST CLOWN: Give me leave. Here lies the water; good. Here stands the man; good. If the man go to this water, and drown himself, it is, will he,° nill he, he goes, mark you that. But if the water come to him and drown him, he drowns not himself. Argal, he that is not guilty of his own death shortens not his own life.

SECOND CLOWN: But is this law?

FIRST CLOWN: Ay, marry, is 't — crowner's quest° law.

SECOND CLOWN: Will you ha' the truth on 't? If this had not been a gentlewoman, she should have been buried out o' Christian burial.

FIRST CLOWN: Why, there thou say'st.° And the more pity that great folk should have count'nance° in this world to drown or hang themselves, more than their even-Christen.° Come, my spade. There is no ancient gentlemen but gard'ners, ditchers, and grave-makers. They hold up Adam's profession.

SECOND CLOWN: Was he a gentleman?

FIRST CLOWN: 'A was the first that ever bore arms.

[SECOND CLOWN: Why, he had none.

FIRST CLOWN: What, art a heathen? How dost thou understand the Scripture? The Scripture says "Adam digg'd." Could he dig without arms?] I'll put another question to thee. If thou answerest me not to the purpose, confess thyself° —

SECOND CLOWN: Go to.

FIRST CLOWN: What is he that builds stronger than either the mason, the shipwright, or the carpenter?

SECOND CLOWN: The gallows-maker, for that frame outlives a thousand tenants.

FIRST CLOWN: I like thy wit well, in good faith. The gallows does well, but how does it well? It does well to those that do ill. Now thou dost ill to say the gallows is built stronger than the church. Argal, the gallows may do well to thee. To 't again, come.

SECOND CLOWN: "Who builds stronger than a mason, a shipwright, or a carpenter?"

FIRST CLOWN: Ay, tell me that, and unyoke.°

SECOND CLOWN: Marry, now I can tell.

FIRST CLOWN: To 't.

SECOND CLOWN: Mass,° I cannot tell.

(*Enter Hamlet and Horatio* [*at a distance*].)

FIRST CLOWN: Cudgel thy brains no more about it, for your dull ass will not mend his pace with beating; and, when you are ask'd this question next, say "a grave-maker." The houses he makes lasts till doomsday. Go, get thee in, and fetch me a stoup° of liquor.

[*Exit Second Clown. First Clown digs.*]
(*Song.*)

"In youth, when I did love, did love,°
    Methought it was very sweet,
To contract — O — the time for — a — my behove,°
    O, methought there — a — was nothing — a — meet."°

HAMLET: Has this fellow no feeling of his business, that 'a sings at grave-making?

HORATIO: Custom hath made it in him a property of easiness.°

HAMLET: 'Tis e'en so. The hand of little employment hath the daintier sense.°

(*Song.*)

FIRST CLOWN: "But age, with his stealing steps,
    Hath claw'd me in his clutch,
And hath shipped me into the land,°
    As if I had never been such."

[*Throws up a skull.*]

HAMLET: That skull had a tongue in it, and could sing once. How the knave jowls° it to the ground, as if 'twere Cain's jaw-bone, that did the first murder! This might be the pate of a politician,° which this ass now o'erreaches,° one that would circumvent God, might it not?

HORATIO: It might, my lord.

---

53. **unyoke:** After this great effort you may unharness the team of your wits.   56. **Mass:** By the Mass.   61. **stoup:** Two-quart measure.   62. **In . . . love:** This and the two following stanzas, with nonsensical variations, are from a poem attributed to Lord Vaux and printed in *Tottel's Miscellany* (1557). The O and a (for "ah") seemingly are the grunts of the digger. 64. **To contract . . . behove:** To make a betrothal agreement for my benefit (?).   65. **meet:** Suitable (i.e., more suitable).   68–69. **property of easiness:** Something he can do easily and without thinking.   71. **daintier sense:** More delicate sense of feeling.   74. **into the land:** Toward my grave (?) (but note the lack of rhyme in *steps, land*).   77. **jowls:** Dashes.   79. **politician:** Schemer, plotter.   80. **o'erreaches:** Circumvents, gets the better of (with a quibble on the literal sense).

V, i. **Location:** A churchyard. [S.D.] *Clowns:* Rustics. 4. **straight:** Straightway, immediately.   **crowner:** Coroner.   9. **se offendendo:** A comic mistake for *se defendendo*, term used in verdicts of justifiable homicide.   12. **Argal:** Corruption of *ergo*, therefore.   17. **will he:** Will he not.   23. **quest:** Inquest.   27. **there thou say'st:** That's right.   28. **count'nance:** Privilege.   30. **even-Christen:** Fellow Christian.   40. **confess thyself:** The saying continues, "and be hanged."

ACT V • SCENE I

HAMLET: Or of a courtier, which could say "Good morrow, sweet lord! How dost thou, sweet lord?" This
85 might be my Lord Such-a-one, that prais'd my Lord
Such-a-one's horse when 'a meant to beg it, might it
not?

HORATIO: Ay, my lord.

HAMLET: Why, e'en so, and now my Lady Worm's
90 chapless,° and knock'd about the mazzard° with a
sexton's spade. Here's fine revolution,° an° we had
the trick to see 't. Did these bones cost no more the
breeding,° but to play at loggats° with them? Mine
ache to think on 't.

                                        (*Song.*)

95 **FIRST CLOWN:** "A pick-axe, and a spade, a spade,
       For and° a shrouding sheet;
    O, a pit of clay for to be made
       For such a guest is meet."

                        [*Throws up another skull.*]

HAMLET: There's another. Why may not that be the
100 skull of a lawyer? Where be his quiddities° now, his
quillities,° his cases, his tenures,° and his tricks? Why
does he suffer this mad knave now to knock him
about the sconce° with a dirty shovel, and will not
tell him of his action of battery? Hum! This fellow
105 might be in 's time a great buyer of land, with his
statutes, his recognizances,° his fines, his double°
vouchers,° his recoveries.° [Is this the fine of his fines,
and the recovery of his recoveries,] to have his fine
pate full of fine dirt?° Will his vouchers vouch him
110 no more of his purchases, and double [ones too],
than the length and breadth of a pair of indentures?°
The very conveyances° of his lands will scarcely lie
in this box,° and must th' inheritor° himself have no
more, ha?

115 **HORATIO:** Not a jot more, my lord.

HAMLET: Is not parchment made of sheep-skins?

HORATIO: Ay, my lord, and of calf-skins too.

90. **chapless:** Having no lower jaw.   **mazzard:** Head (literally,
a drinking vessel).   **91. revolution:** Change.   **an:** If.   **93. the
breeding:** In the breeding, raising.   **loggats:** A game in which
pieces of hardwood are thrown to lie as near as possible to a
stake.   **96. For and:** And moreover.   **100. quiddities:** Subtleties, quibbles (from Latin *quid*, a thing).   **101. quillities:** Verbal
niceties, subtle distinctions (variation of *quiddities*).   **tenures:**
The holding of a piece of property or office; or, the conditions
or period of such holding.   **103. sconce:** Head.   **106. statutes,
recognizances:** Legal documents guaranteeing a debt by attaching land and property.   **106–107. fines, recoveries:** Ways
of converting entailed estates into "fee simple" or freehold.
106. double: Signed by two signatories.   **107. vouchers:** Guarantees of the legality of a title to real estate.   **107–109. fine
of his fines . . . fine pate . . . fine dirt:** End of his legal maneuvers . . . elegant head . . . minutely sifted dirt.   **111. pair of
indentures:** Legal document drawn up in duplicate on a single
sheet and then cut apart on a zigzag line so that each pair was
uniquely matched. (Hamlet may refer to two rows of teeth,
or dentures.)   **112. conveyances:** Deeds.   **113. this box:** The
skull.   **inheritor:** Possessor, owner.

HAMLET: They are sheep and calves which seek out
assurance in that.° I will speak to this fellow.—
Whose grave's this, sirrah?°   120

FIRST CLOWN: Mine, sir.
  [*Sings.*] "O, a pit of clay for to be made
  [For such a guest is meet]."

HAMLET: I think it be thine, indeed, for thou liest in 't.

FIRST CLOWN: You lie out on 't, sir, and therefore 'tis not 125
yours. For my part, I do not lie in 't, yet it is mine.

HAMLET: Thou dost lie in 't, to be in 't and say it is thine.
'Tis for the dead, not for the quick;° therefore thou
liest.

FIRST CLOWN: 'Tis a quick lie, sir; 'twill away again 130
from me to you.

HAMLET: What man dost thou dig it for?

FIRST CLOWN: For no man, sir.

HAMLET: What woman, then?

FIRST CLOWN: For none, neither.   135

HAMLET: Who is to be buried in 't?

FIRST CLOWN: One that was a woman, sir, but, rest her
soul, she's dead.

HAMLET: How absolute° the knave is! We must speak
by the card,° or equivocation° will undo us. By the 140
Lord, Horatio, this three years I have taken note of it:
the age is grown so pick'd° that the toe of the peasant comes so near the heel of the courtier, he galls his
kibe.° How long hast thou been a grave-maker?

FIRST CLOWN: Of all the days i' th' year, I came to 't that 145
day that our last king Hamlet overcame Fortinbras.

HAMLET: How long is that since?

FIRST CLOWN: Cannot you tell that? Every fool can tell
that. It was that very day that young Hamlet was
born—he that is mad, and sent into England. 150

HAMLET: Ay, marry, why was he sent into England?

FIRST CLOWN: Why, because 'a was mad. 'A shall recover
his wits there, or, if 'a do not, 'tis no great matter
there.

HAMLET: Why?   155

FIRST CLOWN: 'Twill not be seen in him there. There the
men are as mad as he.

HAMLET: How came he mad?

FIRST CLOWN: Very strangely, they say.

HAMLET: How strangely?   160

FIRST CLOWN: Faith, e'en with losing his wits.

HAMLET: Upon what ground?

FIRST CLOWN: Why, here in Denmark. I have been sexton
here, man and boy, thirty years.

HAMLET: How long will a man lie i' th' earth ere he rot? 165

FIRST CLOWN: Faith, if 'a be not rotten before 'a die—
as we have many pocky° corses [now-a-days], that

119. **assurance in that:** Safety in legal parchments.   **120. sirrah:**
Term of address to inferiors.   **128. quick:** Living.   **139. absolute:** Positive, decided.   **140. by the card:** By the mariner's card
on which the points of the compass were marked (i.e., with
precision).   **equivocation:** Ambiguity in the use of terms.
142. pick'd: Refined, fastidious.   **143–144. galls his kibe:**
Chafes the courtier's chilblain (a swelling or sore caused by
cold).   **167. pocky:** Rotten, diseased (literally, with the pox, or
syphilis).

will scarce hold the laying in—'a will last you some
eight year or nine year. A tanner will last you nine
170   year.

HAMLET: Why he more than another?

FIRST CLOWN: Why, sir, his hide is so tann'd with his
trade that 'a will keep out water a great while, and
your water is a sore decayer of your whoreson dead
175   body. [*Picks up a skull.*] Here's a skull now hath lain
you° i' th' earth three and twenty years.

HAMLET: Whose was it?

FIRST CLOWN: A whoreson mad fellow's it was. Whose do
you think it was?

180   HAMLET: Nay, I know not.

FIRST CLOWN: A pestilence on him for a mad rogue! 'A
pour'd a flagon of Rhenish° on my head once. This
same skull, sir, was Yorick's skull, the King's jester.

HAMLET: This?

185   FIRST CLOWN: E'en that.

HAMLET: [*Let me see.*] [*Takes the skull*] Alas, poor
Yorick! I knew him, Horatio, a fellow of infinite jest,
of most excellent fancy. He hath borne me on his
back a thousand times; and now, how abhorr'd in
190   my imagination it is! My gorge rises at it. Here hung
those lips that I have kiss'd I know not how oft.
Where be your gibes now? Your gambols, your
songs, your flashes of merriment that were wont to
set the table on a roar? Not one now, to mock your
195   own grinning? Quite chap-fall'n?° Now get you to
my lady's chamber, and tell her, let her paint an inch
thick, to this favor° she must come; make her laugh
at that. Prithee, Horatio, tell me one thing.

HORATIO: What's that, my lord?

200   HAMLET: Dost thou think Alexander look'd o' this fashion i' th' earth?

HORATIO: E'en so.

HAMLET: And smelt so? Pah! [*Puts down the skull.*]

HORATIO: E'en so, my lord.

205   HAMLET: To what base uses we may return, Horatio!
Why may not imagination trace the noble dust of
Alexander, till 'a find it stopping a bung-hole?

HORATIO: 'Twere to consider too curiously,° to consider so.

HAMLET: No, faith, not a jot, but to follow him thither
210   with modesty° enough, and likelihood to lead it.
[*As thus*]: Alexander died, Alexander was buried,
Alexander returneth to dust; the dust is earth; of
earth we make loam;° and why of that loam, whereto
he was converted, might they not stop a beer-barrel?
215   Imperious° Caesar, dead and turn'd to clay,
Might stop a hole to keep the wind away.
O, that that earth which kept the world in awe

Should patch a wall t' expel the winter's flaw!°
But soft, but soft awhile! Here comes the King.

(*Enter King, Queen, Laertes, and the Corse* [*of Ophelia, in procession, with Priest, Lords etc.*].)

The Queen, the courtiers. Who is this they follow?   220
And with such maimed rites? This doth betoken
The corse they follow did with desp'rate hand
Fordo it° own life. 'Twas of some estate.°
Couch° we awhile, and mark.
                    [*He and Horatio conceal themselves.
                    Ophelia's body is taken to the grave.*]

LAERTES: What ceremony else?   225

HAMLET [*to Horatio*]: That is Laertes, a very noble
youth. Mark.

LAERTES: What ceremony else?

PRIEST: Her obsequies have been as far enlarg'd
As we have warranty. Her death was doubtful,
And, but that great command o'ersways the order,   230
She should in ground unsanctified been lodg'd
Till the last trumpet. For° charitable prayers,
Shards,° flints, and pebbles should be thrown on her.
Yet here she is allow'd her virgin crants,°
Her maiden strewments,° and the bringing home   235
Of bell and burial.°

LAERTES: Must there no more be done?

PRIEST: No more be done.
We should profane the service of the dead
To sing a requiem and such rest to her
As to peace-parted souls.

LAERTES: Lay her i' th' earth,   240
And from her fair and unpolluted flesh
May violets° spring! I tell thee, churlish priest,
A minist'ring angel shall my sister be
When thou liest howling!

HAMLET [*to Horatio*]:   What, the fair Ophelia!

QUEEN [*scattering flowers*]: Sweets to the sweet!
Farewell.   245
I hoped thou shouldst have been my Hamlet's wife.
I thought thy bride-bed to have deck'd, sweet maid,
And not have strew'd thy grave.

LAERTES: O, treble woe
Fall ten times treble on that cursed head
Whose wicked deed thy most ingenious sense°   250
Depriv'd thee of! Hold off the earth awhile,
Till I have caught her once more in mine arms.
            [*Leaps into the grave and embraces Ophelia.*]
Now pile your dust upon the quick and dead,
Till of this flat a mountain you have made

---

218. **flaw**: Gust of wind.   223. **Fordo it**: Destroy its.   **estate**: Rank.   224. **Couch**: Hide, lurk.   232. **For**: In place of.
233. **Shards**: Broken bits of pottery.   234. **crants**: Garland.
235. **strewments**: Traditional strewing of flowers.   235–236. **bringing . . . burial**: Laying to rest of the body in consecrated ground, to the sound of the bell.   242. **violets**: See IV, v, 186 and note.   250. **ingenious sense**: Mind endowed with finest qualities.

175–176. **lain you**: Lain.   182. **Rhenish**: Rhine wine.
195. **chap-fall'n**: (1) Lacking the lower jaw; (2) dejected.
197. **favor**: Aspect, appearance.   208. **curiously**: Minutely.
210. **modesty**: Moderation.   213. **loam**: Clay mixture for brickmaking or other clay use.   215. **Imperious**: Imperial.

255   T 'o'ertop old Pelion,° or the skyish head
      Of blue Olympus.°
HAMLET [*coming forward*]: What is he whose grief
      Bears such an emphasis, whose phrase of sorrow
      Conjures the wand'ring stars,° and makes them stand
260   Like wonder-wounded hearers? This is I,
      Hamlet the Dane.°
LAERTES: The devil take thy soul!
                                    [*Grappling with him.*]
HAMLET: Thou pray'st not well.
      I prithee, take thy fingers from my throat;
      For, though I am not splenitive° and rash,
265   Yet have I in me something dangerous,
      Which let thy wisdom fear. Hold off thy hand.
KING: Pluck them asunder.
QUEEN: Hamlet, Hamlet!
ALL: Gentlemen!
HORATIO: Good my lord, be quiet.
                    [*Hamlet and Laertes are parted.*]
HAMLET: Why, I will fight with him upon this theme
270   Until my eyelids will no longer wag.
QUEEN: O my son, what theme?
HAMLET: I lov'd Ophelia. Forty thousand brothers
      Could not with all their quantity of love
      Make up my sum. What wilt thou do for her?
275 KING: O, he is mad, Laertes.
QUEEN: For love of God, forbear him.
HAMLET: 'Swounds,° show me what thou' do.
      Woo 't° weep? Woo 't fight? Woo 't fast? Woo 't
          tear thyself?
      Woo 't drink up eisel?° Eat a crocodile?
280   I'll do 't. Dost thou come here to whine?
      To outface me with leaping in her grave?
      Be buried quick° with her, and so will I.
      And, if thou prate of mountains, let them throw
      Millions of acres on us, till our ground,
285   Singeing his pate° against the burning zone,°
      Make Ossa° like a wart! Nay, an thou 'lt mouth,°
      I'll rant as well as thou.
QUEEN: This is mere° madness,
      And thus a while the fit will work on him;
      Anon, as patient as the female dove
290   When that her golden couplets° are disclos'd,°
      His silence will sit drooping.
HAMLET: Hear you, sir.
      What is the reason that you use me thus?

I lov'd you ever. But it is no matter.
Let Hercules himself do what he may,
The cat will mew, and dog will have his day.°   295
KING: I pray thee, good Horatio, wait upon him.

                    (*Exit Hamlet and Horatio.*)

[*To Laertes.*] Strengthen your patience in° our last
      night's speech;
We'll put the matter to the present push.°—
Good Gertrude, set some watch over your son.—
This grave shall have a living° monument.   300
An hour of quiet shortly shall we see;
Till then, in patience our proceeding be.   (*Exeunt.*)

{Scene II}°

(*Enter Hamlet and Horatio.*)

HAMLET: So much for this, sir; now shall you see the
      other.°
      You do remember all the circumstance?
HORATIO: Remember it, my lord!
HAMLET: Sir, in my heart there was a kind of
      fighting
      That would not let me sleep. Methought I lay   5
      Worse than the mutines° in the bilboes.° Rashly,°
      And prais'd be rashness for it—let us know,°
      Our indiscretion sometime serves us well
      When our deep plots do pall,° and that should
          learn° us
      There's a divinity that shapes our ends,   10
      Rough-hew° them how we will—
HORATIO: That is most certain.
HAMLET: Up from my cabin,
      My sea-gown scarf'd about me, in the dark
      Grop'd I to find out them, had my desire,
      Finger'd° their packet, and in fine° withdrew   15
      To mine own room again, making so bold,
      My fears forgetting manners, to unseal
      Their grand commission; where I found, Horatio—
      Ah, royal knavery!—an exact command,
      Larded° with many several sorts of reasons   20
      Importing° Denmark's health and England's too,
      With, ho, such bugs° and goblins in my life,°
      That, on the supervise,° no leisure bated,°

255, 256. Pelion, Olympus: Mountains in the north of Thessaly; see also the reference to Ossa at line 286. **259. wand'ring stars:** Planets. **261. the Dane:** This title normally signifies the king; see I, i, 15 and note. **264. splenitive:** Quick-tempered. **277. 'Swounds:** By His (Christ's) wounds. **278. Woo 't:** Wilt thou. **279. eisel:** Vinegar. **282. quick:** Alive. **285. his pate:** Its head (i.e., top). **burning zone:** Sun's orbit. **286. Ossa:** Another mountain in Thessaly. (In their war against the Olympian gods, the giants attempted to heap Ossa, Pelion, and Olympus on one another to scale heaven.) **mouth:** Rant. **287. mere:** Utter. **290. golden couplets:** Two baby pigeons, covered with yellow down. **disclos'd:** Hatched.

294–295. Let . . . day: Despite any blustering attempts at interference, every person will sooner or later do what he must do. **297. in:** By recalling. **298. present push:** Immediate test. **300. living:** Lasting; also refers (for Laertes' benefit) to the plot against Hamlet. **V, ii. Location:** The castle. **1. see the other:** Hear the other news. **6. mutines:** Mutineers. **bilboes:** Shackles. **Rashly:** On impulse (this adverb goes with lines 12ff.). **7. know:** Acknowledge. **9. pall:** Fail. **learn:** Teach. **11. Rough-hew:** Shape roughly. **15. Finger'd:** Pilfered, pinched. **in fine:** Finally, in conclusion. **20. Larded:** Enriched. **21. Importing:** Relating to. **22. bugs:** Bugbears, hobgoblins. **in my life:** To be feared if I were allowed to live. **23. supervise:** Reading. **leisure bated:** Delay allowed.

No, not to stay the grinding of the axe,
My head should be struck off.

25 HORATIO: Is 't possible?
HAMLET: Here's the commission; read it at more
    leisure.   [*Gives document.*]
    But wilt thou hear now how I did proceed?
HORATIO: I beseech you.
HAMLET: Being thus benetted round with villainies,
30   Or I could make a prologue to my brains,
    They had begun the play.° I sat me down,
    Devis'd a new commission, wrote it fair.°
    I once did hold it, as our statists° do,
    A baseness° to write fair, and labor'd much
35   How to forget that learning, but, sir, now
    It did me yeoman's° service. Wilt thou know
    Th' effect° of what I wrote?
HORATIO: Ay, good my lord.
HAMLET: An earnest conjuration from the King,
    As England was his faithful tributary,
40   As love between them like the palm might flourish,
    As peace should still her wheaten garland° wear
    And stand a comma° 'tween their amities,
    And many such-like as's° of great charge,°
    That, on the view and knowing of these contents,
45   Without debasement further, more or less,
    He should those bearers put to sudden death,
    Not shriving time° allow'd.
HORATIO: How was this seal'd?
HAMLET: Why, even in that was heaven ordinant.°
    I had my father's signet° in my purse,
50   Which was the model of that Danish seal;
    Folded the writ up in the form of th' other,
    Subscrib'd° it, gave 't th' impression,° plac'd it safely,
    The changeling° never known. Now, the next day
    Was our sea-fight, and what to this was sequent
55   Thou knowest already.
HORATIO: So Guildenstern and Rosencrantz go to 't.
HAMLET: [Why, man, they did make love to this
    employment.]
    They are not near my conscience. Their defeat
    Does by their own insinuation° grow.
60   'Tis dangerous when the baser nature comes
    Between the pass° and fell° incensed points
    Of mighty opposites.
HORATIO: Why, what a king is this!

HAMLET: Does it not, think thee, stand° me now
    upon—
    He that hath killed my king and whor'd my mother,
    Popp'd in between th' election° and my hopes,   65
    Thrown out his angle° for my proper° life,
    And with such coz'nage°—is 't not perfect
    conscience
    [To quit° him with this arm? And is 't not to be
    damn'd
    To let this canker° of our nature come
    In further evil?   70
HORATIO: It must be shortly known to him from
    England
    What is the issue of the business there.
HAMLET: It will be short. The interim is mine,
    And a man's life 's no more than to say "One."°
    But I am very sorry, good Horatio,   75
    That to Laertes I forgot myself,
    For by the image of my cause I see
    The portraiture of his. I'll court his favors.
    But, sure, the bravery° of his grief did put me
    Into a tow'ring passion.
HORATIO: Peace, who comes here?]   80

(*Enter a Courtier* [*Osric*].)

OSRIC: Your lordship is right welcome back to Denmark.
HAMLET: I humbly thank you, sir. [*To Horatio.*] Dost
    know this water-fly?
HORATIO: No, my good lord.
HAMLET: Thy state is the more gracious, for 'tis a vice to   85
    know him. He hath much land, and fertile. Let a
    beast be lord of beasts, and his crib shall stand at the
    King's mess.° 'Tis a chough,° but, as I say, spacious in
    the possession of dirt.
OSRIC: Sweet lord, if your lordship were at leisure, I   90
    should impart a thing to you from his Majesty.
HAMLET: I will receive it, sir, with all diligence of spirit.
    Put your bonnet to his right use; 'tis for the head.
OSRIC: I thank your lordship, it is very hot.
HAMLET: No, believe me, 'tis very cold; the wind is   95
    northerly.
OSRIC: It is indifferent° cold, my lord, indeed.
HAMLET: But yet methinks it is very sultry and hot for
    my complexion.°
OSRIC: Exceedingly, my lord; it is very sultry, as   100
    'twere—I cannot tell how. My lord, his Majesty bade
    me signify to you that 'a has laid a great wager on
    your head. Sir, this is the matter—

30–31. Or . . . play: Before I could consciously turn my brain to
the matter, it had started working on a plan. (*Or* means "ere.")
32. fair: In a clear hand. **33. statists:** Statesmen. **34. baseness:**
Lower-class trait. **36. yeoman's:** Substantial, workmanlike.
37. effect: Purport. **41. wheaten garland:** Symbolic of fruitful
agriculture, of peace. **42. comma:** Indicating continuity, link.
43. as's: (1) The "whereases" of formal document; (2) asses.
charge: (1) Import; (2) burden. **47. shriving time:** Time for
confession and absolution. **48. ordinant:** Directing. **49. signet:** Small seal. **52. Subscrib'd:** Signed. **impression:** With a
wax seal. **53. changeling:** The substituted letter (literally, a
fairy child substituted for a human one). **59. insinuation:** Interference. **61. pass:** Thrust. **fell:** Fierce.

63. stand: Become incumbent. **65. election:** The Danish
monarch was "elected" by a small number of high-
ranking electors. **66. angle:** Fishing line. **proper:** Very.
67. coz'nage: Trickery. **68. quit:** Repay. **69. canker:** Ulcer.
74. a man's . . . "One": To take a man's life requires no more
than to count to one as one duels. **79. bravery:** Bravado.
86–88. Let . . . mess: If a man, no matter how beastlike, is as
rich in possessions as Osric, he may eat at the king's table.
88. chough: Chattering jackdaw. **97. indifferent:** Somewhat.
99. complexion: Temperament.

HAMLET: I beseech you, remember—

[*Hamlet moves him to put on his hat.*]

105   OSRIC: Nay, good my lord; for my ease,° in good faith. Sir, here is newly come to court Laertes—believe me, an absolute gentleman, full of most excellent differences,° of very soft society° and great showing.° Indeed, to speak feelingly° of him, he is the card° or

110   calendar° of gentry,° for you shall find in him the continent of what part° a gentleman would see.

HAMLET: Sir, his definement° suffers no perdition° in you, though, I know, to divide him inventorially° would dozy° th' arithmetic of memory, and yet

115   but yaw° neither° in respect of° his quick sail. But, in the verity of extolment,° I take him to be a soul of great article,° and his infusion° of such dearth and rareness,° as, to make true diction° of him, his semblable° is his mirror, and who else would trace° him,

120   his umbrage,° nothing more.

OSRIC: Your lordship speaks most infallibly of him.

HAMLET: The concernancy,° sir? Why do we wrap the gentleman in our more rawer breath?°

OSRIC: Sir?

125   HORATIO: Is 't not possible to understand in another tongue?° You will do 't,° sir, really.

HAMLET: What imports the nomination° of this gentleman?

OSRIC: Of Laertes?

130   HORATIO [*to Hamlet*]: His purse is empty already; all 's golden words are spent.

HAMLET: Of him, sir.

OSRIC: I know you are not ignorant—

HAMLET: I would you did, sir; yet, in faith, if you did, it

135   would not much approve° me. Well, sir?

OSRIC: You are not ignorant of what excellence Laertes is—

HAMLET: I dare not confess that, lest I should compare° with him in excellence; but to know a man well were to know himself.°   140

OSRIC: I mean, sir, for his weapon; but in the imputation laid on him by them,° in his meed° he's unfellow'd.°

HAMLET: What's his weapon?

OSRIC: Rapier and dagger.

HAMLET: That's two of his weapons—but well.   145

OSRIC: The King, sir, hath wager'd with him six Barbary horses, against the which he has impawn'd,° as I take it, six French rapiers and poniards, with their assigns,° as girdle, hangers,° and so. Three of the carriages,° in faith, are very dear to fancy,° very responsive° to the hilts, most delicate° carriages, and of very liberal conceit.°   150

HAMLET: What call you the carriages?

HORATIO [*to Hamlet*]: I knew you must be edified by the margent° ere you had done.   155

OSRIC: The carriages, sir, are the hangers.

HAMLET: The phrase would be more germane to the matter if we could carry a cannon by our sides; I would it might be hangers till then. But, on: six Barb'ry horses against six French swords, their assigns, and three liberal-conceited carriages; that's the French bet against the Danish. Why is this impawn'd, as you call it?   160

OSRIC: The King, sir, hath laid,° sir, that in a dozen passes° between yourself and him, he shall not exceed you three hits. He hath laid on twelve for nine, and it would come to immediate trial, if your lordship would vouchsafe the answer.   165

HAMLET: How if I answer no?

OSRIC: I mean, my lord, the opposition of your person in trial.   170

HAMLET: Sir, I will walk here in the hall. If it please his Majesty, it is the breathing time° of day with me. Let the foils be brought, the gentleman willing, and the King hold his purpose, I will win for him an I can; if not, I will gain nothing but my shame and the odd hits.   175

---

105. for my ease: A conventional reply declining the invitation to put his hat back on.   **107–108. differences:** Special qualities.   **soft society:** Agreeable manners.   **108. great showing:** Distinguished appearance.   **109. feelingly:** With just perception. **card:** Chart, map.   **110. calendar:** Guide.   **gentry:** Good breeding.   **110–111. the continent . . . part:** One who contains in him all the qualities (a *continent* is that which contains). **112. definement:** Definition. (Hamlet proceeds to mock Osric by using his lofty diction back at him.)   **perdition:** Loss, diminution.   **113. divide him inventorially:** Enumerate his graces. **114. dozy:** Dizzy.   **115. yaw:** To move unsteadily (said of a ship).   **neither:** For all that.   **in respect of:** In comparison with. **116. in . . . extolment:** In true praise (of him).   **117. article:** Moment or importance.   **infusion:** Essence, character imparted by nature.   **117–118. dearth and rareness:** Rarity.   **118. make true diction:** Speak truly.   **119. semblable:** Only true likeness. **who . . . trace:** Any other person who would wish to follow. **120. umbrage:** Shadow.   **122. concernancy:** Import, relevance. **123. breath:** Speech.   **125–126. to understand . . . tongue:** For Osric to understand when someone else speaks in his manner. (Horatio twits Osric for not being able to understand the kind of flowery speech he himself uses when Hamlet speaks in such a vein.)   **126. You will do 't:** You can if you try.   **127. nomination:** Naming.   **135. approve:** Commend.

138. compare: Seem to compete.   **139–140. but . . . himself:** For, to recognize excellence in another man, one must know oneself.   **141–142. imputation . . . them:** Reputation given him by others.   **142. meed:** Merit.   **unfellow'd:** Unmatched.   **147. impawn'd:** Staked, wagered.   **149. assigns:** Appurtenances. **hangers:** Straps on the sword belt (*girdle*) from which the sword hung.   **149–150. carriages:** An affected way of saying *hangers;* literally, gun-carriages.   **150. dear to fancy:** Fancifully designed, tasteful.   **150–151. responsive:** Corresponding closely, matching.   **151. delicate:** I.e., in workmanship. **152. liberal conceit:** Elaborate design.   **155. margent:** Margin of a book, place for explanatory notes.   **164. laid:** Wagered. **165. passes:** Bouts. (The odds of the betting are hard to explain. Possibly the king bets that Hamlet will win at least five out of twelve, at which point Laertes raises the odds against himself by betting he will win nine.)   **173. breathing time:** Exercise period.

OSRIC: Shall I deliver you so?

HAMLET: To this effect, sir—after what flourish your
180   nature will.

OSRIC: I commend my duty to your lordship.

HAMLET: Yours, yours. [*Exit Osric.*] He does well to
commend it himself; there are no tongues else for 's
turn.

185 HORATIO: This lapwing° runs away with the shell on his
head.

HAMLET: 'A did comply, sir, with his dug,° before 'a
suck'd it. Thus has he—and many more of the same
breed that I know the drossy° age dotes on—only
190   got the tune° of the time and, out of an habit of
encounter,° a kind of yesty° collection,° which carries them through and through the most fann'd and
winnow'd° opinions; and do but blow them to their
trial, the bubbles are out.°

(*Enter a Lord.*)

195 LORD: My lord, his Majesty commended him to you by
young Osric, who brings back to him that you attend
him in the hall. He sends to know if your pleasure
hold to play with Laertes, or that you will take longer
time.

200 HAMLET: I am constant to my purposes; they follow the
King's pleasure. If his fitness speaks,° mine is ready;
now or whensoever, provided I be so able as now.

LORD: The King and Queen and all are coming down.

HAMLET: In happy time.°

205 LORD: The Queen desires you to use some gentle enter-
tainment° to Laertes before you fall to play.

HAMLET: She well instructs me.   [*Exit Lord.*]

HORATIO: You will lose, my lord.

HAMLET: I do not think so. Since he went into France, I
210   have been in continual practice; I shall win at the
odds. But thou wouldst not think how ill all's here
about my heart; but it is no matter.

HORATIO: Nay, good my lord—

HAMLET: It is but foolery, but it is such a kind of gain-
215   giving,° as would perhaps trouble a woman.

HORATIO: If your mind dislike anything, obey it. I will
forestall their repair hither, and say you are not fit.

HAMLET: Not a whit, we defy augury. There is special
providence in the fall of a sparrow. If it be now, 'tis
220   not to come; if it be not to come, it will be now, if it

be not now, yet it will come. The readiness is all.
Since no man of aught he leaves knows what is 't to
leave betimes,° let be.

(*A table prepar'd. [Enter] trumpets, drums, and Officers
with cushions; King, Queen, [Osric,] and all the State;
foils, daggers, [and wine borne in;] and Laertes.*)

KING: Come, Hamlet, come, and take this hand from me.
[*The King puts Laertes' hand into Hamlet's.*]

HAMLET: Give me your pardon, sir. I have done you
wrong,   225
But pardon 't, as you are a gentleman.
This presence° knows,
And you must needs have heard, how I am punish'd
With a sore distraction. What I have done
That might your nature, honor, and exception°   230
Roughly awake, I here proclaim was madness.
Was 't Hamlet wrong'd Laertes? Never Hamlet.
If Hamlet from himself be ta'en away,
And when he's not himself does wrong Laertes,
Then Hamlet does it not, Hamlet denies it.   235
Who does it, then? His madness. If 't be so,
Hamlet is of the faction that is wrong'd;
His madness is poor Hamlet's enemy.
[Sir, in this audience,]
Let my disclaiming from a purpos'd evil   240
Free me so far in your most generous thoughts
That I have shot my arrow o'er the house
And hurt my brother.

LAERTES: I am satisfied in nature,°
Whose motive in this case should stir me most
To my revenge. But in my terms of honor   245
I stand aloof, and will no reconcilement
Till by some elder masters of known honor
I have a voice° and precedent of peace
To keep my name ungor'd. But till that time,
I do receive your offer'd love like love,   250
And will not wrong it.

HAMLET: I embrace it freely,
And will this brothers' wager frankly play.
Give us the foils. Come on.

LAERTES: Come, one for me.

HAMLET: I'll be your foil,° Laertes. In mine ignorance
Your skill shall, like a star i' th' darkest night, 255
Stick fiery off° indeed.

LAERTES: You mock me, sir.

HAMLET: No, by this hand.

KING: Give them the foils, young Osric. Cousin Hamlet,
You know the wager?

HAMLET: Very well, my lord.
Your Grace has laid the odds o' th' weaker side.   260

---

185. lapwing: A bird that draws intruders away from its
nest and was thought to run about when newly hatched
with its head in the shell; a seeming reference to Osric's hat.
187. comply . . . dug: Observe ceremonious formality toward
his mother's teat. **189. drossy:** Frivolous. **190. tune:** Temper, mood, manner of speech. **190–191. habit of encounter:**
Demeanor of social intercourse. **191. yesty:** Yeasty, frothy.
collection: I.e., of current phrases. **192–193. fann'd and
winnow'd:** Select and refined. **193–194. blow . . . out:** Put them
to the test, and their ignorance is exposed. **201. If . . . speaks:**
If his readiness answers to the time. **204. In happy time:** A
phrase of courtesy indicating acceptance. **205–206. entertainment:** Greeting. **214–215. gain-giving:** Misgiving.

222–223. what . . . betimes: What is the best time to leave it.
227. presence: Royal assembly. **230. exception:** Disapproval.
243. in nature: As to my personal feelings. **248. voice:**
Authoritative pronouncement. **254. foil:** Thin metal background which sets a jewel off (with pun on the blunted rapier
for fencing). **256. Stick fiery off:** Stand out brilliantly.

KING: I do not fear it; I have seen you both.
  But since he is better'd,° we have therefore odds.
LAERTES: This is too heavy, let me see another.
                            [*Exchanges his foil for another.*]
HAMLET: This likes me well. These foils have all a length?
                               [*They prepare to play.*]
265 OSRIC: Ay, my good lord.
KING: Set me the stoups of wine upon that table.
  If Hamlet give the first or second hit,
  Or quit° in answer of the third exchange,
  Let all the battlements their ordnance fire.
270 The King shall drink to Hamlet's better breath,
  And in the cup an union° shall he throw,
  Richer than that which four successive kings
  In Denmark's crown have worn. Give me the cups,
  And let the kettle° to the trumpet speak,
275 The trumpet to the cannoneer without,
  The cannons to the heavens, the heaven to earth,
  "Now the King drinks to Hamlet." Come, begin.
                     (*Trumpets the while.*)
  And you, the judges, bear a wary eye.
HAMLET: Come on sir.
280 LAERTES: Come, my lord.   [*They play. Hamlet scores
                              a hit.*]
HAMLET: One.
LAERTES: No.
HAMLET: Judgment.
OSRIC: A hit, a very palpable hit.
      (*Drum, trumpets, and shot. Flourish.
                A piece goes off.*)
LAERTES: Well, again.
285 KING: Stay, give me drink. Hamlet, this pearl is thine.
     [*He throws a pearl in Hamlet's cup and drinks.*]
  Here's to thy health. Give him the cup.
HAMLET: I'll play this bout first, set it by awhile.
  Come. [*They play.*] Another hit; what say you?
LAERTES: A touch, a touch. I do confess 't.
KING: Our son shall win.
290 QUEEN: He's fat,° and scant of breath.
  Here, Hamlet, take my napkin,° rub thy brows.
  The Queen carouses° to thy fortune, Hamlet.
HAMLET: Good madam!
KING: Gertrude, do not drink.
295 QUEEN: I will, my lord; I pray you pardon me.
                           [*Drinks.*]
KING [*aside*]: It is the pois'ned cup. It is too late.
HAMLET: I dare not drink yet, madam; by and by.
QUEEN: Come, let me wipe thy face.
LAERTES [*to King*]: My lord, I'll hit him now.
KING: I do not think 't.
LAERTES [*aside*]: And yet it is almost against my
300   conscience.

262. **is better'd:** Has improved; is the odds-on favorite.
268. **quit:** Repay (with a hit).   271. **union:** Pearl (so called, according to Pliny's *Natural History,* IX, because pearls are *unique,* never identical).   274. **kettle:** Kettledrum.   290. **fat:** Not physically fit, out of training.   291. **napkin:** Handkerchief.
292. **carouses:** Drinks a toast.

HAMLET: Come, for the third Laertes. You do but dally.
  I pray you, pass with your best violence;
  I am afeard you make a wanton of me.°
LAERTES: Say you so? Come on.   [*They play.*]
OSRIC: Nothing, neither way.   305
LAERTES: Have at you now!
     [*Laertes wounds Hamlet; then, in scuffling,
       they change rapiers,° and Hamlet wounds
                       Laertes.*]
KING: Part them! They are incens'd.
HAMLET: Nay, come, again.   [*The Queen falls.*]
OSRIC: Look to the Queen there, ho!
HORATIO: They bleed on both sides. How is it, my lord?
OSRIC: How is 't, Laertes?
LAERTES: Why, as a woodcock° to mine own springe,°
  Osric;   310
  I am justly kill'd with mine own treachery.
HAMLET: How does the Queen?
KING: She swoons to see them bleed.
QUEEN: No, no, the drink, the drink—O my dear
  Hamlet—
  The drink, the drink! I am pois'ned.   [*Dies.*]
HAMLET: O villainy! Ho, let the door be lock'd!   315
  Treachery! Seek it out.   [*Laertes falls.*]
LAERTES: It is here, Hamlet. Hamlet, thou art slain.
  No med'cine in the world can do thee good;
  In thee there is not half an hour's life.
  The treacherous instrument is in thy hand,   320
  Unbated° and envenom'd. The foul practice
  Hath turn'd itself on me. Lo, here I lie,
  Never to rise again. Thy mother's pois'ned.
  I can no more. The King, the King's to blame.
HAMLET: The point envenom'd too? Then, venom, to
  thy work.   [*Stabs the King.*] 325
ALL: Treason! Treason!
KING: O, yet defend me, friends; I am but hurt.
HAMLET: Here, thou incestuous, murd'rous, damned
  Dane,
                  [*He forces the King to drink
                     the poisoned cup.*]
  Drink off this potion. Is thy union° here?
  Follow my mother.   [*King dies.*]
LAERTES: He is justly serv'd.   330
  It is a poison temper'd° by himself.
  Exchange forgiveness with me, noble Hamlet.
  Mine and my father's death come not upon thee,
  Nor thine on me!   [*Dies.*]

303. **make . . . me:** Treat me like a spoiled child, holding back to give me an advantage.   306. [s.d.] *in scuffling, they change rapiers:* This stage direction occurs in the Folio. According to a widespread stage tradition, Hamlet receives a scratch, realizes that Laertes' sword is unbated, and accordingly forces an exchange.   310. **woodcock:** A bird, a type of stupidity or decoy. **springe:** Trap, snare.   321. **Unbated:** Not blunted with a button.   329. **union:** Pearl (see line 271; with grim puns on the word's other meanings: marriage, shared death [?]).
331. **temper'd:** Mixed.

335 HAMLET: Heaven make thee free of it! I follow thee.
I am dead, Horatio. Wretched Queen, adieu!
You that look pale and tremble at this chance,
That are but mutes° or audience to this act,
Had I but time—as this fell° sergeant,° Death,
340 Is strict in his arrest—O, I could tell you—
But let it be. Horatio, I am dead;
Thou livest. Report me and my cause aright
To the unsatisfied.
HORATIO: Never believe it.
I am more an antique Roman° than a Dane.
Here's yet some liquor left.
          [*He attempts to drink from the poisoned cup.*
                    Hamlet prevents him.]
345 HAMLET: As th' art a man,
Give me the cup! Let go! By heaven, I'll ha 't.
O God, Horatio, what a wounded name,
Things standing thus unknown, shall I leave
          behind me!
If thou didst ever hold me in thy heart,
350 Absent thee from felicity awhile,
And in this harsh world draw thy breath in pain
To tell my story.
          (*A march afar off* [*and a volley within*].)
                    What warlike noise is this?
OSRIC: Young Fortinbras, with conquest come from
          Poland,
To the ambassadors of England gives
This warlike volley.
355 HAMLET: O, I die, Horatio!
The potent poison quite o'ercrows° my spirit.
I cannot live to hear the news from England,
But I do prophesy th' election lights
On Fortinbras. He has my dying voice.°
360 So tell him, with th' occurrents° more and less
Which have solicited°—the rest is silence.   [*Dies.*]
HORATIO: Now cracks a noble heart. Good night,
          sweet prince;
And flights of angels sing thee to thy rest!
                              [*March within.*]
Why does the drum come hither?

(*Enter Fortinbras, with the* [*English*] *Ambassadors*
[*with drum, colors, and attendants*].)

FORTINBRAS: Where is this sight?
365 HORATIO: What is it you would see?
If aught of woe or wonder, cease your search.
FORTINBRAS: This quarry° cries on havoc.° O proud
          Death.
What feast is toward° in thine eternal cell,

That thou so many princes at a shot
So bloodily hast struck?
FIRST AMBASSADOR: The sight is dismal;   370
And our affairs from England come too late.
The ears are senseless that should give us hearing,
To tell him his commandment is fulfill'd,
That Rosencrantz and Guildenstern are dead.
Where should we have our thanks?
HORATIO: Not from his° mouth,   375
Had it th' ability of life to thank you.
He never gave commandment for their death.
But since, so jump° upon this bloody question,°
You from the Polack wars, and you from England,
Are here arriv'd, give order that these bodies   380
High on a stage° be placed to the view,
And let me speak to th' yet unknowing world
How these things came about. So shall you hear
Of carnal, bloody, and unnatural acts,
Of accidental judgments,° casual° slaughters,   385
Of deaths put on° by cunning and forc'd cause,
And, in this upshot, purposes mistook
Fall'n on th' inventors' heads. All this can I
Truly deliver.
FORTINBRAS: Let us haste to hear it,
And call the noblest to the audience.   390
For me, with sorrow I embrace my fortune.
I have some rights of memory° in this kingdom,
Which now to claim my vantage° doth invite me.
HORATIO: Of that I shall have also cause to speak,
And from his mouth whose voice will draw on
          more.°   395
But let this same be presently° perform'd,
Even while men's minds are wild, lest more
          mischance
On° plots and errors happen.
FORTINBRAS: Let four captains
Bear Hamlet, like a soldier, to the stage,
For he was likely, had he been put on,°   400
To have prov'd most royal; and, for his passage,°
The soldiers' music and the rite of war
Speak loudly for him.
Take up the bodies. Such a sight as this
Becomes the field,° but here shows much amiss.   405
Go, bid the soldiers shoot.
          (*Exeunt* [*marching, bearing off the dead bodies;*
                    a peal of ordnance is shot off].)

---

338. **mutes:** Silent observers. 339. **fell:** Cruel. **sergeant:** Sheriff's officer. 344. **Roman:** It was the Roman custom to follow masters in death. 356. **o'ercrows:** Triumphs over. 359. **voice:** Vote. 360. **occurrents:** Events, incidents. 361. **solicited:** Moved, urged. 367. **quarry:** Heap of dead. **cries on havoc:** Proclaims a general slaughter. 368. **toward:** In preparation.

375. **his:** Claudius's. 378. **jump:** Precisely. **question:** Dispute. 381. **stage:** Platform. 385. **judgments:** Retributions. **casual:** Occurring by chance. 386. **put on:** Instigated. 392. **of memory:** Traditional, remembered. 393. **vantage:** Presence at this opportune moment. 395. **voice . . . more:** Vote will influence still others. 396. **presently:** Immediately. 398. **On:** On the basis of. 400. **put on:** Invested in royal office and so put to the test. 401. **passage:** Death. 405. **field:** I.e., of battle.

COMMENTARIES

The great Shakespearean Andrew Cecil Bradley was professor of poetry at Oxford when he wrote one of the most highly regarded of all critical texts on Shakespeare: *Shakespearean Tragedy* (1904). He limited himself to discussing four plays: *Hamlet, Othello, King Lear,* and *Macbeth*. His insights into all these plays are still useful guides for any reader. In the commentary below, he considers Hamlet's role as the "melancholy Dane."

T. S. Eliot, one of the twentieth century's most important poets and an equally important literary critic, was a great student of Elizabethan and Jacobean drama. His discussion centers on the difficulties he sees with *Hamlet*.

A. C. BRADLEY (1851–1935)

Hamlet's Melancholy   1904

Bradley offers us an analysis of Hamlet's character, with an emphasis on what Shakespeare may have meant by describing him as melancholy. The term today implies little more than sadness, but in the sixteenth and seventeenth centuries it pointed to something quite different. The term suggested that Hamlet was philosophical and capable of inward analysis — it meant that he was, in a modern sense, a deep person. Bradley reviews the ways in which Hamlet seems to fulfill the seventeenth-century concept of Melancholy.

Let us first ask ourselves what we can gather from the play, immediately or by inference, concerning Hamlet as he was just before his father's death. And I begin by observing that the text does not bear out the idea that he was one-sidedly reflective and indisposed to action. Nobody who knew him seems to have noticed this weakness. Nobody regards him as a mere scholar who has "never formed a resolution or executed a deed." In a court which certainly would not much admire such a person he is the observed of all observers. Though he has been disappointed of the throne everyone shows him respect; and he is the favorite of the people, who are not given to worship philosophers. Fortinbras, a sufficiently practical man, considered that he was likely, had he been put on, to have proved most royally. He has Hamlet borne by four captains "like a soldier" to his grave; and Ophelia says that Hamlet *was* a soldier. If he was fond of acting, an aesthetic pursuit, he was equally fond of fencing, an athletic one: he practiced it assiduously even in his worst days.[1] So far as we can conjecture from what we see of him in those bad days, he must normally have been charmingly frank, courteous and kindly to everyone, of whatever rank, whom he liked or respected, but by no means timid or deferential to others; indeed, one would gather that he was rather the reverse, and also that he was apt to be decided and even imperious if thwarted or interfered with. He must always have

---

[1] He says so to Horatio, whom he has no motive for deceiving [V, ii, 209–210]. His contrary statement [II, ii, 301–302] is made to Rosencrantz and Guildenstern.

been fearless—in the play he appears insensible to fear of any ordinary kind. And, finally, he must have been quick and impetuous in action; for it is downright impossible that the man we see rushing after the Ghost, killing Polonius, dealing with the King's commission on the ship, boarding the pirate, leaping into the grave, executing his final vengeance, could *ever* have been shrinking or slow in an emergency. Imagine Coleridge doing any of these things!

If we consider all this, how can we accept the notion that Hamlet's was a weak and one-sided character? "Oh, but he spent ten or twelve years at a University!" Well, even if he did, it is possible to do that without becoming the victim of excessive thought. But the statement that he did rests upon a most insecure foundation.

Where then are we to look for the seeds of danger?

(1) Trying to reconstruct from the Hamlet of the play, one would not judge that his temperament was melancholy in the present sense of the word; there seems nothing to show that; but one would judge that by temperament he was inclined to nervous instability, to rapid and perhaps extreme changes of feeling and mood, and that he was disposed to be, for the time, absorbed in the feeling or mood that possessed him, whether it were joyous or depressed. This temperament the Elizabethans would have called melancholic; and Hamlet seems to be an example of it, as Lear is of a temperament mixedly choleric and sanguine. And the doctrine of temperaments was so familiar in Shakespeare's time—as Burton, and earlier prose writers, and many of the dramatists show—that Shakespeare may quite well have given this temperament to Hamlet consciously and deliberately. Of melancholy in its developed form, a habit, not a mere temperament, he often speaks. He more than once laughs at the passing and half-fictitious melancholy of youth and love; in Don John in *Much Ado* he has sketched the sour and surly melancholy of discontent; in Jaques a whimsical self-pleasing melancholy; in Antonio in the *Merchant of Venice* a quiet but deep melancholy, for which neither the victim nor his friends can assign any cause.[2] He gives to Hamlet a temperament which would not develop into melancholy unless under some exceptional strain, but which still involved a danger. In the play we see the danger realized, and find a melancholy quite unlike any that Shakespeare had as yet depicted, because the temperament of Hamlet is quite different.

(2) Next, we cannot be mistaken in attributing to the Hamlet of earlier days an exquisite sensibility, to which we may give the name "moral," if that word is taken in the wide meaning it ought to bear. This, though it suffers cruelly in later days, as we saw in criticizing the sentimental view of Hamlet, never deserts him; it makes all his cynicism, grossness and hardness appear to us morbidities, and has an inexpressibly attractive and pathetic effect. He had the soul of the youthful poet as Shelley and Tennyson have described it, an unbounded delight and faith in everything good and beautiful. We know this from himself. The world for him was *herrlich wie am ersten Tag*°—"this goodly frame the earth, this most excellent canopy the air, this brave o'erhanging firmament, this majestical roof fretted with golden fire." And not nature only: "What a piece of work is a man! how noble in reason! how infinite in faculty! in form and moving how express and admirable! in action how like an angel! in apprehension how like a god!" This is no commonplace to Hamlet; it is the language of a heart thrilled with wonder and swelling into ecstasy.

[2] The critics have labored to find a cause, but it seems to me Shakespeare simply meant to portray a pathological condition; and a very touching picture he draws. Antonio's sadness, which he describes in the opening lines of the play, would never drive him to suicide, but it makes him indifferent to the issue of the trial, as all his speeches in the trial scene show.

herrlich . . . Tag: As wonderful as the first day.

Doubtless it was with the same eager enthusiasm he turned to those around him. Where else in Shakespeare is there anything like Hamlet's adoration of his father? The words melt into music whenever he speaks of him. And, if there are no signs of any such feeling toward his mother, though many signs of love, it is characteristic that he evidently never entertained a suspicion of anything unworthy in her—characteristic, and significant of his tendency to see only what is good unless he is forced to see the reverse. For we find this tendency elsewhere, and find it going so far that we must call it a disposition to idealize, to see something better than what is there, or at least to ignore deficiencies. He says to Laertes, "I loved you ever," and he describes Laertes as a "very noble youth," which he was far from being. In his first greeting of Rosencrantz and Guildenstern, where his old self revives, we trace the same affectionateness and readiness to take men at their best. His love for Ophelia, too, which seems strange to some, is surely the most natural thing in the world. He saw her innocence, simplicity and sweetness, and it was like him to ask no more; and it is noticeable that Horatio, though entirely worthy of his friendship, is, like Ophelia, intellectually not remarkable. To the very end, however clouded, this generous disposition, this "free and open nature," this unsuspiciousness survive. They cost him his life; for the King knew them, and was sure that he was too "generous and free from all contriving" to "peruse the foils." To the very end, his soul, however sick and tortured it may be, answers instantaneously when good and evil are presented to it, loving the one and hating the other. He is called a skeptic who has no firm belief in anything, but he is never skeptical about *them*.

And the negative side of his idealism, the aversion to evil, is perhaps even more developed in the hero of the tragedy than in the Hamlet of earlier days. It is intensely characteristic. Nothing, I believe, is to be found elsewhere in Shakespeare (unless in the rage of the disillusioned idealist Timon) of quite the same kind as Hamlet's disgust at his uncle's drunkenness, his loathing of his mother's sensuality, his astonishment and horror at her shallowness, his contempt for everything pretentious or false, his indifference to everything merely external. This last characteristic appears in his choice of the friend of his heart, and in a certain impatience of distinctions of rank or wealth. When Horatio calls his father "a goodly king," he answers, surely with an emphasis on "man,"

> He was a man, take him for all in all,
> I shall not look upon his like again.

He will not listen to talk of Horatio being his "servant." When the others speak of their "duty" to him, he answers, "Your love, as mine to you." He speaks to the actor precisely as he does to an honest courtier. He is not in the least a revolutionary, but still, in effect, a king and a beggar are all one to him. He cares for nothing but human worth, and his pitilessness toward Polonius and Osric and his "schoolfellows" is not wholly due to morbidity, but belongs in part to his original character.

Now, in Hamlet's moral sensibility there undoubtedly lay a danger. Any great shock that life might inflict on it would be felt with extreme intensity. Such a shock might even produce tragic results. And, in fact, *Hamlet* deserves the title "tragedy of moral idealism" quite as much as the title "tragedy of reflection."

(3) With this temperament and this sensibility we find, lastly, in the Hamlet of earlier days, as of later, intellectual genius. It is chiefly this that makes him so different from all those about him, good and bad alike, and hardly less different from

most of Shakespeare's other heroes. And this, though on the whole the most important trait in his nature, is also so obvious and so famous that I need not dwell on it at length. But against one prevalent misconception I must say a word of warning. Hamlet's intellectual power is not a specific gift, like a genius for music or mathematics or philosophy. It shows itself, fitfully, in the affairs of life as unusual quickness of perception, great agility in shifting the mental attitude, a striking rapidity and fertility in resource; so that, when his natural belief in others does not make him unwary, Hamlet easily sees through them and masters them, and no one can be much less like the typical helpless dreamer. It shows itself in conversation chiefly in the form of wit or humor; and, alike in conversation and in soliloquy, it shows itself in the form of imagination quite as much as in that of thought in the stricter sense. Further, where it takes the latter shape, as it very often does, it is not philosophic in the technical meaning of the word. There is really nothing in the play to show that Hamlet ever was "a student of philosophies," unless it be the famous lines which, comically enough, exhibit this supposed victim of philosophy as its critic:

> There are more things in heaven and earth, Horatio,
> Than are dreamt of in your philosophy.[3]

His philosophy, if the word is to be used, was, like Shakespeare's own, the immediate product of the wondering and meditating mind; and such thoughts as that celebrated one, "There is nothing either good or bad but thinking makes it so," surely needed no special training to produce them. Or does Portia's remark, "Nothing is good without respect," *i.e.,* out of relation, prove that she had studied metaphysics?

Still Hamlet had speculative genius without being a philosopher, just as he had imaginative genius without being a poet. Doubtless in happier days he was a close and constant observer of men and manners, noting his results in those tables which he afterwards snatched from his breast to make in wild irony his last note of all, that one may smile and smile and be a villain. Again and again we remark that passion for generalization which so occupied him, for instance, in reflections suggested by the King's drunkenness that he quite forgot what it was he was waiting to meet upon the battlements. Doubtless, too, he was always considering things, as Horatio thought, too curiously. There was a necessity in his soul driving him to penetrate below the surface and to question what others took for granted. That fixed habitual look which the world wears for most men did not exist for him. He was forever unmaking his world and rebuilding it in thought, dissolving what to others were solid facts, and discovering what to others were old truths. There were no old truths for Hamlet. It is for Horatio a thing of course that there's a divinity that shapes our ends, but for Hamlet it is a discovery hardly won. And throughout this kingdom of the mind, where he felt that man, who in action is only like an angel, is in apprehension like a god, he moved (we must imagine) more than content, so that even in his dark days he declares he could be bounded in a nutshell and yet count himself a king of infinite space, were it not that he had bad dreams.

If now we ask whether any special danger lurked *here,* how shall we answer? We must answer, it seems to me, "Some danger, no doubt, but, granted the ordinary chances of life, not much." For, in the first place, that idea which so many critics quietly take for granted—the idea that the gift and the habit of meditative and speculative thought tend to produce irresolution in the affairs of life—would be

---

[3] Of course "your" does not mean Horatio's philosophy in particular. "Your" is used as the Gravedigger uses it when he says that "your water is a sore decayer of your . . . dead body."

found by no means easy to verify. Can you verify it, for example, in the lives of the philosophers, or again in the lives of men whom you have personally known to be addicted to such speculation? I cannot. Of course, individual peculiarities being set apart, absorption in *any* intellectual interest, together with withdrawal from affairs, may make a man slow and unskillful in affairs; and doubtless, individual peculiarities being again set apart, a mere student is likely to be more at a loss in a sudden and great practical emergency than a soldier or a lawyer. But in all this there is no difference between a physicist, a historian, and a philosopher; and again, slowness, want of skill, and even helplessness are something totally different from the peculiar kind of irresolution that Hamlet shows. The notion that speculative thinking specially tends to produce *this* is really a mere illusion.

In the second place, even if this notion were true, it has appeared that Hamlet did *not* live the life of a mere student, much less of a mere dreamer, and that his nature was by no means simply or even one-sidedly intellectual, but was healthily active. Hence, granted the ordinary chances of life, there would seem to be no great danger in his intellectual tendency and his habit of speculation; and I would go further and say that there was nothing in them, taken alone, to unfit him even for the extraordinary call that was made upon him. In fact, if the message of the Ghost had come to him within a week of his father's death, I see no reason to doubt that he would have acted on it as decisively as Othello himself, though probably after a longer and more anxious deliberation. And therefore the Schlegel-Coleridge view (apart from its descriptive value) seems to me fatally untrue, for it implies that Hamlet's procrastination was the normal response of an overspeculative nature confronted with a difficult practical problem.

On the other hand, under conditions of a peculiar kind, Hamlet's reflectiveness certainly might prove dangerous to him, and his genius might even (to exaggerate a little) become his doom. Suppose that violent shock to his moral being of which I spoke; and suppose that under this shock, any possible action being denied to him, he began to sink into melancholy; then, no doubt, his imaginative and generalizing habit of mind might extend the effects of this shock through his whole being and mental world. And if, the state of melancholy being thus deepened and fixed, a sudden demand for difficult and decisive action in a matter connected with the melancholy arose, this state might well have for one of its symptoms an endless and futile mental dissection of the required deed. And, finally, the futility of this process, and the shame of his delay, would further weaken him and enslave him to his melancholy still more. Thus the speculative habit would be *one* indirect cause of the morbid state which hindered action; and it would also reappear in a degenerate form as one of the *symptoms* of this morbid state.

Now this is what actually happens in the play. Turn to the first words Hamlet utters when he is alone; turn, that is to say, to the place where the author is likely to indicate his meaning most plainly. What do you hear?

> O, that this too too solid flesh would melt,
> Thaw and resolve itself into a dew!
> Or that the Everlasting had not fix'd
> His canon 'gainst self-slaughter! O God! God!
> How weary, stale, flat and unprofitable,
> Seem to me all the uses of this world!
> Fie on't! ah fie! 'tis an unweeded garden,
> That grows to seed; things rank and gross in nature
> Possess it merely.

Here are a sickness of life, and even a longing for death, so intense that nothing stands between Hamlet and suicide except religious awe. And what has caused them? The rest of the soliloquy so thrusts the answer upon us that it might seem impossible to miss it. It was not his father's death; that doubtless brought deep grief, but mere grief for someone loved and lost does not make a noble spirit loathe the world as a place full only of things rank and gross. It was not the vague suspicion that we know Hamlet felt. Still less was it the loss of the crown; for though the subserviency of the electors might well disgust him, there is not a reference to the subject in the soliloquy, nor any sign elsewhere that it greatly occupied his mind. It was the moral shock of the sudden ghastly disclosure of his mother's true nature, falling on him when his heart was aching with love, and his body doubtless was weakened by sorrow. And it is essential, however disagreeable, to realize the nature of this shock. It matters little here whether Hamlet's age was twenty or thirty: in either case his mother was a matron of mature years. All his life he had believed in her, we may be sure, as such a son would. He had seen her not merely devoted to his father, but hanging on him like a newly wedded bride, hanging on him

> As if increase of appetite had grown
> By what it fed on.

He had seen her following his body "like Niobe, all tears." And then within a month—"O God! a beast would have mourned longer"—she married again, and married Hamlet's uncle, a man utterly contemptible and loathsome in his eyes; married him in what to Hamlet was incestuous wedlock;[4] married him not for any reason of state, nor even out of old family affection, but in such a way that her son was forced to see in her action not only an astounding shallowness of feeling but an eruption of coarse sensuality, "rank and gross,"[5] speeding posthaste to its horrible delight. Is it possible to conceive an experience more desolating to a man such as we have seen Hamlet to be; and is its result anything but perfectly natural? It brings bewildered horror, then loathing, then despair of human nature. His whole mind is poisoned. He can never see Ophelia in the same light again: she is a woman, and his mother is a woman: if she mentions the word "brief" to him, the answer drops from his lips like venom, "as woman's love." The last words of the soliloquy, which is *wholly* concerned with this subject, are,

> But break, my heart, for I must hold my tongue!

He can do nothing. He must lock in his heart, not any suspicion of his uncle that moves obscurely there, but that horror and loathing; and if his heart ever found relief, it was when those feelings, mingled with the love that never died out in him,

---

[4] This aspect of the matter leaves *us* comparatively unaffected, but Shakespeare evidently means it to be of importance. The Ghost speaks of it twice, and Hamlet thrice (once in his last furious words to the King). If, as we must suppose, the marriage was universally admitted to be incestuous, the corrupt acquiescence of the court and the electors to the crown would naturally have a strong effect on Hamlet's mind.

[5] It is most significant that the metaphor of this soliloquy reappears in Hamlet's adjuration to his mother [III, iv, 158–159]:

> Repent what's past; avoid what is to come;
> And do not spread the compost on the weeds
> To make them ranker.

poured themselves forth in a flood as he stood in his mother's chamber beside his father's marriage bed.[6]

If we still wonder, and ask why the effect of this shock should be so tremendous, let us observe that *now* the conditions have arisen under which Hamlet's highest endowments, his moral sensibility and his genius, become his enemies. A nature morally blunter would have felt even so dreadful a revelation less keenly. A slower and more limited and positive mind might not have extended so widely through its world the disgust and disbelief that have entered it. But Hamlet has the imagination which, for evil as well as good, feels and sees all things in one. Thought is the element of his life, and his thought is infected. He cannot prevent himself from probing and lacerating the wound in his soul. One idea, full of peril, holds him fast, and he cries out in agony at it, but is impotent to free himself ("Must I remember?" "Let me not think on't"). And when, with the fading of his passion, the vividness of this idea abates, it does so only to leave behind a boundless weariness and a sick longing for death.

And this is the time which his fate chooses. In this hour of uttermost weakness, this sinking of his whole being toward annihilation, there comes on him, bursting the bounds of the natural world with a shock of astonishment and terror, the revelation of his mother's adultery and his father's murder, and, with this, the demand on him, in the name of everything dearest and most sacred, to arise and act. And for a moment, though his brain reels and totters, his soul leaps up in passion to answer this demand. But it comes too late. It does but strike home the last rivet in the melancholy which holds him bound.

> The time is out of joint! O cursed spite
> That ever I was born to set it right,—

so he mutters within an hour of the moment when he vowed to give his life to the duty of revenge; and the rest of the story exhibits his vain efforts to fulfill this duty, his unconscious self-excuses and unavailing self-reproaches, and the tragic results of his delay.

"Melancholy," I said, not dejection, nor yet insanity. That Hamlet was not far from insanity is very probable. His adoption of the pretense of madness may well have been due in part to fear of the reality; to an instinct of self-preservation, a forefeeling that the pretense would enable him to give some utterance to the load that pressed on his heart and brain, and a fear that he would be unable altogether to repress such utterance. And if the pathologist calls his state melancholia, and even proceeds to determine its species, I see nothing to object to in that; I am grateful to him for emphasizing the fact that Hamlet's melancholy was no mere common depression of spirits; and I have no doubt that many readers of the play would understand it better if they read an account of melancholia in a work on mental diseases. If we like to use the word "disease" loosely, Hamlet's condition may truly be called diseased. No exertion of will could have dispelled it. Even if he had been able at once to do the bidding of the Ghost he would doubtless have still remained for some time under the cloud. It would be absurdly unjust to call *Hamlet* a study of melancholy, but it contains such a study.

---

[6] If the reader will now look at the only speech of Hamlet's that precedes the soliloquy, and is more than one line in length–the speech beginning "Seems, madam! nay, it *is*"–he will understand what, surely, when first we come to it, sounds very strange and almost boastful. It is not, in effect, about Hamlet himself at all; it is about his mother (I do not mean that it is intentionally and consciously so; and still less that she understood it so).

But this melancholy is something very different from insanity, in anything like the usual meaning of that word. No doubt it might develop into insanity. The longing for death might become an irresistible impulse to self-destruction; the disorder of feeling and will might extend to sense and intellect; delusions might arise; and the man might become, as we say, incapable and irresponsible. But Hamlet's melancholy is some way from this condition. It is a totally different thing from the madness which he feigns; and he never, when alone or in company with Horatio alone, exhibits the signs of that madness. Nor is the dramatic use of this melancholy, again, open to the objections which would justly be made to the portrayal of an insanity which brought the hero to a tragic end. The man who suffers as Hamlet suffers—and thousands go about their business suffering thus in greater or less degree—is considered irresponsible neither by other people nor by himself: he is only too keenly conscious of his responsibility. He is therefore, so far, quite capable of being a tragic agent, which an insane person, at any rate according to Shakespeare's practice, is not. And, finally, Hamlet's state is not one which a healthy mind is unable sufficiently to imagine. It is probably not further from average experience, nor more difficult to realize, than the great tragic passions of Othello, Antony or Macbeth.

Let me try to show now, briefly, how much this melancholy accounts for.

It accounts for the main fact, Hamlet's inaction. For the *immediate* cause of that is simply that his habitual feeling is one of disgust at life and everything in it, himself included—a disgust which varies in intensity, rising at times into a longing for death, sinking often into weary apathy, but is never dispelled for more than brief intervals. Such a state of feeling is inevitably adverse to *any* kind of decided action; the body is inert, the mind indifferent or worse; its response is, "it does not matter," "it is not worth while," "it is no good." And the action required of Hamlet is very exceptional. It is violent, dangerous, difficult to accomplish perfectly, on one side repulsive to a man of honor and sensitive feeling, on another side involved in a certain mystery (here come in thus, in their subordinate place, various causes of inaction assigned by various theories). These obstacles would not suffice to prevent Hamlet from acting, if his state were normal; and against them there operate, even in his morbid state, healthy and positive feelings, love of his father, loathing of his uncle, desire of revenge, desire to do duty. But the retarding motives acquire an unnatural strength because they have an ally in something far stronger than themselves, the melancholic disgust and apathy; while the healthy motives, emerging with difficulty from the central mass of diseased feeling, rapidly sink back into it and "lose the name of action." We *see* them doing so; and sometimes the process is quite simple, no analytical reflection on the deed intervening between the outburst of passion and the relapse into melancholy.[7] But this melancholy is perfectly consistent also with that incessant dissection of the task assigned, of which the Schlegel-Coleridge theory makes so much. For those endless questions (as we may imagine them), "Was I deceived by the Ghost? How am I to do the deed? When? Where? What will be the consequence of attempting it—success, my death, utter misunderstanding, mere mischief to the State? Can it be right to do it, or noble to kill a defenseless man? What is the good of doing it in such a world as this?"—all this, and whatever else passed in a sickening round through Hamlet's mind, was not the healthy and right deliberation of a man with such a task, but otiose thinking hardly deserving the name of thought, an unconscious weaving of

---

[7] *E.g.* in the transition, referred to above, from desire for vengeance into the wish never to have been born; in the soliloquy, "O what a rogue"; in the scene at Ophelia's grave. The Schlegel-Coleridge theory does not account for the psychological movement in those passages.

pretexts for inaction, aimless tossings on a sick bed, symptoms of melancholy which only increased it by deepening self-contempt.

Again, (a) this state accounts for Hamlet's energy as well as for his lassitude, those quick decided actions of his being the outcome of a nature normally far from passive, now suddenly stimulated, and producing healthy impulses which work themselves out before they have time to subside. (b) It accounts for the evidently keen satisfaction which some of these actions give to him. He arranges the play scene with lively interest, and exults in its success, not really because it brings him nearer to his goal, but partly because it has hurt his enemy and partly because it has demonstrated his own skill [III, ii, 274–298]. He looks forward almost with glee to countermining the King's designs in sending him away [III, iv, 215], and looks back with obvious satisfaction, even with pride, to the address and vigor he displayed on the voyage [V, ii, 4–55]. These were not *the* action on which his morbid self-feeling had centered; he feels in them his old force, and escapes in them from his disgust. (c) It accounts for the pleasure with which he meets old acquaintances, like his "school-fellows" or the actors. The former observed (and we can observe) in him a "kind of joy" at first, though it is followed by "much forcing of his disposition" as he attempts to keep this joy and his courtesy alive in spite of the misery which so soon returns upon him and the suspicion he is forced to feel. (d) It accounts no less for the painful features of his character as seen in the play, his almost savage irritability on the one hand, and on the other his self-absorption, his callousness, his insensibility to the fates of those whom he despises, and to the feelings even of those whom he loves. These are frequent symptoms of such melancholy, and (e) they sometimes alternate, as they do in Hamlet, with bursts of transitory, almost hysterical, and quite fruitless emotion. It is to these last (of which a part of the soliloquy, "O what a rogue," gives a good example) that Hamlet alludes when, to the Ghost, he speaks of himself as "lapsed in *passion*," and it is doubtless partly his conscious weakness in regard to them that inspires his praise of Horatio as a man who is not "passion's slave."[8]

Finally, Hamlet's melancholy accounts for two things which seem to be explained by nothing else. The first of these is his apathy or "lethargy." We are bound to consider the evidence which the text supplies of this, though it is usual to ignore it. When Hamlet mentions, as one possible cause of his inaction, his "thinking too precisely on the event," he mentions another, "bestial oblivion"; and the thing against which he inveighs in the greater part of that soliloquy (IV, iv) is not the excess or the misuse of reason (which for him here and always is godlike), but this *bestial* oblivion or "*dullness*," this "letting all *sleep*," this allowing of heaven-sent reason to "fust unused":

> What is a man,
> If his chief good and market of his time
> Be but to *sleep* and feed? a *beast,* no more.[9]

---

[8]Hamlet's violence at Ophelia's grave, though probably intentionally exaggerated, is another example of this want of self-control. The Queen's description of him [V, i, 287–291],

> This is mere madness;
> And thus awhile the fit will work on him;
> Anon, as patient as the female dove,
> When that her golden couplets are disclosed,
> His silence will sit drooping,

may be true to life, though it is evidently prompted by anxiety to excuse his violence on the ground of his insanity.

[9]Throughout, I italicize to show the connection of ideas.

So, in the soliloquy in II, ii he accuses himself of being "a *dull* and muddy-mettled rascal," who "peaks [mopes] like John-a-dreams, unpregnant of his cause," dully indifferent to his cause. So, when the Ghost appears to him the second time, he accuses himself of being tardy and lapsed in *time*; and the Ghost speaks of his purpose being almost *blunted,* and bids him not to *forget* (cf. "oblivion"). And so, what is emphasized in those undramatic but significant speeches of the player king and of Claudius is the mere dying away of purpose or of love. Surely what all this points to is not a condition of excessive but useless mental activity (indeed there is, in reality, curiously little about that in the text), but rather one of dull, apathetic, brooding gloom, in which Hamlet, so far from analyzing his duty, is not thinking of it at all, but for the time literally *forgets* it. It seems to me we are driven to think of Hamlet *chiefly* thus during the long time which elapsed between the appearance of the Ghost and the events presented in the Second Act. The Ghost, in fact, had more reason than we suppose at first for leaving with Hamlet as his parting injunction the command, "Remember me," and for greeting him, on reappearing, with the command, "Do not forget." These little things in Shakespeare are not accidents.

T. S. ELIOT (1888–1965)

Hamlet and His Problems   1934

Not only a leading poet of the twentieth-century modernist period, T. S. Eliot also produced extremely interesting criticism of Elizabethan literature. His several collections of essays defined important critical terms that later readers have used to gain insight into great writers. One of those terms is developed here: the objective correlative, which Eliot believes is missing in *Hamlet*. His, argument is provocative and revealing.

Few critics have ever admitted that *Hamlet* the play is the primary problem, and Hamlet the character only secondary. And Hamlet the character has had an especial temptation for that most dangerous type of critic: the critic with a mind which is naturally of the creative order, but which through some weakness in creative power exercises itself in criticism instead. These minds often find in Hamlet a vicarious existence for their own artistic realization. Such a mind had Goethe, who made of Hamlet a Werther; and such had Coleridge, who made of Hamlet a Coleridge; and probably neither of these men in writing about Hamlet remembered that his first business was to study a work of art. The kind of criticism that Goethe and Coleridge produced, in writing of Hamlet, is the most misleading kind possible. For they both possessed unquestionable critical insight, and both make their critical aberrations the more plausible by the substitution—of their own Hamlet for Shakespeare's—which their creative gift effects. We should be thankful that Walter Pater° did not fix his attention on this play.

Two writers of our time, Mr. J. M. Robertson and Professor Stoll of the University of Minnesota, have issued small books which can be praised for moving in the

Walter Pater: English writer and critic (1839–1894). His writings were often overelaborate.

other direction. Mr. Stoll performs a service in recalling to our attention the labors of the critics of the seventeenth and eighteenth centuries, observing that

> they knew less about psychology than more recent Hamlet critics, but they were nearer in spirit to Shakespeare's art; and as they insisted on the importance of the effect of the whole rather than on the importance of the leading character, they were nearer, in their old-fashioned way, to the secret of dramatic art in general.

Qua work of art, the work of art cannot be interpreted; there is nothing to interpret; we can only criticize it according to standards, in comparison to other works of art; and for "interpretation" the chief task is the presentation of relevant historical facts which the reader is not assumed to know. Mr. Robertson points out, very pertinently, how critics have failed in their "interpretation" of *Hamlet* by ignoring what ought to be very obvious: that *Hamlet* is a stratification, that it represents the efforts of a series of men, each making what he could out of the work of his predecessors. The *Hamlet* of Shakespeare will appear to us very differently if, instead of treating the whole action of the play as due to Shakespeare's design, we perceive his *Hamlet* to be superposed upon much cruder material which persists even in the final form.

We know that there was an older play by Thomas Kyd, that extraordinary dramatic (if not poetic) genius who was in all probability the author of two plays so dissimilar as the *Spanish Tragedy* and *Arden of Feversham;* and what this play was like we can guess from three clues: from the *Spanish Tragedy* itself, from the tale of Belleforest upon which Kyd's *Hamlet* must have been based, and from a version acted in Germany in Shakespeare's lifetime which bears strong evidence of having been adapted from the earlier, not from the later, play. From these three sources it is clear that in the earlier play the motive was a revenge motive simply; that the action or delay is caused, as in the *Spanish Tragedy,* solely by the difficulty of assassinating a monarch surrounded by guards; and that the "madness" of Hamlet was feigned in order to escape suspicion, and successfully. In the final play of Shakespeare, on the other hand, there is a motive which is more important than that of revenge, and which explicitly "blunts" the latter; the delay in revenge is unexplained on grounds of necessity or expediency; and the effect of the "madness" is not to lull but to arouse the king's suspicion. The alteration is not complete enough, however, to be convincing. Furthermore, there are verbal parallels so close to the *Spanish Tragedy* as to leave no doubt that in places Shakespeare was merely *revising* the text of Kyd. And finally there are unexplained scenes—the Polonius-Laertes and the Polonius-Reynaldo scenes—for which there is little excuse; these scenes are not in the verse style of Kyd, and not beyond doubt in the style of Shakespeare. These Mr. Robertson believes to be scenes in the original play of Kyd reworked by a third hand, perhaps Chapman,° before Shakespeare touched the play. And he concludes, with very strong show of reason, that the original play of Kyd was, like certain other revenge plays, in two parts of five acts. The upshot of Mr. Robertson's examination is, we believe, irrefragable: that Shakespeare's *Hamlet,* so far as it is Shakespeare's, is a play dealing with the effect of a mother's guilt upon her son, and that Shakespeare was unable to impose this motive successfully upon the "intractable" material of the old play.

Of the intractability there can be no doubt. So far from being Shakespeare's masterpiece, the play is most certainly an artistic failure. In several ways the play is puzzling, and disquieting as is none of the others. Of all the plays it is the longest and is possibly the one on which Shakespeare spent most pains; and yet he has left

---

Chapman: George Chapman (1559?–1634), Elizabethan poet and playwright.

in it superfluous and inconsistent scenes which even hasty revision should have noticed. The versification is variable. Lines like

> Look, the morn, in russet mantle clad,
> Walks o'er the dew of yon high eastern hill,

are of the Shakespeare of *Romeo and Juliet*. The lines in act V, scene ii,

> Sir, in my heart there was a kind of fighting
> That would not let me sleep . . .
> Up from my cabin,
> My sea-gown scarf'd about me, in the dark
> Grop'd I to find out them: had my desire;
> Finger'd their packet;

are of his quite mature. Both workmanship and thought are in an unstable position. We are surely justified in attributing the play, with that other profoundly interesting play of "intractable" material and astonishing versification, *Measure for Measure*, to a period of crisis, after which follow the tragic successes which culminate in *Coriolanus*. *Coriolanus* may be not as "interesting" as *Hamlet*, but it is, with *Antony and Cleopatra*, Shakespeare's most assured artistic success. And probably more people have thought *Hamlet* a work of art because they found it interesting than have found it interesting because it is a work of art. It is the *Mona Lisa* of literature.

The grounds of *Hamlet*'s failure are not immediately obvious. Mr. Robertson is undoubtedly correct in concluding that the essential emotion of the play is the feeling of a son toward a guilty mother:

> [Hamlet's] tone is that of one who has suffered tortures on the score of his mother's degradation. . . . The guilt of a mother is an almost intolerable motive for drama, but it had to be maintained and emphasized to supply a psychological solution, or rather a hint of one.

This, however, is by no means the whole story. It is not merely the "guilt of a mother" that cannot be handled as Shakespeare handled the suspicion of Othello, the infatuation of Antony, or the pride of Coriolanus. The subject might conceivably have expanded into a tragedy like these, intelligible, self-complete, in the sunlight. *Hamlet*, like the sonnets, is full of some stuff that the writer could not drag to light, contemplate, or manipulate into art. And when we search for this feeling, we find it, as in the sonnets, very difficult to localize. You cannot point to it in the speeches; indeed, if you examine the two famous soliloquies, you see the versification of Shakespeare but a content which might be claimed by another, perhaps by the author of the *Revenge of Bussy d'Ambois*,° act V, scene i. We find Shakespeare's Hamlet not in the action, not in any quotations that we might select, so much as in an unmistakable tone which is unmistakably not in the earlier play.

The only way of expressing emotion in the form of art is by finding an "objective correlative"; in other words, a set of objects, a situation, a chain of events which shall be the formula of that *particular* emotion; such that when the external facts, which must terminate in sensory experience, are given, the emotion is immediately evoked. If you examine any of Shakespeare's more successful tragedies, you will find this exact equivalence; you will find that the state of mind of Lady Macbeth walking in her sleep has been communicated to you by a skillful accumulation of imagined sensory impressions; the words of Macbeth on hearing of his wife's death strike us as if, given the sequence of events, these words were

---

Revenge of Bussy d'Ambois: Tragedy (1610–1611) by George Chapman, dealing with the reluctance of Clement d'Ambois to avenge his brother's death.

automatically released by the last event in the series. The artistic "inevitability" lies in this complete adequacy of the external to the emotion; and this is precisely what is deficient in *Hamlet*. Hamlet (the man) is dominated by an emotion which is inexpressible, because it is in *excess* of the facts as they appear. And the supposed identity of Hamlet with his author is genuine to this point: that Hamlet's bafflement at the absence of objective equivalent to his feelings is a prolongation of the bafflement of his creator in the face of his artistic problem. Hamlet is up against the difficulty that his disgust is occasioned by his mother, but that his mother is not an adequate equivalent for it; his disgust envelops and exceeds her. It is thus a feeling which he cannot understand; he cannot objectify it, and it therefore remains to poison life and obstruct action. None of the possible actions can satisfy it; and nothing that Shakespeare can do with the plot can express Hamlet for him. And it must be noticed that the very nature of the *données* of the problem precludes objective equivalence. To have heightened the criminality of Gertrude would have been to provide the formula for a totally different emotion in Hamlet; it is just *because* her character is so negative and insignificant that she arouses in Hamlet the feeling which she is incapable of representing.

The "madness" of Hamlet lay to Shakespeare's hand; in the earlier play a simple ruse, and to the end, we may presume, understood as a ruse by the audience. For Shakespeare it is less than madness and more than feigned. The levity of Hamlet, his repetition of phrase, his puns, are not part of a deliberate plan of dissimulation, but a form of emotional relief. In the character Hamlet it is the buffoonery of an emotion which can find no outlet in action; in the dramatist it is the buffoonery of an emotion which he cannot express in art. The intense feeling, ecstatic or terrible, without an object or exceeding its object, is something which every person of sensibility has known; it is doubtless a subject of study for pathologists. It often occurs in adolescence: the ordinary person puts these feelings to sleep, or trims down his feelings to fit the business world; the artist keeps them alive by his ability to intensify the world to his emotions. The Hamlet of Laforgue° is an adolescent; the Hamlet of Shakespeare is not, he has not that explanation and excuse. We must simply admit that here Shakespeare tackled a problem which proved too much for him. Why he attempted it at all is an insoluble puzzle; under compulsion of what experience he attempted to express the inexpressibly horrible, we cannot ever know. We need a great many facts in his biography; and we should like to know whether, and when, and after or at the same time as what personal experience, he read Montaigne's *Apologie de Raimond Sebond*. We should have, finally, to know something which is by hypothesis unknowable, for we assume it to be an experience which, in the manner indicated, exceeded the facts. We should have to understand things which Shakespeare did not understand himself.

The Tempest

One of Shakespeare's most thought-provoking plays, *The Tempest* links Renaissance Italy, Elizabethan England, and the discoveries of the New World. Shakespeare had an interest in the Virginia Company, an investment group that sent a flotilla of ships to Virginia in 1609. Its flagship, carrying the governor-to-be of Virginia, Sir Thomas Gates, was lost in a July storm and washed up

---

Laforgue: Jules Laforgue (1860–1887), French poet who was an important influence on Eliot.

on Bermuda, then reputed to be the Isle of Devils. Admiral Sir George Somers built new boats and, with Gates and the rest of the crew, continued the journey, arriving in Jamestown in May 1610. All this news was reported in England as Shakespeare was preparing to write a new play for the Globe Theatre. With the "still-vexed Bermudas" of *The Tempest* (not to mention its opening storm), drama now touched on current events in the Elizabethan world of politics and adventure.

There is also a connection between Prospero, the philosopher-magician of *The Tempest,* and the most celebrated Elizabethan magician of the time, John Dee (1527–1608). This learned mathematician was also an astrologer, whom Queen Elizabeth consulted when she wanted to have her horoscope cast. His fame as a necromancer—one who called the spirits to do his bidding—took him as far as Poland to perform magic. While he was there in 1583, an English mob, certain Dee was a dangerous wizard, destroyed his library, furnishings, and laboratories. He was known by reputation to the audiences of the original productions of *The Tempest,* in November 1611 and again in 1612–1613.

King James I, who was almost surely at its first performances, took a special interest in magic. The play was performed at courtly festivities celebrating the marriage of James's daughter Elizabeth. The marriage of Miranda and Ferdinand paralleled this real-life marriage. Moreover, the masque that the spirits perform for Miranda and Ferdinand (act IV, scene i) served as a special wedding celebration, since masques were dedicated to Hymen, the god of marriage.

Apart from relying on current events, *The Tempest* is notable in that it is one of the few plays for which Shakespeare did not use an earlier source from fiction, drama, or history. The plot—the good duke and his daughter being cast adrift by his evil brother and then ending on an island that the duke controls through his magic—seems entirely original. Early critics saw the play as a moral excursion in which the power of good, after great trial, eventually overcomes evil. However, Shakespeare leaves a loose end at the conclusion of the play. While most of those who colluded to remove Prospero from his dukedom are contrite and ashamed—and express honest regret at their earlier actions—Prospero's brother Antonio remains unrepentant at the end. Prospero, whose magic controls everyone on the island, forsakes magic when he declares that he will return to Milan. Thus he leaves himself potentially defenseless against a possible repetition of his brother's crimes. This detail emphasizes the island as a magical place, while reminding us of the existence of evil in the world of Renaissance politics.

The political aspect of the play hints at governmental negligence. Antonio is hungry for power, but Prospero is neglectful of it. Some critics have suggested that Niccoló Machiavelli (1469–1527) may have provided some thematic underpinning for the play in his political treatise *The Prince,* which insists that a prince (or duke) should hold on to power by any means possible. While spending his time cultivating magic, Prospero neglects his political duties, leaving the way open to his usurping brother.

The Tempest in Performance

Curiously, *The Tempest* does not seem to have made a stir when it was first performed in 1611. Unlike *Titus Andronicus, Henry V, Romeo and Juliet, Hamlet,* and thirteen other plays, *The Tempest* was not printed in a convenient small quarto-size book in Shakespeare's lifetime. The quarto (so called because the pages were one quarter the size of the full-size paper fed into printing presses of the time) was a cheap but not always accurate text. Quartos were produced when printers thought the popularity of a play would sell the book. Only in 1623, after Shakespeare's death, was *The Tempest* printed in the First Folio (whose pages were created with a single fold of the full-size paper) by members of his theater company.

In 1642, the Puritans, part of a movement that had been becoming increasingly powerful in London, gained control of the city, at the beginning of what was to be a civil war. The Puritans believed that entertainment was sinful, and in September of that year they ordered all theaters closed. The theaters remained closed for the next eighteen years. After the theaters were closed, *The Tempest* seems not to have been acted in private, although no records survive. After England's restoration of the crown in 1660, the play was revived in the form of a broad adaptation by John Dryden (1631–1700) and William D'Avenant (1606–1668). Their play *The Enchanted Island* (1667) was produced during the Restoration, when women could take roles on stage. Soon after, in 1674, Thomas Shadwell (1642–1692) turned Dryden and D'Avenant's version into an opera, which became one of the most often produced adaptations of *The Tempest*. The original play was not produced successfully in London until 1838. Since then, it has been adapted and revised countless times as an opera and broadly adapted by novelists and poets.

Modern productions of the play are often based on their interpretations of Prospero's role. Late-nineteenth-century actors were not as drawn to the role of Prospero. When Beerbohm Tree, an important Shakespearean actor, produced *The Tempest* in the early 1900s, he took the part of Caliban. He enjoyed the ambiguity of that role, which he played sympathetically.

John Gielgud was the most durable Prospero of the twentieth century, playing the role numerous times, from 1930 at the Old Vic to 1991 in Peter Greenaway's film *Prospero's Books*, an adaptation that used mime and opera. In 1957, Gielgud played Prospero in Peter Brook's first production, which emphasized the theme of revenge. After his second production (1963), Brook said that *The Tempest* "includes all the themes from [Shakespeare's] earlier work—kingship, inheritance, treachery, conscience, identity, love, music, God; he draws them together as if to find the key to it all, but there is no such key. There is no grand order and Prospero returns to Milan not bathed in tranquility, but a wreck."

Peter Hall's 1974 production at London's National Theatre presented Gielgud in makeup that made him resemble John Dee, the Elizabethan magus. The emphasis on magic was clear and powerful. As Prospero, Patrick Stewart began what was supposed to be a limited run in a 1995 production directed by George Wolfe but went on to become a Broadway hit. Stewart was known to the public from the television sci-fi series *Star Trek: The Next Generation,* but his training with the Royal Shakespeare Company was evident in his powerful Prospero. This production also brought out a post-colonial issue—the tension between Ariel and Caliban as two members of oppressed tribes.

Sam Mendes cast Stephen Dillane as Prospero in the Bridge Project's brilliant production at the Brooklyn Academy of Music in February 2010. Julie Taymor's 2010 film *The Tempest* emphasized the colonialist reading of the play but surprised audiences by casting Helen Mirren as Prospera. Ralph Fiennes played Prospero onstage at the Haymarket in London in 2011, in a more traditional reading of the play. This spate of very different interpretations demonstrates the enduring mystery of *The Tempest,* which seems to grow in our imagination rather than diminish.

WILLIAM SHAKESPEARE (1564–1616)

The Tempest 1611

Names of the Actors

ALONSO, *King of Naples*
SEBASTIAN, *his brother*
PROSPERO, *the right Duke of Milan*
ANTONIO, *his brother, the usurping Duke of Milan*
FERDINAND, *son to the King of Naples*
GONZALO, *an honest old councillor*
ADRIAN,
FRANCISCO, } *lords*
CALIBAN, *a savage and deformed slave*
TRINCULO, *a jester*
STEPHANO, *a drunken butler*
MASTER, *of a ship*
BOATSWAIN
MARINERS

MIRANDA, *daughter to Prospero*

ARIEL, *an airy Spirit*
IRIS,
CERES,
JUNO, } *[presented by] Spirits*
NYMPHS,
REAPERS,

[*Other Spirits attending Prospero*]

Scene: *An uninhabited island*

ACT I • Scene I°

(*A tempestuous noise of thunder and lightning heard. Enter a Shipmaster and a Boatswain.*)

MASTER: Boatswain!
BOATSWAIN: Here, Master. What cheer?
MASTER: Good,° speak to the mariners. Fall to 't yarely,° or we run ourselves aground. Bestir,
5 bestir! (*Exit.*)

(*Enter Mariners.*)

BOATSWAIN: Heigh, my hearts! Cheerly,° cheerly, my hearts! Yare, yare! Take in the topsail. Tend° to the

Master's whistle.—Blow° till thou burst thy wind, if room enough!°

(*Enter Alonso, Sebastian, Antonio, Ferdinand, Gonzalo, and others.*)

ALONSO: Good Boatswain, have care. Where's the 10 Master? Play the men.°
BOATSWAIN: I pray now, keep° below.
ANTONIO: Where is the Master, Boatswain?
BOATSWAIN: Do you not hear him? You mar our labor. Keep° your cabins! You do assist the storm. 15
GONZALO: Nay, good,° be patient.
BOATSWAIN: When the sea is. Hence!° What cares these roarers° for the name of king? To cabin! Silence! Trouble us not.
GONZALO: Good, yet remember whom thou hast 20 aboard.
BOATSWAIN: None that I more love than myself. You are a councillor; if you can command these elements to silence and work the peace of the present,° we will not hand° a rope more. Use your authority. If 25 you cannot, give thanks you have lived so long and make yourself ready in your cabin for the mischance° of the hour, if it so hap.°—Cheerly, good hearts!—Out of our way, I say. (*Exit.*)
GONZALO: I have great comfort from this fellow. 30 Methinks he hath no drowning mark upon him; his complexion is perfect gallows.° Stand fast, good Fate, to his hanging! Make the rope of his destiny our cable, for our own doth little advantage.° If he be not born to be hanged, our case is 35 miserable.° (*Exeunt.*)°

I, i. Location: On board ship, off the island's coast.
3. Good: I.e., it's good you've come; or, my good fellow.
4. yarely: Nimbly. **6. Cheerly:** Cheerily. **7. Tend:** Attend.

8. Blow: Addressed to the wind. **8–9. if room enough:** As long as we have sea room enough. **11. Play the men:** Act like men (?), ply, urge the men to exert themselves (?). **12. keep:** Stay. **15. Keep:** Remain in. **16. good:** Good fellow. **17. Hence:** Get away. **18. roarers:** Waves or winds or both; spoken of as though they were "bullies" or "blusterers." **24. work...present:** Bring calm to our present circumstances. **25. hand:** Handle. **28. mischance:** Misfortune. **hap:** Happen. **32. complexion...gallows:** Appearance shows he was born to be hanged (and therefore, according to the proverb, in no danger of drowning). **34–35. our...advantage:** I.e., our own cable is of little benefit. **35–36. case is miserable:** Circumstances are desperate. **36. [s.d.]** *Exeunt:* Latin for "they go out."

233

(Enter Boatswain.)

BOATSWAIN: Down with the topmast! Yare! Lower, lower!
    Bring her to try wi' the main course.° *(A cry within.)*
    A plague upon this howling! They are louder than
40   the weather or our office.°

(Enter Sebastian, Antonio, and Gonzalo.)

    Yet again? What do you here? Shall we give o'er° and
    drown? Have you a mind to sink?
SEBASTIAN: A pox o' your throat, you bawling, blas-
    phemous, incharitable dog!
45 BOATSWAIN: Work you, then.
ANTONIO: Hang, cur! Hang, you whoreson, insolent
    noisemaker! We are less afraid to be drowned than
    thou art.
GONZALO: I'll warrant him for drowning,° though the
50   ship were no stronger than a nutshell and as leaky as
    an unstanched° wench.
BOATSWAIN: Lay her ahold,° ahold! Set her two courses.°
    Off to sea again! Lay her off!

(Enter Mariners, wet.)

MARINERS: All lost! To prayers, to prayers! All lost!
                        [Exeunt Mariners.]
55 BOATSWAIN: What, must our mouths be cold?°
GONZALO: The King and Prince at prayers! Let's
    assist them,
    For our case is as theirs.
SEBASTIAN: I am out of patience.
ANTONIO: We are merely° cheated of our lives by
    drunkards.
    This wide-chapped° rascal! Would thou mightst lie
    drowning
    The washing of ten tides!°
60 GONZALO: He'll be hanged yet,
    Though every drop of water swear against it
    And gape at wid'st° to glut° him.
    (A confused noise within.)   "Mercy on us!"—
    "We split,° we split!"—"Farewell my wife and
    children!"—
    "Farewell, brother!"—"We split, we split, we split!"

                                [Exit Boatswain.]

ANTONIO: Let's all sink wi' the King.   65
SEBASTIAN: Let's take leave of him.

                    (Exit [with Antonio].)

GONZALO: Now would I give a thousand furlongs of sea
    for an acre of barren ground: long heath,° brown
    furze,° anything. The wills above be done! But I
    would fain° die a dry death.   *(Exit.)* 70

Scene II°

(Enter Prospero [in his magic cloak] and Miranda.)

MIRANDA: If by your art,° my dearest father, you
    have
    Put the wild waters in this roar,° allay° them.
    The sky, it seems, would pour down stinking
        pitch,°
    But that the sea, mounting to th' welkin's
        cheek,°
    Dashes the fire out. O, I have suffered   5
    With those that I saw suffer! A brave° vessel,
    Who had, no doubt, some noble creature in her,
    Dashed all to pieces. O, the cry did knock
    Against my very heart! Poor souls, they perished.
    Had I been any god of power, I would   10
    Have sunk the sea within the earth or ere°
    It should the good ship so have swallowed and
    The freighting° souls within her.
PROSPER: Be collected.°
    No more amazement.° Tell your piteous° heart
    There's no harm done.
MIRANDA: O, woe the day!
PROSPERO: No harm.   15
    I have done nothing but° in care of thee,
    Of thee, my dear one, thee, my daughter, who
    Art ignorant of what thou art, naught knowing
    Of whence I am, nor that I am more better°
    Than Prospero, master of a full° poor cell,   20

---

38. **Bring . . . course:** Sail her close to the wind by means of the mainsail. 40. **our office:** I.e., the noise we make at our work. 41. **give o'er:** Give up. 49. **warrant him for drowning:** Guarantee that he will never be drowned. 51. **unstanched:** Insatiable, loose, unrestrained. 52. **ahold:** Ahull, close to the wind. **courses:** Sails (i.e., foresail as well as mainsail), set in an attempt to get the ship back out into open water. 55. **must . . . cold:** I.e., must we drown in the cold sea; or, let us heat up our mouths with liquor. 58. **merely:** Utterly. 59. **wide-chapped:** With mouth wide open. 59–60. **lie . . . tides:** Pirates were hanged on the shore and left until three tides had come in. 62. **at wid'st:** Wide. **glut:** Swallow. 63. **split:** Break apart.

68. **heath:** Heather. 69. **furze:** Gorse, a weed growing on wasteland. 70. **fain:** Rather. **I, ii. Location:** The island. Prospero's cell is visible, and on the Elizabethan stage it presumably remains so throughout the play, although in some scenes the convention of flexible distance allows us to imagine characters in other parts of the island. 1. **art:** Magic 2. **roar:** Uproar. **allay:** Pacify. 3. **pitch:** A thick, viscous substance produced by boiling down tar or turpentine 4. **welkin's cheek:** Sky's face. 6. **brave:** Gallant, splendid. 11. **or ere:** Before. 13. **freighting:** Forming the cargo. **collected:** Calm, composed. 14. **amazement:** Consternation. **piteous:** Pitying. 16. **but:** Except. 19. **more better:** Of higher rank. 20. **full:** Very.

Akiya Henry as Miranda and Joseph Mydell as Prospero at
the Regent's Park Open Air Theatre in London, 2009.

And thy no greater father.

MIRANDA: More to know
Did never meddle° with my thoughts.

PROSPERO: 'Tis time
I should inform thee farther. Lend thy hand
And pluck my magic garment from me. So,
        [*Laying down his magic cloak and staff.*]
Lie there, my art.—Wipe thou thine eyes. Have
25   comfort.
The direful spectacle of the wreck,° which touched
The very virtue° of compassion in thee,
I have with such provision° in mine art
So safely ordered that there is no soul—
30   No, not so much perdition° as an hair
Betid° to any creature in the vessel

Which° thou heardst cry, which thou sawst sink.
    Sit down,
For thou must now know farther.

MIRANDA [*sitting*]:   You have often
Begun to tell me what I am, but stopped
And left me to a bootless inquisition,°   35
Concluding, "Stay, not yet."

PROSPERO: The hour's now come;
The very minute bids thee ope° thine ear.
Obey, and be attentive. Canst thou remember
A time before we came unto this cell?
I do not think thou canst, for then thou wast
    not   40
Out° three years old.

MIRANDA: Certainly, sir, I can.

PROSPERO: By what? By any other house or person?
Of anything the image, tell me, that
Hath kept with thy remembrance.

MIRANDA: 'Tis far off,
And rather like a dream than an assurance   45
That my remembrance warrants.° Had I not
Four or five women once that tended° me?

PROSPERO: Thou hadst, and more, Miranda. But
    how is it
That this lives in thy mind? What seest thou else
In the dark backward and abysm of time?°   50
If thou rememberest aught° ere thou cam'st here,
How thou cam'st here thou mayst.

MIRANDA: But that I do not.

PROSPERO: Twelve year since, Miranda, twelve year
    since,
Thy father was the Duke of Milan and
A prince of power.

MIRANDA: Sir, are not you my father?   55

PROSPERO: Thy mother was a piece° of virtue, and
She said thou wast my daughter; and thy father
Was Duke of Milan, and his only heir
And princess no worse issued.°

MIRANDA: O the heavens!
What foul play had we, that we came from
    thence?   60
Or Blessed was 't we did?

PROSPERO: Both, both, my girl.
By foul play, as thou sayst, were we heaved
    thence,
But blessedly holp° hither.

MIRANDA: O, my heart bleeds
To think o' the teen that I have turned you to,°
Which is from° my remembrance! Please you,
    farther.   65

22. meddle: Mingle. 26. wreck: Shipwreck. 27. virtue:
Essence. 28. provision: Foresight. 30. perdition: Loss.
31. Betid: Happened.

32. **Which:** Whom. 35. **bootless inquisition:** Profitless inquiry. 37. **ope:** Open. 41. **Out:** Fully. 45–46. **assurance . . .
warrants:** Certainty that my memory guarantees. 47. **tended:**
Attended, waited upon. 50. **backward . . . time:** Abyss of
the past. 51. **aught:** Anything. 56. **piece:** Masterpiece,
exemplar. 59. **no worse issued:** No less nobly born, descended.
63. **holp:** Helped. 64. **teen . . . to:** Trouble I've caused you to
remember or put you to. 65. **from:** Out of.

PROSPERO: My brother and thy uncle, called
　　Antonio—
　　I pray thee, mark me, that a brother should
　　Be so perfidious!—he whom next° thyself
　　Of all the world I loved, and to him put
70　The manage° of my state, as at that time
　　Through all the seigniories° it was the first,
　　And Prospero the prime° duke, being so reputed
　　In dignity, and for the liberal arts
　　Without a parallel; those being all my study,
75　The government I cast upon my brother
　　And to my state grew stranger,° being
　　　transported°
　　And rapt in secret studies. Thy false uncle—
　　Dost thou attend me?
MIRANDA:　　　　　　Sir, most heedfully.
PROSPERO: Being once perfected° how to grant suits,
80　How to deny them, who t' advance and who
　　To trash° for overtopping,° new created
　　The creatures° that were mine, I say, or changed
　　　'em
　　Or else new formed 'em;° having both the key°
　　Of officer and office, set all hearts i' the state
85　To what tune pleased his ear, that° now he was
　　The ivy which had hid my princely trunk
　　And sucked my verdure° out on 't.° Thou
　　　attend'st not.
MIRANDA: O, good sir, I do.
PROSPERO:　　　　　I pray thee, mark me.
　　I, thus neglecting worldly ends, all dedicated
90　To closeness° and the bettering of my mind
　　With that which, but by being so retired,
　　O'erprized all popular rate,° in my false brother
　　Awaked an evil nature; and my trust,
　　Like a good parent,° did beget of° him
95　A falsehood in its contrary as great
　　As my trust was, which had indeed no limit,
　　A confidence sans° bound. He being thus lorded°
　　Not only with what my revenue yielded
　　But what my power might else° exact, like one

Who, having into° truth by telling of it,　　　　100
Made such a sinner of his memory
To° credit his own lie,° he did believe
He was indeed the Duke, out o'° the substitution
And executing th' outward face of royalty°
With all prerogative. Hence his ambition
　growing—　　　　　　　　　　　　　　　105
Dost thou hear?
MIRANDA:　　　　Your tale, sir, would cure deafness.
PROSPERO: To have no screen between this part he
　played
And him he played it for,° he needs° will be
Absolute Milan.° Me, poor man, my library
Was dukedom large enough. Of temporal
　royalties°　　　　　　　　　　　　　　　110
He thinks me now incapable; confederates°—
So dry° he was for sway°—wi' the King of
　Naples
To give him° annual tribute, do him homage,
Subject his coronet to his° crown, and bend°
The dukedom yet° unbowed—alas, poor Milan!—　115
To most ignoble stooping.
MIRANDA:　　　　　　O the heavens!
PROSPERO: Mark his condition° and th' event,° then
　tell me
If this might be a brother.
MIRANDA:　　　　　I should sin
To think but° nobly of my grandmother.
Good wombs have borne bad sons.
PROSPERO:　　　　　　Now the condition,　120
This King of Naples, being an enemy
To me inveterate, hearkens° my brother's suit,
Which was that he, in lieu o' the premises°
Of homage and I know not how much tribute,
Should presently extirpate° me and mine　　　　125
Out of the dukedom and confer fair Milan,
With all the honors, on my brother. Whereon
A treacherous army levied, one midnight
Fated to th' purpose did Antonio open
The gates of Milan, and, i' the dead of darkness,　130
The ministers for the purpose° hurried thence°

---

68. **next:** Next to. 70. **manage:** Management, administration. 71. **seigniories:** City-states of northern Italy. 72. **prime:** Of highest rank. 76. **to . . . stranger:** Withdrew from my responsibilities as duke. **transported:** Carried away. 79. **perfected:** Grown skillful. 81. **trash:** Check a hound by tying a cord or weight to its neck. **overtopping:** Running too far ahead of the pack; surmounting, exceeding one's authority. 82. **creatures:** Dependents. 82–83. **or changed . . . formed 'em:** Either changed their loyalties and duties or else created new ones. 83. **key:** (1) Key for unlocking; (2) tool for tuning stringed instruments. 85. **that:** So that. 87. **verdure:** Vitality. **on 't:** Of it. 90. **closeness:** Retirement, seclusion. 91–92. **but . . . rate:** Simply because it was done in such seclusion, had a value not appreciated by popular opinion. 94. **good parent:** Alludes to the proverb that good parents often bear bad children; see also line 120. **of:** In. 97. **sans:** Without. **lorded:** Raised to lordship, with power and wealth. 99. **else:** Otherwise, additionally.

100–102. **Who . . . lie:** Who, by repeatedly telling the lie (that he was indeed Duke of Milan), made his memory such a confirmed sinner against truth that he began to believe his own lie. **into:** Unto, against. **To:** So as to. 103. **out o':** As a result of. 104. **And . . . royalty:** And (as a result of) his carrying out all the ceremonial functions of royalty. 107–108. **To have . . . it for:** To have no separation or barrier between his role and himself. (Antonio wanted to act in his own person, not as substitute.) 108. **needs:** Necessarily. 109. **Absolute Milan:** Unconditional duke of Milan. 110. **temporal royalties:** Practical prerogatives and responsibilities of a sovereign. 111. **confederates:** Conspires, allies himself. 112. **dry:** Thirsty. **sway:** Power. 113. **him:** The King of Naples. 114. **his . . . his:** Antonio's . . . the King of Naples's. **bend:** Make bow down. 115. **yet:** Hitherto. 117. **condition:** Pact. **event:** Outcome. 119. **but:** Other than. 122. **hearkens:** Listens to. 123. **in . . . premises:** In return for the stipulation. 125. **presently extirpate:** At once remove. 131. **ministers . . . purpose:** Agents employed to do this. **thence:** From there.

Me and thy crying self.
MIRANDA: Alack, for pity!
I, not remembering how I cried out then,
Will cry it o'er again. It is a hint°
That wrings° mine eyes to 't.
135 PROSPERO: Hear a little further,
And then I'll bring thee to the present business
Which now's upon 's, without the which this story
Were most impertinent.°
MIRANDA: Wherefore° did they not
That hour destroy us?
PROSPERO: Well demanded,° wench.°
My tale provokes that question. Dear, they durst
140   not,
So dear the love my people bore me, nor set
A mark so bloody° on the business, but
With colors fairer° painted their foul ends.
In few,° they hurried us aboard a bark,°
Bore us some leagues to sea, where they
145   prepared
A rotten carcass of a butt,° not rigged,
Nor tackle,° sail, nor mast; the very rats
Instinctively have quit° it. There they hoist us
To cry to th' sea that roared to us, to sigh
150 To th' winds whose pity, sighing back again,
Did us but loving wrong.°
MIRANDA: Alack, what trouble
Was I then to you!
PROSPERO: O, a cherubin°
Thou wast that did preserve me. Thou didst
      smile,
Infusèd with a fortitude from heaven,
155 When I have decked° the sea with drops full salt,
Under my burden groaned, which° raised in me
An undergoing stomach,° to bear up
Against what should ensue.
MIRANDA: How came we ashore?
160 PROSPERO: By Providence divine.
Some food we had, and some fresh water, that
A noble Neapolitan, Gonzalo,
Out of his charity, who being then appointed
Master of this design, did give us, with
165   Rich garments, linens, stuffs,° and necessaries,

Which since have steaded much.° So, of his
      gentleness,
Knowing I loved my books, he furnished me
From mine own library with volumes that
I prize above my dukedom.
MIRANDA: Would° I might
But ever° see that man!
PROSPERO: Now I arise.   170
[He puts on his magic cloak.]
Sit still and hear the last of our sea sorrow.°
Here in this island we arrived; and here
Have I, thy schoolmaster, made thee more profit°
Than other princess'° can, that have more time
For vainer° hours and tutors not so careful.   175
MIRANDA: Heavens thank you for 't! And now, I
      pray you, sir—
For still 'tis beating in my mind—your reason
For raising this sea storm?
PROSFERO: Know thus far forth:
By accident most strange, bountiful Fortune,
Now my dear lady, hath mine enemies   180
Brought to this shore; and by my prescience
I find my zenith° doth depend upon
A most auspicious star, whose influence°
If now I court not, but omit,° my fortunes
Will ever after droop. Here cease more
      questions.   185
Thou art inclined to sleep. 'Tis a good dullness,°
And give it way.° I know thou canst not choose.
[Miranda sleeps.]
Come away,° servant, come! I am ready now.
Approach, my Ariel, come.

(Enter Ariel.)

ARIEL: All hail, great master, grave sir, hail! I come   190
To answer thy best pleasure; be 't to fly,
To swim, to dive into the fire, to ride
On the curled clouds, to thy strong bidding task°
Ariel and all his quality.°
PROSPERO: Hast thou, spirit,
Performed to point° the tempest that I bade thee?   195
ARIEL: To every article.
I boarded the King's ship. Now on the beak,°
Now in the waist,° the deck,° in every cabin,
I flamed amazement.° Sometimes I'd divide

---

134. hint: Occasion. 135. wrings: (1) Constraints; (2) wrings tears from. 138. impertinent: Irrelevant. Wherefore: Why. 139. demanded: Asked. wench: Here, term of endearment. 141–142. set...bloody: Make obvious their murderous intent (from the practice of marking with the blood of the prey those who have participated in a successful hunt). 143. fairer: Apparently more attractive. 144. few: Few words. bark: Ship. 146. butt: Cask, tub. 147. Nor tackle: Neither rigging (i.e., the pulleys and ropes designed for hoisting sails). 148. quit: Abandoned. 151. loving wrong: I.e., the winds pitied Prospero and Miranda though of necessity they blew them from shore. 152. cherubin: Angel. 155. decked: Covered (with salt tears), adorned. 156. which: I.e., the smile. 157. undergoing stomach: Courage to go on. 165. stuffs: Supplies.

166. steaded much: Been of much use. 169. Would: I wish. 170. But ever: Someday. 171. sea sorrow: Sorrowful adventure at sea. 173. more profit: Profit more. 174. princess': Princesses. (Or the word may be princes, referring to royal children both male and female.) 175. vainer: More foolishly spent. 182. zenith: Height of fortune (astrological term). 183. influence: Astrological power. 184. omit: Ignore. 186. dullness: Drowsiness. 187. give it way: Let it happen (i.e., don't fight it). 188. Come away: Come. 193. task: Make demands upon. 194. quality: (1) Fellow spirits; (2) abilities. 195. to point: To the smallest detail. 197. beak: Prow. 198. waist: Midships. deck: Poop deck at the stern. 199. flamed amazement: Struck terror in the guise of fire (i.e., Saint Elmo's fire).

Julian Bleach as Ariel and
Patrick Stewart as Prospero
in the Royal Shakespeare
Company's 2006 production
directed by Gregory Doran.

200   And burn in many places; on the topmast,
      The yards, and the bowsprit would I flame distinctly,°
      Then meet and join. Jove's lightning, the precursors
      O' the dreadful thunderclaps, more momentary
      And sight-outrunning° were not. The fire and cracks
205   Of sulfurous roaring the most mighty Neptune°
      Seem to besiege and make his bold waves tremble,
      Yea, his dread trident shake.
PROSPERO: My brave spirit!
      Who was so firm, so constant, that this coil°
      Would not infect his reason?
ARIEL: Not a soul
210   But felt a fever of the mad° and played
      Some tricks of desperation. All but mariners
      Plunged in the foaming brine and quit the vessel,
      Then all afire with me. The King's son,
          Ferdinand,
      With hair up-staring°—then like reeds, not hair—
215   Was the first man that leapt; cried, "Hell is empty,
      And all the devils are here!"
PROSPERO: Why, that's my spirit!
      But was not this nigh shore?
ARIEL: Close by, my master.
PROSPERO: But are they, Ariel, safe?
ARIEL: Not a hair perished.
      On their sustaining garments° not a blemish,
220   But fresher than before; and, as thou bad'st° me,

In troops° I have dispersed them 'bout the isle.
The King's son have I landed by himself,
Whom I left cooling of° the air with sighs
In an odd angle° of the isle, and sitting,
His arms in this sad knot.°   [He folds his arms.]
PROSPERO: Of the King's ship,   225
The mariners, say how thou hast disposed,
And all the rest o' the fleet.
ARIEL: Safely in harbor
Is the King's ship; in the deep nook,° where once
Thou calledst me up at midnight to fetch dew
From the still-vexed Bermudas,° there she's hid;   230
The mariners all under hatches stowed,
Who, with a charm joined to their suffered labor,°
I have left asleep. And for the rest o' the fleet,
Which I dispersed, they all have met again
And are upon the Mediterranean float°   235
Bound sadly home for Naples,
Supposing that they saw the King's ship wrecked
And his great person perish.
PROSPERO: Ariel, thy charge
Exactly is performed. But there's more work.
What is the time o' the day?
ARIEL: Past the mid season.°   240
PROSPERO: At least two glasses.° The time twixt six
    and now

201. distinctly: In different places. 204. sight-outrunning:
Swifter than sight. 205. Neptune: Roman god of the sea.
208. coil: Tumult. 210. of the mad: I.e., such as madmen
feel. 214. up-staring: Standing on end. 219. sustaining garments: Garments that buoyed them up in the sea. 220. bad'st:
Ordered.

221. troops: Groups. 223. cooling of: Cooling. 224. angle:
Corner. 225. sad knot: Folded arms are indicative of mel-
ancholy. 228. nook: Bay. 230. still-vexed Bermudas:
Ever-stormy Bermudas. (Perhaps refers to the then-recent
Bermuda shipwreck; see pages 230–231. The Folio text reads
Bermoothes.) 232. with . . . labor: By means of a spell
added to all the labor they have undergone. 235. float: Sea.
240. mid season: Noon. 241. glasses: Hourglasses.

Must by us both be spent most preciously.
ARIEL: Is there more toil? Since thou dost give me pains,°
Let me remember° thee what thou hast promised,
Which is not yet performed me.
245 PROSPERO: How now? Moody?
What is 't thou canst demand?
ARIEL: My liberty.
PROSPERO: Before the time be out? No more!
ARIEL: I prithee,
Remember I have done thee worthy service,
Told thee no lies, made thee no mistakings, served
250 Without or grudge or rumblings. Thou did promise
To bate° me a full year.
PROSPERO: Dost thou forget
From what a torment I did free thee?
ARIEL: No.
PROSPERO: Thou dost, and think'st it much to tread
the ooze
Of the salt deep,
255 To run upon the sharp wind of the north,
To do me° business in the veins° o' the earth
When it is baked° with frost.
ARIEL: I do not, sir.
PROSPERO: Thou liest, malignant thing! Hast thou forgot
The foul witch Sycorax, who with age and envy°
260 Was grown into a hoop?° Hast thou forgot her?
ARIEL: No, sir.
PROSPERO: Thou hast. Where was she born? Speak.
Tell me.
ARIEL: Sir, in Algiers.
PROSPERO: O, was she so? I must
Once in a month recount what thou hast been
Which thou forget'st. This damned witch
265 Sycorax,
For mischiefs manifold and sorceries terrible
To enter human hearing, from Algiers,
Thou know'st, was banished. For one thing she
did°
They would not take her life. Is not this true?
270 ARIEL: Ay, sir.
PROSPERO: This blue-eyed° hag was hither brought
with child°
And here was left by the sailors. Thou, my slave,
As thou report'st thyself, was then her servant;
And, for° thou wast a spirit too delicate
275 To act her earthy and abhorred commands,
Refusing her grand hests,° she did confine thee,
By help of her more potent ministers

And in her most unmitigable rage,
Into a cloven pine, within which rift
Imprisoned thou didst painfully remain   280
A dozen years; within which space she died
And left thee there, where thou didst vent thy
groans
As fast as mill wheels strike.° Then was this
island—
Save° for the son that she did litter° here,
A freckled whelp,° hag-born°—not honored
with   285
A human shape.
ARIEL: Yes, Caliban her son.
PROSPERO: Dull thing, I say so:° he, that Caliban
Whom now I keep in service. Thou best know'st
What torment I did find thee in. Thy groans
Did make wolves howl, and penetrate the breasts 290
Of ever-angry bears. It was a torment
To lay upon the damned, which Sycorax
Could not again undo. It was mine art,
When I arrived and heard thee, that made gape°
The pine and let thee out.
ARIEL: I thank thee, master.   295
PROSPERO: If thou more murmur'st, I will rend an
oak
And peg thee in his° knotty entrails till
Thou hast howled away twelve winters.
ARIEL: Pardon, master.
I will be correspondent° to command
And do my spriting° gently.°   300
PROSPERO: Do so, and after two days
I will discharge thee.
ARIEL: That's my noble master!
What shall I do? Say what? What shall I do?
PROSPERO: Go make thyself like a nymph o' the sea.
Be subject
To no sight but thine and mine, invisible   305
To every eyeball else. Go take this shape
And hither come in 't. Go, hence with diligence!
                              (*Exit* [*Ariel*].)
Awake, dear heart, awake! Thou hast slept well.
Awake!
MIRANDA: The strangeness of your story put
Heaviness° in me.
PROSPERO: Shake it off. Come on,   310
We'll visit Caliban, my slave, who never
Yields us kind answer.
MIRANDA: 'Tis a villain, sir,
I do not love to look on.

---

243. **pains:** Labors. 244. **remember:** Remind. 251. **bate:** Remit, deduct. 256. **do me:** Do for me. **veins:** Veins of minerals; or, underground streams thought to be analogous to the veins of the human body. 257. **baked:** Hardened. 259. **envy:** Malice. 260. **grown into a hoop:** I.e., so bent over with age as to resemble a hoop. 268. **one . . . did:** Perhaps a reference to her pregnancy, for which her life would be spared. 271. **blue-eyed:** With dark circles under the eyes or with blue eyelids, implying pregnancy. **with child:** Pregnant. 274. **for:** Because. 276. **hests:** Commands.

283. **as mill wheels strike:** As the blades of a mill wheel strike the water. 284. **Save:** Except. **litter:** Give birth to. 285. **whelp:** Offspring (used of animals). **hag-born:** Born of a female demon. 287. **Dull . . . so:** I.e., exactly, that's what I said, you dullard. 294. **gape:** Open wide. 297. **his:** Its. 299. **correspondent:** Responsive, submissive. 300. **spriting:** Duties as a spirit. **gently:** Willingly, ungrudgingly. 310. **Heaviness:** Drowsiness.

PROSPERO: But, as 'tis,
  We cannot miss° him. He does make our fire,
315 Fetch in our wood, and serves in offices°
  That profit us.—What ho! Slave! Caliban!
  Thou earth, thou! Speak.
CALIBAN (*within*):   There's wood enough within.
PROSPERO: Come forth, I say! There's other business
    for thee.
  Come, thou tortoise! When?°

(*Enter Ariel like a water nymph.*)

320 Fine apparition! My quaint° Ariel,
  Hark in thine ear.   [*He whispers.*]
ARIEL: My lord, it shall be done.   (*Exit.*)
PROSPERO: Thou poisonous slave, got° by the devil
    himself
  Upon thy wicked dam,° come forth!

(*Enter Caliban.*)

CALIBAN: As wicked° dew as e'er my mother
    brushed
325 With raven's feather from unwholesome fen°
  Drop on you both! A southwest° blow on ye
  And blister you all o'er!
PROSPERO: For this, be sure, tonight thou shalt have
    cramps,
  Side-stitches that shall pen thy breath up. Urchins°
330 Shall forth at vast° of night that they may work
  All exercise on thee. Thou shalt be pinched
  As thick as honeycomb,° each pinch more stinging
  Than bees that made 'em.°
CALIBAN: I must eat my dinner.
  This island's mine, by Sycorax my mother,
  Which thou tak'st from me. When thou cam'st
335   first,
  Thou strok'st me and made much of me, wouldst
    give me
  Water with berries in 't, and teach me how
  To name the bigger light, and how the less,°
  That burn by day and night. And then I loved
    thee
340 And showed thee all the qualities o' th' isle,
  The fresh springs, brine pits, barren place and
    fertile.

Cursed be I that did so! All the charms°
  Of Sycorax, toads, beetles, bats, light on you!
  For I am all the subjects that you have,
  Which first was mine own king; and here you
    sty° me   345
  In this hard rock, whiles you do keep from me
  The rest o' th' island.
PROSPERO: Thou most lying slave,
  Whom stripes° may move, not kindness! I have
    used thee,
  Filth as thou art, with humane° care, and lodged
    thee
  In mine own cell, till thou didst seek to violate   350
  The honor of my child.
CALIBAN: Oho, Oho! Would 't had been done!
  Thou didst prevent me; I had peopled else°
  This isle with Calibans.
MIRANDA: Abhorrèd slave,°
  Which any print° of goodness wilt not take,   355
  Being capable of all ill! I pitied thee,
  Took pains to make thee speak, taught thee each
    hour
  One thing or other. When thou didst not, savage
  Know thine own meaning, but wouldst gabble like
  A thing most brutish, I endowed thy purposes°   360
  With words that made them known. But thy
    vile race,°
  Though thou didst learn, had that in 't which
    good natures
  Could not abide to be with; therefore wast thou
  Deservedly confined into this rock,
  Who hadst deserved more than a prison.   365
CALIBAN: You taught me language, and my profit on 't
  Is I know how to curse. The red plague° rid° you
  For learning° me your language!
PROSPERO: Hagseed,° hence!
  Fetch us in fuel, and be quick, thou'rt best,°
  To answer other business.° Shrugg'st thou,
    malice?   370
  If thou neglect'st or dost unwillingly
  What I command, I'll rack thee with old°
    cramps,
  Fill all thy bones with aches,° make thee roar
  That beasts shall tremble at thy din.
CALIBAN: No, pray thee.
  [*Aside.*] I must obey. His art is of such power   375

---

314. miss: Do without.   **315. offices:** Functions, duties.
319. When: An exclamation of impatience.   **320. quaint:**
Ingenious.   **322. got:** Begotten, sired.   **323. dam:** Mother
(used of animals).   **324. wicked:** Mischievous, harmful.
325. fen: Marsh, bog.   **326. southwest:** I.e., wind thought to
bring disease.   **329. Urchins:** Hedgehogs; here, suggesting goblins in the guise of hedgehogs.   **330. vast:** Lengthy, desolate
time. (Malignant spirits were thought to be restricted to the
hours of darkness.)   **332. As thick as honeycomb:** I.e., all over,
with as many pinches as a honeycomb has cells.   **333. 'em:** I.e.,
the honeycomb.   **338. the bigger . . . less:** I.e., the sun and the
moon. (See Genesis 1:16: "God then made two great lights: the
greater light to rule the day, and the less light to rule the night.")

342. charms: Spells.   **345. sty:** Confine as in a sty.   **348.
stripes:** Lashes.   **349. humane:** Not distinguished as a word
from *human.*   **353. peopled else:** Otherwise populated.
354–365. Abhorrèd . . . prison: These lines are sometimes assigned by editors to Prospero.   **355. print:** Imprint, impression.   **360. purposes:** Meanings, desires.   **361. race:** Natural
disposition; species, nature.   **367. red plague:** Plague characterized by red sores and evacuation of blood.   **rid:** Destroy.
368. learning: Teaching.   **Hagseed:** Offspring of a female demon.   **369. thou'rt best:** You'd be well advised.   **370. answer
other business:** Perform other tasks.   **372. old:** Such as old
people suffer; or, plenty of.   **373. aches:** Pronounced "aitches."

[ABOVE] Helen Mirren as Prospera, Felicity Jones as Miranda, and Djimon Hounsou as Caliban in Julie Taymor's 2010 film.
[BELOW] Stephen Dillane as Prospero and Juliet Rylance as Miranda in a production directed by Sam Mendes at the Old Vic in London, 2010.

It would control my dam's god, Setebos,°
And make a vassal of him.

PROSPERO: So, slave, hence!

(*Exit Caliban.*)

(*Enter Ferdinand; and Ariel, invisible,*° *playing
and singing. [Ferdinand does not see Prospero and
Miranda.]*)

(*Ariel's Song.*)

ARIEL: Come unto these yellow sands,
And then take hands;
380 Curtsied when you have,° and kissed
The wild waves whist,°
Foot it featly° here and there,
And, sweet sprites,° bear
The burden.° Hark, hark!
385 (*Burden, dispersedly*° [*within*].) Bow-wow.
The watchdogs bark.
[*Burden, dispersedly within*]. Bow-wow.
Hark, hark! I hear
The strain of strutting chanticleer
390 Cry Cock-a-diddle-dow.

FERDINAND: Where should this music be? I' th' air or th'
earth?
It sounds no more and sure it waits upon°
Some god o' th' island. Sitting on a bank,°
Weeping again the King my father's wreck,
395 This music crept by me upon the waters,
Allaying both their fury and my passion°
With its sweet air. Thence° I have followed it,
Or it hath drawn me rather. But 'tis gone.
No, it begins again.

(*Ariel's Song.*)

400 ARIEL: Full fathom five thy father lies.
Of his bones are coral made.
Those are pearls that were his eyes.
Nothing of him that doth fade
But doth suffer a sea change
405 Into something rich and strange.
Sea nymphs hourly ring his knell.°
(*Burden* [*within*].) Ding dong.
Hark, now I hear them, ding dong bell.

FERDINAND: The ditty does remember° my drowned
father.
410 This is no mortal business, nor no sound
That the earth owes.° I hear it now above me.

PROSPERO [*to Miranda*]: The fringed curtains of
thine eye advance°
And say what thou seest yond.

MIRANDA: What is 't? A spirit?
Lord, how it looks about! Believe me, sir,
It carries a brave° form. But 'tis a spirit. 415

PROSPERO: No, wench, it eats and sleeps and hath
such senses
As we have, such. This gallant which thou seest
Was in the wreck; and, but° he's something stained°
With grief, that's beauty's canker,° thou mightst
call him
A goodly person. He hath lost his fellows 420
And strays about to find 'em.

MIRANDA: I might call him
A thing divine, for nothing natural
I ever saw so noble.

PROSPERO [*aside*]: It goes on,° I see,
As my soul prompts it.—Spirit, fine spirit, I'll
free thee
Within two days for this.

FERDINAND [*seeing Miranda*]: Most sure, the goddess 425
On whom these airs° attend!—Vouchsafe° my
prayer
May know° if you remain° upon this island,
And that you will some good instruction give
How I may bear me° here. My prime° request,
Which I do last pronounce, is—O you
wonder!°— 430
If you be maid or no?°

MIRANDA: No wonder, sir,
But certainly a maid.

FERDINAND: My language? Heavens!
I am the best° of them that speak this speech,
Were I but where 'tis spoken.

PROSPERO [*coming forward*]: How? The best?
What wert thou if the King of Naples heard thee? 435

FERDINAND: A single° thing, as I am now, that wonders
To hear thee speak of Naples.° He does hear me,°
And that he does I weep.° Myself am Naples,
Who with mine eyes, never since at ebb,° beheld
The King my father wrecked.

MIRANDA: Alack, for mercy! 440

FERDINAND: Yes, faith, and all his lords, the Duke of
Milan

---

376. **Setebos:** A god of the Patagonians, named in Robert Eden's *History of Travel* (1577). 377. [S.D.] *Ariel, invisible:* Ariel wears a garment that by convention indicates he is invisible to the other characters. 380. **Curtsied . . . have:** When you have curtsied. 380–381. **kissed . . . whist:** Kissed the waves into silence; or, kissed while the waves are being hushed. 382. **Foot it featly:** Dance nimbly. 383. **sprites:** Spirits. 384. **burden:** Refrain, undersong. 385. [S.D.] *dispersedly:* From all directions, not in unison. 392. **waits upon:** Serves, attends. 393. **bank:** Sandbank. 396. **passion:** Grief. 397. **Thence:** From the bank on which he sat. 406. **knell:** Announcement of a death by the tolling of a bell. 409. **remember:** Commemorate. 411. **owes:** Owns.

412. **advance:** Raise. 415. **brave:** Excellent. 418. **but:** Except that. **something stained:** Somewhat disfigured. 419. **canker:** Cankerworm (feeding on buds and leaves). 423. **It goes on:** I.e., my plan works. 426. **airs:** Songs. **Vouchsafe:** Grant. 427. **May know:** I.e., that I may know. **remain:** Dwell. 429. **bear me:** Conduct myself. **prime:** Chief. 430. **wonder:** Miranda's name means "to be wondered at." 431. **maid or no:** I.e., a human maiden as opposed to a goddess or married woman. 433. **best:** I.e., in birth. 436. **single:** (1) Solitary, being at once King of Naples and myself; (2) feeble. 437. **Naples:** The King of Naples. **He does hear me:** I.e., the King of Naples does hear my words, for I am King of Naples. 438. **And . . . weep:** I.e., and I weep at this reminder that my father is seemingly dead, leaving me heir. 439. **at ebb:** I.e., dry, not weeping.

And his brave son° being twain.

PROSPERO [*aside*]:   The Duke of Milan
And his more braver° daughter could control°
    thee,
If now 'twere fit to do 't. At the first sight
They have changed eyes.°—Delicate Ariel,   445
I'll set thee free for this. [*To Ferdinand.*] A word,
    good sir.
I fear you have done yourself some wrong.° A word!

MIRANDA [*aside*]: Why speaks my father so
    ungently? This
Is the third man that e'er I saw, the first
That e'er I sighed for. Pity move my father   450
To be inclined my way!

FERDINAND: O, if a virgin,
And your affection not gone forth, I'll make you
The Queen of Naples.

PROSPERO: Soft, sir! One word more.
[*aside.*] They are both in either's° powers; but this
    swift business
I must uneasy° make, lest too light winning   455
Make the prize light.° [*To Ferdinand.*] One word
    more: I charge thee
That thou attend° me. Thou dost here usurp
The name thou ow'st° not, and hast put thyself
Upon this island as a spy, to win it
From me, the lord on 't.°

FERDINAND: No, as I am a man.   460

MIRANDA: There's nothing ill can dwell in such a
    temple.
If the ill spirit have so fair a house,
Good things will strive to dwell with 't.°

PROSPERO: Follow me.—
Speak not you for him, he's a traitor.—Come,
I'll manacle thy neck and feet together.   465
Seawater shalt thou drink; thy food shall be
The fresh-brook mussels, withered roots, and husks
Wherein the acorn cradled. Follow.

FERDINAND: No!
I will resist such entertainment° till
Mine enemy has more power.
    (*He draws and is charmed° from moving.*)   470

MIRANDA: O dear father,
Make not too rash° a trial of him, for
He's gentle,° and not fearful.°

PROSPERO: What, I say,

My foot° my tutor?—Put thy sword up, traitor,
Who mak'st a show but dar'st not strike, thy
    conscience
Is so possessed with guilt. Come from thy ward,°   475
For I can here disarm thee with this stick
And make thy weapon drop.
                        [*He brandishes his staff.*]

MIRANDA [*trying to hinder him*]: Beseech you, father!

PROSPERO: Hence! Hang not on my garments.

MIRANDA: Sir, have pity!
I'll be his surety.°

PROSPERO: Silence! One word more
Shall make me chide thee, if not hate thee.
    What,   480
An advocate for an impostor? Hush!
Thou think'st there is no more such shapes as he,
Having seen but him and Caliban. Foolish wench,
To° the most of men this is a Caliban,
And they to him are angels.

MIRANDA: My affections   485
Are then most humble; I have no ambition
To see a goodlier man.

PROSPERO [*to Ferdinand*]: Come on, obey.
Thy nerves° are in their infancy again
And have no vigor in them.

FERDINAND: So they are.
My spirits,° as in a dream, are all bound up.   490
My father's loss, the weakness which I feel,
The wreck of all my friends, nor this man's threats
To whom I am subdued, are but light° to me
Might I but through my prison once a day
Behold this maid. All corners else° o' th' earth   495
Let liberty make use of; space enough
Have I in such a prison.

PROSPERO [*aside*]: It works. [*To Ferdinand.*] Come
on.—Thou hast done well, fine Ariel! [*To
Ferdinand.*] Follow me.
[*To Ariel.*] Hark what thou else shalt do me.°

MIRANDA [*to Ferdinand*]:   Be of comfort.
My father's of a better nature, sir,   500
Than he appears by speech. This is unwonted°
Which now came from him.

PROSPERO [*to Ariel*]:   Thou shalt be as free
As mountain winds; but then° exactly do
All points of my command.

ARIEL: To th' syllable.

PROSPERO [*to Ferdinand*]: Come, follow. [*To
Miranda.*] Speak not for him.   505

                        (*Exeunt.*)

---

442. son: The only reference in the play to a son of Antonio. 443. more braver: More splendid. control: Refute. 445. changed eyes: Exchanged amorous glances. 447. done . . . wrong: I.e., spoken falsely. 454. both in either's: Each in the other's. 455. uneasy: Difficult. 455–456. light . . . light: Easy . . . cheap. 457. attend: Follow, obey. 458. ow'st: Ownest. 460. on 't: Of it. 463. strive . . . with 't: I.e., expel the evil and occupy the *temple*, the body. 469. entertainment: Treatment. 470. [s.d.] *charmed*: Magically prevented. 471. rash: Harsh. 472. gentle: Well born. fearful: Frightening, dangerous; or, perhaps, cowardly.

473. foot: Subordinate. (Miranda, the foot, presumes to instruct Prospero, the head.) 475. ward: Defensive posture (in fencing). 479. surety: Guarantee. 484. To: Compared to. 488. nerves: Sinews. 490. spirits: Vital powers. 493. light: Unimportant. 495. corners else: Other corners, regions. 499. me: For me. 501. unwonted: Unusual. 503. then: Until then, or if that is to be so.

ACT II • Scene I°

(*Enter Alonso, Sebastian, Antonio, Gonzalo, Adrian, Francisco, and others.*)

GONZALO [*to Alonso*]: Beseech you, sir, be merry. You have cause,
So have we all, of joy, for our escape
Is much beyond° our loss. Our hint of° woe
Is common; every day some sailor's wife,
The masters of some merchant, and the merchant°
Have just° our theme of woe. But for the miracle,
I mean our preservation, few in millions
Can speak like us. Then wisely, good sir, weigh
Our sorrow with° our comfort.

ALONSO: Prithee, peace.

SEBASTIAN [*to Antonio*]: He receives comfort like cold porridge.°

ANTONIO [*to Sebastian*]: The visitor° will not give him o'er° so.

SEBASTIAN: Look, he's winding up the watch of his wit; by and by it will strike.

GONZALO: [*to Alonso*]: Sir—

SEBASTIAN: [*to Antonio*]: One. Tell.°

GONZALO: When every grief is entertained
That's offered, comes to th' entertainer°—

SEBASTIAN: A dollar.°

GONZALO: Dolor comes to him, indeed. You have spoken truer than you purposed.

SEBASTIAN: You have taken it wiselier than I meant you should.

GONZALO [*to Alonso*]: Therefore, my lord—

ANTONIO: Fie, what a spendthrift is he of his tongue!

ALONSO [*To Gonzalo*]: I prithee, spare.°

GONZALO: Well, I have done. But yet—

SEBASTIAN: He will be talking.

ANTONIO: Which, of he or Adrian, for a good wager, first begins to crow?°

SEBASTIAN: The old cock.°

ANTONIO: The cockerel.°

SEBASTIAN: Done. The wager?

ANTONIO: A laughter.°   35

SEBASTIAN: A match!°

ADRIAN: Though this island seem to be desert°—

ANTONIO: Ha, ha, ha!

SEBASTIAN: So, you're paid.°

ADRIAN: Uninhabitable and almost inaccessible—   40

SEBASTIAN: Yet—

ADRIAN: Yet—

ANTONIO: He could not miss 't.°

ADRIAN: It must needs be° of subtle, tender, and delicate temperance.°   45

ANTONIO: Temperance° was a delicate° wench.

SEBASTIAN: Ay, and a subtle,° as he most learnedly delivered.°

ADRIAN: The air breathes upon us here most sweetly.

SEBASTIAN: As if it had lungs, and rotten ones.   50

ANTONIO: Or as 'twere perfumed by a fen.

GONZALO: Here is everything advantageous to life.

ANTONIO: True, save° means to live.

SEBASTIAN: Of that there's none, or little.

GONZALO: How lush and lusty° the grass looks! How green!   55

ANTONIO: The ground indeed is tawny.°

SEBASTIAN: With an eye° of green in 't.

ANTONIO: He misses not much.

SEBASTIAN: No. He doth but° mistake the truth totally. 60

GONZALO: But the rarity of it is—which is indeed almost beyond credit—

SEBASTIAN: As many vouched° rarities are.

GONZALO: That our garments, being, as they were, drenched in the sea, hold notwithstanding their freshness and glosses, being rather new-dyed than stained with salt water.   65

ANTONIO: If but one of his pockets° could speak, would it not say he lies?

II, i. **Location:** Another part of the island.   **3. much beyond:** More remarkable than. **hint of:** Occasion for. **5. masters...the merchant:** Officers of some merchant vessel and the merchant himself, the owner (or else the ship itself). **6. just:** Exactly. **9. with:** Against. **11. porridge:** With a pun on *peace* (line 9) and *peas* or *pease,* a common ingredient of porridge. **12. visitor:** One taking nourishment and comfort to the sick (i.e., Gonzalo). **12–13. give him o'er:** Abandon him. **17. Tell:** Keep count. **18–19. When... entertainer:** When every sorrow that presents itself is accepted without resistance, there comes to the recipient. **20. dollar:** Widely circulated coin, the German thaler and the Spanish piece of eight. (Sebastian puns on *entertainer* in the sense of innkeeper; to Gonzalo, *dollar* suggests *dolor,* grief.) **27. spare:** Forbear, cease. **30–31. Which...crow:** Which of the two, Gonzalo or Adrian, do you bet will speak (crow) first? **32. old cock:** I.e., Gonzalo. **33. cockerel:** I.e., Adrian.

35. laughter: (1) Burst of laughter; (2) sitting of eggs. (When Adrian, the *cockerel,* begins to speak two lines later, Sebastian loses the bet. The Folio speech prefixes in lines 38–39 are here reversed so that Antonio enjoys his laugh as the prize for winning, as in the proverb "He who laughs last laughs best" or "He laughs that wins." The Folio assignment can work in the theater, however, if Sebastian pays for losing with a sardonic laugh of concession.) **36. A match:** A bargain; agreed. **37. desert:** Uninhabited. **39. you're paid:** I.e., you've had your laugh. **43. miss 't:** (1) Avoid saying "Yet"; (2) miss the island. **44. must needs be:** Has to be. **45. Temperance:** Mildness of climate. **46. Temperance:** A girl's name. **delicate:** Here it means "given to pleasure, voluptuous"; in line 44, "pleasant." (Antonio is evidently suggesting that *tender, and delicate temperance* sounds like a Puritan phrase, which Antonio then mocks by applying the words to a woman rather than an island. He began this bawdy comparison with a double entendre on *inaccessible,* line 40.) **47. subtle:** Here it means "tricky, sexually crafty"; in line 44, "delicate." **48. delivered:** Uttered. (Sebastian joins Antonio in baiting the Puritans with his use of the pious cant phrase *learnedly delivered.*) **53. save:** Except. **55. lusty:** Healthy. **57. tawny:** Dull brown, yellowish. **eye:** Tinge or spot (perhaps with reference to Gonzalo's eye or judgment). **60. but:** Merely. **63. vouched:** Certified. **68. pockets:** I.e., because they are muddy.

70 SEBASTIAN: Ay, or very falsely pocket up° his report.°
    GONZALO: Methinks our garments are now as fresh
        as when we put them on first in Afric, at the mar-
        riage of the King's fair daughter Claribel to the
        King of Tunis.
75 SEBASTIAN: 'Twas a sweet marriage, and we prosper well
        in our return.
    ADRIAN: Tunis was never graced before with such a para-
        gon to° their queen.
    GONZALO: Not since widow Dido's° time.
80 ANTONIO: Widow! A pox o' that! How came that
        "widow" in? Widow Dido!
    SEBASTIAN: What if he had said "widower Aeneas" too?
        Good Lord, how you take° it!
    ADRIAN: "Widow Dido" said you? You make me
85   study of° that. She was of Carthage, not of Tunis.
    GONZALO: This Tunis, sir, was Carthage.
    ADRIAN: Carthage?
    GONZALO: I assure you, Carthage.
    ANTONIO: His word is more than the miraculous
90   harp.°
    SEBASTIAN: He hath raised the wall, and houses too.
    ANTONIO: What impossible matter will he make easy
        next?
    SEBASTIAN: I think he will carry this island home in his
95   pocket and give it his son for an apple.
    ANTONIO: And, sowing the kernels° of it in the sea, bring
        forth more islands.
    GONZALO: Ay.°
    ANTONIO: Why, in good time.°
100 GONZALO [to Alonso]: Sir, we were talking° that our gar-
        ments seem now as fresh as when we were at Tunis at
        the marriage of your daughter, who is now queen.
    ANTONIO: And the rarest° that e'er came there.
    SEBASTIAN: Bate,° I beseech you, widow Dido.
105 ANTONIO: O, widow Dido? Ay, widow Dido.
    GONZALO: Is not, sir, my doublet° as fresh as the first day
        I wore it? I mean, in a sort.°
    ANTONIO: That "sort"° was well fished for.

    GONZALO: When I wore it at your daughter's marriage.
    ALONSO: You cram these words into mine ears against   110
        The stomach° of my sense.° Would I had never
        Married° my daughter there! For, coming thence,
        My son is lost and, in my rate,° she too,
        Who is so far from Italy removed
        I ne'er again shall see her. O thou mine heir   115
        Of Naples and of Milan, what strange fish
        Hath made his meal° on thee?
    FRANCISCO: Sir, he may live.
        I saw him beat the surges° under him
        And ride upon their backs. He trod the water,
        Whose enmity he flung aside, and breasted   120
        The surge most swoll'n that met him. His bold head
        'Bove the contentious waves he kept, and oared
        Himself with his good arms in lusty° stroke
        To th' shore, that o'er his wave-worn basis bowed,°
        As° stooping to relieve him. I not° doubt   125
        He came alive to land.°
    ALONSO: No, no, he's gone.
    SEBASTIAN [to Alonso]: Sir, you may thank yourself
        for this great loss,
        That° would not bless our Europe with your
            daughter,
        But rather° loose° her to an African,
        Where she at least is banished from your eye,°   130
        Who hath cause to wet the grief on 't.°
    ALONSO: Prithee, peace.
    SEBASTIAN: You were kneeled to and importuned°
            otherwise
        By all of us, and the fair soul herself
        Weighed between loathness and obedience at
        Which end o' the beam should bow.° We have
            lost your son,   135
        I fear, forever. Milan and Naples have
        More widows in them of this business' making°
        Than we bring men to comfort them.
        The fault's your own.
    ALONSO: So is the dear'st° o' the loss.   140
    GONZALO: My lord Sebastian,
        The truth you speak doth lack some gentleness
        And time° to speak it in. You rub the sore

70. **pocket up:** I.e., conceal, suppress; often used in the sense of "receive unprotestingly, fail to respond to a challenge." **his report:** Sebastian's jest is that the evidence of Gonzalo's soggy and sea-stained pockets would confute Gonzalo's speech and his reputation for truth telling. **78. to:** For. **79. widow Dido:** Queen of Carthage, deserted by Aeneas. (She was in fact a widow when Aeneas, a widower, met her, but Antonio may be amused at Gonzalo's prudish use of the term *widow* to describe a woman deserted by her lover.) **83. take:** Understand, respond to, interpret. **85. study of:** Think about. **89–90. miraculous harp:** Alludes to Amphion's harp, with which he raised the walls of Thebes; Gonzalo has exceeded that deed by creating a modern Carthage—walls *and houses*—mistakenly on the site of Tunis. **96. kernels:** Seeds. **98. Ay:** Gonzalo may be reasserting his point about Carthage, or he may be responding ironically to Antonio, who in turn answers sarcastically. **99. in good time:** An expression of ironical acquiescence or amazement (i.e., "Sure, right away"). **100. talking:** Saying. **103. rarest:** Most remarkable, beautiful. **104. Bate:** Abate, except, leave out. (Sebastian may be saying either "Don't forget Dido" or "Let's have no more talk of Dido.") **106. doublet:** Close-fitting jacket. **107. in a sort:** In a way. **108. "sort":** Antonio plays on the idea of drawing lots.

110–111. **against . . . sense:** I.e., against my will. **stomach:** Appetite. **112. Married:** Given in marriage. **113. rate:** Estimation, opinion. **117. made his meal:** Fed himself. **118. surges:** Waves. **123. lusty:** Vigorous. **124. that . . . bowed:** I.e., that projected out over the base of the cliff that had been eroded by the surf, thus seeming to bend down toward the sea. **125. As:** As if. **I not:** I do not. **126. came . . . land:** Reached land alive. **128. That:** You who. **129. rather:** Would rather. **loose:** (1) Release, let loose; (2) lose. **130. is banished from your eye:** Is not constantly before your eye to serve as a reproachful reminder of what you have done. **131. Who . . . on 't:** I.e., your eye which has good reason to weep because of this; or, Claribel, who has good reason to weep for it. **132. importuned:** Urged, implored. **133–135. the fair . . . bow:** I.e., Claribel herself was poised uncertainly between unwillingness to marry and obedience to her father as to which end of the scale should sink, which should prevail. **137. of . . . making:** On account of this marriage. **140. dear'st:** Heaviest, most costly. **143. time:** Appropriate time.

When you should bring the plaster.°
SEBASTIAN: Very well.
145 ANTONIO: And most chirurgeonly.°
GONZALO [*to Alonso*]:
It is foul weather in us all, good sir,
When you are cloudy.
SEBASTIAN [*to Antonio*]: Fowl° weather?
ANTONIO [*to Sebastian*]:   Very foul.
GONZALO: Had I plantation° of this isle, my lord—
ANTONIO [*to Sebastian*]:
He'd sow 't with nettle seed.
150 SEBASTIAN: Or docks, or mallows.°
GONZALO: And were the king on 't, what would I do?
SEBASTIAN: Scape° being drunk for want° of wine.
GONZALO: I' the commonwealth I would by contraries°
Execute all things; for no kind of traffic°
155 Would I admit; no name of magistrate;
Letters° should not be known; riches, poverty,
And use of service,° none; contract, succession,°
Bourn,° bound of land,° tilth,° vineyard, none;
No use of metal, corn,° or wine, or oil;
160 No occupation; all men idle, all,
And women too, but innocent and pure;
No sovereignty—
SEBASTIAN: Yet he would be king on 't.
ANTONIO: The latter end of his commonwealth forgets
the beginning.
165 GONZALO: All things in common nature should produce
Without sweat or endeavor. Treason, felony,
Sword, pike,° knife, gun, or need of any engine°
Would I not have; but nature should bring forth,
Of its own kind, all foison,° all abundance,
170 To feed my innocent people.
SEBASTIAN: No marrying 'mong his subjects?
ANTONIO: None, man, all idle—whores and knaves.
GONZALO: I would with such perfection govern, sir,
T' excel the Golden Age.°
SEBASTIAN: Save° His Majesty!
ANTONIO: Long live Gonzalo!
175 GONZALO: And—do you mark me, sir?
ALONSO: Prithee, no more. Thou dost talk nothing to me.
GONZALO: I do well believe Your Highness, and did it
to minister occasion° to these gentlemen, who are of

such sensible° and nimble lungs that they always use°
to laugh at nothing.   180
ANTONIO: 'Twas you we laughed at.
GONZALO: Who in this kind of merry fooling am nothing
to you; so you may continue, and laugh at nothing
still.
ANTONIO: What a blow was there given!   185
SEBASTIAN: An° it had not fallen flat-long.°
GONZALO: You are gentlemen of brave mettle:° you
would lift the moon out of her sphere° if she would
continue in it five weeks without changing.

(*Enter Ariel [invisible] playing solemn music.*)

SEBASTIAN: We would so, and then go a-batfowling.°   190
ANTONIO: Nay, good my lord, be not angry.
GONZALO: No, I warrant you, I will not adventure my
discretion so weakly.° Will you laugh me asleep? For
I am very heavy.°
ANTONIO: Go sleep, and hear us.°   195
[*All sleep except Alonso, Sebastian, and
Antonio.*]

ALONSO: What, all so soon asleep? I wish mine eyes
Would, with themselves, shut up my thoughts.° I find
They are inclined to do so.
SEBASTIAN: Please you, sir,
Do not omit° the heavy° offer of it.
It seldom visits sorrow; when it doth,   200
It is a comforter.
ANTONIO: We two, my lord,
Will guard your person while you take your rest,
And watch your safety.
ALONSO: Thank you. Wondrous heavy.
[*Alonso sleeps. Exit Ariel.*]
SEBASTIAN: What a strange drowsiness possesses them!
ANTONIO: It is the quality o' the climate.
SEBASTIAN: Why   205
Doth it not then our eyelids sink? I find not
Myself disposed to sleep.
ANTONIO: Nor I. My spirits are nimble.
They fell together all, as by consent,°
They dropped, as by a thunderstroke. What might,
Worthy Sebastian, O, what might—? No more.   210

144. plaster: A medical application. 145. chirurgeonly: Like a skilled surgeon. (Antonio mocks Gonzalo's medical analogy of a *plaster* applied curatively to a wound.) 148. Fowl: With a pun on *foul*, returning to the imagery of lines 30–35. 149. plantation: Colonization (with subsequent wordplay on the literal meaning). 150. docks, mallows: Weeds used as antidotes for nettle stings. 152. Scape: Escape. want: Lack. (Sebastian jokes sarcastically that this hypothetical ruler would be saved from dissipation only by the barrenness of the island.) 153. by contraries: By what is directly opposite to usual custom. 154. traffic: Trade. 156. Letters: Learning. 157. use of service: Custom of employing servants. succession: Holding of property by right of inheritance. 158. Bourn: Boundaries. bound of land: Landmarks. tilth: Tillage of soil. 159. corn: Grain. 167. pike: Lance. engine: Instrument of warfare. 169. foison: Plenty. 174. the Golden Age: The age, according to Hesiod, when Cronus or Saturn ruled the world; an age of innocence and abundance. Save: God save. 178. minister occasion: Furnish opportunity.

179. sensible: Sensitive. use: Are accustomed. 186. An: If. flat-long: With the flat of the sword—i.e., ineffectually. (Compare "fallen flat.") 187. mettle: Temperament, courage. (The sense of *metal*, indistinguishable as a form from *mettle*, continues the metaphor of the sword.) 188. sphere: Orbit (literally one of the concentric zones occupied by planets in the Ptolemaic astronomy). 190. a-batfowling: Hunting birds at night with lantern and *bat* or stick; also, gulling a simpleton. (Gonzalo is the simpleton, or fowl, and Sebastian will use the moon as his lantern.) 192–193. adventure . . . weakly: Risk my reputation for discretion for so trivial a cause (by getting angry at these sarcastic fellows). 194. heavy: Sleepy. 195. Go . . . us: Let our laughing send you to sleep; or, go to sleep and hear us laugh at you. 197. Would . . . thoughts: Would shut off my melancholy brooding when they close themselves in sleep. 199. omit: Neglect. heavy: Drowsy. 208. consent: Common agreement.

And yet methinks I see it in thy face,
What thou shouldst be. Th' occasion° speaks thee,° and
My strong imagination sees a crown
Dropping upon thy head.
SEBASTIAN: What, art thou waking?
ANTONIO: Do you not hear me speak?
215 SEBASTIAN: I do, and surely
It is a sleepy language, and thou speak'st
Out of thy sleep. What is it thou didst say?
This is a strange repose, to be asleep
With eyes wide open—standing, speaking, moving—
And yet so fast asleep.
220 ANTONIO: Noble Sebastian,
Thou lett'st thy fortune sleep—die, rather; wink'st°
Whiles thou art waking.
SEBASTIAN: Thou dost snore distinctly;°
There's meaning in thy snores.
ANTONIO: I am more serious than my custom. You
225 Must be so too, if heed° me; which to do
Trebles thee o'er.°
SEBASTIAN: Well, I am standing water.°
ANTONIO: I'll teach you how to flow.
SEBASTIAN: Do so. To ebb°
Hereditary sloth° instructs me.
ANTONIO: O,
If you but knew how you the purpose cherish
230 Whiles thus you mock it!° How, in stripping it,
You more invest° it! Ebbing men, indeed,
Most often do so near the bottom° run
By their own fear or sloth.
SEBASTIAN: Prithee, say on.
The setting° of thine eye and cheek proclaim
235 A matter° from thee, and a birth indeed
Which throes° thee much to yield.°
ANTONIO: Thus, sir:
Although this lord° of weak remembrance,° this
Who shall be of as little memory
When he is earthed,° hath here almost persuaded—

For he's a spirit of persuasion, only   240
Professes to persuade°—the King his son's alive,
'Tis as impossible that he's undrowned
As he that sleeps here swims.
SEBASTIAN: I have no hope
That he's undrowned.
ANTONIO: O, out of that "no hope"
What great hope have you! No hope that way° is   245
Another way so high a hope that even
Ambition cannot pierce a wink° beyond,
But doubt discovery there.° Will you grant with
   me
That Ferdinand is drowned?
SEBASTIAN: He's gone.
ANTONIO: Then tell me,
Who's the next heir of Naples?
SEBASTIAN: Claribel.   250
ANTONIO: She that is Queen of Tunis, she that dwells
Ten leagues beyond man's life;° she that from Naples
Can have no note,° unless the sun were post°—
The man i' the moon's too slow—till newborn chins
Be rough and razorable,° she that from° whom   255
We all were sea-swallowed, though some cast°
   again,
And by that destiny to perform an act
Whereof what's past is prologue, what to come
In yours and my discharge.°
SEBASTIAN: What stuff is this? How say you?   260
'Tis true my brother's daughter's Queen of Tunis,
So is she heir of Naples, twixt which regions
There is some space.
ANTONIO: A space whose every cubit°
Seems to cry out, "How shall that Claribel
Measure us° back to Naples? Keep° in Tunis,   265
And let Sebastian wake."° Say this were death
That now hath seized them, why, they were no
   worse
Than now they are. There be° that can rule Naples
As well as he that sleeps, lords that can prate°
As amply and unnecessarily   270
As this Gonzalo. I myself could make
A chough of as deep chat.° O, that you bore
The mind that I do! What a sleep were this
For your advancement! Do you understand me?

212. **occasion:** Opportunity of the moment. **speaks thee:** I.e., calls upon you, proclaims you usurper of Alonso's crown. 221. **wink'st:** (You) shut your eyes. 222. **distinctly:** Articulately. 225. **if heed:** If you heed. 226. **Trebles thee o'er:** Makes you three times as great and rich. **standing water:** Water that neither ebbs nor flows, at a standstill. 227. **ebb:** Recede, decline. 228. **Hereditary sloth:** Natural laziness and the position of younger brother, one who cannot inherit. 229–230. **If . . . mock it:** I.e., if you only knew how much you really enhance the value of ambition even while your words mock your purpose. 230–231. **How . . . invest it:** I.e., how the more you speak flippantly of ambition, the more you in effect affirm it. **invest:** Clothe. (Antonio's paradox is that by skeptically stripping away illusions Sebastian can see the essence of a situation and the opportunity it presents or by disclaiming and deriding his purpose Sebastian shows how he values it.) 232. **the bottom:** I.e., on which unadventurous men may go aground and miss the tide of fortune. 234. **setting:** Set expression (of earnestness). 235. **matter:** Matter of importance. 236. **throes:** Causes pain, as in giving birth. **yield:** Give forth, speak about. 237. **this lord:** I.e., Gonzalo. **remembrance:** (1) Power of remembering; (2) being remembered after his death. 239. **earthed:** Buried.

240–241. **only . . . persuade:** I.e., whose whole function (as a privy councilor) is to persuade. 245. **that way:** I.e., in regard to Ferdinand's being saved. 247–248. **Ambition . . . there:** Ambition itself cannot see any further than that hope (of the crown), but is unsure of itself in seeing even so far, is dazzled by daring to think so high. 247. **wink:** Glimpse. 252. **Ten . . . life:** I.e., it would take more than a lifetime to get there. 253. **note:** News, intimation. **post:** Messenger. 255. **razorable:** Ready for shaving. **from:** On our voyage from. 256. **cast:** Were disgorged (with a pun on *casting* of parts for a play). 259. **discharge:** Performance. 263. **cubit:** Ancient measure of length, about twenty inches. 265. **Measure us:** I.e., traverse the cubits, find her way. **Keep:** Stay (addressed to Claribel). 266. **wake:** I.e., to his good fortune. 268. **There be:** There are those. 269. **prate:** Speak foolishly. 271–272. **I . . . chat:** I could teach a jackdaw to talk as wisely or be such a garrulous talker myself.

SEBASTIAN: Methinks I do.
275 ANTONIO: And how does your content°
Tender° your own good fortune?
SEBASTIAN: I remember
You did supplant your brother Prospero.
ANTONIO: True.
And look how well my garments sit upon me,
Much feater° than before. My brother's servants
280 Were then my fellows. Now they are my men.
SEBASTIAN: But, for your conscience?
ANTONIO: Ay, sir, where lies that? If 'twere a kibe,°
'Twould put me to° my slipper; but I feel not
This deity in my bosom. Twenty consciences
285 That stand twixt me and Milan,° candied° be they°
And melt ere they molest!° Here lies your brother,
No better than the earth he lies upon,
If he were that which now he's like—that's dead,
Whom I, with this obedient steel, three inches of it,
290 Can lay to bed forever; whiles you, doing thus,°
To the perpetual wink° for aye° might put
This ancient morsel, this Sir Prudence, who
Should not° upbraid our course. For all the rest,
They'll take suggestion° as a cat laps milk;
295 They'll tell the clock° to any business that
We say befits the hour.
SEBASTIAN: Thy case, dear friend,
Shall be my precedent. As thou gott'st Milan,
I'll come by Naples. Draw thy sword. One stroke
Shall free thee from the tribute° which thou payest,
And I the king shall love thee.
300 ANTONIO: Draw together;
And when I rear my hand, do you the like
To fall it° on Gonzalo.   [They draw.]
SEBASTIAN: O, but one word.
[They talk apart.]

(Enter Ariel [invisible], with music and song.)

ARIEL: My master through his art foresees the danger
That you, his friend, are in, and sends me forth—
305 For else his project dies—to keep them living.
(Sings in Gonzalo's ear.)
While you here do snoring lie,
Open-eyed conspiracy
His time° doth take.
If of life you keep a care,
310 Shake off slumber, and beware.
Awake, awake!

ANTONIO: Then let us both be sudden.°
GONZALO [waking]: Now, good angels preserve the King!
[The others wake.]
ALONSO: Why, how now, ho, awake? Why are you
drawn?
Wherefore this ghastly looking?
GONZALO: What's the matter? 315
SEBASTIAN: Whiles we stood here securing° your
repose,
Even now, we heard a hollow burst of bellowing
Like bulls, or rather lions. Did 't not wake you?
It struck mine ear most terribly.
ALONSO: I heard nothing.
ANTONIO: O, 'twas a din to fright a monster's ear, 320
To make an earthquake! Sure it was the roar
Of a whole herd of lions.
ALONSO: Heard you this, Gonzalo?
GONZALO: Upon mine honor, sir, I heard a humming,
And that a strange one too, which did awake me. 325
I shaked you, sir, and cried.° As mine eyes opened,
I saw their weapons drawn. There was a noise,
That's verily.° 'Tis best we stand upon our guard,
Or that we quit this place. Let's draw our weapons.
ALONSO: Lead off this ground, and let's make further
search 330
For my poor son.
GONZALO: Heavens keep him from these beasts!
For he is, sure, i' th' island.
ALONSO: Lead away.
ARIEL [aside]: Prospero my lord shall know what I
have done.
So, King, go safely on to seek thy son.
(Exeunt [separately].)

Scene II°

(Enter Caliban with a burden of wood. A noise of
thunder heard.)

CALIBAN: All the infections that the sun sucks up
From bogs, fens, flats,° on Prosper fall, and make him
By inchmeal° a disease! His spirits hear me,
And yet I needs must° curse. But they'll nor° pinch,
Fright me with urchin shows,° pitch me i' the mire, 5
Nor lead me, like a firebrand,° in the dark
Out of my way, unless he bid 'em. But
For every trifle are they set upon me,
Sometimes like apes, that mow° and chatter at me

---

275. **content:** Desire, inclination.   276. **Tender:** Regard, look after.   279. **feater:** More becomingly, fittingly.   282. **kibe:** Chilblain; here, a sore on the heel.   283. **put me to:** Oblige me to wear.   285. **Milan:** The dukedom of Milan. **candied:** Frozen, congealed in crystalline form. **be they:** May they be.   286. **molest:** Interfere.   290. **thus:** The actor makes a stabbing gesture.   291. **wink:** Sleep, closing of eyes. **aye:** Ever.   293. **Should not:** Would not then be able to.   294. **take suggestion:** Respond to prompting.   295. **tell the clock:** I.e., agree, answer appropriately, chime.   299. **tribute:** See I, ii, 113–124.   302. **fall it:** Let it fall.   308. **time:** Opportunity.

312. **sudden:** Quick.   316. **securing:** Standing guard over.   326. **cried:** Called out.   328. **verily:** True.   **II, ii. Location:** Another part of the island.   2. **flats:** Swamps.   3. **By inchmeal:** Inch by inch.   4. **needs must:** Have to. **nor:** neither.   5. **urchin shows:** Elvish apparitions shaped like hedgehogs.   6. **like a firebrand:** In the guise of a will-o'-the-wisp.   9. **mow:** Make faces.

10 And after bite me; then like hedgehogs, which
   Lie tumbling in my barefoot way and mount
   Their pricks at my footfall. Sometimes am I
   All wound with° adders, who with cloven
        tongues
   Do hiss me into madness.

(Enter Trinculo.)

                    Lo, now, lo!
15 Here comes a spirit of his, and to torment me
   For bringing wood in slowly. I'll fall flat.
   Perchance he will not mind° me. [*He lies down.*]
   TRINCULO: Here's neither bush nor shrub to bear off°
   any weather at all. And another storm brewing; I
20 hear it sing i' the wind. Yond same black cloud
   yond huge one, looks like a foul bombard° that
   would shed his° liquor. If it should thunder as it
   did before, I know not where to hide my head.
   Yond same cloud cannot choose but fall by pailfuls.
25 [*Seeing Caliban.*] What have we here, a man or a
   fish? Dead or alive? A fish, he smells like a fish; a
   very ancient and fishlike smell; a kind of not-of-
   the-newest Poor John.° A strange fish! Were I in
   England now, as once I was, and had but this fish
30 painted,° not a holiday fool there but would give
   a piece of silver. There would this monster make
   a man.° Any strange beast there makes a man.
   When they will not give a doit° to relieve a lame
   beggar, they will lay out ten to see a dead Indian.
35 Legged like a man, and his fins like arms! Warm,
   o' my troth!° I do now let loose my opinion, hold
   it° no longer: this is no fish, but an islander, that
   hath lately suffered° by a thunderbolt. [*Thunder.*]
   Alas, the storm is come again! My best way is to
40 creep under his gaberdine.° There is no other shelter
   hereabout. Misery acquaints a man with strange
   bedfellows. I will here shroud° till the dregs° of the
   storm be past.
                    [*He creeps under Caliban's garment.*]

(Enter Stephano, singing, [a bottle in his hand].)

   STEPHANO: "I shall no more to sea, to sea,
45   Here shall I die ashore—"
   This is a very scurvy tune to sing at a man's funeral.

Well, here's my comfort.   (*Drinks.*)
(*Sings.*)
"The master, the swabber,° the boatswain, and I,
     The gunner and his mate,
Loved Mall, Meg, and Marian, and Margery,   50
But none of us cared for Kate.
     For she had a tongue with a tang,°
        Would cry to a sailor, 'Go hang!'
She loved not the savor of tar nor of pitch,
Yet a tailor might scratch her where'er she did itch.° 55
     Then to sea, boys, and let her go hang!"

This is a scurvy tune too. But here's my comfort.
                    (*Drinks.*)

CALIBAN: Do not torment me!° O!
STEPHANO: What's the matter?° Have we devils here?
   Do you put tricks upon 's° with savages and men 60
   of Ind,° ha? I have not scaped drowning to be
   afeard now of your four legs. For it hath been said,
   "As proper° a man as ever went on four legs° cannot make him give ground"; and it shall be said so
   again while Stephano breathes at'° nostrils.   65
CALIBAN: This spirit torments me! O!
STEPHANO: This is some monster of the isle with four
   legs, who hath got, as I take it, an ague.° Where
   the devil should he learn° our language? I will give
   him some relief, if it be but for that.° If I can re- 70
   cover° him and keep him tame and get to Naples
   with him, he's a present for any emperor that ever
   trod on neat's leather.°
CALIBAN: Do not torment me, prithee. I'll bring my
   wood home faster.   75
STEPHANO: He's in his fit now and does not talk after
   the wisest.° He shall taste of my bottle. If he have
   never drunk wine afore,° it will go near to° remove
   his fit. If I can recover° him and keep him tame, I
   will not take too much° for him. He shall pay for 80
   him that hath° him,° and that soundly.

13. **wound with:** Entwined by. 17. **mind:** Notice. 18. **bear off:** Keep off. 21. **foul bombard:** Dirty leather jug. 22. **his:** Its. 28. **Poor John:** Salted fish, type of poor fare. 30. **painted:** I.e., painted on a sign set up outside a booth or tent at a fair. 31–32. **make a man:** (1) Make one's fortune; (2) be indistinguishable from an Englishman. 33. **doit:** Small coin. 36. **o' my troth:** By my faith. 36–37. **hold it:** Hold it in. 38. **suffered:** I.e., died. 40. **gaberdine:** Cloak, loose upper garment. 42. **shroud:** Take shelter. **dregs:** Last remains (as in a *bombard* or jug, line 21).

48. **swabber:** Crew member whose job is to wash the decks. 52. **tang:** Sting. 55. **tailor...itch:** A dig at tailors for their supposed effeminacy and a bawdy suggestion of satisfying a sexual craving. 58. **Do...me:** Caliban assumes that one of Prospero's spirits has come to punish him. 59. **What's the matter:** What's going on here? 60. **put tricks upon 's:** Trick us with conjuring shows. 61. **Ind:** India. 63. **proper:** Handsome. **four legs:** The conventional phrase would supply *two* legs. 65. **at':** At the. 68. **ague:** Fever. (Probably both Caliban and Trinculo are quaking; see lines 58 and 83.) 69. **should he learn:** Could he have learned. 70. **for that:** I.e., for knowing our language. 71. **recover:** Restore. 73. **neat's leather:** Cowhide. 76–77. **after the wisest:** In the wisest fashion. 78. **afore:** Before. **go near to:** Nearly. 79–80. **I will...much:** I.e., no sum can be too much. 80–81. **He shall...hath him:** I.e., anyone who wants him will have to pay dearly for him. 81. **hath:** Possesses, receives.

CALIBAN: Thou does me yet but little hurt; thou wilt anon,° I know it by thy trembling. Now Prosper works upon thee.

85 STEPHANO: Come on your ways. Open your mouth. Here is that which will give language to you, cat. Open your mouth.° This will shake your shaking, I can tell you, and that soundly. [*Giving Caliban a drink.*] You cannot tell who's your friend. Open 90 your chaps° again.

TRINCULO: I should know that voice. It should be— but he is drowned, and these are devils. O, defend me!

STEPHANO: Four legs and two voices—a most deli-95 cate° monster! His forward voice now is to speak well of his friend, his backward voice° is to utter foul speeches and to detract. If all the wine in my bottle will recover him,° I will help° his ague. Come. [*Giving a drink.*] Amen! I will pour some in 100 thy other mouth.

TRINCULO: Stephano!

STEPHANO: Doth thy other mouth call me?° Mercy, mercy! This is a devil, and no monster. I will leave him. I have no long spoon.°

105 TRINCULO: Stephano! If thou beest Stephano, touch me and speak to me, for I am Trinculo—be not afeard—thy good friend Trinculo.

STEPHANO: If thou beest Trinculo, come forth. I'll pull thee by the lesser legs. If any be Trinculo's legs, 110 these are they. [*Pulling him out.*] Thou art very Trinculo indeed! How cam'st thou to be the siege° of this mooncalf?° Can he vent° Trinculos?

TRINCULO: I took him to be killed with a thunder-stroke. But art thou not drowned, Stephano? I 115 hope now thou art not drowned. Is the storm over-blown?° I hid me under the dead mooncalf's gaber-dine for fear of the storm. And art thou living, Stephano? O Stephano, two Neapolitans scaped!

[*He capers with Stephano.*]

STEPHANO: Prithee, do not turn me about. My stomach 120 is not constant.°

CALIBAN: These be fine things, an if° they be not spirits.
That's a brave° god, and bears° celestial liquor.
I will kneel to him.

STEPHANO: How didst thou scape? How cam'st thou hither? Swear by this bottle how thou cam'st 125 hither. I escaped upon a butt of sack° which the sailors heaved o'erboard—by this bottle,° which I made of the bark of a tree with mine own hands since° I was cast ashore.

CALIBAN [*kneeling*]: I'll swear upon that bottle to be 130 thy true subject, for the liquor is not earthly.

STEPHANO: Here. Swear then how thou escapedst.

TRINCULO: Swum ashore, man, like a duck. I can swim like a duck, I'll be sworn.

STEPHANO: Here, kiss the book.° Though thou canst 135 swim like a duck, thou art made like a goose.

[*Giving him a drink.*]

TRINCULO: O Stephano, hast any more of this?

STEPHANO: The whole butt, man. My cellar is in a rock by the seaside, where my wine is hid.—How now, mooncalf? How does thine ague? 140

CALIBAN: Hast thou not dropped from heaven?

STEPHANO: Out o' the moon, I do assure thee. I was the man i' the moon when time was.°

CALIBAN: I have seen thee in her, and I do adore thee.
My mistress showed me thee, and thy dog, and thy bush.° 145

STEPHANO: Come, swear to that. Kiss the book. I will furnish it anon with new contents. Swear.

[*Giving him a drink.*]

TRINCULO: By this good light,° this is a very shallow monster! I afeard of him? A very weak monster! The man i' the moon? A most poor credulous 150 monster! Well drawn,° monster, in good sooth!°

CALIBAN [*to Stephano*]: I'll show thee every fertile inch o'th'island,
And I will kiss thy foot. I prithee, be my god.

TRINCULO: By this light, a most perfidious and drunken monster! When 's god's asleep, he'll rob 155 his bottle.°

83. **anon:** Presently. 86–87. **cat . . . mouth:** Allusion to the proverb "Good liquor will make a cat speak." 90. **chaps:** Jaws. 94–95. **delicate:** Ingenious. 96. **backward voice:** Trinculo and Caliban are facing in opposite directions. Stephano supposes the monster to have a rear end that can emit *foul speeches* or foul-smelling wind at the monster's *other mouth,* line 100. 97–98. **If . . . him:** Even if it takes all the wine in my bottle to cure him. 98. **help:** Cure. 102. **call me:** I.e., call me by name, know supernaturally who I am. 104. **long spoon:** Allusion to the proverb "He that sups with the devil has need of a long spoon." 111. **siege:** Excrement. 112. **mooncalf:** Monstrous or misshapen crea-ture (whose deformity is caused by the malignant influence of the moon). **vent:** Excrete, defecate. 115–116. **overblown:** Blown over. 120. **not constant:** Unsteady.

121. **an if:** If. 122. **brave:** Fine, magnificent. **bears:** He carries. 126. **butt of sack:** Barrel of Canary wine. 127. **by this bottle:** I.e., I swear by this bottle. 128. **since:** After. 135. **book:** I.e., bottle (but with ironic reference to the practice of kissing the Bible in swearing an oath; see *I'll be sworn* in line 134). 143. **when time was:** Once upon a time. 145. **dog . . . bush:** The man in the moon was popularly imagined to have with him a dog and a bush of thorn. 148. **By . . . light:** By God's light, by this good light from heaven. 151. **Well drawn:** Well pulled (on the bottle). **in good sooth:** Truly, indeed. 155–156. **When . . . bottle:** I.e., Caliban wouldn't even stop at robbing his god of his bottle if he could catch him asleep.

CALIBAN: I'll kiss thy foot. I'll swear myself thy
    subject.
STEPHANO: Come on then. Down, and swear.
                                      [*Caliban kneels.*]
160 TRINCULO: I shall laugh myself to death at this puppy-
    headed monster. A most scurvy monster! I could
    find in my heart to beat him—
STEPHANO: Come, kiss.
TRINCULO: But that the poor monster's in drink.° An
165   abominable monster!
CALIBAN: I'll show thee the best springs. I'll pluck
    thee berries.
    I'll fish for thee and get thee wood enough.
    A plague upon the tyrant that I serve!
    I'll bear him no more sticks, but follow thee,
170   Thou wondrous man.
TRINCULO: A most ridiculous monster, to make a
    wonder of a poor drunkard!
CALIBAN: I prithee, let me bring thee where crabs°
    grow;
    And I with my long nails will dig thee pignuts,°
175   Show thee a jay's nest, and instruct thee how
    To snare the nimble marmoset.° I'll bring thee
    To clustering filberts, and sometimes I'll get thee
    Young scamels° from the rock. Wilt thou go with
    me?
STEPHANO: I prithee now, lead the way without any
180   more talking.—Trinculo, the King and all our
    company else° being drowned, we will inherit°
    here.—Here, bear my bottle.—Fellow Trinculo,
    we'll fill him by and by again.
CALIBAN (*sings drunkenly*): Farewell, master, farewell,
185   farewell!
TRINCULO: A howling monster; a drunken monster!
CALIBAN: No more dams I'll make for fish,
    Nor fetch in firing°
    At requiring,
190   Nor scrape trenchering,° nor wash dish.
    'Ban, 'Ban, Ca-Caliban
    Has a new master. Get a new man!°
    Freedom, high-day!° High-day, freedom!
    Freedom, high-day, freedom!
195 STEPHANO: O brave monster! Lead the way.

                                  (*Exeunt.*)

---

164. **in drink:** Drunk. 173. **crabs:** Crab apples; or, perhaps, crabs. 174. **pignuts:** Earthnuts, edible tuberous roots. 176. **marmoset:** Small monkey. 178. **scamels:** Possibly *seamews*, mentioned in William Strachey's report on the shipwreck he endured (see p. 270); possibly shellfish; or, perhaps, from *squamelle*, furnished with little scales. Contemporary French and Italian travel accounts report that the natives of Patagonia in South America ate small fish described as *fort scameux* and *squame*. 181. **else:** In addition, besides ourselves. **inherit:** Take possession. 188. **firing:** Firewood. 190. **trenchering:** Trenchers, wooden plates. 192. **Get a new man:** Addressed to Prospero. 193. **high-day:** Holiday.

ACT III • Scene I°

(*Enter Ferdinand, bearing a log.*)

FERDINAND: There be some sports° are painful,° and their labor
    Delight in them sets off.° Some kinds of baseness°
    Are nobly undergone,° and most poor° matters
    Point to rich ends. This my mean° task
    Would be as heavy to me as odious, but°   5
    The mistress which I serve quickens° what's dead
    And makes my labors pleasures. O, she is
    Ten times more gentle than her father's crabbèd,
    And he's composed of harshness. I must remove
    Some thousands of these logs and pile them up,   10
    Upon a sore injunction.° My sweet mistress
    Weeps when she sees me work and says such baseness
    Had never like executor.° I forget;°
    But these sweet thoughts do even refresh my labors,
    Most busy lest when I do it.°

(*Enter Miranda; and Prospero [at a distance, unseen].*)

MIRANDA: Alas now, pray you,   15
    Work not so hard. I would the lightning had
    Burnt up those logs that you are enjoined° to pile!
    Pray, set it down and rest you. When this° burns,
    'Twill weep° for having wearied you. My father
    Is hard at study. Pray now, rest yourself.   20
    He's safe for these° three hours.
FERDINAND: O most dear mistress,
    The sun will set before I shall discharge°
    What I must strive to do.
MIRANDA: If you'll sit down,
    I'll bear your logs the while. Pray, give me that.
    I'll carry it to the pile.

III, i. Location: Before Prospero's cell. 1. **sports:** Pastimes, activities. **painful:** Laborious. 1–2. **and their ... sets off:** I.e., but the pleasure we get from those pastimes compensates for the effort. 2. **baseness:** Menial activity. 3. **undergone:** Undertaken. **most poor:** Poorest. 4. **mean:** Lowly. 5. **but:** Were it not that. 6. **quickens:** Gives life to. 11. **sore injunction:** Severe command. 13. **Had ... executor:** I.e., was never before undertaken by one of my noble rank. **I forget:** I.e., I forget that I'm supposed to be working; or, I forget my happiness, oppressed by my labor. 15. **Most ... it:** I.e., least troubled by my labor, and most active in my thoughts, when I think of her (?). (The line may be in need of emendation.) 17. **enjoined:** Commanded. 18. **this:** I.e., the log. 19. **weep:** I.e., exude resin. 21. **these:** I.e., the next. 22. **discharge:** Complete.

25 FERDINAND: No, precious creature,
  I had rather crack my sinews, break my back,
  Than you should such dishonor undergo
  While I sit lazy by.
MIRANDA: It would become me
  As well as it does you; and I should do it
30 With much more ease, for my good will is to it,
  And yours it is against.
PROSPERO [*aside*]:   Poor worm, thou art
  infected!
  This visitation° shows it.
MIRANDA: You look wearily.
FERDINAND: No, noble mistress, 'tis fresh morning
  with me
  When you are by° at night. I do beseech you—
35 Chiefly that I might set it in my prayers—
  What is your name?
MIRANDA: Miranda.—O my father,
  I have broke your hest° to say so.
FERDINAND: Admired Miranda!°
  Indeed the top of admiration, worth
  What's dearest° to the world! Full many a lady
40 I have eyed with best regard,° and many a time
  The harmony of their tongues hath into
    bondage
  Brought my too diligent° ear. For several° virtues
  Have I liked several women, never any
  With so full soul but some defect in her
45 Did quarrel with the noblest grace she owed°
  And put it to the foil.° But you, O you,
  So perfect and so peerless, are created
  Of° every creature's best!
MIRANDA: I do not know
  One of my sex; no woman's face remember,
50 Save, from my glass, mine own. Nor have I seen
  More that I may call men than you, good friend,
  And my dear father. How features are abroad°
  I am skilless° of; but, by my modesty,°
  The jewel in my dower, I would nor wish
55 Any companion in the world but you;
  Nor can imagination form a shape,
  Besides yourself, to like of.° But I prattle
  Something° too wildly, and my father's precepts
  I therein do forget.
FERDINAND: I am in my condition°

A prince, Miranda; I do think, a king— 60
  I would, not so!—and would° no more endure
  This wooden slavery° than to suffer
  The flesh-fly° blow° my mouth. Hear my soul
    speak:
  The very instant that I saw you did
  My heart fly to your service; there resides 65
  To make me slave to it, and for your sake
  Am I this patient log-man.
MIRANDA: Do you love me?
FERDINAND: O heaven, O earth, bear witness to this
  sound,
  And crown what I profess with kind event°
  If I speak true! If hollowly,° invert° 70
  What best is boded° me to mischief!° I
  Beyond all limit of what° else i' the world
  Do love, prize, honor you.
MIRANDA [*weeping*]:   I am a fool
  I weep at what I am glad of.
PROSPERO [*aside*]:   Fair encounter
  Of two most rare affections! Heavens rain grace 75
  On that which breeds between 'em!
FERDINAND: Wherefore weep you?
MIRANDA: At mine unworthiness, that dare not
  offer
  What I desire to give, and much less take
  What I shall die° to want.° But this is trifling,
  And all the more it seeks to hide itself 80
  The bigger bulk it shows. Hence, bashful
    cunning,°
  And prompt me, plain and holy innocence!
  I am your wife, if you will marry me;
  If not, I'll die your maid.° To be your fellow°
  You may deny me, but I'll be your servant 85
  Whether you will° or no.
FERDINAND: My mistress,° dearest,
  And I thus humble ever.
MIRANDA: My husband, then?
FERDINAND: Ay, with a heart as willing°
  As bondage e'er of freedom. Here's my hand. 90
MIRANDA [*clasping his hand*]: And mine, with my
  heart in 't. And now farewell
  Till half an hour hence.
FERDINAND: A thousand thousand!°
    (*Exeunt [Ferdinand and Miranda, separately].*)

---

32. visitation: (1) Visit of the sick; (2) visitation of the plague (i.e., infection of love). **34. by:** Nearby. **37. hest:** Command. **Admired Miranda:** Her name means "to be admired or wondered at." **39. dearest:** Most treasured. **40. best regard:** Thoughtful and approving attention. **42. diligent:** Attentive. **several:** Various (also in line 43). **45. owed:** Owned. **46. put . . . foil:** (1) Overthrew it (as in wrestling); (2) served as a *foil*, or contrast, to set it off. **48. Of:** Out of. **52. How . . . abroad:** What people look like in other places. **53. skilless:** Ignorant. **modesty:** Virginity. **57. like of:** Be pleased with, be fond of. **58. Something:** Somewhat. **59. condition:** Rank.

61. would: Wish (it were). **62. wooden slavery:** Being compelled to carry wood. **63. flesh-fly:** Insect that deposits its eggs in dead flesh. **blow:** Befoul with fly eggs. **69. kind event:** Favorable outcome. **70. hollowly:** Insincerely, falsely. **invert:** Turn. **71. boded:** Destined for. **mischief:** Evil. **72. what:** Whatever. **79. die:** Probably with an unconscious sexual meaning that underlies all of lines 77–81. **want:** Lack. **81. bashful cunning:** Coyness. **84. maid:** Handmaiden, servant. **fellow:** Mate, equal. **86. will:** Desire it. **My mistress:** I.e., the woman I adore and serve (not an illicit sexual partner). **89. willing:** Desirous. **92. A thousand thousand:** I.e., a thousand thousand farewells.

PROSPERO: So glad of this as they I cannot be,
95   Who are surprised with all;° but my rejoicing
     At nothing can be more. I'll to my book,
     For yet ere suppertime must I perform
     Much business appertaining.°   (*Exit.*)

Scene II°

(*Enter Caliban, Stephano, and Trinculo.*)

STEPHANO: Tell not me. When the butt is out,° we will
     drink water, not a drop before. Therefore bear up
     and board 'em.° Servant monster, drink to me.
TRINCULO: Servant monster? The folly of° this island!
5   They say there's but five upon this isle. We are
     three of them; if th' other two be brained° like us,
     the state totters.
STEPHANO: Drink, servant monster, when I bid thee.
     Thy eyes are almost set° in thy head.
                                          [*Giving a drink.*]
10   TRINCULO: Where should they be set° else? He were a
     brave° monster indeed if they were set in his tail.
STEPHANO: My man-monster hath drowned his
     tongue in sack. For my part, the sea can-
     not drown me. I swam, ere I could recover° the
15   shore, five and thirty leagues° off and on.° By this
     light,° thou shalt be my lieutenant, monster, or my
     standard.°
TRINCULO: Your lieutenant, if you list.° He's no standard.°
STEPHANO: We'll not run,° Monsieur Monster.
20   TRINCULO: Nor go° neither, but you'll lie° like dogs
     and yet say nothing neither.
STEPHANO: Mooncalf, speak once in thy life, if thou
     beest a good mooncalf.
CALIBAN: How does thy honor? Let me lick thy
     shoe.
25   I'll not serve him. He is not valiant.

TRINCULO: Thou liest, most ignorant monster, I am in
     case to jostle a constable.° Why, thou debauched
     fish, thou, was there ever man a coward that hath
     drunk so much sack° as I today? Wilt thou tell a
     monstrous lie, being but half a fish and half a   30
     monster?
CALIBAN: Lo, how he mocks me! Wilt thou let him,
     my lord?
TRINCULO: "Lord," quoth he? That a monster should
     be such a natural!°
CALIBAN: Lo, lo, again! Bite him to death, I prithee.   35
STEPHANO: Trinculo, keep a good tongue in your
     head. If you prove a mutineer—the next tree!°
     The poor monster's my subject, and he shall not
     suffer indignity.
CALIBAN: I thank my noble lord. Wilt thou be
     pleased   40
     To hearken once again to the suit I made to
     thee?
STEPHANO: Marry,° will I. Kneel and repeat it. I will
     stand, and so shall Trinculo. [*Caliban kneels.*]

(*Enter Ariel, invisible.°*)

CALIBAN: As I told thee before, I am subject to a
     tyrant,
     A sorcerer, that by his cunning hath   45
     Cheated me of the island.
ARIEL [*mimicking Trinculo*]: Thou liest.
CALIBAN: Thou liest, thou jesting monkey, thou!
     I would my valiant master would destroy thee.
     I do not lie.
STEPHANO: Trinculo, if you trouble him any more in 's   50
     tale, by this hand, I will supplant° some of your
     teeth.
TRINCULO: Why, I said nothing.
STEPHANO: Mum, then, and no more.—Proceed.
CALIBAN: I say by sorcery he got this isle;   55
     From me he got it. If thy greatness will
     Revenge it on him—for I know thou dar'st,
     But this thing° dare not—
STEPHANO: That's most certain.
CALIBAN: Thou shalt be lord of it, and I'll serve thee.   60
STEPHANO: How now shall this be compassed?°
     Canst thou bring me to the party?
CALIBAN: Yea, yea, my lord. I'll yield him thee
     asleep,
     Where thou mayst knock a nail into his head.

95. **with all:** By everything that has happened; or, *withal*,
with it. 98. **appertaining:** Related to this. III, ii. Location:
Another part of the island. 1. **out:** Empty. 2–3. **bear . . . 'em:**
Stephano uses the terminology of maneuvering at sea and
boarding a vessel under attack as a way of urging an assault
on the liquor supply. 4. **folly of:** I.e., stupidity found on.
6. **be brained:** Are endowed with intelligence. 9. **set:** Fixed
in a drunken state; or, sunk, like the sun. 10. **set:** Placed.
11. **brave:** Fine, splendid. 14. **recover:** Gain, reach.
15. **leagues:** Units of distance each equaling about three
miles. **off and on:** Intermittently. **By this light:** An oath by
the light of the sun. 16. **standard:** Standard-bearer, ensign (as
distinguished from *lieutenant*, lines 15–17). 17. **list:** Prefer.
17–18. **no standard:** I.e., not able to stand up. 19. **run:** (1)
Retreat; (2) urinate (taking Trinculo's *standard*, line 17, in the
old sense of "conduit"). 20. **go:** Walk. **lie:** (1) Tell lies; (2) lie
prostrate; (3) excrete.

26–27. **in case . . . constable:** I.e., in fit condition, made valiant by drink, to taunt or challenge the police. 29. **sack:**
Spanish white wine. 34. **natural:** (1) Idiot; (2) natural as
opposed to unnatural, monsterlike. 37. **the next tree:** I.e.,
you'll hang. 42. **Marry:** I.e., indeed. (Originally an oath: by
the Virgin Mary.) 43. [S.D.] *invisible:* I.e., wearing a garment to connote invisibility, as at I, ii, 377. 51. **supplant:** Up-
root, displace. 58. **this thing:** I.e., Trinculo. 61. **compassed:**
Achieved.

65 ARIEL: Thou liest; thou canst not.
CALIBAN: What a pied ninny's° this! Thou scurvy
    patch!°—
    I do beseech thy greatness, give him blows
    And take his bottle from him. When that's gone
    He shall drink naught but brine, for I'll not show
    him
70 Where the quick freshes° are.
STEPHANO: Trinculo, run into no further danger. In-
    terrupt the monster one word further° and, by this
    hand, I'll turn my mercy out o' doors° and make a
    stockfish° of thee.
75 TRINCULO: Why, what did I? I did nothing. I'll go far-
    ther off.°
STEPHANO: Didst thou not say he lied?
ARIEL: Thou liest.
STEPHANO: Do I so? Take thou that. [*He beats*
80   *Trinculo.*] As you like this, give me the lie° another
    time.
TRINCULO: I did not give the lie. Out o' your wits and
    hearing too? A pox o' your bottle! This can sack
    and drinking do. A murrain° on your monster, and
85   the devil take your fingers!
CALIBAN: Ha, ha, ha!
STEPHANO: Now, forward with your tale. [*To Trinculo.*]
    Prithee, stand further off.
CALIBAN: Beat him enough. After a little time
    I'll beat him too.
90 STEPHANO: Stand farther.—Come, proceed.
CALIBAN: Why, as I told thee, tis a custom with him
    I' th' afternoon to sleep. There thou mayst brain
    him,
    Having first seized his books; or with a log
    Batter his skull, or paunch° him with a stake,
95   Or cut his weasand° with thy knife. Remember
    First to possess his books, for without them
    He's but a sot,° as I am, nor hath not
    One spirit to command. They all do hate him
    As rootedly as I. Burn but his books.
100 He has brave utensils°—for so he calls them—
    Which, when he has a house, he'll deck withal.°
    And that most deeply to consider is
    The beauty of his daughter. He himself
    Calls her a nonpareil. I never saw a woman
105 But only Sycorax my dam and she;
    But she as far surpasseth Sycorax

As great'st does least.
STEPHANO: Is it so brave° a lass?
CALIBAN: Ay, lord. She will become° thy bed, I
    warrant,
    And bring thee forth brave brood.   110
STEPHANO: Monster, I will kill this man. His daughter
    and I will be king and queen—save Our
    Graces!—and Trinculo and thyself shall be
    viceroys. Dost thou like the plot, Trinculo?
TRINCULO: Excellent.   115
STEPHANO: Give me thy hand. I am sorry I beat thee;
    but, while thou liv'st, keep a good tongue in thy
    head.
CALIBAN: Within this half hour will he be asleep. Wilt
    thou destroy him then?   120
STEPHANO: Ay, on mine honor.
ARIEL [*aside*]: This will I tell my master.
CALIBAN: Thou mak'st me merry; I am full of
    pleasure.
    Let us be jocund.° Will you troll the catch°
    You taught me but whilere?°   125
STEPHANO: At thy request, monster, I will do reason,
    any reason.° Come on, Trinculo, let us sing.
                                              (*Sings.*)
    "Flout° 'em and scout° 'em
    And scout 'em and flout 'em!
    Thought is free."   130
CALIBAN: That's not the tune.
        (*Ariel plays the tune on a tabor° and pipe.*)
STEPHANO: What is this same?
TRINCULO: This is the tune of our catch, played by the
    picture of Nobody.°
STEPHANO: If thou beest a man, show thyself in thy   135
    likeness. If thou beest a devil, take 't as thou list.°
TRINCULO: O, forgive me my sins!
STEPHANO: He that dies pays all debts. I defy thee.
    Mercy upon us!
CALIBAN: Art thou afeard?   140
STEPHANO: No, monster, not I.
CALIBAN: Be not afeard. The isle is full of noises,
    Sounds, and sweet airs, that give delight and hurt
    not.
    Sometimes a thousand twangling instruments
    Will hum about mine ears, and sometimes voices   145
    That, if I then had waked after long sleep,

---

66. **pied ninny:** Fool in motley.   **patch:** Fool.   70. **quick freshes:**
Running springs.   72. **one word further:** I.e., one more time.
73. **turn . . . doors:** I.e., forget about being merciful.
74. **stockfish:** Dried cod beaten before cooking.   76. **off:**
Away.   80. **give me the lie:** Call me a liar to my face.
84. **murrain:** Plague (literally, a cattle disease).   94. **paunch:**
Stab in the belly.   95. **weasand:** Windpipe.   97. **sot:**
Fool.   100. **brave utensils:** Fine furnishings.   101. **deck withal:**
Furnish it with.

108. **brave:** Splendid, attractive.   109. **become:** Suit.
124. **jocund:** Jovial, merry.   **troll the catch:** Sing the round.
125. **but whilere:** Only a short time ago.   126–127. **reason,
any reason:** Anything reasonable.   128. **Flout:** Scoff at.   **scout:**
Deride.   131. [s.d.] **tabor:** Small drum.   134. **picture of Nobody:** Refers to a familiar figure with head, arms, and legs but
no trunk.   136. **take 't . . . list:** I.e., take my defiance as you
please, as best you can.

Will make me sleep again; and then, in dreaming,
The clouds methought would open and show
    riches
Ready to drop upon me, that when I waked
150 I cried to dream° again.
STEPHANO: This will prove a brave kingdom to me,
    where I shall have my music for nothing.
CALIBAN: When Prospero is destroyed.
STEPHANO: That shall be by and by.° I remember the
155   story.
TRINCULO: The sound is going away. Let's follow it, and
    after do our work.
STEPHANO: Lead, monster; we'll follow. I would I could
    see this laborer! He lays it on.°
160 TRINCULO: Wilt come? I'll follow Stephano.
                (*Exeunt [following Ariel's music].*)

Scene III°

(*Enter Alonso, Sebastian, Antonio, Gonzalo, Adrian, Francisco, etc.*)

GONZALO: By 'r lakin,° I can go no further, sir.
  My old bones aches. Here's a maze trod indeed
  Through forthrights and meanders!° By your
    patience,
  I needs must° rest me.
ALONSO: Old lord, I cannot blame thee,
5 Who am myself attached° with weariness,
  To the dulling of my spirits.° Sit down and rest.
  Even here I will put off my hope, and keep it
  No longer for° my flatterer. He is drowned
  Whom thus we stray to find, and the sea mocks
10 Our frustrate° search on land. Well, let him go.
                  [*Alonso and Gonzalo sit.*]
ANTONIO [*aside to Sebastian*]: I am right° glad that
    he's so out of hope.°
  Do not, for° one repulse, forgo the purpose
  That you resolved t' effect.
SEBASTIAN [*to Antonio*]:   The next advantage
  Will we take throughly.°
ANTONIO [*to Sebastian*]:   Let it be tonight,
15 For, now° they are oppressed with travel,° they

Will not, nor cannot, use° such vigilance
As when they are fresh.
SEBASTIAN [*to Antonio*]:   I say tonight. No more.
        (*Solemn and strange music; and
        Prospero on the top,° invisible.*)
ALONSO: What harmony is this? My good friends,
    hark!
GONZALO: Marvelous sweet music!

(*Enter several strange shapes, bringing in a
banquet, and dance about it with gentle actions
of salutations; and, inviting the King, etc., to eat,
they depart.*)

ALONSO: Give us kind keepers,° heavens! What were
    these?   20
SEBASTIAN: A living° drollery.° Now I will believe
  That there are unicorns; that in Arabia
  There is one tree, the phoenix'° throne, one
    phoenix
  At this hour reigning there.
ANTONIO: I'll believe both;
  And what does else want credit,° come to me   25
  And I'll be sworn 'tis true. Travelers ne'er did lie,
  Thou fools at home condemn 'em.
GONZALO: If in Naples
  I should report this now, would they believe me
  If I should say I saw such islanders?
  For, certes,° these are people of the island,   30
  Who though they are of monstrous shape, yet
    note,
  Their manners are more gentle, kind, than of
  Our human generation you shall find
  Many, nay, almost any.
PROSPERO [*aside*]:   Honest lord,
  Thou hast said well, for some of you there
    present   35
  Are worse than devils.
ALONSO: I cannot too much muse°
  Such shapes, such gesture, and such sound,
    expressing—
  Although they want° the use of tongue—a kind
  Of excellent dumb discourse.
PROSPERO [*aside*]:   Praise in departing.°

---

150. **to dream:** Desirous of dreaming.   154. **by and by:** Very soon.   159. **lays it on:** I.e., plays the drum skillfully and energetically.   **III, iii. Location:** Another part of the island.   1. **By 'r lakin:** By our Ladykin, by our Lady.   3. **forthrights and meanders:** Paths straight and crooked.   4. **needs must:** Have to.   5. **attached:** Seized.   6. **To . . . spirits:** To the point of being dull-spirited.   8. **for:** As.   10. **frustrate:** Frustrated.   11. **right:** Very.   **out of hope:** Despairing, discouraged.   12. **for:** Because of.   14. **throughly:** Thoroughly.   15. **now:** Now that.   **travel:** Spelled *trauaile* in the Folio and carrying the sense of labor as well as traveling.

16. **use:** Apply.   17. [S.D.] **on the top:** At some high point of the tiring-house or the theater, on a third level above the gallery.   20. **kind keepers:** Guardian angels.   21. **living:** With live actors.   **drollery:** Comic entertainment, caricature, puppet show.   23. **phoenix:** Mythical bird consumed to ashes every five to six hundred years, only to be renewed into another cycle.   25. **want credit:** Lack credence.   30. **certes:** Certainly.   36. **muse:** Wonder at.   38. **want:** Lack.   39. **Praise in departing:** I.e., save your praise until the end of the performance (proverbial).

FRANCISCO: They vanished strangely.

40 SEBASTIAN: No matter, since
They have left their viands° behind, for we have
   stomachs.°
Will 't please you taste of what is here?

ALONSO: Not I.

GONZALO: Faith, sir, you need not fear. When we
   were boys,
Who would believe that there were
   mountaineers°
Dewlapped° like bulls, whose throats had
45   hanging et 'em
Wallets° of flesh? Or that there were such men
Whose heads stood in their breasts?° Which
   now we find

Each putter-out of five for one° will bring us
Good warrant° of.

ALONSO: I will stand to° and feed,
Although my last°—no matter, since I feel
The best° is past. Brother, my lord the Duke,   50
Stand to, and do as we.

                [They approach the table.]

*(Thunder and lightning. Enter Ariel, like a harpy,° claps
his wings upon the table, and with a quaint device° the
banquet vanishes.°)*

41. **viands:** Provisions. **stomachs:** Appetites. 44. **mountain-eers:** Mountain dwellers. 45. **Dewlapped:** Having a *dewlap*, or fold of skin hanging from the neck, like cattle. 46. **Wallets:** Pendent folds of skin, wattles. 47. **in their breasts:** I.e., like the Anthropophagi described in *Othello*, I, iii, 146.

48. **putter-out . . . one:** One who invests money or gambles on the risks of travel on the condition that, if he returns safely, he is to receive five times the amount deposited; hence, any trav-eler. 49. **Good warrant:** Assurance. **stand to:** Fall to; take the risk. 50. **Although my last:** Even if this were to be my last meal. 51. **best:** Best part of life. 52. [S.D.] *harpy:* A fabulous monster with a woman's face and breasts and a vulture's body, supposed to be a minister of divine vengeance. *quaint device:* Ingenious stage contrivance. *the banquet vanishes:* I.e., the food vanishes; the table remains until line 82.

Christian Camargo as Ariel, directed by Sam Mendes, 2010.

ARIEL: You are three men of sin, whom Destiny—
That hath to° instrument this lower world
55 And what is in 't—the never-surfeited sea
Hath caused to belch up you, and on this island
Where man doth not inhabit, you 'mongst men
Being most unfit to live. I have made you mad;
And even with suchlike valor° men hang and
    drown
Their proper° selves.

*[Alonso, Sebastian, and
Antonio draw their swords.]*

60   You fools! I and my fellows
Are ministers of Fate. The elements
Of whom° your swords are tempered° may as
    well
Wound the loud winds, or with bemocked-at°
    stabs
Kill the still-closing° waters, as diminish
65 One dowl° that's in my plume. My fellow
    ministers
Are like° invulnerable. If° you could hurt,
Your swords are now too massy° for your
    strengths
And will not be uplifted. But remember—
For that's my business to you—that you three
70 From Milan did supplant good Prospero;
Exposed unto the sea, which hath requit° it,
Him and his innocent child; for which foul deed
The powers, delaying, not forgetting, have
Incensed the seas and shores, yea, all the creatures,
75 Against your peace. Thee of thy son, Alonso,
They have bereft; and do pronounce by me
Lingering perdition,° worse than any death
Can be at once, shall step by step attend
You and your ways; whose° wraths to guard you
    from—
80 Which here, in this most desolate isle, else° falls
Upon your heads—is nothing° but heart's
    sorrow
And a clear° life ensuing.

*(He vanishes in thunder; then, to soft music, enter the
shapes again, and dance, with mocks and mows,° and
carrying out the table.)*

PROSPERO: Bravely° the figure of this harpy hast
    thou

Performed, my Ariel; a grace it had devouring.°
Of my instruction hast thou nothing bated°   85
In what thou hadst to say. So,° with good life°
And observation strange,° my meaner° ministers
Their several kinds° have done. My high charms
    work,
And these mine enemies are all knit up
In their distractions. They now are in my power;   90
And in these fits I leave them, while I visit
Young Ferdinand, whom they suppose is drowned,
And his and mine loved darling.   *[Exit above.]*

GONZALO: I' the name of something holy, sir, why°
    stand you
In this strange stare?

ALONSO: O, it° is monstrous, monstrous!   95
Methought the billows° spoke and told me of it;
The winds did sing it to me, and the thunder,
That deep and dreadful organ pipe, pronounced
The name of Prosper; it did bass my trespass.°
Therfor° my son i' th' ooze is bedded; and   100
I'll seek him deeper than e'er plummet° sounded,°
And with him there lie mudded.   *(Exit.)*

SEBASTIAN: But one fiend at a time,
I'll fight their legions o'er.°

ANTONIO: I'll be thy second.

(Exeunt [Sebastian and Antonio].)

GONZALO: All three of them are desperate.° Their   105
    great guilt,
Like poison given to work a great time after,
Now 'gins to bite the spirits.° I do beseech you
That are of suppler joints, follow them swiftly
And hinder them from what this ecstasy°
May now provoke them to.

ADRIAN: Follow, I pray you.   110
(Exeunt omnes.°)

---

54. **to:** I.e., as its. 59. **suchlike valor:** I.e., the reckless valor derived from madness. 60. **proper:** Own. 62. **whom:** Which. **tempered:** Composed and hardened. 63. **bemocked-at:** Scorned. 64. **still-closing:** Always closing again when parted. 65. **dowl:** Soft, fine feather. 66. **like:** Likewise, similarly. **If:** Even if. 67. **massy:** Heavy. 71. **requit:** Requited, avenged. 77. **perdition:** Ruin, destruction. 79. **whose:** Refers to the heavenly powers. 80. **else:** Otherwise. 81. **is nothing:** There is no way. 82. **clear:** Unspotted, innocent. [S.D.] *mocks and mows:* Mocking gestures and grimaces. 83. **Bravely:** Finely, dashingly.

84. **a grace . . . devouring:** I.e., you gracefully caused the banquet to disappear as if you had consumed it (with puns on *grace* meaning "gracefulness" and "a blessing on the meal" and on *devouring* meaning "a literal eating" and "an all-consuming or ravishing grace"). 85. **bated:** Abated, omitted. 86. **So:** In the same fashion. **good life:** Faithful reproduction. 87. **observation strange:** Exceptional attention to detail. **meaner:** I.e., subordinate to Ariel. 88. **several kinds:** Individual parts. 94. **why:** Gonzalo was not addressed in Ariel's speech to the *three men of sin* (line 53) and is not, as they are, in a maddened state; see lines 105–107. 95. **it:** I.e., my sin (also in line 96). 96. **billows:** Waves. 99. **bass my trespass:** Proclaim my trespass like a bass note in music. 100. **Therefor:** In consequence of that. 101. **plummet:** A lead weight attached to a line for testing depth. **sounded:** Probed, tested the depth of. 104. **o'er:** One after another. 105. **desperate:** Despairing and reckless. 107. **bite the spirits:** Sap their vital powers through anguish. 109. **ecstasy:** Mad frenzy. 110. [S.D.] *omnes:* Latin for "all."

ACT IV • Scene I°

(*Enter Prospero, Ferdinand, and Miranda.*)

PROSPERO: If I have too austerely° punished you,
Your compensation makes amends, for I
Have given you here a third° of mine own life,
Or that for which I live; who once again
5   I tender to thy hand. All thy vexations°
Were but my trials of thy love, and thou
Hast strangely° stood the test. Here, afore Heaven,
I ratify this my rich gift. O Ferdinand,
Do not smile at me that I boast her off,°
10   For thou shalt find she will outstrip all praise
And make it halt° behind her.

FERDINAND: I do believe it
Against an oracle.°

PROSPERO: Then, as my gift and thine own
      acquisition
Worthily purchased, take my daughter. But
15   If thou dost break her virgin-knot before
All sanctimonious° ceremonies may
With full and holy rite be ministered,
No sweet aspersion° shall the heavens let fall
To make this contract grow; but barren hate
20   Sour-eyed disdain, and discord shall bestrew
The union of your bed with weeds° so loathly
That you shall hate it both. Therefore take heed,
As Hymen's lamps shall light you.°

FERDINAND: As I hope
For quiet days, fair issue,° and long life,
25   With such love as 'tis now, the murkiest den,
The most opportune place, the strong'st
      suggestion°
Our worser genius° can,° shall never melt
Mine honor into lust, to° take away
The edge° of that day's celebration
30   When I shall think or° Phoebus' steeds are
      foundered°
Or Night kept chained below.

PROSPERO: Fairly spoke.
Sit then and talk with her. She is thine own.
   [*Ferdinand and Miranda sit and talk together.*]
What,° Ariel! My industrious servant, Ariel!

(*Enter Ariel.*)

ARIEL: What would my potent master? Here I am.
PROSPERO: Thou and thy meaner fellows° your last
      service   35
Did worthily perform, and I must use you
In such another trick.° Go bring the rabble,°
O'er whom I give thee power, here to this place.
Incite them to quick motion, for I must
Bestow upon the eyes of this young couple   40
Some vanity° of mine art. It is my promise,
And they expect it from me.

ARIEL: Presently?°
PROSPERO: Ay, with a twink.°
ARIEL: Before you can say "Come" and "Go,"
And breathe twice, and cry "So, so,"   45
Each one, tripping on his toe,
Will be here with mop and mow.°
Do you love me, master? No?

PROSPERO: Dearly, my delicate Ariel. Do not
      approach
Till thou dost hear me call.

ARIEL: Well, I conceive.°   50
                                          (*Exit.*)

PROSPERO: Look thou be true;° do not give dalliance
Too much the rein. The strongest oaths are straw
To the fire i' the blood. Be more abstemious,
Or else good night° your vow!

FERDINAND: I warrant° you, sir,
The white cold virgin snow upon my heart°   55
Abates the ardor of my liver.°

PROSPERO: Well.
Now come, my Ariel! Bring a corollary,°
Rather than want° a spirit. Appear, and
      pertly!°—
No tongue!° All eyes! Be silent.   (*Soft music.*)

(*Enter Iris.°*)

IRIS: Ceres,° most bounteous lady, thy rich leas°   60

IV, i. Location: Before Prospero's cell. **1. austerely:** Severely.
3. a third: I.e., Miranda, into whose education Prospero
has put a third of his life (?) or who represents a large part
of what he cares about, along with his dukedom and his
learned study (?). **5. vexations:** Torments. **7. strangely:**
Extraordinarily. **9. boast her off:** I.e., praise her so; or, perhaps, an error for *boast of her*; the Folio reads *boast her of*.
11. halt: Limp. **12. Against an oracle:** I.e., even if an oracle should declare otherwise. **16. sanctimonious:** Sacred.
18. aspersion: Dew, shower. **21. weeds:** In place of the flowers customarily strewn on the marriage bed. **23. As . . . you:**
I.e., as you long for happiness and concord in your marriage.
(Hymen was the Greek and Roman god of marriage; his
symbolic torches, the wedding torches, were supposed to
burn brightly for a happy marriage, smokily for a troubled
one.) **24. issue:** Offspring. **26. suggestion:** Temptation.
27. worser genius: Evil genius; or, evil attendant spirit. **can:**
Is capable of. **28. to:** So as to. **29. edge:** Keen enjoyment,
sexual ardor. **30. or:** Either. **foundered:** Broken down, made
lame. (Ferdinand will wait impatiently for the bridal night.)

33. What: Now then. **35. meaner fellows:** Subordinates.
37. trick: Device. **rabble:** Band (i.e., the *meaner fellows* of line
35). **41. vanity:** (1) Illusion; (2) trifle; (3) desire for admiration, conceit. **42. Presently:** Immediately. **43. with a twink:**
In the twinkling of an eye, in an instant. **47. mop and mow:**
Gestures and grimaces. **50. conceive:** Understand. **51. true:**
True to your promise. **54. good night:** I.e., say good-bye to.
warrant: Guarantee. **55. The white . . . heart:** I.e., the ideal of
chastity and consciousness of Miranda's chaste innocence en-
shrined in my heart. **56. liver:** As the presumed seat of the
passions. **57. corollary:** Surplus, extra supply. **58. want:**
Lack. **pertly:** Briskly. **59. No tongue:** All the beholders are
to be silent (lest the spirits vanish). [S.D.] ***Iris:*** Goddess of the
rainbow and Juno's messenger. **60. Ceres:** Goddess of the gen-
erative power of nature. **leas:** Meadows.

Of wheat, rye, barley, vetches,° oats, and peas;
Thy turfy mountains, where live nibbling sheep,
And flat meads° thatched with stover,° them to
   keep;
Thy banks with pionèd and twillèd° brims,
65 Which spongy° April at thy hest betrims
To make cold nymphs chaste crowns; and thy
   broom groves,°
Whose shadow the dismissèd bachelor° loves
Being lass-lorn; thy poll-clipped° vineyard;
And thy sea marge,° sterile and rocky hard,
Where thou thyself dost air: the queen o' the
70   sky,°
Whose watery arch° and messenger am I,
Bids thee leave these, and with her sovereign
   grace,
         (*Juno descends° [slowly in her car].*)
Here on this grass plot, in this very place,
To come and sport. Her peacocks° fly amain.°
75 Approach, rich Ceres, her to entertain.°

(*Enter Ceres.*)

CERES: Hail, many-colored messenger, that ne'er
   Dost disobey the wife of Jupiter,
   Who with thy saffron° wings upon my flowers
   Diffusest honeydrops, refreshing showers,
80   And with each end of thy blue bow° dost crown
   My bosky° acres and my unshrubbed down,°
   Rich scarf to my proud earth. Why hath thy
      queen
   Summoned me hither to this short-grassed green?
IRIS: A contract of true love to celebrate,
85   And some donation freely to estate°
   On the blest lovers.
CERES: Tell me, heavenly bow,
   If Venus or her son,° as° thou dost know,
   Do now attend the Queen? Since they did plot
   The means that dusky° Dis my daughter got,°
90   Her° and her blind boy's scandaled° company
   I have forsworn.
IRIS: Of her society°

Be not afraid. I met her deity°
Cutting the clouds towards Paphos,° and her son
Dove-drawn° with her. Here thought they to have done°
Some wanton charm° upon this man and maid,   95
Whose vows are that no bed-right shall be paid
Till Hymen's torch be lighted, but in vain.
Mars's hot minion° is returned° again;
Her waspish-headed° son has broke his arrows,
Swears he will shoot no more, but play with
   sparrows°   100
And be a boy right out.°

[*Juno alights.*]

CERES: Highest Queen of state,°
   Great Juno, comes; I know her by her gait.°
JUNO: How does my bounteous sister? Go with me
   To bless this twain, that they may prosperous be
   And honored in their issue.°   (*They sing.*) 105
JUNO: Honor, riches, marriage blessing,
   Long continuance, and increasing,
   Hourly joys be still° upon you!
   Juno sings her blessings on you,
CERES: Earth's increase, foison plenty,°   110
   Barns and garners° never empty,
   Vines with clustering bunches growing,
   Plants with goodly burden bowing;

   Spring come to you at the farthest
   In the very end of harvest!°   115
   Scarcity and want shall shun you;
   Ceres' blessing so is on you.
FERDINAND: This is a most majestic vision, and
   Harmonious charmingly.° May I be bold
   To think these spirits?
PROSPERO: Spirits, which by mine art   120
   I have from their confines called to enact
   My present fancies.
FERDINAND: Let me live here ever!
   So rare a wondered° father and a wife
   Makes this place Paradise.

         (*Juno and Ceres whisper, and send Iris on
                  employment.*)

PROSPERO: Sweet now, silence!
   Juno and Ceres whisper seriously;   125
   There's something else to do. Hush and be mute.

61. **vetches:** Plants for forage, fodder. 63. **meads:** Meadows. **stover:** Winter fodder for cattle. 64. **pionèd and twillèd:** Undercut by the swift current and protected by roots and branches that tangle to form a barricade. 65. **spongy:** Wet. 66. **broom groves:** Clumps of broom, gorse, yellow-flowered shrub. 67. **dismissèd bachelor:** Rejected male lover. 68. **poll-clipped:** Pruned, looped at the top; or, *pole-clipped,* hedged in with poles. 69. **sea marge:** Shore. 70. **queen o' the sky:** I.e., Juno. 71. **watery arch:** Rainbow. 72. [S.D.] *Juno descends:* I.e., starts her descent from the "heavens" above the stage (?). 74. **peacocks:** Birds sacred to Juno and used to pull her chariot. **amain:** With full speed. 75. **entertain:** Receive. 78. **saffron:** Yellow. 80. **bow:** I.e., rainbow. 81. **bosky:** Wooded. **down:** Upland. 85. **estate:** Bestow. 87. **son:** I.e., Cupid. **as:** As far as. 89. **dusky:** Dark. **Dis...got:** Pluto, or Dis, god of the infernal regions, carried off Persephone, daughter of Ceres, to be his bride in Hades. 90. **Her:** I.e., Venus's. **scandaled:** Scandalous. 91. **society:** Company.

92. **her deity:** I.e., Her highness. 93. **Paphos:** Place on the island of Cyprus sacred to Venus. 94. **Dove-drawn:** Venus's chariot was drawn by doves. **done:** Placed. 95. **wanton charm:** Lustful spell. 98. **Mars's hot minion:** I.e., Venus, the beloved of Mars. **returned:** I.e., returned to Paphos. 99. **waspish-headed:** Fiery, hotheaded, peevish. 100. **sparrows:** Supposed lustful and sacred to Venus. 101. **right out:** Outright. **Highest...state:** Most majestic Queen. 102. **gait:** I.e., majestic bearing. 105. **issue:** Offspring. 108. **still:** Always. 110. **foison plenty:** Plentiful harvest. 111. **garners:** Granaries. 115. **In...harvest:** I.e., with no winter in between. 119. **charmingly:** Enchantingly. 123. **wondered:** Wonder-performing, wondrous.

Or else our spell is marred.

IRIS: You nymphs, called naiads,° of the windring°
    brooks,
  With your sedged° crowns and ever-harmless°
    looks,
  Leave your crisp° channels, and on this green
130   land
  Answer your summons; Juno does command.
  Come, temperate° nymphs, and help to celebrate
  A contract of true love. Be not too late.

(Enter certain nymphs.)

  You sunburnt sicklemen,° of August weary,°
135 Come hither from the furrow° and be merry.
  Make holiday; your rye-straw hats put on,
  And these fresh nymphs encounter° every one
  In country footing.°

*(Enter certain reapers, properly° habited. They join
with the nymphs in a graceful dance, toward the end
whereof Prospero starts suddenly, and speaks; after
which, to a strange, hollow, and confused noise, they
heavily° vanish.)*

PROSPERO [*aside*]: I had forgot that foul conspiracy
140 Of the beast Caliban and his confederates
  Against my life. The minute of their plot
  Is almost come. [*To the Spirits.*] Well done!
    Avoid;° no more!

FERDINAND [*to Miranda*]: This is strange. Your
    father's in some passion
  That works° him strongly.

MIRANDA: Never till this day
145 Saw I him touched with anger so distempered.

PROSPERO: You do look, my son, in a moved sort,°
  As if you were dismayed. Be cheerful, sir.
  Our revels° now are ended. These our actors,
  As I foretold you, were all spirits and
150 Are melted into air, into thin air;
  And, like the baseless° fabric of this vision,
  The cloud-capped towers, the gorgeous palaces,
  The solemn temples, the great globe° itself,
  Yea, all which it inherit,° shall dissolve,
155 And, like this insubstantial pageant faded,
  Leave not a rack° behind. We are such stuff
  As dreams are made on,° and our little life
  Is rounded° with a sleep. Sir, I am vexed.

Bear with my weakness. My old brain is
    troubled.
Be not disturbed with my infirmity.   160
If you be pleased, retire° into my cell
And there repose. A turn or two I'll walk
To still my beating° mind.

FERDINAND, MIRANDA: We wish your peace.
         (Exeunt [Ferdinand and Miranda].)

PROSPERO: Come with a thought!° I thank thee,
  Ariel. Come.

(Enter Ariel.)

ARIEL: Thy thoughts I cleave° to. What's thy pleasure?

PROSPERO: Spirit, 165
  We must prepare to meet with Caliban.

ARIEL: Ay, my commander. When I presented° Ceres,
  I thought to have told thee of it, but I feared
  Lest I might anger thee.

PROSPERO: Say again, where didst thou leave these
    varlets?   170

ARIEL: I told you, sir, they were red-hot with
    drinking,
  So full of valor that they smote the air
  For breathing in their faces, beat the ground
  For kissing of their feet, yet always bending°
  Towards their project. Then I beat my tabor, 175
  At which, like unbacked° colts, they pricked their
    ears,
  Advanced° their eyelids, lifted up their noses
  As° they smelt music. So I charmed their ears
  That calflike they my lowing° followed through
  Toothed briers, sharp furzes, pricking gorse,° and
    thorns,   180
  Which entered their frail shins. At last I left them
  I' the filthy-mantled° pool beyond your cell,
  There dancing up to the chins, that the foul lake
  O'erstunk° their feet.

PROSPERO: This was well done, my bird.
  Thy shape invisible retain thou still.   185
  The trumpery° in my house, go bring it hither,
  For stale° to catch these thieves.

ARIEL: I go. I go.   *(Exit.)*

PROSPERO: A devil, a born devil, on whose nature
  Nurture can never stick; on whom my pains,
  Humanely taken, all, all lost, quite lost!   190
  And as with age his body uglier grows,

---

128. **naiads:** Nymphs of springs, rivers, or lakes. **windring:** Wandering, winding (?). 129. **sedged:** Made of reeds. **ever-harmless:** Ever-innocent. 130. **crisp:** Curled, rippled. 132. **temperate:** Chaste. 134. **sicklemen:** Harvesters, field workers who cut down grain and grass. **weary:** I.e., weary of the hard work of the harvest. 135. **furrow:** I.e., plowed fields. 137. **encounter:** Join. 138. **country footing:** Country dancing. [s.d.] *properly:* Suitably. *heavily:* Slowly, dejectedly. 142. **Avoid:** Depart, withdraw. 144. **works:** Affects, agitates. 146. **moved sort:** Troubled state, condition. 148. **revels:** Entertainment, pageant. 151. **baseless:** Without substance. 153. **great globe:** With a glance at the Globe Theatre. 154. **which it inherit:** Who subsequently occupy it. 156. **rack:** Wisp of cloud. 157. **on:** Of. 158. **rounded:** Surrounded; or, crowned, rounded off.

161. **retire:** Withdraw, go. 163. **beating:** Agitated. 164. **with a thought:** I.e., on the instant or summoned by my thought, no sooner thought of than here. 165. **cleave:** Cling, adhere. 167. **presented:** Acted the part of; or, introduced. 174. **bending:** Aiming. 176. **unbacked:** Unbroken, unridden. 177. **Advanced:** Lifted up. 178. **As:** As if. 179. **lowing:** Mooing. 180. **furzes . . . gorse:** Prickly shrubs. 182. **filthy-mantled:** Covered with a slimy coating. 184. **O'erstunk:** Smelled worse than; or, caused to stink terribly. 186. **trumpery:** Cheap goods, the *glistering apparel* mentioned in the following stage direction. 187. **stale:** (1) Decoy; (2) out-of-fashion garments (with possible further suggestions of *fit for a stale*, or prostitute; *stale*, meaning "horse piss," line 199; and *steal*, pronounced like *stale*).

So his mind cankers.° I will plague them all,
Even to roaring.

(*Enter Ariel, loaden with glistering apparel, etc.*)

                              Come, hang them on this line.°

([*Ariel hangs up the showy finery; Prospero and Ariel
remain,° invisible.*] *Enter Caliban, Stephano, and
Trinculo, all wet.*)

CALIBAN: Pray you, tread softly, that the blind mole
                may
195   Not hear a footfall. We now are near his cell.
STEPHANO: Monster, your fairy, which you say is a
                harmless fairy, has done little better than played the
                jack° with us.
TRINCULO: Monster, I do smell all horse piss, at which
200   my nose is in great indignation.
STEPHANO: So is mine. Do you hear, monster? If I
                should take a displeasure against you, look you—
TRINCULO: Thou wert but a lost monster.
CALIBAN: Good my lord, give me thy favor still.
205   Be patient, for the prize I'll bring thee to
                Shall hoodwink° this mischance.° Therefore
                    speak softly.
                All's hushed as midnight yet.
TRINCULO: Ay, but to lose our bottles in the pool—
STEPHANO: There is not only disgrace and dishonor in
210   that, monster, but an infinite loss.
TRINCULO: That's more to me than my wetting. Yet this is
                your harmless fairy, monster!
STEPHANO: I will fetch off my bottle, though I be o'er
                ears° for my labor.
215   CALIBAN: Prithee, my king, be quiet. Seest thou here,
                This is the mouth o' the cell. No noise, and
                    enter.
                Do that good mischief which may make this
                    island
                Thine own forever, and I thy Caliban
                For aye thy footlicker.
220   STEPHANO: Give me thy hand. I do begin to have bloody
                thoughts.
TRINCULO [*seeing the finery*]: O King Stephano! O
                peer!° O worthy Stephano! Look what a wardrobe
                here is for thee!
225   CALIBAN: Let it alone, thou fool, it is but trash.
TRINCULO: Oho, monster! We know what belongs to
                a frippery.° O King Stephano! [*He takes a gown.*]
STEPHANO: Put off° that gown, Trinculo. By this hand,
                I'll have that gown.
230   TRINCULO: Thy Grace shall have it.

CALIBAN: The dropsy° drown this fool! What do you
                mean
                To dote thus on such luggage?° Let 't alone
                And do the murder first. If he awake,
                From toe to crown° he'll fill our skins with
                    pinches,
                Make us strange stuff.   235
STEPHANO: Be you quiet, monster.—Mistress line,° is
                not this my jerkin?° [*He takes it down.*] Now is the
                jerkin under the line.° Now, jerkin, you are like° to
                lose your hair and prove a bald° jerkin.
TRINCULO: Do, do!° We steal by line and level,° an 't   240
                like° Your Grace.
STEPHANO: I thank thee for that jest. Here's a garment
                for 't. [*He gives a garment.*] Wit shall not go unre-
                warded while I am king of this country. "Steal by
                line and level" is an excellent pass of pate.° There's   245
                another garment for 't.
TRINCULO: Monster, come, put some lime° upon your
                fingers, and away with the rest.
CALIBAN: I will have none on 't. We shall lose our
                time,
                And all be turned to barnacles,° or to apes   250
                With foreheads villainous° low.
STEPHANO: Monster, lay to° your fingers. Help to bear
                this° away where my hogshead° of wine is, or I'll
                turn you out of my kingdom. Go to,° carry this.
TRINCULO: And this.   255
STEPHANO: Ay, and this.
                [*They load Caliban with more and more garments.*]

(*A noise of hunters heard. Enter divers spirits, in shape
of dogs and hounds, hunting them about, Prospero and
Ariel setting them on.*)

PROSPERO: Hey, Mountain, hey!
ARIEL: Silver! There it goes, Silver!

---

192. cankers: Festers, grows malignant. **193. line:** Lime
tree or linden. [s.d.] ***Prospero and Ariel remain:*** The staging is uncertain. They may instead exit here and return with
the spirits at line 256. **198. jack:** (1) Knave; (2) will-o'-the
wisp. **206. hoodwink:** Cover up, make you not see (a hawk-
ing term). **mischance:** Mishap, misfortune. **213–214. o'er
ears:** I.e., totally submerged and perhaps drowned.
222–223. King . . . peer: Alludes to the old ballad beginning
"King Stephen was a worthy peer." **227. frippery:** Place where
cast-off clothes are sold. **228. Put off:** Put down; or, take off.

231. dropsy: Disease characterized by the accumulation of fluid
in the connective tissue of the body. **232. luggage:** Cumber-
some trash. **234. crown:** Head. **236. Mistress line:** Addressed
to the linden or lime tree upon which, at line 193, Ariel hung
the *glistering apparel.* **237. jerkin:** Jacket made of leather.
238. under the line: Under the lime tree (with punning sense of
being south of the equinoctial line or equator; sailors on long
voyages to the southern regions were popularly supposed to lose
their hair from scurvy or other diseases. Stephano also quibbles
handily on losing hair through syphilis, and in *Mistress* and
jerkin). **like:** Likely. **239. bald:** (1) Hairless, napless; (2) meager. **240. Do, do:** I.e., bravo. (Said in response to the jesting or
the taking of the jerkin or both.) **by line and level:** I.e., by means
of plumb line and carpenter's level, methodically (with pun on
line, or lime tree, line 238, and *steal,* pronounced like *stale,* or
prostitute, continuing Stephano's bawdy quibble). **240–241. an
't like:** If it please. **245. pass of pate:** Sally of wit. (The metaphor
is from fencing.) **247. lime:** Birdlime, sticky substance (to give
Caliban sticky fingers). **250. barnacles:** Barnacle geese, formerly supposed to be hatched from seashells attached to trees
and to fall thence into the water; here evidently used, like *apes,*
as types of simpletons. **251. villainous:** Miserably. **252. lay
to:** Start using. **253. this:** I.e., the *glistering apparel.* **hogs-
head:** Large cask. **254. Go to:** An expression of exhortation
or remonstrance.

Ralph Fiennes as Prospero in a production directed by Trevor Nunn at the Theatre Royal Haymarket, 2011.

PROSPERO: Fury, Fury! There, Tyrant, there! Hark! Hark!

[*Caliban, Stephano, and Trinculo are driven out.*]

260   Go, charge my goblins that they grind their joints
    With dry° convulsions,° shorten up their sinews
    With agèd° cramps, and more pinch-spotted make them
    Than pard° or cat o' mountain.°

ARIEL: Hark, they roar!

PROSPERO: Let them be hunted soundly.° At this hour
265   Lies at my mercy all mine enemies.
    Shortly shall all my labors end, and thou
    Shalt have the air at freedom. For a little°
    Follow, and do me service.   (*Exeunt.*)

ACT V • Scene I°

(*Enter Prospero in his magic robes, [with his staff,] and Ariel.*)

PROSPERO: Now does my project gather to a head.
    My charms crack° not, my spirits obey, and Time

Goes upright with his carriage.° How's the day?
ARIEL: On° the sixth hour, at which time, my lord,
    You said our work should cease.
PROSPERO: I did say so,   5
    When first I raised the tempest. Say, my spirit,
    How fares the King and 's followers?
ARIEL: Confined together
    In the same fashion as you gave in charge,
    Just as you left them; all prisoners, sir,
    In the line grove° which weather-fends° your cell.   10
    They cannot budge till your release.° The King,
    His brother, and yours abide all three distracted,°
    And the remainder mourning over them,
    Brim full of sorrow and dismay; but chiefly
    Him that you termed, sir, the good old lord, Gonzalo.   15
    His tears runs down his beard like winter's drops
    From eaves of reeds.° Your charm so strongly works 'em
    That if you now beheld them your affections°
    Would become tender.
PROSPERO: Dost thou think so, spirit?
ARIEL: Mine would, sir, were I human.
PROSPERO: And mine shall.   20
    Hast thou, which art but air, a touch° a feeling
    Of their afflictions, and shall not myself,
    One of their kind, that relish all as sharply
    Passion as they,° be kindlier° moved than thou art?
    Though with their high wrongs I am struck to the quick,   25
    Yet with my nobler reason 'gainst my fury
    Do I take part. The rarer° action is
    In virtue than in vengeance. They being penitent,
    The sole drift of my purpose doth extend
    Not a frown further. Go release them, Ariel.   30
    My charms I'll break, their senses I'll restore,
    And they shall be themselves.
ARIEL: I'll fetch them, sir.
                              (*Exit.*)
    [*Prospero traces a charmed circle with his staff.*]

PROSPERO: Ye elves of hills, brooks, standing lakes, and groves,°
    And ye that on the sands with printless foot
    Do chase the ebbing Neptune, and do fly him   35

261. **dry:** Associated with age, arthritic (?). **convulsions:** Cramps. 262. **agèd:** Characteristic of old age. 263. **pard:** Panther or leopard. **cat o' mountain:** Wildcat. 264. **soundly:** Thoroughly. 267. **little:** Little while longer. V, i. **Location:** Before Prospero's cell. 2. **crack:** Collapse, fail. (The metaphor is probably alchemical, as in *project* and *gather to a head*, line 1.)

3. **his carriage:** Its burden. (Time is no longer heavily burdened and so can go upright, standing straight and unimpeded.) 4. **On:** Approaching. 10. **line grove:** Grove of lime trees. **weather-fends:** Protects from the weather. 11. **your release:** You release them. 12. **distracted:** Out of their wits. 17. **eaves of reeds:** Thatched roofs. 18. **affections:** Feelings. 21. **touch:** Sense, feeling. 23–24. **that . . . they:** I.e., I who am just as sensitive to suffering as they. 24. **kindlier:** (1) More sympathetically; (2) more naturally humanly. 27. **rarer:** Nobler. 33–50. **Ye . . . art:** This famous passage is an embellished paraphrase of Golding's translation of Ovid's *Metamorphoses*, 7, 197–219.

When he comes back; you demi-puppets° that
By moonshine do the green sour ringlets° make,
Whereof the ewe not bites; and you whose
    pastime
Is to make midnight mushrooms,° that rejoice
40 To hear the solemn curfew,° by whose aid,
Weak masters though ye be, I have bedimmed
The noontide sun, called forth the mutinous
    winds,
And twixt the green sea and the azured vault°
Set roaring war; to the dread rattling thunder
45 Have I given fire,° and rifted,° Jove's stout oak
With his own bolt;° the strong-based promontory
Have I made shake, and by the spurs° plucked
    up
The pine and cedar; graves at my command
Have waked their sleepers, oped, and let 'em
    forth
50 By my so potent art. But this rough° magic
I here abjure, and when I have required°
Some heavenly music—which even now I do—
To work mine end upon their senses that°
This airy charm° is for, I'll break my staff,
55 Bury it certain fathoms in the earth,
And deeper than did ever plummet sound
I'll drown my book.   (*Solemn music.*)

(*Here enters Ariel before; then Alonso, with a frantic
gesture, attended by Gonzalo; Sebastian and Antonio
in like manner, attended by Adrian and Francisco. They
all enter the circle which Prospero had made, and there
stand charmed; which Prospero observing, speaks.*)

[*To Alonso.*] A solemn air,° and° the best
    comforter
To an unsettled fancy,° cure thy brains,
Now useless, boiled within thy skull! [*To
60   Sebastian and Antonio.*] There stand,
For you are spell-stopped.—
Holy Gonzalo, honorable man,
Mine eyes, e'en sociable° to the show° of thine,
Fall° fellowly drops. [*Aside.*] The charm dissolves
    apace,
65 And as the morning steals upon the night,
Melting the darkness, so their rising senses
Begin to chase the ignorant fumes° that mantle°

Their clearer° reason.—O good Gonzalo,
My true preserver, and a loyal sir
To him thou follow'st! I will pay thy graces°   70
Home° both in word and deed.—Most cruelly
Didst thou, Alonso, use me and my daughter.
Thy brother was a furtherer° in the act.—
Thou art pinched° for 't now, Sebastian. [*To
    Antonio.*] Flesh and blood,
You, brother mine, that entertained ambition,   75
Expelled remorse° and nature,° whom,° with
    Sebastian,
Whose inward pinches therefore are most strong,
Would here have killed your king, I do forgive
    thee,
Unnatural though thou art.—Their
    understanding
Begins to swell, and the approaching tide   80
Will shortly fill the reasonable shore°
That now lies foul and muddy. Not one of them
That yet looks on me, or would know me.—
    Ariel,
Fetch me the hat and rapier in my cell.

[*Ariel goes to the cell and returns immediately.*]

I will disease° me and myself present   85
As I was sometime Milan.° Quickly, spirit!
Thou shalt ere long be free.

                (*Ariel sings and helps to attire him.*)

ARIEL: Where the bee sucks, there suck I.
    In a cowslip's bell I lie;
    There I couch° when owls do cry.   90
    On the bat's back I do fly
    After° summer merrily.
Merrily, merrily shall I live now
Under the blossom that hangs on the bough.
PROSPERO: Why, that's my dainty Ariel! I shall miss
    thee,   95
But yet thou shalt have freedom. So, so, so.°
To the King's ship, invisible as thou art!
There shalt thou find the mariners asleep
Under the hatches. The Master and the Boatswain
Being awake, enforce them to this place,   100
And presently,° I prithee.
ARIEL: I drink the air before me and return
Or ere° your pulse twice beat.   (*Exit.*)
GONZALO: All torment, trouble, wonder, and
    amazement

---

36. **demi-puppets:** Puppets of half size (i.e., elves and fairies). 37. **green sour ringlets:** Fairy rings, circles in grass (actually produced by mushrooms). 39. **midnight mushrooms:** Mushrooms appearing overnight. 40. **curfew:** Evening bell, usually rung at nine o'clock, ushering in the time when spirits are abroad. 43. **the azured vault:** I.e., the sky. 44–45. **to . . . fire:** I have discharged the dread rattling thunderbolt. 45. **rifted:** Riven, split. 46. **bolt:** Lightning bolt. 47. **spurs:** Roots. 50. **rough:** Violent. 51. **required:** Requested. 53. **their senses that:** The senses of those whom. 54. **airy charm:** I.e., music. 58. **air:** Song. **and:** I.e., which is. 59. **fancy:** Imagination. 63. **sociable:** Sympathetic. **show:** Appearance. 64. **Fall:** Let fall. 67. **ignorant fumes:** Fumes that render them incapable of comprehension. **mantle:** Envelop.

68. **clearer:** Growing clearer. 70. **pay thy graces:** Reward your favors. 71. **Home:** Fully. 73. **furtherer:** Accomplice. 74. **pinched:** Punished, afflicted. 76. **remorse:** Pity. **nature:** Natural feeling. **whom:** I.e., who. 81. **reasonable shore:** Shores of reason—i.e., minds. (Their reason returns like the incoming tide.) 85. **disease:** Disrobe. 86. **As . . . Milan:** In my former appearance as Duke of Milan. 90. **couch:** Lie. 92. **After:** I.e., pursuing. 96. **So, so, so:** Expresses approval of Ariel's help as valet. 101. **presently:** Immediately. 103. **Or ere:** Before.

105 Inhabits here. Some heavenly power guide us
     Out of this fearful° country!
PROSPERO: Behold, sir King,
     The wrongèd Duke of Milan, Prospero.
     For more assurance that a living prince
     Does now speak to thee, I embrace thy body;
110 And to thee and thy company I bid
     A hearty welcome.   [*Embracing him.*]
ALONSO: Whe'er thou be'st he or no,
     Or some enchanted trifle° to abuse° me,
     As late° I have been, I not know. Thy pulse
     Beats as of flesh and blood; and, since I saw
          thee,
115 Th' affliction of my mind amends, with which
     I fear a madness held me. This must crave°—
     An if this be at all°—a most strange story.°
     Thy dukedom I resign,° and do entreat
     Thou pardon me my wrongs.° But how should
          Prospero
     Be living, and be here?
120 PROSPERO [*to Gonzalo*]: First, noble friend,
     Let me embrace thine age,° whose honor cannot
     Be measured or confined.   [*Embracing him.*]
GONZALO: Whether this be
     Or be not, I'll not swear.
PROSPERO: You do yet taste
     Some subtleties° o' th' isle, that will not let you
125 Believe things certain. Welcome, my friends all!
     [*Aside to Sebastian and Antonio.*] But you, my
          brace° of lords, were I so minded,
     I here could pluck His Highness' frown upon
          you
     And justify you° traitors. At this time
     I will tell no tales.
SEBASTIAN: The devil speaks in him.
PROSPERO: No.
     [*To Antonio.*] For you, most wicked sir, whom to
130   call brother
     Would even infect my mouth, I do forgive
     Thy rankest fault—all of them; and require
     My dukedom of thee, which perforce° I know
     Thou must restore.
ALONSO: If thou be'st Prospero,
135 Give us particulars of thy preservation,
     How thou hast met us here, whom° three hours
          Since

Were wrecked upon this shore; where I have
     lost—
How sharp the point of this remembrance is!—
My dear son Ferdinand.
PROSPERO: I am woe° for 't, sir.
ALONSO: Irreparable is the loss, and Patience   140
     Says it is past her cure.
PROSPERO: I rather think
     You have not sought her help, of whose soft
          grace°
     For the like loss I have her sovereign° aid
     And rest myself content.
ALONSO: You the like loss?
PROSPERO: As great to me as late,° and supportable   145
     To make the dear loss, have I° means much
          weaker
     Than you may call to comfort you; for I
     Have lost my daughter.
ALONSO: A daughter?
     O heavens, that they were living both in Naples, 150
     The king and queen there! That° they were, I
          wish
     Myself were mudded° in that oozy bed
     Where my son lies. When did you lose your
          daughter?
PROSPERO: In this last tempest. I perceive these lords
     At this encounter do so much admire°   155
     That they devour their reason° and scarce think
     Their eyes do offices of truth, their words
     Are natural breath.° But, howsoever you have
     Been jostled from your senses, know for certain
     That I am Prospero and that very duke   160
     Which was thrust forth of° Milan, who most
          strangely
     Upon this shore, where you were wrecked, was
          landed
     To be the lord on 't. No more yet of this,
     For 'tis a chronicle of day by day,°
     Not a relation for a breakfast nor   165
     Befitting this first meeting. Welcome, sir.
     This cell's my court. Here have I few attendants,
     And subjects none abroad.° Pray you, look in.
     My dukedom since you have given me again,
     I will requite° you with as good a thing,   170
     At least bring forth a wonder to content ye
     As much as me my dukedom.

---

106. fearful: Frightening. **112. trifle:** Trick of magic. **abuse:** Deceive. **113. late:** Lately. **116. crave:** Require. **117. An ...all:** If this is actually happening. **story:** I.e., explanation. **118. Thy ... resign:** Alonso made an arrangement with Antonio at the time of Prospero's banishment for Milan to pay tribute to Naples; see I, ii, 113–127. **119. wrongs:** Wrongdoings. **121. thine age:** Your venerable self. **124. subtleties:** Illusions, magical powers. **126. brace:** Pair. **128. justify you:** Prove you to be. **133. perforce:** Necessarily. **136. whom:** I.e., who.

139. woe: Sorry. **142. of...grace:** By whose mercy. **143. sovereign:** Efficacious. **145. late:** Recent. **145–146. supportable...have I:** To make the deeply felt loss bearable, I have. **151. That:** So that. **152. mudded:** Buried in the mud. **155. admire:** Wonder. **156. devour their reason:** I.e., are dumbfounded. **156–158. scarce...breath:** Scarcely believe that their eyes inform them accurately what they see or that their words are naturally spoken. **161. of:** From. **164. of day by day:** Requiring days to tell. **168. abroad:** Away from here, anywhere else. **170. requite:** Repay.

(*Here Prospero discovers° Ferdinand and Miranda playing at chess.*)

MIRANDA: Sweet lord, you play me false.
FERDINAND: No, my dearest love,
175 I would not for the world.
MIRANDA: Yes, for a score of kingdoms you should
      wrangle,
     And I would call it fair play.°
ALONSO: If this prove
    A vision° of the island, one dear son
    Shall I twice lose.
SEBASTIAN: A most high miracle!

FERDINAND [*approaching his father*]:
180 Though the seas threaten, they are merciful;
     I have cursed them without cause.   [*He kneels.*]
ALONSO: Now all the blessings
    Of a glad father compass° thee about!
    Arise, and say how thou cam'st here.
                            [*Ferdinand rises.*]
MIRANDA: O, wonder!
    How many goodly creatures are there here!
    How beauteous mankind is! O, brave° new
185   world,
    That has such people in 't!
PROSPERO: 'Tis new to thee.
ALONSO: What is this maid with whom thou wast
      at play?
    Your eld'st° acquaintance cannot be three hours.
    Is she the goddess that hath severed us
    And brought us thus together?
190 FERDINAND: Sir, she is mortal;
    But by immortal Providence she's mine.
    I chose her when I could not ask my father
    For his advice, nor thought I had one. She
    Is daughter to this famous Duke of Milan,
195 Of whom so often I have heard renown
    But never saw before, of whom I have
    Received a second life; and second father
    This lady makes him to me.
ALONSO: I am hers.
    But O, how oddly will it sound that I
    Must ask my child forgiveness!
200 PROSPERO: There, sir, stop.
    Let us not burden our remembrances with

    A heaviness° that's gone.
GONZALO: I have inly° wept,
    Or should have spoke ere this. Look down, you
      gods,
    And on this couple drop a blessèd crown!
    For it is you that have chalked forth the way°   205
    Which brought us hither.
ALONSO: I say amen, Gonzalo!
GONZALO: Was Milan° thrust from Milan that his
      issue
    Should become kings of Naples? O, rejoice
    Beyond a common joy, and set it down
    With gold on lasting pillars: In one voyage   210
    Did Claribel her husband find at Tunis,
    And Ferdinand, her brother, found a wife
    Where he himself was lost; Prospero his dukedom
    In a poor isle; and all of us ourselves
    When no man was his own.°   215
    ALONSO [*to Ferdinand and Miranda*]: Give me your
      hands.
    Let grief and sorrow still° embrace his° heart
    That° doth not wish you joy!
GONZALO: Be it so! Amen!
(*Enter Ariel, with the Master and Boatswain amazedly following.*)
    O, look, sir, look, sir! Here is more of us.
    I prophesied, if a gallows were on land,   220
    This fellow could not drown.—Now, blasphemy,°
    That swear'st grace o'erboard,° not an oath° on
      shore?
    Hast thou no mouth by land? What is the news?
BOATSWAIN: The best news is that we have safely found
    Our King and company; the next, our ship—   225
    Which, but three glasses° since, we gave out° split—
    Is tight and yare° and bravely° rigged as when
    We first put out to sea.
ARIEL [*aside to Prospero*]: Sir, all this service
    Have I done since I went.
PROSPERO [*aside to Ariel*]: My tricksy° spirit!
ALONSO: These are not natural events; they
      strengthen°   230
    From strange to stranger. Say, how came you
      hither?
BOATSWAIN: If I did think, sir, I were well awake,
    I'd strive to tell you. We were dead of sleep,°

172. [S.D.] *discovers:* I.e., by opening a curtain, presumably rear stage. 176–177. Yes . . . play: I.e., yes, even if we were playing for twenty kingdoms, something less than the whole world, you would still contend mightily against me and play me false, and I would let you do it as though it were fair play; or, if you were to play not just for stakes but literally for kingdoms, my accusation of false play would be out of order in that your "wrangling" would be proper. 178. vision: Illusion. 182. compass: Encompass, embrace. 185. brave: Splendid, gorgeously appareled, handsome. 188. eld'st: Longest.

202. heaviness: Sadness. inly: Inwardly. 205. chalked... way: Marked as with a piece of chalk the pathway. 207. Was Milan: Was the Duke of Milan. 214–215. all...own: All of us have found ourselves and our sanity when we all had lost our senses. 217. still: Always. his: That person's. 218. That: Who. 221. blasphemy: I.e., blasphemer. 222. That...o'erboard: I.e., you who banish heavenly grace from the ship by your blasphemies. not an oath: Aren't you going to swear an oath. 226. glasses: I.e., hours. gave out: Reported, professed to be. 227. yare: Ready. bravely: Splendidly. 229. tricksy: Ingenious, sportive. 230. strengthen: Increase. 233. dead of sleep: Deep in sleep.

And—how we know not—all clapped under
   hatches,
Where but even now, with strange and several°
235   noises
Of roaring, shrieking, howling, jingling chains,
And more diversity of sounds, all horrible,
We were awaked; straightway at liberty;
Where we, in all her trim, freshly beheld
240 Our royal, good, and gallant ship, our Master
Cap'ring to eye° her. On a trice,° so please you,
Even in a dream, were we divided from them°
And were brought moping° hither.

ARIEL [*aside to Prospero*]:   Was 't well done?
PROSPERO [*aside to Ariel*]: Bravely, my diligence.
   Thou shalt be free.
245 ALONSO: This is as strange a maze as e'er men trod,
And there is in this business more than nature
Was ever conduct° of. Some oracle
Must rectify our knowledge.

PROSPERO: Sir, my liege,
Do not infest° your mind with beating on°
250 The strangeness of this business. At picked°
   leisure,
Which shall be shortly, single° I'll resolve° you,
Which to you shall seem probable,° of every
These° happened accidents,° till when, be
   cheerful
And think of each thing well.° [*Aside to Ariel.*]
   Come hither, spirit.
255 Set Caliban and his companions free.
Untie the spell. [*Exit Ariel.*] How fares my
   gracious sir?
There are yet missing of your company
Some few odd° lads that you remember not.

(*Enter Ariel, driving in Caliban, Stephano, and Trinculo
in their stolen apparel.*)

STEPHANO: Every man shift° for all the rest,° and let
260 no man take care for himself; for all is but fortune.
Coraggio,° bully monster,° coraggio!
TRINCULO: If these be true spies° which I wear in my
head, here's a goodly sight.
CALIBAN: O Setebos, these be brave° spirits indeed!
265 How fine° my master is! I am afraid
He will chastise me.

SEBASTIAN: Ha, ha!
What things are these, my lord Antonio?
Will money buy 'em?
ANTONIO: Very like. One of them
Is a plain fish, and no doubt marketable.   270
PROSPERO: Mark but the badges° of these men, my
   lords,
Then say if they be true.° This misshapen knave,
His mother was a witch, and one so strong
That could control the moon, make flows and ebbs,
And deal in her command without her power.° 275
These three have robbed me, and this
   demidevil—
For he's a bastard° one—had plotted with them
To take my life. Two of these fellows you
Must know and own.° This thing of darkness I
Acknowledge mine.
CALIBAN: I shall be pinched to death. 280
ALONSO: Is not this Stephano, my drunken butler?
SEBASTIAN: He is drunk now. Where had he wine?
ALONSO: And Trinculo is reeling ripe.° Where
   should they
Find this grand liquor that hath gilded° 'em?
[*To Trinculo.*] How cam'st thou in this pickle?° 285
TRINCULO: I have been in such a pickle since I saw
you last that, I fear me, will never out of my bones.
I shall not fear flyblowing.°
SEBASTIAN: Why, how now, Stephano?
STEPHANO: O, touch me not! I am not Stephano, but 290
a cramp.
PROSPERO: You'd be king o' the isle, sirrah?°
STEPHANO: I should have been a sore° one, then.
ALONSO [*pointing to Caliban*]: This is a strange thing
as e'er I looked on. 295
PROSPERO: He is as disproportioned in his manners
As in his shape.—Go, sirrah, to my cell.
Take with you your companions. As you look
To have my pardon, trim° it handsomely.
CALIBAN: Ay, that I will; and I'll be wise hereafter 300
And seek for grace. What a thrice-double ass
Was I to take this drunkard for a god
And worship this dull fool!
PROSPERO: Go to. Away!
ALONSO: Hence, and bestow your luggage where
   you found it.

---

235. several: Different, diverse. **241. Cap'ring to eye:** Dancing for joy to see. **On a trice:** In an instant. **242. them:** I.e., the other crew members. **243. moping:** In a daze. **247. conduct:** Guide, leader. **249. infest:** Harass, disturb. **beating on:** Worrying about. **250. picked:** Chosen, convenient. **251. single:** I.e., by my own human powers. **resolve:** Satisfy, explain to. **252. probable:** Explicable, plausible. **252–253. of every These:** About every one of these. **253. accidents:** Occurrences. **254. well:** Favorably. **258. odd:** Unaccounted for. **259. shift:** Provide. **for all the rest:** Stephano drunkenly gets wrong the saying "Every man for himself." **261. Coraggio:** Courage. **bully monster:** Gallant monster (ironical). **262. true spies:** Accurate observers (i.e., sharp eyes). **264. brave:** Handsome. **265. fine:** Splendidly attired.

271. badges: Emblems of cloth or silver worn on the arms of retainers. (Prospero refers here to the stolen clothes as emblems of their villainy.) **272. true:** Honest. **275. deal . . . power:** Wield the moon's power, either without her authority or beyond her influence. **277. bastard:** Counterfeit. **279. own:** Recognize, admit as belonging to you. **283. reeling ripe:** Stumblingly drunk. **284. gilded:** (1) Flushed, made drunk; (2) covered with gilt (suggesting the horse urine in IV, i, 181–194, 199–200). **285. pickle:** (1) Fix, predicament; (2) pickling brine (in this case, horse urine). **288. flyblowing:** I.e., being fouled by fly eggs (from which he is saved by being pickled). **292. sirrah:** Standard form of address to an inferior, here expressing reprimand. **293. sore:** (1) Tyrannical; (2) sorry, inept; (3) wracked by pain. **299. trim:** Prepare, decorate.

305   **SEBASTIAN:** Or stole it rather.
                       [*Exeunt Caliban, Stephano, and Trinculo.*]
    PROSPERO: Sir, I invite Your Highness and your train
      To my poor cell, where you shall take your rest
      For this one night; which, part of it, I'll waste°
      With such discourse as, I not doubt, shall make
        it
310   Go quick away: the story of my life,
      And the particular accidents° gone by
      Since I came to this isle. And in the morn
      I'll bring you to your ship, and so to Naples,
      Where I have hope to see the nuptial
315   Of these our dear-belovèd solemnized;
      And thence retire me° to my Milan, where
      Every third thought shall be my grave.
    ALONSO: I long
      To hear the story of your life, which must
      Take° the ear strangely.
    PROSPERO: I'll deliver° all;
320   And promise you calm seas, auspicious gales,
      And sail so expeditious that shall catch
      Your royal fleet far off. [*Aside to Ariel.*] My
        Ariel, chick,
      That is thy charge. Then to the elements
      Be free, and fare thou well!—Please you, draw
        near.°

                           (*Exeunt omnes.*)

308. **waste:** Spend.   311. **accidents:** Occurrences.   316. **retire me:** Return.   319. **Take:** Take effect upon, enchant.   **deliver:** Declare, relate.   324. **draw near:** I.e., enter my cell.

EPILOGUE

(*Spoken by Prospero.*)

    Now my charms are all o'erthrown,
    And what strength I have 's mine own,
    Which is most faint. Now, 'tis true,
    I must be here confined by you
    Or sent to Naples. Let me not,   5
    Since I have my dukedom got
    And pardoned the deceiver, dwell
    In this bare island by your spell,
    But release me from my bands°
    With the help of your good hands.°   10
    Gentle breath° of yours my sails
    Must fill, or else my project fails,
    Which was to please. Now I want°
    Spirits to enforce,° art to enchant,
    And my ending is despair   15
    Unless I be relieved by prayer,°
    Which pierces so that it assaults°
    Mercy itself, and frees° all faults.
    As you from crimes° would pardoned be,
    Let your indulgence° set me free.   (*Exit.*) 20

Epilogue. 9. bands: Bonds. **10. hands:** I.e., applause (the noise of which would break the spell of silence). **11. Gentle breath:** Favorable breeze (produced by hands clapping or favorable comment). **13. want:** Lack. **14. enforce:** Control. **16. prayer:** I.e., Prospero's petition to the audience. **17. assaults:** Rightfully gains the attention of. **18. frees:** Obtains forgiveness for. **19. crimes:** Sins. **20. indulgence:** (1) Humoring, lenient approval; (2) remission of punishment for sin.

Shakespeare's *The Tempest*

Modern-day Shakespeareans find that *The Tempest*'s richness of characterization, impressive theatricality, and complex range of themes definitely support multiple critical perspectives. Early Shakespeare critics would have been surprised by current interpretations of *The Tempest* that posit colonialism as one of the primary themes of the play. Inspired as the play was by the colonizing efforts of the Virginia Company, such a reading is plausible. In these interpretations, Prospero is not seen primarily as a benevolent father or as a magnanimous and forgiving ruler who restores his uninvited guests to their previously "wrecked" ship. Instead, taking Caliban's island from him, putting Caliban into slavery, and demanding his obeisance cast Prospero as a representative of the Europeans who usurped the land of Native Americans and enslaved them.

In part because it is one of Shakespeare's shortest plays and in part because it contains a masterful masque, the wedding celebration for Ferdinand and Miranda, *The Tempest* has been thought of as an elaborate masque in its own right. All the action takes place in one location on one day, observing the Aristotelian unities. And because of Prospero's final speech, renouncing his magic, it has long been thought to be one of the only plays in which Shakespeare was being self-referential. Most early critics focused on the connection between Prospero's magic and Shakespeare's magic on stage. Shortly after writing this play, Shakespeare retired and left London to go home to Stratford, a move paralleling Prospero's return to Milan. Prospero claimed that "graves at my command / Have waked their sleepers," but as the modern critic Stephen Greenblatt says, "It is not Prospero, but Shakespeare who has commanded old Hamlet to burst from the grave."[1] In this sense, the play is not about occult magic, the kind that Sycorax is said to have derived from the devil, but about the dramatic magic that is characteristic of all theaters, in which illusion becomes reality while remaining illusion.

It was conventional for playwrights in Shakespeare's day to derive dramatic material from Italian, French, or other literary sources. Shakespeare's

[1]Stephen Greenblatt, *Will in the World* (New York: W. W. Norton, 2004), p. 376.

early plays about the kings of England relied on histories such as *Holinshed's Chronicles* to provide a structure for the poetry. Scholars have tracked down the original sources for all of Shakespeare's plays except *The Tempest,* which seems to be the only one that did not derive its inspiration from another text, although there are slight echoes of Michel de Montaigne's essay "Of the Cannibals," as well as a few borrowings in one of Prospero's speeches from Ovid's *Metamorphoses.* But scholars early on pointed to reports of a shipwreck that took place in 1610 on the island of Bermuda, which seems to be referenced when Ariel refers to "the still-vexed Bermudas" (I, ii, 230). William Strachey (1572–1621) was a passenger on the wrecked *Sea Venture* and wrote back to England to provide a record of the experience. His was not the only news of the wreck, but scholars have assumed that Shakespeare, who had a financial interest in the Virginia Company, which owned the *Sea Venture,* would have had access to Strachey's report, even though it was suppressed by the company, which did not want to spread bad news. However influential Strachey's report might have been, Shakespeare set his island in the Mediterranean, not in the New World.

Critics such as Samuel Taylor Coleridge and E. K. Chambers focused their comments on the characters in the play, noting, for example, that Ariel may represent the elements of air and fire, while Caliban may represent the elements of earth and water. The four elements were important matters for the early and late Renaissance mind, and accommodating them in a drama was always suggestive of a balance of forces in the universe.

For Robert Browning, Caliban was essentially a monster, part human and part supernatural as a spawn of Sycorax. His poem is a "reading" of Caliban through Caliban's efforts to conceive the nature of God. Browning's Caliban imagines Setebos to be much like himself, willful and capricious, vicious when it suits him, and yet much more powerful. This poem is an experiment in imagining a natural religion as a result of savage reflection. While it may be a critical comment on *The Tempest,* it is also a critical comment on some of the theological questions being raised in Victorian England and continental Europe during the period of great colonial expansion, when the religious beliefs of many non-Europeans were first examined.

Since the 1950s, the general force of critical commentary on the play has centered on issues of colonialism. Ariel seeks his freedom, which Prospero grants only after the tasks he puts him to are complete. Caliban, however, is considered subhuman, and his freedom occurs only with Prospero's abandonment of the island. Aimé Césaire rewrote the play to accommodate his colonialist interpretation of Caliban. Ania Loomba examines Caliban and Sycorax through the lens of colonialism, while Marjorie Garber gives us a contemporary view of the play that honors the complexities introduced by our modern attitudes toward it. Clearly the play can sustain a wide variety of interpretations and is rich enough to accommodate them all.

WILLIAM STRACHEY (1572–1621)

From True Repertory of the Wreck   1610

Strachey was a literary man in the sense that he associated with some of the best writers of the day, especially Ben Jonson, John Donne, John Marston, and George Chapman, all members of the unofficial "club" that met at the Mermaid Tavern. Shakespeare was also associated with that group. Strachey was traveling to Virginia in search of a fortune when the *Sea Venture* ran aground in Bermuda in 1609. Several reports of the event were published in 1610; Strachey's was circulated privately in July 1610. Shakespeare had various connections to the Virginia Company; because the plot of his play reflects events recounted by Strachey and his language is similar to Strachey's, it seems certain that Shakespeare knew of Strachey's report and used it as a source for *The Tempest*.

A most dreadful tempest, the manifold deaths whereof are here to the life described—Their wrack on Bermuda, and the description of those islands.

[. . .]

We had followed this course so long as now we were within seven or eight days at the most, by Captain Newport's reckoning, of making Cape Henry upon the coast of Virginia, when on Saint James his day, July 24, being Monday, preparing for no less all the black night before—the clouds gathering thick upon us, and the winds singing and whistling most unusually, which made us to cast off our pinnace, towing the same until then astern—a dreadful storm and hideous began to blow from out the northeast, which swelling and roaring, as it were, by fits, some hours with more violence than others, at length did beat all light from heaven, which like an hell of darkness turned black upon us, so much the more fuller of horror, as in such cases horror and fear use to overrun the troubled and overmastered senses of all, which, taken up with amazement, the ears-lay so sensible to the terrible cries and murmurs of the winds and distraction of our company, as who was most armed and best prepared was not a little shaken. For surely (noble lady) as death comes not so sudden nor apparent, so he comes not so elvish and painful to men, especially even then in health and perfect habitudes of body, as at sea; who comes at no time so welcome but our frailty (so weak is the hold of hope in miserable demonstrations of danger) it makes guilty of many contrary changes and conflicts. For indeed death is accompanied at no time nor place with circumstances every way so uncapable of particularities of goodness and inward comforts as at sea. For it is most true there arises commonly no such unmerciful tempest, compound of so many contrary and diverse nations, but that it works upon the whole frame of the body, and most loathsomely affects all the powers thereof. And the manner of the sickness it lays upon the body, being so unsufferable, gives not the mind any free and quiet time to use her judgment and empire. Which made the poet say,

> Hostium uxores puerique caecos
> sentiant motus orientis Haedi &
> aequoris nigri fiemitum & trementes
> verbere ripas°

For four and twenty hours the storm in a restless tumult had blown so exceedingly as we could not apprehend in our imaginations any possibility of greater violence. Yet did we still find it not only more terrible but more constant, fury added to fury, and one storm urging a second more outrageous than the former, whether it so wrought upon our fears or indeed met with new forces.

Sometimes strikes in our ship amongst women and passengers not used to such hurly and discomforts made us look one upon the other with troubled hearts and panting bosoms, our clamors drown'd in the winds, and the winds in thunder. Prayers might well be in the heart and lips, but drowned in the outcries of the officers, nothing heard that could give comfort, nothing seen that might encourage hope. It is impossible for me, had I the voice of Stentor, and expression of as many tongues as his throat of voices, to express the outcries and miseries, not languishing but wasting his spirits and art, constant to his own principles, but not prevailing.

Our sails, wound up, lay without their use. And if at any time we bore but a hullock, or half forecourse,° to guide her before the sea, six and sometimes eight men were not enough to hold the whipstaff in the steerage and the tiller below in the gunner room, by which may be imagined the strength of the storm in which the sea swelled above the clouds and gave battle unto heaven.

It could not be said to rain. The waters like whole rivers did flood in the air. And this I did still observe that whereas upon the land when a storm has poured itself forth once in drifts of rain, the wind, as beaten down and vanquished therewith, not long after endures. Here the glut of water, as if throttling the wind erewhile, was no sooner a little emptied and qualified but instantly the winds, as having gotten their mouths now free and at liberty, spake more loud, and grew more tumultuous and malignant. What shall I say?—Winds and seas were as mad as fury and rage could make them. For my own part, I had been in some storms before, as well upon the coast of Barbary and Algier in the Levant, and once more distressful in the Adriatic Gulf, in a bottom of Candy,° so as I may well say, *Ego quid sit ater Adriae novi sinus & quid albus peccet Iapex.°* Yet all that I had ever suffered gathered together might not hold comparison with this. There was not a moment in which the sudden splitting or instant oversetting of the ship was not expected.

Hostium . . . ripas: May our enemies' wives and children feel the blind motions of rising (Haedus) and the roaring of the black sea and the shore quaking with the blow. From Horace, *Europa Ode.*
forecourse: Storm sail.
Candy: Boat in Cyprus.
Ego . . . Iapex: I know what the black gulf of the Adriatic is like and the mischief of the white west-nor'wester.

Howbeit this was not all. It pleased God to bring a greater affliction yet upon us, for in the beginning of the storm we had received likewise a mighty leak, and the ship in every joint almost having spewed out her oakum before we were aware (a casualty more desperate than any other that a voyage by sea draws with it) was grown five foot suddenly deep with water above her ballast, and we almost drowned within while we sat looking when to perish from above. This imparting no less terror than danger ran through the whole ship with much fright and amazement, startled and turned the blood, and took down the braves of the most hardy mariner of them all, insomuch as he that before happily felt not the sorrow of others now began to sorrow for himself when he saw such a pond of water so suddenly broken in, and which he knew could not without present avoiding but instantly sink him, so as joining only for his own sake, not yet worth the saving in the public safety.

There might be seen master, master's mate, boatswain, quartermaster, coopers, carpenters, and who not with candles in their hands, creeping along the ribs viewing the sides, searching every corner, and listening in every place, if they could hear the water run. Many a weeping leak was this way found and hastily stop'd, and at length one in the gunner room made up with I know not how many pieces of beef. But all was to no purpose: The leak (if it were but one) which drunk in our greatest seas and took in our destruction fastest could not then be found, nor ever was, by any labor, counsel, or search. The waters still increasing, and the pumps going, which at length choked with bringing up whole and continual biscuit—and indeed all we had, ten thousand weight it was conceived as most likely that the leak might be sprung in the bread room, whereupon the carpenter went down and rip'd up all the room, but could not find it so.

[. . .]

We found it to be the dangerous and dreaded island, or rather islands, of the Bermuda, whereof let me give Your Ladyship a brief description before I proceed to my narration; and that the rather, because they be so terrible to all that ever touched on them, and such tempests, thunders, and other fearful objects are seen and heard about them that they be called commonly "the Devil's Islands," and are feared and avoided of all sea travelers alive above any other place in the world. Yet it pleased our merciful God to make even this hideous and hated place both the place of our safety and means of our deliverance.

And hereby also I hope to deliver the world from a foul and general error: it being counted of most that they can be no habitation for men, but rather given over to devils and wicked spirits; whereas indeed we find them now by experience to be as habitable and commodious as most countries of the same climate and situation, insomuch as if the entrance into them were as easy as the place itself is contenting, it had long ere this been inhabited as well as other islands. Thus shall we make it appear that truth is the daughter of time, and that men ought not to deny everything which is not subject to their own sense.

[. . .]

This being thus laid,° and by such a one who had gotten an opinion, as I before rememb'red, of religion (when it was declared by those two accusers), not knowing what further ground it had or accomplices, it pleased the governor to let this his factious offense to have a public affront and contestation by these two witnesses

---

This being thus laid: The reference is to Stephen Hopkins, who began a movement to undermine the governor's authority, the beginnings of a mutiny.

before the whole company, who at the tolling of a bell assembled before a *corps du guard,* where the prisoner was brought forth in manacles, and both accused and suffered to make at large to every particular his answer, which was only full of sorrow and tears, pleading simplicity and denial. But he being only found at this time both the captain and the follower of this mutiny, and generally held worthy to satisfy the punishment of his offense with the sacrifice of his life, our governor passed the sentence of a martial court upon him, such as belongs to mutiny and rebellion. But so penitent he was, and made so much moan, alleging the ruin of his wife and children in this his trespass, as it wrought in the hearts of all the better sort of the company, who therefore with humble entreaties and earnest supplications went unto our governor, whom they besought, as likewise did Captain Newport and myself, and never left him until we had got his pardon.

In these dangers and devilish disquiets, while the Almighty God wrought for us and sent us, miraculously delivered from the calamities of the sea, all blessings upon the shore to content and bind us to gratefulness, thus enraged amongst ourselves to the destruction each of other, into what a mischief and misery had we been given up had we not had a governor with his authority to have suppressed the same? Yet was there a worse practice, faction, and conjuration afoot, deadly and bloody, in which the life of our governor with many others were threat'ned, and could not but miscarry in his fall. But such is ever the will of God, who in the execution of His judgments breaks the firebrands upon the head of him who first kindles them!

There were who conceived that our governor indeed neither dared nor had authority to put in execution or pass the act of justice upon anyone, how treacherous or impious soever, their own opinions so much deceiving them for the unlawfulness of any act which they would execute, daring to justify among themselves that if they should be apprehended before the performance, they should happily suffer as martyrs. They persevered therefore not only to draw unto them such a number and associates as they could work into the abandoning of our governor and to the inhabiting of this island, they had now purposed (also) to have made a surprise of the storehouse, and to have forced from thence what was therein either of meal, cloth, cables, arms, sails, oars, or what else it pleased God that we had recovered from the wrack, and was to serve our general necessity and use, either for the relief of us while we stayed here, or for the carrying of us from this place again, when our pinnace should have been furnished.

But as all giddy and lawless attempts have always something of imperfection, and that as well by the property of the action, which holds of disobedience and rebellion (both full of fear), as through the ignorance of the devisers themselves; so in this, besides those defects, there were some of the association who, not strong enough fortified in their own conceits, broke from the plot itself and before the time was ripe for the execution thereof discovered the whole order and every agent and actor thereof; who nevertheless were not suddenly apprehended by reason the confederates were divided and separated in place, some with us, and the chief with Sir George Summers in his island and indeed all his whole company, but good watch passed upon them, every man from thenceforth commanded to wear his weapon, without which before we freely walked from quarter to quarter and conversed among ourselves, and every man advised to stand upon his guard, his own life not being in safety while his next neighbor was not to be trusted.

The sentinels and nightwarders doubled, the passages of both the quarters were carefully observed, by which means nothing was further attempted until a gentleman amongst them, one Henry Paine, the thirteenth of March full of mischief and every hour preparing something or other, stealing swords, adzes, axes, hatchets, saws, augers, planes, mallets, etc. to make good his own bad end his watch night coming about, and being called by the captain of the same to be upon the guard, did not only give his said commander evil language but struck at him, doubled his blows, and when he was not suffered to close with him, went off the guard, scoffing at the double diligence and attendance of the watch appointed by the governor for much purpose, as he said. Upon which the watch telling him if the governor should understand of this his insolence, it might turn him to much blame, and happily be as much as his life were worth, the said Paine replied with a settled and bitter violence, and in such unreverent terms as I should offend the modest ear too much to express it in his own phrase, but the contents were how that the governor had no authority of that quality to justify upon anyone, how mean soever in the colony, an action of that nature, and therefore let the governor (said he) kiss, etc. Which words being with the omitted additions brought the next day unto every common and public discourse, at length they were delivered over to the governor, who examining well the fact the transgression so much the more exemplary and odious as being in a dangerous time, in a confederate, and the success of the same wish'dly listened after with a doubtful conceit what might be the issue of so notorious a boldness and impudency, calling the said Paine before him and the whole company, where, being soon convinced both by the witness of the commander, and many which were upon the watch with him, our governor, who had now the eyes of the whole colony fixed upon him, condemned him to be instantly hanged; and the ladder being ready, after he had made many confessions, he earnestly desired, being a gentleman, that he might be shot to death; and towards the evening he had his desire, the sun and his life setting together.

MICHEL EYQUEM DE MONTAIGNE (1533–1592)

From Of the Cannibals   1580

Montaigne became famous for his essays, which he and his younger contemporary Francis Bacon elevated to the state of literature. Montaigne was enormously influential in Shakespeare's time, especially after John Florio (1553–1625) translated his work in 1603. In this essay, Montaigne discusses the American Indians and their ways of living, as reported by numerous travelers of the age. The passage refers to the occasional habit of eating the flesh of defeated warriors and details some cultural habits of the "savages" of the New World.

They war against the nations that lie beyond their mountains, to which they go naked, having no other weapons than bows or wooden swords, sharp at one end as our broaches are. It is an admirable thing to see the constant resolution of their combats, which never end but by effusion of blood and murder; for they know not what fear or routs are. Every victor brings home the head of the enemy he hath slain as a trophy of his victory and fasteneth the same at the entrance of his dwelling place. After they have long time used and treated their prisoners well and with all commodities they can devise, he that is the master of them, summoning a great assembly of his acquaintance, tieth a cord to one of the prisoner's arms, by the end whereof he holds him fast, with some distance from him for fear he might offend him, and giveth the other arm, bound in like manner, to the dearest friend he hath, and both in the presence of all the assembly kill him with swords. Which done, they roast and then eat him in common and send some slices of him to such of their friends as are absent. It is not, as some imagine, to nourish themselves with it (as anciently the Scythians wont to do), but to represent an extreme and inexpiable revenge.

Which we prove thus: Some of them perceiving the Portugals, who had confederated themselves with their adversaries, to use another kind of death when they took them prisoners—which was to bury them up to the middle, and against the upper part of the body to shoot arrows, and then being almost dead, to hang them up—they supposed that these people of the other world (as they who had sowed the knowledge of many vices amongst their neighbors and were much more cunning in all kinds of evils and mischief than they) undertook not this manner of revenge without cause, and that consequently it was more smartful and cruel than theirs, and thereupon began to leave their old fashion to follow this.

I am not sorry we note the barbarous horror of such an action, but grieved that, prying so narrowly into their faults, we are so blinded in ours. I think there is more barbarism in eating men alive than to feed upon them being dead; to mangle by tortures and torments a body full of lively sense, to roast him in pieces, to make dogs and swine to gnaw and tear him in mammocks° (as we have not only read but seen very lately, yea and [in] our own memory, not amongst ancient enemies but our neighbors and fellow-citizens; and, which is worse, under pretense of piety and religion), than to roast and eat him after he is dead.

Chrysippus and Zeno, archpillars of the Stoic sect, have supposed that it was no hurt at all, in time of need and to what end soever, to make use of our carrion bodies and to feed upon them, as did our forefathers who, being besieged by Caesar in the city of Alexia, resolved to sustain the famine of the siege with the bodies of old men, women, and other persons unserviceable and unfit to fight.

> Gascons (as fame reports)
> Lived with meats of such sorts.
> Juven. *Sat.* XV.93.

And physicians fear not, in all kinds of compositions availful to our health, to make use of it, be it for outward or inward applications. But there was never any opinion found so unnatural and immodest that would excuse treason, treachery, disloyalty, tyranny, cruelty, and suchlike, which are our ordinary faults.

We may then well call them barbarous in regard of reason's rules, but not in respect of us that exceed them in all kind of barbarism. Their wars are noble and generous and have as much excuse and beauty as this human infirmity may admit; they aim at nought so much, and have no other foundation amongst them, but the mere jealousy of virtue. They contend not for the gaining of new lands; for to this day they yet enjoy that natural uberty° and fruitfulness which without laboring toil doth in such plenteous abundance furnish them with all necessary things that they need not enlarge their limits. They are yet in that happy estate as they desire no more than what their natural necessities direct them. Whatsoever is beyond it is to them superfluous. Those that are much about one age do generally inter-call one another

---

mammocks: Shreds.
uberty: Abundance.

brethren, and such as are younger they call children, and the aged are esteemed as fathers to all the rest. These leave this full possession of goods in common and without division to their heirs, without other claim or title but that which nature doth plainly impart unto all creatures, even as she brings them into the world. If their neighbors chance to come over the mountains to assail or invade them, and that they get the victory over them, the victors' conquest is glory and the advantage to be and remain superior in valor and virtue; else have they nothing to do with the goods and spoils of the vanquished, and so return into their country, where they neither want any necessary thing nor lack this great portion, to know how to enjoy their condition happily, and are contented with what nature affordeth them. So do these when their turn cometh. They require no other ransom of their prisoners but an acknowledgment and confession that they are vanquished. And in a whole age a man shall not find one that doth not rather embrace death than either by word or countenance remissly to yield one jot of an invincible courage. There is none seen that would not rather be slain and devoured than sue for life or show any fear. They use their prisoners with all liberty, that they may so much the more hold their lives dear and precious, and commonly entertain them with threats of future death, with the torments they shall endure, with the preparations intended for that purpose, with mangling and slicing of their members, and with the feast that shall be kept at their charge. All which is done to wrest some remiss and exact some faint-yielding speech of submission from them, or to possess them with a desire to escape or run away; that so they may have the advantage to have daunted and made them afraid and to have forced their constancy. For certainly true victory consisteth in that only point.

SAMUEL TAYLOR COLERIDGE (1772–1834)

From The Lectures of 1811–1812, Lecture IX   1812

Coleridge was one of the great Romantic poets, author of *The Rime of the Ancient Mariner, Kubla Khan,* and, with William Wordsworth, the volume *Lyrical Ballads*. In addition to being a major poet, Coleridge was a gifted critic and one of the most profound of Shakespeare interpreters. His lectures, delivered in London between 1810 and 1820, are credited with energizing nineteenth-century interest in Shakespeare, especially *Hamlet*. His comments here about Ariel emphasize that spirit's bondage to Prospero, and those about Miranda emphasize her wonder. Coleridge focuses on a quotation much ridiculed by Alexander Pope (1688–1744) in his critical poem *Peri Bathos, or The Art of Sinking in Poetry*.

But to return to *The Tempest,* and to the wondrous creation of Ariel. If a doubt could ever be entertained whether Shakespeare was a great poet, acting upon laws arising out of his own nature and not without law, as has sometimes been idly asserted, that doubt must be removed by the character of Ariel. The very first words uttered by this being introduce the spirit, not as an angel, above man; not a gnome, or a fiend, below man; but while the poet gives him the faculties and the advantages of reason, he divests him of all mortal character, not positively, it is true, but negatively. In air he lives, from air he derives his being, in air he acts; and all his colors and properties seem to have been obtained from the rainbow and the skies. There is nothing about Ariel that cannot be conceived to exist either at sunrise or at sunset: hence all that belongs to Ariel belongs to the delight the mind is capable of receiving from the most lovely external appearances. His answers to Prospero are directly to the question and nothing beyond; or where he expatiates, which is not unfrequently, it is to himself and upon his own delights, or upon the unnatural situation in which he is placed, though under a kindly power and to good ends.

Shakespeare has properly made Ariel's very first speech characteristic of him. After he has described the manner in which he had raised the storm and produced its harmless consequences, we find that Ariel is discontented—that he has been freed, it is true, from a cruel confinement, but still that he is bound to obey Prospero and to execute any commands imposed upon him. We feel that such a state of bondage is almost unnatural to him, yet we see that it is delightful for him to be so employed. It is as if we were to command one of the winds in a different direction to that which nature dictates, or one of the waves, now rising and now sinking, to recede before it bursts upon the shore: such is the feeling we experience, when we learn that a being like Ariel is commanded to fulfill any mortal behest.

When, however, Shakespeare contrasts the treatment of Ariel by Prospero with that of Sycorax, we are sensible that the liberated spirit ought to be grateful, and Ariel does feel and acknowledge the obligation; he immediately assumes the airy being, with a mind so elastically correspondent that when once a feeling has passed from it, not a trace is left behind.

Is there anything in nature from which Shakespeare caught the idea of this delicate and delightful being, with such childlike simplicity, yet with such preternatural powers? He is neither born of heaven, nor of earth; but, as it were, between both, like a May blossom kept suspended in air by the fanning breeze, which prevents it from falling to the ground, and only finally, and by compulsion, touching earth. This reluctance of the sylph to be under the command even of Prospero is kept up through the whole play, and in the exercise of his admirable judgment Shakespeare has availed himself of it in order to give Ariel an interest in the event, looking forward to that moment when he was to gain his last and only reward—simple and eternal liberty.

Another instance of admirable judgment and excellent preparation is to be found in the creature contrasted with Ariel—Caliban, who is described in such a manner by Prospero as to lead us to expect the appearance of a foul, unnatural monster. He is not seen at once: his voice is heard; this is the preparation; he was too offensive to be seen first in all his deformity, and in nature we do not receive so much disgust from sound as from sight. After we have heard Caliban's voice he does not enter until Ariel has entered like a water nymph. All the strength of contrast is thus acquired without any of the shock of abruptness, or of that unpleasant sensation, which we experience when the object presented is in any way hateful to our vision.

The character of Caliban is wonderfully conceived: he is a sort of creature of the earth, as Ariel is a sort of creature of the air. He partakes of the qualities of the brute, but is distinguished from brutes in two ways: by having mere understanding without moral reason; and by not possessing the instincts which pertain to absolute animals. Still, Caliban is in some respects a noble being: the poet has raised him far above contempt: he is a man in the sense of the imagination: all the images he uses are drawn from nature and are highly poetical; they fit in with the images of Ariel. Caliban gives us images from the earth, Ariel images from the air. Caliban talks of the difficulty of finding fresh water, of the situation of morasses, and of other circumstances which even brute instinct, without reason, could comprehend. No mean figure is employed, no mean passion displayed, beyond animal passion and repugnance to command.

The manner in which the lovers are introduced is equally wonderful, and it is the last point I shall now mention in reference to this, almost miraculous, drama. The same judgment is observable in every scene, still preparing, still inviting, and still gratifying, like a finished piece of music. I have omitted to notice one thing, and you must give me leave to advert to it before I proceed: I mean the conspiracy against the life of Alonzo. I want to show you how well the poet prepares the feelings of the reader for this plot, which was to execute the most detestable of all crimes, and which, in another play, Shakespeare has called "the murder of sleep."

Antonio and Sebastian at first had no such intention: it was suggested by the magical sleep cast on Alonzo and Gonzalo; but they are previously introduced scoffing and scorning at what was said by others, without regard to age or situation—without any sense of admiration for the excellent truths they heard delivered, but giving themselves up entirely to the malignant and unsocial feeling which induced them to listen to everything that was said, not for the sake of profiting by the learning and experience of others, but of hearing something that might gratify vanity and self-love, by making them believe that the person speaking was inferior to themselves.

This, let me remark, is one of the grand characteristics of a villain; and it would not be so much a presentiment as an anticipation of hell for men to suppose that all mankind were as wicked as themselves, or might be so, if they were not too great fools. Pope, you are perhaps aware, objected to this conspiracy; but in my mind, if it could be omitted, the play would lose a charm which nothing could supply.

Many, indeed innumerable, beautiful passages might be quoted from this play, independently of the astonishing scheme of its construction. Everybody will call to mind the grandeur of the language of Prospero in that divine speech, where he takes leave of his magic art; and were I to indulge myself by repetitions of the kind, I should descend from the character of a lecturer to that of a mere reciter. Before I terminate, I may particularly recall one short passage which has fallen under the very severe, but inconsiderate, censure of Pope and Arbuthnot, who pronounce it a piece of the grossest bombast. Prospero thus addresses his daughter, directing her attention to Ferdinand:

> The fringed curtains of thine eye advance,
> And say what thou seest yond.

Taking these words as a periphrase of—"Look what is coming yonder," it certainly may to some appear to border on the ridiculous and to fall under the rule I formerly laid down—that whatever, without injury, can be translated into a foreign language in simple terms, ought to be in simple terms in the original language; but it is to be borne in mind that different modes of expression frequently arise from difference of situation and education: a blackguard would use very different words, to express the same thing, to those a gentleman would employ, yet both would be natural and proper; difference of feeling gives rise to difference of language: a gentleman speaks in polished terms, with due regard to his own rank and position, while a blackguard, a person little better than half a brute, speaks like half a brute, showing no respect for himself nor for others.

But I am content to try the lines I have just quoted by the introduction to them; and then, I think, you will admit, that nothing could be more fit and appropriate than such language. How does Prospero introduce them? He has just told Miranda a wonderful story, which deeply affected her and filled her with surprise and astonishment, and for his own purposes he afterwards lulls her to sleep. When she awakes, Shakespeare has made her wholly inattentive to the present, but wrapped up in the past. An actress who understands the character of Miranda would have her eyes cast down and her eyelids almost covering them, while she was, as it were, living in her dream. At this moment Prospero sees Ferdinand and wishes to point him out to his daughter, not only with great, but with scenic solemnity, he standing before her and before the spectator in the dignified character of a great magician. Something was to appear to Miranda on the sudden, and as unexpectedly as if the hero of a drama were to be on the stage at the instant when the curtain is elevated. It is under such circumstances that Prospero says, in a tone calculated at once to arouse his daughter's attention,

> The fringed curtains of thine eye advance,
> And say what thou seest yond.

Turning from the sight of Ferdinand to his thoughtful daughter, his attention was first struck by the downcast appearance of her eyes and eyelids; and, in my humble opinion, the solemnity of the phraseology assigned to Prospero is completely in character, recollecting his preternatural capacity, in which the most familiar objects in nature present themselves in a mysterious point of view. It is much easier to find fault with a writer by reference to former notions and experience than to sit down and read him, recollecting his purpose, connecting one feeling with another, and judging of his words and phrases in proportion as they convey the sentiments of the persons represented.

Of Miranda we may say that she possesses in herself all the ideal beauties that could be imagined by the greatest poet of any age or country; but it is not my purpose now so much to point out the high poetic powers of Shakespeare as to illustrate his exquisite judgment, and it is solely with this design that I have noticed a passage with which, it seems to me, some critics, and those among the best, have been unreasonably dissatisfied. If Shakespeare be the wonder of the ignorant, he is, and ought to be, much more the wonder of the learned: not only from profundity of thought, but from his astonishing and intuitive knowledge of what man must be at all times and under all circumstances, he is rather to be looked upon as a prophet than as a poet. Yet, with all these unbounded powers, with all this might and majesty of genius, he makes us feel as if he were unconscious of himself and of his high destiny, disguising the half god in the simplicity of a child.

ROBERT BROWNING (1812–1889)

Caliban upon Setebos; or, Natural Theology in the Island   1864

Robert Browning was the most important English poet of his time. One of his specialties was the dramatic monologue, a poem spoken by the protagonist directly to the audience. A dramatic monologue is much like one of Hamlet's soliloquies except that the reader is alone "listening" to the monologue rather than seeing it spoken on stage. Browning, affected by public discussions of Darwin's theory (which had been published in 1859), treats Caliban as a primitive "missing link" who tries to conceive the nature of Setebos, his god. In his search for understanding of theology, Caliban speaks of himself in the third person, then in the first person singular and plural. He imagines Setebos is much like him: whimsical, cruel when necessary, and essentially arbitrary.

'Thou thoughtest that I was altogether such a one as thyself.'

(David, Psalms 50:21)

['Will sprawl, now that the heat of day is best,
Flat on his belly in the pit's much mire,
With elbows wide, fists clenched to prop his chin.
And, while he kicks both feet in the cool slush,
And feels about his spine small eft-things course,
Run in and out each arm, and make him laugh:
And while above his head a pompion-plant,
Coating the cave-top as a brow its eye,
Creeps down to touch and tickle hair and beard,
10   And now a flower drops with a bee inside,
And now a fruit to snap at, catch and crunch,—
He looks out o'er yon sea which sunbeams cross
And recross till they weave a spider-web
(Meshes of fire, some great fish breaks at times)
And talks to his own self, howe'er he please,
Touching that other, whom his dam called God.
Because to talk about Him, vexes—ha,
Could He but know! and time to vex is now,
When talk is safer than in winter-time.
20   Moreover Prosper and Miranda sleep
In confidence he drudges at their task,
And it is good to cheat the pair, and gibe,
Letting the rank tongue blossom into speech.]

Setebos, Setebos, and Setebos!
'Thinketh, He dwelleth i' the cold o' the moon.

'Thinketh He made it, with the sun to match,
But not the stars; the stars came otherwise;
Only made clouds, winds, meteors, such as that:
Also this isle, what lives and grows thereon,
30   And snaky sea which rounds and ends the same.

'Thinketh, it came of being ill at ease:
He hated that He cannot change His cold,
Nor cure its ache. 'Hath spied an icy fish
That longed to 'scape the rock-stream where she lived,
And thaw herself within the lukewarm brine
O' the lazy sea her stream thrusts far amid,
A crystal spike 'twixt two warm walls of wave;
Only, she ever sickened, found repulse
At the other kind of water, not her life
40   (Green-dense and dim-delicious, bred o' the sun)
Flounced back from bliss she was not born to breathe,
And in her old bounds buried her despair,
Hating and loving warmth alike: so He.

'Thinketh, He made thereat the sun, this isle,
Trees and the fowls here, beast and creeping thing.
Yon otter, sleek-wet, black, lithe as a leech;
Yon auk, one fire-eye in a ball of foam,
That floats and feeds; a certain badger brown
He hath watched hunt with that slant white-wedge eye

By moonlight; and the pie with the long tongue   50
That pricks deep into oakwarts for a worm,
And says a plain word when she finds her prize,
But will not eat the ants; the ants themselves
That build a wall of seeds and settled stalks
About their hole—He made all these and more,
Made all we see, and us, in spite: how else?
He could not, Himself, make a second self
To be His mate; as well have made Himself:
He would not make what he mislikes or slights,
An eyesore to Him, or not worth His pains: 60
But did, in envy, listlessness or sport,
Make what Himself would fain, in a manner, be—
Weaker in most points, stronger in a few,
Worthy, and yet mere playthings all the while,
Things He admires and mocks too,—that is it.

Because, so brave, so better though they be,
It nothing skills if He begin to plague.
Look now, I melt a gourd-fruit into mash,
Add honeycomb and pods, I have perceived,
Which bite like finches when they bill and kiss,—   70
Then, when froth rises bladdery, drink up all,
Quick, quick, till maggots scamper through my brain;
Last, throw me on my back i' the seeded thyme,
And wanton, wishing I were born a bird.
Put case, unable to be what I wish,
I yet could make a live bird out of clay:
Would not I take clay, pinch my Caliban
Able to fly?—for, there, see, he hath wings,
And great comb like the hoopoe's to admire,
And there, a sting to do his foes offence,   80
There, and I will that he begin to live,
Fly to yon rock-top, nip me off the horns
Of grigs high up that make the merry din,
Saucy through their veined wings, and mind me not.
In which feat, if his leg snapped, brittle clay,
And he lay stupid-like,—why, I should laugh;
And if he, spying me, should fall to weep,
Beseech me to be good, repair his wrong,
Bid his poor leg smart less or grow again,–
Well, as the chance were, this might take or else   90
Not take my fancy: I might hear his cry,
And give the mankin three sound legs for one,
Or pluck the other off, leave him like an egg,
And lessoned he was mine and merely clay.
Were this no pleasure, lying in the thyme,
Drinking the mash, with brain become alive,
Making and marring clay at will? So He.

'Thinketh, such shows nor right nor wrong in Him,
Nor kind, nor cruel: He is strong and Lord.
'Am strong myself compared to yonder crabs   100
That march now from the mountain to the sea,
'Let twenty pass, and stone the twenty-first,
Loving not, hating not, just choosing so.
'Say, the first straggler that boasts purple spots
Shall join the file, one pincer twisted off;
'Say, this bruised fellow shall receive a worm,
And two worms he whose nippers end in red;
As it likes me each time, I do: so He.

Well then, 'supposeth He is good i' the main,
110   Placable if His mind and ways were guessed,
But rougher than His handiwork, be sure!
Oh, He hath made things worthier than Himself,
And envieth that, so helped, such things do more
Than He who made them! What consoles but this?
That they, unless through Him, do naught at all,
And must submit: what other use in things?
'Hath cut a pipe of pithless elder-joint
That, blown through, gives exact the scream o' the jay
When from her wing you twitch the feathers blue:
120   Sound this, and little birds that hate the jay
Flock within stone's throw, glad their foe is hurt:
Put case such pipe could prattle and boast forsooth
'I catch the birds, I am the crafty thing,
I make the cry my maker cannot make
With his great round mouth; he must blow through mine!'
Would not I smash it with my foot? So He.

But wherefore rough, why cold and ill at ease?
Aha, that is a question! Ask, for that,
What knows,—the something over Setebos
130   That made Him, or He, may be, found and fought,
Worsted, drove off and did to nothing, perchance.
There may be something quiet o'er His head,
Out of His reach, that feels nor joy nor grief,
Since both derive from weakness in some way.
I joy because the quails come; would not joy
Could I bring quails here when I have a mind:
This Quiet, all it hath a mind to, doth.
'Esteemeth stars the outposts of its couch,
But never spends much thought nor care that way.
140   It may look up, work up,—the worse for those
It works on! 'Careth but for Setebos
The many-handed as a cuttle-fish,
Who, making Himself feared through what He does,
Looks up, first, and perceives he cannot soar
To what is quiet and hath happy life;
Next looks down here, and out of very spite
Makes this a bauble-world to ape yon real,
These good things to match those as hips do grapes.
'Tis solace making baubles, ay, and sport.
150   Himself peeped late, eyed Prosper at his books
Careless and lofty, lord now of the isle:
Vexed, 'stitched a book of broad leaves, arrow-shaped,
Wrote thereon, he knows what, prodigious words;
Has peeled a wand and called it by a name;
Weareth at whiles for an enchanter's robe
The eyed skin of a supple oncelot;
And hath an ounce sleeker than youngling mole,
A four-legged serpent he makes cower and couch,
Now snarl, now hold its breath and mind his eye,
160   And saith she is Miranda and my wife:
'Keeps for his Ariel a tall pouch-bill crane
He bids go wade for fish and straight disgorge;
Also a sea-beast, lumpish, which he snared,
Blinded the eyes of, and brought somewhat tame,
And split its toe-webs, and now pens the drudge
In a hole o' the rock and calls him Caliban;
A bitter heart that bides its time and bites.

'Plays thus at being Prosper in a way,
Taketh his mirth with make-believes: so He.

His dam held that the Quiet made all things   170
Which Setebos vexed only: 'holds not so.
Who made them weak, meant weakness He might vex.
Had He meant other, while His hand was in,
Why not make horny eyes no thorn could prick,
Or plate my scalp with bone against the snow,
Or overscale my flesh 'neath joint and joint,
Like an orc's armour? Ay,—so spoil His sport!
He is the One now: only He doth all.

'Saith, He may like, perchance, what profits Him.
Ay, himself loves what does him good; but why?   180
'Gets good no otherwise. This blinded beast
Loves whoso places flesh-meat on his nose,
But, had he eyes, would want no help, but hate
Or love, just as it liked him: He hath eyes.
Also it pleaseth Setebos to work,
Use all His hands, and exercise much craft,
By no means for the love of what is worked.
'Tasteth, himself, no finer good i' the world
When all goes right, in this safe summer-time,
And he wants little, hungers, aches not much,   190
Than trying what to do with wit and strength.
'Falls to make something: 'piled yon pile of turfs,
And squared and stuck mere squares of soft white chalk,
And, with a fish-tooth, scratched a moon on each,
And set up endwise certain spikes of tree,
And crowned the whole with a sloth's skull a-top,
Found dead i' the woods, too hard for one to kill.
No use at all i' the work, for work's sole sake;
'Shall some day knock it down again: so He.

'Saith He is terrible: watch His feats in proof!   200
One hurricane will spoil six good months' hope.
He hath a spite against me, that I know,
Just as He favours Prosper, who knows why?
So it is, all the same, as well I find.
'Wove wattles half the winter, fenced them firm
With stone and stake to stop she-tortoises
Crawling to lay their eggs here: well, one wave,
Feeling the foot of Him upon its neck,
Gaped as a snake does, lolled out its large tongue,
And licked the whole labour flat: so much for spite.   210
'Saw a ball flame down late (yonder it lies)
Where, half an hour before, I slept i' the shade:
Often they scatter sparkles: there is force!
'Dug up a newt He may have envied once
And turned to stone, shut up inside a stone.
Please Him and hinder this?—What Prosper does?
Aha, if He would tell me how! Not He!
There is the sport: discover how or die!
All need not die, for of the things o' the isle
Some flee afar, some dive, some run up trees;   220
Those at His mercy,—why, they please Him most
When . . . when . . . well, never try the same way twice!
Repeat what act has pleased, He may grow wroth.
You must not know His ways, and play Him off,

Sure of the issue. 'Doth the like himself:
'Spareth a squirrel that it nothing fears
But steals the nut from underneath my thumb,
And when I threat, bites stoutly in defence:
'Spareth an urchin that contrariwise,
230   Curls up into a ball, pretending death
For fright at my approach: the two ways please.
But what would move my choler more than this,
That either creature counted on its life
Tomorrow and next day and all days to come,
Saying, forsooth, in the inmost of its heart,
'Because he did so yesterday with me,
And otherwise with such another brute,
So must he do henceforth and always.'—Ay?
Would teach the reasoning couple what 'must' means!
240   'Doth as he likes, or wherefore Lord? So He.

'Conceiveth all things will continue thus,
And we shall have to live in fear of Him
So long as He lives, keeps His strength: no change,
If He have done His best, make no new world
To please Him more, so leave off watching this, –
If He surprise not even the Quiet's self
Some strange day,—or, suppose, grow into it
As grubs grow butterflies: else, here are we,
And there is He, and nowhere help at all.
250   'Believeth with the life, the pain shall stop.
His dam held different, that after death
He both plagued enemies and feasted friends:
Idly! He doth His worst in this our life,
Giving just respite lest we die through pain,
Saving last pain for worst,—with which, an end.
Meanwhile, the best way to escape His ire
Is, not to seem too happy. 'Sees, himself,
Yonder two flies, with purple films and pink,
Bask on the pompion-bell above: kills both.
260   'Sees two black painful beetles roll their ball
On head and tail as if to save their lives:
Moves them the stick away they strive to clear.

Even so, 'would have Him misconceive, suppose
This Caliban strives hard and ails no less,
And always, above all else, envies Him;
Wherefore he mainly dances on dark nights,
Moans in the sun, gets under holes to laugh,
And never speaks his mind save housed as now:
Outside, 'groans, curses. If He caught me here,
270   O'erheard this speech, and asked 'What chuckles at?'
'Would, to appease Him, cut a finger off,
Or of my three kid yearlings burn the best,
Or let the toothsome apples rot on tree,
Or push my tame beast for the ore to taste:
While myself lit a fire, and made a song
And sung it, '*What I hate, be consecrate*
To celebrate Thee and Thy state, no mate
For Thee; what see for envy in poor me?'
Hoping the while, since evils sometimes mend,
280   Warts rub away and sores are cured with slime,
That some strange day, will either the Quiet catch
And conquer Setebos, or likelier He

Decrepit may doze, doze, as good as die.

[What, what? A curtain o'er the world at once!
Crickets stop hissing; not a bird—or, yes,
There scuds His raven that has told Him all!
It was fool's play, this prattling! Ha! The wind
Shoulders the pillared dust, death's house o' the move,
And fast invading fires begin! White blaze—
A tree's head snaps—and there, there, there, there, there,   290
His thunder follows! Fool to gibe at Him!
Lo! 'Lieth flat and loveth Setebos!
'Maketh his teeth meet through his upper lip,
Will let those quails fly, will not eat this month
One little mess of whelks, so he may 'scape!]

E. K. CHAMBERS (1866–1954)

The Tempest   1925

E. K. Chambers is considered one of the most important scholars of Medieval and Renaissance drama. His several volumes on Shakespeare are still important enough to influence twenty-first-century writers on Shakespeare's work. His brief essay on *The Tempest* is drawn from *Shakespeare: A Survey*, in which he devotes a chapter to each play. His critical analysis in the following essay aims at forming a link between Shakespeare the dramatist and Prospero the magician. He sees Shakespeare bidding playwriting a farewell just as Prospero bids magic farewell. Ariel may be the spirit of poetry, but Caliban is an "earthy" creature, similar to those for whom the missionaries labored tirelessly.

The Tempest, among Shakespeare's later plays, is a counterpart to the *Midsummer Night's Dream* of his lyric youth. Here, too, is a dream, or, if you will, a fairy tale, in which the protagonists are not men and women but imagined beings, taken partly from folk-belief and partly from literature, to be the symbols of forces dimly perceived by the poet as ruling that life, which is itself, after all, in another degree, but such stuff as dreams are made on. And, like *A Midsummer Night's Dream*, the play must interest the spectator less through a strictly dramatic appeal to his emotions, than by the strange romantic charm of its setting and its sensuous realization of the delicate and the grotesque in the mysterious personages whom it brings before him. It is, in fact, to be classed as dramatic *spectacle* rather than as drama proper, and the elaboration with which it has been put upon the stage by modern managers may be regarded as not, in this case, wholly out of keeping with the intention of the dramatist.

Apart, indeed, from its Ariel and its Caliban, and tried by the too rigid conception of drama which is blind to everything except just the interplay of human characters in action, *The Tempest* certainly fails to answer satisfactorily to the test. The practical omnipotence which Prospero derives from his magic arts takes all vitality from the plots which he unravels and from the conflict between hero and villains which they represent. And, unless you are sentimentalist inveterate, your emotions will not be more than faintly stirred by the blameless loves at first sight of Ferdinand and Miranda, or by the quite superfluous obstacles, hollow as the property logs that Ferdinand must carry, which are put in their way by the heavy father. The inexperienced but peerless maiden, advancing the fringed curtains of her eyes upon the "brave new world that hath such people in it," only to have them dazzled by the first male being that crossed her path; the gallant but patient lover, of whom she very truly says, "Nothing natural I ever saw so noble"; they have much to answer for, it is to be feared, in the later development of rose-pink drawing-room fiction. Perhaps it would be a little hard to bear them a grudge for this. But even if they are not responsible for their great-great-grandchildren, do they not themselves share something of the colour-less insipidity of their great-great-grandfather and grandmother, Daphnis and Chloe? And if you accept Miranda as a "nonpareil" and "the top of admiration" is it not rather because Shakespeare himself, through the mouths of Prospero and Ferdinand, tells you that that is what she is, than because of anything that she says or does as she stands before you? The device is an effective one in the hands of the novelist; but it is less available for the dramatist, who cannot, after all, escape from sooner or later producing his puppets, and making them speak and act for themselves upon his stage. Incidentally, it is a little curious to observe how the type of Shakespeare's women varies at different periods of his career. Miranda, Imogen, Perdita; set them against Rosalind, Beatrice, Helena. Is one to suppose that Shakespeare, like many more recent dramatists, found himself obliged to write "round" the personality of the "leading lady," who starred it for the time being in his company? Or is he merely following the wavering of the modish taste in heroines, a taste set perhaps, as some think, during the period of his final plays, by the sentimental tragicomedies of Beaumont and Fletcher?°

But if *The Tempest* is not exactly a slice cut straight from the red heart of humanity, still less can it be reasonably interpreted as a deliberate and consistent allegory. To prove, for example, in detail that it is not a formal exposition of the Baconian philosophy would carry me into regions of controversy which I do not propose, now or at any other time, to tread. The dream-formula is the true one. The play is no more than a dream, and as such dispensed from any obligation to logical completeness or continuity; an iridescent bubble, shot across by divers threads of symbolism and suggestion, independent of one other, but all reflecting tendencies of thought and feeling which were dominant in the mind of the poet at the time of its composition. Some of these tendencies may perhaps be indicated without breaking down the filmy texture of fancy by too heavy a burden of external comment.

That the general drift and structure of the play are peculiarly characteristic of Shake-speare's later mood of serene optimism, and that the invincible Prospero, biding his time to charm good out of ill and to make the odds all even, is in particular a kind of concrete embodiment of Providence, have become commonplaces of criticism. I need not labour them, or dwell upon the contrast between the spiritual temper which finds such expres-sion and that which gave birth to the Titanic tragedies of *Macbeth* and *King Lear*. It is one which makes its first appearance in *Pericles*, and dominates *Cymbeline* and *The Winter's Tale*, as well as *The Tempest*. Further, one may readily agree with those who think that the play was written with an eye to the conditions of a court entertainment, rather than to those of the public stage. It is, in fact, a glorified mask. The ship of the first scene repre-sents the "pageant" of carpenter's work, commonly introduced into such devices, and the dances, songs, and disguises of Ariel and his company are balanced, as in an anti-mask, by the clumsy revels of Stephano and his reeling-ripe fellows. The character of the formal mask introduced into the Fourth Act suggests a wedding, and at a Jacobean wedding the plain-spokenness of Prospero's sermon to the lovers would perhaps be neither intolerable nor uncalled for. The parallel to *A Midsummer Night's Dream*, probably performed at a

---

Beaumont and Fletcher: Francis Beaumont (1584–1616) and John Fletcher (1579–1625) were a popular team of playwrights who, along with their works, were known to Shakespeare.

court wedding in 1594 or 1595, and ending with an epithalamium,° is in this point exact. *The Tempest* is known to have been presented before the Princess Elizabeth, afterwards the unfortunate "Queen of Hearts," and Frederick the Elector Palatine, during the festivities accompanying their marriage on the 14th of February, 1613. It has even been supposed that it was originally written for this occasion. But the evidence for an earlier performance in 1611, which has now outlived suspicion, would make this theory untenable, even did Miranda not still more suggest a portrait of Elizabeth as she came into her new-washed world from the seclusion of Combe Abbey in 1611, than a portrait of Elizabeth after two years of court life in 1613. It is possible, however, although not, I think, more than possible, that the play may have been revised in the latter year, and the hymeneal mask, which is not particularly appropriate to its place in the action, inserted as a compliment to the bridal pair. However this may be, the hunt after topical allusions in Shakespeare's plays is surely not pursued with the discretion and saving sense of humour which it demands, when the escape of Ferdinand from drowning is interpreted as a reference to the untimely end of Henry, Prince of Wales, who died, not by drowning, but from typhoid fever, shortly before his sister's marriage. Ferdinand cannot stand both for Henry and for Frederick; nor is it the obvious way of condoling with a father on the death of a son, to point out that somebody else's son did not die. Even less willingly can one be induced to find in the triumphant magic of Prospero a delicate flattery of those political intrigues of James the First which had culminated in the alliance with the Elector. Shakespeare was willing enough, no doubt, to address a passing compliment to the king in *Macbeth*. He had more than once done as much for Gloriana° in earlier plays. But the dignified and patient Prospero is no more likely than Hamlet himself to be intended as a full-length portrait of the meanest and least picturesque of all the Stuarts. And so far, indeed, as there is any personal reference in Prospero at all, is it not clearly to one far greater than James the First, namely William Shakespeare himself? I find it impossible to doubt that in the famous address to the "elves of hills, brooks, standing lakes, and groves," in which Prospero recites how by their aid he has—

> Bedimmed
> The noontide sun, called forth the mutinous winds,
> And 'twixt the green sea and the azured vault
> Set roaring war,

and finally abjures his rough magic, breaks his staff, and drowns his book, Shakespeare is really making his own farewell to the stage and to the arts by which he has exercised a dominion even more elemental than that of the enchanter. This speech gives a key to one at least of the ideas which find expression in the play. Thus Ariel, who from another point of view is the agent and minister of an inscrutable Providence, becomes from this a symbol of the spirit of poetry found pegged in the cloven pine of the pre-Shakespearean drama, brought into the service of the creative imagination, and employed for his term in the fashioning of illusions to delight the eyes and move the hearts of men. And so it is hinted that at the end of the play the insubstantial pageant of the great Shakespearean drama shall fade for ever. Ariel shall have his freedom, and Prospero shall betake himself to the dukedom of Milan—which is Stratford.

Whether I am right in this or not, the scanty evidence available would seem to show that the year 1611, in which *The Tempest* was probably written, was also that in which Shakespeare bade good-bye to London and took up his abode for the rest of his life at New Place. He was then still a comparatively young man, and had been

---

epithalamium: A poem written to celebrate a marriage.
Gloriana: Queen Elizabeth I.

a dramatist for not more than a round score of years. The significance of so early a retirement has perhaps hardly been sufficiently appreciated. No doubt Shakespeare had made money and could afford, like Alleyn,° to enjoy his repose and the responsibilities of a landed proprietor. But his willingness to leave London and his triumphs and to bury himself at the age of forty-eight in the smug obscurity of a petty provincial town certainly suggests that his quality of actor and playwright had lost whatever attraction it may ever have possessed for him. The hints of dissatisfaction with the life of the mime, at a much earlier date, in the *Sonnets*, will not be forgotten. Plays and poems are full of these tantalizing glimpses of the man William Shakespeare behind them, and any attempt at interpretation lands one on the perilous ways of conjectural biography. It is, certainly, a merely conjectural reconstruction of the inadequate data when I suggest that Shakespeare as a lad was "dedicated to closeness and the bettering of his mind" and felt little desire for the career of a farmer and more or less prosperous burgess, which was that laid open to him by the traditions of his family. He cared not to be Duke of Milan. Literary ambitions, aided perhaps by some event capable at least of symbolical representation in a drama as an intrigue against him, drove him to London. But the actual conditions attending the calling of an actor and dramatist spelt disillusion. Shakespeare was more of a *bourgeois* than he had dreamed. The mayor's son, conscious of his father's coat-armour, rebelled against the disrepute attaching to an occupation whose members were only distinguished by a legal fiction from rogues and vagrants. The prospect of retirement was present to his mind from an early period. He saved money, invested it in Stratford, bought a house there, and, as soon as his affairs permitted, he gladly broke his pen, and returned to his rejected dukedom, to enjoy the dignities of New Place, to dig his garden, collect his tithes, sit through sermons, and entertain the preacher to sack and supper.

May one venture to think that something better and more spiritual than this merely respectable instinct helped to account for his flight? Is it possible that, in 1611, Shakespeare heard Warwickshire calling with a voice that would not be denied? London was a growing city in the early seventeenth century, and a note of revolt from urban life, hardly heard since the day of the poets of imperial Rome, was beginning to steal back into literature. Jonson translated his—

Beatus ille, qui procul negotiis,°

although Jonson, if any one, had Fleet Street in his veins; and doubtless many a poet flung himself across a table in the Half-Moon to write an ode about the shepherd's life and its sweet content. But the sentiment was a real one all the same, and there are signs in Shakespeare's latest plays that he shared it. In *The Winter's Tale* it reveals itself in the hints of conventional pastoral, always the townsman's dream of country life. In *The Tempest* it inspires the speculations of Gonzalo, borrowed from Montaigne though these may be, on the golden age and the pleasant liberties of its primitive civilization; and also surely the sweet out-of-doors air of the play, blown through and through with breaths from those voyages of discovery which brought so much romance and such a widening horizon into Elizabethan life.

And so we come to the enigmatic figure of Caliban, about which, it must be admitted, the ingenuity of the commentators has not been idle. I have rejected the temptation to suggest that, just as Ariel symbolizes the spirit of poetry brought by Shakespeare into the service of the creative imagination, so Caliban signifies the spirit of prose, born of Sycorax who is controversial theology, and imperfectly subdued by Shakespeare to the same service. There are some who follow

Alleyn: Edward Alleyn (1566–1626) was one of the best known actors of his age.
Beatus . . . negotiis: Happy those who are away from the business (from Horace, *Odes*).

Renan° in taking Caliban for a type of Demos, and regard his desire to "nor scrape trenchering nor wash dish" as eminently characteristic of political ideals which aim at nothing higher than the escape from reasonable labour. Of any political intention on Shakespeare's part in *The Tempest* I am profoundly sceptical; nor do I feel sure that, in the great political cleavage which was beginning to show itself in his day, he would have been so certainly a foe to Demos as is often assumed. Those who believe in his supposed aristocratic and divine-right sympathies, largely on the basis of the Jack Cade scenes in *Henry the Sixth* which he probably did not design, may be invited to compare the demeanour of the boatswain in the storm with that of the crowd of courtiers whose howling proved louder than the weather or his office. Shakespeare, at least, was the dupe neither of a theory nor of a title. "What cares these roarers for the name of king?"

Browning based on Caliban a semi-ironical disquisition on the genesis of natural religions and their anthropomorphism. Others have seen in him an anticipation of Darwinian theories as to the development of man. It is not necessary to attribute to Shakespeare prophetic gifts in the region of biology; but he does seem to be endeavouring to adumbrate in Caliban such a general conception of primitive humanity as the expanding knowledge of his day had opened out to him. Caliban is an earthy creature. He has the morals and the maliciousness of a troglodyte,° and must be taught the first elements of human knowledge—

> How
> To name the bigger light, and how the less,
> That burn by day and night—

and even the first principles of articulate speech. He will take no print of goodness, and can only be controlled and made serviceable by terror. On the other hand—and here we come back to the cravings after the life according to nature which the play in more than one point suggests—he is akin to earth in another sense. He knows all "the qualities of the isle," where the "quick freshes" are, and where the brine pits; and, in the fervour of his adoration for Stephano, vows—

> I'll show thee the best springs. I'll pluck thee berries.
> I'll fish for thee and get thee wood enough;

and again—

> I prithee, let me bring thee where crabs grow.
> And I with my long nails will dig thee pig-nuts;
> Show thee a jay's nest and instruct thee how
> To snare the nimble marmoset; I'll bring thee
> To clustering filberts and sometimes I'll get thee
> Young scamels from the rock.

And is it upon Caliban or upon the missionaries of European civilization that the irony falls, in his complaint against Prospero—

> You taught me language, and my profit on it
> Is, I know how to curse. The red plague rid you
> For teaching me your language!

or in the Rabelaisian scenes where the monster abases himself in the cult of the *dive bouteille°* and confesses of the drunken lackey who holds it—

> That's a brave god, and bears celestial liquor?

Renan: Ernest Renan (1823–1892) was famous for his *Life of Jesus* (1863), but he also wrote *Caliban* (1878). Demos refers to the common people—in Renan's case, perhaps the peasants.
troglodyte: Literally, a cave dweller, an extremely primitive human.
the cult of the *dive bouteille:* the cult of the "divine bottle" (i.e., the pursuit of drunkenness).

AIMÉ CÉSAIRE (1913–2008)

From A Tempest 1969

TRANSLATED BY RICHARD MILLER

Aimé Césaire was a poet, writer, and politician. He was born in Martinique but educated in Paris at the Sorbonne. In his student days, he associated with other black writers and intellectuals and took part in the development of negritude, a movement championing black thought and black politics. He spent much of his life as a teacher in Martinique. He also wrote important books and several plays condemning colonialism, including *A Season in the Congo* (1966), which he intended as part of a trilogy that ended with his play *A Tempest*. The excerpt below is from the ending of the play, in which Prospero and Caliban are left on the island together, with Prospero aged and Caliban free.

TRINCULO: Raise sail! But that's what we do all the time, Sire, Stephano and I . . . at least, we raise our glasses, from dawn till dusk till dawn. . . . The hard part is putting them down, landing, as you might say.

PROSPERO: Scoundrels! If only life could bring you to the safe harbors of Temperance and Sobriety!

ALONSO: (*indicating Caliban*) That is the strangest creature I've ever seen!

PROSPERO: And the most devilish too!

GONZALO: What's that? Devilish! You've reprimanded him, preached at him, you've ordered and made him obey and you say he is still indomitable!

PROSPERO: Honest Gonzalo, it is as I have said.

GONZALO: Well—and forgive me, Counsellor, if I give counsel—on the basis of my long experience the only thing left is exorcism. "Begone, unclean spirit, in the name of the Father, of the Son and of the Holy Ghost." That's all there is to it!

Caliban bursts out laughing.

GONZALO: You were absolutely right! And more so that you thought . . . He's not just a rebel, he's a real tough customer! (*To Caliban*) So much the worse for you, my friend. I have tried to save you. I give up. I leave you to the secular arm!

PROSPERO: Come here, Caliban. Have you got anything to say in your own defence? Take advantage of my good humor. I'm in a forgiving mood today.

CALIBAN: I'm not interested in defending myself. My only regret is that I've failed.

PROSPERO: What were you hoping for?

CALIBAN: To get back my island and regain my freedom.

PROSPERO: And what would you do all alone here on this island, haunted by the devil, tempest tossed?

CALIBAN: First of all, I'd get rid of you! I'd spit you out, all your works and pomps! Your "white" magic!

PROSPERO: That's a fairly negative program. . . .

CALIBAN: You don't understand it . . . I say I'm going to spit you out, and that's very positive . . .

PROSPERO: Well, the world is really upside down . . . We've seen everything now: Caliban as a dialectician! However, in spite of everything I'm fond of you, Caliban. Come, let's make peace. We've lived together for ten years and worked side by side! Ten years count for something, after all! We've ended up by becoming compatriots!

CALIBAN: You know very well that I'm not interested in peace. I'm interested in being free! Free, you hear?

PROSPERO: It's odd . . . no matter what you do, you won't succeed in making me believe that I'm a tyrant!

CALIBAN: Understand what I say, Prospero:

For years I bowed my head
for years I took it, all of it—

your insults, your ingratitude . . .
and worst of all, more degrading than all the rest,
your condescension.
But now, it's over!
Over, do you hear?
Of course, at the moment
You're still stronger than I am.
But I don't give a damn for your power
or for your dogs or your police or your inventions!
And do you know why?
It's because I know I'll get you.
I'll impale you! And on a stake that you've sharpened yourself!
You'll have impaled yourself!
Prospero, you're a great magician:
you're an old hand at deception.
And you lied to me so much,
about the world, about myself,
that you ended up by imposing on me
an image of myself:
underdeveloped, in your words, undercompetent
that's how you made me see myself!
And I hate that image . . . and it's false!
But now I know you, you old cancer,
And I also know myself!
And I know that one day
my bare fist, just that,
will be enough to crush your world!
The old world is crumbling down!

Isn't it true? Just look!
It even bores you to death.
And by the way . . . you have a chance to get it over with:
You can pick up and leave.
You can go back to Europe.
But the hell you will!
I'm sure you won't leave.
You make me laugh with your "mission"!
Your "vocation"!
Your vocation is to hassle me.
And that's why you'll stay,
just like those guys who founded the colonies
and who now can't live anywhere else.
You're just an old addict, that's what you are!

PROSPERO: Poor Caliban! You know that you're headed towards your own ruin. You're
sliding towards suicide! You know I will be the stronger, and stronger all the time.
I pity you!

CALIBAN: And I hate you!

PROSPERO: Beware! My generosity has its limits.

CALIBAN: (*shouting*)

Shango marches with strength
along his path, the sky!
Shango is a fire-bearer,
his steps shake the heavens
and the earth
Shango, Shango, ho!

PROSPERO: I have uprooted the oak and raised the sea,
I have caused the mountain to tremble and have bared my chest to adversity.
With Jove I have traded thunderbolt for thunderbolt.

Better yet—from a brutish monster I have made man!
But ah! To have failed to find the path to man's heart . . .
if that be where man is.
(*to Caliban*)
Well, I hate you as well!
For it is you who have made me
doubt myself for the first time.
(*to the Nobles*)
. . . My friends, come near. We must say farewell. . . . I shall not be going with you.
My fate is here: I shall not run from it.

ANTONIO: What, Sire?

PROSPERO: Hear me well.
I am not in any ordinary sense a master,
as this savage thinks,
but rather the conductor of a boundless score:
this isle,
summoning voices, I alone,
and mingling them at my pleasure,
arranging out of confusion
one intelligible line.
Without me, who would be able to draw music from all that?
This isle is mute without me.
My duty, thus, is here,
and here I shall stay.

GONZALO: Oh day full rich in miracles!

PROSPERO: Do not be distressed. Antonio, be you the lieutenant of my goods and make use of them as procurator until that time when Ferdinand and Miranda may take effective possession of them, joining them with the Kingdom of Naples. Nothing of that which has been set for them must be postponed: Let their marriage be celebrated at Naples with all royal splendor. Honest Gonzalo, I place my trust in your word. You shall stand as father to our princess at this ceremony.

GONZALO: Count on me, Sire.

PROSPERO: Gentlemen, farewell.

They exit.

And now, Caliban, it's you and me!
What I have to tell you will be brief:
Ten times, a hundred times, I've tried to save you,
above all from yourself.
But you have always answered me with wrath
and venom,
like the opossum that pulls itself up by its own tail
the better to bite the hand that tears it from the darkness.
Well, my boy, I shall set aside my indulgent nature
and henceforth I will answer your violence
with violence!

Time passes, symbolized by the curtain's being lowered halfway and reraised. In semi-darkness Prospero appears, aged and weary. His gestures are jerky and automatic, his speech weak, toneless, trite.

PROSPERO: Odd, but for some time now we seem to be overrun with opossums. They're everywhere. Peccarys, wild boar, all this unclean nature! But mainly opossums. Those eyes! The vile grins they have! It's as though the jungle was laying siege to the cave. . . . But I shall stand firm. . . . I shall not let my work perish! (*Shouting*) I shall protect civilization! (*He fires in all directions.*) They're done for! Now, this way I'll be able to have some peace and quiet for a while. But it's cold. Odd how the climate's changed. Cold on this island . . . Have to think about making a fire . . . Well, Caliban, old fellow, it's just us two now, here on the island . . . only you and me. You and me. You-me . . . me-you! What in the hell is he up to? (*Shouting*) Caliban!

In the distance, above the sound of the surf and the chirping of birds, we hear snatches of Caliban's song:

FREEDOM HI-DAY, FREEDOM HI-DAY!

ANIA LOOMBA

Caliban and Sycorax   1989

Ania Loomba is professor of English and Comparative Literature at the University of Pennsylvania. Educated at the University of New Delhi and the University of Sussex, she specializes in drama, feminism, colonialism, and post-colonialism. Among her works are *Shakespeare, Race and Colonialism* (2002) and *Postcolonial Studies and Beyond* (2005). Her focus in this excerpt from *Gender, Race, Renaissance Drama* (1989) is on colonial preconceptions of Caliban and the position of Sycorax as the only strong female character referenced in the play.

The Black Rapist[1]

One of the reasons for the play's declining pertinence to contemporary third world politics has been identified as

> the difficulty of wresting from it any role for female defiance or leadership in a period when protest is coming increasingly from that quarter. Given that Caliban is without a female counterpart in his oppression and rebellion, and given the largely autobiographical cast of African and Caribbean appropriations of the play, it follows that all the writers who quarried from *The Tempest* an expression of their lot should have been men. (Nixon, p. 577)

It is true that the play poses a problem for a feminist, and especially a nonwestern feminist appropriation, if by "appropriation" we mean an amplification of the anti-colonial voices within the text. But such a difficulty does not arise simply from the lack of a strong female presence, black or white, in the play, but also from the play's representation of black male sexuality.

Caliban contests Prospero's account of his arrival on the island but not the accusation of attempted rape of Miranda. Identifying the political effects of Prospero's accusation, Paul Brown comments that "the issue here is not whether Caliban is actually a rapist or not, since Caliban accepts the charge." On the contrary, I suggest that this acceptance is important for assessing both colonial and anti-colonial readings of the play. An article written in 1892, which later became what Griffiths calls "a standard defence of Caliban" speaks of the rape as "an offence, an unpardonable offence, but *one that he was fated to commit*" (p. 166; emphasis added) and goes on to see Caliban as unfortunate, oppressed, but "like all these lower peoples, easily misled." This implies that sexual violence is part of the

---

[1] I am indebted to work on *The Tempest* by Barker and Hulme, Paul Brown and Rob Nixon, all of which has made this chapter possible.

black man's inferior nature, a view that amalgamates racist common-sense notions about black sexuality and animalism, and sexist assumptions about rape as an inevitable expression of frustrated male desire.

These notions were complexly employed in the influential *Psychologie de la colonisation* (1948) by Octave Mannoni, who seriously reassessed the play in order to propound a controversial view of the psychology of the colonised subject. Mannoni advocated the notion of the "Caliban complex" which he analyzed as the desire for dependency on the part of the native. Caliban (and the Madagascans, whose uprising of 1947–48 provided the impetus for the work) revolts not against slavery but because he is abandoned by Prospero. Analyzing Caliban's speech in Act 2, Mannoni came to the conclusion that "Caliban does not complain of being exploited: he complains of being betrayed." As other Caribbean and African intellectuals pointed out, Mannoni posited Caliban as an eager partner in his own colonization (Nixon, pp. 562–65).

Sycorax

Mannoni, significantly, edited out these opening lines of Caliban's version of Prospero's arrival on the island:

> This island's mine, by Sycorax my mother,
> Which thou tak'st from me.
>
> [I, ii, 334–35]

These lines had elicited the first recorded anti-imperialist response to the play in 1904, which found that in them "the whole case of the aboriginal against aggressive civilisation [was] dramatised before us" (Nixon, pp. 561–62). They were also focused by subsequent Caribbean and African appropriations, but although some of these indicated the matrilinear nature of many pre-colonial societies, gender was hardly ever seized upon by anti-colonial intellectuals as a significant dimension of racial oppression.

Sycorax is more than the justification for Caliban's territorial rights to the island—she operates as a powerful contrast to Miranda. Both Prospero and Caliban testify to her power; the former draws upon the language of misogyny as well as racism to construct her as a "foul witch" [I, ii, 259] the latter invokes her strength to express his hatred of his master [I, ii, 324–26, 342–43]. Prospero's descriptions of Sycorax emphasize both her non-European origins—she's "from Argier"—and her fertility—"This blue-ey'd hag was hither brought with child" [I, ii, 263, 271]. She is also "so strong / That could control the moon, make flows and ebbs, / And deal in her command without her power" [V, i, 272–74]. Hence she stands in complete contrast to the white, virginal and obedient Miranda. Between them they split the patriarchal stereotype of woman as the white devil—virgin and whore, goddess (Miranda is mistaken for one by Ferdinand) and witch.

But Sycorax is also Prospero's "other"; his repeated comparisons between their different magics and their respective reigns of the island are used by him to claim a superior morality, a greater strength and a greater humanity, and hence legitimize his takeover of the island and its inhabitants; but they also betray an anxiety that Sycorax's power has not been fully exorcised, for Caliban still invokes it for his own rebellion: "All the charms / Of Sycorax, toads, beetles, bats, light on you!" [I, ii, 342–43]. As George Lamming pointed out in *The Pleasures of Exile,* while

Miranda is like many an African slave child in never having known her mother, "the actual Caliban of *The Tempest* has the advantage ... of having known the meaning and power of his mother Sycorax" (p. 111).

Prospero's takeover is both *racial* plunder and a transfer to *patriarchy*. The connections between witches and transgressive women, between witch-trials with the process of capital accumulation, and between the economic, ideological and sexual subordination of native women by colonial rule, have already been discussed [in *Gender, Race, Renaissance Drama*, chapters 1 and 3]. The restructuring of the colonized economy not only involved the export of raw material to factories in England, but also a redefinition of men and women's work, which economically dislocated women, and calcified patriarchal tendencies in the native culture.... In Burma, for example, British colonialists acknowledged that Burmese women had property and sexual rights unheard of in England. Accordingly, Fielding Hall, Political Officer in the British Colonial Administration in Burma, suggested that in order to "civilise" the Burmese people:

1. The men must be taught to kill and to fight for the British colonialists.
2. Women must surrender their liberty in the interests of men. (Mies, quoted by Rughani, p. 19)

Colonized women were also subjected to untold sexual harassment, rape, enforced marriage and degradation, both under direct slavery and otherwise. Sycorax's illegitimate pregnancy contrasts with Miranda's chastity and virginity, reminding us that the construction of the promiscuity of non-European women served to legitimize their sexual abuse and to demarcate them from white women.

Therefore Prospero as colonialist consolidates power which is specifically white and male, and constructs Sycorax as a black, wayward and wicked witch in order to legitimize it. If Caliban's version of past events prompts us to question Prospero's story, then this interrogation should include the re-telling of Sycorax's story. The distinctions drawn by generations of critics between his "white magic" and Sycorax's "black magic" only corroborate Prospero's narrative. African appropriations emphasized the brutality of Prospero's "reason" and its historical suppression of black culture, but they did not bring out the gender-value of these terms; they read the story of colonized and colonizing men but not of colonized and colonizing women, which is also told by Miranda's lonely presence on the island.

Brown, Paul, "'This thing of darkness I acknowledge mine': *The Tempest* and the discourse of colonialism," in Dollimore and Sinfield, eds., 1985, pp. 48–71.

Dollimore, Jonathan, and Sinfield, Alan, eds., *Political Shakespeare: New Essays in Cultural Materialism* (Manchester University Press, 1985).

Griffiths, Trevor R., "'This island's mine': Caliban and colonialism," *Yearbook of English Studies* 13 (1983), pp. 159–80.

Lamming, George, *The Pleasures of Exile* (London and New York, Allison and Busby, 1984).

Mies, Maria, *Patriarchy and Accumulation on a World Scale: Women in the International Division of Labour* (London and New Jersey, Zed Books, 1986).

Nixon, Rob, "Caribbean and African appropriations of *The Tempest*," *Critical Inquiry* 13 (Spring 1987), pp. 557–77.

Rughani, Pratap, "Kipling, India and Imperialism" (unpublished paper).

MARJORIE GARBER (b. 1944)

The Tempest and Colonialism   2004

Marjorie Garber is the William R. Kenan, Jr., Professor of English and Chair of the Committee on Dramatic Arts at Harvard University. *Shakespeare After All* (2004), from which the passage below is taken, was selected as one of the five best nonfiction books of the year by *Newsweek*. Garber examines *The Tempest* in detail in an effort to clarify the themes of colonialism that have attracted recent criticism while also examining the geography of the island, whose complexities complicate any absolute connection with the New World—or any world except that of the imagination.

Shakespeare's powerful late romance *The Tempest* has been addressed by modern critics from two important perspectives: as a fable of art and creation, and as a colonialist allegory. These readings very much depend on one's conception of European man's place in the universe, and on whether a figure like Prospero stands for all mankind or for one side of a conflict.

The first interpretation, following upon the ideas of Renaissance humanism and the place of the artist/playwright/magician, offers a story of mankind at the center of the universe, of "man" as creator and authority. Such a reading is, by its nature, at once aesthetic, philosophical, and skeptical. Prospero is man-the-artist, or man-the-scholar: Ariel and Caliban represent his ethereal and material selves—the one airy, imaginative, and swift; the second earthy, gross, and appetitive. Prospero has often been seen as a figure for the artist as creator—as Shakespeare's stand-in, so to speak, or Shakespeare's self-conception, an artist figure unifying the world around him by his "so potent art." By his magic, his *good* magic, or what has been described as *white* (or benevolent) magic, he subdues anarchic figures around him, like Caliban and his mother, Sycorax, the previous ruler of the island, who is also a magician (often thought of as a practitioner of *black*, or malevolent, magic). Prospero's magic books enable him as well to thwart the incipient revolts of both high and low conspirators, and to exact a species of revenge against those who usurped his dukedom and set him adrift on the sea—for *The Tempest* is one of Shakespeare's most compelling "revenge tragedies," turned, at the last moment, toward forgiveness.

But there is something troubling about this idealized picture of a Renaissance man accommodated with arts and crafts, dominance and power, in a little world, a little island, that he takes and makes his own. Many critical observers, especially in the later twentieth century, have seen Prospero as a colonizer of alien territory *not* his own, a European master who comes to an island in the New World, displaces its native ruler, enslaves its indigenous population (in this case emblematized by Caliban), and makes its rightful inhabitants work for him and his family as servants, fetching wood and water, while he and his daughter enjoy all the amenities of the temperate climate and the fertile land. The tensions between the aesthetic and the political lie at the heart of the play.

First staged in 1611, with King James present in the audience, *The Tempest* was subsequently performed as part of the marriage celebration for his daughter, the Princess Elizabeth, whom the King was about to "lose" to her husband, Frederick, the Elector Palatine—just as Prospero "loses" his daughter, Miranda, as he tells Alonso, King of Naples, "in this last tempest," to Ferdinand, the King's son. So the political and social context, the timeliness, of the play may have been evident from the beginning.

Although it takes the form of an extended scene of instruction between Prospero and Miranda, father and daughter, the play is fundamentally built on the continuous contrast between Prospero's two servants, Ariel and Caliban, mind and body, imagination and desire or lust. If Ariel is imagination personified, surely Caliban is something like libido (sexual desire) or id (basic human drives). If one thing is clear on Prospero's island, it is that, for all his anarchic and disruptive qualities, Caliban is *necessary*—like the body itself. "We cannot miss him," says Prospero (meaning, "We cannot do without him"). "He does make our fire, / Fetch in our wood, and serves in offices / That profit us" [I, ii, 314–16]. Later in the play, after Caliban foils the conspiracy against his life, Prospero will say ruefully of him, "This thing of darkness I / Acknowledge mine" [V, i, 278–79]. What Prospero acknowledges in this phrase is not only responsibility (Caliban is my slave), but also identity (Caliban, the "thing of darkness," is part of me).

In one way we might say that *The Tempest* is macrocosmic: Caliban is a spirit of earth and water, Ariel a spirit of fire and air, and together they are elements harnessed by Prospero, here a kind of magician and wonder-worker closely allied to Renaissance science. Together these figures give us a picture of the world. In another way we could say that *The Tempest* is microcosmic, its structural design a mirror of the human psyche: Caliban, who is necessary and burdensome, the libido, the id, a "thing of darkness" who must be acknowledged; Ariel the spirit of imagination incarnate, who cannot be possessed forever, and therefore must be allowed to depart in freedom. And in yet a third way the play's design illustrates the basic doctrines of Renaissance humanist philosophy. Mankind is a creature a little lower than the angels, caught between the bestial and the celestial, a creature of infinite possibilities. In all of these patterns Prospero stands between the poles marked out by Ariel and Caliban.

The second kind of interpretation, the colonial or postcolonial narrative, follows upon early modern voyages of exploration and discovery, "first contact," and the encounters with, and exploitation of, indigenous peoples in the New World. In this interpretive context *The Tempest* is not idealizing, aesthetic, and "timeless," but rather topical, contextual, "political," and in dialogue with the times. Yet manifestly this dichotomy will break down, both in literary analysis and in performance. It is perfectly possible for a play about a mage, artist, and father to be, at the same time, a play about a colonial governor, since Prospero himself is, or was, the Duke of Milan. His neglect of his ducal responsibilities ("rapt in secret studies," he allowed his brother to scheme against him) led first to his usurpation and exile, then to his establishment of an alternative government on the island, displacing and enslaving the native inhabitant Caliban, whose mother, Sycorax, had ruled there before Prospero's arrival and who, as Caliban says, "first was mine own king" [I, ii, 345].

Caliban's name is a variant of "cannibal" (deriving from "Carib," a fierce nation of the West Indies), and Shakespeare's play owes much to Montaigne's essay "Of Cannibals" (1580), which draws trenchant and unflattering comparisons between the supposedly civilized Europeans and the native islanders. "There is nothing savage or barbarous about those peoples, but that every man calls barbarous anything he is not accustomed to," Montaigne writes. Despite the nakedness and unfamiliar ways of these tribes, contemporary European societies "surpass them in every kind of barbarism," like treachery, disloyalty, tyranny, and cruelty, which "are everyday vices in us." As for cannibalism itself, there is "more barbarity in lacerating by rack and torture a body still fully able to feel things, in roasting him little by little . . . than in roasting and eating him after his death."

Colonialist readings have gained force in the last fifty years by analogy with the historical events of postcolonialism, whether in South Asia, Africa, or the Caribbean, but they are also entirely pertinent to Shakespeare's own time. During the years when *The Tempest* was written and first performed, Europe, and England in particular, was in the heyday of the period of colonial exploration. Sir Walter Ralegh is one important and charismatic figure who went from the Elizabethan court to the New World, and in his account, *The Discovery of the Large, Rich, and Beautiful Empire of Guiana* (1596), he describes encounters with native populations of just this kind. Captain John Smith set out with the Virginia colonists in 1606, and his *General History of Virginia, New England, and the Summer Isles* (1624) is another key source for this period, documenting the encounter of Englishmen (for which we may read Prospero's Italians/Europeans) with a native culture and climate in the New World.

There are moments in the play that clearly evoke the local historical context: as, for example, when Trinculo, the drunken jester, stumbling over the recumbent form of Caliban, imagines a fast way to make money, by exhibiting him back in the Old World for a fee:

> Were I in England now, as once I was, and had but this fish painted, not a holiday-fool there but would give a piece of silver. There would this monster make a man. Any strange beast there makes a man. When they will not give a doit to relieve a lame beggar, they will lay out ten to see a dead Indian.
>
> *The Tempest* [II, ii, 26–31]

"Were I in England" is Shakespeare's typical sly wit—an in-joke for the English audience, like the scene in which the gravedigger in *Hamlet* remarks that no one in England would detect Hamlet's infirmity: "There the men are as mad as he" [V, i, 142–43].

Many of the twentieth-century rewritings of *The Tempest* are inspired by New World concerns, and even are written from the point of view of the oppressed. The Uruguayan philosopher and critic José Enrique Rodó wrote his *Ariel* in 1900, calling upon Latin America to retain cultural values unsullied by the materialism of the United States; in 1913 he published *El Mirador de Próspero* (Prospero's Balcony). Martinican playwright Aimé Césaire published the first version of his *Une Tempête*, a radical adaptation of Shakespeare's play, in 1968, and the Cuban revolutionary intellectual Roberto Fernández Retamar wrote his *Calibán* in 1971. The story of *The Tempest* has intersected, repeatedly and always interestingly, with other "political" and colonial moments, through and beyond the postcolonial period of the mid-twentieth century. In many revisionist readings, Caliban becomes a more central and sympathetic figure. In some productions, dating as early as the turn of the last century, he is a loner and a misunderstood "hero," dispossessed of his birthright by the invading Europeans. From W. H. Auden's poem *The Sea and the Mirror* (1944) to Césaire's *Une Tempête*, an adaptation explicitly made "for a Black theater," to films as diverse as *Forbidden Planet* (1956) and *Prospero's Books* (1991), *The Tempest* has retained its power and fascination.

But is Prospero's enchanted island in the Old World or the New World? The play's indebtedness to many New World texts is evident in its descriptions: the storm in the "still-vexed Bermudas"; the native inhabitants, often associated by critics with American Indians; the echoes of Jamestown and the early Virginia tracts, as well as of Montaigne's influential account of New World natives. In literal geographical terms, however, the island must be located in the Mediterranean Sea, not far from the coast of Africa. The King and court party are returning from the wedding of Claribel to an African in Tunis, and Sycorax hails from Algiers ("Argier"). Scholars have also begun to remind us that an even closer island, one actually within the "British isles," was famed for the wildness of its inhabitants, linking Ireland as yet another colonial space evoked by the play's suggestively rich and elusive landscape. That *all* of these associations seem germane is now virtually taken for granted.

What is most magical about the isle, however, is that in being many places at once, geographically, culturally, and mythographically hybrid, it eludes location and becomes a space for poetry, and for dream. It is not found on any map. Prospero's enchanted island, while drawn from real explorations and published accounts, is ultimately a country of the mind. And this is made clear by the very structure of the play, which starts out in medias res,° in clamor, in shipwreck, and in darkness.

As *The Tempest* begins, the audience finds itself in the middle of a storm at sea. All around is confusion: "A tempestuous noise of thunder and lightning heard." Voices cry out, seemingly from nowhere, in disconnected fragments that recall other Shakespearean storms, and other romances.

BOATSWAIN: Keep your cabins; you do assist the storm.
GONZALO: Nay, good, be patient.

[I, i, 12–14]

These lines might have come from the shipwreck scene in *Pericles,* where the nurse Lychorida urges the King in very similar words: "Patience, good sir, do not assist the storm."

"What care these roarers for the name of king?" cries the Boatswain in despair. This is an echo of the storm in *The Winter's Tale,* in which the nobleman Antigonus was torn to pieces by the bear. Those waves, too, "roared," with no regard for such cultural niceties as rank and status. This present tempest, the tempest in the play that bears that name, is thus somehow the quintessential storm, the "perfect" storm, distilled of all the Shakespearean tempests we have weathered before, from *Othello* and *King Lear* to the romances. Indeed, this scene is often played in total darkness, emphasizing the confusion and disorder.

---

in medias res: In the middle of things.

Late-Seventeenth- and Eighteenth-Century Drama

Theater in England continued to thrive after Shakespeare's death, thanks to the efforts of a host of successful playwrights, including John Webster (1580?–1638?), Francis Beaumont (c. 1584–1616) and his collaborator John Fletcher (1579–1625), Philip Massinger (1583–1640), Thomas Middleton (1580–1627), John Ford (1586–c. 1655) and James Shirley (1596–1666). All of these playwrights were busy working independently or in collaboration. Fletcher, chosen successor to Shakespeare at the Globe, furnished the theater with as many as four plays a year. But in 1642, long-standing religious and political conflicts between King Charles I and Parliament finally erupted into civil war, with the Parliament, under the influence of Puritanism, eventually winning.

The Puritans were religious extremists with narrow, specific values. They were essentially an emerging merchant class of well-to-do citizens who viewed the aristocracy as wastrels. Theater for them was associated with both the aristocracy and the low life. Theatergoing was synonymous with wasting time; the theaters were often a focus for immoral activity, and the neighborhoods around the theaters were as unsavory as any in England. Under the Puritan government, all theaters in England were closed for almost twenty years. When the new king, Charles II, was crowned in 1660, those that had not been converted to other uses had become completely outmoded.

As a young prince, Charles, with his mother and brother, had been sent to the Continent in the early stages of the civil war. When his father, Charles I, was beheaded, the future king and his family were in France, where they were in a position to see the remarkable achievements of French comedy and French classical tragedy. Charles II developed a taste for theater that accompanied him back to England. And when he returned in triumph to usher in the exciting and swashbuckling period known as the Restoration, he permitted favorites to build new theaters.

Theater on the Continent: Neoclassicism

Interaction among the leading European countries — England, Spain, and France — was sporadic at best in the seventeenth century because of intermittent wars among the nations, yet the development of theater in all three countries took similar turns throughout the early 1600s.

By the 1630s, the French were aware of Spanish achievements in the theater; Pierre Corneille (1606–1684), who emerged as France's leading playwright of the time, adapted a Spanish story by de Castro that became one of his most important plays, *Le Cid*.

By the time Charles II took up residence in France in the 1640s, the French had developed a suave, polished, and intellectually demanding approach to drama. Corneille and the neoclassicists were part of a large movement in European culture and the arts that tried to codify and emulate the achievement of the ancients. Qualities such as harmony, symmetry, balance in everything structural, and clear moral themes were most sought after. Because **neoclassicism** valued thought over feeling, the thematic material in neoclassical drama was very important. That material was sometimes political, reflecting the values of Augustan Rome — 27 BCE to 17 CE — when Caesar Augustus lived and when it was appropriate to think in terms of subordinating the self to the interests of the state. Neoclassical dramatists focused on honor, moral integrity, self-sacrifice, and heroic political subjects.

French Tragedy

One school of critics held playwrights strictly to the Aristotelian concepts of the unities of time, place, character, and action. These "rules critics" demanded a perfect observance of the unities — that is, they wanted a play to have one plot, a single action that takes place in one day, and a single setting. In most cases the plays that satisfied them are now often thought of as static, cold, limited, and dull. Their perfection is seen today as rigid and emotionally icy.

Corneille's work did not please such critics, and they turned to a much younger competitor, Jean Racine (1639–1699), who brought the tradition of French tragedy to its fullest. Most of Racine's plays are on classical subjects, beginning in 1667 with *Andromache*, continuing with *Britannicus* (1669), *Iphigenia* (1674), and *Mithridate* (1673), and ending in 1677 with his most famous and possibly best play, *Phaedra*.

Phaedra is a deeply passionate, moral play centering on the love of Phaedra for her stepson, Hippolytus. Venus is responsible for her incestuous love — which is the playwright's way of saying that Phaedra is impelled by the gods or by destiny, almost against her will.

The French stage, unlike the English, never substituted boys for female roles, and so plays such as *Phaedra* were opportunities for brilliant actresses. Phaedra, in particular, dominates the stage — she is a commanding and infinitely complex figure. It is no wonder that this play was a favorite of Sarah Bernhardt (1844–1923), one of France's greatest actresses.

French Comedy: Molière

At the same time that Racine commanded the tragic stage, Jean Baptiste Poquelin (1622–1673), known as Molière, began his dominance of the comic stage. He was aware of Racine's achievements and applauded them strongly. His career started with a small theater company that spent most of its time touring the countryside beyond Paris. When the company settled in Paris, its plays were influenced by some of the stock characters and situations of the commedia dell'arte, but they also began to reflect Molière's own genius for composition.

Seeing a performance by Molière's company in 1658, King Louis XIV found it so much to his liking that he installed the company in a theater and demanded to see more of its work. From that time on, Molière wrote, produced, and acted in one comedy after another, most of which have become part of the permanent repertoire of the French stage. Plays such as *The Misanthrope* (1666), *The Miser* (1669), *The Bourgeois Gentleman* (1670), *The Imaginary Invalid* (1673), and his satire on the theme of religious hypocrisy, *Tartuffe* (1669), are also staged all over the world.

Theater in England: The Restoration

The English Restoration began in 1660 with the return of King Charles II to England after nearly two decades in France. The new age craved glitter, excitement, sensuality, and dramatic dazzle. Audiences wanted upbeat comedies that poked fun at stuffed shirts and old-fashioned institutions. Charles was influenced by the French theaters, which were often constructed on a pattern of the French tennis court — a long, narrow, rectangular space that served well for French performances.

The Great Fire of 1666, which destroyed most of London, occasioned extensive reconstruction that, in the 1670s, included the building of new theaters. They too were long and narrow, but, unlike most Elizabethan theaters, they were enclosed and depended on artificial lighting. Restoration theaters operated year-round, and the prices of seats depended on their location. The first-level boxes against the walls were the most expensive seats; the middle-priced seats — actually backless benches — filled the pit before the proscenium-arched stage (Figure 13); and the lowest-priced seats were in the upper ranges of the galleries.

The structure of the new theater permitted realistic scene design, with a receding space that accommodated painted backdrops. Actors could enter and leave by side doors directly on stage or could retreat to the **flies** through the scenic stage. The proscenium was not framed as in later theaters but, rather, permitted actors to move close to those sitting in the pit. The space allotted to the actors in the Drury Lane Theatre was considerable, facilitating rousing fight scenes and crowd scenes. The **apron** also produced an intimacy between actor and audience that encouraged a more natural presentation. The drama-starved audiences favored a new style of comedy—one that was socially observant—and a new style of tragedy—one that may be called heroic, as in the plays of John Dryden (1631–1700), whose *All for Love* was a "rewrite" of Shakespeare's *Antony and Cleopatra*. New plays for the Restoration often consisted of rewritings of great Elizabethan plays (including a version of *King Lear* with a happy ending) or reworkings of plots of French, Italian, and Spanish plays. The age required high fashion, superficial brilliance, and sensual entertainment in the style of a sometimes lewd court and more open society.

Not everyone applauded these developments, however. The clergyman and critic Jeremy Collier, in *A Short View of the Immorality and Profaneness of the English Stage* (1698), attacked the contemporary theater for its immorality, its satiric portrayal of ministers of the church, and its casual references to the Bible. He condemned not only the theater of his age but also the plays of Shakespeare and the great Elizabethan dramatists, whose work was quite different in tone from the contemporary drama. The effect he had on theater

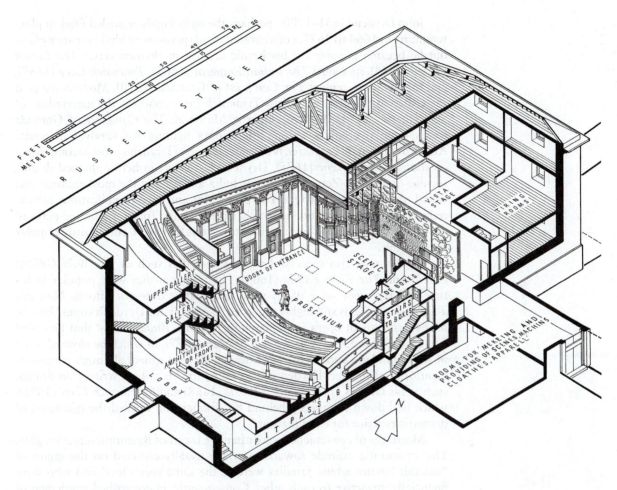

Figure 13. Theatre Royal, Drury Lane, 1676, designed by Sir Christopher Wren.

was extensive, in part because, during his reign a decade earlier, James II had taken up the cry to reform the theater. Major playwrights were fined for their productions, which certainly had a dampening effect on later productions by important actors and companies.

For the full text of Behn's *The Rover*, visit **bedfordstmartins.com/jacobus.**

Among England's notable playwrights from 1660 through the eighteenth century were Aphra Behn (1640–1689), the first professional female playwright on the English stage and author of *The Rover*, one of the most frequently performed plays of the period; William Wycherley (1640–1716), whose best works are thought to be *The Plain Dealer*, indebted to Molière, and *The Country Wife*; William Congreve (1670–1729), whose *The Way of the World* is justly famous; and Richard Brinsley Sheridan (1751–1816), whose *School for Scandal* is still bright, lively, and engaging for modern audiences. Other important playwrights whose work is still performed are George Farquhar (1678–1707), especially known for *The Beaux Stratagem* (1707); John Gay (1685–1732), whose *Beggar's Opera* has been revived repeatedly since its first performance in 1728; and Oliver Goldsmith (1730–1774), author of *She Stoops to Conquer* (1773).

John Dryden (1631–1700), perhaps the most highly regarded English playwright from 1664 to 1677, collaborated in adaptations of Shakespeare's plays, but he became popular for his heroic dramas in rhymed verse: *The Indian Queen* (1664), its sequel *The Indian Emperor* (1665), *Tyrannick Love* (1669), and the two-part, ten-act *The Conquest of Granada* (1670). Montezuma is at the center of the first two plays; *Tyrannick Love* concerns the martyrdom of St. Catherine by the Roman emperor, Maximin. *The Conquest of Granada* traces internal conflicts among the Moors fighting for survival in Spain. Almanzor, the main character, is considered one of Dryden's most accomplished creations. *Aureng-Zebe* (1675), Dryden's last effort in heroic rhymed drama, focuses on Aureng-Zebe, emperor of India and among the most rational and moral of Dryden's characters. The play's plot and love complications are extremely dense and its mood somewhat melancholy. Today the heroic plays of the 1660s resemble high-style melodramas, but they were enormously popular in their time.

Dryden was also successful writing comedies such as *The Wild Gallant* (1663) and *The Rival Ladies* (1664). His tragicomedies were popular in his time and represent some of his most imaginative dramatic efforts. *Marriage à-la-Mode* (1672) is still highly regarded, especially for Dryden's songs. Among his experiments in opera is a version of Milton's *Paradise Lost* that he called *The State of Innocence and the Fall of Man* (1677), in which he rhymed some of Milton's blank verse. This work was never performed, although it remains a curiosity of the age. Dryden is also noted for his critical writing on drama, such as his famous *Of Dramatick Poesie* (1668) and *Of Heroick Plays* (1672), which laid down the theory behind his dramas and opened the questions of dramatic practice for examination.

Marriages of convenience were often the target of Restoration playwrights. The aristocratic attitude toward marriage usually centered on the union of "suitable" mates whose families were of the same social level and who were financially attractive to each other. Consequently, impoverished gentlemen of good name would sometimes seek out wealthy women, and vice versa. Marriages were based sometimes on love but more often on financial or social convenience. As a result, conflicts in choosing marriage partners often involved elaborate dealings between parents and children. Once married, husbands and wives played complex games of adultery and betrayal, negotiating terms of financial settlements while engaging in witty repartee and riposte, as in William Congreve's immortal *The Way of the World*. It is not until the end of the eighteenth century that the sentimental comedy appeared, introducing recognizable emotional responses that appear normal to present-day audiences. Aristocratic attitudes toward marriage are evident in drama as late as the end of the nineteenth century, as in Oscar Wilde's *The Importance of Being Earnest*.

The English playwrights produced a wide range of comedy, to fulfill their audiences' desire for bright, gay, and witty entertainment. The comedies of the period came to be known in the twentieth century as **comedies of manners** because they revealed the foibles of the society that watched them. Society enjoyed laughing at itself. Although some of the English dramas of the eighteenth century developed a moralistic tone and were heavily classical, the earlier **restoration comedies** focused less on reforming the society than on capitalizing on its faults.

Eighteenth-Century Drama

Eighteenth-century Europe absorbed much of the spirit of France and the French neoclassicists. England, like other European countries, began to see the effects of neoclassicism in the arts and literature. Emulation of classical art and classical values was common throughout Europe, and critics established standards of excellence in the arts to guarantee quality.

The most famous name in eighteenth-century English drama is David Garrick (1717–1779), the legendary actor and manager of the Drury Lane Theatre. The theaters, including his own, often reworked French drama and earlier English and Italian drama, but they began to develop a new **sentimental comedy** to balance the neoclassical heroic tragedies of the period. It was comedy that played on, manipulated, and exploited the emotions of the audience to arouse sympathy for the characters in the play.

Sentimental comedy flourished after 1720, but Colley Cibber (1671–1757) is sometimes credited with originating this form with his *Love's Last Shift* (1696). The play centers on Loveless, who wanders from his marriage only to find that his wife has disguised herself as a prostitute to win him back. As in all sentimental comedies, what the audience most wants is what it gets: a certain amount of tears, an equal amount of laughter, and a happy ending. As an actor, Cibber was especially well known for his portrayal of fops, his way of poking satiric fun at his own society and its pretensions.

Sir Richard Steele (1672–1729) wrote one of the best known sentimental comedies, *The Conscious Lovers* (1722). Steele's coauthor on *The Spectator*, Joseph Addison (1672–1719), also distinguished himself with his contribution to the heroic tragedy of the age, the long neoclassical *Cato* (1713). It was considered to be the finest example of the moral heroic style. Today it is not a playable drama because the action is too slow, the speeches too long, and the theme too obscure, although it is a perfect model of what the age preferred in heroic tragedy. George Lillo (1693–1739) in *The London Merchant* (1731) produced a bourgeois tragedy in which the main character was from the middle class. It was one of the most frequently produced plays of its time.

The audiences at the time enjoyed bright, amusing comedies that often criticized wayward youth, overprotective parents, dishonest financial dealings, and social expectations. Their taste in tragedies veered toward a moralizing heroism that extolled the values of the community and self-sacrifice on the part of the hero.

The Seventeenth- and Eighteenth-Century Actor

Although the tradition of acting in England had been interrupted for almost twenty years before the Restoration, some important actors, such as Thomas Betterton (1635–1710), were able to continue many of the features of Shakespeare's staging. Betterton was especially noted for his performances as Hamlet, a part that was popular throughout the eighteenth century. In this period in England, actors received praise if they had fine figures and strong and mellow voices, and used facial expressions to reveal emotion at the proper dramatic moment. Commentary on acting stressed naturalness of expression as a prerequisite for excellence. However, the age's concept of what was natural was much different from ours; the acting of the age would seem grossly exaggerated to us.

In France, women had been on stage for some time, and during the Restoration, actresses appeared on the English stage and proved enormously

Figure 14. Nell Gwynne, the best known actress of her age, in a portrait by Sir Peter Lely (c. 1675).

popular. Actresses were often the most important draw in English theaters in the seventeenth century. Nell Gwynne (1650–1687), one of the most famous actresses of the age (Figure 14), was also mistress to Charles II. She was discovered by her actor husband while selling flowers near a theater at age 15. Her lightheartedness and sometimes risqué manner were part of her stage appeal. The great diarist Samuel Pepys saw her in a comedy and vowed that "so great a performance of a comical part was never, I believe, in the world before." She was so remarkable that John Dryden, poet laureate, wrote comic parts specifically for her.

Actors in this period employed numerous stage tricks, sometimes called **claptraps,** designed to elicit applause because they were conventional theatrical exaggerations. (Hamlet's startled reaction when he first sees his father's ghost is a good example.) Actors often "milked" a scene for applause by using various ingenious means of showing horror and alarm. Even the "pregnant" pause was used by Betterton and others to draw the audience in. Conventions such as broad gestures with the upstage hand and sudden kneeling on the downstage knee were widely employed for dramatic effect, along with impetuous turns to the audience, especially from the apron. Some of the older actors were also skilled at the rant—raising the voice, grotesquely twisting the body, and grimacing while driving home a point. These were tricks that actors such as David Garrick (1717–1779) often railed against in an effort to promote a more subdued style of acting. Although eighteenth-century commentators note that he sometimes used mild forms of the very tricks he disliked, Garrick's purpose was to exhibit a natural style on stage, and he was widely complimented for having done so.

Garrick's greatest role was Richard III, and he was praised for his ability to reveal a variety of emotions in his face, especially in the tent scene on Bosworth field (Figure 15). He practiced moving from joy to horror to surprise to alarm to grief to guilt—and even more emotions, one after another—all in a convincing manner. Garrick and other eighteenth-century actors had the advantage of modern theaters such as the Drury Lane (which he managed), in which the apron was close to the pit. The intimate, enclosed space made it possible for actors to be heard easily and to be seen well enough for their facial expressions to convey reactions that in ages past necessitated broad gesturing. The evolution of the theater's design made it possible for Garrick to achieve the effects for which he was so widely praised. Garrick occasionally went so far as to burlesque the overly theatrical style of some of his competitors, although sometimes only a portion of the audience got the joke.

Many good actors with fine reputations appeared on the stage of the period: James Quin (1693–1766), said to be the finest Falstaff of his age; Charles Macklin (1699–1797), a playwright also known for his sensitive portrayal

Figure 15. David Garrick as Shakespeare's Richard III, in a 1745 portrait by William Hogarth.

of Shylock and his virtual invention of the stage Irishman; Sarah Siddons (1755–1831) and her brother John Philip Kemble (1757–1823), praised for their smooth and careful acting style. Siddons and Kemble sometimes acted together to great acclaim, and their style evolved over time into a melodramatic exaggeration that was to become dominant in the early nineteenth century.

Drama in Japan

During the period of the Tokugawa shogunate (1603–1868), Japan attempted to seal itself off from the Western world. Although the Portuguese had a trading facility in Nagasaki, their influence was limited in range and scope. The great playwrights and actors of the Tokugawa period in Edo (Tokyo), Kyoto, and Osaka were generally unaware of traditions of Western drama, and in some cases they had never read or seen a foreign play.

Although Japan was essentially a military dictatorship at the time, the period was peaceful and prosperous, with a rising merchant middle class that demanded entertainment that represented their own values and interests. The shogun, or leader, was a warrior, and the warrior class—the samurai—had much to say about the forms of entertainment available. They were interested in theater partly because with peacetime came leisure time and the opportunity for indulgence. The pleasure district, or "floating world," of Kyoto permitted prostitution and various theatrical and circus-like entertainments for men. It was in this atmosphere that traditions of kabuki theater and puppet theater flourished.

Kabuki began from a dance performed in 1603 by a female entertainer named Okuni, whose popularity was such that she developed numerous imitators, especially prostitutes who danced kabuki in order to attract customers. The dance was enlarged with sketches from contemporary life accompanied by a popular three-stringed instrument called a *shamisen*. The role of the *shamisen* musician in kabuki plays was to establish the rhythms of speech and help stimulate the motions of the audience. Kabuki quickly drew important actors who used elaborate makeup and brilliant costumes to perform multiact plays over an entire day.

After women were banned from the stage in 1629, men performed all the parts in kabuki plays. Audiences found kabuki exciting because it was designed to stimulate the masses. This popular entertainment form narrated stories of contemporary life and sometimes captured the audience's dissatisfaction with the inequities they perceived in their own society. Kabuki also produced numerous highly gifted actors, many from the samurai class, who became a draw in their own right.

Partly because the actors became difficult and demanding, some of the important playwrights of the time, including Chikamatsu Monzaemon (1653–1725), turned to the *jōruri*, or puppet plays. Unlike actors, puppets made no demands on authors and never stole the show. They were also versatile enough to create remarkably subtle expressions of emotion, thought, and action. Some plays were produced in both kabuki and *jōruri* forms, but because incredible special effects were possible with puppets—effects that could not be achieved with actors—*jōruri* theater flourished in the early eighteenth century.

Chikamatsu, the greatest of Japanese playwrights, was born into a samurai family that had little influence in society. He drifted into kabuki theater and now enjoys the reputation of being Japan's first professional playwright. His early plays were for particularly important kabuki actors. He specialized in history plays, which were popular because they educated people not only about their own history but also about faraway places. His domestic plays, especially his tragedies, which are primarily puppet plays, are more frequently produced today, partly because their subjects—middle-class suffering and emotional longing—seem more modern to us. *The Love Suicides at Sonezaki*, one of a series of love suicide plays, was so influential as to help cause the entire genre to be banned.

During this period, kabuki acting and stagecraft developed quickly, with highly stylized masks, extraordinary costumes, and complex sets. Eventually, complex stage machinery—trap doors and revolving stages—made the drama all the more interesting. The puppet stage depended on a chanter who recited the lines of all the characters and sometimes the narrator. Eventually, puppets operated by a single person gave way to more complex, three-person puppets requiring unusual coordination and skill and producing subtle expressions and effects. Today both forms of theater still exist in Japan and are performed throughout the world.

Late-Seventeenth- and Eighteenth-Century Drama

Date	Theater	Political	Social/Cultural
1600–1700	**1603:** Okuni creates the first kabuki dance.	**1603:** Beginning of the Tokugawa shogunate in Edo, Japan, a long period of peace	**1606–1669:** Rembrandt van Rijn, Dutch painter
	1606–1684: French playwright Pierre Corneille, author of *Le Cid* (1636)	**1605:** Gun Powder Plot in London; execution of Guy Fawkes	**1608–1674:** John Milton, English author
	1622–1673: Molière (born Jean Baptiste Poquelin), French dramatist and actor, author of *The Misanthrope* (1666), *Tartuffe* (1669), and *The Learned Ladies* (1672)		**1610:** Galileo's first observations through a telescope
			1620: Voyage of the *Mayflower*
			1628: William Harvey describes the circulation of blood.
	c. 1634–1691: Sir George Etherege, author of *Love in a Tub* and *The Man of Mode* (1676)		**1631–1700:** John Dryden, English author and playwright
	1635–1710: Thomas Betterton, perhaps the Restoration's most important actor		**1633:** John Donne's *Poems*, the complete collection of his poetry, is published.
	1639–1699: Jean Racine, French playwright, author of *Phaedra* (1677)		**1637:** René Descartes's *Discourse on Method*, an exploration of mathematics and laws
	1640–1689: Aphra Behn, first professional female playwright in the English theater, author of *The Rover* (1677)	**1642:** Beginning of the English Civil War	**1638:** Anne Hutchinson is expelled from the Massachusetts Bay Colony and founds Rhode Island.
	1650–1687: Nell Gwynne, English actress and mistress of Charles II	**1643:** Louis XIV becomes king of France at age four.	**1645:** Gian Lorenzo Bernini begins his *Ecstasy of St. Theresa.*
	1656: First use of Italianate scenery in England in a production of *The Siege of Rhodes,* designed by John Webb	**1649:** Charles I is beheaded by order of Parliament.	**1650:** Anne Bradstreet publishes *The Tenth Muse*, the first collection of poetry from the New World.
	1658: Molière's troupe, the Illustre Théâtre, is invited to perform at the court of Louis XIV. The company is subsequently given permission to remain in Paris, as the Troupe de Monsieur, and allowed to use the Petit Bourbon for public performances.	**1655:** Oliver Cromwell prohibits Anglican church services and divides England into eleven districts governed by major-generals. **1658:** Cromwell dissolves Parliament and then dies in September.	
	1660: Theatrical activity resumes in London (after being halted in 1642) when Charles II issues patents to Thomas Killigrew and William Davenant. Women are permitted on the English stage for the first time.	**1660:** Restoration of the English monarchy and end of the Commonwealth; Charles II, son of the executed Charles I, is crowned.	**1660:** Samuel Pepys begins his diary. **1660:** Dutch Boers settle on the Cape of Good Hope. **1661–1731:** Daniel Defoe, English author

Date	Theater	Political	Social/Cultural
1600–1700 (continued)	**1664:** Japanese playwright Fukui Yagozaemon writes *The Outcast's Revenge,* the first full-length kabuki play. **1670–1729:** William Congreve, author of *Love for Love* (1695) and *The Way of the World* (1700) **1680:** The Comédie-Française, the first national theater, opens in Paris. **1695–1715:** Proliferation of female playwrights in England. Thirty-seven new plays by women are produced on the London stage during this period by playwrights such as Mary Pix (1666–1706), Susanna Centlivre (c. 1670–1723), Mary Delarivière Manley (c. 1672–1724), and Catharine Trotter (1679–1749). **1698:** Jeremy Collier's *A Short View of the Immorality and Profaneness of the English Stage,* the most effective of several attacks on the theater published at the turn of the century	**1664:** The British annex New Amsterdam and rename it New York. **1682:** Louis XIV moves the French court to Versailles. **1682–1725:** Peter the Great reigns as czar of Russia and calls for political and cultural reforms. **1685:** Louis XIV revokes the Edict of Nantes, and persecution of the Huguenots (French Protestants) ensues. **1688:** William of Orange invades England with the encouragement of prominent Protestants, who fear James II's Catholicism. James flees to France. William III and Mary II (daughter of James II) are crowned in 1689. **1690:** An Irish uprising in favor of James II is suppressed by William III at the Battle of the Boyne. **1697:** The last remains of Mayan civilization are destroyed by the Spanish.	**1664–1666:** Isaac Newton (1642–1727), English mathematician and physicist, discovers the law of universal gravitation and begins to develop calculus. **1665:** Plague devastates London. **1666:** Great Fire of London **1685–1750:** J. S. Bach, German composer **1687:** Isaac Newton publishes *Mathematical Principles*. **1688–1704:** Alexander Pope, English poet **1692:** Salem witchcraft trials **1694–1778:** François Marie Arouet de Voltaire, French author often described as the embodiment of the Enlightenment
1700–1800	**1703:** Chikamatsu creates the genre of love suicide plays with *The Love Suicides at Sonezaki*. **1707–1793:** Carlo Goldoni, Italian playwright, author of *The Servant of Two Masters* (1743) **1717–1779:** David Garrick, greatest English actor of the eighteenth century and owner and manager of the Drury Lane Theatre in London **1720–1806:** Carlo Gozzi, Italian playwright, author of *King Stag* (1762) and *Turandot* (1762)	**1703:** Peter the Great lays the foundation for St. Petersburg. **1707:** The Act of Union unites Scotland and England, which become Great Britain. **1714:** The House of Hanover begins its rule of Great Britain with the accession of George I. **1715:** Louis XIV, France's Sun King, dies.	**1703–1758:** Jonathan Edwards, American theologian **1709–1784:** Samuel Johnson, English literary critic, scholar, poet, and lexicographer **1720:** First serialization of novels in newspapers **1724–1804:** Emmanuel Kant, German metaphysics philosopher

Date	Theater	Political	Social/Cultural
1700–1800 (continued)	**1728:** John Gay (1685–1732) writes *The Beggar's Opera,* arguably the most popular English play of the eighteenth century.		**1726:** Jonathan Swift writes *Gulliver's Travels.*
	1730–1774: Oliver Goldsmith, author of *The Vicar of Wakefield*, *The Deserted Village*, and *She Stoops to Conquer*		**1732:** Covent Garden opera house opens in London.
	1729–1781: Gotthold Ephraim Lessing, Germany's first important playwright, author of *Minna von Barnhelm* (1767) and *Emilia Galotti* (1772)		**1732–1809:** Franz Josef Haydn, prolific Austrian composer
	1737: The Licensing Act in England prohibits the performance of any play not previously licensed by the Lord Chamberlain. A number of such laws regulating theatrical activity are enacted throughout the eighteenth century.	**1740:** Frederick the Great introduces freedom of press and worship in Prussia.	**1742:** Cotton factories are established in Birmingham and Northampton, England.
	1749–1832: Johann Wolfgang von Goethe, German writer whose early works include the play *Götz von Berlichingen* (1773) and the novel *The Sorrows of Young Werther* (1774)		**1746–1828:** Francisco de Goya, Spanish painter and political cartoonist
		1756: Frederick begins the Seven Years War, pitting Prussia and Great Britain against Russia, Austria, and France.	**1751:** Denis Diderot, French writer and philosopher, publishes the first volume of his *Encyclopédie.*
	1751–1816: Richard Brinsley Sheridan, playwright and statesman, author of *The School for Scandal* (1777)		**1756–1791:** Wolfgang Amadeus Mozart, Austrian composer
	1762: English actor-manager David Garrick prohibits audience members from sitting on the stage.	**1762:** Catherine the Great (b. 1729) becomes empress of Russia after overthrowing her husband, Peter III; she reigns until her death in 1796.	**1757–1827:** William Blake, Romantic poet and artist, author of *Songs of Innocence* and *Songs of Experience*
		1763: The Treaty of Paris ends the Seven Years War. Prussia emerges as an important European power. France loses many colonial possessions.	**1759–1797:** Mary Wollstonecraft, English writer and early feminist, author of *Vindication of the Rights of Woman* (1792)
		1765: British Parliament passes the Stamp Act. Nine colonies in the New World draw up a declaration of rights and liberties.	**1762:** The Sorbonne library opens in Paris.
	c. 1769: Spectators are banned from sitting on the stage in Paris.	**1766:** Catherine the Great grants freedom of worship in Russia.	
		1776: U.S. Declaration of Independence	**1791:** James Boswell publishes his *Life of Johnson.*

Molière

Molière (1622–1673, born Jean Baptiste Poquelin) came from a family attached to the glittering court of Louis XIV, the Sun King. His father had purchased an appointment to the king, and as a result the family was familiar with the exciting court life of Paris, although not on intimate terms with the courtiers who surrounded the king. Molière's father was a furnisher and upholsterer to the king; the family, while well-to-do and possessing some power, was still apart from royalty and the privileged aristocracy.

Molière's education was exceptional. He went to Jesuit schools and spent more than five years at Collège de Clermont, which he left in 1641, having studied both the humanities and philosophy. His knowledge of philosophy was unusually deep, and his background in the classics was exceptionally strong. He also took a law degree in 1641, at Orléans, but never practiced. His father's dream was that Molière should inherit his father's appointment as furnisher to the king, thereby guaranteeing himself a comfortable future.

That, however, was not to be. Instead of following the law, Molière decided at the last minute to abandon his secure future, change his name so as not to scandalize his family, and take up a career in the theater. He began by joining a company of actors run by the Béjart family. They established a theater based in Paris called the Illustre Théâtre. It was run by Madeleine Béjart, with whom Molière had a professional and personal relationship until she died in 1672.

The famed commedia dell'arte actor Tiberio Fiorillo, known as Scaramouche, was a close friend of Molière and perhaps was responsible for Molière's choice of a career in theater. Scaramouche may have been part of the Illustre Théâtre, or he may have acted in it on occasion. Unfortunately, the Illustre Théâtre lasted only a year. It was one of several Parisian theatrical groups, and none of them prospered.

The company went bankrupt in 1644, and Molière had to be bailed out of debtors' prison. Forced to leave Paris for about thirteen years, he played in the provinces and remote towns. What was left of the Béjart group merged with another company on tour, and Molière became director of that company. During this time he suffered most of the indignities typical of the traveling life, including poverty.

Eventually Molière began writing plays, but only after he had worked extensively as an actor. In October 1658, Louis XIV saw Molière's troupe acting in one of his comedies at the Louvre. The royal court was so impressed with what it saw that the king gave Molière the use of a theater. Molière's work remained immensely popular and controversial. He acted in and produced his own plays and wrote a succession of major works that are still favorites.

Because other companies envied Molière's success and favor with the king, a number of "scandals" arose around his plays. The first play to invite controversy was *The School for Wives* (1662), in which Arnolphe reacts in horror to the infidelities he sees in the wives all around him. He decides that his wife-to-be must be raised far from the world, where she will be ignorant of the wayward lives of the Parisians. A man who intends to seduce her tells Arnolphe

For links to resources about Molière, click on *AuthorLinks* at bedfordstmartins.com/jacobus.

313

(not knowing who he is) how he will get her out of Arnolphe's grasp. The play is highly comic, but groups of theatergoers protested that it was immoral and scandalous. In response Molière wrote *Criticism of the School for Wives* (1663), in which the debate over the play is enacted.

Though not his most comic play, *The Misanthrope* (1666), is one of his most often produced and most thought-provoking. Molière himself acted the part of Alceste, and his wife acted opposite him as Célimène; most of the players realized that the play was making fun of the couple's own marriage. It was not so serious a portrayal as to dampen the spirits of the audience, because Molière introduced enough humor to keep it light. Yet the play had enough substance to keep audiences focused on the opposing sentiments of the couple. Alceste hates society and refuses to be polite and tell people nice things when he feels they deserve rebuke. Célimène loves society and especially loves the way she can dominate it and be its center, enjoying the attention of many suitors.

The Misanthrope examines the character of each person on stage and, by extension, the character of those in the audience—a privileged, refined stratum of society. One reason the play did not satisfy its earliest audiences may be that the lovers adhere to their opposite views of the world and, as a result, do not marry in the end. A conventional comedy would have found a means to join them, but this is not a conventional comedy.

Among Molière's other successes are *The Miser* (1668), *The Bourgeois Gentleman* (1670), and his final play, *The Imaginary Invalid* (1673). Molière had a bad cough for most of the last decade of his life, which onstage he often made to seem the cough of the character he was playing. But Molière was genuinely ill; he died playing the title role in *The Imaginary Invalid*.

Tartuffe

Molière first produced *Tartuffe, or The Hypocrite* in three acts at Versailles at a royal fête in 1664. Although the king recognized the value of the play and liked to have it read at court as a private entertainment, he immediately banned it from public production. While the king was away from court, Molière rewrote the play as *Panulphe, or the Hypocrite,* but that also was deemed too irreverent to be produced publicly.

Because Molière's satirical comedies were already thought to be problematic for French society, the clergy, who wielded considerable power with the king, kept careful watch on Molière's productions. The Society of the Holy Sacrament thought that it was being satirized in *Tartuffe* and protested the play as immoral and an attack on the Church. The Bishop of Autun also believed, perhaps correctly, that he was being satirized in the character of Tartuffe. Molière was denounced as a "demon," and a writ of excommunication was ordered against all who performed in or went to see the play.

In 1669, after the Society of the Holy Sacrament had been dissolved and after the king had managed to assuage the clergy, a permit was issued for the production of the present version of the play in five acts. Its immediate success established it as a permanent repertory piece, and it has been performed regularly ever since. Its satire on religious hypocrisy is timeless and meaningful in virtually all societies.

Tartuffe is a beggar who somehow cons Orgon, a wealthy man with a large estate, into taking him into his home. Tartuffe tricks Orgon by convincing him that he is a man of God who cares nothing for the material goods of the world and whose only duty is to God. Orgon's mother, Madame Pernelle, is thoroughly convinced that Tartuffe is virtuous and that the family must listen to and respect him. Orgon's son Damis sees Tartuffe for a fraud but is silenced and disowned by his father, who will not listen to reason. He has made up his mind and cannot be swayed by argument.

Molière immediately introduces the comic convention of the father forcing his daughter to marry against her will when Orgon announces that Mariane must give up her love for Valère and marry Tartuffe. She is an obedient daughter and seems to comply, though reluctantly. In one of the most amusing scenes in drama (act 2, scene 3), Mariane's maid Dorine cleverly persuades her to disobey her father and marry Valère. The interchange between Mariane and Valère in scene 4 reveals the high spirits of both lovers, who demonstrate their stubbornness and whose irritation with each other is smoothed over by the clever maid, a staple of drama since the Greeks.

Tartuffe, who does not appear until act 3, proposes adultery to Orgon's wife, Elmire, who plays along with him to undo Orgon's plans to marry off Mariane. It is a wonderfully comic scene (act 3, scene 3) marked by memorable lines, such as Tartuffe's "I offer you, my dear Elmire, / Love without scandal, pleasure without fear." Later he adds, "It's scandal, madame, which makes it an offense / And it's no sin to sin in confidence" (act 4, scene 5). Elmire finally plots to expose Tartuffe to her husband by having Orgon hide while Tartuffe tries to seduce her. But the plan almost backfires because Orgon madly signed over his estate to Tartuffe and upbraided his family for abusing a pious man.

The level of satire in the play is broad enough to bring laughter to virtually all audiences, and the portrait of a supposedly pious, religious, and zealous person who is fundamentally a hypocrite and fraud is so brilliantly established that Tartuffe has become the stereotype of the hypocrite. The many such frauds exposed in the press in our own era make it clear that little has changed since Molière's time.

Richard Wilbur's translation, in rhymed couplets, respects the original French, which is also in rhymed couplets. The French verse is twelve-syllable rhymed couplets, called Alexandrines. Rhyming is much easier to do in French than in English, but Wilbur produces some marvelous rhymes, such as Tartuffe's seductive lines "Madam, forget such fears, and be my pupil, / And I shall teach you how to conquer scruple" (act 4, scene 5, 99–100). The artificiality of rhyme mirrors the artificiality of some of the characters and of their society — probably even more effectively in modern English than it did in seventeenth-century France, when it was unusual for plays to be written in prose.

Molière observes the unities in *Tartuffe* by having the action take place in one day, in one setting, with no subplots. The result is that intensity builds relentlessly until the unusual resolution of the action, which comes at the very last minute. As in most comedies, the lovers are permitted to marry, the villain is revealed and chastised, and the family is restored to its rightful position. But in the process, society is exposed as gullible, naive, and easily manipulated. In this sense, the play is a moral play, rather than the dangerous immoral work that the clergy condemned.

Tartuffe in Performance

Molière played the part of Orgon at the first public performance in February 1669, at the Palais Royale in Paris. The Théâtre-Français, which still produces the play regularly, featured Nicholas Auge as Tartuffe in 1776. His first entrance in act 3 was notable for his bringing out a gigantic handkerchief to hide Dorine's bosom, while delivering the line "Hide that breast" with a lustful leer and obvious lecherous looks — a convention later followed and developed by that company throughout the nineteenth century. One of the strangest productions was that of the Athénée theater in Paris in 1950, with Louis Jouvet as a truly pious Tartuffe struggling with himself over the temptation of Elmire! Jouvet's Tartuffe was not a slovenly, fat, lecherous figure with a dangling crucifix, as conventional Tartuffes were. Audiences for that production were annoyed at what they saw as a misreading of the text, and reviews indicate that there were very few laughs. However, the production ran for 139 performances. A similar interpretation in Paris in 1964 with Michel Auclair, a dashing leading man of the era, emphasized a possible unconscious homosexual connection between Tartuffe and Orgon as an explanation for Orgon's strange behavior. The stage was decorated with huge black-and-white religious paintings that depicted a naked Christ, thus introducing the images of flesh even before the play began. In 1965, the Repertory Theatre of Lincoln Center produced the Richard Wilbur translation with Michael O'Sullivan as Tartuffe; the production ran for five months, alternating with an Arthur Miller play. Tyrone Guthrie's 1967 production at the Old Vic starred John Gielgud as Orgon but was criticized for its weak, rural clown Tartuffe. However, it was praised for avoiding modern psychological interpretations and sticking with the text in such a way that the *deus ex machina* of the king's messenger at the end was more intelligible as a force that restores proper order to a disordered world. Freyda Thomas adapted the play at Circle in the Square in New York in 1996 as *Tartuffe: Born Again*. This production portrayed Tartuffe as a modern televangelist, a comparison that begged to be made in the 1990s. In 2002, London's National Theatre produced a rollicking *Tartuffe* with Martin Clunes, a TV sitcom star of considerable girth, playing the role broadly for laughs in a translation that sometimes verged on the scatological. The Yale Repertory Theatre productions took the same approach, first in 1984 and most recently in 2007. Austin Pendleton performed Tartuffe at Yale, and his comic interpretation will be long remembered. The popularity of *Tartuffe* continues, with 2011 productions at Brigham Young University, Dordt College, the Workshop Theatre and Pearl Theatre in New York, the Los Angeles Stage, the Theatricum Botanicum, and the English Touring Theatre, in an adaptation by Roger McGough. Hypocrisy seems to be a lively dramatic subject in any age.

For discussion questions and assignments on *Tartuffe*, visit bedfordstmartins.com/jacobus.

MOLIÈRE (1622–1673)

Tartuffe 1669

TRANSLATED BY RICHARD WILBUR

Characters

MME PERNELLE, *Orgon's mother*
ORGON, *Elmire's husband*
ELMIRE, *Orgon's wife*
DAMIS, *Orgon's son, Elmire's stepson*
MARIANE, *Orgon's daughter, Elmire's stepdaughter, in love with Valère*
VALÈRE, *in love with Mariane*
CLÉANTE, *Orgon's brother-in-law*
TARTUFFE, *a hypocrite*
DORINE, *Mariane's lady's-maid*
M. LOYAL, *a bailiff*
A POLICE OFFICER
FLIPOTE, *Mme Pernelle's maid*

The scene throughout: Orgon's house in Paris.

ACT I • Scene 1

[*Madame Pernelle and Flipote, her maid, Elmire, Mariane, Dorine, Damis, Cléante.*]

MADAME PERNELLE: Come, come, Flipote; it's time I left this place.
ELMIRE: I can't keep up, you walk at such a pace.
MADAME PERNELLE: Don't trouble, child; no need to show me out.
   It's not your manners I'm concerned about.
5 ELMIRE: We merely pay you the respect we owe.
   But, Mother, why this hurry? Must you go?
MADAME PERNELLE: I must. This house appalls me.
      No one in it
   Will pay attention for a single minute.
   Children, I take my leave much vexed in spirit.
10 I offer good advice, but you won't hear it.
   You all break in and chatter on and on.
   It's like a madhouse with the keeper gone.
DORINE: If . . .
MADAME PERNELLE: Girl, you talk too much, and I'm afraid
   You're far too saucy for a lady's-maid.
15 You push in everywhere and have your say.
DAMIS: But . . .
MADAME PERNELLE: You, boy, grow more foolish every day.
   To think my grandson should be such a dunce!
   I've said a hundred times, if I've said it once,
   That if you keep the course on which you've started,

You'll leave your worthy father broken-hearted.   20
MARIANE: I think . . .
MADAME PERNELLE: And you, his sister, seem so pure,
   So shy, so innocent, and so demure.
   But you know what they say about still waters.
   I pity parents with secretive daughters.
ELMIRE: Now, Mother . . .
MADAME PERNELLE: And as for you, child, let me add   25
   That your behavior is extremely bad,
   And a poor example for these children, too.
   Their dear, dead mother did far better than you.
   You're much too free with money, and I'm distressed
   To see you so elaborately dressed.   30
   When it's one's husband that one aims to please,
   One has no need of costly fripperies.
CLÉANTE: Oh, Madam, really . . .
MADAME PERNELLE: You are her brother, Sir,
   And I respect and love you; yet if I were
   My son, this lady's good and pious spouse,   35
   I wouldn't make you welcome in my house.
   You're full of worldly counsels which, I fear,
   Aren't suitable for decent folk to hear.
   I've spoken bluntly, Sir; but it behooves us
   Not to mince words when righteous fervor moves us.   40
DAMIS: Your man Tartuffe is full of holy speeches . . .
MADAME PERNELLE: And practices precisely what he preaches.
   He's a fine man, and should be listened to.
   I will not hear him mocked by fools like you.
DAMIS: Good God! Do you expect me to submit   45
   To the tyranny of that carping hypocrite?
   Must we forgo all joys and satisfactions
   Because that bigot censures all our actions?
DORINE: To hear him talk—and he talks all the time—
   There's nothing one can do that's not a crime.   50
   He rails at everything, your dear Tartuffe.
MADAME PERNELLE: Whatever he reproves deserves reproof.
   He's out to save your souls, and all of you
   Must love him, as my son would have you do.
DAMIS: Ah no, Grandmother, I could never take   55
   To such a rascal, even for my father's sake.
   That's how I feel, and I shall not dissemble.
   His every action makes me seethe and tremble
   With helpless anger, and I have no doubt
   That he and I will shortly have it out.   60
DORINE: Surely it is a shame and a disgrace
   To see this man usurp the master's place—

To see this beggar who, when first he came,
Had not a shoe or shoestring to his name
65　So far forget himself that he behaves
As if the house were his, and we his slaves.

MADAME PERNELLE: Well, mark my words, your souls
　　would fare far better
If you obeyed his precepts to the letter.

DORINE: You see him as a saint. I'm far less awed;
70　In fact, I see right through him. He's a fraud.

MADAME PERNELLE: Nonsense!

DORINE:　　　　　　　　His man Laurent's the same, or
　　worse;
I'd not trust either with a penny purse.

MADAME PERNELLE: I can't say what his servant's
　　morals may be;
His own great goodness I can guarantee.
75　You all regard him with distaste and fear
Because he tells you what you're loath to hear,
Condemns your sins, points out your moral flaws,
And humbly strives to further Heaven's cause.

DORINE: If sin is all that bothers him, why is it
80　He's so upset when folk drop in to visit?
Is Heaven so outraged by a social call
That he must prophesy against us all?
I'll tell you what I think: if you ask me,
He's jealous of my mistress' company.

MADAME PERNELLE: Rubbish! (*To Elmire.*) He's not
85　alone, child, in complaining
Of all your promiscuous entertaining.
Why, the whole neighborhood's upset, I know,
By all these carriages that come and go,
With crowds of guests parading in and out
90　And noisy servants loitering about.
In all of this, I'm sure there's nothing vicious;
But why give people cause to be suspicious?

CLÉANTE: They need no cause; they'll talk in any case.
Madam, this world would be a joyless place
95　If, fearing what malicious tongues might say,
We locked our doors and turned our friends away.
And even if one did so dreary a thing,
D'you think those tongues would cease their
　　chattering?
One can't fight slander; it's a losing battle;
100　Let us instead ignore their tittle-tattle.
Let's strive to live by conscience' clear decrees,
And let the gossips gossip as they please.

DORINE: If there is talk against us, I know the source:
It's Daphne and her little husband, of course.
105　Those who have greatest cause for guilt and shame
Are quickest to besmirch a neighbor's name.
When there's a chance for libel, they never miss it;
When something can be made to seem illicit
They're off at once to spread the joyous news,
110　Adding to fact what fantasies they choose.
By talking up their neighbor's indiscretions
They seek to camouflage their own transgressions,
Hoping that others' innocent affairs
Will lend a hue of innocence to theirs,
115　Or that their own black guilt will come to seem

Part of a general shady color-scheme.

MADAME PERNELLE: All that is quite irrelevant.
　　I doubt
That anyone's more virtuous and devout
Than dear Orante; and I'm informed that she
Condemns your mode of life most vehemently.　120

DORINE: Oh, yes, she's strict, devout, and has no
　　taint
Of worldliness; in short, she seems a saint.
But it was time which taught her that disguise;
She's thus because she can't be otherwise.
So long as her attractions could enthrall,　125
She flounced and flirted and enjoyed it all,
But now that they're no longer what they were
She quits a world which fast is quitting her,
And wears a veil of virtue to conceal
Her bankrupt beauty and her lost appeal.　130
That's what becomes of old coquettes today;
Distressed when all their lovers fall away,
They see no recourse but to play the prude,
And so confer a style on solitude.
Thereafter, they're severe with everyone,　135
Condemning all our actions, pardoning none,
And claiming to be pure, austere, and zealous
When, if the truth were known, they're merely
　　jealous,
And cannot bear to see another know
The pleasures time has forced them to forgo.　140

MADAME PERNELLE (*initially to Elmire*): That sort of
　　talk is what you like to hear;
Therefore you'd have us all keep still, my dear,
While Madam rattles on the livelong day.
Nevertheless, I mean to have my say.
I tell you that you're blest to have Tartuffe　145
Dwelling, as my son's guest, beneath this roof;
That Heaven has sent him to forestall its wrath
By leading you, once more, to the true path;
That all he reprehends is reprehensible,
And that you'd better heed him, and be sensible.　150
These visits, balls, and parties in which you revel
Are nothing but inventions of the Devil.
One never hears a word that's edifying:
Nothing but chaff and foolishness and lying,
As well as vicious gossip in which one's neighbor　155
Is cut to bits with epee, foil, and saber.
People of sense are driven half-insane
At such affairs, where noise and folly reign
And reputations perish thick and fast.
As a wise preacher said on Sunday last,　160
Parties are Towers of Babylon, because
The guests all babble on with never a pause;
And then he told a story which, I think . . .
　　(*To Cléante.*)
I heard that laugh, Sir, and I saw that wink!
Go find your silly friends and laugh some more!　165
Enough; I'm going; don't show me to the door.
I leave this household much dismayed and vexed;
I cannot say when I shall see you next.
　　(*Slapping Flipote.*)

Wake up, don't stand there gaping into space!
170   I'll slap some sense into that stupid face.
Move, move, you slut.

Scene 2   [*Cléante, Dorine.*]

CLÉANTE: I think I'll stay behind;
I want no further pieces of her mind.
How that old lady . . .
DORINE: Oh, what wouldn't she say
If she could hear you speak of her that way!
5   She'd thank you for the *lady,* but I'm sure
She'd find the *old* a little premature.
CLÉANTE: My, what a scene she made, and what a din!
And how this man Tartuffe has taken her in!
DORINE: Yes, but her son is even worse deceived;
10   His folly must be seen to be believed.
In the late troubles, he played an able part
And served his king with wise and loyal heart,
But he's quite lost his senses since he fell
Beneath Tartuffe's infatuating spell.
15   He calls him brother, and loves him as his life,
Preferring him to mother, child, or wife.
In him and him alone will he confide;
He's made him his confessor and his guide;
He pets and pampers him with love more tender
20   Than any pretty mistress could engender,
Gives him the place of honor when they dine,
Delights to see him gorging like a swine,
Stuffs him with dainties till his guts distend,
And when he belches, cries "God bless you, friend!"
25   In short, he's mad; he worships him; he dotes;
His deeds he marvels at, his words he quotes,
Thinking each act a miracle, each word
Oracular as those that Moses heard.
Tartuffe, much pleased to find so easy a victim,
30   Has in a hundred ways beguiled and tricked him,
Milked him of money, and with his permission
Established here a sort of Inquisition.
Even Laurent, his lackey, dares to give
Us arrogant advice on how to live;
35   He sermonizes us in thundering tones
And confiscates our ribbons and colognes.
Last week he tore a kerchief into pieces
Because he found it pressed in a *Life of Jesus:*
He said it was a sin to juxtapose
40   Unholy vanities and holy prose.

Scene 3   [*Elmire, Mariane, Damis, Cléante, Dorine.*]

ELMIRE (*to Cléante*): You did well not to follow; she stood in the door
And said *verbatim* all she'd said before.
I saw my husband coming. I think I'd best
Go upstairs now, and take a little rest.

CLÉANTE: I'll wait and greet him here; then I must go.   5
I've really only time to say hello.
DAMIS: Sound him about my sister's wedding, please,
I think Tartuffe's against it, and that he's
Been urging Father to withdraw his blessing,
As you well know, I'd find that most distressing.   10
Unless my sister and Valère can marry,
My hopes to wed *his* sister will miscarry,
And I'm determined . . .
DORINE: He's coming.

Scene 4   [*Orgon, Cléante, Dorine.*]

ORGON: Ah, Brother, good-day.
CLÉANTE: Well, welcome back. I'm sorry I can't stay,
How was the country? Blooming, I trust, and green?
ORGON: Excuse me, Brother; just one moment.
     (*To Dorine.*)
                  Dorine . . .
     (*To Cleante.*)   5
To put my mind at rest, I always learn
The household news the moment I return.
              (*To Dorine.*)
Has all been well, these two days I've been gone?
How are the family? What's been going on?
DORINE: Your wife, two days ago, had a bad fever,   10
And a fierce headache which refused to leave her.
ORGON: Ah. And Tartuffe?
DORINE: Tartuffe? Why, he's round and red,
Bursting with health, and excellently fed.
ORGON: Poor fellow!
DORINE: That night, the mistress was unable
To take a single bite at the dinner-table.   15
Her headache-pains, she said, were simply hellish.
ORGON: Ah. And Tartuffe?
DORINE: He ate his meal with relish,
And zealously devoured in her presence
A leg of mutton and a brace of pheasants.
ORGON: Poor fellow!
DORINE: Well, the pains continued strong,   20
And so she tossed and tossed the whole night long,
Now icy-cold, now burning like a flame.
We sat beside her bed till morning came.
ORGON: Ah. And Tartuffe?
DORINE: Why, having eaten, he rose
And sought his room, already in a doze,   25
Got into his warm bed, and snored away
In perfect peace until the break of day.
ORGON: Poor fellow!
DORINE: After much ado, we talked her
Into dispatching someone for the doctor.
He bled her, and the fever quickly fell.   30

ORGON: Ah. And Tartuffe?
DORINE: He bore it very well.
   To keep his cheerfulness at any cost,
   And make up for the blood *Madame* had lost,
   He drank, at lunch, four beakers full of port.
ORGON: Poor fellow!
35 DORINE: Both are doing well, in short.
   I'll go and tell *Madame* that you've expressed
   Keen sympathy and anxious interest.

Scene 5   [*Orgon, Cléante.*]

CLÉANTE: That girl was laughing in your face, and
     though
   I've no wish to offend you, even so
   I'm bound to say that she had some excuse.
   How can you possibly be such a goose?
5   Are you so dazed by this man's hocus-pocus
   That all the world, save him, is out of focus?
   You've given him clothing, shelter, food, and care;
   Why must you also . . .
ORGON: Brother, stop right there.
   You do not know the man of whom you speak.
CLÉANTE: I grant you that. But my judgment's not so
10   weak
   That I can't tell, by his effect on others . . .
ORGON: Ah, when you meet him, you two will be
     like brothers!
   There's been no loftier soul since time began.
   He is a man who . . . a man who . . . an excellent man.
15   To keep his precepts is to be reborn,
   And view this dunghill of a world with scorn.
   Yes, thanks to him I'm a changed man indeed.
   Under his tutelage my soul's been freed
   From earthly loves, and every human tie:
20   My mother, children, brother, and wife could die,
   And I'd not feel a single moment's pain.
CLÉANTE: That's a fine sentiment, Brother; most humane.
ORGON: Oh, had you seen Tartuffe as I first knew him,
   Your heart, like mine, would have surrendered to
     him.
25   He used to come into our church each day
   And humbly kneel nearby, and start to pray.
   He'd draw the eyes of everybody there
   By the deep fervor of his heartfelt prayer;
   He'd sigh and weep, and sometimes with a sound
30   Of rapture he would bend and kiss the ground;
   And when I rose to go, he'd run before
   To offer me holy-water at the door.
   His serving-man, no less devout than he,
   Informed me of his master's poverty;
35   I gave him gifts, but in his humbleness
   He'd beg me every time to give him less.
   "Oh, that's too much," he'd cry, "too much by
     twice!
   I don't deserve it. The half, Sir, would suffice."

   And when I wouldn't take it back, he'd share
   Half of it with the poor, right then and there.   40
   At length, Heaven prompted me to take him in
   To dwell with us, and free our souls from sin.
   He guides our lives, and to protect my honor
   Stays by my wife, and keeps an eye upon her;
   He tells me whom she sees, and all she does,   45
   And seems more jealous than I ever was!
   And how austere he is! Why, he can detect
   A mortal sin where you would least suspect;
   In smallest trifles, he's extremely strict.
   Last week, his conscience was severely pricked   50
   Because, while praying, he had caught a flea
   And killed it, so he felt, too wrathfully.
CLÉANTE: Good God, man! Have you lost your
     common sense—
   Or is this all some joke at my expense?
   How can you stand there and in all sobriety . . .   55
ORGON: Brother, your language savors of impiety.
   Too much free-thinking's made your faith unsteady,
   And as I've warned you many times already,
   'Twill get you into trouble before you're through.
CLÉANTE: So I've been told before by dupes like you: 60
   Being blind, you'd have all others blind as well;
   The clear-eyed man you call an infidel,
   And he who sees through humbug and pretense
   Is charged, by you, with want of reverence.
   Spare me your warnings, Brother; I have no fear   65
   Of speaking out, for you and Heaven to hear,
   Against affected zeal and pious knavery.
   There's true and false in piety, as in bravery,
   And just as those whose courage shines the most
   In battle, are the least inclined to boast,   70
   So those whose hearts are truly pure and lowly
   Don't make a flashy show of being holy.
   There's a vast difference, so it seems to me,
   Between true piety and hypocrisy:
   How do you fail to see it, may I ask?   75
   Is not a face quite different from a mask?
   Cannot sincerity and cunning art,
   Reality and semblance, be told apart?
   Are scarecrows just like men, and do you hold
   That a false coin is just as good as gold?   80
   Ah, Brother, man's a strangely fashioned creature
   Who seldom is content to follow Nature,
   But recklessly pursues his inclination
   Beyond the narrow bounds of moderation,
   And often, by transgressing Reason's laws,   85
   Perverts a lofty aim or noble cause.
   A passing observation, but it applies.
ORGON: I see, dear Brother, that you're profoundly wise;
   You harbor all the insight of the age.
   You are our one clear mind, our only sage,   90
   The era's oracle, its Cato° too,
   And all mankind are fools compared to you.

91. Cato: Roman statesman (234–149 BCE) noted for his virtue
and wisdom.

CLÉANTE: Brother, I don't pretend to be a sage,
    Nor have I all the wisdom of the age.
95 There's just one insight I would dare to claim;
    I know that true and false are not the same;
    And just as there is nothing I more revere
    Than a soul whose faith is steadfast and sincere,
    Nothing that I more cherish and admire
100 Than honest zeal and true religious fire,
    So there is nothing that I find more base
    Than specious piety's dishonest face—
    Than these bold mountebanks, these histrios
    Whose impious mummeries and hollow shows
105 Exploit our love of Heaven, and make a jest
    Of all that men think holiest and best;
    These calculating souls who offer prayers
    Not to their Maker, but as public wares,
    And seek to buy respect and reputation
110 With lifted eyes and sighs of exaltation;
    These charlatans, I say, whose pilgrim souls
    Proceed, by way of Heaven, toward earthly goals,
    Who weep and pray and swindle and extort,
    Who preach the monkish life, but haunt the court,
115 Who make their zeal the partner of their vice—
    Such men are vengeful, sly, and cold as ice,
    And when there is an enemy to defame
    They cloak their spite in fair religion's name,
    Their private spleen and malice being made
120 To seem a high and virtuous crusade,
    Until, to mankind's reverent applause,
    They crucify their foe in Heaven's cause.
    Such knaves are all too common; yet, for the wise,
    True piety isn't hard to recognize,
125 And, happily, these present times provide us
    With bright examples to instruct and guide us.
    Consider Ariston and Périandre;
    Look at Oronte, Alcidamas, Clitandre;
    Their virtue is acknowledged; who could
        doubt it?
130 But you won't hear them beat the drum about it.
    They're never ostentatious, never vain,
    And their religion's moderate and humane;
    It's not their way to criticize and chide:
    They think censoriousness a mark of pride,
135 And therefore, letting others preach and rave,
    They show, by deeds, how Christians should
        behave.
    They think no evil of their fellow man,
    But judge of him as kindly as they can.
    They don't intrigue and wangle and conspire;
140 To lead a good life is their one desire;
    The sinner wakes no rancorous hate in them;
    It is the sin alone which they condemn;
    Nor do they try to show a fiercer zeal
    For Heaven's cause than Heaven itself could feel.
145 These men I honor, these men I advocate
    As models for us all to emulate.
    Your man is not their sort at all, I fear:
    And, while your praise of him is quite sincere,

I think that you've been dreadfully deluded.
ORGON: Now then, dear Brother, is your speech
    concluded?   150
CLÉANTE: Why, yes.
ORGON: Your servant, Sir.

[*He turns to go.*]

CLÉANTE: No, Brother; wait.
    There's one more matter. You agreed of late
    That young Valère might have your daughter's
        hand.
ORGON: I did.
CLÉANTE: And set the date, I understand.
ORGON: Quite so.
CLÉANTE: You've now postponed it; is that
        true?   155
ORGON: No doubt.
CLÉANTE: The match no longer pleases you?
ORGON: Who knows?
CLÉANTE: D'you mean to go back on
        your word?
ORGON: I won't say that.
CLÉANTE: Has anything occurred
    Which might entitle you to break your pledge?
ORGON: Perhaps.
CLÉANTE: Why must you hem, and haw, and
        hedge?   160
    The boy asked me to sound you in this affair . . .
ORGON: It's been a pleasure.
CLÉANTE: But what shall I tell
        Valère?
ORGON: Whatever you like.
CLÉANTE: But what have you
        decided?
    What are your plans?
ORGON: I plan, Sir, to be guided
        by Heaven's will.
CLÉANTE: Come, Brother, don't talk rot. 165
    You've given Valère your word; will you keep it,
        or not?
ORGON : Good day.
CLÉANTE: This looks like poor Valère's
        undoing;
    I'll go and warn him that there's trouble brewing.

ACT II • Scene 1   [*Orgon, Mariane.*]

ORGON: Mariane.
MARIANE: Yes, Father?
ORGON: A word with you; come here.
MARIANE: What are you looking for?
ORGON (*peering into a small closet*):
                            Eavesdroppers, dear.
    I'm making sure we shan't be overheard.
    Someone in there could catch our every word.
    Ah, good, we're safe. Now, Mariane, my child,   5

You're a sweet girl who's tractable and mild,
Whom I hold dear, and think most highly of.
MARIANE: I'm deeply grateful, Father, for your love.
ORGON: That's well said, Daughter; and you can
        repay me
10   If, in all things, you'll cheerfully obey me.
MARIANE: To please you, Sir, is what delights me best.
ORGON: Good, good. Now, what d'you think of
        Tartuffe, our guest?
MARIANE: I, Sir?
ORGON: Yes. Weigh your answer; think it through.
MARIANE: Oh, dear. I'll say whatever you wish me to.
ORGON: That's wisely said, my Daughter. Say of him,
15   then,
That he's the very worthiest of men,
And that you're fond of him, and would rejoice
In being his wife, if that should be my choice.
Well?
MARIANE: What?
ORGON: What's that?
MARIANE: I . . .
ORGON: Well?
MARIANE: Forgive me,
        pray.
ORGON: Did you not hear me?
MARIANE: Of *whom*, Sir, must I
20   say
That I am fond of him, and would rejoice
In being his wife, if that should be your choice?
ORGON: Why, of Tartuffe.
MARIANE: But, Father, that's false, you
        know.
Why would you have me say what isn't so?
25 ORGON: Because I am resolved it shall be true.
That it's my wish should be enough for you.
MARIANE: You can't mean, Father . . .
ORGON: Yes, Tartuffe
        shall be
Allied by marriage to this family,
And he's to be your husband, is that clear?
30 It's a father's privilege . . .

Scene 2   [*Dorine, Orgon, Mariane.*]

ORGON (*to Dorine*):   What are you doing in
        here?
Is curiosity so fierce a passion
With you, that you must eavesdrop in this
        fashion?
DORINE: There's lately been a rumor going about—
Based on some hunch or chance remark, no
5   doubt—
That you mean Mariane to wed Tartuffe.
I've laughed it off, of course, as just a spoof.
ORGON: You find it so incredible?
DORINE: Yes, I do.
I won't accept that story, even from you.

ORGON: Well, you'll believe it when the thing is
        done.   10
DORINE: Yes, yes, of course. Go on and have your
        fun.
ORGON: I've never been more serious in my life.
DORINE: Ha!
ORGON: Daughter, I mean it; you're to be his wife.
DORINE: No, don't believe your father; it's all a hoax.
ORGON: See here, young woman . . .
DORINE: Come, Sir, no
        more jokes;   15
You can't fool us.
ORGON: How dare you talk that way?
DORINE: All right, then: we believe you, sad to say.
But how a man like you, who looks so wise
And wears a moustache of such splendid size,
Can be so foolish as to . . .
ORGON: Silence, please!   20
My girl, you take too many liberties.
I'm master here, as you must not forget.
DORINE: Do let's discuss this calmly; don't be upset.
You can't be serious, Sir, about this plan.
What should that bigot want with Mariane?   25
Praying and fasting ought to keep him busy.
And then, in terms of wealth and rank, what
        is he?
Why should a man of property like you
Pick out a beggar son-in-law?
ORGON: That will do.
Speak of his poverty with reverence.   30
His is a pure and saintly indigence
Which far transcends all worldly pride and pelf.
He lost his fortune, as he says himself,
Because he cared for Heaven alone, and so
Was careless of his interests here below.   35
I mean to get him out of his present straits
And help him to recover his estates—
Which, in his part of the world, have no small
        fame.
Poor though he is, he's a gentleman just the same.
DORINE: Yes, so he tells us; and, Sir, it seems to me   40
Such pride goes very ill with piety.
A man whose spirit spurns this dungy earth
Ought not to brag of lands and noble birth;
Such worldly arrogance will hardly square
With meek devotion and the life of prayer.   45
. . . But this approach, I see, has drawn a blank;
Let's speak, then, of his person, not his rank.
Doesn't it seem to you a trifle grim
To give a girl like her to a man like him?
When two are so ill-suited, can't you see   50
What the sad consequence is bound to be?
A young girl's virtue is imperilled, Sir,
When such a marriage is imposed on her;
For if one's bridegroom isn't to one's taste,
It's hardly an inducement to be chaste,   55
And many a man with horns upon his brow
Has made his wife the thing that she is now.
It's hard to be a faithful wife, in short,

To certain husbands of a certain sort,
60   And he who gives his daughter to a man she hates
Must answer for her sins at Heaven's gates.
Think, Sir, before you play so risky a role.
ORGON: This servant-girl presumes to save my soul!
DORINE: You would do well to ponder what I've said.
65   ORGON: Daughter, we'll disregard this dunderhead.
Just trust your father's judgment. Oh, I'm aware
That I once promised you to young Valère;
But now I hear he gambles, which greatly
        shocks me;
What's more, I've doubts about his orthodoxy.
70   His visits to church, I note, are very few.
DORINE: Would you have him go at the same hours
        as you,
And kneel nearby, to be sure of being seen?
ORGON: I can dispense with such remarks, Dorine.
(*To Mariane.*)
Tartuffe, however, is sure of Heaven's blessing,
75   And that's the only treasure worth possessing.
This match will bring you joys beyond all
        measure;
Your cup will overflow with every pleasure;
You two will interchange your faithful loves
Like two sweet cherubs, or two turtle-doves.
80   No harsh word shall be heard, no frown be seen,
And he shall make you happy as a queen.
DORINE: And she'll make him a cuckold, just wait
        and see.
ORGON: What language!
DORINE: Oh, he's a man of destiny;
He's *made* for horns, and what the stars demand
85   Your daughter's virtue surely can't withstand.
ORGON: Don't interrupt me further. Why can't you
        learn
That certain things are none of your concern?
DORINE: It's for your own sake that I interfere.

[*She repeatedly interrupts Orgon just as he is turning to
speak to his daughter.*]

ORGON: Most kind of you. Now, hold your tongue,
        d'you hear?
DORINE: If I didn't love you . . .
ORGON: Spare me your
90   affection.
DORINE: I'll love you, Sir, in spite of your objection.
ORGON: Blast!
DORINE: I can't bear, Sir, for your honor's sake,
To let you make this ludicrous mistake.
ORGON: You mean to go on talking?
DORINE: If I didn't protest
95   This sinful marriage, my conscience couldn't rest.
ORGON: If you don't hold your tongue, you little
        shrew . . .
DORINE: What, lost your temper? A pious man like
        you?
ORGON: Yes! Yes! You talk and talk. I'm maddened
        by it.
Once and for all, I tell you to be quiet.

DORINE: Well, I'll be quiet. But I'll be thinking hard.   100
ORGON: Think all you like, but you had better guard
That saucy tongue of yours, or I'll . . .
(*Turning back to Mariane.*)
                                    Now, child,
I've weighed this matter fully.
DORINE (*aside*):   It drives me wild
that I can't speak.

[*Orgon turns his head, and she is silent.*]

ORGON: Tartuffe is no young dandy,
But, still, his person . . .
DORINE (*aside*):   Is as sweet as candy.   105
ORGON: Is such that, even if you shouldn't care
For his other merits . . .

[*He turns and stands facing Dorine, arms crossed.*]

DORINE (*aside*):   They'll make a lovely pair.
If I were she, no man would marry me
Against my inclination, and go scot-free.
He'd learn, before the wedding-day was over,   110
How readily a wife can find a lover.
ORGON (*to Dorine*): It seems you treat my orders as
        a joke.
DORINE: Why, what's the matter? 'Twas not to you I
        spoke.
ORGON: What *were* you doing?
DORINE: Talking to myself,
        that's all.
ORGON: Ah! (*Aside.*) One more bit of impudence and
        gall,   115
And I shall give her a good slap in the face.

(*He puts himself in position to slap her; Dorine, whenever he glances at her, stands immobile and silent.*)

Daughter, you shall accept, and with good grace,
The husband I've selected . . . Your wedding-day . . .
(*To Dorine.*).
Why don't you talk to yourself?
DORINE: I've nothing to say.
ORGON: Come, just one word.
DORINE: No thank you, Sir, I
        pass.   120
ORGON: Come, speak; I'm waiting.
DORINE: I'd not be such an ass.
ORGON (*turning to Mariane*): In short, dear
        Daughter, I mean to be obeyed,
And you must bow to the sound choice I've made.
DORINE (*moving away*): I'd not wed such a monster,
        even in jest.

[*Orgon attempts to slap her, but misses.*]

ORGON: Daughter, that maid of yours is a thorough
        pest;   125
She makes me sinfully annoyed and nettled.
I can't speak further; my nerves are too
        unsettled.
She's so upset me by her insolent talk,
I'll calm myself by going for a walk.

Scene 3   [*Dorine, Mariane.*]

DORINE (*returning*): Well, have you lost your tongue,
  girl? Must I play
Your part, and say the lines you ought to say?
Faced with a fate so hideous and absurd,
Can you not utter one dissenting word?
MARIANE: What good would it do? A father's power
5 is great.
DORINE: Resist him now, or it will be too late.
MARIANE: But . . .
DORINE: Tell him one cannot love at a
  father's whim,
That you shall marry for yourself, not him;
That once it's you who are to be the bride,
10 It's you, not he, who must be satisfied;
And that if his Tartuffe is so sublime,
He's free to marry him at any time.
MARIANE: I've bowed so long to Father's strict
  control,
I couldn't oppose him now, to save my soul.
DORINE: Come, come, Mariane. Do listen to reason,
15 won't you?
Valère has asked your hand. Do you love him, or
  don't you?
MARIANE: Oh, how unjust of you! What can you
  mean
By asking such a question, dear Dorine?
You know the depth of my affection for him;
20 I've told you a hundred times how I adore him.
DORINE: I don't believe in everything I hear;
Who knows if your professions were sincere?
MARIANE: They were, Dorine, and you do me wrong
  to doubt it;
Heaven knows that I've been all too frank
  about it.
DORINE: You love him, then?
MARIANE: Oh, more than I can
25 express.
DORINE: And he, I take it, cares for you no less?
MARIANE: I think so.
DORINE: And you both, with equal fire,
Burn to be married?
MARIANE: That is our one desire.
DORINE: What of Tartuffe, then? What of your
  father's plan?
MARIANE: I'll kill myself, if I'm forced to wed that
30 man.
DORINE: I hadn't thought of that recourse. How
  splendid!
Just die, and all your troubles will be ended!
A fine solution. Oh, it maddens me
To hear you talk in that self-pitying key.
35 MARIANE: Dorine, how harsh you are! It's most unfair.
You have no sympathy for my despair.
DORINE: I've none at all for people who talk drivel
And, faced with difficulties, whine and snivel.
MARIANE: No doubt I'm timid, but it would be
  wrong . . .

DORINE: True love requires a heart that's firm and
  strong.   40
MARIANE: I'm strong in my affection for Valère,
But coping with my father is his affair.
DORINE: But if your father's brain has grown so
  cracked
Over his dear Tartuffe that he can retract
His blessing, though your wedding-day was
  named,   45
It's surely not Valère who's to be blamed.
MARIANE: If I defied my father, as you suggest,
Would it not seem unmaidenly, at best?
Shall I defend my love at the expense
Of brazenness and disobedience?   50
Shall I parade my heart's desires, and flaunt . . .
DORINE: No, I ask nothing of you. Clearly you want
To be Madame Tartuffe, and I feel bound
Not to oppose a wish so very sound.
What right have I to criticize the match?   55
Indeed, my dear, the man's a brilliant catch.
Monsieur Tartuffe! Now, there's a man of weight!
Yes, yes, Monsieur Tartuffe, I'm bound to state,
Is quite a person; that's not to be denied;
'Twill be no little thing to be his bride.   60
The world already rings with his renown;
He's a great noble—in his native town;
His ears are red, he has a pink complexion,
And all in all, he'll suit you to perfection.
MARIANE: Dear God!
DORINE: Oh, how triumphant you will
  feel   65
At having caught a husband so ideal!
MARIANE: Oh, do stop teasing, and use your
  cleverness
To get me out of this appalling mess.
Advise me, and I'll do whatever you say.
DORINE: Ah no, a dutiful daughter must obey   70
Her father, even if he weds her to an ape.
You've a bright future; why struggle to escape?
Tartuffe will take you back where his family lives,
To a small town aswarm with relatives—
Uncles and cousins whom you'll be charmed to
  meet.   75
You'll be received at once by the elite,
Calling upon the bailiff's wife, no less—
Even, perhaps, upon the mayoress,
Who'll sit you down in the *best* kitchen chair.
Then, once a year, you'll dance at the village fair   80
To the drone of bagpipes—two of them, in fact—
And see a puppet-show, or an animal act.
Your husband . . .
MARIANE: Oh, you turn my blood to ice!
Stop torturing me, and give me your advice.
DORINE (*threatening to go*): Your servant, Madam.
MARIANE: Dorine, I beg of you . . .   85
DORINE: No, you deserve it; this marriage must go
  through.
MARIANE: Dorine!
DORINE: No.

MARIANE: Not Tartuffe! You know I think him . . .
DORINE: Tartuffe's your cup of tea, and you shall
    drink him.
MARIANE: I've always told you everything, and
    relied . . .
90 DORINE: No. You deserve to be tartutified.
MARIANE: Well, since you mock me and refuse to care,
    I'll henceforth seek my solace in despair:
    Despair shall be my counsellor and friend,
    And help me bring my sorrows to an end.
                [*She starts to leave.*]
DORINE: There now, come back; my anger has
95   subsided.
    You do deserve some pity, I've decided.
MARIANE: Dorine, if Father makes me undergo
    This dreadful martyrdom, I'll die, I know.
DORINE: Don't fret; it won't be difficult to discover
    Some plan of action . . . But here's Valère, your
100   lover.

Scene 4   [*Valère, Mariane, Dorine.*]

VALÈRE: Madam. I've just received some wondrous news
    Regarding which I'd like to hear your views.
MARIANE: What news?
VALÈRE: You're marrying Tartuffe.
MARIANE: I find
    That Father does have such a match in mind.
VALÈRE: Your father, Madam . . .
MARIANE: . . . has just this
5   minute said
    That it's Tartuffe he wishes me to wed.
VALÈRE: Can he be serious?
MARIANE: Oh, indeed he can;
    He's clearly set his heart upon the plan.
VALÈRE: And what position do you propose to take,
    Madam?
MARIANE: Why—I don't know.
10 VALÈRE: For heaven's sake—
    You don't know?
MARIANE: No.
VALÈRE: Well, well!
MARIANE: Advise me, do.
VALÈRE: Marry the man. That's my advice to you.
MARIANE: That's your advice?
VALÈRE: Yes.
MARIANE: Truly?
VALÈRE: Oh, absolutely.
    You couldn't choose more wisely, more astutely.
MARIANE: Thanks for this counsel; I'll follow it, of
15   course.
VALÈRE: Do, do; I'm sure 'twill cost you no remorse.
MARIANE: To give it didn't cause your heart to break.
VALÈRE: I gave it, Madam, only for your sake.
MARIANE: And it's for your sake that I take it, Sir.
DORINE (*withdrawing to the rear of the stage*): Let's
20   see which fool will prove the stubborner.

VALÈRE: So! I am nothing to you, and it was flat
    Deception when you . . .
MARIANE: Please, enough of that.
    You've told me plainly that I should agree
    To wed the man my father's chosen for me,
    And since you've deigned to counsel me so wisely, 25
    I promise, Sir, to do as you advise me.
VALÈRE: Ah, no, 'twas not by me that you were
    swayed.
    No, your decision was already made;
    Though now, to save appearances, you protest
    That you're betraying me at my behest.   30
MARIANE: Just as you say.
VALÈRE: Quite so. And I now see
    That you were never truly in love with me.
MARIANE: Alas, you're free to think so if you choose.
VALÈRE: I choose to think so, and here's a bit of news:
    You've spurned my hand, but I know where to
    turn   35
    For kinder treatment, as you shall quickly learn.
MARIANE: I'm sure you do. Your noble qualities
    Inspire affection . . .
VALÈRE: Forget my qualities, please.
    They don't inspire you overmuch, I find.
    But there's another lady I have in mind   40
    Whose sweet and generous nature will not scorn
    To compensate me for the loss I've borne.
MARIANE: I'm no great loss, and I'm sure that you'll
    transfer
    Your heart quite painlessly from me to her.
VALÈRE: I'll do my best to take it in my stride.   45
    The pain I feel at being cast aside
    Time and forgetfulness may put an end to.
    Or if I can't forget, I shall pretend to.
    No self-respecting person is expected
    To go on loving once he's been rejected.   50
MARIANE: Now, that's a fine, high-minded sentiment.
VALÈRE: One to which any sane man would assent.
    Would you prefer it if I pined away
    In hopeless passion till my dying day?
    Am I to yield you to a rival's arms   55
    And not console myself with other charms?
MARIANE: Go then: console yourself; don't hesitate.
    I wish you to; indeed, I cannot wait.
VALÈRE: You wish me to?
MARIANE: Yes.
VALÈRE: That's the final straw.
    Madam, farewell. Your wish shall be my law.   60

[*He starts to leave, and then returns: this repeatedly.*]

MARIANE: Splendid.
VALÈRE (*coming back again*):
                This breach, remember, is of your
    making;
    It's you who've driven me to the step I'm taking.
MARIANE: Of course.
VALÈRE: (*coming back again*):
                Remember, too, that I am merely
    Following your example.

MARIANE: I see that clearly.

65 VALÈRE: Enough. I'll go and do your bidding, then.

MARIANE: Good.

VALÈRE (*coming back again*):
         You shall never see my face again.

MARIANE: Excellent.

VALÈRE (*walking to the door, then turning about*):
         Yes?

MARIANE: What?

VALÈRE: What's that? What did
     you say?

MARIANE: Nothing. You're dreaming.

VALÈRE: Ah. Well, I'm on
     my way.
     Farewell, *Madame.*
     [*He moves slowly away.*]

MARIANE: Farewell.

DORINE (*to Mariane*):   If you ask me,
70   Both of you are as mad as mad can be.
     Do stop this nonsense, now. I've only let you
     Squabble so long to see where it would get you.
     Whoa there, Monsieur Valère!

[*She goes and seizes Valère by the arm; he makes a great show of resistance.*]

VALÈRE: What's this, Dorine?

DORINE: Come here.

VALÈRE: No, no, my heart's too full of
     spleen.
75   Don't hold me back; her wish must be obeyed.

DORINE: Stop!

VALÈRE: It's too late now; my decision's made.

DORINE: Oh, pooh!

MARIANE (*aside*): He hates the sight of me, that's
     plain.
     I'll go, and so deliver him from pain.

DORINE (*leaving Valère, running after Mariane*): And
     now *you* run away! Come back.

MARIANE: No, no.
80   Nothing you say will keep me here. Let go!

VALÈRE (*aside*): She cannot bear my presence, I
     perceive.
     To spare her further torment, I shall leave.

DORINE (*leaving Mariane, running after Valère*):
     Again! You'll not escape, Sir; don't you try it.
     Come here, you two. Stop fussing, and be quiet.

[*She takes Valère by the hand, then Mariane, and draws them together.*]

VALÈRE (*to Dorine*): What do you want of me?

MARIANE (*to Dorine*):   What
85   is the point of this?

DORINE: We're going to have a little armistice.
         (*To Valère.*)
     Now, weren't you silly to get so overheated?

VALÈRE: Didn't you see how badly I was treated?

DORINE (*to Mariane*): Aren't you a simpleton, to have
     lost your head?

90 MARIANE: Didn't you hear the hateful things he said?

DORINE (*to Valère*): You're both great fools. Her sole
     desire, Valère,
     Is to be yours in marriage. To that I'll swear.
         (*To Mariane.*)
     He loves you only, and he wants no wife
     But you, Mariane. On that I'll stake my life.

MARIANE (*to Valère*): Then why you advised me so,
     I cannot see.   95

VALÈRE (*to Mariane*): On such a question, why ask
     advice of *me*?

DORINE: Oh, you're impossible. Give me your hands,
     you two.
         (*To Valère.*)
     Yours first.

VALÈRE (*giving Dorine his hand*):
     But why?

DORINE (*to Mariane*): And now a hand from you.

MARIANE (*also giving Dorine her hand*): What are
     you doing?

DORINE: There: a perfect fit.
     You suit each other better than you'll admit.   100

[*Valère and Mariane hold hands for some time without looking at each other.*]

VALÈRE (*turning toward Mariane*): Ah, come, don't be so
     haughty. Give a man
     A look of kindness, won't you Mariane?
     [*Mariane turns toward Valère and smiles.*]

DORINE: I tell you, lovers are completely mad!

VALÈRE (*to Mariane*): Now come, confess that you
     were very bad
     To hurt my feeling as you did just now.   105
     I have a just complaint, you must allow.

MARIANE: *You* must allow that you were most
     unpleasant . . .

DORINE: Let's table that discussion for the present;
     Your father has a plan which must be stopped.

MARIANE: Advise us, then; what means must we
     adopt?   110

DORINE: We'll use all manner of means, and all at
     once.
         (*To Mariane.*)
     Your father's addled; he's acting like a dunce.
     Therefore you'd better humor the old fossil.
     Pretend to yield to him, be sweet and docile,
     And then postpone, as often as necessary,   115
     The day on which you have agreed to marry.
     You'll thus gain time, and time will turn the trick.
     Sometimes, for instance, you'll be taken sick,
     And that will seem good reason for delay;
     Or some bad omen will make you change the day—   120
     You'll dream of muddy water, or you'll pass
     A dead man's hearse, or break a looking-glass.
     If all else fails, no man can marry you
     Unless you take his ring and say "I do."
     But now, let's separate. If they should find   125
     Us talking here, our plot might be divined.
         (*To Valère.*)

Go to your friends, and tell them what's occurred,
And have them urge her father to keep his word.
Meanwhile, we'll stir her brother into action,
130   And get Elmire, as well, to join our faction.
Good-bye.
VALÈRE (*to Mariane*):
                    Though each of us will do his best,
It's your true heart on which my hopes shall rest.
MARIANE (*to Valère*): Regardless of what Father may
        decide,
None but Valère shall claim me as his bride.
VALÈRE: Oh, how those words content me! Come
135   what will . . .
DORINE: Oh, lovers, lovers! Their tongues are never
        still.
Be off, now.
VALÈRE (*turning to go, then turning back*):
                    One last word . . .
DORINE:
                                        No time to chat:
You leave by this door; and *you* leave by that.

[*Dorine pushes them, by the shoulders, toward opposing doors.*]

ACT III • Scene 1   [*Damis, Dorine.*]

DAMIS: May lightning strike me even as I speak,
May all men call me cowardly and weak,
If any fear or scruple holds me back
From settling things, at once, with that great
        quack!
5   DORINE: Now, don't give way to violent emotion.
Your father's merely talked about this notion,
And words and deeds are far from being one.
Much that is talked about is left undone.
DAMIS: No, I must stop that scoundrel's
        machinations,
10   I'll go and tell him off; I'm out of patience.
DORINE: Do calm down and be practical. I had rather
My mistress dealt with him—and with your father.
She has some influence with Tartuffe, I've noted.
He hangs upon her words, seems most devoted,
15   And may, indeed, be smitten by her charm.
Pray Heaven it's true! 'Twould do our cause no
        harm.
She sent for him, just now, to sound him out
On this affair you're so incensed about;
She'll find out where he stands, and tell him, too,
20   What dreadful strife and trouble will ensue
If he lends countenance to your father's plan.
I couldn't get in to see him, but his man
Says that he's almost finished with his prayers.
Go, now. I'll catch him when he comes
        downstairs.
25   DAMIS: I want to hear this conference, and I will.
DORINE: No, they must be alone.
DAMIS:
                                        Oh, I'll keep still.

DORINE: Not you. I know your temper. You'd start a brawl,
And shout and stamp your foot and spoil it all.
Go on.
DAMIS: I won't; I have a perfect right . . .
DORINE: Lord, you're a nuisance! He's coming; get
        out of sight.   30

[*Damis conceals himself in a closet at the rear of the stage.*]

Scene 2   [*Tartuffe, Dorine.*]

TARTUFFE (*observing Dorine, and calling to his
        manservant offstage*): Hang up my hair-shirt,
        put my scourge in place,
And pray, Laurent, for Heaven's perpetual grace.
I'm going to the prison now, to share
My last few coins with the poor wretches there.
DORINE (*aside*): Dear God, what affectation! What a
        fake!   5
TARTUFFE: You wished to see me?
DORINE: Yes . . .
TARTUFFE (*taking a handkerchief from his pocket*):
                                    For mercy's sake,
Please take this handkerchief, before you speak.
DORINE: What?
TARTUFFE: Cover that bosom, girl. The flesh is weak,
And unclean thoughts are difficult to control.

Debra Gillett as Dorine and Martin Clunes as Tartuffe in the "handkerchief" scene from London's National Theatre production in 2002.

10   Such sights as that can undermine the soul.
    DORINE: Your soul, it seems, has very poor defenses,
    And flesh makes quite an impact on your senses.
    It's strange that you're so easily excited;
    My own desires are not so soon ignited,
15   And if I saw you naked as a beast,
    Not all your hide would tempt me in the least.
    TARTUFFE: Girl, speak more modestly; unless you do,
    I shall be forced to take my leave of you.
    DORINE: Oh, no, it's I who must be on my way;
20   I've just one little message to convey.
    Madame is coming down, and begs you, Sir,
    To wait and have a word or two with her.
    TARTUFFE: Gladly.
    DORINE (*aside*):   *That* had a softening effect!
    I think my guess about him was correct.
    TARTUFFE: Will she be long?
25   DORINE: No: that's her step I hear.
    Ah, here she is, and I shall disappear.

Scene 3   [*Elmire, Tartuffe.*]

    TARTUFFE: May Heaven, whose infinite goodness we
      adore,
    Preserve your body and soul forevermore,
    And bless your days, and answer thus the plea
    Of one who is its humblest votary.
5   ELMIRE: I thank you for that pious wish. But please,
    Do take a chair and let's be more at ease.

[*They sit down.*]

    TARTUFFE: I trust that you are once more well and
      strong?
    ELMIRE: Oh, yes: the fever didn't last for long.
    TARTUFFE: My prayers are too unworthy. I am sure,
    To have gained from Heaven this most gracious
10   cure;
    But lately, Madam, my every supplication
    Has had for object your recuperation.
    ELMIRE: You shouldn't have troubled so. I don't
      deserve it.
    TARTUFFE: Your health is priceless, Madam, and to
      preserve it
15   I'd gladly give my own, in all sincerity.
    ELMIRE: Sir, you outdo us all in Christian charity.
    You've been most kind. I count myself your
      debtor.
    TARTUFFE: 'Twas nothing, Madam. I long to serve
      you better.
    ELMIRE: There's a private matter I'm anxious to
      discuss.
20   I'm glad there's no one here to hinder us.
    TARTUFFE: I too am glad; it floods my heart with bliss
    To find myself alone with you like this.
    For just this chance I've prayed with all my
      power —
    But prayed in vain, until this happy hour.

    ELMIRE: This won't take long, Sir, and I hope
      you'll be   25
    Entirely frank and unconstrained with me.
    TARTUFFE: Indeed, there's nothing I had rather do
    Than bare my inmost heart and soul to you.
    First, let me say that what remarks I've made
    About the constant visits you are paid   30
    Were prompted not by any mean emotion,
    But rather by a pure and deep devotion,
    A fervent zeal . . .
    ELMIRE: No need for explanation.
    Your sole concern, I'm sure, was my salvation.
    TARTUFFE (*taking Elmire's hand and pressing her
      fingertips*): Quite so; and such great fervor
      do I feel . . .   35
    ELMIRE: Ooh! Please! You're pinching!
    TARTUFFE: 'Twas from
      excess of zeal.
    I never meant to cause you pain, I swear.
    I'd rather . . .

[*He places his hand on Elmire's knee.*]

    ELMIRE: What can your hand be doing there?
    TARTUFFE: Feeling your gown; what soft, fine-woven
      stuff!
    ELMIRE: Please, I'm extremely ticklish. That's enough.   40

[*She draws her chair away; Tartuffe pulls his after her.*]

    TARTUFFE (*fondling the lace collar of her gown*): My,
      my, what lovely lacework on your dress!
    The workmanship's miraculous, no less.
    I've not seen anything to equal it.
    ELMIRE: Yes, quite. But let's talk business for a bit.
    They say my husband means to break his word   45
    And give his daughter to you, Sir. Had you heard?
    TARTUFFE: He did once mention it. But I confess
    I dream of quite a different happiness.
    It's elsewhere, Madam, that my eyes discern
    The promise of that bliss for which I yearn.   50
    ELMIRE: I see: you care for nothing here below.
    TARTUFFE: Ah, well—my heart's not made of stone,
      you know.
    ELMIRE: All your desires mount heavenward, I'm
      sure,
    In scorn of all that's earthly and impure.
    TARTUFFE: A love of heavenly beauty does not
      preclude   55
    A proper love for earthly pulchritude;
    Our senses are quite rightly captivated
    By perfect works our Maker has created.
    Some glory clings to all that Heaven has made;
    In you, all Heaven's marvels are displayed.   60
    On that fair face, such beauties have been
      lavished.
    The eyes are dazzled and the heart is ravished;
    How could I look on you, O flawless creature,
    And not adore the Author of all Nature,
    Feeling a love both passionate and pure   65
    For you, his triumph of self-portraiture?

At first, I trembled lest that love should be
A subtle snare that Hell had laid for me;
I vowed to flee the sight of you, eschewing
70 A rapture that might prove my soul's undoing;
But soon, fair being, I became aware
That my deep passion could be made to square
With rectitude, and with my bounden duty.
I thereupon surrendered to your beauty.
75 It is, I know, presumptuous on my part
To bring you this poor offering of my heart,
And it is not my merit, Heaven knows,
But your compassion on which my hopes repose.
You are my peace, my solace, my salvation;
80 On you depends my bliss—or desolation;
I bide your judgment and, as you think best,
I shall be either miserable or blest.
ELMIRE: Your declaration is most gallant, Sir,
But don't you think it's out of character?
85 You'd have done better to restrain your passion
And think before you spoke in such a fashion.
It ill becomes a pious man like you . . .
TARTUFFE: I may be pious, but I'm human too:
With your celestial charms before his eyes,
90 A man has not the power to be wise.
I know such words sound strangely, coming
    from me,
But I'm no angel, nor was meant to be,
And if you blame my passion, you must needs
Reproach as well the charms on which it feeds.
95 Your loveliness I had no sooner seen
Than you became my soul's unrivalled queen;
Before your seraph glance, divinely sweet,
My heart's defenses crumbled in defeat,
And nothing fasting, prayer, or tears might do
100 Could stay my spirit from adoring you.
My eyes, my sighs have told you in the past
What now my lips make bold to say at last,
And if, in your great goodness, you will deign
To look upon your slave, and ease his pain,—
105 If, in compassion for my soul's distress,
You'll stoop to comfort my unworthiness,
I'll raise to you, in thanks for that sweet manna,
An endless hymn, an infinite hosanna.
With me, of course, there need be no anxiety,
110 No fear of scandal or of notoriety.
These young court gallants, whom all the ladies
    fancy,
Are vain in speech, in action rash and chancy;
When they succeed in love, the world soon
    knows it;
No favor's granted them but they disclose it
115 And by the looseness of their tongues profane
The very altar where their hearts have lain.
Men of my sort, however, love discreetly,
And one may trust our reticence completely.
My keen concern for my good name insures
120 The absolute security of yours;
In short, I offer you, my dear Elmire,
Love without scandal, pleasure without fear.

ELMIRE: I've heard your well-turned speeches to
    the end,
And what you urge I clearly apprehend.
Aren't you afraid that I may take a notion   125
To tell my husband of your warm devotion,
And that, supposing he were duly told,
His feelings toward you might grow rather cold?
TARTUFFE: I know, dear lady, that your exceeding
    charity
Will lead your heart to pardon my temerity;   130
That you'll excuse my violent affection
As human weakness, human imperfection;
And that—O fairest!—you will bear in mind
That I'm but flesh and blood, and am not blind.
ELMIRE: Some women might do otherwise, perhaps,   135
But I shall be discreet about your lapse;
I'll tell my husband nothing of what's occurred
If, in return, you'll give your solemn word
To advocate as forcefully as you can
The marriage of Valère and Mariane,   140
Renouncing all desires to dispossess
Another of his rightful happiness,
And . . .

Scene 4 [*Damis, Elmire, Tartuffe.*]

DAMIS (*emerging from the closet where he has been
    hiding*): No! We'll not hush up this vile affair;
I heard it all inside that closet there,
Where Heaven, in order to confound the pride
Of this great rascal, prompted me to hide.
Ah, now I have my long-awaited chance   5
To punish his deceit and arrogance,
And give my father clear and shocking proof
Of the black character of his dear Tartuffe.
ELMIRE: Ah no, Damis; I'll be content if he
Will study to deserve my leniency.   10
I've promised silence—don't make me break my
    word;
To make a scandal would be too absurd.
Good wives laugh off such trifles, and forget them;
Why should they tell their husbands, and upset them?
DAMIS: You have your reasons for taking such a
    course,   15
And I have reasons, too, of equal force.
To spare him now would be insanely wrong.
I've swallowed my just wrath for far too long
And watched this insolent bigot bringing strife
And bitterness into our family life.   20
Too long he's meddled in my father's affairs,
Thwarting my marriage-hopes, and poor Valère's.
It's high time that my father was undeceived,
And now I've proof that can't be disbelieved—
Proof that was furnished me by Heaven above.   25
It's too good not to take advantage of.
This is my chance, and I deserve to lose it
If, for one moment, I hesitate to use it.

ELMIRE: Damis . . .
DAMIS: No, I must do what I think right.
30   Madam, my heart is bursting with delight,
And, say whatever you will, I'll not consent
To lose the sweet revenge on which I'm bent.
I'll settle matters without more ado;
And here, most opportunely, is my cue.

Scene 5   [*Orgon, Damis, Tartuffe, Elmire.*]

DAMIS: Father, I'm glad you've joined us. Let us
     advise you
Of some fresh news which doubtless will surprise
     you.
You've just now been repaid with interest
For all your loving-kindness to our guest.
He's proved his warm and grateful feelings
5   toward you;
It's with a pair of horns he would reward you.
Yes, I surprised him with your wife, and heard
His whole adulterous offer, every word.
She, with her all too gentle disposition,
10   Would not have told you of his proposition;
But I shall not make terms with brazen lechery,
And feel that not to tell you would be treachery.
ELMIRE: And I hold that one's husband's peace of
     mind
Should not be spoilt by tattle of this kind.
15   One's honor doesn't require it: to be proficient
In keeping men at bay is quite sufficient.
These are my sentiments, and I wish, Damis,
That you had heeded me and held your peace.

Scene 6   [*Orgon, Damis, Tartuffe.*]

ORGON: Can it be true, this dreadful thing I hear?
TARTUFFE: Yes, Brother, I'm a wicked man, I fear:
A wretched sinner, all depraved and twisted,
The greatest villain that has ever existed.
My life's one heap of crimes, which grows each
5   minute;
There's naught but foulness and corruption in it;
And I perceive that Heaven, outraged by me,
Has chosen this occasion to mortify me.
Charge me with any deed you wish to name;
10   I'll not defend myself, but take the blame.
Believe what you are told, and drive Tartuffe
Like some base criminal from beneath your roof;
Yes, drive me hence, and with a parting curse:
I shan't protest, for I deserve far worse.
ORGON (*to Damis*): Ah, you deceitful boy, how dare
15   you try
To stain his purity with so foul a lie?
DAMIS: What! Are you taken in by such a bluff?
Did you not hear . . . ?
ORGON: Enough, you rogue, enough!

TARTUFFE: Ah, Brother, let him speak: you're being
     unjust.
Believe his story; the boy deserves your trust.   20
Why, after all, should you have faith in me?
How can you know what I might do, or be?
Is it on my good actions that you base
Your favor? Do you trust my pious face?
Ah, no, don't be deceived by hollow shows;   25
I'm far, alas, from being what men suppose;
Though the world takes me for a man of worth,
I'm truly the most worthless man on earth.
     (*To Damis.*)
Yes, my dear son, speak out now: call me the chief
Of sinners, a wretch, a murderer, a thief;   30
Load me with all the names men most abhor;
I'll not complain; I've earned them all, and more;
I'll kneel here while you pour them on my head
As a just punishment for the life I've led.
ORGON (*to Taruffe*): This is too much, dear Brother.
     (*To Damis.*)
                              Have you no heart?   35
DAMIS: Are you so hoodwinked by this rascal's art . . . ?
ORGON: Be still, you monster.
     (*To Tartuffe.*)
                         Brother, I pray you, rise.
     (*To Damis.*)
Villain!
DAMIS: But . . .
ORGON: Silence!
DAMIS: Can't you realize . . . ?
ORGON: Just one word more, and I'll tear you limb
     from limb.
TARTUFFE: In God's name, Brother, don't be harsh
     with him.   40
I'd rather far be tortured at the stake
Than see him bear one scratch for my poor
     sake.
ORGON (*to Damis*): Ingrate!
TARTUFFE: If I must beg you, on bended knee,
To pardon him . . .
ORGON (*falling to his knees, addressing Tartuffe*):
                    Such goodness cannot be!
     (*To Damis.*)
Now, *there's* true charity!
DAMIS: What, you . . . ?
ORGON: Villain, be still!   45
I know your motives; I know you wish him ill:
Yes, all of you—wife, children, servants, all—
Conspire against him and desire his fall,
Employing every shameful trick you can
To alienate me from this saintly man.   50
Ah, but the more you seek to drive him away,
The more I'll do to keep him. Without delay,
I'll spite this household and confound its pride
By giving him my daughter as his bride.
DAMIS: You're going to force her to accept his hand?   55
ORGON: Yes, and this very night, d'you understand?
I shall defy you all, and make it clear
That I'm the one who gives the orders here.

Come, wretch, kneel down and clasp his blessed feet,
60 And ask his pardon for your black deceit.
DAMIS: I ask that swindler's pardon? Why, I'd
       rather . . .
ORGON: So! You insult him, and defy your father!
   A stick! A stick! (*To Tartuffe.*) No, no—release
   me, do.
   (*To Damis.*)
   Out of my house this minute! Be off with you,
65 And never dare set foot in it again.
DAMIS: Well, I shall go, but . . .
ORGON: Well, go quickly, then
   I disinherit you; an empty purse
   Is all you'll get from me—except my curse!

Scene 7 [*Orgon, Tartuffe.*]

ORGON: How he blasphemed your goodness! What
   a son!
TARTUFFE: Forgive him, Lord, as I've already done.
   (*To Orgon.*)
   You can't know how it hurts when someone
   tries
   To blacken me in my dear Brother's eyes.
ORGON: Ahh!
5 TARTUFFE: The mere thought of such ingratitude
   Plunges my soul into so dark a mood . . .
   Such horror grips my heart . . . I gasp for breath,
   And cannot speak, and feel myself near death.
ORGON:

[*He runs, in tears, to the door through which he has just
driven his son.*]

   You blackguard! Why did I spare you? Why did
   I not
10 Break you in little pieces on the spot?
   Compose yourself, and don't be hurt, dear friend.
TARTUFFE: These scenes, these dreadful quarrels, have
   got to end.
   I've much upset your household, and I perceive
   That the best thing will be for me to leave.
ORGON: What are you saying!
TARTUFFE: They're all against me
15 here;
   They'd have you think me false and insincere.
ORGON: Ah, what of that? Have I ceased believing
   in you?
TARTUFFE: Their adverse talk will certainly continue,
   And charges which you now repudiate
20 You may find credible at a later date.
ORGON: No, Brother, never.
TARTUFFE: Brother, a wife can sway
   Her husband's mind in many a subtle way.
ORGON: No, no.
TARTUFFE: To leave at once is the solution;
   Thus only can I end their persecution.
25 ORGON: No, no, I'll not allow it; you shall remain.

TARTUFFE: Ah, well; 'twill mean much martyrdom
   and pain,
   But if you wish it . . .
ORGON: Ah!
TARTUFFE: Enough; so be it.
   But one thing must be settled, as I see it.
   For your dear honor, and for our friendship's
   sake,
   There's one precaution I feel bound to take.   30
   I shall avoid your wife, and keep away . . .
ORGON: No, you shall not, whatever they may say.
   It pleases me to vex them, and for spite
   I'd have them see you with her day and night.
   What's more, I'm going to drive them to despair   35
   By making you my only son and heir;
   This very day, I'll give to you alone
   Clear deed and title to everything I own.
   A dear, good friend and son-in-law-to-be
   Is more than wife, or child, or kin to me.   40
   Will you accept my offer, dearest son?
TARTUFFE: In all things, let the will of Heaven be
   done.
ORGON: Poor fellow! Come, we'll go draw up
   the deed.
   Then let them burst with disappointed greed!

ACT IV • Scene 1 [*Cléante, Tartuffe.*]

CLÉANTE: Yes, all the town's discussing it, and truly,
   Their comments do not flatter you unduly.
   I'm glad we've met, Sir, and I'll give my view
   Of this sad matter in a word or two.
   As for who's guilty, that I shan't discuss;   5
   Let's say it was Damis who caused the fuss;
   Assuming, then, that you have been ill-used
   By young Damis, and groundlessly accused,
   Ought not a Christian to forgive, and ought
   He not to stifle every vengeful thought?   10
   Should you stand by and watch a father make
   His only son an exile for your sake?
   Again I tell you frankly, be advised:
   The whole town, high and low, is scandalized;
   This quarrel must be mended, and my advice is   15
   Not to push matters to a further crisis.
   No, sacrifice your wrath to God above,
   And help Damis regain his father's love.
TARTUFFE: Alas, for my part I should take great joy
   In doing so. I've nothing against the boy.   20
   I pardon all, I harbor no resentment;
   To serve him would afford me much contentment.
   But Heaven's interest will not have it so:
   If he comes back, then I shall have to go.
   After his conduct—so extreme, so vicious—   25
   Our further intercourse would look suspicious.
   God knows what people would think! Why, they'd
   describe
   My goodness to him as a sort of bribe;

They'd say that out of guilt I made pretense
30   Of loving-kindness and benevolence—
That, fearing my accuser's tongue, I strove
To buy his silence with a show of love.
CLÉANTE: Your reasoning is badly warped and
        stretched,
And these excuses, Sir, are most far-fetched.
35   Why put yourself in charge of Heaven's cause?
Does Heaven need our help to enforce its laws?
Leave vengeance to the Lord, Sir; while we live,
Our duty's not to punish, but forgive;
And what the Lord commands, we should obey
40   Without regard to what the world may say.
What! Shall the fear of being misunderstood
Prevent our doing what is right and good?
No, no; let's simply do what Heaven ordains,
And let no other thoughts perplex our brains.
45   TARTUFFE: Again, Sir, let me say that I've forgiven
Damis, and thus obeyed the laws of Heaven;
But I am not commanded by the Bible
To live with one who smears my name with libel.
CLÉANTE: Were you commanded, Sir, to indulge the
        whim
50   Of poor Orgon, and to encourage him
In suddenly transferring to your name
A large estate to which you have no claim?
TARTUFFE: 'Twould never occur to those who know
        me best
To think I acted from self-interest.
55   The treasures of this world I quite despise;
Their specious glitter does not charm my eyes;
And if I have resigned myself to taking
The gift which my dear Brother insists on
        making,
I do so only, as he well understands,
60   Lest so much wealth fall into wicked hands,
Lest those to whom it might descend in time
Turn it to purposes of sin and crime,
And not, as I shall do, make use of it
For Heaven's glory and mankind's benefit.
CLÉANTE: Forget these trumped-up fears. Your
65   argument
Is one the rightful heir might well resent;
It is a moral burden to inherit
Such wealth, but give Damis a chance to bear it.
And would it not be worse to be accused
70   Of swindling, than to see that wealth misused?
I'm shocked that you allowed Orgon to broach
This matter, and that you feel no self-reproach;
Does true religion teach that lawful heirs
May freely be deprived of what is theirs?
75   And if the Lord has told you in your heart
That you and young Damis must dwell apart,
Would it not be the decent thing to beat
A generous and honorable retreat,
Rather than let the son of the house be sent,
80   For your convenience, into banishment?
Sir, if you wish to prove the honesty
Of your intentions . . .

TARTUFFE: Sir, it is half-past three.
I've certain pious duties to attend to,
And hope my prompt departure won't offend you.
CLÉANTE (alone): Damn.   85

Scene 2   [Elmire, Mariane, Cléante, Dorine.]

DORINE: Stay, Sir, and help Mariane,
        for Heaven's sake!
She's suffering so, I fear her heart will break.
Her father's plan to marry her off tonight
Has put the poor child in a desperate plight.
I hear him coming. Let's stand together, now,   5
And see if we can't change his mind, somehow,
About this match we all deplore and fear.

Scene 3   [Orgon, Elmire, Mariane, Cléante, Dorine.]

ORGON: Halt! Glad to find you all assembled here.
        (To Mariane.)
This contract, child, contains your happiness,
And what it says I think your heart can guess.
MARIANE (falling to her knees): Sir, by that Heaven
        which sees me here distressed,
And by whatever else can move your breast,   5
Do not employ a father's power, I pray you,
To crush my heart and force it to obey you,
Nor by your harsh commands oppress me so
That I'll begrudge the duty which I owe—
And do not so embitter and enslave me   10
That I shall hate the very life you gave me.
If my sweet hopes must perish, if you refuse
To give me to the one I've dared to choose,
Spare me at least—I beg you, I implore—
The pain of wedding one whom I abhor;   15
And do not, by a heartless use of force,
Drive me to contemplate some desperate course.
ORGON (feeling himself touched by her): Be firm, my
        soul. No human weakness, now.
MARIANE: I don't resent your love for him. Allow
Your heart free rein, Sir; give him your property, 20
And if that's not enough, take mine from me;
He's welcome to my money; take it, do,
But don't, I pray, include my person too.
Spare me, I beg you; and let me end the tale
Of my sad days behind a convent veil.   25
ORGON: A convent! Hah! When crossed in their
        amours,
All lovesick girls have the same thought as yours.
Get up! The more you loathe the man, and dread
        him,
The more ennobling it will be to wed him.
Marry Tartuffe, and mortify your flesh!   30
Enough; don't start that whimpering afresh.
DORINE: But why . . . ?

ORGON: Be still, there. Speak when
    you're spoken to.
    Not one more bit of impudence out of you.
CLÉANTE: If I may offer a word of counsel here . . .
35 ORGON: Brother, in counseling you have no peer;
    All your advice is forceful; sound, and clever;
    I don't propose to follow it, however.
ELMIRE (to Orgon): I am amazed, and don't know
    what to say;
    Your blindness simply takes my breath away.
40 You are indeed bewitched, to take no warning
    From our account of what occurred this morning.
ORGON: Madam, I know a few plain facts, and one
    Is that you're partial to my rascal son;
    Hence, when he sought to make Tartuffe the
    victim
45 Of a base lie, you dared not contradict him.
    Ah, but you underplayed your part, my pet;
    You should have looked more angry, more upset.
ELMIRE: When men make overtures, must we reply
    With righteous anger and a battle-cry?
50 Must we turn back their amorous advances
    With sharp reproaches and with fiery glances?
    Myself, I find such offers merely amusing,
    And make no scenes and fusses in refusing;
    My taste is for good-natured rectitude,
55 And I dislike the savage sort of prude
    Who guards her virtue with her teeth and claws,
    And tears men's eyes out for the slightest cause:
    The Lord preserve me from such honor as that,
    Which bites and scratches like an alley-cat!
60 I've found that a polite and cool rebuff
    Discourages a lover quite enough.
ORGON: I know the facts, and I shall not be shaken.
ELMIRE: I marvel at your power to be mistaken.
    Would it, I wonder, carry weight with you
65 If I could *show* you that our tale was true?
ORGON: Show me?
ELMIRE: Yes.
ORGON: Rot.
ELMIRE: Come, what if I found a way
    To make you see the facts as plain as day?
ORGON: Nonsense.
ELMIRE: Do answer me; don't be absurd.
    I'm not now asking you to trust our word.
70 Suppose that from some hiding-place in here
    You learned the whole sad truth by eye and ear—
    What would you say of your good friend, after
    that?
ORGON: Why, I'd say . . . nothing, by Jehoshaphat!
    It can't be true.
ELMIRE: You've been too long deceived,
75 And I'm quite tired of being disbelieved.
    Come now: let's put my statements to the test,
    And you shall see the truth made manifest.
ORGON: I'll take that challenge. Now do your
    uttermost.
    We'll see how you make good your empty boast.
ELMIRE (to Dorine): Send him to me.

DORINE: He's crafty; it
    may be hard   80
    To catch the cunning scoundrel off his guard.
ELMIRE: No, amorous men are gullible. Their conceit
    So blinds them that they're never hard to cheat.
    Have him come down (To Cléante and Mariane.)
    Please leave us, for a bit.

Scene 4   [Elmire, Orgon.]

ELMIRE: Pull up this table, and get under it.
ORGON: What?
ELMIRE: It's essential that you be well-hidden.
ORGON: Why there?
ELMIRE: Oh, Heavens! Just do as you are
    bidden.
    I have my plans; we'll soon see how they fare.
    Under the table, now; and once you're there,   5
    Take care that you are neither seen nor heard.
ORGON: Well, I'll indulge you, since I gave my word
    To see you through this infantile charade.
ELMIRE: Once it is over, you'll be glad we played.

(To her husband, who is now under the table.)

    I'm going to act quite strangely, now, and you   10
    Must not be shocked at anything I do.
    Whatever I may say, you must excuse
    As part of that deceit I'm forced to use.
    I shall employ sweet speeches in the task
    Of making that imposter drop his mask;   15
    I'll give encouragement to his bold desires,
    And furnish fuel to his amorous fires.
    Since it's for your sake, and for his destruction,
    That I shall seem to yield to his seduction,
    I'll gladly stop whenever you decide   20
    That all your doubts are fully satisfied.
    I'll count on you, as soon as you have seen
    What sort of man he is, to intervene,
    And not expose me to his odious lust
    One moment longer than you feel you must.   25
    Remember: you're to save me from my plight
    Whenever . . . He's coming! Hush! Keep out of
    sight!

Scene 5   [Tartuffe, Elmire, Orgon.]

TARTUFFE: You wish to have a word with me, I'm told.
ELMIRE: Yes. I've a little secret to unfold.
    Before I speak, however, it would be wise
    To close that door, and look about for spies.

[Tartuffe goes to the door, closes it, and returns.]

    The very last thing that must happen now   5
    Is a repetition of this morning's row.
    I've never been so badly caught off guard.
    Oh, how I feared for you! You saw how hard

Aaron Hendry as Tartuffe, Misha Bouvion as Elmire, and Ted Barton as Orgon at the Will Geer Theatricum Botanicum, 2011.

I tried to make that troublesome Damis
10   Control his dreadful temper, and hold his peace.
In my confusion, I didn't have the sense
Simply to contradict his evidence;
But as it happened, that was for the best,
And all has worked out in our interest.
15   This storm has only bettered your position;
My husband doesn't have the least suspicion,
And now, in mockery of those who do,
He bids me be continually with you.
And that is why, quite fearless of reproof,
20   I now can be alone with my Tartuffe,
And why my heart—perhaps too quick to yield—
Feels free to let its passion be revealed.
TARTUFFE: Madam, your words confuse me. Not long ago,
You spoke in quite a different style, you know.
25   ELMIRE: Ah, Sir, if that refusal made you smart,
It's little that you know of woman's heart.
Or what that heart is trying to convey
When it resists in such a feeble way!

Always, at first, our modesty prevents
The frank avowal of tender sentiments;   30
However high the passion which inflames us,
Still, to confess its power somehow shames us.
Thus we reluct, at first, yet in a tone
Which tells you that our heart is overthrown,
That what our lips deny, our pulse confesses,   35
And that, in time, all noes will turn to yesses.
I fear my words are all too frank and free,
And a poor proof of woman's modesty;
But since I'm started, tell me, if you will—
Would I have tried to make Damis be still,   40
Would I have listened, calm and unoffended,
Until your lengthy offer of love was ended,
And been so very mild in my reaction,
Had your sweet words not given me satisfaction?
And when I tried to force you to undo   45
The marriage-plans my husband has in view.
What did my urgent pleading signify
If not that I admired you, and that I
Deplored the thought that someone else might own

50   Part of a heart I wished for mine alone?
    TARTUFFE: Madam, no happiness is so complete
      As when, from lips we love, come words so sweet;
      Their nectar floods my every sense, and drains
      In honeyed rivulets through all my veins.
55   To please you is my joy, my only goal;
      Your love is the restorer of my soul;
      And yet I must beg leave, now, to confess
      Some lingering doubts as to my happiness.
      Might this not be a trick? Might not the catch
60   Be that you wish me to break off the match
      With Mariane, and so have feigned to love me?
      I shan't quite trust your fond opinion of me
      Until the feelings you've expressed so sweetly
      Are demonstrated somewhat more concretely,
65   And you have shown, by certain kind concessions,
      That I may put my faith in your professions.
    ELMIRE (*She coughs, to warn her husband*): Why be
      in such a hurry? Must my heart
      Exhaust its bounty at the very start?
      To make that sweet admission cost me dear,
70   But you'll not be content, it would appear,
      Unless my store of favors is disbursed
      To the last farthing, and at the very first.
    TARTUFFE: The less we merit, the less we dare to hope,
      And with our doubts, mere words can never cope.
75   We trust no promised bliss till we receive it;
      Not till a joy is ours can we believe it.
      I, who so little merit your esteem,
      Can't credit this fulfillment of my dream,
      And shan't believe it, Madam, until I savor
80   Some palpable assurance of your favor.
    ELMIRE: My, how tyrannical your love can be,
      And how it flusters and perplexes me!
      How furiously you take one's heart in hand,
      And make your every wish a fierce command!
85   Come, must you hound and harry me to death?
      Will you not give me time to catch my breath?
      Can it be right to press me with such force,
      Give me no quarter, show me no remorse,
      And take advantage, by your stern insistence,
90   Of the fond feelings which weaken my resistance?
    TARTUFFE: Well, if you look with favor upon my love,
      Why, then, begrudge me some clear proof thereof?
    ELMIRE: But how can I consent without offense
      To Heaven, toward which you feel such reverence?
    TARTUFFE: If Heaven is all that holds you back, don't
95   worry.
      I can remove that hindrance in a hurry.
      Nothing of that sort need obstruct our path.
    ELMIRE: Must one not be afraid of Heaven's wrath?
    TARTUFFE: Madam, forget such fears, and be my pupil,
100   And I shall teach you how to conquer scruple.
      Some joys, it's true, are wrong in Heaven's eyes;
      Yet Heaven is not averse to compromise;
      There is a science, lately formulated,
      Whereby one's conscience may be liberated,
105   And any wrongful act you care to mention
      May be redeemed by purity of intention.
      I'll teach you, Madam, the secrets of that science;

      Meanwhile, just place on me your full reliance.
      Assuage my keen desires, and feel no dread:
      The sin, if any, shall be on my head.   110

[*Elmire coughs, this time more loudly.*]

    You've a bad cough.
    ELMIRE: Yes, yes. It's bad indeed.
    TARTUFFE (*producing a little paper bag*): A bit of
      licorice may be what you need.
    ELMIRE: No, I've a stubborn cold, it seems. I'm sure it
      Will take much more than licorice to cure it.
    TARTUFFE: How aggravating.
    ELMIRE: Oh, more than I can say.   115
    TARTUFFE: If you're still troubled, think of things
      this way:
      No one shall know our joys, save us alone,
      And there's no evil till the act is known;
      It's scandal, Madam, which makes it an offense,
      And it's no sin to sin in confidence.   120
    ELMIRE (*having coughed once more*): Well, clearly
      I must do as you require,
      And yield to your importunate desire.
      It is apparent, now, that nothing less
      Will satisfy you, and so I acquiesce.
      To go so far is much against my will;   125
      I'm vexed that it should come to this; but still,
      Since you are so determined on it, since you
      Will not allow mere language to convince you,
      And since you ask for concrete evidence, I
      See nothing for it, now, but to comply.   130
      If this is sinful, if I'm wrong to do it,
      So much the worse for him who drove me to it.
      The fault can surely not be charged to me.
    TARTUFFE: Madam, the fault is mine, if fault there be,
      And . . .
    ELMIRE: Open the door a little, and peek out;   135
      I wouldn't want my husband poking about.
    TARTUFFE: Why worry about the man? Each day he grows
      More gullible; one can lead him by the nose.
      To find us here would fill him with delight,
      And if he saw the worst, he'd doubt his sight.   140
    ELMIRE: Nevertheless, do step out for a minute
      Into the hall, and see that no one's in it.

Scene 6   [*Orgon, Elmire.*]

ORGON (*coming out from under the table*): That man's a
    perfect monster, I must admit!
    I'm simply stunned. I can't get over it.
ELMIRE: What, coming out so soon? How premature!
    Get back in hiding, and wait until you're sure.
    Stay till the end, and be convinced completely;   5
    We mustn't stop till things are proved concretely.
ORGON: Hell never harbored anything so vicious!
ELMIRE: Tut, don't be hasty. Try to be judicious.
    Wait, and be certain that there's no mistake.
    No jumping to conclusions, for Heaven's sake!   10

[*She places Orgon behind her, as Tartuffe re-enters.*]

Scene 7   [*Tartuffe, Elmire, Orgon.*]

TARTUFFE (*not seeing Orgon*): Madam, all things
    have worked out to perfection;
    I've given the neighboring rooms a full inspection;
    No one's about; and now I may at last . . .
ORGON (*intercepting him*): Hold on, my passionate
    fellow, not so fast!
5   I should advise a little more restraint.
    Well, so you thought you'd fool me, my dear saint!
    How soon you wearied of the saintly life—
    Wedding my daughter, and coveting my wife!
    I've long suspected you, and had a feeling
10   That soon I'd catch you at your double-dealing.
    Just now, you've given me evidence galore;
    It's quite enough; I have no wish for more.
ELMIRE (*to Tartuffe*): I'm sorry to have treated you so slyly,
    But circumstances forced me to be wily.
TARTUFFE: Brother, you can't think . . .
15 ORGON: No more talk from you;
    Just leave this household, without more ado.
TARTUFFE: What I intended . . .
ORGON: That seems fairly clear.
    Spare me your falsehoods and get out of here.
TARTUFFE: No, I'm the master, and you're the one to go!
20   This house belongs to me, I'll have you know,
    And I shall show you that you can't hurt *me*
    By this contemptible conspiracy,
    That those who cross me know not what they do,
    And that I've means to expose and punish you,
25   Avenge offended Heaven, and make you grieve
    That ever you dared order me to leave.

Scene 8   [*Elmire, Orgon.*]

ELMIRE: What was the point of all that angry chatter?
ORGON: Dear God, I'm worried. This is no laughing
    matter.
ELMIRE: How so?
ORGON: I fear I understood his drift.
    I'm much disturbed about that deed of gift.
ELMIRE: You gave him . . . ?
ORGON: Yes, it's all been drawn
5   and signed.
    But one thing more is weighing on my mind.
ELMIRE: What's that?
ORGON: I'll tell you; but first let's see if there's
    A certain strong-box in his room upstairs.

ACT V • Scene 1   [*Orgon, Cléante.*]

CLÉANTE: Where are you going so fast?
ORGON: God knows!
CLÉANTE: Then wait;
    Let's have a conference, and deliberate
    On how this situation's to be met.
ORGON: That strong-box has me utterly upset;

    This is the worst of many, many shocks.   5
CLÉANTE: Is there some fearful mystery in that box?
ORGON: My poor friend Argas brought that box to me
    With his own hands, in utmost secrecy;
    'Twas on the very morning of his flight.
    It's full of papers which, if they came to light,   10
    Would ruin him—or such is my impression.
CLÉANTE: Then why did you let it out of your possession?
ORGON: Those papers vexed my conscience, and it
    seemed best
    To ask the counsel of my pious guest.
    The cunning scoundrel got me to agree   15
    To leave the strong-box in his custody,
    So that, in case of an investigation,
    I could employ a slight equivocation
    And swear I didn't have it, and thereby,
    At no expense to conscience, tell a lie.   20
CLÉANTE: It looks to me as if you're out on a limb.
    Trusting him with that box, and offering him
    That deed of gift, were actions of a kind
    Which scarcely indicate a prudent mind.
    With two such weapons, he has the upper hand,   25
    And since you're vulnerable, as matters stand,
    You erred once more in bringing him to bay.
    You should have acted in some subtler way.
ORGON: Just think of it: behind that fervent face,
    A heart so wicked, and a soul so base!   30
    I took him in, a hungry beggar, and then . . .
    Enough, by God! I'm through with pious men:
    Henceforth I'll hate the whole false brotherhood,
    And persecute them worse than Satan could.
CLÉANTE: Ah, there you go—extravagant as ever!   35
    Why can you not be rational? You never
    Manage to take the middle course, it seems,
    But jump, instead, between absurd extremes.
    You've recognized your recent grave mistake
    In falling victim to a pious fake;   40
    Now, to correct that error, must you embrace
    An even greater error in its place,
    And judge our worthy neighbors as a whole
    By what you've learned of one corrupted soul?
    Come, just because one rascal made you swallow   45
    A show of zeal which turned out to be hollow,
    Shall you conclude that all men are deceivers,
    And that, today, there are no true believers?
    Let atheists make that foolish inference;
    Learn to distinguish virtue from pretense,   50
    Be cautious in bestowing admiration,
    And cultivate a sober moderation.
    Don't humor fraud, but also don't asperse
    True piety; the latter fault is worse,
    And it is best to err, if err one must,   55
    As you have done, upon the side of trust.

Scene 2   [*Damis, Orgon, Cléante.*]

DAMIS: Father, I hear that scoundrel's uttered threats
    Against you; that he pridefully forgets
    How, in his need, he was befriended by you,

And means to use your gifts to crucify you.
5   ORGON: It's true, my boy. I'm too distressed for tears.
    DAMIS: Leave it to me, Sir; let me trim his ears.
        Faced with such insolence, we must not waver.
        I shall rejoice in doing you the favor
        Of cutting short his life, and your distress.
10 CLÉANTE: What a display of young hotheadedness!
        Do learn to moderate your fits of rage.
        In this just kingdom, this enlightened age,
        One does not settle things by violence.

Scene 3   [*Madame Pernelle, Mariane, Elmire, Dorine, Damis, Orgon, Cléante.*]

MADAME PERNELLE: I hear strange tales of very strange
        events.
ORGON: Yes, strange events which these two eyes beheld.
        The man's ingratitude is unparalleled.
        I save a wretched pauper from starvation,
5   House him, and treat him like a blood relation,
        Shower him every day with my largesse,
        Give him my daughter, and all that I possess;

Angelika Thomas as Madame Pernelle and Peter Jordan as Orgon in *Der Tartuffe* at the 2006 Salzburg Festival.

And meanwhile the unconscionable knave
Tries to induce my wife to misbehave;
And not content with such extreme rascality,   10
Now threatens me with my own liberality,
And aims, by taking base advantage of
The gifts I gave him out of Christian love,
To drive me from my house, a ruined man,
And make me end a pauper, as he began.   15
DORINE: Poor fellow!
MADAME PERNELLE: No, my son, I'll never bring
        Myself to think him guilty of such a thing.
ORGON: How's that?
MADAME PERNELLE: The righteous always were
        maligned.
ORGON: Speak clearly, Mother. Say what's on your
        mind.
MADAME PERNELLE: I mean that I can smell a rat, my
        dear.   20
        You know how everybody hates him, here.
ORGON: That has no bearing on the case at all.
MADAME PERNELLE: I told you a hundred times, when you
        were small,
        That virtue in this world is hated ever;
        Malicious men may die, but malice never.   25
ORGON: No doubt that's true, but how does it apply?
MADAME PERNELLE: They've turned you against him by
        a clever lie.
ORGON: I've told you, I was there and saw it done.
MADAME PERNELLE: Ah, slanderers will stop at nothing,
        Son.
ORGON: Mother, I'll lose my temper . . . For the last
        time,   30
        I tell you I was witness to the crime.
MADAME PERNELLE: The tongues of spite are busy night
        and noon,
        And to their venom no man is immune.
ORGON: You're talking nonsense. Can't you realize
        I saw it; saw it; saw it with my eyes?   35
        Saw, do you understand me? Must I shout it
        Into your ears before you'll cease to doubt it?
MADAME PERNELLE: Appearances can deceive, my son.
        Dear me,
        We cannot always judge by what we see.
ORGON: Drat! Drat!
MADAME PERNELLE:
                One often interprets things awry;   40
        Good can seem evil to a suspicious eye.
ORGON: Was I to see his pawing at Elmire
        As an act of charity?
MADAME PERNELLE: Till his guilt is clear,
        A man deserves the benefit of the doubt.
        You should have waited, to see how things turned
        out.   45
ORGON: Great God in Heaven, what more proof did
        I need?
        Was I to sit there, watching, until he'd . . .
        You drive me to the brink of impropriety.
MADAME PERNELLE: No, no, a man of such surpassing
        piety
        Could not do such a thing. You cannot shake me.   50

I don't believe it, and you shall not make me.
ORGON: You vex me so that, if you weren't my
        mother,
I'd say to you . . . some dreadful thing or other.
DORINE: It's your turn now, Sir, not to be listened to;
55   You'd not trust us, and now she won't trust you.
CLÉANTE: My friends, we're wasting time which
         should be spent
In facing up to our predicament.
I fear that scoundrel's threats weren't made
       in sport.
DAMIS: Do you think he'd have the nerve to go to
       court?
60 ELMIRE: I'm sure he won't: they'd find it all too crude
A case of swindling and ingratitude.
CLÉANTE: Don't be too sure. He won't be at a loss
To give his claims a high and righteous gloss;
And clever rogues with far less valid cause
65   Have trapped their victims in a web of laws.
I say again that to antagonize
A man so strongly armed was most unwise.
ORGON: I know it; but the man's appalling cheek
Outraged me so, I couldn't control my pique.
70 CLÉANTE: I wish to Heaven that we could devise
Some truce between you, or some compromise.
ELMIRE: If I had known what cards he held, I'd not
Have roused his anger by my little plot.
ORGON (to Dorine, as M. Loyal enters): What is that
       fellow looking for? Who is he?
75   Go talk to him—and tell him that I'm busy.

Scene 4   [*Monsieur Loyal, Madame Pernelle, Orgon, Damis, Mariane, Dorine, Elmire, Cléante.*]

MONSIEUR LOYAL: Good day, dear sister. Kindly let
        me see
Your master.
DORINE: He's involved with company,
And cannot be disturbed just now, I fear.
MONSIEUR LOYAL: I hate to intrude; but what has brought
        me here
5   Will not disturb your master, in any event.
Indeed, my news will make him most content.
DORINE: Your name?
MONSIEUR LOYAL: Just say that I bring greetings
        from
Monsieur Tartuffe, on whose behalf I've come.
DORINE (to Orgon): Sir, he's a very gracious man,
        and bears
10   A message from Tartuffe, which he declares,
Will make you most content.
CLÉANTE: Upon my word,
I think this man had best be seen, and heard.
ORGON: Perhaps he has some settlement to suggest.
How shall I treat him? What manner would be best?
15 CLÉANTE: Control your anger, and if he should mention
Some fair adjustment, give him your full attention.

MONSIEUR LOYAL: Good health to you, good Sir.
        May Heaven confound
Your enemies, and may your joys abound.
ORGON (aside, to Cléante): A gentle salutation: it
        confirms
My guess that he is here to offer terms.   20
MONSIEUR LOYAL: I've always held your family most
        dear;
I served your father, Sir, for many a year.
ORGON: Sir, I must ask your pardon; to my shame,
I cannot now recall your face or name.
MONSIEUR LOYAL: Loyal's my name; I come from
        Normandy,   25
And I'm a bailiff, in all modesty.
For forty years, praise God, it's been my boast
To serve with honor in that vital post,
And I am here, Sir, if you will permit
The liberty, to serve you with this writ . . .   30
ORGON: To—*what*?
MONSIEUR LOYAL: Now, please, Sir, let us have no
        friction:
It's nothing but an order of eviction.
You are to move your goods and family out
And make way for new occupants, without
Deferment or delay, and give the keys . . .   35
ORGON: I? Leave this house?
MONSIEUR LOYAL: Why yes, Sir, if you please.
This house, Sir, from the cellar to the roof,
Belongs now to the good Monsieur Tartuffe,
And he is lord and master of your estate
By virtue of a deed of present date,   40
Drawn in due form, with clearest legal phrasing . . .
DAMIS: Your insolence is utterly amazing!
MONSIEUR LOYAL: Young man, my business here is
        not with you,
But with your wise and temperate father, who,
Like every worthy citizen, stands in awe   45
Of justice, and would never obstruct the law.
ORGON: But . . .
MONSIEUR LOYAL:
                    Not for a million, Sir, would you rebel
Against authority; I know that well.
You'll not make trouble, Sir, or interfere
With the execution of my duties here.   50
DAMIS: Someone may execute a smart tattoo
On that black jacket of yours, before you're through.
MONSIEUR LOYAL: Sir, bid your son be silent. I'd much
        regret
Having to mention such a nasty threat
Of violence, in writing my report.   55
DORINE (aside): This man Loyal's a most disloyal sort!
MONSIEUR LOYAL: I love all men of upright character,
And when I agreed to serve these papers, Sir,
It was your feelings that I had in mind.
I couldn't bear to see the case assigned   60
To someone else, who might esteem you less
And so subject you to unpleasantness.
ORGON: What's more unpleasant than telling a man
        to leave

His house and home?

MONSIEUR LOYAL: You'd like a short reprieve?
65 If you desire it, Sir, I shall not press you,
But wait until tomorrow to dispossess you.
Splendid. I'll come and spend the night here, then,
Most quietly, with half a score of men.
For form's sake, you might bring me, just before
70 You go to bed, the keys to the front door.
My men, I promise, will be on their best
Behavior, and will not disturb your rest.
But bright and early, Sir, you must be quick
And move out all your furniture, every stick:
75 The men I've chosen are both young and strong,
And with their help it shouldn't take you long.
In short, I'll make things pleasant and convenient,
And since I'm being so extremely lenient,
Please show me, Sir, a like consideration,
80 And give me your entire cooperation.

ORGON (*aside*): I may be all but bankrupt, but I vow
I'd give a hundred louis, here and now,
Just for the pleasure of landing one good clout
Right on the end of that complacent snout.

CLÉANTE: Careful; don't make things worse.

85 DAMIS: My bootsole itches
To give that beggar a good kick in the breeches.

DORINE: Monsieur Loyal, I'd love to hear the whack
Of a stout stick across your fine broad back.

MONSIEUR LOYAL: Take care: a woman too may go
to jail if
90 She uses threatening language to a bailiff.

CLÉANTE: Enough, enough, Sir. This must not go on.
Give me that paper, please, and then begone.

MONSIEUR LOYAL: Well, *au revoir*. God give you all
good cheer!

ORGON: May God confound you, and him who sent
you here!

Scene 5   [*Orgon, Cléante, Mariane, Elmire, Madame Pernelle, Dorine, Damis.*]

ORGON: Now, Mother, was I right or not? This
writ
Should change your notion of Tartuffe a bit.
Do you perceive his villainy at last?

MADAME PERNELLE: I'm thunderstruck. I'm utterly
aghast.

5 DORINE: Oh, come, be fair. You mustn't take offense
At this new proof of his benevolence.
He's acting out of selfless love, I know.
Material things enslave the soul, and so
He kindly has arranged your liberation
10 From all that might endanger your salvation.

ORGON: Will you not ever hold your tongue, you
dunce?

CLÉANTE: Come, you must take some action, and at
once.

ELMIRE: Go tell the world of the low trick he's tried.

The deed of gift is surely nullified
By such behavior, and public rage will not   15
Permit the wretch to carry out his plot.

Scene 6   [*Valère, Orgon, Cléante, Elmire, Mariane, Madame Pernelle, Damis, Dorine.*]

VALÈRE: Sir, though I hate to bring you more bad
news,
Such is the danger that I cannot choose.
A friend who is extremely close to me
And knows my interest in your family
Has, for my sake, presumed to violate   5
The secrecy that's due to things of state,
And sends me word that you are in a plight
From which your one salvation lies in flight.
That scoundrel who's imposed upon you so
Denounced you to the King an hour ago   10
And, as supporting evidence, displayed
The strong-box of a certain renegade
Whose secret papers, so he testified,
You had disloyally agreed to hide.
I don't know just what charges may be pressed,   15
But there's a warrant out for your arrest;
Tartuffe has been instructed, furthermore,
To guide the arresting officer to your door.

CLÉANTE: He's clearly done this to facilitate
His seizure of your house and your estate.   20

ORGON: That man, I must say, is a vicious beast!

VALÈRE: Quick, Sir; you mustn't tarry in the least.
My carriage is outside, to take you hence;
This thousand louis should cover all expense.
Let's lose no time, or you shall be undone;   25
The sole defense, in this case, is to run.
I shall go with you all the way, and place you
In a safe refuge to which they'll never trace you.

ORGON: Alas, dear boy, I wish that I could show
you
My gratitude for everything I owe you.   30
But now is not the time; I pray the Lord
That I may live to give you your reward.
Farewell, my dears; be careful . . .

CLÉANTE: Brother, hurry.
We shall take care of things; you needn't worry.

Scene 7   [*The Officer, Tartuffe, Valère, Orgon, Elmire, Mariane, Madame Pernelle, Dorine, Cléante, Damis.*]

TARTUFFE: Gently, Sir, gently; stay right where you are.
No need for haste; your lodging isn't far.
You're off to prison, by order of the Prince.

ORGON: This is the crowning blow, you wretch; and since
It means my total ruin and defeat,   5
Your villainy is now at last complete.

John Beatty's set design (with ensemble cast) for the Roundabout Theatre Company's 2002–2003 production.

TARTUFFE: You needn't try to provoke me; it's no use.
Those who serve Heaven must expect abuse.
CLÉANTE: You are indeed most patient, sweet, and
blameless.
DORINE: How he exploits the name of Heaven! It's
10   shameless.
TARTUFFE: Your taunts and mockeries are all for
naught;
To do my duty is my only thought.
MARIANE: Your love of duty is most meritorious,
And what you've done is little short of glorious.
15 TARTUFFE: All deeds are glorious, Madam, which obey
The sovereign prince who sent me here today.
ORGON: I rescued you when you were destitute;
Have you forgotten that, you thankless brute?
TARTUFFE: No, no, I well remember everything;
20   But my first duty is to serve my King.
That obligation is so paramount
That other claims, beside it, do not count;
And for it I would sacrifice my wife,
My family, my friend, or my own life.
ELMIRE: Hypocrite!
25 DORINE: All that we most revere, he uses
To cloak his plots and camouflage his ruses.
CLÉANTE: If it is true that you are animated
By pure and loyal zeal, as you have stated,
Why was this zeal not roused until you'd sought
30   To make Orgon a cuckold, and been caught?
Why weren't you moved to give your evidence
Until your outraged host had driven you hence?

I shan't say that the gift of all his treasure
Ought to have damped your zeal in any measure;
But if he is a traitor, as you declare,   35
How could you condescend to be his heir?
TARTUFFE (*to the officer*): Sir, spare me all this clamor;
it's growing shrill.
Please carry out your orders, if you will.
OFFICER: Yes, I've delayed too long, Sir. Thank you
kindly.
You're just the proper person to remind me.   40
Come, you are off to join the other boarders
In the King's prison, according to his orders.
TARTUFFE: Who? I, Sir?
OFFICER: Yes.
TARTUFFE: To prison? This can't be true!
OFFICER: I owe an explanation, but not to you.
(*To Orgon.*)
Sir, all is well; rest easy, and be grateful.   45
We serve a Prince to whom all sham is hateful,
A Prince who sees into our inmost hearts,
And can't be fooled by any trickster's arts.
His royal soul, though generous and human,
Views all things with discernment and acumen;   50
His sovereign reason is not lightly swayed,
And all his judgments are discreetly weighed.
He honors righteous men of every kind,
And yet his zeal for virtue is not blind,
Nor does his love of piety numb his wits   55
And make him tolerant of hypocrites.
'Twas hardly likely that this man could cozen

A King who's foiled such liars by the dozen.
With one keen glance, the King perceived
    the whole
60 Perverseness and corruption of his soul,
And thus high Heaven's justice was displayed:
Betraying you, the rogue stood self-betrayed.
The King soon recognized Tartuffe as one
Notorious by another name, who'd done
65 So many vicious crimes that one could fill
Ten volumes with them, and be writing still.
But to be brief: our sovereign was appalled
By this man's treachery toward you, which he
    called
The last, worst villainy of a vile career,
70 And bade me follow the impostor here
To see how gross his impudence could be,
And force him to restore your property.
Your private papers, by the King's command,
I hereby seize and give into your hand.
75 The King, by royal order, invalidates
The deed which gave this rascal your estates,
And pardons, furthermore, your grave offense
In harboring an exile's documents.
By these decrees, our Prince rewards you for
80 Your loyal deeds in the late civil war,
And shows how heartfelt is his satisfaction

In recompensing any worthy action,
How much he prizes merit, and how he makes
More of men's virtues than of their mistakes.
DORINE: Heaven be praised!
MADAME PERNELLE: I breathe again, at last. 85
ELMIRE: We're safe.
MARIANE: I can't believe the danger's past.
ORGON (to Tartuffe): Well, traitor, now you see . . .
CLÉANTE: Ah, Brother, please,
Let's not descend to such indignities.
Leave the poor wretch to his unhappy fate,
And don't say anything to aggravate   90
His present woes; but rather hope that he
Will soon embrace an honest piety,
And mend his ways, and by a true repentance
Move our just King to moderate his sentence.
Meanwhile, go kneel before your sovereign's
    throne   95
And thank him for the mercies he has shown.
ORGON: Well said: let's go at once and, gladly
    kneeling,
Express the gratitude which all are feeling.
Then, when that first great duty has been done,
We'll turn with pleasure to a second one,   100
And give Valère, whose love has proven so true,
The wedded happiness which is his due.

COMMENTARY

MEL GUSSOW (1933–2005)

Review of Tartuffe   1991

Mel Gussow, in his *New York Times* review of the Yale Repertory Theatre's 1991 production of *Tartuffe*, comments on the effects of the stage set, which was dominated by huge mahogany doors, and on the visual elements that help qualify the diminutive stature of Tartuffe as played by the irrepressible Austin Pendleton.

In Walton Jones's production of *Tartuffe* at the Yale Repertory Theatre, a row of large mahogany-like doors is positioned against a *trompe l'oeil* background. The doors are used for quick entrances, exits, and punchlines. They slide across the stage on tracks, swing open and slam on cue, and are filled with concealed crannies for depositing plot-advancing objects.

In using the jack-in-the-box set, the design of Kevin Rupnik, the director offers a well-carpentered, occasionally tricked-up approach to Molière, but with merit in its breathlessness. It is enlivened by several performances, especially by that of Austin Pendleton in the title role.

Mr. Pendleton takes to Tartuffe as a hypocrite to a hairshirt. Although his characterization is larger than life, he is undeniably short, and he uses his lowness to comic effect, even to playing one scene on his knees behind a portable pulpit that is the height of a go-cart. From his first entrance in an itch-provoking gown that almost reaches to his bare feet, he plays Tartuffe like a saint set for martyrdom. When he throws away his propriety and makes an advance on Orgon's wife (Frances Conroy), he does so with a sudden gale of energy. "I may be pious," he proclaims, "but I'm human too," and he raises his hand as if signaling the cavalry into action.

When he is caught in a flagrantly compromising position with the lady of the house, he looks at the almost cuckolded Orgon with the expression of an innocent child. "Brother, you can't think . . . ," says Tartuffe, and the actor takes a long, laughable pause before realizing that his game is up.

The key to Mr. Pendleton's success is that he is portraying a fanatic. This could be regarded as a Pendleton specialty—on stage and also on television, as witness his Mr. Entertainment, a helplessly stagestruck song-and-dance man, the amateur Sinatra of *St. Elsewhere*.

With Tartuffe loose in the household, the interfering maid Dorine (a pert performance by Fran Brill) mobilizes her allies, who include most of the other characters in the play, for an all-out siege on the villain. Subplot humor is provided by her attempt to wake up her employer, Orgon (Jerome Dempsey), a nearsighted fool who holds fast to his astigmatism. Mr. Dempsey is a master of the slow burn, as demonstrated in the scene in which he, aroused from his gullibility, tries to convince his still skeptical mother of Tartuffe's deceit. Patiently he describes the dastard, and she blithely dismisses the charge as slander. His carefully timed delivery of the line "Mother, I'll lose my temper" is done with apoplectic finesse.

Barring a certain amount of busyness—too much swirling through those doors—and a tentativeness at the conclusion, this is a mirthful *Tartuffe* that begins the Yale Repertory season. A final word is due Richard Wilbur's verse translation. In common with his other versions of Molière comedies, it is an eloquent example of the adapter's art.

Chikamatsu Monzaemon

Generally regarded as the most significant Japanese playwright, Chikamatsu Monzaemon (1653–1725) was born in the province of Echizen into a minor samurai family. His family name was Sugimori, but he changed it when he began writing plays. In his lifetime—during the celebrated Tokugawa shogunate (1603–1868)—hundreds of thousands of samurai did not serve the shogun or a *daimyo*, or master. Chikamatsu was among those called *rōnin*, samurai who lived without a master and who were therefore without a clear direction. Trained as warriors and supported by the farmer class in Japan during the extended peace of the period, the samurai had little to do. Some of them left the samurai class and, like Chikamatsu, changed their names and went into theater or into some form of business.

The class structure of Japan at this time consisted essentially of peasant farmers, the samurai, the nobility, and merchants. (Some commentators add a class of artisans.) During the late seventeenth and eighteenth centuries, the merchants grew into a wealthy class and often held power over the nobility through debts and other obligations. Chikamatsu was especially interesting because, although he experienced life as part of the samurai class, he also appears to have been connected with a Buddhist monastery as a youth. He may have taken his pseudonym from the Chikamatsu temple at which he stayed for some time. At age nineteen, he became a page in a noble family and experienced palace life. Some sources suggest that he was employed by nobleman Ogimachi Kimmochi (1653–1733), who wrote puppet plays; others suggest he worked for Lord Ichijo Eikan, a connoisseur of puppet plays. Regardless, it was probably this experience that impelled Chikamatsu to give up his position and become Japan's first professional playwright. In essence, Chikamatsu had personal experience in three of the four primary classes in Japanese culture.

Unfortunately, we do not know a great deal about Chikamatsu. We do not know which was his first play, nor do we know how many plays he wrote. Estimates run from 130 to 140 plays, the majority of which are *jōruri*, or puppet plays, and the rest kabuki plays using live actors.

Kabuki, whose linguistic root implies subversive behavior, began with a dance in the "floating world," or pleasure quarter of Kyoto. This was an area licensed for the entertainment of samurai and nobles and permitting prostitution and many forms of entertainment for men, including theater. If we think of Nō drama as refined and religious at heart, we can think of kabuki as profane and appealing to the masses. Its beginning was in 1603 in the dances of a woman named Okuni. Scholar James Brandon, an expert on classical Japanese theater, says of kabuki, "it was the rock entertainment of the seventeenth century. Okuni performed the first Japanese plays of contemporary urban life: numerous painted screens and scrolls show her outrageously garbed as a handsome young warrior, exotic Christian rosary draped on her bosom, conducting an assignation with a prostitute."[1] Eventually, prostitutes took up the practice

---

[1]James Brandon, *The Cambridge Guide to Asian Theatre* (Cambridge: Cambridge University Press, 1993), p. 147.

of kabuki in narrative plays that were sometimes based on current events and that used live actors aiming at an essentially realistic theatre. The authorities eventually cracked down and in 1629 banned female actors, giving rise to the highly specialized *onnagata*, male actors who represented women on stage.

Chikamatsu was most renowned for his puppet plays, but early in his career he also wrote for the kabuki theater. At that time puppet plays were known as *jōruri*, but the more common term now is *bunraku*. Both forms of theater, kabuki and bunraku, are performed in Japan and elsewhere today. Chikamatsu's earliest plays for the puppet theater were probably written in 1683. The puppet theater relied on chanters—virtuoso speakers with highly trained voices—to deliver the lines of the characters. One of the greatest chanters of this period, Takemoto Gidayū (1651–1714), is known to have produced a number of Chikamatsu's earliest plays, among them *Kagekiyo Victorious* (1686).

Chikamatsu's early kabuki plays seem to have been inspired by especially popular actors, among them the brilliant Sakata Tōjūrō (1647–1709). One problem with kabuki actors in the late seventeenth century was that many grew arrogant and difficult. A cult of personality as strong as anything connected with contemporary film stars grew up around the kabuki actors, resulting in a drama that focused not on the play itself but on the presence of the actor.

The puppet theater had the advantage of eliminating this complication. In addition, during the early part of the eighteenth century, the drama that was possible with puppets was similar to what is possible today with computer-generated imagery (CGI) in animated and live-action films. Impossible situations could be enacted with puppets: caesarian operations, quick transformations, dismemberments, and more. When Chikamatsu was writing *jōruri* plays, each puppet was operated by a single person, usually dressed in black (as they are today) so as to permit the puppets to seem to be acting on their own. Each puppet head was painted in a way that signaled to the audience whether it was a good or a villainous figure. Chikamatsu went beyond these limitations, however, and created characters of some moral ambiguity and considerable complexity.

His works are usually divided into history plays and domestic plays, often domestic tragedies. The most successful of his history plays is *The Battles of Coxinga* (1715), set in China. Because Japan was essentially sealed off from foreigners and no Japanese were allowed to travel at this time, the foreign setting added to its appeal. Chikamatsu also invented the successful genre called *shinjū-mono*, or love-suicide play. *The Love Suicides at Sonezaki* (1703) was the first of a series of love-suicide plays written by Chikamatsu as well as other playwrights of the time. It was based on an actual event that had constituted a minor scandal only weeks before he produced his play. He refined the genre in several more plays, including *The Love Suicides at the Women's Temple* (1708) and the unusually modern and complex *The Love Suicides at Amijima* (c. 1720).

The genre was so popular that it became a societal threat. In response to these plays, a great many people committed their own love-suicides, and consequently the authorities banned all such plays in 1722. (Curiously, a similar cult of suicide developed in Europe after the publication of Goethe's *The Sorrows of Young Werther* [1774].)

After 1705, Chikamatsu moved to Osaka, where he was the resident playwright for Gidayū's puppet theater until his death in 1725. His work matured, and his subtle and complex use of language, especially rhyme patterns and puns, established him as one of Japan's greatest writers. He is noted for a technique known as the "pivot-word"—a word that has a double meaning, functioning one way in the beginning of a line and another way in the rest of the line. His skill as a poet makes reading his plays almost as rewarding as seeing them enacted.

The Love Suicides at Sonezaki

For discussion questions and assignments on *The Love Suicides at Sonezaki*, visit bedfordstmartins.com/jacobus.

Sonezaki shinjū is the first *shinjū-mono*, or love-suicide play. Chikamatsu wrote some dozen such plays himself, and other playwrights contributed their own. Taken from a current event, the story is direct and moving. Tokubei falls in love with Ohatsu, a young prostitute whose freedom he cannot afford to buy. In desperation, Tokubei sees only one way out of their dilemma: suicide.

In this play, Chikamatsu explores a number of interesting issues. It was not uncommon for a visitor to the floating world to fall in love with a courtesan. Japanese society maintained a clear double standard: men were permitted to enjoy the favors of prostitutes in the licensed areas, whereas their wives were threatened with execution if they committed adultery. In some plays a brother and father approved the killing of an unfaithful woman by her husband. Wives who maintained silence in face of such activity were praised. Those who complained or grew jealous were often divorced, and once divorced they were ruined. Prostitutes were unmarried entertainers whose job was to attract the attention of men and to please them. They were owned by the establishments they served and could be purchased for a high price.

One of the first things one notices about *The Love Suicides at Sonezaki* is that the characters are essentially part of what we would think of today as the middle class. The play is a representational drama, a domestic tragedy, that attempts to present characters speaking as they would if they were encountered in actual society. Tokubei works for a company that sells soy sauce. The villain Kuheiji is a powerful oil merchant. One of Ohatsu's customers is a "country bumpkin." Chikamatsu reveals ordinary people experiencing powerful emotions. It would take another 150 years for such serious middle-class drama to appear on European stages.

The play is also interesting because it respects the Aristotelian unities even though Chikamatsu could have known nothing of Aristotle or of any foreign play. The action takes place in a twenty-four-hour period, the characters develop clearly and consistently, and there is no subplot. As a result, the play seems modern to the Western reader.

The popularity of this and other love-suicide plays, which led to a ban on the genre in 1722, continued in the public imagination for a few years after the ban was enacted, but then the form faded into obscurity. After Chikamatsu's death, the puppet theater developed much more technically advanced production values. The development of three-person puppets, which required considerable coordination among the puppeteers, permitted more surprising effects and more subtle and amazing movements. Chikamatsu's plays were sometimes rewritten to take advantage of these and other developments, such as a revolving stage (about a century before a similar development in Europe). Therefore, most of the current texts of the plays have the marks of a modern rewriting. In the text given here, however, Chikamatsu's 1703 version, except for a brief introductory passage, appears as it was originally played.

Because the chanter controls the dialogue in the puppet play, he also acts as a narrator commenting on and advancing the action. The narrator chants some of the most beautiful poetry in the third scene. A passage known as the *michi-yuki*, or "lovers' journey," offers Chikamatsu the opportunity to raise the level of diction and explore the emotions implied in the action of lovers journeying toward their death. It begins,

> Farewell to this world, and to the night farewell.
> We who walk the road to death, to what should we be likened?
> To the frost by the road that leads to the graveyard,
> Vanishing with each step we take ahead:
> How sad is this dream of a dream!

The inclusion of religion, Amida Buddhism, in this and other plays that have at their root erotic content is not unusual. Most of the better kabuki plays treated religion as important. Ohatsu and Tokubei end *The Love Suicides at Sonezaki* with a sense of religious assurance that may seem odd to Western audiences. At the heart of this play and other love-suicide dramas is the conflict of two important values of Japanese society: *giri*, the obligations one has to family and society, and *ninjō*, the personal human feelings to which one responds. Like yin and yang, these elements must be balanced. If one worries only about obligation to others and ignores emotion, one can miss important life experiences. If one is dominated only by personal emotion and desire, society will suffer. In this play Tokubei is torn between his obligation to his master and his feelings for Ohatsu. In addition, he is humiliated by the clever Kuheiji and loses his honor. Ohatsu realizes the situation Tokubei is in and proposes a way out for them both. The narrator, obviously moved by the lovers' situation, sees them as moving toward paradise.

One of the details that makes this play seem so modern, especially in relation to European plays of the eighteenth century, is its emphasis on money. Tokubei seems naïve in lending his money even to a good friend, considering what is at stake. But it is the forfeit of the money through Kuheiji's cleverness that drives Tokubei to the play's ultimate resolution. One way or another, Tokubei seems doomed because of the considerable sum of money he has received from his master.

The Love Suicides at Sonezaki in Performance

A key element of all *jōruri* puppet plays is the musician, who plays a three-string instrument called the *shamisen*. Performers on this instrument were successful entertainers before they collaborated with chanters and puppets, and even today the musician has a prominent role in both kabuki and bunraku (puppet) productions. The chanter stands or sits to the side of the stage, and the handlers of the puppets are usually in a lowered section of the stage so that they remain inconspicuous. In modern performances, the handlers are often dressed in absolute black, including face masks, and from a slight distance they are almost unnoticeable. The puppets are elaborate and capable of expressing considerable emotion, especially in conjunction with the shamisen musician.

The stage itself has grown wider since Chikamatsu's age, but it still relies on painted scenery and realistic representation of the various locations of the drama. Like a number of other important puppet plays, *The Love Suicides at Sonezaki* has also been performed as a kabuki play with living actors, usually wearing masks and elaborate costumes. Contemporary productions of puppet plays, those of both Chikamatsu and other playwrights, take advantage of the scale of large Western theaters, a development that was adopted largely after World War II. These plays are remarkably effective in those spaces.

CHIKAMATSU MONZAEMON (1653–1725)

The Love Suicides at Sonezaki 1703

TRANSLATED BY DONALD KEENE

Cast of Characters

TOKUBEI, *aged 25, employee of a dealer in soy sauce*
KUHEIJI, *an oil merchant*
HOST *of Temma House*
CHŌZŌ, *an apprentice*
CUSTOMER *of Ohatsu*
TOWNSMEN
OHATSU, *aged 19, a courtesan*
HOSTESS
COURTESANS
SERVANTS

Scene One: *The grounds of the Ikudama Shrine in Osaka. Time: May 21, 1703.*

NARRATOR:
This graceful young man has served many springs
With the firm of Hirano in Uchihon Street;
He hides the passion that burns in his breast
Lest word escape and the scandal spread.
He drinks peach wine, a cup at a time,
And combs with care his elegant locks,
"Toku" he is called, and famed for his taste,
But now, his talents buried underground,
He works as a clerk, his sleeves stained with oil,

A slave to his sweet remembrances of love.
Today he makes the rounds of his clients
With a lad who carries a cask of soy:
They have reached the shrine of Ikudama.
A woman's voice calls from a bench inside a refreshment stand.
OHATSU: Tokubei—that's you, isn't it?
NARRATOR: She claps her hands, and Tokubei nods in recognition.
TOKUBEI: Chōzō, I'll be following later. Make the rounds of the temples in Tera Street and the uptown mansions, and then return to the shop. Tell them that I'll be back soon. Don't forget to call on the dyer's in Azuchi Street and collect the money he owes us. And stay away from Dōtombori.
NARRATOR: He watches as long as the boy remains in sight, then lifts the bamboo blinds.
TOKUBEI: Ohatsu—what's the matter?
NARRATOR: He starts to remove his bamboo hat.
OHATSU: Please keep your hat on just now. I have a customer from the country today who's making a pilgrimage to all thirty-three temples of Kwannon. He's been boasting that he intends to spend the whole day drinking. At the moment he's gone off to hear the

impersonators' show, but if he returns and finds us together, there might be trouble. All the chair-bearers know you. It's best you keep your face covered.

But to come back to us. Lately you haven't written me a word. I've been terribly worried but, not knowing what the situation might be in your shop, I couldn't very well write you. I must have called a hundred times at the Tamba House, but they hadn't any news of you either. Somebody—yes, it was Taichi, the blind musician—asked his friends, and they said you'd gone back to the country. I couldn't believe it was true. You've really been too cruel. Didn't you even want to ask about me? Perhaps you hoped things would end that way, but I've been sick with worry. If you think I'm lying, feel this swelling!

NARRATOR: She takes his hand and presses it to her breast, weeping reproachful and entreating tears, exactly as if they were husband and wife. Man though he is, he also weeps.

TOKUBEI: You're right, entirely right, but what good would it have done to tell you and make you suffer? I've been going through such misery that I couldn't be more distracted if Bon, New Year, the Ten Nights, and every other feast in the calendar came all at once. My mind's been in a turmoil, and my finances in chaos. To tell the truth, I went up to Kyoto to raise some money, among other things. It's a miracle I'm still alive. If they make my story into a three-act play, I'm sure the audiences will weep.

NARRATOR: Words fail and he can only sigh.

OHATSU: And is this the comic relief of your tragedy? Why couldn't you have trusted me with your worries when you tell me even trivial little things? You must've had some reason for hiding. Why don't you take me into your confidence?

NARRATOR: She leans over his knee. Bitter tears soak her handkerchief.

TOKUBEI: Please don't cry or be angry with me. I wasn't hiding anything, but it wouldn't have helped to involve you. At any rate, my troubles have largely been settled, and I can tell you the whole story now.

My master has always treated me with particular kindness because I'm his nephew. For my part, I've served him with absolute honesty. There's never been a penny's discrepancy in the accounts. It's true that recently I used his name when I bought on credit a bolt of Kaga silk to make into a summer kimono, but that's the one and only time, and if I have to raise the money on the spot, I can always sell back the kimono without taking a loss. My master has been so impressed by my honesty that he proposed I marry his wife's niece with a dowry of two *kamme,*° and promised to set me up in business. That happened last year, but how could I shift my affections when I have you? I didn't give his suggestion a second thought, but in the meantime my mother—she's really my stepmother—conferred with my master, keeping it a secret from me. She went back

kamme: A considerable sum of money.

to the country with the two *kamme* in her clutches. Fool that I am, I never dreamt what had happened.

The trouble began last month when they tried to force me to marry. I got angry and said, "Master, you surprise me. You know how unwilling I am to get married, and yet you've inveigled my old mother into giving her consent. You've gone too far, master. I can't understand the mistress's attitude either. If I took as my wife this young lady whom I've always treated with the utmost deference and accepted her dowry in the bargain, I'd spend my whole life dancing attendance on my wife. How could I ever assert myself? I've refused once, and even if my father were to return from his grave, the answer would still be no."

The master was furious that I should have answered so bluntly. His voice shook with rage. "I know your real reasons. You're involved with Ohatsu, or whatever her name is, from the Temma House in Dōjima. That's why you seem so averse to my wife's niece. Very well—after what's been said, I'm no longer willing to give you the girl, and since there's to be no wedding, return the money. Settle without fail by the twenty-second of the month and clear your business accounts. I'll chase you from Osaka and never let you set foot here again!"

I too have my pride as a man. "Right you are!" I answered, and rushed off to my village. But my so-called mother wouldn't let the money from her grip, not if this world turned into the next. I went to Kyoto, hoping to borrow the money from the wholesale soy sauce dealers in the Fifth Ward. I've always been on good terms with them. But, as ill luck would have it, they had no money to spare. I retraced my steps to the country, and this time, with the intercession of the whole village, I managed to extract the money from my mother. I intended to return the dowry immediately and settle things for once and for all. But if I can't remain in Osaka, how shall I be able to meet you?

My bones may be crushed to powder, my flesh be torn away, and I may sink, an empty shell, in the slime of Shijimi River. Let that happen if it must, but if I am parted from you, what shall I do?

NARRATOR: He weeps, suffocated by his grief. Ohatsu, holding back the welling tears of sympathy, strengthens and comforts him.

OHATSU: How you've suffered! And when I think that it's been because of me, I feel happy, sad, and most grateful all at once. But please, show more courage. Pull yourself together. Your uncle may have forbidden you to set foot in Osaka again, but you haven't committed robbery or arson. I'll think of some way to keep you here. And if a time should come when we can no longer meet, did our promises of love hold only for this world? Others before us have chosen reunion through death. To die is simple enough—none will hinder and none be hindered on the journey to the Mountain of Death and the River of Three Ways.

NARRATOR: Ohatsu falters among these words of encouragement, choked by tears. She resumes.

OHATSU: The twenty-second is tomorrow. Return the money early, since you must return it anyway. Try to get in your master's good graces again.

TOKUBEI: I want to, and I'm impatient to return the money, but on the thirteenth of the month Kuheiji the oil merchant—I think you know him—begged me desperately for the money. He said he needed it only for one day, and promised to return it by the morning of the eighteenth. I decided to lend him the money since I didn't need it until the twenty-second, and it was for a friend close as a brother. He didn't get in touch with me on the eighteenth or nineteenth. Yesterday he was out and I couldn't see him. I intended to call on him this morning, but I've spent it making the rounds of my customers in order to wind up my business by tomorrow. I'll go to him this evening and settle everything. He's a man of honor and he knows my predicament. I'm sure nothing will go wrong. Don't worry. Oh—look there, Ohatsu!

NARRATOR:
"Hatsuse is far away,
Far too is Naniwa-dera:
So many temples are renowned
For the sound of their bells,
Voices of the Eternal Law.
If, on an evening in spring,
You visit a mountain temple
You will see…"
At the head of a band of revelers

TOKUBEI: Kuheiji! That's a poor performance! You've no business running off on excursions when you haven't cleared up your debt with me. Today we'll settle our account.

NARRATOR: He grasps Kuheiji's arm and restrains him. Kuheiji's expression is dubious.

KUHEIJI: What are you talking about, Tokubei? These people with me are all residents of the ward. We've had a meeting in Ueshio Street to raise funds for a pilgrimage to Ise. We've drunk a little saké, but we're on our way home now. What do you mean by grabbing my arm? Don't be rowdy!

NARRATOR: He removes his wicker hat and glares at Tokubei.

TOKUBEI: I'm not being rowdy. All I ask is that you return the two *kamme* of silver I lent you on the thirteenth, which you were supposed to repay on the eighteenth.

NARRATOR: Before he can finish speaking, Kuheiji bursts out laughing.

KUHEIJI: Are you out of your mind, Tokubei? I can't remember having borrowed a penny from you in all the years I've known you. Don't make any accusations which you'll regret.

NARRATOR: He shakes himself free. His companions also remove their hats. Tokubei pales with astonishment.

TOKUBEI: Don't say that, Kuheiji! You came to me in tears, saying that you couldn't survive your monthly bills, and I thought that this was the kind of emergency for which we'd been friends all these years. I lent you the money as an act of generosity, though I needed it desperately myself. I told you that I didn't even require a receipt, but you insisted on putting your seal to one, for form's sake. You made me write out a promissory note and you sealed it. Don't try to deny it, Kuheiji!

NARRATOR: Tokubei rebukes him heatedly.

KUHEIJI: What's that? I'd like to see the seal.

TOKUBEI: Do you think I'm afraid to show you?

NARRATOR: He produces the paper from his wallet.

TOKUBEI: If these gentlemen are from the ward, I am sure that they will recognize your seal. Will you still dispute it?

NARRATOR: When he unfolds the paper and displays it, Kuheiji claps his hands in recollection.

KUHEIJI: Yes, it's my seal all right. Oh, Tokubei, I never thought you'd do such a thing, not even if you were starving and forced to eat dirt. On the tenth of the month I lost a wallet containing the seal. I advertised for it everywhere, but without success, so as of the sixteenth of this month, as I've informed these gentlemen, I've changed my seal. Could I have affixed the seal I lost on the tenth to a document on the thirteenth? No—what happened was that you found my wallet, wrote the promissory note, and affixed my seal. Now you're trying to extort money from me—that makes you a worse criminal than a forger. You'd do better, Tokubei, to commit out-and-out robbery. You deserve to have your head cut off, but for old times' sake, I'll forgive you. Let's see if you can make any money out of this!

NARRATOR: He throws the note in Tokubei's face and glares at him fiercely in an extraordinary display of feigned innocence. Tokubei, furious, cries aloud.

TOKUBEI: You've been damned clever. You've put one over on me. I'm dishonored. What am I to do? Must I let you take my money brazenly from me? You've planned everything so cleverly that even if I go to court, I'm sure to lose. I'll take back my money with my fists! See here! I'm Tokubei of the Hirano-ya, a man of honor. Do you follow me? I'm not a man to trick a friend out of his money the way you have. Come on!

NARRATOR: He falls on Kuheiji.

KUHEIJI: You impudent little apprentice! I'll knock the insolence out of you!

NARRATOR: He seizes the front of Tokubei's kimono and they grapple, trading blows and shoves. Ohatsu rushes barefoot to them.

OHATSU (*to townsmen*): Please everybody, stop the fight! He's a friend of mine. Where are the chair-bearers? Why don't they do something? Tokubei's being beaten!

NARRATOR: She writhes in anguish, but is helpless. Her customer, country bumpkin that he is, bundles her forcibly into a palanquin.

CUSTOMER: It won't do for you to get hurt.

OHATSU: Please wait just a moment! Oh, I'm so un-happy!

NARRATOR: The palanquin is rushed off, leaving only the echoes of her weeping voice.

Tokubei is alone; Kuheiji has five companions. Men rush out from the nearby booths and drive them all with sticks to the lotus pond. Who tramples Tokubei? Who beats him? There is no way to tell. His hair is disheveled, his sash undone. He stumbles and falls to this side and that.

TOKUBEI: Kuheiji, you swine! Do you think I'll let you escape alive?

NARRATOR: He staggers about searching for Kuheiji, but he has fled and vanished. Tokubei falls heavily in his tracks and, weeping bitterly, he cries aloud.

TOKUBEI (*to bystanders*): I feel humiliated and ashamed that you've seen me this way. There was not a false word in my accusation. I've always treated Kuheiji like a brother, and when he begged me for the money, saying he'd never forget it as long as he lived, I lent it to him, sure that he'd do the same for me, though the money was precious as life, and I knew that without it tomorrow, the twenty-first, I'd have to kill myself. He made me write the note in my own hand, then put his seal to it. But it was a seal which he had already reported as lost, and now he's turned the accusations against me! It's mortifying, infuriating—to be kicked and beaten this way, dishonored and forced to my knees. It would've been better if I had died while smashing and biting him!

NARRATOR: He strikes the ground and gnashes his teeth, clenches his fists and moans, a sight to stir compassion.

TOKUBEI: There's no point in my talking this way. Before three days have passed I, Tokubei, will make amends by showing all Osaka the purity at the bottom of my heart.

NARRATOR: The meaning of these words is later known.

TOKUBEI: I'm sorry to have bothered you all. Please for-give me.

NARRATOR: He speaks his apologies, picks up his bat-tered hat and puts it on. His face, downcast in the sinking rays of the sun, is clouded by tears that en-gulf him. Dejectedly he leaves, a sight too pitiful to behold.

Scene Two: *Inside the Temma House. Time: Evening of the same day.*

NARRATOR:
The breezes of love are all-pervasive
By Shijimi River, where love-drowned guests
Like empty shells, bereft of their senses,
Wander the dark ways of love
Lit each night by burning lanterns,
Fireflies that glow in the four seasons,
Stars that shine on rainy nights.

By Plum Bridge, blossoms show even in summer.
Rustics on a visit, city connoisseurs,
All journey the varied roads of love,
Where adepts wander and novices play:
What a lively place this New Quarter is!

But alas for Ohatsu of the Temma House—even after she returns the day's events still weigh on her. She cannot swallow her saké, she feels on edge. As she sits weeping, some courtesans from the neighbor-ing houses and other friends come for a little chat.

FIRST COURTESAN: Have you heard, Ohatsu? They say that Toku was given a thrashing for something bad he did. Is it true?

SECOND COURTESAN: No, my customer told me that Toku was trampled to death.

NARRATOR: They say he was lettered for fraud or trussed for counterfeiting a seal. Not one decent thing have they to report: every expression of sympathy makes their visit the more painful.

OHATSU: No, please, not another word. The more I hear, the worse my breast pains me. I'm sure I'll be the first to die. I wish I were dead already.

NARRATOR: She can only weep. But amidst her tears she happens to look outside and catches a glimpse of Tokubei, a pathetic figure wearing a wicker hat, even at night. Her heart leaps, and she wants to run to him, but in the sitting room are the master and his wife, and by the entrance stands the cook, while in the kitchen a maid is hovering: with so many sharp eyes watching, she cannot do as she pleases.

OHATSU: I feel terribly depressed. I think I'll step outside for a moment.

NARRATOR: She slips out softly.

OHATSU: What happened? I've heard rumors of every sort about you. They've driven me out of my mind with worry.

NARRATOR: She thrusts her face under the brim of his wicker hat and weeps in secret, soundless, painful tears. He too is lost in tears.

TOKUBEI: I've been made the victim of a clever plot, as no doubt you've heard, and the more I struggle, the worse off I am. Everything has turned against me now. I can't survive this night. I've made up my mind to it.

NARRATOR: As he whispers, voices are heard from within.

VOICES: Come inside, Ohatsu. There's enough gossip about you as it is.

OHATSU: There—did you hear? We can't go on talking. Do as I show you.

NARRATOR: She hides him under the train of her mantle. He crawls behind her to the garden door, where he slips beneath the porch at the step. Ohatsu sits by the entrance and, pulling the tobacco tray to her, lights her pipe. She assumes an air of unconcern.

At this moment Kuheiji and a couple of his loud-mouthed friends burst in, accompanied by a blind musician.

KUHEIJI: Hello, girls. You're looking lonesome. Would you like me for a customer? Hello there, host. I haven't seen you in ages.

NARRATOR: He strides arrogantly into the room.

HOST: Bring a tobacco tray and some saké cups.

NARRATOR: He makes the customary fuss over the guests.

KUHEIJI: No, don't bother about saké. We were drinking before we came. I have something to tell you. Tokubei, the number one customer of your Ohatsu, found a seal I'd lost and tried to cheat me out of two *kamme* in silver with a forged note. The facts were too much for him, and he finally met with some unpleasantness from which he was lucky to escape alive. His reputation has been ruined. Be on your guard if he comes here again. Everybody will tell you that I speak the truth, so even if Tokubei tells you the exact opposite, don't believe him for a moment. You'd do best not to let him in at all. Sooner or later he's bound to end up on the gallows.

NARRATOR: He pours out his words convincingly. Tokubei, underneath the porch, gnashes his teeth and trembles with rage. Ohatsu, afraid that he may reveal himself, calms him with her foot, calms him gently. The host is loath to answer yes or no, for Tokubei's a customer of long standing.

HOST: Well, then, how about some soup?

NARRATOR: Covering his confusion, he leaves the room. Ohatsu, weeping bitterly, exclaims.

OHATSU: You needn't try your clever words on me. Tokubei and I have been intimate for years. We've told each other our inmost secrets. He hasn't a particle of deceit in him, the poor boy. His generosity has been his undoing. He's been tricked, but he hasn't the evidence to prove it. After what has happened Tokubei has no choice but to kill himself. I wish I knew whether or not he was resolved to die.

NARRATOR: She pretends to be talking to herself, but with her foot she questions him. He nods, and taking her ankle, passes it across his throat, to let her know that he is bent on suicide.

OHATSU: I knew it. I knew it. No matter how long one lives, it comes to the same thing. Only death can wipe out the disgrace.

NARRATOR: Kuheiji is startled by her words.

KUHEIJI: What is Ohatsu talking about? Why should Tokubei kill himself? Well, if he kills himself, I'll take good care of you after he is gone! I think you've fallen for me too!

OHATSU: That's most generous of you, I'm sure. But would you object if, by way of thanks for your kindness, I killed you? Could I go on living even a moment if separated from Toku? Kuheiji, you dirty thief! Anyone hearing your silly lies can only suspect you. I'm sure that Toku intends to die with me, as I with him.

NARRATOR: She taps with her foot, and Tokubei, weeping, takes it in his hands and reverently touches it to his forehead. He embraces her knees and sheds tears of love. She too can hardly conceal her emotions. Though no word is spoken, answering each other heart to heart, they silently weep. That no one knows makes it sadder still.

Kuheiji feels uncomfortable.

KUHEIJI: The wind's against us today. Let's get out of here. The whores in this place are certainly peculiar—they seem to have an aversion for customers like ourselves with plenty of money to spend. Let's stop at the Asa House and have a drink there. We'll rattle around a couple of gold pieces, then go home to bed. Oh—my wallet is so heavy I can hardly walk.

NARRATOR: Spewing forth all manner of abuse, they noisily depart. The host and his wife call to the servants.

HOST: It's time to put out the lights for the night. Lay out beds for the guests who are staying on. Ohatsu, you sleep upstairs. Get to bed early.

OHATSU (*to herself*): Master, mistress, I shall probably never see you again. Farewell. Farewell to all the servants too.

NARRATOR: Thus inwardly taking leave, she goes to her bedchamber. Later they will learn that this was a parting for life; how pitiful the foolish hearts of men who do not realize the truth in time!

HOST: See that the fire is out under the kettle. Don't let the mice get at the relishes.

NARRATOR: They shut the place and bar the gate. Hardly have their heads touched their pillows than all are snoring merrily. So short is the night that before they've had a chance to dream, two o'clock in the morning has come. Ohatsu is dressed for death, a black cloak dark as the ways of love thrown over her kimono of spotless white. She tiptoes to the staircase and looks down. Tokubei shows his face from under the porch. He beckons, nods, points, communicating his intent without a word. Below the stairs a servant girl is sleeping. A hanging lantern brightly shines. Ohatsu in desperation attaches her fan to a palm-leaf broom, and from the second step of the staircase attempts in vain to extinguish the flame. At last, by stretching every inch, she puts it out, only to tumble suddenly down the stairs. The lamp is out, and in the darkness the servant girl turns in her sleep. Trembling, the lovers grope for each other—a fearful moment. The host awakens in his room to the back.

HOST: What was that noise just now? Servants! The night lamp has gone out. Get up and light it!

NARRATOR: The servant girl, aroused, sleepily rubs her eyes and gets up from bed stark naked.

SERVANT: I can't find the flint box.

NARRATOR: She wanders about the room searching, and Ohatsu, faint with terror, dodges this way and that to avoid her. At last she catches Tokubei's hand, and softly they creep to the entranceway. They unfasten the latch, but the hinges creak, and frightened by the noise, they hesitate. Just then the maid begins to strike the flints; they time their actions to the rasping sound, and with each rasp open the door farther until, huddled together and their sleeves twisted round them, they pass through the door one after the other, feeling as though they tread on a tiger's tail. They exchange glances and cry out for joy, happy that they are to die—a painful, heart-rending sight. The life left them now is as brief as sparks that fly from blocks of flint.

Scene Three: *The journey from Dōjima to the Sonezaki Shrine.*

NARRATOR:
Farewell to this world, and to the night farewell.
We who walk the road to death, to what should we
  be likened?
To the frost by the road that leads to the graveyard,
Vanishing with each step we take ahead:
How sad is this dream of a dream!

TOKUBEI:
Ah, did you count the bell? Of the seven strokes
That mark the dawn, six have sounded.
The remaining one will be the last echo
We shall hear in this life.

OHATSU:
It will echo the bliss of nirvana.

NARRATOR:
Farewell, and not to the bell alone—
They look a last time on the grass, the trees, the sky.
The clouds, the river go by unmindful of them;
The Dipper's bright reflection shines in the water.

TOKUBEI:
Let's pretend that Umeda Bridge
Is the bridge the magpies built
Across the Milky Way, and make a vow
To be husband and wife stars for eternity.

OHATSU:
I promise. I'll be your wife forever.

NARRATOR:
They cling together—the river waters
Will surely swell with the tears they shed.
Across the river, in a teahouse upstairs,
Some revelers, still not gone to bed,
Are loudly talking under blazing lamps—
No doubt gossiping about the good or bad
Of this year's crop of lovers' suicides;
Their hearts sink to hear these voices.

TOKUBEI:
How strange! but yesterday, even today,
We spoke as if such things did not concern us.
Tomorrow we shall figure in their gossip.
If the world will sing about us, let it sing.

NARRATOR:
This is the song that now they hear.
  "I'm sure you'll never have me for your wife,
    I know my love means nothing to you..."
Yes, for all our love, for all our grieving,
Our lives, our lots, have not been as we wished.
Never, until this very day, have we known
A single night of heart's relaxation—

Instead, the tortures of an ill-starred love.
  "What is this bond between us?
I cannot forget you.
But you would shake me off and go—
I'll never let you!
Kill me with your hands, then go.
I'll never release you!"
So she said in tears.

OHATSU:
Of all the many songs, that one, tonight!

TOKUBEI:
Who is it singing? We who listen

BOTH:
Suffer the ordeal of those before us.

NARRATOR:
They cling to each other, weeping bitterly.
Any other night would not matter
If tonight were only a little longer,
But the heartless summer night, as is its wont,
Breaks as cockcrows hasten their last hour.

TOKUBEI:
It will be worse if we wait for dawn.
Let us die in the wood of Tenjin.

NARRATOR:
He leads her by the hand.
At Umeda Embankment, the night ravens.

TOKUBEI:
Tomorrow our bodies may be their meal.

OHATSU:
It's strange, this is your unlucky year
Of twenty-five, and mine of nineteen.
It's surely proof how deep are our ties
That we who love each other are cursed alike.
All the prayers I have made for this world
To the gods and to the Buddha, I here and now
Direct to the future: in the world to come
May we be reborn on the same lotus!

NARRATOR:
One hundred eight the beads her fingers tell
On her rosary;° tears increase the sum.
No end to her grief, but the road has an end:
Their minds are numbed, the sky is dark, the wind
  still,
They have reached the thick wood of Sonezaki.
  Shall it be here, shall it be there? When they brush
  the grass, the falling dew vanishes even quicker
  than their lives, in this uncertain world a
  lightning flash—or was it something else?

OHATSU: I'm afraid. What was that now?

TOKUBEI: That was a human spirit. I thought we alone would die tonight, but someone else has preceded us. Whoever it may be, we'll have a companion on the journey to the Mountain of Death. *Namu Amida Butsu. Namu Amida Butsu.*°

---

rosary: A Buddhist rosary. ***Namu Amida Butsu:*** Calling the name of the Amida Buddha, an incarnation of Siddhartha Gautama, with sincerity should grant the individual eternal life in The Pure Land—hence Pure Land Buddhism.

NARRATOR: She weeps helplessly.

OHATSU: To think that others are dying tonight too! How heartbreaking!

NARRATOR: Man though he is, his tears fall freely.

TOKUBEI: Those two spirits flying together—do you suppose they belong to anyone else? They must be yours and mine!

OHATSU: Those two spirits? Then, are we dead already?

TOKUBEI: Normally, if we saw a spirit, we'd knot our clothes and murmur prayers to keep our souls with us, but now we hurry towards our end, hoping instead our two souls will find the same dwelling. Do not mistake the way, do not lose me!

NARRATOR: They embrace, flesh to flesh, then fall to the ground and weep—how pitiful they are! Their strings of tears unite like entwining branches, or the pine and palm that grow from a single trunk, a symbol of eternal love. Here the dew of their unhappy lives will at last settle.

TOKUBEI: Let this be the spot.

NARRATOR: He unfastens the sash of his cloak. Ohatsu removes her tear-stained outer robe, and throws it on the palm tree; the frond might now serve as a broom to sweep away the sad world's dust. Ohatsu takes a razor from her sleeve.

OHATSU: I had this razor prepared in case we were overtaken on the way and separated. I was determined not to forfeit our name as lovers. How happy I am that we are to die together as we hoped!

TOKUBEI: How wonderful of you to have thought of that! I am so confident in our love that I have no fears even about death. And yet it would be unfortunate if because of the pain we are to suffer people said that we looked ugly in death. Let us secure our bodies to this twin-trunked tree and die immaculately! We will become an unparalleled example of a lovers' suicide.

OHATSU: Yes, let us do that.

NARRATOR: Alas! She little thought she thus would use her light blue undersash! She draws it taut, and with her razor slashes it through.

OHATSU: The sash is cut, but you and I will never be torn apart.

NARRATOR: She sits, and he binds her twice, thrice to the tree, firmly so that she will not stir.

TOKUBEI: Is it tight?

OHATSU: Very tight.

NARRATOR: She looks at her husband, and he at her—they burst into tears.

BOTH: This is the end of our unhappy lives!

TOKUBEI: No I mustn't give way to grief.

NARRATOR: He lifts his head and joins his hands in prayer.

TOKUBEI: My parents died when I was a boy, and I grew up thanks to the efforts of my uncle, who was my master. It disgraces me to die without repaying his kindness. Instead I shall cause him trouble which will last even after my death. Please forgive my sins.

Soon I shall see my parents in the other world. Father, Mother, welcome me there!

NARRATOR: He weeps. Ohatsu also joins her hands.

OHATSU: I envy you. You say you will meet your parents in the world of the dead. My father and mother are in this world and in good health. I wonder when I shall see them again. I heard from them this spring, but I haven't seen them since the beginning of last autumn. Tomorrow, when word reaches the village of our suicides, how unhappy they will be! Now I must bid farewell for this life to my parents, my brothers and sisters. If at least my thoughts can reach you, please appear before me, if only in dreams. Dear Mother, beloved Father!

NARRATOR: She sobs and wails aloud. Her husband also cries out and sheds incessant tears in all too understandable emotion.

OHATSU: We could talk forever, but it serves no purpose. Kill me, kill me quickly!

NARRATOR: She hastens the moment of death.

TOKUBEI: I'm ready.

NARRATOR: He swiftly draws his dagger.

TOKUBEI: The moment has come. *Namu Amida. Namu Amida.*

NARRATOR: But when he tries to bring the blade against the skin of the woman he's loved, and held and slept with so many months and years, his eyes cloud over, his hand shakes. He tries to steady his weakening resolve, but still he trembles, and when he thrusts, the point misses. Twice or thrice the flashing blade deflects this way and that until a cry tells it has struck her throat.

TOKUBEI: *Namu Amida. Namu Amida. Namu Amida Butsu.*

NARRATOR: He twists the blade deeper and deeper, but the strength has left his arm. When he sees her weaken, he stretches forth his hands. The last agonies of death are indescribable.

TOKUBEI: Must I lag behind you? Let's draw our last breaths together.

NARRATOR: He thrusts and twists the razor in his throat, until it seems the handle or the blade must snap. His eyes grow dim, and his last painful breath is drawn away at its appointed hour. No one is there to tell the tale, but the wind that blows through Sonezaki Wood transmits it, and high and low alike gather to pray for these lovers who beyond a doubt will in the future attain Buddhahood. They have become models of true love.

DONALD H. SHIVELY (1921–2005)

The Development of Theater Buildings 1978

Donald Shively discusses the development of the kabuki theater from 1600, beginning with the theater of Nō drama, through its use of revolving stages in 1830. The experience of the audience was radically altered by the changes in theater design, especially the hanamichi, a runway that took the actor into the audience while still maintaining his distance from both the main action and the onlookers.

The earliest kabuki performances [...] were staged in rudimentary enclosures which could be hastily constructed if subscription nō stages were not already available in the amusement quarters at the edge of the cities. From about 1617 Kyoto began issuing licenses to operate theaters. As was true of houses of prostitution, the theaters were increasingly restricted to certain quarters of the city. In Kyoto they were clustered in the area of Shijō, just east of the river, and although as many as seven licenses were issued by 1669, it is not clear how many were in operation at one time.[1] This concentration parallels the establishment of the large prostitution quarters at Shimabara, several miles to the southwest, in 1641. The Shijō theater area and riverbank was a large amusement center in which kabuki was one of many dozens of diversions. There were smaller playhouses, puppet theaters, and a number of wayside entertainers who recited tales from military epics, the Taiheiki and Heike monogatari. There were fortune-tellers, dentists, sumō wrestlers, jugglers, and tightrope walkers. There were sideshows exhibiting such freaks as the female giant and the armless woman archer. There were exotic animals—tigers, bears, porcupines, eagles and peacocks, performing monkeys, and dancing dogs. Teahouses, restaurants, and refreshment stands lined the streets. Paintings of the period show these establishments crowded together, thronged with people of every description.[2]

Edo performances of women's kabuki and youths' kabuki took place as early as 1617 in the Yoshiwara and the nearby amusement area of Nakabashi. The first theater

---

[1]Dōmoto Kansei (Yatarō), Kamigata engeki shi (Tokyo: Shun'yōdō, 1934), p. 41; Takano Tatsuyuki, Nihon engeki shi (Tokyo: Tōkyō-dō, 1948), II:265–269. Dōmoto believes that seven theaters were licensed as early as 1624, but Takano's opinion that this did not happen until 1669–1670 seems more probable.

[2]There are many illustrations of the scene at the Shijō riverbank, including performances of onna kabuki, wakashu kabuki, and a variety of sideshows in screen paintings of the second quarter of the seventeenth century, as in Kondō Ichitarō, Japanese Genre Painting: The Lively Art of Renaissance Japan, trans. R. A. Miller (Tokyo: Charles E. Tuttle Co., 1961), plates 4, 66–71, pp. 22 and 24; also Kikuchi Sadao et al., eds., Kinsei fūzoku zukan (Tokyo: Mainichi Shimbunsha, 1974), II:109; and Kyoto Kokuritsu Hakubutsukan, comp., Rakuchū rakugai zu (Tokyo: Kadokawa Shoten, 1966), unnumbered plates at back.

to be licensed was the Saruwaka-za in Nakabashi in 1624, later renamed Nakamura-za, which continued to operate at a succession of locations until 1893. It serves as a particularly remarkable example of the exercise of an hereditary license to operate a theater. This and later kabuki theaters were ordered to move from time to time and finally, after the Meireki fire of 1657 forced the Yoshiwara far outside the city, were restricted to Sakai-chō and Kobiki-chō and shortly limited to four in number. The Tokugawa government continued to follow a policy of treating the prostitution and theater quarters as parallel concerns. When the theater quarters burned in 1841, nearly two centuries later, they were ordered to move to Saruwaka-chō in Asakusa, close by the Yoshiwara. In Osaka too, where the issuing of regular licenses to theaters followed the Edo precedent, they were restricted from the 1660s to Dōtombori and Horie.

With the issuing of licenses permitting the construction of permanent theaters, the buildings became gradually more substantial. The mat fence was replaced by solid board walls, and a row of boxes (sajiki) was built along the two sides of the parquet (doma) for spectators who required more comfort and privacy. Later boxes were added at the rear of the parquet. City officials, seeking to keep kabuki a simple form of entertainment, forbade the construction of roofs over the parquet. But resourceful theater owners devised a method of stretching mats across the parquet to serve as makeshift shelters which provided shade from the sun and protection against light showers. Over a period of two centuries the theater buildings became gradually more elaborate and comfortable as the authorities made concessions, alternating between a resigned attitude and a stricter policy of sumptuary regulation.

Set back slightly from the street so as not to obstruct traffic, the theater façade was dominated by a tower on which ornamental spears were mounted to indicate possession of an official license. This spear (or drum) tower was draped with a cloth bunting featuring the large design of the theater's crest. The Nakamura-za first used the wheeling crane (maizuru) design. The Ichimura-za chose a rounded crane within an octagon.[3] Most theaters placed large billboards on the tower, the center board announcing in bold characters the name of the proprietor, those on either side the names of leading actors. Lower billboards, typically four in number if the offering was a four-act play, gave the title of each act. From the 1720s a tableau from each act was painted above the title.

Before these signs stood low platforms where barkers waved their fans to attract the attention of passersby and entice them into the theater. In addition to the cruder techniques of whistling and calling to onlookers, they would attempt to draw a crowd by staging impersonations of the leading actors, imitating their voices as they recited tantalizing lines from the play, and parodying their characteristic poses and gestures. Contemporary paintings record the remarkably exuberant commitment of these kido geisha (entrance performers) to their task.[4]

The early theaters had only one entrance, located in the center of the building under the drum tower. It was a small opening with a high threshold which the customer

[3]The use of the crane became taboo in 1690 because the word for crane (tsuru) was used by the shōgun Tsunayoshi in his daughter's name, Tsuruhime. Thereafter the Nakamura-za used a gingko leaf design, and the Ichimura-za changed its crest to an orange-tree design. Suda Atsuo, Nihon gekijō shi no kenkyū (Tokyo: Sagami Shobō, 1957), p. 330.

[4]The six-fold screen (Tokyo National Museum) of the Nakamura-za with its new gingko-leaf crest and stage, attributed to Hishikawa Moronobu (d. 1694), appears in Kondō, plate 76 (identified inexplicably as the Morita-za); Gunji Masakatsu, Kabuki (New York: Kodansha America, 1969), plate 416; and Suwa Haruo, Kabuki kaika (Tokyo: Kadokawa Shoten, 1970), plate 58.

had to step over while ducking under a low overhead. Aptly called the mouse-entrance (*nezumi kido*), it was a holdover from the enclosures used for subscription *nō* and was presumably designed to make it difficult for anyone to slip in quickly without paying. As the theaters grew larger in the eighteenth century, an entrance was provided on each side of the drum tower for admission to the parquet. The stoop entrance was abandoned and a short curtain (*noren*) hung across the top of the doorway, as is customary in Japanese shops. Tickets were purchased outside and other fees paid within for the rental of a reed mat (*hanjō*) and a length of smoldering cord to light one's pipe. On each side of the front of the building an entrance was added for guests going to boxes in order to avoid jostling by the plebs. Inside, stairs led to the upper level of boxes.

The price of tickets ranged widely between the cheapest and the best seats. In 1714, boxes in Edo theaters commanded 1200 *mon*, single spaces 200 *mon*. Parquet tickets averaged 64 *mon*. When space was available, single-act tickets were sold for 12 *mon*. Rental of a mat was 6 *mon* additional.[5] These prices increased rather steadily through much of the Tokugawa period, probably following the general inflationary trend, but exacerbated at certain times by the escalating salaries of the star actors. Attending a major theater was not cheap. The cost of a box seat in 1828 was 1 *ryō* 2 *bu,* the equivalent of 3 bales (*hyō*) of rice or a servant's salary for three or four months. When a performance was popular, the price of tickets rose abruptly.[6]

While the Nakamura-za in Edo provides a detailed illustration of the physical design of a theater, it should be noted that no two were identical. Theaters were, moreover, periodically rebuilt, for fires frequently ravaged Edo. In the 1690s the outer dimensions of the Nakamura-za were 71.5 feet by 97.5 feet, or 6,971 square feet.[7] At its largest in 1809, it measured 80 feet by 138.5 feet, or 11,080 square feet.[8] The structure remained a fraction of the size of the present Kabuki-za in Tokyo, which has 39,000 square feet of space on the ground floor, seating 1,078 people, approximately the same number as the Tokugawa structure. But the modern building has five floors with 120,000 square feet of floor space and accommodates an additional 1,522 people on the mezzanine and balconies.[9] The Nakamura-za of 1720 had a row of boxes along the two sides and across the back. Although only one tier was allowed at that time, by 1724 a second tier of boxes had been added. It was repeatedly forbidden to hang bamboo blinds across the front of the boxes and to install screens or other partitions which would provide privacy for the occupants. However, a number of paintings from this period show such items in use, partially concealing from the gaze of the populace ladies-in-waiting of the shogun's or daimyo's households, members of the Buddhist clergy, and rich merchants.[10]

The parquet (*doma*) of the Nakamura-za, 52 feet wide and 82.4 feet deep in 1720, had a capacity of 800 persons. Later, the front half with its better seats was divided

[5]Takano, II:242–243.

[6]Gunji Masakatsu, *Kabuki to Yoshiwara* (Tokyo: Awaji Shobo, 1956), pp. 62–63; Gunji (1969), pp. 51–52. Only the large theaters of the three cities are discussed in this chapter, but there were also small, low-priced theaters known as *miyachi shibai* located on temple grounds, which were permitted to give performances for one hundred days during the year. Gunji (1956), pp. 38–42.

[7]Suda, p. 328.

[8]Zushi Yoshihiko, *Nihon no gekijō kaiko* (Tokyo: Sagami Shobō, 1947), p. 61. The largest Kyoto theaters seem to have been somewhat larger, at least in 1689 when one measured 106 by 196 feet, over 20,000 square feet. Suda, p. 330.

[9]Yoshida Teruji, ed., *Kabuki-za* (Tokyo: Kabuki-za Shuppanbu, 1951), p. 324.

[10]Zushi, p. 60; Suda, pp. 331–333; Takano, II:341. Three-tiered boxes are mentioned in 1701, but this perhaps means two tiers raised above the floor, allowing space underneath. Suda, p. 331.

into partitions (*masu*) not quite five feet square which narrowly accommodated seven or eight people.[11] Rear parquet space was unreserved. The last back seats, called the *ōmukō* (greatly beyond) were so far from the stage that they were also known as the "deaf gallery." Thus, including boxes and the cheapest parquet seats, the theater held about 1,200.[12] Operating policy was to crowd in as many as possible. According to a book of 1703, "The people came in pushing and jostling, and eight persons sat knee over knee on a mat. It is very pleasant to see them pressed together like human *sushi*."[13]

By the early eighteenth century, wooden roofs occasionally sheltered part of the pit, although not officially sanctioned until 1724. Thereafter tile roofs were recommended to decrease the danger of fire from flying embers. Even after the theaters added roofs, artificial lighting remained proscribed because of the danger to the wooden structure from the open flame of oil lamps and candles. Performances, expected to end about 5 P.M., depended on natural light from windows with translucent paper-covered *shōji* installed on both sides of the theater behind or above the upper row of boxes.[14]

Dressing rooms, located directly behind the stage, were built in two stories by the 1670s. Before the end of the century the Morita-za in Edo added a third level.[15] This section of the building was built high to take as little ground space as necessary from the stage and parquet. A passageway leading to the dressing room section was constructed behind the boxes. Though intended for use by actors to gain access to the end of the runway (*hanamichi*), it was soon traveled by actors summoned to boxes or patrons visiting dressing rooms.[16] The usual arrangement called for baths and quarters for musicians, writers, and *wakashu* on the first floor, *onnagata* on the second, and players of men's roles on the third. A large rehearsal area also occupied the third level. Leading players had individual dressing rooms, although partitions had not received official sanction.[17]

The early kabuki stage basically recreated the square *nō* stage with pillars in the four corners supporting a thatched roof. The main platform had two narrow appendages, one of the right used by the chorus in the *nō*, the other at the rear for the musicians. Off the left of the stage a "bridge" (*hashigakari*) for entrances and exits extended back at an oblique angle with a railing on each side and a long roof. These features of the *nō* stage were gradually modified in the kabuki theater, although it is surprising how long they persisted. The stage itself was only 19 feet square at the outset. Rather than alter its design, more space was gained by greatly widening the bridge and eliminating its handrails. It then emerged as a secondary performing area, a rectangle set back slightly from the main stage. A platform was appended to the front of the stage (*tsuke-butai*) which jutted into the audience. Though these changes were not completed until the first decades of the eighteenth century, some stages had already become quite large. That of the Nakamura-za measured 32.5 feet by 37.7 feet in 1724. Not until 1796, however, was the roof over the main stage eliminated.[18]

[11] From 1772, wooden partitions replaced ropes to divide the *masu,* and later the size of the *masu* was reduced until finally there was space for only four people. Suda, 339.

[12] Takano, II:343; Iizuka Tomoichirō, *Kabuki gairon* (Tokyo: Hakubunkan, 1928), p. 469; Gunji (1969),p. 50.

[13] *"(Kyō-Ōsaka) Yakusha hyōban iro jamisen,"* in *Kabuki hyōbanki shūsei* (Tokyo: Iwanami Shoten, 1973), III:327a; Takano, II:343.

[14] Suda, p. 333.

[15] Suda, p. 327.

[16] Suda, pp. 327, 329.

[17] Suda, pp. 335, 345.

[18] Suda, p. 337. The present Kabuki-za stage is 77 feet by 95 feet.

One of the most distinctive inventions of the kabuki theater is the *hanamichi*, a five-foot-wide runway which extends from the left side of the stage to the rear of the audience. It is used for more dramatic entrances and exits and as an occasional pivot of activity. Its origins are unclear. The more obvious assumption, that it began as a second *hashigakari* directed through the audience, appears to be incorrect. Perhaps as early as the 1650s a small platform was attached to the stage slightly left of center where members of the audience placed gifts (*hana*) of money or goods for their favorite actors. These were called *hana* because the gift was attached to a flower (*hana*) branch. Such a platform appears in a drawing of the Nakamura-za in 1687.[19] By 1724, at least, the *hanamichi* was a runway 52 feet long, set at an oblique angle, probably ending toward the rear end of the row of boxes on the left side of the hall. Although the word *hanamichi* may originally have meant "a path for gifts," by the 1720s and perhaps several decades earlier, it was used primarily as an extension of the stage. Woodblock prints of the next decade show actors standing or seated upon it. Occasionally a small platform called the *nanori-dai* was added about the midway point where an actor could stand almost dead center of the parquet to announce the name and pedigree (*nanori*) of the character he was portraying. After 1780 another, narrower runway was sometimes erected on the right side of the hall. Perhaps as a result, the main *hanamichi* was set at right angles to the stage, parallel to its narrower companion.[20]

[19] Suda, p. 329. There is some evidence that it was used as part of the stage by 1668. Iizuka, p. 421; Takano, II:361–363.

[20] Suda, pp. 337–341.

Perspective view of Kyogen play stage by artist Okumura Masanobu.

Artist Utagawa Toyokuni III's woodblock print of an eighteenth-century stage, with the galleries at the edges of the stage and the two balconies, the arhat dais and the yoshino.

Most of the physical features of the theater discussed on the preceding pages are illustrated in a woodblock print by Okumura Masanobu (1686–1764) of the Ichimura-za in Edo in 1744. The *nō* stage with its roof and front pillars, the appended *hashigakari* stage right and *tsuke-butai* stage front, and the *hanamichi* are clearly evident. There is a raised walk (*ayumi*) across the hall for easier access by customers and vendors to the front part of the pit. A tea and a food vendor pass through the audience. The stage curtain is drawn to stage right. Boxes of the first tier were known as quail boxes (*uzura sajiki*) because their wooden bars made them resemble crates for keeping quail. The second tier of boxes retained eaves from the days, a few decades earlier, when there was no roof over the pit. Sliding doors of translucent paper let in daylight above the boxes.[21]

In such a theater the play moved easily into the audience. The tiers of boxes at the front of the hall were alongside the stage. Later in the eighteenth century a low balcony intruded behind the left corner of the stage (stage right). Known as the *rakandai* (arhat dais), its tightly lined-up spectators hovered over the stage like the five hundred arhats of a Buddhist painting. A seventeen-syllable satirical poem (*senryū*) observes: "The five hundred went home, having seen the actors' backs."

---

[21] The pillar at stage left bears the name of the play, *Nanakusa wakayagi Soga*, followed by the name of the theater, Ichimura-za. The other pillar gives the name of the scene, "Yaoya Oshichi kyōdai biraki." On the beam joining the pillars we see that the Ichimura-za has reclaimed its crane crest. On stage beside her shop counter stands the vegetable dealer (*yaoya*) Oshichi, played by Segawa Kikujirō in this performance of the first month of 1744. Kichizō, played by Onoe Kikugorō, approaches on the *hanamichi*. A stage attendant waves his fan to quiet the audience. This print is an example of the Western-style perspective picture (*ukie*, "floating picture") which came into vogue about 1736. Yoshida Teruji, *Kabuki-e no kenkyū* (Tokyo: Ryokuen Shobō, 1936, 1963), pp. 98–101. The print is in the collection of the Atami Bijutsu-kan.

A second balcony inevitably grew above this. It was called *tsūten* (passing through to heaven), or Yoshino (a mountain district noted for cherry blossoms), as its perspective barely penetrated the artificial cherry blossoms suspended from the ceiling of the hall. A woodblock print of the last decades of the Tokugawa period shows the plebs, crammed in these galleries at the edge of the stage, watching gleefully, mouths agape, as the actors perform, almost within reach.[22] When the play was a great success, the management, not impervious to the potential boon, seated customers on the stage itself. This practice is recorded by the satirical poems: "A big hit—the action is performed in a six-foot square," and "Spectators and actors are lined up together—a big hit."[23] With an audience thus gathered on three sides of the performers and cheap balcony seating available over one corner of the stage, no concept of a platform-framing proscenium arch emerged.

[22] Detail of a print of a theater interior by Utagawa Toyokuni III (1786–1864), in the collection of the Waseda Daigaku Engeki Hakubutsukan (The Tsubouchi Memorial Theatre Museum, Waseda University). The entire print is reproduced in Gunji (1969), plate 448.

[23] Gunji (1956), pp. 59–60.

Nineteenth-Century Drama through the Turn of the Twentieth Century

The French Revolution of 1789 and the subsequent wars of the early nineteenth century established that century as a period of dynamic and dramatic change in Europe and the Americas. Not only was a democratizing wave surging throughout the western world, but dramatic literature was becoming increasingly serious. The Romantics treated the common people with great sympathy, finding in them sincerity and naturalness, in contrast to the shallow and sometimes cruel behavior of the aristocrats who dominated the social and political landscapes of the eighteenth century. Although Romantic plays were being written and produced in France, England, and Germany even after the end of the Napoleonic Wars in 1814, they have not proved as durable as the Romantic poetry and novels of the time. Later nineteenth-century drama introduced audiences to realism with the work of Henrik Ibsen and August Strindberg, in addition to the well-made melodramas of Dion Boucicault and René Pixérécourt, which were popular in France, Ireland, England, and the United States. The revolutionary movements that continued through the "Springtime of the People"—the revolutions of 1848 in France, Germany, Switzerland, Austria, Brazil, and other nations—pointed to profound social and economic change and the emergence of a considerable new middle class.

The Nineteenth-Century Theater

Technically, theaters changed more during the period between 1800 and 1900 than in any comparable earlier period. The introduction of gas jets early in the century had a major effect. Now, light could be dimmed or raised as needed; the house could be gradually and entirely darkened. With gaslight onstage, selective lighting contributed to the emotional effect of plays and allowed actors to move deeper into the stage instead of playing important scenes on the apron. With the advent of elaborate scenery, as in the Drottningholm Theatre in Sweden, lighting devices were often placed behind the proscenium pillars and scenery so that actors were more visible when they stood within the proscenium. The changes did not take place overnight, but as new theaters were built in the early nineteenth century (and as older theaters were refurbished), the apron shrank and the front doors leading to it disappeared. That change

Figure 16. Elaborately decorated proscenium arch. Auditorium, Chicago, 1889. (Chicago History Museum, HB-31105C, photograph by Hedrich Blessing.)

reinforced the nineteenth-century practice of treating the proscenium opening as the imaginary "fourth wall" of a room. The elaborate framing of Chicago's Auditorium (1889, Figure 16) allowed for complex lighting systems and made the proscenium a "window" into the dramatic action.

Numerous other technical innovations were introduced into the new theaters, such as London's Drury Lane Theatre, which was rebuilt in 1812. Highly sophisticated machinery lifted actors from below the stage, and flies, or fly galleries, above the stage permitted scene changes and other dramatic alterations and effects. At Theatre Royal, Drury Lane (Figure 17), the remodeling changed the shape of the apron and made space for an orchestra. The actors moving forward onto the apron were not able to reach the audience, which necessitated a change in the style of acting. Histrionic gestures were still visible, but intimate expressions of disdain or hatred were not as likely to elicit a response in the audience. Music, especially in the first half of the century, was usually part of the theater experience. In the United States, various kinds of

Figure 17. Theatre Royal, Drury Lane, 1812.

entertainment might share a bill with a play, and the entire experience might last five hours or more. At times it was thought impossible to succeed with a play if there were not dances or music between the acts.

Drury Lane drew a considerable audience from among the middle classes, and the entertainment was lively and often sentimental. However, the great plays of Shakespeare were still being produced—though usually in modified form and often with happy endings, even in the tragedies. France and England naturally influenced each other throughout the century, especially in stage design. The English stage designs in turn influenced North American designs.

The Nineteenth-Century Actor

Throughout the first half of the century in the United States, English actors essentially set the standard for acting. Edmund Kean and William Charles Macready were influenced by David Garrick, whose approach aimed at a "natural" style, although by our standards Kean and Macready still employed an enlarged and overdone mode of acting. Relative to earlier ages, however, it was

Figure 18. Edwin Forrest as Macbeth.

Figure 19. William Charles Macready as Macbeth.

a realistic and emotionally true method of acting that toned down the ranting, as well as the use of broad rhetorical gestures designed to dazzle the audience. English audiences were experienced enough to no longer need the exaggerated style that had appealed to some earlier theatergoers.

American actors, such as Edwin Forrest, Ira Aldrige, and Charlotte Cushman, continued a tradition of broad rhetorical acting, with some of the gestures and exaggerations that in earlier times thrilled English audiences. The English actors believed that the American audiences were less sophisticated and thus much more susceptible to the high drama of an actor such as Forrest.

One of the strangest events in the history of theater occurred on May 10, 1849, when the styles of two actors, the American Edwin Forrest (1806–1872) and the Englishman William Charles Macready (1793–1873) — both playing the role of Macbeth — were the subject of a serious riot! Forrest's American style featured exaggerated gestures and dramatic vocal expostulations — as in Figure 18, which shows his upstage hand gesturing profoundly and his cape rustling in a powerful wind. Macready, by contrast, was typically described as intellectual, cool, and refined in his gestures (Figure 19 shows him as Macbeth in the costume of an older-generation Scots lord). Writing in his diary six years before the riot, when he and Forrest were friends, Macready said of American acting, "From what I can learn the audiences of the United States have been accustomed to exaggeration in all its forms, and have applauded what has been most extravagant; it is not, therefore, surprising that they should bestow such little applause on me, not having their accustomed cues." Of Forrest, whom he had seen as Lear, he said,

> I had a very high opinion of his powers of mind when I saw him exactly seventeen years ago; I said then, if he would cultivate those powers and really study, where, as in England, his taste could be formed, he would make one of the very first actors of this or any day. But I thought he would not do so, as his countrymen were, by their extravagant applause, possessing him with the idea and with the fact, as far as remuneration was concerned, that it was unnecessary. I reluctantly, as far as my feelings towards him are interested, record my opinion that my prophetic soul foresaw the consequence. He has great physical power. But I could discern no imagination, no original thought, no poetry at all in his acting.

The Astor Place Riot took place because Macready's restrained style was thought to be effete and foppish in comparison with Forrest's. The unruly mobs of New York, egged on by several instigators who preferred Forrest over Macready, threw paving stones, rocks, and vegetables in the audience of the Opera House and became so threatening that no one could hear the performance. The police were called in to restore order. When they failed, the National Guard was called up to control the throng of 20,000. Like the police, the Guard faltered for a time, but it eventually gathered itself and fired point blank into the mob after a warning salvo over their heads. The death toll was approximately 20, but upwards of 100 were wounded. This was not the first theater riot, but it was the most famous and the most disastrous. Although Macready never returned, he left his mark on American theater, which began to evolve a more relaxed and realistic style of acting. The generations of actors in melodrama that followed were not always as restrained as Macready, but they were usually not as enthusiastic as Forrest.

Macready is credited with having insisted on several important changes in the production of Shakespeare's plays. He restored them to their original texts—not without criticism—and he insisted on doing considerable research to guarantee the authenticity of costuming and other historical details. In addition, he changed the way actors approached a play. Previously they had memorized their lines in isolation and come to the theater as they pleased, with no special thought to the overall nature of the drama at hand. Macready insisted that the actors respect the spirit of the play and unify their styles so they would be acting in concert. This approach was, ultimately, the beginning of the modern style of acting that dominated the later half of the century.

Romantic Drama

Early-nineteenth-century English Romantic poets produced a variety of plays espousing a new philosophy of the individual, a philosophy of democracy, and a cry for personal liberation, but unfortunately their plays failed to capture the popular stage. William Wordsworth's *The Borderers* (1796–1797), concerning political struggles on the border between England and Scotland, was a failure, perhaps because of its static, declamatory nature, evident in a production at Yale University. Even a play with an inherently dramatic subject—*The Fall of Robespierre* (1794) by Robert Southey and Samuel Taylor Coleridge, concerning the violent excesses of the French Revolution of 1789—could not stir popular audiences. John Keats wrote *Otho the Great* (1819) about a tenth-century dispute between brothers and a father and son. He hoped that the great actor and producer Edmund Kean would want to produce the play, but Kean declined. Percy Bysshe Shelley wrote *The Cenci* (1819) when he was in Italy, hoping it would be produced on the English stage, but it was banned by the censors. The style of Shelley's play has been compared with that of John Webster's *The Dutchess of Malfi* (1613); its themes include violent death and insanity. George Gordon, Lord Byron, wrote several plays that had admirers but were not successful. *Manfred* (1817) is a **closet drama**—a play meant to be read, not produced. It presents a powerful portrait of a brooding intellect comparable, in some ways, to Hamlet. Allardyce Nicoll, the British drama historian and critic, has said of this and other Romantic plays that "audiences and readers familiar with *Lear* and *Macbeth* and *Othello* could not be expected to feel a thrill of wonder and delight in the contemplation of works so closely akin to these in general aim and yet so far removed from them in freshness of imaginative power."

French and German Romantic dramatists were more successful than their English counterparts. Johann Wolfgang von Goethe (1749–1832), one of Germany's most important playwrights, produced a number of successful plays in the late eighteenth century. Then came his masterpiece, *Faust* (1808, 1832), in two parts, with a scope and grandeur of concept that challenged the theaters of his day. The play opens in heaven, with Mephistopheles presenting his plan for tempting Faust; Faust signs over his soul to Mephistopheles in return for one moment of perfect joy. Faust was willing to risk all in his efforts to live life to its fullest, and despite his sins he was admired as a hero. Faust's self-analytic individualism, marked by a love of excess and a capacity for deep feeling and frightening intensity, has fascinated the German mind ever since Goethe redis-covered him. His development of Faust as a psychologically complex character contrasts with Christopher Marlowe's version in *Doctor Faustus*.

Another important force in German theater was Johann Cristoph Friedrich von Schiller (1759–1805), whose early play *The Robbers* (1781) was written when he was twenty-two. This still-popular (and still-produced) play reminds English audiences of the legend of Robin Hood, since its hero, Karl von Moor, is a robber admirable for his generosity and seriousness. His adversary is his evil brother, who dominates the castle, the emblem of local repressive political power. Schiller was a highly successful playwright throughout the late eigh-teenth century. In the early nineteenth century, he produced several popular historical plays, such as *Maria Stuart* (1800) on Scotland's Queen Mary, the ill-fated cousin of Queen Elizabeth I. *The Maid of Orleans* (1801) told the story of Joan of Arc, the French heroine who led her army to victory, only to be burned at the stake to satisfy political and religious exigencies. Both plays evoke deep sympathy for their heroines, and both have been noted for their sentimentality. Schiller's last play, *William Tell* (1804), like *The Robbers*, tells the story of a heroic individual's fight against the oppressive forces of an evil baron. Schiller made the story of William Tell universal, and his theatrical successes were soon known throughout Europe and the Americas.

In France, the Romantic tragedy held sway for some time in the 1830s. Victor Hugo (1802–1885) had a great success in *Hernani* (1830), although critics and writers who insisted on classical rules were so disturbed by its in-novation that they caused disruptions in the theater. They attended only to jeer the pardon of Hernani, an outlaw, by Don Carlos, king of Spain. At the end, Hernani and Donna Sol, his loved one, drink a poison so as to die together because they cannot live together. Alexandre Dumas (1802–1879), soon to be famous as a novelist, produced a number of successful, influential plays, among them *Henry III and His Court* (1829) and *The Tower of Nesle* (1832).

Melodrama

Melodrama developed in Germany and France in the mid- and late eighteenth century. The *melo* in *melodrama* means "song"; incidental music was a hallmark of melodrama. In England, certain regulations separated Covent Garden, Drury Lane, and the Haymarket—the three "major" theaters with exclusive licenses to produce spoken drama—from the "minor" theaters, which had to produce musical plays such as burlettas, which resembled our comic operettas. Eventually, the minor theaters began to produce plays with spoken dialogue and accompanying music, heralding a new, popular style. Melodrama proved to be one of the most durable innovations of the late eighteenth century.

August Friedrich Ferdinand von Kotzebue (1761–1819) and Guilbert de Pixérécourt (1773–1844), who coined the term *melodrama*, began developing the melodramatic play in Germany and France, respectively. Many of these dramas used background music that altered according to the mood of the scene, a tradition that continues today in films and on television. Nineteenth-century melodramas featured familiar crises: the virtuous maiden fallen into the hands of an unscrupulous landlord; the father who, lamenting over a portrait of his dead wife, discovers that he is speaking to his—until then—lost daughter. Nineteenth-century melodramas had well-defined heroes, heroines, and villains. The plots were filled with surprises and unlikely twists designed to amaze and delight the audience. Most of the plays were explicitly sentimental, depending on a strong emotional appeal with clear-cut and relatively decisive endings.

Though not popular later on, the plays of Kotzebue and Pixérécourt pleased their contemporary audiences and helped establish melodrama as a dominant style for the first six decades of the nineteenth century. Kotzebue published thirty-six plays (twenty-two were produced) and enjoyed immense popularity in England and the United States. Translated into several languages, his works influenced later popular playwrights, who admired his ability to invent and resolve complex plot situations. The ending of *La-Peyrouse* (1798) provides a taste of the mode. The hero, cast ashore on a desert island, falls in love with the "savage" Malvina. When he rejoins his wife, Adelaide, he is presented with the problem of what to do with Malvina. Here is the women's solution:

> MALVINA (*turning affectionately, yet with trembling, to Adelaide*): I have prayed for thee, and for myself—let us be sisters!
>
> ADELAIDE: Sisters! (*She remains some moments lost in thought.*) Sisters! Sweet girl, you have awakened a consoling idea in my bosom! Yes, we will be sisters, and this man shall be our brother! Share him we cannot, nor can either possess him singly. (*With enthusiasm.*) We, the sisters, will inhabit one hut, he shall dwell in another. We will educate our children, he shall assist us both—by day we will make but one family, at night we will separate—how say you? will you consent? . . . (*Extending her arms to La-Peyrouse.*) A sisterly embrace!

In France, Pixérécourt produced a similar and highly successful drama that pleased his audiences. Not everyone was pleased, however. Goethe resigned his office in the Weimar Court Theatre when Pixérécourt's *The Dog of Montargis* was produced in 1816 because he did not want to be associated with any play that had a dog as its hero.

Not all these plays have been forgotten. Alexandre Dumas's *La Dame aux camélias* (*Camille*) was a theatrical hit in 1852 and has remained popular ever since, inspiring the Verdi opera *La Traviata* (1853) and revivals and adaptations up to the present, including the British playwright Pam Gems's feminist version (1987), starring Kathleen Turner. Based on a woman Dumas knew in Paris, it is the story of a wealthy young man who falls in love with a courtesan, Marguerite Gauthier. Like Angellica in *The Rover*, she has manipulated men throughout her life, but now she is truly in love with Armand. The young man's father opposes the match, but even he is moved by the majesty of their love. Eventually, the father faces Marguerite and convinces her that if she really loves his son, she will let him go since their union can bring nothing but harm to Armand. She then feigns contempt for Armand and dismisses him, brokenhearted. Later, after they have been separated and she has fallen deathly ill, Armand learns the truth and rushes to her. On her deathbed, Armand professes his love as she dies in his arms.

In the United States, George Aiken produced another long-lasting and influential drama, *Uncle Tom's Cabin* (1852), based on Harriet Beecher Stowe's novel. Stowe, a prominent northern abolitionist, poured all her anger at slavery into her novel. Aiken's stage version played for three hundred nights in its first production and across the nation more than a quarter of a million times. Some of its characters—Uncle Tom, Little Eva, Sambo, Topsy, and Simon Legree—live on in the popular imagination, but despite the contemporary interest in Stowe and in this play, it reflects its era through features like the paternalistic subtitle: *Life among the Lowly*.

The Well-Made Play

Early in the nineteenth century, a Frenchman with an unusual theatrical gift for pleasing popular audiences began a career that spanned fifty successful years. Eugène Scribe (1791–1861) may have produced as many as four or five hundred plays. He employed collaborators and mined novels and stories for his plots, producing tragedies, comedies, opera libretti, and one-act vaudeville pieces. He quickly determined that plot held the attention of the audience and that rambling character studies were of lesser interest. Consequently, he developed a formula for dramatic action and made sure that all his works fit into it. The result was the creation of a "factory" for making plays. Among the elements of Scribe's formula were the following:

1. A careful exposition telling the audience what the situation is, usually including one or more secrets to be revealed later.
2. Surprises, such as letters to be opened at a critical moment and identities to be revealed later.
3. Suspense that builds steadily throughout the play, usually sustained by cliff-hanging situations and characters who miss each other by way of carefully timed entrances and exits. At critical moments, characters lose important papers or misplace identifying jewelry, for instance.
4. A **climax** late in the play when the secrets are revealed and the hero confronts his antagonists and succeeds.
5. A **denouement**, the resolution of the drama, when all the loose ends are drawn together and explanations are made that render all the action plausible.

It should be evident from this description that the **well-made play** still thrives, not only on the stage but also in films and on television. Scribe's emphasis on plot was sensational for his time, and his success was unrivaled; however, none of his plays has survived in contemporary performance. Only one, *Adrienne Lecouvreur* (1849), the story of a famous actress poisoned by a rival, is mentioned by critics as interesting because of its depth of characterization. Scribe was superficial and brilliant—a winning combination in theater at the time. He had numerous imitators and prepared the way for later developments in theater.

The Rise of Realism

Technical changes in theaters during the latter part of the nineteenth century continued at a rapid pace. When limelight was added to gas, the result was bright, intense lighting onstage; in the last decades of the century, electric light heralded a new era in lighting design. Good lighting generally demanded detailed and authentic scenery; the dreamy light produced by gas often hid imperfections that were now impossible to disguise. The new Madison Square Theater (1879) in New York City was built with elevators that allowed its stage, complete with detailed and realistic scenery as well as actors, to be raised into position. European theaters had developed similar capabilities.

In the 1840s, accurate period costumes began to be the norm for historical plays. In the Elizabethan theater, contemporary clothing had been worn onstage, but by the mid-nineteenth century costume designers were researching historical periods and producing costumes that aimed at historical accuracy.

In addition to offering lifelike scenery, lighting, and costumes, the theaters of the latter part of the century also featured plays whose circumstances and language were recognizable, contemporary, and believable. Even the sentimental melodramas seemed more realistic than productions of *King Lear* or *Macbeth,* plays that were still popular. The work of Scribe, including his historical plays, used a relatively prosaic everyday language. The situations may not seem absolutely lifelike to our eyes, but in their day they prepared the way for realism.

Changes in philosophy also contributed to the development of a realistic drama. Émile Zola (1840–1902) preached a doctrine of **naturalism,** demanding that drama avoid the artificiality of convoluted plot and urging a drama of natural, lifelike action. He intended his work to help change social conditions in France. His naturalistic novel *Nana* (1880) focused on a courtesan whose life came to a terrifying end. The play *Thérèse Raquin* (1873), based on Zola's novel of the same name, told the story of a woman and her lover who murder her husband and then commit suicide out of a sense of mutual guilt. There are no twists, surprises, or even much suspense in the play. Zola's subjects seem to have been uniformly grim, and naturalism became associated with the darker side of life.

Realism, which avoided mechanical "clockwork" plots with their artificially contrived conclusions, began to be evident in drama in the later years of the eighteenth century (some scholars claim to see evidence of it even earlier, in the work of Thomas Middleton [1580–1627]) and became progressively more common as the end of the nineteenth century approached. In the realistic plays of Henrik Ibsen (1828–1906) and August Strindberg (1849–1912), the details of the setting, the costuming, and the circumstances of the action were so fully realized as to convince audiences that they were listening in on life itself. (See Figure 20 for an example of a realistic stage setting.)

Figure 20. Realistic setting in a 1941 production of Anton Chekhov's *The Cherry Orchard*.

In Britain, Oscar Wilde (1854–1900), Irish poet, novelist, and playwright, offered an alternative to both melodrama and realistic drama near the end of the century. Wilde had spent much of his literary life promoting the philosophy of art for art's sake. He asserted that the pleasure of poetry was in its sounds, images, and thoughts; poetry and drama did not serve religious, political, social, or even personal goals. For Wilde, art served itself. He was such a brilliant conversationalist that the Irish poet-playwright W. B. Yeats declared him the only person he ever heard who spoke complete, rounded sentences that sounded as if he had written and polished them the night before. His witticisms were often barbed and vicious but always incisive and perceptive. He became famous for his bright, witty comedies. *The Importance of Being Earnest* (1895), sometimes wrongly accused of being about nothing, is the most often performed of Wilde's comedies. It is an unsentimental, witty, and sometimes brittle comedy dissecting English upper-class attitudes that most of his audience would have taken for granted.

Wilde competed with numerous comic playwrights in England and abroad, such as the enormously successful Arthur Wing Pinero (1855–1934) and W. S. Gilbert (1836-1911) in England and Georges Feydeau (1862–1921) in France. None, though, could manage the unusual combination of wit and seriousness that marks Wilde's achievements. Another important competitor was Irish playwright Bernard Shaw (1856–1950), whose plays were also comic and serious, such as *Arms and the Man* (1894), *You Never Can Tell* (1898), and *Pygmalion* (1913). But Shaw is probably best known for his plays of ideas—plays in which an underlying idea or principle drives the action—such as *Mrs. Warren's Profession* (1898), *Man and Superman* (1903), and *Major Barbara* (1905).

After a disappointing beginning as a playwright, Anton Chekhov (1860–1904) worked with the Moscow Art Theatre under the directorship of Konstantin Stanislavski (1865–1938), one of the most influential figures in modern Western drama. Stanislavski emphasized "inner realism," helping the actor become the character even in situations off stage by developing improvisational experiences to let the actor explore the character in situations other than those within the play. The Stanislavski Method helped the actor *become* the part, rather than just play the part. Chekhov and Stanislavski worked together to produce Chekhov's plays at a time when Chekhov believed himself a failure as a dramatist.

The first production of Chekhov's *The Seagull* (1896), his sixth major staged play, was a failure. Stanislavski persuaded Chekhov to give it to his company to produce, resulting in an important triumph. Chekhov then reworked an earlier play into *Uncle Vanya* (1899) for Stanislavski, and it, too, was a hit. *Three Sisters* (1901) was not successful in its first performances, but it later became known as one of Chekhov's finest works. His last play, *The Cherry Orchard* (1904), was put on by Stanislavski's company and has become one of the most important works of twentieth-century drama. Chekhov died of a heart attack soon after the play's first production. Today Chekhov's legacy continues, and all his major plays are staged throughout the world. Thus, one of the most important nineteenth-century writers led the way to new developments in twentieth-century drama that are still evident today on the stage, as well as in films and on television.

Date	Theater	Political	Social/Cultural
1700–1800	**1759–1805:** Friedrich von Schiller, German playwright, author of *The Robbers* (1781) and *Maria Stuart* (1800)		
	1761–1819: August Friedrich Ferdinand von Kotzebue, German playwright and one of the early developers of melodrama	**1775:** The American War of Independence begins at Concord, Massachusetts.	**1770–1827:** Ludwig van Beethoven, German composer
		1776: The Declaration of Independence is signed.	**1775–1817:** Jane Austen, English novelist
	1767–1787: *Sturm und Drang* period in German drama featuring the work of Goethe, Schiller, and others who rebelled against eighteenth-century rationalism	**1783:** Peace of Versailles: Britain recognizes the independence of the United States.	
	1773: The Swedish National Theatre is established in Stockholm.	**1789:** French revolutionaries storm the Bastille as the French revolution sweeps over French society.	**1792–1822:** Percy Bysshe Shelley, English Romantic poet
	1773–1844: Guilbert de Pixérécourt, French playwright generally credited with originating the melodrama	**1793:** Louis XVI and his queen, Marie Antoinette, are guillotined. The Reign of Terror, a purge instituted by the revolutionary government of France, claims 35,000 lives in one year.	**1793:** Eli Whitney (1765–1825) invents the cotton gin.
			1795: British forces occupy the Cape of Good Hope.
	1791–1861: Eugène Scribe, French playwright, developer of the well-made play, author of *Adrienne Lecouvreur* (1849)	**1799:** Napoleon Bonaparte overthrows the Directory of France, the moderate government that replaced the Reign of Terror.	**1795–1821:** John Keats, English Romantic poet
	1793–1873: William Charles Macready, English actor		**1798:** *Lyrical Ballads* is published by Wordsworth and Coleridge.
			1799–1837: Alexander Pushkin, Russian poet
1800–1900	**1806–1872:** Edwin Forrest, America's first great native-born actor	**1803:** The Louisiana Purchase doubles the area of the United States.	**1802–1885:** Victor Hugo, French novelist
		1804: Napoleon I (1769–1821) declares himself emperor of France.	**1803–1882:** Ralph Waldo Emerson, American Transcendental philosopher, clergyman, and author
	1808 and 1832: German writer Johann Wolfgang von Goethe (1749–1832) produces his masterpiece, *Faust* (in two parts).	**1805:** Admiral Horatio Nelson's victory over Napoleon at Trafalgar establishes the supremacy of British naval forces.	**1805:** Gas lighting is introduced in Great Britain.
	1809–1852: Nikolai Gogol, Russian playwright, author of *The Inspector General* (1836)		
	1812: Theatre Royal, Drury Lane, is rebuilt.	**1811–1820:** The Regency period: George, Prince of Wales, acts as regent for George III, who was declared insane.	**1809–1852:** Louis Braille, French inventor of reading system for the blind
	1813–1837: Georg Büchner, German playwright, author of *Danton's Death* (1835) and *Woyzeck* (1836)	**1812:** The United States declares war on Britain.	**1812–1870:** Charles Dickens, English novelist
	1813–1883: Richard Wagner, German composer, among whose works is the four-part *Der Ring des Nibelungen* (1853–1874)	**1814:** Treaty of Ghent ends the War of 1812; Britain is defeated.	

Date	Theater	Political	Social/Cultural
1800–1900 (continued)	**1816:** Chestnut Street Theater in Philadelphia is the first theater to illuminate its stage with gas lighting.	**1815:** Napoleon is decisively defeated at the Battle of Waterloo.	**1816–1855:** Charlotte Brontë, English novelist
	1820–1890: Dion Boucicault, Irish American actor and writer of popular melodramas, among them *The Octoroon* (1859) and *The Colleen Bawn* (1860)	**1818:** Shaka ascends the Zulu throne in Southern Africa and initiates a period of military reform; he is assassinated in 1828.	**1817–1862:** Henry David Thoreau, American Transcendental writer and naturalist
		1820: Accession of George IV	**1820–1906:** Susan B. Anthony, American leader of the women's suffrage movement
	1828–1906: Henrik Ibsen, Norwegian playwright, whose best known works include *A Doll House* (1879) and *Hedda Gabler* (1890)	**1820:** The Missouri Compromise admits Maine as a free state and Missouri as a slave state.	**1821–1881:** Fyodor Dostoevsky, Russian novelist
			1828–1910: Leo Tolstoy, Russian novelist and philosopher
	1830: *Hernani,* by the French novelist and playwright Victor Hugo (1802–1885), traditionally marks the beginning of French romanticism.	**1821:** Mexico declares its independence.	**1830–1886:** Emily Dickinson, American poet
		1823: The Monroe Doctrine closes the American continent to European colonization.	**1831:** William Lloyd Garrison (1805–1879), American abolitionist, founds the *Liberator*.
	1837: William Charles Macready (1793–1873), an English actor, is the first to use the limelight (or Drummond light), a prototype of the spotlight.	**1837:** Queen Victoria begins her sixty-four-year reign in Great Britain.	**1833–1897:** Johannes Brahms, German composer
		1839: The First Opium War between Britain and China begins. The war ends in 1842 with the Treaty of Nanjing, which turns over Hong Kong to Britain and opens several Chinese ports to western trade.	**1839:** Louis Daguerre (1789–1851) invents the daguerreotype, an early type of photograph.
	1840–1902: Émile Zola, French writer and promoter of naturalism in literature, among whose works is the novel (also a play) *Thérèse Raquin* (1873)		**1840–1893:** Peter Ilyich Tchaikovsky, Russian composer
			1843–1916: Henry James, American realist novelist
			1844: The telegraph is used for the first time.
			1845: Frederick Douglass (c. 1817–1895), African American abolitionist, publishes *Narrative of the Life of Frederick Douglass*.
		1846–1848: Mexican War over the United States' annexation of Texas. The Treaty of Guadalupe Hidalgo (1848) cedes Texas to the United States.	**1845–1849:** The great potato famine in Ireland kills nearly a million Irish; 1,600,000 immigrate to the United States.
	1849: The Astor Place Riot in New York is a result of the rivalry between the actors William Charles Macready and Edwin Forrest; twenty-two people are killed.		**1848:** The First U.S. Women's Rights Convention is held in Seneca Falls, New York.
			1848: California gold rush
	1849–1923: Sarah Bernhardt, French performer, perhaps the greatest actress of the nineteenth century		**1848:** Karl Marx, German political philosopher, writes *The Communist Manifesto* with Friedrich Engels.
			1850: Tennyson succeeds Wordsworth as poet laureate of Great Britain.
	1849–1912: August Strindberg, Swedish playwright, among whose works are *Miss Julie* (1888) and *A Dream Play* (1902)		**1851:** Herman Melville (1819–1891) publishes *Moby Dick.*
		1852: Napoleon III declares himself emperor of France and rules until 1871.	**1852:** Harriet Beecher Stowe (1811–1896) publishes *Uncle Tom's Cabin.*

Nineteenth-Century Drama *(continued)*

Date	Theater	Political	Social/Cultural
1800–1900 (continued)	**1854–1900:** Oscar Wilde, Irish writer, whose plays include *A Woman of No Importance* (1893) and *The Importance of Being Earnest* (1895)	**1857:** Czar Alexander II begins emancipation of serfs in Russia.	**1854–1856:** Scottish explorer David Livingstone crosses Africa.
	1856–1950: Bernard Shaw, Irish playwright, among whose works are *Mrs. Warren's Profession* (1898), *Major Barbara* (1905), and *Pygmalion* (1913)	**1860:** Abraham Lincoln is elected president. South Carolina secedes from the Union. **1861:** Italy is unified under Victor Emmanuel II.	
	1860–1904: Anton Chekhov, Russian writer, author of *The Seagull* (1896) and *The Cherry Orchard* (1903)	**1861–1865:** The Civil War is fought in the United States. **1862:** Otto von Bismarck is appointed prime minister of Prussia.	**1859:** Charles Darwin (1809–1882) publishes *On the Origin of Species by Natural Selection.* **1860s:** Louis Pasteur (1822–1895), French chemist, develops pasteurization.
	1870–1900: Golden Age of Peking (Beijing) Opera **1871–1896:** Gilbert and Sullivan write their comic operas, among them *H.M.S. Pinafore* (1878) and *The Pirates of Penzance* (1879).	**1865:** Abraham Lincoln is assassinated by the actor John Wilkes Booth at Ford's Theatre in Washington, D.C. **1869:** The Suez Canal opens.	**1865–1939:** William Butler Yeats, Irish poet and playwright **1869:** The first transcontinental railroad in the United States is completed.
	1876: Opening of Richard Wagner's Festival Theatre in Bayreuth, Germany	**1870–1871:** Franco-Prussian War **1871:** The German Empire is founded under Kaiser Wilhelm I.	**1869–1959:** Frank Lloyd Wright, preeminent American architect **1876:** Alexander Graham Bell (1847–1922) invents the telephone.
	1881: The Savoy Theatre is the first theater in London to be completely illuminated by electric light.	**1876:** At the Battle of the Little Bighorn, the Sioux defeat General George Custer's troops.	**1877:** Thomas Edison (1847–1931) invents the phonograph.
	1887: Théâtre Libre is founded in Paris by André Antoine to pursue naturalism in subject matter and staging.	**1885:** The Congo becomes a personal possession of King Leopold II of Belgium.	**1879:** Thomas Edison invents the lightbulb.
	1890–1930: Vaudeville becomes one of the most popular forms of entertainment in the United States.	**1890:** The Battle of Wounded Knee ends the American Indians' wars of resistance; two hundred Indians are killed by the U.S. Army.	
	1896: The first revolving stage is installed by Karl Lautenschlager at the Residenz Theater in Munich.	**1898:** The Spanish-American War. Cuban patriots demand independence and receive the military support of the United States. The 1898 Treaty of Paris gives Puerto Rico, Guam, the Philippines, and Cuba to the United States.	**1898–1976:** Paul Robeson, African American singer, actor, and civil rights activist
	1898: The Moscow Art Theatre is founded under the direction of Konstantin Stanislavski and Vladimir Nemirovich-Danchenko.	**1899–1902:** The Boer War (South African War) ends British supremacy in South Africa.	

Henrik Ibsen

Using the new style of realism, Henrik Ibsen (1828–1906) slowly and despite many setbacks became the most influential modern dramatist. Subjects that had been ignored on the stage became the center of his work. But his rise to fame was anything but direct. His family was extremely poor, and as a youth he worked in a drugstore in Grimstad, a seaport town in Norway. At seventeen he had an illegitimate child with a servant girl. At twenty-one he wrote his first play, in verse. In 1850, at the age of twenty-two, he left Grimstad for Oslo (then called Christiana) to become a student, but within a year he joined the new National Theatre, where he stayed for six years, writing and directing.

In the 1850s, Ibsen wrote numerous plays that did not bring him recognition: *St. John's Eve* (1853), *Lady Inger of Østraat* (1855), *Olaf Liljekrans* (1857), and *The Vikings at Helgeland* (1857). In the early 1860s, with a wife and daughter to support, he went through a period of serious self-doubt and despair, which was not improved when his first play in five years, *Love's*

Henrik Ibsen at age sixty-eight, seventeen years after the first production of *A Doll House*. He was the most influential playwright in Europe when this photograph was taken in 1896.

Comedy (1862), was turned down for performance. Eventually he got a job with the Christiana Theatre and had a rare success with *The Pretenders* (1864), a historical play about thirteenth-century warriors vying for the vacant throne of Norway.

Ibsen's breakthrough came with the publication in 1866 of the verse play *Brand,* which was written to be read, not performed. (It was first produced in 1885.) It is the portrait of a clergyman who takes the strictures of religion so seriously that he rejects the New Testament doctrine of love and accepts the Old Testament doctrine of the will of God. He destroys himself in the process and ends the play on a mountaintop in the Ice Church, facing an avalanche about to kill him. Out of the clouds comes the answer to his question of whether love or will achieves salvation: "He is the God of Love." *Brand* made Ibsen famous. He followed it with another successful closet drama, *Peer Gynt* (1867), about a character, quite unlike Brand, who avoids the rigors of morality and ends up uncertain whether he has been saved or condemned.

Despite these successes, Ibsen still struggled for recognition. It was not until 1877 that he had his first success in a play that experimented with the new realistic style of drama: *The Pillars of Society,* which probed behind the hypocrisies of Karsten Bernick, a merchant who prospers by all manner of double-dealing and betrayal of his relatives. Eventually, he admits his crimes and, instead of being punished, is welcomed back into society and is more successful than ever. This play gave Ibsen a reputation in Germany, where it was frequently performed, and prepared him for his great successes. *A Doll House* (1879), which he wrote in Italy, came two years later. It was more fully realistic in style than *The Pillars of Society* and, though immensely successful in Scandinavia, did not become widely known elsewhere for another ten years.

Ibsen's next play, *Ghosts* (1881), was denounced violently because it dared to treat a subject that had been taboo on the stage: syphilis. *Ghosts* introduced a respectable family, the Alvings, who harbor the secret that their late father contracted the disease and passed it on to Oswald, his son. In addition, the theme of incest is suggested in the presence of Alving's illegitimate daughter, Regina, who falls in love with Oswald. This kind of material was so foreign to the late-nineteenth-century stage that Ibsen was vilified and isolated by the literary community in Norway. He chose exile for a time in Rome, Amalfi, and Munich.

Ibsen's last years were filled with activity. He wrote some of his best known plays in rapid succession: *An Enemy of the People* (1882), *The Wild Duck* (1884), *Hedda Gabler* (1890), *The Master Builder* (1892), and *John Gabriel Borkman* (1896). In 1891, he returned to live in Norway, where he died fifteen years later.

The most influential European dramatist in the late nineteenth century, Ibsen inspired emerging writers in the United States, Ireland, and many other nations. But his full influence was not felt until the early decades of the twentieth century, when other writers were able to spread the revolutionary doctrine that was implied in realism as practiced by Ibsen and Strindberg. Being direct, honest, and unsparing in treating character and theme became the normal mode of serious drama after Ibsen.

For links to resources about Ibsen, click on *AuthorLinks* at **bedfordstmartins.com/jacobus.**

A Doll House

Once Henrik Ibsen found his voice as a realist playwright, he began to develop plays centering on social problems and the problems of the individual struggling against the demands of society. In *A Doll House* (1879), he focused on the repression of women—a subject that deeply offended conservatives and was very much on the minds of progressive and liberal Scandinavians. It was therefore a rather daring theme. The play opens with the dutiful, eager wife Nora Helmer twittering like a lark and pattering about like a squirrel, pleasing her husband, Torvald. Helmer is obsessed with propriety. As far as he is concerned, Nora is only a woman, an empty-headed ornament in a house designed to keep his life functioning smoothly.

Nora is portrayed as a macaroon-eating, sweet-toothed creature looking for ways to please her husband. When she reveals that she borrowed the money that took them to Italy for a year to save her husband's life, she shows us that she is made of much stronger stuff than anyone has given her credit for. Yet the manner in which she borrowed the money is technically criminal because she had to forge her father's signature, and she now finds herself at the mercy of the lender, Nils Krogstad.

From a modern perspective, Nora's action seems daring and imaginative rather than merely illegal and surreptitious. Torvald Helmer's moralistic position is to us essentially stifling. He condemns people for their crimes without considering their circumstances or motives. He is moralistic rather than moral.

For this 1906 production of Ibsen's *The Wild Duck,* the director, André Antoine, had the set constructed of Norwegian pine to achieve a high degree of realism.

Edvard Munch's 1906 stage design for Max Reinhardt's production of Ibsen's *Ghosts* at the Kammerspiele in Berlin. Although *Ghosts* (1881) was written in Ibsen's realistic style, Munch's expressionistic lines and shadows seem to reflect the tendency in Ibsen's late plays to move beyond realism to a more dreamlike structure.

The atmosphere of the Helmer household is oppressive. Everything is set up to amuse Torvald, and he lacks any awareness that other people might be his equals. Early in the play, Ibsen establishes Nora's longings: she explains that to pay back her loan she had to take in copying work, and, rather than resenting her labor, she observes that it made her feel wonderful, the way a man must feel. Ibsen said that his intention in the play was not primarily to promote the emancipation of women; it was to establish, as Ibsen's biographer Michael Meyer says, "that the primary duty of anyone was to find out who he or she really was and to become that person."

However, the play from the first was seen as addressing the problems of women, especially married women who were treated as their husbands' property. When the play was first performed, the slam of the door at Nora's leaving was much louder than it is today. It was shocking to late-nineteenth-century society, which took Torvald Helmer's attitudes for granted. The first audiences probably were split in their opinions about Nora's actions. As Meyer reminds us, "No play had ever before contributed so momentously to the social debate, or been so widely and furiously discussed among people who were not normally interested in theatrical or even artistic matters." Although the critics in Copenhagen (where the play was first produced) and London were very negative, the audiences were filled with curiosity and flocked to the theaters to see the play.

What the audiences saw was that once Nora is awakened, the kind of life Torvald imagines for her is death to Nora. Torvald cannot see how his self-absorbed concern and fear for his own social standing reveal his limitations and selfishness. Nora sees immediately the limits of his concern, and her only choice is to leave him so that she can grow morally and spiritually.

What she does and where she goes have been a matter of speculation since the play was first performed. Ibsen refused to encourage any specific conjecture. It is enough that she has the courage to leave. But the ending of the play bothered audiences as well as critics, and it was performed in Germany in 1880 with a revised ending that Ibsen himself wrote to forestall anyone else's doing so. Hedwig Niemann-Raabe, the first German actress to play the part, insisted that she would personally never leave her children and therefore would not do the play as written. In the revised version, instead of leaving, Nora is led to the door of her children's room and falls weeping as the curtain goes down. This so-called happy-ending version was played for a while in England and elsewhere. No one was satisfied with this ending, and eventually the play reverted to its original form.

Through the proscenium arch of the theater in Ibsen's day audiences were permitted to eavesdrop on themselves, since Ibsen clearly was analyzing their own mores. In a way the audience was looking at a dollhouse, but instead of containing miniature furniture and miniature people, it contained replicas of those watching. That very sense of intimacy, made possible by the late-nineteenth-century theater, heightened the intensity of the play.

A Doll House in Performance

A Doll House was first produced in the Royal Theatre, Copenhagen, in December 1879. Despite its immediate popular success in Scandinavia and Germany, two years passed before the play appeared elsewhere and ten years before it appeared in England and the United States in a complete and accurate text. An adaptation (also with the happy ending) titled *The Child Wife* was produced in Milwaukee in 1882. The first professional London production of the play in 1889 found favor with the public, but it was attacked in the press for being "unnatural, immoral and, in its concluding scene, essentially undramatic." Among other things, Ibsen was condemned for not providing a vibrant plot.

Among the play's memorable performances was Ethel Barrymore's version in New York in 1905. Barrymore was praised for a brilliant interpretation of "the child wife." Ruth Gordon played the part to acclaim in 1937, as did Claire Bloom in 1971 on the stage and in 1973 in film. Jane Fonda played the role in Joseph Losey's film version of 1973. The Norwegian actress Liv Ullmann performed the role in Lincoln Center in 1975 and was praised as "the most enchanting," the "most honest" Nora that the critic Walter Kerr had seen. Other critics were less kind, but it was a successful run. One of the most riveting of modern productions was Anthony Page's revival of *A Doll House*, starring Janet McTeer. This production began in London in 1997 and transferred to New York for a Broadway run the same year. Ben Brantley of the *New York Times* said of it, "Nothing can prepare you for the initial shock of Ms. McTeer's performance, which transforms the passive Nora Helmer, Ibsen's child-like plaything of a wife, into an electric, even aggressive presence" revealing "previously hidden nuances in Ibsen's landmark work." This production was faithful to the production values of Ibsen's original, using an essentially Victorian-era setting with period costumes. McTeer's energy transformed the play and gave Nora a new dimension that made the audience believe that she would do better than merely survive when she left her home. Lee Breuer's

For discussion questions and assignments on *A Doll House,* visit **bedfordstmartins.com/jacobus.**

2005 production of *Mabou Mines Dollhouse* set the stage as a dollhouse and used actresses who were six feet tall and actors who were five feet tall and shorter. The effect on the audience was to emphasize the power relationships between men and women. Controversy followed the Mabou Mines troupe tour, but it also awakened audiences to some of the underlying forces of the play. The play is performed regularly in college and regional theaters in the United States and elsewhere.

HENRIK IBSEN (1828–1906)

A Doll House   1879

TRANSLATED BY ROLF FJELDE

The Characters

TORVALD HELMER, *a lawyer*
NORA, *his wife*
DR. RANK
MRS. LINDE
NILS KROGSTAD, *a bank clerk*
THE HELMERS' THREE SMALL CHILDREN
ANNE-MARIE, *their nurse*
HELENE, *a maid*
A DELIVERY BOY

The action takes place in Helmer's residence.

ACT I

(*A comfortable room, tastefully but not expensively furnished. A door to the right in the back wall leads to the entryway; another to the left leads to Helmer's study. Between these doors, a piano. Midway in the left-hand wall a door, and further back a window. Near the window a round table with an armchair and a small sofa. In the right-hand wall, toward the rear, a door, and nearer the foreground a porcelain stove with two armchairs and a rocking chair beside it. Between the stove and the side door, a small table. Engravings*

Note: As Fjelde explains in his foreword to the translation, he does not use the possessive "A Doll's House" because "the house is not Nora's, as the possessive implies." Fjelde believes that Ibsen includes Torvald with Nora in the original title, "for the two of them at the play's opening are still posing like the little marzipan bride and groom atop the wedding cake."

on the walls. An étagère° with china figures and other small art objects; a small bookcase with richly bound books; the floor carpeted; a fire burning in the stove. It is a winter day.)

(*A bell rings in the entryway; shortly after we hear the door being unlocked. Nora comes into the room, humming happily to herself; she is wearing street clothes and carries an armload of packages, which she puts down on the table to the right. She has left the hall door open, and through it a Delivery Boy is seen holding a Christmas tree and a basket, which he gives to the Maid who let them in.*)

NORA: Hide the tree well, Helene. The children mustn't get a glimpse of it till this evening, after it's trimmed. (*To the Delivery Boy, taking out her purse.*) How much?

DELIVERY BOY: Fifty, ma'am.

NORA: There's a crown. No, keep the change. (*The Boy thanks her and leaves. Nora shuts the door. She laughs softly to herself while taking off her street things. Drawing a bag of macaroons from her pocket, she eats a couple, then steals over and listens at her husband's study door.*) Yes, he's home. (*Hums again as she moves to the table right.*)

HELMER (*from the study*): Is that my little lark twittering out there?

NORA (*busy opening some packages*): Yes, it is.

HELMER: Is that my squirrel rummaging around?

NORA: Yes!

HELMER: When did my squirrel get in?

NORA: Just now. (*Putting the macaroon bag in her pocket and wiping her mouth.*) Do come in, Torvald, and see what I've bought.

[S.D.] étagère: Cabinet with shelves.

HELMER: Can't be disturbed. (*After a moment he opens the door and peers in, pen in hand.*) Bought, you say? All that there? Has the little spendthrift been out throwing money around again?

NORA: Oh, but Torvald, this year we really should let ourselves go a bit. It's the first Christmas we haven't had to economize.

HELMER: But you know we can't go squandering.

NORA: Oh yes, Torvald, we can squander a little now. Can't we? Just a tiny, wee bit. Now that you've got a big salary and are going to make piles and piles of money.

HELMER: Yes—starting New Year's. But then it's a full three months till the raise comes through.

NORA: Pooh! We can borrow that long.

HELMER: Nora! (*Goes over and playfully takes her by the ear.*) Are your scatterbrains off again? What if today I borrowed a thousand crowns, and you squandered them over Christmas week, and then on New Year's Eve a roof tile fell on my head, and I lay there—

NORA (*putting her hand on his mouth*): Oh! Don't say such things!

HELMER: Yes, but what if it happened—then what?

NORA: If anything so awful happened, then it just wouldn't matter if I had debts or not.

HELMER: Well, but the people I'd borrowed from?

NORA: Them? Who cares about them! They're strangers.

HELMER: Nora, Nora, how like a woman! No, but seriously, Nora, you know what I think about that. No debts! Never borrow! Something of freedom's lost—and something of beauty, too—from a home that's founded on borrowing and debt. We've made a brave stand up to now, the two of us; and we'll go right on like that the little while we have to.

NORA (*going toward the stove*): Yes, whatever you say, Torvald.

HELMER (*following her*): Now, now, the little lark's wings mustn't droop. Come on, don't be a sulky squirrel. (*Taking out his wallet.*) Nora, guess what I have here.

NORA (*turning quickly*): Money!

HELMER: There, see. (*Hands her some notes.*) Good grief, I know how costs go up in a house at Christmastime.

NORA: Ten—twenty—thirty—forty. Oh, thank you, Torvald; I can manage no end on this.

HELMER: You really will have to.

NORA: Oh yes, I promise I will! But come here so I can show you everything I bought. And so cheap! Look, new clothes for Ivar here—and a sword. Here a horse and a trumpet for Bob. And a doll and a doll's bed here for Emmy; they're nothing much, but she'll tear them to bits in no time anyway. And here I have dress material and handkerchiefs for the maids. Old Anne-Marie really deserves something more.

HELMER: And what's in that package there?

NORA (*with a cry*): Torvald, no! You can't see that till tonight!

HELMER: I see. But tell me now, you little prodigal, what have you thought of for yourself?

NORA: For myself? Oh, I don't want anything at all.

HELMER: Of course you do. Tell me just what—within reason—you'd most like to have.

NORA: I honestly don't know. Oh, listen, Torvald—

HELMER: Well?

NORA (*fumbling at his coat buttons, without looking at him*): If you want to give me something, then maybe you could—you could—

HELMER: Come on, out with it.

NORA (*hurriedly*): You could give me money, Torvald. No more than you think you can spare; then one of these days I'll buy something with it.

HELMER: But Nora—

NORA: Oh, please, Torvald darling, do that! I beg you, please. Then I could hang the bills in pretty gilt paper on the Christmas tree. Wouldn't that be fun?

HELMER: What are those little birds called that always fly through their fortunes?

NORA: Oh yes, spendthrifts; I know all that. But let's do as I say, Torvald; then I'll have time to decide what I really need most. That's very sensible, isn't it?

HELMER (*smiling*): Yes, very—that is, if you actually hung onto the money I give you, and you actually used it to buy yourself something. But it goes for the house and for all sorts of foolish things, and then I only have to lay out some more.

NORA: Oh, but Torvald—

HELMER: Don't deny it, my dear little Nora. (*Putting his arm around her waist.*) Spendthrifts are sweet, but they use up a frightful amount of money. It's incredible what it costs a man to feed such birds.

NORA: Oh, how can you say that! Really, I save everything I can.

HELMER (*laughing*): Yes, that's the truth. Everything you can. But that's nothing at all.

NORA (*humming, with a smile of quiet satisfaction*): Hm, if you only knew what expenses we larks and squirrels have, Torvald.

HELMER: You're an odd little one. Exactly the way your father was. You're never at a loss for scaring up money; but the moment you have it, it runs right out through your fingers; you never know what you've done with it. Well, one takes you as you are. It's deep in your blood. Yes, these things are hereditary, Nora.

NORA: Ah, I could wish I'd inherited many of Papa's qualities.

HELMER: And I couldn't wish you anything but just what you are, my sweet little lark. But wait; it seems to me you have a very—what should I call it?—a very suspicious look today—

NORA: I do?

HELMER: You certainly do. Look me straight in the eye.

NORA (*looking at him*): Well?

HELMER (*shaking an admonitory finger*): Surely my sweet tooth hasn't been running riot in town today, has she?

NORA: No. Why do you imagine that?

HELMER: My sweet tooth really didn't make a little detour through the confectioner's?

NORA: No, I assure you, Torvald—

HELMER: Hasn't nibbled some pastry?

NORA: No, not at all.

HELMER: Not even munched a macaroon or two?

NORA: No, Torvald, I assure you, really—

HELMER: There, there now. Of course I'm only joking.

NORA (*going to the table, right*): You know I could never think of going against you.

HELMER: No, I understand that; and you *have* given me your word. (*Going over to her.*) Well, you keep your little Christmas secrets to yourself, Nora darling. I expect they'll come to light this evening, when the tree is lit.

NORA: Did you remember to ask Dr. Rank?

HELMER: No. But there's no need for that, it's assumed he'll be dining with us. All the same, I'll ask him when he stops by here this morning. I've ordered some fine wine. Nora, you can't imagine how I'm looking forward to this evening.

NORA: So am I. And what fun for the children, Torvald!

HELMER: Ah, it's so gratifying to know that one's gotten a safe, secure job, and with a comfortable salary. It's a great satisfaction, isn't it?

NORA: Oh, it's wonderful!

HELMER: Remember last Christmas? Three whole weeks before, you shut yourself in every evening till long after midnight, making flowers for the Christmas tree, and all the other decorations to surprise us. Ugh, that was the dullest time I've ever lived through.

NORA: It wasn't at all dull for me.

HELMER (*smiling*): But the outcome *was* pretty sorry, Nora.

NORA: Oh, don't tease me with that again. How could I help it that the cat came in and tore everything to shreds.

HELMER: No, poor thing, you certainly couldn't. You wanted so much to please us all, and that's what counts. But it's just as well that the hard times are past.

NORA: Yes, it's really wonderful.

HELMER: Now I don't have to sit here alone, boring myself, and you don't have to tire your precious eyes and your fair little delicate hands—

NORA (*clapping her hands*): No, is it really true, Torvald, I don't have to? Oh, how wonderfully lovely to hear! (*Taking his arm.*) Now I'll tell you just how I've thought we should plan things. Right after Christmas—(*The doorbell rings.*) Oh, the bell. (*Straightening the room up a bit.*) Somebody would have to come. What a bore!

HELMER: I'm not at home to visitors, don't forget.

MAID (*from the hall doorway*): Ma'am, a lady to see you—

NORA: All right, let her come in.

MAID (*to Helmer*): And the doctor's just come too.

HELMER: Did he go right to my study?

MAID: Yes, he did.

(*Helmer goes into his room. The Maid shows in Mrs. Linde, dressed in traveling clothes, and shuts the door after her.*)

MRS. LINDE (*in a dispirited and somewhat hesitant voice*): Hello, Nora.

NORA (*uncertain*): Hello—

MRS. LINDE: You don't recognize me.

NORA: No, I don't know—but wait, I think—(*Exclaiming.*) What! Kristine! Is it really you?

MRS. LINDE: Yes, it's me.

NORA: Kristine! To think I didn't recognize you. But then, how could I? (*More quietly.*) How you've changed, Kristine!

MRS. LINDE: Yes, no doubt I have. In nine—ten long years.

NORA: Is it so long since we met? Yes, it's all of that. Oh, these last eight years have been a happy time, believe me. And so now you've come in to town, too. Made the long trip in the winter. That took courage.

MRS. LINDE: I just got here by ship this morning.

NORA: To enjoy yourself over Christmas, of course. Oh, how lovely! Yes, enjoy ourselves, we'll do that. But take your coat off. You're not still cold? (*Helping her.*) There now, let's get cozy here by the stove. No, the easy chair there! I'll take the rocker here. (*Seizing her hands.*) Yes, now you have your old look again; it was only in that first moment. You're a bit more pale, Kristine—and maybe a bit thinner.

MRS. LINDE: And much, much older, Nora.

NORA: Yes, perhaps a bit older; a tiny, tiny bit; not much at all. (*Stopping short; suddenly serious.*) Oh, but thoughtless me, to sit here, chattering away. Sweet, good Kristine, can you forgive me?

MRS. LINDE: What do you mean, Nora?

NORA (*softly*): Poor Kristine, you've become a widow.

MRS. LINDE: Yes, three years ago.

NORA: Oh, I knew it, of course; I read it in the papers. Oh, Kristine, you must believe me; I often thought of writing you then, but I kept postponing it, and something always interfered.

MRS. LINDE: Nora dear, I understand completely.

NORA: No, it was awful of me, Kristine. You poor thing, how much you must have gone through. And he left you nothing?

MRS. LINDE: No.

NORA: And no children?

MRS. LINDE: No.

NORA: Nothing at all, then?

MRS. LINDE: Not even a sense of loss to feed on.

NORA (*looking incredulously at her*): But Kristine, how could that be?

MRS. LINDE (*smiling wearily and smoothing her hair*): Oh, sometimes it happens, Nora.

NORA: So completely alone. How terribly hard that must be for you. I have three lovely children. You can't see them now; they're out with the maid. But now you must tell me everything—

MRS. LINDE: No, no, no, tell me about yourself.

NORA: No, you begin. Today I don't want to be selfish. I want to think only of you today. But there is something I must tell you. Did you hear of the wonderful luck we had recently?

MRS. LINDE: No, what's that?

NORA: My husband's been made manager in the bank, just think!

MRS. LINDE: Your husband? How marvelous!

NORA: Isn't it? Being a lawyer is such an uncertain living, you know, especially if one won't touch any cases that aren't clean and decent. And of course Torvald would never do that, and I'm with him completely there. Oh, we're simply delighted, believe me! He'll join the bank right after New Year's and start getting a huge salary and lots of commissions. From now on we can live quite differently—just as we want. Oh, Kristine, I feel so light and happy! Won't it be lovely to have stacks of money and not a care in the world?

MRS. LINDE: Well, anyway, it would be lovely to have enough for necessities.

NORA: No, not just for necessities, but stacks and stacks of money!

MRS. LINDE (*smiling*): Nora, Nora, aren't you sensible yet? Back in school you were such a free spender.

NORA (*with a quiet laugh*): Yes, that's what Torvald still says. (*Shaking her finger.*) But "Nora, Nora" isn't as silly as you all think. Really, we've been in no position for me to go squandering. We've had to work, both of us.

MRS. LINDE: You too?

NORA: Yes, at odd jobs—needlework, crocheting, embroidery, and such—(*casually*) and other things too. You remember that Torvald left the department when we were married? There was no chance of promotion in his office, and of course he needed to earn more money. But that first year he drove himself terribly. He took on all kinds of extra work that kept him going morning and night. It wore him down, and then he fell deathly ill. The doctors said it was essential for him to travel south.

MRS. LINDE: Yes, didn't you spend a whole year in Italy?

NORA: That's right. It wasn't easy to get away, you know. Ivar had just been born. But of course we had to go. Oh, that was a beautiful trip, and it saved Torvald's life. But it cost a frightful sum, Kristine.

MRS. LINDE: I can well imagine.

NORA: Four thousand, eight hundred crowns it cost. That's really a lot of money.

MRS. LINDE: But it's lucky you had it when you needed it.

NORA: Well, as it was, we got it from Papa.

MRS. LINDE: I see. It was just about the time your father died.

NORA: Yes, just about then. And, you know, I couldn't make that trip out to nurse him. I had to stay here, expecting Ivar any moment, and with my poor sick Torvald to care for. Dearest Papa, I never saw him

again, Kristine. Oh, that was the worst time I've known in all my marriage.

MRS. LINDE: I know how you loved him. And then you went off to Italy?

NORA: Yes. We had the means now, and the doctors urged us. So we left a month after.

MRS. LINDE: And your husband came back completely cured?

NORA: Sound as a drum!

MRS. LINDE: But—the doctor?

NORA: Who?

MRS. LINDE: I thought the maid said he was a doctor, the man who came in with me.

NORA: Yes, that was Dr. Rank—but he's not making a sick call. He's our closest friend, and he stops by at least once a day. No, Torvald hasn't had a sick moment since, and the children are fit and strong, and I am, too. (*Jumping up and clapping her hands.*) Oh, dear God, Kristine, what a lovely thing to live and be happy! But how disgusting of me—I'm talking of nothing but my own affairs. (*Sits on a stool close by Kristine, arms resting across her knees.*) Oh, don't be angry with me! Tell me, is it really true that you weren't in love with your husband? Why did you marry him, then?

MRS. LINDE: My mother was still alive, but bedridden and helpless—and I had my two younger brothers to look after. In all conscience, I didn't think I could turn him down.

NORA: No, you were right there. But was he rich at the time?

MRS. LINDE: He was very well off, I'd say. But the business was shaky, Nora. When he died, it all fell apart, and nothing was left.

NORA: And then—?

MRS. LINDE: Yes, so I had to scrape up a living with a little shop and a little teaching and whatever else I could find. The last three years have been like one endless workday without a rest for me. Now, it's over, Nora. My poor mother doesn't need me, for she's passed on. Nor the boys, either; they're working now and can take care of themselves.

NORA: How free you must feel—

MRS. LINDE: No—only unspeakably empty. Nothing to live for now. (*Standing up anxiously.*) That's why I couldn't take it any longer out in that desolate hole. Maybe here it'll be easier to find something to do and keep my mind occupied. If I could only be lucky enough to get a steady job, some office work—

NORA: Oh, but Kristine, that's so dreadfully tiring, and you already look so tired. It would be much better for you if you could go off to a bathing resort.

MRS. LINDE (*going toward the window*): I have no father to give me travel money, Nora.

NORA (*rising*): Oh, don't be angry with me.

MRS. LINDE (*going to her*): Nora dear, don't you be angry with me. The worst of my kind of situation is all the bitterness that's stored away. No one to work for, and yet you're always having to snap up your opportunities. You have to live; and so you grow self-ish. When you told me the happy change in your lot, do you know I was delighted less for your sakes than for mine?

NORA: How so? Oh, I see. You think maybe Torvald could do something for you.

MRS. LINDE: Yes, that's what I thought.

NORA: And he will, Kristine! Just leave it to me; I'll bring it up so delicately—find something attractive to humor him with. Oh, I'm so eager to help you.

MRS. LINDE: How very kind of you, Nora, to be so concerned over me—doubly kind, considering you really know so little of life's burdens yourself.

NORA: I—? I know so little—?

MRS. LINDE (*smiling*): Well, my heavens—a little needle-work and such—Nora, you're just a child.

NORA (*tossing her head and pacing the floor*): You don't have to act so superior.

MRS. LINDE: Oh?

NORA: You're just like the others. You all think I'm incapable of anything serious—

MRS. LINDE: Come now—

NORA: That I've never had to face the raw world.

MRS. LINDE: Nora dear, you've just been telling me all your troubles.

NORA: Hm! Trivial! (*Quietly.*) I haven't told you the big thing.

MRS. LINDE: Big thing? What do you mean?

NORA: You look down on me so, Kristine, but you shouldn't. You're proud that you worked so long and hard for your mother.

MRS. LINDE: I don't look down on a soul. But it is true: I'm proud—and happy, too—to think it was given to me to make my mother's last days almost free of care.

NORA: And you're also proud thinking of what you've done for your brothers.

MRS. LINDE: I feel I've a right to be.

NORA: I agree. But listen to this, Kristine—I've also got something to be proud and happy for.

MRS. LINDE: I don't doubt it. But whatever do you mean?

NORA: Not so loud. What if Torvald heard! He mustn't, not for anything in the world. Nobody must know, Kristine. No one but you.

MRS. LINDE: But what is it, then?

NORA: Come here. (*Drawing her down beside her on the sofa.*) It's true—I've also got something to be proud and happy for. I'm the one who saved Torvald's life.

MRS. LINDE: Saved—? Saved how?

NORA: I told you about the trip to Italy. Torvald never would have lived if he hadn't gone south—

MRS. LINDE: Of course; your father gave you the means—

NORA (*smiling*): That's what Torvald and all the rest think, but—

MRS. LINDE: But—?

NORA: Papa didn't give us a pin. I was the one who raised the money.

MRS. LINDE: You? That whole amount?

NORA: Four thousand, eight hundred crowns. What do you say to that?

MRS. LINDE: But Nora, how was it possible? Did you win the lottery?

NORA (*disdainfully*): The lottery? Pooh! No art to that.

MRS. LINDE: But where did you get it from then?

NORA (*humming, with a mysterious smile*): Hmm, tra-la-la-la.

MRS. LINDE: Because you couldn't have borrowed it.

NORA: No? Why not?

MRS. LINDE: A wife can't borrow without her husband's consent.

NORA (*tossing her head*): Oh, but a wife with a little business sense, a wife who knows how to manage—

MRS. LINDE: Nora, I simply don't understand—

NORA: You don't have to. Whoever said I *borrowed* the money? I could have gotten it other ways. (*Throwing herself back on the sofa.*) I could have gotten it from some admirer or other. After all, a girl with my ravishing appeal—

MRS. LINDE: You lunatic.

NORA: I'll bet you're eaten up with curiosity, Kristine.

MRS. LINDE: Now listen here, Nora—you haven't done something indiscreet?

NORA (*sitting up again*): Is it indiscreet to save your husband's life?

MRS. LINDE: I think it's indiscreet that without his knowledge you—

NORA: But that's the point: He mustn't know! My Lord, can't you understand? He mustn't ever know the close call he had. It was to *me* the doctors came to say his life was in danger—that nothing could save him but a stay in the south. Didn't I try strategy then! I began talking about how lovely it would be for me to travel abroad like other young wives; I begged and I cried; I told him please to remember my condition, to be kind and indulge me; and then I dropped a hint that he could easily take out a loan. But at that, Kristine, he nearly exploded. He said I was frivolous, and it was his duty as man of the house not to indulge me in whims and fancies—as I think he called them. Aha, I thought, now you'll just have to be saved—and that's when I saw my chance.

MRS. LINDE: And your father never told Torvald the money wasn't from him?

NORA: No, never. Papa died right about then. I'd considered bringing him into my secret and begging him never to tell. But he was too sick at the time—and then, sadly, it didn't matter.

MRS. LINDE: And you've never confided in your husband since?

NORA: For heaven's sake, no! Are you serious? He's so strict on that subject. Besides—Torvald, with all his masculine pride—how painfully humiliating for him if he ever found out he was in debt to me. That would just ruin our relationship. Our beautiful, happy home would never be the same.

MRS. LINDE: Won't you ever tell him?

NORA (*thoughtfully, half smiling*): Yes—maybe sometime years from now, when I'm no longer so attractive. Don't laugh! I only mean when Torvald loves me less than now, when he stops enjoying my dancing and dressing up and reciting for him. Then it might be wise to have something in reserve—(*Breaking off.*) How ridiculous! That'll never happen—Well, Kristine, what do you think of my big secret? I'm capable of something too, hm? You can imagine, of course, how this thing hangs over me. It really hasn't been easy meeting the payments on time. In the business world there's what they call quarterly interest and what they call amortization, and these are always so terribly hard to manage. I've had to skimp a little here and there, wherever I could, you know. I could hardly spare anything from my house allowance, because Torvald has to live well. I couldn't let the children go poorly dressed; whatever I got for them, I felt I had to use up completely—the darlings!

MRS. LINDE: Poor Nora, so it had to come out of your own budget, then?

NORA: Yes, of course. But I was the one most responsible, too. Every time Torvald gave me money for new clothes and such, I never used more than half; always bought the simplest, cheapest outfits. It was a godsend that everything looks so well on me that Torvald never noticed. But it did weigh me down at times, Kristine. It *is* such a joy to wear fine things. You understand.

MRS. LINDE: Oh, of course.

NORA: And then I found other ways of making money. Last winter I was lucky enough to get a lot of copying to do. I locked myself in and sat writing every evening till late in the night. Ah, I was tired so often, dead tired. But still it was wonderful fun, sitting and working like that, earning money. It was almost like being a man.

MRS. LINDE: But how much have you paid off this way so far?

NORA: That's hard to say, exactly. These accounts, you know, aren't easy to figure. I only know that I've paid out all I could scrape together. Time and again I haven't known where to turn. (*Smiling.*) Then I'd sit here dreaming of a rich old gentleman who had fallen in love with me—

MRS. LINDE: What! Who is he?

NORA: Oh, really! And that he'd died, and when his will was opened, there in big letters it said, "All my fortune shall be paid over in cash, immediately, to that enchanting Mrs. Nora Helmer."

MRS. LINDE: But Nora dear—who *was* this gentleman?

NORA: Good grief, can't you understand? The old man never existed; that was only something I'd dream up time and again whenever I was at my wits' end for money. But it makes no difference now; the old fossil can go where he pleases for all I care; I don't need him or his will—because now I'm free. (*Jumping up.*) Oh, how lovely to think of that, Kristine! Carefree! To know you're carefree, utterly carefree; to be

able to romp and play with the children, and to keep up a beautiful, charming home—everything just the way Torvald likes it! And think, spring is coming, with big blue skies. Maybe we can travel a little then. Maybe I'll see the ocean again. Oh yes, it *is* so marvelous to live and be happy!

(*The front doorbell rings.*)

MRS. LINDE (*rising*): There's the bell. It's probably best that I go.

NORA: No, stay. No one's expected. It must be for Torvald.

MAID (*from the hall doorway*): Excuse me, ma'am—there's a gentleman here to see Mr. Helmer, but I didn't know—since the doctor's with him—

NORA: Who is the gentleman?

KROGSTAD (*from the doorway*): It's me, Mrs. Helmer.

(*Mrs. Linde starts and turns away toward the window.*)

NORA (*stepping toward him, tense, her voice a whisper*): You? What is it? Why do you want to speak to my husband?

KROGSTAD: Bank business—after a fashion. I have a small job in the investment bank, and I hear now your husband is going to be our chief—

NORA: In other words, it's—

KROGSTAD: Just dry business, Mrs. Helmer. Nothing but that.

NORA: Yes, then please be good enough to step into the study. (*She nods indifferently as she sees him out by the hall door, then returns and begins stirring up the stove.*)

MRS. LINDE: Nora—who was that man?

NORA: That was a Mr. Krogstad—a lawyer.

MRS. LINDE: Then it really was him.

NORA: Do you know that person?

MRS. LINDE: I did once—many years ago. For a time he was a law clerk in our town.

NORA: Yes, he's been that.

MRS. LINDE: How he's changed.

NORA: I understand he had a very unhappy marriage.

MRS. LINDE: He's a widower now.

NORA: With a number of children. There now, it's burning. (*She closes the stove door and moves the rocker a bit to one side.*)

MRS. LINDE: They say he has a hand in all kinds of business.

NORA: Oh? That may be true; I wouldn't know. But let's not think about business. It's so dull.

(*Dr. Rank enters from Helmer's study.*)

RANK (*still in the doorway*): No, no, really—I don't want to intrude, I'd just as soon talk a little while with your wife. (*Shuts the door, then notices Mrs. Linde.*) Oh, beg pardon. I'm intruding here too.

NORA: No, not at all. (*Introducing him.*) Dr. Rank, Mrs. Linde.

RANK: Well now, that's a name much heard in this house. I believe I passed the lady on the stairs as I came.

MRS. LINDE: Yes, I take the stairs very slowly. They're rather hard on me.

RANK: Uh-hm, some touch of internal weakness?

MRS. LINDE: More overexertion, I'd say.

RANK: Nothing else? Then you're probably here in town to rest up in a round of parties?

MRS. LINDE: I'm here to look for work.

RANK: Is that the best cure for overexertion?

MRS. LINDE: One has to live, Doctor.

RANK: Yes, there's a common prejudice to that effect.

NORA: Oh, come on, Dr. Rank—you really do want to live yourself.

RANK: Yes, I really do. Wretched as I am, I'll gladly prolong my torment indefinitely. All my patients feel like that. And it's quite the same, too, with the morally sick. Right at this moment there's one of those moral invalids in there with Helmer—

MRS. LINDE (*softly*): Ah!

NORA: Who do you mean?

RANK: Oh, it's a lawyer, Krogstad, a type you wouldn't know. His character is rotten to the root—but even he began chattering all-importantly about how he had to live.

NORA: Oh? What did he want to talk to Torvald about?

RANK: I really don't know. I only heard something about the bank.

NORA: I didn't know that Krog—that this man Krogstad had anything to do with the bank.

RANK: Yes, he's gotten some kind of berth down there. (*To Mrs. Linde.*) I don't know if you also have, in your neck of the woods, a type of person who scuttles about breathlessly, sniffing out hints of moral corruption, and then maneuvers his victim into some sort of key position where he can keep an eye on him. It's the healthy these days that are out in the cold.

MRS. LINDE: All the same, it's the sick who most need to be taken in.

RANK (*with a shrug*): Yes, there we have it. That's the concept that's turning society into a sanatorium.

(*Nora, lost in her thoughts, breaks out into quiet laughter and claps her hands.*)

RANK: Why do you laugh at that? Do you have any real idea of what society is?

NORA: What do I care about dreary old society? I was laughing at something quite different—something terribly funny. Tell me, Doctor—is everyone who works in the bank dependent now on Torvald?

RANK: Is that what you find so terribly funny?

NORA (*smiling and humming*): Never mind, never mind! (*Pacing the floor.*) Yes, that's really immensely amusing: that we—that Torvald has so much power now over all those people. (*Taking the bag out of her pocket.*) Dr. Rank, a little macaroon on that?

RANK: See here, macaroons! I thought they were contraband here.

NORA: Yes, but these are some that Kristine gave me.

MRS. LINDE: What? I—?

NORA: Now, now, don't be afraid. You couldn't possibly know that Torvald had forbidden them. You see, he's worried they'll ruin my teeth. But hmp! Just this once! Isn't that so, Dr. Rank? Help yourself! (*Puts a macaroon in his mouth.*) And you too, Kristine. And I'll also have one, only a little one—or two, at the most. (*Walking about again.*) Now I'm really tremendously happy. Now's there's just one last thing in the world that I have an enormous desire to do.

RANK: Well! And what's that?

NORA: It's something I have such a consuming desire to say so Torvald could hear.

RANK: And why can't you say it?

NORA: I don't dare. It's quite shocking.

MRS. LINDE: Shocking?

RANK: Well, then it isn't advisable. But in front of us you certainly can. What do you have such a desire to say so Torvald could hear?

NORA: I have such a huge desire to say—to hell and be damned!

RANK: Are you crazy?

MRS. LINDE: My goodness, Nora!

RANK: Go on, say it. Here he is.

NORA (*hiding the macaroon bag*): Shh, shh, shh!

(*Helmer comes in from his study, hat in hand, overcoat over his arm.*)

NORA (*going toward him*): Well, Torvald dear, are you through with him?

HELMER: Yes, he just left.

NORA: Let me introduce you—this is Kristine, who's arrived here in town.

HELMER: Kristine—? I'm sorry, but I don't know—

NORA: Mrs. Linde, Torvald dear. Mrs. Kristine Linde.

HELMER: Of course. A childhood friend of my wife's, no doubt?

MRS. LINDE: Yes, we knew each other in those days.

NORA: And just think, she made the long trip down here in order to talk with you.

HELMER: What's this?

MRS. LINDE: Well, not exactly—

NORA: You see, Kristine is remarkably clever in office work, and so she's terribly eager to come under a capable man's supervision and add more to what she already knows—

HELMER: Very wise, Mrs. Linde.

NORA: And then when she heard that you'd become a bank manager—the story was wired out to the papers—then she came in as fast as she could and—Really, Torvald, for my sake you can do a little something for Kristine, can't you?

HELMER: Yes, it's not at all impossible. Mrs. Linde, I suppose you're a widow?

MRS. LINDE: Yes.

HELMER: Any experience in office work?

MRS. LINDE: Yes, a good deal.

HELMER: Well, it's quite likely that I can make an opening for you—

NORA (*clapping her hands*): You see, you see!

HELMER: You've come at a lucky moment, Mrs. Linde.

MRS. LINDE: Oh, how can I thank you?

HELMER: Not necessary. (*Putting his overcoat on.*) But today you'll have to excuse me—

RANK: Wait, I'll go with you. (*He fetches his coat from the hall and warms it at the stove.*)

NORA: Don't stay out long, dear.

HELMER: An hour; no more.

NORA: Are you going too, Kristine?

MRS. LINDE (*putting on her winter garments*): Yes, I have to see about a room now.

HELMER: Then perhaps we can all walk together.

NORA (*helping her*): What a shame we're so cramped here, but it's quite impossible for us to—

MRS. LINDE: Oh, don't even think of it! Good-bye, Nora dear, and thanks for everything.

NORA: Good-bye for now. Of course you'll be back this evening. And you too, Dr. Rank. What? If you're well enough? Oh, you've got to be! Wrap up tight now.

(*In a ripple of small talk the company moves out into the hall; children's voices are heard outside on the steps.*)

NORA: There they are! There they are! (*She runs to open the door. The children come in with their nurse, Anne-Marie.*) Come in, come in! (*Bends down and kisses them.*) Oh, you darlings—! Look at them, Kristine. Aren't they lovely!

RANK: No loitering in the draft here.

HELMER: Come, Mrs. Linde—this place is unbearable now for anyone but mothers.

(*Dr. Rank, Helmer, and Mrs. Linde go down the stairs. Anne-Marie goes into the living room with the children. Nora follows, after closing the hall door.*)

NORA: How fresh and strong you look. Oh, such red cheeks you have! Like apples and roses. (*The children interrupt her throughout the following.*) And it was so much fun? That's wonderful. Really? You pulled both Emmy and Bob on the sled? Imagine, all together! Yes, you're a clever boy, Ivar. Oh, let me hold her a bit, Anne-Marie. My sweet little doll baby! (*Takes the smallest from the nurse and dances with her.*) Yes, yes, Mama will dance with Bob as well. What? Did you throw snowballs? Oh, if I'd only been there! No, don't bother, Anne-Marie—I'll undress them myself. Oh yes, let me. It's such fun. Go in and rest; you look half frozen. There's hot coffee waiting for you on the stove. (*The nurse goes into the room to the left. Nora takes the children's winter things off, throwing them about, while the children talk to her all at once.*) Is that so? A big dog chased you? But it didn't bite? No, dogs never bite little, lovely doll babies. Don't peek in the packages, Ivar! What is it? Yes, wouldn't you like to know. No, no, it's an ugly something. Well? Shall we play? What shall we play? Hide-and-seek? Yes, let's play hide-and-seek. Bob must hide first. I must? Yes, let me hide first. (*Laughing and shouting, she and the children play in and out of the living room and*

the adjoining room to the right. At last Nora hides under the table. The children come storming in, search, but cannot find her, then hear her muffled laughter, dash over to the table, lift the cloth up and find her. Wild shouting. She creeps forward as if to scare them. More shouts. Meanwhile, a knock at the hall door; no one has noticed it. Now the door half opens, and Krogstad appears. He waits a moment; the game goes on.*)

KROGSTAD: Beg pardon, Mrs. Helmer—

NORA (*with a strangled cry, turning and scrambling to her knees*): Oh! What do you want?

KROGSTAD: Excuse me. The outer door was ajar; it must be someone forgot to shut it—

NORA (*rising*): My husband isn't home, Mr. Krogstad.

KROGSTAD: I know that.

NORA: Yes—then what do you want here?

KROGSTAD: A word with you.

NORA: With—? (*To the children, quietly.*) Go in to Anne-Marie. What? No, the strange man won't hurt Mama. When he's gone, we'll play some more. (*She leads the children into the room to the left and shuts the door after them. Then, tense and nervous:*) You want to speak to me?

KROGSTAD: Yes, I want to.

NORA: Today? But it's not yet the first of the month—

KROGSTAD: No, it's Christmas Eve. It's going to be up to you how merry a Christmas you have.

NORA: What is it you want? Today I absolutely can't—

KROGSTAD: We won't talk about that till later. This is something else. You do have a moment to spare, I suppose?

NORA: Oh yes, of course—I do, except—

KROGSTAD: Good. I was sitting over at Olsen's Restaurant when I saw your husband go down the street—

NORA: Yes?

KROGSTAD: With a lady.

NORA: Yes. So?

KROGSTAD: If you'll pardon my asking: Wasn't that lady a Mrs. Linde?

NORA: Yes.

KROGSTAD: Just now come into town?

NORA: Yes, today.

KROGSTAD: She's a good friend of yours?

NORA: Yes, she is. But I don't see—

KROGSTAD: I also knew her once.

NORA: I'm aware of that.

KROGSTAD: Oh? You know all about it. I thought so. Well, then let me ask you short and sweet: Is Mrs. Linde getting a job in the bank?

NORA: What makes you think you can cross-examine me, Mr. Krogstad—you, one of my husband's employees? But since you ask, you might as well know—yes, Mrs. Linde's going to be taken on at the bank. And I'm the one who spoke for her, Mr. Krogstad. Now you know.

KROGSTAD: So I guessed right.

NORA (*pacing up and down*): Oh, one does have a tiny bit of influence, I should hope. Just because I am a woman, don't think it means that—When one has a subordinate position, Mr. Krogstad, one really ought to be careful about pushing somebody who—hm—

KROGSTAD: Who has influence?

NORA: That's right.

KROGSTAD (*in a different tone*): Mrs. Helmer, would you be good enough to use your influence on my behalf?

NORA: What? What do you mean?

KROGSTAD: Would you please make sure that I keep my subordinate position in the bank?

NORA: What does that mean? Who's thinking of taking away your position?

KROGSTAD: Oh, don't play the innocent with me. I'm quite aware that your friend would hardly relish the chance of running into me again; and I'm also aware now whom I can thank for being turned out.

NORA: But I promise you—

KROGSTAD: Yes, yes, yes, to the point: There's still time, and I'm advising you to use your influence to prevent it.

NORA: But Mr. Krogstad, I have absolutely no influence.

KROGSTAD: You haven't? I thought you were just saying—

NORA: You shouldn't take me so literally. I! How can you believe that I have any such influence over my husband?

KROGSTAD: Oh, I've known your husband from our student days. I don't think the great bank manager's more steadfast than any other married man.

NORA: You speak insolently about my husband, and I'll show you the door.

KROGSTAD: The lady has spirit.

NORA: I'm not afraid of you any longer. After New Year's, I'll soon be done with the whole business.

KROGSTAD (*restraining himself*): Now listen to me, Mrs. Helmer. If necessary, I'll fight for my little job in the bank as if it were life itself.

NORA: Yes, so it seems.

KROGSTAD: It's not just a matter of income; that's the least of it. It's something else—All right, out with it! Look, this is the thing. You know, just like all the others, of course, that once, a good many years ago, I did something rather rash.

NORA: I've heard rumors to that effect.

KROGSTAD: The case never got into court; but all the same, every door was closed in my face from then on. So I took up those various activities you know about. I had to grab hold somewhere; and I dare say I haven't been among the worst. But now I want to drop all that. My boys are growing up. For their sakes, I'll have to win back as much respect as possible here in town. That job in the bank was like the first rung in my ladder. And now your husband wants to kick me right back down in the mud again.

NORA: But for heaven's sake, Mr. Krogstad, it's simply not in my power to help you.

KROGSTAD: That's because you haven't the will to—but I have the means to make you.

NORA: You certainly won't tell my husband that I owe you money?

KROGSTAD: Hm—what if I told him that?

NORA: That would be shameful of you. (*Nearly in tears.*) This secret—my joy and my pride—that he should learn it in such a crude and disgusting way—learn it from you. You'd expose me to the most horrible unpleasantness—

KROGSTAD: Only unpleasantness?

NORA (*vehemently*): But go on and try. It'll turn out the worse for you, because then my husband will really see what a crook you are, and then you'll never be able to hold your job.

KROGSTAD: I asked if it was just domestic unpleasantness you were afraid of?

NORA: If my husband finds out, then of course he'll pay what I owe at once, and then we'd be through with you for good.

KROGSTAD (*a step closer*): Listen, Mrs. Helmer—you've either got a very bad memory, or else no head at all for business. I'd better put you a little more in touch with the facts.

NORA: What do you mean?

KROGSTAD: When your husband was sick, you came to me for a loan of four thousand, eight hundred crowns.

NORA: Where else could I go?

KROGSTAD: I promised to get you that sum—

NORA: And you got it.

KROGSTAD: I promised to get you that sum, on certain conditions. You were so involved in your husband's illness, and so eager to finance your trip, that I guess you didn't think out all the details. It might just be a good idea to remind you. I promised you the money on the strength of a note I drew up.

NORA: Yes, and that I signed.

KROGSTAD: Right. But at the bottom I added some lines for your father to guarantee the loan. He was supposed to sign down there.

NORA: Supposed to? He did sign.

KROGSTAD: I left the date blank. In other words, your father would have dated his signature himself. Do you remember that?

NORA: Yes, I think—

KROGSTAD: Then I gave you the note for you to mail to your father. Isn't that so?

NORA: Yes.

KROGSTAD: And naturally you sent it at once—because only some five, six days later you brought me the note, properly signed. And with that, the money was yours.

NORA: Well, then; I've made my payments regularly, haven't I?

KROGSTAD: More or less. But—getting back to the point—those were hard times for you then, Mrs. Helmer.

NORA: Yes, they were.

KROGSTAD: Your father was very ill, I believe.

NORA: He was near the end.

KROGSTAD: He died soon after?

NORA: Yes.

KROGSTAD: Tell me, Mrs. Helmer, do you happen to recall the date of your father's death? The day of the month, I mean.

NORA: Papa died the twenty-ninth of September.

KROGSTAD: That's quite correct; I've already looked into that. And now we come to a curious thing—(*taking out a paper*) which I simply cannot comprehend.

NORA: Curious thing? I don't know—

KROGSTAD: This is the curious thing: that your father co-signed the note for your loan three days after his death.

NORA: How—? I don't understand.

KROGSTAD: Your father died the twenty-ninth of September. But look. Here your father dated his signature October second. Isn't that curious, Mrs. Helmer? (*Nora is silent.*) Can you explain it to me? (*Nora remains silent.*) It's also remarkable that the words "October second" and the year aren't written in your father's hand, but rather in one that I think I know. Well, it's easy to understand. Your father forgot perhaps to date his signature, and then someone or other added it, a bit sloppily, before anyone knew of his death. There's nothing wrong in that. It all comes down to the signature. And there's no question about *that,* Mrs. Helmer. It really *was* your father who signed his own name here, wasn't it?

NORA (*after a short silence, throwing her head back and looking squarely at him*): No, it wasn't. I signed Papa's name.

KROGSTAD: Wait, now—are you fully aware that this is a dangerous confession?

NORA: Why? You'll soon get your money.

KROGSTAD: Let me ask you a question—why didn't you send the paper to your father?

NORA: That was impossible. Papa was so sick. If I'd asked him for his signature, I also would have had to tell him what the money was for. But I couldn't tell him, sick as he was, that my husband's life was in danger. That was just impossible.

KROGSTAD: Then it would have been better if you'd given up the trip abroad.

NORA: I couldn't possibly. The trip was to save my husband's life. I couldn't give that up.

KROGSTAD: But didn't you ever consider that this was a fraud against me?

NORA: I couldn't let myself be bothered by that. You weren't any concern of mine. I couldn't stand you, with all those cold complications you made, even though you knew how badly off my husband was.

KROGSTAD: Mrs. Helmer, obviously you haven't the vaguest idea of what you've involved yourself in. But I can tell you this: It was nothing more and nothing worse that I once did—and it wrecked my whole reputation.

NORA: You? Do you expect me to believe that you ever acted bravely to save your wife's life?

KROGSTAD: Laws don't inquire into motives.

NORA: Then they must be very poor laws.

KROGSTAD: Poor or not—if I introduce this paper in court, you'll be judged according to law.

NORA: This I refuse to believe. A daughter hasn't a right to protect her dying father from anxiety and care? A wife hasn't a right to save her husband's life? I don't

Krogstad (Robert Gerringer) explains the seriousness of her actions to Nora.

know much about laws, but I'm sure that somewhere in the books these things are allowed. And you don't know anything about it—you who practice the law? You must be an awful lawyer, Mr. Krogstad.

KROGSTAD: Could be. But business—the kind of business we two are mixed up in—don't you think I know about that? All right. Do what you want now. But I'm telling you *this:* If I get shoved down a second time, you're going to keep me company. (*He bows and goes out through the hall.*)

NORA (*pensive for a moment, then tossing her head*): Oh, really! Trying to frighten me! I'm not so silly as all that. (*Begins gathering up the children's clothes, but soon stops.*) But—? No, but that's impossible! I did it out of love.

THE CHILDREN (*in the doorway, left*): Mama, that strange man's gone out the door.

NORA: Yes, yes, I know it. But don't tell anyone about the strange man. Do you hear? Not even Papa!

THE CHILDREN: No, Mama. But now will you play again?

NORA: No, not now.

Nora (Claire Bloom) is troubled as Helmer (Donald Madden) kisses her in Patrick Garland's 1971 production.

THE CHILDREN: Oh, but Mama, you promised.
NORA: Yes, but I can't now. Go inside; I have too much to do. Go in, go in, my sweet darlings. (*She herds them gently back in the room and shuts the door after them. Settling on the sofa, she takes up a piece of embroidery and makes some stitches, but soon stops abruptly.*) No! (*Throws the work aside, rises, goes to the hall door and calls out.*) Helene! Let me have the tree in here. (*Goes to the table, left, opens the table drawer, and stops again.*) No, but that's utterly impossible!
MAID (*with the Christmas tree*): Where should I put it, ma'am?
NORA: There. The middle of the floor.
MAID: Should I bring anything else?
NORA: No, thanks. I have what I need.

(*The Maid, who has set the tree down, goes out.*)

NORA (*absorbed in trimming the tree*): Candles here— and flowers here. That terrible creature! Talk, talk, talk! There's nothing to it at all. The tree's going to

be lovely. I'll do anything to please you Torvald. I'll sing for you, dance for you—

(*Helmer comes in from the hall, with a sheaf of papers under his arm.*)

NORA: Oh! You're back so soon?
HELMER: Yes. Has anyone been here?
NORA: Here? No.
HELMER: That's odd. I saw Krogstad leaving the front door.
NORA: So? Oh yes, that's true. Krogstad was here a moment.
HELMER: Nora, I can see by your face that he's been here, begging you to put in a good word for him.
NORA: Yes.
HELMER: And it was supposed to seem like your own idea? You were to hide it from me that he'd been here. He asked you that, too, didn't he?
NORA: Yes, Torvald, but—
HELMER: Nora, Nora, and you could fall for that? Talk with that sort of person and promise him anything? And then in the bargain, tell me an untruth.
NORA: An untruth—?
HELMER: Didn't you say that no one had been here? (*Wagging his finger.*) My little songbird must never do that again. A songbird needs a clean beak to warble with. No false notes. (*Putting his arm about her waist.*) That's the way it should be, isn't it? Yes, I'm sure of it. (*Releasing her.*) And so, enough of that. (*Sitting by the stove.*) Ah, how snug and cozy it is here. (*Leafing among his papers.*)
NORA (*busy with the tree, after a short pause*): Torvald!
HELMER: Yes.
NORA: I'm so much looking forward to the Stenborgs' costume party, day after tomorrow.
HELMER: And I can't wait to see what you'll surprise me with.
NORA: Oh, that stupid business!
HELMER: What?
NORA: I can't find anything that's right. Everything seems so ridiculous, so inane.
HELMER: So my little Nora's come to *that* recognition?
NORA (*going behind his chair, her arms resting on its back*): Are you very busy, Torvald?
HELMER: Oh—
NORA: What papers are those?
HELMER: Bank matters.
NORA: Already?
HELMER: I've gotten full authority from the retiring management to make all necessary changes in personnel and procedure. I'll need Christmas week for that. I want to have everything in order by New Year's.
NORA: So that was the reason this poor Krogstad—
HELMER: Hm.
NORA (*still leaning on the chair and slowly stroking the nape of his neck*): If you weren't so very busy, I would have asked you an enormous favor, Torvald.

HELMER: Let's hear. What is it?

NORA: You know, there isn't anyone who has your good taste—and I want so much to look well at the costume party. Torvald, couldn't you take over and decide what I should be and plan my costume?

HELMER: Ah, is my stubborn little creature calling for a lifeguard?

NORA: Yes, Torvald, I can't get anywhere without your help.

HELMER: All right—I'll think it over. We'll hit on something.

NORA: Oh, how sweet of you. (*Goes to the tree again. Pause.*) Aren't the red flowers pretty—? But tell me, was it really such a crime that this Krogstad committed?

HELMER: Forgery. Do you have any idea what that means?

NORA: Couldn't he have done it out of need?

HELMER: Yes, or thoughtlessness, like so many others. I'm not so heartless that I'd condemn a man categorically for just one mistake.

NORA: No, of course not, Torvald!

HELMER: Plenty of men have redeemed themselves by openly confessing their crimes and taking their punishment.

NORA: Punishment—?

HELMER: But now Krogstad didn't go that way. He got himself out by sharp practices, and that's the real cause of his moral breakdown.

NORA: Do you really think that would—?

HELMER: Just imagine how a man with that sort of guilt in him has to lie and cheat and deceive on all sides, has to wear a mask even with the nearest and dearest he has, even with his own wife and children. And with the children, Nora—that's where it's most horrible.

NORA: Why?

HELMER: Because that kind of atmosphere of lies infects the whole life of a home. Every breath the children take in is filled with the germs of something degenerate.

NORA (*coming closer behind him*): Are you sure of that?

HELMER: Oh, I've seen it often enough as a lawyer. Almost everyone who goes bad early in life has a mother who's a chronic liar.

NORA: Why just—the mother?

HELMER: It's usually the mother's influence that's dominant, but the father's works in the same way, of course. Every lawyer is quite familiar with it. And still this Krogstad's been going home year in, year out, poisoning his own children with lies and pretense; that's why I call him morally lost. (*Reaching his hands out toward her.*) So my sweet little Nora must promise me never to plead his cause. Your hand on it. Come, come, what's this? Give me your hand. There, now. All settled. I can tell you it'd be impossible for me to work alongside of him. I literally feel physically revolted when I'm anywhere near such a person.

NORA (*withdraws her hand and goes to the other side of the Christmas tree*): How hot it is here! And I've got so much to do.

The *Mabou Mines Dollhouse*, a 2005 interpretation of Ibsen's play by Lee Breuer and the Mabou Mines troupe, paired female actors at least six feet tall with male actors five feet tall or shorter.

HELMER (*getting up and gathering his papers*): Yes, and I have to think about getting some of these read through before dinner. I'll think about your costume, too. And something to hang on the tree in gilt paper, I may even see about that. (*Putting his hand on her head.*) Oh you, my darling little songbird. (*He goes into his study and closes the door after him.*)

NORA (*softly, after a silence*): Oh, really! It isn't so. It's impossible. It must be impossible.

ANNE-MARIE (*in the doorway left*): The children are begging so hard to come in to Mama.

NORA: No, no, no, don't let them in to me! You stay with them, Anne-Marie.

ANNE-MARIE: Of course, ma'am. (*Closes the door.*)

NORA (*pale with terror*): Hurt my children—! Poison my home? (*A moment's pause; then she tosses her head.*) That's not true. Never. Never in all the world.

ACT II

(*Same room. Beside the piano the Christmas tree now stands stripped of ornament, burned-down candle stubs on its ragged branches. Nora's street clothes lie on the sofa. Nora, alone in the room, moves restlessly about; at last she stops at the sofa and picks up her coat.*)

NORA (*dropping the coat again*): Someone's coming! (*Goes toward the door, listens.*) No—there's no one. Of course—nobody's coming today, Christmas Day—or tomorrow, either. But maybe—(*Opens the door and looks out.*) No, nothing in the mailbox. Quite empty. (*Coming forward.*) What nonsense! He won't do anything serious. Nothing terrible could happen. It's impossible. Why, I have three small children.

(*Anne-Marie, with a large carton, comes in from the room to the left.*)

ANNE-MARIE: Well, at last I found the box with the masquerade clothes.

NORA: Thanks. Put it on the table.

ANNE-MARIE (*does so*): But they're all pretty much of a mess.

NORA: Ahh! I'd love to rip them in a million pieces!

ANNE-MARIE: Oh, mercy, they can be fixed right up. Just a little patience.

NORA: Yes, I'll go get Mrs. Linde to help me.

ANNE-MARIE: Out again now? In this nasty weather? Miss Nora will catch cold—get sick.

NORA: Oh, worse things could happen—How are the children?

ANNE-MARIE: The poor mites are playing with their Christmas presents, but—

NORA: Do they ask for me much?

ANNE-MARIE: They're so used to having Mama around, you know.

NORA: Yes, but Anne-Marie, I *can't* be together with them as much as I was.

ANNE-MARIE: Well, small children get used to anything.

NORA: You think so? Do you think they'd forget their mother if she was gone for good?

ANNE-MARIE: Oh, mercy—gone for good!

NORA: Wait, tell me. Anne-Marie—I've wondered so often—how could you ever have the heart to give your child over to strangers?

ANNE-MARIE: But I had to, you know, to become little Nora's nurse.

NORA: Yes, but how could you *do* it?

ANNE-MARIE: When I could get such a good place? A girl who's poor and who's gotten in trouble is glad enough for that. Because that slippery fish, he didn't do a thing for me, you know.

NORA: But your daughter's surely forgotten you.

ANNE-MARIE: Oh, she certainly has not. She's written to me, both when she was confirmed and when she was married.

NORA (*clasping her about the neck*): You old Anne-Marie, you were a good mother for me when I was little.

ANNE-MARIE: Poor little Nora, with no other mother but me.

NORA: And if the babies didn't have one, then I know that you'd—What silly talk! (*Opening the carton.*) Go in to them. Now I'll have to—Tomorrow you can see how lovely I'll look.

ANNE-MARIE: Oh, there won't be anyone at the party as lovely as Miss Nora. (*She goes off into the room, left.*)

NORA (*begins unpacking the box, but soon throws it aside*): Oh, if I dared to go out. If only nobody would come. If only nothing would happen here while I'm out. What craziness—nobody's coming. Just don't think. This muff—needs a brushing. Beautiful gloves, beautiful gloves. Let it go. Let it go! One, two, three, four, five, six—(*With a cry.*) Oh, there

they are! (*Poises to move toward the door, but remains irresolutely standing. Mrs. Linde enters from the hall, where she has removed her street clothes.*)

NORA: Oh, it's you, Kristine. There's no one else out there? How good that you've come.

MRS. LINDE: I hear you were up asking for me.

NORA: Yes, I just stopped by. There's something you really can help me with. Let's get settled on the sofa. Look, there's going to be a costume party tomorrow evening at the Stenborgs' right above, us, and now Torvald wants me to go as a Neapolitan peasant girl and dance the tarantella that I learned in Capri.

MRS. LINDE: Really, are you giving a whole performance?

NORA: Torvald says yes, I should. See, here's the dress. Torvald had it made for me down there; but now it's all so tattered that I just don't know—

MRS. LINDE: Oh, we'll fix that up in no time. It's nothing more than the trimmings—they're a bit loose here and there. Needle and thread? Good, now we have what we need.

NORA: Oh, how sweet of you!

MRS. LINDE (*sewing*): So you'll be in disguise tomorrow, Nora. You know what? I'll stop by then for a moment and have a look at you all dressed up. But listen, I've absolutely forgotten to thank you for that pleasant evening yesterday.

NORA (*getting up and walking about*): I don't think it was as pleasant as usual yesterday. You should have come to town a bit sooner, Kristine—Yes, Torvald really knows how to give a home elegance and charm.

MRS. LINDE: And you do, too, if you ask me. You're not your father's daughter for nothing. But tell me, is Dr. Rank always so down in the mouth as yesterday?

NORA: No, that was quite an exception. But he goes around critically ill all the time—tuberculosis of the spine, poor man. You know, his father was a disgusting thing who kept mistresses and so on—and that's why the son's been sickly from birth.

MRS. LINDE (*lets her sewing fall to her lap*): But my dearest Nora, how do you know about such things?

NORA (*walking more jauntily*): Hmp! When you've had three children, then you've had a few visits from—from women who know something of medicine, and they tell you this and that.

MRS. LINDE (*resumes sewing; a short pause*): Does Dr. Rank come here every day?

NORA: Every blessed day. He's Torvald's best friend from childhood, and *my* good friend, too. Dr. Rank almost belongs to this house.

MRS. LINDE: But tell me—is he quite sincere? I mean, doesn't he rather enjoy flattering people?

NORA: Just the opposite. Why do you think that?

MRS. LINDE: When you introduced us yesterday, he was proclaiming that he'd often heard my name in this house; but later I noticed that your husband hadn't the slightest idea who I really was. So how could Dr. Rank—?

NORA: But it's all true, Kristine. You see, Torvald loves me beyond words, and, as he puts it, he'd like to keep me all to himself. For a long time he'd almost be jealous if I even mentioned any of my old friends back home. So of course I dropped that. But with Dr. Rank I talk a lot about such things because he likes hearing about them.

MRS. LINDE: Now listen, Nora; in many ways you're still like a child. I'm a good deal older than you, with a little more experience. I'll tell you something: You ought to put an end to all this with Dr. Rank.

NORA: What should I put an end to?

MRS. LINDE: Both parts of it, I think. Yesterday you said something about a rich admirer who'd provide you with money—

NORA: Yes, one who doesn't exist—worse luck. So?

MRS. LINDE: Is Dr. Rank well off?

NORA: Yes, he is.

MRS. LINDE: With no dependents?

NORA: No, no one. But—

MRS. LINDE: And he's over here every day?

NORA: Yes, I told you that.

MRS. LINDE: How can a man of such refinement be so grasping?

NORA: I don't follow you at all.

MRS. LINDE: Now don't try to hide it, Nora. You think I can't guess who loaned you the forty-eight hundred crowns?

NORA: Are you out of your mind? How could you think such a thing! A friend of ours, who comes here every single day. What an intolerable situation that would have been!

MRS. LINDE: Then it really wasn't him.

NORA: No, absolutely not. It never even crossed my mind for a moment—And he had nothing to lend in those days; his inheritance came later.

MRS. LINDE: Well, I think that was a stroke of luck for you, Nora dear.

NORA: No, it never would have occurred to me to ask Dr. Rank—Still, I'm quite sure that if I had asked him—

MRS. LINDE: Which you won't, of course.

NORA: No, of course not. I can't see that I'd ever need to. But I'm quite positive that if I talked to Dr. Rank—

MRS. LINDE: Behind your husband's back?

NORA: I've got to clear up this other thing; *that's* also behind his back. I've *got* to clear it all up.

MRS. LINDE: Yes, I was saying that yesterday, but—

NORA (*pacing up and down*): A man handles these problems so much better than a woman—

MRS. LINDE: One's husband does, yes.

NORA: Nonsense. (*Stopping.*) When you pay everything you owe, then you get your note back, right?

MRS. LINDE: Yes, naturally.

NORA: And can rip it into a million pieces and burn it up—that filthy scrap of paper!

MRS. LINDE (*looking hard at her, laying her sewing aside, and rising slowly*): Nora, you're hiding something from me.

NORA: You can see it in my face?

MRS. LINDE: Something's happened to you since yesterday morning. Nora, what is it?

NORA (*hurrying toward her*): Kristine! (*Listening.*) Shh! Torvald's home. Look, go in with the children a while. Torvald can't bear all this snipping and stitching. Let Anne-Marie help you.

MRS. LINDE (*gathering up some of the things*): All right, but I'm not leaving here until we've talked this out. (*She disappears into the room, left, as Torvald enters from the hall.*)

NORA: Oh, how I've been waiting for you, Torvald dear.

HELMER: Was that the dressmaker?

NORA: No, that was Kristine. She's helping me fix up my costume. You know, it's going to be quite attractive.

HELMER: Yes, wasn't that a bright idea I had?

NORA: Brilliant! But then wasn't I good as well to give in to you?

HELMER: Good—because you give in to your husband's judgment? All right, you little goose, I know you didn't mean it like that. But I won't disturb you. You'll want to have a fitting, I suppose.

NORA: And you'll be working?

HELMER: Yes. (*Indicating a bundle of papers.*) See. I've been down to the bank. (*Starts toward his study.*)

NORA: Torvald.

HELMER (*stops*): Yes.

NORA: If your little squirrel begged you, with all her heart and soul, for something—?

HELMER: What's that?

NORA: Then would you do it?

HELMER: First, naturally, I'd have to know what it was.

NORA: Your squirrel would scamper about and do tricks, if you'd only be sweet and give in.

HELMER: Out with it.

NORA: Your lark would be singing high and low in every room—

HELMER: Come on, she does that anyway.

NORA: I'd be a wood nymph and dance for you in the moonlight.

HELMER: Nora—don't tell me it's that same business from this morning?

NORA (*coming closer*): Yes, Torvald, I beg you, please!

HELMER: And you actually have the nerve to drag that up again?

NORA: Yes, yes, you've got to give in to me; you *have* to let Krogstad keep his job in the bank.

HELMER: My dear Nora, I've slated his job for Mrs. Linde.

NORA: That's awfully kind of you. But you could just fire another clerk instead of Krogstad.

HELMER: This is the most incredible stubbornness! Because you go and give an impulsive promise to speak up for him, I'm expected to—

NORA: That's not the reason, Torvald. It's for your own sake. That man does writing for the worst papers; you said it yourself. He could do you any amount of harm. I'm scared to death of him—

HELMER: Ah, I understand. It's the old memories haunting you.

NORA: What do you mean by that?

HELMER: Of course, you're thinking about your father.

NORA: Yes, all right. Just remember how those nasty gossips wrote in the papers about Papa and slandered him so cruelly. I think they'd have had him dismissed if the department hadn't sent you up to investigate, and if you hadn't been so kind and open-minded toward him.

HELMER: My dear Nora, there's a notable difference between your father and me. Your father's official career was hardly above reproach. But mine is; and I hope it'll stay that way as long as I hold my position.

NORA: Oh, who can ever tell what vicious minds can invent? We could be so snug and happy now in our quiet, carefree home—you and I and the children, Torvald! That's why I'm pleading with you so—

HELMER: And just by pleading for him you make it impossible for me to keep him on. It's already known at the bank that I'm firing Krogstad. What if it's rumored around now that the new bank manager was vetoed by his wife—

NORA: Yes, what then—?

HELMER: Oh yes—as long as our little bundle of stubbornness gets her way—! I should go and make myself ridiculous in front of the whole office—give people the idea I can be swayed by all kinds of outside pressure. Oh, you can bet I'd feel the effects of that soon enough! Besides—there's something that rules Krogstad right out at the bank as long as I'm the manager.

NORA: What's that?

HELMER: His moral failings I could maybe overlook if I had to—

NORA: Yes, Torvald, why not?

HELMER: And I hear he's quite efficient on the job. But he was a crony of mine back in my teens—one of those rash friendships that crop up again and again to embarrass you later in life. Well, I might as well say it straight out: We're on a first-name basis. And that tactless fool makes no effort at all to hide it in front of others. Quite the contrary—he thinks that entitles him to take a familiar air around me, and so every other second he comes booming out with his, "Yes, Torvald!" and "Sure thing, Torvald!" I tell you, it's been excruciating for me. He's out to make my place in the bank unbearable.

NORA: Torvald, you can't be serious about all this.

HELMER: Oh no? Why not?

NORA: Because these are such petty considerations.

HELMER: What are you saying? Petty? You think I'm petty!

NORA: No, just the opposite, Torvald dear. That's exactly why—

HELMER: Never mind. You call my motives petty; then I might as well be just that. Petty! All right! We'll put a stop to this for good. (*Goes to the hall door and calls.*) Helene!

NORA: What do you want?

HELMER (*searching among his papers*): A decision. (*The Maid comes in.*) Look here; take this letter; go out with it at once. Get hold of a messenger and have him deliver it. Quick now. It's already addressed. Wait, here's some money.

MAID: Yes, sir. (*She leaves with the letter.*)

HELMER (*straightening his papers*): There, now, little Miss Willful.

NORA (*breathlessly*): Torvald, what was that letter?

HELMER: Krogstad's notice.

NORA: Call it back, Torvald! There's still time. Oh, Torvald, call it back! Do it for my sake—for your sake, for the children's sake! Do you hear, Torvald; do it! You don't know how this can harm us.

HELMER: Too late.

NORA: Yes, too late.

HELMER: Nora, dear, I can forgive you this panic, even though basically you're insulting me. Yes, you are! Or isn't it an insult to think that *I* should be afraid of a courtroom hack's revenge? But I forgive you anyway, because this shows so beautifully how much you love me. (*Takes her in his arms.*) This is the way it should be, my darling Nora. Whatever comes, you'll see: When it really counts, I have strength and courage enough as a man to take on the whole weight myself.

NORA (*terrified*): What do you mean by that?

HELMER: The whole weight, I said.

NORA (*resolutely*): No, never in all the world.

HELMER: Good. So we'll share it, Nora, as man and wife. That's as it should be. (*Fondling her.*) Are you happy now? There, there, there—not these frightened dove's eyes. It's nothing at all but empty fantasies—Now you should run through your tarantella and practice your tambourine. I'll go to the inner office, and shut both doors, so I won't hear a thing; you can make all the noise you like. (*Turning in the doorway.*) And when Rank comes, just tell him where he can find me. (*He nods to her and goes with his papers into the study, closing the door.*)

NORA (*standing as though rooted, dazed with fright, in a whisper*): He really could do it. He will do it. He'll do it in spite of everything. No, not that, never, never! Anything but that! Escape! A way out—(*The doorbell rings.*) Dr. Rank! Anything but that! Anything, whatever it is! (*Her hands pass over her face, smoothing it; she pulls herself together, goes over and opens the hall door. Dr. Rank stands outside, hanging his fur coat up. During the following scene, it begins getting dark.*)

NORA: Hello, Dr. Rank. I recognized your ring. But you mustn't go in to Torvald yet; I believe he's working.

RANK: And you?

NORA: For you, I always have an hour to spare—you know that. (*He has entered, and she shuts the door after him.*)

RANK: Many thanks. I'll make use of these hours while I can.

NORA: What do you mean by that? While you can?

RANK: Does that disturb you?

NORA: Well, it's such an odd phrase. Is anything going to happen?

RANK: What's going to happen is what I've been expecting so long—but I honestly didn't think it would come so soon.

NORA (*gripping his arm*): What is it you've found out? Dr. Rank, you have to tell me!

RANK (*sitting by the stove*): It's all over with me. There's nothing to be done about it.

NORA (*breathing easier*): Is it you—then—?

RANK: Who else? There's no point in lying to one's self. I'm the most miserable of all my patients, Mrs. Helmer. These past few days I've been auditing my internal accounts. Bankrupt! Within a month I'll probably be laid out and rotting in the churchyard.

NORA: Oh, what a horrible thing to say.

RANK: The thing itself is horrible. But the worst of it is all the other horror before it's over. There's only one final examination left; when I'm finished with that, I'll know about when my disintegration will begin. There's something I want to say. Helmer with his sensitivity has such a sharp distaste for anything ugly. I don't want him near my sickroom.

NORA: Oh, but Dr. Rank—

RANK: I won't have him in there. Under no condition. I'll lock my door to him—As soon as I'm completely sure of the worst, I'll send you my calling card marked with a black cross, and you'll know then the wreck has started to come apart.

NORA: No, today you're completely unreasonable. And I wanted you so much to be in a really good humor.

RANK: With death up my sleeve? And then to suffer this way for somebody else's sins. Is there any justice in that? And in every single family, in some way or another, this inevitable retribution of nature goes on—

NORA (*her hands pressed over her ears*): Oh, stuff! Cheer up! Please—be gay!

RANK: Yes, I'd just as soon laugh at it all. My poor, innocent spine, serving time for my father's gay army days.

NORA (*by the table, left*): He was so infatuated with asparagus tips and pâté de foie gras, wasn't that it?

RANK: Yes—and with truffles.

NORA: Truffles, yes. And then with oysters, I suppose?

RANK: Yes, tons of oysters, naturally.

NORA: And then the port and champagne to go with it. It's so sad that all these delectable things have to strike at our bones.

RANK: Especially when they strike at the unhappy bones that never shared in the fun.

NORA: Ah, that's the saddest of all.

RANK (*looks searchingly at her*): Hm.

NORA (*after a moment*): Why did you smile?

RANK: No, it was you who laughed.

NORA: No, it was you who smiled, Dr. Rank!

RANK (*getting up*): You're even a bigger tease than I'd thought.

NORA: I'm full of wild ideas today.

RANK: That's obvious.

NORA (*putting both hands on his shoulders*): Dear, dear Dr. Rank, you'll never die for Torvald and me.

RANK: Oh, that loss you'll easily get over. Those who go away are soon forgotten.

NORA (*looks fearfully at him*): You believe that?

RANK: One makes new connections, and then—

NORA: Who makes new connections?

RANK: Both you and Torvald will when I'm gone. I'd say you're well under way already. What was that Mrs. Linde doing here last evening?

NORA: Oh, come—you can't be jealous of poor Kristine?

RANK: Oh yes, I am. She'll be my successor here in the house. When I'm down under, that woman will probably—

NORA: Shh! Not so loud. She's right in there.

RANK: Today as well. So you see.

NORA: Only to sew on my dress. Good gracious, how unreasonable you are. (*Sitting on the sofa.*) Be nice now, Dr. Rank. Tomorrow you'll see how beautifully I'll dance; and you can imagine then that I'm dancing only for you—yes, and of course for Torvald, too—that's understood. (*Takes various items out of the carton.*) Dr. Rank, sit over here and I'll show you something.

RANK (*sitting*): What's that?

NORA: Look here. Look.

RANK: Silk stockings.

NORA: Flesh-colored. Aren't they lovely? Now it's so dark here, but tomorrow—No, no, no, just look at the feet. Oh well, you might as well look at the rest.

RANK: Hm—

NORA: Why do you look so critical? Don't you believe they'll fit?

RANK: I've never had any chance to form an opinion on that.

NORA (*glancing at him a moment*): Shame on you. (*Hits him lightly on the ear with the stockings.*) That's for you. (*Puts them away again.*)

RANK: And what other splendors am I going to see now?

NORA: Not the least bit more, because you've been naughty. (*She hunts a little and rummages among her things.*)

RANK (*after a short silence*): When I sit here together with you like this, completely easy and open, then I don't know—I simply can't imagine—whatever would have become of me if I'd never come into this house.

NORA (*smiling*): Yes, I really think you feel completely at ease with us.

RANK (*more quietly, staring straight ahead*): And then to have to go away from it all—

NORA: Nonsense, you're not going away.

RANK (*his voice unchanged*):—and not even be able to leave some poor show of gratitude behind, scarcely a fleeting regret—no more than a vacant place that anyone can fill.

NORA: And if I asked you now for—No—

RANK: For what?

NORA: For a great proof of your friendship—

RANK: Yes, yes?

NORA: No, I mean—for an exceptionally big favor—

RANK: Would you really, for once, make me so happy?

NORA: Oh, you haven't the vaguest idea what it is.

RANK: All right, then tell me.

NORA: No, but I can't, Dr. Rank—it's all out of reason. It's advice and help, too—and a favor—

RANK: So much the better. I can't fathom what you're hinting at. Just speak out. Don't you trust me?

NORA: Of course. More than anyone else. You're my best and truest friend, I'm sure. That's why I want to talk to you. All right, then, Dr. Rank. There's something you can help me prevent. You know how deeply, how inexpressibly dearly Torvald loves me; he'd never hesitate a second to give up his life for me.

RANK (*leaning close to her*): Nora—do you think he's the only one—

NORA (*with a slight start*): Who—?

RANK: Who'd gladly give up his life for you.

NORA (*heavily*): I see.

RANK: I swore to myself you should know this before I'm gone. I'll never find a better chance. Yes, Nora, now you know. And also you know now that you can trust me beyond anyone else.

NORA (*rising, natural and calm*): Let me by.

RANK (*making room for her, but still sitting*): Nora—

NORA (*in the hall doorway*): Helene, bring the lamp in. (*Goes over to the stove.*) Ah, dear Dr. Rank, that was really mean of you.

RANK (*getting up*): That I've loved you just as deeply as somebody else? Was *that* mean?

NORA: No, but that you came out and told me. That was quite unnecessary—

RANK: What do you mean? Have you known—?

(*The Maid comes in with the lamp, sets it on the table, and goes out again.*)

RANK: Nora—Mrs. Helmer—I'm asking you: Have you known about it?

NORA: Oh, how can I tell what I know or don't know? Really, I don't know what to say—Why did you have to be so clumsy, Dr. Rank! Everything was so good.

RANK: Well, in any case, you now have the knowledge that my body and soul are at your command. So won't you speak out?

NORA (*looking at him*): After that?

RANK: Please, just let me know what it is.

NORA: You can't know anything now.

RANK: I have to. You mustn't punish me like this. Give me the chance to do whatever is humanly possible for you.

NORA: Now there's nothing you can do for me. Besides, actually, I don't need any help. You'll see—it's only my fantasies. That's what it is. Of course! (*Sits in the rocker, looks at him, and smiles.*) What a nice one you are, Dr. Rank. Aren't you a little bit ashamed, now that the lamp is here?

RANK: No, not exactly. But perhaps I'd better go—for good?

NORA: No, you certainly can't do that. You must come here just as you always have. You know Torvald can't do without you.

RANK: Yes, but you?

NORA: You know how much I enjoy it when you're here.

RANK: That's precisely what threw me off. You're a mystery to me. So many times I've felt you'd almost rather be with me than with Helmer.

NORA: Yes—you see, there are some people that one loves most and other people that one would almost prefer being with.

RANK: Yes, there's something to that.

NORA: When I was back home, of course I loved Papa most. But I always thought it was so much fun when I could sneak down to the maids' quarters, because they never tried to improve me, and it was always so amusing, the way they talked to each other.

RANK: Aha, so it's their place that I've filled.

NORA (*jumping up and going to him*): Oh, dear, sweet Dr. Rank, that's not what I meant at all. But you can understand that with Torvald it's just the same as with Papa—

(*The Maid enters from the hall.*)

MAID: Ma'am—please! (*She whispers to Nora and hands her a calling card.*)

NORA (*glancing at the card*): Ah! (*Slips it into her pocket.*)

RANK: Anything wrong?

NORA: No, no, not at all. It's only some—it's my new dress—

RANK: Really? But—there's your dress.

NORA: Oh, that. But this is another one—I ordered it—Torvald mustn't know—

RANK: Ah, now we have the big secret.

NORA: That's right. Just go in with him—he's back in the inner study. Keep him there as long as—

RANK: Don't worry. He won't get away. (*Goes into the study.*)

NORA (*to the Maid*): And he's standing waiting in the kitchen?

MAID: Yes, he came up by the back stairs.

NORA: But didn't you tell him somebody was here?

MAID: Yes, but that didn't do any good.

NORA: He won't leave?

MAID: No, he won't go till he's talked with you, ma'am.

NORA: Let him come in, then—but quietly. Helene, don't breathe a word about this. It's a surprise for my husband.

MAID: Yes, yes, I understand—(*Goes out.*)

NORA: This horror—it's going to happen. No, no, no, it can't happen, it mustn't. (*She goes and bolts Helmer's door. The Maid opens the hall door for Krogstad and shuts it behind him. He is dressed for travel in a fur coat, boots, and a fur cap.*)

NORA (*going toward him*): Talk softly. My husband's home.

KROGSTAD: Well, good for him.

NORA: What do you want?

KROGSTAD: Some information.

NORA: Hurry up, then. What is it?

KROGSTAD: You know, of course, that I got my notice.

NORA: I couldn't prevent it, Mr. Krogstad. I fought for you to the bitter end, but nothing worked.

KROGSTAD: Does your husband's love for you run so thin? He knows everything I can expose you to, and all the same he dares to—

NORA: How can you imagine he knows anything about this?

KROGSTAD: Ah, no—I can't imagine it either, now. It's not at all like my fine Torvald Helmer to have so much guts—

NORA: Mr. Krogstad, I demand respect for my husband!

KROGSTAD: Why, of course—all due respect. But since the lady's keeping it so carefully hidden, may I presume to ask if you're also a bit better informed than yesterday about what you've actually done?

NORA: More than you ever could teach me.

KROGSTAD: Yes, I *am* such an awful lawyer.

NORA: What is it you want from me?

KROGSTAD: Just a glimpse of how you are, Mrs. Helmer. I've been thinking about you all day long. A cashier, a night-court scribbler, a—well, a type like me also has a little of what they call a heart, you know.

NORA: Then show it. Think of my children.

KROGSTAD: Did you or your husband ever think of mine? But never mind. I simply wanted to tell you that you don't need to take this thing too seriously. For the present, I'm not proceeding with any action.

NORA: Oh no, really! Well—I knew that.

KROGSTAD: Everything can be settled in a friendly spirit. It doesn't have to get around town at all; it can stay just among us three.

NORA: My husband must never know anything of this.

KROGSTAD: How can you manage that? Perhaps you can pay me the balance?

NORA: No, not right now.

KROGSTAD: Or you know some way of raising the money in a day or two?

NORA: No way that I'm willing to use.

KROGSTAD: Well, it wouldn't have done you any good, anyway. If you stood in front of me with a fistful of bills, you still couldn't buy your signature back.

NORA: Then tell me what you're going to do with it.

KROGSTAD: I'll just hold onto it—keep it on file. There's no outsider who'll even get wind of it. So if you've been thinking of taking some desperate step—

NORA: I have.

KROGSTAD: Been thinking of running away from home—

NORA: I have!

KROGSTAD: Or even of something worse—

NORA: How could you guess that?

KROGSTAD: You can drop those thoughts.

NORA: How could you guess I was thinking of *that*?

KROGSTAD: Most of us think about *that* at first. I thought about it too, but I discovered I hadn't the courage—

NORA (*lifelessly*): I don't either.

KROGSTAD (*relieved*): That's true, you haven't the courage? You too?

NORA: I don't have it—I don't have it.

KROGSTAD: It would be terribly stupid, anyway. After that first storm at home blows out, why, then—I have here in my pocket a letter for your husband—

NORA: Telling everything?

KROGSTAD: As charitably as possible.

NORA (*quickly*): He mustn't ever get that letter. Tear it up. I'll find some way to get money.

KROGSTAD: Beg pardon, Mrs. Helmer, but I think I just told you—

NORA: Oh, I don't mean the money I owe you. Let me know how much you want from my husband, and I'll manage it.

KROGSTAD: I don't want any money from your husband.

NORA: What do you want, then?

KROGSTAD: I'll tell you what. I want to recoup, Mrs. Helmer; I want to get on in the world—and there's where your husband can help me. For a year and a half I've kept myself clean of anything disreputable—all that time struggling with the worst conditions; but I was satisfied, working my way up step by step. Now I've been written right off, and I'm just not in the mood to come crawling back. I tell you, I want to move on. I want to get back in the bank—in a better position. Your husband can set up a job for me—

NORA: He'll never do that!

KROGSTAD: He'll do it. I know him. He won't dare breathe a word of protest. And once I'm in there together with him, you just wait and see! Inside of a year, I'll be the manager's right-hand man. It'll be Nils Krogstad, not Torvald Helmer, who runs the bank.

NORA: You'll never see the day!

KROGSTAD: Maybe you think you can—

NORA: I have the courage now—for *that*.

KROGSTAD: Oh, you don't scare me. A smart, spoiled lady like you—

NORA: You'll see; you'll see!

KROGSTAD: Under the ice, maybe? Down in the freezing, coal-black water? There, till you float up in the spring, ugly, unrecognizable, with your hair falling out—

NORA: You don't frighten me.

KROGSTAD: Nor do you frighten me. One doesn't do these things, Mrs. Helmer. Besides what good would it be? I'd still have him safe in my pocket.

NORA: Afterwards? When I'm no longer—?

KROGSTAD: Are you forgetting that *I'll* be in control then over your final reputation? (*Nora stands speechless, staring at him.*) Good; now I've warned you. Don't do anything stupid. When Helmer's read my letter, I'll be waiting for his reply. And bear in mind that it's your husband himself who's forced me back to my old ways. I'll never forgive him for that. Good-bye, Mrs. Helmer. (*He goes out through the hall.*)

NORA (*goes to the hall door, opens it a crack, and listens*): He's gone. Didn't leave the letter. Oh no, no, that's impossible too! (*Opening the door more and more.*) What's that? He's standing outside—not going downstairs. He's thinking it over? Maybe he'll—? (*A letter falls in the mailbox; then Krogstad's footsteps are heard, dying away down a flight of stairs. Nora gives a muffled cry and runs over toward the sofa table. A short pause.*) In the mailbox. (*Slips warily over to the hall door.*) It's lying there. Torvald, Torvald—now we're lost!

MRS. LINDE (*entering with the costume from the room, left*): There now, I can't see anything else to mend. Perhaps you'd like to try—

NORA (*in a hoarse whisper*): Kristine, come here.

MRS. LINDE (*tossing the dress on the sofa*): What's wrong? You look upset.

NORA: Come here. See that letter? There! Look—through the glass in the mailbox.

MRS. LINDE: Yes, yes, I see it.

NORA: That letter's from Krogstad—

MRS. LINDE: Nora—it's Krogstad who loaned you the money!

NORA: Yes, and now Torvald will find out everything.

MRS. LINDE: Believe me, Nora, it's best for both of you.

NORA: There's more you don't know. I forged a name.

MRS. LINDE: But for heaven's sake—?

NORA: I only want to tell you that, Kristine, so that you can be my witness.

MRS. LINDE: Witness? Why should I—?

NORA: If I should go out of my mind—it could easily happen—

MRS. LINDE: Nora!

NORA: Or anything else occurred—so I couldn't be present here—

MRS. LINDE: Nora, Nora, you aren't yourself at all!

NORA: And someone should try to take on the whole weight, all of the guilt, you follow me—

MRS. LINDE: Yes, of course, but why do you think—?

NORA: Then you're the witness that it isn't true, Kristine. I'm very much myself; my mind right now is perfectly clear; and I'm telling you: Nobody else has known about this; I alone did everything. Remember that.

MRS. LINDE: I will. But I don't understand all this.

NORA: Oh, how could you ever understand it? It's the miracle now that's going to take place.

MRS. LINDE: The miracle?

NORA: Yes, the miracle. But it's so awful, Kristine. It mustn't take place, not for anything in the world.

MRS. LINDE: I'm going right over and talk with Krogstad.

NORA: Don't go near him; he'll do you some terrible harm!

MRS. LINDE: There was a time once when he'd gladly have done anything for me.

NORA: He?

MRS. LINDE: Where does he live?

NORA: Oh, how do I know? Yes. (*Searches in her pocket.*) Here's his card. But the letter, the letter—!

HELMER (*from the study, knocking on the door*): Nora!

NORA (*with a cry of fear*): Oh! What is it? What do you want?

HELMER: Now, now, don't be so frightened. We're not coming in. You locked the door—are you trying on the dress?

NORA: Yes, I'm trying it. I'll look just beautiful, Torvald.

MRS. LINDE (*who has read the card*): He's living right around the corner.

NORA: Yes, but what's the use? We're lost. The letter's in the box.

MRS. LINDE: And your husband has the key?

NORA: Yes, always.

MRS. LINDE: Krogstad can ask for his letter back unread; he can find some excuse—

NORA: But it's just this time that Torvald usually—

MRS. LINDE: Stall him. Keep him in there. I'll be back as quick as I can. (*She hurries out through the hall entrance.*)

NORA (*goes to Helmer's door, opens it, and peers in*): Torvald!

HELMER (*from the inner study*): Well—does one dare set foot in one's own living room at last? Come on, Rank, now we'll get a look—(*In the doorway.*) But what's this?

NORA: What, Torvald dear?

HELMER: Rank had me expecting some grand masquerade.

RANK (*in the doorway*): That was my impression, but I must have been wrong.

NORA: No one can admire me in my splendor—not till tomorrow.

HELMER: But Nora dear, you look so exhausted. Have you practiced too hard?

NORA: No, I haven't practiced at all yet.

HELMER: You know, it's necessary—

NORA: Oh, it's absolutely necessary, Torvald. But I can't get anywhere without your help. I've forgotten the whole thing completely.

HELMER: Ah, we'll soon take care of that.

NORA: Yes, take care of me, Torvald, please! Promise me that? Oh, I'm so nervous. That big party—You must give up everything this evening for me. No business—don't even touch your pen. Yes? Dear Torvald, promise?

HELMER: It's a promise. Tonight I'm totally at your service—you little helpless thing. Hm—but first there's one thing I want to—(*Goes toward the hall door.*)

NORA: What are you looking for?

HELMER: Just to see if there's any mail.

NORA: No, no, don't do that, Torvald!

HELMER: Now what?

NORA: Torvald, please. There isn't any.

HELMER: Let me look, though. (*Starts out. Nora, at the piano, strikes the first notes of the tarantella. Helmer, at the door, stops.*) Aha!

Cheryl Campbell as Nora in the 1981–1982 Royal Shakespeare Company production of *A Doll House.*

NORA: I can't dance tomorrow if I don't practice with you.

HELMER (*going over to her*): Nora dear, are you really so frightened?

NORA: Yes, so terribly frightened. Let me practice right now; there's still time before dinner. Oh, sit down and play for me, Torvald. Direct me. Teach me, the way you always have.

HELMER: Gladly, if it's what you want. (*Sits at the piano.*)

NORA (*snatches the tambourine up from the box, then a long, varicolored shawl, which she throws around herself, whereupon she springs forward and cries out*): Play for me now! Now I'll dance!

(*Helmer plays and Nora dances. Rank stands behind Helmer at the piano and looks on.*)

HELMER (*as he plays*): Slower. Slow down.

NORA: Can't change it.

HELMER: Not so violent, Nora!

NORA: Has to be just like this.

HELMER (*stopping*): No, no, that won't do at all.

NORA (*laughing and swinging her tambourine*): Isn't that what I told you?

RANK: Let me play for her.

HELMER (*getting up*): Yes, go on. I can teach her more easily then.

(*Rank sits at the piano and plays, Nora dances more and more wildly. Helmer has stationed himself by the stove and repeatedly gives her directions; she seems not to hear them; her hair loosens and falls over her shoulders; she does not notice, but goes on dancing. Mrs. Linde enters.*)

MRS. LINDE (*standing dumbfounded at the door*): Ah—!

NORA (*still dancing*): See what fun, Kristine!

HELMER: But Nora darling, you dance as if your life were at stake.

NORA: And it is.

HELMER: Rank, stop! This is pure madness. Stop it, I say!

(*Rank breaks off playing, and Nora halts abruptly.*)

HELMER (*going over to her*): I never would have believed it. You've forgotten everything I taught you.

NORA (*throwing away the tambourine*): You see for yourself.

HELMER: Well, there's certainly room for instruction here.

NORA: Yes, you see how important it is. You've got to teach me to the very last minute. Promise me that, Torvald?

HELMER: You can bet on it.

NORA: You mustn't, either today or tomorrow, think about anything else but me; you mustn't open any letters—or the mailbox—

HELMER: Ah, it's still the fear of that man—

NORA: Oh yes, yes, that too.

HELMER: Nora, it's written all over you—there's already a letter from him out there.

NORA: I don't know. I guess so. But you mustn't read such things now; there mustn't be anything ugly between us before it's all over.

RANK (*quietly to Helmer*): You shouldn't deny her.

HELMER (*putting his arm around her*): The child can have her way. But tomorrow night, after you've danced—

NORA: Then you'll be free.

MAID (*in the doorway, right*): Ma'am, dinner is served.

NORA: We'll be wanting champagne, Helene.

MAID: Very good, ma'am. (*Goes out.*)

HELMER: So—a regular banquet, hm?

NORA: Yes, a banquet—champagne till daybreak! (*Calling out.*) And some macaroons, Helene. Heaps of them—just this once.

HELMER (*taking her hands*): Now, now, now—no hysterics. Be my own little lark again.

NORA: Oh, I will soon enough. But go on in—and you, Dr. Rank. Kristine, help me put up my hair.

RANK (*whispering, as they go*): There's nothing wrong—really wrong, is there?

HELMER: Oh, of course not. It's nothing more than this childish anxiety I was telling you about. (*They go out, right.*)

NORA: Well?

MRS. LINDE: Left town.

NORA: I could see by your face.

MRS. LINDE: He'll be home tomorrow evening. I wrote him a note.

NORA: You shouldn't have. Don't try to stop anything now. After all, it's a wonderful joy, this waiting here for the miracle.

MRS. LINDE: What is it you're waiting for?

NORA: Oh, you can't understand that. Go in to them; I'll be along in a moment.

(*Mrs. Linde goes into the dining room. Nora stands a short while as if composing herself; then she looks at her watch.*)

NORA: Five. Seven hours to midnight. Twenty-four hours to the midnight after, and then the tarantella's done. Seven and twenty-four? Thirty-one hours to live.

HELMER (*in the doorway, right*): What's become of the little lark?

NORA (*going toward him with open arms*): Here's your lark!

ACT III

(*Same scene. The table, with chairs around it, has been moved to the center of the room. A lamp on the table is lit. The hall door stands open. Dance music drifts down from the floor above. Mrs. Linde sits at the table, absently paging through a book, trying to read, but apparently unable to focus her thoughts. Once or twice she pauses, tensely listening for a sound at the outer entrance.*)

MRS. LINDE (*glancing at her watch*): Not yet—and there's hardly any time left. If only he's not—(*Listening again.*) Ah, there it is. (*She goes out in the hall and cautiously opens the outer door. Quiet footsteps are heard on the stairs. She whispers.*) Come in. Nobody's here.

KROGSTAD (*in the doorway*): I found a note from you at home. What's back of all this?

MRS. LINDE: I just *had* to talk to you.

KROGSTAD: Oh? And it just *had* to be here in this house?

MRS. LINDE: At my place it was impossible; my room hasn't a private entrance. Come in, we're all alone. The maid's asleep, and the Helmers are at the dance upstairs.

KROGSTAD (*entering the room*): Well, well, the Helmers are dancing tonight? Really?

MRS. LINDE: Yes, why not?

KROGSTAD: How true—why not?

MRS. LINDE: All right, Krogstad, let's talk.

KROGSTAD: Do we two have anything more to talk about?

MRS. LINDE: We have a great deal to talk about.

KROGSTAD: I wouldn't have thought so.

MRS. LINDE: No, because you've never understood me, really.

KROGSTAD: Was there anything more to understand—except what's all too common in life? A calculating woman throws over a man the moment a better catch comes by.

MRS. LINDE: You think I'm so thoroughly calculating? You think I broke it off lightly?

KROGSTAD: Didn't you?

MRS. LINDE: Nils—is that what you really thought?

KROGSTAD: If you cared, then why did you write me the way you did?

MRS. LINDE: What else could I do? If I had to break off with you, then it was my job as well to root out everything you felt for me.

KROGSTAD (*wringing his hands*): So that was it. And this—all this, simply for money!

MRS. LINDE: Don't forget I had a helpless mother and two small brothers. We couldn't wait for you, Nils; you had such a long road ahead of you then.

KROGSTAD: That may be; but you still hadn't the right to abandon me for somebody else's sake.

MRS. LINDE: Yes—I don't know. So many, many times I've asked myself if I did have that right.

KROGSTAD (*more softly*): When I lost you, it was as if all the solid ground dissolved from under my feet. Look at me; I'm a half-drowned man now, hanging onto a wreck.

MRS. LINDE: Help may be near.

KROGSTAD: It was near—but then you came and blocked it off.

MRS. LINDE: Without my knowing it, Nils. Today for the first time I learned that it's you I'm replacing at the bank.

KROGSTAD: All right—I believe you. But now that you know, will you step aside?

MRS. LINDE: No, because that wouldn't benefit you in the slightest.

KROGSTAD: Not "benefit" me, hm! I'd step aside anyway.

MRS. LINDE: I've learned to be realistic. Life and hard, bitter necessity have taught me that.

KROGSTAD: And life's taught me never to trust fine phrases.

MRS. LINDE: Then life's taught you a very sound thing. But you do have to trust in actions, don't you?

KROGSTAD: What does that mean?

MRS. LINDE: You said you were hanging on like a half-drowned man to a wreck.

KROGSTAD: I've good reason to say that.

MRS. LINDE: I'm also like a half-drowned woman on a wreck. No one to suffer with; no one to care for.

KROGSTAD: You made your choice.

MRS. LINDE: There wasn't any choice then.

KROGSTAD: So—what of it?

MRS. LINDE: Nils, if only we two shipwrecked people could reach across to each other.

KROGSTAD: What are you saying?

MRS. LINDE: Two on one wreck are at least better off than each on his own.

KROGSTAD: Kristine!

MRS. LINDE: Why do you think I came into town?

KROGSTAD: Did you really have some thought of me?

MRS. LINDE: I have to work to go on living. All my born days, as long as I can remember, I've worked, and it's been my best and my only joy. But now I'm completely alone in the world; it frightens me to be so empty and lost. To work for yourself—there's no joy in that. Nils, give me something—someone to work for.

KROGSTAD: I don't believe all this. It's just some hysterical feminine urge to go out and make a noble sacrifice.

MRS. LINDE: Have you ever found me to be hysterical?

KROGSTAD: Can you honestly mean this? Tell me—do you know everything about my past?

MRS. LINDE: Yes.

KROGSTAD: And you know what they think I'm worth around here.

MRS. LINDE: From what you were saying before, it would seem that with me you could have been another person.

KROGSTAD: I'm positive of that.

MRS. LINDE: Couldn't it happen still?

KROGSTAD: Kristine—you're saying this in all seriousness? Yes, you are! I can see it in you. And do you really have the courage, then—?

MRS. LINDE: I need to have someone to care for, and your children need a mother. We both need each other. Nils, I have faith that you're good at heart—I'll risk everything together with you.

KROGSTAD (*gripping her hands*): Kristine, thank you, thank you—Now I know I can win back a place in their eyes. Yes—but I forgot—

MRS. LINDE (*listening*): Shh! The tarantella. Go now! Go on!

KROGSTAD: Why? What is it?

MRS. LINDE: Hear the dance up there? When that's over, they'll be coming down.

KROGSTAD: Oh, then I'll go. But—it's all pointless. Of course, you don't know the move I made against the Helmers.

MRS. LINDE: Yes, Nils, I know.

KROGSTAD: And all the same, you have the courage to—?

MRS. LINDE: I know how far despair can drive a man like you.

KROGSTAD: Oh, if I only could take it all back.

MRS. LINDE: You easily could—your letter's still lying in the mailbox.

KROGSTAD: Are you sure of that?

MRS. LINDE: Positive. But—

KROGSTAD (*looks at her searchingly*): Is that the meaning of it, then? You'll save your friend at any price. Tell me straight out. Is that it?

MRS. LINDE: Nils—anyone who's sold herself for somebody else once isn't going to do it again.

KROGSTAD: I'll demand my letter back.

MRS. LINDE: No, no.

KROGSTAD: Yes, of course. I'll stay here till Helmer comes down; I'll tell him to give me my letter again—that it only involves my dismissal—that he shouldn't read it—

MRS. LINDE: No, Nils, don't call the letter back.

KROGSTAD: But wasn't that exactly why you wrote me to come here?

MRS. LINDE: Yes, in that first panic. But it's been a whole day and night since then, and in that time I've seen such incredible things in this house. Helmer's got to learn everything; this dreadful secret has to be aired; those two have to come to a full understanding; all these lies and evasions can't go on.

KROGSTAD: Well, then, if you want to chance it. But at least there's one thing I can do, and do right away—

MRS. LINDE (*listening*): Go now, go, quick! The dance is over. We're not safe another second.

KROGSTAD: I'll wait for you downstairs.

MRS. LINDE: Yes, please do; take me home.

KROGSTAD: I can't believe it; I've never been so happy. (*He leaves by way of the outer door; the door between the room and the hall stays open.*)

MRS. LINDE (*straightening up a bit and getting together her street clothes*): How different now! How different! Someone to work for, to live for—a home to build. Well, it is worth the try! Oh, if they'd only come! (*Listening.*) Ah, there they are. Bundle up. (*She picks up her hat and coat. Nora's and Helmer's voices can be heard outside; a key turns in the lock, and Helmer brings Nora into the hall almost by force. She is wearing the Italian costume with a large black shawl about her; he has on evening dress, with a black domino open over it.*)

NORA (*struggling in the doorway*): No, no, no, not inside! I'm going up again. I don't want to leave so soon.

HELMER: But Nora dear—

NORA: Oh, I beg you, please, Torvald. From the bottom of my heart, *please*—only an hour more!

HELMER: Not a single minute, Nora darling. You know our agreement. Come on, in we go; you'll catch cold out here. (*In spite of her resistance, he gently draws her into the room.*)

MRS. LINDE: Good evening.

NORA: Kristine!

HELMER: Why, Mrs. Linde—are you here so late?

MRS. LINDE: Yes, I'm sorry, but I did want to see Nora in costume.

NORA: Have you been sitting here, waiting for me?

MRS. LINDE: Yes. I didn't come early enough; you were all upstairs; and then I thought I really couldn't leave without seeing you.

HELMER (*removing Nora's shawl*): Yes, take a good look. She's worth looking at, I can tell you that, Mrs. Linde. Isn't she lovely?

MRS. LINDE: Yes, I should say—

HELMER: A dream of loveliness, isn't she? That's what everyone thought at the party, too. But she's horribly stubborn—this sweet little thing. What's to be done with her? Can you imagine, I almost had to use force to pry her away.

NORA: Oh, Torvald, you're going to regret you didn't indulge me, even for just a half hour more.

HELMER: There, you see. She danced her tarantella and got a tumultuous hand—which was well earned, although the performance may have been a bit too naturalistic—I mean it rather overstepped the proprieties of art. But never mind—what's important is, she made a success, an overwhelming success. You think I could let her stay on after that and spoil the effect? Oh no; I took my lovely little Capri girl—my capricious little Capri girl, I should say—took her under my arm; one quick tour of the ballroom, a curtsy to every side, and then—as they say in novels—the beautiful vision disappeared. An exit should always be effective, Mrs. Linde, but that's what I can't get Nora to grasp. Phew, It's hot in here. (*Flings the domino on a chair and opens the door to his room.*) Why's it dark in here? Oh yes, of course. Excuse me. (*He goes in and lights a couple of candles.*)

NORA (*in a sharp, breathless whisper*): So?

MRS. LINDE (*quietly*): I talked with him.

NORA: And—?

MRS. LINDE: Nora—you must tell your husband everything.

NORA (*dully*): I knew it.

MRS. LINDE: You've got nothing to fear from Krogstad, but you have to speak out.

NORA: I won't tell.

MRS. LINDE: Then the letter will.

NORA: Thanks, Kristine. I know now what's to be done. Shh!

HELMER (*reentering*): Well, then, Mrs. Linde—have you admired her?

MRS. LINDE: Yes, and now I'll say good night.

HELMER: Oh, come, so soon? Is this yours, this knitting?

MRS. LINDE: Yes, thanks. I nearly forgot it.

HELMER: Do you knit, then?

MRS. LINDE: Oh yes.

HELMER: You know what? You should embroider instead.

MRS. LINDE: Really? Why?

HELMER: Yes, because it's a lot prettier. See here, one holds the embroidery so, in the left hand, and then one guides the needle with the right—so—in an easy, sweeping curve—right?

MRS. LINDE: Yes, I guess that's—

HELMER: But, on the other hand, knitting—it can never be anything but ugly. Look, see here, the arms tucked in, the knitting needles going up and down—there's something Chinese about it. Ah, that was really a glorious champagne they served.

MRS. LINDE: Yes, good night, Nora, and don't be stubborn anymore.

HELMER: Well put, Mrs. Linde!

MRS. LINDE: Good night, Mr. Helmer.

HELMER (*accompanying her to the door*): Good night, good night. I hope you get home all right. I'd be very happy to—but you don't have far to go. Good night, good night. (*She leaves. He shuts the door after her and returns.*) There, now, at last we got her out the door. She's a deadly bore, that creature.

NORA: Aren't you pretty tired, Torvald?

HELMER: No, not a bit.

NORA: You're not sleepy?

HELMER: Not at all. On the contrary, I'm feeling quite exhilarated. But you? Yes, you really look tired and sleepy.

NORA: Yes, I'm very tired. Soon now I'll sleep.

HELMER: See! You see! I was right all along that we shouldn't stay longer.

NORA: Whatever you do is always right.

HELMER (*kissing her brow*): Now my little lark talks sense. Say, did you notice what a time Rank was having tonight?

NORA: Oh, was he? I didn't get to speak with him.

HELMER: I scarcely did either, but it's a long time since I've seen him in such high spirits. (*Gazes at her a moment, then comes nearer her.*) Hm—it's marvelous, though, to be back home again—to be completely alone with you. Oh, you bewitchingly lovely young woman!

NORA: Torvald, don't look at me like that!

HELMER: Can't I look at my richest treasure? At all that beauty that's mine, mine alone—completely and utterly.

NORA (*moving around to the other side of the table*): You mustn't talk to me that way tonight.

HELMER (*following her*): The tarantella is still in your blood. I can see—and it makes you even more enticing. Listen. The guests are beginning to go. (*Dropping his voice.*) Nora—it'll soon be quiet through this whole house.

NORA: Yes, I hope so.

HELMER: You do, don't you, my love? Do you realize—when I'm out at a party like this with you—do you know why I talk to you so little, and keep such a distance away; just send you a stolen look now and then—you know why I do it? It's because I'm imagining then that you're my secret darling, my secret young bride-to-be, and that no one suspects there's anything between us.

NORA: Yes, yes; oh, yes, I know you're always thinking of me.

HELMER: And then when we leave and I place the shawl over those fine young rounded shoulders—over that wonderful curving neck—then I pretend that you're my young bride, that we're just coming from the wedding, that for the first time I'm bringing you into my house—that for the first time I'm alone with you—completely alone with you, your trembling young beauty! All this evening I've longed for nothing but you. When I saw you turn and sway in the tarantella—my blood was pounding till I couldn't stand it—that's why I brought you down here so early—

NORA: Go away, Torvald! Leave me alone. I don't want all this.

HELMER: What do you mean? Nora, you're teasing me. You will, won't you? Aren't I your husband—?

(*A knock at the outside door.*)

NORA (*startled*): What's that?

HELMER (*going toward the hall*): Who is it?

RANK (*outside*): It's me. May I come in a moment?

HELMER (*with quiet irritation*): Oh, what does he want now? (*Aloud.*) Hold on. (*Goes and opens the door.*) Oh, how nice that you didn't just pass us by!

RANK: I thought I heard your voice, and then I wanted so badly to have a look in. (*Lightly glancing about.*) Ah, me, these old familiar haunts. You have it snug and cozy in here, you two.

HELMER: You seemed to be having it pretty cozy upstairs, too.

RANK: Absolutely. Why shouldn't I? Why not take in everything in life? As much as you can, anyway, and as long as you can. The wine was superb—

HELMER: The champagne especially.

RANK: You noticed that too? It's amazing how much I could guzzle down.

NORA: Torvald also drank a lot of champagne this evening.

RANK: Oh?

NORA: Yes, and that always makes him so entertaining.

RANK: Well, why shouldn't one have a pleasant evening after a well-spent day?

HELMER: Well spent? I'm afraid I can't claim that.

RANK (*slapping him on the back*): But I can, you see!

NORA: Dr. Rank, you must have done some scientific research today.

RANK: Quite so.

HELMER: Come now—little Nora talking about scientific research!

NORA: And can I congratulate you on the results?

RANK: Indeed you may.

NORA: Then they were good?

RANK: The best possible for both doctor and patient—certainty.

NORA (*quickly and searchingly*): Certainty?

RANK: Complete certainty. So don't I owe myself a gay evening afterwards?

NORA: Yes, you're right, Dr. Rank.

HELMER: I'm with you—just so long as you don't have to suffer for it in the morning.

RANK: Well, one never gets something for nothing in life.

NORA: Dr. Rank—are you very fond of masquerade parties?

RANK: Yes, if there's a good array of odd disguises—

NORA: Tell me, what should we two go as at the next masquerade?

HELMER: You little featherhead—already thinking of the next!

RANK: We two? I'll tell you what: You must go as Charmed Life—

HELMER: Yes, but find a costume for that!

RANK: Your wife can appear just as she looks every day.

HELMER: That was nicely put. But don't you know what you're going to be?

RANK: Yes, Helmer, I've made up my mind.

HELMER: Well?

RANK: At the next masquerade I'm going to be invisible.

HELMER: That's a funny idea.

RANK: They say there's a hat—black, huge—have you never heard of the hat that makes you invisible? You put it on, and then no one on earth can see you.

HELMER (*suppressing a smile*): Ah, of course.

RANK: But I'm quite forgetting what I came for. Helmer, give me a cigar, one of the dark Havanas.

HELMER: With the greatest pleasure. (*Holds out his case.*)

RANK: Thanks. (*Takes one and cuts off the tip.*)

NORA (*striking a match*): Let me give you a light.

RANK: Thank you. (*She holds the match for him; he lights the cigar.*) And now good-bye.

HELMER: Good-bye, good-bye, old friend.

NORA: Sleep well, Doctor.

RANK: Thanks for that wish.

NORA: Wish me the same.

RANK: You? All right, if you like—Sleep well. And thanks for the light. (*He nods to them both and leaves.*)

HELMER (*his voice subdued*): He's been drinking heavily.

NORA (*absently*): Could be. (*Helmer takes his keys from his pocket and goes out in the hall.*) Torvald—what are you after?

HELMER: Got to empty the mailbox; it's nearly full. There won't be room for the morning papers.

NORA: Are you working tonight?

HELMER: You know I'm not. Why—what's this? Someone's been at the lock.

NORA: At the lock—?

HELMER: Yes, I'm positive. What do you suppose—? I can't imagine one of the maids—? Here's a broken hairpin. Nora, it's yours—

NORA (*quickly*): Then it must be the children—

HELMER: You'd better break them of that. Hm, hm—well, opened it after all. (*Takes the contents out and calls into the kitchen.*) Helene! Helene, would you put out the lamp in the hall. (*He returns to the room, shutting the hall door, then displays the handful of mail.*) Look how it's piled up. (*Sorting through them.*) Now what's this?

NORA (*at the window*): The letter! Oh, Torvald, no!

HELMER: Two calling cards—from Rank.

NORA: From Dr. Rank?

HELMER (*examining them*): "Dr. Rank, Consulting Physician." They were on top. He must have dropped them in as he left.

NORA: Is there anything on them?

HELMER: There's a black cross over the name. See? That's a gruesome notion. He could almost be announcing his own death.

NORA: That's just what he's doing.

HELMER: What! You've heard something? Something he's told you?

NORA: Yes. That when those cards came, he'd be taking his leave of us. He'll shut himself in now and die.

HELMER: Ah, my poor friend! Of course I knew he wouldn't be here much longer. But so soon—And then to hide himself away like a wounded animal.

NORA: If it has to happen, then it's best it happens in silence—don't you think so, Torvald?

HELMER (*pacing up and down*): He's grown right into our lives. I simply can't imagine him gone. He with his suffering and loneliness—like a dark cloud setting off our sunlit happiness. Well, maybe it's best this way. For him, at least. (*Standing still.*) And maybe for us too, Nora. Now we're thrown back on each other, completely. (*Embracing her.*) Oh you, my darling wife, how can I hold you close enough? You know what, Nora—time and again I've wished you were in some terrible danger, just so I could stake my life and soul and everything, for your sake.

NORA (*tearing herself away, her voice firm and decisive*): Now you must read your mail, Torvald.

HELMER: No, no, not tonight. I want to stay with you, dearest.

NORA: With a dying friend on your mind?

HELMER: You're right. We've both had a shock. There's ugliness between us—these thoughts of death and corruption. We'll have to get free of them first. Until then—we'll stay apart.

NORA (*clinging about his neck*): Torvald—good night! Good night!

HELMER (*kissing her on the cheek*): Good night, little songbird. Sleep well, Nora. I'll be reading my mail now. (*He takes the letters into his room and shuts the door after him.*)

NORA (*with bewildered glances, groping about, seizing Helmer's domino, throwing it around her, and speaking in short, hoarse, broken whispers*): Never see him again. Never, never. (*Putting her shawl over her head.*) Never see the children either—them, too. Never, never. Oh, the freezing black water! The depths—down—Oh, I wish it were over—He has it now; he's reading it—now. Oh no, no, not yet. Torvald, good-bye, you and the children— (*She starts for the hall; as she does, Helmer throws open his door and stands with an open letter in his hand.*)

HELMER: Nora!

NORA (*screams*): Oh—!

HELMER: What is this? You know what's in this letter?

NORA: Yes, I know. Let me go! Let me out!

HELMER (*holding her back*): Where are you going?

NORA (*struggling to break loose*): You can't save me, Torvald!

HELMER (*slumping back*): True! Then it's true what he writes? How horrible! No, no, it's impossible—it can't be true.

NORA: It *is* true. I've loved you more than all this world.

HELMER: Ah, none of your slippery tricks.

NORA (*taking one step toward him*): Torvald—!

HELMER: What *is* this you've blundered into!

NORA: Just let me loose. You're not going to suffer for my sake. You're not going to take on my guilt.

HELMER: No more playacting. (*Locks the hall door.*) You stay right here and give me a reckoning. You understand what you've done? Answer! You understand?

NORA (*looking squarely at him, her face hardening*): Yes. I'm beginning to understand everything now.

HELMER (*striding about*): Oh, what an awful awakening! In all these eight years—she who was my pride and joy—a hypocrite, a liar—worse, worse—a criminal! How infinitely disgusting it all is! The shame! (*Nora says nothing and goes on looking straight at him. He stops in front of her.*) I should have suspected something of the kind. I should have known. All your father's flimsy values—Be still! All your father's flimsy values have come out in you. No religion, no morals, no sense of duty—Oh, how I'm punished for letting him off! I did it for your sake, and you repay me like this.

NORA: Yes, like this.

HELMER: Now you've wrecked all my happiness—ruined my whole future. Oh, it's awful to think of. I'm in a cheap little grafter's hands; he can do anything he wants with me, ask for anything, play with me like a puppet—and I can't breathe a word. I'll be swept down miserably into the depths on account of a featherbrained woman.

NORA: When I'm gone from this world, you'll be free.

HELMER: Oh, quit posing. Your father had a mess of those speeches too. What good would that ever do me if you were gone from this world, as you say? Not the slightest. He can still make the whole thing known; and if he does, I could be falsely suspected as your accomplice. They might even think that I was behind it—that I put you up to it. And all that I can thank you for—you that I've coddled the whole of our marriage. Can you see now what you've done to me?

NORA (*icily calm*): Yes.

HELMER: It's so incredible, I just can't grasp it. But we'll have to patch up whatever we can. Take off the shawl. I said, take it off! I've got to appease him somehow or other. The thing has to be hushed up at any cost. And as for you and me, it's got to seem like everything between us is just as it was—to the outside world, that is. You'll go right on living in this house, of course. But you can't be allowed to bring up the children; I don't dare trust you with them—Oh, to have to say this to someone I've loved so much! Well, that's done with. From now on happiness doesn't matter; all that matters is saving the bits and pieces, the appearance— (*The doorbell rings. Helmer starts.*) What's that? And so late. Maybe the worst—? You think he'd—? Hide, Nora! Say you're sick. (*Nora remains standing motionless. Helmer goes and opens the door.*)

MAID (*half dressed, in the hall*): A letter for Mrs. Helmer.

HELMER: I'll take it. (*Snatches the letter and shuts the door.*) Yes, it's from him. You don't get it; I'm reading it myself.

NORA: Then read it.

HELMER (*by the lamp*): I hardly dare. We may be ruined, you and I. But—I've got to know. (*Rips open the letter, skims through a few lines, glances at an enclosure, then cries out joyfully.*) Nora! (*Nora looks inquiringly at him.*) Nora! Wait—better check it again—Yes, yes, it's true. I'm saved. Nora, I'm saved!

NORA: And I?

HELMER: You too, of course. We're both saved, both of us. Look. He's sent back your note. He says he's sorry and ashamed—that a happy development in his life—oh, who cares what he says! Nora, we're saved! No one can hurt you. Oh, Nora, Nora—but first, this ugliness all has to go. Let me see—(*Takes a look at the note.*) No, I don't want to see it; I want the whole thing to fade like a dream. (*Tears the note and both letters to pieces, throws them into the stove and watches them burn.*) There—now there's nothing left—He wrote that since Christmas Eve you—Oh, they must have been three terrible days for you, Nora.

NORA: I fought a hard fight.

HELMER: And suffered pain and saw no escape but—No, we're not going to dwell on anything unpleasant. We'll just be grateful and keep on repeating: It's over now, it's over! You hear me, Nora? You don't seem to realize—it's over. What's it mean—that frozen look? Oh, poor little Nora, I understand. You can't believe I've forgiven you. But I have, Nora; I swear I have. I know that what you did, you did out of love for me.

NORA: That's true.

HELMER: You loved me the way a wife ought to love her husband. It's simply the means that you couldn't judge. But you think I love you any the less for not knowing how to handle your affairs? No, no—just lean on me; I'll guide you and teach you. I wouldn't be a man if this feminine helplessness didn't make you twice as attractive to me. You mustn't mind those sharp words I said—that was all in the first confusion of thinking my world had collapsed. I've forgiven you, Nora; I swear I've forgiven you.

NORA: My thanks for your forgiveness. (*She goes out through the door, right.*)

HELMER: No, wait—(*Peers in.*) What are you doing in there?

NORA (*inside*): Getting out of my costume.

HELMER (*by the open door*): Yes, do that. Try to calm yourself and collect your thoughts again, my frightened little songbird. You can rest easy now; I've got wide wings to shelter you with. (*Walking about close by the door.*) How snug and nice our home is, Nora. You're safe here; I'll keep you like a hunted dove I've rescued out of a hawk's claws. I'll bring peace to your poor, shuddering heart. Gradually it'll happen, Nora; you'll see. Tomorrow all this will look different to you; then everything will be as it was. I won't have to go on repeating I forgive you; you'll feel it for yourself. How can you imagine I'd ever conceivably want

to disown you—or even blame you in any way? Ah, you don't know a man's heart, Nora. For a man there's something indescribably sweet and satisfying in knowing he's forgiven his wife—and forgiven her out of a full and open heart. It's as if she belongs to him in two ways now: In a sense he's given her fresh into the world again, and she's become his wife and his child as well. From now on that's what you'll be to me—you little, bewildered, helpless thing. Don't be afraid of anything, Nora; just open your heart to me, and I'll be conscience and will to you both—(*Nora enters in her regular clothes.*) What's this? Not in bed? You've changed your dress?

NORA: Yes, Torvald, I've changed my dress.

HELMER: But why now, so late?

NORA: Tonight I'm not sleeping.

HELMER: But Nora dear—

NORA (*looking at her watch*): It's still not so very late. Sit down, Torvald; we have a lot to talk over. (*She sits at one side of the table.*)

HELMER: Nora—what is this? That hard expression—

NORA: Sit down. This'll take some time. I have a lot to say.

HELMER (*sitting at the table directly opposite her*): You worry me, Nora. And I don't understand you.

NORA: No, that's exactly it. You don't understand me. And I've never understood you either—until tonight. No, don't interrupt. You can just listen to what I say. We're closing out accounts, Torvald.

HELMER: How do you mean that?

NORA (*after a short pause*): Doesn't anything strike you about our sitting here like this?

HELMER: What's that?

NORA: We've been married now eight years. Doesn't it occur to you that this is the first time we two, you and I, man and wife, have ever talked seriously together?

HELMER: What do you mean—seriously?

NORA: In eight whole years—longer even—right from our first acquaintance, we've never exchanged a serious word on any serious thing.

HELMER: You mean I should constantly go and involve you in problems you couldn't possibly help me with?

NORA: I'm not talking of problems. I'm saying that we've never sat down seriously together and tried to get to the bottom of anything.

HELMER: But dearest, what good would that ever do you?

NORA: That's the point right there: You've never understood me. I've been wronged greatly, Torvald—first by Papa, and then by you.

HELMER: What! By us—the two people who've loved you more than anyone else?

NORA (*shaking her head*): You never loved me. You've thought it fun to be in love with me, that's all.

HELMER: Nora, what a thing to say!

NORA: Yes, it's true now, Torvald. When I lived at home with Papa, he told me all his opinions, so I had the same ones too; or if they were different I hid them, since he wouldn't have cared for that. He used to call me his doll-child, and he played with me the way I played with my dolls. Then I came into your house—

Nora and Torvald (Stephen Moore).

HELMER: How can you speak of our marriage like that?

NORA (*unperturbed*): I mean, then I went from Papa's hands into yours. You arranged everything to your own taste, and so I got the same taste as you—or I pretended to; I can't remember. I guess a little of both, first one, then the other. Now when I look back, it seems as if I'd lived here like a beggar—just from hand to mouth. I've lived by doing tricks for you, Torvald. But that's the way you wanted it. It's a great sin what you and Papa did to me. You're to blame that nothing's become of me.

HELMER: Nora, how unfair and ungrateful you are! Haven't you been happy here?

NORA: No, never. I thought so—but I never have.

HELMER: Not—not happy!

NORA: No, only lighthearted. And you've always been so kind to me. But our home's been nothing but a playpen. I've been your doll-wife here, just as at home I was Papa's doll-child. And in turn the children have been my dolls. I thought it was fun when you played with me, just as they thought it fun when I played with them. That's been our marriage, Torvald.

HELMER: There's some truth in what you're saying—under all the raving exaggeration. But it'll all be different after this. Playtime's over; now for the schooling.

NORA: Whose schooling—mine or the children's?

HELMER: Both yours and the children's, dearest.

NORA: Oh, Torvald, you're not the man to teach me to be a good wife to you.

HELMER: And you can say that?

NORA: And I—how am I equipped to bring up children?

HELMER: Nora!

NORA: Didn't you say a moment ago that that was no job to trust me with?

HELMER: In a flare of temper! Why fasten on that?

NORA: Yes, but you were so very right. I'm not up to the job. There's another job I have to do first. I have to try to educate myself. You can't help me with that. I've got to do it alone. And that's why I'm leaving you now.

HELMER (*jumping up*): What's that?

NORA: I have to stand completely alone, if I'm ever going to discover myself and the world out there. So I can't go on living with you.

HELMER: Nora, Nora!

NORA: I want to leave right away. Kristine should put me up for the night—

HELMER: You're insane! You've no right! I forbid you!

NORA: From here on, there's no use forbidding me anything. I'll take with me whatever is mine. I don't want a thing from you, either now or later.

HELMER: What kind of madness is this!

NORA: Tomorrow I'm going home—I mean, home where I came from. It'll be easier up there to find something to do.

HELMER: Oh, you blind, incompetent child!

NORA: I must learn to be competent, Torvald.

HELMER: Abandon your home, your husband, your children! And you're not even thinking what people will say.

NORA: I can't be concerned about that. I only know how essential this is.

HELMER: Oh, it's outrageous. So you'll run out like this on your most sacred vows.

NORA: What do you think are my most sacred vows?

HELMER: And I have to tell you that! Aren't they your duties to your husband and children?

NORA: I have other duties equally sacred.

HELMER: That isn't true. What duties are they?

NORA: Duties to myself.

HELMER: Before all else, you're a wife and a mother.

NORA: I don't believe in that anymore. I believe that before all else, I'm a human being, no less than you—or anyway, I ought to try to become one. I know the majority thinks you're right, Torvald, and plenty of books agree with you, too. But I can't go on believing what the majority says, or what's written in books. I have to think over these things myself and try to understand them.

HELMER: Why can't you understand your place in your own home? On a point like that, isn't there one everlasting guide you can turn to? Where's your religion?

NORA: Oh, Torvald, I'm really not sure what religion is.

HELMER: What—?

NORA: I only know what the minister said when I was confirmed. He told me religion was this thing and that. When I get clear and away by myself, I'll go into that problem too. I'll see if what the minister said was right, or, in any case, if it's right for me.

HELMER: A young woman your age shouldn't talk like that. If religion can't move you, I can try to rouse your conscience. You do have some moral feeling? Or, tell me—has that gone too?

NORA: It's not easy to answer that, Torvald. I simply don't know. I'm all confused about these things. I just know I see them so differently from you. I find out for one thing, that the law's not at all what I'd thought—but I can't get it through my head that the law is fair. A woman hasn't a right to protect her dying father or save her husband's life! I can't believe that.

HELMER: You talk like a child. You don't know anything of the world you live in.

NORA: No, I don't. But now I'll begin to learn for myself. I'll try to discover who's right, the world or I.

HELMER: Nora, you're sick; you've got a fever. I almost think you're out of your head.

NORA: I've never felt more clearheaded and sure in my life.

Janet McTeer as Nora Helmer in Anthony Page's production of *A Doll House* at the Belasco Theater on Broadway, 1997. McTeer's interpretation of the role electrified audiences, who, according to Ben Brantley, found "previously hidden nuances in Ibsen's landmark work."

HELMER: And—clearheaded and sure—you're leaving your husband and children?

NORA: Yes.

HELMER: Then there's only one possible reason.

NORA: What?

HELMER: You no longer love me.

NORA: No. That's exactly it.

HELMER: Nora! You can't be serious!

NORA: Oh, this is so hard, Torvald—you've been so kind to me always. But I can't help it. I don't love you anymore.

HELMER (*struggling for composure*): Are you also clearheaded and sure about that?

NORA: Yes, completely. That's why I can't go on staying here.

HELMER: Can you tell me what I did to lose your love?

NORA: Yes, I can tell you. It was this evening when the miraculous thing didn't come—then I knew you weren't the man I'd imagined.

HELMER: Be more explicit; I don't follow you.

NORA: I've waited now so patiently eight long years—for, my Lord, I know miracles don't come every day. Then this crisis broke over me, and such a certainty filled me: *Now* the miraculous event would occur. While Krogstad's letter was lying out there, I never for an instant dreamed that you could give in to his terms. I was so utterly sure you'd say to him: Go on, tell your tale to the whole wide world. And when he'd done that—

HELMER: Yes, what then? When I'd delivered my own wife into shame and disgrace—!

NORA: When he'd done that, I was so utterly sure that you'd step forward, take the blame on yourself and say: I am the guilty one.

HELMER: Nora—!

NORA: You're thinking I'd never accept such a sacrifice from you? No, of course not. But what good would my protests be against you? That was the miracle I was waiting for, in terror and hope. And to stave that off, I would have taken my life.

HELMER: I'd gladly work for you day and night, Nora—and take on pain and deprivation. But there's no one who gives up honor for love.

NORA: Millions of women have done just that.

HELMER: Oh, you think and talk like a silly child.

NORA: Perhaps. But you neither think nor talk like the man I could join myself to. When your big fright was over—and it wasn't from any threat against me, only for what might damage you—when all the danger was past, for you it was just as if nothing had happened. I was exactly the same, your little lark, your doll, that you'd have to handle with double care now that I'd turned out so brittle and frail. (*Gets up.*) Torvald—in that instant it dawned on me that for eight years I've been living here with a stranger, and that I'd even conceived three children—oh, I can't stand the thought of it! I could tear myself to bits.

HELMER (*heavily*): I see. There's a gulf that's opened between us—that's clear. Oh, but Nora, can't we bridge it somehow?

NORA: The way I am now, I'm no wife for you.

HELMER: I have the strength to make myself over.

NORA: Maybe—if your doll gets taken away.

HELMER: But to part! To part from you! No, Nora, no—I can't imagine it.

NORA (*going out, right*): All the more reason why it has to be. (*She reenters with her coat and a small overnight bag, which she puts on a chair by the table.*)

HELMER: Nora, Nora, not now! Wait till tomorrow.

NORA: I can't spend the night in a strange man's room.

HELMER: But couldn't we live here like brother and sister—

NORA: You know very well how long that would last. (*Throws her shawl about her.*) Good-bye, Torvald. I won't look in on the children. I know they're in better hands than mine. The way I am now, I'm no use to them.

HELMER: But someday, Nora—someday—?

NORA: How can I tell? I haven't the least idea what'll become of me.

HELMER: But you're my wife, now and wherever you go.

NORA: Listen, Torvald—I've heard that when a wife deserts her husband's house just as I'm doing, then the law frees him from all responsibility. In any case, I'm freeing you from being responsible. Don't feel yourself bound, any more than I will. There has to be absolute freedom for us both. Here, take your ring back. Give me mine.

HELMER: That too?

NORA: That too.

HELMER: There it is.

NORA: Good. Well, now it's all over. I'm putting the keys here. The maids know all about keeping up the house—better than I do. Tomorrow, after I've left town, Kristine will stop by to pack up everything that's mine from home. I'd like those things shipped up to me.

HELMER: Over! All over! Nora, won't you ever think about me?

NORA: I'm sure I'll think of you often, and about the children and the house here.

HELMER: May I write you?

NORA: No—never. You're not to do that.

HELMER: Oh, but let me send you—

NORA: Nothing. Nothing.

HELMER: Or help you if you need it.

NORA: No. I accept nothing from strangers.

HELMER: Nora—can I never be more than a stranger to you?

NORA (*picking up the overnight bag*): Ah, Torvald—it would take the greatest miracle of all—

HELMER: Tell me the greatest miracle!

NORA: You and I both would have to transform ourselves to the point that—Oh, Torvald, I've stopped believing in miracles.

HELMER: But I'll believe. Tell me! Transform ourselves to the point that—?

NORA: That our living together could be a true marriage. (*She goes out down the hall.*)

HELMER (*sinks down on a chair by the door, face buried in his hands*): Nora! Nora! (*Looking about and rising.*) Empty. She's gone. (*A sudden hope leaps in him.*) The greatest miracle—?

(*From below, the sound of a door slamming shut.*)

COMMENTARIES

Ibsen wrote about his own work, both in his letters to producers and actors and in his notes describing the development of his plays. Such notes reveal his concern, his insights as he wrote the plays, and his motives. Sometimes what he says about the plays does not completely square with modern interpretations. On the other hand, he explains in his notes that the circumstances of women in modern society were much on his mind when he was working on *A Doll House*.

Ibsen's "Notes for the Modern Tragedy" is remarkable for suggesting a separate sensibility (spiritual law) for men and for women. His observations about the society in which women live—and in which Nora is confounded—sound as if they could have been written a century later than they were. Muriel C. Bradbrook's discussion of *A Doll House* focuses on the moral bankruptcy of Nora's situation, which is to say the situation of all wives of the period.

HENRIK IBSEN (1828–1906)

Notes for the Modern Tragedy   1878

TRANSLATED BY A. G. CHATER

Ibsen's first notes for *A Doll House* were jotted down on October 19, 1878. They show that his thinking on the relations between men and women was quite sophisticated and that the material for the play had been gestating for some time. His comments indicate that the essentially male society he knew was one of his central concerns in the play.

There are two kinds of spiritual law, two kinds of conscience, one in man and another, altogether different, in woman. They do not understand each other; but in practical life the woman is judged by man's law, as though she were not a woman but a man.

The wife in the play ends by having no idea of what is right or wrong; natural feeling on the one hand and belief in authority on the other have altogether bewildered her.

A woman cannot be herself in the society of the present day, which is an exclusively masculine society, with laws framed by men and with a judicial system that judges feminine conduct from a masculine point of view.

She has committed forgery, and she is proud of it; for she did it out of love for her husband, to save his life. But this husband with his commonplace principles of honor is on the side of the law and looks at the question from the masculine point of view.

Spiritual conflicts. Oppressed and bewildered by the belief in authority, she loses faith in her moral right and ability to bring up her children. Bitterness. A mother in modern society, like certain insects who go away and die when she has

409

done her duty in the propagation of the race. Love of life, of home, of husband and children and family. Now and then a womanly shaking off of her thoughts. Sudden return of anxiety and terror. She must bear it all alone. The catastrophe approaches, inexorably, inevitably. Despair, conflict, and destruction.

(Krogstad has acted dishonorably and thereby become well-to-do; now his prosperity does not help him, he cannot recover his honor.)

MURIEL C. BRADBROOK (1909–1993)

A Doll's House: Ibsen the Moralist 1948

In her important study of Ibsen, *Ibsen: The Norwegian*, Muriel C. Bradbrook discusses all the important plays, but she reserves a special place for *A Doll House*. In her analysis she suggests that Nora slowly discovers the fundamental bankruptcy of her marriage. Bradbrook calls it "eight years' prostitution." She also shows the true extent of Torvald's possessiveness and immaturity. As Bradbrook says, the true moment of recognition — in the Greek tragic sense — occurs when Nora sees both herself and Torvald in their true nature. Bradbrook also helps us see the full implication of Nora's leaving her home. She can never hope again for the comforts she has enjoyed as Torvald's wife.

Poor Nora, living by playing her tricks like a little pet animal, sensing how to manage Torvald by those pettinesses in his character she does not know she knows of, is too vulnerably sympathetic to find her life-work in reading John Stuart Mill. At the end she still does not understand the strange world in which she has done wrong by forging a signature. She does understand that she has lived by what Virginia Woolf called "the slow waterlogged sinking of her will into his." And this picture is built up for her and for us by the power of structural implication, a form of writing particularly suited to drama, where the latent possibilities of a long stretch of past time can be thrown into relief by a crisis. In *A Doll's House,* the past is not only lighted up by the present, as a transparency might be lit up with a lamp; the past is changed by the present so that it becomes a different thing. Nora's marriage becomes eight years' prostitution, as she gradually learns the true nature of her relations with Torvald and the true nature of Torvald's feelings for her.

In act I, no less than six different episodes bring out the war that is secretly waged between his masculine dictatorship and her feminine wiles:

Her wheedling him for money with a simple transference: "Let us do as *you* suggest. . . ."

Her promise to Christine: "Just leave it to me: I will broach the matter very cleverly." She is evidently habituated to and aware of her own technique.

Her description of how she tried to coax Torvald into taking the holiday and how she was saving up the story of the bond "for when I am no longer as good-looking as I am now." She knows the precarious nature of her hold.

Her method of asking work for Christine by putting Christine also into a (completely bogus) position of worshiping subservience to Torvald.

Her boast to Krogstad about her influence. Whilst this may be a justifiable triumph over her tormentor, it is an unconscious betrayal of Torvald (witness his fury in act II at the idea of being thought uxorious).

After this faceted exposition, the treatment grows much broader. Nora admits Torvald's jealousy: Yet she flirts with Rank, aware but not acknowledging the grounds of her control. The pressure of implication remains constant throughout: It is comparable with the effect of a dialect, coloring all that is said. To take a few lines at random from the dialogue of Nora and Rank in act II:

> NORA (*putting her hand on his shoulder*): Dear, dear Dr. Rank! Death mustn't take you away from Torvald and me. [Nora is getting demonstrative as she senses Rank's responsiveness, and her hopes of obtaining a loan from him rise. Hence her warmth of feeling, purely seductive.]
>
> RANK: It is a loss you will easily recover from. Those who are gone away are soon forgotten. [Poor Rank is reminded by that "Torvald and me" how little he really counts to Nora.]
>
> NORA (*anxiously*): Do you believe that? [Rank has awakened her thoughts of what may happen if *she* has to go away.]

Her methods grow more desperate—the open appeal to Torvald to keep Krogstad and the frantic expedient of the tarantella. In the last act her fate is upon her; yet in spite of all her terror and Torvald's tipsy amorousness, she still believes in his chivalry and devotion. This extraordinary self-deception is perhaps the subtlest and most telling implication of all. Practice had left her theory unshaken: So when the crash comes, she cries, "I have been living with a strange man," yet it was but the kind of man her actions had always implied him to be. Her vanity had completely prevented her from recognizing what she was doing, even though she had become such an expert at doing it.

Torvald is more gradually revealed. In the first act he appears indulgent, perhaps a trifle inclined to nag about the macaroons and to preach, but virtually a more efficient David Copperfield curbing a rather better-trained Dora. In the second act, his resentment and his pleasure alike uncover the deeper bases of his dominance. His anger at the prospect of being thought under his wife's influence and his fury at the imputation of narrow-mindedness show that it is really based on his own cowardice, the need for something weaker to bully: This is confirmed when he gloats over Nora's panic as evidence of her love for him, and over her agitation in the tarantella ("you little helpless thing!"). His love of order and his fastidiousness, when joined to such qualities, betray a set personality; and the last act shows that he has neither control nor sympathy on the physical level. But he is no fool, and his integrity is not all cowardice. Doubtless, debt or forgery really was abhorrent to him.

The climax of the play comes when Nora sees Torvald and sees herself: It is an *anagnorisis,* a recognition. Her life is cored like an apple. For she has had no life apart from this. Behind the irrelevant program for self-education there stands a woman, pitifully inexperienced, numbed by emotional shock, but with a newfound will to face what has happened, to accept her bankruptcy, as, in a very different way, Peer Gynt had at last accepted his.

"Yes, I am beginning to understand. . . ." she says. "What you did," observes the now magnanimous Torvald, "you did out of love for me." "That is true," says Nora: And she calls him to a "settling of accounts," not in any spirit of hostility but in an attempt to organize vacancy. "I have made nothing of my life. . . . I must stand quite alone . . . it is necessary to me . . . ." That is really the program. *Ainsi tout leur a craqué dans les mains.*°

The spare and laminated speech gains its effect by inference and riddle. But these are the characteristic virtues of Norse. Irony is its natural weapon. Ibsen was working with the grain of the language. It was no accident that it fell to a Norwegian to take that most finely tooled art, the drama, and bring it to a point and precision so nice that literally not a phrase is without its direct contribution to the structure. The unrelenting cohesion of *A Doll's House* is perhaps, like that of the *Oedipus the King,* too hard on the playgoer; he is allowed no relief. Nora cannot coo to her baby without saying: "My sweet little *baby doll!*" or play with her children without choosing, significantly, *Hide and Seek.* Ibsen will not allow the smallest action to escape from the psychopathology of everyday life. However, a play cannot be acted so that every moment is tense with significance, and, in practice, an actor, for the sake of light and shade, will probably slur some of Ibsen's points, deliberately or unconsciously. The tension between the characters is such that the slightest movement of one sets all the others quivering. But this is partly because they are seen with such detachment, like a clear-cut intaglio. The play is, above all, articulated.

That is not to say that it is the mere dissection of a problem. Perhaps Rank and Mrs. Linde would have been more subtly wrought into the action at a later date; but the tight control kept over Nora and Torvald does not mean that they can be exhausted by analysis or staled by custom. They are so far in advance of the characters of *Pillars of Society* that they are capable of the surprising yet inevitable development that marks the character conceived "in the round," the character that is, in Ibsen's phrase, fully "seen."

Consider, for example, Torvald's soliloquy whilst Nora is taking off her masquerade dress. It recalls at one moment Dickens's most unctuous hypocrites — "Here I will protect you like a hunted dove that I have saved from the claws of the hawk!" — at another Meredith's Willoughby Patterne° — "Only be frank and open with me and I will be both will and conscience to you" — yet from broadest caricature to sharpest analysis, it remains the self-glorified strut of the one character, the bank clerk in his pride, cousin to Peer Gynt, that typical Norwegian, and to Hjalmer Ekdal, the toiling breadwinner of the studio.

Whilst the Ibsenites might have conceded that Torvald is Art, they would probably have contended that Nora is Truth. Nora, however, is much more than a Revolting Wife. She is not a sour misanthropist or a fighting suffragette, but a lovely young woman who knows that she still holds her husband firmly infatuated after eight years of marriage. . . .

In leaving her husband Nora is seeking a fuller life as a human being. She is emancipating herself. Yet the seeking itself is also a renunciation, a kind of death — "I must stand alone." No less than Falk, or the hero of *On the Vidda,* she gives up something that has been her whole life. She is as broken as Torvald in the end: But she is a strong character and he is a weak one. In the "happy ending" which Ibsen reluctantly allowed to be used, it was the sight of the children that

---

Ainsi . . . mains: Thus everything has shattered in their hands.
Willoughby Patterne: The protagonist in George Meredith's novel *The Egoist* (1879), an arrogant aristocrat who lacks awareness of the needs and desires of the women in his life.

persuaded her to stay, and unless it is remembered that leaving Torvald means leaving the children, the full measure of Nora's decision cannot be taken. An actress gets her chance to make this point in the reply to Torvald's plea that Nora should stay for the children's sake.

It should be remembered, too, that the seriousness of the step she takes is lost on the present generation. She was putting herself outside society, inviting insult, destitution, and loneliness. She went out into a very dark night.

August Strindberg

The Swedish playwright August Strindberg (1849–1912) wrote fifty-eight plays, more than a dozen novels, and more than a hundred short stories, all collected now in fifty-five volumes. During the time he was producing this astonishing body of work, he was the victim of persistent paranoia, suffered the destruction of three marriages, and lived through a major nervous breakdown.

He was a man of enormous complexity whose work has traditionally been broken into two periods. The first consists of the work he wrote up to 1894, which includes *The Father* (1877), *Miss Julie* (1888), *The Creditors* (1889), and other naturalistic plays. The second consists of work he wrote after 1897, including *To Damascus* (1898–1901), *There Are Crimes and Crimes* (1899), *Easter* and *The Dance of Death* (both 1901), *A Dream Play* (1902), and *Ghost Sonata* (1907); these are largely expressionist plays. **Expressionism** disregarded the strict demands of naturalism to present a "slice of life" without artistic shaping of plot and resolution. Instead, expressionist drama used materials that resembled dreams—or nightmares—and focused on symbolic actions and a subjective interpretation of the world. Strindberg's later drama is often symbolic, taut, and psychological. His novel *Inferno* (1897) not only marks the transition between his early and late work but also gives this period of his life its name. Strindberg's *Inferno* period was a time of madness and paranoic behavior that virtually redirected his life for more than three years. During this time he was convinced that the secrets of life were wrapped in the occult, and his energies went into alchemical experiments and studies of cabalistic lore.

The first period of his dramatic career began with *Master Olof* (1872), a historical drama that he chose to write in prose, which he felt was a more natural medium than verse, the convention for such plays at the time. The play was turned down by the Royal Dramatic Theatre, and he rewrote it in verse in 1876. It was rejected for a second time but was finally produced the following year. At that time, Strindberg recorded, "In 1877 Antoine opened his Théâtre Libre in Paris, and *Thérèse Raquin*, although nothing but an adapted novel, became the dominant model. It was the powerful theme and the concentrated form that showed innovation, although the unity of time was not yet observed, and curtain falls were retained. It was then I wrote my dramas: *Lady Julie, The Father,* and *Creditors*." *Thérèse Raquin,* Émile Zola's naturalistic play, inspired Strindberg to move further toward his own interpretation of naturalism, which is perhaps most evident in *Miss Julie.* Strindberg was more subjective in his approach to naturalism, less scientific and deterministic, than Zola. Whereas Zola's approach might be described as photographic realism, Strindberg's was more selective and impressionistic but no less honest and true. He saw his characters operating out of "a whole series of deeply buried motives." They were not necessarily the product of their biology or their social circumstances, as the naturalists of Zola's stripe sometimes implied. Yet Strindberg saw clearly that class distinctions helped determine the behavior of many people. He seemed to accept the view that people were not created by their class but rather belonged to their class because of the kind of people they were. Strindberg probed deeply into the psychology of his characters, whose emotional lives, rather than outward social qualities, determined their actions.

Strindberg is often described as a woman-hater, a misogynist. For periods of his life he does seem to have been misogynistic, but he was nonetheless extremely contradictory in both behavior and belief. There is no simple way to talk about Strindberg's attitude toward women. On the one hand, he is conventional in his thinking that women belong in the home. On the other hand, he married a highly successful actress, Siri von Essen. As he said in a letter in 1895, "Woman is to me the earth and all its glory, the bond that binds, and of all the evil the worst evil I have seen is the female sex." A decade later, in *A Blue Book,* he wrote, "When I approach a woman as a lover, I look up to her, I see something of the mother in her, and this I respect. I assume a subordinate position, become childish and puerile and actually am subordinate, like most men. . . . I put her on a pedestal." In his views of women, as in many things, including his attitude toward dramatic techniques and style, Strindberg is a mass of contradictions and complexities of the sort sometimes associated with genius.

Miss Julie

For discussion questions and assignments on *Miss Julie,* visit bedfordstmartins.com/jacobus.

Miss Julie, the daughter of a count, and Jean, the count's valet, come from strikingly different social backgrounds. In ordinary circumstances, they might not be on friendly terms, much less become lovers, as they do. But the count is away, and Miss Julie and Jean are drawn into a sexual liaison marked by a struggle for dominance and control. Miss Julie's fiancé has been disposed of before the play begins because he refused to debase himself slavishly to her will. She is a free spirit, but her breeding is suspect because her mother, like her, took a lover and defied the count. Miss Julie's mother rebelled against her husband and punished him by burning their house down after the insurance expired. As further punishment and abasement, she humiliated the count by arranging to have her lover lend him the money to rebuild the house. Thus, Miss Julie's heritage is one of independence, rebellion, and unorthodoxy.

Under her mother's tutelage, Miss Julie was raised to manipulate men, but she cannot accept them totally. She also seems to feel contempt for herself as a woman mixed in with her contempt for men. In his preface to the play, Strindberg says that Julie is a modern "man-hating half-woman" who sells herself for honors of various kinds. (See the commentary on p. 432.)

The play has a mysterious quality. It takes place on Midsummer Eve, when lovers reveal themselves to one another and when almost anything can happen. In primitive fertility rites it was a time associated with sexual awakening. The cook, Kristine, mentions that it is the feast of St. John and alludes to his beheading for spurning Salome's advances. Jean (French for John) in one tense moment of the play beheads Julie's pet bird as a sign of the violence pent up in him. This incident foreshadows Miss Julie's death.

The fairy-tale quality that creeps into the play—as in *A Midsummer Night's Dream,* set on the same day—may seem out of place in a realistic drama, but it is profoundly compelling. It is also typical of Strindberg, who often uses symbolism to suggest a dream quality and deepen the significance of the action. (Dreams are a part of life that modern playwrights have taken great pains to explore.)

The count himself, Julie's father, never appears in the play, but his presence is always felt, ominous and intense, again much as in a fairy tale. Jean tells Miss Julie that he would willingly kill himself if the count were to order it. Kristine, like a witch, demands retribution because she was spurned by Jean, who was once her lover. Near the end of the play she prevents Julie and Jean from running away from the count by impounding the horses in the stable, thus taking revenge on both of them.

Although Julie may be seen as the princess, Jean has very little claim to being Prince Charming of the play, especially since he has little strength of character. He feels superior to his station as a valet, and Strindberg in his preface refers to him as a nobleman. However, like Kristine, he is coarse beneath his outwardly polished appearance. His highest ambition is to be the proprietor of a first-class hotel, a prospect he wants to share with Julie.

One of the most striking passages in the play is the story Jean tells Julie almost reluctantly. He tries to explain to her what it feels like to be "down below," where she has never been. When he was a boy, he thought of the apple trees in her father's garden as part of the "Garden of Eden, guarded by angry angels." He entered this enchanted place with his mother to weed onions and wandered into the outhouse—a building like a Turkish pavilion whose function he could not guess. While he was exploring it, he heard someone coming and had to exit beneath the outhouse and hide himself under a pile of weeds and "wet dirt that stank." From his hiding place he saw Julie in a pink dress and white stockings. He rushed to the millpond and jumped in to wash the filth off himself. Ironically, only a few moments after he tells her this story, he calls her a whore, and she, in response, says, "Oh, God in heaven, end my wretched life! Take me away from the filth I'm sinking into! Save me! Save me!"

Miss Julie falls under the power of her lover and cannot redirect her life; she sinks deeper and deeper into "filth." She has few choices at the end of the play, and the conclusion to *Miss Julie* is swift. The contrast between Julie's willfulness and Jean's caution makes their situation especially desperate. When Julie leaves at the end of the play to seal her fate, we sense the terrible weight of their society's values. Those values are symbolized by the return of the count and the expectations he had of Julie's behavior while he was gone.

Miss Julie in Performance

The first planned professional production of *Miss Julie* was canceled at the last minute by censors in Copenhagen on March 1, 1889. Although the play was performed privately on March 14, 1889, in Copenhagen University's Students' Union, it was not performed professionally in Stockholm until 1906. Some important early productions of the play were in Paris in André Antoine's distinguished Théâtre Libre in 1893 and in Berlin in Max Reinhardt's Kleines Theater in 1904. Reinhardt produced seventeen of Strindberg's plays and was one of his great champions. In 1907, Strindberg produced the play in his own Intimate Theatre in Stockholm, where it ran intermittently for 134 showings. He even arranged a special performance for Bernard Shaw. The first London production was in 1912, but since the 1930s the play has been revived many times, with many distinguished actors in all three major roles.

Among the notable modern productions is the Old Vic's 1966 version directed by Michael Elliott, with Maggie Smith and Albert Finney starring.

The Baxter Theatre of Johannesburg, South Africa, produced the play in 1985 with the black actor John Kani as Jean and the white Afrikaner actress Sandra Prinsloo as Julie. Some white audiences considered that casting outrageous. The sensational Ingmar Bergman production at the Brooklyn Academy of Music in 1991 stretched the play to two hours and made it more of a domestic tragedy—as John Simon said, "more like us, more believable, and, therefore, more terrifying."

Dramatist Frank McGuinness's translation of *Miss Julie* was produced at the Theatre Royal in London in 2000, with Christopher Eccleston and Aisling O'Sullivan in a carefully built period kitchen with period costumes. The sexual dynamic of the play was central to a production designed to attract a younger audience. In New York in 2005, the Rattlestick Playwrights Theatre produced a well-reviewed version, adapted by Craig Lucas, that emphasized the physicality of the protagonists and went so far as to show their lovemaking silhouetted behind a scrim during a scene change.

Filmed at least five times, *Miss Julie* has been televised as well. It is one of the most frequently produced modern plays.

AUGUST STRINDBERG (1849–1912)

Miss Julie   1888

TRANSLATED BY HARRY G. CARLSON

Characters

MISS JULIE, *25 years old*
JEAN, *her father's valet, 30 years old*
KRISTINE, *her father's cook, 35 years old*

(*The action takes place in the Count's kitchen on midsummer eve.*)

Setting: (*A large kitchen, the ceiling and side walls of which are hidden by draperies. The rear wall runs diagonally from down left to up right. On the wall down left are two shelves with copper, iron, and pewter utensils; the shelves are lined with scalloped paper. Visible to the right is most of a set of large, arched glass doors, through which can be seen a fountain with a statue of Cupid, lilac bushes in bloom, and the tops of some Lombardy poplars. At down left is the corner of a large tiled stove; a portion of its hood is showing. At right, one end of the servants' white pine dining table juts out; several chairs stand around it. The stove is decorated with birch branches; juniper twigs are strewn on the floor. On the end of the table stands a large*)

Japanese spice jar, filled with lilac blossoms. An ice box, a sink, and a washstand. Above the door is an old-fashioned bell on a spring; to the left of the door, the mouthpiece of a speaking tube is visible.)

(*Kristine is frying something on the stove. She is wearing a light-colored cotton dress and an apron. Jean enters. He is wearing livery and carries a pair of high riding boots with spurs, which he puts down on the floor where they can be seen by the audience.*)

JEAN: Miss Julie's crazy again tonight; absolutely crazy!

KRISTINE: So you finally came back?

JEAN: I took the Count to the station and when I returned past the barn I stopped in for a dance. Who do I see but Miss Julie leading off the dance with the gamekeeper! But as soon as she saw me she rushed over to ask me for the next waltz. And she's been waltzing ever since—I've never seen anything like it. She's crazy!

KRISTINE: She always has been, but never as bad as the last two weeks since her engagement was broken off.

JEAN: Yes, I wonder what the real story was there. He was a gentleman, even if he wasn't rich. Ah! These people have such romantic ideas. (*Sits at the end of the table.*) Still, it's strange, isn't it? I mean that she'd rather stay home with the servants on midsummer eve instead of going with her father to visit relatives?

KRISTINE: She's probably embarrassed after that row with her fiancé.

JEAN: Probably! He gave a good account of himself, though. Do you know how it happened, Kristine? I saw it, you know, though I didn't let on I had.

KRISTINE: No! You saw it?

JEAN: Yes, I did.———That evening they were out near the stable, and she was "training" him—as she called it. Do you know what she did? She made him jump over her riding crop, the way you'd teach a dog to jump. He jumped twice and she hit him each time. But the third time he grabbed the crop out of her hand, hit her with it across the cheek, and broke it in pieces. Then he left.

KRISTINE: So, that's what happened! I can't believe it!

JEAN: Yes, that's the way it went!———What have you got for me that's tasty, Kristine?

KRISTINE (*serving him from the pan*): Oh, it's only a piece of kidney I cut from the veal roast.

JEAN (*smelling the food*): Beautiful! That's my favorite *délice.*° (*Feeling the plate.*) But you could have warmed the plate!

KRISTINE: You're fussier than the Count himself, once you start! (*She pulls his hair affectionately.*)

JEAN (*angry*): Stop it, leave my hair alone! You know I'm touchy about that.

KRISTINE: Now, now, it's only love, you know that. (*Jean eats. Kristine opens a bottle of beer.*)

JEAN: Beer? On midsummer eve? No thank you! I can do better than that. (*Opens a drawer in the table and takes out a bottle of red wine with yellow sealing wax.*) See that? Yellow seal! Give me a glass! A wine glass! I'm drinking this *pur.*°

KRISTINE (*returns to the stove and puts on a small saucepan*): God help the woman who gets you for a husband! What a fussbudget.

JEAN: Nonsense! You'd be damned lucky to get a man like me. It certainly hasn't done you any harm to have people call me your sweetheart. (*Tastes the wine.*) Good! Very good! Just needs a little warming. (*Warms the glass between his hands.*) We bought this in Dijon. Four francs a liter, not counting the cost of the bottle, or the customs duty.———What are you cooking now? It stinks like hell!

KRISTINE: Oh, some slop Miss Julie wants to give Diana.

JEAN: Watch your language, Kristine. But why should you have to cook for that damn mutt on midsummer eve? Is she sick?

KRISTINE: Yes, she's sick! She sneaked out with the gatekeeper's dog—and now there's hell to pay. Miss Julie won't have it!

JEAN: Miss Julie has too much pride about some things and not enough about others, just like her mother

was. The Countess was most at home in the kitchen and the cowsheds, but a *one-horse* carriage wasn't elegant enough for her. The cuffs of her blouse were dirty, but she had to have her coat of arms on her cufflinks.———And Miss Julie won't take proper care of herself either. If you ask me, she just isn't refined. Just now, when she was dancing in the barn, she pulled the gamekeeper away from Anna and made him dance with her. *We* wouldn't behave like that, but that's what happens when aristocrats pretend they're common people—they get *common!*——— But she is quite a woman! Magnificent! What shoulders, and what—et cetera!

KRISTINE: Oh, don't overdo it! I've heard what Clara says, and she dresses her.

JEAN: Ha, Clara! You're all jealous of each other! I've been out riding with her. . . . And the way she dances!

KRISTINE: Listen, Jean! You're going to dance with me, when I'm finished here, aren't you?

JEAN: Of course I will.

KRISTINE: Promise?

JEAN: Promise? When I say I'll do something, I do it! By the way, the kidney was very good. (*Corks the bottle.*)

JULIE (*in the doorway to someone outside*): I'll be right back! You go ahead for now! (*Jean sneaks the bottle back into the table drawer and gets up respectfully. Miss Julie enters and crosses to Kristine by the stove.*) Well? Is it ready? (*Kristine indicates that Jean is present.*)

JEAN (*gallantly*): Are you ladies up to something secret?

JULIE (*flicking her handkerchief in his face*): None of your business!

JEAN: Hmm! I like the smell of violets!

JULIE (*coquettishly*): Shame on you! So you know about perfumes, too? You certainly know how to dance. Ah, ah! No peeking! Go away.

JEAN (*boldly but respectfully*): Are you brewing up a magic potion for midsummer eve? Something to prophesy by under a lucky star, so you'll catch a glimpse of your future husband!

JULIE (*caustically*): You'd need sharp eyes to see him! (*To Kristine.*) Pour out half a bottle and cork it well.———Come and dance a schottische° with me, Jean . . .

JEAN (*hesitating*): I don't want to be impolite to anyone, and I've already promised this dance to Kristine . . .

JULIE: Oh, she can have another one—can't you, Kristine? Won't you lend me Jean?

KRISTINE: It's not up to me, ma'am. (*To Jean.*) If the mistress is so generous, it wouldn't do for you to say no. Go on, Jean, and thank her for the honor.

JEAN: To be honest, and no offense intended, I wonder whether it's wise for you to dance twice running with the same partner, especially since these people are quick to jump to conclusions . . .

JULIE (*flaring up*): What's that? What sort of conclusions? What do you mean?

___
délice: Delight. *pur:* Pure; the first drink from the bottle.

schottische: A Scottish round dance resembling a polka.

JEAN (*submissively*): If you don't understand, ma'am, I must speak more plainly. It doesn't look good to play favorites with your servants. . . .

JULIE: Play favorites! What an idea! I'm astonished! As mistress of the house, I honor your dance with my presence. And when I dance, I want to dance with someone who can lead, so I won't look ridiculous.

JEAN: As you order, ma'am! I'm at your service!

JULIE (*gently*): Don't take it as an order! On a night like this we're all just ordinary people having fun, so we'll forget about rank. Now, take my arm!———Don't worry, Kristine! I won't steal your sweetheart! (*Jean offers his arm and leads Miss Julie out.*)

Mime

(*The following should be played as if the actress playing Kristine were really alone. When she has to, she turns her back to the audience. She does not look toward them, nor does she hurry as if she were afraid they would grow impatient. Schottische music played on a fiddle sounds in the distance. Kristine hums along with the music. She clears the table, washes the dishes, dries them, and puts them away. She takes off her apron. From a table drawer she removes a small mirror and leans it against the bowl of lilacs on the table. She lights a candle, heats a hairpin over the flame, and uses it to set a curl on her forehead. She crosses to the door and listens, then returns to the table. She finds the handkerchief Miss Julie left behind, picks it up, and smells it. Then, preoccupied, she spreads it out, stretches it, smoothes out the wrinkles, and folds it into quarters, and so forth.*)

JEAN (*enters alone*): God, she really *is* crazy! What a way to dance! Everybody's laughing at her behind her back. What do you make of it, Kristine?

KRISTINE: Ah! It's that time of the month for her, and she always gets peculiar like that. Are you going to dance with me now?

JEAN: You're not mad at me, are you, for leaving . . . ?

KRISTINE: Of course not!———Why should I be, for a little thing like that? Besides, I know my place . . .

JEAN (*puts his arm around her waist*): You're a sensible girl, Kristine, and you'd make a good wife . . .

JULIE (*entering; uncomfortably surprised; with forced good humor*): What a charming escort—running away from his partner.

JEAN: On the contrary, Miss Julie. Don't you see how I rushed back to the partner I abandoned!

JULIE (*changing her tone*): You know, you're a superb dancer!———But why are you wearing livery on a holiday? Take it off at once!

JEAN: Then I must ask you to go outside for a moment. You see, my black coat is hanging over here . . . (*Gestures and crosses right.*)

JULIE: Are you embarrassed about changing your coat in front of me? Well, go in your room then. Either that or stay and I'll turn my back.

JEAN: With your permission, ma'am! (*He crosses right. His arm is visible as he changes his jacket.*)

JULIE (*to Kristine*): Tell me, Kristine—you two are so close—. Is Jean your fiancé?

KRISTINE: Fiancé? Yes, if you wish. We can call him that.

JULIE: What do you mean?

KRISTINE: You had a fiancé yourself, didn't you? So . . .

JULIE: Well, we were properly engaged . . .

KRISTINE: But nothing came of it, did it? (*Jean returns dressed in a frock coat and bowler hat.*)

JULIE: *Très gentil, monsieur Jean! Très gentil!*

JEAN: *Vous voulez plaisanter, madame!*

JULIE: *Et vous voulez parler français!°* Where did you learn that?

JEAN: In Switzerland, when I was wine steward in one of the biggest hotels in Lucerne!

JULIE: You look like a real gentleman in that coat! *Charmant!°* (*Sits at the table.*)

JEAN: Oh, you're flattering me!

JULIE (*offended*): Flattering you?

JEAN: My natural modesty forbids me to believe that you would really compliment someone like me, and so I took the liberty of assuming that you were exaggerating, which polite people call flattering.

JULIE: Where did you learn to talk like that? You must have been to the theater often.

JEAN: Of course. And I've done a lot of traveling.

JULIE: But you come from here, don't you?

JEAN: My father was a farmhand on the district attorney's estate nearby. I used to see you when you were little, but you never noticed me.

JULIE: No! Really?

JEAN: Sure. I remember one time especially . . . but I can't talk about that.

JULIE: Oh, come now! Why not? Just this once!

JEAN: No, I really couldn't, not now. Some other time, perhaps.

JULIE: Why some other time? What's so dangerous about now?

JEAN: It's not dangerous, but there are obstacles.——Her, for example. (*Indicating Kristine, who has fallen asleep in a chair by the stove.*)

JULIE: What a pleasant wife she'll make! She probably snores, too.

JEAN: No, she doesn't, but she talks in her sleep.

JULIE (*cynically*): How do *you* know?

JEAN (*audaciously*): I've heard her! (*Pause, during which they stare at each other.*)

JULIE: Why don't you sit down?

JEAN: I couldn't do that in your presence.

JULIE: But if I order you to?

JEAN: Then I'd obey.

JULIE: Sit down, then.———No, wait. Can you get me something to drink first?

JEAN: I don't know what we have in the ice box. I think there's only beer.

Très gentil . . . français!: Very pleasing, Mr. Jean! Very pleasing. You would trifle with me, madam! And you want to speak French! *Charmant!:* Charming!

JULIE: Why do you say "only"? My tastes are so simple I prefer beer to wine. (*Jean takes a bottle of beer from the ice box and opens it. He looks for a glass and a plate in the cupboard and serves her.*)

JEAN: Here you are, ma'am.

JULIE: Thank you. Won't you have something yourself?

JEAN: I'm not partial to beer, but if it's an order . . .

JULIE: An order?———Surely a gentleman can keep his lady company.

JEAN: You're right, of course. (*Opens a bottle and gets a glass.*)

JULIE: Now, drink to my health! (*He hesitates.*) What? A man of the world—and shy?

JEAN (*in mock romantic fashion, he kneels and raises his glass*): Skål to my mistress!

JULIE: Bravo!———Now kiss my shoe, to finish it properly. (*Jean hesitates, then boldly seizes her foot and kisses it lightly.*) Perfect! You should have been an actor.

JEAN (*rising*): That's enough now, Miss Julie! Someone might come in and see us.

JULIE: What of it?

JEAN: People talk, that's what! If you knew how their tongues were wagging just now at the dance, you'd . . .

JULIE: What were they saying? Tell me!———Sit down!

JEAN (*sits*): I don't want to hurt you, but they were saying things———suggestive things, that, that . . . well, you can figure it out for yourself! You're not a child. If a woman is seen drinking alone with a man—let alone a servant—at night—then . . .

JULIE: Then what? Besides, we're not alone. Kristine is here.

JEAN: Asleep!

JULIE: Then I'll wake her up. (*Rising.*) Kristine! Are you asleep? (*Kristine mumbles in her sleep.*)

JULIE: Kristine!———She certainly can sleep!

KRISTINE (*in her sleep*): The Count's boots are brushed—put the coffee on—right away, right away—uh, huh—oh!

JULIE (*grabbing Kristine's nose*): Will you wake up!

JEAN (*severely*): Leave her alone—let her sleep!

JULIE (*sharply*): What?

JEAN: Someone who's been standing over a stove all day has a right to be tired by now. Sleep should be respected . . .

JULIE (*changing her tone*): What a considerate thought—it does you credit—thank you! (*Offering her hand.*) Come outside and pick some lilacs for me! (*During the following, Kristine awakens and shambles sleepily off right to bed.*)

JEAN: Go with you?

JULIE: With me!

JEAN: We couldn't do that! Absolutely not!

JULIE: I don't understand. Surely you don't imagine . . .

JEAN: No, I don't, but the others might.

JULIE: What? That I've fallen in love with a servant?

JEAN: I'm not a conceited man, but such things happen—and for these people, nothing is sacred.

JULIE: I do believe you're an aristocrat!

JEAN: Yes, I am.

JULIE: And I'm stepping down . . .

JEAN: Don't step down, Miss Julie, take my advice. No one'll believe you stepped down voluntarily. People will always say you fell.

JULIE: I have a higher opinion of people than you. Come and see!———Come! (*She stares at him broodingly.*)

JEAN: You're very strange, do you know that?

JULIE: Perhaps! But so are you!———For that matter, everything is strange. Life, people, everything. Like floating scum, drifting on and on across the water, until it sinks down and down! That reminds me of a dream I have now and then. I've climbed up on top of a pillar. I sit there and see no way of getting down. I get dizzy when I look down, and I must get down, but I don't have the courage to jump. I can't hold on firmly, and I long to be able to fall, but I don't fall. And yet I'll have no peace until I get down, no rest unless I get down, down on the ground! And if I did get down to the ground, I'd want to be under the earth . . . Have you ever felt anything like that?

JEAN: No. I dream that I'm lying under a high tree in a dark forest. I want to get up, up on top, and look out over the bright landscape, where the sun is shining, and plunder the bird's nest up there, where the golden eggs lie. And I climb and climb, but the trunk's so thick and smooth, and it's so far to the first branch. But I know if I just reached that first branch, I'd go right to the top, like up a ladder. I haven't reached it yet, but I will, even if it's only in a dream!

JULIE: Here I am chattering with you about dreams. Come, let's go out! Just into the park! (*She offers him her arm, and they start to leave.*)

JEAN: We'll have to sleep on nine midsummer flowers, Miss Julie, to make our dreams come true! (*They turn at the door. Jean puts his hand to his eye.*)

JULIE: Did you get something in your eye?

JEAN: It's nothing—just a speck—it'll be gone in a minute.

JULIE: My sleeve must have brushed against you. Sit down and let me help you. (*She takes him by the arm and seats him. She tilts his head back and with the tip of a handkerchief tries to remove the speck.*) Sit still, absolutely still! (*She slaps his hand.*) Didn't you hear me?———Why, you're trembling; the big, strong man is trembling! (*Feels his biceps.*) What muscles you have!

JEAN (*warning*): Miss Julie!

JULIE: Yes, *monsieur* Jean.

JEAN: *Attention! Je ne suis qu'un homme!*°

JULIE: Will you sit still!———There! Now it's gone! Kiss my hand and thank me.

JEAN (*rising*): Miss Julie, listen to me!———Kristine has gone to bed!———Will you listen to me!

Attention! Je ne suis qu'un homme!: Watch out! I am only a man!

JULIE: Kiss my hand first!

JEAN: Listen to me!

JULIE: Kiss my hand first!

JEAN: All right, but you've only yourself to blame!

JULIE: For what?

JEAN: For what? Are you still a child at twenty-five? Don't you know that it's dangerous to play with fire?

JULIE: Not for me. I'm insured.

JEAN (*boldly*): No, you're not! But even if you were, there's combustible material close by.

JULIE: Meaning you?

JEAN: Yes! Not because it's me, but because I'm young———

JULIE: And handsome—what incredible conceit! A Don Juan perhaps! Or a Joseph!° Yes, that's it, I do believe you're a Joseph!

JEAN: Do you?

JULIE: I'm almost afraid so. (*Jean boldly tries to put his arm around her waist and kiss her. She slaps his face.*) How dare you?

JEAN: Are you serious or joking?

JULIE: Serious.

JEAN: Then so was what just happened. You play games too seriously, and that's dangerous. Well, I'm tired of games. You'll excuse me if I get back to work. I haven't done the Count's boots yet and it's long past midnight.

JULIE: Put the boots down!

JEAN: No! It's the work I have to do. I never agreed to be your playmate, and never will. It's beneath me.

JULIE: You're proud.

JEAN: In certain ways, but not in others.

JULIE: Have you ever been in love?

JEAN: We don't use that word, but I've been fond of many girls, and once I was sick because I couldn't have the one I wanted. That's right, sick, like those princes in the Arabian Nights—who couldn't eat or drink because of love.

JULIE: Who was she? (*Jean is silent.*) Who was she?

JEAN: You can't force me to tell you that.

JULIE: But if I ask you as an equal, as a—friend! Who was she?

JEAN: You!

JULIE (*sits*): How amusing . . .

JEAN: Yes, if you like! It was ridiculous!———You see, that was the story I didn't want to tell you earlier. Maybe I will now. Do you know how the world looks from down below?———Of course you don't. Neither do hawks and falcons, whose backs we can't see because they're usually soaring up there above us. I grew up in a shack with seven brothers and sisters and a pig, in the middle of a wasteland, where there wasn't a single tree. But from our window I could see the tops of apple trees above the wall of your father's garden. That was the Garden of Eden, guarded by

Don Juan . . . Joseph: Don Juan in Spanish legend is a seducer of women; in Genesis, Joseph resists the advances of Potiphar's wife.

angry angels with flaming swords. All the same, the other boys and I managed to find our way to the Tree of Life.———Now you think I'm contemptible, I suppose.

JULIE: Oh, all boys steal apples.

JEAN: You say that, but you think I'm contemptible anyway. Oh well! One day I went into the Garden of Eden with my mother, to weed the onion beds. Near the vegetable garden was a small Turkish pavilion in the shadow of jasmine bushes and over-grown with honeysuckle. I had no idea what it was used for, but I'd never seen such a beautiful building. People went in and came out again, and one day the door was left open. I sneaked close and saw walls covered with pictures of kings and emperors, and red curtains with fringes at the windows—now you know the place I mean. I———(*Breaks off a sprig of lilac and holds it in front of Miss Julie's nose.*)———I'd never been inside the manor house, never seen anything except the church—but this was more beautiful. From then on, no matter where my thoughts wandered, they returned—there. And gradually I got a longing to experience, just once, the full pleasure of—*enfin*,° I sneaked in, saw, and marveled! But then I heard someone coming! There was only one exit for ladies and gentlemen, but for me there was another, and I had no choice but to take it! (*Miss Julie, who has taken the lilac sprig, lets it fall on the table.*) Afterwards, I started running. I crashed through a raspberry bush, flew over a strawberry patch, and came up onto the rose terrace. There I caught sight of a pink dress and a pair of white stockings—it was you. I crawled under a pile of weeds, and I mean under—under thistles that pricked me and wet dirt that stank. And I looked at you as you walked among the roses, and I thought: If it's true that a thief can enter heaven and be with the angels, then why can't a farm-hand's son here on God's earth enter the manor house garden and play with the Count's daughter?

JULIE (*romantically*): Do you think all poor children would have thought the way you did?

JEAN (*at first hesitant, then with conviction*): If *all* poor—yes—of course. Of course!

JULIE: It must be terrible to be poor!

JEAN (*with exaggerated suffering*): Oh, Miss Julie! Oh!———A dog can lie on the Countess's sofa, a horse can have his nose patted by a young lady's hand, but a servant———(*Changing his tone.*) ———oh, I know—now and then you find one with enough stuff in him to get ahead in the world, but how often?———Anyhow, do you know what I did then?———I jumped in the millstream with my clothes on, was pulled out, and got a beating. But the following Sunday, when my father and all the others went to my grandmother's, I arranged to stay home. I scrubbed myself with soap and water, put on my best clothes, and went to church so that I could see you!

enfin: Finally.

I saw you and returned home, determined to die. But I wanted to die beautifully and pleasantly, without pain. And then I remembered that it was dangerous to sleep under an elder bush. We had a big one, and it was in full flower. I plundered its treasures and bedded down under them in the oat bin. Have you ever noticed how smooth oats are?—and soft to the touch, like human skin . . . ! Well, I shut the lid and closed my eyes. I fell asleep and woke up feeling very sick. But I didn't die, as you can see. What was I after?———I don't know. There was no hope of winning you, of course.———You were a symbol of the hopelessness of ever rising out of the class in which I was born.

JULIE: You're a charming storyteller. Did you ever go to school?

JEAN: A bit, but I've read lots of novels and been to the theater often. And then I've listened to people like you talk—that's where I learned most.

JULIE: Do you listen to what we say?

JEAN: Naturally! And I've heard plenty, too, driving the carriage or rowing the boat. Once I heard you and a friend . . .

JULIE: Oh?———What did you hear?

JEAN: I'd better not say. But I was surprised a little. I couldn't imagine where you learned such words. Maybe at bottom there isn't such a great difference between people as we think.

JULIE: Shame on you! We don't act like you when we're engaged.

JEAN (*staring at her*): Is that true?———You don't have to play innocent with me, Miss . . .

JULIE: The man I gave my love to was a swine.

JEAN: That's what you all say—afterwards.

JULIE: All?

JEAN: I think so. I know I've heard that phrase before, on similar occasions.

JULIE: What occasions?

JEAN: Like the one I'm talking about. The last time . . .

JULIE (*rising*): Quiet! I don't want to hear any more!

JEAN: That's interesting—that's what *she* said, too. Well, if you'll excuse me, I'm going to bed.

JULIE (*gently*): To bed? On midsummer eve?

JEAN: Yes! Dancing with the rabble out there doesn't amuse me much.

JULIE: Get the key to the boat and row me out on the lake. I want to see the sun come up.

JEAN: Is that wise?

JULIE: Are you worried about your reputation?

JEAN: Why not? Why should I risk looking ridiculous and getting fired without a reference, just when I'm trying to establish myself. Besides, I think I owe something to Kristine.

JULIE: So, now it's Kristine . . .

JEAN: Yes, but you, too.———Take my advice, go up and go to bed!

JULIE: Am I to obey you?

JEAN: Just this once—for your own good! Please! It's very late. Drowsiness makes people giddy and liable to lose their heads! Go to bed! Besides—unless I'm mistaken—I hear the others coming to look for me. And if they find us together, you'll be lost!

(*The Chorus approaches, singing.*)

> The swineherd found his true love
> a pretty girl so fair,
> The swineherd found his true love
> but let the girl beware.
>
> For then he saw the princess
> the princess on the golden hill,
> but then saw the princess,
> so much fairer still.
>
> So the swineherd and the princess
> they danced the whole night through,
> and he forgot his first love,
> to her he was untrue.
>
> And when the long night ended,
> and in the light of day, of day,
> the dancing too was ended,
> and the princess could not stay.
>
> Then the swineherd lost his true love,
> and the princess grieves him still,
> and never more she'll wander
> from atop the golden hill.

JULIE: I know all these people and I love them, just as they love me. Let them come in and you'll see.

JEAN: No, Miss Julie, they don't love you. They take your food, but they spit on it! Believe me! Listen to them, listen to what they're singing!———No. don't listen to them!

JULIE (*listening*): What are they singing?

JEAN: It's a dirty song! About you and me!

JULIE: Disgusting! Oh! How deceitful!———

JEAN: The rabble is always cowardly! And in a battle like this, you don't fight; you can only run away!

JULIE: Run away? But where? We can't go out—or into Kristine's room.

JEAN: True. But there's my room. Necessity knows no rules. Besides, you can trust me. I'm your friend and I respect you.

JULIE: But suppose—suppose they look for you in there?

JEAN: I'll bolt the door, and if anyone tries to break in, I'll shoot!———Come! (*On his knees.*) Come!

JULIE (*urgently*): Promise me . . . ?

JEAN: I swear! (*Miss Julie runs off right. Jean hastens after her.*)

Ballet

(*Led by a fiddler, the servants and farm people enter, dressed festively, with flowers in their hats. On the table they place a small barrel of beer and a keg of* schnapps, both garlanded. Glasses are brought out, and the drinking starts. A dance circle is formed and "The Swineherd and the Princess" is sung. When the dance is finished, everyone leaves, singing.)

(Miss Julie enters alone. She notices the mess in the kitchen, wrings her hands, then takes out her powder puff and powders her nose.)

JEAN (enters, agitated): There, you see? And you heard them. We can't possibly stay here now, you know that.
JULIE: Yes, I know. But what can we do?
JEAN: Leave, travel, far away from here.
JULIE: Travel? Yes, but where?
JEAN: To Switzerland, to the Italian lakes. Have you ever been there?
JULIE: No. Is it beautiful?
JEAN: Oh, an eternal summer—oranges growing everywhere, laurel trees, always green . . .
JULIE: But what'll we do there?
JEAN: I'll open a hotel—with first-class service for first-class people.
JULIE: Hotel?
JEAN: That's the life, you know. Always new faces, new languages. No time to worry or be nervous. No hunting for something to do—there's always work to be done: bells ringing night and day, train whistles blowing, carriages coming and going, and all the while gold rolling into the till! That's the life!
JULIE: Yes, it sounds wonderful. But what'll I do?
JEAN: You'll be mistress of the house: the jewel in our crown! With your looks . . . and your manner—oh—success is guaranteed! It'll be wonderful! You'll sit in your office like a queen and push an electric button to set your slaves in motion. The guests will file past your throne and timidly lay their treasures before you.————You have no idea how people tremble when they get their bill.————I'll salt the bills° and you'll sweeten them with your prettiest smile.————Let's get away from here————(Takes a timetable out of his pocket.)————Right away, on the next train!————We'll be in Malmö six-thirty tomorrow morning, Hamburg at eight-forty; from Frankfort to Basel will take a day, then on to Como by way of the St. Gotthard Tunnel, in, let's see, three days. Three days!
JULIE: That's all very well! But Jean—you must give me courage!————Tell me you love me! Put your arms around me!
JEAN (hesitating): I want to—but I don't dare. Not in this house, not again. I love you—never doubt that—you don't doubt it, do you, Miss Julie?
JULIE (shy; very feminine): "Miss!"————Call me Julie! There are no barriers between us anymore. Call me Julie!
JEAN (tormented): I can't! There'll always be barriers between us as long as we stay in this house.————There's the past and there's the Count. I've never met anyone I had such respect for.————When I see his

gloves lying on a chair, I feel small.————When I hear that bell up there ring, I jump like a skittish horse.————And when I look at his boots standing there so stiff and proud, I feel like bowing! (Kicking the boots.) Superstitions and prejudices we learned as children—but they can easily be forgotten. If I can just get to another country, a republic, people will bow and scrape when they see my livery—they'll bow and scrape, you hear, not me! I wasn't born to cringe. I've got stuff in me, I've got character, and if I can only grab onto that first branch, you watch me climb! I'm a servant today, but next year I'll own my own hotel. In ten years I'll have enough to retire. Then I'll go to Rumania and be decorated. I could—mind you I said could—end up a count!
JULIE: Wonderful, wonderful!
JEAN: Ah, in Rumania you just buy your title, and so you'll be a countess after all. My countess!
JULIE: But I don't care about that—that's what I'm putting behind me! Show me you love me, otherwise—otherwise, what am I?
JEAN: I'll show you a thousand times—afterwards! Not here! And whatever you do, no emotional outbursts, or we'll both be lost! We must think this through coolly, like sensible people. (He takes out a cigar, snips the end, and lights it.) You sit there, and I'll sit here. We'll talk as if nothing happened.
JULIE (desperately): Oh, my God! Have you no feelings?
JEAN: Me? No one has more feelings than I do, but I know how to control them.
JULIE: A little while ago you could kiss my shoe—and now!
JEAN (harshly): Yes, but that was before. Now we have other things to think about.
JULIE: Don't speak harshly to me!
JEAN: I'm not—just sensibly! We've already done one foolish thing, let's not have any more. The Count could return any minute, and by then we've got to decide what to do with our lives. What do you think of my plans for the future? Do you approve?
JULIE: They sound reasonable enough. I have only one question: For such a big undertaking you need capital—do you have it?
JEAN (chewing on the cigar): Me? Certainly! I have my professional expertise, my wide experience, and my knowledge of languages. That's capital enough, I should think!
JULIE: But all that won't even buy a train ticket.
JEAN: That's true. That's why I'm looking for a partner to advance me the money.
JULIE: Where will you find one quickly enough?
JEAN: That's up to you, if you want to come with me.
JULIE: But I can't; I have no money of my own. (Pause.)
JEAN: Then it's all off . . .
JULIE: And . . .
JEAN: Things stay as they are.
JULIE: Do you think I'm going to stay in this house as your lover? With all the servants pointing their fingers at me? Do you imagine I can face my father after

salt the bills: Inflate or pad the bills.

Marin Hinkle as Julie and Reg Rogers as Jean in the Rattlestick Playwrights Theatre 2005 production of *Miss Julie,* directed by Craig Lucas.

this? No! Take me away from here, away from shame and dishonor————Oh, what have I done! My God, my God! (*She cries.*)

JEAN: Now, don't start that old song!————What have you done? The same as many others before you.

JULIE (*screaming convulsively*): And now you think I'm contemptible!————I'm falling, I'm falling!

JEAN: Fall down to my level and I'll lift you up again.

JULIE: What terrible power drew me to you? The attraction of the weak to the strong? The falling to the rising? Or was it love? Was this love? Do you know what love is?

JEAN: Me? What do you take me for? You don't think this was my first time, do you?

JULIE: The things you say, the thoughts you think!

JEAN: That's the way I was taught, and that's the way I am! Now don't get excited and don't play the grand lady, because we're in the same boat now!———— Come on, Julie, I'll pour you a glass of something special! (*He opens a drawer in the table, takes out a wine bottle, and fills two glasses already used.*)

JULIE: Where did you get that wine?

JEAN: From the cellar.

JULIE: My father's burgundy!

JEAN: That'll do for his son-in-law, won't it?

JULIE: And I drink beer! Beer!

JEAN: That only shows I have better taste.

JULIE: Thief!

JEAN: Planning to tell?

JULIE: Oh, oh! Accomplice of a common thief! Was I drunk? Have I been walking in a dream the whole evening? Midsummer eve! A time of innocent fun!

JEAN: Innocent, eh?

JULIE (*pacing back and forth*): Is there anyone on earth more miserable than I am at this moment?

JEAN: Why should you be? After such a conquest? Think of Kristine in there. Don't you think she has feelings, too?

JULIE: I thought so awhile ago, but not any more. No, a servant is a servant . . .

JEAN: And a whore is a whore!

JULIE (*on her knees, her hands clasped*): Oh, God in heaven, end my wretched life! Take me away from the filth I'm sinking into! Save me! Save me!

JEAN: I can't deny I feel sorry for you. When I lay in that onion bed and saw you in the rose garden, well . . . I'll be frank . . . I had the same dirty thoughts all boys have.

Helen Mirren as Miss Julie in a 1971 production of Strindberg's play.

JULIE: And you wanted to die for me!

JEAN: In the oat bin? That was just talk.

JULIE: A lie, in other words!

JEAN (*beginning to feel sleepy*): More or less! I got the idea from a newspaper story about a chimney sweep who curled up in a firewood bin full of lilacs because he got a summons for not supporting his illegitimate child . . .

JULIE: So, that's what you're like . . .

JEAN: I had to think of something. And that's the kind of story women always go for.

JULIE: Swine!

JEAN: *Merde!*

JULIE: And now you've seen the hawk's back . . .

JEAN: Not exactly its *back* . . .

JULIE: And I was to be the first branch . . .

JEAN: But the branch was rotten . . .

JULIE: I was to be the sign on the hotel . . .

JEAN: And I the hotel . . .

JULIE: Sit at your desk, entice your customers, pad their bills . . .

JEAN: That I'd do myself . . .

JULIE: How can anyone be so thoroughly filthy?

JEAN: Better clean up then!

JULIE: You lackey, you menial, stand up, when I speak to you!

JEAN: Menial's strumpet, lackey's whore, shut up and get out of here! Who are you to lecture me on coarseness? None of my kind is ever as coarse as you were tonight. Do you think one of your maids would throw herself at a man the way you did? Have you ever seen any girl of my class offer herself like that? I've only seen it among animals and streetwalkers.

JULIE (*crushed*): You're right. Hit me, trample on me. I don't deserve any better. I'm worthless. But help me! If you see any way out of this, help me, Jean, please!

JEAN (*more gently*): I'd be lying if I didn't admit to a sense of triumph in all this, but do you think that a person like me would have dared even to look at someone like you if you hadn't invited it? I'm still amazed . . .

JULIE: And proud . . .

JEAN: Why not? Though I must say it was too easy to be really exciting.

JULIE: Go on, hit me, hit me harder!

JEAN (*rising*): No! Forgive me for what I've said! I don't hit a man when he's down, let alone a woman. I can't deny though, that I'm pleased to find out that what looked so dazzling to us from below was only tinsel, that the hawk's back was only gray, after all, that the lovely complexion was only powder, that those polished fingernails had black edges, and that a dirty handkerchief is still dirty, even if it smells of perfume . . . ! On the other hand, it hurts me to find out that what I was striving for wasn't finer, more substantial. It hurts me to see you sunk so low that you're inferior to your own cook. It hurts like watching flowers beaten down by autumn rains and turned into mud.

JULIE: You talk as if you were already above me.

JEAN: I am. You see, I could make you a countess, but you could never make me a count.

JULIE: But I'm the child of a count—something you could never be!

JEAN: That's true. But I could be the father of counts—if . . .

JULIE: But you're a thief. I'm not.

JEAN: There are worse things than being a thief! Besides, when I'm working in a house, I consider myself sort of a member of the family, like one of the children. And you don't call it stealing when a child snatches a berry off a full bush. (*His passion is aroused again.*) Miss Julie, you're a glorious woman, much too good for someone like me! You were drinking and you lost your head. Now you want to cover up your mistake by telling yourself that you love me! You don't. Maybe there was a physical attraction—but then your love is no better than mine.————I could never be satisfied to be no more than an animal to you, and I could never arouse real love in you.

JULIE: Are you sure of that?

JEAN: You're suggesting it's possible————Oh, I could fall in love with you, no doubt about it. You're beautiful, you're refined————(*approaching and taking her hand*)————cultured, lovable when you want to be, and once you start a fire in a man, it never goes out. (*Putting his arm around her waist.*) You're like hot, spicy wine, and one kiss from you . . . (*He tries to lead her out, but she slowly frees herself.*)

JULIE: Let me go!?————You'll never win me like that.

JEAN: *How* then?————Not like that? Not with caresses and pretty speeches. Not with plans about the future or rescue from disgrace! *How* then?

JULIE: How? How? I don't know!————I have no idea!————I detest you as I detest rats, but I can't escape from you.

JEAN: Escape with me!

JULIE (*pulling herself together*): Escape? Yes, we must escape!————But I'm so tired. Give me a glass of wine? (*Jean pours the wine. She looks at her watch.*) But we must talk first. We still have a little time. (*She drains the glass, then holds it out for more.*)

JEAN: Don't drink so fast. It'll go to your head.

JULIE: What does it matter?

JEAN: What does it matter? It's vulgar to get drunk! What did you want to tell me?

JULIE: We must escape! But first we must talk, I mean I must talk. You've done all the talking up to now. You told about your life, now I want to tell about mine, so we'll know all about each other before we go off together.

JEAN: Just a minute! Forgive me! If you don't want to regret it afterwards, you'd better think twice before revealing any secrets about yourself.

JULIE: Aren't you my friend?

JEAN: Yes, sometimes! But don't rely on me.

JULIE: You're only saying that.————Besides, everyone already knows my secrets.————You see, my mother was a commoner—very humble background. She was brought up believing in social equality, women's rights, and all that. The idea of marriage repelled her. So, when my father proposed, she replied that she would never become his wife, but he could be her lover. He insisted that he didn't want the woman he loved to be less respected than he. But his passion ruled him, and when she explained that the world's respect meant nothing to her, he accepted her conditions.

But now his friends avoided him and his life was restricted to taking care of the estate, which couldn't satisfy him. I came into the world—against my mother's wishes, as far as I can understand. She wanted to bring me up as a child of nature, and, what's more, to learn everything a boy had to learn, so that I might be an example of how a woman can be as good as a man. I had to wear boy's clothes and learn to take care of horses, but I was never allowed in the cowshed. I had to groom and harness the horses and go hunting—and even had to watch them slaughter animals—that was disgusting! On the estate men were put on women's jobs and women on men's jobs—with the result that the property became run down and we became the laughingstock of the district. Finally, my father must have awakened from his trance because he rebelled and changed everything his way. My parents were then married quietly. Mother became ill—I don't know what illness it was—but she often had convulsions, hid in the attic and in the garden, and sometimes stayed out all night. Then came the great fire, which you've heard about. The house, the stables, and the cowshed all burned down, under very curious circumstances, suggesting arson, because the accident happened the day after the insurance had expired. The quarterly premium my father sent in was delayed because of a messenger's carelessness and didn't arrive in time. (*She fills her glass and drinks.*)

JEAN: Don't drink any more!

JULIE: Oh, what does it matter.————We were left penniless and had to sleep in the carriages. My father had no idea where to find money to rebuild the house because he had so slighted his old friends that they had forgotten him. Then my mother suggested that he borrow from a childhood friend of hers, a brick manufacturer who lived nearby. Father got the loan without having to pay interest, which surprised him. And that's how the estate was rebuilt.————(*Drinks again.*) Do you know who started the fire?

JEAN: The Countess, your mother.

JULIE: Do you know who the brick manufacturer was?

JEAN: Your mother's lover?

JULIE: Do you know whose money it was?

JEAN: Wait a moment—no, I don't.

JULIE: It was my mother's.

JEAN: You mean the Count's, unless they didn't sign an agreement when they were married.

JULIE: They didn't.————My mother had a small inheritance which she didn't want under my father's control, so she entrusted it to her—friend.

JEAN: Who stole it!

JULIE: Exactly! He kept it.————All this my father found out, but he couldn't bring it to court, couldn't repay his wife's lover, couldn't prove it was his wife's money! It was my mother's revenge for being forced into marriage against her will. It nearly drove him to suicide—there was a rumor that he tried with a pistol, but failed. So, he managed to live through it and my mother had to suffer for what she'd done. You can imagine that those were a terrible five years for me. I loved my father, but I sided with my mother because I didn't know the circumstances. I learned from her to hate men—you've heard how she hated the whole male sex—and I swore to her I'd never be a slave to any man.

JEAN: But you got engaged to that lawyer.

JULIE: In order to make him my slave.

JEAN: And he wasn't willing?

JULIE: He was willing, all right, but I wouldn't let him. I got tired of him.

JEAN: I saw it—out near the stable.

JULIE: What did you see?

JEAN: I saw—how he broke off the engagement.

JULIE: That's a lie! I was the one who broke it off. Has he said that he did? That swine . . .

JEAN: He was no swine, I'm sure. So, you hate men, Miss Julie?

JULIE: Yes!————Most of the time! But sometimes—when the weakness comes, when passion burns! Oh, God, will the fire never die out?

JEAN: Do you hate me, too?

JULIE: Immeasurably! I'd like to have you put to death, like an animal . . .

JEAN: I see—the penalty for bestiality—the woman gets two years at hard labor and the animal is put to death. Right?

JULIE: Exactly!

JEAN: But there's no prosecutor here—and no animal. So, what'll we do?

JULIE: Go away!

JEAN: To torment each other to death?

JULIE: No! To be happy for—two days, a week, as long as we can be happy, and then—die . . .

JEAN: Die? That's stupid! It's better to open a hotel!

JULIE: (*without listening*):————on the shore of Lake Como, where the sun always shines, where the laurels are green at Christmas and the oranges glow.

JEAN: Lake Como is a rainy hole, and I never saw any oranges outside the stores. But tourists are attracted there because there are plenty of villas to be rented out to lovers, and that's a profitable business.————Do you know why? Because they sign a lease for six months—and then leave after three weeks!

JULIE: (*naively*): Why after three weeks?

JEAN: They quarrel, of course! But they still have to pay the rent in full! And so you rent the villas out again. And that's the way it goes, time after time. There's never a shortage of love—even if it doesn't last long!

JULIE: You don't want to die with me?

JEAN: I don't want to die at all! For one thing, I like living, and for another, I think suicide is a crime against the Providence which gave us life.

JULIE: You believe in God? *You?*

JEAN: Of course I do. And I go to church every other Sunday.————To be honest, I'm tired of all this, and I'm going to bed.

JULIE: Are you? And do you think I can let it go at that? A man owes something to the woman he's shamed.

JEAN (*taking out his purse and throwing a silver coin on the table*): Here! I don't like owing anything to anybody.

JULIE (*pretending not to notice the insult*): Do you know what the law states . . .

JEAN: Unfortunately the law doesn't state any punishment for the woman who seduces a man!

JULIE (*as before*): Do you see any way out but to leave, get married, and then separate?

JEAN: Suppose I refuse such a *mésalliance?*°

JULIE: *Mésalliance* . . .

JEAN: Yes, for me! You see, I come from better stock than you. There's no arsonist in my family.

JULIE: How do you know?

JEAN: You can't prove otherwise. We don't keep charts on our ancestors—there's just the police records! But I've read about your family. Do you know who the founder was? He was a miller who let the king sleep with his wife one night during the Danish War. I don't have any noble ancestors like that. I don't have any noble ancestors at all, but I could become one myself.

JULIE: This is what I get for opening my heart to someone unworthy, for giving my family's honor . . .

JEAN: Dishonor!————Well, I told you so: When people drink, they talk, and talk is dangerous!

JULIE: Oh, how I regret it!————How I regret it!————If you at least loved me.

JEAN: For the last time————what do you want? Shall I cry; shall I jump over your riding crop? Shall I kiss you and lure you off to Lake Como for three weeks, and then God knows what. . . ? What shall I do? What do you want? This is getting painfully embarrassing! But that's what happens when you stick your nose in women's business. Miss Julie! I see that you're unhappy. I know you're suffering, but I can't understand you. We don't have such romantic ideas; there's not this kind of hate between us. Love is a game we play when we get time off from work, but we don't have all day and night, like you. I think you're sick, really sick. Your mother was crazy, and her ideas have poisoned your life.

JULIE: Be kind to me. At least now you're talking like a human being.

JEAN: Be human yourself, then. You spit on me, and you won't let me wipe myself off————

JULIE: Help me! Help me! Just tell me what to do, where to go!

JEAN: In God's name, if I only knew myself!

JULIE: I've been crazy, out of my mind, but isn't there any way out?

JEAN: Stay here and keep calm! No one knows anything!

JULIE: Impossible! The others know and Kristine knows.

JEAN: No they don't, and they'd never believe a thing like that!

JULIE (*hesitantly*): But—it could happen again!

JEAN: That's true!

JULIE: And then?

JEAN (*frightened*): Then?————Why didn't I think about that? Yes, there is only one thing to do—get away from here! Right away! I can't come with you,

---

mésalliance: Misalliance or mismatch, especially regarding relative social status.

then we'd be finished, so you'll have to go alone —away—anywhere!

JULIE: Alone?———Where?———I can't do that!

JEAN: You must! And before the Count gets back! If you stay, you know what'll happen. Once you make a mistake like this, you want to continue because the damage has already been done. . . . Then you get bolder and bolder—until finally you're caught! So leave! Later you can write to the Count and confess everything—except that it was me! He'll never guess who it was, and he's not going to be eager to find out, anyway.

JULIE: I'll go if you come with me.

JEAN: Are you out of your head? Miss Julie runs away with her servant! In two days it would be in the newspapers, and that's something your father would never live through.

JULIE: I can't go and I can't stay! Help me! I'm so tired, so terribly tired.———Order me! Set me in motion—I can't think or act on my own . . .

JEAN: What miserable creatures you people are! You strut around with your noses in the air as if you were the lords of creation! All right, I'll order you. Go upstairs and get dressed! Get some money for the trip, and then come back down!

JULIE (in a half-whisper): Come up with me!

JEAN: To your room?———Now you're crazy again! (Hesitates for a moment.) No! Go, at once! (Takes her hand to lead her out.)

JULIE (as she leaves): Speak kindly to me, Jean!

JEAN: An order always sounds unkind—now you know how it feels. (Jean, alone, sighs with relief. He sits at the table, takes out a notebook and pencil, and begins adding up figures, counting aloud as he works. He continues in dumb show until Kristine enters, dressed for church. She is carrying a white tie and shirt front.)

KRISTINE: Lord Jesus, what a mess! What have you been up to?

JEAN: Oh, Miss Julie dragged everybody in here. You mean you didn't hear anything? You must have been sleeping soundly.

KRISTINE: Like a log.

JEAN: And dressed for church already?

KRISTINE: Of course! You remember you promised to come with me to communion today!

JEAN: Oh, yes, that's right.———And you brought my things. Come on, then! (He sits down. Kristine starts to put on his shirt front and tie. Pause. Jean begins sleepily.) What's the gospel text for today?

KRISTINE: On St. John's Day?—the beheading of John the Baptist, I should think!

JEAN: Ah, that'll be a long one, for sure.———Hey, you're choking me!———Oh, I'm sleepy, so sleepy!

KRISTINE: Yes, what have you been doing, up all night? Your face is absolutely green.

JEAN: I've been sitting here gabbing with Miss Julie.

KRISTINE: She has no idea what's proper, that one! (Pause.)

JEAN: You know, Kristine . . .

KRISTINE: What?

JEAN: It's really strange when you think about it.———Her!

KRISTINE: What's so strange?

JEAN: Everything! (Pause.)

KRISTINE (looking at the half-empty glasses standing on the table): Have you been drinking together, too?

JEAN: Yes.

KRISTINE: Shame on you!———Look me in the eye!

JEAN: Well?

KRISTINE: Is it possible? Is it possible?

JEAN (thinking it over for a moment): Yes, it is.

KRISTINE: Ugh! I never would have believed it! No, shame on you, shame!

JEAN: You're not jealous of her, are you?

KRISTINE: No, not of her! If it had been Clara or Sofie I'd have scratched your eyes out!———I don't know why, but that's the way I feel.———Oh, it's disgusting!

JEAN: Are you angry at her, then?

KRISTINE: No, at you! That was an awful thing to do, awful! Poor girl!———No, I don't care who knows it—I won't stay in a house where we can't respect the people we work for.

JEAN: Why should we respect them?

KRISTINE: You're so clever, you tell me! Do you want to wait on people who can't behave decently? Do you? You disgrace yourself that way, if you ask me.

JEAN: But it's a comfort to know they aren't any better than us.

KRISTINE: Not for me. If they're no better, what do we have to strive for to better ourselves.———And think of the Count! Think of him! As if he hasn't had enough misery in his life! Lord Jesus! No, I won't stay in this house any longer!———And it had to be with someone like you! If it had been that lawyer, if it had been a real gentleman . . .

JEAN: What do you mean?

KRISTINE: Oh, you're all right for what you are, but there are men and gentlemen, after all!———No, this business with Miss Julie I can never forget. She was so proud, so arrogant with men, you wouldn't have believed she could just go and give herself—and to someone like you! And she was going to have poor Diana shot for running after the gatekeepers' mutt!———Yes, I'm giving my notice, I mean it—I won't stay here any longer. On the twenty-fourth of October, I leave!

JEAN: And then?

KRISTINE: Well, since the subject has come up, it's about time you looked around for something since we're going to get married, in any case.

JEAN: Where am I going to look? I couldn't find a job like this if I was married.

KRISTINE: No, that's true. But you can find work as a porter or as a caretaker in some government office. The state doesn't pay much, I know, but it's secure, and there's a pension for the wife and children . . .

JEAN (grimacing): That's all very well, but it's a bit early for me to think about dying for a wife and children. My ambitions are a little higher than that.

KRISTINE: Your ambitions, yes! Well, you have obligations, too! Think about them!

JEAN: Don't start nagging me about obligations. I know what I have to do! (*Listening for something outside.*) Besides, this is something we have plenty of time to think over. Go and get ready for church.

KRISTINE: Who's that walking around up there?

JEAN: I don't know, unless it's Clara.

KRISTINE (*going*): You don't suppose it's the Count, who came home without us hearing him?

JEAN (*frightened*): The Count? No, I don't think so. He'd have rung.

KRISTINE (*going*): Well, God help us! I've never seen anything like this before. (*The sun has risen and shines through the treetops in the park. The light shifts gradually until it slants in through the windows. Jean goes to the door and signals. Miss Julie enters, dressed in travel clothes and carrying a small bird cage, covered with a cloth, which she places on a chair.*)

JULIE: I'm ready now.

JEAN: Shh! Kristine is awake.

JULIE (*very nervous during the following*): Does she suspect something?

JEAN: She doesn't know anything. But my God, you look awful!

JULIE: Why? How do I look?

JEAN: You're pale as a ghost and—excuse me, but your face is dirty.

JULIE: Let me wash up then.————(*She goes to the basin and washes her hands and face.*) Give me a towel!———— Oh———— the sun's coming up.

JEAN: Then the goblins will disappear.

JULIE: Yes, there must have been goblins out last night!————Jean, listen, come with me! I have some money now.

JEAN (*hesitantly*): Enough?

JULIE: Enough to start with. Come with me! I just can't travel alone on a day like this—midsummer day on a stuffy train—jammed in among crowds of people staring at me. Eternal delays at every station, while I'd wish I had wings. No, I can't, I can't! And then there'll be memories, memories of midsummer days when I was little. The church—decorated with birch leaves and lilacs; dinner at the big table with relatives and friends, the afternoons in the park, dancing, music, flowers, and games. Oh, no matter how far we travel, the memories will follow in the baggage car, with remorse and guilt!

JEAN: I'll go with you—but right away, before it's too late. Right this minute!

JULIE: Get dressed, then! (*Picking up the bird cage.*)

JEAN: But no baggage! It would give us away!

JULIE: No, nothing! Only what we can have in the compartment with us.

JEAN (*has taken his hat*): What've you got there? What is it?

JULIE: It's only my greenfinch. I couldn't leave her behind.

JEAN: What? Bring a bird cage with us? You're out of your head! Put it down!

JULIE: It's the only thing I'm taking from my home—the only living being that loves me, since Diana was unfaithful. Don't be cruel! Let me take her!

JEAN: Put the cage down, I said!————And don't talk so loudly—Kristine will hear us!

JULIE: No, I won't leave her in the hands of strangers! I'd rather you killed her.

JEAN: Bring the thing here, then, I'll cut its head off!

JULIE: Oh! But don't hurt her! Don't . . . no, I can't.

JEAN: Bring it here! I can!

JULIE (*taking the bird out of the cage and kissing it*): Oh, my little Serena, must you die and leave your mistress?

JEAN: Please don't make a scene! Your whole future is at stake! Hurry up! (*He snatches the bird from her, carries it over to the chopping block, and picks up a meat cleaver. Miss Julie turns away.*) You should have learned how to slaughter chickens instead of how to fire pistols. (*He chops off the bird's head.*) Then you wouldn't feel faint at the sight of blood.

JULIE (*screaming*): Kill me, too! Kill me! You, who can slaughter an innocent animal without blinking an eye! Oh, how I hate, how I detest you! There's blood between us now! I curse the moment I set eyes on you! I curse the moment I was conceived in my mother's womb!

JEAN: What good does cursing do? Let's go!

JULIE (*approaching the chopping block, as if drawn against her will*): No, I don't want to go yet. I can't . . . until I see . . . Shh! I hear a carriage————(*She listens, but her eyes never leave the cleaver and the chopping block.*) Do you think I can't stand the sight of blood? You think I'm so weak . . . Oh—I'd like to see your blood and your brains on a chopping block!————I'd like to see your whole sex swimming in a sea of blood, like my little bird . . . I think I could drink from your skull! I'd like to bathe my feet in your open chest and eat your heart roasted whole! ————You think I'm weak. You think I love you because my womb craved your seed. You think I want to carry your spawn under my heart and nourish it with my blood—bear your child and take your name! By the way, what is your family name? I've never heard it.————Do you have one? I was to be Mrs. Bootblack—or Madame Pigsty.————You dog, who wears my collar, you lackey, who bears my coat of arms on your buttons—do I have to share you with my cook, compete with my own servant? Oh! Oh! Oh!————You think I'm a coward who wants to run away! No, now I'm staying—and let the storm break! My father will come home . . . to find his desk broken open . . . and his money gone! Then he'll ring—that bell . . . twice for his valet—and then he'll send for the police . . . and then I'll tell everything! Everything! Oh, what a relief it'll be to have it all end—if only it will end!————And then he'll have a stroke and die . . . That'll be the end of all of us—and there'll be peace . . . quiet . . . eternal rest!————And then our coat of arms will be broken against his coffin—the family title extinct—but the valet's line will go on in an orphanage . . . win laurels in the gutter, and end in jail!

JEAN: There's the blue blood talking! Very good, Miss Julie! Just don't let that miller out of the closet! (*Kristine enters, dressed for church, with a psalm-book in her hand.*)

JULIE (*rushing to Kristine and falling into her arms, as if seeking protection*): Help me, Kristine! Help me against this man!

KRISTINE (*unmoved and cold*): What a fine way to behave on a Sunday morning! (*Sees the chopping block.*) And look at this mess!———What does all this mean? Why all this screaming and carrying on?

JULIE: Kristine! You're a woman and my friend! Beware of this swine!

JEAN (*uncomfortable*): While you ladies discuss this, I'll go in and shave. (*Slips off right.*)

JULIE: You must listen to me so you'll understand!

KRISTINE: No, I could never understand such disgusting behavior! Where are you off to in your traveling clothes?———And he had his hat on.———Well?———Well?———

JULIE: Listen to me, Kristine! Listen, and I'll tell you everything———

KRISTINE: I don't want to hear it . . .

JULIE: But you must listen to me . . .

KRISTINE: What about? If it's about this silliness with Jean, I'm not interested, because it's none of my business. But if you're thinking of tricking him into running out, we'll soon put a stop to that!

JULIE (*extremely nervous*): Try to be calm now, Kristine, and listen to me! I can't stay here, and neither can Jean—so we must go away . . .

KRISTINE: Hm, hm!

JULIE (*brightening*): You see, I just had an idea———What if all three of us go—abroad—to Switzerland and start a hotel together?———I have money, you see—and Jean and I could run it—and I thought you, you could take care of the kitchen . . . Wouldn't that be wonderful?———Say yes! And come with us, and then everything will be settled!———Oh, do say yes! (*Embracing Kristine and patting her warmly.*)

KRISTINE (*coolly, thoughtfully*): Hm, hm!

JULIE (*presto tempo*):° You've never traveled, Kristine.———You must get out and see the world. You can't imagine how much fun it is to travel by train—always new faces—new countries.———And when we get to Hamburg, we'll stop off at the zoo—you'll like that.———and then we'll go to the theater and the opera—and when we get to Munich, dear, there we have museums, with Rubens and Raphael, the great painters, as you know.———You've heard of Munich, where King Ludwig lived—the king who went mad.———And then we'll see his castles—they're still there and they're like castles in fairy tales.———And from there it isn't far to Switzerland—and the Alps.———Imagine—the Alps have snow on them even in the middle of summer!———And oranges grow there and laurel trees that

presto tempo: At a rapid pace.

are green all year round———(*Jean can be seen in the wings right, sharpening his razor on a strop which he holds with his teeth and his left hand. He listens to the conversation with satisfaction, nodding now and then in approval. Miss Julie continues tempo prestissimo.*)° And then we'll start a hotel—and I'll be at the desk, while Jean greets the guests . . . does the shopping . . . writes letters.———You have no idea what a life it'll be—the train whistles blowing and the carriages arriving and the bells ringing in the rooms and down in the restaurant.———And I'll make out the bills—and I know how to salt them! . . . You'll never believe how timid travelers are when they have to pay their bills!———And you—you'll be in charge of the kitchen.———Naturally, you won't have to stand over the stove yourself.———And since you're going to be seen by people, you'll have to wear beautiful clothes.———And you, with your looks—no, I'm not flattering you—one fine day you'll grab yourself a husband!———You'll see!—A rich Englishman—they're so easy to——— (*Slowing down.*)———catch—and then we'll get rich—and build ourselves a villa on Lake Como.———It's true it rains there a little now and then, but——— (*Dully.*)———the sun has to shine sometimes—although it looks dark—and then . . . of course we could always come back home again——— (*Pause.*)———here—or somewhere else———

KRISTINE: Listen, Miss Julie, do you believe all this?

JULIE (*crushed*): Do I believe it?

KRISTINE: Yes!

JULIE (*wearily*): I don't know. I don't believe in anything anymore. (*She sinks down on the bench and cradles her head in her arms on the table.*) Nothing! Nothing at all!

KRISTINE (*turning right to where Jean is standing*): So, you thought you'd run out!

JEAN (*embarrassed; puts the razor on the table*): Run out? That's no way to put it. You hear Miss Julie's plan, and even if she is tired after being up all night, it's still a practical plan.

KRISTINE: Now you listen to me! Did you think I'd work as a cook for that . . .

JEAN (*sharply*): You watch what you say in front of your mistress! Do you understand?

KRISTINE: Mistress!

JEAN: Yes!

KRISTINE: Listen to him! Listen to him!

JEAN: Yes, you listen! It'd do you good to listen more and talk less! Miss Julie is your mistress. If you despise her, you have to despise yourself for the same reason!

KRISTINE: I've always had enough self-respect———

JEAN: ———to be able to despise other people!

KRISTINE: ———to stop me from doing anything that's beneath me. You can't say that the Count's cook has been up to something with the groom or the swineherd! Can you?

JEAN: No, you were lucky enough to get hold of a gentleman!

tempo prestissimo: At a very rapid pace.

KRISTINE: Yes, a gentleman who sells the Count's oats from the stable.

JEAN: You should talk—taking a commission from the grocer and bribes from the butcher.

KRISTINE: What?

JEAN: And you say you can't respect your employers any longer. You, you, you!

KRISTINE: Are you coming to church with me, now? You could use a good sermon after your fine deed!

JEAN: No, I'm not going to church today. You'll have to go alone and confess what you've been up to.

KRISTINE: Yes, I'll do that, and I'll bring back enough forgiveness for you, too. The Savior suffered and died on the Cross for all our sins, and if we go to Him with faith and a penitent heart, He takes all our sins on Himself.

JEAN: Even grocery sins?

JULIE: And do you believe that, Kristine?

KRISTINE: It's my living faith, as sure as I stand here. It's the faith I learned as a child, Miss Julie, and kept ever since. "Where sin abounded, grace did much more abound!"

JULIE: Oh, if I only had your faith. If only . . .

KRISTINE: Well, you see, we can't have it without God's special grace, and that isn't given to everyone——

JULIE: Who is it given to then?

KRISTINE: That's the great secret of the workings of grace, Miss Julie, and God is no respecter of persons, for the last shall be the first . . .

JULIE: Then He does respect the last.

KRISTINE (*continuing*): . . . and it is easier for a camel to go through the eye of a needle, than for a rich man to enter the Kingdom of God. That's how it is, Miss Julie! Anyhow, I'm going now—alone, and on the way I'm going to tell the groom not to let any horses out, in case anyone wants to leave before the Count gets back!——Goodbye! (*Leaves.*)

JEAN: What a witch!——And all this because of a greenfinch!——

JULIE (*dully*): Never mind the greenfinch!——Can you see any way out of this? Any end to it?

JEAN (*thinking*): No!

JULIE: What would you do in my place?

JEAN: In your place? Let's see—as a person of position, as a woman who had—fallen. I don't know—wait, now I know.

JULIE (*taking the razor and making a gesture*): You mean like this?

JEAN: Yes! But—understand—I wouldn't do it! That's the difference between us!

JULIE: Because you're a man and I'm a woman? What sort of difference is that?

JEAN: The usual difference—between a man and a woman.

JULIE (*with the razor in her hand*): I want to, but I can't!——My father couldn't either, the time he should have done it.

JEAN: No, he shouldn't have! He had to revenge himself first.

JULIE: And now my mother is revenged again, through me.

JEAN: Didn't you ever love your father, Miss Julie?

JULIE: Oh yes, deeply, but I've hated him, too. I must have done so without realizing it! It was he who brought me up to despise my own sex, making me half woman, half man. Whose fault is what's happened? My father's, my mother's, my own? My own? I don't have anything that's my own. I don't have a single thought that I didn't get from my father, not an emotion that I didn't get from my mother, and this last idea—that all people are equal—I got that from my fiancé.——That's why I called him a swine! How can it be my fault? Shall I let Jesus take on the blame, the way Kristine does?——No, I'm too proud to do that and too sensible—thanks to my father's teachings.——And as for someone rich not going to heaven, that's a lie. But Kristine won't get in—how will she explain the money she has in the savings bank? Whose fault is it?——What does it matter whose fault it is? I'm still the one who has to bear the blame, face the consequences . . .

JEAN: Yes, but . . . (*The bell rings sharply twice. Miss Julie jumps up. Jean changes his coat.*) The Count is back! Do you suppose Kristine—(*He goes to the speaking tube, taps the lid, and listens.*)

JULIE: He's been to his desk!

JEAN: It's Jean, sir! (*Listening; the audience cannot hear the Count's voice.*) Yes, sir! (*Listening.*) Yes, sir! Right away! (*Listening.*) At once, sir! (*Listening.*) I see, in half an hour!

JULIE (*desperately frightened*): What did he say? Dear Lord, what did he say?

JEAN: He wants his boots and his coffee in half an hour.

JULIE: So, in half an hour! Oh, I'm so tired. I'm not able to do anything. I can't repent, can't run away, can't stay, can't live—can't die! Help me now! Order me, and I'll obey like a dog! Do me this last service, save my honor, save his name! You know what I *should* do, but don't have the will to . . . You will it, you order me to do it!

JEAN: I don't know why——but now I can't either——I don't understand.——It's as if this coat made it impossible for me to order you to do anything.——And now, since the Count spoke to me—I—I can't really explain it—but—ah, it's the damn lackey in me!——I think if the Count came down here now—and ordered me to cut my throat, I'd do it on the spot.

JULIE: Then pretend you're he, and I'm you!—— You gave such a good performance before when you knelt at my feet.——You were a real nobleman.——Or—have you ever seen a hypnotist in the theater? (*Jean nods.*) He says to his subject: "Take the broom," and he takes it. He says: "Sweep," and he sweeps——

JEAN: But the subject has to be asleep.

JULIE (*ecstatically*): I'm already asleep.——The whole room is like smoke around me . . . and you look like an iron stove . . . shaped like a man in black, with a tall hat—and your eyes glow like coals when the fire is dying—and your face is a white patch, like ashes————(*The sunlight has reached the floor and now shines on Jean.*)———it's so warm and good———(*She rubs her hands as if warming them before a fire.*)———and bright—and so peaceful!

JEAN (*taking the razor and putting it in her hand*): Here's the broom! Go now while it's bright—out to the barn—and . . . (*Whispers in her ear.*)

JULIE (*awake*): Thank you. I'm going now to rest! But just tell me—that those who are first can also receive the gift of grace. Say it, even if you don't believe it.

JEAN: The first? No, I can't———But wait—Miss Julie—now I know! You're no longer among the first—you're now among—the last!

JULIE: That's true.———I'm among the very last. I'm the last one of all! Oh!———But now I can't go!———Tell me once more to go!

JEAN: No, now I can't either! I can't!

JULIE: And the first shall be the last!

JEAN: Don't think, don't think! You're taking all my strength from me, making me a coward.———What was that? I thought the bell moved!———No! Shall we stuff paper in it?———To be so afraid of a bell!———But it isn't just a bell.———There's someone behind it—a hand sets it in motion—and something else sets the hand in motion.———Maybe if you cover your ears—cover your ears! But then it rings even louder! rings until someone answers.———And then it's too late! And then the police come—and—then———(*The bell rings twice loudly. Jean flinches, then straightens up.*) It's horrible! But there's no other way!———Go! (*Miss Julie walks firmly out through the door.*)

COMMENTARY

AUGUST STRINDBERG (1849–1912)

From the Preface to Miss Julie   1888

TRANSLATED BY HARRY G. CARLSON

Strindberg's preface sets out his intentions in writing *Miss Julie*, a play concerned with the problem of "social climbing or falling, of higher or lower, better or worse, man or woman." He discusses the struggle for dominance between Miss Julie and Jean, and he characterizes Miss Julie as a woman forced to "wreak vengeance" on herself.

Miss Julie is a modern character. Not that the man-hating half-woman has not existed in all ages but because now that she has been discovered, she has come out in the open to make herself heard. The half-woman is a type who pushes her way ahead, selling herself nowadays for power, decorations, honors, and diplomas, as formerly she used to do for money. The type implies a retrogressive step in evolution, an inferior species who cannot endure. Unfortunately, they are able to pass on their wretchedness; degenerate men seem unconsciously to choose their mates from among them. And so they breed, producing an indeterminate sex for whom life is a torture. Fortunately, the offspring go under either because they are out of harmony with reality or because their repressed instincts break out uncontrollably or because their hopes of achieving equality with men are crushed. The type is tragic, revealing the drama of a desperate struggle against Nature, tragic as the romantic heritage now being dissipated by naturalism, which has a contrary aim: happiness, and happiness belongs only to the strong and skillful species.

But Miss Julie is also: a relic of the old warrior nobility now giving way to a new nobility of nerve and intellect, a victim of her own flawed constitution, a victim of the discord caused in a family by a mother's "crime," a victim of the delusions and conditions of her age—and together these are the equivalent of the concept of Destiny, or Universal Law, of antiquity. Guilt has been abolished by the naturalist, along with God, but the consequences of an action—punishment, imprisonment or the fear of it—that he cannot erase, for the simple reason that they remain, whether he pronounces acquittal or not. Those who have been injured are not as kind and understanding as an unscathed outsider can afford to be. Even if her father felt constrained not to seek revenge, his daughter would wreak vengeance upon herself, as she does here, out of an innate or acquired sense of honor, which the upper classes inherit—from where? From barbarism, from the ancient Aryan home of the race, from medieval chivalry. It is a beautiful thing, but nowadays a hindrance to the survival of the race. It is the nobleman's harikari, which compels him to slit open his own stomach when someone insults him and which survives in a modified form in the duel, that privilege of the nobility. That is why Jean, the servant, lives, while Miss Julie cannot live without honor. The slave's advantage over the nobleman is that he lacks this fatal preoccupation with honor. But in all of us Aryans there is something of the nobleman, or a Don Quixote. And so we sympathize with the suicide, whose act means a loss of honor. We are noblemen enough to be pained when we see the mighty fallen and as superfluous as a corpse, yes, even if the fallen should rise again and make amends through an honorable act. The servant Jean is a race-founder, someone in whom the process of differentiation can be detected. Born the son of a tenant farmer, he has educated himself in the things a gentleman should know. He has been quick to learn, has finely developed senses (smell, taste, sight) and a feeling for what is beautiful. He is already moving up in the world and is not embarrassed about using other people's help. He is alienated from his fellow servants, despising them as parts of a past he has already put behind him. He fears and flees them because they know his secrets, pry into his intentions, envy his rise, and look forward eagerly to his fall. Hence his dual, indecisive nature, vacillating between sympathy for people in high social positions and hatred for those who currently occupy those positions. He is an aristocrat, as he himself says, has learned the secrets of good society, is polished on the surface but coarse beneath, wears a frock coat tastefully but without any guarantee that his body is clean.

He has respect for Miss Julie, but is afraid of Kristine because she knows his dangerous secrets. He is sufficiently callous not to let the night's events disturb his plans for the future. With both a slave's brutality and a master's lack of squeamishness, he can see blood without fainting and shake off misfortune easily. Consequently, he comes through the struggle unscathed and will probably end up an innkeeper. And even if *he* does not become a Rumanian count, his son will become a university student and possibly a county police commissioner. . . .

Apart from the fact that Jean is rising in the world, he is superior to Miss Julie because he is a man. Sexually, he is an aristocrat because of his masculine strength, his more keenly developed senses, and his capacity for taking the initiative. His sense of inferiority is mostly due to the social circumstances in which be happens to be living, and he can probably shed it along with his valet's jacket.

His slave mentality expresses itself in the fearful respect he has for the Count (the boots) and his religious superstition; but he respects the Count mainly as the occupant of the kind of high position to which he himself aspires; and the respect remains even after he has conquered the daughter of the house and seen how empty the lovely shell was.

I do not believe that love in any "higher" sense can exist between two people of such different natures, and so I have Miss Julie's love as something she fabricates in order to protect and excuse herself; and I have Jean suppose himself capable of loving her under other social circumstances. I think it is the same with love as with the hyacinth, which must take root in darkness *before* it can produce a sturdy flower. Here a flower shoots up, blooms, and goes to seed all at once, and that is why it dies so quickly.

Oscar Wilde

Oscar Fingal O'Flahertie Wills Wilde (1854–1900) was born to a famous eye surgeon who maintained a home in Dublin's most exclusive neighborhood. Wilde's mother, known by her literary name, Speranza, was noted for collecting Irish folk stories in the western hills in the late 1870s. Her work was important to later literature, but it was especially important for its timing, since most of the storytellers in Ireland were gone by the turn of the century.

Wilde was a brilliant classics scholar at Trinity College, Dublin, where his tutor was the legendary Mahaffy, who later traveled with him in France. After Trinity, he went to Magdalen College, Oxford, where he earned a distinguished degree. Among his influences in Oxford was Slade Professor of Art John Ruskin, with whom Wilde had long walks and talks. Ruskin had published important books on northern Gothic art and on Italian art, especially the art of Venice. Art was one of Wilde's primary passions, especially the decorative arts. He agreed with Walter Pater, a contemporary art critic, that art must best serve the needs of art. He believed, for example, that poetry did not serve religious, political, social, or biographical goals. Its ends were aesthetic and its pleasures were in its sounds, images, and thoughts.

Partly because of his brilliance and partly because he was one of the age's greatest conversationalists, Wilde was soon in the company of the famous and amusing people of his generation. Some of his conversational gift is apparent in his plays.

By his own admission, his life was marked by an overindulgence in sensuality: "What paradox was to me in the sphere of thought, perversity became to me in the sphere of passion." He married Constance Lloyd in 1884, and the couple soon had two sons. But by 1891 Wilde had already had several homosexual liaisons, one of which was to bring him to ruin. His relationship with the much younger Lord Alfred Douglas ended with Douglas's father, the marquis of Queensberry, publicly denouncing Wilde as a sodomite. Wilde sued for libel but lost. As a result, in 1895 he was tried for sodomy, convicted, and sentenced to two years' hard labor. Wilde's actions have been seen as self-destructive, but they are also consistent with his efforts to force society to examine its own hypocrisy. Unfortunately, his efforts in court and prison ruined him, and he died in exile in Paris three years after his release.

His best known novel, *The Picture of Dorian Gray* (1891; expanded 1894), is the story of a young man whose sensual life eats away at him and eventually destroys him. The novel's failure when it was first published led Wilde to try writing for the stage, where he was a signal success. Remarkably, all his plays were written in the period between 1891 and his imprisonment in 1895. Most of his plays—*Salomé* (1891), *Lady Windermere's Fan* (1892), *A Woman of No Importance* (1893), *An Ideal Husband* (1895), and *The Importance of Being Earnest* (1895)—rank as witty, insightful, and sharp commentaries on the upper-class British society Wilde knew best. They owe a great deal to eighteenth-century comedies, such as William Congreve's *The Way of the World*. But they also owe a great deal to British and European farces and comedies of Wilde's own time, many of which he seems to have studied closely. Unlike those plays—many of which have never been published and no longer exist—Wilde's are still funny and still seem pertinent even though the class he criticized has long vanished.

The Importance of Being Earnest was a remarkable success when it opened at the St. James Theatre on Valentine's Day 1895, but it closed in two months after fewer than one hundred performances when the scandal of Wilde's conviction became public. Wilde's reputation as playwright was made and broken in a matter of a few years, and it was not restored until after his death.

The Importance of Being Earnest

For discussion questions and assignments on *The Importance of Being Earnest*, visit **bedfordstmartins.com/jacobus**.

The Importance of Being Earnest was originally written in four acts, but because the producer requested that it be cut, Wilde reworked it into three acts, agreeing that the excisions made the play stronger. Its subtitle, *A Trivial Comedy for Serious People*, has prompted commentators to think of the play as farcical fluff, a play about little or nothing that is nonetheless profoundly amusing. The *New York Times* commented after the play's first U.S. opening, "The thing is as slight in structure and as devoid of purpose as a paper balloon, but it is extraordinarily funny." Recent critics have challenged this view on the grounds that the play's subject matter centers on the questions of identity and reality. One current view is that its surfaces are slight but beneath the surface is a commentary on a society that judges things only by appearance.

The primary characters are Algernon Moncrieff and Jack Worthing, young gentlemen of marriageable age. Among the women are Algernon's cousin Gwendolen Fairfax, who adores the name Ernest and is in love with Jack; Lady Bracknell, her mother; and Cecily Cardew, Jack's ward. Bunbury, referred to by Algernon, seems to be a character, but is instead an invention. He is a convenience for Algernon, a country friend whose illnesses Algernon uses to avoid social events he dislikes, such as Lady Bracknell's dinners. Jack, who lives in the country, has created a similar figure to help him escape to town—an imaginary brother Ernest. In town, Jack pretends to be Ernest, and all his town acquaintances, including Algernon and Gwendolen, know Jack by that name.

The similarities with Restoration comedies are striking. The question of marriage is central in the play, and attitudes toward marriage in Wilde's social class are among the targets of his satire. When Lady Bracknell probes into Jack Worthing's background, she discovers distressing news about his family "line": Jack is a foundling who had been left in a handbag in Victoria Station. His family "line" is the Brighton Line! Gwendolen could also have stepped from a Restoration comedy. She is determined to have Jack Worthing, and when he seems sluggish about proposing she prompts him, offering a critique of his proposal by telling him he seems inexperienced at it.

The play owes perhaps even more to the farces of the 1880s and 1890s and a great deal to the well-made plays of Eugène Scribe and his successors. Critics often compare Wilde to Alexandre Dumas, the author of *La Dame aux camélias* (*Camille*), because both writers fashion their plays with a considerable degree of artificiality, planting information in the first act that would prove the solution to problems in the last act. Dumas also plays with questions of identity, disguise, and revelation at the last minute in much the way Wilde does here when he reveals the identity of Ernest.

In melodramas and well-made plays, the revelation at the end was not that the potential husband had the right name so much as that he had the right background: he was an aristocrat and not the commoner he seemed to be. Wilde has fun with this convention and many others. In an instant, he ridicules the trick of revealing the hero to be "marriageable" because of his birth by emphasizing the triviality of a name. Yet names are of great importance (as Shakespeare tells us in *Romeo and Juliet*), and the earnestness implied in Ernest is one ingredient that helps Jack Worthing succeed.

Critic Kerry Powell has demonstrated that almost every device in *The Importance of Being Earnest* was drawn from a contemporary farce or comedy. The device of the child lost in a piece of luggage was used in *The Lost Child* (1863), and *The Foundling* (1894) actually took place in Brighton. The name Bunbury and the concept of "Bunburying" come from *The Godpapa* (1891). Even the device of baptism was used in *Crimes and Christening* (1891). Wilde was adept at taking the theater conventions his audience was most familiar with and using them to his own ends—to entertain his audience, but at the same time to help him put an extra edge on his satire.

The Importance of Being Earnest in Performance

After the first production closed down in 1895, the play was revived in London in 1898 and 1902. An even more successful production in 1909 saw 324 performances. The benchmark for a truly successful play in those days seems to have been one hundred performances, and Wilde would have felt vindicated by the 1909 production, had he lived to see it. *The Importance of Being Earnest* has been produced so often in Great Britain and the United States that only a few productions can be taken into account here. The first New York production was in 1902. John Gielgud and Edith Evans played in the 1939 London production and then again in 1942. In 1947, Gielgud played in New York with Clifton Webb and Estelle Winwood. The reviews were especially strong, calling the play "as insolently monocled in manner and as killingly high-toned in language as mischievous tomfoolery can make it."

The play inspired at least five musicals between 1927 and 1984. The 1979 production at Stratford, Ontario, was called "a perfect play in a perfect production." A production by the Berlin Play Actors in 1987 used all men and relied on insights drawn from transvestite performers, but it was badly received. University productions of the play are fairly common, although, like the Yale Repertory production in 1986, they are not always able to pull off the comic demands of the play's exacting language. The original four-act version of the play, discovered in 1977 in the New York Public Library, was produced in Ohio in the John Carroll University's Marinello Theater in 1985. It was more a curiosity than a triumph. The 1993 production at the Aldwych in London received great praise for its dazzling sets that "matched Wilde's word pictures with bold stage pictures." Maggie Smith played Lady Bracknell. Sir Peter Hall toured his Theatre Royal Bath company successfully in 2006 with a strikingly energetic Lynn Redgrave as Lady Bracknell. The 2006 production at the Brooklyn Academy of Music was well received, although the Harvey Theatre's stage was faulted for not wholly accommodating the proscenium frame necessary for the drama.

The play is a witty tour de force of language. Its surfaces gleam, and the best productions play it straight. A spate of contemporary films has made Wilde's work available to a wide audience.

OSCAR WILDE (1854–1900)

The Importance of Being Earnest 1895

A Trival Comedy for Serious People

The Persons of the Play

JOHN WORTHING, J.P., *of the Manor House, Woolton, Hertfordshire*
ALGERNON MONCRIEFF, *his friend*
REV. CANON CHASUBLE, D.D., *rector of Woolton*
MERRIMAN, *butler to Mr. Worthing*
LANE, *Mr. Moncrieff's manservant*
LADY BRACKNELL
HON. GWENDOLEN FAIRFAX, *her daughter*
CECILY CARDEW, *John Worthing's ward*
MISS PRISM, *her governess*

The Scenes of the Play

Act I: *Algernon Moncrieff's Flat in Half Moon Street, W.*
Act II: *The Garden at the Manor House, Woolton*
Act III: *Morning Room at the Manor House, Woolton*

ACT I

(*Scene: Morning room in Algernon's flat in Half Moon Street. The room is luxuriously and artistically furnished. The sound of a piano is heard in the adjoining room. Lane is arranging afternoon tea on the table, and after the music has ceased, Algernon enters.*)

ALGERNON: Did you hear what I was playing, Lane?
LANE: I didn't think it polite to listen, sir.
ALGERNON: I'm sorry for that, for your sake. I don't play accurately—anyone can play accurately—but I play with wonderful expression. As far as the piano is concerned, sentiment is my forte. I keep science for Life.
LANE: Yes, sir.
ALGERNON: And, speaking of the science of Life, have you got the cucumber sandwiches cut for Lady Bracknell?
LANE: Yes, sir.   (*Hands them on a salver.*)
ALGERNON (*inspects them, takes two, and sits down on the sofa*): Oh!—by the way, Lane, I see from your book that on Thursday night, when Lord Shoreham and Mr. Worthing were dining with me, eight bottles of champagne are entered as having been consumed.

LANE: Yes, sir; eight bottles and a pint.
ALGERNON: Why is it that at a bachelor's establishment the servants invariably drink the champagne? I ask merely for information.
LANE: I attribute it to the superior quality of the wine, sir. I have often observed that in married households the champagne is rarely of a first-rate brand.
ALGERNON: Good heavens! Is marriage so demoralizing as that?
LANE: I believe it *is* a very pleasant state, sir. I have had very little experience of it myself up to the present. I have only been married once. That was in consequence of a misunderstanding between myself and a young person.
ALGERNON (*languidly*): I don't know that I am much interested in your family life, Lane.
LANE: No, sir; it is not a very interesting subject. I never think of it myself.
ALGERNON: Very natural, I am sure. That will do, Lane, thank you.
LANE: Thank you, sir.   (*Lane goes out.*)
ALGERNON: Lane's views on marriage seem somewhat lax. Really, if the lower orders don't set us a good example, what on earth is the use of them? They seem, as a class, to have absolutely no sense of moral responsibility.

(*Enter Lane.*)

LANE: Mr. Ernest Worthing.

(*Enter Jack. Lane goes out.*)

ALGERNON: How are you, my dear Ernest? What brings you up to town?
JACK: Oh, pleasure, pleasure! What else should bring one anywhere? Eating as usual, I see, Algy!
ALGERNON (*Stiffly*): I believe it is customary in good society to take some slight refreshment at five o'clock. Where have you been since last Thursday?
JACK (*sitting down on the sofa*): In the country.
ALGERNON: What on earth do you do there?
JACK (*pulling off his gloves*): When one is in town one amuses oneself. When one is in the country one amuses other people. It is excessively boring.
ALGERNON: And who are the people you amuse?
JACK (*airily*): Oh, neighbors, neighbors.

ALGERNON: Got nice neighbors in your part of Shropshire?

JACK: Perfectly horrid! Never speak to one of them.

ALGERNON: How immensely you must amuse them! (*Goes over and takes sandwich.*) By the way, Shropshire is your county, is it not?

JACK: Eh? Shropshire? Yes, of course. Hallo! Why all these cups? Why cucumber sandwiches? Why such reckless extravagance in one so young? Who is coming to tea?

ALGERNON: Oh! merely Aunt Augusta and Gwendolen.

JACK: How perfectly delightful!

ALGERNON: Yes, that is all very well; but I am afraid Aunt Augusta won't quite approve of your being here.

JACK: May I ask why?

ALGERNON: My dear fellow, the way you flirt with Gwendolen is perfectly disgraceful. It is almost as bad as the way Gwendolen flirts with you.

JACK: I am in love with Gwendolen. I have come up to town expressly to propose to her.

ALGERNON: I thought you had come up for pleasure? — I call that business.

JACK: How utterly unromantic you are!

ALGERNON: I really don't see anything romantic in proposing. It is very romantic to be in love. But there is nothing romantic about a definite proposal. Why, one may be accepted. One usually is, I believe. Then the excitement is all over. The very essence of romance is uncertainty. If ever I get married, I'll certainly try to forget the fact.

JACK: I have no doubt about that, dear Algy. The Divorce Court was specially invented for people whose memories are so curiously constituted.

ALGERNON: Oh! there is no use speculating on that subject. Divorces are made in heaven — (*Jack puts out his hand to take a sandwich. Algernon at once interferes.*) Please don't touch the cucumber sandwiches. They are ordered specially for Aunt Augusta. (*Takes one and eats it.*)

JACK: Well, you have been eating them all the time.

ALGERNON: That is quite a different matter. She is my aunt. (*Takes plate from below.*) Have some bread and butter. The bread and butter is for Gwendolen. Gwendolen is devoted to bread and butter.

JACK (*advancing to table and helping himself*): And very good bread and butter it is too.

ALGERNON: Well, my dear fellow, you need not eat as if you were going to eat it all. You behave as if you were married to her already. You are not married to her already, and I don't think you ever will be.

JACK: Why on earth do you say that?

ALGERNON: Well, in the first place, girls never marry the men they flirt with. Girls don't think it right.

JACK: Oh, that is nonsense!

ALGERNON: It isn't. It is a great truth. It accounts for the extraordinary number of bachelors that one sees all over the place. In the second place, I don't give my consent.

JACK: Your consent!

ALGERNON: My dear fellow, Gwendolen is my first cousin. And before I allow you to marry her, you will have to clear up the whole question of Cecily.

(*Rings bell.*)

JACK: Cecily! What on earth do you mean? What do you mean, Algy, by Cecily? I don't know anyone of the name of Cecily.

(*Enter Lane.*)

ALGERNON: Bring me that cigarette case Mr. Worthing left in the smoking room the last time he dined here.

LANE: Yes, sir.   (*Lane goes out.*)

JACK: Do you mean to say you have had my cigarette case all this time? I wish to goodness you had let me know. I have been writing frantic letters to Scotland Yard about it. I was very nearly offering a large reward.

ALGERNON: Well, I wish you would offer one. I happen to be more than usually hard up.

JACK: There is no good offering a large reward now that the thing is found.

(*Enter Lane with the cigarette case on a salver. Algernon takes it at once. Lane goes out.*)

ALGERNON: I think that is rather mean of you, Ernest, I must say. (*Opens case and examines it.*) However, it makes no matter, for, now that I look at the inscription inside, I find that the thing isn't yours after all.

JACK: Of course it's mine. (*Moving to him.*) You have seen me with it a hundred times, and you have no right whatsoever to read what is written inside. It is a very ungentlemanly thing to read a private cigarette case.

ALGERNON: Oh! it is absurd to have a hard-and-fast rule about what one should read and what one shouldn't. More than half of modern culture depends on what one shouldn't read.

JACK: I am quite aware of the fact, and I don't propose to discuss modern culture. It isn't the sort of thing one should talk of in private. I simply want my cigarette case back.

ALGERNON: Yes; but this isn't your cigarette case. This cigarette case is a present from someone of the name of Cecily, and you said you didn't know anyone of that name.

JACK: Well, if you want to know, Cecily happens to be my aunt.

ALGERNON: Your aunt!

JACK: Yes. Charming old lady she is, too. Lives at Tunbridge Wells. Just give it back to me, Algy.

ALGERNON (*retreating to back of sofa*): But why does she call herself little Cecily if she is your aunt and lives at Tunbridge Wells? (*Reading.*) "From little Cecily with her fondest love."

JACK (*moving to sofa and kneeling upon it*): My dear fellow, what on earth is there in that? Some aunts are tall, some aunts are not tall. That is a matter that surely an aunt may be allowed to decide for herself. You seem to think that every aunt should be exactly like your aunt! That is absurd! For heaven's sake give me back my cigarette case.

(*Follows Algernon round the room.*)

ALGERNON: Yes. But why does your aunt call you her uncle? "From little Cecily, with her fondest love to her dear Uncle Jack." There is no objection, I admit, to an aunt being a small aunt, but why an aunt, no matter what her size may be, should call her own nephew her uncle, I can't quite make out. Besides, your name isn't Jack at all; it is Ernest.

JACK: It isn't Ernest; it's Jack.

ALGERNON: You have always told me it was Ernest. I have introduced you to everyone as Ernest. You answer to the name of Ernest. You look as if your name was Ernest. You are the most earnest looking person I ever saw in my life. It is perfectly absurd your saying that your name isn't Ernest. It's on your cards. Here is one of them (*taking it from case*) "Mr. Ernest Worthing, B.4, The Albany." I'll keep this as a proof that your name is Ernest if ever you attempt to deny it to me, or to Gwendolen, or to anyone else.

(*Puts the card in his pocket.*)

JACK: Well, my name is Ernest in town and Jack in the country, and the cigarette case was given to me in the country.

ALGERNON: Yes, but that does not account for the fact that your small Aunt Cecily, who lives at Tunbridge Wells, calls you her dear uncle. Come, old boy, you had much better have the thing out at once.

JACK: My dear Algy, you talk exactly as if you were a dentist. It is very vulgar to talk like a dentist when one isn't a dentist. It produces a false impression.

ALGERNON: Well, that is exactly what dentists always do. Now, go on! Tell me the whole thing. I may mention that I have always suspected you of being a confirmed and secret Bunburyist; and I am quite sure of it now.

JACK: Bunburyist? What on earth do you mean by a Bunburyist?

ALGERNON: I'll reveal to you the meaning of that incomparable expression as soon as you are kind enough to inform me why you are Ernest in town and Jack in the country.

JACK: Well, produce my cigarette case first.

ALGERNON: Here it is. (*Hands cigarette case.*) Now produce your explanation, and pray make it improbable.

(*Sits on sofa.*)

JACK: My dear fellow, there is nothing improbable about my explanation at all. In fact it's perfectly ordinary. Old Mr. Thomas Cardew, who adopted me when I was a little boy, made me in his will guardian to his granddaughter, Miss Cecily Cardew. Cecily, who addresses me as her uncle from motives of respect that you could not possibly appreciate, lives at my place in the country under the charge of her admirable governess, Miss Prism.

ALGERNON: Where is that place in the country, by the way?

JACK: That is nothing to you, dear boy. You are not going to be invited—I may tell you candidly that the place is not in Shropshire.

ALGERNON: I suspected that, my dear fellow! I have Bunburyed all over Shropshire on two separate occasions. Now, go on. Why are you Ernest in town and Jack in the country?

JACK: My dear Algy, I don't know whether you will be able to understand my real motives. You are hardly serious enough. When one is placed in the position of guardian, one has to adopt a very high moral tone on all subjects. It's one's duty to do so. And as a high moral tone can hardly be said to conduce very much to either one's health or one's happiness, in order to get up to town I have always pretended to have a younger brother of the name of Ernest, who lives in the Albany, and gets into the most dreadful scrapes. That, my dear Algy, is the whole truth pure and simple.

ALGERNON: The truth is rarely pure and never simple. Modern life would be very tedious if it were either and modern literature a complete impossibility!

JACK: That wouldn't be at all a bad thing.

ALGERNON: Literary criticism is not your forte, my dear fellow. Don't try it. You should leave that to people who haven't been at a university. They do it so well in the daily papers. What you really are is a Bunburyist. I was quite right in saying you were a Bunburyist. You are one of the most advanced Bunburyists I know.

JACK: What on earth do you mean?

ALGERNON: You have invented a very useful younger brother called Ernest, in order that you may be able to come up to town as often as you like. I have invented an invaluable permanent invalid called Bunbury, in order that I may be able to go down into the country whenever I choose. Bunbury is perfectly invaluable. If it wasn't for Bunbury's extraordinary bad health, for instance, I wouldn't be able to dine with you at Willis's tonight, for I have been really engaged to Aunt Augusta for more than a week.

JACK: I haven't asked you to dine with me anywhere tonight.

ALGERNON: I know. You are absurdly careless about sending out invitations. It is very foolish of you. Nothing annoys people so much as not receiving invitations.

JACK: You had much better dine with your Aunt Augusta.

ALGERNON: I haven't the smallest intention of doing anything of the kind. To begin with, I dined there on Monday, and once a week is quite enough to dine with one's own relations. In the second place, whenever I do dine there I am always treated as a member of the family, and sent down with° either no woman at all, or two. In the third place, I know perfectly well whom she will place me next to, tonight. She will place me next Mary Farquhar, who always flirts with her own husband across the dinner table. That is not very pleasant. Indeed, it is not even decent—and that sort of thing is enormously on the increase. The

---

sent down with: Assigned a woman to escort into the dining room for dinner.

amount of women in London who flirt with their own husbands is perfectly scandalous. It looks so bad. It is simply washing one's clean linen in public. Besides, now that I know you to be a confirmed Bunburyist I naturally want to talk to you about Bunburying. I want to tell you the rules.

JACK: I'm not a Bunburyist at all. If Gwendolen accepts me, I am going to kill my brother, indeed I think I'll kill him in any case. Cecily is a little too much interested in him. It is rather a bore. So I am going to get rid of Ernest. And I strongly advise you to do the same with Mr.—with your invalid friend who has the absurd name.

ALGERNON: Nothing will induce me to part with Bunbury, and if you ever get married, which seems to me extremely problematic, you will be very glad to know Bunbury. A man who marries without knowing Bunbury has a very tedious time of it.

JACK: That is nonsense. If I marry a charming girl like Gwendolen, and she is the only girl I ever saw in my life that I would marry, I certainly won't want to know Bunbury.

ALGERNON: Then your wife will. You don't seem to realize, that in married life three is company and two is none.

JACK (*sententiously*): That, my dear young friend, is the theory that the corrupt French drama has been propounding for the last fifty years.

ALGERNON: Yes; and that the happy English home has proved in half the time.

JACK: For heaven's sake, don't try to be cynical. It's perfectly easy to be cynical.

ALGERNON: My dear fellow, it isn't easy to be anything nowadays. There's such a lot of beastly competition about. (*The sound of an electric bell is heard.*) Ah! that must be Aunt Augusta. Only relatives, or creditors, ever ring in that Wagnerian° manner. Now, if I get her out of the way for ten minutes, so that you can have an opportunity for proposing to Gwendolen, may I dine with you tonight at Willis's?

JACK: I suppose so, if you want to.

ALGERNON: Yes, but you must be serious about it. I hate people who are not serious about meals. It is so shallow of them.

(*Enter Lane.*)

LANE: Lady Bracknell and Miss Fairfax.

(*Algernon goes forward to meet them. Enter Lady Bracknell and Gwendolen.*)

LADY BRACKNELL: Good afternoon, dear Algernon, I hope you are behaving very well.

ALGERNON: I'm feeling very well, Aunt Augusta.

LADY BRACKNELL: That's not quite the same thing. In fact the two things rarely go together.

(*Sees Jack and bows to him with icy coldness.*)

Wagnerian: Referring to the operas of Richard Wagner (1813–1883), whose music was popularly thought to be loud.

ALGERNON (*to Gwendolen*): Dear me, you are smart!

GWENDOLEN: I am always smart! Aren't I, Mr. Worthing?

JACK: You're quite perfect, Miss Fairfax.

GWENDOLEN: Oh! I hope I am not that. It would leave no room for developments, and I intend to develop in many directions.

(*Gwendolen and Jack sit down together in the corner.*)

LADY BRACKNELL: I'm sorry if we are a little late Algernon, but I was obliged to call on dear Lady Harbury. I hadn't been there since her poor husband's death. I never saw a woman so altered; she looks quite twenty years younger. And now I'll have a cup of tea, and one of those nice cucumber sandwiches you promised me.

ALGERNON: Certainly, Aunt Augusta.

(*Goes over to tea table.*)

LADY BRACKNELL: Won't you come and sit here, Gwendolen?

GWENDOLEN: Thanks, Mama, I'm quite comfortable where I am.

ALGERNON (*picking up empty plate in horror*): Good heavens! Lane! Why are there no cucumber sandwiches? I ordered them specially.

LANE (*gravely*): There were no cucumbers in the market this morning, sir. I went down twice.

ALGERNON: No cucumbers?

LANE: No, sir. Not even for ready money.

ALGERNON: That will do, Lane, thank you.

LANE: Thank you, sir.   (*Goes out.*)

ALGERNON: I am greatly distressed, Aunt Augusta, about there being no cucumbers, not even for ready money.

LADY BRACKNELL: It really makes no matter, Algernon. I had some crumpets with Lady Harbury, who seems to me to be living entirely for pleasure now.

ALGERNON: I hear her hair has turned quite gold from grief.

LADY BRACKNELL: It certainly has changed its color. From what cause I, of course, cannot say. (*Algernon crosses and hands tea.*) Thank you. I've quite a treat for you tonight, Algernon. I am going to send you down with Mary Farquhar. She is such a nice woman, and so attentive to her husband. It's delightful to watch them.

ALGERNON: I am afraid, Aunt Augusta, I shall have to give up the pleasure of dining with you tonight after all.

LADY BRACKNELL (*frowning*): I hope not, Algernon. It would put my table completely out. Your uncle would have to dine upstairs. Fortunately he is accustomed to that.

ALGERNON: It is a great bore, and, I need hardly say, a terrible disappointment to me, but the fact is I have just had a telegram to say that my poor friend Bunbury is very ill again. (*Exchanges glances with Jack.*) They seem to think I should be with him.

LADY BRACKNELL: It is very strange. This Mr. Bunbury seems to suffer from curiously bad health.

ALGERNON: Yes; poor Bunbury is a dreadful invalid.

LADY BRACKNELL: Well, I must say, Algernon, that I think it is high time that Mr. Bunbury made up his mind whether he was going to live or to die. This shilly-shallying with the question is absurd. Nor do I in any way approve of the modern sympathy with invalids. I consider it morbid. Illness of any kind is hardly a thing to be encouraged in others. Health is the primary duty of life. I am always telling that to your poor uncle, but he never seems to take much notice—as far as any improvement in his ailments goes. I should be much obliged if you would ask Mr. Bunbury, from me, to be kind enough not to have a relapse on Saturday, for I rely on you to arrange my music for me. It is my last reception, and one wants something that will encourage conversation, particularly at the end of the season when everyone has practically said whatever they had to say, which, in most cases, was probably not much.

ALGERNON: I'll speak to Bunbury, Aunt Augusta, if he is still conscious, and I think I can promise you he'll be all right by Saturday. Of course the music is a great difficulty. You see, if one plays good music, people don't listen, and if one plays bad music people don't talk. But I'll run over the program I've drawn out, if you will kindly come into the next room for a moment.

LADY BRACKNELL: Thank you, Algernon. It is very thoughtful of you. (*Rising, and following Algernon.*) I'm sure the program will be delightful, after a few expurgations. French songs I cannot possibly allow. People always seem to think that they are improper, and either look shocked, which is vulgar, or laugh, which is worse. But German sounds a thoroughly respectable language, and indeed, I believe is so. Gwendolen, you will accompany me.

GWENDOLEN: Certainly, Mama.

(*Lady Bracknell and Algernon go into the music room. Gwendolen remains behind.*)

JACK: Charming day it has been, Miss Fairfax.

GWENDOLEN: Pray don't talk to me about the weather Mr. Worthing. Whenever people talk to me about the weather, I always feel quite certain that they mean something else. And that makes me so nervous.

JACK: I do mean something else.

GWENDOLEN: I thought so. In fact, I am never wrong.

JACK: And I would like to be allowed to take advantage of Lady Bracknell's temporary absence—

GWENDOLEN: I would certainly advise you to do so. Mama has a way of coming back suddenly into a room that I have often had to speak to her about.

JACK (*nervously*): Miss Fairfax, ever since I met you I have admired you more than any girl—I have ever met since—I met you.

GWENDOLEN: Yes, I am quite aware of the fact. And I often wish that in public, at any rate, you had been more demonstrative. For me you have always had an irresistible fascination. Even before I met you I was far from indifferent to you. (*Jack looks at her in amazement.*) We live, as I hope you know Mr. Worthing, in an age of ideals. The fact is constantly

mentioned in the more expensive monthly magazines, and has reached the provincial pulpits I am told: And my ideal has always been to love someone of the name of Ernest. There is something in that name that inspires absolute confidence. The moment Algernon first mentioned to me that he had a friend called Ernest, I knew I was destined to love you.

JACK: You really love me, Gwendolen?

GWENDOLEN: Passionately!

JACK: Darling! You don't know how happy you've made me.

GWENDOLEN: My own Ernest!

JACK: But you don't mean to say that you couldn't love me if my name wasn't Ernest?

GWENDOLEN: But your name is Ernest.

JACK: Yes, I know it is. But supposing it was something else? Do you mean to say you couldn't love me then?

GWENDOLEN (*glibly*): Ah! that is clearly a metaphysical speculation, and like most metaphysical speculations has very little reference at all to the actual facts of real life, as we know them.

JACK: Personally, darling, to speak quite candidly, I don't much care about the name of Ernest—I don't think the name suits me at all.

GWENDOLEN: It suits you perfectly. It is a divine name. It has a music of its own. It produces vibrations.

JACK: Well, really, Gwendolen, I must say that I think there are lots of other much nicer names. I think Jack, for instance, a charming name.

GWENDOLEN: Jack?—No, there is very little music in the name Jack, if any at all, indeed. It does not thrill. It produces absolutely no vibrations—I have known several Jacks, and they all, without exception, were more than usually plain. Besides, Jack is a notorious domesticity for John! And I pity any woman who is married to a man called John. She would probably never be allowed to know the entrancing pleasure of a single moment's solitude. The only really safe name is Ernest.

JACK: Gwendolen, I must get christened at once—I mean we must get married at once. There is no time to be lost.

GWENDOLEN: Married, Mr. Worthing?

JACK (*astounded*): Well—surely. You know that I love you, and you led me to believe, Miss Fairfax that you were not absolutely indifferent to me.

GWENDOLEN: I adore you. But you haven't proposed to me yet. Nothing has been said at all about marriage. The subject has not even been touched on.

JACK: Well—may I propose to you now?

GWENDOLEN: I think it would be an admirable opportunity. And to spare you any possible disappointment, Mr. Worthing, I think it only fair to tell you quite frankly beforehand that I am fully determined to accept you.

JACK: Gwendolen!

GWENDOLEN: Yes, Mr. Worthing, what have you got to say to me?

JACK: You know what I have got to say to you.

GWENDOLEN: Yes, but you don't say it.

JACK: Gwendolen, will you marry me?

(Goes on his knees.)

GWENDOLEN: Of course I will, darling. How long you have been about it! I am afraid you have had very little experience in how to propose.

JACK: My own one, I have never loved anyone in the world but you.

GWENDOLEN: Yes, but men often propose for practice. I know my brother Gerald does. All my girlfriends tell me so. What wonderfully blue eyes you have, Ernest! They are quite, quite blue. I hope you will always look at me just like that, especially when there are other people present.

(Enter Lady Bracknell.)

LADY BRACKNELL: Mr. Worthing! Rise, sir, from this semi-recumbent posture. It is most indecorous.

GWENDOLEN: Mama! (He tries to rise; she restrains him.) I must beg you to retire. This is no place for you. Besides, Mr. Worthing has not quite finished yet.

LADY BRACKNELL: Finished what, may I ask?

GWENDOLEN: I am engaged to Mr. Worthing, Mama.

(They rise together.)

LADY BRACKNELL: Pardon me, you are not engaged to anyone. When you do become engaged to someone, I, or your father, should his health permit him, will inform you of the fact. An engagement should come on a young girl as a surprise, pleasant or unpleasant, as the case may be. It is hardly a matter that she could be allowed to arrange for herself—And now I have a few questions to put to you, Mr. Worthing. While I am making these inquiries, you, Gwendolen, will wait for me below in the carriage.

GWENDOLEN (reproachfully): Mama!

LADY BRACKNELL: In the carriage, Gwendolen! (Gwendolen goes to the door. She and Jack blow kisses to each other behind Lady Bracknell's back. Lady Bracknell looks vaguely about as if she could not understand what the noise was. Finally turns round.) Gwendolen, the carriage!

GWENDOLEN: Yes, Mama.

(Goes out, looking back at Jack.)

LADY BRACKNELL (sitting down): You can take a seat, Mr. Worthing.

(Looks in her pocket for notebook and pencil.)

JACK: Thank you, Lady Bracknell, I prefer standing.

LADY BRACKNELL (pencil and notebook in hand): I feel bound to tell you that you are not down on my list of eligible young men, although I have the same list as the dear Duchess of Bolton has. We work together, in fact. However, I am quite ready to enter your name, should your answers be what a really affectionate mother requires. Do you smoke?

JACK: Well, yes, I must admit I smoke.

LADY BRACKNELL: I am glad to hear it. A man should always have an occupation of some kind. There are far too many idle men in London as it is. How old are you?

JACK: Twenty-nine.

LADY BRACKNELL: A very good age to be married at. I have always been of opinion that a man who desires to get married should know either everything or nothing. Which do you know?

JACK (after some hesitation): I know nothing, Lady Bracknell.

LADY BRACKNELL: I am pleased to hear it. I do not approve of anything that tampers with natural ignorance. Ignorance is like a delicate exotic fruit; touch it and the bloom is gone. The whole theory of modern education is radically unsound. Fortunately in England, at any rate, education produces no effect whatsoever. If it did, it would prove a serious danger to the upper classes, and probably lead to acts of violence in Grosvenor Square. What is your income?

JACK: Between seven and eight thousand a year.

LADY BRACKNELL (makes a note in her book): In land, or in investments?

JACK: In investments, chiefly.

LADY BRACKNELL: That is satisfactory. What between the duties expected of one during one's lifetime, and the duties exacted from one after one's death, land has ceased to be either a profit or a pleasure. It gives one position, and prevents one from keeping it up. That's all that can be said about land.

JACK: I have a country house with some land, of course, attached to it, about fifteen hundred acres, I believe; but I don't depend on that for my real income. In fact, as far as I can make out, the poachers are the only people who make anything out of it.

LADY BRACKNELL: A country house! How many bedrooms? Well, that point can be cleared up afterwards. You have a town house, I hope? A girl with a simple, unspoiled nature, like Gwendolen, could hardly be expected to reside in the country.

JACK: Well, I own a house in Belgrave Square, but it is let by the year to Lady Bloxham. Of course, I can get it back whenever I like, at six months' notice.

LADY BRACKNELL: Lady Bloxham? I don't know her.

JACK: Oh, she goes about very little. She is a lady considerably advanced in years.

LADY BRACKNELL: Ah, nowadays that is no guarantee of respectability of character. What number in Belgrave Square?

JACK: 149.

LADY BRACKNELL (shaking her head): The unfashionable side. I thought there was something. However; that could easily be altered.

JACK: Do you mean the fashion, or the side?

LADY BRACKNELL (sternly): Both, if necessary, I presume. What are your politics?

JACK: Well, I am afraid I really have none. I am a Liberal Unionist.

LADY BRACKNELL: Oh, they count as Tories. They dine with us. Or come in the evening, at any rate. Now to minor matters. Are your parents living?

JACK: I have lost both my parents.

LADY BRACKNELL: Both? To lose one parent may be regarded as a misfortune—to lose *both* seems like carelessness. Who was your father? He was evidently a man of some wealth. Was he born in what the Radical papers call the purple of commerce, or did he rise from the ranks of the aristocracy?

JACK: I am afraid I really don't know. The fact is, Lady Bracknell, I said I had lost my parents. It would be nearer the truth to say that my parents seem to have lost me—I don't actually know who I am by birth. I was—well, I was found.

LADY BRACKNELL: Found!

JACK: The late Mr. Thomas Cardew, an old gentleman of a very charitable and kindly disposition, found me, and gave me the name of Worthing, because he happened to have a first-class ticket for Worthing in his pocket at the time. Worthing is a place in Sussex. It is a seaside resort.

LADY BRACKNELL: Where did the charitable gentleman who had a first-class ticket for this seaside resort find you?

JACK (*gravely*): In a handbag.

LADY BRACKNELL: A handbag?

JACK (*very seriously*): Yes, Lady Bracknell. I was in a handbag—a somewhat large, black leather handbag, with handles to it—an ordinary handbag in fact.

LADY BRACKNELL: In what locality did this Mr. James, or Thomas, Cardew come across this ordinary handbag?

JACK: In the cloakroom at Victoria Station. It was given to him in mistake for his own.

LADY BRACKNELL: The cloakroom at Victoria Station?

JACK: Yes. The Brighton line.

LADY BRACKNELL: The line is immaterial. Mr. Worthing, I confess I feel somewhat bewildered by what you have just told me. To be born, or at any rate bred, in a handbag, whether it had handles or not, seems to me to display a contempt for the ordinary decencies of family life that reminds one of the worst excesses of the French Revolution. And I presume you know what that unfortunate movement led to? As for the particular locality in which the handbag was found, a cloakroom at a railway station might serve to conceal a social indiscretion—has probably, indeed, been used for that purpose before now—but it could hardly be regarded as an assured basis for a recognized position in good society.

JACK: May I ask you then what you would advise me to do? I need hardly say I would do anything in the world to ensure Gwendolen's happiness.

LADY BRACKNELL: I would strongly advise you, Mr. Worthing, to try and acquire some relations as soon as possible, and to make a definite effort to produce at any rate one parent of either sex, before the season is quite over.

JACK: Well, I don't see how I could possibly manage to do that. I can produce the handbag at any moment. It is in my dressing room at home. I really think that should satisfy you, Lady Bracknell.

LADY BRACKNELL: Me, sir! What has it to do with me? You can hardly imagine that I and Lord Bracknell would dream of allowing our only daughter—a girl brought up with the utmost care—to marry into a cloakroom, and form an alliance with a parcel? Good morning, Mr. Worthing!

(*Lady Bracknell sweeps out in majestic indignation.*)

JACK: Good morning! (*Algernon, from the other room, strikes up the Wedding March. Jack looks perfectly furious, and goes to the door.*) For goodness' sake don't play that ghastly tune, Algy! How idiotic you are!

(*The music stops, and Algernon enters cheerily.*)

ALGERNON: Didn't it go off all right, old boy? You don't mean to say Gwendolen refused you? I know it is a way she has. She is always refusing people. I think it is most ill-natured of her.

JACK: Oh, Gwendolen is as right as a trivet. As far as she is concerned, we are engaged. Her mother is perfectly unbearable. Never met such a Gorgon°—I don't really know what a Gorgon is like, but I am quite sure that Lady Bracknell is one. In any case, she is a monster, without being a myth, which is rather unfair. I beg your pardon, Algy, I suppose I shouldn't talk about your own aunt in that way before you.

ALGERNON: My dear boy, I love hearing my relations abused. It is the only thing that makes me put up with them at all. Relations are simply a tedious pack of people, who haven't got the remotest knowledge of how to live, nor the smallest instinct about when to die.

JACK: Oh, that is nonsense!

ALGERNON: It isn't!

JACK: Well, I won't argue about the matter. You always want to argue about things.

ALGERNON: That is exactly what things were originally made for.

JACK: Upon my word, if I thought that, I'd shoot myself—(*A pause.*) You don't think there is any chance of Gwendolen becoming like her mother in about a hundred and fifty years, do you Algy?

ALGERNON: All women become like their mothers. That is their tragedy. No man does. That's his.

JACK: Is that clever?

ALGERNON: It is perfectly phrased! and quite as true as any observation in civilized life should be.

JACK: I am sick to death of cleverness. Everybody is clever nowadays. You can't go anywhere without meeting clever people. The thing has become an absolute public nuisance. I wish to goodness we had a few fools left.

Gorgon: In Greek myth, one of three very ugly sisters who had, among other characteristics, serpents for hair.

ALGERNON: We have.

JACK: I should extremely like to meet them. What do they talk about?

ALGERNON: The fools? Oh! about the clever people, of course.

JACK: What fools!

ALGERNON: By the way, did you tell Gwendolen the truth about your being Ernest in town, and Jack in the country?

JACK (in a very patronizing manner): My dear fellow, the truth isn't quite the sort of thing one tells to a nice sweet refined girl. What extraordinary ideas you have about the way to behave to a woman!

ALGERNON: The only way to behave to a woman is to make love to her if she is pretty, and to someone else if she is plain.

JACK: Oh, that is nonsense.

ALGERNON: What about your brother? What about the profligate Ernest?

JACK: Oh, before the end of the week I shall have got rid of him. I'll say he died in Paris of apoplexy. Lots of people die of apoplexy, quite suddenly, don't they?

ALGERNON: Yes, but it's hereditary, my dear fellow. It's a sort of thing that runs in families. You had much better say a severe chill.

JACK: You are sure a severe chill isn't hereditary, or anything of that kind?

ALGERNON: Of course it isn't!

JACK: Very well, then. My poor brother Ernest is carried off suddenly in Paris, by a severe chill. That gets rid of him.

ALGERNON: But I thought you said that—Miss Cardew was a little too much interested in your poor brother Ernest? Won't she feel his loss a good deal?

JACK: Oh, that is all right. Cecily is not a silly romantic girl, I am glad to say. She has got a capital appetite, goes on long walks, and pays no attention at all to her lessons.

ALGERNON: I would rather like to see Cecily.

JACK: I will take very good care you never do. She is excessively pretty, and she is only just eighteen.

ALGERNON: Have you told Gwendolen yet that you have an excessively pretty ward who is only just eighteen?

JACK: Oh! one doesn't blurt these things out to people. Cecily and Gwendolen are perfectly certain to be extremely great friends. I'll bet you anything you like that half an hour after they have met, they will be calling each other sister.

ALGERNON: Women only do that when they have called each other a lot of other things first. Now, my dear boy, if we want to get a good table at Willis's, we really must go and dress. Do you know it is nearly seven?

JACK (irritably): Oh! it always is nearly seven.

ALGERNON: Well, I'm hungry.

JACK: I never knew you when you weren't—

ALGERNON: What shall we do after dinner? Go to a theater?

JACK: Oh, no! I loathe listening.

ALGERNON: Well, let us go to the Club?

JACK: Oh, no! I hate talking.

ALGERNON: Well, we might trot round to the Empire° at ten?

JACK: Oh, no! I can't bear looking at things. It is so silly.

ALGERNON: Well, what shall we do?

JACK: Nothing!

ALGERNON: It is awfully hard work doing nothing. However, I don't mind hard work where there is no definite object of any kind.

(Enter Lane.)

LANE: Miss Fairfax.

(Enter Gwendolen. Lane goes out.)

ALGERNON: Gwendolen, upon my word!

GWENDOLEN: Algy, kindly turn your back. I have something very particular to say to Mr. Worthing.

ALGERNON: Really, Gwendolen, I don't think I can allow this at all.

GWENDOLEN: Algy, you always adopt a strictly immoral attitude towards life. You are not quite old enough to do that.

(Algernon retires to the fireplace.)

JACK: My own darling!

GWENDOLEN: Ernest, we may never be married. From the expression on Mama's face I fear we never shall. Few parents nowadays pay any regard to what their children say to them. The old-fashioned respect for the young is fast dying out. Whatever influence I ever had over Mama, I lost at the age of three. But although she may prevent us from becoming man and wife, and I may marry someone else, and marry often, nothing that she can possibly do can alter my eternal devotion to you.

JACK: Dear Gwendolen!

GWENDOLEN: The story of your romantic origin, as related to me by Mama, with unpleasing comments, has naturally stirred the deeper fibers of my nature. Your Christian name has an irresistible fascination. The simplicity of your character makes you exquisitely incomprehensible to me. Your town address at the Albany I have. What is your address in the country?

JACK: The Manor House, Woolton, Hertfordshire.

(Algernon, who has been carefully listening, smiles to himself, and writes the address on his shirt cuff. Then picks up the Railway Guide.)

GWENDOLEN: There is a good postal service, I suppose? It may be necessary to do something desperate. That of course will require serious consideration. I will communicate with you daily.

JACK: My own one!

Empire: Empire Theatre, a London music hall that was also a rendezvous for prostitutes.

Scene from the Huntington Theatre Company's 1994 production of *The Importance of Being Earnest*.

GWENDOLEN: How long do you remain in town?

JACK: Till Monday.

GWENDOLEN: Good! Algy, you may turn round now.

ALGERNON: Thanks, I've turned round already.

GWENDOLEN: You may also ring the bell.

JACK: You will let me see you to your carriage, my own darling?

GWENDOLEN: Certainly.

JACK (*to Lane, who now enters*): I will see Miss Fairfax out.

LANE: Yes, sir.   (*Jack and Gwendolen go off.*)

(*Lane presents several letters on a salver to Algernon. It is to be surmised that they are bills, as Algernon, after looking at the envelopes, tears them up.*)

ALGERNON: A glass of sherry, Lane.

LANE: Yes, sir.

ALGERNON: Tomorrow, Lane, I'm going Bunburying.

LANE: Yes, sir.

ALGERNON: I shall probably not be back till Monday. You can put up my dress clothes, my smoking jacket, and all the Bunbury suits—

LANE: Yes, sir.   (*Handing sherry.*)

ALGERNON: I hope tomorrow will be a fine day, Lane.

LANE: It never is, sir.

ALGERNON: Lane, you're a perfect pessimist.

LANE: I do my best to give satisfaction, sir.

(*Enter Jack. Lane goes off.*)

JACK: There's a sensible, intellectual girl! the only girl I ever cared for in my life. (*Algernon is laughing immoderately.*) What on earth are you so amused at?

ALGERNON: Oh, I'm a little anxious about poor Bunbury, that is all.

JACK: If you don't take care, your friend Bunbury will get you into a serious scrape some day.

ALGERNON: I love scrapes. They are the only things that are never serious.

JACK: Oh, that's nonsense, Algy. You never talk anything but nonsense.

ALGERNON: Nobody ever does.

(*Jack looks indignantly at him, and leaves the room. Algernon lights a cigarette, reads his shirt cuff, and smiles.*)

ACT II

(*Scene: Garden at the Manor House. A flight of gray stone steps leads up to the house. The garden, an old-fashioned one, full of roses. Time of year, July. Basket chairs, and a table covered with books, are set under a large yew tree. Miss Prism discovered seated at the table. Cecily is at the back watering flowers.*)

MISS PRISM (*calling*): Cecily, Cecily! Surely such a utilitarian occupation as the watering of flowers is rather Moulton's duty than yours? Especially at a moment when intellectual pleasures await you. Your German grammar is on the table. Pray open it at page fifteen. We will repeat yesterday's lesson.

CECILY (*coming over very slowly*): But I don't like German. It isn't at all a becoming language. I know perfectly well that I look quite plain after my German lesson.

MISS PRISM: Child, you know how anxious your guardian is that you should improve yourself in every way. He laid particular stress on your German, as he was leaving for town yesterday. Indeed, he always lays stress on your German when he is leaving for town.

CECILY: Dear Uncle Jack is so very serious! Sometimes he is so serious that I think he cannot be quite well.

MISS PRISM (*drawing herself up*): Your guardian enjoys the best of health, and his gravity of demeanor is especially to be commended in one so comparatively young as he is. I know no one who has a higher sense of duty and responsibility.

CECILY: I suppose that is why he often looks a little bored when we three are together.

MISS PRISM: Cecily! I am surprised at you. Mr. Worthing has many troubles in his life. Idle merriment and triviality would be out of place in his conversation. You must remember his constant anxiety about that unfortunate young man his brother.

CECILY: I wish Uncle Jack would allow that unfortunate young man, his brother, to come down here sometimes. We might have a good influence over him, Miss Prism. I am sure you certainly would. You know German, and geology, and things of that kind influence a man very much.

(*Cecily begins to write in her diary.*)

MISS PRISM (*shaking her head*): I do not think that even I could produce any effect on a character that according to his own brother's admission is irretrievably weak and vacillating. Indeed I am not sure that I would desire to reclaim him. I am not in favor of this modern mania for turning bad people into good people at a moment's notice. As a man sows so let him reap. You must put away your diary, Cecily. I really don't see why you should keep a diary at all.

CECILY: I keep a diary in order to enter the wonderful secrets of my life. If I didn't write them down I should probably forget all about them.

MISS PRISM: Memory, my dear Cecily, is the diary that we all carry about with us.

CECILY: Yes, but it usually chronicles the things that have never happened, and couldn't possibly have happened. I believe that Memory is responsible for nearly all the three-volume novels that Mudie sends us.

MISS PRISM: Do not speak slightingly of the three-volume novel, Cecily. I wrote one myself in earlier days.

CECILY: Did you really, Miss Prism? How wonderfully clever you are! I hope it did not end happily? I don't like novels that end happily. They depress me so much.

MISS PRISM: The good ended happily, and the bad unhappily. That is what Fiction means.

CECILY: I suppose so. But it seems very unfair. And was your novel ever published?

MISS PRISM: Alas! no. The manuscript unfortunately was abandoned. I use the word in the sense of lost or mislaid. To your work, child, these speculations are profitless.

CECILY (*smiling*): But I see dear Dr. Chasuble coming up through the garden.

MISS PRISM (*rising and advancing*): Dr. Chasuble! This is indeed a pleasure.

(*Enter Canon Chasuble.*)

CHASUBLE: And how are we this morning? Miss Prism, you are, I trust, well?

CECILY: Miss Prism has just been complaining of a slight headache. I think it would do her so much good to have a short stroll with you in the park, Dr. Chasuble.

MISS PRISM: Cecily, I have not mentioned anything about a headache.

CECILY: No, dear Miss Prism, I know that, but I felt instinctively that you had a headache. Indeed I was thinking about that, and not about my German lesson, when the Rector came in.

CHASUBLE: I hope, Cecily, you are not inattentive.

CECILY: Oh, I am afraid I am.

CHASUBLE: That is strange. Were I fortunate enough to be Miss Prism's pupil, I would hang upon her lips. (*Miss Prism glares.*) I spoke metaphorically.—My metaphor was drawn from bees. Ahem! Mr. Worthing, I suppose, has not returned from town yet?

MISS PRISM: We do not expect him till Monday afternoon.

CHASUBLE: Ah yes, he usually likes to spend his Sunday in London. He is not one of those whose sole aim is enjoyment, as, by all accounts, that unfortunate young man his brother seems to be. But I must not disturb Egeria° and her pupil any longer.

MISS PRISM: Egeria? My name is Laetitia, Doctor.

CHASUBLE (*bowing*): A classical allusion merely, drawn from the Pagan authors. I shall see you both no doubt at Evensong?

MISS PRISM: I think, dear Doctor, I will have a stroll with you. I find I have a headache after all, and a walk might do it good.

CHASUBLE: With pleasure, Miss Prism, with pleasure. We might go as far as the schools and back.

MISS PRISM: That would be delightful. Cecily, you will read your Political Economy in my absence. The chapter on the Fall of the Rupee° you may omit. It is somewhat too sensational. Even these metallic problems have their melodramatic side.

(*Goes down the garden with Dr. Chasuble.*)

CECILY (*picks up books and throws them back on table*): Horrid Political Economy! Horrid Geography! Horrid, horrid German!

(*Enter Merriman with a card on a salver.*)

MERRIMAN: Mr. Ernest Worthing has just driven over from the station. He has brought his luggage with him.

Egeria: Roman goddess of water.   **Fall of the Rupee:** Reference to the Indian rupee, whose steady deflation between 1873 and 1893 caused the Indian government finally to close the mints.

CECILY (*takes the card and reads it*): "Mr. Ernest Worthing, B.4, The Albany, W." Uncle Jack's brother! Did you tell him Mr. Worthing was in town?

MERRIMAN: Yes, Miss. He seemed very much disappointed. I mentioned that you and Miss Prism were in the garden. He said he was anxious to speak to you privately for a moment.

CECILY: Ask Mr. Ernest Worthing to come here. I suppose you had better talk to the housekeeper about a room for him.

MERRIMAN: Yes, Miss.   (*Merriman goes off.*)

CECILY: I have never met any really wicked person before. I feel rather frightened. I am so afraid he will look just like everyone else.

(*Enter Algernon, very gay and debonair.*)

He does!

ALGERNON (*raising his hat*): You are my little cousin Cecily, I'm sure.

CECILY: You are under some strange mistake. I am not little. In fact, I believe I am more than usually tall for my age. (*Algernon is rather taken aback.*) But I am your cousin Cecily. You, I see from your card, are Uncle Jack's brother, my cousin Ernest, my wicked cousin Ernest.

ALGERNON: Oh! I am not really wicked at all, Cousin Cecily. You mustn't think that I am wicked.

CECILY: If you are not, then you have certainly been deceiving us all in a very inexcusable manner. I hope you have not been leading a double life, pretending to be wicked and being really good all the time. That would be hypocrisy.

ALGERNON (*looks at her in amazement*): Oh! Of course I have been rather reckless.

CECILY: I am glad to hear it.

ALGERNON: In fact, now you mention the subject, I have been very bad in my own small way.

CECILY: I don't think you should be so proud of that, though I am sure it must have been very pleasant.

ALGERNON: It is much pleasanter being here with you.

CECILY: I can't understand how you are here at all. Uncle Jack won't be back till Monday afternoon.

ALGERNON: That is a great disappointment. I am obliged to go up by the first train on Monday morning. I have a business appointment that I am anxious—to miss.

CECILY: Couldn't you miss it anywhere but in London?

ALGERNON: No: the appointment is in London.

CECILY: Well, I know, of course, how important it is not to keep a business engagement, if one wants to retain any sense of the beauty of life, but still I think you had better wait till Uncle Jack arrives. I know he wants to speak to you about your emigrating.

ALGERNON: About my what?

CECILY: Your emigrating. He has gone up to buy your outfit.

ALGERNON: I certainly wouldn't let Jack buy my outfit. He has no taste in neckties at all.

CECILY: I don't think you will require neckties. Uncle Jack is sending you to Australia.

ALGERNON: Australia! I'd sooner die.

CECILY: Well, he said at dinner on Wednesday night, that you would have to choose between this world, the next world, and Australia.

ALGERNON: Oh, well! The accounts I have received of Australia and the next world are not particularly encouraging. This world is good enough for me, Cousin Cecily.

CECILY: Yes, but are you good enough for it?

ALGERNON: I'm afraid I'm not that. That is why I want you to reform me. You might make that your mission, if you don't mind, Cousin Cecily.

CECILY: I'm afraid I've no time, this afternoon.

ALGERNON: Well, would you mind my reforming myself this afternoon?

CECILY: It is rather quixotic° of you. But I think you should try.

ALGERNON: I will. I feel better already.

CECILY: You are looking a little worse.

ALGERNON: That is because I am hungry.

CECILY: How thoughtless of me. I should have remembered that when one is going to lead an entirely new life, one requires regular and wholesome meals. Won't you come in?

ALGERNON: Thank you. Might I have a buttonhole° first? I never have any appetite unless I have a buttonhole first.

CECILY: A Maréchal Niel?°

ALGERNON: No, I'd sooner have a pink rose.

CECILY: Why?   (*Cuts a flower.*)

ALGERNON: Because you are like a pink rose, Cousin Cecily.

CECILY: I don't think it can be right for you to talk to me like that. Miss Prism never says such things to me.

ALGERNON: Then Miss Prism is a shortsighted old lady. (*Cecily puts the rose in his buttonhole.*) You are the prettiest girl I ever saw.

CECILY: Miss Prism says that all good looks are a snare.

ALGERNON: They are a snare that every sensible man would like to be caught in.

CECILY: Oh! I don't think I would care to catch a sensible man. I shouldn't know what to talk to him about.

(*They pass into the house. Miss Prism and Dr. Chasuble return.*)

MISS PRISM: You are too much alone, dear Dr. Chasuble. You should get married. A misanthrope I can understand—a womanthrope, never!

CHASUBLE (*with a scholar's shudder*): Believe me, I do not deserve so neologistic a phrase. The precept as well as the practice of the Primitive Church was distinctly against matrimony.

---

quixotic: Foolishly impractical, from the idealistic hero of Cervantes' *Don Quixote*. buttonhole: Boutonniere. Maréchal Niel: A yellow rose.

MISS PRISM (*sententiously*): That is obviously the reason why the Primitive Church has not lasted up to the present day. And you do not seem to realize, dear Doctor, that by persistently remaining single, a man converts himself into a permanent public temptation. Men should be more careful; this very celibacy leads weaker vessels astray.

CHASUBLE: But is a man not equally attractive when married?

MISS PRISM: No married man is ever attractive except to his wife.

CHASUBLE: And often, I've been told, not even to her.

MISS PRISM: That depends on the intellectual sympathies of the woman. Maturity can always be depended on. Ripeness can be trusted. Young women are green. (*Dr. Chasuble starts.*) I spoke horticulturally. My metaphor was drawn from fruits. But where is Cecily?

CHASUBLE: Perhaps she followed us to the schools.

(*Enter Jack slowly from the back of the garden. He is dressed in the deepest mourning, with crepe hatband and black gloves.*)

MISS PRISM: Mr. Worthing!

CHASUBLE: Mr. Worthing?

MISS PRISM: This is indeed a surprise. We did not look for you till Monday afternoon.

JACK (*shakes Miss Prism's hand in a tragic manner*): I have returned sooner than I expected. Dr. Chasuble, I hope you are well?

CHASUBLE: Dear Mr. Worthing, I trust this garb of woe does not betoken some terrible calamity?

JACK: My brother.

MISS PRISM: More shameful debts and extravagance?

CHASUBLE: Still leading his life of pleasure?

JACK (*shaking his head*): Dead!

CHASUBLE: Your brother Ernest dead?

JACK: Quite dead.

MISS PRISM: What a lesson for him! I trust he will profit by it.

CHASUBLE: Mr. Worthing, I offer you my sincere condolence. You have at least the consolation of knowing that you were always the most generous and forgiving of brothers.

JACK: Poor Ernest! He had many faults, but it is a sad, sad blow.

CHASUBLE: Very sad indeed. Were you with him at the end?

JACK: No. He died abroad, in Paris, in fact. I had a telegram last night from the manager of the Grand Hotel.

CHASUBLE: Was the cause of death mentioned?

JACK: A severe chill, it seems.

MISS PRISM: As a man sows, so shall he reap.

CHASUBLE (*raising his hand*): Charity, dear Miss Prism, charity! None of us are perfect. I myself am peculiarly susceptible to drafts. Will the interment take place here?

JACK: No. He seemed to have expressed a desire to be buried in Paris.

CHASUBLE: In Paris! (*Shakes his head.*) I fear that hardly points to any very serious state of mind at the last. You would no doubt wish me to make some slight allusion to this tragic domestic affliction next Sunday. (*Jack presses his hand convulsively.*) My sermon on the meaning of the manna in the wilderness can be adapted to almost any occasion, joyful, or, as in the present case, distressing. (*All sigh.*) I have preached it at harvest celebrations, christenings, confirmations, on days of humiliation and festal days. The last time I delivered it was in the Cathedral, as a charity sermon on behalf of the Society for the Prevention of Discontent among the Upper Orders. The Bishop, who was present, was much struck by some of the analogies I drew.

JACK: Ah! that reminds me, you mentioned christenings I think, Dr. Chasuble? I suppose you know how to christen all right? (*Dr. Chasuble looks astounded.*) I mean, of course, you are continually christening, aren't you?

MISS PRISM: It is, I regret to say, one of the Rector's most constant duties in this parish. I have often spoken to the poorer classes on the subject. But they don't seem to know what thrift is.

CHASUBLE: But is there any particular infant in whom you are interested, Mr. Worthing? Your brother was, I believe, unmarried, was he not?

JACK: Oh yes.

MISS PRISM (*bitterly*): People who live entirely for pleasure usually are.

JACK: But it is not for any child, dear Doctor. I am very fond of children. No! the fact is, I would like to be christened myself, this afternoon, if you have nothing better to do.

CHASUBLE: But surely, Mr. Worthing, you have been christened already?

JACK: I don't remember anything about it.

CHASUBLE: But have you any grave doubts on the subject?

JACK: I certainly intend to have. Of course I don't know if the thing would bother you in any way, or if you think I am a little too old now.

CHASUBLE: Not at all. The sprinkling, and, indeed, the immersion of adults is a perfectly canonical practice.

JACK: Immersion!

CHASUBLE: You need have no apprehensions. Sprinkling is all that is necessary, or indeed I think advisable. Our weather is so changeable. At what hour would you wish the ceremony performed?

JACK: Oh, I might trot round about five if that would suit you.

CHASUBLE: Perfectly, perfectly! In fact I have two similar ceremonies to perform at that time. A case of twins that occurred recently in one of the outlying cottages on your own estate. Poor Jenkins the carter, a most hardworking man.

JACK: Oh! I don't see much fun in being christened along with other babies. It would be childish. Would half-past five do?

CHASUBLE: Admirably! Admirably! (*Takes out watch.*) And now, dear Mr. Worthing, I will not intrude any longer into a house of sorrow. I would merely beg you not to be too much bowed down by grief. What seem to us bitter trials are often blessings in disguise.

MISS PRISM: This seems to me a blessing of an extremely obvious kind.

(*Enter Cecily from the house.*)

CECILY: Uncle Jack! Oh, I am pleased to see you back. But what horrid clothes you have got on! Do go and change them.

MISS PRISM: Cecily!

CHASUBLE: My child! my child!

(*Cecily goes towards Jack; he kisses her brow in a melancholy manner.*)

CECILY: What is the matter, Uncle Jack? Do look happy! You look as if you had toothache, and I have got such a surprise for you. Who do you think is in the dining room? Your brother!

JACK: Who?

CECILY: Your brother Ernest. He arrived about half an hour ago.

JACK: What nonsense! I haven't got a brother.

CECILY: Oh, don't say that. However badly he may have behaved to you in the past he is still your brother. You couldn't be so heartless as to disown him. I'll tell him to come out. And you will shake hands with him, won't you, Uncle Jack?

(*Runs back into the house.*)

CHASUBLE: These are very joyful tidings.

MISS PRISM: After we had all been resigned to his loss, his sudden return seems to me peculiarly distressing.

JACK: My brother is in the dining room? I don't know what it all means. I think it is perfectly absurd.

(*Enter Algernon and Cecily hand in hand. They come slowly up to Jack.*)

JACK: Good heavens!   (*Motions Algernon away.*)

ALGERNON: Brother John, I have come down from town to tell you that I am very sorry for all the trouble I have given you, and that I intend to lead a better life in the future.

(*Jack glares at him and does not take his hand.*)

CECILY: Uncle Jack, you are not going to refuse your own brother's hand?

JACK: Nothing will induce me to take his hand. I think his coming down here disgraceful. He knows perfectly well why.

CECILY: Uncle Jack, do be nice. There is some good in everyone. Ernest has just been telling me about his poor invalid friend Mr. Bunbury whom he goes to visit so often. And surely there must be much good in one who is kind to an invalid, and leaves the pleasures of London to sit by a bed of pain.

JACK: Oh! he has been talking about Bunbury has he?

CECILY: Yes, he has told me all about poor Mr. Bunbury, and his terrible state of health.

JACK: Bunbury! Well, I won't have him talk to you about Bunbury or about anything else. It is enough to drive one perfectly frantic.

ALGERNON: Of course I admit that the faults were all on my side. But I must say that I think that Brother John's coldness to me is peculiarly painful. I expected a more enthusiastic welcome, especially considering it is the first time I have come here.

CECILY: Uncle Jack, if you don't shake hands with Ernest I will never forgive you.

JACK: Never forgive me?

CECILY: Never, never, never!

JACK: Well, this is the last time I shall ever do it.

(*Shakes hands with Algernon and glares.*)

CHASUBLE: It's pleasant, is it not, to see so perfect a reconciliation? I think we might leave the two brothers together.

MISS PRISM: Cecily, you will come with us.

CECILY: Certainly, Miss Prism. My little task of reconciliation is over.

CHASUBLE: You have done a beautiful action today, dear child.

MISS PRISM: We must not be premature in our judgments.

CECILY: I feel very happy.   (*They all go off.*)

JACK: You young scoundrel, Algy, you must get out of this place as soon as possible. I don't allow any Bunburying here.

(*Enter Merriman.*)

MERRIMAN: I have put Mr. Ernest's things in the room next to yours, sir. I suppose that is all right?

JACK: What?

MERRIMAN: Mr. Ernest's luggage, sir. I have unpacked it and put it in the room next to your own.

JACK: His luggage?

MERRIMAN: Yes, sir. Three portmanteaus, a dressing case, two hatboxes, and a large luncheon basket.

ALGERNON: I am afraid 1 can't stay more than a week this time.

JACK: Merriman, order the dog cart at once. Mr. Ernest has been suddenly called back to town.

MERRIMAN: Yes, sir.   (*Goes back into the house.*)

ALGERNON: What a fearful liar you are, Jack. I have not been called back to town at all.

JACK: Yes, you have.

ALGERNON: I haven't heard anyone call me.

JACK: Your duty as a gentleman calls you back.

ALGERNON: My duty as a gentleman has never interfered with my pleasures in the smallest degree.

JACK: I can quite understand that.

ALGERNON: Well, Cecily is a darling.

JACK: You are not to talk of Miss Cardew like that. I don't like it.

ALGERNON: Well, I don't like your clothes. You look perfectly ridiculous in them. Why on earth don't you go up and change? It is perfectly childish to be in deep mourning for a man who is actually staying for a whole week in your house as a guest. I call it grotesque.

JACK: You are certainly not staying with me for a whole week as a guest or anything else. You have got to leave—by the four-five train.

ALGERNON: I certainly won't leave you so long as you are in mourning. It would be most unfriendly. If I were in mourning you would stay with me, I suppose. I should think it very unkind if you didn't.

JACK: Well, will you go if I change my clothes?

ALGERNON: Yes, if you are not too long. I never saw anybody take so long to dress, and with such little result.

JACK: Well, at any rate, that is better than being always overdressed as you are.

ALGERNON: If I am occasionally a little overdressed, I make up for it by being always immensely overeducated.

JACK: Your vanity is ridiculous, your conduct an outrage, and your presence in my garden utterly absurd. However, you have got to catch the four-five, and I hope you will have a pleasant journey back to town. This Bunburying, as you call it, has not been a great success for you.

(Goes into the house.)

ALGERNON: I think it has been a great success. I'm in love with Cecily, and that is everything.

(Enter Cecily at the back of the garden. She picks up the can and begins to water the flowers.)

But I must see her before I go, and make arrangements for another Bunbury. Ah, there she is.

CECILY: Oh, I merely came back to water the roses. I thought you were with Uncle Jack.

ALGERNON: He's gone to order the dog cart for me.

CECILY: Oh, is he going to take you for a nice drive?

ALGERNON: He's going to send me away.

CECILY: Then have we got to part?

ALGERNON: I am afraid so. It's a very painful parting.

CECILY: It is always painful to part from people whom one has known for a very brief space of time. The absence of old friends one can endure with equanimity. But even a momentary separation from anyone to whom one has just been introduced is almost unbearable.

ALGERNON: Thank you.

(Enter Merriman.)

MERRIMAN: The dog cart is at the door, sir.

(Algernon looks appealingly at Cecily.)

CECILY: It can wait, Merriman—for—five minutes.

MERRIMAN: Yes, miss.   (Exit Merriman.)

ALGERNON: I hope, Cecily, I shall not offend you if I state quite frankly and openly that you seem to me to be in every way the visible personification of absolute perfection.

CECILY: I think your frankness does you great credit, Ernest. If you will allow me I will copy your remarks into my diary.

(Goes over to table and begins writing in diary.)

ALGERNON: Do you really keep a diary? I'd give anything to look at it. May I?

CECILY: Oh no. (Puts her hand over it.) You see, it is simply a very young girl's record of her own thoughts and impressions, and consequently meant for publication. When it appears in volume form I hope you will order a copy. But pray, Ernest, don't stop. I delight in taking down from dictation. I have reached "absolute perfection." You can go on. I am quite ready for more.

ALGERNON (somewhat taken aback): Ahem! Ahem!

CECILY: Oh, don't cough, Ernest. When one is dictating one should speak fluently and not cough. Besides, I don't know how to spell a cough.

(Writes as Algernon speaks.)

ALGERNON (speaking very rapidly): Cecily, ever since I first looked upon your wonderful and incomparable beauty, I have dared to love you wildly, passionately, devotedly, hopelessly.

CECILY: I don't think that you should tell me that you love me wildly, passionately, devotedly, hopelessly. Hopelessly doesn't seem to make much sense, does it?

ALGERNON: Cecily!

(Enter Merriman.)

MERRIMAN: The dog cart is waiting, sir.

ALGERNON: Tell it to come round next week, at the same hour.

MERRIMAN (looks at Cecily, who makes no sign): Yes, sir.
(Merriman retires.)

CECILY: Uncle Jack would be very much annoyed if he knew you were staying on till next week, at the same hour.

ALGERNON: Oh, I don't care about Jack. I don't care for anybody in the whole world but you. I love you, Cecily. You will marry me, won't you?

CECILY: You silly boy! Of course. Why, we have been engaged for the last three months.

ALGERNON: For the last three months?

CECILY: Yes, it will be exactly three months on Thursday.

ALGERNON: But how did we become engaged?

CECILY: Well, ever since dear Uncle Jack first confessed to us that he had a younger brother who was very wicked and bad, you of course have formed the chief topic of conversation between myself and Miss Prism. And of course a man who is much talked about is always very attractive. One feels there must be something in him after all. I daresay it was foolish of me, but I fell in love with you, Ernest.

ALGERNON: Darling! And when was the engagement actually settled?

CECILY: On the 14th of February last. Worn out by your entire ignorance of my existence, I determined to end the matter one way or the other, and after a long struggle with myself I accepted you under this dear old tree here. The next day I bought this little ring in your name, and this is the little bangle with the true lovers' knot I promised you always to wear.

ALGERNON: Did I give you this? It's very pretty, isn't it?

CECILY: Yes, you've wonderfully good taste, Ernest. It's the excuse I've always given for your leading such a bad life. And this is the box in which I keep all your dear letters.

(*Kneels at table, opens box, and produces letters tied up with blue ribbon.*)

ALGERNON: My letters! But my own sweet Cecily, I have never written you any letters.

CECILY: You need hardly remind me of that, Ernest. I remember only too well that I was forced to write your letters for you. I wrote always three times a week, and sometimes oftener.

ALGERNON: Oh, do let me read them, Cecily!

CECILY: Oh, I couldn't possibly. They would make you far too conceited. (*Replaces box.*) The three you wrote me after I had broken off the engagement are so beautiful, and so badly spelled, that even now I can hardly read them without crying a little.

ALGERNON: But was our engagement ever broken off?

CECILY: Of course it was. On the 22nd of last March. You can see the entry if you like. (*Shows diary.*) "Today I broke off my engagement with Ernest. I feel it is better to do so. The weather still continues charming."

ALGERNON: But why on earth did you break it off? What had I done? I had done nothing at all. Cecily, I am very much hurt indeed to hear you broke it off. Particularly when the weather was so charming.

CECILY: It would hardly have been a really serious engagement if it hadn't been broken off at least once. But I forgave you before the week was out.

ALGERNON (*crossing to her, and kneeling*): What a perfect angel you are, Cecily.

CECILY: You dear romantic boy. (*He kisses her; she puts her fingers through his hair.*) I hope your hair curls naturally, does it?

ALGERNON: Yes, darling, with a little help from others.

CECILY: I am so glad.

ALGERNON: You'll never break off our engagement again, Cecily?

CECILY: I don't think I could break it off now that I have actually met you. Besides, of course, there is the question of your name.

ALGERNON (*nervously*): Yes, of course.

CECILY: You must not laugh at me, darling, but it had always been a girlish dream of mine to love someone whose name was Ernest. (*Algernon rises, Cecily also.*) There is something in that name that seems to inspire absolute confidence. I pity any poor married woman whose husband is not called Ernest.

ALGERNON: But, my dear child, do you mean to say you could not love me if I had some other name?

CECILY: But what name?

ALGERNON: Oh, any name you like—Algernon—for instance—

CECILY: But I don't like the name of Algernon.

ALGERNON: Well, my own dear, sweet, loving little darling, I really can't see why you should object to the name of Algernon. It is not at all a bad name. In fact, it is rather an aristocratic name. Half of the chaps who get into the Bankruptcy Court are called Algernon. But seriously, Cecily—(*moving to her*)—if my name was Algy, couldn't you love me?

CECILY (*rising*): I might respect you, Ernest, I might admire your character, but I fear that I should not be able to give you my undivided attention.

ALGERNON: Ahem! Cecily! (*Picking up hat.*) Your Rector here is, I suppose, thoroughly experienced in the practice of all the rites and ceremonials of the Church?

CECILY: Oh yes. Dr. Chasuble is a most learned man. He has never written a single book, so you can imagine how much he knows.

ALGERNON: I must see him at once on a most important christening—I mean on most important business.

CECILY: Oh!

ALGERNON: I shan't be away more than half an hour.

CECILY: Considering that we have been engaged since February the 14th, and that I only met you today for the first time, I think it is rather hard that you should leave me for so long a period as half an hour. Couldn't you make it twenty minutes?

ALGERNON: I'll be back in no time.

(*Kisses her and rushes down the garden.*)

CECILY: What an impetuous boy he is! I like his hair so much. I must enter his proposal in my diary.

(*Enter Merriman.*)

MERRIMAN: A Miss Fairfax has just called to see Mr. Worthing. On very important business Miss Fairfax states.

CECILY: Isn't Mr. Worthing in his library?

MERRIMAN: Mr. Worthing went over in the direction of the Rectory some time ago.

CECILY: Pray ask the lady to come out here; Mr. Worthing is sure to be back soon. And you can bring tea.

MERRIMAN: Yes, miss.   (*Goes out.*)

CECILY: Miss Fairfax! I suppose one of the many good elderly women who are associated with Uncle Jack in some of his philanthropic work in London. I don't quite like women who are interested in philanthropic work. I think it is so forward of them.

(*Enter Merriman.*)

MERRIMAN: Miss Fairfax.

(*Enter Gwendolen. Exit Merriman.*)

CECILY (*advancing to meet her*): Pray let me introduce myself to you. My name is Cecily Cardew.

GWENDOLEN: Cecily Cardew? (*Moving to her and shaking hands.*) What a very sweet name! Something tells me that we are going to great friends. I like you already more than I can say. My first impressions of people are never wrong.

CECILY: How nice of you to like me so much after we have known each other such a comparatively short time. Pray sit down.

GWENDOLEN (*still standing up*): I may call you Cecily, may I not?

CECILY: With pleasure!

GWENDOLEN: And you will always call me Gwendolen, won't you?

CECILY: If you wish.

GWENDOLEN: Then that is all quite settled, is it not?

CECILY: I hope so.

(*A pause. They both sit down together.*)

GWENDOLEN: Perhaps this might be a favorable opportunity for my mentioning who I am. My father is Lord Bracknell. You have never heard of Papa, I suppose?

CECILY: I don't think so.

GWENDOLEN: Outside the family circle, Papa, I am glad to say, is entirely unknown. I think that is quite as it should be. The home seems to me to be the proper sphere for the man. And certainly once a man begins to neglect his domestic duties he becomes painfully effeminate, does he not? And I don't like that. It makes men so very attractive. Cecily, Mama, whose views on education are remarkably strict, has brought me up to be extremely shortsighted; it is part of her system, so do you mind my looking at you through my glasses?

CECILY: Oh! not at all, Gwendolen. I am very fond of being looked at.

GWENDOLEN (*after examining Cecily carefully through a lorgnette*): You are here on a short visit I suppose?

CECILY: Oh no! I live here.

GWENDOLEN (*severely*): Really? Your mother, no doubt, or some female relative of advanced years, resides here also?

CECILY: Oh no! I have no mother, nor, in fact, any relations.

GWENDOLEN: Indeed?

CECILY: My dear guardian, with the assistance of Miss Prism, has the arduous task of looking after me.

GWENDOLEN: Your guardian?

CECILY: Yes, I am Mr. Worthing's ward.

GWENDOLEN: Oh! It is strange he never mentioned to me that he had a ward. How secretive of him! He grows more interesting hourly. I am not sure, however, that the news inspires me with feelings of unmixed delight. (*Rising and going to her.*) I am very fond of you, Cecily; I have liked you ever since I met you! But I am bound to state that now that I know that you are Mr. Worthing's ward, I cannot help expressing a wish you were—well just a little older than you seem to be—and not quite so very alluring in appearance. In fact, if I may speak candidly—

CECILY: Pray do! I think that whenever one has anything unpleasant to say, one should always be quite candid.

GWENDOLEN: Well, to speak with perfect candor, Cecily, I wish that you were fully forty-two, and more than usually plain for your age. Ernest has a strong upright nature. He is the very soul of truth and honor. Disloyalty would be as impossible to him as deception. But even men of the noblest possible moral character are extremely susceptible to the influence of the physical charms of others. Modern, no less than Ancient History, supplies us with many most painful examples of what I refer to. If it were not so, indeed, History would be quite unreadable.

CECILY: I beg your pardon, Gwendolen, did you say Ernest?

GWENDOLEN: Yes.

CECILY: Oh, but it is not Mr. Ernest Worthing who is my guardian. It is his brother—his elder brother.

GWENDOLEN (*sitting down again*): Ernest never mentioned to me that he had a brother.

CECILY: I am sorry to say they have not been on good terms for a long time.

GWENDOLEN: Ah! that accounts for it. And now that I think of it I have never heard any man mention his brother. The subject seems distasteful to most men. Cecily, you have lifted a load from my mind. I was growing almost anxious. It would have been terrible if any cloud had come across a friendship like ours, would it not? Of course you are quite, quite sure that it is not Mr. Ernest Worthing who is your guardian?

CECILY: Quite sure. (*A pause.*) In fact, I am going to be his.

GWENDOLEN (*inquiringly*): I beg your pardon?

CECILY (*rather shy and confidingly*): Dearest Gwendolen, there is no reason why I should make a secret of it to you. Our little county newspaper is sure to chronicle the fact next week. Mr. Ernest Worthing and I are engaged to be married.

GWENDOLEN (*quite politely, rising*): My darling Cecily, I think there must be some slight error. Mr. Ernest Worthing is engaged to me. The announcement will appear in the *Morning Post* on Saturday at the latest.

CECILY (*very politely, rising*): I am afraid you must be under some misconception. Ernest proposed to me exactly ten minutes ago. (*Shows diary.*)

GWENDOLEN (*examines diary through her lorgnette carefully*): It is certainly very curious, for he asked me to be his wife yesterday afternoon at 5:30. If you would care to verify the incident, pray do so. (*Produces diary of her own.*) I never travel without my diary. One should always have something sensational to read in the train. I am so sorry, dear Cecily, if it is any disappointment to you, but I am afraid *I* have the prior claim.

CECILY: It would distress me more than I can tell you, dear Gwendolen, if it caused you any mental or physical anguish, but I feel bound to point out that since Ernest proposed to you he clearly has changed his mind.

GWENDOLEN (*meditatively*): If the poor fellow has been entrapped into any foolish promise I shall consider it my duty to rescue him at once, and with a firm hand.

CECILY (*thoughtfully and sadly*): Whatever unfortunate entanglement my dear boy may have got into, I will never reproach him with it after we are married.

GWENDOLEN: Do you allude to me, Miss Cardew, as an entanglement? You are presumptuous. On an occasion of this kind it becomes more than a moral duty to speak one's mind. It becomes a pleasure.

CECILY: Do you suggest, Miss Fairfax, that I entrapped Ernest into an engagement? How dare you? This is no time for wearing the shallow mask of manners. When I see a spade I call it a spade.

GWENDOLEN (*satirically*): I am glad to say that I have never seen a spade. It is obvious that our social spheres have been widely different.

(*Enter Merriman, followed by the Footman. He carries a salver, tablecloth, and plate stand. Cecily is about to retort. The presence of the servants exercises a restraining influence, under which both girls chafe.*)

MERRIMAN: Shall I lay tea here as usual, miss?
CECILY (*sternly, in a calm voice*): Yes, as usual.

(*Merriman begins to clear table and lay cloth. A long pause. Cecily and Gwendolen glare at each other.*)

GWENDOLEN: Are there many interesting walks in the vicinity, Miss Cardew?

CECILY: Oh! Yes! a great many. From the top of one of the hills quite close one can see five counties.

GWENDOLEN: Five counties! I don't think I should like that. I hate crowds.

CECILY (*sweetly*): I suppose that is why you live in town?

(*Gwendolen bites her lip, and beats her foot nervously with her parasol.*)

GWENDOLEN (*looking round*): Quite a well-kept garden this is, Miss Cardew.

CECILY: So glad you like it, Miss Fairfax.

GWENDOLEN: I had no idea there were any flowers in the country.

CECILY: Oh, flowers are as common here, Miss Fairfax, as people are in London.

GWENDOLEN: Personally I cannot understand how anybody manages to exist in the country, if anybody who is anybody does. The country always bores me to death.

CECILY: Ah! This is what the newspapers call agricultural depression, is it not? I believe the aristocracy are suffering very much from it just at present. It is almost an epidemic amongst them, I have been told. May I offer you some tea, Miss Fairfax?

GWENDOLEN (*with elaborate politeness*): Thank you. (*Aside.*) Detestable girl! But I require tea!

CECILY (*sweetly*): Sugar?

GWENDOLEN (*superciliously*): No, thank you. Sugar is not fashionable anymore.

(*Cecily looks angrily at her, takes up the tongs, and puts four lumps of sugar into the cup.*)

CECILY (*severely*): Cake or bread and butter?

GWENDOLEN (*in a bored manner*): Bread and butter, please. Cake is rarely seen at the best houses nowadays.

CECILY (*cuts a very large slice of cake, and puts it on the tray*): Hand that to Miss Fairfax.

(*Merriman does so, and goes out with Footman. Gwendolen drinks the tea and makes a grimace. Puts down cup at once, reaches out her hand to the bread and butter, looks at it, and finds it is cake. Rises in indignation.*)

GWENDOLEN: You have filled my tea with lumps of sugar, and though I asked most distinctly for bread and butter, you have given me cake. I am known for the gentleness of my disposition, and the extraordinary sweetness of my nature, but I warn you, Miss Cardew, you may go too far.

CECILY (*rising*): To save my poor, innocent, trusting boy from the machinations of any other girl there are no lengths to which I would not go.

GWENDOLEN: From the moment I saw you I distrusted you. I felt that you were false and deceitful. I am never deceived in such matters. My first impressions of people are invariably right.

CECILY: It seems to me, Miss Fairfax, that I am trespassing on your valuable time. No doubt you have many other calls of a similar character to make in the neighborhood.

(*Enter Jack.*)

GWENDOLEN (*catching sight of him*): Ernest! My own Ernest!

JACK: Gwendolen! Darling! (*Offers to kiss her.*)

GWENDOLEN (*drawing back*): A moment! May I ask if you are engaged to be married to this young lady? (*Points to Cecily.*)

JACK (*laughing*): To dear little Cecily! Of course not! What could have put such an idea into your pretty little head?

GWENDOLEN: Thank you. You may!

(*Offers her cheek.*)

CECILY (*very sweetly*): I knew there must be some misunderstanding, Miss Fairfax. The gentleman whose arm is at present round your waist is my dear guardian, Mr. John Worthing.

GWENDOLEN: I beg your pardon?

CECILY: This is Uncle Jack.

GWENDOLEN (*receding*): Jack! Oh!

(*Enter Algernon.*)

CECILY: Here is Ernest.

ALGERNON (*goes straight over to Cecily without noticing anyone else*): My own love!

(*Offers to kiss her.*)

CECILY (*drawing back*): A moment, Ernest! May I ask you—are you engaged to be married to this young lady?

ALGERNON (*looking round*): To what young lady? Good heavens! Gwendolen!

CECILY: Yes! to good heavens, Gwendolen, I mean to Gwendolen.

ALGERNON (*laughing*): Of course not! What could have put such an idea into your pretty little head?

CECILY: Thank you. (*Presenting her cheek to be kissed.*) You may. (*Algernon kisses her.*)

GWENDOLEN: I felt there was some slight error, Miss Cardew. The gentleman who is now embracing you is my cousin, Mr. Algernon Moncrieff.

CECILY (*breaking away from Algernon*): Algernon Moncrieff! Oh!

(*The two girls move towards each other and put their arms round each other's waists as if for protection.*)

CECILY: Are you called Algernon?

ALGERNON: I cannot deny it.

CECILY: Oh!

GWENDOLEN: Is your name really John?

JACK (*standing rather proudly*): I could deny it if I liked. I could deny anything if I liked. But my name certainly is John. It has been John for years.

CECILY (*to Gwendolen*): A gross deception has been practiced on both of us.

GWENDOLEN: My poor wounded Cecily!

CECILY: My sweet wronged Gwendolen!

GWENDOLEN (*slowly and seriously*): You will call me sister, will you not?

(*They embrace. Jack and Algernon groan and walk up and down.*)

CECILY (*rather brightly*): There is just one question I would like to be allowed to ask my guardian.

GWENDOLEN: An admirable idea! Mr. Worthing, there is just one question I would like to be permitted to put to you. Where is your brother Ernest? We are both engaged to be married to your brother Ernest, so it is a matter of some importance to us to know where your brother Ernest is at present.

JACK (*slowly and hesitatingly*): Gwendolen—Cecily—it is very painful for me to be forced to speak the truth. It is the first time in my life that I have ever been reduced to such a painful position, and I am really quite inexperienced in doing anything of the kind. However I will tell you quite frankly that I have no brother Ernest. I have no brother at all. I never had a brother in my life, and I certainly have not the smallest intention of ever having one in the future.

CECILY (*surprised*): No brother at all?

JACK (*cheerily*): None!

GWENDOLEN (*severely*): Had you never a brother of any kind?

JACK (*pleasantly*): Never. Not even of any kind.

GWENDOLEN: I am afraid it is quite clear, Cecily, that neither of us is engaged to be married to anyone.

CECILY: It is not a very pleasant position for a young girl suddenly to find herself in. Is it?

GWENDOLEN: Let us go into the house. They will hardly venture to come after us there.

CECILY: No, men are so cowardly, aren't they?

(*They retire into the house with scornful looks.*)

JACK: This ghastly state of things is what you call Bunburying, I suppose?

ALGERNON: Yes, and a perfectly wonderful Bunbury it is. The most wonderful Bunbury I have ever had in my life.

JACK: Well, you've no right whatsoever to Bunbury here.

ALGERNON: That is absurd. One has a right to Bunbury anywhere one chooses. Every serious Bunburyist knows that.

JACK: Serious Bunburyist! Good heavens!

ALGERNON: Well, one must be serious about something, if one wants to have any amusement in life. I happen to be serious about Bunburying. What on earth you are serious about I haven't got the remotest idea. About everything, I should fancy. You have such an absolutely trivial nature.

JACK: Well, the only small satisfaction I have in the whole of this wretched business is that your friend Bunbury is quite exploded. You won't be able to run down to the country quite so often as you used to do, dear Algy. And a very good thing too.

ALGERNON: Your brother is a little off color, isn't he, dear Jack? You won't be able to disappear to London quite so frequently as your wicked custom was. And not a bad thing either.

JACK: As for your conduct towards Miss Cardew, I must say that your taking in a sweet, simple, innocent girl like that is quite inexcusable. To say nothing of the fact that she is my ward.

ALGERNON: I can see no possible defense at all for your deceiving a brilliant, clever, thoroughly experienced young lady like Miss Fairfax. To say nothing of the fact that she is my cousin.

JACK: I wanted to be engaged to Gwendolen, that is all. I love her.

ALGERNON: Well, I simply wanted to be engaged to Cecily. I adore her.

JACK: There is certainly no chance of your marrying Miss Cardew.

ALGERNON: I don't think there is much likelihood, Jack, of you and Miss Fairfax being united.

JACK: Well, that is no business of yours.

ALGERNON: If it was my business, I wouldn't talk about it. (*Begins to eat muffins.*) It is very vulgar to talk about one's business. Only people like stockbrokers do that, and then merely at dinner parties.

JACK: How you can sit there, calmly eating muffins when we are in this horrible trouble. I can't make out. You seem to me to be perfectly heartless.

ALGERNON: Well, I can't eat muffins in an agitated manner. The butter would probably get on my cuffs. One should always eat muffins quite calmly. It is the only way to eat them.

JACK: I say it's perfectly heartless your eating muffins at all, under the circumstances.

ALGERNON: When I am in trouble, eating is the only thing that consoles me. Indeed, when I am in really great trouble, as anyone who knows me intimately will tell you, I refuse everything except food and drink. At the present moment I am eating muffins because I am unhappy. Besides, I am particularly fond of muffins.
                                                        (*Rising.*)

JACK (*rising*): Well, that is no reason why you should eat them all in that greedy way.

(*Takes muffins from Algernon.*)

ALGERNON (*offering tea cake*): I wish you would have tea cake instead. I don't like tea cake.

JACK: Good heavens! I suppose a man may eat his own muffins in his own garden.

ALGERNON: But you have just said it was perfectly heartless to eat muffins.

JACK: I said it was perfectly heartless of you, under the circumstances. That is a very different thing.

ALGERNON: That may be, but the muffins are the same. (*He seizes the muffin dish from Jack.*)

JACK: Algy, I wish to goodness you would go.

ALGERNON: You can't possibly ask me to go without having some dinner. It's absurd. I never go without my dinner. No one ever does, except vegetarians and people like that. Besides I have just made arrangements, with Dr. Chasuble to be christened at a quarter to six under the name of Ernest.

JACK: My dear fellow, the sooner you give up that nonsense the better. I made arrangements this morning with Dr. Chasuble to be christened myself at 5:30, and I naturally will take the name of Ernest. Gwendolen would wish it. We can't both be christened Ernest. It's absurd. Besides, I have a perfect right to be christened if I like. There is no evidence at all that I ever have been christened by anybody. I should think it extremely probable I never was, and so does Dr. Chasuble. It is entirely different in your case. You have been christened already.

ALGERNON: Yes, but I have not been christened for years.

JACK: Yes, but you have been christened. That is the important thing.

ALGERNON: Quite so. So I know my constitution can stand it. If you are not quite sure about your ever having been christened, I must say I think it rather dangerous your venturing on it now. It might make you very unwell. You can hardly have forgotten that someone very closely connected with you was very nearly carried off this week in Paris by a severe chill.

JACK: Yes, but you said yourself that a severe chill was not hereditary.

ALGERNON: It usen't to be, I know—but I daresay it is now. Science is always making wonderful improvements in things.

JACK (*picking up the muffin dish*): Oh, that is nonsense; you are always talking nonsense.

ALGERNON: Jack, you are at the muffins again! I wish you wouldn't. There are only two left. (*Takes them.*) I told you I was particularly fond of muffins.

JACK: But I hate tea cake.

ALGERNON: Why on earth then do you allow tea cake to be served up for your guests? What ideas you have of hospitality!

JACK: Algernon! I have already told you to go. I don't want you here. Why don't you go!

ALGERNON: I haven't quite finished my tea yet! and there is still one muffin left.

(*Jack groans, and sinks into a chair. Algernon still continues eating.*)

ACT III

(*Scene: Morning room at the Manor House. Gwendolen and Cecily are at the window, looking out into the garden.*)

GWENDOLEN: The fact that they did not follow us at once into the house, as anyone else would have done, seems to me to show that they have some sense of shame left.

CECILY: They have been eating muffins. That looks like repentance.

GWENDOLEN (*after a pause*): They don't seem to notice us at all. Couldn't you cough?

CECILY: But I haven't got a cough.

GWENDOLEN: They're looking at us. What effrontery!

CECILY: They're approaching. That's very forward of them.

GWENDOLEN: Let us preserve a dignified silence.

CECILY: Certainly. It's the only thing to do now.

(*Enter Jack followed by Algernon. They whistle some dreadful popular air from a British opera.*)

GWENDOLEN: This dignified silence seems to produce an unpleasant effect.

CECILY: A most distasteful one.

GWENDOLEN: But we will not be the first to speak.

CECILY: Certainly not.

GWENDOLEN: Mr. Worthing, I have something very particular to ask you. Much depends on your reply.

CECILY: Gwendolen, your common sense is invaluable. Mr. Moncrieff, kindly answer me the following question. Why did you pretend to be my guardian's brother?

ALGERNON: In order that I might have an opportunity of meeting you.

CECILY (*to Gwendolen*): That certainly seems a satisfactory explanation, does it not?

GWENDOLEN: Yes, dear, if you can believe him.

CECILY: I don't. But that does not affect the wonderful beauty of his answer.

GWENDOLEN: True. In matters of grave importance, style, not sincerity is the vital thing. Mr. Worthing, what explanation can you offer to me for pretending to have a brother? Was it in order that you might have an opportunity of coming up to town to see me as often as possible?

JACK: Can you doubt it, Miss Fairfax?

GWENDOLEN: I have the gravest doubts upon the subject. But I intend to crush them. This is not the moment for German skepticism. (*Moving to Cecily.*) Their explanations appear to be quite satisfactory, especially Mr. Worthing's. That seems to me to have the stamp of truth upon it.

CECILY: I am more than content with what Mr. Moncrieff said. His voice alone inspires one with absolute credulity.

GWENDOLEN: Then you think we should forgive them?

CECILY: Yes. I mean no.

GWENDOLEN: True! I had forgotten. There are principles at stake that one cannot surrender. Which of us should tell them? The task is not a pleasant one.

CECILY: Could we not both speak at the same time?

GWENDOLEN: An excellent idea! I nearly always speak at the same time as other people. Will you take the time from me?

CECILY: Certainly.

(*Gwendolen beats time with uplifted finger.*)

GWENDOLEN AND CECILY (*speaking together*): Your Christian names are still an insuperable barrier. That is all!

JACK AND ALGERNON (*speaking together*): Our Christian names! Is that all? But we are going to be christened this afternoon.

GWENDOLEN (*to Jack*): For my sake you are prepared to do this terrible thing?

JACK: I am!

CECILY (*to Algernon*): To please me you are ready to face this fearful ordeal?

ALGERNON: I am!

GWENDOLEN: How absurd to talk of the equality of the sexes! Where questions of self-sacrifice are concerned, men are infinitely beyond us.

JACK: We are! (*Clasps hands with Algernon.*)

CECILY: They have moments of physical courage of which we women know absolutely nothing.

GWENDOLEN (*to Jack*): Darling!

ALGERNON (*to Cecily*): Darling!

(*They fall into each other's arms.*)

(*Enter Merriman. When he enters he coughs loudly, seeing the situation.*)

MERRIMAN: Ahem! Ahem! Lady Bracknell!

JACK: Good heavens!

(*Enter Lady Bracknell. The couples separate, in alarm. Exit Merriman.*)

LADY BRACKNELL: Gwendolen! What does this mean?

GWENDOLEN: Merely that I am engaged to be married to Mr. Worthing, Mama.

LADY BRACKNELL: Come here. Sit down. Sit down immediately. Hesitation of any kind is a sign of mental decay in the young, of physical weakness in the old. (*Turns to Jack.*) Apprised, sir, of my daughter's sudden flight by her trusty maid, whose confidence I purchased by means of a small coin, I followed her at once by a luggage train. Her unhappy father is, I am glad to say, under the impression that she is attending a more than usually lengthy lecture by the University Extension Scheme on the influence of a permanent income on thought. I do not propose to undeceive him. Indeed I have never undeceived him on any question. I would consider it wrong. But of course, you will clearly understand that all communication between yourself and my daughter must cease immediately from this moment. On this point, as indeed on all points, I am firm.

JACK: I am engaged to be married to Gwendolen, Lady Bracknell!

LADY BRACKNELL: You are nothing of the kind, sir. And now, as regards Algernon!—Algernon!

ALGERNON: Yes, Aunt Augusta.

LADY BRACKNELL: May I ask if it is in this house that your invalid friend Mr. Bunbury resides?

ALGERNON (*stammering*): Oh! No! Bunbury doesn't live here. Bunbury is somewhere else at present. In fact, Bunbury is dead.

LADY BRACKNELL: Dead! When did Mr. Bunbury die? His death must have been extremely sudden.

ALGERNON (*airily*): Oh! I killed Bunbury this afternoon. I mean poor Bunbury died this afternoon.

LADY BRACKNELL: What did he die of?

ALGERNON: Bunbury? Oh, he was quite exploded.

LADY BRACKNELL: Exploded! Was he the victim of a revolutionary outrage? I was not aware that Mr. Bunbury was interested in social legislation. If so, he is well punished for his morbidity.

ALGERNON: My dear Aunt Augusta, I mean he was found out! The doctors found out that Bunbury could not live, that is what I mean—so Bunbury died.

LADY BRACKNELL: He seems to have had great confidence in the opinion of his physicians. I am glad, however, that he made up his mind at the last to some definite course of action, and acted under proper medical advice. And now that we have finally got rid of this Mr. Bunbury, may I ask, Mr. Worthing, who is that young person whose hand my nephew Algernon is now holding in what seems to me a peculiarly unnecessary manner?

JACK: That lady is Miss Cecily Cardew, my ward.

(*Lady Bracknell bows coldly to Cecily.*)

ALGERNON: I am engaged to be married to Cecily, Aunt Augusta.

Eric Stoltz and Schuyler Grant propose a toast in the Irish Repertory Theatre's 1996 production of *The Importance of Being Earnest*.

LADY BRACKNELL: I beg your pardon?

CECILY: Mr. Moncrieff and I are engaged to be married, Lady Bracknell.

LADY BRACKNELL (*with a shiver, crossing to the sofa and sitting down*): I do not know whether there is anything peculiarly exciting in the air of this particular part of Hertfordshire, but the number of engagements that go on seems to me considerably above the proper average that statistics have laid down for our guidance. I think some preliminary inquiry on my part would not be out of place. Mr. Worthing, is Miss Cardew at all connected with any of the larger railway stations in London? I merely desire information. Until yesterday I had no idea that there were any families or persons whose origin was a Terminus.

(*Jack looks perfectly furious, but restrains himself.*)

JACK (*in a clear, cold voice*): Miss Cardew is the granddaughter of the late Mr. Thomas Cardew of 149, Belgrave Square, S.W.; Gervase Park, Dorking, Surrey; and the Sporran, Fifeshire, N.B.

LADY BRACKNELL: That sounds not unsatisfactory. Three addresses always inspire confidence, even in tradesmen. But what proof have I of their authenticity?

JACK: I have carefully preserved the Court Guides of the period. They are open to your inspection, Lady Bracknell.

LADY BRACKNELL (*grimly*): I have known strange errors in that publication.

JACK: Miss Cardew's family solicitors are Messrs. Markby, Markby, and Markby.

LADY BRACKNELL: Markby, Markby, and Markby? A firm of the very highest position in their profession. Indeed I am told that one of the Mr. Markbys is occasionally to be seen at dinner parties. So far I am satisfied.

JACK (*very irritably*): How extremely kind of you, Lady Bracknell! I have also in my possession, you will be pleased to hear, certificates of Miss Cardew's birth, baptism, whooping cough, registration, vaccination, confirmation, and the measles; both the German and the English variety.

LADY BRACKNELL: Ah! A life crowded with incident I see; though perhaps somewhat too exciting for a young girl. I am not myself in favor of premature experiences. (*Rises, looks at her watch.*) Gwendolen! the time approaches for our departure. We have not a moment to lose. As a matter of form, Mr. Worthing, I had better ask you if Miss Cardew has any little fortune?

JACK: Oh! about a hundred and thirty thousand pounds in the Funds. That is all. Good-bye, Lady Bracknell. So pleased to have seen you.

LADY BRACKNELL (*sitting down again*): A moment, Mr. Worthing. A hundred and thirty thousand pounds! And in the Funds! Miss Cardew seems to me a most attractive young lady, now that I look at her. Few girls of the present day have any really solid qualities, any of the qualities that last, and improve with time. We live, I regret to say, in an age of surfaces. (*To Cecily.*) Come over here, dear. (*Cecily goes across.*) Pretty child! your dress is sadly simple, and your hair seems almost as Nature might have left it. But we can soon alter all that. A thoroughly experienced French maid produces a really marvelous result in a very brief space of time: I remember recommending one to young Lady Lancing, and after three months her own husband did not know her.

JACK (*aside*): And after six months nobody knew her.

LADY BRACKNELL (*glares at Jack for a few moments. Then bends, with a practiced smile, to Cecily*): Kindly turn round, sweet child. (*Cecily turns completely round.*) No, the side view is what I want. (*Cecily presents her profile.*) Yes, quite as I expected. There are distinct social possibilities in your profile. The two weak points in our age are its want of principle and its want of profile. The chin a little higher, dear. Style largely depends on the way the chin is worn. They are worn very high, just at present. Algernon!

ALGERNON: Yes, Aunt Augusta!

LADY BRACKNELL: There are distinct social possibilities in Miss Cardew's profile.

ALGERNON: Cecily is the sweetest, dearest, prettiest girl in the whole world. And I don't care twopence about social possibilities.

LADY BRACKNELL: Never speak disrespectfully of Society, Algernon. Only people who can't get into it do that. (*To Cecily.*) Dear child, of course you know that Algernon has nothing but his debts to depend upon. But I do not approve of mercenary marriages. When I married Lord Bracknell I had no fortune of any kind. But I never dreamed for a moment of allowing that to stand in my way. Well, I suppose I must give my consent.

ALGERNON: Thank you, Aunt Augusta.

LADY BRACKNELL: Cecily, you may kiss me!

CECILY (*kisses her*): Thank you, Lady Bracknell.

LADY BRACKNELL: You may also address me as Aunt Augusta for the future.

CECILY: Thank you, Aunt Augusta.

LADY BRACKNELL: The marriage, I think, had better take place quite soon.

ALGERNON: Thank you, Aunt Augusta.

CECILY: Thank you, Aunt Augusta.

LADY BRACKNELL: To speak frankly, I am not in favor of long engagements. They give people the opportunity of finding out each other's character before marriage, which I think is never advisable.

JACK: I beg your pardon for interrupting you, Lady Bracknell, but this engagement is quite out of the question. I am Miss Cardew's guardian, and she cannot marry without my consent until she comes of age. That consent I absolutely decline to give.

LADY BRACKNELL: Upon what grounds may I ask? Algernon is an extremely, I may almost say an ostentatiously, eligible young man. He has nothing, but he looks everything. What more can one desire?

JACK: It pains me very much to have to speak frankly to you, Lady Bracknell, about your nephew, but the fact is that I do not approve at all of his moral character. I suspect him of being untruthful.

(*Algernon and Cecily look at him in indignant amazement.*)

LADY BRACKNELL: Untruthful! My nephew Algernon? Impossible! He is an Oxonian.°

JACK: I fear there can be no possible doubt about the matter. This afternoon, during my temporary absence in London on an important question of romance, he obtained admission to my house by means of the false pretense of being my brother. Under an assumed name he drank, I've just been informed by my butler, an entire pint bottle of my Perrier-Jouêt, Brut, '89; a wine I was specially reserving for myself. Continuing his disgraceful deception, he succeeded in the course of the afternoon in alienating the affections of my only ward. He subsequently stayed to tea, and devoured every single muffin. And what makes his conduct all the more heartless is, that he was perfectly well aware from the first that I have no brother, that I never had a brother, and that I don't intend to have a brother, not even of any kind. I distinctly told him so myself yesterday afternoon.

LADY BRACKNELL: Ahem! Mr. Worthing, after careful consideration I have decided entirely to overlook my nephew's conduct to you.

JACK: That is very generous of you, Lady Bracknell. My own decision, however, is unalterable. I decline to give my consent.

LADY BRACKNELL (*to Cecily*): Come here, sweet child. (*Cecily goes over.*) How old are you, dear?

CECILY: Well, I am really only eighteen, but I always admit to twenty when I go to evening parties.

LADY BRACKNELL: You are perfectly right in making some slight alteration. Indeed, no woman should ever be quite accurate about her age. It looks so calculating—(*In a meditative manner.*) Eighteen but admitting to twenty at evening parties. Well, it will not be very long before you are of age and free from the restraints of tutelage. So I don't think your guardian's consent is, after all, a matter of any importance.

JACK: Pray excuse me, Lady Bracknell, for interrupting you again, but it is only fair to tell you that according to the terms of her grandfather's will Miss Cardew does not come legally of age till she is thirty-five.

Oxonian: Educated at Oxford University.

Lady Bracknell (Lynn Redgrave), with Algernon (Robert Petkoff) and Cecily (Charlotte Parry), in Sir Peter Hall's Theatre Royal Bath production, 2006.

LADY BRACKNELL: That does not seem to me to be a grave objection. Thirty-five is a very attractive age. London society is full of women of the very highest birth who have, of their own free choice, remained thirty-five for years. Lady Dumbleton is an instance in point. To my own knowledge she has been thirty-five ever since she arrived at the age of forty, which was many years ago now. I see no reason why our dear Cecily should not be even still more attractive at the age you mention than she is at present. There will be a large accumulation of property.

CECILY: Algy, could you wait for me till I was thirty-five?

ALGERNON: Of course I could, Cecily. You know I could.

CECILY: Yes, I felt it instinctively, but I couldn't wait all that time. I hate waiting even five minutes for anybody. It always makes me rather cross. I am not punctual myself, I know, but I do like punctuality in others, and waiting, even to be married, is quite out of the question.

ALGERNON: Then what is to be done, Cecily?

CECILY: I don't know, Mr. Moncrieff.

LADY BRACKNELL: My dear Mr. Worthing, as Miss Cardew states positively that she cannot wait till she is thirty-five—a remark which I am bound to say seems to me to show a somewhat impatient nature—I would beg of you to reconsider your decision.

JACK: But my dear Lady Bracknell, the matter is entirely in your own hands. The moment you consent to my marriage with Gwendolen, I will most gladly allow your nephew to form an alliance with my ward.

LADY BRACKNELL (*rising and drawing herself up*): You must be quite aware that what you propose is out of the question.

JACK: Then a passionate celibacy is all that any of us can look forward to.

LADY BRACKNELL: That is not the destiny I propose for Gwendolen. Algernon, of course, can choose for himself. (*Pulls out her watch.*) Come, dear; (*Gwendolen rises*) we have already missed five, if not six, trains. To miss any more might expose us to comment on the platform.

(*Enter Dr. Chasuble.*)

CHASUBLE: Everything is quite ready for the christenings.

LADY BRACKNELL: The christenings, sir! Is not that somewhat premature?

CHASUBLE (*looking rather puzzled, and pointing to Jack and Algernon*): Both these gentlemen have expressed a desire for immediate baptism.

LADY BRACKNELL: At their age? The idea is grotesque and irreligious! Algernon, I forbid you to be baptized. I will not hear of such excesses. Lord Bracknell would be highly displeased if he learned that that was the way in which you wasted your time and money.

CHASUBLE: Am I to understand then that there are to be no christenings at all this afternoon?

JACK: I don't think that, as things are now, it would be of much practical value to either of us, Dr. Chasuble.

CHASUBLE: I am grieved to hear such sentiments from you, Mr. Worthing. They savor of the heretical views of the Anabaptists,° views that I have completely refuted in four of my unpublished sermons. However, as your present mood seems to be one peculiarly secular, I will return to the church at once. Indeed, I

Anabaptists: A religious sect founded in the sixteenth century and advocating adult baptism and church membership for adults only.

have just been informed by the pew opener that for the last hour and a half Miss Prism has been waiting for me in the vestry.

LADY BRACKNELL (*starting*): Miss Prism! Did I hear you mention a Miss Prism?

CHASUBLE: Yes, Lady Bracknell. I am on my way to join her.

LADY BRACKNELL: Pray allow me to detain you for a moment. This matter may prove to be one of vital importance to Lord Bracknell and myself. Is this Miss Prism a female of repellent aspect, remotely connected with education?

CHASUBLE (*somewhat indignantly*): She is the most cultivated of ladies, and the very picture of respectability.

LADY BRACKNELL: It is obviously the same person. May I ask what position she holds in your household?

CHASUBLE (*severely*): I am a celibate, madam.

JACK (*interposing*): Miss Prism, Lady Bracknell, has been for the last three years Miss Cardew's esteemed governess and valued companion.

LADY BRACKNELL: In spite of what I hear of her, I must see her at once. Let her be sent for.

CHASUBLE (*looking off*): She approaches; she is nigh.

(*Enter Miss Prism hurriedly.*)

MISS PRISM: I was told you expected me in the vestry, dear Canon. I have been waiting for you there for an hour and three-quarters.

(*Catches sight of Lady Bracknell who has fixed her with a stony glare. Miss Prism grows pale and quails. She looks anxiously round as if desirous to escape.*)

LADY BRACKNELL (*in a severe, judicial voice*): Prism! (*Miss Prism bows her head in shame.*) Come here, Prism! (*Miss Prism approaches in a humble manner.*) Prism! Where is that baby? (*General consternation. The Canon starts back in horror. Algernon and Jack pretend to be anxious to shield Cecily and Gwendolen from hearing the details of a terrible public scandal.*) Twenty-eight years ago, Prism, you left Lord Bracknell's house, Number 104, Upper Grosvenor Street, in charge of a perambulator that contained a baby, of the male sex. You never returned. A few weeks later, through the elaborate investigations of the Metropolitan police, the perambulator was discovered at midnight, standing by itself in a remote corner of Bayswater. It contained the manuscript of a three-volume novel of more than usually revolting sentimentality. (*Miss Prism starts in involuntary indignation.*) But the baby was not there! (*Everyone looks at Miss Prism.*) Prism! Where is that baby? (*A pause.*)

MISS PRISM: Lady Bracknell, I admit with shame that I do not know. I only wish I did. The plain facts of the case are these. On the morning of the day you mention, a day that is forever branded on my memory, I prepared as usual to take the baby out in its perambulator. I had also with me a somewhat old, but capacious handbag in which I had intended to place the manuscript of a work of fiction that I had written during my few unoccupied hours. In a moment of mental abstraction, for which I never can forgive myself, I deposited the manuscript in the bassinette, and placed the baby in the handbag.

JACK (*who has been listening attentively*): But where did you deposit the handbag?

MISS PRISM: Do not ask me, Mr. Worthing.

JACK: Miss Prism, this is a matter of no small importance to me. I insist on knowing where you deposited the handbag that contained that infant.

MISS PRISM: I left it in the cloakroom of one of the larger railway stations in London.

JACK: What railway station?

MISS PRISM (*quite crushed*): Victoria. The Brighton line. (*Sinks into a chair.*)

JACK: I must retire to my room for a moment. Gwendolen, wait here for me.

GWENDOLEN: If you are not too long, I will wait here for you all my life.

(*Exit Jack in great excitement.*)

CHASUBLE: What do you think this means, Lady Bracknell?

LADY BRACKNELL: I dare not even suspect, Dr. Chasuble. I need hardly tell you that in families of high position strange coincidences are not supposed to occur. They are hardly considered the thing.

(*Noises heard overhead as if someone was throwing trunks about. Everyone looks up.*)

CECILY: Uncle Jack seems strangely agitated.

CHASUBLE: Your guardian has a very emotional nature.

LADY BRACKNELL: This noise is extremely unpleasant. It sounds as if he was having an argument. I dislike arguments of any kind. They are always vulgar, and often convincing.

CHASUBLE (*looking up*): It has stopped now. (*The noise is redoubled.*)

LADY BRACKNELL: I wish he would arrive at some conclusion.

GWENDOLEN: This suspense is terrible. I hope it will last.

(*Enter Jack with a handbag of black leather in his hand.*)

JACK (*rushing over to Miss Prism*): Is this the handbag, Miss Prism? Examine it carefully before you speak. The happiness of more than one life depends on your answer.

MISS PRISM (*calmly*): It seems to be mine. Yes, here is the injury it received through the upsetting of a Gower Street omnibus in younger and happier days. Here is the stain on the lining caused by the explosion of a temperance beverage, an incident that occurred at Leamington. And here, on the lock, are my initials. I had forgotten that in an extravagant mood I had had them placed there. The bag is undoubtedly mine. I am delighted to have it so unexpectedly restored to me. It has been a great inconvenience being without it all these years.

JACK (*in a pathetic voice*): Miss Prism, more is restored to you than this handbag. I was the baby you placed in it.

MISS PRISM (*amazed*): You?

JACK (*embracing her*): Yes—mother!

MISS PRISM (*recoiling in indignant astonishment*): Mr. Worthing! I am unmarried!

JACK: Unmarried! I do not deny that is a serious blow. But after all, who has the right to cast a stone against one who has suffered? Cannot repentance wipe out an act of folly? Why should there be one law for men, and another for women? Mother, I forgive you. (*Tries to embrace her again.*)

MISS PRISM (*still more indignant*): Mr. Worthing, there is some error. (*Pointing to Lady Bracknell.*) There is the lady who can tell you who you really are.

JACK (*after a pause*): Lady Bracknell, I hate to seem inquisitive, but would you kindly inform me who I am?

LADY BRACKNELL: I am afraid that the news I have to give you will not altogether please you. You are the son of my poor sister, Mrs. Moncrieff, and consequently Algernon's elder brother.

JACK: Algy's elder brother! Then I have a brother after all. I knew I had a brother! I always said I had a brother! Cecily,—how could you have ever doubted that I had a brother. (*Seizes hold of Algernon.*) Dr. Chasuble, my unfortunate brother. Miss Prism, my unfortunate brother. Gwendolen, my unfortunate brother. Algy, you young scoundrel, you will have to treat me with more respect in the future. You have never behaved to me like a brother in all your life.

ALGERNON: Well, not till today, old boy, I admit. I did my best, however, though I was out of practice.

(*Shakes hands.*)

GWENDOLEN (*to Jack*): My own! But what own are you? What is your Christian name, now that you have become someone else?

JACK: Good heavens!—I had quite forgotten that point. Your decision on the subject of my name is irrevocable, I suppose?

GWENDOLEN: I never change, except in my affections.

CECILY: What a noble nature you have, Gwendolen!

JACK: Then the question had better be cleared up at once. Aunt Augusta, a moment. At the time when Miss Prism left me in the handbag, had I been christened already?

LADY BRACKNELL: Every luxury that money could buy, including christening, had been lavished upon you by your fond and doting parents.

JACK: Then I was christened! That is settled. Now, what name was I given? Let me know the worst.

LADY BRACKNELL: Being the eldest son you were naturally christened after your father.

JACK (*irritably*): Yes, but what was my father's Christian name?

LADY BRACKNELL (*meditatively*): I cannot at the present moment recall what the General's Christian name was. But I have no doubt he had one. He was eccentric, I admit. But only in later years. And that was the result of the Indian climate, and marriage, and indigestion, and other things of that kind.

JACK: Algy! Can't you recollect what our father's Christian name was?

ALGERNON: My dear boy, we were never even on speaking terms. He died before I was a year old.

JACK: His name would appear in the Army Lists of the period, I suppose, Aunt Augusta?

LADY BRACKNELL: The General was essentially a man of peace, except in his domestic life. But I have no doubt his name would appear in any military directory.

JACK: The Army Lists of the last forty years are here. These delightful records should have been my constant study. (*Rushes to bookcase and tears the books out.*) M. Generals—Mallam, Maxbohm, Magley, what ghastly names they have—Markby, Migsby, Mobbs, Moncrieff! Lieutenant 1840, Captain, Lieutenant-Colonel, Colonel, General 1869, Christian names, Ernest John. (*Puts book very quietly down and speaks quite calmly.*) I always told you, Gwendolen, my name was Ernest, didn't I? Well, it is Ernest after all. I mean it naturally is Ernest.

LADY BRACKNELL: Yes, I remember now that the General was called Ernest. I knew I had some particular reason for disliking the name.

GWENDOLEN: Ernest! My own Ernest! I felt from the first that you could have no other name!

JACK: Gwendolen, it is a terrible thing for a man to find out suddenly that all his life he has been speaking nothing but the truth. Can you forgive me?

GWENDOLEN: I can. For I feel that you are sure to change.

JACK: My own one!

CHASUBLE (*to Miss Prism*): Laetitia! (*Embraces her.*)

MISS PRISM (*enthusiastically*): Frederick! At last!

ALGERNON: Cecily! (*Embraces her.*) At last!

JACK: Gwendolen! (*Embraces her.*) At last!

LADY BRACKNELL: My nephew, you seem to be displaying signs of triviality.

JACK: On the contrary, Aunt Augusta, I've now realized for the first time in my life the vital Importance of Being Earnest.

COMMENTARY

JOSEPH DONOHUE (b. 1954)

Interview with Sir Peter Hall, Director of *The Importance of Being Earnest* 2006

The distinguished director is interviewed by professor Joseph Donohue concerning his reasons for directing Wilde's play for contemporary audiences. Hall explains why he believes the play is always timely and what he sees as its central issues. He also explores the gender issues buried in the play.

Q: Is there anything about the present time, the world situation, or our understanding of Oscar Wilde himself that makes mounting a production of *The Importance of Being Earnest* particularly appropriate now?

A: This is the second time I've done the play, and I believe it's an absolutely unique and original object. I don't think that you can write it off as a farce or a farcical comedy; I think it's as original as *Waiting for Godot*, and heaven knows what Wilde would've done if he had been spared, if we hadn't murdered him, because it is absolutely original. In that sense, it's a masterpiece, and in that sense, it's always timely. It's not easy to do, but I think the important thing about Wilde—I've done *Ideal Husband* several times, and *Earnest* twice—the important thing is to understand what his wit is about. It's not about standing on the stage and having like a tennis match of facetiousness of who can win. If you look at Wilde's plays carefully, the wit always covers over something which is very painful, or very extraordinary, something that can't be actually understood or said, for whatever reason. Wilde said, "Give a man a mask and he will tell you the truth," and Wilde's mask, for his characters, is always wit. It's like the English stiff upper lip of the nineteenth century. So you've got to look at *The Importance of Being Earnest* as a deeply serious play about the double life, about sexual desire, about the marriage market, and if you play it very seriously, it's excruciatingly funny. If you don't play it seriously, I think the comedy wears off.

But, why do it now? Well, I think it's always time to do it, in a sense. I don't think there's a deeply contemporary need to do it or anything. Masterpieces need revaluing for each generation.

Q: The original production of *The Importance of Being Earnest*, at George Alexander's St. James Theatre, in London in 1895, featured a three-act play text, cut down—probably mostly by Alexander himself—from the four-act play originally written by Wilde. Earlier, the author had written to Alexander offering him the play and telling him that the two men's parts of Jack and Algy were of equal prominence. In cutting the play to three acts Alexander seems to have made sure that his own part, Jack Worthing, outshone the part of Algy. That choice was memorialized in the first edition of the play. What text do you plan to use for the production? The standard choice is the first edition text, based on Alexander's three-act play, but have you considered using at least some material from the original four-act text? If you chose to do that, would you try to restore more of a balance between the two roles of Jack and Algy, or do you like the greater centrality of Jack as the three-act text presents it? Do you have some other comments about the balancing of pairs of contrasting characters in the play — for example, Gwendolen and Cecily, Miss Prism and Canon Chasuble?

A: We're using the three-act text. When we did the play before, I looked into the fourth act very carefully and actually rehearsed some of it and did some of it, but not in performance. Whoever edited it to the three-act version, whether it was George Alexander or Wilde himself or a collaboration, I personally think they did well. There's something prolix and a little self-indulgent about the fourth act. Of course it's got some good things in it, but I don't think they finally help.

I don't understand the comment about an imbalance between the two roles. Algy is a superb part; he gets all the laughs. Ernest is the center of the play in the sense that Ernest is the man who has not yet come to terms with who he is, not come to terms with his own sexuality, among other things, and therefore needs to lead a double life. I think that's a wonderfully rich and extraordinary part. I don't think that Algy is a supporting role at all.

I think classically, from Plautus onward and certainly [in] Shakespeare, comedy is about couples. Couples who find out they're now mature enough to get married, or relate to each other in terms of love. I think the balancing of the characters is classic comedy.

Q: Is the play essentially a comedy, or essentially a farce? Or is it a mixed breed?

A: I never understand why people need to put some kind of label on things. It's like saying, "Are Shakespeare's late plays romances or comedies, or comedy/romances, or what are they?" They're plays, and they're very original, and as I said, I think *The Importance of Being Earnest* is one of the most original plays in the English language. I certainly don't think it can be dismissed as a farce any more than I think that it can be just looked at as a serious play. It's the most extraordinary combination of critical comedy which illuminates what the people are about, and what their quest is, and what their pains are, and what their anguishes are. It's very serious, but it's excruciatingly funny. I don't know of any label for that; it's why I think Oscar Wilde is so original.

Q: Is the author in the play?

A: Well, the author's in the play. The author's in the play all the while. He's partly Algy always wanting to go off on some secret mission, for some nefarious, probably sexual, purpose. He's also Ernest trying to be a pillar of the community but actually leading a double life. Of course. *Ideal Husband* is another case in point. The first great play in the English language about bisexuality, if you actually look at it. And I don't think any writer leaves himself outside when he sits down to write his play. I think that looking at *The Importance of Being Earnest* as autobiography is altogether too crude. Certainly Wilde is there all the time.

Q: Lady Bracknell is a notorious blocking character—standing in the way, for over two acts, of Jack and Gwendolen's happiness. And yet hers is one of the most delicious roles in all of British comedy—or farce! How do these two aspects of the character factor into your direction of Lynn Redgrave in the role? Will there be some pressure for her to differentiate her approach to the role from such famous portrayers as Edith Evans or Judi Dench?

A: I was fortunate enough to do my other *Importance of Being Earnest* with Judi Dench, so perhaps I'm uniquely qualified to answer the question. I simply don't understand it, actually. I think what's wonderful about Lady Bracknell is that she's such a materialist, such a total exponent of the marriage market. She's out to sell her daughter to the highest bidder. She reveals that [she] had absolutely no money herself, but her marriage enabled her to become rich. She is, in many respects, a monster. But like other monsters, like Fagin, we like the enormity of their desires; we get a charge out of seeing someone behave quite so absolutely. . . . I don't think at all that Lady Bracknell wrecks the play, blocks the play, distorts the play. I think if she's played as a comic turn she wrecks the play; I've seen that happen. But if you understand what a rapacious lady she is, she really makes the serious heart of the play very evident. It's a curious thing, comedy—it has to be highly serious, and that's certainly true of Lady Bracknell.

Anton Chekhov

Anton Chekhov (1860–1904) spent most of his childhood in relative poverty. His family managed to set up household in Moscow after years spent in remote Taganrog, six hundred miles to the south. He studied medicine in Moscow and eventually received his degree. Although he practiced medicine most of his life, he said that if medicine was his wife, literature was his mistress. His earliest literary efforts were for the purpose of relieving his family's poverty; it was not long before he was earning more from writing than from medicine. By 1896 he had written more than three hundred short stories, most of them published in newspapers. Many of them are classics.

His first theatrical works, apart from his short farces, were not successful. *Ivanov* (1887–1889), rushed into production, was a failure, but the revised 1889 version, reflecting much of his personal life, was successful. *The Wood Demon* (1889), also a failure, helped Chekhov eventually produce his great plays: *The Seagull* (1896); *Uncle Vanya* (1897); *Three Sisters* (1901); and his last, *The Cherry Orchard* (1903). These plays essentially reshaped modern drama, creating a style that critic Richard Peace describes as a "subtle blend of naturalism and symbolism."

The Seagull attracted the attention of the Moscow Art Theatre. The play was not a success in its first production in 1896, but two years later it became one of the theater's triumphs. Konstantin Stanislavski, the great Russian director and actor, played Trigorin, the lead character, but Chekhov thought that he was overacting. They often had disagreements about the playwright's work, but the Moscow Art Theatre supported Chekhov fully.

The surfaces of Chekhov's plays are so lifelike that at times one feels his dramatic purposes are submerged, and to an extent that is true. Chekhov is the master of the **subtext,** a technique in which the dialogue on the surface seems innocuous or meandering, but deeper meanings are implied. Madame Ranevskaya's musings about her childhood in act 1 of *The Cherry Orchard* contrast with the purposeful dialogue of Lopakhin. Her long speeches in act 3 about the "millstone" she loves in Paris are also meandering, but they reveal an idealistic character doomed to suffer at the hands of a new generation of realists who have no time for her ramblings and sentimentalism.

Because subtexts are always present, to read Chekhov's work requires close attention. One must constantly probe, analyze, ask what is implied by what is being said. Chekhov resists "explaining" his plays by having key characters give key thematic speeches. Instead, the meaning builds slowly. Our grasp of what a situation or circumstance finally means will change as we read and as we gather more understanding of the subtleties veiled by surfaces.

Chekhov's style is remarkable for its clarity; on its surface, his writing is direct, simple, and effective. Even his short stories have a clear dramatic center, and the characters he chose to observe are exceptionally modern in that they are neither heroes nor villains. The dramatic concept of a larger-than-life Oedipus or of *Hamlet*'s devilish Claudius is nowhere to be seen in his work. Chekhov's characters are limited, recognizable, and in many ways completely ordinary.

Chekhov's genius was in showing such characters' ambitions, pain, and successes. He was quite aware of important social changes taking place in Russia; the old aristocratic classes, who once owned serfs, were being reduced to a genteel impoverishment, while the children of former slaves were beginning to succeed in business and real estate ventures. Since Chekhov's grandfather had been a serf who bought his freedom in 1841, it is likely that Chekhov was especially supportive of such social change; we see evidence of that in his best plays.

The Cherry Orchard

For discussion questions and assignments on *The Cherry Orchard*, visit bedfordstmartins.com/jacobus.

The Cherry Orchard (1903) premiered on Chekhov's birthday, January 17, in 1904. The Moscow Art Theatre performance was directed by Konstantin Stanislavski, an actor-director who pioneered a new method of realistic acting. (Stanislavski is still read and admired the world over. His techniques were modified in the United States and form the basis of **method acting**.) For the subtle effects that Chekhov wanted, however, he found Stanislavski too stagey, flamboyant, and melodramatic. They argued hotly over what should happen in his plays, and often Stanislavski prevailed.

One argument was over whether *The Cherry Orchard* was a tragedy. Chekhov steadfastly called it a comedy, but Stanislavski saw the ruin of Madame Ranevskaya and the destruction of the cherry orchard as tragic. Chekhov perhaps saw it the same way, but he also considered its potential as the impetus for a new, more realistic life for Madame Ranevskaya and her brother Gayev. Their impracticality was an important cause of their having lost their wealth and estate.

How audiences interpret Lopakhin depends on how they view the ambition of the new class of businessmen whose zeal, work, and cleverness earn them the estates that previously they could have hoped only to work on. Social change is fueled by money, which replaces an inherited aristocracy with ambitious moneymakers who earn the power to force changes on the old, less flexible aristocrats. In Russia, massive social change was eventually effected by revolution and the institution of communism. But *The Cherry Orchard* shows that change would have come to Russia in any event.

Perhaps Chekhov's peasant blood helped him see the play as more of a comedy than a tragedy, even though he portrays the characters with greater complexity than we might expect in comedy. Lopakhin is not a simple, unsympathetic character; Trofimov is not a simple dreamer. We need to look closely at what they do and why they do it. For example, when thinking about preserving the beauties of the cherry orchard, Trofimov reminds people that all of Russia is an orchard, that the world is filled with beautiful places. Such a view makes it difficult for him to feel nostalgia for aristocratic privilege.

Trofimov sounds a striking note about the practice of slavery in Russia. He tells Madame Ranevskaya and Gayev that they are living on credit, that they must repay debts to the Russian people. The cherry orchard is beautiful because each tree represents the soul of a serf. The class of beautiful people to which the impractical Madame Ranevskaya belongs owes its beauty and grace to the institution of slavery, and soon the note will be presented for payment. The sound of the breaking string in act 1, repeated at the end of the play, is Chekhov's way of symbolizing the losses and changes represented in the play.

Madame Ranevskaya, however, cannot change. Her habits of mind are fully formed before the play begins; nothing that Lopakhin can say will help change her. Even though she knows she is dangerously in debt, she gives a gold coin to a beggar. *Noblesse oblige* — the duty of the upper class to help the poor — is still part of her ethos, even if it also involves her own ruin.

A sense of tragedy is apparent in Madame Ranevskaya's feelings and her helplessness. She seems incapable of transforming herself, no matter how much she may wish to change. We see her as a victim of fate, a fate that is formed by her expectations and training. But the play also contains comic and nonsensical moments, as, for example, in the by-play of Varya, Yasha, and Yepikhodov over a game of billiards in act 3. In his letters Chekhov mentions that the play is happy and frivolous, "in places even a farce."

The Cherry Orchard in Performance

Since its first production in 1904, *The Cherry Orchard* has played to responsive audiences in Europe and abroad. It was produced in London in 1911, Berlin in 1919, and New York in 1923 (in Russian). Eva Le Gallienne produced it in New York in her English version in 1928. In 1968, she directed the play with Uta Hagen as Madame Ranevskaya. Tyrone Guthrie directed it at the Old Vic in 1933 and again in 1941. John Gielgud, Peggy Ashcroft, Judi Dench, and Dorothy Tutin performed in a powerful and well-reviewed version in London in 1961. When Joseph Papp produced an all-black *Cherry Orchard* in 1973, James Earl Jones was praised as a powerful Lopakhin.

Andrei Serban's 1977 production for Joseph Papp at Lincoln Center in New York was commended for its extraordinary stage effects. According to the reviewer at *Time* magazine,

> Serban's best images effectively magnify the play's conflict between the old order and the bright new world that is its doom: a frieze of peasants laboring beneath modern telegraph wires, a group of aristocrats watching the setting sun silhouette a factory on the horizon.

The American playwright Jean Claude van Italie revised the text for contemporary audiences. His version, produced at the John Drew Theater of Guild Hall in East Hampton in July 1985, was directed by Elinor Renfield. Amanda Plummer played Anya, and Joanna Merlin played Madame Ranevskaya. Peter Brook's 1987 New York production, with Brian Dennehy as a notable Lopakhin, had little scenery beyond a great number of Oriental rugs. It was played without intermissions at breakneck speed. *New York Times* critic Frank Rich said of it, "On this director's magic carpets, *The Cherry Orchard* flies." Other modern treatments of *The Cherry Orchard* include Michael Picardie's adaptation to South Africa and Brian Friel's adaptation to Ireland. In 1997, Galina Volchek staged a Russian-language version in the Martin Beck Theater on Broadway. Critic Peter Marks said the play was "communicated vividly." Theater critic David Finkle described the 2006 production by the Shakespeare Theatre of New Jersey as "the essence of Anton Chekhov." The set of this production, unlike most, included several trees in bloom so that the audience could actually see the orchard that was to be cut away for new housing. Zoë Wanamaker received glowing reviews for her portrayal of Madame Ranevskaya in London's National Theatre production of *The Cherry Orchard*, which was broadcast live in theaters around the world on June 30, 2011, making it the most widely viewed production of Chekhov's drama.

ANTON CHEKHOV (1860–1904)

The Cherry Orchard   1903

TRANSLATED BY ANN DUNNIGAN

Characters

RANEVSKAYA, LYUBOV ANDREYEVNA, *a landowner*
ANYA, *her daughter, seventeen years old*
VARYA, *her adopted daughter, twenty-four years old*
GAYEV, LEONID ANDREYEVICH, *Madame Ranevskaya's brother*
LOPAKHIN, YERMOLAI ALEKSEYEVICH, *a merchant*
TROFIMOV, PYOTR SERGEYEVICH, *a student*
SEMYONOV-PISHCHIK, BORIS BORISOVICH, *a landowner*
CHARLOTTA IVANOVNA, *a governess*
YEPIKHODOV, SEMYON PANTELEYEVICH, *a clerk*
DUNYASHA, *a maid*
FIRS, *an old valet, eighty-seven years old*
YASHA, *a young footman*
A STRANGER
THE STATIONMASTER
A POST-OFFICE CLERK
GUESTS, SERVANTS

The action takes place on Madame Ranevskaya's estate.

ACT I

(*A room that is still called the nursery. One of the doors leads into Anya's room. Dawn; the sun will soon rise. It is May, the cherry trees are in bloom, but it is cold in the orchard; there is a morning frost. The windows in the room are closed. Enter Dunyasha with a candle, and Lopakhin with a book in his hand.*)

LOPAKHIN: The train is in, thank God. What time is it?

DUNYASHA: Nearly two. (*Blows out the candle.*) It's already light.

LOPAKHIN: How late is the train, anyway? A couple of hours at least. (*Yawns and stretches.*) I'm a fine one! What a fool I've made of myself! Came here on purpose to meet them at the station, and then overslept.... Fell asleep in the chair. It's annoying.... You might have waked me.

DUNYASHA: I thought you had gone. (*Listens.*) They're coming now, I think!

LOPAKHIN (*listens*): No ... they've got to get the luggage and one thing and another. (*Pause.*) Lyubov Andreyevna has lived abroad for five years, I don't know what she's like now.... She's a fine person. Sweet-tempered, simple. I remember when I was a boy of fifteen, my late father—he had a shop in the village then—gave me a punch in the face and made my nose bleed.... We had come into the yard here for some reason or other, and he'd had a drop too much. Lyubov Andreyevna—I remember as if it were yesterday—still young, and so slender, led me to the washstand in this very room, the nursery. "Don't cry, little peasant," she said, "it will heal in time for your wedding...." (*Pause.*) Little peasant ... my father was a peasant, it's true, and here I am in a white waistcoat and tan shoes. Like a pig in a pastry shop.... I may be rich, I've made a lot of money, but if you think about it, analyze it, I'm a peasant through and through. (*Turning pages of the book.*) Here I've been reading this book, and I didn't understand a thing. Fell asleep over it. (*Pause.*)

DUNYASHA: The dogs didn't sleep all night: They can tell that their masters are coming.

LOPAKHIN: What's the matter with you, Dunyasha, you're so ...

DUNYASHA: My hands are trembling. I'm going to faint.

Zoë Wanamaker played Madame Ranevskaya in London in 2011.

LOPAKHIN: You're much too delicate, Dunyasha. You dress like a lady, and do your hair like one, too. It's not right. You should know your place.

(*Enter Yepikhodov with a bouquet; he wears a jacket and highly polished boots that squeak loudly. He drops the flowers as he comes in.*)

YEPIKHODOV (*picking up the flowers*): Here, the gardener sent these. He says you're to put them in the dining room. (*Hands the bouquet to Dunyasha.*)

LOPAKHIN: And bring me some kvas.°

DUNYASHA: Yes, sir. (*Goes out.*)

YEPIKHODOV: There's a frost this morning—three degrees—and the cherry trees are in bloom. I cannot approve of our climate. (*Sighs.*) I cannot. Our climate is not exactly conducive. And now, Yermolai Alekseyevich, permit me to append: The day before yesterday I bought myself a pair of boots, which, I venture to assure you, squeak so that it's quite infeasible. What should I grease them with?

LOPAKHIN: Leave me alone. You make me tired.

YEPIKHODOV: Every day some misfortune happens to me. But I don't complain, I'm used to it, I even smile.

(*Dunyasha enters, serves Lopakhin the kvas.*)

YEPIKHODOV: I'm going. (*Stumbles over a chair and upsets it.*) There! (*As if in triumph.*) Now you see, excuse the expression . . . the sort of circumstance, incidentally. . . . It's really quite remarkable! (*Goes out.*)

DUNYASHA: You know, Yermolai Alekseyevich, I have to confess that Yepikhodov has proposed to me.

kvas: A Russian beer.

LOPAKHIN: Ah!

DUNYASHA: And I simply don't know. . . . He's a quiet man, but sometimes, when he starts talking, you can't understand a thing he says. It's nice, and full of feeling, only it doesn't make sense. I sort of like him. He's madly in love with me. But he's an unlucky fellow: Every day something happens to him. They tease him about it around here; they call him Two-and-twenty Troubles.

LOPAKHIN (*listening*): I think I hear them coming . . .

DUNYASHA: They're coming! What's the matter with me? I'm cold all over.

LOPAKHIN: They're really coming. Let's go and meet them. Will she recognize me? It's five years since we've seen each other.

DUNYASHA (*agitated*): I'll faint this very minute . . . oh, I'm going to faint!

(*Two carriages are heard driving up to the house. Lopakhin and Dunyasha go out quickly. The stage is empty. There is a hubbub in the adjoining rooms. Firs hurriedly crosses the stage leaning on a stick. He has been to meet Lyubov Andreyevna and wears old fashioned livery and a high hat. He mutters something to himself, not a word of which can be understood. The noise offstage grows louder and louder. A voice: "Let's go through here. . . ." Enter Lyubov Andreyevna, Anya, Charlotta Ivanovna with a little dog on a chain, all in traveling dress; Varya wearing a coat and kerchief; Gayev, Semyonov-Pishchik, Lopakhin, Dunyasha with a bundle and parasol; servants with luggage—all walk through the room.*)

ANYA: Let's go this way. Do you remember, Mama, what room this is?

LYUBOV ANDREYEVNA (*joyfully, through tears*): The nursery!

VARYA: How cold it is! My hands are numb. (*To Lyubov Andreyevna.*) Your rooms, both the white one and the violet one, are just as you left them, Mama.

LYUBOV ANDREYEVNA: The nursery . . . my dear, lovely nursery. . . . I used to sleep here when I was little. . . . (*Weeps.*) And now, like a child, I . . . (*Kisses her brother, Varya, then her brother again.*) Varya hasn't changed; she still looks like a nun. And I recognized Dunyasha. . . . (*Kisses Dunyasha.*)

GAYEV: The train was two hours late. How's that? What kind of management is that?

CHARLOTTA (*to Pishchik*): My dog even eats nuts.

PISHCHIK (*amazed*): Think of that now!

(*They all go out except Anya and Dunyasha.*)

DUNYASHA: We've been waiting and waiting for you. . . . (*Takes off Anya's coat and hat.*)

ANYA: I didn't sleep for four nights on the road . . . now I feel cold.

DUNYASHA: It was Lent when you went away, there was snow and frost then, but now? My darling! (*Laughs and kisses her.*) I've waited so long for you, my joy, my precious . . . I must tell you at once, I can't wait another minute. . . .

ANYA (*listlessly*): What now?

DUNYASHA: The clerk, Yepikhodov, proposed to me just after Easter.

ANYA: You always talk about the same thing. . . . (*Straightening her hair.*) I've lost all my hairpins. . . . (*She is so exhausted she can hardly stand.*)

DUNYASHA: I really don't know what to think. He loves me—he loves me so!

ANYA (*looking through the door into her room, tenderly*): My room, my windows . . . it's just as though I'd never been away. I am home! Tomorrow morning I'll get up and run into the orchard. . . . Oh, if could only sleep! I didn' sleep during the entire journey, I was so tormented by anxiety.

DUNYASHA: Pyotr Sergeich arrived the day before yesterday.

ANYA (*joyfully*): Petya!

DUNYASHA: He's asleep in the bathhouse, he's staying there. "I'm afraid of being in the way," he said. (*Looks at her pocket watch.*) I ought to wake him up, but Varvara Mikhailovna told me not to. "Don't you wake him," she said.

(*Enter Varya with a bunch of keys at her waist.*)

VARYA: Dunyasha, coffee, quickly . . . Mama's asking for coffee.

DUNYASHA: This very minute. (*Goes out.*)

VARYA: Thank God, you've come! You're home again. (*Caressing her.*) My little darling has come back! My pretty one is here!

ANYA: I've been through so much.

VARYA: I can imagine!

ANYA: I left in Holy Week, it was cold then. Charlotta never stopped talking and doing her conjuring tricks the entire journey. Why did you saddle me with Charlotta?

VARYA: You couldn't have traveled alone, darling. At seventeen!

ANYA: When we arrived in Paris, it was cold, snowing. My French is awful. . . . Mama was living on the fifth floor, and when I got there, she had all sorts of Frenchmen and ladies with her, and an old priest with a little book, and it was full of smoke, dismal. Suddenly I felt sorry for Mama, so sorry. I took her head in my arms and held her close and couldn't let her go. Afterward she kept hugging me and crying. . . .

VARYA (*through her tears*): Don't talk about it, don't talk about it. . . .

ANYA: She had already sold her villa near Mentone, and she had nothing left, nothing. And I hadn't so much as a kopeck left, we barely managed to get there. But Mama doesn't understand! When we had dinner in a station restaurant, she always ordered the most expensive dishes and tipped each of the waiters a ruble. Charlotta is the same. And Yasha also ordered a dinner, it was simply awful. You know, Yasha is Mama's footman; we brought him with us.

VARYA: I saw the rogue.

ANYA: Well, how are things? Have you paid the interest?

VARYA: How could we?

ANYA: Oh, my God, my God!

VARYA: In August the estate will be put up for sale.

ANYA: My God!

(*Lopakhin peeps in at the door and moos like a cow.*)

LOPAKHIN: Moo-o-o! (*Disappears.*)

VARYA (*through her tears*): What I couldn't do to him! (*Shakes her fist.*)

ANYA (*embracing Varya, softly*): Varya, has he proposed to you? (*Varya shakes her head.*) But he loves you. . . . Why don't you come to an understanding, what are you waiting for?

VARYA: I don't think anything will ever come of it. He's too busy, he has no time for me . . . he doesn't even notice me. I've washed my hands of him, it makes me miserable to see him. . . . Everyone talks of our wedding, they all congratulate me, and actually there's nothing to it—it's all like a dream. . . . (*In a different tone.*) You have a brooch like a bee.

ANYA (*sadly*): Mama bought it. (*Goes into her own room; speaks gaily, like a child.*) In Paris I went up in a balloon!

VARYA: My darling is home! My pretty one has come back!

(*Dunyasha has come in with the coffeepot and prepares coffee.*)

VARYA (*stands at the door of Anya's room*): You know, darling, all day long I'm busy looking after the house, but I keep dreaming. If we could marry you to a rich man I'd be at peace. I could go into a hermitage, then to Kiev, to Moscow, and from one holy place to another. . . . I'd go on and on. What a blessing!

ANYA: The birds are singing in the orchard. What time is it?

VARYA: It must be after two. Time you were asleep, darling. (*Goes into Anya's room.*) What a blessing!

(*Yasha enters with a lap robe and a traveling bag.*)

YASHA (*crosses the stage mincingly*): May one go through here?

DUNYASHA: A person would hardly recognize you, Yasha. Your stay abroad has done wonders for you.

YASHA: Hm. . . . And who are you?

DUNYASHA: When you left here I was only that high— (*indicating with her hand*). I'm Dunyasha, Fyodor Kozoyedov's daughter. You don't remember?

YASHA: Hm. . . . A little cucumber! (*Looks around, then embraces her; she cries out and drops a saucer. He quickly goes out.*)

VARYA (*in a tone of annoyance, from the doorway*): What's going on here?

DUNYASHA (*tearfully*): I broke a saucer.

VARYA: That's good luck.

ANYA: We ought to prepare Mama: Petya is here. . . .

VARYA: I gave orders not to wake him.

ANYA (*pensively*): Six years ago Father died, and a month later brother Grisha drowned in the river . . . a pretty little seven-year-old boy. Mama couldn't bear it and went away . . . went without looking back. . . . (*Shudders.*) How I understand her, if she only knew! (*Pause.*) And Petya Trofimov was Grisha's tutor, he may remind her. . . .

(*Enter Firs wearing a jacket and a white waistcoat.*)

FIRS (*goes to the coffeepot, anxiously*): The mistress will have her coffee here. (*Puts on white gloves.*) Is the coffee ready? (*To Dunyasha, sternly.*) You! Where's the cream?

DUNYASHA: Oh, my goodness! (*Quickly goes out.*)

FIRS (*fussing over the coffeepot*): Ah, what an addlepate! (*Mutters to himself.*) They've come back from Paris. . . . The master used to go to Paris . . . by carriage. . . . (*Laughs.*)

VARYA: What is it, Firs?

FIRS: If you please? (*Joyfully.*) My mistress has come home! At last! Now I can die. . . . (*Weeps with joy.*)

(*Enter Lyubov Andreyevna, Gayev, and Semyonov-Pishchik, the last wearing a sleeveless peasant coat of fine cloth and full trousers. Gayev, as he comes in, goes through the motions of playing billiards.*)

LYUBOV ANDREYEVNA: How does it go? Let's see if I can remember . . . cue ball into the corner! Double the rail to center table.

GAYEV: Cut shot into the corner! There was a time, sister, when you and I used to sleep here in this very room, and now I'm fifty-one, strange as it may seem. . . .

LOPAKHIN: Yes, time passes.

GAYEV: How's that?

LOPAKHIN: Time, I say, passes.

GAYEV: It smells of patchouli here.

ANYA: I'm going to bed. Good night, Mama. (*Kisses her mother.*)

LYUBOV ANDREYEVNA: My precious child. (*Kisses her hands.*) Are you glad to be home? I still feel dazed.

ANYA: Good night, Uncle,

GAYEV (*kisses her face and hands*): God bless you. How like your mother you are! (*To his sister.*) At her age you were exactly like her, Lyuba.

(*Anya shakes hands with Lopakhin and Pishchik and goes out, closing the door after her.*)

LYUBOV ANDREYEVNA: She's exhausted.

PISHCHIK: Must have been a long journey.

VARYA: Well, gentlemen? It's after two, high time you were going.

LYUBOV ANDREYEVNA (*laughs*): You haven't changed, Varya. (*Draws Varya to her and kisses her.*) I'll just drink my coffee and then we'll all go. (*Firs places a cushion under her feet.*) Thank you, my dear. I've got used to coffee. I drink it day and night. Thanks, dear old man. (*Kisses him.*)

VARYA: I'd better see if all the luggage has been brought in.

LYUBOV ANDREYEVNA: Is this really me sitting here? (*Laughs.*) I feel like jumping about and waving my arms. (*Buries her face in her hands.*) What if it's only a dream! God knows I love my country, love it dearly. I couldn't look out the train window, I was crying so! (*Through tears.*) But I must drink my coffee. Thank you, Firs, thank you, my dear old friend. I'm so glad you're still alive.

FIRS: The day before yesterday.

GAYEV: He's hard of hearing.

LOPAKHIN: I must go now, I'm leaving for Kharkov about five o'clock. It's so annoying! I wanted to have a good look at you, and have a talk. You're as splendid as ever.

PISHCHIK (*breathing heavily*): Even more beautiful. . . . Dressed like a Parisienne. . . . There goes my wagon, all four wheels!

LOPAKHIN: Your brother here, Leonid Andreich, says I'm a boor, a moneygrubber, but I don't mind. Let him talk. All I want is that you should trust me as you used to, and that your wonderful, touching eyes should look at me as they did then. Merciful God! My father was one of your father's serfs, and your grandfather's, but you yourself did so much for me once, that I've forgotten all that and love you as if you were my own kin—more than my kin.

LYUBOV ANDREYEVNA: I can't sit still, I simply cannot. (*Jumps up and walks about the room in great excitement.*) I cannot bear this joy. . . . Laugh at me, I'm silly. . . . My dear little bookcase . . . (*kisses bookcase*) my little table . . .

GAYEV: Nurse died while you were away.

LYUBOV ANDREYEVNA (*sits down and drinks coffee*): Yes, God rest her soul. They wrote me.

GAYEV: And Anastasy is dead. Petrushka Kosoi left me and is now with the police inspector in town. (*Takes a box of hard candies from his pocket and begins to suck one.*)

PISHCHIK: My daughter, Dashenka . . . sends her regards . . .

LOPAKHIN: I wish I could tell you something very pleasant and cheering. (*Glances at his watch.*) I must go directly, there's no time to talk, but . . . well, I'll say it in a couple of words. As you know, the cherry orchard is to be sold to pay your debts. The auction is set for August twenty-second, but you need not worry, my dear; you can sleep in peace, there is a way out. This is my plan. Now, please listen! Your estate is only twenty versts° from town, the railway runs close by, and if the cherry orchard and the land along the river were cut up into lots and leased for summer cottages, you'd have, at the very least, an income of twenty-five thousand a year.

GAYEV: Excuse me, what nonsense!

LYUBOV ANDREYEVNA: I don't quite understand you, Yermolai Alekseich.

LOPAKHIN: You will get, at the very least, twenty-five rubles a year for a two-and-a-half-acre lot, and if you advertise now, I guarantee you won't have a single plot of ground left by autumn, everything will be snapped up. In short, I congratulate you, you are saved. The site is splendid, the river is deep. Only, of course, the ground must be cleared . . . you must tear down all the old outbuildings, for instance, and this house, which is worthless, cut down the old cherry orchard—

LYUBOV ANDREYEVNA: Cut it down? Forgive me, my dear, but you don't know what you are talking about. If there is one thing in the whole province that is interesting, not to say remarkable, it's our cherry orchard.

LOPAKHIN: The only remarkable thing about this orchard is that it is very big. There's a crop of cherries every other year, and then you can't get rid of them, nobody buys them.

GAYEV: This orchard is even mentioned in the *Encyclopedia.*

LOPAKHIN (*glancing at his watch*): If we don't think of something and come to a decision, on the twenty-second of August the cherry orchard, and the entire estate, will be sold at auction. Make up your minds! There is no other way out, I swear to you. None whatsoever.

FIRS: In the old days, forty or fifty years ago, the cherries were dried, soaked, marinated, and made into jam, and they used to—

GAYEV: Be quiet, Firs.

FIRS: And they used to send cartloads of dried cherries to Moscow and Kharkov. And that brought in money! The dried cherries were soft and juicy in those days, sweet, fragrant. . . . They had a method then . . .

LYUBOV ANDREYEVNA: And what has become of that method now?

FIRS: Forgotten. Nobody remembers. . . .

---

versts: A verst is approximately equal to a kilometer, a little more than half a mile.

PISHCHIK: How was it in Paris? What's it like there? Did you eat frogs?

LYUBOV ANDREYEVNA: I ate crocodiles.

PISHCHIK: Think of that now!

LOPAKHIN: There used to be only the gentry and the peasants living in the country, but now these summer people have appeared. All the towns, even the smallest ones, are surrounded by summer cottages. And it is safe to say that in another twenty years these people will multiply enormously. Now the summer resident only drinks tea on his porch, but it may well be that he'll take to cultivating his acre and then your cherry orchard will be a happy, rich, luxuriant—

GAYEV (*indignantly*): What nonsense!

(*Enter Varya and Yasha.*)

VARYA: There are two telegrams for you, Mama. (*Picks out a key and with a jingling sound opens an old-fashioned bookcase.*) Here they are.

LYUBOV ANDREYEVNA: From Paris. (*Tears up the telegrams without reading them.*) That's all over. . . .

GAYEV: Do you know, Lyuba, how old this bookcase is? A week ago I pulled out the bottom drawer, and what do I see? Some figures burnt into it. The bookcase was made exactly a hundred years ago. What do you think of that? Eh? We could have celebrated its jubilee. It's an inanimate object, but nevertheless, for all that, it's a bookcase.

PISHCHIK: A hundred years . . . think of that now!

GAYEV: Yes . . . that is something. . . . (*Feeling the bookcase.*) Dear, honored bookcase. I salute thy existence, which for over one hundred years has served the glorious ideals of goodness and justice; thy silent appeal to fruitful endeavor, unflagging in the course of a hundred years, tearfully sustaining through generations of our family, courage and faith in a better future, and fostering in us ideals of goodness and social consciousness. . . .

(*A pause.*)

LOPAKHIN: Yes . . .

LYUBOV ANDREYEVNA: You are the same as ever, Lyonya.

GAYEV (*somewhat embarrassed*): Carom into the corner, cut shot to center table.

LOPAKHIN (*looks at his watch*): Well, time for me to go.

YASHA (*hands medicine to Lyubov Andreyevna*): Perhaps you will take your pills now.

PISHCHIK: Don't take medicaments, dearest lady, they do neither harm nor good. Let me have them, honored lady. (*Takes the pillbox, shakes the pills into his hand, blows on them, puts them into his mouth and washes them down with kvas.*) There!

LYUBOV ANDREYEVNA (*alarmed*): Why, you must be mad!

PISHCHIK: I've taken all the pills.

LOPAKHIN: What a glutton!

(*Everyone laughs.*)

FIRS: The gentleman stayed with us during Holy Week . . . ate half a bucket of pickles. . . . (*Mumbles.*)

LYUBOV ANDREYEVNA: What is he saying?

VARYA: He's been muttering like that for three years now. We've grown used to it.

YASHA: He's in his dotage.

(*Charlotta Ivanovna, very thin, tightly laced, in a white dress with a lorgnette at her belt, crosses the stage.*)

LOPAKHIN: Forgive me, Charlotta Ivanovna, I haven't had a chance to say how do you do to you. (*Tries to kiss her hand.*)

CHARLOTTA (*pulls her hand away*): If I permit you to kiss my hand you'll be wanting to kiss my elbow next, then my shoulder.

LOPAKHIN: I have no luck today. (*Everyone laughs.*) Charlotta Ivanovna, show us a trick!

LYUBOV ANDREYEVNA: Charlotta, show us a trick!

CHARLOTTA: No. I want to sleep. (*Goes out.*)

LOPAKHIN: In three weeks we'll meet again. (*Kisses Lyubov Andreyevna's hand.*) Good-bye till then. Time to go. (*To Gayev.*) Good-bye. (*Kisses Pishchik.*) Good bye. (*Shakes hands with Varya, then with Firs and Yasha.*) I don't feel like going. (*To Lyubov Andreyevna.*) If you make up your mind about the summer cottages and come to a decision, let me know; I'll get you a loan of fifty thousand or so. Think it over seriously.

VARYA (*angrily*): Oh, why don't you go!

LOPAKHIN: I'm going, I'm going. (*Goes out.*)

GAYEV: Boor. Oh, pardon. Varya's going to marry him, he's Varya's young man.

VARYA: Uncle dear, you talk too much.

LYUBOV ANDREYEVNA: Well, Varya, I shall be very glad. He's a good man.

PISHCHIK: A man, I must truly say . . . most worthy. . . . And my Dashenka . . . says, too, that . . . says all sorts of things. (*Snores but wakes up at once.*) In any case, honored lady, oblige me . . . a loan of two hundred and forty rubles . . . tomorrow the interest on my mortgage is due. . . .

VARYA (*in alarm*): We have nothing, nothing at all!

LYUBOV ANDREYEVNA: I really haven't any money.

PISHCHIK: It'll turn up. (*Laughs.*) I never lose hope. Just when I thought everything was lost, that I was done for, lo and behold—the railway line ran through my land . . . and they paid me for it. And before you know it, something else will turn up, if not today—tomorrow. . . . Dashenka will win two hundred thousand . . . she's got a lottery ticket.

LYUBOV ANDREYEVNA: The coffee is finished, we can go to bed.

FIRS (*brushing Gayev's clothes, admonishingly*): You've put on the wrong trousers again. What am I to do with you?

VARYA (*softly*): Anya's asleep. (*Quietly opens the window.*) The sun has risen, it's no longer cold. Look, Mama dear, what wonderful trees! Oh, Lord, the air! The starlings are singing!

GAYEV (*opens another window*): The orchard is all white. You haven't forgotten, Lyuba? That long avenue there that runs straight—straight as a stretched-out strap; it gleams on moonlight nights. Remember? You've not forgotten?

LYUBOV ANDREYEVNA (*looking out the window at the orchard*): Oh, my childhood, my innocence! I used to sleep in this nursery, I looked out from here into the orchard, happiness awoke with me each morning, it was just as it is now, nothing has changed. (*Laughing with joy.*) All, all white! Oh, my orchard! After the dark, rainy autumn and the cold winter, you are young again, full of happiness, the heavenly angels have not forsaken you. . . . If I could cast off this heavy stone weighing on my breast and shoulders, if I could forget my past!

GAYEV: Yes, and the orchard will be sold for our debts, strange as it may seem. . . .

LYUBOV ANDREYEVNA: Look, our dead mother walks in the orchard . . . in a white dress! (*Laughs with joy.*) It is she!

GAYEV: Where?

VARYA: God be with you, Mama dear.

LYUBOV ANDREYEVNA: There's no one there, I just imagined it. To the right, as you turn to the summerhouse, a slender white sapling is bent over . . . it looks like a woman.

(*Enter Trofimov wearing a shabby student's uniform and spectacles.*)

LYUBOV ANDREYEVNA: What a wonderful orchard! The white masses of blossoms, the blue sky—

TROFIMOV: Lyubov Andreyevna! (*She looks around at him.*) I only want to pay my respects, then I'll go at once. (*Kisses her hand ardently.*) I was told to wait until morning, but I hadn't the patience.

(*Lyubov Andreyevna looks at him, puzzled.*)

VARYA (*through tears*): This is Petya Trofimov.

TROFIMOV: Petya Trofimov, I was Grisha's tutor. . . . Can I have changed so much?

(*Lyubov Andreyevna embraces him, quietly weeping.*)

GAYEV (*embarrassed*): There, there, Lyuba.

VARYA (*crying*): Didn't I tell you, Petya, to wait till tomorrow?

LYUBOV ANDREYEVNA: My Grisha . . . my little boy . . . Grisha . . . my son. . . .

VARYA: What can we do, Mama dear? It's God's will.

TROFIMOV (*gently, through tears*): Don't, don't. . . .

LYUBOV ANDREYEVNA (*quietly weeping*): My little boy dead, drowned. . . . Why? Why, my friend? (*In a lower voice.*) Anya is sleeping in there, and I'm talking loudly . . . making all this noise. . . . But Petya, why do you look so bad? Why have you grown so old?

TROFIMOV: A peasant woman in the train called me a mangy gentleman.

LYUBOV ANDREYEVNA: You were just a boy then, a charming little student, and now your hair is thin—and spectacles! Is it possible you are still a student? (*Goes toward the door.*)

TROFIMOV: I shall probably be an eternal student.

LYUBOV ANDREYEVNA: (*kisses her brother, then Varya*): Now, go to bed. . . . You've grown older too, Leonid.

PISHCHIK (*follows her*): Well, seems to be time to sleep. . . . Oh, my gout! I'm staying the night. Lyubov Andreyevna, my soul, tomorrow morning . . . two hundred and forty rubles. . . .

GAYEV: He keeps at it.

PISHCHIK: Two hundred and forty rubles . . . to pay the interest on my mortgage.

LYUBOV ANDREYEVNA: I have no money, my friend.

PISHCHIK: My dear, I'll pay it back. . . . It's a trifling sum.

LYUBOV ANDREYEVNA: Well, all right, Leonid will give it to you. . . . Give it to him, Leonid.

GAYEV: Me give it to him! . . . Hold out your pocket!

LYUBOV ANDREYEVNA: It can't be helped, give it to him. . . . He needs it. . . . He'll pay it back.

(*Lyubov Andreyevna, Trofimov, Pishchik, and Firs go out. Gayev, Varya, and Yasha remain.*)

GAYEV: My sister hasn't yet lost her habit of squandering money. (*To Yasha.*) Go away, my good fellow, you smell of the henhouse.

YASHA (*with a smirk*): And you, Leonid Andreyevich, are just the same as ever.

GAYEV: How's that? (*To Varya.*) What did he say?

VARYA: Your mother has come from the village; she's been sitting in the servants' room since yesterday, waiting to see you. . . .

YASHA: Let her wait, for God's sake!

VARYA: Aren't you ashamed?

YASHA: A lot I need her! She could have come tomorrow. (*Goes out.*)

VARYA: Mama's the same as ever, she hasn't changed a bit. She'd give away everything, if she could.

GAYEV: Yes. . . . (*A pause.*) If a great many remedies are suggested for a disease, it means that the disease is incurable. I keep thinking, racking my brains, I have many remedies, a great many, and that means in effect, that I have none. It would be good to receive a legacy from someone, good to marry our Anya to a very rich man, good to go to Yaroslav and try our luck with our aunt, the Countess. She is very, very rich, you know.

VARYA (*crying*): If only God would help us!

GAYEV: Stop bawling. Auntie's very rich, but she doesn't like us. In the first place, sister married a lawyer, not a nobleman . . . (*Anya appears in the doorway.*) She married beneath her, and it cannot be said that she has conducted herself very virtuously. She is good, kind, charming, and I love her dearly, but no matter how much you allow for extenuating circumstances, you must admit she leads a sinful life. You feel it in her slightest movement.

VARYA (*in a whisper*): Anya is standing in the doorway.

GAYEV: What? (*Pause.*) Funny, something got into my right eye . . . I can't see very well. And Thursday, when I was in the district court . . .

(*Anya enters.*)

VARYA: Why aren't you asleep, Anya?

ANYA: I can't get to sleep. I just can't.

GAYEV: My little one! (*Kisses Anya's face and hands.*) My child. . . . (*Through tears.*) You are not my niece, you are my angel, you are everything to me. Believe me, believe . . .

ANYA: I believe you, Uncle. Everyone loves you and respects you, but, Uncle dear, you must keep quiet, just keep quiet. What were you saying just now about my mother, about your own sister? What made you say that?

GAYEV: Yes, yes. . . . (*Covers his face with her hand.*) Really, it's awful! My God! God help me! And today I made a speech to the bookcase . . . so stupid! And it was only when I had finished that I realized it was stupid.

VARYA: It's true, Uncle dear, you ought to keep quiet. Just don't talk, that's all.

ANYA: If you could keep from talking, it would make things easier for you, too.

GAYEV: I'll be quiet. (*Kisses Anya's and Varya's hands.*) I'll be quiet. Only this is about business. On Thursday I was in the district court, well, a group of us gathered together and began talking about one thing and another, this and that, and it seems it might be possible to arrange a loan on a promissory note to pay the interest at the bank.

VARYA: If only God would help us!

GAYEV: On Tuesday I'll go and talk it over again. (*To Varya.*) Stop bawling. (*To Anya.*) Your mama will talk to Lopakhin; he, of course, will not refuse her. . . . And as soon as you've rested, you will go to Yaroslav to the Countess, your great-aunt. In that way we shall be working from three directions—and our business is in the hat. We'll pay the interest, I'm certain of it. . . . (*Puts a candy in his mouth.*) On my honor, I'll swear by anything you like, the estate shall not be sold. (*Excitedly.*) By my happiness, I swear it! Here's my hand on it, call me a worthless, dishonorable man if I let it come to auction! I swear by my whole being!

ANYA (*a calm mood returns to her, she is happy*): How good you are, Uncle, how clever! (*Embraces him.*) Now I am at peace! I'm at peace! I'm happy!

(*Enter Firs.*)

FIRS (*reproachfully*): Leonid Andreich, have you no fear of God? When are you going to bed?

GAYEV: Presently, presently. Go away, Firs, I'll . . . all right, I'll undress myself. Well, children, bye-bye. . . . Details tomorrow, and now go to sleep. (*Kisses Anya and Varya.*) I am a man of the eighties. . . . They don't think much of that period today, nevertheless, I can say that in the course of my life I have suffered not a little for my convictions. It is not for nothing that the peasant loves me. You have to know the peasant! You have to know from what—

ANYA: There you go again, Uncle!

VARYA: Uncle dear, do be quiet.

FIRS (*angrily*): Leonid Andreich!

GAYEV: I'm coming, I'm coming. . . . Go to bed. A clean double rail shot to center table. . . . (*Goes out; Firs hobbles after him.*)

ANYA: I'm at peace now. I would rather not go to Yaroslav, I don't like my great-aunt, but still, I'm at peace, thanks to Uncle. (*She sits down.*)

VARYA: We must get some sleep. I'm going now. Oh, something unpleasant happened while you were away. In the old servants' quarters, as you know, there are only the old people: Yefimushka, Polya, Yevstignei, and, of course, Karp. They began letting in all sorts of rogues to spend the night—I didn't say anything. But then I heard they'd been spreading a rumor that I'd given an order for them to be fed nothing but dried peas. Out of stinginess, you see. . . . It was all Yevstignei's doing. . . . Very well, I think, if that's how it is, you just wait. I send for Yevstignei . . . (*yawning*) he comes. . . . "How is it, Yevstignei," I say, "that you could be such a fool. . . ." (*Looks at Anya.*) She's fallen asleep. (*Takes her by the arm.*) Come to your little bed. . . . Come along. (*Leading her.*) My little darling fell asleep. Come. . . . (*They go.*)

(*In the distance, beyond the orchard, a shepherd is playing on a reed pipe. Trofimov crosses the stage and, seeing Varya and Anya, stops.*)

VARYA: Sh! She's asleep . . . asleep. . . . Come along, darling.

ANYA (*softly, half-asleep*): I'm so tired. . . . Those bells . . . Uncle . . . dear . . . Mama and Uncle . . .

VARYA: Come, darling, come along. (*They go into Anya's room.*)

TROFIMOV (*deeply moved*): My sunshine! My spring!

ACT II

(*A meadow. An old, lopsided, long-abandoned little chapel; near it a well, large stones that apparently were once tombstones, and an old bench. A road to the Gayev manor house can be seen. On one side, where the cherry orchard begins, tall poplars loom. In the distance a row of telegraph poles, and far, far away, on the horizon, the faint outline of a large town, which is visible only in very fine, clear weather. The sun will soon set. Charlotta, Yasha, and Dunyasha are sitting on the bench; Yepikhodov stands near playing something sad on the guitar. They are all lost in thought. Charlotta wears an old forage cap; she has taken a gun from her shoulder and is adjusting the buckle on the sling.*)

CHARLOTTA (*reflectively*): I haven't got a real passport, I don't know how old I am, but it always seems to me that I'm quite young. When I was a little girl, my father and mother used to travel from one fair to another giving performances—very good ones. And I did the *salto mortale*° and all sorts of tricks. Then when papa and Mama died, a German lady took me to live with her and began teaching me. Good. I grew up and became a governess. But where I come from and who I am—I do not know. . . . Who my parents were— perhaps they weren't even married—I don't know.

salto mortale: Somersault.

(*Takes a cucumber out of her pocket and eats it.*) I don't know anything. (*Pause.*) One wants so much to talk, but there isn't anyone to talk to . . . I have no one.

YEPIKHODOV (*plays the guitar and sings*): "What care I for the clamorous world, what's friend or foe to me?" . . . How pleasant it is to play a mandolin!

DUNYASHA: That's a guitar, not a mandolin. (*Looks at herself in a hand mirror and powders her face.*)

YEPIKHODOV: To a madman, in love, it is a mandolin. . . . (*Sings.*) "Would that the heart were warmed by the flame of requited love . . ."

(*Yasha joins in.*)

CHARLOTTA: How horribly these people sing! . . . Pfui! Like jackals!

DUNYASHA (*to Yasha*): Really, how fortunate to have been abroad!

YASHA: Yes, to be sure. I cannot but agree with you there. (*Yawns, then lights a cigar.*)

YEPIKHODOV: It stands to reason. Abroad everything has long since been fully constituted.

YASHA: Obviously.

YEPIKHODOV: I am a cultivated man, I read all sorts of remarkable books, but I am in no way able to make out my own inclinations, what it is I really want, whether, strictly speaking, to live or to shoot myself; nevertheless, I always carry a revolver on me. Here it is. (*Shows revolver.*)

CHARLOTTA: Finished. Now I'm going. (*Slings the gun over her shoulder.*) You're a very clever man, Yepikhodov, and quite terrifying; women must be mad about you. Brrr! (*Starts to go.*) These clever people are all so stupid, there's no one for me to talk to. . . . Alone, always alone, I have no one . . . and who I am, and why I am, nobody knows. . . . (*Goes out unhurriedly.*)

YEPIKHODOV: Strictly speaking, all else aside, I must state regarding myself, that fate treats me unmercifully, as a storm does a small ship. If, let us assume, I am mistaken, then why, to mention a single instance, do I wake up this morning, and there on my chest see a spider of terrifying magnitude? . . . Like that. (*Indicates with both hands.*) And likewise, I take up some kvas to quench my thirst, and there see something in the highest degree unseemly, like a cockroach. (*Pause.*) Have you read Buckle?° (*Pause.*) If I may trouble you, Avdotya Fyodorovna, I should like to have a word or two with you.

DUNYASHA: Go ahead.

YEPIKHODOV: I prefer to speak with you alone. . . . (*Sighs.*)

DUNYASHA (*embarrassed*): Very well . . . only first bring me my little cape . . . you'll find it by the cupboard. . . . It's rather damp here. . . .

YEPIKHODOV: Certainly, ma'ma . . . I'll fetch it, ma'ma. . . . Now I know what to do with my revolver. . . . (*Takes the guitar and goes off playing it.*)

Buckle: Thomas Henry Buckle (1821–1862) was a radical historian who formulated a scientific basis for history emphasizing the interrelationship of climate, food production, population, and wealth.

Laila Robins, Edmond Genest, and Alison Weller in the Shakespeare Theatre of New Jersey's 2006 production of *The Cherry Orchard*, which included a set with trees in bloom.

YASHA: Two-and-twenty Troubles! Between ourselves, a stupid fellow. (*Yawns.*)

DUNYASHA: God forbid that he should shoot himself. (*Pause.*) I've grown so anxious, I'm always worried. I was only a little girl when I was taken into the master's house, and now I'm quite unused to the simple life, and my hands are white as can be, just like a lady's. I've become so delicate, so tender and ladylike, I'm afraid of everything. . . . Frightfully so. And, Yasha, if you deceive me, I just don't know what will become of my nerves.

YASHA (*kisses her*): You little cucumber! Of course, a girl should never forget herself. What I dislike above everything is when a girl doesn't conduct herself properly.

DUNYASHA: I'm passionately in love with you, you're educated, you can discuss anything. (*Pause.*)

YASHA (*yawns*): Yes. . . . As I see it, it's like this: If a girl loves somebody, that means she's immoral. (*Pause.*) Very pleasant smoking a cigar in the open air. . . . (*Listens.*) Someone's coming this way. . . . It's the masters. (*Dunyasha impulsively embraces him.*) You go home, as if you'd been to the river to bathe; take that path, otherwise they'll see you and suspect me of having a rendezvous with you. I can't endure that sort of thing.

DUNYASHA (*with a little cough*): My head is beginning to ache from your cigar. . . . (*Goes out.*)

(*Yasha remains, sitting near the chapel. Lyubov Andreyevna, Gayev, and Lopakhin enter.*)

LOPAKHIN: You must make up your mind once and for all—time won't stand still. The question, after all, is quite simple. Do you agree to lease the land for summer cottages or not? Answer in one word: Yes or no? Only one word!

LYUBOV ANDREYEVNA: Who is it that smokes those disgusting cigars out here? (*Sits down.*)

GAYEV: Now that the railway line is so near, it's made things convenient. (*Sits down.*) We went to town and had lunch . . . cue ball to center! I feel like going to the house first and playing a game.

LYUBOV ANDREYEVNA: Later.

LOPAKHIN: Just one word! (*Imploringly.*) Do give me an answer!

GAYEV (*yawning*): How's that?

LYUBOV ANDREYEVNA (*looks into her purse*): Yesterday I had a lot of money, and today there' hardly any left. My poor Varya tries to economize by feeding everyone milk soup, and in the kitchen the old people get nothing but dried peas, while I squander money foolishly.... (*Drops the purse, scattering gold coins.*) There they go.... (*Vexed.*)

YASHA: Allow me, I'll pick them up in an instant. (*Picks up the money.*)

LYUBOV ANDREYEVNA: Please do, Yasha. And why did I go to town for lunch?... That miserable restaurant of yours with its music, and tablecloths smelling of soap.... Why drink so much, Lyonya? Why eat so much? Why talk so much? Today in the restaurant again you talked too much, and it was all so pointless. About the seventies, about the decadents. And to whom? Talking to waiters about the decadents!

LOPAKHIN: Yes.

GAYEV (*waving his hand*): I'm incorrigible, that's evident.... (*Irritably to Yasha.*) Why do you keep twirling about in front of me?

YASHA (*laughs*): I can't help laughing when I hear your voice.

GAYEV (*to his sister*): Either he or I—

LYUBOV ANDREYEVNA: Go away, Yasha, run along.

YASHA (*hands Lyubov Andreyevna her purse*): I'm going, right away. (*Hardly able to contain his laughter.*) This very instant.... (*Goes out.*)

LOPAKHIN: That rich man, Deriganov, is prepared to buy the estate. They say he's coming to the auction himself.

[ABOVE] The spare set in Ron Daniels's 1993 production of *The Cherry Orchard* at the American Repertory Theatre highlights the characters' emotional isolation.
[RIGHT] Claire Bloom as Madame Ranevskaya.

LYUBOV ANDREYEVNA: Where did you hear that?

LOPAKHIN: That's what they're saying in town.

LYUBOV ANDREYEVNA: Our aunt in Yaroslav promised to send us something, but when and how much, no one knows.

LOPAKHIN: How much do you think she'll send? A hundred thousand? Two hundred?

LYUBOV ANDREYEVNA: Oh . . . ten or fifteen thousand, and we'll be thankful for that.

LOPAKHIN: Forgive me, but I have never seen such frivolous, such queer, unbusinesslike people as you, my friends. You are told in plain language that your estate is to be sold, and it's as though you don't understand it.

LYUBOV ANDREYEVNA: But what are we to do? Tell us what to do.

LOPAKHIN: I tell you every day. Every day I say the same thing. Both the cherry orchard and the land must be leased for summer cottages, and it must be done now, as quickly as possible—the auction is close at hand. Try to understand! Once you definitely decide on the cottages, you can raise as much money as you like, and then you are saved.

LYUBOV ANDREYEVNA: Cottages, summer people—forgive me, but it's so vulgar.

GAYEV: I agree with you, absolutely.

LOPAKHIN: I'll either burst into tears, start shouting, or fall into a faint! I can't stand it! You've worn me out! (*To Gayev.*) You're an old woman!

GAYEV: How's that?

LOPAKHIN: An old woman! (*Starts to go.*)

LYUBOV ANDREYEVNA (*alarmed*): No, don't go, stay, my dear. I beg you. Perhaps we'll think of something!

LOPAKHIN: What is there to think of?

LYUBOV ANDREYEVNA: Don't go away, please. With you here it's more cheerful somehow. . . . (*Pause.*) I keep expecting something to happen, like the house caving in on us.

GAYEV (*in deep thought*): Double rail shot into the corner. . . . Cross table to the center. . . .

LYUBOV ANDREYEVNA: We have sinned so much. . . .

LOPAKHIN: What sins could you have—

GAYEV (*puts a candy into his mouth*): They say I've eaten up my entire fortune in candies. . . . (*Laughs.*)

LYUBOV ANDREYEVNA: Oh, my sins. . . . I've always squandered money recklessly, like a madwoman, and I married a man who did nothing but amass debts. My husband died from champagne—he drank terribly—then, to my sorrow, I fell in love with another man, lived with him, and just at that time—that was my first punishment, a blow on the head—my little boy was drowned . . . here in the river. And I went abroad, went away for good, never to return, never to see this river. . . . I closed my eyes and ran, beside myself, and *he* after me. . . . callously, without pity. I bought a villa near Mentone, becuase he fell ill there, and for three years I had no rest, day or night. The sick man wore me out, my soul dried up. Then last year, when the villa was sold to pay my debts, I went to Paris, and there he stripped me of everything, and left me for another woman; I tried to poison myself. . . . So stupid, so shameful. . . . And suddenly I felt a longing for Russia, for my own country, for my little girl. . . . (*Wipes away her tears.*) Lord, Lord, be merciful, forgive my sins! Don't punish me anymore! (*Takes a telegram out of her pocket.*) This came today from Paris. . . . He asks my forgiveness, begs me to return. . . . (*Tears up telegram.*) Do I hear music? (*Listens.*)

GAYEV: That's our famous Jewish band. You remember, four violins, a flute, and double bass.

LYUBOV ANDREYEVNA: It's still in existence? We ought to send for them sometime and give a party.

LOPAKHIN (*listens*): I don't hear anything. . . . (*Sings softly.*) "The Germans, for pay, will turn Russians into Frenchmen, they say." (*Laughs.*) What a play I saw yesterday at the theater—very funny!

LYUBOV ANDREYEVNA: There was probably nothing funny about it. Instead of going to see plays you ought to look at yourselves a little more often. How drab your lives are, how full of futile talk!

LOPAKHIN: That's true. I must say, this life of ours is stupid. . . . (*Pause.*) My father was a peasant, an idiot; he understood nothing, taught me nothing; all he did was beat me when he was drunk, and always with a stick. As a matter of fact, I'm as big a blockhead and idiot as he was. I never learned anything, my handwriting's disgusting, I write like a pig—I'm ashamed to have people see it.

LYUBOV ANDREYEVNA: You ought to get married, my friend.

LOPAKHIN: Yes . . . that's true.

LYUBOV ANDREYEVNA: To our Varya. She's a nice girl.

LOPAKHIN: Yes.

LYUBOV ANDREYEVNA: She's a girl who comes from simple people, works all day long, but the main thing is she loves you. Besides, you've liked her for a long time now.

LOPAKHIN: Well? I've nothing against it. . . . She's a good girl. (*Pause.*)

GAYEV: I've been offered a place in the bank. Six thousand a year. . . . Have you heard?

LYUBOV ANDREYEVNA: How could you! You stay where you are. . . .

(*Firs enters carrying an overcoat.*)

FIRS (*to Gayev*): If you please, sir, put this on, it's damp.

GAYEV (*puts on the overcoat*): You're a pest, old man.

FIRS: Never mind. . . . You went off this morning without telling me. (*Looks him over.*)

LYUBOV ANDREYEVNA: How you have aged, Firs!

FIRS: What do you wish, madam?

LOPAKHIN: She says you've grown very old!

FIRS: I've lived a long time. They were arranging a marriage for me before your papa was born. . . . (*Laughs.*) I was already head footman when the emancipation came. At that time I wouldn't consent to my freedom, I stayed with the masters. . . . (*Pause.*) I remember, everyone was happy, but what they were happy about, they themselves didn't know.

LOPAKHIN: It was better in the old days. At least they flogged them.

FIRS (*not hearing*): Of course. The peasants kept to the masters, the masters kept to the peasants; but now they have all gone their own ways, you can't tell about anything.

GAYEV: Be quiet, Firs. Tomorrow I must go to town. I've been promised an introduction to a certain general who might let us have a loan.

LOPAKHIN: Nothing will come of it. And you can rest assured, you won't even pay the interest.

LYUBOV ANDREYEVNA: He's raving. There is no such general.

(*Enter Trofimov, Anya, and Varya.*)

GAYEV: Here come our young people.

ANYA: There's Mama.

LYUBOV ANDREYEVNA (*tenderly*): Come, come along, my darlings. (*Embraces Anya and Varya.*) If you only knew how I love you both! Sit here beside me—there, like that.

(*They all sit down.*)

LOPAKHIN: Our eternal student is always with the young ladies.

TROFIMOV: That's none of your business.

LOPAKHIN: He'll soon be fifty, but he's still a student.

TROFIMOV: Drop your stupid jokes.

LOPAKHIN: What are you so angry about, you queer fellow?

TROFIMOV: Just leave me alone.

LOPAKHIN (*laughs*): Let me ask you something: What do you make of me?

TROFIMOV: My idea of you, Yermolai Alekseich, is this: You're a rich man, you will soon be a millionaire. Just as the beast of prey, which devours everything that crosses its path, is necessary in the metabolic process, so are you necessary.

(*Everyone laughs.*)

VARYA: Petya, you'd better tell us something about the planets.

LYUBOV ANDREYEVNA: No, let's go on with yesterday's conversation.

TROFIMOV: What was it about?

GAYEV: About the proud man.

TROFIMOV: We talked a long time yesterday, but we didn't get anywhere. In the proud man, in your sense of the word, there's something mystical. And you may be right from your point of view, but if you look at it simply, without being abstruse, why even talk about pride? Is there any sense in it if, physiologically, man is poorly constructed, if, in the vast majority of cases, he is coarse, ignorant, and profoundly unhappy? We should stop admiring ourselves. We should just work, and that's all.

GAYEV: You die, anyway.

TROFIMOV: Who knows? And what does it mean—to die? It may be that man has a hundred senses, and at his death only the five that are known to us perish, and the other ninety-five go on living.

LYUBOV ANDREYEVNA: How clever you are, Petya!

LOPAKHIN (*ironically*): Terribly clever!

TROFIMOV: Mankind goes forward, perfecting its powers. Everything that is now unattainable will some day be comprehensible and within our grasp, only we must work, and help with all our might those who are seeking the truth. So far, among us here in Russia, only a very few work. The great majority of the intelligentsia that I know seek nothing, do nothing, and as yet are incapable of work. They call themselves the intelligentsia, yet they belittle their servants, treat the peasants like animals, are wretched students, never read anything serious, and do absolutely nothing; they only talk about science and know very little about art. They all look serious, have grim expressions, speak of weighty matters, and philosophize; and meanwhile anyone can see that the workers eat abominably, sleep without pillows, thirty of forty to a room, and everywhere there are bedbugs, stench, dampness, and immorality. . . . It's obvious that all our fine talk is merely to delude ourselves and others. Show me the day nurseries they are always talking about—and where are the reading rooms? They only write about them in novels, but in reality they don't exist. There is nothing but filth, vulgarity, asiaticism.° . . . I'm afraid of those very serious countenances, I don't like them, I'm afraid of serious conversations. We'd do better to remain silent.

LOPAKHIN: You know, I get up before five in the morning, and I work from morning to night; now, I'm always handling money, my own and other people's, and I see what people around me are like. You have only to start doing something to find out how few honest, decent people there are. Sometimes, when I can't sleep, I think: "Lord, Thou gavest us vast forests, boundless fields, broad horizons, and living in their midst we ourselves ought truly to be giants. . . ."

LYUBOV ANDREYEVNA: Now you want giants! They're good only in fairy tales, otherwise they're frightening.

(*Yepikhodov crosses at the rear of the stage, playing the guitar.*)

LYUBOV ANDREYEVNA (*pensively*): There goes Yepikhodov . . .

ANYA (*pensively*): There goes Yepikhodov . . .

GAYEV: The sun has set, ladies and gentlemen.

TROFIMOV: Yes.

GAYEV (*in a low voice, as though reciting*): Oh, Nature, wondrous Nature, you shine with eternal radiance, beautiful and indifferent; you, whom we call mother, unite within yourself both life and death, giving life and taking it away. . . .

---

asiaticism: Trofimov, expressing a common prejudice of the time, refers to Asian apathy.

VARYA (*beseechingly*): Uncle dear!

ANYA: Uncle, you're doing it again!

TROFIMOV: You'd better cue ball into the center.

GAYEV: I'll be silent, silent.

(*All sit lost in thought. The silence is broken only by the subdued muttering of Firs. Suddenly a distant sound is heard, as if from the sky, like the sound of a snapped string mournfully dying away.*)

LYUBOV ANDREYEVNA: What was that?

LOPAKHIN: I don't know. Somewhere far off in a mine shaft a bucket's broken loose. But somewhere very far away.

GAYEV: It might be a bird of some sort ... like a heron.

TROFIMOV: Or an owl ...

LYUBOV ANDREYEVNA (*shudders*): It's unpleasant somehow. ... (*Pause.*)

FIRS: The same thing happened before the troubles: An owl hooted and the samovar hissed continually.

GAYEV: Before what troubles?

FIRS: Before the emancipation.

LYUBOV ANDREYEVNA: Come along, my friends, let us go, evening is falling. (*To Anya.*) There are tears in your eyes—what is it, my little one?

(*Embraces her.*)

ANYA: It's all right, Mama. It's nothing.

TROFIMOV: Someone is coming.

(*A Stranger appears wearing a shabby white forage cap and an overcoat. He is slightly drunk.*)

STRANGER: Permit me to inquire, can I go straight through here to the station?

GAYEV: You can. Follow the road.

STRANGER: I am deeply grateful to you. (*Coughs.*) Splendid weather. ... (*Reciting.*) "My brother, my suffering brother ... come to the Volga, whose groans" ... (*To Varya.*) Mademoiselle, will you oblige a hungry Russian with thirty kopecks?

(*Varya, frightened, cries out.*)

LOPAKHIN (*angrily*): There's a limit to everything.

LYUBOV ANDREYEVNA (*panic-stricken*): Here you are—take this. ... (*Fumbles in her purse.*) I have no silver. ... Never mind, here's a gold piece for you. ...

STRANGER: I am deeply grateful to you. (*Goes off.*)

(*Laughter.*)

VARYA (*frightened*): I'm leaving ... I'm leaving. ... Oh, Mama, dear, there's nothing in the house for the servants to eat, and you give him a gold piece!

LYUBOV ANDREYEVNA: What's to be done with such a silly creature? When we get home I'll give you all I've got. Yermolai Alekseyevich, you'll lend me some more!

LOPAKHIN: At your service.

LYUBOV ANDREYEVNA: Come, my friends, it's time to go. Oh, Varya, we have definitely made a match for you. Congratulations!

VARYA (*through tears*): Mama, that's not something to joke about.

LOPAKHIN: "Aurelia, get thee to a nunnery ... "°

GAYEV: Look, my hands are trembling: It's a long time since I've played a game of billiards.

LOPAKHIN: "Aurelia, O Nymph, in thy orisons, be all my sins remember'd!"

LYUBOV ANDREYEVNA: Let us go, my friends, it will soon be suppertime.

VARYA: He frightened me. My heart is simply pounding.

LOPAKHIN: Let me remind you, ladies and gentlemen: On the twenty-second of August the cherry orchard is to be sold. Think about that!—Think!

(*All go out except Trofimov and Anya.*)

ANYA (*laughs*): My thanks to the stranger for frightening Varya, now we are alone.

TROFIMOV: Varya is so afraid we might suddenly fall in love with each other that she hasn't left us alone for days. With her narrow mind she can't understand that we are above love. To avoid the petty and the illusory, which prevent our being free and happy—that is the aim and meaning of life. Forward! We are moving irresistibly toward the bright star that burns in the distance! Forward! Do not fall behind, friends!

ANYA (*clasping her hands*): How well you talk! (*Pause.*) It's marvelous here today!

TROFIMOV: Yes, the weather is wonderful.

ANYA: What have you done to me, Petya, that I no longer love the cherry orchard as I used to? I loved it so tenderly, it seemed to me there was no better place on earth than our orchard.

TROFIMOV: All Russia is our orchard. It is a great and beautiful land, and there are many wonderful places in it. (*Pause.*) Just think, Anya: Your grandfather, your great-grandfather, and all your ancestors were serf-owners, possessors of living souls. Don't you see that from every cherry tree, from every leaf and trunk, human beings are peering out at you? Don't you hear their voices? To possess living souls—that has corrupted all of you, those who lived before and you who are living now, so that your mother, you, your uncle, no longer perceive that you are living in debt, at someone else's expense, at the expense of those whom you wouldn't allow to cross your threshold. ... We are at least two hundred years behind the times, we have as yet absolutely nothing, we have no definite attitude toward the past, we only philosophize, complain of boredom, or drink vodka. Yet it's quite clear that to begin to live we must first atone for the past, be done with it, and we can atone for it only by suffering, only by extraordinary, unceasing labor. Understand this, Anya.

ANYA: The house we live in hasn't really been ours for a long time, and I shall leave it, I give you my word.

"Aurelia ... nunnery": From Hamlet's famous line rejecting Ophelia (Lopakhin's next line is also from Shakespeare's *Hamlet*).

TROFIMOV: If you have the keys of the household, throw them into the well and go. Be as free as the wind.

ANYA (*in ecstasy*): How well you put that!

TROFIMOV: Believe me, Anya, believe me! I am not yet thirty, I am young, still a student, but I have already been through so much! As soon as winter comes, I am hungry, sick, worried, poor as a beggar, and—where has not fate driven me! Where have I not been? And yet always, every minute of the day and night, my soul was filled with inexplicable premonitions. I have a premonition of happiness, Anya, I can see it . . .

ANYA: The moon is rising.

(*Yepikhodov is heard playing the same melancholy song on the guitar. The moon rises. Somewhere near the poplars Varya is looking for Anya and calling: "Anya, where are you?"*)

TROFIMOV: Yes, the moon is rising. (*Pause*). There it is—happiness . . . It's coming, nearer and nearer, I can hear its footsteps. And if we do not see it, if we do not recognize it, what does it matter? Others will see it.

VARYA'S VOICE: Anya! Where are you?

TROFIMOV: That Varya again! (*Angrily*.) It's revolting!

ANYA: Well? Let's go down to the river. It's lovely there.

TROFIMOV: Come on. (*They go*.)

VARYA'S VOICE: Anya! Anya!

ACT III

(*The drawing room, separated by an arch from the ballroom. The chandelier is lighted. The Jewish band that was mentioned in act II is heard playing in the hall. It is evening. In the ballroom they are dancing a grand rond. The voice of Semyonov-Pishchik: "Promenade à une paire!"° They all enter the drawing room: Pishchik and Charlotta Ivanovna are the first couple, Trofimov and Lyubov Andreyevna the second, Anya and the Post-Office Clerk the third, Varya and the Stationmaster the fourth, etc. Varya, quietly weeping, dries her tears as she dances. Dunyasha is in the last couple. As they cross the drawing room Pishchik calls: "Grand rond, balancez!" and "Les cavaliers à genoux et remerciez vos dames!"° Firs, wearing a dress coat, brings in a tray with seltzer water. Pishchik and Trofimov come into the drawing room.*)

PISHCHIK: I'm a full-blooded man, I've already had two strokes, and dancing's hard work for me, but as they say, "If you run with the pack, you can bark or not, but at least wag your tail." At that, I'm as strong as a horse. My late father—quite a joker he was, God rest his soul—used to say, talking about our origins, that the ancient line of Semyonov-Pishchik was descended from the very horse that Caligula had

"*Promenade à une paire!*": French for "Walk in pairs!"
"*Grand rond . . . dames!*": Instructions in the dance: "Large circle!" and "Gentlemen, kneel down and thank your ladies!"

seated in the Senate.° . . . (*Sits down*.) But the trouble is—no money! A hungry dog believes in nothing but meat. . . . (*Snores but wakes up at once*.) It's the same with me—I can think of nothing but money. . . .

TROFIMOV: You know, there really is something equine about your figure.

PISHCHIK: Well, a horse is a fine animal. . . . You can sell a horse.

(*There is the sound of a billiard game in the next room. Varya appears in the archway.*)

TROFIMOV (*teasing her*): Madame Lopakhina! Madame Lopakhina!

VARYA (*angrily*): Mangy gentleman!

TROFIMOV: Yes, I am a mangy gentleman, and proud of it!

VARYA (*reflecting bitterly*): Here we've hired musicians, and what are we going to pay them with? (*Goes out*.)

TROFIMOV (*to Pishchik*): If the energy you have expended in the course of your life trying to find money to pay interest had gone into something else, ultimately, you might very well have turned the world upside down.

PISHCHIK: Nietzsche . . . the philosopher . . . the greatest, most renowned . . . a man of tremendous intellect . . . says in his works that it is possible to forge banknotes.

TROFIMOV: And have you read Nietzsche?

PISHCHIK: Well . . . Dashenka told me. I'm in such a state now that I'm just about ready for forging. . . . The day after tomorrow I have to pay three hundred and ten rubles . . . I've got a hundred and thirty. . . . (*Feels in his pocket, grows alarmed*.) The money is gone! I've lost the money! (*Tearfully*.) Where is my money? (*Joyfully*.) Here it is, inside the lining. . . . I'm all in a sweat. . . .

(*Lyubov Andreyevna and Charlotta Ivanovna come in.*)

LYUBOV ANDREYEVNA (*humming a Lezginka*):° Why does Leonid take so long? What is he doing in town? (*To Dunyasha*.) Dunyasha, offer the musicians some tea.

TROFIMOV: In all probability, the auction didn't take place.

LYUBOV ANDREYEVNA: It was the wrong time to have the musicians, the wrong time to give a dance. . . . Well, never mind. . . . (*Sits down and hums softly*.)

CHARLOTTA (*gives Pishchik a deck of cards*): Here's a deck of cards for you. Think of a card.

PISHCHIK: I've thought of one.

CHARLOTTA: Now shuffle the pack. Very good. And now, my dear Mr. Pishchik, hand it to me. *Eins, zwei, drei!*° Now look for it—it's in your side pocket.

PISHCHIK: (*takes the card out of his side pocket*): The eight of spades—absolutely right! (*Amazed*.) Think of that, now!

CHARLOTTA (*holding the deck of cards in the palm of her hand, to Trofimov*): Quickly, tell me, which card is on top?

Caligula . . . Senate: Caligula (CE 12–41), a cavalry soldier, was Roman emperor (CE 37–41). Lezginka: A lively Russian tune for a dance. *Eins, zwei, drei!*: "One, two, three!" (German).

TROFIMOV: What? Well, the queen of spades.

CHARLOTTA: Right! (*To Pishchik.*) Now which card is on top?

PISHCHIK: The ace of hearts.

CHARLOTTA: Right! (*Claps her hands and the deck of cards disappears.*) What lovely weather we're having today! (*A mysterious feminine voice, which seems to come from under the floor, answers her: "Oh, yes, splendid weather, madam."*) You are so nice, you're my ideal.... (*The voice: "And I'm very fond of you, too, madam."*)

STATIONMASTER (*applauding*): Bravo, Madame Ventriloquist!

PISHCHIK (*amazed*): Think of that, now! Most enchanting Charlotta Ivanovna...I am simply in love with you....

CHARLOTTA: In love? (*Shrugs her shoulders.*) Is it possible that you can love? *Guter Mensch, aber schlechter Musikant.*°

TROFIMOV (*claps Pishchik on the shoulder*): You old horse, you!

CHARLOTTA: Attention, please! One more trick. (*Takes a lap robe from a chair.*) Here's a very fine lap robe; I should like to sell it. (*Shakes it out.*) Doesn't anyone want to buy it?

PISHCHIK (*amazed*): Think of that, now!

CHARLOTTA: *Eins, zwei, drei!* (*Quickly raises the lap robe, behind it stands Anya, who curtsies, runs to her mother, embraces her, and runs back into the ballroom amid the general enthusiasm.*)

LYUBOV ANDREYEVNA (*applauding*): Bravo, bravo!

CHARLOTTA: Once again! *Eins, zwei, drei.* (*Raises the lap robe; behind it stands Varya, who bows.*)

PISHCHIK (*amazed*): Think of that, now!

CHARLOTTA: The end! (*Throws the robe at Pishchik, makes a curtsy, and runs out of the room.*)

PISHCHIK (*hurries after her*): The minx!...What a woman! What a woman! (*Goes out.*)

LYUBOV ANDREYEVNA: And Leonid still not here. What he is doing in town so long, I do not understand! It must be all over by now. Either the estate is sold, or the auction didn't take place—but why keep us in suspense so long!

VARYA (*trying to comfort her*): Uncle has bought it, I am certain of that.

TROFIMOV (*mockingly*): Yes.

VARYA: Great-aunt sent him power of attorney to buy it in her name and transfer the debt. She's doing it for Anya's sake. And I am sure, with God's help, Uncle will buy it.

LYUBOV ANDREYEVNA: Our great-aunt in Yaroslav sent fifteen thousand to buy the estate in her name—she doesn't trust us—but that's not even enough to pay the interest. (*Covers her face with her hands.*) Today my fate will be decided, my fate...

TROFIMOV (*teasing Varya*): Madame Lopakhina!

Guter Mensch, aber schlechter Musikant: "Good man, but poor musician" (German).

VARYA (*angrily*): Eternal student! Twice already you've been expelled from the university.

LYUBOV ANDREYEVNA: Why are you so cross, Varya? If he teases you about Lopakhin, what of it? Go ahead and marry Lopakhin if you want to. He's a nice man, he's interesting. And if you don't want to, don't. Nobody's forcing you, my pet.

VARYA: To be frank, Mama dear, I regard this matter seriously. He is a good man, I like him.

LYUBOV ANDREYEVNA: Then marry him. I don't know what you're waiting for!

VARYA: Mama, I can't propose to him myself. For the last two years everyone's been talking to me about him; everyone talks, but he is either silent or he jokes. I understand. He's getting rich, he's absorbed in business, he has no time for me. If I had some money, no matter how little, if it were only a hundred rubles, I'd drop everything and go far away. I'd go into a nunnery.

TROFIMOV: A blessing!

VARYA (*to Trofimov*): A student ought to be intelligent! (*In a gentle tone, tearfully.*) How homely you have grown, Petya, how old! (*To Lyubov Andreyevna, no longer crying.*) It's just that I cannot live without work, Mama. I must be doing something every minute.

(*Yasha enters.*)

YASHA (*barely able to suppress his laughter*): Yepikhodov has broken a billiard cue! (*Goes out.*)

VARYA: But why is Yepikhodov here? Who gave him permission to play billiards? I don't understand these people.... (*Goes out.*)

LYUBOV ANDREYEVNA: Don't tease her, Petya. You can see she's unhappy enough without that.

TROFIMOV: She's much too zealous, always meddling in other people's affairs. All summer long she's given Anya and me no peace—afraid a romance might develop. What business is it of hers? Besides, I've given no occasion for it, I am far removed from such banality. We are above love!

LYUBOV ANDREYEVNA: And I suppose I am beneath love. (*In great agitation.*) Why isn't Leonid here? If only I knew whether the estate had been sold or not! The disaster seems to me so incredible that I don't even know what to think, I'm lost.... I could scream this very instant...I could do something foolish. Save me, Petya. Talk to me, say something....

TROFIMOV: Whether or not the estate is sold today—does it really matter? That's all done with long ago; there's no turning back, the path is overgrown. Be calm, my dear. One must not deceive oneself; at least once in one's life one ought to look the truth straight in the eye.

LYUBOV ANDREYEVNA: What truth? You can see where there is truth and where there isn't, but I seem to have lost my sight, I see nothing. You boldly settle all the important problems, but tell me, my dear boy, isn't it because you are young and have not yet had to suffer for a single one of your problems? You boldly look ahead, but isn't it because you neither see nor expect anything dreadful, since life is still hidden from your young eyes? You're bolder, more honest, deeper than we are, but think about it, be just a little bit magnanimous, and spare me. You see, I was born here, my mother and father lived here, and my grandfather. I love this house, without the cherry orchard my life has no meaning for me, and if it must be sold, then sell me with the orchard.... (*Embraces Trofimov and kisses him on the forehead.*) And my son was drowned here.... (*Weeps.*) Have pity on me, you good, kind man.

TROFIMOV: You know I feel for you with all my heart.

LYUBOV ANDREYEVNA: But that should have been said differently, quite differently.... (*Takes out her handkerchief and a telegram falls to the floor.*) My heart is heavy today, you can't imagine. It's so noisy here, my soul quivers at every sound, I tremble all over, and yet I can't go to my room. When I am alone the silence frightens me. Don't condemn me, Petya ... I love you as if you were my own. I would gladly let you marry Anya, I swear it, only you must study, my dear, you must get your degree. You do nothing, fate simply tosses you from place to place—it's so strange.... Isn't that true? Isn't it? And you must do something about your beard, to make it grow somehow.... (*Laughs.*) You're so funny!

TROFIMOV (*picks up the telegram*): I have no desire to be an Adonis.°

LYUBOV ANDREYEVNA: That's a telegram from Paris. I get them every day. One yesterday, one today. That wild man has fallen ill again, he's in trouble again.... He begs my forgiveness, implores me to come, and really, I ought to go to Paris to be near him. Your face is stern, Petya, but what can one do, my dear? What am I to do? He is ill, he's alone and unhappy, and who will look after him there, who will keep him from making mistakes, who will give him his medicine on time? And why hide it or keep silent, I love him, that's clear. I love him, love him.... It's a millstone round my neck, I'm sinking to the bottom with it, but I love that stone, I cannot live without. it. (*Presses Trofimov's hand.*) Don't think badly of me, Petya, and don't say anything to me, don't say anything....

TROFIMOV (*through tears*): For God's sake, forgive my frankness: You know that he robbed you!

LYUBOV ANDREYEVNA: No, no, no, you mustn't say such things! (*Covers her ears.*)

TROFIMOV: But he's a scoundrel! You're the only one who doesn't know it! He's a petty scoundrel, a nonentity—

LYUBOV ANDREYEVNA (*angry, but controlling herself*): You are twenty-six or twenty-seven years old, but you're still a schoolboy!

TROFIMOV: That may be!

LYUBOV ANDREYEVNA: You should be a man, at your age you ought to understand those who love. And you ought to be in love yourself. (*Angrily.*) Yes, yes!

Adonis: From Greek myth, a beautiful young man.

It's not purity with you, it's simply prudery, you're a ridiculous crank, a freak—

TROFIMOV (*horrified*): What is she saying!

LYUBOV ANDREYEVNA: I am above love! You're not above love, you're just an addlepate, as Firs would say. Not to have a mistress at your age!

TROFIMOV (*in horror*): This is awful! What is she saying!.... (*Goes quickly toward the ballroom.*) This is awful ... I can't ... I won't stay here.... (*Goes out, but immediately returns.*) All is over between us! (*Goes out to the hall.*)

LYUBOV ANDREYEVNA (*calls after him*): Petya, wait! You absurd creature, I was joking! Petya!

(*In the hall there is the sound of someone running quickly downstairs and suddenly falling with a crash. Anya and Varya scream, but a moment later laughter is heard.*)

LYUBOV ANDREYEVNA: What was that?

(*Anya runs in.*)

ANYA (*laughing*): Petya fell down the stairs! (*Runs out.*)

LYUBOV ANDREYEVNA: What a funny boy that Petya is!

(*The Stationmaster stands in the middle of the ballroom and recites A. Tolstoy's° "The Sinner." Everyone listens to him, but he has no sooner spoken a few lines than the sound of a waltz is heard from the hall and recitation is broken off. They all dance. Trofimov, Anya, Varya, and Lyubov Andreyevna come in from the hall.*)

LYUBOV ANDREYEVNA: Come, Petya ... come, you pure soul ... please, forgive me.... Let's dance.... (*They dance.*)

(*Anya and Varya dance. Firs comes in, puts his stick by the side door. Yasha also comes into the drawing room and watches the dancers.*)

YASHA: What is it, grandpa?

FIRS: I don't feel well. In the old days, we used to have generals, barons, admirals, dancing at our balls, but now we send for the post office clerk and the stationmaster, and even they are none too eager to come. Somehow I've grown weak. The late master, their grandfather, dosed everyone with sealing wax, no matter what ailed them. I've been taking sealing wax every day for twenty years or more, maybe that's what's kept me alive.

YASHA: You bore me, grandpa. (*Yawns.*) High time you croaked.

FIRS: Ah, you ... addlepate! (*Mumbles.*)

(*Trofimov and Lyubov Andreyevna dance from the ballroom into the drawing room.*)

LYUBOV ANDREYEVNA: *Merci.* I'll sit down a while. (*Sits.*) I'm tired.

(*Anya comes in.*)

A. Tolstoy: Aleksey Konstantinovich Tolstoy (1817–1875), Russian novelist, dramatist, and poet.

ANYA (*excitedly*): There was a man in the kitchen just now saying that the cherry orchard was sold today.

LYUBOV ANDREYEVNA: Sold to whom?

ANYA: He didn't say. He's gone. (*Dances with Trofimov; they go into the ballroom.*)

YASHA: That was just some old man babbling. A stranger.

FIRS: Leonid Andreich is not back yet, still hasn't come. And he's wearing the light, between-seasons overcoat; like enough he'll catch cold. Ah, when they're young they're green.

LYUBOV ANDREYEVNA: This is killing me. Yasha, go and find out who it was sold to.

YASHA: But that old man left long ago. (*Laughs.*)

LYUBOV ANDREYEVNA (*slightly annoyed*): Well, what are you laughing at? What are you so happy about?

YASHA: That Yepikhodov is very funny! Hopeless! Two-and-twenty Troubles.

LYUBOV ANDREYEVNA: Firs, if the estate is sold, where will you go?

FIRS: Wherever you tell me to go, I'll go.

LYUBOV ANDREYEVNA: Why do you look like that? Aren't you well? You ought to go to bed.

FIRS: Yes.... (*With a smirk.*) Go to bed, and without me who will serve, who will see to things? I'm the only one in the whole house.

YASHA (*to Lyubov Andreyevna*): Lyubov Andreyevna! Permit me to make a request, be so kind! If you go back to Paris again, do me the favor of taking me with you. It is positively impossible for me to stay here. (*Looking around, then in a low voice.*) There's no need to say it, you can see for yourself, it's an uncivilized country, the people have no morals, and the boredom! The food they give us in the kitchen is unmentionable, and besides, there's this Firs who keeps walking about mumbling all sorts of inappropriate things. Take me with you, be so kind!

(*Enter Pishchik.*)

PISHCHIK: May I have the pleasure of a waltz with you, fairest lady? (*Lyubov Andreyevna goes with him.*) I really must borrow a hundred and eighty rubles from you, my charmer . . . I really must.... (*Dancing.*) Just a hundred and eighty rubles.... (*They pass into the ballroom.*)

YASHA (*softly sings*): "Wilt thou know my soul's unrest . . ."

(*In the ballroom a figure in a gray top hat and checked trousers is jumping about, waving its arms; there are shouts of "Bravo, Charlotta Ivanovna!"*)

DUNYASHA (*stopping to powder her face*): The young mistress told me to dance—there are lots of gentlemen and not enough ladies—but dancing makes me dizzy, and my heart begins to thump. Firs Nikolayevich, the post office clerk just said something to me that took my breath away.

(*The music grows more subdued.*)

FIRS: What did he say to you?

DUNYASHA: "You," he said, "are like a flower."

YASHA (*yawns*): What ignorance.... (*Goes out.*)

DUNYASHA: Like a flower.... I'm such a delicate girl, I just adore tender words.

FIRS: You'll get your head turned.

(*Enter Yepikhodov.*)

YEPIKHODOV: Avdotya Fyodorovna, you are not desirous of seeing me.... I might almost be some sort of insect. (*Sighs.*) Ah, life!

DUNYASHA: What is it you want?

YEPIKHODOV: Indubitably, you may be right. (*Sighs.*) But, of course, if one looks at it from a point of view, then, if I may so express myself, and you will forgive my frankness, you have completely reduced me to a state of mind. I know my fate, every day some misfortune befalls me, but I have long since grown accustomed to that; I look upon my fate with a smile. But you gave me your word, and although I—

DUNYASHA: Please, we'll talk about it later, but leave me in peace now. Just now I'm dreaming.... (*Plays with her fan.*)

YEPIKHODOV: Every day a misfortune, and yet, if I may so express myself, I merely smile, I even laugh.

(*Varya enters from the ballroom.*)

VARYA: Are you still here, Semyon? What a disrespectful man you are, really! (*To Dunyasha.*) Run along, Dunyasha. (*To Yepikhodov.*) First you play billiards and break a cue, then you wander about the drawing room as though you were a guest.

YEPIKHODOV: You cannot, if I may so express myself, penalize me.

VARYA: I am not penalizing you, I'm telling you. You do nothing but wander from one place to another, and you don't do your work. We keep a clerk, but for what, I don't know.

YEPIKHODOV (*offended*): Whether I work, or wander about, or eat, or play billiards, these are matters to be discussed only by persons of discernment, and my elders.

VARYA: You dare say that to me! (*Flaring up.*) You dare? You mean to say I have no discernment? Get out of here! This instant!

YEPIKHODOV (*intimidated*): I beg you to express yourself in a more delicate manner.

VARYA (*beside herself*): Get out, this very instant! Get out! (*He goes to the door, she follows him.*) Two-and-twenty Troubles! Don't let me set eyes on you again!

YEPIKHODOV (*goes out, his voice is heard behind the door*): I shall lodge a complaint against you!

VARYA: Oh, you're coming back? (*Seizes the stick left near the door by Firs.*) Come, come on.... Come, I'll show you.... Ah, so you're coming, are you? Then take that—(*Swings the stick just as Lopakhin enters.*)

LOPAKHIN: Thank you kindly.

VARYA (*angrily and mockingly*): I beg your pardon.

LOPAKHIN: Not at all. I humbly thank you for your charming reception.

VARYA: Don't mention it. (*Walks away, then looks back and gently asks.*) I didn't hurt you, did I?

LOPAKHIN: No, it's nothing. A huge bump coming up, that's all.

(*Voices in the ballroom: "Lopakhin has come! Yermolai Alekseich!" Pishchik enters.*)

PISHCHIK: As I live and breathe! (*Kisses Lopakhin.*) There is a whiff of cognac about you, dear soul. And we've been making merry here, too.

(*Enter Lyubov Andreyevna.*)

LYUBOV ANDREYEVNA: Is that you, Yermolai Alekseich? What kept you so long? Where's Leonid?

LOPAKHIN: Leonid Andreich arrived with me, he's coming . . .

LYUBOV ANDREYEVNA (*agitated*): Well, what happened? Did the sale take place? Tell me!

LOPAKHIN (*embarrassed, fearing to reveal his joy*): The auction was over by four o'clock. . . . We missed the train, had to wait till half past nine. (*Sighing heavily.*) Ugh! My head is swimming. . . .

(*Enter Gayev; he carries his purchases in one hand and wipes away his tears with the other.*)

LYUBOV ANDREYEVNA: Lyonya, what happened? Well, Lyonya? (*Impatiently, through tears.*) Be quick, for God's sake!

GAYEV (*not answering her, simply waves his hand. To Firs, weeping*): Here, take these. . . . There's anchovies, Kerch herrings. . . . I haven't eaten anything all day. . . . What I have been through! (*The click of billiard balls is heard through the open door to the billiard room, and Yasha's voice: "Seven and eighteen!" Gayev's expression changes, he is no longer weeping.*) I'm terribly tired. Firs, help me change. (*Goes through the ballroom to his own room, followed by Firs.*)

PISHCHIK: What happened at the auction? Come on, tell us!

LYUBOV ANDREYEVNA: Is the cherry orchard sold?

LOPAKHIN: It's sold.

LYUBOV ANDREYEVNA: Who bought it?

LOPAKHIN: I bought it. (*Pause.*)

(*Lyubov Andreyevna is overcome; she would fall to the floor if it were not for the chair and table near which she stands. Varya takes the keys from her belt and throws them on the floor in the middle of the drawing room and goes out.*)

LOPAKHIN: I bought it! Kindly wait a moment, ladies and gentlemen, my head is swimming. I can't talk. . . . (*Laughs.*) We arrived at the auction, Deriganov was already there. Leonid Andreich had only fifteen thousand, and straight off Deriganov bid thirty thousand over and above the mortgage. I saw how the land lay, so I got into the fight and bid forty. He bid forty-five. I bid fifty-five. In other words, he kept raising it by five thousand, and I by ten. Well, it finally came to an end. I bid ninety thousand above the mortgage, and it was knocked down to me. The cherry orchard is now mine! Mine! (*Laughs uproariously.*) Lord! God in heaven! The cherry orchard is mine! Tell me I'm drunk, out of my mind, that I imagine it. . . . (*Stamps his feet.*) Don't laugh at me! If my father and my grandfather could only rise from their graves and see all that has happened, how their Yermolai, their beaten, half-literate Yermolai, who used to run about barefoot in winter, how that same Yermolai has bought an estate, the most beautiful estate in the whole world! I bought the estate where my father and grandfather were slaves, where they weren't even allowed in the kitchen. I'm asleep, this is just some dream of mine, it only seems to be. . . . It's the fruit of your imagination, hidden in the darkness of uncertainty. . . . (*Picks up the keys, smiling tenderly.*) She threw down the keys, wants to show that she's not mistress here anymore. . . . (*Jingles the keys.*) Well, no matter. (*The orchestra is heard tuning up.*) Hey, musicians, play, I want to hear you! Come on, everybody, and see how Yermolai Lopakhin will lay the ax to the cherry orchard, how the trees will fall to the ground! We're going to build summer cottages and our grandsons and great-grandsons will see a new life here. . . . Music! Strike up!

(*The orchestra plays. Lyubov Andreyevna sinks into a chair and weeps bitterly.*)

LOPAKHIN (*reproachfully*): Why didn't you listen to me, why? My poor friend, there's no turning back now. (*With tears.*) Oh, if only all this could be over quickly, if somehow our discordant, unhappy life could be changed!

PISHCHIK (*takes him by the arm; speaks in an undertone*): She's crying. Let's go into the ballroom, let her be alone. . . . Come on. . . . (*Leads him into the ballroom.*)

LOPAKHIN: What's happened? Musicians, play so I can hear you! Let everything be as I want it! (*Ironically.*) Here comes the new master, owner of the cherry orchard! (*Accidentally bumps into a little table, almost upsetting the candelabrum.*) I can pay for everything! (*Goes out with Pishchik.*)

(*There is no one left in either the drawing room or the ballroom except Lyubov Andreyevna, who sits huddled up and weeping bitterly. The music plays softly. Anya and Trofimov enter hurriedly. Anya goes to her mother and kneels before her. Trofimov remains in the doorway of the ballroom.*)

ANYA: Mama! . . . Mama, you're crying! Dear, kind, good Mama, my beautiful one, I love you . . . I bless you. The cherry orchard is sold, it's gone, that's true, true, but don't cry, Mama, life is still before you, you still have your good, pure soul. . . . Come with me, come, darling, we'll go away from here! . . . We'll plant a new orchard, more luxuriant than this one.

You will see it and understand; and joy, quiet, deep joy, will sink into your soul, like the evening sun, and you will smile, Mama! Come, darling, let us go. . . .

ACT IV

(*The scene is the same as act I. There are neither curtains on the windows nor pictures on the walls, and only a little furniture piled up in one corner, as if for sale. There is a sense of emptiness. Near the outer door, at the rear of the stage, suitcases, traveling bags, etc., are piled up. Through the open door on the left the voices of Varya and Anya can be heard. Lopakhin stands waiting. Yasha is holding a tray with little glasses of champagne. In the hall, Yepikhodov is tying up a box. Offstage, at the rear, there is a hum of voices. It is the peasants who have come to say good-bye. Gayev's voice: "Thanks, brothers, thank you."*)*

YASHA: The peasants have come to say good-bye. In my opinion, Yermolai Alekseich, peasants are good-natured, but they don't know much.

(*The hum subsides. Lyubov Andreyevna enters from the hall with Gayev. She is not crying, but she is pale, her face twitches, and she cannot speak.*)

GAYEV: You gave them your purse, Lyuba. That won't do! That won't do!

LYUBOV ANDREYEVNA: I couldn't help it! I couldn't help it! (*They both go out.*)

LOPAKHIN (*in the doorway, calls after them*): Please, do me the honor of having a little glass at parting. I didn't think of bringing champagne from town, and at the station I found only one bottle. Please! What's the matter, friends, don't you want any? (*Walks away from the door.*) If I'd known that, I wouldn't have bought it. Well, then I won't drink any either. (*Yasha carefully sets the tray down on a chair.*) At least you have a glass, Yasha.

YASHA: To those who are departing! Good luck! (*Drinks.*) This champagne is not the real stuff, I can assure you.

LOPAKHIN: Eight rubles a bottle. (*Pause.*) It's devilish cold in here.

YASHA: They didn't light the stoves today; it doesn't matter, since we're leaving. (*Laughs.*)

LOPAKHIN: Why are you laughing?

YASHA: Because I'm pleased.

LOPAKHIN: It's October, yet it's sunny and still outside, like summer. Good for building. (*Looks at his watch, then calls through the door.*) Bear in mind, ladies and gentlemen, only forty-six minutes till train time! That means leaving for the station in twenty minutes. Better hurry up!

(*Trofimov enters from outside wearing an overcoat.*)

TROFIMOV: Seems to me it's time to start. The carriages are at the door. What the devil has become of my rubbers? They're lost. (*Calls through the door.*) Anya, my rubbers are not here. I can't find them.

LOPAKHIN: I've got to go to Kharkov. I'm taking the same train you are. I'm going to spend the winter in Kharkov. I've been hanging around here with you, and I'm sick and tired of loafing. I can't live without work, I don't know what to do with my hands; they dangle in some strange way, as if they didn't belong to me.

TROFIMOV: We'll soon be gone, then you can take up your useful labors again.

LOPAKHIN: Here, have a little drink.

TROFIMOV: No, I don't want any.

LOPAKHIN: So you're off for Moscow?

TROFIMOV: Yes, I'll see them into town, and tomorrow I'll go to Moscow.

LOPAKHIN: Yes. . . . Well, I expect the professors haven't been giving any lectures: They're waiting for you to come!

TROFIMOV: That's none of your business.

LOPAKHIN: How many years is it you've been studying at the university?

TROFIMOV: Can't you think of something new? That's stale and flat. (*Looks for his rubbers.*) You know we'll probably never see each other again, so allow me to give you one piece of advice at parting: Don't wave your arms about! Get out of that habit—of arm-waving. And another thing, building cottages and counting on the summer residents in time becoming independent farmers—that's just another form of arm-waving. Well, when all's said and done, I'm fond of you anyway. You have fine, delicate fingers, like an artist; you have a fine delicate soul.

LOPAKHIN (*embraces him*): Good-bye, my dear fellow. Thank you for everything. Let me give you some money for the journey, if you need it.

TROFIMOV: What for? I don't need it.

LOPAKHIN: But you haven't any!

TROFIMOV: I have. Thank you. I got some money for a translation. Here it is in my pocket. (*Anxiously.*) But where are my rubbers?

VARYA (*from the next room*): Here, take the nasty things! (*Flings a pair of rubbers onto the stage.*)

TROFIMOV: What are you so cross about, Varya? Hm. . . . But these are not my rubbers.

LOPAKHIN: In the spring I sowed three thousand acres of poppies, and now I've made forty thousand rubles clear. And when my poppies were in bloom, what a picture it was! So, I'm telling you, I've made forty thousand, which means I'm offering you a loan because I can afford to. Why turn up your nose? I'm a peasant—I speak bluntly.

TROFIMOV: Your father was a peasant, mine was a pharmacist—which proves absolutely nothing. (*Lopakhin takes out his wallet.*) No, don't—even if you gave me two hundred thousand I wouldn't take it. I'm a free man. And everything that is valued so highly and held so dear by all of you, rich and poor alike, has not the slightest power over me—it's like a feather floating in the air. I can get along without you, I can pass you by, I'm strong and proud.

Mankind is advancing toward the highest truth, the highest happiness attainable on earth, and I am in the front ranks!

LOPAKHIN: Will you get there?

TROFIMOV: I'll get there. (*Pause.*) I'll either get there or I'll show others the way to get there.

(*The sound of axes chopping down trees is heard in the distance.*)

LOPAKHIN: Well, good-bye, my dear fellow. It's time to go. We turn up our noses at one another, but life goes on just the same. When I work for a long time without stopping, my mind is easier, and it seems to me that I, too, know why I exist. But how many there are in Russia, brother, who exist nobody knows why. Well, it doesn't matter, that's not what makes the wheels go round. They say Leonid Andreich has taken a position in the bank, six thousand a year. . . . Only, of course, he won't stick it out, he's too lazy. . . .

ANYA (*in the doorway*): Mama asks you not to start cutting down the cherry orchard until she's gone.

TROFIMOV: Yes, really, not to have had the tact. . . . (*Goes out through the hall.*)

LOPAKHIN: Right away, right away. . . . Ach, what people. . . . (*Follows Trofimov out.*)

ANYA: Has Firs been taken to the hospital?

YASHA: I told them this morning. They must have taken him.

ANYA (*to Yepikhodov, who is crossing the room*): Semyon Panteleich, please find out if Firs has been taken to the hospital.

YASHA (*offended*): I told Yegor this morning. Why ask a dozen times?

YEPIKHODOV: It is my conclusive opinion that the venerable Firs is beyond repair; it's time he was gathered to his fathers. And I can only envy him. (*Puts a suitcase down on a hatbox and crushes it.*) There you are! Of course! I knew it! (*Goes out.*)

YASHA (*mockingly*): Two-and-twenty Troubles!

VARYA (*through the door*): Has Firs been taken to the hospital?

ANYA: Yes, he has.

VARYA: Then why didn't they take the letter to the doctor?

ANYA: We must send it on after them. . . . (*Goes out.*)

VARYA (*from the adjoining room*): Where is Yasha? Tell him his mother has come to say good-bye to him.

YASHA (*waves his hand*): They really try my patience.

(*Dunyasha has been fussing with the luggage; now that Yasha is alone she goes up to him.*)

DUNYASHA: You might give me one little look, Yasha. You're going away . . . leaving me. . . . (*Cries and throws herself on his neck.*)

YASHA: What's there to cry about? (*Drinks champagne.*) In six days I'll be in Paris again. Tomorrow we'll take the express, off we go, and that's the last you'll see of us. I can hardly believe it. *Vive la France!* This place is not for me, I can't live here. . . . It can't be helped.

I've had enough of this ignorance—I'm fed up with it. (*Drinks champagne.*) What are you crying for? Behave yourself properly, then you won't cry.

DUNYASHA (*looks into a small mirror and powders her face*): Send me a letter from Paris. You know, I loved you, Yasha, how I loved you! I'm such a tender creature, Yasha!

YASHA: Here they come. (*Busies himself with the luggage, humming softly.*)

(*Enter Lyubov Andreyevna, Gayev, Charlotta Ivanovna.*)

GAYEV: We ought to be leaving. There's not much time now. (*Looks at Yasha.*) Who smells of herring?

LYUBOV ANDREYEVNA: In about ten minutes we should be getting into the carriages. (*Glances around the room.*) Good-bye, dear house, old grandfather. Winter will pass, spring will come, and you will no longer be here, they will tear you down. How much these walls have seen? (*Kisses her daughter warmly.*) My treasure, you are radiant, your eyes are sparkling like two diamonds. Are you glad? Very?

ANYA: Very! A new life is beginning, Mama!

GAYEV (*cheerfully*): Yes, indeed, everything is all right now. Before the cherry orchard was sold we were all worried and miserable, but afterward, when the question was finally settled once and for all, everybody calmed down and felt quite cheerful. . . . I'm in a bank now, a financier . . . cue ball into the center . . . and you, Lyuba, say what you like, you look better, no doubt about it.

LYUBOV ANDREYEVNA: Yes. My nerves are better, that's true. (*Her hat and coat are handed to her.*) I sleep well. Carry out my things, Yasha, it's time. (*To Anya.*) My little girl, we shall see each other soon. . . . I shall go to Paris and live there on the money your great-aunt sent to buy the estate—long live Auntie!—but that money won't last long.

ANYA: You'll come back soon, Mama, soon . . . won't you? I'll study hard and pass my high school examinations, and then I can work and help you. We'll read all sorts of books together, Mama. . . . Won't we? (*Kisses her mother's hand.*) We'll read in the autumn evenings, we'll read lots of books, and a new and wonderful world will open up before us. . . . (*Dreaming.*) Mama, come back. . . .

LYUBOV ANDREYEVNA: I'll come, my precious. (*Embraces her.*)

(*Enter Lopakhin, Charlotta Ivanovna is softly humming a song.*)

GAYEV: Happy Charlotta: She's singing!

CHARLOTTA (*picks up a bundle and holds it like a baby in swaddling clothes*): Bye, baby, bye. . . . (*A baby's crying is heard, "Wah! Wah!"*) Be quiet, my darling, my dear little boy. ("*Wah! Wah!*") I'm so sorry for you! (*Throws the bundle down.*) You will find me a position, won't you? I can't go on like this.

LOPAKHIN: We'll find something, Charlotta Ivanovna, don't worry.

GAYEV: Everyone is leaving us, Varya's going away . . . all of a sudden nobody needs us.

CHARLOTTA: I have nowhere to go in town. I must go away. (*Hums.*) It doesn't matter . . .

(*Enter Pishchik.*)

LOPAKHIN: Nature's wonder!

PISHCHIK (*panting*): Ugh! Let me catch my breath. . . . I'm exhausted. . . . My esteemed friends. . . . Give me some water. . . .

GAYEV: After money, I suppose? Excuse me, I'm fleeing from temptation. . . . (*Goes out.*)

PISHCHIK: It's a long time since I've been to see you . . . fairest lady. . . . (*To Lopakhin*) So you're here. . . . Glad to see you, you intellectual giant. . . . Here . . . take it . . . four hundred rubles . . . I still owe you eight hundred and forty . . .

LOPAKHIN (*shrugs his shoulders in bewilderment*): I must be dreaming. . . . Where did you get it?

PISHCHIK: Wait . . . I'm hot. . . . A most extraordinary event. Some Englishmen came to my place and discovered some kind of white clay on my land. (*To Lyubov Andreyevna*) And four hundred for you . . . fairest, most wonderful lady. . . . (*Hands her the money.*) The rest later. (*Takes a drink of water.*) Just now a young man in the train was saying that a certain . . . great philosopher recommends jumping off roofs. . . . "Jump!" he says, and therein lies the whole problem. (*In amazement.*) Think of that, now! . . . Water!

LOPAKHIN: Who were those Englishmen?

PISHCHIK: I leased them the tract of land with the clay on it for twenty-four years. . . . And now, excuse me, I have no time . . . I must be trotting along . . . I'm going to Znoikov's . . . to Kardamanov's . . . I owe everybody. (*Drinks.*) Keep well . . . I'll drop in on Thursday . . .

LYUBOV ANDREYEVNA: We're just moving into town, and tomorrow I go abroad . . .

PISHCHIK: What? (*Alarmed.*) Why into town? That's why I see the furniture . . . suitcases. . . . Well, never mind. . . . (*Through tears.*) Never mind. . . . Men of the greatest intellect, those Englishmen. . . . Never mind. . . . Be happy . . . God will help you. . . . Never mind. . . . Everything in this world comes to an end. . . . (*Kisses Lyubov Andreyevna's hand.*) And should the news reach you that my end has come, just remember this old horse, and say: "There once lived a certain Semyonov-Pishchik, God rest his soul." . . . Splendid weather. . . . Yes. . . . (*Goes out greatly disconcerted, but immediately returns and speaks from the doorway.*) Dashenka sends her regards. (*Goes out.*)

LYUBOV ANDREYEVNA: Now we can go. I am leaving with two things on my mind. First—that Firs is sick. (*Looks at her watch.*) We still have about five minutes. . . .

ANYA: Mama, Firs has already been taken to the hospital. Yasha sent him there this morning.

LYUBOV ANDREYEVNA: My second concern is Varya. She's used to getting up early and working, and now, with no work to do, she's like a fish out of water. She's grown pale and thin, and cries all the time, poor girl. . . . (*Pauses.*) You know very well, Yermolai Alekseich, that I dreamed of marrying her to you, and everything pointed to your getting married. (*Whispers to Anya, who nods to Charlotta, and they both go out.*) She loves you, you are fond of her, and I don't know—I don't know why it is you seem to avoid each other. I can't understand it!

LOPAKHIN: To tell you the truth, I don't understand it myself. The whole thing is strange, somehow. . . . If there's still time, I'm ready right now. . . . Let's finish it up—and *basta,*° but without you I feel I'll never be able to propose to her.

LYUBOV ANDREYEVNA: Splendid! After all, it only takes a minute. I'll call her in at once. . . .

LOPAKHIN: And we even have the champagne. (*Looks at the glasses.*) Empty! Somebody's already drunk it. (*Yasha coughs.*) That's what you call lapping it up.

LYUBOV ANDREYEVNA (*animatedly*): Splendid! We'll leave you. . . . Yasha, *allez!*° I'll call her. . . . (*At the door.*) Varya, leave everything and come here. Come! (*Goes out with Yasha.*)

LOPAKHIN (*looking at his watch*): Yes. . . . (*Pause.*)

(*Behind the door there is smothered laughter and whispering; finally Varya enters.*)

VARYA (*looking over the luggage for a long time*): Strange, I can't seem to find it . . .

LOPAKHIN: What are you looking for?

VARYA: I packed it myself, and I can't remember . . . (*Pause.*)

LOPAKHIN: Where are you going now, Varya Mikhailovna?

VARYA: I? To the Ragulins'. . . . I've agreed to go there to look after the house . . . as a sort of housekeeper.

LOPAKHIN: At Yashnevo? That would be about seventy versts from here. (*Pause.*) Well, life in this house has come to an end. . . .

VARYA (*examining the luggage*): Where can it be? . . . Perhaps I put it in the trunk. . . . Yes, life in this house has come to an end . . . there'll be no more . . .

LOPAKHIN: And I'm off for Kharkov . . . by the next train. I have a lot to do. I'm leaving Yepikhodov here . . . I've taken him on.

VARYA: Really!

LOPAKHIN: Last year at this time it was already snowing, if you remember, but now it's still and sunny. It's cold though. . . . About three degrees of frost.

VARYA: I haven't looked. (*Pause.*) And besides, our thermometer's broken. (*Pause.*)

(*A voice from the yard calls: "Yermolai Alekseich!"*)

LOPAKHIN (*as if he had been waiting for a long time for the call*): Coming! (*Goes out quickly.*)

basta: Italian for "enough."   *allez!:* French for "go!"

(*Varya sits on the floor, lays her head on a bundle of clothes, and quietly sobs. The door opens and Lyubov Andreyevna enters cautiously.*)

LYUBOV ANDREYEVNA: Well? (*Pause.*) We must be going.

VARYA (*no longer crying, dries her eyes*): Yes, it's time, Mama dear. I can get to the Ragulins' today, if only we don't miss the train.

LYUBOV ANDREYEVNA (*in the doorway*): Anya, put your things on!

(*Enter Anya, then Gayev and Charlotta Ivanovna. Gayev wears a warm overcoat with a hood. The servants and coachmen come in. Yepikhodov bustles about the luggage.*)

LYUBOV ANDREYEVNA: Now we can be on our way.

ANYA (*joyfully*): On our way!

GAYEV: My friends, my dear, cherished friends! Leaving this house forever, can I pass over in silence, can I refrain from giving utterance, as we say farewell, to those feelings that now fill my whole being—

ANYA (*imploringly*): Uncle!

VARYA: Uncle dear, don't!

GAYEV (*forlornly*): Double the rail off the white to center table...yellow into the side pocket....I'll be quiet....

(*Enter Trofimov, then Lopakhin.*)

TROFIMOV: Well, ladies and gentlemen, it's time to go!

LOPAKHIN: Yepikhodov, my coat!

LYUBOV ANDREYEVNA: I'll sit here just one more minute. It's as though I had never before seen what the walls of this house were like, what the ceilings were like, and now I look at them hungrily, with such tender love...

GAYEV: I remember when I was six years old, sitting on this windowsill on Whitsunday, watching my father going to church...

LYUBOV ANDREYEVNA: Have they taken all the things?

LOPAKHIN: Everything, I think. (*Puts on his overcoat.*) Yepikhodov, see that everything is in order.

YEPIKHODOV (*in a hoarse voice*): Rest assured, Yermolai Alekseich!

LOPAKHIN: What's the matter with your voice?

YEPIKHODOV: Just drank some water...must have swallowed something.

YASHA (*contemptuously*): What ignorance!

LYUBOV ANDREYEVNA: When we go—there won't be a soul left here....

LOPAKHIN: Till spring.

VARYA (*pulls an umbrella out of a bundle as though she were going to hit someone; Lopakhin pretends to be frightened*): Why are you—I never thought of such a thing!

TROFIMOV: Ladies and gentlemen, let's get into the carriages—it's time now! The train will soon be in!

VARYA: Petya, there they are—your rubbers, by the suitcase. (*Tearfully.*) And what dirty old things they are!

TROFIMOV (*putting on his rubbers*): Let's go, ladies and gentlemen!

GAYEV (*extremely upset, afraid of bursting into tears*): The train...the station....Cross table to the center, double the rail...on the white into the corner.

LYUBOV ANDREYEVNA: Let us go!

GAYEV: Are we all here? No one in there? (*Locks the side door on the left.*) There are some things stored in there, we must lock up. Let's go!

ANYA: Good-bye, house! Good-bye, old life!

TROFIMOV: Hail to the new life! (*Goes out with Anya.*)

(*Varya looks around the room and slowly goes out. Yasha and Charlotta with her dog go out.*)

LOPAKHIN: And so, till spring. Come along, my friends.... Till we meet! (*Goes out.*)

(*Lyubov Andreyevna and Gayev are left alone. As though they had been waiting for this, they fall onto each other's necks and break into quiet, restrained sobs, afraid of being heard.*)

GAYEV (*in despair*): My sister, my sister....

LYUBOV ANDREYEVNA: Oh, my dear, sweet, lovely orchard!...My life, my youth, my happiness, good-bye!...Good-bye!

ANYA'S VOICE (*gaily calling*): Mama!

TROFIMOV'S VOICE (*gay and excited*): Aa-oo!

LYUBOV ANDREYEVNA: One last look at these walls, these windows....Mother loved to walk about in this room....

GAYEV: My sister, my sister!

ANYA'S VOICE: Mama!

TROFIMOV'S VOICE: Aa-oo!

LYUBOV ANDREYEVNA: We're coming! (*They go out.*)

(*The stage is empty. There is the sound of doors being locked, then of the carriages driving away. It grows quiet. In the stillness there is the dull thud of an ax on a tree, a forlorn, melancholy sound. Footsteps are heard. From the door on the right Firs appears. He is dressed as always in a jacket and white waistcoat, and wears slippers. He is ill.*)

FIRS (*goes to the door and tries the handle*): Locked. They have gone....(*Sits down on the sofa.*) They've forgotten me....Never mind....I'll sit here awhile....I expect Leonid Andreich hasn't put on his fur coat and has gone off in his overcoat. (*Sighs anxiously.*) And I didn't see to it....When they're young, they're green! (*Mumbles something which cannot be understood.*) I'll lie down awhile....There's no strength left in you, nothing's left, nothing....Ach, you...addlepate! (*Lies motionless.*)

(*A distant sound is heard that seems to come from the sky, the sound of a snapped string mournfully dying away. A stillness falls, and nothing is heard but the thud of the ax on a tree far away in the orchard.*)

ANTON CHEKHOV (1860–1904)

From Letters of Anton Chekov 1888–1903

TRANSLATED BY MICHAEL HENRY HEIM WITH SIMON KARLINSKY

Chekhov, like Ibsen, was an inveterate letter writer. In letters to family members and colleagues, he wrote quite frankly about his hopes, expectations, and difficulties regarding his work. Chekhov's letters concerning his purpose as an artist and his play *The Cherry Orchard* give us some insight into his anxieties and his hopes for his work. His awareness of the difficulties he faced in his writing helps us understand how his plays developed into complex and demanding works.

October 4, 1888

The people I fear are those who look for tendentiousness between the lines and are determined to see me as either liberal or conservative. I am neither liberal, nor conservative, nor gradualist, nor monk, nor indifferentist. I should like to be a free artist and nothing else. That is why I cultivate no particular predilection for policemen, butchers, scientists, writers, or the younger generation. I look upon tags and labels as prejudices. My holy of holies is the human body, health, intelligence, talent, inspiration, love and the most absolute freedom imaginable, freedom from violence and lies.

November 25, 1892

Keep in mind that the writers we call eternal or simply good, the writers who intoxicate us, have one highly important trait in common: They are moving towards something definite and beckon you to follow, and you feel with your entire being, not only with your mind, that they have a certain goal, like the ghost of Hamlet's father, which had a motive for coming and stirring Hamlet's imagination. Depending on their caliber, some have immediate goals—the abolition of serfdom, the liberation of one's country, politics, beauty, or simply vodka . . .—while the goals of others are more remote—God, life after death, the happiness of mankind, etc. The best of them are realistic and describe life as it is, but because each line is saturated with the consciousness of its goal, you feel life as it should be in addition to life as it is, and you are captivated by it. But what about us? Us! We describe life as it is and stop dead right there. We wouldn't lift a hoof if you lit into us with a whip. We have neither immediate nor remote goals, and there is an emptiness in our souls. We have no politics, we don't believe in revolution, there is no God, we're not afraid of ghosts, and I personally am not even afraid of death or blindness. If you want nothing, hope for nothing, and fear nothing, you cannot be an artist.

To K. S. Stanislavsky°
Yalta. Oct. 30, 1903

When I was writing Lopakhin, I thought of it as a part for you. If for any reason you don't care for it, take the part of Gayev. Lopakhin is a merchant, of course, but he is a very decent person in every sense. He must behave with perfect decorum, like an educated man, with no petty ways or tricks of any sort, and it seemed to me this part, the central one of the play, would come out brilliantly in your hands. . . . In choosing an actor for the part you must remember that Varya, a serious and religious girl, is in love with Lopakhin; she wouldn't be in love with a mere money-grubber. . . .

To Vl. I. Nemirovich-Danchenko°
Yalta. Nov. 2, 1903

. . . Pishchik is a Russian, an old man, worn out by the gout, age, and satiety; stout, dressed in a sleeveless undercoat (à la Simov [an actor in the Moscow Art Theatre]), boots without heels. Lopakhin—a white waistcoat, yellow shoes; when walking, swings his arms, a broad stride, thinks deeply while walking, walks as if on a straight line. Hair not short, and therefore often throws back his head; while in thought he passes his hand through his beard, combing it from the back forward, i. e., from the neck toward the mouth. Trofimov, I think, is clear. Varya—black dress, wide belt.

Three years I spent writing "The Cherry Orchard," and for three years I have been telling you that it is necessary to invite an actress for the role of Lyubov Andreyevna. And now you see you are trying to solve a puzzle that won't work out.

To K. S. Alekseyev (Stanislavsky)
Yalta, Nov. 5, 1903

The house in the play is two-storied, a large one. But in the third act does it not speak of a stairway leading down? Nevertheless, this third act worries me. . . . N. has it that the third act takes place in "some kind of hotel"; . . . evidently I made an error in the play. The action does not pass in "some kind of hotel," but in a *drawing room*. If I mention a hotel in the play, which I cannot now doubt, after Vl. Iv.'s [Nemirovich-Danchenko] letter, please telegraph me. We must correct it; we cannot issue it thus, with grave errors distorting its meaning.

The house must be large, solid; wooden (like Aksakov's, which, I think, S. T. Morozov has seen) or stone, it is all the same. It is very old and imposing; country residents do not take such houses; such houses are usually wrecked and the material employed for the construction of a country house. The furniture is ancient, stylish, solid; ruin and debt have not affected the surroundings.

When they buy such a house, they reason thus: it is cheaper and easier to build a new and smaller one than to repair this old one.

Your shepherd played well. That was most essential.

K. S. Stanislavsky: Konstantin Stanislavski (1863–1938), director with the Moscow Art Theatre, which produced most of Chekhov's plays.
Vl. I. Nemirovich-Danchenko: Vladimir Ivanovich Nemirovich-Danchenko (1858–1943), novelist and codirector of the Moscow Art Theatre.

PETER BROOK (b. 1925)

On Chekhov 1987

Peter Brook has established himself as one of the most distinguished directors of recent years. He was educated at Oxford University and has been a director of the Royal Shakespeare Company in England. In 1987, he directed *The Cherry Orchard* at the Brooklyn Academy of Music. Some of his thoughts as he prepared to direct the play are presented here, showing his awareness of Chekhov's "film sense" in a play that was written just as film was emerging as a popular form. He is also aware of Chekhov's personal vision of death and sees it expressed in the circumstances of the play.

Chekhov always looked for what's natural; he wanted performances and productions to be as limpid as life itself. Chekhov's writing is extremely concentrated, employing a minimum of words; in a way, it is similar to Pinter or Beckett. As with them, it is construction that counts, rhythm, the purely theatrical poetry that comes not from beautiful words but from the right word at the right moment. In the theater, someone can say "yes" in such a way that the "yes" is no longer ordinary—it can become a beautiful word, because it is the perfect expression of what cannot be expressed in any other way. With Chekhov, periods, commas, points of suspension are all of a fundamental importance, as fundamental as the "pauses" precisely indicated by Beckett. If one fails to observe them, one loses the rhythm and tensions of the play. In Chekhov's work, the punctuation represents a series of coded messages which record characters' relationships and emotions, the moments at which ideas come together or follow their own course. The punctuation enables us to grasp what the words conceal.

Chekhov is like a perfect filmmaker. Instead of cutting from one image to another—perhaps from one place to another—he switches from one emotion to another just before it gets too heavy. At the precise moment when the spectator risks becoming too involved in a character, an unexpected situation cuts across: Nothing is stable. Chekhov portrays individuals and a society in a state of perpetual change, he is the dramatist of life's movement, simultaneously smiling and serious, amusing and bitter—completely free from the "music," the Slav "nostalgia" that Paris nightclubs still preserve. He often stated that his plays were comedies—this was the central issue of his conflict with Stanislavsky.

But it's wrong to conclude that *The Cherry Orchard* should be performed as a vaudeville. Chekhov is an infinitely detailed observer of the human comedy. As a doctor, he knew the meaning of certain kinds of behavior, how to discern what was essential, to expose what he diagnosed. Although he shows tenderness and an attentive sympathy, he never sentimentalizes. One doesn't imagine a doctor shedding tears over the illnesses of his patients. He learns how to balance compassion with distance.

In Chekhov's work, death is omnipresent—he knew it well—but there is nothing negative or unsavory in its presence. The awareness of death is balanced with a desire to live. His characters possess a sense of the present moment, and the need to taste it fully. As in great tragedies, one finds a harmony between life and death.

Chekhov died young, having traveled, written, and loved enormously, having taken part in the events of his day, in great schemes of social reform. He died shortly after asking for some champagne, and his coffin was transported in a wagon bearing the inscription "Fresh Oysters." His awareness of death, and of the precious moments that could be lived, endows his work with a sense of the relative: in other words, a viewpoint from which the tragic is always a bit absurd.

In Chekhov's work, each character has its own existence: not one of them resembles another, particularly in *The Cherry Orchard,* which presents a microcosm of the political tendencies of the time. There are those who believe in social transformations, others attached to a disappearing past. None of them can achieve satisfaction or plenitude, and seen from outside, their existences might well appear empty, senseless. But they all burn with intense desires. They are not disillusioned, quite the contrary: In their own ways, they are all searching for a better quality of life, emotionally and socially. Their drama is that society—the outside world—blocks their energy. The complexity of their behavior is not indicated in the words, it emerges from the mosaic construction of an infinite number of details. What is essential is to see that these are not plays about lethargic people. They are hypervital people in a lethargic world, forced to dramatize the minutest happening out of a passionate desire to live. They have not given up.

Drama in the Early and Mid-Twentieth Century

The realist tradition in drama has certain expressionist qualities evident in the symbolic actions in Strindberg's *Miss Julie* and certain romantic fantasies seen in later plays of Ibsen. But on the surface the plays appear realistic, consisting of a sequence of events that we might imagine happening in real life. The subject matter is also in the tradition of naturalism because it is drawn from life and not beautified or toned down for the middle-class audience.

But in the early to mid-twentieth century, realistic drama took a new turn, incorporating distortions of reality that border on the unreal or *surreal*. From the time of Anton Chekhov in 1903 to that of Samuel Beckett in the 1950s, drama exploited the possibilities of realism, antirealism, and the poetic expansion of expressionism.

The Heritage of Realism

In the late nineteenth century, realism was often perceived as too severe for an audience that had loved melodrama. Realistic plays forced comfortable audiences to observe psychological and physical problems that their status as members of the middle class usually allowed them to avoid. Audiences often protested loudly at this painful experience.

Early in the twentieth century, Susan Glaspell (1876–1948) began writing plays for the pleasure of having them read in her own living room in Provincetown, Massachusetts. *Trifles* (1916) told the story of a murdered husband in a deadpan fashion without alluding directly to the abusive nature of the husband and the ultimate resistance of the wife. The play may be said to be realistic on the surface, but its deep structure is symbolic, and its indirectness implies an experimental attitude toward the writing of plays.

The technique of realism could, however, be adapted for many different purposes, and eventually realism was reshaped to satisfy middle-class sensibilities by commercial playwrights, who produced popular, pleasant plays. By the 1920s in Europe and the 1930s in the United States, theatergoing audiences expected plays to be realistic. Even the light comedies dominating the commercial stage were in a more or less realistic mode. Anything that disturbed the illusion of realism was thought to be a flaw.

494

Reactions to the comfortable use of realistic techniques were numerous, especially after World War I. One extreme reaction was that of **Dadaism**. Through the Dadaists' chief propagandist, Tristan Tzara (1896–1963), the group promoted an art that was essentially enigmatic and incoherent to the average person. That was its point. The Dadaists blamed World War I on sensible, middle-class people who were logical and well intentioned but never questioned convention. The brief plays that were performed in many Dadaist clubs in Europe often featured actors speaking simultaneously so that nothing they said could be understood. The purpose was to confound the normal expectations of theatergoers.

Other developments were also making it possible for playwrights to experiment and move away from a strict reliance on "comfortable" realism. By World War I, motion pictures had begun to make melodramatic entertainment available to most people in the world. Even when films were silent, they relied on techniques that had been common on the nineteenth-century stage. With their growing domination of popular dramatic entertainment, films provided an outlet for the expectations of middle-class audiences, freeing more imaginative playwrights to experiment and develop in different directions.

Realism and Myth

The incorporation of myth in drama offered new opportunities to expand the limits of realism. Sigmund Freud's theories of psychoanalysis at the turn of the century stimulated a new interest in myth and dreams as psychological links between people. Freud studied Greek myths for clues to the psychic state of his patients, and he published a number of commentaries on Greek plays and on *Hamlet*. (See excerpt on pp. 73–76.) The psychologist Carl Jung, a follower of Freud who eventually split with him, helped give a powerful impetus to the interest in dreams and the symbolism of myth by suggesting that all members of a culture share an inborn knowledge of the basic myths of the culture. Jung postulated a collective unconscious, a repository of mythic material in the mind that all humans inherit as part of their birthright. This theory gave credence to the power of myth in everyday life; along with Freud's theories, it was one of the most important ideas empowering drama and other art forms in the twentieth century. Playwrights who used elements of myth in their plays produced a poetic form of realism that dealt with a level of truth common to all humans.

Myth and Culture

Some non-European drama depends on interpretation of local myth in relation to the culture or cultures that produce it. Wole Soyinka's background as a Nigerian familiar with Yoruba culture and myth, along with his formal education in England, prepared him for a career that expanded the horizons of drama for both Nigerian and European audiences.

Soyinka's experimentation has spanned two traditions—modern European theater and modern ritual theater of the Yoruba people of Nigeria. Traditional Yoruba drama develops from religious celebrations and annual festivals and includes music and dance. Soyinka's plays, including *The Strong Breed* (1962), concern themselves with African traditions and issues, but they often also explore mythic forces that link European and African cultures. His plays have been produced throughout the world and have demonstrated the universality of community and the anxiety it sometimes breeds in the individual. Soyinka has also written critical studies on Yoruba tragedy and has interpreted, translated, and produced Greek tragedy.

Poetic Realism

The Abbey Theatre in Dublin, which functioned with distinction from the turn of the century, produced major works by John Millington Synge, W. B. Yeats, Sean O'Casey, and Lady Gregory. Lady Gregory's peasant plays concentrated on the charming, the amusing, and occasionally the grotesque. She tried to represent the dialect she heard in the west of Ireland, a dialect that was distinctive, poetic, and colorful. She also took advantage of local Irish myths and used some of them for her most powerful plays, such as *Dervorgilla* and *Grania*, both portraits of passionate women from Irish legend and myth.

John Millington Synge, like Lady Gregory, was interested in both myth and peasant dialects. His plays are difficult to fit into a realist mold, although they are sometimes naturalistic on the surface. Some audiences reacted violently to his portrayals of peasant life because they were unflattering. Synge's plays were sometimes directly connected with ancient Irish myth; *Deirdre of the Sorrows* (1910) concerns a willful Irish princess who runs off with a young warrior and his brothers on the eve of her wedding to an old king. The story ends sadly for Deirdre, and she is regarded as a fated heroine, assuming almost the stature of a Greek tragic figure. Synge's most popular one-act play, *Riders to the Sea* (1904), reveals his gift for emulating the Irish way of speaking English in Ireland's western county of Mayo. His creation of peasant dialogue remains one of his most important contributions to modern drama.

In the United States, Eugene O'Neill, influenced by Strindberg, experimented with realism, first by presenting stark, powerful plays that disturbed his audiences. *The Hairy Ape* (1922) portrayed a primitive coal stoker on a passenger liner who awakened base emotions in the more refined passengers. In *The Emperor Jones* (1920), O'Neill produced the first important American expressionist play. The shifting scenery, created by lighting, was dreamlike and at times frightening. The experience of the play reflected the frightening psychic experiences of the main character, Brutus Jones.

O'Neill also experimented with more poetic forms of realism. In *Desire under the Elms* (1924), he explores the myth of Phaedra—centering on her incestuous love for her husband's son—but sets it in rural New England on a rocky farm. In the tradition of realism, the play treats unpleasant themes: a son's distrust and dishonoring of his father, lust between a son and his stepmother, and the murder of a baby to "prove" love. But it is not simply realistic. Without its underpinning of myth, the play would be sordid, but the myth helps us see that fate operates even today, not in terms of messages from the gods but rather in terms of messages from our hearts and bodies. Lust is a force in nature that drives and destroys.

Meanwhile, in Fascist Spain, Federico García Lorca, also a poetic realist, was uncovering dark emotional centers of the psyche in his *House of Bernarda Alba* (1936), which explores erotic forces repressed and then set loose. Lorca was opposed to Fascism and was murdered by a Fascist agent. His plays reveal a bleakness of spirit that helps us imagine the darkness—moral and psychological—that enveloped Europe in the 1940s.

Social Realism

Ten years after *Desire under the Elms* enjoyed popularity, a taste for plays based on **social realism** developed. This was realism with a political conscience. Because the world was in the throes of a depression that had reduced many people to destitution and homelessness, drama began to aim at awakening governments to the consequences of unbridled capitalism and the depressions that freewheeling economies produced.

Plays such as Jack Kirkland's *Tobacco Road* (1933), adapted from Erskine Caldwell's novel, presented a grim portrait of rural poverty in the United States. Sidney Kingsley's *Dead End* (1935) portrayed the lives of virtually homeless boys on the Lower East Side of Manhattan. In the same year, Maxwell Anderson produced a verse tragedy, *Winterset*, with gangsters and gangsterism at its core. Also in 1935, Clifford Odets produced *Waiting for Lefty*, an openly leftist labor drama. These plays' realist credentials lay primarily in their effort to show audiences portraits of life that might shock their middle-class sensibilities.

Realism and Expressionism

O'Neill's later plays shed the underpinnings of myth and developed a powerful realistic style, as seen in *The Iceman Cometh* (1939), set in a dingy bar filled with patrons living on the edge, listening to Theodor Hickman (Hickey) and Harry Hope give their philosophy of life. During this period, O'Neill also wrote a haunting one-act play, *Hughie* (1941), set in a shabby hotel lobby late at night. In it, Erie Smith, a small-time gambler, shares his views of life with the hotel night manager, Charlie Hughes. The play is simple but intense and moving. One of O'Neill's greatest plays, *Long Day's Journey into Night*, completed in 1941 but not published or produced until 1956, took him in a new direction. For the first time, he began an analysis of his own tortured family background, which included alcoholism and drug addiction. The play was so searing and painful that O'Neill sequestered it with Random House, instructing publisher Bennett Cerf not to publish it until twenty-five years after his death. O'Neill's wife, however, broke the will and had the play produced. It has since become the vehicle for some of the best performances of the latter part of the twentieth century.

After Eugene O'Neill's experiments, later American dramatists looked for new ways to expand the resources of realism while retaining its power. The use of **expressionism**—often poetic in language and effect—was one solution that appealed to both Tennessee Williams and Arthur Miller. Expressionism developed in the first and second decades of the twentieth century. The movement began in Germany and was influenced by some of Strindberg's work. Because expressionism takes many forms, there is no simple way to define the term except as an alternative to realistic drama. Instead of having realistic sets, the stage may sometimes be barren or flooded with light or draped. Characters sometimes become symbolic; dialogue is often sharp, abrupt, enigmatic. The German theater saw its earliest developments of expressionism in the work of Frank Wedekind, whose first play, *Spring Awakening*, abandoned a naturalistic style to explore sexual repression. Wedekind's work influenced later German playwrights such as George Kaiser, Ernst Toller, Erwin Piscator, and Bertolt Brecht, whose *Threepenny Opera* (1928) incorporated some of the hallmarks of expressionism, such as a music-hall atmosphere and broadly drawn characters.

Later American playwrights modified the characteristics of expressionism; they melded expressionist elements, such as fantastic sets and highly poetic diction, with a relatively realistic style. Tennessee Williams's *The Glass Menagerie*

Figure 21. Expressionistic setting in Arthur Miller's *Death of a Salesman*.

(1944) and Arthur Miller's *Death of a Salesman* (1949) both use expressionist techniques. Williams's poetic stage directions make clear that he is drawing on nonrealistic dramatic devices. He describes the scene as "memory and . . . therefore nonrealistic." He calls for an interior "rather dim and poetic," and he uses a character who also steps outside the staged action to serve as a narrator—one who "takes whatever license with dramatic convention as is convenient to his purposes." As the narrator tells his story, the walls of the building seem to melt away, revealing the inside of a house and the lives and fantasies of his mother and sister, both caught in their own distorted visions of life.

Arthur Miller's original image for *Death of a Salesman* was the inside of Willy Loman's mind; Jo Mielziner's expressionist set represented his idea as a cross-section of Loman's house. As the action in one room concluded, lights went up to begin action in another (Figure 21). This evocative staging influenced the production of numerous plays by later writers. In the original set, a scrim, or gauze screen, was painted with branches and leaves. When this scrim was lit from the front for memory scenes, the set was transformed to evoke an earlier time when the sons were boys.

Miller used expressionist techniques to create the hallucinatory sequences when Willy talks with Ben, the man who walked into the jungle poor and walked out a millionaire, and when Biff recalls seeing Willy with the woman in Boston.

For Williams and Miller, expressionism offered a way to bring other worlds to bear on the staged action—the worlds of dream and fantasy. And although expressionism made some inroads in American theater, the techniques of realism persisted and developed. Lorraine Hansberry's *A Raisin in the Sun* (1959) uses basically realistic staging and dialogue to portray the difficulties of the members of one family in reaching for opportunity to overcome poverty. Hansberry does not use the expressionist techniques of Miller. Her only exotic touch is the visit of the African young man, Asagai, who offers a moment of cultural counterpoint. Hansberry's realism is essentially conservative.

Antirealism

Surrealism (literally, "beyond realism") in the early twentieth century was based originally on an interpretation of experience not through the lucid mind of the waking person but through the mind of the dreamer, the unconscious mind that Freud described. Surrealism augmented or, for some playwrights, supplanted realism and became a means of distorting reality for emotional purposes.

When Pirandello's six characters come onstage looking for their author in *Six Characters in Search of an Author* (1921), no one believes that they are characters rather than actors. Pirandello's play is an examination of the realities we take for granted in drama. He turns the world of expectation in drama upside down. He reminds us that what we assume to be real is always questionable: we cannot be sure of anything; we must presume that things are true, and in some cases we must take them on faith.

Pirandello's philosophy dominated his stories, plays, and novels. His questioning of the certainty of human knowledge was designed to undermine his audience's faith in an absolute reality. Modern physicists have concurred with philosophers, ancient and modern, who question everyday reality. Pirandello was influenced by the modern theories of relativity that physicists were developing, and he found in them validation of his own attack on certainty.

Epic Theater

Bertolt Brecht (1898–1956) began writing plays just after World War I. He was a political dramatist who rejected the theater of his day, which valued the realistic "well-made play," in which all the parts fit perfectly together and function almost as a machine. His feeling was that such plays were too mechanical, like a "clockwork mouse."

Exploring the style of his predecessor Irwin Piscator, Brecht developed epic theater. The term implies a sequence of actions or episodes of the kind found in Homer's *Iliad*. In epic theater, the sense of dramatic illusion is continually counteracted by reminders from the stage that one is watching a play. Stark, harsh lighting, blank stages, placards announcing changes of scenes, bands playing music onstage, and long, discomfiting pauses make it impossible for an audience to become totally immersed in a realistic illusion. Brecht, offering a genuine alternative to realistic drama, wanted the audience to analyze a play's thematic content rather than to sit back and be entertained. He believed that realistic drama convinced audiences that the play's vision of reality described not just things as they are but things as they must be. Such drama, Brecht asserted, helped maintain the social problems that it portrayed by reinforcing, rather than challenging, their reality.

Brecht's *Mother Courage* (written in 1939) is an antiwar drama staged early in World War II (1941). The use of song, an unreal setting, and an unusual historical perspective (the Thirty Years' War in the seventeenth century) help to achieve the "defamiliarization" that Brecht thought drama ought to produce in its audiences. The techniques of epic theater in *Galileo* (1938–1939) and *The Good Woman of Setzuan* (1943)—a study of the immoralities that prosper under capitalism—were imitated by playwrights in the 1950s. Hardly a major play from that period is free of Brecht's influence.

Absurdist Drama

The critic Martin Esslin coined the term **theater of the absurd** when describing the work of Samuel Beckett (1906–1989), the Irish playwright whose dramas often dispense with almost everything that makes a well-made play well made. Some of his plays have no actors onstage—amplified breathing is the only hint of human presence in one case. Some have little or no plot; others have no words. His theater is minimalist, offering a stage reality that seems cut to the bone, without the usual realistic devices of plot, character development, and intricate setting.

Eugène Ionesco (1909–1994) is said to have been the first of the postwar absurdist dramatists, with his production of *The Bald Soprano* and *The Lesson* (both in 1951). Ionesco called them "anti-plays" because they avoided the normal causal relationship of actions and realistic expectations of conventional drama.

The theater of the absurd assumes that the world is meaningless, that meaning is a human concept, and that individuals must create significance and not rely on institutions or traditions to provide it. The absurdist movement grew out of **existentialism**, a postwar French philosophy demanding that the individual face the emptiness of the universe and create meaning in a life that has no inherent meaning. Beckett's *Waiting for Godot* (1952) captured the modern imagination and established a landmark in absurdist drama.

In *Waiting for Godot,* two tramps, Vladimir and Estragon, meet near a tree where they expect Godot to arrive to talk with them. The play has two acts that both end with a small boy explaining that Godot cannot come today but will come tomorrow. Godot is not coming, and the tramps who wait for Godot will wait forever. While they wait, they entertain themselves with vaudeville routines and eventually are met by a rich man, Pozzo, and his slave, Lucky. Lucky, on the command "Think, pig," speaks in a stream of garbled phrases that evoke Western philosophy and religion but that remain incoherent. Pozzo and Lucky have no interest in joining Vladimir and Estragon in waiting for Godot. They leave the two alone, waiting—afraid to leave for fear of missing Godot, but uncertain that Godot will ever arrive.

Beckett seems to be saying that in an absurd world, such gestures are necessary to create the sense of significance that people need to live. His characters' awareness of an audience and his refusal to create a drama in which an audience can "lose" itself in a comfortable surface of realistic illusion are, in their own way, indebted to Brecht.

Beckett's *Krapp's Last Tape* (1958) places some extraordinary limitations on performance. Krapp is the only person onstage throughout the play, and his dialogues are with tapes of himself made many years before. The situation is absurd, but as Beckett reveals to us, the absurd has its own complexities, and situations such as Krapp's can sustain complex interpretations. Beckett expects his audience to analyze the drama, not merely to be entertained.

The illusion of reality is shed almost entirely in *Endgame* (1957). Hamm cannot move. His parents, both legless, are in trashcans onstage. Clov performs all the play's movement on a barren, cellarlike stage.

Beckett's *Happy Days* (1961) is generally thought to be his most optimistic play. Winnie, who talks almost nonstop throughout, seems mired in trivia and the details of everyday life. Yet, she can pause for philosophical observations on the nature of her existence and position herself thoughtfully in regard to the world. In the first act she is buried in a mound of earth up to her waist, and in the second act she is buried up to her neck, but her positive attitude intensifies. She is doing the best she can. Willy, her husband, hardly says a word and does not begin to act until the last minute of the play, at which time his action is ambiguous. *Happy Days*, while similar to Beckett's other absurdist plays, still intrigues audiences in the twenty-first century. It speaks to the hopeful among us, but it also offers a view of life that is far from sugar coated. It is absurd in the sense that it does not offer an easy answer to the questions raised by the limitations of Winnie's and Willy's existence.

The great plays of this period reflect the values of the cultures from which they spring. They make comments on life in the modern world and question the values that the culture takes for granted. The drama of this part of the twentieth century is a drama of examination.

The Early- and Mid-Twentieth-Century Stage

The physical stage continued its evolution into the twentieth century, although it depended on the proscenium arch and the concept of the "fourth wall" most of the time, especially in the development of the musical theater, which was, to an extent, a substitute for the nineteenth-century melodrama. With early silent films and then mid-century musicals, the popular stage was still home to melodramatic entertainment.

One of the primary aims of early-twentieth-century theater designs was to create spaces in which the audience and the actors became more intimate than in the pure proscenium theater, which treated the audience almost as voyeurs. The smaller theaters, such as the Vieux Colombier (Figure 22), opened the proscenium and extended the stage forward, making it possible for actors to be much closer to the audience and to produce a more involving experience.

In France and England, so-called little theaters developed quickly even before the first world war, taking advantage of this newfound intimacy. In the United States, the growth of "little" theaters led to the founding, in 1915, of the Provincetown Players by George Cram Cook, Eugene O'Neill, and Susan Glaspell. This company held its early performances at the end of a wharf in an old abandoned fish house in Provincetown, Massachusetts (see Figure 23).

Eventually the Provincetown Players moved to New York City, where the Provincetown Playhouse still exists, now connected with New York University. Most major cities (Boston, New York, Chicago, and Detroit) and even some smaller cities produced plays in "little" theaters, some of which still exist. The Theatre Guild formed in 1919 in the United States for the purpose of producing plays that were not likely to have a broad commercial appeal. It became one of the most distinguished theater companies of its time.

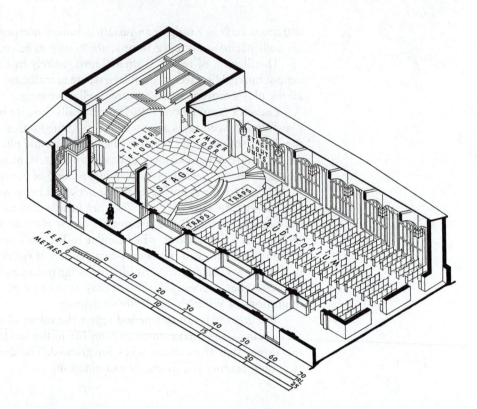

Figure 22. The Vieux Colombier, Paris, 1920.

Although he worked directly on stage in Paris for only a few years in the 1920s, Antonin Artaud (1896–1948) made a lasting impression on drama theory and theatrical space. His concept of the **theater of cruelty** helped shape the modern theater as we know it. The cruelty he prosposed was psychological in that he wanted the audience to relinquish its comfortable and privileged position in the theater and to feel the discomfort produced by facing unpleasant ideas and events. This was a complete departure from the goal of earlier melodrama, which soothed the audience with happy endings and avoided raising profound and unanswerable questions. Artaud proposed avoiding standard theaters altogether and moving drama into a barn or warehouse or similar open space. Even today, many small theater companies follow his lead and perform in such spaces as garages and storefronts.

Technical developments in larger theaters naturally continued throughout the early part of the century, with improved lighting, revolving stages, and complex arrangements of flies that lowered and then raised elaborate scenery for set changes. Some experiments in staging brought the audience to all sides of the stage so that they were virtually "involved" in such necessary activities as entrances and exits. Theater in the round developed in the 1930s, and it helped create some of the most intense experiences in the mid-century, particularly those that depended on surrealist effects. Artaud was a proponent of theater in the round because the audience could never feel separated from the action, as it would in a proscenium theater. Many of the stage settings in the larger theaters in Europe and the United States generated exciting visual designs for expressionist and surrealist plays that are still talked about as visionary productions.

Figure 23. The original theater of the Provincetown Players was a converted fishing shack on Lewis Wharf, in Provincetown, Massachusetts.

Expressionist drama, such as *Miss Julie* and other late-nineteenth-century experimental works, often attempted to examine transformations of the inner life of characters through the use of symbolism. Expressionist plays favored a certain form of abstraction, represented in their stage settings, that attempted to be emotionally representational rather than realistic in the usual sense. The stage settings for O'Neill's plays, as well as those for Elmer Rice's *The Adding Machine* (1923), have been interpreted in many interesting ways, but they are often described as symbolic. In a Queens College production of Rice's *The Adding Machine*, the primary character is Mr. Zero, who eventually kills Boss. The sets allude visually to the machine, as in Figure 24, where the interior of the machine suggests a virtual cave as Mr. Zero approaches Heaven. The play itself is a commentary on the influence of the machine on modern life, and it may be even more relevant in the twenty-first century than it was in the twentieth.

The Early- and Mid-Twentieth-Century Actor

From the Moscow Art Theater in the late 1890s to the Group Theatre in the United States in 1931, the most persistent influence on acting and acting theory was Constantin Stanislavski (1863–1938) (Figure 25). Stanislavski, a name

Figure 24. Elmer Rice's *The Adding Machine*, Queens College Drama, Theatre, and Dance Production, 1999.

adopted for the stage, was born into a prosperous Russian family but decided to make his own way acting and directing. His productions of Gorky and Chekhov were legendary, and it was while working on these plays that he developed acting techniques that actors are still using today. He wished above all to encourage a natural style of acting that would be instantly recognized as offering insight into the truth of life. Years of successful melodramas had produced an exaggerated mode of acting, both "theatrical" in the pejorative sense and rhetorical in its demand for attention. It was against this "star" system, which relied entirely on stars of the magnitude of Edwin Forrest, William Macready, Edmund Kean, Junius Brutus Booth, William Gillette, Sarah Bernhardt, and others, that Stanislavski rebelled.

Instead, Stanislavski insisted that the actor prepare for a role using a method rooted in modern psychology—searching for the subconscious energy that would inform the actor and permit him or her to understand a character's most profound feelings. Applying Stanislavski's method, the actor should first analyze the scenes carefully to establish the underlying motive of the character and then attempt to recreate within himself or herself the motivation and the emotional content of the action by reflecting on his or her own life and drawing from a personal store of emotional experience. Only then was the actor ready to go on stage and perform the scene.

Stanislavski also developed exercises for actors, some of which he discusses in *An Actor Prepares* (1936). One of the exercises on his principle of concentration of attention requires that the actor concentrate on something

Figure 25. Constantin Stanislavski as Gayev in Chekhov's *The Cherry Orchard*, 1923.

on stage—it must arrest the actor's attention and utterly absorb the actor in order to generate the closeness to truth that Stanislavski demanded from his company. As he said, "Here we are dealing with powers of observation that are subconscious in their origin. Our ordinary type of attention is not sufficiently far-reaching to carry out the process of penetrating another person's soul." Some of the most famous actors of the twentieth century, including Marlon Brando, Al Pacino, Jane Fonda, and Jack Nicholson, employed the basic principles of "The Method," which they learned as students of Lee Strasberg's Actor's Studio in New York City in the 1940s and 1950s.

Some form of naturalism was dominant on the stage in the first half of the century, but expressionist plays such as O'Neill's *The Emperor Jones* (1920), *The Hairy Ape* (1922), and *The Great God Brown* (1926) depended on a style of acting that verged on distortion and exaggeration. The characters were meant to be larger than life, so the style of acting followed suit, but it could not be described as overly theatrical in the style that Stanislavski and others condemned. Many of the best actors of the period also worked in films. Examples include Emile Jannings (1887–1950), Sir Cedric Hardwicke (1893–1964), Sibyl Thorndike (1882–1976), John Barrymore (1882–1942), and Laurette Taylor (1884–1946). Each was renowned, but much of their best work was done in film and not on the stage. Most of these distinguished actors relied on conventional acting training rather than following Stanislavski, although most of them were aware of his ideas and were, if only indirectly, affected by them.

On a theoretical level, the work of Bertolt Brecht (1898–1956) reinforced Artaud's ideas about acting and the structure of drama in Europe and elsewhere between the two world wars. Brecht's concept of epic theater and the "alienation effect" took root and influenced theaters and actors everywhere. For example, Brecht insisted on controlling the amount of empathy an actor on stage might evoke. He also wished to avoid "magic" on stage, by which he meant the creation of an illusion of reality. In this sense, he was anti-Aristotelian. He said,

> On the Epic stage, no attempt is made to create the atmosphere of a particular place (a room at evening, a street in autumn), or to generate a mood by a broken speech-rhythm. The actor does not warm the audience up by unloosing a flood of temperament, nor cast a spell over them by tightening his muscles. In short, no effort is made to put the audience into a trance and give them the illusion of witnessing natural, unrehearsed events.

Brecht's staging often was symbolic in nature, and his actors often were outfitted in oversized clothing and spoke in an unnatural fashion. His staging employed dance and/or music as needed. A Communist protesting the brutalities of the Nazis, Brecht expressed a political message between the wars, as in his extraordinary play *Galileo*, which was written in 1938 and 1939 and was first produced in Hollywood in 1947, with Charles Laughton in the title role. Galileo had been punished by the Catholic Church for his discovery that the earth revolves around the sun, not the other way around. Brecht's *Galileo* became a symbol for people resisting tyranny of all kinds. Brecht, like many other playwrights in the first half of the twentieth century, was searching for ways to express serious ideas through the medium of drama. They knew they could not rely on the ordinary realistic styles of the late nineteenth century, so they had to invent new ways to write and new ways to act.

Date	Theater	Political	Social/Cultural
1850–1900	**1853–1931:** David Belasco, American producer who uses pictorial realism in staging and creates "stars" on the New York stage	**1857:** Sepoy mutiny in India against British officers	**1853:** U.S. Navy arrives in Tokyo Bay to negotiate a trade treaty.
	1862–1928: Adolphe Appia, influential Swiss designer	**1861–1865:** Civil War in the United States	**1861:** Russia emancipates its serfs.
	1863–1938: Constantin Stanislavski, Russian actor and director	**1867:** Dominion of Canada is formed.	**1863:** U.S. Emancipation Proclamation frees slaves.
	1871–1909: John Millington Synge, Irish playwright, author of *Riders to the Sea* (1904) and *The Playboy of the Western World* (1907)	**1868–1912:** Meiji period in Japan	**1869:** The Suez Canal opens.
		1871: Feudalism in Japan ends.	
	1872–1966: Edward Gordon Craig, influential English theatrical designer		
	1873–1943: Max Reinhardt, Austrian director, producer, and theorist		**1876:** General George Custer's troops are destroyed at Little Big Horn by Sioux-Cheyennes.
	1880–1964: Sean O'Casey, Irish playwright, author of *Juno and the Paycock* (1924) and *The Plough and the Stars* (1926)		**1880–1914:** All of Africa (except Ethiopia) is rapidly colonized by European and Turkish authorities.
	1887–1954: Robert Edmond Jones, revolutionary American scenic designer		
	1888–1953: Eugene O'Neill, American playwright among whose works are *Desire under the Elms* (1924), *Mourning Becomes Electra* (1931), and *Long Day's Journey into Night* (1939–1941)	**1889:** First Japanese Constitution is enacted.	
	1896–1948: Antonin Artaud, French playwright, poet, actor, and director	**1895:** China is defeated in war by Japan. Korea becomes independent.	
	1898–1956: Bertolt Brecht, German playwright, author of *The Threepenny Opera* (1928), *Mother Courage* (1941), and *The Good Woman of Setzuan* (1943)	**1898:** Spanish-American War. Cuba is freed from Spain.	
	1898: The Irish Literary Society is founded by W. B. Yeats (1865–1939) and Lady Augusta Gregory (1852–1932). The group leads the way in creating an indigenous Irish theater.	**1899–1902:** Boer War in South Africa	

Date	Theater	Political	Social/Cultural
1900–1950	**1901–1976:** Jo Mielziner, set designer	**1900:** The Boxer Rebellion attempts to curtail Western commercial interests in China.	**1900:** Sigmund Freud (1856–1939) writes *The Interpretation of Dreams.*
	1904: The Abbey Theatre, evolved from the Irish Literary Society founded by Yeats and Lady Gregory, opens in Dublin.	**1901:** Queen Victoria of Great Britain dies and is succeeded by her son Edward VII.	**1900s:** Ragtime music becomes popular in the United States.
	1905–1984: Lillian Hellman, American playwright, author of *The Children's Hour* (1934) and *The Little Foxes* (1939). Other important American female playwrights of the period include Rachel Crothers (1878–1958), Zona Gale (1874–1938), and Susan Glaspell (1876–1948).	**1904–1905:** Russo-Japanese War. Russia is defeated, and Japan emerges as a world power.	**1901–1971:** Louis Armstrong, African American jazz trumpet player
		1905: The Sinn Fein party is founded in Dublin.	**1903:** Wilbur and Orville Wright make their first flight.
			1905–1914: More than 10 million immigrants arrive in the United States.
	1906–1989: Samuel Beckett, Irish playwright who wrote some of his plays in French, including *Waiting for Godot* (1952) and *Endgame* (1957)		**1906:** An earthquake and subsequent fire ravage San Francisco.
	1909–1994: Eugène Ionesco, playwright		**1907:** Picasso (1881–1973) paints *Les Demoiselles d'Avignon,* one of the earliest instances of the cubism movement in art.
	1911–1983: Tennessee Williams, American playwright, author of *The Glass Menagerie* (1944), *A Streetcar Named Desire* (1947), and *Cat on a Hot Tin Roof* (1955)		**1908:** Henry Ford (1863–1947) designs the Model T.
			1909: W. E. B. DuBois (1868–1963), African American civil rights leader and author, establishes the NAACP.
		1912: Sun Yat Sen is elected president of the Republic of China and founds the Kuomintang.	**1912:** The ocean liner *Titanic* sinks, killing 1,513 passengers.
	1915: George Cram Cook, Eugene O'Neill, and Susan Glaspell found the Provincetown Players in Provincetown, Massachusetts.	**1914:** World War I begins with the assassination of Austrian Archduke Franz Ferdinand in Sarajevo.	**1913:** Niels Bohr (1885–1962) formulates his theory of atomic structure.
	1915–2005: Arthur Miller, American playwright, among whose works are *Death of a Salesman* (1949) and *The Crucible* (1953)	**1916:** The Easter Rising in Ireland is suppressed by the British.	**1914:** The Panama Canal is completed.
			1915: D. W. Griffith's film *The Birth of a Nation* is released.
	1917: J. L. Williams's *Why Marry?* receives the first Pulitzer Prize for drama.	**1917:** The Russian Revolution overthrows the czar and establishes Bolshevik control under V. I. Lenin.	**c. 1916:** Albert Einstein (1879–1955) formulates his theory of relativity.
	1918: The Theatre Guild is formed in New York City.	**1919:** The Treaty of Versailles formally ends World War I.	**1918–1922:** Influenza epidemic kills 22 million people worldwide.
	1919: Actors Equity Association is officially recognized as a union in the United States.	**1920:** The Nineteenth Amendment recognizes the right of American women to vote.	**1919:** The Bauhaus, an influential school of art and architecture, is established by Walter Gropius in Germany.
	1920: Théâtre National Populaire is founded in Paris.	**1921:** Southern Ireland becomes the independent Republic of Ireland.	**1920:** Prohibition begins in the United States. It will continue until 1933.
			1920s: Jazz music evolves in New Orleans, Chicago, and New York City.

Date	Theater	Political	Social/Cultural
1900–1950 (continued)	**1921:** Italian playwright Luigi Pirandello (1867–1936) writes *Six Characters in Search of an Author*. **1923–1924:** Moscow Art Theater visits the United States for the first time. **1927:** Neil Simon is born. His plays include *The Odd Couple* (1965), *Chapter Two* (1979), and *Biloxi Blues* (1984). **1928:** Bertolt Brecht and Kurt Weill produce *The Threepenny Opera* in Berlin. **1930–1965:** Lorraine Hansberry, African American playwright, author of *A Raisin in the Sun* (1959) **1931:** The Group Theatre is founded by Harold Clurman, Cheryl Crawford, and Lee Strasberg. It will operate for ten years. **1934:** Wole Soyinka, Nigerian playwright, is born. His works include *The Strong Breed* (1962) and *A Play of Giants* (1984). **1934:** Socialist realism is declared the official artistic policy in Soviet theater.	**1921:** Ku Klux Klan activities become violent throughout the southern United States. **1921:** Sacco and Vanzetti, Italian anarchists, are sentenced to death in the United States. **1922:** Fascist dictator Benito Mussolini gains power in Italy. **1925:** Adolf Hitler reorganizes the Nazi Party and publishes volume 1 of *Mein Kampf*. **1928:** The Kellogg-Briand Pact, outlawing war, is signed in Paris by 65 states. **c. 1928:** Joseph Stalin comes to power in the Soviet Union. **1929:** The U.S. stock market crash begins the Great Depression. **1933:** New Deal economic reforms attempt to stimulate recovery from the Depression. **1933:** Adolf Hitler comes to power in Germany. German labor unions and political parties other than the Nazi Party are suppressed. Nazis erect their first concentration camp; persecution of Jews begins in Germany. **1935:** Roosevelt signs the U.S. Social Security Act. **1935:** The Nuremberg laws in Nazi Germany deprive German Jews of their citizenship and civil rights. **1935–1936:** Italy's conquest of Ethiopia **1936:** Chiang Kai-shek declares war on Japan.	**1920s:** Harlem Renaissance: African American literature, music, and art flourish in New York City. Langston Hughes (1902–1967), Zora Neale Hurston (1891–1960), Jean Toomer (1894–1967), and many others publish. **1922:** T. S. Eliot (1888–1965) publishes *The Waste Land*. **1922:** James Joyce (1882–1941) publishes *Ulysses*. **1923:** George Gershwin (1898–1937) performs *Rhapsody in Blue*. **1925:** F. Scott Fitzgerald (1896–1940) publishes *The Great Gatsby*. **1925:** Margaret Sanger (1879–1966) organizes the first international birth control conference. **1925:** John T. Scopes, schoolteacher, is tried for violating a Tennessee law that prohibits the teaching of the theory of evolution. **1926:** Ernest Hemingway (1899–1961) publishes *The Sun Also Rises*. **1926:** Duke Ellington's (1899–1974) first records appear. **1927:** *The Jazz Singer* is the first "talkie" movie. **1927:** Charles Lindbergh (1902–1974) makes the first solo nonstop transatlantic flight. **1927:** Virginia Woolf (1882–1941), English novelist, publishes *To the Lighthouse*. **1929:** William Faulkner (1897–1962) publishes *The Sound and the Fury*. **1931:** Robert Frost (1874–1963) wins the Pulitzer Prize for *Collected Poems*. **1931:** The Empire State Building in New York City is completed. **1932:** Aldous Huxley (1894–1963) publishes *Brave New World*.

Date	Theater	Political	Social/Cultural
1900–1950 (continued)	**1935:** The American plays *Dead End* by Sidney Kingsley, *Winterset* by Maxwell Anderson, and *Waiting for Lefty* by Clifford Odets are produced.	**1936–1939:** Civil War in Spain results in Generalissimo Franco's consolidation of power.	**1937:** Amelia Earhart (1897–1937), the first woman to fly across the Atlantic, vanishes over the Pacific Ocean.
	1935–1939: The Federal Theatre Project operates in the United States under the auspices of the Works Progress Administration.	**1939:** Germany invades Poland.	**1938:** Joe Louis (1914–1981), African American heavyweight boxer, defeats German Max Schmeling.
	1936: Federico García Lorca (1898–1936), Spanish playwright, writes *The House of Bernarda Alba*.	**1939:** Great Britain and France declare war on Germany and its allies.	
	1938: Antonín Artaud, French playwright and theorist, writes *The Theater and Its Double*.	**1940:** Germany invades France.	
	1940s: The era of great musical theater begins in the United States, featuring the songs of Cole Porter (1891–1964), Richard Rodgers (1902–1979), and Oscar Hammerstein (1895–1960), among many others.	**1941:** Japan attacks Pearl Harbor, and the United States enters World War II.	
		1942: Germany begins killing Jews and others in gas chambers.	
		1942: The U.S. Army interns Japanese Americans in prison camps.	**1943:** Penicillin is first used in the treatment of chronic diseases.
		1944: Allies liberate France.	
	1946: The Living Theatre is founded by Judith Malina and Julian Beck.	**1945:** Hitler commits suicide in Berlin, and Germany surrenders.	
		1945: The United States drops atomic bombs on Hiroshima and Nagasaki, Japan.	
		1946: Juan Perón is elected president of Argentina.	
	1947: The Actors Studio is founded in New York City by Robert Lewis, Elia Kazan, and Cheryl Crawford. Lee Strasberg assumes control by 1948.	**1947:** India proclaims independence and is divided into Pakistan and India.	**1947:** Jackie Robinson (1919–1972) becomes the first African American to sign a contract with a major league baseball club.
	1947–1950: The regional theater movement begins in the United States. Margo Jones opens an arena theater in Dallas, Nina Vance founds the Alley Theatre in Houston, and the Arena Stage opens in Washington, D.C.	**1948:** The Republic of Israel is proclaimed by Jewish leaders in Palestine.	
		1948: Indian leader Mahatma Gandhi is assassinated.	
	1949: The Berliner Ensemble is founded in East Berlin.	**1949:** Mao Zedong announces the establishment of the People's Republic of China.	
		1949: The North Atlantic Treaty Organization unites Canada, Western Europe, and the United States as allies.	
		1949: The apartheid system is established in South Africa.	

Susan Glaspell

"The biggest stories are written about the things which draw human beings closer together."

–Susan Glaspell

Susan Glaspell (1876–1948) was already established as a novelist when she became an important figure in early-twentieth-century drama. She was born in Davenport, Iowa, graduated from Drake University in Des Moines, and went to work as a reporter on the *Des Moines Daily News* in 1899. While there she began writing short fiction and novels, and with the beginnings of publishing success, she returned to Davenport to write. Her first novel, *The Glory of the Conquered: The Story of a Great Love* (1909), earned enough for her to spend a year in Paris. *The Visioning* (1911) was set on an army base and presented a less sentimentalized world than her first book. Back in the United States in 1911, she published her book of short stories, *Lifted Masks* (1912). One of her best novels, *Fidelity*, published in 1915, tells the story of a woman who leaves her loving husband and family to run off with a married man.

In 1908, Glaspell first met her future husband, George Cram (Jig) Cook, a traveled intellectual and Harvard graduate who was teaching at Iowa University. After that initial meeting, Cook married another woman, but five years later he was divorced for the second time. Glaspell and Cook were reintroduced in 1913 by mutual friends and eventually came to believe they were fated for each other. Because the scandal of Cook's divorces made it virtually impossible for them to live in Iowa, the couple moved to New York and Provincetown, Massachusetts.

In Provincetown, Cook wanted to involve himself in a new kind of drama, and the two of them wrote *Suppressed Desires* (1915), which they first produced in their living room. They eventually relocated to a neglected fish house on a wharf, and this playhouse was a local success. *Suppressed Desires* was a satire that poked fun at the trend of using Freudian theories to explain everyday life. In a letter to the *New York Times* (February 13, 1920), Glaspell wrote that the play "is having fun with the people who went off their heads about psychoanalysis—went 'bugs'—when this subject reached the first circle in New York to know of it." *Trifles*, written entirely by Glaspell, followed in 1916. Its story line developed from a murder in Des Moines that Glaspell was familiar with from her days as a journalist.

The Provincetown Players, which Glaspell and Cook founded with Eugene O'Neill, quickly became an influential platform for a number of important American writers, such as Edna St. Vincent Millay and Eugene O'Neill, whose first play, *Bound East for Cardiff*, was produced at the Wharf Theatre in 1916. Eventually the Provincetown Players relocated to New York, where they attracted other important playwrights and produced additional plays by Glaspell and O'Neill.

Glaspell's one-act plays, including *Close the Book* (1917), *A Woman's Honor* (1918), and *Tickless Time* (1919), were collected in 1920. Her first full-length play, *Bernice* (1919), centered on interpreting the character of a dead woman. Its success led to another full-length play, *The Verge* (1921), about a woman who tries to make a new reality around herself and begins with creating new kinds of plants. Some critics saw the protagonist as an admirable new woman; others saw her as neurotic. *The Inheritors* (1921), also a full-length

For links to resources about Glaspell, click on *AuthorLinks* at bedfordstmartins.com/jacobus.

drama, focuses on the third-generation inheritors of a Midwestern college who clash because one family has liberal views and one has conservative views. Glaspell's last play, winner of the Pulitzer Prize, was *Alison's House* (1930), based on the life of Emily Dickinson. The latter part of Glaspell's life was spent writing fiction, especially four novels set in the Midwest that traced the struggles of women to maintain their ideals and values. *The Morning Is Near Us* sold over 100,000 copies in 1940 and was only one of her best-selling novels.

Jig Cook, a writer himself and a partner in many of Glaspell's ventures, spent the last two years of his life living in Delphi, Greece, in the manner of the peasants living on Mount Parnassus near the temple of Apollo. He died in 1924, and when Glaspell returned to the United States, she wrote a memoir of their life together called *The Road to the Temple*. In 1925, she broke with the Provincetown Players, who had moved in directions she did not approve of under the directorship of Eugene O'Neill. O'Neill tried to mollify Glaspell, but she never accepted his use of the theater company she and her husband had cofounded with him. When she died in 1948, she and O'Neill were essentially unreconciled.

Trifles

Trifles (1916) was apparently written as a companion piece for Eugene O'Neill's first produced play, the one-act *Bound East for Cardiff*. The two were performed together to make a complete evening presentation. In one sense *Trifles* is a murder mystery, but in another it is a critique of the gender-rigid attitudes of the officials whose responsibility it is to investigate the death of John Wright. Its main character, Minnie Foster Wright, is never presented but only described as a sweet woman who loved to sing when she was young but who married a man who slowly stifled her joy in living.

The setting of the play is a kitchen where the women, Mrs. Peters and Mrs. Hale, remain throughout the action. They examine the condition of the room and, by extension, the condition of Minnie Foster Wright. The men, examining the crime scene, the upstairs bedroom, spend much of the time offstage. They believe they are examining the important evidence, yet when they return with their findings, they are unable to understand what led to the death of John Wright, who to them seems quite a normal farmer.

The women, however, by examining the messy condition of the kitchen, the state of Minnie's preserves, and the quilt she was working on, begin to understand the motive behind Wright's murder. When they get to the dead body of the songbird Minnie had valued, they understand things in a way that the men cannot. The men observe that women are concerned with trifles, things of no importance. But the truth is that the women understand the fate of Minnie Foster Wright and John Wright in a way that would be almost impossible for the men, given their sense of what is significant and what is a trifle.

For discussion questions and assignments on *Trifles*, visit bedfordstmartins.com/jacobus.

In many ways the play is a study of gender differences and the way men's expectations and their sense of reality can distort the truth and deform a woman's life. In 1917, Glaspell wrote a short story using all the same material, called "A Jury of Her Peers," implying that the only peers of Minnie Foster Wright would be women like Mrs. Hale and Mrs. Peters. In 1917, however, women could not vote and in most states could not serve on juries.

Trifles in Performance

The original production, which may have included Eugene O'Neill among its cast members, was well received, but after Glaspell's death, most of her work fell out of fashion. *The Verge*, however, is still highly regarded in England and is often performed there. *Trifles* was neglected until the early 1960s, when feminist interest helped revive Glaspell's plays. Teacher and writer Sylvan Barnet included the play in his drama anthology, helping to bring it to the attention of contemporary viewers. Now produced most often by school and college groups, the play enjoys considerable popularity.

SUSAN GLASPELL (1876–1948)

Trifles   1916

Characters

GEORGE HENDERSON, *county attorney*
HENRY PETERS, *sheriff*
LEWIS HALE, *a neighboring farmer*
MRS. PETERS
MRS. HALE

Scene: *The kitchen in the now abandoned farmhouse of John Wright, a gloomy kitchen, and left without having been put in order — the walls covered with a faded wall paper. Down right is a door leading to the parlor. On the right wall above this door is a built-in kitchen cupboard with shelves in the upper portion and drawers below. In the rear wall at right, up two steps is a door opening onto stairs leading to the second floor. In the rear wall at left is a door to the shed and from there to the outside. Between these two doors is an old-fashioned black iron stove. Running along the left wall from the shed door is an old iron sink and sink shelf, in which is set a hand pump. Downstage of the sink is an uncurtained window. Near the window is an old wooden rocker. Center stage is an unpainted wooden kitchen table with straight chairs on either side. There is a small chair down right. Unwashed pans under the sink, a loaf of bread outside the breadbox, a dish towel on the table — other signs of incompleted work. At the rear the shed door opens and the Sheriff comes* in followed by the County Attorney and Hale. The Sheriff and Hale are men in middle life, the County Attorney is a young man; all are much bundled up and go at once to the stove. They are followed by the two women — the Sheriff's wife, Mrs. Peters, first: she is a slight wiry woman, a thin nervous face. Mrs. Hale is larger and would ordinarily be called more comfortable looking, but she is disturbed now and looks fearfully about as she enters. The women have come in slowly, and stand close together near the door.

COUNTY ATTORNEY (*at stove rubbing his hands*): This feels good. Come up to the fire, ladies.

MRS. PETERS (*after taking a step forward*): I'm not — cold.

SHERIFF (*unbuttoning his overcoat and stepping away from the stove to right of table as if to mark the beginning of official business*): Now, Mr. Hale, before we move things about, you explain to Mr. Henderson just what you saw when you came here yesterday morning.

COUNTY ATTORNEY (*crossing down to left of the table*): By the way, has anything been moved? Are things just as you left them yesterday?

SHERIFF (*looking about*): It's just about the same. When it dropped below zero last night I thought I'd better send Frank out this morning to make a fire for us — (*sits right of center table*) no use getting pneumonia with a big case on, but I told him not to touch anything except the stove—and you know Frank.

COUNTY ATTORNEY: Somebody should have been left here yesterday.

SHERIFF: Oh—yesterday. When I had to send Frank to Morris Center for that man who went crazy—I want you to know I had my hands full yesterday. I knew you could get back from Omaha by today and as long as I went over everything here myself———

COUNTY ATTORNEY: Well, Mr. Hale, tell just what happened when you came here yesterday morning.

HALE (crossing down to above table): Harry and I had started to town with a load of potatoes. We came along the road from my place and as I got here I said, "I'm going to see if I can't get John Wright to go in with me on a party telephone." I spoke to Wright about it once before and he put me off, saying folks talked too much anyway, and all he asked was peace and quiet—I guess you know about how much he talked himself; but I thought maybe if I went to the house and talked about it before his wife, though I said to Harry that I didn't know as what his wife wanted made much difference to John———

COUNTY ATTORNEY: Let's talk about that later, Mr. Hale. I do want to talk about that, but tell now just what happened when you got to the house.

HALE: I didn't hear or see anything; I knocked at the door, and still it was all quiet inside. I knew they must be up, it was past eight o'clock. So I knocked again, and I thought I heard someone say, "Come in." I wasn't sure, I'm not sure yet, but I opened the door—this door (indicating the door by which the two women are still standing) and there in that rocker—(pointing to it) sat Mrs. Wright. (They all look at the rocker down left.)

COUNTY ATTORNEY: What—was she doing?

HALE: She was rockin' back and forth. She had her apron in her hand and was kind of—pleating it.

COUNTY ATTORNEY: And how did she—look?

HALE: Well, she looked queer.

COUNTY ATTORNEY: How do you mean—queer?

HALE: Well, as if she didn't know what she was going to do next. And kind of done up.

COUNTY ATTORNEY (takes out notebook and pencil and sits left of center table): How did she seem to feel about your coming?

HALE: Why, I don't think she minded—one way or other. She didn't pay much attention. I said, "How do, Mrs. Wright, it's cold, ain't it?" And she said, "Is it?"—and went on kind of pleating at her apron. Well, I was surprised: she didn't ask me to come up to the stove, or to set down, but just sat there, not even looking at me, so I said, "I want to see John." And then she—laughed. I guess you would call it a laugh. I thought of Harry and the team outside, so I said a little sharp: "Can't I see John?" "No," she says, kind o' dull like. "Ain't he home?" says I. "Yes," says she, "he's home." "Then why can't I

see him?" I asked her, out of patience. "'Cause he's dead," says she. "Dead?" says I. She just nodded her head, not getting a bit excited, but rockin' back and forth. "Why—where is he?" says I, not knowing what to say. She just pointed upstairs—like that. (Himself pointing to the room above.) I started for the stairs, with the idea of going up there. I walked from there to here—then I says, "Why, what did he die of?" "He died of a rope round his neck," says she, and just went on pleatin' at her apron. Well, I went out and called Harry. I thought I might—need help. We went upstairs and there he was lyin'———

COUNTY ATTORNEY: I think I'd rather have you go into that upstairs, where you can point it all out. Just go on now with the rest of the story.

HALE: Well, my first thought was to get that rope off. It looked . . . (stops: his face twitches) . . . but Harry, he went up to him, and he said, "No, he's dead all right, and we'd better not touch anything." So we went right back downstairs. She was still sitting that same way. "Has anybody been notified?" I asked. "No," says she, unconcerned. "Who did this, Mrs. Wright?" said Harry. He said it businesslike—and she stopped pleatin' of her apron. "I don't know," she says. "You don't know?" says Harry. "No," says she. "Weren't you sleepin' in the bed with him?" says Harry. "Yes," says she, "but I was on the inside." "Somebody slipped a rope round his head and strangled him and you didn't wake up?" says Harry. "I didn't wake up," she said after him. We must 'a' looked as if we didn't see how that could be, for after a minute she said, "I sleep sound." Harry was going to ask her more questions but I said maybe we ought to let her tell her story first to the coroner, or the sheriff, so Harry went fast as he could to Rivers' place, where there's a telephone.

COUNTY ATTORNEY: And what did Mrs. Wright do when she knew that you had gone for the coroner?

HALE: She moved from the rocker to that chair over there (pointing to a small chair in the down right corner) and just sat there with her hands held together and looking down. I got a feeling that I ought to make some conversation, so I said I had come in to see if John wanted to put in a telephone, and at that she started to laugh, and then she stopped and looked at me—scared. (The County Attorney, who has had his notebook out, makes a note.) I dunno, maybe it wasn't scared. I wouldn't like to say it was. Soon Harry got back, and then Dr. Lloyd came and you, Mr. Peters, and so I guess that's all I know that you don't.

COUNTY ATTORNEY (rising and looking around): I guess we'll go upstairs first—and then out to the barn and around there. (To the Sheriff.) You're convinced that there was nothing important here—nothing that would point to any motive?

SHERIFF: Nothing here but kitchen things. (The County Attorney, after again looking around the kitchen,

An early performance by the Provincetown Players of *Trifles* shows the small space and simple staging of the Wharf Theatre.

opens the door of a cupboard closet in right wall. He brings a small chair from right—gets on it and looks on a shelf. Pulls his hand away, sticky.)

COUNTY ATTORNEY: Here's a nice mess. (*The women draw nearer up to center.*)

MRS. PETERS (*to the other woman*): Oh, her fruit; it did freeze. (To the Lawyer.) She worried about that when it turned so cold. She said the fire'd go out and her jars would break.

SHERIFF (*rises*): Well, can you beat the woman! Held for murder and worryin' about her preserves.

COUNTY ATTORNEY (*getting down from chair*): I guess before we're through she may have something more serious than preserves to worry about. (*Crosses down right center.*)

HALE: Well, women are used to worrying over trifles. (*The two women move a little closer together.*)

COUNTY ATTORNEY (*with the gallantry of a young politician*): And yet, for all their worries, what would we do without the ladies? (*The women do not unbend. He goes below the center table to the sink, takes a dipperful of water from the pail, and pouring it into a basin, washes his hands. While he is doing this the Sheriff and Hale cross to cupboard, which they inspect. The County Attorney starts to wipe his hands on the roller towel, turns it for a cleaner place.*) Dirty towels! (*Kicks his foot against the pans under the sink.*) Not much of a housekeeper, would you say, ladies?

MRS. HALE (*stiffly*): There's a great deal of work to be done on a farm.

COUNTY ATTORNEY: To be sure. And yet (*with a little bow to her*) I know there are some Dickson County farmhouses which do not have such roller towels. (*He gives it a pull to expose its full-length again.*)

MRS. HALE: Those towels get dirty awful quick. Men's hands aren't always clean as they might be.

COUNTY ATTORNEY: Ah, loyal to your sex, I see. But you and Mrs. Wright were neighbors. I suppose you were friends, too.

MRS. HALE (*shaking her head*): I've not seen much of her of late years. I've not been in this house—it's more than a year.

COUNTY ATTORNEY (*crossing to women up center*): And why was that? You didn't like her?

MRS. HALE: I liked her all well enough. Farmer's wives have their hands full, Mr. Henderson. And then———

COUNTY ATTORNEY: Yes———?

MRS. HALE (*looking about*): It never seemed a very cheerful place.

COUNTY ATTORNEY: No—it's not cheerful. I shouldn't say she had the homemaking instinct.

MRS. HALE: Well, I don't know as Wright had, either.

COUNTY ATTORNEY: You mean that they didn't get on very well?

MRS. HALE: No, I don't mean anything. But I don't think a place'd be any cheerfuller for John Wright's being in it.

COUNTY ATTORNEY: I'd like to talk more of that a little later. I want to get the lay of things upstairs now. (*He goes past the women to up right where the steps lead to a stair door.*)

SHERIFF: I suppose anything Mrs. Peters does'll be all right. She was to take in some clothes for her, you know, and a few little things. We left in such a hurry yesterday.

COUNTY ATTORNEY: Yes, but I would like to see what you take, Mrs. Peters, and keep an eye out for anything that might be of use to us.

MRS. PETERS: Yes, Mr. Henderson. (*The men leave by up right door to stairs. The women listen to the men's steps on the stairs, then look about the kitchen.*)

MRS. HALE (*crossing left to sink*): I'd hate to have men coming into my kitchen, snooping around and criticizing. (*She arranges the pans under sink which the lawyer had shoved out of place.*)

MRS. PETERS: Of course it's no more than their duty. (*Crosses to cupboard up right.*)

MRS. HALE: Duty's all right, but I guess that deputy sheriff that came out to make the fire might have got a little of this on. (*Gives the roller towel a pull.*) Wish I'd thought of that sooner. Seems mean to talk about her for not having things slicked up when she had to come away in such a hurry. (*Crosses right to Mrs. Peters at cupboard.*)

MRS. PETERS (*who has been looking through cupboard, lifts one end of towel that covers a pan*): She had bread set. (*Stands still.*)

MRS. HALE (*eyes fixed on a loaf of bread beside the breadbox, which is on a low shelf of the cupboard*): She was going to put this in there. (*Picks up loaf, abruptly drops it. In a manner of returning to familiar things.*) It's a shame about her fruit. I wonder if it's all gone. (*Gets up on chair and looks.*) I think there's some here that's all right, Mrs. Peters. Yes—here; (*holding it toward the window*) this is cherries, too. (*Looking again.*) I declare I believe that's the only one. (*Gets down, jar in hand. Goes to the sink and wipes it off on the outside.*) She'll feel awful bad after all her hard work in the hot weather. I remember the afternoon I put up my cherries last summer. (*She puts the jar on the big kitchen table, center of the room. With a sigh, is about to sit down in the rocking chair. Before she is seated realizes what chair it is; with a slow look at it, steps back. The chair which she has touched rocks back and forth. Mrs. Peters moves to center table and they both watch the chair rock for a moment or two.*)

MRS. PETERS (*shaking off the mood which the empty rocking chair has evoked. Now in a businesslike manner she speaks*): Well I must get those things from the front room closet. (*She goes to the door at the right but, after looking into the other room, steps back.*) You coming with me, Mrs. Hale? You could help me carry them. (*They go in the other room; reappear, Mrs. Peters carrying a dress, petticoat, and skirt, Mrs. Hale following with a pair of shoes.*) My, it's cold in there. (*She puts the clothes on the big table and hurries to the stove.*)

MRS. HALE (*right of center table examining the skirt*): Wright was close. I think maybe that's why she kept so much to herself. She didn't even belong to the Ladies' Aid. I suppose she felt she couldn't do her part, and then you don't enjoy things when you feel shabby. I heard she used to wear pretty clothes and be lively, when she was Minnie Foster, one of the town girls singing in the choir. But that—oh, that was thirty years ago. This all you want to take in?

MRS. PETERS: She said she wanted an apron. Funny thing to want, for there isn't much to get you dirty in jail, goodness knows. But I suppose just to make her feel more natural. (*Crosses to cupboard.*) She said they was in the top drawer in this cupboard. Yes, here. And then her little shawl that always hung behind the door. (*Opens stair door and looks.*) Yes, here it is. (*Quickly shuts door leading upstairs.*)

MRS. HALE (*abruptly moving toward her*): Mrs. Peters?

MRS. PETERS: Yes, Mrs. Hale? (*At up right door.*)

MRS. HALE: Do you think she did it?

MRS. PETERS (*in a frightened voice*): Oh, I don't know.

MRS. HALE: Well, I don't think she did. Asking for an apron and her little shawl. Worrying about her fruit.

MRS. PETERS (*starts to speak, glances up, where footsteps are heard in the room above. In a low voice*): Mr. Peters says it looks bad for her. Mr. Henderson is awful sarcastic in a speech and he'll make fun of her sayin' she didn't wake up.

MRS. HALE: Well, I guess John Wright didn't wake when they was slipping that rope under his neck.

MRS. PETERS (*crossing slowly to table and placing shawl and apron on table with other clothing*): No, it's strange. It must have been done awful crafty and still. They say it was such a—funny way to kill a man, rigging it all up like that.

MRS. HALE (*crossing to left of Mrs. Peters at table*): That's just what Mr. Hale said. There was a gun in the house. He says that's what he can't understand.

MRS. PETERS: Mr. Henderson said coming out that what was needed for the case was a motive: something to show anger, or—sudden feeling.

MRS. HALE (*who is standing by the table*): Well, I don't see any signs of anger around here. (*She puts her hand on the dish towel, which lies on the table, stands looking down at table, one-half of which is clean, the other half messy.*) It's wiped to here. (*Makes a move as if to finish work, then turns and looks at loaf of bread outside the breadbox. Drops towel. In that voice of coming back to familiar things.*) Wonder how they are finding things upstairs. (*Crossing below table to down right.*) I hope she had it a little more red-up° up there. You know, it seems kind of sneaking. Locking her up in town and then coming out here and trying to get her own house to turn against her!

MRS. PETERS: But, Mrs. Hale, the law is the law.

MRS. HALE: I s'pose 'tis. (*Unbuttoning her coat.*) Better loosen up your things, Mrs. Peters. You won't feel them when you go out. (*Mrs. Peters takes off her fur tippet, goes to hang it on chair back left of table, stands looking at the work basket on floor near down left window.*)

---

red-up: (slang) Ready for company

MRS. PETERS: She was piecing a quilt. (*She brings the large sewing basket to the center table and they look at the bright pieces, Mrs. Hale above the table and Mrs. Peters left of it.*)

MRS. HALE: It's a log cabin pattern. Pretty, isn't it? I wonder if she was goin' to quilt it or just knot it? (*Footsteps have been heard coming down the stairs. The Sheriff enters followed by Hale and the County Attorney.*)

SHERIFF: They wonder if she was going to quilt it or just knot it! (*The men laugh, the women look abashed.*)

COUNTY ATTORNEY (*rubbing his hands over the stove*): Frank's fire didn't do much up there, did it? Well, let's go out to the barn and get that cleared up. (*The men go outside by up left door.*)

MRS. HALE (*resentfully*): I don't know as there's anything so strange, our takin' up our time with little things while we're waiting for them to get the evidence. (*She sits in chair right of table smoothing out a block with decision.*) I don't see as it's anything to laugh about.

MRS. PETERS (*apologetically*): Of course they've got awful important things on their minds. (*Pulls up a chair and joins Mrs. Hale at the left of the table.*)

MRS. HALE (*examining another block*): Mrs. Peters, look at this one. Here, this is the one she was working on, and look at the sewing! All the rest of it has been so nice and even. And look at this! It's all over the place! Why, it looks as if she didn't know what she was about! (*After she has said this they look at each other, then start to glance back at the door. After an instant Mrs. Hale has pulled at a knot and ripped the sewing.*)

MRS. PETERS: Oh, what are you doing, Mrs. Hale?

MRS. HALE (*mildly*): Just pulling out a stitch or two that's not sewed very good. (*Threading a needle.*) Bad sewing always made me fidgety.

MRS. PETERS (*with a glance at the door, nervously*): I don't think we ought to touch things.

MRS. HALE: I'll just finish up this end. (*Suddenly stopping and leaning forward.*) Mrs. Peters?

MRS. PETERS: Yes, Mrs. Hale?

MRS. HALE: What do you suppose she was so nervous about?

MRS. PETERS: Oh—I don't know. I don't know as she was nervous. I sometimes sew awful queer when I'm just tired. (*Mrs. Hale starts to say something, looks at Mrs. Peters, then goes on sewing.*) Well, I must get these things wrapped up. They may be through sooner than we think. (*Putting apron and other things together.*) I wonder where I can find a piece of paper, and string. (*Rises.*)

MRS. HALE: In that cupboard, maybe.

MRS. PETERS (*crosses right looking in cupboard*): Why, here's a bird-cage. (*Holds it up.*) Did she have a bird, Mrs. Hale?

MRS. HALE: Why, I don't know whether she did or not—I've not been here for so long. There was a

Mrs. Hale (Sarah Einerson) and Mrs. Peters (Mary-Margaret Pyeatt) discovering the truth about the dead songbird in the 2000 Echo Theatre production of Susan Glaspell's *Trifles*, performed in Dallas, Texas, and directed by Ellen Locy. The production was an entry in Dallas's second annual Festival of Independent Theaters (FIT).

man around last year selling canaries cheap, but I don't know as she took one; maybe she did. She used to sing real pretty herself.

MRS. PETERS (*glancing around*): Seems funny to think of a bird here. But she must have had one, or why would she have a cage? I wonder what happened to it?

MRS. HALE: I s'pose maybe the cat got it.

MRS. PETERS: No, she didn't have a cat. She's got that feeling some people have about cats—being afraid of them. My cat got in her room and she was real upset and asked me to take it out.

MRS. HALE: My sister Bessie was like that. Queer, ain't it?

MRS. PETERS (*examining the cage*): Why, look at this door. It's broke. One hinge is pulled apart. (*Takes a step down to Mrs. Hale's right.*)

MRS. HALE (*looking too*): Looks as if someone must have been rough with it.

MRS. PETERS: Why, yes. (*She brings the cage forward and puts it on the table.*)

MRS. HALE (*glancing toward up left door*): I wish if they're going to find any evidence they'd be about it. I don't like this place.

MRS. PETERS: But I'm awful glad you came with me, Mrs. Hale. It would be lonesome for me sitting here alone.

MRS. HALE: It would, wouldn't it? (*Dropping her sewing.*) But I tell you what I do wish, Mrs. Peters. I wish I had come over sometimes when *she* was here. I—(*looking around the room*)—wish I had.

MRS. PETERS: But of course you were awful busy, Mrs. Hale—your house and your children.

MRS. HALE (*rises and crosses left*): I could've come. I stayed away because it weren't cheerful—and that's why I ought to have come. I—(*looking out left window*)—I've never liked this place. Maybe it's because it's down in a hollow and you don't see the road. I dunno what it is, but it's a lonesome place and always was. I wish I had come over to see Minnie Foster sometimes. I can see now—(*Shakes her head.*)

MRS. PETERS (*left of table and above it*): Well, you mustn't reproach yourself, Mrs. Hale. Somehow we just don't see how it is with other folks until— something turns up.

MRS. HALE: Not having children makes less work—but it makes a quiet house, and Wright out to work all day, and no company when he did come in. (*Turning from window.*) Did you know John Wright, Mrs. Peters?

MRS. PETERS: Not to know him; I've seen him in town. They say he was a good man.

MRS. HALE: Yes—good; he didn't drink, and kept his word as well as most, I guess, and paid his debts. But he was a hard man, Mrs. Peters. Just to pass the time of day with him—(*Shivers.*) Like a raw wind that gets to the bone. (*Pauses, her eye falling on the cage.*) I should think she would 'a' wanted a bird. But what do you suppose went with it?

MRS. PETERS: I don't know, unless it got sick and died. (*She reaches over and swings the broken door, swings it again, both women watch it.*)

MRS. HALE: You weren't raised round here, were you? (*Mrs. Peters shakes her head.*) You didn't know— her?

MRS. PETERS: Not till they brought her yesterday.

MRS. HALE: She—come to think of it, she was kind of like a bird herself—real sweet and pretty, but kind of timid and—fluttery. How—she—did—change. (*Silence: then as if struck by a happy thought and relieved to get back to everyday things. Crosses right above Mrs. Peters to cupboard, replaces small chair used to stand on to its original place down right.*) Tell you what, Mrs. Peters, why don't you take the quilt in with you? It might take up her mind.

MRS. PETERS: Why, I think that's a real nice idea, Mrs. Hale. There couldn't possibly be any objection to it could there? Now, just what would I take? I wonder if her patches are in here—and her things. (*They look in the sewing basket.*)

MRS. HALE (*crosses to right of table*): Here's some red. I expect this has got sewing things in it. (*Brings out a fancy box.*) What a pretty box. Looks like something somebody would give you. Maybe her scissors are in here. (*Opens box. Suddenly puts her hand to her nose.*) Why——(*Mrs. Peters bends nearer, then turns her face away.*) There's something wrapped up in this piece of silk.

MRS. PETERS: Why, this isn't her scissors.

MRS. HALE (*lifting the silk*): Oh, Mrs. Peters—it's—— (*Mrs. Peters bends closer.*)

MRS. PETERS: It's the bird.

MRS. HALE: But, Mrs. Peters—look at it! Its neck! Look at its neck! It's all—other side *to.*

MRS. PETERS: Somebody—wrung—its—neck. (*Their eyes meet. A look of growing comprehension, of horror. Steps are heard outside. Mrs. Hale slips box under quilt pieces, and sinks into her chair. Enter Sheriff and County Attorney. Mrs. Peters steps down left and stands looking out of window.*)

COUNTY ATTORNEY (*as one turning from serious things to little pleasantries*): Well, ladies, have you decided whether she was going to quilt it or knot it? (*Crosses to center above table.*)

MRS. PETERS: We think she was going to—knot it. (*Sheriff crosses to right of stove, lifts stove lid, and glances at fire, then stands warming hands at stove.*)

COUNTY ATTORNEY: Well, that's interesting, I'm sure. (*Seeing the bird-cage.*) Has the bird flown?

MRS. HALE (*putting more quilt pieces over the box*): We think the—cat got it.

COUNTY ATTORNEY (*preoccupied*): Is there a cat? (*Mrs. Hale glances in a quick covert way at Mrs. Peters.*)

MRS. PETERS (*turning from window takes a step in*): Well, not *now.* They're superstitious, you know. They leave.

COUNTY ATTORNEY (*to Sheriff Peters, continuing an inter- rupted conversation*): No sign at all of anyone having come from the outside. Their own rope. Now let's go up again and go over it piece by piece. (*They start upstairs.*) It would have to have been someone who knew just the——(*Mrs. Peters sits down left of table. The two women sit there not looking at one another, but as if peering into something and at the same time holding back. When they talk now it is in the manner of feeling their way over strange ground, as if afraid of what they are saying, but as if they can- not help saying it.*)

MRS. HALE (*hesistatively and in hushed voice*): She liked the bird. She was going to bury it in that pretty box.

MRS. PETERS (*in a whisper*): When I was a girl—my kitten—there was a boy took a hatchet, and before my eyes—and before I could get there————(*Covers her face an instant.*) If they hadn't held me back I would have—(*catches herself, looks upstairs where steps are heard, falters weakly*)—hurt him.

MRS. HALE (*with a slow look around her*): I wonder how it would seem never to have had any children around. (*Pause.*) No, Wright wouldn't like the bird—a thing that sang. She used to sing. He killed that, too.

MRS. PETERS (*moving uneasily*): We don't know who killed the bird.

MRS. HALE: I knew John Wright.

MRS. PETERS: It was an awful thing was done in this house that night, Mrs. Hale. Killing a man while he slept, slipping a rope around his neck that choked the life out of him.

MRS. HALE: His neck. Choked the life out of him. (*Her hand goes out and rests on the bird-cage.*)

MRS. PETERS (*with rising voice*): We don't know who killed him. We don't know.

MRS. HALE (*her own feelings not interrupted*): If there'd been years and years of nothing, then a bird to sing to you, it would be awful—still, after the bird was still.

MRS. PETERS (*something within her speaking*): I know what stillness is. When we homesteaded in Dakota, and my first baby died—after he was two years old, and me with no other then————

MRS. HALE (*moving*): How soon do you suppose they'll be through looking for the evidence?

MRS. PETERS: I know what stillness is. (*Pulling herself back.*) The law has got to punish crimes, Mrs. Hale.

MRS. HALE (*not as if answering that*): I wish you'd seen Minnie Foster when she wore a white dress with blue ribbons and stood up there in the choir and sang. (*A look around the room.*) Oh, I *wish* I'd come over here once in a while! That was a crime! That was a crime! Who's going to punish that?

MRS. PETERS (*looking upstairs*): We mustn't—take on.

MRS. HALE: I might have known she needed help! I know how things can be—for women. I tell you, it's queer, Mrs. Peters. We live close together and we live far apart. We all go through the same things—it's all just a different kind of the same thing. (*Brushes her eyes, noticing the jar of fruit, reaches out for it.*) If I was you I wouldn't tell her her fruit was gone. Tell her it *ain't*. Tell her it's all right. Take this in to prove it to her. She—she may never know whether it was broke or not.

MRS. PETERS (*takes the jar, looks about for something to wrap it in; takes petticoat from the clothes brought from the other room, very nervously begins winding this around the jar. In a false voice*): My, it's a good thing the men couldn't hear us. Wouldn't they just laugh! Getting all stirred up over a little thing like a—dead canary. As if that could have anything to do with—with—wouldn't they *laugh!* (*The men are heard coming downstairs.*)

MRS. HALE (*under her breath*): Maybe they would—maybe they wouldn't.

COUNTY ATTORNEY: No, Peters, it's all perfectly clear except a reason for doing it. But you know juries when it comes to women. If there was some definite thing. (*Crosses slowly to above table. Sheriff crosses down right. Mrs. Hale and Mrs. Peters remain seated at either side of table.*) Something to show—something to make a story about—a thing that would connect up with this strange way of doing it————(*The women's eyes meet for an instant. Enter Hale from outer door.*)

HALE (*remaining by door*): Well, I've got the team around. Pretty cold out there.

COUNTY ATTORNEY: I'm going to stay awhile by myself. (*To the Sheriff.*) You can send Frank out for me, can't you? I want to go over everything. I'm not satisfied that we can't do better.

SHERIFF: Do you want to see what Mrs. Peters is going to take in? (*The Lawyer picks up the apron, laughs.*)

COUNTY ATTORNEY: Oh, I guess they're not very dangerous things the ladies have picked out. (*Moves a few things about, disturbing the quilt pieces which cover the box. Steps back.*) No, Mrs. Peters doesn't need supervising. For that matter a sheriff's wife is married to the law. Ever think of it that way, Mrs. Peters?

MRS. PETERS: Not—just that way.

SHERIFF (*chuckling*): Married to the law. (*Moves to down right door to the other room.*) I just want you to come in here a minute, George. We ought to take a look at these windows.

COUNTY ATTORNEY (*scoffingly*): Oh, windows!

SHERIFF: We'll be right out, Mr. Hale. (*Hale goes outside. The Sheriff follows the County Attorney into the room. Then Mrs. Hale rises, hands tight together, looking intensely at Mrs. Peters, whose eyes make a slow turn, finally meeting Mrs. Hale's. A moment Mrs. Hale holds her, then her own eyes point the way to where the box is concealed. Suddenly Mrs. Peters throws back quilt pieces and tries to put the box in the bag she is carrying. It is too big. She opens box, starts to take bird out, cannot touch it, goes to pieces, stands there helpless. Sound of a knob turning in the other room. Mrs. Hale snatches the box and puts it in the pocket of her big coat. Enter County Attorney and Sheriff, who remains down right.*)

COUNTY ATTORNEY (*crosses to up left door facetiously*): Well, Henry, at least we found out that she was not going to quilt it. She was going to—what is it you call it, ladies?

MRS. HALE (*standing center below table facing front, her hand against her pocket*): We call it—knot it, Mr. Henderson.

CHRISTINE DYMKOWSKI (b. 1950)

On the Edge: The Plays
of Susan Glaspell 1988

Christine Dymkowski sees *Trifles* as a play that occupies the edge — the marginalized space reserved for women. The male figures in the play assume that their interests are central to the murder investigation, whereas Glaspell demonstrates that the most significant issues in the investigation are on the edge of men's attention, where they can never see them.

The paradoxically central nature of the edge informs Glaspell's theatrical methods and themes. Her first play, *Trifles* (1916), illustrates its use in several ways, the irony of the title already having been noted. The plot revolves around the visit to a farmhouse by County Attorney Henderson and Sheriff Peters to investigate the murder of John Wright; they are accompanied by the farmer who discovered the murder and, almost incidentally, by the farmer's and sheriff's wives. The men's assumption is that Minnie Wright, already in custody for the crime, has killed her husband, and they are there to search the house for clues to a motive. The audience undoubtedly sees them as protagonists at the start of the play.

The stage directions immediately call attention to the women's marginality: the men, "much bundled up" against the freezing cold, "go at once to the stove" in the Wrights' kitchen, while the women who follow them in do so "slowly, and stand close together near the door." The separateness of the female and male worlds is thus immediately established visually and then reinforced by the dialogue:

MRS. PETERS (*to the other woman*): Oh, her fruit; it did freeze. (*To the Lawyer.*)
    She worried about that when it turned so cold. . . .
SHERIFF: Well, can you beat the women [*sic*]! Held for murder and worryin' about
    her preserves.
COUNTY ATTORNEY: I guess before we're through she may have something more
    serious than preserves to worry about.
HALE: Well, women are used to worrying over trifles.
    (*The two women move a little closer together.*)

Not surprisingly, the women are relegated to the kitchen, while the men's attention turns to the rest of the house, particularly the bedroom where the crime was committed: "You're convinced that there was nothing important here—nothing that would point to any motive," Henderson asks Peters, and is assured that there is "Nothing here but kitchen things." However, while the men view the kitchen as marginal to their purpose, the drama stays centered there where the women are: contrary to expectation, it becomes the central focus of the play.

Ironically, it is the kitchen that holds the clues to the desperation and loneliness of Minnie's life and yields the women the answers for which the men search in vain; moreover, the understanding that they do reach goes beyond the mere solving of the crime to a redefinition of what the crime was. Mrs. Hale blames herself for a failure of imagination: "Oh, I *wish* I'd come over here once in a while! That was a crime! That was a crime! Who's going to punish that? . . . I might have known she needed help! I know how things can be—for women. I tell you, it's queer, Mrs. Peters. We live close together and we live far apart. We all go through the same things—it's all just a different kind of the same thing." The empathy both women feel for Minnie leads them to suppress the evidence they have found, patiently enduring the men's condescension instead of competing with them on their own ground. Conventional moral values are overturned, just as the expected form of the murder mystery is ignored: the play differentiates between justice and law and shows that the traditional "solution" is no such thing.

Just as Glaspell sets the play in the seemingly marginal kitchen, she makes the absent Minnie Wright its focus, a tactic she was to use again in *Bernice* and *Alison's House;* although noted by critics, this use of an absent central character has not received much comment. It is yet another way in which Glaspell makes central the apparently marginal—indeed, in stage terms, the nonexistent.

Luigi Pirandello

Luigi Pirandello (1867–1936) was an Italian short-story writer and novelist, a secondary school teacher, and finally a playwright. His life was complicated by business failures that wiped out his personal income and threw his wife into a psychological depression that Pirandello quite bluntly described as madness. Out of his acquaintance with madness—he remained with his wife for fourteen years after she lost touch with reality—Pirandello claimed to have developed much of his attitude toward the shifting surfaces of appearances.

Pirandello's short stories and novels show the consistent pattern of his plays: a deep examination of what we know to be real and a questioning of our confidence in our beliefs. His novel *Shoot* (1915) questions the surfaces of cinema reality, which contemporary Italy had embraced with great enthusiasm. His relentless examination of the paradoxes of experience has given him a reputation for pessimism. He himself said, "I think of life as a very sad piece of buffoonery," and he insisted that people bear within them a deep need to deceive themselves "by creating a reality . . . which . . . is discovered to be vain and illusory."

For most of his early career, Pirandello was not a popular playwright in Italy, and therefore much of his dramatic work was first performed abroad. In 1923, he was known as an important novelist and came to the attention of Benito Mussolini (1883–1945), the Fascist dictator of Italy. Pirandello joined the Italian Fascist party as a means of establishing the National Art Theatre in Rome, which enjoyed considerable state support. When asked why he was a Fascist, he said, "I am a Fascist because I am an Italian." After Pirandello won the Nobel Prize for literature in 1934, one account has him breaking with Fascism entirely over the Italian invasion of Ethiopia, and another account has him giving over his Nobel medal to be melted down for the Ethiopian campaign. Profound uncertainties about his behavior, as well as about some of his dramas, persist to this day.

Pirandello's influence in modern theater resulted from his experimentation with the concept of realism that dominated drama from the time of Strindberg and Ibsen. The concept of the imaginary "fourth wall" of the stage through which the audience observed the action of characters in their living rooms had become the norm in theater. Pirandello, however, questioned all thought of norms by subjecting the very idea of reality to philosophical scrutiny. His questioning helped playwrights around the world expand their approaches to theater in the early part of the twentieth century. Pirandello was one of the first, and one of the best, experimentalists.

For links to resources about
Pirandello, click on
AuthorLinks at
bedfordstmartins.com/jacobus.

Six Characters in Search of an Author

Pirandello's play is part of a trilogy: *Six Characters in Search of an Author* (1921), *Each in His Own Way* (1924), and *Tonight We Improvise* (1930). These plays all examine the impossibility of knowing reality. There is no objective truth to know, Pirandello tells us, and what we think of as reality is totally subjective, something that each of us maintains independently of other people and that none of us can communicate. We are, in other words, apart—each of us sealed into his or her own limited world.

These ideas were hardly novel. Playwrights had dealt with them before, even during the Elizabethan age, at a time when—because of the Protestant Reformation—the absolute hold of the definitions of reality promoted by the Roman Catholic Church had crumbled. Pirandello's plays were produced during the 1920s, when people were uncertain, frightened, and still reeling in shock from the destruction of World War I. In this depressed time, Pirandello's audience saw in his work a reflection of their own dispirited, fearful selves.

In a sense, *Six Characters in Search of an Author* is about the relationship between art and life, and especially about the relationship between drama and life. The premise of the play is absurd. In the middle of a rehearsal of a Pirandello play, several characters appear and request that an author be found to cobble them into a play. The stage manager assumes that they are presenting themselves as actors to be in a play, but they explain that they are not actors. They are real characters. This implies a paradox: that characters are independent of the actors who play them (we are used to the characters being only on paper). When the characters demand actors to represent them, we know that one limit of impossibility has been reached.

The characters who appear are, in a sense, types: a father, a mother, a stepdaughter, a son, two silent figures—the boy and the child—and, finally, a milliner, Madame Pace. They share the stage with the actors of the company, who are rehearsing the Pirandello play *Mixing It Up*. The six characters have been abandoned by their creator, the author who has absconded, leaving them in search of a substitute. The stepdaughter, late in the play, surmises that their author abandoned them "in a fit of depression, of disgust for the ordinary theater as the public knows it and likes it."

Pirandello uses his characters and their situation to comment on the life of the theater in the 1920s, and he also uses them to begin a series of speculations on the relationship of a public to the actors they see in plays, the characters the actors play, and the authors who create them. To an extent, the relationship between an author and his or her characters is always a metaphor for the relationship between a creator and all creation. It is tempting to think of Samuel Beckett years later in his *Waiting for Godot* imagining an "author" having abandoned his creations because they failed to satisfy him. The six characters—or creations—who invade the stage in Pirandello's play have a firm sense of themselves and their actions. They bring with them a story—as all characters in plays do—and they invite the manager to participate in their stories, just as characters invite audiences to become one with their narratives.

One of the more amusing scenes depicts the characters' reactions to seeing actors play their parts. Since they are "real" characters, they have the utmost authority regarding how their parts should be played, and they end up laughing at the inept efforts of the actors in act 2. When the manager disputes with them, wondering why they protest so vigorously, they explain that they want to make sure the truth is told. The truth: the concept seems so simple on the

For discussion questions and assignments on *Six Characters in Search of an Author,* visit **bedfordstmartins.com/jacobus**.

surface, but in the situation that Pirandello has conceived, it is loaded with complexities that the stage manager cannot fathom.

By the time the question of truth has been raised, the manager has begun to get a sense of the poignancy of the story that these characters have to tell. He has also begun to see that he must let them continue to tell their story—except that they are not telling it, they are living it. When the climax of their story is reached in the last moments of the play, the line between what is acted and what is lived onstage has become almost completely blurred. When the play ends, it is difficult to know what has truly occurred and what has truly been acted out.

Six Characters in Search of an Author has endured because it still rings true in its examination of the relationship between art and life, illusion and reality. The very word *illusion* is rejected by the characters—as characters, they are part of the illusion of reality. They reject the thought that they are literature, asserting, "This is Life, this is passion!"

Six Characters in Search of an Author in Performance

The first production of *Six Characters in Search of an Author* in Rome in May 1921 resulted in a riot that threatened the author and his daughter. The calmer London production in March 1922 in the Kingsway Theater garnered positive reviews, and the audiences, although at times puzzled, were responsive to what the *Christian Science Monitor* called "one of the freshest and most original productions seen for a long time." The first production in New York was directed by Brock Pemberton at the Princess Theatre in October 1922 with the distinguished American actress Florence Eldridge as the stepdaughter. One newspaper critic said, "Pirandello turns a powerful microscope on the dramatist's mental workshop—the modus operandi of play production—and after having destroyed our illusion, like a prestidigitator who shows us how a trick is done, expects us to believe in him."

Pirandello directed the play in Italian in London in 1925, and despite the audience's general inability to understand the language, the New Oxford Theatre was filled for every night of its run. He brought the company to the United States after the British censor determined that the play was "unsuitable for English audiences" and closed the play in London. It was not officially licensed for performance in England again until 1928.

Revivals of the play have been numerous. Three productions in New York in the 1930s preceded revivals in 1948 and 1955. London saw productions in February 1932 and November 1950. By the 1930s audience confusion had diminished, and in 1932 one London critic declared, "Repetition cannot dull the brilliance of the play's attack on theatrical shams." In 1955, Tyrone Guthrie's Phoenix Theatre used a translation and adaptation by Guthrie and Michael Wager. The production was not successful, although critics liked the translation. Sir Ralph Richardson performed in London's West End production in 1963. Robert Brustein received extraordinary praise for his American Repertory Theater (ART) production in 1985. Instead of interrupting a Pirandello play, the six characters interrupt the rehearsal of a Molière play, *Sganarelle*, which has roots in Italian commedia dell'arte and which had been a highly successful ART production. This self-reference—in Pirandellian fashion—helped to blur the line between the realities on and off the stage. Boston critic Kevin

Kelly said of the performance, "Brustein immediately links the paradox in Pirandello's theme about reality in illusion / illusion in reality to . . . the pragmatic fantasy of theater itself." The play was revived by Brustein and ART once more in 1996 to great acclaim. The 2008 production directed by Rupert Goold in the Gielgud Theatre in London's West End had the six characters interrupt a conference of film people discussing how to finish their upcoming documentary about an English boy who successfully sought euthanasia in Norway. This production added the question of life and death to the question of appearance and reality.

LUIGI PIRANDELLO (1867–1936)

Six Characters in Search of an Author   1921
A Comedy in the Making

TRANSLATED BY EDWARD STORER

Characters of the Comedy in the Making

THE FATHER
THE MOTHER
THE STEPDAUGHTER
THE SON
THE BOY ⎫
THE CHILD ⎭ *do not speak*
MADAME PACE

Actors of the Company

THE MANAGER
LEADING LADY
LEADING MAN
SECOND LADY LEAD
L'INGÉNUE
JUVENILE LEAD
OTHER ACTORS AND ACTRESSES
PROPERTY MAN
PROMPTER
MACHINIST
MANAGER'S SECRETARY
DOOR-KEEPER
SCENE SHIFTERS

Scene: *Daytime. The stage of a theater.*

(N.B.: *The Comedy is without acts or scenes. The performance is interrupted once, without the curtain being lowered, when the Manager and the chief characters withdraw to arrange a scenario. A second interruption of the action takes place when, by mistake, the stage hands let the curtain down.*)

ACT I

(*The spectators will find the curtain raised and the stage as it usually is during the daytime. It will be half dark, and empty, so that from the beginning the public may have the impression of an impromptu performance.*)

(*Prompter's box and a small table and chair for the Manager*)

(*Two other small tables and several chairs scattered about as during rehearsals.*)

(*The Actors and Actresses of the company enter from the back of the stage: first one, then another, then two together; nine or ten in all. They are about to rehearse a Pirandello play: Mixing It Up. Some of the company move off toward their dressing rooms. The Prompter, who has the "book" under his arm, is waiting for the Manager in order to begin the rehearsal.*)

(*The Actors and Actresses, some standing, some sitting, chat and smoke. One perhaps reads a paper; another cons his part.*)

(*Finally, the Manager enters and goes to the table prepared for him. His Secretary brings him his mail, through which he glances. The Prompter takes his seat, turns on a light, and opens the "book."*)

THE MANAGER (*throwing a letter down on the table*): I can't see. (*To Property Man.*) Let's have a little light, please!

PROPERTY MAN: Yes, sir, yes, at once. (*A light comes down on to the stage.*)

THE MANAGER (*clapping his hands*): Come along! Come along! Second act of "Mixing It Up." (*Sits down.*)

(*The Actors and Actresses go from the front of the stage to the wings, all except the three who are to begin the rehearsal.*)

THE PROMPTER (*reading the "book"*): "Leo Gala's house. A curious room serving as dining-room and study."

THE MANAGER (*to Property Man*): Fix up the old red room.

PROPERTY MAN (*noting it down*): Red set. All right!

THE PROMPTER (*continuing to read from the "book"*): "Table already laid and writing desk with books and papers. Bookshelves. Exit rear to Leo's bedroom. Exit left to kitchen. Principal exit to right."

THE MANAGER (*energetically*): Well, you understand: The principal exit over there; here, the kitchen. (*Turning to actor who is to play the part of Socrates.*) You make your entrances and exits here. (*To Property Man.*) The baize doors at the rear, and curtains.

PROPERTY MAN (*noting it down*): Right!

PROMPTER (*reading as before*): "When the curtain rises, Leo Gala, dressed in cook's cap and apron, is busy beating an egg in a cup. Philip, also dressed as a cook, is beating another egg. Guidi Venanzi is seated and listening."

LEADING MAN (*to Manager*): Excuse me, but must I absolutely wear a cook's cap?

THE MANAGER (*annoyed*): I imagine so. It says so there anyway. (*Pointing to the "book."*)

LEADING MAN: But it's ridiculous!

THE MANAGER (*jumping up in a rage*): Ridiculous? Ridiculous? Is it my fault if France won't send us any more good comedies, and we are reduced to putting on Pirandello's works, where nobody understands anything, and where the author plays the fool with us all? (*The Actors grin. The Manager goes to Leading Man and shouts.*) Yes sir, you put on the cook's cap and beat eggs. Do you suppose that with all this egg-beating business you are on an ordinary stage? Get that out of your head. You represent the shell of the eggs you are beating! (*Laughter and comments among the Actors.*) Silence! and listen to my explanations, please! (*To Leading Man.*) "The empty form of reason without the fullness of instinct, which is blind."—You stand for reason, your wife is instinct.

It's a mixing up of the parts, according to which you who act your own part become the puppet of yourself. Do you understand?

LEADING MAN: I'm hanged if I do.

THE MANAGER: Neither do I. But let's get on with it. It's sure to be a glorious failure anyway. (*Confidentially.*) But I say, please face three-quarters. Otherwise, what with the abstruseness of the dialogue, and the public that won't be able to hear you, the whole thing will go to hell. Come on! come on!

PROMPTER: Pardon sir, may I get into my box? There's a bit of a draft.

THE MANAGER: Yes, yes, of course!

(*At this point, the Door-Keeper has entered from the stage door and advances toward the Manager's table, taking off his braided cap. During this maneuver, the Six Characters enter, and stop by the door at back of stage, so that when the Door-Keeper is about to announce their coming to the Manager, they are already on the stage. A tenuous light surrounds them, almost as if irradiated by them—the faint breath of their fantastic reality.*)

(*This light will disappear when they come forward toward the actors. They preserve, however, something of the dream lightness in which they seem almost suspended; but this does not detract from the essential reality of their forms and expressions.*)

(*He who is known as the Father is a man of about 50: hair, reddish in color, thin at the temples; he is not bald, however, thick mustaches, falling over his still fresh mouth, which often opens in an empty and uncertain smile. He is fattish, pale; with an especially wide forehead. He has blue, oval-shaped eyes, very clear and piercing. Wears light trousers and a dark jacket. He is alternatively mellifluous and violent in his manner.*)

(*The Mother seems crushed and terrified as if by an intolerable weight of shame and abasement. She is dressed in modest black and wears a thick widow's veil of crepe. When she lifts this, she reveals a waxlike face. She always keeps her eyes downcast.*)

(*The Stepdaughter is dashing, almost impudent, beautiful. She wears mourning too, but with great elegance. She shows contempt for the timid half-frightened manner of the wretched Boy (14 years old, and also dressed in black); on the other hand, she displays a lively tenderness for her little sister, the Child (about four), who is dressed in white, with a black silk sash at the waist.*)

(*The Son (22) is tall, severe in his attitude of contempt for the Father, supercilious and indifferent to the Mother. He looks as if he had come on the stage against his will.*)

DOOR-KEEPER (*cap in hand*): Excuse me, sir . . .

THE MANAGER (*rudely*): Eh? What is it?

DOOR-KEEPER (*timidly*): These people are asking for you, sir.

THE MANAGER (*furious*): I am rehearsing, and you know perfectly well no one's allowed to come in during rehearsals! (*Turning to the Characters.*) Who are you, please? What do you want?

THE FATHER (*coming forward a little, followed by the others who seem embarrassed*): As a matter of fact . . . we have come here in search of an author . . .

THE MANAGER (*half angry, half amazed*): An author? What author?

THE FATHER: Any author, sir.

THE MANAGER: But there's no author here. We are not rehearsing a new piece.

THE STEPDAUGHTER (*vivaciously*): So much the better, so much the better! We can be your new piece.

AN ACTOR (*coming forward from the others*): Oh, do you hear that?

THE FATHER (*to Stepdaughter*): Yes, but if the author isn't here . . . (*To Manager.*) unless you would be willing . . .

THE MANAGER: You are trying to be funny.

THE FATHER: No, for Heaven's sake, what are you saying? We bring you a drama, sir.

THE STEPDAUGHTER: We may be your fortune.

THE MANAGER: Will you oblige me by going away? We haven't time to waste with mad people.

THE FATHER (*mellifluously*): Oh sir, you know well that life is full of infinite absurdities, which, strangely enough, do not even need to appear plausible, since they are true.

THE MANAGER: What the devil is he talking about?

THE FATHER: I say that to reverse the ordinary process may well be considered a madness: that is, to create credible situations, in order that they may appear true. But permit me to observe that if this be madness, it is the sole *raison d'être*° of your profession, gentlemen. (*The Actors look hurt and perplexed.*)

THE MANAGER (*getting up and looking at him*): So our profession seems to you one worthy of madmen then?

THE FATHER: Well, to make seem true that which isn't true . . . without any need . . . for a joke as it were . . . Isn't that your mission, gentlemen: to give life to fantastic characters on the stage?

THE MANAGER (*interpreting the rising anger of the Company*): But I would beg you to believe, my dear sir, that the profession of the comedian is a noble one. If today, as things go, the playwrights give us stupid comedies to play and puppets to represent instead of men, remember we are proud to have given life to immortal works here on these very boards! (*The Actors, satisfied, applaud their Manager.*)

THE FATHER (*interrupting furiously*): Exactly, perfectly, to living beings more alive than those who breathe and wear clothes: beings less real perhaps, but truer! I agree with you entirely. (*The Actors look at one another in amazement.*)

THE MANAGER: But what do you mean? Before, you said . . .

THE FATHER: No, excuse me, I meant it for you, sir, who were crying out that you had no time to lose with madmen, while no one better than yourself knows that nature uses the instrument of human fantasy in order to pursue her high creative purpose.

raison d'être: French for "reason to exist."

THE MANAGER: Very well,—but where does all this take us?

THE FATHER: Nowhere! It is merely to show you that one is born to life in many forms, in many shapes, as tree, or as stone, as water, as butterfly, or as woman. So one may also be born a character in a play.

THE MANAGER (*with feigned comic dismay*): So you and these other friends of yours have been born characters?

THE FATHER: Exactly, and alive as you see! (*Manager and Actors burst out laughing.*)

THE FATHER (*hurt*): I am sorry you laugh, because we carry in us a drama, as you can guess from this woman here veiled in black.

THE MANAGER (*losing patience at last and almost indignant*): Oh, chuck it! Get away please! Clear out of here! (*To Property Man.*) For Heaven's sake, turn them out!

THE FATHER (*resisting*): No, no, look here, we . . .

THE MANAGER (*roaring*): We come here to work, you know.

LEADING ACTOR: One cannot let oneself be made such a fool of.

THE FATHER (*determined, coming forward*): I marvel at your incredulity, gentlemen. Are you not accustomed to see the characters created by an author spring to life in yourselves and face each other? Just because there is no "book" (*pointing to the Prompter's box*) which contains us, you refuse to believe . . .

THE STEPDAUGHTER (*advances toward Manager, smiling and coquettish*): Believe me, we are really six most interesting characters, sir; sidetracked however.

THE FATHER: Yes, that is the word! (*To Manager all at once.*) In the sense, that is, that the author who created us alive no longer wished, or was no longer able, materially to put us into a work of art. And this was a real crime, sir, because he who has had the luck to be born a character can laugh even at death. He cannot die. The man, the writer, the instrument of the creation will die, but his creation does not die. And to live for ever, it does not need to have extraordinary gifts or to be able to work wonders. Who was Sancho Panza? Who was Don Abbondio?° Yet they live eternally because—live germs as they were—they had the fortune to find a fecundating matrix, a fantasy which could raise and nourish them: make them live for ever!

THE MANAGER: That is quite all right. But what do you want here, all of you?

THE FATHER: We want to live.

THE MANAGER (*ironically*): For Eternity?

THE FATHER: No, sir, only for a moment . . . in you.

AN ACTOR: Just listen to him!

LEADING LADY: They want to live, in us . . . !

Sancho Panza . . . Don Abbondio: Memorable characters in novels: the squire in Cervantes's *Don Quixote* and the priest in Manzoni's *I Promessi Sposi* (*The Betrothed*), respectively.

JUVENILE LEAD (*pointing to the Stepdaughter*): I've no objection, as far as that one is concerned!

THE FATHER: Look here! look here! The comedy has to be made. (*To the Manager.*) But if you and your actors are willing, we can soon concert it among ourselves.

THE MANAGER (*annoyed*): But what do you want to concert? We don't go in for concerts here. Here we play dramas and comedies!

THE FATHER: Exactly! That is just why we have come to you.

THE MANAGER: And where is the "book"?

THE FATHER: It is in us! (*The Actors laugh.*) The drama is in us, and we are the drama. We are impatient to play it. Our inner passion drives us on to this.

THE STEPDAUGHTER (*disdainful, alluring, treacherous, full of impudence*): My passion, sir! Ah, if you only knew! My passion for him! (*Points to the Father and makes a pretense of embracing him. Then she breaks out into a loud laugh.*)

THE FATHER (*angrily*): Behave yourself! And please don't laugh in that fashion.

THE STEPDAUGHTER: With your permission, gentlemen, I, who am a two months orphan, will show you how I can dance and sing. (*Sings and then dances Prenez garde à Tchou-Tchin-Tchou.*)

Les chinois sont un peuple malin,
De Shangaï à Pékin,
Ils ont mis des écriteaux partout:
Prenez garde à Tchou-Tchin-Tchou.°

ACTORS AND ACTRESSES: Bravo! Well done! Tip-top!

THE MANAGER: Silence! This isn't a café concert, you know! (*Turning to the Father in consternation.*) Is she mad?

THE FATHER: Mad? No, she's worse than mad.

THE STEPDAUGHTER (*to Manager*): Worse? Worse? Listen! Stage this drama for us at once! Then you will see that at a certain moment I . . . when this little darling here. . . . (*Takes the Child by the hand and leads her to the Manager.*) Isn't she a dear? (*Takes her up and kisses her.*) Darling! Darling! (*Puts her down again and adds feelingly.*) Well, when God suddenly takes this dear little child away from that poor mother there; and this imbecile here (*seizing hold of the Boy roughly and pushing him forward*) does the stupidest things, like the fool he is, you will see me run away. Yes, gentlemen, I shall be off. But the moment hasn't arrived yet. After what has taken place between him and me (*indicates the Father with a horrible wink*) I can't remain any longer in this society, to have to witness the anguish of this mother here for that fool. . . . (*Indicates the Son.*) Look at him! Look at him! See how indifferent, how frigid he is, because he is the legitimate son. He despises me, despises him (*pointing to the Boy*), despises this baby

Prenez . . . Tchou: This French popular song is an adaptation of "Chu-Chin-Chow," an old Broadway show tune. "The Chinese are a sly people; / From Shanghai to Peking, / They've stuck up warning signs: / Beware of Tchou-Tchin-Tchou." (The words are funnier in French because *chou* means "cabbage.")

here; because . . . we are bastards. (*Goes to the Mother and embraces her.*) And he doesn't want to recognize her as his mother—she who is the common mother of us all. He looks down upon her as if she were only the mother of us three bastards. Wretch! (*She says all this very rapidly, excitedly. At the word "bastards" she raises her voice, and almost spits out the final "Wretch!"*)

THE MOTHER (*to the Manager, in anguish*): In the name of these two little children, I beg you. . . . (*She grows faint and is about to fall.*) Oh God!

THE FATHER (*coming forward to support her as do some of the Actors*): Quick, a chair, a chair for this poor widow!

THE ACTORS: Is it true? Has she really fainted?

THE MANAGER: Quick, a chair! Here!

(*One of the Actors brings a chair, the others proffer assistance. The Mother tries to prevent the Father from lifting the veil which covers her face.*)

THE FATHER: Look at her! Look at her!

THE MOTHER: No, no; stop it please!

THE FATHER (*raising her veil*): Let them see you!

THE MOTHER (*rising and covering her face with her hands, in desperation*): I beg you, sir, to prevent this man from carrying out his plan which is loathsome to me.

THE MANAGER (*dumbfounded*): I don't understand at all. What is the situation? (*To the Father.*) Is this lady your wife?

THE FATHER: Yes, gentlemen: my wife!

THE MANAGER: But how can she be a widow if you are alive? (*The Actors find relief for their astonishment in a loud laugh.*)

THE FATHER: Don't laugh! Don't laugh like that, for Heaven's sake. Her drama lies just here in this: she has had a lover, a man who ought to be here.

THE MOTHER (*with a cry*): No! No!

THE STEPDAUGHTER: Fortunately for her, he is dead. Two months ago as I said. We are in mourning, as you see.

THE FATHER: He isn't here, you see, not because he is dead. He isn't here—look at her a moment and you will understand—because her drama isn't a drama of the love of two men for whom she was incapable of feeling anything except possibly a little gratitude—gratitude not for me but for the other. She isn't a woman, she is a mother, and her drama—powerful, sir, I assure you—lies, as a matter of fact, all in these four children she has had by two men.

THE MOTHER: I had them? Have you got the courage to say that I wanted them? (*To the Company.*) It was his doing. It was he who gave me that other man, who forced me to go away with him.

THE STEPDAUGHTER: It isn't true.

THE MOTHER (*startled*): Not true, isn't it?

THE STEPDAUGHTER: No, it isn't true, it just isn't true.

THE MOTHER: And what can you know about it?

THE STEPDAUGHTER: It isn't true. Don't believe it. (*To Manager.*) Do you know why she says so? For that fellow there. (*Indicates the Son.*) She tortures herself, destroys herself on account of the neglect of that son there, and she wants him to believe that if she abandoned him when he was only two years old, it was because he (*indicates the Father*) made her do so.

THE MOTHER (*vigorously*): He forced me to it, and I call God to witness it. (*To the Manager.*) Ask him (*indicates Husband*) if it isn't true. Let him speak. You (*to Daughter*) are not in a position to know anything about it.

THE STEPDAUGHTER: I know you lived in peace and happiness with my father while he lived. Can you deny it?

THE MOTHER: No, I don't deny it. . . .

THE STEPDAUGHTER: He was always full of affection and kindness for you. (*To the Boy, angrily.*) It's true, isn't it? Tell them! Why don't you speak, you little fool?

THE MOTHER: Leave the poor boy alone. Why do you want to make me appear ungrateful, daughter? I don't want to offend your father. I have answered him that I didn't abandon my house and my son through any fault of mine, nor from any wilful passion.

THE FATHER: It is true. It was my doing.

LEADING MAN (*to the Company*): What a spectacle!

LEADING LADY: We are the audience this time.

JUVENILE LEAD: For once, in a way.

THE MANAGER (*beginning to get really interested*): Let's hear them out. Listen!

THE SON: Oh yes, you're going to hear a fine bit now. He will talk to you of the Demon of Experiment.

THE FATHER: You are a cynical imbecile. I've told you so already a hundred times. (*To the Manager.*) He tries to make fun of me on account of this expression which I have found to excuse myself with.

THE SON (*with disgust*): Yes, phrases! phrases!

THE FATHER: Phrases! Isn't everyone consoled when faced with a trouble or fact he doesn't understand, by a word, some simple word, which tells us nothing and yet calms us?

THE STEPDAUGHTER: Even in the case of remorse. In fact, especially then.

THE FATHER: Remorse? No, that isn't true. I've done more than use words to quiet the remorse in me.

THE STEPDAUGHTER: Yes, there was a bit of money too. Yes, yes, a bit of money. There were the hundred lire he was about to offer me in payment, gentlemen. . . . (*Sensation of horror among the Actors.*)

THE SON (*to the Stepdaughter*): This is vile.

THE STEPDAUGHTER: Vile? There they were in a pale blue envelope on a little mahogany table in the back of Madame Pace's shop. You know Madame Pace—one of those ladies who attract poor girls of good family into their ateliers, under the pretext of their selling *robes et manteaux.*°

THE SON: And he thinks he has bought the right to tyrannize over us all with those hundred lire he was going to pay; but which, fortunately—note this, gentlemen—he had no chance of paying.

robes et manteaux: French for "dresses and capes."

THE STEPDAUGHTER: It was a near thing, though, you know! (*Laughs ironically.*)

THE MOTHER (*protesting*): Shame, my daughter, shame!

THE STEPDAUGHTER: Shame indeed! This is my revenge! I am dying to live that scene . . . The room . . . I see it . . . Here is the window with the mantles exposed, there the divan, the looking-glass, a screen, there in front of the window the little mahogany table with the blue envelope containing one hundred lire. I see it. I see it. I could take hold of it. . . . But you, gentlemen, you ought to turn your backs now: I am almost nude, you know. But I don't blush: I leave that to him. (*Indicating Father.*)

THE MANAGER: I don't understand this at all.

THE FATHER: Naturally enough. I would ask you, sir, to exercise your authority a little here, and let me speak before you believe all she is trying to blame me with. Let me explain.

THE STEPDAUGHTER: Ah yes, explain it in your own way.

THE FATHER: But don't you see that the whole trouble lies here? In words, words. Each one of us has within him a whole world of things, each man of us his own special world. And how can we ever come to an understanding if I put in the words I utter the sense and value of things as I see them; while you who listen to me must inevitably translate them according to the conception of things each one of you has within himself. We think we understand each other, but we never really do. Look here! This woman (*indicating the Mother*) takes all my pity for her as a specially ferocious form of cruelty.

THE MOTHER: But you drove me away.

THE FATHER: Do you hear her? I drove her away! She believes I really sent her away.

THE MOTHER: You know how to talk, and I don't but, believe me, sir (*to Manager*), after he had married me . . . who knows why? . . . I was a poor insignificant woman. . . .

THE FATHER: But, good Heavens! it was just for your humility that I married you. I loved this simplicity in you. (*He stops when he sees she makes signs to contradict him, opens his arms wide in sign of desperation, seeing how hopeless it is to make himself understood.*) You see she denies it. Her mental deafness, believe me, is phenomenal, the limit: (*touches his forehead*) deaf, deaf, mentally deaf! She has plenty of feeling. Oh yes, a good heart for the children; but the brain—deaf, to the point of desperation—!

THE STEPDAUGHTER: Yes, but ask him how his intelligence has helped us.

THE FATHER: If we could see all the evil that may spring from good, what should we do? (*At this point the Leading Lady, who is biting her lips with rage at seeing the Leading Man flirting with the Stepdaughter, comes forward and speaks to the Manager.*)

LEADING LADY: Excuse me, but are we going to rehearse today?

THE MANAGER: Of course, of course; but let's hear them out.

JUVENILE LEAD: This is something quite new.

L'INGÉNUE: Most interesting!

LEADING LADY: Yes, for the people who like that kind of thing. (*Casts a glance at Leading Man.*)

THE MANAGER (*to Father*): You must please explain yourself quite clearly. (*Sits down.*)

THE FATHER: Very well then: listen! I had in my service a poor man, a clerk, a secretary of mine, full of devotion, who became friends with her. (*Indicating the Mother.*) They understood one another, were kindred souls in fact, without, however, the least suspicion of any evil existing. They were incapable even of thinking of it.

THE STEPDAUGHTER: So he thought of it—for them!

THE FATHER: That's not true. I meant to do good to them—and to myself, I confess, at the same time. Things had come to the point that I could not say a word to either of them without their making a mute appeal, one to the other, with their eyes. I could see them silently asking each other how I was to be kept in countenance, how I was to be kept quiet. And this, believe me, was just about enough of itself to keep me in a constant rage, to exasperate me beyond measure.

THE MANAGER: And why didn't you send him away then—this secretary of yours?

THE FATHER: Precisely what I did, sir. And then I had to watch this poor woman drifting forlornly about the house like an animal without a master, like an animal one has taken in out of pity.

THE MOTHER: Ah yes . . . !

THE FATHER (*suddenly turning to the Mother*): It's true about the son anyway, isn't it?

THE MOTHER: He took my son away from me first of all.

THE FATHER: But not from cruelty. I did it so that he should grow up healthy and strong by living in the country.

THE STEPDAUGHTER (*pointing to him ironically*): As one can see.

THE FATHER (*quickly*): Is it my fault if he has grown up like this? I sent him to a wet nurse in the country, a peasant, as *she* did not seem to me strong enough, though she is of humble origin. That was, anyway, the reason I married her. Unpleasant all this may be, but how can it be helped? My mistake possibly, but there we are! All my life I have had these confounded aspirations towards a certain moral sanity. (*At this point the Stepdaughter bursts into a noisy laugh.*) Oh, stop it! Stop it! I can't stand it.

THE MANAGER: Yes, please stop it, for Heaven's sake.

THE STEPDAUGHTER: But imagine moral sanity from him, if you please—the client of certain ateliers like that of Madame Pace!

THE FATHER: Fool! That is the proof that I am a man! This seeming contradiction, gentlemen, is the strongest proof that I stand here a live man before you. Why, it is just for this very incongruity in my nature that I have had to suffer what I have. I could not live by the side of that woman (*indicating the Mother*) any longer; but not so much for the boredom she inspired me with as for the pity I felt for her.

THE MOTHER: And so he turned me out—.

THE FATHER: —well provided for! Yes, I sent her to that man, gentlemen . . . to let her go free of me.

THE MOTHER: And to free himself.

THE FATHER: Yes, I admit it. It was also a liberation for me. But great evil has come of it. I meant well when I did it, and I did it more for her sake than mine. I swear it. (*Crosses his arms on his chest; then turns suddenly to the Mother.*) Did I ever lose sight of you until that other man carried you off to another town, like the angry fool he was? And on account of my pure interest in you . . . my pure interest, I repeat, that had no base motive in it . . . I watched with the tenderest concern the new family that grew up around her. She can bear witness to this. (*Points to the Stepdaughter.*)

THE STEPDAUGHTER: Oh yes, that's true enough. When I was a kiddie so so high, you know, with plaits over my shoulders and knickers longer than my skirts, I used to see him waiting outside the school for me to come out. He came to see how I was growing up.

THE FATHER: This is infamous, shameful!

THE STEPDAUGHTER: No. Why?

THE FATHER: Infamous! infamous! (*Then excitedly to Manager, explaining.*) After she (*indicating the Mother*) went away, my house seemed suddenly empty. She was my incubus, but she filled my house. I was like a dazed fly alone in the empty rooms. This boy here (*indicating the Son*) was educated away from home, and when he came back, he seemed to me to be no more mine. With no mother to stand between him and me, he grew up entirely for himself, on his own, apart, with no tie of intellect or affection binding him to me. And then—strange but true—I was driven, by curiosity at first and then by some tender sentiment, towards her family, which had come into being through my will. The thought of her began gradually to fill up the emptiness I felt all around me. I wanted to know if she were happy in living out the simple daily duties of life. I wanted to think of her as fortunate and happy because far away from the complicated torments of my spirit. And so, to have proof of this, I used to watch that child coming out of school.

THE STEPDAUGHTER: Yes, yes. True. He used to follow me in the street and smiled at me, waved his hand, like this. I would look at him with interest, wondering who he might be. I told my mother, who guessed at once. (*The Mother agrees with a nod.*) Then she didn't want to send me to school for some days; and when I finally went back, there he was again—looking so ridiculous—with a paper parcel in his hands. He came close to me, caressed me, and drew out a fine straw hat from the parcel, with a bouquet of flowers—all for me!

THE MANAGER: A bit discursive this, you know!

THE SON (*contemptuously*): Literature! Literature!

Scene from the 1985 American Repertory Theater production of *Six Characters in Search of an Author,* directed by Robert Brustein.

THE FATHER: Literature indeed! This is life, this is passion!

THE MANAGER: It may be, but it won't act.

THE FATHER: I agree. This is only the part leading up. I don't suggest this should be staged. She (*pointing to the Stepdaughter*), as you see, is no longer the flapper with plaits down her back—

THE STEPDAUGHTER: —and knickers showing below the skirt!

THE FATHER: The drama is coming now, sir; something new, complex, most interesting.

THE STEPDAUGHTER: As soon as my father died . . .

THE FATHER: —there was absolute misery for them. They came back here, unknown to me. Through her stupidity! (*Pointing to the Mother.*) It is true she can barely write her own name; but she could anyhow have got her daughter to write to me that they were in need . . .

THE MOTHER: And how was I to divine all this sentiment in him?

THE FATHER: That is exactly your mistake, never to have guessed any of my sentiments.

THE MOTHER: After so many years apart, and all that had happened . . .

THE FATHER: Was it my fault if that fellow carried you away? It happened quite suddenly, for after he had obtained some job or other, I could find no trace of them; and so, not unnaturally, my interest in them dwindled. But the drama culminated unforeseen and violent on their return, when I was impelled by my miserable flesh that still lives. . . . Ah! what misery, what wretchedness is that of the man who is alone and disdains debasing *liaisons!* Not old enough to do without women, and not young enough to go and look for one without shame. Misery? It's worse than misery; it's a horror; for no woman can any longer give him love; and when a man feels this. . . . One ought to do without, you say? Yes, yes, I know. Each of us when he appears before his fellows is clothed in a certain dignity. But every man knows what unconfessable things pass within the secrecy of his own heart. One gives way to the temptation, only to rise from it again, afterwards, with a great eagerness to reestablish one's dignity, as if it were a tombstone to place on the grave of one's shame, and a monument to hide and sign the memory of our weaknesses. Everybody's in the same case. Some folks haven't the courage to say certain things, that's all!

THE STEPDAUGHTER: All appear to have the courage to do them though.

THE FATHER: Yes, but in secret. Therefore, you want more courage to say these things. Let a man but speak these things out, and folks at once label him a cynic. But it isn't true. He is like all the others, better indeed, because he isn't afraid to reveal with the light of the intelligence the red shame of human bestiality on which most men close their eyes so as not to see it.

Woman—for example, look at her case! She turns tantalizing inviting glances on you. You seize her. No sooner does she feel herself in your grasp than she closes her eyes. It is the sign of her mission, the sign by which she says to man: "Blind yourself, for I am blind."

THE STEPDAUGHTER: Sometimes she can close them no more: when she no longer feels the need of hiding her shame to herself, but dry-eyed and dispassionately, sees only that of the man who has blinded himself without love. Oh, all these intellectual complications make me sick, disgust me—all this philosophy that uncovers the beast in man, and then seeks to save him, excuse him . . . I can't stand it, sir. When a man seeks to "simplify" life bestially, throwing aside every relic of humanity, every chaste aspiration, every pure feeling, all sense of ideality, duty, modesty, shame . . . then nothing is more revolting and nauseous than a certain kind of remorse—crocodiles' tears, that's what it is.

THE MANAGER: Let's come to the point. This is only discussion.

THE FATHER: Very good, sir! But a fact is like a sack which won't stand up when it's empty. In order that it may stand up, one has to put into it the reason and sentiment which have caused it to exist. I couldn't possibly know that after the death of that man, they had decided to return here, that they were in misery, and that she (*pointing to the Mother*) had gone to work as a modiste,° and at a shop of the type of that of Madame Pace.

THE STEPDAUGHTER: A real high-class modiste, you must know, gentlemen. In appearance, she works for the leaders of the best society; but she arranges matters so that these elegant ladies serve her purpose . . . without prejudice to other ladies who are . . . well . . . only so so.

THE MOTHER: You will believe me, gentlemen, that it never entered my mind that the old hag offered me work because she had her eye on my daughter.

THE STEPDAUGHTER: Poor mamma! Do you know, sir, what that woman did when I brought her back the work my mother had finished? She would point out to me that I had torn one of my frocks, and she would give it back to my mother to mend. It was I who paid for it, always I; while this poor creature here believed she was sacrificing herself for me and these two children here, sitting up at night sewing Madame Pace's robes.

THE MANAGER: And one day you met there . . .

THE STEPDAUGHTER: Him, him. Yes sir, an old client. There's a scene for you to play! Superb!

THE FATHER: She, the Mother arrived just then . . .

THE STEPDAUGHTER (*treacherously*): Almost in time!

THE FATHER (*crying out*): No, in time! in time! Fortunately I recognized her . . . in time. And I took them back home with me to my house. You can imagine now her position and mine; she, as you see her; and I who cannot look her in the face.

THE STEPDAUGHTER: Absurd! How can I possibly be expected—after that—to be a modest young miss, a fit person to go with his confounded aspirations for "a solid moral sanity"?

modiste: A person who makes fashionable clothing for women.

THE FATHER: For the drama lies all in this—in the conscience that I have, that each one of us has. We believe this conscience to be a single thing, but it is many-sided. There is one for this person, and another for that. Diverse consciences. So we have this illusion of being one person for all, of having a personality that is unique in all our acts. But it isn't true. We perceive this when, tragically perhaps, in something we do, we are as it were, suspended, caught up in the air on a kind of hook. Then we perceive that all of us was not in that act, and that it would be an atrocious injustice to judge us by that action alone, as if all our existence were summed up in that one deed. Now do you understand the perfidy of this girl? She surprised me in a place, where she ought not to have known me, just as I could not exist for her; and she now seeks to attach to me a reality such as I could never suppose I should have to assume for her in a shameful and fleeting moment of my life. I feel this above all else. And the drama, you will see, acquires a tremendous value from this point. Then there is the position of the others . . . his. . . . (*Indicating the Son.*)

THE SON (*shrugging his shoulders scornfully*): Leave me alone! I don't come into this.

THE FATHER: What? You don't come into this?

THE SON: I've got nothing to do with it, and don't want to have; because you know well enough I wasn't made to be mixed up in all this with the rest of you.

THE STEPDAUGHTER: We are only vulgar folk! He is the fine gentleman. You may have noticed, Mr. Manager, that I fix him now and again with a look of scorn while he lowers his eyes—for he knows the evil he has done me.

THE SON (*scarcely looking at her*): I?

THE STEPDAUGHTER: You! you! I owe my life on the streets to you. Did you or did you not deny us, with your behavior, I won't say the intimacy of home, but even that mere hospitality which makes guests feel at their ease? We were intruders who had come to disturb the kingdom of your legitimacy. I should like to have you witness, Mr. Manager, certain scenes between him and me. He says I have tyrannized over everyone. But it was just his behavior which made me insist on the reason for which I had come into the house,—this reason he calls "vile"—into his house, with my mother who is his mother too. And I came as mistress of the house.

THE SON: It's easy for them to put me always in the wrong. But imagine, gentlemen, the position of a son, whose fate it is to see arrive one day at his home a young woman of impudent bearing, a young woman who inquires for his father, with whom who knows what business she has. This young man has then to witness her return bolder than ever, accompanied by that child there. He is obliged to watch her treat his father in an equivocal and confidential manner. She asks for money of him in a way that lets one suppose he must give it to her, *must,* do you understand, because he has every obligation to do so.

THE FATHER: But I have, as a matter of fact, this obligation. I owe it to your mother.

THE SON: How should I know? When had I ever seen or heard of her? One day there arrive with her (*indicating Stepdaughter*) that lad and this baby here. I am told: "This is *your* mother too, you know." I divine from her manner (*indicating Stepdaughter again*) why it is they have come home. I had rather not say what I feel and think about it. I shouldn't even care to confess to myself. No action can therefore be hoped for from me in this affair. Believe me, Mr. Manager, I am an "unrealized" character, dramatically speaking; and I find myself not at all at ease in their company. Leave me out of it, I beg you.

THE FATHER: What? It is just because you are so that . . .

THE SON: How do you know what I am like? When did you ever bother your head about me?

THE FATHER: I admit it. I admit it. But isn't that a situation in itself? This aloofness of yours which is so cruel to me and to your mother, who returns home and sees you almost for the first time grown up, who doesn't recognize you but knows you are her son. . . . (*Pointing out the Mother to the Manager.*) See, she's crying!

THE STEPDAUGHTER (*angrily, stamping her foot*): Like a fool!

THE FATHER (*indicating Stepdaughter*): She can't stand him, you know. (*Then referring again to the Son.*) He says he doesn't come into the affair, whereas he is really the hinge of the whole action. Look at that lad who is always clinging to his mother, frightened and humiliated. It is on account of this fellow here. Possibly his situation is the most painful of all. He feels himself a stranger more than the others. The poor little chap feels mortified, humiliated at being brought into a home out of charity as it were. (*In confidence.*) He is the image of his father. Hardly talks at all. Humble and quiet.

THE MANAGER: Oh, we'll cut him out. You've no notion what a nuisance boys are on the stage. . . .

THE FATHER: He disappears soon, you know. And the baby too. She is the first to vanish from the scene. The drama consists finally in this: when that mother reenters my house, her family born outside of it, and shall we say superimposed on the original, ends with the death of the little girl, the tragedy of the boy and the flight of the elder daughter. It cannot go on, because it is foreign to its surroundings. So after much torment, we three remain: I, the mother, that son. Then, owing to the disappearance of that extraneous family, we too find ourselves strange to one another. We find we are living in an atmosphere of mortal desolation which is the revenge, as he (*indicating Son*) scornfully said of the Demon of Experiment, that unfortunately hides in me. Thus, sir, you see when faith is lacking, it becomes impossible to create certain states of happiness, for we lack the necessary humility. Vaingloriously, we try to substitute ourselves for this faith, creating thus for the rest of the world a reality which we believe after their fashion, while, actually, it doesn't exist. For each one of us has his own reality to be respected before God, even when it is harmful to one's very self.

THE MANAGER: There is something in what you say. I assure you all this interests me very much. I begin to think there's the stuff for a drama in all this, and not a bad drama either.

THE STEPDAUGHTER (*coming forward*): When you've got a character like me . . .

THE FATHER (*shutting her up, all excited to learn the decision of the Manager*): You be quiet!

THE MANAGER (*reflecting, heedless of interruption*): It's new . . . hem . . . yes. . . .

THE FATHER: Absolutely new!

THE MANAGER: You've got a nerve though, I must say, to come here and fling it at me like this . . .

THE FATHER: You will understand, sir, born as we are for the stage . . .

THE MANAGER: Are you amateur actors then?

THE FATHER: No, I say born for the stage, because . . .

THE MANAGER: Oh, nonsense. You're an old hand, you know.

THE FATHER: No sir, no. We act that role for which we have been cast, that role which we are given in life. And in my own case, passion itself, as usually happens, becomes a trifle theatrical when it is exalted.

THE MANAGER: Well, well, that will do. But you see, without an author. . . . I could give you the address of an author if you like . . .

THE FATHER: No, no. Look here! You must be the author.

THE MANAGER: I? What are you talking about?

THE FATHER: Yes, you, you! Why not?

THE MANAGER: Because I have never been an author: that's why.

THE FATHER: Then why not turn author now? Everybody does it. You don't want any special qualities. Your task is made much easier by the fact that we are all here alive before you. . . .

THE MANAGER: It won't do.

THE FATHER: What? When you see us live our drama. . . .

THE MANAGER: Yes, that's all right. But you want someone to write it.

THE FATHER: No, no. Someone to take it down, possibly, while we play it, scene by scene! It will be enough to sketch it out at first, and then try it over.

THE MANAGER: Well . . . I am almost tempted. It's a bit of an idea. One might have a shot at it.

THE FATHER: Of course. You'll see what scenes will come out of it. I can give you one, at once . . .

THE MANAGER: By Jove, it tempts me. I'd like to have a go at it. Let's try it out. Come with me to my office. (*Turning to the Actors.*) You are at liberty for a bit, but don't step out of the theater for long. In a quarter of an hour, twenty minutes, all back here again! (*To the Father.*) We'll see what can be done. Who knows if we don't get something really extraordinary out of it?

THE FATHER: There's no doubt about it. They (*indicating the Characters*) had better come with us too, hadn't they?

THE MANAGER: Yes, yes. Come on! come on! (*Moves away and then turning to the Actors.*) Be punctual, please! (*Manager and the Six Characters cross the stage and go off. The other Actors remain, looking at one another in astonishment.*)

LEADING MAN: Is he serious? What the devil does he want to do?

JUVENILE LEAD: This is rank madness.

THIRD ACTOR: Does he expect to knock up a drama in five minutes?

JUVENILE LEAD: Like the improvisers!

LEADING LADY: If he thinks I'm going to take part in a joke like this. . . .

JUVENILE LEAD: I'm out of it anyway.

FOURTH ACTOR: I should like to know who they are. (*Alludes to Characters.*)

THIRD ACTOR: What do you suppose? Madmen or rascals!

JUVENILE LEAD: And he takes them seriously!

L'INGÉNUE: Vanity! He fancies himself as an author now.

LEADING MAN: It's absolutely unheard of. If the stage has come to this . . . well I'm . . .

FIFTH ACTOR: It's rather a joke.

THIRD ACTOR: Well, we'll see what's going to happen next.

(*Thus talking, the Actors leave the stage, some going out by the little door at the back, others retiring to their dressing rooms.*)

   (*The curtain remains up.*)

   (*The action of the play is suspended for twenty minutes.*)

ACT II

(*The stage call-bells ring to warn the company that the play is about to begin again.*)

   (*The Stepdaughter comes out of the Manager's office along with the Child and the Boy. As she comes out of the office, she cries: —*)

   Nonsense! nonsense! Do it yourselves! I'm not going to mix myself up in this mess. (*Turning to the Child and coming quickly with her on to the stage.*) Come on, Rosetta, let's run!

(*The Boy follows them slowly, remaining a little behind and seeming perplexed.*)

THE STEPDAUGHTER (*stops, bends over the Child and takes the latter's face between her hands*): My little darling! You're frightened, aren't you? You don't know where we are, do you? (*Pretending to reply to a question of the Child.*) What is the stage? It's a place, baby, you know, where people play at being serious, a place where they act comedies. We've got to act a comedy now, dead serious, you know; and

you're in it also, little one. (*Embraces her, pressing the little head to her breast, and rocking the Child for a moment.*) Oh darling, darling, what a horrid comedy you've got to play! What a wretched part they've found for you! A garden . . . a fountain . . . look . . . just suppose, kiddie, it's here. Where, you say? Why, right here in the middle. It's all pretense you know. That's the trouble, my pet: it's all make-believe here. It's better to imagine it though, because if they fix it up for you, it'll only be painted cardboard, painted cardboard for the rockery, the water, the plants. . . . Ah, but I think a baby like this one would sooner have a make-believe fountain than a real one, so she could play with it. What a joke it'll be for the others! But for you, alas! not quite such a joke: you who are real, baby dear, and really play by a real fountain that is big and green and beautiful, with ever so many bamboos around it that are reflected in the water, and a whole lot of little ducks swimming about. . . . No, Rosetta, no, your mother doesn't bother about you on account of that wretch of a son there. I'm in the devil of a temper, and as for that lad. . . . (*Seizes Boy by the arm to force him to take one of his hands out of his pockets.*) What have you got there? What are you hiding? (*Pulls his hand out of his pocket, looks into it, and catches the glint of a revolver.*) Ah! where did you get this? (*The Boy, very pale in the face, looks at her, but does not answer.*) Idiot! If I'd been in your place, instead of killing myself, I'd have shot one of those two, or both of them: father and son.

(*The Father enters from the office, all excited from his work. The Manager follows him.*)

THE FATHER: Come on, come on dear! Come here for a minute! We've arranged everything. It's all fixed up.

THE MANAGER (*also excited*): If you please, young lady, there are one or two points to settle still. Will you come along?

THE STEPDAUGHTER (*following him toward the office*): Ouff! what's the good, if you've arranged everything.

(*The Father, Manager, and Stepdaughter go back into the office again [off] for a moment. At the same time, the Son, followed by the Mother, comes out.*)

THE SON (*looking at the three entering office*): Oh this is fine, fine! And to think I can't even get away!

(*The Mother attempts to look at him, but lowers her eyes immediately when he turns away from her. She then sits down. The Boy and the Child approach her. She casts a glance again at the Son, and speaks with humble tones, trying to draw him into conversation.*)

THE MOTHER: And isn't my punishment the worst of all? (*Then seeing from the Son's manner that he will not bother himself about her.*) My God! Why are you so cruel? Isn't it enough for one person to support all this torment? Must you then insist on others seeing it also?

THE SON (*half to himself, meaning the Mother to hear, however*): And they want to put it on the stage! If there was at least a reason for it! He thinks he has got at the meaning of it all. Just as if each one of us in every circumstance of life couldn't find his own explanation of it! (*Pauses.*) He complains he was discovered in a place where he ought not to have been seen, in a moment of his life which ought to have remained hidden and kept out of the reach of that convention which he has to maintain for other people. And what about my case? Haven't I had to reveal what no son ought ever to reveal: how father and mother live and are man and wife for themselves quite apart from that idea of father and mother which we give them? When this idea is revealed, our life is then linked at one point only to that man and that woman; and as such it should shame them, shouldn't it?

(*The Mother hides her face in her hands. From the dressing rooms and the little door at the back of the stage the Actors and Stage Manager return, followed by the Property Man and the Prompter. At the same moment, the Manager comes out of his office, accompanied by the Father and the Stepdaughter.*)

THE MANAGER: Come on, come on, ladies and gentlemen! Heh! you there, machinist!

MACHINIST: Yes sir?

THE MANAGER: Fix up the parlor with the floral decorations. Two wings and a drop with a door will do. Hurry up!

(*The Machinist runs off at once to prepare the scene and arranges it while the Manager talks with the Stage Manager, the Property Man, and the Prompter on matters of detail.*)

THE MANAGER (*to Property Man*): Just have a look, and see if there isn't a sofa or a divan in the wardrobe . . .

PROPERTY MAN: There's the green one.

THE STEPDAUGHTER: No no! Green won't do. It was yellow, ornamented with flowers—very large! and most comfortable!

PROPERTY MAN: There isn't one like that.

THE MANAGER: It doesn't matter. Use the one we've got.

THE STEPDAUGHTER: Doesn't matter? It's most important!

THE MANAGER: We're only trying it now. Please don't interfere. (*To Property Man.*) See if we've got a shop window—long and narrowish.

THE STEPDAUGHTER: And the little table! The little mahogany table for the pale blue envelope!

PROPERTY MAN (*to Manager*): There's that little gilt one.

THE MANAGER: That'll do fine.

THE FATHER: A mirror.

THE STEPDAUGHTER: And the screen! We must have a screen. Otherwise how can I manage?

PROPERTY MAN: That's all right, Miss. We've got any amount of them.

THE MANAGER (*to the Stepdaughter*): We want some clothes pegs too, don't we?

THE STEPDAUGHTER: Yes, several, several!

THE MANAGER: See how many we've got and bring them all.

PROPERTY MAN: All right!

(*The Property Man hurries off to obey his orders. While he is putting the things in their places, the Manager talks to the Prompter and then with the Characters and the Actors.*)

THE MANAGER (*to Prompter*): Take your seat. Look here: this is the outline of the scenes, act by act. (*Hands him some sheets of paper.*) And now I'm going to ask you to do something out of the ordinary.

PROMPTER: Take it down in shorthand?

THE MANAGER (*pleasantly surprised*): Exactly! Can you do shorthand?

PROMPTER: Yes, a little.

THE MANAGER: Good! (*Turning to a Stage Hand.*) Go and get some paper from my office, plenty, as much as you can find.

(*The Stage Hand goes off and soon returns with a handful of paper which he gives to the Prompter.*)

THE MANAGER (*to Prompter*): You follow the scenes as we play them, and try and get the points down, at any rate the most important ones. (*Then addressing the Actors.*) Clear the stage, ladies and gentlemen! Come over here (*pointing to the left*) and listen attentively.

LEADING LADY: But, excuse me, we . . .

THE MANAGER (*guessing her thought*): Don't worry! You won't have to improvise.

LEADING MAN: What have we to do then?

THE MANAGER: Nothing. For the moment you just watch and listen. Everybody will get his part written out afterwards. At present we're going to try the thing as best we can. They're going to act now.

THE FATHER (*as if fallen from the clouds into the confusion of the stage*): We? What do you mean, if you please, by a rehearsal?

THE MANAGER: A rehearsal for them. (*Points to the Actors.*)

THE FATHER: But since we are the characters . . .

THE MANAGER: All right: "characters" then, if you insist on calling yourselves such. But here, my dear sir, the characters don't act. Here the actors do the acting. The characters are there, in the "book" (*pointing toward Prompter's box*)—when there is a "book"!

THE FATHER: I won't contradict you; but excuse me, the actors aren't the characters. They want to be, they pretend to be, don't they? Now if these gentlemen here are fortunate enough to have us alive before them . . .

THE MANAGER: Oh, this is grand! You want to come before the public yourselves then?

THE FATHER: As we are. . . .

THE MANAGER: I can assure you it would be a magnificent spectacle!

LEADING MAN: What's the use of us here anyway then?

THE MANAGER: You're not going to pretend that you can act? It makes me laugh! (*The Actors laugh.*) There, you see, they are laughing at the notion. But, by the way, I must cast the parts. That won't be difficult. They cast themselves. (*To the Second Lady Lead.*) You play the Mother. (*To the Father.*) We must find her a name.

THE FATHER: Amalia, sir.

THE MANAGER: But that is the real name of your wife. We don't want to call her by her real name.

THE FATHER: Why ever not, if it is her name? . . . Still, perhaps, if that lady must . . . (*Makes a slight motion of the hand to indicate the Second Lady Lead.*) I see this woman here (*means the Mother*) as Amalia. But do as you like. (*Gets more and more confused.*) I don't know what to say to you. Already, I begin to hear my own words ring false, as if they had another sound . . .

THE MANAGER: Don't you worry about it. It'll be our job to find the right tones. And as for her name, if you want her Amalia, Amalia it shall be; and if you don't like it, we'll find another! For the moment though, we'll call the characters in this way: (*To Juvenile Lead.*) You are the Son. (*To the Leading Lady.*) You naturally are the Stepdaughter. . . .

THE STEPDAUGHTER (*excitedly*): What? what? I, that woman there? (*Bursts out laughing.*)

THE MANAGER (*angry*): What is there to laugh at?

LEADING LADY (*indignant*): Nobody has ever dared to laugh at me. I insist on being treated with respect; otherwise I go away.

THE STEPDAUGHTER: No, no, excuse me . . . I am not laughing at you. . . .

THE MANAGER (*to Stepdaughter*): You ought to feel honored to be played by . . .

LEADING LADY (*at once, contemptuously*): "That woman there" . . .

THE STEPDAUGHTER: But I wasn't speaking of you, you know. I was speaking of myself—whom I can't see at all in you! That is all. I don't know . . . but . . . you . . . aren't in the least like me. . . .

THE FATHER: True. Here's the point. Look here, sir, our temperaments, our souls. . . .

THE MANAGER: Temperament, soul, be hanged! Do you suppose the spirit of the piece is in you? Nothing of the kind!

THE FATHER: What, haven't we our own temperaments, our own souls?

THE MANAGER: Not at all. Your soul or whatever you like to call it takes shape here. The actors give body and form to it, voice and gesture. And my actors—I may tell you—have given expression to much more lofty material than this little drama of yours, which may or may not hold up on the stage. But if it does, the merit of it, believe me, will be due to my actors.

THE FATHER: I don't dare contradict you, sir, but, believe me, it is a terrible suffering for us who are as we are, with these bodies of ours, these features to see. . . .

THE MANAGER (*cutting him short and out of patience*): Good heavens! The make-up will remedy all that, man, the make-up. . . .

THE FATHER: Maybe. But the voice, the gestures . . .

THE MANAGER: Now, look here! On the stage, you as yourself, cannot exist. The actor here acts you, and that's an end to it!

THE FATHER: I understand. And now I think I see why our author who conceived us as we are, all alive, didn't want to put us on the stage after all. I haven't the least desire to offend your actors. Far from it! But when I think that I am to be acted by . . . I don't know by whom. . . .

LEADING MAN (*on his dignity*): By me, if you've no objection!

THE FATHER (*humbly, mellifluously*): Honored, I assure you, sir. (*Bows.*) Still, I must say that try as this gentleman may, with all his good will and wonderful art, to absorb me into himself. . . .

LEADING MAN: Oh chuck it! "Wonderful art!" Withdraw that, please!

THE FATHER: The performance he will give, even doing his best with make-up to look like me. . . .

LEADING MAN: It will certainly be a bit difficult! (*The Actors laugh.*)

THE FATHER: Exactly! It will be difficult to act me as I really am. The effect will be rather—apart from the make-up—according as to how he supposes I am, as he senses me—if he does sense me—and not as I inside of myself feel myself to be. It seems to me then that account should be taken of this by everyone whose duty it may become to criticize us. . . .

THE MANAGER: Heavens! The man's starting to think about the critics now! Let them say what they like. It's up to us to put on the play if we can. (*Looking around.*) Come on! come on! Is the stage set? (*To the Actors and Characters.*) Stand back—stand back! Let me see, and don't let's lose any more time! (*To the Stepdaughter.*) Is it all right as it is now?

THE STEPDAUGHTER: Well, to tell the truth, I don't recognize the scene.

THE MANAGER: My dear lady, you can't possibly suppose that we can construct that shop of Madame Pace piece by piece here? (*To the Father.*) You said a white room with flowered wallpaper, didn't you?

THE FATHER: Yes.

THE MANAGER: Well then. We've got the furniture right more or less. Bring that little table a bit further forward. (*The Stage Hands obey the order. To Property Man.*) You go and find an envelope, if possible, a pale blue one; and give it to that gentleman. (*Indicates Father.*)

PROPERTY MAN: An ordinary envelope?

MANAGER AND FATHER: Yes, yes, an ordinary envelope.

PROPERTY MAN: At once, sir. (*Exit.*)

THE MANAGER: Ready, everyone! First scene—the Young Lady. (*The Leading Lady comes forward.*) No, no, you must wait. I meant her. (*Indicating the Stepdaughter.*) You just watch—

THE STEPDAUGHTER (*adding at once*): How I shall play it, how I shall live it! . . .

LEADING LADY (*offended*): I shall live it also, you may be sure, as soon as I begin!

THE MANAGER (*with his hands to his head*): Ladies and gentlemen, if you please! No more useless discussions! Scene I: the Young Lady with Madame Pace: Oh! (*Looks around as if lost.*) And this Madame Pace, where is she?

THE FATHER: She isn't with us, sir.

THE MANAGER: Then what the devil's to be done?

THE FATHER: But she is alive too.

THE MANAGER: Yes, but where is she?

THE FATHER: One minute. Let me speak! (*Turning to the Actresses.*) If these ladies would be so good as to give me their hats for a moment. . . .

THE ACTRESSES (*half surprised, half laughing, in chorus*): What? Why? Our hats? What does he say?

THE MANAGER: What are you going to do with the ladies' hats? (*The Actors laugh.*)

THE FATHER: Oh nothing. I just want to put them on these pegs for a moment. And one of the ladies will be so kind as to take off her mantle. . . .

THE ACTORS: Oh, what d'you think of that? Only the mantle? He must be mad.

SOME ACTRESSES: But why? Mantles as well?

THE FATHER: To hang them up here for a moment. Please be so kind, will you?

THE ACTRESSES (*taking off their hats, one or two also their cloaks, and going to hang them on the racks*): After all, why not? There you are! This is really funny. We've got to put them on show.

THE FATHER: Exactly; just like that, on show.

THE MANAGER: May we know why?

THE FATHER: I'll tell you. Who knows if, by arranging the stage for her, she does not come here herself, attracted by the very articles of her trade? (*Inviting the Actors to look toward the exit at back of stage.*) Look! Look!

(*The door at the back of stage opens and Madame Pace enters and takes a few steps forward. She is a fat, oldish woman with puffy oxygenated hair. She is rouged and powdered, dressed with a comical elegance in black silk. Round her waist is a long silver chain from which hangs a pair of scissors. The Stepdaughter runs over to her at once amid the stupor of the Actors.*)

THE STEPDAUGHTER (*turning toward her*): There she is! There she is!

THE FATHER (*radiant*): It's she! I said so, didn't I! There she is!

THE MANAGER (*conquering his surprise, and then becoming indignant*): What sort of a trick is this?

LEADING MAN (*almost at the same time*): What's going to happen next?

JUVENILE LEAD: Where does she come from?

L'INGÉNUE: They've been holding her in reserve, I guess.

LEADING LADY: A vulgar trick!

THE FATHER (*dominating the protests*): Excuse me, all of you! Why are you so anxious to destroy in the name of a vulgar, commonplace sense of truth, this reality which comes to birth attracted and formed by the magic of the stage itself, which has indeed more right to live here than you, since it is much truer than you—if you don't mind my saying so? Which is the actress among you who is to play Madame Pace? Well, here is Madame Pace herself. And you will allow, I fancy, that the actress who acts her will be less true than this woman here, who is herself in person. You see my daughter recognized her and went over to her at once. Now you're going to witness the scene!

(*But the scene between the Stepdaughter and Madame Pace has already begun despite the protest of the Actors and the reply of the Father. It has begun quietly, naturally, in a manner impossible for the stage. So when the Actors, called to attention by the Father, turn round and see Madame Pace, who has placed one hand under the Stepdaughter's chin to raise her head, they observe her at first with great attention, but hearing her speak in an unintelligible manner their interest begins to wane.*)

THE MANAGER: Well? well?

LEADING MAN: What does she say?

LEADING LADY: One can't hear a word.

JUVENILE LEAD: Louder! Louder please!

THE STEPDAUGHTER (*leaving Madame Pace, who smiles a Sphinx-like smile, and advancing toward the Actors*): Louder? Louder? What are you talking about? These aren't matters which can be shouted at the top of one's voice. If I have spoken them out loud, it was to shame him and have my revenge. (*Indicates Father.*) But for Madame it's quite a different matter.

THE MANAGER: Indeed? indeed? But here, you know people have got to make themselves heard, my dear. Even we who are on the stage can't hear you. What will it be when the public's in the theater? And anyway, you can very well speak up now among yourselves, since we shan't be present to listen to you as we are now. You've got to pretend to be alone in a room at the back of a shop where no one can hear you.

(*The Stepdaughter coquettishly and with a touch of malice makes a sign of disagreement two or three times with her finger.*)

THE MANAGER: What do you mean by no?

THE STEPDAUGHTER (*sotto voce,° mysteriously*): There's someone who will hear us if she (*indicating Madame Pace*) speaks out loud.

THE MANAGER (*in consternation*): What? Have you got someone else to spring on us now? (*The Actors burst out laughing.*)

THE FATHER: No, no sir. She is alluding to me. I've got to be here—there behind that door, in waiting; and

sotto voce: In a soft voice or stage whisper.

Madame Pace knows it. In fact, if you will allow me, I'll go there at once, so I can be quite ready. (*Moves away.*)

THE MANAGER (*stopping him*): No! wait! wait! We must observe the conventions of the theater. Before you are ready . . .

THE STEPDAUGHTER (*interrupting him*): No, get on with it at once! I'm just dying, I tell you, to act this scene. If he's ready, I'm more than ready.

THE MANAGER (*shouting*): But, my dear young lady, first of all, we must have the scene between you and this lady. . . . (*Indicates Madame Pace.*) Do you understand?

THE STEPDAUGHTER: Good Heavens! She's been telling me what you know already: that mama's work is badly done again, that the material's ruined; and that if I want her to continue to help us in our misery I must be patient. . . .

MADAME PACE (*coming forward with an air of great importance*): Yes indeed, sir, I no wanta take advantage of her, I no wanta be hard. . . .

(*Note: Madame Pace is supposed to talk in a jargon half Italian, half English.*)

THE MANAGER (*alarmed*): What? What? She talks like that? (*The Actors burst out laughing again.*)

THE STEPDAUGHTER (*also laughing*): Yes yes, that's the way she talks, half English, half Italian! Most comical it is!

MADAME PACE: Itta seem not verra polite gentlemen laugha atta me eeff I trya best speaka English.

THE MANAGER: *Diamine!°* Of course! Of course! Let her talk like that! Just what we want. Talk just like that, Madame, if you please! The effect will be certain. Exactly what was wanted to put a little comic relief into the crudity of the situation. Of course she talks like that! Magnificent!

THE STEPDAUGHTER: Magnificent? Certainly! When certain suggestions are made to one in language of that kind, the effect is certain, since it seems almost a joke. One feels inclined to laugh when one hears her talk about an "old signore" "who wanta talka nicely with you." Nice old signore, eh, Madame?

MADAME PACE: Not so old my dear, not so old! And even if you no like him, he won't make any scandal!

THE MOTHER (*jumping up amid the amazement and consternation of the Actors, who had not been noticing her. They move to restrain her*): You old devil! You murderess!

THE STEPDAUGHTER (*running over to calm her Mother*): Calm yourself, Mother, calm yourself! Please don't. . . .

THE FATHER (*going to her also at the same time*): Calm yourself! Don't get excited! Sit down now!

THE MOTHER: Well then, take that woman away out of my sight!

Diamine!: Italian for "Well, I'll be damned!"

THE STEPDAUGHTER (*to Manager*): It is impossible for my mother to remain here.

THE FATHER (*to Manager*): They can't be here together. And for this reason, you see: that woman there was not with us when we came. . . . If they are on together, the whole thing is given away inevitably, as you see.

THE MANAGER: It doesn't matter. This is only a first rough sketch—just to get an idea of the various points of the scene, even confusedly. . . . (*Turning to the Mother and leading her to her chair.*) Come along, my dear lady, sit down now, and let's get on with the scene. . . .

(*Meanwhile, the Stepdaughter, coming forward again, turns to Madame Pace.*)

THE STEPDAUGHTER: Come on, Madame, come on!

MADAME PACE (*offended*): No, no, *grazie*. I do not do anything witha your mother present.

THE STEPDAUGHTER: Nonsense! Introduce this "old signore" who wants to talk nicely to me. (*Addressing the Company imperiously.*) We've got to do this scene one way or another, haven't we? Come on! (*To Madame Pace.*) You can go!

MADAME PACE: Ah yes! I go'way! I go'way! Certainly! (*Exits furious.*)

THE STEPDAUGHTER (*to the Father*): Now you make your entry. No, you needn't go over there. Come here. Let's suppose you've already come in. Like that, yes! I'm here with bowed head, modest like. Come on! Out with your voice! Say "Good morning, Miss" in that peculiar tone, that special tone. . . .

THE MANAGER: Excuse me, but are you the Manager, or am I? (*To the Father, who looks undecided and perplexed.*) Get on with it, man! Go down there to the back of the stage. You needn't go off. Then come right forward here.

(*The Father does as he is told, looking troubled and perplexed at first. But as soon as he begins to move, the reality of the action affects him, and he begins to smile and to be more natural. The Actors watch intently.*)

THE MANAGER (*sotto voce, quickly to the Prompter in his box*): Ready! ready! Get ready to write now.

THE FATHER (*coming forward and speaking in a different tone*): Good afternoon, Miss!

THE STEPDAUGHTER (*head bowed down slightly, with restrained disgust*): Good afternoon!

THE FATHER (*looks under her hat which partly covers her face. Perceiving she is very young, he makes an exclamation, partly of surprise, partly of fear lest he compromise himself in a risky adventure*): Ah . . . but . . . ah . . . I say . . . this is not the first time that you have come here, is it?

THE STEPDAUGHTER (*modestly*): No sir.

THE FATHER: You've been here before, eh? (*Then seeing her nod agreement.*) More than once? (*Waits for her to answer, looks under her hat, smiles, and then says:*) Well then, there's no need to be so shy, is there? May I take off your hat?

THE STEPDAUGHTER (*anticipating him and with veiled disgust*): No sir . . . I'll do it myself. (*Takes it off quickly.*)

(*The Mother, who watches the progress of the scene with the Son and the other two children who cling to her, is on thorns; and follows with varying expressions of sorrow, indignation, anxiety, and horror the words and actions of the other two. From time to time she hides her face in her hands and sobs.*)

THE MOTHER: Oh, my God, my God!

THE FATHER (*playing his part with a touch of gallantry*): Give it to me! I'll put it down. (*Takes hat from her hands.*) But a dear little head like yours ought to have a smarter hat. Come and help me choose one from the stock, won't you?

L'INGÉNUE (*interrupting*): I say . . . those are our hats you know.

THE MANAGER (*furious*): Silence! silence! Don't try and be funny, if you please. . . . We're playing the scene now, I'd have you notice. (*To the Stepdaughter.*) Begin again, please!

THE STEPDAUGHTER (*continuing*): No thank you, sir.

THE FATHER: Oh, come now. Don't talk like that. You must take it. I shall be upset if you don't. There are some lovely little hats here; and then— Madame will be pleased. She expects it, anyway, you know.

THE STEPDAUGHTER: No, no! I couldn't wear it!

THE FATHER: Oh, you're thinking about what they'd say at home if they saw you come in with a new hat? My dear girl, there's always a way round these little matters, you know.

THE STEPDAUGHTER (*all keyed up*): No, it's not that. I couldn't wear it because I am . . . as you see . . . you might have noticed . . .

(*Showing her black dress.*)

THE FATHER: . . . in mourning! Of course: I beg your pardon: I'm frightfully sorry. . . .

THE STEPDAUGHTER (*forcing herself to conquer her indignation and nausea*): Stop! Stop! It's I who must thank you. There's no need for you to feel mortified or specially sorry. Don't think any more of what I've said. (*Tries to smile.*) I must forget that I am dressed so. . . .

THE MANAGER (*interrupting and turning to the Prompter*): Stop a minute! Stop! Don't write that down. Cut out that last bit. (*Then to the Father and Stepdaughter.*) Fine! it's going fine! (*To the Father only.*) And now you can go on as we arranged. (*To the Actors.*) Pretty good that scene, where he offers her the hat, eh?

THE STEPDAUGHTER: The best's coming now. Why can't we go on?

THE MANAGER: Have a little patience! (*To the Actors.*) Of course, it must be treated rather lightly.

LEADING MAN: Still, with a bit of go in it!

LEADING LADY: Of course! It's easy enough! (*To Leading Man.*) Shall you and I try it now?

LEADING MAN: Why, yes! I'll prepare my entrance. (*Exit in order to make his entrance.*)

THE MANAGER (*to Leading Lady*): See here! The scene between you and Madame Pace is finished. I'll have it written out properly after. You remain here . . . oh, where are you going?

LEADING LADY: One minute. I want to put my hat on again. (*Goes over to hatrack and puts her hat on her head.*)

THE MANAGER: Good! You stay here with your head bowed down a bit.

THE STEPDAUGHTER: But she isn't dressed in black.

LEADING LADY: But I shall be, and much more effectively than you.

THE MANAGER (*to Stepdaughter*): Be quiet please, and watch! You'll be able to learn something. (*Clapping his hands.*) Come on! come on! Entrance, please!

(*The door at rear of stage opens, and the Leading Man enters with the lively manner of an old gallant. The rendering of the scene by the Actors from the very first words is seen to be quite a different thing, though it has not in any way the air of a parody. Naturally, the Stepdaughter and the Father, not being able to recognize themselves in the Leading Lady and the Leading Man, who deliver their words in different tones and with a different psychology, express, sometimes with smiles, sometimes with gestures, the impression they receive.*)

LEADING MAN: Good afternoon, Miss . . .

THE FATHER (*at once unable to contain himself*): No! no!

(*The Stepdaughter, noticing the way the Leading Man enters, bursts out laughing.*)

THE MANAGER (*furious*): Silence! And you, please, just stop that laughing. If we go on like this, we shall never finish.

THE STEPDAUGHTER: Forgive me, sir but it's natural enough. This lady (*indicating Leading Lady*) stands there still; but if she is supposed to be me, I can assure you that if I heard anyone say "Good afternoon" in that manner and in that tone, I should burst out laughing as I did.

THE FATHER: Yes, yes, the manner, the tone . . .

THE MANAGER: Nonsense! Rubbish! Stand aside and let me see the action.

LEADING MAN: If I've got to represent an old fellow who's coming into a house of an equivocal character . . .

THE MANAGER: Don't listen to them, for Heaven's sake! Do it again! It goes fine. (*Waiting for the Actors to begin again.*) Well?

LEADING MAN: Good afternoon, Miss.

LEADING LADY: Good afternoon.

LEADING MAN (*imitating the gesture of the Father when he looked under the hat, and then expressing quite clearly first satisfaction and then fear*): Ah, but . . . I say . . . this is not the first time that you have come here, is it?

THE MANAGER: Good, but not quite so heavily. Like this. (*Acts himself.*) "This isn't the first time that you have come here" . . . (*To Leading Lady.*) And you say: "No, sir."

LEADING LADY: No, sir.

LEADING MAN: You've been here before, more than once.

THE MANAGER: No, no, stop! Let her nod "yes" first. "You've been here before, eh?" (*The Leading Lady lifts up her head slightly and closes her eyes as though in disgust. Then she inclines her head twice.*)

THE STEPDAUGHTER (*unable to contain herself*): Oh my God! (*Puts a hand to her mouth to prevent herself from laughing.*)

THE MANAGER (*turning round*): What's the matter?

THE STEPDAUGHTER: Nothing, nothing!

THE MANAGER (*to Leading Man*): Go on!

LEADING MAN: You've been here before, eh? Well then, there's no need to be so shy, is there? May I take off your hat?

(*The Leading Man says this last speech in such a tone and with such gestures that the Stepdaughter, though she has her hand to her mouth, cannot keep from laughing.*)

LEADING LADY (*indignant*): I'm not going to stop here to be made a fool of by that woman there.

LEADING MAN: Neither am I! I'm through with it!

THE MANAGER (*shouting to Stepdaughter*): Silence! for once and all, I tell you!

THE STEPDAUGHTER: Forgive me! forgive me!

THE MANAGER: You haven't any manners: that's what it is! You go too far.

THE FATHER (*endeavoring to intervene*): Yes, it's true, but excuse her . . .

THE MANAGER: Excuse what? It's absolutely disgusting.

THE FATHER: Yes, sir, but believe me, it has such a strange effect when . . .

THE MANAGER: Strange? Why strange? Where is it strange?

THE FATHER: No, sir; I admire your actors—this gentleman here, this lady; but they are certainly not us!

THE MANAGER: I should hope not. Evidently they cannot be you, if they are actors.

THE FATHER: Just so: actors! Both of them act our parts exceedingly well. But, believe me, it produces quite a different effect on us. They want to be us, but they aren't, all the same.

THE MANAGER: What is it then anyway?

THE FATHER: Something that is . . . that is theirs—and no longer ours . . .

THE MANAGER: But naturally, inevitably, I've told you so already.

THE FATHER: Yes, I understand . . . I understand . . .

THE MANAGER: Well then, let's have no more of it! (*Turning to the Actors.*) We'll have the rehearsals by ourselves, afterwards, in the ordinary way. I never could stand rehearsing with the author present. He's never satisfied! (*Turning to Father and Stepdaughter.*) Come on! Let's get on with it again; and try and see if you can't keep from laughing.

THE STEPDAUGHTER: Oh, I shan't laugh any more. There's a nice little bit coming from me now: you'll see.

THE MANAGER: Well then: when she says "Don't think any more of what I've said, I must forget, etc.," you (*addressing the Father*) come in sharp with "I understand"; and then you ask her . . .

THE STEPDAUGHTER (*interrupting*): What?

THE MANAGER: Why she is in mourning.

THE STEPDAUGHTER: Not at all! See here: when I told him that it was useless for me to be thinking about my wearing mourning, do you know how he answered me? "Ah well," he said, "then let's take off this little frock."

THE MANAGER: Great! Just what we want, to make a riot in the theater!

THE STEPDAUGHTER: But it's the truth!

THE MANAGER: What does that matter? Acting is our business here. Truth up to a certain point, but no further.

THE STEPDAUGHTER: What do you want to do then?

THE MANAGER: You'll see, you'll see! Leave it to me.

THE STEPDAUGHTER: No sir! What you want to do is to piece together a little romantic sentimental scene out of my disgust, out of all the reasons, each more cruel and viler than the other, why I am what I am. He is to ask me why I'm in mourning; and I'm to answer with tears in my eyes, that it is just two months since papa died. No sir, no! He's got to say to me, as he did say, "Well, let's take off this little dress at once." And I, with my two months' mourning in my heart, went there behind that screen, and with these fingers tingling with shame . . .

THE MANAGER (*running his hands through his hair*): For Heaven's sake! What are you saying?

THE STEPDAUGHTER (*crying out excitedly*): The truth! The truth!

THE MANAGER: It may be. I don't deny it, and I can understand all your horror; but you must surely see that you can't have this kind of thing on the stage. It won't go.

THE STEPDAUGHTER: Not possible, eh? Very well! I'm much obliged to you—but I'm off.

THE MANAGER: Now be reasonable! Don't lose your temper!

THE STEPDAUGHTER: I won't stop here! I won't! I can see you fixed it all up with him in your office. All this talk about what is possible for the stage . . . I understand! He wants to get at his complicated "cerebral drama," to have his famous remorses and torments acted; but I want to act my part, *my part*!

THE MANAGER: (*annoyed, shaking his shoulders*): Ah! Just *your* part! But, if you will pardon me, there are other parts than yours: His (*indicating the Father*) and hers (*indicating the Mother*)! On the stage you can't have a character becoming too prominent and overshadowing all the others. The thing is to pack them all into a neat little framework and then act what is actable. I am aware of the fact that everyone has his own interior life which he wants very much to put forward. But the difficulty lies in this fact: to set out just so much as is necessary for the stage, taking the other characters into consideration, and at the same time hint at the unrevealed interior life of each. I am willing to admit, my dear young lady, that from your point of view it would be a fine idea if each character could tell the public all his troubles in a nice monologue or a regular one hour lecture. (*Good humoredly.*) You must restrain yourself, my dear, and in your own interest, too; because this fury of yours, this exaggerated disgust you show, may make a bad impression, you know. After you have confessed to me that there were others before him at Madame Pace's and more than once . . .

THE STEPDAUGHTER (*bowing her head, impressed*): It's true. But remember those others mean him for me all the same.

THE MANAGER (*not understanding*): What? The others? What do you mean?

THE STEPDAUGHTER: For one who has gone wrong, sir, he who was responsible for the first fault is responsible for all that follow. He is responsible for my faults, was, even before I was born. Look at him, and see if it isn't true!

THE MANAGER: Well, well! And does the weight of so much responsibility seem nothing to you? Give him a chance to act it, to get it over!

THE STEPDAUGHTER: How? How can he act all his "noble remorses," all his "moral torments," if you want to spare him the horror of being discovered one day—after he had asked her what he did ask her—in the arms of her, that already fallen woman, that child, sir, that child he used to watch come out of school? (*She is moved.*)

(*The Mother at this point is overcome with emotion and breaks out into a fit of crying. All are touched. A long pause.*)

THE STEPDAUGHTER (*as soon as the Mother becomes a little quieter, adds resolutely and gravely*): At present, we are unknown to the public. Tomorrow, you will act us as you wish, treating us in your own manner. But do you really want to see drama, do you want to see it flash out as it really did?

THE MANAGER: Of course! That's just what I do want, so I can use as much of it as is possible.

THE STEPDAUGHTER: Well then, ask that Mother there to leave us.

THE MOTHER (*changing her low plaint into a sharp cry*): No! No! Don't permit it, sir, don't permit it!

THE MANAGER: But it's only to try . . .

THE MOTHER: I can't bear it. I can't.

THE MANAGER: But since it has happened already . . . I don't understand!

THE MOTHER: It's taking place now. It happens all the time. My torment isn't a pretended one. I live and feel every minute of my torture. Those two children there—have you heard them speak? They can't speak anymore. They cling to me to keep my torment

actual and vivid for me. But for themselves, they do not exist, they aren't anymore. And she (*indicating the Stepdaughter*) has run away, she has left me, and is lost. If I now see her here before me, it is only to renew for me the tortures I have suffered for her too.

THE FATHER: The eternal moment! She (*indicating the Stepdaughter*) is here to catch me, fix me, and hold me eternally in the stocks for that one fleeting and shameful moment of my life. She can't give it up! And you, sir, cannot either fairly spare me . . .

THE MANAGER: I never said I didn't want to act it. It will form, as a matter of fact, the nucleus of the whole first act right up to her surprise. (*Indicates the Mother.*)

THE FATHER: Just so! This is my punishment: the passion in all of us that must culminate in her final cry.

THE STEPDAUGHTER: I can hear it still in my ears. It's driven me mad, that cry!—You can put me on as you like; it doesn't matter. Fully dressed, if you like—provided I have at least the arm bare; because, standing like this (*she goes close to the Father and leans her head on his breast*) with my head so, and my arms round his neck, I saw a vein pulsing in my arm here; and then, as if that live vein had awakened disgust in me, I closed my eyes like this, and let my head sink on his breast. (*Turning to the Mother.*) Cry out, mother! Cry out! (*Buries head in Father's breast, and with her shoulders raised as if to prevent her hearing the cry, adds in tones of intense emotion.*) Cry out as you did then!

THE MOTHER (*coming forward to separate them*): No! My daughter, my daughter! (*And after having pulled her away from him.*) You brute! you brute! She is my daughter! Don't you see she's my daughter?

THE MANAGER (*walking backward toward footlights*): Fine! fine! Damned good! And then, of course—curtain!

THE FATHER (*going toward him excitedly*): Yes, of course, because that's the way it really happened.

THE MANAGER (*convinced and pleased*): Oh, yes, no doubt about it. Curtain here, curtain!

(*At the reiterated cry of the Manager, the Machinist lets the curtain down, leaving the Manager and the Father in front of it before the footlights.*)

THE MANAGER: The darned idiot! I said "curtain" to show the act should end there, and he goes and lets it down in earnest. (*To the Father, while he pulls the curtain back to go on to the stage again.*) Yes, yes, it's all right. Effect certain! That's the right ending. I'll guarantee the first act at any rate.

ACT III

(*When the curtain goes up again, it is seen that the stage hands have shifted the bit of scenery used in the last part and have rigged up instead at the back of the stage a drop, with some trees, and one or two wings. A portion of a fountain basin is visible. The Mother is sitting on the right with the two children by her side. The Son is on the same side, but away from the others. He seems bored, angry, and full of shame. The Father and the Stepdaughter are also seated toward the right front. On the other side (left) are the Actors, much in the positions they occupied before the curtain was lowered. Only the Manager is standing up in the middle of the stage, with his hand closed over his mouth, in the act of meditating.)*

THE MANAGER (*shaking his shoulders after a brief pause*): Ah yes: the second act! Leave it to me, leave it all to me as we arranged, and you'll see! It'll go fine!

THE STEPDAUGHTER: Our entry into his house (*indicates Father*) in spite of him . . . (*Indicates the Son.*)

THE MANAGER (*out of patience*): Leave it to me, I tell you!

THE STEPDAUGHTER: Do let it be clear, at any rate, that it is in spite of my wishes.

THE MOTHER (*from her corner, shaking her head*): For all the good that's come of it . . .

THE STEPDAUGHTER (*turning toward her quickly*): It doesn't matter. The more harm done us, the more remorse for him.

THE MANAGER (*impatiently*): I understand! Good Heavens! I understand! I'm taking it into account.

THE MOTHER (*supplicatingly*): I beg you, sir, to let it appear quite plain that for conscience' sake I did try in every way . . .

THE STEPDAUGHTER (*interrupting indignantly and continuing for the Mother*): . . . to pacify me, to dissuade me from spiting him. (*To Manager.*) Do as she wants: satisfy her, because it is true! I enjoy it immensely. Anyhow, as you can see, the meeker she is, the more she tries to get at his heart, the more distant and aloof does he become.

THE MANAGER: Are we going to begin this second act or not?

THE STEPDAUGHTER: I'm not going to talk any more now. But I must tell you this: you can't have the whole action take place in the garden, as you suggest. It isn't possible!

THE MANAGER: Why not?

THE STEPDAUGHTER: Because he (*indicates the Son again*) is always shut up alone in his room. And then there's all the part of that poor dazed-looking boy there which takes place indoors.

THE MANAGER: Maybe! On the other hand, you will understand—we can't change scenes three or four times in one act.

LEADING MAN: They used to once.

THE MANAGER: Yes, when the public was up to the level of that child there.

LEADING LADY: It makes the illusion easier.

THE FATHER (*irritated*): The illusion! For Heaven's sake, don't say illusion. Please don't use that word, which is particularly painful for . . .

THE MANAGER (*astounded*): And why, if you please?

THE FATHER: It's painful, cruel, really cruel; and you ought to understand that.

THE MANAGER: But why? What ought we to say then? The illusion, I tell you, sir, which we've got to create for the audience. . . .

LEADING MAN: With our acting.

THE MANAGER: The illusion of a reality.

THE FATHER: I understand; but you, perhaps, do not understand us. Forgive me! You see . . . here for you and your actors, the thing is only—and rightly so . . . a kind of game. . . .

LEADING LADY (*interrupting indignantly*): A game! We're not children here, if you please! We are serious actors.

THE FATHER: I don't deny it. What I mean is the game, or play, of your art, which has to give, as the gentleman says, a perfect illusion of reality.

THE MANAGER: Precisely—!

THE FATHER: Now, if you consider the fact that we (*indicates himself and the other five Characters*), as we are, have no other reality outside of this illusion. . . .

THE MANAGER (*astonished, looking at his Actors, who are also amazed*): And what does that mean?

THE FATHER (*after watching them for a moment with a wan smile*): As I say, sir, that which is a game of art for you is our sole reality. (*Brief pause. He goes a step or two nearer the Manager and adds.*) But not only for us, you know, by the way. Just you think it over well. (*Looks him in the eyes.*) Can you tell me who you are?

THE MANAGER (*perplexed, half-smiling*): What? Who am I? I am myself.

THE FATHER: And if I were to tell you that that isn't true, because you and I . . . ?

THE MANAGER: I should say you were mad—! (*The Actors laugh.*)

THE FATHER: You're quite right to laugh: because we are all making believe here. (*To Manager.*) And you can therefore object that it's only for a joke that that gentleman there (*indicates the Leading Man*), who naturally is himself, has to be me, who am on the contrary myself—this thing you see here. You see I've caught you in a trap! (*The Actors laugh.*)

THE MANAGER (*annoyed*): But we've had all this over once before. Do you want to begin again?

THE FATHER: No, no! That wasn't my meaning! In fact, I should like to request you to abandon this game of art (*looking at the Leading Lady as if anticipating her*) which you are accustomed to play here with your actors, and to ask you seriously once again who are you?

THE MANAGER (*astonished and irritated, turning to his Actors*): If this fellow here hasn't got a nerve! A man who calls himself a character comes and asks me who I am!

THE FATHER (*with dignity, but not offended*): A character, sir, may always ask a man who he is. Because a character has really a life of his own, marked with his especial characteristics; for which reason he is always "somebody." But a man—I'm not speaking of you now—may very well be "nobody."

THE MANAGER: Yes, but you are asking these questions of me, the boss, the manager! Do you understand?

THE FATHER: But only in order to know if you, as you really are now, see yourself as you once were with all the illusions that were yours then, with all the things both inside and outside of you as they seemed to you—as they were then indeed for you. Well, sir, if you think of all those illusions that mean nothing to you now, of all those things which don't even *seem* to you to exist anymore, while once they *were* for you, don't you feel that—I won't say these boards—but the very earth under your feet is sinking away from you when you reflect that in the same way this *you* as you feel it today—all this present reality of yours—is fated to seem a mere illusion to you tomorrow?

THE MANAGER (*without having understood much, but astonished by the specious argument*): Well, well! And where does all this take us anyway?

THE FATHER: Oh, nowhere! It's only to show you that if we (*indicating the Characters*) have no other reality beyond the illusion, you too must not count overmuch on your reality as you feel it today, since, like that of yesterday, it may prove an illusion for you tomorrow.

THE MANAGER (*determining to make fun of him*): Ah, excellent! Then you'll be saying next that you, with this comedy of yours that you brought here to act, are truer and more real than I am.

THE FATHER (*with the greatest seriousness*): But of course, without doubt!

THE MANAGER: Ah, really?

THE FATHER: Why, I thought you'd understand that from the beginning.

THE MANAGER: More real than I?

THE FATHER: If your reality can change from one day to another. . . .

THE MANAGER: But everyone knows it can change. It is always changing, the same as anyone else's.

THE FATHER (*with a cry*): No, sir, not ours! Look here! That is the very difference! Our reality doesn't change: it can't change! It can't be other than what it is, because it is already fixed for ever. It's terrible. Ours is an immutable reality which should make you shudder when you approach us if you are really conscious of the fact that your reality is a mere transitory and fleeting illusion, taking this form today and that tomorrow, according to the conditions, according to your will, your sentiments, which in turn are controlled by an intellect that shows them to you today in one manner and tomorrow . . . who knows how? . . . Illusions of reality represented in this fatuous comedy of life that never ends, nor can ever end! Because if tomorrow it were to end . . . then why, all would be finished.

THE MANAGER: Oh for God's sake, will you *at least* finish with this philosophizing and let us try and shape this comedy which you yourself have brought me here? You argue and philosophize a bit too much, my dear sir. You know you seem to me almost, almost . . . (*Stops and looks him over from head to foot.*) Ah, by the way, I think you introduced yourself to me as a—what shall . . . we say—a "character," created by an author who did not afterward care to make a drama of his own creations.

THE FATHER: It is the simple truth, sir.

THE MANAGER: Nonsense! Cut that out, please! None of us believes it, because it isn't a thing, as you must recognize yourself, which one can believe seriously. If you want to know, it seems to me you are trying to imitate the manner of a certain author whom I heartily detest—I warn you—although I have unfortunately bound myself to put on one of his works. As a matter of fact, I was just starting to rehearse it, when you arrived. (*Turning to the Actors.*) And this is what we've gained—out of the frying-pan into the fire!

THE FATHER: I don't know to what author you may be alluding, but believe me I feel what I think; and I seem to be philosophizing only for those who do not think what they feel, because they blind themselves with their own sentiment. I know that for many people this self-blinding seems much more "human"; but the contrary is really true. For man never reasons so much and becomes so introspective as when he suffers, since he is anxious to get at the cause of his sufferings, to learn who has produced them, and whether it is just or unjust that he should have to bear them. On the other hand, when he is happy, he takes his happiness as it comes and doesn't analyze it, just as if happiness were his right. The animals suffer without reasoning about their sufferings. But take the case of a man who suffers and begins to reason about it. Oh no! it can't be allowed! Let him suffer like an animal, and then—ah yes, he is "human"!

THE MANAGER: Look here! Look here! You're off again, philosophizing worse than ever.

THE FATHER: Because I suffer, sir! I'm not philosophizing: I'm crying aloud the reason of my sufferings.

THE MANAGER (*makes brusque movement as he is taken with a new idea*): I should like to know if anyone has ever heard of a character who gets right out of his part and perorates and speechifies as you do. Have you ever heard of a case? I haven't.

THE FATHER: You have never met such a case, sir, because authors, as a rule, hide the labor of their creations. When the characters are really alive before their author, the latter does nothing but follow them in their action, in other words, in the situations which they suggest to him; and he has to will them the way they will themselves—for there's trouble if he doesn't. When a character is born, he acquires at once such an independence, even of his own author, that he can be imagined by everybody even in many other situations where the author never dreamed of placing him; and so he acquires for himself a meaning which the author never thought of giving him.

THE MANAGER: Yes, yes, I know this.

THE FATHER: What is there then to marvel at in us? Imagine such a misfortune for characters as I have described to you: to be born of an author's fantasy, and be denied life by him; and then answer me if these characters left alive, and yet without life, weren't right in doing what they did do and are doing now, after they have attempted everything in their power to persuade him to give them their stage life. We've all tried him in turn, I, she (*indicating the Stepdaughter*) and she (*indicating the Mother*).

THE STEPDAUGHTER: It's true. I too have sought to tempt him, many, many times, when he has been sitting at his writing table, feeling a bit melancholy, at the twilight hour. He would sit in his armchair too lazy to switch on the light, and all the shadows that crept into his room were full of our presence coming to tempt him. (*As if she saw herself still there by the writing table, and was annoyed by the presence of the Actors.*) Oh, if you would only go away, go away and leave us alone—mother here with that son of hers—I with that child—that boy there always alone—and then I with him (*just hints at the Father*)—and then I alone, alone . . . in those shadows! (*Makes a sudden movement as if in the vision she has of herself illuminating those shadows she wanted to seize hold of herself.*) Ah! my life! my life! Oh, what scenes we proposed to him—and I tempted him more than any of the others!

THE FATHER: Maybe. But perhaps it was your fault that he refused to give us life: because you were too insistent, too troublesome.

THE STEPDAUGHTER: Nonsense! Didn't he make me so himself? (*Goes close to the Manager to tell him as if in confidence.*) In my opinion he abandoned us in a fit of depression, of disgust for the ordinary theater as the public knows it and likes it.

THE SON: Exactly what it was, sir; exactly that!

THE FATHER: Not at all! Don't believe it for a minute. Listen to me! You'll be doing quite right to modify, as you suggest, the excesses both of this girl here, who wants to do too much, and of this young man, who won't do anything at all.

THE SON: No, nothing!

THE MANAGER: You too get over the mark occasionally, my dear sir, if I may say so.

THE FATHER: I? When? Where?

THE MANAGER: Always! Continuously! Then there's this insistence of yours in trying to make us believe you are a character. And then too, you must really argue and philosophize less, you know, much less.

THE FATHER: Well, if you want to take away from me the possibility of representing the torment of my spirit which never gives me peace, you will be suppressing me: that's all. Every true man, sir, who is a little above the level of the beasts and plants does not live for the sake of living, without knowing how to live; but he lives so as to give a meaning and a value of his own to life. For me this is *everything*. I cannot give up this, just to represent a mere fact as she (*indicating the Stepdaughter*) wants. It's all very well for

her, since her "vendetta" lies in the "fact." I'm not going to do it. It destroys my *raison d'être*.

THE MANAGER: Your *raison d'être*! Oh, we're going ahead fine! First she starts off, and then you jump in. At this rate, we'll never finish.

THE FATHER: Now, don't be offended! Have it your own way—provided, however, that within the limits of the parts you assign us each one's sacrifice isn't too great.

THE MANAGER: You've got to understand that you can't go on arguing at your own pleasure. Drama is action, sir, action and not confounded philosophy.

THE FATHER: All right. I'll do just as much arguing and philosophizing as everybody does when he is considering his own torments.

THE MANAGER: If the drama permits! But for Heaven's sake, man, let's get along and come to the scene.

THE STEPDAUGHTER: It seems to me we've got too much action with our coming into his house. (*Indicating Father.*) You said, before, you couldn't change the scene every five minutes.

THE MANAGER: Of course not. What we've got to do is to combine and group up all the facts in one simultaneous, close-knit action. We can't have it as you want, with your little brother wandering like a ghost from room to room, hiding behind doors and meditating a project which—what did you say it did to him?

THE STEPDAUGHTER: Consumes him, sir, wastes him away!

THE MANAGER: Well, it may be. And then at the same time, you want the little girl there to be playing in the garden . . . one in the house, and the other in the garden; isn't that it?

THE STEPDAUGHTER: Yes, in the sun, in the sun! That is my only pleasure: to see her happy and careless in the garden after the misery and squalor of the horrible room where we all four slept together. And I had to sleep with her—I, do you understand?—with my vile contaminated body next to hers; with her holding me fast in her loving little arms. In the garden, whenever she spied me, she would run to take me by the hand. She didn't care for the big flowers, only the little ones; and she loved to show me them and pet me.

THE MANAGER: Well then, we'll have it in the garden. Everything shall happen in the garden; and we'll group the other scenes there. (*Calls a Stage Hand.*) Here, a backcloth with trees and something to do as a fountain basin. (*Turning round to look at the back of the stage.*) Ah, you've fixed it up. Good! (*To Stepdaughter.*) This is just to give an idea, of course. The Boy, instead of hiding behind the doors, will wander about here in the garden, hiding behind the trees. But it's going to be rather difficult to find a child to do that scene with you where she shows you the flowers. (*Turning to the Boy.*) Come forward a little, will you please? Let's try it now! Come along! come along! (*Then seeing him come shyly forward, full of fear and looking lost.*) It's a nice business, this lad here. What's the matter with him? We'll have to give him a word or two to say. (*Goes close to him, puts a hand on his shoulders, and leads him behind one of the trees.*) Come on! come on! Let me see you a little! Hide here . . . yes, like that. Try and show your head just a little as if you were looking for some-one. . . . (*Goes back to observe the effect, when the Boy at once goes through the action.*) Excellent! fine! (*Turning to Stepdaughter.*) Suppose the little girl there were to surprise him as he looks round, and run over to him, so we could give him a word or two to say?

THE STEPDAUGHTER: It's useless to hope he will speak, as long as that fellow there is here. . . . (*Indicates the Son.*) You must send him away first.

THE SON (*jumping up*): Delighted! Delighted! I don't ask for anything better. (*Begins to move away.*)

THE MANAGER (*at once stopping him*): No! No! Where are you going? Wait a bit!

(*The Mother gets up alarmed and terrified at the thought that he is really about to go away. Instinctively she lifts her arms to prevent him, without, however, leaving her seat.*)

THE SON (*to Manager, who stops him*): I've got nothing to do with this affair. Let me go, please! Let me go!

THE MANAGER: What do you mean by saying you've got nothing to do with this?

THE STEPDAUGHTER (*calmly, with irony*): Don't bother to stop him: he won't go away.

THE FATHER: He has to act the terrible scene in the garden with his mother.

THE SON (*suddenly resolute and with dignity*): I shall act nothing at all. I've said so from the very beginning. (*To the Manager.*) Let me go!

THE STEPDAUGHTER (*going over to the Manager*): Allow me? (*Puts down the Manager's arm which is restraining the Son.*) Well, go away then, if you want to! (*The Son looks at her with contempt and hatred. She laughs and says.*) You see, he can't, he can't go away! He is obliged to stay here, indissolubly bound to the chain. If I, who fly off when that happens which has to happen because I can't bear him—if I am still here and support that face and expression of his, you can well imagine that he is unable to move. He has to remain here, has to stop with that nice father of his, and that mother whose only son he is. (*Turning to the Mother.*) Come on, mother, come along! (*Turning to Manager to indicate her.*) You see, she was getting up to keep him back. (*To the Mother, beckoning her with her hand.*) Come on, come on! (*Then to Manager.*) You can imagine how little she wants to show these actors of yours what she really feels; but so eager is she to get near him that. . . . There, you see? She is willing to act her part. (*And in fact, the Mother approaches him; and as soon as the Stepdaughter has finished speaking, opens her arms to signify that she consents.*)

THE SON (*suddenly*): No! no! If I can't go away, then I'll stop here; but I repeat: I act nothing!

THE FATHER (*to Manager excitedly*): You can force him, sir.

THE SON: Nobody can force me.

THE FATHER: I can.

THE STEPDAUGHTER: Wait a minute, wait . . . First of all, the baby has to go to the fountain. . . . (*Runs to take the Child and leads her to the fountain.*)

THE MANAGER: Yes, yes of course; that's it. Both at the same time.

(*The Second Lady Lead and the Juvenile Lead at this point separate themselves from the group of Actors. One watches the Mother attentively; the other moves about studying the movements and manner of the Son whom he will have to act.*)

THE SON (*to Manager*): What do you mean by both at the same time? It isn't right. There was no scene between me and her. (*Indicates the Mother.*) Ask her how it was!

THE MOTHER: Yes, it's true. I had come into his room. . . .

THE SON: Into my room, do you understand? Nothing to do with the garden.

THE MANAGER: It doesn't matter. Haven't I told you we've got to group the action?

THE SON (*observing the Juvenile Lead studying him*): What do you want?

JUVENILE LEAD: Nothing! I was just looking at you.

THE SON (*turning toward the Second Lady Lead*): Ah! she's at it too: to re-act her part! (*Indicating the Mother.*)

THE MANAGER: Exactly! And it seems to me that you ought to be grateful to them for their interest.

THE SON: Yes, but haven't you yet perceived that it isn't possible to live in front of a mirror which not only freezes us with the image of ourselves, but throws our likeness back at us with a horrible grimace?

THE FATHER: That is true, absolutely true. You must see that.

THE MANAGER (*to Second Lady Lead and Juvenile Lead*): He's right! Move away from them!

THE SON: Do as you like. I'm out of this!

THE MANAGER: Be quiet, you, will you? And let me hear your mother! (*To Mother.*) You were saying you had entered. . . .

THE MOTHER: Yes, into his room, because I couldn't stand it any longer. I went to empty my heart to him of all the anguish that tortures me. . . . But as soon as he saw me come in. . . .

THE SON: Nothing happened! There was no scene. I went away, that's all! I don't care for scenes!

THE MOTHER: It's true, true. That's how it was.

THE MANAGER: Well now, we've got to do this bit between you and him. It's indispensable.

THE MOTHER: I'm ready . . . when you are ready. If you could only find a chance for me to tell him what I feel here in my heart.

THE FATHER (*going to Son in a great rage*): You'll do this for your mother, for your mother, do you understand?

THE SON (*quite determined*): I do nothing!

THE FATHER (*taking hold of him and shaking him*): For God's sake, do as I tell you! Don't you hear your mother asking you for a favor? Haven't you even got the guts to be a son?

THE SON (*taking hold of the Father*): No! No! And for God's sake stop it, or else.... (*General agitation. The Mother, frightened, tries to separate them.*)

THE MOTHER (*pleading*): Please! please!

THE FATHER (*not leaving hold of the Son*): You've got to obey, do you hear?

THE SON (*almost crying from rage*): What does it mean, this madness you've got? (*They separate.*) Have you no decency, that you insist on showing everyone our shame? I won't do it! I won't! And I stand for the will of our author in this. He didn't want to put us on the stage, after all!

THE MANAGER: Man alive! You came here . . .

THE SON (*indicating Father*): He did! I didn't!

THE MANAGER: Aren't you here now?

THE SON: It was his wish, and he dragged us along with him. He's told you not only the things that did happen, but also things that have never happened at all.

THE MANAGER: Well, tell me then what did happen. You went out of your room without saying a word.

THE SON: Without a word, so as to avoid a scene!

THE MANAGER: And then what did you do?

THE SON: Nothing . . . walking in the garden. . . . (*Hesitates for a moment with expression of gloom.*)

THE MANAGER (*coming closer to him, interested by his extraordinary reserve*): Well, well . . . walking in the garden. . . .

THE SON (*exasperated*): Why on earth do you insist? It's horrible!

(*The Mother trembles, sobs, and looks toward the fountain.*)

THE MANAGER (*slowly observing the glance and turning toward the Son with increasing apprehension*): The baby?

THE SON: There in the fountain. . . .

THE FATHER (*pointing with tender pity to the Mother*): She was following him at the moment. . . .

THE MANAGER (*to the Son anxiously*): And then you . . .

THE SON: I ran over to her; I was jumping in to drag her out when I saw something that froze my blood . . . the boy standing stock still, with eyes like a madman's, watching his little drowned sister, in the fountain! (*The Stepdaughter bends over the fountain to hide the Child. She sobs.*) Then. . . . (*A revolver shot rings out behind the trees where the Boy is hidden.*)

THE MOTHER (*with a cry of terror runs over in that direction together with several of the Actors amid general confusion*): My son! My son! (*Then amid the cries and exclamations one hears her voice.*) Help! Help!

THE MANAGER (*pushing the Actors aside while they lift up the Boy and carry him off*): Is he really wounded?

SOME ACTORS: He's dead! dead!

OTHER ACTORS: No, no, it's only make-believe, it's only pretense!

THE FATHER (*with a terrible cry*): Pretense? Reality, sir, reality!

THE MANAGER: Pretense? Reality? To hell with it all! Never in my life has such a thing happened to me. I've lost a whole day over these people, a whole day!

Eugene O'Neill

Eugene O'Neill (1888–1953) is a major figure in American drama. His enormous output began in the tradition of realism established by Strindberg and Ibsen, and his early plays, such as *Anna Christie* (1921), introduced Americans to the techniques of the great European realists. Realism for Americans was a move away from the sentimental comedies and the melodramas that dominated the American stage from before the Civil War to World War I. Some of O'Neill's plays, such as *Strange Interlude* (1928) and *Dynamo* (1929), were expressionist in style, demonstrating his considerable range. O'Neill rejected the kind of theater in which his father had thrived. James O'Neill had long been a stage star, traveling across the country in his production of *The Count of Monte Cristo*, which had made him rich but had also made him a prisoner of a single role.

Eugene O'Neill won the Pulitzer Prize for drama three times in the 1920s and once posthumously in 1957 for *Long Day's Journey into Night*, which had been completed in 1941. He won the Nobel Prize for literature in 1936. Although not popular successes in his own day, his plays—including those published posthumously—are now mainstays of the American theater. Some of the finest American actors have taken a strong interest in his work, both producing his plays and acting in them on the stage and on television. From the 1950s to the 1990s, the late Colleen Dewhurst and Jason Robards, Jr., in particular, gave some magnificent performances and interpretations of O'Neill's work.

The young O'Neill was a romantic in the popular sense of the word. After a year at Princeton University, he began to travel on the sea. His jaunts took him to South America, and he once wound up virtually broke and without resources in Buenos Aires. When he returned to the United States, he studied for a year at Harvard with George Pierce Baker, the most famous drama teacher of his day. Eventually, O'Neill took up residence in Provincetown, Massachusetts, where a group of people dedicated to theater—including the playwright Susan Glaspell—began to put on plays in their living rooms. When their audiences spilled over, the group created the Provincetown Playhouse, the theater in which some of O'Neill's earliest pieces were first performed.

The subjects of many of O'Neill's plays were not especially appealing to general theater audiences. Those who hoped for light comedy and a good laugh or light melodrama and a good cry found the intensity of his dark vision of the world to be overwhelming. They came for mere entertainment, and he was providing them with frightening visions of the soul's interior. The glum and painful surroundings of *Anna Christie* (1921) and the brutality of the lower-class coal stoker in *The Hairy Ape* (1922) were foreign to the comfortable middle-class audiences who supported commercial theater in the United States. They found O'Neill's characters to be haunted by family agonies, affections never given, ambitions never realized, pains never assuaged. Despite his remarkable abilities and the power of his drama, audiences often did not know what to make of him. To a large extent, his acceptance came on waves of shock, as had the acceptance of the Scandinavian realists.

O'Neill's early work is marked by a variety of experiments with theatrical effects and moods. He tried to use the primary influences of Greek drama in such plays as *Desire under the Elms* (1924), which has been described by critics as Greek tragedy, and *Mourning Becomes Electra* (1931), based on the *Oresteia*, which took three days to perform. But many of his early plays now seem dated and strange. His most impressive plays are his later work, such as *Ah, Wilderness!* (1933), *The Iceman Cometh* (1939), *Long Day's Journey into Night* (1939–1941), *A Moon for the Misbegotten* (1943), and *A Touch of the Poet* (1935–1942), which was performed posthumously in 1957.

O'Neill's personal life had been darkened by the alcoholism of his father and brother and the drug addiction of his mother. O'Neill himself had to fight alcoholism and depression brought on by the instability of his life and family. The darkness of his dramas may or may not be related to his personal life experiences, but the dramas reflect his understanding of the human condition. His experiments with Greek concepts of fate are tempered and strengthened by his interpretation of Freud's theories about the unconscious, the ruling force of the sexual drive, and the effects of trauma on childhood. *Desire under the Elms* brings together all these elements with the influence of the land—the environment of Puritan New England—and illustrates perfectly his awareness of the limits of human free will and the power of the forces that work on us all.

Desire under the Elms

Desire under the Elms (1924) is Eugene O'Neill's first effort at writing in the style of Greek tragedy. He did not follow the Greek tradition of choosing a great figure of noble birth whose mystery the fates unravel. Rather, he was deliberately democratic, choosing a New England farmer and his family as the protagonists of his drama. Just as fate animates a Greek tragedy, the emotional forces of jealousy, resentment, lust, and incestuous love animate *Desire under the Elms*.

O'Neill set his play on typically rocky New England soil, which in many ways bears a striking resemblance to the rocky soil of Athens and the Greek coastline. The unyielding toughness of life on that land contrasts with the easy life to be made from gold mining in California. Ephraim Cabot, the seventy-five-year-old father, has been made hard and physically powerful by his work. He has just taken a third wife, the young and scheming Abbie. His youngest son, Eben, has decided to stay on the farm, whereas his two other sons plan to put New England behind them and go to California.

The sense of having been dispossessed of his farm by his new stepmother drives Eben to hate Abbie, who has married the elder Cabot merely to inherit his farm. At first the sparring between Abbie and Eben is based on calculating self-interest, but eventually their feelings overpower them. Lust turns to love, and the son they produce is passed off as old Cabot's, although the townspeople have no illusion about whose child it is.

The farm itself is a powerful presence in the play. Whenever old Cabot thinks he should give up and follow the promise of easy money in California, he feels God's presence urging him to stay. God operates for Ephraim as the oracle in *Oedipus Rex* does, giving him a message that is painful but must be

For discussion questions and assignments on *Desire under the Elms*, visit bedfordstmartins.com/jacobus.

obeyed. The rocks on the farm are unforgiving, and so is the fate that Abbie and Eben face. Theirs is an impossible love; everything they do to prove their love condemns them even more. The forces of fate center on the farm. When the play opens, Eben says of it, "God! Purty!" When the play ends, the sheriff praises the farm and says he surely would like to own it, striking a clear note of irony: the agony of the play is rooted in lust—lust for the farm that parallels the lust between Abbie and Eben.

The play is haunted by the ghost of Eben's mother, whom Ephraim married primarily for her farm. Her ghost is exorcised only after the cycle of retribution has begun. Old Cabot has committed a crime against her, and now he must become the victim.

The language of the dialogue is that of New England in the mid-nineteenth century. Living in New England, O'Neill understood the ways and the language of its people. He seems to have imagined the "downeast" flavor of Maine in the language, and he has been careful to build the proper pronunciation into the dialogue. This folksy way of speaking helps emphasize the peasantlike qualities in these New England farmers. O'Neill's careful use of language is reminiscent of Synge's masterful representation of the Irish-English speech in *Riders to the Sea*.

The language of O'Neill's characters has a rocky toughness at times. Characters are laconic—they often answer in a single word: "Ay-eh." Faithful to his vision of the simple speech of country folk, O'Neill avoids giving them elaborate poetic soliloquies. Instead, he shows how, despite their limited language, rural people feel profound emotions and act on them.

O'Neill carefully links Abbie with Queen Phaedra, who in Euripides' play *Hippolytus* and in Racine's seventeenth-century play *Phaedra* finds herself uncontrollably desiring her husband's son as a lover. Racine and his audience could easily imagine such intense emotions overwhelming a noblewoman, because they thought that members of the nobility felt and lived more intensely than ordinary people. But O'Neill is trying to make his audience see that even unlettered farm people can feel as deeply as tragic heroes of any age do. The Cabots are victims of passion. They share their fate with the great families of the Greek tragedies.

Desire under the Elms in Performance

Desire under the Elms was first performed in Greenwich Village in 1924 under the auspices of the Provincetown Players. A year later, it appeared on Broadway for thirty-six weeks, a long run for a tragedy. Its first reviewers were courteous but puzzled. They compared the play with earlier O'Neill works, remarking on its "tragic gloom and irony" and praising its language. At the Los Angeles production in 1926, the cast was arrested for "giving an obscene play." The sexual themes offended theatergoers in California, and even those who defended the play admitted that the text would be offensive to some members of the audience.

Because the English censor banned the play until 1938, its first European production was in Prague's National Theatre in 1925. Its Czech title translated as "The Farm under the Elms." The director used a highly stylized set influenced by the Moscow Art Theatre and later described as "a sort of two-storied wooden edifice . . . rather like a log cabin multiplied by four."

Other European productions followed in Moscow in 1932, in Stockholm in 1933, and finally in London in 1940. The 1952 New York revival was not successful. The 1963 revival at the Circle in the Square in New York starred George C. Scott and his wife, Colleen Dewhurst. José Quintero, a notable interpreter of O'Neill, directed. Critics complained about "awkward" echoes of Greek tragedy while admitting that the play had an uncanny power despite its flaws. It ran for 380 performances.

The play has often been revived: in Boston in 1967; at the Berkshire Theater Festival in 1974; at the Roundabout Theatre in New York, directed by Terry Schrieber, in 1984; and by numerous local theater groups. In 1978, Edward Thomas staged it at Connecticut College in New London as an opera. A creditable production, it emphasized the play's American folk qualities. Dan Wackerman directed an off-Broadway production in 1997 adding an African American character named Silent Woman. She did not speak but added the issue of race to this issue-laden play. In 2005, the American Repertory Theater staged the play under the direction of János Szász with an innovative, expressionistic set designed by Riccardo Hernandez. Brian Dennehy, who has become the most distinguished current interpreter of O'Neill, appeared as Ephraim Cabot in a production directed by Robert Falls that played at the Goodman Theatre in Chicago before moving to the St. James Theater in New York in 2009. The reviews were enthusiastic, and critic Charles Isherwood said, "Mr. Dennehy exudes the hungry malice of a jackal tearing away at a rodent."

EUGENE O'NEILL (1888–1953)

Desire under the Elms   1924

Characters

EPHRAIM CABOT
SIMEON }
PETER   } his sons
EBEN   }
ABBIE PUTNAM
YOUNG GIRL, TWO FARMERS, the FIDDLER, a SHERIFF, and other folk from the neighboring farms.

Scene: *The action of the entire play takes place in, and immediately outside of, the Cabot farmhouse in New England, in the year 1850. The south end of the house faces front to a stone wall with a wooden gate at center opening on a country road. The house is in good condition but in need of paint. Its walls are a sickly grayish, the green of the shutters faded. Two enormous elms are on each side of the house. They bend their trailing branches down over the roof. They appear to protect and at the same time subdue. There is a sinister maternity in their aspect, a crushing, jealous absorption. They have developed from their intimate contact with the life of man in the house an appalling humanness. They brood oppressively over the house. They are like exhausted women resting their sagging breasts and hands and hair on its roof, and when it rains their tears trickle down monotonously and rot on the shingles.*

There is a path running from the gate around the right corner of the house to the front door. A narrow porch is on this side. The end wall facing us has two windows in its upper story, two larger ones on the floor below. The two upper are those of the father's bedroom and that of the brothers. On the left, ground floor, is the kitchen—on the right, the parlor, the shades of which are always drawn down.

PART I • Scene I

(*Exterior of the farmhouse. It is sunset of a day at the beginning of summer in the year 1850. There is no wind and everything is still. The sky above the roof is suffused with deep colors, the green of the elms glows, but the house is in shadow, seeming pale and washed out by contrast.*)

(*A door opens and Eben Cabot comes to the end of the porch and stands looking down the road to the right. He has a large bell in his hand and this he swings mechanically, awakening a deafening clangor. Then he puts his hands on his hips and stares up at the sky. He sighs with a puzzled awe and blurts out with halting appreciation.*)

EBEN: God! Purty! (*His eyes fall and he stares about him frowningly. He is twenty-five, tall and sinewy. His face is well formed, good-looking, but its expression is resentful and defensive. His defiant, dark eyes remind one of a wild animal's in captivity. Each day is a cage in which he finds himself trapped but inwardly unsubdued. There is a fierce repressed vitality about him. He has black hair, mustache, a thin curly trace of beard. He is dressed in rough farm clothes.*)

(*He spits on the ground with intense disgust, turns, and goes back into the house.*)

(*Simeon and Peter come in from their work in the fields. They are tall men, much older than their half-brother [Simeon is thirty-nine and Peter thirty-seven], built on a squarer, simpler model, fleshier in body, more bovine and homelier in face, shrewder and more practical. Their shoulders stoop a bit from years of farm work. They clump heavily along in their clumsy thick-soled boots caked with earth. Their clothes, their faces, hands, bare arms, and throats are earth-stained. They smell of earth. They stand together for a moment in front of the house and, as if with the one impulse, stare dumbly up at the sky, leaning on their hoes. Their faces have a compressed, unresigned expression. As they look upward, this softens.*)

SIMEON (*grudgingly*): Purty.

PETER: Ay-eh.

SIMEON (*suddenly*): Eighteen year ago.

PETER: What?

SIMEON: Jenn. My woman. She died.

PETER: I'd fergot.

SIMEON: I rec'lect—now an' agin. Makes it lonesome. She'd hair long's a hoss' tail—an' yeller like gold!

PETER: Waal—she's gone. (*This with indifferent finality—then after a pause.*) They's gold in the West, Sim.

SIMEON (*still under the influence of sunset—vaguely*): In the sky?

PETER: Waal—in a manner o' speakin'—that's the promise. (*Growing excited.*) Gold in the sky—in the West—Golden Gate—Californi-a!—Goldest West!—fields o' gold!

SIMEON (*excited in his turn*): Fortunes layin' just atop o' the ground waitin' t' be picked! Solomon's mines, they says! (*For a moment they continue looking up at the sky—then their eyes drop.*)

PETER (*with sardonic bitterness*): Here—it's stones atop o' the ground—stones atop o' stones—makin' stone walls—year atop o' year—him 'n' yew 'n' me 'n' then Eben—makin' stone walls fur him to fence us in!

SIMEON: We've wuked. Give our strength. Give our years. Plowed 'em under in the ground—(*He stamps rebelliously.*)—rottin'—makin' soil for his crops! (*A pause.*) Waal—the farm pays good for hereabouts.

PETER: If we plowed in Californi-a, they'd be lumps o' gold in the furrow!

SIMEON: Californi-a's t'other side o' earth, a'most. We got t' calc'late—

PETER (*after a pause*): 'Twould be hard fur me, too, to give up what we've 'arned here by our sweat. (*A pause. Eben sticks his head out of the dining room window, listening.*)

SIMEON: Ay-eh. (*A pause.*) Mebbe—he'll die soon.

PETER (*doubtfully*): Mebbe.

SIMEON: Mebbe—fur all we knows—he's dead now.

PETER: Ye'd need proof.

SIMEON: He's been gone two months—with no word.

PETER: Left us in the fields an evenin' like this. Hitched up an' druv off into the West. That's plum onnateral. He hadn't never been off this farm 'ceptin' t' the village in thirty year or more, not since he married Eben's maw. (*A pause. Shrewdly.*) I calc'late we might git him declared crazy by the court.

SIMEON: He skinned 'em too slick. He got the best o' all on 'em. They'd never b'lieve him crazy. (*A pause.*) We got t' wait—till he's underground.

EBEN (*with a sardonic chuckle*): Honor thy father! (*They turn startled, and stare at him. He grins, then scowls.*) I pray he's died. (*They stare at him. He continues matter-of-factly.*) Supper's ready.

SIMEON AND PETER (*together*): Ay-eh.

EBEN (*gazing up at the sky*): Sun's downin' purty.

SIMEON AND PETER (*together*): Ay-eh. They's gold in the West.

EBEN: Ay-eh. (*Pointing.*) Yonder atop o' the hill pasture, ye mean?

SIMEON AND PETER (*together*): In Californi-a!

EBEN: Hunh? (*Stares at them indifferently for a second, then drawls.*) Waal—supper's gittin' cold. (*He turns back into kitchen.*)

SIMEON (*startled—smacks his lips*): I air hungry!

PETER (*sniffing*): I smells bacon!

SIMEON (*with hungry appreciation*): Bacon's good!

PETER (*in same tone*): Bacon's bacon! (*They turn, shouldering each other, their bodies bumping and rubbing together as they hurry clumsily to their food, like two*

Riccardo Hernandez's set model for the American Repertory Theater's 2004–2005 production of *Desire under the Elms*.

friendly oxen toward their evening meal. They disappear around the right corner of house and can be heard entering the door.)

Scene II

(*The color fades from the sky. Twilight begins. The interior of the kitchen is now visible. A pine table is at center, a cook-stove in the right rear corner, four rough wooden chairs, a tallow candle on the table. In the middle of the rear wall is fastened a big advertising poster with a ship in full sail and the word "California" in big letters. Kitchen utensils hang from nails. Everything is neat and in order but the atmosphere is of a men's camp kitchen rather than that of a home.*)

(*Places for three are laid. Eben takes boiled potatoes and bacon from the stove and puts them on the table, also a loaf of bread and a crock of water. Simeon and Peter shoulder in, slump down in their chairs without a word. Eben joins them. The three eat in silence for a moment, the two elder as naturally unrestrained as beasts of the field, Eben picking at his food without appetite, glancing at them with a tolerant dislike.*)

SIMEON (*suddenly turns to Eben*): Looky here! Ye'd oughtn't t' said that, Eben.

PETER: 'Twa'n't righteous.

EBEN: What?

SIMEON: Ye prayed he'd died.

EBEN: Waal—don't yew pray it? (*A pause.*)

PETER: He's our Paw.

EBEN (*violently*): Not mine!

SIMEON (*dryly*): Ye'd not let no one else say that about yer Maw! Ha! (*He gives one abrupt sardonic guffaw. Peter grins.*)

EBEN (*very pale*): I meant—I hain't his'n—I hain't like him—he hain't me!

PETER (*dryly*): Wait till ye've growed his age!

EBEN (*intensely*): I'm Maw—every drop o' blood! (*A pause. They stare at him with indifferent curiosity.*)

PETER (*reminiscently*): She was good t' Sim 'n' me. A good Stepmaw's scurse.

SIMEON: She was good t' everyone.

EBEN (*greatly moved, gets to his feet and makes an awkward bow to each of them—stammering*): I be thankful t' ye. I'm her—her heir. (*He sits down in confusion.*)

PETER (*after a pause—judicially*): She was good even t' him.

EBEN (*fiercely*): An' fur thanks he killed her!

SIMEON (*after a pause*): No one never kills nobody. It's allus somethin'. That's the murderer.

EBEN: Didn't he slave Maw t' death?

552

PETER: He's slaved himself t' death. He's slaved Sim 'n' me 'n' yew t' death—on'y none o' us hain't died—yit.

SIMEON: It's somethin'—drivin' him—t' drive us!

EBEN (*vengefully*): Waal—I hold him t' jedgment! (*Then scornfully.*) Somethin'! What's somethin'?

SIMEON: Dunno.

EBEN (*sardonically*): What's drivin' yew to Californi-a, mebbe? (*They look at him in surprise.*) Oh, I've heerd ye! (*Then, after a pause.*) But ye'll never go t' the gold fields!

PETER (*assertively*): Mebbe!

EBEN: Whar'll ye git the money?

PETER: We kin walk. It's an a'mighty ways—Californi-a—but if yew was t' put all the steps we've walked on this farm end t' end we'd be in the moon!

EBEN: The Injuns'll skulp ye on the plains.

SIMEON (*with grim humor*): We'll mebbe make 'em pay a hair fur a hair!

EBEN (*decisively*): But t'aint that. Ye won't never go because ye'll wait here fur yer share o' the farm, thinkin' allus he'll die soon.

SIMEON (*after a pause*): We've a right.

PETER: Two-thirds belongs t'us.

EBEN (*jumping to his feet*): Ye've no right! She wa'n't yewr Maw! It was her farm! Didn't he steal it from her? She's dead. It's my farm.

SIMEON (*sardonically*): Tell that t' Paw—when he comes! I'll bet ye a dollar he'll laugh—fur once in his life. Ha! (*He laughs himself in one single mirthless bark.*)

PETER (*amused in turn, echoes his brother*): Ha!

SIMEON (*after a pause*): What've ye got held agin us, Eben? Year arter year it's skulked in yer eye—somethin'.

PETER: Ay-eh.

EBEN: Ay-eh. They's somethin'. (*Suddenly exploding.*) Why didn't ye never stand between him 'n' my Maw when he was slavin' her to her grave—t' pay her back fur the kindness she done t' yew? (*There is a long pause. They stare at him in surprise.*)

SIMEON: Waal—the stock'd got t' be watered.

PETER: 'R they was woodin' t' do.

SIMEON: 'R plowin'.

PETER: 'R hayin'.

SIMEON: 'R spreadin' manure.

PETER: 'R weedin'.

SIMEON: 'R prunin'.

PETER: 'R milkin'.

EBEN (*breaking in harshly*): An' makin' walls—stone atop o' stone—makin' walls till yer heart's a stone ye heft up out o' the way o' growth onto a stone wall t' wall in yer heart!

SIMEON (*matter-of-factly*): We never had no time t' meddle.

PETER (*to Eben*): Yew was fifteen afore yer Maw died—an' big fur yer age. Why didn't ye never do nothin'?

EBEN (*harshly*): They was chores t' do, wasn't they? (*A pause—then slowly.*) It was on'y arter she died I come to think o' it. Me cookin'—doin' her work—that made me know her, suffer her sufferin'—she'd come back t' help—come back t' bile potatoes—come back t' fry bacon—come back t' bake biscuits—come back all cramped up t' shake the fire, an' carry ashes, her eyes weepin' an' bloody with smoke an' cinders same's they used t' be. She still comes back—stands by the stove thar in the evenin'—she can't find it nateral sleepin' an' restin' in peace. She can't git used t' bein' free—even in her grave.

SIMEON: She never complained none.

EBEN: She'd got too tired. She'd got too used t' bein' too tired. That was what he done. (*With vengeful passion.*) An' sooner'r later, I'll meddle. I'll say the thin's I didn't say then t' him! I'll yell 'em at the top o' my lungs. I'll see t' it my Maw gits some rest an' sleep in her grave! (*He sits down again, relapsing into a brooding silence. They look at him with a queer indifferent curiosity.*)

PETER (*after a pause*): Whar in tarnation d'ye s'pose he went, Sim?

SIMEON: Dunno. He druv off in the buggy, all spick an' span, with the mare all breshed an' shiny, druv off clackin' his tongue an' wavin' his whip. I remember it right well. I was finishin' plowin', it was spring an' May an' sunset, an' gold in the West, an' he druv off into it. I yells "Whar ye goin', Paw?" an' he hauls up by the stone wall a jiffy. His old snake's eyes was glitterin' in the sun like he'd been drinkin' a jugful an' he says with a mule's grin: "Don't ye run away till I come back!"

PETER: Wonder if he knowed we was wantin' fur Californi-a?

SIMEON: Mebbe. I didn't say nothin' and he says, lookin' kinder queer an' sick: "I been hearin' the hens cluckin' an' the roosters crowin' all the durn day. I been listenin't' the cows lowin' an' everythin' else kickin' up till I can't stand it no more. It's spring an' I'm feelin' damned," he says. "Damned like an old bare hickory tree fit on'y fur burnin'," he says. An' then I calc'late I must've looked a mite hopeful, fur he adds real spry and vicious: "But don't git no fool idee I'm dead. I've sworn t' live a hundred an' I'll do it, if on'y t' spite yer sinful greed! An' now I'm ridin' out t' learn God's message t' me in the spring, like the prophets done. An' yew git back t' yer plowin'," he says. An' he druv off singin' a hymn. I thought he was drunk—'r I'd stopped him goin'.

EBEN (*scornfully*): No, ye wouldn't! Ye're scared o' him. He's stronger—inside—than both o' ye put together!

PETER (*sardonically*): An' yew—be yew Samson?°

EBEN: I'm gittin' stronger. I kin feel it growin' in me—growin' an' growin'—till it'll bust out—! (*He gets up and puts on his coat and a hat. They watch him, gradually breaking into grins. Eben avoids their eyes sheepishly.*) I'm goin' out fur a spell—up the road.

Samson: A biblical hero known for his great physical strength.

PETER: T' the village.

SIMEON: T' see Minnie?

EBEN (*defiantly*): Ay-eh!

PETER (*jeeringly*): The Scarlet Woman!

SIMEON: Lust—that's what's growin' in ye!

EBEN: Waal—she's purty!

PETER: She's been purty fur twenty year.

SIMEON: A new coat o' paint'll make a heifer out of forty.

EBEN: She hain't forty!

PETER: If she hain't, she's teeterin' on the edge.

EBEN (*desperately*): What d'yew know—

PETER: All they is . . . Sim knew her—an' then me arter—

SIMEON: An' Paw kin tell yew somethin' too! He was fust!

EBEN: D'ye mean t' say he . . . ?

SIMEON (*with a grin*): Ay-eh! We air his heirs in everythin'!

EBEN (*intensely*): That's more to it! That grows on it! It'll bust soon! (*Then violently.*) I'll go smash my fist in her face! (*He pulls open the door in rear violently.*)

SIMEON (*with a wink at Peter—drawlingly*): Mebbe—but the night's wa'm—purty—by the time ye git thar mebbe ye'll kiss her instead!

PETER: Sart'n he will! (*They both roar with coarse laughter. Eben rushes out and slams the door—then the outside front door—comes around the corner of the house and stands still by the gate, staring up at the sky.*)

SIMEON (*looking after him*): Like his Paw.

PETER: Dead spit an' image!

SIMEON: Dog'll eat dog!

PETER: Ay-eh. (*Pause. With yearning.*) Mebbe a year from now we'll be in Californi-a.

SIMEON: Ay-eh. (*A pause. Both yawn.*) Let's git t'bed. (*He blows out the candle. They go out door in rear. Eben stretches his arms up to the sky—rebelliously.*)

EBEN: Waal—thar's a star, an' somewhar's they's him, an' here's me, an' thar's Min up the road—in the same night. What if I does kiss her? She's like t'night, she's soft 'n' wa'm, her eyes kin wink like a star, her mouth's wa'm, her arms're wa'm, she smells like a wa'm plowed field, she's purty . . . Ay-eh! By God A'mighty she's purty, an' I don't give a damn how many sins she's sinned afore mine or who she's sinned 'em with, my sin's as purty as any one on 'em! (*He strides off down the road to the left.*)

Scene III

(*It is the pitch darkness just before dawn. Eben comes in from the left and goes around to the porch, feeling his way, chuckling bitterly and cursing half-aloud to himself.*)

EBEN: The cussed old miser! (*He can be heard going in the front door. There is a pause as he goes upstairs,*

then a loud knock on the bedroom door of the brothers.*) Wake up!

SIMEON (*startledly*): Who's thar?

EBEN (*Pushing open the door and coming in, a lighted candle in his hand. The bedroom of the brothers is revealed. Its ceiling is the sloping roof. They can stand upright only close to the center dividing wall of the upstairs. Simeon and Peter are in a double bed, front. Eben's cot is to the rear. Eben has a mixture of silly grin and vicious scowl on his face.*): I be!

PETER (*angrily*): What in hell's-fire . . . ?

EBEN: I got news fur ye! Ha! (*He gives one abrupt sardonic guffaw.*)

SIMEON (*angrily*): Couldn't ye hold it 'til we'd got our sleep?

EBEN: It's nigh sunup. (*Then explosively.*) He's gone an' married agen!

SIMEON AND PETER (*explosively*): Paw?

EBEN: Got himself hitched to a female 'bout thirty-five—an' purty, they says . . .

SIMEON (*aghast*): It's a durn lie!

PETER: Who says?

SIMEON: They been stringin' ye!

EBEN: Think I'm a dunce, do ye? The hull village says. The preacher from New Dover, he brung the news—told it t'our preacher—New Dover, that's whar the old loon got himself hitched—that's whar the woman lived—

PETER (*no longer doubting—stunned*): Waal . . . !

SIMEON (*the same*): Waal . . . !

EBEN (*sitting down on a bed—with vicious hatred*): Ain't he a devil out o' hell? It's jest t' spite us—the damned old mule!

PETER (*after a pause*): Everythin'll go t'her now.

SIMEON: Ay-eh. (*A pause—dully.*) Waal—if it's done—

PETER: It's done us. (*Pause—then persuasively.*) They's gold in the fields o' Californi-a, Sim. No good a-stayin' here now.

SIMEON: Jest what I was a-thinkin'. (*Then with decision.*) S'well fust's last! Let's light out and git this mornin'.

PETER: Suits me.

EBEN: Ye must like walkin'.

SIMEON (*sardonically*): If ye'd grow wings on us we'd fly thar!

EBEN: Ye'd like ridin' better—on a boat, wouldn't ye? (*Fumbles in his pocket and takes out a crumpled sheet of foolscap.*) Waal, if ye sign this ye kin ride on a boat. I've had it writ out an' ready in case ye'd ever go. It says fur three hundred dollars t' each ye agree yewr shares o' the farm is sold t' me. (*They look suspiciously at the paper. A pause.*)

SIMEON (*wonderingly*): But if he's hitched agen—

PETER: An' whar'd yew git that sum o' money, anyways?

EBEN (*cunningly*): I know whar it's hid. I been waitin'—Maw told me. She knew whar it lay fur years, but she was waitin' . . . It's her'n—the money he hoarded from her farm an' hid from Maw. It's my money by rights now.

PETER: Whar's it hid?

EBEN (*cunningly*): Whar yew won't never find it without me. Maw spied on him—'r she'd never knowed. (*A pause. They look at him suspiciously, and he at them.*) Waal, is it fa'r trade?

SIMEON: Dunno.

PETER: Dunno.

SIMEON (*looking at window*): Sky's grayin'.

PETER: Ye better start the fire, Eben.

SIMEON: An' fix some vittles.

EBEN: Ay-eh. (*Then with a forced jocular heartiness.*) I'll git ye a good one. If ye're startin' t' hoof it t' Californi-a ye'll need somethin' that'll stick t' yer ribs. (*He turns to the door, adding meaningly.*) But ye kin ride on a boat if ye'll swap. (*He stops at the door and pauses. They stare at him.*)

SIMEON (*suspiciously*): Whar was ye all night?

EBEN (*defiantly*): Up t' Min's. (*Then slowly.*) Walkin' thar, fust I felt 's if I'd kiss her; then I got a-thinkin' o' what ye'd said o' him an' her an' I says, I'll bust her nose fur that! Then I got t' the village an' heerd the news an' I got madder'n hell an' run all the way t' Min's not knowin' what I'd do—(*He pauses—then sheepishly but more defiantly.*) Waal—when I seen her, I didn't hit her—nor I didn't kiss her nuther—I begun t' beller like a calf an' cuss at the same time, I was so durn mad—an' she got scared—an' I jest grabbed holt an' tuk her! (*Proudly.*) Yes, sirree! I tuk her. She may've been his'n—an' your'n, too—but she's mine now!

SIMEON (*dryly*): In love, air yew?

EBEN (*with lofty scorn*): Love! I don't take no stock in sech slop!

PETER (*winking at Simeon*): Mebbe Eben's aimin' t' marry, too.

SIMEON: Min'd make a true faithful he'pmeet! (*They snicker.*)

EBEN: What do I care fur her—'ceptin' she's round an' wa'm? The p'int is she was his'n—an' now she b'longs t' me! (*He goes to the door—then turns—rebelliously.*) An' Min hain't sech a bad un. They's worse'n Min in the world, I'll bet ye! Wait'll we see this cow the Old Man's hitched t'! She'll beat Min, I got a notion! (*He starts to go out.*)

SIMEON (*suddenly*): Mebbe ye'll try t' make her your'n, too?

PETER: Ha! (*He gives a sardonic laugh of relish at this idea.*)

EBEN (*spitting with disgust*): Her—here—sleepin' with him—stealin' my Maw's farm! I'd as soon pet a skunk 'r kiss a snake! (*He goes out. The two stare after him suspiciously. A pause. They listen to his steps receding.*)

PETER: He's startin' the fire.

SIMEON: I'd like t' ride t' Californi-a—but—

PETER: Min might o' put some scheme in his head.

SIMEON: Mebbe it's all a lie 'bout Paw marryin'. We'd best wait an' see the bride.

PETER: An' don't sign nothin' till we does!

SIMEON: Nor till we've tested it's good money! (*Then with a grin.*) But if Paw's hitched we'd be sellin' Eben somethin' we'd never git nohow!

PETER: We'll wait an' see. (*Then with sudden vindictive anger.*) An' till he comes, let's yew 'n' me not wuk a lick, let Eben tend to thin's if he's a mind t', let's us jest sleep an' eat an' drink likker, an' let the hull damned farm go t' blazes!

SIMEON (*excitedly*): By God, we've 'arned a rest! We'll play rich fur a change. I hain't a-going to stir outa bed till breakfast's ready.

PETER: An' on the table!

SIMEON (*after a pause—thoughtfully*): What d'ye calc'late she'll be like—our new Maw? Like Eben thinks?

PETER: More'n' likely.

SIMEON (*vindictively*): Waal—I hope she's a she-devil that'll make him wish he was dead an' livin' in the pit o' hell fur comfort!

PETER (*fervently*): Amen!

SIMEON (*imitating his father's voice*): "I'm ridin' out t' learn God's message t' me in the spring like the prophets done," he says. I'll bet right then an' thar he knew plumb well he was goin' whorin', the stinkin' old hypocrite!

Scene IV

(*Same as scene II—shows the interior of the kitchen with a lighted candle on table. It is gray dawn outside. Simeon and Peter are just finishing their breakfast. Eben sits before his plate of untouched food, brooding frowningly.*)

PETER (*glancing at him rather irritably*): Lookin' glum don't help none.

SIMEON (*sarcastically*): Sorrowin' over his lust o' the flesh!

PETER (*with a grin*): Was she yer fust?

EBEN (*angrily*): None o'yer business. (*A pause.*) I was thinkin' o' him. I got a notion he's gittin' near—I kin feel him comin' on like yew kin feel malaria chill afore it takes ye.

PETER: It's too early yet.

SIMEON: Dunno. He'd like t' catch us nappin'—jest t' have somethin' t' boss us 'round over.

PETER (*mechanically gets to his feet. Simeon does the same.*): Waal—let's git t'wuk. (*They both plod mechanically toward the door before they realize. Then they stop short.*)

SIMEON (*grinning*): Ye're a cussed fool, Pete—and I be wuss! Let him see we hain't wukin'! We don't give a durn!

PETER (*as they go back to the table*): Not a damned durn! It'll serve t' show him we're done with him. (*They sit down again. Eben stares from one to the other with surprise.*)

SIMEON (*grins at him*): We're aimin' t' start bein' lilies o' the field.

PETER: Nary a toil 'r spin 'r lick o' wuk do we put in!

SIMEON: Ye're sole owner—till he comes—that's what ye wanted. Waal, ye got t' be sole hand, too.

PETER: The cows air bellerin'. Ye better hustle at the milkin'.

EBEN (*with excited joy*): Ye mean ye'll sign the paper?

SIMEON (*dryly*): Mebbe.

PETER: Mebbe.

SIMEON: We're considerin'. (*Peremptorily.*) Ye better git t' wuk.

EBEN (*with queer excitement*): It's Maw's farm agen! It's my farm! Them's my cows! I'll milk my durn fingers off fur cows o' mine! (*He goes out door in rear, they stare after him indifferently.*)

SIMEON: Like his Paw.

PETER: Dead spit 'n' image!

SIMEON: Waal—let dog eat dog! (*Eben comes out of front door and around the corner of the house. The sky is beginning to grow flushed with sunrise. Eben stops by the gate and stares around him with glowing, possessive eyes. He takes in the whole farm with his embracing glance of desire.*)

EBEN: It's purty! It's damned purty! It's mine! (*He suddenly throws his head back boldly and glares with hard, defiant eyes at the sky.*) Mine, d'ye hear? Mine! (*He turns and walks quickly off left, rear, toward the barn. The two brothers light their pipes.*)

SIMEON (*putting his muddy boots up on the table, tilting back his chair, and puffing defiantly*): Waal—this air solid comfort—fur once.

PETER: Ay-eh. (*He follows suit. A pause. Unconsciously they both sigh.*)

SIMEON (*suddenly*): He never was much o' a hand at milkin', Eben wa'n't.

PETER (*with a snort*): His hands air like hoofs! (*A pause.*)

SIMEON: Reach down the jug thar! Let's take a swaller. I'm feelin' kind o' low.

PETER: Good idee! (*He does so—gets two glasses—they pour out drinks of whisky.*) Here's t' the gold in Californi-a!

SIMEON: An' luck t' find it! (*They drink—puff resolutely—sigh—take their feet down from the table.*)

PETER: Likker don't pear t' sot right.

SIMEON: We hain't used t' it this early. (*A pause. They become very restless.*)

PETER: Gittin' close in this kitchen.

SIMEON (*with immense relief*): Let's git a breath o' air. (*They arise briskly and go out rear—appear around house and stop by the gate. They stare up at the sky with a numbed appreciation.*)

PETER: Purty!

SIMEON: Ay-eh. Gold's t' the East now.

PETER: Sun's startin' with us fur the Golden West.

SIMEON (*staring around the farm, his compressed face tightened, unable to conceal his emotion*): Waal—it's our last mornin'—mebbe.

PETER (*the same*): Ay-eh.

SIMEON (*stamps his foot on the earth and addresses it desperately*): Waal—ye've thirty year o' me buried in ye—spread out over ye—blood an' bone an' sweat—rotted away—fertilizin' ye—richin' yer soul—prime manure, by God, that's what I been t' ye!

PETER: Ay-eh! An' me.

SIMEON: An' yew, Peter. (*He sighs—then spits.*) Waal—no use'n cryin' over spilt milk.

PETER: They's gold in the West—an' freedom, mebbe. We been slaves t' stone walls here.

SIMEON (*defiantly*): We hain't nobody's slaves from this out—nor nothin's slaves nuther. (*A pause—restlessly.*) Speaking o' milk, wonder how Eben's managin'?

PETER: I s'pose he's managin'.

SIMEON: Mebbe we'd ought t' help—this once.

PETER: Mebbe. The cows knows us.

SIMEON: An' likes us. They don't know him much.

PETER: An' the hosses, an' pigs, an' chickens. They don't know him much.

SIMEON: They knows us like brothers—an' likes us! (*Proudly.*) Hain't we raised 'em t' be fust-rate, number one prize stock?

PETER: We hain't—not no more.

SIMEON (*dully*): I was fergittin'. (*Then resignedly.*) Waal, let's go help Eben a spell an' git waked up.

PETER: Suits me. (*They are starting off down left, rear, for the barn when Eben appears from there hurrying toward them, his face excited.*)

EBEN (*breathlessly*): Waal—har they be! The old mule an' the bride! I seen 'em from the barn down below at the turnin'.

PETER: How could ye tell that far?

EBEN: Hain't I as far-sight as he's near-sight? Don't I know the mare 'n' buggy, an' two people settin' in it? Who else . . . ? An' I tell ye I kin feel 'em a'comin', too! (*He squirms as if he had the itch.*)

PETER (*beginning to be angry*): Waal—let him do his own unhitchin'!

SIMEON (*angry in his turn*): Let's hustle in an' git our bundles an' be a-goin' as he's a-comin'. I don't want never t' step inside the door agen arter he's back. (*They both start back around the corner of the house. Eben follows them.*)

EBEN (*anxiously*): Will ye sign it afore ye go?

PETER: Let's see the color o' the old skinflint's money an' we'll sign. (*They disappear left. The two brothers clump upstairs to get their bundles. Eben appears in the kitchen, runs to window, peers out, comes back and pulls up a strip of flooring in under stove, takes out a canvas bag and puts it on table, then sets the floorboard back in place. The two brothers appear a moment after. They carry old carpetbags.*)

EBEN (*puts his hand on bag guardingly*): Have ye signed?

SIMEON (*shows paper in his hand*): Ay-eh. (*Greedily.*) Be that the money?

EBEN (*opens bag and pours out pile of twenty-dollar gold pieces*): Twenty-dollar pieces—thirty of 'em. Count 'em. (*Peter does so, arranging them in stacks of five, biting one or two to test them.*)

PETER: Six hundred. (*He puts them in bag and puts it inside his shirt carefully.*)

SIMEON (*handing paper to Eben*): Har ye be.

EBEN (*after a glance, folds it carefully and hides it under his shirt—gratefully*): Thank yew.

PETER: Thank yew fur the ride.

SIMEON: We'll send ye a lump o' gold fur Christmas. (*A pause. Eben stares at them and they at him.*)

PETER (*awkwardly*): Waal—we're a-goin'.

SIMEON: Comin' out t' the yard?

EBEN: No. I'm waitin' in here a spell. (*Another silence. The brothers edge awkwardly to door in rear—then turn and stand.*)

SIMEON: Waal—good-by.

PETER: Good-by.

EBEN: Good-by. (*They go out. He sits down at the table, faces the stove and pulls out the paper. He looks from it to the stove. His face, lighted up by the shaft of sunlight from the window, has an expression of trance. His lips move. The two brothers come out to the gate.*)

PETER (*looking off toward barn*): Thar he be—unhitchin'.

SIMEON (*with a chuckle*): I'll bet ye he's riled!

PETER: An thar she be.

SIMEON: Let's wait 'n' see what our new Maw looks like.

PETER (*with a grin*): An' give him our partin' cuss!

SIMEON (*grinning*): I feel like raisin' fun. I feel light in my head an' feet.

PETER: Me, too. I feel like laffin' till I'd split up the middle.

SIMEON: Reckon it's the likker?

PETER: No. My feet feel itchin' t' walk an' walk—an' jump high over thin's—an'. . . .

SIMEON: Dance? (*A pause.*)

PETER (*puzzled*): It's plumb onnateral.

SIMEON (*a light coming over his face*): I calc'late it's 'cause school's out. It's holiday. Fur once we're free!

PETER (*dazedly*): Free?

SIMEON: The halter's broke—the harness is busted—the fence bars is down—the stone walls air crumblin' an' tumblin'! We'll be kickin' up an' tearin' away down the road!

PETER (*drawing a deep breath—oratorically*): Anybody that wants this stinkin' old rock-pile of a farm kin hev it. T'ain't our'n, no sirree!

SIMEON (*takes the gate off its hinges and puts it under his arm*): We harby 'bolishes shet gates, an' open gates, an' all gates, by thunder!

PETER: We'll take it with us fur luck an' let 'er sail free down some river.

SIMEON (*as a sound of voices comes from left, rear*): Har they comes! (*The two brothers congeal into two stiff, grim-visaged statues. Ephraim Cabot and Abbie Putnam come in. Cabot is seventy-five, tall and gaunt, with great, wiry, concentrated power, but stoop-shouldered from toil. His face is as hard as if it were hewn out of a boulder, yet there is a weakness in it, a*

petty pride in its own narrow strength. His eyes are small, close together, and extremely near-sighted, blinking continually in the effort to focus on objects, their stare having a straining, ingrowing quality. He is dressed in his dismal black Sunday suit. Abbie is thirty-five, buxom, full of vitality. Her round face is pretty but marred by its rather gross sensuality. There is strength and obstinacy in her jaw, a hard determination in her eyes, and about her whole personality the same unsettled, untamed, desperate quality which is so apparent in Eben.*)

CABOT (*as they enter—a queer strangled emotion in his dry cracking voice*): Har we be t' hum, Abbie.

ABBIE (*with lust for the word*): Hum! (*Her eyes gloating on the house without seeming to see the two stiff figures at the gate.*) It's purty—purty! I can't b'lieve it's r'ally mine.

CABOT (*sharply*): Yewr'n? Mine! (*He stares at her penetratingly. She stares back. He adds relentingly.*) Our'n—mebbe! It was lonesome too long. I was growin' old in the spring. A hum's got t' hev a woman.

ABBIE (*her voice taking possession*): A woman's got t' hev a hum!

CABOT (*nodding uncertainly*): Ay-eh. (*Then irritably.*) Whar be they? Ain't thar nobody about—'r wukin'—'r nothin'?

ABBIE (*Sees the brothers. She returns their stare of cold appraising contempt with interest—slowly.*): Thar's two men loafin' at the gate an' starin' at me like a couple o' strayed hogs.

CABOT (*straining his eyes*): I kin see 'em—but I can't make out. . . .

SIMEON: It's Simeon.

PETER: It's Peter.

CABOT (*exploding*): Why hain't ye wukin'?

SIMEON (*dryly*): We're waitin' t' welcome ye hum—yew an' the bride!

CABOT (*confusedly*): Huh? Waal—this be yer new Maw, boys. (*She stares at them and they at her.*)

SIMEON (*turns away and spits contemptuously*): I see her!

PETER (*spits also*): An I see her!

ABBIE (*with the conqueror's conscious superiority*): I'll go in an' look at *my* house. (*She goes slowly around to porch.*)

SIMEON (*with a snort*): Her house!

PETER (*calls after her*): Ye'll find Eben inside. Ye better not tell him it's *yewr* house.

ABBIE (*mouthing the name*): Eben. (*Then quietly.*) I'll tell Eben.

CABOT (*with a contemptuous sneer*): Ye needn't heed Eben. Eben's a dumb fool—like his Maw—soft an' simple!

SIMEON (*with his sardonic burst of laughter*): Ha! Eben's a chip o' yew—spit 'n' image—hard 'n' bitter's a hickory tree! Dog'll eat dog. He'll eat ye yet, old man!

CABOT (*commandingly*): Ye git t' wuk.

SIMEON (*as Abbie disappears in house—winks at Peter and says tauntingly*): So that thar's our new Maw, be it? Whar in hell did ye dig her up? (*He and Peter laugh.*)

PETER: Ha! Ye'd better turn her in the pen with the other sows. (*They laugh uproariously, slapping their thighs.*)

CABOT (*so amazed at their effrontery that he stutters in confusion*): Simeon! Peter! What's come over ye? Air ye drunk?

SIMEON: We're free, old man—free o' yew an' the hull damned farm! (*They grow more and more hilarious and excited.*)

PETER: An' we're startin' out fur the gold fields o' Californi-a!

SIMEON: Ye kin take this place an' burn it!

PETER: An' bury it—fur all we cares!

SIMEON: We're free, old man! (*He cuts a caper.*)

PETER: Free! (*He gives a kick in the air.*)

SIMEON (*in a frenzy*): Whoop!

PETER: Whoop! (*They do an absurd Indian war dance about the old man who is petrified between rage and the fear that they are insane.*)

SIMEON: We're free as Injuns! Lucky we don't skulp ye!

PETER: An' burn yer barn an' kill the stock!

SIMEON: An' rape yer new woman! Whoop! (*He and Peter stop their dance, holding their sides, rocking with wild laughter.*)

CABOT (*edging away*): Lust fur gold—fur the sinful, easy gold o' Californi-a! It's made ye mad!

SIMEON (*tauntingly*): Wouldn't ye like us to send ye back some sinful gold, ye old sinner?

PETER: They's gold besides what's in Californi-a! (*He retreats back beyond the vision of the old man and takes the bag of money and flaunts it in the air above his head, laughing.*)

SIMEON: And sinfuller, too!

PETER: We'll be voyagin' on the sea! Whoop! (*He leaps up and down.*)

SIMEON: Livin' free! Whoop! (*He leaps in turn.*)

CABOT (*suddenly roaring with rage*): My cuss on ye!

SIMEON: Take our'n in trade fur it! Whoop!

CABOT: I'll hev ye both chained up in the asylum!

PETER: Ye old skinflint! Good-by!

SIMEON: Ye old blood sucker! Good-by!

CABOT: Go afore I . . . !

PETER: Whoop! (*He picks a stone from the road. Simeon does the same.*)

SIMEON: Maw'll be in the parlor.

PETER: Ay-eh! One! Two!

CABOT (*frightened*): What air ye . . . ?

PETER: Three! (*They both throw, the stones hitting the parlor window with a crash of glass, tearing the shade.*)

SIMEON: Whoop!

PETER: Whoop!

CABOT (*in a fury now, rushing toward them*): If I kin lay hands on ye—I'll break yer bones fur ye! (*But they beat a capering retreat before him, Simeon with the gate still under his arm. Cabot comes back, panting with impotent rage. Their voices as they go off take up the song of the gold-seekers to the old tune of "Oh, Susannah!"*)

"I jumped aboard the Liza ship,
And traveled on the sea,
And every time I thought of home
I wished it wasn't me!
Oh! Californi-a,
That's the land fur me!
I'm off to Californi-a!
With my wash bowl on my knee."

(*In the meantime, the window of the upper bedroom on right is raised and Abbie sticks her head out. She looks down at Cabot—with a sigh of relief.*)

ABBIE: Waal—that's the last o' them two, hain't it? (*He doesn't answer. Then in possessive tones.*) This here's a nice bedroom, Ephraim. It's a r'al nice bed. Is it my room, Ephraim?

CABOT (*grimly—without looking up*): Our'n! (*She cannot control a grimace of aversion and pulls back her head slowly and shuts the window. A sudden horrible thought seems to enter Cabot's head.*) They been up to somethin'! Mebbe—mebbe they've pizened the stock—'r somethin'! (*He almost runs off down toward the barn. A moment later the kitchen door is slowly pushed open and Abbie enters. For a moment she stands looking at Eben. He does not notice her at first. Her eyes take him in penetratingly with a calculating appraisal of his strength as against hers. But under this her desire is dimly awakened by his youth and good looks. Suddenly he becomes conscious of her presence and looks up. Their eyes meet. He leaps to his feet, glowering at her speechlessly.*)

ABBIE (*in her most seductive tones which she uses all through this scene*): Be you—Eben? I'm Abbie—(*She laughs.*) I mean, I'm yer new Maw.

EBEN (*viciously*): No, damn ye!

ABBIE (*as if she hadn't heard—with a queer smile*): Yer Paw's spoke a lot o' yew. . . .

EBEN: Ha!

ABBIE: Ye mustn't mind him. He's an old man. (*A long pause. They stare at each other.*) I don't want t' pretend playin' Maw t' ye, Eben. (*Admiringly.*) You're too big an' too strong fur that. I want t' be frens with ye. Mebbe with me fur a fren ye'd find ye'd like livin' here better. I kin make it easy fur ye with him, mebbe. (*With a scornful sense of power.*) I calc'late I kin git him t' do most anythin' fur me.

EBEN (*with bitter scorn*): Ha! (*They stare again, Eben obscurely moved, physically attracted to her—in forced stilted tones.*) Yew kin go t' the devil!

ABBIE (*calmly*): If cussin' me does ye good, cuss all ye've a mind t'. I'm all prepared t' have ye agin me—at fust. I don't blame ye nuther. I'd feel the same at any stranger comin' t' take my Maw's place. (*He shudders. She is watching him carefully.*) Yew must've cared a lot fur yewr Maw, didn't ye? My Maw died afore I'd growed. I don't remember her none. (*A pause.*) But yew won't hate me long, Eben. I'm not the wust in the world—an' yew an' me've got a lot in common. I kin tell that by lookin' at ye. Waal—I've had a hard life, too—oceans o' trouble an' nuthin' but wuk fur reward. I was a orphan early an' had t' wuk fur others in other folks' hums. Then I married an' he turned out a drunken spreer an' so he had to wuk fur others an' me too agen in other folks' hums, an' the baby died, an' my husband got sick an' died too, an' I was glad sayin' now I'm free fur once, on'y I diskivered right away all I was free fur was t'wuk agen in other folks' hums, doin' other folks' wuk till I'd most give up hope o' ever doin' my own wuk in my own hum, an' then your Paw come ... (*Cabot appears returning from the barn. He comes to the gate and looks down the road the brothers have gone. A faint strain of their retreating voices is heard: "Oh, Californi-a! That's the place for me." He stands glowering, his fist clenched, his face grim with rage.*)

EBEN (*fighting against his growing attraction and sympathy—harshly*): An' bought yew—like a harlot! (*She is stung and flushes angrily. She has been sincerely moved by the recital of her troubles. He adds furiously.*) An' the price he's payin' ye—this farm—was my Maw's, damn ye!—an' mine now!

ABBIE (*with a cool laugh of confidence*): Yewr'n? We'll see 'bout that! (*Then strongly.*) Waal—what if I did need a hum? What else'd I marry an old man like him fur?

EBEN (*maliciously*): I'll tell him ye said that!

ABBIE (*smiling*): I'll say ye're lyin' a-purpose—an' he'll drive ye off the place!

EBEN: Ye devil!

ABBIE (*defying him*): This be my farm—this be my hum—this be my kitchen—!

EBEN (*furiously, as if he were going to attack her*): Shut up, damn ye!

ABBIE (*walks up to him—a queer coarse expression of desire in her face and body—slowly*): An' upstairs—that be my bedroom—an' my bed! (*He stares into her eyes, terribly confused and torn. She adds softly.*) I hain't bad nor mean—'ceptin' fur an enemy—but I got t' fight fur what's due me out o' life, if I ever 'spect t' git it. (*Then putting her hand on his arm—seductively.*) Let's yew 'n' me be frens, Eben.

EBEN (*stupidly—as if hypnotized*): Ay-eh. (*Then furiously flinging off her arm.*) No, ye durned old witch! I hate ye! (*He rushes out the door.*)

ABBIE (*looks after him smiling satisfiedly—then half to herself, mouthing the word*): Eben's nice. (*She looks at the table, proudly.*) I'll wash up *my* dishes now. (*Eben appears outside, slamming the door behind him. He comes around corner, stops on seeing his father, and stands staring at him with hate.*)

CABOT (*raising his arms to heaven in the fury he can no longer control*): Lord God o' Hosts, smite the undutiful sons with Thy wust cuss!

EBEN (*breaking in violently*): Yew 'n' yewr God! Allus cussin' folks—allus naggin' 'em!

CABOT (*oblivious to him—summoningly*): God o' the old! God o' the lonesome!

EBEN (*mockingly*): Naggin' His sheep t' sin! T' hell with yewr God! (*Cabot turns. He and Eben glower at each other.*)

CABOT (*harshly*): So it's yew. I might've knowed it. (*Shaking his finger threateningly at him.*) Blasphemin' fool! (*Then quickly.*) Why hain't ye t' wuk?

EBEN: Why hain't yew? They've went. I can't wuk it all alone.

CABOT (*contemptuously*): Nor noways! I'm wuth ten o' ye yit, old's I be! Ye'll never be more'n half a man! (*Then, matter-of-factly.*) Waal—let's git t' the barn. (*They go. A last faint note of the "Californi-a" song is heard from the distance. Abbie is washing her dishes.*)

PART II • Scene I

(*The exterior of the farmhouse, as in part I—a hot Sunday afternoon two months later. Abbie, dressed in her best, is discovered sitting in a rocker at the end of the porch. She rocks listlessly, enervated by the heat, staring in front of her with bored, half-closed eyes.*)

(*Eben sticks his head out of his bedroom window. He looks around furtively and tries to see—or hear—if anyone is on the porch, but although he has been careful to make no noise, Abbie has sensed his movement. She stops rocking, her face grows animated and eager, she waits attentively. Eben seems to feel her presence, he scowls back his thoughts of her and spits with exaggerated disdain—then withdraws back into the room. Abbie waits, holding her breath as she listens with passionate eagerness for every sound within the house.*)

(*Eben comes out. Their eyes meet; his falter. He is confused, he turns away and slams the door resentfully. At this gesture, Abbie laughs tantalizingly, amused but at the same time piqued and irritated. He scowls, strides off the porch to the path and starts to walk past her to the road with a grand swagger of ignoring her existence. He is dressed in his store suit, spruced up, his face shines from soap and water. Abbie leans forward on her chair, her eyes hard and angry now, and, as he passes her, gives a sneering, taunting chuckle.*)

EBEN (*stung—turns on her furiously*): What air yew cacklin' 'bout?

ABBIE (*triumphant*): Yew!

EBEN: What about me?

ABBIE: Ye look all slicked up like a prize bull.

EBEN (*with a sneer*): Waal—ye hain't so durned purty yerself, be ye? (*They stare into each other's eyes, his held by hers in spite of himself, hers glowingly possessive. Their physical attraction becomes a palpable force quivering in the hot air.*)

ABBIE (*softly*): Ye don't mean that, Eben. Ye may think ye mean it, mebbe, but ye don't. Ye can't. It's agin nature, Eben. Ye been fightin' yer nature ever since the day I come—tryin' t' tell yourself I hain't purty t'ye. (*She laughs a low humid laugh without taking her eyes from his. A pause—her body squirms desirously—she murmurs languorously.*) Hain't the sun strong an' hot? Ye kin feel it burnin' into the earth—Nature—makin' thin's grow—bigger 'n' bigger—burnin' inside ye—makin' ye want t' grow—into somethin' else—till ye're jined with it—an' it's your'n—but it owns ye, too—ant makes ye grow bigger—like a tree—like them elums—(*She laughs again softly, holding his eyes. He takes a step toward her, compelled against his will.*) Nature'll beat ye, Eben. Ye might's well own up t' it fust 's last.

EBEN (*trying to break from her spell—confusedly*): If Paw'd hear ye goin' on.... (*Resentfully.*) But ye've made such a damned idjit out o' the old devil...! (*Abbie laughs.*)

ABBIE: Waal—hain't it easier fur yew with him changed softer?

EBEN (*defiantly*): No. I'm fightin' him—fightin' yew—fightin' fur Maw's rights t' her hum! (*This breaks her spell for him. He glowers at her.*) An' I'm onto ye. Ye hain't foolin' me a mite. Ye're aimin' t' swaller up everythin' an' make it your'n. Waal, you'll find I'm a heap sight bigger hunk nor yew kin chew! (*He turns from her with a sneer.*)

ABBIE (*trying to regain her ascendancy—seductively*): Eben!

EBEN: Leave me be! (*He starts to walk away.*)

ABBIE (*more commandingly*): Eben!

EBEN (*stops—resentfully*): What d'ye want?

ABBIE (*trying to conceal a growing excitement*): Whar air ye goin'?

EBEN (*with malicious nonchalance*): Oh—up the road a spell.

ABBIE: T' the village?

EBEN (*airily*): Mebbe.

ABBIE (*excitedly*): T' see that Min, I s'pose?

EBEN: Mebbe.

ABBIE (*weakly*): What d'ye want t' waste time on her fur?

EBEN (*revenging himself now—grinning at her*): Ye can't beat Nature, didn't ye say? (*He laughs and again starts to walk away.*)

ABBIE (*bursting out*): An ugly old hake!

EBEN (*with a tantalizing sneer*): She's purtier'n yew be!

ABBIE: That every wuthless drunk in the country has....

EBEN (*tauntingly*): Mebbe—but she's better'n yew. She owns up fa'r 'n' squar' t' her doin's.

ABBIE (*furiously*): Don't ye dare compare....

EBEN: She don't go sneakin' an' stealin'—what's mine.

ABBIE (*savagely seizing on his weak point*): Your'n? Yew mean—my farm?

EBEN: I mean the farm yew sold yourself fur like any other old whore—my farm!

ABBIE (*stung—fiercely*): Ye'll never live t' see the day when even a stinkin' weed on it'll belong t' ye! (*Then in a scream.*) Git out o' my sight! Go on t' yer slut—disgracin' yer Paw 'n' me! I'll git yer Paw t' horsewhip ye off the place if I want t'! Ye're only livin'

here 'cause I tolerate ye! Git along! I hate the sight o' ye! (*She stops, panting and glaring at him.*)

EBEN (*returning her glance in kind*): An' I hate the sight o' yew! (*He turns and strides off up the road. She follows his retreating figure with concentrated hate. Old Cabot appears coming up from the barn. The hard, grim expression of his face has changed. He seems in some queer way softened, mellowed. His eyes have taken on a strange, incongruous dreamy quality. Yet there is no hint of physical weakness about him—rather he looks more robust and younger. Abbie sees him and turns away quickly with unconcealed aversion. He comes slowly up to her.*)

CABOT (*mildly*): War yew an' Eben quarrelin' agen?

ABBIE (*shortly*): No.

CABOT: Ye was talkin' a'mighty loud. (*He sits down on the edge of porch.*)

ABBIE (*snappishly*): If ye heerd us they hain't no need askin' questions.

CABOT: I didn't hear what ye said.

ABBIE (*relieved*): Waal—it wa'n't nothin' t' speak on.

CABOT (*after a pause*): Eben's queer.

ABBIE (*bitterly*): He's the dead spit 'n' image o' yew!

CABOT (*queerly interested*): D'ye think so, Abbie? (*After a pause, ruminatingly.*) Me 'n' Eben's allus fit 'n' fit. I never could b'ar him noways. He's so thunderin' soft—like his Maw.

ABBIE (*scornfully*): Ay-eh! 'Bout as soft as yew be!

CABOT (*as if he hadn't heard*): Mebbe I been too hard on him.

ABBIE (*jeeringly*): Waal—ye're gittin' soft now—soft as slop! That's what Eben was sayin'.

CABOT (*his face instantly grim and ominous*): Eben was sayin'? Waal, he'd best not do nothin' t' try me 'r he'll soon diskiver.... (*A pause. She keeps her face turned away. His gradually softens. He stares up at the sky.*) Purty, hain't it?

ABBIE (*crossly*): I don't see nothin' purty.

CABOT: The sky. Feels like a wa'm field up thar.

ABBIE (*sarcastically*): Air yew aimin' t' buy up over the farm too? (*She snickers contemptuously.*)

CABOT (*strangely*): I'd like t' own my place up thar. (*A pause.*) I'm gittin' old, Abbie. I'm gittin' ripe on the bough. (*A pause. She stares at him mystified. He goes on.*) It's allus lonesome cold in the house—even when it's bilin' hot outside. Hain't yew noticed?

ABBIE: No.

CABOT: It's wa'm down t' the barn—nice smellin' an' warm—with the cows. (*A pause.*) Cows is queer.

ABBIE: Like yew?

CABOT: Like Eben. (*A pause.*) I'm gittin' t' feel resigned t' Eben—jest as I got t' feel 'bout his Maw. I'm gittin' t' learn to b'ar his softness—jest like her'n. I calc'late I c'd a'most take t' him—if he wa'n't sech a dumb fool! (*A pause.*) I s'pose it's old age a-creepin' in my bones.

ABBIE (*indifferently*): Waal—ye hain't dead yet.

CABOT (*roused*): No, I hain't, yew bet—not by a hell of a sight—I'm sound 'n' tough as hickory! (*Then moodily.*) But arter three score and ten the Lord warns ye t' prepare. (*A pause.*) That's why Eben's come in my head. Now that his cussed sinful brothers is gone their path t' hell, they's no one left but Eben.

ABBIE (*resentfully*): They's me, hain't they? (*Agitatedly.*) What's all this sudden likin' ye've tuk to Eben? Why don't ye say nothin' 'bout me? Hain't I yer lawful wife?

CABOT (*simply*): Ay-eh. Ye be. (*A pause—he stares at her desirously—his eyes grow avid—then with a sudden movement he seizes her hands and squeezes them, declaiming in a queer camp meeting preacher's tempo.*) Yew air my Rose o' Sharon! Behold, yew air fair; yer eyes air doves; yer lips air like scarlet; yer two breasts air like two fawns; yer navel be like a round goblet; yer belly be like a heap o' wheat.... (*He covers her hand with kisses. She does not seem to notice. She stares before her with hard angry eyes.*)

ABBIE (*jerking her hands away—harshly*): So ye're plannin' t' leave the farm t' Eben, air ye?

CABOT (*dazedly*): Leave ...? (*Then with resentful obstinacy.*) I hain't a-givin' it t' no one!

ABBIE (*remorselessly*): Ye can't take it with ye.

CABOT (*thinks a moment—then reluctantly*): No, I calc'late not. (*After a pause—with a strange passion.*) But if I could, I would, by the Eternal! 'R if I could, in my dyin' hour, I'd set it afire an' watch it burn—this house an' every ear o' corn an' every tree down t' the last blade o' hay! I'd sit an' know it was all a-dying with me an' no one else'd ever own what was mine, what I'd made out o' nothin' with my own sweat 'n' blood! (*A pause—then he adds with a queer affection.*) 'Ceptin' the cows. Them I'd turn free.

ABBIE (*harshly*): An' me?

CABOT (*with a queer smile*): Ye'd be turned free, too.

ABBIE (*furiously*): So that's the thanks I git fur marryin' ye—t' have ye change kind to Eben who hates ye, an' talk o' turnin' me out in the road.

CABOT (*hastily*): Abbie! Ye know I wa'n't....

ABBIE (*vengefully*): Just let me tell ye a thing or two 'bout Eben! Whar's he gone? T' see that harlot, Min! I tried fur t' stop him. Disgracin' yew an' me—on the Sabbath, too!

CABOT (*rather guiltily*): He's a sinner—nateral-born. It's lust eatin' his heart.

ABBIE (*enraged beyond endurance—wildly vindictive*): An' his lust fur me! Kin ye find excuses fur that?

CABOT (*stares at her—after a dead pause*): Lust—fur yew?

ABBIE (*defiantly*): He was tryin' t' make love t' me—when ye heerd us quarrelin'.

CABOT (*stares at her—then a terrible expression of rage comes over his face—he springs to his feet shaking all over*): By the A'mighty God—I'll end him!

ABBIE (*frightened now for Eben*): No! Don't ye!

CABOT (*violently*): I'll git the shotgun an' blow his soft brains t' the top o' them elums!

ABBIE (*throwing her arms around him*): No, Ephraim!

CABOT (*pushing her away violently*): I will, by God!

ABBIE (*in a quieting tone*): Listen, Ephraim. 'Twa'n't nothin' bad—on'y a boy's foolin'—'twa'n't meant serious—jest jokin' an' teasin'....

CABOT: Then why did ye say—lust?

ABBIE: It must hev sounded wusser'n I meant. An' I was mad at thinkin'—ye'd leave him the farm.

CABOT (*quieter but still grim and cruel*): Waal then, I'll horsewhip him off the place if that much'll content ye.

ABBIE (*reaching out and taking his hand*): No. Don't think o' me! Ye mustn't drive him off. 'Tain't sensible. Who'll ye get to help ye on the farm? They's no one hereabouts.

CABOT (*considers this—then nodding his appreciation*): Ye got a head on ye. (*Then irritably.*) Waal, let him stay. (*He sits down on the edge of the porch. She sits beside him. He murmurs contemptuously.*) I oughtn't t' git riled so—at that 'ere fool calf. (*A pause.*) But har's the p'int. What son o' mine'll keep on here t' the farm—when the Lord does call me? Simeon an' Peter air gone t' hell—an' Eben's follerin' 'em.

ABBIE: They's me.

CABOT: Ye're on'y a woman.

ABBIE: I'm yewr wife.

CABOT: That hain't me. A son is me—my blood—mine. Mine ought t' git mine. An' then it's still mine—even though I be six foot under. D'ye see?

ABBIE (*giving him a look of hatred*): Ay-eh. I see. (*She becomes very thoughtful, her face growing shrewd, her eyes studying Cabot craftily.*)

CABOT: I'm gittin' old—ripe on the bough. (*Then with a sudden forced reassurance.*) Not but what I hain't a hard nut t' crack even yet—an' fur many a year t' come! By the Etarnal, I kin break most o' the young fellers' backs at any kind o' work any day o' the year!

ABBIE (*suddenly*): Mebbe the Lord'll give us a son.

CABOT (*turns and stares at her eagerly*): Ye mean—a son—t' me 'n' yew?

ABBIE (*with a cajoling smile*): Ye're a strong man yet, hain't ye? 'Tain't noways impossible, be it? We know that. Why d'ye stare so? Hain't ye never thought o' that afore? I been thinkin' o' it all along. Ay-eh—an' I been prayin' it'd happen, too.

CABOT (*his face growing full of joyous pride and a sort of religious ecstasy*): Ye been prayin', Abbie?—fur a son?—t' us?

ABBIE: Ay-eh. (*With a grim resolution.*) I want a son now.

CABOT (*excitedly clutching both of her hands in his*): It'd be the blessin' o' God, Abbie—the blessin' o' God A'mighty on me—in my old age—in my lonesomeness! They hain't nothin' I wouldn't do fur ye then, Abbie. Ye'd hev on'y t' ask it—anythin' ye'd a mind t'!

ABBIE (*interrupting*): Would ye will the farm t' me then—t' me an' it ...?

CABOT (*vehemently*): I'd do anythin' ye axed, I tell ye! I swar it! May I be everlastin' damned t' hell if I wouldn't! (*He sinks to his knees pulling her down with him. He trembles all over with the fervor of his hopes.*) Pray t' the Lord agen, Abbie. It's the Sabbath! I'll jine ye! Two prayers air better nor one. "An' God hearkened unto Rachel"! An' God hearkened unto Abbie! Pray, Abbie! Pray fur him to hearken! (*He bows his head, mumbling. She pretends to do likewise but gives him a side glance of scorn and triumph.*)

Scene II

(*About eight in the evening. The interior of the two bedrooms on the top floor is shown. Eben is sitting on the side of his bed in the room on the left. On account of the heat he has taken off everything but his undershirt and pants. His feet are bare. He faces front, brooding moodily, his chin propped on his hands, a desperate expression on his face.*)

   (*In the other room Cabot and Abbie are sitting side by side on the edge of their bed, an old four-poster with feather mattress. He is in his nightshirt, she in her nightdress. He is still in the queer, excited mood into which the notion of a son has thrown him. Both rooms are lighted dimly and flickeringly by tallow candles.*)

CABOT: The farm needs a son.

ABBIE: I need a son.

CABOT: Ay-eh. Sometimes ye air the farm an' sometimes the farm be yew. That's why I clove t'ye in my lonesomeness. (*A pause. He pounds his knee with his fist.*) Me an' the farm has got t' beget a son!

ABBIE: Ye'd best go t' sleep. Ye're gittin' thin's all mixed.

CABOT (*with an impatient gesture*): No, I hain't. My mind's clear's a well. Ye don't know me, that's it. (*He stares hopelessly at the floor.*)

ABBIE (*indifferently*): Mebbe. (*In the next room Eben gets up and paces up and down distractedly. Abbie hears him. Her eyes fasten on the intervening wall with concentrated attention. Eben stops and stares. Their hot glances seem to meet through the wall. Unconsciously he stretches out his arms for her and she half rises. Then aware, he mutters a curse at himself and flings himself face downward on the bed, his clenched fists above his head, his face buried in the pillow. Abbie relaxes with a faint sigh but her eyes remain fixed on the wall; she listens with all her attention for some movement from Eben.*)

CABOT (*suddenly raises his head and looks at her—scornfully*): Will ye ever know me—'r will any man 'r woman? (*Shaking his head.*) No. I calc'late wa'n't t' be. (*He turns away. Abbie looks at the wall. Then, evidently unable to keep silent about his thoughts, without looking at his wife, he puts out his hand and clutches her knee. She starts violently, looks at him, sees he is not watching her, concentrates again on the wall, and pays no attention to what he says.*) Listen, Abbie. When I come here fifty odd year ago—I was jest twenty an' the strongest an' hardest ye ever seen—ten times as strong an' fifty times as hard as Eben. Waal—this place was nothin' but fields o' stones. Folks laughed when I tuk it. They couldn't know what I knowed. When ye kin make corn sprout out o' stones, God's livin' in yew! They wa'n't strong enuf fur that! They reckoned God was easy. They laughed. They don't laugh no more. Some died hereabouts. Some went West an' died. They're all underground—fur follerin' arter an easy God. God hain't easy. (*He shakes his head slowly.*) An' I growed hard. Folks kept allus sayin' he's a hard man like 'twas sinful t' be hard, so's at last I said back at 'em: Waal then, by thunder, ye'll git me hard an' see how ye like it! (*Then suddenly.*) But I give in t' weakness once. 'Twas arter I'd been here two year. I got weak—despairful—they was so many stones. They was a party leavin', givin' up, goin' West. I jined 'em. We tracked on 'n on. We come t' broad medders, plains, whar the soil was black an' rich as gold. Nary a stone. Easy. Ye'd on'y to plow an' sow an' then set an' smoke yer pipe an' watch thin's grow. I could o' been a rich man—but somethin' in me fit me an' fit me—the voice o' God sayin': "This hain't wuth nothin' t' Me. Git ye back t' hum!" I got afeerd o' that voice an' I lit out back t' hum here, leavin' my claim an' crops t' whoever'd a mind t' take 'em. Ay-eh. I actoolly give up what was rightful mine! God's hard, not easy! God's in the stones! Build my church on a rock—out o' stones an' I'll be in them! That's what He meant t' Peter! (*He sighs heavily—a pause.*) Stones. I picked 'em up an' piled 'em into walls. Ye kin read the years o' my life in them walls, every day a hefted stone, climbin' over the hills up and down, fencin' in the fields that was mine, whar I'd made thin's grow out o' nothin'—like the will o' God, like the servant o' His hand. It wa'n't easy. It was hard an' He made me hard fur it. (*He pauses.*) All the time I kept gittin' lonesomer. I tuk a wife. She bore Simeon an' Peter. She was a good woman. She wuked hard. We was married twenty year. She never knowed me. She helped but she never knowed what she was helpin'. I was allus lonesome. She died. After that it wa'n't so lonesome fur a spell. (*A pause.*) I lost count o' the years. I had no time t' fool away countin' 'em. Sim an' Peter helped. The farm growed. It was all mine! When I thought o' that I didn't feel lonesome. (*A pause.*) But ye can't hitch yer mind t' one thin' day an' night. I tuk another wife—Eben's Maw. Her folks was contestin' me at law over my deeds t' the farm—my farm! That's why Eben keeps a-talkin' his fool talk o' this bein' his Maw's farm. She bore Eben. She was purty—but soft. She tried t' be hard. She couldn't. She never knowed me nor nothin'. It was lonesomer 'n hell with her. After a matter o' sixteen odd years, she died. (*A pause.*) I lived with the boys. They hated me 'cause I was hard. I hated them 'cause they was soft. They coveted the farm without knowin' what it meant. It made me bitter 'n wormwood. It aged me—them coveting what I'd made fur

Abbie in the 1988 Pushkin Theatre (Moscow) production of *Desire under the Elms*, directed by Mark Lamos of the Hartford Stage Company.

mine. Then this spring the call come—the voice o' God cryin' in my wilderness, in my lonesomeness—t' go out an' seek an' find! (*Turning to her with strange passion.*) I sought ye an' I found ye! Yew air my Rose o' Sharon! Yer eyes air like. . . . (*She has turned a blank face, resentful eyes to his. He stares at her for a moment—then harshly.*) Air ye any the wiser fur all I've told ye?

ABBIE (*confusedly*): Mebbe.

CABOT (*pushing her away from him—angrily*): Ye don't know nothin'—nor never will. If ye don't hev a son t' redeem ye. . . . (*This in a tone of cold threat.*)

ABBIE (*resentfully*): I've prayed, hain't I?

CABOT (*bitterly*): Pray agen—fur understandin'!

ABBIE (*a veiled threat in her tone*): Ye'll have a son out o' me, I promise ye.

CABOT: How kin ye promise?

ABBIE: I got second-sight mebbe. I kin foretell. (*She gives a queer smile.*)

CABOT: I believe ye have. Ye give me the chills sometimes. (*He shivers.*) It's cold in this house. It's oneasy. They's thin's pokin' about in the dark—in the corners. (*He pulls on his trousers, tucking in his nightshirt, and pulls on his boots.*)

ABBIE (*surprised*): Whar air ye goin'?

CABOT (*queerly*): Down whar it's restful—whar it's warm—down t' the barn. (*Bitterly.*) I kin talk t'

the cows. They know. They know the farm an' me. They'll give me peace. (*He turns to go out the door.*)

ABBIE (*a bit frightenedly*): Air ye ailin' tonight, Ephraim?

CABOT: Growin'. Growin' ripe on the bough. (*He turns and goes, his boots clumping down the stairs. Eben sits up with a start, listening. Abbie is conscious of his movement and stares at the wall. Cabot comes out of the house around the corner and stands by the gate, blinking at the sky. He stretches up his hands in a tortured gesture.*) God A'mighty, call from the dark! (*He listens as if expecting an answer. Then his arms drop, he shakes his head and plods off toward the barn. Eben and Abbie stare at each other through the wall. Eben sighs heavily and Abbie echoes it. Both become terribly nervous, uneasy. Finally Abbie gets up and listens, her ear to the wall. He acts as if he saw every move she was making, he becomes resolutely still. She seems driven into a decision—goes out the door in rear determinedly. His eyes follow her. Then as the door of his room is opened softly, he turns away, waits in an attitude of strained fixity. Abbie stands for a second staring at him, her eyes burning with desire. Then with a little cry she runs over and throws her arms about his neck, she pulls his head back and covers his mouth with kisses. At first, he submits dumbly; then he puts his arms about her neck and returns her kisses, but finally, suddenly aware of his hatred, he hurls her away*

563

from him, springing to his feet. They stand speechless and breathless, panting like two animals.)

ABBIE (*at last—painfully*): Ye shouldn't, Eben—ye shouldn't—I'd make ye happy!

EBEN (*harshly*): I don't want t' be happy—from yew!

ABBIE (*helplessly*): Ye do, Eben! Ye do! Why d'ye lie?

EBEN (*viciously*): I don't take t'ye, I tell ye! I hate the sight o' ye!

ABBIE (*with an uncertain troubled laugh*): Waal, I kissed ye anyways—an' ye kissed back—yer lips was burnin'—ye can't lie 'bout that! (*Intensely.*) If ye don't care, why did ye kiss me back—why was yer lips burnin'?

EBEN (*wiping his mouth*): It was like pizen on 'em. (*Then tauntingly.*) When I kissed ye back, mebbe I thought 'twas someone else.

ABBIE (*wildly*): Min?

EBEN: Mebbe.

ABBIE (*torturedly*): Did ye go t' see her? Did ye r'ally go? I thought ye mightn't. Is that why ye throwed me off jest now?

EBEN (*sneeringly*): What if it be?

ABBIE (*raging*): Then ye're a dog, Eben Cabot!

EBEN (*threateningly*): Ye can't talk that way t' me!

ABBIE (*with a shrill laugh*): Can't I? Did ye think I was in love with ye—a weak thin' like yew? Not much! I on'y wanted ye fur a purpose o' my own—an' I'll hev ye fur it yet 'cause I'm stronger'n yew be!

EBEN (*resentfully*): I knowed well it was on'y part o' yer plan t' swaller everythin'!

ABBIE (*tauntingly*): Mebbe!

EBEN (*furious*): Git out o' my room!

ABBIE: This air my room an' ye're on'y hired help!

EBEN (*threateningly*): Git out afore I murder ye!

ABBIE (*quite confident now*): I hain't a mite afeerd. Ye want me, don't ye? Yes, ye do! An' yer Paw's son'll never kill what he wants! Look at yer eyes! They's lust fur me in 'em, burnin' 'em up! Look at yer lips now! They're tremblin' an' longin' t' kiss me, an' yer teeth t' bite! (*He is watching her now with a horrible fascination. She laughs a crazy triumphant laugh.*) I'm a-goin' t' make all o' this hum my hum! They's one room hain't mine yet, but it's a-goin' t' be tonight. I'm a-goin' down now an' light up! (*She makes him a mocking bow.*) Won't ye come courtin' me in the best parlor, Mister Cabot?

EBEN (*staring at her—horribly confused—dully*): Don't ye dare! It hain't been opened since Maw died an' was laid out thar! Don't ye . . . ! (*But her eyes are fixed on his so burningly that his will seems to wither before hers. He stands swaying toward her helplessly.*)

ABBIE (*holding his eyes and putting all her will into her words as she backs out the door*): I'll expect ye afore long, Eben.

EBEN (*Stares after her for a while, walking toward the door. A light appears in the parlor window. He murmurs.*): In the parlor? (*This seems to arouse connotations, for he comes back and puts on his white shirt, collar, half ties the tie mechanically, puts on coat, takes his hat, stands barefooted looking about him in bewilderment, mutters wonderingly.*) Maw! Whar air yew? (*Then goes slowly toward the door in rear.*)

Scene III

(*A few minutes later. The interior of the parlor is shown. A grim, repressed room like a tomb in which the family has been interred alive. Abbie sits on the edge of the horsehair sofa. She has lighted all the candles and the room is revealed in all its preserved ugliness. A change has come over the woman. She looks awed and frightened now, ready to run away.*)

(*The door is opened and Eben appears. His face wears an expression of obsessed confusion. He stands staring at her, his arms hanging disjointedly from his shoulders, his feet bare, his hat in his hand.*)

ABBIE (*after a pause—with a nervous, formal politeness*): Won't ye set?

EBEN (*dully*): Ay-eh. (*Mechanically he places his hat carefully on the floor near the door and sits stiffly beside her on the edge of the sofa. A pause. They both remain rigid, looking straight ahead with eyes full of fear.*)

ABBIE: When I fust come in—in the dark—they seemed somethin' here.

EBEN (*simply*): Maw.

ABBIE: I kin still feel—somethin'. . . .

EBEN: It's Maw.

ABBIE: At fust I was feered o' it. I wanted t' yell an' run. Now—since yew come—seems like it's growin' soft an' kind t' me. (*Addressing the air—queerly.*) Thank yew.

EBEN: Maw allus loved me.

ABBIE: Mebbe it knows I love yew, too. Mebbe that makes it kind t' me.

EBEN (*dully*): I dunno. I should think she'd hate ye.

ABBIE (*with certainty*): No. I kin feel it don't—not no more.

EBEN: Hate ye fur stealin' her place—here in her hum—settin' in her parlor whar she was laid—(*He suddenly stops, staring stupidly before him.*)

ABBIE: What is it, Eben?

EBEN (*in a whisper*): Seems like Maw didn't want me t' remind ye.

ABBIE (*excitedly*): I knowed, Eben! It's kind t' me! It don't b'ar me no grudges fur what I never knowed an' couldn't help!

EBEN: Maw b'ars him a grudge.

ABBIE: Waal, so does all o' us.

EBEN: Ay-eh. (*With passion.*) I does, by God!

ABBIE (*taking one of his hands in hers and patting it*): Thar! Don't git riled thinkin' o' him. Think o' yer Maw who's kind t' us. Tell me about yer Maw, Eben.

Raymond J. Barry and Amelia Campbell in the American Repertory Theater's 2004–2005 production of *Desire under the Elms*, directed by János Szász.

EBEN: They hain't nothin' much. She was kind. She was good.

ABBIE (*Putting one arm over his shoulder. He does not seem to notice—passionately.*): I'll be kind an' good t' ye!

EBEN: Sometimes she used t' sing fur me.

ABBIE: I'll sing fur ye!

EBEN: This was her hum. This was her farm.

ABBIE: This is my hum! This is my farm!

EBEN: He married her t' steal 'em. She was soft an' easy. He couldn't 'preciate her.

ABBIE: He can't 'preciate me!

EBEN: He murdered her with his hardness.

ABBIE: He's murderin' me!

EBEN: She died. (*A pause.*) Sometimes she used to sing fur me. (*He bursts into a fit of sobbing.*)

ABBIE (*both her arms around him—with wild passion*): I'll sing fur ye! I'll die fur ye! (*In spite of her overwhelming desire for him, there is a sincere maternal love in her manner and voice—a horribly frank mixture of lust and mother love.*) Don't cry, Eben! I'll take yer Maw's place! I'll be everythin' she was t' ye! Let me kiss ye, Eben! (*She pulls his head around. He*

makes a bewildered pretense of resistance. She is tender.*) Don't be afeered! I'll kiss ye pure, Eben—same 's if I was a Maw t' ye—an' ye kin kiss me back 's if yew was my son—my boy—sayin' good-night t' me! Kiss me, Eben. (*They kiss in restrained fashion. Then suddenly wild passion overcomes her. She kisses him lustfully again and again and he flings his arms about her and returns her kisses. Suddenly, as in the bedroom, he frees himself from her violently and springs to his feet. He is trembling all over, in a strange state of terror. Abbie strains her arms toward him with fierce pleading.*) Don't ye leave me, Eben! Can't ye see it hain't enuf—lovin' ye like a Maw—can't ye see it's got t' be that an' more—much more—a hundred times more—fur me t' be happy—fur yew t' be happy?

EBEN (*to the presence he feels in the room*): Maw! Maw! What d'ye want? What air ye tellin' me?

ABBIE: She's tellin' ye t' love me. She knows I love ye an' I'll be good t' ye. Can't ye feel it? Don't ye know? She's tellin' ye t' love me, Eben!

EBEN: Ay-eh. I feel—mebbe she—but—I can't figger out—why—when ye've stole her place—here in her hum—in the parlor whar she was—

ABBIE (*fiercely*): She knows I love ye!

EBEN (*his face suddenly lighting up with a fierce, triumphant grin*): I see it! I sees why. It's her vengeance on him—so's she kin rest quiet in her grave!

ABBIE (*wildly*): Vengeance o' God on the hull o' us! What d'we give a durn? I love ye, Eben! God knows I love ye! (*She stretches out her arms for him.*)

EBEN (*throws himself on his knees beside the sofa and grabs her in his arms—releasing all his pent-up passion*): An' I love ye, Abbie!—now I kin say it! I been dyin' fur want o' ye—every hour since ye come! I love ye! (*Their lips meet in a fierce, bruising kiss.*)

Scene IV

(*Exterior of the farmhouse. It is just dawn. The front door at right is opened and Eben comes out and walks around to the gate. He is dressed in his working clothes. He seems changed. His face wears a bold and confident expression, he is grinning to himself with evident satisfaction. As he gets near the gate, the window of the parlor is heard opening and the shutters are flung back and Abbie sticks her head out. Her hair tumbles over her shoulders in disarray, her face is flushed, she looks at Eben with tender, languorous eyes and calls softly.*)

ABBIE: Eben. (*As he turns—playfully.*) Jest one more kiss afore ye go. I'm goin' to miss ye fearful all day.

EBEN: An' me yew, ye kin bet! (*He goes to her. They kiss several times. He draws away, laughingly.*) Thar. That's enuf, hain't it? Ye won't hev none left fur next time.

ABBIE: I got a million o' 'em left fur yew! (*Then a bit anxiously.*) D'ye r'ally love me, Eben?

EBEN (*emphatically*): I like ye better'n any gal I ever knowed! That's gospel!

ABBIE: Likin' hain't lovin'.

EBEN: Waal then—I love ye. Now air yew satisfied?

ABBIE: Ay-eh, I be. (*She smiles at him adoringly.*)

EBEN: I better git t' the barn. The old critter's liable t' suspicion an' come sneakin' up.

ABBIE (*with a confident laugh*): Let him! I kin allus pull the wool over his eyes. I'm goin' t' leave the shutters open and let in the sun 'n' air. This room's been dead long enuf. Now it's goin' t' be my room!

EBEN (*frowning*): Ay-eh.

ABBIE (*hastily*): I meant—our room.

EBEN: Ay-eh.

ABBIE: We made it our'n last night, didn't we? We give it life—our lovin' did. (*A pause.*)

EBEN (*with a strange look*): Maw's gone back t' her grave. She kin sleep now.

ABBIE: May she rest in peace! (*Then tenderly rebuking.*) Ye oughtn't t' talk o' sad thin's—this mornin'.

EBEN: It jest come up in my mind o' itself.

ABBIE: Don't let it. (*He doesn't answer. She yawns.*) Waal, I'm a-goin' t' steal a wink o' sleep. I'll tell the Old Man I hain't feelin' pert. Let him git his own vittles.

EBEN: I see him comin' from the barn. Ye better look smart an' git upstairs.

ABBIE: Ay-eh. Good-by. Don't ferget me. (*She throws him a kiss. He grins—then squares his shoulders and awaits his father confidently. Cabot walks slowly up from the left, staring up at the sky with a vague face.*)

EBEN (*jovially*): Mornin', Paw. Star-gazin' in daylight?

CABOT: Purty, hain't it?

EBEN (*looking around him possessively*): It's a durned purty farm.

CABOT: I mean the sky.

EBEN (*grinning*): How d'ye know? Them eyes o' your'n can't see that fur. (*This tickles his humor and he slaps his thigh and laughs.*) Ho-ho! That's a good un!

CABOT (*grimly sarcastic*): Ye're feelin' right chipper, hain't ye? Whar'd ye steal the likker?

EBEN (*good-naturedly*): 'Tain't likker. Jest life. (*Suddenly holding out his hand—soberly.*) Yew 'n' me is quits. Let's shake hands.

CABOT (*suspiciously*): What's come over ye?

EBEN: Then don't. Mebbe it's jest as well. (*A moment's pause.*) What's come over me? (*Queerly.*) Didn't ye feel her passin'—goin' back t' her grave?

CABOT (*dully*): Who?

EBEN: Maw. She kin rest now an' sleep content. She's quit with ye.

CABOT (*confusedly*): I rested. I slept good—down with the cows. They know how t' sleep. They're teachin' me.

EBEN (*suddenly jovial again*): Good fur the cows! Waal—ye better git t' work.

CABOT (*grimly amused*): Air yew bossin' me, ye calf?

EBEN (*beginning to laugh*): Ay-eh! I'm bossin' yew! Ha-ha-ha! See how ye like it! Ha-ha-ha! I'm the prize rooster o' this roost. Ha-ha-ha! (*He goes off toward the barn laughing.*)

CABOT (*looks after him with scornful pity*): Soft-headed. Like his Maw. Dead spit 'n' image. No hope in him! (*He spits with contemptuous disgust.*) A born fool! (*Then matter-of-factly.*) Waal—I'm gittin' peckish. (*He goes toward door.*)

PART III • Scene I

(*A night in late spring the following year. The kitchen and the two bedrooms upstairs are shown. The two bedrooms are dimly lighted by a tallow candle in each. Eben is sitting on the side of the bed in his room, his chin propped on his fists, his face a study of the struggle he is making to understand his conflicting emotions. The noisy laughter and music from below where a kitchen dance is in progress annoy and distract him. He scowls at the floor.*)

(*In the next room a cradle stands beside the double bed.*)

(*In the kitchen all is festivity. The stove has been taken down to give more room to the dancers. The chairs, with wooden benches added, have been pushed back against the walls. On these are seated, squeezed in tight against one another, farmers and their wives and their young folks of both sexes from the neighboring farms. They are all chattering and laughing loudly. They evidently have some secret joke in common. There is no end of winking, of nudging, of meaning nods of the head toward Cabot who, in a state of extreme hilarious excitement increased by the amount he has drunk, is standing near the rear door where there is a small keg of whisky and serving drinks to all the men. In the left corner, front, dividing the attention with her husband, Abbie is sitting in a rocking chair, a shawl wrapped about her shoulders. She is very pale, her face is thin and drawn, her eyes are fixed anxiously on the open door in rear as if waiting for someone.*)

(*The musician is tuning up his fiddle, seated in the far right corner. He is a lanky young fellow with a long, weak face. His pale eyes blink incessantly and he grins about him slyly with a greedy malice.*)

ABBIE (*suddenly turning to a young girl on her right*): Whar's Eben?

YOUNG GIRL (*eyeing her scornfully*): I dunno, Mrs. Cabot. I hain't seen Eben in ages. (*Meaningly.*) Seems like he's spent most o' his time t' hum since yew come.

ABBIE (*vaguely*): I tuk his Maw's place.

YOUNG GIRL: Ay-eh. So I've heerd. (*She turns away to retail this bit of gossip to her mother sitting next to her. Abbie turns to her left to a big stoutish middle-aged man whose flushed face and starting eyes show the amount of "likker" he has consumed.*)

ABBIE: Ye hain't seen Eben, hev ye?

MAN: No, I hain't. (*Then he adds with a wink.*) If yew hain't, who would?

ABBIE: He's the best dancer in the county. He'd ought t' come an' dance.

MAN (*with a wink*): Mebbe he's doin' the dutiful an' walkin' the kid t' sleep. It's a boy, hain't it?

ABBIE (*nodding vaguely*): Ay-eh—born two weeks back—purty's a picter.

MAN: They all is—t' their Maws. (*Then in a whisper, with a nudge and a leer.*) Listen, Abbie—if ye ever git tired o' Eben, remember me! Don't fergit now! (*He looks at her uncomprehending face for a second—then grunts disgustedly.*) Waal—guess I'll likker agin. (*He goes over and joins Cabot who is arguing noisily with an old farmer over cows. They all drink.*)

ABBIE (*this time appealing to nobody in particular*): Wonder what Eben's a-doin'? (*Her remark is repeated down the line with many a guffaw and titter until it reaches the fiddler. He fastens his blinking eyes on Abbie.*)

FIDDLER (*raising his voice*): Bet I kin tell ye, Abbie, what Eben's doin'! He's down t' the church offerin' up prayers o' thanksgivin'. (*They all titter expectantly.*)

A MAN: What fur? (*Another titter.*)

FIDDLER: 'Cause unto him a—(*He hesitates just long enough.*) brother is born! (*A roar of laughter. They all look from Abbie to Cabot. She is oblivious, staring at the door. Cabot, although he hasn't heard the words, is irritated by the laughter and steps forward, glaring about him. There is an immediate silence.*)

CABOT: What're ye all bleatin' about—like a flock o' goats? Why don't ye dance, damn ye? I axed ye here t' dance—t' eat, drink an' be merry—an' thar ye set cacklin' like a lot o' wet hens with the pip! Ye've swilled my likker an' guzzled my vittles like hogs, hain't ye? Then dance fur me, can't ye? That's fa'r an' squar', hain't it? (*A grumble of resentment goes around but they are all evidently in too much awe of him to express it openly.*)

FIDDLER (*slyly*): We're waitin' fur Eben. (*A suppressed laugh.*)

CABOT (*with a fierce exultation*): T'hell with Eben! Eben's done fur now! I got a new son! (*His mood switching with drunken suddenness.*) But ye needn't t' laugh at Eben, none o' ye! He's my blood, if he be a dumb fool. He's better nor any o' yew! He kin do a day's work a'most up t' what I kin—an' that'd put any o' yew pore critters t' shame!

FIDDLER: An' he kin do a good night's work, too! (*A roar of laughter.*)

CABOT: Laugh, ye damn fools! Ye're right jist the same, Fiddler. He kin work day an' night too, like I kin, if need be!

OLD FARMER (*from behind the keg where he is weaving drunkenly back and forth—with great simplicity*): They hain't many t' touch ye, Ephraim—a son at seventy-six. That's a hard man fur ye! I be on'y sixty-eight an' I couldn't do it. (*A roar of laughter in which Cabot joins uproariously.*)

CABOT (*slapping him on the back*): I'm sorry fur ye, Hi. I'd never suspicion sech weakness from a boy like yew!

OLD FARMER: An' I never reckoned yew had it in ye nuther, Ephraim. (*There is another laugh.*)

CABOT (*suddenly grim*): I got a lot in me—a hell of a lot—folks don't know on. (*Turning to the fiddler.*) Fiddle 'er up, durn ye! Give 'em somethin' t' dance t'! What air ye, an ornament? Hain't this a celebration? Then grease yer elbow an' go it!

FIDDLER (*seizes a drink which the Old Farmer holds out to him and downs it*): Here goes! (*He starts to fiddle "Lady of the Lake." Four young fellows and four girls form in two lines and dance a square dance. The Fiddler shouts directions for the different movements, keeping his words in the rhythm of the music and interspersing them with jocular personal remarks to the dancers themselves. The people seated along the walls stamp their feet and clap their hands in unison. Cabot is especially active in this respect. Only Abbie remains apathetic, staring at the door as if she were alone in a silent room.*)

FIDDLER: Swing your partner t' the right! That's it, Jim! Give her a b'ar hug. Her Maw hain't lookin'. (*Laughter.*) Change partners! That suits ye, don't it, Essie, now ye got Reub afore ye? Look at her redden up, will ye? Waal, life is short an' so's love, as the feller says. (*Laughter.*)

CABOT (*excitedly, stamping his foot*): Go it, boys! Go it, gals!

FIDDLER (*with a wink at the others*): Ye're the spryest seventy-six ever I sees, Ephraim! Now if ye'd on'y good eyesight . . . ! (*Suppressed laughter. He gives Cabot no chance to retort but roars.*) Promenade! Ye're walkin' like a bride down the aisle, Sarah! Waal, while they's life they's allus hope, I've heerd tell. Swing your partner to the left! Gosh A'mighty, look at Johnny Cook high-steppin'! They hain't goin' t' be much strength left fur howin' in the corn lot t'morrow. (*Laughter.*)

CABOT: Go it! Go it! (*Then suddenly, unable to restrain himself any longer, he prances into the midst of the dancers, scattering them, waving his arms about wildly.*) Ye're all hoofs! Git out o' my road! Give me room! I'll show ye dancin'. Ye're all too soft! (*He pushes them roughly away. They crowd back toward the walls, muttering, looking at him resentfully.*)

FIDDLER (*jeeringly*): Go it, Ephraim! Go it! (*He starts "Pop, Goes the Weasel," increasing the tempo with every verse until at the end he is fiddling crazily as fast as he can go.*)

CABOT (*Starts to dance, which he does very well and with tremendous vigor. Then he begins to improvise, cuts incredibly grotesque capers, leaping up and cracking his heels together, prancing around in a circle with body bent in an Indian war dance, then suddenly straightening up and kicking as high as he can with both legs. He is like a monkey on a string. And all the while he intersperses his antics with shouts and derisive comments.*): Whoop! Here's dancin' fur ye! Whoop! See that! Seventy-six, if I'm a day! Hard as iron yet! Beatin' the young 'uns like I allus done! Look at me! I'd invite ye t' dance on my hundredth birthday on'y ye'll all be dead by then. Ye're a sickly generation! Yer hearts air pink, not red! Yer veins is full o' mud an' water! I be the on'y man in the county! Whoop! See that! I'm a Injun! I've killed Injuns in the West afore ye was born—an' skulped 'em too! They's a arrer wound on my backside I c'd show ye! The hull tribe chased me. I outrun 'em all—with the arrer stuck in me! An' I tuk vengeance on 'em. Ten eyes fur an eye, that was my motter! Whoop! Look at me! I kin kick the ceilin' off the room! Whoop!

FIDDLER (*stops playing—exhaustedly*): God A'mighty, I got enuf. Ye got the devil's strength in ye.

CABOT (*delightedly*): Did I beat yew, too? Waal, ye played smart. Hev a swig. (*He pours whisky for himself and Fiddler. They drink. The others watch Cabot silently with cold, hostile eyes. There is a dead pause. The Fiddler rests. Cabot leans against the keg, panting, glaring around him confusedly. In the room above, Eben gets to his feet and tiptoes out the door in rear, appearing a moment later in the other bedroom. He moves silently, even frightenedly, toward the cradle and stands there looking down at the baby. His face is as vague as his reactions are confused, but there is a trace of tenderness, of interested discovery. At the same moment that he reaches the cradle, Abbie seems to sense something. She gets up weakly and goes to Cabot.*)

ABBIE: I'm goin' up t' the baby.

CABOT (*with real solicitation*): Air ye able fur the stairs? D'ye want me t' help ye, Abbie?

ABBIE: No. I'm able. I'll be down agen soon.

CABOT: Don't ye git wore out! He needs ye, remember— our son does! (*He grins affectionately, patting her on the back. She shrinks from his touch.*)

ABBIE (*dully*): Don't—tech me. I'm goin'—up. (*She goes. Cabot looks after her. A whisper goes around the room. Cabot turns. It ceases. He wipes his forehead streaming with sweat. He is breathing pantingly.*)

CABOT: I'm a-goin' out t' git fresh air. I'm feelin' a mite dizzy. Fiddle up thar! Dance, all o' ye! Here's likker fur them as wants it. Enjoy yerselves. I'll be back. (*He goes, closing the door behind him.*)

FIDDLER (*sarcastically*): Don't hurry none on our account! (*A suppressed laugh. He imitates Abbie.*) Whar's Eben? (*More laughter.*)

A WOMAN (*loudly*): What's happened in this house is plain as the nose on yer face! (*Abbie appears in the doorway upstairs and stands looking in surprise and adoration at Eben who does not see her.*)

A MAN: Ssshh! He's li'ble t' be listenin' at the door. That'd be like him. (*Their voices die to an intensive whispering. Their faces are concentrated on this gossip. A noise as of dead leaves in the wind comes from the room. Cabot has come out from the porch and stands by the gate, leaning on it, staring at the sky blinkingly. Abbie comes across the room silently. Eben does not notice her until quite near.*)

EBEN (*starting*): Abbie!

ABBIE: Ssshh! (*She throws her arms around him. They kiss—then bend over the cradle together.*) Ain't he purty?—dead spit 'n' image o' yew!

EBEN (*pleased*): Air he? I can't tell none.

ABBIE: E-zactly like!

EBEN (*frowningly*): I don't like this. I don't like lettin' on what's mine's his'n. I been doin' that all my life. I'm gittin' t' the end o' b'arin' it!

ABBIE (*putting her finger on his lips*): We're doin' the best we kin. We got t' wait. Somethin's bound t' happen. (*She puts her arms around him.*) I got t' go back.

EBEN: I'm goin' out. I can't b'ar it with the fiddle playin' an' the laughin'.

ABBIE: Don't git feelin' low. I love ye, Eben. Kiss me. (*He kisses her. They remain in each other's arms.*)

CABOT (*at the gate, confusedly*): Even the music can't drive it out—somethin'. Ye kin feel it droppin' off the elums, climbin' up the roof, sneakin' down the chimney, pokin' in the corners! They's no peace in houses, they's no rest livin' with folks. Somethin's always livin' with ye. (*With a deep sigh.*) I'll go t' the barn an' rest a spell. (*He goes wearily toward the barn.*)

FIDDLER (*tuning up*): Let's celebrate the old skunk gittin' fooled! We kin have some fun now he's went. (*He starts to fiddle "Turkey in the Straw." There is real merriment now. The young folks get up to dance.*)

Scene II

(*A half hour later—exterior—Eben is standing by the gate looking up at the sky, an expression of dumb pain bewildered by itself on his face. Cabot appears, returning from the barn, walking wearily, his eyes on the ground. He sees Eben and his whole mood immediately changes. He becomes excited, a cruel, triumphant grin comes to his lips, he strides up and slaps Eben on the back. From within comes the whining of the fiddle and the noise of stamping feet and laughing voices.*)

CABOT: So har ye be!

EBEN (*startled, stares at him with hatred for a moment— then dully*): Ay-eh.

CABOT (*surveying him jeeringly*): Why hain't ye been in t' dance? They was all axin' fur ye.

EBEN: Let 'em ax!

CABOT: They's a hull passel o' purty gals.

EBEN: T' hell with 'em!

CABOT: Ye'd ought t' be marryin' one o' 'em soon.

EBEN: I hain't marryin' no one.

CABOT: Ye might 'arn a share o' a farm that way.

EBEN (*with a sneer*): Like yew did, ye mean? I hain't that kind.

CABOT (*stung*): Ye lie! 'Twas yer Maw's folks aimed t' steal my farm from me.

EBEN: Other folks don't say so. (*After a pause—defiantly.*) An' I got a farm, anyways!

CABOT (*derisively*): Whar?

EBEN (*stamps a foot on the ground*): Har!

CABOT (*throws his head back and laughs coarsely*): Ho-ho! Ye hev, hev ye? Waal, that's a good un!

EBEN (*controlling himself—grimly*): Ye'll see!

CABOT (*stares at him suspiciously, trying to make him out—a pause—then with scornful confidence*): Ay-eh. I'll see. So'll ye. It's ye that's blind—blind as a mole underground. (*Eben suddenly laughs, one short sardonic bark: "Ha." A pause. Cabot peers at him with renewed suspicion.*) What air ye hawin' 'bout? (*Eben turns away without answering. Cabot grows angry.*) God A'mighty, yew air a dumb dunce! They's nothin' in that thick skull o' your'n but noise—like an empty keg it be! (*Eben doesn't seem to hear. Cabot's rage grows.*) Yewr farm! God A'mighty! If ye wa'n't a born donkey ye'd know ye'll never own stick nor stone on it, specially now arter him bein' born. It's his'n, I tell ye—his'n arter I die—but I'll live a hundred jest t' fool ye all—an' he'll be growed then—yewr age a'most! (*Eben laughs again his sardonic "Ha." This drives Cabot into a fury.*) Ha? Ye think ye kin git 'round that someways, do ye? Waal, it'll be her'n, too—Abbie's—ye won't git 'round her—she knows yer tricks—she'll be too much fur ye—she wants the farm her'n—she's afeerd o' ye—she told me ye was sneakin' 'round tryin' t' make love t' her t' git her on yer side ... ye ... ye mad fool, ye! (*He raises his clenched fists threateningly.*)

EBEN (*is confronting him, choking with rage*): Ye lie, ye old skunk! Abbie never said no sech thing!

CABOT (*suddenly triumphant when he sees how shaken Eben is*): She did. An' I says, I'll blow his brains t' the top o' them elums—an' she says no that hain't sense, who'll ye git t'help ye on the farm in his place—an' then she says yew'n me ought t' have a son—I know we kin, she says—an' I says, if we do, ye kin have anythin' I've got ye've a mind t'. An' she says, I wants Eben cut off so's this farm'll be mine when ye die! (*With terrible gloating.*) An' that's what's happened, hain't it? An' the farm's her'n! An' the dust o' the road—that's you'rn! Ha! Now who's hawin'?

EBEN (*has been listening, petrified with grief and rage—suddenly laughs wildly and brokenly*): Ha-ha-ha! So that's her sneakin' game—all along!—like I suspicioned at fust—t' swaller it all—an' me, too ...! (*Madly.*) I'll murder her! (*He springs toward the porch but Cabot is quicker and gets in between.*)

CABOT: No, ye don't!

EBEN: Git out o' my road! (*He tries to throw Cabot aside. They grapple in what becomes immediately a murderous struggle. The old man's concentrated strength is too much for Eben. Cabot gets one hand on his throat and presses him back across the stone*

wall. At the same moment, Abbie comes out on the porch. With a stifled cry she runs toward them.*)

ABBIE: Eben! Ephraim! (*She tugs at the hand on Eben's throat.*) Let go, Ephraim! Ye're chokin' him!

CABOT (*Removes his hand and flings Eben sideways full length on the grass, gasping and choking. With a cry, Abbie kneels beside him, trying to take his head on her lap, but he pushes her away. Cabot stands looking down with fierce triumph.*): Ye needn't t've fret, Abbie, I wa'n't aimin' t' kill him. He hain't wuth hangin' fur—not by a hell of a sight! (*More and more triumphantly.*) Seventy-six an' him not thirty yit—an' look whar he be fur thinkin' his Paw was easy! No, by God, I hain't easy! An' him upstairs, I'll raise him t' be like me! (*He turns to leave them.*) I'm goin' in an' dance!—sing an' celebrate! (*He walks to the porch—then turns with a great grin.*) I don't cal-c'late it's left in him, but if he gits pesky, Abbie, ye jest sing out. I'll come a-runnin' an' by the Etarnal, I'll put him across my knee an' birch him! Ha-ha-ha! (*He goes into the house laughing. A moment later his loud "whoop" is heard.*)

ABBIE (*tenderly*): Eben. Air ye hurt? (*She tries to kiss him but he pushes her violently away and struggles to a sitting position.*)

EBEN (*gaspingly*): T'hell—with ye!

ABBIE (*not believing her ears*): It's me, Eben—Abbie—don't ye know me?

EBEN (*glowering at her with hatred*): Ay-eh—I know ye—now! (*He suddenly breaks down, sobbing weakly.*)

ABBIE (*fearfully*): Eben—what's happened t' ye—why did ye look at me 's if ye hated me?

EBEN (*violently, between sobs and gasps*): I do hate ye! Ye're a whore—a damn trickin' whore!

ABBIE (*shrinking back horrified*): Eben! Ye don't know what ye're sayin'!

EBEN (*scrambling to his feet and following her—accusingly*): Ye're nothin' but a stinkin' passel o' lies! Ye've been lyin' t' me every word ye spoke, day an' night, since we fust—done it. Ye've kept sayin' ye loved me....

ABBIE (*frantically*): I do love ye! (*She takes his hand but he flings hers away.*)

EBEN (*unheeding*): Ye've made a fool o' me—a sick, dumb fool—a-purpose! Ye've been on'y playin' yer sneakin', stealin' game all along—gittin' me t' lie with ye so's ye'd hev a son he'd think was his'n, an' makin' him promise he'd give ye the farm and let me eat dust, if ye did git him a son! (*Staring at her with anguished, bewildered eyes.*) They must be a devil livin' in ye! T'ain't human t' be as bad as that be!

ABBIE (*stunned—dully*): He told yew ...?

EBEN: Hain't it true? It hain't no good in yew lyin'.

ABBIE (*pleadingly*): Eben, listen—ye must listen—it was long ago—afore we done nothin'—yew was scornin' me—goin' t' see Min—when I was lovin' ye—an' I said it t' him t' git vengeance on ye!

EBEN (*Unheedingly. With tortured passion.*): I wish ye was dead! I wish I was dead along with ye afore this come! (*Ragingly.*) But I'll git my vengeance too! I'll pray Maw t' come back t' help me—t' put her cuss on yew an' him!

ABBIE (*brokenly*): Don't ye, Eben! Don't ye! (*She throws herself on her knees before him, weeping.*) I didn't mean t' do bad t'ye! Fergive me, won't ye?

EBEN (*not seeming to hear her—fiercely*): I'll git squar' with the old skunk—an' yew! I'll tell him the truth 'bout the son he's so proud o'! Then I'll leave ye here t' pizen each other—with Maw comin' out o' her grave at nights—an' I'll go t' the gold fields o' Californi-a whar Sim an' Peter be!

ABBIE (*terrified*): Ye won't—leave me? Ye can't!

EBEN (*with fierce determination*): I'm a-goin', I tell ye! I'll git rich thar an' come back an' fight him fur the farm he stole—an' I'll kick ye both out in the road—t' beg an' sleep in the woods—an' yer son along with ye—t' starve an' die! (*He is hysterical at the end.*)

ABBIE (*with a shudder—humbly*): He's yewr son, too, Eben.

EBEN (*torturedly*): I wish he never was born! I wish he'd die this minit! I wish I'd never sot eyes on him! It's him—yew havin' him—a-purpose t' steal—that's changed everythin'!

ABBIE (*gently*): Did ye believe I loved ye—afore he come?

EBEN: Aye-eh—like a dumb ox!

ABBIE: An' ye don't believe no more?

EBEN: B'lieve a lyin' thief! Ha!

ABBIE (*shudders—then humbly*): An' did ye r'ally love me afore?

EBEN (*brokenly*): Ay-eh—an' ye was trickin' me!

ABBIE: An' ye don't love me now!

EBEN (*violently*): I hate ye, I tell ye!

ABBIE: An' ye're truly goin' West—goin' t' leave me—all account o' him being born?

EBEN: I'm a-goin' in the mornin'—or may God strike me t' hell!

ABBIE (*after a pause—with a dreadful cold intensity—slowly*): If that's what his comin's done t' me—killin' yewr love—takin' yew away—my on'y joy—the on'y joy I ever knowed—like heaven t' me—purtier'n heaven—then I hate him, too, even if I be his Maw!

EBEN (*bitterly*): Lies! Ye love him! He'll steal the farm fur ye! (*Brokenly.*) But t'ain't the farm so much—not no more—it's yew foolin' me—gittin' me t' love ye—lyin' yew loved me—jest t' git a son t' steal!

ABBIE (*distractedly*): He won't steal! I'd kill him fust! I do love ye! I'll prove t' ye . . . !

EBEN (*harshly*): T'ain't no use lyin' no more. I'm deaf t' ye! (*He turns away.*) I hain't seein' ye agen. Good-by!

ABBIE (*pale with anguish*): Hain't ye even goin' t' kiss me—not once—arter all we loved?

EBEN (*in a hard voice*): I hain't wantin' t' kiss ye never agen! I'm wantin' t' forgit I ever sot eyes on ye!

ABBIE: Eben!—ye mustn't—wait a spell—I want t' tell ye. . . .

EBEN: I'm a-goin' in t' git drunk. I'm a-goin' t' dance.

ABBIE (*clinging to his arm—with passionate earnestness*): If I could make it—'s if he'd never come up between us—if I could prove t' ye I wa'n't schemin' t' steal from ye—so's everythin' could be jest the same with us, lovin' each other jest the same, kissin' an' happy the same's we've been happy afore he come—if I could do it—ye'd love me agen, wouldn't ye? Ye'd kiss me agen? Ye wouldn't never leave me, would ye?

EBEN (*moved*): I calc'late not. (*Then shaking her hand off his arm—with a bitter smile.*) But ye hain't God, be ye?

ABBIE (*exultantly*): Remember ye've promised! (*Then with strange intensity.*) Mebbe I kin take back one thin' God does!

EBEN (*peering at her*): Ye're gittin' cracked, hain't ye? (*Then going toward door.*) I'm a-goin' t' dance.

ABBIE (*calls after him intensely*): I'll prove t' ye! I'll prove I love ye better'n. . . . (*He goes in the door, not seeming to hear. She remains standing where she is, looking after him—then she finishes desperately.*) Better'n everythin' else in the world!

Scene III

(*Just before dawn in the morning—shows the kitchen and Cabot's bedroom. In the kitchen, by the light of a tallow candle on the table, Eben is sitting, his chin propped on his hands, his drawn face blank and expressionless. His carpetbag is on the floor beside him. In the bedroom, dimly lighted by a small whale-oil lamp, Cabot lies asleep. Abbie is bending over the cradle, listening, her face full of terror yet with an undercurrent of desperate triumph. Suddenly, she breaks down and sobs, appears about to throw herself on her knees beside the cradle, but the old man turns restlessly, groaning in his sleep, and she controls herself, and, shrinking away from the cradle with a gesture of horror, backs swiftly toward the door in rear and goes out. A moment later she comes into the kitchen and, running to Eben, flings her arms about his neck and kisses him wildly. He hardens himself, he remains unmoved and cold, he keeps his eyes straight ahead.*)

ABBIE (*hysterically*): I done it, Eben! I told ye I'd do it! I've proved I love ye—better'n everythin'—so's ye can't never doubt me no more!

EBEN (*dully*): Whatever ye done, it hain't no good now.

ABBIE (*wildly*): Don't ye say that! Kiss me, Eben, won't ye? I need ye t' kiss me arter what I done! I need ye t' say ye love me!

EBEN (*kisses her without emotion—dully*): That's fur good-by. I'm a-goin' soon.

ABBIE: No! No! Ye won't go—not now!

EBEN (*going on with his own thoughts*): I been a-thinkin'—an' I hain't goin' t' tell Paw nothin'. I'll leave Maw t' take vengeance on ye. If I told him, the old skunk'd jest be stinkin' mean enuf to take it out on that baby. (*His voice showing emotion in spite of him.*) An' I don't want nothin' bad t' happen t' him. He hain't t' blame fur yew. (*He adds with a certain queer pride.*) An' he looks like me! An' by God, he's mine! An' some day I'll be a-comin' back an' ... !

ABBIE (*too absorbed in her own thoughts to listen to him—pleadingly*): They's no cause fur ye t' go now—they's no sense—it's all the same's it was—they's nothin' come b'tween us now—arter what I done!

EBEN (*Something in her voice arouses him. He stares at her a bit frightenedly.*): Ye look mad, Abbie. What did ye do?

ABBIE: I—I killed him, Eben.

EBEN (*amazed*): Ye killed him?

ABBIE (*dully*): Ay-eh.

EBEN (*recovering from his astonishment—savagely*): An' serves him right! But we got t' do somethin' quick t' make it look s'if the old skunk'd killed himself when he was drunk. We kin prove by 'em all how drunk he got.

ABBIE (*wildly*): No! No! Not him! (*Laughing distract-edly.*) But that's what I ought t' done, hain't it? I oughter killed him instead! Why didn't ye tell me?

EBEN (*appalled*): Instead? What d'ye mean?

ABBIE: Not him.

EBEN (*his face grown ghastly*): Not—not that baby!

ABBIE (*dully*): Ay-eh!

EBEN (*falls to his knees as if he'd been struck—his voice trembling with horror*): Oh, God A'mighty! A'mighty God! Maw, whar was ye, why didn't ye stop her?

ABBIE (*simply*): She went back t' her grave that night we fust done it, remember? I hain't felt her about since. (*A pause. Eben hides his head in his hands, trembling all over as if he had the ague. She goes on dully.*) I left the piller over his little face. Then he killed himself. He stopped breathin'. (*She begins to weep softly.*)

EBEN (*rage beginning to mingle with grief*): He looked like me. He was mine, damn ye!

ABBIE (*slowly and brokenly*): I didn't want t' do it. I hated myself fur doin' it. I loved him. He was so purty—dead spit 'n' image o' yew. But I loved yew more—an' yew was goin' away—far off whar I'd never see ye agen, never kiss ye, never feel ye pressed agin me agen—an' ye said ye hated me fur havin' him—ye said ye hated him an' wished he was dead—ye said if it hain't been fur him comin' it'd be the same's afore between us.

EBEN (*unable to endure this, springs to his feet in a fury, threatening her, his twitching fingers seeming to reach out for her throat*): Ye lie! I never said—I never dreamed ye'd—I'd cut off my head afore I'd hurt his finger!

ABBIE (*piteously, sinking on her knees*): Eben, don't ye look at me like that—hatin' me—not after what I done fur ye—fur us—so's we could be happy agen—

EBEN (*furiously now*): Shut up, or I'll kill ye! I see yer game now—the same old sneakin' trick—ye're aimin' t' blame me fur the murder ye done!

ABBIE (*moaning—putting her hands over her ears*): Don't ye, Eben! Don't ye! (*She grasps his legs.*)

EBEN (*his mood suddenly changing to horror, shrinks away from her*): Don't ye tech me! Ye're pizen! How could ye—t' murder a pore little critter—Ye must've swapped yer soul t' hell! (*Suddenly raging.*) Ha! I kin see why ye done it! Not the lies ye jest told—but 'cause ye wanted t' steal agen—steal the last thin' ye'd left me—my part o' him—no, the hull o' him—ye saw he looked like me—ye knowed he was all mine—an' ye couldn't b'ar it—I know ye! Ye killed him fur bein' mine! (*All this has driven him almost insane. He makes a rush past her for the door—then turns—shaking both fists at her, violently.*) But I'll take vengeance now! I'll git the Sheriff! I'll tell him everythin'! Then I'll sing "I'm off to Californi-a!" an' go—gold—Golden Gate—gold sun—fields o' gold in the West! (*This last he half shouts, half croons incoherently, suddenly breaking off passionately.*) I'm a-goin' fur the Sheriff t' come an' git ye! I want ye tuk away, locked up from me! I can't stand t' luk at ye! Murderer an' thief 'r not, ye still tempt me! I'll give ye up t' the Sheriff! (*He turns and runs out, around the corner of house, panting and sobbing, and breaks into a swerving sprint down the road.*)

ABBIE (*struggling to her feet, runs to the door, calling after him*): I love ye, Eben! I love ye! (*She stops at the door weakly, swaying, about to fall.*) I don't care what ye do—if ye'll on'y love me agen—(*She falls limply to the floor in a faint.*)

Scene IV

(*About an hour later. Same as scene III. Shows the kitchen and Cabot's bedroom. It is after dawn. The sky is brilliant with the sunrise. In the kitchen, Abbie sits at the table, her body limp and exhausted, her head bowed down over her arms, her face hidden. Upstairs, Cabot is still asleep but awakens with a start. He looks toward the window and gives a snort of surprise and irritation—throws back the covers and begins hurriedly pulling on his clothes. Without looking behind him, he begins talking to Abbie whom he supposes beside him.*)

CABOT: Thunder 'n' lightin', Abbie! I hain't slept this late in fifty year! Looks 's if the sun was full riz a'most. Must've been the dancin' an' likker. Must be gittin' old. I hope Eben's t' wuk. Ye might've tuk the trouble t' rouse me, Abbie. (*He turns—sees no one there—surprised.*) Waal—whar air she? Gittin' vittles, I calc'late. (*He tiptoes to the cradle and peers down—proudly.*) Mornin', sonny. Purty's a picter! Sleepin' sound. He don't beller all night like most o' 'em. (*He goes quietly out the door in rear—a few*

Paolo Schreiber (left) and Brian Dennehy play father and son, and Carla Gugino the father's new wife, in the production of *Desire under the Elms* directed by Robert Falls at the St. James Theater, 2009.

moments later enters kitchen—sees Abbie—with satisfaction.) So thar ye be. Ye got any vittles cooked?

ABBIE (*without moving*): No.

CABOT (*coming to her, almost sympathetically*): Ye feelin' sick?

ABBIE: No.

CABOT (*Pats her on shoulder. She shudders.*): Ye'd best lie down a spell. (*Half jocularly.*) Yer son'll be needin' ye soon. He'd ought t' wake up with a gnashin' appetite, the sound way he's sleepin'.

ABBIE (*shudders—then in a dead voice*): He hain't never goin' t' wake up.

CABOT (*jokingly*): Takes after me this mornin'. I hain't slept so late in . . .

ABBIE: He's dead.

CABOT (*stares at her—bewilderedly*): What. . . .

ABBIE: I killed him.

CABOT (*stepping back from her—aghast*): Air ye drunk—'r crazy—'r . . . ?

ABBIE (*suddenly lifts her head and turns on him—wildly*): I killed him, I tell ye! I smothered him. Go up an' see if ye don't b'lieve me!

(*Cabot stares at her a second, then bolts out the rear door, can be heard bounding up the stairs, and rushes into the bedroom and over to the cradle. Abbie has sunk back lifelessly into her former position. Cabot puts his hand down on the body in the crib. An expression of fear and horror comes over his face.*)

CABOT (*shrinking away—tremblingly*): God A'mighty! God A'mighty. (*He stumbles out the door—in a short while returns to the kitchen—comes to Abbie, the stunned expression still on his face—hoarsely.*) Why did ye do it? Why? (*As she doesn't answer, he grabs her violently by the shoulder and shakes her.*) I ax ye why ye done it! Ye'd better tell me 'r . . . !

ABBIE (*gives him a furious push which sends him staggering back and springs to her feet—with wild rage and hatred*): Don't ye dare tech me! What right hev ye t' question me 'bout him? He wa'n't yewr son! Think I'd have a son by yew? I'd die fust! I hate the sight o' ye an' allus did! It's yew I should've murdered, if I'd had good sense! I hate ye! I love Eben. I did from the fust. An' he was Eben's son—mine an' Eben's—not your'n!

CABOT (*stands looking at her dazedly—a pause—finding his words with an effort—dully*): That was it—what I felt—pokin' round the corners—while ye lied—holdin' yerself from me—sayin' ye'd already conceived—(*He lapses into crushed silence—then with a strange emotion.*) He's dead, sart'n. I felt his heart. Pore little critter! (*He blinks back one tear, wiping his sleeve across his nose.*)

ABBIE (*hysterically*): Don't ye! Don't ye! (*She sobs unrestrainedly.*)

CABOT (*with a concentrated effort that stiffens his body into a rigid line and hardens his face into a stony mask—through his teeth to himself*): I got t' be—like a stone—a rock o' jedgment! (*A pause. He gets *complete control over himself—harshly.*) If he was Eben's, I be glad he air gone! An' mebbe I suspicioned it all along. I felt they was somethin' onnateral—somewhars—the house got so lonesome—an' cold—drivin' me down t' the barn—t' the beasts o' the field. . . . Ay-eh. I must've suspicioned—somethin'. Ye didn't fool me—not altogether, leastways—I'm too old a bird—growin' ripe on the bough. . . . (*He becomes aware he is wandering, straightens again, looks at Abbie with a cruel grin.*) So ye'd liked t' hev murdered me 'steed o' him, would ye? Waal, I'll live to a hundred! I'll live t' see ye hung! I'll deliver ye up t' the jedgment o' God an' the law! I'll git the Sheriff now. (*Starts for the door.*)

ABBIE (*dully*): Ye needn't. Eben's gone fur him.

CABOT (*amazed*): Eben—gone fur the Sheriff?

ABBIE: Ay-eh.

CABOT: T' inform agen ye?

ABBIE: Ay-eh.

CABOT (*considers this—a pause—then in a hard voice*): Waal, I'm thankful fur him savin' me the trouble. I'll git t' wuk. (*He goes to the door—then turns—in a voice full of strange emotion.*) He'd ought t' been my son, Abbie. Ye'd ought t' loved me. I'm a man. If ye'd loved me, I'd never told no Sheriff on ye no matter what ye did, if they was t' brile me alive!

ABBIE (*defensively*): They's more to it nor yew know, makes him tell.

CABOT (*dryly*): Fur yewr sake, I hope they be. (*He goes out—comes around to the gate—stares up at the sky. His control relaxes. For a moment he is old and weary. He murmurs despairingly.*) God A'mighty, I be lonesomer'n ever! (*He hears running footsteps from the left, immediately is himself again. Eben runs in, panting exhaustedly, wild-eyed and mad looking. He lurches through the gate. Cabot grabs him by the shoulder. Eben stares at him dumbly.*) Did ye tell the Sheriff?

EBEN (*nodding stupidly*): Ay-eh.

CABOT (*gives him a push away that sends him sprawling—laughing with withering contempt*): Good fur ye! A prime chip o' yer Maw ye be! (*He goes toward the barn, laughing harshly. Eben scrambles to his feet. Suddenly Cabot turns—grimly threatening.*) Git off this farm when the Sheriff takes her—or, by God, he'll have t' come back an' git me fur murder, too! (*He stalks off. Eben does not appear to have heard him. He runs to the door and comes into the kitchen. Abbie looks up with a cry of anguished joy. Eben stumbles over and throws himself on his knees beside her sobbing brokenly.*)

EBEN: Fergive me!

ABBIE (*happily*): Eben! (*She kisses him and pulls his head over against her breast.*)

EBEN: I love ye! Fergive me!

ABBIE (*ecstatically*): I'd fergive ye all the sins in hell fur sayin' that! (*She kisses his head, pressing it to her with a fierce passion of possession.*)

EBEN (*brokenly*): But I told the Sheriff. He's comin' fur ye!

ABBIE: I kin b'ar what happens t' me—now!

EBEN: I woke him up. I told him. He says, wait 'til I git dressed. I was waiting. I got to thinkin' o' yew. I got to thinkin' how I'd loved ye. It hurt like somethin' was bustin' in my chest an' head. I got t' cryin'. I knowed sudden I loved ye yet, an' allus would love ye!

ABBIE (*caressing his hair—tenderly*): My boy, hain't ye?

EBEN: I begun t' run back. I cut across the fields an' through the woods. I thought ye might have time t' run away—with me—an' . . .

ABBIE (*shaking her head*): I got t' take my punishment—t' pay fur my sin.

EBEN: Then I want t' share it with ye.

ABBIE: Ye didn't do nothin'.

EBEN: I put it in yer head. I wisht he was dead! I as much as urged ye t' do it!

ABBIE: No. It was me alone!

EBEN: I'm as guilty as yew be! He was the child o' our sin.

ABBIE (*lifting her head as if defying God*): I don't repent that sin! I hain't askin' God t' fergive that!

EBEN: Nor me—but it led up t' the other—an' the murder ye did, ye did 'count o' me—an' it's my murder, too, I'll tell the Sheriff—an' if ye deny it, I'll say we planned it t'gether—an' they'll all b'lieve me, fur they suspicion everythin' we've done, an' it'll seem likely an' true to 'em. An' it is true—way down. I did help ye—somehow.

ABBIE (*laying her head on his—sobbing*): No! I don't want yew t' suffer!

EBEN: I got t' pay fur my part o' the sin! An' I'd suffer wuss leavin' ye, goin' West, thinkin' o' ye day an' night, bein' out when yew was in—(*lowering his voice*) 'r bein' alive when yew was dead. (*A pause.*) I want t' share with ye, Abbie—prison 'r death 'r hell 'r anythin'! (*He looks into her eyes and forces a trembling smile.*) If I'm sharin' with ye, I won't feel lonesome, leastways.

ABBIE (*weakly*): Eben! I won't let ye! I can't let ye!

EBEN (*kissing her—tenderly*): Ye can't he'p yerself. I got ye beat fur once!

ABBIE (*forcing a smile—adoringly*): I hain't beat—s'long's I got ye!

EBEN (*hears the sound of feet outside*): Ssshh! Listen! They've come t' take us!

ABBIE: No, it's him. Don't give him no chance to fight ye, Eben. Don't say nothin'—no matter what he says. An' I won't neither. (*It is Cabot. He comes up from the barn in a great state of excitement and strides into the house and then into the kitchen. Eben is kneeling beside Abbie, his arm around her, hers around him. They stare straight ahead.*)

CABOT (*Stares at them, his face hard. A long pause—vindictively.*): Ye make a slick pair o' murderin' turtle doves! Ye'd ought t' be both hung on the same limb an' left thar t' swing in the breeze an' rot—a warnin' t' old fools like me t' b'ar their lonesomeness alone—an' fur young fools like ye t' hobble their lust.

(*A pause. The excitement returns to his face, his eyes snap, he looks a bit crazy.*) I couldn't work today. I couldn't take no interest. T' hell with the farm! I'm leavin' it! I've turned the cows an' other stock loose! I've druv 'em into the woods whar they kin be free! By freein' 'em, I'm freein' myself! I'm quittin' here today! I'll set fire t' house an' barn an' watch 'em burn, an' I'll leave yer Maw t' haunt the ashes, an' I'll will the fields back t' God, so that nothin' human kin never touch 'em! I'll be a-goin' to Californi-a—t' jine Simeon an' Peter—true sons o' mine if they be dumb fools—an' the Cabots'll find Solomon's Mines t'gether! (*He suddenly cuts a mad caper.*) Whoop! What was the song they sung? "Oh, Californi-a! That's the land fur me." (*He sings this—then gets on his knees by the floorboard under which the money was hid.*) An' I'll sail thar on one o' the finest clippers I kin find! I've got the money! Pity ye didn't know whar this was hidden so's ye could steal. . . . (*He has pulled up the board. He stares—feels—stares again. A pause of dead silence. He slowly turns, slumping into a sitting position on the floor, his eyes like those of a dead fish, his face the sickly green of an attack of nausea. He swallows painfully several times—forces a weak smile at last.*) So—ye did steal it!

EBEN (*emotionlessly*): I swapped it t' Sim an' Peter fur their share o' the farm—t' pay their passage t' Californi-a.

CABOT (*with one sardonic*): Ha! (*He begins to recover. Gets slowly to his feet—strangely.*) I calc'late God give it to 'em—not yew! God's hard, not easy! Mebbe they's easy gold in the West but it hain't God's gold. It hain't fur me. I kin hear His voice warnin' me agen t' be hard an' stay on my farm. I kin see his hand usin' Eben t' steal t' keep me from weakness. I kin feel I be in the palm o' His hand, His fingers guidin' me. (*A pause—then he mutters sadly.*) It's a-goin' t' be lonesomer now than ever it war afore—an' I'm gittin'

old, Lord—ripe on the bough. . . . (*Then stiffening.*) Waal—what d'ye want? God's lonesome, hain't He? God's hard an' lonesome! (*A pause. The Sheriff with two men comes up the road from the left. They move cautiously to the door. The Sheriff knocks on it with the butt of his pistol.*)

SHERIFF: Open in the name o' the law! (*They start.*)

CABOT: They've come fur ye. (*He goes to the rear door.*) Come in, Jim! (*The three men enter. Cabot meets them in doorway.*) Jest a minit, Jim. I got 'em safe here. (*The Sheriff nods. He and his companions remain in the doorway.*)

EBEN (*suddenly calls*): I lied this mornin', Jim. I helped her to do it. Ye kin take me, too.

ABBIE (*brokenly*): No!

CABOT: Take 'em both. (*He comes forward—stares at Eben with a trace of grudging admiration.*) Purty good—fur yew! Waal, I got t' round up the stock. Good-by.

EBEN: Good-by.

ABBIE: Good-by. (*Cabot turns and strides past the men—comes out and around the corner of the house, his shoulders squared, his face stony, and stalks grimly toward the barn. In the meantime the Sheriff and men have come into the room.*)

SHERIFF (*embarrassedly*): Waal—we'd best start.

ABBIE: Wait. (*Turns to Eben.*) I love ye, Eben.

EBEN: I love ye, Abbie. (*They kiss. The three men grin and shuffle embarrassedly. Eben takes Abbie's hand. They go out the door in rear, the men following, and come from the house, walking hand in hand to the gate. Eben stops there and points to the sunrise sky.*) Sun's a-rizin'. Purty, hain't it?

ABBIE: Ay-eh. (*They both stand for a moment looking up raptly in attitudes strangely aloof and devout.*)

SHERIFF (*looking around at the farm enviously—to his companions*): It's a jim-dandy farm, no denyin'. Wished I owned it!

COMMENTARY

ROGER ASSELINEAU 1915–2002

The Quest for God in *Desire Under the Elms* 1969

Roger Asselineau was a professor of American literature at the Sorbonne in Paris. In this excerpt from his essay "*Desire Under the Elms*: A Phase of Eugene O'Neill's Philosophy," he explores the play as "a philosophical tragedy" about the relationship between man and God.

Though to all appearances O'Neill was primarily a playwright and an experimenter with dramatic forms who never considered himself a thinker, he was in fact desperately trying to express "something" in all his plays. He chose drama as a medium, but, for all his interest in technique, he never considered it an end in itself, but rather a means to live by proxy a certain number of problems which obsessed him. In *Lazarus Laughed*, he speaks of men as "those haunted heroes." Actually this is less a definition of mankind than a description of himself. He composed plays because he *had* to write in order to liberate himself and exorcise ghosts. It was a compulsion. The result was plays because of his environment, because his father was an actor and he was an "enfant de la balle," but it might have been novels just as well, and he would probably have written better novels than plays, for he was constantly hampered by the limitations of the stage. In his case literary creation was not a gratuitous activity, but an intense imaginative experience, an "*Erlebnis*." He lived it. It was a passionate answer to the problems which tormented him with excruciating strength. This is no mere figure of speech. He roamed the world for years in search of a solution, trying to find a remedy for his fundamental despair, giving up the comfort and security of family life and nearly losing his health and life in the process.

After his wandering years, his *Wanderjahre,* when his health broke down and he was obliged to bring his restless comings-and-goings to a close, he went on exploring the world in imagination, not as a dilettante or a tourist in the realms of thought, but as a passionate pilgrim in quest of a shrine at which to worship. Though brought up a Roman Catholic, he lost his faith as an adolescent. Yet his nature abhorred this spiritual vacuum and he ardently looked for a substitute ever after. His religious faith was killed by rationalism and scientific materialism, but the restlessness and violence of his quest for a personal religion sprang from no coldly rational intellect.

Each of his plays is thus not only an experiment in craftsmanship, but also an attempt to find God or at least some justification for the flagrant inconsistencies of the human condition. His interest was less in psychology than in metaphysics. He said so himself in a letter to Joseph Wood Krutch: "Most modern plays are concerned with the relation between man and man, but that does not interest me at all. I am interested only in the relation between man and God."

In spite of its apparent dramatic directness therefore, *Desire Under the Elms* is essentially, like his other plays, a philosophical tragedy about man and God rather than a naturalistic chunk of life depicting the mores of a bunch of clumsy New England rustics.

Animal Nature of Man

Reduced to essentials in this very primitive setting man appears primarily as an animal. The first specimens whom we have a chance to observe when the curtain rises, Eben and especially Simeon and Peter, look like oxen, eat, work and behave like a team of oxen, and feel tied up to the other animals of the farm by bonds of brotherhood: ". . . the cows knows us . . . An' the hosses, an' pigs, an' chickens . . . They knows us like brothers—and likes us" (Part I, scene 4). They obey their instincts blindly and think only of drinking, eating and fornicating. Their lust is quite literally bestial as is shown by Eben's account of his visit to Min: "I begun t'beller like a calf an' cuss at the same time . . . an' she got scared, an' I just grabbled holt an' tuk her" (Part I, scene 3). When Abbie courts Eben, the scene is not much different.

She kisses him greedily and at first he submits dumbly, but soon, after returning her kisses he hurls her away from him and, O'Neill tells us, "they stand speechless and breathless, panting like two animals" (Part II, scene 2).

These inarticulate, animal-like creatures differ from their dumb brothers in only one respect (but it is hardly an improvement): they are possessed with the mania of owning things, whether gold or land. They all crave for money or title-deeds. In short, they bear a strong family likeness to Swift's Yahoos. They have only one redeeming feature: an embryonic sense of beauty which makes them exclaim "purty" in a rather monotonous manner whenever they notice the beauty of their surroundings. The only exception is the sheriff, who at the very end of the play passes very matter-of-fact and anti-climactic comments on the salable value of the farm while Eben and Abbie admire the beauty of the sunrise.

Man Trapped by Circumstance

Far from being a free agent, man is thus by and large the slave of his instincts and O'Neill here revives the old Calvinistic dogma of predestination. As early as his very first play, *The Web*, of the transparent title, he attempted to show that man is caught in a web of circumstances, a web that is not of his own weaving. At the end of *The Web*, O'Neill tells us that Rose, the prostitute, "seems to be aware of something in the room which none of the others can see—perhaps the personification of the ironic life force that has crushed her." In *Desire Under the Elms* Eben feels trapped in exactly the same way: "Each day," the stage directions inform us, "is a cage in which he finds himself trapped." He is indeed trapped by circumstances—tied up to that bleak New England farm which he somehow considers part of his mother, and he is also psychologically trapped by an all-powerful mother-complex which unknown to him determines his whole behavior towards his father as well as towards women in general. His temperament is wholly determined by his heredity: it is a combination of his mother's softness and lack of will, as his father again and again points out, and of his father's aggressiveness and obstinacy, as his two elder brothers repeatedly tell us: "he is a chip off the old block, the spitting image of his father. . . ."

As to Abbie, she is just as trapped as he is. When she enters the stage, we are warned that she has "the same unsettled, untamed, desperate quality which is so apparent in Eben." And shortly afterwards we learn that she "was a orphan early an' had t'wuk fur others in other folks' hums" and her first husband "turned out a drunken spreer" and got sick and died. She then felt free again only to discover that all she was free for was to work again "in other folks' hums, doin' other folks' wuk" till she had almost given up hope of ever doing her own work in her own home (Part I, scene 4).

Ephraim Cabot himself, for all his will-power and vigor, is caught in the same web as the others. His whole behavior is conditioned by his Puritan upbringing. He cannot think of anything but work, hard work on a barren New England farm. "*Laborare est orare*," Carlyle claimed, "work is worship." Ephraim Cabot is a degenerate Puritan. Work has ceased to be a form of worship for him, yet he believes in its virtue and absolute value because he has been brought up that way. He once tried to escape this self-imposed serfdom. Like many other New Englanders, he went West and in the broad meadows of the central plains found black soil as rich as gold, without a stone. He had only to plough and sow and then sit and smoke his pipe and watch things grow. He could have become a rich man and led an easy and idle life, but he preferred to give it up and return to his New England farm and to hard work on a stony soil, which proves the extraordinary strength of his Puritan compulsions. They practically deprived him of his freedom of choice.

So, at the start at least, the three major characters of *Desire Under the Elms* are not free. They bear psychological or moral chains. Consequently, they cannot be held responsible for their actions, and Simeon with his peasant shrewdness is perfectly aware of it. When Eben accuses his father of killing his "Maw," Simeon retorts: "No one never kills nobody. It's allus somethin' that's the murderer" (Part I, scene 2). "Somethin'," that is to say one of those mysterious things which impel men to act this way or that, whether they like it or not, whether they are aware of it or not. This is a modified form of Puritan pessimism: all men are sinners in the clutches of Satan—or of God who is always "nagging his sheep to sin" (Part I, scene 4), the better to punish them afterwards, always ready to smite his undutiful sons with his worst curse.

The Redeeming Power of Passion

How can a man save his soul under such circumstances? Though, theoretically, O'Neill's approach is strictly nontheological and he is not concerned with the problem of salvation, he is constantly obsessed with it all the same and in this particular play, he gives it a Nietzschean answer: passion. Passion alone, he suggests, can enable man to transcend his animal nature. He repeatedly exalts the purity and transfiguring power of love. Eben's passion for Abbie which at first is mere lust soon becomes love—and there is a difference in kind between the two. The passage from lust to love is similar to the transmutation of lead into gold. Whereas lust, which is tied to the body, is finite and transient, love, which transcends the body, is infinite and eternal. Abbie kills her infant son to prove her love to Eben, and at the end of scene 3 of Part III proclaims that her love for Eben will never change, whatever he does to her. The play ends on an apotheosis of love. The two lovers stand "looking up raptly in attitudes strangely aloof and devout" at the "purty" rising sun, which contrasts with the pallid setting sun that lit up the opening of the play, at a time when everything took place on the plane of coarse material things and lust.

Man can thus be redeemed by a great passion and save his soul and attain grandeur. The farm under the elms, which looked so sordid when the curtain rose, witnesses a sublime *dénouement* and at the end almost becomes one of those places where the spirit bloweth.

The reason for this extraordinary change is that, in Hamlet's words:

There are more things in heaven and earth . . .
Than are dreamt of in all [our] philosophy,

as Cabot again and again feels, for all his hardness and insensitivity: "They's thin's pokin' about in the dark—in the corners" (Part II, scene 2). "Even the music can't drive it out—somethin'. Ye kin feel it droppin' off the elums, climbin' up the roof, sneakin' down the chimney, pokin' in the corners. They's no peace in houses, they's no rest livin' with folks. Somethin's always livin' with ye . . ." (Part III, scene 2).

God in Nature

What is that "somethin'" whose presence disturbs him? It is the "Desire" of the title—an irresistible life-force (somewhat similar to G. B. Shaw's), which flows through the elms and through old Cabot himself sometimes, as when it makes him leave his farm in spring and go in search of a new wife. But it is especially powerful in Eben and Abbie. It is that thing which makes Eben look like a wild animal in captivity when he enters the stage and feel "inwardly unsubdued." It is quite impersonal and Eben refers to it in the neuter: "I kin feel it growin' in me—growin' an' growin'—till it'll bust out" (Part I, scene 2). It is the magnetic force which draws Eben to Abbie through walls and partitions (Part II, scene 2). It is Nature—and Abbie intones a hymn to her—or it—in her own inarticulate way when she presses Eben to yield to his passion: "Hain't the sun strong an' hot? Ye kin feel it burnin' into the earth—Nature—makin' thin's grow—bigger 'n' bigger—burnin' inside ye—makin' ye want t'grow—into somethin' else—till ye are jined with it—an' it's your'n—but it owns ye—too—an' makes ye grow bigger—like a tree—like them elums" (Part II, scene 1).

In short, the "Desire" which flows through the elms and drips from them and pervades everything under them is God—though the word is never used. It is not, however, the God of the Christians, but rather a dynamic, impersonal, pantheistic or panpsychistic deity present in all things, whether animate or inanimate, breaking barriers between individuals as in the case of Eben and Abbie, dissolving their lonesomeness and making them feel one. In a way it is a pagan God, a Dionysian deity, for it partly manifests itself in the form of carnal desire. Under its influence, Eben and Cabot become inspired poets (in prose) and sing woman, the lovely incarnation of the soft and warm goddess of fertility and life: "She's like t'night, she's soft 'n' warm, her eyes kin wink like a star, her mouth's wa'm, her arms're wa'm. She smells like a wa'm plowed field, she's purty" (Part I, scene 2). "Yew air my Rose o' Sharon! Behold! yew air fair; yer eyes air doves; yer lips air like scarlet; yer two breasts air like two fawns; yer navel be like a round goblet; yer belly be like a heap o' wheat," exclaims old Cabot echoing chapters 4 and 7 of the Song of Solomon.

This omnipresent God is fundamentally a cosmic sexual urge, spontaneous, beautiful, unselfish and amoral. In this perspective the notion of sin becomes meaningless. "He was the child of our sin," says Eben of the baby, but Abbie proudly answers "as if defying God" (the God of the Christians): "I don't repent that sin. I ain't askin' God t'fergive that" (Part III, scene 4). The two lovers have gone back to the Garden of Eden from which Adam and Eve were expelled. They have become "Children of Adam," to take up Walt Whitman's phrase.

The life-force, the desire which circulates through the elms as well as through the *dramatis personae* is the very reverse of the God worshipped by Ephraim Cabot, which has the hardness and immobility of a stone—and the sterility of one (Part II, scene 2). His God is the God of repression and lonesomeness and hard work—the God humorously called up by Robert Frost in "Of the Stones of the Place" and to some extent a duplicate of Robinson Jeffers's anti-human God.

Abbie, on the contrary, recommends to yield to the life impulse, to let Nature speak at every hazard "without check with original energy." It is against nature, it is impious, she claims, to resist its will: "It's agin nature, Eben. Ye been fightin' yer nature ever since the day I come. . . ." (Part II, scene 1).

This is a combination of Nietzsche's Dionysian philosophy and Freudianism and in *Desire Under the Elms* it leads—in spite of the Dostoevskian quality of the *Crime and Punishment* situation at the end of the play—to an optimistic conclusion: the couple Eben-Abbie is not crushed by adverse circumstances. They have fulfilled themselves, they have fully lived and, far from being driven to despair by their trials, they are full of a strange "hopeless hope" when the curtain falls.

Bertolt Brecht

Among the most inventive and influential of modern playwrights, Bertolt Brecht (1898–1956) left a legacy of important plays and theories about how those plays should be produced. Throughout most of his career, he believed that drama should inform and awaken sensibilities, not just entertain or anesthetize an audience. Most of his plays concern philosophical and political issues, and some of them so threatened the Nazi regime that his works were burned publicly in Germany during the Third Reich.

At nineteen, Brecht worked as an orderly in a hospital during the last months of World War I. Seeing so much carnage and misery in the medical wards made him a lifelong pacifist. After the war, while a student in Munich, he began writing plays. His first successes in the Munich theater took the form of commentary on returned war veterans and on the questions of duty and heroism—two concepts that Brecht viewed negatively. His rejection of spiritual concepts was influenced by his reading of Hegel and of Marx's doctrine of dialectical materialism. Marx's theories predicted class struggles and based most social values in economic realities. Brecht eventually moved to Berlin, the theatrical center of Germany, and by 1926 was on his way to becoming a Communist.

Finding the political pressures in early Nazi Germany too frightening and dangerous for his writing, Brecht went into exile in 1933. He lived for a time in Scandinavia and later in the United States. After World War II Brecht and his wife returned to Berlin where, in 1949, he founded the Berliner Ensemble, which produced most of his later work. Brecht chose East Berlin as his home, in part because he believed his work could best be understood in a Communist setting. One irony is that his work has been even more widely appreciated and accepted in the West than in the countries of the former Communist eastern bloc.

In 1928 Brecht wrote his most popular play, a musical on which he collaborated with the German composer Kurt Weill: *The Threepenny Opera*. The model for this play, the English writer John Gay's 1728 ballad opera *The Beggar's Opera*, provided Brecht with a perfect platform for commenting satirically on the political and economic circumstances in Germany two hundred years after Gay wrote. The success of the Brecht–Weill collaboration—the work is still performed regularly—is due in part to Brecht's capacity to create appealing underworld characters such as Polly Peachum and Macheath, known as Mack the Knife. Brecht's wife, Helene Weigel, played Mrs. Peachum, the madam of the brothel in which the action takes place. Kurt Weill's second wife, Lotte Lenya, was an overnight sensation in the part of Jenny. She had a highly acclaimed reprise in New York almost twenty-five years after the play's premiere.

Brecht's most successful plays are *Galileo* (1938–1939), *Mother Courage and Her Children* (1941), *The Good Woman of Setzuan* (1943), *The Private Lives of the Master Race* (1945), and *The Caucasian Chalk Circle* (1948). But these represent only a tiny fraction of a mass of work that includes plays, poetry, criticism, and fiction. Brecht's output is extraordinary in volume and quality. It includes plays adapted from the work not only of Gay but also of Sophocles, Molière, Gorky, Shakespeare, and John Webster, among others.

Brecht developed a number of theories regarding drama. He used the term *epic theater* to distinguish his own theater from traditional Aristotelian drama. Brecht expected his audience to observe critically, to draw conclusions, and to participate in an intellectual argument with the work at hand. The confrontational relationship he intended was designed to engage the audience in analyzing what they saw rather than in identifying with the main characters or in enjoying a wash of sentimentality or emotion.

One of the ways Brecht achieved his ends was by making a production's props, lights, sets, and equipment visible, thereby reminding the members of the audience that they were seeing a play. He used the term **alienation** to define the effect he wanted his theater to have on an audience. He hoped that by alienating his audience from the drama, he would keep them emotionally detached and intellectually alert. Brecht's theater was political. He saw a connection between an audience that could analyze theater critically and an audience that could analyze reality critically—and see that social, political, and economic conditions were not "natural" or fixed immutably but could (and should) be changed.

Brecht's theories produced interesting results and helped stimulate audiences that expected to be entertained by realistic or sentimental plays. His style spread rapidly throughout the world of theater, and it is still being used and developed by contemporary playwrights such as Suzan-Lori Parks and Tony Kushner.

Mother Courage and Her Children

Since *Mother Courage and Her Children* was first produced in 1941 in Zurich, it has become a classic of modern theater, performed successfully in the United States and most other Western countries. Brecht conceived of the drama as a powerful antiwar play. He set it in Germany during the Thirty Years' War, in which German Protestants, supported by countries such as France, Denmark, and England, fought against the Hapsburg empire, which was allied with the Holy Roman Empire and the German Catholic princes. The war was actually a combination of many wars fought during the period of thirty years. It was bloody and seemingly interminable, devastating Germany's towns and citizenry as well as its agriculture and commerce. The armies fought to control territory and economic markets; also underlying the war were longstanding religious differences between German Lutherans and Roman Catholics.

Brecht was not interested in the immediate causes of the Thirty Years' War. He was making a case against war entirely, regardless of its cause. To do this, he deliberately avoided making his play realistic. The stage setting is essentially barren, and the play is structured in scenes that are very intense but that avoid any sense of continuity of action. Audiences cannot become involved in unfolding action; they must always remain conscious of themselves as audience.

For discussion questions and assignments on *Mother Courage,* visit **bedfordstmartins.com/jacobus**.

Moreover, the lighting is high-intensity, almost cruel at times, spotlighting the action in a way that is completely unnatural. In the early productions, Brecht included slide projections of the headings that accompany each of the twelve scenes so that the audience was always reminded of the presence of the playwright and the fact that they were seeing a play. These headings provided yet another break in the continuity of the action.

Although the printed text does not convey it, the play as Brecht produced it employed long silences, some of which were unsettling to the audience. When Swiss Cheese, Mother Courage's "honest son," has a moment of rest in scene 3, he is in an intense ring of stage light as he comments on sitting in the sun in his shirtsleeves. As Swiss Cheese relaxes for the last time, the intense light becomes an ironic device; it seems to expose him as a thief, and he is dragged off to his death. Although he is Mother Courage's "honest son," circumstances make it seem that he has been corrupted by the war, like everyone else.

Mother Courage herself lives off the war by selling goods to the soldiers. She and her children haul their wagon across the battlefields with no concern for who is winning, who is losing, or even where they are. Her only ambition is to stock her wagon, sell her goods, and make sure she does not get stuck with any useless inventory. When the chaplain tells her that peace has broken out, she laments their condition—without war the family has no livelihood.

As Mother Courage continues to pull her wagon across field after field, she learns how to survive. But she also loses her children, one by one, to the war. Eilif, seduced into joining the army by a recruitment officer, is led into battle thinking that war is a heroic adventure. Swiss Cheese thinks he has found a good deal in a paymaster's uniform. Both are wrong; there is no security in war, and they eventually perish.

Kattrin, the daughter, is likewise a victim of the violence of war. Having been violated by a Swedish soldier, she becomes mute. Near the end of the play she is treated violently again, and the terrible scar on her face leaves her unmarriageable. At the end Kattrin dies while sounding an alarm to warn the sleeping town of an imminent attack.

Finally, Mother Courage is left alone. She picks up her wagon and finds that she can maneuver it herself. The play ends as she circles the stage, with everything around her consumed by war.

Brecht's stated intentions were somewhat thwarted by the reactions of the play's first audiences. They were struck by the power of Brecht's characterization of Mother Courage and treated her with immense sympathy. They saw her as an indomitable woman whose strength in the face of adversity was so great that she could not be overwhelmed. But Brecht intended the audience to analyze Mother Courage further and to see in her a reflection of society's wrong values. She conducts business on the field of battle, paying no attention to the moral question of war itself. She makes her living from the war but cannot see that it is the war that causes her anguish.

In response to audiences' sympathetic reactions, Brecht revised the play, adding new lines to help audiences see the venality of Mother Courage's motives. But subsequent audiences have continued to treat her as a survivor—almost a biblical figure. Brecht's German critics saw her as one whose endurance of all the terrors of war testifies to the resilience of humankind. No matter how one decides to interpret her, Mother Courage remains one of the most unusual and haunting characters in modern drama.

Mother Courage and Her Children in Performance

Brecht wrote *Mother Courage* in three months, beginning in September 1939, while he and Helene Weigel were in Sweden, in exile from Nazi Germany. Its first production was on April 19, 1941, in Zurich, Switzerland, while Brecht waited in Sweden for entry papers to the United States. Brecht and Weigel returned to Europe after the war. In 1948 they went to East Berlin to work with a new theater group explicitly to produce *Mother Courage* with Helene Weigel in the title role; the production opened in January 1949. In October 1950 Brecht directed Thérèsa Giehse as Courage in Munich. Other productions were staged in provincial German towns and in other European cities, such as Rotterdam and Paris, both in 1951.

Brecht's productions are sometimes regarded as "canonical," although contemporary directors often modify his original plans. He usually began the performance with a half-curtain and a four-person orchestra playing an overture. Next, an unseen record player played a song associated with Courage; as Courage came on stage, she sang the second verse of her song herself. The stage had only a **cyclorama**, a large curved curtain used as a backdrop, and a circle marked on the floor. This defined the space that was Mother Courage's world, and various sets were placed on the circle to accommodate successive scenes. The circle itself was a revolving turntable on which the wagon moved, going essentially nowhere. Brecht used placards to signal changes in time and place as well as to indicate events in the life of Mother Courage and her children. The lighting was generally bright, and the effect was lively and colorful.

Brecht's plays were not widely produced in the West during the cold war, but Leon Epp directed *Mother Courage* at the Volkstheater in Vienna in 1963. In the same year Jerome Robbins produced the play at the Martin Beck Theatre on Broadway, with sets by Ming Cho Lee. Anne Bancroft played Mother Courage, and Zohra Lampert was Kattrin. The reviews praised Bancroft for achievhing a "lonely magnificence" at the end of the play and maintained that Brecht generated a considerable emotional intensity despite his theoretical distaste for such effects.

The next year Joseph Slowik produced the play in the Goodman Theatre in Chicago with students playing some of the roles and the distinguished Eugenie Leontovich as Mother Courage. In England *Mother Courage* was produced twice in the 1950s in London. In 1961 and 1965 it was produced by the Old Vic. Numerous local theaters put on the play in the late 1960s and 1970s. In 1980 Ntozake Shange adapted the play for its second New York production, resetting it in the period after the American Civil War; Gloria Foster and Morgan Freeman had the major roles. Frank Rich praised the acting and the energy of the play but feared that Brecht's original vision had been altered almost beyond recognition: Mother Courage becomes "an innocent victim of an entire system," which is exactly what Brecht argued against.

The Royal Shakespeare Company produced the play in London in 1984 with Judi Dench as Courage and Zoë Wanamaker as Kattrin. Both received fine reviews, as did the production itself. Diana Rigg was Mother Courage in the production at the Olivier Theatre in London (November 1995–January 1996), which featured a new colloquial translation by the playwright David Hare and reset the play in the period of World War I. Like all productions of the play, this one maintained the circular set that Brecht had originally used and experimented with Brecht's theories of alienation and distancing.

Gwendolyn Mulamba played Mother Courage in the Classical Theatre of Harlem's production in New York City in February 2004. Christopher McElroen directed. In the summer of 2006, Kevin Kline and Meryl Streep starred in George Wolfe's production of *Mother Courage* at Shakespeare in the Park Public Theater, based on a new translation of the play by Tony Kushner. Clearly, Brecht's play speaks to all of us in the twenty-first century.

BERTOLT BRECHT (1898–1956)

Mother Courage and Her Children   1941
A Chronicle of the Thirty Years' War

TRANSLATED BY TONY KUSHNER

Characters

MOTHER COURAGE
KATTRIN, *her mute daughter*
EILIF, *her oldest son*
SWISS CHEESE, *her youngest son*
THE SERGEANT *in Scene One*
THE ARMY RECRUITER
THE COOK
THE GENERAL
THE CHAPLAIN
THE QUARTERMASTER
YVETTE POTTIER
THE ONE WITH THE EYEPATCH
THE COLONEL
THE SERGEANT *in Scene Three*
THE CLERK
THE YOUNG SOLDIER
THE OLDER SOLDIER
THE FARMER *in Scene Five*
THE FARMER'S WIFE *in Scene Five*
THE REGIMENTAL SECRETARY
THE OLD WOMAN
THE YOUNG MAN
THE VOICE INSIDE
THE LIEUTENANT
THE FARMER *in Scene Eleven*
THE FARMER'S WIFE *in Scene Eleven*
THE FARMER'S SON
SOLDIERS

ONE

Spring 1624. The Protestant King of Sweden invades Catholic Poland. Recruiters for the Swedish General Oxenstjerna° search in Dalarna° for soldiers. The merchant, Anna Fierling, who goes by the name Mother Courage, loses a son.

A road outside of town.

A Sergeant and an Army Recruiter stand waiting, shivering.

THE ARMY RECRUITER: How's a recruiter going to find recruits in a place like this? Orders from the General Staff, *four fresh companies* in two weeks time! I contemplate suicide, Sergeant. And the people here are so lacking in fundamental decency they've given me insomnia! Imagine if you will some jerk, concave chest, veiny legs, a total zero. I buy him beers till he's shit-faced, he signs up, and then: I'm paying the tab, he's off to take a leak, he says, I try to keep an eye on him because I've learned the smell of rat, and sure enough, zzzzzzzip! Jump up and fled like a louse flees louse-powder. A handshake's meaningless, honour and duty

---

Oxenstjerna: Axel Oxenstierna (1583–1654) was Governor-General of Prussia during the Thirty Years' War (1618–1648), which was largely a war between Catholics and Protestants and resulted in the destruction of more lives per capita than any war since.   **Dalarna:** A province of Sweden.

are empty words. A place like this, you lose your conviction in the Inner Goodness of Man, Sergeant.

THE SERGEANT: The problem with these people is they haven't had enough war. Where else do morals come from? War! Everything rots in peacetime. People turn into carefree rutting animals and nobody fucking cares. Everyone overeats, whatever they want, 'Oh I'll just sit down now and eat a big cheese and fatback sandwich on fluffy white bread.' Think these people know how many young men and horses they've got? Why count? It's peacetime! I've been in some towns that've gone seventy years without any war whatsoever, people hadn't even bothered naming their children, no one knew whose was whose. You need a bit of butchery to get them counting and listing and naming: big piles of empty boots, corn bagged for portage, man and cow alike stamped and mobilised. War makes order, order makes war.

THE ARMY RECRUITER: Amen.

THE SERGEANT: It isn't easy, starting a war, but nothing worthwhile is easy. And once you're in, you're hooked like a gambler, you can't afford to walk away from the crapshoot once you're deep into it. You become as afraid of peace as you ever were of war, no one really wants the fighting to end. You just have to get people used to the idea. Everyone's scared of anything changing.

THE ARMY RECRUITER: Heads up, a wagon. Two boys appropriate age. Tell 'em to pull over. If this goes bust I'm packing it in, I'm kissing the April wind goodbye.

(*A Jew's harp offstage. A canteen wagon comes down the road. It's pulled by two young men, Eilif and Swiss Cheese. In the wagon, driving it, Mother Courage; seated beside her, playing the Jew's harp, her mute daughter Kattrin.*)

MOTHER COURAGE: Morning, Sergeant.

(*The Sergeant blocks the wagon.*)

THE SERGEANT: Morning, people. Declare yourselves!

MOTHER COURAGE: Retail!

(*She sings:*)
To feed a war you have to pillage,
But let your soldiers rest a bit:
For what they need, here's Mother Courage,
With woolen coats and boots that fit!
Their heads ablaze with lice and liquor,
The boys are marching to the beat!
I guarantee they'll step it quicker
With boots upon their blistered feet!

MOTHER COURAGE AND HER SONS (*singing*):
Now Spring has come, and Winter's dead.
The snow has gone, so draw a breath!
Let Christian souls crawl out of bed,
Pull on their socks and conquer death!

MOTHER COURAGE (*singing*):
Unless his belly's full of porridge,
A soldier's sure to turn and run.
Buy him some grub from Mother Courage—
So he'll know where to point his gun.
They fight for God and legal tender,
I'll see them clothed, and feed them well,

And bless the boys, in all their splendour,
As they march down the road to hell.

MOTHER COURAGE AND HER SONS (*singing*):
Now Spring has come, and Winter's dead.
The snow has gone, so draw a breath!
Let Christian souls crawl out of bed,
Pull on their socks and conquer death!

(*The wagon starts to roll again. Again the Sergeant blocks it.*)

THE SERGEANT: Hang on a minute, garbage. What's your regiment?

EILIF: Second Finnish.

THE SERGEANT: Paperwork!

MOTHER COURAGE: Paperwork?

SWISS CHEESE: She's Mother Courage.

THE SERGEANT: I never heard of her. Why's she called 'Courage'?

MOTHER COURAGE: They called me Courage because I was scared of financial ruin, Sergeant, so I drove my wagon straight through the cannon fire at Riga, with fifty loaves of bread turning mouldy—I didn't see that I had a choice.

THE SERGEANT: Fascinating, now I know your life's story, gimme your paperwork.

(*Mother Courage reaches behind her, finds a battered tin box, removes a big stack of tattered paper. She climbs down off the wagon.*)

MOTHER COURAGE: Here's paper, all I possess. A prayer book I bought in Alt-Ötting,° I use the pages to wrap pickles, and a map of Moravia, will I ever get to Moravia? God knows. If I don't the map's for the cat to shit on. And here, official proof my horse doesn't have hoof-and-mouth disease, which is swell except the horse is dead, poor thing, fifteen guilders she cost, although praise Jesus, not *my* fifteen guilders. I have more paper if you want it.

THE SERGEANT: What I want is, I want your licence to sell. You want my boot up your ass?

MOTHER COURAGE: Excuse me but you may not discuss my ass in front of my children, that's disgusting. And my ass is not for you. The Second Finnish Regiment never required any licence besides my patent honesty which, if you had a better character, you could read off my face.

THE ARMY RECRUITER: Sergeant, I think this woman's insubordinate. The King's army needs discipline.

MOTHER COURAGE: And sausages!

THE SERGEANT: Name.

MOTHER COURAGE: Anna Fierling.

THE SERGEANT: And these others are Fierlings?

MOTHER COURAGE: Who? I'm Fierling. Not them.

THE SERGEANT: They're your children.

MOTHER COURAGE: They are. What's your problem? (*Pointing to her elder son.*) Take him for example, he's Finnish, he's Eilif Nojocki, why? His father was Kojocki or Mojocki so I split the difference. The boy's got fond memories of his father, only it's not actually his father he remembers but a French guy with

---

Alt-Ötting: A small town in Bavaria, Germany.

a goatee. Regardless, he inherited the Kojocki or Mojocki brains; that man could steal a farmer's socks without removing the boots first. None of us has the same name.

THE SERGEANT: None of you?

MOTHER COURAGE: Four points on the compass and I've been pricked in every direction.

THE SERGEANT (*pointing at the youngest son*): I bet. Was his father Chinese?

MOTHER COURAGE: Bad guess. Swiss.

THE SERGEANT: He came along after the French guy?

MOTHER COURAGE: French guy? I never knew any French guys, try to follow or we'll be here till night falls. His father was Swiss, as in Switzerland, but *his* name's Fejos because he's not named after his father, who built fortresses, drunk.

(*Swiss Cheese smiles proudly, nodding. Kattrin hides a laugh.*)

THE SERGEANT: Then who was Fejos?

MOTHER COURAGE: I don't mean to be rude, but you're entirely devoid of imagination, aren't you? I more or less had to call him Fejos because when he came out I was with a Hungarian. He couldn't care less, the Hungarian, he was dying, his kidneys shrivelled up even though he was abstemious. A nice man, the boy looks just like him.

THE SERGEANT: But he wasn't the father.

MOTHER COURAGE: Nevertheless. His big talent is pulling the wagon, so I call him Swiss Cheese. (*Pointing to her daughter.*) She's Kattrin Haupt. Half-German.

THE SERGEANT: Jesus. A nice wholesome family.

MOTHER COURAGE: We are. I've crossed the wide world in this wagon.

THE SERGEANT: You're Bavarian. I'm guessing Bamberg. What're you doing in Sweden?

MOTHER COURAGE: There's no war in Bamberg, is there? Was I supposed to wait?

THE ARMY RECRUITER: So, Jacob and Esau Ox.° Does she ever unstrap the rig and turn you loose to graze?

EILIF: Mama, can I punch this asshole in the mouth? Please?

MOTHER COURAGE: Can you stay where you are and keep quiet, please? Now, Officers, how's about a good pistol, or a belt buckle? Sergeant, your buckle's all bent.

THE SERGEANT: How's about you tell me instead why these two boys who are solid as birch trees with chests and legs like Arabian chargers aren't in the army.

MOTHER COURAGE (*quick*): Drop it, Sergeant, my kids aren't suited for war work.

THE ARMY RECRUITER: They look suitable to me. Make a little money, get famous. Selling shoes, that's for women. (*To Eilif.*) Come here. You talk big. But maybe you're a chicken.

MOTHER COURAGE: He is. He's a chicken. Look at him cross-eyed, he'll faint.

THE ARMY RECRUITER: I'm crossing my eyes, he still looks good to me!

(*The Army Recruiter gestures to Eilif to follow him.*)

MOTHER COURAGE: He's mine, not yours.

Jacob and Esau Ox: A reference to brothers working together.

THE ARMY RECRUITER: He called me an asshole. I invite him to accompany me to the field over there so I can clobber him.

EILIF: Glad to. Don't fret, Mama, I'll be right back.

MOTHER COURAGE: Don't you move, you brawling lump! (*To the Army Recruiter, pointing at Eilif.*) Watch out, he's got a knife sheathed in his boot!

THE ARMY RECRUITER: A knife, huh? I'll extract it easy as a baby tooth. This way, baby boy.

MOTHER COURAGE (*to the Sergeant*): You listen to me, your Captain has been ogling my daughter, and I'm going to tell him you're making her unhappy and he'll clap you in the stocks.

THE SERGEANT (*to the Army Recruiter*): No fighting, OK? (*To Mother Courage.*) What's so terrible about a job in the army? Bet his daddy was a soldier! Died a hero or something?

MOTHER COURAGE: Or something, dead at any rate, and (*pointing at Eilif*) he's just a child! I know your kind, you'll get a five-guilder fee and he'll get slaughtered!

THE ARMY RECRUITER: We'll give him a soldier's snazzy hat and brand new regulation boots when he signs.

EILIF: I don't want you to give me shit.

MOTHER COURAGE: Hey hey hey, I got a fun idea, let's you and me go fishing said the fisherman to the worm. (*To Swiss Cheese.*) Run tell the Captain they're stealing your brother! (*She pulls a knife.*)

He's mine! He's not going to war! I'll poke your eyes out first, you cannibals. We're merchants, we sell ham and shirts and we're friendly people.

THE SERGEANT: Yeah, you look friendly. Put up the knife, you old cunt. If there's a war, there have to be soldiers, right?

MOTHER COURAGE: Somebody else's kids, not mine.

THE SERGEANT: And there it is, your brood gets fat off the war but you think it's a one-way transaction. Maybe your sons have courage even if you don't.

EILIF: The war doesn't scare me.

THE SERGEANT: Why would it? See any bruises on me? I joined at seventeen!

MOTHER COURAGE: Let's see how close you get to seventy.

THE SERGEANT: What're you insinuating? I'm gonna get killed?

MOTHER COURAGE: You look marked to me. What if you're just a cadaver who hasn't heard the bad news, hmm?

SWISS CHEESE: She can see things, everyone knows that, she sees into the future.

THE ARMY RECRUITER: Tell the Sergeant his future then. He likes a good laugh.

THE SERGEANT: That's crap. Seeing things.

MOTHER COURAGE: Give me your helmet.

(*He does.*)

THE SERGEANT: Whatever you're doing, it means as much as dried turds in dead grass. (*Mother Courage looks at him, asking if she should continue.*)

Go ahead, it'll make a good story.

(*She tears a piece of paper in two.*)

MOTHER COURAGE: Eilif, Swiss Cheese, Kattrin, we'll all be torn to scrap like this, if we let the war pull us in too deeply. (*To the Sergeant.*) For a friend I do it for free. I make a black cross on the paper. Black is death.

SWISS CHEESE: And see the other piece of paper's empty.

MOTHER COURAGE: I fold them, I tumble 'em together, topsy turvy as we all tumble together, the marked and unremarkable, from mother love onward, and now draw and now you'll know.

(*The Sergeant hesitates.*)

THE ARMY RECRUITER (*to Eilif*): I'm the pickiest recruiter in the Swedish Army, most don't come close to making the cut but maybe you've got the grit, the beans, that special fire.

(*The Sergeant reaches in the helmet.*)

THE SERGEANT: It's all gobbledegook, oooh, the scales are falling from my eyes!

(*He draws a piece of paper, unfolds it.*)

SWISS CHEESE: Uh-oh! The black cross! He's going away!

THE ARMY RECRUITER: There are more soldiers than bullets. Don't let them scare you.

THE SERGEANT (*hoarse*): You cheated me.

MOTHER COURAGE: You did that to yourself the day you enlisted. Now we'll get going, it isn't every day there's a war on, we don't want to miss out on the fun.

THE SERGEANT: Hell and the Devil, you cheated me, bitch, but you'll be sorry you did! Your bastard's a soldier now!

EILIF: I wanna go with them, Mama.

MOTHER COURAGE: Shut your mouth, nasty!

EILIF: Swiss Cheese too, he wants to be a soldier too!

MOTHER COURAGE: You think so? Says who? Draw your own papers from the helmet, all three of you, then we'll see what's what.

(*She goes behind the wagon, where she tears paper and marks slips with crosses.*)

THE ARMY RECRUITER (*to Eilif*): And I've heard the enemy propaganda, in the Swedish Army it's Bible study and hymn singing night and day, but between us, the army's the army and once you're in you're washed clean of sin, and you can sing any song you like.

(*Mother Courage returns with the helmet.*)

MOTHER COURAGE: Time to abandon mother, huh, my two terrors? War is irresistible to young knuckleheads like you. Draw, draw and see what a welcome the world has in store. You bet I'm terrified, Sergeant, you would be too if you'd given birth to 'em, each one has a horrible personality defect. (*To Eilif.*) Here. Fish out your ticket. (*Eilif picks a slip of paper. She snatches it from him and unfolds it.*)

Oh I'm an unlucky mother! My womb only ever gave me grief after grief after grief! So young, into the army and then rotting in the ground, grass waving over him, it's hideously clear. You see, you see! A cross! Marked! Your father was a brazen idiot, like you, but you learned from me: think or die. Just like the paper shows. (*She flattens Eilif.*)

ARE YOU GOING TO THINK???!!!

EILIF: Sure, why not?

MOTHER COURAGE: And if they laugh and call you a chicken just cluck at them, who cares?

THE ARMY RECRUITER: If you've crapped your pants we can take your brother instead.

MOTHER COURAGE: Cluck! Cluck! Laugh right back! (*To Swiss Cheese.*) Now you, Swiss Cheese, fish for it. I'm not much worried about you, honest as you are. (*Swiss Cheese draws a slip from the helmet. He stares at it.*)

It's empty, isn't it? It can't be you pulled a black cross, that I'm losing you too, can't be. (*She takes the slip from him.*)

A cross! I guess because he's the simple son? Swiss Cheese, you're also going down unless you're always honest, like I taught you when you were a tiny kid—always bring back exact change from the baker. Otherwise you're lost. See, Sergeant, a black cross, yeah?

THE SERGEANT: Yeah. But I don't get it. I stay back, I never go near the fighting, why'd I get one? (*To the Army Recruiter.*) She's not a swindler, even her own kids get marked.

SWISS CHEESE: Even I'm marked. But I get it, I'm obedient.

MOTHER COURAGE (*to Kattrin*): You're safe, I know it, you won't draw a cross because you are the cross I bear: your good heart. (*She holds the helmet up to Kattrin, but she snatches the slip out herself before Kattrin has a chance.*)

I'm completely desperate. Something's wrong, maybe the way I stirred them. You can't be so kind, Kattrin, not any more, a cross stands athwart the road for you too. Stay quiet always, that should be easy for a mute. So now you all know, safety first, all of you. Back to the wagon and let's get far away from here.

(*Mother Courage hands the Sergeant his helmet and climbs back up on the wagon.*)

THE ARMY RECRUITER (*to the Sergeant*): Do something!

THE SERGEANT: I feel funny.

THE ARMY RECRUITER: You have to wear your hat in wind like this, now you're getting sick. Catch her up in some haggling. (*Loud.*) At least take a look at the merchandise, Sergeant, these nice people have to make a living, right? Wait a minute, lady, the Sergeant here wants a buckle.

MOTHER COURAGE: A half-guilder. Though buckles like mine are worth two guilders easy.

(*She climbs down from the wagon, pulls out a box of belt buckles.*)

THE SERGEANT: It looks like it was chewed on. I'm shivering with this wind, let me look it over back here.

(*He goes behind the wagon.*)

MOTHER COURAGE: Doesn't seem windy to me.

THE SERGEANT: A half-guilder, maybe, it's silver.

MOTHER COURAGE (*going behind the wagon*): Solid six ounces.

THE ARMY RECRUITER (*to Eilif*): And now let's go get drunk, you and me, man to man, I have a pocket full of change.

(*Eilif hesitates, undecided.*)

MOTHER COURAGE: OK, a half-guilder, done deal.

THE SERGEANT: I just don't get it. I stay in the rear, I find a safe place, a sergeant's prerogative, I let the others go for the glory. Now I won't manage to keep my lunch down, I can tell, I'm queasy all of a sudden.

MOTHER COURAGE: Don't let it ruin your appetite. Here, take a slug of schnapps, man, and stick to the rear.

(*She gives him a drink. The Army Recruiter has taken Eilif's arm and is leading him away.*)

THE ARMY RECRUITER: Ten guilders up front, and you're a brave warrior for the King, and all the women go for you. And you can punch me in the mouth for insulting you.

(*They go out. Dumb Kattrin jumps down from the wagon and starts making wild loud noises.*)

MOTHER COURAGE: Wait Kattrin, wait a minute. The Sergeant's paying. (*She bites the half-guilder the Sergeant's given her.*)

I've been burned, Sergeant, never learned to trust money. And now—where's Eilif?

SWISS CHEESE: With the recruiter. Gone.

MOTHER COURAGE (*stands frozen, then*): You're simplicity itself, you are. (*To Kattrin.*) I know, I know, you can't speak, it isn't your fault.

THE SERGEANT: Give yourself a little schnapps, Mama. So goes the world. It's not so terrible, a soldier's life.

MOTHER COURAGE: You have to help your brother pull, Kattrin.

(*Side by side, brother and sister harness themselves to the wagon and pull it away. Mother Courage walks alongside. They exit.*)

THE SERGEANT (*watching them leave*):

If off the war you hope to live,
Take what you can. You'll also give.

TWO

From 1625 to 1626 Mother Courage follows the Swedish Army as it crosses Poland. Near the fort at Wallhof she sees her son again. The lucky sale of a chicken and a great day for the brave son.

The General's tent.

Beside the tent, the kitchen. Cannon fire in the distance. The Cook argues with Mother Courage who hopes to sell him a chicken.

THE COOK: Sixty hellers for that scraggly hen?

MOTHER COURAGE: Scraggly? This fat beast? What, your General, who can outeat anyone from Sweden to Poland and back again, and woe unto the cook who serves him up a skimpy table, he can't up sixty little hellers?

THE COOK: For ten hellers on any street corner I can fetch a dozen birds better looking than that.

MOTHER COURAGE: Sure, sure you can get a fat chicken like this on a street corner with everyone from miles about all withered and skeletal. You'll fetch a rat from the fields, maybe, *maybe,* if you can find one, they've all been eaten, I saw five men chase one rat for hours. Fifty hellers for this, this, what, would you call it, well it's practically a turkey, it's so big. And in the middle of a siege.

THE COOK: We're not in the middle of a siege, it's them up in the fort that are in the middle of the siege, we're the besiegers. Try to keep it straight.

MOTHER COURAGE: Why bother, the besiegers have less food than the besieged. They hauled all the crops and cattle up to the fort before they locked themselves in.

I hear they're swimming in sauce and beer up there. Down here, well, I've been to the farms. Grim. Zilch.

THE COOK: They've got it, the farmers. They hide it.

MOTHER COURAGE (*playing her trump*): They've got nothing, starving, I've seen them, digging roots up out of the ground and sucking their fingers after a meal of boiled leather. And I'm supposed to sell a gourmet capon for forty hellers.

THE COOK: I offered thirty, not forty.

MOTHER COURAGE: This isn't any workaday chicken. He was musically gifted, he'd eat only to the tune of his favorite marches, and he could do arithmetic. All that for forty hellers. If you don't have something to serve him, your General's liable to eat your head.

THE COOK: Know why I'm not worried? (*He spears a piece of beef with his knife and lifts it up.*)

A roast for roasting. I've tendered you my final offer.

MOTHER COURAGE: Roast it, but hurry, it's been dead three weeks and it stinks.

THE COOK: I saw it running across the fields yesterday.

MOTHER COURAGE: Praise Jesus, a dead dog, running around. It's a miracle.

THE COOK: It was a cow, not a dog, and after two hours in a stewpot, it'll be tender as a tit.

MOTHER COURAGE: After five hours, it'll be glue, but say a prayer if the general comes hungry, and keep the pepper handy, I'm telling you, it stinks.

(*The General, a Chaplain and Eilif enter the General's tent. The General claps Eilif's shoulder.*)

THE GENERAL: Come on, son, sit at the right hand of your General. You're a hero and a real Christian and this is a war for God and what's done is done because God wants it done and you did it and I feel fantastic! When we take the goddamned fort I'm going to give you a gold bracelet. We come to set their souls free, and what do they do, these farmers who've happily let centuries of their beefsteak disappear down the gullets of fat Polish priests? They decide to turn their livestock loose so we can't eat. Savages. Ingrates. Stinky little shitpeople. But they'll remember what they learned from you, boy! (*He pours wine into two tin cups, then offers one to Eilif.*)

Here's a can of my best red, we'll bolt it down together. (*Eilif and General gulp down the wine.*)

Chaplain can lap up the dregs, like the suffering Christ he is. Now what's for lunch, heart of my hearts?

EILIF: Umm . . . steak!

THE GENERAL (*screaming to the kitchen*): Cook! Meat!

THE COOK: He knows we're out of everything so he brings guests.

(*Mother Courage gestures to him to be silent, so she can hear what's happening in the tent.*)

EILIF: You really work up an appetite, butchering peasants.

MOTHER COURAGE: Jesus, it's my Eilif.

THE COOK: Who?

MOTHER COURAGE: My eldest. Haven't laid eyes on him for two years, stolen from me on the open road, and he must be in great good favour with the General, his special lunch guest, and what're you going to feed them, nothing! You heard the General: meat! My advice: buy the chicken. Price: one hundred hellers.

THE GENERAL: Lunch, Lamb, you beast-who-barely-learned-to-cook, or I'll hook and gut you!

THE COOK: Oh hell, give it, it's blackmail.

MOTHER COURAGE: This shabby bird?

THE COOK: Just give it to me, it's a sin, fifty hellers for scraggle like that.

MOTHER COURAGE: I said a hundred, one whole guilder. Nothing's too nice for my eldest, the General's special guest.

(*The Cook gives her the money.*)

THE COOK: Plucking included. While I get the fire up.

MOTHER COURAGE (*sitting down, plucking*): The look on his face when he sees it's me! He's my brave, clever boy. I've got another one, stupid but honest. The girl's nothing. At least she's quiet, at least there's that.

(*The General pours another drink. They keep drinking, getting drunker.*)

THE GENERAL: Have another, son, a lip-smacking Falernian,° only one or maybe two kegs left, but I don't begrudge my best for my true believers. Who act! Not like this watery-eyed old simp of a soul-shepherd, he preaches sunup to sundown till the whole church is out cold and snoring but we still haven't taken the goddamned fort and don't ask him how to do it, or how to do anything. You, Eilif, my son, on the other hand, you showed an initiative which eventuated in the requisitioning of twenty head of cattle from some farmers. Which will arrive soon I hope.

EILIF: By morning.

MOTHER COURAGE: That's thoughtful of my Eilif, delivering the oxen tomorrow, otherwise I doubt my chicken would've had such an enthusiastic reception.

THE GENERAL: Regale us!

EILIF: Yep, well, this is the way it went: I heard the farmers were sneaking out at night all hush-hush to round up these cows they were hiding in a woods. They'd arranged a sale of the cows with the people up in the fort. I held back, let the farmers do all the work rounding up the cows—they're good at herding, saved me the work. Meanwhile I got my men good and ready, for two days I fed them only bread and water, so they got crazy for meat, they'd drool if they just heard the word 'meat', if they even heard a word beginning with 'M', like ... um ... 'meat'!

THE GENERAL: You're smart.

EILIF: I dunno. After that it was basically one-two-three. Except the farmers had huge clubs and they outnumbered us three to one and when they saw we wanted their cows they came after us like murder. Four of them got me backed up against a thornbush and one of them clouted the sword from out of my hand and they were hollering 'give up' and I thought right, I give up and you pound me to paste.

THE GENERAL: What'd you do?

EILIF: I started laughing.

THE GENERAL: What?

EILIF: I laughed. So then they wanted to discuss that. So I start bargaining: 'You're fucking kidding, twenty guilders for that ox? More like fifteen tops!' Like we're doing business. Which confuses them, they're scratching their heads. And that's when I picked up my cutlass and I cut their heads off, HUH! HUH! HUH! HUH! All four of them. Necessity trumps the commandments. Right?

THE GENERAL: Want to rule on that, you pious pedant?

THE CHAPLAIN: There's no such exemption in the Bible, in the literal sense, but back then Our Lord could take five loaves of bread and make five hundred, so there was no necessity per se. You can command people to love their neighbours and if they're full of bread they may comply. That was then and this is now.

THE GENERAL (*laughing*): You can say that again. Here, you need to whet your whistle after that, Pharisee.° (*He pours the Chaplain a glass of wine.*)

(*To Eilif.*) You massacred the farmers and now my brave boys'll bite down on a bit of real red meat, and how could God gripe about that? Doesn't His Holy Writ say 'Whateversoever thou dost for the least of My brethren is done for Me'? It'll be like in the old days again, a bit of beef, a gulp of wine and then fight for God.

EILIF: I snatched up my sword and I split their skulls in two!

THE GENERAL: You're a Caesar in the making. You ought to meet His Majesty.

EILIF: I saw him once, distantly. He kind of gives off light. I want to be just like him.

THE GENERAL: You already are. I treasure you, Eilif, brave soldier boy, you're my own son, that's how I'll handle you. (*He leads Eilif to a big map.*)

Here's the picture, Eilif, the whole campaign. So much to do.

(*In the kitchen, Courage stops eavesdropping and resumes plucking the chicken, furious.*)

MOTHER COURAGE: That's one lousy General.

THE COOK: No he's not, he eats to excess but he's good at what he does.

MOTHER COURAGE: If he knew what he was doing he wouldn't need brave soldiers, he could make do with ordinary soldiers. It's when the General's a moron the soldiers have to be brave. It's when the King's pinching his pennies and doesn't hire enough soldiers, every soldier has to be hard-working. You only need brave hard-working patriot soldiers when the country's coming unglued. In a decent country that's properly managed with decent kings and generals, people can be just what people are, common and of middling intelligence and for all I care every one of them a shivering coward. In a decent country that's properly managed.

THE GENERAL: A man like you was born a soldier.

EILIF: My daddy was. A soldier. My mother taught me a song about it.

THE GENERAL: Sing it for me! (*Hollering.*) Where's my goddamn food?!

EILIF: It's called 'The Song about the Soldier and His Wife'.

Falernian: A highly valued wine.

Pharisee: Used to imply that the chaplain is a hypocrite.

(*He sings, doing a sabre dance:*)
'Your gun is precise, and your bayonet's nice—
But the ice on the river won't hold you.
You'll drown in a trice if you march on the ice.
And lonely cold death shall enfold you!'

Thus spoke his wife, as he whetted his knife;
Hoisting his pack he said, 'Marching's my life!
When you're marching no woman can scold you.
When you're marching no woman can scold you.
We're marching into Poland,
Then we're marching off to Spain!
With your bayonet sharpened—
With your sharp bayonet you've no need to explain!
No woman ever controlled you!'

Oh bitter her tears, she was younger in years,
But wiser than he, so she told him.
March off if he must, it will all come to dust—
For only a coffin shall hold him.
Off goes her man, he will write when he can,
And women have wept since the world first began,
And her weeping has often consoled him.
The sound of her sorrow consoled him.

With the moon on the shingles,
Icy white on the snow,
Wave goodbye to your husband!
So long to your husband and then back home you go,
Where you'll wait for the fate you foretold him!
(*Mother Courage, in the kitchen, takes up his song, beating time on a pot with spoon.*)
MOTHER COURAGE (*singing*):
It isn't a joke. Your life is like smoke.
And someday you'll wish you had tarried.
Oh, how quickly you'll fall. Oh God. Help us all.
Soldiers should never get married.
EILIF: Who's that?
MOTHER COURAGE (*singing*):
He tumbled the dice and he soon paid the price:
They gave him his orders to march on the ice.
And the water rose up all around him.
And the water rose up and it drowned him.
Through Poland, through Spain, his poor wife
  searched in vain.
But he'd vanished, and she never found him.
He was gone and his wife never found him.
THE GENERAL: Who told them they could sing in my kitchen?
(*Eilif goes into the kitchen. He sees his mother. He embraces her.*)
EILIF: I missed you! Where's everybody else?
(*Mother Courage stays in his embrace.*)
MOTHER COURAGE: Everyone's fine, stout as trout in a brook. Swiss Cheese is paymaster for the Second Regiment; that keeps him away from fighting, even if I couldn't keep him out of the army.
EILIF: How are your feet?
MOTHER COURAGE: Too swollen for shoes in the morning.
(*The General has joined them.*)

Lotte Lenya as Mother Courage, pulling her wagon in Brecht's 1979 Berliner Ensemble production of his play.

THE GENERAL: So you're his mother! Got any more sons like this one?
EILIF: That's what my luck's like. You happen to be sitting in the kitchen so you can hear your son called a hero.
MOTHER COURAGE: You're goddamned right I heard.
(*She slaps Eilif.*)
EILIF (*holding his cheek*): For taking the oxen?
MOTHER COURAGE: For not surrendering! Four peasants!? Are you nuts?! I taught you always to watch out for yourself! You brazen sticky-fingered fork-tongued son of a Finn!
(*The General and the Chaplain laugh.*)

THREE

Three years later, Mother Courage and the Remnants of the Second Finnish Regiment, still in Poland, are made prisoners of war. Her daughter is saved, and also her wagon, but her honest son dies.
  The army camp.

Afternoon. The regimental flag hangs from a flag-pole. A clothes line stretches from Mother Courage's wagon to the pole, and a variety of merchandise is hanging from it. Near the wagon is a large cannon, on which laundry has been draped for drying. Mother Courage is simultaneously folding clothes that have dried with Kattrin and negotiating the purchase of a sack of bullets with a Quartermaster. Swiss Cheese, in his paymaster's uniform, is watching all this.

Yvette Pottier, a pretty woman, sits nearby drinking brandy and sewing vivid things to her hat. She's in her stocking feet, her red high-heeled shoes lying nearby.

THE QUARTERMASTER: Two guilders. That's cheap for bullets, but I need money now, the Colonel's been on a two-day bender, celebrating with his staff, they drank us dry and where am I supposed to get money for more liquor?

MOTHER COURAGE: Not from me. That's official ammunition, they catch me holding a bag of that, I'll be court-martialled and shot. You crooks sell the soldiers' ammo out from under them, in the thick of battle what're they supposed to do? Throw rocks?

THE QUARTERMASTER: What am I supposed to do when he wants his wine, serve rainwater?

MOTHER COURAGE: It's immoral. I don't want army ammunition. Not for two guilders.

THE QUARTERMASTER: Two little guilders, come on, buy them from me then sell them to the Fourth Regiment's quartermaster, the Fourth's clean out of bullets, he'll give you five guilders for them, eight guilders if you make him out a receipt says he paid twelve guilders, and one hand washes the other and who isn't happy?

MOTHER COURAGE: Go to the Fourth's quartermaster on your own, why do you need me?

THE QUARTERMASTER: I don't trust him and he doesn't trust me, we've been friends for years.

MOTHER COURAGE: Give. (*She takes the sack and gives it to Kattrin.*)

(*To Kattrin*): Stow this in the back and give the man one and a half guilders. (*The Quartermaster starts to complain; she stops him.*)

No more discussion. (*Kattrin drags the sack behind the wagon. The Quartermaster follows her.*)

(*To Swiss Cheese*): Here's your woolens, look after them, it's October and frosty soon, at any rate it should be, who knows, you can't expect anything with any certainty, not even fall following summer. Only one thing must be as must be: and that's your regimental cash box, whatever else is awry, you keep their cash pin-tidy. Is it pin-tidy?

SWISS CHEESE: Yes, Mama.

MOTHER COURAGE: They made you paymaster because you're honest, you're not brave like your brother, they like it that you're too feeble-minded to get your mind around the idea of stealing it. Which puts my mind at ease. Cash in the cash box and where do the woolies go?

SWISS CHEESE: Under my mattress, Mama, except when I'm wearing 'em.

(*He starts to go.*)

THE QUARTERMASTER: Wait for me, paymaster, I'll go with you.

MOTHER COURAGE: Don't teach him your tricks.

(*The Quartermaster walks off with Swiss Cheese. Yvette waves to the Quartermaster as he leaves. He doesn't wave back.*)

YVETTE: Whatever happened to 'So long, nice to meet you'?

MOTHER COURAGE (*to Yvette*): I don't want my Swiss Cheese consorting with people like him, I don't even like to see them walking together, it makes me worry, though in general everything's OK, the war's going well, every other day fresh countries are joining in, it'll last four or five years easily. Thinking ahead and no impulsive moves, I can build a good business. And you, with your disease, don't you know you should lay off the booze?

YVETTE: What disease, it's a lie, who says so?

MOTHER COURAGE: Everybody does.

YVETTE: Everybody lies. I'm panicked, Mother Courage, customers avoid me like the plague, it's like I hung a sign over my cootch saying 'Remember you must die.' Why the hell am I stitching new crap to this fucking hat? (*She throws it to the ground.*)

I never used to drink in the morning, it gives you crow's feet, but so what? Pride isn't for people like us. If you can't learn to eat shit and like it, down you go.

MOTHER COURAGE: Here it comes, the why-oh-why and woe-is-me, your Piping Pieter and how he done you dirt. Just don't start your filthy yowling where my innocent daughter can hear you.

YVETTE: Let her listen, she should learn what it's like to lose a man and spend ten bad years looking everywhere for him, never finding him, she should learn what love is.

MOTHER COURAGE: That's something they never learn.

YVETTE: Then I'll talk just for the relief of talking, I need some relief. It started in Flanders because I was a girl there, if I'd been a girl someplace else I wouldn't have seen him that day, Dutch, blond and thin, and now I'm in Poland just because he cooked for the army, a thin cook. What I didn't know then, Kattrin, is stay away from the thin boys, and also I didn't know he had another girlfriend or that they called him Piping Pieter because even when he did it, he kept his pipe in his mouth, with him doing it was just a casual thing.

(*Yvette sings 'The Song of Fraternisation'.*)
We hated the soldiers,
Their army took our town.
I was sixteen. The foreign occupier
Grinned as he loosened my nightgown.
    May mornings are so bright.
    But comes the dark May night . . .
    The Captain shouts 'You're all dismissed!'
    Then boys with mischief in their eyes
    Will find the girls who fraternise.
    How could I hate him when we kissed?

The foreign occupation
Brought sorrows—and a cook!
By day I would despise him, then when night fell,

I loved the liberties that he took!
    May mornings are so bright.
    But comes the dark May night . . .
    The Captain shouts 'Boys, hit the hay!'
    But one with something on his mind
    Knows just the kind of girl to find.
    We fraternised till day.

My oppressor and my lover
For me were one and the same.
Everyone said, 'Her love's just convenient.'
What we agreed on was my shame.
    A cloud that hid the sun
    Announced my joy was done.
    You have your fun but troops move on.
    You wait all night. Where can he be?
    Your lover and your enemy?
    His army's marching, and he's . . . gone.

(*She stumbles back behind the wagon. As she goes:*)

MOTHER COURAGE: Your hat.

YVETTE: Anyone wants it, be my guest.

(*She goes behind the wagon.*)

MOTHER COURAGE: You heard, Kattrin? Don't start up with soldiers. He tells you he wants to kiss the ground over which your delicate feet have trod—and did you wash your delicate feet yesterday, as long as we're talking about feet—and bang, you're his goat cow mule and whatever else he's itching after. Be happy you're a mute, when you've finally got a husband you'll never contradict yourself or bite your tongue because you told the truth, it's a blessing from God, being dumb. And here comes the General's cook, what brought him?

(*The Cook and the Chaplain enter.*)

THE CHAPLAIN: I bring a message from your son, Eilif, and the cook wanted to accompany me, you've made an impression.

THE COOK: I accompanied you for the exercise and air.

MOTHER COURAGE: Air's free so breathe all you want, just mind your manners, and if you forget, I'm ready for you. (*To the Chaplain.*) So what's Eilif want? I have no extra money.

THE CHAPLAIN: Truth to be told the message is for his brother, Mr Paymaster.

MOTHER COURAGE: He isn't his brother's paymaster. And he's gone, so he can't get led into temptation by bright ideas. (*She takes money from her money belt and hands it to the Chaplain.*)

Give this to him, it's a sin, calculating on maternal instinct and he should be ashamed of himself.

THE COOK: His regiment's marching out, who knows, maybe off to die. Add a little to that pittance, lady, or later on you'll regret. You women come on hard, but later on, you regret. A guy pleads for a glass of brandy, but you're not feeling generous, so the brandy isn't flowing, and he goes off dry, next thing he's dead under the green green ground in some place far away and, oh, you wish you could serve him that brandy now, but forget it, he's gone where you'll never claw him up.

THE CHAPLAIN: Any soldier who falls in a religious war will go straight to heaven, where he can have all the brandy he wants.

THE COOK: Point taken, though still the woman who turns him away without a little brandy to burn his belly should burn with shame, and not because he's a holy kind of soldier—she shouldn't turn him away unrefreshed even if he was just your normal undistinguished infidel infantryman off to meet St Peter with all his venality, shooting and looting, and don't forget a rape here and there, completely unexculpated by virtue of his having done all those things but in the service of his Protestant faith. Thirsty's thirsty is my point.

THE CHAPLAIN (*to Mother Courage, indicating the Cook*): I didn't want him to come with me but he says he's dreaming about you.

THE COOK (*lighting his pipe*): Brandy poured by a slender hand, nothing contemptible on my mind.

MOTHER COURAGE: Who'd say no to a drink?

THE CHAPLAIN: Temptation! shrieked the Bishop, and fell. (*Looking at Kattrin.*) And who is this comely young lady?

MOTHER COURAGE: She isn't comely, she's stay-at-homely and I don't want clergy sniffing up my daughter.

THE COOK: Keep a gimlet eye on this dirty dog, you oughta hear his jokes! Revolting!

(*The Chaplain and the Cook go behind the wagon with Mother Courage. Kattrin watches them leave, then she leaves her washing and goes to Yvette's hat. She puts it on, then sits and puts on the red shoes. From behind the wagon Mother Courage is heard talking politics with the Chaplain and the Cook.*)

MOTHER COURAGE: What's the news from the front?

THE COOK: Nobody knows where that is.

MOTHER COURAGE: It's a mess. It was a nice peaceful invasion, the Swedish king rolled in with his troops and horses and wagons, waving the Protestant flag, he rolled here, he rolled there, he's ready to roll back to Sweden and now, now the Poles break the peace and look, blood's poured down on their heads.

THE COOK: The way I see it is, I knew you'd serve exquisite brandy, I never misread a face.

THE CHAPLAIN: All our King ever wanted was to set Poland free from the tyranny of the Pope and his crony the Kaiser.

(*In front of the wagon, Kattrin, checking to make sure she's not being seen, wearing the hat and shoes, begins imitating Yvette's provocative walk. As she continues she abandons the imitation; she becomes more confident, more mature, a pretty young woman. She even dances a little. The talk behind the wagon is continuous.*)

THE COOK: Absolutely. Liberty! Everybody craves liberty, the human body needs it like it needs water or bread or salt. Who knows why we need liberty? What humans need is a mystery. Who knows why we need salt? We need what we need.

THE CHAPLAIN: Amen.

THE COOK: But it's expensive, liberty, especially when you start exporting it to other countries, so the King has to levy a tax on salt back home in Sweden, so his own subjects are free but they can't afford salt, or, well, the poor can't afford it, the rich can afford anything, even when it's taxed and pricey, and even better, the rich get tax exemptions!

THE CHAPLAIN: You shouldn't mock liberty. It's—

THE COOK: Who's mocking?

MOTHER COURAGE: He isn't mocking anything, he's a cook, cooks have an intellectual bent, not like preachers.

THE COOK: I'm talking about the human body.

MOTHER COURAGE: Right.

THE COOK: A lovely thing, the human body.

THE CHAPLAIN: Created in God's image.

THE COOK: You bet. Given half a chance, it'll do a little jig. It's stubborn, though. The body. Or is that the soul? Preacher I get confused.

THE CHAPLAIN: I'm sure you do.

THE COOK: It's the wanting that makes 'em stubborn, is my point. So sometimes you have to torture the people—which by the way adds to the cost of the war, since contrary to expectations the Poles have preferred to remain unliberated, the King's tried everything, the rack and the screw and prisons are expensive, and when the King discovered they didn't want to be free, even after torture, he stopped having any fun. But God told our King to fight, He didn't say it'd be fun, and it isn't much fun, is it, though since I cook for the General I have table salt at least, and the rest of it's beyond me, what bodies want and what bodies get, and it's a good thing the King's got God going for him. Or else people might suspect that he's just in it for what he can take out of it. But he's always had his principles, our King, and with his clear conscience he doesn't get depressed.

MOTHER COURAGE: Long live Gustavus Adolphus, the Hero-King. About whom a certain kind of talk is unhealthy.

THE CHAPLAIN (to the Cook): You eat his bread.

THE COOK: I don't eat it, I bake it.

MOTHER COURAGE: The King will never be defeated, and why, his people believe in him, and why? Precisely because everyone knows he's in the war to make a profit. If he wasn't, little people like me would smell disaster in the war and steer away from it. If it's business, it makes sense.

THE COOK: Here's to the little people like you.

THE CHAPLAIN: Hey, Dutchman, it would be advisable to cast a glance at the Swedish flag that's flying overhead before sharing your opinions so liberally.

MOTHER COURAGE: No harm done. Nobody here but us Protestants! Alley-oop!

(They toast and drink, we hear the clink of their glasses. Suddenly cannon thunder and rifle shots are heard. Mother Courage, the Cook and the Chaplain rush around from behind the wagon, the Cook and Chaplain with brandy glasses in hand.)

MOTHER COURAGE: What's happened? (The Quartermaster and a Soldier rush in and begin to wheel the cannon away, clothes hanging all over it.)
I have to take the laundry down first, you idiots.

(She scrambles to retrieve her laundry.)

THE QUARTERMASTER: The Catholics! Attacking! There wasn't any warning, I don't know if we have time to— (An increase in the sound of fighting, drums and alarms.)
(To the soldier.) Do something about the cannon!

(The Quartermaster runs away. The Soldier tries with all his might to move the cannon, which won't budge.)

THE COOK: Better get back to my General, if they haven't shot him he'll be screaming for dinner. Look for me, Courage, I'll be back for more political debate.

(He starts to leave.)

MOTHER COURAGE: You're leaving your pipe!

THE COOK (exiting): Keep it for me, I'll need it.

MOTHER COURAGE: Of course, just when we're starting to clear a profit the sky falls in.

THE CHAPLAIN: I'll be making tracks myself, if the enemy breaks through there's apt to be serious trouble. Blessed are the peaceable, that's my battle cry. I need a big cloak for camouflage.

MOTHER COURAGE: I'm not lending cloaks or anything else, not if it costs your life. I've gone that route before.

THE CHAPLAIN: But my religious calling puts me in particular jeopardy.

(She hands him a cloak.)

MOTHER COURAGE: This rubs against my better impulses. Now get lost.

THE CHAPLAIN: Many thanks, it's big-hearted of you, but on further consideration it might be better to settle here for a bit.

MOTHER COURAGE (turning to the Soldier struggling with the cannon): Drop it you donkey, who's paying you to do that? I'll watch it for you, it's not worth your life.

THE SOLDIER (running away): You can tell them I tried!

MOTHER COURAGE: I'll swear on the Bible. (She sees her daughter with Yvette's hat.)
What're you doing in that hooker's hat? Take that off, are you cracked? Now, with the enemy coming? (She tears the hat off Kattrin's head.)
You want them stumbling across you and making you their whore? And you've put on the shoes too, haven't you, you scarlet Babylonian?! Take 'em off, now now now! (Courage tries to yank the shoes off Kattrin's feet. Then she turns to the Chaplain.)
Jesus, help me, Pastor, get her shoes off. I'll be back in a minute.

(She runs to the wagon. Yvette comes in, powdering herself.)

YVETTE: Is it the Catholics? Oh please God let it be the Catholics! Where's my hat? (She sees the hat on the ground.) Who stomped on it? I can't run around in that, not if it's Catholics, they're finnicky about costumes. I gotta get to a mirror. And where are the shoes? (She looks around for them, not seeing them, because Kattrin has hidden her feet under her skirt.)
They were here when I left them. I'll have to walk back to my tent barefoot. It's mortifying. (To the Chaplain.) What do you think? Too heavy with the make-up?

THE CHAPLAIN: You're perfect.

(*Yvette leaves. Swiss Cheese runs in, carrying a metal cash box. Mother Courage comes out of the wagon, her hands full of soot.*)

MOTHER COURAGE (*to Kattrin*): Here. Soot. For you. (*To Swiss Cheese.*) What're you lugging there?

SWISS CHEESE: It's the regimental cash box.

MOTHER COURAGE: Get rid of that! You're not the pay-master any more.

SWISS CHEESE: I am. It's my responsibility.

(*He goes behind the wagon.*)

MOTHER COURAGE (*to the Chaplain*): Take off your cleri-cal get-up, Pastor, they'll see it under the cloak. (*She rubs soot all over Kattrin's face.*)

Hold still! A little filth, a little bit safer. What a di-saster! Bet the sentries guarding the camp got drunk. Hide your light under a bushel, just like they say. A soldier sees a girl with a clean face, watch out! When he's done raping her, he calls for his buddies. (*Looking at Kattrin's face.*) That oughta do it. Let me look. Not bad. Like you've been rolling in shit. Don't shiver. Now nothing will happen to you. (*To Swiss Cheese.*) Where'd you leave the cash box?

SWISS CHEESE: I figured it should go in the wagon.

MOTHER COURAGE (*horrified*): In my wagon? Of all the godforsaken blockheadedness. If I don't watch every second! They'll hang us, all three of us!

SWISS CHEESE: Then I'll put it someplace else, or I could take it and run away.

MOTHER COURAGE: Stay here, too late for that.

(*The Chaplain, changing his clothes, notices the regimental flag.*)

THE CHAPLAIN: Oh my goodness, the flag!

(*Mother Courage takes down the flag.*)

MOTHER COURAGE: Holy crap! Blinded by habit! I've flown it for twenty-five years. (*The cannons' thunder gets louder.*)

(*Mid-morning, three days later. The cannon that had been next to the wagon is gone. Mother Courage, Kattrin, Swiss Cheese and the Chaplain, nervous, bur-dened, eating together.*)

SWISS CHEESE: It's three days now and I'm wasting time sitting around and the Sergeant, who was always nice to me even when I made mistakes, has finally got to be asking himself: where's that Swiss Cheese gone with the regimental cash box?

MOTHER COURAGE: Just be glad they haven't come sniff-ing around here.

THE CHAPLAIN: Amen. Unobjectionable is our only hope. He whose heart is full of woe must sing out loud, as they say, but God and all the apostles forfend I should start singing now! I don't know any Latin hymns.

MOTHER COURAGE: One's got his cash box and the other's got an ecclesiastical sense of humour and I'm stuck between the two and I don't know which is worse.

THE CHAPLAIN: Even now God's watching over us.

MOTHER COURAGE: Which explains why I'm not sleeping well. God and your cash box keep me awake. I think I've straightened my own position out. I told them

I was a good Catholic and adamantly opposed to Satan, I'd seen him, Satan, he's a Swede with ram's horns. I stopped to ask if they knew where I could buy votive candles. I've got that churchy talk down pat. I know they knew I was lying but they don't have any commissary wagons, so they squint a little. It could still work out well for us. We're prisoners, but so are head lice.

THE CHAPLAIN: It's good milk. Albeit available only in small quantities, we may have to curb our Swedish appetites. Since we're defeated.

MOTHER COURAGE: Victory, defeat, depends on your per-spective. Defeat is frequently profitable for underdogs. Honour's lost, but what's that? What works out best for us is what they call paralysis, a shot here, a shot there, one step forward, one back, and troops going no place needing provisions. (*To Swiss Cheese.*) Eat!

SWISS CHEESE: I don't want to eat. How's the Sergeant going to pay the soldiers?

MOTHER COURAGE: They're retreating, they don't get paid when they're retreating.

SWISS CHEESE: If they don't get paid to do it they shouldn't retreat.

MOTHER COURAGE: Swiss Cheese, your conscientiousness is terrifying. Since you're stupid I decided to raise you to be honest but really it's getting out of hand. Now I'm taking the Chaplain to buy a Catholic flag and some meat. Nobody noses out good meat like the Chaplain, when there's good meat anywhere in the area you can tell because there are little spit bubbles in the corners of his mouth and his lips get shiny. Everything's going to be all right as long as they let me do business. Prot-estant pants cover your ass same as any other.

THE CHAPLAIN: Martin Luther met a priest who was beg-ging for alms by the side of the road. Luther said to the beggar priest, 'After I turn the world inside out we won't need priests!' 'Maybe not,' said the priest, 'but you'll still need beggars,' and he went on his way. (*Mother Courage has gone into the wagon.*)

That cash box is weighing on her. Everyone thinks we all belong to the wagon, but how long before they come to investigate?

SWISS CHEESE: I can take it someplace else.

THE CHAPLAIN: That could mean trouble for us all if they catch you doing it. They've got spies everywhere. Yes-terday morning I was relieving myself in an open-air latrine. I'd just started to squat when a spy jumped up! Right out of the latrine!

SWISS CHEESE: He was in the latrine?

THE CHAPLAIN: Yes! *In* the latrine!

SWISS CHEESE: Why was he in the latrine?

THE CHAPLAIN: Sniffing out Protestants! Probably sleeps down there. This one was a little stump of a man with a patch over his eye. I screamed and almost ejaculated a prayer in Swedish, which would have been the end of me.

(*Mother Courage climbs down from the wagon with a basket.*)

MOTHER COURAGE: And what have I found, you shame-less nothing? (*In triumph she holds up the red shoes.*) Yvette's red shoes! She's a cold-blooded thief! (*To the

Chaplain.) You led her straight into this, telling her she was comely! (*Putting the shoes in her basket.*) I'm returning them. Stealing Yvette's shoes! She does what she does to make a living, I understand that. But you'll give it for nothing, hoping for a little fun. But until peace comes you have no business having hopes, you hear me? None!

THE CHAPLAIN: Everyone's entitled to have hopes.

MOTHER COURAGE: Not her! I'm her mother, not you! Let her be like a stone in Darlarna. One grey stone among many grey stones as far as the eye can see, and all silent, that's how I want it with her. That way nothing ever happens to her. (*To Swiss Cheese.*) Listen up you, leave that cash box right where it is. And keep a close eye on your sister, she needs watching. Raising kids! It'd be easier turning weasels into house pets.

(*She leaves with the Chaplain. Kattrin clears the dishes from their meal.*)

SWISS CHEESE: Not many days left when people can sit out in the sun in their shirtsleeves. (*Kattrin points to a tree.*)

That's what I mean, the leaves turned yellow. (*Kattrin gestures to ask him if he wants something to drink.*)

I won't drink. I have to think. (*Pause.*)

She said she isn't sleeping. I should take the cash box someplace else, I found a secret place for it. All right, now I will have a drink. (*Kattrin goes behind the wagon.*)

There are mole rills down by the river, I'll stick it down into one, then I'll fetch it back. Maybe tonight just before morning and I'll take it to the regiment. It's been three days, how far have they retreated? The Sergeant's eyes are going to bug out of his head. 'Swiss Cheese, I am pleasantly disappointed,' is what he's going to say. 'I trusted you would take care of the regimental cash box and you did.'

(*Kattrin is coming from behind the wagon with a glass of brandy when she runs into two men suddenly standing there. One is a Sergeant, and the other, bowing, sweeps the ground before him with his hat. He wears an eyepatch over one eye.*)

THE ONE WITH THE EYEPATCH: Nominy dominy, pretty girlie. Seen anyone around here from the HQ of the Second Finnish Regiment?

(*Kattrin, badly frightened, runs to Swiss Cheese at the front of the wagon, spilling brandy, making gestures, including something about an eyepatch. The two men look at one another and, after seeing Swiss Cheese, they disappear.*)

SWISS CHEESE (*startled out of a reverie*): You spilled half of it. Why are you being silly? Did you stab yourself in the eye? I don't understand. I have to go someplace else, I decided, that's what I have to do. (*He stands to leave. She frantically tries to explain the danger to him, to stop him. He gets around her.*)

I wish I knew what you mean. It's something important, you poor mutt, you just can't explain what. Don't worry about the brandy, I'm sure I'll have lots of chances to drink brandy, a little spilt brandy, so what? (*He goes into the wagon and returns with the cash box, which he stuffs under his jacket. Kattrin grabs him.*)

I'll be back in two shakes. Don't hold on to me, or else I'll have to pinch you. Probably you mean something important. I wish you could talk.

(*He kisses her and pulls himself away. He leaves. Kattrin runs back and forth, gesticulating frantically, grunting, trying to make words. The Chaplain and Mother Courage return. Kattrin storms around her mother.*)

MOTHER COURAGE: What then, what then? You're falling into pieces. Did somebody do something to you? Where's Swiss Cheese? (*Trying to calm her.*) One thing, and then the next thing, Kattrin, not all jumbled. Your mother understands you. The biscuit-brains took the money box? I'll twist his ears right off him! Slow down and stop all this flurry, use your hands, I hate it when you moan like a dog, what's the pastor going to think? You'll make his skin crawl. There was a one-eyed man?

THE CHAPLAIN: The one with one eye, he's a spy. They arrested Swiss Cheese? (*Kattrin nods 'yes'.*)

It's over.

(*Mother Courage takes the Catholic flag out of her basket.*)

MOTHER COURAGE: Raise the new flag!

(*The Chaplain affixes it to the flagpole.*)

THE CHAPLAIN (*bitterly*): Good Catholics now, root and branches.

(*Voices are heard. The two men drag in Swiss Cheese.*)

SWISS CHEESE: Let me go, I'm not carrying anything. Stop yanking on my shoulder, I didn't do anything wrong.

THE SERGEANT: He came from here. You know each other.

MOTHER COURAGE: We do? From where?

SWISS CHEESE: I don't know them. Who knows who they are? I don't know anything about them. I bought my lunch from them, ten hellers it cost me. Maybe you saw me sitting here, too salty to boot.

THE SERGEANT: Who are you, huh?

MOTHER COURAGE: Ordinary people. It's just like he said, he bought lunch. For him it was oversalted.

THE SERGEANT: You want me to believe you don't know each other?

MOTHER COURAGE: Why should I know him? I don't know everyone. I don't ask names or if someone's a heathen; if you pay up, you're not a heathen. (*To Swiss Cheese.*) Are you a heathen?

SWISS CHEESE: Not at all.

THE CHAPLAIN: He was an orderly customer and he never opened his mouth, except when he ate. Then you more or less have to.

THE SERGEANT: And who are you?

MOTHER COURAGE: He serves my liquor. And you're thirsty, he'll fetch you a glass of brandy, you've got to be parched and melting.

THE SERGEANT: No booze when we're working. (*To Swiss Cheese.*) You had something with you. You hid it near the river. Your shirt was all puffed out when you left here.

MOTHER COURAGE: You're sure it was him?

SWISS CHEESE: Must've been somebody else. I saw a guy run away from here in a big puffy shirt. But that wasn't me.

MOTHER COURAGE: I agree with him, you're confused, that can happen. I know a good person when I see one, I'm Courage, you've probably heard of me, everybody knows me, and I'm telling you, he seems honest to me.

THE SERGEANT: We're after the cash box of the Second Finnish Regiment. And we know what he looks like, the guy responsible for it. We've been looking for him for two days. You're it.

SWISS CHEESE: I'm not it.

THE SERGEANT: And if you don't hand it over you're dead, you know that. Where is it?

MOTHER COURAGE (*urgent*): Of course he'd give it to you if he knew his life depended on it. Right here, he'd say, I have it, you're stronger than me. He's not that dumb. Do it already, you goose, the Sergeant here is trying to help you.

SWISS CHEESE: If I don't have it.

THE SERGEANT: Let's go, then. We'll help you find it.

(*The two men drag Swiss Cheese away.*)

MOTHER COURAGE (*calling after them*): He'd tell you. He's not that stupid. And don't wrench his shoulder like that! (*She runs after them.*)

(*Evening of the same day. The Chaplain and dumb Kattrin are washing glasses and polishing knives.*)

THE CHAPLAIN: These traps into which one falls, they're not unfamiliar from our Devotional tales. It reminds me a little of the Passion of our Lord and Saviour. There's a very old song about that.

(*He sings the 'Song of the Hours'.*)
In the first hour of the day
Our Lord finally knows that
Like a murderer he'll be judged by
Heathen Pontius Pilate.

Pilate shall refuse the blame
Wash his hands in water
Then the innocent condemned
Sent off to the slaughter.

In the third hour God's own son
Flails and scourges flayed him
On his head a thorny crown
That the soldiers made him.

Dressed in rags and mockery
They beat him and deride him
And the cross of his own death
He'll drag along beside him.

In the sixth hour, naked, cold
On the cross they staved him
As his blood spilled down he prayed
For his father to save him.

One thief laughed and one thief wept
As he died beside them
While the sun withdrew its light
Hoping thus to hide them.

Jesus screamed by hour nine
Why does God forsake him
In his mouth a bitter gall
Vinegar to slake him.

At last he gave up the ghost
Mountains disassembled
Temple veils were rent in twain
And the whole world trembled.

Dark and sudden night time fell
The mocking crowd was scattered
Jesus's sides were torn by spears
The two thieves' bones were shattered.

Still the blood and water flows
Sill their mocking laughter
Thus befell the Son of Man
And many people after.

(*Mother Courage comes in, very worried, upset.*)

MOTHER COURAGE: He's strung up between life and death. But the Sergeant's still open to talking. And taking. Only we can't let on that Swiss Cheese is ours, they'll say we helped him. It's just about money. But where are we going to get money? Yvette's snagged herself a colonel, maybe he's interested in getting her started selling merchandise. Where is she? She said she'd hurry.

THE CHAPLAIN: You're going to sell her the wagon?

MOTHER COURAGE: How else get the money the Sergeant's demanding?

THE CHAPLAIN: How will you make a living?

MOTHER COURAGE: That's it, isn't it?

(*Yvette comes in with a decrepit Colonel. She embraces Mother Courage.*)

YVETTE: Courage, my love, long time no see! (*Whispering.*) It's a go. (*Loud again.*) This is my dear pal and business advisor, Poldi. Poldi, Courage. I hear you're looking to sell your wagon owing to exigent circumstances. It got me thinking.

MOTHER COURAGE: Pawn it, not sell it, don't trip over yourself, it's not so easy to find a good wagon in war-time. Two hundred guilders.

YVETTE (*disappointed*): Pawn? I thought it was for sale. (*To the Colonel.*) What's your opinion?

THE COLONEL: Your opinion's my opinion, honey.

MOTHER COURAGE: It's only up for pawning.

YVETTE: I thought you needed the money.

MOTHER COURAGE (*decisively*): No way around it, the wagon's our life. This is a good thing for you, Yvette, who knows when something like this'll come your way again? You front me the money and when I redeem the pawn, you pocket a tidy profit, you never made such easy money, your nice old pal there agrees with me. (*To the Colonel.*) I'm right, huh? What's his name? Mouldy?

YVETTE: Poldi. And he thinks we should keep looking for something we can buy. Don't you, Poldi?

THE COLONEL: That's what I think.

MOTHER COURAGE: You keep looking then, maybe you'll find something you want, two or three weeks of looking is all it should take, just pray Poldi holds up, but you better hurry, he looks wobbly to me.

YVETTE: I'm happy shopping with you, Poldi. You don't mind looking around for a few weeks, do you, so long as we're always together? There are lots of places to look.

THE COLONEL (*to Mother Courage*): Well, baby girl, my knees go all stiff in this weather, I—

MOTHER COURAGE: I'll pay it back, quick as possible, with interest.

YVETTE: I'm all confused, Poldi, *chéri*, advise me. (*She takes the Colonel aside.*)
    We should give her the cash, let her pawn it, we'll own the wagon outright in the end, where's she gonna get two hundred guilders from to redeem it? I don't have two hundred guilders, but I can get money from that young blond lieutenant with the enormous feet. Know who I mean, Poldi? He's always waving it at me!

THE COLONEL: You don't need him, I told you I'd buy it for you, didn't I, baby bunny?

YVETTE: Oh, but it's indecent taking money from someone you love when you aren't married to him, though if in your opinion the lieutenant is inclined to exploit a situation, I'll let you do it.

THE COLONEL: I insist.

YVETTE: I'll find some way to pay you back.

THE COLONEL: I hate that lieutenant!

YVETTE: I know. (*She goes back to Mother Courage.*)
    My friend advises me to accept. Write out a receipt that the wagon's mine, after two weeks, and everything in it. I'll bring your two hundred guilders straight away. (*To the Colonel.*) Run back to the camp, I'll be right behind you. I just want to take stock so nothing'll go missing from my wagon. (*She kisses the Colonel and he leaves. She climbs up into the wagon.*)
    (*Inside the wagon.*) You've got boots, but not many.

MOTHER COURAGE: Yvette, there's no time for that! You have to go talk to that Sergeant, tell him the money's coming, there's not a minute to spare.

YVETTE (*inside the wagon*): Let me just take a second count of these linen shirts.

(*Mother Courage grabs hold of Yvette's skirt and pulls her down from the wagon.*)

MOTHER COURAGE: Leave it for now, jackal, or it's over for Swiss Cheese. And not a word who's making this offer. It came from your lover, swear that on God's good name, otherwise we'll all be implicated, his accomplices, we sheltered him.

YVETTE: Calm down, I'll take care of it, One-Eye's meeting me behind those trees, over there.

THE CHAPLAIN: And when you make your first offer, it doesn't have to be the whole two hundred up front, start with one hundred and fifty, that's perfectly ample.

MOTHER COURAGE (*to the Chaplain*): It's your money? Please, butt out. You'll still get your soup, now go haggle somewhere else, this is his life.

(*She shoos Yvette on her way.*)

THE CHAPLAIN: Apologies for interfering, but if you give them the full two hundred, how are you going to live, to earn money? With your unemployable daughter hanging around your neck.

MOTHER COURAGE: I'm counting on that regimental cash box, genius. When Swiss Cheese is free he'll bring it back to us, we can take out money to cover expenses.

I'll redeem the pawn, we'll get the wagon back when we get the cash box. (*To Kattrin.*) You, polish the knives, use the pumice stone. (*To the Chaplain.*) And you, leave off posing like Christ on Mount Olive, wash the glasses, by evening we'll have fifty suppers to serve. Thank God they're corrupt. They aren't wolves, they're just men after money. Corruption is the human equivalent of God's Mercy. As long as someone's on the take you can buy lighter sentences, so even the innocent have a shot at justice.

(*Yvette enters, winded.*)

YVETTE: Two hundred even. I'll go get the money from my Colonel, fast, soon it'll be too late, already he's sentenced to die. They used the thumbscrews, he confessed that he had the cash box. He told them when he saw he was being followed he threw it in the river.

MOTHER COURAGE: The cash box? He threw it in the . . .

YVETTE: It's gone. I'm gonna run and get the money from my Colonel.

MOTHER COURAGE: But if the cash box is gone, how will I get back my two hundred guilders?

YVETTE: Oh, of course, damn I'm stupid, you were hoping to take it outa that cash box! I shoulda known you'd find an angle. Well, give that up, you'll have to pay if you want Swiss Cheese back, or maybe you want to forget the whole deal, and you can keep your wagon?

MOTHER COURAGE: I hadn't anticipated this. Don't panic, you'll get the wagon, it's lost, I had it seventeen years. I need more time to think, what to do, I can't do two hundred, you should've bargained them down. If I'm left without anything, any stranger who wants to can have me in a ditch. Go and tell them I can't do two hundred, I'll give them a hundred twenty guilders, the wagon's lost regardless.

YVETTE: They're not going to agree. One-Eye's rushing me, he keeps looking with that one eye to see if someone's watching. He's scared. I have to offer the whole two hundred!

MOTHER COURAGE (*despairing*): I can't! I worked thirty years. She's twenty-five and she hasn't got a husband. She's mine as well. Stop tearing at me, I know what I'm doing. Tell them a hundred twenty and that's that.

YVETTE: Your choice.

(*She leaves. Mother Courage, avoiding looking at the Chaplain or her daughter, sits and helps Kattrin with the knives.*)

MOTHER COURAGE (*to the Chaplain*): Don't break any glasses, they don't belong to us now. (*To Kattrin.*) Pay attention, you'll cut yourself. Swiss Cheese will be back, I'll pay the two hundred if that's the only way. You'll get your brother back. With eighty guilders we can provision a rucksack with goods and start over. It's same game everywhere, you want to cook, you cook with water.

THE CHAPLAIN: The Lord will steer us right, as they say.

MOTHER COURAGE: Dry them carefully.

(*They scour the knives, silent. Suddenly Kattrin bursts into tears, hurries behind the wagon. Yvette runs in.*)

YVETTE: They said no deal. I warned you. One-Eye wants to drop the whole business, he says it's nearly over, in a minute we're going to hear the drums, the rifles are loaded. I went up to one hundred fifty. He didn't budge, not a flicker. I begged him to wait till I talked to you.

MOTHER COURAGE: Tell him I'll pay two hundred. Run. (*Yvette runs out. They sit in silence. The Chaplain has stopped cleaning the glasses.*)

Seems to me, I haggled too long.

(*Drums are heard in the distance. The Chaplain stands and goes behind the wagon. Courage remains seated. It gets dark. The drumroll stops. Then it gets light again. Mother Courage sits, motionless. Yvette enters, ashen.*)

YVETTE: Look what you've done with your haggling and hanging on. He got eleven bullets, eleven bullets, it was enough. It's not worth it, worrying about the likes of you. But they don't believe he threw the cash box in the river. They suspect it's been here all along, that you were working with him. So they're bringing him here, maybe you'll give yourself away when you see him. I warn you, you don't know him, or you're all dead. Should I take Kattrin away?

(*Mother Courage shakes her head 'no'.*)

MOTHER COURAGE: She knows. Fetch her.

(*Yvette gets Kattrin, who goes to her mother and stands beside her. Mother Courage takes her hand. Two soldiers enter with a stretcher on which something is lying, covered with a sheet. The Sergeant follows. They put the stretcher on the ground.*)

THE SERGEANT: Here's somebody, we don't know his name. It's got to be entered in the record, everything in its place. He bought a meal from you. Look and see if you know him. (*He takes the sheet away.*)

Know him? (*Mother Courage shakes her head.*)

You never saw him before you served him supper? (*Mother Courage shakes her head.*)

Lift him up. Throw him in the pit. He's got no one who knows him. (*They carry him away.*)

FOUR

Mother Courage sings 'The Song of the Great Capitulation'.

In front of an officer's tent. Mother Courage is waiting. A Clerk looks out from inside the tent.

THE CLERK: I know you. You're the one who was hiding that Protestant paymaster. Think twice before you make any complaints.

MOTHER COURAGE: I'm making a complaint. I hid nobody, and if I just take what they did to me it'll look like I think I'm guilty of something. They cut my wagon and my entire inventory to ribbons with their sabres, and then they charged me a five thaler fine, and all for having done nothing, less than nothing.

THE CLERK: Listen to what I'm telling you, it's for your own good: we don't have many merchandise wagons, so we'll let you stay in business, provided you assuage your guilty conscience by paying the necessary fines. And keep your mouth shut.

MOTHER COURAGE: I want to make a complaint.

THE CLERK: Be my guest. Wait here for the Captain's convenience.

(*He goes back into the tent. A Young Soldier enters, furious. An Older Soldier is running after him.*)

THE YOUNG SOLDIER: By the Holy Virgin's Flowerbush where's that goddamned sonofabitch of a Captain who withheld my bonus and then spent it on his whores' bar tab? Time to pay up!

THE OLDER SOLDIER: Aw Jesus, they're gonna slam you in the stocks!

THE YOUNG SOLDIER: Come out, you crook! I'm gonna butcher you! Refusing me my bonus after I was the only one willing to swim that river, the only one in the whole battalion, and I can't even buy a beer for myself. I'm not letting myself get fucked like this. You come outside now and let me cut your fucking head off!

(*The Older Soldier restrains the Young Soldier, who's trying to get into the tent.*)

THE OLDER SOLDIER: Sweet Christ, he's gonna mess everything up for himself.

MOTHER COURAGE: They screwed him out of his bonus?

THE YOUNG SOLDIER: Let go of me or I'll murder you too, he's gonna get hung out to dry, it's gotta happen.

THE OLDER SOLDIER: He rescued the Colonel's horse but then they didn't give the bonus like they're supposed to. He's young, he hasn't learned.

MOTHER COURAGE: Let him loose, he's not a dog, a man doesn't have to be put on a leash. A bonus is a bonus and it's perfectly reasonable to expect to be paid. Why else bother being brave?

THE YOUNG SOLDIER: He's drinking in there! You all shit yourselves for fear of him. I stepped up and stood out and now I get my bonus pay!

MOTHER COURAGE: Don't bark at me, son. I've got problems of my own, and anyway you should spare your big fine voice—if all you can do is whisper when the Captain comes out, he won't haul your ass to the stocks. People who shout the way you're shouting are hoarse in half an hour and so exhausted anyone can sing them to sleep.

THE YOUNG SOLDIER: I'm not exhausted and who could sleep this hungry? The bread's made out of acorn mash and hemp seed and now they're cutting back on that. He spent my bonus on whores and I'm starving. He's gonna pay!

MOTHER COURAGE: I get it, you're hungry. I remember last year when your general ordered you guys to march back and forth across the cornfields—I could've sold boots for ten guilders a pair if I'd had any boots to sell. He planned to be elsewhere by now, but here he is, a year later, bogged down, and there's no corn and everyone's starving. I get it, you're angry.

THE YOUNG SOLDIER: Stop talking to me, I don't give a shit about any of that, I won't let myself be treated unfairly.

MOTHER COURAGE: How long? How long will you refuse to be treated unfairly? An hour, two? See, never occurs to you to ask yourself that, and that's the first thing you should ask, 'cause it's no good figuring it out later, after all the skin on your back has been flayed off with the whipping you'll get for insubordination, after the whip's blistered all the skin off you and you're raw and bleeding, in chains praying for death it hurts so bad, then it's a little late to realise that maybe, on second thoughts, actually you can live with being treated unfairly.

THE YOUNG SOLDIER: Why am I listening to you? By the Holy Mother's Bush! CAPTAIN!

MOTHER COURAGE: I'll tell you why you're listening: I'm right and you know it, your fury's just a lightning bolt that splits the air, bright, noisy, then BANG!—all over. It was short-lived anger, when what you needed was long-burning rage, but where would you get something like that?

THE YOUNG SOLDIER: You're saying I don't have a right to get paid what I'm owed?

MOTHER COURAGE: Just the opposite. You have a right, but you have a short-lived anger and that'll never get you what you want. If you had long-lasting rage, I'd cheer you on. Hack the sonofabitch to death, I'm right behind you, but what if you cool down smack in the middle of it, and he doesn't get hacked up, because your hard-on's gone all of a sudden? There I am, standing there, you've slunk off and the Captain blames me.

THE OLDER SOLDIER: You're right, he'll settle down, he just went a little crazy.

THE YOUNG SOLDIER: You'll see, I'm gonna cut his throat. (He draws his sword.)

As soon as he sets his foot out here I'm gonna do it. (The Clerk comes out.)

THE CLERK: The Captain'll be out soon. Sit.

(The Young Soldier sits.)

MOTHER COURAGE: They say sit, he sits. Like I said. Sitting pretty. They know us so well, what makes us tick. Sit! And we sit. And sitting people don't make trouble. (The Young Soldier starts to stand.)

Better not stand up again, you won't be standing the way you did before. (He sits back down.)

Hope you're not embarrassed on my account, I'm not better than you, worse if anything. We had gumption. They bought it, all of it. Why kick, might hurt business. It's called the Great Capitulation.

(She sings 'The Song of the Great Capitulation'.)
Back when I was young, fresh as grass and innocent,
Any day, I'd fly away on butterfly wings.

(Speaking.) Not just a peddler's daughter, me with my good looks and my talent and my longing for a better life!

(Singing.)
If my soup was cold, or the meat they served me
    wasn't succulent,
Back it went, it's worth the wait for nicer things.

(Speaking.) All or nothing, next best is no good at all, everyone makes her own luck, I don't take orders from anyone.

(Singing.)
Birdsong up above:
Push comes to shove.

Soon you fall down from the grandstand
And join the players in the band
Who tootle out that melody:
Wait, wait and see.
And then: it's all downhill.
Your fall was God's will.
Better let it be.

But within a year, I would eat what I was served.
And I learned, you smile and take your medicine.

(Speaking.) Two kids hanging on my neck and the price of bread and everything it takes from you.

(Singing.)
I'd accepted that I only got the shit that I deserved
On my ass, or on my knees, I took it with a grin.

(Speaking.) You have to learn to make deals with people, one hand washes the other one, your head's not hard enough to knock over a wall.

(Singing.)
Birdsong from above:
Push comes to shove.
Soon you fall down from your grandstand
And join the players in the band
Who tootle out that melody:
Wait, wait and see.
And then: it's all downhill.
Your fall was God's will.
Better let it be.

Many folk I've known planned to scale the highest peak.
Off they go, the starry sky high overhead.

(Speaking.) To the victor the spoils, where there's a will there's a way, at least act like you own the store.

(Singing.)
Stone by stone you climb, but your efforts only
    leave you worn and weak,
Broken down, you barely make it back to bed.

(Speaking.) If the shoe fits, wear it.

(Singing.)
From the God of Love:
Push comes to shove.
And you fall down from that grandstand
And join the players in the band
Who tootle out that melody:
Wait, wait and see.
And then; it just goes downhill,
Who knows? It's God's will.
Best to leave it be.

(Speaking, to the Young Soldier.) Stay here with your sword ready if your anger is great enough, because you're in the right, I know you are, but if your anger's only a flash, better to run away.

THE YOUNG SOLDIER: Go fuck yourself in hell.

(He stumbles out, the Older Soldier following him. The Clerk sticks his head out of the tent.)

THE CLERK: The Captain's ready. You can make your complaint now.

MOTHER COURAGE: I've thought it over. I'm not complaining. (*She leaves.*)

Interval.

FIVE

Two years have gone by. The war has expanded over ever wider territory. Mother Courage's little wagon travels ceaselessly, crossing Poland, Moravia, Bavaria, Italy, and Bavaria again. 1631. Tilly's victory at Magdeburg costs Mother Courage four officers' shirts.

Mother Courage's wagon has set up in a village that's been wrecked by cannon fire. Military marches sound in the distance. Two Soldiers stand at the wagon's bar, served by Kattrin and Mother Courage. One of the Soldiers has a woman's fur coat draped over his shoulders.

MOTHER COURAGE: Why can't you pay? No money, no schnapps. If I'm hearing a victory march, the soldiers ought to have enough back pay to pay a bar tab.

SOLDIER: C'mon, schnapps! I was delayed and I missed the looting. The general only allowed one hour of looting, one hour for a whole city! It'd be inhuman to allow more, he said; the city must've bribed him, the treacherous fuck.

(*The Chaplain stumbles in.*)

THE CHAPLAIN: In the farmyard, they're lying there. A family. Somebody help me. I need linen.

(*The Second Soldier goes with him. Kattrin, agitated, beseeches her mother to bring out linen.*)

MOTHER COURAGE: I'm out. I sold every bandage in stock to the regiment. What should I do, tear up good officers' shirts to bandage farmers?

THE CHAPLAIN (*calling from offstage*): I said I need linen.

(*Mother Courage sits on the steps to the wagon so Kattrin can't go in.*)

MOTHER COURAGE: I'm giving nothing. They'll never pay and here's why, because they've got nothing.

(*The Chaplain is bent over a woman he's carried from the yard.*)

THE CHAPLAIN (*to the woman*): Why did you stay after the shooting started?

THE FARMER'S WIFE (*very weak*): Farm.

MOTHER COURAGE: Them let go of what's theirs? Oh no never! And I should be left holding the bill. Not me, no way.

FIRST SOLDIER: Too bad they wouldn't convert.

MOTHER COURAGE: They would have if anyone'd asked. They'd whistle any tune you wanted. The farm's everything to farmers.

SECOND SOLDIER: Anyway, not a one of them is Protestant. These are Catholics, same as us.

FIRST SOLDIER: That's the trouble with artillery shells, they're indiscriminate.

(*The Chaplain has carried the Farmer from the yard.*)

FARMER: My arm's ripped open.

THE CHAPLAIN: Where's the linen?

(*Everyone looks at Mother Courage who doesn't move.*)

MOTHER COURAGE: Taxes, tolls, penalties and payoffs! I can't spare a thing. (*Growling, Kattrin picks up a plank and threatens her mother with it.*)

Have you snapped your tether? You put that plank down now or I'll slap your face off you, you cramp! I'm giving nothing, no one can make me, I've got myself to think about. (*The Chaplain lifts her off the steps and puts her on the ground. He goes into the wagon and comes out with linen shirts, which he proceeds to tear into strips.*)

Oh not my shirts! That's half a guilder I paid per. I'm ruined!

(*A baby is heard screaming in terror inside the house.*)

THE FARMER: Baby's still inside!

(*Kattrin rushes into the house. The Farmer's Wife tries to sit up, the Chaplain restrains her.*)

THE CHAPLAIN (*to the Farmer's Wife*): Stay, stay, they've gone in to get it.

MOTHER COURAGE: Stop her, the roof might collapse.

THE CHAPLAIN: I'm not going in there again.

MOTHER COURAGE: Leave off my poor linen, you jackass.

(*Kattrin emerges from the rubble, carrying an infant.*)

Oh what luck, who's found herself another suckling to haul around? You give it back to its mother one-two-three before you get attached and I have to spend hours pulling it away, you hear me? (*To the Second Soldier.*) Stop gawping, go tell them they can stop that music, I don't need to hear about it, I can see they've had a victory. I've had only losses from your victory.

(*The Chaplain is bandaging wounds.*)

THE CHAPLAIN: This isn't stopping the bleeding.

(*Kattrin rocks the baby, singing a cradle song in her thick inarticulate way.*)

MOTHER COURAGE: Look at her, joy sitting in the midst of misery, now give it back, its mother's coming to. (*She grabs the First Soldier, who's been pouring himself drinks and is now trying to get away with the whole bottle.*)

Pay up, pig, no victories for you here animal! Pay up.

FIRST SOLDIER: With what?

(*She tears the fur coat off his shoulders.*)

MOTHER COURAGE: Leave me the coat, which anyway you stole somewhere.

THE CHAPLAIN: Someone's still inside.

SIX

Near the Bavarian city of Ingolstadt Mother Courage observes the funeral of the fallen Imperial Field Marshal Tilly. Discussions take place regarding war heroes and the duration of the war. The Chaplain complains that he's wasting his talents, and dumb Kattrin gets the red shoes. The year's recorded: 1632.

Inside a canteen tent Mother Courage has set up. A bar in the back is open to serve people outside. Rain. Drumrolls and sad music in the distance. The Chaplain and the Regimental Secretary are playing a board game. Mother Courage and her daughter are taking stock.

THE CHAPLAIN: The funeral cortege has set forth.

MOTHER COURAGE: Too bad about the Field Marshal—twenty-two pairs of socks—he was up at the front before the battle, inspiring yet another regiment, don't fear death and that sort of thing, then he headed back to HQ but there was fog on the meadows and he got turned around and ended up in the middle of the slaughter and he caught a musket ball in the gut—we've only got four lanterns left. (*Someone outside whistles and Mother Courage goes to tend the bar.*)

You guys are shameless, he was your Field Marshal and you're skipping his funeral!

(*She serves them drinks.*)

THE REGIMENTAL SECRETARY: It was a mistake, paying them before the funeral. Now instead of attending, they're all getting soused.

THE CHAPLAIN (*to the Regimental Secretary*): Shouldn't you be at the funeral?

THE REGIMENTAL SECRETARY: I wanted to go but it's raining.

MOTHER COURAGE: You've got an excuse, the rain'd ruin your uniform. They're saying they wanted to ring church bells for the funeral, the way you ought to, but the Field Marshal blew up every steeple in Ingolstadt, so no bells for the poor bastard as his coffin's dropped down to the worms. They'll fire off the cannons, just to keep it from getting too sober seventeen bullet belts.

(*Calls from outside, men at the bar:*)

VOICES OUTSIDE: COME ON! SERVICE! BRANDY!!

MOTHER COURAGE: Show me your money first. And no one comes inside, you're not mucking up my tent with your filthy boots. You'll drink outside, rain rain go away. (*To the Regimental Secretary.*) Only commissioned officers get in. On a memorable occasion such as this you want classier company.

(*A funeral march. Everyone looks outside.*)

THE CHAPLAIN: They're filing past the estimable corpse.

MOTHER COURAGE: It grieves me in a special way when it's a field marshal or a king who dies, someone who dreamed of doing things that'll still be talked about ages hence, whose strivings fell flat all because big dreamers need common people to do the sweaty work, and common people have no aspirations, a cold mug of beer in some friendly saloon and they're happy. Look at those men out there, drinking brandy in the rain. It's pathetic is what it is, that tiny-mindedness.

THE CHAPLAIN: Oh, they're not so bad. Soldiers. They do what they're told. They'll fight for a hundred more years if they're ordered to. Two hundred years. Tell 'em to do it and they'll fight for ever.

MOTHER COURAGE: Think the war will end now?

THE CHAPLAIN: Why? Because a field marshal died? Don't be silly. Food's scarce, not field marshals.

MOTHER COURAGE: Seriously, for me it's not a casual question, I could really beef up the inventory, I've got cash and prices are low, but then if the war ends, no demand, I'll be sunk.

THE CHAPLAIN: Very well then, my earnest opinion. There are always people who run around and say, 'Some day the war will end.' I say no one can say whether the war will end. There will of course be brief pauses, intermissions if you will. The war might meet with an accident, same as the Field Marshal. There are risks in every enterprise, the earth is under heaven and nothing's perfect upon it. Wars get stuck in ruts, no one saw it coming, no one can think of everything, maybe there's been short-sighted planning and all at once your war's a big mess. But the Emperor or the King or the Pope reliably provides what's necessary to get it going again. This war's got no significant worries as far as I can see, a long life lies ahead of it.

(*A soldier is singing at the bar.*)

THE SOLDIER (*singing*):
A schnapps, landlord, and fast!
A soldier's never last!
His fists are even faster!

(*Speaking.*) Make mine a double, today's a holiday!

MOTHER COURAGE: I must be getting tired, or it's the rain or the funeral or something, uncertainty's never bothered me before.

THE CHAPLAIN: What's uncertain? What will ever stop the war?

THE SOLDIER (*singing*):
Your tits, girl, show 'em fast!
A soldier's heart is vast!
But please don't tell the pastor!

THE REGIMENTAL SECRETARY (*abruptly*): And peace, whatever happened to that? I'm from Bohemia and I want to go home.

THE CHAPLAIN: Oh, yes, peace indeed. It's the hole in the cheese, we search high and low for it after we've eaten.

THE SOLDIER (*singing*):
Your cards, comrades, and fast!
A soldier's not tight-assed!
He smiles at disaster!

Your prayer, good priest, and fast!
A soldier's die is cast!
He's mincemeat for his master!

THE REGIMENTAL SECRETARY: People can't live without peace.

THE CHAPLAIN: True, but just because there's war doesn't mean there's no peace, war has its moments of peace. War satisfies every human need, even for peace, it's got to or why else would we have wars? You can take a dump in wartime exactly as you do when things are peaceful, and between one battle and the next have a beer. Even when you're dog weary on the march you can prop your head up on your elbows and catch a nap in a ditch. While it's true that in the thick of battle you can't play cards, you can't do that in the thick of peacetime either, when you're ploughing furrows in the field, hour by hour day after day—after a battle, at least, if you win, there are possibilities. Your leg's shot up, maybe, and first thing you scream, then you calm down, then a glass of schnapps, then in the end you're hopping about like a regular flea and the war's still the war, unperturbed by your misadventure. And what's to stop you from multiplying in the midst of slaughter, behind a barn or anyplace, breeding like maggots in raw meat, nothing stops that, and then the war takes the kids you produce and on and on it goes on and on and on. No, war always finds a way. Why should it ever end?

(*Kattrin has stopped working. She's holding a basket full of bottles and is staring at the Chaplain.*)

MOTHER COURAGE: OK, I'm buying more goods. On your say-so. (*Kattrin suddenly throws the basket to the ground and runs off.*)
Kattrin! (*Laughing.*) Jesus, she's waiting for peace. I promised her she'd get a husband when peace arrives.

(*Mother Courage runs after her. The Regimental Secretary stands up.*)

THE REGIMENTAL SECRETARY: While you chattered I paid attention to the game. I win. Pay up.

(*Mother Courage returns with Kattrin.*)

MOTHER COURAGE: A little more war, a little more money, peace'll be sweeter for the wait. You go to town, ten minutes' walk, get our package at the Golden Lion, the pricey things, the rest we'll pick up with the wagon. They expect you, and the Regimental Secretary here will accompany you. Most everyone's at the Field Marshal's funeral, nothing can happen to you. Hang tight to the package, anyone says they'll help carry it no thanks, think about your trousseau.

(*Kattrin covers her head with a scarf and leaves with the Regimental Secretary.*)

THE CHAPLAIN: You think it's a good idea, letting her go with him?

MOTHER COURAGE: She should be so pretty that a man like him pays attention to her.

THE CHAPLAIN: Often I sit back and watch you, amazed. Your quick mind, your indomitable spirit, it's the right name for you, Courage.

MOTHER COURAGE: You're talkative today. I'm not courageous. Only poor people need courage. Why, because they're hopeless. To get out of bed each morning, or plough a potato field in wartime, or bring kids with no prospects into the world—to live poor, that takes courage. Consider how easily and often they murder each other, they need courage just to look one another in the face. They trudge along, uncomplainingly carrying the Emperor and his heavy throne and the Pope and his stone cathedral, they stagger, starving, bearing the whole thundering weight of the great wealth of the wealthy on their broad stupid backs, and is that courage? Must be, but it's perverted courage, because what they carry on their backs will cost them their lives. (*She sits, takes a small pipe from a pocket, lights it and smokes.*)
You could be chopping up kindling.

(*The Chaplain reluctantly takes off his coat, picks up a hatchet and a bundle of branches, and starts chopping kindling, standing over a chopping block, hacking the branches into smaller sticks.*)

THE CHAPLAIN: I'm a pastor, not a woodcutter.

MOTHER COURAGE: I don't have a soul so I don't need a pastor. I have a stove, and it needs firewood.

THE CHAPLAIN: Where'd you get that stubby little pipe?

MOTHER COURAGE: It's a pipe, who knows?

THE CHAPLAIN: It's not a pipe, or rather not just a pipe, it's special.

MOTHER COURAGE: Is it?

THE CHAPLAIN: It's the stubby little pipe of the cook from the Oxenstjerna Regiment.

MOTHER COURAGE: If you know, why're you asking, hypocrite?

THE CHAPLAIN: Because I don't know whether you pay attention to what you smoke. Could be you just fish around in your pockets like some people do and any stumpy grubby snub of a pipe your fingers come across, you'll pop it in your mouth from sheer absent-mindedness.

MOTHER COURAGE: As long as I can suck smoke out of it, I'm not fussy.

THE CHAPLAIN: Perhaps, only I don't think so. Not you. You know what you're smoking.

MOTHER COURAGE: This is going somewhere?

THE CHAPLAIN: Listen to me, Courage. It's my obligation as your minister. It's hardly likely you'll meet up with that character again, and you know what character I mean, but that's luck not loss.

MOTHER COURAGE: Seemed nice enough to me. Who cares what you think?

THE CHAPLAIN: Good, you think he was nice, I think he wasn't, I think he's maybe not actually evil, but nice, definitely not. A Don Juan, exceedingly well-oiled. Take a look at that pipe, it exposes him, his personality.

MOTHER COURAGE: I'm looking at it.

THE CHAPLAIN: The stem of which has been half chewed through. As if a rat had attacked it. The gnawed-upon pipe of a boorish violent rat of a man, you can see it for yourself if you haven't lost your last lick of horse sense.

MOTHER COURAGE: You're really going to town with that hatchet.

THE CHAPLAIN: I'm not trained to do this, I'm trained to preach. I went to divinity school. My gifts, my abilities are squandered on physical activity. It's an inappropriate application of God-given talents. Which is sinful. You never heard me preach. I can so intoxicate a battalion they think the enemy army's a grazing flock of fine fat mutton. When I preach, a soldier's life's no more to him than an old *fershtunkeneh*° footwrap he casts away as he marches off to glory. God gave me a mighty tongue. When I preach people fall dumb and go blind.

MOTHER COURAGE: Jesus, that's sort of terrifying.

THE CHAPLAIN: Courage, I've been waiting for this opportunity to talk to you.

MOTHER COURAGE: Maybe if we're quiet we'll hear more funeral music.

THE CHAPLAIN: Beneath your customarily brusque and businesslike manner you're human, a woman, you need warmth.

fershtunkeneh: Used.

MOTHER COURAGE: I'm warm, and all it takes is a steady supply of chopped wood.

THE CHAPLAIN: Kindling aside, Courage, shouldn't we make our relationship a closer one? I mean, consider how the whirligig of war has whirled us two together.

MOTHER COURAGE: I think we've whirled close as we're ever going to get. I cook, you eat what I cook, you do this and that and when you feel like it you chop kindling.

(The Chaplain moves towards her.)

THE CHAPLAIN: You know perfectly well that when I use the word 'close' I don't mean cooking or eating or kindling.

MOTHER COURAGE: Don't come at me waving that axe.

THE CHAPLAIN: I'm not a figure of fun. You make me a figure of fun. I'm a man with his dignity and I'm tendering you a considered, legitimate proposal. I'm proposing! Respond to my proposal!

MOTHER COURAGE: Give it a rest, Pastor. We get along, don't make me dunk your head in a pail. I want nothing more than for me and my children to get through all this with our wagon. I have nothing to give anyone, and anyway there's no room inside me for private dramas. It's drama enough, stocking up with the Field Marshal fallen and everyone talking about peace. If my business folds, where would you be? Look, you hesitate, you don't know. If you make kindling we'll be warm come evening, and that's a lot, these days. (She stands up.) What's that? (Kattrin enters, a large cut across her forehead and over an eye. She carries many packages, leather goods, a drum and other things as well.)

What, what, did somebody attack you? On your way back? Someone attacked her on the way back! Bet it was that soldier who was getting drunk! I shouldn't have sent you. Drop those things! It's not so terrible, a bad scratch. I'll bandage you up and in a week you're healed. They're not human, none of 'em, every one of them's swine.

(She bandages Kattrin's wounds.)

THE CHAPLAIN: Blame the ones who start the wars. They don't rape back home.

MOTHER COURAGE: I'll blame who I want and the hell they don't. Why didn't the Regimental Secretary walk you back? Probably he figured an upstanding person such as yourself wouldn't get bothered by anyone. The wound's not deep, it won't leave a mark. Done and done, wrapped tight. You just rest, calm yourself. I've got a secret something to show you, you'll see. (She gets a sack from which she takes Yvette's red shoes.)

All right, look! See? You've been dreaming about them. They're yours. Put them on quick, before I have second thoughts. You won't be scarred, though there are worse things than that. If you're pretty you've got to be afraid of what's hiding behind every bush, your life's a nightmare. It's the ones no one warns who manage to have a life, like with trees, the tall beautiful trees get felled for roof beams, but the crippled and crooked trees get overlooked and go on living.

You have to know how to recognise good luck. The shoes are ready to be worn, I've been shining them on the sly.

(Kattrin leaves the shoes and crawls into the wagon.)

THE CHAPLAIN: Hopefully she won't be disfigured.

MOTHER COURAGE: It'll scar. Peace will never come for her.

THE CHAPLAIN: She didn't let them take your merchandise.

MOTHER COURAGE: I shouldn't have made such a fuss about that maybe. I wish I knew what it looked like inside her head! She stayed out all night just once in all these years. After that she stumped around the way she does, only she started to work herself till she dropped, every day. She'd never tell me about it, what adventures she'd had. I clubbed my forehead with my fists for a long time over that one. (She picks up the goods Kattrin dropped and angrily inspects them.)

War! A great way to make a living!

(Cannon fire.)

THE CHAPLAIN: Now they're burying the Field Marshal. A moment in history.

MOTHER COURAGE: The only history I know is today's the day they hit my daughter in the eye. She's more than halfway to done-for now, no husband for her now, and her such a great fool for children, she's mute because of the war, that too, when she was little a soldier stuffed something in her mouth. I'll never see Swiss Cheese again, and where Eilif is only God knows. It's a curse, this fucking war.

SEVEN

Mother Courage at the height of her business career.

A highway. The Chaplain and Kattrin are pulling the wagon, festooned with new wares. Mother Courage walks alongside, wearing a necklace made of silver thalers.

MOTHER COURAGE: I won't let you knock the war. Everyone says the weak are exterminated, but the weak don't fare any better in peacetime. War feeds its people better.

(She sings:)
It overwhelms all opposition,
it needs to grow or else it dies.
What else is war but competition,
A profit-building enterprise?

(Speaking.) You can't hide from it. The ones who hide are the first it finds.

War isn't nice, you hope to shirk it,
You hope you'll find someplace to hide.
But if you've courage you can work it,
And put a tidy sum aside.
The refugees? Oh sure, I've seen 'em,
the thousands fleeing from the war!
They've not a scrap of bread between 'em.
I wonder what they're running for?
The Spring has come, and Winter's dead.

The snow has gone, so draw a breath!
Let Christian souls crawl out of bed,
pull on their socks and conquer death!
(*They keep pulling.*)

EIGHT

In the same year the Swedish king, Gustavus Adolphus, falls in the battle of Lutzen. Peace threatens to ruin Mother Courage's business. Her brave son does one heroic deed too many and comes to an ignominious end.

An army camp. A summer's morning. Outside the wagon, an Old Woman and a Young Man, her son, are waiting. The son is carrying a heavy mattress.

MOTHER COURAGE'S VOICE (*inside the wagon*): Does it have to be so goddamned early?

THE YOUNG MAN: We've been walking all night, twenty miles, we have to get back today.

MOTHER COURAGE'S VOICE (*inside the wagon*): Who's buying mattresses? People don't have houses.

THE YOUNG MAN: Come look at it.

THE OLD WOMAN: She doesn't want it, no one does. Let's go home.

THE YOUNG MAN: Home's forfeit if we can't pay the taxes. She'll give us at least three guilders for the bed if we include your crucifix. (*Bells start ringing.*)
    Listen, Mama!

OFFSTAGE VOICES: Peace! The Swedish King is dead!

(*Mother Courage sticks her head out of the wagon. Her hair's an uncombed mess.*)

MOTHER COURAGE: What's with the bells? It's Wednesday!

(*The Chaplain crawls out from under the wagon.*)

THE CHAPLAIN: What's the shouting about?

MOTHER COURAGE: Don't tell me peace has broken out. I've just replenished my entire stock.

THE CHAPLAIN (*shouting to the rear*): Is it peace?

A VOICE: The war was over three weeks ago, they're saying, it took three weeks for the news to get here!

ANOTHER VOICE: In town, a whole heap of Lutherans arrived in their carts, they brought the news with them.

THE YOUNG MAN: Ma, it's peace! (*The Old Woman collapses. Her son rushes to her.*)
    Ma? MA!

(*Mother Courage goes back inside the wagon.*)

MOTHER COURAGE: Mary and Joseph! Kattrin, it's peace! Put your black dress on! We'll go find a Protestant church. We should pray for Swiss Cheese. I can't believe it!

THE YOUNG MAN: They wouldn't be saying it if it wasn't true. They made peace. (*To his mother.*) Can you stand up? (*The Old Woman stands.*)
    I'll start making saddles again, I'll open up the shop. I promise you. Everything will go back to what it was. We'll bring back Daddy's bedding. Can you walk? (*To the Chaplain.*) It hit her hard. The news. She decided long ago the war would last for ever. (*To his mother.*) Daddy always said otherwise. Let's get home.

(*The mother and son leave.*)

MOTHER COURAGE (*inside the wagon*): Give the old woman a schnapps!

THE CHAPLAIN: Gone. Gone.

MOTHER COURAGE (*inside the wagon*): What're they up to in the camp?

THE CHAPLAIN: There's a huge crowd. I'll go over. Think I should put on my evangelical garb?

MOTHER COURAGE (*inside the wagon*): If it was me, I'd inquire a little more precisely as to the state of things before I went into a Catholic army camp dressed as the Antichrist. I'm so happy it's peace, I don't care if I'm ruined. At least two of my children survived the war, I saw to that. Bet I'll see my Eilif soon.

(*The Cook enters, haggard, carrying a bundle.*)

THE CHAPLAIN: And look what peace already dragged in. It's the General's cook!

THE COOK: What's this apparition I see before me? The Holy Ghost? No, it's the General's chaplain, same as ever, pale as a snail's sticky underbelly!

THE CHAPLAIN: Courage, a visitor!

(*Mother Courage climbs down from the wagon.*)

MOTHER COURAGE: The General's cook. After all these years.

THE COOK: At the first opportunity, as promised, a visit, a little intelligent conversation, some unforgettable brandy, Mrs Fierling, a man's only as good as his word.

MOTHER COURAGE: Where's Eilif, my eldest?

THE COOK: He left before I did, on his way here same as me. Funny he isn't here yet, he's so robust.

THE CHAPLAIN: I'm putting on my pastoral vestments, don't say anything interesting till I get back.

(*He goes behind the wagon.*)

MOTHER COURAGE: He's robust but he dawdles. He'll show up any minute, I can feel it! (*Calling into the wagon.*) Kattrin, Eilif's coming! Bring the cook a glass of brandy, Kattrin! (*Kattrin doesn't come out.*)
    (*Calling into the wagon.*) Comb your bangs down over it, it's enough already! Mr Lamb isn't a stranger. (*She gets the brandy herself.*)
    She won't come out, what does peace mean to her? It took its time coming and it came too late. They hit her, right above the eye, you can barely see the scar now, but to her mind people stare.

THE COOK: War.

(*They sit.*)

MOTHER COURAGE: You're showing up at an unlucky moment for me, Cook. Ruined. I took the Chaplain's advice and I've overstocked, forked over all my cash for goods I'll be sitting on, the troops'll be packing up and heading home.

THE COOK: A woman your age listening to a preacher? For shame. I meant to warn you back when to give that dried-up-twig of a chaplain a wide berth but there wasn't time, and you—you fell for his big words.

MOTHER COURAGE: I fell for nothing. He's chief dishwasher and assistant drayhorse and that's it.

THE COOK: You must be hard up for drayhorses. You tell you any of his sideways jokes, he's sort of got a careless opinion of women, I tried to use my influence for moral improvements but in vain, the man's absolutely unsolid.

MOTHER COURAGE: You're solid, huh?

THE COOK: If I'm anything, I'm solid. (*Toasting her.*) Skol!

MOTHER COURAGE: *Prosit!*°

THE COOK: *A votre santé!*°

MOTHER COURAGE: Mud in yer eye. I've only been with one solid man, thank God. Soon as spring arrived for a little extra pocket money he stripped the blankets from the kids' beds, then he told me my harmonica wasn't a Christian instrument.

THE COOK: I like a woman who knows how to handle a harmonica.

MOTHER COURAGE: Maybe later, if the mood strikes me, I might play a snatch.

THE COOK: Here we sit, together again, and the bells are chiming peace, peace peace . . . And then there's your indelible brandy, your unimpeachable hospitality.

MOTHER COURAGE: Did you get paid before you deserted?

THE COOK (*hesitantly*): Not exactly, no, they've been out of cash all year. So I didn't desert, non-payment of our salaries inspired us to dissolve our regiment on our own authority.

MOTHER COURAGE: You're broke.

THE COOK: Oh really you know, they could stop that fucking din. I'm not broke, I'm between money, looking for something to which I can apply these capable hands, I've lost my appetite as it were for army cooking, they give me roots and boots for the soup pot then they throw the consequences piping hot in my face. I begged to be transferred to the infantry, and now, peacetime. (*The Chaplain appears in his pastor's coat.*) (*To Mother Courage.*) Later.

THE CHAPLAIN: Apart from the occasional moth hole, it's perfectly presentable.

THE COOK: But not worth the effort, putting it on. No more soldiers to inflame. And I have another chicken to pluck with you, if you've the time, because thanks to you this lady purchased surplus goods under the illusion you peddled her that the war will go on eternally.

THE CHAPLAIN (*heatedly*): I'm going to have to ask you how this is any concern of yours?

THE COOK: It's unscrupulous, what you did! Interfering in the way other people manage their affairs with unasked-for advice.

THE CHAPLAIN: I interfered? Who says I interfered? (*To Mother Courage.*) Did you say I interfered?

MOTHER COURAGE: Don't get excited, the Cook's entitled to his personal opinion.

THE CHAPLAIN: I didn't know you owed him perusal of your accounts.

MOTHER COURAGE: I owe him quatsch, and I owe you quatsch, and his point is your war was a bust, and he's got a point. You ruined me.

THE CHAPLAIN: The way you talk about peace, Courage, it's a sin. You're a hyena of the battlefields.

Prosit!: "Cheers." *A votre santé!*: "To your health."

MOTHER COURAGE: I'm what?

THE COOK: He who insults my friend deals with me.

THE CHAPLAIN: I wasn't talking to you. You have transparent intentions. (*To Mother Courage.*) But when I see you picking up peace disdainfully betwixt your thumb and forefinger as if it were a, a, a snot-rag, my humanity's affronted; I see you as you are, a woman who hates peace and loves war, as long as you can make money off it, but don't forget the old saying, 'If you want to dine with the Devil bring a long spoon!'

MOTHER COURAGE: I didn't ask the war to linger and it didn't linger any longer than it wanted to. And anybody calls me a hyena is looking for a divorce.

THE CHAPLAIN: The whole world's finally, finally able to draw a deep breath and you alone, you, carping about peace because, because what, because of that load of tattery antiquated crap in your wagon?!

MOTHER COURAGE: My wares aren't crap, and I survived by selling them, and you survived by leeching off me.

THE CHAPLAIN: By leeching off war! My point! Right!

THE COOK (*to the Chaplain*): Adults should neither give nor receive advice, according to someone or other. Who probably knew what he was talking about. (*To Mother Courage.*) Sell quick before prices fall much farther. Dress up and get going, there isn't a second to spare!

MOTHER COURAGE: Sharp thinking. I like it, I'll do it.

THE CHAPLAIN: On his say-so?

MOTHER COURAGE: Better his than yours! Anyone asks, I'm off to the market.

(*She goes into the wagon.*)

THE COOK: Score one for me, Pastor. You don't think quick on your feet. You should have said, 'When did I ever advise you? A little political hypothesising was all it was!' You're outflanked. Cockfighting doesn't suit men who're dressed like that.

THE CHAPLAIN: If you don't shut up, whether or not it suits my clothes, I'm going to murder you.

(*The Cook takes his shoes off and unwinds the rags wrapped around his feet.*)

THE COOK: If the war hadn't turned you into the secular wreck I see before me, you could've found a parsonage to settle in, what with peace and all. No one needs a cook when there's no food, but folks still believe in things they can't see, nothing changes that.

THE CHAPLAIN: Mr Lamb, please, I'm asking you, don't push me out. I am a wreck, you're right, I've been brought low, humiliated, debased. But I . . . I like myself better now. Even if you handed me a nice metropolitan pulpit with a sinecure, I don't think I could preach. Washing bottles is better work than saving souls, the bottles come clean. Tell her to keep me.

(*Yvette comes in, dressed in black, but bedizened, walking with a cane. She's much older, fatter, and she wears gobs of make-up. A serving man walks behind her. The Cook turns away and busies himself with something.*)

YVETTE: Hey hey, everyone! Is this Mother Courage's?

THE CHAPLAIN: Is, was, and always will be.

YVETTE: Where's Courage? Could you please announce that she has a guest, Madame Colonel Starhemberg.

THE CHAPLAIN (*calling into the wagon*): Madame Colonel Starhemberg wants to speak with you!

MOTHER COURAGE (*from inside*): Be right out!

YVETTE: I'm Yvette!

MOTHER COURAGE (*excited, from inside*): Aaaaccchh! Yvette!

YVETTE: Popped over to see what's up! (*The Cook turns around.*)
     Pieter!

THE COOK: Yvette!

YVETTE: Holy shit! Since when! How come you're here?

THE COOK: As opposed to where?

THE CHAPLAIN: How well do you know each other?

YVETTE: Too well! (*She gives the Cook the once-over.*)
     Fat!

THE COOK: You've been slimmer yourself.

YVETTE: You're fat and I'm fat and how-de-do, you scalded hog. How many years has it been I've been waiting to tell you what I think of you?

THE CHAPLAIN: Many, many years, from the look of it, but if you could wait just a minute longer and start telling him when Courage is here.

(*Mother Courage comes out of the wagon, hauling merchandise.*)

MOTHER COURAGE: Yvette! (*They embrace.*)
     You're in mourning?

YVETTE: Looks nice, huh? My husband the Colonel died a few years back.

MOTHER COURAGE: The old guy who wanted to buy you my wagon?

YVETTE: No, his father!

MOTHER COURAGE: You look nice all right, not bad, not bad at all! At least somebody got something out of the war.

YVETTE: Touch and go, that's how I do it, up and down and up and down and etcetera.

MOTHER COURAGE: Yeah, but you hooked a colonel and we have to hand it those colonels, they made hay.

THE CHAPLAIN (*to the Cook*): Heaven forfend I offer advice, but you might want to consider getting back in your boots. (*To Yvette.*) Madame Colonel, you had something you were about to say about this barefoot man.

THE COOK: Don't make a stink, Yvette.

MOTHER COURAGE: Yvette, let me introduce you to a friend of mine.

YVETTE: No, no, let me introduce you! Courage, meet Piping Pieter.

MOTHER COURAGE (*laughing*): Piping Pieter!

THE COOK: An old nickname, forget it.

MOTHER COURAGE: Who made the girls throw their skirts over their heads!

THE COOK: My name's Lamb.

MOTHER COURAGE: Look, I hung on to your pipe.

THE CHAPLAIN: Rarely took it out of her mouth.

YVETTE: Fling his poxy pipe away, Courage, this is the nastiest fish ever to wash up on the Flanders shore. Every one of his fingers has brought misery to a different miserable girl.

THE COOK: Years ago. A man can change.

YVETTE: Stand up when a lady talks to you, poodle. God how I loved this man!

THE COOK: I was the best thing ever happened to you, I helped you find your calling.

YVETTE: Shut your mouth, you tragic disaster! (*To Mother Courage.*) After he disappeared and left me, um, broken-hearted, I found four other girls in town in a similar condition and it was a very small town! Maybe you're thinking time and dissipation has ground down his teeth and horns, but you listen to me, be careful, there's danger in the ruins. If he's here hoping to hitch a ride on your wagon, show him the highway and bless his scabby backside with your boot!

MOTHER COURAGE (*to Yvette*): You come with me to the market, I've got to unload this stuff before the prices hit bottom. You must know the whole regiment, tell me who to talk to. (*Calling into the wagon.*) Never mind church, Kattrin. I am going to market. As soon as Eilif shows, give him something to drink.

(*She leaves with Yvette. As they go, Yvette says:*)

YVETTE: It amazes me, a picked-over carcass of man like you was enough to overturn my apple cart. I've got my lucky star to thank, I got every fucking apple back, and then some! I've saved this woman from the catastrophe of your company, and that'll go down to my credit in the world to come. And now at very long last, Piping Pieter, you can kiss my ass!

(*They leave.*)

THE CHAPLAIN: I suddenly find my tongue freed, I can sermonise again! I take as our text today: 'The mills of God grind slowly. And they grind small.'

THE COOK: I never had a lucky star. It's just . . . well, I'd hoped there might be a warm meal. I'm starving. I haven't had food in two days. Now they're cluckling about me, and she'll form a more-or-less completely false impression. It discombobulates me, a woman's cold shoulder. I'll leave before she's back.

THE CHAPLAIN: Better part of valour. Amen.

THE COOK: Peace is as heavy as a millstone. I miss the General, you know, God knows where he is, I could be basting a fat roasted capon with mustard sauce, served with yellow carrots.

THE CHAPLAIN: Red cabbage. Red cabbage with a capon.

THE COOK: I know, I know, but he insisted on carrots.

THE CHAPLAIN: The man was an appalling ignoramus.

THE COOK: You never mentioned that when you were sitting next to him stuffing your face.

THE CHAPLAIN: I swallowed my pride.

THE COOK: You swallowed more than that. Who knew we'd long for those days?

THE CHAPLAIN: Nostalgic for the war. Peace seems less hospitable, somehow.

THE COOK: You're finished here same as me, you called her a hyena. You—what are you staring at?

THE CHAPLAIN: I think it's Eilif. (*A grim contingent of Soldiers with pikes leading Eilif, whose hands are tied. He's chalk-white.*)
     What's happened?

EILIF: Where's my mother?

THE CHAPLAIN: In town.

EILIF: I heard she was here. They let me come to see her.

THE COOK (to the Soldiers): Where are you taking him?

A SOLDIER: Noplace good.

THE CHAPLAIN: What did he do?

THE SOLDIER: He broke into a farmhouse. The wife— (Gestures to indicate she's dead.)

THE CHAPLAIN: You did that? How could you do that?

EILIF: Same as I've always done.

THE COOK: But it's peacetime. You can't—

EILIF: Shut up. Can I sit till she comes back?

THE SOLDIER: We don't have time for that.

THE CHAPLAIN: During the war he got medals for things like this, he was fearless, they said, brave, he was summoned to sit at the General's right hand. Couldn't we talk to your commander?

THE SOLDIER: Why bother? Stealing some farmer's cow, that's brave?

THE COOK: It was idiotic!

EILIF: If I was an idiot I'd have starved long before this, you asshole.

THE COOK: So you used your brains and now they're going to cut your head off.

THE CHAPLAIN: At least let's get Kattrin.

EILIF: No! Don't! Leave her. Give me a taste of schnapps.

THE SOLDIER: You don't have time for that, come on!

THE CHAPLAIN: What should we tell your mother?

EILIF: Tell her it wasn't different. Tell her it was the same. Or don't tell her anything.

(The Soldiers shove him and he starts to walk.)

THE CHAPLAIN: I'll walk with you on your hard path.

EILIF: I don't need you, black crow.

THE CHAPLAIN: You don't know what you may need.

(The Soldiers shove Eilif again and they leave. The Chaplain follows them.)

THE COOK (calling after the Chaplain): I have to tell her, she'll want to see him!

THE CHAPLAIN: Better not say anything. Or he was here and he'll be back, tomorrow possibly. When I get back I'll find some way to explain.

(The Chaplain runs off after them. The Cook watches them leave, shakes his head, then finally goes to the wagon. He calls in.)

THE COOK: Hey! Don't you want to come out? I understand you, I think, peace comes and you crawl under the rug. Me too. It's terrifying. I was the General's cook, remember? I'm asking myself if maybe there's a scrap left over from your breakfast, just to tide me over till your mother returns? A little ham or some bread, we might have a bit of a wait. (He looks inside.) She's thrown the blanket over her head.

(In the distance, cannonfire. Mother Courage runs in, still carrying all her wares, out of breath.)

MOTHER COURAGE: Cook! Peace is finished! The war's been back on three whole days. I was just about to sell at a loss when I heard the news! Thank God! In town they're shooting at the Lutherans and the Lutherans are shooting back. We've got to get on our way with the wagon. Kattrin, pack! (To the Cook.) Look me in the eye. What's the matter?

THE COOK: Nothing.

MOTHER COURAGE: Bullshit, it's something, something's wrong.

THE COOK: War's started up, maybe that's it. And it'll probably be tomorrow evening before I get hot food in my stomach.

MOTHER COURAGE: You're lying, Cook.

THE COOK: Eilif was here. He couldn't stay.

MOTHER COURAGE: He was here? Then we'll find him on the march. From now on I'm pulling right behind the soldiers, like I was official, it's safer. Did he look all right?

THE COOK: As always.

MOTHER COURAGE: He's always the same as always, smart. That one the war couldn't take from me. Help me pack? (She starts packing. The Cook helps.) Did he have any news? Is he still the General's favourite? Any more heroism?

THE COOK (grim): Yes, apparently, only recently.

MOTHER COURAGE: Tell me about it once we're under way. (Kattrin comes out of the wagon and takes her place at the axle shaft, ready to pull.) Peace is already over, Kattrin. We're on the move again. (To the Cook.) And you?

THE COOK: Find my regiment, sign up.

MOTHER COURAGE: You could do that I guess or . . . Where's his Holiness?

THE COOK: He went towards town with Eilif.

MOTHER COURAGE: Come along, Lamb, for a bit. I need a helper.

THE COOK: All that stuff Yvette was saying . . .

MOTHER COURAGE: Didn't do you discredit in my eyes. The opposite. I've always admired vitality; don't worry as much as I used to over the shape it chooses to take. Interested?

THE COOK: I'm not saying no.

MOTHER COURAGE: The Twelfth Regiment's already headed out. Take hold and pull. Here's a slice of bread. We'll have to go the long way around to catch up with the Lutherans. I might see Eilif this very night. I love him best of all. It was a short peace. Let's get going.

(Kattrin and the Cook in harness start to pull the wagon while Mother Courage sings:)
From Ulm to Metz . . .

THE COOK (singing):
. . . from Metz to Maähren!

MOTHER COURAGE (singing):
The goddamned army's on its feet!
What if the land is burnt and barren?

THE COOK (singing):
The war needs men, and men must eat!

MOTHER COURAGE (singing):
The war will feed you steel and fire
If you sign up for bloody deeds!
It's only blood that wars require!
So come and feed it what it needs!

NINE

The Great War of Religion has been going on for six-teen years. Over half the inhabitants of Germany have perished. Widespread plague kills those the war spares. In once fertile countries, famine. Wolves prowl through the burnt-out cities. In the autumn of 1634 we meet Courage in the German mountains called Fichtelbirge, off the route of the Swedish Army. Winter this year has come early and is severe. Business is terrible, and beg-ging is all that remains. The Cook gets a letter from Utrecht and is bid farewell.

Outside a half-ruined parsonage. Grey morning in early winter. Wind is blasting. Mother Courage and the Cook in ratty sheepskins, the wagon nearby.

THE COOK: It's pitch black, nobody's up.

MOTHER COURAGE: It's a parsonage. The bells will have to be rung and the Father's got to crawl to it. Then he'll have hot soup.

THE COOK: You're talking nonsense, the village was burnt to the ground.

MOTHER COURAGE: Someone's living here, there was a dog barking.

THE COOK: If the parson's got anything, he won't give it away.

MOTHER COURAGE: Maybe if we sing something.

THE COOK: I've had more than my share of this. (*He takes a letter from his pocket.*) A letter from Utrecht, my mother's dead from cholera, her inn belongs to me now. Read the letter if you don't believe me. (*He proffers the letter, Mother Courage reaches to take it, he snatches it back.*)

From my aunt, the handwriting's a little primitive. But . . . there's stuff about what a wretched little bas-tard I always was, that's family matters, skip that, read here, the salient part.

(*He hands her the letter, which she takes and reads. She stops reading, looks at him.*)

MOTHER COURAGE: Lamb, I can't take the open road any more either. Look at us begging. My whole life, I never begged before. I feel like a slaughterhouse dog, red meat for paying customers but nothing for me. I have nothing to sell any more and no one has anything to pay with. In Saxony one of those raggedy beggars offered me a parcel of precious books wrapped in greaseproof parchment, just for two eggs, and for a little bag of salt in Würtenburg they wanted to give me their plough. What's the use of ploughing? Nothing grows but nettles. In Pomerania I've heard there's vil-lagers so ravenous they've eaten little children.

THE COOK: The world's dying.

MOTHER COURAGE: Sometimes I see myself pulling that wagon through the streets of hell, selling burning pitch. Or making a living in purgatory, offering my wares to the wandering souls till the last trumpet blast. If me and my children could find a place where no one's shooting, I wouldn't mind a few years' rest, a few years of calm.

THE COOK: We could make a go of it at the inn. Give it serious consideration, Anna. Last night I made my final decision, I'm going to Utrecht with you or alone, today.

MOTHER COURAGE: I have to talk it over with Kattrin. It's a little abrupt, and I'm usually averse to making big decisions when I'm freezing and there's nothing in my belly. Kattrin! (*Kattrin climbs down from the wagon.*)

Kattrin, we have to talk about something. The Cook and I want to go to Utrecht. He's inherited an inn. You'd have a home, make acquaintances. There are many men who'd want a competent somebody who helped run an inn, good looks aren't everything. It's a good deal. The Cook and I get along. I will say this about him: he tucks his head between his shoulders and goes about his business. We'd know where our next meal came from, and when to expect it, that'd be a change, huh, nice? And your own bed, you'd sleep better, right? Finally, life on the road isn't life. Look at us, you're fall-ing apart. Lice are eating you alive. We have to decide, all right, Utrecht or, or we could just keep on, go where the Swede soldiers are, the army up north. (*She gestures vaguely to the left.*) We could go find the army again, but . . . I think we'll go with cook, Kattrin.

THE COOK: Anna, I have to talk to you alone.

MOTHER COURAGE: Go back in the wagon, Kattrin.

(*Kattrin climbs back into the wagon.*)

THE COOK: I interrupted you because you didn't under-stand me. I thought I was clear but I guess I wasn't, so: you can't bring her. I think that's clear enough.

(*Kattrin positions herself inside so she can listen.*)

MOTHER COURAGE: What do you mean, leave Kattrin?

THE COOK: Think. There's not enough room for her. It's not a big place. If we screw our hind legs to the floor we might keep it open and running, but three people, the inn can't support that. Kattrin can take over the wagon.

MOTHER COURAGE: I was thinking she'd find a husband in Utrecht.

THE COOK: That's a laugh! Dumb, a scarred face, and old as she is?

MOTHER COURAGE: Don't talk so loud!

THE COOK: What is, is, loud or soft. And come to think of it, there's the paying guests at the inn, who'd want to look up from supper and see that waiting to clear the table? How do you think this could work?

MOTHER COURAGE: I said shut up, I said don't talk so loud.

THE COOK: Someone's lit a candle in the parsonage. Let's sing.

MOTHER COURAGE: Cook, how'd she pull that wagon on her own? She's frightened by the war. She couldn't manage. The dreams she must have! I hear her groaning nights. After battles especially. What she sees in those dreams, I can't imagine. She suffers because she pities. A few days back I found a hedgehog we'd killed, the wagon, an ac-cident. She'd hidden it in her blanket.

THE COOK: The inn's too small. (*Shouting.*) Worthy gentle-men, servants, and all who dwell within! In the hope of procuring a little leftover food, we will now give you a lecture in the form of a song, the Song of Solomon,

Julius Caesar and other men possessed of a gigantic spirit, which proved to be of little use to them. All of this so you can see that we're decent obedient people and we are having a hard time getting by, especially this winter!

(*He sings:*)
No doubt you've heard of Solomon,
The wisest man on earth!
He saw with perfect clarity,
He would spit on the cursed hour of his birth
And say that all was vanity.
How deep and wise was Solomon!
And see, before the night descends,
He longed to taste oblivion!
He started wise but as a fool he ends.
Oh, wisdom's fine; we're glad we've none.

(*Shouting.*) All virtues are dangerous in a world like this, as our beautiful song shows, you're better off having an easy life and breakfast, in our opinion, hot soup. I for instance, I've got none and I'd like some, I'm a soldier, but what use was it to me, my bravery in all those battles, nix, nil, starvation, and if I'd stayed home shitting myself I'd be better off. This is why:

(*Sings:*)
Then Julius Caesar, mighty one,
Raised high his royal rod,
So brave he tore the world apart,
So they voted and changed their Caesar to a God,
Then drove a dagger through his heart.
How loud he screamed: 'You too, my son!'
And see, before the night descends,
His reign had only just begun,
So brave, but screaming out in fear he ends.
Brave hearts are grand! We're fine with none.

(*Muttering.*) They're hiding in there, the bastards. (*Shouting.*) Worthy gentlemen, servants and the whole household! You aren't responding, you're sitting in there by your fire, and maybe you're saying to yourself sure, bravery's not much when you need a hot meal, I agree, but maybe if you were honest you wouldn't be so bad off! Maybe if you were honest someone would feed you or at least not leave you completely sober.

Let's test this proposition!

(*Sings:*)
And Socrates, that paragon,
Who always told the truth—
They mixed a bitter poison drink
Made of hemlock; they said he's done things to our youth
And now we hate the way they think!
His truth was a phenomenon.
And see, before his night descends,
No longer dazzled by the sun,
He pays his bills and with a sip, he ends.
Truths are lovely; we know none.

(*Shouting.*) You still don't want to give, and it's not surprising, who wants to give anyone anything? Sure, they tell us to give unto others, but what if you've got nothing to give? And the ones who give are left empty-handed, and that can't feel very good either, and that's why sacrifice is the rarest of all the virtues, because in the end it makes everyone feel like crap.

(*Sings:*)
St Martin° sang his benison,
His pity flowereth.
He met a man lost in the snows
Who was freezing, so Martin shared with him his clothes.
Of course the two men froze to death.
The pearly gates no doubt he won!
And see, before the night descends,
So kind beyond comparison!
Warm-hearted but beneath the ice he ends.
Oh, pity's great; thank God we've none.

(*Shouting.*) And that's how it is with us! Law-abiding people, loyal to each other, we don't steal, murder or burn down houses! And like the song says, down we're going, deeper in the hole, and soup's a rare commodity, and if we were thieves and murderers we might eat! So if you've no food for us you better pray our patience holds out, because we know! It's not virtue that pays in this world, but wickedness, that's how the world is and it shouldn't be that way!

(*Sings:*)
At last our final yarn's been spun.
We ask you, gentle souls,
What use our loving heaven's been?
While you sit safe and soft within,
We stand without, with empty bowls.
God's love has left us here, undone.
And see, before the night descends
The way the meek are overrun.
Our virtues led us to our wretched ends.
And folk do better who have none.

A VOICE FROM ABOVE (*inside the house*): You out there! Come inside! We'll give you some hot marrow stew.
MOTHER COURAGE: I'd choke on anything I tried to swallow now, Lamb. I can't argue with anything you've said but is it your final word? We've always had a good understanding.
THE COOK: My last word. Take some time to decide.
MOTHER COURAGE: I don't need it. I'm not leaving her here.
THE COOK: That's pure senselessness, but nothing I can do about it. I'm not a monster, it's a small inn. Let's go inside before there's no more soup, we'll have sung in the cold in vain.
MOTHER COURAGE: I'll get Kattrin.
THE COOK: Come get it and bring it out to her. If it's three of us tramping in, they might get scared.
(*They go into the house. Kattrin climbs down from the wagon, carrying a bundle. She looks to make sure the others have gone in. She drapes, over a wheel of the wagon where it can't be missed, one of her mother's*

St Martin: The patron saint of soldiers (316–397).

skirts, and then atop the skirt, an old pair of the cook's pants. As she's leaving with her bundle, Mother Courage comes out of the house, carrying a bowl of hot soup.)

MOTHER COURAGE: Kattrin! Wait! Kattrin! Stop! What's the bundle and where are you off to? Have you turned your back on God and all his angels? (*She grabs the bundle away from Kattrin and opens it.*)

She's packed her belongings! You heard? I told him to fuck himself, with the shitty tiny tavern and Utrecht, what would we do in Utrecht? We don't know anything about innkeeping. The war's still got a great deal in store for us. (*She sees the skirt and pants.*)

You're an idiot. What do you think I'd have done, seeing that and you just gone? (*Kattrin tries to go, but Mother Courage won't let her.*)

Don't be so quick, it wasn't for your sake I handed him his walking papers. It's the wagon. I'm never giving up that wagon. It's mine, it's what I'm used to, it's not about you in the least. We'll go now, we'll go the opposite direction of Utrecht and find the army and leave the cook's stuff here where he'll trip over it, the stupid man. (*She climbs up and then throws out a few things to lie near the trousers.*)

There, the partnership's dissolved, and I'm not taking anyone else into the business ever. We'll both go on. The winter will be over some day, like all the other winters. Get in the harness, snow's coming.

(*They strap themselves into the harnesses, turn the wagon in another direction and pull it away. The Cook comes out of the house. He sees his things on the ground. And stands there, dumbstruck.*)

TEN

The entire year 1635 Mother Courage and her daughter Kattrin pull across central German highways, following behind ever more ragged armies.

A highway. Mother Courage and Kattrin are pulling the wagon. They come to a small farmhouse. Someone inside is singing. Mother Courage and Kattrin stop to listen.

A VOICE INSIDE (*singing*):
We've got a rosebush glowing
Within our garden wall.
When April winds come calling
They set the blossoms blowing
And petals will go falling,
All white and red the petals fall
When April winds come calling.

When wild geese go flying
Before the winter storm,
The autumn roses dying,
Our roof's in need of fixing!
Of moss and straw we're mixing
The stuff to keep the parlour warm
For when wild geese go flying.

(*Mother Courage and Kattrin start to pull again.*)

ELEVEN

January 1636. Imperial troops threaten the Protestant city of Halle. The stone begins to speak. Mother Courage loses her daughter and continues alone. The war goes on, no sign that it will end.

The wagon, beaten up, stands forlornly alongside a farmhouse with a huge thatched roof which leans against a cliff. It's night. A Lieutenant and three Soldiers in heavy armour step out of the nearby woods.

THE LIEUTENANT: I don't want any noise. Somebody even looks like shouting, gut 'em.

(*One of the Soldiers knocks on the door of the house. A farm woman comes out. He covers her mouth with his hand. The other two Soldiers go into the house. They come out with the farmer and his son. Kattrin has put her head out of the wagon to see what's happening. The Lieutenant points at her.*)

THE LIEUTENANT: There's someone else. (*One of the Soldiers pulls Kattrin out of the wagon.*)

Who else lives here?

THE FARMER: That's our son.

THE FARMER'S WIFE: She's a dumb girl.

THE FARMER: Her mother's marketing in town.

THE FARMER'S WIFE: For their provisioning business, salespeople, people are fleeing and they're hunting bargains.

THE FARMER: They're migrants.

THE LIEUTENANT: All right enough, you have to stay quiet all of you, the first noise from any of you I'm going to tell my boys to shove bayonets through your thick stupid country-ass heads. I need one of you to show us the path into town. (*Pointing to the Farmer's Son.*) You.

THE FARMER'S SON: I don't know where the path is.

SECOND SOLDIER (*grinning*): Doesn't know where his dick is. Fucking peasants.

THE FARMER'S SON: There's no path for Catholics.

THE LIEUTENANT (*to the Second Soldier*): You gonna take that from him?

(*The Soldiers force the Farmer's Son to his knees and the Second Soldier holds a bayonet to his throat.*)

THE FARMER'S SON: Cut my throat. I won't help you.

FIRST SOLDIER (*to his comrades*): Watch this. (*The First Soldier goes to the barn door and looks in.*)

Two cows and an ox. Before the army I was a butcher's apprentice.

THE FARMER'S SON: Don't!

THE FARMER'S WIFE (*crying*): Captain, please, leave our animals alone.

THE LIEUTENANT: Help us out or we'll eat your ox. (*Indicating the Farmer's Son.*) Hope you didn't raise stubborn children.

FIRST SOLDIER: Wish I'd brought my bone saw. Here goes.

THE FARMER'S SON (*to his father*): What do I do? (*The Farmer's Wife looks at her son.*)

(*To the Soldiers.*) All right, all right. Let's go.

THE FARMER'S WIFE: And many thanks, Captain, for not butchering them, for ever and amen.

(*The Farmer stops his wife from continuing to thank the Lieutenant.*)

FIRST SOLDIER: It's the ox before everything, then the cows, then their kid, farm priorities.

(*The Lieutenant and the Soldiers leave, led by the Farmer's Son.*)

THE FARMER: What're they planning? Nothing good.

THE FARMER'S WIFE: Probably they're just scouting around— (*The Farmer has got a ladder and is propping it against the wall of the house.*)

   What in God's name?

THE FARMER: I want to see how many. (*He climbs up to the roof.*) The woods are full of 'em. To the quarry. I can see armoured men in the clearing, and there's cannons, it's more than a regiment. God help the city and everyone in it.

THE FARMER'S WIFE: Any lights on?

THE FARMER: None. Everyone's sleeping. (*He climbs down.*) They'll kill everyone.

THE FARMER'S WIFE: The town sentries.

THE FARMER: Probably killed the men in the watchtower in the cliffs, or else we'd have heard their horns.

THE FARMER'S WIFE: If we had a few more of us . . .

THE FARMER: More than just us all the way up here, us and this cripple.

THE FARMER'S WIFE: What should we do then? Anything?

THE FARMER: Nothing.

THE FARMER'S WIFE: Even if we dared to, it's night and we couldn't run.

THE FARMER: They're all over the hill like ants.

THE FARMER'S WIFE: So there's no way to signal?

THE FARMER: Not unless you want to get killed.

THE FARMER'S WIFE (*to Kattrin*): Pray, you poor dumb beast, pray. We can't stop the slaughter, but we can pray to God and maybe because you're a cripple He'll listen better. (*They all kneel. Kattrin kneels behind the farm couple.*)

   Our Father who art in heaven, don't let them murder the people in the city, who're asleep and don't know that death's come so near, at least wake them up, Father, so they can see the spears and rifles and the siege engines and fires, the enemy in the night. (*Nodding towards Kattrin.*) Remember her mother, Lord, who's gone there and remember to keep the night watchman wakeful, maybe he'll sound the alarm, and remember and protect my brother-in-law and the four kids my late sister's left him, may her soul rest, poor thing, save the four kids who never did nothing wrong. (*Kattrin groans.*)

   The little one isn't two yet, the eldest only seven. (*Kattrin stands, very upset. As the Farmer's Wife keeps praying, Kattrin moves quietly to the wagon, takes something from it, goes to the ladder and climbs to the roof.*)

   We have no defence but you, Lord. In your wisdom you saw fit to leave us helpless and now we ask you to show us mercy, save our son and save our animals and the crops and the sleeping people in the town, the little children and old people especially, death's come in the night, Heavenly Father, and all your children are in dreadful need.

THE FARMER: And we hope to be forgiven our sins as we try to forgive them who sin against us. Amen.

(*On the roof, Kattrin starts banging the drum she's taken from the wagon.*)

THE FARMER'S WIFE: Jesus what is she doing?

THE FARMER: Lost her wits!

THE FARMER'S WIFE: Drag her down from there, quick! (*The Farmer moves towards the ladder, but Kattrin pulls it up on the roof and resumes her drumming.*) Oh, this is disastrous!

THE FARMER: Stop that pounding, you cripple!

THE FARMER'S WIFE: The Kaiser's whole army's going to come crashing down on us! (*Kattrin keeps drumming, looking towards the city.*)

   (*To her husband.*) I warned you about letting gypsies put up here, think they care if the soldiers take our last cow?

(*The Lieutenant and his Soldiers and the Farmer's Son run in.*)

THE LIEUTENANT: I'll fucking murder you!

THE FARMER'S WIFE: Mr Officer sir, please, it's not us, she—

FIRST SOLDIER: Jesus Christ.

SECOND SOLDIER: Fucking hell.

THE LIEUTENANT: Where's the ladder? Where's the goddamn—

THE FARMER: It's on the roof, with her.

FIRST SOLDIER: She— (*To the Second Soldier.*) Get the— get the gun, do you—

THIRD SOLDIER: You told me not to, it's heavy, you—fuck, listen to her.

THE FARMER'S WIFE: She got up there without our noticing.

FIRST SOLDIER: Hey girl, get down or we're gonna come up and get you!

SECOND SOLDIER: Yeah, get down here and suck my—

THE LIEUTENANT (*to Kattrin*): All right, all right, stay calm, stay calm, this is—

THE FARMER'S WIFE: She's a total stranger.

THE LIEUTENANT: Shut up! This is an order! Throw the drum down. (*Kattrin keeps drumming.*)

   (*To the Farmer.*) You planned this, you're responsible, if she—

THE FARMER: There's some tall pine trees they cut down in the woods.

THE LIEUTENANT: So what?

THE FARMER: I dunno, maybe if somehow we could . . . you know, we could hoist one of the tall tree trunks somehow and use one end to sort of shove her off and—

FIRST SOLDIER (*to the Lieutenant*): Can I try something sir? (*The Lieutenant nods. The First Soldier calls to Kattrin:*) Hey! Girl! We wanna make a deal with you, friends, right?

SECOND SOLDIER: They're gonna hear that, they're bound to—kill the bitch.

THIRD SOLDIER: Should I go back and get the—

FIRST SOLDIER (*to the Third Soldier*): QUIET, goddamn it! (*To Kattrin.*) You, you listening?

SECOND SOLDIER: Hey! Hey you, listen to him, he's trying to—

FIRST SOLDIER: We're friends, we . . . Get down, right, if you get down we'll take you with us, we promise we won't touch you—

SECOND SOLDIER: Who'd want to touch an ugly fucking—

FIRST SOLDIER: We'll take you into town with us and you point out your mother and she won't get hurt.

(*Kattrin keeps drumming. The Lieutenant shoves the First Soldier aside.*)

THE LIEUTENANT (*calling up to Kattrin*): You don't believe him, you aren't stupid, you know we're not friends and anyway, who'd trust someone with a face like his? But will you believe me if I give you my word as an officer of His Majesty the Emperor's army? My sacred word?

(*Kattrin drums harder.*)

THIRD SOLDIER (*muttering*): Well that was effective. Jesus Christ.

FIRST SOLDIER: You better do something, sir.

SECOND SOLDIER: They're gonna hear that in town.

THE LIEUTENANT: We've gotta—

THIRD SOLDIER: Torch the house!

THE LIEUTENANT: Make some sort of noise!

SECOND SOLDIER: You told us not to make any noise, we—

THE LIEUTENANT: Drown out the—

FIRST SOLDIER: I thought we weren't supposed to make any—

THE LIEUTENANT: Drown out the drumming, a, a normal noise, you goddamned imbecile, a peacetime sound, like—

THE FARMER: Wood chopping!

THE LIEUTENANT: Good, do it, start chopping! (*The Farmer takes up his axe and starts chopping at a log lying on the ground.*)

Can't you chop any harder than that? (*Kattrin drums a little softer, distracted by the chopping sound, but then she realises what's happening and starts drumming all the harder.*)

(*To the Farmer.*) Louder dammit! (*To the First Soldier.*) You too! Start chopping!

THE FARMER: There's just the one axe.

THE LIEUTENANT: Torch it, torch the house.

(*The Farmer stops chopping.*)

THE FARMER: They'll see the fire in town, that's a bad idea.

(*Kattrin, still drumming, laughs.*)

THE LIEUTENANT: That does it, she's laughing at us. Get the gun, shoot her down, I don't care, shoot her!

(*Two of the Soldiers run out. Kattrin drums harder.*)

THE FARMER'S WIFE: That wagon over there's all they have. Take the axe to that and she'll have to stop.

(*The Lieutenant hands the axe to the Farmer's Son.*)

THE LIEUTENANT: Do it, you heard your mother, chop that wagon to splinters. (*To Kattrin.*) You want him to take an axe to your wagon? Then stop!

(*The Lieutenant signals to the Farmer's Son, who hits the wagon with the axe, a few tepid blows.*)

THE FARMER'S WIFE (*screaming up to Kattrin*): STOP IT YOU DUMB COW!

(*As the boy hits the wagon, Kattrin watches with a stricken expression, making a few low groaning sounds. But she doesn't stop drumming.*)

THE LIEUTENANT: Where are those lazy cunts with the rifle?

FIRST SOLDIER: LISTEN! (*Everyone, including Kattrin, stops and listens. Silence.*)

They're not hearing her in town, there'd be alarm bells if they did.

THE LIEUTENANT (*to Kattrin*): Nobody's hearing you, it's not working, and now you're going to get shot and killed for nothing. One last time: throw down that drum!

(*The Farmer's Son throws the axe down and calls out abruptly:*)

THE FARMER'S SON: Keep drumming! They'll kill them all! Drum! Drum! Drum!

(*Kattrin resumes her drumming. The First Soldier knocks the Farmer's Son to the ground and clubs him brutally, with the butt end of his spear. Kattrin starts crying but keeps drumming.*)

THE FARMER'S WIFE: Oh God, please stop hitting him in the back, you're killing him!

(*The Soldiers run in with a large musket on a tripod.*)

SECOND SOLDIER: The Colonel's foaming at the mouth, Lieutenant. We're gonna get court-martialled.

THE LIEUTENANT: Set it up! Hurry! (*They set up the musket. The Lieutenant calls up to Kattrin while this is being done:*)

All right this is the final warning: Stop drumming! (*Kattrin is crying and drumming as hard as she can.*)

STOP IT! STOP IT! STOP THE— (*He turns to his Soldiers.*) Fire! (*The Soldiers fire. Kattrin is hit. She strikes the drum weakly a few more times, then collapses, slowly.*)

No more noise.

(*From the city, a cannon's shot answers Kattrin's last drumbeat. Alarm bells and cannonfire sounding all together is heard in the distance.*)

FIRST SOLDIER: Listen. It worked. She did it.

TWELVE

Night, nearly dawn. Trumpets and drums and fifes, an army departing.

Alongside the wagon, Mother Courage sits, bent down over her daughter. The farm couple stand nearby.

THE FARMER (*angrily*): You have to go now, lady. Only one last regiment left and then that's it. You wanna travel alone?

MOTHER COURAGE: Maybe she's sleeping.

(*Sings:*)
Eia popeia,°
Who sleeps in the hay?
The neighbour's brat's crying
While my children play.
The neighbour's kid's shabby
But my kids look nice,
With shirts like the angels wear
In paradise.

Neighbour can't feed 'em
But mine shall have cake,

Eia popeia: Lullaby.

The sweetest and choicest
The baker can bake.

Eia popeia,
I see your eyes close.
One kid lies in Poland.
The other—well, who knows?

(*Speaking*) You should never have told her about your brother-in-law's children.

THE FARMER: You had to go to town to hunt for bargains, maybe if you'd been here none of this would have happened.

MOTHER COURAGE: Now she's sleeping.

THE FARMER'S WIFE: She isn't sleeping, stop saying that and look, she's gone.

THE FARMER: And you have to go too. There are wolves around here, and people who're worse than the wolves.

MOTHER COURAGE: Yes.

(*She goes to the wagon and brings out a sheet.*)

THE FARMER'S WIFE: Do you have anyone left? Anyone you could go to?

MOTHER COURAGE: One left. Eilif.

(*She uses the sheet to wrap Kattrin's body.*)

THE FARMER: You've got to go find him then. We'll take care of her, she'll have a decent burial. Don't worry.

MOTHER COURAGE: Here's money for what it costs.

(*She gives the Farmer some money. The Farmer and his son shake her hand and carry Kattrin's body away. The Farmer's Wife follows them. She turns as she leaves and says to Mother Courage:*)

THE FARMER'S WIFE: Hurry.

(*She leaves.*)

MOTHER COURAGE (*harnessing herself to the wagon*): Hopefully I'll manage to pull the wagon alone. I bet I can do it, not much in it any more. I have to get back in business.

(*The fife and drums of another regiment marching by. Soldiers are singing in the distance. As they sing, Mother Courage begins to pull her wagon, pursuing them.*)

SOLDIERS (*offstage, singing*):
Sometimes there's luck, and always worry.
The war goes on, and perseveres!
For war is never in a hurry,
And it can last a thousand years.

The day of wrath will come like thunder
But who has time to make amends?
You march in line, but never wonder
How it began and where it ends.

The Spring has come, and Winter's dead!

MOTHER COURAGE (*over the singing*): Take me with you!

SOLDIERS (*singing over her, offstage*):
The snow has gone, so draw a breath!
Let Christian souls crawl out of bed,
Pull on their socks and conquer death!

The world will end, and time will cease!
And while we live we buy and sell!
And in our graves we shall find peace—
Unless the war goes on in Hell!

COMMENTARIES

BERTOLT BRECHT (1898–1956)

The Alienation Effect 1964

TRANSLATED BY JOHN WILLETT

In this short description, Brecht explains some of his theories of staging and acting. His alienation effect (A-effect) reminds the audience that the characters on stage are dramatic constructs, not real people suffering real emotions. As he explains, the A-effect is the opposite of traditional acting, which is designed to produce an empathy between actor and audience. The A-effect rejects that empathy.

What follows represents an attempt to describe a technique of acting which was applied in certain theaters with a view to taking the incidents portrayed and alienating them from the spectator. The aim of this technique, known as the alienation effect, was to make the spectator adopt an attitude of inquiry and criticism in his approach to the incident. The means were artistic.

The first condition for the A-effect's application to this end is that stage and auditorium must be purged of everything "magical" and that no "hypnotic tensions" should be set up. This ruled out any attempt to make the stage convey the flavor of a particular place (a room at evening, a road in the autumn), or to create atmosphere by relaxing the tempo of the conversation. The audience was not "worked up" by a display of temperament or "swept away" by acting with tautened muscles; in short, no attempt was made to put it in a trance and give it the illusion of watching an ordinary unrehearsed event. As will be seen presently, the audience's tendency to plunge into such illusions has to be checked by specific artistic means.

The first condition for the achievement of the A-effect is that the actor must invest what he has to show with a definite gest of showing. It is of course necessary to drop the assumption that there is a fourth wall cutting the audience off from the stage and the consequent illusion that the stage action is taking place in reality and without an audience. That being so, it is possible for the actor in principle to address the audience directly.

It is well known that contact between audience and stage is normally made on the basis of empathy. Conventional actors devote their efforts so exclusively to bringing about this psychological operation that they may be said to see it as the principal aim of their art. Our introductory remarks will already have made it clear that the technique which produces an A-effect is the exact opposite of that which aims at empathy. The actor applying it is bound not to try to bring about the empathy operation.

Yet in his efforts to reproduce particular characters and show their behavior he need not renounce the means of empathy entirely. He uses these means just as any normal person with no particular acting talent would use them if he wanted to portray someone else, i.e., show how he behaves. This showing of other people's behavior happens time and again in ordinary life (witnesses of an accident demonstrating to newcomers how the victim behaved, a facetious person imitating a friend's walk, etc.), without those involved making the least effort to subject their spectators to an illusion. At the same time they do feel their way into their characters' skins with a view to acquiring their characteristics.

As has already been said, the actor too will make use of this psychological operation. But whereas the usual practice in acting is to execute it during the actual performance, in the hope of stimulating the spectator into a similar operation, he will achieve it only at an earlier stage, at some time during rehearsals.

To safeguard against an unduly "impulsive," frictionless and uncritical creation of characters and incidents, more reading rehearsals can be held than usual. The actor should refrain from living himself into the part prematurely in any way, and should go on functioning as long as possible as a reader (which does not mean a reader-aloud). An important step is memorizing one's first impressions.

When reading his part the actor's attitude should be one of a man who is astounded and contradicts. Not only the occurrence of the incidents, as he reads about them, but the conduct of the man he is playing, as he experiences it, must be weighed up by him and their peculiarities understood; none can be taken as given, as something that "was bound to turn out that way," that was "only to be expected from a character like that." Before memorizing the words he must memorize what he felt astounded at and where he felt impelled to contradict. For these are dynamic forces that he must preserve in creating his performance.

When he appears on the stage, besides what he actually is doing he will at all essential points discover, specify, imply what he is not doing; that is to say he will act in such a way that the alternative emerges as clearly as possible, that his acting allows the other possibilities to be inferred and only represents one out of the possible variants. He will say for instance "You'll pay for that," and not say "I forgive you." He detests his children; it is not the case that he loves them. He moves down stage left and not up stage right. Whatever he doesn't do must be contained and conserved in what he does. In this way every sentence and every gesture signifies a decision; the character remains under observation and is tested. The technical term for this procedure is "fixing the 'not . . . but.'"

The actor does not allow himself to become completely transformed on the stage into the character he is portraying. He is not Lear, Harpagon, Schweik; he shows them. He reproduces their remarks as authentically as he can; he puts forward their way of behaving to the best of his abilities and knowledge of men; but he never tries to persuade himself (and thereby others) that this amounts to a complete transformation. Actors will know what it means if I say that a typical kind of acting without this complete transformation takes place when a producer or colleague shows one how to play a particular passage. It is not his own part, so he is not completely transformed; he underlines the technical aspect and retains the attitude of someone just making suggestions.

Once the idea of total transformation is abandoned the actor speaks his part not as if he were improvising it himself but like a quotation. At the same time he obviously has to render all the quotation's overtones, the remark's full human and concrete shape; similarly the gesture he makes must have the full substance of a human gesture even though it now represents a copy.

Given this absence of total transformation in the acting there are three aids which may help to alienate the actions and remarks of the characters being portrayed:

1. Transposition into the third person.
2. Transposition into the past.
3. Speaking the stage directions out loud.

Using the third person and the past tense allows the actor to adopt the right attitude of detachment. In addition he will look for stage directions and remarks that comment on his lines, and speak them aloud at rehearsal ("He stood up and exclaimed angrily, not having eaten: . . . ," or "He had never been told so before, and didn't know if it was true or not," or "He smiled, and said with forced non-chalance: . . ."). Speaking the stage directions out loud in the third person results in a clash between two tones of voice, alienating the second of them, the text proper. This style of acting is further alienated by taking place on the stage after having already been outlined and announced in words. Transposing it into the past gives the speaker a standpoint from which he can look back at his sentence. The sentence too is thereby alienated without the speaker adopting an unreal point of view; unlike the spectator, he has read the play right through and is better placed to judge the sentence in accordance with the ending, with its consequences, than the former, who knows less and is more of a stranger to the sentence.

This composite process leads to an alienation of the text in the rehearsals which generally persists in the performance too. The directness of the relationship with the audience allows and indeed forces the actual speech delivery to be varied in accordance with the greater or smaller significance attaching to the sentences. Take the case of witnesses addressing a court. The underlinings, the characters' insistence on their remarks, must be developed as a piece of effective virtuosity. If the actor turns to the audience it must be a whole-hearted turn rather than the asides and soliloquizing technique of the old-fashioned theater. To get the full A-effect from the poetic medium the actor should start at rehearsal by paraphrasing the verse's content in vulgar prose, possibly accompanying this by the gestures designed for the verse. A daring and beautiful handling of verbal media will alienate the text. (Prose can be alienated by translation into the actor's native dialect.)

Gesture will be dealt with below, but it can at once be said that everything to do with the emotions has to be externalized; that is to say, it must be developed into a gesture. The actor has to find a sensibly perceptible outward expression for his character's emotions, preferably some action that gives away what is going on inside him. The emotion in question must be brought out, must lose all its restrictions so that it can be treated on a big scale. Special elegance, power and grace of gesture bring about the A-effect.

A masterly use of gesture can be seen in Chinese acting. The Chinese actor achieves the A-effect by being seen to observe his own movements.

Whatever the actor offers in the way of gesture, verse structure, etc., must be finished and bear the hallmarks of something rehearsed and rounded-off. The impression to be given is one of ease, which is at the same time one of difficulties overcome. The actor must make it possible for the audience to take his own art, his mastery of technique, lightly too. He puts an incident before the spectator with perfection and as he thinks it really happened or might have happened. He does not conceal the fact that he has rehearsed it, any more than an acrobat conceals his training, and he emphasizes that it is his own (actor's) account, view, version of the incident.

Because he doesn't identify himself with him he can pick a definite attitude to adopt towards the character whom he portrays, can show what he thinks of him and invite the spectator, who is likewise not asked to identify himself, to criticize the character portrayed.

The attitude which he adopts is a socially critical one. In his exposition of the incidents and in his characterization of the person he tries to bring out those features which come within society's sphere. In this way his performance becomes a discussion (about social conditions) with the audience he is addressing. He prompts the spectator to justify or abolish these conditions according to what class he belongs to.

The object of the A-effect is to alienate the social gest underlying every incident. By social gest is meant the mimetic and gestural expression of the social relationships prevailing between people of a given period.

It helps to formulate the incident for society, and to put it across in such a way that society is given the key, if titles are thought up for the scenes. These titles must have a historical quality.

This brings us to a crucial technical device: historicization.

The actor must play the incidents as historical ones. Historical incidents are unique, transitory incidents associated with particular periods. The conduct of the persons involved in them is not fixed and "universally human"; it includes elements that have been or may be overtaken by the course of history, and is subject to criticism from the immediately following period's point of view. The conduct of those born before us is alienated[1] from us by an incessant evolution.

---

[1]*Entfremdet.*

It is up to the actor to treat present-day events and modes of behavior with the same detachment as the historian adopts with regard to those of the past. He must alienate these characters and incidents from us.

Characters and incidents from ordinary life, from our immediate surroundings, being familiar, strike us as more or less natural. Alienating them helps to make them seem remarkable to us. Science has carefully developed a technique of getting irritated with the everyday, "self-evident," universally accepted occurrence, and there is no reason why this infinitely useful attitude should not be taken over by art. It is an attitude which arose in science as a result of the growth in human productive powers. In art the same motive applies.

As for the emotions, the experimental use of the A-effect in the epic theater's German productions indicated that this way of acting too can stimulate them, though possibly a different class of emotion is involved from those of the orthodox theater. A critical attitude on the audience's part is a thoroughly artistic one. Nor does the actual practice of the A-effect seem anything like so unnatural as its description. Of course it is a way of acting that has nothing to do with stylization as commonly practiced. The main advantage of the epic theater with its A-effect, intended purely to show the world in such a way that it becomes manageable, is precisely its quality of being natural and earthly, its humor and its renunciation of all the mystical elements that have stuck to the orthodox theater from the old days.

BERTOLT BRECHT

Notes for *Mother Courage*, Scene 12   1949

TRANSLATED BY ERIC BENTLEY AND HUGO SCHMIDT

For some of his work, Brecht produced booklets that supply a great deal of background information that does not appear in the text of the plays. Brecht's manner of producing his plays was important to him. Although he did not expect every successive production to adhere strictly to the standards he established in commentaries such as this, he hoped his intentions would be substantially respected.

Twelfth Scene

Courage Moves On

The peasants have to convince Courage that Kattrin is dead. Kattrin's lullaby. Mother Courage pays for Kattrin's funeral and receives the expressions of sympathy of the peasants. Mother Courage harnesses herself to her empty covered wagon. Still hoping to get back into business, she follows the tattered army.

Basic Arrangement

The wagon stands on the empty stage. Mother Courage holds dead Kattrin's head in her lap. The peasants stand at the foot of the dead girl, huddled together and hostile. Courage talks as if her daughter were only sleeping, and deliberately overhears the reproach of the peasants that she was to blame for Kattrin's death.

Kattrin's lullaby. The mother's face is bent low over the face of the daughter. The song does not conciliate those who listen.

Mother Courage pays for Kattrin's funeral and receives expressions of sympathy from the peasants. After she has realized that her last child is dead, Courage gets up laboriously and hobbles around the corpse (right), along the footlights, behind the wagon. She returns with a tent cloth, and answers over her shoulder the peasant's question whether she had no one to turn to: "Oh yes, one. Eilif." And places the cloth over the body, with her back toward the footlights. At the head of the corpse, she pulls the cloth all the way over the face, then again takes her place behind the corpse. The peasant and his son shake hands with her and bow ceremoniously before carrying the body out (to the right). The peasant woman, too, shakes hands with Courage, walks to the right and stops once more, undecided. The two women exchange a few words, then the peasant woman exits.

Mother Courage harnesses herself to her empty covered wagon. Still hoping to get back into business, she follows the tattered army. Slowly, the old woman walks to the wagon, rolls up the rope which Dumb Kattrin had been pulling to this point, takes a stick, looks at it, slips it through the sling of the second rope, tucks the stick under her arm, and starts pulling. The turntable begins to move, and Courage circles the stage once. The curtain closes when she is upstage right for the second time.

The Peasants

The attitude of the peasants toward Courage is hostile. She got them into difficulties, and they will be saddled with her if she does not catch up with the regiments. Besides, she is to blame for the accident herself, in their opinion. And moreover the canteen woman is not part of the resident population, and now, in time of war, she belongs to the fleecers, cutthroats, and marauders in the wake of the armies. When they condole with her by shaking her hand, they merely follow custom.

The Bow

During this entire scene, Weigel, as Courage, showed an almost animal indifference. All the more beautiful was the deep bow that she made when the body was carried away.

The Lullaby

The lullaby must be sung without sentimentality and without the desire to arouse sentimentality. Otherwise, its significance does not get across. The thought that is the basis of this song is a murderous one: the child of this mother was supposed to be better off than other children of other mothers. Through a slight stress on the "you," Weigel revealed the treacherous hope of Courage to get her child, and perhaps only hers, through the war alive. The child to whom the most common things were denied was promised the uncommon.

Paying for the Funeral

Even when paying for the funeral, Weigel gave another hint at the character of Courage. She fished a few coins from her leather purse, put one back, and gave the rest to the peasant. The overpowering impression she gave of having been destroyed was not in the least diminished by this.

The Last Verse

While Courage slowly harnessed herself to her wagon, the last verse of her song
was sung from the box in which the band had been placed. It expresses one more
time her undestroyed hope to get something out of war anyway. It becomes more
impressive in that it does not aim at the illusion that the song is actually sung by
army units moving past in the distance.

Giehse in the Role of Courage

When covering up the body, Giehse put her head under the cloth, looking at her
daughter one more time, before finally dropping it over her face.

Before she began pulling away her covered wagon—another beautiful
variant—she looked into the distance, to figure out where to go, and before she
started pulling, she blew her nose with her index finger.

Take Your Time

At the end of the play it is necessary that one see the wagon roll away. Naturally,
the audience gets the idea when the wagon starts. If the movement is extended, a
moment of irritation arises ("that's long enough, now"). If it is prolonged even
further, deeper understanding sets in.

Pulling the Wagon in the Last Scene

For the 12th scene, farm house and stable with roof (of the 11th scene) were cleared
away, and only the wagon and Dumb Kattrin's body were left. The act of dragging the
wagon off—the large letters "Saxony" were pulled up (out of sight) when the music
begins—took place on a completely empty stage: whereby one remembered the setting
of the first scene. Courage and her wagon moved in a complete circle on the revolving
stage. She passed the footlights once more. As usual, the stage was bathed in light.

Discoveries of the Realists

Wherein lies the effectiveness of Weigel's gesture when she mechanically puts one coin
back into her purse, after having fished her money out, as she hands the peasant the
funeral money for dead Kattrin? She shows that this tradeswoman, in all her grief, does
not completely forget to count, since money is so hard to come by. And she shows this
as a discovery about human nature that is shaped by certain conditions. This little feature has the power and the suddenness of a discovery. The art of the realists consists of
digging out the truth from under the rubble of the evident, of connecting the particular
with the general, of pinning down the unique within the larger process.

A Change of Text

After "I'll manage, there isn't much in it now," Courage added, in the Munich and
then also in the Berlin production: "I must start up again in business."

Mother Courage Learns Nothing

In the last scene, Weigel's Courage appeared like an eighty-year-old woman. And
she comprehends nothing. She reacts only to the statements that are connected with

war, such as that one must not remain behind. She overhears the crude reproach of the peasants that Kattrin's death was her fault.

Courage's inability to learn from the unproductiveness of war was a prophecy in the year 1938 when the play was written. At the Berlin production in 1948 the desire was voiced that Courage should at least come to a realization in the play. To make it possible for the spectator to get something out of this realistic play, i.e., to make the spectator learn a lesson, theaters have to arrive at an acting style that does not seek an identification of the spectator with the protagonist.

Judging on the basis of reports of spectators and newspaper reviews, the Zurich world premiere—although artistically on a high level—presented only the image of war as a natural catastrophe and an inevitable fate, and thereby it underscored to the middle-class spectator in the orchestra his own indestructibility, his ability to survive. But even to the likewise middle-class Courage, the decision "Join in or don't join in" was always left open in the play. The production, it seems, must also have presented Courage's business dealings, profiteering, willingness to take risks, as quite natural, "eternally human" behavior, so that she had no other choice. Today, it is true, the man of the middle class can no longer stay out of war, as Courage could have. To him, a production of the play can probably teach nothing but a real hatred of war, and a certain insight into the fact that the big deals of which war consists are not made by the little people. In that sense, the play is more of a lesson than reality is, because here in the play the situation of war is more of an experimental situation, made for the sake of insights. I.e., the spectator attains the attitude of a student—as long as the acting style is correct. The part of the audience that belongs to the proletariat, i.e., the class that actually can struggle against and overcome war, should be given insight into the connection between business and war (again provided the acting style is correct): the proletariat as a class can do away with war by doing away with capitalism. Of course, as far as the proletarian part of the audience is concerned, one must also take into consideration the fact that this class is busy drawing its own conclusions—inside as well as outside the theater.

The Epic Element

The Epic element was certainly visible in the production at the Deutsches Theater—in the arrangement, in the presentation of the characters, in the minute execution of details, and in the pacing of the entire play. Also, contradictory elements were not eliminated but stressed, and the parts, visible as such, made a convincing whole. However, the goal of Epic Theater was not reached. Much became clear, but clarification was in the end absent. Only in a few recasting-rehearsals did it clearly emerge, for then the actors were only "pretending," i.e., they only showed to the newly added colleague the positions and intonations, and then the whole thing received that preciously loose, unlabored, non-urgent element that incites the spectator to have his own independent thoughts and feelings.

That the production did not have an Epic foundation was never remarked, however: which was probably the reason the actors did not dare provide one.

Concerning the Notes Themselves

We hope that the present notes, offering various explanations and inventions essential to the production of a play, will not have an air of spurious seriousness. It is admittedly hard to establish the lightness and casualness that are of the essence of theater. The arts, even when they are instructive, are forms of amusement.

Tennessee Williams

Tennessee Williams (1911–1983) was one of a handful of post–World War II American playwrights to achieve an international reputation. He was born Thomas Lanier Williams in Columbus, Mississippi, the first son of a traveling shoe salesman who eventually moved the family to a dark and dreary tenement in St. Louis. A precocious child, Williams was given a typewriter by his mother when he was eleven years old. The instrument helped him create fantasy worlds that seemed more real, more important to him than the dark and sometimes threatening world in which he lived. His parents, expecting a third child, their son Dakin, moved out of the tenement and bought a house whose gloominess depressed virtually everyone in it. His mother and father found themselves arguing, and his older sister, Rose, took refuge from the real world by closeting herself with a collection of glass animals.

Both Rose and Tennessee responded badly to their environment, and both had breakdowns. Tennessee was so ill that he suffered a partial paralysis of his legs, a disorder that made him a victim of bullies at school and a disappointment to his father at home. He could never participate in sports and was always somewhat frail; however, he was very advanced intellectually and published his first story when he was sixteen.

His education was sporadic. He attended the University of Missouri but, failing ROTC because of his physical limitations, soon dropped out to work in a shoe company. He then went to Washington University in St. Louis but dropped out again. Finally, he earned a bachelor's degree in playwriting at the State University of Iowa when he was twenty-four. During this time he was writing plays, some of which were produced at Washington University. Two years after he graduated, the Theatre Guild produced his first commercial play, *Battle of Angels* (1940), in Boston. It was such a distinct failure that he feared his fledgling career was stunted, but he kept writing and managed to live for a few years on foundation grants. It was not until the production of *The Glass Menagerie* (1944 in Chicago, 1945 in New York) that he achieved the kind of notice he knew he deserved. His first real success, the play was given the New York Drama Critics' Circle Award, the sign of his having achieved a measure of professional recognition and financial independence.

Having tried several jobs that did not work out, including an unsuccessful attempt at screenwriting, Williams had no more worries about work after *The Glass Menagerie* ran on Broadway for 561 performances. In 1947, his second success, *A Streetcar Named Desire*, starring the then-unknown Marlon Brando, was an even bigger box-office smash. It ran for 855 performances and won the Pulitzer Prize. By the time Tennessee Williams was thirty-six, he was regarded as one of the most important playwrights in the United States.

Williams followed these successes with a number of plays that were not all as well received as his first works. *Summer and Smoke* (1948), *The Rose Tattoo* (1951), and *Camino Real* (1953) were met with measured enthusiasm from the public, although the critics thought highly of Williams's work. These plays were followed by another success, *Cat on a Hot Tin Roof*, the saga of a southern family, which won all the major drama prizes in 1955, including the Pulitzer.

620

Williams's energy was unfailing over the next several years. He authored a screenplay, *Baby Doll*, with the legendary director Elia Kazan, in 1956. In 1958 he wrote a one-act play, *Suddenly Last Summer*, and in 1959 *Sweet Bird of Youth*. Some of his later plays are *The Night of the Iguana* (1961), *The Milk Train Doesn't Stop Here Anymore* (1963), and *Small Craft Warnings* (1972). He also wrote a novel and several volumes of short stories, establishing himself as an important writer in many genres. His sudden death in 1983 was a blow to the theater world.

Cat on a Hot Tin Roof

For discussion questions and assignments on *Cat on a Hot Tin Roof*, visit **bedfordstmartins.com/jacobus**.

The title *Cat on a Hot Tin Roof* comes from an offhand remark made by Tennessee Williams's father, Cornelius Williams, who told his wife that she sometimes made him "as nervous as a cat on a hot tin roof." In speaking about the play's first production, Williams said that he saw his father in the character of Big Daddy. Reminiscence and family memory are as apparent in this play as in most of Williams's work. The secret ingredient in the play, the secret that haunts Brick and torments Maggie, is homosexuality and Brick's relationship with his now-dead friend Skipper. Maggie seduced Skipper to find out what his relation with Brick was, and when he was unable to perform sexually with her, she felt she knew the truth. The theme of homosexuality extends to the previous inhabitants of Maggie and Brick's bedroom, the bachelors Jack Straw and Peter Ochello, the original owners of the plantation. Williams's note that the two "shared this room all their lives together" implies that their relationship was that of lovers. Williams had already become fully aware of his own homosexuality, although he revealed that personal element only obliquely, in works such as *Cat on a Hot Tin Roof*, until he "came out" during a television interview with David Frost in 1970.

Williams said in his *Memoirs* that this play was his favorite: "I believe that in *Cat* I reached beyond myself, in the second act, to a kind of crude eloquence of expression in Big Daddy that I have managed to give no other character of my creation." Critics have said that one reason Williams liked the play is that he was able to observe the unities of time, place, and action. Brick is confined to his room because he has broken his ankle in a drunken competition at the high school track. The central action of the play, the celebration of Big Daddy's sixty-fifth birthday, is thus brought to the bedroom, which is also at the center of one of the principal tensions in the play.

Big Daddy owns a cotton plantation, and both his sons are a disappointment to him. Gooper, with his ambitious wife and his five "no-neck monsters," is weak and unappealing. Even though Gooper has become a lawyer and produced children in an effort to please his father, Big Daddy sees him as possessing none of the masculine qualities he expects in his heir. Brick, a former football player and Big Daddy's favorite, slipped into debilitating alcoholism after Skipper's death. At the time of the play, he has no career and few prospects. Maggie sees that the only way she can secure Big Daddy's blessing in the form of Brick's inheritance is by having a child. And with Brick keeping a sexual distance from her, she has to find a way to help him overcome his grief.

Because Williams made Brick's homosexuality more or less ambiguous, some critics asserted that the play's structure was inconclusive. For example, they reasoned that one sexual failure did not prove anything about Skipper's sexual preference. They also pointed out that Maggie and Brick's sexual efforts after the curtain falls on the last act may not be successful at all.

Williams's original version of the play—before it was performed—differed from his final version. Originally, Big Daddy did not appear after act 2, and Maggie and Brick did not vow to have a child or to get together at all. The play was changed because its first director, Elia Kazan, believed that Big Daddy was too brilliant a character to leave out of act 3. He argued with Williams until, against his will, Williams revised act 3 to imply a more positive ending, to bring back Big Daddy—who tells an elephant joke that caused the censor to complain in 1955—and to make Maggie a softer, less acerbic, and much more appealing character. Williams later said that he agreed that the revision made the play stronger, although he preferred his original ending. He later published the play with two versions of act 3 so that regional and other theaters could choose the ending they preferred.

Cat on a Hot Tin Roof in Performance

The play premiered at the Morosco Theatre in New York in March 1955 with Burl Ives, then known best as a folk singer, as Big Daddy, Barbara Bel Geddes as Maggie, Ben Gazzara as Brick, and Mildred Dunnock as Big Mama. This powerful cast made the play a huge success. After 694 performances in New York, the play toured for another 268 performances. It won Williams his second Pulitzer Prize and his third Drama Critics' Circle Award for best play of the season. Elia Kazan not only directed the play but worked hard to help Williams alter his conception. Williams believed that the play should have a realistic production, since in his mind it was a realistic play. Kazan saw it otherwise and introduced soft lighting and a dreamy setting that established the play as moderately expressionistic.

London theaters were forbidden to put on the play as written, but a theater club produced it to mixed reviews in 1956. The film version originally was to have Grace Kelly as Maggie, but Elizabeth Taylor got the role, and Paul Newman played Brick. The film version removed all suggestions of homosexuality, focusing instead on Brick's immaturity and his need to grow up to the responsibilities of marriage. It was a highly successful film for its time.

Numerous revivals of the play have appeared in many countries, including a production in Tokyo in 1970. Williams revised the ending once more—putting back the elephant joke—for a restaging of the play in 1974 in Stratford, Connecticut, and then took it to New York for twenty weeks with Elizabeth Ashley as Maggie and Keir Dullea as Brick. That version (which we use in this book) was made into a television production in 1984 with Rip Torn as Big Daddy, Kim Stanley as Big Mama, Tommy Lee Jones as Brick, and Jessica Lange as Maggie. TV critic Richard Zoglin said, "The net effect is to retain the beefed-up dimensions of Maggie and Big Daddy from Broadway, but to leave Brick, at the end, a little more stuck in what Williams describes as a 'state of spiritual despair.'" Kathleen Turner was nominated for a Tony Award for her acclaimed performance as Maggie in the 1990 revival of the play at the Eugene O'Neill Theatre on Broadway. Polly Holliday won the Tony for her portrayal of Big Mama. But theater critic Frank Rich said the play would be best remembered for the performance of Charles Durning as Big Daddy.

Ned Beatty, as Big Daddy, and Margo Martindale, as Big Mama, were both praised in reviews for their performances in the 2003 revival at the Music Box Theatre on Broadway. Ashley Judd as Maggie and Jason Patric as Brick also got strong reviews for their performances. In 2004, the play was performed at the Kennedy Center in Washington, D.C., with George Grizzard as Big Daddy, Dana Ivey as Big Mama, and Mary Stuart Masterson as Maggie. Both of these productions were successful and much anticipated. Debbie Allen's 2008 Broadway production featured an all African American cast, including Anika Noni Rose as Maggie, James Earl Jones as Big Daddy, Terrence Howard as Brick, and Phylicia Rashad as Big Mama. The production was well heralded but not warmly reviewed in New York. However, when it moved to London, where it featured Sanaa Lathan as Maggie and Adrian Lester as Brick, the reviews were excellent. Jones was described as leaving "the critics breathless." In 2011, Vienna's English Theatre in Austria produced the play in celebration of Williams's one-hundredth birthday.

TENNESSEE WILLIAMS (1911–1983)

Cat on a Hot Tin Roof   1955

Characters

MARGARET
BRICK
MAE, *sometimes called Sister Woman*
BIG MAMA
DIXIE, *a little girl*
BIG DADDY
REVEREND TOOKER
GOOPER, *sometimes called Brother Man*
DOCTOR BAUGH, *pronounced "Baw"*
LACEY, *a Negro servant*
SOOKEY, *another*
CHILDREN

Notes for the Designer: *The set is the bed-sitting-room of a plantation home in the Mississippi Delta. It is along an upstairs gallery which probably runs around the entire house; it has two pairs of very wide doors opening onto the gallery, showing white balustrades against a fair summer sky that fades into dusk and night during the course of the play, which occupies*

precisely the time of its performance, excepting, of course, the fifteen minutes of intermission.

Perhaps the style of the room is not what you would expect in the home of the Delta's biggest cotton planter. It is Victorian with a touch of the Far East. It hasn't changed much since it was occupied by the original owners of the place, Jack Straw and Peter Ochello, a pair of old bachelors who shared this room all their lives together. In other words, the room must evoke some ghosts; it is gently and poetically haunted by a relationship that must have involved a tenderness which was uncommon. This may be irrelevant or unnecessary, but I once saw a reproduction of a faded photograph of the verandah of Robert Louis Stevenson's home on that Samoan Island where he spent his last years, and there was a quality of tender light on weathered wood, such as porch furniture made of bamboo and wicker, exposed to tropical suns and tropical rains, which came to mind when I thought about the set for this play, bringing also to mind the grace and comfort of light, the reassurance it gives, on a late and fair afternoon in summer, the way that no matter what, even dread of death, is gently touched and soothed by it. For the set is the background for a play that deals with human extremities of emotion, and it needs that softness behind it.

The bathroom door, showing only pale-blue tile and silver towel racks, is in one side wall; the hall door in the opposite wall. Two articles of furniture need mention: a big double bed which staging should make a functional part of the set as often as suitable, the surface of which should be slightly raked to make figures on it seen more easily; and against the wall space between the two huge double doors upstage: a monumental monstrosity peculiar to our times, a huge console combination of radio-phonograph (hi-fi with three speakers), TV set, and liquor cabinet, bearing and containing many glasses and bottles, all in one piece, which is a composition of muted silver tones, and the opalescent tones of reflecting glass, a chromatic link, this thing, between the sepia (tawny gold) tones of the interior and the cool (white and blue) tones of the gallery and sky. This piece of furniture (?!), this monument, is a very complete and compact little shrine to virtually all the comforts and illusions behind which we hide from such things as the characters in the play are faced with. . . .

The set should be far less realistic than I have so far implied in this description of it. I think the walls below the ceiling should dissolve mysteriously into air; the set should be roofed by the sky; stars and moon suggested by traces of milky pallor, as if they were observed through a telescope lens out of focus.

Anything else I can think of? Oh, yes, fanlights (transoms shaped like an open glass fan) above all the doors in the set, with panes of blue and amber, and above all, the designer should take as many pains to give the actors room to move about freely (to show their restlessness, their passion for breaking out) as if it were a set for a ballet.

An evening in summer. The action is continuous with two intermissions.

ACT 1

(At the rise of the curtain someone is taking a shower in the bathroom, the door of which is half open. A pretty young woman, with anxious lines in her face, enters the bedroom and crosses to the bathroom door.)

MARGARET *(shouting above roar of water)*: One of those no-neck monsters hit me with a hot buttered biscuit so I have t' change!

(Margaret's voice is both rapid and drawling. In her long speeches she has the vocal tricks of a priest delivering a liturgical chant, the lines are almost sung, always continuing a little beyond her breath so she has to gasp for another. Sometimes she intersperses the lines with a little wordless singing, such as "Da-da-daaaa!")

(Water turns off and Brick calls out to her, but is still unseen. A tone of politely feigned interest, masking indifference, or worse, is characteristic of his speech with Margaret.)

BRICK: Wha'd you say, Maggie? Water was on s' loud I couldn't hearya. . . .

MARGARET: Well, I!—just remarked that!—one of th' no-neck monsters messed up m' lovely lace dress so I got t'—cha-a-ange. . . .

(She opens and kicks shut drawers of the dresser.)

BRICK: Why d'ya call Gooper's kiddies no-neck monsters?

MARGARET: Because they've got no necks! Isn't that a good enough reason?

BRICK: Don't they have any necks?

MARGARET: None visible. Their fat little heads are set on their fat little bodies without a bit of connection.

BRICK: That's too bad.

MARGARET: Yes, it's too bad because you can't wring their necks if they've got no necks to wring! Isn't that right, honey?

(She steps out of her dress, stands in a slip of ivory satin and lace.)

Yep, they're no-neck monsters, all no-neck people are monsters . . .

(Children shriek downstairs.)

Hear them? Hear them screaming? I don't know where their voice boxes are located since they don't have necks. I tell you I got so nervous at that table tonight I thought I would throw back my head and utter a scream you could hear across the Arkansas border an' parts of Louisiana an' Tennessee. I said to your charming sister-in-law, Mae, honey, couldn't you feed those precious little things at a separate table with an oilcloth cover? They make such a mess an' the lace cloth looks *so* pretty! She made enormous eyes at me and said, "Ohhh, noooooo! On Big Daddy's birthday? Why, he would never forgive me!" Well, I want you to know, Big Daddy hadn't been at the table two minutes with those five no-neck monsters slobbering and drooling over their food before he threw down his fork an' shouted, "Fo' God's sake, Gooper, why don't you put them pigs at a trough in th' kitchen?"—Well, I swear, I simply could have di-eed!

Think of it, Brick, they've got five of them and number six is coming. They've brought the whole bunch down here like animals to display at a county fair. Why, they have those children doin' tricks all the time! "Junior, show Big Daddy how you do this, show Big Daddy how you do that, say your little piece fo' Big Daddy, Sister. Show your dimples, Sugar. Brother, show Big Daddy how you stand on your head!"—It goes on all the time, along with constant little remarks and innuendos about the fact that you and I have not produced any children, are totally childless and therefore totally useless!—Of course it's comical but it's also disgusting since it's so obvious what they're up to!

BRICK (*without interest*): What are they up to, Maggie?

MARGARET: Why you know what they're up to!

BRICK (*appearing*): No, I don't know what they're up to.

(*He stands there in the bathroom doorway drying his hair with a towel and hanging onto the towel rack because one ankle is broken, plastered and bound. He is still slim and firm as a boy. His liquor hasn't started tearing him down outside. He has the additional charm of that cool air of detachment that people have who have given up the struggle. But now and then, when disturbed, something flashes behind it, like lightning in a fair sky, which shows that at some deeper level he is far from peaceful. Perhaps in a stronger light he would show some signs of deliquescence, but the fading, still warm light from the gallery treats him gently.*)

MARGARET: I'll tell you what they're up to, boy of mine!—They're up to cutting you out of your father's estate, and—

(*She freezes momentarily before her next remark. Her voice drops as if it were somehow a personally embarrassing admission.*)

—Now we know that Big Daddy's dyin' of—*cancer*. . . .

(*There are voices on the lawn below: long-drawn calls across distance. Margaret raises her lovely bare arms and powders her armpits with a light sigh.*)

(*She adjusts the angle of a magnifying mirror to straighten an eyelash, then rises fretfully saying:*)

There's so much light in the room it—

BRICK (*softly but sharply*): Do we?

MARGARET: Do we what?

BRICK: Know Big Daddy's dyin' of cancer?

MARGARET: Got the report today.

BRICK: Oh . . .

MARGARET (*letting down bamboo blinds which cast long, gold-fretted shadows over the room*): Yep, got th' report just now . . . it didn't surprise me, Baby. . . .

(*Her voice has range, and music; sometimes it drops low as a boy's and you have a sudden image of her playing boy's games as a child.*)

I recognized the symptoms soon's we got here last spring and I'm willin' to bet you that Brother Man and his wife were pretty sure of it, too. That more than likely explains why their usual summer migration to the coolness of the Great Smokies was passed up this summer in favor of—hustlin' down here

ev'ry whipstitch with their whole screamin' tribe! And why so many allusions have been made to Rainbow Hill lately. You know what Rainbow Hill is? Place that's famous for treatin' alcoholics an' dope fiends in the movies!

BRICK: I'm not in the movies.

MARGARET: No, and you don't take dope. Otherwise you're a perfect candidate for Rainbow Hill, Baby, and that's where they aim to ship you—over my dead body! Yep, over my dead body they'll ship you there, but nothing would please them better. Then Brother Man could get a-hold of the purse strings and dole out remittances to us, maybe get power of attorney and sign checks for us and cut off our credit wherever, whenever he wanted! Son-of-a-bitch!—How'd you like that, Baby?—Well, you've been doin' just about ev'rything in your power to bring it about, you've just been doin' ev'rything you can think of to aid and abet them in this scheme of theirs! Quittin' work, devoting yourself to the occupation of drinkin'!—Breakin' your ankle last night on the high school athletic field: doin' what? Jumpin' hurdles? At two or three in the morning? Just fantastic! Got in the paper. *Clarksdale Register* carried a nice little item about it, human interest story about a well-known former athlete stagin' a one-man track meet on the Glorious Hill High School athletic field last night, but was slightly out of condition and didn't clear the first hurdle! Brother Man Gooper claims he exercised his influence t' keep it from goin' out over AP or UP or every goddamn "P."

But, Brick? You still have one big advantage!

(*During the above swift flood of words, Brick has reclined with contrapuntal leisure on the snowy surface of the bed and has rolled over carefully on his side or belly.*)

BRICK (*wryly*): Did you *say* something, Maggie?

MARGARET: Big Daddy dotes on you, honey. And he can't stand Brother Man and Brother Man's wife, that monster of fertility, Mae. Know how I know? By little expressions that flicker over his face when that woman is holding fo'th on one of her choice topics such as—how she refused twilight sleep!°—when the twins were delivered! Because she feels motherhood's an experience that a woman ought to experience fully!—in order to fully appreciate the wonder and beauty of it! HAH!—and how she made Brother Man come in an' stand beside her in the delivery room so he would not miss out on the "wonder and beauty" of it either!—producin' those no-neck monsters. . . .

(*A speech of this kind would be antipathetic from almost anybody but Margaret; she makes it oddly funny, because her eyes constantly twinkle and*

twilight sleep: Anesthesia.

her voice shakes with laughter which is basically indulgent.)

—Big Daddy shares my attitude toward those two! As for me, well—I give him a laugh now and then and he tolerates me. In fact!—I sometimes suspect that Big Daddy harbors a little unconscious "lech" fo' me. . . .

BRICK: What makes you think that Big Daddy has a lech for you, Maggie?

MARGARET: Way he always drops his eyes down my body when I'm talkin' to him, drops his eyes to my boobs an' licks his old chops! Ha ha!

BRICK: That kind of talk is disgusting.

MARGARET: Did anyone ever tell you that you're an ass-aching Puritan, Brick?

I think it's mighty fine that that ole fellow, on the doorstep of death, still takes in my shape with what I think is deserved appreciation!

And you wanta know something else? Big Daddy didn't know how many little Maes and Goopers had been produced! "How many kids have you got?" he asked at the table, just like Brother Man and his wife were new acquaintances to him! Big Mama said he was jokin', but that ole boy wasn't jokin', Lord, no!

And when they infawmed him that they had five already and were turning out number six!—the news seemed to come as a sort of unpleasant surprise . . .

(*Children yell below.*)
Scream, monsters!
(*Turns to Brick with a sudden, gay, charming smile which fades as she notices that he is not looking at her but into fading gold space with a troubled expression.*)
(*It is constant rejection that makes her humor "bitchy."*)

Yes, you should of been at that supper-table, Baby.

(*Whenever she calls him "baby" the word is a soft caress.*)

Y'know, Big Daddy, bless his ole sweet soul, he's the dearest ole thing in the world, but he does hunch over his food as if he preferred not to notice anything else. Well, Mae an' Gooper were side by side at the table, direckly across from Big Daddy, watchin' his face like hawks while they jawed an' jabbered about the cuteness an' brilliance of th' no-neck monsters!

(*She giggles with a hand fluttering at her throat and her breast and her long throat arched.*)
(*She comes downstage and recreates the scene with voice and gesture.*)

And the no-neck monsters were ranged around the table, some in high chairs and some on th' *Books of Knowledge*, all in fancy little paper caps in honor of Big Daddy's birthday, and all through dinner, well, I want you to know that Brother Man an' his partner never once, for one moment, stopped exchanging pokes an' pinches an' kicks an' signs an' signals!—Why, they were like a couple of cardsharps fleecing a sucker.—Even Big Mama, bless her ole sweet soul, she isn't th' quickest an' brightest thing in the world, she finally noticed, at last, an' said to Gooper, "Gooper, what are you an' Mae makin' all these signs at each other about?"—I swear t' goodness, I nearly choked on my chicken!

(*Margaret, back at the dressing table, still doesn't see Brick. He is watching her with a look that is not quite definable—Amused? shocked? contemptuous?—part of those and part of something else.*)

Y'know—your brother Gooper still cherishes the illusion he took a giant step up on the social ladder when he married Miss Mae Flynn of the Memphis Flynns.

But I have a piece of Spanish news for Gooper. The Flynns never had a thing in this world but money and they lost that, they were nothing at all but fairly successful climbers. Of course, Mae Flynn came out in Memphis eight years before I made my debut in Nashville, but I had friends at Ward-Belmont who came from Memphis and they used to come to see me and I used to go to see them for Christmas and spring vacations, and so I know who rates an' who doesn't rate in Memphis society. Why, y'know ole Papa Flynn, he barely escaped doing time in the Federal pen for shady manipulations on th' stock market when his chain stores crashed, and as for Mae having been a cotton carnival queen, as they remind us so often, lest we forget, well, that's one honor that I don't envy her for!—Sit on a brass throne on a tacky float an' ride down Main Street, smilin', bowin', and blowin' kisses to all the trash on the street—

(*She picks out a pair of jeweled sandals and rushes to the dressing table.*)

Why, year before last, when Susan McPheeters was singled out fo' that honor, y'know what happened to her? Y'know what happened to poor little Susie McPheeters?

BRICK (*absently*): No. What happened to little Susie McPheeters?

MARGARET: Somebody spit tobacco juice in her face.

BRICK (*dreamily*): Somebody spit tobacco juice in her face?

MARGARET: That's right, some old drunk leaned out of a window in the Hotel Gayoso and yelled, "Hey, Queen, hey, hey, there, Queenie!" Poor Susie looked up and flashed him a radiant smile and he shot out a squirt of tobacco juice right in poor Susie's face.

BRICK: Well, what d'you know about that.

MARGARET (*gaily*): What do I know about it? I was there, I saw it!

BRICK (*absently*): Must have been kind of funny.

MARGARET: Susie didn't think so. Had hysterics. Screamed like a banshee. They had to stop th' parade an' remove her from her throne an' go on with—

(*She catches sight of him in the mirror, gasps slightly, wheels about to face him. Count ten.*)

—Why are you looking at me like that?

BRICK (*whistling softly, now*): Like what, Maggie?

MARGARET (*intensely, fearfully*): The way y' were lookin' at me just now, befo' I caught your eye in the mirror and you started t' whistle! I don't know how t' describe it but it froze my blood!—I've caught you lookin' at me like that so often lately. What are you thinkin' of when you look at me like that?

BRICK: I wasn't conscious of lookin' at you, Maggie.

MARGARET: Well, I was conscious of it! What were you thinkin'?

BRICK: I don't remember thinking of anything, Maggie.

MARGARET: Don't you think I know that—? Don't you—?—Think I know that—?

BRICK (*cooly*): Know *what*, Maggie?

MARGARET (*struggling for expression*): That I've gone through this—*hideous!*—transformation, become—*hard! Frantic!*

(*Then she adds, almost tenderly:*)

—cruel!!

That's what you've been observing in me lately. How could y' help but observe it? That's all right. I'm not—thin-skinned any more, can't afford t' be thin-skinned any more.

(*She is now recovering her power.*)

—But Brick? Brick?

BRICK: Did you say something?

MARGARET: I was *goin*' t' say something: that I get—lonely. Very!

BRICK: Ev'rybody gets that . . .

MARGARET: Living with someone you love can be lonelier—than living entirely *alone!*—if the one that y' love doesn't love you. . . .

(*There is a pause. Brick hobbles downstage and asks, without looking at her:*)

BRICK: Would you like to live alone, Maggie?

(*Another pause: then—after she has caught a quick, hurt breath:*)

MARGARET: *No!—God!—I wouldn't!*

(*Another gasping breath. She forcibly controls what must have been an impulse to cry out. We see her deliberately, very forcibly, going all the way back to the world in which you can talk about ordinary matters.*)

Did you have a nice shower?

BRICK: Uh-huh.

MARGARET: Was the water cool?

BRICK: No.

MARGARET: But it made y' feel fresh, huh?

BRICK: Fresher. . . .

MARGARET: I know something would make y' feel *much* fresher!

BRICK: What?

MARGARET: An alcohol rub. Or cologne, a rub with cologne!

BRICK: That's good after a workout but I haven't been workin' out, Maggie.

MARGARET: You've kept in good shape, though.

BRICK: (*indifferently*): You think so, Maggie?

MARGARET: I always thought drinkin' men lost their looks, but I was plainly mistaken.

BRICK (*wryly*): Why, thanks, Maggie.

MARGARET: You're the only drinkin' man I know that it never seems t' put fat on.

BRICK: I'm gettin' softer, Maggie.

MARGARET: Well, sooner or later it's bound to soften you up. It was just beginning to soften up Skipper when—

(*She stops short.*)

I'm sorry. I never could keep my fingers off a sore—I wish you *would* lose your looks. If you did it would make the martyrdom of Saint Maggie a little more bearable. But no such goddamn luck. I actually believe you've gotten better looking since you've gone on the bottle. Yeah, a person who didn't know you would think you'd never had a tense nerve in your body or a strained muscle.

(*There are sounds of croquet on the lawn below: the click of mallets, light voices, near and distant.*)

Of course, you always had that detached quality as if you were playing a game without much concern over whether you won or lost, and now that you've lost the game, not lost but just quit playing, you have that rare sort of charm that usually only happens in very old or hopelessly sick people, the charm of the defeated.—You look so cool, so cool, so enviably cool.

REVEREND TOOKER (*offstage right*): Now looka here, boy, lemme show you how to get outa that!

MARGARET: They're playing croquet. The moon has appeared and it's white, just beginning to turn a little bit yellow. . . .

You were a wonderful lover. . . .

Such a wonderful person to go to bed with, and I think mostly because you were really indifferent to it. Isn't that right? Never had any anxiety about it, did it naturally, easily, slowly, with absolute confidence and perfect calm, more like opening a door for a lady or seating her at a table than giving expression to any longing for her. Your indifference made you wonderful at lovemaking—*strange?*—but true. . . .

REVEREND TOOKER: Oh! That's a beauty.

DOCTOR BAUGH: Yeah. I got you boxed.

MARGARET: You know, if I thought you would never, never, *never* make love to me again—I would go downstairs to the kitchen and pick out the longest and sharpest knife I could find and stick it straight into my heart, I swear that I would!

REVEREND TOOKER: Watch out, you're gonna miss it.

DOCTOR BAUGH: You just don't know me, boy!

MARGARET: But one thing I don't have is the charm of the defeated, my hat is still in the ring, and I am determined to win!

(*There is the sound of croquet mallets hitting croquet balls.*)

REVEREND TOOKER: Mmm—You're too slippery for me.

MARGARET: —What is the victory of a cat on a hot tin roof?—I wish I knew. . . .
Just staying on it, I guess, as long as she can. . . .

DOCTOR BAUGH: Jus' like an eel, boy, jus' like an eel!

(*More croquet sounds.*)

MARGARET: Later tonight I'm going to tell you I love you an' maybe by that time you'll be drunk enough to believe me. Yes, they're playing croquet. . . .
Big Daddy is dying of cancer. . . .
What were you thinking of when I caught you looking at me like that? Were you thinking of Skipper?

(*Brick takes up his crutch, rises.*)

Oh, excuse me, forgive me, but laws of silence don't work! No, laws of silence don't work. . . .

(*Brick crosses to the bar, takes a quick drink, and rubs his head with a towel.*)

Laws of silence don't work. . . .
When something is festering in your memory or your imagination, laws of silence don't work, it's just like shutting a door and locking it on a house on fire in hope of forgetting that the house is burning. But not facing a fire doesn't put it out. Silence about a thing just magnifies it. It grows and festers in silence, becomes malignant. . . .

(*He drops his crutch.*)

BRICK: Give me my crutch.

(*He has stopped rubbing his hair dry but still stands hanging onto the towel rack in a white towel-cloth robe.*)

MARGARET: Lean on me.

BRICK: No, just give me my crutch.

MARGARET: Lean on my shoulder.

BRICK: *I don't want to lean on your shoulder, I want my crutch!*

(*This is spoken like sudden lightning.*)

Are you going to give me my crutch or do I have to get down on my knees on the floor and—

MARGARET: *Here, here, take it, take it!*

(*She has thrust the crutch at him.*)

BRICK (*hobbling out*): Thanks . . .

MARGARET: We mustn't scream at each other, the walls in this house have ears. . . .

(*He hobbles directly to liquor cabinet to get a new drink.*)

—but that's the first time I've heard you raise your voice in a long time, Brick. A crack in the wall?—Of composure?
—I think that's a good sign. . . .
A sign of nerves in a player on the defensive!

(*Brick turns and smiles at her coolly over his fresh drink.*)

BRICK: It just hasn't happened yet, Maggie.

MARGARET: What?

BRICK: The click I get in my head when I've had enough of this stuff to make me peaceful. . . .
Will you do me a favor?

MARGARET: Maybe I will. What favor?

BRICK: Just, just keep your voice down!

MARGARET (*in a hoarse whisper*): I'll do you that favor, I'll speak in a whisper, if not shut up completely, if *you* will do *me* a favor and make that drink your last one till after the party.

BRICK: What party?

MARGARET: Big Daddy's birthday party.

BRICK: Is this Big Daddy's birthday?

MARGARET: You know this is Big Daddy's birthday!

BRICK: No, I don't, I forgot it.

MARGARET: Well, I remembered it for you . . .

(*They are both speaking as breathlessly as a pair of kids after a fight, drawing deep exhausted breaths and looking at each other with faraway eyes, shaking and panting together as if they had broken apart from a violent struggle.*)

BRICK: Good for you, Maggie.

MARGARET: You just have to scribble a few lines on this card.

BRICK: You scribble something, Maggie.

MARGARET: It's got to be your handwriting; it's your present, I've given him my present; it's got to be your handwriting!

(*The tension between them is building again, the voices becoming shrill once more.*)

BRICK: I didn't get him a present.

MARGARET: I got one for you.

BRICK: All right. You write the card, then.

MARGARET: And have him know you didn't remember his birthday?

BRICK: I didn't remember his birthday.

MARGARET: You don't have to prove you didn't!

BRICK: I don't want to fool him about it.

MARGARET: Just write "Love, Brick!" for God's—

BRICK: No.

MARGARET: You've *got* to!

BRICK: I don't have to do anything I don't want to do. You keep forgetting the conditions on which I agreed to stay on living with you.

MARGARET (*out before she knows it*): I'm not living with you. We occupy the same cage.

BRICK: You've got to remember the conditions agreed on.

SONNY (*offstage*): Mommy, give it to me. I had it first.

MAE: Hush.

MARGARET: They're impossible conditions!

BRICK: Then why don't you—?

SONNY: I want it, I want it!

MAE: Get away!

MARGARET: HUSH! Who is out there? Is somebody at the door?

(*There are footsteps in hall.*)

MAE (*outside*): May I enter a moment?

MARGARET: Oh, *you!* Sure. Come in, Mae.

(*Mae enters bearing aloft the bow of a young lady's archery set.*)

MAE: Brick, is this thing yours?

MARGARET: Why, Sister Woman—that's my Diana Trophy. Won it at the intercollegiate archery contest on the Ole Miss campus.

MAE: It's a mighty dangerous thing to leave exposed round a house full of nawmal rid-blooded children attracted t'weapons.

MARGARET: "Nawmal rid-blooded children attracted t'weapons" ought t'be taught to keep their hands off things that don't belong to them.

MAE: Maggie, honey, if you had children of your own you'd know how funny that is. Will you please lock this up and put the key out of reach?

MARGARET: Sister Woman, nobody is plotting the destruction of your kiddies.—Brick and I still have our special archers' license. We're goin' deer-huntin' on Moon Lake as soon as the season starts. I love to run with dogs through chilly woods, run, run leap over obstructions—

(*She goes into the closet carrying the bow.*)

MAE: How's the injured ankle, Brick?

BRICK: Doesn't hurt. Just itches.

MAE: Oh, my! Brick—Brick, you should've been downstairs after supper! Kiddies put on a show. Polly played the piano, Buster an' Sonny drums, an' then they turned out the lights an' Dixie an' Trixie puhfawmed a toe dance in fairy costume with *spahkluhs!* Big Daddy just beamed! He just beamed!

MARGARET (*from the closet with a sharp laugh*): Oh, I bet. It breaks my heart that we missed it!

(*She reenters.*)

But Mae? Why did y'give dawgs' names to all your kiddies?

MAE: *Dogs'* names?

MARGARET (*sweetly*): Dixie, Trixie, Buster, Sonny, Polly!—Sounds like four dogs and a parrot . . .

MAE: Maggie?

(*Margaret turns with a smile.*)

Why are you so catty?

MARGARET: Cause I'm a cat! But why can't *you* take a joke, Sister Woman?

MAE: Nothin' pleases me more than a joke that's funny. You know the real names of our kiddies. Buster's real name is Robert. Sonny's real name is Saunders. Trixie's real name is Marlene and Dixie's—

(*Gooper downstairs calls for her. "Hey, Mae! Sister Woman, intermission is over!"—She rushes to door, saying:*)

Intermission is over! See ya later!

MARGARET: I wonder what Dixie's real name is?

BRICK: Maggie, being catty doesn't help things any . . .

MARGARET: I know! *WHY!*—Am I so catty?—Cause I'm consumed with envy an' eaten up with longing?—Brick, I'm going to lay out your beautiful Shantung silk suit from Rome and one of your monogrammed silk shirts. I'll put your cuff links in it, those lovely star sapphires I get you to wear so rarely. . . .

BRICK: I can't get trousers on over this plaster cast.

MARGARET: Yes, you can, I'll help you.

BRICK: I'm not going to get dressed, Maggie.

MARGARET: Will you just put on a pair of white silk pajamas?

BRICK: Yes, I'll do that, Maggie.

MARGARET: *Thank* you, thank you so *much!*

BRICK: Don't mention it.

MARGARET: *Oh, Brick!* How long does it have t' go on? This punishment? Haven't I done time enough, haven't I served my term, can't I apply for a—pardon?

BRICK: Maggie, you're spoiling my liquor. Lately your voice always sounds like you'd been running upstairs to warn somebody that the house was on fire!

MARGARET: Well, no wonder, no wonder. Y'know what I feel like, Brick?

I feel all the time like a cat on a hot tin roof!

BRICK: Then jump off the roof, jump off it, cats can jump off roofs and land on their four feet uninjured!

MARGARET: Oh, yes!

BRICK: Do it!—fo' God's sake, do it . . .

MARGARET: Do what?

BRICK: Take a lover!

MARGARET: I can't see a man but you! Even with my eyes closed, I just see you! Why don't you get ugly, Brick, why don't you please get fat or ugly or something so I could stand it?

Maggie (Barbara Bel Geddes)
and Brick (Ben Gazzara) in
the original 1955 Broadway
production of *Cat on a Hot
Tin Roof.*

Barbara Bel Geddes as Maggie.

Maggie (Anika Noni Rose) attempts to seduce Brick (Terrence Howard) in the 2008 New York production of *Cat on a Hot Tin Roof*, directed by Debbie Allen.

(*She rushes to hall door, opens it, listens.*)

The concert is still going on! Bravo, no-necks, bravo!

(*She slams and locks door fiercely.*)

BRICK: What did you lock the door for?
MARGARET: To give us a little privacy for a while.
BRICK: You know better, Maggie.
MARGARET: No, I don't know better. . . .

(*She rushes to gallery doors, draws the rose-silk drapes across them.*)

BRICK: Don't make a fool of yourself.
MARGARET: I don't mind makin' a fool of myself over you!
BRICK: I mind, Maggie. I feel embarrassed for you.
MARGARET: Feel embarrassed! But don't continue my torture. I can't live on and on under these circumstances.
BRICK: You agreed to—
MARGARET: I know but—
BRICK:—Accept that condition!
MARGARET: *I CAN'T! CAN'T! CAN'T!*

(*She seizes his shoulder.*)

BRICK: Let go!

(*He breaks away from her and seizes the small boudoir chair and raises it like a lion-tamer facing a big circus cat.*)

(*Count five. She stares at him with her fist pressed to her mouth, then bursts into shrill, almost hysterical laughter. He remains grave for a moment, then grins and puts the chair down.*)

(*Big Mama calls through closed door.*)

BIG MAMA: Son? Son? Son?
BRICK: What is it, Big Mama?
BIG MAMA (*outside*): Oh, son! We got the most wonderful news about Big Daddy. I just had t' run up an' tell you right this—

(*She rattles the knob.*)

—What's this door doin', locked, faw? You all think there's robbers in the house?
MARGARET: Big Mama, Brick is dressin', he's not dressed yet.
BIG MAMA: That's all right, it won't be the first time I've seen Brick not dressed. Come on, open this door!

(*Margaret, with a grimace, goes to unlock and open the hall door, as Brick hobbles rapidly to the bathroom and kicks the door shut. Big Mama has disappeared from the hall.*)

MARGARET: Big Mama?

(*Big Mama appears through the opposite gallery doors behind Margaret, huffing and puffing like an old bulldog. She is a short, stout woman; her sixty years and 170 pounds have left her somewhat breathless most of the time; she's always tensed like a boxer, or rather, a*

Japanese wrestler. Her "family" was maybe a little superior to Big Daddy's, but not much. She wears a black or silver lace dress and at least half a million in flashy gems. She is very sincere.)

BIG MAMA (*loudly, startling Margaret*): Here—I come through Gooper's and Mae's gall'ry door. Where's Brick? *Brick*—Hurry on out of there son, I just have a second and want to give you the news about Big Daddy.—I hate locked doors in a house . . .

MARGARET (*with affected lightness*): I've noticed you do, Big Mama, but people have got to have *some* moments of privacy, don't they?

BIG MAMA: No, ma'am, not in *my* house. (*Without pause.*) Whacha took off you' dress faw? I thought that little lace dress was so sweet on yuh, honey.

MARGARET: I thought it looked sweet on me, too, but one of m' cute little table-partners used it for a napkin so—!

BIG MAMA (*picking up stockings on floor*): What?

MARGARET: You know, Big Mama, Mae and Gooper's so touchy about those children—thanks, Big Mama . . .

(Big Mama has thrust the picked-up stockings in Margaret's hand with a grunt.)

—that you just don't dare to suggest there's any room for improvement in their—

BIG MAMA: Brick, hurry out!—Shoot, Maggie, you just don't like children.

MARGARET: I do SO like children! Adore them!—well brought up!

BIG MAMA (*gentle—loving*): Well, why don't you have some and bring them up well, then, instead of all the time pickin' on Gooper's an' Mae's?

GOOPER (*shouting up the stairs*): Hey, hey, Big Mama, Betsy an' Hugh got to go, waitin' t' tell yuh g'by!

BIG MAMA: Tell 'em to hold their hawses, I'll be right down in a jiffy!

GOOPER: Yes ma'am!

(She turns to the bathroom door and calls out.)

BIG MAMA: Son? Can you hear me in there?

(There is a muffled answer.)

We just got the full report from the laboratory at the Ochsner Clinic, completely negative, son, ev'rything negative, right on down the line! Nothin' a-tall's wrong with him but some little functional thing called a spastic colon. Can you hear me, son?

MARGARET: He can hear you, Big Mama.

BIG MAMA: Then why don't he say something? God Almighty, a piece of news like that should make him shout. It made *me* shout, I can tell you. I shouted and sobbed and fell right down on my knees!—Look!

(She pulls up her skirt.)

See the bruises where I hit my kneecaps? Took both doctors to haul me back on my feet!

(She laughs—she always laughs like hell at herself.)

Big Daddy was furious with me! But ain't that wonderful news?

(Facing bathroom again, she continues:)

After all the anxiety we been through to git a report like that on Big Daddy's birthday? Big Daddy tried to hide how much of a load that news took off his mind, but didn't fool *me*. He was mighty close to crying about it *himself*!

(Good-byes are shouted downstairs, and she rushes to door.)

GOOPER: Big Mama!

BIG MAMA: *Hold those people down there, don't let them go!*—Now, git dressed we're all comin' up to this room fo' Big Daddy's birthday party because of your ankle.—How's his ankle, Maggie?

MARGARET: Well, he broke it, Big Mama.

BIG MAMA: I know he broke it.

(A phone is ringing in hall. A Negro voice answers: "Mistuh Polly's res'dence.")

I mean does it hurt him much still.

MARGARET: I'm afraid I can't give you that information, Big Mama. You'll have to ask Brick if it hurts much still or not.

SOOKEY (*in the hall*): It's Memphis, Mizz Polly, it's Miss Sally in Memphis.

BIG MAMA: Awright, Sookey.

(Big Mama rushes into the hall and is heard shouting on the phone:)

Hello, Miss Sally. How are you, Miss Sally?—Yes, well, I was just gonna call you about it. *Shoot!*—

MARGARET: Brick, don't!

(Big Mama raises her voice to a bellow.)

BIG MAMA: *Miss Sally? Don't ever call me from the Gayoso Lobby, too much talk goes on in that hotel lobby, no wonder you can't hear me!* Now listen, Miss Sally. They's nothin' serious wrong with Big Daddy. We got the report just now, they's nothin' wrong but a thing called a—spastic! SPASTIC!—colon . . .

(She appears at the hall door and calls to Margaret.)

—Maggie, come out here and talk to that fool on the phone. I'm shouted breathless!

MARGARET (*goes out and is heard sweetly at phone*): Miss Sally? This is Brick's wife, Maggie. So nice to hear your voice. Can you hear *mine*? Well, good!—Big Mama just wanted you to know that they've got the report from the Ochsner Clinic and what Big Daddy has is a spastic colon. Yes. Spastic colon, Miss Sally. That's right, spastic colon. G'bye, Miss Sally, hope I'll see you real soon!

(Hangs up a little before Miss Sally was probably ready to terminate the talk. She returns through the hall door.)

She heard me perfectly. I've discovered with deaf people the thing to do is not shout at them but just enunciate clearly. My rich old Aunt Cornelia was deaf as the dead but I could make her hear me just by sayin' each word slowly, distinctly, close to her ear. I read her the *Commercial Appeal* ev'ry night, read her the classified ads in it, even, she never missed a word of it. But was she a mean ole thing! Know what I got when she died? Her unexpired subscriptions to five magazines and the Book-of-the-Month Club and a LIBRARY full of ev'ry dull book ever written! All else went to her hellcat of a sister . . . meaner than she was, even!

(*Big Mama has been straightening things up in the room during this speech.*)

BIG MAMA (*closing closet door on discarded clothes*): Miss Sally sure is a case! Big Daddy says she's always got her hand out fo' something. He's not mistaken. That poor ole thing always has her hand out fo' somethin'. I don't think Big Daddy gives her as much as he should.

GOOPER: Big Mama! Come on now! Betsy and Hugh can't wait no longer!

BIG MAMA (*shouting*): I'm comin'!

(*She starts out. At the hall door, turns and jerks a forefinger, first toward the bathroom door, then toward the liquor cabinet, meaning: "Has Brick been drinking?" Margaret pretends not to understand, cocks her head and raises her brows as if the pantomimic performance was completely mystifying to her.*)

(*Big Mama rushes back to Margaret:*)

Shoot! Stop playin' so dumb!—I mean has he been drinkin' that stuff much yet?

MARGARET (*with a little laugh*): Oh! I think he had a highball after supper.

BIG MAMA: Don't laugh about it!—Some single men stop drinkin' when they git married and others start! Brick never touched liquor before he—!

MARGARET (*crying out*): THAT'S NOT FAIR!

BIG MAMA: Fair or not fair I want to ask you a question, one question: D'you make Brick happy in bed?

MARGARET: Why don't you ask if he makes *me* happy in bed?

BIG MAMA: Because I know that—

MARGARET: *It works both ways!*

BIG MAMA: Something's not right! You're childless and my son drinks!

GOOPER: Come on, Big Mama!

(*Gooper has called her downstairs and she has rushed to the door on the line above. She turns at the door and points at the bed.*)

—When a marriage goes on the rocks, the rocks are there, right *there!*

MARGARET: *That's*—

(*Big Mama has swept out of the room and slammed the door.*)

—not—*fair* . . .

(*Margaret is alone, completely alone, and she feels it. She draws in, bunches her shoulders, raises her arms with fists clenched, shuts her eyes tight as a child about to be stabbed with a vaccination needle. When she opens her eyes again, what she sees is the long oval mirror and she rushes straight to it, stares into it with a grimace and says: "Who are you?"—Then she crouches a little and answers herself in a different voice which is high, thin, mocking: "I am Maggie the Cat!"—Straightens quickly as bathroom door opens a little and Brick calls out to her.*)

BRICK: Has Big Mama gone?
MARGARET: She's gone.

(*He opens the bathroom door and hobbles out, with his liquor glass now empty, straight to the liquor cabinet. He is whistling softly. Margaret's head pivots on her long, slender throat to watch him.*)

(*She raises a hand uncertainly to the base of her throat, as if it was difficult for her to swallow, before she speaks:*)

You know, our sex life didn't just peter out in the usual way, it was cut off short, long before the natural time for it to, and it's going to revive again, just as sudden as that. I'm confident of it. That's what I'm keeping myself attractive for. For the time when you'll see me again like other men see me. Yes, like other men see me. They still see me, Brick, and they like what they see. Uh-huh. Some of them would give their—

Look, Brick!

(*She stands before the long oval mirror, touches her breast and then her hips with her two hands.*)

How high my body stays on me!—Nothing has fallen on me—not a fraction. . . .

(*Her voice is soft and trembling: a pleading child's. At this moment as he turns to glance at her—a look which is like a player passing a ball to another player, third down and goal to go—she has to capture the audience in a grip so tight that she can hold it till the first intermission without any lapse of attention.*)

Other men still want me. My face looks strained, sometimes, but I've kept my figure as well as you've kept yours, and men admire it. I still turn heads on the street. Why, last week in Memphis everywhere that I went men's eyes burned holes in my clothes, at the country club and in restaurants and department stores, there wasn't a man I met or walked by that didn't just eat me up with his eyes and turn around when I passed him and look back at me. Why, at Alice's party for her New York cousins, the best-lookin' man in the crowd—followed me upstairs and tried to force his way in the powder room with me, followed me to the door and tried to force his way in!

BRICK: Why didn't you let him, Maggie?

MARGARET: Because I'm not that common, for one thing. Not that I wasn't almost tempted to. You like to know who it was? It was Sonny Boy Maxwell, that's who!

BRICK: Oh, yeah, Sonny Boy Maxwell, he was a good end-runner but had a little injury to his back and had to quit.

MARGARET: He has no injury now and has no wife and still has a lech for me!

BRICK: I see no reason to lock him out of a powder room in that case.

MARGARET: And have someone catch me at it? I'm not that stupid. Oh, I might sometime cheat on you with someone, since you're so insultingly eager to have me do it!—But if I do, you can be damned sure it will be in a place and a time where no one but me and the man could possibly know. Because I'm not going to give you any excuse to divorce me for being unfaithful or anything else. . . .

BRICK: Maggie, I wouldn't divorce you for being unfaithful or anything else. Don't you know that? Hell. I'd be relieved to know that you'd found yourself a lover.

MARGARET: Well, I'm taking no chances. No, I'd rather stay on this hot tin roof.

BRICK: A hot tin roof's 'n uncomfo'table place t' stay on. . . .

(*He starts to whistle softly.*)

MARGARET (*through his whistle*): Yeah, but I can stay on it just as long as I have to.

BRICK: You could leave me, Maggie.

(*He resumes whistle. She wheels about to glare at him.*)

MARGARET: *Don't want to and will not!* Besides if I did, you don't have a cent to pay for it but what you get from Big Daddy and he's dying of cancer!

(*For the first time a realization of Big Daddy's doom seems to penetrate to Brick's consciousness, visibly, and he looks at Margaret.*)

BRICK: Big Mama just said he *wasn't*, that the report was okay.

MARGARET: That's what she thinks because she got the same story that they gave Big Daddy. And was just as taken in by it as he was, poor ole things. . . .

But tonight they're going to tell her the truth about it. When Big Daddy goes to bed, they're going to tell her that he is dying of cancer.

(*She slams the dresser drawer.*)

—It's malignant and it's terminal.

BRICK: Does Big Daddy know it?

MARGARET: Hell, do they *ever* know it? Nobody says, "You're dying." You have to fool them. They have to fool *themselves*.

BRICK: Why?

MARGARET: *Why?* Because human beings dream of life everlasting, that's the reason! But most of them want it on earth and not in heaven.

(*He gives a short, hard laugh at her touch of humor.*)

Well. . . . (*She touches up her mascara.*) That's how it is, anyhow. . . . (*She looks about.*) Where did I put down my cigarette? Don't want to burn up the homeplace, at least not with Mae and Gooper and their five monsters in it!

(*She has found it and sucks at it greedily. Blows out smoke and continues:*)

So this is Big Daddy's last birthday. And Mae and Gooper, they know it, oh, *they* know it, all right. They got the first information from the Ochsner Clinic. That's why they rushed down here with their no-neck monsters. Because. Do you know something? Big Daddy's made no will? Big Daddy's never made out any will in his life, and so this campaign's afoot to impress him, forcibly as possible, with the fact that you drink and I've borne no children!

(*He continues to stare at her a moment, then mutters something sharp but not audible and hobbles rather rapidly out onto the long gallery in the fading, much faded, gold light.*)

MARGARET (*continuing her liturgical chant*): Y'know, I'm *fond* of Big Daddy, I am genuinely fond of that old man, I really *am*, you know. . . .

BRICK (*faintly, vaguely*): Yes, I know you are. . . .

MARGARET: I've always sort of admired him in spite of his coarseness, his four-letter words and so forth. Because Big Daddy *is* what he *is*, and he makes no bones about it. He hasn't turned gentleman farmer, he's still a Mississippi redneck, as much of a redneck as he must have been when he was just overseer here on the old Jack Straw and Peter Ochello place. But he got hold of it an' built it into th' biggest an' finest plantation in the Delta.—I've always *liked* Big Daddy. . . .

(*She crosses to the proscenium.*)

Well, this is Big Daddy's last birthday. I'm sorry about it. But I'm facing the facts. It takes money to take care of a drinker and that's the office that I've been elected to lately.

BRICK: You don't have to take care of me.

MARGARET: Yes, I do. Two people in the same boat have got to take care of each other. At least you want money to buy more Echo Spring when this supply is exhausted, or will you be satisfied with a ten-cent beer?

Mae an' Gooper are plannin' to freeze us out of Big Daddy's estate because you drink and I'm childless. But we can defeat that plan. We're *going* to defeat that plan!

Brick, y'know, I've been so God damn disgustingly poor all my life!—That's the *truth*, Brick!

BRICK: I'm not sayin' it isn't.

MARGARET: Always had to suck up to people I couldn't stand because they had money and I was poor as

Job's turkey. You don't know what that's like. Well, I'll tell you, it's like you would feel a thousand miles away from Echo Spring!—And had to get back to it on that broken ankle . . . without a crutch!

That's how it feels to be as poor as Job's turkey and have to suck up to relatives that you hated because they had money and all you had was a bunch of hand-me-down clothes and a few old moldy three-percent government bonds. My daddy loved his liquor, he fell in love with his liquor the way you've fallen in love with Echo Spring!—And my poor Mama, having to maintain some semblance of social position, to keep appearances up, on an income of one hundred and fifty dollars a month on those old government bonds!

When I came out, the year that I made my debut, I had just two evening dresses! One Mother made me from a pattern in *Vogue*, the other a hand-me-down from a snotty rich cousin I hated!

—The dress that I married you in was my grandmother's weddin' gown. . . .

So that's why I'm like a cat on a hot tin roof!

(*Brick is still on the gallery. Someone below calls up to him in a warm Negro voice, "Hiya, Mistuh Brick, how yuh feelin'?" Brick raises his liquor glass as if that answered the question.*)

MARGARET: You can be young without money, but you can't be old without it. You've got to be old *with* money because to be old without it is just too awful, you've got to be one or the other, either *young* or *with money*, you can't be old and *without* it.—That's the *truth*, Brick. . . .

(*Brick whistles softly, vaguely.*)

Well, now I'm dressed, I'm all dressed, there's nothing else for me to do.

(*Forlornly, almost fearfully.*)

I'm dressed, all dressed, nothing else for me to do . . .

(*She moves about restlessly, aimlessly, and speaks, as if to herself.*)

What am I—? Oh!—my bracelets. . . .

(*She starts working a collection of bracelets over her hands onto her wrists, about six on each, as she talks.*)

I've thought a whole lot about it and now I know when I made my mistake. Yes, I made my mistake when I told you the truth about that thing with Skipper. Never should have confessed it, a fatal error, tellin' you about that thing with Skipper.

BRICK: Maggie, shut up about Skipper. I mean it, Maggie; you got to shut up about Skipper.

MARGARET: You ought to understand that Skipper and I—

BRICK: You don't think I'm serious, Maggie? You're fooled by the fact that I am saying this quiet? Look,

Maggie. What you're doing is a dangerous thing to do. You're—you're—you're—foolin' with something that—nobody ought to fool with.

MARGARET: This time I'm going to finish what I have to say to you. Skipper and I made love, if love you could call it, because it made both of us feel a little bit closer to you. You see, you son of a bitch, you asked too much of people, of me, of him, of all the unlucky poor damned sons of bitches that happen to love you, and there was a whole pack of them, yes, there was a pack of them besides me and Skipper, you asked too goddamn much of people that loved you, you—superior creature!—you godlike being!—And so we made love to each other to dream it was you, both of us! Yes, yes, yes! Truth, truth! What's so awful about it? I like it, I think the truth is—yeah! I shouldn't have told you. . . .

BRICK (*holding his head unnaturally still and uptilted a bit*): It was Skipper that told me about it. Not you, Maggie.

MARGARET: I told you!

BRICK: After he told me!

MARGARET: What does it matter who—?

DIXIE: I got your mallet, I got your mallet.

TRIXIE: Give it to me, give it to me. IT's mine.

(*Brick turns suddenly out upon the gallery and calls:*)

BRICK: Little girl! Hey, little girl!

LITTLE GIRL (*at a distance*): What, Uncle Brick?

BRICK: Tell the folks to come up!—Bring everybody upstairs!

TRIXIE: It's mine, it's mine.

MARGARET: I can't stop myself! I'd go on telling you this in front of them all, if I had to!

BRICK: Little girl! Go on, go on, will you? Do what I told you, call them!

DIXIE: Okay.

MARGARET: Because it's got to be told and you, you!—you never let me!

(*She sobs, then controls herself, and continues almost calmly.*)

It was one of those beautiful, ideal things they tell about in the Greek legends, it couldn't be anything else, you being you, and that's what made it so sad, that's what made it so awful, because it was love that never could be carried through to anything satisfying or even talked about plainly.

BRICK: Maggie, you gotta stop this.

MARGARET: Brick, I tell you, you got to believe me, Brick, I *do* understand all about it! I—I think it was—*noble!* Can't you tell I'm sincere when I say I respect it? My only point, the only point that I'm making, is life has got to be allowed to continue even after the *dream* of life is—all—over. . . .

(*Brick is without his crutch. Leaning on furniture, he crosses to pick it up as she continues as if possessed by a will outside herself:*)

Why I remember when we double-dated at college, Gladys Fitzgerald and I and you and Skipper, it was more like a date between you and Skipper. Gladys and I were just sort of tagging along as if it was necessary to chaperone you!—to make a good public impression—

BRICK (*turns to face her, half lifting his crutch*): Maggie, you want me to hit you with this crutch? Don't you know I could kill you with this crutch?

MARGARET: Good Lord, man, d' you think I'd care if you did?

BRICK: One man has one great good true thing in his life. One great good thing which is true!—I had friendship with Skipper.—You are naming it dirty!

MARGARET: I'm not naming it dirty! I am naming it clean.

BRICK: Not love with you, Maggie, but friendship with Skipper was that one great true thing, and you are naming it dirty!

MARGARET: Then you haven't been listenin', not understood what I'm saying! I'm naming it so damn clean that it killed poor Skipper!—You two had something that had to be kept on ice, yes, incorruptible, yes!—and death was the only icebox where you could keep it....

BRICK: I married you, Maggie. Why would I marry you, Maggie, if I was—?

MARGARET: Brick, let me finish!—I know, believe me I know, that it was only Skipper that harbored even any *unconscious* desire for anything not perfectly pure between you two!—Now let me skip a little. You married me early that summer we graduated out of Ole Miss, and we were happy, weren't we, we were blissful, yes, hit heaven together ev'ry time that we loved! But that fall you an' Skipper turned down wonderful offers of jobs in order to keep on bein' football heroes—pro-football heroes. You organized the Dixie Stars that fall, so you could keep on bein' teammates forever! But somethin' was not right with it!—*Me included!*—between you. Skipper began hittin' the bottle ... you got a spinal injury—couldn't play the Thanksgivin' game in Chicago, watched it on TV from a traction bed in Toledo. I joined Skipper. The Dixie Stars lost because poor Skipper was drunk. We drank together that night all night in the bar of the Blackstone and when cold day was comin' up over the Lake an' we were comin' out drunk to take a dizzy look at it, I said, "SKIPPER! STOP LOVIN' MY HUSBAND OR TELL HIM HE'S GOT TO LET YOU ADMIT IT TO HIM!"—one way or another!

HE SLAPPED ME HARD ON THE MOUTH!—then turned and ran without stopping once, I am sure, all the way back into his room at the Blackstone....

—When I came to his room that night, with a little scratch like a shy little mouse at his door, he made that pitiful, ineffectual little attempt to prove that what I had said wasn't true....

(*Brick strikes at her with crutch, a blow that shatters the gemlike lamp on the table.*)

—In this way, I destroyed him, by telling him truth that he and his world which he was born and raised in, yours and his world, had told him could not be told?

—From then on Skipper was nothing at all but a receptacle for liquor and drugs....

—*Who shot cock robin? I with my*—

(*She throws back her head with tight shut eyes.*)

—*merciful arrow!*

(*Brick strikes at her; misses.*)

Missed me!—Sorry,—I'm not tryin' to whitewash my behavior, Christ, no! Brick, I'm not good. I don't know why people have to pretend to be good, nobody's good. The rich or the well-to-do can afford to respect moral patterns, conventional moral patterns, but I could never afford to, yeah, but—I'm honest! Give me credit for just that, will you *please?*—Born poor, raised poor, expect to die poor unless I manage to get us something out of what Big Daddy leaves when he dies of cancer! But Brick?!—*Skipper is dead! I'm alive!* Maggie the cat is—

(*Brick hops awkwardly forward and strikes at her again with his crutch.*)

—*alive! I am alive, alive! I am* ...

(*He hurls the crutch at her, across the bed she took refuge behind, and pitches forward on the floor as she completes her speech.*)

—*alive!*

(*A little girl, Dixie, bursts into the room, wearing an Indian war bonnet and firing a cap pistol at Margaret and shouting: "Bang, bang, bang!"*)

(*Laughter downstairs floats through the open hall door. Margaret had crouched gasping to bed at child's entrance. She now rises and says with cool fury:*)

Little girl, your mother or someone should teach you—(*gasping*)—to knock at a door before you come into a room. Otherwise people might think that you—lack—good breeding....

DIXIE: Yanh, yanh, yanh, what is Uncle Brick doin' on th' floor?

BRICK: I tried to kill your Aunt Maggie, but I failed—and I fell. Little girl, give me my crutch so I can get up off th' floor.

MARGARET: Yes, give your uncle his crutch, he's a cripple, honey, he broke his ankle last night jumping hurdles on the high school athletic field!

DIXIE: What were you jumping hurdles for, Uncle Brick?

BRICK: Because I used to jump them, and people like to do what they used to do, even after they've stopped being able to do it....

MARGARET: That's right, that's your answer, now go away, little girl.

(*Dixie fires cap pistol at Margaret three times.*)

> Stop, you stop that, monster! You little no-neck monster!

(*She seizes the cap pistol and hurls it through gallery doors.*)

DIXIE (*with a precocious instinct for the cruelest thing*): You're *jealous!*—You're just jealous because you can't have babies!

(*She sticks out her tongue at Margaret as she sashays past her with her stomach stuck out, to the gallery. Margaret slams the gallery doors and leans panting against them. There is a pause. Brick has replaced his spilt drink and sits, faraway, on the great four-poster bed.*)

MARGARET: You see?—they gloat over us being childless, even in front of their five little no-neck monsters!

(*Pauses. Voices approach on the stairs.*)

> Brick?—I've been to a doctor in Memphis, a—a gynecologist....
> I've been completely examined, and there is no reason why we can't have a child whenever we want one. And this is my time by the calendar to conceive. Are you listening to me? Are you? Are you LISTENING TO ME!

BRICK: Yes. I hear you, Maggie.

(*His attention returns to her inflamed face.*)

> —But how in hell on earth do you imagine—that you're going to have a child by a man that can't stand you?

MARGARET: That's a problem that I will have to work out.

(*She wheels about to face the hall door.*)

MAE (*offstage left*): Come on, Big Daddy. We're all goin' up to Brick's room.

(*From offstage left, voices: Reverend Tooker, Doctor Baugh, Mae.*)

MARGARET: *Here they come!*

(*The lights dim.*)

ACT 2

(*There is no lapse of time. Margaret and Brick are in the same positions they held at the end of act 1.*)

MARGARET (*at door*): Here they come!

(*Big Daddy appears first, a tall man with a fierce, anxious look, moving carefully not to betray his weakness even, or especially, to himself.*)

GOOPER: I read in the *Register* that you're getting a new memorial window.

(*Some of the people are approaching through the hall, others along the gallery: voices from both directions. Gooper and Reverend Tooker become visible outside gallery doors, and their voices come in clearly.*)
(*They pause outside as Gooper lights a cigar.*)

REVEREND TOOKER (*vivaciously*): Oh, but St. Paul's in Grenada has three memorial windows, and the latest one is a Tiffany stained-glass window that cost twenty-five hundred dollars, a picture of Christ the Good Shepherd with a Lamb in His arms.

MARGARET: Big Daddy.

BIG DADDY: Well, Brick.

BRICK: Hello Big Daddy.—Congratulations!

BIG DADDY:—Crap....

GOOPER: Who give that window, Preach?

REVEREND TOOKER: Clyde Fletcher's widow. Also presented St. Paul's with a baptismal font.

GOOPER: Y'know what somebody ought t' give your church is a *coolin'* system, Preach.

MAE (*almost religiously*):—Let's see now, they've had their *tyyy*-phoid shots, and their tetanus shots, their diphtheria shots and their hepatitis shots and their polio shots, they got *those* shots every month from May through September, and—Gooper? Hey! Gooper!—What all have the kiddies been shot faw?

REVEREND TOOKER: Yes, siree, Bob! And y'know what Gus Hamma's family gave in his memory to the church at Two Rivers? A complete new stone parish-house with a basketball court in the basement and a—

BIG DADDY (*uttering a loud barking laugh which is far from truly mirthful*): Hey, Preach! What's all this talk about memorials, Preach? Y' think somebody's about t' kick off around here? 'S that it?

(*Startled by this interjection, Reverend Tooker decides to laugh at the question almost as loud as he can.*)
(*How he would answer the question we'll never know, as he's spared that embarrassment by the voice of Gooper's wife, Mae, rising high and clear as she appears with "Doc" Baugh, the family doctor, through the hall door.*)

MARGARET (*overlapping a bit*): Turn on the hi-fi, Brick! Let's have some music t' start off th' party with!

BRICK: You turn it on, Maggie.

(*The talk becomes so general that the room sounds like a great aviary of chattering birds. Only Brick remains unengaged, leaning upon the liquor cabinet with his faraway smile, an ice cube in a paper napkin with which he now and then rubs his forehead. He doesn't respond to Margaret's command. She bounds forward and stoops over the instrument panel of the console.*)

GOOPER: We gave 'em that thing for a third anniversary present, got three speakers in it.

(*The room is suddenly blasted by the climax of a Wagnerian opera or a Beethoven symphony.*)

BIG DADDY: *Turn that damn thing off!*

(*Almost instant silence, almost instantly broken by the shouting charge of Big Mama, entering through hall door like a charging rhino.*)

BIG MAMA: *Wha's my Brick, wha's mah precious baby!!*
BIG DADDY: *Sorry! Turn it back on!*

(*Everyone laughs very loud. Big Daddy is famous for his jokes at Big Mama's expense, and nobody laughs louder at these jokes than Big Mama herself, though sometimes they're pretty cruel and Big Mama has to pick up or fuss with something to cover the hurt that the loud laugh doesn't quite cover.*)
   (*On this occasion, a happy occasion because the dread in her heart has also been lifted by the false report on Big Daddy's condition, she giggles, grotesquely, coyly, in Big Daddy's direction and bears down upon Brick, all very quick and alive.*)

BIG MAMA: Here he is, here's my precious baby! What's that you've got in your hand? You put that liquor down, son, your hand was made fo' holdin' somethin' better than that!
GOOPER: Look at Brick put it down!

(*Brick has obeyed Big Mama by draining the glass and handing it to her. Again everyone laughs, some high, some low.*)

BIG MAMA: Oh, you bad boy, you, you're my bad little boy. Give Big Mama a kiss, you bad boy, you!—Look at him shy away, will you? Brick never liked bein' kissed or made a fuss over, I guess because he's always had too much of it!
Son, you turn that thing off!

(*Brick has switched on the TV set.*)

I can't stand TV, radio was bad enough but TV has gone it one better, I mean—(*plops wheezing in chair*)—one worse, ha ha! Now what'm I sittin' down here faw? I want t' sit next to my sweetheart on the sofa, hold hands with him and love him up a little!

(*Big Mama has on a black and white figured chiffon. The large irregular patterns, like the markings of some massive animal, the luster of her great diamonds and many pearls, the brilliants set in the silver frames of her glasses, her riotous voice, booming laugh, have dominated the room since she entered. Big Daddy has been regarding her with a steady grimace of chronic annoyance.*)

BIG MAMA (*still louder*): Preacher, Preacher, hey, Preach! Give me you' hand an' help me up from this chair!
REVEREND TOOKER: None of your tricks, Big Mama!
BIG MAMA: What tricks? You give me you' hand so I can get up an'—

(*Reverend Tooker extends her his hand. She grabs it and pulls him into her lap with a shrill laugh that spans an octave in two notes.*)

Ever seen a preacher in a fat lady's lap? Hey, hey, folks! Ever seen a preacher in a fat lady's lap?

(*Big Mama is notorious throughout the Delta for this sort of inelegant horseplay. Margaret looks on with indulgent humor, sipping Dubonnet "on the rocks" and watching Brick, but Mae and Gooper exchange signs of humorless anxiety over these antics, the sort of behavior which Mae thinks may account for their failure to quite get in with the smartest young married set in Memphis, despite all. One of the Negroes, Lacey or Sookey, peeks in, cackling. They are waiting for a sign to bring in the cake and champagne. But Big Daddy's not amused. He doesn't understand why, in spite of the infinite mental relief he's received from the doctor's report, he still has these same old fox teeth in his guts. "This spastic condition is something else," he says to himself, but aloud he roars at Big Mama:*)

BIG DADDY: *BIG MAMA, WILL YOU QUIT HORSIN'?*—You're too old an' too fat fo' that sort of crazy kid stuff an' besides a woman with your blood pressure—she had two hundred last spring!—is riskin' a stroke when you mess around like that....

(*Mae blows on a pitch pipe.*)

BIG MAMA: *Here comes Big Daddy's birthday!*

(*Negroes in white jackets enter with an enormous birthday cake ablaze with candles and carrying buckets of champagne with satin ribbons about the bottle necks.*)
   (*Mae and Gooper strike up song, and everybody, including the Negroes and Children, joins in. Only Brick remains aloof.*)

EVERYONE: Happy birthday to you.
   Happy birthday to you.
   Happy birthday, Big Daddy—

(*Some sing: "Dear, Big Daddy!"*)

   Happy birthday to you.

(*Some sing: "How old are you?"*)
   (*Mae has come down center and is organizing her children like a chorus. She gives them a barely audible: "One, two, three!" and they are off in the new tune.*)

CHILDREN: Skinamarinka—dinka—dink
   Skinamarinka—do
   We love you.
   Skinamarinka—dinka—dink
   Skinamarinka—do.

(*All together, they turn to Big Daddy.*)

   Big Daddy, you!

(*They turn back front, like a musical comedy chorus.*)

   We love you in the morning;
   We love you in the night.

James Earl Jones as Big Daddy and Phylicia Rashad as Big Mama in Debbie Allen's production at the Novello Theatre in London, 2009.

We love you when we're with you,
And we love you out of sight.
Skinamarinka — dinka — dink
Skinamarinka — do.

(*Mae turns to Big Mama.*)

Big Mama, too!

(*Big Mama bursts into tears. The Negroes leave.*)

BIG DADDY: Now Ida, what the hell is the matter with you?
MAE: She's just so happy.
BIG MAMA: I'm just so happy, Big Daddy, I have to cry or something.

(*Sudden and loud in the hush:*)

Brick, do you know the wonderful news that Doc Baugh got from the clinic about Big Daddy? Big Daddy's one hundred percent!
MARGARET: Isn't that wonderful?
BIG MAMA: He's just one hundred percent. Passed the examination with flying colors. Now that we know there's nothing wrong with Big Daddy but a spastic colon, I can tell you something. I was worried sick half out of my mind, for fear that Big Daddy might have a thing like—

(*Margaret cuts through this speech, jumping up and exclaiming shrilly:*)

MARGARET: Brick, honey, aren't you going to give Big Daddy his birthday present?

(*Passing by him, she snatches his liquor glass from him.*)
(*She picks up a fancily wrapped package.*)

Here it is, Big Daddy, this is from Brick!
BIG MAMA: This is the biggest birthday Big Daddy's ever had, a hundred presents and bushels of telegrams from—
MAE (*at same time*): What is it, Brick?
GOOPER: I bet 500 to 50 that Brick don't *know* what it is.
BIG MAMA: The fun of presents is not knowing what they are till you open the package. Open your present, Big Daddy.
BIG DADDY: Open it you'self. I want to ask Brick somethin'! Come here, Brick!
MARGARET: Big Daddy's callin' you, Brick.

(*She is opening the package.*)

BRICK: Tell Big Daddy I'm crippled.
BIG DADDY: I see you're crippled. I want to know how you got crippled.
MARGARET (*making diversionary tactics*): Oh, look, oh, look, why, it's a cashmere robe!

(*She holds the robe up for all to see.*)

MAE: You sound surprised, Maggie.
MARGARET: I never saw one before.
MAE: That's funny.—Hah!
MARGARET (*turning on her fiercely, with a brilliant smile*): Why is it funny? All my family ever had was family—and luxuries such as cashmere robes still surprise me!

BIG DADDY (*ominously*): Quiet!

MAE (*heedless in her fury*): I don't see how you could be so surprised when you bought it yourself at Loewenstein's in Memphis last Saturday. You know how I know?

BIG DADDY: I said, Quiet!

MAE: —I know because the salesgirl that sold it to you waited on me and said, Oh, Mrs. Pollitt, your sister-in-law just bought a cashmere robe for your husband's father!

MARGARET: Sister Woman! Your talents are wasted as a housewife and mother, you really ought to be with the FBI or—

BIG DADDY: QUIET!

(*Reverend Tooker's reflexes are slower than the others'. He finishes a sentence after the bellow.*)

REVEREND TOOKER (*to Doc Baugh*): —the Stork and the Reaper are running neck and neck!

(*He starts to laugh gaily when he notices the silence and Big Daddy's glare. His laugh dies falsely.*)

BIG DADDY: Preacher, I hope I'm not butting in on more talk about memorial stained-glass windows, am I, Preacher?

(*Reverend Tooker laughs feebly, then coughs dryly in the embarrassed silence.*)

Preacher?

BIG MAMA: Now, Big Daddy, don't you pick on Preacher!

BIG DADDY (*raising his voice*): You ever hear that expression all hawk and no spit? You bring that expression to mind with that little dry cough of yours, all hawk an' no spit. . . .

(*The pause is broken only by a short startled laugh from Margaret, the only one there who is conscious of and amused by the grotesque.*)

MAE (*raising her arms and jangling her bracelets*): I wonder if the mosquitoes are active tonight?

BIG DADDY: What's that, Little Mama? Did you make some remark?

MAE: Yes, I said I wondered if the mosquitoes would eat us alive if we went out on the gallery for a while.

BIG DADDY: Well, if they do, I'll have your bones pulverized for fertilizer!

BIG MAMA (*quickly*): Last week we had an airplane spraying the place and I think it done some good, at least I haven't had a—

BIG DADDY (*cutting her speech*): Brick, they tell me, if what they tell me is true, that you done some jumping last night on the high school athletic field?

BIG MAMA: Brick, Big Daddy is talking to you, son.

BRICK (*smiling vaguely over his drink*): What was that, Big Daddy?

BIG DADDY: They said you done some jumping on the high school track field last night.

BRICK: That's what they told me, too.

BIG DADDY: Was it jumping or humping that you were doing out there? What were you doing out there at three A.M., layin' a woman on that cinder track?

BIG MAMA: Big Daddy, you are off the sick-list, now, and I'm not going to excuse you for talkin' so—

BIG DADDY: Quiet!

BIG MAMA: —*nasty* in front of Preacher and—

BIG DADDY: QUIET!—I ast you, Brick, if you was cut-in' you'self a piece o' poon-tang last night on that cinder track? I thought maybe you were chasin' poon-tang on that track an' tripped over something in the heat of the chase—'sthat it?

(*Gooper laughs, loud and false, others nervously following suit. Big Mama stamps her foot, and purses her lips, crossing to Mae and whispering something to her as Brick meets his father's hard, intent, grinning stare with a slow, vague smile that he offers all situations from behind the screen of his liquor.*)

BRICK: No, sir, I don't think so. . . .

MAE (*at the same time, sweetly*): Reverend Tooker, let's you and I take a stroll on the widow's walk.

(*She and the preacher go out on the gallery as Big Daddy says:*)

BIG DADDY: Then what the hell were you doing out there at three o'clock in the morning?

BRICK: Jumping the hurdles, Big Daddy, runnin' and jumpin' the hurdles, but those high hurdles have gotten too high for me, now.

BIG DADDY: Cause you was drunk?

BRICK (*his vague smile fading a little*): Sober I wouldn't have tried to jump the *low* ones. . . .

BIG MAMA (*quickly*): Big Daddy, blow out the candles on your birthday cake!

MARGARET (*at the same time*): I want to propose a toast to Big Daddy Pollitt on his sixty-fifth birthday, the biggest cotton planter in—

BIG DADDY (*bellowing with fury and disgust*): I told you to stop it, now stop it, quit this—!

BIG MAMA (*coming in front of Big Daddy with the cake*): Big Daddy, I will not allow you to talk that way, not even on your birthday, I—

BIG DADDY: I'll talk like I want to on my birthday, Ida, or any other goddamn day of the year and anybody here that don't like it knows what they can do!

BIG MAMA: You don't mean that!

BIG DADDY: What makes you think I don't mean it?

(*Meanwhile various discreet signals have been exchanged and Gooper has also gone out on the gallery.*)

BIG MAMA: I just know you don't mean it.

BIG DADDY: You don't know a goddamn thing and you never did!

BIG MAMA: Big Daddy, you don't mean that.

BIG DADDY: Oh, yes, I do, oh, yes, I do, I mean it! I put up with a whole lot of crap around here because I thought I was dying. And you thought I was dying and you started taking over, well, you can stop taking over now, Ida, because I'm not gonna die, you can just stop now this business of taking over because you're not taking over because I'm not dying, I went through the laboratory and the goddamn exploratory operation and there's nothing wrong with me but a spastic colon. And I'm not dying of cancer which you thought I was dying of. Ain't that so? Didn't you think that I was dying of cancer, Ida?

(*Almost everybody is out on the gallery but the two old people glaring at each other across the blazing cake.*)
(*Big Mama's chest heaves and she presses a fat fist to her mouth.*)
(*Big Daddy continues, hoarsely:*)

Ain't that so, Ida? Didn't you have an idea I was dying of cancer and now you could take control of this place and everything on it? I got that impression, I seemed to get that impression. Your loud voice everywhere, your fat old body butting in here and there!

BIG MAMA: Hush! The Preacher!
BIG DADDY: Fuck the goddamn preacher!

(*Big Mama gasps loudly and sits down on the sofa which is almost too small for her.*)

Did you hear what I said? I said fuck the goddamn preacher!

(*Somebody closes the gallery doors from outside just as there is a burst of fireworks and excited cries from the children.*)

BIG MAMA: I never seen you act like this before and I can't think what's got in you!
BIG DADDY: I went through all that laboratory and operation and all just so I would know if you or me was boss here! Well, now it turns out that I am and you ain't—and that's my birthday present—and my cake and champagne!—because for three years now you been gradually taking over. Bossing. Talking. Sashaying your fat old body around the place I made! I made this place! I was overseer on it! I was the overseer on the old Straw and Ochello plantation. I quit school at ten! I quit school at ten years old and went to work like a nigger in the fields. And I rose to be overseer of the Straw and Ochello plantation. And old Straw died and I was Ochello's partner and the place got bigger and bigger and bigger and bigger and bigger! I did all that myself with no goddamn help from you, and now you think you're just about to take over. Well, I am just about to tell you that you are not just about to take over, you are not just about to take over a God damn thing. Is that clear to you, Ida? Is that very plain to you, now? Is that understood completely? I been through the laboratory from A to Z. I've had the goddamn exploratory operation, and nothing is wrong with me but a spastic colon—made spastic, I guess, by *disgust!* By all the goddamn lies and liars that I have had to put up with and all the goddamn hypocrisy

that I lived with all these forty years that we been livin' together!

Hey! Ida!! Blow out the candles on the birthday cake! Purse up your lips and draw a deep breath and blow out the goddamn candles on the cake!

BIG MAMA: Oh, Big Daddy, oh, oh, oh, Big Daddy!
BIG DADDY: What's the matter with you?
BIG MAMA: *In all these years you never believed that I loved you??*
BIG DADDY: Huh?
BIG MAMA: *And I did, I did so much, I did love you!*—I even loved your hate and your hardness, Big Daddy!

(*She sobs and rushes awkwardly out onto the gallery.*)

BIG DADDY (*to himself*): *Wouldn't it be funny if that was true. . . .*

(*A pause is followed by a burst of light in the sky from the fireworks.*)

BRICK! HEY, BRICK!

(*He stands over his blazing birthday cake.*)
(*After some moments, Brick hobbles in on his crutch, holding his glass.*)
(*Margaret follows him with a bright, anxious smile.*)

I didn't call you, Maggie. I called Brick.
MARGARET: I'm just delivering him to you.

(*She kisses Brick on the mouth which he immediately wipes with the back of his hand. She flies girlishly back out. Brick and his father are alone.*)

BIG DADDY: Why did you do that?
BRICK: Do what, Big Daddy?
BIG DADDY: Wipe her kiss off your mouth like she'd spit on you.
BRICK: I don't know. I wasn't conscious of it.
BIG DADDY: That woman of yours has a better shape on her than Gooper's but somehow or other they got the same look about them.
BRICK: What sort of look is that, Big Daddy?
BIG DADDY: I don't know how to describe it but it's the same look.
BRICK: They don't look peaceful, do they?
BIG DADDY: No, they sure in hell don't.
BRICK: They look nervous as cats?
BIG DADDY: That's right, they look nervous as cats.
BRICK: Nervous as a couple of cats on a hot tin roof?
BIG DADDY: That's right, boy, they look like a couple of cats on a hot tin roof. It's funny that you and Gooper being so different would pick out the same type of woman.
BRICK: Both of us married into society, Big Daddy.
BIG DADDY: Crap . . . I wonder what gives them both that look?
BRICK: Well. They're sittin' in the middle of a big piece of land, Big Daddy, twenty-eight thousand acres is a pretty big piece of land and so they're squaring off on it, each determined to knock off a bigger piece of it than the other whenever you let it go.

BIG DADDY: I got a surprise for those women. I'm not gonna let it go for a long time yet if that's what they're waiting for.

BRICK: That's right, Big Daddy. You just sit tight and let them scratch each other's eyes out....

BIG DADDY: You bet your life I'm going to sit tight on it and let those sons of bitches scratch their eyes out, ha ha ha....

But Gooper's wife's a good breeder, you got to admit she's fertile. Hell, at supper tonight she had them all at the table and they had to put a couple of extra leafs in the table to make room for them, she's got five head of them, now, and another one's comin'.

BRICK: Yep, number six is comin' . . .

BIG DADDY: Six hell, she'll probably drop a litter next time. Brick, you know, I swear to God, I don't know the way it happens.

BRICK: The way what happens, Big Daddy?

BIG DADDY: You git you a piece of land, by hook or crook, an' things start growin' on it, things accumulate on it, and the first thing you know it's completely out of hand, completely out of hand!

BRICK: Well, they say nature hates a vacuum, Big Daddy.

BIG DADDY: That's what they say, but sometimes I think that a vacuum is a hell of a lot better than some of the stuff that nature replaces it with.

Is someone out there by that door?

GOOPER: Hey Mae.

BRICK: Yep.

BIG DADDY: Who?

(*He has lowered his voice.*)

BRICK: Someone int'rested in what we say to each other.

BIG DADDY: Gooper?—*GOOPER!*

(*After a discreet pause, Mae appears in the gallery door.*)

MAE: Did you call Gooper, Big Daddy?

BIG DADDY: Aw, it was you.

MAE: Do you want Gooper, Big Daddy?

BIG DADDY: No, and I don't want you. I want some privacy here, while I'm having a confidential talk with my son Brick. Now it's too hot in here to close them doors, but if I have to close those fuckin' doors in order to have a private talk with my son Brick, just let me know and I'll close 'em. Because I hate eavesdroppers, I don't like any kind of sneakin' an' spyin'.

MAE: Why, Big Daddy—

BIG DADDY: You stood on the wrong side of the moon, it threw your shadow!

MAE: I was just—

BIG DADDY: You was just nothing but *spyin'* an' you *know* it!

MAE (*begins to sniff and sob*): Oh, Big Daddy, you're so unkind for some reason to those that really love you!

BIG DADDY: Shut up, shut up, shut up! I'm going to move you and Gooper out of that room next to this! It's none of your goddamn business what goes on in here at night between Brick an' Maggie. You listen at night like a couple of rutten peekhole spies and

go and give a report on what you hear to Big Mama an' she comes to me and says they say such and such and so and so about what they heard goin' on between Brick an' Maggie, and Jesus, it makes me sick. I'm goin' to move you an' Gooper out of that room, I can't stand sneakin' an' spyin', it makes me puke....

(*Mae throws back her head and rolls her eyes heavenward and extends her arms as if invoking God's pity for this unjust martyrdom; then she presses a handkerchief to her nose and flies from the room with a loud swish of skirts.*)

BRICK (*now at the liquor cabinet*): They listen, do they?

BIG DADDY: Yeah. They listen and give reports to Big Mama on what goes on in here between you and Maggie. They say that—

(*He stops as if embarrassed.*)

—You won't sleep with her, that you sleep on the sofa. Is that true or not true? If you don't like Maggie, get rid of Maggie!—What are you doin' there now?

BRICK: Fresh'nin' up my drink.

BIG DADDY: Son, you know you got a real liquor problem?

BRICK: Yes, sir, yes, I know.

BIG DADDY: Is that why you quit sports-announcing, because of this liquor problem?

BRICK: Yes, sir, yes, sir, I guess so.

(*He smiles vaguely and amiably at his father across his replenished drink.*)

BIG DADDY: Son, don't guess about it, it's too important.

BRICK (*vaguely*): Yes, sir.

BIG DADDY: And listen to me, don't look at the damn chandelier....

(*Pause. Big Daddy's voice is husky.*)

—Somethin' else we picked up at th' big fire-sale in Europe.

(*Another pause.*)

Life is important. There's nothing else to hold onto. A man that drinks is throwing his life away. Don't do it, hold onto your life. There's nothing else to hold onto....

Sit down over here so we don't have to raise our voices, the walls have ears in this place.

BRICK (*hobbling over to sit on the sofa beside him*): All right, Big Daddy.

BIG DADDY: Quit!—how'd that come about? Some disappointment?

BRICK: I don't know. Do you?

BIG DADDY: I'm askin' you, God damn it! How in hell would I know if you don't?

BRICK: I just got out there and found that I had a mouth full of cotton. I was always two or three beats behind what was goin' on on the field and so I—

BIG DADDY: Quit!

BRICK (*amiably*): Yes, quit.

BIG DADDY: Son?

BRICK: Huh?

BIG DADDY (*inhales loudly and deeply from his cigar; then bends suddenly a little forward, exhaling loudly and raising a hand to his forehead*):—Whew!—ha ha!—I took in too much smoke, it made me a little lightheaded. . . .

(*The mantel clock chimes.*)

Why is it so damn hard for people to talk?

BRICK: Yeah. . . .

(*The clock goes on sweetly chiming till it has completed the stroke of ten.*)

—Nice peaceful-soundin' clock, I like to hear it all night. . . .

(*He slides low and comfortable on the sofa; Big Daddy sits up straight and rigid with some unspoken anxiety. All his gestures are tense and jerky as he talks. He wheezes and pants and sniffs through his nervous speech, glancing quickly, shyly, from time to time, at his son.*)

BIG DADDY: We got that clock the summer we wint to Europe, me an' Big Mama on that damn Cook's Tour, never had such an awful time in my life, I'm tellin' you, son, those gooks over there, they gouge your eyeballs out in their grand hotels. And Big Mama bought more stuff than you could haul in a couple of boxcars, that's no crap. Everywhere she wint on this whirlwind tour, she bought, bought, bought. Why, half that stuff she bought is still crated up in the cellar, under water last spring!

(*He laughs.*)

That Europe is nothin' on earth but a great big auction, that's all it is, that bunch of old worn-out places, it's just a big fire-sale, the whole fuckin' thing, an' Big Mama wint wild in it, why, you couldn't hold that woman with a mule's harness! Bought, bought, bought!—lucky I'm a rich man, yes siree, Bob, an' half that stuff is mildewin' in th' basement. It's lucky I'm a rich man, it sure is lucky, well, I'm a rich man, Brick, yep, I'm a mighty rich man.

(*His eyes light up for a moment.*)

Y'know how much I'm worth? Guess, Brick! Guess how much I'm worth!

(*Brick smiles vaguely over his drink.*)

Close on ten million in cash an' blue-chip stocks, outside, mind you, of twenty-eight thousand acres of the richest land this side of the valley Nile!

But a man can't buy his life with it, he can't buy back his life with it when his life has been spent, that's one thing not offered in the Europe fire-sale or in the American markets or any markets on earth, a man can't buy his life with it, he can't buy back his life when his life is finished. . . .

That's a sobering thought, a very sobering thought, and that's a thought that I was turning over in my head, over and over and over—until today. . . .

I'm wiser and sadder, Brick, for this experience which I just gone through. They's one thing else that I remember in Europe.

BRICK: What is that, Big Daddy?

BIG DADDY: The hills around Barcelona in the country of Spain and the children running over those bare hills in their bare skins beggin' like starvin' dogs with howls and screeches, and how fat the priests are on the streets of Barcelona, so many of them and so fat and so pleasant, ha ha!—Y'know I could feed that country? I got money enough to feed that goddamn country, but the human animal is a selfish beast and I don't reckon the money I passed out there to those howling children in the hills around Barcelona would more than upholster the chairs in this room, I mean pay to put a new cover on this chair!

Hell, I threw them money like you'd scatter feed corn for chickens, I threw money at them just to get rid of them long enough to climb back into th' car and—drive away. . . .

And then in Morocco, them Arabs, why, I remember one day in Marrakech, that old walled Arab city, I set on a broken-down wall to have a cigar, it was fearful hot there and this Arab woman stood in the road and looked at me till I was embarrassed, she stood stock still in the dusty hot road and looked at me till I was embarrassed. But listen to this. She had a naked child with her, a little naked girl with her, barely able to toddle, and after a while she set this child on the ground and give her a push and whispered something to her.

This child come toward me, barely able t' walk, come toddling up to me and—

Jesus, it makes you sick t' remember a thing like this! It stuck out its hand and tried to unbutton my trousers!

That child was not yet five! Can you believe me? Or do you think that I am making this up? I wint back to the hotel and said to Big Mama, Git packed! We're clearing out of this country. . . .

BRICK: Big Daddy, you're on a talkin' jag tonight.

BIG DADDY (*ignoring this remark*): Yes, sir, that's how it is, the human animal is a beast that dies but the fact that he's dying don't give him pity for others, no, sir, it—

—Did you say something?

BRICK: Yes.

BIG DADDY: What?

BRICK: Hand me over that crutch so I can get up.

BIG DADDY: Where you goin?

BRICK: I'm takin' a little short trip to Echo Spring.

BIG DADDY: To where?

BRICK: Liquor cabinet. . . .

BIG DADDY: Yes, sir, boy—

(*He hands Brick the crutch.*)

—the human animal is a beast that dies and if he's got money he buys and buys and buys and I think the reason he buys everything he can buy is that in the back of his mind he has the crazy hope that one of his purchases will be life everlasting!—Which it never can be.... The human animal is a beast that—

BRICK (*at the liquor cabinet*): Big Daddy, you sure are shootin' th' breeze here tonight.

(*There is a pause and voices are heard outside.*)

BIG DADDY: I been quiet here lately, spoke not a word, just sat and stared into space. I had something heavy weighing on my mind but tonight that load was took off me. That's why I'm talking.—The sky looks diff'rent to me....

BRICK: You know what I like to hear most?

BIG DADDY: What?

BRICK: Solid quiet. Perfect unbroken quiet.

BIG DADDY: Why?

BRICK: Because it's more peaceful.

BIG DADDY: Man, you'll hear a lot of that in the grave.

(*He chuckles agreeably.*)

BRICK: Are you through talkin' to me?

BIG DADDY: Why are you so anxious to shut me up?

BRICK: Well, sir, ever so often you say to me, Brick, I want to have a talk with you, but when we talk, it never materializes. Nothing is said. You sit in a chair and gas about this and that and I look like I listen. I try to look like I listen, but I don't listen, not much. Communication is—awful hard between people an'—somehow between you and me, it just don't—happen.

BIG DADDY: Have you ever been scared? I mean have you ever felt downright terror of something?

(*He gets up.*)

Just one moment.

(*He looks off as if he were going to tell an important secret.*)

Brick?

BRICK: What?

BIG DADDY: Son, I thought I had it!

BRICK: Had what? Had what, Big Daddy?

BIG DADDY: Cancer!

BRICK: Oh...

BIG DADDY: I thought the old man made out of bones had laid his cold and heavy hand on my shoulder!

BRICK: Well, Big Daddy, you kept a tight mouth about it.

BIG DADDY: A pig squeals. A man keeps a tight mouth about it, in spite of a man not having a pig's advantage.

BRICK: What advantage is that?

BIG DADDY: Ignorance—of mortality—is a comfort. A man don't have that comfort, he's the only living thing that conceives of death, that knows what it is. The others go without knowing, which is the way that anything living should go, go without knowing, without any knowledge of it, and yet a pig squeals, but a man sometimes, he can keep a tight mouth about it. Sometimes he—

(*There is a deep, smoldering ferocity in the old man.*)

—can keep a tight mouth about it. I wonder if—

BRICK: What, Big Daddy?

BIG DADDY: A whiskey highball would injure this spastic condition?

BRICK: No, sir, it might do it good.

BIG DADDY (*grins suddenly, wolfishly*): Jesus, I can't tell you! The sky is open! Christ, it's open again! It's open, boy, it's open!

(*Brick looks down at his drink.*)

BRICK: You feel better, Big Daddy?

BIG DADDY: Better? Hell! I can breathe!—All of my life I been like a doubled up fist....

(*He pours a drink.*)

—Poundin', smashin', drivin'!—now I'm going to loosen these doubled-up hands and touch things *easy* with them....

(*He spreads his hands as if caressing the air.*)

You know what I'm contemplating?

BRICK (*vaguely*): No, sir. What are you contemplating?

BIG DADDY: Ha ha!—*Pleasure!*—pleasure with *women!*

(*Brick's smile fades a little but lingers.*)

—Yes, boy. I'll tell you something that you might not guess. I still have desire for women and this is my sixty-fifth birthday.

BRICK: I think that's mighty remarkable, Big Daddy.

BIG DADDY: Remarkable?

BRICK: *Admirable*, Big Daddy.

BIG DADDY: You're damn right it is, remarkable and admirable both. I realize now that I never had me enough. I let many chances slip by because of scruples about it, scruples, convention—crap.... All that stuff is bull, bull, bull!—It took the shadow of death to make me see it. Now that shadow's lifted, I'm going to cut loose and have, what is it they call it, have me a—ball!

BRICK: A ball, huh?

BIG DADDY: That's right, a ball, a ball! Hell!—I slept with Big Mama till, let's see, five years ago, till I was sixty and she was fifty-eight, and never even liked her, never did!

(*The phone has been ringing down the hall. Big Mama enters, exclaiming:*)

BIG MAMA: Don't you men hear that phone ring? I heard it way out on the gall'ry.

BIG DADDY: There's five rooms off this front gall'ry that you could go through. Why do you go through this one?

(*Big Mama makes a playful face as she bustles out the hall door.*)

Hunh!—Why, when Big Mama goes out of a room, I can't remember what that woman looks like—

BIG MAMA: Hello.

BIG DADDY: —But when Big Mama comes back into the room, boy, then I see what she looks like, and I wish I didn't!

(*Bends over laughing at this joke till it hurts his guts and he straightens with a grimace. The laugh subsides to a chuckle as he puts the liquor glass a little distrustfully down on the table.*)

BIG MAMA: Hello, Miss Sally.

(*Brick has risen and hobbled to the gallery doors.*)

BIG DADDY: Hey! Where you goin'?

BRICK: Out for a breather.

BIG DADDY: Not yet you ain't. Stay here till this talk is finished, young fellow.

BRICK: I thought it was finished, Big Daddy.

BIG DADDY: It ain't even begun.

BRICK: My mistake. Excuse me. I just wanted to feel that river breeze.

BIG DADDY: Set back down in that chair.

(*Big Mama's voice rises, carrying down the hall.*)

BIG MAMA: Miss Sally, you're a case! You're a caution, Miss Sally.

BIG DADDY: Jesus, she's talking to my old maid sister again.

BIG MAMA: Why didn't you give me a chance to explain it to you?

BIG DADDY: Brick, this stuff burns me.

BIG MAMA: Well, good-bye, now, Miss Sally. You come down real soon. Big Daddy's dying to see you.

BIG DADDY: Crap!

BIG MAMA: Yaiss, good-bye, Miss Sally. . . .

(*She hangs up and bellows with mirth. Big Daddy groans and covers his ears as she approaches.*)

(*Bursting in:*)

Big Daddy, that was Miss Sally callin' from Memphis again! You know what she done, Big Daddy? She called her doctor in Memphis to git him to tell her what that spastic thing is! Ha-*HAAAA!*—And called back to tell me how relieved she was that—Hey! Let me in!

(*Big Daddy has been holding the door half closed against her.*)

BIG DADDY: Naw I ain't. I told you not to come and go through this room. You just back out and go through those five other rooms.

BIG MAMA: Big Daddy? Big Daddy? Oh, Big Daddy!— You didn't mean those things you said to me, did you?

(*He shuts door firmly against her but she still calls.*)

Sweetheart? Sweetheart? Big Daddy? You didn't mean those awful things you said to me?—I know you didn't. I know you didn't mean those things in your heart. . . .

(*The childlike voice fades with a sob and her heavy footsteps retreat down the hall. Brick has risen once more on his crutches and starts for the gallery again.*)

BIG DADDY: All I ask of that woman is that she leave me alone. But she can't admit to herself that she makes me sick. That comes of having slept with her too many years. Should of quit much sooner but that old woman she never got enough of it—and I was good in bed . . . I never should of wasted so much of it on her. . . . They say you got just so many and each one is numbered. Well, I got a few left in me, a few, and I'm going to pick me a good one to spend 'em on! I'm going to pick me a choice one, I don't care how much she costs, I'll smother her in—minks! Ha ha! I'll strip her naked and smother her in minks and choke her with diamonds! Ha ha! I'll strip her naked and choke her with diamonds and smother her with minks and hump her from hell to breakfast. *Ha aha ha ha ha!*

MAE: (*gaily at door*): Who's that laughin' in there?

GOOPER: Is Big Daddy laughin' in there?

BIG DADDY: Crap!—them two—*drips*. . . .

(*He goes over and touches Brick's shoulder.*)

Yes, son. Brick, boy.—I'm—*happy!* I'm happy, son, I'm happy!

(*He chokes a little and bites his under lip, pressing his head quickly, shyly against his son's head and then, coughing with embarrassment, goes uncertainly back to the table where he set down the glass. He drinks and makes a grimace as it burns his guts. Brick sighs and rises with effort.*)

What makes you so restless? Have you got ants in your britches?

BRICK: Yes, sir . . .

BIG DADDY: Why?

BRICK: —Something—hasn't—happened. . . .

BIG DADDY: Yeah? What is that!

BRICK (*sadly*): —the click. . . .

BIG DADDY: Did you say click?

BRICK: Yes, click.

BIG DADDY: What click?

BRICK: A click that I get in my head that makes me peaceful.

BIG DADDY: I sure in hell don't know what you're talking about, but it disturbs me.

BRICK: It's just a mechanical thing.

BIG DADDY: What is a mechanical thing?

BRICK: This click that I get in my head that makes me peaceful. I got to drink till I get it. It's just a mechanical thing, something like a—like a—like a—

BIG DADDY: Like a—

BRICK: Switch clicking off in my head, turning the hot light off and the cool night on and—

(*He looks up, smiling sadly.*)

   —all of a sudden there's—peace!

BIG DADDY (*whistles long and soft with astonishment; he goes back to Brick and clasps his son's two shoulders*): Jesus! I didn't know it had gotten that bad with you. Why, boy, you're—*alcoholic!*

BRICK: That's the truth, Big Daddy. I'm alcoholic.

BIG DADDY: This shows how I—let things go!

BRICK: I have to hear that little click in my head that makes me peaceful. Usually I hear it sooner than this, sometimes as early as—noon, but—
   —Today it's—dilatory....
   I just haven't got the right level of alcohol in my bloodstream yet!

(*This last statement is made with energy as he freshens his drink.*)

BIG DADDY: Uh—huh. Expecting death made me blind. I didn't have no idea that a son of mine was turning into a drunkard under my nose.

BRICK (*gently*): Well, now you do, Big Daddy, the news has penetrated.

BIG DADDY: UH-huh, yes, now I do, the news has—penetrated....

BRICK: And so if you'll excuse me—

BIG DADDY: No, I won't excuse you.

BRICK: —I'd better sit by myself till I hear that click in my head, it's just a mechanical thing but it don't happen except when I'm alone or talking to no one....

BIG DADDY: You got a long, long time to sit still, boy, and talk to no one, but now you're talkin' to me. At least I'm talking to you. And you set there and listen until I tell you the conversation is over!

BRICK: But this talk is like all the others we've ever had together in our lives! It's nowhere, nowhere!—it's—it's *painful,* Big Daddy....

BIG DADDY: All right, then let it be painful, but don't you move from that chair!—I'm going to remove that crutch....

(*He seizes the crutch and tosses it across room.*)

BRICK: I can hop on one foot, and if I fall, I can crawl!

BIG DADDY: If you ain't careful you're gonna crawl off this plantation and then, by Jesus, you'll have to hustle your drinks along Skid Row!

BRICK: That'll come, Big Daddy.

BIG DADDY: Naw, it won't. You're my son and I'm going to straighten you out; now that *I'm* straightened out, I'm going to straighten out you!

BRICK: Yeah?

BIG DADDY: Today the report come in from Ochsner Clinic. Y'know what they told me?

(*His face glows with triumph.*)

The only thing that they could detect with all the instruments of science in that great hospital is a little spastic condition of the colon! And nerves torn to pieces by all that worry about it.

(*A little girl bursts into room with a sparkler clutched in each fist, hops and shrieks like a monkey gone mad and rushes back out again as Big Daddy strikes at her.*)
(*Silence. The two men stare at each other. A woman laughs gaily outside.*)

I want you to know I breathed a sigh of relief almost as powerful as the Vicksburg tornado!

(*There is laughter outside, running footsteps, the soft, plushy sound and light of exploding rockets.*)
(*Brick stares at him soberly for a long moment; then makes a sort of startled sound in his nostrils and springs up on one foot and hops across the room to grab his crutch, swinging on the furniture for support. He gets the crutch and flees as if in horror for the gallery. His father seizes him by the sleeve of his white silk pajamas.*)

Stay here, you son of a bitch!—till I say go!

BRICK: I can't.

BIG DADDY: You sure in hell will, God damn it.

BRICK: No, I can't. We talk, you talk, in—circles! We get no where, no where! It's always the same, you say you want to talk to me and don't have a fuckin' thing to say to me!

BIG DADDY: Nothin' to say when I'm tellin' you I'm going to live when I thought I was dying?!

BRICK: Oh—*that!*—Is that what you have to say to me?

BIG DADDY: Why, you son of a bitch! Ain't that, ain't that—*important?!*

BRICK: Well, you said that, that's said, and now I—

BIG DADDY: Now you set back down.

BRICK: You're all balled up, you—

BIG DADDY: I ain't balled up!

BRICK: You are, you're all balled up!

BIG DADDY: Don't tell me what I am, you drunken whelp! I'm going to tear this coat sleeve off if you don't set down!

BRICK: Big Daddy—

BIG DADDY: Do what I tell you! I'm the boss here, now! I want you to know I'm back in the driver's seat now!

(*Big Mama rushes in, clutching her great heaving bosom.*)

BIG MAMA: Big Daddy!

BIG DADDY: What in hell do you want in here, Big Mama?

BIG MAMA: Oh, Big Daddy! Why are you shouting like that? I just cain't *stainnnnnnnd*—it....

BIG DADDY (*raising the back of his hand above his head*): GIT!—outa here.

(*She rushes back out, sobbing.*)

BRICK (*softly, sadly*): Christ....

BIG DADDY (*fiercely*): Yeah! Christ!—is right....

(*Brick breaks loose and hobbles toward the gallery.*)

(*Big Daddy jerks his crutch from under Brick so he steps with the injured ankle. He utters a hissing cry of anguish, clutches a chair and pulls it over on top of him on the floor.*)

Son of a—tub of—hog fat. . . .

BRICK: Big Daddy! Give me my crutch.

(*Big Daddy throws the crutch out of reach.*)

Give me that crutch, Big Daddy.

BIG DADDY: Why do you drink?

BRICK: Don't know, give me my crutch!

BIG DADDY: You better think why you drink or give up drinking!

BRICK: Will you please give me my crutch so I can get up off this floor?

BIG DADDY: First you answer my question. Why do you drink? Why are you throwing your life away, boy, like somethin' disgusting you picked up on the street?

BRICK (*getting onto his knees*): Big Daddy, I'm in pain, I stepped on that foot.

BIG DADDY: Good! I'm glad you're not too numb with the liquor in you to feel some pain!

BRICK: You—spilled my—drink . . .

BIG DADDY: I'll make a bargain with you. You tell me why you drink and I'll hand you one. I'll pour you the liquor myself and hand it to you.

BRICK: Why do I drink?

BIG DADDY: Yea! Why?

BRICK: Give me a drink and I'll tell you.

BIG DADDY: Tell me first!

BRICK: I'll tell you in one word.

BIG DADDY: What word?

BRICK: DISGUST!

(*The clock chimes softly, sweetly. Big Daddy gives it a short, outraged glance.*)

Now how about that drink?

BIG DADDY: What are you disgusted with? You got to tell me that, first. Otherwise being disgusted don't make no sense!

BRICK: Give me my crutch.

BIG DADDY: You heard me, you got to tell me what I asked you first.

BRICK: I told you, I said to kill my disgust!

BIG DADDY: DISGUST WITH WHAT!

BRICK: You strike a hard bargain.

BIG DADDY: What are you disgusted with?—an' I'll pass you the liquor.

BRICK: I can hop on one foot, and if I fall, I can crawl.

BIG DADDY: You want liquor that bad?

BRICK (*dragging himself up, clinging to bedstead*): Yeah, I want it that bad.

BIG DADDY: If I give you a drink, will you tell me what it is you're disgusted with, Brick?

BRICK: Yes, sir, I will try to.

(*The old man pours him a drink and solemnly passes it to him.*)

(*There is silence as Brick drinks.*)

Have you ever heard the word "mendacity"?

BIG DADDY: Sure. Mendacity is one of them five dollar words that cheap politicians throw back and forth at each other.

BRICK: You know what it means?

BIG DADDY: Don't it mean lying and liars?

BRICK: Yes, sir, lying and liars.

BIG DADDY: Has someone been lying to you?

CHILDREN (*chanting in chorus offstage*):
  We want Big Dad-dee!
  We want Big Dad-dee!

(*Gooper appears in the gallery door.*)

GOOPER: Big Daddy, the kiddies are shouting for you out there.

BIG DADDY (*fiercely*): Keep out, Gooper!

GOOPER: 'Scuse *me*!

(*Big Daddy slams the doors after Gooper.*)

BIG DADDY: Who's been lying to you, has Margaret been lying to you, has your wife been lying to you about something, Brick?

BRICK: Not her. That wouldn't matter.

BIG DADDY: Then who's been lying to you, and what about?

BRICK: No one single person and no one lie. . . .

BIG DADDY: Then what, what then, for Christ's sake?

BRICK: —The whole, the whole—thing. . . .

BIG DADDY: Why are you rubbing your head? You got a headache?

BRICK: No, I'm tryin' to—

BIG DADDY: —Concentrate, but you can't because your brain's all soaked with liquor, is that the trouble? Wet brain!

(*He snatches the glass from Brick's hand.*)

What do you know about this mendacity thing? Hell! I could write a book on it! Don't you know that? I could write a book on it and still not cover the subject? Well, I could, I could write a goddamn book on it and still not cover the subject anywhere near enough!!—Think of all the lies I got to put up with!—Pretenses! Ain't that mendacity? Having to pretend stuff you don't think or feel or have any idea of? Having for instance to act like I care for Big Mama!—I haven't been able to stand the sight, sound, or smell of that woman for forty years now!—even when I *laid* her!—regular as a piston. . . .

Pretend to love that son of a bitch of a Gooper and his wife Mae and those five same screechers out there like parrots in a jungle? Jesus! Can't stand to look at 'em!

Church!—it bores the bejesus out of me but I go!—I go an' sit there and listen to the fool preacher!

Clubs!—Elks! Masons! Rotary!—*crap*!

(*A spasm of pain makes him clutch his belly. He sinks into a chair and his voice is softer and hoarser.*)

You I *do* like for some reason, did always have some kind of real feeling for—affection—respect—yes, always. . . .

You and being a success as a planter is all I ever had any devotion to in my whole life!—and that's the truth. . . .

I don't know why, but it is!

I've lived with mendacity!—Why can't *you* live with it? Hell, you *got* to live with it, there's nothing *else* to *live* with except mendacity, is there?

BRICK: Yes, sir. Yes, sir there is something else that you can live with!

BIG DADDY: What?

BRICK (*lifting his glass*): This!—Liquor. . . .

BIG DADDY: That's not living, that's dodging away from life.

BRICK: I want to dodge away from it.

BIG DADDY: Then why don't you kill yourself, man?

BRICK: I like to drink. . . .

BIG DADDY: Oh, God, I can't talk to you. . . .

BRICK: I'm sorry, Big Daddy.

BIG DADDY: Not as sorry as I am. I'll tell you something. A little while back when I thought my number was up—

(*This speech should have torrential pace and fury.*)

—before I found out it was just this—spastic—colon. I thought about you. Should I or should I not, if the jig was up, give you this place when I go—since I hate Gooper an' Mae an' know that they hate me, and since all five same monkeys are little Maes an' Goopers.—And I thought, No!—Then I thought, Yes!—I couldn't make up my mind. I hate Gooper and his five same monkeys and that bitch Mae! Why should I turn over twenty-eight thousand acres of the richest land this side of the valley Nile to not my kind?—But why in hell, on the other hand, Brick—should I subsidize a goddamn fool on the bottle?—Liked or not liked, well, maybe even—*loved!*—Why should I do that?—Subsidize worthless behavior? Rot? Corruption?

BRICK (*smiling*): I understand.

BIG DADDY: Well, if you do, you're smarter than I am, God damn it, because I don't understand. And this I will tell you frankly. I didn't make up my mind at all on that question and still to this day I ain't made out no will!—Well, now I don't *have* to. The pressure is gone. I can just wait and see if you pull yourself together or if you don't.

BRICK: That's right, Big Daddy.

BIG DADDY: You sound like you thought I was kidding.

BRICK (*rising*): No, sir, I know you're not kidding.

BIG DADDY: But you don't care—?

BRICK (*hobbling toward the gallery door*): No, sir, I don't care. . . .

(*He stands in the gallery doorway as the night sky turns pink and green and gold with successive flashes of light.*)

BIG DADDY: *WAIT!*—Brick. . . .

(*His voice drops. Suddenly there is something shy, almost tender, in his restraining gesture.*)

Don't let's—leave it like this, like them other talks we've had, we've always—talked around things, we've—just talked around things for some fuckin' reason, I don't know what, it's always like something was left not spoken, something avoided because neither of us was honest enough with the—other. . . .

BRICK: I never lied to you, Big Daddy.

BIG DADDY: Did I ever to *you?*

BRICK: No, sir. . . .

BIG DADDY: Then there is at least two people that never lied to each other.

BRICK: But we've never *talked* to each other.

BIG DADDY: We can *now*.

BRICK: Big Daddy, there don't seem to be anything much to say.

BIG DADDY: You say that you drink to kill your disgust with lying.

BRICK: You said to give you a reason.

BIG DADDY: Is liquor the only thing that'll kill this disgust?

BRICK: Now. Yes.

BIG DADDY: But not once, huh?

BRICK: Not when I was still young an' believing. A drinking man's someone who wants to forget he isn't still young an' believing.

BIG DADDY: Believing what?

BRICK: Believing. . . .

BIG DADDY: Believing *what?*

BRICK (*stubbornly evasive*): Believing. . . .

BIG DADDY: I don't know what the hell you mean by believing and I don't think you know what you mean by believing, but if you still got sports in your blood, go back to sports announcing and—

BRICK: Sit in a glass box watching games I can't play? Describing what I can't do while players do it? Sweating out their disgust and confusion in contests I'm not fit for? Drinkin' a coke, half bourbon, so I can stand it? That's no goddamn good any more, no help—time just outran me, Big Daddy—got there first . . .

BIG DADDY: I think you're passing the buck.

BRICK: You know many drinkin' men?

BIG DADDY (*with a slight, charming smile*): I have known a fair number of that species.

BRICK: Could any of them tell you why he drank?

BIG DADDY: Yep, you're passin' the buck to things like time and disgust with "mendacity" and—crap!—if you got to use that kind of language about a thing, it's ninety-proof bull, and I'm not buying any.

BRICK: I had to give you a reason to get a drink!

BIG DADDY: You started drinkin' when your friend Skipper died.

(*Silence for five beats. Then Brick makes a startled movement, reaching for his crutch.*)

BRICK: What are you suggesting?
BIG DADDY: I'm suggesting nothing.

(*The shuffle and clop of Brick's rapid hobble away from his father's steady, grave attention.*)

—But Gooper an' Mae suggested that there was something not right exactly in your—
BRICK (*stopping short downstage as if backed to a wall*): "Not right"?
BIG DADDY: Not, well, exactly *normal* in your friendship with—
BRICK: They suggested that, too? I thought that was Maggie's suggestion.

(*Brick's detachment is at last broken through. His heart is accelerated; his forehead sweat-beaded; his breath becomes more rapid and his voice hoarse. The thing they're discussing, timidly and painfully on the side of Big Daddy, fiercely, violently on Brick's side, is the inadmissible thing that Skipper died to disavow between them. The fact that if it existed it had to be disavowed to "keep face" in the world they lived in, may be at the heart of the "mendacity" that Brick drinks to kill his disgust with. It may be the root of his collapse. Or maybe it is only a single manifestation of it, not even the most important. The bird that I hope to catch in the net of this play is not the solution of one man's psychological problem. I'm trying to catch the true quality of experience in a group of people, that cloudy, flickering, evanescent—fiercely charged!—interplay of live human beings in the thundercloud of a common crisis. Some mystery should be left in the revelation of character in a play, just as a great deal of mystery is always left in the revelation of character in life, even in one's own character to himself. This does not absolve the playwright of his duty to observe and probe as clearly and deeply as he legitimately can: But it should steer him away from "pat" conclusions, facile definitions which make a play just a play, not a snare for the truth of human experience.*)

(*The following scene should be played with great concentration, with most of the power leashed but palpable in what is left unspoken.*)

Who else's suggestion is it, is it *yours?* How many others thought that Skipper and I were—
BIG DADDY (*gently*): Now, hold on, hold on a minute, son.—I knocked around in my time.
BRICK: What's that got to do with—
BIG DADDY: I said "Hold on!"—I bummed, I bummed this country till I was—
BRICK: Whose suggestion, who else's suggestion is it?
BIG DADDY: Slept in hobo jungles and railroad Y's and flophouses in all cities before I—
BRICK: Oh, *you* think so, too, you call me your son and a queer. Oh! Maybe that's why you put Maggie and me in this room that was Jack Straw's and Peter

Ochello's, in which that pair of old sisters slept in a double bed where both of 'em died!
BIG DADDY: *Now just don't go throwing rocks at*—

(*Suddenly Reverend Tooker appears in the gallery doors, his head slightly, playfully, fatuously cocked, with a practiced clergyman's smile, sincere as a birdcall blown on a hunter's whistle, the living embodiment of the pious, conventional lie.*)
(*Big Daddy gasps a little at this perfectly timed, but incongruous, apparition.*)

—What're you lookin' for, preacher?
REVEREND TOOKER: The gentleman's lavatory, ha ha!—heh, heh . . .
BIG DADDY (*with strained courtesy*):—Go back out and walk down to the other end of the gallery, Reverend Tooker, and use the bathroom connected with my bedroom, and if you can't find it, ask them where it is!
REVEREND TOOKER: Ah, thanks.

(*He goes out with a deprecatory chuckle.*)

BIG DADDY: It's hard to talk in this place . . .
BRICK: Son of a—!
BIG DADDY (*leaving a lot unspoken*):—I seen all things and understood a lot of them, till 1910. Christ, the year that—I had worn my shoes through, hocked my—I hopped off a yellow dog freight car half a mile down the road, slept in a wagon of cotton outside the gin—Jack Straw an' Peter Ochello took me in. Hired me to manage this place which grew into this one.—When Jack Straw died—why, old Peter Ochello quit eatin' like a dog does when its master's dead, and died, too!
BRICK: Christ!
BIG DADDY: I'm just saying I understand such—
BRICK (*violently*): Skipper is dead. I have not quit eating!
BIG DADDY: No, but you started drinking.

(*Brick wheels on his crutch and hurls his glass across the room shouting.*)

BRICK: YOU THINK SO, TOO?

(*Footsteps run on the gallery. There are women's calls.*)
(*Big Daddy goes toward the door.*)
(*Brick is transformed, as if a quiet mountain blew suddenly up in volcanic flame.*)

BRICK: You think so, too? You think so, too? You think me an' Skipper did, did, did!—*sodomy!*—together?
BIG DADDY: Hold—!
BRICK: That what you—
BIG DADDY:—ON—a minute!
BRICK: You think we did dirty things between us, Skipper an'—
BIG DADDY: Why are you shouting like that? Why are you—

BRICK:—Me, is that what you think of Skipper, is that—

BIG DADDY:—so excited? I don't think nothing. I don't know nothing. I'm simply telling you what—

BRICK: You think that Skipper and me were a pair of dirty old men?

BIG DADDY: Now that's—

BRICK: Straw? Ochello? A couple of—

BIG DADDY: Now just—

BRICK:—fucking sissies? Queers? Is that what you—

BIG DADDY: Shhh.

BRICK:—think?

(*He loses his balance and pitches to his knees without noticing the pain. He grabs the bed and drags himself up.*)

BIG DADDY: Jesus!—Whew. . . .Grab my hand!

BRICK: Naw, I don't want your hand. . . .

BIG DADDY: Well, I want yours. Git up!

(*He draws him up, keeps an arm about him with concern and affection.*)

You broken out in a sweat! You're panting like you'd run a race with—

BRICK (*freeing himself from his father's hold*): Big Daddy, you shock me, Big Daddy, you, you—*shock* me! Talkin' so—

(*He turns away from his father.*)

—casually!—about a—thing like that . . .
    —Don't you know how people *feel* about things like that? How, how *disgusted* they are by things like that? Why, at Ole Miss when it was discovered a pledge to our fraternity, Skipper's and mine, did a, *attempted* to do a, unnatural thing with—
    We not only dropped him like a hot rock!—We told him to git off the campus, and he did, he got!—All the way to—

(*He halts, breathless.*)

BIG DADDY:—Where?

BRICK:—North Africa, last I heard!

BIG DADDY: Well, I have come back from further away than that, I have just now returned from the other side of the moon, death's country, son, and I'm not easy to shock by anything here.

(*He comes downstage and faces out.*)

Always, anyhow, lived with too much space around me to be infected by ideas of other people. One thing you can grow on a big place more important than cotton!—is *tolerance!*—I grown it.

(*He returns toward Brick.*)

BRICK: Why can't exceptional friendship, *real, real, deep, deep friendship!* between two men be respected as something clean and decent without being thought of as—

BIG DADDY: It can, it is, for God's sake.

BRICK:—*Fairies.* . . .

(*In his utterance of this word, we gauge the wide and profound reach of the conventional mores he got from the world that crowned him with early laurel.*)

BIG DADDY: I told Mae an' Gooper—

BRICK: Frig Mae and Gooper, frig all dirty lies and liars!—Skipper and me had a clean, true thing between us!—had a clean friendship, practically all our lives, till Maggie got the idea you're talking about. Normal? No!—It was too rare to be normal, any true thing between two people is too rare to be normal. Oh, once in a while he put his hand on my shoulder or I'd put mine on his, oh, maybe even, when we were touring the country in pro-football an' shared hotel rooms we'd reach across the space between the two beds and shake hands to say goodnight, yeah, one or two times we—

BIG DADDY: Brick, nobody thinks that that's not normal!

BRICK: Well, they're mistaken, it was! It was a pure an' true thing an' that's not normal.

MAE (*offstage*): Big Daddy, they're startin' the fireworks.

(*They both stare straight at each other for a long moment. The tension breaks and both turn away as if tired.*)

BIG DADDY: Yeah, it's—hard t'—talk. . . .

BRICK: All right, then, let's—let it go. . . .

BIG DADDY: Why did Skipper crack up? Why have you?

(*Brick looks back at his father again. He has already decided, without knowing that he has made this decision, that he is going to tell his father that he is dying of cancer. Only this could even the score between them: one inadmissible thing in return for another.*)

BRICK (*ominously*): All right. You're asking for it, Big Daddy. We're finally going to have that real true talk you wanted. It's too late to stop it, now, we got to carry it through and cover every subject.

(*He hobbles back to the liquor cabinet.*)

Uh-huh.

(*He opens the ice bucket and picks up the silver tongs with slow admiration of their frosty brightness.*)

Maggie declares that Skipper and I went into pro-football after we left Ole Miss because we were scared to grow up . . .

(*He moves downstage with the shuffle and clop of a cripple on a crutch. As Margaret did when her speech became "recitative," he looks out into the house, commanding its attention by his direct, concentrated gaze—a broken, "tragically elegant" figure telling simply as much as he knows of "the Truth":*)

—Wanted to—keep on tossing—those long, long!—high, high!—passes that—couldn't be intercepted except by time, the aerial attack that made us famous! And so we did, we did, we kept it up for one season, that aerial attack, we held it high!—Yeah, but—

—that summer, Maggie, she laid the law down to me, said, Now or never, and so I married Maggie. . . .

BIG DADDY: How was Maggie in bed?

BRICK (*wryly*): Great! the greatest!

(*Big Daddy nods as if he thought so.*)

She went on the road that fall with the Dixie Stars. Oh, she made a great show of being the world's best sport. She wore a—wore a—tall bearskin cap! A shako, they call it, a dyed moleskin coat, a moleskin coat dyed red!—Cut up crazy! Rented hotel ballrooms for victory celebrations, wouldn't cancel them when it—turned out—defeat. . . .

MAGGIE THE CAT! Ha ha!

(*Big Daddy nods.*)

—But Skipper, he had some fever which came back on him which doctors couldn't explain and I got that injury—turned out to be just a shadow on the X-ray plate—and a touch of bursitis. . . .

I lay in a hospital bed, watched our games on TV, saw Maggie on the bench next to Skipper when he was hauled out of a game for stumbles, fumbles!—Burned me up the way she hung on his arm!—Y'know, I think that Maggie had always felt sort of left out because she and me never got any closer together than two people just get in bed, which is not much closer than two cats on a—fence humping. . . .

So! She took this time to work on poor dumb Skipper. He was a less than average student at Ole Miss, you know that, don't you?!—Poured in his mind the dirty, false idea that what we were, him and me, was a frustrated case of that ole pair of sisters that lived in this room, Jack Straw and Peter Ochello!—He, poor Skipper, went to bed with Maggie to prove it wasn't true, and when it didn't work out, he thought it *was* true!—Skipper broke in two like a rotten stick—nobody ever turned so fast to a lush—or died of it so quick. . . .

—Now are you satisfied?

(*Big Daddy has listened to this story, dividing the grain from the chaff. Now he looks at his son.*)

BIG DADDY: Are *you* satisfied?

BRICK: With what?

BIG DADDY: That half-ass story!

BRICK: What's half-ass about it?

BIG DADDY: Something's left out of that story. What did you leave out?

(*The phone has started ringing in the hall.*)

GOOPER (*offstage*): Hello.

(*As if it reminded him of something, Brick glances suddenly toward the sound and says:*)

BRICK: Yes!—I left out a long-distance call which I had from Skipper—

GOOPER: Speaking, go ahead.

BRICK:—In which he made a drunken confession to me and on which I hung up!

GOOPER: No.

BRICK:—Last time we spoke to each other in our lives . . .

GOOPER: No, sir.

BIG DADDY: You musta said something to him before you hung up.

BRICK: What could I say to him?

BIG DADDY: Anything. Something.

BRICK: Nothing.

BIG DADDY: Just hung up?

BRICK: Just hung up.

BIG DADDY: Uh-huh. Anyhow now!—we have tracked down the lie with which you're disgusted and which you are drinking to kill your disgust with, Brick. You been passing the buck. This disgust with mendacity is disgust with yourself.

You!—dug the grave of your friend and kicked him in it!—before you'd face truth with him!

BRICK: *His* truth, not *mine!*

BIG DADDY: His truth, okay! But you wouldn't face it with him!

BRICK: Who *can* face truth? Can *you?*

BIG DADDY: Now don't start passin' the rotten buck again, boy!

BRICK: How about these birthday congratulations, these many, many happy returns of the day, when ev'rybody knows there won't be any except you!

(*Gooper, who has answered the hall phone, lets out a high, shrill laugh; the voice becomes audible saying: "No, no, you got it all wrong! Upside down! Are you crazy?"*)

(*Brick suddenly catches his breath as he realizes that he has made a shocking disclosure. He hobbles a few paces, then freezes, and without looking at his father's shocked face says:*)

Let's, let's—go out, now, and—watch the fireworks. Come on, Big Daddy.

(*Big Daddy moves suddenly forward and grabs hold of the boy's crutch like it was a weapon for which they were fighting for possession.*)

BIG DADDY: Oh, no, no! No one's going out! What did you start to say?

BRICK: I don't remember.

BIG DADDY: "Many happy returns when they know there won't be any"?

BRICK: Aw, hell, Big Daddy, forget it. Come on out on the gallery and look at the fireworks they're shooting off for your birthday. . . .

BIG DADDY: First you finish that remark you were makin' before you cut off. "Many happy returns when they know there won't be any"?—Ain't that what you just said?

BRICK: Look, now. I can get around without that crutch if I have to but it would be a lot easier on the furniture an' glassware if I didn't have to go swinging along like Tarzan of th'—

BIG DADDY: FINISH! WHAT YOU WAS SAYIN'!

(*An eerie green glow shows in sky behind him.*)

BRICK (*sucking the ice in his glass, speech becoming thick*): Leave th' place to Gooper and Mae an' their five little same little monkeys. All I want is—

BIG DADDY: "LEAVE TH' PLACE," did you say?

BRICK (*vaguely*): All twenty-eight thousand acres of the richest land this side of the valley Nile.

BIG DADDY: Who said I was "leaving the place" to Gooper or anybody? This is my sixty-fifth birthday! I got fifteen years or twenty years left in me! I'll outlive *you!* I'll bury you an' have to pay for your coffin!

BRICK: Sure. Many happy returns. Now let's go watch the fireworks, come on, let's—

BIG DADDY: Lying, have they been lying? About the report from th'—clinic? Did they, did they—find something?—*Cancer.* Maybe?

BRICK: Mendacity is a system that we live in. Liquor is one way out an' death's the other....

(*He takes the crutch from Big Daddy's loose grip and swings out on the gallery leaving the doors open.*)
(*A song, "Pick a Bale of Cotton," is heard.*)

MAE (*appearing in door*): Oh, Big Daddy, the field hands are singin' fo' you!

BRICK: I'm sorry, Big Daddy. My head don't work any more and it's hard for me to understand how anybody could care if he lived or died or was dying or cared about anything but whether or not there was liquor left in the bottle and so I said what I said without thinking. In some ways I'm no better than the others, in some ways worse because I'm less alive. Maybe it's being alive that makes them lie, and being almost *not* alive makes me sort of accidentally truthful—I don't know but—anyway—we've been friends . . .
    —And being friends is telling each other the truth. . . .

(*There is a pause.*)

    You told *me!* I told *you!*

BIG DADDY (*slowly and passionately*): CHRIST—DAMN—

GOOPER (*offstage*): Let her go!

(*Fireworks offstage right.*)

BIG DADDY:—ALL—LYING SONS OF—LYING BITCHES!

(*He straightens at last and crosses to the inside door. At the door he turns and looks back as if he had some*

desperate question he couldn't put into words. Then he nods reflectively and says in a hoarse voice:*)

    Yes, all liars, all liars, all lying dying liars!

(*This is said slowly, slowly, with a fierce revulsion. He goes on out.*)

    —Lying! Dying! Liars!

(*Brick remains motionless as the lights dim out and the curtain falls.*)

ACT 3

(*There is no lapse of time. Big Daddy is seen leaving as at the end of act 2.*)

BIG DADDY: ALL LYIN'—DYIN'!—LIARS! LIARS!—LIARS!

(*Margaret enters.*)

MARGARET: Brick, what in the name of God was goin' on in this room?

(*Dixie and Trixie enter through the doors and circle around Margaret shouting. Mae enters from the lower gallery window.*)

MAE: Dixie, Trixie, you quit that!

(*Gooper enters through the doors.*)

    Gooper, will y' please get these kiddies to bed right now!

GOOPER: Mae, you seen Big Mama?

MAE: Not yet.

(*Gooper and kids exit through the doors. Reverend Tooker enters through the windows.*)

REVEREND TOOKER: Those kiddies are so full of vitality. I think I'll have to be starting back to town.

MAE: Not yet, Preacher. You know we regard you as a member of this family, one of our closest an' dearest, so you just got t' be with us when Doc Baugh gives Big Mama th' actual truth about th' report from the clinic.

MARGARET: Where do you think you're going?

BRICK: Out for some air.

MARGARET: Why'd Big Daddy shout "Liars"?

MAE: Has Big Daddy gone to bed, Brick?

GOOPER (*entering*): Now where is that old lady?

REVEREND TOOKER: I'll look for her.

(*He exits to the gallery.*)

MAE: Cain'tcha find her, Gooper?

GOOPER: She's avoidin' this talk.

MAE: I think she senses somethin'.

MARGARET (*going out on the gallery to Brick*): Brick, they're goin' to tell Big Mama the truth about Big Daddy and she's goin' to need you.

DOCTOR BAUGH: This is going to be painful.

MAE: Painful things caint always be avoided.

REVEREND TOOKER: I see Big Mama.

GOOPER: Hey, Big Mama, come here.

MAE: Hush, Gooper, don't holler.

BIG MAMA (*entering*): Too much smell of burnt fireworks makes me feel a little bit sick at my stomach.—Where is Big Daddy?

MAE: That's what I want to know, where has Big Daddy gone?

BIG MAMA: He must have turned in, I reckon he went to baid . . .

GOOPER: Well, then, now we can talk.

BIG MAMA: What *is* this talk, *what* talk?

(*Margaret appears on the gallery, talking to Doctor Baugh.*)

MARGARET (*musically*): My family freed their slaves ten years before abolition. My great-great-grandfather gave his slaves their freedom five years before the War between the States started!

MAE: Oh, for God's sake! Maggie's climbed back up in her family tree!

MARGARET (*sweetly*): What, Mae?

(*The pace must be very quick: great Southern animation.*)

BIG MAMA (*addressing them all*): I think Big Daddy was just worn out. He loves his family, he loves to have them around him, but it's a strain on his nerves. He wasn't himself tonight, Big Daddy wasn't himself, I could tell he was all worked up.

REVEREND TOOKER: I think he's remarkable.

BIG MAMA: Yaisss! Just remarkable. Did you all notice the food he ate at that table? Did you all notice the supper he put away? Why he ate like a hawss!

GOOPER: I hope he doesn't regret it.

BIG MAMA: What? Why that man—ate a huge piece of cawn bread with molasses on it! Helped himself twice to hoppin' John.

MARGARET: Big Daddy loves hoppin' John.—We had a real country dinner.

BIG MAMA (*overlapping Margaret*): Yaiss, he simply adores it! an' candied yams? Son? That man put away enough food at that table to stuff a *field* hand!

GOOPER (*with grim relish*): I hope he don't have to pay for it later on . . .

BIG MAMA (*fiercely*): What's *that,* Gooper?

MAE: Gooper says he hopes Big Daddy doesn't suffer tonight.

BIG MAMA: Oh, shoot, Gooper says, Gooper says! Why should Big Daddy suffer for satisfying a normal appetite? There's nothin' wrong with that man but nerves, he's sound as a dollar! And now he knows he is an' that's why he ate such a supper. He had a big load off his mind, knowin' he wasn't doomed t'—what he thought he was doomed to . . .

MARGARET (*sadly and sweetly*): Bless his old sweet soul . . .

BIG MAMA (*vaguely*): Yais, bless his heart, where's Brick?

MAE: Outside.

GOOPER:—Drinkin' . . .

BIG MAMA: I know he's drinkin'. Cain't I see he's drinkin' without you continually tellin' me that boy's drinkin'?

MARGARET: Good for you, Big Mama!

(*She applauds.*)

BIG MAMA: Other people *drink* and *have* drunk an' will *drink,* as long as they make that stuff an' put it in bottles.

MARGARET: That's the truth. I never trusted a man that didn't drink.

BIG MAMA: *Brick? Brick!*

MARGARET: He's still on the gall'ry. I'll go bring him in so we can talk.

BIG MAMA (*worriedly*): I don't know what this mysterious family conference is about.

(*Awkward silence. Big Mama looks from face to face, then belches slightly and mutters, "Excuse me . . ." She opens an ornamental fan suspended about her throat. A black lace fan to go with her black lace gown, and fans her wilting corsage, sniffing nervously and looking from face to face in the uncomfortable silence as Margaret calls "Brick?" and Brick sings to the moon on the gallery.*)

MARGARET: Brick, they're gonna tell Big Mama the truth an' she's gonna need you.

BIG MAMA: I don't know what's wrong here, you all have such long faces! Open that door on the hall and let some air circulate through here, will you please, Gooper?

MAE: I think we'd better leave that door closed, Big Mama, till after the talk.

MARGARET: Brick!

BIG MAMA: Reveren' Tooker, will *you* please open that door?

REVEREND TOOKER: I sure will, Big Mama.

MAE: I just didn't think we ought t' take any chance of Big Daddy hearin' a word of this discussion.

BIG MAMA: *I swan!* Nothing's going to be said in Big Daddy's house that he caint hear if he want to!

GOOPER: Well, Big Mama, it's—

(*Mae gives him a quick, hard poke to shut him up. He glares at her fiercely as she circles before him like a burlesque ballerina, raising her skinny bare arms over her head, jangling her bracelets, exclaiming:*)

MAE: *A breeze! A breeze!*

REVEREND TOOKER: I think this house is the coolest house in the Delta.—Did you all know that Halsey Banks's widow put air-conditioning units in the church and rectory at Friar's Point in memory of Halsey?

(*General conversation has resumed; everybody is chatting so that the stage sounds like a bird cage.*)

GOOPER: Too bad nobody cools your church off for you. I bet you sweat in that pulpit these hot Sundays, Reverend Tooker.

REVEREND TOOKER: Yes, my vestments are drenched. Last Sunday the gold in my chasuble faded into the purple.

GOOPER: Reveren', you musta been preachin' hell's fire last Sunday.

MAE (*at the same time to Doctor Baugh*): You reckon those vitamin B12 injections are what they're cracked up t' be, Doc Baugh?

DOCTOR BAUGH: Well, if you want to be stuck with something I guess they're as good to be stuck with as anything else.

BIG MAMA (*at the gallery door*): Maggie, Maggie, aren't you comin' with Brick?

MAE (*suddenly and loudly, creating a silence*): I have a strange feeling, I have a peculiar feeling!

BIG MAMA (*turning from the gallery*): What feeling?

MAE: That Brick said somethin' he shouldn't of said t' Big Daddy.

BIG MAMA: Now what on earth could Brick of said t' Big Daddy that he shouldn't say?

GOOPER: Big Mama, there's somethin'—

MAE: NOW, WAIT!

(*She rushes up to Big Mama and gives her a quick hug and kiss. Big Mama pushes her impatiently off.*)

DOCTOR BAUGH: In my day they had what they call the Keeley cure for heavy drinkers.

BIG MAMA: Shoot!

DOCTOR BAUGH: But now I understand they just take some kind of tablets.

GOOPER: They call them "Annie Bust" tablets.

BIG MAMA: *Brick* don't need to take *nothin'*.

(*Brick and Margaret appear in gallery doors, Big Mama unaware of his presence behind her.*)

That boy is just broken up over Skipper's death. You know how poor Skipper died. They gave him a big, big dose of that sodium amytal stuff at his home and then they called the ambulance and give him another big, big dose of it at the hospital and that and all of the alcohol in his system fo' months an' months just proved too much for his heart . . . I'm scared of needles! I'm more scared of a needle than the knife . . . I think more people have been needled out of this world than—

(*She stops short and wheels about.*)

Oh—here's Brick! My precious baby—

(*She turns upon Brick with short, fat arms extended, at the same time uttering a loud, short sob, which is both comic and touching. Brick smiles and bows slightly, making a burlesque gesture of gallantry for Margaret to pass before him into the room. Then he hobbles on his crutch directly to the liquor cabinet and there is absolute silence, with everybody looking*

at Brick as everybody has always looked at Brick when he spoke or moved or appeared. One by one he drops ice cubes in his glass, then suddenly, but not quickly, looks back over his shoulder with a wry, charming smile, and says:)

BRICK: I'm sorry! Anyone else?

BIG MAMA (*sadly*): No, son. I *wish* you wouldn't!

BRICK: I wish I didn't have to, Big Mama, but I'm still waiting for that click in my head which makes it all smooth out!

BIG MAMA: Ow, Brick, you—BREAK MY HEART!

MARGARET (*at same time*): Brick, go sit with Big Mama!

BIG MAMA: I just cain't staiiiiii-nnnnnnnd-it . . .

(*She sobs.*)

MAE: Now that we're all assembled—

GOOPER: We kin talk . . .

BIG MAMA: Breaks my heart . . .

MARGARET: Sit with Big Mama, Brick, and hold her hand.

(*Big Mama sniffs very loudly three times, almost like three drumbeats in the pocket of silence.*)

BRICK: You do that, Maggie. I'm a restless cripple. I got to stay on my crutch.

(*Brick hobbles to the gallery door; leans there as if waiting.*)

(*Mae sits beside Big Mama, while Gooper moves in front and sits on the end of the couch, facing her. Reverend Tooker moves nervously into the space between them; on the other side, Doctor Baugh stands looking at nothing in particular and lights a cigar. Margaret turns away.*)

BIG MAMA: Why're you all *surroundin'* me—like this? Why're you all starin' at me like this an' makin' signs at each other?

(*Reverend Tooker steps back startled.*)

MAE: Calm yourself, Big Mama.

BIG MAMA: Calm you'self, *you'self*, Sister Woman. How could I calm myself with everyone starin' at me as if big drops of blood had broken out on m'face? What's this all about, annh! What?

(*Gooper coughs and takes a center position.*)

GOOPER: Now, Doc Baugh.

MAE: Doc Baugh?

GOOPER: Big Mama wants to know the complete truth about the report we got from the Ochsner Clinic.

MAE (*eagerly*):—on Big Daddy's condition!

GOOPER: Yais, on Big Daddy's condition, we got to face it.

DOCTOR BAUGH: Well . . .

BIG MAMA (*terrified, rising*): Is there? Something? Something that I? Don't—know?

(*In these few words, this startled, very soft, question, Big Mama reviews the history of her forty-five years with Big Daddy, her great, almost embarrassingly true-hearted and simple-minded devotion to Big Daddy, who must have had something Brick has, who made himself loved so much by the "simple expedient" of not loving enough to disturb his charming detachment, also once coupled, like Brick, with virile beauty.)*

(Big Mama has a dignity at this moment; she almost stops being fat.)

DOCTOR BAUGH *(after a pause, uncomfortably)*: Yes?—Well—

BIG MAMA: I!!!—want to—*knowwwwww . . .*

(Immediately she thrusts her fist to her mouth as if to deny that statement. Then for some curious reason, she snatches the withered corsage from her breast and hurls it on the floor and steps on it with her short, fat feet.)

Somebody must be lyin'!—I want to know!

MAE: Sit down, Big Mama, sit down on this sofa.

MARGARET: Brick, go sit with Big Mama.

BIG MAMA: *What is it, what is it?*

DOCTOR BAUGH: I never have seen a more thorough examination than Big Daddy Pollitt was given in all my experience with the Ochsner Clinic.

GOOPER: It's one of the best in the country.

MAE: It's THE best in the country—bar *none!*

(For some reason she gives Gooper a violent poke as she goes past him. He slaps at her hand without removing his eyes from his mother's face.)

DOCTOR BAUGH: Of course they were ninety-nine and nine-tenths percent sure before they even started.

BIG MAMA: Sure of what, sure of what, sure of—*what?*—*what?*

(She catches her breath in a startled sob. Mae kisses her quickly. She thrusts Mae fiercely away from her, staring at the Doctor.)

MAE: Mommy, be a brave girl!

BRICK *(in the doorway, softly)*: "By the light, by the light, Of the sil-ve-ry mo-oo-n . . ."

GOOPER: Shut up!—Brick.

BRICK: Sorry . . .

(He wanders out on the gallery.)

DOCTOR BAUGH: But now, you see, Big Mama, they cut a piece of this growth, a specimen of the tissue and—

BIG MAMA: Growth? You told Big Daddy—

DOCTOR BAUGH: Now wait.

BIG MAMA *(fiercely)*: You told me and Big Daddy there wasn't a thing wrong with him but—

MAE: Big Mama, they always—

GOOPER: Let Doc Baugh talk, will yuh?

BIG MAMA: —little spastic condition of—

(Her breath gives out in a sob.)

DOCTOR BAUGH: Yes, that's what we told Big Daddy. But we had this bit of tissue run through the laboratory and I'm sorry to say the test was positive on it. It's—well—malignant . . .

(Pause.)

BIG MAMA: —Cancer?! Cancer?!

(Doctor Baugh nods gravely. Big Mama gives a long gasping cry.)

MAE AND GOOPER: Now, now, now, Big Mama, you had to know . . .

BIG MAMA: WHY DIDN'T THEY CUT IT OUT OF HIM? HANH? HANH?

DOCTOR BAUGH: Involved too much, Big Mama, too many organs affected.

MAE: Big Mama, the liver's affected and so's the kidneys, both! It's gone way past what they call a—

GOOPER: A surgical risk.

MAE: —Uh-huh . . .

(Big Mama draws a breath like a dying gasp.)

REVEREND TOOKER: Tch, tch, tch, tch, tch!

DOCTOR BAUGH: Yes it's gone past the knife.

MAE: *That's why he's turned yellow, Mommy!*

BIG MAMA: *Git away from me, git away from me, Mae!*

(She rises abruptly.)

I want Brick! Where's Brick? Where is my only son?

MAE: Mama! Did she say *"only son"*?

GOOPER: What does that make *me*?

MAE: A sober responsible man with five precious children!—*Six!*

BIG MAMA: I want Brick to tell me! Brick! Brick!

MARGARET *(rising from her reflections in a corner)*: Brick was so upset he went back out.

BIG MAMA: *Brick!*

MARGARET: Mama, let *me* tell you!

BIG MAMA: No, no, leave me alone, you're not my blood!

GOOPER: *Mama, I'm your son! Listen to me!*

MAE: Gooper's your son, he's your first-born!

BIG MAMA: Gooper never liked Daddy.

MAE *(as if terribly shocked)*: That's not TRUE!

(There is a pause. The minister coughs and rises.)

REVEREND TOOKER *(to Mae)*: I think I'd better slip away at this point.

(Discreetly.)

Good night, good night, everybody, and God bless you all . . . on this place . . .

(He slips out.)

(Mae coughs and points at Big Mama.)

GOOPER: Well, Big Mama . . .

(He sighs.)

BIG MAMA: It's all a mistake, I know it's just a bad dream.

DOCTOR BAUGH: We're gonna keep Big Daddy as comfortable as we can.

BIG MAMA: Yes, it's just a bad dream, that's all it is, it's just an awful dream.

GOOPER: In my opinion Big Daddy is having some pain but won't admit that he has it.

BIG MAMA: Just a dream, a bad dream.

DOCTOR BAUGH: That's what lots of them do, they think if they don't admit they're having the pain they can sort of escape the fact of it.

GOOPER (*with relish*): Yes, they get sly about it, they get real sly about it.

MAE: Gooper and I think—

GOOPER: Shut up, Mae! Big Mama, I think—Big Daddy ought to be started on morphine.

BIG MAMA: Nobody's going to give Big Daddy morphine.

DOCTOR BAUGH: Now, Big Mama, when that pain strikes it's going to strike mighty hard and Big Daddy's going to need the needle to bear it.

BIG MAMA: I tell you, nobody's going to give him morphine.

MAE: Big Mama, you don't want to see Big Daddy suffer, you know you—

(*Gooper, standing beside her, gives her a savage poke.*)

DOCTOR BAUGH (*placing a package on the table*): I'm leaving this stuff here, so if there's a sudden attack you all won't have to send out for it.

MAE: I know how to give a hypo.

BIG MAMA: Nobody's gonna give Big Daddy morphine.

GOOPER: Mae took a course in nursing during the war.

MARGARET: Somehow I don't think Big Daddy would want Mae to give him a hypo.

MAE: You think he'd want *you* to do it?

DOCTOR BAUGH: Well . . .

(*Doctor Baugh rises.*)

GOOPER: Doctor Baugh is goin'.

DOCTOR BAUGH: Yes, I got to be goin'. Well, keep your chin up, Big Mama.

GOOPER (*with jocularity*): She's gonna keep *both* chins up, aren't you, Big Mama?

(*Big Mama sobs.*)

Now stop that, Big Mama.

GOOPER (*at the door with Doctor Baugh*): Well, Doc, we sure do appreciate all you done. I'm telling you, we're surely obligated to you for—

(*Doctor Baugh has gone out without a glance at him.*)

—I guess that doctor has got a lot on his mind but it wouldn't hurt him to act a little more human . . .

(*Big Mama sobs.*)

Now be a brave girl, Mommy.

BIG MAMA: It's not true, I know that it's just not true!

GOOPER: Mama, those tests are infallible!

BIG MAMA: Why are you so determined to see your father daid?

MAE: Big Mama!

MARGARET (*gently*): I know what Big Mama means.

MAE (*fiercely*): Oh, do you?

MARGARET (*quietly and very sadly*): Yes, I think I do.

MAE: For a newcomer in the family you sure do show a lot of understanding.

MARGARET: Understanding is needed on this place.

MAE: I guess you must have needed a lot of it in your family, Maggie, with your father's liquor problem and now you've got Brick with his!

MARGARET: Brick does not have a liquor problem at all. Brick is devoted to Big Daddy. This thing is a terrible strain on him.

BIG MAMA: Brick is Big Daddy's boy, but he drinks too much and it worries me and Big Daddy, and, Margaret, you've got to cooperate with us, you've got to cooperate with Big Daddy and me in getting Brick straightened out. Because it will break Big Daddy's heart if Brick don't pull himself together and take hold of things.

MAE: Take hold of *what* things, Big Mama?

BIG MAMA: The place.

(*There is a quick violent look between Mae and Gooper.*)

GOOPER: Big Mama, you've had a shock.

MAE: Yais, we've all had a shock, but . . .

GOOPER: Let's be realistic—

MAE: —Big Daddy would never, would *never*, be foolish enough to—

GOOPER: —put this place in irresponsible hands!

BIG MAMA: Big Daddy ain't going to leave the place in anybody's hands; Big Daddy is *not* going to die. I want you to get that in your heads, all of you!

MAE: Mommy, Mommy, Big Mama, we're just as hopeful an' optimistic as you are about Big Daddy's prospects, we have faith in *prayer*—but nevertheless there are certain matters that have to be discussed an' dealt with, because otherwise—

GOOPER: Eventualities have to be considered and now's the time . . . Mae, will you please get my brief case out of our room?

MAE: Yes, honey.

(*She rises and goes out through the hall door.*)

GOOPER (*standing over Big Mama*): Now, Big Mom. What you said just now was not at all true and you know it. I've always loved Big Daddy in my own quiet way. I never made a show of it, and I know that Big Daddy has always been fond of me in a quiet way, too, and he never made a show of it neither.

(*Mae returns with Gooper's brief case.*)

MAE: Here's your brief case, Gooper, honey.

GOOPER (*handing the brief case back to her*): Thank you . . . Of cou'se, my relationship with Big Daddy is different from Brick's.

MAE: You're eight years older'n Brick an' always had t' carry a bigger load of th' responsibilities than Brick ever had t' carry. He never carried a thing in his life but a football or a highball.

GOOPER: Mae, will y' let me talk, please?

MAE: Yes, honey.

GOOPER: Now, a twenty-eight-thousand-acre plantation's a mighty big thing t' run.

MAE: Almost singlehanded.

(*Margaret has gone out onto the gallery and can be heard calling softly to Brick.*)

BIG MAMA: You never had to run this place! What are you talking about? As if Big Daddy was dead and in his grave, you had to run it? Why, you just helped him out with a few business details and had your law practice at the same time in Memphis!

MAE: Oh, Mommy, Mommy, Big Mommy! Let's be fair!

MARGARET: Brick!

MAE: Why, Gooper has given himself body and soul to keeping this place up for the past five years since Big Daddy's health started failing.

MARGARET: Brick!

MAE: Gooper won't say it, Gooper never thought of it as a duty, he just did it. And what did Brick do? Brick kept living in his past glory at college! Still a football player at twenty-seven!

MARGARET (*returning alone*): Who are you talking about now? Brick? A football player? He isn't a football player and you know it. Brick is a sports announcer on TV and one of the best-known ones in the country!

MAE: I'm talking about what he was.

MARGARET: Well, I wish you would just stop talking about my husband.

GOOPER: I've got a right to discuss my brother with other members of MY OWN family, which don't include *you*. Why don't you go out there and drink with Brick?

MARGARET: I've never seen such malice toward a brother.

GOOPER: How about his for me? Why, he can't stand to be in the same room with me!

MARGARET: This is a deliberate campaign of vilification for the most disgusting and sordid reason on earth, and I know what it is! It's *avarice, avarice, greed, greed!*

BIG MAMA: *Oh, I'll scream! I will scream in a moment unless this stops!*

(*Gooper has stalked up to Margaret with clenched fists at his sides as if he would strike her. Mae distorts her face again into a hideous grimace behind Margaret's back.*)

BIG MAMA (*sobs*): Margaret. Child. Come here. Sit next to Big Mama.

MARGARET: Precious Mommy. I'm sorry, I'm sorry, I—!

(*She bends her long graceful neck to press her forehead to Big Mama's bulging shoulder under its black chiffon.*)

MAE: How beautiful, how touching, this display of devotion! Do you know why she's childless? She's childless because that big beautiful athlete husband of hers won't go to bed with her!

GOOPER: You jest won't let me do this in a nice way, will yah? Aw right—I don't give a goddamn if Big Daddy likes me or don't like me or did or never did or will or will never! I'm just appealing to a sense of common decency and fair play. I'll tell you the truth. I've resented Big Daddy's partiality to Brick ever since Brick was born, and the way I've been treated like I was just barely good enough to spit on and sometimes not even good enough for that. Big Daddy is dying of cancer, and it's spread all through him and it's attacked all his vital organs including the kidneys and right now he is sinking into uremia, and you all know what uremia is, it's poisoning of the whole system due to the failure of the body to eliminate its poisons.

MARGARET (*to herself, downstage, hissingly*): Poisons, poisons! Venomous thoughts and words! In hearts and minds!—That's poisons!

GOOPER (*overlapping her*): I am asking for a square deal, and, by God, I expect to get one. But if I don't get one, if there's any peculiar shenanigans going on around here behind my back, well, I'm not a corporation lawyer for nothing, I know how to protect my own interests.

(*Brick enters from the gallery with a tranquil, blurred smile, carrying an empty glass with him.*)

BRICK: Storm coming up.

GOOPER: Oh! A late arrival!

MAE: Behold the conquering hero comes!

GOOPER: The fabulous Brick Pollitt! Remember him?—Who could forget him!

MAE: He looks like he's been injured in a game!

GOOPER: Yep, I'm afraid you'll have to warm the bench at the Sugar Bowl this year, Brick!

(*Mae laughs shrilly.*)

Or was it the Rose Bowl that he made that famous run in?—

(*Thunder.*)

MAE: The punch bowl, honey. It was in the punch bowl, the cut-glass punch bowl!

GOOPER: Oh, that's right, I'm getting the bowls mixed up!

MARGARET: Why don't you stop venting your malice and envy on a sick boy?

BIG MAMA: *Now you two hush, I mean it, hush, all of you, hush!*

DAISY, SOOKEY: Storm! Storm comin'! Storm! Storm!

LACEY: Brightie, close them shutters.

GOOPER: Lacey, put the top up on my Cadillac, will yuh?

LACEY: Yes, suh, Mistah Pollitt!

GOOPER (*at the same time*): Big Mama, you know it's necessary for me t' go back to Memphis in th' mornin' t' represent the Parker estate in a lawsuit.

(*Mae sits on the bed and arranges papers she has taken from the brief case.*)

BIG MAMA: Is it, Gooper?

MAE: Yaiss.

GOOPER: That's why I'm forced to—to bring up a problem that—

MAE: Somethin' that's too important t' be put off!

GOOPER: If Brick was sober, he ought to be in on this.

MARGARET: Brick is present; we're present.

GOOPER: Well, good. I will now give you this outline my partner, Tom Bullitt, an' me have drawn up—a sort of dummy—trusteeship.

MARGARET: Oh, that's it! You'll be in charge an' dole out remittances, will you?

GOOPER: This we did as soon as we got the report on Big Daddy from th' Ochsner Laboratories. We did this thing, I mean we drew up this dummy outline with the advice and assistance of the Chairman of the Boa'd of Directors of th' Southern Plantahs Bank and Trust Company in Memphis, C. C. Bellowes, a man who handles estates for all th' prominent fam'lies in West Tennessee and th' Delta.

BIG MAMA: Gooper?

GOOPER (crouching in front of Big Mama): Now this is not—not final, or anything like it. This is just a preliminary outline. But it does provide a basis—a design—a—possible, feasible—plan!

MARGARET: Yes, I'll bet it's a plan.

(Thunder.)

MAE: It's a plan to protect the biggest estate in the Delta from irresponsibility an'—

BIG MAMA: Now you listen to me, all of you, you listen here! They's not goin' to be any more catty talk in my house! And Gooper, you put that away before I grab it out of your hand and tear it right up! I don't know what the hell's in it, and I don't want to know what the hell's in it. I'm talkin' in Big Daddy's language now; I'm his wife, not his widow, I'm still his wife! And I'm talkin' to you in his language an'—

GOOPER: Big Mama, what I have here is—

MAE (at the same time): Gooper explained that it's just a plan . . .

BIG MAMA: I don't care what you got there. Just put it back where it came from, an' don't let me see it again, not even the outside of the envelope of it! Is that understood? Basis! Plan! Preliminary! Design! I say—what is it Big Daddy always says when he's disgusted?

BRICK (from the bar): Big Daddy says "crap" when he's disgusted.

BIG MAMA (rising): That's right—CRAP! I say CRAP too, like Big Daddy!

(Thunder.)

MAE: Coarse language doesn't seem called for in this—

GOOPER: Somethin' in me is deeply outraged by hearin' you talk like this.

BIG MAMA: Nobody's goin' to take nothin'!—till Big Daddy lets go of it—maybe, just possibly, not—not even then! No, not even then!

(Thunder.)

MAE: Sookey, hurry up an' git that po'ch furniture covahed; want th' paint to come off?

GOOPER: Lacey, put mah car away!

LACEY: Caint, Mistah Pollitt, you got the keys!

GOOPER: Naw, you got 'em, man. Where th' keys to th' car, honey?

MAE: You got 'em in your pocket!

BRICK: "You can always hear me singin' this song, Show me the way to go home."

(Thunder distantly.)

BIG MAMA: Brick! Come here, Brick, I need you. Tonight Brick looks like he used to look when he was a little boy, just like he did when he played wild games and used to come home when I hollered myself hoarse for him, all sweaty and pink cheeked and sleepy, with his—red curls shining . . .

(Brick draws aside as he does from all physical contact and continues the song in a whisper, opening the ice bucket and dropping in the ice cubes one by one as if he were mixing some important chemical formula.)
(Distant thunder.)

Time goes by so fast. Nothin' can outrun it. Death commences too early—almost before you're half acquainted with life—you meet the other . . . Oh, you know we just got to love each other an' stay together, all of us, just as close as we can, especially now that such a black thing has come and moved into this place without invitation.

(Awkwardly embracing Brick, she presses her head to his shoulder.)
(A dog howls offstage.)

Oh, Brick, son of Big Daddy, Big Daddy does so love you. Y'know what would be his fondest dream come true? If before he passed on, if Big Daddy has to pass on . . .

(A dog howls.)

. . . you give him a child of yours, a grandson as much like his son as his son is like Big Daddy . . .

MARGARET: I know that's Big Daddy's dream.

BIG MAMA: That's his dream.

MAE: Such a pity that Maggie and Brick can't oblige.

BIG DADDY (off downstage right on the gallery): Looks like the wind was takin' liberties with this place.

SERVANT (offstage): Yes, sir, Mr. Pollitt.

MARGARET (crossing to the right door): Big Daddy's on the gall'ry.

(Big Mama has turned toward the hall door at the sound of Big Daddy's voice on the gallery.)

BIG MAMA: I can't stay here. He'll see somethin' in my eyes.

(Big Daddy enters the room from upstage right.)

BIG DADDY: Can I come in?

(He puts his cigar in an ash tray.)

MARGARET: Did the storm wake you up, Big Daddy?

BIG DADDY: Which stawm are you talkin' about—th' one outside or th' hullballoo in here?

(*Gooper squeezes past Big Daddy.*)

GOOPER: 'Scuse me.

(*Mae tries to squeeze past Big Daddy to join Gooper, but Big Daddy puts his arm firmly around her.*)

BIG DADDY: I heard some mighty loud talk. Sounded like somethin' important was bein' discussed. What was the powwow about?

MAE (*flustered*): Why—nothin', Big Daddy . . .

BIG DADDY (*crossing to extreme left center, taking Mae with him*): What is that pregnant-lookin' envelope you're puttin' back in your brief case, Gooper?

GOOPER (*at the foot of the bed, caught, as he stuffs papers into envelope*): That? Nothin', suh—nothin' much of anythin' at all . . .

BIG DADDY: Nothin'? It looks like a whole lot of nothin'!

(*He turns upstage to the group.*)

You all know th' story about th' young married couple—

GOOPER: Yes, sir!

BIG DADDY: Hello, Brick—

BRICK: Hello, Big Daddy.

(*The group is arranged in a semicircle above Big Daddy, Margaret at the extreme right, then Mae and Gooper, then Big Mama, with Brick at the left.*)

BIG DADDY: Young married couple took Junior out to th' zoo one Sunday, inspected all of God's creatures in their cages, with satisfaction.

GOOPER: Satisfaction.

BIG DADDY (*crossing to upstage center, facing front*): This afternoon was a warm afternoon in spring an' that ole elephant had somethin' else on his mind which was bigger'n peanuts. You know this story, Brick?

(*Gooper nods.*)

BRICK: No, sir, I don't know it.

BIG DADDY: Y'see, in th' cage adjoinin' they was a young female elephant in heat!

BIG MAMA (*at Big Daddy's shoulder*): Oh, Big Daddy!

BIG DADDY: What's the matter, preacher's gone, ain't he? All right. That female elephant in the next cage was permeatin' the atmosphere about her with a powerful and excitin' odor of female fertility! Huh! Ain't that a nice way to put it, Brick?

BRICK: Yes, sir, nothin' wrong with it.

BIG DADDY: Brick says th's nothin' wrong with it!

BIG MAMA: Oh, Big Daddy!

BIG DADDY (*crossing to downstage center*): So this ole bull elephant still had a couple of fornications left in him. He reared back his trunk an' got a whiff of that elephant lady next door!—began to paw at the dirt in his cage an' butt his head against the separatin' partition and, first thing y'know, there was a conspicuous change in his *profile*—very *conspicuous*! Ain't I tellin' this story in decent language, Brick?

BRICK: Yes, sir, too fuckin' decent!

BIG DADDY: So, the little boy pointed at it and said, "What's that?" His mama said, "Oh, that's—nothin'!"—His papa said, "She's spoiled!"

(*Big Daddy crosses to Brick at left.*)

You didn't laugh at that story, Brick.

(*Big Mama crosses to downstage right crying. Margaret goes to her. Mae and Gooper hold upstage right center.*)

BRICK: No, sir, I didn't laugh at that story.

BIG DADDY: What is the smell in this room? Don't you notice it, Brick? Don't you notice a powerful and obnoxious odor of mendacity in this room?

BRICK: Yes, sir, I think I do, sir.

GOOPER: Mae, Mae . . .

BIG DADDY: There is nothing more powerful. Is there, Brick?

BRICK: No, sir. No, sir, there isn't, an' nothin' more obnoxious.

BIG DADDY: Brick agrees with me. The odor of mendacity is a powerful and obnoxious odor an' the stawm hasn't blown it away from this room yet. You notice it, Gooper?

GOOPER: What, sir?

BIG DADDY: How about you, Sister Woman? You notice the unpleasant odor of mendacity in this room?

MAE: Why, Big Daddy, I don't even know what that is.

BIG DADDY: You can smell it. Hell it smells like death!

(*Big Mama sobs. Big Daddy looks toward her.*)

What's wrong with that fat woman over there, loaded with diamonds? Hey, what's-you-name, what's the matter with you?

MARGARET (*crossing toward Big Daddy*): She had a slight dizzy spell, Big Daddy.

BIG DADDY: You better watch that, Big Mama. A stroke is a bad way to go.

MARGARET (*crossing to Big Daddy at center*): Oh, Brick, Big Daddy has on your birthday present to him, Brick, he has on your cashmere robe, the softest material I have ever felt.

BIG DADDY: Yeah, this is my soft birthday, Maggie . . . Not my gold or my silver birthday, but my soft birthday, everything's got to be soft for Big Daddy on this soft birthday.

(*Maggie kneels before Big Daddy at center.*)

MARGARET: Big Daddy's got on his Chinese slippers that I gave him, Brick. Big Daddy, I haven't given you my big present yet, but now I will, now's the time for me to present it to you! I have an announcement to make!

MAE: What? What kind of announcement?

GOOPER: A sports announcement, Maggie?

MARGARET: Announcement of life beginning! A child is coming, sired by Brick, and out of Maggie the Cat! I have Brick's child in my body, an' that's my birthday present to Big Daddy on this birthday!

(*Big Daddy looks at Brick who crosses behind Big Daddy to downstage portal, left.*)

BIG DADDY: Get up, girl, get up off your knees, girl.

(*Big Daddy helps Margaret to rise. He crosses above her, to her right, bites off the end of a fresh cigar, taken from his bathrobe pocket, as he studies Margaret.*)

Uh-huh, this girl has life in her body, that's no lie!

BIG MAMA: BIG DADDY'S DREAM COME TRUE!

BRICK: JESUS!

BIG DADDY (*crossing right below wicker stand*): Gooper, I want my lawyer in the mornin'.

BRICK: Where are you goin', Big Daddy?

BIG DADDY: Son, I'm goin' up on the roof, to the belvedere on th' roof to look over my kingdom before I give up my kingdom—twenty-eight thousand acres of th' richest land this side of the valley Nile!

(*He exits through right doors, and down right on the gallery.*)

BIG MAMA (*following*): Sweetheart, sweetheart, sweetheart—can I come with you?

(*She exits downstage right.*)
(*Margaret is downstage center in the mirror area. Mae has joined Gooper and she gives him a fierce poke, making a low hissing sound and a grimace of fury.*)

GOOPER (*pushing her aside*): Brick, could you possibly spare me one small shot of that liquor?

BRICK: Why, help yourself, Gooper boy.

GOOPER: I will.

MAE (*shrilly*): Of course we know that this is—a lie.

GOOPER: Be still, Mae.

MAE: I won't be still! I know she's made this up!

GOOPER: Goddamn it, I said shut up!

MARGARET: Gracious! I didn't know that my little announcement was going to provoke such a storm!

MAE: *That* woman isn't *pregnant!*

GOOPER: Who said she was?

MAE: *She* did.

GOOPER: The doctor didn't. Doc Baugh didn't.

MARGARET: I haven't gone to Doc Baugh.

GOOPER: Then who'd you go to, Maggie?

MARGARET: One of the best gynecologists in the South.

GOOPER: Uh huh, uh huh!—I see . . .

(*He takes out a pencil and notebook.*)

—May we have his name, please?

MARGARET: No, you may not, Mister Prosecuting Attorney!

MAE: He doesn't have any name, he doesn't exist!

MARGARET: Oh, he exists all right, and so does my child, Brick's baby!

MAE: You can't conceive a child by a man that won't sleep with you unless you think you're—

(*Brick has turned on the phonograph. A scat song cuts Mae's speech.*)

GOOPER: *Turn that off!*

MAE: We know it's a lie because we hear you in here; he won't sleep with you, we hear you! So don't imagine you're going to put a trick over on us, to fool a dying man with a—

(*A long drawn cry of agony and rage fills the house. Margaret turns the phonograph down to a whisper. The cry is repeated.*)

MAE: Did you hear that, Gooper, did you hear that?

GOOPER: Sounds like the pain has struck.

MAE: Go see, Gooper!

GOOPER: Come along and leave these lovebirds together in their nest!

(*He goes out first. Mae follows but turns at the door, contorting her face and hissing at Margaret.*)

MAE: *Liar!*

(*She slams the door.*)
(*Margaret exhales with relief and moves a little unsteadily to catch hold of Brick's arm.*)

MARGARET: Thank you for—keeping still . . .

BRICK: O.K., Maggie.

MARGARET: It was gallant of you to save my face!

(*He now pours down three shots in quick succession and stands waiting, silent. All at once he turns with a smile and says:*)

BRICK: *There!*

MARGARET: What?

BRICK: The *click* . . .

(*His gratitude seems almost infinite as he hobbles out on the gallery with a drink. We hear his crutch as he swings out of sight. Then, at some distance, he begins singing to himself a peaceful song. Margaret holds the big pillow forlornly as if it were her only companion, for a few moments, then throws it on the bed. She rushes to the liquor cabinet, gathers all the bottles in her arms, turns about undecidedly, then runs out of the room with them, leaving the door ajar on the dim yellow hall. Brick is heard hobbling back along the gallery, singing his peaceful song. He comes back in, sees the pillow on the bed, laughs lightly, sadly, picks it up. He has it under his arm as Margaret returns to the room. Margaret softly shuts the door and leans against it, smiling softly at Brick.*)

MARGARET: Brick, I used to think that you were stronger than me and I didn't want to be overpowered by you. But now, since you've taken to liquor—you know what?—I guess it's bad, but now I'm stronger than you and I can love you more truly! Don't—move that pillow. I'll move it right back if you do!—Brick?

(*She turns out all the lamps but a single rose-silk-shaded one by the bed.*)

I really have been to a doctor and I know what to do and—Brick?—this is my time by the calendar to conceive?

BRICK: Yes, I understand, Maggie. But how are you going to conceive a child by a man in love with his liquor?

MARGARET: By locking his liquor up and making him satisfy my desire before I unlock it!

BRICK: Is that what you've done, Maggie?

MARGARET: Look and see. That cabinet's mighty empty compared to before!

BRICK: Well, I'll be a son of a—

(*He reaches for his crutch but she beats him to it and rushes out on the gallery, hurls the crutch over the rail, and comes back in, panting.*)

MARGARET: And so tonight we're going to make the lie true, and when that's done, I'll bring the liquor back here and we'll get drunk together, here, tonight, in this place that death has come into . . .—What do you say?

BRICK: I don't say anything. I guess there's nothing to say.

MARGARET: Oh, you weak people, you weak, beautiful people!—who give up with such grace. What you want is someone to—

(*She turns out the rose-silk lamp.*)

—take hold of you.—Gently, gently with love hand your life back to you, like somethin' gold you let go of. I *do* love you, Brick, I *do*!

BRICK (*smiling with charming sadness*): Wouldn't it be funny if that was true?

COMMENTARIES

TENNESSEE WILLIAMS (1911–1983)

From Memoirs 1972

Tennessee Williams published *Memoirs* in 1972, after establishing himself as one of the most successful American playwrights. The excerpts included here concern his feelings about *Cat on a Hot Tin Roof* and his feelings about being a writer.

Well, now, about plays, what about them? Plays are written and then, if they are lucky, they are performed, and if their luck still holds, which is not too frequently the case, their performance is so successful that both audience and critics at the first night are aware that they are being offered a dramatic work which is both honest and entertaining and also somehow capable of engaging their aesthetic appreciation.

I have never liked to talk about the professional side of my life. Am I afraid that it is a bird that will be startled away by discussion, as by a hawk's shadow? Something like that, I suppose.

People are always asking me, at those symposia to which I've been subjected in recent years, which is my favorite among the plays I have written, the number of which eludes my recollection, and I either say to them, "Always the latest" or I succumb to my instinct for the truth and say, "I suppose it must be the published version of *Cat on a Hot Tin Roof*."

That play comes closest to being both a work of art and a work of craft. It is really very well put together, in my opinion, and all its characters are amusing and credible and touching. Also it adheres to the valuable edict of Aristotle that a tragedy must have unity of time and place and magnitude of theme.

The set in *Cat* never changes and its running time is exactly the time of its action, meaning that one act, timewise, follows directly upon the other, and I know of no other modern American play in which this is accomplished.

However my reasons for liking *Cat* best are deeper than that. I believe that in *Cat* I reached beyond myself, in the second act, to a kind of crude eloquence of expression in Big Daddy that I have managed to give no other character of my creation.

The story of *Cat's* production in 1954 and the disaster that followed upon its enormous success must be told now.

[Director Elia] Kazan immediately shared Audrey's [Wood, Williams's agent] enthusiasm for *Cat* but he said that it was faulty in one act. I assumed that he meant the first act, but no, it was the third act. He wanted a more admirable heroine than the Maggie offered in the original script.

Inwardly I disagreed. I thought that in Maggie I had presented a very true and moving portrait of a young woman whose frustration in love and whose practicality drove her to the literal seduction of an unwilling young man. Seduction is too soft a word. Brick was literally forced back to bed by Maggie, when she confiscated his booze . . .

Then I also had to violate my own intuition by having Big Daddy re-enter the stage in Act Three. I saw nothing for him to do in that act when he re-entered and I did not think that it was dramatically proper that he should re-enter. Consequently I had him tell "the elephant story." This was assaulted by censors. I was told it must be removed. The material which I then had to put in its place was always offensive to me.

I would not tell you this except for the consequences to me as a writer after *Cat* had received its Critics' Award and its Pulitzer.

Even though I always go crazy on opening nights, the New York opening of *Cat* was particularly dreadful. I thought it was a failure, a distortion of what I had intended. After the show was over I thought I had heard coughs all during the performance. I suppose there weren't that many, probably the usual number. And it did become my biggest, my longest-running play. But after the show was over on opening night, Kazan said, "Let's go to my apartment until the reviews are out." He was totally confident that it would be a hit. I met Audrey Wood outside, and at the time I was totally dependent on her for any creative confidence; and so I said, "Audrey, we're all going up to the Kazans' to wait for the notices." She said, "Oh no, I have other plans." I was hurt, and said something mean. . . .

What is it like being a writer? I would say it is like being free.

I know that some writers aren't free, they are professionally employed, which is quite a different thing.

Professionally, they are probably better writers in the conventional sense of "better." They have an ear to the ground of best-seller demands: They please their publishers and presumably their public as well.

But they are not free and so they are not what I regard a true writer as being.

To be free is to have achieved your life.

It means any number of freedoms.

It means the freedom to stop when you please, to go where and when you please, it means to be voyager here and there, one who flees many hotels, sad or happy, without obstruction and without much regret.

It means the freedom of being. And someone has wisely observed, if you can't be yourself, what's the point of being anything at all?

I am not a frequent reader nor quoter of Scriptures and yet I love a piece of advice which occurs among them:
"Let thy light so shine among men that they see thy good works and glorify thy Father which is in heaven."
There is a New Journalism, there is a New Criticism, there is a new look and style of cinema and theater, of practically everything that we live with, but what I think we most need is a New Morality.
And I think we've arrived at a point where that is a necessity of continued and bearable existence.

BRENDA MURPHY (b. 1950)

Tennessee Williams and Elia Kazan Collaborate on *Cat* 1991

Theater is a collaborative art, and numerous plays have been altered because of suggestions of a director or actor. The collaboration of Tennessee Williams and director Elia Kazan was special because both were powerful personalities and each respected the other. The *Cat on a Hot Tin Roof* that we know is much different from the one that Williams first wrote. He was willing to make many of the creative changes suggested by Kazan.

[Director Elia Kazan's] imagination stimulated by Big Daddy's rhetorical power, Kazan developed the production around the impetus of direct communication between the characters and the audience. At the beginning of Act 2, for example, he made a note to himself to have Big Daddy come downstage facing the audience and talk straight out to them while the others remained way upstage, even out on the gallery. Williams agreed with Kazan about the power of Big Daddy's character and the centrality of words in the play. In *Memoirs* he wrote, "In *Cat* I reached beyond myself, in the second act, to a kind of crude eloquence of expression in Big Daddy that I have managed to give no other character of my creation."[1]

Although Williams had incorporated the idea of addressing the audience in the "recitative" speeches of Maggie and Brick in the early scripts, he had not counted on what was in 1955 the radical concept that Kazan devised for the production. As Kazan noted in a later interview, the conventions of representational realism were so entrenched in the Broadway theater of the fifties that foregrounding the production's theatricality to the extent of having the characters address the audience directly had been considered anathema for many years. The last time he could remember it being done was in the production of *Our Town*° in 1938.[2]

[1]Tennessee Williams, *Memoirs* (Garden City: Doubleday, 1975).
[2]Michel Ciment, *Kazan on Kazan* (New York: Viking, 1974) 47.
Our Town: In this play the Stage Manager speaks to the audience.

Kazan's pride in this rejection of realistic convention and his continuing interest in subjectifying theatrical experience were evident in an interview he gave in the early sixties:

> I was busting out of the goddamned proscenium theater uptown. In *Cat on a Hot Tin Roof* I had everybody address the audience continually. Every time they had one of those long speeches they'd turn and say it to the audience. Nobody thought anything of it once we opened. But there was a hell of a lot of bitching about it before. . . . The whole second act of *Cat* was a long address by Burl Ives to the audience. I had him address various members of the audience . . . "what would *you* do?" is implicit in this kind of staging. It sucks the audience into the experience and emotion of that moment.[3]

Kazan wrote in his autobiography that he had to convince Williams to accept his notion of how Burl Ives would play the part of Big Daddy. When Kazan said he was going to bring Ives right down to the edge of the forestage, have him "look the audience right in the eye, and speak it directly to them," Williams protested that *Cat* was a realistic play, and should be kept within the representational conventions. When pressed by Kazan to say whether old cotton planters actually talked that eloquently and that long without interruption, Williams replied that they did. After all, who would dare interrupt them?[4] Nonetheless Kazan pursued his concept for the production in the face of Williams's skepticism, if not his opposition.

The Design

When the central dynamic of the production had been established as direct communication between the characters and the audience, it had to imbue all the elements of the stage language. Here Kazan reports that he did run into opposition from Williams, who had a clear idea of what he thought the set should be like, an image that had evolved as he had revised the play. In the notes for the designer he prepared for the script preceding the November pre-rehearsal version, Williams described the basic plan of the set that was eventually used for the production: a bed–sitting room in a Mississippi Delta plantation, opening onto an upstairs gallery and showing white balustrades against a fair summer sky that fades into dusk and night during the course of the play. This is what is needed to support the action of the play which, as Williams was fond of pointing out, observed the unities of time and place, the action of the play being confined to the single set and occupying exactly the amount of time it took to enact on stage. The lighting was obviously crucial for this play, to show the passage of time that is a central thematic concern as well as a structural one.

Beyond this, however, Williams's original image of the set was strikingly different from the set Kazan and Jo Mielziner eventually devised between them. Williams described the room as Victorian, with a touch of the Far East, and poetically haunted by the tender relationship of Jack Straw and Peter Ochello. He noted that the room should not have changed much since Straw and Ochello's time. To suggest the style for the design, Williams referred the designer to the reproduction he had seen of a faded photograph of the verandah of Robert Louis Stevenson's home in Samoa: "There was a quality of tender light on weathered wood, such as porch-furniture made of bamboo and wicker, exposed to tropical suns and tropical rains,

---

[3]Quoted in Richard Schechner and Theodore Hoffman, " 'Look, There's the American Theatre': An Interview with Elia Kazan," *Tulane Drama Review*, 9 (Winter 1964): 71.

[4]Elia Kazan, *Elia Kazan: A Life* (New York: Knopf, 1988) 541–42.

which came to mind when I thought about the set for this play" (RV xiii).° The photograph, he wrote, also brought to mind "the grace and comfort of light, the reassurance it gives, on a late and fair afternoon in summer, the way that no matter what, even dread of death, is gently touched and soothed by it. For the set is the background for a play that deals with human extremities of emotion and needs that softness behind it" (RV xiii).

Williams described in detail the big, slightly raked, double bed and the "entertainment center" that were the most significant objects in the set, and then he cautioned the designer, lest he feel that the previous description confined him to literal realism. As in the published "Note for the Designer," Williams envisioned that "the set should be far less realistic than I have so far implied in this description of it": The walls should dissolve mysteriously into the air below the ceiling; the set should be roofed by the sky; stars and moon suggested by traces of milky pallor, as if they were observed through a telescope lens out of focus (RV xiv). The original note, however, added the idea that a spiral nebula might be faintly suggested in order to suggest the "mystery of the cosmos," which Williams thought should be a visible presence in the play, almost as present as an actor in it. He also thought that the cloud effects and the sound effects for the windstorm in Act 3 should be as unrealistic as the set. As he revised the script, however, Williams began to reconceptualize the set as well. In November he sent off a rewrite of the scene description suggesting that the room should appear to have been remodeled since Straw and Ochello's time, and now had an open, Japanese effect. The canopied bed, he suggested, could appear to have been removed from an Italian renaissance palazzo when Big Daddy and Big Mama raided Europe a few years previously.

When Kazan and Mielziner began talking about the design, their concept of a production that foregrounded the characters' rhetorical appeals to the audience became the central element in their discussion. Kazan has written:

> Jo Mielziner and I had read the play in the same way; we saw its great merit was its brilliant rhetoric and its theatricality. Jo didn't see the play as realistic any more than I did. If it was to be done realistically, I would have to contrive stage business to keep the old man talking those great second-act speeches turned out front and pretend that it was just another day in the life of the Pollitt family. This would, it seemed to me, amount to an apology to the audience for the glory of the author's language. It didn't seem like just another day in the life of a cotton planter's family to Jo or to me; it seemed like the best kind of theater, the kind we were interested in encouraging, the theater theatrical, not pretending any longer that an audience wasn't out there to be addressed but having a performer as great as Burl Ives acknowledge their presence at all times and even make eye contact with individuals.[5]

Accordingly, Kazan wrote, "I caused Jo to design our setting as I wished, a large, triangular platform, tipped toward the audience and holding only one piece of furniture, an ornate bed. This brought the play down to its essentials and made it impossible for it to be played any way except as I preferred."[6]

The set was not quite so spare as Kazan remembered it, but the central point of his statement, that the presentational impulse was the dominant aesthetic factor in

[5]Kazan 542–43.
[6]Kazan 543.
RV: The reading version of the play (New York: New American Library, 1958), which has both versions of the third act.

creating the design, has been fully corroborated by Mielziner. In his memoir, Mielziner described their discussion about the design much as Kazan did. Asked how he thought the "elephant story" should be handled proxemically, Mielziner told Kazan that he thought it should receive as much emphasis as possible: "I suggested that we have an area of the stage on which Big Daddy could come down close to the audience and deliver the lines with dramatic force." Mielziner wrote that Kazan was delighted with his answer, and "from this discussion grew the idea of creating a stage within the stage. It would be steeply raked toward the audience with one corner actually jutting out over the footlights. In its final form it turned out to be a sort of thrust stage."[7]

Mielziner's design was a departure from the subjective realism he had employed in *Menagerie*, *Streetcar*, and *Summer and Smoke*, in that he did not try to suggest through the material elements of the stage language that the events unfolding on stage were filtered through the mind of one of the characters. Instead, the design of the set projected the action out toward the audience, forcing it to become involved as though it were one of the characters. Extremely spare, the set was composed of two platforms, a large diamond-shaped one, a corner of which projected beyond the proscenium, and a smaller rectangle a foot lower at stage right. There were no doors, such actions as opening doors and looking into the mirror being mimed in this production. The only items of furniture Mielziner drew in his sketches were the primary material signifiers: the large bed, which signified both Maggie and Brick's failing marriage and the lingering memory of Straw and Ochello; the entertainment center, which signified both Brick's immediate goal of escape from reality and the vacuous materialism that Williams saw in the fifties; and the daybed, which signified Brick's withdrawal from Maggie, their marriage, and life in general. The actual set, however, also held a wicker night table and a large wicker armchair which could accommodate either Burl Ives or two of the other actors. The overall effect was of a large playing space down front where the actors could address the audience as if from a bare platform.

The lines of the design contributed to this effect. The perspective was such that the corner of the ceiling came down to a point slightly to the left of upstage center, helping to focus the audience's attention on the point of the diamond where the characters addressed the audience. Mielziner took Williams's hints to give lighting a central function in the play, running a scrim from floor to ceiling along two sides of the set with strips of black velour indicating the lines of the columns outside the windows of the room when the light of the moon was projected through them. To signify sunlight, slide projections of blinds were thrown on the scrims, while the gallery and the lawn beyond the windows were blocked out. When characters on the gallery or the lawn were to be seen, the lights behind the scrim were brought up, making the actors visible to the audience, as had been done with *Streetcar*.

Two follow-spots were used in the production. One, on the audience's left, highlighted Maggie throughout Act 1 and picked up Big Mama, Maggie, and Brick in Act 2, as they were in turn nominally being addressed by Big Daddy, who was downstage talking to the audience. In Act 3 the light again shone on Maggie almost without interruption. The follow-spot on the audience's right highlighted the characters Maggie was addressing in Act 1, chiefly Brick, as she had her turn at "recitative." It shone on Big Daddy throughout Act 2 and picked up Brick, Big Mama,

---

[7]*Designing for Theatre: A Memoir and a Portfolio* (New York: Bram Hall House, 1965) 183.

Gooper, Mae, and Maggie at various times during Act 3, emphasizing a significant entrance or a significant reaction indexically as it occurred. Contributing to the generally "golden" look of the production's lighting, the follow-spots were amber except when a character went out onto the gallery, when they were changed to blue. The follow-spots not only helped to avoid confusion by focusing the audience's attention where Kazan wanted it to be, they also contributed to the foregrounding of the theatricality in the production by "framing" specific characters and pieces of action. Kazan stylized the composition of his stage picture in *Cat,* and encoded a great deal of meaning through gesture, movement, and pose in the production. Using the follow-spots to highlight these formal compositions emphasized that what was happening onstage was not real life but theater.

In designing the furniture, both Kazan and Mielziner took their cue from Williams's earlier description of the set, emphasizing the qualities he had seen in the Robert Louis Stevenson photograph. Kazan had underlined elements of this description in his copy of the script. Listed together, they indicate quite well the direction Mielziner took with the design after their conferences:

> Delta's biggest cotton planter
> Far East
> The room must evoke some ghosts
> Gently . . . poetically haunted by a relationship . . . a tenderness which was uncommon
> Samoan Island
> tender light on weathered wood
> Bamboo . . . wicker
> [the entertainment center] monument . . . very complete . . . compact little shrine . . . all the comforts . . . illusions . . . hide [written in the margin, "Brick hides"] such things as the characters in the play are faced with (RV xii-xiv)

From these suggestions came the old wicker headboard with its huge and fantastically shaped design of two cornucopias, the matching wicker furniture, the carpet with its lushly fertile design of oversized flowers and vines, and the one object in the room that competed with the fertility symbol of the bed for the audience's attention, the oversized bar, hi-fi, radio, and television with its sleekly modern fifties lines. This object realized Williams's description of a compact modern shrine to all the comforts and illusions of contemporary life and signified Brick's retreat from human contact.

Kazan has said more than once that Williams did not like the set that Mielziner finally developed for *Cat* because he thought his play should be performed realistically. Kazan has also indicated that the set was a material signifier of his aesthetic vision in opposition to Williams's:

> I had the setting I'd asked for; Jo had given me what I wanted. Tennessee had approved of it earlier, when he was ready to approve of damn near anything I asked for, because I was the director he wanted. Now the setting was up onstage, too late to change, and on that setting there was only one way for any human to conduct himself: "out front" it's called. Dear Tennessee was stuck with my vision, like it or not.[8]

[8]Kazan 543.

Arthur Miller

Arthur Miller (1915–2005) was the dean of American playwrights after the opening of *Death of a Salesman* in 1949. His steady output as a writer and a playwright began with his first publications after college in 1939, when he worked in the New York Federal Theatre Project, a branch of the Works Progress Administration (WPA), Franklin D. Roosevelt's huge Depression-era effort to put Americans back to work.

Miller, the son of a Jewish immigrant, was born in the Harlem section of Manhattan and raised first there and later in Brooklyn, after his father's business failed. In high school Miller thought of himself more as an athlete than as a student, and he had trouble getting teachers' recommendations for college. After considerable struggle and waiting, he entered the University of Michigan, where his talent as a playwright emerged under the tutelage of Kenneth Rowe, his playwriting professor. His undergraduate plays won important university awards, and he became noticed by the Theatre Guild, a highly respected theater founded to present excellent plays (not necessarily commercial successes). His career was under way.

From 1939 to 1947 Miller wrote radio plays, screenplays, articles, stories, and a novel. His work covered a wide range of material, much of it growing out of his childhood memories of a tightly knit and somewhat eccentric family that provided him with a large gallery of characters. But he also dealt with political issues and problems of anti-Semitism, which was widespread in the 1930s and 1940s. Miller's political concerns were a presence in his work throughout his career.

All My Sons (1947) was his first successful play. It ran on Broadway for three hundred performances, a remarkable record for a serious drama. The story centers on a man who knowingly produces defective parts for airplanes and then blames the subsequent crashes on his business partner, who is ruined and imprisoned. When the guilty man's son finds out the truth, he confronts his father and rebukes him. Ultimately, the man realizes not only that he has lost his son because of his deceit but that the dead pilots were also "all my sons." The play won the New York Drama Critics' Circle Award.

Miller's next play, *Death of a Salesman* (1949), was written in eight weeks. Focusing on the American ideal of business success, the play in its conclusions challenged standard American business values. Willy Loman, first performed by Lee J. Cobb, was intended to be a warning for Americans in the postwar period of the cost of growing wealth and affluence.

Miller's next play, *The Crucible* (1953), portrayed witch hunts of seventeenth-century New England, but most people recognized the subtext: it was about contemporary anti-Communist witch hunts. In the late 1940s and early 1950s, the House Un-American Activities Committee (HUAC) held hearings to uncover suspected Communists in all areas of American life, particularly the arts. Many writers, artists, and performers came under close, often unfair, scrutiny by HUAC for their own political views and allegiances and were asked to testify against their friends. Many were blacklisted (prevented from working in commercial theaters and movie companies), some were imprisoned for not testifying at others' trials, and some had their reputations and careers destroyed.

Arthur Miller was fearless in facing down HUAC, and he was convicted of contempt of court for not testifying against his friends. For a time he too was

For links to resources about Miller, click on *AuthorLinks* at bedfordstmartins.com/jacobus.

blacklisted, but his contempt citation was reversed, and he was not imprisoned. Given his personal political stance during that dangerous time, it is not a surprise that he usually wrote about matters of social concern.

In the 1990s, Miller became the darling of the London stage, while at the same time being somewhat neglected in the United States. One full-scale play, *Broken Glass* (1994), played in regional theater before a brief run on Broadway and then a longer run in London's West End. The play concerns a woman who becomes paralyzed in response to *Kristallnacht* ("night of broken glass"), a night of violent rampages against Jews and Jewish property in Germany that resulted in 91 Jewish dead, hundreds injured, and 7,500 businesses and 177 synagogues gutted. After November 9, 1938, it was clear that Jews were no longer safe in Hitler's Germany. The subject of Miller's play is intense, significant, and still timely.

The Ride Down Mount Morgan had its premiere in London in 1991; it then took seven years to open in New York in 1998. Its protagonist, Lyman Felt, played by Patrick Stewart in New York, was conceived as a Reaganite go-getter of the late 1980s: economically rapacious, sexually voracious, and amoral. When Felt's Porsche crashes on a ride down Mount Morgan, his two wives discover each other at the hospital. The play proceeds from there, examining the ethical values that permit Felt to live as he does. George Wolfe produced the play at the Joseph Papp Public Theater. The Broadway production opened at the Ambassador Theater in April 2000, again with Patrick Stewart. The play was nominated for a Tony Award.

Death of a Salesman

Death of a Salesman (1949) was a hit from its first performances and has remained at the center of modern American drama ever since. Everywhere this play has touched the hearts and minds of its audiences. The success of this American drama has been phenomenal.

The play was first performed in an experimental environment. Miller had originally conceived of a model of a man's head as the stage setting. He said, "The first image that occurred to me which was to result in *Death of a Salesman* was of an enormous face the height of the proscenium arch which would appear and then open up, and we would see the inside of a man's head. In fact, *The Inside of His Head* was the first title." This technique was not used, but when Miller worked with the director and producer of the first production, he helped develop a setting that became a model for the "American style" in drama. The multilevel set permitted the play to shift from Willy Loman and his wife, Linda, having a conversation in their kitchen to their sons' bedroom on the second level of the house. The set permitted portions of the stage to be reserved for Willy's visions of his brother, Ben, and for scenes outside the house, such as Willy's interlude with the woman in Boston.

In a way, the setup of the stage respected Miller's original plan, but instead of portraying a cross section of Willy's head, it presented a metaphor for a cross section of his life. The audience was looking in not on just a living room, as in the nineteenth-century Ibsenist approach, but on an entire house and an entire life.

Using a cross section of a house as a metaphor was an especially important device in this play because of the play's allusions to Greek tragedy. The great

For discussion questions and assignments on *Death of a Salesman*, visit bedfordstmartins.com/jacobus.

Greek tragedies usually portray the destruction of a house—such as the house of Atreus—in which "house" stands for a whole family, not a building. When Shakespeare's Hamlet dies, for example, his entire line—his house—dies with him. The death in *Death of a Salesman* implies the destruction of a family holding certain beliefs that have been wrong from the start.

The life of the salesman has given Willy a sense of dignity and worth, and he imagines that the modern world has corrupted that sense by robbing salesmen of the value of their personality. He thinks that the modern world has failed him, but he is wrong. His original belief—that what counts is not *what* you know but *whom* you know and how well you are liked—lies at the heart of his failure. When the play opens, he already has failed at the traveling salesman's job because he can no longer drive to his assigned territory. He cannot sell what he needs to sell.

Willy has inculcated his beliefs in his sons, Happy and Biff, and both are as ineffectual as their father. Willy doted on Biff and encouraged him to become a high school football star at the expense of his studies. But when Biff cannot pass an important course, and his plans to make up the work are subverted by his disillusionment in his father, his dreams of a college football career vanish. He cannot change and recover from this defeat. Happy, like his father, builds castles in the air and assumes somehow that he will be successful, though he has nothing with which to back up this assumption. He wants the glory—and he spends time in fanciful imaginings, as Willy does—but he cannot do the basic work that makes it possible to achieve glory. Ironically, it is the "anemic" Bernard—who studies hard, stresses personal honesty and diligence, and never brags—who is successful.

Linda supports Willy's illusions, allowing him to be a fraud by sharing—or pretending to believe—in his dream. Willy has permitted himself to believe that integrity, honesty, and fidelity are not as important as being well liked.

The play ends with Willy still unable to face the deceptions he has perpetuated. He commits suicide, believing that his sons will be able to follow in his footsteps and succeed where he did not; he thinks that his insurance money will save the house and the family. What he does not realize is that his sons are no more capable than he is. They have been corrupted by his thinking, his values, his beliefs. And they cannot solve the problems that overwhelmed him.

Death of a Salesman has been given a privileged position in American drama because it is a modern tragedy. Aristotle believed that only characters of noble birth could be tragic heroes, but Miller confounds this theory, as Eugene O'Neill did, by showing the human integrity in even the most humble characters. Miller's Willy Loman is not a peasant, nor is he noble. In fact, Miller took a frightening risk in creating a character whom we find hard to like. Willy wants to be well liked, but as an audience we find it difficult to like a person who whines, complains, and accepts petty immorality as a normal way of life. Despite his character, we are awed by his fate.

One Chinese commentator said, after seeing Miller's Chinese production of the play in 1983, that China is filled with such dreamers as Willy. Certainly the United States has been filled with them. Willy stands as an aspect of our culture, commercial and otherwise, that is at the center of our reflection of ourselves. Perhaps we react so strongly to Willy because we are afraid that we might easily become a Willy Loman if we are not vigilant about our moral views, our psychological well-being, and the limits of our commitment to success. Willy Loman has mesmerized U.S. audiences under many different economic circumstances: prosperity, recession, rapid growth, and cautious development. No matter what those circumstances, we have looked at the play as if looking in a mirror. What we have seen has always involved us, although it has not always made us pleased with ourselves.

Death of a Salesman in Performance

Death of a Salesman opened on Broadway on February 10, 1949, and won virtually every prize available for drama, including the Pulitzer Prize and the New York Drama Critics' Circle Award for best play. It ran on Broadway for an incredible 742 performances. Elia Kazan, director, was instrumental in establishing the play's innovative staging. Lee J. Cobb was cast as Willy, Mildred Dunnock as Linda, Arthur Kennedy as Biff, and Cameron Mitchell as Happy. Robert Coleman said of the New York production: "An explosion of emotional dynamite was set off last evening in the Morosco [Theatre]. . . . In fashioning *Death of a Salesman* for them, author Arthur Miller and director Elia Kazan have collaborated on as exciting and devastating a theatrical blast as the nerves of modern playgoers can stand." Of Cobb, Howard Barnes said, "Cobb contributes a mammoth and magnificent portrayal of the central character. In his hands the salesman's frustration and final suicide are a matter of tremendous import."

The London production in July 1949, with Paul Muni as Willy and Kevin McCarthy as Biff, lasted 204 performances. An all-black production was directed by Lee Sankowich in Baltimore in 1972. Miller, in the audience on that production's opening night, commented that the play had been well received in "many countries and cultures" and that the Baltimore production further underscored the universality of the play. George C. Scott was praised for the power of his performance as Willy in New York's Circle in the Square production in 1975. A Chinese production directed by Arthur Miller was enormously successful in 1983. In the most celebrated revival of the play, Dustin Hoffman portrayed Willy, John Malkovich played Biff, and Michael Rudman directed at the Broadhurst Theatre in New York in 1984. The critic Benedict Nightingale said of that production, "Somewhere at the core of him [Willy] an elaborate battle is being fought between dishonesty and honesty, glitter and substance, appearance and reality, between the promises or supposed promises of society and the claims of the self, between what Willy professes to value and what, perhaps without knowing it, he actually does value." In 1985, Dustin Hoffman brought his production of Miller's play to television, where it was viewed by an estimated twenty-five million people.

On February 10, 1999, exactly fifty years to the day from its original opening, a major production opened with Brian Dennehy as Willy Loman. The production was conceived in Chicago by the Goodman Theatre Company, and Dennehy was praised by critics and theater-goers alike for presenting a powerful portrayal of Willy Loman for a new generation. With Claire Higgins as Linda, Dennehy brought the play to London's Lyric Theatre in 2005 to resounding reviews. Critics praised the timelessness of the drama—ultimately crowning it an American classic.

The 2012 revival of the play at the Ethel Barrymore Theatre in New York featured Philip Seymour Hoffman as Willy Loman in Mike Nichols's production. In his review in the *New York Times*, Ben Brantley described it as "an immaculate monument to a great American play." Nichols, who saw the play in 1949, tried to honor the designs of Jo Mielziner and the spirit of the original production.

ARTHUR MILLER (1915–2005)

Death of a Salesman   1949

Certain Private Conversations in Two Acts and a Requiem

Characters

WILLY LOMAN	UNCLE BEN
LINDA	HOWARD WAGNER
BIFF	JENNY
HAPPY	STANLEY
BERNARD	MISS FORSYTHE
THE WOMAN	LETTA
CHARLEY	

The action takes place in Willy Loman's house and yard and in various places he visits in the New York and Boston of today.

(Throughout the play, in the stage directions, left and right mean stage left and stage right.)

ACT I

(A melody is heard, played upon a flute. It is small and fine, telling of grass and trees and the horizon. The curtain rises.)

(Before us is the Salesman's house. We are aware of towering, angular shapes behind it, surrounding it on all sides. Only the blue light of the sky falls upon the house and forestage; the surrounding area shows an angry glow of orange. As more light appears, we see a solid vault of apartment houses around the small, fragile-seeming home. An air of the dream clings to the place, a dream rising out of reality. The kitchen at center seems actual enough, for there is a kitchen table with three chairs, and a refrigerator. But no other fixtures are seen. At the back of the kitchen there is a draped entrance, which leads to the living room. To the right of the kitchen, on a level raised two feet, is a bedroom furnished only with a brass bedstead and a straight chair. On a shelf over the bed a silver athletic trophy stands. A window opens onto the apartment house at the side.)

(Behind the kitchen, on a level raised six and a half feet, is the boys' bedroom, at present barely visible. Two beds are dimly seen, and at the back of the room a dormer window. [This bedroom is above the unseen living room.] At the left a stairway curves up to it from the kitchen.)

(The entire setting is wholly or, in some places, partially transparent. The roofline of the house is one-dimensional; under and over it we see the apartment buildings. Before the house lies an apron, curving beyond the forestage into the orchestra. This forward area serves as the back yard as well as the locale of all Willy's imaginings and of his city scenes. Whenever the action is in the present the actors observe the imaginary wall-lines, entering the house only through its door at the left. But in the scenes of the past these boundaries are broken, and characters enter or leave a room by stepping "through" a wall onto the forestage.)

(From the right, Willy Loman, the Salesman, enters, carrying two large sample cases. The flute plays on. He hears but is not aware of it. He is past sixty years of age, dressed quietly. Even as he crosses the stage to the doorway of the house, his exhaustion is apparent. He unlocks the door, comes into the kitchen, and thankfully lets his burden down, feeling the soreness of his palms. A word-sigh escapes his lips—it might be "Oh, boy, oh, boy." He closes the door then carries his cases out into the living room, through the draped kitchen doorway.)

(Linda, his wife, has stirred in her bed at the right. She gets out and puts on a robe, listening. Most often jovial, she has developed an iron repression of her exceptions to Willy's behavior—she more than loves him, she admires him, as though his mercurial nature, his temper, his massive dreams and little cruelties, served her only as sharp reminders of the turbulent longings within him, longings which she shares but lacks the temperament to utter and follow to their end.)

LINDA (*hearing Willy outside the bedroom, calls with some trepidation*): Willy!

WILLY: It's all right. I came back.

LINDA: Why? What happened? (*Slight pause.*) Did something happen, Willy?

WILLY: No, nothing happened.

LINDA: You didn't smash the car, did you?

WILLY (*with casual irritation*): I said nothing happened. Didn't you hear me?

LINDA: Don't you feel well?

WILLY: I'm tired to the death. (*The flute has faded away. He sits on the bed beside her, a little numb.*) I couldn't make it. I just couldn't make it, Linda.

LINDA (*very carefully, delicately*): Where were you all day? You look terrible.

WILLY: I got as far as a little above Yonkers. I stopped for a cup of coffee. Maybe it was the coffee.

LINDA: What?

WILLY (*after a pause*): I suddenly couldn't drive anymore. The car kept going off onto the shoulder, y'know?

LINDA (*helpfully*): Oh. Maybe it was the steering again. I don't think Angelo knows the Studebaker.

WILLY: No, it's me, it's me. Suddenly I realize I'm goin' sixty miles an hour and I don't remember the last five minutes. I'm—I can't seem to—keep my mind to it.

LINDA: Maybe it's your glasses. You never went for your new glasses.

WILLY: No, I see everything. I came back ten miles an hour. It took me nearly four hours from Yonkers.

LINDA (*resigned*): Well, you'll just have to take a rest, Willy, you can't continue this way.

WILLY: I just got back from Florida.

LINDA: But you didn't rest your mind. Your mind is over-active, and the mind is what counts, dear.

WILLY: I'll start out in the morning. Maybe I'll feel better in the morning. (*She is taking off his shoes.*) These goddam arch supports are killing me.

LINDA: Take an aspirin. Should I get you an aspirin? It'll soothe you.

WILLY (*with wonder*): I was driving along, you understand? And I was fine. I was even observing the scenery. You can imagine, me looking at scenery, on the road every week of my life. But it's so beautiful up there, Linda, the trees are so thick, and the sun is warm. I opened the windshield and just let the warm air bathe over me. And then all of a sudden I'm goin' off the road! I'm tellin' ya, I absolutely forgot I was driving. If I'd've gone the other way over the white line I might've killed somebody. So I went on again—and five minutes later I'm dreamin' again, and I nearly—(*He presses two fingers against his eyes.*) I have such thoughts, I have such strange thoughts.

LINDA: Willy, dear. Talk to them again. There's no reason why you can't work in New York.

WILLY: They don't need me in New York. I'm the New England man. I'm vital in New England.

LINDA: But you're sixty years old. They can't expect you to keep traveling every week.

WILLY: I'll have to send a wire to Portland. I'm supposed to see Brown and Morrison tomorrow morning at ten o'clock to show the line. Goddammit, I could sell them! (*He starts putting on his jacket.*)

LINDA (*taking the jacket from him*): Why don't you go down to the place tomorrow and tell Howard you've simply got to work in New York? You're too accommodating, dear.

WILLY: If old man Wagner was alive I'd a been in charge of New York now! That man was a prince, he was a masterful man. But that boy of his, that Howard, he don't appreciate. When I went north the first time, the Wagner Company didn't know where New England was!

LINDA: Why don't you tell those things to Howard, dear?

WILLY (*encouraged*): I will, I definitely will. Is there any cheese?

LINDA: I'll make you a sandwich.

WILLY: No, go to sleep. I'll take some milk. I'll be up right away. The boys in?

LINDA: They're sleeping. Happy took Biff on a date tonight.

WILLY (*interested*): That so?

LINDA: It was so nice to see them shaving together, one behind the other, in the bathroom. And going out together. You notice? The whole house smells of shaving lotion.

WILLY: Figure it out. Work a lifetime to pay off a house. You finally own it, and there's nobody to live in it.

LINDA: Well, dear, life is a casting off. It's always that way.

WILLY: No, no, some people—some people accomplish something. Did Biff say anything after I went this morning?

LINDA: You shouldn't have criticized him, Willy, especially after he just got off the train. You mustn't lose your temper with him.

WILLY: When the hell did I lose my temper? I simply asked him if he was making any money. Is that a criticism?

LINDA: But, dear, how could he make any money?

WILLY (*worried and angered*): There's such an undercurrent in him. He became a moody man. Did he apologize when I left this morning?

LINDA: He was crestfallen, Willy. You know how he admires you. I think if he finds himself, then you'll both be happier and not fight any more.

WILLY: How can he find himself on a farm? Is that a life? A farmhand? In the beginning, when he was young, I thought, well, a young man, it's good for him to tramp around, take a lot of different jobs. But it's more than ten years now and he has yet to make thirty-five dollars a week!

LINDA: He's finding himself, Willy.

WILLY: Not finding yourself at the age of thirty-four is a disgrace!

LINDA: Shh!

WILLY: The trouble is he's lazy, goddammit!

LINDA: Willy, please!

WILLY: Biff is a lazy bum!

LINDA: They're sleeping. Get something to eat. Go on down.

WILLY: Why did he come home? I would like to know what brought him home.

LINDA: I don't know. I think he's still lost, Willy. I think he's very lost.

WILLY: Biff Loman is lost. In the greatest country in the world a young man with such—personal attractiveness, gets lost. And such a hard worker. There's one thing about Biff—he's not lazy.

LINDA: Never.

WILLY (*with pity and resolve*): I'll see him in the morning; I'll have a nice talk with him. I'll get him a job selling. He could be big in no time. My God! Remember how they used to follow him around in high school? When he smiled at one of them their faces lit up. When he walked down the street . . . (*He loses himself in reminiscences.*)

LINDA (*trying to bring him out of it*): Willy, dear, I got a new kind of American-type cheese today. It's whipped.

WILLY: Why do you get American when I like Swiss?

LINDA: I just thought you'd like a change—

WILLY: I don't want a change! I want Swiss cheese. Why am I always being contradicted?

LINDA (*with a covering laugh*): I thought it would be a surprise.

WILLY: Why don't you open a window in here, for God's sake?

LINDA (*with infinite patience*): They're all open, dear.

WILLY: The way they boxed us in here. Bricks and windows, windows and bricks.

LINDA: We should've bought the land next door.

WILLY: The street is lined with cars. There's not a breath of fresh air in the neighborhood. The grass don't grow anymore, you can't raise a carrot in the back yard. They should've had a law against apartment houses. Remember those two beautiful elm trees out there? When I and Biff hung the swing between them?

LINDA: Yeah, like being a million miles from the city.

WILLY: They should've arrested the builder for cutting those down. They massacred the neighborhood. (*Lost.*) More and more I think of those days, Linda. This time of year it was lilac and wisteria. And then the peonies would come out, and the daffodils. What fragrance in this room!

LINDA: Well, after all, people had to move somewhere.

WILLY: No, there's more people now.

LINDA: I don't think there's more people. I think—

WILLY: There's more people! That's what's ruining this country! Population is getting out of control. The competition is maddening! Smell the stink from that apartment house! And another one on the other side . . . How can they whip cheese?

(*On Willy's last line, Biff and Happy raise themselves up in their beds, listening.*)

LINDA: Go down, try it. And be quiet.

WILLY (*turning to Linda, guiltily*): You're not worried about me, are you, sweetheart?

BIFF: What's the matter?

HAPPY: Listen!

LINDA: You've got too much on the ball to worry about.

WILLY: You're my foundation and my support, Linda.

LINDA: Just try to relax, dear. You make mountains out of molehills.

WILLY: I won't fight with him any more. If he wants to go back to Texas, let him go.

LINDA: He'll find his way.

WILLY: Sure. Certain men just don't get started till later in life. Like Thomas Edison, I think. Or B. F. Goodrich. One of them was deaf. (*He starts for the bedroom doorway.*) I'll put my money on Biff.

LINDA: And Willy—if it's warm Sunday we'll drive in the country. And we'll open the windshield, and take lunch.

WILLY: No, the windshields don't open on the new cars.

LINDA: But you opened it today.

WILLY: Me? I didn't. (*He stops.*) Now isn't that peculiar! Isn't that a remarkable—(*He breaks off in amazement and fright as the flute is heard distantly.*)

LINDA: What, darling?

WILLY: That is the most remarkable thing.

LINDA: What, dear?

WILLY: I was thinking of the Chevvy. (*Slight pause.*) Nineteen twenty-eight . . . when I had that red Chevvy—(*Breaks off.*) That funny? I coulda sworn I was driving that Chevvy today.

LINDA: Well, that's nothing. Something must've reminded you.

WILLY: Remarkable. Ts. Remember those days? The way Biff used to simonize that car? The dealer refused to believe there was eighty thousand miles on it. (*He shakes his head.*) Heh! (*To Linda.*) Close your eyes, I'll be right up. (*He walks out of the bedroom.*)

HAPPY (*to Biff*): Jesus, maybe he smashed up the car again!

LINDA (*calling after Willy*): Be careful on the stairs, dear! The cheese is on the middle shelf! (*She turns, goes over to the bed, takes his jacket, and goes out of the bedroom.*)

(*Light has risen on the boys' room. Unseen, Willy is heard talking to himself, "Eighty thousand miles," and a little laugh. Biff gets out of bed, comes downstage a bit, and stands attentively. Biff is two years older than his brother Happy, well built, but in these days bears a worn air and seems less self-assured. He has succeeded less, and his dreams are stronger and less acceptable than Happy's. Happy is tall, powerfully made. Sexuality is like a visible color on him, or a scent that many women have discovered. He, like his brother, is lost, but in a different way, for he has never allowed himself to turn his face toward defeat and is thus more confused and hard-skinned, although seemingly more content.*)

HAPPY (*getting out of bed*): He's going to get his license taken away if he keeps that up. I'm getting nervous about him, y'know, Biff?

BIFF: His eyes are going.

HAPPY: No, I've driven with him. He sees all right. He just doesn't keep his mind on it. I drove into the city with him last week. He stops at a green light and then it turns red and he goes. (*He laughs.*)

BIFF: Maybe he's color-blind.

HAPPY: Pop? Why he's got the finest eye for color in the business. You know that.

BIFF (*sitting down on his bed*): I'm going to sleep.

HAPPY: You're not still sour on Dad, are you, Biff?

BIFF: He's all right, I guess.

WILLY (*underneath them, in the living room*): Yes, sir, eighty thousand miles—eighty-two thousand!

BIFF: You smoking?

HAPPY (*holding out a pack of cigarettes*): Want one?

BIFF (*taking a cigarette*): I can never sleep when I smell it.

WILLY: What a simonizing job, heh!

HAPPY (*with deep sentiment*): Funny, Biff, y'know? Us sleeping in here again? The old beds. (*He pats his bed affectionately.*) All the talk that went across those two beds, huh? Our whole lives.

BIFF: Yeah. Lotta dreams and plans.

HAPPY (*with a deep and masculine laugh*): About five hundred women would like to know what was said in this room.

(*They share a soft laugh.*)

BIFF: Remember that big Betsy something—what the hell was her name—over on Bushwick Avenue?

HAPPY (*combing his hair*): With the collie dog!

BIFF: That's the one. I got you in there, remember?

HAPPY: Yeah, that was my first time—I think. Boy, there was a pig. (*They laugh, almost crudely.*) You taught me everything I know about women. Don't forget that.

BIFF: I bet you forgot how bashful you used to be. Especially with girls.

HAPPY: Oh, I still am, Biff.

BIFF: Oh, go on.

HAPPY: I just control it, that's all. I think I got less bashful and you got more so. What happened, Biff? Where's the old humor, the old confidence? (*He shakes Biff's knee. Biff gets up and moves restlessly about the room.*) What's the matter?

BIFF: Why does Dad mock me all the time?

HAPPY: He's not mocking you, he—

BIFF: Everything I say there's a twist of mockery on his face. I can't get near him.

HAPPY: He just wants you to make good, that's all. I wanted to talk to you about Dad for a long time, Biff. Something's—happening to him. He—talks to himself.

BIFF: I noticed that this morning. But he always mumbled.

HAPPY: But not so noticeable. It got so embarrassing I sent him to Florida. And you know something? Most of the time he's talking to you.

BIFF: What's he say about me?

HAPPY: I can't make it out.

BIFF: What's he say about me?

HAPPY: I think the fact that you're not settled, that you're still kind of up in the air . . .

BIFF: There's one or two other things depressing him, Happy.

HAPPY: What do you mean?

BIFF: Never mind. Just don't lay it all to me.

HAPPY: But I think if you just got started—I mean—is there any future for you out there?

BIFF: I tell ya, Hap, I don't know what the future is. I don't know—what I'm supposed to want.

HAPPY: What do you mean?

BIFF: Well, I spent six or seven years after high school trying to work myself up. Shipping clerk, salesman, business of one kind or another. And it's a measly manner of existence. To get on that subway on the hot mornings in summer. To devote your whole life to keeping stock, or making phone calls, or selling or buying. To suffer fifty weeks of the year for the sake of a two-week vacation, when all you really desire is to be outdoors, with your shirt off. And always to have to get ahead of the next fella. And still—that's how you build a future.

HAPPY: Well, you really enjoy it on a farm? Are you content out there?

BIFF (*with rising agitation*): Hap, I've had twenty or thirty different kinds of jobs since I left home before the war, and it always turns out the same. I just realized it lately. In Nebraska when I herded cattle, and the Dakotas, and Arizona, and now in Texas. It's why I came home now, I guess, because I realized it. This farm I work on, it's spring there now, see? And they've got about fifteen new colts. There's nothing more inspiring or—beautiful than the sight of a mare and a new colt. And it's cool there now, see? Texas is cool now, and it's spring. And whenever spring comes to where I am, I suddenly get the feeling, my God, I'm not gettin' anywhere! What the hell am I doing, playing around with horses, twenty-eight dollars a week! I'm thirty-four years old, I oughta be makin' my future. That's when I come running home. And now, I get here, and I don't know what to do with myself. (*After a pause.*) I've always made a point of not wasting my life, and every time I come back here I know that all I've done is to waste my life.

HAPPY: You're a poet, you know that, Biff? You're a—you're an idealist!

BIFF: No, I'm mixed up very bad. Maybe I oughta get married. Maybe I oughta get stuck into something. Maybe that's my trouble. I'm like a boy. I'm not married, I'm not in business, I just—I'm like a boy. Are you content, Hap? You're a success, aren't you? Are you content?

HAPPY: Hell, no!

BIFF: Why? You're making money, aren't you?

HAPPY (*moving about with energy, expressiveness*): All I can do now is wait for the merchandise manager to die. And suppose I get to be merchandise manager? He's a good friend of mine, and he just built a terrific estate on Long Island. And he lived there about two months and sold it, and now he's building another one. He can't enjoy it once it's finished. And I know that's just what I would do. I don't know what the hell I'm workin' for. Sometimes I sit in my apartment—all alone. And I think of the rent I'm paying. And it's crazy. But then, it's what I always wanted. My own apartment, a car, and plenty of women. And still, goddammit, I'm lonely.

BIFF (*with enthusiasm*): Listen, why don't you come out West with me?

HAPPY: You and I, heh?

BIFF: Sure, maybe we could buy a ranch. Raise cattle, use our muscles. Men built like we are should be working out in the open.

HAPPY (*avidly*): The Loman Brothers, heh?

BIFF (*with vast affection*): Sure, we'd be known all over the counties!

HAPPY (*enthralled*): That's what I dream about, Biff. Sometimes I want to just rip my clothes off in the middle of the store and outbox that goddam merchandise manager. I mean I can outbox, outrun and outlift anybody in that store, and I have to take orders from those common, petty sons-of-bitches till I can't stand it anymore.

BIFF: I'm tellin' you, kid, if you were with me I'd be happy out there.

HAPPY (*enthused*): See, Biff, everybody around me is so false that I'm constantly lowering my ideals . . .

BIFF: Baby, together we'd stand up for one another, we'd have someone to trust.

HAPPY: If I were around you—

BIFF: Hap, the trouble is we weren't brought up to grub for money. I don't know how to do it.

HAPPY: Neither can I!

BIFF: Then let's go!

HAPPY: The only thing is—what can you make out there?

BIFF: But look at your friend. Builds an estate and then hasn't the peace of mind to live in it.

HAPPY: Yeah, but when he walks into the store the waves part in front of him. That's fifty-two thousand dollars a year coming through the revolving door, and I got more in my pinky finger than he's got in his head.

BIFF: Yeah, but you just said—

HAPPY: I gotta show some of those pompous, self-important executives over there that Hap Loman can make the grade. I want to walk into the store the way he walks in. Then I'll go with you, Biff. We'll be together yet, I swear. But take those two we had tonight. Now weren't they gorgeous creatures?

BIFF: Yeah, yeah, most gorgeous I've had in years.

HAPPY: I get that any time I want, Biff. Whenever I feel disgusted. The only trouble is, it gets like bowling or something. I just keep knockin' them over and it doesn't mean anything. You still run around a lot?

BIFF: Naa. I'd like to find a girl—steady, somebody with substance.

HAPPY: That's what I long for.

BIFF: Go on! You'd never come home.

HAPPY: I would! Somebody with character, with resistance! Like Mom, y'know? You're gonna call me a bastard when I tell you this. That girl Charlotte I was with tonight is engaged to be married in five weeks. (*He tries on his new hat.*)

BIFF: No kiddin'!

HAPPY: Sure, the guy's in line for the vice-presidency of the store. I don't know what gets into me, maybe I just have an overdeveloped sense of competition or something, but I went and ruined her, and furthermore I can't get rid of her. And he's the third executive I've done that to. Isn't that a crummy characteristic? And to top it all, I go to their weddings! (*Indignantly, but laughing.*) Like I'm not supposed to take bribes. Manufacturers offer me a hundred-dollar bill now and then to throw an order their way. You know how honest I am, but it's like this girl, see. I hate myself for it. Because I don't want the girl, and, still, I take it and—I love it!

BIFF: Let's go to sleep.

HAPPY: I guess we didn't settle anything, heh?

BIFF: I just got one idea that I think I'm going to try.

HAPPY: What's that?

BIFF: Remember Bill Oliver?

HAPPY: Sure, Oliver is very big now. You want to work for him again?

BIFF: No, but when I quit he said something to me. He put his arm on my shoulder, and he said, "Biff, if you ever need anything, come to me."

HAPPY: I remember that. That sounds good.

BIFF: I think I'll go to see him. If I could get ten thousand or even seven or eight thousand dollars I could buy a beautiful ranch.

HAPPY: I bet he'd back you. 'Cause he thought highly of you, Biff. I mean, they all do. You're well liked, Biff. That's why I say to come back here, and we both have the apartment. And I'm tellin' you, Biff, any babe you want . . .

BIFF: No, with a ranch I could do the work I like and still be something. I just wonder though. I wonder if Oliver still thinks I stole that carton of basketballs.

HAPPY: Oh, he probably forgot that long ago. It's almost ten years. You're too sensitive. Anyway, he didn't really fire you.

BIFF: Well, I think he was going to. I think that's why I quit. I was never sure whether he knew or not. I know he thought the world of me, though. I was the only one he'd let lock up the place.

WILLY (*below*): You gonna wash the engine, Biff?

HAPPY: Shh!

(*Biff looks at Happy, who is gazing down, listening. Willy is mumbling in the parlor.*)

HAPPY: You hear that?

(*They listen. Willy laughs warmly.*)

BIFF (*growing angry*): Doesn't he know Mom can hear that?

WILLY: Don't get your sweater dirty, Biff!

(*A look of pain crosses Biff's face.*)

HAPPY: Isn't that terrible? Don't leave again, will you? You'll find a job here. You gotta stick around. I don't know what to do about him, it's getting embarrassing.

WILLY: What a simonizing job!

BIFF: Mom's hearing that!

WILLY: No kiddin', Biff, you got a date? Wonderful!

HAPPY: Go on to sleep. But talk to him in the morning, will you?

BIFF (*reluctantly getting into bed*): With her in the house. Brother!

HAPPY (*getting into bed*): I wish you'd have a good talk with him.

(*The light on their room begins to fade.*)

BIFF (*to himself in bed*): That selfish, stupid . . .

HAPPY: Sh . . . Sleep, Biff.

(*Their light is out. Well before they have finished speaking, Willy's form is dimly seen below in the darkened kitchen. He opens the refrigerator, searches in there, and takes out a bottle of milk. The apartment houses are fading out, and the entire house and surroundings become covered with leaves. Music insinuates itself as the leaves appear.*)

WILLY: Just wanna be careful with those girls, Biff, that's all. Don't make any promises. No promises of any kind. Because a girl, y'know, they always believe what you tell 'em, and you're very young, Biff, you're too young to be talking seriously to girls.

(*Light rises on the kitchen. Willy, talking, shuts the refrigerator door and comes downstage to the kitchen table. He pours milk into a glass. He is totally immersed in himself, smiling faintly.*)

WILLY: Too young entirely, Biff. You want to watch your schooling first. Then when you're all set, there'll be plenty of girls for a boy like you. (*He smiles broadly at a kitchen chair.*) That so? The girls pay for you? (*He laughs.*) Boy, you must really be makin' a hit.

(*Willy is gradually addressing—physically—a point offstage, speaking through the wall of the kitchen, and his voice has been rising in volume to that of a normal conversation.*)

WILLY: I been wondering why you polish the car so careful. Ha! Don't leave the hubcaps, boys. Get the chamois to the hubcaps. Happy, use newspaper on the windows, it's the easiest thing. Show him how to do it, Biff! You see, Happy? Pad it up, use it like a pad. That's it, that's it, good work. You're doin' all right, Hap. (*He pauses, then nods in approbation for a few seconds, then looks upward.*) Biff, first thing we gotta do when we get time is clip that big branch over the house. Afraid it's gonna fall in a storm and hit the roof. Tell you what. We get a rope and sling her around, and then we climb up there with a couple of saws and take her down. Soon as you finish the car, boys, I wanna see ye. I got a surprise for you, boys.

BIFF (*offstage*): Whatta ya got, Dad?

WILLY: No, you finish first. Never leave a job till you're finished—remember that. (*Looking toward the "big trees."*) Biff, up in Albany I saw a beautiful hammock. I think I'll buy it next trip, and we'll hang it right between those two elms. Wouldn't that be something! Just swingin' there under those branches. Boy, that would be . . .

(*Young Biff and Young Happy appear from the direction Willy was addressing. Happy carries rags and a pail of water. Biff, wearing a sweater with a block "S," carries a football.*)

BIFF (*pointing in the direction of the car offstage*): How's that, Pop, professional?

WILLY: Terrific. Terrific job, boys. Good work, Biff.

HAPPY: Where's the surprise, Pop?

WILLY: In the back seat of the car.

HAPPY: Boy! (*He runs off.*)

BIFF: What is it, Dad? Tell me, what'd you buy?

WILLY (*laughing, cuffs him*): Never mind, something I want you to have.

BIFF (*turns and starts off*): What is it, Hap?

HAPPY (*offstage*): It's a punching bag!

BIFF: Oh, Pop!

WILLY: It's got Gene Tunney's signature on it!

(*Happy runs onstage with a punching bag.*)

BIFF: Gee, how'd you know we wanted a punching bag?

WILLY: Well, it's the finest thing for the timing.

HAPPY (*lies down on his back and pedals with his feet*): I'm losing weight, you notice, Pop?

WILLY (*to Happy*): Jumping rope is good too.

BIFF: Did you see the new football I got?

WILLY (*examining the ball*): Where'd you get a new ball?

BIFF: The coach told me to practice my passing.

WILLY: That so? And he gave you the ball, heh?

BIFF: Well, I borrowed it from the locker room. (*He laughs confidentially.*)

WILLY (*laughing with him at the theft*): I want you to return that.

HAPPY: I told you he wouldn't like it!

BIFF (*angrily*): Well, I'm bringing it back!

WILLY (*stopping the incipient argument, to Happy*): Sure, he's gotta practice with a regulation ball, doesn't he? (*To Biff.*) Coach'll probably congratulate you on your initiative!

BIFF: Oh, he keeps congratulating my initiative all the time, Pop.

WILLY: That's because he likes you. If somebody else took that ball there'd be an uproar. So what's the report, boys, what's the report?

BIFF: Where'd you go this time, Dad? Gee we were lonesome for you.

WILLY (*pleased, puts an arm around each boy and they come down to the apron*): Lonesome, heh?

BIFF: Missed you every minute.

WILLY: Don't say? Tell you a secret, boys. Don't breathe it to a soul. Someday I'll have my own business, and I'll never have to leave home anymore.

HAPPY: Like Uncle Charley, heh?

WILLY: Bigger than Uncle Charley! Because Charley is not liked. He's liked, but he's not—well liked.

BIFF: Where'd you go this time, Dad?

WILLY: Well, I got on the road, and I went north to Providence. Met the Mayor.

BIFF: The Mayor of Providence!

WILLY: He was sitting in the hotel lobby.

BIFF: What'd he say?

WILLY: He said, "Morning!" And I said, "You got a fine city here, Mayor." And then he had coffee with me. And then I went to Waterbury. Waterbury is a fine city. Big clock city, the famous Waterbury clock. Sold a nice bill there. And then Boston—Boston is the cradle of the Revolution. A fine city. And a couple of other towns in Mass., and on to Portland and Bangor and straight home!

BIFF: Gee, I'd love to go with you sometime, Dad.

WILLY: Soon as summer comes.

HAPPY: Promise?

WILLY: You and Hap and I, and I'll show you all the towns. America is full of beautiful towns and fine, upstanding people. And they know me, boys, they

Biff (Kevin Anderson), Willy (Brian Dennehy), and Happy (Ted Koch) in a bright moment in Robert Falls's 1999 Broadway revival of *Death of a Salesman*.

know me up and down New England. The finest people. And when I bring you fellas up, there'll be open sesame for all of us, 'cause one thing, boys: I have friends. I can park my car in any street in New England, and the cops protect it like their own. This summer, heh?

BIFF AND HAPPY (*together*): Yeah! You bet!

WILLY: We'll take our bathing suits.

HAPPY: We'll carry your bags, Pop!

WILLY: Oh, won't that be something! Me comin' into the Boston stores with you boys carryin' my bags. What a sensation!

(*Biff is prancing around, practicing passing the ball.*)

WILLY: You nervous, Biff, about the game?

BIFF: Not if you're gonna be there.

WILLY: What do they say about you in school, now that they made you captain?

HAPPY: There's a crowd of girls behind him every time the classes change.

BIFF (*taking Willy's hand*): This Saturday, Pop, this Saturday—just for you, I'm going to break through for a touchdown.

HAPPY: You're supposed to pass.

BIFF: I'm takin' one play for Pop. You watch me, Pop, and when I take off my helmet, that means I'm brea-kin' out. Then you watch me crash through that line!

WILLY (*kisses Biff*): Oh, wait'll I tell this in Boston!

(*Bernard enters in knickers. He is younger than Biff, earnest and loyal, a worried boy.*)

BERNARD: Biff, where are you? You're supposed to study with me today.

WILLY: Hey, looka Bernard. What're you lookin' so ane-mic about, Bernard?

BERNARD: He's gotta study, Uncle Willy. He's got Regents next week.

HAPPY (*tauntingly, spinning Bernard around*): Let's box, Bernard!

BERNARD: Biff! (*He gets away from Happy.*) Listen, Biff, I heard Mr. Birnbaum say that if you don't start studyin' math he's gonna flunk you, and you won't graduate. I heard him!

WILLY: You better study with him, Biff. Go ahead now.

BERNARD: I heard him!

BIFF: Oh, Pop, you didn't see my sneakers! (*He holds up a foot for Willy to look at.*)

WILLY: Hey, that's a beautiful job of printing!

BERNARD (*wiping his glasses*): Just because he printed University of Virginia on his sneakers doesn't mean they've got to graduate him, Uncle Willy!

WILLY (*angrily*): What're you talking about? With scholarships to three universities they're gonna flunk him?

BERNARD: But I heard Mr. Birnbaum say—

WILLY: Don't be a pest, Bernard! (*To his boys.*) What an anemic!

BERNARD: Okay, I'm waiting for you in my house, Biff.

(*Bernard goes off. The Lomans laugh.*)

WILLY: Bernard is not well liked, is he?

BIFF: He's liked, but he's not well liked.

HAPPY: That's right, Pop.

WILLY: That's just what I mean. Bernard can get the best marks in school, y'understand, but when he gets out in the business world, y'understand, you are going to be five times ahead of him. That's why I thank Almighty God you're both built like Adonises. Because the man who makes an appearance in the business world, the man who creates personal interest, is the man who gets ahead. Be liked and you will never want. You take me, for instance. I never have to wait in line to see a buyer. "Willy Loman is here!" That's all they have to know, and I go right through.

BIFF: Did you knock them dead, Pop?

WILLY: Knocked 'em cold in Providence, slaughtered 'em in Boston.

HAPPY (*on his back, pedaling again*): I'm losing weight, you notice, Pop?

(*Linda enters as of old, a ribbon in her hair, carrying a basket of washing.*)

LINDA (*with youthful energy*): Hello, dear!

WILLY: Sweetheart!

LINDA: How'd the Chevvy run?

WILLY: Chevrolet, Linda, is the greatest car ever built. (*To the boys.*) Since when do you let your mother carry wash up the stairs?

BIFF: Grab hold there, boy!

HAPPY: Where to, Mom?

LINDA: Hang them up on the line. And you better go down to your friends, Biff. The cellar is full of boys. They don't know what to do with themselves.

BIFF: Ah, when Pop comes home they can wait!

WILLY (*laughs appreciatively*): You better go down and tell them what to do, Biff.

BIFF: I think I'll have them sweep out the furnace room.

WILLY: Good work, Biff.

BIFF (*goes through wall-line of kitchen to doorway at back and calls down*): Fellas! Everybody sweep out the furnace room! I'll be right down!

VOICES: All right! Okay, Biff.

BIFF: George and Sam and Frank, come out back! We're hangin' up the wash! Come on, Hap, on the double! (*He and Happy carry out the basket.*)

LINDA: The way they obey him!

WILLY: Well, that's training, the training. I'm tellin' you, I was sellin' thousands and thousands, but I had to come home.

LINDA: Oh, the whole block'll be at that game. Did you sell anything?

WILLY: I did five hundred gross in Providence and seven hundred gross in Boston.

LINDA: No! Wait a minute, I've got a pencil. (*She pulls pencil and paper out of her apron pocket.*) That makes your commission . . . Two hundred—my God! Two hundred and twelve dollars!

WILLY: Well, I didn't figure it yet, but . . .

LINDA: How much did you do?

WILLY: Well, I—I did—about a hundred and eighty gross in Providence. Well, no—it came to—roughly two hundred gross on the whole trip.

LINDA (*without hesitation*): Two hundred gross. That's . . . (*She figures.*)

WILLY: The trouble was that three of the stores were half-closed for inventory in Boston. Otherwise I woulda broke records.

LINDA: Well, it makes seventy dollars and some pennies. That's very good.

WILLY: What do we owe?

LINDA: Well, on the first there's sixteen dollars on the refrigerator—

WILLY: Why sixteen?

LINDA: Well, the fan belt broke, so it was a dollar eighty.

WILLY: But it's brand new.

LINDA: Well, the man said that's the way it is. Till they work themselves in, y'know.

(*They move through the wall-line into the kitchen.*)

WILLY: I hope we didn't get stuck on that machine.

LINDA: They got the biggest ads of any of them!

WILLY: I know, it's a fine machine. What else?

LINDA: Well, there's nine-sixty for the washing machine. And for the vacuum cleaner there's three and a half due on the fifteenth. Then the roof, you got twenty-one dollars remaining.

WILLY: It don't leak, does it?

LINDA: No, they did a wonderful job. Then you owe Frank for the carburetor.

WILLY: I'm not going to pay that man! That goddam Chevrolet, they ought to prohibit the manufacture of that car!

LINDA: Well, you owe him three and a half. And odds and ends, comes to around a hundred and twenty dollars by the fifteenth.

WILLY: A hundred and twenty dollars! My God, if business don't pick up I don't know what I'm gonna do!

LINDA: Well, next week you'll do better.

WILLY: Oh, I'll knock 'em dead next week. I'll go to Hartford. I'm very well liked in Hartford. You know, the trouble is, Linda, people don't seem to take to me.

(*They move onto the forestage.*)

LINDA: Oh, don't be foolish.

WILLY: I know it when I walk in. They seem to laugh at me.

LINDA: Why? Why would they laugh at you? Don't talk that way, Willy.

(*Willy moves to the edge of the stage. Linda goes into the kitchen and starts to darn stockings.*)

WILLY: I don't know the reason for it, but they just pass me by. I'm not noticed.

LINDA: But you're doing wonderful, dear. You're making seventy to a hundred dollars a week.

WILLY: But I gotta be at it ten, twelve hours a day. Other men—I don't know—they do it easier. I don't know why—I can't stop myself—I talk too much. A man oughta come in with a few words. One thing about Charley. He's a man of few words, and they respect him.

LINDA: You don't talk too much, you're just lively.

WILLY (*smiling*): Well, I figure, what the hell, life is short, a couple of jokes. (*To himself.*) I joke too much! (*The smile goes.*)

LINDA: Why? You're—

WILLY: I'm fat. I'm very—foolish to look at, Linda. I didn't tell you, but Christmas time I happened to be calling on F. H. Stewarts, and a salesman I know, as I was going in to see the buyer I heard him say something about—walrus. And I—I cracked him right across the face. I won't take that. I simply will not take that. But they do laugh at me. I know that.

LINDA: Darling . . .

WILLY: I gotta overcome it. I know I gotta overcome it. I'm not dressing to advantage, maybe.

LINDA: Willy, darling, you're the handsomest man in the world—

WILLY: Oh, no, Linda.

LINDA: To me you are. (*Slight pause.*) The handsomest.

(*From the darkness is heard the laughter of a woman. Willy doesn't turn to it, but it continues through Linda's lines.*)

LINDA: And the boys, Willy. Few men are idolized by their children the way you are.

(*Music is heard as behind a scrim, to the left of the house, The Woman, dimly seen, is dressing.*)

WILLY (*with great feeling*): You're the best there is, Linda, you're a pal, you know that? On the road—on the road I want to grab you sometimes and just kiss the life outa you.

(*The laughter is loud now, and he moves into a brightening area at the left, where The Woman has come from behind the scrim and is standing, putting on her hat, looking into a "mirror" and laughing.*)

WILLY: 'Cause I get so lonely—especially when business is bad and there's nobody to talk to. I get the feeling that I'll never sell anything again, that I won't make a living for you, or a business, a business for the boys. (*He talks through The Woman's subsiding laughter; The Woman primps at the "mirror."*) There's so much I want to make for—

THE WOMAN: Me? You didn't make me, Willy. I picked you.

WILLY (*pleased*): You picked me?

THE WOMAN (*who is quite proper-looking, Willy's age*): I did. I've been sitting at that desk watching all the salesmen go by, day in, day out. But you've got such a sense of humor, and we do have such a good time together, don't we?

WILLY: Sure, sure. (*He takes her in his arms.*) Why do you have to go now?

THE WOMAN: It's two o'clock . . .

WILLY: No, come on in! (*He pulls her.*)

THE WOMAN: . . . my sisters'll be scandalized. When'll you be back?

WILLY: Oh, two weeks about. Will you come up again?

THE WOMAN: Sure thing. You do make me laugh. It's good for me. (*She squeezes his arm, kisses him.*) And I think you're a wonderful man.

WILLY: You picked me, heh?

THE WOMAN: Sure. Because you're so sweet. And such a kidder.

WILLY: Well, I'll see you next time I'm in Boston.

THE WOMAN: I'll put you right through to the buyers.

WILLY (*slapping her bottom*): Right. Well, bottoms up!

THE WOMAN (*slaps him gently and laughs*): You just kill me, Willy. (*He suddenly grabs her and kisses her roughly.*) You kill me. And thanks for the stockings. I love a lot of stockings. Well, good night.

WILLY: Good night. And keep your pores open!

THE WOMAN: Oh, Willy!

(*The Woman bursts out laughing, and Linda's laughter blends in. The Woman disappears into the dark. Now the area at the kitchen table brightens. Linda is sitting where she was at the kitchen table, but now is mending a pair of her silk stockings.*)

LINDA: You are, Willy. The handsomest man. You've got no reason to feel that—

WILLY (*coming out of The Woman's dimming area and going over to Linda*): I'll make it all up to you, Linda, I'll—

LINDA: There's nothing to make up, dear. You're doing fine, better than—

WILLY (*noticing her mending*): What's that?

LINDA: Just mending my stockings. They're so expensive—

WILLY (*angrily, taking them from her*): I won't have you mending stockings in this house! Now throw them out!

(*Linda puts the stockings in her pocket.*)

BERNARD (*entering on the run*): Where is he? If he doesn't study!

WILLY (*moving to the forestage, with great agitation*): You'll give him the answers!

BERNARD: I do, but I can't on a Regents! That's a state exam! They're liable to arrest me!

WILLY: Where is he? I'll whip him, I'll whip him!

LINDA: And he'd better give back that football, Willy, it's not nice.

WILLY: Biff! Where is he? Why is he taking everything?

LINDA: He's too rough with the girls, Willy. All the mothers are afraid of him!

WILLY: I'll whip him!

BERNARD: He's driving the car without a license!

(*The Woman's laugh is heard.*)

WILLY: Shut up!

LINDA: All the mothers—

WILLY: Shut up!

BERNARD (*backing quietly away and out*): Mr. Birnbaum says he's stuck up.

WILLY: Get outa here!

BERNARD: If he doesn't buckle down he'll flunk math! (*He goes off.*)

LINDA: He's right, Willy, you've gotta—

WILLY (*exploding at her*): There's nothing the matter with him! You want him to be a worm like Bernard? He's got spirit, personality . . .

(*As he speaks, Linda, almost in tears, exits into the living room. Willy is alone in the kitchen, wilting and staring. The leaves are gone. It is night again, and the apartment houses look down from behind.*)

WILLY: Loaded with it. Loaded! What is he stealing? He's giving it back, isn't he? Why is he stealing? What did I tell him? I never in my life told him anything but decent things.

(*Happy in pajamas has come down the stairs; Willy suddenly becomes aware of Happy's presence.*)

HAPPY: Let's go now, come on.

WILLY (*sitting down at the kitchen table*): Huh! Why did she have to wax the floors herself? Everytime she waxes the floors she keels over. She knows that!

HAPPY: Shh! Take it easy. What brought you back tonight?

WILLY: I got an awful scare. Nearly hit a kid in Yonkers. God! Why didn't I go to Alaska with my brother Ben that time! Ben! That man was a genius, that man was success incarnate! What a mistake! He begged me to go.

HAPPY: Well, there's no use in—

WILLY: You guys! There was a man started with the clothes on his back and ended up with diamond mines!

HAPPY: Boy, someday I'd like to know how he did it.

WILLY: What's the mystery? The man knew what he wanted and went out and got it! Walked into a jungle, and comes out, the age of twenty-one, and he's rich! The world is an oyster, but you don't crack it open on a mattress!

HAPPY: Pop, I told you I'm gonna retire you for life.

WILLY: You'll retire me for life on seventy goddam dollars a week? And your women and your car and your apartment, and you'll retire me for life! Christ's sake, I couldn't get past Yonkers today! Where are you guys, where are you? The woods are burning! I can't drive a car!

(*Charley has appeared in the doorway. He is a large man, slow of speech, laconic, immovable. In all he says, despite what he says, there is pity, and, now, trepidation. He has a robe over pajamas, slippers on his feet. He enters the kitchen.*)

CHARLEY: Everything all right?

HAPPY: Yeah, Charley, everything's . . .

WILLY: What's the matter?

CHARLEY: I heard some noise. I thought something happened. Can't we do something about the walls? You sneeze in here, and in my house hats blow off.

HAPPY: Let's go to bed, Dad. Come on.

(*Charley signals to Happy to go.*)

WILLY: You go ahead, I'm not tired at the moment.

HAPPY (*to Willy*): Take it easy, huh? (*He exits.*)

WILLY: What're you doin' up?

CHARLEY (*sitting down at the kitchen table opposite Willy*): Couldn't sleep good. I had a heartburn.

WILLY: Well, you don't know how to eat.

CHARLEY: I eat with my mouth.

WILLY: No, you're ignorant. You gotta know about vitamins and things like that.

CHARLEY: Come on, let's shoot. Tire you out a little.

WILLY (*hesitantly*): All right. You got cards?

CHARLEY (*taking a deck from his pocket*): Yeah, I got them. Someplace. What is it with those vitamins?

WILLY (*dealing*): They build up your bones. Chemistry.

CHARLEY: Yeah, but there's no bones in a heartburn.

WILLY: What are you talkin' about? Do you know the first thing about it?

CHARLEY: Don't get insulted.

WILLY: Don't talk about something you don't know anything about.

(*They are playing. Pause.*)

CHARLEY: What're you doin' home?

WILLY: A little trouble with the car.

CHARLEY: Oh. (*Pause.*) I'd like to take a trip to California.

WILLY: Don't say.

CHARLEY: You want a job?

WILLY: I got a job, I told you that. (*After a slight pause.*) What the hell are you offering me a job for?

CHARLEY: Don't get insulted.

WILLY: Don't insult me.

CHARLEY: I don't see no sense in it. You don't have to go on this way.

WILLY: I got a good job. (*Slight pause.*) What do you keep comin' in here for?

CHARLEY: You want me to go?

WILLY (*after a pause, withering*): I can't understand it. He's going back to Texas again. What the hell is that?

CHARLEY: Let him go.

WILLY: I got nothin' to give him, Charley, I'm clean, I'm clean.

CHARLEY: He won't starve. None a them starve. Forget about him.

WILLY: Then what have I got to remember?

CHARLEY: You take it too hard. To hell with it. When a deposit bottle is broken you don't get your nickel back.

WILLY: That's easy enough for you to say.

CHARLEY: That ain't easy for me to say.

WILLY: Did you see the ceiling I put up in the living room?

CHARLEY: Yeah, that's a piece of work. To put up a ceiling is a mystery to me. How do you do it?

WILLY: What's the difference?

CHARLEY: Well, talk about it.

WILLY: You gonna put up a ceiling?

CHARLEY: How could I put up a ceiling?

WILLY: Then what the hell are you bothering me for?

CHARLEY: You're insulted again.

WILLY: A man who can't handle tools is not a man. You're disgusting.

CHARLEY: Don't call me disgusting, Willy.

(*Uncle Ben, carrying a valise and an umbrella, enters the forestage from around the right corner of the house. He is a stolid man, in his sixties, with a mustache and an authoritative air. He is utterly certain of his destiny, and there is an aura of far places about him. He enters exactly as Willy speaks.*)

WILLY: I'm getting awfully tired, Ben.

(*Ben's music is heard. Ben looks around at everything.*)

CHARLEY: Good, keep playing; you'll sleep better. Did you call me Ben?

(*Ben looks at his watch.*)

WILLY: That's funny. For a second there you reminded me of my brother Ben.

BEN: I only have a few minutes. (*He strolls, inspecting the place. Willy and Charley continue playing.*)

CHARLEY: You never heard from him again, heh? Since that time?

WILLY: Didn't Linda tell you? Couple of weeks ago we got a letter from his wife in Africa. He died.

CHARLEY: That so.

BEN (*chuckling*): So this is Brooklyn, eh?

CHARLEY: Maybe you're in for some of his money.

WILLY: Naa, he had seven sons. There's just one opportunity I had with that man . . .

BEN: I must make a train, William. There are several properties I'm looking at in Alaska.

WILLY: Sure, sure! If I'd gone with him to Alaska that time, everything would've been totally different.

CHARLIE: Go on, you'd froze to death up there.

WILLY: What're you talking about?

BEN: Opportunity is tremendous in Alaska, William. Surprised you're not up there.

WILLY: Sure, tremendous.

CHARLEY: Heh?

WILLY: There was the only man I ever met who knew the answers.

CHARLEY: Who?

BEN: How are you all?

WILLY (*taking a pot, smiling*): Fine, fine.

CHARLEY: Pretty sharp tonight.

BEN: Is Mother living with you?

WILLY: No, she died a long time ago.

CHARLEY: Who?

BEN: That's too bad. Fine specimen of a lady, Mother.

WILLY (*to Charley*): Heh?

BEN: I'd hoped to see the old girl.

CHARLEY: Who died?

BEN: Heard anything from Father, have you?

WILLY (*unnerved*): What do you mean, who died?

CHARLEY (*taking a pot*): What're you talkin' about?

BEN (*looking at his watch*): William, it's half-past eight!

WILLY (*as though to dispel his confusion he angrily stops Charley's hand*): That's my build!

CHARLEY: I put the ace—

WILLY: If you don't know how to play the game I'm not gonna throw my money away on you!

CHARLEY (*rising*): It was my ace, for God's sake!

WILLY: I'm through, I'm through!

BEN: When did Mother die?

WILLY: Long ago. Since the beginning you never knew how to play cards.

CHARLEY (*picks up the cards and goes to the door*): All right! Next time I'll bring a deck with five aces.

WILLY: I don't play that kind of game!

CHARLEY (*turning to him*): You ought to be ashamed of yourself!

WILLY: Yeah?

CHARLEY: Yeah! (*He goes out.*)

WILLY (*slamming the door after him*): Ignoramus!

BEN (*as Willy comes toward him through the wall-line of the kitchen*): So you're William.

WILLY (*shaking Ben's hand*): Ben! I've been waiting for you so long! What's the answer? How did you do it?

BEN: Oh, there's a story in that.

(*Linda enters the forestage, as of old, carrying the wash basket.*)

LINDA: Is this Ben?

BEN (*gallantly*): How do you do, my dear.

LINDA: Where've you been all these years? Willy's always wondered why you—

WILLY (*pulling Ben away from her impatiently*): Where is Dad? Didn't you follow him? How did you get started?

BEN: Well, I don't know how much you remember.

WILLY: Well, I was just a baby, of course, only three or four years old—

BEN: Three years and eleven months.

WILLY: What a memory, Ben!

BEN: I have many enterprises, William, and I have never kept books.

WILLY: I remember I was sitting under the wagon in—was it Nebraska?

BEN: It was South Dakota, and I gave you a bunch of wild flowers.

WILLY: I remember you walking away down some open road.

BEN (*laughing*): I was going to find Father in Alaska.

WILLY: Where is he?

BEN: At that age I had a very faulty view of geography, William. I discovered after a few days that I was heading due south, so instead of Alaska, I ended up in Africa.

LINDA: Africa!

WILLY: The Gold Coast!

BEN: Principally diamond mines.

LINDA: Diamond mines!

BEN: Yes, my dear. But I've only a few minutes—

WILLY: No! Boys! Boys! (*Young Biff and Happy appear.*) Listen to this. This is your Uncle Ben, a great man! Tell my boys, Ben!

BEN: Why, boys, when I was seventeen I walked into the jungle, and when I was twenty-one I walked out. (*He laughs.*) And by God I was rich.

WILLY (*to the boys*): You see what I been talking about? The greatest things can happen!

BEN (*glancing at his watch*): I have an appointment in Ketchikan Tuesday week.

WILLY: No, Ben! Please tell about Dad. I want my boys to hear. I want them to know the kind of stock they spring from. All I remember is a man with a big beard, and I was in Mamma's lap, sitting around a fire, and some kind of high music.

BEN: His flute. He played the flute.

WILLY: Sure, the flute, that's right!

(*New music is heard, a high, rollicking tune.*)

BEN: Father was a very great and a very wild-hearted man. We would start in Boston, and he'd toss the whole family into the wagon, and then he'd drive the team right across the country; through Ohio, and Indiana, Michigan, Illinois, and all the Western states. And we'd stop in the towns and sell the flutes that he'd made on the way. Great inventor Father. With one gadget he made more in a week than a man like you could make in a lifetime.

WILLY: That's just the way I'm bringing them up, Ben—rugged, well liked, all-around.

BEN: Yeah? (*To Biff.*) Hit that, boy—hard as you can. (*He pounds his stomach.*)

BIFF: Oh, no, sir!

BEN (*taking boxing stance*): Come on, get to me! (*He laughs.*)

WILLY: Go to it, Biff! Go ahead, show him!

BIFF: Okay! (*He cocks his fists and starts in.*)

LINDA (*to Willy*): Why must he fight, dear?

BEN (*sparring with Biff*): Good boy! Good boy!

WILLY: How's that, Ben, heh?

HAPPY: Give him the left, Biff!

LINDA: Why are you fighting?

BEN: Good boy! (*Suddenly comes in, trips Biff, and stands over him, the point of his umbrella poised over Biff's eye.*)

LINDA: Look out, Biff!

BIFF: Gee!

BEN (*patting Biff's knee*): Never fight fair with a stranger, boy. You'll never get out of the jungle that way. (*Taking Linda's hand and bowing.*) It was an honor and a pleasure to meet you, Linda.

LINDA (*withdrawing her hand coldly, frightened*): Have a nice—trip.

BEN (*to Willy*): And good luck with your—what do you do?

WILLY: Selling.

BEN: Yes. Well . . . (*He raises his hand in farewell to all.*)

WILLY: No, Ben, I don't want you to think . . . (*He takes Ben's arm to show him.*) It's Brooklyn, I know, but we hunt too.

BEN: Really, now.

WILLY: Oh, sure, there's snakes and rabbits and—that's why I moved out here. Why, Biff can fell any one of these trees in no time! Boys! Go right over to where they're building the apartment house and get some sand. We're gonna rebuild the entire front stoop right now! Watch this, Ben!

BIFF: Yes, sir! On the double, Hap!

HAPPY (*as he and Biff run off*): I lost weight, Pop, you notice?

(*Charley enters in knickers, even before the boys are gone.*)

CHARLEY: Listen, if they steal any more from that building the watchman'll put the cops on them!

LINDA (*to Willy*): Don't let Biff . . .

(*Ben laughs lustily.*)

WILLY: You shoulda seen the lumber they brought home last week. At least a dozen six-by-tens worth all kinds a money.

CHARLEY: Listen, if that watchman—

WILLY: I gave them hell, understand. But I got a couple of fearless characters there.

CHARLEY: Willy, the jails are full of fearless characters.

BEN (*clapping Willy on the back, with a laugh at Charley*): And the stock exchange, friend!

WILLY (*joining in Ben's laughter*): Where are the rest of your pants?

CHARLEY: My wife bought them.

WILLY: Now all you need is a golf club and you can go upstairs and go to sleep. (*To Ben.*) Great athlete! Between him and his son Bernard they can't hammer a nail!

BERNARD (*rushing in*): The watchman's chasing Biff!

WILLY (*angrily*): Shut up! He's not stealing anything!

LINDA (*alarmed, hurrying off left*): Where is he? Biff, dear! (*She exits.*)

WILLY (*moving toward the left, away from Ben*): There's nothing wrong. What's the matter with you?

BEN: Nervy boy. Good!

WILLY (*laughing*): Oh, nerves of iron, that Biff!

CHARLEY: Don't know what it is. My New England man comes back and he's bleedin', they murdered him up there.

WILLY: It's contacts, Charley, I got important contacts!

CHARLEY (*sarcastically*): Glad to hear it, Willy. Come in later, we'll shoot a little casino. I'll take some of your Portland money. (*He laughs at Willy and exits.*)

WILLY (*turning to Ben*): Business is bad, it's murderous. But not for me, of course.

BEN: I'll stop by on my way back to Africa.

WILLY (*longingly*): Can't you stay a few days? You're just what I need, Ben, because I—I have a fine position here, but I—well, Dad left when I was such a baby and I never had a chance to talk to him and I still feel—kind of temporary about myself.

BEN: I'll be late for my train.

(*They are at opposite ends of the stage.*)

WILLY: Ben, my boys—can't we talk? They'd go into the jaws of hell for me, see, but I—

BEN: William, you're being first-rate with your boys. Outstanding, manly chaps!

WILLY (*hanging on to his words*): Oh, Ben, that's good to hear! Because sometimes I'm afraid that I'm not teaching them the right kind of—Ben, how should I teach them?

BEN (*giving great weight to each word, and with a certain vicious audacity*): William, when I walked into the jungle, I was seventeen. When I walked out I was twenty-one. And, by God, I was rich! (*He goes off into darkness around the right corner of the house.*)

WILLY: . . . was rich! That's just the spirit I want to imbue them with! To walk into a jungle! I was right! I was right! I was right!

(*Ben is gone, but Willy is still speaking to him as Linda, in nightgown and robe, enters the kitchen, glances around for Willy, then goes to the door of the house, looks out and sees him. Comes down to his left. He looks at her.*)

LINDA: Willy, dear? Willy?

WILLY: I was right!

LINDA: Did you have some cheese? (*He can't answer.*) It's very late, darling. Come to bed, heh?

WILLY (*looking straight up*): Gotta break your neck to see a star in this yard.

LINDA: You coming in?

WILLY: Whatever happened to that diamond watch fob? Remember? When Ben came from Africa that time? Didn't he give me a watch fob with a diamond in it?

LINDA: You pawned it, dear. Twelve, thirteen years ago. For Biff's radio correspondence course.

WILLY: Gee, that was a beautiful thing. I'll take a walk.

LINDA: But you're in your slippers.

WILLY (*starting to go around the house at the left*): I was right! I was! (*Half to Linda, as he goes, shaking his head.*) What a man! There was a man worth talking to. I was right!

LINDA (*calling after Willy*): But in your slippers, Willy!

(*Willy is almost gone when Biff, in his pajamas, comes down the stairs and enters the kitchen.*)

BIFF: What is he doing out there?

LINDA: Sh!

BIFF: God Almighty, Mom, how long has he been doing this?

LINDA: Don't, he'll hear you.

BIFF: What the hell is the matter with him?

LINDA: It'll pass by morning.

BIFF: Shouldn't we do anything?

LINDA: Oh, my dear, you should do a lot of things, but there's nothing to do, so go to sleep.

(*Happy comes down the stair and sits on the steps.*)

HAPPY: I never heard him so loud, Mom.

LINDA: Well, come around more often, you'll hear him. (*She sits down at the table and mends the lining of Willy's jacket.*)

BIFF: Why didn't you ever write me about this, Mom?

LINDA: How would I write to you? For over three months you had no address.

BIFF: I was on the move. But you know I thought of you all the time. You know that, don't you, pal?

LINDA: I know, dear, I know. But he likes to have a letter. Just to know that there's still a possibility for better things.

BIFF: He's not like this all the time, is he?

LINDA: It's when you come home he's always the worst.

BIFF: When I come home?

LINDA: When you write you're coming, he's all smiles and talks about the future, and—he's just wonderful. And then the closer you seem to come, the more shaky he gets, and then, by the time you get here, he's arguing, and he seems angry at you. I think it's just that maybe he can't bring himself to—to open up to you. Why are you so hateful to each other? Why is that?

BIFF (*evasively*): I'm not hateful, Mom.

LINDA: But you no sooner come in the door than you're fighting!

BIFF: I don't know why. I mean to change. I'm tryin', Mom, you understand?

LINDA: Are you home to stay now?

BIFF: I don't know. I want to look around, see what's goin'.

LINDA: Biff, you can't look around all your life, can you?

BIFF: I just can't take hold, Mom. I can't take hold of some kind of a life.

LINDA: Biff, a man is not a bird, to come and go with the springtime.

BIFF: Your hair . . . (*He touches her hair.*) Your hair got so gray.

LINDA: Oh, it's been gray since you were in high school. I just stopped dyeing it, that's all.

BIFF: Dye it again, will ye? I don't want my pal looking old. (*He smiles.*)

LINDA: You're such a boy! You think you can go away for a year and . . . You've got to get it into your head now that one day you'll knock on this door and there'll be strange people here—

BIFF: What are you talking about? You're not even sixty, Mom.

LINDA: But what about your father?

BIFF (*lamely*): Well, I meant him too.

HAPPY: He admires Pop.

LINDA: Biff, dear, if you don't have any feeling for him, then you can't have any feeling for me.

BIFF: Sure I can, Mom.

LINDA: No. You can't just come to see me, because I love him. (*With a threat, but only a threat, of tears.*) He's the dearest man in the world to me, and I won't have anyone making him feel unwanted and low and blue. You've got to make up your mind now, darling, there's no leeway any more. Either he's your father and you pay him that respect, or else you're not to come here. I know he's not easy to get along with—nobody knows that better than me—but . . .

WILLY (*from the left, with a laugh*): Hey, hey, Biffo!

BIFF (*starting to go out after Willy*): What the hell is the matter with him? (*Happy stops him.*)

LINDA: Don't—don't go near him!

BIFF: Stop making excuses for him! He always, always wiped the floor with you. Never had an ounce of respect for you.

HAPPY: He's always had respect for—

BIFF: What the hell do you know about it?

HAPPY (*surlily*): Just don't call him crazy!

BIFF: He's got no character—Charley wouldn't do this. Not in his own house—spewing out that vomit from his mind.

HAPPY: Charley never had to cope with what he's got to.

BIFF: People are worse off than Willy Loman. Believe me, I've seen them!

LINDA: Then make Charley your father, Biff. You can't do that, can you? I don't say he's a great man. Willy Loman never made a lot of money. His name was never in the paper. He's not the finest character that ever lived. But he's a human being, and a terrible thing is happening to him. So attention must be paid. He's not to be allowed to fall into his grave like an old dog. Attention, attention must be finally paid to such a person. You called him crazy—

BIFF: I didn't mean—

LINDA: No, a lot of people think he's lost his—balance. But you don't have to be very smart to know what his trouble is. The man is exhausted.

HAPPY: Sure!

LINDA: A small man can be just as exhausted as a great man. He works for a company thirty-six years this March, opens up unheard-of territories to their trademark, and now in his old age they take his salary away.

HAPPY (*indignantly*): I didn't know that, Mom.

LINDA: You never asked, my dear! Now that you get your spending money someplace else you don't trouble your mind with him.

HAPPY: But I gave you money last—

LINDA: Christmas time, fifty dollars! To fix the hot water it cost ninety-seven fifty! For five weeks he's been on straight commission, like a beginner, an unknown!

BIFF: Those ungrateful bastards!

LINDA: Are they any worse than his sons? When he brought them business, when he was young, they were glad to see him. But now his old friends, the old buyers that loved him so and always found some order to hand him in a pinch—they're all dead, retired. He used to be able to make six, seven calls a day in Boston. Now he takes his valises out of the car and puts them back and takes them out again and he's exhausted. Instead of walking he talks now. He

drives seven hundred miles, and when he gets there no one knows him anymore, no one welcomes him. And what goes through a man's mind, driving seven hundred miles home without having earned a cent? Why shouldn't he talk to himself? Why? When he has to go to Charley and borrow fifty dollars a week and pretend to me that it's his pay? How long can that go on? How long? You see what I'm sitting here and waiting for? And you tell me he has no character? The man who never worked a day but for your benefit? When does he get the medal for that? Is this his reward—to turn around at the age of sixty-three and find his sons, who he loved better than his life, one a philandering bum—

HAPPY: Mom!

LINDA: That's all you are, my baby! (*To Biff.*) And you! What happened to the love you had for him? You were such pals! How you used to talk to him on the phone every night! How lonely he was till he could come home to you!

BIFF: All right, Mom. I'll live here in my room, and I'll get a job. I'll keep away from him, that's all.

LINDA: No, Biff. You can't stay here and fight all the time.

BIFF: He threw me out of this house, remember that.

LINDA: Why did he do that? I never knew why.

BIFF: Because I know he's a fake and he doesn't like anybody around who knows!

LINDA: Why a fake? In what way? What do you mean?

BIFF: Just don't lay it all at my feet. It's between me and him—that's all I have to say. I'll chip in from now on. He'll settle for half my pay check. He'll be all right. I'm going to bed. (*He starts for the stairs.*)

LINDA: He won't be all right.

BIFF (*turning on the stairs, furiously*): I hate this city and I'll stay here. Now what do you want?

LINDA: He's dying, Biff.

(*Happy turns quickly to her, shocked.*)

BIFF (*after a pause*): Why is he dying?

LINDA: He's been trying to kill himself.

BIFF (*with great horror*): How?

LINDA: I live from day to day.

BIFF: What're you talking about?

LINDA: Remember I wrote you that he smashed up the car again? In February?

BIFF: Well?

LINDA: The insurance inspector came. He said that they have evidence. That all these accidents in the last year—weren't—weren't—accidents.

HAPPY: How can they tell that? That's a lie.

LINDA: It seems there's a woman . . . (*She takes a breath as*

BIFF (*sharply but contained*): } What woman?
LINDA (*simultaneously*):   { . . . and this woman . . .

LINDA: What?

BIFF: Nothing. Go ahead.

LINDA: What did you say?

BIFF: Nothing. I just said what woman?

HAPPY: What about her?

LINDA: Well, it seems she was walking down the road and saw his car. She says that he wasn't driving fast at all, and that he didn't skid. She says he came to that little bridge, and then deliberately smashed into the railing, and it was only the shallowness of the water that saved him.

BIFF: Oh, no, he probably just fell asleep again.

LINDA: I don't think he fell asleep.

BIFF: Why not?

LINDA: Last month . . . (*With great difficulty.*) Oh, boys, it's so hard to say a thing like this! He's just a big stupid man to you, but I tell you there's more good in him than in many other people. (*She chokes, wipes her eyes.*) I was looking for a fuse. The lights blew out, and I went down the cellar. And behind the fuse box—it happened to fall out—was a length of rubber pipe—just short.

HAPPY: No kidding!

LINDA: There's a little attachment on the end of it. I knew right away. And sure enough, on the bottom of the water heater there's a new little nipple on the gas pipe.

HAPPY (*angrily*): That—jerk.

BIFF: Did you have it taken off?

LINDA: I'm—I'm ashamed to. How can I mention it to him? Every day I go down and take away that little rubber pipe. But, when he comes home, I put it back where it was. How can I insult him that way? I don't know what to do. I live from day to day, boys. I tell you, I know every thought in his mind. It sounds so old-fashioned and silly, but I tell you he put his whole life into you and you've turned your backs on him. (*She is bent over in the chair, weeping, her face in her hands.*) Biff, I swear to God! Biff, his life is in your hands!

HAPPY (*to Biff*): How do you like that damned fool!

BIFF (*kissing her*): All right, pal, all right. It's all settled now. I've been remiss. I know that, Mom. But now I'll stay, and I swear to you, I'll apply myself. (*Kneeling in front of her, in a fever of self-reproach.*) It's just—you see, Mom, I don't fit in business. Not that I won't try. I'll try, and I'll make good.

HAPPY: Sure you will. The trouble with you in business was you never tried to please people.

BIFF: I know, I—

HAPPY: Like when you worked for Harrison's. Bob Harrison said you were tops, and then you go and do some damn fool thing like whistling whole songs in the elevator like a comedian.

BIFF (*against Happy*): So what? I like to whistle sometimes.

HAPPY: You don't raise a guy to a responsible job who whistles in the elevator!

LINDA: Well, don't argue about it now.

HAPPY: Like when you'd go off and swim in the middle of the day instead of taking the line around.

BIFF (*his resentment rising*): Well, don't you run off? You take off sometimes, don't you? On a nice summer day?

HAPPY: Yeah, but I cover myself!

LINDA: Boys!

HAPPY: If I'm going to take a fade the boss can call any number where I'm supposed to be and they'll swear to him that I just left. I'll tell you something that I hate to say, Biff, but in the business world some of them think you're crazy.

BIFF (*angered*): Screw the business world!

HAPPY: All right, screw it! Great, but cover yourself!

LINDA: Hap, Hap!

BIFF: I don't care what they think! They've laughed at Dad for years, and you know why? Because we don't belong in this nuthouse of a city! We should be mixing cement on some open plain, or—or carpenters. A carpenter is allowed to whistle!

(*Willy walks in from the entrance of the house, at left.*)

WILLY: Even your grandfather was better than a carpenter. (*Pause. They watch him.*) You never grew up. Bernard does not whistle in the elevator, I assure you.

BIFF (*as though to laugh Willy out of it*): Yeah, but you do, Pop.

WILLY: I never in my life whistled in an elevator! And who in the business world thinks I'm crazy?

BIFF: I didn't mean it like that, Pop. Now don't make a whole thing out of it, will ye?

WILLY: Go back to the West! Be a carpenter, a cowboy, enjoy yourself!

LINDA: Willy, he was just saying—

WILLY: I heard what he said!

HAPPY (*trying to quiet Willy*): Hey, Pop, come on now . . .

WILLY (*continuing over Happy's line*): They laugh at me, heh? Go to Filene's, go to the Hub, go to Slattery's, Boston. Call out the name Willy Loman and see what happens! Big shot!

BIFF: All right, Pop.

WILLY: Big!

BIFF: All right!

WILLY: Why do you always insult me?

BIFF: I didn't say a word. (*To Linda.*) Did I say a word?

LINDA: He didn't say anything, Willy.

WILLY (*going to the doorway of the living room*): All right, good night, good night.

LINDA: Willy, dear, he just decided . . .

WILLY (*to Biff*): If you get tired hanging around tomorrow, paint the ceiling I put up in the living room.

BIFF: I'm leaving early tomorrow.

HAPPY: He's going to see Bill Oliver, Pop.

WILLY (*interestedly*): Oliver? For what?

BIFF (*with reserve, but trying, trying*): He always said he'd stake me. I'd like to go into business, so maybe I can take him up on it.

LINDA: Isn't that wonderful?

WILLY: Don't interrupt. What's wonderful about it? There's fifty men in the City of New York who'd stake him. (*To Biff.*) Sporting goods?

BIFF: I guess so. I know something about it and—

WILLY: He knows something about it! You know sporting goods better than Spalding, for God's sake! How much is he giving you?

BIFF: I don't know, I didn't even see him yet, but—

WILLY: Then what're you talkin' about?

BIFF (*getting angry*): Well, all I said was I'm gonna see him, that's all!

WILLY (*turning away*): Ah, you're counting your chickens again.

BIFF (*starting left for the stairs*): Oh, Jesus, I'm going to sleep!

WILLY (*calling after him*): Don't curse in this house!

BIFF (*turning*): Since when did you get so clean?

HAPPY (*trying to stop them*): Wait a . . .

WILLY: Don't use that language to me! I won't have it!

HAPPY (*grabbing Biff, shouts*): Wait a minute! I got an idea. I got a feasible idea. Come here, Biff, let's talk this over now, let's talk some sense here. When I was down in Florida last time, I thought of a great idea to sell sporting goods. It just came back to me. You and I, Biff—we have a line, the Loman Line. We train a couple of weeks, and put on a couple of exhibitions, see?

WILLY: That's an idea!

HAPPY: Wait! We form two basketball teams, see? Two water polo teams. We play each other. It's a million dollars' worth of publicity. Two brothers, see? The Loman Brothers. Displays in the Royal Palms—all the hotels. And banners over the ring and the basketball court: "Loman Brothers." Baby, we could sell sporting goods!

WILLY: That is a one-million-dollar idea!

LINDA: Marvelous!

BIFF: I'm in great shape as far as that's concerned.

HAPPY: And the beauty of it is, Biff, it wouldn't be like a business. We'd be out playin' ball again . . .

BIFF (*enthused*): Yeah, that's . . .

WILLY: Million-dollar . . .

HAPPY: And you wouldn't get fed up with it, Biff. It'd be the family again. There'd be the old honor, and comradeship, and if you wanted to go off for a swim or somethin'—well, you'd do it! Without some smart cooky gettin' up ahead of you!

WILLY: Lick the world! You guys together could absolutely lick the civilized world.

BIFF: I'll see Oliver tomorrow. Hap, if we could work that out . . .

LINDA: Maybe things are beginning to—

WILLY (*wildly enthused, to Linda*): Stop interrupting! (*To Biff.*) But don't wear sport jacket and slacks when you see Oliver.

BIFF: No, I'll—

WILLY: A business suit, and talk as little as possible, and don't crack any jokes.

BIFF: He did like me. Always liked me.

LINDA: He loved you!

WILLY (*to Linda*): Will you stop! (*To Biff.*) Walk in very serious. You are not applying for a boy's job. Money is to pass. Be quiet, fine, and serious. Everybody likes a kidder, but nobody lends him money.

HAPPY: I'll try to get some myself, Biff. I'm sure I can.

WILLY: I see great things for you kids, I think your troubles are over. But remember, start big and you'll end big. Ask for fifteen. How much you gonna ask for?

BIFF: Gee, I don't know—

WILLY: And don't say "Gee." "Gee" is a boy's word. A man walking in for fifteen thousand dollars does not say "Gee!"

BIFF: Ten, I think, would be top though.

WILLY: Don't be so modest. You always started too low. Walk in with a big laugh. Don't look worried. Start off with a couple of your good stories to lighten things up. It's not what you say, it's how you say it—because personality always wins the day.

LINDA: Oliver always thought the highest of him—

WILLY: Will you let me talk?

BIFF: Don't yell at her, Pop, will ye?

WILLY (*angrily*): I was talking, wasn't I?

BIFF: I don't like you yelling at her all the time, and I'm tellin' you, that's all.

WILLY: What're you, takin' over this house?

LINDA: Willy—

WILLY (*turning to her*): Don't take his side all the time, goddammit!

BIFF (*furiously*): Stop yelling at her!

WILLY (*suddenly pulling on his cheek, beaten down, guilt ridden*): Give my best to Bill Oliver—he may remember me. (*He exits through the living room doorway.*)

LINDA (*her voice subdued*): What'd you have to start that for? (*Biff turns away.*) You see how sweet he was as soon as you talked hopefully? (*She goes over to Biff.*) Come up and say good night to him. Don't let him go to bed that way.

HAPPY: Come on, Biff, let's buck him up.

LINDA: Please, dear. Just say good night. It takes so little to make him happy. Come. (*She goes through the living room doorway, calling upstairs from within the living room.*) Your pajamas are hanging in the bathroom, Willy!

HAPPY (*looking toward where Linda went out*): What a woman! They broke the mold when they made her. You know that, Biff?

BIFF: He's off salary. My God, working on commission!

HAPPY: Well, let's face it: he's no hot-shot selling man. Except that sometimes, you have to admit, he's a sweet personality.

BIFF (*deciding*): Lend me ten bucks, will ye? I want to buy some new ties.

HAPPY: I'll take you to a place I know. Beautiful stuff. Wear one of my striped shirts tomorrow.

BIFF: She got gray. Mom got awful old. Gee, I'm gonna go in to Oliver tomorrow and knock him for a—

HAPPY: Come on up. Tell that to Dad. Let's give him a whirl. Come on.

BIFF (*steamed up*): You know, with ten thousand bucks, boy!

HAPPY (*as they go into the living room*): That's the talk, Biff, that's the first time I've heard the old confidence out of you! (*From within the living room, fading off.*) You're gonna live with me, kid, and any babe you want just say the word . . . (*The last lines are hardly heard. They are mounting the stairs to their parents' bedroom.*)

LINDA (*entering her bedroom and addressing Willy, who is in the bathroom. She is straightening the bed for him.*): Can you do anything about the shower? It drips.

WILLY (*from the bathroom*): All of a sudden everything falls to pieces. Goddam plumbing, oughta be sued, those people. I hardly finished putting it in and the thing . . . (*His words rumble off.*)

LINDA: I'm just wondering if Oliver will remember him. You think he might?

WILLY (*coming out of the bathroom in his pajamas*): Remember him? What's the matter with you, you crazy? If he'd've stayed with Oliver he'd be on top by now! Wait'll Oliver gets a look at him. You don't know the average caliber any more. The average young man today—(*he is getting into bed*)—is got a caliber of zero. Greatest thing in the world for him was to bum around.

(*Biff and Happy enter the bedroom. Slight pause.*)

WILLY (*stops short, looking at Biff*): Glad to hear it, boy.

HAPPY: He wanted to say good night to you, sport.

WILLY (*to Biff*): Yeah. Knock him dead, boy. What'd you want to tell me?

BIFF: Just take it easy, Pop. Good night. (*He turns to go.*)

WILLY (*unable to resist*): And if anything falls off the desk while you're talking to him—like a package or something—don't you pick it up. They have office boys for that.

LINDA: I'll make a big breakfast—

WILLY: Will you let me finish? (*To Biff.*) Tell him you were in the business in the West. Not farm work.

BIFF: All right, Dad.

LINDA: I think everything—

WILLY (*going right through her speech*): And don't undersell yourself. No less than fifteen thousand dollars.

BIFF (*unable to bear him*): Okay. Good night, Mom. (*He starts moving.*)

WILLY: Because you got a greatness in you, Biff, remember that. You got all kinds of greatness . . . (*He lies back, exhausted. Biff walks out.*)

LINDA (*calling after Biff*): Sleep well, darling!

HAPPY: I'm gonna get married, Mom. I wanted to tell you.

LINDA: Go to sleep, dear.

HAPPY (*going*): I just wanted to tell you.

WILLY: Keep up the good work. (*Happy exits.*) God . . . remember that Ebbets Field game? The championship of the city?

LINDA: Just rest. Should I sing to you?

WILLY: Yeah. Sing to me. (*Linda hums a soft lullaby.*) When that team came out—he was the tallest, remember?

LINDA: Oh, yes. And in gold.

(*Biff enters the darkened kitchen, takes a cigarette, and leaves the house. He comes downstage into a golden pool of light. He smokes, staring at the night.*)

WILLY: Like a young god. Hercules—something like that. And the sun, the sun all around him. Remember how he waved to me? Right up from the field, with the representatives of three colleges standing by? And the buyers I brought, and the cheers when he came out—Loman, Loman, Loman! God Almighty, he'll be great yet. A star like that, magnificent, can never really fade away!

(*The light on Willy is fading. The gas heater begins to glow through the kitchen wall, near the stairs, a blue flame beneath red coils.*)

LINDA (*timidly*): Willy dear, what has he got against you?

WILLY: I'm so tired. Don't talk anymore.

(*Biff slowly returns to the kitchen. He stops, stares toward the heater.*)

LINDA: Will you ask Howard to let you work in New York?

WILLY: First thing in the morning. Everything'll be all right.

(*Biff reaches behind the heater and draws out a length of rubber tubing. He is horrified and turns his head toward Willy's room, still dimly lit, from which the strains of Linda's desperate but monotonous humming rise.*)

WILLY (*staring through the window into the moonlight*): Gee, look at the moon moving between the buildings!

(*Biff wraps the tubing around his hand and quickly goes up the stairs.*)

ACT II

(*Music is heard, gay and bright. The curtain rises as the music fades away. Willy, in shirt sleeves, is sitting at the kitchen table, sipping coffee, his hat in his lap. Linda is filling his cup when she can.*)

WILLY: Wonderful coffee. Meal in itself.

LINDA: Can I make you some eggs?

WILLY: No. Take a breath.

LINDA: You look so rested, dear.

WILLY: I slept like a dead one. First time in months. Imagine, sleeping till ten on a Tuesday morning. Boys left nice and early, heh?

LINDA: They were out of here by eight o'clock.

WILLY: Good work!

LINDA: It was so thrilling to see them leaving together. I can't get over the shaving lotion in this house!

WILLY (*smiling*): Mmm—

LINDA: Biff was very changed this morning. His whole attitude seemed to be hopeful. He couldn't wait to get downtown to see Oliver.

WILLY: He's heading for a change. There's no question, there simply are certain men that take longer to get—solidified. How did he dress?

LINDA: His blue suit. He's so handsome in that suit. He could be a—anything in that suit!

(*Willy gets up from the table. Linda holds his jacket for him.*)

WILLY: There's no question, no question at all. Gee, on the way home tonight I'd like to buy some seeds.

LINDA (*laughing*): That'd be wonderful. But not enough sun gets back there. Nothing'll grow any more.

WILLY: You wait, kid, before it's all over we're gonna get a little place out in the country, and I'll raise some vegetables, a couple of chickens . . .

LINDA: You'll do it yet, dear.

(*Willy walks out of his jacket. Linda follows him.*)

WILLY: And they'll get married, and come for a weekend. I'd build a little guest house. 'Cause I got so many fine tools, all I'd need would be a little lumber and some peace of mind.

LINDA (*joyfully*): I sewed the lining . . .

WILLY: I could build two guest houses, so they'd both come. Did he decide how much he's going to ask Oliver for?

LINDA (*getting him into the jacket*): He didn't mention it, but I imagine ten or fifteen thousand. You going to talk to Howard today?

WILLY: Yeah. I'll put it to him straight and simple. He'll just have to take me off the road.

LINDA: And Willy, don't forget to ask for a little advance, because we've got the insurance premium. It's the grace period now.

WILLY: That's a hundred . . . ?

LINDA: A hundred and eight, sixty-eight. Because we're a little short again.

WILLY: Why are we short?

LINDA: Well, you had the motor job on the car . . .

WILLY: That goddam Studebaker!

LINDA: And you got one more payment on the refrigerator . . .

WILLY: But it just broke again!

LINDA: Well, it's old, dear.

WILLY: I told you we should've bought a well-advertised machine. Charley bought a General Electric and it's twenty years old and it's still good, that son-of-a-bitch.

LINDA: But, Willy—

WILLY: Whoever heard of a Hastings refrigerator? Once in my life I would like to own something outright before it's broken! I'm always in a race with the junkyard! I just finished paying for the car and it's on its last legs. The refrigerator consumes belts like a goddamn maniac. They time those things. They time them so when you finally paid for them, they're used up.

LINDA (*buttoning up his jacket as he unbuttons it*): All told, about two hundred dollars would carry us, dear. But that includes the last payment on the mortgage. After this payment, Willy, the house belongs to us.

WILLY: It's twenty-five years!

LINDA: Biff was nine years old when we bought it.

WILLY: Well, that's a great thing. To weather a twenty-five year mortgage is—

LINDA: It's an accomplishment.

WILLY: All the cement, the lumber, the reconstruction I put in this house! There ain't a crack to be found in it anymore.

LINDA: Well, it served its purpose.

WILLY: What purpose? Some stranger'll come along, move in, and that's that. If only Biff would take this house, and raise a family . . . (*He starts to go.*) Goodby, I'm late.

LINDA (*suddenly remembering*): Oh, I forgot! You're supposed to meet them for dinner.

WILLY: Me?

LINDA: At Frank's Chop House on Forty-eighth near Sixth Avenue.

WILLY: Is that so! How about you?

LINDA: No, just the three of you. They're gonna blow you to a big meal!

WILLY: Don't say! Who thought of that?

LINDA: Biff came to me this morning, Willy, and he said, "Tell Dad, we want to blow him to a big meal." Be there six o'clock. You and your two boys are going to have dinner.

WILLY: Gee whiz! That's really somethin'. I'm gonna knock Howard for a loop, kid. I'll get an advance, and I'll come home with a New York job. Goddammit, now I'm gonna do it!

LINDA: Oh, that's the spirit, Willy!

WILLY: I will never get behind a wheel the rest of my life!

LINDA: It's changing, Willy, I can feel it changing!

WILLY: Beyond a question. G'by, I'm late. (*He starts to go again.*)

LINDA (*calling after him as she runs to the kitchen table for a handkerchief*): You got your glasses?

WILLY (*feels for them, then comes back in*): Yeah, yeah, got my glasses.

LINDA (*giving him the handkerchief*): And a handkerchief.

WILLY: Yeah, handkerchief.

LINDA: And your saccharine?

WILLY: Yeah, my saccharine.

LINDA: Be careful on the subway stairs.

(*She kisses him, and a silk stocking is seen hanging from her hand. Willy notices it.*)

WILLY: Will you stop mending stockings? At least while I'm in the house. It gets me nervous. I can't tell you. Please.

(*Linda hides the stocking in her hand as she follows Willy across the forestage in front of the house.*)

LINDA: Remember, Frank's Chop House.

WILLY (*passing the apron*): Maybe beets would grow out there.

LINDA (*laughing*): But you tried so many times.

WILLY: Yeah. Well, don't work hard today. (*He disappears around the right corner of the house.*)

LINDA: Be careful!

(*As Willy vanishes, Linda waves to him. Suddenly the phone rings. She runs across the stage and into the kitchen and lifts it.*)

LINDA: Hello? Oh, Biff! I'm so glad you called, I just . . . Yes, sure, I just told him. Yes, he'll be there for dinner at six o'clock, I didn't forget. Listen, I was just dying to tell you. You know that little rubber pipe I told you about? That he connected to the gas heater? I finally decided to go down the cellar this morning and take it away and destroy it. But it's gone! Imagine? He took it away himself, it isn't there! (*She listens.*) When? Oh, then you took it. Oh—nothing, it's just that I'd hoped he'd taken it away himself. Oh, I'm not worried, darling, because this morning he left in such high spirits, it was like the old days! I'm not afraid any more. Did Mr. Oliver see you? . . . Well, you wait there then. And make a nice impression on him, darling. Just don't perspire too much before you see him. And have a nice time with Dad. He may have big news too! . . . That's right, a New York job. And be sweet to him tonight, dear. Be loving to him. Because he's only a little boat looking for a harbor. (*She is trembling with sorrow and joy.*) Oh, that's wonderful, Biff, you'll save his life. Thanks, darling. Just put your arm around him when he comes into the restaurant. Give him a smile. That's the boy . . . Good-by, dear. . . . You got your comb? . . . That's fine. Good-by, Biff dear.

(*In the middle of her speech, Howard Wagner, thirty-six, wheels in a small typewriter table on which is a wire-recording machine and proceeds to plug it in. This is on the left forestage. Light slowly fades on Linda as it rises on Howard. Howard is intent on threading the machine and only glances over his shoulder as Willy appears.*)

WILLY: Pst! Pst!

HOWARD: Hello, Willy, come in.

WILLY: Like to have a little talk with you, Howard.

HOWARD: Sorry to keep you waiting. I'll be with you in a minute.

WILLY: What's that, Howard?

HOWARD: Didn't you ever see one of these? Wire recorder.

WILLY: Oh. Can we talk a minute?

HOWARD: Records things. Just got delivery yesterday. Been driving me crazy, the most terrific machine I ever saw in my life. I was up all night with it.

WILLY: What do you do with it?

HOWARD: I bought it for dictation, but you can do anything with it. Listen to this. I had it home last night. Listen to what I picked up. The first one is my daughter. Get this. (*He flicks the switch and "Roll out the Barrel" is heard being whistled.*) Listen to that kid whistle.

WILLY: That is lifelike, isn't it?

HOWARD: Seven years old. Get that tone.

WILLY: Ts, ts. Like to ask a little favor if you . . .

(*The whistling breaks off, and the voice of Howard's daughter is heard.*)

HIS DAUGHTER: Now you, Daddy.

HOWARD: She's crazy for me! (*Again the same song is whistled.*) That's me! Ha! (*He winks.*)

WILLY: You're very good!

(*The whistling breaks off again. The machine runs silent for a moment.*)

HOWARD: Sh! Get this now, this is my son.

HIS SON: "The capital of Alabama is Montgomery; the capital of Arizona is Phoenix; the capital of Arkansas is Little Rock; the capital of California is Sacramento . . ." (*and on, and on.*)

HOWARD (*holding up five fingers*): Five years old, Willy!

WILLY: He'll make an announcer some day!

HIS SON (*continuing*): "The capital . . . "

HOWARD: Get that—alphabetical order! (*The machine breaks off suddenly.*) Wait a minute. The maid kicked the plug out.

WILLY: It certainly is a—

HOWARD: Sh, for God's sake!

HIS SON: "It's nine o'clock, Bulova watch time. So I have to go to sleep."

WILLY: That really is—

HOWARD: Wait a minute! The next is my wife.

(*They wait.*)

HOWARD'S VOICE: "Go on, say something." (*Pause.*) "Well, you gonna talk?"

HIS WIFE: "I can't think of anything."

HOWARD'S VOICE: "Well, talk—it's turning."

HIS WIFE (*shyly, beaten*): "Hello." (*Silence.*) "Oh, Howard, I can't talk into this . . . "

HOWARD (*snapping the machine off*): That was my wife.

WILLY: That is a wonderful machine. Can we—

HOWARD: I tell you, Willy, I'm gonna take my camera, and my bandsaw, and all my hobbies, and out they go. This is the most fascinating relaxation I ever found.

WILLY: I think I'll get one myself.

HOWARD: Sure, they're only a hundred and a half. You can't do without it. Supposing you wanna hear Jack Benny, see? But you can't be at home at that hour. So you tell the maid to turn the radio on when Jack Benny comes on, and this automatically goes on with the radio . . .

WILLY: And when you come home you . . .

HOWARD: You can come home twelve o'clock, one o'clock, any time you like, and you get yourself a Coke and sit yourself down, throw the switch, and there's Jack Benny's program in the middle of the night!

WILLY: I'm definitely going to get one. Because lots of times I'm on the road, and I think to myself, what I must be missing on the radio!

HOWARD: Don't you have a radio in the car?

WILLY: Well, yeah, but who ever thinks of turning it on?

HOWARD: Say, aren't you supposed to be in Boston?

WILLY: That's what I want to talk to you about, Howard. You got a minute? (*He draws a chair in from the wing.*)

HOWARD: What happened? What're you doing here?

WILLY: Well . . .

HOWARD: You didn't crack up again, did you?

WILLY: Oh, no. No . . .

HOWARD: Geez, you had me worried there for a minute. What's the trouble?

WILLY: Well, tell you the truth, Howard. I've come to the decision that I'd rather not travel anymore.

HOWARD: Not travel! Well, what'll you do?

WILLY: Remember, Christmas time, when you had the party here? You said you'd try to think of some spot for me here in town.

HOWARD: With us?

WILLY: Well, sure.

HOWARD: Oh, yeah, yeah. I remember. Well, I couldn't think of anything for you, Willy.

WILLY: I tell ya, Howard. The kids are all grown up, y'know. I don't need much anymore. If I could take home—well, sixty-five dollars a week, I could swing it.

HOWARD: Yeah, but Willy, see I—

WILLY: I tell ya why, Howard. Speaking frankly and between the two of us, y'know—I'm just a little tired.

HOWARD: Oh, I could understand that, Willy. But you're a road man, Willy, and we do a road business. We've only got a half-dozen salesmen on the floor here.

WILLY: God knows, Howard, I never asked a favor of any man. But I was with the firm when your father used to carry you in here in his arms.

HOWARD: I know that, Willy, but—

WILLY: Your father came to me the day you were born and asked me what I thought of the name Howard, may he rest in peace.

HOWARD: I appreciate that, Willy, but there just is no spot here for you. If I had a spot I'd slam you right in, but I just don't have a single solitary spot.

(*He looks for his lighter. Willy has picked it up and gives it to him. Pause.*)

WILLY (*with increasing anger*): Howard, all I need to set my table is fifty dollars a week.

HOWARD: But where am I going to put you, kid?

WILLY: Look, it isn't a question of whether I can sell merchandise, is it?

HOWARD: No, but it's business, kid, and everybody's gotta pull his own weight.

WILLY (*desperately*): Just let me tell you a story, Howard—

HOWARD: 'Cause you gotta admit, business is business.

WILLY (*angrily*): Business is definitely business, but just listen for a minute. You don't understand this. When I was a boy—eighteen, nineteen—I was already on the road. And there was a question in my mind as to whether selling had a future for me. Because in those days I had a yearning to go to Alaska. See, there were three gold strikes in one month in Alaska, and I felt like going out. Just for the ride, you might say.

HOWARD (*barely interested*): Don't say.

WILLY: Oh, yeah, my father lived many years in Alaska. He was an adventurous man. We've got quite a little streak of self-reliance in our family. I thought I'd go out with my older brother and try to locate him, and maybe settle in the North with the old man. And I was almost decided to go, when I met a salesman in the Parker House. His name was Dave Singleman. And he was eighty-four years old, and he'd drummed merchandise in thirty-one states. And old Dave, he'd go up to his room, y'understand, put on his green velvet slippers—I'll never forget—and pick up his phone and call the buyers, and without ever leaving his room, at the age of eighty-four, he made his living. And when I saw that, I realized that selling was the greatest career a man could want. 'Cause what could be more satisfying than to be able to go, at the age of eighty-four, into twenty or thirty different cities, and pick up a phone, and be remembered and loved and helped by so many different people? Do you know? When he died—and by the way he died the death of a salesman, in his green velvet slippers in the smoker of the New York, New Haven and Hartford, going into Boston—when he died, hundreds of salesmen and buyers were at his funeral. Things were sad on a lotta trains for months after that. (*He stands up. Howard has not looked at him.*) In those days there was personality in it, Howard. There was respect and comradeship, and gratitude in it. Today, it's all cut and dried, and there's no chance for bringing friendship to bear—or personality. You see what I mean? They don't know me any more.

HOWARD (*moving away, to the right*): That's just the thing, Willy.

WILLY: If I had forty dollars a week—that's all I'd need. Forty dollars, Howard.

HOWARD: Kid, I can't take blood from a stone, I—

WILLY (*desperation is on him now*): Howard, the year Al Smith was nominated, your father came to me and—

HOWARD (*starting to go off*): I've got to see some people, kid.

WILLY (*stopping him*): I'm talking about your father! There were promises made across this desk! You mustn't tell me you've got people to see—I put thirty-four years into this firm, Howard, and now I can't pay my insurance! You can't eat the orange and throw the peel away—a man is not a piece of fruit! (*After a pause.*) Now pay attention. Your father—in 1928 I had a big year. I averaged a hundred and seventy dollars a week in commissions.

HOWARD (*impatiently*): Now, Willy, you never averaged—

WILLY (*banging his hand on the desk*): I averaged a hundred and seventy dollars a week in the year of 1928! And your father came to me—or rather I was in the office here—it was right over this desk—and he put his hand on my shoulder—

HOWARD (*getting up*): You'll have to excuse me, Willy, I gotta see some people. Pull yourself together. (*Going out.*) I'll be back in a little while.

(*On Howard's exit, the light on his chair grows very bright and strange.*)

WILLY: Pull myself together! What the hell did I say to him? My God, I was yelling at him! How could I? (*Willy breaks off, staring at the light, which occupies the chair, animating it. He approaches this chair, standing across the desk from it.*) Frank, Frank, don't you remember what you told me that time? How you put your hand on my shoulder, and Frank . . . (*He leans on the desk and as he speaks the dead man's name he accidentally switches on the recorder, and instantly)*

HOWARD'S SON: "... of New York is Albany. The capital of Ohio is Cincinnati, the capital of Rhode Island is ... " (*The recitation continues.*)

WILLY (*leaping away with fright, shouting*): Ha! Howard! Howard! Howard!

HOWARD (*rushing in*): What happened?

WILLY (*pointing at the machine, which continues nasally, childishly, with the capital cities*): Shut it off! Shut it off!

HOWARD (*pulling the plug out*): Look, Willy . . .

WILLY (*pressing his hands to his eyes*): I gotta get myself some coffee. I'll get some coffee . . .

(*Willy starts to walk out. Howard stops him.*)

HOWARD (*rolling up the cord*): Willy, look . . .

WILLY: I'll go to Boston.

HOWARD: Willy, you can't go to Boston for us.

WILLY: Why can't I go?

HOWARD: I don't want you to represent us. I've been meaning to tell you for a long time now.

WILLY: Howard, are you firing me?

HOWARD: I think you need a good long rest, Willy.

WILLY: Howard—

HOWARD: And when you feel better, come back, and we'll see if we can work something out.

WILLY: But I gotta earn money, Howard. I'm in no position to—

HOWARD: Where are your sons? Why don't your sons give you a hand?

WILLY: They're working on a very big deal.

HOWARD: This is no time for false pride, Willy. You go to your sons and you tell them that you're tired. You've got two great boys, haven't you?

WILLY: Oh, no question, no question, but in the meantime . . .

HOWARD: Then that's that, heh?

WILLY: All right, I'll go to Boston tomorrow.

HOWARD: No, no.

WILLY: I can't throw myself on my sons. I'm not a cripple!

HOWARD: Look, kid, I'm busy this morning.

WILLY (*grasping Howard's arm*): Howard, you've got to let me go to Boston!

HOWARD (*hard, keeping himself under control*): I've got a line of people to see this morning. Sit down, take five minutes, and pull yourself together, and then go home, will ya? I need the office, Willy. (*He starts to go, turns, remembering the recorder, starts to push off the table holding the recorder.*) Oh, yeah. Whenever you can this week, stop by and drop off the samples. You'll feel better, Willy, and then come back and we'll talk. Pull yourself together, kid, there's people outside.

(*Howard exits, pushing the table off left. Willy stares into space, exhausted. Now the music is heard—Ben's music—first distantly, then closer, closer. As Willy speaks, Ben enters from the right. He carries valise and umbrella.*)

WILLY: Oh, Ben, how did you do it? What is the answer? Did you wind up the Alaska deal already?

BEN: Doesn't take much time if you know what you're doing. Just a short business trip. Boarding ship in an hour. Wanted to say good-by.

WILLY: Ben, I've got to talk to you.

BEN (*glancing at his watch*): Haven't the time, William.

WILLY (*crossing the apron to Ben*): Ben, nothing's working out. I don't know what to do.

BEN: Now, look here, William. I've bought timberland in Alaska and I need a man to look after things for me.

WILLY: God, timberland! Me and my boys in those grand outdoors!

BEN: You've a new continent at your doorstep, William. Get out of these cities, they're full of talk and time payments and courts of law. Screw on your fists and you can fight for a fortune up there.

WILLY: Yes, yes! Linda, Linda!

(*Linda enters as of old, with the wash.*)

LINDA: Oh, you're back?

BEN: I haven't much time.

WILLY: No, wait! Linda, he's got a proposition for me in Alaska.

LINDA: But you've got—(*To Ben.*) He's got a beautiful job here.

WILLY: But in Alaska, kid, I could—

LINDA: You're doing well enough, Willy!

BEN (*to Linda*): Enough for what, my dear?

LINDA (*frightened of Ben and angry at him*): Don't say those things to him! Enough to be happy right here, right now. (*To Willy, while Ben laughs.*) Why must everybody conquer the world? You're well liked, and the boys love you, and someday—(*To Ben*)—why, old man Wagner told him just the other day that if he keeps it up he'll be a member of the firm, didn't he, Willy?

WILLY: Sure, sure. I am building something with this firm, Ben, and if a man is building something he must be on the right track, mustn't he?

BEN: What are you building? Lay your hand on it. Where is it?

WILLY (*hesitantly*): That's true, Linda, there's nothing.

LINDA: Why? (*To Ben.*) There's a man eighty-four years old—

WILLY: That's right, Ben, that's right. When I look at that man I say, what is there to worry about?

BEN: Bah!

WILLY: It's true, Ben. All he has to do is go into any city, pick up the phone, and he's making his living and you know why?

BEN (*picking up his valise*): I've got to go.

WILLY (*holding Ben back*): Look at this boy!

(*Biff, in his high school sweater, enters carrying suitcase. Happy carries Biff's shoulder guards, gold helmet, and football pants.*)

WILLY: Without a penny to his name, three great universities are begging for him, and from there the sky's the limit, because it's not what you do, Ben. It's who you know and the smile on your face! It's contacts, Ben, contacts! The whole wealth of Alaska passes over the lunch table at the Commodore Hotel, and that's the wonder, the wonder of this country, that a man can end with diamonds here on the basis of being liked! (*He turns to Biff.*) And that's why when you get out on that field today it's important. Because thousands of people will be rooting for you and loving you. (*To Ben, who has again begun to leave.*) And Ben! when he walks into a business office his name will sound out like a bell and all the doors will open to him! I've seen it, Ben, I've seen it a thousand times! You can't feel it with your hand like timber, but it's there!

BEN: Good-by, William.

WILLY: Ben, am I right? Don't you think I'm right? I value your advice.

BEN: There's a new continent at your doorstep, William. You could walk out rich. Rich! (*He is gone.*)

WILLY: We'll do it here, Ben! You hear me? We're gonna do it here!

(*Young Bernard rushes in. The gay music of the Boys is heard.*)

BERNARD: Oh, gee, I was afraid you left already!

WILLY: Why? What time is it?

BERNARD: It's half-past one!

WILLY: Well, come on, everybody! Ebbets Field next stop! Where's the pennants? (*He rushes through the wall-line of the kitchen and out into the living room.*)

LINDA (*to Biff*): Did you pack fresh underwear?

BIFF (*who has been limbering up*): I want to go!

BERNARD: Biff, I'm carrying your helmet, ain't I?

HAPPY: No, I'm carrying the helmet.

BERNARD: Oh, Biff, you promised me.

HAPPY: I'm carrying the helmet.

BERNARD: How am I going to get in the locker room?

LINDA: Let him carry the shoulder guards. (*She puts her coat and hat on in the kitchen.*)

BERNARD: Can I, Biff? 'Cause I told everybody I'm going to be in the locker room.

HAPPY: In Ebbets Field it's the clubhouse.

BERNARD: I meant the clubhouse. Biff!

HAPPY: Biff!

BIFF (*grandly, after a slight pause*): Let him carry the shoulder guards.

HAPPY (*as he gives Bernard the shoulder guards*): Stay close to us now.

(*Willy rushes in with the pennants.*)

WILLY (*handing them out*): Everybody wave when Biff comes out on the field. (*Happy and Bernard run off.*) You set now, boy?

(*The music has died away.*)

BIFF: Ready to go, Pop. Every muscle is ready.

WILLY (*at the edge of the apron*): You realize what this means?

BIFF: That's right, Pop.

WILLY (*feeling Biff's muscles*): You're comin' home this afternoon captain of the All-Scholastic Championship Team of the City of New York.

BIFF: I got it, Pop. And remember, pal, when I take off my helmet, that touchdown is for you.

WILLY: Let's go! (*He is starting out, with his arm around Biff, when Charley enters, as of old, in knickers.*) I got no room for you, Charley.

CHARLEY: Room? For what?

WILLY: In the car.

CHARLEY: You goin' for a ride? I wanted to shoot some casino.

WILLY (*furiously*): Casino! (*Incredulously.*) Don't you realize what today is?

LINDA: Oh, he knows, Willy. He's just kidding you.

WILLY: That's nothing to kid about!

CHARLEY: No, Linda, what's goin' on?

LINDA: He's playing in Ebbets Field.

CHARLEY: Baseball in this weather?

WILLY: Don't talk to him. Come on, come on! (*He is pushing them out.*)

CHARLEY: Wait a minute, didn't you hear the news?

WILLY: What?

CHARLEY: Don't you listen to the radio? Ebbets Field just blew up.

WILLY: You go to hell! (*Charley laughs. Pushing them out.*) Come on, come on! We're late.

CHARLEY (*as they go*): Knock a homer, Biff, knock a homer!

WILLY (*the last to leave, turning to Charley*): I don't think that was funny, Charley. This is the greatest day of his life.

CHARLEY: Willy, when are you going to grow up?

WILLY: Yeah, heh? When this game is over, Charley, you'll be laughing out of the other side of your face. They'll be calling him another Red Grange. Twenty-five thousand a year.

CHARLEY (*kidding*): Is that so?

WILLY: Yeah, that's so.

CHARLEY: Well, then, I'm sorry, Willy. But tell me something.

WILLY: What?

CHARLEY: Who is Red Grange?

WILLY: Put up your hands. Goddam you, put up your hands!

(*Charley, chuckling, shakes his head and walks away, around the left corner of the stage. Willy follows him. The music rises to a mocking frenzy.*)

WILLY: Who the hell do you think you are, better than everybody else? You don't know everything, you big, ignorant, stupid . . . Put up your hands!

(*Light rises, on the right side of the forestage, on a small table in the reception room of Charley's office. Traffic sounds are heard. Bernard, now mature, sits whistling to himself. A pair of tennis rackets and an overnight bag are on the floor beside him.*)

WILLY (*offstage*): What are you walking away for? Don't walk away! If you're going to say something say it to my face! I know you laugh at me behind my back. You'll laugh out of the other side of your god-dam face after this game. Touchdown! Touchdown! Eighty thousand people! Touchdown! Right between the goal posts.

(*Bernard is a quiet, earnest, but self-assured young man. Willy's voice is coming from right upstage now. Bernard lowers his feet off the table and listens. Jenny, his father's secretary, enters.*)

JENNY (*distressed*): Say, Bernard, will you go out in the hall?

BERNARD: What is that noise? Who is it?

JENNY: Mr. Loman. He just got off the elevator.

BERNARD (*getting up*): Who's he arguing with?

JENNY: Nobody. There's nobody with him. I can't deal with him anymore, and your father gets all upset everytime he comes. I've got a lot of typing to do, and your father's waiting to sign it. Will you see him?

WILLY (*entering*): Touchdown! Touch—(*He sees Jenny.*) Jenny, Jenny, good to see you. How're ya? Workin'? Or still honest?

JENNY: Fine. How've you been feeling?

WILLY: Not much any more, Jenny. Ha, ha! (*He is surprised to see the rackets.*)

BERNARD: Hello, Uncle Willy.

WILLY (*almost shocked*): Bernard! Well, look who's here! (*He comes quickly, guiltily, to Bernard and warmly shakes his hand.*)

BERNARD: How are you? Good to see you.

WILLY: What are you doing here?

BERNARD: Oh, just stopped by to see Pop. Get off my feet till my train leaves. I'm going to Washington in a few minutes.

WILLY: Is he in?

BERNARD: Yes, he's in his office with the accountant. Sit down.

WILLY (*sitting down*): What're you going to do in Washington?

BERNARD: Oh, just a case I've got there, Willy.

WILLY: That so? (*Indicating the rackets.*) You going to play tennis there?

BERNARD: I'm staying with a friend who's got a court.

WILLY: Don't say. His own tennis court. Must be fine people, I bet.

BERNARD: They are, very nice. Dad tells me Biff's in town.

WILLY (*with a big smile*): Yeah, Biff's in. Working on a very big deal, Bernard.

BERNARD: What's Biff doing?

WILLY: Well, he's been doing very big things in the West. But he decided to establish himself here. Very big. We're having dinner. Did I hear your wife had a boy?

BERNARD: That's right. Our second.

WILLY: Two boys! What do you know!

BERNARD: What kind of a deal has Biff got?

WILLY: Well, Bill Oliver—very big sporting-goods man—he wants Biff very badly. Called him in from the West. Long distance, carte blanche, special deliveries. Your friends have their own private tennis court?

BERNARD: You still with the old firm, Willy?

WILLY (*after a pause*): I'm—I'm overjoyed to see how you made the grade, Bernard, overjoyed. It's an encouraging thing to see a young man really—really—Looks very good for Biff—very—(*He breaks off, then.*) Bernard—(*He is so full of emotion, he breaks off again.*)

BERNARD: What is it, Willy?

WILLY (*small and alone*): What—what's the secret?

BERNARD: What secret?

WILLY: How—how did you? Why didn't he ever catch on?

BERNARD: I wouldn't know that, Willy.

WILLY (*confidentially, desperately*): You were his friend, his boyhood friend. There's something I don't understand about it. His life ended after that Ebbets Field game. From the age of seventeen nothing good ever happened to him.

BERNARD: He never trained himself for anything.

WILLY: But he did, he did. After high school he took so many correspondence courses. Radio mechanics; television; God knows what, and never made the slightest mark.

BERNARD (*taking off his glasses*): Willy, do you want to talk candidly?

WILLY (*rising, faces Bernard*): I regard you as a very brilliant man, Bernard. I value your advice.

BERNARD: Oh, the hell with the advice, Willy. I couldn't advise you. There's just one thing I've always wanted to ask you. When he was supposed to graduate, and the math teacher flunked him—

WILLY: Oh, that son-of-a-bitch ruined his life.

BERNARD: Yeah, but, Willy, all he had to do was go to summer school and make up that subject.

WILLY: That's right, that's right.

BERNARD: Did you tell him not to go to summer school?

WILLY: Me? I begged him to go. I ordered him to go!

BERNARD: Then why wouldn't he go?

WILLY: Why? Why! Bernard, that question has been trailing me like a ghost for the last fifteen years. He flunked the subject, and laid down and died like a hammer hit him!

BERNARD: Take it easy, kid.

WILLY: Let me talk to you—I got nobody to talk to. Bernard, Bernard, was it my fault? Y'see? It keeps going around in my mind, maybe I did something to him. I got nothing to give him.

BERNARD: Don't take it so hard.

WILLY: Why did he lay down? What is the story there? You were his friend!

BERNARD: Willy, I remember, it was June, and our grades came out. And he'd flunked math.

WILLY: That son-of-a-bitch!

BERNARD: No, it wasn't right then. Biff just got very angry, I remember, and he was ready to enroll in summer school.

WILLY (*surprised*): He was?

BERNARD: He wasn't beaten by it at all. But then, Willy, he disappeared from the block for almost a month. And I got the idea that he'd gone up to New England to see you. Did he have a talk with you then?

(*Willy stares in silence.*)

BERNARD: Willy?

WILLY (*with a strong edge of resentment in his voice*): Yeah, he came to Boston. What about it?

BERNARD: Well, just that when he came back—I'll never forget this, it always mystifies me. Because I'd thought so well of Biff, even though he'd always taken advantage of me. I loved him, Willy, y'know? And he came back after that month and took his sneakers—remember those sneakers with "University of Virginia" printed on them? He was so proud of those, wore them every day. And he took them down in the cellar, and burned them up in the furnace. We had a fist fight. It lasted at least half an hour. Just the two of us, punching each other down the cellar, and crying right through it. I've often thought of how strange it was that I knew he'd given up his life. What happened in Boston, Willy?

(*Willy looks at him as at an intruder.*)

BERNARD: I just bring it up because you asked me.

WILLY (*angrily*): Nothing. What do you mean, "What happened?" What's that got to do with anything?

BERNARD: Well, don't get sore.

WILLY: What are you trying to do, blame it on me? If a boy lays down is that my fault?

BERNARD: Now, Willy, don't get—

WILLY: Well, don't—don't talk to me that way! What does that mean, "What happened?"

(*Charley enters. He is in his vest, and he carries a bottle of bourbon.*)

CHARLEY: Hey, you're going to miss that train. (*He waves the bottle.*)

BERNARD: Yeah, I'm going. (*He takes the bottle.*) Thanks, Pop. (*He picks up his rackets and bag.*) Good-by, Willy, and don't worry about it. You know, "If at first you don't succeed . . ."

WILLY: Yes, I believe in that.

BERNARD: But sometimes, Willy, it's better for a man just to walk away.

WILLY: Walk away?

BERNARD: That's right.

WILLY: But if you can't walk away?

BERNARD (*after a slight pause*): I guess that's when it's tough. (*Extending his hand.*) Good-by, Willy.

WILLY (*shaking Bernard's hand*): Good-by, boy.

CHARLEY (*an arm on Bernard's shoulder*): How do you like this kid? Gonna argue a case in front of the Supreme Court.

BERNARD (*protesting*): Pop!

WILLY (*genuinely shocked, pained, and happy*): No! The Supreme Court!

BERNARD: I gotta run. "By, Dad!

CHARLEY: Knock 'em dead, Bernard!

(*Bernard goes off.*)

WILLY (*as Charley takes out his wallet*): The Supreme Court! And he didn't even mention it!

CHARLEY (*counting out money on the desk*): He don't have to—he's gonna do it.

WILLY: And you never told him what to do, did you? You never took any interest in him.

CHARLEY: My salvation is that I never took any interest in anything. There's some money—fifty dollars. I got an accountant inside.

WILLY: Charley, look . . . (*With difficulty.*) I got my insurance to pay. If you can manage it—I need a hundred and ten dollars.

(*Charley doesn't reply for a moment; merely stops moving.*)

WILLY: I'd draw it from my bank but Linda would know, and I . . .

CHARLEY: Sit down, Willy.

WILLY (*moving toward the chair*): I'm keeping an account of everything, remember. I'll pay every penny back. (*He sits.*)

CHARLEY: Now listen to me, Willy.

WILLY: I want you to know I appreciate . . .

CHARLEY (*sitting down on the table*): Willy, what're you doin'? What the hell is goin' on in your head?

WILLY: Why? I'm simply . . .

CHARLEY: I offered you a job. You make fifty dollars a week. And I won't send you on the road.

WILLY: I've got a job.

CHARLEY: Without pay? What kind of a job is a job without pay? (*He rises.*) Now, look, kid, enough is enough. I'm no genius but I know when I'm being insulted.

WILLY: Insulted!

CHARLEY: Why don't you want to work for me?

WILLY: What's the matter with you? I've got a job.

CHARLEY: Then what're you walkin' in here every week for?

WILLY (*getting up*): Well, if you don't want me to walk in here—

CHARLEY: I'm offering you a job.

WILLY: I don't want your goddam job!

CHARLEY: When the hell are you going to grow up?

WILLY (*furiously*): You big ignoramus, if you say that to me again I'll rap you one! I don't care how big you are! (*He's ready to fight.*)

(*Pause.*)

CHARLEY (*kindly, going to him*): How much do you need, Willy?

WILLY: Charley, I'm strapped. I'm strapped. I don't know what to do. I was just fired.

CHARLEY: Howard fired you?

WILLY: That snotnose. Imagine that? I named him. I named him Howard.

CHARLEY: Willy, when're you gonna realize that them things don't mean anything? You named him Howard, but you can't sell that. The only thing you got in this world is what you can sell. And the funny thing is that you're a salesman, and you don't know that.

WILLY: I've always tried to think otherwise, I guess. I always felt that if a man was impressive, and well liked, that nothing—

CHARLEY: Why must everybody like you? Who liked J. P. Morgan?° Was he impressive? In a Turkish bath he'd look like a butcher. But with his pockets on he was very well liked. Now listen, Willy, I know you don't like me, and nobody can say I'm in love with you, but I'll give you a job because—just for the hell of it, put it that way. Now what do you say?

WILLY: I—I just can't work for you, Charley.

CHARLEY: What're you, jealous of me?

WILLY: I can't work for you, that's all, don't ask me why.

CHARLEY (*angered, takes out more bills*): You been jealous of me all your life, you dammed fool! Here, pay your insurance. (*He puts the money in Willy's hand.*)

WILLY: I'm keeping strict accounts.

CHARLEY: I've got some work to do. Take care of yourself. And pay your insurance.

WILLY (*moving to the right*): Funny, y'know? After all the highways, and the trains, and the appointments, and the years, you end up worth more dead than alive.

CHARLEY: Willy, nobody's worth nothin' dead. (*After a slight pause.*) Did you hear what I said?

(*Willy stands still, dreaming.*)

CHARLEY: Willy!

WILLY: Apologize to Bernard for me when you see him. I didn't mean to argue with him. He's a fine boy. They're all fine boys, and they'll end up big—all of them. Someday they'll all play tennis together. Wish me luck, Charley. He saw Bill Oliver today.

CHARLEY: Good luck.

WILLY (*on the verge of tears*): Charley, you're the only friend I got. Isn't that a remarkable thing? (*He goes out.*)

CHARLEY: Jesus!

(*Charley stares after him a moment and follows. All light blacks out. Suddenly raucous music is heard, and a red glow rises behind the screen at right. Stanley, a young waiter, appears, carrying a table, followed by Happy, who is carrying two chairs.*)

STANLEY (*putting the table down*): That's all right, Mr. Loman, I can handle it myself. (*He turns and takes the chairs from Happy and places them at the table.*)

HAPPY (*glancing around*): Oh, this is better.

STANLEY: Sure, in the front there you're in the middle of all kinds of noise. Whenever you got a party, Mr. Loman, you just tell me and I'll put you back here. Y'know, there's a lotta people they don't like it private, because when they go out they like to see a lotta action around them because they're sick and tired to stay in the house by theirself. But I know you, you ain't from Hackensack. You know what I mean?

HAPPY (*sitting down*): So how's it coming, Stanley?

STANLEY: Ah, it's a dog life. I only wish during the war they'd a took me in the Army. I coulda been dead by now.

HAPPY: My brother's back, Stanley.

STANLEY: Oh, he come back, heh? From the Far West.

HAPPY: Yeah, big cattle man, my brother, so treat him right. And my father's coming too.

STANLEY: Oh, your father too!

HAPPY: You got a couple of nice lobsters?

STANLEY: Hundred percent, big.

HAPPY: I want them with the claws.

STANLEY: Don't worry, I don't give you no mice. (*Happy laughs.*) How about some wine? It'll put a head on the meal.

HAPPY: No. You remember, Stanley, that recipe I brought you from overseas? With the champagne in it?

STANLEY: Oh, yeah, sure. I still got it tacked up yet in the kitchen. But that'll have to cost a buck apiece anyways.

HAPPY: That's all right.

STANLEY: What'd you, hit a number or somethin'?

HAPPY: No, it's a little celebration. My brother is—I think he pulled off a big deal today. I think we're going into business together.

STANLEY: Great! That's the best for you. Because a family business, you know what I mean?—that's the best.

HAPPY: That's what I think.

STANLEY: 'Cause what's the difference? Somebody steals? It's in the family. Know what I mean? (*Sotto voce.*°) Like this bartender here. The boss is goin' crazy what kinda leak he's got in the cash register. You put it in but it don't come out.

HAPPY (*raising his head*): Sh!

STANLEY: What?

HAPPY: You notice I wasn't lookin' right or left, was I?

STANLEY: No.

HAPPY: And my eyes are closed.

STANLEY: So what's the—?

HAPPY: Strudel's comin'.

STANLEY (*catching on, looks around*): Ah, no, there's no—

(*He breaks off as a furred, lavishly dressed girl enters and sits at the next table. Both follow her with their eyes.*)

STANLEY: Geez, how'd ya know?

HAPPY: I got radar or something. (*Staring directly at her profile.*) Oooooooo . . . Stanley.

STANLEY: I think that's for you, Mr. Loman.

HAPPY: Look at that mouth. Oh, God. And the binoculars.

STANLEY: Geez, you got a life, Mr. Loman.

HAPPY: Wait on her.

STANLEY (*going to the girl's table*): Would you like a menu, ma'am?

GIRL: I'm expecting someone, but I'd like a—

HAPPY: Why don't you bring her—excuse me, miss, do you mind? I sell champagne, and I'd like you to try my brand. Bring her a champagne, Stanley.

GIRL: That's awfully nice of you.

HAPPY: Don't mention it. It's all company money. (*He laughs.*)

GIRL: That's a charming product to be selling, isn't it?

HAPPY: Oh, gets to be like everything else. Selling is selling, y'know.

J. P. Morgan: Wealthy financier and art collector (1837–1913), whose money was made chiefly in banking, railroads, and steel.

Sotto voce: In a soft voice or stage whisper.

GIRL: I suppose.

HAPPY: You don't happen to sell, do you?

GIRL: No, I don't sell.

HAPPY: Would you object to a compliment from a stranger? You ought to be on a magazine cover.

GIRL (*looking at him a little archly*): I have been.

(*Stanley comes in with a glass of champagne.*)

HAPPY: What'd I say before, Stanley? You see? She's a cover girl.

STANLEY: Oh, I could see, I could see.

HAPPY (*to the Girl*): What magazine?

GIRL: Oh, a lot of them. (*She takes the drink.*) Thank you.

HAPPY: You know what they say in France, don't you? "Champagne is the drink of the complexion"—Hya, Biff!

(*Biff has entered and sits with Happy.*)

BIFF: Hello, kid. Sorry I'm late.

HAPPY: I just got here. Uh, Miss—?

GIRL: Forsythe.

HAPPY: Miss Forsythe, this is my brother.

BIFF: Is Dad here?

HAPPY: His name is Biff. You might've heard of him. Great football player.

GIRL: Really? What team?

HAPPY: Are you familiar with football?

GIRL: No, I'm afraid I'm not.

HAPPY: Biff is quarterback with the New York Giants.

GIRL: Well, that is nice, isn't it? (*She drinks.*)

HAPPY: Good health.

GIRL: I'm happy to meet you.

HAPPY: That's my name. Hap. It's really Harold, but at West Point they called me Happy.

GIRL (*now really impressed*): Oh, I see. How do you do? (*She turns her profile.*)

BIFF: Isn't Dad coming?

HAPPY: You want her?

BIFF: Oh, I could never make that.

HAPPY: I remember the time that idea would never come into your head. Where's the old confidence, Biff?

BIFF: I just saw Oliver—

HAPPY: Wait a minute. I've got to see that old confidence again. Do you want her? She's on call.

BIFF: Oh, no. (*He turns to look at the Girl.*)

HAPPY: I'm telling you. Watch this. (*Turning to the Girl*): Honey? (*She turns to him.*) Are you busy?

GIRL: Well, I am . . . but I could make a phone call.

HAPPY: Do that, will you, honey? And see if you can get a friend. We'll be here for a while. Biff is one of the greatest football players in the country.

GIRL (*standing up*): Well, I'm certainly happy to meet you.

HAPPY: Come back soon.

GIRL: I'll try.

HAPPY: Don't try, honey, try hard.

(*The Girl exits. Stanley follows, shaking his head in bewildered admiration.*)

HAPPY: Isn't that a shame now? A beautiful girl like that? That's why I can't get married. There's not a good woman in a thousand. New York is loaded with them, kid!

BIFF: Hap, look—

HAPPY: I told you she was on call!

BIFF (*strangely unnerved*): Cut it out, will ya? I want to say something to you.

HAPPY: Did you see Oliver?

BIFF: I saw him all right. Now look, I want to tell Dad a couple of things and I want you to help me.

HAPPY: What? Is he going to back you?

BIFF: Are you crazy? You're out of your goddam head, you know that?

HAPPY: Why? What happened?

BIFF (*breathlessly*): I did a terrible thing today, Hap. It's been the strangest day I ever went through. I'm all numb, I swear.

HAPPY: You mean he wouldn't see you?

BIFF: Well, I waited six hours for him, see? All day. Kept sending my name in. Even tried to date his secretary so she'd get me to him, but no soap.

HAPPY: Because you're not showin' the old confidence Biff. He remembered you, didn't he?

BIFF (*stopping Happy with a gesture*): Finally, about five o'clock, he comes out. Didn't remember who I was or anything. I felt like such an idiot, Hap.

HAPPY: Did you tell him my Florida idea?

BIFF: He walked away. I saw him for one minute. I got so mad I could've torn the walls down! How the hell did I ever get the idea I was a salesman there? I even believed myself that I'd been a salesman for him! And then he gave me one look and—I realized what a ridiculous lie my whole life has been! We've been talking in a dream for fifteen years. I was a shipping clerk.

HAPPY: What'd you do?

BIFF (*with great tension and wonder*): Well, he left, see. And the secretary went out. I was all alone in the waiting room. I don't know what came over me, Hap. The next thing I know I'm in his office—paneled walls, everything. I can't explain it. I—Hap, I took his fountain pen.

HAPPY: Geez, did he catch you?

BIFF: I ran out. I ran down all eleven flights. I ran and ran and ran.

HAPPY: That was an awful dumb—what'd you do that for?

BIFF (*agonized*): I don't know, I just—wanted to take something, I don't know. You gotta help me, Hap. I'm gonna tell Pop.

HAPPY: You crazy? What for?

BIFF: Hap, he's got to understand that I'm not the man somebody lends that kind of money to. He thinks I've been spiting him all these years and it's eating him up.

HAPPY: That's just it. You tell him something nice.

BIFF: I can't.

HAPPY: Say you got a lunch date with Oliver tomorrow.

BIFF: So what do I do tomorrow?

HAPPY: You leave the house tomorrow and come back at night and say Oliver is thinking it over. And he thinks it over for a couple of weeks, and gradually it fades away and nobody's the worse.

BIFF: But it'll go on forever!

HAPPY: Dad is never so happy as when he's looking forward to something!

(*Willy enters.*)

HAPPY: Hello, scout!

WILLY: Gee, I haven't been here in years!

(*Stanley has followed Willy in and sets a chair for him. Stanley starts off but Happy stops him.*)

HAPPY: Stanley!

(*Stanley stands by, waiting for an order.*)

BIFF (*going to Willy with guilt, as to an invalid*): Sit down, Pop. You want a drink?

WILLY: Sure, I don't mind.

BIFF: Let's get a load on.

WILLY: You look worried.

BIFF: N-no. (*To Stanley.*) Scotch all around. Make it doubles.

STANLEY: Doubles, right. (*He goes.*)

WILLY: You had a couple already, didn't you?

BIFF: Just a couple, yeah.

WILLY: Well, what happened, boy? (*Nodding affirmatively, with a smile.*) Everything go all right?

BIFF (*takes a breath, then reaches out and grasps Willy's hand*): Pal . . . (*He is smiling bravely, and Willy is smiling too.*) I had an experience today.

HAPPY: Terrific, Pop.

WILLY: That so? What happened?

BIFF (*high, slightly alcoholic, above the earth*): I'm going to tell you everything from first to last. It's been a strange day. (*Silence. He looks around, composes himself as best he can, but his breath keeps breaking the rhythm of his voice.*) I had to wait quite a while for him, and—

WILLY: Oliver?

BIFF: Yeah, Oliver. All day, as a matter of cold fact. And a lot of—instances—facts, Pop, facts about my life came back to me. Who was it, Pop? Who ever said I was a salesman with Oliver?

WILLY: Well, you were.

BIFF: No, Dad, I was a shipping clerk.

WILLY: But you were practically—

BIFF (*with determination*): Dad, I don't know who said it first, but I was never a salesman for Bill Oliver.

WILLY: What're you talking about?

BIFF: Let's hold on to the facts tonight, Pop. We're not going to get anywhere bullin' around. I was a shipping clerk.

WILLY (*angrily*): All right, now listen to me—

BIFF: Why don't you let me finish?

WILLY: I'm not interested in stories about the past or any crap of that kind because the woods are burning, boys, you understand? There's a big blaze going on all around. I was fired today.

BIFF (*shocked*): How could you be?

WILLY: I was fired, and I'm looking for a little good news to tell your mother, because the woman has waited and the woman has suffered. The gist of it is that I haven't got a story left in my head, Biff. So don't give me a lecture about facts and aspects. I am not interested. Now what've you got to say to me?

(*Stanley enters with three drinks. They wait until he leaves.*)

WILLY: Did you see Oliver?

BIFF: Jesus, Dad!

WILLY: You mean you didn't go up there?

HAPPY: Sure he went up there.

BIFF: I did. I—saw him. How could they fire you?

WILLY (*on the edge of his chair*): What kind of a welcome did he give you?

BIFF: He won't even let you work on commission?

WILLY: I'm out! (*Driving.*) So tell me, he gave you a warm welcome?

HAPPY: Sure, Pop, sure!

BIFF (*driven*): Well, it was kind of—

WILLY: I was wondering if he'd remember you. (*To Happy.*) Imagine, man doesn't see him for ten, twelve years and gives him that kind of a welcome!

HAPPY: Damn right!

BIFF (*trying to return to the offensive*): Pop, look—

WILLY: You know why he remembered you, don't you? Because you impressed him in those days.

BIFF: Let's talk quietly and get this down to the facts, huh?

WILLY (*as though Biff had been interrupting*): Well, what happened? It's great news, Biff. Did he take you into his office or'd you talk in the waiting room?

BIFF: Well, he came in, see, and—

WILLY (*with a big smile*): What'd he say? Betcha he threw his arm around you.

BIFF: Well, he kinda—

WILLY: He's a fine man. (*To Happy.*) Very hard man to see, y'know.

HAPPY (*agreeing*): Oh, I know.

WILLY (*to Biff*): Is that where you had the drinks?

BIFF: Yeah, he gave me a couple of—no, no!

HAPPY (*cutting in*): He told him my Florida idea.

WILLY: Don't interrupt. (*To Biff.*) How'd he react to the Florida idea?

BIFF: Dad, will you give me a minute to explain?

WILLY: I've been waiting for you to explain since I sat down here! What happened? He took you into his office and what?

BIFF: Well—I talked. And—and he listened, see.

WILLY: Famous for the way he listens, y'know. What was his answer?

BIFF: His answer was—(*He breaks off, suddenly angry.*) Dad, you're not letting me tell you what I want to tell you!

WILLY (*accusing, angered*): You didn't see him, did you?

BIFF: I did see him!

WILLY: What'd you insult him or something? You insulted him, didn't you?

BIFF: Listen, will you let me out of it, will you just let me out of it!

HAPPY: What the hell!

WILLY: Tell me what happened!

BIFF (to Happy): I can't talk to him!

(A single trumpet note jars the ear. The light of green leaves stains the house, which holds the air of night and a dream. Young Bernard enters and knocks on the door of the house.)

YOUNG BERNARD (frantically): Mrs. Loman, Mrs. Loman!

HAPPY: Tell him what happened!

BIFF (to Happy): Shut up and leave me alone!

WILLY: No, no! You had to go and flunk math!

BIFF: What math? What're you talking about?

YOUNG BERNARD: Mrs. Loman, Mrs. Loman!

(Linda appears in the house, as of old.)

WILLY (wildly): Math, math, math!

BIFF: Take it easy, Pop!

YOUNG BERNARD: Mrs. Loman!

WILLY (furiously): If you hadn't flunked you'd've been set by now!

BIFF: Now, look, I'm gonna tell you what happened, and you're going to listen to me.

YOUNG BERNARD: Mrs. Loman!

BIFF: I waited six hours—

HAPPY: What the hell are you saying?

BIFF: I kept sending in my name but he wouldn't see me. So finally he . . . (He continues unheard as light fades low on the restaurant.)

YOUNG BERNARD: Biff flunked math!

LINDA: No!

YOUNG BERNARD: Birnbaum flunked him! They won't graduate him!

LINDA: But they have to. He's gotta go to the university. Where is he? Biff! Biff!

YOUNG BERNARD: No, he left. He went to Grand Central.

LINDA: Grand—You mean he went to Boston!

YOUNG BERNARD: Is Uncle Willy in Boston?

LINDA: Oh, maybe Willy can talk to the teacher. Oh, the poor, poor boy!

(Light on house area snaps out.)

BIFF (at the table, now audible, holding up a gold fountain pen): . . . so I'm washed up with Oliver, you understand? Are you listening to me?

WILLY (at a loss): Yeah, sure. If you hadn't flunked—

BIFF: Flunked what? What're you talking about?

WILLY: Don't blame everything on me! I didn't flunk math—you did! What pen?

HAPPY: That was awful dumb, Biff, a pen like that is worth—

WILLY (seeing the pen for the first time): You took Oliver's pen?

BIFF (weakening): Dad, I just explained it to you.

WILLY: You stole Bill Oliver's fountain pen!

BIFF: I didn't exactly steal it! That's just what I've been explaining to you!

HAPPY: He had it in his hand and just then Oliver walked in, so he got nervous and stuck it in his pocket!

WILLY: My God, Biff!

BIFF: I never intended to do it, Dad!

OPERATOR'S VOICE: Standish Arms, good evening!

WILLY (shouting): I'm not in my room!

BIFF (frightened): Dad, what's the matter? (He and Happy stand up.)

OPERATOR: Ringing Mr. Loman for you!

WILLY: I'm not there, stop it!

BIFF (horrified, gets down on one knee before Willy): Dad, I'll make good, I'll make good. (Willy tries to get to his feet. Biff holds him down.) Sit down now.

WILLY: No, you're no good, you're no good for anything.

BIFF: I am, Dad, I'll find something else, you understand? Now don't worry about anything. (He holds up Willy's face.) Talk to me, Dad.

OPERATOR: Mr. Loman does not answer. Shall I page him?

WILLY (attempting to stand, as though to rush and silence the Operator): No, no, no!

HAPPY: He'll strike something, Pop.

WILLY: No, no . . .

BIFF (desperately, standing over Willy): Pop, listen! Listen to me! I'm telling you something good. Oliver talked to his partner about the Florida idea. You listening? He—he talked to his partner, and he came to me . . . I'm going to be all right, you hear? Dad, listen to me, he said it was just a question of the amount!

WILLY: Then you . . . got it?

HAPPY: He's gonna be terrific, Pop!

WILLY (trying to stand): Then you got it, haven't you? You got it! You got it!

BIFF (agonized, holds Willy down): No, no. Look, Pop. I'm supposed to have lunch with them tomorrow. I'm just telling you this so you'll know that I can still make an impression, Pop. And I'll make good somewhere, but I can't go tomorrow, see?

WILLY: Why not? You simply—

BIFF: But the pen, Pop!

WILLY: You give it to him and tell him it was an oversight!

HAPPY: Sure, have lunch tomorrow!

BIFF: I can't say that—

WILLY: You were doing a crossword puzzle and accidentally used his pen!

BIFF: Listen, kid, I took those balls years ago, now I walk in with his fountain pen? That clinches it, don't you see? I can't face him like that! I'll try elsewhere.

PAGE'S VOICE: Paging Mr. Loman!

WILLY: Don't you want to be anything?

BIFF: Pop, how can I go back?

WILLY: You don't want to be anything, is that what's behind it?

BIFF (now angry at Willy for not crediting his sympathy): Don't take it that way! You think it was easy walking into that office after what I'd done to him? A team of horses couldn't have dragged me back to Bill Oliver!

WILLY: Then why'd you go?

BIFF: Why did I go? Why did I go! Look at you! Look at what's become of you!

(*Off left, The Woman laughs.*)

WILLY: Biff, you're going to go to that lunch tomorrow, or—

BIFF: I can't go. I've got no appointment!

HAPPY: Biff, for . . . !

WILLY: Are you spiting me?

BIFF: Don't take it that way! Goddammit!

WILLY (*strikes Biff and falters away from the table*): You rotten little louse! Are you spiting me?

THE WOMAN: Someone's at the door, Willy!

BIFF: I'm no good, can't you see what I am?

HAPPY (*separating them*): Hey, you're in a restaurant! Now cut it out, both of you! (*The girls enter.*) Hello, girls, sit down.

(*The Woman laughs, off left.*)

MISS FORSYTHE: I guess we might as well. This is Letta.

THE WOMAN: Willy, are you going to wake up?

BIFF (*ignoring Willy*): How're ya, miss, sit down. What do you drink?

MISS FORSYTHE: Letta might not be able to stay long.

LETTA: I gotta get up very early tomorrow. I got jury duty. I'm so excited! Were you fellows ever on a jury?

BIFF: No, but I been in front of them! (*The girls laugh.*) This is my father.

LETTA: Isn't he cute? Sit down with us, Pop.

HAPPY: Sit him down, Biff!

BIFF (*going to him*): Come on, slugger, drink us under the table. To hell with it! Come on, sit down, pal.

(*On Biff's last insistence, Willy is about to sit.*)

THE WOMAN (*now urgently*): Willy, are you going to answer the door!

(*The Woman's call pulls Willy back. He starts right, befuddled.*)

BIFF: Hey, where are you going?

WILLY: Open the door.

BIFF: The door?

WILLY: The washroom . . . the door . . . where's the door?

BIFF (*leading Willy to the left*): Just go straight down.

(*Willy moves left.*)

THE WOMAN: Willy, Willy, are you going to get up, get up, get up, get up?

(*Willy exits left.*)

LETTA: I think it's sweet you bring your daddy along.

MISS FORSYTHE: Oh, he isn't really your father!

BIFF (*at left, turning to her resentfully*): Miss Forsythe, you've just seen a prince walk by. A fine, troubled prince. A hard-working, unappreciated prince. A pal, you understand? A good companion. Always for his boys.

LETTA: That's so sweet.

HAPPY: Well, girls, what's the program? We're wasting time. Come on, Biff. Gather round. Where would you like to go?

BIFF: Why don't you do something for him?

HAPPY: Me!

BIFF: Don't you give a damn for him, Hap?

HAPPY: What're you talking about? I'm the one who—

BIFF: I sense it, you don't give a good goddam about him. (*He takes the rolled-up hose from his pocket and puts it on the table in front of Happy.*) Look what I found in the cellar, for Christ's sake. How can you bear to let it go on?

HAPPY: Me? Who goes away? Who runs off and—

BIFF: Yeah, but he doesn't mean anything to you. You could help him—I can't! Don't you understand what I'm talking about? He's going to kill himself, don't you know that?

HAPPY: Don't I know it! Me!

BIFF: Hap, help him! Jesus . . . help him . . . Help me, help me, I can't bear to look at his face! (*Ready to weep, he hurries out, up right.*)

HAPPY (*starting after him*): Where are you going?

MISS FORSYTHE: What's he so mad about?

HAPPY: Come on, girls, we'll catch up with him.

MISS FORSYTHE (*as Happy pushes her out*): Say, I don't like that temper of his!

HAPPY: He's just a little overstrung, he'll be all right!

WILLY (*off left, as The Woman laughs*): Don't answer! Don't answer!

LETTA: Don't you want to tell your father—

HAPPY: No, that's not my father. He's just a guy. Come on, we'll catch Biff, and, honey, we're going to paint this town! Stanley, where's the check! Hey, Stanley!

(*They exit. Stanley looks toward left.*)

STANLEY (*calling to Happy indignantly*): Mr. Loman! Mr. Loman!

(*Stanley picks up a chair and follows them off. Knocking is heard off left. The Woman enters, laughing. Willy follows her. She is in a black slip; he is buttoning his shirt. Raw, sensuous music accompanies their speech.*)

WILLY: Will you stop laughing? Will you stop?

THE WOMAN: Aren't you going to answer the door? He'll wake the whole hotel.

WILLY: I'm not expecting anybody.

THE WOMAN: Whyn't you have another drink, honey, and stop being so damn self-centered?

WILLY: I'm so lonely.

THE WOMAN: You know you ruined me, Willy? From now on, whenever you come to the office, I'll see that you go right through to the buyers. No waiting at my desk anymore, Willy. You ruined me.

WILLY: That's nice of you to say that.

THE WOMAN: Gee, you are self-centered! Why so sad? You are the saddest, self-centeredest soul I ever did see-saw. (*She laughs. He kisses her.*) Come on inside, drummer boy. It's silly to be dressing in the middle of the night. (*As knocking is heard.*) Aren't you going to answer the door?

WILLY: They're knocking on the wrong door.

THE WOMAN: But I felt the knocking. And he heard us talking in here. Maybe the hotel's on fire!

WILLY (*his terror rising*): It's a mistake.

THE WOMAN: Then tell him to go away!

WILLY: There's nobody there.

THE WOMAN: It's getting on my nerves, Willy. There's somebody standing out there and it's getting on my nerves!

WILLY (*pushing her away from him*): All right, stay in the bathroom here, and don't come out. I think there's a law in Massachusetts about it, so don't come out. It may be that new room clerk. He looked very mean. So don't come out. It's a mistake, there's no fire.

(*The knocking is heard again. He takes a few steps away from her, and she vanishes into the wing. The light follows him, and now he is facing Young Biff, who carries a suitcase. Biff steps toward him. The music is gone.*)

BIFF: Why didn't you answer?

WILLY: Biff! What are you doing in Boston?

BIFF: Why didn't you answer? I've been knocking for five minutes, I called you on the phone—

WILLY: I just heard you. I was in the bathroom and had the door shut. Did anything happen home?

BIFF: Dad—I let you down.

WILLY: What do you mean?

BIFF: Dad . . .

WILLY: Biffo, what's this about? (*Putting his arm around Biff.*) Come on, let's go downstairs and get you a malted.

BIFF: Dad, I flunked math.

WILLY: Not for the term?

BIFF: The term. I haven't got enough credits to graduate.

WILLY: You mean to say Bernard wouldn't give you the answers?

BIFF: He did, he tried, but I only got a sixty-one.

WILLY: And they wouldn't give you four points?

BIFF: Birnbaum refused absolutely. I begged him, Pop, but he won't give me those points. You gotta talk to him before they close the school. Because if he saw the kind of man you are, and you just talked to him in your way, I'm sure he'd come through for me. The class came right before practice, see, and I didn't go enough. Would you talk to him? He'd like you, Pop. You know the way you could talk.

WILLY: You're on. We'll drive right back.

BIFF: Oh, Dad, good work! I'm sure he'll change it for you!

WILLY: Go downstairs and tell the clerk I'm checkin' out. Go right down.

BIFF: Yes, sir! See, the reason he hates me, Pop—one day he was late for class so I got up at the blackboard and imitated him. I crossed my eyes and talked with a lithp.

WILLY (*laughing*): You did? The kids like it?

BIFF: They nearly died laughing!

WILLY: Yeah? What'd you do?

BIFF: The thquare root of thixthy twee is . . . (*Willy bursts out laughing; Biff joins.*) And in the middle of it he walked in!

(*Willy laughs and The Woman joins in offstage.*)

WILLY (*without hesitation*): Hurry downstairs and—

BIFF: Somebody in there?

WILLY: No, that was next door.

(*The Woman laughs offstage.*)

BIFF: Somebody got in your bathroom!

WILLY: No, it's the next room, there's a party—

THE WOMAN (*enters, laughing. She lisps this.*): Can I come in? There's something in the bathtub, Willy, and it's moving!

(*Willy looks at Biff, who is staring open-mouthed and horrified at The Woman.*)

WILLY: Ah—you better go back to your room. They must be finished painting by now. They're painting her room so I let her take a shower here. Go back, go back . . . (*He pushes her.*)

THE WOMAN (*resisting*): But I've got to get dressed, Willy, I can't—

WILLY: Get out of here! Go back, go back . . . (*Suddenly striving for the ordinary.*) This is Miss Francis, Biff, she's a buyer. They're painting her room. Go back, Miss Francis, go back . . .

THE WOMAN: But my clothes, I can't go out naked in the hall!

WILLY (*pushing her offstage*): Get outa here! Go back, go back!

(*Biff slowly sits down on his suitcase as the argument continues offstage.*)

THE WOMAN: Where's my stockings? You promised me stockings, Willy!

WILLY: I have no stockings here!

THE WOMAN: You had two boxes of size nine sheers for me, and I want them!

WILLY: Here, for God's sake, will you get outa here!

THE WOMAN (*enters holding a box of stockings*): I just hope there's nobody in the hall. That's all I hope. (*To Biff.*) Are you football or baseball?

BIFF: Football.

THE WOMAN (*angry, humiliated*): That's me too. G'night. (*She snatches her clothes from Willy, and walks out.*)

WILLY (*after a pause*): Well, better get going. I want to get to the school first thing in the morning. Get my suits out of the closet. I'll get my valise. (*Biff doesn't move.*) What's the matter! (*Biff remains motionless, tears falling.*) She's a buyer. Buys for J. H. Simmons. She lives down the hall—they're painting. You don't imagine—(*He breaks off. After a pause.*) Now listen, pal, she's just a buyer. She sees merchandise in her room and they have to keep it looking just so . . . (*Pause. Assuming command.*) All right, get my suits. (*Biff doesn't move.*) Now stop crying and do as I say. I gave you an order. Biff, I gave you an order! Is that what you do when I give you an order? How dare you cry! (*Putting his arm around Biff.*) Now look, Biff, when you grow up you'll understand about these things. You mustn't—you mustn't overemphasize a thing like this. I'll see Birnbaum first thing in the morning.

BIFF: Never mind.

WILLY (*getting down beside Biff*): Never mind! He's going to give you those points. I'll see to it.

BIFF: He wouldn't listen to you.

WILLY: He certainly will listen to me. You need those points for the U. of Virginia.

BIFF: I'm not going there.

WILLY: Heh? If I can't get him to change that mark you'll make it up in summer school. You've got all summer to—

BIFF (*his weeping breaking from him*): Dad . . .

WILLY (*infected by it*): Oh, my boy . . .

BIFF: Dad . . .

WILLY: She's nothing to me, Biff. I was lonely, I was terribly lonely.

BIFF: You—you gave her Mama's stockings! (*His tears break through and he rises to go.*)

WILLY (*grabbing for Biff*): I gave you an order!

BIFF: Don't touch me, you—liar!

WILLY: Apologize for that!

BIFF: You fake! You phony little fake! You fake! (*Overcome, he turns quickly and weeping fully goes out with his suitcase. Willy is left on the floor on his knees.*)

WILLY: I gave you an order! Biff, come back here or I'll beat you! Come back here! I'll whip you!

(*Stanley comes quickly in from the right and stands in front of Willy.*)

WILLY (*shouts at Stanley*): I gave you an order . . .

STANLEY: Hey, let's pick it up, pick it up, Mr. Loman. (*He helps Willy to his feet.*) Your boys left with the chippies. They said they'll see you home.

(*A second waiter watches some distance away.*)

WILLY: But we were supposed to have dinner together.

(*Music is heard, Willy's theme.*)

STANLEY: Can you make it?

WILLY: I'll—sure, I can make it. (*Suddenly concerned about his clothes.*) Do I—I look all right?

STANLEY: Sure, you look all right. (*He flicks a speck off Willy's lapel.*)

WILLY: Here—here's a dollar.

STANLEY: Oh, your son paid me. It's all right.

WILLY (*putting it in Stanley's hand*): No, take it. You're a good boy.

STANLEY: Oh, no, you don't have to . . .

WILLY: Here—here's some more, I don't need it anymore. (*After a slight pause.*) Tell me—is there a seed store in the neighborhood?

STANLEY: Seeds? You mean like to plant?

(*As Willy turns, Stanley slips the money back into his jacket pocket.*)

WILLY: Yes. Carrots, peas . . .

STANLEY: Well, there's hardware stores on Sixth Avenue, but it may be too late now.

WILLY (*anxiously*): Oh, I'd better hurry. I've got to get some seeds. (*He starts off to the right.*) I've got to get some seeds, right away. Nothing's planted. I don't have a thing in the ground.

(*Willy hurries out as the light goes down. Stanley moves over to the right after him, watches him off. The other waiter has been staring at Willy.*)

STANLEY (*to the waiter*): Well, whatta you looking at?

(*The waiter picks up the chairs and moves off right. Stanley takes the table and follows him. The light fades on this area. There is a long pause, the sound of the flute coming over. The light gradually rises on the kitchen, which is empty. Happy appears at the door of the house, followed by Biff. Happy is carrying a large bunch of long-stemmed roses. He enters the kitchen, looks around for Linda. Not seeing her, he turns to Biff, who is just outside the house door, and makes a gesture with his hands, indicating "Not here, I guess." He looks into the living room and freezes. Inside, Linda, unseen, is seated, Willy's coat on her lap. She rises ominously and quietly and moves toward Happy, who backs up into the kitchen, afraid.*)

HAPPY: Hey, what're you doing up? (*Linda says nothing but moves toward him implacably.*) Where's Pop? (*He keeps backing to the right, and now Linda is in full view in the doorway to the living room.*) Is he sleeping?

LINDA: Where were you?

HAPPY (*trying to laugh it off*): We met two girls, Mom, very fine types. Here, we brought you some flowers. (*Offering them to her.*) Put them in your room, Ma.

(*She knocks them to the floor at Biff's feet. He has now come inside and closed the door behind him. She stares at Biff, silent.*)

HAPPY: Now what'd you do that for? Mom, I want you to have some flowers—

LINDA (*cutting Happy off, violently to Biff*): Don't you care whether he lives or dies?

HAPPY (*going to the stairs*): Come upstairs, Biff.

BIFF (*with a flare of disgust, to Happy*): Go away from me! (*To Linda.*) What do you mean, lives or dies? Nobody's dying around here, pal.

LINDA: Get out of my sight! Get out of here!

BIFF: I wanna see the boss.

LINDA: You're not going near him!

BIFF: Where is he? (*He moves into the living room and Linda follows.*)

LINDA (*shouting after Biff*): You invite him for dinner. He looks forward to it all day—(*Biff appears in his parents' bedroom, looks around, and exits*)—and then you desert him there. There's no stranger you'd do that to!

HAPPY: Why? He had a swell time with us. Listen, when I—(*Linda comes back into the kitchen*)—desert him I hope I don't outlive the day!

LINDA: Get out of here!

HAPPY: Now look, Mom . . .

LINDA: Did you have to go to women tonight? You and your lousy rotten whores!

(*Biff reenters the kitchen.*)

HAPPY: Mom, all we did was follow Biff around trying to cheer him up! (*To Biff.*) Boy, what a night you gave me!

LINDA: Get out of here, both of you, and don't come back! I don't want you tormenting him any more. Go on now, get your things together! (*To Biff.*) You can sleep in his apartment. (*She starts to pick up the flowers and stops herself.*) Pick up this stuff, I'm not your maid anymore. Pick it up, you bum, you!

(*Happy turns his back to her in refusal. Biff slowly moves over and gets down on his knees, picking up the flowers.*)

LINDA: You're a pair of animals! Not one, not another living soul would have had the cruelty to walk out on that man in a restaurant!

BIFF (*not looking at her*): Is that what he said?

LINDA: He didn't have to say anything. He was so humiliated he nearly limped when he came in.

HAPPY: But, Mom, he had a great time with us—

BIFF (*cutting him off violently*): Shut up!

(*Without another word, Happy goes upstairs.*)

LINDA: You! You didn't even go in to see if he was all right!

BIFF (*still on the floor in front of Linda, the flowers in his hand; with self-loathing*): No. Didn't. Didn't do a damned thing. How do you like that, heh? Left him babbling in a toilet.

LINDA: You louse. You . . .

BIFF: Now you hit it on the nose! (*He gets up, throws the flowers in the wastebasket.*) The scum of the earth, and you're looking at him!

LINDA: Get out of here!

BIFF: I gotta talk to the boss, Mom. Where is he?

LINDA: You're not going near him. Get out of this house!

BIFF (*with absolute assurance, determination*): No. We're gonna have an abrupt conversation, him and me.

LINDA: You're not talking to him.

(*Hammering is heard from outside the house, off right. Biff turns toward the noise.*)

LINDA (*suddenly pleading*): Will you please leave him alone?

BIFF: What's he doing out there?

LINDA: He's planting the garden!

BIFF (*quietly*): Now? Oh, my God!

(*Biff moves outside, Linda following. The light dies down on them and comes up on the center of the apron as Willy walks into it. He is carrying a flashlight, a hoe, and a handful of seed packets. He raps the top of the hoe sharply to fix it firmly, and then moves to the left, measuring off the distance with his foot. He holds the flashlight to look at the seed packets, reading off the instructions. He is in the blue of night.*)

WILLY: Carrots . . . quarter-inch apart. Rows . . . one-foot rows. (*He measures it off.*) One foot. (*He puts down a package and measures off.*) Beets. (*He puts down another package and measures again.*) Lettuce. (*He reads the package, puts it down.*) One foot—(*He breaks off as Ben appears at the right and moves slowly down to him.*) What a proposition, ts, ts. Terrific, terrific. 'Cause she's suffered, Ben, the woman has suffered. You understand me? A man can't go out the way he came in, Ben, a man has got to add up to something. You can't, you can't—(*Ben moves toward him as though to interrupt.*) You gotta consider, now. Don't answer so quick. Remember, it's a guaranteed twenty-thousand-dollar proposition. Now look, Ben, I want you to go through the ins and outs of this thing with me. I've got nobody to talk to, Ben, and the woman has suffered, you hear me?

BEN (*standing still, considering*): What's the proposition?

WILLY: It's twenty thousand dollars on the barrelhead. Guaranteed, gilt-edged, you understand?

BEN: You don't want to make a fool of yourself. They might not honor the policy.

WILLY: How can they dare refuse? Didn't I work like a coolie to meet every premium on the nose? And now they don't pay off? Impossible!

BEN: It's called a cowardly thing, William.

WILLY: Why? Does it take more guts to stand here the rest of my life ringing up a zero?

BEN (*yielding*): That's a point, William. (*He moves, thinking, turns.*) And twenty thousand—that is something one can feel with the hand, it is there.

WILLY (*now assured, with rising power*): Oh, Ben, that's the whole beauty of it! I see it like a diamond, shining in the dark, hard and rough, that I can pick up and touch in my hand. Not like—like an appointment! This would not be another damned-fool appointment, Ben, and it changes all the aspects. Because he thinks I'm nothing, see, and so he spites me. But the funeral—(*Straightening up.*) Ben, that funeral will be massive! They'll come from Maine, Massachusetts, Vermont, New Hampshire! All the old-timers with the strange license plates—that boy will be thunderstruck, Ben, because he never realized—I am known! Rhode Island, New York, New Jersey—I am known, Ben and he'll see it with his eyes once and for all. He'll see what I am, Ben! He's in for a shock, that boy!

BEN (*coming down to the edge of the garden*): He'll call you a coward.

WILLY (*suddenly fearful*): No, that would be terrible.

BEN: Yes. And a damned fool.

WILLY: No, no, he mustn't, I won't have that! (*He is broken and desperate.*)

BEN: He'll hate you, William.

(*The gay music of the Boys is heard.*)

WILLY: Oh, Ben, how do we get back to all the great times? Used to be so full of light, and comradeship, the sleigh-riding in winter, and the ruddiness on his cheeks. And always some kind of good news coming up, always something nice coming up ahead. And never even let me carry the valises in the house, and simonizing, simonizing that little red car! Why, why can't I give him something and not have him hate me?

BEN: Let me think about it. (*He glances at his watch.*) I still have a little time. Remarkable proposition, but you've got to be sure you're not making a fool of yourself.

(*Ben drifts off upstage and goes out of sight. Biff comes down from the left.*)

WILLY (*suddenly conscious of Biff, turns and looks up at him, then begins picking up the packages of seeds in confusion*): Where the hell is that seed? (*Indignantly.*) You can't see nothing out here! They boxed in the whole goddam neighborhood!

BIFF: There are people all around here. Don't you realize that?

WILLY: I'm busy. Don't bother me.

BIFF (*taking the hoe from Willy*): I'm saying good-by to you, Pop. (*Willy looks at him, silent, unable to move.*) I'm not coming back any more.

WILLY: You're not going to see Oliver tomorrow?

BIFF: I've got no appointment, Dad.

WILLY: He put his arm around you, and you've got no appointment?

BIFF: Pop, get this now, will you? Everytime I've left it's been a fight that sent me out of here. Today I realized something about myself and I tried to explain it to you and I—I think I'm just not smart enough to make any sense out of it for you. To hell with whose fault it is or anything like that. (*He takes Willy's arm.*) Let's just wrap it up, heh? Come on in, we'll tell Mom. (*He gently tries to pull Willy to left.*)

WILLY (*frozen, immobile, with guilt in his voice*): No, I don't want to see her.

BIFF: Come on! (*He pulls again, and Willy tries to pull away.*)

WILLY (*highly nervous*): No, no, I don't want to see her.

BIFF (*tries to look into Willy's face, as if to find the answer there*): Why don't you want to see her?

WILLY (*more harshly now*): Don't bother me, will you?

BIFF: What do you mean, you don't want to see her? You don't want them calling you yellow, do you? This isn't your fault; it's me, I'm a bum. Now come inside! (*Willy strains to get away.*) Did you hear what I said to you?

(*Willy pulls away and quickly goes by himself into the house. Biff follows.*)

LINDA (*to Willy*): Did you plant, dear?

BIFF (*at the door, to Linda*): All right, we had it out. I'm going and I'm not writing any more.

LINDA (*going to Willy in the kitchen*): I think that's the best way, dear. 'Cause there's no use drawing it out, you'll just never get along.

(*Willy doesn't respond.*)

BIFF: People ask where I am and what I'm doing, you don't know, and you don't care. That way it'll be off your mind and you can start brightening up again. All right? That clears it, doesn't it? (*Willy is silent, and Biff goes to him.*) You gonna wish me luck, scout? (*He extends his hand.*) What do you say?

LINDA: Shake his hand, Willy.

WILLY (*turning to her, seething with hurt*): There's no necessity to mention the pen at all, y'know.

BIFF (*gently*): I've got no appointment, Dad.

WILLY (*erupting fiercely*): He put his arm around . . . ?

BIFF: Dad, you're never going to see what I am, so what's the use of arguing? If I strike oil I'll send you a check. Meantime forget I'm alive.

WILLY (*to Linda*): Spite, see?

BIFF: Shake hands, Dad.

WILLY: Not my hand.

BIFF: I was hoping not to go this way.

WILLY: Well, this is the way you're going. Good-by.

(*Biff looks at him a moment, then turns sharply and goes to the stairs.*)

WILLY (*stops him with*): May you rot in hell if you leave this house!

BIFF (*turning*): Exactly what is it that you want from me?

WILLY: I want you to know, on the train, in the mountains, in the valleys, wherever you go, that you cut down your life for spite!

BIFF: No, no.

WILLY: Spite, spite, is the word of your undoing! And when you're down and out, remember what did it. When you're rotting somewhere beside the railroad tracks, remember, and don't you dare blame it on me!

BIFF: I'm not blaming it on you!

WILLY: I won't take the rap for this, you hear?

(*Happy comes down the stairs and stands on the bottom step, watching.*)

BIFF: That's just what I'm telling you!

WILLY (*sinking into a chair at a table, with full accusation*): You're trying to put a knife in me—don't think I don't know what you're doing!

BIFF: All right, phony! Then let's lay it on the line. (*He whips the rubber tube out of his pocket and puts it on the table.*)

HAPPY: You crazy . . .

LINDA: Biff! (*She moves to grab the hose, but Biff holds it down with his hand.*)

BIFF: Leave it there! Don't move it!

WILLY (*not looking at it*): What is that?

BIFF: You know goddam well what that is.

WILLY (*caged, wanting to escape*): I never saw that.

BIFF: You saw it. The mice didn't bring it into the cellar! What is this supposed to do, make a hero out of you? This supposed to make me sorry for you?

WILLY: Never heard of it.

BIFF: There'll be no pity for you, you hear it? No pity!

WILLY (*to Linda*): You hear the spite!

BIFF: No, you're going to hear the truth—what you are and what I am!

LINDA: Stop it!

WILLY: Spite!

HAPPY (*coming down toward Biff*): You cut it now!

BIFF (*to Happy*): The man don't know who we are! The man is gonna know! (*To Willy.*) We never told the truth for ten minutes in this house!

Dustin Hoffman as
Willy Loman in the 1985
television version of *Death of a
Salesman.*

HAPPY: We always told the truth!

BIFF (*turning on him*): You big blow, are you the assistant buyer? You're one of the two assistants to the assistant, aren't you?

HAPPY: Well, I'm practically . . .

BIFF: You're practically full of it! We all are! and I'm through with it. (*To Willy.*) Now hear this, Willy, this is me.

WILLY: I know you!

BIFF: You know why I had no address for three months? I stole a suit in Kansas City and I was in jail. (*To Linda, who is sobbing.*) Stop crying. I'm through with it.

(*Linda turns away from them, her hands covering her face.*)

WILLY: I suppose that's my fault!

BIFF: I stole myself out of every good job since high school!

WILLY: And whose fault is that?

BIFF: And I never got anywhere because you blew me so full of hot air I could never stand taking orders from anybody! That's whose fault it is!

WILLY: I hear that!

LINDA: Don't, Biff!

BIFF: It's goddam time you heard that! I had to be boss big shot in two weeks, and I'm through with it!

WILLY: Then hang yourself! For spite, hang yourself!

BIFF: No! Nobody's hanging himself, Willy! I ran down eleven flights with a pen in my hand today. And suddenly I stopped, you hear me? And in the middle of that office building, do you hear this? I stopped in the middle of that building and I saw—the sky. I saw the things that I love in this world. The work and the food and time to sit and smoke. And I looked at the pen and said to myself, what the hell am I grabbing this for? Why am I trying to become what I don't want to be? What am I doing in an office, making a contemptuous begging fool of myself, when all I want is out there, waiting for me the minute I say I know who I am! Why can't I say that, Willy? (*He tries to make Willy face him, but Willy pulls away and moves to the left.*)

WILLY (*with hatred, threateningly*): The door of your life is wide open!

BIFF: Pop! I'm a dime a dozen, and so are you!

WILLY (*turning on him now in an uncontrolled outburst*): I am not a dime a dozen! I am Willy Loman, and you are Biff Loman!

(*Biff starts for Willy, but is blocked by Happy. In his fury, Biff seems on the verge of attacking his father.*)

BIFF: I am not a leader of men, Willy, and neither are you. You were never anything but a hard-working drummer who landed in the ash can like all the rest of them! I'm one dollar an hour, Willy! I tried seven states and couldn't raise it. A buck an hour! Do you gather my meaning? I'm not bringing home any prizes any more, and you're going to stop waiting for me to bring them home!

WILLY (*directly to Biff*): You vengeful, spiteful mutt!

(*Biff breaks from Happy. Willy, in fright, starts up the stairs. Biff grabs him.*)

BIFF (*at the peak of his fury*): Pop, I'm nothing! I'm nothing, Pop. Can't you understand that? There's no spite in it any more. I'm just what I am, that's all.

(*Biff's fury has spent itself and he breaks down, sobbing, holding on to Willy, who dumbly fumbles for Biff's face.*)

WILLY (*astonished*): What're you doing? What're you doing? (*To Linda.*) Why is he crying?

BIFF (*crying, broken*): Will you let me go, for Christ's sake? Will you take that phony dream and burn it before something happens? (*Struggling to contain himself he pulls away and moves to the stairs.*) I'll go in the morning. Put him—put him to bed. (*Exhausted, Biff moves up the stairs to his room.*)

WILLY (*after a long pause, astonished, elevated*): Isn't that—isn't that remarkable? Biff—he likes me!

LINDA: He loves you, Willy!

HAPPY (*deeply moved*): Always did, Pop.

WILLY: Oh, Biff! (*Staring wildly.*) He cried! Cried to me. (*He is choking with his love, and now cries out his promise.*) That boy—that boy is going to be magnificent!

(*Ben appears in the light just outside the kitchen.*)

BEN: Yes, outstanding, with twenty thousand behind him.

LINDA (*sensing the racing of his mind, fearfully, carefully*): Now come to bed, Willy. It's all settled now.

WILLY (*finding it difficult not to rush out of the house*): Yes, we'll sleep. Come on. Go to sleep, Hap.

BEN: And it does take a great kind of a man to crack the jungle.

(*In accents of dread, Ben's idyllic music starts up.*)

HAPPY (*his arm around Linda*): I'm getting married, Pop, don't forget it. I'm changing everything. I'm gonna run that department before the year is up. You'll see, Mom. (*He kisses her.*)

BEN: The jungle is dark but full of diamonds, Willy.

(*Willy turns, moves, listening to Ben.*)

LINDA: Be good. You're both good boys, just act that way, that's all.

HAPPY: 'Night, Pop. (*He goes upstairs.*)

LINDA (*to Willy*): Come, dear.

BEN (*with greater force*): One must go in to fetch a diamond out.

WILLY (*to Linda, as he moves slowly along the edge of kitchen, toward the door*): I just want to get settled down, Linda. Let me sit alone for a little.

LINDA (*almost uttering her fear*): I want you upstairs.

WILLY (*taking her in his arms*): In a few minutes, Linda. I couldn't sleep right now. Go on, you look awful tired. (*He kisses her.*)

BEN: Not like an appointment at all. A diamond is rough and hard to the touch.

WILLY: Go on now. I'll be right up.

LINDA: I think this is the only way, Willy.

WILLY: Sure, it's the best thing.

BEN: Best thing!

WILLY: The only way. Everything is gonna be—go on, kid, get to bed. You look so tired.

LINDA: Come right up.

WILLY: Two minutes.

(*Linda goes into the living room, then reappears in her bedroom. Willy moves just outside the kitchen door.*)

WILLY: Loves me. (*Wonderingly.*) Always loved me. Isn't that a remarkable thing? Ben, he'll worship me for it!

BEN (*with promise*): It's dark there, but full of diamonds.

WILLY: Can you imagine that magnificence with twenty thousand dollars in his pocket?

LINDA (*calling from her room*): Willy! Come up!

WILLY (*calling into the kitchen*): Yes! yes. Coming! It's very smart, you realize that, don't you, sweetheart? Even Ben sees it. I gotta go, baby. 'By! 'By! (*Going

Biff (Kevin Anderson) and Willy (Brian Dennehy) try to console each other in Robert Falls's 1999 production of *Death of a Salesman.*

over to Ben, almost dancing.) Imagine? When the mail comes he'll be ahead of Bernard again!

BEN: A perfect proposition all around.

WILLY: Did you see how he cried to me? Oh, if I could kiss him, Ben!

BEN: Time, William, time!

WILLY: Oh, Ben, I always knew one way or another we were gonna make it, Biff and I!

BEN (*looking at his watch*): The boat. We'll be late. (*He moves slowly off into the darkness.*)

WILLY (*elegiacally, turning to the house*): Now when you kick off, boy, I want a seventy-yard boot, and get right down the field under the ball, and when you hit, hit low and hit hard, because it's important, boy. (*He swings around and faces the audience.*) There's all kinds of important people in the stands, and the first thing you know . . . (*Suddenly realizing he is alone.*) Ben! Ben, where do I . . . ? (*He makes a sudden movement of search.*) Ben, how do I . . . ?

LINDA (*calling*): Willy, you coming up?

WILLY (*uttering a gasp of fear, whirling about as if to quiet her*): Sh! (*He turns around as if to find his way; sounds, faces, voices, seem to be swarming in upon him and he flicks at them, crying, Sh! Sh! Suddenly music, faint and high, stops him. It rises in intensity, almost to an unbearable scream. He goes up and down on his toes, and rushes off around the house.*) Shhh!

LINDA: Willy?

(*There is no answer. Linda waits. Biff gets up off his bed. He is still in his clothes. Happy sits up. Biff stands listening.*)

LINDA (*with real fear*): Willy, answer me! Willy!

(*There is the sound of a car starting and moving away at full speed.*)

LINDA: No!

BIFF (*rushing down the stairs*): Pop!

(*As the car speeds off, the music crashes down in a frenzy of sound, which becomes the soft pulsation of a single cello string. Biff slowly returns to his bedroom. He and Happy gravely don their jackets. Linda slowly walks out of her room. The music has developed into a dead march. The leaves of day are appearing over everything. Charley and Bernard, somberly dressed, appear and knock on the kitchen door. Biff and Happy slowly descend the stairs to the kitchen as Charley and Bernard enter. All stop a moment when Linda, in clothes of mourning, bearing a little bunch of roses, comes through the draped doorway into the kitchen. She goes to Charley and takes his arm. Now all move toward the audience, through the wall-line of the kitchen. At the limit of the apron, Linda lays down the flowers, kneels, and sits back on her heels. All stare down at the grave.*)

REQUIEM

CHARLEY: It's getting dark, Linda.

(*Linda doesn't react. She stares at the grave.*)

BIFF: How about it, Mom? Better get some rest, heh? They'll be closing the gate soon.

(*Linda makes no move. Pause.*)

HAPPY (*deeply angered*): He had no right to do that. There was no necessity for it. We would've helped him.

CHARLEY (*grunting*): Hmmm.

BIFF: Come along, Mom.

LINDA: Why didn't anybody come?

CHARLEY: It was a very nice funeral.

LINDA: But where are all the people he knew? Maybe they blame him.

CHARLEY: Naa. It's a rough world, Linda. They wouldn't blame him.

LINDA: I can't understand it. At this time especially. First time in thirty-five years we were just about free and clear. He only needed a little salary. He was even finished with the dentist.

CHARLEY: No man only needs a little salary.

LINDA: I can't understand it.

BIFF: There were a lot of nice days. When he'd come home from a trip; or on Sundays, making the stoop; finishing the cellar; putting on the new porch; when he built the extra bathroom; and put up the garage. You know something, Charley, there's more of him in that front stoop than in all the sales he ever made.

CHARLEY: Yeah. He was a happy man with a batch of cement.

LINDA: He was so wonderful with his hands.

BIFF: He had the wrong dreams. All, all, wrong.

HAPPY (*almost ready to fight Biff*): Don't say that!

BIFF: He never knew who he was.

CHARLEY (*stopping Happy's movement and reply. To Biff*): Nobody dast blame this man. You don't understand: Willy was a salesman. And for a salesman, there is no rock bottom to the life. He don't put a bolt to a nut, he don't tell you the law or give you medicine. He's a man way out there in the blue, riding on a smile and a shoeshine. And when they start not smiling back—that's an earthquake. And then you get yourself a couple of spots on your hat, and you're finished. Nobody dast blame this man. A salesman is got to dream, boy. It comes with the territory.

BIFF: Charley, the man didn't know who he was.

HAPPY (*infuriated*): Don't say that!

BIFF: Why don't you come with me, Happy?

HAPPY: I'm not licked that easily. I'm staying right in this city, and I'm gonna beat this racket! (*He looks at Biff, his chin set.*) The Loman Brothers!

BIFF: I know who I am, kid.

HAPPY: All right, boy. I'm gonna show you and everybody else that Willy Loman did not die in vain. He had a good dream. It's the only dream you can have—to come out number-one man. He fought it out here, and this is where I'm gonna win it for him.

BIFF (*with a hopeless glance at Happy, bends toward his mother*): Let's go, Mom.

LINDA: I'll be with you in a minute. Go on, Charley. (*He hesitates.*) I want to, just for a minute. I never had a chance to say good-by.

(*Charley moves away, followed by Happy. Biff remains a slight distance up and left of Linda. She sits there, summoning herself. The flute begins, not far away, playing behind her speech.*)

LINDA: Forgive me, dear. I can't cry. I don't know what it is, but I can't cry. I don't understand it. Why did you ever do that? Help me, Willy, I can't cry. It seems to me that you're just on another trip. I keep expecting you. Willy, dear, I can't cry. Why did you do it? I search and search and I search, and I can't understand it, Willy. I made the last payment on the house today. Today, dear. And there'll be nobody home. (*A sob rises in her throat.*) We're free and clear. (*Sobbing more fully, released.*) We're free. (*Biff comes slowly toward her.*) We're free . . . We're free . . .

(*Biff lifts her to her feet and moves out up right with her in his arms. Linda sobs quietly. Bernard and Charley come together and follow them, followed by Happy. Only the music of the flute is left on the darkening stage as over the house the hard towers of the apartment buildings rise into sharp focus, and the curtain falls.*)

ARTHUR MILLER (1915–2005)

Tragedy and the Common Man   1949

One of the curious debates that arose around *Death of a Salesman* was the question of whether it was a genuine tragedy. One of the traditional requirements for tragedy is that the hero be of noble birth. Miller countered that notion with a clear statement of modern purpose regarding tragedy.

In this age few tragedies are written. It has often been held that the lack is due to a paucity of heroes among us, or else that modern man has had the blood drawn out of his organs of belief by the skepticism of science, and the heroic attack on life cannot feed on an attitude of reserve and circumspection. For one reason or another, we are often held to be below tragedy—or tragedy above us. The inevitable conclusion is, of course, that the tragic mode is archaic, fit only for the very highly placed, the kings or the kingly, and where this admission is not made in so many words it is most often implied.

I believe that the common man is as apt a subject for tragedy in its highest sense as kings were. On the face of it this ought to be obvious in the light of modern psychiatry, which bases its analysis upon classic formulations, such as the Oedipus and Orestes complexes, for instance, which were enacted by royal beings, but which apply to everyone in similar emotional situations.

More simply, when the question of tragedy in art is not at issue, we never hesitate to attribute to the well-placed and the exalted the very same mental processes as the lowly. And finally, if the exaltation of tragic action were truly a property of the high-bred character alone, it is inconceivable that the mass of mankind should cherish tragedy above all other forms, let alone be capable of understanding it.

As a general rule, to which there may be exceptions unknown to me, I think the tragic feeling is evoked in us when we are in the presence of a character who is ready to lay down his life, if need be, to secure one thing—his sense of personal dignity. From Orestes to Hamlet, Medea to Macbeth, the underlying struggle is that of the individual attempting to gain his "rightful" position in his society.

Sometimes he is one who has been displaced from it, sometimes one who seeks to attain it for the first time, but the fateful wound from which the inevitable events spiral is the wound of indignity, and its dominant force is indignation. Tragedy, then, is the consequence of a man's total compulsion to evaluate himself justly.

In the sense of having been initiated by the hero himself, the tale always reveals what has been called his "tragic flaw," a failing that is not peculiar to grand or elevated characters. Nor is it necessarily a weakness. The flaw, or crack in the character, is really nothing—and need be nothing—but his inherent unwillingness to remain passive in the face of what he conceives to be a challenge to his dignity, his image of his rightful status. Only the passive, only those who accept their lot without active retaliation, are "flawless." Most of us are in that category.

But there are among us today, as there always have been, those who act against the scheme of things that degrades them, and in the process of action everything we have accepted out of fear or insensitivity or ignorance is shaken before us and examined, and from this total onslaught by an individual against the seemingly stable cosmos surrounding us—from this total examination of the "unchangeable" environment—comes the terror and the fear that is classically associated with tragedy.

More important, from this total questioning of what has previously been unquestioned, we learn. And such a process is not beyond the common man. In revolutions around the world, these past thirty years, he has demonstrated again and again this inner dynamic of all tragedy.

Insistence upon the rank of the tragic hero, or the so-called nobility of his character, is really but a clinging to the outward forms of tragedy. If rank or nobility of character was indispensable, then it would follow that the problems of those with rank were the particular problems of tragedy. But surely the right of one monarch to capture the domain from another no longer raises our passions, nor are our concepts of justice what they were to the mind of an Elizabethan king.

The quality in such plays that does shake us, however, derives from the underlying fear of being displaced, the disaster inherent in being torn away from our chosen image of what and who we are in this world. Among us today this fear is as strong, and perhaps stronger, than it ever was. In fact, it is the common man who knows this fear best.

Now, if it is true that tragedy is the consequence of a man's total compulsion to evaluate himself justly, his destruction in the attempt posits a wrong or an evil in his environment. And this is precisely the morality of tragedy and its lesson. The discovery of the moral law, which is what the enlightenment of tragedy consists of, is not the discovery of some abstract or metaphysical quantity.

The tragic right is a condition of life, a condition in which the human personality is able to flower and realize itself. The wrong is the condition which suppresses man, perverts the flowing out of his love and creative instinct. Tragedy enlightens— and it must, in that it points the heroic finger at the enemy of man's freedom. The thrust for freedom is the quality in tragedy which exalts. The revolutionary questioning of the stable environment is what terrifies. In no way is the common man debarred from such thoughts or such actions.

Seen in this light, our lack of tragedy may be partially accounted for by the turn which modern literature has taken toward the purely psychiatric view of life, or the purely sociological. If all our miseries, our indignities, are born and bred within our minds, then all action, let alone the heroic action, is obviously impossible.

And if society alone is responsible for the cramping of our lives, then the protagonist must needs be so pure and faultless as to force us to deny his validity as a character. From neither of these views can tragedy derive, simply because neither represents a balanced concept of life. Above all else, tragedy requires the finest appreciation by the writer of cause and effect.

No tragedy can therefore come about when its author fears to question absolutely everything, when he regards any institution, habit, or custom as being either everlasting, immutable, or inevitable. In the tragic view the need of man to wholly realize himself is the only fixed star, and whatever it is that hedges his nature and lowers it is ripe for attack and examination. Which is not to say that tragedy must preach revolution.

The Greeks could probe the very heavenly origin of their ways and return to confirm the rightness of laws. And Job could face God in anger, demanding his right, and end in submission. But for a moment everything is in suspension, nothing is accepted, and in this stretching and tearing apart of the cosmos, in the very action of so doing, the character gains "size," the tragic stature which is spuriously attached to the royal or the highborn in our minds. The commonest of men may take on that stature to the extent of his willingness to throw all he has into the contest, the battle to secure his rightful place in his world.

There is a misconception of tragedy with which I have been struck in review after review, and in many conversations with writers and readers alike. It is the idea that tragedy is of necessity allied to pessimism. Even the dictionary says nothing more about the word than that it means a story with a sad or unhappy ending. This impression is so firmly fixed that I almost hesitate to claim that in truth tragedy implies more optimism in its author than does comedy, and that its final result ought to be the reinforcement of the onlooker's brightest opinions of the human animal.

For, if it is true to say that in essence the tragic hero is intent upon claiming his whole due as a personality, and if this struggle must be total and without reservation, then it automatically demonstrates the indestructible will of man to achieve his humanity.

The possibility of victory must be there in tragedy. Where pathos rules, where pathos is finally derived, a character has fought a battle he could not possibly have won. The pathetic is achieved when the protagonist is, by virtue of his witlessness, his insensitivity, or the very air he gives off, incapable of grappling with a much superior force.

Pathos truly is the mode for the pessimist. But tragedy requires a nicer balance between what is possible and what is impossible. And it is curious, although edifying, that the plays we revere, century after century, are the tragedies. In them, and in them alone, lies the belief—optimistic, if you will—in the perfectibility of man.

It is time, I think, that we who are without kings, took up this bright thread of our history and followed it to the only place it can possibly lead in our time—the heart and spirit of the average man.

Death of a Salesman

The original staging of *Death of a Salesman* presented enormous challenges to everyone involved with the production. In many ways the play was radical in conception. Not only was the theory of tragedy challenged by the choice of a traveling salesman as the hero, but the approach to the drama itself—the sense that one needed to get inside Willy Loman's head—made the first production quite different from what theatergoers in 1949 would have expected. Arthur Miller's original title for the play, *The Inside of His Head,* was a rough guide to staging problems. The final production designs bestowed a novel transparency on the Lomans' house, so that the audience was not just looking through a fourth wall, as in conventional stagings, but looking through a small world.

The designer for the stage, Jo Mielziner (1901–1976), was committed to innovation in stage design even before he was given the chance to work with director Elia Kazan on this project. In his notes, he discusses the ways in which the illusional realistic theater seemed to be limited in spite of extraordinary technical resources—the use of projections, film (or video), and multilevel staging—all of which could achieve effects that could only be suggested previously. He approached the problems of the play enthusiastically, as his journal excerpts reveal. While working on *Death of a Salesman,* he was approached by Josh Logan to work on *South Pacific,* an upbeat and timeless American musical that must have provided Mielziner with an emotional relief of sorts while he dealt with the complexities of Miller's dark play.

It is perhaps unfair to refer to the play as dark, but when Miller sent the script to Elia Kazan, already a distinguished director, Kazan called him and said, "What a sad play." Miller thought that Kazan was rejecting the play. At that time Miller was famous as the author of *All My Sons,* but he was not at all confident that his new play would be acceptable for the stage. However, Kazan, whose voice sounded almost funereal, went on to talk about his own father; Miller later said Kazan was the first of many people who saw their own fathers in Willy Loman. The conversation with Kazan ended with a commitment to produce the play within the year. Kazan's "Directing

Death of a Salesman" essay offers an overview of his experience as the play's director.

The problem of finding the right actor to play Willy Loman naturally challenged Kazan, who had Lee J. Cobb in mind right away, even though Miller believed that the actor who played the part should be small in stature. Cobb was so large a man that Miller referred to him as "the walrus," and for a very long time Miller had no confidence in Cobb's ability to play the part. Deep into rehearsals, Cobb internalized the role and shocked Miller into seeing him as perfect. From the beginning, Cobb was convinced that this play was a masterpiece and that it would alter theater history.

Casting for the play involved a great deal of thought and agreement between the author and the director. Arthur Miller, in his essay "The American Theater," gives us some interesting insights into the complexities and challenges that both actors and producers face. He includes an engrossing description of the way Mildred Dunnock, a distinguished and well-known actress, kept coming back for auditions even after being told she was not right for the role of Linda. What this demonstrates is that minds can be changed even when firm decisions have been made—and that people can misjudge the ability of actors to do the work that needs to be done. As it turned out, Mildred Dunnock was perfect for the part and breathed life into it as few actresses have done since.

As June Schlueter and James K. Flanagan point out, Willy Loman might well be the most memorable character in modern theater. Consequently, it is no surprise that a great variety of significant actors have played the role of Willy. Dustin Hoffman was notable as Willy and, because of his small size, close to what Miller had originally intended. Interestingly, Hoffman played Bernard in 1965, with Lee J. Cobb as Willy, when they produced a long-playing-record version of the play. Hume Cronyn and Brian Dennehy were both important in the part also, although Cronyn was almost *too* small in stature. Arthur Miller describes Ying Ruocheng, who translated the play into Chinese for Miller's 1983 production in Beijing, as a "brilliant" Willy.

All-black productions of the play, as well as versions in which some of the characters were played by black actors, presented their own issues. Brenda Murphy considers some of the questions that those renditions raised in her essay "Racial Consciousness in Casting *Death of a Salesman*." Any view that sees Willy Loman as restricted to a specific place and time seems to have been contradicted by the remarkable range of productions and producers, all of which have faced considerable problems in staging and casting.

Some of the interesting questions concerning the universality of the play were answered in the Asian productions, which have been enthusiastically received. One such production was the Taiwanese production reviewed by professor and director Catherine Diamond. The Beijing production was especially exciting because it came at a time when China's attitude toward capitalism was beginning to shift.

Perhaps the only generalization that can really be made is that the challenges the play presents seem to have inspired a boundless upswelling of creativity.

JO MIELZINER (1901–1976)

Designing a Play: *Death of a Salesman* 1948–1949

A seasoned and already respected set designer when he began work on the play, Jo Mielziner reveals the detailed and demanding work that went into making the innovative designs for the first production of *Death of a Salesman*. The late nights; the collaboration with electricians and carpenters, not to mention those with the director and the producer; and all the worries and difficulties of conception — all these are revealed in the journal Mielziner kept as a record of his work on the play.

Figure 26. Jo Mielziner's early sketch for the design of the original 1949 production of *Death of a Salesman*.

Figure 27. Jo Mielziner's painting of the original set, showing the backdrop of apartment buildings.

December 15, 1948

During my midweek check-up of unfinished *Salesman* chores, I realized that a large number of basic decisions still had to be made about the small scenes outside Willy Loman's house. Since rehearsals were due to start a couple of days after Christmas, I appealed to Kazan for a good long session.

During the previous weeks I had been receiving from Arthur Miller, scene by scene, the final version of the rehearsal script. Although he had done the basic rewriting, he had made no attempt to say how the transitions from one scene to another would be made. This was a problem for the director and the designer to work out together as we studied the model, the ground plan, and the cut-out cardboard symbols representing the props.

I pointed out to Kazan how difficult it would be in an office scene, for instance, to remove two desks, two chairs, and a hat rack (which the present script called for) and at the same time have an actor walk quickly across the stage and appear in "a hotel room in Boston where he meets a girl." I urged him to do even more cutting, not in the text but in the props called for in this latest version of the script. We finally got the office pared down to one desk and one chair. Then I suggested going so far as to use the same desk for both office scenes—first in Heiser's office and then, with a change of other props, in Charley's office. As usual, Kazan's imagination rose to the suggestion. He replied, "Sure, let's cut this down to the bone—we can play on practically anything." This is effective abstraction, giving the spectator the opportunity to "fill in."

I had felt from the outset that the cemetery scene at the end of the play would be done on the forestage, and I had actually drawn up a design for a trick trapdoor out of which would rise the small gravestone that we had thought necessary for this scene. I had shown Kazan the working drawing for the gravestone, explained how

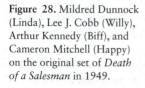

Figure 28. Mildred Dunnock (Linda), Lee J. Cobb (Willy), Arthur Kennedy (Biff), and Cameron Mitchell (Happy) on the original set of *Death of a Salesman* in 1949.

it would operate, and mentioned that because of union rules the man operating this mechanism would be doing this and nothing else, thereby adding a member to the crew for the sake of one effect. I had also mentioned that since the trap would be very close to the audience the sound of its opening might disturb the solemnity of the scene.

With some malice aforethought, I had also done a drawing showing the Salesman's widow sitting on the step leading to the forestage, with her two sons standing behind her, their heads bowed; on the floor at her feet was a small bouquet of flowers. The whole scene was bathed in a magic-lantern projection of autumn leaves. Here, again, leaves were symbolic. With this kind of lighting I thought I could completely obliterate the house in the background and evoke a sense of sadness and finality that might enable us to eliminate the gravestone itself.

My hints were not lost. "I get your point," Kazan said. "Let's do it without the gravestone. No matter how quietly you move it into place, everybody nearby is going to be so busy thinking, 'How is that done?' that they'll miss the mood of the scene."

I felt that this extreme simplicity would be the best theatre possible, and later, in dress rehearsal, it proved to be the right answer.

Kazan and I went over all the prop problems, especially the small hand props—who would bring them on, what actors would be handling them, were stagehands necessary on the set, how long could we black out the stage successfully for the changes?

A blackout is always difficult. As a rule, only a few seconds are permissible for a well-rehearsed stagehand to cross the stage in the darkness, pick up a prop, and exit without being seen by the audience. The eyes of those seated close to the stage soon become used to the sudden change of light, and figures onstage can be observed after six or eight seconds of the dark; gradually, everyone in the theatre can make them out. Stage blackouts are never complete anyway because there are masked and dimmed lights in the wings that must stay on for the control of the switchboard, the stage manager's desk with its telephones and master cue sheets, and the prop tables where the master property man gives hand props to actors waiting for entrance cues.

When we came to the scene in the Boston hotel room, Kazan said, "I don't need anything; just give me the feeling of a hotel room." I showed him a sketch of a panel of cheap wallpaper which I planned to project from the theatre balcony onto a background that was really a section of the trellis at one side of the Salesman's house. Projected images used in conjunction with scenery can be very valuable. In this case, the associations evoked by faded old wallpaper gave the audience a complete picture. Both the house and the exterior trellis faded away. The audience saw the Salesman in that cheap hotel room with that woman. I stress the phrase "in that room." Actors should never play against a scenic background but within the setting.

Kazan felt that the right actress cast in the role of the girl who visits Willy Loman in the hotel room, dressed in the right costume, plus the visual image of the wallpaper, would be enough to make this short scene come alive. There is no question that when a good actor is backed up by simple scenic treatment, his strong qualities are stressed. Of course, this can work in reverse, but Arthur Miller was lucky in the casting of *Salesman;* even the bit roles were played by vivid actors.

During these last weeks before rehearsals began, the producer's office was finishing the always difficult financing of the production, arranging details in preparation for the tryout and the New York run, organizing theatre parties, completing the casting. Arthur Miller was correcting and polishing the rehearsal version of the script. And Kazan was in constant communication with the author as well as the technical staff. I was busy enough myself. Although my wife and children were enjoying Christmas vacation in the country, I wasn't to join them until the day before Christmas.

January 19, 1949

This day was all mine. The stage was ready for me to set the lighting levels for the entire production. Backstage, property men were still unpacking and arranging hand props, and carpenters were finishing the masking of light leaks and cleaning up the paraphernalia; the acting company was still in New York for final run-throughs and costume fittings. The production stage manager had come down to Philadelphia to make notes from my lighting cues and to take over running the crew backstage; one of his assistants stayed in New York to be with Kazan and the company. The company manager was already in Philadelphia and had reported happily that advance sales were promising.

I had asked Del Hughes, the production stage manager, to enlist a couple of local drama students as volunteer stand-ins for my lighting rehearsal. For this process, without the company on hand, I always try to have someone on the set each time I set a light. It is easy to become so absorbed in lighting an empty stage that you wind up illuminating the scenery for its own sake; if I have stand-ins, not only can I see exactly what they themselves look like in the acting light, but I have figures in the foreground to give perspective when I am lighting the background.

I began by taking out every light in the theatre except those over the fire exits. We had to find out how much light the electricians needed on their boards, how much the fly men needed in the fly loft, and how much the property man needed in the wings; with these necessities as a base, I would know how much light there was to start with. Then, with my assistant sitting in back of me, the complete blueprint in my hands which showed the number of each pipe and area, and a speaker in front of me, I called out to Richard Raven, the chief electrician, "Light first pipe playing area right, blue circuit."

As the process went on, I could judge two things: what my predetermined color would look like on the set, and how well my assistant and the crew had angled the units. One by one, I looked at every group of lamps, every individual spot, every color, and every circuit. Then I looked at each projection individually.

The next phase was to create the mood of the background. For the opening of the play I had decided to start with lights behind the drop, which would illuminate the windows of the neighboring buildings painted on the face of the drop. I always start by telling my electrician, "When I call for something, don't bring it on full power, but start with it low on the dimmer." Dimmer controls have markings from one to ten, one being full power, nine and ten being lowest intensity. In this case, I said on the intercom, "Bring the tenth pipe amber up slowly from the bottom." When it reached about halfway, I said, "Hold it." Then I went to the lights on the face of the drop; for this we had two pipes of border lights. I had planned one to cover the top half of the drop; the other was to pick up and carry the bottom half. Each of these pipes contained three colors; one color at a time, I brought the lights up to a certain level, blending the three elements. In this way I gradually established the mood for the opening scene.

I next worked with a series of light pipes that gave a blue backlighting to the Loman house; this brought out the plastic element in that part of the set which was built three-dimensionally. When I had established these, I called backstage on the intercom to the chief electrician, "Mark it up carefully." It takes patience to sit in the dark of the auditorium and wait for what seems an endless time; but the boys on the switchboard, in this case three of them, have to look at each one of the many dimmer handles and mark meticulously at just what point I had called out to hold. This has to be checked and double-checked and then written down on each one of their cue sheets.

Because of the refusal of theatre owners to provide modern electronic lighting systems, almost all of the professional theatres in America are still forced to use the same manual switchboards that were in use fifty and more years ago. While university theatres and community playhouses throughout the country are decades ahead, the professional theatre still hauls in antiquated, heavy (even if serviceable) manual boards. All this, of course, means extra money for the management of a play. In this respect a theatrical producer is not unlike a person who might rent an expensive Fifth Avenue apartment and find a kitchen with an outlet plug for a stove and a refrigerator, but no stove or refrigerator. In most of the New York theatres even the outlets are inadequate in power for modern lighting. Many a time, not only in New York but in try out on the road, I have had every fuse in the place blow out because the electric service was being taxed beyond the limit.

I welcomed the chief electrician's voice on the intercom, saying, "O.K., Mr. M., we're all marked up; what next?" I was ready now for the playing areas, and the stage manager brought on the two young people who were going to stand in for the actors. I placed them first in the bedroom. The opening scene occurs late at night when the Salesman arrives home; I wanted just enough glow to bring out the forms in bed. I then traced through the entrance of Willy Loman and had the electricians mark down the "pre-set," the lights that can be set behind the curtain before it rises. When this was done, I planned the "follow-up"; this is the next cue, which the stage manager gives when he sees that the house curtain is all the way up and the lights in the auditorium can be brought up; these lights, of course, cannot be pre-set, since their beams would hit the house curtain when it was down, creating ugly patterns on its surface.

I had to be careful to judge the effect of light on the faces of people who were not in make-up and costume. For instance, the young lady stand-in had appeared in a white blouse, and I had borrowed a throw from the bed to put around her shoulders. The mere presence of that much white would have given me the illusion that I was getting much more light than was actually there. When I finished with a scene and was waiting for it to be noted on the electricians' cue sheets, I had the property man bring out the props that went with the scene at hand; this gave me a chance to see them not only in terms of distance but also in relationship to their surroundings. The color of the "oilcloth" on the kitchen table, for example, proved to be satisfactory on the surfaces facing the audience but too light on the top surface, where the bounce from the overhead spotlights brought it into competition with the actors' faces. This was swiftly remedied by spraying down the table top.

Knowing that we had about a hundred and fifty light cues to set, we decided to work straight through the night until we had at least a basic scheme and a basic cue for every part of the production. There was no time for polishing or for going back to rehearse the timing of cues, things I usually have been able to do on this day. As it was, we worked until midnight, sent out for coffee and sandwiches for all, and didn't finish the final scene until 4:30 in the morning. This added up to twenty and a half hours of pretty intense work, and the week had just begun.

During the afternoon Alex North and the musicians had arrived from New York, and I used what little time I had, while waiting for the electrical crew to do their mark-ups, to work out some details about the music. I checked to see that the dressing room which was to be the "sound studio" was properly equipped with microphones and a communication system. We had to put blankets on the floor and on the walls before North was satisfied with the quality of the sound as it came into the auditorium over the speaker system. At the same time the assistant electrician rigged a signal-and-sound system for the musicians so that the stage manager's voice announcing cue warnings and cues would be clear and unmistakable.

The process of lighting a musical is basically the same as for a play like *Death of a Salesman,* but there is less refinement in the musical because the picture is broader and the contrasts greater; less subtlety is needed, more vitality desired. Another difference is that in a legitimate play, with the acting areas more limited and the sets fewer, there is much greater need for extreme control of lighting equipment. During this day of setting the lighting for *Salesman* I occasionally had the two follow-spot men turn on their new and beautifully engineered lights, and the effect was fascinating. In the opening scene, for instance, when the Salesman makes his tiptoe entrance carrying his bags, we dimmed the follow-spot far down and played the beam just on the face of the stand-in. The effect was magical; there was so little light that there was no shadow behind him, and yet there was enough warmth in it so that the face stood out in the gray-blue night light. I was sure that this new experiment would come through very serviceably indeed.

How different this subtle and complex lighting was from earlier times! When I designed *Of Thee I Sing* in 1931 for Sam Harris, he was disturbed that I was not willing to use the 1900 type of stage lighting that had characterized his previous productions. This consisted of border lights, footlights, and old-fashioned flood-lights for what were known as "entrances." There was no control of any segment of the stage, only a system of dimming and raising lights for the total acting area, with all people, all objects, and all scenery treated alike.

After Harris had finally agreed to let me try out "modern lighting," I was busy one day with the electrician, who had laid out several dozen new spotlights on the stage in preparation for hanging them. Harris walked on, gave a quizzical glance at the equipment, started to leave, and then turned and said, "You know, kid, my name is Sam Harris, not Uncle Sam." But the lighting stayed in and Harris' productions started to look like their contemporaries.

January 24, 1949

At last: Opening Night. Nerves take over backstage on this night of nights, and it is the rare actor or stage manager who isn't in a cold sweat until the performance moves into high gear. But from the very beginning of my career I have been favored. As I sit out front, I become fatalistic: I've done what I've done; good, bad, or indifferent, there it stands. I can no longer do anything about it. If something goes wrong, I may cringe, but I rarely get up to go backstage.

One of the fascinating aspects of theatre is the feeling I get when I am watching a familiar performance as a member of an audience for the first time. I do not mean an audience of fellow professionals or the people with whom I have been working for weeks on the production, but an audience of ordinary theatre-goers who are seeing the show for the first time. I become intensely aware of their response, and my own reactions, both intellectual and emotional, change completely from what they were the night before when only my fellow workers were around me. I become part of a community of 800 people, and my responses reflect the communal atmosphere.

The first public performance of *Death of a Salesman* gave us all the feeling that the play had it. There were scenes that didn't go well; others seemed a little long, and would later be cut or changed. But from the very beginning, long before any applause, there was a sense that the play really held the audience. There is nothing esoteric about being able to make a fairly reliable verdict on whether a show is going to be a hit after seeing an out-of-town performance. If there are serious doubts, the chances are that the play will not succeed. Of course, some plays received coolly out of town can become moderate successes on Broadway, but out of the more than 250 productions I have designed I cannot remember one really first-rate show that did not reveal its strength on first exposure.

ELIA KAZAN (1909–2003)

Directing *Death of a Salesman*   1988

Kazan speaks very personally about his involvement with *Death of a Salesman*, beginning with his first reading of the script. He explains that the experience was like that of a brother speaking to him, someone who had shared his life experiences. And although he had directed the plays of Tennessee Williams and films such as *On the Waterfront*, *Death of a Salesman* was his favorite. The way in which he internalized the play may well parallel the responses of many readers and theater-goers, who might go home and wonder, as Kazan did, "Was I a good father? No? Why hadn't I done better?"

Of all the plays I've directed, *Death of a Salesman* is my favorite. When I read it again recently, it hit me as hard as it had when I read it the first time, thirty-eight years ago—just as hard and in the same place, immediately, on page two! I am a man who has trained himself to let no pain show, but I felt tears coming as I turned that page. I suppose the play revives the memory, long at rest, of my father, a salesman of another product, of his hopes for his sons in this new country and the gently twisted Anatolian° smile on his face when he'd ask me, a muddle-headed kid of sixteen, "Who going support me my old age? Hey, you Elia, what you saying to that?" When I had nothing to say to that, but looked away, feeling

---

Anatolian: Of the main portion of Turkey, in western Asia. Kazan was born Elia Kazanjoglous to a Greek family in Istanbul, then the capital of the multiethnic Turkish Ottoman Empire.

threatened, he'd shrug and mutter—I'd hear it—"Hopeh-less case." That and more from those years of my life, as well as other memories, without words or faces, lying in wait with their burden of sadness, swarmed up when I read that damned disturbing play last week, just as they had when Art Miller, the day after he finished it in 1948, gave it to me.

After I'd read it that first time, I didn't wait for the next morning to see if I'd have a more "balanced" judgment, didn't delay as I generally did in those years to hear what Molly° might say about it, but called Art as I turned the back cover and told him his play had "killed" me. "I wrote it in eight weeks," he replied.

When I say this was my favorite play, I don't mean it was the best play. I am not a critic, and I do believe Williams wrote better. They were both Puritans, they were both concerned with morality—Tennessee more open about his "sins" and his problems, Miller more guarded. Still *Salesman* is the play that got to me most deeply. It's as if a brother was speaking of our common experience, a man who'd been through precisely the same life with his family that I had with mine. Art does an extraordinary thing there; he shows us a man who represents everything Art believes to be misguided about the system we live in, then goes on to make us feel affection and concern, pity and even love for this man. Then he goes deeper and we are aware of a tragic weight. Is it for the Salesman? Is it for ourselves? And along with arousing this sympathetic pain, his horrendous hero is able to make us laugh. He is ridiculous and he is tragic all at once. How is that accomplished? I don't know any other play in any other language that does all these things at the same time. But Arthur Miller did them all—that one time and never again.

I believe the reason he was able to do this was not that he was more understanding than anyone else about his fellow Americans and the system we live in, or knew better than the rest of us what was wrong with our civilization. It was because of his uncle. I remember—and I hope I remember correctly— that he derived Willy Loman from his uncle, "a very small man," the original stage direction reads, "who wears little shoes and little vests . . . " and "His emotions, in a word, are mercurial." Which is the way Art expected the part would be cast, not with Lee Cobb, certainly not great lumbering Leo Jacob Cobb. Art had this most ambivalent feeling about an actual person, thought him completely wrongheaded, believed he'd misguided his family and that everything he said that was meant to be serious was rubbish, but he still felt great affection for him and enjoyed his company and relished his passionate, nonsensical talk. The man made Art laugh, and Art likes to laugh. In short, he had the living model with that impossible combination of qualities in his own family, and he was smart enough, Art was, and talented enough to recognize that he had a character who could arouse affection and pity at the same time he evoked total condemnation and that both these reactions were significant separately, but together, in the same person, they were much more meaningful; together they could be tragic; together they were all of us.

Studying the play, as I was preparing to direct it, I began to see my father differently; I stopped being angry at him. I was ready at last to forget what I'd considered tyrannical and appreciate what he'd done for me. To gain an understanding of the play, one of the first things I did was sum up the similarities of my father to

---

Molly: His wife, Molly Day Thatcher (1907–1963).

Willy Loman. George Kazan was a man full of violence that he dared release only at home, where it was safe to be angry. But the possibility that he might blow up at any time kept us all in terrible fear.

He also had about him, my father along with Willy, the euphoria of a salesman. When it came time to seduce a customer, he was expressive to a theatrical degree. "Feel it!" I remember him shouting at a buyer, as he lifted the end of a large Kashan carpet and thrust it into the man's hand. "Go on, take it in your hand. Give yourself the pleasure. No charge. Like butter, right? Eh? What you say? Like sweet butter! Tell me where you find piece goods like this piece goods, tell me that much." And so on. People in the trade said he was a great salesman. But when I watched these mercantile revels, they embarrassed me.

"Baba" dressed as a salesman and had his shoes shined every day. Even when he went to my aunt's apple farm in the Catskills for a weekend's vacation, he'd bring along other rug merchants, to talk about prices and the market and the sources "on the other side," then to play poker or pinochle most of the night. Sundays, when he would supervise the shish-ke-bab, bending over the hot wood coals and carefully turning the spits thrust through the cubes of well-marinated lamb leg, he wore a hard collar and a bow tie. Sometimes he even wore the jacket of his business suit and a flat-brimmed straw hat. In the Catskills on a Sunday, he was a merchant waiting for Monday.

It's the essence of the salesman's philosophy that your success or failure depends on your impressing others not only with the goods you have for sale but with yourself. You must gain their approval of your personality, make them believe that anything you say is true, even when you know it's grossly exaggerated or even totally false. That is how my father lived, by saying with the passion of unqualified conviction what was useful in winning a customer. Come to think of it, it was not different from what actors do on stage; they must make an audience believe the poetry and the nonsense, even when they don't believe it themselves. They are rewarded not with a sale but with applause.

Like Willy, my father considered his eldest son a special failure and oh, God, this hurt him! And me! But how could I blame him for what he expected of me and didn't get? Obviously what his wife had produced for him, this silent, secretive, mysteriously sullen son, was not going to rally to his side and sell rugs, not any to anyone, ever. Father preferred his next two boys: one was bound to study medicine—Father already called him "the doctor"—and the other actually did show, for a time, an interest in the business that had been my father's life. But he was afraid to tell himself the truth about his eldest son, the truth being that I didn't give a damn about the Oriental rug trade and, despite his persisting hopes, would never go into it; and if I did, would soon defect; and if I stayed, be no damn good. But just as Willy did, George Kazan kept pumping up hope, and the burden of that hope was on my back.

Willy had Linda, ever-faithful, fiercely devoted Linda; my father had my mother, Athena. She'd stand behind him every night as he gulped the dinner she'd spent the day preparing, would sit to eat her own meal only after he'd moved to the sofa; typically Anatolian that, taking a quick nap after his *yehmek*.° Old lions sleep after eating what the lioness provides.

There is an unarticulated tragedy when a woman discovers that the man she married is not what she hoped he was when she married him. Both Linda and

---

yehmek: Meal.

Willy's best friend, Charley, saw through him but still loved him. Like Linda, my mother would not tolerate any criticism of my father from me; not while he was alive. If I indicated some disaffection, she'd turn on me and tell me he was a good man; "he never goes to other woman," she'd say, and someday I'd come to appreciate what he'd done for us all. He'd brought her to America, you see, not found her here, and she appreciated this. She protected him until the day he died; but when he was finally quiet in the grave, she surprised me one day by saying, "Your father was a stupid man." And soon afterward she said, "These years"—those following his death—"are best years of my life."

Art's play had such deep value for me because it forced me to understand my parents better. Even recently, when I read the play again, it made me wonder about the way I was treating my youngest son, ask myself if I was being as understanding of him as I should be. It disturbed me that I'd discovered my father's traits—even his facial expressions!—in myself. It disturbed me greatly when my youngest son told me that for years he'd lived in terror of my anger. I was repeating the pressure patterns of my father, and I was ashamed when I read Art's play and realized this. That damned play cut me where I was most vulnerable: Was I a good father? No? Why hadn't I done better?

I know it did this for many men; it was the only play I ever directed where men in the audience cried. I recall hearing sobs at the end of a performance, and they were mostly from men.

All the critics rushed to nail down the theme of the play, and Miller helped them with what's in the dialogue: "The man didn't know who he was," spoken over the grave, and a line even closer to the meaning, "He had the wrong dream," which is stated and restated. But it seemed to me that I, as the director, had to take another step and ask what that "wrong dream" was. I came to believe that the point was far more lethal than anything Art put into words. It's in the very fabric of the work, in the legend itself, which is where a theme should be. The Christian faith of this God-fearing civilization says we should love our brother as ourselves. Miller's story tells us that actually—as we have to live—we live by an opposite law, by which the purpose of life is to get the better of your brother, destroying him if necessary, yes, by in effect killing him. Even sex becomes a kind of aggression—to best your boss by taking his woman! That contrast between the ideal and the practice specific to our time is the sense in which the play is a "social drama," and this theme, so shameful and so final, permeates the work's fabric and is projected through the example of human behavior so there can be no avoiding it. Here is an antisystem play that is not "agitprop." We are out of the thirties at last—the audience does not have to suffer instruction or correction. The essence of our society, the capitalist system, is being destroyed not by rhetoric but by that unchallengeable vocabulary, action between people, which makes you believe that the terrible things that happen are true, are inevitable, and concern us all. Furthermore, the conflict we watch is between people who have every traditional reason to love each other. Miller makes us reach out for the lesson; it is not thrust down our throats. The question remains: Why do we live by that law when we know—and Art shows us this—that the result is so humanly destructive?

Art was trained first of all by Henrik Ibsen. The play has a strong structure. The viewer is immediately made aware, first by the title, then by Willy's revealing that he found himself driving off the road, that we are gathered together to watch the course of a suicide. That promise of terror and tragedy lies under every scene in the action that follows and makes the tension continuous. You wait in anxiety as you watch this ridiculous, tragic, misguided, frantically obsessed man—whether Cobb plays him, or the actor is a smaller man like Miller's uncle, doesn't matter. What you watch is yourself, struggling against the fate you've made for yourself.

This production became the other half (with *Streetcar*)° of a theatre legend. The fascinating game of what is fact and what is public relations buildup began to be played. In the accounts of the production and in the remeasuring of the people involved, what had actually happened was replaced by what a hungry press needed—good copy!—and what the imaginations of the people who saw the production were prepared to believe. Furthermore, within each of the people involved there was a swell of confidence. We became convinced of our ability to do anything we chose to do. Success seemed the natural course for us all, the inevitable reward of our efforts. The great success of the play certified our worth. Truth was soon out of sight; we all puffed up. Our producers, Bloomgarden and Fried, Lee Cobb, Arthur Miller, and Elia Kazan were never the same again.

The play became, to the surprise of many theatre people, including its producers, a great success, selling out immediately. Kermit Bloomgarden, an excellent "line" producer, who had the ability to see to it that everything necessary for mounting a show arrived on time and in good working order, was now offered to the public as something more, the leading producer of "class" plays that no one else dared produce on Broadway. His pressman immediately set about creating an enlarged reputation. But how Kermit was able to acquire *Death of a Salesman* and what he thought of it is more interesting than this "puff." Daring is not a feature of the true story; luck is.

At the end of the triumphant opening night performance, Eddie Kook, who'd provided the equipment for lighting the show, was sitting behind Cheryl Crawford, listening to the applause storm. Eddie noticed tears in Cheryl's eyes and commented on the play's power. "That's not why I'm crying," she said. "I had this play and let it get away." This was true. When Art and I weren't sure which producer to entrust it to, I suggested we give it to Cheryl. To my surprise, the force it would have with an audience did not strike her. She hesitated; the time allowed for hesitation in the theatre is brief. Cheryl seemed especially dubious about the play's commercial potential. She'd given it to friends to read; they hadn't been sure either. Since a lively enthusiasm is a necessity for a successful ride through the obstacle course of a Broadway production, and Cheryl didn't show any, I told her to forget the play.

Now luck was loose. Art and I decided to pass the script on to another good friend, Kermit, and his associate, Walter Fried. They'd accepted the play for production, but, as had been the case with Cheryl, they were not sure of its box office strength. Kermit told me he'd consulted theatre owners and box-office treasurers, and everyone had cautioned him that the word "Death" in a title invited death to the ticket window; this had been proven time and again, so they maintained.

Streetcar: A Streetcar Named Desire by Tennessee Williams, which Kazan directed earlier in 1947. It was still running when *Death of a Salesman* opened.

One morning when I was in Kermit's side office, working on casting, he burst in and declared that he was convinced the title of the play had to be changed. He said there was an "upbeat" phrase in the play that would make a fine title, commercial as well as meaningful. Fried and he were determined that *Free and Clear* should be our title. When my reaction was negative, then obdurate, then — when they persisted — scornful, they asked if I'd mind if they talked to Miller without me there. I don't know why I was so damned gracious, because my emotions were violently hostile, but I did say, "Go ahead," and they summoned the author quickly for consultation. Art had to pass the small office where I was waiting with the door open. When he came by, I pulled him in, and without telling him what their proposal was, I said, "They want to talk to you about something I'm dead against. Don't you dare say yes." Art went in, they talked without me; our title was not changed.

But Kermit was a man who made it a matter of pride that he never changed his mind. Perhaps he thought that I, along with others who knew his original concerns about Miller's title, might think him weak if he altered his stand. Kermit had a horror of appearing weak. On opening night, he was cornered by Irving Hoffman, who wrote theatre reviews for the *Hollywood Reporter,* and although Irving didn't ask him what he thought of the title, Kermit volunteered, "I still don't like the title, but it's Arthur Miller's play and he wants the title we have and that's all right with me." Perhaps Kermit was throwing up a defense for himself in case Hoffman didn't like the title either. His anxiety about what Hoffman might think was not altogether unfounded. The "head" of the review in the *Hollywood Reporter* read: "Tragically We Roll Along."

The imaginative qualities of Art's play, the nonrealistic aspects, worked successfully on stage and added a great deal to the force of the theme. They were indeed innovative, and Art deserved all the praise he's been given. How they came to be in the production, however, is a story that brings credit to the theatre as an institution, as well as confirming a string of influences. As Tennessee Williams admired and was stirred by *All My Sons* ("It has the kind of eloquence we need now," he'd written me), so did Art benefit from *A Streetcar Named Desire*. I remember the night he came to see *Streetcar*. After the performance he appeared to be full of wonder at the theatre's expressive possibilities. He told me he was amazed at how simply and successfully the nonrealistic elements in the play — "*Flores! Flores para los muertos!*"° — blended with the realistic ones. These two men, completely different humans who never mixed socially, influenced each other's work and owed each other a debt.

After *Death of a Salesman* had made theatre history, it was published, and the sentence that follows "The Curtain rises" on the first printed pages is: "Before us is the Salesman's home . . . an air of a dream clings to the place, a dream rising out of reality." However, the stage direction in the original manuscript that Art gave me to read directly he'd finished it does not mention a home as a scenic element. It reads: "A pinpoint travelling spot lights a small area on stage left. The Salesman is revealed. He takes out his keys and opens an invisible door." It was a play waiting for a directorial solution.

Flores! . . . muertos!: Flowers! Flowers for the dead!

The concept of a house standing like a specter behind all the scenes of the play, always present as it might be always present in Willy's mind, wherever his travels take him, even behind the office he visits, even behind the Boston hotel room and above his grave plot, is not even suggested in the original script. Although the spectral home is a directorial vision, it was not my idea any more than it was Art's. It was urged on us by the scenic designer, Jo Mielziner. I went for it—it solved many problems for me—and when we took it to Miller, he approved of it. In this production, it was the single most critically important contribution and the key to the way I directed the play. Both Miller and I were praised for what Jo had conceived; he never got the credit he deserved. Art rewrote his stage direction for the book based on Jo's design. A published play is often the record of a collaboration: The director's stage directions are incorporated, as are some of the contributions of others working on the show—actors' "business," designer's solutions, and so on. The theatre is not an exclusively literary form. Although the playscript is the essentially important element, after that is finished, actors, designers, directors, technicians "write" the play together.

Lee J. Cobb became the great star of that season; people marveled at his power and his brilliance. This adulation may have done him more harm than good. When I recommended that we cast Cobb as Willy, I knew him well from our days in the Group° and a road tour we'd played of *Golden Boy*. Our friendship had started close, but like many actors' friendships, it thinned out. I knew him for a mass of contradictions: loving and hateful, anxious yet still supremely pleased with himself, smug but full of doubt, guilty and arrogant, fiercely competitive but very withdrawn, publicly private, suspicious but always reaching for trust, boastful with a modest air, begging for total acceptance no matter what he did to others. In other words, the part was him; I knew that Willy was in Cobb, there to be pulled out.

When he received his fabulous notices, Lee awarded himself a status even higher than any the theatre world gave him. He was great as Willy Loman until he was told he was great and believed it—then he was less great. He was at his best during the last week of the tryout in Philadelphia, before his New York triumph. After we opened on Broadway, he began to share the audience's admiration for his performance and their pity for the character he played. Life on Broadway would not, because it could not, satisfy this man's hunger for unqualified recognition. He withdrew from our play before he should have, claiming that he was dangerously exhausted—which we might have appreciated except that we all saw he was dramatizing it beyond its measure. He said he was on the verge of a breakdown and demanded that I consult with his analyst. I did; we had a bad scene. I still don't know how serious Lee's trouble was; he was a very good actor and determined to prove that he had to leave the show.

Once he was "available" again, no more parts like Willy came his way. He began to masquerade as a martyr to an unappreciative theatre. Something pouting in his character waited for "justice," meaning that a role of great worth was his due and had to come soon. He'd certainly be the Lear of our time, he boasted. Friends agreed. But the theatre is no more just than life, and nothing came along that he found acceptable. Today, Cobb is remembered for Willy Loman and that is all; it became the story of his life.

Group: The Group Theatre was founded in New York in 1931.

Many actors are remembered because of a single great performance, but this comfort from history did not satisfy Cobb. When another season's crop of new plays came along with nothing for him, he decided to return west and to films. I brought him back east to my "location" in Hoboken, to play the corrupt labor boss in *Waterfront,* and he did well, even had an Academy Award nomination. But after that the roles offered him in films were beneath his talent. He felt aggrieved and insulted, and found that the people who dominated the film community were no less arrogant than I. To save his pride, he responded with arrogance. To release his tensions, he gambled more frequently and more seriously. I know only what I heard, the outside of the story. He disappeared from my view. Then suddenly he was dead, too young and—I agree—insufficiently rewarded. What a waste!

Thinkers who think about the theatre have said that success is a problem more difficult than failure—an astonishing thought to anyone who'd been hungry for recognition as long as I'd been. I didn't find success a problem; I was not uncomfortable sitting on a peak. I was credited with all kinds of magic and became the coy object of artistic temptation and commercial seduction. Every play of worth intended for Broadway was offered me first. I had to shrug them off. In films it was only a matter of what I wanted to do, name it. I could see no limit to what I might accomplish. I began to make notes on ambitious future projects, those I'd once only dreamed of. Now they were within reach; all I had to do was extend my hand. And work! That was easy; I had perfect health and boundless energy. I enjoyed the devotion and the intimate friendship of the two best playwrights of the day; one was writing a play, the other a film, both intended for me. I didn't have an enemy, not that I knew of; no, nothing but admiring followers. I was so successful there was no reason for anyone to be jealous of me: I was too far ahead of the pack. I was certain all this would endure—why would it not?—sure that my success would swell, my friendships deepen, my creative associations become richer. No longer suffering from self-doubt, I quit my analyst.

In time I had to confront some facts. I am a mediocre director except when a play or a film touches a part of my life's experience. Other times my cleverness and facility will not overcome my inadequacies. When I rely on mechanics, I do only what a good stage manager should be able to do. I am not catholic in my tastes. I dislike Beckett—his work. I am not an intellectual. I don't have great range. I am no good with music or with spectacles. The classics are beyond me. I enjoy humor and the great clowns, but I can't make up jokes or amusing bits of byplay and visual humor. What I need I steal. I have no ear for poetry. I have a pretty good eye but not a great eye. I do have courage, even some daring. I am able to talk to actors; I don't fear them and their questions. I've been able to arouse them to better work. I have strong, even violent, feelings, and they are assets. I am not shy about ripping the cover-guard off my own experiences; this encourages actors to overcome their inhibitions. I enjoy working with performers; they sense this and have been happy as well as successful with me. This is useful.

Molly used to say that I was too hard on myself. But I don't feel the above is inaccurate. I prefer this measure to the pumped-up state of fame I had after *Death of a Salesman* and *A Streetcar Named Desire.* It took me some years to face what I was as a director; in fact, it took a painful defeat at the Lincoln Center Repertory Theatre. At the time I'm writing about, I was mired in media mud; I'm afraid that for a time I believed what I read. When I see my photographs from that period, I don't like what I see. For three years I was on the very top, then life twisted, as it will; by surviving a great deal of pain and trouble, I became a different person. But that's looking too far ahead.

ARTHUR MILLER (1915–2005)

From "The American Theater" 1978

Reflecting on the process of casting both the main character, Willy, and Willy's wife, Linda, Miller considers some of the reasons for choosing one actor over another. He reminds us that the choices that producers and directors make are usually sound and sensible. Some actors have a great track record and recommend themselves in terms of their recent successes. Others have a quality that a director remembers and sees as appropriate for a part. In addition, there are actors who see themselves as the only viable choice for the part they want; their job, perhaps the most difficult, is to persuade the decision makers that they are the right choice.

The basis upon which actors are hired or not hired is sometimes quite sound; for example, they may have been seen recently in a part which leads the director to believe they are right for the new role; but quite as often a horde of applicants is waiting beyond the door of the producer's private office and neither he nor the director nor the author has the slightest knowledge of any of them. It is at this point that things become painful, for the strange actor sits before them, so nervous and frightened that he either starts talking and can't stop, and sometimes says he can't stop, or is unable to say anything at all and says that. During the casting of one of my plays there entered a middle-aged woman who was so frightened she suddenly started to sing. The play being no musical, this was slightly beside the point, but the producer, the director, and myself, feeling so guilty ourselves, sat there and heard her through.

To further complicate matters there is each year the actor or actress who suddenly becomes what they call "hot." A hot performer is one not yet well-known, but who, for some mysterious reason, is generally conceded to be a coming star. It is possible, naturally, that a hot performer really has talent, but it is equally possible, and much more likely, that she or he is not a whit more attractive or more talented than a hundred others. Nevertheless, there comes a morning when every producer in these five blocks—some of them with parts the performer could never play—simply has to have him or her. Next season, of course, nobody hears about the new star and it starts all over again with somebody else.

All that is chancy in life, all that is fortuitous, is magnified to the bursting point at casting time; and that, I suspect, is one of the attractions of this whole affair, for it makes the ultimate winning of a part so much more zesty. It is also, to many actors, a most degrading process and more and more of them refuse to submit to these interviews until after the most delicate advances of friendship and hospitality are made to them. And their use of agents as intermediaries is often an attempt to soften the awkwardness of their applying for work.

The theatrical agents, in keeping with the unpredictable lunacy of the business, may be great corporations like the Music Corporation of America, which has an entire building on Madison Avenue, and will sell you anything from a tap dancer to a movie star, a symphony orchestra, saxophonists, crooners, scene designers, actors, and playwrights, to a movie script complete with cast; or they may be like Jane Broder, who works alone and can spread out her arms and touch both walls of her office. They may even be like Carl Cowl, who lives around the corner from me in Brooklyn. Carl is an ex-seaman who still ships out when he has no likely scripts on hand to sell, and when things get too nerve-racking he stays up all night playing Mozart on his flute. MCA has antique desks, English eighteenth-century prints, old broken clocks and inoperative antique barometers hanging on its paneled walls, but Carl Cowl had a hole in his floor that the cat got into, and when he finally got the landlord to repair it he was happy and sat down to play his flute again; but he heard meowing, and they had to rip the floor open again to let out the cat. Still, Carl is not incapable of landing a hit play and neither more nor less likely than MCA to get it produced, and that is another handicraft aspect of this much publicized small business, a quality of opportunity which keeps people coming into it. The fact is that theatrical agents do not sell anyone or anything in the way one sells merchandise. Their existence is mainly due to the need theater people have for a home, some semblance of order in their lives, some sense of being wanted during the long periods when they have nothing to do. To have an agent is to have a kind of reassurance that you exist. The actor is hired, however, mainly because he is wanted for the role.

By intuition, then, by rumor, on the recommendation of an agent—usually heartfelt; out of sheer exhaustion, and upsurge of sudden hope or what not, several candidates for each role are selected in the office of the producer, and are called for readings on the stage of a theater.

It is here that the still unsolved mystery begins, the mystery of what makes a stage performer. There are persons who, in an office, seem exciting candidates for a role, but as soon as they step onto a stage the observers out front—if they are experienced—know that the blessing was not given them. For myself, I know it when, regardless of how well the actor is reading, my eyes begin to wander up to the brick wall back of the stage. Conversely, there are many who make little impression in an office, but once on the stage it is impossible to take one's attention from them. It is a question neither of technique nor of ability, I think, but some quality of surprise inherent in the person.

For instance, when we were searching for a woman to play Linda, the mother in *Death of a Salesman*, a lady came in whom we all knew but could never imagine in the part. We needed a woman who looked as though she had lived in a house dress all her life, even somewhat coarse and certainly less than brilliant. Mildred Dunnock insisted she was that woman, but she was frail, delicate, not long ago a teacher in a girl's college, and a cultivated citizen who probably would not be out of place in a cabinet post. We told her this, in effect, and she understood, and left.

And the next day the line of women formed again in the wings, and suddenly there was Milly again. Now she had padded herself from neck to hem line to look a bit bigger, and for a moment none of us recognized her, and she read again. As soon as she spoke we started to laugh at her ruse; but we saw, too, that she *was* a little more worn now, and seemed less well-maintained, and while she was not quite ordinary, she reminded you of women who were. But we all agreed, when she was finished reading, that she was not right, and she left.

Next day she was there again in another getup, and the next and the next, and each day she agreed with us that she was wrong; and to make a long story short when it came time to make the final selection it had to be Milly, and she turned out to be magnificent. But in this case we had known her work; there was no doubt that she was an excellent actress. The number of talented applicants who are turned down because they are unknown is very large. Such is the crap-shooting chanciness of the business, its chaos, and part of its charm. In a world where one's fate so often seems machined and standardized, and unlikely to suddenly change, these five blocks are like a stockade inside which are people who insist that the unexpected, the sudden chance, must survive. And to experience it they keep coming on all the trains.

But to understand its apparently deathless lure for so many it is necessary, finally, to have participated in the first production of a new play. When a director takes his place at the beaten-up wooden table placed at the edge of the stage, and the cast for the first time sit before him in a semicircle, and he gives the nod to the actor who has the opening lines, the world seems to be filling with a kind of hope, a kind of regeneration that, at the time, anyway, makes all the sacrifices worth while.

The production of a new play, I have often thought, is like another chance in life, a chance to emerge cleansed of one's imperfections. Here, as when one was very young, it seems possible again to attain even greatness, or happiness, or some otherwise unattainable joy. And when production never loses that air of hope through all its three-and-a-half-week rehearsal period, one feels alive as at no other imaginable occasion. At such a time, it seems to all concerned that the very heart of life's mystery is what must be penetrated. They watch the director and each other and they listen with the avid attention of deaf mutes who have suddenly learned to speak and hear. Above their heads there begins to form a tantalizing sort of cloud, a question, a challenge to penetrate the mystery of why men move and speak and act.

It is a kind of glamour that can never be reported in a newspaper column, and yet it is the center of all the lure theater has. It is a kind of soul-testing that ordinary people rarely experience except in the greatest emergencies. The actor who has always regarded himself as a strong spirit discovers now that his vaunted power somehow sounds querulous, and he must look within himself to find his strength. The actress who has made her way on her charm discovers that she appears not charming so much as shallow now, and must evaluate herself all over again, and create anew what she always took for granted. And the great performers are merely those who have been able to face themselves without remorse.

In the production of a good play with a good cast and a knowing director a kind of banding together occurs; there is formed a fraternity whose members share a mutual sense of destiny. In these five blocks, where the rapping of the tap-dancer's feet and the bawling of the phonographs in the record-shop doorways mix with the roar of the Broadway traffic; where the lonely, the perverted, and the lost wander like the souls in Dante's hell and the life of the spirit seems impossible, there are still little circles of actors in the dead silence of empty theaters, with a director in their center, and a new creation of life taking place.

There are always certain moments in such rehearsals, moments of such wonder that the memory of them serves to further entrap all who witness them into this most insecure of all professions. Remembering such moments the resolution to leave and get a "real" job vanishes, and they are hooked again.

I think of Lee Cobb, the greatest dramatic actor I ever saw, when he was creating the role of Willy Loman in *Death of a Salesman*. When I hear people scoffing at actors as mere exhibitionists, when I hear them ask why there must be a theater if it cannot support itself as any business must, when I myself grow sick and weary of the endless waste and the many travesties of this most abused of all arts, I think then of Lee Cobb making that role and I know that the theater can yet be one of the chief glories of mankind.

He sat for days on the stage like a great lump, a sick seal, a mourning walrus. When it came his time to speak lines, he whispered meaninglessly. Kazan, the director, pretended certainty, but from where I sat he looked like an ant trying to prod an elephant off his haunches. Ten days went by. The other actors were by now much further advanced: Milly Dunnock, playing Linda, was already creating a role; Arthur Kennedy as Biff had long since begun to reach for his high notes; Cameron Mitchell had many scenes already perfected; but Cobb stared at them, heavy-eyed, morose, even persecuted, it seemed.

And then, one afternoon, there on the stage of the New Amsterdam way up on top of a movie theater on Forty-second Street (this roof theater had once been Ziegfeld's private playhouse in the gilded times, and now was barely heated and misty with dust), Lee rose from his chair and looked at Milly Dunnock and there was a silence. And then he said, "I was driving along, you understand, and then all of a sudden I'm going off the road. . . ."

And the theater vanished. The stage vanished. The chill of an age-old recognition shuddered my spine; a voice was sounding in the dimly lit air up front, a created spirit, an incarnation, a Godlike creation was taking place; a new human being was being formed before all our eyes, born for the first time on this earth, made real by an act of will, by an artist's summoning up of all his memories and his intelligence; a birth was taking place above the meaningless traffic below; a man was here transcending the limits of his body and his own history. Through the complete concentration of his mind he had even altered the stance of his body, which now was strangely not the body of Lee Cobb (he was thirty-seven then) but of a sixty-year-old salesman; a mere glance of his eye created a window beside him, with the gentle touch of his hand on this empty stage a bed appeared, and when he glanced up at the emptiness above him a ceiling was there, and there was even a crack in it where his stare rested.

I knew then that something astounding was being made here. It would have been almost enough for me without even opening the play. The actors, like myself and Kazan and the producer, were happy, of course, that we might have a hit; but there was a good deal more. There was a new fact of life, there was an alteration of history for all of us that afternoon.

There is a certain immortality involved in theater, not created by monuments and books, but through the knowledge the actor keeps to his dying day that on a certain afternoon, in an empty and dusty theater, he cast a shadow of a being that was not himself but the distillation of all he had ever observed; all the unsingable heartsong the ordinary man may feel but never utter, he gave voice to. And by that he somehow joins the ages.

And that is the glamour that remains, but it will not be found in the gossip columns. And it is enough, once discovered, to make people stay with the theater, and others to come seeking it.

I think also that people keep coming into these five blocks because the theater is still so simple, so old-fashioned. And that is why, however often its obsequies are intoned, it somehow never really dies. Because underneath our shiny fronts of stone, our fascination with gadgets, and our new toys that can blow the earth into a million stars, we are still outside the doorway through which the great answers wait. Not all the cameras in Christendom nor all the tricky lights will move us one step closer to a better understanding of ourselves, but only, as it always was, the truly written word, the profoundly felt gesture, the naked and direct contemplation of man which is the enduring glamour of the stage.

BRENDA MURPHY (b. 1950)
Racial Consciousness in Casting
Death of a Salesman   1995

A number of interesting issues came to the surface when the 1972 Baltimore production of *Death of a Salesman* cast all black actors. Race-blind casting had been common with other classic American plays and often with Shakespeare and other European plays. This play provided unexpected surprises, however, as Murphy explains.

The Center Stage production in 1972 brought to the fore the issue of race and ethnicity in casting the play. Although it was the first professional production cast with African-Americans, it was not the first to raise the color issue. As early as 1960, Miller had turned down a request from Terry Carter to do a "Negro version" of *Salesman* Off-Broadway. Although Carter assured Miller that care would be taken to avoid interracial casting that might "distort" the play—the entire Loman family, as well as The Woman, Miss Forsythe, and Letta were to be played by black actors—the request was refused, presumably because of Miller's ban on professional productions in New York.[1] According to Miller, however, he approved a production in New York during the sixties that would have featured African-American Frederick O'Neal as Willy, although the production never materialized.[2] O'Neal had played Willy in a 1962 production directed by Esther Merle Jackson at Clark College in Atlanta with an all-black cast.

The Center Stage production featured Richard Ward, who had been a hit in *Ceremonies of Dark Old Men* at the theatre in the previous year. Miller attended the opening night of the all-black production, and contributed a note to the program, saying:

> I have felt for many years that particularly with this play, which has been so well received in so many countries and cultures, the black actor would have an opportunity, if indeed that is needed anymore, to demonstrate to all his common humanity and his talent.[3]

[1]Unpublished letter from Terry Carter to Kay Brown, January 1960, HRHRC. [Harry Ransom Humanities Research Center]
[2]Unpublished letter from Arthur Miller to George [C. Scott], 28 April 1975, HRHRC.
[3]Quoted in Mel Gussow, "Stage: Black *Salesman*," *New York Times*, 9 April 1972: 69.

The production was not particularly successful, chiefly because some inexperienced actors were cast in the minor roles. In several interviews, Ward made it clear that he had wanted to do the play with an integrated cast, particularly with Charley played by a white man, showing that "a white man and a black man can live next door to each other and care for each other . . . their children can grow up together and love each other."[4] Miller also was quoted as saying he would like to see the play done with an integrated cast, just because it would allow a greater selection of players.[5] The producers reported that they had thought about an integrated cast, but decided that it "might be an attempt to make a statement that's not in the play." They had wanted to make Charley white, "but some black leaders in Baltimore pointed out that the neighbor ends up success[ful], and that a 'be white, be a success' message might come across."[6]

Not surprisingly, the production was analyzed almost exclusively in terms of the race issue. Mel Gussow asserted in the *New York Times* that "Black time has caught up to *Salesman*," and contended that "what makes this more than just an intriguing experiment, but an exciting concept, is not only what it tells us about *Death of a Salesman*, but what it tells us about the black experience."[7] In Gussow's view, "Willy Loman's values are white values—the elevation of personality, congeniality, conformity, salesmanship in the sense of selling oneself, so that in the context of an all-black production, Willy becomes a black man embracing the white world as an example to be emulated."[8] Hollie West of the *Washington Post* found the concept less revealing. Putting black actors "in roles written for whites," she contended, required the actors to "shed the badge of their color. Without the nuances of black dialogue and a consciousness reflecting the unique customs and traditions of black life, such actors may ask the question: Am I playing a white black man?"[9] West did not think the production succeeded in transferring the circumstances of the lower-middle-class white family in New York during the 1930s and 1940s to "the black circumstances of the same period."[10] Although she found Ward's performance as Willy entirely convincing, she found historical and social reality impinging on the dramatic illusion of the other characters: "Have black women been willing to play secondary roles when their husbands were failing, as in the case of Mrs. Loman?" she asked. "Would Biff have been considered an outcast among thousands of similar black men a generation ago?"[11]

Despite his support for Richard Ward's desire for interracial casting in the Baltimore production, Miller made it clear three years later that he found the question of race in casting an extremely complex one. A year after taking over the direction of the Philadelphia Drama Guild production from Scott, Miller approved an Off-Broadway revival of *Salesman* at the Circle in the Square Theatre that Scott was to direct, with himself in the title role. When he learned that Scott was planning to cast a black actor as Charley, Miller wrote him a four-page single-spaced

[4]Quoted in Carl Schoettler, "Actor in *Death of a Salesman* Went on Stage at Age 13," *Baltimore Evening Sun*, 3 April 1972: C6. See also Larry Siddons, "A Black Willy Loman Talks of *Salesman*'s Soul," *New York Post*, 4 April 1972: 60.

[5]Quoted in Siddons, "A Black Willy Loman."

[6]*Ibid.*

[7]Gussow, "Black *Salesman*."

[8]*Ibid.*

[9]Hollie I. West, "*Death of a Salesman*," *Washington Post*, 14 April 1972: D1.

[10]*Ibid.*, D7.

[11]*Ibid.*

letter, warning him to consider carefully what the implications of this casting would be. So-called color-blind casting, he believed, only worked when it was entirely color-blind, with Biff black and Happy white, for example. This, however, took the play out of the realm of realism, and made its relation to the social reality it depicted purely metaphorical, a conception which needed to be thoroughly thought through.[12]

In 1975, casting one "white" role with a black actor immediately foregrounded the issue of race. In the case of Charley, Miller did not think this would work. It would suggest that Willy, in daring to have a black man for his best friend during the thirties, would have it in him to rebel against accepted social values and prejudices, a quality antithetical to his character. It would also take away the sense that Charley is fundamentally the same as Willy, except for Willy's ruling passion, which destroys him. Miller felt that Charley should face the same conditions in life that Willy does, that he should be a representative of the American system when it functions as it should. He felt that adding the issue of race to this relationship would distort its dynamics as he had intended them to work.

JUNE SCHLUETER (b. 1948) and JAMES K. FLANAGAN

Memorable Willy   1987

The authors contend that there may be no more memorable character on the modern stage than Willy Loman. To an extent they base their statement on the effect that Willy has on the audience's imagination. Audiences in the 1970s and 1980s seem to have been affected by Willy Loman even more than the original 1949 audience. The society had changed in a direction that made Willy's values seem less connected with the Depression of the 1930s and more connected with the affluence of the 1970s.

When Walter Goodman reviewed the 1975 revival of *Death of a Salesman*, in which George C. Scott replaced Lee J. Cobb as the self-deluded drummer, he claimed that the play, though applauded in 1949 as the great American tragedy, might well mean more in 1975. Goodman argues that the sympathetic reception of so unmitigated a failure as Willy Loman could be expected from a people who had lived through the Great Depression and World War II, but identification with this loser of a salesman could not have lasted beyond the two-hour life of the play. For this audience was on its way to becoming the Affluent Society; in 1949, Willy Loman was "an anachronism, a relic of a Depression mentality." By 1975, however, America had again become a society ready to acknowledge that "attention must be paid," even to this unlikable, inept failure, whose condition rather than personality was moving. For the 1975 audience had lived through an unpopular, unnecessary war, which brought none of the enthusiasm or the nationalism of World War II; and it was disillusioned with two decades of an

---

[12]Unpublished letter from Arthur Miller to George [C. Scott], 28 April 1975, HRHRC.

energetic prosperity that could not pause for failures nor accommodate a man who yearned to plant seeds or look at the moon.[1]

In 1984, Willy Loman appeared once again on the Broadway stage, this time a bit thinner and a bit smaller—more like the original "shrimp" Miller had created than the "walrus" into which Willy was metamorphosed when Lee J. Cobb was cast. Dustin Hoffman's portrayal of Willy was powerful and convincing, suggesting that the method actor had clearly found some coincidence between himself and the character that enabled him to create the role. But where America was in the mid-1980s did not seem to concern the critics. *Death of a Salesman* was no longer being viewed as time-bound commentary on capitalism and its victims, and audience response was not being judged in terms of economic or social circumstance. Miller's play had clearly earned its author's description of it as a play that raises "questions . . . whose answers define humanity,"[2] a description dramatically endorsed in 1983 when the play opened at the Beijing People's Art Theatre in China.

That production, the first in China of an American play directed by an American, challenged the assumption that *Salesman* was culture-bound, meeting with enthusiastic responses in a country where peasants constitute 90 percent of the population and where there are no salesmen. Speaking of the opening in *"Salesman" in Beijing*, Miller noticed the odd laughs, the cruel laughs, beneath which he sensed "a comprehension of Willy's character, a recognition. Which I suppose means they share these embarrassing weaknesses?"[3] Harry Moses, producer of the Bill Moyers show on PBS, which ran a special program on the production of *Death of a Salesman* in Beijing, told Miller the day after opening night that the last shot on the program would be of a young Chinese who spoke English, saying that "China was full of Willys, dreamers of the dream."[4]

But the problem with Willy—aside from his self-delusion, his ineptness, his self-pity, his misplaced pride, and his fraudulent morality—is that he has dreamed the wrong dream. About to be fired from his job, Willy cries out to the young upstart Howard, "You can't eat the orange and throw the peel away—a man is not a piece of fruit!" Though only the peel of Willy's dream remains, he refuses to discard it, deluding himself into believing that the dream of being a salesman with green velvet slippers, who was not only liked but well liked by the hundreds who mourned his death, was right for him.

There may well be no character in modern drama more memorable than Willy Loman. The image of the tired salesman, valise in hand, shoulders sloping, suit jacket hanging loosely about his weary frame, which appeared on the jacket of the Viking edition of the play for years, has sustained its power in the imagination of the theatergoing public. It has become a symbol of the pursuer of the American—and the universal—dream who met with the harsh consequences of not being able to keep up. Willy Loman is indeed a low man; no tragic hero of high degree, he is circumstantially and psychologically down. Surrounded by high-rise apartment buildings that deflect the sun from the backyard, Willy's little house

[1]Walter Goodman, "Miller's *Salesman*, Created in 1949, May Mean More to 1975." *New York Times*, June 15, 1975, pp. 1, 5.

[2]Arthur Miller, introduction to *Arthur Miller's Collected Plays* (New York: Viking Press, 1957), p. 32.

[3]Arthur Miller, *"Salesman" in Beijing* (New York: Viking Press, 1984), p. 238.

[4]Miller, *"Salesman" in Beijing*, p. 245.

in Brooklyn stands as a symbol of time past, when the world still had room for vegetable gardens and for salesmen who carried on their trade on the strength of a smile. There is a collective guilt in Willy's failure in which every theatergoer participates; it is a guilt occasioned by the knowledge that society cannot accommodate its failures in a system that relentlessly demands success.

CATHERINE DIAMOND (b. 1951)
Death of a Salesman in Taipei   1993

Diamond, who is a professor and director of the only English-language theater in Taiwan, asserts that a 1992 Taiwanese production of *Death of a Salesman* reflected Chinese values almost as much as it did American values. The political complexities of the production give some indication of the difficulties that the National Theater of Taipei had to overcome in order to produce the play. Diamond points to some of the interesting cultural differences that might be invisible to an American audience but that would be of considerable importance to the Chinese.

> **DEATH OF A SALESMAN.** By Arthur Miller. The Performance Workshop. The National Theater, Taipei, Taiwan, Republic of China. 18–26 April 1992.

In 1987, Yang Shipeng, director of the Hong Kong Repertory Theatre, was invited to direct a play at Taiwan's new National Theater. He requested permission from Arthur Miller to use a Taiwanese translation of *Death of a Salesman* because he could not use the Ying Ruocheng translation Miller used in Beijing. Miller initially gave his permission with the caveat that the translation be used only in Taiwan. The production was postponed and later, Yang heard from Miller's agent that only the Ying Ruocheng translation was acceptable. The reason for this change of mind has never been clearly determined, but the Taiwan press put the blame on Miller, insinuating his pro-communist sympathies. On the other hand, perhaps Miller, irritated that Taiwan's refusal of the mainland translation was based purely on political rather than artistic grounds, revoked his initial permission.

In 1991, Yang again wrote to Miller, asking whether he could use the Ying Ruocheng translation with some of his own emendations. Miller answered affirmatively. In both his alteration of the translation, in which he substituted Taipei idiom for the original Beijing idiom, and in his directing style, Yang strove for what he believed would appear most natural to the Taipei audience, neither emphasizing the play's Americanisms nor trying to adapt the story to a Taiwanese locale.

The actors played the essence of relationships rather than their specifically American manifestations. However, there were some fundamental differences in social values that made it difficult for the audience to comprehend Willy's character and to sympathize with him. For example, virtually no Chinese father harbors aspirations for his son to become a professional sportsman, but desires instead for him to go to university—an American school preferably—and become a professor, doctor, manager, or lawyer. As an actor in Miller's *Salesman in Beijing* expressed it: "Every man wants his son to be a dragon." The audience clearly understood

Figure 29. The 1992 Chinese production of *Death of a Salesman,* at the National Theater in Taipei, Taiwan, directed by Yang Shipeng.

Willy's hopes for Biff and his ensuing disappointment, but since Taiwanese society so clearly admires the path taken by Willy's neighbor, the successful businessman Charley and his bookish son Bernard, people laughed at Willy's delusions, often failing to empathize with his particular dreams of success.

Despite some confusion caused by Willy's highly individualized character, other aspects of the play were almost written for modern day Taipei. The similarities between the United States in the wheeling-dealing 1920s and laissez faire capitalism in 1990s Taiwan are uncanny. Out-of-town extramarital affairs, children suffering from parental expectations, the high cost of housing, overcrowding, disappearance of green spaces, job obsolescence, increasing competition for jobs, and the struggle to maintain the esteem of others while facing failure are well-known phenomena in the postindustrial, newly wealthy metropolis of Taipei. Yet the production did not challenge the audience to reflect upon these problems or the social values that cause them.

Director Yang had a clearcut goal of presenting an American play without any concessions to the Chinese actors or the Chinese audience, yet certain changes were inevitable. In the translation itself, the flavor of individual characters' speech gets attenuated, especially Happy's, which is slangy.

Another significant difference was in acting style. Modern Chinese stage acting tends to be broad, exaggerated and emphatic. This has roots in the traditional drama and is reinforced by television dramas which tend to be either contemporary soap operas or historical melodramas. Consequently the male actors in particular engaged in a great deal of demonstrative acting—pointing, waving their hands around, and touching each other to get attention. Seasoned stage actor Li Lichun played Willy's poignant scenes with admirable restraint, but Deng Chenghui, as the loyal wife Linda, evoked more sympathy. Her voice never broke until her last line at Willy's grave: "We're free . . . we're free," and, because she held back her tears until the very end, the audience wept with her, moved more by her devotion than Willy's fall and final sacrifice.

In his Beijing production, Miller initially felt apprehensive that his play might be reduced to a political message—an indictment of American capitalism. This aspect was wholly absent from the Taipei production, where it might have been more justified. Instead, both director and actors stressed the pathos of the Loman family. Yang Shipeng wanted to move the audience, but to what end, his production never made clear.

Samuel Beckett

Samuel Beckett (1906–1989) was born in Dublin to an upper-middle-class Protestant family. After a privileged education at the Portora Royal School, he went to Trinity College, Dublin, where he studied French and Italian. He was an exceptionally good student and, in 1928 after graduation, taught English at the École Normale Supérieure in Paris.

Beckett early on straddled two literary cultures: Irish and Anglo-Irish. Most of the literary energy in Ireland in the 1920s and 1930s was split between the essentially conservative Anglo-Irish Protestants, such as W. B. Yeats and Lady Gregory, and the more avant-garde Catholics, such as James Joyce, with whom Beckett formed an enduring personal and literary friendship in Paris. Although much younger than Joyce, Beckett developed a close artistic sympathy with him. Beckett's first published work (1929) was one of the earliest critical essays on Joyce's most radical literary composition, the not-yet-published *Finnegans Wake*.

When he was first in France, Beckett's reading of French philosophers, especially Descartes, exerted a strong influence on his work. Beckett's earliest writings appeared in Eugene Jolas's avant-garde literary journal *transition,* which put him in the center of Parisian literary activity in the late 1920s. After 1930, his series of short stories published under the title *More Pricks Than Kicks* (1934) established him as an important writer. After settling in Paris in 1937, Beckett wrote the novel *Murphy* (1938), on a recognizably Irish theme of economic impoverishment, alienation, and inward meditation and spiritual complexity.

When World War II began in 1939, Beckett took up the cause of the French Resistance. After his activity caught the eye of the Gestapo, for two years he lay low in unoccupied France by working as a farmhand and also writing another novel, *Watt* (written in 1944 but published in 1953). After the war, he took up residence again in Paris and began writing most of his work in French. His greatest novels were written in the five years after the war, and they are often referred to as his trilogy: *Molloy, Malone Dies,* and *The Unnamable.* These three novels are about men who have become disaffected with society and who have strange and compelling urgencies to be alone and to follow exacting and repetitive patterns of behavior. In a sense, they are archetypes of the kinds of protagonists that Beckett created in most of his work.

Beckett's first published play, *Waiting for Godot* (1952), was produced in Paris (1953), in London (1955), and in Miami (1956). From the first, its repetitive, whimsical, and sometimes nonsensical style established the play as a major postwar statement. In a barren setting, Vladimir and Estragon, two tramps who echo the comic vision of Charlie Chaplin, wait for Godot to come. They amuse themselves by doing vaudeville routines, but their loneliness and isolation are painfully apparent to the audience. Godot has promised to come, and as they wait, Vladimir and Estragon speculate on whether or not he will.

The comic moments in the play, along with the enigma of Vladimir and Estragon's fruitless waiting, combined to capture the imagination of audiences and the press. They saw the play as a modern statement about the condition of humankind, although there was never any agreement on just what the statement was. Godot sends a boy to say that he will indeed come, but when the play ends, he has not arrived. The implication seems to be that he will never arrive. Most audiences saw Godot as a metaphor for God. Despite the critics' constant inquiries, Beckett never confirmed the view that Godot was God and kept Godot's identity open-ended.

The play itself was open-ended, as Beckett had hoped, and therefore could be interpreted in many ways. One interpretation was to see the play as a commentary on the futility of religion; another was to suggest that the play underscored the loneliness of humankind in an empty universe; yet a third implied that it was up to individuals, represented by the hapless Vladimir and Estragon, to shape the significance of their own lives, and their waiting represented that effort.

Many of the themes in *Waiting for Godot* are apparent in Beckett's later plays. The radio play *All That Fall* (1957) was followed by the very successful *Krapp's Last Tape* (1958). Also in 1957, *Endgame,* a play on the theme of the end of the world, was produced, followed in 1961 by *Happy Days*. Beckett experimented with minimalist approaches to drama, including minimalism in setting, props, and — in mime plays such as *Act without Words I* and *Act without Words II* — even words.

Beckett's plays reveal the deep influence of French postwar philosophers such as Albert Camus and Jean-Paul Sartre, both existentialists. Their philosophy declares that people are not essentially good, bad, kind, or anything else but are what they make of themselves. Beckett's adaptation of existentialism sometimes borders on pessimism, because his vision seems to negate many of the consolations of religious and secular philosophy. His style is antirealist, but the search for beliefs that are reasonable and plausible in a fundamentally absurd world and the plight of individuals who must make their own meanings are central to most of his work.

Beckett's view of the world is not cheerful. But his vision is consistent, honest, and sympathetic to the persistence of his characters, who endure even in the face of apparent defeat. The significance of Beckett's achievements was recognized in 1969 when he was awarded the Nobel Prize for literature.

Endgame

For discussion questions and assignments on *Endgame,* visit bedfordstmartins.com/jacobus.

The title *Endgame* derives from the game of chess, which has three different strategies to mark the opening, the middle game, and the endgame. The strategy of the endgame focuses on the protection of the king and depends on very few pieces being left on the board — the king and sometimes a rook and a pawn. The moves in the endgame are always restricted, often repetitive, and limited by the fact that the king, if it can move at all, cannot move more than one space at a time. In Beckett's *Endgame,* Hamm is the king and the central character in the drama; however, he cannot move or even stand by himself. Beckett described Hamm as "a king in the chess game lost from the start." Hamm's parents, Nagg and Nell, stuck immobile in ashcans, resemble rooks, who protect the king by controlling spaces forward, backward, and side to side but have little reason themselves to move. Clov, who most closely resembles a pawn, cannot sit down and is the only character in the play who can move. He is also the only means by which Hamm can move.

World politics in 1957, when the play was written, were dominated by the threat of nuclear war and the possible extinction of the human race. The circumstances of *Endgame* suggest that the play portrays a version of the end of the world. Clov's description of the world outside the window implies desolation and grief. At one point as Clov looks out the window, Hamm tells him to use his "glass" (his telescope) and to report back to him. Clov says all is "Zero," and Hamm asks, "All is what?" "In a word?" says Clov. "Is that what you want to know?" And in a moment he reports his one word: "Corpsed."

Unlike Hamm and Clov, who seem rooted only in the present, Nagg and Nell have a past. They remember rowing on Lake Como on an April afternoon after they were engaged. Nell remembers it as a moment in which she was happy. But they also remember the day they crashed on their tandem bicycle and lost their legs. Nagg recalls it was in the Ardennes forest on the road to Sedan. Beckett is alluding to the French forest at Ardennes, site of the most appalling and murderous fighting in World War I, and to the French town of Sedan, the place where Napoleon III surrendered to the Germans in a battle during the Franco-Prussian war.

Ruby Cohn and other critics have noted that the characters' names have associations with hammers and nails: Nell is a homophone for *nail*; Hamm is a shortened form of *hammer*; Nagg is from the German *nagel*, for *nail*; and Clov is from the French *clou*, also for *nail*. The characters thus seem to be equipped to rebuild their society, but they refuse to do so. By using English, French, and German versions of *nail,* Beckett alludes to the principal combatants of modern European wars.

Some critics have observed that Beckett's drama often focuses on elements of play. Plays are play; life is play. In chess an endgame is played. In Beckett's drama, characters' actions seem to be performed as if they were part of a game. Clov exercises great precision, for example, in placing Hamm exactly where he wishes to be. When Clov has done the rounds and moved Hamm's chair back to its position, Hamm says, "I feel a little too far to the left. Now I feel a little too far to the right." In a game of chess, it would matter if he were too far to the left or right. In an endgame the king might move to one square and then move back again and again. The movements of Hamm and Clov are repetitious and meaningful only within the "system" of the drama and its space, just as all moves in an endgame are meaningful only within the "system" of the game of chess. Clov continually enters and exits with his ladder and looks out the windows, only to find that nothing has changed. He picks up the lids of Nagg and Nell's ashcans and replaces them several times. He pushes Hamm's chair along the wall, making minute adjustments, for no apparent reason, when he returns the chair to the center of the room. His moves are part of an endgame, and *Endgame* is a play.

Beckett critic Ted Estess said that "in Beckett's literature 'existence is play,'" implying absurdity of the kind Martin Esslin talks about in his discussion of theater of the absurd. (See the commentary on p. 1220.) The absurd implies nonmeaning, such as the meaningless movements of Hamm by Clov. The meaning of those moves is in the action itself, which strikes those in the audience as absurd. Beckett's use of the absurd helps him move away from the well-made play with its clearly marked beginning, middle, and end. In the process he pokes fun at that concept by embedding the end in the beginning of *Endgame*. As the lights go up and Clov removes the sheets from the ashcans and from Hamm in his chair, he intones to the audience: "Finished." The audience is meant to sense this irony. It is the endgame when the action—and the play—are expected to stop, but as Hamm says: "The end is in the beginning and yet you go on."

Endgame in Performance

Endgame was first produced in 1957. The year before, *Waiting for Godot* had been produced in Miami and New York, establishing Beckett as an important figure in modern absurdist drama. *Endgame,* his next major play, satisfied the critics but baffled the public. The first London production was in French, at the Royal Court Theatre, which was known for producing experimental plays. Roger Blin directed. The first Paris production began three weeks later, April 26, 1957, in the Studio des Champs-Élysées. The New York production, directed by Beckett's friend and interpreter Alan Schneider, opened on January 28, 1958. A number of important revivals of the play have attested to its continuing power. In 1964, *Endgame* was produced at The Royal Shakespeare Company's Aldwych Theatre. Beckett himself directed the play at the Schiller Theatre in Berlin in September 1967. In the 1970 Open Theater Production at the Loeb Theater in Cambridge, Massachusetts, Joseph Chaikin as Hamm created a richly nuanced performance:

> Joseph Chaikin as the chairbound Hamm throws an eerie light over the play. . . . He is sensual, domineering, crafty, and infinitely tender; he prattles and tells macabre stories and his dominion over the dwindling lives of his family is like the last hoarse gasp of King Lear over the strangled body of Cordelia.   (Samuel Hirsch, *Herald Traveler*, Boston, May 13, 1970)

Andre Gregory directed the play at the Manhattan Project in 1973. Clive Barnes noted the unusual staging of this production:

> Mr. Gregory has built himself a strange, bullring of a theater. It is hexagonal, and the audience is on two levels. The audience is placed in cubicles—each holding four chairs. Each cubicle is insulated from the stage and from the world by chicken wire.   (*New York Times*, February 9, 1973)

The Royal Court presented *Endgame* in English during its Beckett Festival in 1976. Beckett directed the play again in London at the Young Vic in January 1980 and then in Chicago's Goodman Theater with the San Quentin Workshop in September 1980. In 1984, JoAnn Akalaitis staged a controversial *Endgame* at the American Repertory Theater in Cambridge, Massachusetts. She set the play in a burned-out subway tunnel and commissioned an eerie musical score by minimalist composer Philip Glass. Grove Press, Beckett's representative, complained that the production disregarded "the playwright's sparse, rigorous scenic demands" and added uncalled-for music. The production was allowed to continue after the American Repertory Theater agreed to include a program insert, signed by Beckett, "decrying the interpretation."

The 2008 production directed by Andrei Belgrader at the Brooklyn Academy of Music starred John Turturro as Hamm, Max Casella as Clov, Elaine

Stritch as Nell, and Alvin Epstein as Nagg. It followed Beckett's stage directions carefully. Mark Rylance played Hamm in a warmly reviewed London production at the Duchess Theatre in October 2009; Simon McBurney directed and played the role of Clov. Again, Beckett's stage directions were adhered to in every detail. Clearly, audiences of recent productions here and abroad identify with the anxiety that inspired the first production.

SAMUEL BECKETT (1906–1989)

Endgame   1957
A Play in One Act

The Characters

NAGG   HAMM
NELL   CLOV

(*Bare interior.*)
   (*Gray light.*)
   (*Left and right back, high up, two small windows, curtains drawn.*)
   (*Front right, a door. Hanging near door, its face to wall, a picture.*)
   (*Front left, touching each other, covered with an old sheet, two ashbins.°*)
   (*Center, in an armchair on casters, covered with an old sheet, Hamm.*)
   (*Motionless by the door, his eyes fixed on Hamm, Clov. Very red face.*)
   (*Brief tableau.*)

(*Clov goes and stands under window left. Stiff, staggering walk. He looks up at window left. He turns and looks at window right. He goes and stands under window right. He looks up at window right. He turns and looks at window left. He goes out, comes back immediately with a small stepladder, carries it over and sets it down under window left, gets up on it, draws back curtain. He gets down, takes six steps (for example) towards window right, goes back for ladder, carries it over and sets it down under window right, gets up on it, draws back curtain. He gets down, takes three steps towards window left, goes back for ladder, carries it over and sets it down under window left, gets up on it, looks out of window. Brief laugh. He gets down, takes one step towards window right, goes back for ladder, carries it over and sets it down under window right, gets the*

ladder and carries it out. Pause. Hamm stirs. He yawns under the handkerchief. He removes the handkerchief from his face. Very red face. Black glasses.*)

HAMM: Me—(*he yawns*)—to play.

(*He holds the handkerchief spread out before him.*)

   Old Stancher!°

(*He takes off his glasses, wipes his eyes, his face, the glasses, puts them on again, folds the handkerchief and puts it back neatly in the breast pocket of his dressing gown. He clears his throat, joins the tips of his fingers.*)

   Can there be misery—(*he yawns*)—loftier than mine? No doubt. Formerly. But now?

(*Pause.*)

   My father?

(*Pause.*)

   My mother?

(*Pause.*)

   My . . . dog?

(*Pause.*)

   Oh I am willing to believe they suffer as much as such creatures can suffer. But does that mean their sufferings equal mine? No doubt.

(*Pause.*)

   No, all is a—(*he yawns*)—bsolute, (*proudly*) the bigger a man is the fuller he is.

(*Pause. Gloomily.*)

---

ashbins: Trash cans.

stancher: Item that stops, or stanches, the flow of blood.

And the emptier.

(*He sniffs.*)

Clov!

(*Pause.*)

No, alone.

(*Pause.*)

What dreams! Those forests!

(*Pause.*)

Enough, it's time it ended, in the shelter too.

(*Pause.*)

And yet I hesitate, I hesitate to . . . to end. Yes there it is, it's time it ended and yet I hesitate to—(*he yawns*)—to end.

(*Yawns.*)

God, I'm tired, I'd be better off in bed.

(*He whistles. Enter Clov immediately. He halts beside the chair.*)

You pollute the air!

(*Pause.*)

Get me ready, I'm going to bed.

CLOV: I've just got you up.

HAMM: And what of it?

CLOV: I can't be getting you up and putting you to bed every five minutes, I have things to do.

(*Pause.*)

HAMM: Did you ever see my eyes?

CLOV: No.

HAMM: Did you never have the curiosity, while I was sleeping, to take off my glasses and look at my eyes?

CLOV: Pulling back the lids?

(*Pause.*)

No.

HAMM: One of these days I'll show them to you.

(*Pause.*)

It seems they've gone all white.

(*Pause.*)

What time is it?

CLOV: The same as usual.

HAMM (*gesture towards window right*): Have you looked?

CLOV: Yes.

HAMM: Well?

CLOV: Zero.

HAMM: It'd need to rain.

CLOV: It won't rain.

(*Pause.*)

HAMM: Apart from that, how do you feel?

CLOV: I don't complain.

HAMM: You feel normal?

CLOV (*irritably*): I tell you I don't complain.

HAMM: I feel a little queer.

(*Pause.*)

Clov!

CLOV: Yes.

HAMM: Have you not had enough?

CLOV: Yes!

(*Pause.*)

Of what?

HAMM: Of this . . . this . . . thing.

CLOV: I always had.

(*Pause.*)

Not you?

HAMM (*gloomily*): Then there's no reason for it to change.

CLOV: It may end.

(*Pause.*)

All life long the same questions, the same answers.

HAMM: Get me ready.

(*Clov does not move.*)

Go and get the sheet.

(*Clov does not move.*)

Clov!

CLOV: Yes.

HAMM: I'll give you nothing more to eat.

CLOV: Then we'll die.

HAMM: I'll give you just enough to keep you from dying. You'll be hungry all the time.

CLOV: Then we won't die.

(*Pause.*)

I'll go and get the sheet.

(*He goes towards the door.*)

HAMM: No!

(*Clov halts.*)

I'll give you one biscuit per day.

(*Pause.*)

One and a half.

(*Pause.*)

Why do you stay with me?

CLOV: Why do you keep me?

HAMM: There's no one else.

CLOV: There's nowhere else.

(*Pause.*)

HAMM: You're leaving me all the same.

CLOV: I'm trying.

HAMM: You don't love me.

CLOV: No.

HAMM: You loved me once.

CLOV: Once!

HAMM: I've made you suffer too much.

(*Pause.*)

Haven't I?

CLOV: It's not that.

HAMM (*shocked*): I haven't made you suffer too much?

CLOV: Yes!

HAMM (*relieved*): Ah you gave me a fright!

(*Pause. Coldly.*)

Forgive me.

(*Pause. Louder.*)

I said, Forgive me.

CLOV: I heard you.

(*Pause.*)

Have you bled?

HAMM: Less.

(*Pause.*)

Is it not time for my painkiller?

CLOV: No.

(*Pause.*)

HAMM: How are your eyes?

CLOV: Bad.

HAMM: How are your legs?

CLOV: Bad.

HAMM: But you can move.

CLOV: Yes.

HAMM (*violently*): Then move!

(*Clov goes to back wall, leans against it with his forehead and hands.*)

Where are you?

CLOV: Here.

HAMM: Come back!

(*Clov returns to his place beside the chair.*)

Where are you?

CLOV: Here.

HAMM: Why don't you kill me?

CLOV: I don't know the combination of the cupboard.

(*Pause.*)

HAMM: Go and get two bicycle wheels.

CLOV: There are no more bicycle wheels.

HAMM: What have you done with your bicycle?

CLOV: I never had a bicycle.

HAMM: The thing is impossible.

CLOV: When there were still bicycles I wept to have one. I crawled at your feet. You told me to go to hell. Now there are none.

HAMM: And your rounds? When you inspected my paupers. Always on foot?

CLOV: Sometimes on horse.

(*The lid of one of the bins lifts and the hands of Nagg appear, gripping the rim. Then his head emerges. Nightcap. Very white face. Nagg yawns, then listens.*)

I'll leave you, I have things to do.

HAMM: In your kitchen?

CLOV: Yes.

HAMM: Outside of here it's death.

(*Pause.*)

All right, be off.

(*Exit Clov. Pause.*)

We're getting on.

NAGG: Me pap!

HAMM: Accursed progenitor!

NAGG: Me pap!

HAMM: The old folks at home! No decency left! Guzzle, guzzle, that's all they think of.

(*He whistles. Enter Clov. He halts beside the chair.*)

Well! I thought you were leaving me.

CLOV: Oh not just yet, not just yet.

NAGG: Me pap!

HAMM: Give him his pap.

CLOV: There's no more pap.

HAMM (*to Nagg*): Do you hear that? There's no more pap. You'll never get any more pap.

NAGG: I want me pap!

HAMM: Give him a biscuit.

(*Exit Clov.*)

Accursed fornicator! How are your stumps?

NAGG: Never mind me stumps.

(*Enter Clov with biscuit.*)

CLOV: I'm back again, with the biscuit.

(*He gives biscuit to Nagg who fingers it, sniffs it.*)

NAGG (*plaintively*): What is it?

CLOV: Spratt's medium.

NAGG (*as before*): It's hard! I can't!

HAMM: Bottle him!

(*Clov pushes Nagg back into the bin, closes the lid.*)

CLOV (*returning to his place beside the chair*): If age but knew!

HAMM: Sit on him!

CLOV: I can't sit.

HAMM: True. And I can't stand.

CLOV: So it is.

HAMM: Every man his speciality.

(*Pause.*)

No phone calls?

(*Pause.*)

Don't we laugh?

CLOV (*after reflection*): I don't feel like it.

HAMM (*after reflection*): Nor I.

(*Pause.*)

Clov!

CLOV: Yes.

HAMM: Nature has forgotten us.

CLOV: There's no more nature.

HAMM: No more nature! You exaggerate.

CLOV: In the vicinity.

HAMM: But we breathe, we change! We lose our hair, our teeth! Our bloom! Our ideals!

CLOV: Then she hasn't forgotten us.

HAMM: But you say there is none.

CLOV (*sadly*): No one that ever lived ever thought so crooked as we.

HAMM: We do what we can.

CLOV: We shouldn't.

(*Pause.*)

HAMM: You're a bit of all right, aren't you?

CLOV: A smithereen.

(*Pause.*)

HAMM: This is slow work.

(*Pause.*)

Is it not time for my painkiller?

CLOV: No.

(*Pause.*)

I'll leave you, I have things to do.

HAMM: In your kitchen?

CLOV: Yes.

HAMM: What, I'd like to know.

CLOV: I look at the wall.

HAMM: The wall! And what do you see on your wall? Mene, mene?° Naked bodies?

CLOV: I see my light dying.

HAMM: Your light dying! Listen to that! Well, it can die just as well here, *your* light. Take a look at me and then come back and tell me what you think of *your* light.

(*Pause.*)

CLOV: You shouldn't speak to me like that.

(*Pause.*)

HAMM (*coldly*): Forgive me.

(*Pause. Louder.*)

I said, Forgive me.

CLOV: I heard you.

(*The lid of Nagg's bin lifts. His hands appear, gripping the rim. Then his head emerges. In his mouth the biscuit. He listens.*)

HAMM: Did your seeds come up?

CLOV: No.

HAMM: Did you scratch round them to see if they had sprouted?

CLOV: They haven't sprouted.

HAMM: Perhaps it's still too early.

CLOV: If they were going to sprout they would have sprouted.

(*Violently.*)

They'll never sprout!

(*Pause. Nagg takes biscuit in his hand.*)

HAMM: This is not much fun.

Mene, mene: The handwriting on the wall in Daniel 5:25 indicating the end of King Belshazzar's reign: "MENE, MENE, TEKEL, and PARSIN."

(*Pause.*)

But that's always the way at the end of the day, isn't it, Clov?

CLOV: Always.

HAMM: It's the end of the day like any other day, isn't it, Clov?

CLOV: Looks like it.

(*Pause.*)

HAMM (*anguished*): What's happening, what's happening?

CLOV: Something is taking its course.

(*Pause.*)

HAMM: All right, be off.

(*He leans back in his chair, remains motionless. Clov does not move, heaves a great groaning sigh. Hamm sits up.*)

I thought I told you to be off.

CLOV: I'm trying.

(*He goes to door, halts.*)

Ever since I was whelped.

(*Exit Clov.*)

HAMM: We're getting on.

(*He leans back in his chair, remains motionless. Nagg knocks on the lid of the other bin. Pause. He knocks harder. The lid lifts and the hands of Nell appear, gripping the rim. Then her head emerges. Lace cap. Very white face.*)

NELL: What is it, my pet?

(*Pause.*)

Time for love?

NAGG: Were you asleep?

NELL: Oh no!

NAGG: Kiss me.

NELL: We can't.

NAGG: Try.

(*Their heads strain towards each other, fail to meet, fall apart again.*)

NELL: Why this farce, day after day?

(*Pause.*)

NAGG: I've lost me tooth.

NELL: When?

NAGG: I had it yesterday.

NELL (*elegiac*): Ah yesterday!

(*They turn painfully towards each other.*)

NAGG: Can you see me?

NELL: Hardly. And you?

NAGG: What?

NELL: Can you see me?

NAGG: Hardly.

NELL: So much the better, so much the better.

NAGG: Don't say that.

(*Pause.*)

Our sight has failed.

NELL: Yes.

(*Pause. They turn away from each other.*)

From left, Elaine Stritch (Nell), Alvin Epstein (Nagg), and John Turturro (Hamm) in the Brooklyn Academy of Music production of *Endgame* in 2008.

NAGG: Can you hear me?
NELL: Yes. And you?
NAGG: Yes.

(*Pause.*)

Our hearing hasn't failed.
NELL: Our what?
NAGG: Our hearing.
NELL: No.

(*Pause.*)

Have you anything else to say to me?
NAGG: Do you remember—
NELL: No.
NAGG: When we crashed on our tandem and lost our shanks.

(*They laugh heartily.*)

NELL: It was in the Ardennes.

(*They laugh less heartily.*)

NAGG: On the road to Sedan.

(*They laugh still less heartily.*)

Are you cold?
NELL: Yes, perished. And you?
NAGG:

(*Pause.*)

I'm freezing.

(*Pause.*)

Do you want to go in?
NELL: Yes.
NAGG: Then go in.

(*Nell does not move.*)

Why don't you go in?
NELL: I don't know.

(*Pause.*)

NAGG: Has he changed your sawdust?
NELL: It isn't sawdust.

(*Pause. Wearily.*)

Can you not be a little accurate, Nagg?
NAGG: Your sand then. It's not important.
NELL: It is important.

(*Pause.*)

NAGG: It was sawdust once.
NELL: Once!
NAGG: And now it's sand.

(*Pause.*)

From the shore.

(*Pause. Impatiently.*)

Now it's sand he fetches from the shore.

NELL: Now it's sand.
NAGG: Has he changed yours?
NELL: No.
NAGG: Nor mine.

(*Pause.*)

    I won't have it!

(*Pause. Holding up the biscuit.*)

    Do you want a bit?
NELL: No.

(*Pause.*)

    Of what?
NAGG: Biscuit. I've kept you half.

(*He looks at the biscuit. Proudly.*)

    Three quarters. For you. Here.

(*He proffers the biscuit.*)

    No?

(*Pause.*)

    Do you not feel well?
HAMM (*wearily*): Quiet, quiet, you're keeping me awake.

(*Pause.*)

    Talk softer.

(*Pause.*)

    If I could sleep I might make love. I'd go into the woods. My eyes would see . . . the sky, the earth. I'd run, run, they wouldn't catch me.

(*Pause.*)

    Nature!

(*Pause.*)

    There's something dripping in my head.

(*Pause.*)

    A heart, a heart in my head.

(*Pause.*)

NAGG (*soft*): Do you hear him? A heart in his head!

(*He chuckles cautiously.*)

NELL: One mustn't laugh at those things, Nagg. Why must you always laugh at them?
NAGG: Not so loud!
NELL (*without lowering her voice*): Nothing is funnier than unhappiness, I grant you that. But—
NAGG (*shocked*): Oh!
NELL: Yes, yes, it's the most comical thing in the world. And we laugh, we laugh, with a will, in the beginning. But it's always the same thing. Yes, it's like the funny story we have heard too often, we still find it funny, but we don't laugh anymore.

(*Pause.*)

    Have you anything else to say to me?

NAGG: No.
NELL: Are you quite sure?

(*Pause.*)

    Then I'll leave you.
NAGG: Do you not want your biscuit?

(*Pause.*)

    I'll keep it for you.

(*Pause.*)

    I thought you were going to leave me.
NELL: I am going to leave you.
NAGG: Could you give me a scratch before you go?
NELL: No.

(*Pause.*)

    Where?
NAGG: In the back.
NELL: No.

(*Pause.*)

    Rub yourself against the rim.
NAGG: It's lower down. In the hollow.
NELL: What hollow?
NAGG: The hollow!

(*Pause.*)

    Could you not?

(*Pause.*)

    Yesterday you scratched me there.
NELL (*elegiac*): Ah yesterday!
NAGG: Could you not?

(*Pause.*)

    Would you like me to scratch you?

(*Pause.*)

    Are you crying again?
NELL: I was trying.

(*Pause.*)

HAMM: Perhaps it's a little vein.

(*Pause.*)

NAGG: What was that he said?
NELL: Perhaps it's a little vein.
NAGG: What does that mean?

(*Pause.*)

    That means nothing.

(*Pause.*)

    Will I tell you the story of the tailor?
NELL: No.

(*Pause.*)

    What for?

NAGG: To cheer you up.
NELL: It's not funny.
NAGG: It always made you laugh.

(*Pause.*)

The first time I thought you'd die.
NELL: It was on Lake Como.

(*Pause.*)

One April afternoon.

(*Pause.*)

Can you believe it?
NAGG: What?
NELL: That we once went out rowing on Lake Como.

(*Pause.*)

One April afternoon.
NAGG: We had got engaged the day before.
NELL: Engaged!
NAGG: You were in such fits that we capsized. By rights we should have been drowned.
NELL: It was because I felt happy.
NAGG (*indignant*): It was not, it was not, it was my story and nothing else. Happy! Don't you laugh at it still? Every time I tell it. Happy!
NELL: It was deep, deep. And you could see down to the bottom. So white. So clean.
NAGG: Let me tell it again.

(*Raconteur's voice.*)

An Englishman, needing a pair of striped trousers in a hurry for the New Year festivities, goes to his tailor who takes his measurements.

(*Tailor's voice.*)

"That's the lot, come back in four days, I'll have it ready." Good. Four days later.

(*Tailor's voice.*)

"So sorry, come back in a week, I've made a mess of the seat." Good, that's all right, a neat seat can be very ticklish. A week later.

(*Tailor's voice.*)

"Frightfully sorry, come back in ten days, I've made a hash of the crotch." Good, can't be helped, a snug crotch is always a teaser. Ten days later.

(*Tailor's voice.*)

"Dreadfully sorry, come back in a fortnight, I've made a balls of the fly." Good, at a pinch, a smart fly is a stiff proposition.

(*Pause. Normal voice.*)

I never told it worse.

(*Pause. Gloomy.*)

I tell this story worse and worse.

(*Pause. Raconteur's voice.*)

Well, to make it short, the bluebells are blowing and he ballockses the buttonholes.

(*Customer's voice.*)

"God damn you to hell, Sir, no, it's indecent, there are limits! In six days, do you hear me, six days, God made the world. Yes Sir, no less Sir, the WORLD! And you are not bloody well capable of making me a pair of trousers in three months!"

(*Tailor's voice, scandalized.*)

"But my dear Sir, my dear Sir, look—(*disdainful gesture, disgustedly*)—at the world—(*pause*) and look—(*loving gesture, proudly*)—at my TROUSERS!"

(*Pause. He looks at Nell who has remained impassive, her eyes unseeing, breaks into a high forced laugh, cuts it short, pokes his head towards Nell, launches his laugh again.*)

HAMM: Silence!

(*Nagg starts, cuts short his laugh.*)

NELL: You could see down to the bottom.
HAMM (*exasperated*): Have you not finished? Will you never finish?

(*With sudden fury.*)

Will this never finish?

(*Nagg disappears into his bin, closes the lid behind him. Nell does not move. Frenziedly.*)

My kingdom for a nightman!

(*He whistles. Enter Clov.*)

Clear away this muck! Chuck it in the sea!

(*Clov goes to bins, halts.*)

NELL: So white.
HAMM: What? What's she blathering about?

(*Clov stoops, takes Nell's hand, feels her pulse.*)

NELL (*to Clov*): Desert!

(*Clov lets go her hand, pushes her back in the bin, closes the lid.*)

CLOV (*returning to his place beside the chair*): She has no pulse.
HAMM: What was she driveling about?
CLOV: She told me to go away, into the desert.
HAMM: Damn busybody! Is that all?
CLOV: No.
HAMM: What else?
CLOV: I didn't understand.
HAMM: Have you bottled her?
CLOV: Yes.
HAMM: Are they both bottled?

CLOV: Yes.

HAMM: Screw down the lids.

(*Clov goes towards door.*)

Time enough.

(*Clov halts.*)

My anger subsides, I'd like to pee.

CLOV (*with alacrity*): I'll go and get the catheter.

(*He goes towards door.*)

HAMM: Time enough.

(*Clov halts.*)

Give me my painkiller.

CLOV: It's too soon.

(*Pause.*)

It's too soon on top of your tonic, it wouldn't act.

HAMM: In the morning they brace you up and in the evening they calm you down. Unless it's the other way round.

(*Pause.*)

That old doctor, he's dead naturally?

CLOV: He wasn't old.

HAMM: But he's dead?

CLOV: Naturally.

(*Pause.*)

You ask *me* that?

(*Pause.*)

HAMM: Take me for a little turn.

(*Clov goes behind the chair and pushes it forward.*)

Not too fast!

(*Clov pushes chair.*)

Right round the world!

(*Clov pushes chair.*)

Hug the walls, then back to the center again.

(*Clov pushes chair.*)

I was right in the center, wasn't I?

CLOV (*pushing*): Yes.

HAMM: We'd need a proper wheelchair. With big wheels. Bicycle wheels!

(*Pause.*)

Are you hugging?

CLOV (*pushing*): Yes.

HAMM (*groping for wall*): It's a lie! Why do you lie to me?

Clov (*bearing closer to wall*): There! There!

HAMM: Stop!

(*Clov stops chair close to back wall. Hamm lays his hand against wall.*)

Old wall!

(*Pause.*)

Beyond is the . . . other hell.

(*Pause. Violently.*)

Closer! Closer! Up against!

CLOV: Take away your hand.

(*Hamm withdraws his hand. Clov rams chair against wall.*)

There!

(*Hamm leans towards wall, applies his ear to it.*)

HAMM: Do you hear?

(*He strikes the wall with his knuckles.*)

Do you hear? Hollow bricks!

(*He strikes again.*)

All that's hollow!

(*Pause. He straightens up. Violently.*)

That's enough. Back!

CLOV: We haven't done the round.

HAMM: Back to my place!

(*Clov pushes chair back to center.*)

Is that my place?

CLOV: Yes, that's your place.

HAMM: Am I right in the center?

CLOV: I'll measure it.

HAMM: More or less! More or less!

CLOV (*moving chair slightly*): There!

HAMM: I'm more or less in the center?

CLOV: I'd say so.

HAMM: You'd say so! Put me right in the center!

CLOV: I'll go and get the tape.

HAMM: Roughly! Roughly!

(*Clov moves chair slightly.*)

Bang in the center!

CLOV: There!

(*Pause.*)

HAMM: I feel a little too far to the left.

(*Clov moves chair slightly.*)

Now I feel a little too far to the right.

(*Clov moves chair slightly.*)

I feel a little too far forward.

(*Clov moves chair slightly.*)

Now I feel a little too far back.

(*Clov moves chair slightly.*)

Don't stay there (*i.e., behind the chair*), you give me the shivers.

(*Clov returns to his place beside the chair.*)

CLOV: If I could kill him I'd die happy.

(*Pause.*)

HAMM: What's the weather like?
CLOV: As usual.
HAMM: Look at the earth.
CLOV: I've looked.
HAMM: With the glass?
CLOV: No need of the glass.
HAMM: Look at it with the glass.
CLOV: I'll go and get the glass.

(*Exit Clov.*)

HAMM: No need of the glass!

(*Enter Clov with telescope.*)

CLOV: I'm back again, with the glass.

(*He goes to window right, looks up at it.*)

I need the steps.
HAMM: Why? Have you shrunk?

(*Exit Clov with telescope.*)

I don't like that, I don't like that.

(*Enter Clov with ladder, but without telescope.*)

CLOV: I'm back again, with the steps.

(*He sets down ladder under window right, gets up on it, realizes he has not the telescope, gets down.*)

I need the glass.

(*He goes towards door.*)

HAMM (*violently*): But you have the glass!
CLOV (*halting, violently*): No, I haven't the glass!

(*Exit Clov.*)

HAMM: This is deadly.

(*Enter Clov with telescope. He goes towards ladder.*)

CLOV: Things are livening up.

(*He gets up on ladder, raises the telescope, lets it fall.*)

I did it on purpose.

(*He gets down, picks up the telescope, turns it on auditorium.*)

I see . . . a multitude . . . in transports . . . of joy.

(*Pause.*)

That's what I call a magnifier.

(*He lowers the telescope, turns towards Hamm.*)

Well? Don't we laugh?
HAMM (*after reflection*): I don't.
CLOV (*after reflection*): Nor I.

(*He gets up on ladder, turns the telescope on the without.*)

Let's see.

(*He looks, moving the telescope.*)

Zero . . . (*he looks*) . . . zero . . . (*he looks*) . . . and zero.
HAMM: Nothing stirs. All is—
CLOV: Zer—
HAMM (*violently*): Wait till you're spoken to!

(*Normal voice.*)

All is . . . all is . . . all is what?

(*Violently.*)

All is what?
CLOV: What all is? In a word? Is that what you want to know? Just a moment.

(*He turns the telescope on the without, looks, lowers the telescope, turns towards Hamm.*)

Corpsed.

(*Pause.*)

Well? Content?
HAMM: Look at the sea.
CLOV: It's the same.
HAMM: Look at the ocean!

(*Clov gets down, takes a few steps towards window left, goes back for ladder, carries it over and sets it down under window left, gets up on it, turns the telescope on the without, looks at length. He starts, lowers the telescope, examines it, turns it again on the without.*)

CLOV: Never seen anything like that!
HAMM (*anxious*): What? A sail? A fin? Smoke?
CLOV (*looking*): The light is sunk.
HAMM (*relieved*): Pah! We all knew that.
CLOV (*looking*): There was a bit left.
HAMM: The base.
CLOV (*looking*): Yes.
HAMM: And now?
CLOV (*looking*): All gone.
HAMM: No gulls?
CLOV (*looking*): Gulls!
HAMM: And the horizon? Nothing on the horizon?
CLOV (*lowering the telescope, turning towards Hamm, exasperated*): What in God's name could there be on the horizon?

(*Pause.*)

HAMM: The waves, how are the waves?
CLOV: The waves?

(*He turns the telescope on the waves.*)

Lead.
HAMM: And the sun?
CLOV (*looking*): Zero.
HAMM: But it should be sinking. Look again.
CLOV (*looking*): Damn the sun.
HAMM: Is it night already then?
CLOV (*looking*): No.

HAMM: Then what is it?
CLOV (*looking*): Gray.

(*Lowering the telescope, turning towards Hamm, louder.*)

Gray!

(*Pause. Still louder.*)

GRRAY!

(*Pause. He gets down, approaches Hamm from behind, whispers in his ear.*)

HAMM (*starting*): Gray! Did I hear you say gray?
CLOV: Light black. From pole to pole.
HAMM: You exaggerate.

(*Pause.*)

Don't stay there, you give me the shivers.

(*Clov returns to his place beside the chair.*)

CLOV: Why this farce, day after day?
HAMM: Routine. One never knows.

(*Pause.*)

Last night I saw inside my breast. There was a big sore.
CLOV: Pah! You saw your heart.
HAMM: No, it was living.

(*Pause. Anguished.*)

Clov!
CLOV: Yes.
HAMM: What's happening?
CLOV: Something is taking its course.

(*Pause.*)

HAMM: Clov!
CLOV (*impatiently*): What is it?
HAMM: We're not beginning to . . . to . . . mean something?
CLOV: Mean something! You and I, mean something!

(*Brief laugh.*)

Ah that's a good one!
HAMM: I wonder.

(*Pause.*)

Imagine if a rational being came back to earth, wouldn't he be liable to get ideas into his head if he observed us long enough.

(*Voice of rational being.*)

Ah, good, now I see what it is, yes, now I understand what they're at!

(*Clov starts, drops the telescope and begins to scratch his belly with both hands. Normal voice.*)

And without going so far as that, we ourselves . . .(*with emotion*) . . . we ourselves . . . at certain moments . . .

(*Vehemently.*)

To think perhaps it won't all have been for nothing!
CLOV (*anguished, scratching himself*): I have a flea!

HAMM: A flea! Are there still fleas?
CLOV: On me there's one.

(*Scratching.*)

Unless it's a crablouse.
HAMM (*very perturbed*): But humanity might start from there all over again! Catch him, for the love of God!
CLOV: I'll go and get the powder.

(*Exit Clov.*)

HAMM: A flea! This is awful! What a day!

(*Enter Clov with a sprinkling tin.*)

CLOV: I'm back again, with the insecticide.
HAMM: Let him have it!

(*Clov loosens the top of his trousers, pulls it forward and shakes powder into the aperture. He stoops, looks, waits, starts, frenziedly shakes more powder, stoops, looks, waits.*)

CLOV: The bastard!
HAMM: Did you get him?
CLOV: Looks like it.

(*He drops the tin and adjusts his trousers.*)

Unless he's laying doggo.°
HAMM: Laying! Lying you mean. Unless he's *lying* doggo.
CLOV: Ah? One says lying? One doesn't say laying?
HAMM: Use your head, can't you. If he was laying we'd be bitched.
CLOV: Ah.

(*Pause.*)

What about that pee?
HAMM: I'm having it.
CLOV: Ah that's the spirit, that's the spirit!

(*Pause.*)

HAMM (*with ardor*): Let's go from here, the two of us! South! You can make a raft and the currents will carry us away, far away, to other . . . mammals!
CLOV: God forbid!
HAMM: Alone, I'll embark alone! Get working on that raft immediately. Tomorrow I'll be gone forever.
CLOV (*hastening towards door*): I'll start straight away.
HAMM: Wait!

(*Clov halts.*)

Will there be sharks, do you think?
CLOV: Sharks? I don't know. If there are there will be.

(*He goes towards door.*)

HAMM: Wait!

(*Clov halts.*)

Is it not yet time for my painkiller?
CLOV (*violently*): No!

(*He goes towards door.*)

doggo: In hiding.

HAMM: Wait!

(*Clov halts.*)

How are your eyes?

CLOV: Bad.

HAMM: But you can see.

CLOV: All I want.

HAMM: How are your legs?

CLOV: Bad.

HAMM: But you can walk.

CLOV: I come . . . and go.

HAMM: In my house.

(*Pause. With prophetic relish.*)

One day you'll be blind, like me. You'll be sitting there, a speck in the void, in the dark, forever, like me.

(*Pause.*)

One day you'll say to yourself, I'm tired, I'll sit down, and you'll go and sit down. Then you'll say, I'm hungry, I'll get up and get something to eat. But you won't get up. You'll say, I shouldn't have sat down, but since I have I'll sit on a little longer, then I'll get up and get something to eat. But you won't get up and you won't get anything to eat.

(*Pause.*)

You'll look at the wall a while, then you'll say, I'll close my eyes, perhaps have a little sleep, after that I'll feel better, and you'll close them. And when you open them again there'll be no wall anymore.

(*Pause.*)

Infinite emptiness will be all around you, all the resurrected dead of all the ages wouldn't fill it, and there you'll be like a little bit of grit in the middle of the steppe.

(*Pause.*)

Yes, one day you'll know what it is, you'll be like me, except that you won't have anyone with you, because you won't have had pity on anyone and because there won't be anyone left to have pity on.

(*Pause.*)

CLOV: It's not certain.

(*Pause.*)

And there's one thing you forget.

HAMM: Ah?

CLOV: I can't sit down.

HAMM (*impatiently*): Well you'll lie down then, what the hell! Or you'll come to a standstill, simply stop and stand still, the way you are now. One day you'll say, I'm tired, I'll stop. What does the attitude matter?

(*Pause.*)

CLOV: So you all want me to leave you.

HAMM: Naturally.

CLOV: Then I'll leave you.

HAMM: You can't leave us.

CLOV: Then I won't leave you.

(*Pause.*)

HAMM: Why don't you finish us?

(*Pause.*)

I'll tell you the combination of the cupboard if you promise to finish me.

CLOV: I couldn't finish you.

HAMM: Then you won't finish me.

(*Pause.*)

CLOV: I'll leave you, I have things to do.

HAMM: Do you remember when you came here?

CLOV: No. Too small, you told me.

HAMM: Do you remember your father?

CLOV (*wearily*): Same answer.

(*Pause.*)

You've asked me these questions millions of times.

HAMM: I love the old questions.

(*With fervor.*)

Ah the old questions, the old answers, there's nothing like them!

(*Pause.*)

It was I was a father to you.

CLOV: Yes.

(*He looks at Hamm fixedly.*)

You were that to me.

HAMM: My house a home for you.

CLOV: Yes.

(*He looks about him.*)

This was that for me.

HAMM (*proudly*): But for me (*gesture towards himself*), no father. But for Hamm (*gesture towards surroundings*), no home.

(*Pause.*)

CLOV: I'll leave you.

HAMM: Did you ever think of one thing?

CLOV: Never.

HAMM: That here we're down in a hole.

(*Pause.*)

But beyond the hills? Eh? Perhaps it's still green. Eh?

(*Pause.*)

Flora! Pomona!

(*Ecstatically.*)

Ceres!°

(*Pause.*)

Flora . . . Ceres: Three Roman goddesses — Flora, of flowers; Pomona, of fruit; Ceres, of agriculture.

Perhaps you won't need to go very far.

CLOV: I can't go very far.

(*Pause.*)

I'll leave you.

HAMM: Is my dog ready?

CLOV: He lacks a leg.

HAMM: Is he silky?

CLOV: He's a kind of Pomeranian.

HAMM: Go and get him.

CLOV: He lacks a leg.

HAMM: Go and get him!

(*Exit Clov.*)

We're getting on.

(*Enter Clov holding by one of its three legs a black toy dog.*)

CLOV: Your dogs are here.

(*He hands the dog to Hamm who feels it, fondles it.*)

HAMM: He's white, isn't he?

CLOV: Nearly.

HAMM: What do you mean, nearly? Is he white or isn't he?

CLOV: He isn't.

(*Pause.*)

HAMM: You've forgotten the sex.

CLOV (*vexed*): But he isn't finished. The sex goes on at the end.

(*Pause.*)

HAMM: You haven't put on his ribbon.

CLOV (*angrily*): But he isn't finished, I tell you! First you finish your dog and then you put on his ribbon!

(*Pause.*)

HAMM: Can he stand?

CLOV: I don't know.

HAMM: Try.

(*He hands the dog to Clov who places it on the ground.*)

Well?

CLOV: Wait!

(*He squats down and tries to get the dog to stand on its three legs, fails, lets it go. The dog falls on its side.*)

HAMM (*impatiently*): Well?

CLOV: He's standing.

HAMM (*groping for the dog*): Where? Where is he?

(*Clov holds up the dog in a standing position.*)

CLOV: There.

(*He takes Hamm's hand and guides it towards the dog's head.*)

HAMM (*his hand on the dog's head*): Is he gazing at me?

CLOV: Yes.

HAMM (*proudly*): As if he were asking me to take him for a walk?

CLOV: If you like.

HAMM (*as before*): Or as if he were begging me for a bone.

(*He withdraws his hand.*)

Leave him like that, standing there imploring me.

(*Clov straightens up. The dog falls on its side.*)

CLOV: I'll leave you.

HAMM: Have you had your visions?

CLOV: Less.

HAMM: Is Mother Pegg's light on?

CLOV: Light! How could anyone's light be on?

HAMM: Extinguished!

CLOV: Naturally it's extinguished. If it's not on it's extinguished.

HAMM: No, I mean Mother Pegg.

CLOV: But naturally she's extinguished!

(*Pause.*)

What's the matter with you today?

HAMM: I'm taking my course.

(*Pause.*)

Is she buried?

CLOV: Buried! Who would have buried her?

HAMM: You.

CLOV: Me! Haven't I enough to do without burying people?

HAMM: But you'll bury me.

CLOV: No I won't bury you.

(*Pause.*)

HAMM: She was bonny once, like a flower of the field.

(*With reminiscent leer.*)

And a great one for the men!

CLOV: We too were bonny—once. It's a rare thing not to have been bonny—once.

(*Pause.*)

HAMM: Go and get the gaff.

(*Clov goes to door, halts.*)

CLOV: Do this, do that, and I do it. I never refuse. Why?

HAMM: You're not able to.

CLOV: Soon I won't do it anymore.

HAMM: You won't be able to anymore.

(*Exit Clov.*)

Ah the creatures, the creatures, everything has to be explained to them.

(*Enter Clov with gaff.*)

CLOV: Here's your gaff. Stick it up.

(*He gives the gaff to Hamm who, wielding it like a puntpole,° tries to move his chair.*)

HAMM: Did I move?
CLOV: No.

(*Hamm throws down the gaff.*)

HAMM: Go and get the oilcan.
CLOV: What for?
HAMM: To oil the casters.
CLOV: I oiled them yesterday.
HAMM: Yesterday! What does that mean? Yesterday!
CLOV (*violently*): That means that bloody awful day, long ago, before this bloody awful day. I use the words you taught me. If they don't mean anything anymore, teach me others. Or let me be silent.

(*Pause.*)

HAMM: I once knew a madman who thought the end of the world had come. He was a painter—and engraver. I had a great fondness for him. I used to go and see him, in the asylum. I'd take him by the hand and drag him to the window. Look! There! All that rising corn! And there! Look! The sails of the herring fleet! All that loveliness!

(*Pause.*)

He'd snatch away his hand and go back into his corner. Appalled. All he had seen was ashes.

(*Pause.*)

He alone had been spared.

(*Pause.*)

Forgotten.

(*Pause.*)

It appears the case is . . . was not so . . . so unusual.
CLOV: A madman? When was that?
HAMM: Oh way back, way back, you weren't in the land of the living.
CLOV: God be with the days!

(*Pause. Hamm raises his toque.*)

HAMM: I had a great fondness for him.

(*Pause. He puts on his toque again.*)

He was a painter—and engraver.
CLOV: There are so many terrible things.
HAMM: No, no, there are not so many now.

(*Pause.*)

Clov!
CLOV: Yes.
HAMM: Do you not think this has gone on long enough?
CLOV: Yes!

---

puntpole: A pole used to propel a punt, a flat-bottomed boat, through the water.

(*Pause.*)

What?
HAMM: This . . . this . . . thing.
CLOV: I've always thought so.

(*Pause.*)

You not?
HAMM (*gloomily*): Then it's a day like any other day.
CLOV: As long as it lasts.

(*Pause.*)

All life long the same inanities.
HAMM: I can't leave you.
CLOV: I know. And you can't follow me.

(*Pause.*)

HAMM: If you leave me how shall I know?
CLOV (*briskly*): Well you simply whistle me and if I don't come running it means I've left you.

(*Pause.*)

HAMM: You won't come and kiss me good-bye?
CLOV: Oh I shouldn't think so.

(*Pause.*)

HAMM: But you might be merely dead in your kitchen.
CLOV: The result would be the same.
HAMM: Yes, but how would I know, if you were merely dead in your kitchen?
CLOV: Well . . . sooner or later I'd start to stink.
HAMM: You stink already. The whole place stinks of corpses.
CLOV: The whole universe.
HAMM (*angrily*): To hell with the universe.

(*Pause.*)

Think of something.
CLOV: What?
HAMM: An idea, have an idea.

(*Angrily.*)

A bright idea!
CLOV: Ah good.

(*He starts pacing to and fro, his eyes fixed on the ground, his hands behind his back. He halts.*)

The pains in my legs! It's unbelievable! Soon I won't be able to think anymore.
HAMM: You won't be able to leave me.

(*Clov resumes his pacing.*)

What are you doing?
CLOV: Having an idea.

(*He paces.*)

Ah!

(*He halts.*)

HAMM: What a brain!

(*Pause.*)

Well?

CLOV: Wait!

(*He meditates. Not very convinced.*)

Yes . . .

(*Pause. More convinced.*)

Yes!

(*He raises his head.*)

I have it! I set the alarm.

(*Pause.*)

HAMM: This is perhaps not one of my bright days, but
frankly—

CLOV: You whistle me. I don't come. The alarm rings. I'm
gone. It doesn't ring. I'm dead.

(*Pause.*)

HAMM: Is it working?

(*Pause. Impatiently.*)

The alarm, is it working?

CLOV: Why wouldn't it be working?

HAMM: Because it's worked too much.

CLOV: But it's hardly worked at all.

HAMM (*angrily*): Then because it's worked too little!

CLOV: I'll go and see.

(*Exit Clov. Brief ring of alarm off. Enter Clov with
alarm clock. He holds it against Hamm's ear and
releases alarm. They listen to it ringing to the end.
Pause.*)

Fit to wake the dead! Did you hear it?

HAMM: Vaguely.

CLOV: The end is terrific!

HAMM: I prefer the middle.

(*Pause.*)

Is it not time for my painkiller?

CLOV: No!

(*He goes to door, turns.*)

I'll leave you.

HAMM: It's time for my story. Do you want to listen to
my story?

CLOV: No.

HAMM: Ask my father if he wants to listen to my story.

(*Clov goes to bins, raises the lid of Nagg's, stoops,
looks into it. Pause. He straightens up.*)

CLOV: He's asleep.

HAMM: Wake him.

(*Clov stoops, wakes Nagg with the alarm. Unintelligible words. Clov straightens up.*)

CLOV: He doesn't want to listen to your story.

HAMM: I'll give him a bonbon.

(*Clov stoops. As before.*)

CLOV: He wants a sugarplum.

HAMM: He'll get a sugarplum.

(*Clov stoops. As before.*)

CLOV: It's a deal.

(*He goes towards door. Nagg's hands appear, gripping
the rim. Then the head emerges. Clov reaches door,
turns.*)

Do you believe in the life to come?

HAMM: Mine was always that.

(*Exit Clov.*)

Got him that time!

NAGG: I'm listening.

HAMM: Scoundrel! Why did you engender me?

NAGG: I didn't know.

HAMM: What? What didn't you know?

NAGG: That it'd be you.

(*Pause.*)

You'll give me a sugarplum?

HAMM: After the audition.

NAGG: You swear?

HAMM: Yes.

NAGG: On what?

HAMM: My honor.

(*Pause. They laugh heartily.*)

NAGG: Two.

HAMM: One.

NAGG: One for me and one for—

HAMM: One! Silence!

(*Pause.*)

Where was I?

(*Pause. Gloomily.*)

It's finished, we're finished.

(*Pause.*)

Nearly finished.

(*Pause.*)

There'll be no more speech.

(*Pause.*)

Something dripping in my head, ever since the
fontanelles.°

(*Stifled hilarity of Nagg.*)

Splash, splash, always on the same spot.

(*Pause.*)

Perhaps it's a little vein.

since the fontanelles: Since soft membranes linked the incom-
pletely developed skull bones in his infant head.

(*Pause.*)

A little artery.

(*Pause. More animated.*)

Enough of that, it's story time, where was I?

(*Pause. Narrative tone.*)

The man came crawling towards me, on his belly. Pale, wonderfully pale and thin, he seemed on the point of—

(*Pause. Normal tone.*)

No, I've done that bit.

(*Pause. Narrative tone.*)

I calmly filled my pipe—the meerschaum, lit it with . . . let us say a vesta,° drew a few puffs. Aah!

(*Pause.*)

Well, what is it *you* want?

(*Pause.*)

It was an extraordinarily bitter day, I remember, zero by the thermometer. But considering it was Christmas Eve there was nothing . . . extraordinary about that. Seasonable weather, for once in a way.

(*Pause.*)

Well, what ill wind blows you my way? He raised his face to me, black with mingled dirt and tears.

(*Pause. Normal tone.*)

That should do it.

(*Narrative tone.*)

No no, don't look at me, don't look at me. He dropped his eyes and mumbled something, apologies I presume.

(*Pause.*)

I'm a busy man, you know, the final touches, before the festivities, you know what it is.

(*Pause. Forcibly.*)

Come on now, what is the object of this invasion?

(*Pause.*)

It was a glorious bright day, I remember, fifty by the heliometer,° but already the sun was sinking down into the . . . down among the dead.

(*Normal tone.*)

Nagg, it's nice of Mine all Perceived I hadn't been me if would. been something else but

vesta: Wooden match.   heliometer: A telescope for measuring the apparent diameter of the sun.

Nicely put, that.

(*Narrative tone.*)

Come on now, come on, present your petition and let me resume my labors.

(*Pause. Normal tone.*)

There's English for you. Ah well . . .

(*Narrative tone.*)

It was then he took the plunge. It's my little one, he said. Tsstss, a little one, that's bad. My little boy, he said, as if the sex mattered. Where did he come from? He named the hole. A good half-day, on horse. What are you insinuating? That the place is still inhabited? No, no, not a soul, except himself and the child— assuming he existed. Good. I inquired about the situation at Kov, beyond the gulf. Not a sinner. Good. And you expect me to believe you have left your little one back there, all alone, and alive into the bargain? Come now!

(*Pause.*)

It was a howling wild day, I remember, a hundred by the anemometer.° The wind was tearing up the dead pines and sweeping them . . . away.

(*Pause. Normal tone.*)

A bit feeble, that.

(*Narrative tone.*)

Come on, man, speak up, what is it you want from me, I have to put up my holly.

(*Pause.*)

Well to make it short it finally transpired that what he wanted from me was . . . bread for his brat? Bread? But I have no bread, it doesn't agree with me. Good. Then perhaps a little corn?

(*Pause. Normal tone.*)

That should do it.

(*Narrative tone.*)

Corn, yes, I have corn, it's true, in my granaries. But use your head. I give you some corn, a pound, a pound and a half, you bring it back to your child and you make him—if he's still alive—a nice pot of porridge, (*Nagg reacts*) a nice pot and a half of porridge, full of nourishment. Good. The colors come back into his little cheeks—perhaps. And then?

(*Pause.*)

I lost patience.

anemometer: An instrument for measuring wind speed.

(*Violently.*)

Use your head, can't you, use your head, you're on earth, there's no cure for that!

(*Pause.*)

It was an exceedingly dry day, I remember, zero by the hygrometer.° Ideal weather, for my lumbago.

(*Pause. Violently.*)

But what in God's name do you imagine? That the earth will awake in spring? That the rivers and seas will run with fish again? That there's manna in heaven still for imbeciles like you?

(*Pause.*)

Gradually I cooled down, sufficiently at least to ask him how long he had taken on the way. Three whole days. Good. In what condition he had left the child. Deep in sleep.

(*Forcibly.*)

But deep in what sleep, deep in what sleep already?

(*Pause.*)

Well to make it short I finally offered to take him into my service. He had touched a chord. And then I imagined already that I wasn't much longer for this world.

(*He laughs. Pause.*)

Well?

(*Pause.*)

Well? Here if you were careful you might die a nice natural death, in peace and comfort.

(*Pause.*)

Well?

(*Pause.*)

In the end he asked me would I consent to take in the child as well—if he were still alive.

(*Pause.*)

It was the moment I was waiting for.

(*Pause.*)

Would I consent to take in the child . . .

(*Pause.*)

I can see him still, down on his knees, his hands flat on the ground, glaring at me with his mad eyes, in defiance of my wishes.

(*Pause. Normal tone.*)

hygrometer: Device for measuring humidity.

I'll soon have finished with this story.

(*Pause.*)

Unless I bring in other characters.

(*Pause.*)

But where would I find them?

(*Pause.*)

Where would I look for them?

(*Pause. He whistles. Enter Clov.*)

Let us pray to God.
NAGG: Me sugarplum!
CLOV: There's a rat in the kitchen!
HAMM: A rat! Are there still rats?
CLOV: In the kitchen there's one.
HAMM: And you haven't exterminated him?
CLOV: Half. You disturbed us.
HAMM: He can't get away?
CLOV: No.
HAMM: You'll finish him later. Let us pray to God.
CLOV: Again!
NAGG: Me sugarplum!
HAMM: God first!

(*Pause.*)

Are you right?
CLOV (*resigned*): Off we go.
HAMM (*to Nagg*): And you?
NAGG (*clasping his hands, closing his eyes, in a gabble*): Our Father which art—
HAMM: Silence! In silence! Where are your manners?

(*Pause.*)

Off we go.

(*Attitudes of prayer. Silence. Abandoning his attitude, discouraged.*)

Well?
CLOV (*abandoning his attitude*): What a hope! And you?
HAMM: Sweet damn all!

(*To Nagg.*)

And you?
NAGG: Wait!

(*Pause. Abandoning his attitude.*)

Nothing doing!
HAMM: The bastard! He doesn't exist!
CLOV: Not yet.
NAGG: Me sugarplum!
HAMM: There are no more sugarplums!

(*Pause.*)

NAGG: It's natural. After all I'm your father. It's true if it hadn't been me it would have been someone else. But that's no excuse.

(*Pause.*)

Turkish Delight,° for example, which no longer exists, we all know that, there is nothing in the world I love more. And one day I'll ask you for some, in return for a kindness, and you'll promise it to me. One must live with the times.

(*Pause.*)

Whom did you call when you were a tiny boy, and were frightened, in the dark? Your mother? No. Me. We let you cry. Then we moved you out of earshot, so that we might sleep in peace.

(*Pause.*)

I was asleep, as happy as a king, and you woke me up to have me listen to you. It wasn't indispensable, you didn't really need to have me listen to you.

(*Pause.*)

I hope the day will come when you'll really need to have me listen to you, and need to hear my voice, any voice.

(*Pause.*)

Yes, I hope I'll live till then, to hear you calling me like when you were a tiny boy, and were frightened, in the dark, and I was your only hope.

(*Pause. Nagg knocks on lid of Nell's bin. Pause.*)

Nell!

(*Pause. He knocks louder. Pause. Louder.*)

Nell!

(*Pause. Nagg sinks back into his bin, closes the lid behind him. Pause.*)

HAMM: Our revels now are ended.

(*He gropes for the dog.*)

The dog's gone.
CLOV: He's not a real dog, he can't go.
HAMM (*groping*): He's not there.
CLOV: He's lain down.
HAMM: Give him up to me.

(*Clov picks up the dog and gives it to Hamm. Hamm holds it in his arms. Pause. Hamm throws away the dog.*)

Dirty brute!

(*Clov begins to pick up the objects lying on the ground.*)

What are you doing?
CLOV: Putting things in order.

(*He straightens up. Fervently.*)

I'm going to clear everything away!

(*He starts picking up again.*)

HAMM: Order!

Turkish Delight: Gummy candy.

CLOV (*straightening up*): I love order. It's my dream. A world where all would be silent and still and each thing in its last place, under the last dust.

(*He starts picking up again.*)

HAMM (*exasperated*): What in God's name do you think you are doing?
CLOV (*straightening up*): I'm doing my best to create a little order.
HAMM: Drop it!

(*Clov drops the objects he has picked up.*)

CLOV: After all, there or elsewhere.

(*He goes towards door.*)

HAMM (*irritably*): What's wrong with your feet?
CLOV: My feet?
HAMM: Tramp! Tramp!
CLOV: I must have put on my boots.
HAMM: Your slippers were hurting you?

(*Pause.*)

CLOV: I'll leave you.
HAMM: No!
CLOV: What is there to keep me here?
HAMM: The dialogue.

(*Pause.*)

I've got on with my story.

(*Pause.*)

I've got on with it well.

(*Pause. Irritably.*)

Ask me where I've got to.
CLOV: Oh, by the way, your story?
HAMM (*surprised*): What story?
CLOV: The one you've been telling yourself all your days.
HAMM: Ah you mean my chronicle?
CLOV: That's the one.

(*Pause.*)

HAMM (*angrily*): Keep going, can't you, keep going!
CLOV: You've got on with it, I hope.
HAMM (*modestly*): Oh not very far, not very far.

(*He sighs.*)

There are days like that, one isn't inspired.

(*Pause.*)

Nothing you can do about it, just wait for it to come.

(*Pause.*)

No forcing, no forcing, it's fatal.

(*Pause.*)

I've got on with it a little all the same.

(*Pause.*)

Technique, you know.

(*Pause. Irritably.*)

I say I've got on with it a little all the same.

CLOV (*admiringly*): Well I never! In spite of everything you were able to get on with it!

HAMM (*modestly*): Oh not very far, you know, not very far, but nevertheless, better than nothing.

CLOV: Better than nothing! Is it possible?

HAMM: I'll tell you how it goes. He comes crawling on his belly—

CLOV: Who?

HAMM: What?

CLOV: Who do you mean, he?

HAMM: Who do I mean! Yet another.

CLOV: Ah him! I wasn't sure.

HAMM: Crawling on his belly, whining for bread for his brat. He's offered a job as gardener. Before—

(*Clov bursts out laughing.*)

What is there so funny about that?

CLOV: A job as gardener!

HAMM: Is that what tickles you?

CLOV: It must be that.

HAMM: It wouldn't be the bread?

CLOV: Or the brat.

(*Pause.*)

HAMM: The whole thing is comical, I grant you that. What about having a good guffaw the two of us together?

CLOV (*after reflection*): I couldn't guffaw again today.

HAMM (*after reflection*): Nor I.

(*Pause.*)

I continue then. Before accepting with gratitude he asks if he may have his little boy with him.

CLOV: What age?

HAMM: Oh tiny.

CLOV: He would have climbed the trees.

HAMM: All the little odd jobs.

CLOV: And then he would have grown up.

HAMM: Very likely.

(*Pause.*)

CLOV: Keep going, can't you, keep going!

HAMM: That's all. I stopped there.

(*Pause.*)

CLOV: Do you see how it goes on.

HAMM: More or less.

CLOV: Will it not soon be the end?

HAMM: I'm afraid it will.

CLOV: Pah! You'll make up another.

HAMM: I don't know.

(*Pause.*)

I feel rather drained.

(*Pause.*)

The prolonged creative effort.

(*Pause.*)

If I could drag myself down to the sea! I'd make a pillow of sand for my head and the tide would come.

CLOV: There's no more tide.

(*Pause.*)

HAMM: Go and see is she dead.

(*Clov goes to bins, raises the lid of Nell's, stoops, looks into it. Pause.*)

CLOV: Looks like it.

(*He closes the lid, straightens up. Hamm raises his toque. Pause. He puts it on again.*)

HAMM (*with his hand to his toque*): And Nagg?

(*Clov raises lid of Nagg's bin, stoops, looks into it. Pause.*)

CLOV: Doesn't look like it.

(*He closes the lid, straightens up.*)

HAMM (*letting go his toque*): What's he doing?

(*Clov raises lid of Nagg's bin, stoops, looks into it. Pause.*)

CLOV: He's crying.

(*He closes lid, straightens up.*)

HAMM: Then he's living.

(*Pause.*)

Did you ever have an instant of happiness?

CLOV: Not to my knowledge.

(*Pause.*)

HAMM: Bring me under the window.

(*Clov goes towards chair.*)

I want to feel the light on my face.

(*Clov pushes chair.*)

Do you remember, in the beginning, when you took me for a turn? You used to hold the chair too high. At every step you nearly tipped me out.

(*With senile quaver.*)

Ah great fun, we had, the two of us, great fun.

(*Gloomily.*)

And then we got into the way of it.

(*Clov stops the chair under window right.*)

There already?

(*Pause. He tilts back his head.*)

Is it light?

CLOV: It isn't dark.

HAMM (*angrily*): I'm asking you is it light.

CLOV: Yes.

(*Pause.*)

HAMM: The curtain isn't closed?

CLOV: No.

HAMM: What window is it?

CLOV: The earth.

HAMM: I knew it!

(*Angrily.*)

But there's no light there! The other!

(*Clov pushes chair towards window left.*)

The earth!

(*Clov stops the chair under window left. Hamm tilts back his head.*)

That's what I call light!

(*Pause.*)

Feels like a ray of sunshine.

(*Pause.*)

No?

CLOV: No.

HAMM: It isn't a ray of sunshine I feel on my face?

CLOV: No.

(*Pause.*)

HAMM: Am I very white?

(*Pause. Angrily.*)

I'm asking you am I very white!

CLOV: Not more so than usual.

(*Pause.*)

HAMM: Open the window.

CLOV: What for?

HAMM: I want to hear the sea.

CLOV: You wouldn't hear it.

HAMM: Even if you opened the window?

CLOV: No.

HAMM: Then it's not worthwhile opening it?

CLOV: No.

HAMM (*violently*): Then open it!

(*Clov gets up on the ladder, opens the window. Pause.*)

Have you opened it?

CLOV: Yes.

(*Pause.*)

HAMM: You swear you've opened it?

CLOV: Yes.

(*Pause.*)

HAMM: Well . . . !

(*Pause.*)

It must be very calm.

(*Pause. Violently.*)

I'm asking you is it very calm!

CLOV: Yes.

HAMM: It's because there are no more navigators.

(*Pause.*)

You haven't much conversation all of a sudden. Do you not feel well?

CLOV: I'm cold.

HAMM: What month are we?

(*Pause.*)

Close the window, we're going back.

(*Clov closes the window, gets down, pushes the chair back to its place, remains standing behind it, head bowed.*)

Don't stay there, you give me the shivers!

(*Clov returns to his place beside the chair.*)

Father!

(*Pause. Louder.*)

Father!

(*Pause.*)

Go and see did he hear me.

(*Clov goes to Nagg's bin, raises the lid, stoops. Unintelligible words. Clov straightens up.*)

CLOV: Yes.

HAMM: Both times?

(*Clov stoops. As before.*)

CLOV: Once only.

HAMM: The first time or the second?

(*Clov stoops. As before.*)

CLOV: He doesn't know.

HAMM: It must have been the second.

CLOV: We'll never know.

(*He closes lid.*)

HAMM: Is he still crying?

CLOV: No.

HAMM: The dead go fast.

(*Pause.*)

What's he doing?

CLOV: Sucking his biscuit.

HAMM: Life goes on.

(*Clov returns to his place beside the chair.*)

Give me a rug,° I'm freezing.

CLOV: There are no more rugs.

(*Pause.*)

HAMM: Kiss me.

(*Pause.*)

Will you not kiss me?

CLOV: No.

HAMM: On the forehead.

CLOV: I won't kiss you anywhere.

(*Pause.*)

HAMM (*holding out his hand*): Give me your hand at least.

(*Pause.*)

Will you not give me your hand?

CLOV: I won't touch you.

rug: A small blanket to cover the lap, legs, and feet.

(*Pause.*)

HAMM: Give me the dog.

(*Clov looks round for the dog.*)

No!

CLOV: Do you not want your dog?

HAMM: No.

CLOV: Then I'll leave you.

HAMM (*head bowed, absently*): That's right.

(*Clov goes to door, turns.*)

CLOV: If I don't kill that rat he'll die.

HAMM (*as before*): That's right.

(*Exit Clov. Pause.*)

Me to play.

(*He takes out his handkerchief, unfolds it, holds it spread out before him.*)

We're getting on.

(*Pause.*)

You weep, and weep, for nothing, so as not to laugh, and little by little . . . you begin to grieve.

(*He folds the handkerchief, puts it back in his pocket, raises his head.*)

All those I might have helped.

(*Pause.*)

Helped!

(*Pause.*)

Saved.

(*Pause.*)

Saved!

(*Pause.*)

The place was crawling with them!

(*Pause. Violently.*)

Use your head, can't you, use your head, you're on earth, there's no cure for that!

(*Pause.*)

Get out of here and love one another! Lick your neighbor as yourself!

(*Pause. Calmer.*)

When it wasn't bread they wanted it was crumpets.

(*Pause. Violently.*)

Out of my sight and back to your petting parties!

(*Pause.*)

All that, all that!

(*Pause.*)

Not even a real dog!

(*Calmer.*)

The end is in the beginning and yet you go on.

(*Pause.*)

Perhaps I could go on with my story, end it and begin another.

(*Pause.*)

Perhaps I could throw myself out on the floor.

(*He pushes himself painfully off his seat, falls back again.*)

Dig my nails into the cracks and drag myself forward with my fingers.

(*Pause.*)

It will be the end and there I'll be, wondering what can have brought it on and wondering what can have . . . (*he hesitates*) . . . why it was so long coming.

(*Pause.*)

There I'll be, in the old shelter, alone against the silence and . . . (*he hesitates*) . . . the stillness. If I can hold my peace, and sit quiet, it will be all over with sound, and motion, all over and done with.

(*Pause.*)

I'll have called my father and I'll have called my . . . (*he hesitates*) . . . my son. And even twice, or three times, in case they shouldn't have heard me, the first time, or the second.

(*Pause.*)

I'll say to myself, He'll come back.

(*Pause.*)

And then?

(*Pause.*)

And then?

(*Pause.*)

He couldn't, he has gone too far.

(*Pause.*)

And then?

(*Pause. Very agitated.*)

All kinds of fantasies! That I'm being watched! A rat! Steps! Breath held and then . . .

(*He breathes out.*)

Then babble, babble, words, like the solitary child who turns himself into children, two, three, so as to be together, and whisper together, in the dark.

(*Pause.*)

Moment upon moment, pattering down, like the millet grains of . . . (*he hesitates*) . . . that old Greek, and all life long you wait for that to mount up to a life.

(*Pause. He opens his mouth to continue, renounces.*)

Ah let's get it over!

(*He whistles. Enter Clov with alarm clock. He halts beside the chair.*)

What? Neither gone nor dead?
CLOV: In spirit only.
HAMM: Which?
CLOV: Both.
HAMM: Gone from me you'd be dead.
CLOV: And vice versa.
HAMM: Outside of here it's death!

(*Pause.*)

And the rat?
CLOV: He's got away.
HAMM: He can't go far.

(*Pause. Anxious.*)

Eh?
CLOV: He doesn't need to go far.

(*Pause.*)

HAMM: Is it not time for my painkiller?
CLOV: Yes.
HAMM: Ah! At last! Give it to me! Quick!

(*Pause.*)

CLOV: There's no more painkiller.

(*Pause.*)

HAMM (*appalled*): Good . . . !

(*Pause.*)

No more painkiller!
CLOV: No more painkiller. You'll never get any more painkiller.

(*Pause.*)

HAMM: But the little round box. It was full!
CLOV: Yes. But now it's empty.

(*Pause. Clov starts to move about the room. He is looking for a place to put down the alarm clock.*)

HAMM (*soft*): What'll I do?

(*Pause. In a scream.*)

What'll I do?

(*Clov sees the picture, takes it down, stands it on the floor with its face to the wall, hangs up the alarm clock in its place.*)

What are you doing?
CLOV: Winding up.
HAMM: Look at the earth.
CLOV: Again!
HAMM: Since it's calling to you.
CLOV: Is your throat sore?

(*Pause.*)

Would you like a lozenge?

(*Pause.*)

Simon McBurney as Clov and Mark Rylance as Hamm in the production directed by McBurney at the Duchess Theatre in London, 2009.

No.

(*Pause.*)

Pity.

(*Clov goes, humming, towards window right, halts before it, looks up at it.*)

HAMM: Don't sing.

CLOV (*turning towards Hamm*): One hasn't the right to sing anymore?

HAMM: No.

CLOV: Then how can it end?

HAMM: You want it to end?

CLOV: I want to sing.

HAMM: I can't prevent you.

(*Pause. Clov turns towards window right.*)

CLOV: What did I do with that steps?

(*He looks around for ladder.*)

You didn't see that steps?

(*He sees it.*)

Ah, about time.

(*He goes towards window left.*)

Sometimes I wonder if I'm in my right mind. Then it passes over and I'm as lucid as before.

(*He gets up on ladder, looks out of window.*)

Christ, she's under water!

(*He looks.*)

How can that be?

(*He pokes forward his head, his hand above his eyes.*)

It hasn't rained.

(*He wipes the pane, looks. Pause.*)

Ah what a fool I am! I'm on the wrong side!

(*He gets down, takes a few steps towards window right.*)

Under water!

(*He goes back for ladder.*)

What a fool I am!

(*He carries ladder towards window right.*)

Sometimes I wonder if I'm in my right senses. Then it passes off and I'm as intelligent as ever.

(*He sets down ladder under window right, gets up on it, looks out of window. He turns towards Hamm.*)

Any particular sector you fancy? Or merely the whole thing?

HAMM: Whole thing.

CLOV: The general effect? Just a moment.

(*He looks out of window. Pause.*)

HAMM: Clov.

CLOV (*absorbed*): Mmm.

HAMM: Do you know what it is?

CLOV (*as before*): Mmm.

HAMM: I was never there.

(*Pause.*)

Clov!

CLOV (*turning towards Hamm, exasperated*): What is it?

HAMM: I was never there.

CLOV: Lucky for you.

(*He looks out of window.*)

HAMM: Absent, always. It all happened without me. I don't know what's happened.

(*Pause.*)

Do you know what's happened?

(*Pause.*)

Clov!

CLOV (*turning towards Hamm, exasperated*): Do you want me to look at this muckheap, yes or no?

HAMM: Answer me first.

CLOV: What?

HAMM: Do you know what's happened?

CLOV: When? Where?

HAMM (*violently*): When! What's happened? Use your head, can't you! What has happened?

CLOV: What for Christ's sake does it matter?

(*He looks out of window.*)

HAMM: I don't know.

(*Pause. Clov turns towards Hamm.*)

CLOV (*harshly*): When old Mother Pegg asked you for oil for her lamp and you told her to get out to hell, you knew what was happening then, no?

(*Pause.*)

You know what she died of, Mother Pegg? Of darkness.

HAMM (*feebly*): I hadn't any.

CLOV (*as before*): Yes, you had.

(*Pause.*)

HAMM: Have you the glass?

CLOV: No, it's clear enough as it is.

HAMM: Go and get it.

(*Pause. Clov casts up his eyes, brandishes his fists. He loses balance, clutches on to the ladder. He starts to get down, halts.*)

CLOV: There's one thing I'll never understand.

(*He gets down.*)

Why I always obey you. Can you explain that to me?

HAMM: No. . . . Perhaps it's compassion.

Clov (Max Casella) strikes Hamm (John Turturro) in the Brooklyn Academy of Music production, 2008.

(*Pause.*)

A kind of great compassion.

(*Pause.*)

Oh you won't find it easy, you won't find it easy.

(*Pause. Clov begins to move about the room in search of the telescope.*)

CLOV: I'm tired of our goings on, very tired.

(*He searches.*)

You're not sitting on it?

(*He moves the chair, looks at the place where it stood, resumes his search.*)

HAMM (*anguished*): Don't leave me there!

(*Angrily Clov restores the chair to its place.*)

Am I right in the center?

CLOV: You'd need a microscope to find this—

(*He sees the telescope.*)

Ah, about time.

(*He picks up the telescope, gets up on the ladder, turns the telescope on the without.*)

HAMM: Give me the dog.

CLOV (*looking*): Quiet!

HAMM (*angrily*): Give me the dog!

(*Clov drops the telescope, clasps his hands to his head. Pause. He gets down precipitately, looks for the dog, sees it, picks it up, hastens towards Hamm and strikes him violently on the head with the dog.*)

CLOV: There's your dog for you!

(*The dog falls to the ground. Pause.*)

HAMM: He hit me!

CLOV: You drive me mad, I'm mad!

HAMM: If you must hit me, hit me with the axe.

(*Pause.*)

Or with the gaff, hit me with the gaff. Not with the dog. With the gaff. Or with the axe.

(*Clov picks up the dog and gives it to Hamm who takes it in his arms.*)

CLOV (*imploringly*): Let's stop playing!

HAMM: Never!

(*Pause.*)

Put me in my coffin.

CLOV: There are no more coffins.

HAMM: Then let it end!

(*Clov goes towards ladder.*)

With a bang!

(*Clov gets up on ladder, gets down again, looks for telescope, sees it, picks it up, gets up ladder, raises telescope.*)

Of darkness! And me? Did anyone ever have pity on me?

CLOV (*lowering the telescope, turning towards Hamm*): What?

(*Pause.*)

Is it me you're referring to?

HAMM (*angrily*): An aside, ape! Did you never hear an aside before?

(*Pause.*)

I'm warming up for my last soliloquy.

CLOV: I warn you. I'm going to look at this filth since it's an order. But it's the last time.

(*He turns the telescope on the without.*)

Let's see.

(*He moves the telescope.*)

Nothing . . . nothing . . . good . . . good . . . nothing . . . goo—

(*He starts, lowers the telescope, examines it, turns it again on the without. Pause.*)

Bad luck to it!

HAMM: More complications!

(*Clov gets down.*)

Not an underplot, I trust.

(*Clov moves ladder nearer window, gets up on it, turns telescope on the without.*)

CLOV (*dismayed*): Looks like a small boy!

HAMM (*sarcastic*): A small . . . boy!

CLOV: I'll go and see.

(*He gets down, drops the telescope, goes towards door, turns.*)

I'll take the gaff.

(*He looks for the gaff, sees it, picks it up, hastens towards door.*)

HAMM: No!

(*Clov halts.*)

CLOV: No? A potential procreator?

HAMM: If he exists he'll die there or he'll come here. And if he doesn't . . .

(*Pause.*)

CLOV: You don't believe me? You think I'm inventing?

(*Pause.*)

HAMM: It's the end, Clov, we've come to the end. I don't need you anymore.

(*Pause.*)

CLOV: Lucky for you.

(*He goes towards door.*)

HAMM: Leave me the gaff.

(*Clov gives him the gaff, goes towards door, halts, looks at alarm clock, takes it down, looks round for a better place to put it, goes to bins, puts it on lid of Nagg's bin. Pause.*)

CLOV: I'll leave you.

(*He goes towards door.*)

HAMM: Before you go . . .

(*Clov halts near door.*)

. . . say something.

CLOV: There is nothing to say.

HAMM: A few words . . . to ponder . . . in my heart.

CLOV: Your heart!

HAMM: Yes.

(*Pause. Forcibly.*)

Yes!

(*Pause.*)

With the rest, in the end, the shadows, the murmurs, all the trouble, to end up with.

(*Pause.*)

Clov. . . . He never spoke to me. Then, in the end, before he went, without my having asked him, he spoke to me. He said . . .

CLOV (*despairingly*): Ah . . . !

HAMM: Something . . . from your heart.

CLOV: My heart!

HAMM: A few words . . . from your heart.

(*Pause.*)

CLOV (*fixed gaze, tonelessly, towards auditorium*): They said to me, That's love, yes, yes, not a doubt, now you see how—

HAMM: Articulate!

CLOV (*as before*): How easy it is. They said to me, That's friendship, yes, yes, no question, you've found it. They said to me, Here's the place, stop, raise your head and look at all that beauty. That order! They said to me, Come now, you're not a brute beast, think upon these things and you'll see how all becomes clear. And simple! They said to me, What skilled attention they get, all these dying of their wounds.

HAMM: Enough!

CLOV (*as before*): I say to myself—sometimes, Clov, you must learn to suffer better than that if you want them to weary of punishing you—one day. I say to myself—sometimes, Clov, you must be there better than that if you want them to let you go—one day. But I feel too old, and too far, to form new habits. Good, it'll never end, I'll never go.

(*Pause.*)

Then one day, suddenly, it ends, it changes, I don't understand, it dies, or it's me, I don't understand, that either. I ask the words that remain—sleeping, waking, morning, evening. They have nothing to say.

(*Pause.*)

I open the door of the cell and go. I am so bowed I only see my feet, if I open my eyes, and between my legs a little trail of black dust. I say to myself that the earth is extinguished, though I never saw it lit.

(*Pause.*)

It's easy going.

(*Pause.*)

When I fall I'll weep for happiness.

(*Pause. He goes towards door.*)

HAMM: Clov!
(*Clov halts, without turning.*)
    Nothing.

(*Clov moves on.*)

    Clov!

(*Clov halts, without turning.*)

CLOV: This is what we call making an exit.
HAMM: I'm obliged to you, Clov. For your services.
CLOV (*turning, sharply*): Ah pardon, it's I am obliged to you.
HAMM: It's we are obliged to each other.

(*Pause. Clov goes towards door.*)

    One thing more.

(*Clov halts.*)

    A last favor.

(*Exit Clov.*)

    Cover me with the sheet.

(*Long pause.*)

    No? Good.

(*Pause.*)

    Me to play.

(*Pause. Wearily.*)

    Old endgame lost of old, play and lose and have done with losing.

(*Pause. More animated.*)

    Let me see.

(*Pause.*)

    Ah yes!

(*He tries to move the chair, using the gaff as before. Enter Clov, dressed for the road. Panama hat, tweed coat, raincoat over his arm, umbrella, bag. He halts by

the door and stands there, impassive and motionless, his eyes fixed on Hamm, till the end. Hamm gives up.*)

    Good.

(*Pause.*)

    Discard.

(*He throws away the gaff, makes to throw away the dog, thinks better of it.*)

    Take it easy.

(*Pause.*)

    And now?

(*Pause.*)

    Raise hat.

(*He raises his toque.*)

    Peace to our . . . arses.

(*Pause.*)

    And put on again.

(*He puts on his toque.*)

    Deuce.

(*Pause. He takes off his glasses.*)

    Wipe.

(*He takes out his handkerchief and, without unfolding it, wipes his glasses.*)

    And put on again.

(*He puts on his glasses, puts back the handkerchief in his pocket.*)

    We're coming. A few more squirms like that and I'll call.

(*Pause.*)

    A little poetry.

(*Pause.*)

    You prayed—

(*Pause. He corrects himself.*)

    You CRIED for night; it comes—

(*Pause. He corrects himself.*)

    It FALLS: now cry in darkness.

(*He repeats, chanting.*)

    You cried for night; it falls: now cry in darkness.

(*Pause.*)

    Nicely put, that.

(*Pause.*)

    And now?

(*Pause.*)

Moments for nothing, now as always, time was never and time is over, reckoning closed and story ended.

(*Pause. Narrative tone.*)

If he could have his child with him. . . .

(*Pause.*)

It was the moment I was waiting for.

(*Pause.*)

You don't want to abandon him? You want him to bloom while you are withering? Be there to solace your last million last moments?

(*Pause.*)

He doesn't realize, all he knows is hunger, and cold, and death to crown it all. But you! You ought to know what the earth is like, nowadays. Oh I put him before his responsibilities!

(*Pause. Normal tone.*)

Well, there we are, there I am, that's enough.

(*He raises the whistle to his lips, hesitates, drops it. Pause.*)

Yes, truly!

(*He whistles. Pause. Louder. Pause.*)

Good.

(*Pause.*)

Father!

(*Pause. Louder.*)

Father!

(*Pause.*)

Good.

(*Pause.*)

We're coming.

(*Pause.*)

And to end up with?

(*Pause.*)

Discard.

(*He throws away the dog. He tears the whistle from his neck.*)

With my compliments.

(*He throws whistle towards auditorium. Pause. He sniffs. Soft.*)

Clov!

(*Long pause.*)

No? Good.

(*He takes out the handkerchief.*)

Since that's the way we're playing it . . . (*he unfolds handkerchief*) . . . let's play it that way . . . (*he unfolds*) . . . and speak no more about it . . . (*he finishes unfolding*) . . . speak no more.

(*He holds handkerchief spread out before him.*)

Old stancher!

(*Pause.*)

You . . . remain.

(*Pause. He covers his face with handkerchief, lowers his arms to armrests, remains motionless.*)

(*Brief tableau.*)

COMMENTARY

MARTIN ESSLIN (1918–2002)

The Theater of the Absurd 1960

Martin Esslin was a drama critic whose work has had wide currency. He was the first to write extensively about the theater of the absurd, and with this essay he defined the term that has come to describe the plays of Samuel Beckett and a number of other post–World War II playwrights such as Eugène Ionesco and Harold Pinter. The essay tries to establish the character of absurd drama, its limits, and its importance.

Audiences were certainly baffled by Beckett's work, starting with his very successful *Waiting for Godot* and including *Krapp's Last Tape* and *Happy Days*. All these plays are restricted in space and in action. Their very essence is restriction. Esslin shows the possible range of significance in Beckett's plays and explains that if we see the plays properly, we can understand how they interpret experience. The question of what use playwrights make of the absurd and why it is an appropriate term to reflect Beckett's achievement is explored briefly in this excerpt.

The Theater of the Absurd shows the world as an incomprehensible place. The spectators see the happenings on the stage entirely from the outside, without ever understanding the full meaning of these strange patterns of events, as newly arrived visitors might watch life in a country of which they have not yet mastered the language. The confrontation of the audience with characters and happenings which they are not quite able to comprehend makes it impossible for them to share the aspirations and emotions depicted in the play. Brecht's famous "Verfremdungs-effekt" (alienation effect), the inhibition of any identification between spectator and actor, which Brecht could never successfully achieve in his own highly rational theater, really comes into its own in the Theater of the Absurd. It is impossible to identify oneself with characters one does not understand or whose motives remain a closed book, and so the distance between the public and the happenings on the stage can be maintained. Emotional identification with the characters is replaced by a puzzled, critical attention. For while the happenings on the stage are absurd, they yet remain recognizable as somehow related to real life with *its* absurdity, so that eventually the spectators are brought face to face with the irrational side of their existence. Thus, the absurd and fantastic goings-on of the Theater of the Absurd will, in the end, be found to reveal the irrationality of the human condition and the illusion of what we thought was its apparent logical structure.

If the dialogue in these plays consists of meaningless clichés and the mechanical, circular repetition of stereotyped phrases—how many meaningless clichés and stereotyped phrases do we use in our day-to-day conversation? If the characters change their personality halfway through the action, how consistent and truly integrated are the people we meet in our real life? And if people in these plays appear as mere marionettes, helpless puppets without any will of their own, passively at the mercy of blind fate and meaningless circumstance, do we, in fact, in our overorganized world, still possess any genuine initiative or power to decide our own destiny? The spectators of the Theater of the Absurd are thus confronted with a grotesquely heightened picture of their own world: a world without faith, meaning, and genuine freedom of will. In this sense, the Theater of the Absurd is the true theater of our time.

The theater of most previous epochs reflected an accepted moral order, a world whose aims and objectives were clearly present to the minds of all its public, whether it was the audience of the medieval mystery plays with their solidly accepted faith in the Christian world order or the audience of the drama of Ibsen, Shaw, or Hauptmann with their unquestioned belief in evolution and progress. To such audiences, right and wrong were never in doubt, nor did they question the then accepted goals of human endeavor. Our own time, at least in the Western world, wholly lacks such a generally accepted and completely integrated world picture. The decline of religious faith, the destruction of the belief in automatic social and biological progress, the discovery of vast areas of irrational and unconscious forces within the human psyche, the loss of a sense of control over rational human development in an age of totalitarianism and weapons of mass destruction, have all contributed to the erosion of the basis for a dramatic convention in which the action proceeds within a fixed and self-evident framework of generally accepted values. Faced with the vacuum left by the destruction of a universally accepted and unified set of beliefs, most serious playwrights have felt the need to fit their work into the frame of values and objectives expressed in one of the contemporary ideologies: Marxism, psychoanalysis, aestheticism, or nature worship. But these, in the eyes of a writer like Adamov, are nothing but superficial rationalizations which try to hide the depth of man's predicament, his loneliness and his anxiety. Or, as Ionesco puts it:

> As far as I am concerned, I believe sincerely in the poverty of the poor, I deplore it; it is real; it can become a subject for the theatre; I also believe in the anxieties and serious troubles the rich may suffer from; but it is neither in the misery of the former nor in the melancholia of the latter, that I, for one, find my dramatic subject matter. Theatre is for me the outward projection onto the stage of an inner world; it is in my dreams, in my anxieties, in my obscure desires, in my internal contradictions that I, for one, reserve for myself the right of finding my dramatic subject matter. As I am not alone in the world, as each of us, in the depth of his being, is at the same time part and parcel of all others, my dreams, my desires, my anxieties, my obsessions do not belong to me alone. They form part of an ancestral heritage, a very ancient storehouse which is a portion of the common property of all mankind. It is this, which, transcending their outward diversity, reunites all human beings and constitutes our profound common patrimony, the universal language.[1]

In other words, the commonly acceptable framework of beliefs and values of former epochs which has now been shattered is to be replaced by the community of dreams and desires of a collective unconscious. And, to quote Ionesco again:

> ... the new dramatist is one ... who tries to link up with what is most ancient; new language and subject matter in a dramatic structure which aims at being clearer, more stripped of inessentials and more purely theatrical; the rejection of traditionalism to rediscover tradition; a synthesis of knowledge and invention, of the real and imaginary, of the particular and the universal, or as they say now, of the individual and the collective. ... By expressing my deepest obsessions, I express my deepest humanity. I become one with all others, spontaneously, over and above all the barriers of caste and different psychologies. I express my solitude and become one with all other solitudes.[2]

What is the tradition with which the Theater of the Absurd—at first sight the most revolutionary and radically new movement—is trying to link itself? It is in fact a very ancient and a very rich tradition, nourished from many and varied sources: the verbal exuberance and extravagant inventions of Rabelais, the age-old clowning of the Roman mimes and the Italian *Commedia dell'Arte*, the knock-about humor of circus clowns like Grock; the wild, archetypal symbolism of English nonsense verse, the baroque horror of Jacobean dramatists like Webster or Tourneur, the harsh, incisive and often brutal tones of the German drama of Grabbe, Büchner, Kleist, and Wedekind with its delirious language and grotesque inventiveness; and the Nordic paranoia of the dreams and persecution fantasies of Strindberg.

[1] Eugène Ionesco, "L'Impromptu de l'Alma," *Théâtre II*, Paris, 1958.
[2] Ionesco, "The Avant-Garde Theatre," *World Theatre*, 8.3 (Autumn 1959).

Lorraine Hansberry

"That's where Lorraine Hansberry came from and August Wilson. Out of what life had given them, they turned it into something beautiful."

–Ruben Santiago-
  Hudson, Actor

Lorraine Hansberry (1930–1965), like John Millington Synge, died tragically young. The loss to the American stage is incalculable; her successes were only beginning, and at her death she seemed on the verge of a remarkable career.

Hansberry grew up in a middle-class black family in Chicago. Her father, who was successful in real estate, founded one of the first banks in Chicago to solicit black patronage. However, he spent much of his life vainly trying to find a way to make a decent life for himself and his family. He eventually gave up on the United States, and when he died in 1945, he was scouting for a place in Mexico where he and his family could move to live comfortably.

Lorraine Hansberry went to college after her father died, and her first ambition was to become a visual artist. She attended the Art Institute of Chicago and numerous other schools before moving to New York. Once there, she became interested in some drama groups and soon married the playwright Howard Nemiroff. She began writing, sharing parts of her first play with friends in her own living room. They helped raise money to stage the play, and, with black director Lloyd Richards and little-known Sidney Poitier as Walter Lee Younger, *A Raisin in the Sun* (1959) thrust Hansberry into the drama spotlight.

In 1959, only twenty-nine years old, Hansberry was the most promising woman writing for the American stage. She was also the first black American to win the New York Drama Critics' Circle Award for the best play of the year. She died of cancer the day her second produced play, *The Sign in Sidney Brustein's Window,* closed. She had finished a third play, *Les Blancs,* which was brought to Broadway by Nemiroff in 1970. Neither of her other plays was as popular as *Raisin,* but the two later plays demonstrate a deepening concern for and understanding of some of the key issues of racial and sexual politics that interested her throughout her career.

The hero in *The Sign in Sidney Brustein's Window* is a Jewish intellectual in the 1950s in Greenwich Village. Believing that all the gains of radical struggle of the 1930s have been lost, he agitates for personal involvement, for emotional and intellectual action. This idealistic play anticipates the political agitation in the United States during the mid-1960s and early 1970s. *Les Blancs* takes as its central character a black African intellectual, Tshembe, and explores his relationship to both Europe and Africa. In his uneasiness with both cultures he discovers that he cannot live outside his own history. *Les Blancs* reveals some of Hansberry's deep interest in Pan-Africanism and the search for a personal heritage.

A posthumous work was put together by Howard Nemiroff from Hansberry's notes, letters, and early writings. Titled *To Be Young, Gifted, and Black* (1971), it has helped solidify her achievements. Although we will never know just how Hansberry's career would have developed had she lived, her gifts were so remarkable that we can only lament that she is not writing for the stage today.

For links to resources about Hansberry, click on *AuthorLinks* at bedfordstmartins.com/jacobus.

A Raisin in the Sun

When produced on Broadway in 1959, *A Raisin in the Sun* was somewhat prophetic. Lorraine Hansberry's themes of blacks pressing forward with legitimate demands and expressing interest in their African heritage were to become primary themes of black culture in the 1960s, in the 1970s, and, indeed, to this day. The title of her play is from a poem by Langston Hughes, one of the poets of the Harlem Renaissance. The poem warns of the social explosions that might occur if society permits blacks to remain unequal and unfree.

Hansberry's work appeared at the beginning of renewed political activity on the part of African Americans; it reveals its historical position in the use of the word *Negro,* which black activists rejected in the 1960s as an enslaving euphemism. This play illustrates the American dream as it is understood not just by African Americans but by all Americans: if you work hard, save your money, are honorable, and hope, then you can one day buy your own home and have the kind of space and privacy that permit people to live with dignity. Yet this very theme has plagued the play from the beginning: its apparent emphasis on middle-class, bourgeois values. On the surface, it seems to celebrate a mild form of consumerism—the desire for the house in the suburbs with the TV set inside to anesthetize its occupants. Hansberry was shocked when such criticisms, from black critics as well as white, were leveled at the play. She had written it very carefully to explore just those issues in a context that demonstrated that black families' needs paralleled those of white families, while also having a different dimension that most white families could not understand.

Hansberry was quick to admit that Walter Lee Younger was affected by the same craziness influencing all Americans who lusted after possessions and the power they might confer. Walter wants to take his father's insurance money to buy a liquor store in partnership with a con man. Lena Younger argues against her son's plan as a profanation of her husband's memory as well as an abuse of the American dream: she believes that the product of a liquor store will further poison the community. What she wants is not a consumer product but the emblem of identity and security that she feels her family deserves.

Hansberry is painfully honest in this play. Walter Lee's weaknesses are recognizable. His male chauvinistic behavior undoes him. He is caught up in the old, failing pattern of male dominance over women. But none of the women in his life will tolerate his behavior. Hansberry also admits the social distinctions among African Americans. George Murchison is a young man from a wealthy black family, and when Beneatha tells Lena that she will not marry George, she says, "The only people in the world who are more snobbish than rich white people are rich colored people." Beneatha's desire to be a doctor is obviously not rooted in consumerism any more than in the middle-class need to be comfortable and rich.

The confusion caused in the family by a native African, Asagai, is realistically portrayed. In the early days of the Pan-African movement in the 1960s, blacks were often bemused by the way Africans presented themselves.

For a Drama in Depth tutorial on *A Raisin in the Sun*, click on *VirtualLit Drama Tutorials* at bedfordstmartins.com/jacobus.

Interest in Africa on the part of American blacks was distorted by Tarzan movies and *National Geographic* articles, none of which presented black Africans as role models. Therefore, the adjustment to black African pride, though it was made swiftly, was not without difficulties. The Youngers are presented as no more sophisticated about black Africans than the rest of black society would be.

The dignity of the Younger family finally triumphs. When Walter Lee stands up for himself, he is asserting not macho domination but black manhood—a manhood that needs no domination over women. He is expressing not a desire for a big house—as he had done when he reflected on the possessions of his rich employer—but a desire to demonstrate to members of the Clybourne Park Improvement Association that the Youngers are their social equals and that they have a right to live wherever they choose.

A Raisin in the Sun in Performance

Lloyd Richards directed the first production at the Ethel Barrymore Theater in New York on March 11, 1959. The play won major prizes, and Sidney Poitier as a passionate Walter Lee Younger was a signal success. *New York Times* critic Brooks Atkinson said, "Since the performance is also honest and since Sidney Poitier is a candid actor, *A Raisin in the Sun* has vigor as well as veracity and is likely to destroy the complacency of any one who sees it." Critics were astonished that a first play could have the sophistication and depth they saw onstage.

The Theatre Guild staged the play in 1960 in Boston with a different cast, but the production received similar reviews. The film version, with most of the New York cast, was directed by Daniel Petrie in 1961. A revival in Chicago in 1983 at the Art Institute of Chicago—Hansberry's alma mater—was not altogether successful, but critics agreed the text held up well. The Chicago revival, like the 1985 Merrimack Repertory Theater revival in Lowell, Massachusetts, demonstrated that the play needs strong actors to have the desired impact. A twenty-fifth-anniversary production was directed by Lloyd Richards at the Yale Repertory Theatre in 1983. This production was taken to New York in 1986 and enjoyed a successful run. The setting was a realistic interior, emphasizing the play's realistic style. Critic Mel Gussow asserted that the revival demonstrated that the play is "an enduring work of contemporary theater." The production also revealed that Hansberry's language had not become dated, nor had the social issues of the play become any less critical and important twenty-five years later. In fact, a production starring hip-hop artist and fashion mogul Sean "P. Diddy" Combs and Audra McDonald during the 2004 season in New York City got good reviews. This production was shown on television in 2008 in a version that gained the play a brand-new audience. Like the proletarian plays of Sean O'Casey, who inspired Lorraine Hansberry, this play continues to move us because the problems it examines are serious and still remain with us.

LORRAINE HANSBERRY (1930–1965)

A Raisin in the Sun   1959

Harlem (A Dream Deferred)

What happens to a dream deferred?

> *Does it dry up*
> *like a raisin in the sun?*
> *Or fester like a sore —*
> *And then run?*
> *Does it stink like rotten meat?*

Or crust and sugar over —
like a syrupy sweet?

> *Maybe it just sags*
> *like a heavy load.*

Or does it explode?   — LANGSTON HUGHES

Characters

RUTH YOUNGER
TRAVIS YOUNGER
WALTER LEE YOUNGER (*brother*)
BENEATHA YOUNGER
LENA YOUNGER (*Mama*)
JOSEPH ASAGAI
GEORGE MURCHISON
MRS. JOHNSON
KARL LINDNER
BOBO
MOVING MEN

The action of the play is set in Chicago's Southside, sometime between World War II and the present.

Act I

Scene I: *Friday morning.*
Scene II: *The following morning.*

Act II

Scene I: *Later, the same day.*
Scene II: *Friday night, a few weeks later.*
Scene III: *Moving day, one week later.*

Act III

An hour later.

ACT I • Scene I

(The Younger living room would be a comfortable and well-ordered room if it were not for a number of indestructible contradictions to this state of being. Its furnishings are typical and undistinguished and their primary feature now is that they have clearly had to accommodate the living of too many people for too many years—and they are tired. Still, we can see that at some time, a time probably no longer remembered

by the family [except perhaps for Mama], the furnishings of this room were actually selected with care and love and even hope—and brought to this apartment and arranged with taste and pride.)

(That was a long time ago. Now the once loved pattern of the couch upholstery has to fight to show itself from under acres of crocheted doilies and couch covers which have themselves finally come to be more important than the upholstery. And here a table or a chair has been moved to disguise the worn places in the carpet; but the carpet has fought back by showing its weariness, with depressing uniformity, elsewhere on its surface.)

(Weariness has, in fact, won in this room. Everything has been polished, washed, sat on, used, scrubbed too often. All pretenses but living itself have long since vanished from the very atmosphere of this room.)

(Moreover, a section of this room, for it is not really a room unto itself, though the landlord's lease would make it seem so, slopes backward to provide a small kitchen area, where the family prepares the meals that are eaten in the living room proper, which must also serve as dining room. The single window that has been provided for these "two" rooms is located in this kitchen area. The sole natural light the family may enjoy in the course of a day is only that which fights its way through this little window.)

(At left, a door leads to a bedroom which is shared by Mama and her daughter, Beneatha. At right, opposite, is a second room [which in the beginning of the life of this apartment was probably a breakfast room] which serves as a bedroom for Walter and his wife, Ruth.)

(Time: Sometime between World War II and the present.)

(Place: Chicago's Southside.)

(At rise: It is morning dark in the living room. Travis is asleep on the make-down bed at center. An alarm clock sounds from within the bedroom at right, and presently Ruth enters from that room and closes the door behind her. She crosses sleepily toward the window.

As she passes her sleeping son she reaches down and shakes him a little. At the window she raises the shade and a dusky Southside morning light comes in feebly. She fills a pot with water and puts it on to boil. She calls to the boy, between yawns, in a slightly muffled voice.)

(*Ruth is about thirty. We can see that she was a pretty girl, even exceptionally so, but now it is apparent that life has been little that she expected, and disappointment has already begun to hang in her face. In a few years, before thirty-five even, she will be known among her people as a "settled woman."*)

(*She crosses to her son and gives him a good, final, rousing shake.*)

RUTH: Come on now, boy, it's seven thirty! (*Her son sits up at last, in a stupor of sleepiness.*) I say hurry up, Travis! You ain't the only person in the world got to use a bathroom! (*The child, a sturdy, handsome little boy of ten or eleven, drags himself out of the bed and almost blindly takes his towels and "today's clothes" from drawers and a closet and goes out to the bathroom, which is in an outside hall and which is shared by another family or families on the same floor. Ruth crosses to the bedroom door at right and opens it and calls in to her husband.*) Walter Lee! . . . It's after seven thirty! Lemme see you do some waking up in there now! (*She waits.*) You better get up from there, man! It's after seven thirty I tell you. (*She waits again.*) All right, you just go ahead and lay there and next thing you know Travis be finished and Mr. Johnson'll be in there and you'll be fussing and cussing round here like a madman! And be late too! (*She waits, at the end of patience.*) Walter Lee—it's time for you to GET UP!

(*She waits another second and then starts to go into the bedroom, but is apparently satisfied that her husband has begun to get up. She stops, pulls the door to, and returns to the kitchen area. She wipes her face with a moist cloth and runs her fingers through her sleep-disheveled hair in a vain effort and ties an apron around her housecoat. The bedroom door at right opens and her husband stands in the doorway in his pajamas, which are rumpled and mismated. He is a lean, intense young man in his middle thirties, inclined to quick nervous movements and erratic speech habits—and always in his voice there is a quality of indictment.*)

WALTER: Is he out yet?

RUTH: What you mean *out?* He ain't hardly got in there good yet.

WALTER (*wandering in, still more oriented to sleep than to a new day*): Well, what was you doing all that yelling for if I can't even get in there yet? (*Stopping and thinking.*) Check coming today?

RUTH: They *said* Saturday and this is just Friday and I hopes to God you ain't going to get up here first thing this morning and start talking to me 'bout no money—'cause I 'bout don't want to hear it.

WALTER: Something the matter with you this morning?

RUTH: No—I'm just sleepy as the devil. What kind of eggs you want?

WALTER: Not scrambled. (*Ruth starts to scramble eggs.*) Paper come? (*Ruth points impatiently to the rolled up Tribune on the table, and he gets it and spreads it out and vaguely reads the front page.*) Set off another bomb yesterday.

RUTH (*maximum indifference*): Did they?

WALTER (*looking up*): What's the matter with you?

RUTH: Ain't nothing the matter with me. And don't keep asking me that this morning.

WALTER: Ain't nobody bothering you. (*Reading the news of the day absently again.*) Say Colonel McCormick is sick.

RUTH (*affecting tea-party interest*): Is he now? Poor thing.

WALTER (*sighing and looking at his watch*): Oh, me. (*He waits.*) Now what is that boy doing in that bathroom all this time? He just going to have to start getting up earlier. I can't be being late to work on account of him fooling around in there.

RUTH (*turning on him*): Oh, no he ain't going to be getting up no earlier no such thing! It ain't his fault that he can't get to bed no earlier nights 'cause he got a bunch of crazy good-for-nothing clowns sitting up running their mouths in what is supposed to be his bedroom after ten o'clock at night . . .

WALTER: That's what you mad about, ain't it? The things I want to talk about with my friends just couldn't be important in your mind, could they?

(*He rises and finds a cigarette in her handbag on the table and crosses to the little window and looks out, smoking and deeply enjoying this first one.*)

RUTH (*almost matter of factly, a complaint too automatic to deserve emphasis*): Why you always got to smoke before you eat in the morning?

WALTER (*at the window*): Just look at 'em down there . . . Running and racing to work . . . (*He turns and faces his wife and watches her a moment at the stove, and then, suddenly.*) You look young this morning, baby.

RUTH (*indifferently*): Yeah?

WALTER: Just for a second—stirring them eggs. Just for a second it was—you looked real young again. (*He reaches for her; she crosses away. Then, drily.*) It's gone now—you look like yourself again!

RUTH: Man, if you don't shut up and leave me alone.

WALTER (*looking out to the street again*): First thing a man ought to learn in life is not to make love to no colored woman first thing in the morning. You all some eeeevil people at eight o'clock in the morning.

(*Travis appears in the hall doorway, almost fully dressed and quite wide awake now, his towels and pajamas across his shoulders. He opens the door and signals for his father to make the bathroom in a hurry.*)

TRAVIS (*watching the bathroom*): Daddy, come on!

(*Walter gets his bathroom utensils and flies out to the bathroom.*)

RUTH: Sit down and have your breakfast, Travis.

TRAVIS: Mama, this is Friday. (*Gleefully.*) Check coming tomorrow, huh?

RUTH: You get your mind off money and eat your breakfast.

TRAVIS (*eating*): This is the morning we supposed to bring the fifty cents to school.

RUTH: Well, I ain't got no fifty cents this morning.

TRAVIS: Teacher say we have to.

RUTH: I don't care what teacher say. I ain't got it. Eat your breakfast, Travis.

TRAVIS: I *am* eating.

RUTH: Hush up now and just eat!

(*The boy gives her an exasperated look for her lack of understanding and eats grudgingly.*)

TRAVIS: You think Grandmama would have it?

RUTH: No! And I want you to stop asking your grandmother for money, you hear me?

TRAVIS (*outraged*): Gaaaleee! I don't ask her, she just gimme it sometimes!

RUTH: Travis Willard Younger—I got too much on me this morning to be—

TRAVIS: Maybe Daddy—

RUTH: *Travis!*

(*The boy hushes abruptly. They are both quiet and tense for several seconds.*)

TRAVIS (*presently*): Could I maybe go carry some groceries in front of the supermarket for a little while after school then?

RUTH: Just hush, I said. (*Travis jabs his spoon into his cereal bowl viciously and rests his head in anger upon his fists.*) If you through eating, you can get over there and make up your bed.

(*The boy obeys stiffly and crosses the room, almost mechanically, to the bed and more or less folds the bedding into a heap, then angrily gets his books and cap.*)

TRAVIS (*sulking and standing apart from her unnaturally*): I'm gone.

RUTH (*looking up from the stove to inspect him automatically*): Come here. (*He crosses to her and she studies his head.*) If you don't take this comb and fix this here head, you better! (*Travis puts down his books with a great sigh of oppression and crosses to the mirror. His mother mutters under her breath about his "slubbornness."*) 'Bout to march out of here with that head looking just like chickens slept in it! I just don't know where you get your slubborn ways . . . And get your jacket, too. Looks chilly out this morning.

TRAVIS (*with conspicuously brushed hair and jacket*): I'm gone.

RUTH: Get carfare and milk money—(*waving one finger*)—and not a single penny for no caps, you hear me?

TRAVIS (*with sullen politeness*): Yes'm.

(*He turns in outrage to leave. His mother watches after him as in his frustration he approaches the door almost comically. When she speaks to him, her voice has become a very gentle tease.*)

RUTH (*mocking; as she thinks he would say it*): Oh, Mama makes me so mad sometimes, I don't know what to do! (*She waits and continues to his back as he stands stock-still in front of the door.*) I wouldn't kiss that woman good-bye for nothing in this world this morning! (*The boy finally turns around and rolls his eyes at her, knowing the mood has changed and he is vindicated; he does not, however, move toward her yet.*) Not for nothing in this world! (*She finally laughs aloud at him and holds out her arms to him and we see that it is a way between them, very old and practiced. He crosses to her and allows her to embrace him warmly but keeps his face fixed with masculine rigidity. She holds him back from her presently and looks at him and runs her fingers over the features of his face. With utter gentleness—*) Now—whose little old angry man are you?

TRAVIS (*the masculinity and gruffness start to fade at last*): Aw gaalee—Mama . . .

RUTH (*mimicking*): Aw—gaaaaalleeeee, Mama! (*She pushes him, with rough playfulness and finality, toward the door.*) Get on out of here or you going to be late.

TRAVIS (*in the face of love, new aggressiveness*): Mama, could I *please* go carry groceries?

RUTH: Honey, it's starting to get so cold evenings.

WALTER (*coming in from the bathroom and drawing a make-believe gun from a make-believe holster and shooting at his son*): What is it he wants to do?

RUTH: Go carry groceries after school at the supermarket.

WALTER: Well, let him go . . .

TRAVIS (*quickly, to the ally*): I have to—she won't gimme the fifty cents . . .

WALTER (*to his wife only*): Why not?

RUTH (*simply, and with flavor*): 'Cause we don't have it.

WALTER (*to Ruth only*): What you tell the boy things like that for? (*Reaching down into his pants with a rather important gesture.*) Here, son—

(*He hands the boy the coin, but his eyes are directed to his wife's. Travis takes the money happily.*)

TRAVIS: Thanks, Daddy.

(*He starts out. Ruth watches both of them with murder in her eyes. Walter stands and stares back at her with defiance and suddenly reaches into his pocket again on an afterthought.*)

WALTER (*without even looking at his son, still staring hard at his wife*): In fact, here's another fifty cents . . . Buy yourself some fruit today—or take a taxicab to school or something!

TRAVIS: Whoopee—

(*He leaps up and clasps his father around the middle with his legs, and they face each other in mutual appreciation; slowly Walter Lee peeks around the boy*) *to catch the violent rays from his wife's eyes and draws his head back as if shot.*)

WALTER: You better get down now—and get to school, man.

TRAVIS (*at the door*): O.K. Good-bye.

(*He exits.*)

WALTER (*after him, pointing with pride*): That's my boy. (*She looks at him in disgust and turns back to her work.*) You know what I was thinking 'bout in the bathroom this morning?

RUTH: No.

WALTER: How come you always try to be so pleasant!

RUTH: What is there to be pleasant 'bout!

WALTER: You want to know what I was thinking 'bout in the bathroom or not!

RUTH: I know what you thinking 'bout.

WALTER (*ignoring her*): 'Bout what me and Willy Harris was talking about last night.

RUTH (*immediately—a refrain*): Willy Harris is a good-for-nothing loudmouth.

WALTER: Anybody who talks to me has got to be a good-for-nothing loudmouth, ain't he? And what you know about who is just a good-for-nothing loudmouth? Charlie Atkins was just a "good-for-nothing loudmouth" too, wasn't he! When he wanted me to go in the dry-cleaning business with him. And now—he's grossing a hundred thousand a year. A hundred thousand dollars a year! You still call *him* a loudmouth!

RUTH (*bitterly*): Oh, Walter Lee . . .

(*She folds her head on her arms over the table.*)

WALTER (*rising and coming to her and standing over her*): You tired, ain't you? Tired of everything. Me, the boy, the way we live—this beat-up hole—everything. Ain't you? (*She doesn't look up, doesn't answer.*) So tired—moaning and groaning all the time, but you wouldn't do nothing to help, would you? You couldn't be on my side that long for nothing, could you?

RUTH: Walter, please leave me alone.

WALTER: A man needs for a woman to back him up . . .

RUTH: Walter—

WALTER: Mama would listen to you. You know she listen to you more than she do me and Bennie. She think more of you. All you have to do is just sit down with her when you drinking your coffee one morning and talking 'bout things like you do and—(*He sits down beside her and demonstrates graphically what he thinks her methods and tone should be.*)—you just sip your coffee, see, and say easy like that you been thinking 'bout that deal Walter Lee is so interested in, 'bout the store and all, and sip some more coffee, like what you saying ain't really that important to you—And the next thing you know, she be listening good and asking you questions and when I come home—I can tell her the details. This ain't no fly-by-night proposition, baby. I mean we figured it out, me and Willy and Bobo.

RUTH (*with a frown*): Bobo?

WALTER: Yeah. You see, this little liquor store we got in mind cost seventy-five thousand and we figured the initial investment on the place be 'bout thirty thousand, see. That be ten thousand each. Course, there's a couple of hundred you got to pay so's you don't spend your life just waiting for them clowns to let your license get approved—

RUTH: You mean graft?

WALTER (*frowning impatiently*): Don't call it that. See there, that just goes to show you what women understand about the world. Baby, don't *nothing* happen for you in this world 'less you pay *somebody* off!

RUTH: Walter, leave me alone! (*She raises her head and stares at him vigorously—then says, more quietly.*) *Eat* your eggs, they gonna be cold.

WALTER (*straightening up from her and looking off*): That's it. There you are. Man say to his woman: I got me a dream. His woman say: Eat your eggs. (*Sadly, but gaining in power.*) Man say: I got to take hold of this here world, baby! And a woman will say: Eat your eggs and go to work. (*Passionately now.*) Man say: I got to change my life, I'm choking to death, baby! And his woman say—(*in utter anguish as he brings his fists down on his thighs*)—Your eggs is getting cold!

RUTH (*softly*): Walter, that ain't none of our money.

WALTER (*not listening at all or even looking at her*): This morning, I was lookin' in the mirror and thinking about it . . . I'm thirty-five years old; I been married eleven years and I got a boy who sleeps in the living room—(*very, very quietly*)—and all I got to give him is stories about how rich white people live . . .

RUTH: Eat your eggs, Walter.

WALTER (*slams the table and jumps up*):—DAMN MY EGGS—DAMN ALL THE EGGS THAT EVER WAS!

RUTH: Then go to work.

WALTER (*looking up at her*): See—I'm trying to talk to you 'bout myself—(*shaking his head with the repetition*)—and all you can say is eat them eggs and go to work.

RUTH (*wearily*): Honey, you never say nothing new. I listen to you every day, every night and every morning, and you never say nothing new. (*Shrugging.*) So you would rather *be* Mr. Arnold than be his chauffeur. So—I would *rather* be living in Buckingham Palace.

WALTER: That is just what is wrong with the colored woman in this world . . . Don't understand about building their men up and making 'em feel like they somebody. Like they can do something.

RUTH (*drily, but to hurt*): There *are* colored men who do things.

WALTER: No thanks to the colored woman.

RUTH: Well, being a colored woman, I guess I can't help myself none.

(*She rises and gets the ironing board and sets it up and attacks a huge pile of rough-dried clothes, sprinkling them in preparation for the ironing and then rolling them into tight fat balls.*)

WALTER (*mumbling*): We one group of men tied to a race of women with small minds!

(*His sister Beneatha enters. She is about twenty, as slim and intense as her brother. She is not as pretty as her sister-in-law, but her lean, almost intellectual face has a handsomeness of its own. She wears a bright red flannel nightie, and her thick hair stands wildly about her head. Her speech is a mixture of many things; it is different from the rest of the family's insofar as education has permeated her sense of English—and perhaps the Midwest rather than the South has finally—at last—won out in her inflection; but not altogether, because over all of it is a soft slurring and transformed use of vowels which is the decided influence of the Southside. She passes through the room without looking at either Ruth or Walter and goes to the outside door and looks, a little blindly, out to the bathroom. She sees that it has been lost to the Johnsons. She closes the door with a sleepy vengeance and crosses to the table and sits down a little defeated.*)

BENEATHA: I am going to start timing those people.

WALTER: You should get up earlier.

BENEATHA (*Her face in her hands. She is still fighting the urge to go back to bed.*): Really—would you suggest dawn? Where's the paper?

WALTER (*pushing the paper across the table to her as he studies her almost clinically, as though he has never seen her before*): You a horrible-looking chick at this hour.

BENEATHA (*drily*): Good morning, everybody.

WALTER (*senselessly*): How is school coming?

BENEATHA (*in the same spirit*): Lovely. Lovely. And you know, biology is the greatest. (*Looking up at him.*) I dissected something that looked just like you yesterday.

WALTER: I just wondered if you've made up your mind and everything.

BENEATHA (*gaining in sharpness and impatience*): And what did I answer yesterday morning—and the day before that?

RUTH (*from the ironing board, like someone disinterested and old*): Don't be so nasty, Bennie.

BENEATHA (*still to her brother*): And the day before that and the day before that!

WALTER (*defensively*): I'm interested in you. Something wrong with that? Ain't many girls who decide—

WALTER AND BENEATHA (*in unison*):—"to be a doctor."

(*Silence.*)

WALTER: Have we figured out yet just exactly how much medical school is going to cost?

RUTH: Walter Lee, why don't you leave that girl alone and get out of here to work?

BENEATHA (*exits to the bathroom and bangs on the door*): Come on out of there, please!

(*She comes back into the room.*)

WALTER (*looking at his sister intently*): You know the check is coming tomorrow.

BENEATHA (*turning on him with a sharpness all her own*): That money belongs to Mama, Walter, and it's for her to decide how she wants to use it. I don't care if she wants to buy a house or a rocketship or just nail it up somewhere and look at it. It's hers. Not ours—hers.

WALTER (*bitterly*): Now ain't that fine! You just got your mother's interest at heart, ain't you, girl? You such a nice girl—but if Mama got that money she can always take a few thousand and help you through school too—can't she?

BENEATHA: I have never asked anyone around here to do anything for me!

WALTER: No! And the line between asking and just accepting when the time comes is big and wide—ain't it!

BENEATHA (*with fury*): What do you want from me, Brother—that I quit school or just drop dead, which!

WALTER: I don't want nothing but for you to stop acting holy 'round here. Me and Ruth done made some sacrifices for you—why can't you do something for the family?

RUTH: Walter, don't be dragging me in it.

WALTER: You are in it—Don't you get up and go work in somebody's kitchen for the last three years to help put clothes on her back?

RUTH: Oh, Walter—that's not fair . . .

WALTER: It ain't that nobody expects you to get on your knees and say thank you, Brother; thank you, Ruth; thank you, Mama—and thank you, Travis, for wearing the same pair of shoes for two semesters—

BENEATHA (*dropping to her knees*): Well—I do—all right?—thank everybody! And forgive me for ever wanting to be anything at all! (*Pursuing him on her knees across the floor.*) FORGIVE ME, FORGIVE ME, FORGIVE ME!

RUTH: Please stop it! Your mama'll hear you.

WALTER: Who the hell told you you had to be a doctor? If you so crazy 'bout messing 'round with sick people—then go be a nurse like other women—or just get married and be quiet . . .

BENEATHA: Well—you finally got it said . . . It took you three years but you finally got it said. Walter, give up; leave me alone—it's Mama's money.

WALTER: *He was my father, too!*

BENEATHA: So what? He was mine, too—and Travis' grandfather—but the insurance money belongs to Mama. Picking on me is not going to make her give it to you to invest in any liquor stores—(*under breath, dropping into a chair*)—and I for one say, God bless Mama for that!

WALTER (*to Ruth*): See—did you hear? Did you hear!

RUTH: Honey, please go to work.

WALTER: Nobody in this house is ever going to understand me.

BENEATHA: Because you're a nut.

WALTER: Who's a nut?

BENEATHA: You—you are a nut. Thee is mad, boy.

Claudia McNeil as Lena (Mama) and Sidney Poitier as Walter in the 1961 film version of *A Raisin in the Sun.*

WALTER (*looking at his wife and his sister from the door, very sadly*): The world's most backward race of people, and that's a fact.

BENEATHA (*turning slowly in her chair*): And then there are all those prophets who would lead us out of the wilderness—(*Walter slams out of the house.*)—into the swamps!

RUTH: Bennie, why you always gotta be pickin' on your brother? Can't you be a little sweeter sometimes? (*Door opens. Walter walks in. He fumbles with his cap, starts to speak, clears throat, looks everywhere but at Ruth. Finally.*)

WALTER (*to Ruth*): I need some money for carfare.

RUTH (*looks at him, then warms; teasing, but tenderly*): Fifty cents? (*She goes to her bag and gets money.*) Here—take a taxi!

(*Walter exits. Mama enters. She is a woman in her early sixties, full-bodied and strong. She is one of those women of a certain grace and beauty who wear it so unobtrusively that it takes a while to notice. Her dark brown face is surrounded by the total whiteness of her hair, and, being a woman who has adjusted to many things in life and overcome many more, her face is full of strength. She has, we can see, wit and faith of a kind that keep her eyes lit and full of interest and expectancy. She is, in a word, a beautiful woman. Her bearing is perhaps most like the noble bearing of the women of the Hereros of Southwest Africa—rather as if she imagines that as she walks she still bears a basket or a vessel upon her head. Her speech, on the other hand, is* as careless as her carriage is precise—she is inclined to slur everything—but her voice is perhaps not so much quiet as simply soft.)

MAMA: Who that 'round here slamming doors at this hour?

(*She crosses through the room, goes to the window, opens it, and brings in a feeble little plant growing doggedly in a small pot on the window sill. She feels the dirt and puts it back out.*)

RUTH: That was Walter Lee. He and Bennie was at it again.

MAMA: My children and they tempers. Lord, if this little old plant don't get more sun than it's been getting it ain't never going to see spring again. (*She turns from the window.*) What's the matter with you this morning, Ruth? You looks right peaked. You aiming to iron all them things? Leave some for me. I'll get to 'em this afternoon. Bennie honey, it's too drafty for you to be sitting 'round half dressed. Where's your robe?

BENEATHA: In the cleaners.

MAMA: Well, go get mine and put it on.

BENEATHA: I'm not cold, Mama, honest.

MAMA: I know—but you so thin . . .

BENEATHA (*irritably*): Mama, I'm not cold.

MAMA (*seeing the make-down bed as Travis has left it*): Lord have mercy, look at that poor bed. Bless his heart—he tries, don't he?

(*She moves to the bed Travis has sloppily made up.*)

Ester Rolle as Lena Younger comforts her daughter-in-law Ruth in the Huntington Theatre Company's 1994 production of *A Raisin in the Sun*. Also in the scene are Marguerite Hannah as Ruth and B. W. Gonzalez as Beneatha.

RUTH: No—he don't half try at all 'cause he knows you going to come along behind him and fix everything. That's just how come he don't know how to do nothing right now—you done spoiled that boy so.

MAMA (*folding bedding*): Well—he's a little boy. Ain't supposed to know 'bout housekeeping. My baby, that's what he is. What you fix for his breakfast this morning?

RUTH (*angrily*): I feed my son, Lena!

MAMA: I ain't meddling—(*Under breath; busybodyish.*) I just noticed all last week he had cold cereal, and when it starts getting this chilly in the fall a child ought to have some hot grits or something when he goes out in the cold—

RUTH (*furious*): I gave him hot oats—is that all right!

MAMA: I ain't meddling. (*Pause.*) Put a lot of nice butter on it? (*Ruth shoots her an angry look and does not reply.*) He likes lots of butter.

RUTH (*exasperated*): Lena—

MAMA (*To Beneatha. Mama is inclined to wander conversationally sometimes.*): What was you and your brother fussing 'bout this morning?

BENEATHA: It's not important, Mama.

(*She gets up and goes to look out at the bathroom, which is apparently free, and she picks up her towels and rushes out.*)

MAMA: What was they fighting about?

RUTH: Now you know as well as I do.

MAMA (*shaking her head*): Brother still worrying hisself sick about that money?

RUTH: You know he is.

MAMA: You had breakfast?

RUTH: Some coffee.

MAMA: Girl, you better start eating and looking after yourself better. You almost thin as Travis.

RUTH: Lena—

MAMA: Un-hunh?

RUTH: What are you going to do with it?

MAMA: Now don't you start, child. It's too early in the morning to be talking about money. It ain't Christian.

RUTH: It's just that he got his heart set on that store—

MAMA: You mean that liquor store that Willy Harris want him to invest in?

RUTH: Yes—

MAMA: We ain't no business people, Ruth. We just plain working folks.

RUTH: Ain't nobody business people till they go into business. Walter Lee say colored people ain't never going to start getting ahead till they start gambling on some different kinds of things in the world— investments and things.

MAMA: What done got into you, girl? Walter Lee done finally sold you on investing.

RUTH: No. Mama, something is happening between Walter and me. I don't know what it is—but he needs something—something I can't give him anymore. He needs this chance, Lena.

MAMA (*frowning deeply*): But liquor, honey—

RUTH: Well—like Walter say—I spec people going to always be drinking themselves some liquor.

MAMA: Well—whether they drinks it or not ain't none of my business. But whether I go into business selling it to 'em *is*, and I don't want that on my ledger this late in life. (*Stopping suddenly and studying her daughter-in-law.*) Ruth Younger, what's the matter with you today? You look like you could fall over right there.

RUTH: I'm tired.

MAMA: Then you better stay home from work today.

RUTH: I can't stay home. She'd be calling up the agency and screaming at them, "My girl didn't come in today—send me somebody! My girl didn't come in!" Oh, she just have a fit . . .

MAMA: Well, let her have it. I'll just call her up and say you got the flu—

RUTH (*laughing*): Why the flu?

MAMA: 'Cause it sounds respectable to 'em. Something white people get, too. They know 'bout the flu. Otherwise they think you been cut up or something when you tell 'em you sick.

RUTH: I got to go in. We need the money.

MAMA: Somebody would of thought my children done all but starved to death the way they talk about money here late. Child, we got a great big old check coming tomorrow.

RUTH (*sincerely, but also self-righteously*): Now that's your money. It ain't got nothing to do with me. We all feel like that—Walter and Bennie and me—even Travis.

MAMA (*thoughtfully, and suddenly very far away*): Ten thousand dollars—

RUTH: Sure is wonderful.

MAMA: Ten thousand dollars.

RUTH: You know what you should do, Miss Lena? You should take yourself a trip somewhere. To Europe or South America or someplace—

MAMA (*throwing up her hands at the thought*): Oh, child!

RUTH: I'm serious. Just pack up and leave! Go on away and enjoy yourself some. Forget about the family and have yourself a ball for once in your life—

MAMA (*drily*): You sound like I'm just about ready to die. Who'd go with me? What I look like wandering 'round Europe by myself?

RUTH: Shoot—these here rich white women do it all the time. They don't think nothing of packing up they suitcases and piling on one of them big steamships and—swoosh!—they gone, child.

MAMA: Something always told me I wasn't no rich white woman.

RUTH: Well—what are you going to do with it then?

MAMA: I ain't rightly decided. (*Thinking. She speaks now with emphasis.*) Some of it got to be put away for Beneatha and her schoolin'—and ain't nothing going to touch that part of it. Nothing. (*She waits several seconds, trying to make up her mind about something, and looks at Ruth a little tentatively before going on.*) Been thinking that we maybe could meet the notes on a little old two-story somewhere, with a yard where Travis could play in the summertime, if we use part of the insurance for a down payment and everybody kind of pitch in. I could maybe take on a little day work again, few days a week—

RUTH (*studying her mother-in-law furtively and concentrating on her ironing, anxious to encourage without seeming to*): Well, Lord knows, we've put enough rent into this here rat trap to pay for four houses by now . . .

MAMA (*looking up at the words "rat trap" and then looking around and leaning back and sighing—in a suddenly reflective mood—*): "Rat trap"—yes, that's all it is. (*Smiling.*) I remember just as well the day me and Big Walter moved in here. Hadn't been married but two weeks and wasn't planning on living here no more than a year. (*She shakes her head at the dissolved dream.*) We was going to set away, little by little, don't you know, and buy a little place out in Morgan Park. We had even picked out the house. (*Chuckling a little.*) Looks right dumpy today. But Lord, child, you should know, all the dreams I had 'bout buying that house and fixing it up and making me a little garden in the back—(*She waits and stops smiling.*) And didn't none of it happen.

(*Dropping her hands in a futile gesture.*)

RUTH (*keeps her head down, ironing*): Yes, life can be a barrel of disappointments, sometimes.

MAMA: Honey, Big Walter would come in here some nights back then and slump down on that couch there and just look at the rug, and look at me and look at the rug and then back at me—and I'd know he was down then . . . really down. (*After a second very long and thoughtful pause; she is seeing back to times that only she can see.*) And then, Lord, when I lost that baby—little Claude—I almost thought I was going to lose Big Walter too. Oh, that man grieved hisself! He was one man to love his children.

RUTH: Ain't nothin' can tear at you like losin' your baby.

MAMA: I guess that's how come that man finally worked hisself to death like he done. Like he was fighting his own war with this here world that took his baby from him.

RUTH: He sure was a fine man, all right. I always liked Mr. Younger.

MAMA: Crazy 'bout his children! God knows there was plenty wrong with Walter Younger—hard-headed, mean, kind of wild with women—plenty wrong with him. But he sure loved his children. Always wanted them to have something—be something. That's where Brother gets all these notions, I reckon. Big Walter used to say, he'd get right wet in the eyes sometimes, lean his head back with the water standing in his eyes and say, "Seem like God didn't see fit to give the black man nothing but dreams—but He did give us children to make them dreams seem worthwhile." (*She smiles.*) He could talk like that, don't you know.

RUTH: Yes, he sure could. He was a good man, Mr. Younger.

MAMA: Yes, a fine man—just couldn't never catch up with his dreams, that's all.

(*Beneatha comes in, brushing her hair and looking up to the ceiling, where the sound of a vacuum cleaner has started up.*)

BENEATHA: What could be so dirty on that woman's rugs that she has to vacuum them every single day?

RUTH: I wish certain young women 'round here who I could name would take inspiration about certain rugs in a certain apartment I could also mention.

BENEATHA (*shrugging*): How much cleaning can a house need, for Christ's sakes.

MAMA (*not liking the Lord's name used thus*): Bennie!

RUTH: Just listen to her—just listen!

BENEATHA: Oh, God!

MAMA: If you use the Lord's name just one more time—

BENEATHA (*a bit of a whine*): Oh, Mama—

RUTH: Fresh—just fresh as salt, this girl!

BENEATHA (*drily*): Well—if the salt loses its savor—

MAMA: Now that will do. I just ain't going to have you 'round here reciting the scriptures in vain—you hear me?

BENEATHA: How did I manage to get on everybody's wrong side by just walking into a room?

RUTH: If you weren't so fresh—

BENEATHA: Ruth, I'm twenty years old.

MAMA: What time you be home from school today?

BENEATHA: Kind of late. (*With enthusiasm.*) Madeline is going to start my guitar lessons today.

(*Mama and Ruth look up with the same expression.*)

MAMA: Your *what* kind of lessons?

BENEATHA: Guitar.

RUTH: Oh, Father!

MAMA: How come you done taken it in your mind to learn to play the guitar?

BENEATHA: I just want to, that's all.

MAMA (*smiling*): Lord, child, don't you know what to do with yourself? How long it going to be before you get tired of this now—like you got tired of that little play-acting group you joined last year? (*Looking at Ruth.*) And what was it the year before that?

RUTH: The horseback-riding club for which she bought that fifty-five-dollar riding habit that's been hanging in the closet ever since!

MAMA (*to Beneatha*): Why you got to flit so from one thing to another, baby?

BENEATHA (*sharply*): I just want to learn to play the guitar. Is there anything wrong with that?

MAMA: Ain't nobody trying to stop you. I just wonders sometimes why you has to flit so from one thing to another all the time. You ain't never done nothing with all that camera equipment you brought home—

BENEATHA: I don't flit! I—I experiment with different forms of expression—

RUTH: Like riding a horse?

BENEATHA: —People have to express themselves one way or another.

MAMA: What is it you want to express?

BENEATHA (*angrily*): Me! (*Mama and Ruth look at each other and burst into raucous laughter.*) Don't worry—I don't expect you to understand.

MAMA (*to change the subject*): Who you going out with tomorrow night?

BENEATHA (*with displeasure*): George Murchison again.

MAMA (*pleased*): Oh—you getting a little sweet on him?

RUTH: You ask me, this child ain't sweet on nobody but herself—(*Under breath.*) Express herself!

(*They laugh.*)

BENEATHA: Oh—I like George all right, Mama. I mean I like him enough to go out with him and stuff, but—

RUTH (*for devilment*): What does *and stuff* mean?

BENEATHA: Mind your own business.

MAMA: Stop picking at her now, Ruth. (*She chuckles—then a suspicious sudden look at her daughter as she turns in her chair for emphasis.*) What DOES it mean?

BENEATHA (*wearily*): Oh, I just mean I couldn't ever really be serious about George. He's—he's so shallow.

RUTH: Shallow—what do you mean he's shallow? He's *Rich*!

MAMA: Hush, Ruth.

BENEATHA: I know he's rich. He knows he's rich, too.

RUTH: Well—what other qualities a man got to have to satisfy you, little girl?

BENEATHA: You wouldn't even begin to understand. Anybody who married Walter could not possibly understand.

MAMA (*outraged*): What kind of way is that to talk about your brother?

BENEATHA: Brother is a flip—let's face it.

MAMA (*to Ruth, helplessly*): What's a flip?

RUTH (*glad to add kindling*): She's saying he's crazy.

BENEATHA: Not crazy. Brother isn't really crazy yet—he—he's an elaborate neurotic.

MAMA: Hush your mouth!

BENEATHA: As for George. Well. George looks good—he's got a beautiful car and he takes me to nice places and, as my sister-in-law says, he is probably the richest boy I will ever get to know and I even like him sometimes—but if the Youngers are sitting around waiting to see if their little Bennie is going to tie up the family with the Murchisons, they are wasting their time.

RUTH: You mean you wouldn't marry George Murchison if he asked you someday? That pretty, rich thing? Honey, I knew you was odd—

BENEATHA: No I would not marry him if all I felt for him was what I feel now. Besides, George's family wouldn't really like it.

MAMA: Why not?

BENEATHA: Oh, Mama—The Murchisons are honest-to-God-real-*live*-rich colored people, and the only people in the world who are more snobbish than rich white people are rich colored people. I thought everybody knew that. I've met Mrs. Murchison. She's a scene!

MAMA: You must not dislike people 'cause they well off, honey.

BENEATHA: Why not? It makes just as much sense as disliking people 'cause they are poor, and lots of people do that.

RUTH (*A wisdom-of-the-ages manner. To Mama.*): Well, she'll get over some of this—

BENEATHA: Get over it? What are you talking about, Ruth? Listen, I'm going to be a doctor. I'm not worried about who I'm going to marry yet—if I ever get married.

MAMA AND RUTH: *If!*

MAMA: Now, Bennie—

BENEATHA: Oh, I probably will . . . but first I'm going to be a doctor, and George, for one, still thinks that's pretty funny. I couldn't be bothered with that. I am going to be a doctor and everybody around here better understand that!

MAMA (*kindly*): 'Course you going to be a doctor, honey, God willing.

BENEATHA (*drily*): God hasn't got a thing to do with it.

MAMA: Beneatha—that just wasn't necessary.

BENEATHA: Well—neither is God. I get sick of hearing about God.

MAMA: Beneatha!

BENEATHA: I mean it! I'm just tired of hearing about God all the time. What has He got to do with anything? Does he pay tuition?

MAMA: You 'bout to get your fresh little jaw slapped!

RUTH: That's just what she needs, all right!

BENEATHA: Why? Why can't I say what I want to around here, like everybody else?

MAMA: It don't sound nice for a young girl to say things like that—you wasn't brought up that way. Me and your father went to trouble to get you and Brother to church every Sunday.

BENEATHA: Mama, you don't understand. It's all a matter of ideas, and God is just one idea I don't accept. It's not important. I am not going out and be immoral or commit crimes because I don't believe in God. I don't even think about it. It's just that I get tired of Him getting credit for all the things the human race achieves through its own stubborn effort. There simply is no blasted God—there is only man and it is *he* who makes miracles!

(*Mama absorbs this speech, studies her daughter and rises slowly and crosses to Beneatha and slaps her powerfully across the face. After, there is only silence and the daughter drops her eyes from her mother's face, and Mama is very tall before her.*)

MAMA: Now—you say after me, in my mother's house there is still God. (*There is a long pause and Beneatha stares at the floor wordlessly. Mama repeats the phrase with precision and cool emotion.*) In my mother's house there is still God.

BENEATHA: In my mother's house there is still God.

(*A long pause.*)

MAMA (*Walking away from Beneatha, too disturbed for triumphant posture. Stopping and turning back to her daughter.*): There are some ideas we ain't going to have in this house. Not long as I am at the head of this family.

BENEATHA: Yes, ma'am.

(*Mama walks out of the room.*)

RUTH (*almost gently, with profound understanding*): You think you a woman, Bennie—but you still a little girl. What you did was childish—so you got treated like a child.

BENEATHA: I see. (*Quietly.*) I also see that everybody thinks it's all right for Mama to be a tyrant. But all the tyranny in the world will never put a God in the heavens!

(*She picks up her books and goes out. Pause.*)

RUTH (*goes to Mama's door*): She said she was sorry.

MAMA (*coming out, going to her plant*): They frightens me, Ruth. My children.

RUTH: You got good children, Lena. They just a little off sometimes—but they're good.

MAMA: No—there's something come down between me and them that don't let us understand each other and

I don't know what it is. One done almost lost his mind thinking 'bout money all the time and the other done commence to talk about things I can't seem to understand in no form or fashion. What is it that's changing, Ruth?

RUTH (*soothingly, older than her years*): Now . . . you taking it all too seriously. You just got strong-willed children and it takes a strong woman like you to keep 'em in hand.

MAMA (*looking at her plant and sprinkling a little water on it*): They spirited all right, my children. Got to admit they got spirit—Bennie and Walter. Like this little old plant that ain't never had enough sunshine or nothing—and look at it . . .

(*She has her back to Ruth, who has had to stop ironing and lean against something and put the back of her hand to her forehead.*)

RUTH (*trying to keep Mama from noticing*): You . . . sure . . . loves that little old thing, don't you? . . .

MAMA: Well, I always wanted me a garden like I used to see sometimes at the back of the houses down home. This plant is close as I ever got to having one. (*She looks out of the window as she replaces the plant.*) Lord, ain't nothing as dreary as the view from this window on a dreary day, is there? Why ain't you singing this morning, Ruth? Sing that "No Ways Tired." That song always lifts me up so—(*She turns at last to see that Ruth has slipped quietly to the floor, in a state of semiconsciousness.*) Ruth! Ruth honey—what's the matter with you . . . Ruth!

Scene II

(*It is the following morning; a Saturday morning, and house cleaning is in progress at the Youngers'. Furniture has been shoved hither and yon and Mama is giving the kitchen-area walls a washing down. Beneatha, in dungarees, with a handkerchief tied around her face, is spraying insecticide into the cracks in the walls. As they work, the radio is on and a Southside disk jockey program is inappropriately filling the house with a rather exotic saxophone blues. Travis, the sole idle one, is leaning on his arms, looking out of the window.*)

TRAVIS: Grandmama, that stuff Bennie is using smells awful. Can I go downstairs, please?

MAMA: Did you get all them chores done already? I ain't seen you doing much.

TRAVIS: Yes'm—finished early. Where did Mama go this morning?

MAMA (*looking at Beneatha*): She had to go on a little errand.

(*The phone rings. Beneatha runs to answer it and reaches it before Walter, who has entered from bedroom.*)

TRAVIS: Where?

MAMA: To tend to her business.

BENEATHA: Haylo . . . (*Disappointed.*) Yes, he is. (*She tosses the phone to Walter, who barely catches it.*) It's Willie Harris again.

WALTER (*as privately as possible under Mama's gaze*): Hello, Willie. Did you get the papers from the lawyer? . . . No, not yet. I told you the mailman doesn't get here till ten-thirty . . . No, I'll come there . . . Yeah! Right away. (*He hangs up and goes for his coat.*)

BENEATHA: Brother, where did Ruth go?

WALTER (*as he exits*): How should I know!

TRAVIS: Aw come on, Grandma. Can I go outside?

MAMA: Oh, I guess so. You stay right in front of the house, though, and keep a good lookout for the postman.

TRAVIS: Yes'm. (*He darts into bedroom for stickball and bat, reenters, and sees Beneatha on her knees spraying under sofa with behind upraised. He edges closer to the target, takes aim, and lets her have it. She screams.*) Leave them poor little cockroaches alone, they ain't bothering you none! (*He runs as she swings the spraygun at him viciously and playfully.*) Grandma! Grandma!

MAMA: Look out there, girl, before you be spilling some of that stuff on that child!

TRAVIS (*safely behind the bastion of Mama*): That's right—look out, now! (*He exits.*)

BENEATHA (*drily*): I can't imagine that it would hurt him—it has never hurt the roaches.

MAMA: Well, little boys' hides ain't as tough as Southside roaches. You better get over there behind the bureau. I seen one marching out of there like Napoleon yesterday.

BENEATHA: There's really only one way to get rid of them, Mama—

MAMA: How?

BENEATHA: Set fire to this building! Mama, where did Ruth go?

MAMA (*looking at her with meaning*): To the doctor, I think.

BENEATHA: The doctor? What's the matter? (*They exchange glances.*) You don't think—

MAMA (*with her sense of drama*): Now I ain't saying what I think. But I ain't never been wrong 'bout a woman neither.

(*The phone rings.*)

BENEATHA (*at the phone*): Hay-lo . . . (*Pause, and a moment of recognition.*) Well—when did you get back! . . . And how was it? . . . Of course I've missed you—in my way . . . This morning? No . . . house cleaning and all that and Mama hates it if I let people come over when the house is like this . . . You *have*? Well, that's different . . . What is it—Oh, what the hell, come on over . . . Right, see you then. *Arrivederci.*

(*She hangs up.*)

MAMA (*who has listened vigorously, as is her habit*): Who is that you inviting over here with this house looking like this? You ain't got the pride you was born with!

BENEATHA: Asagai doesn't care how houses look, Mama—he's an intellectual.

MAMA: *Who?*

BENEATHA: Asagai—Joseph Asagai. He's an African boy I met on campus. He's been studying in Canada all summer.

MAMA: What's his name?

BENEATHA: Asagai, Joseph. Ah-sah-guy . . . He's from Nigeria.

MAMA: Oh, that's the little country that was founded by slaves way back . . .

BENEATHA: No, Mama—that's Liberia.

MAMA: I don't think I never met no African before.

BENEATHA: Well, do me a favor and don't ask him a whole lot of ignorant questions about Africans. I mean, do they wear clothes and all that—

MAMA: Well, now, I guess if you think we so ignorant 'round here maybe you shouldn't bring your friends here—

BENEATHA: It's just that people ask such crazy things. All anyone seems to know about when it comes to Africa is Tarzan—

MAMA (*indignantly*): Why should I know anything about Africa?

BENEATHA: Why do you give money at church for the missionary work?

MAMA: Well, that's to help save people.

BENEATHA: You mean save them from *heathenism*—

MAMA (*innocently*): Yes.

BENEATHA: I'm afraid they need more salvation from the British and the French.

(*Ruth comes in forlornly and pulls off her coat with dejection. They both turn to look at her.*)

RUTH (*dispiritedly*): Well, I guess from all the happy faces—everybody knows.

BENEATHA: You pregnant?

MAMA: Lord have mercy, I sure hope it's a little old girl. Travis ought to have a sister.

(*Beneatha and Ruth give her a hopeless look for this grandmotherly enthusiasm.*)

BENEATHA: How far along are you?

RUTH: Two months.

BENEATHA: Did you mean to? I mean did you plan it or was it an accident?

MAMA: What do you know about planning or not planning?

BENEATHA: Oh, Mama.

RUTH (*wearily*): She's twenty years old, Lena.

BENEATHA: Did you plan it, Ruth?

RUTH: Mind your own business.

BENEATHA: It is my business—where is he going to live, on the *roof?* (*There is silence following the remark as the three women react to the sense of it.*) Gee—I

didn't mean that, Ruth, honest. Gee, I don't feel like that at all. I—I think it is wonderful.

RUTH (*dully*): Wonderful.

BENEATHA: Yes—really.

MAMA (*looking at Ruth, worried*): Doctor say everything going to be all right?

RUTH (*far away*): Yes—she says everything is going to be fine . . .

MAMA (*immediately suspicious*): "She"—What doctor you went to?

(*Ruth folds over, near hysteria.*)

MAMA (*worriedly hovering over Ruth*): Ruth honey—what's the matter with you—you sick?

(*Ruth has her fists clenched on her thighs and is fighting hard to suppress a scream that seems to be rising in her.*)

BENEATHA: What's the matter with her, Mama?

MAMA (*working her fingers in Ruth's shoulders to relax her*): She be all right. Women gets right depressed sometimes when they get her way. (*Speaking softly, expertly, rapidly.*) Now you just relax. That's right . . . just lean back, don't think 'bout nothing at all . . . nothing at all—

RUTH: I'm all right . . .

(*The glassy-eyed look melts and then she collapses into a fit of heavy sobbing. The bell rings.*)

BENEATHA: Oh, my God—that must be Asagai.

MAMA (*to Ruth*): Come on now, honey. You need to lie down and rest awhile . . . then have some nice hot food.

(*They exit, Ruth's weight on her mother-in-law. Beneatha, herself profoundly disturbed, opens the door to admit a rather dramatic-looking young man with a large package.*)

ASAGAI: Hello, Alaiyo—

BENEATHA (*holding the door open and regarding him with pleasure*): Hello . . . (*Long pause.*) Well—come in. And please excuse everything. My mother was very upset about my letting anyone come here with the place like this.

ASAGAI (*coming into the room*): You look disturbed too . . . Is something wrong?

BENEATHA (*still at the door, absently*): Yes . . . we've all got acute ghetto-itus. (*She smiles and comes toward him, finding a cigarette and sitting.*) So—sit down! No! Wait! (*She whips the spraygun off the sofa where she had left it and puts the cushions back. At last perches on arm of sofa. He sits.*) So, how was Canada?

ASAGAI (*a sophisticate*): Canadian.

BENEATHA (*looking at him*): Asagai, I'm very glad you are back.

ASAGAI (*looking back at her in turn*): Are you really?

BENEATHA: Yes—very.

ASAGAI: Why?—you were quite glad when I went away. What happened?

BENEATHA: You went away.

ASAGAI: Ahhhhhhhh.

BENEATHA: Before—you wanted to be so serious before there was time.

ASAGAI: How much time must there be before one knows what one feels?

BENEATHA (*Stalling this particular conversation. Her hands pressed together, in a deliberately childish gesture.*): What did you bring me?

ASAGAI (*handing her the package*): Open it and see.

BENEATHA (*eagerly opening the package and drawing out some records and the colorful robes of a Nigerian woman*): Oh, Asagai! . . . You got them for me! . . . How beautiful . . . and the records too! (*She lifts out the robes and runs to the mirror with them and holds the drapery up in front of herself.*)

ASAGAI (*coming to her at the mirror*): I shall have to teach you how to drape it properly. (*He flings the material about her for the moment and stands back to look at her.*) Ah—Oh-pay-gay-day, oh-gbah-mu-shay. (*A Yoruba exclamation for admiration.*) You wear it well . . . very well . . . mutilated hair and all.

BENEATHA (*turning suddenly*): My hair—what's wrong with my hair?

ASAGAI (*shrugging*): Were you born with it like that?

BENEATHA (*reaching up to touch it*): No . . . of course not.

(*She looks back to the mirror, disturbed.*)

ASAGAI (*smiling*): How then?

BENEATHA: You know perfectly well how . . . as crinkly as yours . . . that's how.

ASAGAI: And it is ugly to you that way?

BENEATHA (*quickly*): Oh, no—not ugly . . . (*More slowly, apologetically.*) But it's so hard to manage when it's, well—raw.

ASAGAI: And so to accommodate that—you mutilate it every week?

BENEATHA: It's not mutilation!

ASAGAI (*laughing aloud at her seriousness*): Oh . . . please! I am only teasing you because you are so very serious about these things. (*He stands back from her and folds his arms across his chest as he watches her pulling at her hair and frowning in the mirror.*) Do you remember the first time you met me at school? . . . (*He laughs.*) You came up to me and you said—and I thought you were the most serious little thing I had ever seen—you said: (*He imitates her.*) "Mr. Asagai—I want very much to talk with you. About Africa. You see, Mr. Asagai, I am looking for my *identity*!"

(*He laughs.*)

BENEATHA (*turning to him, not laughing*): Yes—

(*Her face is quizzical, profoundly disturbed.*)

ASAGAI (*still teasing and reaching out and taking her face in his hands and turning her profile to him*): Well . . . it is true that this is not so much a profile of a Hollywood queen as perhaps a queen of the Nile—(*A mock dismissal of the importance of the question.*) But what does it matter? Assimilationism is so popular in your country.

BENEATHA (*wheeling, passionately, sharply*): I am not an assimilationist!

ASAGAI (*the protest hangs in the room for a moment and Asagai studies her, his laughter fading*): Such a serious one. (*There is a pause.*) So—you like the robes? You must take excellent care of them—they are from my sister's personal wardrobe.

BENEATHA (*with incredulity*): You—you sent all the way home—for me?

ASAGAI (*with charm*): For you—I would do much more . . . Well, that is what I came for. I must go.

BENEATHA: Will you call me Monday?

ASAGAI: Yes . . . We have a great deal to talk about. I mean about identity and time and all that.

BENEATHA: Time?

ASAGAI: Yes. About how much time one needs to know what one feels.

BENEATHA: You see! You never understood that there is more than one kind of feeling which can exist between a man and a woman—or, at least, there should be.

ASAGAI (*shaking his head negatively but gently*): No. Between a man and a woman there need be only one kind of feeling. I have that for you . . . Now even . . . right this moment . . .

BENEATHA: I know—and by itself—it won't do. I can find that anywhere.

ASAGAI: For a woman it should be enough.

BENEATHA: I know—because that's what it says in all the novels that men write. But it isn't. Go ahead and laugh—but I'm not interested in being someone's little episode in America or—(*with feminine vengeance*)—one of them! (*Asagai has burst into laughter again.*) That's funny as hell, huh!

ASAGAI: It's just that every American girl I have known has said that to me. White—black—in this you are all the same. And the same speech, too!

BENEATHA (*angrily*): Yuk, yuk, yuk!

ASAGAI: It's how you can be sure that the world's most liberated women are not liberated at all. You all talk about it too much!

(*Mama enters and is immediately all social charm because of the presence of a guest.*)

BENEATHA: Oh—Mama—this is Mr. Asagai.

MAMA: How do you do?

ASAGAI (*total politeness to an elder*): How do you do, Mrs. Younger. Please forgive me for coming at such an outrageous hour on a Saturday.

MAMA: Well, you are quite welcome. I just hope you understand that our house don't always look like this. (*Chatterish.*) You must come again. I would love to hear all about—(*not sure of the name*)—your country. I think it's so sad the way our American Negroes don't know nothing about Africa 'cept Tarzan and all that. And all that money they pour into these churches when they ought to be helping you people over there drive out them French and Englishmen done taken away your land.

(*The mother flashes a slightly superior look at her daughter upon completion of the recitation.*)

ASAGAI (*taken aback by this sudden and acutely unrelated expression of sympathy*): Yes . . . yes . . .

MAMA (*smiling at him suddenly and relaxing and looking him over*): How many miles is it from here to where you come from?

ASAGAI: Many thousands.

MAMA (*looking at him as she would Walter*): I bet you don't half look after yourself, being away from your mama either. I spec you better come 'round here from time to time to get yourself some decent home-cooked meals . . .

ASAGAI (*moved*): Thank you. Thank you very much. (*They are all quiet, then*—) Well . . . I must go. I will call you Monday, Alaiyo.

MAMA: What's that he call you?

ASAGAI: Oh—"Alaiyo." I hope you don't mind. It is what you would call a nickname, I think. It is a Yoruba word. I am a Yoruba.

MAMA (*looking at Beneatha*): I—I thought he was from—(*Uncertain.*)

ASAGAI (*understanding*): Nigeria is my country. Yoruba is my tribal origin—

BENEATHA: You didn't tell us what Alaiyo means . . . for all I know, you might be calling me Little Idiot or something . . .

ASAGAI: Well . . . let me see . . . I do not know how just to explain it . . . The sense of a thing can be so different when it changes languages.

BENEATHA: You're evading.

ASAGAI: No—really it is difficult . . . (*Thinking.*) It means . . . it means One for Whom Bread—Food—Is Not Enough. (*He looks at her.*) Is that all right?

BENEATHA (*understanding, softly*): Thank you.

MAMA (*looking from one to the other and not understanding any of it*): Well . . . that's nice . . . You must come see us again—Mr.——

ASAGAI: Ah-sah-guy . . .

MAMA: Yes . . . Do come again.

ASAGAI: Good-bye.

(*He exits.*)

MAMA (*after him*): Lord, that's a pretty thing just went out here! (*Insinuatingly, to her daughter.*) Yes, I guess I see why we done commence to get so interested in Africa 'round here. Missionaries my aunt Jenny!

(*She exits.*)

BENEATHA: Oh, Mama! . . .

(*She picks up the Nigerian dress and holds it up to her in front of the mirror again. She sets the headdress on haphazardly and then notices her hair again and clutches at it and then replaces the headdress and frowns at herself. Then she starts to wriggle in front of the mirror as she thinks a Nigerian woman might. Travis enters and stands regarding her.*)

TRAVIS: What's the matter, girl, you cracking up?

BENEATHA: Shut up.

(*She pulls the headdress off and looks at herself in the mirror and clutches at her hair again and squinches her eyes as if trying to imagine something. Then, suddenly, she gets her raincoat and kerchief and hurriedly prepares for going out.*)

MAMA (*coming back into the room*): She's resting now. Travis, baby, run next door and ask Miss Johnson to please let me have a little kitchen cleanser. This here can is empty as Jacob's kettle.

TRAVIS: I just came in.

MAMA: Do as you told. (*He exits and she looks at her daughter.*) Where you going?

BENEATHA (*halting at the door*): To become a queen of the Nile!

(*She exits in a breathless blaze of glory. Ruth appears in the bedroom doorway.*)

MAMA: Who told you to get up?

RUTH: Ain't nothing wrong with me to be lying in no bed for. Where did Bennie go?

MAMA (*drumming her fingers*): Far as I could make out—to Egypt. (*Ruth just looks at her.*) What time is it getting to?

RUTH: Ten twenty. And the mailman going to ring that bell this morning just like he done every morning for the last umpteen years.

(*Travis comes in with the cleanser can.*)

TRAVIS: She say to tell you that she don't have much.

MAMA (*angrily*): Lord, some people I could name sure is tight-fisted! (*Directing her grandson.*) Mark two cans of cleanser down on the list there. If she that hard up for kitchen cleanser, I sure don't want to forget to get her none!

RUTH: Lena—maybe the woman is just short on cleanser—

MAMA (*not listening*):—Much baking powder as she done borrowed from me all these years, she could of done gone into the baking business!

(*The bell sounds suddenly and sharply and all three are stunned—serious and silent—mid-speech. In spite of all the other conversations and distractions of the morning, this is what they have been waiting for, even Travis, who looks helplessly from his mother to his grandmother. Ruth is the first to come to life again.*)

RUTH (*to Travis*): Get down them steps, boy!

(*Travis snaps to life and flies out to get the mail.*)

MAMA (*her eyes wide, her hand to her breast*): You mean it done really come?

RUTH (*excited*): Oh, Miss Lena!

MAMA (*collecting herself*): Well . . . I don't know what we all so excited about 'round here for. We known it was coming for months.

RUTH: That's a whole lot different from having it come and being able to hold it in your hands . . . a piece of paper worth ten thousand dollars . . . (*Travis bursts back into the room. He holds the envelope high above his head, like a little dancer, his face is radiant and he is breathless. He moves to his grandmother with sudden slow ceremony and puts the envelope into her hands. She accepts it, and then merely holds it and looks at it.*) Come on! Open it . . . Lord have mercy, I wish Walter Lee was here!

TRAVIS: Open it, Grandmama!

MAMA (*staring at it*): Now you all be quiet. It's just a check.

RUTH: Open it . . .

MAMA (*still staring at it*): Now don't act silly . . . We ain't never been no people to act silly 'bout no money—

RUTH (*swiftly*): We ain't never had none before—OPEN IT!

(*Mama finally makes a good strong tear and pulls out the thin blue slice of paper and inspects it closely. The boy and his mother study it raptly over Mama's shoulders.*)

MAMA: *Travis!* (*She is counting off with doubt.*) Is that the right number of zeros.

TRAVIS: Yes'm . . . ten thousand dollars. Gaalee, Grandmama, you rich.

MAMA (*She holds the check away from her, still looking at it. Slowly her face sobers into a mask of unhappiness.*): Ten thousand dollars. (*She hands it to Ruth.*) Put it away somewhere, Ruth. (*She does not look at Ruth; her eyes seem to be seeing something somewhere very far off.*) Ten thousand dollars they give you. Ten thousand dollars.

TRAVIS (*to his mother, sincerely*): What's the matter with Grandmama—don't she want to be rich?

RUTH (*distractedly*): You go on out and play now, baby. (*Travis exits. Mama starts wiping dishes absently, humming intently to herself. Ruth turns to her, with kind exasperation.*) You've gone and got yourself upset.

MAMA (*not looking at her*): I spec if it wasn't for you all . . . I would just put that money away or give it to the church or something.

RUTH: Now what kind of talk is that. Mr. Younger would just be plain mad if he could hear you talking foolish like that.

MAMA (*stopping and staring off*): Yes . . . he sure would. (*Sighing.*) We got enough to do with that money, all right. (*She halts then, and turns and looks at her daughter-in-law hard; Ruth avoids her eyes and Mama wipes her hands with finality and starts to speak firmly to Ruth.*) Where did you go today, girl?

RUTH: To the doctor.

MAMA (*impatiently*): Now, Ruth . . . you know better than that. Old Doctor Jones is strange enough in his way but there ain't nothing 'bout him make somebody slip and call him "she"—like you done this morning.

RUTH: Well, that's what happened—my tongue slipped.

MAMA: You went to see that woman, didn't you?

RUTH (*defensively, giving herself away*): What woman you talking about?

MAMA (*angrily*): That woman who—

(*Walter enters in great excitement.*)

WALTER: Did it come?

MAMA (*quietly*): Can't you give people a Christian greeting before you start asking about money?

WALTER (*to Ruth*): Did it come? (*Ruth unfolds the check and lays it quietly before him, watching him intently with thoughts of her own. Walter sits down and grasps it close and counts off the zeros.*) Ten thousand dollars— (*He turns suddenly, frantically to his mother and draws some papers out of his breast pocket.*) Mama—look. Old Willy Harris put everything on paper—

MAMA: Son—I think you ought to talk to your wife . . . I'll go on out and leave you alone if you want—

WALTER: I can talk to her later—Mama, look—

MAMA: Son—

WALTER: WILL SOMEBODY PLEASE LISTEN TO ME TODAY!

MAMA (*quietly*): I don't 'low no yellin' in this house, Walter Lee, and you know it—(*Walter stares at them in frustration and starts to speak several times.*) And there ain't going to be no investing in no liquor stores.

WALTER: But, Mama, you ain't even looked at it.

MAMA: I don't aim to have to speak on that again.

(*A long pause.*)

WALTER: You ain't looked at it and you don't aim to have to speak on that again? You ain't even looked at it and *you* have decided—(*Crumpling his papers.*) Well, *you* tell that to my boy tonight when you put him to sleep on the living room couch . . . (*Turning to Mama and speaking directly to her.*) Yeah—and tell it to my wife, Mama, tomorrow when she has to go out of here to look after somebody else's kids. And tell it to *me*, Mama, every time we need a new pair of curtains and I have to watch *you* go out and work in somebody's kitchen. Yeah, you tell me then!

(*Walter starts out.*)

RUTH: Where you going?

WALTER: I'm going out!

RUTH: Where?

WALTER: Just out of this house somewhere—

RUTH (*getting her coat*): I'll come too.

WALTER: I don't want you to come!

RUTH: I got something to talk to you about, Walter.

WALTER: That's too bad.

MAMA (*still quietly*): Walter Lee—(*She waits and he finally turns and looks at her.*) Sit down.

WALTER: I'm a grown man, Mama.

MAMA: Ain't nobody said you wasn't grown. But you still in my house and my presence. And as long as you are—you'll talk to your wife civil. Now sit down.

RUTH (*suddenly*): Oh, let him go on out and drink himself to death! He makes me sick to my stomach! (*She flings her coat against him and exits to bedroom.*)

WALTER (*violently flinging the coat after her*): And you turn mine too, baby! (*The door slams behind her.*) That was my biggest mistake—

MAMA (*still quietly*): Walter, what is the matter with you?

WALTER: Matter with me? Ain't nothing the matter with *me!*

MAMA: Yes there is. Something eating you up like a crazy man. Something more than me not giving you this money. The past few years I been watching it happen to you. You get all nervous acting and kind of wild in the eyes—(*Walter jumps up impatiently at her words.*) I said sit there now, I'm talking to you!

WALTER: Mama—I don't need no nagging at me today.

MAMA: Seem like you getting to a place where you always tied up in some kind of knot about something. But if anybody ask you 'bout it you just yell at 'em and bust out the house and go out and drink somewheres. Walter Lee, people can't live with that. Ruth's a good, patient girl in her way—but you getting to be too much. Boy, don't make the mistake of driving that girl away from you.

WALTER: Why—what she do for me?

MAMA: She loves you.

WALTER: Mama—I'm going out. I want to go off somewhere and be by myself for a while.

MAMA: I'm sorry 'bout your liquor store, son. It just wasn't the thing for us to do. That's what I want to tell you about—

WALTER: I got to go out, Mama—

(*He rises.*)

MAMA: It's dangerous, son.

WALTER: What's dangerous?

MAMA: When a man goes outside his home to look for peace.

WALTER (*beseechingly*): Then why can't there never be no peace in this house then?

MAMA: You done found it in some other house?

WALTER: No—there ain't no woman! Why do women always think there's a woman somewhere when a man gets restless. (*Picks up the check.*) Do you know what this money means to me? Do you know what this money can do for us? (*Puts it back.*) Mama—Mama—I want so many things . . .

MAMA: Yes, son—

WALTER: I want so many things that they are driving me kind of crazy . . . Mama—look at me.

MAMA: I'm looking at you. You a good-looking boy. You got a job, a nice wife, a fine boy and—

WALTER: A job. (*Looks at her.*) Mama, a job? I open and close car doors all day long. I drive a man around in his limousine and I say, "Yes, sir; no, sir; very good, sir; shall I take the Drive, sir?" Mama, that ain't no kind of job . . . that ain't nothing at all. (*Very quietly.*) Mama, I don't know if I can make you understand.

MAMA: Understand what, baby?

WALTER (*quietly*): Sometimes it's like I can see the future stretched out in front of me—just plain as day. The future, Mama. Hanging over there at the edge of my days. Just waiting for me—a big, looming blank space—full of *nothing*. Just waiting for *me*. But it don't have to be. (*Pause. Kneeling beside her chair.*) Mama—sometimes when I'm downtown and I pass them cool, quiet-looking restaurants where them white boys are sitting back and talking 'bout things . . . sitting there turning deals worth millions of dollars . . . sometimes I see guys don't look much older than me—

MAMA: Son—how come you talk so much 'bout money?

WALTER (*with immense passion*): Because it is life, Mama!

MAMA (*quietly*): Oh—(*Very quietly.*) So now it's life. Money is life. Once upon a time freedom used to be life—now it's money. I guess the world really do change . . .

WALTER: No—it was always money, Mama. We just didn't know about it.

MAMA: No . . . something has changed. (*She looks at him.*) You something new, boy. In my time we was worried about not being lynched and getting to the North if we could and how to stay alive and still have a pinch of dignity too . . . Now here come you and Beneatha—talking 'bout things we ain't never even thought about hardly, me and your daddy. You ain't satisfied or proud of nothing we done. I mean that you had a home, that we kept you out of trouble till you was grown, that you don't have to ride to work on the back of nobody's streetcar—You my children—but how different we done become.

WALTER (*A long beat. He pats her hand and gets up.*): You just don't understand, Mama, you just don't understand.

MAMA: Son—do you know your wife is expecting another baby? (*Walter stands, stunned, and absorbs what his mother has said.*) That's what she wanted to talk to you about. (*Walter sinks down into a chair.*) This ain't for me to be telling—but you ought to know. (*She waits.*) I think Ruth is thinking 'bout getting rid of that child.

WALTER (*slowly understanding*):—No—no—Ruth wouldn't do that.

MAMA: When the world gets ugly enough—a woman will do anything for her family. *The part that's already living.*

WALTER: You don't know Ruth, Mama, if you think she would do that.

(*Ruth opens the bedroom door and stands there a little limp.*)

RUTH (*beaten*): Yes I would too, Walter. (*Pause.*) I gave her a five-dollar down payment.

(*There is total silence as the man stares at his wife and the mother stares at her son.*)

MAMA (*presently*): Well—(*Tightly.*) Well—son, I'm waiting to hear you say something . . . (*She waits.*) I'm waiting to hear how you be your father's son. Be the man he was . . . (*Pause. The silence shouts.*) Your wife says she going to destroy your child. And I'm waiting to hear you talk like him and say we a people who give children life, not who destroys them—(*She rises.*) I'm waiting to see you stand up and look like your daddy and say we done give up one baby to poverty and that we ain't going to give up nary another one . . . I'm waiting.

WALTER: Ruth—(*He can say nothing.*)

MAMA: If you a son of mine, tell him! (*Walter picks up his keys and his coat and walks out. She continues, bitterly.*) You . . . you are a disgrace to your father's memory. Somebody get me my hat!

ACT II • Scene I

(*Time: Later the same day.*)

(*At rise: Ruth is ironing again. She has the radio going. Presently Beneatha's bedroom door opens and Ruth's mouth falls and she puts down the iron in fascination.*)

RUTH: What have we got on tonight!

BENEATHA (*emerging grandly from the doorway so that we can see her thoroughly robed in the costume Asagai brought*): You are looking at what a well-dressed Nigerian woman wears—(*She parades for Ruth, her hair completely hidden by the headdress; she is coquettishly fanning herself with an ornate oriental fan, mistakenly more like Butterfly° than any Nigerian that ever was.*) Isn't it beautiful? (*She promenades to the radio and, with an arrogant flourish, turns off the good loud blues that is playing.*) Enough of this assimilationist junk! (*Ruth follows her with her eyes as she goes to the phonograph and puts on a record and turns and waits ceremoniously for the music to come up. Then, with a shout—*) OCOMOGOSIAY!

(*Ruth jumps. The music comes up, a lovely Nigerian melody. Beneatha listens, enraptured, her eyes far away—"back to the past." She begins to dance. Ruth is dumbfounded.*)

RUTH: What kind of dance is that?

BENEATHA: A folk dance.

RUTH (*Pearl Bailey*): What kind of folks do that, honey?

BENEATHA: It's from Nigeria. It's a dance of welcome.

RUTH: Who you welcoming?

BENEATHA: The men back to the village.

RUTH: Where they been?

BENEATHA: How should I know—out hunting or something. Anyway, they are coming back now . . .

RUTH: Well, that's good.

BENEATHA (*with the record*): Alundi, alundi
   Alundi alunya
   Jop pu a jeepua
   Ang gu soooooooooo

   Ai yai yue . . .
   Ayehaye—alundi . . .

Butterfly: Madame Butterfly, the title character in the opera by Puccini, set in Japan.

(*Walter comes in during this performance; he has obviously been drinking. He leans against the door heavily and watches his sister, at first with distaste. Then his eyes look off—"back to the past"—as he lifts both his fists to the roof, screaming.*)

WALTER: YEAH . . . AND ETHIOPIA STRETCH FORTH HER HANDS AGAIN! . . .

RUTH (*drily, looking at him*): Yes—and Africa sure is claiming her own tonight. (*She gives them both up and starts ironing again.*)

WALTER (*all in a drunken, dramatic shout*): Shut up! . . . I'm digging them drums . . . them drums move me! . . . (*He makes his weaving way to his wife's face and leans in close to her.*) In my *heart of hearts*—(*he thumps his chest*)—I am much warrior!

RUTH (*without even looking up*): In your heart of hearts you are much drunkard.

WALTER (*coming away from her and starting to wander around the room, shouting*): Me and Jomo . . . (*Intently, in his sister's face. She has stopped dancing to watch him in this unknown mood.*) That's my man, Kenyatta. (*Shouting and thumping his chest.*) FLAMING SPEAR! HOT DAMN! (*He is suddenly in possession of an imaginary spear and actively spearing enemies all over the room.*) OCOMOGOSIAY . . .

BENEATHA (*to encourage Walter, thoroughly caught up with this side of him*): OCOMOGOSIAY, FLAMING SPEAR!

WALTER: THE LION IS WAKING . . . OWIMOWEH! (*He pulls his shirt open and leaps up on the table and gestures with his spear.*)

BENEATHA: OWIMOWEH!

WALTER (*On the table, very far gone, his eyes pure glass sheets. He sees what we cannot, that he is a leader of his people, a great chief, a descendant of Chaka, and that the hour to march has come.*): Listen, my black brothers—

BENEATHA: OCOMOGOSIAY!

WALTER:—Do you hear the waters rushing against the shores of the coastlands—

BENEATHA: OCOMOGOSIAY!

WALTER:—Do you hear the screeching of the cocks in yonder hills beyond where the chiefs meet in council for the coming of the mighty war—

BENEATHA: OCOMOGOSIAY!

(*And now the lighting shifts subtly to suggest the world of Walter's imagination, and the mood shifts from pure comedy. It is the inner Walter speaking: the Southside chauffeur has assumed an unexpected majesty.*)

WALTER:—Do you hear the beating of the wings of the birds flying low over the mountains and the low places of our land—

BENEATHA: OCOMOGOSIAY!

WALTER:—Do you hear the singing of the women singing the war songs of our fathers to the babies in the great houses? Singing the sweet war songs! (*The doorbell rings.*) OH, DO YOU HEAR, MY *BLACK* BROTHERS!

Sean "P. Diddy" Combs as Walter in the 2004 Broadway production of *A Raisin in the Sun* at the Royale Theater.

BENEATHA (*completely gone*): We hear you, Flaming Spear—

(*Ruth shuts off the phonograph and opens the door. George Murchison enters.*)

WALTER: Telling us to prepare for the GREATNESS OF THE TIME! (*Lights back to normal. He turns and sees George.*) Black Brother!

(*He extends his hand for the fraternal clasp.*)

GEORGE: Black Brother, hell!

RUTH (*having had enough, and embarrassed for the family*): Beneatha, you got company—what's the matter with you? Walter Lee Younger, get down off that table and stop acting like a fool . . .

(*Walter comes down off the table suddenly and makes a quick exit to the bathroom.*)

RUTH: He's had a little to drink . . . I don't know what her excuse is.

GEORGE (*to Beneatha*): Look honey, we're going *to* the theater—we're not going to be *in* it . . . so go change, huh?

(*Beneatha looks at him and slowly, ceremoniously, lifts her hands and pulls off the headdress. Her hair is close-cropped and unstraightened. George freezes mid-sentence and Ruth's eyes all but fall out of her head.*)

GEORGE: What in the name of—

RUTH (*touching Beneatha's hair*): Girl, you done lost your natural mind? Look at your head!

GEORGE: What have you done to your head—I mean your hair!

BENEATHA: Nothing—except cut it off.

RUTH: Now that's the truth—it's what ain't been done to it! You expect this boy to go out with you with your head all nappy like that?

BENEATHA (*looking at George*): That's up to George. If he's ashamed of his heritage—

GEORGE: Oh, don't be so proud of yourself, Bennie—just because you look eccentric.

BENEATHA: How can something that's natural be eccentric?

GEORGE: That's what being eccentric means—being natural. Get dressed.

BENEATHA: I don't like that, George.

RUTH: Why must you and your brother make an argument out of everything people say?

BENEATHA: Because I hate assimilationist Negroes!

RUTH: Will somebody please tell me what assimila-whoever means!

GEORGE: Oh, it's just a college girl's way of calling people Uncle Toms—but that isn't what it means at all.

RUTH: Well, what does it mean?

BENEATHA (*cutting George off and staring at him as she replies to Ruth*): It means someone who is willing to give up his own culture and submerge himself completely in the dominant, and in this case *oppressive* culture!

GEORGE: Oh, dear, dear, dear! Here we go! A lecture on the African past! On our Great West African Heritage! In one second we will hear all about the great Ashanti empires; the great Songhay civilizations; and the great sculpture of Bénin—and then some poetry in the Bantu—and the whole monologue will end with the word *heritage!* (*Nastily.*) Let's face it, baby, your heritage is nothing but a bunch of raggedy-assed spirituals and some grass huts!

BENEATHA: GRASS HUTS! (*Ruth crosses to her and forcibly pushes her toward the bedroom.*) See there . . . you are standing there in your splendid ignorance talking about people who were the first to smelt iron on the face of the earth! (*Ruth is pushing her through the door.*) The Ashanti were performing surgical operations when the English—(*Ruth pulls the door to, with Beneatha on the other side, and smiles graciously at George. Beneatha opens the door and shouts the end of the sentence defiantly at George*)—were still tatooing themselves with blue dragons! (*She goes back inside.*)

RUTH: Have a seat, George. (*They both sit. Ruth folds her hands rather primly on her lap, determined to demonstrate the civilization of the family.*) Warm, ain't it? I mean for September. (*Pause.*) Just like they always say about Chicago weather: If it's too hot or cold for you, just wait a minute and it'll change. (*She smiles happily at this cliché of clichés.*) Everybody say it's got to do with them bombs and things they keep setting off. (*Pause.*) Would you like a nice cold beer?

GEORGE: No, thank you. I don't care for beer. (*He looks at his watch.*) I hope she hurries up.

RUTH: What time is the show?

GEORGE: It's an eight-thirty curtain. That's just Chicago, though. In New York standard curtain time is eight forty.

(*He is rather proud of this knowledge.*)

RUTH (*properly appreciating it*): You get to New York a lot?

GEORGE (*offhand*): Few times a year.

RUTH: Oh—that's nice. I've never been to New York.

(*Walter enters. We feel he has relieved himself, but the edge of unreality is still with him.*)

WALTER: New York ain't got nothing Chicago ain't. Just a bunch of hustling people all squeezed up together—being "Eastern."

(*He turns his face into a screw of displeasure.*)

GEORGE: Oh—you've been?

WALTER: *Plenty* of times.

RUTH (*shocked at the lie*): Walter Lee Younger!

WALTER (*staring her down*): Plenty! (*Pause.*) What we got to drink in this house? Why don't you offer this man some refreshment. (*To George.*) They don't know how to entertain people in this house, man.

GEORGE: Thank you—I don't really care for anything.

WALTER (*feeling his head; sobriety coming*): Where's Mama?

RUTH: She ain't come back yet.

WALTER (*looking Murchison over from head to toe, scrutinizing his carefully casual tweed sports jacket over cashmere V-neck sweater over soft eyelet shirt and tie, and soft slacks, finished off with white buckskin shoes*): Why all you college boys wear them faggoty-looking white shoes?

RUTH: Walter Lee!

(*George Murchison ignores the remark.*)

WALTER (*to Ruth*): Well, they look crazy as hell—white shoes, cold as it is.

RUTH (*crushed*): You have to excuse him—

WALTER: No he don't! Excuse me for what? What you always excusing me for! I'll excuse myself when I needs to be excused! (*A pause.*) They look as funny as them black knee socks Beneatha wears out of here all the time.

RUTH: It's the college *style*, Walter.

WALTER: Style, hell. She looks like she got burnt legs or something!

RUTH: Oh, Walter—

WALTER (*an irritable mimic*): Oh, Walter! Oh, Walter! (*To Murchison.*) How's your old man making out? I understand you all going to buy that big hotel on the Drive? (*He finds a beer in the refrigerator, wanders over to Murchison, sipping and wiping his lips with the back of his hand, and straddling a chair backward to talk to the other man.*) Shrewd move. Your old man is all right, man. (*Tapping his head and half winking for emphasis.*) I mean he knows how to operate. I mean he thinks *big*, you know what I mean, I mean for a *home*, you know? But I think he's kind of running out of ideas now. I'd like to talk to him. Listen, man, I got some plans that could turn this city upside down. I mean think like he does. *Big.* Invest big, gamble big, hell, lose *big* if you have to, you know what I mean. It's hard to find a man on this whole Southside who understands my kind of thinking—you dig? (*He scrutinizes Murchison again, drinks his beer, squints his eyes, and leans in close, confidential, man to man.*) Me and you ought to sit down and talk sometimes, man. Man, I got me some ideas . . .

MURCHISON (*with boredom*): Yeah—sometimes we'll have to do that, Walter.

WALTER (*understanding the indifference, and offended*): Yeah—well, when you get the time, man. I know you a busy little boy.

RUTH: Walter, please—

WALTER (*bitterly, hurt*): I know ain't nothing in this world as busy as you colored college boys with your fraternity pins and white shoes . . .

RUTH (*covering her face with humiliation*): Oh, Walter Lee—

WALTER: I see you all all the time—with the books tucked under your arms—going to your (*British A—a mimic*) "clahsses." And for what! What the hell you learning over there? Filling up your heads—(*counting off on his fingers*)—with the sociology and the psychology—but they teaching you how to be a man? How to take over and run the world? They teaching you how to run a rubber plantation or a steel mill? Naw—just to talk proper and read books and wear them faggoty-looking white shoes . . .

GEORGE (*looking at him with distaste, a little above it all*): You're all wacked up with bitterness, man.

WALTER (*intently, almost quietly, between the teeth, glaring at the boy*): And you—ain't you bitter, man? Ain't you just about had it yet? Don't you see no stars gleaming that you can't reach out and grab? You happy?—You contented son-of-a-bitch—you happy? You got it made? Bitter? Man, I'm a volcano. Bitter? Here I am a giant—surrounded by ants! Ants who can't even understand what it is the giant is talking about.

RUTH (*passionately and suddenly*): Oh, Walter—ain't you with nobody!

WALTER (*violently*): No! 'Cause ain't nobody with me! Not even my own mother!

RUTH: Walter, that's a terrible thing to say!

(*Beneatha enters, dressed for the evening in a cocktail dress and earrings, hair natural.*)

GEORGE: Well—hey—(*Crosses to Beneatha; thoughtful, with emphasis, since this is a reversal.*) You look great!

WALTER (*seeing his sister's hair for the first time*): What's the matter with your head?

BENEATHA (*tired of the jokes now*): I cut it off, Brother.

WALTER (*coming close to inspect it and walking around her*): Well, I'll be damned. So that's what they mean by the African bush . . .

BENEATHA: Ha ha. Let's go, George.

GEORGE (*looking at her*): You know something? I like it. It's sharp. I mean it really is. (*Helps her into her wrap.*)

RUTH: Yes—I think so, too. (*She goes to the mirror and starts to clutch at her hair.*)

WALTER: Oh no! You leave yours alone, baby. You might turn out to have a pin-shaped head or something!

BENEATHA: See you all later.

RUTH: Have a nice time.

GEORGE: Thanks. Good night. (*Half out the door, he reopens it. To Walter.*) Good night, Prometheus!°

(*Beneatha and George exit.*)

WALTER (*to Ruth*): Who is Prometheus?

RUTH: I don't know. Don't worry about it.

WALTER (*in fury, pointing after George*): See there—they get to a point where they can't insult you man to man—they got to go talk about something ain't nobody never heard of!

RUTH: How do you know it was an insult? (*To humor him.*) Maybe Prometheus is a nice fellow.

WALTER: Prometheus! I bet there ain't even no such thing! I bet that simple-minded clown—

RUTH: Walter—

(*She stops what she is doing and looks at him.*)

WALTER (*yelling*): Don't start!

RUTH: Start what?

WALTER: Your nagging! Where was I? Who was I with? How much money did I spend?

RUTH (*plaintively*): Walter Lee—why don't we just try to talk about it . . .

WALTER (*not listening*): I been out talking with people who understand me. People who care about the things I got on my mind.

RUTH (*wearily*): I guess that means people like Willy Harris.

WALTER: Yes, people like Willy Harris.

RUTH (*with a sudden flash of impatience*): Why don't you all just hurry up and go into the banking business and stop talking about it!

WALTER: Why? You want to know why? 'Cause we all tied up in a race of people that don't know how to do nothing but moan, pray, and have babies!

Prometheus: Defiantly inventive Titan who stole fire from the gods and gave it to humans.

(*The line is too bitter even for him and he looks at her and sits down.*)

RUTH: Oh, Walter . . . (*Softly.*) Honey, why can't you stop fighting me?

WALTER (*without thinking*): Who's fighting you? Who even cares about you?

(*This line begins the retardation of his mood.*)

RUTH: Well—(*She waits a long time, and then with resignation starts to put away her things.*) I guess I might as well go on to bed . . . (*More or less to herself.*) I don't know where we lost it . . . but we have . . . (*Then, to him.*) I—I'm sorry about this new baby, Walter. I guess maybe I better go on and do what I started . . . I guess I just didn't realize how bad things was with us . . . I guess I just didn't really realize—(*She starts out to the bedroom and stops.*) You want some hot milk?

WALTER: Hot milk?

RUTH: Yes—hot milk.

WALTER: Why hot milk?

RUTH: 'Cause after all that liquor you come home with you ought to have something hot in your stomach.

WALTER: I don't want no milk.

RUTH: You want some coffee then?

WALTER: No, I don't want no coffee. I don't want nothing hot to drink. (*Almost plaintively.*) Why you always trying to give me something to eat?

RUTH (*standing and looking at him helplessly*): What else can I give you, Walter Lee Younger?

(*She stands and looks at him and presently turns to go out again. He lifts his head and watches her going away from him in a new mood which began to emerge when he asked her "Who cares about you?"*)

WALTER: It's been rough, ain't it, baby? (*She hears and stops but does not turn around and he continues to her back.*) I guess between two people there ain't never as much understood as folks generally thinks there is. I mean like between me and you—(*She turns to face him.*) How we gets to the place where we scared to talk softness to each other. (*He waits, thinking hard himself.*) Why you think it got to be like that? (*He is thoughtful, almost as a child would be.*) Ruth, what is it gets into people ought to be close?

RUTH: I don't know, honey. I think about it a lot.

WALTER: On account of you and me, you mean? The way things are with us. The way something done come down between us.

RUTH: There ain't so much between us, Walter . . . Not when you come to me and try to talk to me. Try to be with me . . . a little even.

WALTER (*total honesty*): Sometimes . . . sometimes . . . I don't even know how to try.

RUTH: Walter—

WALTER: Yes?

RUTH (*coming to him, gently and with misgiving, but coming to him*): Honey . . . life don't have to be like this. I mean sometimes people can do things so that things are better . . . You remember how we used to talk when Travis was born . . . about the way we were going to live . . . the kind of house . . . (*She is stroking his head.*) Well, it's all starting to slip away from us . . .

(*He turns her to him and they look at each other and kiss, tenderly and hungrily. The door opens and Mama enters—Walter breaks away and jumps up. A beat.*)

WALTER: Mama, where have you been?

MAMA: My—them steps is longer than they used to be. Whew! (*She sits down and ignores him.*) How you feeling this evening, Ruth?

(*Ruth shrugs, disturbed at having been interrupted and watching her husband knowingly.*)

WALTER: Mama, where have you been all day?

MAMA (*still ignoring him and leaning on the table and changing to more comfortable shoes*): Where's Travis?

RUTH: I let him go out earlier and he ain't come back yet. Boy, is he going to get it!

WALTER: Mama!

MAMA (*as if she has heard him for the first time*): Yes, son?

WALTER: Where did you go this afternoon?

MAMA: I went downtown to tend to some business that I had to tend to.

WALTER: What kind of business?

MAMA: You know better than to question me like a child, Brother.

WALTER (*rising and bending over the table*): Where were you, Mama? (*Bringing his fists down and shouting.*) Mama, you didn't go do something with that insurance money, something crazy?

(*The front door opens slowly, interrupting him, and Travis peeks his head in, less than hopefully.*)

TRAVIS (*to his mother*): Mama, I—

RUTH: "Mama I" nothing! You're going to get it, boy! Get on in that bedroom and get yourself ready!

TRAVIS: But I—

MAMA: Why don't you all never let the child explain hisself.

RUTH: Keep out of it now, Lena.

(*Mama clamps her lips together, and Ruth advances toward her son menacingly.*)

RUTH: A thousand times I have told you not to go off like that—

MAMA (*holding out her arms to her grandson*): Well—at least let me tell him something. I want him to be the first one to hear . . . Come here, Travis. (*The boy obeys, gladly.*) Travis—(*she takes him by the shoulder and looks into his face*)—you know that money we got in the mail this morning?

TRAVIS: Yes'm—

MAMA: Well—what you think your grandmama gone and done with that money?

TRAVIS: I don't know, Grandmama.

MAMA (*putting her finger on his nose for emphasis*): She went out and she bought you a house! (*The explosion comes from Walter at the end of the revelation and he jumps up and turns away from all of them in a fury. Mama continues, to Travis.*) You glad about the house? It's going to be yours when you get to be a man.

TRAVIS: Yeah—I always wanted to live in a house.

MAMA: All right, gimme some sugar then—(*Travis puts his arms around her neck as she watches her son over the boy's shoulder. Then, to Travis, after the embrace.*) Now when you say your prayers tonight, you thank God and your grandfather—'cause it was him who give you the house—in his way.

RUTH (*taking the boy from Mama and pushing him toward the bedroom*): Now you get out of here and get ready for your beating.

TRAVIS: Aw, Mama—

RUTH: Get on in there—(*Closing the door behind him and turning radiantly to her mother-in-law.*) So you went and did it!

MAMA (*quietly, looking at her son with pain*): Yes, I did.

RUTH (*raising both arms classically*): PRAISE GOD! (*Looks at Walter a moment, who says nothing. She crosses rapidly to her husband.*) Please, honey—let me be glad . . . you be glad too. (*She has laid her hands on his shoulders, but he shakes himself free of her roughly, without turning to face her.*) Oh, Walter . . . a home . . . a home. (*She comes back to Mama.*) Well—where is it? How big is it? How much it going to cost?

MAMA: Well—

RUTH: When we moving?

MAMA (*smiling at her*): First of the month.

RUTH (*throwing back her head with jubilance*): Praise God!

MAMA (*tentatively, still looking at her son's back turned against her and Ruth*): It's—it's a nice house too . . . (*She cannot help speaking directly to him. An imploring quality in her voice, her manner, makes her almost like a girl now.*) Three bedrooms—nice big one for you and Ruth . . . Me and Beneatha still have to share our room, but Travis have one of his own and (*with difficulty*) I figure if the—new baby—is a boy, we could get one of them double-decker outfits . . . And there's a yard with a little patch of dirt where I could maybe get to grow me a few flowers . . . And a nice big basement . . .

RUTH: Walter honey, be glad—

MAMA (*still to his back, fingering things on the table*): 'Course I don't want to make it sound fancier than it is . . . It's just a plain little old house—but it's made good and solid—and it will be *ours*. Walter Lee—it makes a difference in a man when he can walk on floors that belong to *him* . . .

RUTH: Where is it?

MAMA (*frightened at this telling*): Well—well—it's out there in Clybourne Park—

(*Ruth's radiance fades abruptly, and Walter finally turns slowly to face his mother with incredulity and hostility.*)

RUTH: Where?

MAMA (*matter-of-factly*): Four o six Clybourne Street, Clybourne Park.

RUTH: Clybourne Park? Mama, there ain't no colored people living in Clybourne Park.

MAMA (*almost idiotically*): Well, I guess there's going to be some now.

WALTER (*bitterly*): So that's the peace and comfort you went out and bought for us today!

MAMA (*raising her eyes to meet his finally*): Son—I just tried to find the nicest place for the least amount of money for my family.

RUTH (*trying to recover from the shock*): Well—well— 'course I ain't one never been 'fraid of no crackers,° mind you—but—well, wasn't there no other houses nowhere?

MAMA: Them houses they put up for colored in them areas way out all seem to cost twice as much as other houses. I did the best I could.

RUTH (*struck senseless with the news, in its various degrees of goodness and trouble, she sits a moment, her fists propping her chin in thought, and then she starts to rise, bringing her fists down with vigor, the radiance spreading from cheek to cheek again*): Well—well—All I can say is—if this is my time in life—MY TIME—to say good-bye—(*and she builds with momentum as she starts to circle the room with an exuberant, almost tearfully happy release*)—to these Goddamned cracking walls!—(*she pounds the walls*)—and these marching roaches!—(*she wipes at an imaginary army of marching roaches*)—and this cramped little closet which ain't now or never was no kitchen! . . . then I say it loud and good, HALLELU-JAH! AND GOOD-BYE MISERY . . . I DON'T NEVER WANT TO SEE YOUR UGLY FACE AGAIN! (*She laughs joyously, having practically destroyed the apartment, and flings her arms up and lets them come down happily, slowly, reflectively, over her abdomen, aware for the first time perhaps that the life therein pulses with happiness and not despair.*) Lena?

MAMA (*moved, watching her happiness*): Yes, honey?

RUTH (*looking off*): Is there—is there a whole lot of sunlight?

MAMA (*understanding*): Yes, child, there's a whole lot of sunlight.

(*Long pause.*)

RUTH (*collecting herself and going to the door of the room Travis is in*): Well—I guess I better see 'bout Travis. (*To Mama.*) Lord, I sure don't feel like whipping nobody today!

(*She exits.*)

crackers: White people, often used to refer disparagingly to poor whites.

MAMA (*the mother and son are left alone now and the mother waits a long time, considering deeply, before she speaks*): Son—you—you understand what I done, don't you? (*Walter is silent and sullen.*) I—I just seen my family falling apart today . . . just falling to pieces in front of my eyes . . . We couldn't of gone on like we was today. We was going backwards 'stead of forwards—talking 'bout killing babies and wishing each other was dead . . . When it gets like that in life—you just got to do something different, push on out and do something bigger . . . (*She waits.*) I wish you say something, son . . . I wish you'd say how deep inside you you think I done the right thing—

WALTER (*crossing slowly to his bedroom door and finally turning there and speaking measuredly*): What you need me to say you done right for? *You* the head of this family. You run our lives like you want to. It was your money and you did what you wanted with it. So what you need for me to say it was all right for? (*Bitterly, to hurt her as deeply as he knows is possible.*) So you butchered up a dream of mine—you—who always talking 'bout your children's dreams . . .

MAMA: Walter Lee—

(*He just closes the door behind him. Mama sits alone, thinking heavily.*)

Scene II

(*Time: Friday night. A few weeks later.*)

(*At rise: Packing crates mark the intention of the family to move. Beneatha and George come in, presumably from an evening out again.*)

GEORGE: O.K. . . . O.K., whatever you say . . . (*They both sit on the couch. He tries to kiss her. She moves away.*) Look, we've had a nice evening; let's not spoil it, huh? . . .

(*He again turns her head and tries to nuzzle in and she turns away from him, not with distaste but with momentary lack of interest; in a mood to pursue what they were talking about.*)

BENEATHA: I'm *trying* to talk to you.

GEORGE: We always talk.

BENEATHA: Yes—and I love to talk.

GEORGE (*exasperated; rising*): I know it and I don't mind it sometimes . . . I want you to cut it out, see—The moody stuff, I mean. I don't like it. You're a nice-looking girl . . . all over. That's all you need, honey, forget the atmosphere. Guys aren't going to go for the atmosphere—they're going to go for what they see. Be glad for that. Drop the Garbo routine. It doesn't go with you. As for myself, I want a nice— (*groping*)—simple (*thoughtfully*)—sophisticated girl . . . not a poet—O.K.?

(*He starts to kiss her, she rebuffs him again, and he jumps up.*)

BENEATHA: Why are you angry, George?

GEORGE: Because this is stupid! I don't go out with you to discuss the nature of "quiet desperation" or to hear all about your thoughts—because the world will go on thinking what it thinks regardless—

BENEATHA: Then why read books? Why go to school?

GEORGE (*with artificial patience, counting on his fingers*): It's simple. You read books—to learn facts—to get grades—to pass the course—to get a degree. That's all—it has nothing to do with thoughts.

(*A long pause.*)

BENEATHA: I see. (*He starts to sit.*) Good night, George.

(*George looks at her a little oddly and starts to exit. He meets Mama coming in.*)

GEORGE: Oh—hello, Mrs. Younger.

MAMA: Hello, George, how you feeling?

GEORGE: Fine—fine, how are you?

MAMA: Oh, a little tired. You know them steps can get you after a day's work. You all have a nice time tonight?

GEORGE: Yes—a fine time. A fine time.

MAMA: Well, good night.

GEORGE: Good night. (*He exits. Mama closes the door behind her.*)

MAMA: Hello, honey. What you sitting like that for?

BENEATHA: I'm just sitting.

MAMA: Didn't you have a nice time?

BENEATHA: No.

MAMA: No? What's the matter?

BENEATHA: Mama, George is a fool—honest. (*She rises.*)

MAMA (*Hustling around unloading the packages she has entered with. She stops.*): Is he, baby?

BENEATHA: Yes.

(*Beneatha makes up Travis's bed as she talks.*)

MAMA: You sure?

BENEATHA: Yes.

MAMA: Well—I guess you better not waste your time with no fools.

(*Beneatha looks up at her mother, watching her put groceries in the refrigerator. Finally she gathers up her things and starts into the bedroom. At the door she stops and looks back at her mother.*)

BENEATHA: Mama—

MAMA: Yes, baby—

BENEATHA: Thank you.

MAMA: For what?

BENEATHA: For understanding me this time.

(*She exits quickly and the mother stands, smiling a little, looking at the place where Beneatha just stood. Ruth enters.*)

RUTH: Now don't you fool with any of this stuff, Lena—

MAMA: Oh, I just thought I'd sort a few things out. Is Brother here?

RUTH: Yes.

MAMA (*with concern*): Is he—

RUTH (*reading her eyes*): Yes.

(*Mama is silent and someone knocks on the door. Mama and Ruth exchange weary and knowing glances and Ruth opens it to admit the neighbor, Mrs. Johnson,° who is a rather squeaky wide-eyed lady of no particular age, with a newspaper under her arm.*)

MAMA (*changing her expression to acute delight and a ringing cheerful greeting*): Oh—hello there, Johnson.

JOHNSON (*this is a woman who decided long ago to be enthusiastic about EVERYTHING in life and she is inclined to wave her wrist vigorously at the height of her exclamatory comments*): Hello there, yourself! H'you this evening, Ruth?

RUTH (*not much of a deceptive type*): Fine, Mis' Johnson, h'you?

JOHNSON: Fine. (*Reaching out quickly, playfully, and patting Ruth's stomach.*) Ain't you starting to poke out none yet! (*She mugs with delight at the over-familiar remark and her eyes dart around looking at the crates and packing preparation; Mama's face is a cold sheet of endurance.*) Oh, ain't we getting ready round here, though! Yessir! Lookathere! I'm telling you the Youngers is really getting ready to "move on up a little higher!"—Bless God!

MAMA (*a little drily, doubting the total sincerity of the Blesser*): Bless God.

JOHNSON: He's good, ain't He?

MAMA: Oh yes, He's good.

JOHNSON: I mean sometimes He works in mysterious ways . . . but He works, don't He!

MAMA (*the same*): Yes, he does.

JOHNSON: I'm just soooooo happy for y'all. And this here child—(*about Ruth*) looks like she could just pop open with happiness, don't she. Where's all the rest of the family?

MAMA: Bennie's gone to bed—

JOHNSON: Ain't no . . . (*the implication is pregnancy*) sickness done hit you—I hope . . . ?

MAMA: No—she just tired. She was out this evening.

JOHNSON (*all is a coo, an emphatic coo*): Aw—ain't that lovely. She still going out with the little Murchison boy?

MAMA (*drily*): Ummmm huh.

JOHNSON: That's lovely. You sure got lovely children, Younger. Me and Isaiah talks all the time 'bout what fine children you was blessed with. We sure do.

MAMA: Ruth, give Mis' Johnson a piece of sweet potato pie and some milk.

JOHNSON: Oh honey, I can't stay hardly a minute—I just dropped in to see if there was anything I could

---

Mrs. Johnson: This character and the scene of her visit were cut from the original production and early editions of the play.

do. (*Accepting the food easily.*) I guess y'all seen the news what's all over the colored paper this week . . .

MAMA: No—didn't get mine yet this week.

JOHNSON (*lifting her head and blinking with the spirit of catastrophe*): You mean you ain't read 'bout them colored people that was bombed out their place out there?

(*Ruth straightens with concern and takes the paper and reads it. Johnson notices her and feeds commentary.*)

JOHNSON: Ain't it something how bad these here white folks is getting here in Chicago! Lord, getting so you think you right down in Mississippi! (*With a tremendous and rather insincere sense of melodrama.*) 'Course I thinks it's wonderful how our folks keeps on pushing out. You hear some of these Negroes round here talking 'bout how they don't go where they ain't wanted and all that—but not me, honey! (*This is a lie.*) Wilhemenia Othella Johnson goes anywhere, any time she feels like it! (*With head movement for emphasis.*) Yes I do! Why if we left it up to these here crackers the poor niggers wouldn't have nothing—(*She clasps her hand over her mouth.*) Oh, I always forgets you don't 'low that word in your house.

MAMA (*quietly, looking at her*): No—I don't 'low it.

JOHNSON (*vigorously again*): Me neither! I was just telling Isaiah yesterday when he come using it in front of me—I said, "Isaiah, it's just like Mis' Younger says all the time—"

MAMA: Don't you want some more pie?

JOHNSON: No—no thank you; this was lovely. I got to get on over home and have my midnight coffee. I hear some people say it don't let them sleep but I finds I can't close my eyes right lessen I done had that laaaast cup of coffee . . . (*She waits. A beat. Undaunted.*) My Good-night coffee, I calls it!

MAMA (*with much eye-rolling and communication between herself and Ruth*): Ruth, why don't you give Mis' Johnson some coffee.

(*Ruth gives Mama an unpleasant look for her kindness.*)

JOHNSON (*accepting the coffee*): Where's Brother tonight?

MAMA: He's lying down.

JOHNSON: Mmmmmmm, he sure gets his beauty rest, don't he? Good-looking man. Sure is a good-looking man! (*Reaching out to pat Ruth's stomach again.*) I guess that's how come we keep on having babies around here. (*She winks at Mama.*) One thing 'bout Brother, he always know how to have a *good* time. And soooooo ambitious! I bet it was his idea y'all moving out to Clybourne Park. Lord—I bet this time next month y'all's names will have been in the papers plenty—(*Holding up her hands to mark off each word of the headline she can see in front of her.*) "NEGROS INVADE CLYBOURNE PARK—BOMBED!"

MAMA (*she and Ruth look at the woman in amazement*): We ain't exactly moving out there to get bombed.

JOHNSON: Oh, honey—you know I'm praying to God every day that don't nothing like that happen! But you have to think of life like it is—and these here Chicago peckerwoods is some baaaad peckerwoods.

MAMA (*wearily*): We done thought about all that Mis' Johnson.

(*Beneatha comes out of the bedroom in her robe and passes through to the bathroom. Mrs. Johnson turns.*)

JOHNSON: Hello there, Bennie!

BENEATHA (*crisply*): Hello, Mrs. Johnson.

JOHNSON: How is school?

BENEATHA (*crisply*): Fine, thank you. (*She goes out.*)

JOHNSON (*insulted*): Getting so she don't have much to say to nobody.

MAMA: The child was on her way to the bathroom.

JOHNSON: I know—but sometimes she act like ain't got time to pass the time of day with nobody ain't been to college. Oh—I ain't criticizing her none. It's just—you know how some of our young people gets when they get a little education. (*Mama and Ruth say nothing, just look at her.*) Yes—well. Well, I guess I better get on home. (*Unmoving.*) 'Course I can understand how she must be proud and everything—being the only one in the family to make something of herself. I know just being a chauffeur ain't never satisfied Brother none. He shouldn't feel like that, though. Ain't nothing wrong with being a chauffeur.

MAMA: There's plenty wrong with it.

JOHNSON: What?

MAMA: Plenty. My husband always said being any kind of a servant wasn't a fit thing for a man to have to be. He always said a man's hands was made to make things, or to turn the earth with—not to drive nobody's car for 'em—or—(*she looks at her own hands*) carry they slop jars. And my boy is just like him—he wasn't meant to wait on nobody.

JOHNSON (*rising, somewhat offended*): Mmmmmmmmm. The Youngers is too much for me! (*She looks around.*) You sure one proud-acting bunch of colored folks. Well—I always thinks like Booker T. Washington said that time—"Education has spoiled many a good plow hand"—

MAMA: Is that what old Booker T. said?

JOHNSON: He sure did.

MAMA: Well, it sounds just like him. The fool.

JOHNSON (*indignantly*): Well—he was one of our great men.

MAMA: Who said so?

JOHNSON (*nonplussed*): You know, me and you ain't never agreed about some things, Lena Younger. I guess I better be going—

RUTH (*quickly*): Good night.

JOHNSON: Good night. Oh—(*Thrusting it at her.*) You can keep the paper! (*With a trill.*) 'Night.

MAMA: Good night, Mis' Johnson.

(*Mrs. Johnson exits.*)

RUTH: If ignorance was gold . . .

MAMA: Shush. Don't talk about folks behind their backs.

RUTH: You do.

MAMA: I'm old and corrupted. (*Beneatha enters.*) You was rude to Mis' Johnson, Beneatha, and I don't like it at all.

BENEATHA (*at her door*): Mama, if there are two things we, as a people, have got to overcome, one is the Klu Klux Klan—and the other is Mrs. Johnson. (*She exits.*)

MAMA: Smart aleck.

(*The phone rings.*)

RUTH: I'll get it.

MAMA: Lord, ain't this a popular place tonight.

RUTH (*at the phone*): Hello—Just a minute. (*Goes to door.*) Walter, it's Mrs. Arnold. (*Waits. Goes back to the phone. Tense.*) Hello. Yes, this is his wife speaking . . . He's lying down now. Yes . . . well, he'll be in tomorrow. He's been very sick. Yes—I know we should have called, but we were so sure he'd be able to come in today. Yes—yes, I'm very sorry. Yes . . . Thank you very much. (*She hangs up. Walter is standing in the doorway of the bedroom behind her.*) That was Mrs. Arnold.

WALTER (*indifferently*): Was it?

RUTH: She said if you don't come in tomorrow that they are getting a new man . . .

WALTER: Ain't that sad—ain't that crying sad.

RUTH: She said Mr. Arnold has had to take a cab for three days . . . Walter, you ain't been to work for three days! (*This is a revelation to her.*) Where you been, Walter Lee Younger? (*Walter looks at her and starts to laugh.*) You're going to lose your job.

WALTER: That's right . . . (*He turns on the radio.*)

RUTH: Oh, Walter, and with your mother working like a dog every day—

(*A steamy, deep blues pours into the room.*)

WALTER: That's sad too—Everything is sad.

MAMA: What you been doing for these three days, son?

WALTER: Mama—you don't know all the things a man what got leisure can find to do in this city . . . What's this—Friday night? Well—Wednesday I borrowed Willy Harris's car and I went for a drive . . . just me and myself and I drove and drove . . . Way out . . . way past South Chicago, and I parked the car and I sat and looked at the steel mills all day long. I just sat in the car and looked at them big black chimneys for hours. Then I drove back and I went to the Green Hat. (*Pause.*) And Thursday—Thursday I borrowed the car again and I got in it and I pointed it the other way and I drove the other way—for hours—way, way up to Wisconsin, and I looked at the farms. I just drove and looked at the farms. Then I drove back and I went to the Green Hat. (*Pause.*) And today—today I didn't get the car. Today I just walked. All over the Southside. And I looked at the Negroes and they looked at me and finally I just sat down on the curb at Thirty-ninth and South Parkway and I just sat there and watched the Negroes go by. And then I went to the Green Hat. You all sad? You all depressed? And you know where I am going right now—

(*Ruth goes out quietly.*)

MAMA: Oh, Big Walter, is this the harvest of our days?

WALTER: You know what I like about the Green Hat? I like this little cat they got there who blows a sax . . . He blows. He talks to me. He ain't but 'bout five feet tall and he's got a conked head and his eyes is always closed and he's all music—

MAMA (*rising and getting some papers out of her handbag*): Walter—

WALTER: And there's this other guy who plays the piano . . . and they got a sound. I mean they can work on some music . . . They got the best little combo in the world in the Green Hat . . . You can just sit there and drink and listen to them three men play and you realize that don't nothing matter worth a damn, but just being there—

MAMA: I've helped do it to you, haven't I, son? Walter I been wrong.

WALTER: Naw—you ain't never been wrong about nothing, Mama.

MAMA: Listen to me, now. I say I been wrong, son. That I been doing to you what the rest of the world been doing to you. (*She turns off the radio.*) Walter—(*She stops and he looks up slowly at her and she meets his eyes pleadingly.*) What you ain't never understood is that I ain't got nothing, don't own nothing, ain't never really wanted nothing that wasn't for you. There ain't nothing as precious to me . . . There ain't nothing worth holding on to, money, dreams, nothing else—if it means—if it means it's going to destroy my boy. (*She takes an envelope out of her handbag and puts it in front of him and he watches her without speaking or moving.*) I paid the man thirty-five hundred dollars down on the house. That leaves sixty-five hundred dollars. Monday morning I want you to take this money and take three thousand dollars and put it in a savings account for Beneatha's medical schooling. The rest you put in a checking account—with your name on it. And from now on any penny that come out of it or that go in it is for you to look after. For you to decide. (*She drops her hands a little helplessly.*) It ain't much, but it's all I got in the world and I'm putting it in your hands. I'm telling you to be the head of this family from now on like you supposed to be.

WALTER (*stares at the money*): You trust me like that, Mama?

MAMA: I ain't never stop trusting you. Like I ain't never stop loving you.

(*She goes out, and Walter sits looking at the money on the table. Finally, in a decisive gesture, he gets up and, in mingled joy and desperation, picks up the money. At the same moment, Travis enters for bed.*)

TRAVIS: What's the matter, Daddy? You drunk?

WALTER (*sweetly, more sweetly than we have ever known him*): No, Daddy ain't drunk. Daddy ain't going to never be drunk again . . .

TRAVIS: Well, good night, Daddy.

(*The father has come from behind the couch and leans over, embracing his son.*)

WALTER: Son, I feel like talking to you tonight.

TRAVIS: About what?

WALTER: Oh, about a lot of things. About you and what kind of man you going to be when you grow up. . . . Son—son, what do you want to be when you grow up?

TRAVIS: A bus driver.

WALTER (*laughing a little*): A what? Man, that ain't nothing to want to be!

TRAVIS: Why not?

WALTER: 'Cause, man—it ain't big enough—you know what I mean.

TRAVIS: I don't know then. I can't make up my mind. Sometimes Mama asks me that too. And sometimes when I tell her I just want to be like you—she says she don't want me to be like that and sometimes she says she does. . . .

WALTER (*gathering him up in his arms*): You know what, Travis? In seven years you going to be seventeen years old. And things is going to be very different with us in seven years Travis. . . . One day when you are seventeen I'll come home—home from my office downtown somewhere—

TRAVIS: You don't work in no office, Daddy.

WALTER: No—but after tonight. After what your daddy gonna do tonight, there's going to be offices—a whole lot of offices. . . .

TRAVIS: What you gonna do tonight, Daddy?

WALTER: You wouldn't understand yet, son, but your daddy's gonna make a transaction . . . a business transaction that's going to change our lives. . . . That's how come one day when you 'bout seventeen years old I'll come home and I'll be pretty tired, you know what I mean, after a day of conferences and secretaries getting things wrong the way they do . . . 'cause an executive's life is hell man—(*The more he talks the farther away he gets.*) And I'll pull the car up on the driveway . . . just a plain black Chrysler, I think, with white walls—no—black tires. More elegant. Rich people don't have to be flashy . . . though I'll have to get something a little sportier for Ruth—maybe a Cadillac convertible to do her shopping in. . . . And I'll come up the steps to the house and the gardener will be clipping away at the hedges and he'll say, "Good evening, Mr. Younger." And I'll say, "Hello, Jefferson, how are you this evening?" And I'll go inside and Ruth will come downstairs and meet me at the door and we'll kiss each other and she'll take my arm and we'll go up to your room to see you sitting on the floor with the catalogues of all the great schools in America around you. . . . All the great schools in the world! And—and I'll say, all right son—it's your seventeenth birthday, what is it you've decided? . . . Just tell me where you want to go to school and you'll go. Just tell me, what it is you want to be—and you'll *be* it. . . . Whatever you want to be—Yessir! (*He holds his arms open for Travis.*) You just name it, son . . . (*Travis leaps into them*) and I hand you the world!

(*Walter's voice has risen in pitch and hysterical promise and on the last line he lifts Travis high.*)

Scene III

(*Time: Saturday, moving day, one week later.*)

(*Before the curtain rises, Ruth's voice, a strident, dramatic church alto, cuts through the silence.*)

(*It is, in the darkness, a triumphant surge, a penetrating statement of expectation: "Oh, Lord, I don't feel no ways tired! Children, oh, glory hallelujah!"*)

(*As the curtain rises we see that Ruth is alone in the living room, finishing up the family's packing. It is moving day. She is nailing crates and tying cartons. Beneatha enters, carrying a guitar case, and watches her exuberant sister-in-law.*)

RUTH: Hey!

BENEATHA (*putting away the case*): Hi.

RUTH (*pointing at a package*): Honey—look in that package there and see what I found on sale this morning at the South Center. (*Ruth gets up and moves to the package and draws out some curtains.*) Lookahere—hand-turned hems!

BENEATHA: How do you know the window size out there?

RUTH (*who hadn't thought of that*): Oh—Well, they bound to fit something in the whole house. Anyhow, they was too good a bargain to pass up. (*Ruth slaps her head, suddenly remembering something.*) Oh, Bennie—I meant to put a special note on that carton over there. That's your mama's good china and she wants 'em to be very careful with it.

BENEATHA: I'll do it.

(*Beneatha finds a piece of paper and starts to draw large letters on it.*)

RUTH: You know what I'm going to do soon as I get in that new house?

BENEATHA: What?

RUTH: Honey—I'm going to run me a tub of water up to here . . . (*With her fingers practically up to her nostrils.*) And I'm going to get in it—and I am going to sit . . . and sit . . . and sit in that hot water and the first person who knocks to tell *me* to hurry up and come out—

BENEATHA: Gets shot at sunrise.

RUTH (*laughing happily*): You said it, sister! (*Noticing how large Beneatha is absent-mindedly making the note.*) Honey, they ain't going to read that from no airplane.

BENEATHA (*laughing herself*): I guess I always think things have more emphasis if they are big, somehow.

RUTH (*looking up at her and smiling*): You and your brother seem to have that as a philosophy of life. Lord, that man—done changed so 'round here. You know—you know what we did last night? Me and Walter Lee?

BENEATHA: What?

RUTH (*smiling to herself*): We went to the movies. (*Looking at Beneatha to see if she understands.*) We went to the movies. You know the last time me and Walter went to the movies together?

BENEATHA: No.

RUTH: Me neither. That's how long it been. (*Smiling again.*) But we went last night. The picture wasn't much good, but that didn't seem to matter. We went—and we held hands.

BENEATHA: Oh, Lord!

RUTH: We held hands—and you know what?

BENEATHA: What?

RUTH: When we come out of the show it was late and dark and all the stores and things was closed up . . . and it was kind of chilly and there wasn't many people on the streets . . . and we was still holding hands, me and Walter.

BENEATHA: You're killing me.

(*Walter enters with a large package. His happiness is deep in him; he cannot keep still with his newfound exuberance. He is singing and wiggling and snapping his fingers. He puts his package in a corner and puts a phonograph record which he has brought in with him, on the record player. As the music, soulful and sensuous, comes up he dances over to Ruth and tries to get her to dance with him. She gives in at last to his raunchiness and in a fit of giggling allows herself to be drawn into his mood. They dip and she melts into his arms in a classic, body-melding "slow drag.*")

BENEATHA (*regarding them a long time as they dance, then drawing in her breath for a deeply exaggerated comment which she does not particularly mean*): Talk about—olddddddddd—fashionedddddddd—Negroes!

WALTER (*stopping momentarily*): What kind of Negroes?

(*He says this in fun. He is not angry with her today, nor with anyone. He starts to dance with his wife again.*)

BENEATHA: Old-fashioned.

WALTER (*as he dances with Ruth*): You know, when these *New Negroes* have their convention—(*pointing at his sister*)—that is going to be the chairman of the Committee on Unending Agitation. (*He goes on dancing, then stops.*) Race, race, race! . . . Girl, I do believe you are the first person in the history of the entire human race to successfully brainwash yourself. (*Beneatha breaks up and he goes on dancing. He stops again, enjoying his tease.*) Damn, even

the N double A C P takes a holiday sometimes! (*Beneatha and Ruth laugh. He dances with Ruth some more and starts to laugh and stops and pantomimes someone over an operating table.*) I can just see that chick someday looking down at some poor cat on an operating table and before she starts to slice him, she says . . . (*pulling his sleeves back maliciously*) "By the way, what are your views on civil rights down there? . . ."

(*He laughs at her again and starts to dance happily. The bell sounds.*)

BENEATHA: Sticks and stones may break my bones but . . . words will never hurt me!

(*Beneatha goes to the door and opens it as Walter and Ruth go on with the clowning. Beneatha is somewhat surprised to see a quiet-looking middle-aged white man in a business suit holding his hat and a briefcase in his hand and consulting a small piece of paper.*)

MAN: Uh—how do you do, miss. I am looking for a Mrs.—(*he looks at the slip of paper*) Mrs. Lena Younger? (*He stops short, struck dumb at the sight of the oblivious Walter and Ruth.*)

BENEATHA (*smoothing her hair with slight embarrassment*): Oh—yes, that's my mother. Excuse me. (*She closes the door and turns to quiet the other two.*) Ruth! Brother! (*Enunciating precisely but soundlessly: "There's a white man at the door!" They stop dancing, Ruth cuts off the phonograph, Beneatha opens the door. The man casts a curious quick glance at all of them.*) Uh—come in please.

MAN (*coming in*): Thank you.

BENEATHA: My mother isn't here just now. Is it business?

MAN: Yes . . . well, of a sort.

WALTER (*freely, the Man of the House*): Have a seat. I'm Mrs. Younger's son. I look after most of her business matters.

(*Ruth and Beneatha exchange amused glances.*)

MAN (*regarding Walter, and sitting*): Well—My name is Karl Lindner . . .

WALTER (*stretching out his hand*): Walter Younger. This is my wife—(*Ruth nods politely*)—and my sister.

LINDNER: How do you do.

WALTER (*amiably, as he sits himself easily on a chair, leaning forward on his knees with interest and looking expectantly into the newcomer's face*): What can we do for you, Mr. Lindner?

LINDNER (*some minor shuffling of the hat and briefcase on his knees*): Well—I am a representative of the Clybourne Park Improvement Association—

WALTER (*pointing*): Why don't you sit your things on the floor?

LINDNER: Oh—yes. Thank you. (*He slides the briefcase and hat under the chair.*) And as I was saying—I am from the Clybourne Park Improvement Association and we have had it brought to our attention at the last meeting that you people—or at least your mother—has bought a piece of residential property at—(*he digs for the slip of paper again*)—four o six Clybourne Street . . .

WALTER: That's right. Care for something to drink? Ruth, get Mr. Lindner a beer.

LINDNER (*upset for some reason*): Oh—no, really. I mean thank you very much, but no thank you.

RUTH: (*innocently*): Some coffee?

LINDNER: Thank you, nothing at all.

(*Beneatha is watching the man carefully.*)

LINDNER: Well, I don't know how much you folks know about our organization. (*He is a gentle man; thoughtful and somewhat labored in his manner.*) It is one of these community organizations set up to look after—oh, you know, things like block upkeep and special projects and we also have what we call our New Neighbors Orientation Committee . . .

BENEATHA (*drily*): Yes—and what do they do?

LINDNER (*turning a little to her and then returning the main force to Walter*): Well—it's what you might call a sort of welcoming committee, I guess. I mean they, we—I'm the chairman of the committee—go around and see the new people who move into the neighborhood and sort of give them the lowdown on the way we do things out in Clybourne Park.

BENEATHA (*with appreciation of the two meanings, which escape Ruth and Walter*): Un-huh.

LINDNER: And we also have the category of what the association calls—(*he looks elsewhere*)—uh—special community problems . . .

BENEATHA: Yes—and what are some of those?

WALTER: Girl, let the man talk.

LINDNER (*with understated relief*): Thank you. I would sort of like to explain this thing in my own way. I mean I want to explain to you in a certain way.

WALTER: Go ahead.

LINDNER: Yes. Well. I'm going to try to get right to the point. I'm sure we'll all appreciate that in the long run.

BENEATHA: Yes.

WALTER: Be still now!

LINDNER: Well—

RUTH (*still innocently*): Would you like another chair—you don't look comfortable.

LINDNER (*more frustrated than annoyed*): No, thank you very much. Please. Well—to get right to the point I—(*a great breath, and he is off at last*) I am sure you people must be aware of some of the incidents which have happened in various parts of the city when colored people have moved into certain areas—(*Beneatha exhales heavily and starts tossing a piece of fruit up and down in the air.*) Well—because we have what I think is going to be a unique type of organization in American community life—not only do we deplore that kind of thing—but we are trying to do something about it. (*Beneatha stops tossing and turns with a new and quizzical interest to the*

man.*) We feel—(*gaining confidence in his mission because of the interest in the faces of the people he is talking to*)—we feel that most of the trouble in this world, when you come right down to it—(*he hits his knee for emphasis*)—most of the trouble exists because people just don't sit down and talk to each other.

RUTH (*nodding as she might in church, pleased with the remark*): You can say that again, mister.

LINDNER (*more encouraged by such affirmation*): That we don't try hard enough in this world to understand the other fellow's problem. The other guy's point of view.

RUTH: Now that's right.

(*Beneatha and Walter merely watch and listen with genuine interest.*)

LINDNER: Yes—that's the way we feel out in Clybourne Park. And that's why I was elected to come here this afternoon and talk to you people. Friendly like, you know, the way people should talk to each other and see if we couldn't find some way to work this thing out. As I say, the whole business is a matter of *caring* about the other fellow. Anybody can see that you are a nice family of folks, hard-working and honest I'm sure. (*Beneatha frowns slightly, quizzically, her head tilted regarding him.*) Today everybody knows what it means to be on the outside of *something.* And of course, there is always somebody who is out to take advantage of people who don't always understand.

WALTER: What do you mean?

LINDNER: Well—you see our community is made up of people who've worked hard as the dickens for years to build up that little community. They're not rich and fancy people; just hard-working, honest people who don't really have much but those little homes and a dream of the kind of community they want to raise their children in. Now, I don't say we are perfect and there is a lot wrong in some of the things they want. But you've got to admit that a man, right or wrong, has the right to want to have the neighborhood he lives in a certain kind of way. And at the moment the overwhelming majority of our people out there feel that people get along better, take more of a common interest in the life of the community, when they share a common background. I want you to believe me when I tell you that race prejudice simply doesn't enter into it. It is a matter of the people of Clybourne Park believing, rightly or wrongly, as I say, that for the happiness of all concerned that our Negro families are happier when they live in their *own* communities.

BENEATHA (*with a grand and bitter gesture*): This, friends, is the Welcoming Committee!

WALTER (*dumfounded, looking at Lindner*): Is this what you came marching all the way over here to tell us?

LINDNER: Well, now we've been having a fine conversation. I hope you'll hear me all the way through.

WALTER (*tightly*): Go ahead, man.

LINDNER: You see—in the face of all the things I have said, we are prepared to make your family a very generous offer . . .

BENEATHA: Thirty pieces and not a coin less!

WALTER: Yeah!

LINDNER (*putting on his glasses and drawing a form out of the briefcase*): Our association is prepared, through the collective effort of our people, to buy the house from you at a financial gain to your family.

RUTH: Lord have mercy, ain't this the living gall!

WALTER: All right, you through?

LINDNER: Well, I want to give you the exact terms of the financial arrangement—

WALTER: We don't want to hear no exact terms of no arrangements. I want to know if you got any more to tell us 'bout getting together?

LINDNER (*taking off his glasses*): Well—I don't suppose that you feel . . .

WALTER: Never mind how I feel—you got any more to say 'bout how people ought to sit down and talk to each other? . . . Get out of my house, man.

(*He turns his back and walks to the door.*)

LINDNER (*looking around at the hostile faces and reaching and assembling his hat and briefcase*): Well—I don't understand why you people are reacting this way. What do you think you are going to gain by moving into a neighborhood where you just aren't wanted and where some elements—well—people can get awful worked up when they feel that their whole way of life and everything they've ever worked for is threatened.

WALTER: Get out.

LINDNER (*at the door, holding a small card*): Well—I'm sorry it went like this.

WALTER: Get out.

LINDNER (*almost sadly regarding Walter*): You just can't force people to change their hearts, son.

(*He turns and puts his card on a table and exits. Walter pushes the door to with stinging hatred, and stands looking at it. Ruth just sits and Beneatha just stands. They say nothing. Mama and Travis enter.*)

MAMA: Well—this all the packing got done since I left out of here this morning. I testify before God that my children got all the energy of the *dead!* What time the moving men due?

BENEATHA: Four o'clock. You had a caller, Mama.

(*She is smiling, teasingly.*)

MAMA: Sure enough—who?

BENEATHA (*her arms folded saucily*): The Welcoming Committee.

(*Walter and Ruth giggle.*)

MAMA (*innocently*): Who?

BENEATHA: The Welcoming Committee. They said they're sure going to be glad to see you when you get there.

WALTER (*devilishly*): Yeah, they said they can't hardly wait to see your face.

(*Laughter.*)

MAMA (*sensing their facetiousness*): What's the matter with you all?

WALTER: Ain't nothing the matter with us. We just telling you 'bout the gentleman who came to see you this afternoon. From the Clybourne Park Improvement Association.

MAMA: What he want?

RUTH (*in the same mood as Beneatha and Walter*): To welcome you, honey.

WALTER: He said they can't hardly wait. He said the one thing they don't have, that they just *dying* to have out there is a fine family of fine colored people! (*To Ruth and Beneatha.*) Ain't that right!

RUTH (*mockingly*): Yeah! He left his card—

BENEATHA (*handing card to Mama*): In case.

(*Mama reads and throws it on the floor—understanding and looking off as she draws her chair up to the table on which she has put her plant and some sticks and some cord.*)

MAMA: Father, give us strength. (*Knowingly—and without fun.*) Did he threaten us?

BENEATHA: Oh—Mama—they don't do it like that anymore. He talked Brotherhood. He said everybody ought to learn how to sit down and hate each other with good Christian fellowship.

(*She and Walter shake hands to ridicule the remark.*)

MAMA (*sadly*): Lord, protect us . . .

RUTH: You should hear the money those folks raised to buy the house from us. All we paid and then some.

BENEATHA: What they think we going to do—eat 'em?

RUTH: No, honey, marry 'em.

MAMA (*shaking her head*): Lord, Lord, Lord . . .

RUTH: Well—that's the way the crackers crumble. (*A beat.*) Joke.

BENEATHA (*laughingly noticing what her mother is doing*): Mama, what are you doing?

MAMA: Fixing my plant so it won't get hurt none on the way . . .

BENEATHA: Mama, you going to take *that* to the new house?

MAMA: Un-huh—

BENEATHA: That raggedy-looking old thing?

MAMA (*stopping and looking at her*): It expresses ME!

RUTH (*with delight, to Beneatha*): So there, Miss Thing!

(*Walter comes to Mama suddenly and bends down behind her and squeezes her in his arms with all his strength. She is overwhelmed by the suddenness of it and, though delighted, her manner is like that of Ruth and Travis.*)

MAMA: Look out now, boy! You make me mess up my thing here!

WALTER (*his face lit, he slips down on his knees beside her, his arms still about her*): Mama . . . you know what it means to climb up in the chariot?

MAMA (*gruffly, very happy*): Get on away from me now . . .

RUTH (*near the gift-wrapped package, trying to catch Walter's eye*): Psst—

WALTER: What the old song say, Mama . . .

RUTH: Walter—Now?

(*She is pointing at the package.*)

WALTER (*speaking the lines, sweetly, playfully, in his mother's face*): I got wings . . . you got wings . . . All God's Children got wings . . .

MAMA: Boy—get out of my face and do some work . . .

WALTER: When I get to heaven gonna put on my wings, Gonna fly all over God's heaven . . .

BENEATHA (*teasingly, from across the room*): Everybody talking 'bout heaven ain't going there!

WALTER (*to Ruth, who is carrying the box across to them*): I don't know, you think we ought to give her that . . . Seems to me she ain't been very appreciative around here.

MAMA (*eyeing the box, which is obviously a gift*): What is that?

WALTER (*taking it from Ruth and putting it on the table in front of Mama*): Well—what you all think? Should we give it to her?

RUTH: Oh—she was pretty good today.

MAMA: I'll good you—

(*She turns her eyes to the box again.*)

BENEATHA: Open it, Mama.

(*She stands up, looks at it, turns, and looks at all of them, and then presses her hands together and does not open the package.*)

WALTER (*sweetly*): Open it, Mama. It's for you. (*Mama looks in his eyes. It is the first present in her life without its being Christmas. Slowly she opens her package and lifts out, one by one, a brand-new sparkling set of gardening tools. Walter continues, prodding.*) Ruth made up the note—read it . . .

MAMA (*picking up the card and adjusting her glasses*): "To our own Mrs. Miniver—Love from Brother, Ruth and Beneatha." Ain't that lovely . . .

TRAVIS (*tugging at his father's sleeve*): Daddy, can I give her mine now?

WALTER: All right, son. (*Travis flies to get his gift.*)

MAMA: Now I don't have to use my knives and forks no more . . .

WALTER: Travis didn't want to go in with the rest of us, Mama. He got his own. (*Somewhat amused.*) We don't know what it is . . .

TRAVIS (*racing back in the room with a large hatbox and putting it in front of his grandmother*): Here!

MAMA: Lord have mercy, baby. You done gone and bought your grandmother a hat?

TRAVIS (*very proud*): Open it!

(*She does and lifts out an elaborate, but very elaborate, wide gardening hat, and all the adults break up at the sight of it.*)

RUTH: Travis, honey, what is that?

TRAVIS (*who thinks it is beautiful and appropriate*): It's a gardening hat! Like the ladies always have on in the magazines when they work in their gardens.

BENEATHA (*giggling fiercely*): Travis—we were trying to make Mama Mrs. Miniver—not Scarlett O'Hara!

MAMA (*indignantly*): What's the matter with you all! This here is a beautiful hat! (*Absurdly.*) I always wanted me one just like it!

(*She pops it on her head to prove it to her grandson, and the hat is ludicrous and considerably oversized.*)

RUTH: Hot dog! Go, Mama!

WALTER (*doubled over with laughter*): I'm sorry, Mama—but you look like you ready to go out and chop you some cotton sure enough!

(*They all laugh except Mama, out of deference to Travis's feelings.*)

MAMA (*gathering the boy up to her*): Bless your heart—this is the prettiest hat I ever owned—(*Walter, Ruth, and Beneatha chime in—noisily, festively, and insincerely congratulating Travis on his gift.*) What are we all standing around here for? We ain't finished packin' yet. Bennie, you ain't packed one book.

(*The bell rings.*)

BENEATHA: That couldn't be the movers . . . it's not hardly two good yet—

(*Beneatha goes into her room. Mama starts for door.*)

WALTER (*turning, stiffening*): Wait—wait—I'll get it.

(*He stands and looks at the door.*)

MAMA: You expecting company, son?

WALTER (*just looking at the door*): Yeah—yeah . . .

(*Mama looks at Ruth, and they exchange innocent and unfrightened glances.*)

MAMA (*not understanding*): Well, let them in, son.

BENEATHA (*from her room*): We need some more string.

MAMA: Travis—you run to the hardware and get me some string cord.

(*Mama goes out and Walter turns and looks at Ruth. Travis goes to a dish for money.*)

RUTH: Why don't you answer the door, man?

WALTER (*suddenly bounding across the floor to embrace her*): 'Cause sometimes it hard to let the future begin! (*Stooping down in her face.*) I got wings! You got wings! All God's children got wings!

(*He crosses to the door and throws it open. Standing there is a very slight little man in a not too prosperous business suit and with haunted frightened eyes and a hat pulled down tightly, brim up, around his forehead. Travis passes between the men and exits. Walter leans deep in the man's face, still in his jubilance.*) When I get to heaven gonna put on my wings, Gonna fly all over

God's heaven . . . (*The little man just stares at him.*) Heaven—(*Suddenly he stops and looks past the little man into the empty hallway.*) Where's Willy, man?

BOBO: He ain't with me.

WALTER (*not disturbed*): Oh—come on in. You know my wife.

BOBO (*dumbly, taking off his hat*): Yes—h'you, Miss Ruth.

RUTH (*quietly, a mood apart from her husband already, seeing Bobo*): Hello, Bobo.

WALTER: You right on time today . . . Right on time. That's the way! (*He slaps Bobo on his back.*) Sit down . . . lemme hear.

(*Ruth stands stiffly and quietly in back of them, as though somehow she senses death, her eyes fixed on her husband.*)

BOBO (*his frightened eyes on the floor, his hat in his hands*): Could I please get a drink of water, before I tell you about it, Walter Lee?

(*Walter does not take his eyes off the man. Ruth goes blindly to the tap and gets a glass of water and brings it to Bobo.*)

WALTER: There ain't nothing wrong, is there?

BOBO: Lemme tell you—

WALTER: Man—didn't nothing go wrong?

BOBO: Lemme tell you—Walter Lee. (*Looking at Ruth and talking to her more than to Walter.*) You know how it was. I got to tell you how it was. I mean first I got to tell you how it was all the way . . . I mean about the money I put in, Walter Lee . . .

WALTER (*with taut agitation now*): What about the money you put in?

BOBO: Well—it wasn't much as we told you—me and Willy—(*He stops.*) I'm sorry, Walter. I got a bad feeling about it. I got a real bad feeling about it . . .

WALTER: Man, what you telling me about all this for? . . . Tell me what happened in Springfield . . .

BOBO: Springfield.

RUTH (*like a dead woman*): What was supposed to happen in Springfield?

BOBO (*to her*): This deal that me and Walter went into with Willy—Me and Willy was going to go down to Springfield and spread some money 'round so's we wouldn't have to wait so long for the liquor license . . . That's what we were going to do. Everybody said that was the way you had to do, you understand, Miss Ruth?

WALTER: Man—what happened down there?

BOBO (*a pitiful man, near tears*): I'm trying to tell you, Walter.

WALTER (*screaming at him suddenly*): THEN TELL ME, GODDAMMIT . . . WHAT'S THE MATTER WITH YOU?

BOBO: Man . . . I didn't go to no Springfield, yesterday.

WALTER (*halted, life hanging in the moment*): Why not?

BOBO (*the long way, the hard way to tell*): 'Cause I didn't have no reasons to . . .

WALTER: Man, what are you talking about!

BOBO: I'm talking about the fact that when I got to the train station yesterday morning—eight o'clock like we planned . . . Man—*Willy didn't never show up.*

WALTER: Why . . . where was he . . . where is he?

BOBO: That's what I'm trying to tell you . . . I don't know . . . I waited six hours . . . I called his house . . . and I waited . . . six hours . . . I waited in that train station six hours . . . (*Breaking into tears.*) That was all the extra money I had in the world . . . (*Looking up at Walter with the tears running down his face.*) Man, *Willy is gone.*

WALTER: Gone, what you mean Willy is gone? Gone where? You mean he went by himself. You mean he went off to Springfield by himself—to take care of getting the license—(*Turns and looks anxiously at Ruth.*) You mean maybe he didn't want too many people in on the business down there? (*Looks to Ruth again, as before.*) You know Willy got his own ways. (*Looks back to Bobo.*) Maybe you was late yesterday and he just went on down there without you. Maybe—maybe—he's been callin' you at home tryin' to tell you what happened or something. Maybe—maybe—he just got sick. He's somewhere—he's got to be somewhere. We just got to find him—me and you got to find him. (*Grabs Bobo senselessly by the collar and starts to shake him.*) We got to!

BOBO (*in sudden angry, frightened agony*): What's the matter with you, Walter! *When a cat take off with your money he don't leave you no road maps!*

WALTER (*turning madly, as though he is looking for Willy in the very room*): Willy! . . . Willy . . . don't do it . . . Please don't do it . . . Man, not with that money . . . Man, please, not with that money . . . Oh, God . . . Don't let it be true . . . (*He is wandering around, crying out for Willy and looking for him or perhaps for help from God.*) Man . . . I trusted you . . . Man, I put my life in your hands . . . (*He starts to crumple down on the floor as Ruth just covers her face in horror. Mama opens the door and comes into the room, with Beneatha behind her.*) Man . . . (*He starts to pound the floor with his fists, sobbing wildly.*) THAT MONEY IS MADE OUT MY FATHER'S FLESH——

BOBO (*standing over him helplessly*): I'm sorry, Walter . . . (*Only Walter's sobs reply. Bobo puts on his hat.*) I had my life staked on this deal, too . . .

(*He exits.*)

MAMA (*to Walter*): Son—(*She goes to him, bends down to him, talks to his bent head.*) Son . . . Is it gone? Son, I gave you sixty-five hundred dollars. Is it gone? All of it? Beneatha's money too?

WALTER (*lifting his head slowly*): Mama . . . I never . . . went to the bank at all . . .

MAMA (*not wanting to believe him*): You mean . . . your sister's school money . . . you used that too . . . Walter? . . .

WALTER: Yessss! All of it . . . It's all gone . . .

(*There is total silence. Ruth stands with her face covered with her hands; Beneatha leans forlornly against a wall, fingering a piece of red ribbon from the mother's gift. Mama stops and looks at her son without recognition and then, quite without thinking about it, starts to beat him senselessly in the face. Beneatha goes to them and stops it.*)

BENEATHA: Mama!

(*Mama stops and looks at both of her children and rises slowly and wanders vaguely, aimlessly away from them.*)

MAMA: I seen...him...night after night...come in...and look at that rug...and then look at me...the red showing in his eyes...the veins moving in his head...I seen him grow thin and old before he was forty...working and working and working like somebody's old horse...killing himself...and you—you give it all away in a day—(*She raises her arms to strike him again.*)

BENEATHA: Mama—

MAMA: Oh, God...(*She looks up to Him.*) Look down here—and show me the strength.

BENEATHA: Mama—

MAMA (*folding over*): Strength...

BENEATHA (*plaintively*): Mama...

MAMA: Strength!

ACT III

(*An hour later.*)

(*At curtain, there is a sullen light of gloom in the living room, gray light not unlike that which began the first scene of act I. At left we can see Walter within his room, alone with himself. He is stretched out on the bed, his shirt out and open, his arms under his head. He does not smoke, he does not cry out, he merely lies there, looking up at the ceiling, much as if he were alone in the world.*)

(*In the living room Beneatha sits at the table, still surrounded by the now almost ominous packing crates. She sits looking off. We feel that this is a mood struck perhaps an hour before, and it lingers now, full of the empty sound of profound disappointment. We see on a line from her brother's bedroom the sameness of their attitudes. Presently the bell rings and Beneatha rises without ambition or interest in answering. It is Asagai, smiling broadly, striding into the room with energy and happy expectation and conversation.*)

ASAGAI: I came over...I had some free time. I thought I might help with the packing. Ah, I like the look of packing crates! A household in preparation for a journey! It depresses some people...but for me...it is another feeling. Something full of the flow of life, do you understand? Movement, progress...It makes me think of Africa.

BENEATHA: Africa!

ASAGAI: What kind of a mood is this? Have I told you how deeply you move me?

BENEATHA: He gave away the money, Asagai...

ASAGAI: Who gave away what money?

BENEATHA: The insurance money. My brother gave it away.

ASAGAI: Gave it away?

BENEATHA: He made an investment! With a man even Travis wouldn't have trusted with his most worn-out marbles.

ASAGAI: And it's gone?

BENEATHA: Gone!

ASAGAI: I'm very sorry...And you, now?

BENEATHA: Me?...Me?...Me, I'm nothing...Me. When I was very small...we used to take our sleds out in the wintertime and the only hills we had were the ice-covered stone steps of some houses down the street. And we used to fill them in with snow and make them smooth and slide down them all day...and it was very dangerous, you know...far too steep...and sure enough one day a kid named Rufus came down too fast and hit the sidewalk and we saw his face just split open right there in front of us...And I remember standing there looking at his bloody open face thinking that was the end of Rufus. But the ambulance came and they took him to the hospital and they fixed the broken bones and they sewed it all up...and the next time I saw Rufus he just had a little line down the middle of his face...I never got over that...

ASAGAI: What?

BENEATHA: That that was what one person could do for another, fix him up—sew up the problem, make him all right again. That was the most marvelous thing in the world...I wanted to do that. I always thought it was the one concrete thing in the world that a human being could do. Fix up the sick, you know—and make them whole again. This was truly being God...

ASAGAI: You wanted to be God?

BENEATHA: No—I wanted to cure. It used to be so important to me. I wanted to cure. It used to matter. I used to care. I mean about people and how their bodies hurt...

ASAGAI: And you've stopped caring?

BENEATHA: Yes—I think so.

ASAGAI: Why?

BENEATHA (*bitterly*): Because it doesn't seem deep enough, close enough to what ails mankind! It was a child's way of seeing things—or an idealist's.

ASAGAI: Children see things very well sometimes—and idealists even better.

BENEATHA: I know that's what you think. Because you are still where I left off. You with all your talk and dreams about Africa! You still think you can patch up the world. Cure the Great Sore of Colonialism—(*loftily, mocking it*) with the Penicillin of Independence—!

ASAGAI: Yes!

BENEATHA: Independence *and then what?* What about all the crooks and thieves and just plain idiots who will come into power and steal and plunder the same as before—only now they will be black and do it in the name of the new Independence—WHAT ABOUT THEM?!

ASAGAI: That will be the problem for another time. First we must get there.

BENEATHA: And where does it end?

ASAGAI: End? Who even spoke of an end? To life? To living?

BENEATHA: An end to misery! To stupidity! Don't you see there isn't any real progress, Asagai, there is only one large circle that we march in, around and around, each of us with our own little picture in front of us—our own little mirage that we think is the future.

ASAGAI: That is the mistake.

BENEATHA: What?

ASAGAI: What you just said—about the circle. It isn't a circle—it is simply a long line—as in geometry, you know, one that reaches into infinity. And because we cannot see the end—we also cannot see how it changes. And it is very odd but those who see the changes—who dream, who will not give up—are called idealists . . . and those who see only the circle—we call *them* the "realists"!

BENEATHA: Asagai, while I was sleeping in that bed in there, people went out and took the future right out of my hands! And nobody asked me, nobody consulted me—they just went out and changed my life!

ASAGAI: Was it your money?

BENEATHA: What?

ASAGAI: Was it your money he gave away?

BENEATHA: It belonged to all of us.

ASAGAI: But did you earn it? Would you have had it at all if your father had not died?

BENEATHA: No.

ASAGAI: Then isn't there something wrong in a house—in a world—where all dreams, good or bad, must depend on the death of a man? I never thought to see *you* like this, Alaiyo. You! Your brother made a mistake and you are grateful to him so that now you can give up the ailing human race on account of it! You talk about what good is struggle, what good is anything! Where are we all going and why are we bothering!

BENEATHA: AND YOU CANNOT ANSWER IT!

ASAGAI (*shouting over her*): I LIVE THE ANSWER! (*Pause.*) In my village at home it is the exceptional man who can even read a newspaper . . . or who ever sees a book at all. I will go home and much of what I will have to say will seem strange to the people of my village. But I will teach and work and things will happen, slowly and swiftly. At times it will seem that nothing changes at all . . . and then again the sudden dramatic events which make history leap into the future. And then quiet again. Retrogression even. Guns, murder, revolution. And I even will have moments when I wonder if the quiet was not better than all that death and hatred. But I will look about my village at the illiteracy and disease and ignorance and I will not wonder long. And perhaps . . . perhaps I will be a great man . . . I mean perhaps I will hold on to the substance of truth and find my way always with the right course . . . and perhaps for it I will be butchered in my bed some night by the servants of empire . . .

BENEATHA: *The martyr!*

ASAGAI (*he smiles*): . . . or perhaps I shall live to be a very old man, respected and esteemed in my new nation . . . And perhaps I shall hold office and this is what I'm trying to tell you, Alaiyo: Perhaps the things I believe now for my country will be wrong and outmoded, and I will not understand and do terrible things to have things my way or merely to keep my power. Don't you see that there will be young men and women—not British soldiers then, but my own black countrymen—to step out of the shadows some evening and slit my then useless throat? Don't you see they have always been there . . . that they always will be. And that such a thing as my own death will be an advance? They who might kill me even . . . actually replenish all that I was.

BENEATHA: Oh, Asagai, I know all that.

ASAGAI: Good! Then stop moaning and groaning and tell me what you plan to do.

BENEATHA: Do?

ASAGAI: I have a bit of a suggestion.

BENEATHA: What?

ASAGAI (*rather quietly for him*): That when it is all over—that you come home with me—

BENEATHA (*staring at him and crossing away with exasperation*): Oh—Asagai—at this moment you decide to be romantic!

ASAGAI (*quickly understanding the misunderstanding*): My dear, young creature of the New World—I do not mean across the city—I mean across the ocean: home—to Africa.

BENEATHA (*slowly understanding and turning to him with murmured amazement*): To Africa?

ASAGAI: Yes! . . . (*Smiling and lifting his arms playfully.*) Three hundred years later the African Prince rose up out of the seas and swept the maiden back across the middle passage over which her ancestors had come—

BENEATHA (*unable to play*): To—to Nigeria?

ASAGAI: Nigeria. Home. (*Coming to her with genuine romantic flippancy.*) I will show you our mountains and our stars; and give you cool drinks from gourds and teach you the old songs and the ways of our people—and, in time, we will pretend that—(*very softly*)—you have only been away for a day. Say that you'll come—(*He swings her around and takes her full in his arms in a kiss which proceeds to passion.*)

BENEATHA (*pulling away suddenly*): You're getting me all mixed up—

ASAGAI: Why?

BENEATHA: Too many things—too many things have happened today. I must sit down and think. I don't know what I feel about anything right this minute.

(*She promptly sits down and props her chin on her fist.*)

ASAGAI (*charmed*): All right, I shall leave you. No—don't get up. (*Touching her, gently, sweetly.*) Just sit awhile and think ... Never be afraid to sit awhile and think. (*He goes to door and looks at her.*) How often I have looked at you and said, "Ah—so this is what the New World hath finally wrought ..."

(*He exits. Beneatha sits on alone. Presently Walter enters from his room and starts to rummage through things, feverishly looking for something. She looks up and turns in her seat.*)

BENEATHA (*hissingly*): Yes—just look at what the New World hath wrought! ... Just look! (*She gestures with bitter disgust.*) There he is! *Monsieur le petit bourgeois noir*°—himself! There he is—Symbol of a Rising Class! Entrepreneur! Titan° of the system! (*Walter ignores her completely and continues frantically and destructively looking for something and hurling things to the floor and tearing things out of their place in his search. Beneatha ignores the eccentricity of his actions and goes on with the monologue of insult.*) Did you dream of yachts on Lake Michigan, Brother? Did you see yourself on that Great Day sitting down at the Conference Table, surrounded by all the mighty bald-headed men in America? All halted, waiting, breathless, waiting for your pronouncements on industry? Waiting for you—Chairman of the Board! (*Walter finds what he is looking for—a small piece of white paper—and pushes it in his pocket and puts on his coat and rushes out without ever having looked at her. She shouts after him.*) I look at you and I see the final triumph of stupidity in the world!

(*The door slams and she returns to just sitting again. Ruth comes quickly out of Mama's room.*)

RUTH: Who was that?
BENEATHA: Your husband.
RUTH: Where did he go?
BENEATHA: Who knows—maybe he has an appointment at U.S. Steel.
RUTH (*anxiously, with frightened eyes*): You didn't say nothing bad to him, did you?
BENEATHA: Bad? Say anything bad to him? No—I told him he was a sweet boy and full of dreams and everything is strictly peachy keen, as the ofay° kids say!

(*Mama enters from her bedroom. She is lost, vague, trying to catch hold, to make some sense of her former command of the world, but it still eludes her. A sense*

Monsieur ... noir: Mr. Black Lower Middle Class. Titan: Person of great power; originally, a god. ofay: White person, usually used disparagingly.

of waste overwhelms her gait; a measure of apology rides on her shoulders. She goes to her plant, which has remained on the table, looks at it, picks it up and takes it to the window sill and sits it outside, and she stands and looks at it a long moment. Then she closes the window, straightens her body with effort, and turns around to her children.*)

MAMA: Well—ain't it a mess in here, though? (*A false cheerfulness, a beginning of something.*) I guess we all better stop moping around and get some work done. All this unpacking and everything we got to do. (*Ruth raises her head slowly in response to the sense of the line; and Beneatha in similar manner turns very slowly to look at her mother.*) One of you all better call the moving people and tell 'em not to come.
RUTH: Tell 'em not to come?
MAMA: Of course, baby. Ain't no need in 'em coming all the way here and having to go back. They charges for that too. (*She sits down, fingers to her brow, thinking.*) Lord, ever since I was a little girl, I always remembers people saying, "Lena—Lena Eggleston, you aims too high all the time. You needs to slow down and see life a little more like it is. Just slow down some." That's what they always used to say down home—"Lord, that Lena Eggleston is a high-minded thing. She'll get her due one day!"
RUTH: No, Lena ...
MAMA: Me and Big Walter just didn't never learn right.
RUTH: Lena, no! We gotta go. Bennie—tell her ... (*She rises and crosses to Beneatha with her arms outstretched. Beneatha doesn't respond.*) Tell her we can still move ... the notes ain't but a hundred and twenty-five a month. We got four grown people in this house—we can work ...
MAMA (*to herself*): Just aimed too high all the time—
RUTH (*turning and going to Mama fast—the words pouring out with urgency and desperation*): Lena—I'll work ... I'll work twenty hours a day in all the kitchens in Chicago ... I'll strap my baby on my back if I have to and scrub all the floors in America and wash all the sheets in America if I have to—but we got to MOVE! We got to get OUT OF HERE!!

(*Mama reaches out absently and pats Ruth's hand.*)

MAMA: No—I sees things differently now. Been thinking 'bout some of the things we could do to fix this place up some. I seen a second-hand bureau over on Maxwell Street just the other day that could fit right there. (*She points to where the new furniture might go. Ruth wanders away from her.*) Would need some new handles on it and then a little varnish and it look like something brand-new. And—we can put up them new curtains in the kitchen ... Why this place be looking fine. Cheer us all up so that we forget trouble ever come ... (*To Ruth.*) And you could get some nice screens to put up in your room round the baby's bassinet ... (*She looks at both of them, pleadingly.*)

Sometimes you just got to know when to give up some things . . . and hold on to what you got. . . .

(*Walter enters from the outside, looking spent and leaning against the door, his coat hanging from him.*)

MAMA: Where you been, son?

WALTER (*breathing hard*): Made a call.

MAMA: To who, son?

WALTER: To The Man. (*He heads for his room.*)

MAMA: What man, baby?

WALTER (*stops in the door*): The Man, Mama. Don't you know who The Man is?

RUTH: Walter Lee?

WALTER: *The Man.* Like the guys in the streets say—The Man. Captain Boss—Mistuh Charley . . . Old Cap'n Please Mr. Bossman . . .

BENEATHA (*suddenly*): Lindner!

WALTER: That's right! That's good. I told him to come right over.

BENEATHA (*fiercely, understanding*): For what? What do you want to see him for!

WALTER (*looking at his sister*): We going to do business with him.

MAMA: What you talking 'bout, son?

WALTER: Talking 'bout life, Mama. You all always telling me to see life like it is. Well—I laid in there on my back today . . . and I figured it out. Life just like it is. Who gets and who don't get. (*He sits down with his coat on and laughs.*) Mama, you know it's all divided up. Life is. Sure enough. Between the takers and the "tooken." (*He laughs.*) I've figured it out finally. (*He looks around at them.*) Yeah. Some of us always getting "tooken." (*He laughs.*) People like Willy Harris, they don't never get "tooken." And you know why the rest of us do? 'Cause we all mixed up. Mixed up bad. We get to looking 'round for the right and the wrong; and we worry about it and cry about it and stay up nights trying to figure out 'bout the wrong and the right of things all the time . . . And all the time, man, them takers is out there operating, just taking and taking. Willy Harris? Shoot—Willy Harris don't even count. He don't even count in the big scheme of things. But I'll say one thing for old Willy Harris . . . he's taught me something. He's taught me to keep my eye on what counts in this world. Yeah—(*Shouting out a little.*) Thanks, Willy!

RUTH: What did you call that man for, Walter Lee?

WALTER: Called him to tell him to come on over to the show. Gonna put on a show for the man. Just what he wants to see. You see, Mama, the man came here today and he told us that them people out there where you want to move—well they so upset they willing to pay us *not* to move! (*He laughs again.*) And—and oh, Mama—you would of been proud of the way me and Ruth and Bennie acted. We told him to get out . . . Lord have mercy! We told the man to get out! Oh, we was some proud folks this afternoon, yeah. (*He lights a cigarette.*) We were still full of that old-time stuff . . .

RUTH (*coming toward him slowly*): You talking 'bout taking them people's money to keep us from moving in that house?

WALTER: I ain't just talking 'bout it, baby—I'm telling you that's what's going to happen!

BENEATHA: Oh, God! Where is the bottom! Where is the real honest-to-God bottom so he can't go any farther!

WALTER: See—that's the old stuff. You and that boy that was here today. You all want everybody to carry a flag and a spear and sing some marching songs, huh? You wanna spend your life looking into things and trying to find the right and the wrong part, huh? Yeah. You know what's going to happen to that boy someday—he'll find himself sitting in a dungeon, locked in forever—and the takers will have the key! Forget it, baby! There ain't no causes—there ain't nothing but taking in this world, and he who takes most is smartest—and it don't make a damn bit of difference *how*.

MAMA: You making something inside me cry, son. Some awful pain inside me.

WALTER: Don't cry, Mama. Understand. That white man is going to walk in that door able to write checks for more money than we ever had. It's important to him and I'm going to help him . . . I'm going to put on the show, Mama.

MAMA: Son—I come from five generations of people who was slaves and sharecroppers—but ain't nobody in my family never let nobody pay 'em no money that was a way of telling us we wasn't fit to walk the earth. We ain't never been that poor. (*Raising her eyes and looking at him.*) We ain't never been that—dead inside.

BENEATHA: Well—we are dead now. All the talk about dreams and sunlight that goes on in this house. It's all dead now.

WALTER: What's the matter with you all! I didn't make this world! It was give to me this way! Hell, yes, I want me some yachts someday! Yes, I want to hang some real pearls 'round my wife's neck. Ain't she supposed to wear no pearls? Somebody tell me—tell me, who decides which women is suppose to wear pearls in this world. I tell you I am a *man*—and I think my wife should wear some pearls in this world!

(*This last line hangs a good while and Walter begins to move about the room. The word "Man" has penetrated his consciousness; he mumbles it to himself repeatedly between strange agitated pauses as he moves about.*)

MAMA: Baby, how you going to feel on the inside?

WALTER: Fine! . . . Going to feel fine . . . a man . . .

MAMA: You won't have nothing left then, Walter Lee.

WALTER (*coming to her*): I'm going to feel fine, Mama. I'm going to look that son-of-a-bitch in the eyes and say—(*he falters*)—and say, "All right, Mr. Lindner—(*he falters even more*)—that's *your* neighborhood out there! You got the right to keep it like you want! You got the right to have it like you want! Just write the check and—the house is yours." And—and

I am going to say—(*His voice almost breaks.*) "And you—you people just put the money in my hand and you won't have to live next to this bunch of stinking niggers! . . ." (*He straightens up and moves away from his mother, walking around the room.*) And maybe—maybe I'll just get down on my black knees . . . (*He does so; Ruth and Bennie and Mama watch him in frozen horror.*) "Captain, Mistuh, Bossman—(*Groveling and grinning and wringing his hands in profoundly anguished imitation of the slow-witted movie stereotype.*) A-hee-hee-hee! Oh, yassuh boss! Yasssssuh! Great white—(*voice breaking, he forces himself to go on*)—Father, just gi' us-sen de money, fo' God's sake, and we's—we's ain't gwine come out deh and dirty up yo' white folks neighborhood . . ." (*He breaks down completely.*) And I'll feel fine! Fine! fine! (*He gets up and goes into the bedroom.*)

BENEATHA: That is not a man. That is nothing but a toothless rat.

MAMA: Yes—death done come in this here house. (*She is nodding, slowly, reflectively.*) Done come walking in my house on the lips of my children. You what supposed to be my beginning again. You—what supposed to be my harvest. (*To Beneatha.*) You—you mourning your brother?

BENEATHA: He's no brother of mine.

MAMA: What you say?

BENEATHA: I said that that individual in that room is no brother of mine.

MAMA: That's what I thought you said. You feeling like you better than he is today? (*Beneatha does not answer.*) Yes? What you tell him a minute ago? That he wasn't a man? Yes? You give him up for me? You done wrote his epitaph too—like the rest of the world? Well, who give you the privilege?

BENEATHA: Be on my side for once! You saw what he just did, Mama! You saw him—down on his knees. Wasn't it you who taught me to despise any man who would do that? Do what he's going to do?

MAMA: Yes—I taught you that. Me and your daddy. But I thought I taught you something else too . . . I thought I taught you to love him.

BENEATHA: Love him? There is nothing left to love.

MAMA: There is *always* something left to love. And if you ain't learned that, you ain't learned nothing. (*Looking at her.*) Have you cried for that boy today? I don't mean for yourself and for the family 'cause we lost the money. I mean for him: what he been through and what it done to him. Child, when do you think is the time to love somebody the most? When they done good and made things easy for everybody? Well then, you ain't through learning—because that ain't the time at all. It's when he's at his lowest and can't believe in hisself 'cause the world done whipped him so! When you starts measuring somebody, measure him right, child, measure him right. Make sure you done taken into account what hills and valleys he come through before he got to wherever he is.

(*Travis bursts into the room at the end of the speech, leaving the door open.*)

TRAVIS: Grandmama—the moving men are downstairs! The truck just pulled up.

MAMA (*turning and looking at him*): Are they, baby? They downstairs?

(*She sighs and sits. Lindner appears in the doorway. He peers in and knocks lightly, to gain attention, and comes in. All turn to look at him.*)

LINDNER (*hat and briefcase in hand*): Uh—hello . . .

(*Ruth crosses mechanically to the bedroom door and opens it and lets it swing open freely and slowly as the lights come up on Walter within, still in his coat, sitting at the far corner of the room. He looks up and out through the room to Lindner.*)

RUTH: He's here.

(*A long minute passes and Walter slowly gets up.*)

LINDNER (*coming to the table with efficiency, putting his briefcase on the table and starting to unfold papers and unscrew fountain pens*): Well, I certainly was glad to hear from you people. (*Walter has begun the trek out of the room, slowly and awkwardly, rather like a small boy, passing the back of his sleeve across his mouth from time to time.*) Life can really be so much simpler than people let it be most of the time. Well—with whom do I negotiate? You, Mrs. Younger, or your son here? (*Mama sits with her hands folded on her lap and her eyes closed as Walter advances. Travis goes closer to Lindner and looks at the papers curiously.*) Just some official papers, sonny.

RUTH: Travis, you go downstairs—

MAMA (*opening her eyes and looking into Walter's*): No. Travis, you stay right here. And you make him understand what you doing, Walter Lee. You teach him good. Like Willy Harris taught you. You show where our five generations done come to. (*Walter looks from her to the boy, who grins at him innocently.*) Go ahead, son—(*She folds her hands and closes her eyes.*) Go ahead.

WALTER (*at last crosses to Lindner, who is reviewing the contract*): Well, Mr. Lindner. (*Beneatha turns away.*) We called you—(*there is a profound, simple groping quality in his speech*)—because, well, me and my family (*he looks around and shifts from one foot to the other*) Well—we are very plain people . . .

LINDNER: Yes—

WALTER: I mean—I have worked as a chauffeur most of my life—and my wife here, she does domestic work in people's kitchens. So does my mother. I mean—we are plain people . . .

LINDNER: Yes, Mr. Younger—

WALTER (*really like a small boy, looking down at his shoes and then up at the man*): And—uh—well, my father, well, he was a laborer most of his life. . . .

LINDNER (*absolutely confused*): Uh, yes—yes, I understand. (*He turns back to the contract.*)

WALTER (*a beat; staring at him*): And my father—(*With sudden intensity.*) My father almost *beat a man to death* once because this man called him a bad name or something, you know what I mean?

LINDNER (*looking up, frozen*): No, no, I'm afraid I don't—

WALTER (*A beat. The tension hangs; then Walter steps back from it.*): Yeah. Well—what I mean is that we come from people who had a lot of *pride.* I mean—we are very proud people. And that's my sister over there and she's going to be a doctor—and we are very proud—

LINDNER: Well—I am sure that is very nice, but—

WALTER: What I am telling you is that we called you over here to tell you that we are very proud and that this—(*Signaling to Travis.*) Travis, come here. (*Travis crosses and Walter draws him before him facing the man.*) This is my son, and he makes the sixth generation of our family in this country. And we have all thought about your offer—

LINDNER: Well, good . . . good—

WALTER: And we have decided to move into our house because my father—my father—he earned it for us brick by brick. (*Mama has her eyes closed and is rocking back and forth as though she were in church, with her head nodding the Amen yes.*) We don't want to make no trouble for nobody or fight no causes, and we will try to be good neighbors. And that's *all* we got to say about that. (*He looks the man absolutely in the eyes.*) We don't want your money. (*He turns and walks away.*)

LINDNER (*looking around at all of them*): I take it then—that you have decided to occupy . . .

BENEATHA: That's what the man said.

LINDNER (*to Mama in her reverie*): Then I would like to appeal to you, Mrs. Younger. You are older and wiser and understand things better I am sure . . .

MAMA: I am afraid you don't understand. My son said we was going to move and there ain't nothing left for me to say. (*Briskly.*) You know how these young folks is nowadays, mister. Can't do a thing with 'em! (*As he opens his mouth, she rises.*) Goodbye.

LINDNER (*folding up his materials*): Well—if you are that final about it . . . there is nothing left for me to say. (*He finishes, almost ignored by the family, who are concentrating on Walter Lee. At the door Lindner halts and looks around.*) I sure hope you people know what you're getting into.

(*He shakes his head and exits.*)

RUTH (*looking around and coming to life*): Well, for God's sake—if the moving men are here—LET'S GET THE HELL OUT OF HERE!

MAMA (*into action*): Ain't it the truth! Look at all this here mess. Ruth, put Travis's good jacket on him . . . Walter Lee, fix your tie and tuck your shirt in, you look like somebody's hoodlum! Lord have mercy, where is my plant? (*She flies to get it amid* the general bustling of the family, who are deliberately trying to ignore the nobility of the past moment.*) You all start on down . . . Travis child, don't go empty-handed . . . Ruth, where did I put that box with my skillets in it? I want to be in charge of it myself . . . I'm going to make us the biggest dinner we ever ate tonight . . . Beneatha, what's the matter with them stockings? Pull them things up, girl . . .

(*The family starts to file out as two moving men appear and begin to carry out the heavier pieces of furniture, bumping into the family as they move about.*)

BENEATHA: Mama, Asagai asked me to marry him today and go to Africa—

MAMA (*in the middle of her getting-ready activity*): He did? You ain't old enough to marry nobody—(*Seeing the moving men lifting one of her chairs precariously.*) Darling, that ain't no bale of cotton, please handle it so we can sit in it again! I had that chair twenty-five years . . .

(*The movers sigh with exasperation and go on with their work.*)

BENEATHA (*girlishly and unreasonably trying to pursue the conversation*): To go to Africa, Mama—be a doctor in Africa . . .

MAMA (*distracted*): Yes, baby—

WALTER: *Africa!* What he want you to go to Africa for?

BENEATHA: To practice there . . .

WALTER: Girl, if you don't get all them silly ideas out your head! You better marry yourself a man with some loot . . .

BENEATHA (*angrily, precisely as in the first scene of the play*): What have you got to do with who I marry!

WALTER: Plenty. Now I think George Murchison—

BENEATHA: *George Murchison!* I wouldn't marry him if he was Adam and I was Eve!

(*Walter and Beneatha go out yelling at each other vigorously and the anger is loud and real till their voices diminish. Ruth stands at the door and turns to Mama and smiles knowingly.*)

MAMA (*fixing her hat at last*): Yeah—they something all right, my children . . .

RUTH: Yeah—they're something. Let's go, Lena.

MAMA (*stalling, starting to look around at the house*): Yes—I'm coming. Ruth—

RUTH: Yes?

MAMA (*quietly, woman to woman*): He finally come into his manhood today, didn't he? Kind of like a rainbow after the rain . . .

RUTH (*biting her lip lest her own pride explode in front of Mama*): Yes, Lena.

(*Walter's voice calls for them raucously.*)

WALTER (*offstage*): Y'all come on! These people charges by the hour you know!

MAMA (*waving Ruth out vaguely*): All right, honey—go on down. I be down directly.

(*Ruth hesitates, then exits. Mama stands, at last alone in the living room, her plant on the table before her as the lights start to come down. She looks around at all the walls and ceilings and suddenly, despite herself, while the children call below, a great heaving thing rises in her and she puts her fist to her mouth to stifle it, takes a final desperate look, pulls her coat about her, pats her hat, and goes out. The lights dim down. The door opens and she comes back in, grabs her plant, and goes out for the last time.*)

Contemporary Drama

The experimentation in drama that flourished in the first half of the twentieth century has continued in contemporary drama. In fact, the achievements of Tennessee Williams, Arthur Miller, Samuel Beckett, and other midcentury playwrights encouraged later playwrights to experiment more daringly with mixing media such as film, video, opera, rock, and other music with live actors. Mixed-media approaches are still options for playwrights in the twenty-first century, but most contemporary plays celebrated by critics and audiences have been relatively traditional. They build on the achievements of nineteenth-century realism and twentieth-century expressionism.

Experimentation

Most of the interesting late-twentieth-century experimental theater was done in groups such as Richard Schechner's Performance Group, which created what Schechner called **environmental theater** in New York City in the late 1960s, and Jerzy Grotowski's Polish Laboratory Theatre in Wroclaw, Poland, during the same period. Ensembles like the Bread and Puppet Theater, the San Francisco Mime Troupe, and Luis Valdez's El Teatro Campesino on the West Coast combined a radical political message with theatrical experimentation. The work of these groups is effective primarily at the performance level; their texts are not representative of their impact on audiences.

Theater of Cruelty

The ensembles of the 1960s and 1970s were strongly influenced by the work of Antonin Artaud (1896–1948), a French actor, director, and theorist of theater. In creating what came to be known as the **theater of cruelty**, he insisted on removing the comforting distance between actors and audience. Thus the audience was involved in a direct, virtually physical fashion with the dramatic action. Artaud designed theater to be a total experience—a sensational spectacle that did not depend on coherent plot or development. He concentrated on what he called total theater, which emphasized movement, gesture, music, sound, light, and other nonverbal elements to intensify the experience.

Artaud's manifestos, collected in a work entitled *The Theater and Its Double* (1938), inspired some of the most important twentieth-century theater practitioners, including Peter Brook and Robert Wilson. Artaud's notion of a "serious" theater is at the root of his influence:

> Our long habit of seeking diversion has made us forget the idea of a serious theater, which, overturning all our preconceptions, inspires us with the fiery magnetism of its images and acts upon us like a spiritual therapeutics whose touch can never be forgotten.
>
> Everything that acts is a cruelty. It is upon this idea of extreme action, pushed beyond all limits, that theater must be rebuilt.

Artaud compared the theater artist he envisioned to a victim "burnt at the stake, signaling through the flames."

Environmental Theater

Richard Schechner's most famous production, based on Euripides' *The Bacchae*, was *Dionysus in 69* (1968), in which Pentheus is torn to pieces in an impassioned frenzy. Part of the point of Schechner's production was to inspire the audience so much that they would take to the stage, becoming indistinguishable from the actors. *Dionysus in 69* was an effort to draw on the same spiritual energies tapped by Greek drama by connecting with the feasts of Dionysus, god of wine and ecstasy. The play was a spontaneous and partly improvised performance piece rather than a text meant to be read. At one point the audience and actors disrobed in a simulation of a Greek religious orgy, and Schechner's goal of involving audience and actors in a pagan ritual was realized night after night during the run.

In a similar way Julian Beck and Judith Malina's Living Theatre maintained a special relationship with the audience. Beck's plays were designed to break down the absolutes of dramatic space and audience space by having the actors roam through the audience and interact apparently at random with audience members. *Paradise Now* (1968) is his best-known play. Like Schechner's *Dionysus in 69*, it was essentially a performance piece. Certain segments were improvised; therefore, as a reading text, it has relatively little power.

"Poor Theater"

Jerzy Grotowski called his work "poor theater" because it was meant to contrast with the "rich theater" of the commercial stage, with its expensive lighting, decorated stages, rich costumes, numerous props, and elaborate settings. Grotowski's Laboratory Theatre, begun in 1959, relied on preexisting texts but interpreted them broadly through a total reconception of their meaning. For example, Grotowski's *Akropolis* (1962; revised frequently from 1963 to 1975) adapted an older Polish drama by Stanislaw Wyspiański (1904) and reset it in modern times in Auschwitz with the actors, dressed in ragged sackcloth prison uniforms, looking wretched and starving. At the end of the play the prisoners follow a headless puppet-corpse, Christ, into an afterlife. They march in an eerie ritual procession offstage into the waiting prison camp ovens.

Grotowski's theater has been influential worldwide. When the Polish government clamped down on the Solidarity° movement in the late 1970s, Grotowski left Poland. After 1970 Grotowski shifted his focus from public performances to small, intense group workshops and to the ritual performances of cultures from all over the world. The first phase of his work with the Laboratory Theatre has remained the most influential. One of his actors, Richard Cieslak, traveled widely, training people in Grotowski's methods.

Theater of Images

Robert Wilson experimented from the 1970s through the 1990s with repetitive narratives that sometimes take eight hours to perform. His multimedia dramas involve huge casts and ordinarily cover an immense historical range (Figure 30). One of his most extraordinary successes was *Einstein on the Beach* (1976), an opera written in collaboration with composer Philip Glass. Eight hours long, it was originally produced in a conventional theater, but it uses dramatic techniques that involve extensive patterns of repetition, the creation of enigmatic and evocative images, and characters who are cartoonlike caricatures of historical people. The overall effect is hypnotic; one of the points of Wilson's work seems to be to induce a trancelike state in his audience. One of his multimedia productions, *CIVIL warS* (1983), continued to develop this concept of massive theater that transcends conventional dramatic boundaries. In 1994 Wilson produced a monologue version of *Hamlet* that received some acclaim.

Gay and Lesbian Theater and Other New Ensembles

Some of the most energetic theater of the late twentieth century came from groups that were excluded for long periods from representation in mainstream theater. Gay, lesbian, African American, Hispanic American, and Native American groups have been virtually ignored by commercial theater and as a result have formed their own collectives and groups.

Through the 1970s, 1980s, and 1990s, numerous black theatrical groups developed in many parts of the world. An important Afro-Caribbean theater group was formed in the Keskidee Centre in North London, with Edgar White (b. 1947) as one of its directors. White's plays are often centered in Caribbean mystical experiences, including Rastafarianism. *The Nine Night* (1983), produced in London, focuses on a Jamaican funeral tradition designed to help the deceased enter the gates of heaven.

One reason for the development of gay theater in the United States and Great Britain in the 1960s was the decriminalization of homosexuality, beginning in 1967 in Boston. The first openly gay play was Mart Crowley's *The Boys in the Band* (1968), a popular success produced just after the repeal of a New York law prohibiting homosexuality from being represented on stage. Depiction of homosexual love onstage waited even longer, until the Gay Workshop began producing plays in London in 1976.

The Ridiculous Theatrical Company, founded by Charles Ludlam (1940–1987) in 1969, produced a formidable body of work rooted in the experiences of the homosexual community of New York. Its influence spread to many parts of the world. One of Ludlam's catchphrases was "plays without the stink of art." His plays were often ridiculously funny. *Bluebeard* (1970),

---

Solidarity: A labor-organizing movement in Communist Poland led by Lech Walesa.

Figure 30. Multimedia effects in Robert Wilson's *CIVIL warS*.

for example, focused on creating a third gender by inventing a third genital. *Camille* (1973), starring Ludlam himself in the title role, hilariously spoofed not only Dumas's play but most of the "Hallmark card" conventions about romantic love. A gifted female impersonator, Ludlam played Hedda Gabler at the American Ibsen Theater in Pittsburgh. For a few years, under the direction of Ludlam's partner, Everett Quinton, the Ridiculous Theatrical Company continued to produce Ludlam's plays as well as new plays in his tradition.

Some of the most highly praised plays of the 1980s and 1990s addressed the issues of AIDS and its ravaging of the gay community. Harvey Fierstein's *Torch Song Trilogy* (1982) was named best play of the year and appeared several years later on television. *As Is* by William M. Hoffman (1985) has been described by Don Shewey as the "best gay play anyone has written on AIDS yet." Tony Kushner dazzled New York with *Angels in America Part One: Millennium Approaches* (1992) and *Part Two: Perestroika* (1992). This two-part drama approached the problems of gay life in America on both a personal and a public, political level. The plays are called a "fantasia" and use a free-form, nonrealistic style of presentation. In late 2003, HBO produced an award-winning version for television starring Al Pacino and Meryl Streep.

Lesbian theatrical groups have sprung up in the United States and Great Britain. They often merge with women's theater groups and address issues such as male violence, societal restrictions on women, and women's opportunities. A number of important collectives, such as the Rhode Island Women's Theater and At the Foot of the Mountain in Minneapolis, treated general women's issues in the 1970s. Groups such as Medusa's Revenge (founded 1976) and Atlanta's Red Dyke Theater (1974) centered more on lesbian experience. These last two groups disbanded after a few years of successful productions. Megan Terry's Omaha Magic Theatre, founded with Jo Ann Schmidman, has been a long-lasting theater focusing on women's issues. Other groups such as Spiderwoman, consisting of three Native American sisters, and the highly successful Split Britches consider WOW Cafe Theatre in New York's East Village to be the home of lesbian theater. Gay and lesbian theater groups have often been concerned with erasing stereotypes while also celebrating gay and lesbian lifestyles. Plays that once played only to gay and lesbian audiences—such as Martin Sherman's (b. 1939) *Bent* (1977) and Larry Kramer's (b. 1935) *The Normal Heart* (1985)—are now performed in theaters worldwide.

Contemporary Women Playwrights

The contemporary female writers whose plays appear in this collection are among a throng of powerful playwrights who have helped shape theater in the twenty-first century. María Irene Fornés's *Fefu and Her Friends* (1977) is a sprawling play featuring women in roles traditionally reserved for men. Her later play, *Conduct of Life* (1985), is a cruel parody of macho values in a Latin American dictatorship. Caryl Churchill's *Cloud Nine* (1979) critiques colonialism and gender stereotyping. *Top Girls* (1982), one of her most successful plays, centers on an employment agency for women but has as its premise the introduction of famous women from the past of several cultures. *Fen* (1983), a verse play called *Serious Money* (1987), and *The Skriker* (1994) have solidified Churchill's reputation as an experimental, powerful dramatist. Suzan-Lori Parks's *Topdog/Underdog* (2001) won the Pulitzer Prize for drama, the first for an African American female playwright. Her earlier plays, *The Death of the Last Black Man in the Whole Entire World* (1990), *The American Play* (1993), *Venus* (1996), and *In the Blood* (1999), are all powerful pieces that are frequently revived.

Lynn Nottage's *Crumbs from the Table of Joy* (1995), *Intimate Apparel* (2004), and *Ruined* (2010) have established her as one of the most important modern African American playwrights. Sarah Ruhl's plays *Eurydice* (2003), *The Clean House* (2004), and *In the Next Room: or, The Vibrator Play* (2009) have been international successes. Paula Vogel, author of *How I Learned to Drive* (1997), is not only a distinguished playwright but also a remarkable teacher who has been a mentor to both Nottage and Ruhl.

Of course, there are many exceptional contemporary female writers whose work is not included here. Among the most distinguished is Marsha Norman, author of the prison drama *Getting Out* (1977); *'night Mother* (1982), about a daughter who says goodnight to her mother and commits suicide; and *The Secret Garden* (1991). Emily Mann's *Execution of Justice* (1984) retells the trial of Dan White, who murdered Harvey Milk, an openly gay San Francisco city councilman. Irish playwright Anne Devlin's *Ourselves Alone* (1986) is set against the background of an Irish hunger strike. Lynn Siefert's *Coyote Ugly* (1986), about a painfully and comically dysfunctional Southwestern family, may have spawned a similarly named bar in New York. Anna Deveare Smith produces one-woman dramas that are *tours de force;* she personates as many as forty different characters in plays such as *Fires in the Mirror: Crown Heights, Brooklyn and Other Identities* (1991), about ethnic disturbances after a child is killed in Crown Heights; *Twilight: Los Angeles 1992* (1992), about the riots in Los Angeles following the trial of police officers charged in the beating of Rodney King; and *Let Me Down Easy* (2011), a critique of the current medical establishment. All of these playwrights have enhanced the stature of women in contemporary theater.

Experimentation within the Tradition

Much of the powerful and lasting drama of the 1980s, 1990s, and early years of the twenty-first century has been achieved in a proscenium theater, using traditional methods of **dramaturgy** (the craft or techniques of dramatic composition). Contemporary dramatists are by no means shy about experimentation, but they are also sensitive to the continuing resources of the traditional stage as it was conceived by Chekhov and Ibsen and Miller. Marsha Norman, who wrote *'night, Mother,* has said that her plays are "wildly traditional. I'm a purist about structure. Plays are like plane rides. You [the audience] buy the ticket and you have to get where the ticket takes you. Or else you've been had."

Drama in the United States

Sam Shepard (b. 1943), one of the most prolific modern playwrights in the United States, experiments with his material, much of which premiered in small theaters in Greenwich Village, such as the La Mama Experimental Theatre Club. But his most widely known plays, among them *Buried Child* (1978), are produced easily on conventional stages. Shepard's work is wide-ranging and challenging. His language is coarse, a representation of the way real people speak, and the violence he portrays onstage is strong enough to alienate many in the audience. Shepard, important as he is, has not found a popular commercial audience for his plays. At root, his work is always experimental.

Although she claims to be a traditionalist, Marsha Norman (b. 1947) has written experimental plays, including her first success, *Getting Out* (1977), which portrays the same character at two periods in her life—as an adolescent and as an adult—on separate parts of the stage at the same time. Norman's *'night, Mother* is a more traditionally structured play. It respects the Aristotelian unities of time, place, and action, and it is confrontational. Thelma and her daughter, Jessie, are in a power struggle over Jessie's right to commit suicide. The technique is naturalistic, and the play's subject matter, like that of Strindberg and Ibsen, is discomforting to contemporary audiences.

August Wilson's (1945–2005) Pittsburgh Cycle treats the subject of black life in modern America. He completed this series of ten plays just before he died in 2005, and each of the first four won the New York Drama Critics' Circle Award for best play of the year. All of Wilson's plays have explored how the heritage of blacks enables them to live intelligently in the present, with understanding and dignity. People in his plays have lost touch with the past and, for that reason, risk a loss of self-understanding. Wilson's plays also show the pain endured by blacks in a country that is supposedly the land of opportunity. Like Arthur Miller in *Death of a Salesman* and Lorraine Hansberry in *A Raisin in the Sun*, Wilson explores the nature and consequences of the American dream, especially for those effectively excluded from this dream. Blacks' frustration, exploitation, and suffering are presented through Wilson's powerful characters, such as Troy Maxson in *Fences* (1985). Troy is a garbage collector who was a star baseball player at a time when blacks could not play in the major leagues. The play centers on Maxson's anger, his pride in his family, and his concerns for his son, who is growing up into a world in which he must empower himself to achieve what he most wants for himself. Cory, Troy's son, does not see the same kind of discrimination and has not felt the unfairness that was Troy's primary experience in growing up. Showing the world as Troy Maxson sees it is one of the functions of the play.

Wilson's plays have a naturalistic surface, but they also allude to the supernatural, as in *The Piano Lesson* (1990). Some of the roots of this tradition are in the black church and some in African religion, a source shared by Soyinka and Wilson, among others.

Among current playwrights is David Henry Hwang (b. 1957), who has been active in writing for both stage and film. His work often centers on Chinese Americans and the problems they encounter in their experiences in the United States. Hwang has sensitized audiences to subjects about which playwrights had hitherto been silent. His first success, *FOB* (1980), focused on how new immigrants were viewed by Chinese Americans who had already assimilated. The play's title is an acronym for "fresh off the boat." Hwang's most successful play, *M. Butterfly* (1987), is about a romance between a French diplomat and a transvestite Chinese opera singer. *Yellow Face* (2009) is his most personal play, with a protagonist named DHH fuming about the choice of a white actor for the main Eurasian character in *Miss Saigon*. *Yellow Face* exposes David Henry Hwang's shortcomings as explicitly as it exposes the stresses caused by ethnic categories in contemporary theater.

Since his short but intense *The Zoo Story* (1958) came out, Edward Albee (b. 1928) has been a powerful force in American theater. He has won three Pulitzer Prizes for drama: for *A Delicate Balance* (1966), *Seascape* (1974), and *Three Tall Women* (1991). He is better known for *Who's Afraid of Virginia Woolf?* (1961), however, a portrait of a violent, alcohol-filled marriage between academics George and Martha, portrayed memorably by Richard Burton and Elizabeth Taylor in Mike Nichols's 1966 film version. Not all of Albee's plays have been successful, but throughout his career he has maintained a reputation as an important experimentalist. His Tony Award–winning play *The Goat, or Who Is Sylvia?* (2002) is a complex portrait of a prize-winning architect who falls in love with a goat. Albee thus pushes beyond the questions of heterosexuality and homosexuality into the taboo of bestiality. Beneath the surface, however, he presses the issues of tragedy as it is expressed in a modern situation.

David Mamet (b. 1947) responds to a social situation in *Oleanna* (1992). The characters, a male college professor and a female student, at first adopt an ordinary teacher-student relationship; eventually, though, that relationship alters. Mamet explores questions of power and issues of sexual harassment. As the lines he draws shift back and forth, the audience never knows exactly how clear the lines are meant to be. The issues in the play are thus subject to a number of different interpretations. Widely considered Mamet's best play, *Glengarry Glen Ross* (1983) offers a savage portrait of the masculine world of salesmanship. Deception, competition, and outright theft dominate the play, demonstrating a failure of values of the main characters, all of whom feel justified in their willingness to push property on those who do not want or need it. Mamet's language carries the weight of a philosophy that scorns the get-ahead attitude of the salesman.

Tony Kushner's two-part drama *Angels in America: Millennium Approaches* (1992) and *Perestroika* (1992) explores issues in modern American history, with an emphasis on religion, politics, and a variety of hysterias. The plays explore homophobia, red-baiting politics, and the impact of AIDS on contemporary society. The open, dynamic structure of the work is enormously powerful. The entire drama lasts six and a half hours and has been seen not only in San Francisco, where it opened, but also in New York, London, other European cities, and regional theaters throughout the United States. The Golden Globe Award–winning 2003 HBO production introduced the play to many millions of viewers and expanded some of Kushner's vision for the drama. His *Homebody/Kabul* (2001), which examines the political circumstances in Afghanistan in 1998 after U.S. bombing raids, reflects his continuing interest in exploring contemporary historical events; his chamber opera *Caroline, or Change* (2003) considers racial issues in Louisiana in 1963.

In the late 1990s, young men and women made important contributions to theater. Jose Rivera (b. 1955) presented two plays that drew on the tradition of magic realism that is prominent in Latin American fiction. *Marisol* (1992) and *Cloud Tectonics* (1995) are visually and emotionally impressive pieces that work counter to the Ibsenist tradition of realism. As especially theatrical pieces, they give the director a considerable degree of freedom in staging. Rivera's *Boleros for the Disenchanted,* staged at the Yale Repertory Theatre in May 2008, treats the subjects of love, aging, and marriage.

Paula Vogel (b. 1951) created a portrait of an adolescent girl, Li'l Bit, involved with an incestuous Uncle Peck in *How I Learned to Drive* (1997). The play won the 1998 Pulitzer Prize and established Vogel as one of the most important American playwrights. Her play *The Long Christmas Ride Home* (2003) continued her experimentation in the realm of puppet theater. The effect recalls techniques of Japanese Bunraku theater.

Nilo Cruz (b. 1961) won the Pulitzer Prize in 2003 for *Anna in the Tropics.* He was the first Hispanic Pulitzer winner in drama. Among his many plays is *Lorca in a Green Dress* (2003); it and *Beauty of the Father* (2007) are experiments in literary allusion.

Moisés Kaufman's Tectonic Theater Project began *The Laramie Project* in 1998, after Matthew Shepard, a young gay man, was brutally beaten, tied to a fence, and left to die in Laramie, Wyoming. The group conducted interviews of townspeople for a year and a half and presented the play, which is in some ways a portrait of the community, in Laramie in 2000. It has been televised and seen across the country.

Doug Wright (b. 1962) created a play called *I Am My Own Wife,* about Charlotte von Mahlsdorf, a transvestite who survived the Nazis and the Russians in Berlin. Directed by Moisés Kaufman, *I Am My Own Wife* won every major award in 2004, including the Pulitzer. The single actor on stage, Jefferson Mays, played dozens of characters, all convincingly.

Neil LaBute (b. 1963) makes films as well as writing plays. His *The Shape of Things* (2001) uses a highly experimental approach to language in which silences play a profound role as he explores the dark side of femininity and the complexities of art.

John Patrick Shanley (b. 1950) won the Pulitzer Prize in 2005 for *Doubt,* a play about a Catholic nun's suspicions about the behavior of a priest who befriends a young boy. The staging of the play was traditional, but the subject matter struck a painful note for some audiences.

Rolin Jones's (b. 1972) experimental and enormously entertaining *The Intelligent Design of Jenny Chow* (2006) resembles a video game, with Jenny creating a robotic other who crosses continents. Suzan-Lori Parks's (b. 1963) extraordinary experiment *365 Days/365 Plays* involved her writing a play every day for a year. She has permitted groups to stage the plays without paying royalties, and projects have been established to produce the plays across the country.

Rajiv Joseph (b. 1974) spent several years with the Peace Corps in Senegal; his best-known play is *Bengal Tiger at the Baghdad Zoo* (2009), starring Robin Williams as the tiger. A powerful political drama set in Iraq, it was a finalist for the Pulitzer Prize. Aditi Brennan Kapil's *Agnes under the Big Top: A Tall Tale* (2011) addresses the pain of immigrants in the United States and features a subway train driven by a former Bulgarian ringmaster. Much of the play is dark, set in a subway with a remarkable variety of ethnic and handicapped characters.

Katori Hall (b. 1981) has had a remarkable first success with *The Mountaintop* (2011), which portrays a very human Dr. Martin Luther King on the night before he was assassinated. Amy Herzog (b. 1978) has written *After the Revolution* (2010), which portrays a family of aging lefties holding on to earlier ideals, and *Belleville* (2011), about an expatriate couple in Paris whose marriage falls apart when their deceptions catch up with them. Quiara Alegría Hudes (b. 1977) was nominated for a Pulitzer Prize for the book of the musical *In the Heights* (2008) and won the prize for her 2011 play, *Water by the Spoonful*, which focuses on the return of Iraq veterans. These and many other excellent playwrights are making contemporary American drama a powerful force all over the globe.

Drama in Europe: England, Ireland, and France

English playwright Harold Pinter's (1930–2008) distinctive style, developed in the late 1950s and early 1960s, was connected with some of the absurdist experiments in drama. His dialogue was acerbic, repetitive, sometimes apparently aimless. However, he was able to produce intense emotional situations, such as in *The Dumb Waiter* (1957), in which two "hit men" wait for instructions in a basement room. *The Caretaker* (1960) and *The Homecoming* (1965), Pinter's first commercial successes, established him as a major figure in modern theater. He was also a screenwriter for such films as *The Quiller Memorandum* (1966), *The French Lieutenant's Woman* (1981), and *The Handmaid's Tale* (1990). His experiments with time and sequence in his full-length play *Betrayal* (1978), for which he also wrote the screenplay, have inspired other playwrights, such as Paula Vogel, to experiment with the backward movement of action.

Some of Caryl Churchill's (b. 1938) plays, emphasizing themes of socialism, colonialism, and feminism, were developed in workshops and collaborations with actors and directors. Early in the first stages of writing a play, Churchill experiments by spending time in the environments her play depicts. When she was working on *Top Girls* (1982), she came up with the idea of setting the action in an employment agency after she had talked with many people who work in the business world. For *Serious Money* (1987), she and the group developing the play spent time at the London Stock Exchange, absorbing the atmosphere of frenetic buying and selling.

Jez Butterworth's (b. 1969) *Jerusalem* (2009) opened to impressive reviews in London and in New York. Mark Rylance starred as a wildly eccentric "lord of misrule" trying to keep a piece of land away from the local town council, whose aim was to clean up the area, evict him, and erect new dwellings.

Irish playwright Brian Friel (b. 1929) began his career as an experimentalist in *Philadelphia, Here I Come!* (1964), in which Gar O'Donnell, the main character, appears both as his public self, represented by one actor, and as his private self, represented by another actor. This experimental drama ran for 326 performances on Broadway. Friel's political drama *Freedom of the City* (1974) addresses the "troubles" in Northern Ireland at a time of bombings and threats. *Translations* (1980) experiments with language—having Irish-speaking characters speak Irish to one another to baffle the British characters, while we "listen in" as if the Irish were being translated for us. *Faith Healer* (1979) presents characters onstage one at a time—with no interaction—telling us their stories in a powerful way. Throughout his career, Friel has been on the cutting edge of experimentation.

Marina Carr (b. 1964) is one of Ireland's most respected playwrights. *Portia Coughlan* (1996), which opened in Dublin and London, won the Susan Smith Blackburn Prize; *By the Bog of Cats* (1998) is a retelling of the story of Medea; *On Raftery's Hill* (2000) is a tale of madness and incest in Ireland's isolating west country. Another Irish playwright, Moira Buffini (b. 1965), wrote *Silence* (1999), which won the Susan Smith Blackburn Prize for best play by a woman. Buffini's *Welcome to Thebes* (2010) echoes Greek drama in a play about African political instability in which a political cadre of men comes to a ravaged nation now in the hands of women and tries to tell them how they must run their government. A stunning production, with a huge cast, was mounted at the enormous Olivier Theatre on London's South Bank.

Martin McDonagh (b. 1970) startled the London theater scene with his Leenane trilogy: *The Beauty Queen of Leenane* (1996), *A Skull in Connemara* (1997), and *The Lonesome West* (1997). These three plays and his *The Cripple of Inishmaan* (1996) were produced at the same time in London, a record for a twenty-seven-year-old playwright. His *The Lieutenant of Inishmore* (2003) is a brutal farce centering on IRA terrorism. His 2003 play *The Pillowman* had pedophilia as its subject. McDonagh is one of the most productive modern playwrights.

French playwright Yasmina Reza (b. 1959) had great success in France, England, the United States, and many other nations with her award-winning comedy *"Art,"* which raises unexpected questions about taste and friendship. *God of Carnage* (2006) has also been produced in many countries, solidifying her stature as a major modern playwright. Both of these plays have been made into films, and both are startling in part because they seem so normal at first and then develop in shocking ways.

Drama in Asia and Africa

China's most distinguished modern playwright, Gao Xingjian (b. 1940), now lives and writes in Paris, after having lived through the Cultural Revolution of the 1960s, when all his plays and manuscripts were destroyed and he was forced to work as a laborer for several years. His work has been banned in China because it is seen as critical of the communist system in that country. Having lived in France since 1987, Gao has been influenced by playwrights such as Samuel Beckett and Bertolt Brecht. His *Bus Stop* (1983) resembles Beckett's *Waiting for Godot* in that the characters wait patiently for the bus to come—a symbol of a positive change in their lives—but it never arrives. *The Other Shore* (1986) explores the religious aspirations of the characters from a perspective of Pure Land Buddhism, the other shore being the land of the dead, a world with ambiguous virtues. Gao is also a novelist and wrote *Soul Mountain* (1989), a best-seller in its English translation (1999). Gao won the Nobel Prize for literature in 2000.

Athol Fugard (b. 1932), a South African, writes powerful plays that work well on conventional proscenium stages. Like Shepard's, his subject matter is not the kind that permits an audience to sit back, relax, and appreciate the drama with a sense of detachment. Instead, the plays usually disturb audiences. His primary subject matter is the devastation—for blacks and whites—caused by apartheid in South Africa. Fugard's work with black actors in South Africa produced a vital experimental theater out of which his best early work grew. Fugard's *The Blood Knot* (1961) and *Boesman and Lena* (1969), part of a trilogy on South Africa, are based on the theme of racial discrimination. But other plays, such as *A Lesson from Aloes* (1978) and *My Children! My Africa!* (1989), highlight the problems of individuals in relation to their political world. Fugard is in many ways a traditional playwright, except for his subject matter. His characters are thoroughly developed, but with great economy. In *"MASTER HAROLD" . . . and the boys,* for example, we are given a deep understanding of Hally and Sam, whose relationship, past, present, and future, is the center of the play. Fugard is not writing the well-made play, any more than the other contemporary playwrights in this collection are. There is nothing "mechanical" in Fugard's work; rather, it conveys a sense of organic growth, of actions arising from perceptible conditions and historical circumstances. These contribute to the sense of integrity that his plays communicate. Fugard's three recent plays, *Coming Home* (2009), *Have You Seen Us* (2009), and *The Train Driver* (2010), take us from Capetown to Los Angeles, but they remain powerful statements of political and social reality in the tradition of most of his work. His plays have been performed in South Africa, Europe, and North and South America.

The plays of Nobel Prize winner Wole Soyinka (b. 1934) have enjoyed international celebrity far from his native Nigeria. *The Strong Breed* (1964), *Madmen and Specialists* (1971), *The Bacchae of Euripides* (1973), and *Death and the King's Horseman* (1975) are all extraordinary by virtue of Soyinka's inclusion of African themes and Yoruba rituals as well as his emphasis on the African sense of community. He has demonstrated the universality of his characters and their circumstances.

Just as Soyinka reinterpreted Euripides' *The Bacchae*, Aimé Césaire (1913–2008), from Martinique, completely reinterpreted Shakespeare's *Tempest* into his own *A Tempest* (1993), using Shakespeare's characters and an ending that satisfied him much more than the original. Césaire produced a remarkable body of work including drama, poetry, and essays. *A Season in the Congo* (1990) is only one of his pointedly political plays.

Bernard Dadié (b. 1916), from the Ivory Coast, is also interested in political drama. His *Monsieur Thôgô-gnini* (1970) is a satire on political oppression featuring an African king in 1840. The name means "one who will stop at nothing," and the play begins ironically with the sound of "Old Man River," as a white trader enters to begin doing business. Most of Dadié's plays were written originally in French. He is famous for a poem that begins, "Thank God for creating me black."

The range of African drama has been extraordinary and continues to challenge theater spaces throughout the world.

The Contemporary Theater

In the major cities of the world, most theaters comparable to those on Broadway and London's West End are compatible with the needs of nineteenth-century realist plays, many of which still entertain a wide range of audiences. However, modern theaters are not limited to large urban centers, and those that have been built since the 1950s recognize the needs of experimental drama as well as traditional drama.

Theater in the round, which seats audience members on all sides of the actors, has been exceptionally powerful for certain plays. Peter Weiss's *The Persecution and Assassination of Jean-Paul Marat as Performed by the Inmates of the Asylum of Charenton under the Direction of the Marquis de Sade* (1964) was especially effective in this format. Many contemporary theaters attempt to accommodate the needs of theater in the round, the thrust theater (which is virtually in the round), and the proscenium theater, all in one place. Such a theater is illustrated in Figure 31: the Questors Theatre in Ealing, London, built in 1964.

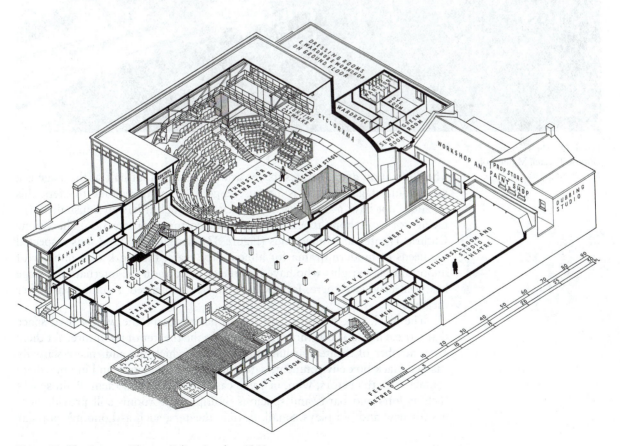

Figure 31. The Questors Theatre, Ealing, London, 1964.

Figure 32. The Tyrone Guthrie Theater, Minneapolis, Minnesota, 1963.

The illustration demonstrates its versatility, showing that half of the stage is a proscenium stage and half is a thrust stage. Like many regional theaters, this one does not have a large seating capacity, although it has an unusually large facility for workshops, rehearsal spaces, and costume construction. The Tyrone Guthrie Theater in Minneapolis (Figure 32), designed in 1963, has respected the needs of modern drama for almost fifty years; the work of a number of important playwrights who have become significant on the international stage has been produced there. Its flexible plan has influenced a number of newer theaters.

The black box theater seems not to have become the widely used space that writers in the 1960s thought it might, as the theater of the future. Yet there are a number of theaters around the world in which the audience essentially sits in a black box environment, with only a minimal setting and in immediate contact with the actors, who, in some cases, work around them. Plain spaces such as lofts and barns and spacious multipurpose rooms still provide venues for new and old plays. Small, flexible theaters, such as London's popular

Cottlesloe, seat three hundred at most; their intimacy intensifies the effect of the drama.

Other theatrical experiments have explored the power of spaces one would not have thought appropriate for drama. For example, Wladimir Pereira Cardoso designed an elaborate welded-steel set for a production of Jean Genet's *The Balcony* in the Ruth Escobar Theater in São Paulo, Brazil. The set was a huge suspended cone, in which people sat looking inward at the actors, who were suspended in the spherical space before them. The production was first staged in 1969 and was seen through 1971 and most of 1972 by many thousands of people. The set was constructed of eighty tons of iron assembled like a trellis and requiring 500,000 welds. The entire inside of the theater was torn out to accommodate the new set. The audience of 250 was seated on circular platforms, and the actors moved through the space on ramps, on suspended cables, and on moving platforms. The same theater produced *The Voyage,* an adaptation of the epic poem *The Lusiads,* about the origin of the Portuguese people. That set used open welded platforms suggesting ships' decks. In Dubrovnik, Croatia, a replica of Columbus's *Santa Maria*—built much larger than the original—was used to stage Miroslav Krleza's expressionist play *Christopher Columbus,* written in 1917. The ship was docked in Dubrovnik Harbor for the performances.

Richard Foreman's (b. 1937) Ontological-Hysteric Theater performs in a loft in New York City with all audience members facing in the same direction. This is not fundamentally different from the traditional proscenium theater, but the open loft space and the visible movements of actors offstage create a new relationship to the action. Foreman's work, such as *Sophia = (Wisdom)* (1970 and later), which has been performed in many parts, offers none of the usually accepted narrative clues to its action. Rather, it explores hitherto hidden aspects of experience, such as sexual taboos and unorthodox relationships. The relationship of the author to the performance is also experimental in Foreman's theater, since he directs his actors as if they were extensions of his will, often using a loud buzzer. His work, begun in the 1960s, continues to this day. He collaborated in the staging of Suzan-Lori Parks's *Venus* (1996).

Proscenium theaters probably make up the largest number of dramatic spaces even today, because of the large number of restored theaters whose designs generally date to the era of the Drury Lane Theatre renovations in the late eighteenth and early nineteenth centuries. Many technical innovations, such as portable microphones, elaborate methods for allowing actors to fly (Figure 33), and stage effects such as fog and stage flooding, have made it possible for audiences in larger theaters to feel closely connected with the dramatic action. Techniques that create a striking effect—such as the simulation of heavy rainfall in Sarah Ruhl's *Eurydice* when Eurydice, and later Orpheus, descending to the underworld, arrives in a stunning downpour in an elevator—would have been difficult, if not impossible, in earlier centuries.

Music and dance are central to some contemporary dramas that are not considered musicals, such as Wole Soyinka's *The Lion and the Jewel* (1963). Sound systems in modern theaters can accommodate the most difficult audio challenges. Video, too, is common in contemporary theater, whether in the

Figure 33. Visual effects and technical apparatus featured prominently in the rock musical *Spider-Man: Turn Off the Dark* (2011). In this scene, Spider-Man and the Green Goblin fly over the audience.

form of projections on scrims or working television sets in living rooms or bedrooms on stage. Complex lighting and shifting scene changes can be made convincingly realistic. What Aristotle called "spectacle" has been available in most ages in the theater, but the technology of the digital age provides resources never before possible. Even so, a great many successful dramatists insist on the simplest of dramatic effects and the simplest of theatrical spaces.

The Contemporary Actor

For the most part, the ambition of eighteenth-century British actor David Garrick to create a style of acting that is as natural as everyday life has been the goal for most contemporary actors. Marlon Brando put Stanislavski's theories of acting to work in Tennessee Williams's *A Streetcar Named Desire* and became celebrated as a Method actor. He studied at the Actors Studio, which was founded by Elia Kazan and others but later run and developed by Lee Strasberg with other important teachers such as Sanford Meisner. The modern Method involved relaxation techniques, memory exercises, and a great deal of self-analysis. The point, as Stanislavski said, was to re-create in oneself the life of the character on stage.

Marlon Brando became the first widely celebrated Method actor, and his particular style, of mumbling lines or moodily half-articulating them, became associated unfairly with Method acting. James Dean, who was a film star rather than a stage star, emulated him and made it seem all the more certain that Brando's style was that of the Method actor. But other Method

Figure 34. Al Pacino as salesman Erie Smith in Eugene O'Neill's *Hughie* (1996) at Circle in the Square Theatre.

actors, such as Al Pacino (Figure 34), who has done some important stage work, particularly in Eugene O'Neill's *Hughie* in 1996, also studied with Lee Strasberg. Pacino can be seen online in a video on YouTube reading and discussing the play.

Among the great actors to have worked in the Actors Studio, Lee J. Cobb is one who seems to have influenced a number of later actors, such as George C. Scott in the 1960s. Robert de Niro, Ellen Burstyn, Jane Fonda, Paul Newman, Joanne Woodward, Maureen Stapleton, Rod Steiger, Christopher Walken, Mickey Rourke, Julia Roberts, Harvey Keitel, Sidney Poitier, Jack Nicholson, Steve McQueen, and Marilyn Monroe were all products of the Actors Studio. The influence of the Method is still present in contemporary drama.

In England, however, the traditional training of actors continues. Whereas Method acting concentrates on the inner potential of the actor's psyche, the Royal Academy of Dramatic Arts in London and the London Academy of Music and Dramatic Arts train actors in the traditional basics, such as dance and movement, voice and projection, analysis of texts, and the study of the techniques of the best historical actors. John Gielgud, Laurence Olivier, Jeremy Irons, and Judi Dench (Figure 35) are products of such training. Sometimes their techniques are described as being external—they are "applied" outwardly as a means of creating the character on stage—as opposed to the internal process

Figure 35. Judi Dench as Viola with Gordon Reid as Sebastian in the 1969 production of *Twelfth Night* at the Royal Shakespeare Theatre.

of the Method actor. Both techniques work well on the modern stage, and some actors (such as Johnny Depp and Julianne Moore) use them both.

The purpose of the actor is to create character in the hope that we will believe the character rather than the actor. And in the dramas that disregard psychological realism, the purpose of the actor is to stimulate the audience into a recognition of the power of the drama itself and to interpret the action in an authentic and honest fashion.

Timeline Contemporary Drama

Date	Theater	Political	Social/Cultural
1950–1960	**1950:** Anna Deavere Smith, African American playwright and actress, is born. Among her works are *Fires in the Mirror* (1991) and *Twilight: Los Angeles, 1992* (1992).	**1950:** U.S. Senator Joseph McCarthy begins his war on Communism by investigating the alleged "un-American activities" of hundreds of U.S. citizens.	
	1951: Lee Strasberg becomes artistic director of the Actors Studio in New York.	**1951:** The USSR explodes its first atomic bomb.	**1952:** Ralph Ellison (1914–1994), African American novelist, publishes *Invisible Man*.
		1953: Joseph Stalin dies.	
	1954: Joseph Papp founds the New York Shakespeare festival.	**1954:** *Brown v. Board of Education* finds school segregation unconstitutional.	**1953:** The English translation of French author Simone de Beauvoir's *The Second Sex* (1949) is published in the United States.
	1956: John Osborne's *Look Back in Anger* is produced in London.	**1954:** Senator Joseph McCarthy's witch hunt for Communist infiltration in the United States ends.	**1954:** Elvis Presley (1935–1977) makes his first recording at Sun Studios.
	1956: Tony Kushner, American playwright, is born. He is best known for the plays *Angels in America, Parts One and Two* (1992).	**1955:** Communist Eastern European allies sign the Warsaw Pact.	
		1955: Montgomery, Alabama, bus boycott	
		1958: Fidel Castro begins total war against Batista in Cuba; in 1959 he becomes premier.	**1957:** Jack Kerouac (1922–1969) publishes *On the Road*.
	1959: Jerzy Grotowski establishes the Laboratory Theatre in Poland. In 1968 he publishes *Towards a Poor Theatre*.	**1958–1969:** Charles de Gaulle is president of France.	
1960–1970	**1960s:** Off-off-Broadway flourishes with the formation of such groups as Café Cino (1958), La Mama ETC (1962), the Open Theatre (1963), and the Performance Group (1967).	**1960:** The Belgian Congo is granted independence.	
		1961: The Berlin Wall blocks movement to and from East and West Germany.	
	1962: Peter Schumann founds the Bread and Puppet Theater, an influential political ensemble, in New York City.	**1962:** The cold war reaches one of its tensest moments when the United States confronts the USSR over Soviet nuclear missile bases in Cuba.	**1962:** James Watson and Francis Crick share the Nobel Prize for defining the 3-D molecular structure of DNA.
	1963: The National Theatre is established in London under the direction of Laurence Olivier.	**1962:** The first U.S. combat troops are sent to fight in South Vietnam.	**1962:** César Chávez (1927–1993) organizes California migrant farm workers.
	1964: Ariane Mnouchkine forms the Théâtre du Soleil in Paris.	**1963:** President John F. Kennedy is assassinated in Dallas.	**1962:** Alexander Solzhenitsyn's *One Day in the Life of Ivan Denisovich* describes life in the Soviet gulag.
	1964: Peter Brook's production of Peter Weiss's *Marat/Sade* opens at the Royal Shakespeare Company.	**1965:** Malcolm X is assassinated in New York.	**1964:** The Beatles appear on *The Ed Sullivan Show*.
			1965: The National Endowment for the Arts is established by the U.S. government.

Contemporary Drama (*continued*)

Date	Theater	Political	Social/Cultural
1960–1970 (continued)	**1968:** The Negro Ensemble Company is established in the United States under the direction of Douglas Turner Ward.	**1967:** In the Six-Day War, Israel responds to Arab provocation by capturing territory from Egypt, Syria, and Jordan.	**1966:** The National Organization for Women (NOW) is established to end discrimination against women.
	1968: The Living Theatre produces its highly influential experimental work *Paradise Now*.	**1967:** Thurgood Marshall (1908–1993) is the first African American appointed to the U.S. Supreme Court.	**1967:** Dr. Christiaan N. Barnard performs the world's first human heart transplant operation in South Africa.
	1968: Theatrical censorship, in place since the Licensing Act of 1737, is finally abolished in England.	**1968:** The American civil rights leader Martin Luther King Jr. is assassinated.	
	1968: *Hair!*, the first rock musical, hits Broadway; it is followed by *Jesus Christ Superstar* in 1971.	**1968:** Students demonstrate throughout France.	**1969:** U.S. astronaut Neil Armstrong walks on the moon.
	1968: The Performance Group produces *Dionysus in 69* under the direction of Richard Schechner.		**1969:** New York City police raid the Stonewall Inn, a gay bar, and the resulting three-day protest becomes a symbol for the emerging gay rights movement.
1970–1980	**1970:** Peter Brook's acclaimed production of *A Midsummer Night's Dream* opens at the Royal Shakespeare Company.	**1970–1975:** Civil war is fought in Cambodia; Communist leader Pol Pot takes power in 1975 and begins genocidal campaign.	**1970:** First celebration of Earth Day in the United States
	1971: Peter Stein, influential German director, produces *Peer Gynt*.	**1972:** U.S. President Richard Nixon and Soviet leader Leonid Brezhnev sign the Strategic Arms Limitation Treaty (SALT).	
		1972: Philippine President Ferdinand Marcos declares martial law and assumes dictatorial powers.	
		1973: U.S. troops are withdrawn from Vietnam.	**1973:** In *Roe v. Wade,* the U.S. Supreme Court legalizes abortion.
		1974: President Nixon resigns from office as a result of the Watergate scandal.	
	1975: Michael Bennett's musical *A Chorus Line* opens on Broadway and runs until 1990.	**1975:** The Spanish dictator Francisco Franco dies.	
		1976: The Chinese Communist leader Mao Zedong dies. Deng Xiaoping emerges as the new Chinese leader in 1978.	**1976:** The Episcopal Church approves the ordination of women to be priests and bishops.
	1977: María Irene Fornés's *Fefu and Her Friends* is produced.	**1976:** Waves of violence against apartheid in Cape Town, Soweto, and Johannesburg, South Africa	
	1978: Harold Pinter's *Betrayal* premieres at the National Theatre in London.		

Date	Theater	Political	Social/Cultural
1970–1980 (continued)	**1979:** Caryl Churchill's *Cloud Nine* premieres. **1979:** Stephen Sondheim's *Sweeney Todd* opens on Broadway. Other musicals by the prolific composer include *Sunday in the Park with George* (1984), *Into the Woods* (1987), and *Passion* (1995).	**1979:** After the overthrow of Shah Mohammad Reza Pahlavi, the Ayatollah Khomeini establishes the Islamic Republic of Iran.	
1980–1990	**1980:** Sam Shepard's *True West* premieres. **1982:** Athol Fugard's *"MASTER HAROLD" . . . and the boys* premieres at the Yale Repertory Theatre. **1983:** Marsha Norman's *'night, Mother* opens at New York's Golden Theatre and wins the Pulitzer Prize. **1985:** August Wilson's *Fences* premieres at the Yale Repertory Theatre and wins the Pulitzer Prize in 1987. **1987:** The immensely popular Broadway adaptation of Victor Hugo's *Les Misérables* opens, ultimately closing in March 2003.	**1980:** The Iran-Iraq War begins when Iraq invades Iran; the war lasts for eight years. **1981:** General Idi Amin begins his eight-year reign of terror in Uganda. **1981:** Egyptian leader Anwar Sadat is assassinated by Muslim extremists. **1985:** Mikhail Gorbachev becomes the leader of the Soviet Union and institutes a policy of *glasnost* (openness). **1989:** A student demonstration in Beijing's Tiananmen Square results in bloodshed. **1989:** Communism crumbles in Eastern Europe, and the Berlin Wall is torn down.	**1981:** Sandra Day O'Connor becomes the first woman appointed to the U.S. Supreme Court. **1981:** IBM markets its first personal computer. **1982:** Wisconsin becomes the first state to protect gays and lesbians under civil rights legislation. **1986:** In *Bowers v. Hardwick,* the U.S. Supreme Court upholds the constitutionality of the Georgia state law against sodomy. **1986:** The U.S. space shuttle *Challenger* explodes seconds after liftoff, killing all seven on board.
1990–2000	**1990s:** In a proliferation of Shakespeare on film, new versions of *Hamlet, Henry V, Much Ado about Nothing, Othello,* and *Richard III* are released.	**1990:** Iraq invades Kuwait, which leads to the Gulf War in 1991. **1990:** East and West Germany reunite after 45 years of separation. **1990:** The South African nationalist leader Nelson Mandela is released from prison. **1990–1991:** South Africa repeals its apartheid laws. **1991:** The Soviet Union collapses. U.S. President George H. W. Bush officially recognizes the twelve new countries created as a result.	**1990:** Octavio Paz, Mexican poet, receives the Nobel Prize for literature. **1990:** The National Endowment for the Arts is attacked when controversial awards are publicized.

Date	Theater	Political	Social/Cultural
1990–2000 (continued)	**1992:** David Mamet's *Oleanna* premieres off-Broadway and runs for over 250 performances.	**1991:** Yugoslavia dissolves. Croatia, Slovenia, Bosnia-Herzegovina, and Macedonia declare independence, and bitter fighting ensues for several years. **1994:** Nelson Mandela is elected the first black president of South Africa after that nation's first multiracial elections. **1994:** Chechnya declares independence from Russia, and Russian troops invade the republic. Russia invades again in 1999.	**1993:** Toni Morrison (b. 1931), African American novelist, is awarded the Nobel Prize for literature. **mid-1990s:** *Internet* and *World Wide Web* become household words.
	1996: Jonathan Larson's *Rent*, a musical based on Puccini's *La Bohème*, wins the Pulitzer Prize. **1997:** Martin McDonagh, at age 27, has four plays running simultaneously in London. **1998:** Paula Vogel's play *How I Learned to Drive* wins the Pulitzer Prize. **1998:** Yasmina Reza's *"Art"* wins a Tony Award for best play.	**1995:** The Israeli leader Yitzhak Rabin is assassinated. **1997:** Hong Kong is returned to China after 156 years as a British colony. **1998:** Asian nations face a dramatic recession after economic booms of the 1980s and early 1990s. **1999:** Congress impeaches President Clinton for his improper conduct in the White House, but the president remains in office. **1999:** U.N. troops keep a tentative peace between ethnic Albanians and Serbian Albanians in Kosovo. **1999:** The United States transfers the Panama Canal to Panama.	**1995:** Shannon Faulkner is the first woman to be admitted to the Citadel military academy. **1995:** The National Endowment for the Arts budget is slashed by the newly elected Republican Congress. The Public Broadcasting Corporation and the National Endowment for the Humanities also come under fire. **1996:** In *Rome v. Evans,* the U.S. Supreme Court rules that the equal protection clause of the Constitution applies to lesbians and gay men. **1997:** Scottish scientist Ian Wilmot clones a sheep.
2000–present	**2000:** Lee Blessing's *Cobb* makes a political statement about baseball. **2002:** Suzan-Lori Parks's *Topdog/Underdog* wins the Pulitzer Prize. **2002:** Edward Albee's *The Goat, or Who Is Sylvia?* wins the Drama Desk Award for best play. **2003:** Nilo Cruz's *Anna in the Tropics* wins the Pulitzer Prize. **2004:** Doug Wright's *I Am My Own Wife* wins the Pulitzer Prize. **2007:** David Lindsay-Abaire's *Rabbit Hole* wins the Pulitzer Prize.	**2000:** Boris Yeltsin resigns as president of Russia. **2001:** On September 11, Al Qaeda terrorists destroy the World Trade Center with two airliners. A third plane damages the Pentagon, and a fourth crashes in Pennsylvania. **2002:** U.S. attacks Taliban forces in Afghanistan. **2003:** U.S. attacks Saddam Hussein in Iraq, bringing down his government.	**2000:** Gao Xingjian wins the Nobel Prize for literature. **2001:** The human genome is decoded. **2003:** A law barring "partial-birth" abortions comes under fire with legal challenges. **2004:** *Spirit* and *Rover* explore the surface of Mars, sending back 3-D images. **2007:** China launches its first lunar orbiter in preparation for sending an astronaut to the moon in 2020.

Date	Theater	Political	Social/Cultural
2000–present (continued)	**2008:** Conor McPherson's *The Seafarer* is produced on Broadway.	**2008:** America's first black president, Barack Obama (b. 1961), is elected.	**2008:** Housing bubble bursts in United States; global economy is in recession.
	2008: Tracy Letts's *August: Osage County* wins the Pulitzer Prize.	**2009:** The Tea Party movement gains popularity in the United States.	**2009:** Barack Obama wins the Nobel Peace Prize.
	2009: Lynn Nottage's *Ruined* wins the Pulitzer Prize.		**2010:** Apple introduces the iPad line of tablet computers.
	2009: Rajiv Joseph's *Bengal Tiger at the Baghdad Zoo* and Sarah Ruhl's *In the Next Room: or, The Vibrator Play* are produced.		
	2011: Bruce Norris's *Clybourne Park* wins the Pulitzer Prize.	**2011:** The Arab Spring, a wave of pro-democracy demonstrations, overthrows the governments of Tunisia, Egypt, and Libya; Syria reaches the brink of civil war.	**2011:** *Time* magazine names "The Protester" its "Person of the Year."
			2011: Facebook has more than 840 million users.
		2011: Osama bin Laden, leader of Al Qaeda, is killed by the United States military.	
		2011: Euro-zone debt crisis escalates.	

Caryl Churchill

Caryl Churchill (b. 1938) is in many ways a conventional middle-class woman. She was born in London to a comfortable family; her father was a political cartoonist and her mother a model. During World War II, her family emigrated to Canada, and much of her growing up was done in Montreal. She returned to England for college, receiving her degree in English literature at Oxford.

Churchill says that through all these years she did all the right things. She was a proper intellectual, a proper student, a proper person. She began writing plays at Oxford, where they were produced by students. After college, she married David Harter, also from Oxford, who became a lawyer in London. She raised three sons and at the same time tried to keep alive her dream of being a writer. Most of her early work was written for radio, and many of the plays were short. With so many children in the house, she says, it was difficult to sustain a long project.

Churchill's social conscience has been a significant part of her playwriting and her life. She found herself sometimes depressed by the dullness of the middle-class life demanded of the wife of a lawyer, and much of her early drama is satire directed at what many people thought was an enviable lifestyle.

Her husband left a very lucrative law practice in the early 1970s and has since devoted himself to helping the poor at a nearby legal aid center. Churchill has become involved in theater groups, among them a group of women called Monstrous Regiment. She is closely aligned with the Royal Court Theatre in London, noted for producing satiric, biting, experimental drama with a punch.

Churchill's first play staged at the Royal Court Theatre was a farcical but serious drama called *Owners* (1972). It attacks the way the concept of ownership destroys potential relationships. Churchill's basic socialist views are very apparent in the play, which is a critique of the values that most capitalists take for granted: being aggressive, getting ahead, doing well. Although this play is not explicitly feminist, Churchill combines socialism and feminism in most of her plays, thus often producing an unusual approach to her subject matter. *Owners* has been criticized for its Brechtian use of disconnected scenes and its loose plot, but when it was produced off Broadway in 1973, it marked Churchill as a serious playwright.

After a year as a playwright in residence at the Royal Court Theatre, Churchill produced *Objections to Sex and Violence* (1975). The play was not immensely successful, but it introduced themes of feminism into her work, among other themes. The play examines in depth the domination of women by men and the relationship of violence to sex roles.

In 1976 Churchill produced *Vinegar Tom*, a play about witch hunts set in the seventeenth century. After researching witch trials, Churchill concluded that women were convenient scapegoats for men when times became difficult. A companion play also set in the seventeenth century is *Light Shining in Buckinghamshire,* which studies revolutions. The play was developed by the Joint Stock Theatre Group and produced at the Royal Court Theatre to uniformly positive reviews.

Churchill's first play to receive wide notice was *Cloud Nine* (1979). It treats several themes simultaneously, among them colonization. The first act is set in the Victorian era in a British colony in Africa. The play is broadly satirical, involving farcical moments in the relationships of colonizer and native, master and servant, and man and woman. Churchill cast certain parts of the play in a cross-gender fashion: A woman plays a sensitive schoolboy, and a man plays an unfulfilled wife. The effect is both comic and instructive, since one of Churchill's most important purposes is to cast some light on gender distinctions. She said that she saw "parallels between the way colonizers treat the colonized and the way men tended to treat women in our own society." *Cloud Nine* was produced in the Lucille Lortel Theatre, where it ran for two years off Broadway and won an Obie award.

Top Girls (1982) played at the Royal Court Theatre in London and at the Public Theater in New York, where the reviews were mixed. The play, essentially feminist in theme, was praised in England for being "the best British play ever from a woman dramatist." *Fen* (1983) was warmly praised by critics and audiences alike. A study of the effects of poverty on women, the play was developed with the Joint Stock Theatre Group and set in the area of England called the Fens, a flat country prone to flooding, where women work the fields and most of the people are poor.

Churchill's *Serious Money* (1987) is a verse play (like her first Oxford play) about the London stock market. It ran on Broadway to exceptional acclaim, partly because it played just after the stock market crash of October 1987. The play is a satiric study of those for whom only greed and getting ahead matter.

Churchill has written a number of plays for radio and television, such as *Lovesick, Abortive, Not Not Not Not Not Enough Oxygen, Schreber's Nervous Illness, The Hospital at the Time of the Revolution,* and *The Judge's Wife.* These are gathered in a volume called *Shorts* (1990). *The Skriker* (1994) is an experiment in fantasy, with a spirit world that parallels the real world. *Blue Heart* (1999) consists of two one-act plays: *Heart's Desire* and *Blue Kettle.* These are relatively realistic domestic dramas. *Heart's Desire* is a satire set in a sparkling kitchen where Alice and Brian wait, with Brian's sister Maisie, for the return of their daughter from Australia. Their peaceful setting is invaded by alcoholics and terrorists, among others, and yet the play has been described as "achingly, aggressively funny." *Blue Kettle* features a young man who searches for women who have given up children for adoption and then claims to be their lost son. It is a somber play that deals with the failure of language.

Among Churchill's later plays, *Far Away* (2000) is a dark piece on the subject of modern life and modern politics as seen in the context of the millennium. *A Number* (2002) treats the relationship of fathers and sons in a remarkably unusual way. A man has his son cloned twenty-one times and, in this play, interacts with two of those clones. *A Dream Play* (2005) is an adaptation of a Strindberg play with the addition of Freudian implications. *Drunk Enough to Say I Love You?* (2006) focuses on world domination, torture, and war, but from the perspective of a computer game. Jack (Union Jack), a British man, goes to the United States to live with Sam (Uncle Sam), and the two plot to control the world. One review said simply that it was the best value in London theater during its run. Churchill's ten-minute play *Seven Jewish Children* (2009), a very brief history of Israel, was written to give support to Palestinians living in Gaza. A very controversial political play, it has been released to any theater group that wishes to produce it, as long as it gathers funds for those living in Gaza. Churchill is one of the most prolific of modern playwrights and continues to stir audiences all over the world.

Cloud Nine

Cloud Nine (1979) was commissioned by London's Joint Stock Theatre Group and developed with the help of director Max Stafford-Clark, who ran the Royal Court Theatre, one of London's most exciting experimental theaters. Many of Churchill's later plays were also developed at the Royal Court, and they helped establish it as one of the centers of new drama in England. The central subject of *Cloud Nine* is sex, but the drama draws us into the worlds of politics, gender definition, and social mores.

The play is divided into two acts that are more disconnected than unified. Some of the same characters appear in both acts, but the actors trade parts in act 2. Such a disjunction is so striking—especially to the first audiences who saw the play in 1979—that we realize Churchill is telling us something radical about the psychological continuity of characters and thus about psychological realism. Also, the first act is set in British imperial Africa in the 1870s, while the second act is set in London in the 1970s, so it seems reasonable that different actors should play these characters in view of the time difference.

But there is more. The characters in act 1 play recognizable types. Clive is the patriarch of a Victorian family who rules his environment, sometimes with a whip. His wife Betty is played in both acts by a man, implying that in the Victorian world of act 1 the British woman was really a male ideal or in fact a male and was expected to act as one, while in the contemporary London of act 2 gender liberation is within the realm of possibility. Act 1 is a study of the world of Victorian sexual repression and the system of gender expectations—the social construction of conventional gender behavior. Such expectations are spoofed by nine-year-old Edward, played by a grown woman, who holds his two-year-old sister's doll for safekeeping. He wants the doll for himself but tells his parents that he is "minding" his sister's doll, not playing with it. His merely holding the doll, however, unsettles his father, who insists that Edward do something more manly, such as riding with Harry Bagley, the mythic adventurer. Harry Bagley turns out to be bisexual and involved with the black servant, who is played by a white actor.

Part of the social comment of act 1 involves a critique of British colonial rule. Joshua, the servant, regards himself as inferior, while Clive, the representative of British authority, comports himself with no thought for the feelings of the "natives." British rule is intentionally oppressive. The sound of native drums implies a threatening "jungle" environment with the potential for an uprising. The situation is self-consciously developed as a cliché in a conventional romantic mode—typical of thrillers of the Victorian period.

But in addition to a commentary on the colonial ethos of the British, the play offers a critique of Victorian repression. Clive and others are sexually promiscuous. His relationship with Mrs. Saunders is conducted almost farcically. Other characters engage in homosexual relationships in secret. All sexuality is essentially relegated to secret hideaways, while on the surface society maintains total conventionality. Churchill includes moments of comic relief, as when Ellen and Betty are attracted to each other, and Betty instructs her son Edward to go and play with Uncle Harry, whom the audience knows is a pederast. That such sexual relationships occurred in 1870s England is now well known, but the image that survives of the period is one of absolute moral rectitude.

For discussion questions and assignments on *Cloud Nine,* visit bedfordstmartins.com/jacobus.

When act 2 introduces us to the sexual mores of 1970s London, it becomes clear that the period's usual reputation for sexual liberation is no more accurate than the official version we have of Victorian England. Two mothers, Victoria and Lin, introduce us to the modern world. Their children play with guns while Victoria remarks that in Sweden such toys are banned. Lin replies that she will give her daughter, Cathy, a rifle for Christmas with the suggestion that she shoot Victoria's son, Tommy. Victoria hardly hears when Lin says that she is a lesbian and has left her husband or notices her making sexual advances. At the end of the first scene Victoria and Lin may or may not have sex with each other.

Scene 2 reveals a casual sexual encounter between two men, Edward and Gerry, on the train from Victoria to Clapham (two coded destinations that imply the distance from Victorian England to the modern world). Sex is casual, and Martin tells Victoria and Betty that he's ready for almost anything: "Whatever you want to do, I'll be delighted." The comedy reaches an amusing moment at the end of scene 2 when Edward decides he is probably a lesbian because he thinks he likes women more than men.

Scene 3 looks further back into history at ancient cults, many of whose priestesses allegedly were interested in unusual sexual relationships. It is as if Churchill is suggesting that the more things change the more they remain the same. In the play the sexual liberation of the 1970s appears to be less radical and novel than it once seemed.

Cloud Nine in Performance

The first production of *Cloud Nine* was in the Dartington College of Arts in February 1979. The play quickly went on tour and then to the Royal Court Theatre in London. The earliest versions of the play were revised based on contributions from the director and actors, and Churchill revised the text even after its first publication in 1979. The current version reflects changes made in performance and development until at least 1984.

Although much of the play is serious in tone, most productions have emphasized its burlesque elements. Some productions have approached the drama as if it were farce, using a broad comic style and producing much laughter. Segments of act 1 have been compared with sketches by Monty Python, some of whose purposes may have been similar to Churchill's.

The cross-casting—men playing women, women playing men, and adults playing children—was one of the striking elements of the earliest performances. The first act has been played with pith helmets and other emblems of the British empire. In one version a rhinoceros horn was positioned on the wall in such a way as to appear to be a phallic symbol. The 1979 production in the Royal Court Theatre established the play as a significant part of the modern English repertory.

Eighteen years later, after performances in many countries around the world, Peter Hall included *Cloud Nine* in a series of seven classic plays at the Old Vic in London. He believed the play ranked with Shakespeare's *King Lear* and Chekhov's *The Seagull*. Not everyone agreed with him, but the Old Vic production in 1997 demonstrated that the play was still timely and potentially powerful. Theater critic Alastair Macaulay said of the second act: "It is shot through with mystery, it proceeds with dreamlike fluency, and, most beautifully, it allows each character, even while he or she grows more complex and more poignant, to remain an unanswered question." *Cloud Nine* remains a popular play, having been produced in Philadelphia at the Wilma Theater in 2006, in London at the Almeida Theatre in 2007, and in Los Angeles, Seattle, and Chicago in 2011. It has proven to be a durable and important play, just as Churchill has proven to be one of contemporary theater's most important playwrights.

CARYL CHURCHILL (b. 1938)

Cloud Nine   1979

Characters

(Act One)
CLIVE, *a colonial administrator*
BETTY, *his wife, played by a man*
JOSHUA, *his black servant, played by a white*
EDWARD, *his son, played by a woman*
VICTORIA, *his daughter, a dummy*
MAUD, *his mother-in-law*
ELLEN, *Edward's governess*
HARRY BAGLEY, *an explorer*
MRS. SAUNDERS, *a widow*

(Act Two)
BETTY
EDWARD, *her son*
VICTORIA, *her daughter*
MARTIN, *Victoria's husband*
LIN
CATHY, *Lin's daughter age 5, played by a man*
GERRY, *Edward's lover*

(*Except for Cathy, characters in Act Two are played by actors of their own sex.*)
(*Act One takes place in a British colony in Africa in Victorian times.*)
(*Act Two takes place in London in 1979. But for the characters it is twenty-five years later.*)

ACT ONE • Scene One

(*Low bright sun. Verandah. Flagpole with Union Jack. The Family—Clive, Betty, Edward, Victoria, Maud, Ellen, Joshua.*)

ALL (*sing*): Come gather, sons of England, come gather
     in your pride.
   Now meet the world united, now face it side by side;
   Ye who the earth's wide corners, from veldt to prai-
     rie, roam.
   From bush and jungle muster all who call old
     England "home."
   Then gather round for England,
   Rally to the flag,
   From North and South and East and West
   Come one and all for England!
CLIVE: This is my family. Though far from home
   We serve the Queen wherever we may roam
   I am a father to the natives here,
   And father to my family so dear.

(*He presents Betty. She is played by a man.*)

   My wife is all I dreamt a wife should be,
   And everything she is she owes to me.
BETTY: I live for Clive. The whole aim of my life
   Is to be what he looks for in a wife.
   I am a man's creation as you see,
   And what men want is what I want to be.

(*Clive presents Joshua. He is played by a white.*)

CLIVE: My boy's a jewel. Really has the knack.
   You'd hardly notice that the fellow's black.
JOSHUA: My skin is black but oh my soul is white.
   I hate my tribe. My master is my light.
   I only live for him. As you can see,
   What white men want is what I want to be.

(*Clive presents Edward. He is played by a woman.*)

CLIVE: My son is young. I'm doing all I can
   To teach him to grow up to be a man.
EDWARD: What father wants I'd dearly like to be.
   I find it rather hard as you can see.

(*Clive presents Victoria, who is a dummy, Maud, and Ellen.*)

CLIVE: No need for any speeches by the rest.
   My daughter, mother-in-law, and governess.

The casts of *Cloud Nine* from [TOP] the Panasonic Theatre in Toronto in 2010 and [BOTTOM] the Almeida Theatre in London in 2007.

ALL (*sing*): O'er countless numbers she, our Queen,
Victoria reigns supreme;
O'er Afric's sunny plains, and o'er
Canadian frozen stream;
The forge of war shall weld the chains of brother-
hood secure;
So to all time in ev'ry clime our Empire shall endure.

Then gather round for England,
Rally to the flag,
From North and South and East and West
Come one and all for England!

(*All go except Betty. Clive comes.*)

BETTY: Clive?
CLIVE: Betty. Joshua!

(*Joshua comes with a drink for Clive.*)

BETTY: I thought you would never come. The day's so long without you.
CLIVE: Long ride in the bush.
BETTY: Is anything wrong? I heard drums.
CLIVE: Nothing serious. Beauty is a damned good mare. I must get some new boots sent from home. These ones have never been right. I have a blister.
BETTY: My poor dear foot.
CLIVE: It's nothing.
BETTY: Oh but it's sore.
CLIVE: We are not in this country to enjoy ourselves. Must have ridden fifty miles. Spoke to three different headmen who would all gladly chop off each other's heads and wear them round their waists.
BETTY: Clive!
CLIVE: Don't be squeamish, Betty, let me have my joke. And what has my little dove done today?
BETTY: I've read a little.
CLIVE: Good. Is it good?
BETTY: It's poetry.
CLIVE: You're so delicate and sensitive.
BETTY: And I played the piano. Shall I send for the children?
CLIVE: Yes, in a minute. I've a piece of news for you.
BETTY: Good news?
CLIVE: You'll certainly think it's good. A visitor.
BETTY: From home?
CLIVE: No. Well of course originally from home.
BETTY: Man or woman?
CLIVE: Man.
BETTY: I can't imagine.
CLIVE: Something of an explorer. Bit of a poet. Odd chap but brave as a lion. And a great admirer of yours.
BETTY: What do you mean? Whoever can it be?
CLIVE: With an H and a B. And does conjuring tricks for little Edward.
BETTY: That sounds like Mr. Bagley.
CLIVE: Harry Bagley.
BETTY: He certainly doesn't admire me, Clive, what a thing to say. How could I possibly guess from that. He's hardly explored anything at all, he's just been up a river, he's done nothing at all compared to what

you do. You should have said a heavy drinker and a bit of a bore.
CLIVE: But you like him well enough. You don't mind him coming?
BETTY: Anyone at all to break the monotony.
CLIVE: But you have your mother. You have Ellen.
BETTY: Ellen is a governess. My mother is my mother.
CLIVE: I hoped when she came to visit she would be company for you.
BETTY: I don't think mother is on a visit. I think she lives with us.
CLIVE: I think she does.
BETTY: Clive you are so good.
CLIVE: But are you bored my love?
BETTY: It's just that I miss you when you're away. We're not in this country to enjoy ourselves. If I lack society that is my form of service.
CLIVE: That's a brave girl. So today has been all right? No fainting? No hysteria?
BETTY: I have been very tranquil.
CLIVE: Ah what a haven of peace to come home to. The coolth, the calm, the beauty.
BETTY: There is one thing, Clive, if you don't mind.
CLIVE: What can I do for you, my dear?
BETTY: It's about Joshua.
CLIVE: I wouldn't leave you alone here with a quiet mind if it weren't for Joshua.
BETTY: Joshua doesn't like me.
CLIVE: Joshua has been my boy for eight years. He has saved my life. I have saved his life. He is devoted to me and to mine. I have said this before.
BETTY: He is rude to me. He doesn't do what I say. Speak to him.
CLIVE: Tell me what happened.
BETTY: He said something improper.
CLIVE: Well, what?
BETTY: I don't like to repeat it.
CLIVE: I must insist.
BETTY: I had left my book inside on the piano. I was in the hammock. I asked him to fetch it.
CLIVE: And did he not fetch it?
BETTY: Yes, he did eventually.
CLIVE: And what did he say?
BETTY: Clive—
CLIVE: Betty.
BETTY: He said Fetch it yourself. You've got legs under that dress.
CLIVE: Joshua!

(*Joshua comes.*)

Joshua, madam says you spoke impolitely to her this afternoon.
JOSHUA: Sir?
CLIVE: When she asked you to pass her book from the piano.
JOSHUA: She has the book, sir.
BETTY: I have the book now, but when I told you—
CLIVE: Betty, please, let me handle this. You didn't pass it at once?

JOSHUA: No sir, I made a joke first.

CLIVE: What was that?

JOSHUA: I said my legs were tired, sir. That was funny because the book was very near, it would not make my legs tired to get it.

BETTY: That's not true.

JOSHUA: Did madam hear me wrong?

CLIVE: She heard something else.

JOSHUA: What was that, madam?

BETTY: Never mind.

CLIVE: Now Joshua, it won't do you know. Madam doesn't like that kind of joke. You must do what madam says, just do what she says and don't answer back. You know your place, Joshua. I don't have to say any more.

JOSHUA: No sir.

BETTY: I expect an apology.

JOSHUA: I apologise, madam.

CLIVE: There now. It won't happen again, my dear. I'm very shocked Joshua, very shocked.

(*Clive winks at Joshua, unseen by Betty. Joshua goes.*)

CLIVE: I think another drink, and send for the children, and isn't that Harry riding down the hill? Wave, wave. Just in time before dark. Cuts it fine, the blighter. Always a hothead, Harry.

BETTY: Can he see us?

CLIVE: Stand further forward. He'll see your white dress. There, he waved back.

BETTY: Do you think so? I wonder what he saw. Sometimes sunset is so terrifying I can't bear to look.

CLIVE: It makes me proud. Elsewhere in the empire the sun is rising.

BETTY: Harry looks so small on the hillside.

(*Ellen comes.*)

ELLEN: Shall I bring the children?

BETTY: Shall Ellen bring the children?

CLIVE: Delightful.

BETTY: Yes, Ellen, make sure they're warm. The night air is deceptive. Victoria was looking pale yesterday.

CLIVE: My love.

(*Maud comes from inside the house.*)

MAUD: Are you warm enough Betty?

BETTY: Perfectly.

MAUD: The night air is deceptive.

BETTY: I'm quite warm. I'm too warm.

MAUD: You're not getting a fever, I hope? She's not strong, you know, Clive. I don't know how long you'll keep her in this climate.

CLIVE: I look after Her Majesty's domains. I think you can trust me to look after my wife.

(*Ellen comes carrying Victoria, age 2. Edward, aged 9, lags behind.*)

BETTY: Victoria, my pet, say good evening to papa.

(*Clive takes Victoria on his knee.*)

CLIVE: There's my sweet little Vicky. What have we done today?

BETTY: She wore Ellen's hat.

CLIVE: Did she wear Ellen's big hat like a lady? What a pretty.

BETTY: And Joshua gave her a piggy back. Tell papa. Horsy with Joshy?

ELLEN: She's tired.

CLIVE: Nice Joshy played horsy. What a big strong Joshy. Did you have a gallop? Did you make him stop and go? Not very chatty tonight are we?

BETTY: Edward, say good evening to papa.

CLIVE: Edward my boy. Have you done your lessons well?

EDWARD: Yes papa.

CLIVE: Did you go riding?

EDWARD: Yes papa.

CLIVE: What's that you're holding?

BETTY: It's Victoria's doll. What are you doing with it, Edward?

EDWARD: Minding her.

BETTY: Well I should give it to Ellen quickly. You don't want papa to see you with a doll.

CLIVE: No, we had you with Victoria's doll once before, Edward.

ELLEN: He's minding it for Vicky. He's not playing with it.

BETTY: He's not playing with it, Clive. He's minding it for Vicky.

CLIVE: Ellen minds Victoria, let Ellen mind the doll.

ELLEN: Come, give it to me.

(*Ellen takes the doll.*)

EDWARD: Don't pull her about. Vicky's very fond of her. She likes me to have her.

BETTY: He's a very good brother.

CLIVE: Yes, it's manly of you Edward, to take care of your little sister. We'll say no more about it. Tomorrow I'll take you riding with me and Harry Bagley. Would you like that?

EDWARD: Is he here?

CLIVE: He's just arrived. There Betty, take Victoria now. I must go and welcome Harry.

(*Clive tosses Victoria to Betty, who gives her to Ellen.*)

EDWARD: Can I come, papa?

BETTY: Is he warm enough?

EDWARD: Am I warm enough?

CLIVE: Never mind the women, Ned. Come and meet Harry.

(*They go. The women are left. There is a silence.*)

MAUD: I daresay Mr. Bagley will be out all day and we'll see nothing of him.

BETTY: He plays the piano. Surely he will sometimes stay at home with us.

MAUD: We can't expect it. The men have their duties and we have ours.

BETTY: He won't have seen a piano for a year. He lives a very rough life.

ELLEN: Will it be exciting for you, Betty?

MAUD: Whatever do you mean, Ellen?

ELLEN: We don't have very much society.

BETTY: Clive is my society.

MAUD: It's time Victoria went to bed.

ELLEN: She'd like to stay up and see Mr. Bagley.

MAUD: Mr. Bagley can see her tomorrow.

(*Ellen goes.*)

MAUD: You let that girl forget her place, Betty.

BETTY: Mother, she is governess to my son. I know what her place is. I think my friendship does her good. She is not very happy.

MAUD: Young women are never happy.

BETTY: Mother, what a thing to say.

MAUD: Then when they're older they look back and see that comparatively speaking they were ecstatic.

BETTY: I'm perfectly happy.

MAUD: You are looking very pretty tonight. You were such a success as a young girl. You have made a most fortunate marriage. I'm sure you will be an excellent hostess to Mr. Bagley.

BETTY: I feel quite nervous at the thought of entertaining.

MAUD: I can always advise you if I'm asked.

BETTY: What a long time they're taking. I always seem to be waiting for the men.

MAUD: Betty you have to learn to be patient. I am patient. My mama was very patient.

(*Clive approaches, supporting Caroline Saunders.*)

CLIVE: It is a pleasure. It is an honor. It is positively your duty to seek my help. I would be hurt, I would be insulted by any show of independence. Your husband would have been one of my dearest friends if he had lived. Betty, look who has come, Mrs. Saunders. She has ridden here all alone, amazing spirit. What will you have? Tea or something stronger? Let her lie down, she is overcome. Betty, you will know what to do.

(*Mrs. Saunders lies down.*)

MAUD: I knew it. I heard drums. We'll be killed in our beds.

CLIVE: Now, please, calm yourself.

MAUD: I am perfectly calm. I am just outspoken. If it comes to being killed I shall take it as calmly as anyone.

CLIVE: There is no cause for alarm. Mrs. Saunders has been alone since her husband died last year, amazing spirit. Not surprisingly, the strain has told. She has come to us as her nearest neighbors.

MAUD: What happened to make her come?

CLIVE: This is not an easy country for a woman.

MAUD: Clive, I heard drums. We are not children.

CLIVE: Of course you heard drums. The tribes are constantly at war, if the term is not too grand to grace their squabbles. Not unnaturally Mrs. Saunders would like the company of white women. The piano. Poetry.

BETTY: We are not her nearest neighbors.

CLIVE: We are among her nearest neighbors and I was a dear friend of her late husband. She knows that she will find a welcome here. She will not be disappointed. She will be cared for.

MAUD: Of course we will care for her.

BETTY: Victoria is in bed. I must go and say goodnight. Mother, please, you look after Mrs. Saunders.

CLIVE: Harry will be here at once.

(*Betty goes.*)

MAUD: How rash to go out after dark without a shawl.

CLIVE: Amazing spirit. Drink this.

MRS. SAUNDERS: Where am I?

MAUD: You are quite safe.

MRS. SAUNDERS: Clive? Clive? Thank God. This is very kind. How do you do? I am sorry to be a nuisance. Charmed. Have you a gun? I have a gun.

CLIVE: There is no need for guns I hope. We are all friends here.

MRS. SAUNDERS: I think I will lie down again.

(*Harry Bagley and Edward have approached.*)

MAUD: Ah, here is Mr. Bagley.

EDWARD: I gave his horse some water.

CLIVE: You don't know Mrs. Saunders, do you Harry? She has at present collapsed, but she is recovering thanks to the good offices of my wife's mother who I think you've met before. Betty will be along in a minute. Edward will go home to school shortly. He is quite a young man since you saw him.

HARRY: I hardly knew him.

MAUD: What news have you for us, Mr. Bagley?

CLIVE: Do you know Mrs. Saunders, Harry? Amazing spirit.

EDWARD: Did you hardly know me?

HARRY: Of course I knew you. I mean you have grown.

EDWARD: What do you expect?

HARRY: That's quite right, people don't get smaller.

MAUD: Edward. You should be in bed.

EDWARD: No, I'm not tired, I'm not tired am I Uncle Harry?

HARRY: I don't think he's tired.

CLIVE: He is overtired. It is past his bedtime. Say goodnight.

EDWARD: Goodnight, sir.

CLIVE: And to your grandmother.

EDWARD: Goodnight, grandmother.

(*Edward goes.*)

MAUD: Shall I help Mrs. Saunders indoors? I'm afraid she may get a chill.

CLIVE: Shall I give her an arm?

MAUD: How kind of you Clive. I think I am strong enough.

(*Maud helps Mrs. Saunders into the house.*)

CLIVE: Not a word to alarm the women.

HARRY: Absolutely.

CLIVE: I did some good today I think. Kept up some alliances. There's a lot of affection there.

HARRY: They're affectionate people. They can be very cruel of course.

CLIVE: Well they are savages.

HARRY: Very beautiful people many of them.

CLIVE: Joshua! (*To Harry.*) I think we should sleep with guns.

HARRY: I haven't slept in a house for six months. It seems extremely safe.

(*Joshua comes.*)

CLIVE: Joshua, you will have gathered there's a spot of bother. Rumors of this and that. You should be armed I think.

JOSHUA: There are many bad men, sir. I pray about it. Jesus will protect us.

CLIVE: He will indeed and I'll also get you a weapon. Betty, come and keep Harry company. Look in the barn, Joshua, every night.

(*Clive and Joshua go. Betty comes.*)

HARRY: I wondered where you were.

BETTY: I was singing lullabies.

HARRY: When I think of you I always think of you with Edward in your lap.

BETTY: Do you think of me sometimes then?

HARRY: You have been thought of where no white woman has ever been thought of before.

BETTY: It's one way of having adventures. I suppose I will never go in person.

HARRY: That's up to you.

BETTY: Of course it's not. I have duties.

HARRY: Are you happy, Betty?

BETTY: Where have you been?

HARRY: Built a raft and went up the river. Stayed with some people. The king is always very good to me. They have a lot of skulls around the place but not white men's I think. I made up a poem one night. If I should die in this forsaken spot, There is a loving heart without a blot, Where I will live—and so on.

BETTY: When I'm near you it's like going out into the jungle. It's like going up the river on a raft. It's like going out in the dark.

HARRY: And you are safety and light and peace and home.

BETTY: But I want to be dangerous.

HARRY: Clive is my friend.

BETTY: I am your friend.

HARRY: I don't like dangerous women.

BETTY: Is Mrs. Saunders dangerous?

HARRY: Not to me. She's a bit of an old boot.

(*Joshua comes, unobserved.*)

BETTY: Am I dangerous?

HARRY: You are rather.

BETTY: Please like me.

HARRY: I worship you.

BETTY: Please want me.

HARRY: I don't want to want you. Of course I want you.

BETTY: What are we going to do?

HARRY: I should have stayed on the river. The hell with it.

(*He goes to take her in his arms, she runs away into the house. Harry stays where he is. He becomes aware of Joshua.*)

HARRY: Who's there?

JOSHUA: Only me sir.

HARRY: Got a gun now have you?

JOSHUA: Yes sir.

HARRY: Where's Clive?

JOSHUA: Going round the boundaries sir.

HARRY: Have you checked there's nobody in the barns?

JOSHUA: Yes sir.

HARRY: Shall we go in a barn and fuck? It's not an order.

JOSHUA: That's all right, yes.

(*They go off.*)

Scene Two

(*An open space some distance from the house. Mrs. Saunders alone, breathless. She is carrying a riding crop. Clive arrives.*)

CLIVE: Why? Why?

MRS. SAUNDERS: Don't fuss, Clive, it makes you sweat.

CLIVE: Why ride off now? Sweat, you would sweat if you were in love with somebody as disgustingly capricious as you are. You will be shot with poisoned arrows. You will miss the picnic. Somebody will notice I came after you.

MRS. SAUNDERS: I didn't want you to come after me. I wanted to be alone.

CLIVE: You will be raped by cannibals.

MRS. SAUNDERS: I just wanted to get out of your house.

CLIVE: My God, what women put us through. Cruel, cruel. I think you are the sort of woman who would enjoy whipping somebody. I've never met one before.

MRS. SAUNDERS: Can I tell you something, Clive?

CLIVE: Let me tell you something first. Since you came to the house I have had an erection twenty-four hours a day except for ten minutes after the time we had intercourse.

MRS. SAUNDERS: I don't think that's physically possible.

CLIVE: You are causing me appalling physical suffering. Is this the way to treat a benefactor?

MRS. SAUNDERS: Clive, when I came to your house the other night I came because I was afraid. The cook was going to let his whole tribe in through the window.

CLIVE: I know that, my poor sweet. Amazing—

MRS. SAUNDERS: I came to you although you are not my nearest neighbor—

CLIVE: Rather than to the old major of seventy-two.

MRS. SAUNDERS: Because the last time he came to visit me I had to defend myself with a shotgun and I thought you would take no for an answer.

CLIVE: But you've already answered yes.

MRS. SAUNDERS: I answered yes once. Sometimes I want to say no.

CLIVE: Women, my God. Look the picnic will start, I have to go to the picnic. Please Caroline—

MRS. SAUNDERS: I think I will have to go back to my own house.

CLIVE: Caroline, if you were shot with poisoned arrows do you know what I'd do? I'd fuck your dead body and poison myself. Caroline, you smell amazing. You terrify me. You are dark like this continent. Mysterious. Treacherous. When you rode to me through the night. When you fainted in my arms. When I came to you in your bed, when I lifted the mosquito netting, when I said let me in, let me in. Oh don't shut me out, Caroline, let me in.

(*He has been caressing her feet and legs. He disappears completely under her skirt.*)

MRS. SAUNDERS: Please stop. I can't concentrate. I want to go home. I wish I didn't enjoy the sensation because I don't like you, Clive. I do like living in your house where there's plenty of guns. But I don't like you at all. But I do like the sensation. Well I'll have it then. I'll have it, I'll have it—

(*Voices are heard singing* The First Noël.)

Don't stop. Don't stop.

(*Clive comes out from under her skirt.*)

CLIVE: The Christmas picnic. I came.
MRS. SAUNDERS: I didn't.
CLIVE: I'm all sticky.
MRS. SAUNDERS: What about me? Wait.
CLIVE: All right, are you? Come on. We mustn't be found.
MRS. SAUNDERS: Don't go now.
CLIVE: Caroline, you are so voracious. Do let go. Tidy yourself up. There's a hair in my mouth.

(*Clive and Mrs. Saunders go off. Betty and Maud come, with Joshua carrying hamper.*)

MAUD: I never would have thought a guinea fowl could taste so like a turkey.
BETTY: I had to explain to the cook three times.
MAUD: You did very well dear.

(*Joshua sits apart with gun. Edward and Harry with Victoria on his shoulder, singing* The First Noël. *Maud and Betty are unpacking the hamper. Clive arrives separately.*)

MAUD: This tablecloth was one of my mama's.
BETTY: Uncle Harry playing horsy.
EDWARD: Crackers crackers.
BETTY: Not yet, Edward.
CLIVE: And now the moment we have all been waiting for.

(*Clive opens champagne. General acclaim.*)

CLIVE: Oh dear, stained my trousers, never mind.
EDWARD: Can I have some?
MAUD: Oh no Edward, not for you.
CLIVE: Give him half a glass.
MAUD: If your father says so.
CLIVE: All rise please. To Her Majesty Queen Victoria, God bless her, and her husband and all her dear children.
ALL: The Queen.
EDWARD: Crackers crackers.

(*General cracker pulling, hats. Clive and Harry discuss champagne.*)

HARRY: Excellent, Clive, wherever did you get it?
CLIVE: I know a chap in French Equatorial Africa.
EDWARD: I won, I won mama.

(*Ellen arrives.*)

BETTY: Give a hat to Joshua, he'd like it.

(*Edward takes hat to Joshua. Betty takes a ball from the hamper and plays catch with Ellen. Murmurs of surprise and congratulations from the men whenever they catch the ball.*)

EDWARD: Mama, don't play. You know you can't catch a ball.

BETTY: He's perfectly right. I can't throw either.

(*Betty sits down. Ellen has the ball.*)

EDWARD: Ellen, don't you play either. You're no good. You spoil it.

(*Edward takes Victoria from Harry and gives her to Ellen. He takes the ball and throws it to Harry. Harry, Clive, and Edward play ball.*)

BETTY: Ellen come and sit with me. We'll be spectators and clap.

(*Edward misses the ball.*)

CLIVE: Butterfingers.
EDWARD: I'm not.
HARRY: Throw straight now.
EDWARD: I did, I did.
CLIVE: Keep your eye on the ball.
EDWARD: You can't throw.
CLIVE: Don't be a baby.
EDWARD: I'm not, throw a hard one, throw a hard one—
CLIVE: Butterfingers. What will Uncle Harry think of you?
EDWARD: It's your fault. You can't throw. I hate you.

(*He throws the ball wildly in the direction of Joshua.*)

CLIVE: Now you've lost the ball. He's lost the ball.
EDWARD: It's Joshua's fault. Joshua's butterfingers.
CLIVE: I don't think I want to play any more. Joshua, find the ball will you?
EDWARD: Yes, please play. I'll find the ball. Please play.
CLIVE: You're so silly and you can't catch. You'll be no good at cricket.
MAUD: Why don't we play hide and seek?
EDWARD: Because it's a baby game.
BETTY: You've hurt Edward's feelings.
CLIVE: A boy has no business having feelings.
HARRY: Hide and seek. I'll be it. Everybody must hide. This is the base, you have to get home to base.
EDWARD: Hide and seek, hide and seek.
HARRY: Can we persuade the ladies to join us?
MAUD: I'm playing. I love games.
BETTY: I always get found straight away.
ELLEN: Come on, Betty, do. Vicky wants to play.
EDWARD: You won't find me ever.

(*They all go except Clive, Harry, Joshua.*)

HARRY: It is safe, I suppose?
CLIVE: They won't go far. This is very much my territory and it's broad daylight. Joshua will keep an open eye.
HARRY: Well I must give them a hundred. You don't know what this means to me, Clive. A chap can only go on so long alone. I can climb mountains and go down rivers, but what's it for? For Christmas and England and games and women singing. This is the empire, Clive. It's not me putting a flag in new lands. It's you. The empire is one big family. I'm one of its black sheep, Clive. And I know you think my life is rather dashing. But I want you to know I admire you. This is the empire, Clive, and I serve it. With all my heart.

CLIVE: I think that's about a hundred.
HARRY: Ready or not, here I come!

(*He goes.*)

CLIVE: Harry Bagley is a fine man, Joshua. You should be proud to know him. He will be in history books.
JOSHUA: Sir, while we are alone.
CLIVE: Joshua of course, what is it? You always have my ear. Any time.
JOSHUA: Sir, I have some information. The stable boys are not to be trusted. They whisper. They go out at night. They visit their people. Their people are not my people. I do not visit my people.
CLIVE: Thank you, Joshua. They certainly look after Beauty. I'll be sorry to have to replace them.
JOSHUA: They carry knives.
CLIVE: Thank you, Joshua.
JOSHUA: And, sir.
CLIVE: I appreciate this, Joshua, very much.
JOSHUA: Your wife.
CLIVE: Ah, yes?
JOSHUA: She also thinks Harry Bagley is a fine man.
CLIVE: Thank you, Joshua.
JOSHUA: Are you going to hide?
CLIVE: Yes, yes I am. Thank you. Keep your eyes open Joshua.
JOSHUA: I do, sir.

(*Clive goes. Joshua goes. Harry and Betty race back to base.*)

BETTY: I can't run, I can't run at all.
HARRY: There, I've caught you.
BETTY: Harry, what are we going to do?
HARRY: It's impossible, Betty.
BETTY: Shall we run away together?

(*Maud comes.*)

MAUD: I give up. Don't catch me. I have been stung.
HARRY: Nothing serious I hope.
MAUD: I have ointment in my bag. I always carry ointment. I shall just sit down and rest. I am too old for all this fun. Hadn't you better be seeking, Harry?

(*Harry goes. Maud and Betty are alone for some time. They don't speak. Harry and Edward race back.*)

EDWARD: I won, I won, you didn't catch me.
HARRY: Yes I did.
EDWARD: Mama, who was first?
BETTY: I wasn't watching. I think it was Harry.
EDWARD: It wasn't Harry. You're no good at judging. I won, didn't I grandma?
MAUD: I expect so, since it's Christmas.
EDWARD: I won, Uncle Harry. I'm better than you.
BETTY: Why don't you help Uncle Harry look for the others?
EDWARD: Shall I?
HARRY: Yes, of course.
BETTY: Run along then. He's just coming.

(*Edward goes.*)

Harry, I shall scream.
HARRY: Ready or not, here I come.

(*Harry runs off.*)

BETTY: Why don't you go back to the house, mother, and rest your insect-bite?
MAUD: Betty, my duty is here. I don't like what I see. Clive wouldn't like it, Betty. I am your mother.
BETTY: Clive gives you a home because you are my mother.

(*Harry comes back.*)

HARRY: I can't find anyone else. I'm getting quite hot.
BETTY: Sit down a minute.
HARRY: I can't do that. I'm he. How's your sting?
MAUD: It seems to be swelling up.
BETTY: Why don't you go home and rest? Joshua will go with you. Joshua!
HARRY: I could take you back.
MAUD: That would be charming.
BETTY: You can't go. You're he.

(*Joshua comes.*)

BETTY: Joshua, my mother wants to go back to the house. Will you go with her please.
JOSHUA: Sir told me I have to keep an eye.
BETTY: I am telling you to go back to the house. Then you can come back here and keep an eye.
MAUD: Thank you Betty. I know we have our little differences, but I always want what is best for you.

(*Joshua and Maud go.*)

HARRY: Don't give way. Keep calm.
BETTY: I shall kill myself.
HARRY: Betty, you are a star in my sky. Without you I would have no sense of direction. I need you, and I need you where you are, I need you to be Clive's wife. I need to go up rivers and know you are sitting here thinking of me.
BETTY: I want more than that. Is that wicked of me?
HARRY: Not wicked, Betty. Silly.

(*Edward calls in the distance.*)

EDWARD: Uncle Harry, where are you?
BETTY: Can't we ever be alone?
HARRY: You are a mother. And a daughter. And a wife.
BETTY: I think I shall go and hide again.

(*Betty goes. Harry goes. Clive chases Mrs. Saunders across the stage. Edward and Harry call in the distance.*)

EDWARD: Uncle Harry!
HARRY: Edward!

(*Edward comes.*)

EDWARD: Uncle Harry!

(*Harry comes.*)

There you are. I haven't found anyone, have you?
HARRY: I wonder where they all are.
EDWARD: Perhaps they're lost forever. Perhaps they're dead. There's trouble going on isn't there, and nobody says because of not frightening the women and children.

HARRY: Yes, that's right.

EDWARD: Do you think we'll be killed in our beds?

HARRY: Not very likely.

EDWARD: I can't sleep at night. Can you?

HARRY: I'm not used to sleeping in a house.

EDWARD: If I'm awake at night can I come and see you? I won't wake you up. I'll only come in if you're awake.

HARRY: You should try to sleep.

EDWARD: I don't mind being awake because I make up adventures. Once we were on a raft going down to the rapids. We've lost the paddles because we used them to fight off the crocodiles. A crocodile comes at me and I stab it again and again and the blood is everywhere and it tips up the raft and it has you by the leg and it's biting your leg right off and I take my knife and stab it in the throat and rip open its stomach and it lets go of you but it bites my hand but it's dead. And I drag you onto the river bank and I'm almost fainting with pain and we lie there in each other's arms.

HARRY: Have I lost my leg?

EDWARD: I forgot about the leg by then.

HARRY: Hadn't we better look for the others?

EDWARD: Wait. I've got something for you. It was in mama's box but she never wears it.

(*Edward gives Harry a necklace.*)

You don't have to wear it either but you might like it to look at.

HARRY: It's beautiful. But you'll have to put it back.

EDWARD: I wanted to give it to you.

HARRY: You did. It can go back in the box. You still gave it to me. Come on now, we have to find the others.

EDWARD: Harry, I love you.

HARRY: Yes I know. I love you too.

EDWARD: You know what we did when you were here before. I want to do it again. I think about it all the time. I try to do it to myself but it's not as good. Don't you want to any more?

HARRY: I do, but it's a sin and a crime and it's also wrong.

EDWARD: But we'll do it anyway won't we?

HARRY: Yes of course.

EDWARD: I wish the others would all be killed. Take it out now and let me see it.

HARRY: No.

EDWARD: Is it big now?

HARRY: Yes.

EDWARD: Let me touch it.

HARRY: No.

EDWARD: Just hold me.

HARRY: When you can't sleep.

EDWARD: We'd better find the others then. Come on.

HARRY: Ready or not, here we come.

(*They go out with whoops and shouts. Betty and Ellen come.*)

BETTY: Ellen, I don't want to play any more.

ELLEN: Nor do I, Betty.

BETTY: Come and sit here with me. Oh Ellen, what will become of me?

ELLEN: Betty, are you crying? Are you laughing?

BETTY: Tell me what you think of Harry Bagley.

ELLEN: He's a very fine man.

BETTY: No, Ellen, what you really think.

ELLEN: I think you think he's very handsome.

BETTY: And don't you think he is? Oh Ellen, you're so good and I'm so wicked.

ELLEN: I'm not so good as you think.

(*Edward comes.*)

EDWARD: I've found you.

ELLEN: We're not hiding Edward.

EDWARD: But I found you.

ELLEN: We're not playing, Edward, now run along.

EDWARD: Come on, Ellen, do play. Come on, mama.

ELLEN: Edward, don't pull your mama like that.

BETTY: Edward, you must do what your governess says. Go and play with Uncle Harry.

EDWARD: Uncle Harry!

(*Edward goes.*)

BETTY: Ellen, can you keep a secret?

ELLEN: Oh yes, yes please.

BETTY: I love Harry Bagley. I want to go away with him. There, I've said it, it's true.

ELLEN: How do you know you love him?

BETTY: I kissed him.

ELLEN: Betty.

BETTY: He held my hand like this. Oh I want him to do it again. I want him to stroke my hair.

ELLEN: Your lovely hair. Like this, Betty?

BETTY: I want him to put his arm around my waist.

ELLEN: Like this, Betty?

BETTY: Yes, oh I want him to kiss me again.

ELLEN: Like this Betty?

(*Ellen kisses Betty.*)

BETTY: Ellen, whatever are you doing? It's not a joke.

ELLEN: I'm sorry, Betty. You're so pretty. Harry Bagley doesn't deserve you. You wouldn't really go away with him?

BETTY: Oh Ellen, you don't know what I suffer. You don't know what love is. Everyone will hate me, but it's worth it for Harry's love.

ELLEN: I don't hate you, Betty, I love you.

BETTY: Harry says we shouldn't go away. But he says he worships me.

ELLEN: I worship you Betty.

BETTY: Oh Ellen, you are my only friend.

(*They embrace. The others have all gathered together. Maud has rejoined the party, and Joshua.*)

CLIVE: Come along everyone, you mustn't miss Harry's conjuring trick.

(*Betty and Ellen go to join the others.*)

MAUD: I didn't want to spoil the fun by not being here.

Harry pulls the British flag from his sleeve in the 2010 production of *Cloud Nine* at the Panasonic Theatre in Toronto, Canada.

HARRY: What is it that flies all over the world and is up my sleeve?

(*Harry produces a Union Jack from up his sleeve. General acclaim.*)

CLIVE: I think we should have some singing now. Ladies, I rely on you to lead the way.

ELLEN: We have a surprise for you. I have taught Joshua a Christmas carol. He has been singing it at the piano but I'm sure he can sing it unaccompanied, can't you, Joshua?

JOSHUA: In the deep midwinter
Frosty wind made moan,
Earth stood hard as iron,
Water like a stone.
Snow had fallen snow on snow
Snow on snow,
In the deep midwinter
Long long ago.

What can I give him
Poor as I am?
If I were a shepherd
I would bring a lamb.
If I were a wise man
I would do my part
What I can I give him,
Give my heart.

Scene Three

(*Inside the house. Betty, Mrs. Saunders, Maud with Victoria. The blinds are down so the light isn't bright though it is day outside. Clive looks in.*)

CLIVE: Everything all right? Nothing to be frightened of. (*Clive goes. Silence.*)

MAUD: Clap hands, daddy comes, with his pockets full of plums. All for Vicky.

(*Silence.*)

MRS. SAUNDERS: Who actually does the flogging?

MAUD: I don't think we want to imagine.

MRS. SAUNDERS: I imagine Joshua.

BETTY: Yes I think it would be Joshua. Or would Clive do it himself?

MRS. SAUNDERS: Well we can ask them afterwards.

MAUD: I don't like the way you speak of it, Mrs. Saunders.

MRS. SAUNDERS: How should I speak of it?

MAUD: The men will do it in the proper way, whatever it is. We have our own part to play.

MRS. SAUNDERS: Harry Bagley says they should just be sent away. I don't think he likes to see them beaten.

BETTY: Harry is so tender hearted. Perhaps he is right.

MAUD: Harry Bagley is not altogether—He has lived in this country a long time without any responsibilities. It is part of his charm but it hasn't improved his judgment. If the boys were just sent away they would go back to the village and make more trouble.

MRS. SAUNDERS: And what will they say about us in the village if they've been flogged?

BETTY: Perhaps Clive should keep them here.

MRS. SAUNDERS: That is never wise.

BETTY: Whatever shall we do?

MAUD: I don't think it is up to us to wonder. The men don't tell us what is going on among the tribes, so how can we possibly make a judgment?

MRS. SAUNDERS: I know a little of what is going on.

BETTY: Tell me what you know. Clive tells me nothing.

MAUD: You would not want to be told about it, Betty. It is enough for you that Clive knows what is happening. Clive will know what to do. Your father always knew what to do.

BETTY: Are you saying you would do something different, Caroline?

MRS. SAUNDERS: I would do what I did at my own home. I left. I can't see any way out except to leave. I will leave here. I will keep leaving everywhere I suppose.

MAUD: Luckily this household has a head. I am squeamish myself. But luckily Clive is not.

BETTY: You are leaving here then, Caroline?

MRS. SAUNDERS: Not immediately. I'm sorry.

847

(*Silence.*)

MRS. SAUNDERS: I wonder if it's over.

(*Edward comes in.*)

BETTY: Shouldn't you be with the men, Edward?
EDWARD: I didn't want to see any more. They got what they deserved. Uncle Harry said I could come in.
MRS. SAUNDERS: I never allowed the servants to be beaten in my own house. I'm going to find out what's happening.

(*Mrs. Saunders goes out.*)

BETTY: Will she go and look?
MAUD: Let Mrs. Saunders be a warning to you, Betty. She is alone in the world. You are not, thank God. Since your father died, I know what it is to be unprotected. Vicky is such a pretty little girl. Clap hands, daddy comes, with his pockets full of plums. All for Vicky.

(*Edward, meanwhile, has found the doll and is playing clap hands with her.*)

BETTY: Edward, what have you got there?
EDWARD: I'm minding her.
BETTY: Edward, I've told you before, dolls are for girls.
MAUD: Where is Ellen? She should be looking after Edward. (*She goes to the door.*) Ellen! Betty, why do you let that girl mope about in her own room? That's not what she's come to Africa for.
BETTY: You must never let the boys at school know you like dolls. Never, never. No one will talk to you, you won't be on the cricket team, you won't grow up to be a man like your papa.
EDWARD: I don't want to be like papa. I hate papa.
MAUD: Edward! Edward!
BETTY: You're a horrid wicked boy and papa will beat you. Of course you don't hate him, you love him. Now give Victoria her doll at once.
EDWARD: She's not Victoria's doll, she's my doll. She doesn't love Victoria and Victoria doesn't love her. Victoria never even plays with her.
MAUD: Victoria will learn to play with her.
EDWARD: She's mine and she loves me and she won't be happy if you take her away, she'll cry, she'll cry, she'll cry.

(*Betty takes the doll away, slaps him, bursts into tears. Ellen comes in.*)

BETTY: Ellen, look what you've done. Edward's got the doll again. Now, Ellen, will you please do your job.
ELLEN: Edward, you are a wicked boy. I am going to lock you in the nursery until supper time. Now go upstairs this minute.

(*She slaps Edward, who bursts into tears and goes out.*)

I do try to do what you want. I'm so sorry.

(*Ellen bursts into tears and goes out.*)

MAUD: There now, Vicky's got her baby back. Where did Vicky's naughty baby go? Shall we smack her? Just a little smack. (*Maud smacks the doll hard.*) There, now she's a good baby. Clap hands, daddy comes, with his pockets full of plums. All for Vicky's baby. When I was a child we honored our parents. My mama was an angel.

(*Joshua comes in. He stands without speaking.*)

BETTY: Joshua?
JOSHUA: Madam?
BETTY: Did you want something?
JOSHUA: Sent to see the ladies are all right, madam.

(*Mrs. Saunders comes in.*)

MRS. SAUNDERS: We're very well thank you, Joshua, and how are you?
JOSHUA: Very well thank you, Mrs. Saunders.
MRS. SAUNDERS: And the stable boys?
JOSHUA: They have had justice, madam.
MRS. SAUNDERS: So I saw. And does your arm ache?
MAUD: This is not a proper conversation, Mrs. Saunders.
MRS. SAUNDERS: You don't mind beating your own people?
JOSHUA: Not my people, madam.
MRS. SAUNDERS: A different tribe?
JOSHUA: Bad people.

(*Harry and Clive come in.*)

CLIVE: Well this is all very gloomy and solemn. Can we have the shutters open? The heat of the day has gone, we could have some light, I think. And cool drinks on the verandah, Joshua. Have some lemonade yourself. It is most refreshing.

(*Sunlight floods in as the shutters are opened. Edward comes.*)

EDWARD: Papa, papa, Ellen tried to lock me in the nursery. Mama is going to tell you of me. I'd rather tell you myself. I was playing with Vicky's doll again and I know it's very bad of me. And I said I didn't want to be like you and I said I hated you. And it's not true and I'm sorry, I'm sorry and please beat me and forgive me.
CLIVE: Well there's a brave boy to own up. You should always respect and love me, Edward, not for myself, I may not deserve it, but as I respected and loved my own father, because he was my father. Through our father we love our Queen and our God, Edward. Do you understand? It is something men understand.
EDWARD: Yes papa.
CLIVE: Then I forgive you and shake you by the hand. You spend too much time with the women. You may spend more time with me and Uncle Harry, little man.
EDWARD: I don't like women. I don't like dolls. I love you, papa, and I love you, Uncle Harry.

CLIVE: There's a fine fellow. Let us go out onto the verandah.

(*They all start to go. Edward takes Harry's hand and goes with him. Clive draws Betty back. They embrace.*)

BETTY: Poor Clive.

CLIVE: It was my duty to have them flogged. For you and Edward and Victoria, to keep you safe.

BETTY: It is terrible to feel betrayed.

CLIVE: You can tame a wild animal only so far. They revert to their true nature and savage your hand. Sometimes I feel the natives are the enemy. I know that is wrong. I know I have a responsibility towards them, to care for them and bring them all to be like Joshua. But there is something dangerous. Implacable. This whole continent is my enemy. I am pitching my whole mind and will and reason and spirit against it to tame it, and I sometimes feel it will break over me and swallow me up.

BETTY: Clive, Clive, I am here. I have faith in you.

CLIVE: Yes, I can show you my moments of weakness, Betty, because you are my wife and because I trust you. I trust you, Betty, and it would break my heart if you did not deserve that trust. Harry Bagley is my friend. It would break my heart if he did not deserve my trust.

BETTY: I'm sorry, I'm sorry. Forgive me. It is not Harry's fault, it is all mine. Harry is noble. He has rejected me. It is my wickedness, I get bored, I get restless, I imagine things. There is something so wicked in me, Clive.

CLIVE: I have never thought of you having the weakness of your sex, only the good qualities.

BETTY: I am bad, bad, bad—

CLIVE: You are thoughtless, Betty, that's all. Women can be treacherous and evil. They are darker and more dangerous than men. The family protects us from that, you protect me from that. You are not that sort of woman. You are not unfaithful to me, Betty. I can't believe you are. It would hurt me so much to cast you off. That would be my duty.

BETTY: No, no, no.

CLIVE: Joshua has seen you kissing.

BETTY: Forgive me.

CLIVE: But I don't want to know about it. I don't want to know. I wonder of course, I wonder constantly. If Harry Bagley was not my friend I would shoot him. If I shot you every British man and woman would applaud me. But no. It was a moment of passion such as women are too weak to resist. But you must resist it, Betty, or it will destroy us. We must fight against it. We must resist this dark female lust, Betty, or it will swallow us up.

BETTY: I do, I do resist. Help me. Forgive me.

CLIVE: Yes I do forgive you. But I can't feel the same about you as I did. You are still my wife and we still have duties to the household.

(*They go out arm in arm. As soon as they have gone Edward sneaks back to get the doll, which has been dropped on the floor. He picks it up and comforts it. Joshua comes through with a tray of drinks.*)

JOSHUA: Baby. Sissy. Girly.

(*Joshua goes. Betty calls from off.*)

BETTY: Edward?

(*Betty comes in.*)

BETTY: There you are, my darling. Come, papa wants us all to be together. Uncle Harry is going to tell how he caught a crocodile. Mama's sorry she smacked you.

(*They embrace. Joshua comes in again, passing through.*)

BETTY: Joshua, fetch me some blue thread from my sewing box. It is on the piano.

JOSHUA: You've got legs under that skirt.

BETTY: Joshua.

JOSHUA: And more than legs.

BETTY: Edward, are you going to stand there and let a servant insult your mother?

EDWARD: Joshua, get my mother's thread.

JOSHUA: Oh little Eddy, playing at master. It's only a joke.

EDWARD: Don't speak to my mother like that again.

JOSHUA: Ladies have no sense of humor. You like a joke with Joshua.

EDWARD: You fetch her sewing at once, do you hear me? You move when I speak to you, boy.

JOSHUA: Yes sir, master Edward sir.

(*Joshua goes.*)

BETTY: Edward, you were wonderful.

(*She goes to embrace him but he moves away.*)

EDWARD: Don't touch me.

SONG (*"A Boy's Best Friend"—All*): While plodding on our way, the toilsome road of life,
How few the friends that daily there we meet.
Not many will stand in trouble and in strife,
With counsel and affection ever sweet.
But there is one whose smile will ever on us beam,
Whose love is dearer far than any other;
And wherever we may turn
This lesson we will learn
A boy's best friend is his mother.

Then cherish her with care
And smooth her silv'ry hair,
When gone you will never get another.
And wherever we may turn
This lesson we shall learn,
A boy's best friend is his mother.

Scene Four

The verandah as in Scene One. Early morning. Nobody there. Joshua comes out of the house slowly and stands for some time doing nothing. Edward comes out.

EDWARD: Tell me another bad story, Joshua. Nobody else is even awake yet.

JOSHUA: First there was nothing and then there was the great goddess. She was very large and she had golden eyes and she made the stars and the sun and the earth. But soon she was miserable and lonely and she cried like a great waterfall and her tears made all the rivers in the world. So the great spirit sent a terrible monster, a tree with hundreds of eyes and a long green tongue, and it came chasing after her and she jumped into a lake and the tree jumped in after her, and she jumped right up into the sky. And the tree couldn't follow, he was stuck in the mud. So he picked up a big handful of mud and he threw it at her, up among the stars, and hit her on the head. And she fell down onto the earth into his arms and the ball of mud is the moon in the sky. And then they had children which is all of us.

EDWARD: It's not true, though.

JOSHUA: Of course it's not true. It's a bad story. Adam and Eve is true. God made man white like him and gave him the bad woman who liked the snake and gave us all this trouble.

(Clive and Harry come out.)

CLIVE: Run along now, Edward. No, you may stay. You mustn't repeat anything you hear to your mother or your grandmother or Ellen.

EDWARD: Or Mrs. Saunders?

CLIVE: Mrs. Saunders is an unusual woman and does not require protection in the same way. Harry, there was trouble last night where we expected it. But it's all over now. Everything is under control but nobody should leave the house today I think.

HARRY: Casualties?

CLIVE: No, none of the soldiers hurt thank God. We did a certain amount of damage, set a village on fire and so forth.

HARRY: Was that necessary?

CLIVE: Obviously, it was necessary, Harry, or it wouldn't have happened. The army will come and visit, no doubt. You'll like that, eh, Joshua, to see the British army? And a treat for you, Edward, to see the soldiers. Would you like to be a soldier?

EDWARD: I'd rather be an explorer.

CLIVE: Ah, Harry, like you, you see. I didn't know an explorer at his age. Breakfast, I think, Joshua.

(Clive and Joshua go in. Harry is following.)

EDWARD: Uncle.

(Harry stops.)

EDWARD: Harry, why won't you talk to me?

HARRY: Of course I'll talk to you.

EDWARD: If you won't be nice to me I'll tell father.

HARRY: Edward, no, not a word, never, not to your mother, nobody, please. Edward, do you understand? Please.

EDWARD: I won't tell. I promise I'll never tell. I've cut my finger and sworn.

HARRY: There's no need to get so excited Edward. We can't be together all the time. I will have to leave soon anyway, and go back to the river.

EDWARD: You can't, you can't go. Take me with you.

ELLEN: Edward!

HARRY: I have my duty to the Empire.

(Harry goes in. Ellen comes out.)

ELLEN: Edward, breakfast time. Edward.

EDWARD: I'm not hungry.

ELLEN: Betty, please come and speak to Edward.

(Betty comes.)

BETTY: Why what's the matter?

ELLEN: He won't come in for breakfast.

BETTY: Edward, I shall call your father.

EDWARD: You can't make me eat.

(He goes in. Betty is about to follow.)

ELLEN: Betty.

(Betty stops.)

ELLEN: Betty, when Edward goes to school will I have to leave?

BETTY: Never mind, Ellen dear, you'll get another place. I'll give you an excellent reference.

ELLEN: I don't want another place, Betty. I want to stay with you forever.

BETTY: If you go back to England you might get married, Ellen. You're quite pretty, you shouldn't despair of getting a husband.

ELLEN: I don't want a husband. I want you.

BETTY: Children of your own, Ellen, think.

ELLEN: I don't want children, I don't like children. I just want to be alone with you, Betty, and sing for you and kiss you because I love you, Betty.

BETTY: I love you too, Ellen. But women have their duty as soldiers have. You must be a mother if you can.

ELLEN: Betty, Betty, I love you so much. I want to stay with you forever, my love for you is eternal, stronger than death. I'd rather die than leave you, Betty.

BETTY: No you wouldn't, Ellen, don't be silly. Come, don't cry. You don't feel what you think you do. It's the loneliness here and the climate is very confusing. Come and have breakfast, Ellen dear, and I'll forget all about it.

(Ellen goes, Clive comes.)

BETTY: Clive, please forgive me.
CLIVE: Will you leave me alone?

(*Betty goes back into the house. Harry comes.*)

CLIVE: Women, Harry. I envy you going into the jungle, a man's life.
HARRY: I envy you.
CLIVE: Harry, I know you do. I have spoken to Betty.
HARRY: I assure you, Clive—
CLIVE: Please say nothing about it.
HARRY: My friendship for you—
CLIVE: Absolutely. I know the friendship between us, Harry, is not something that could be spoiled by the weaker sex. Friendship between men is a fine thing. It is the noblest form of relationship.
HARRY: I agree with you.
CLIVE: There is the necessity of reproduction. The family is all important. And there is the pleasure. But what we put ourselves through to get that pleasure, Harry. When I heard about our fine fellows last night fighting those savages to protect us I thought yes, that is what I aspire to. I tell you Harry, in confidence, I suddenly got out of Mrs. Saunders' bed and came out here on the verandah and looked at the stars.
HARRY: I couldn't sleep last night either.
CLIVE: There is something dark about women, that threatens what is best in us. Between men that light burns brightly.
HARRY: I didn't know you felt like that.
CLIVE: Women are irrational, demanding, inconsistent, treacherous, lustful, and they smell different from us.
HARRY: Clive—
CLIVE: Think of the comradeship of men, Harry, sharing adventures, sharing danger, risking their lives together.

(*Harry takes hold of Clive.*)

CLIVE: What are you doing?
HARRY: Well, you said—
CLIVE: I said what?
HARRY: Between men.

(*Clive is speechless.*)

I'm sorry, I misunderstood, I would never have dreamt, I thought—
CLIVE: My God, Harry, how disgusting.
HARRY: You will not betray my confidence.
CLIVE: I feel contaminated.
HARRY: I struggle against it. You cannot imagine the shame. I have tried everything to save myself.
CLIVE: The most revolting perversion. Rome fell, Harry, and this sin can destroy an empire.
HARRY: It is not a sin, it is a disease.
CLIVE: A disease more dangerous than diphtheria. Effeminacy is contagious. How I have been deceived. Your face does not look degenerate. Oh Harry, how did you sink to this?

HARRY: Clive, help me, what am I to do?
CLIVE: You have been away from England too long.
HARRY: Where can I go except into the jungle to hide?
CLIVE: You don't do it with the natives, Harry? My God, what a betrayal of the Queen.
HARRY: Clive, I am like a man born crippled. Please help me.
CLIVE: You must repent.
HARRY: I have thought of killing myself.
CLIVE: That is a sin too.
HARRY: There is no way out. Clive, I beg of you, do not betray my confidence.
CLIVE: I cannot keep a secret like this. Rivers will be named after you, it's unthinkable. You must save yourself from depravity. You must get married. You are not unattractive to women. What a relief that you and Betty were not after all—good God, how disgusting. Now Mrs. Saunders. She's a woman of spirit, she could go with you on your expeditions.
HARRY: I suppose getting married wouldn't be any worse than killing myself.
CLIVE: Mrs. Saunders! Mrs. Saunders! Ask her now, Harry. Think of England.

(*Mrs. Saunders comes. Clive withdraws. Harry goes up to Mrs. Saunders.*)

HARRY: Mrs. Saunders, will you marry me?
MRS. SAUNDERS: Why?
HARRY: We are both alone.
MRS. SAUNDERS: I choose to be alone, Mr. Bagley. If I can look after myself, I'm sure you can. Clive, I have something important to tell you. I've just found Joshua putting earth on his head. He tells me his parents were killed last night by the British soldiers. I think you owe him an apology on behalf of the Queen.
CLIVE: Joshua! Joshua!
MRS. SAUNDERS: Mr. Bagley, I could never be a wife again. There is only one thing about marriage that I like.

(*Joshua comes.*)

CLIVE: Joshua, I am horrified to hear what has happened. Good God!
MRS. SAUNDERS: His father was shot. His mother died in the blaze.
　　　　　　　　　　　　　　　　(*Mrs. Saunders goes.*)
CLIVE: Joshua, do you want a day off? Do you want to go to your people?
JOSHUA: Not my people, sir.
CLIVE: But you want to go to your parents' funeral?
JOSHUA: No sir.
CLIVE: Yes, Joshua, yes, your father and mother. I'm sure they were loyal to the crown. I'm sure it was all a terrible mistake.
JOSHUA: My mother and father were bad people.
CLIVE: Joshua, no.
JOSHUA: You are my father and mother.

CLIVE: Well really. I don't know what to say. That's very decent of you. Are you sure there's nothing I can do? You can have the day off you know.

(*Betty comes out followed by Edward.*)

BETTY: What's the matter? What's happening?

CLIVE: Something terrible has happened. No, I mean some relatives of Joshua's met with an accident.

JOSHUA: May I go sir?

CLIVE: Yes, yes of course. Good God, what a terrible thing. Bring us a drink will you Joshua?

(*Joshua goes.*)

EDWARD: What? What?

BETTY: Edward, go and do your lessons.

EDWARD: What is it, Uncle Harry?

HARRY: Go and do your lessons.

ELLEN: Edward, come in here at once.

EDWARD: What's happened, Uncle Harry?

(*Harry has moved aside, Edward follows him. Ellen comes out.*)

HARRY: Go away. Go inside. Ellen!

ELLEN: Go inside, Edward. I shall tell your mother.

BETTY: Go inside, Edward at once. I shall tell your father.

CLIVE: Go inside, Edward. And Betty you go inside too.

(*Betty, Edward, and Ellen go. Maud comes out.*)

CLIVE: Go inside. And Ellen, you come outside.

(*Ellen comes out.*)

Mr. Bagley has something to say to you.

HARRY: Ellen. I don't suppose you would marry me?

ELLEN: What if I said yes?

CLIVE: Run along now, you two want to be alone.

(*Harry and Ellen go out. Joshua brings Clive a drink.*)

JOSHUA: The governess and your wife, sir.

CLIVE: What's that, Joshua?

JOSHUA: She talks of love to your wife, sir. I have seen them. Bad women.

CLIVE: Joshua, you go too far. Get out of my sight.

Scene Five

(*The verandah. A table with a white cloth. A wedding cake and a large knife. Bottles and glasses. Joshua is putting things on the table. Edward has the doll. Joshua sees him with it. He holds out his hand. Edward gives him the doll. Joshua takes the knife and cuts the doll open and shakes the sawdust out of it. Joshua throws the doll under the table.*)

MAUD: Come along Edward, this is such fun.

(*Everyone enters, triumphal arch for Harry and Ellen.*)

MAUD: Your mama's wedding was a splendid occasion, Edward. I cried and cried.

(*Ellen and Betty go aside.*)

ELLEN: Betty, what happens with a man? I don't know what to do.

BETTY: You just keep still.

ELLEN: And what does he do?

BETTY: Harry will know what to do.

ELLEN: And is it enjoyable?

BETTY: Ellen, you're not getting married to enjoy yourself.

ELLEN: Don't forget me, Betty.

(*Ellen goes.*)

BETTY: I think my necklace has been stolen Clive. I did so want to wear it at the wedding.

EDWARD: It was Joshua. Joshua took it.

CLIVE: Joshua?

EDWARD: He did, he did, I saw him with it.

HARRY: Edward, that's not true.

EDWARD: It is, it is.

HARRY: Edward, I'm afraid you took it yourself.

EDWARD: I did not.

HARRY: I have seen him with it.

CLIVE: Edward, is that true? Where is it? Did you take your mother's necklace? And to try and blame Joshua, good God.

(*Edward runs off.*)

BETTY: Edward, come back. Have you got my necklace?

HARRY: I should leave him alone. He'll bring it back.

BETTY: I wanted to wear it. I wanted to look my best at your wedding.

HARRY: You always look your best to me.

BETTY: I shall get drunk.

(*Mrs. Saunders comes.*)

MRS. SAUNDERS: The sale of my property is completed. I shall leave tomorrow.

CLIVE: That's just as well. Whose protection will you seek this time?

MRS. SAUNDERS: I shall go to England and buy a farm there. I shall introduce threshing machines.

CLIVE: Amazing spirit.

(*He kisses her. Betty launches herself on Mrs. Saunders. They fall to the ground.*)

CLIVE: Betty—Caroline—I don't deserve this—Harry, Harry.

(*Harry and Clive separate them. Harry holding Mrs. Saunders, Clive Betty.*)

CLIVE: Mrs. Saunders, how can you abuse my hospitality? How dare you touch my wife? You must leave here at once.

BETTY: Go away, go away. You are a wicked woman.

MAUD: Mrs. Saunders, I am shocked. This is your hostess.

CLIVE: Pack your bags and leave the house this instant.

MRS. SAUNDERS: I was leaving anyway. There's no place for me here. I have made arrangements to leave tomorrow, and tomorrow is when I will leave. I wish you joy, Mr. Bagley.

(*Mrs. Saunders goes.*)

CLIVE: No place for her anywhere I should think. Shocking behavior.

BETTY: Oh Clive, forgive me, and love me like you used to.

CLIVE: Were you jealous my dove? My own dear wife!

MAUD: Ah, Mr. Bagley, one flesh, you see.

(*Edward comes back with the necklace.*)

CLIVE: Good God, Edward, it's true.

EDWARD: I was minding it for mama because of the troubles.

CLIVE: Well done, Edward, that was very manly of you. See Betty? Edward was protecting his mama's jewels from the rebels. What a hysterical fuss over nothing. Well done, little man. It is quite safe now. The bad men are dead. Edward, you may do up the necklace for mama.

(*Edward does up Betty's necklace, supervised by Clive, Joshua is drinking steadily. Ellen comes back.*)

MAUD: Ah, here's the bride. Come along, Ellen, you don't cry at your own wedding, only at other people's.

CLIVE: Now, speeches, speeches. Who is going to make a speech? Harry, make a speech.

HARRY: I'm no speaker. You're the one for that.

ALL: Speech, speech.

HARRY: My dear friends—what can I say—the empire—the family—the married state to which I have always aspired—your shining example of domestic bliss—my great good fortune in winning Ellen's love—happiest day of my life.

(*Applause.*)

CLIVE: Cut the cake, cut the cake.

(*Harry and Ellen take the knife to cut the cake. Harry steps on the doll under the table.*)

HARRY: What's this?

ELLEN: Oh look.

BETTY: Edward.

EDWARD: It was Joshua. It was Joshua. I saw him.

CLIVE: Don't tell lies again.

(*He hits Edward across the side of the head.*)

Unaccustomed as I am to public speaking—

(*Cheers.*)

Harry, my friend. So brave and strong and supple.
Ellen, from neath her veil so shyly peeking.
I wish you joy. A toast—the happy couple.
Dangers are past. Our enemies are killed.
—Put your arm round her, Harry, have a kiss—

All murmuring of discontent is stilled.
Long may you live in peace and joy and bliss.

(*While he is speaking Joshua raises his gun to shoot Clive. Only Edward sees. He does nothing to warn the others. He puts his hands over his ears.*)
(*Black.*)

ACT TWO • Scene One

(*Winter afternoon. Inside the hut of a one o'clock club, a children's playcenter in a park, Victoria and Lin, mothers. Cathy, Lin's daughter, age 5, played by a man, clinging to Lin. Victoria reading a book.*)

CATHY: Yum yum bubblegum.
Stick it up your mother's bum.
When it's brown
Pull it down
Yum yum bubblegum.

LIN: Like your shoes, Victoria.

CATHY: Jack be nimble, Jack be quick,
Jack jump over the candlestick.
Silly Jack, he should jump higher,
Goodness gracious, great balls of fire.

LIN: Cathy, do stop. Do a painting.

CATHY: You do a painting.

LIN: You do a painting.

CATHY: What shall I paint?

LIN: Paint a house.

CATHY: No.

LIN: Princess.

CATHY: No.

LIN: Pirates.

CATHY: Already done that.

LIN: Spacemen.

CATHY: I never paint spacemen. You know I never.

LIN: Paint a car crash and blood everywhere.

CATHY: No, don't tell me. I know what to paint.

LIN: Go on then. You need an apron, where's an apron. Here.

CATHY: Don't want an apron.

LIN: Lift up your arms. There's a good girl.

CATHY: I don't want to paint.

LIN: Don't paint. Don't paint.

CATHY: What shall I do? You paint. What shall I do mum?

VICTORIA: There's nobody on the big bike, Cathy, quick.

(*Cathy goes out. Victoria is watching the children playing outside.*)

VICTORIA: Tommy, it's Jimmy's gun. Let him have it. What the hell.

(*She goes on reading. She reads while she talks.*)

LIN: I don't know how you can concentrate.

VICTORIA: You have to or you never do anything.

LIN: Yeh, well. It's really warm in here, that's one thing. It's better than standing out there. I got chilblains last winter.

VICTORIA: It is warm.

LIN: I suppose Tommy doesn't let you read much. I expect he talks to you while you're reading.

VICTORIA: Yes, he does.

LIN: I didn't get very far with that book you lent me.

VICTORIA: That's all right.

LIN: I was glad to have it, though. I sit with it on my lap while I'm watching telly. Well, Cathy's off. She's frightened I'm going to leave her. It's the baby-minder didn't work out when she was two, she still remembers. You can't get them used to other people if you're by yourself. It's no good blaming me. She clings round my knees every morning up the nursery and they don't say anything but they make you feel you're making her do it. But I'm desperate for her to go to school. I did cry when I left her the first day. You wouldn't, you're too fucking sensible. You'll call the teacher by her first name. I really fancy you.

VICTORIA: What?

LIN: Put your book down will you for five minutes. You didn't hear a word I said.

VICTORIA: I don't get much time to myself.

LIN: Do you ever go to the movies?

VICTORIA: Tommy's very funny who he's left with. My mother babysits sometimes.

LIN: Your husband could babysit.

VICTORIA: But then we couldn't go to the movies.

LIN: You could go to the movies with me.

VICTORIA: Oh I see.

LIN: Couldn't you?

VICTORIA: Well yes, I could.

LIN: Friday night?

VICTORIA: What film are we talking about?

LIN: Does it matter what film?

VICTORIA: Of course it does.

LIN: You choose then. Friday night.

(*Cathy comes in with gun, shoots them saying Kiou kiou kiou, and runs off again.*)

Not in a foreign language, ok. You don't go in the movies to read.

(*Lin watches the children playing outside.*)

Don't hit him, Cathy, kill him. Point the gun, kiou, kiou, kiou. That's the way.

VICTORIA: They've just banned war toys in Sweden.

LIN: The kids'll just hit each other more.

VICTORIA: Well, psychologists do differ in their opinions as to whether or not aggression is innate.

LIN: Yeh?

VICTORIA: I'm afraid I do let Tommy play with guns and just hope he'll get it out of his system and not end up in the army.

LIN: I've got a brother in the army.

VICTORIA: Oh I'm sorry. Whereabouts is he stationed?

LIN: Belfast.

VICTORIA: Oh dear.

LIN: I've got a friend who's Irish and we went on a Troops Out march. Now my dad won't speak to me.

VICTORIA: I don't get on too well with my father either.

LIN: And your husband? How do you get on with him?

VICTORIA: Oh, fine. Up and down. You know. Very well. He helps with the washing up and everything.

LIN: I left mine two years ago. He let me keep Cathy and I'm grateful for that.

VICTORIA: You shouldn't be grateful.

LIN: I'm a lesbian.

VICTORIA: You still shouldn't be grateful.

LIN: I'm grateful he didn't hit me harder than he did.

VICTORIA: I suppose I'm very lucky with Martin.

LIN: Don't get at me about how I bring up Cathy, ok?

VICTORIA: I didn't.

LIN: Yes you did. War toys. I'll give her a rifle for Christmas and blast Tommy's pretty head off for a start.

(*Victoria goes back to her book.*)

LIN: I hate men.

VICTORIA: You have to look at it in a historical perspective in terms of learnt behavior since the industrial revolution.

LIN: I just hate the bastards.

VICTORIA: Well it's a point of view.

(*By now Cathy has come back in and started painting in many colors, without an apron. Edward comes in.*)

EDWARD: Victoria, mother's in the park. She's walking round all the paths very fast.

VICTORIA: By herself?

EDWARD: I told her you were here.

VICTORIA: Thanks.

EDWARD: Come on.

VICTORIA: Ten minutes talking to my mother and I have to spend two hours in a hot bath.

(*Victoria goes out.*)

LIN: Shit, Cathy, what about an apron. I don't mind you having paint on your frock but if it doesn't wash off just don't tell me you can't wear your frock with paint on, ok?

CATHY: Ok.

LIN: You're gay, aren't you?

EDWARD: I beg your pardon?

LIN: I really fancy your sister. I thought you'd understand. You do but you can go on pretending you don't, I don't mind. That's lovely Cathy, I like the green bit.

EDWARD: Don't go around saying that. I might lose my job.

LIN: The last gardener was ever so straight. He used to flash at all the little girls.

EDWARD: I wish you hadn't said that about me. It's not true.

LIN: It's not true and I never said it and I never thought it and I never will think it again.

EDWARD: Someone might have heard you.

LIN: Shut up about it then.

(*Betty and Victoria come up.*)

BETTY: It's quite a nasty bump.

VICTORIA: He's not even crying.

BETTY: I think that's very worrying. You and Edward always cried. Perhaps he's got concussion.

VICTORIA: Of course he hasn't mummy.

BETTY: That other little boy was very rough. Should you speak to somebody about him?

VICTORIA: Tommy was hitting him with a spade.

BETTY: Well he's a real little boy. And so brave not to cry. You must watch him for signs of drowsiness. And nausea. If he's sick in the night, phone an ambulance. Well, you're looking very well darling, a bit tired, a bit peaky. I think the fresh air agrees with Edward. He likes the open air life because of growing up in Africa. He misses the sunshine, don't you, darling? We'll soon have Edward back on his feet. What fun it is here.

VICTORIA: This is Lin. And Cathy.

BETTY: Oh Cathy what a lovely painting. What is it? Well I think it's a house on fire. I think all that red is a fire. Is that right? Or do I see legs, is it a horse? Can I have the lovely painting or is it for mummy? Children have such imagination, it makes them so exhausting. (*To Lin.*) I'm sure you're wonderful, just like Victoria. I had help with my children. One does need help. That was in Africa of course so there wasn't the servant problem. This is my son Edward. This is—

EDWARD: Lin.

BETTY: Lin, this is Lin. Edward is doing something such fun, he's working in the park as a gardener. He does look exactly like a gardener.

EDWARD: I am a gardener.

BETTY: He's certainly making a stab at it. Well it will be a story to tell. I expect he will write a novel about it, or perhaps a television series. Well what a pretty child Cathy is. Victoria was a pretty child just like a little doll—you can't be certain how they'll grow up. I think Victoria's very pretty but she doesn't make the most of herself, do you darling, it's not the fashion I'm told but there are still women who dress out of *Vogue,* well we hope that's not what Martin looks for, though in many ways I wish it was, I don't know what it is Martin looks for and nor does he I'm afraid poor Martin. Well I am rattling on. I like your skirt dear but your shoes won't do at all. Well do they have lady gardeners, Edward, because I'm going to leave your father and I think I might need to get a job, not a gardener really of course. I haven't got green fingers I'm afraid, everything I touch shrivels straight up. Vicky gave me a poinsettia last Christmas and the leaves all fell off on Boxing Day. Well good heavens, look what's happened to that lovely painting.

(*Cathy has slowly and carefully been going over the whole sheet with black paint. She has almost finished.*)

LIN: What you do that for silly? It was nice.

CATHY: I like your earrings.

VICTORIA: Did you say you're leaving Daddy?

BETTY: Do you darling? Shall I put them on you? My ears aren't pierced, I never wanted that, they just clip on the lobe.

LIN: She'll get paint on you, mind.

BETTY: There's a pretty girl. It doesn't hurt does it? Well you'll grow up to know you have to suffer a little bit for beauty.

CATHY: Look mum I'm pretty, I'm pretty, I'm pretty.

LIN: Stop showing off Cathy.

VICTORIA: It's time we went home. Tommy, time to go home. Last go then, all right.

EDWARD: Mum did I hear you right just now?

CATHY: I want my ears pierced.

BETTY: Ooh, not till you're big.

CATHY: I know a girl got her ears pierced and she's three. She's got real gold.

BETTY: I don't expect she's English, darling. Can I give her a sweety? I know they're not very good for the teeth, Vicky gets terribly cross with me. What does mummy say?

LIN: Just one, thank you very much.

CATHY: I like your beads.

BETTY: Yes they are pretty. Here you are.

(*It is the necklace from Act One.*)

CATHY: Look at me, look at me. Vicky, Vicky, Vicky look at me.

LIN: You look lovely, come on now.

CATHY: And your hat, and your hat.

LIN: No, that's enough.

BETTY: Of course she can have my hat.

CATHY: Yes, yes, hat, hat. Look look look.

LIN: That's enough, please, stop it now. Hat off, bye bye hat.

CATHY: Give me my hat.

LIN: Bye bye beads.

BETTY: It's just fun.

LIN: It's very nice of you.

CATHY: I want my beads.

LIN: Where's the other earring?

CATHY: I want my beads.

(*Cathy has the other earring in her hand. Meanwhile Victoria and Edward look for it.*)

EDWARD: Is it on the floor?

VICTORIA: Don't step on it.

EDWARD: Where?

CATHY: I want my beads. I want my beads.

LIN: You'll have a smack.

(*Lin gets the earring from Cathy.*)

CATHY: I want my beads.

BETTY: Oh dear oh dear. Have you got the earring? Thank you darling.

CATHY: I want my beads, you're horrid, I hate you, mum, you smell.

BETTY: This is the point you see where one had help. Well it's been lovely seeing you dears and I'll be off again on my little walk.

VICTORIA: You're leaving him? Really?

BETTY: Yes you hear aright, Vicky, yes. I'm finding a little flat, that will be fun.

(*Betty goes.*)

Bye bye Tommy, granny's going now. Tommy don't hit that little girl, say goodbye to granny.

VICTORIA: Fucking hell.

EDWARD: Puking Jesus.

LIN: That was news was it, leaving your father?

EDWARD: They're going to want so much attention.

VICTORIA: Does everybody hate their mothers?

EDWARD: Mind you, I wouldn't live with him.

LIN: Stop snivelling, pigface. Where's your coat? Be quiet now and we'll have doughnuts for tea and if you keep on we'll have dogshit on toast.

(*Cathy laughs so much she lies on the floor.*)

VICTORIA: Tommy, you've had two last goes. Last last last last go.

LIN: Not that funny, come on, coat on.

EDWARD: Can I have your painting?

CATHY: What for?

EDWARD: For a friend of mine.

CATHY: What's his name?

EDWARD: Gerry.

CATHY: How old is he?

EDWARD: Thirty-two.

CATHY: You can if you like. I don't care. Kiou kiou kiou kiou.

(*Cathy goes out. Edward takes the painting and goes out.*)

LIN: Will you have sex with me?

VICTORIA: I don't know what Martin would say. Does it count as adultery with a woman?

LIN: You'd enjoy it.

Scene Two

(*Spring. Swing, bench, pond nearby. Edward is gardening. Gerry sitting on a bench.*)

EDWARD: I sometimes pretend we don't know each other. And you've come to the park to eat your sandwiches and look at me.

GERRY: That would be more interesting, yes. Come and sit down.

EDWARD: If the superintendent comes I'll be in trouble. It's not my dinner time yet. Where were you last night? I think you owe me an explanation. We always do tell each other everything.

GERRY: Is that a rule?

EDWARD: It's what we agreed.

GERRY: It's a habit we've got into. Look, I was drunk. I woke up at 4 o'clock on somebody's floor. I was sick. I hadn't any money for a cab. I went back to sleep.

EDWARD: You could have phoned.

GERRY: There wasn't a phone.

EDWARD: Sorry.

GERRY: There was a phone and I didn't phone you. Leave it alone, Eddy, I'm warning you.

EDWARD: What are you going to do to me, then?

GERRY: I'm going to the pub.

EDWARD: I'll join you in ten minutes.

GERRY: I didn't ask you to come. (*Edward goes.*) Two years I've been with Edward. You have to get away sometimes or you lose sight of yourself. The train from Victoria to Clapham still has those compartments without a corridor. As soon as I got on the platform I saw who I wanted. Slim hips, tense shoulders, trying not to look at anyone. I put my hand on my packet just long enough so that he couldn't miss it. The train came in. You don't want to get in too fast or some straight dumbo might get in with you. I sat by the window. I couldn't see where the fuck he'd got to. Then just as the whistle went he got in. Great. It's a six-minute journey so you can't start anything you can't finish. I stared at him and he unzipped his flies. Then he stopped. So I stood up and took my cock out. He took me in his mouth and shut his eyes tight. He was sort of mumbling it about as if he wasn't sure what to do, so I said, "A bit tighter son" and he said "Sorry" and then got on with it. He was jerking off with his left hand, and I could see he'd got a fairsized one. I wished he'd keep still so I could see his watch. I was getting really turned on. What if we pulled into Clapham Junction now. Of course by the time we sat down again the train was just slowing up. I felt wonderful. Then he started talking. It's better if nothing is said. Once you find he's a librarian in Walthamstow with a special interest in science fiction and lives with his aunt, then forget it. He said I hope you don't think I do this all the time. I said I hope you will from now on. He said he would if I was on the train, but why don't we go out for a meal? I opened the door before the train stopped. I told him I live with somebody, I don't want to know. He was jogging sideways to keep up. He said "What's your phone number, you're my ideal physical type, what sign of the zodiac are you? Where do you live? Where are you going now?" It's not fair, I saw him at Victoria a couple of months later and I went straight down to the end of the platform and I picked up somebody really great who never said a word, just smiled.

(*Cathy is on the swing.*)

CATHY: Batman and Robin
Had a batmobile.
Robin done a fart
And paralyzed the wheel.
The wheel couldn't take it,
The engine fell apart,
All because of Robin
And his supersonic fart.

(*Cathy goes. Martin, Victoria and Betty walking slowly.*)

MARTIN: Tom!

BETTY: He'll fall in.

VICTORIA: No he won't.

MARTIN: Don't go too near the edge Tom. Throw the bread from there. The ducks can get it.

BETTY: I'll never be able to manage. If I can't even walk down the street by myself. Everything looks so fierce.

VICTORIA: Just watch Tommy feeding the ducks.

BETTY: He's going to fall in. Make Martin make him move back.

VICTORIA: He's not going to fall in.

BETTY: It's since I left your father.

VICTORIA: Mummy, it really was the right decision.

BETTY: Everything comes at me from all directions. Martin despises me.

VICTORIA: Of course he doesn't, mummy.

BETTY: Of course he does.

MARTIN: Throw the bread. That's the way. The duck can get it. Quack quack quack quack quack.

BETTY: I don't want to take pills. Lin says you can't trust doctors.

VICTORIA: You're not taking pills. You're doing very well.

BETTY: But I'm so frightened.

VICTORIA: What are you frightened of?

BETTY: Victoria, you always ask that as if there was suddenly going to be an answer.

VICTORIA: Are you all right sitting there?

BETTY: Yes, yes. Go and be with Martin.

(*Victoria joins Martin, Betty stays sitting on the bench.*)

MARTIN: You take the job, you go to Manchester. You turn it down, you stay in London. People are making decisions like this every day of the week. It needn't be for more than a year. You get long vacations. Our relationship might well stand the strain of that, and if it doesn't we're better out of it. I don't want to put any pressure on you. I'd just like to know so we can sell the house. I think we're moving into an entirely different way of life if you go to Manchester because it won't end there. We could keep the house as security for Tommy but he might as well get used to the fact that life nowadays is insecure. You should ask your mother what she thinks and then do the opposite. I could just take that room in Barbara's house, and then we could babysit for each other. You think that means I want to fuck Barbara. I don't. Well, I do, but I won't. And even if I did, what's a fuck between friends? What are we meant to do it with, strangers? Whatever you want to do, I'll be delighted. If you could just let me know what it is I'm to be delighted about. Don't cry again, Vicky, I'm not the sort of man who makes women cry.

(*Lin has come in and sat down with Betty, Cathy joins them. She is wearing a pink dress and carrying a rifle.*)

LIN: I've bought her three new frocks. She won't wear jeans to school any more because Tracy and Mandy called her a boy.

CATHY: Tracy's got a perm.

LIN: You should have shot them.

CATHY: They're coming to tea and we've got to have trifle. Not trifle you make, trifle out of a packet. And you've got to wear a skirt. And tights.

LIN: Tracy's mum wears jeans.

CATHY: She does not. She wears velvet.

BETTY: Well I think you look very pretty. And if that gun has caps in it please take it a long way away.

CATHY: It's got red caps. They're louder.

MARTIN: Do you think you're well enough to do this job? You don't have to do it. No one's going to think any the less of you if you stay here with me. There's no point being so liberated you make yourself cry all the time. You stay and we'll get everything sorted out. What it is about sex, when we talk while it's happening I get to feel it's like a driving lesson. Left, right, a little faster, carry on, slow down—

(*Cathy shoots Victoria.*)

CATHY: You're dead Vicky.

VICTORIA: Aaaargh.

CATHY: Fall over.

VICTORIA: I'm not falling over, the ground's wet.

CATHY: You're dead.

VICTORIA: Yes, I'm dead.

CATHY: The Dead Hand Gang fall over. They said I had to fall over in the mud or I can't play. That duck's a mandarin.

MARTIN: Which one? Look, Tommy.

CATHY: That's a diver. It's got a yellow eye and it dives. That's a goose. Tommy doesn't know it's a goose, he thinks it's a duck. The babies get eaten by weasels. Kiou kiou.

(*Cathy goes.*)

MARTIN: So I lost my erection last night not because I'm not prepared to talk, it's just that taking in technical information is a different part of the brain and also I don't like to feel that you do it better to yourself. I have read the Hite report. I do know that women have to learn to get their pleasure despite our clumsy attempts at expressing undying devotion and ecstasy, and that what we spent our adolescence thinking was an animal urge we had to suppress is in fact a fine art we have to acquire. I'm not like whatever percentage of American men have become impotent as a direct result of women's liberation, which I am totally in favor of, more I sometimes think than you are yourself. Nor am I one of your villains who sticks it in, bangs away, and falls asleep. My one aim is to give you pleasure. My one aim is to give you rolling orgasms like I do other women. So why the hell don't you have them? My analysis for what it's worth is that despite all my efforts you still feel dominated by me. I in fact think it's very sad that you don't feel able to take that job. It makes me feel very guilty. I don't want you to do it just because I encourage you to do it. But don't you think you'd feel better if you did take the job? You're the one who's talked about freedom. You're the one who's experimenting with bisexuality, and I don't stop you, I think women have something to give each other. You seem to need the mutual support. You find me too overwhelming. So follow it through, go away, leave me and Tommy alone for a bit, we can manage perfectly well without you. I'm not putting any pressure on you but I don't think you're being a whole person. God knows I do everything I can to make you stand on your own two feet. Just be yourself. You don't seem to realize how insulting it is to me that you can't get yourself together.

(Martin and Victoria go.)

BETTY: You must be very lonely yourself with no husband. You don't miss him?

LIN: Not really, no.

BETTY: Maybe you like being on your own.

LIN: I'm seeing quite a lot of Vicky. I don't live alone. I live with Cathy.

BETTY: I would have been frightened when I was your age. I thought, the poor children, their mother all alone.

LIN: I've a lot of friends.

BETTY: I find when I'm making tea I put out two cups. It's strange not having a man in the house. You don't know who to do things for.

LIN: Yourself.

BETTY: Oh, that's very selfish.

LIN: Have you any women friends?

BETTY: I've never been so short of men's company that I've had to bother with women.

LIN: Don't you like women?

BETTY: They don't have such interesting conversations as men. There has never been a woman composer of genius. They don't have a sense of humor. They spoil things for themselves with their emotions. I can't say I do like women very much, no.

LIN: But you're a woman.

BETTY: There's nothing says you have to like yourself.

LIN: Do you like me?

BETTY: There's no need to take it personally, Lin.

(Martin and Victoria come back.)

MARTIN: Did you know if you put cocaine on your prick you can keep it up all night? The only thing is of course it goes numb so you don't feel anything. But you would, that's the main thing. I just want to make you happy.

BETTY: Vicky, I'd like to go home.

VICTORIA: Yes, mummy, of course.

BETTY: I'm sorry, dear.

VICTORIA: I think Tommy would like to stay out a bit longer.

LIN: Hello, Martin. We do keep out of each other's way.

MARTIN: I think that's the best thing to do.

BETTY: Perhaps you'd walk home with me, Martin. I do feel safer with a man. The park is so large the grass seems to tilt.

MARTIN: Yes, I'd like to go home and do some work. I'm writing a novel about women from the women's point of view.

(Martin and Betty go. Lin and Victoria are alone. They embrace.)

VICTORIA: Why the hell can't he just be a wife and come with me? Why does Martin make me tie myself in knots? No wonder we can't just have a simple fuck. No, not Martin, why do I make myself tie myself in knots. It's got to stop, Lin. I'm not like that with you. Would you love me if I went to Manchester?

LIN: Yes.

VICTORIA: Would you love me if I went on a climbing expedition in the Andes mountains?

LIN: Yes.

VICTORIA: Would you love me if my teeth fell out?

LIN: Yes.

VICTORIA: Would you love me if I loved ten other people?

LIN: And me?

VICTORIA: Yes.

LIN: Yes.

VICTORIA: And I feel apologetic for not being quite so subordinate as I was. I am more intelligent than him. I am brilliant.

LIN: Leave him Vic. Come and live with me.

VICTORIA: Don't be silly.

LIN: Silly, Christ, don't then. I'm not asking because I need to live with someone. I'd enjoy it, that's all, we'd both enjoy it. Fuck you. Cathy, for fuck's sake stop throwing stones at the ducks. The man's going to get you.

VICTORIA: What man? Do you need a man to frighten your child with?

LIN: My mother said it.

VICTORIA: You're so inconsistent, Lin.

LIN: I've changed who I sleep with, I can't change everything.

VICTORIA: Like when I had to stop you getting a job in a boutique and collaborating with sexist consumerism.

LIN: I should have got that job, Cathy would have liked it. Why shouldn't I have some decent clothes? I'm sick of dressing like a boy, why can't I look sexy, wouldn't you love me?

VICTORIA: Lin, you've no analysis.

LIN: No but I'm good at kissing aren't I? I give Cathy guns, my mum didn't give me guns. I dress her in jeans, she wants to wear dresses. I don't know. I can't work it out, I don't want to. You read too many books, you get at me all the time, you're worse to me than Martin is to you, you piss me off, my brother's been killed. I'm sorry to win the argument that way but there it is.

VICTORIA: What do you mean win the argument?

LIN: I mean be nice to me.

VICTORIA: In Belfast?

LIN: I heard this morning. Don't don't start. I've hardly seen him for two years. I rung my father. You'd think I'd shot him myself. He doesn't want me to go to the funeral.

(Cathy approaches.)

VICTORIA: What will you do?

LIN: Go of course.

CATHY: What is it? Who's killed? What?

LIN: It's Bill. Your uncle. In the army. Bill that gave you the blue teddy.

CATHY: Can I have his gun?

LIN: It's time we went home. Time you went to bed.

CATHY: No it's not.

LIN: We go home and you have tea and you have a bath and you go to bed.

CATHY: Fuck off.

LIN: Cathy, shut up.

VICTORIA: It's only half past five, why don't we—

LIN: I'll tell you why she has to go to bed—

VICTORIA: She can come home with me.

LIN: Because I want her out of the fucking way.

VICTORIA: She can come home with me.

CATHY: I'm not going to bed.

LIN: I want her home with me not home with you, I want her in bed, I want today over.

CATHY: I'm not going to bed.

(Lin hits Cathy, Cathy cries.)

LIN: And shut up or I'll give you something to cry for.

CATHY: I'm not going to bed.

VICTORIA: Cathy—

LIN: You keep out of it.

VICTORIA: Lin for God's sake.

(They are all shouting. Cathy runs off. Lin and Victoria are silent. Then they laugh and embrace.)

LIN: Where's Tommy?

VICTORIA: What? Didn't he go with Martin?

LIN: Did he?

VICTORIA: God oh God.

LIN: Cathy! Cathy!

VICTORIA: I haven't thought about him. How could I not think about him? Tommy!

LIN: Cathy! Come on, quick, I want some help.

VICTORIA: Tommy! Tommy!

(Cathy comes back.)

LIN: Where's Tommy? Have you seen him? Did he go with Martin? Do you know where he is?

CATHY: I showed him the goose. We went in the bushes.

LIN: Then what?

CATHY: I came back on the swing.

VICTORIA: And Tommy? Where was Tommy?

CATHY: He fed the ducks.

LIN: No that was before.

CATHY: He did a pee in the bushes. I helped him with his trousers.

VICTORIA: And after that?

CATHY: He fed the ducks.

VICTORIA: No no.

CATHY: He liked the ducks. I expect he fell in.

LIN: Did you see him fall in?

VICTORIA: Tommy! Tommy!

LIN: What's the last time you saw him?

CATHY: He did a pee.

VICTORIA: Mummy said he would fall in. Oh God, Tommy!

LIN: We'll go round the pond. We'll go opposite ways round the pond.

ALL *(shout)*: Tommy!

(Victoria and Lin go off opposite sides. Cathy climbs the bench.)

CATHY: Georgie Best, superstar
    Walks like a woman and wears a bra.
    There he is! I see him! Mum! Vicky! There he is! He's in the bushes.

(Lin comes back.)

LIN: Come on Cathy love, let's go home.

CATHY: Vicky's got him.

LIN: Come on.

CATHY: Is she cross?

LIN: No. Come on.

CATHY: I found him.

LIN: Yes. Come on.

(Cathy gets off the bench. Cathy and Lin hug.)

CATHY: I'm watching telly.

LIN: Ok.

CATHY: After the news.

LIN: Ok.

CATHY: I'm not going to bed.

LIN: Yes you are.

CATHY: I'm not going to bed now.

LIN: Not now but early.

CATHY: How early?

LIN: Not late.

CATHY: How not late?

LIN: Early.

CATHY: How early?

LIN: Not late.

(They go off together. Gerry comes on. He waits. Edward comes.)

EDWARD: I've got some fish for dinner. I thought I'd make a cheese sauce.

GERRY: I won't be in.

EDWARD: Where are you going?

GERRY: For a start I'm going to a sauna. Then I'll see.

EDWARD: All right. What time will you be back? We'll eat then.

GERRY: You're getting like a wife.

EDWARD: I don't mind that.

GERRY: Why don't I do the cooking sometime?

EDWARD: You can if you like. You're just not so good at it that's all. Do it tonight.

GERRY: I won't be in tonight.

EDWARD: Do it tomorrow. If we can't eat it we can always go to a restaurant.

GERRY: Stop it.

EDWARD: Stop what?

GERRY: Just be yourself.

EDWARD: I don't know what you mean. Everyone's always tried to stop me being feminine and now you are too.

GERRY: You're putting it on.

EDWARD: I like doing the cooking. I like being fucked. You do like me like this really.

GERRY: I'm bored, Eddy.

EDWARD: Go to the sauna.

GERRY: And you'll stay home and wait up for me.

EDWARD: No, I'll go to bed and read a book.

GERRY: Or knit. You could knit me a pair of socks.

EDWARD: I might knit. I like knitting.

GERRY: I don't mind if you knit. I don't want to be married.

EDWARD: I do.

GERRY: Well I'm divorcing you.

EDWARD: I wouldn't want to keep a man who wants his freedom.

GERRY: Eddy, do stop playing the injured wife, it's not funny.

EDWARD: I'm not playing. It's true.

GERRY: I'm not the husband so you can't be the wife.

EDWARD: I'll always be here, Gerry, if you want to come back. I know you men like to go off by yourselves. I don't think I could love deeply more than once. But I don't think I can face life on my own so don't leave it too long or it may be too late.

GERRY: What are you trying to turn me into?

EDWARD: A monster, darling, which is what you are.

GERRY: I'll collect my stuff from the flat in the morning.

(*Gerry goes. Edward sits on the bench. It gets darker. Victoria comes.*)

VICTORIA: Tommy dropped a toy car somewhere, you haven't seen it? It's red. He says it's his best one. Oh the hell with it. Martin's reading him a story. There, isn't it quiet?

(*They sit on the bench, holding hands.*)

EDWARD: I like women.

VICTORIA: That should please mother.

EDWARD: No listen Vicky. I'd rather be a woman. I wish I had breasts like that, I think they're beautiful. Can I touch them?

VICTORIA: What, pretending they're yours?

EDWARD: No, I know it's you.

VICTORIA: I think I should warn you I'm enjoying this.

EDWARD: I'm sick of men.

VICTORIA: I'm sick of men.

EDWARD: I think I'm a lesbian.

Scene Three

(*The park. Summer night. Victoria, Lin, and Edward drunk.*)

LIN: Where are you?

VICTORIA: Come on.

EDWARD: Do we sit in a circle?

VICTORIA: Sit in a triangle.

EDWARD: You're good at mathematics. She's good at mathematics.

VICTORIA: Give me your hand. We all hold hands.

EDWARD: Do you know what to do?

LIN: She's making it up.

VICTORIA: We start off by being quiet.

EDWARD: What?

LIN: Hush.

EDWARD: Will something appear?

VICTORIA: It was your idea.

EDWARD: It wasn't my idea. It was your book.

LIN: You said call up the goddess.

EDWARD: I don't remember saying that.

LIN: We could have called her on the telephone.

EDWARD: Don't be so silly, this is meant to be frightening.

LIN: Kiss me.

VICTORIA: Are we going to do it?

LIN: We're doing it.

VICTORIA: A ceremony.

LIN: It's very sexy, you said it is. You said the women were priests in the temples and fucked all the time. I'm just helping.

VICTORIA: As long as it's sacred.

LIN: It's very sacred.

VICTORIA: Innin, Innana, Nana, Nut, Anat, Anahita, Istar, Isis.

LIN: I can't remember all that.

VICTORIA: Lin! Innin, Innana, Nana, Nut, Anat, Anahita, Istar, Isis.

(*Lin and Edward join in and continue the chant under Victoria's speech.*)

Goddess of many names, oldest of the old, who walked in chaos and created life, hear us calling you back through time, before Jehovah, before Christ, before men drove you out and burnt your temples, hear us, Lady, give us back what we were, give us the history we haven't had, make us the women we can't be.

ALL: Innin, Innana, Nana, Nut, Anat, Anahita, Istar, Isis.

(*Chant continues under other speeches.*)

LIN: Come back, goddess.

VICTORIA: Goddess of the sun and the moon her brother, little goddess of Crete with snakes in your hands.

LIN: Goddess of breasts.

VICTORIA: Goddess of cunts.

LIN: Goddess of fat bellies and babies. And blood blood blood.

(*Chant continues.*)

I see her.

EDWARD: What?

(*They stop chanting.*)

LIN: I see her. Very tall. Snakes in her hands. Light light light—look out! Did I give you a fright?

EDWARD: I was terrified.

VICTORIA: Don't spoil it Lin.

LIN: It's all out of a book.

VICTORIA: Innin Innana—I can't do it now. I was really enjoying myself.

LIN: She won't appear with a man here.

VICTORIA: They had men, they had sons and lovers.

EDWARD: They had eunuchs.

LIN: Don't give us ideas.

VICTORIA: There's Attis and Tammuz, they're torn to pieces.

EDWARD: Tear me to pieces, Lin.

VICTORIA: The priestess chose a lover for a year and he was king because she chose him and then he was killed at the end of the year.

EDWARD: Hurray.

VICTORIA: And the women had the children and nobody knew it was done by fucking so they didn't know about fathers and nobody cared who the father was and the property was passed down through the maternal line—

LIN: Don't turn it into a lecture, Vicky, it's meant to be an orgy.

VICTORIA: It never hurts to understand the theoretical background. You can't separate fucking and economics.

LIN: Give us a kiss.

EDWARD: Shut up, listen.

LIN: What?

EDWARD: There's somebody there.

LIN: Where?

EDWARD: There.

VICTORIA: The priestesses used to make love to total strangers.

LIN: Go on then, I dare you.

EDWARD: Go on, Vicky.

VICTORIA: He won't know it's a sacred rite in honor of the goddess.

EDWARD: We'll know.

LIN: We can tell him.

EDWARD: It's not what he thinks, it's what we think.

LIN: Don't tell him till after, he'll run a mile.

VICTORIA: Hello. We're having an orgy. Do you want me to suck your cock?

(*The stranger approaches. It is Martin.*)

MARTIN: There you are. I've been looking everywhere. What the hell are you doing? Do you know what the time is? You're all pissed out of your minds.

(*They leap on Martin, pull him down and start to make love to him.*)

MARTIN: Well that's all right. If all we're talking about is having a lot of sex there's no problem. I was all for the sixties when liberation just meant fucking.

(*Another stranger approaches.*)

LIN: Hey you, come here. Come and have sex with us.

VICTORIA: Who is it?

(*The stranger is a soldier.*)

LIN: It's my brother.

EDWARD: Lin, don't.

LIN: It's my brother.

VICTORIA: It's her sense of humor, you get used to it.

LIN: Shut up Vicky, it's my brother. Isn't it? Bill?

SOLDIER: Yes it's me.

LIN: And you are dead.

SOLDIER: Fucking dead all right yeh.

LIN: Have you come back to tell us something?

SOLDIER: No I've come for a fuck. That was the worst thing in the fucking army. Never fucking let out. Can't fucking talk to Irish girls. Fucking bored out of my fucking head. That or shit scared. For five minutes I'd be glad I wasn't bored, then I was fucking scared. Then we'd come in and I'd be glad I wasn't scared and then I was fucking bored. Spent the day reading fucking porn and the fucking night wanking. Man's fucking life in the fucking army? No fun when the fucking kids hate you. I got so I fucking wanted to kill someone and I got fucking killed myself and I want a fuck.

LIN: I miss you. Bill. Bill.

(*Lin collapses. Soldier goes. Victoria comforts Lin.*)

EDWARD: Let's go home.

LIN: Victoria, come home with us. Victoria's coming to live with me and Edward.

MARTIN: Tell me about it in the morning.

LIN: It's true.

VICTORIA: It is true.

MARTIN: Tell me when you're sober.

(*Edward, Lin, Victoria go off together. Martin goes off alone. Gerry comes on.*)

GERRY: I come here sometimes at night and pick somebody up. Sometimes I come here at night and don't pick anybody up. I do also enjoy walking about at night. There's never any trouble finding someone. I can have sex any time. You might not find the type you most fancy every day of the week, but there's plenty of people about who just enjoy having a good time. I quite like living alone. If I live with someone I get annoyed with them. Edward always put on Capital radio when he got up. The silence gets wasted. I wake up at four o'clock sometimes. Birds. Silence. If I bring somebody home I never let them stay the night. Edward! Edward!

(*Edward from Act One comes on.*)

EDWARD: Gerry I love you.

GERRY: Yes, I know. I love you, too.

EDWARD: You know what we did? I want to do it again. I think about it all the time. Don't you want to any more?

GERRY: Yes, of course.

SONG (“*Cloud Nine*”—*All*):

It'll be fine when you reach Cloud Nine.

Mist was rising and the night was dark.
Me and my baby took a walk in the park.
He said Be mine and you're on Cloud Nine.

Better watch out when you're on Cloud Nine.

Smoked some dope on the playground swings
Higher and higher on true love's wings
He said Be mine and you're on Cloud Nine.

Twenty-five years on the same Cloud Nine.

Who did she meet on her first blind date?
The guys were no surprise but the lady was great
They were women in love, they were on Cloud Nine.

Two the same, they were on Cloud Nine.

The bride was sixty-five, the groom was seventeen,
They fucked in the back of the black limousine.
It was divine in their silver Cloud Nine.

Simply divine in their silver Cloud Nine.

The wife's lover's children and my lover's wife,
Cooking in my kitchen, confusing my life.
And it's upside down when you reach Cloud Nine.

Upside down when you reach Cloud Nine.

Scene Four

(*The park. Afternoon in late summer. Martin, Cathy, Edward.*)

CATHY: Under the bramble bushes,
    Under the sea boom boom boom,
    True love for you my darling,
    True love for me my darling,
    When we are married,
    We'll raise a family.
    Boy for you, girl for me,
    Boom tiddley oom boom
    SEXY.
EDWARD: You'll have Tommy and Cathy tonight then ok? Tommy's still on antibiotics, do make him finish the bottle, he takes it in Ribena. It's no good in orange, he spits it out. Remind me to give you Cathy's swimming things.
CATHY: I did six strokes, didn't I Martin? Did I do a width? How many strokes is a length? How many miles is a swimming pool? I'm going to take my bronze and silver and gold and diamond.
MARTIN: Is Tommy still wetting the bed?
EDWARD: Don't get angry with him about it.
MARTIN: I just need to go to the launderette so I've got a spare sheet. Of course I don't get fucking angry,

Eddy, for God's sake. I don't like to say he is my son but he is my son. I'm surprised I'm not wetting the bed myself.
CATHY: I don't wet the bed ever. Do you wet the bed Martin?
MARTIN: No.
CATHY: You said you did.

(*Betty comes.*)

BETTY: I do miss the sun living in England but today couldn't be more beautiful. You appreciate the weekend when you're working. Betty's been at work this week, Cathy. It's terrible tiring, Martin, I don't know how you've done it all these years. And the money, I feel like a child with the money, Clive always paid everything but I do understand it perfectly well. Look Cathy let me show you my money.
CATHY: I'll count it. Let me count it. What's that?
BETTY: Five pounds, Five and five is—?
CATHY: One two three—
BETTY: Five and five is ten, and five—
CATHY: If I get it right can I have one?
EDWARD: No you can't.

(*Cathy goes on counting the money.*)

BETTY: I never like to say anything, Martin, or you'll think I'm being a mother-in-law.
EDWARD: Which you are.
BETTY: Thank you, Edward, I'm not talking to you. Martin, I think you're being wonderful. Vicky will come back. Just let her stay with Lin till she sorts herself out. It's very nice for a girl to have a friend; I had friends at school, that was very nice. But I'm sure Lin and Edward don't want her with them all the time. I'm not at all shocked that Lin and Edward aren't married and she already has a child, we all know first marriages don't always work out. But really Vicky must be in the way. And poor little Tommy. I hear he doesn't sleep properly and he's had a cough.
MARTIN: No, he's fine, Betty, thank you.
CATHY: My bed's horrible. I want to sleep in the big bed with Lin and Vicky and Eddy and I do get in if I've got a bad dream, and my bed's got a bump right in my back. I want to sleep in a tent.
BETTY: Well Tommy has got a nasty cough, Martin, whatever you say.
EDWARD: He's over that. He's got some medicine.
MARTIN: He takes it in Ribena.
BETTY: Well I'm glad to hear it. Look what a lot of money, Cathy, and I sit behind a desk of my own and I answer the telephone and keep the doctor's appointment book and it really is great fun.
CATHY: Can we go camping, Martin, in a tent? We could take the Dead Hand Gang.
BETTY: Not those big boys, Cathy? They're far too big and rough for you. They climb back into the park after dark. I'm sure mummy doesn't let you play with them, does she Edward? Well I don't know.

(*Ice cream bells.*)

CATHY: Ice cream. Martin you promised. I'll have a double ninety-nine. No I'll have a shandy lolly. Betty, you have a shandy lolly and I'll have a lick. No, you have a double ninety-nine and I'll have the chocolate.

(*Martin, Cathy, and Betty go, leaving Edward. Gerry comes.*)

GERRY: Hello, Eddy. Thought I might find you here.
EDWARD: Gerry.
GERRY: Not working today then?
EDWARD: I don't work here any more.
GERRY: Your mum got you into a dark suit?
EDWARD: No of course not. I'm on the dole. I am working, though, I do housework.
GERRY: Whose wife are you now then?
EDWARD: Nobody's. I don't think like that any more. I'm living with some women.
GERRY: What women?
EDWARD: It's my sister, Vic, and her lover. They go out to work and I look after the kids.
GERRY: I thought for a moment you said you were living with women.
EDWARD: We do sleep together, yes.
GERRY: I was passing the park anyway so I thought I'd look in. I was in the sauna the other night and I saw someone who looked like you but it wasn't. I had sex with him anyway.
EDWARD: I do go to the sauna sometimes.

(*Cathy comes, gives Edward an ice cream, goes.*)

GERRY: I don't think I'd like living with children. They make a lot of noise don't they?
EDWARD: I tell them to shut up and they shut up. I wouldn't want to leave them at the moment.
GERRY: Look why don't we go for a meal sometime?
EDWARD: Yes I'd like that. Where are you living now?
GERRY: Same place.
EDWARD: I'll come round for you tomorrow night about 7:30.
GERRY: Great.

(*Edward goes. Harry comes. Harry and Gerry pick each other up. They go off. Betty comes back.*)

BETTY: No, the ice cream was my treat, Martin. Off you go. I'm going to have a quiet sit in the sun.

(*Maud comes.*)

MAUD: Let Mrs. Saunders be a warning to you, Betty. I know what it is to be unprotected.
BETTY: But mother, I have a job. I earn money.
MAUD: I know we have our little differences but I always want what is best for you.

(*Ellen comes.*)

ELLEN: Betty, what happens with a man?
BETTY: You just keep still.
ELLEN: And is it enjoyable? Don't forget me, Betty.
(*Maud and Ellen go.*)

BETTY: I used to think Clive was the one who liked sex. But then I found I missed it. I used to touch myself when I was very little, I thought I'd invented something wonderful. I used to do it to go to sleep with or to cheer myself up, and one day it was raining and I was under the kitchen table, and my mother saw me with my hand under my dress rubbing away, and she dragged me out so quickly I hit my head and it bled and I was sick, and nothing was said, and I never did it again till this year. I thought if Clive wasn't looking at me there wasn't a person there. And one night in bed in my flat I was so frightened I started touching myself. I thought my hand might go through space. I touched my face, it was there, my arm, my breast, and my hand went down where I thought it shouldn't, and I thought well there is somebody there. It felt very sweet, it was a feeling from very long ago, it was very soft, just barely touching, and I felt myself gathering together more and more and I felt angry with Clive and angry with my mother and I went on and on defying them, and there was this vast feeling growing in me and all round me and they couldn't stop me and no one could stop me and I was there and coming and coming. Afterwards I thought I'd betrayed Clive. My mother would kill me. But I felt triumphant because I was a separate person from them. And I cried because I didn't want to be. But I don't cry about it any more. Sometimes I do it three times in one night and it really is great fun.

(*Victoria and Lin come in.*)

VICTORIA: So I said to the professor, I don't think this is an occasion for invoking the concept of structural causality—oh hello mummy.
BETTY: I'm going to ask you a question, both of you. I have a little money from your grandmother. And the three of you are living in that tiny flat with two children. I wonder if we could get a house and all live in it together? It would give you more room.
VICTORIA: But I'm going to Manchester anyway.
LIN: We'd have a garden, Vicky.
BETTY: You do seem to have such fun all of you.
VICTORIA: I don't want to.
BETTY: I didn't think you would.
LIN: Come on, Vicky, she knows we sleep together, and Eddy.
BETTY: I think I've known for quite a while but I'm not sure. I don't usually think about it, so I don't know if I know about it or not.
VICTORIA: I don't want to live with my mother.
LIN: Don't think of her as your mother, think of her as Betty.
VICTORIA: But she thinks of herself as my mother.
BETTY: I am your mother.
VICTORIA: But mummy we don't even like each other.
BETTY: We might begin to.

(*Cathy comes on howling with a nosebleed.*)

LIN: Oh Cathy what happened?
BETTY: She's been assaulted.

VICTORIA: It's a nosebleed.
CATHY: Took my ice cream.
LIN: Who did?
CATHY: Took my money.

(*Martin comes.*)

MARTIN: Is everything all right?
LIN: I thought you were looking after her.
CATHY: They hit me. I can't play. They said I'm a girl.
BETTY: Those dreadful boys, the gang, the Dead Hand.
MARTIN: What do you mean you thought I was looking after her?
LIN: Last I saw her she was with you getting an ice cream. It's your afternoon.
MARTIN: Then she went off to play. She goes off to play. You don't keep an eye on her every minute.
LIN: She doesn't get beaten up when I'm looking after her.
CATHY: Took my money.
MARTIN: Why the hell should I look after your child anyway? I just want Tommy. Why should he live with you and Vicky all week?
LIN: I don't mind if you don't want to look after her but don't say you will and then this happens.
VICTORIA: When I get to Manchester everything's going to be different anyway, Lin's staying here, and you're staying here, we're all going to have to sit down and talk it through.
MARTIN: I'd really enjoy that.
CATHY: Hit me on the face.
LIN: You were the one looking after her and look at her now, that's all.
MARTIN: I've had enough of you telling me.
LIN: Yes you know it all.
MARTIN: Now stop it. I work very hard at not being like this, I could do with some credit.
LIN: Ok you're quite nice, try and enjoy it. Don't make me sorry for you, Martin, it's hard for me too. We've better things to do than quarrel. I've got to go and sort those little bastards out for a start. Where are they, Cathy?
CATHY: Don't kill them, mum, hit them. Give them a nosebleed, mum.

(*Lin goes.*)

VICTORIA: Tommy's asleep in the pushchair. We'd better wake him up or he won't sleep tonight.
MARTIN: Sometimes I keep him up watching television till he falls asleep on the sofa so I can hold him. Come on, Cathy, we'll get another ice cream.
CATHY: Chocolate sauce and nuts.
VICTORIA: Betty, would you like an ice cream?
BETTY: No thank you, the cold hurts my teeth, but what a nice thought, Vicky, thank you.

(*Victoria goes. Betty alone. Gerry comes.*)

BETTY: I think you used to be Edward's flatmate.
GERRY: You're his mother. He's talked about you.
BETTY: Well never mind. Children are always wrong about their parents. It's a great problem knowing where to live and who to share with. I live by myself just now.

GERRY: Good. So do I. You can do what you like.
BETTY: I don't really know what I like.
GERRY: You'll soon find out.
BETTY: What do you like?
GERRY: Waking up at four in the morning.
BETTY: I like listening to music in bed and sometimes for supper I just have a big piece of bread and dip it in very hot lime pickle. So you don't get lonely by yourself? Perhaps you have a lot of visitors. I've been thinking I should have some visitors, I could give a little dinner party. Would you come? There wouldn't just be bread and lime pickle.
GERRY: Thank you very much.
BETTY: Or don't wait to be asked to dinner. Just drop in informally. I'll give you the address shall I? I don't usually give strange men my address but then you're not a strange man, you're a friend of Edward's. I suppose I seem a different generation to you but you are older than Edward. I was married for so many years it's quite hard to know how to get acquainted. But if there isn't a right way to do things you have to invent one. I always thought my mother was far too old to be attractive but when you get to an age yourself it feels quite different.
GERRY: I think you could be quite attractive.
BETTY: If what?
GERRY: If you stop worrying.
BETTY: I think when I do more about things I worry about them less. So perhaps you could help me do more.
GERRY: I might be going to live with Edward again.
BETTY: That's nice, but I'm rather surprised if he wants to share a flat. He's rather involved with a young woman he lives with, or two young women, I don't understand Edward but never mind.
GERRY: I'm very involved with him.
BETTY: I think Edward did try to tell me once but I didn't listen. So what I'm being told now is that Edward is "gay" is that right? And you are too. And I've been making rather a fool of myself. But Edward does also sleep with women.
GERRY: He does, yes, I don't.
BETTY: Well people always say it's the mother's fault but I don't intend to start blaming myself. He seems perfectly happy.
GERRY: I could still come and see you.
BETTY: So you could, yes. I'd like that. I've never tried to pick up a man before.
GERRY: Not everyone's gay.
BETTY: No, that's lucky isn't it.

(*Gerry goes. Clive comes.*)

CLIVE: You are not that sort of woman, Betty. I can't believe you are. I can't feel the same about you as I did. And Africa is to be communist I suppose. I used to be proud to be British. There was a high ideal. I came out onto the verandah and looked at the stars.

(*Clive goes. Betty from Act One comes. Betty and Betty embrace.*)

Athol Fugard

Athol Fugard (b. 1932) was an actor before becoming a playwright. Fugard's wife, the actress Sheila Meiring, stimulated his interest in theater, and in 1956 he began working with a theater group called the Serpent Company in Cape Town, South Africa. The group included both black and white actors at a time when racial mixing was illegal, and it went on to make a notable contribution to world drama.

Fugard, who is white, met Zakes Mokae (1934–2009), a black musician and actor, in the early days of the Serpent players, and the two collaborated on several works. Mokae said that the tradition in Africa was not so much for a solitary playwright to compose a work that others would act out as it was for people to develop a communal approach to drama, crafting a dramatic piece through their interaction. To some extent, Fugard in his early efforts did just that. He worked with actors, watched the developments among them, and then shaped the drama accordingly.

In 1960 Fugard began to write a two-person play called *The Blood Knot* while he was in England trying to establish a theater group there. This play was part of a trilogy called *The Family,* with *Hello and Goodbye* (1965) and *Boesman and Lena* (1969). *The Blood Knot* was given its first performance in Dorkay House in Johannesburg, South Africa, late in 1961. As Fugard has said, the entire production, which starred Fugard and Mokae, was put together so quickly that the government never had time to stop it. The play is about two brothers, one black and the other light-skinned enough to pass for white. It is exceptionally powerful, and the play's first performances in Johannesburg were a sensation. It toured South Africa and had a revival in New Haven and in New York in 1984 and 1985.

While they toured South Africa, Fugard and Mokae were victims of the country's apartheid policies. They could not travel in the same train car: Fugard went first class, and Mokae had to go in special cars for blacks. After *The Blood Knot*'s success, the government passed laws making it all but impossible for black and white actors to work together on the stage.

Fugard has had a considerable number of plays produced in New York and London over the years. *Sizwe Banzi Is Dead* (1972), written with black actors John Kani and Winston Ntshona, is about a man who exchanges identities with a corpse as a way of avoiding the racial laws of South Africa; it was well received. *The Island* (1975), also written with Kani and Ntshona, starred the latter two, who have become associated with Fugard and his work. They portray prisoners who, while putting on *Antigone,* become immersed in the political themes of the play, seeing it as an example of the political repression they experience in their own lives. A revival in New York in April 2003, with Kani and Ntshona in a mildly revised version, received excellent reviews.

Fugard's plays *A Lesson from Aloes* (1978) and *The Road to Mecca* (1984) were successful in their first U.S. productions at the Yale Repertory Theatre and on Broadway. Fugard's works are not always concerned with racial problems, but they usually center on political issues and the stress that individuals feel in trying to be themselves in an intolerant society.

The situation in South Africa has improved since *"MASTER HAROLD" . . . and the boys* was first produced in 1982. Apartheid has been abolished, and the government is in the hands of the African National Congress. The shift has been more successful than white South Africans expected, although political tensions still exist. Fugard's attachment and commitment to South Africa remain deep. He has been criticized by black writers for dealing with themes they believe belong to them, while also being criticized by whites for his sympathies toward blacks. In the new South Africa some of these problems have begun to sort themselves out. *Valley Song* (1996), produced at London's Royal Court Theatre, explores the problems and the promise of the new South Africa.

In May 1998, *The Captain's Tiger* was directed by Fugard, who also acted in the role of Tiger, a character on board a ship. Fugard himself had left university to work on ships around Africa. In May 2001, Fugard directed *Sorrows and Rejoicing,* a play about a man whose white wife and colored mistress meet at his funeral. Fugard's *Exits and Entrances* (2004) was written for the Fountain Theatre in Los Angeles; it is a one-act meditation on Fugard's life in the theater. Another play, *The Abbess* (2000), is based on the life of Saint Hildegard of Bingen (1098–1179), a Benedictine abbess known for her correspondence, for her work in medicine, and for her music, poems, writing, and drama. The Long Wharf Theatre in New Haven, Connecticut, premiered Fugard's three most recent plays: *Coming Home* (2009) tells of Veronica, a hopeful young African who, after failing in her singing career, returns to her pre-apartheid family home in South Africa to raise her son; *Have You Seen Us* (2009) is set in southern California, where Fugard now lives, and focuses on anti-Semitism; *The Train Driver* (2010) tells the story of a white South African train driver who feels guilty after seeing an African woman and her child step in front of his train. All of these plays continue Fugard's concern for the welfare of those who are marginalized in one way or another.

"MASTER HAROLD" . . . and the boys

For discussion questions and assignments on *"MASTER HAROLD" . . . and the boys,* visit bedfordstmartins.com/jacobus.

Athol Fugard has said that *"MASTER HAROLD" . . . and the boys* (1982) is a very personal play in which he exorcises personal guilt. As a white South African (Fugard's entire name is Harold Athol Lannigan Fugard), he has written numerous plays that represent the racial circumstances of life in that troubled nation. This play won international distinction and made a reputation for its stars, especially Zakes Mokae, with whom Fugard worked for more than forty years.

Hally, the teenage son, reveals throughout the play (which is set in 1950) that he is more attached emotionally to Sam, the black waiter who has befriended him, than he is even to his own parents, owners of the restaurant where Sam works. His attitude toward his father is complicated by his father's alcoholism and confinement. At that time in South Africa, even a white alcoholic was considered superior to a black man such as Sam, even though Sam is intelligent, quick, thoughtful, and generous. When Hally reveals his anxiety about his father, Sam warns him that it is dishonorable to treat one's father the way he does, and Sam's presumption in admonishing Hally triggers Hally's meanspirited outburst toward him.

Zakes Mokae, who created the role of Sam in the first performance of the play at the Yale Repertory Theatre, commented extensively about his role and the character of Sam. He observed that some black audience members called out during a performance that he should beat up Hally the minute Hally demands that Sam call him Master Harold. But other black audience members spoke with him after the performance and agreed that, because Sam had never taken that kind of stand against Harold or his father, he was getting what he deserved. Mokae himself pointed out that Sam is probably not living in Port Elizabeth legally and that to have taken action, even if he had wanted to, would have ended with his ejection from the town into exile.

Zakes Mokae understood the character from his perspective as a black South African, and he realized Sam's limits. But he said that in his version of the play, Sam would give Hally a beating and "suffer the consequences." He pointed out, however, that, as an urban South African, unlike Sam, he had an attitude quite different from anything that Sam would have understood. As an urban black, Mokae could not have been sent into exile, although he could certainly have been punished, for beating a white boy.

On the question of whether the play made a positive contribution to white-black relations in South Africa, Mokae pointed out that a play cannot change people's minds. Audiences were not likely to seek to change the government of South Africa simply because they had seen a play. At the same time, however, he believed that it was productive to talk about apartheid and racial distrust in South Africa.

Unfortunately, the government of South Africa decided the play was too inflammatory for performance in that country, and it was banned briefly from performance in Johannesburg and other theatrical centers in South Africa. This suggests that although Zakes Mokae did not believe one play would have much impact on injustices in South Africa, the government feared otherwise.

In an important way, *"MASTER HAROLD" . . . and the boys* is a personal statement by Fugard that establishes the extent to which apartheid damages even a person sympathetic to black rights. It is astonishing in retrospect to think, as one interviewer, Heinrich von Staden, once said, that Hally could grow up to be Athol himself. If this is true, then it is also true that the play is hopeful.

One sign of hope is that the violence in the play is restrained. Sam does not beat Hally for humiliating him, although he probably would like to. And no one in the play makes a move to be physically threatening to Sam. However faint, these are signs of hope. And as Zakes Mokae said about the situation in his homeland, "One is always optimistic. It can't go on forever." He was right. On June 5, 1991, Parliament abandoned apartheid, and South Africa had a new beginning.

"MASTER HAROLD" . . . and the boys in Performance

The world premiere of *"MASTER HAROLD" . . . and the boys* was at the Yale Repertory Theatre in March 1982. Fugard himself directed the play, with Zakes Mokae as Sam, Danny Glover as Willie, and Željko Ivanek as Hally. It was the first of Fugard's plays to premiere outside South Africa. Fugard chose New Haven, Connecticut, in part because the play's setting was so personal that he feared it might disturb his brother and sister if it were produced first in

South Africa. The setting was a bright tea room—a restaurant that serves light meals—interpreted to look like the tea room Fugard's mother actually ran in Port Elizabeth when he was a child. The space was open, the walls a whitish hue, everything simple and plain in decoration.

New York Times critic Frank Rich reviewed the premiere, saying, "'*MASTER HAROLD*'... *and the boys* is only an anecdote, really, and it's often as warm and musical as the men's dance. But somewhere along the way it rises up and breaks over the audience like a storm." Alan Stern of the *Boston Phoenix* linked the play with Greek tragedy:

> One reason for the play's potency is that, as in Greek tragedy, the events seem preordained—they're the by-product of social forces and human nature. Even as he spits in Sam's face, Hally realizes the magnitude of his action, that he is the one who will be harmed by it. And yet he can't help himself. Power corrupts, and in a society that sanctions the domination of one man—or set of men—over another, all relationships, even the promising ones, are poisoned.

Zakes Mokae and Danny Glover starred in the Broadway production in May 1982. After a brief period in which it was banned, the play was produced in Johannesburg, South Africa, in March 1983 with a South African cast. Joseph Lelyveld, in the *New York Times,* said of that production, "Athol Fugard's confessional drama about a white adolescent's initiation in the uses of racial power has come home to South Africa, and it left its multiracial audience... visibly shaken and stunned.... Many, blacks and whites, were crying."

The play was televised in 1984 with Matthew Broderick as Hally. It has been revived several times: in 1985 by the Trinity Repertory Company in Providence, in 1986 by the Boston Shakespeare Company, and in 1987 at the American Stage Festival in Milford, New Hampshire. These productions, although without Fugard's direction and without a "star" cast, had the same effect on their audiences as the major productions in New York and Johannesburg. Clifford Gallo in the *Boston Globe* called the American Stage Festival production "a devastating look at the loss of racial innocence in a nation where political and social inequality are the norm." Danny Glover revived the play in June 2003 in New York's Royale Theatre. This time he played Sam, whereas twenty years before he had played Willie. In the 2010 production at the TimeLine Theatre in Chicago, the play was presented together with *The Island* and *Sizwe Banzi Is Dead,* directed by O. J. Parson. The Dayton Playhouse in Cincinnati produced "*MASTER HAROLD*" in November 2011. Its production by the Palm Beach Dramaworks in April 2012 indicates that the durability of this play is remarkable, and its appearance on regional stages here and abroad makes us aware that its message is universal.

ATHOL FUGARD (b. 1932)

"Master Harold" . . . and the boys   1982

Characters

WILLIE
SAM
HALLY

The St. George's Park Tea Room on a wet and windy Port Elizabeth afternoon.

Tables and chairs have been cleared and are stacked on one side except for one which stands apart with a single chair. On this table a knife, fork, spoon and side plate in anticipation of a simple meal, together with a pile of comic books.

Other elements: a serving counter with a few stale cakes under glass and a not very impressive display of sweets, cigarettes and cool drinks, etc.; a few cardboard advertising handouts—Cadbury's Chocolate, Coca-Cola—and a blackboard on which an untrained hand has chalked up the prices of Tea, Coffee, Scones, Milkshakes—all flavors—and Cool Drinks; a few sad ferns in pots; a telephone; an old-style jukebox.

There is an entrance on one side and an exit into a kitchen on the other.

Leaning on the solitary table, his head cupped in one hand as he pages through one of the comic books, is Sam. A black man in his mid-forties. He wears the white coat of a waiter. Behind him on his knees, mopping down the floor with a bucket of water and a rag, is Willie. Also black and about the same age as Sam. He has his sleeves and trousers rolled up.

The year: 1950.

WILLIE (*singing as he works*): "She was scandalizin'
        my name,
    She took my money
    She called me honey
    But she was scandalizin' my name.
    Called it love but was playin' a game. . . . "

(*He gets up and moves the bucket. Stands thinking for a moment, then, raising his arms to hold an imaginary partner, he launches into an intricate ballroom dance step. Although a mildly comic figure, he reveals a reasonable degree of accomplishment.*)

    Hey, Sam.

(*Sam, absorbed in the comic book, does not respond.*)

    Hey, Boet° Sam!

(*Sam looks up.*)

Boet: Brother.

I'm getting it. The quickstep. Look now and tell me. (*He repeats the step.*) Well?

SAM (*encouragingly*): Show me again.

WILLIE: Okay, count for me.

SAM: Ready?

WILLIE: Ready.

SAM: Five, six, seven, eight. . . . (*Willie starts to dance.*) A-n-d one two three four . . . and one two three four. . . . (*Ad libbing as Willie dances.*) Your shoulders, Willie . . . your shoulders! Don't look down! Look happy, Willie! Relax, Willie!

WILLIE (*desperate but still dancing*): I am relax.

SAM: No, you're not.

WILLIE (*he falters*): Ag no man, Sam! Mustn't talk. You make me make mistakes.

SAM: But you're stiff.

WILLIE: Yesterday I'm not straight . . . today I'm too stiff!

SAM: Well, you are. You asked me and I'm telling you.

WILLIE: Where?

SAM: Everywhere. Try to glide through it.

WILLIE: Glide?

SAM: Ja, make it smooth. And give it more style. It must look like you're enjoying yourself.

WILLIE (*emphatically*): I wasn't.

SAM: Exactly.

WILLIE: How can I enjoy myself? Not straight, too stiff and now it's also glide, give it more style, make it smooth. . . . Haai! Is hard to remember all those things, Boet Sam.

SAM: That's your trouble. You're trying too hard.

WILLIE: I try hard because it *is* hard.

SAM: But don't let me see it. The secret is to make it look easy. Ballroom must look happy, Willie, not like hard work. It must. . . . Ja! . . . it must look like romance.

WILLIE: Now another one! What's romance?

SAM: Love story with happy ending. A handsome man in tails, and in his arms, smiling at him, a beautiful lady in evening dress!

WILLIE: Fred Astaire, Ginger Rogers.

SAM: You got it. Tapdance or ballroom, it's the same. Romance. In two weeks' time when the judges look at you and Hilda, they must see a man and a woman who are dancing their way to a happy ending. What I saw was you holding her like you were frightened she was going to run away.

WILLIE: Ja! Because that is what she wants to do! I got no romance left for Hilda anymore, Boet Sam.

SAM: Then pretend. When you put your arms around Hilda, imagine she is Ginger Rogers.

WILLIE: With no teeth? You try.

SAM: Well, just remember, there's only two weeks left.

WILLIE: I know, I know! (*To the jukebox.*) I do it better with music. You got sixpence for Sarah Vaughan?

SAM: That's a slow foxtrot. You're practicing the quickstep.

WILLIE: I'll practice slow foxtrot.

SAM (*shaking his head*): It's your turn to put money in the jukebox.

WILLIE: I only got bus fare to go home. (*He returns disconsolately to his work.*) Love story and happy ending! She's doing it all right, Boet Sam, but is not me she's giving happy endings. Fuckin' whore! Three nights now she doesn't come practice. I wind up gramophone, I get record ready and I sit and wait. What happens? Nothing. Ten o'clock I start dancing with my pillow. You try and practice romance by yourself, Boet Sam. Struesgod, she doesn't come tonight I take back my dress and ballroom shoes and I find me new partner. Size twenty-six. Shoes size seven. And now she's also making trouble for me with the baby again. Reports me to Child Wellfed, that I'm not giving her money. She lies! Every week I am giving her money for milk. And how do I know is my baby? Only his hair looks like me. She's fucking around all the time I turn my back. Hilda Samuels is a bitch! (*Pause.*) Hey, Sam!

SAM: Ja.

WILLIE: You listening?

SAM: Ja.

WILLIE: So what you say?

SAM: About Hilda?

WILLIE: Ja.

SAM: When did you last give her a hiding?

WILLIE (*reluctantly*): Sunday night.

SAM: And today is Thursday.

WILLIE (*he knows what's coming*): Okay.

SAM: Hiding on Sunday night, then Monday, Tuesday, and Wednesday she doesn't come to practice . . . and you are asking me why?

WILLIE: I said okay, Boet Sam!

SAM: You hit her too much. One day she's going to leave you for good.

WILLIE: So? She makes me the hell-in too much.

SAM (*emphasizing his point*): *Too* much and *too* hard. You had the same trouble with Eunice.

WILLIE: Because she also make the hell-in, Boet Sam. She never got the steps right. Even the waltz.

SAM: Beating her up every time she makes a mistake in the waltz? (*Shaking his head.*) No, Willie! That takes the pleasure out of ballroom dancing.

WILLIE: Hilda is not too bad with the waltz, Boet Sam. Is the quickstep where the trouble starts.

SAM (*teasing him gently*): How's your pillow with the quickstep?

WILLIE (*ignoring the tease*): Good! And why? Because it got no legs. That's her trouble. She can't move them quick enough, Boet Sam. I start the record and before halfway Count Basie is already winning. Only time we catch up with him is when gramophone runs down. (*Sam laughs.*) Haaikona, Boet Sam, is not funny.

SAM (*snapping his fingers*): I got it! Give her a handicap.

WILLIE: What's that?

SAM: Give her a ten-second start and then let Count Basie go. Then I put my money on her. Hot favorite in the Ballroom Stakes: Hilda Samuels ridden by Willie Malopo.

WILLIE (*turning away*): I'm not talking to you no more.

SAM (*relenting*): Sorry, Willie. . . .

WILLIE: It's finish between us.

SAM: Okay, okay . . . I'll stop.

WILLIE: You can also fuck off.

SAM: Willie, listen! I want to help you!

WILLIE: No more jokes?

SAM: I promise.

WILLIE: Okay. Help me.

SAM (*his turn to hold an imaginary partner*): Look and learn. Feet together. Back straight. Body relaxed. Right hand placed gently in the small of her back and wait for the music. Don't start worrying about making mistakes or the judges or the other competitors. It's just you, Hilda and the music, and you're going to have a good time. What Count Basie do you play?

WILLIE: "You the cream in my coffee, you the salt in my stew."

SAM: Right. Give it to me in strict tempo.

WILLIE: Ready?

SAM: Ready.

WILLIE: A-n-d . . . (*Singing.*)
"You the cream in my coffee.
You the salt in my stew.
You will always be my necessity.
I'd be lost without you. . . ." (*etc.*)

(*Sam launches into the quickstep. He is obviously a much more accomplished dancer than Willie. Hally enters. A seventeen-year-old white boy. Wet raincoat and school case. He stops and watches Sam. The demonstration comes to an end with a flourish. Applause from Hally and Willie.*)

HALLY: Bravo! No question about it. First place goes to Mr. Sam Semela.

WILLIE (*in total agreement*): You was gliding with style, Boet Sam.

HALLY (*cheerfully*): How's it, chaps?

SAM: Okay, Hally.

WILLIE (*springing to attention like a soldier and saluting*): At your service, Master Harold!

HALLY: Not long to the big event, hey!

SAM: Two weeks.

HALLY: You nervous?

SAM: No.

HALLY: Think you stand a chance?

SAM: Let's just say I'm ready to go out there and dance.

HALLY: It looked like it. What about you, Willie?

(*Willie groans.*)

What's the matter?

SAM: He's got leg trouble.

HALLY (*innocently*): Oh, sorry to hear that, Willie.

WILLIE: Boet Sam! You promised. (*Willie returns to his work.*)

(*Hally deposits his school case and takes off his rain-coat. His clothes are a little neglected and untidy: black blazer with school badge, gray flannel trousers in need of an ironing, khaki shirt and tie, black shoes. Sam has fetched a towel for Hally to dry his hair.*)

HALLY: God, what a lousy bloody day. It's coming down cats and dogs out there. Bad for business, chaps. . . . (*Conspiratorial whisper.*) . . . but it also means we're in for a nice quiet afternoon.

SAM: You can speak loud. Your Mom's not here.

HALLY: Out shopping?

SAM: No. The hospital.

HALLY: But it's Thursday. There's no visiting on Thursday afternoons. Is my Dad okay?

SAM: Sounds like it. In fact, I think he's going home.

HALLY (*stopped short by Sam's remark*): What do you mean?

SAM: The hospital phoned.

HALLY: To say what?

SAM: I don't know. I just heard your Mom talking.

HALLY: So what makes you say he's going home?

SAM: It sounded as if they were telling her to come and fetch him.

(*Hally thinks about what Sam has said for a few seconds.*)

HALLY: When did she leave?

SAM: About an hour ago. She said she would phone you. Want to eat?

(*Hally doesn't respond.*)

Hally, want your lunch?

HALLY: I suppose so. (*His mood has changed.*) What's on the menu? . . . as if I don't know.

SAM: Soup, followed by meat pie and gravy.

HALLY: Today's?

SAM: No.

HALLY: And the soup?

SAM: Nourishing pea soup.

HALLY: Just the soup. (*The pile of comic books on the table.*) And these?

National Theatre of London's 1983 production of *"MASTER HAROLD" . . . and the boys* with (from left to right) Ramolao Makhene as Willie, Duart Sylwain as Hally, and John Kani as Sam.

SAM: For your Dad. Mr. Kempston brought them.

HALLY: You haven't been reading them, have you?

SAM: Just looking.

HALLY (examining the comics): Jungle Jim . . . Batman and Robin . . . Tarzan . . . God, what rubbish! Mental pollution. Take them away.

(Sam exits waltzing into the kitchen. Hally turns to Willie.)

HALLY: Did you hear my Mom talking on the telephone, Willie?

WILLIE: No, Master Hally. I was at the back.

HALLY: And she didn't say anything to you before she left?

WILLIE: She said I must clean the floors.

HALLY: I mean about my Dad.

WILLIE: She didn't say nothing to me about him, Master Hally.

HALLY (with conviction): No! It can't be. They said he needed at least another three weeks of treatment. Sam's definitely made a mistake. (Rummages through his school case, finds a book and settles down at the table to read.) So, Willie!

WILLIE: Yes, Master Hally! Schooling okay today?

HALLY: Yes, okay. . . . (He thinks about it.) . . . No, not really. Ag, what's the difference? I don't care. And Sam says you've got problems.

WILLIE: Big problems.

HALLY: Which leg is sore?

(Willie groans.)

Both legs.

WILLIE: There is nothing wrong with my legs. Sam is just making jokes.

HALLY: So then you will be in the competition.

WILLIE: Only if I can find a partner.

HALLY: But what about Hilda?

SAM (returning with a bowl of soup): She's the one who's got trouble with her legs.

HALLY: What sort of trouble, Willie?

SAM: From the way he describes it, I think the lady has gone a bit lame.

HALLY: Good God! Have you taken her to see a doctor?

SAM: I think a vet would be better.

HALLY: What do you mean?

SAM: What do you call it again when a racehorse goes very fast?

HALLY: Gallop?

SAM: That's it!

WILLIE: Boet Sam!

HALLY: "A gallop down the homestretch to the winning post." But what's that got to do with Hilda?

SAM: Count Basie always gets there first.

(Willie lets fly with his slop rag. It misses Sam and hits Hally.)

HALLY (furious): For Christ's sake, Willie! What the hell do you think you're doing?

WILLIE: Sorry, Master Hally, but it's him. . . .

HALLY: Act your bloody age! (Hurls the rag back at Willie.) Cut out the nonsense now and get on with your work. And you too, Sam. Stop fooling around.

(Sam moves away.)

No. Hang on. I haven't finished! Tell me exactly what my Mom said.

SAM: I have. "When Hally comes, tell him I've gone to the hospital and I'll phone him."

HALLY: She didn't say anything about taking my Dad home?

SAM: No. It's just that when she was talking on the phone. . . .

HALLY (interrupting him): No, Sam. They can't be discharging him. She would have said so if they were. In any case, we saw him last night and he wasn't in good shape at all. Staff nurse even said there was talk about taking more X-rays. And now suddenly today he's better? If anything, it sounds more like a bad turn to me . . . which I sincerely hope it isn't. Hang on . . . how long ago did you say she left?

SAM: Just before two . . . (His wrist watch.) . . . hour and a half.

HALLY: I know how to settle it. (Behind the counter to the telephone. Talking as he dials.) Let's give her ten minutes to get to the hospital, ten minutes to load him up, another ten, at the most, to get home, and another ten to get him inside. Forty minutes. They should have been home for at least half an hour already. (Pause—he waits with the receiver to his ear.) No reply, chaps. And you know why? Because she's at his bedside in hospital helping him pull through a bad turn. You definitely heard wrong.

SAM: Okay.

(As far as Hally is concerned, the matter is settled. He returns to his table, sits down, and divides his attention between the book and his soup. Sam is at his school case and picks up a textbook.)

Modern Graded Mathematics for Standards Nine and Ten. (Opens it at random and laughs at something he sees.) Who is this supposed to be?

HALLY: Old fart-face Prentice.

SAM: Teacher?

HALLY: Thinks he is. And believe me, that is not a bad likeness.

SAM: Has he seen it?

HALLY: Yes.

SAM: What did he say?

HALLY: Tried to be clever, as usual. Said I was no Leonardo da Vinci and that bad art had to be punished. So, six of the best, and his are bloody good.

SAM: On your bum?

HALLY: Where else? The days when I got them on my hands are gone forever, Sam.

SAM: With your trousers down!

HALLY: No. He's not quite that barbaric.

SAM: That's the way they do it in jail.

HALLY (flicker of morbid interest): Really?

SAM: Ja. When the magistrate sentences you to "strokes with a light cane."

HALLY: Go on.

SAM: They make you lie down on a bench. One policeman pulls down your trousers and holds your ankles, another one pulls your shirt over your head and holds your arms . . .

HALLY: Thank you! That's enough.

SAM: . . . and the one that gives you the strokes talks to you gently and for a long time between each one. (*He laughs.*)

HALLY: I've heard enough, Sam! Jesus! It's a bloody awful world when you come to think of it. People can be real bastards.

SAM: That's the way it is, Hally.

HALLY: It doesn't *have* to be that way. There is something called progress, you know. We don't exactly burn people at the stake anymore.

SAM: Like Joan of Arc.

HALLY: Correct. If she was captured today, she'd be given a fair trial.

SAM: And then the death sentence.

HALLY (*a world-weary sigh*): I know, I know! I oscillate between hope and despair for this world as well, Sam. But things will change, you wait and see. One day somebody is going to get up and give history a kick up the backside and get it going again.

SAM: Like who?

HALLY (*after thought*): They're called social reformers. Every age, Sam, has got its social reformer. My history book is full of them.

SAM: So where's ours?

HALLY: Good question. And I hate to say it, but the answer is: I don't know. Maybe he hasn't even been born yet. Or is still only a babe in arms at his mother's breast. God, what a thought.

SAM: So we just go on waiting.

HALLY: Ja, looks like it. (*Back to his soup and the book.*)

SAM (*reading from the textbook*): "Introduction: In some mathematical problems only the magnitude . . ." (*He mispronounces the word "magnitude."*)

HALLY (*correcting him without looking up*): Magnitude.

SAM: What's it mean?

HALLY: How big it is. The size of the thing.

SAM (*reading*): " . . . magnitude of the quantities is of importance. In other problems we need to know whether these quantities are negative or positive. For example, whether there is a debit or credit bank balance . . ."

HALLY: Whether you're broke or not.

SAM: " . . . whether the temperature is above or below Zero. . . . "

HALLY: Naught degrees. Cheerful state of affairs! No cash and you're freezing to death. Mathematics won't get you out of that one.

SAM: "All these quantities are called . . . " (*spelling the word*): . . . s-c-a-l . . .

HALLY: Scalars.

SAM: Scalars! (*Shaking his head with a laugh.*) You understand all that?

HALLY (*turning a page*): No. And I don't intend to try.

SAM: So what happens when the exams come?

HALLY: Failing a maths exam isn't the end of the world, Sam. How many times have I told you that examination results don't measure intelligence?

SAM: I would say about as many times as you've failed one of them.

HALLY (*mirthlessly*): Ha, ha, ha.

SAM (*simultaneously*): Ha, ha, ha.

HALLY: Just remember Winston Churchill didn't do particularly well at school.

SAM: You've also told me that one many times.

HALLY: Well, it just so happens to be the truth.

SAM (*enjoying the word*): Magnitude! Magnitude! Show me how to use it.

HALLY (*after thought*): An intrepid social reformer will not be daunted by the magnitude of the task he has undertaken.

SAM (*impressed*): Couple of jaw-breakers in there!

HALLY: I gave you three for the price of one. Intrepid, daunted, and magnitude. I did that once in an exam. Put five of the words I had to explain in one sentence. It was half a page long.

SAM: Well, I'll put my money on you in the English exam.

HALLY: Piece of cake. Eighty percent without even trying.

SAM (*another textbook from Hally's case*): And history?

HALLY: So-so. I'll scrape through. In the fifties if I'm lucky.

SAM: You didn't do too badly last year.

HALLY: Because we had World War One. That at least has some action. You try to find that in the South African Parliamentary system.

SAM (*reading from the history textbook*): "Napoleon and the principle of equality." Hey! This sounds interesting. "After concluding peace with Britain in 1802, Napoleon used a brief period of calm to in-sti-tute . . . "

HALLY: Introduce.

SAM: " . . . many reforms. Napoleon regarded all people as equal before the law and wanted them to have equal opportunities for advancement. All ves-ti-ges of the feu-dal sys-tem with its oppression of the poor were abol-ished." Vestiges, feudal system, and abolished. I'm all right on oppression.

HALLY: I'm thinking. He swept away . . . abol-ished . . . the last remains . . . vestiges . . . of the bad old days . . . feudal system.

SAM: Ha! There's the social reformer we're waiting for. He sounds like a man of some magnitude.

HALLY: I'm not so sure about that. It's a damn good title for a book, though. A man of magnitude!

SAM: He sounds pretty big to me, Hally.

HALLY: Don't confuse historical significance with greatness. But maybe I'm being a bit prejudiced. Have a look in there and you'll see he's two chapters long. And hell! . . . has he only got dates, Sam, all of which you've got to remember! This campaign and that campaign, and then, because of all the fighting, the next thing is we get Peace Treaties all over the place. And what's the end of the story? Battle of Waterloo, which he loses. Wasn't worth it. No, I don't know about him as a man of magnitude.

SAM: Then who would you say was?

HALLY: To answer that, we need a definition of greatness, and I suppose that would be somebody who ... somebody who benefited all mankind.

SAM: Right. But like who?

HALLY (*he speaks with total conviction*): Charles Darwin. Remember him? That big book from the library. *The Origin of the Species.*

SAM: Him?

HALLY: Yes. For his Theory of Evolution.

SAM: You didn't finish it.

HALLY: I ran out of time. I didn't finish it because my two weeks was up. But I'm going to take it out again after I've digested what I read. It's safe. I've hidden it away in the Theology section. Nobody ever goes in there. And anyway who are you to talk? You hardly even looked at it.

SAM: I tried. I looked at the chapters in the beginning and I saw one called "The Struggle for an Existence." Ah ha, I thought. At last! But what did I get? Something called the mistiltoe which needs the apple tree and there's too many seeds and all are going to die except one ...! No, Hally.

HALLY (*intellectually outraged*): What do you mean, No! The poor man had to start somewhere. For God's sake, Sam, he revolutionized science. Now we know.

SAM: What?

HALLY: Where we come from and what it all means.

SAM: And that's a benefit to mankind? Anyway, I still don't believe it.

HALLY: God, you're impossible. I showed it to you in black and white.

SAM: Doesn't mean I got to believe it.

HALLY: It's the likes of you that kept the Inquisition in business. It's called bigotry. Anyway, that's my man of magnitude. Charles Darwin! Who's yours?

SAM (*without hesitation*): Abraham Lincoln.

HALLY: I might have guessed as much. Don't get sentimental, Sam. You've never been a slave, you know. And anyway we freed your ancestors here in South Africa long before the Americans. But if you want to thank somebody on their behalf, do it to Mr. William Wilberforce.° Come on. Try again. I want a real genius.

(*Now enjoying himself, and so is Sam. Hally goes behind the counter and helps himself to a chocolate.*)

SAM: William Shakespeare.

HALLY (*no enthusiasm*): Oh. So you're also one of them, are you? You're basing that opinion on only one play,

Mr. William Wilberforce: British statesman (1759–1833) who supported a bill outlawing the slave trade and suppressing slavery in the British Empire.

you know. You've only read my *Julius Caesar* and even I don't understand half of what they're talking about. They should do what they did with the old Bible: bring the language up to date.

SAM: That's all you've got. It's also the only one *you've* read.

HALLY: I know. I admit it. That's why I suggest we reserve our judgment until we've checked up on a few others. I've got a feeling, though, that by the end of this year one is going to be enough for me, and I can give you the names of twenty-nine other chaps in the Standard Nine class of the Port Elizabeth Technical College who feel the same. But if you want him, you can have him. My turn now. (*Pacing.*) This is a damned good exercise, you know! It started off looking like a simple question and here it's got us really probing into the intellectual heritage of our civilization.

SAM: So who is it going to be?

HALLY: My next man ... and he gets the title on two scores: social reform and literary genius ... is Leo Nikolaevich Tolstoy.

SAM: That Russian.

HALLY: Correct. Remember the picture of him I showed you?

SAM: With the long beard.

HALLY (*trying to look like Tolstoy*): And those burning, visionary eyes. My God, the face of a social prophet if ever I saw one! And remember my words when I showed it to you? Here's a *man*, Sam!

SAM: Those were words, Hally.

HALLY: Not many intellectuals are prepared to shovel manure with the peasants and then go home and write a "little book" called *War and Peace*. Incidentally, Sam, he was somebody else who, to quote, " ... did not distinguish himself scholastically."

SAM: Meaning?

HALLY: He was also no good at school.

SAM: Like you and Winston Churchill.

HALLY (*mirthlessly*): Ha, ha, ha.

SAM (*simultaneously*): Ha, ha, ha.

HALLY: Don't get clever, Sam. That man freed his serfs of his own free will.

SAM: No argument. He was a somebody, all right. I accept him.

HALLY: I'm sure Count Tolstoy will be very pleased to hear that. Your turn. Shoot. (*Another chocolate from behind the counter.*) I'm waiting, Sam.

SAM: I've got him.

HALLY: Good. Submit your candidate for examination.

SAM: Jesus.

HALLY (*stopped dead in his tracks*): Who?

SAM: Jesus Christ.

HALLY: Oh, come on, Sam!

SAM: The Messiah.

HALLY: Ja, but still ... No, Sam. Don't let's get started on religion. We'll just spend the whole afternoon arguing again. Suppose I turn around and say Mohammed?

SAM: All right.

HALLY: You can't have them both on the same list!

SAM: Why not? You like Mohammed, I like Jesus.

HALLY: I *don't* like Mohammed. I never have. I was merely being hypothetical. As far as I'm concerned, the Koran is as bad as the Bible. No. Religion is out! I'm not going to waste my time again arguing with you about the existence of God. You know perfectly well I'm an atheist . . . and I've got homework to do.

SAM: Okay, I take him back.

HALLY: You've got time for one more name.

SAM (*after thought*): I've got one I know we'll agree on. A simple straightforward great Man of Magnitude . . . and no arguments. And *he* really *did* benefit all mankind.

HALLY: I wonder. After your last contribution I'm beginning to doubt whether anything in the way of an intellectual agreement is possible between the two of us. Who is he?

SAM: Guess.

HALLY: Socrates? Alexandre Dumas? Karl Marx? Dostoevsky? Nietzsche?

(*Sam shakes his head after each name.*)

Give me a clue.

SAM: The letter *P* is important . . .

HALLY: Plato!

SAM: . . . and his name begins with an *F*.

HALLY: I've got it. Freud and Psychology.

SAM: No. I didn't understand him.

HALLY: That makes two of us.

SAM: Think of moldy apricot jam.

HALLY (*after a delighted laugh*): Penicillin and Sir Alexander Fleming! And the title of the book: *The Microbe Hunters*. (*Delighted.*) Splendid, Sam! Splendid. For once we are in total agreement. The major breakthrough in medical science in the Twentieth Century. If it wasn't for him, we might have lost the Second World War. It's deeply gratifying, Sam, to know that I haven't been wasting my time in talking to you. (*Strutting around proudly.*) Tolstoy may have educated his peasants, but I've educated you.

SAM: Standard Four to Standard Nine.

HALLY: Have we been at it as long as that?

SAM: Yep. And my first lesson was geography.

HALLY (*intrigued*): Really? I don't remember.

SAM: My room there at the back of the old Jubilee Boarding House. I had just started working for your Mom. Little boy in short trousers walks in one afternoon and asks me seriously: "Sam, do you want to see South Africa?" Hey man! Sure I wanted to see South Africa!

HALLY: Was that me?

SAM: . . . So the next thing I'm looking at a map you had just done for homework. It was your first one and you were very proud of yourself.

HALLY: Go on.

SAM: Then came my first lesson. "Repeat after me, Sam: Gold in the Transvaal, mealies in the Free State, sugar in Natal, and grapes in the Cape." I still know it!

HALLY: Well, I'll be buggered. So that's how it all started.

SAM: And your next map was one with all the rivers and the mountains they came from. The Orange, the Vaal, the Limpopo, the Zambezi. . . .

HALLY: You've got a phenomenal memory!

SAM: You should be grateful. That is why you started passing your exams. You tried to be better than me.

(*They laugh together. Willie is attracted by the laughter and joins them.*)

HALLY: The old Jubilee Boarding House. Sixteen rooms with board and lodging, rent in advance and one week's notice. I haven't thought about it for donkey's years . . . and I don't think that's an accident. God, was I glad when we sold it and moved out. Those years are not remembered as the happiest ones of an unhappy childhood.

WILLIE (*knocking on the table and trying to imitate a woman's voice*): "Hally, are you there?"

HALLY: Who's that supposed to be?

WILLIE: "What you doing in there, Hally? Come out at once!"

HALLY (*to Sam*): What's he talking about?

SAM: Don't you remember?

WILLIE: "Sam, Willie . . . is he in there with you boys?"

SAM: Hiding away in our room when your mother was looking for you.

HALLY (*another good laugh*): Of course! I used to crawl and hide under your bed! But finish the story, Willie. Then what used to happen? You chaps would give the game away by telling her I was in there with you. So much for friendship.

SAM: We couldn't lie to her. She knew.

HALLY: Which meant I got another rowing for hanging around the "servants' quarters." I think I spent more time in there with you chaps than anywhere else in that dump. And do you blame me? Nothing but bloody misery wherever you went. Somebody was always complaining about the food, or my mother was having a fight with Micky Nash because she'd caught her with a petty officer in her room. Maud Meiring was another one. Remember those two? They were prostitutes, you know. Soldiers and sailors from the troopships. Bottom fell out of the business when the war ended. God, the flotsam and jetsam that life washed up on our shores! No joking, if it wasn't for your room, I would have been the first certified ten-year-old in medical history. Ja, the memories are coming back now. Walking home from school and thinking: "What can I do this afternoon?" Try out a few ideas, but sooner or later I'd end up in there with you fellows. I bet you I could still find my way to your room with my eyes closed. (*He does exactly that.*) Down the corridor . . . telephone on the right, which my Mom keeps locked because somebody is using it on the sly and not paying . . . past the kitchen and unappetizing cooking smells . . . around the corner into the backyard, hold my breath again because there are more smells coming when I pass your lavatory, then into that little passageway, first door on the right and into your room. How's that?

SAM: Good. But, as usual, you forgot to knock.

HALLY: Like that time I barged in and caught you and Cynthia . . . at it. Remember? God, was I embarrassed! I didn't know what was going on at first.

SAM: Ja, that taught you a lesson.

HALLY: And about a lot more than knocking on doors, I'll have you know, and I don't mean geography either. Hell, Sam, couldn't you have waited until it was dark?

SAM: No.

HALLY: Was it that urgent?

SAM: Yes, and if you don't believe me, wait until your time comes.

HALLY: No, thank you. I am not interested in girls. (*Back to his memories. . . . Using a few chairs he re-creates the room as he lists the items.*) A gray little room with a cold cement floor. Your bed against that wall . . . and I now know why the mattress sags so much! . . . Willie's bed . . . it's propped up on bricks because one leg is broken . . . that wobbly little table with the washbasin and jug of water . . . Yes! . . . stuck to the wall above it are some pin-up pictures from magazines. Joe Louis . . . .

WILLIE: Brown Bomber. World Title. (*Boxing pose.*) Three rounds and knockout.

HALLY: Against who?

SAM: Max Schmeling.

HALLY: Correct. I can also remember Fred Astaire and Ginger Rogers, and Rita Hayworth in a bathing costume which always made me hot and bothered when I looked at it. Under Willie's bed is an old suitcase with all his clothes in a mess, which is why I never hide there. Your things are neat and tidy in a trunk next to your bed, and on it there is a picture of you and Cynthia in your ballroom clothes, your first silver cup for third place in a competition and an old radio which doesn't work anymore. Have I left out anything?

SAM: No.

HALLY: Right, so much for the stage directions. Now the characters. (*Sam and Willie move to their appropriate positions in the bedroom.*) Willie is in bed, under his blankets with his clothes on, complaining nonstop about something, but we can't make out a word of what he's saying because he's got his head under the blankets as well. You're on your bed trimming your toenails with a knife—not a very edifying sight—and as for me . . . . What am I doing?

SAM: You're sitting on the floor giving Willie a lecture about being a good loser while you get the checkerboard and pieces ready for a game. Then you go to Willie's bed, pull off the blankets and make him play with you first because you know you're going to win, and that gives you the second game with me.

HALLY: And you certainly were a bad loser, Willie!

WILLIE: Haai!

HALLY: Wasn't he, Sam? And so slow! A game with you almost took the whole afternoon. Thank God I gave up trying to teach you how to play chess.

WILLIE: You and Sam cheated.

HALLY: I never saw Sam cheat, and mine were mostly the mistakes of youth.

WILLIE: Then how is it you two was always winning?

HALLY: Have you ever considered the possibility, Willie, that it was because we were better than you?

WILLIE: Every time better?

HALLY: Not every time. There were occasions when we deliberately let you win a game so that you would stop sulking and go on playing with us. Sam used to wink at me when you weren't looking to show me it was time to let you win.

WILLIE: So then you two didn't play fair.

HALLY: It was for your benefit, Mr. Malopo, which is more than being fair. It was an act of self-sacrifice. (*To Sam.*) But you know what my best memory is, don't you?

SAM: No.

HALLY: Come on, guess. If your memory is so good, you must remember it as well.

SAM: We got up to a lot of tricks in there, Hally.

HALLY: This one was special, Sam.

SAM: I'm listening.

HALLY: It started off looking like another of those useless nothing-to-do afternoons. I'd already been down to Main Street looking for adventure, but nothing had happened. I didn't feel like climbing trees in the Donkin Park or pretending I was a private eye and following a stranger . . . so as usual: See what's cooking in Sam's room. This time it was you on the floor. You had two thin pieces of wood and you were smoothing them down with a knife. It didn't look particularly interesting, but when I asked you what you were doing, you just said, "Wait and see, Hally. Wait . . . and see" . . . in that secret sort of way of yours, so I knew there was a surprise coming. You teased me, you bugger, by being deliberately slow and not answering my questions!

(*Sam laughs.*)

And whistling while you worked away! God, it was infuriating! I could have brained you! It was only when you tied them together in a cross and put that down on the brown paper that I realized what you were doing. "Sam is making a kite?" And when I asked you and you said, "Yes" . . . ! (*Shaking his head with disbelief.*) The sheer audacity of it took my breath away. I mean, seriously, what the hell does a black man know about flying a kite? I'll be honest with you, Sam, I had no hopes for it. If you think I was excited and happy, you got another guess coming. In fact, I was shit-scared that we were going to make fools of ourselves. When we left the boarding house to go up onto the hill, I was praying quietly that there wouldn't be any other kids around to laugh at us.

SAM (*enjoying the memory as much as Hally*): Ja, I could see that.

HALLY: I made it obvious, did I?

SAM: Ja. You refused to carry it.

HALLY: Do you blame me? Can you remember what the poor thing looked like? Tomato-box wood and brown paper! Flour and water for glue! Two of my mother's old stockings for a tail, and then all those bits and pieces of string you made me tie together so that we could fly it! Hell, no, that was now only asking for a miracle to happen.

SAM: Then the big argument when I told you to hold the string and run with it when I let go.

HALLY: I was prepared to run, all right, but straight back to the boarding house.

SAM (*knowing what's coming*): So what happened?

HALLY: Come on, Sam, you remember as well as I do.

SAM: I want to hear it from you.

(*Hally pauses. He wants to be as accurate as possible.*)

HALLY: You went a little distance from me down the hill, you held it up ready to let it go. . . . "This is it," I thought. "Like everything else in my life, here comes another fiasco." Then you shouted, "Go, Hally!" and I started to run. (*Another pause.*) I don't know how to describe it, Sam. Ja! The miracle happened! I was running, waiting for it to crash to the ground, but instead suddenly there was something alive behind me at the end of the string, tugging at it as if it wanted to be free. I looked back . . . (*Shakes his head.*) . . . I still can't believe my eyes. It was flying! Looping around and trying to climb even higher into the sky. You shouted to me to let it have more string. I did, until there was none left and I was just holding that piece of wood we had tied it to. You came up and joined me. You were laughing.

SAM: So were you. And shouting, "It works, Sam! We've done it!"

HALLY: And we had! I was so proud of us! It was the most splendid thing I had ever seen. I wished there were hundreds of kids around to watch us. The part that scared me, though, was when you showed me how to make it dive down to the ground and then just when it was on the point of crashing, swoop up again!

SAM: You didn't want to try yourself.

HALLY: Of course not! I would have been suicidal if anything had happened to it. Watching you do it made me nervous enough. I was quite happy just to see it up there with its tail fluttering behind it. You left me after that, didn't you? You explained how to get it down, we tied it to the bench so that I could sit and watch it, and you went away. I wanted you to stay, you know. I was a little scared of having to look after it by myself.

SAM (*quietly*): I had work to do, Hally.

HALLY: It was sort of sad bringing it down, Sam. And it looked sad again when it was lying there on the ground. Like something that had lost its soul. Just tomato-box wood, brown paper and two of my mother's old stockings! But, hell, I'll never forget that first moment when I saw it up there. I had a stiff neck the next day from looking up so much.

(*Sam laughs. Hally turns to him with a question he never thought of asking before.*)

Why did you make that kite, Sam?

SAM (*evenly*): I can't remember.

HALLY: Truly?

SAM: Too long ago, Hally.

HALLY: Ja, I suppose it was. It's time for another one, you know.

SAM: Why do you say that?

HALLY: Because it feels like that. Wouldn't be a good day to fly it, though.

SAM: No. You can't fly kites on rainy days.

HALLY (*He studies Sam. Their memories have made him conscious of the man's presence in his life.*): How old are you, Sam?

SAM: Two score and five.

HALLY: Strange, isn't it?

SAM: What?

HALLY: Me and you.

SAM: What's strange about it?

HALLY: Little white boy in short trousers and a black man old enough to be his father flying a kite. It's not every day you see that.

SAM: But why strange? Because the one is white and the other black?

HALLY: I don't know. Would have been just as strange, I suppose, if it had been me and my Dad . . . cripple man and a little boy! Nope! There's no chance of me flying a kite without it being strange. (*Simple statement of fact—no self-pity.*) There's a nice little short story there. "The Kite-Flyers." But we'd have to find a twist in the ending.

SAM: Twist?

HALLY: Yes. Something unexpected. The way it ended with us was too straightforward . . . me on the bench and you going back to work. There's no drama in that.

WILLIE: And me?

HALLY: You?

WILLIE: Yes me.

HALLY: You want to get into the story as well, do you? I got it! Change the title: "Afternoons in Sam's Room" . . . expand it and tell all the stories. It's on its way to being a novel. Our days in the old Jubilee. Sad in a way that they're over. I almost wish we were still in that little room.

SAM: We're still together.

HALLY: That's true. It's just that life felt the right size in there . . . not too big and not too small. Wasn't so hard to work up a bit of courage. It's got so bloody complicated since then.

(The telephone rings. Sam answers it.)

SAM: St. George's Park Tea Room . . . Hello, Madam . . . Yes, Madam, he's here. . . . Hally, it's your mother.

HALLY: Where is she phoning from?

SAM: Sounds like the hospital. It's a public telephone.

HALLY *(relieved)*: You see! I told you. *(The telephone.)* Hello, Mom . . . Yes . . . Yes no fine. Everything's under control here. How's things with poor old Dad? . . . Has he had a bad turn? . . . What? . . . Oh, God! . . . Yes, Sam told me, but I was sure he'd made a mistake. But what's this all about, Mom? He didn't look at all good last night. How can he get better so quickly? . . . Then very obviously you must say no. Be firm with him. You're the boss. . . . You know what it's going to be like if he comes home. . . . Well then, don't blame me when I fail my exams at the end of the year. . . . Yes! How am I expected to be fresh for school when I spend half the night massaging his gammy leg? . . . So am I! . . . So tell him a white lie. Say Dr. Colley wants more X-rays of his stump. Or bribe him. We'll sneak in double tots of brandy in future. . . . What? . . . Order him to get back into bed at once! If he's going to behave like a child, treat him like one. . . . All right, Mom! I was just trying to . . . I'm sorry. . . . I said I'm sorry. . . . Quick, give me your number. I'll phone you back. *(He hangs up and waits a few seconds.)* Here we go again! *(He dials.)* I'm sorry, Mom. . . . Okay. . . . But now listen to me carefully. All it needs is for you to put your foot down. Don't take no for an answer. . . . Did you hear me? And whatever you do, don't discuss it with him. . . . Because I'm frightened you'll give in to him. . . . Yes, Sam gave me lunch. . . . I ate all of it! . . . No, Mom not a soul. It's still raining here. . . . Right, I'll tell them. I'll just do some homework and then lock up. . . . But remember now, Mom. Don't listen to anything he says. And phone me back and let me know what happens. . . . Okay. Bye, Mom. *(He hangs up. The men are staring at him.)* My Mom says that when you're finished with the floors you must do the windows. *(Pause.)* Don't misunderstand me, chaps. All I want is for him to get better. And if he was, I'd be the first person to say: "Bring him home." But he's not, and we can't give him the medical care and attention he needs at home. That's what hospitals are there for. *(Brusquely.)* So don't just stand there! Get on with it!

(Sam clears Hally's table.)

You heard right. My Dad wants to go home.

SAM: Is he better?

HALLY *(sharply)*: No! How the hell can he be better when last night he was groaning with pain? This is not an age of miracles!

SAM: Then he should stay in hospital.

HALLY *(seething with irritation and frustration)*: Tell me something I don't know, Sam. What the hell do you think I was saying to my Mom? All I can say is fuck-it-all.

SAM: I'm sure he'll listen to your Mom.

HALLY: You don't know what she's up against. He's already packed his shaving kit and pajamas and is sitting on his bed with his crutches, dressed and ready to go. I know him when he gets in that mood. If she tries to reason with him, we've had it. She's no match for him when it comes to a battle of words. He'll tie her up in knots. *(Trying to hide his true feelings.)*

SAM: I suppose it gets lonely for him in there.

HALLY: With all the patients and nurses around? Regular visits from the Salvation Army? Balls! It's ten times worse for him at home. I'm at school and my mother is here in the business all day.

SAM: He's at least got you at night.

HALLY *(before he can stop himself)*: And we've got him! Please! I don't want to talk about it anymore. *(Unpacks his school case, slamming down books on the table.)* Life is just a plain bloody mess, that's all. And people are fools.

SAM: Come on, Hally.

HALLY: Yes, they are! They bloody well deserve what they get.

SAM: Then don't complain.

HALLY: Don't try to be clever, Sam. It doesn't suit you. Anybody who thinks there's nothing wrong with this world needs to have his head examined. Just when things are going along all right, without fail someone or something will come along and spoil everything. Somebody should write that down as a fundamental law of the Universe. The principle of perpetual disappointment. If there is a God who created this world, he should scrap it and try again.

SAM: All right, Hally, all right. What you got for homework?

HALLY: Bullshit, as usual. *(Opens an exercise book and reads.)* "Write five hundred words describing an annual event of cultural or historical significance."

SAM: That should be easy enough for you.

HALLY: And also plain bloody boring. You know what he wants, don't you? One of their useless old ceremonies. The commemoration of the landing of the 1820 Settlers, or if it's going to be culture, Carols by Candlelight every Christmas.

SAM: It's an impressive sight. Make a good description, Hally. All those candles glowing in the dark and the people singing hymns.

HALLY: And it's called religious hysteria. *(Intense irritation.)* Please, Sam! Just leave me alone and let me get on with it. I'm not in the mood for games this afternoon. And remember my Mom's orders . . . you're to help Willie with the windows. Come on now, I don't want any more nonsense in here.

SAM: Okay, Hally, okay.

(Hally settles down to his homework; determined preparations . . . pen, ruler, exercise book, dictionary, another cake . . . all of which will lead to nothing.)

(Sam waltzes over to Willie and starts to replace tables and chairs. He practices a ballroom step while doing so. Willie watches. When Sam is finished, Willie tries.)

Good! But just a little bit quicker on the turn and only move in to her after she's crossed over. What about this one?

(Another step. When Sam is finished, Willie again has a go.)

Much better. See what happens when you just relax and enjoy yourself? Remember that in two weeks' time and you'll be all right.

WILLIE: But I haven't got partner, Boet Sam.

SAM: Maybe Hilda will turn up tonight.

WILLIE: No, Boet Sam. *(Reluctantly.)* I gave her a good hiding.

SAM: You mean a bad one.

WILLIE: Good bad one.

SAM: Then you mustn't complain either. Now you pay the price for losing your temper.

WILLIE: I also pay two pounds ten shilling entrance fee.

SAM: They'll refund you if you withdraw now.

WILLIE *(appalled)*: You mean, don't dance?

SAM: Yes.

WILLIE: No! I wait too long and I practice too hard. If I find me new partner, you think I can be ready in two weeks? I ask Madam for my leave now and we practice every day.

SAM: Quickstep nonstop for two weeks. World record, Willie, but you'll be mad at the end.

WILLIE: No jokes, Boet Sam.

SAM: I'm not joking.

WILLIE: So then what?

SAM: Find Hilda. Say you're sorry and promise you won't beat her again.

WILLIE: No.

SAM: Then withdraw. Try again next year.

WILLIE: No.

SAM: Then I give up.

WILLIE: Haaikona, Boet Sam, you can't.

SAM: What do you mean, I can't? I'm telling you: I give up.

WILLIE *(adamant)*: No! *(Accusingly.)* It was you who start me ballroom dancing.

SAM: So?

WILLIE: Before that I use to be happy. And is you and Miriam who bring me to Hilda and say here's partner for you.

SAM: What are you saying, Willie?

WILLIE: You!

SAM: But me what? To blame?

WILLIE: Yes.

SAM: Willie . . . ? *(Bursts into laughter.)*

WILLIE: And now all you do is make jokes at me. You wait. When Miriam leaves you is my turn to laugh. Ha! Ha! Ha!

SAM *(he can't take Willie seriously any longer)*: She can leave me tonight! I know what to do. *(Bowing before an imaginary partner.)* May I have the pleasure? *(He dances and sings.)*
"Just a fellow with his pillow . . .
Dancin' like a willow . . .
In an autumn breeze. . . . "

WILLIE: There you go again!

(Sam goes on dancing and singing.)

Boet Sam!

SAM: There's the answer to your problem! Judges' announcement in two weeks' time: "Ladies and gentlemen, the winner in the open section . . . Mr. Willie Malopo and his pillow!"

(This is too much for a now really angry Willie. He goes for Sam, but the latter is too quick for him and puts Hally's table between the two of them.)

HALLY *(exploding)*: For Christ's sake, you two!

WILLIE *(still trying to get at Sam)*: I donner you, Sam! Struesgod!

SAM *(still laughing)*: Sorry, Willie . . . Sorry. . . .

HALLY: Sam! Willie! *(Grabs his ruler and gives Willie a vicious whack on the bum.)* How the hell am I supposed to concentrate with the two of you behaving like bloody children!

WILLIE: Hit him too!

HALLY: Shut up, Willie.

WILLIE: He started jokes again.

HALLY: Get back to your work. You too, Sam. *(His ruler.)* Do you want another one, Willie?

(Sam and Willie return to their work. Hally uses the opportunity to escape from his unsuccessful attempt at homework. He struts around like a little despot, ruler in hand, giving vent to his anger and frustration.)

Suppose a customer had walked in then? Or the Park Superintendent. And seen the two of you behaving like a pair of hooligans. That would have been the end of my mother's license, you know. And your jobs? Well, this is the end of it. From now on there will be no more of your ballroom nonsense in here. This is a business establishment, not a bloody New Brighton dancing school. I've been far too lenient with the two of you. *(Behind the counter for a green cool drink and a dollop of ice cream. He keeps up his tirade as he prepares it.)* But what really makes me bitter is that I allow you chaps a little freedom in here when business is bad and what do you do with it? The foxtrot! Specially you, Sam. There's more to life than trotting around a dance floor and I thought at least you knew it.

SAM: It's a harmless pleasure, Hally. It doesn't hurt anybody.

HALLY: It's also a rather simple one, you know.

SAM: You reckon so? Have you ever tried?

HALLY: Of course not.

SAM: Why don't you? Now.

HALLY: What do you mean? Me dance?

SAM: Yes. I'll show you a simple step—the waltz—then you try it.

HALLY: What will that prove?

SAM: That it might not be as easy as you think.

HALLY: I didn't say it was easy. I said it was simple—like in simple-minded, meaning mentally retarded. You can't exactly say it challenges the intellect.

SAM: It does other things.

HALLY: Such as?

SAM: Make people happy.

HALLY (the glass in his hand): So do American cream sodas with ice cream. For God's sake, Sam, you're not asking me to take ballroom dancing serious, are you?

SAM: Yes.

HALLY (sigh of defeat): Oh, well, so much for trying to give you a decent education. I've obviously achieved nothing.

SAM: You still haven't told me what's wrong with admiring something that's beautiful and then trying to do it yourself.

HALLY: Nothing. But we happen to be talking about a foxtrot, not a thing of beauty.

SAM: But that is just what I'm saying. If you were to see two champions doing, two masters of the art . . . !

HALLY: Oh God, I give up. So now it's also art!

SAM: Ja.

HALLY: There's a limit, Sam. Don't confuse art and entertainment.

SAM: So then what is art?

HALLY: You want a definition?

SAM: Ja.

HALLY (He realizes he has got to be careful. He gives the matter a lot of thought before answering.): Philosophers have been trying to do that for centuries. What is Art? What is Life? But basically I suppose it's . . . the giving of meaning to matter.

SAM: Nothing to do with beautiful?

HALLY: It goes beyond that. It's the giving of form to the formless.

SAM: Ja, well, maybe it's not art, then. But I still say it's beautiful.

HALLY: I'm sure the word you mean to use is entertaining.

SAM (adamant): No. Beautiful. And if you want proof come along to the Centenary Hall in New Brighton in two weeks' time.

(The mention of the Centenary Hall draws Willie over to them.)

HALLY: What for? I've seen the two of you prancing around in here often enough.

SAM (he laughs): This isn't the real thing, Hally. We're just playing around in here.

HALLY: So? I can use my imagination.

SAM: And what do you get?

HALLY: A lot of people dancing around and having a so-called good time.

SAM: That all?

HALLY: Well, basically it is that, surely.

SAM: No, it isn't. Your imagination hasn't helped you at all. There's a lot more to it than that. We're getting ready for the championships, Hally, not just another dance. There's going to be a lot of people, all right, and they're going to have a good time, but they'll only be spectators, sitting around and watching. It's just the competitors out there on the dance floor. Party decorations and fancy lights all around the walls! The ladies in beautiful evening dresses!

HALLY: My mother's got one of those, Sam, and, quite frankly, it's an embarrassment every time she wears it.

SAM (undeterred): Your imagination left out the excitement.

(Hally scoffs.)

Oh, yes. The finalists are not going to be out there just to have a good time. One of those couples will be the 1950 Eastern Province Champions. And your imagination left out the music.

WILLIE: Mr. Elijah Gladman Guzana and his Orchestral Jazzonions.

SAM: The sound of the big band, Hally. Trombone, trumpet, tenor and alto sax. And then, finally, your imagination also left out the climax of the evening when the dancing is finished, the judges have stopped whispering among themselves and the Master of Ceremonies collects their scorecards and goes up onto the stage to announce the winners.

HALLY: All right. So you make it sound like a bit of a do. It's an occasion. Satisfied?

SAM (victory): So you admit that!

HALLY: Emotionally yes, intellectually no.

SAM: Well, I don't know what you mean by that, all I'm telling you is that it is going to be the event of the year in New Brighton. It's been sold out for two weeks already. There's only standing room left. We've got competitors coming from Kingwilliamstown, East London, Port Alfred.

(Hally starts pacing thoughtfully.)

HALLY: Tell me a bit more.

SAM: I thought you weren't interested . . . intellectually.

HALLY (mysteriously): I've got my reasons.

SAM: What do you want to know?

HALLY: It takes place every year?

SAM: Yes. But only every third year in New Brighton. It's East London's turn to have the championships next year.

HALLY: Which, I suppose, makes it an even more significant event.

SAM: Ah ha! We're getting somewhere. Our "occasion" is now a "significant event."

HALLY: I wonder.

SAM: What?

HALLY: I wonder if I would get away with it.

SAM: But what?

HALLY (to the table and his exercise book): "Write five hundred words describing an annual event of cultural or historical significance." Would I be stretching poetic license a little too far if I called your ballroom championships a cultural event?

SAM: You mean . . . ?

HALLY: You think we could get five hundred words out of it, Sam?

SAM: Victor Sylvester has written a whole book on ballroom dancing.

WILLIE: You going to write about it, Master Hally?

HALLY: Yes, gentlemen, that is precisely what I am considering doing. Old Doc Bromely—he's my English teacher—is going to argue with me, of course. He doesn't like natives. But I'll point out to him that in strict anthropological terms the culture of a primitive black society includes its dancing and singing. To put my thesis in a nutshell: The war-dance has been replaced by the waltz. But it still amounts to the same thing: the release of primitive emotions through movement. Shall we give it a go?

SAM: I'm ready.

WILLIE: Me also.

HALLY: Ha! This will teach the old bugger a lesson. (*Decision taken.*) Right. Let's get ourselves organized. (*This means another cake on the table. He sits.*) I think you've given me enough general atmosphere, Sam, but to build the tension and suspense I need facts. (*Pencil poised.*)

WILLIE: Give him facts, Boet Sam.

HALLY: What you called the climax . . . how many finalists?

SAM: Six couples.

HALLY (*making notes*): Go on. Give me the picture.

SAM: Spectators seated right around the hall. (*Willie becomes a spectator.*)

HALLY: . . . and it's a full house.

SAM: At one end, on the stage, Gladman and his Orchestral Jazzonions. At the other end is a long table with the three judges. The six finalists go onto the dance floor and take up their positions. When they are ready and the spectators have settled down, the Master of Ceremonies goes to the microphone. To start with, he makes some jokes to get people laughing. . . .

HALLY: Good touch. (*As he writes.*) ". . . creating a relaxed atmosphere which will change to one of tension and drama as the climax is approached."

SAM (*onto a chair to act out the M.C.*): "Ladies and gentlemen, we come now to the great moment you have all been waiting for this evening . . . The finals of the 1950 Eastern Province Open Ballroom Dancing Championships. But first let me introduce the finalists! Mr. and Mrs. Welcome Tchabalala from Kingwilliamstown . . ."

WILLIE (*he applauds after every name*): Is when the people clap their hands and whistle and make a lot of noise, Master Hally.

SAM: "Mr. Mulligan Njikelane and Miss Nomhle Nkonyeni of Grahamstown; Mr. and Mrs. Norman Nchinga from Port Alfred; Mr. Fats Bokolane and Miss Dina Plaatjies from East London; Mr. Sipho

Danny Glover, who played Willie in the 1982 Broadway production, played the older waiter, Sam, in the 2003 New York revival of *"MASTER HAROLD" . . . and the boys*, directed by Lonny Price.

Dugu and Mrs. Mable Magada from Peddie; and from New Brighton our very own Mr. Willie Malopo and Miss Hilda Samuels."

(*Willie can't believe his ears. He abandons his role as spectator and scrambles into position as a finalist.*)

WILLIE: Relaxed and ready to romance!

SAM: The applause dies down. When everybody is silent, Gladman lifts up his sax, nods at the Orchestral Jazzonions. . . .

WILLIE: Play the jukebox please, Boet Sam!

SAM: I also only got bus fare, Willie.

HALLY: Hold it, everybody. (*Heads for the cash register behind the counter.*) How much is in the till, Sam?

SAM: Three shillings. Hally . . . Your Mom counted it before she left.

(*Hally hesitates.*)

HALLY: Sorry, Willie. You know how she carried on the last time I did it. We'll just have to pool our combined imaginations and hope for the best. (*Returns to the table.*) Back to work. How are the points scored, Sam?

SAM: Maximum of ten points each for individual style, deportment, rhythm, and general appearance.

WILLIE: Must I start?

HALLY: Hold it for a second, Willie. And penalties?

SAM: For what?

HALLY: For doing something wrong. Say you stumble or bump into somebody . . . do they take off any points?

SAM (*aghast*): Hally . . . !

HALLY: When you're dancing. If you and your partner collide into another couple.

(*Hally can get no further. Sam has collapsed with laughter. He explains to Willie.*)

SAM: If me and Miriam bump into you and Hilda . . . .

(*Willie joins him in another good laugh.*)

Hally, Hally . . . !

HALLY (*perplexed*): Why? What did I say?

SAM: There's no collisions out there, Hally. Nobody trips or stumbles or bumps into anybody else. That's what that moment is all about. To be one of those finalists on that dance floor is like . . . like being in a dream about a world in which accidents don't happen.

HALLY (*genuinely moved by Sam's image*): Jesus, Sam! That's beautiful!

WILLIE (*can endure waiting no longer*): I'm starting!

(*Willie dances while Sam talks.*)

SAM: Of course it is. That's what I've been trying to say to you all afternoon. And it's beautiful because that is what we want life to be like. But instead, like you said, Hally, we're bumping into each other all the time. Look at the three of us this afternoon: I've bumped into Willie, the two of us have bumped into you, you've bumped into your mother, she bumping into your Dad. . . . None of us knows the steps and there's no music playing. And it doesn't stop with us. The whole world is doing it all the time. Open a newspaper and what do you read? America has bumped into Russia, England is bumping into India, rich man bumps into poor man. Those are big collisions, Hally. They make for a lot of bruises. People get hurt in all that bumping, and we're sick and tired of it now. It's been going on for too long. Are we never going to get it right? . . . Learn to dance life like champions instead of always being just a bunch of beginners at it?

HALLY (*deep and sincere admiration of the man*): You've got a vision, Sam!

SAM: Not just me. What I'm saying to you is that everybody's got it. That's why there's only standing room left for the Centenary Hall in two weeks' time. For as long as the music lasts, we are going to see six couples get it right, the way we want life to be.

HALLY: But is that the best we can do, Sam . . . watch six finalists dreaming about the way it should be?

SAM: I don't know. But it starts with that. Without the dream we won't know what we're going for. And anyway I reckon there are a few people who have got past just dreaming about it and are trying for something real. Remember that thing we read once in the paper about the Mahatma Gandhi? Going without food to stop those riots in India?

HALLY: You're right. He certainly was trying to teach people to get the steps right.

SAM: And the Pope.

HALLY: Yes, he's another one. Our old General Smuts° as well, you know. He's also out there dancing. You know, Sam, when you come to think of it, that's what the United Nations boils down to . . . a dancing school for politicians!

SAM: And let's hope they learn.

HALLY (*a little surge of hope*): You're right. We mustn't despair. Maybe there's some hope for mankind after all. Keep it up, Willie. (*Back to his table with determination.*) This is a lot bigger than I thought. So what have we got? Yes, our title: "A World Without Collisions."

SAM: That sounds good! "A World Without Collisions."

HALLY: Subtitle: "Global Politics on the Dance Floor." No. A bit too heavy, hey? What about "Ballroom Dancing as a Political Vision"?

(*The telephone rings. Sam answers it.*)

SAM: St. George's Park Tea Room . . . Yes, Madam . . . Hally, it's your Mom.

HALLY (*back to reality*): Oh, God, yes! I'd forgotten all about that. Shit! Remember my words, Sam? Just when you're enjoying yourself, someone or something will come along and wreck everything.

SAM: You haven't heard what she's got to say yet.

HALLY: Public telephone?

SAM: No.

HALLY: Does she sound happy or unhappy?

SAM: I couldn't tell. (*Pause.*) She's waiting, Hally.

HALLY (*to the telephone*): Hello, Mom . . . No, everything is okay here. Just doing my homework. . . . What's your news? . . . You've what? . . . (*Pause. He takes the receiver away from his ear for a few seconds. In the course of Hally's telephone conversation, Sam and Willie discreetly position the stacked tables and chairs. Hally places the receiver back to his ear.*) Yes, I'm still here. Oh, well, I give up now. Why did you do it, Mom? . . . Well, I just hope you know what you've let us in for. . . . (*Loudly.*) I said I hope you know what you've let us in for! It's the end of the peace and quiet we've been having. (*Softly.*) Where is he? (*Normal voice.*) He can't hear us from in there. But for God's

General Smuts: South African statesman (1870–1950), who fought the British in the Boer War in 1899, was instrumental in forming the Union of South Africa in 1910, and was active in the creation of the United Nations.

sake, Mom, what happened? I told you to be firm with him. . . . Then you and the nurses should have held him down, taken his crutches away. . . . I know only too well he's my father! . . . I'm not being disrespectful, but I'm sick and tired of emptying stinking chamber pots full of phlegm and piss. . . . Yes, I do! When you're not there, he asks *me* to do it. . . . If you really want to know the truth, that's why I've got no appetite for my food. . . . Yes! There's a lot of things you don't know about. For your information, I still haven't got that science textbook I need. And you know why? He borrowed the money you gave me for it. . . . Because I didn't want to start another fight between you two. . . . He says that every time. . . . All right, Mom! (*Viciously.*) Then just remember to start hiding your bag away again, because he'll be at your purse before long for money for booze. And when he's well enough to come down here, you better keep an eye on the till as well, because that is also going to develop a leak. . . . Then don't complain to me when he starts his old tricks. . . . Yes, you do. I get it from you on one side and from him on the other, and it makes life hell for me. I'm not going to be the peacemaker anymore. I'm warning you now: when the two of you start fighting again, I'm leaving home. . . . Mom, if you start crying, I'm going to put down the receiver. . . . Okay. . . . (*Lowering his voice to a vicious whisper.*) Okay, Mom. I heard you. (*Desperate.*) No. . . . Because I don't want to. I'll see him when I get home! Mom! . . . (*Pause. When he speaks again, his tone changes completely. It is not simply pretense. We sense a genuine emotional conflict.*) Welcome home, chum! . . . What's that? . . . Don't be silly, Dad. You being home is just about the best news in the world. . . . I bet you are. Bloody depressing there with everybody going on about their ailments, hey! . . . How you feeling? . . . Good. . . . Here as well, pal. Coming down cats and dogs. . . . That's right. Just the day for a kip° and a toss in your old Uncle Ned. . . . Everything's just hunky-dory on my side, Dad. . . . Well, to start with, there's a nice pile of comics for you on the counter. . . . Yes, old Kemple brought them in. *Batman and Robin, Submariner* . . . just your cup of tea. . . . I will. . . . Yes, we'll spin a few yarns tonight. . . . Okay, chum, see you in a little while. . . . No, I promise. I'll come straight home. . . . (*Pause—his mother comes back on the phone.*) Mom? Okay. I'll lock up now. . . . What? . . . Oh, the brandy . . . Yes, I'll remember! . . . I'll put it in my suitcase now, for God's sake. I know well enough what will happen if he doesn't get it. . . . (*Places a bottle of brandy on the counter.*) I *was* kind to him, Mom. I didn't say anything nasty! . . . All right. Bye. (*End of telephone conversation. A desolate Hally doesn't move. A strained silence.*)

kip: Nap.

SAM (*quietly*): That sounded like a bad bump, Hally.

HALLY (*Having a hard time controlling his emotions. He speaks carefully.*): Mind your own business, Sam.

SAM: Sorry. I wasn't trying to interfere. Shall we carry on? Hally? (*He indicates the exercise book. No response from Hally.*)

WILLIE (*also trying*): Tell him about when they give out the cups, Boet Sam.

SAM: Ja! That's another big moment. The presentation of the cups after the winners have been announced. You've got to put that in.

(*Still no response from Hally.*)

WILLIE: A big silver one, Master Hally, called floating trophy for the champions.

SAM: We always invite some big-shot personality to hand them over. Guest of honor this year is going to be His Holiness Bishop Jabulani of the All African Free Zionist Church.

(*Hally gets up abruptly, goes to his table, and tears up the page he was writing on.*)

HALLY: So much for a bloody world without collisions.

SAM: Too bad. It was on its way to being a good composition.

HALLY: Let's stop bullshitting ourselves, Sam.

SAM: Have we been doing that?

HALLY: Yes! That's what all our talk about a decent world has been . . . just so much bullshit.

SAM: We did say it was still only a dream.

HALLY: And a bloody useless one at that. Life's a fuckup and it's never going to change.

SAM: Ja, maybe that's true.

HALLY: There's no maybe about it. It's a blunt and brutal fact. All we've done this afternoon is waste our time.

SAM: Not if we'd got your homework done.

HALLY: I don't give a shit about my homework, so, for Christ's sake, just shut up about it. (*Slamming books viciously into his school case.*) Hurry up now and finish your work. I want to lock up and get out of here. (*Pause.*) And then go where? Home-sweet-fucking-home. Jesus, I hate that word.

(*Hally goes to the counter to put the brandy bottle and comics in his school case. After a moment's hesitation, he smashes the bottle of brandy. He abandons all further attempts to hide his feelings. Sam and Willie work away as unobtrusively as possible.*)

Do you want to know what is really wrong with your lovely little dream, Sam? It's not just that we are all bad dancers. That does happen to be perfectly true, but there's more to it than just that. You left out the cripples.

SAM: Hally!

HALLY (*now totally reckless*): Ja! Can't leave them out, Sam. That's why we always end up on our backsides on the dance floor. They're also out there dancing . . . like a bunch of broken spiders trying to do the quickstep! (*An ugly attempt at laughter.*) When you come to think of it, it's a bloody comical sight. I mean, it's bad enough on two legs . . . but one and a pair of crutches! Hell, no, Sam. That's guaranteed to turn that dance floor into a shambles. Why you shaking your head? Picture it, man. For once this afternoon let's use our imaginations sensibly.

SAM: Be careful, Hally.

HALLY: Of what? The truth? I seem to be the only one around here who is prepared to face it. We've had the pretty dream, it's time now to wake up and have a good long look at the way things really are. Nobody knows the steps, there's no music, the cripples are also out there tripping up everybody and trying to get into the act, and it's all called the All-Comers-How-to-Make-a-Fuckup-of-Life Championships. (*Another ugly laugh.*) Hang on, Sam! The best bit is still coming. Do you know what the winner's trophy is? A beautiful big chamber pot with roses on the side, and it's full to the brim with piss. And guess who I think is going to be this year's winner.

SAM (*almost shouting*): Stop now!

HALLY (*suddenly appalled by how far he has gone*): Why?

SAM: Hally? It's your father you're talking about.

HALLY: So?

SAM: Do you know what you've been saying?

(*Hally can't answer. He is rigid with shame. Sam speaks to him sternly.*)

No, Hally, you mustn't do it. Take back those words and ask for forgiveness! It's a terrible sin for a son to mock his father with jokes like that. You'll be punished if you carry on. Your father is your father, even if he is a . . . cripple man.

WILLIE: Yes, Master Hally. Is true what Sam say.

SAM: I understand how you are feeling, Hally, but even so. . . .

HALLY: No, you don't!

SAM: I think I do.

HALLY: And I'm telling you you don't. Nobody does. (*Speaking carefully as his shame turns to rage at Sam.*) It's your turn to be careful, Sam. Very careful! You're treading on dangerous ground. Leave me and my father alone.

SAM: I'm not the one who's been saying things about him.

HALLY: What goes on between me and my Dad is none of your business!

SAM: Then don't tell me about it. If that's all you've got to say about him, I don't want to hear.

(*For a moment Hally is at loss for a response.*)

HALLY: Just get on with your bloody work and shut up.

SAM: Swearing at me won't help you.

HALLY: Yes, it does! Mind your own fucking business and shut up!

SAM: Okay. If that's the way you want it, I'll stop trying.

(*He turns away. This infuriates Hally even more.*)

HALLY: Good. Because what you've been trying to do is meddle in something you know nothing about. All that concerns you in here, Sam, is to try and do what you get paid for—keep the place clean and serve the customers. In plain words, just get on with your job. My mother is right. She's always warning me about allowing you to get too familiar. Well, this time you've gone too far. It's going to stop right now.

(*No response from Sam.*)

You're only a servant in here, and don't forget it.

(*Still no response. Hally is trying hard to get one.*)

And as far as my father is concerned, all you need to remember is that he is your boss.

SAM (*needled at last*): No, he isn't. I get paid by your mother.

HALLY: Don't argue with me, Sam!

SAM: Then don't say he's my boss.

HALLY: He's a white man and that's good enough for you.

SAM: I'll try to forget you said that.

HALLY: Don't! Because you won't be doing me a favor if you do. I'm telling you to remember it.

(*A pause. Sam pulls himself together and makes one last effort.*)

SAM: Hally, Hally . . . ! Come on now. Let's stop before it's too late. You're right. We *are* on dangerous ground. If we're not careful, somebody is going to get hurt.

HALLY: It won't be me.

SAM: Don't be so sure.

HALLY: I don't know what you're talking about, Sam.

SAM: Yes, you do.

HALLY (*furious*): Jesus, I wish you would stop trying to tell me what I do and what I don't know.

(*Sam gives up. He turns to Willie.*)

SAM: Let's finish up.

HALLY: Don't turn your back on me! I haven't finished talking.

(*He grabs Sam by the arm and tries to make him turn around. Sam reacts with a flash of anger.*)

SAM: Don't do that, Hally! (*Facing the boy.*) All right, I'm listening. Well? What do you want to say to me?

HALLY (*pause as Hally looks for something to say*): To begin with, why don't you also start calling me Master Harold, like Willie.

SAM: Do you mean that?

HALLY: Why the hell do you think I said it?

SAM: And if I don't?

HALLY: You might just lose your job.

SAM (*quietly and very carefully*): If you make me say it once, I'll never call you anything else again.

HALLY: So? (*The boy confronts the man.*) Is that meant to be a threat?

SAM: Just telling you what will happen if you make me do that. You must decide what it means to you.

HALLY: Well, I have. It's good news. Because that is exactly what Master Harold wants from now on.

Think of it as a little lesson in respect, Sam, that's long overdue, and I hope you remember it as well as you do your geography. I can tell you now that somebody who will be glad to hear I've finally given it to you will be my Dad. Yes! He agrees with my Mom. He's always going on about it as well. "You must teach the boys to show you more respect, my son."

SAM: So now you can stop complaining about going home. Everybody is going to be happy tonight.

HALLY: That's perfectly correct. You see, you mustn't get the wrong idea about me and my Dad, Sam. We also have our good times together. Some bloody good laughs. He's got a marvelous sense of humor. Want to know what our favorite joke is? He gives out a big groan, you see, and says: "It's not fair, is it, Hally?" Then I have to ask: "What, chum?" And then he says: "A nigger's arse" . . . and we both have a good laugh.

(*The men stare at him with disbelief.*)

What's the matter, Willie? Don't you catch the joke? You always were a bit slow on the uptake. It's what is called a pun. You see, fair means both light in color and to be just and decent. (*He turns to Sam.*) I thought *you* would catch it, Sam.

SAM: Oh ja, I catch it all right.

HALLY: But it doesn't appeal to your sense of humor.

SAM: Do you really laugh?

HALLY: Of course.

SAM: To please him? Make him feel good?

HALLY: No, for heavens sake! I laugh because I think it's a bloody good joke.

SAM: You're really trying hard to be ugly, aren't you? And why drag poor old Willie into it? He's done nothing to you except show you the respect you want so badly. That's also not being fair, you know . . . and *I* mean just or decent.

WILLIE: It's all right, Sam. Leave it now.

SAM: It's me you're after. You should just have said "Sam's arse" . . . because that's the one you're trying to kick. Anyway, how do you know it's not fair? You've never seen it. Do you want to? (*He drops his trousers and underpants and presents his backside for Hally's inspection.*) Have a good look. A real Basuto arse . . . which is about as nigger as they can come. Satisfied? (*Trousers up.*) Now you can make your Dad even happier when you go home tonight. Tell him I showed you my arse and he is quite right. It's not fair. And if it will give him an even better laugh next time, I'll also let *him* have a look. Come, Willie, let's finish up and go.

(*Sam and Willie start to tidy up the tea room. Hally doesn't move. He waits for a moment when Sam passes him.*)

HALLY (*quietly*): Sam . . .

(*Sam stops and looks expectantly at the boy. Hally spits in his face. A long and heartfelt groan from Willie. For a few seconds Sam doesn't move.*)

SAM (*taking out a handkerchief and wiping his face*): It's all right, Willie.

(*To Hally.*)

Ja, well, you've done it . . . Master Harold. Yes, I'll start calling you that from now on. It won't be difficult anymore. You've hurt yourself, Master Harold. I saw it coming. I warned you, but you wouldn't listen. You've just hurt yourself *bad*. And you're a coward, Master Harold. The face you should be spitting in is your father's . . . but you used mine, because you think you're safe inside your fair skin . . . and this time I don't mean just or decent. (*Pause, then moving violently toward Hally.*) Should I hit him, Willie?

WILLIE (*stopping Sam*): No, Boet Sam.

SAM (*violently*): Why not?

WILLIE: It won't help, Boet Sam.

SAM: I don't want to help! I want to hurt him.

WILLIE: You also hurt yourself.

SAM: And if he had done it to you, Willie?

WILLIE: Me? Spit at me like I was a dog? (*A thought that had not occurred to him before. He looks at Hally.*) Ja. Then I want to hit him. I want to hit him hard!

(*A dangerous few seconds as the men stand staring at the boy. Willie turns away, shaking his head.*)

But maybe all I do is go cry at the back. He's little boy, Boet Sam. Little *white* boy. Long trousers now, but he's still little boy.

SAM (*his violence ebbing away into defeat as quickly as it flooded*): You're right. So go on, then: groan again, Willie. You do it better than me. (*To Hally.*) You don't know all of what you've just done . . . Master Harold. It's not just that you've made me feel dirtier than I've ever been in my life . . . I mean, how do I wash off yours and your father's filth? . . . I've also failed. A long time ago I promised myself I was going to try and do something, but you've just shown me . . . Master Harold . . . that I've failed. (*Pause.*) I've also got a memory of a little white boy when he was still wearing short trousers and a black man, but they're not flying a kite. It was the old Jubilee days, after dinner one night. I was in my room. You came in and just stood against the wall, looking down at the ground, and only after I'd asked you what you wanted, what was wrong, I don't know how many times, did you speak and even then so softly I almost didn't hear you. "Sam, please help me to go and fetch my Dad." Remember? He was dead drunk on the floor of the Central Hotel Bar. They'd phoned for your Mom, but you were the only one at home. And do you remember how we did it? You went in first by yourself to ask permission for me to go into the bar. Then I loaded him onto my back like a baby and carried him back to the boarding house with you following behind carrying his crutches. (*Shaking his head as he remembers.*) A crowded Main Street with all the people watching a little white boy following his drunk father on a nigger's back! I felt for that little boy . . . Master Harold. I felt for him. After that we still had to clean him up, remember? He'd messed in his trousers, so we had to clean him up and get him into bed.

HALLY (*great pain*): I love him, Sam.

SAM: I know you do. That's why I tried to stop you from saying these things about him. It would have been so simple if you could have just despised him for being a weak man. But he's your father. You love him and you're ashamed of him. You're ashamed of so much! . . . And now that's going to include yourself. That was the promise I made to myself: to try and stop that happening. (*Pause.*) After we got him to bed you came back with me to my room and sat in a corner and carried on just looking down at the ground. And for days after that! You hadn't done anything wrong, but you went around as if you owed the world an apology for being alive. I didn't like seeing that! That's not the way a boy grows up to be a man! . . . But the one person who should have been teaching you what that means was the cause of your shame. If you really want to know, that's why I made you that kite. I wanted you to look up, be proud of something, of yourself . . . (*bitter smile at the memory*) . . . and you certainly were that when I left you with it up there on the hill. Oh, ja . . . something else! . . . If you ever do write it as a short story, there *was* a twist in our ending. I couldn't sit down there and stay with you. It was a "Whites Only" bench. You were too young, too excited to notice then. But not anymore. If you're not careful . . . Master Harold . . . you're going to be sitting up there by yourself for a long time to come, and there won't be a kite in the sky. (*Sam has got nothing more to say. He exits into the kitchen, taking off his waiter's jacket.*)

WILLIE: Is bad. Is all bad in here now.

HALLY (*books into his school case, raincoat on*): Willie . . . (*It is difficult to speak.*) Will you lock up for me and look after the keys?

WILLIE: Okay.

(*Sam returns. Hally goes behind the counter and collects the few coins in the cash register. As he starts to leave . . . .*)

SAM: Don't forget the comic books.

(*Hally returns to the counter and puts them in his case. He starts to leave again.*)

SAM (*to the retreating back of the boy*): Stop . . . Hally. . . .

(*Hally stops, but doesn't turn to face him.*)

Hally . . . I've got no right to tell you what being a man means if I don't behave like one myself, and I'm not doing so well at that this afternoon. Should we try again, Hally?

HALLY: Try what?

SAM: Fly another kite, I suppose. It worked once, and this time I need it as much as you do.

HALLY: It's still raining, Sam. You can't fly kites on rainy days, remember.

SAM: So what do we do? Hope for better weather tomorrow?

HALLY (*helpless gesture*): I don't know. I don't know anything anymore.

SAM: You sure of that, Hally? Because it would be pretty hopeless if that was true. It would mean nothing has been learnt in here this afternoon, and there was a hell of a lot of teaching going on . . . one way or the other. But anyway, I don't believe you. I reckon there's one thing you know. You don't *have* to sit up there by yourself. You know what that bench means now, and you can leave it any time you choose. All you've got to do is stand up and walk away from it.

(*Hally leaves. Willie goes up quietly to Sam.*)

WILLIE: Is okay, Boet Sam. You see. Is . . . (*he can't find any better words*) . . . is going to be okay tomorrow. (*Changing his tone.*) Hey, Boet Sam! (*He is trying hard.*) You right. I think about it and you right. Tonight I find Hilda and say sorry. And make promise I won't beat her no more. You hear me, Boet Sam?

SAM: I hear you, Willie.

WILLIE: And when we practice I relax and romance with her from beginning to end. Nonstop! You watch! Two weeks' time: "First prize for promising newcomers: Mr. Willie Malopo and Miss Hilda Samuels." (*Sudden impulse.*) To hell with it! I walk home. (*He goes to the jukebox, puts in a coin and selects a record. The machine comes to life in the gray twilight, blushing its way through a spectrum of soft, romantic colors.*) How did you say it, Boet Sam? Let's dream. (*Willie sways with the music and gestures for Sam to dance.*)

(*Sarah Vaughan sings.*)

"Little man you're crying,
I know why you're blue,
Someone took your kiddy car away;
Better go to sleep now,
Little man you've had a busy day." (*etc., etc.*)
You lead. I follow.

(*The men dance together.*)

"Johnny won your marbles,
Tell you what we'll do;
Dad will get you new ones right away;
Better go to sleep now,
Little man you've had a busy day."

COMMENTARY

ATHOL FUGARD (b. 1932)

From Notebooks 1960–1977 1983

Like most playwrights, Athol Fugard is a journal writer. His notebooks contain scraps of memories that have special meaning to him. In one entry for March 1961, long before he began to write *"MASTER HAROLD" . . . and the boys* (1982), he describes one of his childhood memories. It concerns the real-life Sam, and it recounts — very painfully — the personal crime that Fugard's play deals with. His gesture of contempt for the man who was like a grandfather to him became a demon that had to be exorcised.

Sam Semela — Basuto — with the family fifteen years. Meeting him again when he visited Mom set off string of memories.

The kite which he produced for me one day during those early years when Mom ran the Jubilee Hotel and he was a waiter there. He had made it himself: brown paper, its ribs fashioned from thin strips of tomato-box plank which he had smoothed down, a paste of flour and water for glue. I was surprised and bewildered that he had made it for me.

I vaguely recall shyly "haunting" the servants' quarters in the well of the hotel — cold, cement-gray world — the pungent mystery of the dark little rooms — a world I didn't understand. Frightened to enter any of the rooms. Sam, broad-faced, broader based — he smelled of woodsmoke. The "kaffir smell" of South Africa is the smell of poverty — wood smoke and sweat.

Later, when he worked for her at the Park café, Mom gave him the sack: " . . . he became careless. He came late for work. His work went to hell. He didn't seem to care no more." I was about thirteen and served behind the counter while he waited on table.

Realize now he was the most significant — the only — friend of my boyhood years. On terrible windy days when no one came to swim or walk in the park, we would sit together and talk. Or I was reading — Introductions to Eastern Philosophy or Plato and Socrates — and when I had finished he would take the book back to New Brighton.

Can't remember now what precipitated it, but one day there was a rare quarrel between Sam and myself. In a truculent silence we closed the café, Sam set off home to New Brighton on foot and I followed a few minutes later on my bike. I saw him walking ahead of me and, coming out of a spasm of acute loneliness, as I rode up behind him I called his name, he turned in mid-stride to look back and, as I cycled past, I spat in his face. Don't suppose I will ever deal with the shame that overwhelmed me the second after I had done that.

Now he is thin. We had a long talk. He told about the old woman ("Ma") whom he and his wife have taken in to look after their house while he goes to work — he teaches ballroom dancing. "Ma" insists on behaving like a domestic — making Sam feel guilty and embarrassed. She brings him an early morning cup of coffee. Sam: "No, Ma, you mustn't, man." Ma: "I must." Sam: "Look, Ma, if I want it, I can make it." Ma: "No, I must."

Occasionally, when she is doing something, Sam feels like a cup of tea but is too embarrassed to ask her, and daren't make one for himself. Similarly, with his washing. After three days or a week away in other towns, giving dancing lessons, he comes back with underclothes that are very dirty. He is too shy to give them out to be washed so washes them himself. When Ma sees this she goes and complains to Sam's wife that he doesn't trust her, that it's all wrong for him to do the washing.

Of tsotsis,° he said: "They grab a old man, stick him with a knife, and ransack him. And so he must go to hospital and his kids is starving with hungry." Of others: "He's got some little moneys. So he is facing starvation for the weekend."

Of township snobs, he says there are the educational ones: "If you haven't been to the big school, like Fort Hare, what you say isn't true." And the money ones: "If you aren't selling shops or got a business or a big car, man, you're nothing."

Sam's incredible theory about the likeness of those "with the true seed of love." Starts with Plato and Socrates—they were round. "Man is being shrinking all the time. An Abe Lincoln, him too, taller, but that's because man is shrinking." Basically, those with the true seed of love look the same—"It's in the eyes."

He spoke admiringly of one man, a black lawyer in East London, an educated man—university background—who was utterly without snobbery, looking down on no one—any man, educated or ignorant, rich or poor, was another *man* to him, another human being, to be respected, taken seriously, to be talked to, listened to.

"They" won't allow Sam any longer to earn a living as a dancing teacher. "You must get a job!" One of his fellow teachers was forced to work at Fraser's Quarries.

---

tsotsis: Gang members.

August Wilson

August Wilson (1945–2005) was born in Pittsburgh, the son of a white father who abandoned his family and a black mother who had come from North Carolina to a Pittsburgh slum, where she worked to keep her family together. Wilson's early childhood was spent in an environment very similar to that of his play *Fences*, and Troy Maxson seems to be patterned somewhat on Wilson's stepfather.

Wilson's writing is rooted to a large extent in music, specifically the blues. As a poet, writing over several years, Wilson became interested in the speech patterns and rhythms that were familiar to him from black neighborhoods, but the value of those patterns became clearer to him when he grew older and moved from Pittsburgh to Minneapolis. From a distance, he was able to see more clearly what had attracted him to the language and begin to use it more fully in his work.

In the 1960s and 1970s, Wilson became involved in the civil rights movement and began to describe himself as a black nationalist, a term he said he felt comfortable with. He began writing plays in the 1960s in Pittsburgh and then took a job in St. Paul writing dramatic skits for the Science Museum of Minnesota. He founded the Playwrights Center in Minneapolis and wrote a play, *Jitney,* about a gypsy cab station. *Jitney* was first produced in 1982; a revised version was staged in New York in April 2000 at the Second Stage Theatre. *Fullerton Street,* about Pittsburgh, was another play written in this early period. Wilson's first commercial success, *Ma Rainey's Black Bottom,*

August Wilson in a portrait by David Cooper made in 2004, just one year before Wilson's untimely death.

premiered at the Yale Repertory Theatre in 1984 and then went to Broadway, where it enjoyed 275 performances and won the New York Drama Critics' Circle Award.

Ma Rainey's Black Bottom was the first of a planned sequence of ten plays based on the black American experience. As Wilson said, "I think the black Americans have the most dramatic story of all mankind to tell." The concept of such a vast project echoes Eugene O'Neill's projected group of eleven plays based on the Irish American experience. Unfortunately, O'Neill destroyed all but three of the plays (*A Touch of the Poet, More Stately Mansions,* and part of *Calms of Capricorn*) in his series. Wilson's project, however, was completed and produced some of the most successful plays in the recent American theater.

Ma Rainey is about the legendary black blues singer, who preceded Bessie Smith and Billie Holiday. The play is about the ways in which Rainey was exploited by white managers and recording executives and how she dealt with her exploitation. In the cast of the play are several black musicians in the backup band. Levee, the trumpet player, has a dream of leading his own band and establishing himself as an important jazz musician. But he is haunted by memories of seeing his mother raped by a gang of white men when he was a boy. He wants to "improve" the session he's playing by making the old jazz tune "Black Bottom" swing in the new jazz style, but Ma Rainey keeps him in tow and demands that they play the tune in the old way. Levee finally cracks under the pressure, and the play ends painfully.

Fences opened at the Yale Repertory Theatre in 1985 and in New York in early 1987, where it won the Pulitzer Prize as well as the New York Drama Critics' Circle Award. This long-running success firmly established Wilson as an important writer. *Joe Turner's Come and Gone* opened at the Yale Repertory Theatre in late 1986 and moved to New York in early 1988, where it too was hailed as an important play, winning its author another New York Drama Critics' Circle Award. Set in a rooming house in Pittsburgh in 1911, *Joe Turner* is a study of the children of former slaves. They have come north to look for work, and some of them have been found by the legendary bounty hunter Joe Turner. As a study of a people in transition, the play is a quiet masterpiece. It incorporates a number of important African traditions, especially religious rituals of healing as performed by Bynum, the "bone man," a seer and a medicine man. In this play and others, Wilson makes a special effort to highlight the elements of African heritage that white society strips away from blacks.

The next play in Wilson's series, *The Piano Lesson,* which premiered at the Yale Repertory Theatre in 1987, also portrays the complexity of black attitudes toward the past and black heritage. The piano represents two kinds of culture: the white culture that produced the musical instrument and the black culture, in the form of Papa Boy Willie, who carved into it images from black Africa. The central question in the play is whether Boy Willie should sell the piano and use the money for a down payment on land and therefore on the future. Or should he follow his sister Berniece's advice and keep it because it is too precious to sell? The conflict is deep, and the play ultimately focuses on a profound moment of spiritual exorcism. How one exorcises the past — how one lives with it or without it — is a central theme in Wilson's work.

His next play, *Two Trains Running,* is set in 1969, in the decade that saw the Vietnam War, racial and political riots, and the assassinations of John and Robert Kennedy, Malcolm X, and Martin Luther King Jr. The play premiered at the Yale Repertory Theatre in 1990 and opened on Broadway at the Walter Kerr Theatre in April 1992, directed by Lloyd Richards. The characters remain in Memphis Lee's diner—scheduled for demolition—throughout the play. The two trains in the title are heading to Africa and to the old South, but the characters are immobile and seem indifferent to both of them. Wilson moved away from the careful structure of the well-made play in this work and produced an open-ended conclusion, leaving the racial and philosophical tensions unresolved.

Seven Guitars (1995) takes place in a backyard in Pittsburgh in 1948 on the eve of the landmark boxing match between Joe Louis and "Jersey" Joe Walcott. The play focuses on a blues musician, Floyd Barton, who hopes to regain his lost love, put his band back together, and move to Chicago to make his second recording. *Seven Guitars* emphasizes the blues, especially in its long first act, with Barton's friends gathered in his backyard to mourn his death and the loss of his talent. People did much the same when Joe Louis, the "Brown Bomber," lost his fight, a loss that punctuated the end of an era. The second act focuses on Hedley, a West Indian boarder, whom critic Margo Jefferson describes as "half madman and half prophet." Hedley recites a litany of racial injustices and gives voice to a torrent of wrongs. Hedley's voice is a counterpoint to the blues; he gives us a powerful range of responses to the condition of being black in Pittsburgh in the late 1940s.

King Hedley II (1999), set in 1985, picks up some of the characters of *Seven Guitars,* including Hedley, and develops further the experience of living in the Hill District of Pittsburgh. Wilson described the play as focusing on "the breakdown of the black community's extended-family structure." Wilson, then living in Seattle, returned to his hometown for the December 1999 premiere of *King Hedley II,* the first play produced in the new O'Reilly Theater by the Pittsburgh Public Theater. It moved to the Seattle Repertory Theatre in 2000 and to Broadway in 2001.

At this point, the sequence of plays detailing the African American experience for each decade of the twentieth century needed only the first and last decades' plays. *Gem of the Ocean,* set in 1904, introduced Aunt Ester, who had been alluded to in earlier plays. Her birthday, more than 280 years before, coincides with the introduction of African slaves into the United States. She has a healing power that helps cleanse some of the characters of their sense of guilt. The production, directed by Marion McClinton, featured Phylicia Rashad as Aunt Ester and won the Tony Award for best play of 2005. It ran for 72 performances. The final play in the cycle is *Radio Golf,* which premiered at Yale Repertory Theatre before Wilson's death in 2005 and then moved to the Cort Theatre on Broadway in April 2007. It too won a Tony, for best play of 2007, but it ran for only 64 performances. The play is set in 1997 and focuses on the Bedford Hills Redevelopment company, a storefront on Centre Street in Pittsburgh. This company's project involves the total demolition and reconstruction of the Hill District, including the destruction of Aunt Ester's home, the setting of *Gem of the Ocean.* The struggle between doing what is right and doing what is profitable and practicable is central to the drama. Wilson died of liver cancer, knowing his project was complete.

For links to resources about Wilson, click on *AuthorLinks* at bedfordstmartins.com/jacobus.

Fences

For discussion questions and assignments on *Fences,* visit bedfordstmartins.com/jacobus.

Fences (1985), like most of August Wilson's plays, was directed by Lloyd Richards, who also directed the first production of Lorraine Hansberry's *A Raisin in the Sun*. Richards was, until 1991, the dean of the School of Drama at Yale University and ran the Yale Repertory Theatre, where he directed the first several of the plays Wilson wrote in his ten-play cycle about black American life.

Fences presents a slice of life in a black tenement in Pittsburgh in the 1950s. Its main character, Troy Maxson, is a garbage collector who has taken great pride in keeping his family together and providing for them. When the play opens, he and his friend Bono are talking about Troy's challenge to the company and the union about blacks' ability to do the same "easy" work that whites do. Troy's rebellion and frustration set the tone for the entire play; he is looking for his rights, and, at age fifty-three, he has missed many opportunities to get what he deserves.

Troy's struggle for fairness becomes virtually mythic as he describes his wrestling with death during a bout of pneumonia in 1941. He describes a three-day struggle in which he eventually overcame his foe. Troy—a good baseball player who was relegated to the Negro leagues—sees death as nothing but a fastball, and he could always deal with a fastball. Both Bono and Troy's wife, Rose, show an intense admiration for him as he describes his ordeal.

The father-son relationship that begins to take a central role in the drama is complicated by strong feelings of pride and independence on both sides. Troy's son Cory wants to play football, and Troy wants him to work on the fence he's mending. Cory's youthful enthusiasm probably echoes Troy's own youthful innocence, but Troy resents it in Cory, seeing it as partly responsible for his own predicament. Cory cannot see his father's point of view and believes that he is exempt from the kind of prejudice his father suffered.

The agony of the father-son relationship and their misperceptions of each other persist through the play. Rose's capacity to cope with the deepest of Troy's anxieties—his fear of death—is one of her most important achievements in the play. At the end of the play, Rose demands that Cory give Troy the respect he deserves, although Cory's anger and inexperience make it all but impossible for him to see his father as anything other than an oppressor. Cory thinks that he must say no to his father once, but Rose will not let him deny his father. When the play ends with Gabriel's fantastic ritualistic dance, the audience feels a sense of closure, of spiritual finish.

Fences in Performance

Like many of the best American plays, *Fences* began in a workshop production. Its first version was performed as a reading, rather than as a full production—no sets, no full lighting, actors working "on book" instead of fully memorizing the play—in the summer of 1983 at the Eugene O'Neill Center in Waterford, Connecticut. This early version was four hours long.

Once Wilson found the focus of his play, it premiered in 1985 at the Yale Repertory Theatre in New Haven. Lloyd Richards, then dean of Yale Drama School, directed this as well as the New York production. The New York opening on March 27, 1987, starred Mary Alice, James Earl Jones, and Ray Aranha, the cast from New Haven. Frank Rich at the *New York Times* praised James Earl Jones, congratulating him on finding "what may be the best role of his career." Rich also said, "*Fences* leaves no doubt that Mr. Wilson is a major writer, combining a poet's ear for vernacular with a robust sense of humor (political and sexual), a sure instinct for crackling dramatic incident and a passionate commitment to a great subject." The play ran for 575 performances.

From the first, *Fences* was recognized as an important play. It won four Tony Awards: best play, best actor, best actress in a supporting role, and best director. It also won the New York Drama Critics' Circle Award for best play and the Pulitzer Prize. Before the New York production, it had traveled to Chicago, San Francisco, and Seattle. It has been performed numerous times since. The most recent major production, in April 2010, featured Denzel Washington as Troy Maxson and Viola Davis as Rose at the Cort Theatre on Broadway. Reviewers reminded audiences that Washington is physically much smaller than James Earl Jones and therefore less imposing, but they admitted that he had built a powerful Troy Maxson "brick by brick." Denzel Washington and Viola Davis won Tony Awards for best actor and best actress, and the play won the Tony for best revival. The production was nominated for ten Tony Awards in all.

AUGUST WILSON (1945–2005)

Fences   1987

Characters

TROY MAXSON
JIM BONO, *Troy's friend*
ROSE, *Troy's wife*
LYONS, *Troy's oldest son by previous marriage*
GABRIEL, *Troy's brother*
CORY, *Troy and Rose's son*
RAYNELL, *Troy's daughter*

Setting: *The setting is the yard which fronts the only entrance to the Maxson household, an ancient two-story brick house set back off a small alley in a big-city neighborhood. The entrance to the house is gained by two or three steps leading to a wooden porch badly in need of paint.*

A relatively recent addition to the house and running its full width, the porch lacks congruence. It is a sturdy porch with a flat roof. One or two chairs of dubious value sit at one end where the kitchen window opens onto the porch. An old-fashioned icebox stands silent guard at the opposite end.

The yard is a small dirt yard, partially fenced, except for the last scene, with a wooden sawhorse, a pile of lumber, and other fence-building equipment set off to the side. Opposite is a tree from which hangs a ball made of rags. A baseball bat leans against the tree. Two oil drums serve as garbage receptacles and sit near the house at right to complete the setting.

The Play: *Near the turn of the century, the destitute of Europe sprang on the city with tenacious claws and an honest and solid dream. The city devoured them. They swelled its belly until it burst into a thousand furnaces and sewing machines, a thousand butcher shops and bakers' ovens, a thousand churches and hospitals and funeral parlors and money-lenders. The city grew. It nourished itself and offered each man a partnership limited only by his talent, his guile, and his willingness and capacity for hard work. For the immigrants of Europe, a dream dared and won true.*

The descendants of African slaves were offered no such welcome or participation. They came from places called the Carolinas and the Virginias, Georgia, Alabama, Mississippi, and Tennessee. They came strong, eager, searching. The city rejected them and they fled and settled along the riverbanks and under bridges in shallow, ramshackle houses made of sticks and tar-paper. They collected rags and wood. They sold the use of their muscles and their bodies. They cleaned houses and washed clothes, they shined shoes, and in quiet desperation and vengeful pride, they stole, and lived in pursuit of their own dream. That they could breathe free, finally, and stand to meet life with the force of dignity and whatever eloquence the heart could call upon.

By 1957, the hard-won victories of the European immigrants had solidified the industrial might of America. War had been confronted and won with new energies that used loyalty and patriotism as its fuel. Life was rich, full, and flourishing. The Milwaukee Braves won the World Series, and the hot winds of change that would make the sixties a turbulent, racing, dangerous, and provocative decade had not yet begun to blow full.

ACT I • Scene I

(It is 1957. Troy and Bono enter the yard, engaged in conversation. Troy is fifty-three years old, a large man with thick, heavy hands; it is this largeness that he strives to fill out and make an accommodation with. Together with his blackness, his largeness informs his sensibilities and the choices he has made in his life.)

(Of the two men, Bono is obviously the follower. His commitment to their friendship of thirty-odd years is rooted in his admiration of Troy's honesty, capacity for hard work, and his strength, which Bono seeks to emulate.)

(It is Friday night, payday, and the one night of the week the two men engage in a ritual of talk and drink. Troy is usually the most talkative and at times he can be crude and almost vulgar, though he is capable of rising to profound heights of expression. The men carry lunch buckets and wear or carry burlap aprons and are dressed in clothes suitable to their jobs as garbage collectors.)

BONO: Troy, you ought to stop that lying!

TROY: I ain't lying! The nigger had a watermelon this big.

(He indicates with his hands.)

Talking about . . . "What watermelon, Mr. Rand?" I liked to fell out! "What watermelon, Mr. Rand?" . . . And it sitting there big as life.

BONO: What did Mr. Rand say?

TROY: Ain't said nothing. Figure if the nigger too dumb to know he carrying a watermelon, he wasn't gonna get much sense out of him. Trying to hide that great big old watermelon under his coat. Afraid to let the white man see him carry it home.

BONO: I'm like you . . . I ain't got no time for them kind of people.

TROY: Now what he look like getting mad cause he see the man from the union talking to Mr. Rand?

BONO: He come to me talking about . . . "Maxson gonna get us fired." I told him to get away from me with that. He walked away from me calling you a trouble-maker. What Mr. Rand say?

TROY: Ain't said nothing. He told me to go down the Commissioner's office next Friday. They called me down there to see them.

BONO: Well, as long as you got your complaint filed, they can't fire you. That's what one of them white fellows tell me.

TROY: I ain't worried about them firing me. They gonna fire me cause I asked a question? That's all I did. I went to Mr. Rand and asked him, "Why? Why you got the white mens driving and the colored lifting?" Told him "what's the matter, don't I count? You think only white fellows got sense enough to drive a truck. That ain't no paper job! Hell, anybody can drive a truck. How come you got all whites driving and the colored lifting?" He told me "take it to the union." Well, hell, that's what I done! Now they wanna come up with this pack of lies.

BONO: I told Brownie if the man come and ask him any questions . . . just tell the truth! It ain't nothing but something they done trumped up on you cause you filed a complaint on them.

TROY: Brownie don't understand nothing. All I want them to do is change the job description. Give everybody a chance to drive the truck. Brownie can't see that. He ain't got that much sense.

BONO: How you figure he be making out with that gal be up at Taylors' all the time . . . that Alberta gal?

TROY: Same as you and me. Getting just as much as we is. Which is to say nothing.

BONO: It is, huh? I figure you doing a little better than me . . . and I ain't saying what I'm doing.

TROY: Aw, nigger, look here . . . I know you. If you had got anywhere near that gal, twenty minutes later you be looking to tell somebody. And the first one you gonna tell . . . that you gonna want to brag to . . . is gonna be me.

BONO: I ain't saying that. I see where you be eyeing her.

TROY: I eye all the women. I don't miss nothing. Don't never let nobody tell you Troy Maxson don't eye the women.

BONO: You been doing more than eyeing her. You done bought her a drink or two.

TROY: Hell yeah, I bought her a drink! What that mean? I bought you one, too. What that mean cause I buy her a drink? I'm just being polite.

BONO: It's all right to buy her one drink. That's what you call being polite. But when you wanna be buying two or three . . . that's what you call eyeing her.

TROY: Look here, as long as you known me . . . you ever known me to chase after women?

BONO: Hell yeah! Long as I done known you. You forgetting I knew you when.

TROY: Naw, I'm talking about since I been married to Rose?

BONO: Oh, not since you been married to Rose. Now, that's the truth, there. I can say that.

TROY: All right then! Case closed.

BONO: I see you be walking up around Alberta's house. You supposed to be at Taylors' and you be walking up around there.

TROY: What you watching where I'm walking for? I ain't watching after you.

BONO: I seen you walking around there more than once.

TROY: Hell, you liable to see me walking anywhere! That don't mean nothing cause you see me walking around there.

BONO: Where she come from anyway? She just kinda showed up one day.

TROY: Tallahassee. You can look at her and tell she one of them Florida gals. They got some big healthy women down there. Grow them right up out the ground. Got a little bit of Indian in her. Most of them niggers down in Florida got some Indian in them.

BONO: I don't know about that Indian part. But she damn sure big and healthy. Woman wear some big stockings. Got them great big old legs and hips as wide as the Mississippi River.

TROY: Legs don't mean nothing. You don't do nothing but push them out of the way. But them hips cushion the ride!

BONO: Troy, you ain't got no sense.

TROY: It's the truth! Like you riding on Goodyears!

(*Rose enters from the house. She is ten years younger than Troy, her devotion to him stems from her recognition of the possibilities of her life without him: a succession of abusive men and their babies, a life of partying and running the streets, the Church, or aloneness with its attendant pain and frustration. She recognizes Troy's spirit as a fine and illuminating one and she either ignores or forgives his faults, only some of which she recognizes. Though she doesn't drink, her presence is an integral part of the Friday night rituals. She alternates between the porch and the kitchen, where supper preparations are under way.*)

ROSE: What you all out here getting into?

TROY: What you worried about what we getting into for? This is men talk, woman.

ROSE: What I care what you all talking about? Bono, you gonna stay for supper?

BONO: No, I thank you, Rose. But Lucille say she cooking up a pot of pigfeet.

TROY: Pigfeet! Hell, I'm going home with you! Might even stay the night if you got some pigfeet. You got something in there to top them pigfeet, Rose?

ROSE: I'm cooking up some chicken. I got some chicken and collard greens.

TROY: Well, go on back in the house and let me and Bono finish what we was talking about. This is men talk. I got some talk for you later. You know what kind of talk I mean. You go on and powder it up.

ROSE: Troy Maxson, don't you start that now!

TROY (*puts his arm around her*): Aw, woman...come here. Look here, Bono...when I met this woman... I got out that place, say, "Hitch up my pony, saddle up my mare...there's a woman out there for me somewhere. I looked here. Looked there. Saw Rose and latched on to her." I latched on to her and told her—I'm gonna tell you the truth—I told her, "Baby, I don't wanna marry, I just wanna be your man." Rose told me...tell him what you told me, Rose.

ROSE: I told him if he wasn't the marrying kind, then move out the way so the marrying kind could find me.

TROY: That's what she told me. "Nigger, you in my way. You blocking the view! Move out the way so I can

find me a husband." I thought it over two or three days. Come back—

ROSE: Ain't no two or three days nothing. You was back the same night.

TROY: Come back, told her..."Okay, baby...but I'm gonna buy me a banty rooster and put him out there in the backyard...and when he see a stranger come, he'll flap his wings and crow..." Look here, Bono, I could watch the front door by myself...it was that back door I was worried about.

ROSE: Troy, you ought not talk like that. Troy ain't doing nothing but telling a lie.

TROY: Only thing is...when we first got married... forget the rooster...we ain't had no yard!

BONO: I hear you tell it. Me and Lucille was staying down there on Logan Street. Had two rooms with the outhouse in the back. I ain't mind the outhouse none. But when that goddamn wind blow through there in the winter...that's what I'm talking about! To this day I wonder why in the hell I ever stayed down there for six long years. But see, I didn't know I could do no better. I thought only white folks had inside toilets and things.

ROSE: There's a lot of people don't know they can do no better than they doing now. That's just something you got to learn. A lot of folks still shop at Bella's.

TROY: Ain't nothing wrong with shopping at Bella's. She got fresh food.

ROSE: I ain't said nothing about if she got fresh food. I'm talking about what she charge. She charge ten cents more than the A&P.

TROY: The A&P ain't never done nothing for me. I spends my money where I'm treated right. I go down to Bella, say, "I need a loaf of bread, I'll pay you Friday." She give it to me. What sense that make when I got money to go and spend it somewhere else and ignore the person who done right by me? That ain't in the Bible.

ROSE: We ain't talking about what's in the Bible. What sense it make to shop there when she overcharge?

TROY: You shop where you want to. I'll do my shopping where the people been good to me.

ROSE: Well, I don't think it's right for her to overcharge. That's all I was saying.

BONO: Look here...I got to get on. Lucille going be raising all kind of hell.

TROY: Where you going, nigger? We ain't finished this pint. Come here, finish this pint.

BONO: Well, hell, I am...if you ever turn the bottle loose.

TROY (*hands him the bottle*): The only thing I say about the A&P is I'm glad Cory got that job down there. Help him take care of his school clothes and things. Gabe done moved out and things getting tight around here. He got that job....He can start to look out for himself.

ROSE: Cory done went and got recruited by a college football team.

TROY: I told that boy about that football stuff. The white man ain't gonna let him get nowhere with that football. I told him when he first come to me with it. Now you come telling me he done went and got more tied up in it. He ought to go and get recruited in how to fix cars or something where he can make a living.

ROSE: He ain't talking about making no living playing football. It's just something the boys in school do. They gonna send a recruiter by to talk to you. He'll tell you he ain't talking about making no living playing football. It's a honor to be recruited.

TROY: It ain't gonna get him nowhere. Bono'll tell you that.

BONO: If he be like you in the sports . . . he's gonna be all right. Ain't but two men ever played baseball as good as you. That's Babe Ruth and Josh Gibson.° Them's the only two men ever hit more home runs than you.

TROY: What it ever get me? Ain't got a pot to piss in or a window to throw it out of.

ROSE: Times have changed since you was playing baseball, Troy. That was before the war. Times have changed a lot since then.

TROY: How in hell they done changed?

ROSE: They got lots of colored boys playing ball now. Baseball and football.

BONO: You right about that, Rose. Times have changed, Troy. You just come along too early.

TROY: There ought not never have been no time called too early! Now you take that fellow . . . what's that fellow they had playing right field for the Yankees back then? You know who I'm talking about, Bono. Used to play right field for the Yankees.

ROSE: Selkirk?

TROY: Selkirk! That's it! Man batting .269, understand? .269. What kind of sense that make? I was hitting .432 with thirty-seven home runs! Man batting .269 and playing right field for the Yankees! I saw Josh Gibson's daughter yesterday. She walking around with raggedy shoes on her feet. Now I bet you Selkirk's daughter ain't walking around with raggedy shoes on her feet! I bet you that!

ROSE: They got a lot of colored baseball players now. Jackie Robinson was the first. Folks had to wait for Jackie Robinson.

TROY: I done seen a hundred niggers play baseball better than Jackie Robinson. Hell, I know some teams Jackie Robinson couldn't even make! What you talking about Jackie Robinson. Jackie Robinson wasn't nobody. I'm talking about if you could play ball then they ought to have let you play. Don't care what color you were. Come telling me I come along too early. If you could play . . . then they ought to have let you play.

(*Troy takes a long drink from the bottle.*)

ROSE: You gonna drink yourself to death. You don't need to be drinking like that.

Josh Gibson: Powerful black baseball player (1911–1947) known in the 1930s as the Babe Ruth of the Negro leagues.

TROY: Death ain't nothing. I done seen him. Done wrassled with him. You can't tell me nothing about death. Death ain't nothing but a fastball on the outside corner. And you know what I'll do to that! Lookee here, Bono . . . am I lying? You get one of them fastballs, about waist high, over the outside corner of the plate where you can get the meat of the bat on it . . . and good god! You can kiss it goodbye. Now, am I lying?

BONO: Naw, you telling the truth there. I seen you do it.

TROY: If I'm lying . . . that 450 feet worth of lying!

(*Pause.*)

That's all death is to me. A fastball on the outside corner.

ROSE: I don't know why you want to get on talking about death.

TROY: Ain't nothing wrong with talking about death. That's part of life. Everybody gonna die. You gonna die, I'm gonna die. Bono's gonna die. Hell, we all gonna die.

ROSE: But you ain't got to talk about it. I don't like to talk about it.

TROY: You the one brought it up. Me and Bono was talking about baseball . . . you tell me I'm gonna drink myself to death. Ain't that right, Bono? You know I don't drink this but one night out of the week. That's Friday night. I'm gonna drink just enough to where I can handle it. Then I cuts it loose. I leave it alone. So don't you worry about me drinking myself to death. 'Cause I ain't worried about Death. I done seen him. I done wrestled with him.

Look here, Bono . . . I looked up one day and Death was marching straight at me. Like Soldiers on Parade! The Army of Death was marching straight at me. The middle of July, 1941. It got real cold just like it be winter. It seem like Death himself reached out and touched me on the shoulder. He touch me just like I touch you. I got cold as ice and Death standing there grinning at me.

ROSE: Troy, why don't you hush that talk.

TROY: I say . . . What you want, Mr. Death? You be wanting me? You done brought your army to be getting me? I looked him dead in the eye. I wasn't fearing nothing. I was ready to tangle. Just like I'm ready to tangle now. The Bible say be ever vigilant. That's why I don't get but so drunk. I got to keep watch.

ROSE: Troy was right down there in Mercy Hospital. You remember he had pneumonia? Laying there with a fever talking plumb out of his head.

TROY: Death standing there staring at me . . . carrying that sickle in his hand. Finally he say, "You want bound over for another year?" See, just like that . . . "You want bound over for another year?" I told him, "Bound over hell! Let's settle this now!"

It seem like he kinda fell back when I said that, and all the cold went out of me. I reached down and grabbed that sickle and threw it just as far as I could throw it . . . and me and him commenced to wrestling.

We wrestled for three days and three nights. I can't say where I found the strength from. Every time it seemed like he was gonna get the best of me, I'd reach way down deep inside myself and find the strength to do him one better.

ROSE: Every time Troy tell that story he find different ways to tell it. Different things to make up about it.

TROY: I ain't making up nothing. I'm telling you the facts of what happened. I wrestled with Death for three days and three nights and I'm standing here to tell you about it.

(*Pause.*)

All right. At the end of the third night we done weakened each other to where we can't hardly move. Death stood up, throwed on his robe . . . had him a white robe with a hood on it. He threw on that robe and went off to look for his sickle. Say, "I'll be back." Just like that. "I'll be back." I told him, say, "Yeah, but . . . you gonna have to find me!" I wasn't no fool. I wan't going looking for him. Death ain't nothing to play with. And I know he's gonna get me. I know I got to join his army . . . his camp followers. But as long as I keep my strength and see him coming . . . as long as I keep up my vigilance . . . he's gonna have to fight to get me. I ain't going easy.

BONO: Well, look here, since you got to keep up your vigilance . . . let me have the bottle.

TROY: Aw hell, I shouldn't have told you that part. I should have left out that part.

ROSE: Troy be talking that stuff and half the time don't even know what he be talking about.

TROY: Bono know me better than that.

BONO: That's right. I know you. I know you got some Uncle Remus° in your blood. You got more stories than the devil got sinners.

TROY: Aw hell, I done seen him too! Done talked with the devil.

ROSE: Troy, don't nobody wanna be hearing all that stuff.

(*Lyons enters the yard from the street. Thirty-four years old, Troy's son by a previous marriage, he sports a neatly trimmed goatee, sport coat, white shirt, tieless and buttoned at the collar. Though he fancies himself a musician, he is more caught up in the rituals and "idea" of being a musician than in the actual practice of the music. He has come to borrow money from Troy, and while he knows he will be successful, he is uncertain as to what extent his lifestyle will be held up to scrutiny and ridicule.*)

LYONS: Hey, Pop.

TROY: What you come "Hey, Popping" me for?

LYONS: How you doing, Rose?

(*He kisses her.*)

Mr. Bono. How you doing?

° **Uncle Remus:** Black storyteller who recounts traditional African American tales in the book by Joel Chandler Harris.

BONO: Hey, Lyons . . . how you been?

TROY: He must have been doing all right. I ain't seen him around here last week.

ROSE: Troy, leave your boy alone. He come by to see you and you wanna start all that nonsense.

TROY: I ain't bothering Lyons.

(*Offers him the bottle.*)

Here . . . get you a drink. We got an understanding. I know why he come by to see me and he know I know.

LYONS: Come on, Pop . . . I just stopped by to say hi . . . see how you was doing.

TROY: You ain't stopped by yesterday.

ROSE: You gonna stay for supper, Lyons? I got some chicken cooking in the oven.

LYONS: No, Rose . . . thanks. I was just in the neighborhood and thought I'd stop by for a minute.

TROY: You was in the neighborhood all right, nigger. You telling the truth there. You was in the neighborhood cause it's my payday.

LYONS: Well, hell, since you mentioned it . . . let me have ten dollars.

TROY: I'll be damned! I'll die and go to hell and play blackjack with the devil before I give you ten dollars.

BONO: That's what I wanna know about . . . that devil you done seen.

LYONS: What . . . Pop done seen the devil? You too much, Pops.

TROY: Yeah, I done seen him. Talked to him too!

ROSE: You ain't seen no devil. I done told you that man ain't had nothing to do with the devil. Anything you can't understand, you want to call it the devil.

TROY: Look here, Bono . . . I went down to see Hertzberger about some furniture. Got three rooms for two-ninety-eight. That what it say on the radio. "Three rooms . . . two-ninety-eight." Even made up a little song about it. Go down there . . . man tell me I can't get no credit. I'm working every day and can't get no credit. What to do? I got an empty house with some raggedy furniture. Cory ain't got no bed. He's sleeping on a pile of rags on the floor. Working every day and can't get no credit. Come back here—Rose'll tell you—madder than hell. Sit down . . . try to figure what I'm gonna do. Come a knock on the door. Ain't been living here but three days. Who know I'm here? Open the door . . . devil standing there bigger than life. White fellow . . . got on good clothes and everything. Standing there with a clipboard in his hand. I ain't had to say nothing. First words come out of his mouth was . . . "I understand you need some furniture and can't get no credit." I liked to fell over. He say, "I'll give you all the credit you want, but you got to pay the interest on it." I told him, "Give me three rooms worth and charge whatever you want." Next day a truck pulled up here and two men unloaded them three rooms. Man what drove the truck give me a book. Say send ten dollars, first of every month to the address in the book and everything will be all right. Say if I miss a payment the devil was coming back and it'll be hell to pay. That was fifteen years ago. To this day ... the first of the month I send my ten dollars, Rose'll tell you.

ROSE: Troy lying.

TROY: I ain't never seen that man since. Now you tell me who else that could have been but the devil? I ain't sold my soul or nothing like that, you understand. Naw, I wouldn't have truck with the devil about nothing like that. I got my furniture and pays my ten dollars the first of the month just like clockwork.

BONO: How long you say you been paying this ten dollars a month?

TROY: Fifteen years!

BONO: Hell, ain't you finished paying for it yet? How much the man done charged you.

TROY: Ah hell, I done paid for it. I done paid for it ten times over! The fact is I'm scared to stop paying it.

ROSE: Troy lying. We got that furniture from Mr. Glickman. He ain't paying no ten dollars a month to nobody.

TROY: Aw hell, woman. Bono know I ain't that big a fool.

LYONS: I was just getting ready to say ... I know where there's a bridge for sale.

TROY: Look here, I'll tell you this ... it don't matter to me if he was the devil. It don't matter if the devil give credit. Somebody has got to give it.

ROSE: It ought to matter. You going around talking about having truck with the devil ... God's the one you gonna have to answer to. He's the one gonna be at the Judgment.

LYONS: Yeah, well, look here, Pop ... let me have that ten dollars. I'll give it back to you. Bonnie got a job working at the hospital.

TROY: What I tell you, Bono? The only time I see this nigger is when he wants something. That's the only time I see him.

LYONS: Come on, Pop, Mr. Bono don't want to hear all that. Let me have the ten dollars. I told you Bonnie working.

TROY: What that mean to me? "Bonnie working." I don't care if she working. Go ask her for the ten dollars if she working. Talking about "Bonnie working." Why ain't you working?

LYONS: Aw, Pop, you know I can't find no decent job. Where am I gonna get a job at? You know I can't get no job.

TROY: I told you I know some people down there. I can get you on the rubbish if you want to work. I told you that the last time you came by here asking me for something.

LYONS: Naw, Pop ... thanks. That ain't for me. I don't wanna be carrying nobody's rubbish. I don't wanna be punching nobody's time clock.

TROY: What's the matter, you too good to carry people's rubbish? Where you think that ten dollars you talking about come from? I'm just supposed to haul people's rubbish and give my money to you cause you too lazy to work. You too lazy to work and wanna know why you ain't got what I got.

ROSE: What hospital Bonnie working at? Mercy?

LYONS: She's down at Passavant working in the laundry.

TROY: I ain't got nothing as it is. I give you that ten dollars and I got to eat beans the rest of the week. Naw ... you ain't getting no ten dollars here.

LYONS: You ain't got to be eating no beans. I don't know why you wanna say that.

TROY: I ain't got no extra money. Gabe done moved over to Miss Pearl's paying her the rent and things done got tight around here. I can't afford to be giving you every payday.

LYONS: I ain't asked you to give me nothing. I asked you to loan me ten dollars. I know you got ten dollars.

TROY: Yeah, I got it. You know why I got it? Cause I don't throw my money away out there in the streets. You living the fast life ... wanna be a musician ... running around in them clubs and things ... then, you learn to take care of yourself. You ain't gonna find me going and asking nobody for nothing. I done spent too many years without.

LYONS: You and me is two different people, Pop.

TROY: I done learned my mistake and learned to do what's right by it. You still trying to get something for nothing. Life don't owe you nothing. You owe it to yourself. Ask Bono. He'll tell you I'm right.

LYONS: You got your way of dealing with the world ... I got mine. The only thing that matters to me is the music.

TROY: Yeah, I can see that! It don't matter how you gonna eat ... where your next dollar is coming from. You telling the truth there.

LYONS: I know I got to eat. But I got to live too. I need something that gonna help me to get out of the bed in the morning. Make me feel like I belong in the world. I don't bother nobody. I just stay with my music cause that's the only way I can find to live in the world. Otherwise there ain't no telling what I might do. Now I don't come criticizing you and how you live. I just come by to ask you for ten dollars. I don't wanna hear all that about how I live.

TROY: Boy, your mamma did a hell of a job raising you.

LYONS: You can't change me, Pop. I'm thirty-four years old. If you wanted to change me, you should have been there when I was growing up. I come by to see you ... ask for ten dollars and you want to talk about how I was raised. You don't know nothing about how I was raised.

ROSE: Let the boy have ten dollars, Troy.

TROY (to Lyons): What the hell you looking at me for? I ain't got no ten dollars. You know what I do with my money.

(To Rose.)

Give him ten dollars if you want him to have it.

ROSE: I will. Just as soon as you turn it loose.

TROY (*handing Rose the money*): There it is. Seventy-six dollars and forty-two cents. You see this, Bono? Now, I ain't gonna get but six of that back.

ROSE: You ought to stop telling that lie. Here, Lyons.

(*She hands him the money.*)

LYONS: Thanks, Rose. Look . . . I got to run . . . I'll see you later.

TROY: Wait a minute. You gonna say, "thanks, Rose" and ain't gonna look to see where she got that ten dollars from? See how they do me, Bono?

LYONS: I know she got it from you, Pop. Thanks. I'll give it back to you.

TROY: There he go telling another lie. Time I see that ten dollars . . . he'll be owing me thirty more.

LYONS: See you, Mr. Bono.

BONO: Take care, Lyons!

LYONS: Thanks, Pop. I'll see you again.

(*Lyons exits the yard.*)

TROY: I don't know why he don't go and get him a decent job and take care of that woman he got.

BONO: He'll be all right, Troy. The boy is still young.

TROY: The *boy* is thirty-four years old.

ROSE: Let's not get off into all that.

BONO: Look here . . . I got to be going. I got to be getting on. Lucille gonna be waiting.

TROY (*puts his arm around Rose*): See this woman, Bono? I love this woman. I love this woman so much it hurts. I love her so much . . . I done run out of ways of loving her. So I got to go back to basics. Don't you come by my house Monday morning talking about time to go to work . . . 'cause I'm still gonna be stroking!

ROSE: Troy! Stop it now!

BONO: I ain't paying him no mind, Rose. That ain't nothing but gin-talk. Go on, Troy. I'll see you Monday.

TROY: Don't you come by my house, nigger! I done told you what I'm gonna be doing.

(*The lights go down to black.*)

Scene II

(*The lights come up on Rose hanging up clothes. She hums and sings softly to herself. It is the following morning.*)

ROSE (*sings*): Jesus, be a fence all around me every day
Jesus, I want you to protect me as I travel on my way.
Jesus, be a fence all around me every day.

(*Troy enters from the house.*)

Jesus, I want you to protect me
As I travel on my way.

(*To Troy.*) 'Morning. You ready for breakfast? I can fix it soon as I finish hanging up these clothes.

TROY: I got the coffee on. That'll be all right. I'll just drink some of that this morning.

ROSE: That 651 hit yesterday. That's the second time this month. Miss Pearl hit for a dollar . . . seem like those that need the least always get lucky. Poor folks can't get nothing.

TROY: Them numbers don't know nobody. I don't know why you fool with them. You and Lyons both.

ROSE: It's something to do.

TROY: You ain't doing nothing but throwing your money away.

ROSE: Troy, you know I don't play foolishly. I just play a nickel here and a nickel there.

TROY: That's two nickels you done thrown away.

ROSE: Now I hit sometimes . . . that makes up for it. It always comes in handy when I do hit. I don't hear you complaining then.

TROY: I ain't complaining now. I just say it's foolish. Trying to guess out of six hundred ways which way the number gonna come. If I had all the money niggers, these Negroes, throw away on numbers for one week — just one week — I'd be a rich man.

ROSE: Well, you wishing and calling it foolish ain't gonna stop folks from playing numbers. That's one thing for sure. Besides . . . some good things come from playing numbers. Look where Pope done bought him that restaurant off of numbers.

TROY: I can't stand niggers like that. Man ain't had two dimes to rub together. He walking around with his shoes all run over bumming money for cigarettes. All right. Got lucky there and hit the numbers . . .

ROSE: Troy, I know all about it.

TROY: Had good sense, I'll say that for him. He ain't throwed his money away. I seen niggers hit the numbers and go through two thousand dollars in four days. Man bought him that restaurant down there . . . fixed it up real nice . . . and then didn't want nobody to come in it! A Negro go in there and can't get no kind of service. I seen a white fellow come in there and order a bowl of stew. Pope picked all the meat out the pot for him. Man ain't had nothing but a bowl of meat! Negro come behind him and ain't got nothing but the potatoes and carrots. Talking about what numbers do for people, you picked a wrong example. Ain't done nothing but make a worser fool out of him than he was before.

ROSE: Troy, you ought to stop worrying about what happened at work yesterday.

TROY: I ain't worried. Just told me to be down there at the Commissioner's office on Friday. Everybody think they gonna fire me. I ain't worried about them firing me. You ain't got to worry about that.

(*Pause.*)

Where's Cory? Cory in the house? (*Calls.*) Cory?

ROSE: He gone out.

TROY: Out, huh? He gone out 'cause he know I want him to help me with this fence. I know how he is. That boy scared of work.

(*Gabriel enters. He comes halfway down the alley and, hearing Troy's voice, stops.*)

TROY (*continues*): He ain't done a lick of work in his life.

ROSE: He had to go to football practice. Coach wanted them to get in a little extra practice before the season start.

TROY: I got his practice . . . running out of here before he get his chores done.

ROSE: Troy, what is wrong with you this morning? Don't nothing set right with you. Go on back in there and go to bed . . . get up on the other side.

TROY: Why something got to be wrong with me? I ain't said nothing wrong with me.

ROSE: You got something to say about everything. First it's the numbers . . . then it's the way the man runs his restaurant . . . then you done got on Cory. What's it gonna be next? Take a look up there and see if the weather suits you . . . or is it gonna be how you gonna put up the fence with the clothes hanging in the yard.

TROY: You hit the nail on the head then.

ROSE: I know you like I know the back of my hand. Go on in there and get you some coffee . . . see if that straighten you up. 'Cause you ain't right this morning.

(*Troy starts into the house and sees Gabriel. Gabriel starts singing. Troy's brother, he is seven years younger than Troy. Injured in World War II, he has a metal plate in his head. He carries an old trumpet tied around his waist and believes with every fiber of his being that he is the Archangel Gabriel. He carries a chipped basket with an assortment of discarded fruits and vegetables he has picked up in the strip district and which he attempts to sell.*)

GABRIEL (*singing*): Yes, ma'am, I got plums
You ask me how I sell them
Oh ten cents apiece
Three for a quarter
Come and buy now
'Cause I'm here today
And tomorrow I'll be gone

(*Gabriel enters.*)

Hey, Rose!

ROSE: How you doing, Gabe?

GABRIEL: There's Troy . . . Hey, Troy!

TROY: Hey, Gabe.

(*Exit into kitchen.*)

ROSE (*to Gabriel*): What you got there?

GABRIEL: You know what I got, Rose. I got fruits and vegetables.

ROSE (*looking in basket*): Where's all these plums you talking about?

GABRIEL: I ain't got no plums today, Rose. I was just singing that. Have some tomorrow. Put me in a big order for plums. Have enough plums tomorrow for St. Peter and everybody.

(*Troy reenters from kitchen, crosses to steps.*)
(*To Rose.*)

Troy's mad at me.

TROY: I ain't mad at you. What I got to be mad at you about? You ain't done nothing to me.

GABRIEL: I just moved over to Miss Pearl's to keep out from in your way. I ain't mean no harm by it.

TROY: Who said anything about that? I ain't said anything about that.

GABRIEL: You ain't mad at me, is you?

TROY: Naw . . . I ain't mad at you, Gabe. If I was mad at you I'd tell you about it.

GABRIEL: Got me two rooms. In the basement. Got my own door too. Wanna see my key?

(*He holds up a key.*)

That's my own key! Ain't nobody else got a key like that. That's my key! My two rooms!

TROY: Well, that's good, Gabe. You got your own key . . . that's good.

ROSE: You hungry, Gabe? I was just fixing to cook Troy his breakfast.

GABRIEL: I'll take some biscuits. You got some biscuits? Did you know when I was in heaven . . . every morning me and St. Peter would sit down by the gate and eat some big fat biscuits? Oh, yeah! We had us a good time. We'd sit there and eat us them biscuits and then St. Peter would go off to sleep and tell me to wake him up when it's time to open the gates for the judgment.

ROSE: Well, come on . . . I'll make up a batch of biscuits.

(*Rose exits into the house.*)

GABRIEL: Troy . . . St. Peter got your name in the book. I seen it. It say . . . Troy Maxson. I say . . . I know him! He got the same name like what I got. That's my brother!

TROY: How many times you gonna tell me that, Gabe?

GABRIEL: Ain't got my name in the book. Don't have to have my name. I done died and went to heaven. He got your name though. One morning St. Peter was looking at his book . . . marking it up for the judgment . . . and he let me see your name. Got it in there under M. Got Rose's name . . . I ain't seen it like I seen yours . . . but I know it's in there. He got a great big book. Got everybody's name what was ever been born. That's what he told me. But I seen your name. Seen it with my own eyes.

TROY: Go on in the house there. Rose going to fix you something to eat.

GABRIEL: Oh, I ain't hungry. I done had breakfast with Aunt Jemimah. She come by and cooked me up a whole mess of flapjacks. Remember how we used to eat them flapjacks?

TROY: Go on in the house and get you something to eat now.

GABRIEL: I got to go sell my plums. I done sold some tomatoes. Got me two quarters. Wanna see?

(*He shows Troy his quarters.*)

I'm gonna save them and buy me a new horn so St. Peter can hear me when it's time to open the gates.

(*Gabriel stops suddenly. Listens.*)

Hear that? That's the hellhounds. I got to chase them out of here. Go on get out of here! Get out!

(*Gabriel exits singing.*)

Better get ready for the judgment
Better get ready for the judgment
My Lord is coming down

(*Rose enters from the house.*)

TROY: He gone off somewhere.

GABRIEL (*offstage*): Better get ready for the judgment
Better get ready for the judgment morning
Better get ready for the judgment
My God is coming down

ROSE: He ain't eating right. Miss Pearl say she can't get him to eat nothing.

TROY: What you want me to do about it, Rose? I done did everything I can for the man. I can't make him get well. Man got half his head blown away . . . what you expect?

ROSE: Seem like something ought to be done to help him.

TROY: Man don't bother nobody. He just mixed up from that metal plate he got in his head. Ain't no sense for him to go back into the hospital.

ROSE: Least he be eating right. They can help him take care of himself.

TROY: Don't nobody wanna be locked up, Rose. What you wanna lock him up for? Man go over there and fight the war . . . messin' around with them Japs, get half his head blown off . . . and they give him a lousy three thousand dollars. And I had to swoop down on that.

ROSE: Is you fixing to go into that again?

TROY: That's the only way I got a roof over my head . . . cause of that metal plate.

ROSE: Ain't no sense you blaming yourself for nothing. Gabe wasn't in no condition to manage that money. You done what was right by him. Can't nobody say you ain't done what was right by him. Look how long you took care of him . . . till he wanted to have his own place and moved over there with Miss Pearl.

TROY: That ain't what I'm saying, woman! I'm just stating the facts. If my brother didn't have that metal plate in his head . . . I wouldn't have a pot to piss in or a window to throw it out of. And I'm fifty-three years old. Now see if you can understand that!

(*Troy gets up from the porch and starts to exit the yard.*)

ROSE: Where you going off to? You been running out of here every Saturday for weeks. I thought you was gonna work on this fence?

TROY: I'm gonna walk down to Taylors'. Listen to the ball game. I'll be back in a bit. I'll work on it when I get back.

(*He exits the yard. The lights go to black.*)

Scene III

(*The lights come up on the yard. It is four hours later. Rose is taking down the clothes from the line. Cory enters carrying his football equipment.*)

ROSE: Your daddy like to had a fit with you running out of here this morning without doing your chores.

CORY: I told you I had to go to practice.

ROSE: He say you were supposed to help him with this fence.

CORY: He been saying that the last four or five Saturdays, and then he don't never do nothing but go down to Taylors'. Did you tell him about the recruiter?

ROSE: Yeah, I told him.

CORY: What he say?

ROSE: He ain't said nothing too much. You get in there and get started on your chores before he gets back. Go on and scrub down them steps before he gets back here hollering and carrying on.

CORY: I'm hungry. What you got to eat, Mama?

ROSE: Go on and get started on your chores. I got some meat loaf in there. Go on and make you a sandwich . . . and don't leave no mess in there.

(*Cory exits into the house. Rose continues to take down the clothes. Troy enters the yard and sneaks up and grabs her from behind.*)

Troy! Go on, now. You liked to scared me to death. What was the score of the game? Lucille had me on the phone and I couldn't keep up with it.

TROY: What I care about the game? Come here, woman. (*He tries to kiss her.*)

ROSE: I thought you went down Taylors' to listen to the game. Go on, Troy! You supposed to be putting up this fence.

TROY (*attempting to kiss her again*): I'll put it up when I finish with what is at hand.

ROSE: Go on, Troy. I ain't studying you.

TROY (*chasing after her*): I'm studying you . . . fixing to do my homework!

ROSE: Troy, you better leave me alone.

TROY: Where's Cory? That boy brought his butt home yet?

ROSE: He's in the house doing his chores.

TROY (*calling*): Cory! Get your butt out here, boy!

(*Rose exits into the house with the laundry. Troy goes over to the pile of wood, picks up a board, and starts sawing. Cory enters from the house.*)

TROY: You just now coming in here from leaving this morning?

CORY: Yeah, I had to go to football practice.

TROY: Yeah, what?

CORY: Yessir.

TROY: I ain't but two seconds off you noway. The garbage sitting in there overflowing . . . you ain't done none of your chores . . . and you come in here talking about "Yeah."

CORY: I was just getting ready to do my chores now, Pop...

TROY: Your first chore is to help me with this fence on Saturday. Everything else come after that. Now get that saw and cut them boards.

(*Cory takes the saw and begins cutting the boards. Troy continues working. There is a long pause.*)

CORY: Hey, Pop... why don't you buy a TV?

TROY: What I want with a TV? What I want one of them for?

CORY: Everybody got one. Earl, Ba Bra... Jesse!

TROY: I ain't asked you who had one. I say what I want with one?

CORY: So you can watch it. They got lots of things on TV. Baseball games and everything. We could watch the World Series.

TROY: Yeah... and how much this TV cost?

CORY: I don't know. They got them on sale for around two hundred dollars.

TROY: Two hundred dollars, huh?

CORY: That ain't that much, Pop.

TROY: Naw, it's just two hundred dollars. See that roof you got over your head at night? Let me tell you something about that roof. It's been over ten years since that roof was last tarred. See now... the snow come this winter and sit up there on that roof like it is... and it's gonna seep inside. It's just gonna be a little bit... ain't gonna hardly notice it. Then the next thing you know, it's gonna be leaking all over the house. Then the wood rot from all that water and you gonna need a whole new roof. Now, how much you think it cost to get that roof tarred?

CORY: I don't know.

TROY: Two hundred and sixty-four dollars... cash money. While you thinking about a TV, I got to be thinking about the roof... and whatever else go wrong around here. Now if you had two hundred dollars, what would you do... fix the roof or buy a TV?

CORY: I'd buy a TV. Then when the roof started to leak... when it needed fixing... I'd fix it.

TROY: Where you gonna get the money from? You done spent it for a TV. You gonna sit up and watch the water run all over your brand new TV.

CORY: Aw, Pop. You got money. I know you do.

TROY: Where I got it at, huh?

CORY: You got it in the bank.

TROY: You wanna see my bankbook? You wanna see that seventy-three dollars and twenty-two cents I got sitting up in there.

CORY: You ain't got to pay for it all at one time. You can put a down payment on it and carry it on home with you.

TROY: Not me. I ain't gonna owe nobody nothing if I can help it. Miss a payment and they come and snatch it right out your house. Then what you got? Now, soon as I get two hundred dollars clear, then I'll buy a TV. Right now, as soon as I get two hundred and sixty-four dollars, I'm gonna have this roof tarred.

CORY: Aw... Pop!

TROY: You go on and get you two hundred dollars and buy one if ya want it. I got better things to do with my money.

CORY: I can't get no two hundred dollars. I ain't never seen two hundred dollars.

TROY: I'll tell you what... you get you a hundred dollars and I'll put the other hundred with it.

CORY: All right, I'm gonna show you.

TROY: You gonna show me how you can cut them boards right now.

(*Cory begins to cut the boards. There is a long pause.*)

CORY: The Pirates won today. That makes five in a row.

TROY: I ain't thinking about the Pirates. Got an all-white team. Got that boy... that Puerto Rican boy... Clemente. Don't even half-play him. That boy could be something if they give him a chance. Play him one day and sit him on the bench the next.

CORY: He gets a lot of chances to play.

TROY: I'm talking about playing regular. Playing every day so you can get your timing. That's what I'm talking about.

CORY: They got some white guys on the team that don't play every day. You can't play everybody at the same time.

TROY: If they got a white fellow sitting on the bench... you can bet your last dollar he can't play! The colored guy got to be twice as good before he get on the team. That's why I don't want you to get all tied up in them sports. Man on the team and what it get him? They got colored on the team and don't use them. Same as not having them. All them teams the same.

CORY: The Braves got Hank Aaron and Wes Covington. Hank Aaron hit two home runs today. That makes forty-three.

TROY: Hank Aaron ain't nobody. That's what you supposed to do. That's how you supposed to play the game. Ain't nothing to it. It's just a matter of timing... getting the right follow-through. Hell, I can hit forty-three home runs right now!

CORY: Not off no major-league pitching, you couldn't.

TROY: We had better pitching in the Negro leagues. I hit seven home runs off of Satchel Paige.° You can't get no better than that!

CORY: Sandy Koufax. He's leading the league in strike-outs.

TROY: I ain't thinking of no Sandy Koufax.

CORY: You got Warren Spahn and Lew Burdette. I bet you couldn't hit no home runs off of Warren Spahn.

TROY: I'm through with it now. You go on and cut them boards.

(*Pause.*)

Satchel Paige: Legendary black pitcher (1906–1982) in the Negro leagues.

Your mama tell me you done got recruited by a college football team? Is that right?

CORY: Yeah. Coach Zellman say the recruiter gonna be coming by to talk to you. Get you to sign the permission papers.

TROY: I thought you supposed to be working down there at the A&P. Ain't you suppose to be working down there after school?

CORY: Mr. Stawicki say he gonna hold my job for me until after the football season. Say starting next week I can work weekends.

TROY: I thought we had an understanding about this football stuff? You suppose to keep up with your chores and hold that job down at the A&P. Ain't been around here all day on a Saturday. Ain't none of your chores done . . . and now you telling me you done quit your job.

CORY: I'm gonna be working weekends.

TROY: You damn right you are! And ain't no need for nobody coming around here to talk to me about signing nothing.

CORY: Hey, Pop . . . you can't do that. He's coming all the way from North Carolina.

TROY: I don't care where he coming from. The white man ain't gonna let you get nowhere with that football noway. You go on and get your book-learning so you can work yourself up in that A&P or learn how to fix cars or build houses or something, get you a trade. That way you have something can't nobody take away from you. You go on and learn how to put your hands to some good use. Besides hauling people's garbage.

CORY: I get good grades, Pop. That's why the recruiter wants to talk with you. You got to keep up your grades to get recruited. This way I'll be going to college. I'll get a chance . . .

TROY: First you gonna get your butt down there to the A&P and get your job back.

CORY: Mr. Stawicki done already hired somebody else 'cause I told him I was playing football.

TROY: You a bigger fool than I thought . . . to let somebody take away your job so you can play some football. Where you gonna get your money to take out your girlfriend and whatnot? What kind of foolishness is that to let somebody take away your job?

CORY: I'm still gonna be working weekends.

TROY: Naw . . . naw. You getting your butt out of here and finding you another job.

CORY: Come on, Pop! I got to practice. I can't work after school and play football too. The team needs me. That's what Coach Zellman say . . .

TROY: I don't care what nobody else say. I'm the boss . . . you understand? I'm the boss around here. I do the only saying what counts.

CORY: Come on, Pop!

TROY: I asked you . . . did you understand?

CORY: Yeah . . .

TROY: What?!

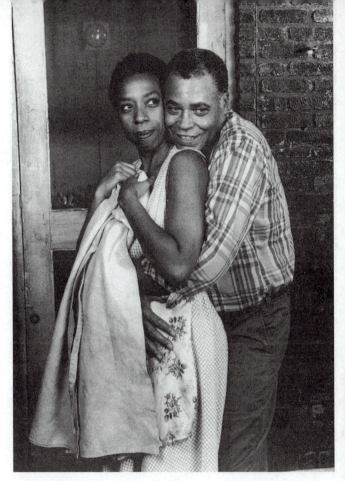

Lynn Thigpen and James Earl Jones in the 1987 production of *Fences*.

CORY: Yessir.

TROY: You go on down there to that A&P and see if you can get your job back. If you can't do both . . . then you quit the football team. You've got to take the crookeds with the straights.

CORY: Yessir.

(*Pause.*)

Can I ask you a question?

TROY: What the hell you wanna ask me? Mr. Stawicki the one you got the questions for.

CORY: How come you ain't never liked me?

TROY: Liked you? Who the hell say I got to like you? What law is there say I got to like you? Wanna stand up in my face and ask a damn fool-ass question like that. Talking about liking somebody. Come here, boy, when I talk to you.

(*Cory comes over to where Troy is working. He stands slouched over and Troy shoves him on his shoulder.*)

Straighten up, goddammit! I asked you a question . . . what law is there say I got to like you?

CORY: None.

TROY: Well, all right then! Don't you eat every day?

(*Pause.*)

Answer me when I talk to you! Don't you eat every day?

CORY: Yeah.

TROY: Nigger, as long as you in my house, you put that sir on the end of it when you talk to me!

CORY: Yes ... sir.

TROY: You eat every day.

CORY: Yessir!

TROY: Got a roof over your head.

CORY: Yessir!

TROY: Got clothes on your back.

CORY: Yessir.

TROY: Why you think that is?

CORY: Cause of you.

TROY: Ah, hell I know it's 'cause of me ... but why do you think that is?

CORY (*hesitant*): Cause you like me.

TROY: Like you? I go out of here every morning ... bust my butt ... putting up with them crackers° every day ... cause I like you? You about the biggest fool I ever saw.

(*Pause.*)

It's my job. It's my responsibility! You understand that? A man got to take care of his family. You live

crackers: White people (derogatory).

[ABOVE] James Earl Jones as Troy Maxson in *Fences*. [RIGHT] Jones and Courtney Vance as his son Cory.

in my house . . . sleep you behind on my bed-clothes . . . fill you belly up with my food . . . cause you my son. You my flesh and blood. Not 'cause I like you! Cause it's my duty to take care of you. I owe a responsibility to you! Let's get this straight right here . . . before it go along any further . . . I ain't got to like you. Mr. Rand don't give me my money come payday cause he likes me. He gives me cause he owe me. I done give you everything I had to give you. I gave you your life! Me and your mama worked that out between us. And liking your black ass wasn't part of the bargain. Don't you try and go through life worrying about if somebody like you or not. You best be making sure they doing right by you. You understand what I'm saying, boy?

CORY: Yessir.

TROY: Then get the hell out of my face, and get on down to that A&P.

(*Rose has been standing behind the screen door for much of the scene. She enters as Cory exits.*)

ROSE: Why don't you let the boy go ahead and play football, Troy? Ain't no harm in that. He's just trying to be like you with the sports.

TROY: I don't want him to be like me! I want him to move as far away from my life as he can get. You the only decent thing that ever happened to me. I wish him that. But I don't wish him a thing else from my life. I decided seventeen years ago that boy wasn't getting involved in no sports. Not after what they did to me in the sports.

ROSE: Troy, why don't you admit you was too old to play in the major leagues? For once . . . why don't you admit that?

TROY: What do you mean too old? Don't come telling me I was too old. I just wasn't the right color. Hell, I'm fifty-three years old and can do better than Selkirk's .269 right now!

ROSE: How's was you gonna play ball when you were over forty? Sometimes I can't get no sense out of you.

TROY: I got good sense, woman. I got sense enough not to let my boy get hurt over playing no sports. You been mothering that boy too much. Worried about if people like him.

ROSE: Everything that boy do . . . he do for you. He wants you to say "Good job, son." That's all.

TROY: Rose, I ain't got time for that. He's alive. He's healthy. He's got to make his own way. I made mine. Ain't nobody gonna hold his hand when he get out there in that world.

ROSE: Times have changed from when you was young, Troy. People change. The world's changing around you and you can't even see it.

TROY (*slow, methodical*): Woman . . . I do the best I can do. I come in here every Friday. I carry a sack of potatoes and a bucket of lard. You all line up at the door with your hands out. I give you the lint from my pockets. I give you my sweat and my blood. I ain't got no tears. I done spent them. We go upstairs in that room at night . . . and I fall down on you and try to blast a hole into forever. I get up Monday morning . . . find my lunch on the table. I go out. Make my way. Find my strength to carry me through to the next Friday.

(*Pause.*)

That's all I got, Rose. That's all I got to give. I can't give nothing else.

(*Troy exits into the house. The lights go down to black.*)

Scene IV

(*It is Friday. Two weeks later. Cory starts out of the house with his football equipment. The phone rings.*)

CORY (*calling*): I got it!

(*He answers the phone and stands in the screen door talking.*)

Hello? Hey, Jesse. Naw . . . I was just getting ready to leave now.

ROSE (*calling*): Cory!

CORY: I told you, man, them spikes is all tore up. You can use them if you want, but they ain't no good. Earl got some spikes.

ROSE (*calling*): Cory!

CORY (*calling to Rose*): Mam? I'm talking to Jesse.

(*Into phone.*)

When she say that? (*Pause.*) Aw, you lying, man. I'm gonna tell her you said that.

ROSE (*calling*): Cory, don't you go nowhere!

CORY: I got to go to the game, Ma!

(*Into the phone.*)

Yeah, hey, look, I'll talk to you later. Yeah, I'll meet you over Earl's house. Later. Bye, Ma.

(*Cory exits the house and starts out the yard.*)

ROSE: Cory, where you going off to? You got that stuff all pulled out and thrown all over your room.

CORY (*in the yard*): I was looking for my spikes. Jesse wanted to borrow my spikes.

ROSE: Get up there and get that cleaned up before your daddy get back in here.

CORY: I got to go to the game! I'll clean it up *when I get back.*

(*Cory exits.*)

ROSE: That's all he need to do is see that room all messed up.

(*Rose exits into the house. Troy and Bono enter the yard. Troy is dressed in clothes other than his work clothes.*)

BONO: He told him the same thing he told you. Take it to the union.

TROY: Brownie ain't got that much sense. Man wasn't thinking about nothing. He wait until I confront them on it . . . then he wanna come crying seniority.

(*Calls.*)

Hey, Rose!

BONO: I wish I could have seen Mr. Rand's face when he told you.

TROY: He couldn't get it out of his mouth! Liked to bit his tongue! When they called me down there to the Commissioner's office . . . he thought they was gonna fire me. Like everybody else.

BONO: I didn't think they was gonna fire you. I thought they was gonna put you on the warning paper.

TROY: Hey, Rose!

(*To Bono.*)

Yeah, Mr. Rand like to bit his tongue.

(*Troy breaks the seal on the bottle, takes a drink, and hands it to Bono.*)

BONO: I see you run right down to Taylors' and told that Alberta gal.

TROY (*calling*): Hey, Rose! (*To Bono.*) I told everybody. Hey, Rose! I went down there to cash my check.

ROSE (*entering from the house*): Hush all that hollering, man! I know you out here. What they say down there at the Commissioner's office?

TROY: You supposed to come when I call you, woman. Bono'll tell you that.

(*To Bono.*)

Don't Lucille come when you call her?

ROSE: Man, hush your mouth. I ain't no dog . . . talk about "come when you call me."

TROY (*puts his arm around Rose*): You hear this Bono? I had me an old dog used to get uppity like that. You say, "C'mere, Blue!" . . . and he just lay there and look at you. End up getting a stick and chasing him away trying to make him come.

ROSE: I ain't studying you and your dog. I remember you used to sing that old song.

TROY (*he sings*): Hear it ring! Hear it ring! I had a dog his name was Blue.

ROSE: Don't nobody wanna hear you sing that old song.

TROY (*sings*): You know Blue was mighty true.

ROSE: Used to have Cory running around here singing that song.

BONO: Hell, I remember that song myself.

TROY (*sings*): You know Blue was a good old dog. Blue treed a possum in a hollow log.

That was my daddy's song. My daddy made up that song.

ROSE: I don't care who made it up. Don't nobody wanna hear you sing it.

TROY (*makes a song like calling a dog*): Come here, woman.

ROSE: You come in here carrying on, I reckon they ain't fired you. What they say down there at the Commissioner's office?

TROY: Look here, Rose . . . Mr. Rand called me into his office today when I got back from talking to them people down there . . . it come from up top . . . he called me in and told me they was making me a driver.

ROSE: Troy, you kidding!

TROY: No I ain't. Ask Bono.

ROSE: Well, that's great, Troy. Now you don't have to hassle them people no more.

(*Lyons enters from the street.*)

TROY: Aw hell, I wasn't looking to see you today. I thought you was in jail. Got it all over the front page of the *Courier* about them raiding Sefus' place . . . where you be hanging out with all them thugs.

LYONS: Hey, Pop . . . that ain't got nothing to do with me. I don't go down there gambling. I go down there to sit in with the band. I ain't got nothing to do with the gambling part. They got some good music down there.

TROY: They got some rogues . . . is what they got.

LYONS: How you been, Mr. Bono? Hi, Rose.

BONO: I see where you playing down at the Crawford Grill tonight.

ROSE: How come you ain't brought Bonnie like I told you. You should have brought Bonnie with you, she ain't been over in a month of Sundays.

LYONS: I was just in the neighborhood . . . thought I'd stop by.

TROY: Here he come . . .

BONO: Your daddy got a promotion on the rubbish. He's gonna be the first colored driver. Ain't got to do nothing but sit up there and read the paper like them white fellows.

LYONS: Hey, Pop . . . if you knew how to read you'd be all right.

BONO: Naw . . . naw . . . you mean if the nigger knew how to *drive* he'd be all right. Been fighting with them people about driving and ain't even got a license. Mr. Rand know you ain't got no driver's license?

TROY: Driving ain't nothing. All you do is point the truck where you want it to go. Driving ain't nothing.

BONO: Do Mr. Rand know you ain't got no driver's license? That's what I'm talking about. I ain't asked if driving was easy. I asked if Mr. Rand know you ain't got no driver's license.

TROY: He ain't got to know. The man ain't got to know my business. Time he find out, I have two or three driver's licenses.

LYONS (*going into his pocket*): Say, look here, Pop . . .

TROY: I knew it was coming. Didn't I tell you, Bono? I know what kind of "Look here, Pop" that was.

The nigger fixing to ask me for some money. It's Friday night. It's my payday. All them rogues down there on the avenue . . . the ones that ain't in jail . . . and Lyons is hopping in his shoes to get down there with them.

LYONS: See, Pop . . . if you give somebody else a chance to talk sometime, you'd see that I was fixing to pay you back your ten dollars like I told you. Here . . . I told you I'd pay you when Bonnie got paid.

TROY: Naw . . . you go ahead and keep that ten dollars. Put it in the bank. The next time you feel like you wanna come by here and ask me for something . . . you go on down there and get that.

LYONS: Here's your ten dollars, Pop. I told you I don't want you to give me nothing. I just wanted to borrow ten dollars.

TROY: Naw . . . you go on and keep that for the next time you want to ask me.

LYONS: Come on, Pop . . . here go your ten dollars.

ROSE: Why don't you go on and let the boy pay you back, Troy?

LYONS: Here you go, Rose. If you don't take it I'm gonna have to hear about it for the next six months.

(*He hands her the money.*)

ROSE: You can hand yours over here too, Troy.

TROY: You see this, Bono. You see how they do me.

BONO: Yeah, Lucille do me the same way.

(*Gabriel is heard singing offstage. He enters.*)

GABRIEL: Better get ready for the Judgment! Better get ready for . . . Hey! . . . Hey! . . . There's Troy's boy!

LYONS: How are you doing, Uncle Gabe?

GABRIEL: Lyons . . . The King of the Jungle! Rose . . . hey, Rose. Got a flower for you.

(*He takes a rose from his pocket.*)

Picked it myself. That's the same rose like you is!

ROSE: That's right nice of you, Gabe.

LYONS: What you been doing, Uncle Gabe?

GABRIEL: Oh, I been chasing hellhounds and waiting on the time to tell St. Peter to open the gates.

LYONS: You been chasing hellhounds, huh? Well . . . you doing the right thing, Uncle Gabe. Somebody got to chase them.

GABRIEL: Oh, yeah . . . I know it. The devil's strong. The devil ain't no pushover. Hellhounds snipping at everybody's heels. But I got my trumpet waiting on the judgment time.

LYONS: Waiting on the Battle of Armageddon, huh?

GABRIEL: Ain't gonna be too much of a battle when God get to waving that Judgment sword. But the people's gonna have a hell of a time trying to get into heaven if them gates ain't open.

LYONS (*putting his arm around Gabriel*): You hear this, Pop. Uncle Gabe, you all right!

GABRIEL (*laughing with Lyons*): Lyons! King of the Jungle.

ROSE: You gonna stay for supper, Gabe. Want me to fix you a plate?

GABRIEL: I'll take a sandwich, Rose. Don't want no plate. Just wanna eat with my hands. I'll take a sandwich.

ROSE: How about you, Lyons? You staying? Got some short ribs cooking.

LYONS: Naw, I won't eat nothing till after we finished playing.

(*Pause.*)

You ought to come down and listen to me play, Pop.

TROY: I don't like that Chinese music. All that noise.

ROSE: Go on in the house and wash up, Gabe . . . I'll fix you a sandwich.

GABRIEL (*to Lyons, as he exits*): Troy's mad at me.

LYONS: What you mad at Uncle Gabe for, Pop.

ROSE: He thinks Troy's mad at him cause he moved over to Miss Pearl's.

TROY: I ain't mad at the man. He can live where he want to live at.

LYONS: What he move over there for? Miss Pearl don't like nobody.

ROSE: She don't mind him none. She treats him real nice. She just don't allow all that singing.

TROY: She don't mind that rent he be paying . . . that's what she don't mind.

ROSE: Troy, I ain't going through that with you no more. He's over there cause he want to have his own place. He can come and go as he please.

TROY: Hell, he could come and go as he please here. I wasn't stopping him. I ain't put no rules on him.

ROSE: It ain't the same thing, Troy. And you know it.

(*Gabriel comes to the door.*)

Now, that's the last I wanna hear about that. I don't wanna hear nothing else about Gabe and Miss Pearl. And next week . . .

GABRIEL: I'm ready for my sandwich, Rose.

ROSE: And next week . . . when that recruiter come from that school . . . I want you to sign that paper and go on and let Cory play football. Then that'll be the last I have to hear about that.

TROY (*to Rose as she exits into the house*): I ain't thinking about Cory nothing.

LYONS: What . . . Cory got recruited? What school he going to?

TROY: That boy walking around here smelling his piss . . . thinking he's grown. Thinking he's gonna do what he want, irrespective of what I say. Look here, Bono . . . I left the Commissioner's office and went down to the A&P . . . that boy ain't working down there. He lying to me. Telling me he got his job back . . . telling me he working weekends . . . telling me he working after school . . . Mr. Stawicki tell me he ain't working down there at all!

LYONS: Cory just growing up. He's just busting at the seams trying to fill out your shoes.

TROY: I don't care what he's doing. When he get to the point where he wanna disobey me . . . then it's time for him to move on. Bono'll tell you that. I bet he ain't never disobeyed his daddy without paying the consequences.

BONO: I ain't never had a chance. My daddy came on through . . . but I ain't never knew him to see him . . . or what he had on his mind or where he went. Just moving on through. Searching out the New Land. That's what the old folks used to call it. See a fellow moving around from place to place . . . woman to woman . . . called it searching out the New Land. I can't say if he ever found it. I come along, didn't want no kids. Didn't know if I was gonna be in one place long enough to fix on them right as their daddy. I figured I was going searching too. As it turned out I been hooked up with Lucille near about as long as your daddy been with Rose. Going on sixteen years.

TROY: Sometimes I wish I hadn't known my daddy. He ain't cared nothing about no kids. A kid to him wasn't nothing. All he wanted was for you to learn how to walk so he could start you to working. When it come time for eating . . . he ate first. If there was anything left over, that's what you got. Man would sit down and eat two chickens and give you the wing.

LYONS: You ought to stop that, Pop. Everybody feed their kids. No matter how hard times is . . . everybody care about their kids. Make sure they have something to eat.

TROY: The only thing my daddy cared about was getting them bales of cotton in to Mr. Lubin. That's the only thing that mattered to him. Sometimes I used to wonder why he was living. Wonder why the devil hadn't come and got him. "Get them bales of cotton in to Mr. Lubin" and find out he owe him money . . .

LYONS: He should have just went on and left when he saw he couldn't get nowhere. That's what I would have done.

TROY: How he gonna leave with eleven kids? And where he gonna go? He ain't knew how to do nothing but farm. No, he was trapped and I think he knew it. But I'll say this for him . . . he felt a responsibility toward us. Maybe he ain't treated us the way I felt he should have . . . but without that responsibility he could have walked off and left us . . . made his own way.

BONO: A lot of them did. Back in those days what you talking about . . . they walk out their front door and just take on down one road or another and keep on walking.

LYONS: There you go! That's what I'm talking about.

BONO: Just keep on walking till you come to something else. Ain't you never heard of nobody having the walking blues? Well, that's what you call it when you just take off like that.

TROY: My daddy ain't had them walking blues! What you talking about? He stayed right there with his family. But he was just as evil as he could be. My mama couldn't stand him. Couldn't stand that evilness. She run off when I was about eight. She sneaked off one night after he had gone to sleep. Told me she was coming back for me. I ain't never seen her no

more. All his women run off and left him. He wasn't good for nobody.

When my turn come to head out, I was fourteen and got to sniffing around Joe Canewell's daughter. Had us an old mule we called Greyboy. My daddy sent me out to do some plowing and I tied up Greyboy and went to fooling around with Joe Canewell's daughter. We done found us a nice little spot, got real cozy with each other. She about thirteen and we done figured we was grown anyway . . . so we down there enjoying ourselves . . . ain't thinking about nothing. We didn't know Greyboy had got loose and wandered back to the house and my daddy was looking for me. We down there by the creek enjoying ourselves when my daddy come up on us. Surprised us. He had them leather straps off the mule and commenced to whupping me like there was no tomorrow. I jumped up, mad and embarrassed. I was scared of my daddy. When he commenced to whupping on me . . . quite naturally I run to get out of the way.

(Pause.)

Now I thought he was mad cause I ain't done my work. But I see where he was chasing me off so he could have the gal for himself. When I see what the matter of it was, I lost all fear of my daddy. Right there is where I become a man . . . at fourteen years of age.

(Pause.)

Now it was my turn to run him off. I picked up them same reins that he had used on me. I picked up them reins and commenced to whupping on him. The gal jumped up and run off . . . and when my daddy turned to face me, I could see why the devil had never come to get him . . . cause he was the devil himself. I don't know what happened. When I woke up, I was laying right there by the creek, and Blue . . . this old dog we had . . . was licking my face. I thought I was blind. I couldn't see nothing. Both my eyes were swollen shut. I layed there and cried. I didn't know what I was gonna do. The only thing I knew was the time had come for me to leave my daddy's house. And right there the world suddenly got big. And it was a long time before I could cut it down to where I could handle it.

Part of that cutting down was when I got to the place where I could feel him kicking in my blood and knew that the only thing that separated us was the matter of a few years.

(Gabriel enters from the house with a sandwich.)

LYONS: What you got there, Uncle Gabe?

GABRIEL: Got me a ham sandwich. Rose gave me a ham sandwich.

TROY: I don't know what happened to him. I done lost touch with everybody except Gabriel. But I hope he's dead. I hope he found some peace.

LYONS: That's a heavy story, Pop. I didn't know you left home when you was fourteen.

TROY: And didn't know nothing. The only part of the world I knew was the forty-two acres of Mr. Lubin's land. That's all I knew about life.

LYONS: Fourteen's kinda young to be out on your own. (*Phone rings.*) I don't even think I was ready to be out on my own at fourteen. I don't know what I would have done.

TROY: I got up from the creek and walked on down to Mobile. I was through with farming. Figured I could do better in the city. So I walked the two hundred miles to Mobile.

LYONS: Wait a minute . . . you ain't walked no two hundred miles, Pop. Ain't nobody gonna walk no two hundred miles. You talking about some walking there.

BONO: That's the only way you got anywhere back in them days.

LYONS: Shhh. Damn if I wouldn't have hitched a ride with somebody!

TROY: Who you gonna hitch it with? They ain't had no cars and things like they got now. We talking about 1918.

ROSE (*entering*): What you all out here getting into?

TROY (*to Rose*): I'm telling Lyons how good he got it. He don't know nothing about this I'm talking.

ROSE: Lyons, that was Bonnie on the phone. She say you supposed to pick her up.

LYONS: Yeah, okay, Rose.

TROY: I walked on down to Mobile and hitched up with some of them fellows that was heading this way. Got up here and found out . . . not only couldn't you get a job . . . you couldn't find no place to live. I thought I was in freedom. Shhh. Colored folks living down there on the riverbanks in whatever kind of shelter they could find for themselves. Right down there under the Brady Street Bridge. Living in shacks made of sticks and tarpaper. Messed around there and went from bad to worse. Started stealing. First it was food. Then I figured, hell, if I steal money I can buy me some food. Buy me some shoes too! One thing led to another. Met your mama. I was young and anxious to be a man. Met your mama and had you. What I do that for? Now I got to worry about feeding you and her. Got to steal three times as much. Went out one day looking for somebody to rob . . . that's what I was, a robber. I'll tell you the truth. I'm ashamed of it today. But it's the truth. Went to rob this fellow . . . pulled out my knife . . . and he pulled out a gun. Shot me in the chest. It felt just like somebody had taken a hot branding iron and laid it on me. When he shot me I jumped at him with my knife. They told me I killed him and they put me in the penitentiary and locked me up for fifteen years. That's where I met Bono. That's where I learned how to play baseball. Got out that place and your mama had taken you and went on to make life without me. Fifteen years was a long time for her to wait. But that fifteen years cured me of that robbing stuff. Rose'll tell you. She asked me when I met her if I had gotten all that foolishness out of my system. And I told her, "Baby, it's you and baseball all what count with me." You hear me, Bono? I meant it too. She say "Which one comes first?" I told her, "Baby, ain't no doubt it's baseball . . . but you stick and get old with me and we'll both outlive this baseball." Am I right, Rose? And it's true.

ROSE: Man, hush your mouth. You ain't said no such thing. Talking about, "Baby, you know you'll always be number one with me." That's what you was talking.

TROY: You hear that, Bono. That's why I love her.

BONO: Rose'll keep you straight. You get off the track, she'll straighten you up.

ROSE: Lyons, you better get on up and get Bonnie. She waiting on you.

LYONS (*gets up to go*): Hey, Pop, why don't you come on down to the Grill and hear me play?

TROY: I ain't going down there. I'm too old to be sitting around in them clubs.

BONO: You got to be good to play down at the Grill.

LYONS: Come on, Pop . . .

TROY: I got to get up in the morning.

LYONS: You ain't got to stay long.

TROY: Naw, I'm gonna get my supper and go on to bed.

LYONS: Well, I got to go. I'll see you again.

TROY: Don't you come around my house on my payday.

ROSE: Pick up the phone and let somebody know you coming. And bring Bonnie with you. You know I'm always glad to see her.

LYONS: Yeah, I'll do that, Rose. You take care now. See you, Pop. See you, Mr. Bono. See you, Uncle Gabe.

GABRIEL: Lyons! King of the Jungle!

(*Lyons exits.*)

TROY: Is supper ready, woman? Me and you got some business to take care of. I'm gonna tear it up too.

ROSE: Troy, I done told you now!

TROY (*puts his arm around Bono*): Aw hell, woman . . . this is Bono. Bono like family. I done known this nigger since . . . how long I done know you?

BONO: It's been a long time.

TROY: I done known this nigger since Skippy was a pup. Me and him done been through some times.

BONO: You sure right about that.

TROY: Hell, I done know him longer than I known you. And we still standing shoulder to shoulder. Hey, look here, Bono . . . a man can't ask for no more than that.

(*Drinks to him.*)

I love you, nigger.

BONO: Hell, I love you too . . . but I got to get home see my woman. You got yours in hand. I got to go get mine.

(*Bono starts to exit as Cory enters the yard, dressed in his football uniform. He gives Troy a hard, uncompromising look.*)

CORY: What you do that for, Pop?

(*He throws his helmet down in the direction of Troy.*)

ROSE: What's the matter? Cory . . . what's the matter?

CORY: Papa done went up to the school and told Coach Zellman I can't play football no more. Wouldn't even let me play the game. Told him to tell the recruiter not to come.

ROSE: Troy . . .

TROY: What you Troying me for. Yeah, I did it. And the boy know why I did it.

CORY: Why you wanna do that to me? That was the one chance I had.

ROSE: Ain't nothing wrong with Cory playing football, Troy.

TROY: The boy lied to me. I told the nigger if he wanna play football . . . to keep up his chores and hold down that job at the A&P. That was the conditions. Stopped down there to see Mr. Stawicki . . .

CORY: I can't work after school during the football season, Pop! I tried to tell you that Mr. Stawicki's holding my job for me. You don't never want to listen to nobody. And then you wanna go and do this to me!

TROY: I ain't done nothing to you. You done it to yourself.

CORY: Just cause you didn't have a chance! You just scared I'm gonna be better than you, that's all.

TROY: Come here.

ROSE: Troy . . .

(*Cory reluctantly crosses over to Troy.*)

TROY: All right! See. You done made a mistake.

CORY: I didn't even do nothing!

TROY: I'm gonna tell you what your mistake was. See . . . you swung at the ball and didn't hit it. That's strike one. See, you in the batter's box now. You swung and you missed. That's strike one. Don't you strike out!

(*Lights fade to black.*)

ACT II • Scene I

(*The following morning. Cory is at the tree hitting the ball with the bat. He tries to mimic Troy, but his swing is awkward, less sure. Rose enters from the house.*)

ROSE: Cory, I want you to help me with this cupboard.

CORY: I ain't quitting the team. I don't care what Poppa say.

ROSE: I'll talk to him when he gets back. He had to go see about your Uncle Gabe. The police done arrested him. Say he was disturbing the peace. He'll be back directly. Come on in here and help me clean out the top of this cupboard.

(*Cory exits into the house. Rose sees Troy and Bono coming down the alley.*)

Troy . . . what they say down there?

TROY: Ain't said nothing. I give them fifty dollars and they let him go. I'll talk to you about it. Where's Cory?

ROSE: He's in there helping me clean out these cupboards.

TROY: Tell him to get his butt out here.

(*Troy and Bono go over to the pile of wood. Bono picks up the saw and begins sawing.*)

TROY (*to Bono*): All they want is the money. That makes six or seven times I done went down there and got him. See me coming they stick out their *hands*.

BONO: Yeah. I know what you mean. That's all they care about . . . that money. They don't care about what's right.

(*Pause.*)

Nigger, why you got to go and get some hard wood? You ain't doing nothing but building a little old fence. Get you some soft pine wood. That's all you need.

TROY: I know what I'm doing. This is outside wood. You put pine wood inside the house. Pine wood is inside wood. This here is outside wood. Now you tell me where the fence is gonna be?

BONO: You don't need this wood. You can put it up with pine wood and it'll stand as long as you gonna be here looking at it.

TROY: How you know how long I'm gonna be here, nigger? Hell, I might just live forever. Live longer than old man Horsely.

BONO: That's what Magee used to say.

TROY: Magee's a damn fool. Now you tell me who you ever heard of gonna pull their own teeth with a pair of rusty pliers.

BONO: The old folks . . . my granddaddy used to pull his teeth with pliers. They ain't had no dentists for the colored folks back then.

TROY: Get clean pliers! You understand? Clean pliers! Sterilize them! Besides we ain't living back then. All Magee had to do was walk over to Doc Goldblum's.

BONO: I see where you and that Tallahassee gal . . . that Alberta . . . I see where you all done got tight.

TROY: What you mean "got tight"?

BONO: I see where you be laughing and joking with her all the time.

TROY: I laughs and jokes with all of them, Bono. You know me.

BONO: That ain't the kind of laughing and joking I'm talking about.

(*Cory enters from the house.*)

CORY: How you doing, Mr. Bono?

TROY: Cory? Get that saw from Bono and cut some wood. He talking about the wood's too hard to cut. Stand back there, Jim, and let that young boy show you how it's done.

BONO: He's sure welcome to it.

(*Cory takes the saw and begins to cut the wood.*)

Whew-e-e! Look at that. Big old strong boy. Look like Joe Louis. Hell, must be getting old the way I'm watching that boy whip through that wood.

CORY: I don't see why Mama want a fence around the yard noways.

TROY: Damn if I know either. What the hell she keeping out with it? She ain't got nothing nobody want.

BONO: Some people build fences to keep people out ... and other people build fences to keep people in. Rose wants to hold on to you all. She loves you.

TROY: Hell, nigger, I don't need nobody to tell me my wife loves me, Cory ... go on in the house and see if you can find that other saw.

CORY: Where's it at?

TROY: I said find it! Look for it till you find it!

(*Cory exits into the house.*)

What's that supposed to mean? Wanna keep us in?

BONO: Troy ... I done known you seem like damn near my whole life. You and Rose both. I done know both of you all for a long time. I remember when you met Rose. When you was hitting them baseball out the park. A lot of them old gals was after you then. You had the pick of the litter. When you picked Rose, I was happy for you. That was the first time I knew you had any sense. I said ... My man Troy knows what he's doing ... I'm gonna follow this nigger ... he might take me somewhere. I been following you too. I done learned a whole heap of things about life watching you. I done learned how to tell where the shit lies. How to tell it from the alfalfa. You done learned me a lot of things. You showed me how to not make the same mistakes ... to take life as it comes along and keep putting one foot in front of the other.

(*Pause.*)

Rose a good woman, Troy.

TROY: Hell, nigger, I know she a good woman. I been married to her for eighteen years. What you got on your mind, Bono?

BONO: I just say she a good woman. Just like I say anything. I ain't got to have nothing on my mind.

TROY: You just gonna say she a good woman and leave it hanging out there like that? Why you telling me she a good woman?

BONO: She loves you, Troy. Rose loves you.

TROY: You saying I don't measure up. That's what you trying to say. I don't measure up cause I'm seeing this other gal. I know what you trying to say.

BONO: I know what Rose means to you, Troy. I'm just trying to say I don't want to see you mess up.

TROY: Yeah, I appreciate that, Bono. If you was messing around on Lucille I'd be telling you the same thing.

BONO: Well, that's all I got to say. I just say that because I love you both.

TROY: Hell, you know me ... I wasn't out there looking for nothing. You can't find a better woman than Rose. I know that. But seems like this woman just stuck onto me where I can't shake her loose. I done wrestled with it, tried to throw her off me ... but she just stuck on tighter. Now she's stuck on for good.

BONO: You's in control ... that's what you tell me all the time. You responsible for what you do.

TROY: I ain't ducking the responsibility of it. As long as it sets right in my heart ... then I'm okay. Cause that's all I listen to. It'll tell me right from wrong every time. And I ain't talking about doing Rose no bad turn. I love Rose. She done carried me a long ways and I love and respect her for that.

BONO: I know you do. That's why I don't want to see you hurt her. But what you gonna do when she find out? What you got then? If you try and juggle both of them ... sooner or later you gonna drop one of them. That's common sense.

TROY: Yeah, I hear what you saying, Bono. I been trying to figure a way to work it out.

BONO: Work it out right, Troy. I don't want to be getting all up between you and Rose's business ... but work it so it come out right.

TROY: Ah hell, I get all up between you and Lucille's business. When you gonna get that woman that refrigerator she been wanting? Don't tell me you ain't got no money now. I know who your banker is. Mellon don't need that money bad as Lucille want that refrigerator. I'll tell you that.

BONO: Tell you what I'll do ... when you finish building this fence for Rose ... I'll buy Lucille that refrigerator.

TROY: You done stuck your foot in your mouth now!

(*Troy grabs up a board and begins to saw. Bono starts to walk out the yard.*)

Hey, nigger ... where you going?

BONO: I'm going home. I know you don't expect me to help you now. I'm protecting my money. I wanna see you put that fence up by yourself. That's what I want to see. You'll be here another six months without me.

TROY: Nigger, you ain't right.

BONO: When it comes to my money ... I'm right as fireworks on the Fourth of July.

TROY: All right, we gonna see now. You better get out your bankbook.

(*Bono exits, and Troy continues to work. Rose enters from the house.*)

ROSE: What they say down there? What's happening with Gabe?

TROY: I went down there and got him out. Cost me fifty dollars. Say he was disturbing the peace. Judge set up a hearing for him in three weeks. Say to show cause why he shouldn't be recommitted.

ROSE: What was he doing that cause them to arrest him?

TROY: Some kids was teasing him and he run them off home. Say he was howling and carrying on. Some folks seen him and called the police. That's all it was.

ROSE: Well, what's you say? What'd you tell the judge?

TROY: Told him I'd look after him. It didn't make no sense to recommit the man. He stuck out his big greasy palm and told me to give him fifty dollars and take him on home.

ROSE: Where's he at now? Where'd he go off to?

TROY: He's gone on about his business. He don't need nobody to hold his hand.

ROSE: Well, I don't know. Seem like that would be the best place for him if they did put him into the hospital. I know what you're gonna say. But that's what I think would be best.

TROY: The man done had his life ruined fighting for what? And they wanna take and lock him up. Let him be free. He don't bother nobody.

ROSE: Well, everybody got their own way of looking at it I guess. Come on and get your lunch. I got a bowl of lima beans and some cornbread in the oven. Come on get something to eat. Ain't no sense you fretting over Gabe.

(*Rose turns to go into the house.*)

TROY: Rose . . . got something to tell you.

ROSE: Well, come on . . . wait till I get this food on the table.

TROY: Rose!

(*She stops and turns around.*)

I don't know how to say this.

(*Pause.*)

I can't explain it none. It just sort of grows on you till it gets out of hand. It starts out like a little bush . . . and the next thing you know it's a whole forest.

ROSE: Troy . . . what is you talking about?

TROY: I'm talking, woman, let me talk. I'm trying to find a way to tell you . . . I'm gonna be a daddy. I'm gonna be somebody's daddy.

ROSE: Troy . . . you're not telling me this? You're gonna be . . . what?

TROY: Rose . . . now . . . see . . .

ROSE: You telling me you gonna be somebody's daddy? You telling your *wife* this?

(*Gabriel enters from the street. He carries a rose in his hand.*)

GABRIEL: Hey, Troy! Hey, Rose!

ROSE: I have to wait eighteen years to hear something like this.

GABRIEL: Hey, Rose . . . I got a flower for you.

(*He hands it to her.*)

That's a rose. Same rose like you is.

ROSE: Thanks, Gabe.

GABRIEL: Troy, you ain't mad at me is you? Them bad mens come and put me away. You ain't mad at me is you?

TROY: Naw, Gabe, I ain't mad at you.

ROSE: Eighteen years and you wanna come with this.

GABRIEL (*takes a quarter out of his pocket*): See what I got? Got a brand new quarter.

TROY: Rose . . . it's just . . .

ROSE: Ain't nothing you can say, Troy. Ain't no way of explaining that.

GABRIEL: Fellow that give me this quarter had a whole mess of them. I'm gonna keep this quarter till it stop shining.

ROSE: Gabe, go on in the house there. I got some watermelon in the frigidaire. Go on and get you a piece.

GABRIEL: Say, Rose . . . you know I was chasing hellhounds and them bad mens come and get me and take me away. Troy helped me. He come down there and told them they better let me go before he beat them up. Yeah, he did!

ROSE: You go on and get you a piece of watermelon, Gabe. Them bad mens is gone now.

GABRIEL: Okay, Rose . . . gonna get me some watermelon. The kind with the stripes on it.

(*Gabriel exits into the house.*)

ROSE: Why, Troy? Why? After all these years to come dragging this in to me now. It don't make no sense at your age. I could have expected this ten or fifteen years ago, but not now.

TROY: Age ain't got nothing to do with it, Rose.

ROSE: I done tried to be everything a wife should be. Everything a wife could be. Been married eighteen years and I got to live to see the day you tell me you been seeing another woman and done fathered a child by her. And you know I ain't never wanted no half nothing in my family. My whole family is half. Everybody got different fathers and mothers . . . my two sisters and my brother. Can't hardly tell who's who. Can't never sit down and talk about Papa and Mama. It's your papa and your mama and my papa and my mama . . .

TROY: Rose . . . stop it now.

ROSE: I ain't never wanted that for none of my children. And now you wanna drag your behind in here and tell me something like this.

TROY: You ought to know. It's time for you to know.

ROSE: Well, I don't want to know, goddamn it!

TROY: I can't just make it go away. It's done now. I can't wish the circumstance of the thing away.

ROSE: And you don't want to either. Maybe you want to wish me and my boy away. Maybe that's what you want? Well, you can't wish us away. I've got eighteen years of my life invested in you. You ought to have stayed upstairs in my bed where you belong.

TROY: Rose . . . now listen to me . . . we can get a handle on this thing. We can talk this out . . . come to an understanding.

ROSE: All of a sudden it's "we." Where was "we" at when you was down there rolling around with some godforsaken woman? "We" should have come to an understanding before you started making a damn fool of yourself. You're a day late and a dollar short when it comes to an understanding with me.

TROY: It's just . . . She gives me a different idea . . . a different understanding about myself. I can step out of this house and get away from the pressures and problems . . . be a different man. I ain't got to wonder how I'm gonna pay the bills or get the roof fixed. I can just be a part of myself that I ain't never been.

ROSE: What I want to know . . . is do you plan to continue seeing her. That's all you can say to me.

TROY: I can sit up in her house and laugh. Do you understand what I'm saying. I can laugh out loud . . . and it feels good. It reaches all the way down to the bottom of my shoes.

(*Pause.*)

Rose, I can't give that up.

ROSE: Maybe you ought to go on and stay down there with her . . . if she's a better woman than me.

TROY: It ain't about nobody being a better woman or nothing. Rose, you ain't the blame. A man couldn't ask for no woman to be a better wife than you've been. I'm responsible for it. I done locked myself into a pattern trying to take care of you all that I forgot about myself.

ROSE: What the hell was I there for? That was my job, not somebody else's.

TROY: Rose, I done tried all my life to live decent . . . to live a clean . . . hard . . . useful life. I tried to be a good husband to you. In every way I knew how. Maybe I come into the world backwards, I don't know. But . . . you born with two strikes on you before you come to the plate. You got to guard it closely . . . always looking for the curve ball on the inside corner. You can't afford to let none get past you. You can't afford a call strike. If you going down . . . you going down swinging. Everything lined up against you. What you gonna do. I fooled them, Rose. I bunted. When I found you and Cory and a halfway decent job . . . I was safe. Couldn't nothing touch me. I wasn't gonna strike out no more. I wasn't going back to the penitentiary. I wasn't gonna lay in the streets with a bottle of wine. I was safe. I had me a family. A job. I wasn't gonna get that last strike. I was on first looking for one of them boys to knock me in. To get me home.

ROSE: You should have stayed in my bed, Troy.

TROY: Then when I saw that gal . . . she firmed up my backbone. And I got to thinking that if I tried . . . I just might be able to steal second. Do you understand after eighteen years I wanted to steal second.

ROSE: You should have held me tight. You should have grabbed me and held on.

TROY: I stood on first base for eighteen years and I thought . . . well, goddamn it . . . go on for it!

ROSE: We're not talking about baseball! We're talking about you going off to lay in bed with another woman . . . and then bring it home to me. That's what we're talking about. We ain't talking about no baseball.

TROY: Rose, you're not listening to me. I'm trying the best I can to explain it to you. It's not easy for me to admit that I been standing in the same place for eighteen years.

ROSE: I been standing with you! I been right here with you, Troy. I got a life too. I gave eighteen years of my life to stand in the same spot with you. Don't you think I ever wanted other things? Don't you think I had dreams and hopes? What about my life? What about me? Don't you think it ever crossed my mind to want to know other men? That I wanted to lay up somewhere and forget about my responsibilities? That I wanted someone to make me laugh so I could feel good? You not the only one who's got wants and needs. But I held on to you, Troy. I took all my feelings, my wants and needs, my dreams . . . and I buried them inside you. I planted a seed and watched and prayed over it. I planted myself inside you and waited to bloom. And it didn't take me no eighteen years to find out the soil was hard and rocky and it wasn't never gonna bloom.

But I held on to you, Troy. I held you tighter. You was my husband. I owed you everything I had. Every part of me I could find to give you. And upstairs in that room . . . with the darkness falling in on me . . . I gave everything I had to try and erase the doubt that you wasn't the finest man in the world. And wherever you was going . . . I wanted to be there with you. Cause you was my husband. Cause that's the only way I was gonna survive as your wife. You always talking about what you give . . . and what you don't have to give. But you take too. You take . . . and don't even know nobody's giving!

(*Rose turns to exit into the house; Troy grabs her arm.*)

TROY: You say I take and don't give!

ROSE: Troy! You're hurting me!

TROY: You say I take and don't give.

ROSE: Troy . . . you're hurting my arm! Let go!

TROY: I done give you everything I got. Don't you tell that lie on me.

ROSE: Troy!

TROY: Don't you tell that lie on me!

(*Cory enters from the house.*)

CORY: Mama!

ROSE: Troy. You're hurting me.

TROY: Don't you tell me about no taking and giving.

(*Cory comes up behind Troy and grabs him. Troy, surprised, is thrown off balance just as Cory throws a glancing blow that catches him on the chest and knocks him down. Troy is stunned, as is Cory.*)

ROSE: Troy. Troy. No!

(*Troy gets to his feet and starts at Cory.*)

Troy . . . no. Please! Troy!

(*Rose pulls on Troy to hold him back. Troy stops himself.*)

TROY (*to Cory*): All right. That's strike two. You stay away from around me, boy. Don't you strike out. You living with a full count. Don't you strike out.

(*Troy exits out the yard as the lights go down.*)

Scene II

(*It is six months later, early afternoon. Troy enters from the house and starts to exit the yard. Rose enters from the house.*)

ROSE: Troy, I want to talk to you.

TROY: All of a sudden, after all this time, you want to talk to me, huh? You ain't wanted to talk to me for months. You ain't wanted to talk to me last night. You ain't wanted no part of me then. What you wanna talk to me about now?

ROSE: Tomorrow's Friday.

TROY: I know what day tomorrow is. You think I don't know tomorrow's Friday? My whole life I ain't done nothing but look to see Friday coming and you got to tell me it's Friday.

ROSE: I want to know if you're coming home.

TROY: I always come home, Rose. You know that. There ain't never been a night I ain't come home.

ROSE: That ain't what I mean . . . and you know it. I want to know if you're coming straight home after work.

TROY: I figure I'd cash my check . . . hang out at Taylors' with the boys . . . maybe play a game of checkers . . .

ROSE: Troy, I can't live like this. I won't live like this. You livin' on borrowed time with me. It's been going on six months now you ain't been coming home.

TROY: I be here every night. Every night of the year. That's 365 days.

ROSE: I want you to come home tomorrow after work.

TROY: Rose . . . I don't mess up my pay. You know that now. I take my pay and I give it to you. I don't have no money but what you give me back. I just want to have a little time to myself . . . a little time to enjoy life.

ROSE: What about me? When's my time to enjoy life?

TROY: I don't know what to tell you, Rose. I'm doing the best I can.

ROSE: You ain't been home from work but time enough to change your clothes and run out . . . and you wanna call that the best you can do?

TROY: I'm going over to the hospital to see Alberta. She went into the hospital this afternoon. Look like she might have the baby early. I won't be gone long.

ROSE: Well, you ought to know. They went over to Miss Pearl's and got Gabe today. She said you told them to go ahead and lock him up.

TROY: I ain't said no such thing. Whoever told you that is telling a lie. Pearl ain't doing nothing but telling a big fat lie.

ROSE: She ain't had to tell me. I read it on the papers.

TROY: I ain't told them nothing of the kind.

ROSE: I saw it right there on the papers.

TROY: What it say, huh?

ROSE: It said you told them to take him.

TROY: Then they screwed that up, just the way they screw up everything. I ain't worried about what they got on the paper.

ROSE: Say the government send part of his check to the hospital and the other part to you.

TROY: I ain't got nothing to do with that if that's the way it works. I ain't made up the rules about how it work.

ROSE: You did Gabe just like you did Cory. You wouldn't sign the paper for Cory . . . but you signed for Gabe. You signed that paper.

(*The telephone is heard ringing inside the house.*)

TROY: I told you I ain't signed nothing, woman! The only thing I signed was the release form. Hell, I can't read, I don't know what they had on that paper! I ain't signed nothing about sending Gabe away.

ROSE: I said send him to the hospital . . . you said let him be free . . . now you done went down there and signed him to the hospital for half his money. You went back on yourself, Troy. You gonna have to answer for that.

TROY: See now . . . you been over there talking to Miss Pearl. She done got mad cause she ain't getting Gabe's rent money. That's all it is. She's liable to say anything.

ROSE: Troy, I seen where you signed the paper.

TROY: You ain't seen nothing I signed. What she doing got papers on my brother anyway? Miss Pearl telling a big fat lie. And I'm gonna tell her about it too! You ain't seen nothing I signed. Say . . . you ain't seen nothing I signed.

(*Rose exits into the house to answer the telephone. Presently she returns.*)

ROSE: Troy . . . that was the hospital. Alberta had the baby.

TROY: What she have? What is it?

ROSE: It's a girl.

TROY: I better get on down to the hospital to see her.

ROSE: Troy . . .

TROY: Rose . . . I got to go see her now. That's only right . . . what's the matter . . . the baby's all right, ain't it?

ROSE: Alberta died having the baby.

TROY: Died . . . you say she's dead? Alberta's dead?

ROSE: They said they done all they could. They couldn't do nothing for her.

TROY: The baby? How's the baby?

ROSE: They say it's healthy. I wonder who's gonna bury her.

TROY: She had family, Rose. She wasn't living in the world by herself.

ROSE: I know she wasn't living in the world by herself.

TROY: Next thing you gonna want to know if she had any insurance.

ROSE: Troy, you ain't got to talk like that.

TROY: That's the first thing that jumped out your mouth. "Who's gonna bury her?" Like I'm fixing to take on that task for myself.

ROSE: I am your wife. Don't push me away.

TROY: I ain't pushing nobody away. Just give me some space. That's all. Just give me some room to breathe.

(*Rose exits into the house. Troy walks about the yard.*)

TROY (*with a quiet rage that threatens to consume him*): All right . . . Mr. Death. See now . . . I'm gonna tell you what I'm gonna do. I'm gonna take and build me a fence around this yard. See? I'm gonna build me a fence around what belongs to me. And then I want you to stay on the other side. See? You stay over there until you're ready for me. Then you come on. Bring your army. Bring your sickle. Bring your wrestling clothes. I ain't gonna fall down on my vigilance this time. You ain't gonna sneak up on me no more. When you ready for me . . . when the top of your list say Troy Maxson . . . that's when you come around here. You come up and knock on the front door. Ain't nobody else got nothing to do with this. This is between you and me. Man to man. You stay on the other side of that fence until you ready for me. Then you come up and knock on the front door. Anytime you want. I'll be ready for you.

(*The lights go down to black.*)

Scene III

(*The lights come up on the porch. It is late evening three days later. Rose sits listening to the ball game waiting for Troy. The final out of the game is made and Rose switches off the radio. Troy enters the yard carrying an infant wrapped in blankets. He stands back from the house and calls.*)

    (*Rose enters and stands on the porch. There is a long, awkward silence, the weight of which grows heavier with each passing second.*)

TROY: Rose . . . I'm standing here with my daughter in my arms. She ain't but a wee bittie little old thing. She don't know nothing about grownups' business. She innocent . . . and she ain't got no mama.

ROSE: What you telling me for, Troy?

(*She turns and exits into the house.*)

TROY: Well . . . I guess we'll just sit out here on the porch.

(*He sits down on the porch. There is an awkward indelicateness about the way he handles the baby. His largeness engulfs and seems to swallow it. He speaks loud enough for Rose to hear.*)

    A man's got to do what's right for him. I ain't sorry for nothing I done. It felt right in my heart.

(*To the baby.*)

    What you smiling at? Your daddy's a big man. Got these great big old hands. But sometimes he's scared. And right now your daddy's scared cause we sitting out here and ain't got no home. Oh, I been homeless before. I ain't had no little baby with me. But I been homeless. You just be out on the road by your lonesome and you see one of them trains coming and you just kinda go like this . . .

(*He sings as a lullaby.*)

    Please, Mr. Engineer let a man ride the line
    Please, Mr. Engineer let a man ride the line
    I ain't got no ticket please let me ride the blinds

(*Rose enters from the house. Troy hearing her steps behind him, stands and faces her.*)

    She's my daughter, Rose. My own flesh and blood. I can't deny her no more than I can deny them boys.

(*Pause.*)

    You and them boys is my family. You and them and this child is all I got in the world. So I guess what I'm saying is . . . I'd appreciate it if you'd help me take care of her.

ROSE: Okay, Troy . . . you're right. I'll take care of your baby for you . . . cause . . . like you say . . . she's innocent . . . and you can't visit the sins of the father upon the child. A motherless child has got a hard time.

(*She takes the baby from him.*)

    From right now . . . this child got a mother. But you a womanless man.

(*Rose turns and exits into the house with the baby. Lights go down to black.*)

Scene IV

(*It is two months later. Lyons enters from the street. He knocks on the door and calls.*)

LYONS: Hey, Rose! (*Pause.*) Rose!

ROSE (*from inside the house*): Stop that yelling. You gonna wake up Raynell. I just got her to sleep.

LYONS: I just stopped by to pay Papa this twenty dollars I owe him. Where's Papa at?

ROSE: He should be here in a minute. I'm getting ready to go down to the church. Sit down and wait on him.

LYONS: I got to go pick up Bonnie over her mother's house.

ROSE: Well, sit it down there on the table. He'll get it.

LYONS (*enters the house and sets the money on the table*): Tell Papa I said thanks. I'll see you again.

ROSE: All right, Lyons. We'll see you.

(*Lyons starts to exit as Cory enters.*)

CORY: Hey, Lyons.

LYONS: What's happening, Cory. Say man, I'm sorry I missed your graduation. You know I had a gig and couldn't get away. Otherwise, I would have been there, man. So what you doing?

CORY: I'm trying to find a job.

LYONS: Yeah I know how that go, man. It's rough out here. Jobs are scarce.

CORY: Yeah, I know.

LYONS: Look here, I got to run. Talk to Papa . . . he know some people. He'll be able to help get you a job. Talk to him . . . see what he say.

CORY: Yeah . . . all right, Lyons.

LYONS: You take care. I'll talk to you soon. We'll find some time to talk.

(*Lyons exits the yard. Cory wanders over to the tree, picks up the bat, and assumes a batting stance. He studies an imaginary pitcher and swings. Dissatisfied with the result, he tries again. Troy enters. They eye each other for a beat. Cory puts the bat down and exits the yard. Troy starts into the house as Rose exits with Raynell. She is carrying a cake.*)

TROY: I'm coming in and everybody's going out.

ROSE: I'm taking this cake down to the church for the bake sale. Lyons was by to see you. He stopped by to pay you your twenty dollars. It's laying in there on the table.

TROY (*going into his pocket*): Well . . . here go this money.

ROSE: Put it in there on the table, Troy. I'll get it.

TROY: What time you coming back?

ROSE: Ain't no use in you studying me. It don't matter what time I come back.

TROY: I just asked you a question, woman. What's the matter . . . can't I ask you a question?

ROSE: Troy, I don't want to go into it. Your dinner's in there on the stove. All you got to do is heat it up. And don't you be eating the rest of them cakes in there. I'm coming back for them. We having a bake sale at the church tomorrow.

(*Rose exits the yard. Troy sits down on the steps, takes a pint bottle from his pocket, opens it, and drinks. He begins to sing.*)

TROY: Hear it ring! Hear it ring!
    Had an old dog his name was Blue
    You know Blue was mighty true
    You know Blue as a good old dog
    Blue trees a possum in a hollow log
    You know from that he was a good old dog

(*Bono enters the yard.*)

BONO: Hey, Troy.

TROY: Hey, what's happening, Bono?

BONO: I just thought I'd stop by to see you.

TROY: What you stop by and see me for? You ain't stopped by in a month of Sundays. Hell, I must owe you money or something.

BONO: Since you got your promotion I can't keep up with you. Used to see you every day. Now I don't even know what route you working.

TROY: They keep switching me around. Got me out in Greentree now . . . hauling white folks' garbage.

BONO: Greentree, huh? You lucky, at least you ain't got to be lifting them barrels. Damn if they ain't getting heavier. I'm gonna put in my two years and call it quits.

TROY: I'm thinking about retiring myself.

BONO: You got it easy. You can *drive* for another five years.

TROY: It ain't the same, Bono. It ain't like working the back of the truck. Ain't got nobody to talk to . . . feel like you working by yourself. Naw, I'm thinking about retiring. How's Lucille?

BONO: She all right. Her arthritis get to acting up on her sometime. Saw Rose on my way in. She going down to the church, huh?

TROY: Yeah, she took up going down there. All them preachers looking for somebody to fatten their pockets.

(*Pause.*)

    Got some gin here.

BONO: Naw, thanks. I just stopped by to say hello.

TROY: Hell, nigger . . . you can take a drink. I ain't never known you to say no to a drink. You ain't got to work tomorrow.

BONO: I just stopped by. I'm fixing to go over to Skinner's. We got us a domino game going over his house every Friday.

TROY: Nigger, you can't play no dominoes. I used to whup you four games out of five.

BONO: Well, that learned me. I'm getting better.

TROY: Yeah? Well, that's all right.

BONO: Look here . . . I got to be getting on. Stop by sometime, huh?

TROY: Yeah, I'll do that, Bono. Lucille told Rose you bought her a new refrigerator.

BONO: Yeah, Rose told Lucille you had finally built your fence . . . so I figured we'd call it even.

TROY: I knew you would.

BONO: Yeah . . . okay. I'll be talking to you.

TROY: Yeah, take care, Bono. Good to see you. I'm gonna stop over.

BONO: Yeah. Okay, Troy.

(*Bono exits. Troy drinks from the bottle.*)

TROY: Old Blue died and I dig his grave
    Let him down with a golden chain
    Every night when I hear old Blue bark
    I know Blue treed a possum in Noah's Ark.
    Hear it ring! Hear it ring!

(*Cory enters the yard. They eye each other for a beat. Troy is sitting in the middle of the steps. Cory walks over.*)

CORY: I got to get by.

TROY: Say what? What's you say?

CORY: You in my way. I got to get by.

TROY: You got to get by where? This is my house. Bought and paid for. In full. Took me fifteen years. And if you wanna go in my house and I'm sitting on the steps . . . you say excuse me. Like your mama taught you.

CORY: Come on, Pop . . . I got to get by.

(*Cory starts to maneuver his way past Troy. Troy grabs his leg and shoves him back.*)

TROY: You just gonna walk over top of me?

CORY: I live here too!

TROY (*advancing toward him*): You just gonna walk over top of me in my own house?

CORY: I ain't scared of you.

TROY: I ain't asked if you was scared of me. I asked you if you was fixing to walk over top of me in my own house? That's the question. You ain't gonna say excuse me? You just gonna walk over top of me?

CORY: If you wanna put it like that.

TROY: How else am I gonna put it?

CORY: I was walking by you to go into the house cause you sitting on the steps drunk, singing to yourself. You can put it like that.

TROY: Without saying excuse me???

(*Cory doesn't respond.*)

I asked you a question. Without saying excuse me???

CORY: I ain't got to say excuse me to you. You don't count around here no more.

TROY: Oh, I see . . . I don't count around here no more. You ain't got to say excuse me to your daddy. All of a sudden you done got so grown that your daddy don't count around here no more . . . Around here in his own house and yard that he done paid for with the sweat of his brow. You done got so grown to where you gonna take over. You gonna take over my house. Is that right? You gonna wear my pants. You gonna go in there and stretch out on my bed. You ain't got to say excuse me cause I don't count around here no more. Is that right?

CORY: That's right. You always talking this dumb stuff. Now, why don't you just get out my way.

TROY: I guess you got someplace to sleep and something to put in your belly. You got that, huh? You got that? That's what you need. You got that, huh?

CORY: You don't know what I got. You ain't got to worry about what I got.

TROY: You right! You one hundred percent right! I done spent the last seventeen years worrying about what you got. Now it's your turn, see? I'll tell you what to do. You grown . . . we done established that. You a man. Now, let's see you act like one. Turn your behind around and walk out this yard. And when you get out there in the alley . . . you can forget about this house. See? 'Cause this is my house. You go on and be a man and get your own house. You can forget about this. 'Cause this is mine. You go on and get yours 'cause I'm through with doing for you.

CORY: You talking about what you did for me . . . what'd you ever give me?

TROY: Them feet and bones! That pumping heart, nigger! I give you more than anybody else is ever gonna give you.

CORY: You ain't never gave me nothing! You ain't never done nothing but hold me back. Afraid I was gonna be better than you. All you ever did was try and make me scared of you. I used to tremble every time you called my name. Every time I heard your footsteps in the house. Wondering all the time . . . what's Papa gonna say if I do this? . . . What's he gonna say if I do that? . . . What's Papa gonna say if I turn on the radio? And Mama, too . . . she tries . . . but she's scared of you.

TROY: You leave your mama out of this. She ain't got nothing to do with this.

CORY: I don't know how she stand you . . . after what you did to her.

TROY: I told you to leave your mama out of this!

(*He advances toward Cory.*)

CORY: What you gonna do . . . give me a whupping? You can't whup me no more. You're too old. You just an old man.

TROY (*shoves him on his shoulder*): Nigger! That's what you are. You just another nigger on the street to me!

CORY: You crazy! You know that?

TROY: Go on now! You got the devil in you. Get on away from me!

CORY: You just a crazy old man . . . talking about I got the devil in me.

TROY: Yeah, I'm crazy! If you don't get on the other side of that yard . . . I'm gonna show you how crazy I am! Go on . . . get the hell out of my yard.

CORY: It ain't your yard. You took Uncle Gabe's money he got from the army to buy this house and then you put him out.

TROY (*Troy advances on Cory*): Get your black ass out of my yard!

(*Troy's advance backs Cory up against the tree. Cory grabs up the bat.*)

CORY: I ain't going nowhere! Come on . . . put me out! I ain't scared of you.

TROY: That's my bat!

CORY: Come on!

TROY: Put my bat down!

CORY: Come on, put me out.

(*Cory swings at Troy, who backs across the yard.*)

What's the matter? You so bad . . . put me out!

(*Troy advances toward Cory.*)

CORY (*backing up*): Come on! Come on!

TROY: You're gonna have to use it! You wanna draw that bat back on me . . . you're gonna have to use it.

CORY: Come on! . . . Come on!

(*Cory swings the bat at Troy a second time. He misses. Troy continues to advance toward him.*)

TROY: You're gonna have to kill me! You wanna draw that bat back on me. You're gonna have to kill me.

(*Cory, backed up against the tree, can go no farther. Troy taunts him. He sticks out his head and offers him a target.*)

Come on! Come on!

(*Cory is unable to swing the bat. Troy grabs it.*)

TROY: Then I'll show you.

(*Cory and Troy struggle over the bat. The struggle is fierce and fully engaged. Troy ultimately is the stronger and takes the bat from Cory and stands over him ready to swing. He stops himself.*)

Go on and get away from around my house.

(*Cory, stung by his defeat, picks himself up, walks slowly out of the yard and up the alley.*)

CORY: Tell Mama I'll be back for my things.
TROY: They'll be on the other side of that fence.

(*Cory exits.*)

TROY: I can't taste nothing. Helluljah! I can't taste nothing no more. (*Troy assumes a batting posture and begins to taunt Death, the fastball on the outside corner.*) Come on! It's between you and me now! Come on! Anytime you want! Come on! I be ready for you . . . but I ain't gonna be easy.

(*The lights go down on the scene.*)

Scene V

(*The time is 1965. The lights come up in the yard. It is the morning of Troy's funeral. A funeral plaque with a light hangs beside the door. There is a small garden plot off to the side. There is noise and activity in the house as Rose, Gabriel, and Bono have gathered. The door opens and Raynell, seven years old, enters dressed in a flannel nightgown. She crosses to the garden and pokes around with a stick. Rose calls from the house.*)

ROSE: Raynell!
RAYNELL: Mam?
ROSE: What you doing out there?
RAYNELL: Nothing.

(*Rose comes to the door.*)

ROSE: Girl, get in here and get dressed. What you doing?
RAYNELL: Seeing if my garden growed.
ROSE: I told you it ain't gonna grow overnight. You got to wait.
RAYNELL: It don't look like it never gonna grow. Dag!
ROSE: I told you a watched pot never boils. Get in here and get dressed.
RAYNELL: This ain't even no pot, Mama.
ROSE: You just have to give it a chance. It'll grow. Now you come on and do what I told you. We got to be getting ready. This ain't no morning to be playing around. You hear me?
RAYNELL: Yes, mam.

(*Rose exits into the house. Raynell continues to poke at her garden with a stick. Cory enters. He is dressed in a Marine corporal's uniform, and carries a duffel bag. His posture is that of a military man, and his speech has a clipped sternness.*)

CORY (*to Raynell*): Hi.

(*Pause.*)

I bet your name is Raynell.
RAYNELL: Uh huh.
CORY: Is your mama home?

(*Raynell runs up on the porch and calls through the screen door.*)

RAYNELL: Mama . . . there's some man out here. Mama?

(*Rose comes to the door.*)

ROSE: Cory? Lord have mercy! Look here, you all!

(*Rose and Cory embrace in a tearful reunion as Bono and Lyons enter from the house dressed in funeral clothes.*)

BONO: Aw, looka here . . .
ROSE: Done got all grown up!
CORY: Don't cry, Mama. What you crying about?
ROSE: I'm just so glad you made it.
CORY: Hey Lyons. How you doing, Mr. Bono.

(*Lyons goes to embrace Cory.*)

LYONS: Look at you, man. Look at you. Don't he look good, Rose. Got them Corporal stripes.
ROSE: What took you so long.
CORY: You know how the Marines are, Mama. They got to get all their paperwork straight before they let you do anything.
ROSE: Well, I'm sure glad you made it. They let Lyons come. Your Uncle Gabe's still in the hospital. They don't know if they gonna let him out or not. I just talked to them a little while ago.
LYONS: A Corporal in the United States Marines.
BONO: Your daddy knew you had it in you. He used to tell me all the time.
LYONS: Don't he look good, Mr. Bono?
BONO: Yeah, he remind me of Troy when I first met him.

(*Pause.*)

Say, Rose, Lucille's down at the church with the choir. I'm gonna go down and get the pallbearers lined up. I'll be back to get you all.
ROSE: Thanks, Jim.
CORY: See you, Mr. Bono.
LYONS (*with his arm around Raynell*): Cory . . . look at Raynell. Ain't she precious? She gonna break a whole lot of hearts.
ROSE: Raynell, come and say hello to your brother. This is your brother, Cory. You remember Cory.
RAYNELL: No, Mam.
CORY: She don't remember me, Mama.
ROSE: Well, we talk about you. She heard us talk about you. (*To Raynell.*) This is your brother, Cory. Come on and say hello.
RAYNELL: Hi.
CORY: Hi. So you're Raynell. Mama told me a lot about you.
ROSE: You all come on into the house and let me fix you some breakfast. Keep up your strength.

CORY: I ain't hungry, Mama.

LYONS: You can fix me something, Rose. I'll be in there in a minute.

ROSE: Cory, you sure you don't want nothing. I know they ain't feeding you right.

CORY: No, Mama . . . thanks. I don't feel like eating. I'll get something later.

ROSE: Raynell . . . get on upstairs and get that dress on like I told you.

(*Rose and Raynell exit into the house.*)

LYONS: So . . . I hear you thinking about getting married.

CORY: Yeah, I done found the right one, Lyons. It's about time.

LYONS: Me and Bonnie been split up about four years now. About the time Papa retired. I guess she just got tired of all them changes I was putting her through.

(*Pause.*)

I always knew you was gonna make something out yourself. Your head was always in the right direction. So . . . you gonna stay in . . . make it a career . . . put in your twenty years?

CORY: I don't know. I got six already, I think that's enough.

LYONS: Stick with Uncle Sam and retire early. Ain't nothing out here. I guess Rose told you what happened with me. They got me down the workhouse. I thought I was being slick cashing other people's checks.

CORY: How much time you doing?

LYONS: They give me three years. I got that beat now. I ain't got but nine more months. It ain't so bad. You learn to deal with it like anything else. You got to take the crookeds with the straights. That's what Papa used to say. He used to say that when he struck out. I seen him strike out three times in a row . . . and the next time up he hit the ball over the grandstand. Right out there in Homestead Field. He wasn't satisfied hitting in the seats . . . he want to hit it over everything! After the game he had two hundred people standing around waiting to shake his hand. You got to take the crookeds with the straights. Yeah, Papa was something else.

CORY: You still playing?

LYONS: Cory . . . you know I'm gonna do that. There's some fellows down there we got us a band . . . we gonna try and stay together when we get out . . . but yeah, I'm still playing. It still helps me to get out of bed in the morning. As long as it do that I'm gonna be right there playing and trying to make some sense out of it.

ROSE (*calling*): Lyons, I got these eggs in the pan.

LYONS: Let me go on and get these eggs, man. Get ready to go bury Papa.

(*Pause.*)

How you doing? You doing all right?

(*Cory nods. Lyons touches him on the shoulder and they share a moment of silent grief. Lyons exits into the house. Cory wanders about the yard. Raynell enters.*)

RAYNELL: Hi.

CORY: Hi.

RAYNELL: Did you used to sleep in my room?

CORY: Yeah . . . that used to be my room.

RAYNELL: That's what Papa call it. "Cory's room." It got your football in the closet.

(*Rose comes to the door.*)

ROSE: Raynell, get in there and get them good shoes on.

RAYNELL: Mama, can't I wear these. Them other one hurt my feet.

ROSE: Well, they just gonna have to hurt your feet for a while. You ain't said they hurt your feet when you went down to the store and got them.

RAYNELL: They didn't hurt then. My feet done got bigger.

ROSE: Don't you give me no backtalk now. You get in there and get them shoes on.

(*Raynell exits into the house.*)

Ain't too much changed. He still got that piece of rag tied to that tree. He was out here swinging that bat. I was just ready to go back in the house. He swung that bat and then he just fell over. Seem like he swung it and stood there with this grin on his face . . . and then he just fell over. They carried him on down to the hospital, but I knew there wasn't no need . . . why don't you come on in the house?

CORY: Mama . . . I got something to tell you. I don't know how to tell you this . . . but I've got to tell you . . . I'm not going to Papa's funeral.

ROSE: Boy, hush your mouth. That's your daddy you talking about. I don't want hear that kind of talk this morning. I done raised you to come to this? You standing there all healthy and grown talking about you ain't going to your daddy's funeral?

CORY: Mama . . . listen . . .

ROSE: I don't want to hear it, Cory. You just get that thought out of your head.

CORY: I can't drag Papa with me everywhere I go. I've got to say no to him. One time in my life I've got to say no.

ROSE: Don't nobody have to listen to nothing like that. I know you and your daddy ain't seen eye to eye, but I ain't got to listen to that kind of talk this morning. Whatever was between you and your daddy . . . the time has come to put it aside. Just take it and set it over there on the shelf and forget about it. Disrespecting your daddy ain't gonna make you a man, Cory. You got to find a way to come to that on your own. Not going to your daddy's funeral ain't gonna make you a man.

CORY: The whole time I was growing up . . . living in his house . . . Papa was like a shadow that followed you everywhere. It weighed on you and sunk into your flesh. It would wrap around you and lay there until you couldn't tell which one was you anymore. That shadow digging in your flesh. Trying to crawl in. Trying to live through you. Everywhere I looked, Troy Maxson was staring back at me ... hiding under the bed ... in the closet. I'm just saying I've got to find a way to get rid of that shadow, Mama.

ROSE: You just like him. You got him in you good.

CORY: Don't tell me that, Mama.

ROSE: You Troy Maxson all over again.

CORY: I don't want to be Troy Maxson. I want to be me.

ROSE: You can't be nobody but who you are, Cory. That shadow wasn't nothing but you growing into yourself. You either got to grow into it or cut it down to fit you. But that's all you got to make life with. That's all you got to measure yourself against that world out there. Your daddy wanted you to be everything he wasn't ... and at the same time he tried to make you into everything he was. I don't know if he was right or wrong ... but I do know he meant to do more good than he meant to do harm. He wasn't always right. Sometimes when he touched he bruised. And sometimes when he took me in his arms he cut.

When I first met your daddy I thought ... Here is a man I can lay down with and make a baby. That's the first thing I thought when I seen him. I was thirty years old and had done seen my share of men. But when he walked up to me and said "I can dance a waltz that'll make you dizzy," I thought, Rose Lee, here is a man that you can open yourself up to and be filled to bursting. Here is a man that can fill all them empty spaces you been tipping around the edges of. One of them empty spaces was being somebody's mother.

I married your daddy and settled down to cooking his supper and keeping clean sheets on the bed. When your daddy walked through the house he was so big he filled it up. That was my first mistake. Not to make him leave some room for me. For my part in the matter. But at that time I wanted that. I wanted a house that I could sing in. And that's what your daddy gave me. I didn't know to keep up his strength I had to give up little pieces of mine. I did that. I took on his life as mine and mixed up the pieces so that you couldn't hardly tell which was which anymore. It was my choice. It was my life and I didn't have to live it like that. But that's what life offered me in the way of being a woman and I took it. I grabbed hold of it with both hands.

By the time Raynell came into the house, me and your daddy had done lost touch with one another. I didn't want to make my blessing off of nobody's misfortune ... but I took on to Raynell like she was all them babies I had wanted and never had.

(*The phone rings.*)

Like I'd been blessed to relive a part of my life. And if the Lord see fit to keep up my strength ... I'm gonna do her just like your daddy did you ... I'm gonna give her the best of what's in me.

RAYNELL (*entering, still with her old shoes*): Mama ... Reverend Tollivier on the phone.

(*Rose exits into the house.*)

RAYNELL: Hi.

CORY: Hi.

RAYNELL: You in the Army or the Marines?

CORY: Marines.

RAYNELL: Papa said it was the Army. Did you know Blue?

CORY: Blue? Who's Blue?

RAYNELL: Papa's dog what he sing about all the time.

CORY (*singing*): Hear it ring! Hear it ring!
   I had a dog his name was Blue
   You know Blue was mighty true
   You know Blue was a good old dog
   Blue treed a possum in a hollow log
   You know from that he was a good old dog.
   Hear it ring! Hear it ring!

(*Raynell joins in singing.*)

CORY AND RAYNELL: Blue treed a possum out on a limb
   Blue looked at me and I looked at him
   Grabbed that possum and put him in a sack
   Blue stayed there till I came back
   Old Blue's feets was big and round
   Never allowed a possum to touch the ground.

   Old Blue died and I dug his grave
   I dug his grave with a silver spade
   Let him down with a golden chain
   And every night I call his name
   Go on Blue, you good dog you
   Go on Blue, you good dog you

RAYNELL: Blue laid down and died like a man
   Blue laid down and died ...

BOTH: Blue laid down and died like a man
   Now he's treeing possums in the Promised Land
   I'm gonna tell you this to let you know
   Blue's gone where the good dogs go
   When I hear old Blue bark
   When I hear old Blue bark
   Blue treed a possum in Noah's Ark
   Blue treed a possum in Noah's Ark.

(*Rose comes to the screen door.*)

ROSE: Cory, we gonna be ready to go in a minute.

CORY (*to Raynell*): You go on in the house and change them shoes like Mama told you so we can go to Papa's funeral.

RAYNELL: Okay, I'll be back.

(*Raynell exits into the house. Cory gets up and crosses over to the tree. Rose stands in the screen door watching him. Gabriel enters from the alley.*)

GABRIEL (*calling*): Hey, Rose!

ROSE: Gabe?

GABRIEL: I'm here, Rose. Hey Rose, I'm here!

(*Rose enters from the house.*)

ROSE: Lord . . . Look here, Lyons!

LYONS: See, I told you, Rose . . . I told you they'd let him come.

CORY: How you doing, Uncle Gabe?

LYONS: How you doing, Uncle Gabe?

GABRIEL: Hey, Rose. It's time. It's time to tell St. Peter to open the gates. Troy, you ready? You ready, Troy. I'm gonna tell St. Peter to open the gates. You get ready now.

(*Gabriel, with great fanfare, braces himself to blow. The trumpet is without a mouthpiece. He puts the end of it into his mouth and blows with great force, like a man who has been waiting some twenty-odd years for this single moment. No sound comes out of the trumpet. He braces himself and blows again with the same result. A third time he blows. There is a weight of impossible description that falls away and leaves him bare and exposed to a frightful realization. It is a trauma that a sane and normal mind would be unable to withstand. He begins to dance. A slow, strange dance, eerie and life-giving. A dance of atavistic signature and ritual. Lyons attempts to embrace him. Gabriel pushes Lyons away. He begins to howl in what is an attempt at song, or perhaps a song turning back into itself in an attempt at speech. He finishes his dance and the gates of heaven stand open as wide as God's closet.*)

That's the way that go!

COMMENTARY

JOAN HERRINGTON (b. 1960)

The Development of *Fences*   1998

Among the interesting things we know about Wilson's decision to write *Fences* is the fact that he was struck by some of the criticism of *Ma Rainey's Black Bottom* for its unusual structure. With *Fences* Wilson decided to write a play that respected the unities of time, place, and action. He also wanted to write a play about family, and in the process he chose baseball and its attendant mythologies as the all-American game. Wilson struggled with clarifying the relationship of Troy Maxson with his sons and their differing needs. He also struggled with Troy's relationship with his wife through many stages of revision. Herrington gives us a good view of what was involved in the writing of the play.

Troy's relationship with his second son, Cory, is a vital part of the play as Wilson examines Troy's attempt to guide the boy into a responsible life. A high school senior, Cory has been recruited to play college football. But Troy will not sign the papers to permit this.

Although Wilson presents Cory's position sympathetically, he supports Troy's decision. "Blacks who received sports scholarships to go to school were exploited. Very few got an education. Troy makes the right choice when he tells his son that football won't lead anywhere. He's telling his son to get a job so he won't have to carry garbage."

Despite Wilson's implicit endorsement of Troy's decision, he fully understands its negative impact on his son. And as Wilson worked on *Fences,* he continually labored over his portrayal of their relationship. In the first version of the play, there is an extended scene between Cory and Troy in which they discuss the purchase of a new television set. Cory doesn't understand why they cannot buy a TV, and Troy tries to explain the financial management of a household. The scene concludes with Troy offering to pay half if Cory can come up with the other half. Here we have an opportunity to see father and son interact in a nonconfrontational manner, and also to see Troy exercising a fatherly concern for his son beyond feeding and clothing him. During work at the O'Neill Conference, this section was effectively moved from the second to the first half of the play, where it serves as groundwork to inform the later conflicts between Troy and Cory.

At the Yale Rep, however, the entire section was dropped in an effort to shorten the work. But the omission of the exchange between Troy and Cory left too large a gap in the portrayal of Troy's exercise of familial responsibility. At the conclusion of the play, in all the drafts, Cory complains of a lack of understanding and emotional support from Troy, and he provokes Troy by asking him what he ever gave to his son. Troy responds: "Them feet and bones. That pumping heart. I give you more than anybody else is ever gonna give you."

Troy is angry with Cory's implication that he has somehow failed the boy, for he believes that he has fulfilled his obligation to his son. With the long scene about the television having been cut, however, we can see only that Troy has provided Cory the bare bones. But Wilson wanted the audience to know that Troy has, in fact, provided more—more guidance, more support, more sympathy—and he restored the television scene in the final version.

While doing so, Wilson also gave Troy the opportunity to explain more fully his attitude toward Cory's college recruitment. In earlier drafts, Troy had challenged Cory, in anger, to give up football: "You go on and get your book learning where you can learn to do something besides carry people's garbage." In Wilson's final revision, Troy is more patient, more loving and concerned, and his speech has a more inspirational quality. Wilson moved Troy from an expression of bitterness over his own life to an expression of a positive dream for his son.

> You go on and get your book learning so you can work yourself up in that A&P or learn how to fix cars or build houses or something, get you a trade. That way you have something can't nobody take away from you. You go on and learn how to put your hands to some good use. Besides hauling people's garbage.

It is important to see that Troy has good intentions even as the play reveals his failings. As a younger man, Troy pursued his personal destiny in baseball at the cost of his family. Now, later in life, he professes to have made responsibility to others his priority. But Troy's efforts are neither wholehearted nor entirely successful, and Wilson uses Cory to make this point. As he revised the play, Wilson gave Cory a more mature understanding of the workings and failings of his family, particularly his father.

In early drafts, Cory was angry at his father and revealed his emotions in naive, sophomoric outbursts: "I hate your blood in me." As the drafts progressed, Cory challenges Troy on substantive issues. At the play's close, in the final draft, Cory upbraids Troy for his mistreatment of Rose, "I don't know how [Rose] stand you . . . after what you did to her." Although Cory's understanding of the issue is not complete, it goes straight to the core of Troy's view of himself as a responsible man, forcing him to come to terms with the fact that he put himself, his own fulfillment, before his responsibility to his wife.

The structure of the play leads to a dramatic confrontation, both physical and emotional, between Troy and Cory. Recognizing the flaws in his father and needing to make his own choices, Cory has become a man. There isn't room in the house for two men, and a simple argument about Troy moving over on the steps so that Cory can pass into the house blows up into the final exchange between them.

In early drafts, this final scene was potentially more violent. In the first versions, at the height of the confrontation, when Cory picks up Troy's baseball bat, Troy brings out a gun, points it at his son, and the stage directions read that he cocks the trigger. Wilson dropped this detail before the Yale Rep production when he read that Marvin Gaye° had been shot by his father. In the later drafts, the only weapon in the scene is the baseball bat, symbolically more powerful in its meaning to Troy, and dramatically more powerful, too, since it can be used as a weapon only when two people are in close physical proximity to each other.

The conflict between father and son continued to change in other ways, too. In the production at the Yale Rep, Cory swings the bat once and then retreats into the alley as Troy continues to approach. The conflict is interrupted by the arrival of Rose, prompting Cory to leave the yard.

Wilson realized that the interruption left the conflict unresolved. Thus, in the final version, Rose does not enter, and the climax of the play is more meaningful as the complex relationship between father and son is more intricately explored. Cory swings the bat once and misses. Then he swings again and misses. Troy offers him the chance to swing a third time, having positioned himself as a target impossible to miss. Now, Cory cannot swing. The two men struggle for the bat, and Troy takes it away. Troy prepares to swing, but he stops himself. Defeated, Cory leaves the yard and does not return until after Troy's death, years later. In this final version the anger between Cory and Troy is the most visceral. And yet it is in this version where we clearly see that neither one can intentionally injure the other.

Whether Cory becomes like his father or learns to be different is explored by Wilson in the final "interaction" between the two. The play concludes after a passage of eight years and the death of Troy. The issue of Cory's sense of responsibility is explored one last time through his indecision about whether to attend Troy's funeral. Wilson, like his character, changed his mind many times about whether Cory would go.

In the first draft, Cory does not attend his father's funeral. He expresses his continued bitterness to Lyons in an extensive exchange. Then, as a casualty of Wilson's feeling that the exchange between the half-brothers did not ring true, as well as his concern for the running time of the show, this long discussion was cut before the first performance at the O'Neill Conference. Cory merely wanders away during a discussion between Lyons and Rose and does not return. Dissatisfied with Cory's disrespectful choice, the audience responded negatively. For the second O'Neill performance, Cory's discussion with Lyons and his subsequent departure were dropped, leaving the implication that Cory does attend the funeral.

Both of these versions were unsatisfactory to Wilson. So, in the Yale Rep version, Cory tells Rose that he is not going to the funeral and Rose, playing the role Wilson had previously assigned to Lyons, urges Cory to attend. Wilson also rearranged the scene so that the entire family surrounds the young man at the moment of his decision. Cory knows he must go to the funeral, and in this final draft, Wilson

Marvin Gaye: Popular American songwriter killed April 1, 1984.

provides Cory a subtle acknowledgment of his choice as he says to his half-sister Raynell, "You go on in the house and change them shoes like Mama told you so we can go to Papa's funeral."

Rose, having survived the most damaging kind of betrayal from Troy, is a powerful spokesperson for remaining true to one's commitments even without the expectation of reciprocity. In progressive drafts, Wilson carefully refined her character so that as she moved toward greater forgiveness and understanding, Troy's betrayal appeared all the more dramatic.

The most significant change in Rose was in her day-to-day relationship with Troy and how this, in turn, affects his relationship with Alberta. In the early version of the play, Rose is much more a nagging wife. She bothers Troy constantly about his drinking (which is considerably greater in the early drafts). She reprimands Troy for his neglect of Cory, and when she is tired of Troy's shouting, she tells him to go shout somewhere else. Although certainly none of these faults warrants Troy's infidelity, they perhaps provide him an excuse. As the versions progress, this side of Rose almost completely disappears, and Troy's affair seems less excusable, more stark a violation of his marital responsibility.

But Rose is tolerant—more and more so as the drafts of the play progressed. In the early versions of the play, Troy's announcement that he will be a father comes as a complete surprise to Rose. In later versions of the play, Rose suspects that he is having an affair as she catches inconsistencies in his explanations of his whereabouts, but she says nothing.

When Troy finally tells his wife about Alberta, Rose preaches the bible of familial responsibility.

> I gave eighteen years of my life to stand in the same spot with you. Don't you think I ever wanted things? Don't you think I had dreams and hopes? . . . Don't you think it ever crossed my mind to want to know other men? That I wanted to lay up somewhere and forget about my responsibilities? . . . But I held on to you, Troy . . . I took all my feelings, my wants and needs, my dreams . . . and I buried them inside you . . . I held on to you, Troy.

In the second, third, and fourth drafts of the script, there is no further mention of the affair until Troy brings home the baby. But in the final version, Wilson chose to extend the duration of Rose's tolerance by reinserting an original scene which had been cut to shorten the script. Here, six months after Rose learns of Troy's infidelity, she confronts him about his continuing attention to Alberta, telling him he's living on "borrowed time" with her. Rose retains her composure and her emotional charge as she points out the fallacy in Troy's theory that his physical presence in bed at the end of every night fulfills his obligation to his household regardless of where he has been up to that time.

As Rose grows more philosophical, even under the burden of a betrayal that she understands to be ongoing, our sympathy for her becomes stronger. And Rose's eventual decision to accept Troy's bastard child but to sexually renounce its father—the same in all drafts of the play—makes more sense as the action of a woman who, over time, has come to recognize the impossibility of change in her husband.

Rose stands in the center of the play as a model of responsibility but also as an example of the cost of responsibility to others at the expense of self. In response to Troy's explanation of his affair, Rose responds that she also has needs and wants not satisfied at home. But ultimately she sees no options for herself simply because, as she explains to Troy, "You my husband."

Rose's selflessness moves toward an ultimate commitment outside of herself—that is, to the church. In successive versions of the play, Rose becomes more involved with the church, participates more in its events, sings more of its hymns, and ends the final version of the play completely engrossed in the institution.

Troy remains independent, somehow able to reconcile to his own satisfaction a complex range of conflicting needs and desires. Wilson performed a complicated balancing act of his own to get the audience to be sympathetic to the choices Troy makes, even to support them. He accomplished this through careful selection of the details, choosing those that would highlight Troy's concern with personal autonomy, dignity, self-realization.

Tony Kushner

Tony Kushner was born in 1956 in New York City, but his family soon moved to Louisiana, where his father ran the family lumberyard. His parents were classical musicians, and their home was filled with art. Kushner dates his interest in theater to early memories of seeing his mother onstage. He also recollects from childhood "fairly clear memories of being gay since I was six." He did not, however, "come out" until after he had tried psychotherapy to change his sexual orientation.

After finishing his undergraduate education at Columbia University, Kushner studied directing in graduate school at New York University, partly because he was not confident of his chances to become a playwright. Among his early plays are *Yes, Yes, No, No* (1985), a children's play produced in St. Louis; *Stella* (1987), an adaptation from Goethe produced in New York; *A Bright Room Called Day* (1987), produced in San Francisco; and *The Illusion* (1988), adapted from Corneille, produced in New York and then in Hartford in 1990. He worked with Argentinian playwright Ariel Dorfman to adapt Dorfman's *Widows,* produced in Los Angeles in 1991. *A Bright Room Called Day,* about left-wing politics in Nazi Germany, was not well reviewed on its New York production in 1991. Frank Rich, for example, said that it was "an early front-runner for the most infuriating play of 1991." But some people saw in it the power that was to show up later in Kushner's work. The Eureka Theatre in San Francisco commissioned him to write a play that ultimately turned out to be *Angels in America: A Gay Fantasia on National Themes* (1992), the play that catapulted him to international prominence.

Among Kushner's projects is a series of three plays that he describes as having money as its subject—meaning, in part, the effects of economic status, both poverty and wealth, on individuals. The first of these plays, titled *Henry Box Brown* (1997), centers on the true story of a black American who escaped slavery by being smuggled out of the South in a crate. Brown eventually made his way to England, where he joined with a number of other former slaves in producing dramatic "panoramas" intended to discourage the English from buying slave-picked cotton, on which their textile industry largely relied. Kushner has said, "I've always been drawn to writing historical characters. . . . The best stories are the ones you find in history."

Kushner's play *Homebody/Kabul* (2001) seems connected with history, too. It is set in London and Afghanistan in 1998, after a U.S. bombing raid. Some of the dialogue is in Pashto. It was described by Paul Taylor, a London critic, as "a deeply felt expansively ruminative drama."

Among Kushner's many projects is a chamber opera about a black maid working for a Jewish family in Louisiana, *Caroline, or Change* (2003), written in collaboration with Jeanine Tesori and performed at the Joseph Papp Public Theater in New York.

In June 2006, Opera Unlimited produced *Angels in America* at the Calderwood Pavilion in the Boston Center for the Arts. The music was written by Peter Eotvos and the libretto was by Mari Mezei. In another interesting development, Kushner translated Brecht's *Mother Courage* for an August

2006 production at the Public Theater at the Delacorte Theater Central Park, New York. Meryl Streep was an extraordinarily energetic Mother Courage, Kevin Kline was the cook, and Austin Pendleton was the chaplain. Kushner's activism and energy have helped fuel anticipation of his next contribution to contemporary drama.

Angels in America: Millennium Approaches

Kushner began work on *Angels in America* shortly after Oskar Eustis of the Eureka Theatre commissioned a two-and-a-half-hour play with songs. Once Kushner had developed a presentable version, he showed it to Eustis and realized that, even incomplete, it was already longer than a one-evening play. Eventually, *Millennium Approaches* and *Perestroika*, the second part of *Angels* (not included here), grew to be more than seven hours long. Although the two parts are thematically linked and contain many of the same characters, both parts of *Angels* stand on their own as complete plays. Kushner said that he never expected to see his play produced anywhere but in a small theater in San Francisco; certainly he never expected it to be a smash hit on Broadway. It won the 1993 Pulitzer Prize for drama, another surprise.

Angels in America has epic, Brechtian proportions. Kushner has said that he set out to write a play on "AIDS, Mormons, and Roy Cohn." He chose AIDS because it is a scourge that has destroyed large numbers of the gay community. He chose Mormons because he saw in them a group that valued goodness and godliness but that could not tolerate gays. He chose Roy Cohn because, when Cohn was an aide to Senator Joseph McCarthy during the anti-Communist hysteria of the 1950s, he persecuted gays even though he was himself a closeted homosexual. His homosexuality did not become public until he contracted AIDS and died in 1986. In Cohn, Kushner had found a villain whose rapacious individualism and unquenchable thirst for power helped symbolize the selfishness of the 1980s. In the New York production of *Angels*, Ron Liebman was an overbearingly powerful Cohn, shouting orders and raising hypocrisy to an art form, with depths of contempt matching a profound love of power.

Kushner indicated that his play was a "fantasia on national themes," and it certainly lives up to its title. Kushner set his play in 1985, during the second presidential term of Ronald Reagan. He critiques the values of the Reagan years and politics in general. Jews, WASPs, and Mormons all suffer under Kushner's scrutiny. Moreover, he goes beyond national themes and introduces cosmological themes, notably with the introduction of an angel descending through the ceiling at the end of *Millennium Approaches*.

The play also focuses on problems of individuals. Cohn's friend and protégé Joe Pitt works for the Reagan administration and struggles with his growing awareness that he is gay. A conservative Mormon, Joe faces these complex, threatening feelings honestly and painfully. Harper, Joe's wife, relies on pills,

For discussion questions and assignments on *Angels in America*, visit bedfordstmartins.com/jacobus.

listens all day to talk shows, and has no job but thinks of herself as part of a traditional marriage and fights to hold on to it. Louis Ironson, a liberal but not especially political gay man, is in a relationship with Prior Walter, who is dying from AIDS. Louis has hidden his sexuality from his family and finds it impossible to stay with Prior as his lover's illness worsens. Kushner makes sure that we see all these sets of people interrelated throughout the play, despite their distinctness and the unlikelihood of their ever knowing one another.

Though the scope of the play is enormous, its focus is essentially on politics. Kushner's own views contrast sharply with Cohn's conservative politics, and he is surprised that both conservatives and liberals found the play rewarding, because he constructed it to be a pointed attack on conservative values.

Angels in America in Performance

The 1991 premiere of *Millennium Approaches* was in a workshop version at the Eureka Theatre in San Francisco. Its first full-scale production came in July 1992 at London's Royal National Theatre, where it was a sensation. Some reviewers speculated that in London the political theater of Caryl Churchill and other playwrights such as David Hare and David Edgar prepared the way for this play. The audiences were enormously enthusiastic, and the positive reviews the play received attracted attention in the United States. Despite Kushner's relatively unknown status, the two parts of the drama (over seven hours long) were staged in the Mark Taper Forum in Los Angeles in 1992, directed by Oskar Eustis and Tony Taccone. *Millennium Approaches* appeared on Broadway in April 1993 at the Walter Kerr Theatre, directed by George C. Wolfe. Frank Rich gave it a strong, positive review in the *New York Times*, saying "When first seen a year or so ago, the play seemed defined by its anger at the reigning political establishment, which tended to reward the Roy Cohns and ignore the Prior Walters. Mr. Kushner has not revised the text since — a crony of Cohn's still boasts of a Republican lock on the White House until the year 2000 — but the shift in Washington has had the subliminal effect of making *Angels in America* seem more focused on what happens next than on the past."

The second part of the work, *Perestroika*, arrived on Broadway in November 1993. Frank Rich in the *New York Times* said it was "also a true millennial work of art, uplifting, hugely comic and pantheistically religious in a very American style." After its Broadway run, the play moved to regional theaters, touring throughout the United States. The staging of the drama includes moments that may be described as magic realism, featuring ghosts, hallucinations, and other illusions. But Kushner has said, "The play benefits from a pared-down style of presentation, with minimal scenery and scene shifts done rapidly (no blackouts!), employing the cast as well as stagehands — which makes for an actor-driven event, as this must be." He said that it was not a problem if "wires showed," "but the magic should at the same time be thoroughly amazing."

One of Kushner's signal successes in 2003 was seeing *Angels in America* air in a six-part production over two evenings on Home Box Office (HBO) cable television, directed by Mike Nichols and starring Al Pacino in the role of Roy Cohn, Meryl Streep as both Hannah Pitt and Ethel Rosenberg, and Emma Thompson as the Angel. The production was beautifully done and won a Golden Globe Award. Kushner made more inroads into television with the 2004 HBO production of *Homebody/Kabul* (2001). The Signature Theatre Company's production of *Angels in America* in 2010 at the Peter Norton Space in New York was directed by Michael Greif. It was successful, but reviewers admitted that the shock value of the original production was inevitably lost despite the imaginative theatrical effects.

TONY KUSHNER (b. 1956)

Angels in America: Millennium Approaches   1992

A Gay Fantasia on National Themes

In a murderous time
     the heart breaks and breaks
          and lives by breaking.   — STANLEY KUNITZ, "THE TESTING-TREE"

Characters

ROY M. COHN, *a successful New York lawyer and unofficial power broker*

JOSEPH PORTER PITT, *chief clerk for Justice Theodore Wilson of the Federal Court of Appeals, Second Circuit*

HARPER AMATY PITT, *Joe's wife, an agoraphobic with a mild Valium addiction*

LOUIS IRONSON, *a word processor working for the Second Circuit Court of Appeals*

PRIOR WALTER, *Louis's boyfriend. Occasionally works as a club designer or caterer, otherwise lives very modestly but with great style off a small trust fund.*

HANNAH PORTER PITT, *Joe's mother, currently residing in Salt Lake City, living off her deceased husband's army pension*

BELIZE, *a former drag queen and former lover of Prior's. A registered nurse. Belize's name was originally Norman Arriaga; Belize is a drag name that stuck.*

THE ANGEL, *four divine emanations, Fluor, Phosphor, Lumen and Candle; manifest in One: the Continental Principality of America. She has magnificent steel-gray wings.*

Other Characters in Part One:

RABBI ISIDOR CHEMELWITZ, *an orthodox Jewish rabbi, played by the actor playing Hannah*

MR. LIES, *Harper's imaginary friend, a travel agent, who in style of dress and speech suggests a jazz musician; he always wears a large lapel badge emblazoned "IOTA" (The International Order of Travel Agents). He is played by the actor playing Belize.*

THE MAN IN THE PARK, *played by the actor playing Prior*

THE VOICE, *the voice of The Angel*

HENRY, *Roy's doctor, played by the actor playing Hannah*

EMILY, *a nurse, played by the actor playing The Angel*

MARTIN HELLER, *a Reagan Administration Justice Department flackman, played by the actor playing Harper*

SISTER ELLA CHAPTER, *a Salt Lake City real-estate saleswoman, played by the actor playing The Angel*

PRIOR 1, *the ghost of a dead Prior Walter from the 13th century, played by the actor playing Joe. He is a blunt, gloomy medieval farmer with a guttural Yorkshire accent.*

PRIOR 2, *the ghost of a dead Prior Walter from the 17th century, played by the actor playing Roy. He is a Londoner, sophisticated, with a High British accent.*

THE ESKIMO, *played by the actor playing Joe*

THE WOMAN IN THE SOUTH BRONX, *played by the actor playing The Angel*

ETHEL ROSENBERG, *played by the actor playing Hannah*

Playwright's Notes

A Disclaimer: Roy M. Cohn, the character, is based on the late Roy M. Cohn (1927–1986), who was all too real; for the most part the acts attributed to the character Roy, such as his illegal conferences with Judge Kaufmann during the trial of Ethel Rosenberg, are to be found in the historical record. But this Roy is a work of dramatic fiction; his words are my invention, and liberties have been taken.

A Note about the Staging: The play benefits from a pared-down style of presentation, with minimal scenery and scene shifts done rapidly (no blackouts!), employing the cast as well as stagehands—which makes for an actor-driven event, as this must be. The moments of magic—the appearance and disappearance of Mr. Lies and the ghosts, the Book hallucination, and the ending—are to be fully realized, as bits of wonderful theatrical illusion—which means it's OK if the wires show, and maybe it's good that they do, but the magic should at the same time be thoroughly amazing.

ACT 1
BAD NEWS •
October–November 1985

Scene 1

(*The last days of October. Rabbi Isidor Chemelwitz alone onstage with a small coffin. It is a rough pine box with two wooden pegs, one at the foot and one at the head, holding the lid in place. A prayer shawl embroidered with a Star of David is draped over the lid, and by the head a yarzheit candle is burning.*)

RABBI ISIDOR CHEMELWITZ (*he speaks sonorously, with a heavy Eastern European accent, unapologetically consulting a sheet of notes for the family names*): Hello and good morning. I am Rabbi Isidor Chemelwitz of the Bronx Home for Aged Hebrews. We are here this morning to pay respects at the passing of Sarah Ironson, devoted wife of Benjamin Ironson, also deceased, loving and caring mother of her sons Morris, Abraham, and Samuel, and her daughters Esther and Rachel; beloved grandmother of Max, Mark, Louis, Lisa, Maria . . . uh . . . Lesley, Angela, Doris, Luke and Eric. (*Looks more closely at paper.*) Eric? This is a Jewish name? (*Shrugs.*) Eric. A large and loving family. We assemble that we may mourn collectively this good and righteous woman.

(*He looks at the coffin.*)

This woman. I did not know this woman. I cannot accurately describe her attributes, nor do justice to her dimensions. She was . . . . Well, in the Bronx Home of Aged Hebrews are many like this, the old, and to many I speak but not to be frank with this one. She preferred silence. So I do not know her and yet I know her. She was . . .

(*he touches the coffin*)

. . . not a person but a whole kind of person, the ones who crossed the ocean, who brought with us to America the villages of Russia and Lithuania—and how we struggled, and how we fought, for the family, for the Jewish home, so that you would not grow up *here*, in this strange place, in the melting pot where nothing melted. Descendants of this immigrant

woman, you do not grow up in America, you and your children and their children with the goyische names. You do not live in America. No such place exists. Your clay is the clay of some Litvak shtetl, your air the air of the steppes—because she carried the old world on her back across the ocean, in a boat, and she put it down on Grand Concourse Avenue, or in Flatbush, and she worked that earth into your bones, and you pass it to your children, this ancient, ancient culture and home.

(*Little pause.*)

You can never make that crossing that she made, for such Great Voyages in this world do not any more exist. But every day of your lives the miles that voyage between that place and this one you cross. Every day. You understand me? In you that journey is.

So . . .

She was the last of the Mohicans, this one was. Pretty soon . . . all the old will be dead.

Scene 2

(*Same day. Roy and Joe in Roy's office. Roy at an impressive desk, bare except for a very elaborate phone system, rows and rows of flashing buttons which bleep and beep and whistle incessantly, making chaotic music underneath Roy's conversations. Joe is sitting, waiting. Roy conducts business with great energy, impatience and sensual abandon: gesticulating, shouting, cajoling, crooning, playing the phone, receiver and hold button with virtuosity and love.*)

ROY (*hitting a button*): Hold. (*To Joe.*) I wish I was an octopus, a fucking octopus. Eight loving arms and all those suckers. Know what I mean?

JOE: No, I . . .

ROY (*gesturing to a deli platter of little sandwiches on his desk*): You want lunch?

JOE: No, that's OK really I just . . .

ROY (*hitting a button*): Ailene? Roy Cohn. Now what kind of a greeting is . . . . I thought we were friends, Ai. . . . Look Mrs. Soffer you don't have to get . . . . You're upset. You're yelling. You'll aggravate your condition, you shouldn't yell, you'll pop little blood vessels in your face if you yell. . . . No that was a joke, Mrs. Soffer, I was joking. . . . I already apologized sixteen times for that, Mrs. Soffer, you . . . (*While she's fulminating, Roy covers the mouthpiece with his hand and talks to Joe.*) This'll take a minute, *eat* already, what is this tasty sandwich here it's—(*He takes a bite of a sandwich.*) Mmmmm, liver or some . . . . Here.

(*He pitches the sandwich to Joe, who catches it and returns it to the platter.*)

ROY (*back to Mrs. Soffer*): Uh huh, uh huh. . . . No, I already told you, it wasn't a vacation, it was business, Mrs. Soffer, I have clients in Haiti, Mrs. Soffer,

I . . . . Listen, Ailene, YOU THINK I'M THE ONLY GODDAM LAWYER IN HISTORY EVER MISSED A COURT DATE? Don't make such a big fucking . . . . Hold. (*He hits the hold button.*) You HAG!

JOE: If this is a bad time . . .

ROY: *Bad* time? This is a *good* time! (*Button.*) Baby doll, get me . . . . Oh fuck, wait . . . (*Button, button.*) Hello? Yah. Sorry to keep you holding, Judge Hollins, I . . . . Oh *Mrs.* Hollins, sorry dear deep voice you got. Enjoying your visit? (*Hand over mouthpiece again, to Joe.*) She sounds like a truckdriver and he sounds like Kate Smith, very confusing. Nixon appointed him, all the geeks are Nixon appointees . . . (*To Mrs. Hollins.*) Yeah yeah right good so how many tickets dear? Seven. For what, *Cats, 42nd Street,* what? No you wouldn't like *La Cage,* trust me, I know. Oh for godsake . . . . Hold. (*Button, button.*) Baby doll, seven for *Cats* or something, anything hard to get, I don't give a fuck what and neither will they. (*Button; to Joe.*) You see *La Cage?*

JOE: No, I . . .

ROY: Fabulous. Best thing on Broadway. Maybe ever. (*Button.*) Who? Aw, Jesus H. Christ, Harry, *no,* Harry, Judge John Francis Grimes, Manhattan Family Court. Do I have to do every goddam thing myself? *Touch* the bastard, Harry, and don't call me on this line again, I told you not to . . .

JOE (*starting to get up*): Roy, uh, should I wait outside or . . .

ROY (*to Joe*): Oh sit. (*To Harry.*) You hold. I pay you to hold fuck you Harry you jerk. (*Button.*) Halfwit dick-brain. (*Instantly philosophical.*) I see the universe, Joe, as a kind of sandstorm in outer space with winds of mega-hurricane velocity, but instead of grains of sand it's shards and splinters of glass. You ever feel that way? Ever have one of those days?

JOE: I'm not sure I . . .

ROY: So how's life in Appeals? How's the Judge?

JOE: He sends his best.

ROY: He's a good man. Loyal. Not the brightest man on the bench, but he has manners. And a nice head of silver hair.

JOE: He gives me a lot of responsibility.

ROY: Yeah, like writing his decisions and signing his name.

JOE: Well . . .

ROY: He's a nice guy. And you cover admirably.

JOE: Well, thanks, Roy, I . . .

ROY (*button*): Yah? Who is *this?* Well who the fuck are *you?* Hold—(*button*) Harry? Eighty-seven grand, something like that. Fuck him. Eat me. New Jersey, chain of porno film stores in, uh, Weehawken. That's—Harry, that's the beauty of the law. (*Button.*) So, baby doll, what? *Cats?* Bleah. (*Button.*) *Cats!* It's about cats. Singing cats, you'll love it. Eight o'clock, the theatre's always at eight. (*Button.*) Fucking tourists. (*Button, then to Joe.*) Oh live a little, Joe, *eat* something for Christ sake—

JOE: Um, Roy, could you . . .

ROY: What? (*To Harry.*) Hold a minute. (*Button.*) Mrs. Soffer? Mrs. . . . (*Button.*) God-fucking-dammit to hell, where is . . .

JOE (*overlapping*): Roy, I'd really appreciate it if . . .

ROY (*overlapping*): Well she was here a minute ago, baby doll, see if . . .

(*The phone starts making three different beeping sounds, all at once.*)

ROY (*smashing buttons*): Jesus fuck this goddam thing . . .

JOE (*overlapping*): I really wish you wouldn't . . .

ROY (*overlapping*): Baby doll? Ring the *Post* get me Suzy see if . . .

(*The phone starts whistling loudly.*)

ROY: CHRIST!

JOE: *Roy.*

ROY (*into receiver*): Hold. (*Button; to Joe.*) *What?*

JOE: Could you please not take the Lord's name in vain
    (*Pause.*)
    I'm sorry. But please. At least while I'm . . .

ROY (*laughs, then*): Right. Sorry. Fuck. Only in America. (*Punches a button.*) Baby doll, tell 'em all to fuck off. Tell 'em I died. You handle Mrs. Soffer. Tell her it's on the way. Tell her I'm schtupping the judge. I'll call her back. I *will* call her. I *know* how much I borrowed. She's got four hundred times that stuffed up her . . . . Yeah, tell her I said that. (*Button. The phone is silent.*) So, Joe.

JOE: I'm sorry Roy, I just . . .

ROY: No no no no, principles count, I respect principles, I'm not religious but I like God and God likes me. Baptist, Catholic?

JOE: Mormon.

ROY: Mormon. Delectable. Absolutely. Only in America. So, Joe. Whattya think?

JOE: It's . . . well . . .

ROY: Crazy life.

JOE: Chaotic.

ROY: Well but God bless chaos. Right?

JOE: Ummm . . .

ROY: Huh. Mormons. I knew Mormons, in, um, Nevada.

JOE: Utah, mostly.

ROY: No, these Mormons were in Vegas.
    So. So, how'd you like to go to Washington and work for the Justice Department?

JOE: Sorry?

ROY: How'd you like to go to Washington and work for the Justice Department? All I gotta do is pick up the phone, talk to Ed, and you're in.

JOE: In . . . what, exactly?

ROY: Associate Assistant Something Big. Internal Affairs, heart of the woods, something nice with clout.

JOE: Ed . . . ?

ROY: Meese. The Attorney General.

JOE: Oh.

ROY: I just have to pick up the phone . . .

JOE: I have to think.

ROY: Of course.

> (*Pause.*)
>
> It's a great time to be in Washington, Joe.

JOE: Roy, it's incredibly exciting . . .

ROY: And it would mean something to me. You understand?

(*Little pause.*)

JOE: I . . . can't say how much I appreciate this Roy, I'm sort of . . . well, stunned, I mean . . . . Thanks, Roy. But I have to give it some thought. I have to ask my wife.

ROY: Your wife. Of course.

JOE: But I really appreciate . . .

ROY: Of course. Talk to your wife.

Scene 3

(*Later that day. Harper at home, alone. She is listening to the radio and talking to herself, as she often does. She speaks to the audience.*)

HARPER: People who are lonely, people left alone, sit talking nonsense to the air, imagining . . . beautiful systems dying, old fixed orders spiraling apart . . .

When you look at the ozone layer, from outside, from a spaceship, it looks like a pale blue halo, a gentle, shimmering aureole encircling the atmosphere encircling the earth. Thirty miles above our heads, a thin layer of three-atom oxygen molecules, product of photosynthesis, which explains the fussy vegetable preference for visible light, its rejection of darker rays and emanations. Danger from without. It's a kind of gift, from God, the crowning touch to the creation of the world: guardian angels, hands linked, make a spherical net, a blue-green nesting orb, a shell of safety for life itself. But everywhere, things are collapsing, lies surfacing, systems of defense giving way. . . . This is why, Joe, this is why I shouldn't be left alone.

> (*Little pause.*)
>
> I'd like to go traveling. Leave you behind to worry. I'll send postcards with strange stamps and tantalizing messages on the back. "Later maybe." "Nevermore . . ."

(*Mr. Lies, a travel agent, appears.*)

HARPER: Oh! You startled me!

MR. LIES: Cash, check or credit card?

HARPER: I remember you. You're from Salt Lake. You sold us the plane tickets when we flew here. What are you doing in Brooklyn?

MR. LIES: You said you wanted to travel . . .

HARPER: And here you are. How thoughtful.

MR. LIES: Mr. Lies. Of the International Order of Travel Agents. We mobilize the globe, we set people adrift, we stir the populace and send nomads eddying across the planet. We are adepts of motion, acolytes of the flux. Cash, check or credit card. Name your destination.

HARPER: Antarctica, maybe. I want to see the hole in the ozone. I heard on the radio . . .

MR. LIES (*he has a computer terminal in his briefcase*): I can arrange a guided tour. Now?

HARPER: Soon. Maybe soon. I'm not safe here you see. Things aren't right with me. Weird stuff happens . . .

MR. LIES: Like?

HARPER: Well, like you, for instance. Just appearing. Or last week . . . well never mind.

People are like planets, you need a thick skin. Things get to me, Joe stays away and now . . . . Well look. My dreams are talking back to me.

MR. LIES: It's the price of rootlessness. Motion sickness. The only cure: to keep moving.

HARPER: I'm undecided. I feel . . . that something's going to give. It's 1985. Fifteen years till the third millennium. Maybe Christ will come again. Maybe seeds will be planted, maybe there'll be harvests then, maybe early figs to eat, maybe new life, maybe fresh blood, maybe companionship and love and protection, safety from what's outside, maybe the door will hold, or maybe . . . maybe the troubles will come, and the end will come, and the sky will collapse and there will be terrible rains and showers of poison light, or maybe my life is really fine, maybe Joe loves me and I'm only crazy thinking otherwise, or maybe not, maybe it's even worse than I know, maybe . . . I want to know, maybe I don't. The suspense, Mr. Lies, it's killing me.

MR. LIES: I suggest a vacation.

HARPER (*hearing something*): That was the elevator. Oh God, I should fix myself up, I . . . . You have to go, you shouldn't be here . . . you aren't even real.

MR. LIES: Call me when you decide . . .

HARPER: Go!

(*The Travel Agent vanishes as Joe enters.*)

JOE: Buddy?

Buddy? Sorry I'm late. I was just . . . out. Walking. Are you mad?

HARPER: I got a little anxious.

JOE: Buddy kiss.

(*They kiss.*)

JOE: Nothing to get anxious about.

So. So how'd you like to move to Washington?

Scene 4

(*Same day. Louis and Prior outside the funeral home, sitting on a bench, both dressed in funereal finery, talking. The funeral service for Sarah Ironson has just concluded and Louis is about to leave for the cemetery.*)

LOUIS: My grandmother actually saw Emma Goldman speak. In Yiddish. But all Grandma could remember was that she spoke well and wore a hat.
    What a weird service. That rabbi . . .

PRIOR: A definite find. Get his number when you go to the graveyard. I want him to bury me.

LOUIS: Better head out there. Everyone gets to put dirt on the coffin once it's lowered in.

PRIOR: Oooh. Cemetery fun. Don't want to miss that.

LOUIS: It's an old Jewish custom to express love. Here, Grandma, have a shovelful. Latecomers run the risk of finding the grave completely filled.
    She was pretty crazy. She was up there in that home for ten years, talking to herself. I never visited. She looked too much like my mother.

PRIOR (hugs him): Poor Louis. I'm sorry your grandma is dead.

LOUIS: Tiny little coffin, huh?
    Sorry I didn't introduce you to . . . . I always get so closety at these family things.

PRIOR: Butch. You get butch. (Imitating.) "Hi Cousin Doris, you don't remember me I'm Lou, Rachel's boy." Lou, not Louis, because if you say Louis they'll hear the sibilant S.

LOUIS: I don't have a . . .

PRIOR: I don't blame you, hiding. Bloodlines. Jewish curses are the worst. I personally would dissolve if anyone ever looked me in the eye and said "Feh." Fortunately WASPs don't say "Feh." Oh and by the way, darling, cousin Doris is a dyke.

LOUIS: No.
    Really?

PRIOR: You don't notice anything. If I hadn't spent the last four years fellating you I'd swear you were straight.

LOUIS: You're in a pissy mood. Cat still missing?

(Little pause.)

PRIOR: Not a furball in sight. It's your fault.

LOUIS: It is?

PRIOR: I warned you, Louis. Names are important. Call an animal "Little Sheba" and you can't expect it to stick around. Besides, it's a dog's name.

LOUIS: I wanted a dog in the first place, not a cat. He sprayed my books.

PRIOR: He was a female cat.

LOUIS: Cats are stupid, high-strung predators. Babylonians sealed them up in bricks. Dogs have brains.

PRIOR: Cats have intuition.

LOUIS: A sharp dog is as smart as a really dull two-year-old child.

PRIOR: Cats know when something's wrong.

LOUIS: Only if you stop feeding them.

PRIOR: They know. That's why Sheba left, because she knew.

LOUIS: Knew what?

(Pause.)

PRIOR: I did my best Shirley Booth this morning, floppy slippers, housecoat, curlers, can of Little Friskies; "Come back, Little Sheba, come back. . . ." To no avail. Le chat, elle ne reviendra jamais, jamais . . .°
    (He removes his jacket, rolls up his sleeve, shows Louis a dark-purple spot on the underside of his arm near the shoulder.)
    See.

LOUIS: That's just a burst blood vessel.

PRIOR: Not according to the best medical authorities.

LOUIS: What?
    (Pause.)
    Tell me.

PRIOR: K.S., baby. Lesion number one. Lookit. The wine-dark kiss of the angel of death.

LOUIS (very softly, holding Prior's arm): Oh please . . .

PRIOR: I'm a lesionnaire. The Foreign Lesion. The American Lesion. Lesionnaire's disease.

LOUIS: Stop.

PRIOR: My troubles are lesion.

LOUIS: Will you stop.

PRIOR: Don't you think I'm handling this well?
    I'm going to die.

LOUIS: Bullshit.

PRIOR: Let go of my arm.

LOUIS: No.

PRIOR: Let go.

LOUIS (grabbing Prior, embracing him ferociously): No.

PRIOR: I can't find a way to spare you baby. No wall like the wall of hard scientific fact. K.S. Wham. Bang your head on that.

LOUIS: Fuck you. (Letting go.) Fuck you fuck you fuck you.

PRIOR: Now that's what I like to hear. A mature reaction.
    Let's go see if the cat's come home.
    Louis?

LOUIS: When did you find this?

PRIOR: I couldn't tell you.

LOUIS: Why?

PRIOR: I was scared, Lou.

LOUIS: Of what?

PRIOR: That you'll leave me.

LOUIS: Oh.

(Little pause.)

PRIOR: Bad timing, funeral and all, but I figured as long as we're on the subject of death . . .

LOUIS: I have to go bury my grandma.

PRIOR: Lou?
    (Pause.)
    Then you'll come home?

LOUIS: Then I'll come home.

Le chat . . . jamais: The cat will never ever return.

Scene 5

(Same day, later on. Split scene: Joe and Harper at home; Louis at the cemetery with Rabbi Isidor Chemelwitz and the little coffin.)

HARPER: Washington?

JOE: It's an incredible honor, buddy, and ...

HARPER: I have to think.

JOE: Of course.

HARPER: Say no.

JOE: You said you were going to think about it.

HARPER: I don't want to move to Washington.

JOE: Well I do.

HARPER: It's a giant cemetery, huge white graves and mausoleums everywhere.

JOE: We could live in Maryland. Or Georgetown.

HARPER: We're happy here.

JOE: That's not really true, buddy, we ...

HARPER: Well happy enough! Pretend-happy. That's better than nothing.

JOE: It's time to make some changes, Harper.

HARPER: No changes. Why?

JOE: I've been chief clerk for four years. I make twenty-nine thousand dollars a year. That's ridiculous. I graduated fourth in my class and I make less than anyone I know. And I'm ... I'm tired of being a clerk, I want to go where something good is happening.

HARPER: Nothing good happens in Washington. We'll forget church teachings and buy furniture at ... at *Conran's* and become yuppies. I have too much to do here.

JOE: Like what?

HARPER: I *do* have things ...

JOE: What things?

HARPER: I have to finish painting the bedroom.

JOE: You've been painting in there for over a year.

HARPER: I know, I .... It just isn't done because I never get time to finish it.

JOE: Oh that's ... that doesn't make sense. You have all the time in the world. You could finish it when I'm at work.

HARPER: I'm afraid to go in there alone.

JOE: Afraid of what?

HARPER: I heard someone in there. Metal scraping on the wall. A man with a knife, maybe.

JOE: There's no one in the bedroom, Harper.

HARPER: Not now.

JOE: Not this morning either.

HARPER: How do you know? You were at work this morning. There's something creepy about this place. Remember *Rosemary's Baby*?

JOE: *Rosemary's Baby*?

HARPER: Our apartment looks like that one. Wasn't that apartment in Brooklyn?

JOE: No, it was ...

HARPER: Well, it looked like this. It did.

JOE: Then let's move.

HARPER: Georgetown's worse. *The Exorcist* was in Georgetown.

JOE: The devil, everywhere you turn, huh, buddy.

HARPER: Yeah. Everywhere.

JOE: How many pills today, buddy?

HARPER: None. One. Three. Only three.

LOUIS *(pointing at the coffin)*: Why are there just two little wooden pegs holding the lid down?

RABBI ISIDOR CHEMELWITZ: So she can get out easier if she wants to.

LOUIS: I hope she stays put.

I pretended for years that she was already dead. When they called to say she had died it was a surprise. I abandoned her.

RABBI ISIDOR CHEMELWITZ: "Sharfer vi di tson fun a shlang iz an umdankbar kind!"

LOUIS: I don't speak Yiddish.

RABBI ISIDOR CHEMELWITZ: Sharper than the serpent's tooth is the ingratitude of children. Shakespeare. *King Lear*.

LOUIS: Rabbi, what does the Holy Writ say about someone who abandons someone he loves at a time of great need?

RABBI ISIDOR CHEMELWITZ: Why would a person do such a thing?

LOUIS: Because he has to. Maybe because this person's sense of the world, that it will change for the better with struggle, maybe a person who has this neo-Hegelian positivist sense of constant historical progress towards happiness or perfection or something, who feels very powerful because he feels connected to these forces, moving uphill all the time ... maybe that person can't, um, incorporate sickness into his sense of how things are supposed to go. Maybe vomit ... and sores and disease ... really frighten him, maybe ... he isn't so good with death.

RABBI ISIDOR CHEMELWITZ: The Holy Scriptures have nothing to say about such a person.

LOUIS: Rabbi, I'm afraid of the crimes I may commit.

RABBI ISIDOR CHEMELWITZ: Please, mister. I'm a sick old rabbi facing a long drive home to the Bronx. You want to confess, better you should find a priest.

LOUIS: But I'm not a Catholic, I'm a Jew.

RABBI ISIDOR CHEMELWITZ: Worse luck for you, bubbulah. Catholics believe in forgiveness. Jews believe in Guilt. *(He pats the coffin tenderly.)*

LOUIS: You just make sure those pegs are in good and tight.

RABBI ISIDOR CHEMELWITZ: Don't worry, mister. The life she had, she'll stay put. She's better off.

JOE: Look, I know this is scary for you. But try to understand what it means to me. Will you try?

HARPER: Yes.

JOE: Good. Really try.

I think things are starting to change in the world.

HARPER: But I don't want ...

JOE: Wait. For the good. Change for the good. America has rediscovered itself. Its sacred position among nations. And people aren't ashamed of that like they used to be. This is a great thing. The truth restored. Law restored. That's what President Reagan's done, Harper. He says "Truth exists and can be spoken proudly." And the country responds to him. We become better. More good. I need to be a part of that, I need something big to lift me up. I mean, six years ago the world seemed in decline, horrible, hopeless, full of unsolvable problems and crime and confusion and hunger and . . .

HARPER: But it still seems that way. More now than before. They say the ozone layer is . . .

JOE: Harper . . .

HARPER: And today out the window on Atlantic Avenue there was a schizophrenic traffic cop who was making these . . .

JOE: Stop it! I'm trying to make a point.

HARPER: So am I.

JOE: You aren't even making sense, you . . .

HARPER: My point is the world seems just as . . .

JOE: It only seems that way to you because you never go out in the world, Harper, and you have emotional problems.

HARPER: I do so get out in the world.

JOE: You don't. You stay in all day, fretting about imaginary . . .

HARPER: I get out. I do. You don't know what I do.

JOE: You don't stay in all day.

HARPER: No.

JOE: Well. . . . Yes you do.

HARPER: That's what you think.

JOE: Where do you go?

HARPER: Where do you go? When you walk.
    (*Pause, then angrily.*) And I DO NOT have emotional problems.

JOE: I'm sorry.

HARPER: And if I do have emotional problems it's from living with you. Or . . .

JOE: I'm sorry buddy, I didn't mean to . . .

HARPER: Or if you do think I do then you should never have married me. You have all these secrets and lies.

JOE: I want to be married to you, Harper.

HARPER: You shouldn't. You never should.
    (*Pause.*)
    Hey buddy. Hey buddy.

JOE: Buddy kiss . . .

(*They kiss.*)

HARPER: I heard on the radio how to give a blowjob.

JOE: What?

HARPER: You want to try?

JOE: You really shouldn't listen to stuff like that.

HARPER: Mormons can give blowjobs.

JOE: *Harper.*

HARPER (*imitating his tone*): Joe.
    It was a little Jewish lady with a German accent. This is a good time. For me to make a baby.

(*Little pause. Joe turns away.*)

HARPER: Then they went on to a program about holes in the ozone layer. Over Antarctica. Skin burns, birds go blind, icebergs melt. The world's coming to an end.

Scene 6

(*First week of November. In the men's room of the offices of the Brooklyn Federal Court of Appeals; Louis is crying over the sink; Joe enters.*)

JOE: Oh, um. . . . Morning.

LOUIS: Good morning, counselor.

JOE (*he watches Louis cry*): Sorry, I . . . I don't know your name.

LOUIS: Don't bother. Word processor. The lowest of the low.

JOE (*holding out hand*): Joe Pitt. I'm with Justice Wilson . . .

LOUIS: Oh, I know that. Counselor Pitt. Chief Clerk.

JOE: Were you . . . are you OK?

LOUIS: Oh, yeah. Thanks. What a nice man.

JOE: Not so nice.

LOUIS: What?

JOE: Not so nice. Nothing. You sure you're . . .

LOUIS: Life sucks shit. Life . . . just sucks shit.

JOE: What's wrong?

LOUIS: Run in my nylons.

JOE: Sorry . . . ?

LOUIS: Forget it. Look, thanks for asking.

JOE: Well . . .

LOUIS: I mean it really is nice of you.
    (*He starts crying again.*)
    Sorry, sorry, sick friend . . .

JOE: Oh, I'm sorry.

LOUIS: Yeah, yeah, well, that's sweet.
    Three of your colleagues have preceded you to this baleful sight and you're the first one to ask. The others just opened the door, saw me, and fled. I hope they had to pee real bad.

JOE (*handing him a wad of toilet paper*): They just didn't want to intrude.

LOUIS: Hah. Reaganite heartless macho asshole lawyers.

JOE: Oh, that's unfair.

LOUIS: What is? Heartless? Macho? Reaganite? Lawyer?

JOE: I voted for Reagan.

LOUIS: You did?

JOE: Twice.

LOUIS: Twice? Well, oh boy. A Gay Republican.

JOE: Excuse me?

LOUIS: Nothing.

JOE: I'm not . . .
    Forget it.

LOUIS: Republican? Not Republican? Or . . .

JOE: What?

LOUIS: What?

JOE: Not gay. I'm not gay.

LOUIS: Oh. Sorry.
    (*Blows his nose loudly.*) It's just . . .
JOE: Yes?
LOUIS: Well, sometimes you can tell from the way a person sounds that . . . I mean you *sound* like a . . .
JOE: No I don't. Like what?
LOUIS: Like a Republican.

(*Little pause. Joe knows he's being teased; Louis knows he knows. Joe decides to be a little brave.*)

JOE (*making sure no one else is around*): Do I? Sound like a . . . ?
LOUIS: What? Like a . . . ? Republican, or . . . ? Do I?
JOE: Do you what?
LOUIS: Sound like a . . . ?
JOE: Like a . . . ?
    I'm . . . confused.
LOUIS: Yes.
    My name is Louis. But all my friends call me Louise. I work in Word Processing. Thanks for the toilet paper.

(*Louis offers Joe his hand, Joe reaches, Louis feints and pecks Joe on the cheek, then exits.*)

Scene 7

(*A week later. Mutual dream scene. Prior is at a fantastic makeup table, having a dream, applying the face. Harper is having a pill-induced hallucination. She has these from time to time. For some reason, Prior has appeared in this one. Or Harper has appeared in Prior's dream. It is bewildering.*)

PRIOR (*alone, putting on makeup, then examining the results in the mirror; to the audience*): "I'm ready for my closeup, Mr. DeMille."
    One wants to move through life with elegance and grace, blossoming infrequently but with exquisite taste, and perfect timing, like a rare bloom, a zebra orchid. . . . One wants . . . . But one so seldom gets what one wants, does one? No. One does not. One gets fucked. Over. One . . . dies at thirty, robbed of . . . decades of majesty.
    Fuck this shit. Fuck this shit.
(*He almost crumbles; he pulls himself together; he studies his handiwork in the mirror.*)
    I look like a corpse. A corpsette. Oh my queen; you know you've hit rock-bottom when even drag is a drag.

(*Harper appears.*)

HARPER: Are you . . . . Who are you?
PRIOR: Who are you?
HARPER: What are you doing in my hallucination?
PRIOR: I'm not in your hallucination. You're in my dream.
HARPER: You're wearing makeup.
PRIOR: So are you.

HARPER: But you're a man.
PRIOR (*feigning dismay, shock, he mimes slashing his throat with his lipstick and dies, fabulously tragic. Then*): The hands and feet give it away.
HARPER: There must be some mistake here. I don't recognize you. You're not . . . . Are you my . . . some sort of imaginary friend?
PRIOR: No. Aren't you too old to have imaginary friends?
HARPER: I have emotional problems. I took too many pills. Why are you wearing makeup?
PRIOR: I was in the process of applying the face, trying to make myself feel better—I swiped the new fall colors at the Clinique counter at Macy's. (*Showing her.*)
HARPER: You stole these?
PRIOR: I was out of cash; it was an emotional emergency!
HARPER: Joe will be so angry. I promised him. No more pills.
PRIOR: These pills you keep alluding to?
HARPER: Valium. I take Valium. Lots of Valium.
PRIOR: And you're dancing as fast as you can.
HARPER: I'm not *addicted*. I don't believe in addiction, and I never . . . well, I never drink. And I *never* take drugs.
PRIOR: Well, smell *you*, Nancy Drew.
HARPER: Except Valium.
PRIOR: Except Valium; in wee fistfuls.
HARPER: It's terrible. Mormons are not supposed to be addicted to anything. I'm a Mormon.
PRIOR: I'm a homosexual.
HARPER: Oh! In my church we don't believe in homosexuals.
PRIOR: In my church we don't believe in Mormons.
HARPER: What church do . . . oh! (*She laughs.*) I get it.
    I don't understand this. If I didn't ever see you before and I don't think I did then I don't think you should be here, in this hallucination, because in my experience the mind, which is where hallucinations come from, shouldn't be able to make up anything that wasn't there to start with, that didn't enter it from experience, from the real world. Imagination can't create anything new, can it? It only recycles bits and pieces from the world and reassembles them into visions. . . . Am I making sense right now?
PRIOR: Given the circumstances, yes.
HARPER: So when we think we've escaped the unbearable ordinariness and, well, untruthfulness of our lives, it's really only the same old ordinariness and falseness rearranged into the appearance of novelty and truth. Nothing unknown is knowable. Don't you think it's depressing?
PRIOR: The limitations of the imagination?
HARPER: Yes.
PRIOR: It's something you learn after your second theme party: It's All Been Done Before.
HARPER: The world. Finite. Terribly, terribly . . . . Well . . .

This is the most depressing hallucination I've ever had.

PRIOR: Apologies. I do try to be amusing.

HARPER: Oh, well, don't apologize, you .... I can't expect someone who's really sick to entertain me.

PRIOR: How on earth did you know ...

HARPER: Oh that happens. This is the very threshold of revelation sometimes. You can see things ... how sick you are. Do you see anything about me?

PRIOR: Yes.

HARPER: What?

PRIOR: You are amazingly unhappy.

HARPER: Oh big deal. You meet a Valium addict and you figure out she's unhappy. That doesn't count. Of course I .... Something else. Something surprising.

PRIOR: Something surprising.

HARPER: Yes.

PRIOR: Your husband's a homo.

(*Pause.*)

HARPER: Oh, ridiculous.
    (*Pause, then very quietly.*)
    Really?

PRIOR (*shrugs*): Threshold of revelation.

HARPER: Well I don't like your revelations. I don't think you intuit well at all. Joe's a very normal man, he ...
    Oh God. Oh God. He .... Do homos take, like, lots of long walks?

PRIOR: Yes. We do. In stretch pants with lavender coifs. I just looked at you, and there was ...

HARPER: A sort of blue streak of recognition.

PRIOR: Yes.

HARPER: Like you knew me incredibly well.

PRIOR: Yes.

HARPER: Yes.
    I have to go now, get back, something just ... fell apart.
    Oh God, I feel so sad ...

PRIOR: I ... I'm sorry. I usually say, "Fuck the truth," but mostly, the truth fucks you.

HARPER: I see something else about you ...

PRIOR: Oh?

HARPER: Deep inside you, there's a part of you, the most inner part, entirely free of disease. I can see that.

PRIOR: Is that .... That isn't true.

HARPER: Threshold of revelation.
    Home ...

(*She vanishes.*)

PRIOR: People come and go so quickly here ...
    (*To himself in the mirror.*) I don't think there's any uninfected part of me. My heart is pumping polluted blood. I feel dirty.

(*He begins to wipe makeup off with his hands, smearing it around. A large gray feather falls from up above. Prior stops smearing the makeup and looks at the feather. He goes to it and picks it up.*)

A VOICE (*it is an incredibly beautiful voice*): Look up!

PRIOR (*looking up, not seeing anyone*): Hello?

A VOICE: Look up!

PRIOR: Who is that?

A VOICE: Prepare the way!

PRIOR: I don't see any ...

(*There is a dramatic change in lighting, from above.*)

A VOICE: Look up, look up,
    prepare the way
    the infinite descent
    A breath in air
    floating down
    Glory to ...

(*Silence.*)

PRIOR: Hello? Is that it? Helloooo!
    What the fuck ...? (*He holds himself.*)
    Poor me. Poor poor me. Why me? Why poor poor me? Oh I don't feel good right now. I really don't.

Scene 8

(*That night. Split scene: Harper and Joe at home; Prior and Louis in bed.*)

HARPER: Where were you?

JOE: Out.

HARPER: Where?

JOE: Just out. Thinking.

HARPER: It's late.

JOE: I had a lot to think about.

HARPER: I burned dinner.

JOE: Sorry.

HARPER: Not my dinner. My dinner was fine. Your dinner. I put it back in the oven and turned everything up as high as it could go and I watched till it burned black. It's still hot. Very hot. Want it?

JOE: You didn't have to do that.

HARPER: I know. It just seemed like the kind of thing a mentally deranged sex-starved pill-popping housewife would do.

JOE: Uh huh.

HARPER: So I did it. Who knows anymore what I have to do?

JOE: How many pills?

HARPER: A bunch. Don't change the subject.

JOE: I won't talk to you when you ...

HARPER: No. No. Don't do that! I'm ... I'm fine, pills are not the problem, not our problem, I WANT TO KNOW WHERE YOU'VE BEEN! I WANT TO KNOW WHAT'S GOING ON!

JOE: Going on with what? The job?

HARPER: Not the job.

JOE: I said I need more time.

HARPER: Not the job!

JOE: Mr. Cohn, I talked to him on the phone, he said I had to hurry ...

HARPER: Not the ...

JOE: But I can't get you to talk sensibly about anything so ...

HARPER: SHUT UP!

JOE: Then what?

HARPER: Stick to the subject.

JOE: I don't know what that is. You have something you want to ask me? Ask me. Go.

HARPER: I . . . can't. I'm scared of you.

JOE: I'm tired, I'm going to bed.

HARPER: Tell me without making me ask. Please.

JOE: This is crazy, I'm not . . .

HARPER: When you come through the door at night your face is never exactly the way I remembered it. I get surprised by something . . . mean and hard about the way you look. Even the weight of you in the bed at night, the way you breathe in your sleep seems unfamiliar.

You terrify me.

JOE (*cold*): I know who you are.

HARPER: Yes. I'm the enemy. That's easy. That doesn't change.

You think you're the only one who hates sex; I do; I hate it with you; I do. I dream that you batter away at me till all my joints come apart, like wax, and I fall into pieces. It's like a punishment. It was wrong of me to marry you. I knew it . . . (*She stops herself.*) It's a sin, and it's killing us both.

JOE: I can always tell when you've taken pills because it makes you red-faced and sweaty and frankly that's very often why I don't want to . . .

HARPER: Because . . .

JOE: Well, you aren't pretty. Not like this.

HARPER: I have something to ask you.

JOE: Then ASK! ASK! What in hell are you . . .

HARPER: Are you a homo?

(*Pause.*)

Are you? If you try to walk out right now I'll put your dinner back in the oven and turn it up so high the whole building will fill with smoke and everyone in it will asphyxiate. So help me God I will.

Now answer the question.

JOE: What if I . . .

(*Small pause.*)

HARPER: Then tell me, please. And we'll see.

JOE: No. I'm not.

I don't see what difference it makes.

LOUIS: Jews don't have any clear textual guide to the afterlife; even that it exists. I don't think much about it. I see it as a perpetual rainy Thursday afternoon in March. Dead leaves.

PRIOR: Eeeugh. Very Greco-Roman.

LOUIS: Well for us it's not the verdict that counts, it's the act of judgment. That's why I could never be a lawyer. In court all that matters is the verdict.

PRIOR: You could never be a lawyer because you are oversexed. You're too distracted.

LOUIS: Not distracted; *ab*stracted. I'm trying to make a point:

PRIOR: Namely:

LOUIS: It's the judge in his or her chambers, weighing, books open, pondering the evidence, ranging freely over categories: good, evil, innocent, guilty; the judge in the chamber of circumspection, not the judge on the bench with the gavel. The shaping of the law, not its execution.

PRIOR: The point, dear, the point . . .

LOUIS: That it should be the questions and shape of a life, its total complexity gathered, arranged and considered, which matters in the end, not some stamp of salvation or damnation which disperses all the complexity in some unsatisfying little decision—the balancing of the scales . . .

PRIOR: I like this; very zen; it's . . . reassuringly incomprehensible and useless. We who are about to die thank you.

LOUIS: You are not about to die.

PRIOR: It's not going well, really . . . two new lesions. My leg hurts. There's protein in my urine, the doctor says, but who knows what the fuck that portends. Anyway it shouldn't be there, the protein. My butt is chapped from diarrhea and yesterday I shat blood.

LOUIS: I really hate this. You don't tell me . . .

PRIOR: You get too upset, I wind up comforting you. It's easier . . .

LOUIS: Oh thanks.

PRIOR: If it's bad I'll tell you.

LOUIS: Shitting blood sounds bad to me.

PRIOR: And I'm telling you.

LOUIS: And I'm handling it.

PRIOR: Tell me some more about justice.

LOUIS: I *am* handling it.

PRIOR: Well Louis you win Trooper of the Month.

(*Louis starts to cry.*)

PRIOR: I take it back. You aren't Trooper of the Month. This isn't working . . .

Tell me some more about justice.

LOUIS: You are not about to die.

PRIOR: Justice . . .

LOUIS: . . . is an immensity, a confusing vastness. Justice is God.

Prior?

PRIOR: Hmmm?

LOUIS: You love me.

PRIOR: Yes.

LOUIS: What if I walked out on this? Would you hate me forever?

(*Prior kisses Louis on the forehead.*)

PRIOR: Yes.

JOE: I think we ought to pray. Ask God for help. Ask him together . . .

HARPER: God won't talk to me. I have to make up people to talk to me.

JOE: You have to keep asking.

HARPER: I forgot the question.

Oh yeah. God, is my husband a . . .

JOE (*scary*): Stop it. Stop it. I'm warning you.

Does it make any difference? That I might be one thing deep within, no matter how wrong or ugly that thing is, so long as I have fought, with everything I have, to kill it. What do you want from me? What do you want from me, Harper? More than that? For God's sake, there's nothing left, I'm a shell. There's nothing left to kill.

As long as my behavior is what I know it has to be. Decent. Correct. That alone in the eyes of God.

HARPER: No, no, not that, that's Utah talk, Mormon talk, I hate it, Joe, tell me, say it . . .

JOE: All I will say is that I am a very good man who has worked very hard to become good and you want to destroy that. You want to destroy me, but I am not going to let you do that.

(*Pause.*)

HARPER: I'm going to have a baby.

JOE: Liar.

HARPER: You liar.

A baby born addicted to pills. A baby who does not dream but who hallucinates, who stares up at us with big mirror eyes and who does not know who we are.

(*Pause.*)

JOE: Are you really . . .

HARPER: No. Yes. No. Yes. Get away from me.

Now we both have a secret.

PRIOR: One of my ancestors was a ship's captain who made money bringing whale oil to Europe and returning with immigrants—Irish mostly, packed in tight, so many dollars per head. The last ship he captained foundered off the coast of Nova Scotia in a winter tempest and sank to the bottom. He went down with the ship—la Grande Geste—but his crew took seventy women and kids in the ship's only longboat, this big, open rowboat, and when the weather got too rough, and they thought the boat was overcrowded, the crew started lifting people up and hurling them into the sea. Until they got the ballast right. They walked up and down the longboat, eyes to the water-line, and when the boat rode low in the water they'd grab the nearest passenger and throw them into the sea. The boat was leaky, see; seventy people; they arrived in Halifax with nine people on board.

LOUIS: Jesus.

PRIOR: I think about that story a lot now. People in a boat, waiting, terrified, while implacable, unsmiling men, irresistibly strong, seize . . . maybe the person next to you, maybe you, and with no warning at all, with time only for a quick intake of air you are pitched into freezing, turbulent water and salt and darkness to drown.

I like your cosmology, baby. While time is running out I find myself drawn to anything that's suspended, that lacks an ending—but it seems to me that it lets you off scot-free.

LOUIS: What do you mean?

PRIOR: No judgment, no guilt or responsibility.

LOUIS: For me.

PRIOR: For anyone. It was an editorial "you."

LOUIS: Please get better. Please.

Please don't get any sicker.

Scene 9

(*Third week in November. Roy and Henry, his doctor, in Henry's office.*)

HENRY: Nobody knows what causes it. And nobody knows how to cure it. The best theory is that we blame a retrovirus, the Human Immunodeficiency Virus. Its presence is made known to us by the useless antibodies which appear in reaction to its entrance into the bloodstream through a cut, or an orifice. The antibodies are powerless to protect the body against it. Why, we don't know. The body's immune system ceases to function. Sometimes the body even attacks itself. At any rate it's left open to a whole horror house of infections from microbes which it usually defends against.

Like Kaposi's sarcomas. These lesions. Or your throat problem. Or the glands.

We think it may also be able to slip past the blood-brain barrier into the brain. Which is of course very bad news.

And it's fatal in we don't know what percent of people with suppressed immune responses.

(*Pause.*)

ROY: This is very interesting, Mr. Wizard, but why the fuck are you telling me this?

(*Pause.*)

HENRY: Well, I have just removed one of three lesions which biopsy results will probably tell us is a Kaposi's sarcoma lesion. And you have a pronounced swelling of glands in your neck, groin, and armpits—lymphadenopathy is another sign. And you have oral candidiasis and maybe a little more fungus under the fingernails of two digits on your right hand. So that's why . . .

ROY: This disease . . .

HENRY: Syndrome.

ROY: Whatever. It afflicts mostly homosexuals and drug addicts.

HENRY: Mostly. Hemophiliacs are also at risk.

ROY: Homosexuals and drug addicts. So why are you implying that I . . .

(*Pause.*)

What are you implying, Henry?

HENRY: I don't . . .

ROY: I'm not a drug addict.

HENRY: Oh come on Roy.

ROY: What, what, come on Roy what? Do you think I'm a junkie, Henry, do you see tracks?

HENRY: This is absurd.

ROY: Say it.

HENRY: Say what?

ROY: Say, "Roy Cohn, you are a . . . "

HENRY: Roy.

ROY: "You are a . . . ." Go on. Not "Roy Cohn you are a drug fiend." "Roy Marcus Cohn, you are a . . . "

Go on, Henry, it starts with an "H."

HENRY: Oh I'm not going to . . .

ROY: *With an "H,"* Henry, and it isn't "Hemophiliac." Come on . . .

HENRY: What are you doing, Roy?

ROY: No, say it. I mean it. Say: "Roy Cohn, you are a homosexual."

(*Pause.*)

And I will proceed, systematically, to destroy your reputation and your practice and your career in New York State, Henry. Which you know I can do.

(*Pause.*)

HENRY: Roy, you have been seeing me since 1958. Apart from the facelifts I have treated you for everything from syphilis . . .

ROY: From a whore in Dallas.

HENRY: From syphilis to venereal warts. In your rectum. Which you may have gotten from a whore in Dallas, but it wasn't a female whore.

(*Pause.*)

ROY: So say it.

HENRY: Roy Cohn, you are . . .

You have had sex with men, many many times, Roy, and one of them, or any number of them, has made you very sick. You have AIDS.

ROY: AIDS.

Your problem, Henry, is that you are hung up on words, on labels, that you believe they mean what they seem to mean. AIDS. Homosexual. Gay. Lesbian. You think these are names that tell you who someone sleeps with, but they don't tell you that.

HENRY: No?

ROY: No. Like all labels they tell you one thing and one thing only: where does an individual so identified fit in the food chain, in the pecking order? Not ideology, or sexual taste, but something much simpler: clout. Not who I fuck or who fucks me, but who will pick up the phone when I call, who owes me favors. This is what a label refers to. Now to someone who does not understand this, homosexual is what I am because I have sex with men. But really this is wrong. Homosexuals are not men who sleep with other men. Homosexuals are men who in fifteen years of trying cannot get a pissant antidiscrimination bill through City Council. Homosexuals are men who know nobody and who nobody knows. Who have zero clout. Does this sound like me, Henry?

HENRY: No.

ROY: No. I have clout. A lot. I can pick up this phone, punch fifteen numbers, and you know who will be on the other end in under five minutes, Henry?

HENRY: The President.

ROY: Even better, Henry. His wife.

HENRY: I'm impressed.

ROY: I don't want you to be impressed. I want you to understand. This is not sophistry. And this is not hypocrisy. This is reality. I have sex with men. But unlike nearly every other man of whom this is true, I bring the guy I'm screwing to the White House and President Reagan smiles at us and shakes his hand. Because *what* I am is defined entirely by *who* I am. Roy Cohn is not a homosexual. Roy Cohn is a heterosexual man, Henry, who fucks around with guys.

HENRY: OK, Roy.

ROY: And what is my diagnosis, Henry?

HENRY: You have AIDS, Roy.

ROY: No, Henry, no. AIDS is what homosexuals have. I have liver cancer.

(*Pause.*)

HENRY: Well, whatever the fuck you have, Roy, it's very serious, and I haven't got a damn thing for you. The NIH in Bethesda has a new drug called AZT with a two-year waiting list that not even I can get you onto. So get on the phone, Roy, and dial the fifteen numbers, and tell the First Lady you need in on an experimental treatment for liver cancer, because you can call it any damn thing you want, Roy, but what it boils down to is very bad news.

ACT 2
IN VITRO •
December 1985–January 1986

Scene 1

(*Night, the third week in December. Prior alone on the floor of his bedroom; he is much worse.*)

PRIOR: Louis, Louis, please wake up, oh God.

(*Louis runs in.*)

PRIOR: I think something horrible is wrong with me I can't breathe . . .

LOUIS (*starting to exit*): I'm calling the ambulance.

PRIOR: No, wait, I . . .

LOUIS: *Wait?* Are you fucking crazy? Oh God you're on fire, your head is on fire.

PRIOR: It hurts, it hurts . . .

LOUIS: I'm calling the ambulance.

PRIOR: I don't want to go to the hospital, I don't want to go to the hospital please let me lie here, just . . .

LOUIS: No, no, God, Prior, stand up . . .

PRIOR: DON'T TOUCH MY LEG!

LOUIS: We have to . . . oh God this is so crazy.

PRIOR: I'll be OK if I just lie here Lou, really, if I can only sleep a little . . .

(*Louis exits.*)

PRIOR: Louis?

> *NO! NO!* Don't call, you'll send me there and I won't come back, please, please Louis I'm begging, baby, please . . .
>
> (*Screams.*) LOUIS!!

LOUIS (*from off; hysterical*): WILL YOU SHUT THE FUCK UP!

PRIOR (*trying to stand*): Aaaah. I have . . . to go to the bathroom. Wait. Wait, just . . . oh. Oh God. (*He shits himself.*)

LOUIS (*entering*): Prior? They'll be here in . . .

> Oh my God.

PRIOR: I'm sorry, I'm sorry.

LOUIS: What did . . . ? What?

PRIOR: I had an accident.

(*Louis goes to him.*)

LOUIS: This is blood.

PRIOR: Maybe you shouldn't touch it . . . me. . . . I . . . (*He faints.*)

LOUIS (*quietly*): Oh help. Oh help. Oh God oh God oh God help me I can't I can't I can't.

Scene 2

(*Same night. Harper is sitting at home, all alone, with no lights on. We can barely see her. Joe enters, but he doesn't turn on the lights.*)

JOE: Why are you sitting in the dark? Turn on the light.

HARPER: No. I heard the sounds in the bedroom again. I know someone was in there.

JOE: No one was.

HARPER: Maybe actually in the bed, under the covers with a knife.

> Oh, boy. Joe. I, um, I'm thinking of going away. By which I mean: I think I'm going off again. You . . . you know what I mean?

JOE: Please don't. Stay. We can fix it. I pray for that. This is my fault, but I can correct it. You have to try too . . .

(*He turns on the light. She turns it off again.*)

HARPER: When you pray, what do you pray for?

JOE: I pray for God to crush me, break me up into little pieces and start all over again.

HARPER: Oh. Please. Don't pray for that.

JOE: I had a book of Bible stories when I was a kid. There was a picture I'd look at twenty times every day: Jacob wrestles with the angel. I don't really remember the story, or why the wrestling—just the picture. Jacob is young and very strong. The angel is . . . a beautiful man, with golden hair and wings, of course. I still dream about it. Many nights. I'm . . . . It's me. In that struggle. Fierce, and unfair. The angel is not human, and it holds nothing back, so how could

anyone human win, what kind of a fight is that? It's not just. Losing means your soul thrown down in the dust, your heart torn out from God's. But you can't not lose.

HARPER: In the whole entire world, you are the only person, the only person I love or have ever loved. And I love you terribly. Terribly. That's what's so awfully, irreducibly real. I can make up anything but I can't dream that away.

JOE: Are you . . . are you really going to have a baby?

HARPER: It's my time, and there's no blood. I don't really know. I suppose it wouldn't be a great thing. Maybe I'm just not bleeding because I take too many pills. Maybe I'll give birth to a pill. That would give a new meaning to pill-popping, huh?

> I think you should go to Washington. Alone. Change, like you said.

JOE: I'm not going to leave you, Harper.

HARPER: Well maybe not. But I'm going to leave you.

Scene 3

(*One AM, the next morning. Louis and a nurse, Emily, are sitting in Prior's room in the hospital.*)

EMILY: He'll be all right now.

LOUIS: No he won't.

EMILY: No. I guess not. I gave him something that makes him sleep.

LOUIS: Deep asleep?

EMILY: Orbiting the moons of Jupiter.

LOUIS: A good place to be.

EMILY: Anyplace better than here. You his . . . uh?

LOUIS: Yes. I'm his uh.

EMILY: This must be hell for you.

LOUIS: It is. Hell. The After Life. Which is not at all like a rainy afternoon in March, by the way, Prior. A lot more vivid than I'd expected. Dead leaves, but the crunchy kind. Sharp, dry air. The kind of long, luxurious dying feeling that breaks your heart.

EMILY: Yeah, well we all get to break our hearts on this one.

> He seems like a nice guy. Cute.

LOUIS: Not like this.

> Yes, he is. Was. Whatever.

EMILY: Weird name. Prior Walter. Like, "The Walter before this one."

LOUIS: Lots of Walters before this one. Prior is an old old family name in an old old family. The Walters go back to the Mayflower and beyond. Back to the Norman Conquest. He says there's a Prior Walter stitched into the Bayeux tapestry.

EMILY: Is that impressive?

LOUIS: Well, it's old. Very old. Which in some circles equals impressive.

EMILY: Not in my circle. What's the name of the tapestry?

LOUIS: The Bayeux tapestry. Embroidered by La Reine Mathilde.

EMILY: I'll tell my mother. She embroiders. Drives me nuts.

LOUIS: Manual therapy for anxious hands.

EMILY: Maybe you should try it.

LOUIS: Mathilde stitched while William the Conqueror was off to war. She was capable of . . . more than loyalty. Devotion.

> She waited for him, she stitched for years. And if he had come back broken and defeated from war, she would have loved him even more. And if he had returned mutilated, ugly, full of infection and horror, she would still have loved him; fed by pity, by a sharing of pain, she would love him even more, and even more, and she would never, never have prayed to God, please let him die if he can't return to me whole and healthy and able to live a normal life. . . . If he had died, she would have buried her heart with him.
>
> So what the fuck is the matter with me?
> (*Little pause.*)
> Will he sleep through the night?

EMILY: At least.

LOUIS: I'm going.

EMILY: It's one A.M. Where do you have to go at . . .

LOUIS: I know what time it is. A walk. Night air, good for the . . . . The park.

EMILY: Be careful.

LOUIS: Yeah. Danger.

> Tell him, if he wakes up and you're still on, tell him goodbye, tell him I had to go.

Scene 4

(*An hour later. Split scene. Joe and Roy in a fancy [straight] bar; Louis and a Man in the Rambles in Central Park. Joe and Roy are sitting at the bar; the place is brightly lit. Joe has a plate of food in front of him but he isn't eating. Roy occasionally reaches over the table and forks small bites off Joe's plate. Roy is drinking heavily, Joe not at all. Louis and the Man are eyeing each other, each alternating interest and indifference.*)

JOE: The pills were something she started when she miscarried or . . . no, she took some before that. She had a really bad time at home, when she was a kid, her home was really bad. I think a lot of drinking and physical stuff. She doesn't talk about that, instead she talks about . . . the sky falling down, people with knives hiding under sofas. Monsters. Mormons. Everyone thinks Mormons don't come from homes like that, we aren't supposed to behave that way, but we do. It's not lying, or being two-faced. Everyone tries very hard to live up to God's strictures, which are very . . . um . . .

ROY: Strict.

JOE: I shouldn't be bothering you with this.

ROY: No, please. Heart to heart. Want another . . . . What is that, seltzer?

JOE: The failure to measure up hits people very hard. From such a strong desire to be good they feel very far from goodness when they fail.

> What scares me is that maybe what I really love in her is the part of her that's farthest from the light, from God's love; maybe I was drawn to that in the first place. And I'm keeping it alive because I need it.

ROY: Why would you need it?

JOE: There are things . . . . I don't know how well we know ourselves. I mean, what if? I know I married her because she . . . because I loved it that she was always wrong, always doing something wrong, like one step out of step. In Salt Lake City that stands out. I never stood out, on the outside, but inside, it was hard for me. To pass.

ROY: Pass?

JOE: Yeah.

ROY: Pass as what?

JOE: Oh. Well. . . . As someone cheerful and strong. Those who love God with an open heart unclouded by secrets and struggles are cheerful; God's easy simple love for them shows in how strong and happy they are. The saints.

ROY: But you had secrets? Secret struggles . . .

JOE: I wanted to be one of the elect, one of the Blessed. You feel you ought to be, that the blemishes are yours by choice, which of course they aren't. Harper's sorrow, that really deep sorrow, she didn't choose that. But it's there.

ROY: You didn't put it there.

JOE: No.

ROY: You sound like you think you did.

JOE: I am responsible for her.

ROY: Because she's your wife.

JOE: That. And I do love her.

ROY: Whatever. She's your wife. And so there are obligations. To her. But also to yourself.

JOE: She'd fall apart in Washington.

ROY: Then let her stay here.

JOE: She'll fall apart if I leave her.

ROY: Then bring her to Washington.

JOE: I just can't, Roy. She needs me.

ROY: Listen, Joe. I'm the best divorce lawyer in the business.

(*Little pause.*)

JOE: Can't Washington wait?

ROY: You do what you need to do, Joe. What *you* need. *You*. Let her life go where it wants to go. You'll both be better for that. *Somebody* should get what they want.

MAN: What do you want?

LOUIS: I want you to fuck me, hurt me, make me bleed.

MAN: I want to.

LOUIS: Yeah?

MAN: I want to hurt you.

LOUIS: Fuck me.

MAN: Yeah?

LOUIS: Hard.

MAN: Yeah? You been a bad boy?

(*Pause. Louis laughs, softly.*)

LOUIS: Very bad. Very bad.

MAN: You need to be punished, boy?

LOUIS: Yes. I do.

MAN: Yes what?

(*Little pause.*)

LOUIS: Um, I . . .

MAN: Yes *what*, boy?

LOUIS: Oh. Yes sir.

MAN: I want you to take me to your place, boy.

LOUIS: No, I can't do that.

MAN: No *what*?

LOUIS: No sir, I can't, I . . .
      I don't live alone, sir.

MAN: Your lover know you're out with a man tonight, boy?

LOUIS: No sir, he . . .
      My lover doesn't know.

MAN: Your lover know you . . .

LOUIS: Let's change the subject, OK? Can we go to your place?

MAN: I live with my parents.

LOUIS: Oh.

ROY: Everyone who makes it in this world makes it because somebody older and more powerful takes an interest. The most precious asset in life, I think, is the ability to be a good son. You have that, Joe. Somebody who can be a good son to a father who pushes them farther than they would otherwise go. I've had many fathers, I owe my life to them, powerful, powerful men. Walter Winchell, Edgar Hoover. Joe McCarthy most of all. He valued me because I am a good lawyer, but he loved me because I was and am a good son. He was a very difficult man, very guarded and cagey; I brought out something tender in him. He would have died for me. And me for him. Does this embarrass you?

JOE: I had a hard time with my father.

ROY: Well sometimes that's the way. Then you have to find other fathers, substitutes, I don't know. The father-son relationship is central to life. Women are for birth, beginning, but the father is continuance. The son offers the father his life as a vessel for carrying forth his father's dream. Your father's living?

JOE: Um, dead.

ROY: He was . . . what? A difficult man?

JOE: He was in the military. He could be very unfair. And cold.

ROY: But he loved you.

JOE: I don't know.

ROY: No, no, Joe, he did, I know this. Sometimes a father's love has to be very, very hard, unfair even, cold to make his son grow strong in a world like this. This isn't a good world.

MAN: Here, then.

LOUIS: I . . . . Do you have a rubber?

MAN: I don't use rubbers.

LOUIS: You should. (*He takes one from his coat pocket.*) Here.

MAN: I don't use them.

LOUIS: Forget it, then. (*He starts to leave.*)

MAN: No, wait.
      Put it on me. Boy.

LOUIS: Forget it, I have to get back. Home. I must be going crazy.

MAN: Oh come on please he won't find out.

LOUIS: It's cold. Too cold.

MAN: It's never too cold, let me warm you up. Please?

(*They begin to fuck.*)

MAN: Relax.

LOUIS (*a small laugh*): Not a chance.

MAN: It . . .

LOUIS: What?

MAN: I think it broke. The rubber. You want me to keep going? (*Little pause.*) Pull out? Should I . . .

LOUIS: Keep going.
      Infect me.
      I don't care. I don't care.

(*Pause. The Man pulls out.*)

MAN: I . . . um, look, I'm sorry, but I think I want to go.

LOUIS: Yeah.
      Give my best to mom and dad.

(*The Man slaps him.*)

LOUIS: Ow!

(*They stare at each other.*)

LOUIS: It was a joke.

(*The Man leaves.*)

ROY: How long have we known each other?

JOE: Since 1980.

ROY: Right. A long time. I feel close to you, Joe. Do I advise you well?

JOE: You've been an incredible friend, Roy, I . . .

ROY: I want to be family. Familia, as my Italian friends call it. La Familia. A lovely word. It's important for me to help you, like I was helped.

JOE: I owe practically everything to you, Roy.

ROY: I'm dying, Joe. Cancer.

JOE: Oh my God.

ROY: Please. Let me finish.
      Few people know this and I'm telling you this only because . . . . I'm not afraid of death. What can death bring that I haven't faced? I've lived; life is the worst. (*Gently mocking himself.*) Listen to me, I'm a philosopher.
      Joe. You must do this. You must must must. Love; that's a trap. Responsibility; that's a trap too. Like a father to a son I tell you this: Life is full of horror; nobody escapes, nobody; save yourself. Whatever

pulls on you, whatever needs from you, threatens you. Don't be afraid; people are so afraid; don't be afraid to live in the raw wind, naked, alone.... Learn at least this: What you are capable of. Let nothing stand in your way.

Scene 5

(*Three days later. Prior and Belize in Prior's hospital room. Prior is very sick but improving. Belize has just arrived.*)

PRIOR: Miss Thing.

BELIZE: Ma cherie bichette.

PRIOR: Stella.

BELIZE: Stella for star. Let me see. (*Scrutinizing Prior.*) You look like shit, why yes indeed you do, comme la merde!°

PRIOR: Merci.

BELIZE (*taking little plastic bottles from his bag, handing them to Prior*): Not to despair, Belle Reeve. Lookie! Magic goop!

PRIOR (*opening a bottle, sniffing*): Pooh! What kinda crap is that?

BELIZE: Beats me. Let's rub it on your poor blistered body and see what it does.

PRIOR: This is not Western medicine, these bottles . . .

BELIZE: Voodoo cream. From the botanica° 'round the block.

PRIOR: And you a registered nurse.

BELIZE (*sniffing it*): Beeswax and cheap perfume. Cut with Jergen's Lotion. Full of good vibes and love from some little black Cubana witch in Miami.

PRIOR: Get that trash away from me, I am immune-suppressed.

BELIZE: I *am* a health professional. I *know* what I'm doing.

PRIOR: It stinks. Any word from Louis?

(*Pause. Belize starts giving Prior a gentle massage.*)

PRIOR: Gone.

BELIZE: He'll be back. I know the type. Likes to keep a girl on edge.

PRIOR: It's been . . .

(*Pause.*)

BELIZE (*trying to jog his memory*): How long?

PRIOR: I don't remember.

BELIZE: How long have you been here?

PRIOR (*getting suddenly upset*): I don't remember, I don't give a fuck. I want Louis. I want my fucking boyfriend, where the fuck is he? I'm dying, I'm dying, where's Louis?

BELIZE: Shhhh, shhh . . .

PRIOR: This is a very strange drug, this drug. Emotional lability, for starters.

BELIZE: Save a tab or two for me.

PRIOR: Oh no, not this drug, ce n'est pas pour la joyeux noël et la bonne année, this drug she is serious poisonous chemistry, ma pauvre bichette.°
    And not just disorienting. I hear things. Voices.

BELIZE: Voices.

PRIOR: A voice.

BELIZE: Saying what?

(*Pause.*)

PRIOR: I'm not supposed to tell.

BELIZE: You better tell the doctor. Or I will.

PRIOR: No no don't. Please. I want the voice; it's wonderful. It's all that's keeping me alive. I don't want to talk to some intern about it.
    You know what happens? When I hear it, I get hard.

BELIZE: Oh my.

PRIOR: Comme ça. (*He uses his arm to demonstrate.*) And you know I am slow to rise.

BELIZE: My jaw aches at the memory.

PRIOR: And would you deny me this little solace—betray my concupiscence to Florence Nightingale's storm troopers?

BELIZE: Perish the thought, ma bébé.°

PRIOR: They'd change the drug just to spoil the fun.

BELIZE: You and your boner can depend on me.

PRIOR: Je t'adore, ma belle nègre.°

BELIZE: All this girl-talk shit is politically incorrect, you know. We should have dropped it back when we gave up drag.

PRIOR: I'm sick, I get to be politically incorrect if it makes me feel better. You sound like Lou.
    (*Little pause.*)
    Well, at least I have the satisfaction of knowing he's in anguish somewhere. I loved his anguish. Watching him stick his head up his asshole and eat his guts out over some relatively minor moral conundrum—it was the best show in town. But Mother warned me: if they get overwhelmed by the little things . . .

BELIZE: They'll be belly-up bustville when something big comes along.

PRIOR: Mother warned me.

BELIZE: And they do come along.

PRIOR: But I didn't listen.

BELIZE: No. (*Doing Hepburn.*) Men are beasts.

PRIOR (*also Hepburn*): The absolute lowest.

BELIZE: I have to go. If I want to spend my whole lonely life looking after white people I can get underpaid to do it.

PRIOR: You're just a Christian martyr.

BELIZE: Whatever happens, baby, I will be here for you.

PRIOR: Je t'aime.°

---

comme la merde: Like shit.   botanica: Shop that sells magic charms and herbs.

ce n'est pas . . . bichette: This drug isn't for a merry Christmas or a happy New Year . . . my poor little bitch.   ma bébé: My baby.   Je t'adore . . . nègre: I adore you, my beautiful negro.   Je t'aime: I love you.

BELIZE: Je t'aime. Don't go crazy on me, girlfriend, I already got enough crazy queens for one lifetime. For two. I can't be bothering with dementia.

PRIOR: I promise.

BELIZE (*touching him; softly*): Ouch.

PRIOR: Ouch. Indeed.

BELIZE: Why'd they have to pick on you?
   And eat more, girlfriend, you really do look like shit.

(*Belize leaves.*)

PRIOR (*after waiting a beat*): He's gone.
   Are you still . . .

VOICE: I can't stay. I will return.

PRIOR: Are you one of those "Follow me to the other side" voices?

VOICE: No. I am no nightbird. I am a messenger . . .

PRIOR: You have a beautiful voice, it sounds . . . like a viola, like a perfectly tuned, tight string, balanced, the truth. . . . Stay with me.

VOICE: Not now. Soon I will return, I will reveal myself to you; I am glorious, glorious; my heart, my countenance and my message. You must prepare.

PRIOR: For what? I don't want to . . .

VOICE: No death, no:
   A marvelous work and a wonder we undertake, an edifice awry we sink plumb and straighten, a great Lie we abolish, a great error correct, with the rule, sword and broom of Truth!

PRIOR: What are you talking about, I . . .

VOICE: I am on my way; when I am manifest, our Work begins:
   Prepare for the parting of the air,
   The breath, the ascent,
   Glory to . . .

Scene 6

(*The second week of January. Martin, Roy and Joe in a fancy Manhattan restaurant.*)

MARTIN: It's a revolution in Washington, Joe. We have a new agenda and finally a real leader. They got back the Senate but we have the courts. By the nineties the Supreme Court will be block-solid Republican appointees, and the Federal bench—Republican judges like land mines, everywhere, everywhere they turn. Affirmative action? Take it to court. Boom! Land mine. And we'll get our way on just about everything: abortion, defense, Central America, family values, a live investment climate. We have the White House locked till the year 2000. And beyond. A permanent fix on the Oval Office? It's possible. By '92 we'll get the Senate back, and in ten years the South is going to give us the House. It's really the end of Liberalism. The end of New Deal Socialism. The end of ipso facto secular humanism. The dawning of a genuinely American political personality. Modeled on Ronald Wilson Reagan.

JOE: It sounds great, Mr. Heller.

MARTIN: Martin. And Justice is the hub. Especially since Ed Meese took over. He doesn't specialize in Fine Points of the Law. He's a flatfoot, a cop. He reminds me of Teddy Roosevelt.

JOE: I can't wait to meet him.

MARTIN: Too bad, Joe, he's been dead for sixty years!

(*There is a little awkwardness. Joe doesn't respond.*)

MARTIN: Teddy Roosevelt. You said you wanted to . . . . Little joke. It reminds me of the story about the . . .

ROY (*smiling, but nasty*): Aw shut the fuck up Martin.
   (*To Joe.*) You see that? Mr. Heller here is one of the mighty, Joseph, in D.C. he sitteth on the right hand of the man who sitteth on the right hand of The Man. And yet I can say "shut the fuck up" and he will take no offense. Loyalty. He . . .
   Martin?

MARTIN: Yes, Roy?

ROY: Rub my back.

MARTIN: Roy . . .

ROY: No no really, a sore spot, I get them all the time now, these . . . . Rub it for me darling, would you do that for me?

(*Martin rubs Roy's back. They both look at Joe.*)

ROY (*to Joe*): How do you think a handful of Bolsheviks turned St. Petersburg into Leningrad in one afternoon? *Comrades*. Who do for each other. Marx and Engels. Lenin and Trotsky. Josef Stalin and Franklin Delano Roosevelt.

(*Martin laughs.*)

ROY: *Comrades*, right Martin?

MARTIN: This man, Joe, is a Saint of the Right.

JOE: I know, Mr. Heller, I . . .

ROY: And you see what I mean, Martin? He's special, right?

MARTIN: Don't embarrass him, Roy.

ROY: Gravity, decency, smarts! His strength is as the strength of ten because his heart is pure! And he's a Royboy, one hundred percent.

MARTIN: We're on the move, Joe. On the move.

JOE: Mr. Heller, I . . .

MARTIN (*ending backrub*): We can't wait any longer for an answer.

(*Little pause.*)

JOE: Oh. Um, I . . .

ROY: Joe's a married man, Martin.

MARTIN: Aha.

ROY: With a wife. She doesn't care to go to D.C., and so Joe cannot go. And keeps us dangling. We've seen that kind of thing before, haven't we? These men and their wives.

MARTIN: Oh yes. Beware.

JOE: I really can't discuss this under . . .

MARTIN: Then *don't* discuss. Say yes, Joe.

ROY: Now.

MARTIN: Say yes I will.

ROY: Now.

Now. I'll hold my breath till you do, I'm turning blue waiting.... *Now*, goddammit!

MARTIN: Roy, calm down, it's not . . .

ROY: Aw, fuck it. (*He takes a letter from his jacket pocket, hands it to Joe.*)

Read. Came today.

(*Joe reads the first paragraph, then looks up.*)

JOE: Roy. This is . . . Roy, this is terrible.

ROY: You're telling me.

A letter from the New York State Bar Association, Martin.

They're gonna try and disbar me.

MARTIN: Oh my.

JOE: Why?

ROY: Why, Martin?

MARTIN: Revenge.

ROY: The whole Establishment. Their little rules. Because I know no rules. Because I don't see the Law as a dead and arbitrary collection of antiquated dictums, thou shall, thou shalt not, because, because I know the Law's a pliable, breathing, sweating . . . *organ*, because, because . . .

MARTIN: Because he borrowed half a million from one of his clients.

ROY: Yeah, well, there's that.

MARTIN: *And* he forgot to *return* it.

JOE: Roy, that's . . . . You borrowed money from a client?

ROY: I'm deeply ashamed.

(*Little pause.*)

JOE (*very sympathetic*): Roy, you know how much I admire you. Well I mean I know you have unorthodox ways, but I'm sure you only did what you thought at the time you needed to do. And I have faith that . . .

ROY: Not so damp, please. I'll deny it was a loan. She's got no paperwork. Can't prove a fucking thing.

(*Little pause. Martin studies the menu.*)

JOE (*handing back the letter, more official in tone*): Roy I really appreciate your telling me this, and I'll do whatever I can to help.

ROY (*holding up a hand, then, carefully*): I'll tell you what you can do.

I'm about to be tried, Joe, by a jury that is not a jury of my peers. The disbarment committee: genteel gentleman Brahmin lawyers, country-club men. I offend them, to these men . . . I'm what, Martin, some sort of filthy little Jewish troll?

MARTIN: Oh well, I wouldn't go so far as . . .

ROY: Oh well I would.

Very fancy lawyers, these disbarment committee lawyers, fancy lawyers with fancy corporate clients and complicated cases. Antitrust suits. Deregulation.

Environmental control. Complex cases like these need Justice Department cooperation like flowers need the sun. Wouldn't you say that's an accurate assessment, Martin?

MARTIN: I'm not here, Roy. I'm not hearing any of this.

ROY: No. Of course not.

Without the light of the sun, Joe, these cases, and the fancy lawyers who represent them, will wither and die.

A well-placed friend, someone in the Justice Department, say, can turn off the sun. Cast a deep shadow on my behalf. Make them shiver in the cold. If they overstep. They would fear that.

(*Pause.*)

JOE: Roy. I don't understand.

ROY: You do.

(*Pause.*)

JOE: You're not asking me to . . .

ROY: Sssshhhh. Careful.

JOE (*a beat, then*): Even if I said yes to the job, it would be illegal to interfere. With the hearings. It's unethical. No. I can't.

ROY: Un-ethical.

Would you excuse us, Martin?

MARTIN: Excuse you?

ROY: Take a walk, Martin. For real.

(*Martin leaves.*)

ROY: Un-ethical. Are you trying to embarrass me in front of my friend?

JOE: Well it is unethical, I can't . . .

ROY: Boy, you are really something. What the fuck do you think this is, Sunday School?

JOE: No, but Roy this is . . .

ROY: This is . . . this is gastric juices churning, this is enzymes and acids, this is intestinal is what this is, bowel movement and blood-red meat — this stinks, this is *politics*, Joe, the game of being alive. And you think you're . . . . What? Above that? Above alive is what? Dead! In the clouds! You're on earth, goddammit! Plant a foot, stay a while.

I'm sick. They smell I'm weak. They want blood this time. I must have eyes in Justice. In Justice you will protect me.

JOE: Why can't Mr. Heller . . .

ROY: Grow up, Joe. The administration can't get involved.

JOE: But I'd be part of the administration. The same as him.

ROY: Not the same. Martin's Ed's man. And Ed's Reagan's man. So Martin's Reagan's man.

And you're mine.

(*Little pause. He holds up the letter.*)

This will never be. Understand me?

(*He tears the letter up.*)

I'm gonna be a lawyer, Joe, I'm gonna be a lawyer, Joe, I'm gonna be a goddam motherfucking legally licensed member of the bar lawyer, just like my daddy was, till my last bitter day on earth, Joseph, until the day I die.

(*Martin returns.*)

ROY: Ah, Martin's back.
MARTIN: So are we agreed?
ROY: Joe?

(*Little pause.*)

JOE: I will think about it.
    (*To Roy.*) I will.
ROY: Huh.
MARTIN: It's the fear of what comes after the doing that makes the doing hard to do.
ROY: Amen.
MARTIN: But you can almost always live with the consequences.

Scene 7

(*That afternoon. On the granite steps outside the Hall of Justice, Brooklyn. It is cold and sunny. A Sabrett wagon is selling hot dogs. Louis, in a shabby overcoat, is sitting on the steps contemplatively eating one. Joe enters with three hot dogs and a can of Coke.*)

JOE: Can I . . . ?
LOUIS: Oh sure. Sure. Crazy cold sun.
JOE (*sitting*): Have to make the best of it.
    How's your friend?
LOUIS: My . . . ? Oh. He's worse. My friend is worse.
JOE: I'm sorry.
LOUIS: Yeah, well. Thanks for asking. It's nice. You're nice. I can't believe you voted for Reagan.
JOE: I hope he gets better.
LOUIS: Reagan?
JOE: Your friend.
LOUIS: He won't. Neither will Reagan.
JOE: Let's not talk politics, OK?
LOUIS (*pointing to Joe's lunch*): You're eating *three* of those?
JOE: Well . . . I'm . . . hungry.
LOUIS: They're really terrible for you. Full of rat-poo and beetle legs and wood shavings 'n' shit.
JOE: Huh.
LOUIS: And . . . um . . . irridium, I think. Something toxic.
JOE: You're eating one.
LOUIS: Yeah, well, the shape, I can't help myself, plus I'm *trying* to commit suicide, what's your excuse?
JOE: I don't have an excuse. I just have Pepto-Bismol.

(*Joe takes a bottle of Pepto-Bismol and chugs it. Louis shudders audibly.*)

JOE: Yeah I know but then I wash it down with Coke.

(*He does this. Louis mimes barfing in Joe's lap. Joe pushes Louis's head away.*)

JOE: Are you *always* like this?
LOUIS: I've been worrying a lot about his kids.
JOE: Whose?
LOUIS: Reagan's. Maureen and Mike and little orphan Patti and Miss Ron Reagan Jr., the you-should-pardon-the-expression heterosexual.
JOE: Ron Reagan Jr. is *not* . . . . You shouldn't just make these assumptions about people. How do you know? About him? What he is? You don't know.
LOUIS (*doing Tallulah*): Well darling he never sucked *my* cock but . . .
JOE: Look, if you're going to get vulgar . . .
LOUIS: No no really I mean . . . . What's it like to be the child of the Zeitgeist? To have the American Animus as your dad? It's not really a *family*, the Reagans, I read *People*, there aren't any connections there, no love, they don't ever even speak to each other except through their agents. So what's it like to be Reagan's kid? Enquiring minds want to know.
JOE: You can't believe everything you . . .
LOUIS (*looking away*): But . . . I think we all know what that's like. Nowadays. No connections. No responsibilities. All of us . . . falling through the cracks that separate what we owe to our selves and . . . and what we owe to love.
JOE: You just . . . . Whatever you feel like saying or doing, you don't care, you just . . . do it.
LOUIS: Do what?
JOE: It. Whatever. Whatever it is you want to do.
LOUIS: Are you trying to tell me something?

(*Little pause, sexual. They stare at each other. Joe looks away.*)

JOE: No, I'm just observing that you . . .
LOUIS: Impulsive.
JOE: Yes, I mean it must be scary, you . . .
LOUIS (*shrugs*): Land of the free. Home of the brave. Call me irresponsible.
JOE: It's kind of terrifying.
LOUIS: Yeah, well, freedom is. Heartless, too.
JOE: Oh you're not heartless.
LOUIS: You don't know.
    Finish your weenie.

(*He pats Joe on the knee, starts to leave.*)

JOE: Um . . .

(*Louis turns, looks at him. Joe searches for something to say.*)

JOE: Yesterday was Sunday but I've been a little unfocused recently and I thought it was Monday. So I came here like I was going to work. And the whole place was empty. And at first I couldn't figure out why, and I had this moment of incredible . . . fear and also . . . . It just flashed through my mind: The whole Hall of Justice, it's empty, it's deserted, it's gone out of business. Forever. The people that make it run have up and abandoned it.
LOUIS (*looking at the building*): Creepy.

JOE: Well yes but. I felt that I was going to scream. Not because it was creepy, but because the emptiness felt so *fast*.

And . . . well, good. A . . . happy scream.

I just wondered what a thing it would be . . . if overnight everything you owe anything to, justice, or love, had really gone away. Free.

It would be . . . heartless terror. Yes. Terrible, and . . .

Very great. To shed your skin, every old skin, one by one and then walk away, unencumbered, into the morning.

(*Little pause. He looks at the building.*)

I can't go in there today.

LOUIS: Then don't.

JOE (*not really hearing Louis*): I can't go in, I need . . .

(*He looks for what he needs. He takes a swig of Pepto-Bismol.*)

I can't *be* this anymore. I need . . . a change, I should just . . .

LOUIS (*not a come-on, necessarily; he doesn't want to be alone*): Want some company? For whatever?

(*Pause. Joe looks at Louis and looks away, afraid. Louis shrugs.*)

LOUIS: Sometimes, even if it scares you to death, you have to be willing to break the law. Know what I mean?

(*Another little pause.*)

JOE: Yes.

(*Another little pause.*)

LOUIS: I moved out. I moved out on my . . .

I haven't been sleeping well.

JOE: Me neither.

(*Louis goes up to Joe, licks his napkin and dabs at Joe's mouth.*)

LOUIS: Antacid moustache.

(*Points to the building.*) Maybe the court won't convene. Ever again. Maybe we are free. To do whatever.

Children of the new morning, criminal minds. Selfish and greedy and loveless and blind. Reagan's children.

You're scared. So am I. Everybody is in the land of the free. God help us all.

Scene 8

(*Late that night. Joe at a payphone phoning Hannah at home in Salt Lake City.*)

JOE: Mom?

HANNAH: Joe?

JOE: Hi.

HANNAH: You're calling from the street. It's . . . it must be four in the morning. What's happened?

JOE: Nothing, nothing, I . . .

HANNAH: It's Harper. Is Harper . . . . Joe? Joe?

JOE: Yeah, hi. No, Harper's fine. Well, no, she's . . . not fine. How are you, Mom?

HANNAH: What's happened?

JOE: I just wanted to talk to you. I, uh, wanted to try something out on you.

HANNAH: Joe, you haven't . . . have you been drinking, Joe?

JOE: Yes ma'am. I'm drunk.

HANNAH: That isn't like you.

JOE: No. I mean, who's to say?

HANNAH: Why are you out on the street at four A.M.? In that crazy city. It's dangerous.

JOE: Actually, Mom, I'm not on the street. I'm near the boathouse in the park.

HANNAH: What park?

JOE: Central Park.

HANNAH: CENTRAL PARK! Oh my Lord. What on earth are you doing in Central Park at this time of night? Are you . . .

Joe, I think you ought to go home right now. Call me from home.

(*Little pause.*)

Joe?

JOE: I come here to watch, Mom. Sometimes. Just to watch.

HANNAH: Watch what? What's there to watch at four in the . . .

JOE: Mom, did Dad love me?

HANNAH: What?

JOE: Did he?

HANNAH: You ought to go home and call from there.

JOE: Answer.

HANNAH: Oh now really. This is maudlin. I don't like this conversation.

JOE: Yeah, well, it gets worse from here on.

(*Pause.*)

HANNAH: Joe?

JOE: Mom. Momma. I'm a homosexual, Momma.

Boy, did that come out awkward.

(*Pause.*)

Hello? Hello?

I'm a homosexual.

(*Pause.*)

Please, Momma. Say something.

HANNAH: You're old enough to understand that your father didn't love you without being ridiculous about it.

JOE: What?

HANNAH: You're ridiculous. You're being ridiculous.

JOE: I'm . . .

What?

HANNAH: You really ought to go home now to your wife. I need to go to bed. This phone call . . . . We will just forget this phone call.

JOE: Mom.

HANNAH: No more talk. Tonight. This . . .

(*Suddenly very angry.*) Drinking is a sin! A sin! I raised you better than that. (*She hangs up.*)

Scene 9

(*The following morning, early. Split scene: Harper and Joe at home; Louis and Prior in Prior's hospital room. Joe and Louis have just entered. This should be fast and obviously furious; overlapping is fine; the proceedings may be a little confusing but not the final results.*)

HARPER: Oh God. Home. The moment of truth has arrived.

JOE: Harper.

LOUIS: I'm going to move out.

PRIOR: The fuck you are.

JOE: Harper. Please listen. I still love you very much. You're still my best buddy; I'm not going to leave you.

HARPER: No, I don't like the sound of this. I'm leaving.

LOUIS: I'm leaving.
        I already have.

JOE: Please listen. Stay. This is really hard. We have to talk.

HARPER: We are talking. Aren't we. Now please shut up. OK?

PRIOR: Bastard. Sneaking off while I'm flat out here, that's low. If I could get up now I'd beat the holy shit out of you.

JOE: Did you take pills? How many?

HARPER: No pills. Bad for the . . . (*Pats stomach.*)

JOE: You aren't pregnant. I called your gynecologist.

HARPER: I'm seeing a new gynecologist.

PRIOR: You have no right to do this.

LOUIS: Oh, that's ridiculous.

PRIOR: No right. It's criminal.

JOE: Forget about that. Just listen. You want the truth. This is the truth.
        I knew this when I married you. I've known this I guess for as long as I've known anything, but . . . I don't know, I thought maybe that with enough effort and will I could change myself . . . but I can't . . .

PRIOR: Criminal.

LOUIS: There oughta be a law.

PRIOR: There is a law. You'll see.

JOE: I'm losing ground here, I go walking, you want to know where I walk, I . . . go to the park, or up and down 53rd Street, or places where . . . . And I keep swearing I won't go walking again, but I just can't.

LOUIS: I need some privacy.

PRIOR: That's new.

LOUIS: Everything's new, Prior.

JOE: I try to tighten my heart into a knot, a snarl, I try to learn to live dead, just numb, but then I see someone I want, and it's like a nail, like a hot spike right through my chest, and I know I'm losing.

PRIOR: Apartment too small for three? Louis and Prior comfy but not Louis and Prior and Prior's disease?

LOUIS: Something like that.
        I won't be judged by you. This isn't a crime, just—the inevitable consequence of people who run out of—whose limitations . . . .

PRIOR: Bang bang bang. The court will come to order.

LOUIS: I mean let's talk practicalities, schedules; I'll come over if you want, spend nights with you when I can, I can . . .

PRIOR: Has the jury reached a verdict?

LOUIS: I'm doing the best I can.

PRIOR: Pathetic. Who cares?

JOE: My whole life has conspired to bring me to this place, and I can't despise my whole life. I think I believed when I met you I could save you, you at least if not myself, but . . .
        I don't have any sexual feelings for you, Harper. And I don't think I ever did.

(*Little pause.*)

HARPER: I think you should go.

JOE: Where?

HARPER: Washington. Doesn't matter.

JOE: What are you talking about?

HARPER: Without me.
        Without me, Joe. Isn't that what you want to hear?

(*Little pause.*)

JOE: Yes.

LOUIS: You can love someone and fail them. You can love someone and not be able to . . .

PRIOR: You *can*, theoretically, yes. A person can, maybe an editorial "you" can love, Louis, but not *you*, specifically you, I don't know, I think you are excluded from that general category.

HARPER: You were going to save me, but the whole time you were spinning a lie. I just don't understand that.

PRIOR: A person could theoretically love and maybe many do but we both know now you can't.

LOUIS: I do.

PRIOR: You can't even say it.

LOUIS: I love you, Prior.

PRIOR: I repeat. Who cares?

HARPER: This is so scary, I want this to stop, to go back . . .

PRIOR: We have reached a verdict, your honor. This man's heart is deficient. He loves, but his love is worth nothing.

JOE: Harper . . .

HARPER: Mr. Lies, I want to get away from here. Far away. Right now. Before he starts talking again. Please, please . . .

JOE: As long as I've known you Harper you've been afraid of . . . Of men hiding under the bed, men hiding under the sofa, men with knives.

PRIOR (*shattered; almost pleading; trying to reach him*): I'm dying! You stupid fuck! Do you know what that is! Love! Do you know what love means? We lived together four-and-a-half years, you animal, you idiot.

LOUIS: I have to find some way to save myself.

JOE: Who are these men? I never understood it. Now I know.

HARPER: What?

JOE: It's me.

HARPER: It is?

PRIOR: GET OUT OF MY ROOM!

JOE: I'm the man with the knives.

HARPER: You are?

PRIOR: If I could get up now I'd kill you. I would. Go away. Go away or I'll scream.

HARPER: Oh God . . .

JOE: I'm sorry . . .

HARPER: It is you.

LOUIS: Please don't scream.

PRIOR: Go.

HARPER: I recognize you now.

LOUIS: Please . . .

JOE: Oh. Wait, I . . . . Oh!

(*He covers his mouth with his hand, gags, and removes his hand, red with blood.*)

I'm bleeding.

(*Prior screams.*)

HARPER: Mr. Lies.

MR. LIES (*appearing, dressed in antarctic explorer's apparel*): Right here.

HARPER: I want to go away. I can't see him anymore.

MR. LIES: Where?

HARPER: Anywhere. Far away.

MR. LIES: Absolutamento.

(*Harper and Mr. Lies vanish. Joe looks up, sees that she's gone.*)

PRIOR (*closing his eyes*): When I open my eyes you'll be gone.

(*Louis leaves.*)

JOE: Harper?

PRIOR (*opening his eyes*): Huh. It worked.

JOE (*calling*): Harper?

PRIOR: I hurt all over. I wish I was dead.

Scene 10

(*The same day, sunset. Hannah and Sister Ella Chapter, a real-estate saleswoman, Hannah Pitt's closest friend, in front of Hannah's house in Salt Lake City.*)

SISTER ELLA CHAPTER: Look at that view! A view of heaven. Like the living city of heaven, isn't it, it just fairly glimmers in the sun.

HANNAH: Glimmers.

SISTER ELLA CHAPTER: Even the stone and brick it just glimmers and glitters like heaven in the sunshine. Such a nice view you get, perched up on a canyon rim. Some kind of beautiful place.

HANNAH: It's just Salt Lake, and you're selling the house *for* me, not *to* me.

SISTER ELLA CHAPTER: I like to work up an enthusiasm for my properties.

HANNAH: Just get me a good price.

SISTER ELLA CHAPTER: Well, the market's off.

HANNAH: At least fifty.

SISTER ELLA CHAPTER: Forty'd be more like it.

HANNAH: Fifty.

SISTER ELLA CHAPTER: Wish you'd wait a bit.

HANNAH: Well I can't.

SISTER ELLA CHAPTER: Wish you would. You're about the only friend I got.

HANNAH: Oh well now.

SISTER ELLA CHAPTER: Know why I decided to like you? I decided to like you 'cause you're the only unfriendly Mormon I ever met.

HANNAH: Your wig is crooked.

SISTER ELLA CHAPTER: Fix it.

(*Hannah straightens Sister Ella's wig.*)

SISTER ELLA CHAPTER: New York City. All they got there is tiny rooms.

I always thought: People ought to stay put. That's why I got my license to sell real estate. It's a way of saying: Have a house! Stay put! It's a way of saying traveling's no good. Plus I needed the cash. (*She takes a pack of cigarettes out of her purse, lights one, offers pack to Hannah.*)

HANNAH: Not out here, anyone could come by.

There's been days I've stood at this ledge and thought about stepping over.

It's a hard place, Salt Lake: baked dry. Abundant energy; not much intelligence. That's a combination that can wear a body out. No harm looking some-place else. I don't need much room.

My sister-in-law Libby thinks there's radon gas in the basement.

SISTER ELLA CHAPTER: Is there gas in the . . .

HANNAH: Of course not. Libby's a fool.

SISTER ELLA CHAPTER: 'Cause I'd have to include that in the description.

HANNAH: There's no gas, Ella. (*Little pause.*) Give a puff. (*She takes a furtive drag of Ella's cigarette.*) Put it away now.

SISTER ELLA CHAPTER: So I guess it's goodbye.

HANNAH: You'll be all right, Ella, I wasn't ever much of a friend.

SISTER ELLA CHAPTER: I'll say something but don't laugh, OK?

This is the home of saints, the godliest place on earth, they say, and I think they're right. That mean there's no evil here? No. Evil's everywhere. Sin's everywhere. But this . . . is the spring of sweet water in the desert, the desert flower. Every step a Believer takes away from here is a step fraught with peril. I fear for you, Hannah Pitt, because you are my friend. Stay put. This is the right home of saints.

HANNAH: Latter-day saints.

SISTER ELLA CHAPTER: Only kind left.

HANNAH: But still. Late in the day . . . for saints and everyone. That's all. That's all.

  Fifty thousand dollars for the house, Sister Ella Chapter; don't undersell. It's an impressive view.

ACT 3
NOT-YET-CONSCIOUS, FORWARD DAWNING •
January 1986

Scene 1

(*Late night, three days after the end of act 2. The stage is completely dark. Prior is in bed in his apartment, having a nightmare. He wakes up, sits up and switches on a nightlight. He looks at his clock. Seated by the table near the bed is a man dressed in the clothing of a 13th-century British squire.*)

PRIOR (*terrified*): Who are you?
PRIOR 1: My name is Prior Walter.

(*Pause.*)

PRIOR: My name is Prior Walter.
PRIOR 1: I know that.
PRIOR: Explain.
PRIOR 1: You're alive. I'm not. We have the same name. What do you want me to explain?
PRIOR: A ghost?
PRIOR 1: An ancestor.
PRIOR: Not *the* Prior Walter? The Bayeux tapestry Prior Walter?
PRIOR 1: His great-great grandson. The fifth of the name.
PRIOR: I'm the thirty-fourth, I think.
PRIOR 1: Actually the thirty-second.
PRIOR: Not according to Mother.
PRIOR 1: She's including the two bastards, then; I say leave them out. I say no room for bastards. The little things you swallow . . .
PRIOR: Pills.
PRIOR 1: Pills. For the pestilence. I too . . .
PRIOR: Pestilence. . . . You too what?
PRIOR 1: The pestilence in my time was much worse than now. Whole villages of empty houses. You could look outdoors and see Death walking in the morning, dew dampening the ragged hem of his black robe. Plain as I see you now.
PRIOR: You died of the plague.
PRIOR 1: The spotty monster. Like you, alone.
PRIOR: I'm not alone.
PRIOR 1: You have no wife, no children.
PRIOR: I'm gay.
PRIOR 1: So? Be gay, dance in your altogether for all I care, what's that to do with not having children?
PRIOR: Gay homosexual, not bonny, blithe and . . . never mind.
PRIOR 1: I had twelve. When I died.

(*The second ghost appears, this one dressed in the clothing of an elegant 17th-century Londoner.*)

PRIOR 1 (*pointing to Prior 2*): And I was three years younger than him.

(*Prior sees the new ghost, screams.*)

PRIOR: Oh God another one.
PRIOR 2: Prior Walter. Prior to you by some seventeen others.
PRIOR 1: He's counting the bastards.
PRIOR: Are we having a convention?
PRIOR 2: We've been sent to declare her fabulous incipience. They love a well-paved entrance with lots of heralds, and . . .
PRIOR 1: The messenger come. Prepare the way. The infinite descent, a breath in air . . .
PRIOR 2: They chose us, I suspect, because of the mortal affinities. In a family as long-descended as the Walters there are bound to be a few carried off by plague.
PRIOR 1: The spotty monster.
PRIOR 2: Black Jack. Came from a water pump, half the city of London, can you imagine? His came from fleas. Yours, I understand, is the lamentable consequence of venery . . .
PRIOR 1: Fleas on rats, but who knew that?
PRIOR: Am I going to die?
PRIOR 2: We aren't allowed to discuss . . .
PRIOR 1: When you do, you don't get ancestors to help you through it. You may be surrounded by children but you die alone.
PRIOR: I'm afraid.
PRIOR 1: You should be. There aren't even torches, and the path's rocky, dark and steep.
PRIOR 2: Don't alarm him. There's good news before there's bad.

  We two come to strew rose petal and palm leaf before the triumphal procession. Prophet. Seer. Revelator. It's a great honor for the family.
PRIOR 1: He hasn't got a family.
PRIOR 2: I meant for the Walters, for the family in the larger sense.
PRIOR (*singing*): All I want is a room somewhere,
  Far away from the cold night air . . .
PRIOR 2 (*putting a hand on Prior's forehead*): Calm, calm, this is no brain fever . . .

(*Prior calms down, but keeps his eyes closed. The lights begin to change. Distant Glorious Music.*)

PRIOR 1 (*low chant*): Adonai, Adonai,
  Olam ha-yichud,
  Zefirot, Zazahot,
  Ha-adam, ha-gadol
  Daughter of Light,
  Daughter of Splendors,
  Fluor! Phosphor!
  Lumen! Candle!
PRIOR 2 (*simultaneously*): Even now,
  From the mirror-bright halls of heaven,

Across the cold and lifeless infinity of space,
The Messenger comes
Trailing orbs of light,
Fabulous, incipient,
Oh Prophet,
To you . . .
PRIOR 1 AND PRIOR 2: Prepare, prepare,
The Infinite Descent,
A breath, a feather,
Glory to . . .

(*They vanish.*)

Scene 2

(*The next day. Split scene. Louis and Belize in a coffee shop. Prior is at the outpatient clinic at the hospital with Emily, the nurse; she has him on a pentamidine IV drip.*)

LOUIS: Why has democracy succeeded in America? Of course by succeeded I mean comparatively, not literally, not in the present, but what makes for the prospect of some sort of radical democracy spreading outward and growing up? Why does the power that was once so carefully preserved at the top of the pyramid by the original framers of the Constitution seem drawn inexorably downward and outward in spite of the best effort of the Right to stop this? I mean it's the really hard thing about being Left in this country, the American Left can't help but trip over all these petrified little fetishes: freedom, that's the worst; you know, *Jeane Kirkpatrick*° for God's sake will go on and on about freedom and so what does that mean, the word freedom, when she talks about it, or human rights; you have Bush talking about human rights, and so what are these people talking about, they might as well be talking about the mating habits of Venusians, these people don't begin to know what, ontologically, freedom is or human rights, like they see these bourgeois property-based Rights-of-Man-type rights but that's not enfranchisement, not democracy, not what's implicit, what's potential within the idea, not the idea with blood in it. That's just liberalism, the worst kind of liberalism, really, bourgeois tolerance, and what I think is that what AIDS shows us is the limits of tolerance, that it's not enough to be tolerated, because when the shit hits the fan you find out how much tolerance is worth. Nothing. And underneath all the tolerance is intense, passionate hatred.
BELIZE: Uh huh.
LOUIS: Well don't you think that's true?
BELIZE: Uh huh. It is.

Jeane Kirkpatrick: Ardent anti-Communist (1920–2006) and former U.S. ambassador to the United Nations.

LOUIS: *Power* is the object, not being tolerated. Fuck assimilation. But I mean in spite of all this the thing about America, I think, is that ultimately we're different from every other nation on earth, in that, with people here of every race, we can't . . . . Ultimately what defines us isn't race, but politics. Not like any European country where there's an insurmountable fact of a kind of racial, or ethnic, monopoly, or monolith, like all Dutchmen, I mean Dutch people, are well, Dutch, and the Jews of Europe were never Europeans, just a small problem. Facing the monolith. But here there are so many small problems, it's really just a collection of small problems, the monolith is missing. Oh, I mean, of course I suppose there's the monolith of White America. White Straight Male America.
BELIZE: Which is not unimpressive, even among monoliths.
LOUIS: Well, no, but when the race thing gets taken care of, and I don't mean to minimalize how major it is, I mean I know it is, this is a really, really incredibly racist country but it's like, well, the British. I mean, all these blue-eyed pink people. And it's just weird, you know, I mean I'm not all that Jewish-looking, or . . . well, maybe I am but, you know, in New York, everyone is . . . well, not everyone, but so many are but so but in England, in London I walk into bars and I feel like Sid the Yid, you know I mean like Woody Allen in *Annie Hall*, with the payess and the gabardine coat, like never, never anywhere so much — I mean, not actively despised, not like they're Germans, who I think are still terribly anti-Semitic, and racist too, I mean black-racist, they pretend otherwise but, anyway, in London, there's just . . . and at one point I met this black gay guy from Jamaica who talked with a lilt but he said his family'd been living in London since before the Civil War — the American one — and how the English never let him forget for a minute that he wasn't blue-eyed and pink and I said yeah, me too, these people are anti-Semites and he said yeah but the British Jews have the clothing business all sewed up and blacks there can't get a foothold. And it was an incredibly awkward moment of just . . . . I mean there we were, in this bar that was gay but it was a *pub*, you know, the beams and the plaster and those horrible little, like, two-day-old fish and egg sandwiches — and just so British, so *old*, and I felt, well, there's no way out of this because both of us are, right now, too much immersed in this history, hope is dissolved in the sheer age of this place, where race is what counts and there's no real hope of change — it's the racial destiny of the Brits that matters to them, not their political destiny, whereas in America . . .
BELIZE: Here in America race doesn't count.
LOUIS: No, no, that's not . . . . I mean you *can't* be hearing that . . .
BELIZE: I . . .
LOUIS: It's — look, race, yes, but ultimately race here is a political question, right? Racists just try to use race

here as a tool in a political struggle. It's not really about race. Like the spiritualists try to use that stuff, are you enlightened, are you centered, channeled, whatever, this reaching out for a spiritual past in a country where no indigenous spirits exist—only the Indians, I mean Native American spirits and we killed them off so now, there are no gods here, no ghosts and spirits in America, there are no angels in America, no spiritual past, no racial past, there's only the political, and the decoys and the ploys to ma-neuver around the inescapable battle of politics, the shifting downwards and outwards of political power to the people . . .

BELIZE: POWER to the People! AMEN! (*Looking at his watch.*) *OH MY GOODNESS!* Will you look at the time, I gotta . . .

LOUIS: Do you . . . . You think this is, what, racist or naive or something?

BELIZE: Well it's certainly *something*. Look, I just remem-bered I have an appointment . . .

LOUIS: What? I mean I really don't want to, like, speak from some position of privilege and . . .

BELIZE: I'm sitting here, thinking, eventually he's *got* to run out of steam, so I let you rattle on and on say-ing about maybe seven or eight things I find really offensive.

LOUIS: What?

BELIZE: But I know you, Louis, and I know the guilt fuel-ing this peculiar tirade is obviously already swollen bigger than your hemorrhoids.

LOUIS: I don't have hemorrhoids.

BELIZE: I hear different. May I finish?

LOUIS: Yes, but I don't have hemorrhoids.

BELIZE: So finally, when I . . .

LOUIS: Prior told you, he's an asshole, he shouldn't have . . .

BELIZE: You promised, Louis. Prior is not a subject.

LOUIS: You brought him up.

BELIZE: I brought up hemorrhoids.

LOUIS: So it's indirect. Passive-aggressive.

BELIZE: Unlike, I suppose, banging me over the head with your theory that America doesn't have a race problem.

LOUIS: Oh be fair I never said that.

BELIZE: Not exactly, but . . .

LOUIS: I said . . .

BELIZE: . . . but it was close enough, because if it'd been that blunt I'd've just walked out and . . .

LOUIS: You deliberately misinterpreted! I . . .

BELIZE: Stop interrupting! I haven't been able to . . .

LOUIS: Just let me . . .

BELIZE: NO! What, *talk*? You've been running your mouth nonstop since I got here, yaddadda yaddadda blah blah blah, up the hill, down the hill, playing with your MONOLITH . . .

LOUIS (*overlapping*): Well, you could have joined in at any time instead of . . .

BELIZE (*continuing over Louis*): . . . and girlfriend it is truly an *awesome* spectacle but I got better things to

do with my time than sit here listening to this racist bullshit just because I feel sorry for you that . . .

LOUIS: I am not a racist!

BELIZE: Oh come on . . .

LOUIS: So maybe I am a racist but . . .

BELIZE: Oh I really hate that! It's no fun picking on you Louis; you're so guilty, it's like throwing darts at a glob of jello, there's no satisfying hits, just quivering, the darts just blop in and vanish.

LOUIS: I just think when you are discussing lines of op-pression it gets very complicated and . . .

BELIZE: Oh is that a fact? You know, we black drag queens have a rather intimate knowledge of the com-plexity of the lines of . . .

LOUIS: *Ex*-black drag queen.

BELIZE: Actually ex-ex.

LOUIS: You're doing drag again?

BELIZE: I don't . . . . Maybe. I don't have to tell you. Maybe.

LOUIS: I think it's sexist.

BELIZE: I didn't ask you.

LOUIS: Well it is. The gay community, I think, has to adopt the same attitude towards drag as black women have to take towards black women blues singers.

BELIZE: Oh my we *are* walking dangerous tonight.

LOUIS: Well, it's all internalized oppression, right, I mean the masochism, the stereotypes, the . . .

BELIZE: Louis, are you deliberately trying to make me hate you?

LOUIS: No, I . . .

BELIZE: I mean, are you deliberately transforming your-self into an arrogant, sexual-political Stalinist-slash-racist flag-waving thug for my benefit?

(*Pause.*)

LOUIS: You know what I think?

BELIZE: What?

LOUIS: You hate me because I'm a Jew.

BELIZE: I'm leaving.

LOUIS: It's true.

BELIZE: You have no basis except your . . .

Louis, it's good to know you haven't changed; you are still an honorary citizen of the Twilight Zone, and after your pale, pale white polemics on behalf of racial insensitivity you have a flaming *fuck* of a lot of nerve calling me an anti-Semite. Now I really gotta go.

LOUIS: You called me Lou the Jew.

BELIZE: That was a joke.

LOUIS: I didn't think it was funny. It was hostile.

BELIZE: It was three years ago.

LOUIS: So?

BELIZE: You just called yourself Sid the Yid.

LOUIS: That's not the same thing.

BELIZE: Sid the Yid is different from Lou the Jew.

LOUIS: Yes.

BELIZE: Someday you'll have to explain that to me, but right now . . .

You hate me because you hate black people.

LOUIS: I do not. But I do think most black people are anti-Semitic.

BELIZE: "Most black people." *That's* racist, Louis, and I think most Jews . . .

LOUIS: Louis Farrakhan.

BELIZE: Ed Koch.

LOUIS: Jesse Jackson.

BELIZE: Jackson. Oh really, Louis, this is . . .

LOUIS: Hymietown! Hymietown!

BELIZE: Louis, you voted for Jesse Jackson. You send checks to the Rainbow Coalition.

LOUIS: I'm ambivalent. The checks bounced.

BELIZE: All your checks bounce, Louis; you're ambivalent about everything.

LOUIS: What's that supposed to mean?

BELIZE: You may be dumber than shit but I refuse to believe you can't figure it out. Try.

LOUIS: I was never ambivalent about Prior. I love him. I do. I really do.

BELIZE: Nobody said different.

LOUIS: Love and ambivalence are . . . . Real love isn't ambivalent.

BELIZE: "Real love isn't ambivalent." I'd swear that's a line from my favorite bestselling paperback novel, *In Love with the Night Mysterious*, except I don't think you ever read it.

(*Pause.*)

LOUIS: I never read it, no.

BELIZE: You ought to. Instead of spending the rest of your life trying to get through *Democracy in America*. It's about this white woman whose Daddy owns a plantation in the Deep South in the years before the Civil War—the American one—and her name is Margaret, and she's in love with her Daddy's number-one slave, and his name is Thaddeus, and she's married but her white slave-owner husband has AIDS: Antebellum Insufficiently Developed Sex-organs. And there's a lot of hot stuff going down when Margaret and Thaddeus can catch a spare torrid ten under the cotton-picking moon, and then of course the Yankees come, and they set the slaves free, and the slaves string up old Daddy, and so on. Historical fiction. Somewhere in there I recall Margaret and Thaddeus find the time to discuss the nature of love; her face is reflecting the flames of the burning plantation—you know, the way white people do—and his black face is dark in the night and she says to him, "Thaddeus, real love isn't ever ambivalent."

(*Little pause. Emily enters and turns off IV drip.*)

BELIZE: Thaddeus looks at her; he's contemplating her thesis; and he isn't sure he agrees.

EMILY (*removing IV drip from Prior's arm*): Treatment number . . . (*consulting chart*) four.

PRIOR: Pharmaceutical miracle. Lazarus breathes again.

LOUIS: Is he . . . . How bad is he?

BELIZE: You want the laundry list?

EMILY: Shirt off, let's check the . . .

(*Prior takes his shirt off. She examines his lesions.*)

BELIZE: There's the weight problem and the shit problem and the morale problem.

EMILY: Only six. That's good. Pants.

(*He drops his pants. He's naked. She examines.*)

BELIZE: And. He thinks he's going crazy.

EMILY: Looking good. What else?

PRIOR: Ankles sore and swollen, but the leg's better. The nausea's mostly gone with the little orange pills. BM's pure liquid but not bloody anymore, for now, my eye doctor says everything's OK, for now, my dentist says "Yuck!" when he sees my fuzzy tongue, and now he wears little condoms on his thumb and forefinger. And a mask. So what? My dermatologist is in Hawaii and my mother . . . well leave my mother out of it. Which is usually where my mother is, out of it. My glands are like walnuts, my weight's holding steady for week two, and a friend died two days ago of bird tuberculosis; bird tuberculosis; that scared me and I didn't go to the funeral today because he was an Irish Catholic and it's probably open casket and I'm afraid of . . . something, the bird TB or seeing him or . . . . So I guess I'm doing OK. Except for of course I'm going nuts.

EMILY: We ran the toxoplasmosis series and there's no indication . . .

PRIOR: I know, I know, but I feel like something terrifying is on its way, you know, like a missile from outer space, and it's plummeting down towards the earth, and I'm ground zero, and . . . I am generally known where I am known as one cool, collected queen. And I am ruffled.

EMILY: There's really nothing to worry about. I think that shochen bamromim hamtzeh menucho nechono al kanfey haschino.

PRIOR: What?

EMILY: Everything's fine. Bemaalos k'doshim ut'horim kezohar horokeea mazhirim . . .

PRIOR: Oh I don't understand what you're . . .

EMILY: Es nishmas Prior sheholoch leolomoh, baavur she-nodvoo z'dokoh b'ad hazkoras nishmosoh.

PRIOR: Why are you doing that?! Stop it! Stop it!

EMILY: Stop what?

PRIOR: You were just . . . weren't you just speaking in Hebrew or something.

EMILY: *Hebrew?* (*Laughs.*) I'm basically Italian-American. No. I didn't speak in Hebrew.

PRIOR: Oh no, oh God please I really think I . . .

EMILY: Look, I'm sorry, I have a waiting room full of . . . . I think you're one of the lucky ones, you'll live for years, probably—you're pretty healthy for someone with no immune system. Are you seeing someone? Loneliness is a danger. A therapist?

PRIOR: No, I don't need to see anyone, I just . . .

EMILY: Well think about it. You aren't going crazy. You're just under a lot of stress. No wonder . . . (*She starts to write in his chart.*)

(*Suddenly there is an astonishing blaze of light, a huge chord sounded by a gigantic choir, and a great book with steel pages mounted atop a molten-red pillar pops up from the stage floor. The book opens; there is a large Aleph inscribed on its pages, which bursts into flames. Immediately the book slams shut and disappears instantly under the floor as the lights become normal again. Emily notices none of this, writing. Prior is agog.*)

EMILY (*laughing, exiting*): Hebrew . . .

(*Prior flees.*)

LOUIS: Help me.

BELIZE: I beg your pardon?

LOUIS: You're a nurse, give me something, I . . . don't know what to do anymore, I . . . . Last week at work I screwed up the Xerox machine like permanently and so I . . . then I tripped on the subway steps and my glasses broke and I cut my forehead, here, see, and now I can't see much and my forehead . . . it's like the Mark of Cain,° stupid, right, but it won't heal and every morning I see it and I think, Biblical things, Mark of Cain, Judas Iscariot° and his silver and his noose, people who . . . in betraying what they love betray what's truest in themselves, I feel . . . nothing but cold for myself, just cold, and every night I miss him, I miss him so much but then . . . those sores, and the smell and . . . where I thought it was going. . . . I could be . . . I could be . . . sick too, maybe I'm sick too. I don't know.
    Belize. Tell him I love him. Can you do that?

BELIZE: I've thought about it for a very long time, and I still don't understand what love is. Justice is simple. Democracy is simple. Those things are unambivalent. But love is very hard. And it goes bad for you if you violate the hard law of love.

LOUIS: I'm dying.

BELIZE: He's dying. You just wish you were.
    Oh cheer up, Louis. Look at that heavy sky out there.

LOUIS: Purple.

BELIZE: *Purple?* Boy, what kind of a homosexual are you, anyway? That's not purple, Mary, that color up there is (*very grand*) mauve.
    All day today it's felt like Thanksgiving. Soon, this . . . ruination will be blanketed white. You can smell it—can you smell it?

LOUIS: Smell what?

BELIZE: Softness, compliance, forgiveness, grace.

LOUIS: No . . .

BELIZE: I can't help you learn that. I can't help you, Louis. You're not my business. (*He exits.*)

(*Louis puts his head in his hands, inadvertently touching his cut forehead.*)

Mark of Cain: In Genesis, Cain murdered his brother Abel and subsequently was marked on his forehead by God. **Judas Iscariot:** An apostle who betrayed Jesus for thirty pieces of silver.

LOUIS: Ow FUCK! (*He stands slowly, looks towards where Belize exited.*) Smell what?
    (*He looks both ways to be sure no one is watching, then inhales deeply, and is surprised.*) Huh. Snow.

Scene 3

(*Same day. Harper in a very white, cold place, with a brilliant blue sky above; a delicate snowfall. She is dressed in a beautiful snowsuit. The sound of the sea, faint.*)

HARPER: Snow! Ice! Mountains of ice! Where am I? I . . .
    I feel better, I do, I . . . feel better. There are ice crystals in my lungs, wonderful and sharp. And the snow smells like cold, crushed peaches. And there's something . . . some current of blood in the wind, how strange, it has that iron taste.

MR. LIES: Ozone.

HARPER: Ozone! Wow! Where am I?

MR. LIES: The Kingdom of Ice, the bottommost part of the world.

HARPER (*looking around, then realizing*): Antarctica. This is Antarctica!

MR. LIES: Cold shelter for the shattered. No sorrow here, tears freeze.

HARPER: Antarctica, Antarctica, oh boy oh boy, LOOK at this, I . . . . Wow, I must've really snapped the tether, huh?

MR. LIES: Apparently

HARPER: That's great. I want to stay here forever. Set up camp. Build things. Build a city, an enormous city made up of frontier forts, dark wood and green roofs and high gates made of pointed logs and bonfires burning on every street corner. I should build by a river. Where are the forests?

MR. LIES: No timber here. Too cold. Ice, no trees.

HARPER: Oh details! I'm sick of details! I'll plant them and grow them. I'll live off caribou fat, I'll melt it over the bonfires and drink it from long, curved goat-horn cups. It'll be great. I want to make a new world here. So that I never have to go home again.

MR. LIES: As long as it lasts. Ice has a way of melting . . .

HARPER: No. Forever. I can have anything I want here—maybe even companionship, someone who has . . . desire for me. You, maybe.

MR. LIES: It's against the by-laws of the International Order of Travel Agents to get involved with clients. Rules are rules. Anyway, I'm not the one you really want.

HARPER: There isn't anyone . . . maybe an Eskimo. Who could ice-fish for food. And help me build a nest for when the baby comes.

MR. LIES: There are no Eskimo in Antarctica. And you're not really pregnant. You made that up.

HARPER: Well all of this is made up. So if the snow feels cold I'm pregnant. Right? Here, I can be pregnant. And I can have any kind of a baby I want.

MR. LIES: This is a retreat, a vacuum, its virtue is that it lacks everything; deep-freeze for feelings. You can be numb and safe here, that's what you came for. Respect the delicate ecology of your delusions.

HARPER: You mean like no Eskimo in Antarctica.

MR. LIES: Correcto. Ice and snow, no Eskimo. Even hallucinations have laws.

HARPER: Well then who's that?

(*The Eskimo appears.*)

MR. LIES: An Eskimo.

HARPER: An antarctic Eskimo. A fisher of the polar deep.

MR. LIES: There's something wrong with this picture.

(*The Eskimo beckons.*)

HARPER: I'm going to like this place. It's my own National Geographic Special! Oh! Oh! (*She holds her stomach.*) I think . . . I think I felt her kicking. Maybe I'll give birth to a baby covered with thick white fur, and that way she won't be cold. My breasts will be full of hot cocoa so she doesn't get chilly. And if it gets really cold, she'll have a pouch I can crawl into. Like a marsupial. We'll mend together. That's what we'll do; we'll mend.

Scene 4

(*Same day. An abandoned lot in the South Bronx. A homeless Woman is standing near an oil drum in which a fire is burning. Snowfall. Trash around. Hannah enters dragging two heavy suitcases.*)

HANNAH: Excuse me? I said excuse me? Can you tell me where I am? Is this Brooklyn? Do you know a Pineapple Street? Is there some sort of bus or train or . . . ?

I'm lost, I just arrived from Salt Lake. City. Utah? I took the bus that I was told to take and I got off—well it was the very last stop, so I had to get off, and I *asked* the driver was this Brooklyn, and he nodded yes but he was from one of those foreign countries where they think it's good manners to nod at everything even if you have no idea what it is you're nodding at, and in truth I think he spoke no English at all, which I think would make him ineligible for employment on public transportation. The public being English-speaking, mostly. Do you speak English?

(*The Woman nods.*)

HANNAH: I was supposed to be met at the airport by my son. He didn't show and I don't wait more than three and three-quarters hours for *anyone*. I should have been patient, I guess, I . . . . Is this . . .

WOMAN: Bronx.

HANNAH: Is that . . . . The *Bronx*? Well how in the name of Heaven did I get to the Bronx when the bus driver said . . .

WOMAN (*talking to herself*): Slurp slurp slurp will you STOP that disgusting slurping! YOU DISGUSTING SLURPING FEEDING ANIMAL! Feeding yourself, just feeding yourself, what would it matter, to you or to ANYONE, if you just stopped. Feeding. And DIED?

(*Pause.*)

HANNAH: Can you just tell me where I . . .

WOMAN: Why was the Kosciusko Bridge named after a Polack?

HANNAH: I don't know what you're . . .

WOMAN: That was a joke.

HANNAH: Well what's the punchline?

WOMAN: I don't know.

HANNAH (*looking around desperately*): Oh for pete's sake, is there anyone else who . . .

WOMAN (*again, to herself*): Stand further off you fat loathsome whore, you can't have any more of this soup, slurp slurp slurp you animal, and the—I know you'll just go pee it all away and where will you do that? Behind what bush? It's FUCKING COLD out here and I . . .

Oh that's right, because it was supposed to have been a tunnel!

That's not very funny.

Have you read the prophecies of Nostradamus?

HANNAH: Who?

WOMAN: Some guy I went out with once somewhere, Nostradamus. Prophet, outcast, eyes like . . . . Scary shit, he . . .

HANNAH: Shut up. Please. Now I want you to stop jabbering for a minute and pull your wits together and tell me how to get to Brooklyn. Because you know! And you are going to tell me! Because there is no one else around to tell me and I am wet and cold and I am very angry! So I am sorry you're psychotic but just make the effort—take a deep breath—DO IT!

(*Hannah and the Woman breathe together.*)

HANNAH: That's good. Now exhale.

(*They do.*)

HANNAH: Good. Now how do I get to Brooklyn?

WOMAN: Don't know. Never been. Sorry. Want some soup?

HANNAH: Manhattan? Maybe you know . . . I don't suppose you know the location of the Mormon Visitor's . . .

WOMAN: 65th and Broadway.

HANNAH: How do you . . .

WOMAN: Go there all the time. Free movies. Boring, but you can stay all day.

HANNAH: Well. . . . So how do I.

WOMAN: Take the D Train. Next block make a right.

HANNAH: Thank you.

WOMAN: Oh yeah. In the new century I think we will all be insane.

Scene 5

(*Same day. Joe and Roy in the study of Roy's brown-stone. Roy is wearing an elegant bathrobe. He has made a considerable effort to look well. He isn't well, and he hasn't succeeded much in looking it.*)

JOE: I can't. The answer's no. I'm sorry.
ROY: Oh, well, apologies . . .
    I can't see that there's anyone asking for apologies.

(*Pause.*)

JOE: I'm sorry, Roy.
ROY: Oh, well, apologies.
JOE: My wife is missing, Roy. My mother's coming from Salt Lake to . . . to help look, I guess. I'm supposed to be at the airport now, picking her up but . . . . I just spent two days in a hospital, Roy, with a bleeding ulcer, I was spitting up blood.
ROY: Blood, huh? Look, I'm very busy here and . . .
JOE: It's just a job.
ROY: A job? A *job*? *Washington*! Dumb Utah Mormon hick shit!
JOE: Roy . . .
ROY: *WASHINGTON!* When Washington called me I was younger than you, you think I said "Aw fuck no I can't go I got two fingers up my asshole and a little moral nosebleed to boot!" When Washington calls you my pretty young punk friend you go or you can go fuck yourself sideways 'cause the train has pulled out of the station, and you are *out*, nowhere, out in the cold. Fuck you, Mary Jane, get outta here.
JOE: Just let me . . .
ROY: Explain? Ephemera. You broke my heart. Explain that. Explain that.
JOE: I love you. Roy.
    There's so much that I want, to be . . . what you see in me, I want to be a participant in the world, in your world, Roy, I want to be capable of that, I've tried, really I have but . . . I can't do this. Not because I don't believe in you, but because I believe in you so much, in what you stand for, at heart, the order, the decency. I would give anything to protect you, but . . . . There are laws I can't break. It's too ingrained. It's not me. There's enough damage I've already done.
    Maybe you were right, maybe I'm dead.
ROY: You're not dead, boy, you're a sissy.
    You love me; that's moving, I'm moved. It's nice to be loved. I warned you about her, didn't I, Joe? But you don't listen to me, why, because you say Roy is smart and Roy's a friend but Roy . . . well, he isn't nice, and you wanna be nice. Right? A nice, nice man!
    (*Little pause.*)
    You know what my greatest accomplishment was, Joe, in my life, what I am able to look back on and be proudest of? And I have helped make Presidents and unmake them and mayors and more goddam judges than anyone in NYC ever—AND several million

dollars, tax-free—and what do you think means the most to me?
    You ever hear of Ethel Rosenberg? Huh, Joe, huh?
JOE: Well, yeah, I guess I . . . . Yes.
ROY: Yes. Yes. You have heard of Ethel Rosenberg. Yes. Maybe you even read about her in the history books.
    If it wasn't for me, Joe, Ethel Rosenberg would be alive today, writing some personal-advice column for *Ms.* magazine. She isn't. Because during the trial, Joe, I was on the phone every day, talking with the judge . . .
JOE: Roy . . .
ROY: Every day, doing what I do best, talking on the telephone, making sure that timid Yid nebbish on the bench did his duty to America, to history. That sweet unprepossessing woman, two kids, boo-hoo-hoo, reminded us all of our little Jewish mamas—she came this close to getting life; I pleaded till I wept to put her in the chair. Me. I did that. I would have fucking pulled the switch if they'd have let me. Why? Because I fucking hate traitors. Because I fucking hate communists. Was it legal? Fuck legal. Am I a nice man? Fuck nice. They say terrible things about me in the *Nation*. Fuck the *Nation*. You want to be Nice, or you want to be Effective? Make the law, or subject to it. Choose. Your wife chose. A week from today, she'll be back. SHE knows how to get what SHE wants. Maybe I ought to send *her* to Washington.
JOE: I don't believe you.
ROY: Gospel.
JOE: You can't possibly mean what you're saying.
    Roy, you were the Assistant United States Attorney on the Rosenberg case, ex-parte communication with the judge during the trial would be . . . censurable, at least, probably conspiracy and . . . in a case that resulted in execution, it's . . .
ROY: What? Murder?
JOE: You're not well is all.
ROY: What do you mean, not well? Who's not well?

(*Pause.*)

JOE: You said . . .
ROY: No I didn't. I said what?
JOE: Roy, you have cancer.
ROY: No I don't.

(*Pause.*)

JOE: You told me you were dying.
ROY: What the fuck are you talking about, Joe? I never said that. I'm in perfect health. There's not a goddam thing wrong with me.
    (*He smiles.*)
    Shake?

(*Joe hesitates. He holds out his hand to Roy. Roy pulls Joe into a close, strong clinch.*)

ROY (*more to himself than to Joe*): It's OK that you hurt me because I love you, baby Joe. That's why I'm so rough on you.

(*Roy releases Joe. Joe backs away a step or two.*)

ROY: Prodigal son. The world will wipe its dirty hands all over you.

JOE: It already has, Roy.

ROY: Now go.

(*Roy shoves Joe, hard. Joe turns to leave. Roy stops him, turns him around.*)

ROY (*smoothing Joe's lapels, tenderly*): I'll always be here, waiting for you . . .
  (*Then again, with sudden violence, he pulls Joe close, violently.*)
  What did you want from me, what was all this, what do you want, treacherous ungrateful little . . .

(*Joe, very close to belting Roy, grabs him by the front of his robe, and propels him across the length of the room. He holds Roy at arm's length, the other arm ready to hit.*)

ROY (*laughing softly, almost pleading to be hit*): Transgress a little, Joseph.

(*Joe releases Roy.*)

ROY: There are so many laws; find one you can break.

(*Joe hesitates, then leaves, backing out. When Joe has gone, Roy doubles over in great pain, which he's been hiding throughout the scene with Joe.*)

ROY: Ah, Christ . . .
  Andy! Andy! Get in here! Andy!

(*The door opens, but it isn't Andy. A small Jewish Woman dressed modestly in a fifties hat and coat stands in the doorway. The room darkens.*)

ROY: Who the fuck are you? The new nurse?

(*The figure in the doorway says nothing. She stares at Roy. A pause. Roy looks at her carefully, gets up, crosses to her. He crosses back to the chair, sits heavily.*)

ROY: Aw, fuck. Ethel.

ETHEL ROSENBERG (*her manner is friendly, her voice is ice-cold*): You don't look good, Roy.

ROY: Well, Ethel. I don't feel good.

ETHEL ROSENBERG: But you lost a lot of weight. That suits you. You were heavy back then. Zaftig, mit hips.

ROY: I haven't been that heavy since 1960. We were all heavier back then, before the body thing started. Now I look like a skeleton. They stare.

ETHEL ROSENBERG: The shit's really hit the fan, huh, Roy?

(*Little pause. Roy nods.*)

ETHEL ROSENBERG: Well the fun's just started.

ROY: What is this, Ethel, Halloween? You trying to scare me?

(*Ethel says nothing.*)

ROY: Well you're wasting your time! I'm scarier than you any day of the week! So beat it, Ethel! BOOO!

BETTER DEAD THAN RED! Somebody trying to shake me up? HAH HAH! From the throne of God in heaven to the belly of hell, you can all fuck yourselves and then go jump in the lake because I'M NOT AFRAID OF YOU OR DEATH OR HELL OR ANYTHING!

ETHEL ROSENBERG: Be seeing you soon, Roy. Julius sends his regards.

ROY: Yeah, well send this to Julius!

(*He flips the bird in her direction, stands and moves towards her. Halfway across the room he slumps to the floor, breathing laboriously, in pain.*)

ETHEL ROSENBERG: You're a very sick man, Roy.

ROY: Oh God . . . ANDY!

Ron Liebman as Roy Cohn in the Broadway production of *Angels in America: Millennium Approaches.*

ETHEL ROSENBERG: Hmmm. He doesn't hear you, I guess. We should call the ambulance.

(*She goes to the phone.*)

Hah! Buttons! Such things they got now. What do I dial, Roy?

(*Pause. Roy looks at her, then:*)

ROY: 911.

ETHEL ROSENBERG (*dials the phone*): It sings!

(*Imitating dial tones.*) La la la . . .

Huh.

Yes, you should please send an ambulance to the home of Mister Roy Cohn, the famous lawyer. What's the address, Roy?

ROY (*a beat, then*): 244 East 87th.

ETHEL ROSENBERG: 244 East 87th Street. No apartment number, he's got the whole building.

My name? (*A beat.*) Ethel Greenglass Rosenberg.

(*Small smile.*) Me? No I'm not related to Mr. Cohn. An old friend.

(*She hangs up.*)

They said a minute.

ROY: I have all the time in the world.

ETHEL ROSENBERG: You're immortal.

ROY: I'm immortal. Ethel. (*He forces himself to stand.*)

I have *forced* my way into history. I ain't never gonna die.

ETHEL ROSENBERG (*a little laugh, then*): History is about to crack wide open. Millennium approaches.

Scene 6

(*Late that night. Prior's bedroom. Prior 1 watching Prior in bed, who is staring back at him, terrified. Tonight Prior 1 is dressed in weird alchemical robes*

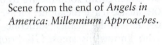

Scene from the end of *Angels in America: Millennium Approaches.*

and hat over his historical clothing and he carries a long palm-leaf bundle.)

PRIOR 1: Tonight's the night! Aren't you excited? Tonight she arrives! Right through the roof! Ha-adam, Ha-gadol . . .

PRIOR 2 (*appearing, similarly attired*): Lumen! Phosphor! Fluor! Candle! An unending billowing of scarlet and . . .

PRIOR: Look. Garlic. A mirror. Holy water. A crucifix. FUCK OFF! Get the fuck out of my room! GO!

PRIOR 1 (*to Prior 2*): Hard as a hickory knob, I'll bet.

PRIOR 2: We all tumesce when they approach. We wax full, like moons.

PRIOR 1: Dance.

PRIOR: Dance?

PRIOR 1: Stand up, dammit, give us your hands, dance!

PRIOR 2: Listen . . .

(A lone oboe begins to play a little dance tune.)

PRIOR 2: Delightful sound. Care to dance?

PRIOR: Please leave me alone, please just let me sleep . . .

PRIOR 2: Ah, he wants someone familiar. A partner who knows his steps. (*To Prior.*) Close your eyes. Imagine . . .

PRIOR: I don't . . .

PRIOR 2: Hush. Close your eyes.

(Prior does.)

PRIOR 2: Now open them.

(Prior does. Louis appears. He looks gorgeous. The music builds gradually into a full-blooded, romantic dance tune.)

PRIOR: Lou.

LOUIS: Dance with me.

PRIOR: I can't, my leg, it hurts at night . . .
    Are you . . . a ghost, Lou?

LOUIS: No. Just spectral. Lost to myself. Sitting all day on cold park benches. Wishing I could be with you. Dance with me, babe . . .

(Prior stands up. The leg stops hurting. They begin to dance. The music is beautiful.)

PRIOR 1 (*to Prior 2*): Hah. Now I see why he's got no children. He's a sodomite.

PRIOR 2: Oh be quiet, you medieval gnome, and let them dance.

PRIOR 1: I'm not interfering, I've done my bit. Hooray, hooray, the messenger's come, now I'm blowing off. I don't like it here.

(Prior 1 vanishes.)

PRIOR 2: The twentieth century. Oh dear, the world has gotten so terribly, terribly old.

(Prior 2 vanishes. Louis and Prior waltz happily. Lights fade back to normal. Louis vanishes.
    Prior dances alone.
    Then suddenly, the sound of wings fills the room.)

Scene 7

(Split scene. Prior alone in his apartment; Louis alone in the park.
    Again, a sound of beating wings.)

PRIOR: Oh don't come in here don't come in . . . LOUIS!!
    No. My name is Prior Walter, I am . . . the scion of an ancient line, I am . . . abandoned I . . . no, my name is . . . is . . . Prior and I live . . . *here and now,* and . . . in the dark, in the dark, the Recording Angel opens its hundred eyes and snaps the spine of the Book of Life and . . . hush! Hush!
    I'm talking nonsense, I . . .
    No more mad scene, hush, hush.

(Louis in the park on a bench. Joe approaches, stands at a distance. They stare at each other, then Louis turns away.)

LOUIS: Do you know the story of Lazarus?

JOE: Lazarus?

LOUIS: Lazarus. I can't remember what happens, exactly.

JOE: I don't. . . . Well, he was dead, Lazarus, and Jesus breathed life into him. He brought him back from death.

LOUIS: Come here often?

JOE: No. Yes. Yes.

LOUIS: Back from the dead. You believe that really happened?

JOE: I don't know anymore what I believe.

LOUIS: This is quite a coincidence. Us meeting.

JOE: I followed you.
    From work. I . . . followed you here.

(Pause.)

LOUIS: You followed me.
    You probably saw me that day in the washroom and thought: there's a sweet guy, sensitive, cries for friends in trouble.

JOE: Yes.

LOUIS: You thought maybe I'll cry for you.

JOE: Yes.

LOUIS: Well I fooled you. Crocodile tears. Nothing . . .
    (*He touches his heart, shrugs.*)

(Joe reaches tentatively to touch Louis's face.)

LOUIS (*pulling back*): What are you doing? Don't do that.

JOE (*withdrawing his hand*): Sorry. I'm sorry.

LOUIS: I'm . . . just not . . . I think, if you touch me, your hand might fall off or something. Worse things have happened to people who have touched me.

JOE: Please.
    Oh, boy . . .
    Can I . . .
    I . . . want . . . to touch you. Can I please just touch you . . . um, here?
    (*He puts his hand on one side of Louis's face. He holds it there.*)
    I'm going to hell for doing this.

LOUIS: Big deal. You think it could be any worse than New York City?

(*He puts his hand on Joe's hand. He takes Joe's hand away from his face, holds it for a moment, then:*) Come on.

JOE: Where?

LOUIS: Home. With me.

JOE: This makes no sense. I mean I don't know you.

LOUIS: Likewise.

JOE: And what you do know about me you don't like.

LOUIS: The Republican stuff?

JOE: Yeah, well for starters.

LOUIS: I don't not like that. I *hate* that.

JOE: So why on earth should we . . .

(*Louis goes to Joe and kisses him.*)

LOUIS: Strange bedfellows. I don't know. I never made it with one of the damned before.

I would really rather not have to spend tonight alone.

JOE: I'm a pretty terrible person, Louis.

LOUIS: Lou.

JOE: No, I really really am. I don't think I deserve being loved.

LOUIS: There? See? We already have a lot in common.

(*Louis stands, begins to walk away. He turns, looks back at Joe. Joe follows. They exit.*)

(*Prior listens. At first no sound, then once again, the sound of beating wings, frighteningly near.*)

PRIOR: That sound, that sound, it . . . . What is that, like birds or something, like a *really* big bird, I'm frightened, I . . . no, no fear, find the anger, find the . . . anger, my blood is clean, my brain is fine, I can handle pressure, I am a gay man and I am used to pressure, to trouble, I am tough and strong and . . . . Oh. Oh my

goodness. I . . . (*He is washed over by an intense sexual feeling.*) Ooohhhh. . . . I'm hot, I'm . . . so . . . aw Jeez what is going on here I . . . must have a fever I . . .

(*The bedside lamp flickers wildly as the bed begins to roll forward and back. There is a deep bass creaking and groaning from the bedroom ceiling, like the timbers of a ship under immense stress, and from above a fine rain of plaster dust.*)

PRIOR: OH!

PLEASE, OH PLEASE! Something's coming in here, I'm scared, I don't like this at all, something's approaching and I . . . . OH!

(*There is a great blaze of triumphal music, heralding. The light turns an extraordinary harsh, cold, pale blue, then a rich, brilliant warm golden color, then a hot, bilious green, and then finally a spectacular royal purple. Then silence.*)

PRIOR (*an awestruck whisper*): God almighty . . . Very Steven Spielberg.

(*A sound, like a plummeting meteor, tears down from very, very far above the earth, hurtling at an incredible velocity towards the bedroom; the light seems to be sucked out of the room as the projectile approaches; as the room reaches darkness, we hear a terrifying CRASH as something immense strikes earth; the whole building shudders and a part of the bedroom ceiling, lots of plaster and lathe and wiring, crashes to the floor. And then in a shower of unearthly white light, spreading great opalescent gray-silver wings, the Angel descends into the room and floats above the bed.*)

ANGEL: Greetings, Prophet;
The Great Work begins:
The Messenger has arrived.

(*Blackout.*)

COMMENTARY

ANDREA BERNSTEIN

Interview with Tony Kushner   1995

Andrea Bernstein, a freelance cultural critic, engaged Tony Kushner in a discussion of the politics in his plays. Kushner's responses to her questions establish his credentials as a left-thinking critic of contemporary political life. His discussion of his work is centered much more in political reality than it is in dramatic technique or concern for theater. Yet Kushner is able to zero in on the dramatic moment and present contemporary politics as a dialectical struggle.

Tony Kushner, a gay Jewish socialist who was raised in Louisiana, won a Pulitzer Prize and two Tony Awards for his two-part, seven-hour Broadway production of *Angels in America: A Gay Fantasia on National Themes.* Other plays, *A Bright Room Called Day* (1985) and *Slavs!* (1994), are also concerned with the moral responsibilities of people in politically repressive times. Such concerns may be especially relevant in America today, where, as he observes: "What used to be called liberal is now called radical, what used to be called radical is now called insane, what used to be called reactionary is now called moderate, and what used to be called insane is now called solid conservative thinking."

Q: *Angels in America* opened on Broadway just months after the Clinton inauguration. It ends with a very hopeful speech about healing. Do you still feel that hope?

A: You have to have hope. It's irresponsible to give *false* hope, which I think a lot of playwrights are guilty of. But I also think it's irresponsible to simply be a nihilist, which quite a lot of playwrights, especially playwrights younger than me, have become guilty of. I don't believe you would bother to write a play if you really had no hope. That passage was one of the very first things I ever wrote when I was working on *Angels.* I read it to the woman who I was originally writing the part of the angel for, who died of breast cancer before the play was finished. In one of my last conversations with her, she told me that she thought about that image a lot and that she hoped I would include it in the play. I think I wouldn't have included it otherwise, but I'm glad I did now.

Q: *Angels in America* was a political play—and that's something Americans and critics frequently resist. How did you overcome that resistance?

A: What I found in the audience response is a huge hunger for political issues and political discussion. So I always wonder: Is it that Americans don't like politics, or is it that so much theater that is political isn't well done? One of the things I learned in *Slavs!* is that it's much easier to talk about being gay than it is to talk about being a socialist. People are afraid of socialism, and plays that deal with economics are scarier to them. I'll learn more about that—my next three plays are all about money.

Also, *Angels* is very entertaining. It does things formally that are new, and people were excited by the size and the scope. It's a good play and that makes all the difference.

Thelma and Louise, for instance, is a really terrific movie, and genuinely left in its political sensibilities. It's well-made, so the fact that it is unquestionably coming from a feminist perspective didn't make it absolutely marginal the way you would expect such a film to be. It had guns—that probably helped.

Q: People loved *Forrest Gump,* too.

A: People shouldn't trust artists and they shouldn't trust art. Part of the fun of art is that it invites you to interpret it.

There's a very complicated relationship between form and content and between aesthetics and politics. Good politics will produce good aesthetics, really good politics will produce really good aesthetics, and really good aesthetics, if somebody's really asking the hard questions and answering them honestly, they'll probably produce truth, which is to say progressive politics.

Q: Is it hard to write characters that are not caricatures and to overcome the barrier that people have about listening to politics from a character on stage?

A: I think that a character's politics have to live in the same sort of relationship to the character's psyche that people's politics live in relationship to their own psyches. People are never consistent. People will always do surprising things, both good and bad, and the way that people surprise themselves and their audience are the most interesting moments of human behavior. The space between what we'd like to be and what we actually are is where you find out the most interesting things.

Q: Do you see your plays as part of a political movement?

A: I do. I would hate to write anything that wasn't. I would like my plays to be of use to progressive people. I think preaching to the converted is exactly what art ought to do.

I am happiest when people who are politically engaged in the world say, "Your play meant a lot to me; it helped me think about something, or made me feel like I wasn't the only person who felt this way."

It's the way you feel when you go to a demo, which is the only way to keep sane a lot of the time. You need to remind yourself there are many bodies who are as angry about something as you are.

When I teach writing, I always tell my students you should assume that the audience you're writing for is smarter than you. You can't write if you don't think they're on your side, because then you start to yell at them or preach down to them.

Q: The character Prelapsarianov — the "world's oldest living Bolshevik" — gives the same speech in both *Angels* and *Slavs!*: "How are we to proceed without theory? Is it enough to reject the past, is it wise to move forward in this blind fashion, without the cold brilliant light of theory to guide the way? . . . You who live in this sour little age cannot imagine the sheer grandeur of the prospect we gazed upon."

A: In both *Perestroika* [part two of *Angels*] and *Slavs!*, the whole play proceeds from the question: If you don't know where you're going, can you move? And do you even have a choice, or do you just dive in and work it out as you're going?

That speech came out of a fight I had with my friend Oskar Eustis about Gorbachev. Oskar's point, which became the basis of Prelapsarianov's speech, is that if you don't have a theory to start with — Gorbachev pretended to be about democratic socialism but actually sort of was and sort of wasn't; he was also sort of about preserving the Communist Party power elite — what do you do? It's one of those big conundrums.

Q: So what *do* you do?

A: You can't stay back. The fundamental question is: Are we made by history or do we make history — and the answer is yes. I was rereading Marx's *Eighteenth Brumaire of Louis Bonaparte* recently. The whole tradition in socialist struggle is looking to the past for an antecedent form upon which the present revolutionary response is to be modeled. We may need to stop doing that.

Q: Why does the play *Slavs!* end with the question: "What is to be done?"

A: I wanted someone to ask the question: What if this really is the end of history? What if there really is literally nothing to be done, and we're simply stuck with capitalism—although I don't really think it is a possibility.

I still believe in a dialectical ordering of the universe. There is a dynamic principle at work—it isn't always mechanically moving things toward the good, but there's always either some sort of progress or decay. And there's too much misery in the world. That is not something that can hold.

Q: What do you think is to be done?

A: I'm 38 now. One of the painful rites of passage that everyone on the left goes through is to realize it's a lifelong struggle. What we're dealing with from Nixon on as a counter-reaction to the '60s is a very widespread, long-term historical trend. It's going to take many years and probably a few decades to reverse. People need to be willing to take an issue that they feel passionately about, address themselves to it as extensively as they are capable of and build common cause between issue groups.

Everybody on the left needs to start talking about how to create, first on local levels and eventually on a national level, a third party or at least a party that could establish some kind of position in Congress. That's the eternal dream of the left.

Q: You think there's no hope for revitalizing the Democratic Party?

A: It's a waste of time at this point. There's a famous story about Paul Wellstone refusing to shake Jesse Helms' hand and being chastised by everyone in the Senate because he wouldn't do it—he was told this is a gentlemen's club where we're all colleagues. That's what's wrong.

Q: One of the characters in *A Bright Room Called Day* keeps saying—as Nazism progressively snatches power and the Weimar Republic falls—that each turn for the worse would be the essential spur for people to rise up and oppose fascism. That didn't happen. Do you see parallels today?

A: You don't want to be opportunistic about it and say, "Oh, goody, millions of people are going to be thrown out of their homes—now we'll really get things cooking." It's like people saying the AIDS epidemic helped organize the gay and lesbian community.

Q: Speaking of which, there's a lot of discussion now about the second wave of the AIDS epidemic, and about gay men not practicing safer sex. Where do you weigh in?

A: It's very difficult to ask people to abstain from pleasure indefinitely, especially sexual erotic pleasure, which is so incredibly important to human beings and the enjoyment of which among homosexuals is so much of a political battlefield. There is absolutely no question that safer sex is not as gratifying and that given all the despair and the unbelievably imponderable weight of loss that the community has had to deal with, self-destructive behaviors are going to be engaged in.

Q: Do you think the gay community should be discussing this publicly?

A: Of course it's going to be discussed publicly. But you have to be smart. When you make a public utterance you are responsible for being responsible. We're still an embattled community, and if you're stupid about it you'll give aid to the enemy.

Q: Do you have that conundrum as a playwright?

A: You have to say: What am I feeding into? I think you should ask yourself that question and then make the decision based on the answers you come up with. I regret having made the only black person in *Angels* a nurse; that was an inept thing to do.

   I was very scared about writing a play where there's a couple, one has AIDS and the other walks out. I thought, this is transgressive and scary and am I going to become public enemy number one in the gay community for having written a character like Louis?

   On the other hand, you have to be willing to scare the horses. You have to be interesting and you have to be daring and you have to be willing to write things that shock. Shock is part of art. Art that's polite is not much fun.

Suzan-Lori Parks

Suzan-Lori Parks (b. 1964) was named by Mel Gussow in the *New York Times* as the "year's most promising playwright" in 1989. Currently she serves as the Master Writer Chair at the Public Theater in New York and as a visiting professor of dramatic writing at New York University's Tisch School of the Arts. Parks's work has been supported by grants from numerous foundations, including the Rockefeller and Ford Foundations and the National Endowment for the Arts, from which she has twice received a playwriting fellowship. She also received a MacArthur Award in 2001. In 2002 she became the first African American woman to win the Pulitzer Prize in drama, for *Topdog/Underdog* (2001).

Parks is the daughter of an army officer and grew up in several locations. She says, "I've heard horrible stories about twelve-step groups for army people. But I had a great childhood. My parents were really into experiencing the places we lived." She lived, for example, in a small town in Germany and attended German schools, studying in German. She went to Mt. Holyoke College and took courses at nearby Hampshire College, where she studied writing with James Baldwin. After that experience she went to London for a year to study acting. "It really made a difference in my writing. It dawned on me that a lot of people write with ideas in mind. . . . But I never really have ideas, per se. I have these movements, these gestures. Then I figure out how to put those gestures into words."

Parks is aware of being influenced by a number of important literary figures, among them Gertrude Stein, James Joyce, William Faulkner, and Samuel Beckett, but echoes of other writers such as Shakespeare and Richard Wright can be heard in *The Death of the Last Black Man in the Whole Entire World* (1990). Parks's approach to language is partly vernacular, as she attempts to reproduce speech both as it is spoken and as her audience assumes it may be spoken. But she is interested in the hypnotic and musical value of words, which accounts for much of the patterning of repetition that marks her work.

Parks's early short plays are *Betting on the Dust Commander* (1990), *Fishes* (1987), *The Sinners' Place* (1984), and *The America Play* (1994). Her full-length play *Imperceptible Mutabilities in the Third Kingdom* (1989), directed by her longtime collaborator Liz Diamond, won the Obie Award for the best off-Broadway play of 1990. One section of *Mutabilities* takes place on Emancipation Day in 1865 and is played in whiteface by African American actors. Another section, "Greeks," makes reference to her own family, with a character called Mr. Sergeant Smith. Parts of the play have been described as "like a choral poem."

Parks produced a film, *Anemone Me* (1990), that has been shown in New York. Her *Devotees in the Garden of Love* (1992) premiered at the Actors Theatre of Louisville, Kentucky. Her next play, *Venus* (1996), was a coproduction of the Joseph Papp Public Theater and Yale Repertory Theatre. It was directed by Richard Foreman, the founder of the Ontological-Hysteric Theater. The play focuses on the life of a black woman brought to England as the Venus Hottentot, a sideshow freak displaying "an intensely ugly figure, distorted beyond all European notions of beauty." The authorities put an end to the sideshow, and Parks explores this mysterious woman's life. Parks also wrote *Girl 6* (1996), a film directed by Spike Lee.

Parks has said that characters stay with her, and she feels free to create new plays on old themes. *In the Blood* (1999) focuses on Hester, a mother of five who faces poverty, the welfare system's workfare, and sterilization. The play examines attitudes toward poverty and responsibility. Hester appears again in *Fucking A* (2000), based on Nathaniel Hawthorne's novel *The Scarlet Letter* but with the A standing for abortion rather than adultery. *The America Play* (1994) features a black Lincoln impersonator, a character who later inspired *Topdog/Underdog*.

In 2003 Parks published her first novel, *Getting Mother's Body*, which was inspired by a novel by William Faulkner. She next produced a remarkably daring sequence of plays, each written in one day and each performed in one day, called *365 Days/365 Plays*. The work was performed by more than 700 theater companies and arts organizations from November 13, 2006, to November 12, 2007. *Ray Charles Live! A New Musical* (2007) won the NAACP Theatre Award in 2008 and opened on Broadway in 2010 with the title *Unchain My Heart: The Ray Charles Musical. Book of Grace* (2010) played in the Public Theater in New York to good reviews that likened its portrait of a dysfunctional family to a portrait of the nation at large. In 2011 Parks, with director Diane Paulus, adapted *The Gershwins' Porgy and Bess,* adding a positive ending and a number of new scenes. The first performances were at the American Repertory Theater in Boston; the musical opened on Broadway in 2012.

Parks is an energetic and carefully focused playwright with a special interest in the language of speech and the language of gesture—in almost equal measure.

Topdog/Underdog

Although Lincoln is listed as the top dog and Booth as the underdog, Parks has said they shift from moment to moment in this drama. John Wilkes Booth shot and killed Abraham Lincoln in 1865, but Booth was hunted down twelve days later and either shot or burned to death by federal troops. Lincoln is history's top dog, but the real Booth believed that Lincoln was a tyrant who needed to be put to death not only because the South lost the war but also because Lincoln planned to give blacks citizenship and voting rights in addition to their freedom. Modern historians have pointed out that Lincoln's personal views on matters of race were complex and sometimes contradictory. He believed, for example, that only very bright blacks should have voting rights. He also believed that blacks and whites would probably not be able to live together as social equals, and, as a result, he hoped that the white race would essentially be top dog in the future.

Naturally, it is a striking irony to have Lincoln, the elder brother in the play, play the part of Abraham Lincoln in an entertainment arcade, where he sits staring at a shiny metal electrical box while customers pay for the privilege of shooting him with a pistol loaded with blanks. He plays the part in whiteface and gets less pay than the previous "Lincoln," a white man. Nevertheless, he believes the job is an opportunity. He likes the work and hopes to continue and build something for himself. For Lincoln, this job represents a way out of the pattern of hustling and petty crime that has been his heritage. The fact that he is let go because of belt-tightening on the part of the arcade owners is emblematic of patterns of black hiring: "last hired, first fired."

Lincoln's younger brother, Booth, has a real gun. He carries it with him, and it remains a threatening presence throughout the play. He spends much of his time "boosting" goods from stores. He also practices the street con card game three-card monte, in which the dealer throws down three cards and then permits a "mark" to gamble on finding the ace of spades among the cards. It's a dishonest game, using sleight of hand and a number of sidekicks who act as shills, or make-believe players. Lincoln is the very best at the game, but he has left the street and wants to make a go of the "straight" life with a job that has potential and benefits. He has abandoned his game and refuses in act 1 to touch the cards. Booth, on the other hand, has no plans of going straight and pleads with Lincoln to teach him how the game works. He expects to be the best ever at three-card monte. Booth is even willing to change his name to Three-Card, and he envisions getting Lincoln's "old gang" together again to work with him.

Over the course of the play, the brothers examine their backgrounds, beginning with the fact that their parents separated and individually left them to fend for themselves when Lincoln was sixteen and Booth was thirteen. Booth points out that each of them got an inheritance from their parents of $500. The money that his mother gave Booth, we learn in act 2, is safe in a stocking that he has never opened. The final struggle in the last act seems focused on that "bequest," although it also has its roots in jealousy and brotherly competition of the kind found in the Bible's story of Cain and Abel.

The fact that they were abandoned as children weighs on both brothers, as does the fact that they were named Lincoln and Booth by their father as a joke. In other words, they were burdened by a violent history, unaware that, as the Chinese saying goes, "One's name is one's fate." In addition to reliving the personal history of Lincoln and Booth (both in the arcade and beyond it), however, they also live through the history of slavery and its aftermath. Their heritage is one of hustling and insecurity, and when Lincoln tries to emulate the virtues of his namesake—"Honest Abe"—he finds that, indeed, he likes the feeling of being honest and making an honest living. He does not want to go back to the street hustle, whereas Booth sees no hope of finding himself a role in the working world. He does not even try. In the end, however, Lincoln, having tried and temporarily succeeded, finds himself replaced because of cutbacks not by another actor, but by a wax dummy—essentially a wax machine that sits there and is shot, combined with a recording apparatus that can cry out appropriately at the proper moment.

In his review of the second New York performance in the *New York Times*, critic Ben Brantley said, "Brotherly love and hatred is translated into the terms of men who have known betrayal since their youth, when their parents walked out on them, and who will never be able entirely to trust anyone, including (and especially) each other. Implicit in their relationship is the idea that to live is to con."

Topdog/Underdog **in Performance**

The first production of *Topdog/Underdog* was on July 22, 2001, at the Joseph Papp Public Theater/New York Shakespeare Festival. George C. Wolfe was the producer and director. Don Cheadle played Booth and Jeffrey Wright played Lincoln. With the success of this production, the play moved to the larger Ambassador Theater on Broadway in April 2002, with Jeffrey Wright as Lincoln and the hip-hop artist Mos Def as Booth. The reviews of the production cited the intensity and brilliance of this performance. The energy displayed by Mos Def was extraordinary, and the interplay with Jeffrey Wright was so powerful that at times one wondered how they could contain themselves to get to the end of the play. The setting, by Riccardo Hernández, suggested the gloominess of a mid-nineteenth-century rooming house, adding to the tension and darkness of the drama.

Despite the demands of the play, it has been performed to considerable acclaim in London and in regional theaters in the United States and Canada. The Canadian premiere at the Shaw Festival at Niagara-on-the-Lake in 2011 received strong reviews that cited the special power of the play in "the Obama era." It has become noticed widely as a very important play.

SUZAN-LORI PARKS (b. 1964)

Topdog/Underdog   2001

I am God in nature;
I am a weed by the wall. — RALPH WALDO EMERSON, FROM "CIRCLES," *ESSAYS: FIRST SERIES* (1841)

The Players

LINCOLN, *the topdog*
BOOTH *(aka 3-Card), the underdog*

Author's Notes: From the "Elements of Style"

I'm continuing the use of my slightly unconventional theatrical elements. Here's a road map.

- *(Rest)*
  Take a little time, a pause, a breather; make a transition.

- A Spell
  An elongated and heightened *(Rest)*. Denoted by repetition of figures' names with no dialogue. Has sort of an architectural look:

  LINCOLN
  BOOTH
  LINCOLN
  BOOTH

  This is a place where the figures experience their pure true simple state. While no action or stage business is necessary, directors should fill this moment as they best see fit.

- [Brackets in the text indicate optional cuts for production.]

- (Parentheses around dialogue indicate softly spoken passages (asides; sotto voce)).

SCENE ONE

Thursday evening, A seedily furnished rooming house room. A bed, a reclining chair, a small wooden chair, some other stuff but not much else. Booth, a black man in his early 30s, practices his 3-card monte scam on the classic setup: 3 playing cards and the cardboard playing board atop 2 mismatched milk crates. His moves and accompanying patter are, for the most part, studied and awkward.

BOOTH: Watch me close watch me close now: who-see-thuh-red-card-who-see-thuh-red-card?

I-see-thuh-red-card. Thuh-red-card-is-thuh-winner.
Pick-thuh-red-card-you-pick-uh-winner. Pick-uh-
black-card-you-pick-uh-loser. Theres-thuh-loser, yeah,
theres-thuh-black-card, theres-thuh-other-loser-and-
theres-thuh-red-card, thuh-winner.

(*Rest*)

Watch me close watch me close now: 3-Card-
throws-thuh-cards-lightning-fast. 3-Card-thats-me-
and-Ima-last. Watch-me-throw-cause-here-I-go.
One-good-pickll-get-you-in, 2-good-picks-and-you-
gone-win. See-thuh-red-card-see-thuh-red-card-who-
see-thuh-red-card?

(*Rest*)

Dont touch my cards, man, just point to thuh one you
want. You-pick-that-card-you-pick-a-loser, yeah, that-
cards-a-loser. You-pick-that-card-thats-thuh-other-
loser. You-pick-that-card-you-pick-a-winner. Follow
that card. You gotta chase that card. You-pick-thuh-
dark-deuce-thats-a-loser-other-dark-deuces-thuh-
other-loser, red-deuce, thuh-deuce-of-heartsll-win-it-all.
Follow thuh red card.

(*Rest*)

Ima show you thuh cards: 2 black cards but only one
heart. Now watch me now. Who-sees-thuh-red-card-
who-knows-where-its-at? Go on, man, point to thuh
card. Put yr money down cause you aint no clown. No?
Ah you had thuh card, but you didnt have thuh heart.

(*Rest*)

You wanna bet? 500 dollars? Shoot. You musta
been watching 3-Card real close. Ok. Lay the cash
in my hand cause 3-Cards thuh man. Thank you,
mister. This card you say?

(*Rest*)

Wrong! Sucker! Fool! Asshole! Bastard! I bet yr daddy
heard how stupid you was and drank himself to death
just cause he didnt wanna have nothing to do witchu!
I bet yr mama seen you when you comed out and she
walked away from you with thuh afterbirth still hanging from out twixt her legs, sucker! Ha Ha Ha! And
3-Card, once again, wins all thuh money!!

(*Rest*)

What? Cops looking my way? Fold up thuh game, and
walk away. Sneak outa sight. Set up on another corner.

(*Rest*)

Yeah.

(*Rest*)

*Having won the imaginary loot and dodged the imagi-
nary cops, Booth sets up his equipment and starts practicing his scam all over again. Lincoln comes in quietly.
He is a black man in his later 30s. He is dressed in an
antique frock coat and wears a top hat and fake beard,
that is, he is dressed to look like Abraham Lincoln.
He surreptitiously walks into the room to stand right*

*behind Booth, who, engrossed in his cards, does not
notice Lincoln right away.*

BOOTH: Watch me close watch me close now: who-
see-thuh-red-card-who-see-thuh-red-card?
I-see-thuh-red-card. Thuh-red-card-is-thuh-
winner. Pick-thuh-red-card-you-pick-uh-winner.
Pick-uh-black-card-you-pick-uh-loser. Theres-
thuh-loser-yeah-theres-thuh-black-card, theres-thuh-
other-loser-and-theres-thuh-red-card, thuh-winner.
Dont touch my cards, man, dont—

(*Rest*)

Dont do that shit. Dont do that shit. Dont do that shit!

*Booth, sensing someone behind him, whirls around,
pulling a gun from his pants. While the presence of
Lincoln doesnt surprise him, the Lincoln costume does.*

BOOTH: And woah, man dont *ever* be doing that shit!
Who thuh fuck you think you is coming in my shit
all spooked out and shit. You pull that one more time
I'll shoot you!
LINCOLN: I only had a minute to make the bus.
BOOTH: Bullshit.
LINCOLN: Not completely. I mean, its either bull or shit,
but not a complete lie so it aint bullshit, right?

(*Rest*)

Put yr gun away.
BOOTH: Take off the damn hat at least.

*Lincoln takes off the stovepipe hat. Booth puts his gun
away.*

LINCOLN: Its cold out there. This thing kept my head
warm.
BOOTH: I dont like you wearing that bullshit, that shit that
bull that disguise that getup that motherdisfuckinguise
anywhere in the vicinity of my humble abode.

Lincoln takes off the beard.

LINCOLN: Better?
BOOTH: Take off the damn coat too. Damn, man. Bad
enough you got to wear that shit all day you come
up in here wearing it. What my women gonna say?
LINCOLN: What women?
BOOTH: I got a date with Grace tomorrow. Shes in love with
me again but she dont know it yet. Aint no man can
love her the way I can. She sees you in that getup its
gonna reflect bad on me. She coulda seen you coming
down the street. Shit. Could be standing outside right
now taking her ring off and throwing it on the sidewalk.

Booth takes a peek out the window.

BOOTH: I got her this ring today. Diamond. Well, dia-
mond-esque, but it looks just as good as the real
thing. Asked her what size she wore. She say 7 so I
go boost a size 6 and a half, right? Show it to her and
she loves it and I shove it on her finger and its a tight
fit right, so she cant just take it off on a whim, like
she did the last one I gave her. Smooth, right?

Booth takes another peek out the window.

LINCOLN: She out there?

BOOTH: Nope. Coast is clear.

LINCOLN: You boosted a ring?

BOOTH: Yeah. I thought about spending my inheritance on it but—take off that damn coat, man, you make me nervous standing there looking like a spook, and that damn face paint, take it off. You should take all of it off at work and leave it there.

LINCOLN: I don't bring it home someone might steal it.

BOOTH: At least take it *off* there, then.

LINCOLN: Yeah.

(*Rest*)

Lincoln takes off the frock coat and applies cold cream, removing the whiteface.

LINCOLN: I was riding the bus. Really I only had a minute to make my bus and I was sitting in the arcade thinking, should I change into my street clothes or should I make the bus? Nobody was in there today anyway. Middle of week middle of winter. Not like on weekends. Weekends the place is packed. So Im riding the bus home. And this kid asked me for my autograph. I pretended I didnt hear him at first. I'd had a long day. But he kept asking. Theyd just done Lincoln in history class and he knew all about him, he'd been to the arcade but, I dunno, for some reason he was tripping cause there was Honest Abe right beside him on the bus. I wanted to tell him to go fuck hisself. But then I got a look at him. A little rich kid. Born on easy street, you know the type. So I waited until I could tell he really wanted it, the autograph, and I told him he could have it for 10 bucks. I was gonna say *5*, cause of the Lincoln connection but something in me made me ask for 10.

BOOTH: But he didnt have a 10. All he had was a penny. So you took the penny.

LINCOLN: All he had was a *20*. So I took the 20 and told him to meet me on the bus tomorrow and Honest Abe would give him the change.

BOOTH: Shit.

LINCOLN: Shit is right.

(*Rest*)

BOOTH: Whatd you do with thuh 20?

LINCOLN: Bought drinks at Luckys. A round for everybody. They got a kick out of the getup.

BOOTH: You shoulda called me down.

LINCOLN: Next time, bro.

(*Rest*)

You making bookshelves? With the milk crates, you making bookshelves?

BOOTH: Yeah, big bro, Im making bookshelves.

LINCOLN: Whats the cardboard part for?

BOOTH: Versatility.

LINCOLN: Oh.

BOOTH: I was thinking we dont got no bookshelves we dont got no dining room table so lm making a sorta modular unit you put the books in the bottom and the table top on top. We can eat and store our books. We could put the photo album in there.

Booth gets the raggedy family photo album and puts it in the milk crate.

BOOTH: Youd sit there, I'd sit on the edge of the bed. Gathered around the dinner table. Like old times.

LINCOLN: We just gotta get some books but thats great, Booth, thats real great.

BOOTH: Dont be calling me Booth no more, K?

LINCOLN: You changing yr name?

BOOTH: Maybe.

LINCOLN

BOOTH

LINCOLN: What to?

BOOTH: Im not ready to reveal it yet.

LINCOLN: You already decided on something?

BOOTH: Maybe.

LINCOLN: You gonna call yrself something african? That be cool. Only pick something thats easy to spell and pronounce, man, cause you know, some of them african names, I mean, ok, Im down with the power to the people thing, but, no ones gonna hire you if they cant say yr name. And some of them fellas who got they african names, no one can say they names and they cant say they names neither. I mean, you dont want yr new handle to obstruct yr employment possibilities.

BOOTH

LINCOLN

BOOTH: You bring dinner?

LINCOLN: "Shango" would be a good name. The name of the thunder god. If you aint decided already Im just throwing it in the pot. I brought Chinese.

BOOTH: Lets try the table out.

LINCOLN: Cool.

They both sit at the new table. The food is far away near the door.

LINCOLN

BOOTH

LINCOLN: I buy it you set it up. Thats the deal. Thats the deal, right?

BOOTH: You like this place?

LINCOLN: Ssallright.

BOOTH: But a little cramped sometimes, right?

LINCOLN: You dont hear me complain. Although that recliner sometimes Booth, man—no Booth, right—man, Im too old to be sleeping in that chair.

BOOTH: Its my place. You dont got a place. Cookie, she threw you out. And you cant seem to get another woman. Yr lucky I let you stay.

LINCOLN: Every Friday you say *mi casa es su casa.*°

BOOTH: Every Friday you come home with yr paycheck. Today is Thursday and I tell you brother, its a long way from Friday to Friday. All kinds of things can happen. All kinds of bad feelings can surface and erupt while yr little brother waits for you to bring in yr share.

(*Rest*)

I got my Thursday head on, Link. Go get the food.

Lincoln doesnt budge.

mi . . . casa: My house is your house.

[ABOVE] Don Cheadle as Booth
and Jeffrey Wright as Lincoln
in the original 2001 production
of *Topdog/Underdog* at
the Joseph Papp Public Theater
in New York, directed and
produced by George C. Wolfe.
[RIGHT] Mos Def as Booth,
playing three-card monte in the
2002 New York production
at the Ambassador Theater on
Broadway.

LINCOLN: You dont got no running water in here, man.

BOOTH: So?

LINCOLN: You dont got no toilet you dont got no sink.

BOOTH: Bathrooms down the hall.

LINCOLN: You living in thuh Third World, fool! Hey, I'll get thuh food.

Lincoln goes to get the food. He sees a stray card on the floor and examines it without touching it. He brings the food over, putting it nicely on the table.

LINCOLN: You been playing cards?

BOOTH: Yeah.

LINCOLN: Solitaire?

BOOTH: Thats right. Im getting pretty good at it.

LINCOLN: Thats soup and thats sauce. I got you the meat and I got me the skrimps.

BOOTH: I wanted the skrimps.

LINCOLN: You said you wanted the meat. This morning when I left you said you wanted the meat.

(Rest)

Here man, take the skrimps. No sweat.

They eat. Chinese food, from styrofoam containers, cans of the soda, fortune cookies. Lincoln eats slowly and carefully, Booth eats ravenously.

LINCOLN: Yr getting good at solitaire?

BOOTH: Yeah. How about we play a hand after eating?

LINCOLN: Solitaire?

BOOTH: Poker or rummy or something.

LINCOLN: You know I dont touch thuh cards, man.

BOOTH: Just for fun.

LINCOLN: I dont touch thuh cards.

BOOTH: How about for money?

LINCOLN: You dont got no money. All the money you got I bring in here.

BOOTH: I got my inheritance.

LINCOLN: Thats like saying you dont got no money cause you aint never gonna do nothing with it so its like you dont got it.

BOOTH: At least I still got mines. You blew yrs.

LINCOLN

BOOTH

LINCOLN: You like the skrimps?

BOOTH: Ssallright.

LINCOLN: Whats yr fortune?

BOOTH: "Waste not want not." Whats yrs?

LINCOLN: "Your luck will change!"

Booth finishes eating. He turns his back to Lincoln and fiddles around with the cards, keeping them on the bed, just out of Lincolns sight. He mutters the 3-card patter under his breath. His moves are still clumsy. Every once and a while he darts a look over at Lincoln who does his best to ignore Booth.

((((Watch me close watch me close now: who-see-thuh-red-card who-see-thuh-red-card? I-see-thuh-red-card. Thuh-red-card-is-thuh-winner. Pick-thuh-red-card-you-pick-uh-winner.

Pick-uh-black-card-and-you-pick-uh-loser. Theres-thuh-loser, yeah, theres-thuh-black-card, theres-thuh-other-loser-and-theres-thuh-red-card, thuh-winner! Cop C, Stick, Cop C! Go on—))))

LINCOLN: ((Shit.))

BOOTH: (((((((One-good-pickll-get-you-in, 2-good-picks-and-you-gone-win. Dont touch my cards, man, just point to thuh one you want. You-pick-that-card-you-pick-uh-loser, yeah, that-cards-uh-loser, You-pick-that-card-thats-thuh-other-loser. You-pick-that-card-you-pick-uh-winner. Follow-that-card. You-gotta-chase-that-card!)))))))

LINCOLN: You wanna hustle 3-card monte, you gotta do it right, you gotta break it down. Practice it in smaller bits. Yr trying to do the whole thing at once thats why you keep fucking it up.

BOOTH: Show me.

LINCOLN: No. Im just saying you wanna do it you gotta do it right and if you gonna do it right you gotta work on it in smaller bits, thatsall.

BOOTH: You and me could team up and do it together. We'd clean up, Link.

LINCOLN: I'll clean up—bro.

Lincoln cleans up. As he clears the food, Booth goes back to using the "table" for its original purpose.

BOOTH: My new names 3-Card. 3-Card, got it? You wanted to know it so now you know it. 3-card monte by 3-Card. Call me 3-Card from here on out.

LINCOLN: 3-Card. Shit.

BOOTH: Im getting everybody to call me 3-Card. Grace likes 3-Card better than Booth. She says 3-Cards got something to it. Anybody not calling me 3-Card gets a bullet.

LINCOLN: Yr too much, man.

BOOTH: Im making a point.

LINCOLN: Point made, 3-Card. Point made.

Lincoln picks up his guitar. Plays at it.

BOOTH: Oh, come on, man, we could make money you and me. Throwing down the cards. 3-Card and Link: look out! We could clean up you and me. You would throw the cards and I'd be yr Stickman. The one in the crowd who looks like just an innocent passerby, who looks like just another player, like just another customer, but who gots intimate connections with you, the Dealer, the one throwing the cards, the main man. I'd be the one who brings in the crowd, I'd be the one who makes them want to put they money down, you do yr moves and I do mines. You turn yr head and I turn the card—

LINCOLN: It aint as easy as all that. Theres—

BOOTH: We could be a team, man. Rake in the money! Sure thered be some cats out there with fast eyes, some brothers and sisters who would watch real close and pick the right card, and so thered be some days when we would lose money, but most of the days we would come out on top! Pockets bulging, plenty of cash! And the ladies would be thrilling! You could afford to get laid! Grace would be all over me again.

LINCOLN: I thought you said she was all over you.

BOOTH: She is she is. Im seeing her tomorrow but today we gotta solidify the shit twixt you and me. Big brother Link and little brother Booth—

LINCOLN: 3-Card.

BOOTH: Yeah. Scheming and dreaming. No one throws the cards like you, Link. And with yr moves and my magic, and we get Grace and a girl for you to round out the posse. We'd be golden, bro! Am I right?

LINCOLN

BOOTH

BOOTH: Am I right?

LINCOLN: I dont touch thuh cards, 3-Card. I dont touch thuh cards no more.

LINCOLN

BOOTH

LINCOLN

BOOTH

BOOTH: You know what Mom told me when she was packing to leave? You was at school motherfucker you was at school. You got up that morning and sat down in yr regular place and read the cereal box while Dad read the sports section and Mom brought you yr dick toast and then you got on the damn school bus cause you didnt have the sense to do nothing else you was so into yr own shit that you didnt have the sense to feel nothing else going on. I had the sense to go back cause I was feeling something going on man, I was feeling something changing. So I—

LINCOLN: Cut school that day like you did almost every day—

BOOTH: She was putting her stuff in bags. She had all them nice suitcases but she was putting her stuff in bags.

(Rest)

Packing up her shit. She told me to look out for you. I told her I was the little brother and the big brother should look out after the little brother. She just said it again. That I should look out for you. Yeah. So who gonna look out for me. Not like you care. Here I am interested in an economic opportunity, willing to work hard, willing to take risks and all you can say you shiteating motherfucking pathetic limpdick uncle tom, all you can tell me is how you dont do no more what I be wanting to do. Here I am trying to earn a living and you standing in my way. YOU STANDING IN MY WAY, LINK!

LINCOLN: Im sorry.

BOOTH: Yeah, you sorry all right.

LINCOLN: I cant be hustling no more, bro.

BOOTH: What you do all day aint no hustle?

LINCOLN: Its honest work.

BOOTH: Dressing up like some crackerass white man, some dead president and letting people shoot at you sounds like a hustle to me.

LINCOLN: People know the real deal. When people know the real deal it aint a hustle.

BOOTH: We do the card game people will know the real deal. Sometimes we will win sometimes they will win. They fast they win, we faster we win.

LINCOLN: I aint going back to that, bro. I aint going back.

BOOTH: You play Honest Abe. You aint going back but you going all the way back. Back to way back then when folks was slaves and shit.

LINCOLN: Dont push me.

BOOTH

LINCOLN

BOOTH: You gonna have to leave.

LINCOLN: I'll be gone tomorrow.

BOOTH: Good. Cause this was only supposed to be a temporary arrangement.

LINCOLN: I will be gone tomorrow.

BOOTH: Good.

Booth sits on his bed. Lincoln, sitting in his easy chair with his guitar, plays and sings.

LINCOLN:

My dear mother left me, my fathers gone away
My dear mother left me and my fathers gone away
I dont got no money, I dont got no place to stay.

My best girl, she threw me out into the street
My favorite horse, they ground him into meat
Im feeling cold from my head down to my feet.

My luck was bad but now it turned to worse
My luck was bad but now it turned to worse
Dont call me up a doctor, just call me up a hearse.

BOOTH: You just made that up?

LINCOLN: I had it in my head for a few days.

BOOTH: Sounds good.

LINCOLN: Thanks.

(Rest)

Daddy told me once why we got the names we do.

BOOTH: Yeah?

LINCOLN: Yeah.

(Rest)

He was drunk when he told me, or maybe I was drunk when he told me. Anyway he told me, may not be true, but he told me. Why he named us both. Lincoln and Booth.

BOOTH: How come. How come, man?

LINCOLN: It was his idea of a joke.

Both men relax back as the lights fade.

SCENE TWO

Friday evening. The very next day. Booth comes in looking like he is bundled up against the cold. He makes sure his brother isnt home, then stands in the middle of the room. From his big coat sleeves he pulls out one new shoe then another, from another sleeve come two more shoes. He then slithers out a belt from each sleeve. He removes his coat. Underneath he wears a very nice new suit. He removes the jacket and pants revealing another new suit underneath. The suits still have the price tags on them. He takes two neckties from his pockets and two folded shirts from the back of his pants. He pulls a magazine from the front of his pants. Hes clearly had a busy day of shoplifting. He lays one suit out on Lincolns easy chair. The other he lays out on his own bed. He goes out into the hall returning with a folding screen which he sets up between the bed and the recliner creating 2 separate spaces. He takes out a bottle of whiskey and two glasses, setting them on the two stacked milk crates. He hears footsteps and sits down in the small wooden chair reading the magazine. Lincoln, dressed in street clothes, comes in.

LINCOLN: Taaaaadaaaaaaaaa!

BOOTH: Lordamighty, Pa, I smells money!

LINCOLN: Sho nuff, Ma. Poppas brung home thuh bacon.

BOOTH: Bringitherebringitherebringithere.

With a series of very elaborate moves Lincoln brings the money over to Booth.

BOOTH: Put it in my hands, Pa!

LINCOLN: I want ya tuh smells it first, Ma!

BOOTH: Put it neath my nose then, Pa!

LINCOLN: Take yrself a good long whiff of them greenbacks.

BOOTH: Oh lordamighty Ima faint, Pa! Get me muh med-sin!

Lincoln quickly pours two large glasses of whiskey.

LINCOLN: Dont die on me, Ma!

BOOTH: Im fading fast, Pa!

LINCOLN: Thinka thuh children, Ma! Thinka thuh farm!

BOOTH: 1-2-3.

Both men gulp down their drinks simultaneously.

LINCOLN AND BOOTH: AAAAAAAAAAAAAAAAAAA AAH!

Lots of laughing and slapping on the backs.

LINCOLN: Budget it out man budget it out.

BOOTH: You in a hurry?

LINCOLN: Yeah. I wanna see how much we got for the week.

BOOTH: You rush in here and dont even look around. Could be a fucking A-bomb in the middle of the floor you wouldnt notice. Yr wife, Cookie—

LINCOLN: X-wife—

BOOTH: —could be in my bed you wouldnt notice—

LINCOLN: She was once—

BOOTH: Look the fuck around please.

Lincoln looks around and sees the new suit on his chair.

LINCOLN: Wow.

BOOTH: Its yrs.

LINCOLN: Shit.

BOOTH: Got myself one too.

LINCOLN: Boosted?

BOOTH: Yeah, I boosted em. Theys stole from a big-ass department store. That store takes in more money in one day than we will in our whole life. I stole and I stole generously. I got one for me and I got one for you. Shoes belts shirts ties socks in the shoes and everything. Got that screen too.

LINCOLN: You all right, man.

BOOTH: Just cause I aint good as you at cards dont mean I cant do nothing.

LINCOLN: Lets try em on.

They stand in their separate sleeping spaces. Booth near his bed, Lincoln near his recliner, and try on their new clothes.

BOOTH: Ima wear mine tonight. Gracell see me in this and *she* gonna ask me tuh marry *her*.

(Rest)

I got you the blue and I got me the brown. I walked in there and walked out and they didnt as much as bat an eye. Thats how smooth lil bro be, Link.

LINCOLN: You did good. You did real good, 3-Card.

BOOTH: All in a days work.

LINCOLN: They say the clothes make the man. All day long I wear that getup. But that dont make me who I am. Old black coat not even real old just fake old. Its got worn spots on the elbows, little raggedy places thatll break through into holes before the winters out. Shiny strips around the cuffs and the collar. Dust from the cap guns on the left shoulder where they shoot him, where they shoot me I should say but I never feel like they shooting me. The fella who had the gig before I had it wore the same coat. When I got the job they had the getup hanging there waiting for me. Said thuh fella before me just took it off one day and never came back.

(Rest)

Remember how Dads clothes used to hang in the closet?

BOOTH: Until you took em outside and burned em.

(Rest)

He had some nice stuff. What he didnt spend on booze he spent on women. What he didnt spend on them two he spent on clothes. He had some nice stuff I would look at his stuff and calculate thuh how long it would take till I was big enough to fit it. Then you went and burned it all up.

LINCOLN: I got tired of looking at em without him in em.

(Rest)

They said thuh fella before me—he took off the getup one day, hung it up real nice, and never came back. And as they offered me thuh job, saying of course I would have to wear a little makeup and accept less than what they would offer a—another guy—

BOOTH: Go on, say it. "White." Theyd pay you less than theyd pay a white guy.

LINCOLN: I said to myself thats exactly what I would do: wear it out and then leave it hanging there and not come back. But until then, I would make a living at it. But it dont make me. Worn suit coat, not even worn by the fool that Im supposed to be playing, but making fools out of all those folks who come crowding in for they chance to play at something great. Fake beard. Top hat. Dont make me into no Lincoln. I was Lincoln on my own before any of that.

The men finish dressing. They style and profile.

BOOTH: Sharp, huh?

LINCOLN: Very sharp.

BOOTH: You look sharp too, man. You look like the real you. Most of the time you walking around all bedraggled and shit. You look good. Like you used to look back in thuh day when you had Cookie in love with you and all the women in the world was eating out of yr hand.

LINCOLN: This is real nice, man. I dont know where Im gonna wear it but its real nice.

BOOTH: Just wear it around. Itll make you feel good and when you feel good yll meet someone nice. Me I aint interested in meeting no one nice, I mean, I only got eyes for Grace. You think she'll go for me in this?

LINCOLN: I think thuh tie you gave me'll go better with what you got on.

BOOTH: Yeah?

LINCOLN: Grace likes bright colors dont she? My ties bright, yrs is too subdued.

BOOTH: Yeah. Gimmie yr tie.

LINCOLN: You gonna take back a gift?

BOOTH: I stole the damn thing didnt I? Gimmie yrs! I'll give you mines.

They switch neckties. Booth is pleased. Lincoln is more pleased.

LINCOLN: Do thuh budget.

BOOTH: Right. Ok lets see: we got 314 dollars. We put 100 aside for the rent. 100 a week times 4 weeks makes the rent and—

LINCOLN AND BOOTH: —we dont want thuh rent spent.

BOOTH: That leaves 214. We put aside 30 for the electric leaving 184. We put aside 50 for thuh phone leaving 134.

LINCOLN: We dont got a phone.

BOOTH: We pay our bill theyll turn it back on.

LINCOLN: We dont need no phone.

BOOTH: How you gonna get a woman if you dont got a phone? Women these days are more cautious, more whaddacallit, more circumspect. You go into a club looking like a fast daddy, you get a filly to give you her numerophono and gone is the days when she just gives you her number and dont ask for yrs.

LINCOLN: Like a woman is gonna call me.

BOOTH: She dont wanna call you she just doing a preliminary survey of the property. Shit, Link, you dont know nothin no more.

(*Rest*)

She gives you her number and she asks for yrs. You give her yr number. The phone number of yr home. Thereby telling her 3 things: 1) you got a home, that is, you aint no smooth talking smooth dressing *homeless* joe; 2) that you is in possession of a telephone and a working telephone number which is to say that you got thuh cash and thuh wherewithal to acquire for yr self the worlds most revolutionary communication apparatus and you together enough to pay yr bills!

LINCOLN: Whats 3?

BOOTH: You give her yr number you telling her that its cool to call if she should so please, that is, that you aint got no wife or wife approximation on the premises.

(*Rest*)

50 for the phone leaving 134. We put aside 40 for "med-sin."

LINCOLN: The price went up. 2 bucks more a bottle.

BOOTH: We'll put aside 50, then. That covers the bills. We got 84 left. 40 for meals together during the week leaving 44. 30 for me 14 for you. I got a woman I gotta impress tonight.

LINCOLN: You didnt take out for the phone last week.

BOOTH: Last week I was depressed. This week things is looking up. For both of us.

LINCOLN: Theyre talking about cutbacks at the arcade. I only been there 8 months, so—

BOOTH: Dont sweat it man, we'll find something else.

LINCOLN: Not nothing like this. I like the job. This is sit down, you know, easy work. I just gotta sit there all day. Folks come in kill phony Honest Abe with the phony pistol. I can sit there and let my mind travel.

BOOTH: Think of women.

LINCOLN: Sometimes.

(*Rest*)

All around the whole arcade is buzzing and popping. Thuh whirring of thuh duckshoot, baseballs smacking the back wall when someone misses the stack of cans, some woman getting happy cause her fella just won the ring toss. The Boss playing the barker talking up the fake freaks. The smell of the ocean and cotton candy and rat shit. And in thuh middle of all that, I can just sit and let my head go quiet. Make up songs, make plans. Forget.

(*Rest*)

You should come down again.

BOOTH: Once was plenty, but thanks.

(*Rest*)

Yr Best Customer, he come in today?

LINCOLN: Oh, yeah, he was there.

BOOTH: He shoot you?

LINCOLN: He shot Honest Abe, yeah.

BOOTH: He talk to you?

LINCOLN: In a whisper. Shoots on the left whispers on the right.

BOOTH: Whatd he say this time?

LINCOLN: "Does thuh show stop when no ones watching or does thuh show go on?"

BOOTH: Hes getting deep.

LINCOLN: Yeah.

BOOTH: Whatd he say, that one time? " Yr only yrself—"

LINCOLN: "—when no ones watching," yeah.

BOOTH: Thats deep shit.

(*Rest*)

Hes a brother, right?

LINCOLN: I think so.

BOOTH: He know yr a brother?

LINCOLN: I dunno. Yesterday he had a good one. He shoots me, Im playing dead, and he leans in close then goes: "God aint nothing but a parasite."

BOOTH: Hes one *deep* black brother.

LINCOLN: Yeah. He makes the day interesting.

BOOTH (*Rest*): Thats a fucked-up job you got.

LINCOLN: Its a living.

BOOTH: But you aint living.

LINCOLN: Im alive aint I?

(*Rest*)

One day I was throwing the cards. Next day Lonny died. Somebody shot him. I knew I was next, so I quit. I saved my life.

(*Rest*)

The arcade gig is the first lucky break Ive ever had. And Ive actually grown to like the work. And now theyre talking about cutting me.

BOOTH: You was lucky with thuh cards.

LINCOLN: Lucky? Aint nothing lucky about cards. Cards aint luck. Cards is work. Cards is skill. Aint never nothing lucky about cards.

(*Rest*)

I dont wanna lose my job.

BOOTH: Then you gotta jazz up yr act. Elaborate yr moves, you know. You was always too stiff with it. You cant just sit there! Maybe, when they shoot you, you know, leap up flail yr arms then fall down and wiggle around and shit so they gotta shoot you more than once. Blam Blam Blam! Blam!

LINCOLN: Help me practice. I'll sit here like I do at work and you be like one of the tourists.

BOOTH: No thanks.

LINCOLN: My paychecks on the line, man.

BOOTH: I got a date. Practice on yr own.

(*Rest*)

I got a rendezvous with Grace. Shit she so sweet she makes my teeth hurt.

(*Rest*)

Link, uh, howbout slipping me an extra 5 spot. Its the biggest night of my life.

LINCOLN

BOOTH

Lincoln gives Booth a 5er.

BOOTH: Thanks.

LINCOLN: No sweat.

BOOTH: Howabout I run through it with you when I get back. Put on yr getup and practice till then.

LINCOLN: Sure.

Booth leaves. Lincoln stands there alone. He takes off his shoes, giving them a shine. He takes off his socks and his fancy suit, hanging it neatly over the little wooden chair. He takes his getup out of his shopping bag. He puts it on, slowly, like an actor preparing for a great role: frock coat, pants, beard, top hat, necktie. He leaves his feet bare. The top hat has an elastic band which he positions securely underneath his chin. He picks up the white pancake makeup but decides against it. He sits. He pretends to get shot, flings himself on the floor and thrashes around. He gets up, considers giving the new moves another try, but instead pours himself a big glass of whiskey and sits there drinking.

SCENE THREE

Much later that same Friday evening. The recliner is reclined to its maximum horizontal position and Lincoln lies there asleep. He wakes with a start. He is horrific, bleary eyed and hungover, in his full Lincoln regalia. He takes a deep breath, realizes where he is and reclines again, going back to sleep. Booth comes in full of swagger. He slams the door trying to wake his brother who is dead to the world. He opens the door and slams it again. This time Lincoln wakes up, as hungover and horrid as before. Booth swaggers about, his moves are exaggerated, rooster-like. He walks round and round Lincoln making sure his brother sees him.

LINCOLN: You hurt yrself?

BOOTH: I had me "an evening to remember."

LINCOLN: You look like you hurt yrself.

BOOTH: Grace Grace Grace. *Grace.* She wants me back. She wants me back so bad she wiped her hand over the past where we wasnt together just so she could say we aint never been apart. She wiped her hand over our breakup. She wiped her hand over her childhood, her teenage years, her first boyfriend, just so she could say that she been mine since the dawn of time.

LINCOLN: Thats great, man.

BOOTH: And all the shit I put her through: she wiped it clean. And the women I saw while I was seeing her—

LINCOLN: Wiped clean too?

BOOTH: Mister Clean, Mister, Mister Clean!

LINCOLN: Whered you take her?

BOOTH: We was over at her place. I brought thuh food, Stopped at the best place I could find and stuffed my coat with only the best. We had candlelight, we had music we had—

LINCOLN: She let you do it?

BOOTH: Course she let me do it.

LINCOLN: She let you do it without a rubber?

BOOTH: —Yeah.

LINCOLN: Bullshit.

BOOTH: I put my foot down—and she *melted*. And she was—huh—she was something else. I dont wanna get you jealous, though.

LINCOLN: Go head, I dont mind.

BOOTH (*Rest*): Well, you know what she looks like.

LINCOLN: She walks on by and the emergency room fills up cause all the guys get whiplash from lookin at her.

BOOTH: Thats right thats right. Well—she comes to the door wearing nothing but her little nightie, eats up the food I'd brought like there was no tomorrow and then goes and eats on me.

(*Rest*)

LINCOLN: Go on.

BOOTH: I dont wanna make you feel bad, man.

LINCOLN: Ssallright. Go on.

BOOTH (*Rest*): Well, uh, you know what shes like. Wild. Goodlooking. So sweet my teeth hurt.

LINCOLN: Sexmachine.

BOOTH: Yeah.

LINCOLN: Hotsy-Totsy.

BOOTH: Yeah.

LINCOLN: Amazing Grace.

BOOTH: Amazing Grace! Yeah. Thats right. She let me do her how I wanted. And no rubber.

(*Rest*)

LINCOLN: Go on.

BOOTH: You dont wanna hear the mushy shit.

LINCOLN: Sure I do.

BOOTH: You hate mushy shit. You always hated thuh mushy shit.

LINCOLN: Ive changed. Go head. You had "an evening to remember," remember? I was just here alone sitting here. Drinking. Go head. Tell Link thuh stink.

(*Rest*)

Howd ya do her?

BOOTH: Dogstyle.

LINCOLN: Amazing Grace.

BOOTH: In front of a mirror.

LINCOLN: So you could see her. Her face her breasts her back her ass. Graces got a great ass.

BOOTH: Its all right.

LINCOLN: Amazing Grace!

Booth goes into his bed area and takes off his suit, tossing the clothes on the floor.

BOOTH: She said next time Ima have to use a rubber. She let me have my way this time but she said that next time I'd have to put my boots on.

LINCOLN: Im sure you can talk her out of it.

BOOTH: Yeah.

(*Rest*)

What kind of rubbers you use, I mean, when you was with Cookie.

LINCOLN: We didnt use rubbers. We was married, man.

BOOTH: Right. But you had other women on the side. What kind you use when you was with them?

LINCOLN: Magnums.

BOOTH: Thats thuh kind I picked up. For next time. Grace was real strict about it.

While Booth sits on his bed fiddling with his box of condoms, Lincoln sits in his chair and resumes drinking.

LINCOLN: Im sure you can talk her out of it. You put yr foot down and she'll melt.

BOOTH: She was real strict. Sides I wouldnt wanna be taking advantage of her or nothing. Putting my foot down and her melting all over thuh place.

LINCOLN: Magnums then.

(*Rest*)

Theyre for "the larger man."

BOOTH: Right. Right.

Lincoln keeps drinking as Booth, sitting in the privacy of his bedroom, fiddles with the condoms, perhaps trying to put one on.

LINCOLN: Thats right.

BOOTH: Graces real different from them fly-by-night gals I was making do with. Shes in school. Making something of herself. Studying cosmetology. You should see what she can do with a womans hair and nails.

LINCOLN: Too bad you aint a woman.

BOOTH: What?

LINCOLN: You could get yrs done for free, I mean.

BOOTH: Yeah. She got this way of sitting. Of talking. Everything she does is. Shes just so hot.

(*Rest*)

We was together 2 years. Then we broke up. I had my little employment difficulty and she needed time to think.

LINCOLN: And shes through thinking now.

BOOTH: Thats right.

LINCOLN

BOOTH

LINCOLN: Whatcha doing back there?

BOOTH: Resting. That girl wore me out.

LINCOLN: You want some med-sin?

BOOTH: No thanks.

LINCOLN: Come practice my moves with me, then.

BOOTH: Lets hit it tomorrow, K?

LINCOLN: I been waiting. I got all dressed up and you said if I waited up—come on, man, they gonna replace me with a wax dummy.

BOOTH: No shit.

LINCOLN: Thats what theyre talking about. Probably just talk, but—come on, man, I even lent you 5 bucks.

BOOTH: Im tired.

LINCOLN: You didnt get shit tonight.

BOOTH: You jealous, man. You just jail-us.

LINCOLN: You laying over there yr balls blue as my boosted suit. Laying over there waiting for me to go back to sleep or black out so I wont hear you rustling thuh pages of yr fuck book.

BOOTH: Fuck you, man.

LINCOLN: I was over there looking for something the other week and theres like 100 fuck books under yr bed and theyre matted together like a bad fro, bro, cause you spunked in the pages and didnt wipe them off.

BOOTH: Im hot. I need constant sexual release. If I wasnt taking care of myself by myself I would be out there running around on thuh town which costs cash that I dont have so I would be doing worse: I'd be out there doing who knows what, shooting people and shit. Out of a need for unresolved sexual release. I'm a hot man. I aint apologizing for it. When I dont got a woman, I gotta make do. Not like you, Link. When you dont got a woman you just sit there. Letting yr shit fester. Yr dick, if it aint failed off yet, is hanging there between yr legs, little whiteface shriveled-up blank-shooting grub worm. As goes thuh man so goes thuh mans dick. Thats what I say. Least my shits intact.

(Rest)

You a limp dick jealous whiteface motherfucker whose wife dumped him cause he couldnt get it up and she told me so. Came crawling to me cause she needed a man.

(Rest)

I gave it to Grace good tonight. So goodnight.

LINCOLN (Rest): Goodnight.

LINCOLN
BOOTH
LINCOLN
BOOTH
LINCOLN
BOOTH

Lincoln sitting in his chair. Booth lying in bed. Time passes. Booth pecks out to see if Lincoln is asleep. Lincoln is watching for him.

LINCOLN: You can hustle 3-card monte without me you know.

BOOTH: Im planning to.

LINCOLN: I could contact my old crew. You could work with them. Lonny aint around no more but theres the rest of them. Theyre good.

BOOTH: I can get my own crew. I dont need yr crew. Buncha has-beens. I can get my own crew.

LINCOLN: My crews experienced. We usedta pull down a thousand a day. Thats 7 G a week. That was years ago. They probably do twice, 3 times that now.

BOOTH: I got my own connections, thank you.

LINCOLN: Theyd take you on in a heartbeat. With my say. My say still counts with them. They know you from before, when you tried to hang with us but—wernt ready yet. They know you from then, but I'd talk you up. I'd say yr my bro, which they know, and I'd say youd been working the west coast. Little towns. Mexican border. Taking tourists. I'd tell them you got moves like I dreamed of having. Meanwhile youd be working out yr shit right here, right in this room, getting good and getting better every day so when I did do the reintroductions youd have some marketable skills. Youd be passable.

BOOTH: I'd be more than passable, I'd be the be all end all.

LINCOLN: Youd be the be all end all. And youd have my say. If yr interested.

BOOTH: Could do.

LINCOLN: Youd have to get a piece. They all pack pistols, bro.

BOOTH: I *got* a piece.

LINCOLN: Youd have to be packing something more substantial than that pop gun, 3-Card. These hustlers is upper echelon hustlers they pack upper echelon heat, not no Saturday night shit, now.

BOOTH: Whata you know of heat? You aint hung with those guys for 6, 7 years. You swore off em. Threw yr heat in thuh river and you "Dont touch thuh cards." I know more about heat than you know about heat.

LINCOLN: Im around guns every day. At the arcade. Theyve all been reworked so they only fire caps but I see guns every day. Lots of guns.

BOOTH: What kinds?

LINCOLN: You been there, you seen them. Shiny deadly metal each with their own deadly personality.

BOOTH: Maybe I *could* visit you over there. I'd boost one of them guns and rework it to make it shoot for real again. What kind you think would best suit my personality?

LINCOLN: You aint stealing nothing from the arcade.

BOOTH: I go in there and steal if I want to go in there and steal I go in there and steal.

LINCOLN: It aint worth it. They dont shoot nothing but blanks.

BOOTH: Yeah, like you. Shooting blanks.

(Rest)

(Rest)

You ever wonder if someones gonna come in there with a real gun? A real gun with real slugs? Someone with uh axe tuh grind or something?

LINCOLN: No.

BOOTH: Someone who hates you come in there and guns you down and gets gone before anybody finds out.

LINCOLN: I dont got no enemies.

BOOTH: Yr X.

LINCOLN: Cookie dont hate me.

BOOTH: Yr Best Customer? Some miscellaneous stranger?

LINCOLN: I cant be worrying about the actions of miscellaneous strangers.

BOOTH: But there they come day in day out for a chance to shoot Honest Abe.

(*Rest*)

Who are they mostly?

LINCOLN: I dont really look.

BOOTH: You must see something.

LINCOLN: Im supposed to be staring straight ahead. Watching a play, like Abe was.

BOOTH: All day goes by and you never ever take a sneak peek at who be pulling the trigger.

Pulled in by his own curiosity, Booth has come out of his bed area to stand on the dividing line between the two spaces.

LINCOLN: Its pretty dark. To keep thuh illusion of thuh whole thing.

(*Rest*)

But on thuh wall opposite where I sit theres a little electrical box, like a fuse box. Silver metal. Its got uh dent in it like somebody hit it with they fist. Big old dent so everything reflected in it gets reflected upside down. Like yr looking in uh spoon. And thats where I can see em. The assassins.

(*Rest*)

Not behind me yet but I can hear him coming. Coming in with his gun in hand, thuh gun he already picked out up front when he paid his fare. Coming on in. But not behind me yet. His dress shoes making too much noise on the carpet, the carpets too thin, Boss should get a new one but hes cheap. Not behind me yet. Not behind me yet. Cheap lightbulb just above my head.

(*Rest*)

And there he is. Standing behind me. Standing in position. Standing upside down. Theres some feet shapes on the floor so he knows just where he oughta stand. So he wont miss. Thuh gun is always cold. Winter or summer thuh gun is always cold. And when the gun touches me he can feel that Im warm and he knows Im alive. And if Im alive then he can shoot me dead. And for a minute, with him hanging back there behind me, its real. Me looking at him upside down and him looking at me looking like Lincoln. Then he shoots.

(*Rest*)

I slump down and close my eyes. And he goes out thuh other way. More come in. Uh whole day full. Bunches of kids, little good for nothings, in they school uniforms. Businessmen smelling like two for one martinis. Tourists in they theme park t-shirts trying to catch it on film. Housewives with they mouths closed tight, shooting more than once.

(*Rest*)

They all get so into it. I do my best for them. And now they talking bout replacing me with uh wax dummy. Itll cut costs.

BOOTH: You just gotta show yr boss that you can do things a wax dummy cant do. You too dry with it. You gotta add spicy shit.

LINCOLN: Like what.

BOOTH: Like when they shoot you, I dunno, scream or something.

LINCOLN: Scream?

Booth plays the killer without using his gun.

BOOTH: Try it. I'll be the killer. Bang!

LINCOLN: Aaaah!

BOOTH: Thats good.

LINCOLN: A wax dummy can scream. They can put a voicebox in it and make it like its screaming.

BOOTH: You can curse. Try it. Bang!

LINCOLN: Motherfucking cocksucker!

BOOTH: Thats good, man.

LINCOLN: They aint going for that, though.

BOOTH: You practice rolling and wiggling on the floor?

LINCOLN: A little.

BOOTH: Lemmie see. Bang!

Lincoln slumps down, falls on the floor and silently wiggles around.

BOOTH: You look more like a worm on the sidewalk. Move yr arms. Good. Now scream or something.

LINCOLN: Aaaah! Aaaaah! Aaaah!

BOOTH: A little tougher than that, you sound like yr fucking.

LINCOLN: Aaaaaah!

BOOTH: Hold yr head or something, where I shotcha. Good. And look at me! I am the assassin! *I am Booth!!* Come on man this is life and death! Go all out!

Lincoln goes all out.

BOOTH: Cool, man thats cool. Thats enough.

LINCOLN: Whatdoyathink?

BOOTH: I dunno, man. Something about it. I dunno. It was looking too real or something.

LINCOLN: They dont want it looking too real. I'd scare the customers. Then I'd be out for sure. Yr trying to get me fired.

BOOTH: Im trying to help. Cross my heart.

LINCOLN: People are funny about they Lincoln shit. Its historical. People like they historical shit in a certain way. They like it to unfold the way they folded it up. Neatly like a book. Not raggedy and bloody and screaming. You trying to get me fired.

(Rest)

I am uh brother playing Lincoln. Its uh screech for anyones imagination. And it aint easy for me neither. Every day I put on that shit, I leave my own shit at the door and I put on that shit and I go out there and I make it work. I make it look easy but its hard. That shit is hard. But it works. Cause I work it. And you trying to get me fired.

(Rest)

I swore off them cards. Took nowhere jobs. Drank. Then Cookie threw me out. What thuh fuck was I gonna do? I seen that "Help Wanted" sign and I went up in there and I looked good in the getup and agreed to the whiteface and they really dug it that me and Honest Abe got the same name.

(Rest)

Its a sit down job. With benefits. I dont wanna get fired. They wont give me a good reference if I get fired.

BOOTH: Iffen you was tuh get fired, then, well—then you and me could—hustle the cards together. We'd have to support ourselves somehow.

(Rest)

Just show me how to do the hook part of the card hustle, man. The part where the Dealer looks away but somehow he sees—

LINCOLN: I couldnt remember if I wanted to.

BOOTH: Sure you could.

LINCOLN: No.

(Rest)

Night, man.

BOOTH: Yeah.

Lincoln stretches out in his recliner. Booth stands over him waiting for him to get up, to change his mind. But Lincoln is fast asleep. Booth covers him with a blanket then goes to his bed, turning off the lights as he goes. He quietly rummages underneath his bed for a girlie magazine which, as the lights fade, he reads with great interest.

SCENE FOUR

Saturday. Just before dawn. Lincoln gets up. Looks around. Booth is fast asleep, dead to the world.

LINCOLN: No fucking running water.

He stumbles around the room looking for something which he finally finds: a plastic cup, which he uses as a urinal. He finishes peeing and finds an out of the way place to stow the cup. He claws at his Lincoln getup, removing it and tearing it in the process. He strips down to his t-shirt and shorts.

LINCOLN: Hate falling asleep in this damn shit. Shit. Ripped the beard. I can just hear em tomorrow.

Busiest day of the week. They looking me over to make sure Im presentable. They got a slew of guys working but Im the only one they look over every day. "Yr beards ripped, pal. Sure, we'll getcha new one but its gonna be coming outa yr pay." Shit. I should quit right then and there. I'd yank off the beard, throw it on the ground and stomp it, then go strangle the fucking boss. Thatd be good. My hands around his neck and his bug eyes bugging out. You been ripping me off since I took this job and now Im gonna have to take it outa *yr* pay, mother-fucker. Shit.

(Rest)

Sit down job. With benefits.

(Rest)

Hustling. Shit, I was good. I was great. Hell I was the be all end all. I was throwing cards like throwing cards was made for me. Made for me and me alone. I was the best anyone ever seen. Coast to coast. Everybody said so. And I never lost. Not once. Not one time. Not never. Thats how much them cards was mines. I was the be all end all. I was that good.

(Rest)

Then you woke up one day and you didnt have the taste for it no more. Like something in you knew—. Like something in you knew it was time to quit. Quit while you was still ahead. Something in you was telling you—. But hells no. Not Link thuh stink. So I went out there and threw one more time. What thuh fuck. And Lonny died.

(Rest)

Got yrself a good job. And when the arcade lets you go yll get another good job. I dont gotta spend my whole life hustling. Theres more to Link than that. More to me than some cheap hustle. More to life than cheating some idiot out of his paycheck or his life savings.

(Rest)

Like that joker and his wife from out of town. Always wanted to see the big city. I said you could see the bigger end of the big city with a little more cash. And if they was fast enough, faster than me, and here I slowed down my moves I slowed em way down and my Lonny, my right hand, my Stickman, Spanish guy who looked white and could draw a customer in like nothing else, Lonny could draw a fly from fresh shit, he could draw Adam outa Eve just with that look he had, Lonny always got folks playing.

(Rest)

Somebody shot him. They dont know who. Nobody knows nobody cares.

(Rest)

We took that man and his wife for hundreds. No, thousands. We took them for everything they had and everything they ever wanted to have. We took a father for the money he was gonna get his kids new bike with and he cried in the street while we vanished. We took a mothers welfare check, she pulled a knife on us and we ran. She threw it but her aim werent shit. People shopping. Greedy. Thinking they could take me and they got took instead.

(*Rest*)

Swore off thuh cards. Something inside me telling me—. But I was good.

LINCOLN

LINCOLN

He sees a packet of cards. He studies them like an alcoholic would study a drink. Then he reaches for them, delicately picking them up and choosing 3 cards.

LINCOLN: Still got my moves. Still got my touch. Still got my chops. Thuh feel of it. And I aint hurting no one, God. Link is just here hustling hisself.

(*Rest*)

Lets see whatcha got.

He stands over the monte setup. Then he bends over it placing the cards down and moving them around. Slowly at first, aimlessly, as if hes just making little ripples in water. But then the game draws him in. Unlike Booth, Lincolns patter and moves are deft, dangerous, electric.

LINCOLN: (((Lean in close and watch me now: who see thuh black card who see thuh black card I see thuh black card black cards thuh winner pick thuh black card thats thuh winner pick thuh red card thats thuh loser pick thuh other red card thats thuh other loser pick thuh black card you pick thuh winner. Watch me as I throw thuh cards. Here we go.)))

(*Rest*)

(((Who see thuh black card who see thuh black card? You pick thuh red card you pick a loser you pick that red card you pick a loser you pick thuh black card thuh deuce of spades you pick a winner who sees thuh deuce of spades thuh one who sees it never fades watch me now as I throw thuh cards. Red losers black winner follow thuh deuce of spades chase thuh black deuce. Dark deuce will get you thuh win.)))

Even though Lincoln speaks softly, Booth wakes and, unbeknownst to Lincoln, listens intently.

(*Rest*)

LINCOLN: ((10 will get you 20, 20 will get you 40.))

(*Rest*)

((Ima show you thuh cards: 2 red cards but only one spade. Dark winner in thuh center and thuh red losers on thuh sides. Pick uh red card you got a loser

pick thuh other red card you got a loser pick thuh black card you got a winner. One good pickll get you in, 2 good picks and you gone win. Watch me come on watch me now.))

(*Rest*)

((Who sees thuh winner who knows where its at? You do? You sure? Go on then, put yr money where yr mouth is. Put yr money down you aint no clown. No? Ah, you had thuh card but you didnt have thuh heart.))

(*Rest*)

((Watch me now as I throw thuh cards watch me real close. Ok, man, you know which card is the deuce of spades? Was you watching Links lightning fast express? Was you watching Link cause he the best? So you sure, huh? Point it out first, then place yr bet and Linkll show you yr winner.))

(*Rest*)

((500 dollars? You thuh man of thuh hour you thuh man with thuh power. You musta been watching Link real close. You must be thuh man who know thuh most. Ok. Lay the cash in my hand cause Link the man. Thank you, mister. This card you say?))

(*Rest*)

((Wrong! Ha!))

(*Rest*)

((Thats thuh show. We gotta go.))

Lincoln puts the cards down. He moves away from the monte setup. He sits on the edge of his easy chair, but he can't take his eyes off the cards.

Intermission

SCENE FIVE

Several days have passed. Its now Wednesday night. Booth is sitting in his brand-new suit. The monte setup is nowhere in sight. In its place is a table with two nice chairs. The table is covered with a lovely tablecloth and there are nice plates, silverware, champagne glasses and candles. All the makings of a very romantic dinner for two. The whole apartment in fact takes its cue from the table. Its been cleaned up considerably. New curtains on the windows, a doily-like object on the recliner. Booth sits at the table darting his eyes around, making sure everything is looking good.

BOOTH: Shit.

He notices some of his girlie magazines visible from underneath his bed. He goes over and nudges them out of sight. He sits back down. He notices that theyre still visible. He goes over and nudges them some more, kicking at them finally. Then he takes the spread from his bed and pulls it down, hiding them. He sits back

Jeffrey Wright and Mos Def in the 2002 production at the Ambassador Theater.

down. He gets up. Checks the champagne on much melted ice. Checks the food.

BOOTH: Foods getting cold, Grace!! Dont worry man, she'll get here, she'll get here.

He sits back down. He goes over to the bed. Checks it for springiness. Smoothes down the bedspread. Double-checks 2 matching silk dressing gowns, very expensive, marked "His" and "Hers." Lays the dressing gowns across the bed again, He sits back down. He cant help but notice the visibility of the girlie magazines again. He goes to the bed, kicks them fiercely, then on his hands and knees shoves them. Then he begins to get under the bed to push them, but he remembers his nice cloth-ing and takes off his jacket. After a beat he removes his pants and, in this half-dressed way, he crawls under the bed to give those telltale magazines a good and final shove. Lincoln comes in. At first Booth, still stripped down to his underwear, thinks its his date. When he realizes its his brother, he does his best to keep Lincoln from entering the apartment. Lincoln wears his frock coat and carries the rest of his getup in a plastic bag.

LINCOLN: You in the middle of it?

BOOTH: What the hell you doing here?

LINCOLN: If yr in thuh middle of it I can go. Or I can just be real quiet and just—sing a song in my head or something.

BOOTH: The casas off limits to you tonight.

LINCOLN: You know when we lived in that 2-room place with the cement backyard and the frontyard with nothing but trash in it, Mom and Pops would do it in the middle of the night and I would always hear them but I would sing in my head, cause, I dunno, I couldnt bear to listen.

BOOTH: You gotta get out of here.

LINCOLN: I would make up all kinds of songs. Oh, sorry, yr all up in it. No sweat, bro. No sweat. Hey, Grace, howyadoing?!

BOOTH: She aint here yet, man. Shes running late. And its a good thing too cause I aint all dressed yet. Yr gonna spend thuh night with friends?

LINCOLN: Yeah.

Booth waits for Lincoln to leave. Lincoln stands his ground.

LINCOLN: I lost my job.

BOOTH: Hunh.

LINCOLN: I come in there right on time like I do every day and that motherfucker gives me some song and dance about cutbacks and too many folks complaining.

BOOTH: Hunh.

LINCOLN: Showd me thuh wax dummy—hes buying it right out of a catalog.

(Rest)

I walked out still wearing my getup.

(Rest)

I could go back in tomorrow. I could tell him I'll take another pay cut. Thatll get him to take me back.

BOOTH: Link. Yr free. Dont go crawling back. Yr free at last! Now you can do anything you want. Yr not tied down by that job. You can—you can do something else. Something that pays better maybe.

LINCOLN: You mean Hustle.

BOOTH: Maybe. Hey, Graces on her way. You gotta go.

Lincoln flops into his chair. Booth is waiting for him to move. Lincoln doesnt budge.

LINCOLN: I'll stay until she gets here. I'll act nice. I wont embarrass you.

BOOTH: You gotta go.

LINCOLN: What time she coming?

BOOTH: Shes late. She could be here any second.

LINCOLN: I'll meet her. I met her years ago. I'll meet her again.

(Rest)

How late is she?

BOOTH: She was supposed to be here at 8.

LINCOLN: Its after 2 a.m. Shes—shes late.

(Rest)

Maybe when she comes you could put the blanket over me and I'll just pretend like Im not here.

(Rest)

I'll wait. And when she comes I'll go. I need to sit down. I been walking around all day.

BOOTH

LINCOLN

Booth goes to his bed and dresses hurriedly.

BOOTH: Pretty nice, right? The china thuh silver thuh crystal.

LINCOLN: Its great.

(Rest)

Boosted?

BOOTH: Yeah.

LINCOLN: Thought you went and spent yr inheritance for a minute, you had me going I was thinking shit, Booth—3-Card—that 3-Cards gone and spent his inheritance and the gal is—late.

BOOTH: Its boosted. Every bit of it.

(Rest)

Fuck this waiting bullshit.

LINCOLN: She'll be here in a minute. Dont sweat it.

BOOTH: Right.

Booth comes to the table. Sits. Relaxes as best he can.

BOOTH: How come I got a hand for boosting and I dont got a hand for throwing cards? Its sorta the same thing—you gotta be quick—and slick. Maybe yll show me yr moves sometime.

LINCOLN

BOOTH

LINCOLN

BOOTH

LINCOLN: Look out the window. When you see Grace coming, I'll go.

BOOTH: Cool. Cause youd jinx it, youd really jinx it. Maybe you being here has jinxed it already. Naw. Shes just a little late. You aint jinxed nothing.

Booth sits by the window, glancing out, watching for his date. Lincoln sits in his recliner. He finds the whiskey bottle, sips from it. He then rummages around, finding the raggedy photo album. He looks through it.

LINCOLN: There we are at that house. Remember when we moved in?

BOOTH: No.

LINCOLN: You were 2 or 3.

BOOTH: I was 5.

LINCOLN: I was 8. We all thought it was the best fucking house in the world.

BOOTH: Cement backyard and a frontyard full of trash, yeah, dont be going down memory lane man, yll jinx thuh vibe I got going in here. Gracell be walking in here and wrinkling up her nose cause you done jinxed up thuh joint with yr raggedy recollections.

LINCOLN: We had some great times in that house, bro. Selling lemonade on thuh corner, thuh treehouse out back, summers spent lying in thuh grass and looking at thuh stars.

BOOTH: We never did none of that shit.

LINCOLN: But we had us some good times. That row of nails I got you to line up behind Dads car so when he backed out the driveway to work—

BOOTH: He came back that night, only time I ever seen his face go red, 4 flat tires and yelling bout how thuh white man done sabotaged him again.

LINCOLN: And neither of us flinched. Neither of us let on that itd been us.

BOOTH: It was at dinner, right? What were we eating?

LINCOLN: Food.

BOOTH: We was eating pork chops, mashed potatoes and peas. I remember cause I had to look at them peas real hard to keep from letting on. And I would glance over at you, not really glancing not actually turning my head, but I was looking at you out thuh corner of my eye. I was sure he was gonna find us out and then he woulda whipped us good. But I kept glancing at yon and you was cool, man. Like nothing was going on. You was coooooool.

(Rest)

What time is it?

LINCOLN: After 3.

(Rest)

You should call her. Something mighta happened.

BOOTH: No man, Im cool. She'll be here in a minute. Patience is a virtue. She'll be here.

LINCOLN: You look sad.
BOOTH: Nope. Im just, you know, Im just—
LINCOLN: Cool.
BOOTH: Yeah. Cool.

Booth comes over, takes the bottle of whiskey and pours himself a big glassful. He returns to the window looking out and drinking.

BOOTH: They give you a severance package, at thuh job?
LINCOLN: A weeks pay.
BOOTH: Great.
LINCOLN: I blew it. Spent it all.
BOOTH: On what?
LINCOLN: —. Just spent it.

(*Rest*)

It felt good, spending it. Felt really good. Like back in thuh day when I was really making money. Throwing thuh cards all day and strutting and rutting all night. Didnt have to take no shit from no fool, didnt have to worry about getting fired in favor of some damn wax dummy. I was thuh shit and they was my fools.

(*Rest*)

Back in thuh day.

(*Rest*)

(*Rest*)

Why you think they left us, man?
BOOTH: Mom and Pops? I dont think about it too much.
LINCOLN: I dont think they liked us.
BOOTH: Naw. That aint it.
LINCOLN: I think there was something out there that they liked more than they liked us and for years they was struggling against moving towards that more liked something. Each of them had a special something that they was struggling against. Moms had hers. Pops had his. And they was struggling. We moved out of that nasty apartment into a house. A whole house. It wernt perfect but it was a house and theyd bought it and they brought us there and everything we owned, figuring we could be a family in that house and them things, them two separate things each of them was struggling against, would just leave them be. Them things would see thuh house and be impressed and just leave them be. Would see thuh job Pops had and how he shined his shoes every night before he went to bed, shining them shoes whether they needed it or not, and thuh thing he was struggling against would see all that and just let him be, and thuh thing Moms was struggling against, it would see the food on the table every night and listen to her voice when she'd read to us sometimes, the clean clothes, the buttons sewed on all right and it would just let her be. Just let us all be, just regular people living in a house. That wernt too much to ask.
BOOTH: Least we was grown when they split.
LINCOLN: 16 and 13 aint grown.

BOOTH: 16s grown. Almost. And I was ok cause you were there.

(*Rest*)

Shit man, it aint like they both one day both together packed all they shit up and left us so they could have fun in thuh sun on some tropical island and you and me would have to grub in thuh dirt forever. They didnt leave together. That makes it different. She left. 2 years go by. Then he left. Like neither of them couldnt handle it no more. She split then he split. Like thuh whole family mortgage bills going to work thing was just too much. And I dont blame them. You dont see me holding down a steady job. Cause its bullshit and I know it. I seen how it cracked them up and I aint going there.

(*Rest*)

It aint right me trying to make myself into a one woman man just because she wants me like that. One woman rubber-wearing motherfucker. Shit. Not me. She gonna walk in here looking all hot and shit trying to see how much she can get me to sweat, how much she can get me to give her before she gives me mines. Shit.

LINCOLN
BOOTH
LINCOLN: Moms told me I shouldnt never get married.
BOOTH: She told me thuh same thing.
LINCOLN: They gave us each 500 bucks then they cut out.
BOOTH: Thats what Im gonna do. Give my kids 500 bucks then cut out. Thats thuh way to do it.
LINCOLN: You dont got no kids.
BOOTH: Im gonna have kids then Im gonna cut out.
LINCOLN: Leaving each of yr offspring 500 bucks as yr splitting.
BOOTH: Yeah.

(*Rest*)

Just goes to show Mom and Pops had some agreement between them.
LINCOLN: How so.
BOOTH: Theyd stopped talking to eachother. Theyd stopped *screwing* eachother. But they had an agreement. Somewhere in there when it looked like all they had was hate they sat down and did thuh "split" budget.

(*Rest*)

When Moms splits she gives me 5 hundred-dollar bills rolled up and tied up tight in one of her nylon stockings. She tells me to put it in a safe place, to spend it only in case of an emergency, and not to tell nobody I got it, not even you. 2 years later Pops splits and before he goes —
LINCOLN: He slips me 10 fifties in a clean handkerchief: "Hide this somewheres good, dont go blowing it, dont tell no one you got it, especially that Booth."

BOOTH: Theyd been scheming together all along. They left separately but they was in agreement. Maybe they arrived at the same place at the same time, maybe they renewed they wedding vows, maybe they got another family.

LINCOLN: Maybe they got 2 new kids. 2 boys. Different than us, though. Better.

BOOTH: Maybe.

Their glasses are empty. The whiskey bottle is empty too. Booth takes the champagne bottle front the ice tub. He pops the cork and pours drinks for his brother and himself.

BOOTH: I didnt mind them leaving cause you was there. Thats why Im hooked on us working together. If we could work together it would be like old times. They split and we got that room downtown. You was done with school and I stopped going. And we had to run around doing odd jobs just to keep the lights on and the heat going and thuh child protection bitch off our backs. It was you and me against thuh world, Link. It could be like that again.

LINCOLN

BOOTH

LINCOLN

BOOTH

LINCOLN: Throwing thuh cards aint as easy as it looks.

BOOTH: I aint stupid.

LINCOLN: When you hung with us back then, you was just on thuh sidelines. Thuh perspective from thuh sidelines is thuh perspective of a customer. There was all kinds of things you didnt know nothing about.

BOOTH: Lonny would entice folks into thuh game as they walked by. Thuh 2 folks on either side of ya looked like they was playing but they was only pretending tuh play. Just tuh generate excitement. You was moving thuh cards as fast as you could hoping that yr hands would be faster than yr customers eyes. Sometimes you won sometimes you lost what else is there to know?

LINCOLN: Thuh customer is actually called the "Mark." You know why?

BOOTH: Cause hes thuh one you got yr eye on. You mark him in with yr eye.

LINCOLN

LINCOLN

BOOTH: Im right, right?

LINCOLN: Lemmie show you a few moves. If you pick up these yll have a chance.

BOOTH: Yr playing.

LINCOLN: Get thuh cards and set it up.

BOOTH: No shit.

LINCOLN: Set it up set it up.

In a flash, Booth clears away the romantic table setting by gathering it all up in the tablecloth and tossing it aside. As he does so he reveals the "table" underneath: the 2 stacked monte milk crates and the cardboard playing surface. Lincoln lays out the cards. The brothers are ready. Lincoln begins to teach Booth in earnest.

LINCOLN: Thuh deuce of spades is thuh card tuh watch.

BOOTH: I work with thuh deuce of hearts. But spades is cool.

LINCOLN: Theres thuh Dealer, thuh Stickman, thuh Sides, thuh Lookout and thuh Mark. I'll be thuh Dealer.

BOOTH: I'll be thuh Lookout. Lemmie be thuh Lookout, right? I'll keep an eye for thuh cops. I got my piece on me.

LINCOLN: You got it on you right now?

BOOTH: I always carry it.

LINCOLN: Even on a date? In yr own home?

BOOTH: You never know, man.

(Rest)

So Im thuh Lookout.

LINCOLN: Gimmie yr piece.

Booth gives Lincoln his gun. Lincoln moves the little wooden chair to face right in front of the setup. He then puts the gun on the chair.

LINCLON: We dont need nobody standing on the corner watching for cops cause there aint none.

BOOTH: I'll be thuh Stickman, then.

LINCOLN: Stickman knows the game inside out. You aint there yet. But you will be. You wanna learn good, be my Sideman. Playing along with the Dealer, moving the Mark to lay his money down. You wanna learn, right?

BOOTH: I'll be thuh Side.

LINCOLN: Good.

(Rest)

First thing you learn is what is. Next thing you learn is what aint. You dont know what is you dont know what aint, you dont know shit.

BOOTH: Right.

LINCOLN

BOOTH

BOOTH: Whatchu looking at?

LINCOLN: Im sizing you up.

BOOTH: Oh yeah?!

LINCOLN: Dealer always sizes up thuh crowd.

BOOTH: Im yr Side, Link, Im on yr team, you dont go sizing up yr own team. You save looks like that for yr Mark.

LINCOLN: Dealer always sizes up thuh crowd. Everybody out there is part of the crowd. His crew is part of the crowd, he himself is part of the crowd. Dealer always sizes up thuh crowd.

Lincoln looks Booth over some more then looks around at an imaginary crowd.

BOOTH: Then what then what?

LINCOLN: Dealer dont wanna play.

BOOTH: Bullshit man! Come on you promised!

LINCOLN: Thats thuh Dealers attitude. He *acts* like he dont wanna play. He holds back and thuh crowd, with their eagerness to see his skill and their willingness to take a chance, and their greediness to win his cash, the larceny in their hearts, all goad him on and push him to throw his cards, although of course the Dealer has been wanting to throw his cards all along. Only he dont never show it.

BOOTH: Thats some sneaky shit, Link.

LINCOLN: It sets thuh mood. You wanna have them in yr hand before you deal a hand, K?

BOOTH: Cool.—K.

LINCOLN: Right.

LINCOLN

BOOTH

BOOTH: You sizing me up again?

LINCOLN: Theres 2 parts to throwing thuh cards. Both parts are fairly complicated. Thuh moves and thuh grooves, thuh talk and thuh walk, thuh patter and thuh pitter pat, thuh flap and thuh rap: what yr doing with yr mouth and what yr doing with yr hands.

BOOTH: I got thuh words down pretty good.

LINCOLN: You need to work on both.

BOOTH: K.

LINCOLN: A goodlooking walk and a dynamite talk captivates their entire attention. The Mark focuses with 2 organs primarily: his eyes and his ears. Leave one out you lose yr shirt. Captivate both, yr golden.

BOOTH: So them times I seen you lose, them times I seen thuh Mark best you, that was a time when yr hands werent fast enough or yr patter werent right.

LINCOLN: You could say that.

BOOTH: So, there was plenty of times—

Lincoln moves the cards around.

LINCOLN: You see what Im doing? Dont look at my hands, man, look at my eyes. Know what is and know what aint.

BOOTH: What is?

LINCOLN: My eyes.

BOOTH: What aint?

LINCOLN: My hands. Look at my eyes not my hands. And you standing there thinking how thuh fuck I gonna learn how tuh throw thuh cards if I be looking in his eyes? Look into my eyes and get yr focus. Dont think about learning how tuh throw thuh cards. Dont think about nothing. Just look into my eyes. Focus.

BOOTH: Theyre red.

LINCOLN: Look into my eyes.

BOOTH: You been crying?

LINCOLN: Just look into my eyes, fool. Now. Look down at thuh cards. I been moving and moving and moving them around. Ready?

BOOTH: Yeah.

LINCOLN: Ok, Sideman, thuh Marks got his eye on you. Yr gonna show him its easy.

BOOTH: K.

LINCOLN: Pick out thuh deuce of spades. Dont pick it up just point to it.

BOOTH: This one, right?

LINCOLN: Dont ask thuh Dealer if yr right, man, point to yr card with confidence.

Booth points.

BOOTH: That one.

(*Rest*)

Flip it over, man.

Lincoln flips over the card. It is in fact the deuce of spades. Booth struts around gloating like a rooster. Lincoln is mildly crestfallen.

BOOTH: Am I right or am I right?! Make room for 3-Card! Here comes thuh champ!

LINCOLN: Cool. Stay focused. Now we gonna add the second element. Listen.

Lincoln moves the cards and speaks in a low hypnotic voice.

LINCOLN: Lean in close and watch me now: who see thuh black card who see thuh black card I see thuh black card black cards thuh winner pick thuh black card thats thuh winner pick thuh red card thats thuh loser pick thuh other red card thats thuh other loser pick thuh black card you pick thuh winner. Watch me as I throw thuh cards. Here we go.

(*Rest*)

Who see thuh black card who see thuh black card? You pick thuh red card you pick a loser you pick that red card you pick a loser you pick thuh black card thuh deuce of spades you pick a winner who sees thuh deuce of spades thuh one who sees it never fades watch me now as I throw thuh cards. Red losers black winner follow thuh deuce of spades chase thuh black deuce. Dark deuce will get you thuh win. One good pickll get you in 2 good picks you gone win. 10 will get you 20, 20 will get you 40.

(*Rest*)

Ima show you thuh cards: 2 red cards but only one spade. Dark winner in thuh center and thuh red losers on thuh sides. Pick uh red card you got a loser pick thuh other red card you got a loser pick thuh black card you got a winner. Watch me watch me watch me now.

(*Rest*)

Ok, 3-Card, you know which cards thuh deuce of spades?

BOOTH: Yeah.

LINCOLN: You sure? Yeah? You sure you sure or you just think you sure? Oh you sure you sure huh? Was you watching Links lightning fast express? Was you watching Link cause he the best? So you sure, huh? Point it out. Now, place yr bet and Linkll turn over yr card.

BOOTH: What should I bet?

LINCOLN: Dont bet nothing man, we just playing. Slap me 5 and point out thuh deuce.

Booth slaps Lincoln 5, then points out a card which Lincoln flips over. It is in fact again the deuce of spades.

BOOTH: Yeah, baby! 3-Card got thuh moves! You didnt know lil bro had thuh stuff, huh? Think again, Link, think again.

LINCOLN: You wanna learn or you wanna run yr mouth?

BOOTH: Thought you had fast hands. Wassup? What happened tuh "Links Lightning Fast Express"? Turned into uh local train looks like tuh me.

LINCOLN: Thats yr whole motherfucking problem. Yr so busy running yr mouth you aint never gonna learn nothing! You think you something but you aint shit.

BOOTH: I aint shit, I am *The* Shit. Shit. Wheres thuh dark deuce? Right there! Yes, baby!

LINCOLN: Ok, 3-Card. Cool. Lets switch. Take thuh cards and show me whatcha got. Go on. Dont touch thuh cards too heavy just—its a light touch. Like yr touching Graces skin. Or, whatever, man, just a light touch. Like uh whisper.

BOOTH: Like uh whisper.

Booth moves the cards around, in an awkward imitation of his brother.

LINCOLN: Good.

BOOTH: Yeah. All right. Look into my eyes.

Booths speech is loud and his movements are jerky. He is doing worse than when he threw the cards at the top of the play.

BOOTH: Watch-me-close-watch-me-close-now: who-see-thuh-dark-card-who-see-thuh-dark-card? I-see-thuh-dark-card. Here-it-is. Thuh-dark-card-is-thuh-winner. Pick-thuh-dark-card-and-you-pick-uh-winner. Pick-uh-red-card-and-you-pick-uh-loser. Theres-thuh-loser-yeah-theres-thuh-red-card, theres-thuh-other-loser-and-theres-thuh-black-card, thuh-winner. Watch-me-close-watch-me-close-now: 3-Card-throws-thuh-cards-lightning-fast. 3-Card-thats-me-and-Ima-last. Watch-me-throw-cause-here-I-go. See thuh black card? Yeah? Who see I see you see thuh black card?

LINCOLN: Hahahahhahahahahahahah!

Lincoln doubles over laughing. Booth puts on his coat and pockets his gun.

BOOTH: What?

LINCOLN: Nothing, man, nothing.

BOOTH: *What?!*

LINCOLN: Yr just, yr just a little wild with it. You talk like that on thuh street cards or no cards and theyll lock you up, man. Shit. Reminds me of that time when you hung with us and we let you try being thuh Stick cause you wanted to so bad. Thuh hustle was so simple. Remember? I told you that when I put my hand in my left pocket you was to get thuh Mark tuh pick thuh card on that side. You got to thinking something like Links left means my left some dyslexic shit and turned thuh wrong card. There was 800 bucks on the line and you fucked it up.

(Rest)

But it was cool, little bro, cause we made the money back. It worked out cool.

(Rest)

So, yeah, I said a light touch, little bro. Throw thuh cards light. Like uh whisper.

BOOTH: Like Graces skin.

LINCOLN: Like Graces skin.

BOOTH: What time is it?

Lincoln holds up his watch. Booth takes a look.

BOOTH: Bitch. *Bitch!* She said she was gonna show up around 8. 8-a-fucking-clock.

LINCOLN: Maybe she meant 8 *a.m.*

BOOTH: Yeah. She gonna come all up in my place talking bout how she *love* me. How she cant stop *thinking* bout me. Nother mans shit up in her nother mans thing in her nother mans dick on her breath.

LINCOLN: Maybe something happened to her.

BOOTH: Something happened to her all right. She trying to make a chump outa me. I aint her chump. I aint nobodys chump.

LINCOLN: Sit. I'll go to the payphone on the corner. I'll—

BOOTH: Thuh world puts its foot in yr face and you dont move. You tell thuh world tuh keep on stepping. But Im my own man, Link. I aint you.

Booth goes out, slamming the door behind him.

LINCOLN: You got that right.

After a moment Lincoln picks up the cards. He moves them around fast, faster, faster.

SCENE SIX

Thursday night. The room looks empty, as if neither brother is home. Lincoln comes in. Hes fairly drunk. He strides in, leaving the door slightly ajar.

LINCOLN: Taaadaaaa!

(Rest)

(Rest)

Taadaa, motherfucker. Taadaa!

(Rest)

Booth—uh, 3-Card—you here? Nope. Good. Just as well. HaHa *Ha Ha Ha*!

He pulls an enormous wad of money from his pocket. He counts it, slowly and luxuriously, arranging and smoothing the bills and sounding the amounts under his breath. He neatly rolls up the money, secures it with a rubber band and puts it back in his pocket. He relaxes in his chair. Then he takes the money out again, counting it all over again, but this time quickly, with the touch of an expert hustler.

LINCOLN: You didnt go back, Link, you got back, you got it back you got yr shit back in thuh saddle, man, you got back in business. Walking in Luckys and you seen how they was looking at you? Lucky starts pouring for you when you walk in. And the women. You see how they was looking at you? Bought drinks for everybody. Bought drinks for Lucky. Bought drinks for Luckys damn dog. Shit. And thuh women be hanging on me and purring. And I be feeling that old call of thuh wild calling. I got more phone numbers in my pockets between thuh time I walked out that door and thuh time I walked back in than I got in my whole life. Cause my shit is *back*. And back better than it was when it left too. Shoot. Who thuh man? Link. Thats right. Purrrrring all up on me and letting me touch them and promise them shit. 3 of them sweethearts in thuh restroom on my dick all at once and I was *there* my shit was there. And Cookie just went out of my mind which is cool which is very cool. 3 of them. Fighting over it. Shit. Cause they knew I'd been throwing thuh cards. Theyd seen me on thuh corner with thuh old crew or if they aint seed me with they own eyes theyd heard word. Links thuh stink! Theyd heard word and they seed uh sad face on some poor sucker or a tear in thuh eye of some stupid fucking tourist and they figured it was me whod just took thuh suckers last dime, it was me who had all thuh suckers loot. They knew. They knew.

Booth appears, in the room. He was standing behind the screen, unseen all this time. He goes to the door, soundlessly, just stands there.

LINCOLN: And they was all in Luckys. Shit. And they was waiting for me to come in from my last throw. Cant take too many fools in one day, its bad luck, Link, so they was all waiting in there for me to come in thuh door and let thuh liquor start flowing and thuh music start going and let thuh boys who dont have thuh balls to get nothing but a regular job and uh weekly paycheck, let them crowd around and get in somehow on thuh excitement, and make way for thuh ladies, so they can run they hands on my clothes and feel thuh magic and imagine thuh man, with plenty to go around, living and breathing underneath.

(Rest)

They all thought I was down and out! They all thought I was some NoCount HasBeen LostCause motherfucker. But I got my shit back. Thats right. They stepped on me and kept right on stepping. Not no more. Who thuh man?! Goddamnit, who thuh—

Booth closes the door.

LINCOLN

BOOTH

(Rest)

LINCOLN: Another evening to remember, huh?

BOOTH *(Rest)*: Uh—yeah, man, yeah. Thats right, thats right.

LINCOLN: Had me a memorable evening myself.

BOOTH: I got news.

(Rest)

What you been up to?

LINCOLN: Yr news first.

BOOTH: Its good.

LINCOLN: Yeah?

BOOTH: Yeah.

LINCOLN: Go head then.

BOOTH *(Rest)*: Grace got down on her knees. Down on her knees, man. Asked *me* tuh marry *her*.

LINCOLN: Shit.

BOOTH: Amazing Grace!

LINCOLN: Lucky you, man.

BOOTH: And guess where she was, I mean, while I was here waiting for her. She was over at her house watching tv. I'd told her come over Thursday and I got it all wrong and was thinking I said Wednesday and here I was sitting waiting my ass off and all she was doing was over at her house just watching tv.

LINCOLN: Howboutthat.

BOOTH: She wants to get married right away. Shes tired of waiting. Feels her clock ticking and shit. Wants to have my baby. But dont look so glum man, we gonna have a boy and we gonna name it after you.

LLNCOLN: Thats great, man. Thats really great.

BOOTH

LINCOLN

BOOTH: Whats yr news?

LINCOLN *(Rest)*: Nothing.

BOOTH: Mines good news, huh?

LINCOLN: Yeah. Real good news, bro.

BOOTH: Bad news is—well, shes real set on us living together. And she always did like this place.

(Rest)

Yr gonna have to leave. Sorry.

LINCOLN: No sweat.

BOOTH: This was only a temporary situation anyhow.

LINCOLN: No sweat man. You got a new life opening up for you, no sweat. Graces moving in today? I can leave right now.

BOOTH: I dont mean to put you out.

LINCOLN: No sweat. I'll just pack up.

Lincoln rummages around finding a suitcase and begins to pack his things.

BOOTH: Just like that, huh? "No sweat"?! Yesterday you lost yr damn job. You dont got no cash. You dont got no friends, no nothing, but you clearing out just like that and its "no sweat"?!

LINCOLN: Youve been real generous and you and Grace need me gone and its time I found my own place.

BOOTH: No sweat.

LINCOLN: No sweat.

(Rest)

K. I'll spill it. I got another job, so getting my own place aint gonna be so bad.

BOOTH: You got a new job! Doing what?

LINCOLN: Security guard.

BOOTH (Rest): Security guard. Howaboutthat.

Lincoln continues packing the few things he has.
He picks up a whiskey bottle.

BOOTH: Go head, take thuh med-sin, bro. You gonna need it more than me. I got, you know, I got my love to keep me warm and shit.

LINCOLN: You gonna have to get some kind of work, or are you gonna let Grace support you?

BOOTH: I got plans.

LINCOLN: She might want you now but she wont want you for long if you dont get some kind of job. Shes a smart chick. And she cares about you. But she aint gonna let you treat her like some pack mule while shes out working her ass off and yr laying up in here scheming and dreaming to cover up thuh fact that you dont got no skills.

BOOTH: Grace is very cool with who I am and where Im at, thank you.

LINCOLN: It was just some advice. But, hey, yr doing great just like yr doing.

LINCOLN

BOOTH

LINCOLN

BOOTH

BOOTH: When Pops left he didnt take nothing with him. I always thought that was fucked-up.

LINCOLN: He was a drunk. Everything he did was always half regular and half fucked-up.

BOOTH: Whyd he leave his clothes though? Even drunks gotta wear clothes.

LINCOLN: Whyd he leave his clothes whyd he leave us? He was uh drunk, bro. He—whatever, right? I mean, you aint gonna figure it out by thinking about it. Just call it one of thuh great unsolved mysteries of existence.

BOOTH: Moms had a man on thuh side.

LINCOLN: Yeah? Pops had side shit going on too. More than one. He would take me with him when he went to visit them. Yeah.

(Rest)

Sometimes he'd let me meet the ladies. They was all very nice. Very polite. Most of them real pretty. Sometimes he'd let me watch. Most of thuh time I was just outside on thuh porch or in thuh lobby or in thuh car waiting for him but sometimes he'd let me watch.

BOOTH: What was it like?

LINCOLN: Nothing. It wasnt like nothing. He made it seem like it was this big deal this great thing he was letting me witness but it wasnt like nothing.

(Rest)

One of his ladies liked me, so I would do her after he'd done her. On thuh sly though. He'd be laying there, spent and sleeping and snoring and her and me would be sneaking it.

BOOTH: Shit.

LINCOLN: It was alright.

BOOTH

LINCOLN

Lincoln takes his crumpled Abe Lincoln getup from the closet. Isnt sure what to do with it.

BOOTH: Im gonna miss you coming home in that getup. I dont even got a picture of you in it for the album.

LINCOLN (Rest): Hell, I'll put it on. Get thuh camera get thuh camera.

BOOTH: Yeah?

LINCOLN: What thuh fuck, right?

BOOTH: Yeah, what thuh fuck.

Booth scrambles around the apartment and finds the camera. Lincoln quickly puts on the getup, including 2 thin smears of white pancake makeup, more like war paint than whiteface.

LINCOLN: They didnt fire me cause I wasnt no good. They fired me cause they was cutting back. Me getting dismissed didnt have no reflection on my performance. And I was a damn good Honest Abe considering.

BOOTH: Yeah. You look great man, really great. Fix yr hat. Get in thuh light. Smile.

LINCOLN: Lincoln didnt never smile.

BOOTH: Sure he smiled.

LINCOLN: No he didnt, man, you seen thuh pictures of him. In all his pictures he was real serious.

BOOTH: You got a new job, yr having a good day, right?

LINCOLN: Yeah.

BOOTH: So smile.

LINCOLN: Snapshots gonna look pretty stupid with me—

Booth takes a picture.

BOOTH: Thisll look great in thuh album.

LINCOLN: Lets take one together, you and me.

BOOTH: No thanks. Save the film for the wedding.

LINCOLN: This wasnt a bad job. I just outgrew it. I could put in a word for you down there, maybe when business picks up again theyd hire you.

BOOTH: No thanks. That shit aint for me. I aint into pretending Im someone else all day.

LINCOLN: I was just sitting there in thuh getup. I wasnt pretending nothing.

BOOTH: What was going on in yr head?

LINCOLN: I would make up songs and shit.

BOOTH: And think about women.

LINCOLN: Sometimes.

BOOTH: Cookie.

LINCOLN: Sometimes.

BOOTH: And how she came over here one night looking for you.

LINCOLN: I was at Luckys.

BOOTH: She didnt know that.

LINCOLN: I was drinking.

BOOTH: All she knew was you couldnt get it up. You couldnt get it up with her so in her head you was tired of her and had gone out to screw somebody new and this time maybe werent never coming back.

(Rest)

She had me pour her a drink or 2. I didnt want to. She wanted to get back at you by having some fun of her own and when I told her to go out and have it, she said she wanted to have her fun right here. With me.

(Rest)

[And then, just like that, she changed her mind.

(Rest)

But she'd hooked me. That bad part of me that I fight down everyday. You beat yrs down and it stays there dead but mine keeps coming up for another round. And she hooked the bad part of me. And the bad part of me opened my mouth and started promising her things. Promising her things I knew she wanted and you couldnt give her. And the bad part of me took her clothing off and carried her into thuh bed and had her, Link, yr Cookie. It wasnt just thuh bad part of me it was all of me, man,] I had her. Yr damn wife. Right in that bed.

LINCOLN: I used to think about her all thuh time but I dont think about her no more.

BOOTH: I told her if she dumped you I'd marry her but I changed my mind.

LINCOLN: I dont think about her no more.

BOOTH: You dont go back.

LINCOLN: Nope.

BOOTH: Cause you cant. No matter what you do you cant get back to being who you was. Best you can do is just pretend to be yr old self.

LINCOLN: Yr outa yr mind.

BOOTH: Least Im still me!

LINCOLN: Least I work. You never did like to work. You better come up with some kinda way to bring home the bacon or Gracell drop you like a hot rock.

BOOTH: I got plans!

LINCOLN: Yeah, you gonna throw thuh cards, right?

BOOTH: Thats right!

LINCOLN: You a double left-handed motherfucker who dont stand a chance in all get out there throwing no cards.

BOOTH: You scared.

LINCOLN: Im gone.

Lincoln goes to leave.

BOOTH: Fuck that!

LINCOLN: Yr standing in my way.

BOOTH: You scared I got yr shit.

LINCOLN: The only part of my shit you got is the part of my shit you think you got and that aint shit.

BOOTH: Did I pick right them last times? Yes. Oh, I got yr shit.

LINCOLN: Set up the cards.

BOOTH: Thought you was gone.

LINCOLN: Set it up.

BOOTH: I got yr shit and Ima go out there and be thuh man and you aint gonna be nothin.

LINCOLN: Set it up!

Booth hurriedly sets up the milk crates and cardboard top. Lincoln throws the cards.

LINCOLN: Lean in close and watch me now: who see thuh black card who see thuh black card I see thuh black card black cards thuh winner pick thuh black card thats thuh winner pick thuh red card thats thuh loser pick thuh other red card thats thuh other loser pick thuh black card you pick thuh winner. Who see thuh black card who see thuh black card? You pick thuh red card you pick a loser you pick that red card you pick a loser you pick thuh black card thuh deuce of spades you pick a winner who sees thuh deuce of spades thuh one who sees it never fades watch me now as I throw thuh cards. Red losers black winner follow thuh deuce of spades chase thuh black deuce. Dark deuce will get you thuh win. 10 will get you 20, 20 will get you 40. One good pickll get you in 2 good picks and you gone win.

(Rest)

Ok, man, wheres thuh black deuce?

Booth points to a card. Lincoln flips it over. It is the deuce of spades.

BOOTH: Who thuh man?!

Lincoln turns over the other 2 cards, looking at them confusedly.

LINCOLN: Hhhhh.

BOOTH: Who thuh man, Link?! Huh? Who thuh man, Link?!?!

LINCOLN: You thuh man, man.

BOOTH: I got yr shit down.

LINCOLN: Right.

BOOTH: "Right"? All you saying is "right"?

(Rest)

You was out on the street throwing. Just today. Werent you? You wasnt gonna tell me.

LINCOLN: Tell you what?

BOOTH: That you was out throwing.

LINCOLN: I was gonna tell you, sure. Cant go and leave my little bro out thuh loop, can I? Didnt say nothing cause I thought you heard. Did all right today but Im still rusty, I guess. But hey—yr getting good.

BOOTH: But I'll get out there on thuh street and still fuck up, wont I?

LINCOLN: You seem pretty good, bro.

BOOTH: You gotta do it for real, man.

LINCOLN: I am doing it for real. And yr getting good.

BOOTH: I dunno. It didnt feel real. Kinda felt—well it didnt feel real.

LINCOLN: We're missing the essential elements. The crowd, the street, thuh traffic sounds, all that.

BOOTH: We missing something else too, thuh thing thatll really make it real.

LINCOLN: Whassat, bro?

BOOTH: Thuh cash. Its just bullshit without thuh money. Put some money down on thuh table then itd be real, then youd do it for real, then I'd win it for real.

(*Rest*)

And dont be looking all glum like that. I know you got money. A whole pocketful. Put it down.

LINCOLN
BOOTH

BOOTH: You scared of losing it to thuh man, chump? Put it down, less you think thuh kid who got two left hands is gonna give you uh left hook. Put it down, bro, put it down.

Lincoln takes the roll of bills from his pocket and places it on the table.

BOOTH: How much you got there?

LINCOLN: 500 bucks.

BOOTH: Cool.

(*Rest*)

Ready?

LINCOLN: Does it feel real?

BOOTH: Yeah. Clean slate. Take it from the top. "One good pickll get you in 2 good picks and you gone win."

(*Rest*)

Go head.

LINCOLN: Watch me now.

BOOTH: Woah, man, woah.

(*Rest*)

You think Ima chump.

LINCOLN: No I dont.

BOOTH: You aint going full out.

LINCOLN: I was just getting started.

BOOTH: But when you got good and started you wasnt gonna go full out. Ye wasnt gonna go all out. You was gonna do thuh pussy shit, not thuh real shit.

LINCOLN: I put my money down. Money makes it real.

BOOTH: But not if I dont put no money down tuh match it.

LINCOLN: You dont got no money.

BOOTH: I got money!

LINCOLN: You aint worked in years. You dont got shit.

BOOTH: I got money.

LINCOLN: Whatcha been doing, skimming off my weekly paycheck and squirreling it away?

BOOTH: I got money.

(*Rest*)

They stand there sizing each other up. Booth breaks away, going over to his hiding place from which he gets

an old nylon stocking with money in the toe, a knot holding the money secure.

LINCOLN
BOOTH

BOOTH: You know she was putting her stuff in plastic bags? She was just putting her stuff in plastic bags not putting but shoving. She was shoving her stuff in plastic bags and I was standing in thuh doorway watching her and she was so busy shoving thuh shit she didnt see me. "I aint made of money," thats what he always saying. The guy she had on the side. I would catch them together sometimes. Thuh first time I cut school I got tired of hanging out so I goes home—figured I could tell Mom I was sick and cover my ass. Come in thuh house real slow cause Im sick and moving slow and quiet. He had her bent over. They both had all they clothes on like they was about to do something like go out dancing cause they was dressed to thuh 9s but at thuh last minute his pants had fallen down and her dress had flown up and theyd ended up doing something else.

(*Rest*)

They didnt see me come in, they didnt see me watching them, they didnt see me going out. That was uh Thursday. Something told me tuh cut school thuh next Thursday and sure enough—. He was her Thursday man. Every Thursday. Yeah. And Thursday nights she was always all cleaned up and fresh and smelling nice. Serving up dinner. And Pops would grab her cause she was all bright and she would look at me, like she didnt know that I knew but she was asking me not to tell nohow. She was asking me to—oh who knows.

(*Rest*)

She was talking with him one day, her sideman, her Thursday dude, her backdoor man, she needed some money for something, thered been some kind of problem some kind of mistake had been made some kind of mistake that needed cleaning up and she was asking Mr. Thursday for some money to take care of it. "I aint made of money," he says. He was putting his foot down. And then there she was 2 months later not showing yet, maybe she'd got rid of it maybe she hadnt maybe she'd stuffed it along with all her other things in them plastic bags while he waited outside in thuh car with thuh motor running. She musta known I was gonna walk in on her this time cause she had my payoff—my *inheritance*—she had it all ready for me. 500 dollars in a nylon stocking. Huh.

He places the stuffed nylon stocking on the table across from Lincolns money roll.

BOOTH: Now its real.

LINCOLN: Dont put that down.

BOOTH: Throw thuh cards.

LINCOLN: I dont want to play.

BOOTH: Throw thuh fucking cards, man!!

LINCOLN (*Rest*): 2 red cards but only one black. Pick thuh black you pick thuh winner. All thuh cards are face down you point out thuh cards and then you move them around. Now watch me now, now watch me real close. Put thuh winning deuce down in the center put thuh loser reds on either side then you just move thuh cards around. Move them slow or move them fast, Links thuh king he gonna last.

(*Rest*)

Wheres thuh deuce of spades?

Booth chooses a card and chooses correctly.

BOOTH: HA!

LINCOLN: One good pickll get you in 2 good picks and you gone win.

BOOTH: I know man I know.

LINCOLN: Im just doing thuh talk.

BOOTH: Throw thuh fucking cards!

Lincoln throws the cards.

LINCOLN: Lean in close and watch me now: who see thuh black card who see thuh black card I see thuh black card black cards thuh winner pick thuh black card thats thuh winner pick thuh red card thats thuh loser pick thuh other red card thats thuh other loser pick thuh black card you pick thuh winner. Watch me as I throw thuh cards. Here we go.

(*Rest*)

Ima show you thuh cards: 2 red cards but only one spade. Dark winner in thuh center and thuh red losers on thuh sides. Pick uh red card you got a loser pick thuh other red card you got a loser pick thuh black card you got a winner. Watch me watch me watch me now.

(*Rest*)

Who see thuh black card who see thuh black card? You pick thuh red card you pick a loser you pick that red card you pick a loser you pick thuh black card thuh deuce of spades you pick a winner who sees thuh deuce of spades thuh one who sees it never fades watch me now as I throw thuh cards. Red losers black winner follow thuh deuce of spades chase thuh black deuce. Dark deuce will get you thuh win.

(*Rest*)

Ok, 3-Card, you know which cards thuh deuce of spades? This is for real now, man. You pick wrong Im in yr wad and I keep mines.

BOOTH: I pick right I got yr shit.

LINCOLN: Yeah.

BOOTH: Plus I beat you for real.

LINCOLN: Yeah.

(*Rest*)

You think we're really brothers?

BOOTH: Huh?

LINCOLN: I know we *brothers,* but is we really brothers, you know, blood brothers or not, you and me, what-duhyathink?

BOOTH: I think we're brothers.

BOOTH

LINCOLN

BOOTH

LINCOLN

BOOTH

LINCOLN

LINCOLN: Go head man, wheres thuh deuce?

In a flash Booth points out a card.

LINCOLN: You sure?

BOOTH: Im sure!

LINCOLN: Yeah? Dont touch thuh cards, now.

BOOTH: Im sure.

The 2 brothers lock eyes. Lincoln turns over the card that Booth selected and Booth, in a desperate break of concentration, glances down to see that he has chosen the wrong card.

LINCOLN: Deuce of hearts, bro. Im sorry. Thuh deuce of spades was this one.

(*Rest*)

I guess all this is mines.

He slides the money toward himself.

LINCOLN: You were almost right. Better luck next time.

(*Rest*)

Aint yr fault if yr eyes aint fast. And you cant help it if you got 2 left hands, right? Throwing cards aint thuh whole world. You got other shit going for you. You got Grace.

BOOTH: Right.

LINCOLN: Whassamatter?

BOOTH: Mm.

LINCOLN: Whatsup?

BOOTH: Nothing.

LINCOLN:

(*Rest*)

It takes a certain kind of understanding to be able to play this game.

(*Rest*)

I still got thuh moves, dont I?

BOOTH: Yeah you still got thuh moves.

Lincoln cant help himself. He chuckles.

LINCOLN: I aint laughing at you, bro, Im just laughing. Shit there is so much to this game. This game is—there is just so much to it.

Lincoln, still chuckling, flops down in the easy chair. He takes up the nylon stocking and fiddles with the knot.

LINCOLN: Woah, she sure did tie this up tight, didnt she?

BOOTH: Yeah. I aint opened it since she gived it to me.

LINCOLN: Yr kidding. 500 and you aint never opened it? Shit. Sure is tied tight. She said heres 500 bucks and you didnt undo thuh knot to get a look at the cash? You aint needed to take a peek in all these years? Shit. I woulda opened it right away. Just a little peek.

BOOTH: I been saving it.

(*Rest*)

Oh, dont open it, man.

LINCOLN: How come?

BOOTH: You won it man, you dont gotta go opening it.

LINCOLN: We gotta see whats in it.

BOOTH: We *know* whats in it. Dont open it.

LINCOLN: You are a chump, bro. There could be millions in here! There could be nothing! I'll open it.

BOOTH: Dont.

LINCOLN

BOOTH

(*Rest*)

LINCOLN: Shit this knot aint coming out. I could cut it, but that would spoil the whole effect, wouldnt it? Shit. Sorry. I aint laughing at you Im just laughing. Theres so much about those cards. You think you can learn them just by watching and just by playing but there is more to them cards than that. And—. Tell me something, Mr. 3-Card, she handed you this stocking and she said there was money in it and then she split and you say you didnt open it. Howd you know she was for real?

BOOTH: She was for real.

LINCOLN: How you know? She coulda been jiving you, bro. Jiving you that there really *was* money in this thing. Jiving you big time. Its like thuh cards. And ooooh you certainly was persistent. But you was in such a hurry to learn thuh last move that you didnt bother learning thuh first one. That was yr mistake. Cause its thuh first move that separates thuh Player from thuh Played. And thuh first move is to know that there aint no winning. It may look like you got a chance but the only time yon pick right is when thuh man lets you. And when its thuh real deal, when its thuh real fucking deal, bro, and thuh moneys on thuh line, thats when thuh man wont want you picking right. He will want you picking wrong so he will make you pick wrong. Wrong wrong wrong. Ooooh, you thought you was finally happening, didnt you? You thought yr ship had come in or some shit, huh? Thought you was uh player. But I played you, bro.

BOOTH: Fuck you. Fuck you FUCK YOU *FUCK YOU*!!

LINCOLN: Whatever, man. Damn this knot is tough. Ima cut it.

Lincoln reaches in his boot, pulling out a knife. He chuckles all the while.

LINCOLN: Im not laughing at you, bro, Im just laughing.

Booth chuckles with him. Lincoln holds the knife high ready to cut the stocking.

LINCOLN: Turn yr head. You may not wanna look.

Booth turns away slightly. They both continue laughing. Lincoln brings the knife down to cut the stocking.

BOOTH: I popped her.

LINCOLN: Huh?

BOOTH: Grace. I popped her. Grace.

(*Rest*)

Who thuh fuck she think she is doing me like she done? Telling me I dont got nothing going on. I showed her what I got going on. Twice. 3 times. Whatever. Popped her good.

(*Rest*)

She aint dead.

(*Rest*)

She werent wearing my ring I gived her. Said it was too small. Fuck that. Said it hurt her. Fuck that. Said she was into bigger things. *Fuck* that. Shes alive not to worry, she aint going out that easy, shes alive shes shes—.

LINCOLN: Dead. Shes—

BOOTH: Dead.

LINCOLN: Ima give you back yr stocking, man. Here, bro—

BOOTH: Only so long I can stand that little brother shit. Can only take it so long. Im telling you—

LINCOLN: Take it back, man—

BOOTH: That little bro shit had to go—

LINCOLN: Cool—

BOOTH: Like Booth went—

LINCOLN: Here, 3-Card—

BOOTH: That Booth shit is over. 3-Cards thuh man now—

LINCOLN: Ima give you yr stocking back, 3-Card—

BOOTH: Who thuh man now, huh? Who thuh man now?! Think you can fuck with me, motherfucker think again motherfucker think again! Think you can take me like Im just some chump some two left-handed pussy dickbreath chump who you can take and then go laugh at. Aint laughing at me you was just laughing bunch uh bullshit and you know it.

LINCOLN: Here. Take it.

BOOTH: I aint gonna be needing it. Go on. You won it you open it.

LINCOLN: No thanks.

BOOTH: Open it open it open it open it. *OPEN IT!!!*

(*Rest*)

Open it up, bro.

LINCOLN

BOOTH

Lincoln brings the knife down to cut the stocking. In a flash, Booth grabs Lincoln from behind. He pulls his

gun and thrusts it into the left side of Lincolns neck.
They stop there poised.

LINCOLN: Dont.

Booth shoots Lincoln. Lincoln slumps forward, falling
out of his chair and onto the floor. He lies there dead.
Booth paces back and forth, like a panther in a cage,
holding his gun.

BOOTH: Think you can take my shit? My shit. That shit
was mines. I kept it. Saved it. All this while. Through
thick and through thin. Through fucking thick and
through fucking thin, motherfucker. And you just
gonna come up in here and mock my shit and call
me two lefthanded talking bout how she coulda been
jiving me then go steal from me? My *inheritance*. You
stole my *inheritance*, man. That aint right. That aint
right and you know it. You had yr own. And you
blew it. You *blew* it, motherfucker! I saved mines and
you blew yrs. Thinking you all that and blew yr shit.
And I *saved* mines.

(Rest)

You aint gonna be needing yr fucking money-roll no
more, dead motherfucker, so I will pocket it thank
you.

(Rest)

Watch me close watch me close now: lma go out there
and make a name for myself that dont have nothing
to do with you. And 3-Cards gonna be in everybodys
head and in everybodys mouth like Link was.

(Rest)

Ima take back my inheritance too. It was mines
anyhow. Even when you stole it from me it was still
mines cause she gave it to me. She didnt give it to
you. And I been saving it all this while.

He bends to pick up the money-filled stocking. Then
he just crumples. As he sits beside Lincolns body, the
money-stocking falls away. Booth holds Lincolns body,
hugging him close. He sobs.

BOOTH: *AAAAAAAAAAAAAAAAAAAAH!*

Sarah Ruhl

Although she is from Chicago, Sarah Ruhl (b. 1974) now lives in New York City and is married to a physician at New York University. She studied with Paula Vogel at Brown University and, in 2006, won a MacArthur Fellowship, which provided her with $100,000 a year for five years—freeing her to write without financial concerns. Since the production of *The Clean House* (2004), which won the Susan Smith Blackburn Award for the best play of the year by a woman and was a finalist for the 2005 Pulitzer Prize, her plays are eagerly anticipated. In almost record time, Ruhl has become a powerful force in modern theater. Paula Vogel said that her work takes us "back to the importance of theatre as myth, the importance of theatre as community."

Some of her earlier plays, such as *Melancholy Play* (2002), deal with psychological issues. Ruhl explores melancholy and sadness in this play, with a special perspective on the medication that often masks such emotions. Not all sadness is depression, she argues, and using Prozac and other such drugs to treat sadness is not necessarily valid. One need not always be "up," and moments of sadness are normal human feelings, not medical emergencies.

Late: A Cowboy Song was given a reading in 2002 in Dallas, Texas, but a full production did not occur until 2005 in Houston at Stages Repertory Theatre. Set in Pittsburgh, the play examines questions of identity and focuses on a man and woman who change their lives after a chance meeting with a cowgirl. Unfortunately, the reviews were not kind to this play. By contrast, the reviews of *Eurydice* (2003) have been overwhelmingly positive, and the staging has been praised as highly original. The play is an adaptation of the myth of Orpheus and Eurydice, in which the poet Orpheus sings so beautifully that the very rocks feel emotion.

The Clean House (2004) not only was successful in its premiere at Yale Repertory Theatre, and in its later production in New York, but also has gone on to become one of the most produced plays of the past several years. In it, Matilde is a Portuguese woman who cleans house for Lane and her husband Charles, both doctors. Matilde was born laughing and spends her time searching for the perfect joke. Secretly, she does not enjoy cleaning house. Lane's sister Virginia visits and discovers Matilde's secret, and then she creates a secret of her own by cleaning Lane's house herself without Lane's knowledge. Cleaning together, Matilde and Virginia discover that Charles is having an affair with one of his patients who is dying of cancer. The complications that arise from these circumstances are deftly woven together in such a way as to involve every character and to produce changes that surprise everyone.

Ruhl's next work, *Passion Play* (2007), developed over a period of ten years. It began when, as a student in Providence, Rhode Island, Ruhl saw a performance of the passion play and began writing an undergraduate thesis. A traditional play that has been performed for centuries in one form or another, the passion play tells the story of the crucifixion of Jesus Christ. The production in Oberammergau, Germany, has been put on regularly since the Middle Ages, and because it has changed little in all that time, it is often accused of contributing to European anti-Semitism. What Ruhl did with the play, which was produced by the Goodman Theatre in Chicago in September 2007, was to explore it in different contexts, both historically and geographically. The play is told in three parts. The first is set in England in 1571 during the reign of Queen Elizabeth, in the period during which there was a very severe crackdown on Roman Catholics, who were thought to be a threat to the English Crown. The second part is set in Germany in 1934, when Hitler especially approved of the passion play at Oberammergau because it fueled his hatred of the Jews, helped spread anti-Semitism, and made it politically easier for him to begin murdering Europe's Jews. The third part is set in Spearfish, South Dakota, in the 1980s, during Ronald Reagan's presidency, at the Black Hills passion play. This event is a huge outdoor undertaking that reenacts the last days of Jesus's life using period costumes, dozens of players, and a great deal of sophisticated technology in a pageant described as the most impressive of its kind.

Ruhl's play merges religion and politics to demonstrate the ways in which the religious material of the passion play can be molded into a political message appropriate for its time. She comments on both religion and politics at a time when they have once again merged as a force in the modern world.

Dead Man's Cell Phone (2007), commissioned by and performed at Playwrights Horizons in New York, starred Mary-Louise Parker, Kathleen Chalfant, and Anne Bogart. This play deals with moral issues and the way people connect with one another. It centers on a woman who answers a cell phone, only to discover that the owner is dead and that the man's life was strange and challenging in ways that she could never have imagined.

In the Next Room: or, The Vibrator Play premiered at the Berkeley Repertory Theatre in Berkeley, California, in February 2009, then moved to the Lyceum Theatre in New York in October, thus becoming Ruhl's first play with a Broadway opening. Michael Cerveris and Maria Dizzia starred. The play is set in the 1880s, when electricity began to be available in households. The play focuses on the assumption among some psychologists and doctors at that time that what most women suffered from could be cured by the application of the vibrator so as to produce an orgasm. What Ruhl reveals in the play is not that the doctors are prurient, but that the sexual relationships between the husbands and wives in the play are distorted by the social values of the age, when sexual issues could not be frankly discussed even by married couples. *In the Next Room: or, The Vibrator Play* was nominated for the Pulitzer Prize and a Tony Award.

Eurydice

Eurydice is about the terrible power of loss. In the myth of Orpheus and Eurydice, as told by Ovid in his *Metamorphoses,* Orpheus, the most famous musician in classical literature, has the reputation of charming even the stones when he sings. In Ovid's version, Eurydice steps on a snake in the grass at her wedding to Orpheus and dies of its bite. In another version of the myth, Eurydice attracts the attention of a satyr, who attempts to assault her. In trying to get away, she runs through tall grass and arouses a viper that gives her a fatal bite. In both versions, Orpheus, coming upon her, sings a lamentation that reduces all to tears. One of the wedding guests suggests he visit the underworld and persuade Persephone, goddess of the underworld, to return his wife. Orpheus goes to the underworld and sings so plaintively that Persephone permits

Eurydice to return on the condition that she follow Orpheus to the upper world without Orpheus's looking back at her. But when Orpheus reaches daylight, he is startled and turns around before Eurydice has also reached the upper world. She then disappears and Orpheus loses her forever. The poignancy of the myth inspired the very first opera, Monteverdi's *Orfeo* (1607), and many subsequent operas.

Ruhl focuses on the fact that Eurydice dies not once, but twice. She explores Eurydice's love for Orpheus by studying their sense of each other. Eurydice, for example, loves reading and loves books. Orpheus, in contrast, loves music and very little more. At their wedding, Eurydice expects to meet more interesting people, but she does not. Orpheus tries to teach her something about music, but she has no sense of rhythm and cannot sing on pitch.

The stranger who attracts Eurydice to his high-rise apartment with a letter from her recently deceased father seems at first to be an interesting person. But we know from the myth that he is a stand-in for the satyr in one version and the snake in another. He is a sexual predator. In the version staged by the Yale Repertory Theatre, he appears on a tricycle, which seems to foreshadow his reappearance later as a child in the underworld. Eurydice dies by falling from the high-rise apartment. In a brilliant scene (movement 2, scene 1), Eurydice arrives in the underworld in an elevator in which it is raining, carrying an umbrella. Water is an emblem throughout the play, referred to frequently in the stage directions, and this scene establishes its power. When Eurydice arrives, she must swim across Lethe, the classical river of forgetfulness. As a result, she can no longer read the works of Shakespeare, nor does she even know what to do with a book, yet she has not totally forgotten the world. She meets her father, who remembers her and tells her about the past and helps her to read. This section of the play explores the powerful bond between father and daughter, also illustrated by allusions to King Lear and Cordelia. Ruhl, in dedicating the play to her father, seems to be establishing the importance of the father-daughter relationship and the pain of their separation through death.

After Orpheus arrives in the raining elevator and has won Eurydice's release, they proceed to the upper world, but in Ruhl's version, the loss of Eurydice is not caused by Orpheus's inattention—it is caused by Eurydice's uncertainty. Throughout the last section of the play she is uncertain of her husband's name, even while being advised by her father to return to her husband. When she seems to have gone back to the upper world, her father dips himself in the river and loses the memory of the world and of his daughter. When Eurydice returns, expecting to find her father, she is cast into mourning and chastised by the stones, who have given her direction throughout her time in Hades. After writing a letter to Orpheus and his next wife, Eurydice lies down beside her father and dips herself into the river along with him.

Eurydice in Performance

The play is intentionally Greek in character, with the lines often resembling the poetic forms expected from playwrights like Euripides. Along with three principal characters and two minor characters, there is a chorus of stones. In performance, the sense of tragic intensity is very clear. The most impressive theatrical effect is achieved by the use of the elevator and the rain on the stage. An elevator (without rain) was first used in Jacques Offenbach's operetta *Orpheus in the Underworld* (1874).

The world premiere of *Eurydice* was at the Madison Repertory Theatre in 2003, directed by Richard Corley. The Berkeley Repertory Theatre in Berkeley,

California, produced the play, directed by Les Waters, in October 2004. The Yale Repertory Theatre production was in October 2006, also directed by Les Waters and starring Maria Dizzia as Eurydice. The play has been performed throughout the United States and abroad many times since then, in Denver's Curious Theatre in 2006, in London's Young Vic Theatre in 2010, and in Chicago's Filament Theatre Ensemble production and Toronto's Summer Festival in 2011. In his *New York Times* review, Charles Isherwood said of *Eurydice*, "It may just be the most moving exploration of the theme of loss that the American theater has produced since the events of September 11, 2001."

SARAH RUHL (b. 1974)

Eurydice   2003

Characters

EURYDICE
HER FATHER
ORPHEUS
A NASTY INTERESTING MAN/THE LORD OF THE UNDERWORLD
A CHORUS OF STONES:
　BIG STONE
　LITTLE STONE
　LOUD STONE

Setting: *The set contains a raining elevator,*
a water-pump,
some rusty exposed pipes,
an abstracted River of Forgetfulness,
an old-fashioned glow-in-the-dark globe.

Notes

Eurydice and Orpheus should be played as though they are a little too young and a little too in love. They should resist the temptation to be "classical."

The underworld should resemble the world of Alice in Wonderland more than it resembles Hades.

The stones might be played as though they are nasty children at a birthday party.

When people compose letters in this play they needn't actually scribble them—they can speak directly to the audience.

The play should be performed without an intermission.

FIRST MOVEMENT • Scene 1

A young man—Orpheus—
and a young woman—Eurydice.

They wear swimming outfits from the 1950s.
Orpheus makes a sweeping gesture with his arm,
indicating the sky.

EURYDICE: All those birds?

He nods.

EURYDICE: For me? Thank you.

They make a quarter turn and he makes a sweeping
gesture.
He makes a gesture of giving the sea to Eurydice.

EURYDICE: And—the sea! Now?

Orpheus opens his hands.

EURYDICE: It's mine already?

Orpheus nods.

EURYDICE: Wow.

They kiss. He indicates the sky.

EURYDICE: Surely not—surely not the sky and the stars too.

Orpheus nods.

EURYDICE: That's very generous.

Orpheus nods.

EURYDICE: Perhaps too generous?

Orpheus shakes his head.

EURYDICE: Thank you.

She crawls on top of him and kisses his eyes.

EURYDICE: What are you thinking about?
ORPHEUS: Music.
EURYDICE: How can you think about music? You either hear it or you don't.
ORPHEUS: I'm hearing it then.
EURYDICE: Oh.

(Pause.)

　　I read a book today.

ORPHEUS: Did you?

EURYDICE: Yes. It was very interesting.

ORPHEUS: That's good.

EURYDICE: Don't you want to know what it was about?

ORPHEUS: Of course.

EURYDICE: There were—stories—about people's lives—how some come out well—and others come out badly.

ORPHEUS: Do you love the book?

EURYDICE: Yes—I think so.

ORPHEUS: Why?

EURYDICE: It can be interesting to see if other people—like dead people who wrote books—agree or disagree with what you think.

ORPHEUS: Why?

EURYDICE: Because it makes you—a larger part of the human community. It had very interesting arguments.

ORPHEUS: Oh. And arguments that are interesting are good arguments?

EURYDICE: Well—yes.

ORPHEUS: I didn't know an argument should be interesting. I thought it should be right or wrong.

EURYDICE: Well, these particular arguments were very interesting.

ORPHEUS: Maybe you should make up your own thoughts. Instead of reading them in a book.

EURYDICE: I do. I do think up my own thoughts.

ORPHEUS: I know you do. I love how you love books. Don't be mad.

Pause.

ORPHEUS: I made up a song for you today.

EURYDICE: Did you!?

ORPHEUS: Yup. It's not *interesting* or *not*-interesting. It just—is.

EURYDICE: Will you sing it for me?

ORPHEUS: It has too many parts.

EURYDICE: Let's go in the water.

They start walking, arm in arm,
on extensive unseen boardwalks, towards the water.

ORPHEUS: Wait—remember this melody.

He hums a bar of melody.

EURYDICE: I'm bad at remembering melodies. Why don't you remember it?

ORPHEUS: I have eleven other ones in my head, making for a total of twelve.
　　You have it?

EURYDICE: Yes. I think so.

ORPHEUS: Let's hear it.

She sings the melody.
She misses a few notes.
She's not the best singer in the world.

ORPHEUS: Pretty good. The rhythm's a little off. Here—clap it out.

She claps.
He claps the rhythmic sequence for her.
She tries to imitate.
She is still off.

EURYDICE: Is that right?

ORPHEUS: We'll practice.

EURYDICE: I don't need to know about rhythm. I have my books.

ORPHEUS: Don't books have rhythm?

EURYDICE: Kind of. Let's go in the water.

ORPHEUS: Will you remember my melody under the water?

EURYDICE: Yes! I WILL ALWAYS REMEMBER YOUR MELODY! It will be imprinted on my heart like wax.

ORPHEUS: Thank you.

EURYDICE: You're welcome. When are you going to play me the whole song?

ORPHEUS: When I get twelve instruments.

EURYDICE: Where are you going to get twelve instruments?

ORPHEUS: I'm going to make each strand of your hair into an instrument. Your hair will stand on end as it plays my music and become a hair orchestra. It will fly you up into the sky.

EURYDICE: I don't know if I want to be an instrument.

ORPHEUS: Why?

EURYDICE: Won't I fall down when the song ends?

ORPHEUS: That's true. But the clouds will be so moved by your music that they will fill up with water until they become heavy and you'll sit on one and fall gently down to earth. How about that?

EURYDICE: Okay.

They gaze at each other.

ORPHEUS: It's settled then.

EURYDICE: What is?

ORPHEUS: Your hair will be my orchestra and—I love you.

EURYDICE: I love you too.

ORPHEUS: How will you remember?

EURYDICE: That I love you?

ORPHEUS: Yes.

EURYDICE: That's easy. I can't help it.

ORPHEUS: You never know. I'd better tie a string around your finger to remind you.

EURYDICE: Is there string at the ocean?

ORPHEUS: I always have string. In case I come upon a broken instrument.

He takes out a string from his pocket.
He takes her left hand.

ORPHEUS: This hand.

He wraps string deliberately around her fourth finger.

ORPHEUS: Is this too tight?

EURYDICE: No—it's fine.

ORPHEUS: There—now you'll remember.

EURYDICE: That's a very particular finger.

ORPHEUS: Yes.

EURYDICE: You're aware of that?
ORPHEUS: Yes.
EURYDICE: How aware?
ORPHEUS: Very aware.
EURYDICE: Orpheus—are we?
ORPHEUS: You tell me.
EURYDICE: Yes.
  I think so.
ORPHEUS: You *think* so?
EURYDICE: I wasn't thinking.
  I mean—Yes. Just: Yes.
ORPHEUS: Yes?
EURYDICE: Yes.
ORPHEUS: Yes!
EURYDICE: Yes!
ORPHEUS: May our lives be full of music!

Music.
He picks her up and throws her into the sky.

EURYDICE: Maybe you could also get me another ring—a
  gold one—to put over the string one. You know?
ORPHEUS: Whatever makes you happy. Do you still have
  my melody?
EURYDICE: It's right here.

She points to her temple.
They look at each other. A silence.

EURYDICE: What are you thinking about?
ORPHEUS: Music.

Her face falls.

ORPHEUS: Just kidding. I was thinking about you. And
  music.
EURYDICE: Let's go in the water. I'll race you!

She puts on her swimming goggles.

ORPHEUS: I'll race *you!*
EURYDICE: I'll race *you!*
ORPHEUS: I'll race *you!*
EURYDICE: I'll race *you!*

They race towards the water.

Scene 2

The Father, dressed in a grey suit, reads from a letter.

FATHER: Dear Eurydice,

  A letter for you on your wedding day.

  There is no choice of any importance in life but the
  choosing of a beloved. I haven't met Orpheus, but he
  seems like a serious young man. I understand he's a
  musician.

  (*The father thinks—oh, dear.*)

  If I were to give a speech at your wedding I would
  start with one or two funny jokes and then I might
  offer some words of advice. I would say:

Cultivate the arts of dancing and small talk.

Everything in moderation.

Court the companionship and respect of dogs.

Grilling a fish or toasting bread without burning requires singleness of purpose, vigilance and steadfast watching.

Keep quiet about politics, but vote for the right man.

Take care to change the light bulbs.

Continue to give yourself to others because that's the ultimate satisfaction in life—to love, accept, honor and help others.

As for me, this is what it's like being dead: the atmosphere smells. And there are strange high pitched noises—like a tea kettle always boiling over. But it doesn't seem to bother anyone. And, for the most part, there is a pleasant atmosphere and you can work and socialize, much like at home. I'm working in the business world and it seems that, here, you can better see the far reaching consequences of your actions.

Also, I am one of the few dead people who still remembers how to read and write. That's a secret. If anyone finds out, they might dip me in the River again.

I write you letters. I don't know how to get them to you.

Love,
Your father

He drops the letter as though into a mail slot.
It falls on the ground.

Wedding music.
In the underworld, the father walks in a straight line as though he is walking his daughter down the aisle.

He is affectionate, then solemn, then glad, then solemn, then amused, then solemn.

He looks at his imaginary daughter; he looks straight ahead; he acknowledges the guests at the wedding; he gets choked up; he looks at his daughter and smiles an embarrassed smile for getting choked up.

He looks straight ahead, calm.
He walks.

Suddenly, he checks his watch.
He exits, in a hurry.

Scene 3

Eurydice, by a water pump.
The noise of a party, from far off.

EURYDICE: I hate parties.
  And a wedding party is the biggest party of all.
  All the guests arrived and Orpheus is taking a shower.
  He's always taking a shower when the guests arrive
  so he doesn't have to greet them.

Then I have to greet them.

A wedding is for daughters and fathers. The mothers all dress up, trying to look like young women. But a wedding is for a father and a daughter. They stop being married to each other on that day.

I always thought there would be more interesting people at my wedding.

She drinks water from the water pump.
The Nasty Interesting Man, wearing a trench coat, appears and sees Eurydice cupping her hands full of water.

MAN: Are you a homeless person?

EURYDICE: No.

MAN: Oh. I'm on my way to a party where there are really very interesting people. Would you like to join me?

EURYDICE: No. I just left my own party.

MAN: You were giving a party and you just—left?

EURYDICE: I was thirsty.

MAN: You must be a very interesting person, to leave your own party like that.

EURYDICE: Thank you.

MAN: You mustn't care at all what other people think of you. I always say that's a mark of a really interesting person, don't you?

EURYDICE: I guess.

MAN: So would you like to accompany me to this interesting affair?

EURYDICE: No, thank you. I just got married, you see.

MAN: Oh—lots of people do that.

EURYDICE: That's true—lots of people do.

MAN: What's your name?

EURYDICE: Eurydice.

He looks at her, hungry.

MAN: Eurydice.

EURYDICE: Good-bye, then.

MAN: Good-bye.

She exits. He sits by the water pump.
He notices a letter on the ground.
He picks it up and reads it.

MAN: (*to himself*) Dear Eurydice.

Musty dripping sounds.

Scene 4

The father tries to remember how to do the jitterbug in the underworld.
He does the jitterbug with an imaginary partner.
He has fun.

Orpheus and Eurydice dance together at their wedding.
They are happy.
They have had some champagne.
They sing together.

ORPHEUS AND EURYDICE: Don't sit under the apple tree

with anyone else but me
anyone else but me
anyone else but me
no no no
Don't sit under the apple tree
with anyone else but me,
'til I come marching home . . .

On the other side of the stage,
the Father checks his watch.
He stops doing the jitterbug.
He exits, in a hurry.

EURYDICE: I'm warm; are you warm?

ORPHEUS: Yes!

EURYDICE: I'm going to get a drink of water.

ORPHEUS: Don't go.

EURYDICE: I'll be right back.

ORPHEUS: Promise?

EURYDICE: Yes.

ORPHEUS: I can't stand to let you out of my sight tonight.

EURYDICE: Silly goose.

They kiss.

Scene 5

Eurydice at the water pump,
getting a glass of water.
The Interesting Man appears.

EURYDICE: Oh—you're still here.

MAN: Yes. I forgot to tell you something. I have a letter. Addressed to Eurydice—that's you—from your father.

EURYDICE: That's not possible.

MAN: He wrote down some thoughts—for your wedding day.

EURYDICE: Let me see.

MAN: I left it at home. It got delivered to my elegant high-rise apartment by mistake.

EURYDICE: Why didn't you say so before?

MAN: You left in such a hurry.

EURYDICE: From my father?

MAN: Yes.

EURYDICE: You're sure?

MAN: Yes.

EURYDICE: I knew he'd send something!

MAN: It'll just take a moment. I live around the block. What an interesting dress you're wearing.

EURYDICE: Thank you.

Scene 6

Orpheus, from the water pump.

ORPHEUS: Eurydice?
   Eurydice!

Scene 7

The sound of a door closing.
The Interesting Apartment—a giant loft space with no furniture.
Eurydice and the Man enter, panting.

MAN: Voila.
EURYDICE: You're very high up.
MAN: Yes. I am.
EURYDICE: I feel a little faint.
MAN: It'll pass.
EURYDICE: Have you ever thought about installing an elevator?
MAN: No. I prefer stairs. I think architecture is so interesting, don't you?
EURYDICE: Oh, yes. So, where's the letter?
MAN: But isn't this an interesting building?
EURYDICE: It's so—high up.
MAN: Yes.
EURYDICE: There's no one here. I thought you were having a party.
MAN: I like to celebrate things quietly. With a few other interesting people. Don't you?

She tilts her head to the side and stares at him.

   Would you like some champagne?
EURYDICE: Maybe some water.
MAN: Water it is! Make yourself comfortable.

He gestures to the floor.
He switches on Brazilian mood music.
She looks around.

EURYDICE: I can't stay long!

She looks out the window. She is very high up.

EURYDICE: I can see my wedding from here!
   The people are so small—they're dancing!
   There's Orpheus!
   He's not dancing.
MAN: (*shouting from off-stage*) So, who's this guy you're marrying?
EURYDICE: (*shouting*) His name is Orpheus.
MAN: (*as he attempts to open the champagne, off-stage*) Orpheus. Not a very interesting name. I've heard it before.
EURYDICE: (*shouting*) Maybe you've heard of him. He's kind of famous. He plays the most beautiful music in the world, actually.
MAN: I can't hear you!
EURYDICE: (*shouting*) So the letter was delivered—here—today?
MAN: That's right.
EURYDICE: Through the post?
MAN: It was—mysterious.

The sound of champagne popping.
He enters with one glass of champagne.

MAN: Voila.

He drinks the champagne.

   So. Eurydice. Tell me one thing. Name me one person you find interesting.
EURYDICE: Why?
MAN: Just making conversation.

He sways a little, to the music.

EURYDICE: Right. Um—all the interesting people I know are dead or speak French.
MAN: Well, I don't speak French, Eurydice.

He takes one step toward her.
She takes one step back.

EURYDICE: I'm sorry. I have to go. There's no letter, is there?
MAN: Of course there's a letter. It's right here.

He pats his breast pocket.

MAN: Eurydice. I'm not interesting, but I'm strong. You could teach me to be interesting. I would listen. Orpheus is too busy listening to his own thoughts. There's music in his head. Try to pluck the music out and it bites you. I'll bet you had an interesting thought today, for instance.

She tilts her head to the side, quizzical.

   I bet you're always having them, the way you tilt your head to the side and stare . . .

She jerks her head back up.
Musty dripping sounds.

EURYDICE: I feel dizzy all of a sudden. I want my husband. I think I'd better go now.
MAN: You're free to go, whenever you like.
EURYDICE: I know.
   I think I'll go now, in fact. I'll just take my letter first, if you don't mind.

She holds out her hand for the letter.
He takes her hand.

MAN: Relax.

She takes her hand away.

EURYDICE: Good-bye.

She turns to exit.
He blocks the doorway.

MAN: Wait. Eurydice. Don't go. I love you.
EURYDICE: Oh no.
MAN: You need to get yourself a real man. A man with broad shoulders like me. Orpheus has long fingers that would tremble to pet a bull or pluck a bee from a hive—
EURYDICE: How do you know about my husband's fingers?
MAN: A man who can put his big arm around your little shoulders as he leads you through the crowd, a man who answers the door at parties. . . . A man with big hands, with big stupid hands like potatoes, a man who can carry a cow in labor.

The man backs Eurydice against the wall.

MAN: My lips were meant to kiss your eyelids, that's obvious!

EURYDICE: Close your eyes, then!

He closes his eyes, expecting a kiss.
She takes the letter from his breast pocket.
She slips under him and opens the door to the stairwell.
He opens his eyes.
She looks at the letter.

EURYDICE: It's his handwriting!

MAN: Of course it is!

He reaches for her.

EURYDICE: Good-bye.

She runs for the stairs.
She wavers, off-balance, at the top of the stairwell.

MAN: Don't do that, you'll trip!

EURYDICE: Orpheus!

From the water pump:

ORPHEUS: EURYDICE!

She runs, trips and pitches down the stairs, holding her letter.
She follows the letter down, down down . . .
Blackout. A clatter. Strange sounds—xylophones, brass bands, sounds of falling, sounds of vertigo.
Sounds of breathing.

SECOND MOVEMENT

The underworld.
There is no set change.
Strange watery noises.
Drip, drip, drip.
The movement to the underworld is marked by the entrance of stones.

Scene 1

THE STONES: We are a chorus of stones.

LITTLE STONE: I'm a little stone.

BIG STONE: I'm a big stone.

LOUD STONE: I'm a loud stone.

THE STONES: We are all three stones.

LITTLE STONE: We live with the dead people in the land of the dead.

BIG STONE: Eurydice was a great musician. Orpheus was his wife.

LOUD STONE: (*correcting Big Stone*) Orpheus was a great musician. Eurydice was his wife. She died.

LITTLE STONE: Then he played the saddest music. Even we—

THE STONES: The stones—

LITTLE STONE: Cried when we heard it.

The sound of three drops of water hitting a pond.

LITTLE STONE: Oh, look,
    she is coming into the land of the dead now.

BIG STONE: Oh!

LOUD STONE: Oh!

LITTLE STONE: Oh!
    We might say—"Poor Eurydice"—

LOUD STONE: But stones don't feel bad for dead people.

The sound of an elevator ding.
An elevator door opens.
Inside the elevator, it is raining.
Eurydice gets rained on inside the elevator.
She carries a suitcase and an umbrella.
She is dressed in the kind of 1930s suit that women wore when they eloped.
She looks bewildered.

Ramiz Monsef as Big Stone, Gian-Murray Gianino as Loud Stone, and Carla Harting as Little Stone in the 2006 production of *Eurydice* directed by Les Waters at the Yale Repertory Theatre.

Eurydice (Ony Uhiara) arrives in the underworld in a production directed by Bijan Sheibani at the Young Vic Theatre in London, 2010.

The sound of an elevator ding.
Eurydice steps out of the elevator.
The elevator door closes.

She walks towards the audience and opens her mouth,
trying to speak.
There is a great humming noise.
She closes her mouth.
The humming noise stops.
She opens her mouth for the second time,
attempting to tell her story to the audience.
There is a great humming noise.
She closes her mouth—the humming noise stops.
She has a tantrum of despair.

STONES: Eurydice wants to speak to you.
    But she can't speak your language anymore.
    She talks in the language of dead people now.
LITTLE STONE: It's a very quiet language.
LOUD STONE: Like if the pores in your face opened up
   and talked.

BIG STONE: Like potatoes sleeping in the dirt.

The stones look at Big Stone as though that were a
dumb thing to say.

LITTLE STONE: Pretend that you understand her
   or she'll be embarrassed.
BIG STONE: Yes—pretend for a moment
   that you understand
   the language of stones.
LOUD STONE: Listen to her the way you would listen
   to your own daughter
   if she died too young
   and tried to speak to you
   across long distances.

Eurydice shakes out her umbrella.
She approaches the audience.
This time, she can speak.

EURYDICE: There was a roar, and a coldness—
   I think my husband was with me.
   What was my husband's name?

Eurydice turns to the stones.

   My husband's name? Do you know it?

The stones shrug their shoulders.

   How strange. I don't remember.
   It was horrible to see his face
   when I died. His eyes were
   two black birds
   and they flew to me.
   I said no—stay where you are—
   he needs you in order to see!
   When I got through the cold
   they made me swim in a river
   and I forgot his name.
   I forgot all the names.
   I know his name starts with my mouth
   shaped like a ball of twine—
   Oar—oar.
   I forget.
   They took me to a tiny boat.
   I only just fit inside.
   I looked at the oars
   and I wanted to cry.
   I tried to cry but I just drooled a little.
   I'll try now.

She tries to cry and finds that she can't.

EURYDICE: What happiness it would be to cry.

(*She takes a breath.*)

   I was not lonely
   only alone with myself
   begging myself not to leave my own body
   but I *was* leaving.

Good-bye, head—I said—
it inclined itself a little, as though to nod to me
in a solemn kind of way.

(*She turns to the stones.*)

How do you say good-bye to yourself?

They shake their heads.
A train whistle.
Eurydice steps onto a platform, surveying a large
crowd.

EURYDICE: A train!
LITTLE STONE: The station is like a train but there is no
    train.
BIG STONE: The train has wheels that are not wheels.
LOUD STONE: There is the opposite of a wheel and the
    opposite of smoke and the opposite of a train.

A train pulls away.

EURYDICE: Oh! I'm waiting for someone to meet me, I
    think.

Eurydice's Father approaches and takes her baggage.

FATHER: Eurydice.
EURYDICE: (*to the stones*) At last, a porter to meet me!

    (*to the father*) Do you happen to know where the
    bank is? I need money. I've just arrived. I need to
    exchange my money at the Bureau de Change. I
    didn't bring traveler's checks because I left in such
    a hurry. They didn't even let me pack my suitcase.
    There's nothing in it! That's funny, right? Funny—ha
    ha! I suppose I can buy new clothes here. I would
    really love a bath.
FATHER: Eurydice!
EURYDICE: What is that language you're speaking? It
    gives me tingles. Say it again.
FATHER: Eurydice!
EURYDICE: Oooh—it's like a fruit! Again!
FATHER: Eurydice—I'm your father!
EURYDICE: (*strangely imitating*) Eurydice—I'm your
    father. How funny! You remind me of something
    but I can't understand a word you're saying. Say
    it again!
FATHER: Your father.
STONES: (*to the father*) Shut up, shut up!
    She doesn't understand you.
    She's dead now too.
    You have to speak in the language of stones.
FATHER: You're dead now. I'm dead, too.
EURYDICE: Yes, that's right. I need a reservation. For the
    fancy hotel.
FATHER: When you were alive, I was your father.
STONES: Father is not a word that dead people
    understand.
BIG STONE: He is what we call subversive.

FATHER: When you were alive, I was your tree.
EURYDICE: My tree! Yes, the tall one in the back yard! I
    used to sit all day in its shade!

She sits at the feet of her father.

EURYDICE: Ah—there—shade!
LITTLE STONE: There is a problem here.
EURYDICE: Is there any entertainment at the hotel? Any
    dancing ladies? Like with the great big fans?
FATHER: I named you Eurydice: Your mother named all
    the other children. But Eurydice I chose for you.
BIG STONE: Be careful, sir.
FATHER: Eurydice. I wanted to remember your name.
    I asked the stones. They said: Forget the names—the
    names make you remember.
LOUD STONE: We told you how it works!
FATHER: One day it would not stop raining.

    I heard your name inside the rain—somewhere
    between the drops—I saw falling letters. Each letter
    of your name—I began to translate.

    E—I remembered elephants. U—I remembered
    ulcers and under. R—I remembered reindeers.
    I saw them putting their black noses into snow.
    Y—youth and yellow. D—dog, dig, daughter,
    day. Time poured into my head. The days of the
    week. Hours, months. . . .
EURYDICE: The tree talks so beautifully.
STONES: Don't listen!
EURYDICE: I feel suddenly hungry! Where is the porter
    who met me at the station?
FATHER: Here I am.
EURYDICE: I would like a continental breakfast, please.
    Maybe some rolls and butter. Oh—and jam. Please
    take my suitcase to my room, if you would.
FATHER: I'm sorry, Miss, but there are no rooms here.
EURYDICE: What? No rooms? Where do people sleep?
FATHER: People don't sleep here.
EURYDICE: I have to say I'm very disappointed. It's been
    such a tiring day. I've been traveling all day—first
    on a river, then on an elevator that rained, then on
    a train . . . I thought someone would meet me at the
    station . . .

Eurydice is on the verge of tears.

STONES: Don't cry! Don't cry!
EURYDICE: I don't know where I am and there are all
    these stones and I hate them! They're horrible! I
    want a bath! I thought someone would meet me at
    the station!
FATHER: Don't be sad. I'll take your luggage to your
    room.
STONES: THERE ARE NO ROOMS!

He picks up her luggage.
He gives the stones a dirty look.
The sound of water in rusty pipes.

Scene 2

Orpheus writes a letter to Eurydice.

ORPHEUS: Dear Eurydice,

I miss you. No—that's not enough.

He crumples up the letter.
He writes a new letter.
He thinks.
He writes:

ORPHEUS: Dear Eurydice,
    Symphony for twelve instruments.

(*A pause.*
He hears the music in his head.
He conducts.)

    Love, Orpheus

He drops the letter as though into a mail slot.

Scene 3

The father creates a room out of string for Eurydice.

He makes four walls and a door out of string.
Time passes.
It takes time to build a room out of string.

Eurydice observes the underworld.
There isn't much to observe.
She plays hop-scotch without chalk.

Every so often,
the father looks at her,
happy to see her,
while he makes her room out of string.
She looks back at him, polite.

Scene 4

The father has completed the string room.
He gestures for Eurydice to enter.
She enters.

EURYDICE: Thank you. That will do.

She nods to her father.
He doesn't leave.

EURYDICE: Oh.
    I suppose you want a tip.

He shakes his head.

EURYDICE: Would you run a bath for me?
FATHER: Yes, miss.

He exits the string room.
Eurydice opens her suitcase.
She is surprised that nothing is inside.
She sits down inside her suitcase.

Scene 5

ORPHEUS: Dear Eurydice,

I love you. I'm going to find you. I play the saddest music now that you're gone. You know I hate writing letters. I'll give this letter to a worm. I hope he finds you.

Love,
Orpheus

He drops the letter as though into a mail slot.

Scene 6

The father enters the string room with a letter on a silver tray.

FATHER: There is a letter for you, miss.
EURYDICE: A letter?

He nods.

FATHER: A letter.

He hands her the letter.

FATHER: It's addressed to you.
EURYDICE: There's dirt on it.

Eurydice wipes the dirt off the letter.
She opens it.
She scrutinizes it.
She does not know how to read it.
She puts it on the ground, takes off her shoes,
stands on the letter, and shuts her eyes.
She thinks, without language for the thought,
the melody: There's no place like home . . .

FATHER: Miss.
EURYDICE: What is it?
FATHER: Would you like me to *read* you the letter?
EURYDICE: "Read you the letter"?
FATHER: You can't do it with your feet.

(*The father guides her off the letter, picks it up and begins to read.*)

    It's addressed to Eurydice. That's you.
EURYDICE: That's you.
FATHER: You.
    It says: I love you.

EURYDICE: I love you?
FATHER: It's like your tree.
EURYDICE: Tall?

The father considers.

EURYDICE: Green?
FATHER: It's like sitting in the shade.
EURYDICE: Oh.
FATHER: It's like sitting in the shade with no clothes on.
EURYDICE: Oh!—yes.
FATHER: (*reading*) I'm going to find you. I play the saddest music—
EURYDICE: Music?

He whistles a note.

FATHER: It's like that.

She smiles.

EURYDICE: Go on.
FATHER: You know I hate writing letters. I'll give this letter to a worm. I hope he finds you.

   Love,
   Orpheus
EURYDICE: Orpheus?
FATHER: Orpheus.

A pause.

EURYDICE: That word!
   It's like—I can't breathe.
   Orpheus! My husband.

Eurydice looks at her father.
She recognizes him.

EURYDICE: Oh!

She embraces her father.

Scene 7

ORPHEUS: Dear Eurydice,

   Last night I dreamed that we climbed Mount Olympus and we started to make love and all the strands of your hair were little faucets and water was streaming out of your head and I said, why is water coming out of your hair? And you said, gravity is very compelling.

   And then we jumped off Mount Olympus and flew through the clouds and you held your knee to your chest because you skinned it on a sharp cloud and then we fell into a salty lake. Then I woke up and the window frightened me and I thought: Eurydice is dead. Then I thought—who is Eurydice? Then the whole room started to float and I thought: what are people? Then my bed clothes smiled at me with a crooked green mouth and I thought: who am I? It scares me, Eurydice. Please come back.

   Love,
   Orpheus

Scene 8

Eurydice and her Father in the string room.

FATHER: Did you get my letters?
EURYDICE: No! You wrote me letters?
FATHER: Every day.
EURYDICE: What did they say?
FATHER: Oh—nothing much. The usual stuff.
EURYDICE: Tell me the names of my mother and brothers and sisters.
FATHER: I don't think that's a good idea. It will make you sad.
EURYDICE: I want to know.
FATHER: It's a long time to be sad.
EURYDICE: I'd rather be sad.
THE STONES: Being sad is not allowed! Act like a stone.

Scene 9

Time shifts. Drops of water.
Eurydice and her father in the string room.

EURYDICE: Teach me another.
FATHER: Ostracize.
EURYDICE: What does it mean?
FATHER: To exclude. The Greeks decided who to banish. They wrote the name of the banished person on a white piece of pottery called ostrakon.
EURYDICE: Ostrakon.

   Another.
FATHER: Peripatetic. From the Greek. It means to walk slowly, speaking of weighty matters, in bare feet.
EURYDICE: Peripatetic: a learned fruit, wandering through the snow.

   Another.
FATHER: Defunct.
EURYDICE: Defunct.
FATHER: It means dead in a very abrupt way. Not the way I died, which was slowly. But all at once, in cowboy boots.
EURYDICE: Tell me a story of when you were little.
FATHER: Well, there was the time your uncle shot at me with a bee-bee gun and I was mad at him so I swallowed a nail.

   Then there was the time I went to a dude ranch and I was riding a horse and I lassoed a car. The lady driving the car got out and spanked me. And your grandmother spanked me too.
EURYDICE: Remember the Christmas when she gave me a doll and I said, "If I see one more doll I'm going to throw up"?
FATHER: I think grammy was a little surprised when you said that.
EURYDICE: Tell me a story about your mother.
FATHER: The most vivid recollection I have of mother was seeing her at parties and in the house playing piano. When she was younger she was extremely animated.

She could really play the piano. She could play every-thing by ear. They called her Flaming Sally.

EURYDICE: I never saw grammy play the piano.

FATHER: She was never the same after my father died. My father was a very gentle man.

EURYDICE: Tell me a story about your father.

FATHER: My father and I used to duck hunt. By the Mississippi River. He would call up old Frank the night before and ask, "Where are the ducks moving tonight?" Old Frank, he could really call the ducks.

It was hard for me to kill the poor little ducks, but you get caught up in the fervor of it. You'd get as many as ten ducks.

If you went over the limit—there were only so many ducks per person—father would throw the ducks to the side of the creek we were paddling on and make sure there was no game warden. If the war-den was gone, he'd run back and get the extra ducks and throw them in the back of the car. My father was never a great conversationalist—but he loved to rhapsodize about hunting. He would always say, if I ever have to die, it's in a duck pond. And he did.

EURYDICE: There was something I always wanted to ask you. A story—or someone's name—I forget.

FATHER: Don't worry. You'll remember. There's plenty of time.

Scene 10

Orpheus writes a letter.

ORPHEUS: Dear Eurydice,

I wonder if you miss reading books in the underworld.

Orpheus holds the Collected Works of Shakespeare with a long string attached.
He drops it slowly to the ground.

Scene 11

Eurydice holds the Collected Works of Shakespeare.

EURYDICE: What is this?

She opens it. She doesn't understand it.
She throws the book on the ground.

EURYDICE: What are you?

She is wary of it, as though it might bite her.
She tries to understand the book.
She tries to make the book do something.

EURYDICE: (*to the book*) What do you do?
  What do you DO?!
  Say something!
  I hate you!

She stands on the book, trying to read it.

EURYDICE: Damn you!

She throws the book.
She lies down in the string room.
Drops of water. Time passes.
The Father picks up the book.
He brushes it off.
In the string room,
the father teaches Eurydice how to read.
She looks over his shoulder as he reads out loud from King Lear.

FATHER: We two alone will sing like birds in the cage.
  When thou dost ask my blessing, I'll kneel down
  And ask of thee forgiveness; so we'll live,
  And pray and sing. . . .°

Scene 12

Orpheus, with a telephone.

ORPHEUS: For Eurydice—E, U, R, Y—that's right. No, there's no last name. It's not like that. What? No, I don't know the country. I don't know the city either. I don't know the street. I don't know—it probably starts with a vowel. Could you just—would you mind checking please—I would really appreciate it. You can't enter a name without a city? Why not? Well, thank you for trying. Wait—miss—it's a spe-cial case. She's dead. Well, thank you for trying. You have a nice day too.

He hangs up.

I'll find you. Don't move!

He fingers a glow-in-the-dark globe, looking for her.

Scene 13

Eurydice and her father in the string room.

EURYDICE: Tell me another story of when you were little.

FATHER: Well, there was my first piano recital. I was play-ing "I Got Rhythm." I played the first few chords and I couldn't remember the rest. I ran out of the room and locked myself in the bathroom.

EURYDICE: Then what happened?

FATHER: Your grandmother pulled me out of the bath-room and made me apologize to everyone in the auditorium. I never played piano after that. But I still know the first four chords—let's see—

We two alone . . . : In Shakespeare's *King Lear* (V, viii, 6–9), the mad Lear speaks these words to his still living daughter Cordelia, expecting them both to be placed in prison.

(*He plays the chords in the air with his hands*)

    Da Da *Dee* Da
    Da Da *Dee* Da
    Da Da *Dee* Da . . .

EURYDICE: What are the words?
FATHER: I can't remember.
    Let's see . . .
    Da da Dee Da
    Da da Dee da . . .

They both start singing to the tune of I Got Rhythm.

FATHER AND EURYDICE: Da da *Dee* Da
    Da da Dee Da
    Da da Dee Da
    Da dee da da doo dee dee da.
    Da da Da da
    Da da Da da
    Da Da da Da
    Da da da . . .
    Da da Dee Da
    Da da dee da . . .

STONES: WHAT IS THAT NOISE?
LITTLE STONE: Stop singing!
LOUD STONE: STOP SINGING!
BIG STONE: Neither of you can carry a tune.
LITTLE STONE: It's awful.
STONES: DEAD PEOPLE CAN'T SING!
EURYDICE: I'm not a very good singer.
FATHER: Neither am I.

Scene 14

The Father leaves for work.
He takes his briefcase.
He waves to Eurydice.
She waves back.
She is alone in the string room.
She touches the string.

The Lord of the Underworld enters on his red tricycle.
Music from a heavy metal band accompanies his entrance.
His clothes and his hat are too small for him.
He stops pedaling at the entrance to the string room.

CHILD: Knock, knock.
EURYDICE: Who's there?
CHILD: I am Lord of the Underworld.
EURYDICE: Very funny.
CHILD: I am.
EURYDICE: Prove it.
CHILD: I can do chin-ups inside your bones. Close your
    eyes.

She closes her eyes.

EURYDICE: Ow.
CHILD: See?
    You're pretty.

EURYDICE: You're little.
CHILD: I grow downward. Like a turnip.
EURYDICE: What do you want?
CHILD: I wanted to see if you were comfortable.
    You're not itchy?
EURYDICE: No.
CHILD: That's good. Sometimes our residents get itchy.
    Then I scratch them.
EURYDICE: I'm not itchy.
CHILD: What's all this string?
EURYDICE: It's my room.
CHILD: Rooms are not allowed!

(*To the stones.*)

    Tell her.
STONES: ROOMS ARE NOT ALLOWED!
CHILD: Who made your room?
EURYDICE: My father.
CHILD: Fathers are not allowed! Where is he?
EURYDICE: He's at work.
CHILD: We'll have to dip you in the river again and make
    sure you're good and dunked.
EURYDICE: Please, don't.
CHILD: Oooh—say that again. It's nice.
EURYDICE: Please, don't.
CHILD: Say it in my ear.
EURYDICE: (*towards his ear*) Please, don't.
CHILD: I like that.

(*A seduction:*)

    I'll huff and I'll puff and I'll blow your house down!

(*He blows on her face.*)

    I mean that in the nicest possible way.
EURYDICE: I have a husband.
CHILD: Husbands are for children. You need a lover. I'll
    be back.

(*To the stones.*)

    See that she's . . . comfortable.
STONES: We will!
CHILD: Good-bye.
EURYDICE: Good-bye.
STONES: Good-bye.
CHILD: I'm growing. Can you tell? I'm growing!

He laughs his hysterical laugh and speeds away on his
red tricycle.

Scene 15

A big storm. The sound of rain on a roof.
Orpheus in a rain slicker.

ORPHEUS: (*shouting above the storm*) If a drop of water
    enters the soil
    at a particular angle, with a particular pitch,
    what's to say a man can't ride one note
    into the earth like a fireman's pole?

He puts a bucket on the ground to catch rain falling.
He looks at the rain falling into the bucket.
He tunes his guitar, trying to make the pitch of each
note correspond with the pitch of each water drop.

Orpheus wonders if one particular pitch
might lead him to the underworld.
Orpheus wonders if the pitch
he is searching for might
correspond to the pitch of a drop
of rain, as it enters the soil.
A pitch.

ORPHEUS: Eurydice—did you hear that?

Another pitch.

Eurydice? That's the note. That one, right there.

Scene 16

Eurydice and her father in the string room.

EURYDICE: Orpheus never liked words. He had his music. He would get a funny look on his face and I would say what are you thinking about and he would always be thinking about music.

If we were in a restaurant sometimes Orpheus would look sullen and wouldn't talk to me and I thought people felt sorry for me. I should have realized that women envied me. Their husbands talked too much.

But I wanted to talk to him about my notions. I was working on a new philosophical system. It involved hats.

This is what it is to love an artist: The moon is always rising above your house. The houses of your neighbors look dull and lacking in moonlight. But he is always going away from you. Inside his head there is always something more beautiful.

Orpheus said the mind is a slide ruler. It can fit around anything. Words can mean anything. Show me your body, he said. It only means one thing.

Scene 17

ORPHEUS: Eurydice!

Before I go down there, I won't practice my music. Some say practice. But practice is a word invented by cowards. The animals don't have a word for practice. A gazelle does not run for practice. He runs because he is scared or he is hungry. A bird doesn't sing for practice. She sings because she's happy or sad. So I say: store it up. The music sounds better in my head than it does in the world. When songs are pressing against my throat, then, only then, I will go down and sing for the devils and they will cry through their parched throats.

Eurydice, don't kiss a dead man. Their lips look red and tempting but put your tongue in their mouths and it tastes like oatmeal. I know how much you hate oatmeal.

I'm going the way of death.

Here is my plan: Tonight, when I go to bed, I will turn off the light and put a straw in my mouth. When I fall asleep, I will crawl through the straw and my breath will push me like a great wind into the darkness and I will sing your name and I will arrive. I have consulted the almanacs, the footstools, and the architects, and everyone agrees: I found the right note. Wait for me.

Love,
Orpheus

Scene 18

EURYDICE: I got a letter. From Orpheus.
FATHER: What did he say?
EURYDICE: He says he's going to come find me.
FATHER: How?
EURYDICE: He's going to sing.

Scene 19

Darkness.
An unearthly light surrounds Orpheus.
He holds a straw up to his lips in slow motion.

He blows into the straw.

The sound of breath.
He disappears.

Scene 20

The sound of a knock.

LITTLE STONE: Someone is knocking!
BIG STONE: Who is it?
LOUD STONE: Who is it?

The sound of three loud knocks, insistent.

STONES: NO ONE KNOCKS AT THE DOOR OF THE DEAD!

THIRD MOVEMENT • Scene 1

Orpheus stands at the gates of hell.
He opens his mouth.

He looks like he's singing, but he's silent.
Music surrounds him.
The melody Orpheus hummed in the first scene,
repeated over and over again.

Raspberries, peaches and plums drop from the ceiling into the River. Perhaps only in our imagination.
Orpheus keeps singing.

The stones weep.
They look at their tears, bewildered.
Orpheus keeps singing.

A child comes out of a trap door.

CHILD: Who are you?
ORPHEUS: I am Orpheus.
CHILD: I am Lord of the Underworld.
ORPHEUS: But you're so young!
CHILD: Don't be rude.
ORPHEUS: Sorry.
    Did you like my music?
CHILD: No, I prefer happy music with a nice beat.
ORPHEUS: Oh.
CHILD: You've come for Eurydice.
ORPHEUS: Yes!
CHILD: And you thought singing would get you through the gates of hell.
ORPHEUS: See here. I want my wife.
    What do I have to do?
CHILD: You'll have to do more than sing.
ORPHEUS: I'm not sure what you mean, sir.
CHILD: Start walking home. Your wife just might be on the road behind you. We make it real nice here. So people want to stick around. As you walk, keep your eyes facing front. If you look back at her—poof! She's gone.
ORPHEUS: I can't look at her?
CHILD: No.
ORPHEUS: Why?
CHILD: Because.
ORPHEUS: Because?
CHILD: Because!
ORPHEUS: I look straight ahead. That's all?
CHILD: Yes.
ORPHEUS: That's easy.
CHILD: Good.

The child smiles. He exits.

Scene 2

Eurydice and her father.

EURYDICE: I hear him at the gates! That's his music! He's come to save me!
FATHER: Do you want to go with him?
EURYDICE: Yes, of course!

She sees that his face falls a little.

EURYDICE: Oh—you'll be lonely, won't you?
FATHER: No, no. You should go to your husband. You should have grandchildren. You'll all come down and meet me one day.
EURYDICE: Are you sure?
FATHER: You should love your family until the grapes grow dust on their purple faces.
    I'll take you to him.
EURYDICE: Now?
FATHER: It's for the best.

He takes her arm.
They process, arm in arm, as at a wedding.
Wedding music.
They are solemn and glad.
They walk.
They see Orpheus up ahead.

FATHER: Is that him?
EURYDICE: Yes—I think so—
FATHER: His shoulders aren't very broad. Can he take care of you?

Eurydice nods.

FATHER: Are you sure?
EURYDICE: Yes.
FATHER: There's one thing you need to know. If he turns around and sees you, you'll die a second death. Those are the rules. So step quietly. And don't cry out.
EURYDICE: I won't.
FATHER: Good-bye.

They embrace.

EURYDICE: I'll come back to you. I seem to keep dying.
FATHER: Don't let them dip you in the River too long, the second time. Hold your breath.
EURYDICE: I'll look for a tree.
FATHER: I'll write you letters.
EURYDICE: Where will I find them?
FATHER: I don't know yet. I'll think of something. Good-bye, Eurydice.
EURYDICE: Good-bye.

They move away.
The father waves.
She waves back,
as though on an old steamer ship.
The father exits.
Eurydice takes a deep breath. She takes a big step forward towards the audience, on an unseen gangplank.
She is brave.
She takes another step forward.
She hesitates.
She is all of a sudden not so brave.
She is afraid.
SHE LOOKS BACK.
She turns in the direction of her father, her back to the audience. He's out of sight.

EURYDICE: Wait, come back!
LITTLE STONE: You can't go back now, Eurydice.
LOUD STONE: Face forward!
BIG STONE: Keep walking.
EURYDICE: I'm afraid!
LOUD STONE: Your husband is waiting for you, Eurydice.
EURYDICE: I don't recognize him! That's a stranger!
LITTLE STONE: Go on. It's him.
EURYDICE: I want to go home! I want my father!
LOUD STONE: You're all grown up now. You have a husband.
STONES: TURN AROUND!
EURYDICE: Why?

STONES: BECAUSE!

EURYDICE: That's a stupid reason.

LITTLE STONE: Orpheus braved the gates of hell
    to find you.

LOUD STONE: He played the saddest music.

BIG STONE: Even we—

STONES: The stones—

LITTLE STONE: cried when we heard it.

She turns slowly, facing front.

EURYDICE: That's Orpheus?

STONES: Yes, that's him!

EURYDICE: Where's his music?

STONES: It's in your head.

*Orpheus walks slowly, in a straight line, with the focus
of a tight-rope walker.
Eurydice moves to follow him.
She follows him, several steps behind.
THEY WALK.
Eurydice follows him with precision, one step for every
step he takes.
She makes a decision.
She increases her pace.
She takes two steps for every step that Orpheus takes.
She catches up to him.*

EURYDICE: Orpheus?

*HE TURNS TOWARDS HER, STARTLED.
ORPHEUS LOOKS AT EURYDICE.
EURYDICE LOOKS AT ORPHEUS.
THE WORLD FALLS AWAY.*

ORPHEUS: You startled me.

*A small sound—ping.
They turn their faces away from each other,
matter-of-fact, compelled.
The lights turn blue.*

EURYDICE: I'm sorry.

ORPHEUS: Why?

EURYDICE: I don't know.

ORPHEUS: *(syncopated)*	EURYDICE:
You always clapped your hands	I could never spell the word
on the third beat	rhythm—
you couldn't wait for the fourth.	it is such a difficult
Remember—	word to spell—
I tried to teach you—	r—y—no—
	there's an H
	in it—
you were always one step ahead	somewhere—a
of the music	breath—
your sense of rhythm—	rhy—rhy—
it was—off—	rhy—

ORPHEUS: I would say clap on the down-beat—
    no, the down-beat—
    It's dangerous not

to have a sense of rhythm.
    You LOSE things when you can't
    keep a simple beat—
    why'd you have to say my name—
    Eurydice—

EURYDICE: I'm sorry.

ORPHEUS: I know we used to fight—
    it seems so silly now—if—

EURYDICE: If ifs and ands were pots and pans
    there'd be no need for tinkers—

ORPHEUS: Why?

*They begin walking away from each other
on extensive unseen boardwalks,
their figures long shadows,
looking straight ahead.*

EURYDICE: If ifs and ands were pots and pans
    there'd be no need for tinkers—

ORPHEUS: Eurydice—

EURYDICE: I think I see the gates.
    The stones—the boat—
    it looks familiar—
    the stones look happy to see me—

ORPHEUS: Don't look—

EURYDICE: Wow! That's the happiest I've ever seen them!

ORPHEUS: *(syncopated)*	EURYDICE:
Think of things we did:	Everything is so grey—
	it looks familiar—
we went ice skating—	like home—
	our house was—
I wore a red sweater—	grey—with a red door—
	we had two cats
	and two dogs
	and two fish
	that died—

ORPHEUS: Will you talk to me!

EURYDICE: The train looks like
    the opposite of a train—

ORPHEUS: Eurydice!
    WE'VE KNOWN EACH OTHER FOR CENTURIES!
    I want to reminisce!
    Remember when you wanted your name in a song
    so I put your name in a song—
    When I played my music
    at the gates of hell
    I was singing your name
    over and over and over again.
    Eurydice.

*He grows quiet.
They walk away from each other on extended lines
until they are out of sight.*

Scene 3

THE STONES: Finally.
    Some peace.

LOUD STONE: And quiet.

THE STONES: Like the old days.
>No music.
>No conversation.
>How about that.

A pause.

FATHER: With Eurydice gone it will be a second death for me.
LITTLE STONE: Oh, please, sir—
BIG STONE: We're tired.
FATHER: Do you understand the love a father has for his daughter?
LITTLE STONE: Love is a big, funny word.
BIG STONE: Dead people should be seen and not heard.

The father looks at the stones.
He looks at the string room.
He dismantles the string room,
matter-of-fact.
There's nothing else to do.
This can take time.
It takes time to dismantle a room made of string.
Music.
He sits down in what used to be the string room.

FATHER: How does a person remember to forget. It's difficult.
LOUD STONE: It's not difficult.
LITTLE STONE: We told you how it works.
LOUD STONE: Dip yourself in the river.
BIG STONE: Dip yourself in the river.
LITTLE STONE: Dip yourself in the river.
FATHER: I need directions.
LOUD STONE: That's ridiculous.
BIG STONE: There are no directions.

A pause.
The father thinks.

FATHER: I remember.
>Take Tri-State South—294—
>to Route 88 West.
>Take Route 88 West to Route 80.
>You'll go over a bridge.
>Go three miles and you'll come
>to the exit for Middle Road.
>Proceed 3 to 4 miles.
>Duck Creek Park will be on the right.
>Take a left on Fernwood Avenue.

>Continue straight on Fernwood past
>two intersections.
>Fernwood will curve to the right leading
>you to Forest Road.
>Take a left on Forest Road.
>Go two blocks.
>Pass the first entrance to the alley on the right.
>Take the second entrance.
>You'll go about 100 yards.
>A red brick house will
>be on the right.
>Look for Illinois license plates.

>Go inside the house.
>In the living room,
>look out the window.
>You'll see the lights on the Mississippi River.
>Take off your shoes.
>Walk down the hill.
>You'll pass a tree good for climbing on the right.
>Cross the road.
>Watch for traffic.
>Cross the train tracks.
>Catfish are sleeping in the mud, on your left.
>Roll up your jeans.
>Count to ten.
>Put your feet in the river
>and swim.

He dips himself in the river.
A small metallic sound of forgetfulness—ping.
The sound of water.
He lies down on the ground,
curled up, asleep.

Eurydice returns and sees that her string room is gone.

EURYDICE: Where's my room?

The stones are silent.

EURYDICE: (*to the stones*) WHERE IS MY ROOM? Answer me!
LITTLE STONE: It's none of our business.
LOUD STONE: What are you doing here?
BIG STONE: You should be with your husband.
LOUD STONE: Up there.
EURYDICE: Where's my father?

The stones point to the father.

EURYDICE: (*to the stones*) Why is he sleeping?

The stones shrug their shoulders.

EURYDICE: (*to her father*) I've come back!
LOUD STONE: He can't hear you.
LITTLE STONE: It's too late.
EURYDICE: What are you talking about?
BIG STONE: He dipped himself in the River.
EURYDICE: My father did not dip himself in the River.
STONES: He did!
>We saw him!
LOUD STONE: He wanted some peace and quiet.
EURYDICE: (*to the stones*) HE DID NOT!

(*To her father.*)

>Listen. I'll teach you the words. Then we'll know each other again. Ready? We'll start with my name. Eurydice. E U R Y . . . .
BIG STONE: He can't hear you.
LOUD STONE: He can't see you.
LITTLE STONE: He can't remember you.
EURYDICE: (*to the stones*) I hate you! I've always hated you!
>Shut up! Shut up! Shut up!

(*To her father.*)

Listen. I'll tell you a story.

LITTLE STONE: Try speaking in the language of stones.

LOUD STONE: It's a very quiet language.
Like if the pores in your
face opened up and wanted to talk.

EURYDICE: Stone.
Rock.
Tree. Rock. Stone.

It doesn't work.
She holds her father.

LOUD STONE: Didn't you already mourn for your father, young lady?

LITTLE STONE: Some things should be left well enough alone.

BIG STONE: To mourn twice is excessive.

LITTLE STONE: To mourn three times a sin.

LOUD STONE: Life is like a good meal.

BIG STONE: Only gluttons want more food when they finish their helping.

LITTLE STONE: Learn to be more moderate.

BIG STONE: It's weird for a dead person to be morbid.

LITTLE STONE: We don't like to watch it!

LOUD STONE: We don't like to see it!

BIG STONE: It makes me uncomfortable.

Eurydice cries.

STONES: Don't cry!
Don't cry!

BIG STONE: Learn the art of keeping busy!

EURYDICE: IT'S HARD TO KEEP BUSY WHEN YOU'RE DEAD!

STONES: It is not hard!
We keep busy
and we like it
We're busy busy busy stones
Watch us work
Keeping still
Keeping quiet
It's hard work
to be a stone
No time for crying
No no no!

EURYDICE: I HATE YOU! I'VE ALWAYS HATED YOU!

She runs towards them and tries to hit them.

STONES: Go ahead.
Try to hit us.

LITTLE STONE: You'll hurt your fist.

BIG STONE: You'll break your hand.

STONES: Ha ha ha!

Enter the child.
He has grown.
He is now at least ten feet tall.
His voice sounds suspiciously
like the Nasty Interesting Man's.

CHILD: Is there a problem here?

STONES: No, sir.

CHILD: (*to Eurydice*) You chose to stay with us, huh? Good.

(*He looks her over.*)

Perhaps to be my bride?

EURYDICE: I told you. You're too young.

CHILD: I'll be the judge of that.
I've grown.

EURYDICE: Yes—I see that.

CHILD: I'm ready to be a man now. I'm ready—to be—a man.

EURYDICE: Please. Leave me alone.

CHILD: I'll have them start preparing the satins and silks. You can't refuse me. I've made my choice.

EURYDICE: Can I have a moment to prepare myself?

CHILD: Don't be long. The wedding songs are already being written. They're very quiet. Inaudible, you might say. A dirt-filled orchestra for my bride. Don't trouble the songs with your music, I say. A song is two dead bodies rubbing under the covers to keep warm.

Orpheus (played by Joseph Parks) descending into the underworld in a rainy elevator in the Yale Repertory Theatre's 2006 performance of Sarah Ruhl's *Eurydice*.

He exits.

STONES: Well, well, well!

LITTLE STONE: You had better prepare yourself.

EURYDICE: There is nothing to prepare.

BIG STONE: You had better comb your hair.

LOUD STONE: You had better find a veil.

EURYDICE: I don't need a veil. I need a pen!

LITTLE STONE: Pens are forbidden here.

EURYDICE: I need a pencil then.

LOUD STONE: Pencils, too.

EURYDICE: Damn you! I'll dip you in the river!

BIG STONE: Too late, too late!

EURYDICE: There must be a pen. There are. There must be.

She remembers the pen and paper in the breast pocket
of her father's coat.
She takes them out.
She holds the pen up to show the stones.

EURYDICE: A pen.

She writes a letter.

EURYDICE: Dear Orpheus,

I'm sorry. I don't know what came over me. I was afraid.
I'm not worthy of you. But I still love you, I think. Don't
try to find me again. You would be lonely for music. I
want you to be happy. I want you to marry again. I am
going to write out instructions for your next wife.

To my Husband's Next Wife:

Be gentle.
Be sure to comb his hair when it's wet.
Do not fail to notice
that his face flushes pink
like a bride's
when you kiss him.

Give him lots to eat.
He forgets to eat and he gets cranky.

When he's sad,
kiss his forehead and I will thank you.
Because he is a young prince
and his robes are too heavy on him.
His crown falls down
around his ears.

I'll give this letter to a worm. I hope he finds you.

Love,
Eurydice.

She puts the letter on the ground.
She dips herself in the river.
A small metallic sound of forgetfulness—ping.
The sound of water.
She lies down next to her father, as though asleep.

The sound of an elevator—ding.
Orpheus appears in the elevator.
He sees Eurydice.
He is happy.
The elevator starts raining on Orpheus.
He forgets.
He steps out of the elevator.

He sees the letter on the ground.
He picks it up.
He scrutinizes it.
He can't read it.
He stands on it.
He closes his eyes.
The sound of water.
Then silence.

The end.

John Patrick Shanley

John Patrick Shanley (b. 1950) grew up in the Bronx, New York, and his experiences in school were marked by difficulties. He was expelled from kindergarten, and in St. Anthony's, a school run by the Sisters of Charity, he was restricted from the lunch program for life. At Cardinal Spellman High School, he rebelled against the strict program and was eventually asked to leave. He then attended Thomas More, a private Catholic school in New Hampshire, where his talent for writing was discovered and nurtured. He went to New York University for a semester, but was asked to leave. He then joined the Marines during the Vietnam War. After returning home, he finished his degree at New York University and began his professional writing career with his first play, *Saturday Night at the War* (1978). His academic difficulties were not an indication of a lack of intelligence—he was the valedictorian of his class at NYU—but of a certain lack of judgment that Shanley said later helped him in working out dramatic problems.

Shanley's screenwriting experience earned him an Oscar for his original script, *Moonstruck* (1988), starring Cher and Nicholas Cage. He produced several more scripts that attracted famous stars, such as Tom Hanks and Meg Ryan, but while he was writing screenplays and directing, he continued writing off-Broadway plays. Shanley has said that his four early plays are essentially one long play: *Danny and the Deep Blue Sea* (1983), *Savage in Limbo* (1984), *The Dreamer Examines His Pillow* (1985), and *Italian-American Reconciliation* (1986). While there is a great deal of humor in these plays, Shanley also works out a number of personal issues related to family and the stress of relationships. For example, *Italian-American Reconciliation*, which premiered in New York in 1988 at the Manhattan Theatre Club, starring John Turturro, explores the virtual insanity of a character who turns his back on a loving woman to attempt a reconciliation with his impossible ex-wife. Shanley has been married twice and now lives with his two adopted sons. His plays, he has hinted, come from a deep reservoir of personal experiences.

Critics have not always been kind to Shanley, and one of their early complaints was that his plays are too "talky." In his own defense, Shanley says he uses the language of his plays to discuss difficult and important issues. He makes every effort to have his characters talk the way he has heard real people talk and to be clear about the truth. He tries to avoid clichés that give people the sense that they know the truth about something when, in fact, they do not. Political slogans, for example, are a clichéd kind of shorthand for positions that are only vaguely understood, and Shanley believes that there are "middlemen"—journalists, politicians, and others—who appropriate language in such a way as to keep people confused about important issues in their lives.

One result of Shanley's Catholic education and his experience in the Marine Corps is that he developed an understanding of and respect for the nature of authority. But he also came to understand that the certainty imparted to him by his early experiences was not absolute. His desire to discover the truth about important issues in life could not be satisfied by accepting without question everything he was told.

Shanley's plays often show us wounded people in situations of stress. *Kissing Christine* (1996) introduces two differently traumatized people on a first date; *Psychopathia Sexualis* (1998) is about a man with an argyle sock fetish who wishes to marry a woman who defies their psychiatrist; and *Where's My Money?* (2001) treats sexual infidelity in marriage and the opinions people rush to in judging others. His most quoted line is from *Where's My Money?*: "Monogamy is like a 40-watt bulb. It works, but it's not enough."

The idea for *Doubt* (2004) came to Shanley as he was rehearsing another play. Fearing that it was too close to current headlines exposing child molestation in the Roman Catholic Church, he hesitated. But he knew that the idea depended on his own experience in Catholic school, and in an interview he said that when he thought of the scene in which a child's mother, Mrs. Muller, talks with Sister Aloysius, he knew that he had a real play, not a hint of journalism.

For links to resources about Shanley, click on *AuthorLinks* at **bedfordstmartins.com/jacobus**.

Doubt: A Parable

In his preface to the play, Shanley says, "We are living in a culture of extreme advocacy, of confrontation, of judgment, and of verdict." *Doubt* is, in many ways, an illustration of that statement. Sister Aloysius has arrived at a verdict with respect to Father Flynn, who she believes is molesting a young student, Donald Muller. Flynn himself delivers a sermon on the question of doubt related to the assassination of President Kennedy. He later delivers a sermon on the consequences of malicious gossip, using a simple parable to illustrate his point. Sister James is much younger than Sister Aloysius and by nature tends to be much less confrontational and judgmental. She is, as Sister Aloysius tells her, innocent, and as a result turns out to be easily led by her superior to suspect Father Flynn.

Father Flynn's first sermon arises in response to the despair people felt after the assassination of President Kennedy. Interestingly, he ends the sermon with a story about a figure on the open ocean who sets his course and then begins to doubt whether he has set it truly. Flynn likens this situation to a crisis in faith, which at that point seems to be the center of doubt for members of the church. Flynn says, "Doubt can be a bond as powerful and sustaining as certainty." The bond he refers to is a bond of a community, whether a community of two or a community of dozens. When he speaks later of the force of gossip and its effects on a community, he speaks in reference not to a public action, but to the specific action of Sister Aloysius and her attempt to destroy his reputation. In both of his sermons, Father Flynn adds a parable to his message, a practice that recalls the sermons of Jesus Christ.

The structure of the play depends on the absolute certainty of Sister Aloysius in her conviction that Father Flynn's behavior with his students is dangerous. The fact that Father Flynn takes Donald Muller under his wing is, for her, evidence of his inappropriate treatment of the student. Although she admits that there is no real evidence, nothing specific or provable that would indict Father Flynn, she insists that she knows the truth. Her personal experience, combined with her suspicions and observations, makes her totally convinced. Nothing that Father Flynn can say to her will change her mind. From her position of power she comes close to converting Sister James to her point of view. It is only in the presence of Father Flynn himself that Sister James becomes uncertain and then decides that he may not be guilty of child molestation.

When Mrs. Muller comes for a conference with Sister Aloysius, we discover additional complexities in the situation. Mrs. Muller is confounded by the fact that Sister Aloysius makes her son pay for the aberrant behavior of a priest, when she should remove the priest, not the student. Mrs. Muller explains how important this school is for her son, how he had been beaten up by students in his other school. She implies that Donald might be gay and for that reason her husband beats Donald. The fact that Father Flynn has taken an interest in Donald is for Mrs. Muller something positive. Yet her sense of what her son needs and the benefits he receives from the school do not move Sister Aloysius, who remains certain of herself.

Audience members cannot be certain why Father Flynn accepts a promotion and leaves the school, nor can they be certain why Sister Aloysius resorts to lying to Father Flynn about her phone call "investigating" his former appointments. John Patrick Shanley leaves us with doubts.

For discussion questions and assignments on *Doubt*, visit bedfordstmartins.com/jacobus.

Doubt: A Parable in Performance

Doubt premiered off-Broadway at the Manhattan Theatre Club in New York in November 2004, because Lynne Meadow, artistic director of the Manhattan Theatre Club, asked to produce it. Since Shanley had produced so many plays off-Broadway, the venue seemed a natural choice to him. The play soon transferred to the Walter Kerr Theatre on Broadway in response to intense audience approval. Doug Hughes directed in March 2005, with Brían O'Byrne as Father Flynn and Cherry Jones as Sister Aloysius. Interestingly, Shanley invited his first-grade teacher, also named Sister James, to sit with him at both openings. The critics were uniformly positive, with a great many of them naming it the number one show of the year. The play won the Tony Award for best play, the New York Drama Critics' Circle Award, the Lucille Lortel Award, and the Pulitzer Prize for drama. *Doubt* was made into a film in 2008 starring Meryl Streep, Philip Seymour Hoffman, and Amy Adams. The film received five Academy Award nominations, including one for best writing.

From 2006 to the present, the play has been performed regionally and internationally. It went on tour in the United States in 2006 and 2007. It played in the Philippines, in Paris (directed by Roman Polanski), in Poland, in Australia at the Sidney Opera House, and in many other venues throughout the world. The play has been called "actor proof" and continues to be produced in high schools as well as university theaters.

JOHN PATRICK SHANLEY (b. 1950)

Doubt
A Parable

2004

ONE

A priest, Father Flynn, in his late thirties, in green and gold vestments, gives a sermon. He is working class, from the Northeast.

FLYNN: What do you do when you're not sure? That's the topic of my sermon today. You look for God's direction and can't find it. Last year when President Kennedy was assassinated, who among us did not experience the most profound disorientation. Despair. "What now? Which way? What do I say to my kids? What do I tell myself?" It was a time of people sitting together, bound together by a common feeling of hopelessness. But think of that! Your *bond* with your fellow beings was your *despair*. It was a public experience, shared by everyone in our society. It was awful, but we were in it together! How much worse is it then for the lone man, the lone woman, stricken by a private calamity? "No one knows I'm sick. No one knows I've lost my last real friend. No one knows I've done something wrong." Imagine the isolation. You see the world as through a window. On the one side of the glass: happy, untroubled people. On the other side: you. Something has happened, you have to carry it, and it's incommunicable. For those so afflicted, only God knows their pain. Their secret. The secret of their alienating sorrow. And when such a person, as they must, howls to the sky, to God: "Help me!" What if no answer comes? Silence. I want to tell you a story. A cargo ship sank, and all her crew was drowned. Only this one sailor survived. He made a raft of some spars and, being of a nautical discipline, turned his eyes to the Heavens and read the stars. He set a course for his home and, exhausted, fell asleep. Clouds rolled in and blanketed the sky. For the next twenty nights, as he floated on the vast ocean, he could no longer see the stars. He thought he was on course, but there was no way to be certain. As the days rolled on, and he wasted away with fevers, thirst and starvation, he began to have doubts. Had he set his course right? Was he still going on towards his home? Or was he horribly lost and doomed to a terrible death? No way to know. The message of the constellations—had he imagined it because of his desperate circumstance? Or had he seen Truth once and now had to hold on to it without further reassurance? That was his dilemma on a voyage without apparent end. There are those of you in church today who know exactly the crisis of faith I describe. I want to say to you. Doubt can be a bond as powerful and sustaining as certainty. When you are lost, you are not alone. In the name of the Father, the Son, and the Holy Ghost. Amen. (*He exits.*)

TWO

The lights crossfade to a corner office in a Catholic school in the Bronx. The principal, Sister Aloysius Beauvier, sits at her desk, writing in a ledger with a fountain pen. She is in her fifties or sixties. She is watchful, reserved, unsentimental. She is of the order of the Sisters of Charity. She wears a black bonnet and floor-length black habit, rimless glasses. A knock at the door.

SISTER ALOYSIUS: Come in. (*Sister James, also of the Sisters of Charity, pokes her head in. She is in her twenties. There's a bit of sunshine in her heart, though she's reserved as well.*)
SISTER JAMES: Have you a moment, Sister Aloysius?
SISTER ALOYSIUS: Come in, Sister James. (*She enters.*) Who's watching your class?
SISTER JAMES: They're having Art.
SISTER ALOYSIUS: Art. Waste of time.
SISTER JAMES: It's only an hour a week.
SISTER ALOYSIUS: Much can be accomplished in sixty minutes.
SISTER JAMES: Yes, Sister Aloysius. I wondered if I might know what you did about William London?
SISTER ALOYSIUS: I sent him home.
SISTER JAMES: Oh dear. So he's still bleeding?
SISTER ALOYSIUS: Oh yes.
SISTER JAMES: His nose just let loose and started gushing during the Pledge of Allegiance.
SISTER ALOYSIUS: Was it spontaneous?
SISTER JAMES: What else would it be?
SISTER ALOYSIUS: Self-induced.
SISTER JAMES: You mean, you think he might've intentionally given himself a nosebleed?
SISTER ALOYSIUS: Exactly.
SISTER JAMES: No!

SISTER ALOYSIUS: You are a very innocent person, Sister James. William London is a fidgety boy and if you do not keep right on him, he will do anything to escape his chair. He would set his foot on fire for half a day out of school.

SISTER JAMES: But why?

SISTER ALOYSIUS: He has a restless mind.

SISTER JAMES: But that's good.

SISTER ALOYSIUS: No, it's not. His father's a policeman, and the last thing he wants is a rowdy boy. William London is headed for trouble. Puberty has got hold of him. He will be imagining all the wrong things, and I strongly suspect he will not graduate high school. But that's beyond our jurisdiction. We simply have to get him through, out the door, and then he's somebody else's project. Ordinarily, I assign my most experienced sisters to eighth grade, but I'm working within constraints. Are you in control of your class?

SISTER JAMES: I think so.

SISTER ALOYSIUS: Usually more children are sent down to me.

SISTER JAMES: I try to take care of things myself.

SISTER ALOYSIUS: That can be an error. You are answerable to me, I to the monsignor, he to the bishop, and so on up to the Holy Father. There's a chain of discipline. Make use of it.

SISTER JAMES: Yes, Sister.

SISTER ALOYSIUS: How's Donald Muller doing?

SISTER JAMES: Steady.

SISTER ALOYSIUS: Good. Has anyone hit him?

SISTER JAMES: No.

SISTER ALOYSIUS: Good. That girl, Linda Conte, have you seated her away from the boys?

SISTER JAMES: As far as space permits. It doesn't do much good.

SISTER ALOYSIUS: Just get her through. Intact. (*Pause, Sister Aloysius is staring absently at Sister James. A silence falls.*)

SISTER JAMES: So. Should I go? (*No answer.*) Is something the matter?

SISTER ALOYSIUS: No. Why? Is something the matter?

SISTER JAMES: I don't think so.

SISTER ALOYSIUS: Then nothing's the matter then.

SISTER JAMES: Well. Thank you, Sister. I just wanted to check on William's nose. (*She starts to go.*)

SISTER ALOYSIUS: He had a ballpoint pen.

SISTER JAMES: Excuse me, Sister?

SISTER ALOYSIUS: William London had a ballpoint pen. He was fiddling with it while he waited for his mother. He's not using it for assignments, I hope.

SISTER JAMES: No, of course not.

SISTER ALOYSIUS: I'm sorry I allowed even cartridge pens into the school. The students really should only be learning script with true fountain pens. Always the easy way out these days. What does that teach? Every easy choice today will have its consequence tomorrow. Mark my words.

SISTER JAMES: Yes, Sister.

SISTER ALOYSIUS: Ballpoints make them press down, and when they press down, they write like monkeys.

SISTER JAMES: I don't allow them ballpoint pens.

SISTER ALOYSIUS: Good. Penmanship is dying all across the country. You have some time. Sit down. (*Sister James hesitates and sits down.*) We might as well have a talk. I've been meaning to talk to you. I observed your lesson on the New Deal at the beginning of the term. Not bad. But I caution you. Do not idealize Franklin Delano Roosevelt. He was a good president, but he did attempt to pack the Supreme Court. I do not approve of making heroes of lay historical figures. If you want to talk about saints, do it in Religion.

SISTER JAMES: Yes, Sister.

SISTER ALOYSIUS: Also. I question your enthusiasm for History.

SISTER JAMES: But I love History!

SISTER ALOYSIUS: That is exactly my meaning. You favor History and risk swaying the children to value it over their other subjects. I think this is a mistake.

SISTER JAMES: I never thought of that. I'll try to treat my other lessons with more enthusiasm.

SISTER ALOYSIUS: No. Give them their History without putting sugar all over it. That's the point. Now. Tell me about your class. How would you characterize the condition of 8-B?

SISTER JAMES: I don't know where to begin. What do you want to know?

SISTER ALOYSIUS: Let's begin with Stephen Inzio.

SISTER JAMES: Stephen Inzio has the highest marks in the class.

SISTER ALOYSIUS: Noreen Horan?

SISTER JAMES: Second highest marks.

SISTER ALOYSIUS: Brenda McNulty?

SISTER JAMES: Third highest.

SISTER ALOYSIUS: You see I am making a point, Sister James. I know that Stephen Inzio, Noreen Horan and Brenda McNulty are one, two and three in your class. School-wide, there are forty-eight such students each grade period. I make it my business to know all forty-eight of their names. I do not say this to aggrandize myself, but to illustrate the importance of paying attention. You must pay attention as well.

SISTER JAMES: Yes, Sister Aloysius.

SISTER ALOYSIUS: I cannot be everywhere.

SISTER JAMES: Am I falling short, Sister?

SISTER ALOYSIUS: These three students with the highest marks. Are they the most intelligent children in your class?

SISTER JAMES: No, I wouldn't say they are. But they work the hardest.

SISTER ALOYSIUS: Very good! That's right! That's the ethic. What good's a gift if it's left in the box? What good is a high IQ if you're staring out the window with your mouth agape? Be hard on the bright ones, Sister James. Don't be charmed by cleverness. Not theirs. And not yours. I think you are a competent teacher, Sister James, but maybe not our best teacher.

The best teachers do not perform, they cause the students to perform.

SISTER JAMES: Do I perform?

SISTER ALOYSIUS: As if on a Broadway stage.

SISTER JAMES: Oh dear. I had no conception!

SISTER ALOYSIUS: You're showing off. You like to see yourself ten feet tall in their eyes. Another thing occurs to me. Where were you before?

SISTER JAMES: Mount St. Margaret's.

SISTER ALOYSIUS: All girls.

SISTER JAMES: Yes.

SISTER ALOYSIUS: I feel I must remind you. Boys are made of gravel, soot and tar paper. Boys are a different breed.

SISTER JAMES: I feel I know how to handle them.

SISTER ALOYSIUS: But perhaps you are wrong. And perhaps you are not working hard enough.

SISTER JAMES: Oh. (*Sister James cries a little.*)

SISTER ALOYSIUS: No tears.

SISTER JAMES: I thought you were satisfied with me.

SISTER ALOYSIUS: Satisfaction is a vice. Do you have a handkerchief?

SISTER JAMES: Yes.

SISTER ALOYSIUS: Use it. Do you think that Socrates was satisfied? Good teachers are never content. We have some three hundred and seventy-two students in this school. It is a society which requires constant educational, spiritual and human vigilance. I cannot afford an excessively innocent instructor in my eighth grade class. It's self-indulgent. Innocence is a form of laziness. Innocent teachers are easily duped. You must be canny, Sister James.

SISTER JAMES: Yes, Sister.

SISTER ALOYSIUS: When William London gets a nosebleed, be skeptical. Don't let a little blood fuddle your judgment. God gave you a brain and a heart. The heart is warm, but your wits must be cold. Liars should be frightened to lie to you. They should be uncomfortable in your presence. I doubt they are.

SISTER JAMES: I don't know. I've never thought about it.

SISTER ALOYSIUS: The children should think you see right through them.

SISTER JAMES: Wouldn't that be a little frightening?

SISTER ALOYSIUS: Only to the ones that are up to no good.

SISTER JAMES: But I want my students to feel they can talk to me.

SISTER ALOYSIUS: They're children. They can talk to each other. It's more important they have a fierce moral guardian. You stand at the door, Sister. You are the gatekeeper. If you are vigilant, they will not need to be.

SISTER JAMES: I'm not sure what you want me to do.

SISTER ALOYSIUS: And if things occur in your classroom which you sense require understanding, but you don't understand, come to me.

SISTER JAMES: Yes, Sister.

SISTER ALOYSIUS: That's why I'm here. That's why I'm the principal of this school. Do you stay when the specialty instructors come in?

SISTER JAMES: Yes.

SISTER ALOYSIUS: But you're here now while the Art class is going on.

SISTER JAMES: I was a little concerned about William's nose.

SISTER ALOYSIUS: Right. So you have Art in class.

SISTER JAMES: She comes in. Mrs. Bell. Yes.

SISTER ALOYSIUS: And you take them down to the basement for Dance with Mrs. Shields.

SISTER JAMES: On Thursdays.

SISTER ALOYSIUS: Another waste of time.

SISTER JAMES: Oh, but everyone loves the Christmas pageant.

SISTER ALOYSIUS: I don't love it. Frankly it offends me. Last year the girl playing Our Lady was wearing lipstick. I was waiting in the wings for that little jade.

SISTER JAMES: Then there's Music.

SISTER ALOYSIUS: That strange woman with the portable piano. What's wrong with her neck?

SISTER JAMES: Some kind of goiter. Poor woman.

SISTER ALOYSIUS: Yes. Mrs. Carolyn.

SISTER JAMES: That's right.

SISTER ALOYSIUS: We used to have a Sister teaching that. Not enough Sisters. What else?

SISTER JAMES: Physical Education and Religion.

SISTER ALOYSIUS: And for that we have Father Flynn. Two hours a week. And you stay for those?

SISTER JAMES: Mostly. Unless I have reports to fill out or . . .

SISTER ALOYSIUS: What do you think of Father Flynn?

SISTER JAMES: Oh, he's a brilliant man. What a speaker!

SISTER ALOYSIUS: Yes. His sermon this past Sunday was poetic.

SISTER JAMES: He's actually very good, too, at teaching basketball. I was surprised. I wouldn't think a man of the cloth the personality type for basketball, but he has a way he has, very natural with dribbling and shooting.

SISTER ALOYSIUS: What do you think that sermon was about?

SISTER JAMES: What?

SISTER ALOYSIUS: This past Sunday. What was he talking about?

SISTER JAMES: Well, Doubt. He was talking about Doubt.

SISTER ALOYSIUS: Why?

SISTER JAMES: Excuse me, Sister?

SISTER ALOYSIUS: Well, sermons come from somewhere, don't they? Is Father Flynn in Doubt, is he concerned that someone else is in Doubt?

SISTER JAMES: I suppose you'd have to ask him.

SISTER ALOYSIUS: No. That would not be appropriate. He is my superior. And if he were troubled, he should confess it to a fellow priest, or the monsignor. We do not share intimate information with priests. (*A pause.*)

SISTER JAMES: I'm a little concerned. (*Sister Aloysius leans forward.*)

SISTER ALOYSIUS: About what?

SISTER JAMES: The time. Art class will be over in a few minutes. I should go up.

SISTER ALOYSIUS: Have you noticed anything, Sister James?

SISTER JAMES: About what?

SISTER ALOYSIUS: I want you to be alert.

SISTER JAMES: I don't believe I'm following you, Sister.

SISTER ALOYSIUS: I'm sorry I'm not more forthright, but I must be careful not to create something by saying it. I can only say I am concerned, perhaps needlessly, about matters in St. Nicholas School.

SISTER JAMES: Academically?

SISTER ALOYSIUS: I wasn't inviting a guessing game. I want you to pay attention to your class.

SISTER JAMES: Well, of course I'll pay attention to my class, Sister. And I'll try not to perform. And I'll try to be less innocent. I'm sorry you're disappointed in me. Please know that I will try my best. Honestly.

SISTER ALOYSIUS: Look at you. You'd trade anything for a warm look. I'm telling you here and now, I want to see the starch in your character cultivated. If you are looking for reassurance, you can be fooled. If you forget yourself and study others, you will not be fooled. It's important. One final matter and then you really must get back. Sister Veronica is going blind.

SISTER JAMES: Oh how horrible!

SISTER ALOYSIUS: This is not generally known, and I don't want it known. If they find out in the rectory, she'll be gone. I cannot afford to lose her. But now if you see her making her way down those stone stairs into the courtyard, for the love of Heaven, lightly take her hand as if in fellowship and see that she doesn't destroy herself. All right, go.

THREE

The lights crossfade to Father Flynn, whistle around his neck, in a sweatshirt and pants, holding a basketball.

FLYNN: All right, settle down, boys. Now the thing about shooting from the foul line: It's psychological. The rest of the game you're cooperating with your teammates, you're competing against the other team. But at the foul line, it's you against yourself. And the danger is: You start to think. When you think, you stop breathing. Your body locks up. So you have to remember to relax. Take a breath, unlock your knees—this is something for you to watch, Jimmy. You stand like a parking meter. Come up with a routine of what you do. Shift your weight, move your hips . . . You think that's funny, Ralph? What's funny is you never getting a foul shot. Don't worry if you look silly. They won't think you're silly if you get the basket. Come up with a routine, concentrate on the routine, and you'll forget to get tensed up. Now on another matter, I've noticed several of you guys have dirty nails. I don't want to see that. I'm not talking about the length of your nails, I'm talking about cleanliness. See? Look at my nails. They're long, I like them a little long, but look at how clean they are. That makes it okay. There was a kid I grew up with, Timmy Mathisson, never had clean nails, and he'd stick his fingers up his nose, in his mouth.— This is a true story, learn to listen! He got spinal meningitis and died a horrible death. Sometimes it's the little things that get you. You try to talk to a girl with those filthy paws, Mr. Conroy, she's gonna take off like she's being chased by the Red Chinese! (*Reacting genially to laughter*) All right, all right. You guys, what am I gonna do with you? Get dressed, come on over to the rectory, have some Kool-Aid and cookies, we'll have a bull session. (*Blows his whistle.*) Go!

FOUR

Crossfade to a bit of garden, a bench, brick walls. Sister Aloysius, in full habit and a black shawl, is wrapping a pruned rosebush in burlap. Sister James enters.

SISTER JAMES: Good afternoon, Sister.

SISTER ALOYSIUS: Good afternoon, Sister James. Mr. McGinn pruned this bush, which was the right thing to do, but he neglected to protect it from the frost.

SISTER JAMES: Have we had a frost?

SISTER ALOYSIUS: When it comes, it's too late.

SISTER JAMES: You know about gardening?

SISTER ALOYSIUS: A little. Where is your class?

SISTER JAMES: The girls are having Music.

SISTER ALOYSIUS: And the boys?

SISTER JAMES: They're in the rectory. (*Sister James indicates the rectory, which is out of view, just on the other side of the garden.*)

SISTER ALOYSIUS: With Father Flynn.

SISTER JAMES: Yes. He's giving them a talk.

SISTER ALOYSIUS: On what subject?

SISTER JAMES: How to be a man.

SISTER ALOYSIUS: Well, if Sisters were permitted in the rectory, I would be interested to hear that talk. I don't know how to be a man. I would like to know what's involved. Have you ever given the girls a talk on how to be a woman?

SISTER JAMES: No. I wouldn't be competent.

SISTER ALOYSIUS: Why not?

SISTER JAMES: I just don't think I would. I took my vows at the beginning . . . Before . . . At the beginning.

SISTER ALOYSIUS: The founder of our order, the Blessed Mother Seton, was married and had five children before embarking on her vows.

SISTER JAMES: I've often wondered how she managed so much in one life.

SISTER ALOYSIUS: Life perhaps is longer than you think and the dictates of the soul more numerous. I was married.

SISTER JAMES: You were! (*Sister Aloysius smiles for the first time.*)

Heather Goldenhersh as Sister James and Cherry Jones as Sister Aloysius in the 2005 Broadway production of *Doubt* at the Walter Kerr Theatre in New York.

SISTER ALOYSIUS: You could at least hide your astonishment.

SISTER JAMES: I . . . didn't know.

SISTER ALOYSIUS: When one takes on the habit, one must close the door on secular things. My husband died in the war against Adolph Hitler.

SISTER JAMES: Really! Excuse me, Sister.

SISTER ALOYSIUS: But I'm like you. I'm not sure I would feel competent to lecture tittering girls on the subject of womanhood. I don't come into this garden often. What is it, forty feet across? The convent here, the rectory there. We might as well be separated by the Atlantic Ocean. I used to potter around out here, but Monsignor Benedict does his reverie at quixotic times, and we are rightly discouraged from crossing paths with priests unattended. He is seventy-nine, but nevertheless.

SISTER JAMES: The monsignor is very good, isn't he?

SISTER ALOYSIUS: Yes. But he is oblivious.

SISTER JAMES: To what?

SISTER ALOYSIUS: I don't believe he knows who's President of the United States. I mean him no disrespect of course. It's just that he's otherworldly in the extreme.

SISTER JAMES: Is it that he's innocent, Sister Aloysius?

SISTER ALOYSIUS: You have a slyness at work, Sister James. Be careful of it. How is your class? How is Donald Muller?

SISTER JAMES: He is thirteenth in class.

SISTER ALOYSIUS: I know. That's sufficient. Is he being accepted?

SISTER JAMES: He has no friends.

SISTER ALOYSIUS: That would be a lot to expect after only two months. Has anyone hit him?

SISTER JAMES: No.

SISTER ALOYSIUS: Someone will. And when it happens, send them right down to me.

SISTER JAMES: I'm not so sure anyone will.

SISTER ALOYSIUS: There is a statue of St. Patrick on one side of the church altar and a statue of St. Anthony on the other. This parish serves Irish and Italian families. Someone will hit Donald Muller.

SISTER JAMES: He has a protector.

SISTER ALOYSIUS: Who?

SISTER JAMES: Father Flynn. (*Sister Aloysius, who has been fussing with mulch, is suddenly rigid. She rises.*)

SISTER ALOYSIUS: What?

SISTER JAMES: He's taken an interest. Since Donald went on the altar boys. (*Pause.*) I thought I should tell you.

SISTER ALOYSIUS: I told you to come to me, but I hoped you never would.

SISTER JAMES: Maybe I shouldn't have.

SISTER ALOYSIUS: I knew once you did, something would be set in motion. So it's happened.

SISTER JAMES: What?! I'm not telling you that! I'm not even certain what you mean.

SISTER ALOYSIUS: Yes, you are.

SISTER JAMES: I've been trying to become more cold in my thinking as you suggested . . . I feel as if I've lost my way a little, Sister Aloysius. I had the most terrible dream last night. I want to be guided by you and responsible to the children, but I want my peace of mind. I must tell you I have been longing for the return of my peace of mind.

SISTER ALOYSIUS: You may not have it. It is not your place to be complacent. That's for the children. That's what we give them.

SISTER JAMES: I think I'm starting to understand you a little. But it's so unsettling to look at things and people with suspicion. It feels as if I'm less close to God.

SISTER ALOYSIUS: When you take a step to address wrongdoing, you are taking a step away from God, but in His service. Dealing with such matters is hard and thankless work.

SISTER JAMES: I've become more reserved in class. I feel separated from the children.

SISTER ALOYSIUS: That's as it should be.

SISTER JAMES: But I feel. Wrong. And about this other matter, I don't have any evidence. I'm not at all certain that anything's happened.

SISTER ALOYSIUS: We can't wait for that.

SISTER JAMES: But what if it's nothing?

SISTER ALOYSIUS: Then it's nothing. I wouldn't mind being wrong. But I doubt I am.

SISTER JAMES: Then what's to be done?

SISTER ALOYSIUS: I don't know.

SISTER JAMES: You'll know what to do.

SISTER ALOYSIUS: I don't know what to do. There are parameters which protect him and hinder me.

SISTER JAMES: But he can't be safe if it's established. I doubt he could recover from the shame.

SISTER ALOYSIUS: What have you seen?

SISTER JAMES: I don't know.

SISTER ALOYSIUS: What have you seen?

SISTER JAMES: He took Donald to the rectory.

SISTER ALOYSIUS: What for?

SISTER JAMES: A talk.

SISTER ALOYSIUS: Alone?

SISTER JAMES: Yes.

SISTER ALOYSIUS: When?

SISTER JAMES: A week ago.

SISTER ALOYSIUS: Why didn't you tell me?

SISTER JAMES: I didn't think there was anything wrong with it. It never came into my mind that he . . . that there could be anything wrong.

SISTER ALOYSIUS: Of all the children. Donald Muller. I suppose it makes sense.

SISTER JAMES: How does it make sense?

SISTER ALOYSIUS: He's isolated. The little sheep lagging behind is the one the wolf goes for.

SISTER JAMES: I don't know that anything's wrong!

SISTER ALOYSIUS: Our first Negro student. I thought there'd be fighting, a parent or two to deal with . . . I should've foreseen this possibility.

SISTER JAMES: How could you imagine it?

SISTER ALOYSIUS: It is my job to outshine the fox in cleverness! That's my job!

SISTER JAMES: But maybe it's nothing!

SISTER ALOYSIUS: Then why do you look like you've seen the Devil?

SISTER JAMES: It's just the way the boy acted when he came back to class.

SISTER ALOYSIUS: He said something?

SISTER JAMES: No. It was his expression. He looked frightened and . . . he put his head on the desk in the most peculiar way. (*Struggles.*) And one other thing. I think there was alcohol on his breath. There was alcohol on his breath. (*Sister Aloysius looks toward the rectory.*)

SISTER ALOYSIUS: Eight years ago at St. Boniface we had a priest who had to be stopped. But I had Monsignor Scully then . . . whom I could rely on. Here, there's no man I can go to, and men run everything. We are going to have to stop him ourselves.

SISTER JAMES: Can't you just . . . report your suspicions?

SISTER ALOYSIUS: To Monsignor Benedict? The man's guileless! He would just ask Father Flynn!

SISTER JAMES: Well, would that be such a bad idea?

SISTER ALOYSIUS: And he would believe whatever Father Flynn told him. He would think the matter settled.

SISTER JAMES: But maybe that is all that needs to be done. If it's true. If I had done something awful, and I was confronted with it, I'd be so repentant.

SISTER ALOYSIUS: Sister James, my dear, you must try to imagine a very different kind of person than yourself. A man who would do this has already denied a great deal. If I tell the monsignor and he is satisfied with Father Flynn's rebuttal, the matter is suppressed.

SISTER JAMES: Well then, tell the bishop.

SISTER ALOYSIUS: The hierarchy of the Church does not permit my going to the bishop. No. Once I tell the monsignor, it's out of my hands, I'm helpless. I'm going to have to come up with a pretext, get Father Flynn into my office. Try to force it. You'll have to be there.

SISTER JAMES: Me? No! Why? Oh no, Sister! I couldn't!

SISTER ALOYSIUS: I can't be closeted alone with a priest. Another Sister must be in attendance, and it has to be you. The circle of confidence mustn't be made any wider. Think of the boy if this gets out.

SISTER JAMES: I can't do it!

SISTER ALOYSIUS: Why not? You're squeamish?

SISTER JAMES: I'm not equipped! It's . . . I would be embarrassed. I couldn't possibly be present if the topic were spoken of!

SISTER ALOYSIUS: Please, Sister, do not indulge yourself in witless adolescent scruples. I assure you I would prefer a more seasoned confederate. But you are the one who came to me.

SISTER JAMES: You told me to!

SISTER ALOYSIUS: Would you rather leave the boy to be exploited? And don't think this will be the only story. If you close your eyes, you will be a party to all that comes after.

SISTER JAMES: You're supposed to tell the monsignor!

SISTER ALOYSIUS: That you saw a look in a boy's eye? That perhaps you smelled something on his breath? Monsignor Benedict thinks the sun rises and sets on Father Flynn. You'd be branded an hysteric and transferred.

SISTER JAMES: We can ask him.

SISTER ALOYSIUS: Who?

SISTER JAMES: The boy. Donald Muller.

SISTER ALOYSIUS: He'll deny it.

SISTER JAMES: Why?

SISTER ALOYSIUS: Shame.

SISTER JAMES: You can't know that.

SISTER ALOYSIUS: And if he does point the finger, how do you think that will be received in this community? A black child. (*No answer.*) I am going to think this through. Then I'm going to invite Father Flynn to my office on an unrelated matter. You will be there.

SISTER JAMES: But what good can I do?

SISTER ALOYSIUS: Aside from the unacceptability of a priest and nun being alone, I need a witness.

SISTER JAMES: To what?

SISTER ALOYSIUS: He may tell the truth and lie afterwards. (*Sister James looks toward the rectory.*)

SISTER JAMES: The boys are coming out of the rectory. They look happy enough.

SISTER ALOYSIUS: They look smug. Like they have a secret.

SISTER JAMES: There he is.

SISTER ALOYSIUS: If I could, Sister James, I would certainly choose to live in innocence. But innocence can only be wisdom in a world without evil. Situations arise, and we are confronted with wrongdoing and the need to act.

SISTER JAMES: I have to take the boys up to class.

SISTER ALOYSIUS: Go on, then. Take them. I will be talking to you. (*The sound of wind. Sister Aloysius pulls her shawl tightly about her and goes. After a moment, Sister James goes as well.*)

FIVE

The principal's office. A phone rings, Sister Aloysius enters with a pot of tea, walking quickly to answer the phone.

SISTER ALOYSIUS: Hello, St. Nicholas School? Oh yes, Mr. McGinn. Thank you for calling back. That was quite a windstorm we had last night. No, I didn't know there was a Great Wind in Ireland and you were there for it. That's fascinating. Yes, I was wondering if you would be so kind as to remove a tree limb that's fallen in the courtyard of the church. Sister Veronica tripped on it this morning and fell on her face. I think she's all right. She doesn't look any worse, Mr. McGinn. Thank you, Mr. McGinn. (*She hangs up the phone and looks at her watch, a bit anxious. A knock at the door.*) Come in. (*The door opens. Father Flynn is standing there in his black cassock. He doesn't come in.*)

FLYNN: Good morning, Sister Aloysius! How are you today?

SISTER ALOYSIUS: Good morning, Father Flynn. Very well. Good of you to come by. (*Father Flynn takes a step into the office.*)

FLYNN: Are we ready for the meeting?

SISTER ALOYSIUS: We're just short Sister James. (*Father Flynn steps back into the doorway.*) Did you hear that wind last night?

FLYNN: I certainly did. Imagine what it must've been like in the frontier days when a man alone in the woods sat by a fire in his buckskins and listened to a sound like that. Imagine the loneliness! The immense darkness pressing in! How frightening it must've been!

SISTER ALOYSIUS: If one lacked faith in God's protection, I suppose it would be frightening.

FLYNN: Did I hear Sister Veronica had an accident?

SISTER ALOYSIUS: Yes. Sister Veronica fell on a piece of wood this morning and practically killed herself.

FLYNN: Is she all right?

SISTER ALOYSIUS: Oh, she's fine.

FLYNN: Her sight isn't good, is it?

SISTER ALOYSIUS: Her sight is fine. Nuns fall, you know.

FLYNN: No, I didn't know that.

SISTER ALOYSIUS: It's the habit. It catches us up more often than not. What with our being in black and white, and so prone to falling, we're more like dominos than anything else. (*Sister James appears at the door, breathless.*)

SISTER JAMES: Am I past the time? (*Father Flynn takes a step into the office.*)

FLYNN: Not at all. Sister Aloysius and I were just having a nice chat.

SISTER JAMES: Good morning, Father Flynn. Good morning, Sister. I'm sorry I was delayed. Mr. McGinn has closed the courtyard to fix something so I had to go back through the convent and out the side door, and then I ran into Sister Veronica.

FLYNN: How is she?

SISTER JAMES: She has a bit of a bloody nose.

SISTER ALOYSIUS: I'm beginning to think you're punching people.

SISTER JAMES: Sister?

SISTER ALOYSIUS: Well, after the incident with . . . Never mind. Well, come in, please. Sit down. (*They come in and sit down. Father Flynn takes Sister Aloysius' chair. He's sitting at her desk. She reacts but says nothing.*) I actually have a hot pot of tea. (*Closes the door but for an inch.*) And close this but not quite, for form's sake. Would you have a cup of tea, Father?

FLYNN: I would love a cup of tea.

SISTER ALOYSIUS: Perhaps you could serve him, Sister?

SISTER JAMES: Of course.

SISTER ALOYSIUS: And yourself, of course.

SISTER JAMES: Would you like tea, Sister Aloysius?

SISTER ALOYSIUS: I've already had my cup.

FLYNN: Is there sugar?

SISTER ALOYSIUS: Sugar? Yes! (*Rummages in her desk.*) It's here somewhere. I put it in the drawer for Lent last year and never remembered to take it out.

FLYNN: It mustn't have been much to give up then.

SISTER ALOYSIUS: No, I'm sure you're right. Here it is. I'll serve you, though for want of practice, I'm ... [clumsy] (*She's got the sugar bowl and is poised to serve him a lump of sugar with a small pair of tongs when she sees his nails.*) Your fingernails.

FLYNN: I wear them a little long. The sugar?

SISTER ALOYSIUS: Oh yes. One?

FLYNN: Three.

SISTER ALOYSIUS: Three. (*She's appalled but tries to hide it.*)

FLYNN: Sweet tooth.

SISTER ALOYSIUS: One, two, three. Sister, do you take sugar? (*Sister Aloysius looks at Sister James.*)

SISTER JAMES: (*To Sister Aloysius.*) Never! (*To Father Flynn.*) Not that there's anything wrong with sugar. (*To Sister Aloysius again.*) Thank you. (*Sister Aloysius puts the sugar away in her desk.*)

SISTER ALOYSIUS: Well, thank you, Father, for making the time for us. We're at our wit's end.

FLYNN: I think it's an excellent idea to rethink the Christmas pageant. Last year's effort was a little woebegone.

SISTER JAMES: No! I loved it! (*Becomes self-conscious.*) But I love all Christmas pageants. I just love the Nativity. The birth of the Savior. And the hymns of course. "O Little Town of Bethlehem," "O Come, O Come, Emmanuel" ...

SISTER ALOYSIUS: Thank you, Sister James. Sister James will be co-directing the pageant with Mrs. Shields this year. So what do you think, Father Flynn? Is there something new we could do?

FLYNN: Well, we all love the Christmas hymns, but it might be jolly to include a secular song.

SISTER ALOYSIUS: Secular.

FLYNN: Yes. "It's Beginning to Look a Lot Like Christmas." Something like that.

SISTER ALOYSIUS: What would be the point of performing a secular song?

FLYNN: Fun.

SISTER JAMES: Or "Frosty the Snowman."

FLYNN: That's a good one. We could have one of the boys dress as a snowman and dance around.

SISTER ALOYSIUS: Which boy?

FLYNN: We'd do tryouts.

SISTER ALOYSIUS: "Frosty the Snowman" espouses a pagan belief in magic. The snowman comes to life when an enchanted hat is put on his head. If the music were more somber, people would realize the images are disturbing and the song heretical. (*Sister James and Father Flynn exchange a look.*)

SISTER JAMES: I've never thought about "Frosty the Snowman" like that.

SISTER ALOYSIUS: It should be banned from the airwaves.

FLYNN: So. Not "Frosty the Snowman." (*Father Flynn writes something in a small notebook.*)

SISTER ALOYSIUS: I don't think so. "It's Beginning to Look a Lot Like Christmas" would be fine, I suppose. The parents would like it. May I ask what you wrote down? With that ballpoint pen.

FLYNN: Oh. Nothing. An idea for a sermon.

SISTER ALOYSIUS: You had one just now?

FLYNN: I get them all the time.

SISTER ALOYSIUS: How fortunate.

FLYNN: I forget them, so I write them down.

SISTER ALOYSIUS: What is the idea?

FLYNN: Intolerance. (*Sister James tries to break a bit of tension.*)

SISTER JAMES: Would you like a little more tea, Father?

FLYNN: Not yet. I think a message of the Second Ecumenical Council° was that the Church needs to take on a more familiar face. Reflect the local community. We should sing a song from the radio now and then. Take the kids out for ice cream.

SISTER ALOYSIUS: Ice cream.

FLYNN: Maybe take the boys on a camping trip. We should be friendlier. The children and the parents should see us as members of their family rather than emissaries from Rome. I think the pageant should be charming, like a community theatre doing a show.

SISTER ALOYSIUS: But we are not members of their family. We're different.

FLYNN: Why? Because of our vows?

SISTER ALOYSIUS: Precisely.

FLYNN: I don't think we're so different. (*To Sister James.*) You know, I would take some more tea, Sister. Thank you.

SISTER ALOYSIUS: And they think we're different. The working-class people of this parish trust us to be different.

FLYNN: I think we're getting off the subject.

SISTER ALOYSIUS: Yes, you're right, back to it. The Christmas pageant. We must be careful how Donald Muller is used in the pageant. (*Sister James shakes as she pours the tea.*)

FLYNN: Easy there, Sister, you don't spill.

SISTER JAMES: Oh, uh, yes, Father.

FLYNN: What about Donald Muller?

SISTER ALOYSIUS: We must be careful, in the pageant, that we neither hide Donald Muller nor put him forward.

FLYNN: Because of the color of his skin.

Second Ecumenical Council: The Second Vatican Council, opened by Pope John XXIII in 1962, addressed the Church's recognition of modern life and its need to respond to the contemporary world.

Sister James, Father Flynn (Brían F. O'Byrne), and Sister Aloysius meet over tea in the principal's office in the 2005 Broadway production.

SISTER ALOYSIUS: That's right.

FLYNN: Why?

SISTER ALOYSIUS: Come, Father. You're being disingenuous.

FLYNN: I think he should be treated like every other boy.

SISTER ALOYSIUS: You yourself singled the boy out for special attention. You held a private meeting with him at the rectory. (*Turning to Sister James.*) A week ago?

SISTER JAMES: Yes. (*He realizes something's up.*)

FLYNN: What are we talking about?

SISTER JAMES: Donald Muller?

SISTER ALOYSIUS: The boy acted strangely when he returned to class. (*Father Flynn turns to Sister James.*)

FLYNN: He did?

SISTER JAMES: When he returned from the rectory. A little odd, yes.

SISTER ALOYSIUS: Can you tell us why?

FLYNN: How did he act strangely?

SISTER JAMES: I'm not sure how to explain it. He laid his head on the desk . . .

FLYNN: You mean you had some impression?

SISTER JAMES: Yes.

FLYNN: And he'd come from the rectory so you're asking me if I know anything about it?

SISTER JAMES: That's it.

FLYNN: Hmmm. Did you want to discuss the pageant, is that why I'm here, or is this what you wanted to discuss?

SISTER ALOYSIUS: This.

FLYNN: Well. I feel a little uncomfortable.

SISTER ALOYSIUS: Why?

FLYNN: Why do you think? Something about your tone.

SISTER ALOYSIUS: I would prefer a discussion of fact rather than tone.

FLYNN: Well. If I had judged my conversation with Donald Muller to be of concern to you, Sister, I would have sat you down and talked to you about it. But I did not judge it to be of concern to you.

SISTER ALOYSIUS: Perhaps you are mistaken in your understanding of what concerns me. The boy is in my school, and his well-being is my responsibility.

FLYNN: His well-being is not at issue.

SISTER ALOYSIUS: I am not satisfied that that is true. He was upset when he returned to class.

FLYNN: Did he say something?

SISTER JAMES: No.

SISTER ALOYSIUS: What happened in the rectory?

FLYNN: Happened? Nothing happened. I had a talk with a boy.

SISTER ALOYSIUS: What about?

FLYNN: It was a private matter.

SISTER ALOYSIUS: He's twelve years old. What could be private?

FLYNN: I'll say it again, Sister. I object to your tone.

SISTER ALOYSIUS: This is not about my tone or your tone, Father Flynn. It's about arriving at the truth.

FLYNN: Of what?

SISTER ALOYSIUS: You know what I'm talking about. Don't you? You're controlling the expression on your face right now. Aren't you?

FLYNN: My face? You said you wanted to talk about the pageant, Sister. That's why I'm here. Am I to understand that you brought me into your office to confront me in some way? It's outrageous. I'm not answerable to you. What exactly are you accusing me of?

SISTER ALOYSIUS: I am not accusing you of anything, Father Flynn. I am asking you to tell me what happened in the rectory. (Father Flynn stands.)

FLYNN: I don't wish to continue this conversation at all further. And if you are dissatisfied with that, I suggest you speak to Monsignor Benedict. I can only imagine that your unfortunate behavior this morning is the result of overwork. Perhaps you need a leave of absence. I may suggest it. Have a good morning. (To Sister James.) Sister?

SISTER JAMES: Good morning, Father. (Sister Aloysius' next words stop him.)

SISTER ALOYSIUS: There was alcohol on his breath. (He turns.) When he returned from his meeting with you. (He comes back and sits down. He rubs his eyes.)

FLYNN: Alcohol.

SISTER JAMES: I did smell it on his breath.

SISTER ALOYSIUS: Well?

FLYNN: Can't you let this alone?

SISTER ALOYSIUS: No.

FLYNN: I see there's no way out of this.

SISTER JAMES: Take your time, Father. Would you like some more tea?

FLYNN: You should've let it alone.

SISTER ALOYSIUS: Not possible.

FLYNN: Donald Muller served as altar boy last Tuesday morning. After Mass, Mr. McGinn caught him in the sacristy drinking altar wine. When I found out, I sent for him. There were tears. He begged not to be removed from the altar boys. And I took pity on him.

I told him if no one else found out, I would let him stay on. (Sister James is overjoyed. Sister Aloysius is unmoved.)

SISTER JAMES: Oh, what a relief! That explains everything! Thanks be to God! Oh, Sister, look, it's all a mistake!

SISTER ALOYSIUS: And if I talk to Mr. McGinn?

FLYNN: Talk to Mr. McGinn by all means. But now that the boy's secret's out, I'm going to have to remove him from the altar boys. Which I think is too bad. That's what I was trying to avoid.

SISTER JAMES: You were trying to protect the boy!

FLYNN: That's right.

SISTER JAMES: I might've done the same thing! (To Sister Aloysius.) Is there a way Donald could stay on the altar boys?

SISTER ALOYSIUS: No. If the boy drank altar wine, he cannot continue as an altar boy.

FLYNN: Of course you're right. I'm just not the disciplinarian you are, Sister. And he is the only Negro in the school. That did affect my thinking on the matter. It will be commented on that he's no longer serving at Mass. It's a public thing. A certain ignorant element in the parish will be confirmed in their beliefs.

SISTER ALOYSIUS: He must be held to the same standard as the others.

FLYNN: Of course. Do we need to discuss the pageant or was that just . . .

SISTER ALOYSIUS: No, this was the issue.

FLYNN: Are you satisfied?

SISTER ALOYSIUS: Yes.

FLYNN: Then I'll be going. I have some writing to do.

SISTER ALOYSIUS: Intolerance.

FLYNN: That's right. (He goes, then stops at the door.) I'm not pleased with how you handled this, Sister. Next time you are troubled by dark ideas, I suggest you speak to the monsignor. (He goes. After a moment, Sister James weakly launches into optimism.)

SISTER JAMES: Well. What a relief! He cleared it all up.

SISTER ALOYSIUS: You believe him?

SISTER JAMES: Of course.

SISTER ALOYSIUS: Isn't it more that it's easier to believe him?

SISTER JAMES: But we can corroborate his story with Mr. McGinn!

SISTER ALOYSIUS: Yes. These types of people are clever. They're not so easily undone.

SISTER JAMES: Well, I'm convinced!

SISTER ALOYSIUS: You're not. You just want things to be resolved so you can have simplicity back.

SISTER JAMES: I want no further part of this.

SISTER ALOYSIUS: I'll bring him down. With or without your help.

SISTER JAMES: How can you be so sure he's lying?

SISTER ALOYSIUS: Experience.

SISTER JAMES: You just don't like him! You don't like it that he uses a ballpoint pen. You don't like it that he takes three lumps of sugar in his tea. You don't like it that he likes "Frosty the Snowman." And you're letting that convince you of something terrible, just terrible! Well, I like "Frosty the Snowman"! And it would be nice if this school weren't run like a prison! And I think it's a good thing that I love to teach History and that I might inspire my students to love it, too! And if you judge that to mean I'm not fit to be a teacher, then so be it!

SISTER ALOYSIUS: Sit down. (*Sister James does.*) In ancient Sparta, important matters were decided by who shouted loudest. Fortunately, we are not in ancient Sparta. Now. Do you honestly find the students in this school to be treated like inmates in a prison?

SISTER JAMES: (*Relenting.*) No, I don't. Actually, by and large, they seem to be fairly happy. But they're all uniformly terrified of you!

SISTER ALOYSIUS: Yes. That's how it works. Sit there. (*Sister Aloysius looks in a notebook, picks up the phone, dials.*) Hello, this is Sister Aloysius Beauvier, the principal of St. Nicholas. Is this Mrs. Muller? I'm calling about your son, Donald. I would like you and your husband to come down here for a talk. When would be convenient? (*Lights fade.*)

SIX

Father Flynn, in blue and white vestments, is at the pulpit.

FLYNN: A woman was gossiping with a friend about a man she hardly knew—I know none of you have ever done this—and that night she had a dream. A great hand appeared over her and pointed down at her. She was immediately seized with an overwhelming sense of guilt. The next day she went to confession. She got the old parish priest, Father O'Rourke, and she told him the whole thing. "Is gossiping a sin?" she asked the old man. "Was that the Hand of God Almighty pointing a finger at me? Should I be asking your absolution? Father, tell me, have I done something wrong?" (*Irish brogue.*) "Yes!" Father O'Rourke answered her. "Yes, you ignorant, badly brought-up female! You have borne false witness against your neighbor, you have played fast and loose with his reputation, and you should be heartily ashamed!" So the woman said she was sorry and asked forgiveness. "Not so fast!" says O'Rourke. "I want you to go home, take a pillow up on your roof, cut it open with a knife, and return here to me!" So she went home, took the pillow off her bed, a knife from the drawer, went up the fire escape to the roof, and stabbed the pillow. Then she went back to the old priest as instructed. "Did you gut the pillow with the knife?" he says. "Yes, Father." "And what was the result?" "Feathers," she said. "Feathers?" he repeated. "Feathers everywhere, Father!" "Now I want you to go back and gather up every last feather that flew out on the wind!" "Well," she says, "it can't be

done. I don't know where they went. The wind took them all over." "And that," said Father O'Rourke, "is gossip!" In the name of the Father, Son, and the Holy Ghost, Amen.

SEVEN

The lights crossfade to the garden. A crow caws.
Sister James sits on the bench, deep in thought. Father Flynn enters.

FLYNN: Good afternoon, Sister James.

SISTER JAMES: Good afternoon, Father.

FLYNN: What is that bird complaining about? What kind of bird is that? A starling? A grackle?

SISTER JAMES: A crow?

FLYNN: Of course it is. Are you praying? I didn't mean to interrupt.

SISTER JAMES: I'm not praying, no.

FLYNN: You seem subdued.

SISTER JAMES: Oh. I can't sleep.

FLYNN: Why not?

SISTER JAMES: Bad dreams. Actually one bad dream, and then I haven't slept right since.

FLYNN: What about?

SISTER JAMES: I looked in a mirror and there was a darkness where my face should be. It frightened me.

FLYNN: I can't sleep on occasion.

SISTER JAMES: No? Do you see that big hand pointing a finger at you?

FLYNN: Yes. Sometimes.

SISTER JAMES: Was your sermon directed at anyone in particular?

FLYNN: What do you think?

SISTER JAMES: Did you make up that story about the pillow?

FLYNN: Yes. You make up little stories to illustrate. In the tradition of the parable.

SISTER JAMES: Aren't the things that actually happen in life more worthy of interpretation than a made-up story?

FLYNN: No. What actually happens in life is beyond interpretation. The truth makes for a bad sermon. It tends to be confusing and have no clear conclusion.

SISTER JAMES: I received a letter from my brother in Maryland yesterday. He's very sick.

FLYNN: Maybe you should go and see him.

SISTER JAMES: I can't leave my class.

FLYNN: How's Donald Muller doing?

SISTER JAMES: I don't know.

FLYNN: You don't see him?

SISTER JAMES: I see him every day, but I don't know how he's doing. I don't know how to judge these things. Now.

FLYNN: I stopped speaking to him for fear of it being misunderstood. Isn't that a shame? I actually avoided him the other day when I might've passed him in the hall. He doesn't understand why. I noticed you didn't come to me for confession.

SISTER JAMES: No. I went to Monsignor Benedict. He's very kind.

FLYNN: I wasn't?

SISTER JAMES: It wasn't that. As you know. You know why.

FLYNN: You're against me?

SISTER JAMES: No.

FLYNN: You're not convinced?

SISTER JAMES: It's not for me to be convinced, one way or the other. It's Sister Aloysius.

FLYNN: Are you just an extension of her?

SISTER JAMES: She's my superior.

FLYNN: But what about you?

SISTER JAMES: I wish I knew nothing whatever about it. I wish the idea had never entered my mind.

FLYNN: How did it enter your mind?

SISTER JAMES: Sister Aloysius.

FLYNN: I feel as if my reputation has been damaged through no fault of my own. But I'm reluctant to take the steps necessary to repair it for fear of doing further harm. It's frustrating, I can tell you that.

SISTER JAMES: Is it true?

FLYNN: What?

SISTER JAMES: You know what I'm asking.

FLYNN: No, it's not true.

SISTER JAMES: Oh, I don't know what to believe.

FLYNN: How can you take sides against me?

SISTER JAMES: It doesn't matter.

FLYNN: It does matter! I've done nothing. There's no substance to any of this. The most innocent actions can appear sinister to the poisoned mind. I had to throw that poor boy off the altar. He's devastated. The only reason I haven't gone to the monsignor is I don't want to tear apart the school. Sister Aloysius would most certainly lose her position as principal if I made her accusations known. Since they're baseless. You might lose your place as well.

SISTER JAMES: Are you threatening me?

FLYNN: What do you take me for? No.

SISTER JAMES: I want to believe you.

FLYNN: Then do. It's as simple as that.

SISTER JAMES: It's not me that has to be convinced.

FLYNN: I don't have to prove anything to her.

SISTER JAMES: She's determined.

FLYNN: To what?

SISTER JAMES: Protect the boy.

FLYNN: It's me that cares about that boy, not her. Has she ever reached out a hand to that child or any child in this school? She's like a block of ice! Children need warmth, kindness, understanding! What does she give them? Rules. That black boy needs a helping hand or he's not going to make it here! But if she has her way, he'll be left to his own undoing. Why do you think he was in the sacristy drinking wine that day? He's in trouble! She sees me talk in a human way to these children and she immediately assumes there must be something wrong with it. Something dirty.

Well, I'm not going to let her keep this parish in the Dark Ages! And I'm not going to let her destroy my spirit of compassion!

SISTER JAMES: I'm sure that's not her intent.

FLYNN: I care about this congregation!

SISTER JAMES: I know you do.

FLYNN: Like you care about your class! You love them, don't you?

SISTER JAMES: Yes.

FLYNN: That's natural. How else would you relate to children? I can look at your face and know your philosophy: kindness.

SISTER JAMES: I don't know. I mean, of course.

FLYNN: What is Sister Aloysius' philosophy do you suppose? (*A pause.*)

SISTER JAMES: I don't have to suppose. She's told me. She discourages . . . warmth. She's suggested I be more . . . formal.

FLYNN: There are people who go after your humanity, Sister James, who tell you the light in your heart is a weakness. That your soft feelings betray you. I don't believe that. It's an old tactic of cruel people to kill kindness in the name of virtue. Don't believe it. There's nothing wrong with love.

SISTER JAMES: Of course not, but . . .

FLYNN: Have you forgotten that was the message of the Savior to us all. Love. Not suspicion, disapproval and judgment. Love of people. Have you found Sister Aloysius a positive inspiration?

SISTER JAMES: I don't want to misspeak, but no. She's taken away my joy of teaching. And I loved teaching more than anything. (*She cries a little. He pats her uneasily, looking around.*)

FLYNN: It's all right. You're going to be all right.

SISTER JAMES: I feel as if everything is upside down.

FLYNN: It isn't though. There are just times in life when we feel lost. You're not alone with it. It happens to many of us.

SISTER JAMES: A bond. (*Becomes self-conscious.*) I'd better go in.

FLYNN: I'm sorry your brother is ill.

SISTER JAMES: Thank you, Father. (*Starts to go, stops.*) I don't believe it!

FLYNN: You don't?

SISTER JAMES: No.

FLYNN: Thank you, Sister. That's a great relief to me. Thank you very much. (*She goes. He takes out his little black book and writes in it. The crow caws. He yells at it:*) Oh, be quiet. (*Then he opens a prayer book and walks away.*)

EIGHT

Crossfade to the principal's office. Sister Aloysius is sitting looking out the window, very still. A knock at the door. She doesn't react. A second knock, louder. She pulls a small earplug out of her ear and scurries to the door. She opens it. There stands Mrs. Muller, a black woman of about thirty-eight, in her Sunday best, dressed for church. She's on red alert.

SISTER ALOYSIUS: Mrs. Muller?

MRS. MULLER: Yes.

SISTER ALOYSIUS: Come in. (*Sister Aloysius closes the door.*) Please have a seat.

MRS. MULLER: I thought I might a had the wrong day when you didn't answer the door.

SISTER ALOYSIUS: Oh. Yes. Well, just between us, I was listening to a transistor radio with an earpiece. (*She shows Mrs. Muller a very small transistor radio.*) Look at how tiny they're making them now. I confiscated it from one of the students, and now I can't stop using it.

MRS. MULLER: You like music?

SISTER ALOYSIUS: Not really. News reports. Years ago I used to listen to all the news reports because my husband was in Italy in the war. When I came into possession of this little radio, I found myself doing it again. Though there is no war and the voices have changed.

MRS. MULLER: You were a married woman?

SISTER ALOYSIUS: Yes. But then he was killed. Is your husband coming?

MRS. MULLER: Couldn't get off work.

SISTER ALOYSIUS: I see. Of course. It was a lot to ask.

MRS. MULLER: How's Donald doing?

SISTER ALOYSIUS: He's passing his subjects. He has average grades.

MRS. MULLER: Oh. Good. He was upset about getting taken off the altar boys.

SISTER ALOYSIUS: Did he explain why?

MRS. MULLER: He said he was caught drinking wine.

SISTER ALOYSIUS: That is the reason.

MRS. MULLER: Well, that seems fair. But he's a good boy, Sister. He fell down there, but he's a good boy pretty much down the line. And he knows what an opportunity he has here. I think the whole thing was just a bit much for him.

SISTER ALOYSIUS: What do you mean, the whole thing?

MRS. MULLER: He's the only colored here. He's the first in this school. That'd be a lot for a boy.

SISTER ALOYSIUS: I suppose it is. But he has to do the work of course.

MRS. MULLER: He is doing it though, right?

SISTER ALOYSIUS: Yes. He's getting by. He's getting through. How is he at home?

MRS. MULLER: His father beat the hell out of him over that wine.

SISTER ALOYSIUS: He shouldn't do that.

MRS. MULLER: You don't tell my husband what to do. You just stand back. He didn't want Donald to come here.

SISTER ALOYSIUS: Why not?

MRS. MULLER: Thought he'd have a lot of trouble with the other boys. But that hasn't really happened as far as I can make out.

SISTER ALOYSIUS: Good.

MRS. MULLER: That priest, Father Flynn, been watching out for him.

SISTER ALOYSIUS: Yes. Have you met Father Flynn?

MRS. MULLER: Not exactly, no. I seen him on the altar, but I haven't met him face to face. No. Just, you know, heard from Donald.

SISTER ALOYSIUS: What does he say?

MRS. MULLER: You know, Father Flynn, Father Flynn. He looks up to him. The man gives him his time, which is what the boy needs. He needs that.

SISTER ALOYSIUS: Mrs. Muller, we may have a problem.

MRS. MULLER: Well, I thought you must a had a reason for asking me to come in. Principal's a big job. If you stop your day to talk to me, must be something. I just want to say though, it's just till June.

SISTER ALOYSIUS: Excuse me?

MRS. MULLER: Whatever the problem is, Donald just has to make it here till June. Then he's off into high school.

SISTER ALOYSIUS: Right.

MRS. MULLER: If Donald can graduate from here, he has a better chance of getting into a good high school. And that would mean an opportunity at college. I believe he has the intelligence. And he wants it, too.

SISTER ALOYSIUS: I don't see anything at this time standing in the way of his graduating with his class.

MRS. MULLER: Well, that's all I care about. Anything else is all right with me.

SISTER ALOYSIUS: I doubt that.

MRS. MULLER: Try me.

SISTER ALOYSIUS: I'm concerned about the relationship between Father Flynn and your son.

MRS. MULLER: You don't say. Concerned. What do you mean, concerned?

SISTER ALOYSIUS: That it may not be right.

MRS. MULLER: Uh-huh. Well, there's something wrong with everybody, isn't that so? Got to be forgiving.

SISTER ALOYSIUS: I'm concerned, to be frank, that Father Flynn may have made advances on your son.

MRS. MULLER: *May* have made.

SISTER ALOYSIUS: I can't be certain.

MRS. MULLER: No evidence?

SISTER ALOYSIUS: No.

MRS. MULLER: Then maybe there's nothing to it?

SISTER ALOYSIUS: I think there is something to it.

MRS. MULLER: Well, I would prefer not to see it that way if you don't mind.

SISTER ALOYSIUS: I can understand that this is hard to hear. I think Father Flynn gave Donald that altar wine.

MRS. MULLER: Why would he do that?

SISTER ALOYSIUS: Has Donald been acting strangely?

MRS. MULLER: No.

SISTER ALOYSIUS: Nothing out of the ordinary?

MRS. MULLER: He's been himself.

SISTER ALOYSIUS: All right.

MRS. MULLER: Look, Sister, I don't want any trouble, and I feel like you're on the march somehow.

SISTER ALOYSIUS: I'm not sure you completely understand.

MRS. MULLER: I think I understand the kind of thing you're talking about. But I don't want to get into it.

SISTER ALOYSIUS: What's that?

MRS. MULLER: Not to be disagreeing with you, but if we're talking about something floating around between this priest and my son, that ain't my son's fault.

SISTER ALOYSIUS: I'm not suggesting it is.

MRS. MULLER: He's just a boy.

SISTER ALOYSIUS: I know.

MRS. MULLER: Twelve years old. If somebody should be taking blame for anything, it should be the man, not the boy.

SISTER ALOYSIUS: I agree with you completely.

MRS. MULLER: You're agreeing with me but I'm sitting in the principal's office talking about my son. Why isn't the priest in the principal's office, if you know what I'm saying and you'll excuse my bringing it up.

SISTER ALOYSIUS: You're here because I'm concerned about Donald's welfare.

MRS. MULLER: You think I'm not?

SISTER ALOYSIUS: Of course you are.

MRS. MULLER: Let me ask you something. You honestly think that priest gave Donald that wine to drink?

SISTER ALOYSIUS: Yes, I do.

MRS. MULLER: Then how come my son got kicked off the altar boys if it was the man that gave it to him?

SISTER ALOYSIUS: The boy got caught, the man didn't.

MRS. MULLER: How come the priest didn't get kicked off the priesthood?

SISTER ALOYSIUS: He's a grown man, educated. And he knows what's at stake. It's not so easy to pin someone like that down.

MRS. MULLER: So you give my son the whole blame. No problem my son getting blamed and punished. That's easy. You know why that is?

SISTER ALOYSIUS: Perhaps you should let me talk. I think you're getting upset.

MRS. MULLER: That's because that's the way it is. You're just finding out about it, but that's the way it is and the way it's been, Sister. You're not going against no *man* in a *robe* and win, Sister. He's got the position.

SISTER ALOYSIUS: And he's got your son.

MRS. MULLER: Let him have 'im then.

SISTER ALOYSIUS: What?

MRS. MULLER: It's just till June.

SISTER ALOYSIUS: Do you know what you're saying?

MRS. MULLER: Know more about it than you.

SISTER ALOYSIUS: I believe this man is creating or has already brought about an improper relationship with your son.

MRS. MULLER: I don't know.

SISTER ALOYSIUS: I know I'm right.

MRS. MULLER: Why you need to know something like that for sure when you don't? Please, Sister. You got some kind a righteous cause going with this priest, and now you want to drag my boy into it. My son doesn't need additional difficulties. Let him take the good and leave the rest when he leaves this place in June. He knows how to do that, I taught him how to do that.

SISTER ALOYSIUS: What kind of mother are you?

MRS. MULLER: Excuse me, but you don't know enough about life to say a thing like that, Sister.

SISTER ALOYSIUS: I know enough.

MRS. MULLER: You know the rules maybe, but that don't cover it.

SISTER ALOYSIUS: I know what I won't accept!

MRS. MULLER: You accept what you gotta accept, and you work with it. That's the truth I know. Sorry to be so sharp, but you're in here in this room…

SISTER ALOYSIUS: This man is in my school.

MRS. MULLER: Well, he's gotta be somewhere, and maybe he's doing some good too. You ever think of that?

SISTER ALOYSIUS: He's after the boys.

MRS. MULLER: Well, maybe some of them boys want to get caught. Maybe what you don't know maybe is my son is … that way. That's why his father beat him up. Not the wine. He beat Donald for being what he is.

SISTER ALOYSIUS: What are you telling me?

MRS. MULLER: I'm his mother. I'm talking about his nature now, not anything he's done. But you can't hold a child responsible for what God gave him to be.

SISTER ALOYSIUS: Listen to me with care, Mrs. Muller. I'm only interested in actions. It's hopeless to discuss a child's possible inclination. I'm finding it difficult enough to address a man's deeds. This isn't about what the boy may be, but what the man is. It's about the man.

MRS. MULLER: But there's the boy's nature.

SISTER ALOYSIUS: Let's leave that out of it.

MRS. MULLER: Forget it then. You're the one forcing people to say these things out loud. Things are in the air and you leave them alone if you can. That's what I know. My boy came to this school 'cause they were gonna kill him at the public school. So we were lucky enough to get him in here for his last year. Good. His father don't like him. He comes here, the kids don't like him. One man is good to him. This priest. Puts out a hand to the boy. Does the man have his reasons? Yes. Everybody has their reasons. *You* have your reasons. But do I ask the man why he's good to my son? No. I don't care why. My son needs some man to care about him and see him through to where he wants to go. And thank God, this educated man with some kindness in him wants to do just that.

SISTER ALOYSIUS: This will not do.

MRS. MULLER: It's just till June. Sometimes things aren't black and white.

SISTER ALOYSIUS: And sometimes they are. I'll throw your son out of this school. Make no mistake.

MRS. MULLER: But why would you do that? If nothing started with him?

SISTER ALOYSIUS: Because I will stop this whatever way I must.

MRS. MULLER: You'd hurt my son to get your way?

SISTER ALOYSIUS: It won't end with your son. There will be others, if there aren't already.

MRS. MULLER: Throw the priest out then.

SISTER ALOYSIUS: I'm trying to do just that.

MRS. MULLER: Well, what do you want from me? (*A pause.*)

SISTER ALOYSIUS: Nothing. As it turns out. I was hoping you might know something that would help me, but it seems you don't.

MRS. MULLER: Please leave my son out of this. My husband would kill that child over a thing like this.

SISTER ALOYSIUS: I'll try. (*Mrs. Muller stands up.*)

MRS. MULLER: I don't know, Sister. You may think you're doing good, but the world's a hard place. I don't know that you and me are on the same side. I'll be standing with my son and those who are good with my son. It'd be nice to see you there. Nice talking with you, Sister. Good morning. (*She goes, leaving the door open behind her. Sister Aloysius is shaken. After a moment, Father Flynn appears at the door. He's in a controlled fury.*)

FLYNN: May I come in?

SISTER ALOYSIUS: We would require a third party.

Father Flynn (Brían F. O'Byrne) confronts Sister Aloysius (Cherry Jones) in the original production of *Doubt* by the Manhattan Theatre Club in 2004.

FLYNN: What was Donald's mother doing here?

SISTER ALOYSIUS: We were having a chat.

FLYNN: About what?

SISTER ALOYSIUS: A third party is truly required, Father.

FLYNN: No Sister. No third party. You and me are due for a talk. (*He comes in and slams the door behind him. They face each other.*) You have to stop this campaign against me!

SISTER ALOYSIUS: You can stop it at any time.

FLYNN: How?

SISTER ALOYSIUS: Confess and resign.

FLYNN: You are attempting to destroy my reputation! But the result of all this is going to be your removal, not mine!

SISTER ALOYSIUS: What are you doing in this school?

FLYNN: I am trying to do good!

SISTER ALOYSIUS: Or even more to the point, what are you doing in the priesthood?

FLYNN: You are single-handedly holding this school and this parish back!

SISTER ALOYSIUS: From what?

FLYNN: Progressive education and a welcoming church.

SISTER ALOYSIUS: You can't distract me, Father Flynn. This isn't about my behavior, it's about yours.

FLYNN: It's about your unfounded suspicions.

SISTER ALOYSIUS: That's right. I have suspicions.

FLYNN: You know what I haven't understood through all this? Why do you suspect me? What have I done?

SISTER ALOYSIUS: You gave that boy wine to drink. And you let him take the blame.

FLYNN: That's completely untrue! Did you talk to Mr. McGinn?

SISTER ALOYSIUS: All McGinn knows is the boy drank wine. He doesn't how he came to drink it.

FLYNN: Did his mother have something to add to that?

SISTER ALOYSIUS: No.

FLYNN: So that's it. There's nothing there.

SISTER ALOYSIUS: I'm not satisfied.

FLYNN: Well, if you're not satisfied, ask the boy then!

SISTER ALOYSIUS: No, he'd protect you. That's what he's been doing.

FLYNN: Oh, and why would he do that?

SISTER ALOYSIUS: Because you have seduced him.

FLYNN: You're insane! You've got it in your head that I've corrupted this child after giving him wine, and nothing I say will change that.

SISTER ALOYSIUS: That's right.

FLYNN: But correct me if I'm wrong. This has nothing to do with the wine, not really. You had a fundamental mistrust of me before this incident! It was you that warned Sister James to be on the lookout, wasn't it?

SISTER ALOYSIUS: That's true.

FLYNN: So you admit it!

SISTER ALOYSIUS: Certainly.

FLYNN: Why?

SISTER ALOYSIUS: I know people.

FLYNN: That's not good enough!

SISTER ALOYSIUS: It won't have to be.

FLYNN: How's that?

SISTER ALOYSIUS: You will tell me what you've done.

FLYNN: Oh I will?

SISTER ALOYSIUS: Yes.

FLYNN: I'm not one of your truant boys, you know. Sister James is convinced I'm innocent.

SISTER ALOYSIUS: So you talked to Sister James? Well, of course you talked to Sister James.

FLYNN: Did you know that Donald's father beats him?

SISTER ALOYSIUS: Yes.

FLYNN: And might that not account for the odd behavior Sister James noticed in the boy?

SISTER ALOYSIUS: It might.

FLYNN: Then what is it? What? What did you hear, what did you see that convinced you so thoroughly?

SISTER ALOYSIUS: What does it matter?

FLYNN: I want to know.

SISTER ALOYSIUS: On the first day of the school year, I saw you touch William London's wrist. And I saw him pull away.

FLYNN: That's all?

SISTER ALOYSIUS: That was all.

FLYNN: But that's nothing. (*He writes in his book.*)

SISTER ALOYSIUS: What are you writing now?

FLYNN: You leave me no choice, I'm writing down what you say. I tend to get too flustered to remember the details of an upsetting conversation, and this may be important. When I talk to the monsignor and explain why you have to be removed as the principal of this school.

SISTER ALOYSIUS: This morning, before I spoke with Mrs. Muller, I took the precaution of calling the last parish to which you were assigned.

FLYNN: What did he say?

SISTER ALOYSIUS: Who?

FLYNN: The pastor?

SISTER ALOYSIUS: I did not speak to the pastor. I spoke to one of the nuns.

FLYNN: You should've spoken to the pastor.

SISTER ALOYSIUS: I spoke to a nun.

FLYNN: That's not the proper route for you to have taken, Sister! The Church is very clear. You're supposed to go through the pastor.

SISTER ALOYSIUS: Why? Do you have an understanding, you and he? Father Flynn, you have a history.

FLYNN: You have no right to go rummaging through my past!

SISTER ALOYSIUS: This is your third parish in five years.

FLYNN: Call the pastor and ask him why I left! It was perfectly innocent.

SISTER ALOYSIUS: I'm not calling the pastor.

FLYNN: I am a good priest! And there is nothing in my record to suggest otherwise.

SISTER ALOYSIUS: You will go after another child and another, until you are stopped.

FLYNN: What nun did you speak to?

SISTER ALOYSIUS: I won't say.

FLYNN: I've not touched a child.

SISTER ALOYSIUS: You have.

FLYNN: You have not the slightest proof of anything.

SISTER ALOYSIUS: But I have my certainty, and armed with that, I will go to your last parish, and the one before that if necessary. I will find a parent, Father Flynn! Trust me I will. A parent who probably doesn't know that you are still working with children! And once I do that, you will be exposed. You may even be attacked, metaphorically or otherwise.

FLYNN: You have no right to act on your own! You are a member of a religious order. You have taken vows, obedience being one! You answer to us! You have no right to step outside the Church!

SISTER ALOYSIUS: I will step outside the Church if that's what needs to be done, though the door should shut behind me! I will do what needs to be done, Father, if it means I'm damned to Hell! You should understand that, or you will mistake me. Now, did you give Donald Muller wine to drink?

FLYNN: Have you never done anything wrong?

SISTER ALOYSIUS: I have.

FLYNN: Mortal sin?

SISTER ALOYSIUS: Yes.

FLYNN: And?

SISTER ALOYSIUS: I confessed it! Did you give Donald Muller wine to drink?

FLYNN: Whatever I have done, I have left in the healing hands of my confessor. As have you! We are the same!

SISTER ALOYSIUS: We are not the same! A dog that bites is a dog that bites! I do not justify what I do wrong and go on. I admit it, desist, and take my medicine. Did you give Donald Muller wine to drink?

FLYNN: No.

SISTER ALOYSIUS: Mental reservation?

FLYNN: No.

SISTER ALOYSIUS: You lie. Very well then. If you won't leave my office, I will. And once I go, I will not stop. (*She goes to the door. Suddenly, a new tone comes into his voice.*)

FLYNN: Wait!

SISTER ALOYSIUS: You will request a transfer from this parish. You will take a leave of absence until it is granted.

FLYNN: And do what for the love of God? My life is here.

SISTER ALOYSIUS: Don't.

FLYNN: Please! Are we people? Am I a person flesh and blood like you? Or are we just ideas and convictions. I can't say everything. Do you understand? There are things I can't say. Even if you can't imagine the explanation, Sister, remember that there are circumstances beyond your knowledge. Even if you feel certainty, it is an emotion and not a fact. In the spirit of charity, I appeal to you. On behalf of my life's work. You have to behave responsibly. I put myself in your hands.

SISTER ALOYSIUS: I don't want you.

FLYNN: My reputation is at stake.

SISTER ALOYSIUS: You can preserve your reputation.

FLYNN: If you say these things, I won't be able to do my work in the community.

SISTER ALOYSIUS: Your work in the community should be discontinued.

FLYNN: You'd leave me with nothing.

SISTER ALOYSIUS: That's not true. It's Donald Muller who has nothing, and you took full advantage of that.

FLYNN: I have not done anything wrong. I care about that boy very much.

SISTER ALOYSIUS: Because you smile at him and sympathize with him, and talk to him as if you were the same?

FLYNN: That child needed a friend!

SISTER ALOYSIUS: You are a cheat. The warm feeling you experienced when that boy looked at you with trust was not the sensation of virtue. It can be got by a drunkard from his tot of rum. You're a disgrace to the collar. The only reason you haven't been thrown out of the Church is the decline in vocations.

FLYNN: I can fight you.

SISTER ALOYSIUS: You will lose.

FLYNN: You can't know that.

SISTER ALOYSIUS: I know.

FLYNN: Where's your compassion?

SISTER ALOYSIUS: Nowhere you can get at it. Stay here. Compose yourself. Use the phone if you like. Good day, Father. I have no sympathy for you. I know you're invulnerable to true regret. (*Starts to go. Pause.*) And cut your nails. (*She goes, closing the door behind her. After a moment, he goes to the phone and dials.*)

FLYNN: Yes. This is Father Brendan Flynn of St. Nicholas parish. I need to make an appointment to see the bishop. (*Lights fade.*)

NINE

The lights crossfade to Sister Aloysius walking into the garden. It's a sunny day. She sits on the bench. Sister James enters.

SISTER ALOYSIUS: How's your brother?

SISTER JAMES: Better. Much better.

SISTER ALOYSIUS: I'm very glad. I prayed for him.

SISTER JAMES: It was good to get away. I needed to see my family. It had been too long.

SISTER ALOYSIUS: Then I'm glad you did it.

SISTER JAMES: And Father Flynn is gone.

SISTER ALOYSIUS: Yes.

SISTER JAMES: Where?

SISTER ALOYSIUS: St. Jerome's.

SISTER JAMES: So you did it. You got him out.

SISTER ALOYSIUS: Yes.

SISTER JAMES: Donald Muller is heartbroken that he's gone.

SISTER ALOYSIUS: Can't be helped. It's just till June.

SISTER JAMES: I don't think Father Flynn did anything wrong.

SISTER ALOYSIUS: No? He convinced you?

SISTER JAMES: Yes, he did.

SISTER ALOYSIUS: Hmmm.

SISTER JAMES: Did you ever prove it?

SISTER ALOYSIUS: What?

SISTER JAMES: That he interfered with Donald Muller?

SISTER ALOYSIUS: Did I ever prove it to whom?

SISTER JAMES: Anyone but yourself?

SISTER ALOYSIUS: No.

SISTER JAMES: But you were sure.

SISTER ALOYSIUS: Yes.

SISTER JAMES: I wish I could be like you.

SISTER ALOYSIUS: Why?

SISTER JAMES: Because I can't sleep at night anymore. Everything seems uncertain to me.

SISTER ALOYSIUS: Maybe we're not supposed to sleep so well. They've made Father Flynn the pastor of St. Jerome.

SISTER JAMES: Who?

SISTER ALOYSIUS: The bishop appointed Father Flynn the pastor of St. Jerome Church and School. It's a promotion.

SISTER JAMES: You didn't tell them?

SISTER ALOYSIUS: I told our good Monsignor Benedict. I crossed the garden and told him. He did not believe it to be true.

SISTER JAMES: Then why did Father Flynn leave? What did you say to him to make him go?

SISTER ALOYSIUS: That I had called a nun in his previous parish. That I had found out his prior history of infringements.

SISTER JAMES: So you did prove it!

SISTER ALOYSIUS: I was lying. I made no such call.

SISTER JAMES: You lied?

SISTER ALOYSIUS: Yes. But if he had no such history, the lie wouldn't have worked. His resignation was his confession. He was what I thought he was. And he's gone.

SISTER JAMES: I can't believe you lied.

SISTER ALOYSIUS: In the pursuit of wrongdoing, one steps away from God. Of course there's a price.

SISTER JAMES: I see. So now he's in another school.

SISTER ALOYSIUS: Yes. Oh, Sister James!

SISTER JAMES: What is it, Sister?

SISTER ALOYSIUS: I have doubts! I have such doubts! (*Sister Aloysius is bent with emotion. Sister James comforts her. Lights fade.*)

Lynn Nottage

Lynn Nottage, born in 1964 in Brooklyn, New York, was educated at Brown University and then at the Yale School of Drama, where she has served as a visiting lecturer in playwriting. After graduating from Yale, she spent four years working for Amnesty International, learning firsthand about international injustice. She left Amnesty International during the period of the Rwandan genocide, in which the Hutu and Tutsi people slaughtered each other. Her pain over this tragedy was intensified by the realization that the outside world was not going to attempt to stop the genocide. Nothing was being done, while people were dying by the hundreds of thousands throughout the country. Her interest in Africa and in injustice would infuse her later work.

One of Nottage's earliest works is also one of her most unusual. *Poof!* (1993) is a ten-minute play that was produced at the Humana Festival at the Actors Theatre of Louisville. In it an abusive husband experiences spontaneous human combustion. In this satire, Loureen begins the play by damning her husband Samuel, who then suddenly explodes and leaves a pile of ash. Loureen and her friend Florence discuss what she should do, a conversation that ultimately leads her to put off calling the police. The play is vigorous and comic but with a serious undertone. *Por'Knockers* (1995) is also a satire. The pork knockers of the title are people of mixed ethnicity who have subsisted by panning for gold in remote South American regions and who are now disappearing. The play, which was written prior to the Oklahoma City bombing, focuses on the plans and rationale of a group called the People's Diasporatic Party, who blow up a federal building that they mistakenly think is empty.

The play that brought Nottage to the attention of major critics is *Crumbs from the Table of Joy* (1995), a memory play featuring an adolescent girl, Ernestine, whose conventional African American family lives in Brooklyn in the 1950s. Ernestine's mother has died, and her aunt Lily has come to visit the family. Ermina, Ernestine's younger sister, and their father, Godfrey, take Lily in without understanding her agenda. Lily thinks that because she is the sister of Ernestine's dead mother, she has a claim on Godfrey. Lily, however, is a fast, boisterous woman who frightens Godfrey, a devotee of Father Divine, the black evangelist who was among the most popular religious figures of the 1950s. The play moves in a new direction when Godfrey brings home a white woman, a German émigrée, whom he decides to marry, thus rejecting Lily entirely. The portrait of a mixed-race marriage in this period is handled with delicacy and understanding. And although the play is not a bright and cheerful portrait of any of the characters, it is touching and significant.

Mud, River, Stone (1996) was produced in New York in 1997 at Playwrights Horizons and directed by Roger Rees. It is set in both New York and southeast Africa and concerns a hostage situation in which a white neo-colonialist, an African aid worker, an African American couple, and a United Nations worker—none of whom knew one another—discuss the situation in Africa as they understand it.

In an interesting departure, Nottage's next play was *Las Meninas* (2002), a historical comedy that focuses on an illegitimate daughter of Marie Therese, the wife of Louis XIV, who had an affair with an African dwarf named Nabo. The daughter was sent off to a convent and became a nun, while Nabo was sent away. The play was produced in 2002 at the San Jose Repertory Theatre in California.

Nottage won the Drama Critics' Circle Award for best play in 2004 with *Intimate Apparel,* set in Lower Manhattan in 1905, during the building of the Panama Canal and after the Spanish-American War. In this play, Esther, a shy, virginal thirty-five-year-old seamstress who has virtually given up hope of marriage, sews beautiful intimate garments for the girls in Mrs. Dickson's rooming house who leave to get married. When Esther gets a letter from George Armstrong, a laborer on the Panama Canal, she slowly begins to see her opportunity for a truly intimate relationship.

After the opening of *Fabulation: or The Re-Education of Undine* in 2004, for which Nottage won the Obie Award for Playwriting, she traveled to Uganda with director Kate Whoriskey to search for material for a drama on the subject of the refugee women and girls who had fled the Sudan and the Democratic Republic of the Congo—women who had been raped and sometimes mutilated and who had lost virtually everything. The resulting play, *Ruined,* set in a brothel in the Congo, won the Pulitzer Prize for drama in 2009. Nottage's most recent play, *By the Way, Meet Vera Stark* (2011), tells the story of a black woman who acted in films from the 1930s on, but in somewhat demeaning roles as a maid or even a slave in plantation dramas. Both plays illustrate why Nottage is known for her sharp intelligence and her powerful narratives.

For links to resources about Nottage, click on *AuthorLinks* at **bedfordstmartins.com/jacobus.**

Ruined

After spending time in Africa interviewing women survivors of the civil war in the Democratic Republic of the Congo, Lynn Nottage returned to the United States to write about her experiences. *Ruined* focuses on the effects of brutal rape and enslavement of women by violent soldiers on both sides of a civil conflict that has been going on for years. The main character in the play is Mama Nadi, who runs a supply store and brothel that caters to local miners as well as to both Commander Osembenga, the government troop commander, and Jerome Kisembe, the leader of the rebels. Mama Nadi's shop is on the edge of a rain forest that is now being cut down by miners searching for coltan, an ore that produces tantalum, a metal used in mobile phones, DVD players, and gaming systems.

Nottage says nothing in the play about the uses of coltan, but her own view is that one of the sources of the problems that have produced the terrible military actions in the Congo is the need of the developed nations for the natural resources of Africa. Coltan is, in fact, being mined in the Congo, and the mining has had a serious effect on the cultures of the people who live near the source of the ores that are so important to China and other industrial nations. The presence in the play of the coltan mines provides the reason for the conflict between government and rebel troops in the area of Mama Nadi's business.

Mama Nadi at first seems indifferent to either side in the war. She provides what both sides need: sex and beer. Because she is a businesswoman, she attracts people like Christian, who travels with supplies and repeatedly asks her to leave everything and come away with him. Christian has a concern for the women who are in the midst of the war and brings both Salima and Sophie to Mama Nadi's. He has to persuade her to take his niece, Sophie, into her brothel even though she is "ruined," a term meaning that the soldiers have raped her so brutally and so often that she is mutilated and cannot give a man sexual satisfaction. She is ruined as a woman, but it turns out that her ability to keep the books is enough to save her. Mr. Harari, an entrepreneur and diamond merchant with contacts in the larger cities in the Congo, offers help when Mama Nadi needs it. He enjoys the pleasures of her establishment and also has earned her trust as an honest man.

The women in her house understand that they survive because of Mama Nadi's protection, based on her ability to manipulate commanders on both sides of the battle. Salima, pregnant, has been enslaved and raped repeatedly and is afraid to return to her husband because of the shame involved in being used by the soldiers. Josephine's attitude is different from Salima's. The daughter of a village chieftain, she is a survivor, like Mama Nadi, and manages to deal with the miners and the soldiers. Mama Nadi takes special care of Sophie because she is ruined. Late in the play we discover that Mama Nadi has her own secrets, which have placed her in the difficult situation she has somehow managed to take advantage of to maintain her store.

Mama Nadi has been compared with Mother in Brecht's *Mother Courage* because both businesswomen deal with warriors on both sides of the battle. Both women are damaged, but both keep on because they have survived. Yet Mama Nadi seems to have much more feeling for those around her and more of a capacity to change than Brecht's character.

For discussion questions and assignments on *Ruined*, visit bedfordstmartins.com/jacobus.

Ruined in Performance

Ruined premiered as a joint production of the Goodman Theatre and the Manhattan Theatre Club at the Goodman Theatre in Chicago in November 2008. It opened in February 2009 off-Broadway at the City Center Stage I in New York. The director of both productions was Kate Whoriskey, who had worked with Lynn Nottage earlier on *Fabulation*. Mama Nadi was played by Saidah Arrika Ekulona and Sophie by Condola Rashad, both of whom received special praise in the reviews. The play won the Pulitzer Prize for drama in 2009. *Ruined* garnered good reviews in its London production by the Almeida Theatre Company in 2010. London theater critic Philip Fisher said, "This is the kind of work that makes the supposedly civilized world understand what is going on in countries that are far too rarely featured in the media or the arts." The Arena Stage in Washington, D.C., produced *Ruined* in April 2011. In her review in the *Baltimore Sun,* Mary Carole McCauley said, "This is the first time *Ruined* has been staged in the round, and the seating arrangement has two [salutary] results: Theatergoers are brought close to the action, and a perception is created that the characters on stage are surrounded and trapped." The play has gone on to be one of the most frequently performed plays at regional theaters in recent seasons.

LYNN NOTTAGE (b. 1964)

Ruined   2008

Characters

SALIMA
JOSEPHINE
JEROME KISEMBE
MAMA NADI
SIMON
FORTUNE
CHRISTIAN
COMMANDER OSEMBENGA
MR. HARARI
LAURENT
SOPHIE
AID WORKER
SOLDIERS
MINERS

Place: *A small mining town in the Democratic Republic of the Congo.*

ACT ONE • Scene 1

A small mining town. The sounds of the tropical Ituri rain forest. Democratic Republic of the Congo.

A bar with makeshift furniture and a rundown pool table. A lot of effort has gone into making the worn bar cheerful. A stack of plastic washtubs rests in the corner. An old car battery powers the lights and audio system, a covered birdcage conspicuously sits in the corner of the room.

Mama Nadi, early forties, an attractive woman with an arrogant stride and majestic air, watches Christian, early forties, a perpetually cheerful traveling salesman, knock back a Fanta. His good looks have been worn down by hard living on the road. He wears a suit that might have been considered stylish when new, but it's now nearly ten years old and overly loved. He brushes travel dust from his clothing, and takes a generous sip of his soda.

CHRISTIAN: Ah. Cold. The only cold Fanta in twenty-five kilometers. You don't know how good this tastes. (*Mama flashes a warm, flirtatious smile, then pours herself a Primus beer.*)

MAMA: And where the hell have you been?

CHRISTIAN: It was no easy task getting here.

MAMA: I've been expecting you for the last three weeks. How am I supposed do business? No soap, no cigarettes, no condoms. Not even a half liter of petrol for the generator.

CHRISTIAN: Why are you picking a fight with me already? I didn't create this damn chaos. Nobody, and I'm telling you, nobody could get through on the main road. Every two kilometers a boy with a Kalashnikov and pockets that need filling. Toll, tax, tariff. They invent reasons to lighten your load.

MAMA: Then why does Mr. Harari always manage to get through?

CHRISTIAN: Mr. Harari doesn't bring you things you need, does he? Mr. Harari has interests that supercede his safety. Me, I still hope to have a family one day. (*Christian laughs, heartily.*)

MAMA: And my lipstick?

CHRISTIAN: Your lipstick? Aye! Did you ask me for lipstick?

MAMA: Of course, I did, you idiot!

CHRISTIAN: Look at the way you speak to me, *Chérie. Comment est-ce possible?* You should be happy I made it here in one piece. (*Christian produces a tube of lipstick from his pocket.*) Play nice or I'll give this to Josephine. She knows how to show her appreciation.

MAMA: Yes, but you always take home a little more than you ask for with Josephine. I hope you know how to use a condom. (*Christian laughs.*)

CHRISTIAN: Are you jealous?

MAMA: Leave me alone, you're too predictable. (*Mama turns away, dismissive.*)

CHRISTIAN: Where are you going? Hey, hey what are you doing? (*Teasingly.*) *Chérie,* I know you wanted me to forget, so you could yell at me, but you won't get the pleasure this time. (*Christian taunts her with the lipstick. Mama resists the urge to smile.*)

MAMA: Oh shut up and give it to me. (*He passes her the lipstick.*) Thank you, Christian.

CHRISTIAN: I didn't hear you—

MAMA: Don't press your luck. And it better be red. (*Mama grabs a sliver of a broken mirror from behind the rough-hewn bar, and gracefully applies the lipstick.*)

CHRISTIAN: You don't have to say it. I know you want a husband.

MAMA: Like a hole in my head.

CHRISTIAN: (*Reciting.*)

What, is this love?
An unexpected wind,
A fluctuation,
fronting the coming of a storm.

Resolve, a thorny bush
Blown asunder and swept away
There, *Chérie.* I give you a poem in lieu of the kiss you won't allow me. (*Christian laughs, warmly. Mama puts out a bowl of peanuts.*)

MAMA: Here. I saved you some groundnuts, *Professor.*

CHRISTIAN: That's all you saved for me?

MAMA: Be smart, and I'll show you the door in one second. (*Mama scolds him with her eyes.*)

CHRISTIAN: Ach, ach . . . why are you wearing my Grand-mama's face? (*Christian mocks her expression. Mama laughs and downs her beer.*)

MAMA: You sure you don't want a beer?

CHRISTIAN: You know me better than that, *Chérie,* I haven't had a drop of liquor in four years.

MAMA: (*Teasing.*) It's cold.

CHRISTIAN: Tst! (*Christian cracks open a few peanuts, and playfully pops them into his mouth. The parrot squawks.*) What's there? In the cage?

MAMA: Oh, that, a grey parrot. Old Papa Batunga passed.

CHRISTIAN: When?

MAMA: Last Thursday. No one wanted the damn bird. It complains too much.

CHRISTIAN: (*Amused.*) Yeah, what does it say? (*Christian walks to the birdcage, and peers under the covering.*)

MAMA: Who the hell knows? It speaks pygmy. He . . . Old Papa was the last of his tribe. That stupid bird was the only thing he had left to talk to.

CHRISTIAN: (*To bird.*) Hello?

MAMA: He believed as long as the words of the forest people were spoken the spirits would stay alive.

CHRISTIAN: For true? (*Christian pokes his finger into the cage. To Mama.*) What are you going to do with him?

MAMA: Sell it. I don't want it. It stinks. (*Christian pokes at the birdcage.*)

CHRISTIAN: (*To bird.*) Hello.

MAMA: Hey, hey don't put your fingers in there.

CHRISTIAN: Look. He likes me. So Mama, you haven't asked me what else I've brought for you? Go see. (*Christian quickly withdraws his finger.*) Ow. Shit. He bit me.

MAMA: Well, you shouldn't be messing with it. (*Mama laughs.*)

CHRISTIAN: Ow, damn it.

MAMA: (*Impatiently.*) Don't be a crybaby, what did you bring me? Well? . . . Are you going to keep me guessing?

CHRISTIAN: Go on. Take a peek in the truck. And don't say I don't think about you. (*Mama smiles.*)

MAMA: How many?

CHRISTIAN: Three.

MAMA: Three? But, I can't use three right now. You know that.

CHRISTIAN: Of course you can. And I'll give you a good price if you take all of them. (*Mama goes to the doorway, and peers out at the offerings, unimpressed.*)

MAMA: I don't know. They look used. Worn.

CHRISTIAN: C'mon, Mama. Take another look. A full look. You've said it yourself business is good. (*Mama considers, then finally.*)

MAMA: Okay, one. That one in front. (*Points into the distance.*)

CHRISTIAN: Three. C'mon, don't make me travel back with them.

MAMA: Just one. How much?

CHRISTIAN: Do you know how difficult it was getting here? The road was completely washed out—

MAMA: All right, all right. I don't need the whole damn saga. Just tell me, how much for the one?

CHRISTIAN: The same as usual plus twenty-five, because . . . because . . . You understand it wasn't easy to get here with the—

MAMA: I'll give you fifteen.

CHRISTIAN: Ahh! Fifteen? No. That's nothing. Twenty-two. C'mon.

MAMA: Twenty. My best offer. (*Christian mulls it over. He's reluctant.*)

CHRISTIAN: Aye. Okay. Okay. Damn it. Yes. Yes. But I expect another cold Fanta. One from the bottom this time. (*Christian, defeated, exits. Mama smiles victoriously, and retrieves another soda from the refrigerator. She reapplies lipstick for good measure, then counts out her money. Christian re-enters proudly bearing two cartons of Ugandan cigarettes. A moment later two women in ragged clothing step tentatively into the bar: Sophie, a luminous beauty with an air of defiance, and Salima, a sturdy peasant woman whose face betrays a world weariness. They hold hands. Mama studies the women, then—*)

MAMA: I said one. That one. (*She points to Sophie.*)

CHRISTIAN: It's been a good week, and I'll tell you what, I'll give you two for the price of one. Why not?

MAMA: Are you deaf? No. Tst! I don't need two more mouths to feed and pester me. (*Mama continues to examine each woman.*)

CHRISTIAN: Take both. Feed them as one. Please, Mama, I'll throw in the cigarettes for cost.

MAMA: But, I'll only pay for one.

CHRISTIAN: Of course. We agree, why are we arguing?

MAMA: (*Yelling.*) Josephine! Josephine! Where is that stupid woman? (*Josephine, a sexy woman in a short Western-style miniskirt and high heels, appears in the beaded doorway. She surveys the new women with obvious contempt.*) Take them out back. Get them washed and some proper clothing.

JOSEPHINE: *Njoo.* [Come.] (*Beat.*) *Sasa.* [Quick.] (*Josephine beckons to the women. They reluctantly follow.*)

MAMA: Wait. (*Mama gestures to Salima, who clings to Sophie.*) You. Come here. (*Salima doesn't move.*) Come. (*Salima clings to Sophie, then slowly walks toward Mama.*) What's your name?

SALIMA: (*Whispers.*) Salima.

MAMA: What?

SALIMA: Salima. (*Mama examines Salima's rough hands.*)

MAMA: Rough. (*With disdain.*) A digger. We'll have to do something about that. (*Salima yanks her hand away. Mama registers the bold gesture.*) And you, come. You're a pretty thing, what's your name?

SOPHIE: (*Gently.*) Sophie.

MAMA: Do you have a smile?

SOPHIE: Yes.

MAMA: Then let me see it. (*Sophie struggles to find a defiant smile.*) Good. Go get washed up. (*A moment.*)

JOSEPHINE: (*Snaps.*) C'mon, now! (*Salima looks to Sophie. She follows. The women follow behind Josephine. Sophie walks with some pain.*)

MAMA: Did you at least tell them this time?

CHRISTIAN: Yes. They know and they came willingly.

MAMA: And—?

CHRISTIAN: Salima is from a tiny village. No place really. She was captured by rebel soldiers, Mayi-mayi; the poor thing spent nearly five months in the bush as their concubine.

MAMA: And what of her people?

CHRISTIAN: She says her husband is a farmer, and from what I understand, her village won't have her back. Because . . . But she's a simple girl, she doesn't have much learning, I wouldn't worry about her.

MAMA: And the other?

CHRISTIAN: Sophie. Sophie is . . .

MAMA: Is what?

CHRISTIAN: . . . is . . . ruined. (*A moment.*)

MAMA: (*Enraged.*) You brought me a girl that's ruined?

CHRISTIAN: She cost you nothing.

MAMA: I paid money for her, not the other one. The other one is plain. I have a half a dozen girls like her, I don't need to feed another plain girl.

CHRISTIAN: I know this, okay, don't get worked up. Sophie is a good girl, she won't trouble you.

MAMA: How do I know that?

CHRISTIAN: (*Defensively.*) Because I am telling you. She's seen some very bad times.

MAMA: Yeah? And why is that my concern?

CHRISTIAN: Take her on, just for a month. You'll see she's a good girl. Hard worker. (*Mama gestures toward her genitals.*)

MAMA: But damaged, am I right?

CHRISTIAN: . . . Yes . . . Look, militia did ungodly things to the child, took her with . . . a bayonet and then left her for dead. And she was—

MAMA: (*Snaps.*) I don't need to hear it. Are you done?

CHRISTIAN: (*Passionately.*) Things are gonna get busy, Mama. All along the road people are talking about how this red dirt is rich with Coltan.° Suddenly everyone has a shovel, and wants to stake a claim since that boastful pygmy dug up his fortune in the reserve. I guarantee there'll be twice as many miners here by September. And you know all those bastards will be thirsty. So, take her, put her to work for you.

MAMA: And what makes you think I have any use for her?

Coltan: An ore that produces tantalum, a metal used in mobile phones and electronic gadgets.

CHRISTIAN: (*Pleads.*) The girl cooks, cleans, and she sings like an angel. And you . . . you haven't had nice music here since that one, that beauty Camille got the AIDS.

MAMA: No. A girl like this is bad luck. I can't have it. Josephine! Josephine!

CHRISTIAN: And Mama, she's pretty pretty. She'll keep the miner's eyes happy. I promise.

MAMA: Stop it already, no. You're like a hyena. Won't you shut up, now. (*Josephine enters, put-upon.*)

JOSEPHINE: Yes, Mama.

MAMA: Bring the girl, Sophie, back.

CHRISTIAN: Wait. Give us a minute, Josephine. (*Josephine doesn't move.*) Mama, please. Look, okay, I'm asking you to do me this favor. I've done many things for you over the years. And I don't ask you for a lot in return. Please. The child has no place else to go.

MAMA: I'm sorry, but I'm running a business, not a mission. Take her to the sisters in Bunia, let her weave baskets for them. Josephine, why are you standing there like a fool . . . go get the girl.

CHRISTIAN: Wait. (*Josephine addresses both of them.*)

JOSEPHINE: (*Annoyed.*) Do you want me to stay or to go?

MAMA: (*Snaps.*) Get her! (*Josephine sucks her teeth and exits.*)

CHRISTIAN: (*With a tinge of resentment.*) Tst! I remembered your lipstick and everything.

MAMA: Don't look at me that way. I open my doors, and tomorrow I'm a refugee camp overrun with suffering. Everyone has their hand open since this damned war began. I can't do it. I keep food in the mouths of eight women, when half the country's starving, so don't give me shit about taking on one more girl.

CHRISTIAN: Look. Have anything you want off of my truck. Anything! I even have some . . . some Belgian chocolate.

MAMA: You won't let up. Why are you so damn concerned with this girl? Huh?

CHRISTIAN: C'mon, Mama, please.

MAMA: Chocolate. I always ask you for chocolate, and you always tell me it turns in this heat. How many times have you refused me this year. Huh? But, she must be very very important to you. I see that. Do you want to fuck her or something? (*A moment.*)

CHRISTIAN: She's my sister's only daughter. Okay? I told my family I'd find a place for her . . . And here at least I know she'll be safe. Fed. (*He stops himself and gulps down his soda.*) And as you know the village isn't a place for a girl who has been . . . ruined. It brings shame, dishonor to the family.

MAMA: (*Ironically.*) But it's okay for her to be here, huh? I'm sorry, but, I can't. I don't have room for another broken girl.

CHRISTIAN: She eats like a bird. Nothing. (*Sophie enters.*)

SOPHIE: Madame.

MAMA: (*Defensively.*) It's Mademoiselle. (*A moment. Mama stares at Sophie, thinking, her resolve slowly softening.*) Come here. (*Sophie walks over to Mama.*) How old are you? (*Sophie meets Mama's eyes.*)

SOPHIE: Eighteen.

MAMA: Yeah? Do you have a beau?

SOPHIE: No. (*Mama's surprised by her haughtiness.*)

MAMA: Are you a student?

SOPHIE: Yes, I was to sit for the university exam.

MAMA: I bet you were good at your studies. Am I right?

SOPHIE: Yes.

MAMA: A *petit* bureaucrat in the making. (*Sophie shifts with discomfort. Her body aches, tears escape her eyes. Mama uses the cloth from her skirt to wipe Sophie's eyes.*) Did they hurt you badly?

SOPHIE: (*Whispered.*) . . . Yes.

MAMA: I bet they did. (*Mama studies Sophie. Considers, and then decides.*) Christian, go get me the chocolate.

CHRISTIAN: Does that mean . . . ?

MAMA: I'm doing this for you, 'cuz you've been good to me. (*Whispers to Christian.*) But this is the last time you bring me damaged goods. Understood? It's no good for business.

CHRISTIAN: Thank you. It's the last time. I promise. Thank you.

MAMA: You sing?

SOPHIE: (*Softly.*) Yes.

MAMA: Do you know any popular songs?

SOPHIE: Yes. A few.

CHRISTIAN: Speak up! (*Christian exits.*)

SOPHIE: Yes, Mad— (*Catching herself.*) . . . emoiselle.

MAMA: Mama. You do math? Stuff like that?

SOPHIE: Yes, Mama.

MAMA: Good. (*Mama lifts Sophie's chin with her fingers, enviously examining her face.*) Yes, you're very pretty. I can see how that caused you problems. Do you know what kind of place this is?

SOPHIE: Yes, Mama. I think so.

MAMA: Good. (*Mama carefully applies red lipstick to Sophie's mouth.*) Then we have no problems. I expect my girls to be well-behaved and clean. That's all. I provide a bed, food, and clothing. If things are good, everyone gets a little. If things are bad, then Mama eats first. Am I making myself clear? (*Sophie nods.*) Good. Red is your color. (*Sophie doesn't respond.*) Thank you, Mama.

SOPHIE: Thank you, Mama. (*Mama pours a glass of local home-brewed liquor. She holds it out.*)

MAMA: Here. It'll help the pain down below. I know it hurts, because it smells like the rot of meat. So wash good. (*Sophie takes the glass, and slowly drinks the liquor down.*) Don't get too dependent on drink. It'll make you sloppy, and I have no tolerance for sloppiness. Understood? (*Christian, put-upon, reenters with a faded, but pretty, box of chocolates.*)

CHRISTIAN: Handmade. Imported. *Très bon.* I hope you're impressed. A Belgian shopkeeper in Bunia ordered them. Real particular. I had a hell of a time trying to find these Goddamn chocolates. And then poof, she's gone. And now I'm stuck with twenty boxes. I tried to pawn them off on Pastor Robbins, but apparently he's on a diet. (*Mama opens the box, surveying the chocolates. She's in seventh heaven. She offers a piece to Sophie, who timidly selects a chocolate.*)

Mama Nadi (Saidah Arrika Ekulona) applies lipstick to Sophie (Condola Rashad) in the Manhattan Theatre Club production of *Ruined* at City Center Stage I in New York, directed by Kate Whoriskey in 2009.

SOPHIE: *Merci.* (*Mama bites into the chocolate.*)

MAMA: Mmm.

CHRISTIAN: Happy? That's what the good life in Belgium tastes like.

MAMA: Caramel. (*Savoring.*) Good God, I haven't had caramel in ages. You bastard, you've been holding out on me! Mmm. Smell 'em, the smell reminds me of my mother. She'd take me and my brothers to Kisangani. And she'd buy us each an enormous bag of caramels wrapped in that impossible plastic. You know why? So we wouldn't tell my grandfather about all of the uncles she visited in the big town. She'd sit us on the bank of the river, watching the boats and eating sweaty caramels, while she "visited with uncles." And as long as there were sweets, we didn't breathe a word, not a murmur, to old Papa. (*Sophie eats her chocolate, smiling for the first time. Christian reaches for a chocolate, but Mama quickly slaps his hand and shuts the box.*)

CHRISTIAN: What about me?

MAMA: What about you?

CHRISTIAN: Don't I get one?

MAMA: No! (*This amuses Sophie. She smiles.*)

CHRISTIAN: Why are you smiling? You're a lucky girl. You're lucky you have such a good uncle. A lot of men would've left you for dead. (*Sophie's smile disappears.*)

MAMA: Never mind him. (*To Christian.*) Go, all ready and bring the other stuff in before the vultures steal it!

CHRISTIAN: Sophie. I'm . . . you . . . you be a good girl. Don't make Mama angry.

SOPHIE: I won't, Uncle. (*Christian exits with apology in his posture. Sophie licks her chocolate-covered fingers as the lights fade.*)

Scene 2

A month later.

The bar. Josephine cranks the generator, and colorful Christmas lights flicker on. The birdcage rests in the back of the bar; periodically the bird makes a raucous squawk.

At the bar, drunk and disheveled rebel soldiers drain their beers and laugh too loudly. Salima, wearing a shiny gold midriff, a colorful traditional wrap, and mismatched yellow heels, shoots pool doing her best to ignore the occasional lustful leers of the soldiers.

Jerome Kisembe, the rebel leader dressed in military uniform, holds court. Mama, toting bowls of peanuts, wears a bright red kerchief around her neck, in recognition of the rebel leaders' colors.

Josephine dirty-dances for Mr. Harari, a handsome tipsy Lebanese mineral merchant sporting a surprisingly pristine safari suit. He is barefoot.

Sophie plows through an upbeat dance song, accompanied by a guitar and drums.

SOPHIE: (*Sings.*)
> The liquid night slowly pours in.
> Languor peels away like a curtain.
> Spirits rise, and tongues loosen
> And the weary ask to be forgiven
>
> You come here to forget,
> You say drive away all regret.
> And dance like it's the ending
> The ending of the war.
>
> The day's heavy door closes quick
> Leaving the scold of the sun behind
> Dusk ushers in the forest's music
> And your body's free to unwind

(*Josephine dances for the men.*)

> You come here to forget,
> You say drive away all regret
> And dance like it's the ending
> The ending of the war.
>
> But, can the music be all forgiving
> Purge the wear and tear of the living?
> Will the sound drown out your sorrow,
> So you'll remember nothing tomorrow?

(*A drunk rebel soldier stands and demands attention.*)

REBEL SOLDIER #1: Another! Hey!

MAMA: I hear you! I hear you!

REBEL SOLDIER #1: C'mon! Another! (*He clumsily slams the bottle on the counter, and gestures to Sophie.*) Psst! You! Psst! Psst! (*Another rebel soldier gives Sophie a cat-call. Sophie ignores him. Rebel Soldier #1 turns his attention back to Mama.*) Her! Why won't she come talk to me?

MAMA: You want to talk to her. Behave, and let me see your money. (*Jerome Kisembe, the haughty rebel leader, lets out a roar of a laugh.*)

REBEL SOLDIER #1: The damn beer drained my pocket. It cost too much! You're a fucking thief!

MAMA: Then go somewhere else, and mind your tongue. (*Mama turns away.*)

REBEL SOLDIER #1: Hey. Wait. Wait. I want her to talk to me. Mama, lookie! I have this. (*Rebel Soldier #1 proudly displays a cloth filled with little chunks of ore.*)

MAMA: What is it? Huh? Coltan? Where'd you get it?

REBEL SOLDIER #1: (*Boasting.*) From a miner on the reserve.

MAMA: He just gave it to you?

REBEL SOLDIER #1: (*Snickering.*) Yeah, he give it to me. Dirty poacher been diggin' up our forest, we run 'em off. Run 'em good, gangsta-style, "muthafucka run!," left 'em for the fucking scavengers. (*Rebel Soldier #1 strikes a hip-hop "gangsta-style" pose. The other rebel soldiers laugh. Mr. Harari, unamused, ever so slightly registers the conversation. Mama laughs.*)

MAMA: Coltan? Let me see. Ah, that's nothing, it's worthless, my friend. A month ago, yes, but now you can't get a handful of meal for it. Too many prospectors. Every miner that walks in here has a bucket of it. Bring me a gram of gold, then we talk.

REBEL SOLDIER #1: What do you mean? Liar! In the city this would fetch me plenty.

MAMA: This ain't the city, is it, soldier? (*He aggressively grabs Mama's wrist.*) This is a nice place for a drink. Yeah? I don't abide by bush laws. If you want to drink like a man, you drink like a man, you want to behave like a gorilla, then go back into the bush. (*The rebel soldiers laugh. He unhands Mama.*)

REBEL SOLDIER #1: C'mon Mama, this is worth plenty! Yeah? (*Again, he gestures to Sophie. He's growing increasingly belligerent.*) Bitch. Why won't she talk to me? (*Frustrated, Rebel Soldier #1 puts the cloth back in his pocket. He broods, silently watching Sophie sway to the music. Then all of sudden he collects himself, and drunkenly makes his way toward her.*) I'll teach her manners! Respect me! (*Rebel Soldier #1 pounds his chest, the other rebel soldier goads him on. Sophie stiffens. Mama quickly steps between them. The musicians stop playing.*)

MAMA: But . . . as the Coltan is all you have. I'll take it this time. Now go sit down. Sit down. Please.

REBEL SOLDIER #1: (*Excited.*) Yeah? Now, I want her to talk to me! Will she talk to me?

MAMA: Okay. Okay. Sit. (*Rebel Soldier #1 pulls out the cloth. He gently removes several pieces of the ore.*) Don't be stingy. Tst! Let me see all of it. (*Rebel Soldier #1 reluctantly relinquishes the weathered cloth to Mama. Smiling.*) Salima! Salima, come! (*Salima, disgusted, bristles at the sound of her name. She reluctantly approaches Rebel Soldier #1.*)

REBEL SOLDIER #1: What about her? (*He gestures to Sophie.*)

MAMA: Salima is a better dancer. I promise. Okay. Everyone is happy.

KISEMBE: Soldier, everyone is happy! (*Salima sizes up the drunken Rebel Soldier #1.*)

SALIMA: So, "gangsta," you wanna dance with me? (*She places his arms around her waist. He longingly looks over at Sophie, then pulls Salima close. He leads aggressively.*) Easy.

MAMA: Sophie. (*Sophie, relieved, resumes singing.*)

SOPHIE: (*Sings.*)

Have another beer, my friend,
Douse the fire of your fears, my friend,
Get drunk and foolish on the moment,
Brush aside the day's heavy judgment

Yes, have another beer, my friend
Wipe away the angry tears, my friend
Get drunk and foolish on the moment,
Brush aside the day's heavy judgment.

'Cuz, you come here to forget,
You say drive away all regret.
And dance like it's the ending
The ending of the war.
The ending of the war.
The ending of the war.

(*Applause. Mama, having quenched the fire, fetches her lockbox from a hiding place beneath the counter and puts the ore inside.*)

MR. HARARI: That one, she's pretty. (*He gestures to Sophie.*)

JOSEPHINE: (*With disdain.*) Sophie?! She's broken. All of the girls think she's bad luck. (*Josephine leads Mr. Harari to the table, they sit.*)

MR. HARARI: What are you wearing? Where's the dress I bought you?

JOSEPHINE: If I had known you were coming, I'd have put it on.

MR. HARARI: Then what are you waiting for, my darling? (*Josephine exits quickly. Mama, toting her lockbox, joins Mr. Harari at his table.*)

MAMA: What happened to your shoes, Mr. Harari?

MR. HARARI: Your fucking country, some drunk child doing his best impersonation of a rebel soldier liberated my shoes. (*Laughter from pool table.*) Every time I come here I have to buy a new fucking pair of shoes.

MAMA: You're lucky he only wanted your shoes. Santé. Cheers. (*Rebel Soldier #1 gets too friendly with Salima. She lurches away.*)

REBEL SOLDIER #1: Hey!

KISEMBE: Ach, ach, quiet, I'm trying to play here. (*Rebel Soldier #1 grabs Salima onto his lap. Mr. Harari watches the Rebel Soldier #1 and Salima.*)

MR. HARARI: You took that poor man's Coltan. Shame on you. He probably doesn't know what he gave away for the taste of that woman. (*To Rebel Soldier #1.*) Savor it! The toll to enter that tunnel was very expensive, my friend. (*To Mama.*) We both know how much it would fetch on the market.

MAMA: Six months ago it was just more black dirt. I don't get why everyone's crawling over each other for it.

MR. HARARI: Well, my darling, in this damnable age of the mobile phone it's become quite the precious ore, no? And for whatever reason God has seen fit to bless your backward country with an abundance of it. Now, if that young man had come to me, I would've given him enough money to buy pussy for a month. Even yours. So who's the bigger thief, you or him?

MAMA: He give it to me, you saw. So, does that make me a thief or merely more clever than you. (*Mr. Harari laughs.*)

MR. HARARI: My darling, you'd do well in Kisangani.

MAMA: I do well here, and I'd get homesick in Kisangani. It's a filthy city full of bureaucrats and thieves.

MR. HARARI: Very funny, but I imagine you'd enjoy it, terribly. And I mean that as compliment.

MAMA: Do you have a minute?

MR. HARARI: Of course.

KISEMBE: Soldier! Soldier!

REBEL SOLDIER #2: Chief.

KISEMBE: Bring me my mobile! What're you, an old man? Hurry! (*Mama empties a bag containing a precious stone onto a cloth on the table.*)

MAMA: What do you think? Huh?

MR. HARARI: (*Referring to rough stones.*) Just looking, I can tell you, most of these are worthless. I'm sorry. (*Mama takes out another stone. She discreetly shows it to Mr. Harari.*)

MAMA: What about that one? (*Mr. Harari examines the diamond on the table, then meticulously places a loupe to his eye and examines the stone more closely.*)

MR. HARARI: Hm. It's a rough diamond. Where'd you get this?

MAMA: Don't you worry. I'm holding it for someone. (*Mr. Harari continues to examine the diamond.*)

MR. HARARI: Nice. Yes, you see, there. It carries the light very well.

MAMA: Yeah, yeah, but is it worth anything?

MR. HARARI: . . . Well—

MAMA: Well—

MR. HARARI: Depends. (*Mama smiles.*) It's raw, and the market—

MAMA: Yeah, yeah but, how much are we talking? A new generator or a plot of land? (*Mr. Harari chuckles.*)

MR. HARARI: Slow down, I can offer you a fairly good price. But, be reasonable, darling, I'm an independent with a family that doesn't appreciate how hard I work. (*Mama takes back the diamond.*)

MAMA: You sound like my old Papa. He was like you, Mr. Harari, work too much, always want more, no rest. He drove his farm hard, too hard. When there was famine our bananas were rotting. He used to say as long as the forest grows a man will never starve.

MR. HARARI: Yes, but does he still have the farm? (*Mama smiles to herself.*)

MAMA: You know better, Mr. Harari, you're in the Congo. Things slip from our fingers like butter. No. When I was eleven, this white man turned up with a piece of paper. It say he have rights to my family land. (*With acid.*) Just like that. Taken! And you want to hear a joke? Poor old Papa bought magic from a friend, he thought a hand full of powder would give him back his land. Everyone talk talk diamonds, but I . . . I want a powerful slip of paper that says I can cut down forests and dig holes and build to the moon if I choose. I don't want someone to turn up at my door, and take my life from me. Not ever again. But how does a woman get a piece of land, without having to pick up a fucking gun? (*Mr. Harari watches the soldiers.*)

MR. HARARI: I wish I could tell you, but I can't even hold onto a fucking pair of shoes. These idiots keep changing the damn rules. You file papers, and the next day the office is burned down. You buy land, and the next day the Chief's son has built a fucking house on it. I don't know why anybody bothers. Madness. And look now, a hungry pygmy digs a hole in the forest, and suddenly every two-bit militia is battling for the keys to hell.

MAMA: True, but someone must provide them with beer and distractions. (*Mr. Harari laughs. Mama scoops up the diamonds and places them back into her lockbox. Mr. Harari removes the loupe.*)

MR. HARARI: But, be careful; where will I drink if anything happens to you? (*Mr. Harari gives Mama a friendly kiss.*)

MAMA: Don't worry about me. Everything is beautiful. (*Josephine enters proudly sporting an elegant traditional dress. Mr. Harari watches Sophie.*)

JOSEPHINE: What do you think? (*Mr. Harari shifts his gaze to Josephine.*)

MR. HARARI: Such loveliness. Doesn't she look beautiful?

MAMA: Yes, very. Excuse me. *Karibu.*°

MR. HARARI: I just might have to take you home with me.

JOSEPHINE: (*Excited.*) Promise.

MR. HARARI: Of course. (*Josephine hitches up her dress, straddles Mr. Harari, and kisses him.*)

KISEMBE: (*Shouts.*) Mama! Mama!

MAMA: Okay, okay, chief, *sawa sawa.* [Okay okay.]

KISEMBE: Two more Primus.° And Mama, why can't I get mobile service in this pit?

Karibu: Welcome.   **Primus:** A brand of beer.

MAMA: You tell me, you're important, go make it happen!

MR. HARARI: Who's that?

JOSEPHINE: Him? Jerome Kisembe, leader of the rebel militia. He's very powerful. He have sorcerer that give him a charm so he can't be touched by bullet. He's fearless. He is the boss man, the government and the church and anything else he wants to be. (*Harari studies Kisembe.*) Don't look so hard at a man like that. (*Josephine grabs Mr. Harari's face and kisses him. Mama clears the beer bottles from Kisembe's table. The rebel soldier gropes at Salima, then he nips her on the neck.*)

SALIMA: Ow! You jackass. (*Salima pulls away from the rebel soldier and heads for the door. Mama races after her, catching her arm forcefully.*)

MAMA: What's your problem?

SALIMA: Did you see what he did?

MAMA: You selfish girl. Now get back to him. (*Mama shoves Salima toward the rebel soldier. Sophie, watching, walks over to Salima.*)

SOPHIE: Are you all right, Salima?

SALIMA: The dog bit me. (*Whispered.*) I'm not going back over there.

SOPHIE: You have to.

SALIMA: He's filth! It's a man like him that—

SOPHIE: Don't. Mama's looking. (*Tears well up in Salima's eyes.*)

SALIMA: Do you know what he said to me—

SOPHIE: They'll say anything to impress a lady. Half of them are lies. Dirty fucking lies! Go back, don't listen. I'll sing the song you like. (*Sophie gives Salima a kiss on the cheek. Salima's eyes shoot daggers at Mama, and she reluctantly returns to the drunken soldier. Sophie launches into. Josephine dirty-dances for Mr. Harari. Sophie sings.*)

Have another beer, my friend
Wipe away the angry tears, my friend
Get drunk and foolish on the moment,
Brush aside the day's heavy judgment.

'Cuz,
You come here to forget,
You say drive away all regret.
And dance like it's the ending,
The ending, The ending, The ending,
And dance like it's the ending.

(*Mama watches Salima like a hawk. Lights fade.*)

Scene 3

Morning.

  Living quarters behind the bar. Ragged wood and straw beds. A poster of a popular African-American pop star hangs over Josephine's bed. Sophie paints Salima's fingernails, as she peruses a worn fashion magazine. Salima shifts in place, agitated.

SALIMA: (*Impatiently.*) C'mon, c'mon, c'mon, Sophie. Finish before she comes back.

SOPHIE: Keep still, will ya. Stop moving. She's with Mr. Harari.

SALIMA: She's gonna kill me if she find out I use her nail polish.

SOPHIE: Well, keep it up, and she's gonna find out one of these days.

SALIMA: But, not today. So hurry! (*Sophie makes a mistake with Salima's nails. Salima yanks her hand away.*) Aye girl, look what you did! *Pumbafu!* [Stupid!]

SOPHIE: What's your problem?!

SALIMA: Nothing. Nothing. I'm fine. (*Salima, frustrated, stands up and walks away.*)

SOPHIE: Yeah? You've been short with me all morning? Don't turn away. I'm talking to you.

SALIMA: "Smile, Salima. Talk pretty." Them soldiers don't respect nothing. Them miners, they easy, they want drink, company, and it's over. But the soldiers, they want more of you, and—

SOPHIE: Did that man do something to hurt you?

SALIMA: You know what he say? He say fifteen Hema° men were shot dead and buried in their own mining pit, in mud so thick it swallow them right into the ground without mercy. He say, one man stuff the Coltan into his mouth to keep the soldiers from stealing his hard work, and they split his belly open with a machete. "It'll show him for stealing," he say, bragging like I should be congratulating him. And then he fucked me, and when he was finished he sat on the floor and wept. He wanted me to hold him. Comfort him.

SOPHIE: And, did you?

SALIMA: No. I'm Hema. One of those men could be my brother.

SOPHIE: Don't even say that. (*Salima is overcome by the possibility.*)

SALIMA: I . . . I . . . miss my family. My husband. My baby—

SOPHIE: Stop it! We said we wouldn't talk about it.

SALIMA: Just then I was thinking about Beatrice and how much she liked banana. I feed her like this, I squeeze banana between my fingers and let her suck them, and she'd make a funny little face. Such delight. Delight. (*Emotionally.*) Delight! Delight!

SOPHIE: Shhh! Lower your voice.

SALIMA: Please, let me say my baby's name, Beatrice.

SOPHIE: Shhh!

SALIMA: I wanna go home!

SOPHIE: Now, look at me. Look here, if you leave, where will you go? Huh? Sleep in the bush? Scrounge for food in a stinking refugee camp.

SALIMA: But I wanna—!

Hema: An ethnic group in the Congo related to the Bantu people. Their northern neighbors are the Lendu people.

SOPHIE: What? Be thrown back out there? Where will you go? Huh? Your husband? Your village? How much goodness did they show you?

SALIMA: (*Wounded.*) Why did you say that?

SOPHIE: I'm sorry, but you know it's true. There is a war going on, and it isn't safe for a woman alone. You know this! It's better this way. Here.

SALIMA: You, you don't have to be with them. Sometimes their hands are so full of rage that it hurts to be touched. This night, I look over at you singing, and you seem almost happy like a sunbird that can fly away if you reach out to touch it.

SOPHIE: Is that what you think? While I'm singing, I'm praying the pain will be gone, but what those men did to me lives inside of my body. Every step I take I feel them in me. Punishing me. And it will be that way for the rest of my life. (*Salima touches Sophie's face.*)

SALIMA: I'm pregnant.

SOPHIE: What?

SALIMA: I'm pregnant. I can't tell Mama. (*Tears fill her eyes. Sophie hugs Salima.*)

SOPHIE: No. Shh. Shh. Okay. Okay. (*Sophie breaks away from Salima.*)

SALIMA: I can't tell Mama, she'll turn me out. (*Sophie digs in a basket for a book.*) What are you doing?

SOPHIE: Shh. Be quiet. I want to show you something. Look, look. (*Sophie pulls money from between the pages of the book.*)

SALIMA: Sophie?!

SOPHIE: Shhh. This is for us. We won't be here forever. Okay.

SALIMA: Where'd you get . . . the money?

SOPHIE: Don't worry. Mama may be many things, but she don't count so good. And when there's enough we'll get a bus to Bunia. I promise. But you can't say anything, not even to Josephine. Okay?

SALIMA: But if Mama finds out that you're—

SOPHIE: Shhh. She won't. (*Josephine, bedraggled, enters and throws herself on the bed.*)

JOSEPHINE: What you two whispering about?

SALIMA AND SOPHIE: Nothing. (*Sophie hides the nail polish and book beneath the mattress, and places the fashion magazine back on Josephine's bed.*)

JOSEPHINE: God, I'm starving. I thought you were going to save me some fufu.

SOPHIE: I did, I put it on the shelf under the cloth.

SALIMA: I bet that stupid monkey took it again. Pesky creature.

JOSEPHINE: It ain't the monkey, it's Emeline's nasty child. He's a menace. That boy's buttocks would be raw if he were mine. (*Josephine takes off her shirt revealing an enormous disfiguring black scar circumventing her stomach. She tries to hide it. Sophie's eyes are drawn to the scar. To Salima.*) But, if it's you who's been pinching my supper don't think I won't find out. I ain't the only one who's noticed that you getting fat fat off the same food we eating. (*To Sophie.*) What are you looking at? (*A moment.*) No questions. Hang up my shirt! *Sasa!* (*Sophie hangs Josephine's shirt on a nail.*)

SALIMA: Tst.

JOSEPHINE: And what's wrong with you?

SALIMA: Nothing. Tst. (*Josephine suspiciously sniffs the air. Then puts on a traditional colorful wrap. A moment. Salima sits back on the bed. Josephine notices her magazine on the bed.*)

JOSEPHINE: Hey, girl, why is my fashion magazine here? Huh?

SALIMA: I . . . I had a quick look.

JOSEPHINE: What do you want with it? Can you even read?

SALIMA: Oh shut your mouth, I like looking at the photographs.

JOSEPHINE: Oh c'mon, girl, you've seen them a dozen times. It's the same photographs that were there yesterday.

SALIMA: So why do you care if I look at them?

SOPHIE: *Atsha, makelle.* [Stop the noise.] Let her see it, Josephine. Let's not have the same argument.

JOSEPHINE: There.

SALIMA: (*Whispered.*) Bitch.

JOSEPHINE: What?

SALIMA: Thank you.

JOSEPHINE: Yeah, that's what I thought. (*Josephine tosses the magazine at Salima.*) Girl, I really should charge you for all the times your dirty fingers fuss with it. (*Josephine sucks her teeth.*)

SOPHIE: Oh, give us peace, she doesn't feel well.

JOSEPHINE: No? (*Salima moping, thumbs through the magazine doing her best to ignore Josephine.*)

SALIMA: The only reason I don't read is 'cuz my younger sister get school, and I get good husband.

JOSEPHINE: So where is he?! (*Josephine, ignoring her, turns on the portable radio hanging over her bed.*)

ANNOUNCER: (*Voiceover.*) *Nous avons reçu des rapports que les bandits armés de Lendu et des groupes rivaux de Hema combattent pour la commande de la ville—*°

SALIMA: What's he say?

SOPHIE: Lendu and Hema, fighting near Bunia. (*Josephine quickly turns the radio dial. American R&B music plays. She does a few quick suggestive steps, then lights a cigarette.*)

JOSEPHINE: Hey. Hey. Guess what? Guess what? I'm going to Kisangani next month.

SOPHIE: What?

JOSEPHINE: Mr. Harari is going to take me. Watch out, *Chérie*, he's promised to set me up in a high-rise apartment. Don't hate, all of this fineness belongs in the city.

SOPHIE: For true?

JOSEPHINE: What, you think I'm lying?

Nous . . . la ville: We have received reports that armed Lendu bandits and rival groups of Hema are fighting for possession of the city.

Condola Rashad as Sophie, Cherise Boothe as Josephine, and Quincy Tyler Bernstine as Salima in *Ruined*, in 2009.

SOPHIE: No, no that's real cool, Josephine. The big town. Yeah, what's it like? Have you been?

JOSEPHINE: Me? . . . No. No. (*To Salima.*) And I know you haven't.

SALIMA: How do you know? Huh? I was planning to go sometime next year. My husband—

JOSEPHINE: (*Sarcastically.*) What, he was going to sell his yams in the market?

SALIMA: I'll ask you not to mention my family.

JOSEPHINE: And if I do?

SALIMA: I'm asking you kindly this time. (*Josephine recognizes the weight of her words.*)

JOSEPHINE: I'm tired of hearing about your family. (*Josephine blows smoke at Salima.*)

SALIMA: Mention them again, and I swear to God I'll beat your ass.

JOSEPHINE: Yeah?

SALIMA: Yeah. You don't know what the hell you're talking about.

JOSEPHINE: I don't? All right. Digger! I'm stupid! I don't! You are smarter than all of us. Yeah? That's what you think, huh? *Kiwele wele.* [Dummy.] You wait, girl. I'll forgive you, I will, when you say "Josephine you were so so right."

SOPHIE: Just shut up!

JOSEPHINE: Hey, I'm done. (*Josephine blows a kiss, and throws herself across the bed. Salima, enraged, starts for the door.*)

SOPHIE: Salima, Salima.

JOSEPHINE: (*Taunting.*) Salima! (*Josephine falls on the bed laughing.*)

SOPHIE: What's wrong with you? What did Salima do to you? You make me sick. (*Sophie flicks off the radio.*)

JOSEPHINE: Hey, *jolie fille.* (*Josephine makes kissing sounds.*)

SOPHIE: Don't talk to me.

JOSEPHINE: I can't talk to you? Who put you on the top shelf? You flutter about here as if God touched only you. What you seem to forget is that this is a whorehouse, *Chérie.*

SOPHIE: Yeah, but, I'm not a whore.

JOSEPHINE: A mere trick of fate. I'm sorry, but let me say what we all know, you are something worse than a whore. So many men have had you that you're worthless. (*A moment. Sophie, wounded, turns and walks away silently.*)

JOSEPHINE: Am I wrong?

SOPHIE: . . . Yes.

JOSEPHINE: Am I wrong?

SOPHIE: Yes.

JOSEPHINE: My father was chief! (*Sophie heads for the door, Josephine blocks her.*) My father was chief! The most important man in the villages, and when the soldiers raided us, who was kind to me? Huh? Not his second wife. "There she is the chief's daughter!" Or the cowards who pretended not to know me, and did any of them bring a blanket to cover me, did anyone move to help me? NO! So you see, you ain't special! (*Lights fade.*)

Scene 4

Dusk. Generator hums. The bar bustles with activity: miners, prostitutes, and government soldiers. Laughter. Salima and Josephine sit at a table with two government soldiers. Sophie sings.

SOPHIE: (*Sings.*)
A rare bird on a limb
sings a song heard by a few.
A few patient and distant listeners.

Hear, its sweet call,
a sound that haunts the forest
A cry that tells a story,
harmonious, but time forgotten.

To be seen, is to be doomed
It must evade capture,
And yet the bird
Still cries out to be heard.

And yet the bird
Still cries out to be heard.

And yet the bird
Still cries out to be heard.

(*Mama feeds the parrot.*)

MAMA: Hello. Talk to me. You hungry? Yes?

CHRISTIAN: Mama! (*Mama is surprised by Christian, her face lights up.*)

MAMA: Ah, Professor! (*Mama cracks open a couple of sodas. Christian places a box of chocolates and several cartons of cigarettes on the counter. The music stops, and he launches into a poem.*)

CHRISTIAN:
The tidal dance,
a nasty tug of war,
two equally implacable partners
Day fighting night . . .

And so forth and so on.

Forgive me, I bring you an early poem, but I'm afraid it's running away from my memory. I still hope one day you will hear the music and dance with me.

MAMA: (*Dismissive.*) You're a ridiculous man. (*Mama passes a cold soda to Christian. He blows a kiss to Sophie.*)

CHRISTIAN: Lovely, *Chérie.* It's what I've been waiting for.

MAMA: You're the only man I know who doesn't crave a cold beer at the end of a long drive.

CHRISTIAN: Last time I had a drink, I lost several years of my life. (*Mama hands him a list.*) What's this?

MAMA: A list of everything I know you forgot to bring me. (*Christian examines the list.*)

CHRISTIAN: What? When'd you learn to spell so good?

MAMA: Oh, close your mouth. Sophie wrote it down for me. She's a smart girl, been helping me here and there. (*Christian laughs.*)

CHRISTIAN: You see how things work out. And you, you wanted to turn her away—

MAMA: Are you finished? (*The government soldiers break into loud laughter.*) Those soldiers want a full meal, but never want to pay. Tst. (*The government soldiers laugh. Flirtatiously.*) Professor, I looked out for you on Friday. What the hell happened?

CHRISTIAN: I had to deliver supplies to the mission. Have you heard? Pastor Robbin's been missing for a couple days. (*Sophie and a government soldier laugh.*) I told them I'd ask about.

MAMA: The white preacher? I'm not surprised. He's got a big fucking mouth. The mission's better off without him, the only thing that old bastard ever did was pass out flaky aspirin and maybe a round of penicillin if you were dying.

CHRISTIAN: Well, the rumor is the pastor's been treating wounded rebel soldiers.

MAMA: (*Concerned.*) Really?

CHRISTIAN: That's what I'm hearing. Things are getting ugly over that way.

MAMA: Since when?

CHRISTIAN: Last week. The militias are battling for control of the area. It is impossible.

MAMA: What about Yaka-Yaka mine? Has the fighting scared off the miners?

CHRISTIAN: I don't know about the miners, but it's scaring me. (*Salima and miner laugh.*) I was just by Yaka-Yaka. When I was there six months ago, it was a forest filled with noisy birds, now it looks like God spooned out heaping mouthfuls of earth! And every stupid bastard is trying to get a taste of it. It's been ugly, *Chérie*, but never like this. Not here.

MAMA: No more talk. (*She's spooked, but doesn't want to show it. She signals for the musicians to play an upbeat song. ["Rare Bird."] The song plays softly. Josephine leads a government soldier to the back.*) There will always be squabbles, ancient and otherwise. Me, I thank God for deep dirty holes like Yaka-Yaka. In my house I try to keep everyone happy.

CHRISTIAN: Don't fool yourself!

MAMA: Hey, hey Professor, are you worried about me? (*Christian gently takes Mama's hand.*)

CHRISTIAN: Of course, *Chérie*. I am a family man at heart. A lover, baby. We could build a nice business together. I have friends in Kampala, I have friends in Bamako, I even have friends in Paris, the city of love. (*Mama laughs, and withdraws her hand away from Christian. His affection throws her off balance.*)

MAMA: You . . . are . . . a stupid . . . man . . . with a running tongue. And look here, I have my own business, and I'm not leaving it for a jackass who doesn't have enough sense to buy a new suit.

CHRISTIAN: You are too proud and stubborn, you know that. This is a good suit, *très chic*, so who cares if it's old? And . . . don't pretend, *Chérie*, eventually you'll grace me with . . . a dance.

MAMA: Have a cold beer, it'll flush out some of your foolishness.

CHRISTIAN: Ach, ach, woman! Liquor is not a dance partner I choose. (*Christian does a few seductive dance steps. Just then Commander Osembenga, a pompous peacock of a man in dark sunglasses, a gold chain, and a jogging suit, struts into the bar. He wears a pistol in a harness. Christian nods deferentially. He is accompanied by a government soldier in uniform.*) *Monsieur*. (*Osembenga stands erect waiting to be acknowledged. Everyone grows silent.*)

MAMA: (*Flirtatiously.*) Good evening.

OSEMBENGA: It is now. (*He gives the place a once-over.*)

MAMA: Can I get you something?

OSEMBENGA: Bring me a cold Primus. A pack of cigarettes, fresh. (*Mama produces a chair for Osembenga, then she fishes into the cooler for a beer.*)

MAMA: *Monsieur*, I must ask you to leave your bullets at the bar, otherwise you don't come in.

OSEMBENGA: And if I choose not to. (*Mama holds the cold beer in her hand.*)

MAMA: Then you don't get served. I don't want any mischief in here. Is that clear? (*Osembenga is charmed by her tenacity. He laughs with the robust authority of a man in charge.*)

OSEMBENGA: Do you know who I am?

MAMA: I'm afraid you must edify me. And then forgive me, if it makes absolutely no difference. Once you step through my door, then you're in my house. And I make the rules here. (*Osembenga laughs again.*)

OSEMBENGA: All right, Mama. Forgive me. (*Osembenga makes a show of removing the bullets from his gun and placing them on the table.*) And who said I don't respect the rule of law? (*Josephine, laughing, runs in from the back. A drunk government soldier chases her. His pants are unzipped.*)

GOVERNMENT SOLDIER #1: Commander, beg my pardon.

OSEMBENGA: Take it easy, young man. Take it easy. We're all off duty. Clean up. We're in Mama's house. (*Osembenga sits down, and unzips his jacket. Mama opens a pack of cigarettes and passes them to Osembenga.*)

MAMA: *Monsieur*, I don't recall seeing you here before.

OSEMBENGA: No. (*Mama lights Osembenga's cigarette.*)

MAMA: What brings you to *mon hotel*?

OSEMBENGA: Jerome Kisembe, the rebel leader. (*Osembenga studies her face to gauge the response.*) You know him, of course.

MAMA: I know of him. We all know of him. His name is spoken here at least several times a day. We've felt the sting of his reputation.

OSEMBENGA: So, you do know him.

MAMA: No, as I said I know of him. His men control the road east and the forest to the north of here. (*Osembenga turns his attention to everyone. Scrutiny. Suspicion.*)

OSEMBENGA: Is that so?

MAMA: Yes, but you must know that. (*Osembenga speaks to Mama, but he is clearly addressing everyone.*)

OSEMBENGA: This Jerome Kisembe is a dangerous man. You hide him and his band of renegades in your villages. Give them food, and say you're protecting your liberator. What liberator? What will he give the people? That is what I want to know. What has he given you, Mama? Hm? A new roof? Food? Peace?

MAMA: Me, I don't need a man to give me anything.

OSEMBENGA: Make a joke, but Kisembe has one goal and that is to make himself rich on your back, Mama. (*Osembenga grows loud and more forthright as he speaks. The bar grows quiet.*) He will burn your crops, steal your women, and make slaves of your men all in the name of peace and reconciliation. Don't believe him. He, and men like him, these careless militias wage a diabolical campaign. They leave stains everywhere they go. And remember the land he claims as his own, it is a national reserve, it is the people's land, our land. And yet he will tell you the government has taken everything, though we're actually paving the way for democracy.

MAMA: I know that, but the government needs to let him know that. But you, I'm only seeing you for the first time. Kisembe I hear his name every day.

OSEMBENGA: Then hear my name, Commander Prestige de Bembe Osembenga, *Banga Liwa*. [Fear death.] (*A moment. Mama absorbs the news, she seems genuinely humbled. Christian retreats to the bar.*) You will hear my name quite a bit from now on.

MAMA: Commander Osembenga, forgive me for not knowing your name. *Karibu.* [Welcome.] It's a pleasure to have such an important man in our company. Allow me to pour you a glass of our very best whiskey. From the U.S of A.

OSEMBENGA: Thank you. A clean glass.

MAMA: Of course. (*Mama fetches Osembenga a glass of whiskey. She makes a show of wiping out the cloudy glass. She pours him a generous glass of whiskey and places the bottle in front of him. Seductively.*) Karibu! We take good care of our visitors. And we offer very good company. Clean company, not like other places. You are safe here. If you need something, anything, while—

OSEMBENGA: You are a practical woman, I know that you have the sense to keep your doors closed to rebel dogs. Am I right?

MAMA: Of course. (*Osembenga gently takes Mama's hand. She allows the intimacy. Christian looks on. Contempt. Jealousy. A miner enters covered in mud.*) Hey, hey my friend. Wash your hands and feet in the bucket outside! (*The miner, annoyed, exits.*) These fucking miners have no respect for nothing. I have to tell that one every time. (*Christian sits at the bar, fuming. Osembenga notices him. Obsequiously.*) Anything you need.

OSEMBENGA: I will keep that in mind. (*Mama politely pulls her hand away from Osembenga. She beckons to Josephine and Salima, who join Osembenga at the table. The government soldiers groan.*)

MAMA: Ladies.

JOSEPHINE: Commander. (*Josephine places her hand on his knee.*)

MAMA: Excuse me a moment. (*Christian grabs Mama's arm as she passes.*)

CHRISTIAN: (*Whispers.*) Watch that one.

MAMA: What? It's always good to have friends in the government, no? (*Mama clears bottles from the government soldiers' tables. The miner reenters, and sits at the bar.*)

GOVERNMENT SOLDIER #1: Another.

MAMA: Show me your money. (*The government soldier holds up his money.*) Sophie! Sophie! What are you standing around for? I'm losing money as I speak. Quick. Quick. Two beers. (*Sophie cracks open two beers, and carries them over to the government soldiers. The government soldier places his money on the table. Sophie picks it up, and quickly slips it into her shirt. She doesn't realize Mama is watching her. The government soldier grabs her onto his lap. Christian protectively rises. Sophie skillfully*

extracts herself from the government soldier's lap, and exits.)

CHRISTIAN: Are you okay?

SOPHIE: Yes. (*Christian smiles to himself, and lights a cigarette. A drunken government soldier plops down next to Christian.*)

GOVERNMENT SOLDIER #1: *Ça va*, Papa?°

CHRISTIAN: *Bien merci.* (*The government soldier stares down Christian.*)

GOVERNMENT SOLDIER #1: You give me a cigarette, my friend?

CHRISTIAN: (*Nervously.*) Sorry, this is my last one.

GOVERNMENT SOLDIER #1: Yeah? You, buy me cigarette.

CHRISTIAN: What?

GOVERNMENT SOLDIER #1: (*Showing off.*) Buy me cigarette!

CHRISTIAN: Sure. (*Christian reluctantly digs into his pocket, and places money on the counter. Mama places a cigarette on the counter. The government soldier scoops it up triumphantly, and walks away.*) And? *Merci?* (*The government soldier stops short, and menacingly stares down Christian.*)

OSEMBENGA: Soldier, show this good man the bush hasn't robbed you of your manners. (*A moment.*)

GOVERNMENT SOLDIER #1: *Merci.* (*Christian acknowledges Commander.*)

OSEMBENGA: Of course. (*The government soldier, embarrassed, angrily drives the miner out of his bar seat. The miner retreats. Christian thankfully acknowledges Osembenga with a nod. Osembenga smiles, and gestures to Mama.*)

MAMA: Yes, Commander.

OSEMBENGA: (*Whispered.*) Who is he?

MAMA: Passing through.

OSEMBENGA: What's his business?

MAMA: Salesman. He's nobody.

OSEMBENGA: I don't trust him.

MAMA: Does he look dangerous to you?

OSEMBENGA: Everyone looks dangerous to me, until I've shared a drink with them. (*Osembenga sizes up Christian. Deciding.*) Give him a glass of whiskey, and tell him I hope he finds success here. (*Mama pours a glass of whiskey, and walks over to Christian.*)

MAMA: Good news, you've made a friend, the Commander has bought you a drink of whiskey and hopes that you'll find prosperity.

CHRISTIAN: That's very generous, but you know I don't drink. Please, tell him thanks, but no thanks. (*A moment.*)

MAMA: The Commander is buying you a drink. (*Mama places the glass in Christian's hand.*) Raise your glass to him, and smile.

CHRISTIAN: Thank you, but I don't drink.

MAMA: (*Whispered.*) Oh you most certainly do, today. You will drink every last drop of what he offers, and when he buys you another round you'll drink that as well. You will drink until he decides you've had enough.

Ça va, **Papa?**: How is it going, Pop?

(*Christian looks over at the smiling Osembenga. He raises his glass to Osembenga across the room, contemplating the drink for a long hard moment.*)

OSEMBENGA: Drink up! (*The government soldiers encourage Christian.*)

CHRISTIAN: I—

MAMA: Please. (*Whispered.*) He's a very important man. So when he offers you a drink, you drink it.

CHRISTIAN: Please, Mama.

MAMA: He can help us, or he can cause us many problems. It's your decision. Remember, if you don't step on the dog's tail, he won't bite you.

OSEMBENGA: Drink up! (*Nervous, Christian slowly and with difficulty drinks back the liquor, wincing. Osembenga laughs, and signals for Mama to pour him another. She does. The government soldiers cheer Christian on.*) Good. (*Shouts.*) To health and prosperity! (*Christian looks at the second drink. Osembenga encourages him to drink up. Christian nervously knocks back the second shot of whiskey, and winces. Osembenga laughs. The soldiers cheer. Mama pours him another.*)

CHRISTIAN: Don't make—

MAMA: Trust me. (*She places the glass in his hand. Christian walks over to Osembenga's table. We aren't sure whether he's going to throw the drink in Osembenga's face or toast him. He forcefully thrusts his drink into the air.*)

Scene 5

Morning. Bar.
    Sophie reads from the pages of a romance novel. Josephine and Salima sit listening, rapt.

SOPHIE: (*Reading.*) "The others had left the party, they were alone. She was now painfully aware that there was only the kiss left between them. She felt herself stiffen as he leaned into her. The hairs on her forearms stood on end, and the room suddenly grew several degrees warmer."

JOSEPHINE: Oh, kiss her!

SALIMA: Shh!

SOPHIE: "His lips met hers. She could taste him, smell him, and all at once her body was infused with—" (*Mama enters with the lockbox. Sophie protectively slips the book behind her back. Mama grabs it.*)

MAMA: What's this?

SOPHIE: . . . A romance, Uncle Christian bought it.

MAMA: A romance?

SOPHIE: Yes. (*Mama examines the book. The women's eyes plead with her not to take it.*)

MAMA: Josephine, we need water in the back, and Salima, the broom is waiting for you in the yard.

SALIMA: Ah Mama, let her finish the chapter.

MAMA: Are you giving me lip? I didn't think so. Come here. Hurry. (*Salima reluctantly walks over to Mama.*

Mama grabs her wrist and runs her hand over Salima's stomach.) You must be happy here. You're getting fat fat!

SALIMA: I didn't notice.

MAMA: Well, I have. (*Salima, petrified, isn't sure what Mama's going to do. Then.*) You did good last night.

SALIMA: Thank you. (*Mama tosses the book back to Sophie.*)

JOSEPHINE: You don't care for romance, Mama?

MAMA: Me? No, the problem is I already know how it's going to end. There'll be kissing, fucking, a betrayal, and then the woman will foolishly surrender her heart to an undeserving man. Okay. Move. Move. Ach. Ach. Sophie wait. (*Salima grabs the broom and exits.*)

JOSEPHINE: (*Gesturing to Sophie.*) What about her? How come she never has to fetch water?

MAMA: I need Sophie's help.

JOSEPHINE: Tst!

MAMA: You have a problem with that? You count good? (*Josephine stares down Sophie. Sophie isn't having it. Mama laughs. Salima pokes her head in the door.*)

SALIMA: Mama. Someone's coming around the bend.

MAMA: (*Surprised.*) So early?

JOSEPHINE: Tst! Another stupid miner looking to get his cock wet.

SALIMA: No, I think it's Mr. Harari. (*Josephine runs to the door. Salima smiles, jokingly, at Sophie.*)

JOSEPHINE: What?

SALIMA: "Come with me to the city, my darling."

JOSEPHINE: Don't hate!

SOPHIE: "I'm going to buy you a palace in Lebanon, my darling." (*This strikes a nerve. The women laugh.*)

JOSEPHINE: Hey, hey. At least I have somebody, I take care of him good. And he comes back. (*Josephine seductively approaches Sophie. She grabs her close.*) Joke, laugh, *jolie fille*, but we all know a man wants a woman who's complete.

SOPHIE: Okay, stop—

JOSEPHINE: He wants her to open up and allow him to release himself, he wants to pour the whole world into her.

SOPHIE: I said stop!

JOSEPHINE: Can you be that woman?

MAMA: Let her alone. Go get the water!

JOSEPHINE: I was firstborn child! My father was chief!

MAMA: Yeah, and my father was whoever put money in my Mama's pocket! Chief, farmer, who the hell cares? Go! (*A moment. Josephine exits. Salima follows.*) Give Josephine a good smack in the mouth, and she won't bother you no more. (*Mama places the lockbox on the table.*) Here. Count the money from last night. Let me know how we did. (*Sophie opens the lockbox and holds up. Mama skillfully funnels water into the whiskey bottle.*) I don't know all these men are coming from, but I'm happy for it. (*Sophie pulls out the money, a worn ribbon, and then a small stone.*)

SOPHIE: Why do you keep this pebble?

MAMA: That? It doesn't look like anything. Stupid man, give it to me to hold for a one night of company and four beers not even cold enough to quench his thirst. He said he'd be back for it and he'd pay me. It's a rough diamond. It probably took him a half year of sifting through mud to dig it up, and he promised his simple wife a Chinese motor scooter and fabric from Senegal. And here it is, in my hand, some unfortunate woman's dream. (*Mama places the stone in her lockbox.*)

SOPHIE: What will you do with it? (*Mama chuckles to herself.*)

MAMA: Do? Ha! (*Mama knocks back a shot of watered-down whiskey.*) It still tastes like whiskey. I don't know, but as long as they are foolish enough to give it to me, I'll keep accepting it. My mother taught me that you can follow behind everyone and walk in the dust, or you can walk ahead through the unbroken thorny brush. You may get blood on your ankles, but you arrive first and not covered in the residue of others. This land is fertile and blessed in many regards, and the men are not the only ones entitled to its bounty.

SOPHIE: But what if the man comes back for his stone?

MAMA: A lot of people would sell it, run away. But it is my insurance policy, it is what keeps me from becoming like them. There must always be a part of you that this war can't touch. It'll be here, if he comes back. It's a damn shame, but I keep it for that stupid woman. Too many questions, how'd we do?

SOPHIE: Good. If we—

MAMA: We?

SOPHIE: Charged a little more for the beer, a few more francs, by the end of the year you'll have enough to buy a new generator.

MAMA: Yeah? A new generator? Good. You're quick with numbers. You counted everything from last night?

SOPHIE: Yes.

MAMA: Your tips?

SOPHIE: Yes.

MAMA: Yes? (*A moment. Mama grabs Sophie and reaches into her dress, producing a fold of money.*) Is this yours?

SOPHIE: Yes. I was—

MAMA: So tell me what you're planning to do with my money. (*With edge.*) 'Cuz it's my money.

SOPHIE: I—

MAMA: I, I, I . . . what?

SOPHIE: It's not what you think, Mama.

MAMA: "Take her in, give her food." Your uncle begged me. What am I supposed to do? I trust you. Everyone say, she bad luck, but I think this is a smart girl, maybe Mama won't have to do everything by herself. You read books, you speak good like white man—but is this who you want to be?

SOPHIE: I'm sorry, Mama.

MAMA: No. No. I will put you out on your ass. I will let you walk naked down that road, let every scavenger dog have a piece of you, is that what you want? What did you think you were going to do with my money?! (*Mama grabs Sophie and pulls her to the door.*)

SOPHIE: Mama! Please! . . .

MAMA: You want to be out there? Huh? Huh? Then go! Go! (*Sophie struggles, terrified.*) That's what I thought. (*A beat.*) Now tell me, what were you going to do?

SOPHIE: A woman that come in here said she can help me. She said there is an operation for girls.

MAMA: Don't you lie to me.

SOPHIE: Listen, listen, please listen, they can repair the damage. (*A moment. Mama releases Sophie.*)

MAMA: An operation?

SOPHIE: Yes, she give me this pamphlet. Look, look.

MAMA: And it can make it better?

SOPHIE: Yes. (*Mama puts the money into her lockbox.*)

MAMA: Hm. Congratulations! You're the first girl bold enough to steal from me. (*Laughs.*) Where are your books?

SOPHIE: Under my bed.

MAMA: Go bring them to me. I know you better than you think, girl. (*Lights fade.*)

Scene 6

Bar. Morning light pours in. Josephine struggles with a drunk miner. She finally manages to push him out of the bar, then exits into the back. Salima quickly sneaks food from under the counter. She stuffs fufu into her mouth. The bird squawks as if to tell on her.

SALIMA: Shh! Shh! (*Christian, winded and on edge, comes rushing into the bar.*) Professor!

CHRISTIAN: Get Mama! (*Salima exits quickly. Christian paces. Mama enters.*)

MAMA: (*She lights up.*) Professor! (*Beat.*) What, what is it?

CHRISTIAN: The white pastor's dead.

MAMA: What? (*Christian sits, then immediately stands.*)

CHRISTIAN: He was dead for over a week before anyone found his body. He was only a hundred meters from the chapel. The cook said it was Osembenga's soldiers. They accused the pastor of aiding rebels. They cut him up beyond recognition. Cut out his eyes and tongue. (*He's nauseated by the notion.*)

MAMA: The pastor? I'm sorry to hear that. (*Mama pours herself a whiskey.*)

CHRISTIAN: Can I have one of those, please?

MAMA: Are you sure?

CHRISTIAN: Just give it to me, damn it! (*Mama hesitantly pours Christian a drink. She stares at him.*) What? (*He gulps it down.*) The policeman said there were no witnesses. No one saw anything, and so there is nothing he can do. Bury him, he said. Me? I barely know the man, and people who worked with him for years were mute, no one knew anything. He was butchered, and no one knows anything.

MAMA: Take it easy.

CHRISTIAN: These ignorant country boys, who wouldn't be able to tell left from right, they put on a uniform and suddenly they're making decisions for us. *Mambo kama hayo siyawezi, Mama! Yani hata kidogo! Siyawezi kabisa! Kabisa!* [Things like these I can't take, Mama! Not even one bit. I can't, just can't.] Get me another.

MAMA: The Fantas are cold.

CHRISTIAN: I don't want a Fanta. (*Mama goes behind the counter, and reluctantly pours Christian another drink. His hand slightly quivers as he knocks back the liquor.*) They've killed a white man. Do you know what that means? A missionary. They won't think twice about killing us.

MAMA: A dead pastor is just another dead man, and people here see that every day. I can't think about it right now. I have ten girls to feed, and a business to run. (*Mama buries her face in her palms, overwhelmed.*)

CHRISTIAN: We'll go West where there's no trouble. Between the two of us . . . The two of us. We'll open a small place. Serve food, drink, dancing. Come with me, Mama. (*Mama isn't convinced. Christian reaches for the bottle of whiskey, Mama snatches it away. Christian slams the bar and goes to a table. Meanwhile two men, Fortune and Simon, silently enter, fatigued and ragged. They carry beat-up rifles and wear dirty, ill-fitting uniforms. Fortune also carries an iron pot. The men are very nervous, which makes Mama uneasy.*)

MAMA: Yes?

FORTUNE: Is this the place of Mama Nadi?

MAMA: Yes, that is me. What can I do for you?

FORTUNE: We'll have a meal and a beer.

MAMA: Okay, no problem. I have fish and fufu from last night.

FORTUNE: Yeah. Good. Good.

MAMA: It ain't hot.

SIMON: We'll have it. (*Mama eyes the men suspiciously. Christian glares at them.*)

MAMA: Please don't be offended, but I'll need to see your money. (*Fortune removes a pile of worn bills from his pocket. The men move to sit.*) Hey. Hey. Hey. Empty your weapons. (*The men hesitate.*)

SIMON: No, our wea—

MAMA: It's the rule. If you want to be fed. (*The men reluctantly remove their clips from their guns and hand them to Mama.*)

FORTUNE: (*To Christian.*) Good morning.

CHRISTIAN: Good morning.

SIMON: Do you have a place for us to wash up?

FORTUNE: In the back maybe. (*A moment.*)

MAMA: (*Suspicious.*) I can bring you a basin of water. (*They sit at the table. Sophie enters. She's surprised to find Christian and Simon.*)

SOPHIE: Uncle.

CHRISTIAN: *Bonjour, mon amour.*° (*She is leery of the men.*)

SOPHIE: What happened to—

Bonjour, mon amour: Good day, my love.

CHRISTIAN: Shh. I'm okay. (*Sophie notes the caution in his tone.*)

FORTUNE/SIMON: Good morning. How are you? (*The men politely rise.*)

SOPHIE: Good morning. (*The men sit.*)

MAMA: Bring some water for the basin.

FORTUNE: Please. (*Sophie exits with the basin while Mama serves the beer.*) Thank you.

MAMA: You come from the east?

FORTUNE: No.

MAMA: Farmers?

FORTUNE: NO! We're soldiers! We follow Commander Osembenga! (*Sophie returns with the full basin but Christian signals for her to leave. Christian grows increasingly nervous. He watches the men like a hawk.*)

MAMA: Easy. I don't mean to insult you, soldier. But you look like good men. Men who don't follow trouble. (*Fortune seems reluctant to speak.*)

SIMON: We are—

FORTUNE: I'm told there is a woman here named Salima. Is that true?

CHRISTIAN: There— (*Christian starts to speak, Mama cuts him off.*)

MAMA: Why? Who is looking for her?

FORTUNE: Is she here!? I asked you, is she here!?

MAMA: I'd adjust your tone, Mister.

FORTUNE: Please, I'm looking for a woman named Salima.

MAMA: I have to ask inside. (*Christian and Mama exchange a look.*)

FORTUNE: She's from Kaligili. She has a small scar on her right cheek. Just so.

MAMA: A lot of women come and go. I'll ask around. And may I say who's looking for her?

FORTUNE: Fortune, her husband. (*Christian registers this discovery.*)

MAMA: Excuse me. I'll go ask inside. (*Mama exits. Christian disappears into his drink.*)

SIMON: We'll find her, Fortune. C'mon. Drink up. When was your last cold beer?

FORTUNE: I'm not thirsty. (*Simon drinks.*)

SIMON: Ah, that's nice. It's nice, man. (*Fortune isn't interested.*)

FORTUNE: Come on, come on, where is she?

SIMON: Be patient. Man, if she's here we'll find her.

FORTUNE: Why is it taking so long?

SIMON: Take it easy.

FORTUNE: You heard it, the man on the road described Salima. It is her. (*Simon laughs.*) What? (*Fortune paces.*)

SIMON: You say that every time. Maybe it is, maybe it isn't. We've been walking for months, and in every village there is a Salima. You are certain. So please, don't— (*Mama reemerges.*)

MAMA: There is no Salima here.

FORTUNE: (*Shocked.*) What? No! She is here!

MAMA: I'm sorry, you are mistaken. You got bad information.

FORTUNE: Salima! Salima Mukengeshayi!

MAMA: I said she is not here.

FORTUNE: You lying witch! Salima!

MAMA: Call me names, but there's still no Salima here. I think maybe the woman you're looking for is dead.

FORTUNE: She is here! Goddamn you, she is here. (*Fortune flips the table. Mama grabs a machete. Christian brandishes the whiskey bottle like a weapon.*)

MAMA: Please, I said she is not here. And if you insist I will show you how serious I am.

SIMON: We don't want trouble.

MAMA: Now go. Get out! Get the hell out of here.

FORTUNE: Tell Salima, I will be back for her. (*Fortune storms out, Simon follows. The birds raise hell. Christian scolds Mama with his eyes. Blackout.*)

ACT TWO • Scene 1

Fortune in his ill-fitting uniform stands outside the bar, like a centurion guarding the gates.
Josephine teases two drunk government soldiers and a miner. Guitar. Drums. Mama and Sophie sing a dance song. Mr. Harari and Christian watch. Festive.

MAMA: (*Sings.*)
Hey, hey Monsieur.
Come play, Monsieur,
Hey, hey Monsieur.
Come play, Monsieur,
The Congo sky rages electric,
As bullets fly like hell's rain,
Wild flowers wilt, and the forest decays.
But here we're pouring Champagne.

MAMA AND SOPHIE:
'Cuz a warrior knows no peace,
When a hungry lion's awake.
But when that lion's asleep
The warrior is free to play.

SOPHIE:
Drape your weariness on my shoulder,
Sweep travel dust from your heart.
Villagers die as soldiers grow bolder.
We party as the world falls apart.

MAMA AND SOPHIE:
'Cuz a warrior knows no peace,
When a hungry lion's awake.
But when that lion's asleep
The warrior is free to play.

(*The drum beats a furious rhythm. Josephine answers with a dance, which begins playfully, seductively, then slowly becomes increasingly frenzied. She releases her anger, her pain . . . everything. The men cheer her on, a mob growing louder and more demanding. Josephine desperately grabs at the air as if trying to hold on to something. Her dance becomes uglier, more frantic. She abruptly stops, overwhelmed. Sophie goes to her aid.*)

MAMA:
Hey, Monsieur.
Come play, Monsieur,

Hey, Monsieur.
Come play, Monsieur
The door never closes at Mama's place.
The door never closes at Mama's place.

(*Distant gunfire. The bar grows still. A moment.*)

The door never closes at Mama's place.

(*Lights fade.*)

Scene 2

Back room. Josephine is asleep.
Salima quickly pulls down her shirt hiding her pregnant stomach as Mama enters eating a mango.

MAMA: (*To Salima.*) Are you going to hang here in the shadows until forever? I have a thirsty miner with a good day in his pockets.

SALIMA: Sorry, Mama, but—

MAMA: I need one of you to go make him happy, show him his hard work isn't for naught. (*Mama clicks her tongue.*) C'mon. C'mon.

SALIMA: (*Whispered.*) But . . .

MAMA: Josephine!

JOSEPHINE: Ah! Why is it always me? (*Josephine rises, and exits in a huff, as Sophie enters from bathing. Salima nervously looks to the door.*)

SALIMA: Is Fortune still outside?

MAMA: Your husband? Yes. He's still standing there, he couldn't be more quiet than if he were a stake driven into the ground. I don't like quiet men.

SALIMA: He's always been so.

MAMA: Well, I wish he wouldn't be "so" outside of my door. (*Salima involuntarily smiles, then . . .*)

SALIMA: Why won't he go already? I don't want him to see me.

SOPHIE: He's not leaving until he sees you, Salima. (*Sophie gets dressed.*)

MAMA: Ha. What for? So he can turn his lip up at her again.

SOPHIE: No. C'mon, he's been out there for two nights. If he doesn't love you, why would he still be there.

SALIMA: Yeah?

MAMA: Tst! Both of you are so stupid. He'll see you, love will flood into his eyes, he'll tell you everything you want to hear, and then one morning, I know how it happens, he will begin to ask ugly questions, but he won't be able to hear the answers. And no matter what you say, he won't be satisfied. I know. And *Chérie*, don't look away from me, will you be able to tell him the truth? Huh? We know, don't we? The woman he loved is dead.

SOPHIE: That's not true. He—

MAMA: (*To Salima.*) He left her for dead. (*A moment. Mama's words hit home.*) See. This is your home now. Mama takes care of you. (*Mama takes Salima in her arms.*) But if you want to go back out there, go, but they, your village, your people, they won't

Saidah Arrika Ekulona as Mama Nadi and Quincy Tyler Bernstine as Salima in *Ruined*, in 2009.

understand. Oh, they'll say they will, but they won't. Because, you know, underneath everything, they will be thinking, "She's damaged. She's been had by too many men. She let them, those dirty men, touch her. She's a whore." And Salima, are you strong enough to stomach their hate? It will be worse than anything you've felt yet.

SOPHIE: But he—

MAMA: I'm not being cruel, but your simple life, the one you remember, that . . . Yeah the one you're so fond of . . . it's vapor, *Chérie*. It's gone. (*Tears flood Salima's eyes.*) Now, uh-uh, don't cry. We keep our faces pretty. I will send him away. Okay? Okay?

SALIMA: Okay.

MAMA: We'll make him go away. Yeah?

SALIMA: Okay. Good.

SOPHIE: No, Mama, please, let her at least talk to him. He wants to take her home.

MAMA: You read too many of those romance novels where everything is forgiven with a kiss. Enough, my

miner is waiting. So c'mon, one of you! (*Mama suspiciously eyes Salima's belly and exits.*)

SOPHIE: If you don't want to see him, then at least go out there and tell him. He's been sitting outside in the rain for two days, and he's not going to leave.

SALIMA: Let him sit.

SOPHIE: Go, talk to him. Maybe you'll feel differently.

SALIMA: He doesn't know that I'm pregnant. When he sees me, he'll hate me all over again.

SOPHIE: You don't know that. He came all this way. (*A moment.*)

SALIMA: Stupid man. Why did he have to come?

SOPHIE: All you ever talk about is wanting to get away from here. Go with him, Salima. Get the hell out of here! Go!

SALIMA: He called me a filthy dog, and said I tempted them. Why else would it happen? Five months in the bush, passed between the soldiers like a wash rag. Used. I was made poison by their fingers, that is what he said. He had no choice but to turn away from me, because I dishonored him.

SOPHIE: He was hurting. It was sour pride.

SALIMA: Why are you defending him!? Then you go with him!

SOPHIE: I'm not def—

SALIMA: Do you know what I was doing on that morning? I was working in our garden picking the last of the sweet tomatoes. I put Beatrice down in the shade of a frangipani tree, because my back was giving me some trouble. Forgiven? Where was Fortune? He was in town fetching a new iron pot. "Go," I said. "Go, today, man, or you won't have dinner tonight!" I had been after him for a new pot for a month. And finally on that day the damn man had to go and get it. A new pot. The sun was about to crest, but I had to put in another hour before it got too hot. It was such a clear and open sky. This splendid bird, a peacock, had come into the garden to taunt me, and was showing off its feathers. I stooped down and called to the bird. "Wssht, Wssht." And I felt a shadow cut across my back, and when I stood four men were there over me, smiling, wicked schoolboy smiles. "Yes?" I said. And the tall soldier slammed the butt of his gun into my cheek. Just like that. It was so quick, I didn't even know I'd fallen to the ground. Where did they come from? How could I not have heard them?

SOPHIE: You don't have to—

SALIMA: One of the soldiers held me down with his foot. He was so heavy, thick like an ox and his boot was cracked and weathered like it had been left out in the rain for weeks. His boot was pressing my chest and the cracks in the leather had the look of drying sorghum. His foot was so heavy and it was all I could see, as the others . . . "took" me. My baby was crying. She was a good baby. Beatrice never cried, but she was crying, screaming. "Shhh," I said. "Shhh." And right then (*Salima closes her eyes.*) a soldier stomped on her head with his boot. And she was quiet. (*A moment. Salima releases.*) Where was everybody? WHERE WAS EVERYBODY? (*Sophie hugs Salima.*)

SOPHIE: It's okay. Take a breath.

SALIMA: I fought them!

SOPHIE: I know.

SALIMA: I did!

SOPHIE: I know.

SALIMA: But they still took me from my home. They took me through the bush, raiding thieves. Fucking demons! "She is for everyone, soup to be had before dinner," that is what someone said. They tied me to a tree by my foot, and the men came whenever they wanted soup. I make fires, I cook food, I listen to their stupid songs, I carry bullets, I clean wounds, I wash blood from their clothing, and, and, and . . . I lay there as they tore me to pieces, until I was raw . . . five months. Five months. Chained like a goat. These men fighting . . . fighting for our liberation. Still I close my eyes and I see such terrible things. Things, I cannot stand to have in my head. How can men be this way? (*A moment.*) It was such a clear and open sky. So, so beautiful. How could I not hear them coming?

SOPHIE: Those men were on a path and we were there. It happened.

SALIMA: A peacock wandered into my garden, and the tomatoes were ripe beyond belief. Our fields of red sorghum were so perfect, it was going to be a fine season. Fortune thought so too, and we could finally think about planning a trip on the ferry to visit his brother. Oh God please give me back that morning. "Forget the pot, Fortune. Stay, . . . stay," that's what I would tell him. How did I get in the middle of their fight? What did I do, Sophie? I must have done something.

SOPHIE: You were picking sweet tomatoes. That's all. You didn't do anything wrong. (*Sophie kisses Salima on the cheek.*)

SALIMA: It isn't his baby. It's the child of a monster, and there's no telling what it will be. Now, he's willing to forgive me, and is it that simple, Sophie? But what happens when the baby is born, will he be able to forgive the child, will I? And, and . . . and even if I do, I don't think I'll be able to forgive him.

SOPHIE: You can't know that until you speak to him.

SALIMA: I walked into the family compound expecting wide open arms. An embrace. Five months, suffering. I suffered every single second of it. And my family gave me the back of their heads. And he, the man I loved since I was fourteen, chased me away with a green switch. He beat my ankles raw. And I dishonored him? I dishonored him?! Where was he? Buying a pot? He was too proud to bear my shame . . . but not proud enough to protect me from it. Let him sit in the rain.

SOPHIE: Is that really what you want?

SALIMA: Yes.

SOPHIE: He isn't going to leave.

SALIMA: Then I'm sorry for him. (*Lights shift to moonlight.*)

Scene 3

Rain. Moonlight. Outside of the bar.
   Fortune stands in the rain. His posture is erect. Music and laughter pours out of the bar. Mama stands seductively in the doorway.

MAMA: The sky doesn't look like it's gonna let up for a long time. My mama used to say, "Careful of the cold rain it carries more men to their death than a storm of arrows."

FORTUNE: Why won't you let me see her?

MAMA: Young man, the woman you're looking for isn't here. But if you want company I have plenty of that. What do you like? (*Seductively.*) I know the challenges of a soldier's life, I hear stories from men every day. And there's nothing better than a gentle hand to pluck out the thorns, and heal the heart. (*Mama runs her hand up her thigh and laughs. Fortune turns away, disgusted. Mama smiles.*)

FORTUNE: Please, tell my wife I love her.

MAMA: Yeah. Yeah. I've heard it before. You're not the first man to come here for his wife. But soldier, are you sure this is the place you want to be looking for her?

FORTUNE: Here. Give this to her. (*Fortune lifts an iron pot.*)

MAMA: A pot? (*Mama laughs.*)

FORTUNE: Yes, please. Just give it to her.

MAMA: Very charming. A pot. Is this how you intend to woo a lady? (*Fortune shoves it into her hand. A moment. She refuses the pot.*) You're a nice-looking young man. You seem decent. Go from here. Take care of your land and your mother. (*Two tipsy government soldiers tumble out of the bar.*)

GOVERNMENT SOLDIER #2: Just one more time. One. More. Time.

GOVERNMENT SOLDIER #3: Shut up! That girl doesn't want you.

GOVERNMENT SOLDIER #2: Oh yes, she do. She don't know it, but she do. Let me go.

GOVERNMENT SOLDIER #3: I'm not touching you. (*Drunk, Government Soldier #2 crumples to the ground; the other government soldier finds it hysterically funny.*)

MAMA: (*To Fortune.*) Go home. Have I made myself clear? (*Mama goes into the bar. Fortune fumes.*)

FORTUNE: (*To Government Soldier #3.*) Idiot! Pick him up! God is watching you. (*Government Soldier #3 lifts up his friend, as Simon, out of breath, comes running up to Fortune. Josephine seductively fills the doorway.*)

JOSEPHINE: Ay! Ay! Don't leave me so soon. Where are you going?

SIMON: Fortune! Fortune! (*The two government soldiers disappear into the night.*)

JOSEPHINE: Come back! Let me show you something sweet and pretty. Come. (*Josephine laughs.*)

SIMON: Fortune! (*Simon doubles over, out of breath.*) The Commander is gathering everyone. We march out tomorrow morning. The militia is moving on the next village.

FORTUNE: What about Salima? I can't leave her.

SIMON: But we have our orders. We have to go.

JOSEPHINE: (*Seductively.*) Hello, baby. Come say hello to me. (*His face lights up.*)

SIMON: God help me, look at that sweetness. (*Simon licks his lips. Josephine does several down-and-dirty pelvic thrusts. Fortune tries not to smile.*) Quick. Let me hold some money, so I can go inside and talk to this good time girl. C'mon. C'mon . . . C'mon, Fortune. What's your name?

JOSEPHINE: Josephine. Come inside, baby.

FORTUNE: Don't let the witch tempt you.

SIMON: Let's enjoy ourselves, Man, tonight . . . At least let me have one more taste of pleasure. A little taste. Just the tip of my tongue. C'mon, man, let me hold some money. (*Simon laughs. Fortune does not respond. Josephine laughs and disappears inside. Fortune silently prays.*) How long are you gonna do this? Huh? We've been up and down the road. It's time to consider that maybe she's dead.

FORTUNE: Then leave! (*A moment. Simon, frustrated, starts to leave, then.*)

SIMON: This makes no sense. You can't stay here, the rebel militia are moving this way. And if they find you, they'll kill you. We have to go by morning, with or without her.

FORTUNE: Go!

SIMON: Are you sure? You're becoming like Emmanuel Bwiza whose wife drowned in the river when we were children. Remember, the old fool got drunk on bitterness and lost heself. Look here, Fortune, they're making a joke of you. The men are saying "Why won't the man just take another woman." "Why is he chasing a damaged girl?" (*Fortune impulsively grabs Simon around the neck. The friends struggle. Fortune turns Simon loose.*)

FORTUNE: (*Challenges.*) Say it again!

SIMON: It is not me saying it. It is the other men in the brigade.

FORTUNE: Who?

SIMON: If I tell you, are you going to fight all of them?

FORTUNE: Tell me who!

SIMON: Everyone. Every damn one of them. Okay. (*Fortune releases Simon.*) Man, *Mavi Yako!* [Shit!] It's time to forget her. I'm your cousin, and for three months I've been walking with you, right? Got dirty, got bloody with you. But now, I'm begging you, stop looking. It's time.

FORTUNE: No, I've prayed on this.

SIMON: Come out of the rain. We'll go inside and spend the last of our money, and forget her. C'mon, Fortune. Let's get stupid drunk. Huh? Huh? C'mon. (*Simon tries to drag Fortune into the bar. He resists. Fortune, fuming, raises his fist to Simon.*) If you are angry, then be angry at the men who took her. Think about how they did you, they reached right into your pocket and stole from you. I know Salima since we were children. I love her the same as you. She'd want

you to avenge her honor. That is the only way to heal your soul. (*Fortune contemplates his words.*)

FORTUNE: Kill?

SIMON: Yes. (*Fortune laughs ironically.*)

FORTUNE: We are farmers. What are we doing? They tell us shoot and we shoot. But for what are we getting? Salima? A better crop? No, man, we're moving further and further away from home. I want my wife! That's all. I want my family.

SIMON: The Commander gave us orders to kill all deserters.

FORTUNE: Are you going to kill me?

SIMON: I wouldn't have said it a month ago, but I'll say it now. She's gone. (*Simon runs into the darkness. Fortune stands outside of the bar in the pouring rain. Gunfire. A fire fight. The sounds of the forest.*)

Scene 4

The bar.
   Christian, drunk and haggard, is in the middle of an energetic story. He stands at the bar nursing a beer. Mr. Harari, Sophie, and Mama stand around listening with urgency.

CHRISTIAN: (*With urgency.*) No, no, no . . . listen, listen to me, I've just come from there, and it's true. I saw a boy take a machete to a man, sever his neck, a clean blow and lift the head in the air like a trophy. May God be my witness. Men were hollering. "We strong warriors, we taste victory. We will kill!"

MAMA: Shh, keep it down?!

CHRISTIAN: Oh shit, my hand, my hand is still shaking. This . . . this man Osembenga is evil. He plays at democracy. This word we all bandy about. Democracy, and the first opportunity we get, we spit on our neighbors and why? Because he has cattle and I don't. Because he is a fisherman and I am not. But nobody has and nobody will have, except for men like you, Mr. Harari, who have the good sense to come and go, and not give a damn.

MAMA: Oh, hush up.

CHRISTIAN: But we have to pretend that all this ugliness means nothing. We wash the blood off with buckets of frigid water, and whitewash our walls. Our leaders tell us, follow my rules your life will be better, their doctors say take this pill your life will be better, plant these seeds your life will be better, read this book your life will be better, kill your neighbor your life will be better—

MAMA: Stop. Take it outside. You know I don't allow this talk in here. My doors are open to everybody. And that way trouble doesn't settle here.

CHRISTIAN: Well, someone has to say it, otherwise what? We let it go on. Huh?

MAMA: Professor, enough! Stop it now. Leave the philoso-phizing and preaching to the wretched politicians. I mean it! I won't have it here!

CHRISTIAN: One day it will be at your door, Mama.

MAMA: And then I'll shut it. People come here to leave behind whatever mess they've made out there. That includes you, Professor. (*Two rebel soldiers appear from the back in various stages of undress. Josephine and Jerome Kisembe enter from the back. She buttons his shirt. He pushes her away.*) Sophie, turn on the music. (*Sophie turns on the radio. Congolese hip-hop music plays. Christian attempts to disappear behind his drink. Sophie stands behind the bar drying glasses. Mama walks over to greet the men. The parrot squawks.*) Colonel Kisembe, I hope my girls gave you good company.

KISEMBE: Very. It is good to be back, Mama. Where's everyone?

MAMA: You tell me. It's been this way for a week. I haven't seen but a handful of miners. I bake bread and it goes stale.

KISEMBE: It is Commander Osembenga. He is giving us some trouble.

CHRISTIAN: He's a crazy bastard!

KISEMBE: His men set fire to several of our mining vil-lages, now everyone has fled deeper into the bush.

MAMA: I saw smoke over the trees.

REBEL SOLDIER #3: The mission. They're burning everything to save bullets. (*Sophie gasps and covers her mouth.*)

KISEMBE: They took machetes to anything that moves. This is their justice. (*Kisembe sits at the table. Josephine spots Mr. Harari and is torn between where to place her affection.*) Believe me, when we find Osembenga and his collaborators, he will be shown the same mercy he showed our people. It's what they deserve. (*To Christian.*) Am I right? Am I right?

CHRISTIAN: (*Reluctantly.*) You are right. But—

KISEMBE: I'm sorry. It's how it has to be. They have done this to us. I see you agree, Mama.

MAMA: Of course. (*Everyone in the bar grows uneasy, afraid of Kisembe's intense erratic energy. They're barely listening to his rhetoric, instead focused on trying not to set him off. Jerome addresses everyone with growing intensity.*)

KISEMBE: They say we are the renegades. We don't re-spect the rule of law . . . but how else do we protect ourselves against their aggression? Huh? How do we feed our families? Ay? They bring soldiers from Uganda, drive us from our land and make us refu-gees . . . and then turn us into criminals when we pro-test or try to protect ourselves. How can we let the government carve up our most valuable land to serve to companies in China? It's our land. Ask the Mbuti,° they can describe every inch of the forest as if it were their own flesh. Am I telling the truth?

Mbuti: A pygmy group.

MAMA: Here's to the truth! (*Kisembe, pleased with his own words, places a cigarette in his mouth. A young rebel soldier quickly lights it for him. Kisembe stares hard at Christian, who averts his gaze, and nervously raises his glass.*)

CHRISTIAN: The truth! (*Mr. Harari uses the awkward si-lence to interject.*)

MR. HARARI: Has Osembenga shut down production at Yaka-Yaka mine?

KISEMBE: And you are?

MR. HARARI: I'm sorry, Colonel, may I offer you my card? (*Mr. Harari passes Kisembe his card. The rebel leader examines it.*)

KISEMBE: Ha-ra-i?

MR. HARARI: Harari. Yes. Please. Let me buy you a drink. (*Mr. Harari signals Sophie to bring a bottle of whis-key over to Kisembe.*) I handle mostly minerals, some precious stones, but I have contacts for everything. My mobile is always on. (*Sophie pours two glasses.*)

KISEMBE: Thank you. (*Kisembe takes the bottle of whis-key and slips the card into his pocket, by way of dis-missing Mr. Harari, who backs away. Mama wraps her arms around Kisembe's shoulders.*)

MAMA: Come, gentlemen. You will be treated like war-riors, here. (*Kisembe signals to his men. They follow him toward the door.*)

KISEMBE: I wish we could stay all day, but duty calls.

MAMA: No! So soon? (*Mama signals to Josephine, who refuses to budge, instead sits on Mr. Harari's lap. Mr. Harari tenses.*)

MR. HARARI: (*Whispers.*) Go!

JOSEPHINE: No. (*Kisembe and his men collect their guns and leave. A moment. Relief. Christian slaps his thigh and stands up. He does a spot-on imitation of the haughty swagger of the rebel leader.*)

CHRISTIAN: Girl. Quick. Quick. Bring me a beer, so I can wash it down with Osembenga's blood. (*Sophie and Josephine laugh. Mr. Harari is too nervous to enjoy the show.*)

SOPHIE: Yes, Colonel.

CHRISTIAN: (*Imitating Kisembe.*) Woman, are you addressing me as Colonel?

SOPHIE: Yes. Colonel.

CHRISTIAN: Don't you know who I am? I am from here on in, to be known as the Great Commander of All Things Wise and Wonderful, with the Heart of a Hundred Lions in Battle.

SOPHIE: I'm so sorry, Great Commander of All Things Wise and—

CHRISTIAN: Wonderful with the Heart of a Hundred Lions in Battle. Don't you forget that! (*Christian does a play-ful mocking warrior dance. Sophie taps out a rhythm on the counter. The drummer joins in. Mama laughs.*)

MAMA: You are a fool! (*Mama carries empty bottles to the back. Unseen, the formidable Commander Osembenga and a sullen soldier, Laurent, enter. They wear black berets and muddy uniforms. A moment. Christian stops his dance abruptly.*)

OSEMBENGA: Don't stop you. Go on.

CHRISTIAN: Commander Osembenga.

OSEMBENGA: Continue. (*Christian finishes his dance, now drained of its verve and humor. Osembenga smiles, and claps his hands. Christian dances until Osembenga stops clapping, releasing him from the dance. Osembenga acknowledges Mr. Harari with a polite nod. The two soldiers ritualistically empty the bullets from their guns.*) Where is Mama?

SOPHIE: She's in the back. (*Yells.*) Mama! Mama!

OSEMBENGA: (*Suspiciously.*) I saw a truck leaving? Whose was it? (*A moment.*)

CHRISTIAN: (*Lying.*) Uh . . . aid worker.

OSEMBENGA: Oh? Good-looking vehicle. Expensive. Eight cylinders.

CHRISTIAN: Yes.

OSEMBENGA: Sturdy. It looked like it could take the road during rainy season.

CHRISTIAN: Probably. (*Osembenga approves.*)

SOPHIE: Mama!

MAMA: (*Annoyed.*) Why are you calling me?! You know I'm busy. (*Mama stops short when she sees Osembenga. She conjures a warm smile.*) Commander Osembenga. Karibu. (*Nervously.*) We . . . how are you? (*Mama glances at the door.*)

OSEMBENGA: Run ragged, if the truth be told. Two Primus, cold, and a pack of cigarettes. (*Mama directs Sophie to get beers for the men. Osembenga strokes Mama's backside. She playfully swats away his hand.*) You look good today.

MAMA: You should have seen me yesterday.

OSEMBENGA: I wish I had, but I was otherwise engaged.

MAMA: Yeah? We heard you had some trouble. Kisembe.

OSEMBENGA: Is that what is being said? Not trouble! Slight irritation. But you'd be pleased to know, we're close to shutting down Kisembe and his militia. We finally have him on the run. He won't be troubling the people here very much longer.

MAMA: Is that so?

OSEMBENGA: My guess, he's heading east. He'll need to come through here. He can't hide from me. It's the only passable road.

MAMA: I saw smoke over the trees.

OSEMBENGA: That bastard and his cronies attacked the hospital.

MR. HARARI: The hospital? Why?

OSEMBENGA: Because they are imbeciles. I don't know. Looking for medicine. Morphine. Who the hell knows? They rounded up and killed mostly Hema patients. (*To Sophie.*) Tsst. Tsst. You, bring me some groundnuts. (*To Mama.*) It was chaos. When we arrived we found the hospital staff tied by their hands and cut up like meat.

LAURENT: One man's heart was missing. (*Sophie covers her mouth with disgust.*)

MAMA: (*Disgusted.*) What?

OSEMBENGA: And he accuses us of being the barbarians? Don't worry, I've given my soldiers the liberty to control the situation. And control it they will. I am afraid this is what must be done. They force our hand. (*Osembenga takes sadistic delight in this notion. Sophie cringes as she places beer and peanuts on the table for Osembenga. He grabs Sophie's wrist and pulls her toward him. Laughing.*) Come here, you pretty pretty thing. (*Osembenga aggressively grabs Sophie around the buttocks and pulls her onto his lap. Laughing.*) What? You don't like what I'm wearing? (*Sophie tries to gently pry herself loose. Christian, sensing tension, moves toward them. Laurent intervenes.*) You don't like men in uniforms? You don't like men, maybe. Is that it? (*A moment. Sophie struggles to free herself. Mama, sensing the tension.*)

MAMA: Sophie, come here. Let—

OSEMBENGA: (*Smiling, Osembenga pulls Sophie onto his lap.*) Hey. We are talking. We are talking, yeah? (*Osembenga gently runs his hand up her leg.*) Jolie fille! Je connais pas votre nom. [Pretty girl! I do not know your name.] (*Sophie tenses. Osembenga moves his hand up her skirt. Sophie gasps and struggles harder.*)

SOPHIE: (*Hisses.*) Let go of me! (*Sophie pushes away, shocked, from Osembenga. Christian rushes in to protect her, as Osembenga lunges for her. Mama blocks him. Laurent rushes to aid Osembenga.*)

MAMA: Sophie, shush! Enough. Commander, ignore her, there are other girls for you. Come. Come.

OSEMBENGA: Bring this girl around back, my men will teach her a lesson. She needs proper schooling. (*Laurent shoves Christian out of the way and grabs Sophie. This is the first time we've seen Mama scared. Sophie spits on Osembenga's feet.*)

MAMA: Sophie. (*Mama, horrified bends down and wipes the spit from Osembenga's shoes. Osembenga glares at Sophie. She shouts as if possessed.*)

SOPHIE: I am dead.

MAMA: No!

SOPHIE: (*Possessed.*) I am dead! Shetani! [Satan!] Fuck a corpse! What would that make you? (*Osembenga is thrown. Christian quickly pulls Sophie away.*)

OSEMBENGA: I'm trying to bring order here, and this girl spits on my feet. You see, this is what I have to deal with. This is the problem.

MAMA: Gentlemen, Commander, this is not our way . . . we want you to be comfortable and happy here, let me show you the pleasures of Mama Nadi's. (*A moment. A standoff.*)

OSEMBENGA: Then Mama you show me. (*Osembenga checks his anger. He smiles, and blows a kiss at Sophie. He takes Mama's arm, and pulls her to the back with his man. Sophie desperately scrubs her hands in the basin. Mr. Harari pours himself a healthy drink.*)

MR. HARARI: Okay. Let's not overreact. Everything's going to be fine.

Ruined at the Almeida Theatre in London, 2010: from left to right, Steve Toussaint as Osembenga, Jenny Jules as Mama Nadi, Kehinde Fadipe as Josephine, Pippa Bennett-Warner as Sophie, and Joel Kangudi as a soldier.

CHRISTIAN: (*Whispers.*) Sophie, are you crazy? What are you doing? (*Josephine stops Sophie, who is scrubbing her hands raw.*)

JOSEPHINE: Stop it. Stop it. (*Josephine hugs Sophie tightly.*) Shh. Shhh. (*Mama furiously enters. She slaps Sophie across the face.*)

MAMA: (*Enraged.*) Next time I will put you out for the vultures. I don't care if that was the man who slit your mother's throat. Do you understand me? You could have gotten all of us killed. What do you have to say to me?

SOPHIE: . . . Sorry, Mama.

MAMA: You're lucky the Commander is generous. I had to plead with him to give you another chance. Now you go in there and make sure that his cock is clean. Am I making myself clear?

SOPHIE: Please—

MAMA: Now get outta my sight. (*Mama grabs Sophie and thrusts her into the back. Mr. Harari, Christian and Josephine stare at Mama. A moment. Mama goes behind the bar and pours herself a drink.*) What?

CHRISTIAN: Don't make her do that!

MAMA: What if Osembenga had been more than offended? What then? Who would protect my business, if he turned on me? It is but for the grace of God, that he didn't beat her to the ground. And now I have to give away business to keep him and his filthy soldiers happy.

CHRISTIAN: But if—

MAMA: Not a word from you. You have a problem, then leave.

CHRISTIAN: Business. Just then when you said it, it sounded vulgar, polluted.

MAMA: Are you going to lecture me, Professor? Turn your dirty finger away from me. (*Christian is stung by her words.*)

CHRISTIAN: Mama?

MAMA: What, *Chérie*? (*Mama laughs.*)

CHRISTIAN: (*Wounded.*) Forget it! Bring me another beer. There's my money. (*Christian slams the money down on the counter.*) You understand that, don't you? You like that? There's your fucking money. (*Mama slowly picks up the money and puts it in her apron. She ceremoniously cracks open a beer and places it in front of Christian.*)

MAMA: Drink up, you fucking drunk.

CHRISTIAN: What's wrong with you? (*Christian snatches up his beer and retreats into the corner. He drinks it down quickly.*)

MAMA: You men kill me. You come in here, drink your beer, take your pleasure, and then wanna judge the way I run my "business." The front door swings both ways. I don't force anyone's hand. My girls, ask them, Emilene, Mazima, Josephine, ask them, they'd rather be here, any day, than back out there in their villages where they are taken without regard. They're safer with me, than in their own homes, because this country is picked clean, while men, poets like you, drink beer, eat nuts, and look for someplace to disappear. And I am without mercy, is that what you're saying? Because I give them something other than a beggar's cup. (*With ferocity.*) I didn't come to this place as Mama Nadi, I found her the same way miners find their wealth in the muck. I stumbled off of that road without two twigs to start a fire. I turned a basket of sweets and soggy biscuits into a business. I don't give a damn what any of you think. This is my place, Mama Nadi's. (*Christian begins to exit.*) Of course. (*Mama's words stop him. He walks up to Mama.*)

CHRISTIAN:
     The black rope of water
     towing
     a rusted ferry
     fighting the current of time
     an insatiable flow,
     Drifting, without enough kerosene to get
     through the dark nights.
     The destination
     always a port away

MAMA: (*She spits.*) It's wind. If you can't place it on a scale, it's nothing. (*Christian heads for the door.*) You'll be back when you need another beer.

CHRISTIAN: I don't think so. (*Christian absorbs the blow, then storms outside in a huff. Josephine leads Mr. Harari to the back. Mama is left alone onstage to weigh the enormity of what she has done. Lights fade.*)

Scene 5

Outside of the bar.
     Osembenga and Laurent stumble out of Mama Nadi's place, laughing.

OSEMBENGA: I always like the taste of something new.

FORTUNE: Commander! Commander!

OSEMBENGA: Yes?

FORTUNE: I'm sorry to disturb you, but I . . .

OSEMBENGA: Yes?

FORTUNE: I saw Jerome Kisembe.

OSEMBENGA: Who are you?

FORTUNE: I am Fortune Mukengeshayi, I'm with your brigade.

OSEMBENGA: Jerome Kisembe?

FORTUNE: Yes . . . He was inside Mama Nadi's.

OSEMBENGA: Inside here?

FORTUNE: Yes, I saw him. She was hiding him. I heard him say the rebels are heading south along this road. He will join them tomorrow.

OSEMBENGA: Mama Nadi's?! Here?!

FORTUNE: He just drove south in a white truck! Please, she is holding my wife. I just want to get her back.

OSEMBENGA: (*To Laurent.*) Quick, quick. We'll go after him. Call ahead, prepare the brigade to move out. I'll deal with Mama later! (*They exit with haste.*)

Scene 6

The bar. Dawn.
     Morning light pours into the bar. Mr. Harari paces. His traveling bag is perched near the door. Mama enters, catching him off guard.

MAMA: Would you like a drink while you wait? (*Artillery fire, closer than expected.*)

MR. HARARI: Yes. Thank you. A little palm wine. (*Mama settles her nerves, and pours them both a palm wine.*)

MAMA: It's raining hard, you might wanna wait until—

MR. HARARI: I can't. Thank goodness, I found a lift with one of the aid workers. My driver, fucking idiot, took off last night. (*Jokes.*) Apparently he doesn't care for the sound of gunfire.

MAMA: I told you, you didn't pay him enough.

MR. HARARI: This fucking war, *ya Allah ya azim.*° It's everybody's and nobody's.

MAMA: Tst!

MR. HARARI: It keeps fracturing and redefining itself, militias form overnight and suddenly a drunken footsoldier with a tribal vendetta is a rebel leader and in possession of half of the enriched land, but you can't reason with him, because he's only thinking as far as his next drink.

MAMA: Yes, and what is new?

MR. HARARI: The man I shake hands with in the morning is my enemy by sundown, and why? His whims. Because?! His witch doctor says I'm the enemy. I don't know whose hand to grease other than the one directly in front of me. At least I understood Mobutu's° brand of chaos. Now, I'm a relative beginner, I must relearn the terms every few months, and make new friends, but who? It's difficult to say, so I must befriend everybody and nobody. And it's utterly exhausting.

MAMA: Let all the mother-hating soldiers fight it out. 'Cuz in the end do you think that will change anything here?

MR. HARARI: God only knows. The main road is crowded with folks heading east. There is no shame in leaving, Mama. Part of being in business is knowing when to cut your losses and get out.

MAMA: I have the only pool table in fifty kilometers. Where will people drink if anything happens to me?

MR. HARARI: Eventually you must fly your colors. Take a side.

---

ya Allah ya azim: Literally, by Allah the Supreme Glory.
Mobutu: Mobutu Sese Seko (1930–1997), president of the Democratic Republic of the Congo when it was known as Zaire.

MAMA: He pays me in gold, he pays me in Coltan. What is worth more? You tell me. What is their argument? I don't know. Who will win? Who cares? There's an old proverb: "Two hungry birds fight over a kernel, just then a third one swoops down and carries it off. Whoops!"

MR. HARARI: You are the most devilish of optimists. You, I don't worry so much about you. But what about a lovely girl like Sophie? (*His words weigh heavily on Mama. Mr. Harari knocks back his drink, and heads for the door looking out for his ride.*) Until next time! (*Distant gunfire. Mr. Harari anxiously goes to the doorway. Mama goes to the bar; she appears conflicted. An internal battle.*)

MAMA: Ah . . . One thing, Mr. Harari, before you leave can I ask you a favor.

MR. HARARI: Of course. (*Mama opens the lockbox, and carefully lays out the diamond.*)

MAMA: This. (*Mr. Harari's eyes light up.*)

MR. HARARI: Ah. Your insurance policy.

MAMA: (*With irony.*) Yes. My house, my garden to dig in, and a chief's fortune of cows.

MR. HARARI: You are ready to sell?

MAMA: Yes. Take this. (*Hands him the pamphlet.*) It has the name of a man in Bunia, a doctor. He won't trouble you with questions. Use my name.

MR. HARARI: Slow, slow, what do you want me—

MAMA: Just listen. I want you to take her to—

MR. HARARI: (*Confused.*) Josephine? (*Genuinely surprised.*) Be realistic, how would a girl like Josephine survive in the city?

MAMA: No, listen.

MR. HARARI: I can't. She is a country thing, not refined at all.

MAMA: No, listen . . . I'm talking about Sophie. This will raise enough money for an operation, and whatever she needs to get settled.

MR. HARARI: Sophie?

MAMA: Yes.

MR. HARARI: Why? Operation? What?

MAMA: It's a long conversation, and there isn't time.

MR. HARARI: This is more than—

MAMA: Enough for a life. I know.

MR. HARARI: Are you sure? This diamond will fetch a fairly decent price, you can settle over the border in Uganda. Start fresh.

MAMA: I have ten girls here. What will I do with them? Is there enough room for all of us in the car? No. I can't go. Since I was young, people have found reasons to push me out of my home, men have laid claim to my possessions, but I am not running now. This is my place. Mama Nadi's.

MR. HARARI: But I'm not—

MAMA: You do this for me. I don't want the other women to know. So let's do this quickly.

MR. HARARI: And the doctor's name is on the paper. I'm to call when I get there.

MAMA: Yes. And you give Sophie the money. The money for the stone. Understand. Promise me. It's important. All of it.

MR. HARARI: . . . Yes. Are you sure?

MAMA: . . . Yes. (*Mama reluctantly passes the diamond to Mr. Harari.*) Thank you. I'll get her. (*Mama exits. Mr. Harari examines the diamond with absolute delight. An aid worker comes rushing in.*)

AID WORKER: I'm loaded. We have to go now! Now! Three vehicles are coming in fast. We can't be here.

MR. HARARI: But . . . What about—

AID WORKER: (*Panicked.*) Now! I can't wait. C'mon. C'mon. (*Distant gunfire.*)

MR. HARARI: I have to—

AID WORKER: They'll be okay. Us, men, they'll come after us—

MR. HARARI: (*Calls to.*) One minute. Mama! Mama! Come! Mama! I—

AID WORKER: I hafta go! I can't wait. (*The aid worker doesn't have time to listen, he races out. The engine revs.*)

MR. HARARI: Mama! Mama! (*Mr. Harari seems torn, a moment, then he decides. He places the diamond in his pocket and leaves. Silence. Distant gunfire. Mama enters, frantically pulling Sophie.*)

MAMA: When you get there, he has the money to take care of everything. Settle. Make a good life, you hear.

SOPHIE: Why are you doing this for me?

MAMA: Stop, don't ask me stupid questions, just go. Go! (*She tucks a piece of paper into Sophie's hand.*) This is my cousin's wife, all I have is her address. But a motorbike will take you. You say that I am your friend.

SOPHIE: Thank you, Mama, I—

MAMA: No time. You send word through Mr. Harari. Let me know that everything goes well. Okay. (*Sophie hugs Mama. She exits. Mama, elated, goes to pour herself a celebratory drink. She doesn't see Sophie reenter.*)

SOPHIE: He's gone. (*The stage is flooded with intense light. The sound of chaos, shouting, gunfire grows with intensity. Government soldiers pour in. A siege. A white-hot flash. The generator blows. Streams of natural light pour in to the bar. Fortune, Osembenga, Simon, and government soldiers stand over Sophie and Mama.*)

FORTUNE: He was here! I saw him here! (*Osembenga stands over Mama.*)

OSEMBENGA: This soldier said he saw Jerome Kisembe here.

MAMA: This soldier is liar.

FORTUNE: I swear to you! He was here with two men. The same night you were here, Commander!

MAMA: We are friends. Why would I lie to you? This soldier has been menacing us for days. He's crazy. A liar!

FORTUNE: This woman is the devil! She's a witch! She enchanted my wife.

OSEMBENGA: Again. Where is Kisembe?

MAMA: I don't know. Why would I play these games? Don't you think I know better. He is a simple digger. And me, I wouldn't give him what he wants, so he tells tales. Commander, we are friends. You know me. I am with you. Of course. Come, let me get you some whiskey.

OSEMBENGA: *Funga kinua yaké.* [Shut her mouth.] (*Osembenga signals to his soldiers. They ransack the bar. The parrot squawks. Osembenga calmly sits and watches from a chair. He pours himself a whiskey, lights a cigarette as the men turn the place upside down.*)

MAMA: No! (*Fortune takes pleasure in restraining Mama. A soldier drags Josephine from the back. It is chaos. Frightening. Menacing.*)

OSEMBENGA: This can stop. Tell me where, I can find Kisembe.

MAMA: . . . I don't know where he is.

OSEMBENGA: (*Points to Josephine.*) Take that one. (*A soldier grabs Josephine and bends her over the table poised to violate her. The women scream.*)

JOSEPHINE: No! No! Tell him, Mama. He was here.

MAMA: Please! (*Salima enters. A pool of blood forms in the middle of her dress.*)

SALIMA: (*Screams.*) STOP! Stop it!

FORTUNE: Salima!

SALIMA: (*Screams.*) For the love of God, stop this! Haven't you done enough to us? Enough! Enough! (*The soldiers stop abruptly, shocked by Salima's defiant voice.*)

MAMA: What did you do?! (*Fortune violently pushes the soldiers out of the way, and races to Salima.*)

FORTUNE: Salima! Salima!

SALIMA: Fortune. (*Fortune scoops Salima into his arms. Mama breaks away from the soldiers.*)

MAMA: Quick go get some hot water and cloth. Salima look at me. You have to look at me, keep your eyes on me. Don't think of anything else. C'mon look at me. (*Salima smiles triumphantly, she takes Fortune's hand. She turns to Osembenga.*)

SALIMA: (*To soldiers and Osembenga.*) You will not fight your battles on my body anymore. (*Salima collapses to the floor. Fortune cradles Salima in his arms. She dies. Blackout.*)

Scene 7

The sounds of the tropical Ituri rain forest. Bar. The birds quietly chatter.

Sophie methodically sweeps the dirt floor with a thatched broom. Josephine washes the countertop. Mama stands in the doorway anxiously watching the road.

SOPHIE: (*Sings.*)
Have another beer, my friend,
Douse the fire of your fears, my friend.
Get drunk and foolish on the moment,
Brush aside the day's heavy judgment.

(*Excited, Mama spots a passing truck.*)

'Cuz you come here to forget,
You say drink away all regret,
And dance like it's the ending.

MAMA: Dust rising.

JOSEPHINE: (*Eagerly.*) Who is it?

MAMA: (*Excited.*) I don't know. Blue helmets heading north. Hello? Hello? (*Mama seductively waves. Nothing. Disappointed, she retreats to the table.*) Damn them. How the hell are we supposed to do business? They're draining our blood.

JOSEPHINE: Hey Sophie, give me a hand. (*Josephine and Sophie pick up the basin of water and exit. Mama buries her face in her hands. Christian enters. He whistles. Mama looks up, doing her best to contain her excitement. Christian brushes the travel dust from his brand-new brown suit.*)

MAMA: Look who it is. The wind could have brought me a paying customer, but instead I get you.

CHRISTIAN: Lovely. I'm glad to see after all these months you haven't lost any of your wonderful charm. You're looking fine as ever.

MAMA: Yeah? I'm making do with nothing. (*Christian smiles.*) Who'd you bribe to get past the road block?

CHRISTIAN: I have my ways, and as it turns out the officer on duty has a fondness for Nigerian soap operas and Belgian chocolates. (*Mama finally smiles.*) I'm surprised to find you're still here.

MAMA: Were you expecting me to disappear into the forest and live off roots with the Mbuti? I'm staying put. The war's on the back of the golddiggers; you follow them, you follow trouble. What are you wearing?

CHRISTIAN: You like?

MAMA: They didn't have your size?

CHRISTIAN: Very funny. *Chérie*, your eyes tell me everything I need to know.

MAMA: Tst!

CHRISTIAN: What you have something in your teeth?

MAMA: Business must be good. Yeah?

CHRISTIAN: No, but a man's got to have at least one smart change of clothing, even in times like these . . . I heard what happened. (*A moment.*)

MAMA: *C'est la vie.*° Salima was a good girl. (*Sophie enters.*)

SOPHIE: Uncle! (*They exchange a long hug.*)

CHRISTIAN: Sophie, *mon amour.* I have something for you.

SOPHIE: *Un livre?*

CHRISTIAN: . . . Yes.

SOPHIE: *Merci.* (*She rips open the brown paper. She pulls out a handful of magazines and a book. A moment.*)

CHRISTIAN: And this. A letter from your mother. Don't expect too much. (*Sophie, shocked, grabs the letter.*)

SOPHIE: (*Overwhelmed.*) Excuse me.

CHRISTIAN: Go! (*Sophie exits.*)

MAMA: I'm surprised to see you. I thought you were through with me.

CHRISTIAN: I was. I didn't come here to see you.

MAMA: (*Wounded.*) Oh?

CHRISTIAN: And—

MAMA: Yes? (*A moment.*) . . . Hello, yes?

C'est la vie: That's life.

CHRISTIAN: (*Hesitantly, but genuinely.*) I . . . I debated whether even to come, but damn it, I missed you. (*Mama laughs.*) You have nothing to say to me?

MAMA: Do you really want me to respond to your foolishness?

CHRISTIAN: (*Wounded.*) You are a mean-spirited woman. I don't know why I expect the sun to shine where only mold thrives. (*His frankness catches Mama off guard.*)

MAMA: I don't like your tone.

CHRISTIAN: We have unfinished "business"!

MAMA: Look around, there's no business here. There's nothing left. (*Christian looks around. He looks at Mama, shakes his head and smiles.*)

CHRISTIAN: (*Blurts.*) Then Mama, settle down with me.

MAMA: Go home!

CHRISTIAN: What?!

MAMA: You heard me, go the hell home. I don't wanna hear it. I have too much on my mind for this shit.

CHRISTIAN: That's all you have to say. I looked death in the eye on the river road. A boy nearly took out my liver with a bayonet. I'm serious, I drop and kiss the ground that he was a romantic, and spared me when I told him I was man on a mission. (*Mama cracks open a cold beer.*)

MAMA: It's cold, why can't you be happy with that?

CHRISTIAN: Because, it isn't what I want? Bring me a Fanta, please. (*Mama smiles and gets him a Fanta.*)

MAMA: I'll put on some music.

CHRISTIAN: What's the point, you never dance with me. (*Mama laughs.*)

MAMA: Oh shut up, relax, I'll roast some groundnuts. Huh? (*A moment.*)

CHRISTIAN: Why not us?

MAMA: What would we do, Professor? How would it work? The two of us? Imagine. You'd wander. I'd get impatient. I see how men do. We'd argue, fight, and I'd grow resentful. You'd grow jealous. We know this story. It's tiresome.

CHRISTIAN: You know everything, don't you? And if I said, I'd stay, help you run things. Make a legitimate business. A shop. Fix the door. Hang the mirror. Protect you. Make love to you.

MAMA: Do I look like I need protection?

CHRISTIAN: No, but you look like you need someone to make love to you.

MAMA: Do I, now?

CHRISTIAN: Yes. How long has it been, Mama, since you allowed a man to touch you? Huh? A man like me, who isn't looking through you for a way home.

MAMA: Enough. God. You're getting pathetic.

CHRISTIAN: Maybe. But damn it against my better judgement . . . I love you.

MAMA: (*With contempt.*) Love. What's the point in all this shit? Love is too fragile a sentiment for out here. Think about what happens to the things we "love." It isn't worth it. Love. It is a poisonous word. It will cost us more than it returns. Don't you think? It'll be an unnecessary burden for people like us. And it'll eventually strangle us!

CHRISTIAN: Do you hear what you're saying?

MAMA: It's the truth. Deal with it!

CHRISTIAN: Hm . . . Why do I bother. If you can't put it on a scale it is nothing, right?! Pardon me. (*Christian, flustered by her response, walks to the door.*)

MAMA: Where are you going?! (*Mama watches suddenly panicked.*) Hey! You heard me. Don't be a baby. (*Christian stops before exiting.*)

CHRISTIAN: We joke. It's fun. But honestly, I'm worn bare. I've been driving this route a long time and I'm getting to the age where I'd like to sleep in the same bed every night. I need familiar company, food that is predictable, conversation that's too easy. If you don't know what I'm talking about, then I'll go. But, please, I'd like to have the truth . . . why not us? (*A moment. Mama says nothing. Christian starts to leave, but her words catch him—*)

MAMA: (*With surprising vulnerability.*) I'm ruined. (*Louder.*) I'm ruined. (*He absorbs her words.*)

CHRISTIAN: God, I don't know what those men did to you, but I'm sorry for it. I may be an idiot for saying so, but I think we, and I speak as a man, can do better. (*He goes to comfort her, she pulls away until he's forced to hold her in a tight embrace.*)

MAMA: No! Don't touch me! No! (*She struggles to free herself eventually succumbing to his heartfelt embrace. He kisses her. Sophie walks in.*)

SOPHIE: Oh, I'm sorry. (*Sophie smiles to herself. Mama pulls away.*)

MAMA: Why are you standing there looking like a lost elephant?

SOPHIE: Sorry, Mama. (*Sophie slips out.*)

MAMA: Don't think this changes anything.

CHRISTIAN: Wait, there.

MAMA: Where are you going? (*Christian straightens his suit.*)

CHRISTIAN: I swear to you, this is the last time I'll ask. (*Recites.*)

> A branch lists to and fro,
> An answer to the insurgent wind,
> A circle dance, grace nearly broken,
> But it ends peacefully, stillness welcome.

(*He holds his hand out to Mama. A long moment. Finally, she takes his hand and he pulls her into his arms. They begin to dance. At first she's a bit stiff and resistant, but slowly gives in. Guitar music: "Rare Bird." Sophie pulls Josephine into the doorway. They watch the pair dance, incredulously.*)

JOSEPHINE: (*Smiling, whispers.*) Go, Mama.

PARROT: Mama! Primus! Mama! Primus! (*Mama and Christian continue their measured dance. Lights slowly fade.*)

COMMENTARY

RANDY GENER

In Defense of *Ruined:* Five Elements That Shape Lynn Nottage's Masterwork 2010

Randy Gener is a senior editor for *American Theatre* magazine and a winner of the 2010 George Jean Nathan Award for best theatrical criticism in the United States. He has won several other awards for his theater writing and is known as an arts curator and an international cultural advisor. His article on *Ruined* examines five major points of contention that help illuminate the significance of the drama.

1. Salima

Seated in the living room of the brownstone in Brooklyn where she grew up and still lives, surrounded by the African and African-American art her parents collected, Lynn Nottage is talking about *Ruined.* She lays emphasis on a precept that guided her in giving flesh-and-blood character to the women and girls in the Democratic Republic of Congo whose experience of being brutally raped is the play's central subject. In using the true stories of these African women, the playwright drew careful lines between documentary reality and theatrical fiction. "The women told me their stories—they didn't *give* me their stories to tell," she says. "I didn't want to write a verbatim play. It would've been a different relationship if they knew I was going to put their exact words on the stage. They would have censored themselves more, become much more self-conscious. Those are their stories, and they are sacred."

It is early summer of 2005, and Nottage is preparing to embark on a second journey to East Africa in order to collect more narratives of these refugee women, all survivors of war, rape and torture at the hands of armed forces. Supported by a Guggenheim Fellowship, accompanied by her husband, filmmaker Tony Gerber, as well as her father and daughter, she is planning to visit refugee camps in Kenya and Uganda for a little over a month. She'd already been there in the summer of 2004, with director Kate Whoriskey, who would help shape and direct the play, but this time around Nottage wants to stay longer. On the first trip, the two women couldn't enter the Congo, because war was still raging in the Ituri Rainforest area and Congolese refugees kept flowing over the border into Uganda. Having worked as a press officer for Amnesty International, Nottage was aware that virtually none of the media narratives provided by Western reporters had investigated the plight of raped and mutilated women whose numbers have continuously risen since the war's official end in 2003. (That situation has worsened, with recent reports of sexual violation of some men and boys.) "I had no idea what play I would find in that war-torn landscape," Nottage says, "but I traveled to the region because I wanted to paint a three-dimensional portrait of the women caught in the middle of armed conflicts; I wanted to understand who they were, beyond their status as victims."

An air of ease and ebullience naturally surrounds Nottage, and that lightness of spirit feels especially disarming when her anecdotes swerve into dark alleys or when her uneasy or fearful reactions to past experiences surface. She recalls the very first Congolese woman who spoke with her, through tears and in a voice barely above a whisper. Her name was Salima. "She related her story in such graphic detail that I remember wanting to cry out for her to stop, but I knew that she had a need to be heard," Nottage says. "She'd walked miles from her refugee camp to share her story with a willing listener." Salima described being dragged from her home, arrested and wrongfully imprisoned by men seeking to arrest her husband. In prison she was beaten and raped by five soldiers. Eventually she found a way to bribe her way out of jail, only to discover that her husband and two of her four children had been abducted. At the time of the interview, Salima still had not learned her family's whereabouts. Her memories so astonished Nottage that "they entered my body in a totally unexpected way," the writer says.

Back in Brooklyn some three years later, as *Ruined* wended its way to a 2008 premiere at the Goodman Theatre of Chicago and the Manhattan Theatre Club, Nottage would sum up her African sojourns in tender language: "I found my play in the painful narratives of Salima and the other Congolese women, in their gentle cadences and the monumental space between their gasps and sighs. I also found my play in the way they occasionally accessed their smiles, as if glimpsing beyond their wounds into the future."

Ruined, which will be one of the most-produced plays of the 2010–11 season, performed this past summer at the Intiman Theatre of Seattle, where Whoriskey recently became artistic director. The Seattle company, which gathers the leading cast members and design team from her original 2008–09 production, remounts the play through Oct. 17 at the Geffen Playhouse in Los Angeles. The play will eventually be brought to South Africa's Market Theatre, where the story will be shared with Congolese refugees in Johannesburg. Ironically, Nottage has yet to set foot in the Congo.

2. Acknowledging Brecht

Allow me to cut the umbilical cord: An original creation, *Ruined* is not—as a few articles and reviews would have it—an adaptation, a version nor a loose recasting of *Mother Courage and Her Children*, Bertolt Brecht's 1939 classic. "People always enter from the thing that is familiar to them," Nottage conjectures. "I am probably to blame for saying, 'Oh, it was inspired by *Mother Courage*'—which it was. But *Ruined* is a huge departure. I didn't want to use a Western theatrical construct. I felt that was totally the antithesis of what I wanted to do with the play." *Ruined* neither apes the thematic concerns nor mimics the gestural interruptions of action in *Mother Courage*. Although the name of *Ruined*'s embittered Mama Nadi dimly echoes the central character's name in Brecht's intellectual epic, that resemblance is merely a tip of the hat. Mama Nadi's courage or cowardice is not a quagmire *Ruined* asks to confront.

There are many ways to define war, just as there are many ways to violate a woman's body. War is, however, a persistent disease whose symptoms recur and break out, like an opportunistic virus. The Congolese women whom Nottage interviewed did indeed react, in French, with mournful pride upon hearing the words "mother" and "courage" spoken together. But the personal resonances those women felt bear no relation to the great capitulation—the totality and finality of defeat—that is Brecht's great subject. The women of *Ruined* are fictional composites of real survivors of sexual violence. As a tribute to the first woman she interviewed, Nottage named one of these composites Salima. She is a simple and uneducated farmer's wife who spent nearly five months in the bush as the sex slave of rebel soldiers. Her monologue recounting the calamitous but "bright and beautiful" day when the men abducted her from her home, and how she was shunned by her husband, her family and her village, is the heartbreaking crux of Act 2.

Ruined takes place entirely in a combination nightclub and brothel in a small mining town in the Congo. Mama Nadi, the club's haughty owner and madam, need only stay put, since the war in the Congo keeps tossing "girls" at her—women in this context are not only less human than men, they are fundamentally the spoils and the discards of the conflict. Like Mother Courage, Mama Nadi profits by taking no sides in the war but her own, yet her actions do not mirror Brecht's template of a wily woman who loses everything, including her children, in a drawn-out war—unlike Mother Courage, Mama Nadi's maternity is merely figurative. She does use her own idiosyncratic ethics ("I put food in the mouths of eight women," she says) to exploit young women for personal gain and political advantage. And yet, although Mama Nadi states that nothing will ever stand in the way of business, her affection for her girls grows in the play, and her actions toward the most damaged of them, 18-year-old Sophie, the chanteuse who is useless for sex, belie her frequent pronouncements.

"I think my play is written from a woman's point of view, so there's much more compassion, there's much more optimism, than in *Mother Courage*," Nottage contends. "Mama embodies the role of 'mama' in a much more traditional way."

Brecht wrote a socialist epic about business during a time of war, where goodness and virtues are not rewarded. Nottage crafted a hard-hitting humanist exposé about the brutalization of women's bodies during the armed conflicts in the Congo. To expose this brutalization, Nottage strives *not* to distance us from its subject. A seamless synthesis of social-justice politics, edge-of-your-seat suspense and uncommon love story, *Ruined* brings audiences emotionally close to the realities of a region where women have been violated and mutilated with sticks and bayonets by soldiers, where families have driven rape victims from their communities, where sexual torture has resulted in sterility or infection or death.

At the same time, *Ruined* sustains, with as much depth and humor as Nottage could muster, the aspects of dignity, integrity, earthbound simplicity and (most emphatically) the implacability she found during her two trips to East Africa. Except for the tellingly named traveling salesman Christian, nobody is allowed to talk politics in Mama Nadi's place. Soldiers must unload their weapons before being serviced. Mama Nadi constantly insists that her bar be treated as a haven of escape and respite for rough-handed miners and drunken soldiers. There's live music and occasional dancing, signs that life goes on no matter what. "The mess is outside," she contends, but the promise of sex in the brothel can never shut out the nation's civil war, which encroaches closer and closer with the appearance of soldiers from various factions, all thoroughly convinced of their murderous righteousness.

3. Politics

None of *Ruined*'s richly drawn characters is an African-American. Nevertheless, *Ruined* earned the 2009 Pulitzer Prize for Drama, normally reserved for plays by an American author, "preferably original in its source and dealing with American life." Perhaps not coincidentally, *Ruined*'s consecration took place during those same heart-stopping months that Barack Obama, whose immigrant father was Kenyan, became our president. In American culture, when blacks advance beyond historically assigned roles, it is usually a point of intrigue. The victory of an American president with African origins sparked a degree of hope abroad that tribal divisions might someday be recognized (if not crumble) and that improved international diplomacy might combat U.S. aggression.

The surge of Iraq-themed plays and anti-war dramas (both fictional and documentary) during the later George W. Bush years mostly vented feelings of ideological upset and political helplessness. Recent U.S. plays about conflict zones—such as Eve Ensler's *Necessary Targets*, about the Bosnian conflict; J.T. Rogers's *The Overwhelming*, about the Rwandan genocide; and practically every U.S. play about the wars in Iraq and Afghanistan—depend on American characters as narrators and protagonists (often they are journalists) as a means of audience entry. *Ruined* commands our respect, because it takes up the cause of the global voiceless who reside outside U.S. boundaries. Nottage's un-chic dramaturgy of naturalism allows sufficient freedom to stir a far-flung narrative into vibrant life.

Sexual violence against women as a side effect of civil war in Africa is, for most Americans, a remote subject. We might shake our heads in horror or numbly watch at the awful reports. Here is a play about gender inequality that transcends our more common hot-button squabbles about pay differentials and glass ceilings and old-boy networks—the stuff we Westerners get anxious or angry or organize tea-parties about. Here is a drama about a phenomenon (Ensler calls it "femicide") that is so extensive, so common, so entrenched as to seem perpetually old news even while it is happening so hellishly.

This tradition of objectifying women during conflicts, dramatized as far back as the extant Greek plays, has stepped up to new levels: Fighters have systematically used rape and murder in the former Yugoslavia, in Rwanda in the 1990s, and currently in Darfur—with the intent to eliminate ethnic groups and to induce forced displacement. The prevalence of rape and other sexual violations in Eastern Congo has been described as the worst in the world. Women, children and even some men are being attacked by multiple assailants, often in public and in front of their neighbors. Even the United Nations' peacekeeping forces have been accused of rape. Sexual violence wasn't recognized as a war crime until June 2008 when the UN Security Council passed Resolution 1820, a small step toward ending what Jan Egeland, the former humanitarian-affairs chief, described as "one of the biggest conspiracies of silence in history."

Ruined's realist zeal prefers, at first, to woo and coax us, because the acts of sexual violence being committed are ghastly and often indescribable. When Nottage lends the most vulnerable of her characters, Salima, a line that crosses the border from the suggestive to direct protest—"You will not fight your battles on my body anymore"—her outcry is desperate and appropriate and hard-won. It works. In black aesthetics, political struggle *is* cultural struggle. Anything less than a cry of rage would mean the worst sort of betrayal; anything other than those words would render women like Salima once again voiceless and unworthy of tragic ennoblement.

4. Hearts of Coltan

Several days before the 2009 opening of *Ruined*, I interviewed Nottage at a Times Square diner.

RANDY GENER: The second time you went to Africa, you interviewed men. What was that experience like?

LYNN NOTTAGE: It was really fascinating, because we traveled throughout the Great Lakes region. In this case, it wasn't Congolese men I talked to. In the northern part of Uganda, we met quite a few mobilized men from the Lord's Resistance Army in a refugee camp. A lot of them divorced themselves of the responsibility. They said, "We put on this uniform. We were given these orders, but we had to comply. That's not who we really are." I expected them to be contrite, apologetic and ashamed. I was shocked, because they could tell their stories divorced of emotion: "And we cut off their lips, and we. . . ." Also I was shocked that people would be around them listening. I thought, "These are war criminals. Why isn't someone arresting them?" But they were listening and not horrified in the way that I was horrified. We interviewed refugee camp members who had been victims of these LRA soldiers and were coexisting with them. That coexistence really confused me.

RANDY GENER: You told me you were making plans to visit the all-female Kenyan village of Umoja, a sanctuary for women escaping violence, genital mutilation and forced marriages.

LYNN NOTTAGE: When I heard about Umoja, I was fascinated by its founder, Rebecca Lolosoli, this woman who started a village of women who had all been shunned by their families or their husbands or had been forced out of their communities because they had been raped, or they rejected hysterectomy for a host of reasons. She managed to form, in the center of this arid northern region of Kenya, a village that is committed to sustaining and nurturing an all-female community. Mama Nadi is not Rebecca. Rebecca is a far more altruistic and nurturing woman than Mama. But I was interested in the dynamics of that: how this woman chief defied odds in this country defined by men. Rebecca is an extremely articulate and passionate advocate for her community. She's been able to get national attention and raise money. I'm part of this women's group; we managed to raise $1,700 worth of supplies and clothing that was sent to her schoolhouse in Umoja.

RANDY GENER: What does Africa mean to you as a playwright or as a citizen of the world?

LYNN NOTTAGE: I want Americans to understand that they have a very deep investment in what happens in Africa and in the Congo. We're beneficiaries of the abundance of resources that exists there. About 90 percent of coltan, the semi-conductive mineral that's used to fuel cell phones and laptops, comes from the Congo. We're invested in the instability there. As long as they can extract coltan cheaply, we continue to buy our cell phones and laptops for very little. I want Americans to acknowledge that we have a stake in the war that's being fought there.

5. Possibility

Trapped in the fear-ridden illogic and dense moral thickets of a hellish war, Mama Nadi thrives. Hers is an act of defiance waged not just over women's bodies but over the ruined body of the Congo herself. "Love is too fragile a sentiment for out here," says Mama Nadi. But it's love and humanity that moves her to action by the play's end. The persistent criticism of Nottage's achievement is that offering Mama Nadi the possibility for romantic love at the play's climax may be too upbeat or false a conclusion for a play about war, rape and survival. The Pulitzer board noted this emotional appeal, characterizing the play as an "affirmation of life and hope amid hopelessness."

The criticism that *Ruined*, emotionally scorching as it is, lacks the ruthless logic of the Brechtian prototype fails to acknowledge that Nottage is a confident yet individual artist who writes big-hearted political stories about the ways of women in the world. The struggle to move on is *Ruined*'s great subject. Yes (without fully giving away the plot), Christian and Mama Nadi do reach some sort of resolution at the close of *Ruined*, but it is a strange denouement, because real happiness remains the dimmest certainty, given the violent outbreaks and bleak realities of war-torn Congo. Will these two find ultimate peace together? Nowhere does the play hint anything as pat as redemption. Christian's entreaties end on a dance of hesitancy.

Righting gender inequality in the developing world, *Ruined* reminds us, continues to be the moral battle of the 21st century. And yet, like others who have seen and documented Africa's horrors firsthand, Nottage offers up in her implacable play a promise of life: Yes, perhaps, the violence will continue to roll on, but this does not mean there are no Congolese men like Christian who are nurturing and loving and supportive, men who will want to form families and relationships with women like Mama Nadi. Nottage does not demonize all African men. Humanist to the core, she seeks to demonstrate that what's obdurate is, in fact, assailable—that although the consequences of gender inequality in Africa are so vast and the statistics those consequences generate are so huge, theatre is still a place that can enlarge our collective feelings of connection and political agency.

Nottage aspires to do more than document what might seem unbearable, outrageous hardships. For the Congolese women and girls Nottage portrays in *Ruined*, gender inequality is far more elemental. It issues from a belief so fixed as to be unimpeachable: that women are less human than men. If we argue, as some critics have, that the damaged women of the Congo aren't capable of change and healing—if we insist that a playwright cannot, as Nottage hopes, "glimpse beyond the wounds into the future"—might it mean that in some deep place most of us believe that ruined women are less than human, too?

Let us hope not. Yes, it's a vicious world. Attitudes change slowly. Good intentions are not enough. Even so. Small steps taken against tragic problems, actions such as writing a play, are the opposite of a vicious circle. And they can be resounding.

Writing about Drama

The act of writing involves making a commitment to ideas, and that commitment helps clarify your thinking. Writing forces you to examine the details, the elements of a play that might otherwise pass unnoticed, and it helps you develop creative interpretations that enrich your appreciation of the plays you read. Besides deepening your own understanding, your writing can contribute to that of your peers and readers, as the commentaries in this book are meant to do.

Because every reader of plays has a unique experience and background, every reader can contribute something to the experience and awareness of others. You will see things that others do not. You will interpret things in a way that others will not. Naturally, every reader's aim is to respect the text, but it is not reasonable to think that there is only one "correct" way to interpret a text. One of the most interesting aspects of writing about drama is that it is usually preceded by discussion, through which a range of possible interpretations begin to appear. When you start to write, you commit yourself to working with certain ideas, and you deepen your thinking about those ideas as you write.

Writing Criticism about Drama

Ordinarily, when you are asked to write about a play, you are expected to produce a critical and analytical study. A critical essay will go beyond simply describing your subjective experience and include a discussion of what the play achieves and how it does so. If you have a choice, you should choose a play that you admire and enjoy. If you have background material on that play, such as a playbill or a newspaper article, or if you have seen a production, these aids will be especially useful in writing.

For a critical study you will need to go far beyond retelling the events of the play. You may have to describe what you believe happens in a given scene or moment, but simply rewriting the plot of the play in your own words does not constitute an interpretation. A critical reading of a play demands that you isolate evidence and comment on it. For example, you may want to quote passages of dialogue or stage directions to point out an essential idea in the drama, but do so in moderation. A string of quotations linked together with a small amount of your commentary will not suffice. Further, make sure that the quotations you use in fact illustrate your point; explain clearly their importance to your discussion.

Approaches to Criticism

Many critical approaches are available to the reader of drama. One approach is to emphasize the response of audience members or readers, recognizing that the audience brings a great deal to a play even before the action begins. The audience's or reader's previous experience with drama influences expectations about what will happen on stage and about how the central characters will behave. Personal and cultural biases also influence how an audience member reacts to the unfolding drama. Reader response criticism pays close attention to these responses and to what causes them.

Another critical approach is to treat the play as the coherent work of a playwright who intends the audience to perceive certain meanings in the play. This approach assumes that a careful analysis, or close reading, of the play will reveal the author's meanings.

Either approach can lead to engaging essays on drama. In the pages that follow, you will find directions on how to pay attention to your responses as an audience member or reader and advice about how to read a play with close attention to dialogue, images, and patterns of action.

Reader Response Criticism

Response criticism depends on a full experience of the text—a good understanding of its meaning as well as of its conventions of staging and performance.

Your responses to various elements of the drama, whether the characters, the setting, the theme, or the dialogue, may change and grow as you see a play or read it through. You might have a very different reaction to a play during a second reading or viewing of it. Keeping a careful record of your responses as you read is a first step in response criticism.

There is, however, a big difference between recording your responses and examining them. Douglas Atkins of the University of Kansas speaks not only of reader response in criticism but also of reader responsibility, by which he means that readers have the responsibility to respond on more than a superficial level when they read drama. This book helps you reach deeper critical levels because you can read each play in light of the history of drama. This book also gives you important background material and commentary from the playwrights and from professional critics. Reading such criticism helps you understand what the critic's role is and what a critic might say about drama.

Reading drama in a historical perspective is important because it can highlight similarities between plays of different eras. Anyone who has read *Oedipus Rex* and *Antigone* will be better prepared to respond to *Hamlet*. The variety of styles and subject matter of the plays presented in this book gives you the opportunity to read and respond to a broad range of drama. The more plays you read carefully, the better you will become at responding to drama and writing about it.

When you write response criticism, keep these guidelines in mind:

1. As you read, make note of the important effects the text has on you. Annotate in the margins moments that are especially effective. Do you find yourself alarmed? Disturbed? Sympathetic or unsympathetic to a character? Do you sense suspense, or are you confused about what is happening? Do you feel personally involved with the action, or does it seem to have nothing to do with you? Do you find the situation funny? What overall response do you find yourself experiencing?

2. By analyzing the following two elements of your response, establish why the play had the effects you experienced. Do you think it would have those effects on others? Have you observed that it does?

   First, determine what it is about the play that causes you to have the response you do. Is it the structure of the play, the way the characters behave or talk? Is it an unusual use of language, allusions to literature you know (or don't know)? Is the society portrayed especially familiar (or especially unfamiliar) to you? What does the author seem to expect the audience to know before the play begins?

Second, determine what it is about you, the reader, that causes you to respond as you do. Were you prepared for the dramatic conventions of the play, in terms of its genre as tragedy, comedy, or tragicomedy or in terms of its place in the history of drama? How did your preparation affect your response? Did you have difficulty interpreting the language of the play? Are you especially responsive to certain kinds of plays because of familiarity?

3. What do your responses to the play tell you about your own limitations, your own expertise, your own values, and your own attitudes toward social behavior, uses of language, and your sense of what is "normal"? Be sure to be willing to face your limitations as well as your strengths.[1]

Reader response criticism is a flexible and useful way to explore possible interpretations of a text. Everyone is capable of responding to drama, and everyone's response will differ depending on his or her preparation and background.

Close Reading

Analyzing a play by close reading means examining the text in detail, looking for patterns that might not be evident with a less attentive approach to the text. Annotation is the key to close reading, since the critic's job is to keep track of elements in the play that, incidental though they may seem alone, imply a greater significance when seen together.

Close reading implies rereading, because the first time through a text, you do not know just what will be meaningful as the play unfolds, and you will want to read it again to confirm and deepen your impressions. You will usually make only a few discoveries the first time through. However, it is important to annotate the text even the first time you read it.

In annotating a play, try following these guidelines:

1. Underline all the speeches and images you think are important. Look for dialogue that you think reveals the play's themes, the true nature of the characters, and the position of the playwright.
2. Watch for repetition of imagery (such as the garden and weed imagery in *Hamlet*) and keep track of it through annotation. Do the same for repeated ideas in the dialogue and for repeated comments on government or religion or psychology. Such repetitions will reveal the importance of such imagery and ideas to the playwright.
3. Highlight in color (or use some other system) to identify various patterns in the text; then examine each pattern before you begin to plan your essay.

Criticism that uses the techniques of close reading pays very careful attention to the elements of drama—plot, characterization, setting, dialogue (use of

---

[1]Adapted from Kathleen McCormick, "Theory in the Reader: Bleich, Holland, and Beyond," *College English* 47 (1985): 838.

language), movement, and theme—that were discussed in the first part of the book in relation to Lady Gregory's *The Rising of the Moon*. As you read a play, keep track of its chief elements; often, they will give you useful ideas for your paper. You may find it helpful to refer to the earlier discussion of the elements in *The Rising of the Moon* (pp. 23–29), because a short critical essay about that play is presented here (pp. 1078–1079).

Annotating the special use of any of the primary elements will help you decide how important they are and whether a close study of them might contribute to an interesting interpretation of the play. You may not want to discuss all the elements in an essay—or, if you do, only one may be truly dominant—but you should be aware of them in any play you write about.

From Prewriting to Final Draft: A Sample Essay on *The Rising of the Moon*

Most good writing results from good planning. When you write criticism about drama, consider these important stages:

1. When possible, choose a play that you enjoy.
2. Annotate the play very carefully.
3. Spend time prewriting.
4. Write a good first draft, then revise for content, organization, style, and mechanics.

The essay on Lady Gregory's *The Rising of the Moon* later in this section involved several stages of writing. First, the writer read and annotated the play. In the process of doing so, she noticed the unusual stage direction beginning the play, *Moonlight*, and noticed also that when the two policemen leave the Sergeant, they take the lantern, but the Sergeant reminds them that it is very lonely waiting there "with nothing but the moon." Second, the writer used the stage directions regarding moonlight to guide her in several important techniques of prewriting, including brainstorming, clustering, freewriting, drafting a trial thesis, and outlining.

The first technique, brainstorming, involved listing ideas, words, or phrases suggested by reading the play. The idea of moonlight and the moon recurred often. Then the writer practiced clustering: beginning with *moon*, a key term developed from brainstorming, then radiating from it all the associations that naturally suggested themselves. (See the cluster diagram on p. 1077.)

Next the writer chose the term *romance,* which had come to mind during her brainstorming, and performed a freewriting exercise around that term. Freewriting is a technique in which a writer takes four or five minutes to write whatever comes to mind. The technique is intended to be done quickly, so the conscious censor has to be turned off. Anything you write in freewriting may be useful, because you may produce ideas you did not know you had.

The following passage is part of the freewriting the student did using *romance* as a key term. The passage is also an example of "invisible writing": the writing was done on a computer and the student turned off the monitor so that she could not censor or erase what she was writing. She could only go forward, as fast as possible!

The setting of the play is completely romantic. In a lot of ways the play wouldn't work in a different setting. When you think about it the moon in the title is what makes all the action possible. Moon associated with darkness, underworld, world of fairies, so the moon is what makes all the action possible. Moon makes Sergeant look at things differently. The moon is the rebel moon — that's what title means. Rebel moon is rising, always rising. So the world the policeman lives in — sun lights up everything in practical and nonromantic way — is like lantern that second policeman brings to dockside. It shows things in a harsh light. Moon shows things in soft light. Without the moon there would be a different play.

The freewriting gave the writer a new direction — discussing the setting of the play, especially the role of light. Thus, the writer's clustering began with the moon, veered off to the concept of the romantic elements in the play, and then came back to the way the moon and the lantern function in the play. The writer was now ready to work up a trial thesis:

Lady Gregory uses light to create a romantic setting that helps us understand the relationship between the rebel and the Sergeant and the values that they each stand for.

Because a writer drafts a thesis before writing an essay, the thesis is like a trial balloon. It may work or it may not. At this point it gives the writer direction.

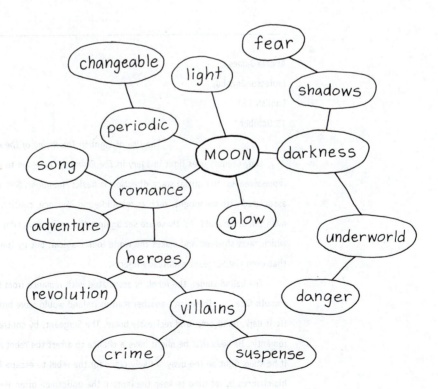

Next, the student outlined her essay. Because she did not know the outcome of the essay yet, her outline was necessarily sketchy:

I. Moonlight is associated with romance and rebellion; harsh light of lantern is associated with repressiveness of police.

    A. Rebel is associated with romance.

    B. Sergeant is associated with practicality and the law.

II. Without the lantern the Sergeant is under the influence of the romantic moon and the rebel.

    A. Sergeant feels resentment about his job.

    B. Rebel sings forbidden song and Sergeant reveals his former sympathies.

    C. Sergeant admits he was romantic when young.

III. Sergeant must choose between moon and lantern.

    A. Sergeant seems ready to arrest rebel.

    B. When police return with lantern the Sergeant sends them away.

    C. Rebel escapes and Sergeant remains in moonlight.

The prewriting strategies of brainstorming, clustering, freewriting, drafting a thesis, and outlining helped the student generate ideas and material for her first draft. After writing this draft, she revised it carefully for organization, clarity, expression, punctuation, and format. What follows is her final draft.

Andrea James

Professor Jacobus

English 233

19 October

The Use of Light in *The Rising of the Moon*

Lady Gregory uses light imagery in *The Rising of the Moon* to contrast rebellion and repressiveness. Her initial stage direction is basic: *Moonlight.* She suggests some of the values associated with moonlight, such as rebellion and romance, caution and secrecy, daring exploits, and even the underworld. All these are set against the policemen, who are governed not by the moon, which casts shadows and makes the world look magical, but by the lantern, which casts a harsh light that even the Sergeant eventually rejects.

The ballad singer, the rebel, is associated with romance from the start: "Dark hair — dark eyes, smooth face. . . . There isn't another man in Ireland would have broken jail the way he did" (26). He is dark, handsome, and recklessly brave. The Sergeant, by contrast, is a practical man, no romantic. He sees that he might have a chance to arrest the rebel and gain the reward for his capture if he stays right on the quay, a likely place for the rebel to escape from. But he unknowingly spoils his chances by refusing to keep the lantern the policemen offer. He tells the policemen, "You can take the lantern. Don't be too long now. It's very lonesome here with nothing but the moon" (26).

What he does not realize is that with the lantern as his guiding light, he will behave like a proper Sergeant. But with the moon to guide him, he will side with the rebel.

It takes only a few minutes for the rebel to show up on the scene. At first, the Sergeant is very tough and abrupt with the rebel, who is disguised as "Jimmy Walsh, a ballad singer." The rebel tells the Sergeant that he is a traveler, that he is from Ennis, and that he has been to Cork. Unlike the Sergeant, who has stayed in one place and is a family man, the ballad singer appears to be a romantic figure, in the sense that he follows his mind to go where he wants to, sings what he wants to, and does what he wants to.

When the ballad singer begins singing, the Sergeant reacts badly, telling the singer, "Stop that noise" (26). Maybe he is envious of the ballad singer's freedom. When the Sergeant tries to make the rebel leave, the rebel instead begins telling stories about the man the Sergeant is looking for. He reminds the Sergeant of deeds done that would frighten anyone. "It was after the time of the attack on the police barrack at Kilmallock. . . . Moonlight . . . just like this" (27). The moonlight of the tale and the moonlight of the setting combine to add mystery and suspense to the situation.

The effect of the rebel's talk — and of the moonlight — is to make the Sergeant feel sorry for himself in a thankless job. "It's little we get but abuse from the people, and no choice but to obey our orders," he says bitterly while sitting on the barrel sharing a pipe with the singer (27). When the rebel sings an illegal song, the Sergeant corrects a few words, revealing his former sympathies with the people. The rebel realizes this, telling the Sergeant, "It was with the people you were, and not with the law you were, when you were a young man" (28). The Sergeant admits that when he was young he too was a romantic, but now that he is older he is practical and law-abiding: "Well, if I was foolish then, that time's gone. . . . I have my duties and I know them" (28).

Pulled by his past and his present, the Sergeant is suddenly forced to choose when the ballad singer's signal to his friend reveals the singer's identity to the Sergeant. He must decide whether his heart is with the world of moonlight or the world of the lantern. He seizes the rebel's hat and wig and seems about to arrest him when the policemen, with their lantern, come back. The Sergeant orders the policemen back to the station, and they offer to leave the lantern with him. But the Sergeant refuses. We know that he will not turn the rebel in. He has chosen the world of moonlight, of the rebel.

Before they leave the policemen try to make the world of the lantern seem the right choice. Policeman B says:

> Well, I thought it might be a comfort to you. I often think when I have it in my hand and can be flashing it about into every dark corner (*doing so*) that it's the same as being beside the fire at home, and the bits of bogwood blazing up now and again. (*Flashes it about, now on the barrel, now on Sergeant.*) (29)

The Sergeant reacts furiously and tells them to get out — "yourselves and your lantern!"

The play ends with the Sergeant giving the hat and wig back to the rebel, obviously having chosen the side of the people. When the rebel leaves, the Sergeant wonders if he himself was crazy for losing his chance at the reward. But as the curtain goes down, the Sergeant is still in the moonlight.

Writing a Review

A review is more than a critical essay because it covers an actual performance of a play. As a reviewer, you write after digesting an evening's entertainment and observing how actors and a director present a production for your enjoyment. Your responsibility is to respond both to the production and to the text of the play; thus, you will discuss the quality of the acting, the effectiveness of the setting, the interpretation of the text, and the power of the direction.

What Is the Purpose of a Review?

Reviews of plays ordinarily appear in daily newspapers or in weekly or semi-weekly publications timely enough to help a prospective playgoer decide whether to see the play. Considering the cost of tickets in contemporary theater, the best reviewers perform a valuable service by letting readers know what they believe is most worth seeing. Regular reviewers, such as Ben Brantley and Charles Isherwood in the *New York Times,* Daniel Mendelsohn of *The New York Review of Books,* and Michael Billington of *The Guardian,* develop their own followings, because playgoers know from experience whether they can rely on these reviewers' judgments.

Another purpose of theater reviews is to set a standard to which producers can aspire. Criticism can promote excellence because experienced and demanding critics force producers of drama to maintain high standards. The power of theater critics in major cities is legendary: more than a few plays have closed prematurely after savage reviews in London, New York, Chicago, and elsewhere. Knowing that they will undergo scrutiny by knowledgeable reviewers convinces writers, directors, actors, and producers to do their best.

What You Need to Write a Good Review

The best reviewers bring three qualifications to their work: experience in the theater, a knowledge of theatrical history, and a sensitivity to dramatic production. Some reviewers have had experience onstage as actors or as production assistants. They are familiar with the process of preparing a play for the stage and in some cases may actually have written for the stage. Other reviewers who have not had such experience have, instead, spent hours in the theater watching plays; their rich experience of seeing a variety of plays enables them to make useful comparisons.

Knowledge of the basics of theater history is indispensable to being a good reviewer. New plays that borrow from the traditions of the Greek chorus or plays that emulate medieval pageants or nineteenth-century melodrama need reviewers who understand their sources. Playwright Suzan-Lori Parks, for example, admits that her work is influenced by that of Bertolt Brecht and Samuel Beckett. She expects her audience to recognize some of that influence, but she knows that her reviewers will spot most or all of it. This book is structured around the history of drama so that readers will better understand drama's roots and evolution. In that sense this book can help a theater enthusiast become a competent reviewer.

Besides knowing the history of drama, a reviewer must also be extremely well read. Some reviewers, for example, have not had the opportunity to see productions of all of Shakespeare's plays, but a good reviewer will have read most of them and can refer to them as necessary. The same is true of the plays of Bernard Shaw, many of which have not been produced in over a dozen years.

In the case of contemporary playwrights, it is common for a reviewer to refer to the playwright's earlier work to put the current production in a useful context. A knowledgeable reviewer knows not only the history of theater but also the work of other playwrights that may be relevant to the play under review.

Most students of theater have enough sensitivity to dramatic productions to write adequate reviews. The most sensitive reviewers will pay close attention to the suitability of the acting and often consider the acting to be of greatest importance, especially if the play is well known. Most contemporary reviews single out actors and comment on their performance in some detail. Reviewers usually know the work of the busiest actors, and in some cases they will make comparisons with an actor's performance in earlier roles. They will also indicate whether the actor has developed further as an artist or has walked mechanically through the part. The reviewer's sensitivity to individual actors is developed in part from past experience, providing a benchmark against which to measure a performance.

No reviewer is going to review *Oedipus Rex* with an eye toward telling us whether it is a good or a bad play; the history of criticism has already done that. The reviewer of *Oedipus Rex,* like the reviewer of any of Sophocles' great plays, will aim to tell us about the quality of the acting or the effectiveness of the setting. Being sensitive to the effective use of lighting, props, costumes, and stage design is essential for any reviewer, but it is even more crucial for a reviewer of classic theater.

Preparing to Review a Classic Play

If you have the opportunity to review a play that is well established—like most of the plays in this collection—you need special preparation. Before seeing the play, besides having read the text, you need to imagine how the play *should* be staged. Once you understand what the play is about and what its implications may be, you need to consult reviews or descriptions of earlier productions. You may do so by referring to the index of any major newspaper or to *New York Theatre Critics' Reviews,* which includes multiple reviews of important productions over the years. The point is to come to the experience of the drama as a fully informed viewer. Knowing how the play has been staged in the past will help you see the innovations and special interpretation of the current production.

Preparing to Review a New Play

Sometime you may have the opportunity to review a new play—one that playgoers, including reviewers, have not had the chance to read in advance. In that case, you need to pay special attention to the dialogue, taking notes when necessary, to follow the development of the drama's ideas and issues. You are still responsible for commenting on the acting and the production, but in the case of a new play, your main responsibility shifts to preparing the prospective audience to understand and respond to the play. They will need to know what the play is about, how it presents the primary issues in the drama, and what is at stake. You may need to refer to the plot, but always do so with an eye toward not giving too much away, especially if the play involves suspense. Ask yourself how much the reader needs to know to decide whether to see the play.

Reviewers of new plays usually include commentary on a new or relatively unknown playwright. The most important information here would be about any previous work of the playwright. The best reviewers will have seen that work and will be prepared to discuss how it relates to the new play at hand. Reviewers of August Wilson, for example, spent time in the late 1980s establishing his credentials as a playwright. Later, when a new play of his was produced, reviewers would usually attempt to describe how the new play fit into the growing body of his work. Because Wilson was in the process of writing a series of plays on African American life, centering on specific decades of the twentieth century, reviewers did readers a service by explaining how each new play fit into Wilson's overall scheme.

Guidelines for Writing Reviews

Good reviewers approach the job of writing reviews from many different angles. Some of the reviews in this book begin with a generalization on a play's theme. Some begin with a personal observation about the play at hand or a personal experience in the theater. Others begin with a note on the background of the playwright, the actors, or the director. There are many ways to write a review. The following suggestions can help you structure your reaction.

1. If you are reviewing a professionally produced play, request a press kit from the theater. These kits usually include a great deal of information that could interest readers.

2. In your review, provide any necessary background on a playwright who is contemporary or relatively unknown. The press kit should contain some information; if not, the program may do so. Check with the press representative or with the box office manager to see whether the playwright is in the house. If so, before the play begins, you may be able to arrange an interview.

3. Before attending a play, be sure to set up a checklist based on this one so that you record the important information:

Author and title of play	Description of the action
What the play is about	Director of the play
The play's main issues	Theater and dates of
The actors, with comments	performance
Your final recommendation	The setting and its
to your readers	effectiveness

Take the list to the theater with you and keep your notes on it. When you begin writing your review, look at the reviews in this book or in your local newspaper. Your review should aim at providing a valuable service for your readers by telling them whether or not you recommend that they attend the performance.

Sample Review

Mel Gussow, in reviewing the Yale Repertory Theatre's production of Molière's *Tartuffe* in 1991 (page 341), focuses not only on the set design but also on the actor playing the title role. Gussow begins by complimenting the director, Walton Jones, by name and then goes on to call attention to the "large mahoganylike doors" that expedite the quick entrances and exits that keep the action of the play moving. Gussow is interested in them because they function in special ways that make them uniquely effective for this play. The man responsible for the "jack-in-the-box" set, Kevin Rupnick, is given credit as well.

In terms of the rhythm of the play, Gussow reminds readers more than once that there is a "breathlessness" to the production because of the speed with which things happen. Directors of a classic play like *Tartuffe* can have a tendency to be so respectful of the text that they let the play drag—but not the director of this production. Gussow does imply a negative criticism in calling the production a "tricked-up approach to Molière," but he quickly explains that it "is enlivened by several performances" and then credits the star playing Tartuffe, Austin Pendleton.

Several paragraphs of the review are about Pendleton's creditable performance. Pendleton is a short man, and Gussow seems amused when he tells us that Pendleton used his stature to good effect, "playing one scene on his knees behind a portable pulpit that is the height of a go-cart." When Gussow tells us that Pendleton's success lies in playing the part as a fanatic, he also tells us that this must be "regarded as a Pendleton specialty" and then cites Pendleton's performance in another drama. A good reviewer will have seen many plays and, when appropriate, call attention to the other achievements of a major figure like Pendleton, which we can compare to the current performance.

Again, because *Tartuffe* is so well known among theatergoers, Gussow tells us almost nothing about what happens. If this play were being performed for the first time, however, he would need to tell us something of what the play is about, describing the action without giving away the entire plot.

Glossary of Dramatic Terms

Act. A major division in the action of a play. Most plays from the Elizabethan era until the nineteenth century were divided into five acts by the playwrights or by later editors. In the nineteenth century many writers began to write four-act plays. Today one-, two-, and three-act plays are most common.

Action. What happens in a play; the events that make up the **plot**.

Agon. The Greek word for "contest." In Greek tragedy the *agon* was often a formal debate in which the **chorus** divided and took the sides of the disputants.

Alienation effect. In his epic drama, Bertolt Brecht (1898–1956) tried to make the familiar unfamiliar (or to alienate it) to show the audience that familiar, seemingly "natural," and therefore unalterable social conditions could be changed. Different devices achieved the alienation effect by calling attention to the theater as theater—stage lights brought in front of the curtain, musicians put onstage instead of hidden in an orchestra pit, placards indicating scene changes and interrupting the linear flow of the action, actors distancing themselves from their characters to invite the audience to analyze and criticize the characters instead of empathizing with them. These alienating devices prevented the audience from losing itself in the illusion of reality. (See **epic drama**.)

Allegory. A literary work that is coherent on at least two levels simultaneously: a literal level consisting of recognizable characters and events and an allegorical level on which the literal characters and events represent moral, political, religious, or other ideas and meanings.

Anagnorisis. Greek term for a character's discovery or recognition of someone or something previously unknown. *Anagnorisis* often paves the way for a reversal of fortune (see *peripeteia*). An example in *Oedipus Rex* is Oedipus's discovery of his true identity.

Antagonist. A character or force in conflict with the **protagonist**. The antagonist is often another character but may also be an intangible force such as nature or society. The dramatic conflict can even take the form of a protagonist's struggle against his or her own character.

Anticlimax. See **plot**.

Antimasque. A parody of the court **masque** developed by Ben Jonson, featuring broad humor, grotesque characters, and ludicrous actions.

Antistrophe. The second of the three parts of the verse ode sung by the **chorus** in Greek drama. While singing the **strophe**, the chorus moved in a dance rhythm from right to left; during the **antistrophe**, it moved from left to right back to its original position. The third part, the **epode**, was sung standing still.

Apron stage. The apron is the part of the stage extending in front of the **proscenium arch**. A stage is an apron stage if all or most of it is in front of any framing structures. The Elizabethan stage, which the audience surrounded on three sides, is an example of an apron stage.

Arena theater. A theater in which the stage is surrounded on all sides by the audience and actors make exits and entrances through the aisles. Used for **theater in the round**.

Arras. A curtain hung at the back of an Elizabethan playhouse to partition off an alcove or booth. The curtain could be pulled back to reveal a room or a cave.

Aside. A short speech made by a character to the audience which, by **convention**, the other characters onstage cannot hear.

Atellan farce. Broad and sometimes coarse popular humor indigenous to the town of Atella in Italy. By the third century BCE, the Romans had imported the Atellan farce, which they continued to modify and develop.

Blank verse. An unrhymed verse form often used in writing drama. Blank verse is composed of ten-syllable lines accented on the second, fourth, sixth, eighth, and tenth syllables (**iambic pentameter**).

Bombast. A loud, pompous speech whose inflated diction is disproportionate to the subject matter it expresses.

Bourgeois drama. Drama that treats middle-class subject matter or characters rather than the lives of the rich and powerful.

Braggart soldier. A **stock character** in comedy who is usually cowardly, parasitical, pompous, and easily victimized by practical jokers. Sir John Falstaff in Shakespeare's *Henry IV* (parts 1, 2) is an example.

Burla (plural, *burle*). Jests or practical jokes that were part of the comic **stage business** in the **commedia dell'arte**.

Buskin. A thick-soled boot possibly worn by Greek tragedians to increase their stature. Later called a *cothurnus* or *kothornos*.

Catastrophe. See **plot.**

Catharsis. The feeling of emotional purgation or release that, according to Aristotle, an audience should feel after watching a tragedy.

Ceremonial drama. Egyptian passion play about the god Osiris.

Character. Any person appearing in a drama or narrative. (Also see **stock character.**)

Chiton. Greek tunic worn by Roman actors.

Choregos. An influential citizen chosen to pay for the training and costuming of the **chorus** in Greek drama competitions. He probably also paid for the musicians and met other financial demands of production not paid for by the state.

Chorus. A masked group that sang and danced in Greek tragedy. The chorus usually chanted in unison, offering advice and commentary on the action but rarely participating. (See **strophe, antistrophe,** and **epode.**)

City Dionysia. The most important of the four Athenian festivals in honor of **Dionysus.** This spring festival was the occasion for the first tragedy competitions; comedy was associated with the winter festival, the Lenaea. Also called Great or Greater Dionysia.

Claptrap. A dramatic device designed to get the audience clapping; it is not usually connected to the core of the drama.

Climax. See **plot.**

Closet drama. A drama, usually in verse, meant for reading rather than for performance. Hrosvitha's *Dulcitius,* Percy Bysshe Shelley's *Prometheus Unbound,* and John Milton's *Samson Agonistes* are examples.

Comedy. A type of drama intended to interest and amuse rather than to concern the audience deeply. Although characters experience various discomfitures, the audience feels confident that they will overcome their ill fortune and find happiness at the end.

Comedy of humors. Form of comedy developed by Ben Jonson in the seventeenth century in which characters' actions are determined by the preponderance in their systems of one of the four bodily fluids, or humors—blood, phlegm, choler (yellow bile), and melancholy (black bile). Characters' dispositions are exaggerated and stereotyped; common types are the melancholic and the belligerent bully.

Comedy of manners. Realistic, often satiric comedy concerned with the manners and conventions of high society. Usually refers to the Restoration comedies of late-seventeenth-century England, which feature witty dialogue, or **repartee.** An example is William Congreve's *The Way of the World.*

Drawing room comedy. A type of comedy of manners concerned with life in polite society. The action generally takes place in a drawing room.

Farce. A short dramatic work that depends for its comic effect on exaggerated improbable situations, incongruities, coarse wit, and horseplay.

High comedy. Comedy that appeals to the intellect, often focusing on the pretensions, foolishness, and incongruity of human behavior. Comedy of manners, with its witty dialogue, is a type of high comedy.

Low comedy. Comedy that lacks the intellectual appeal of high comedy, depending instead on boisterous buffoonery, "gags," and jokes for its comic effect.

Middle Comedy. A transitional style of Greek comedy that extended from 400 to about 320 BCE. It marks a change, especially in language, which grew less formal and closer to the way people spoke. Little evidence of Middle Comedy exists, but from surviving statuettes we can surmise that costumes on stage resembled what Athenians actually wore on the street.

New Comedy. Emerging between the fourth and third centuries BCE in ancient Greece, the style that replaced the farcical Old Comedy. New Comedy, usually associated with Menander, is witty and intellectually engaging; it is often thought of as the first high comedy.

Old Comedy. Greek comedy of the fifth century BCE that uses bawdy farce to attack social, religious, and political institutions satirically. Old Comedy is usually associated with Aristophanes.

Sentimental comedy. Comedy populated by stereotypical virtuous **protagonists** and villainous **antagonists** that resolves the domestic trials of middle-class people in a pat, happy ending.

Slapstick. Low comedy that involves little plot or character development but rather consists of physical horseplay or practical jokes.

Comic relief. The use of humorous characters, speeches, or scenes in an otherwise serious or tragic drama.

Commedia dell'arte. Italian low comedy dating from around the mid-sixteenth century in which professional actors playing **stock characters** improvised dialogue to fit a given scenario.

Complication. See **plot.**

Conflict. See **plot**.

Convention. Any feature of a literary work that has become standardized over time, such as the **aside** or the **stock character**. Often refers to an unrealistic device (such as Danish characters speaking English in *Hamlet*) that the audience tacitly agrees to accept.

Coryphaeus. See *koryphaios*.

Cosmic irony. See **irony**.

Cothurnus. See **buskin**.

Craft play. Medieval sacred drama based on Old and New Testament stories. Craft plays were performed outside the church by members of a particular trade guild, and their subject matter often reflected the guild's trade. The fishermen's guild, for example, might present the story of Noah and the flood.

Crisis. Another term for *climax*. See **plot**.

Cycle. A group of medieval **mystery plays** written in the vernacular (the language in common use rather than Latin) for performance outside the church. Cycles, each of which treated biblical stories from creation through the last judgment, are named after the town in which they were produced. Most extant mystery plays are from the York, Chester, Wakefield (Towneley), and N-Town cycles.

Cyclorama. A large painted backdrop, usually curved and covering all of the stage with a complex scene against which the action takes place.

Dadaism. A post–World War I art movement that was in part anti-art; a revolt against pretension in the arts.

Decorum. A quality that exists when the style of a work is appropriate to the speaker, the occasion, and the subject matter. Kings should speak in a "high style" and clowns in a "low style," according to many Renaissance authors. Decorum was a guiding critical principle in **neoclassicism**.

Defamiliarization effect (or *Verfremdungseffekt*). See **alienation effect**.

Denouement. See **plot**.

Deus ex machina. Latin for "a god out of a machine." In Greek drama, a mechanical device called a *mekane* could lower "gods" onto the stage to solve the seemingly unsolvable problems of mortal characters. Also used to describe a playwright's use of a forced or improbable solution to plot complications—for example, the discovery of a lost will or an inheritance that will pay off the evil landlord.

Dialogue. Spoken interchange or conversation between two or more characters. Also see **soliloquy**.

Diction. A playwright's choice of words or the match between language and subject matter. Also refers collectively to an actor's phrasing, enunciation, and manner of speaking.

Dionysus. Greek nature god of wine, mystic revelry, and irrational impulse. Greek tragedy probably evolved from dramatized ritual choral celebrations in honor of Dionysus. (Also see **City Dionysia**.)

Director. The person responsible for a play's interpretation and staging and for the guidance of the actors.

Disguising. Medieval entertainment featuring a procession of masked actors performing short plays in pantomime; probably the origin of the court **masque**.

Dithyramb. Ancient Greek choral hymn sung and danced to honor **Dionysus**. Originally divided into an improvised story sung by a choral leader and a traditional refrain sung by the **chorus**, it is believed by some to be the origin of Greek tragedy.

Domestic tragedy. A serious play usually focusing on a family and depicting the fall of a middle-class **protagonist** rather than of a powerful or noble hero. An example is Arthur Miller's *Death of a Salesman*, which traces the emotional collapse and eventual suicide of Willy Loman, a traveling salesman. Also called *bourgeois tragedy*.

Double plot. See **plot**.

Drama. A play written in prose or verse that tells a story through **dialogue** and actions performed by actors impersonating the characters of the story.

Dramatic illusion. The illusion of reality created by drama and accepted by the audience for the duration of the play.

Dramatic irony. See **irony**.

Dramatist. The author of a play; playwright.

Dramaturge. One who represents the playwright and guides the production. In some cases, the dramaturge researches different aspects of a production or earlier productions of a play.

Dramaturgy. The art of writing plays.

Drawing room comedy. See **comedy**.

Empathy. The sense of feeling *with* a character. (Distinct from sympathy, which is feeling *for* a character.)

Ensemble acting. Performance by a group of actors, usually members of a **repertory** company, in which the integrated acting of all members is emphasized over individual star performances. The famous nineteenth-century director Constantin Stanislavski promoted this type of acting in the Moscow Art Theatre.

Environmental theater. A term used by Richard Schechner, director of the Performance Group in the late 1960s and early 1970s, to describe his work and the work of other theater companies, including the Bread and Puppet Theatre, Open Theatre, and Living Theatre. He also used the term to describe the indigenous theater of Africa and Asia. Environmental theater occupies the whole of a performance space; it is not confined to a stage separated from the audience. Action can take place in and around the audience, and audience members are often encouraged to participate in the theater event.

Epic theater. A type of theater first associated with German director Erwin Piscator (1893–1966). Bertolt Brecht (1898–1956) used the term to distinguish his own theater from the "dramatic" theater that created the illusion of reality and invited the audience to identify and empathize with the characters. Brecht criticized the dramatic theater for encouraging the audience to believe that social conditions were "natural" and therefore unalterable. According to Brecht, the theater should show human beings as dependent on certain political and economic factors and at the same time as capable of altering them. "The spectator is given the chance to criticize human behavior from a social point of view, and the scene is played as a piece of history," he wrote. Epic drama calls attention to itself as theater, bringing the stage lights in front of the curtain and interrupting the linear flow of the action to help the audience analyze the action and characters onstage. (Also see **alienation effect.**)

Epilogue. A final speech added to the end of a play. An example is Puck's "If we shadows have offended..." speech that ends Shakespeare's *A Midsummer Night's Dream.*

Epitasis. Ancient term for the rising action of a plot. (See **plot.**)

Epode. The third of the three parts of the verse ode sung by the **chorus** in a Greek drama. The epode follows the **strophe** and **antistrophe.**

Existentialism. A post–World War II philosophy that insisted humans had to give their lives value and significance because nothing outside themselves could do so.

Exodos. The concluding scene of a Greek drama, which includes the exit of all characters and the **chorus.**

Exposition. See **plot.**

Expressionism. Early-twentieth-century literary movement in Germany that posited that art should represent powerful emotional states and moods. Expressionists abandon **realism** and **verisimilitude,** producing distorted, nightmarish images of the individual unconscious.

Falling action. See **plot.**

Farce. See **comedy.**

First Folio. The first collected edition of thirty-six of Shakespeare's plays, collected by two of his fellow actors and published posthumously in 1623.

Flies. Space over a stage used to store scenery, lights, curtains, and the like, so that they can be raised and lowered as necessary.

Foil. A character who, through difference or similarity, brings out a particular aspect of another character. Laertes, reacting to the death of his father, acts as a foil for Hamlet.

Foreshadowing. Ominous hints of events to come that help to create an air of suspense in a drama.

Frons scaena. The elaborately decorated facade of the *scaena,* or stage house, used in presenting Roman drama. Also called *scaena frons.*

Hamartia. An error or wrong act through which the fortunes of the **protagonist** are reversed in a tragedy.

High comedy. See **comedy.**

History play. A drama set in a time other than that in which it was written. The term usually refers to Elizabethan drama, such as Shakespeare's Henry plays, that draws its plots from English historical materials, such as Holinshed's *Chronicles.*

Hubris (or *hybris*). Excessive pride or ambition. In ancient Greek tragedy, hubris often causes the **protagonist's** fall.

Humor character. A stereotyped character in the comedy of humors (see **comedy**). Clever plots often play on the character's personality distortions (caused by an imbalance of humors), revealing his or her absurdity.

Iambic pentameter. A poetic meter that divides a line into five parts (or feet), each part containing an unaccented syllable followed by an accented syllable. The line "When I consider everything that grows" is an example of iambic pentameter verse.

Imitation. See *mimesis.*

Impressionism. A highly personal style of writing in which an author presents characters, scenes, or moods as they appear to him or her at a particular moment rather than striving for an objectively realistic description.

Interlude. A short play, usually either farcical or moralistic, performed between the courses of a feast or between the acts of a longer play. The interlude thrived during the late fifteenth and early sixteenth centuries in England.

Irony. The use of words to suggest a meaning that is the opposite of the literal meaning, as in "I can't wait to take the exam." Irony is present in a literary work that gives expression to contradictory attitudes or impulses to entertain ambiguity or to maintain detachment.

Cosmic irony. Irony present when destiny or the gods seem to be in favor of the **protagonist** but are actually engineering his or her downfall. Also known as *irony of fate.*

Dramatic irony. Irony present when the outcome of an event or situation is the opposite of what a character expects.

Tragic irony. Irony that exists when a character's lack of complete knowledge or understanding (which the audience possesses) results in his or her fall or has tragic consequences for loved ones. An example from *Oedipus Rex* is Oedipus's declaration that he will stop at nothing to banish King Laios's murderer, whom the audience knows to be Oedipus himself.

Jongleur. Early medieval French musical entertainer who recited lyrics, ballads, and stories. Forerunner of the minstrel.

Koryphaios (or *coryphaeus*). The leader of the **chorus** in Greek drama. Also called the *choragos.*

Kothornos. See **buskin.**

Lazzo (plural, *lazzi*). Comic routines or **stage business** associated with the stock situations and characters of the Italian **commedia dell'arte.** A scenario might, for example, call for the *lazzo* of fear.

Liturgical drama. Short dramatized sections of the medieval church service. Some scholars believe that these playlets evolved into the vernacular **mystery plays,** which were performed outside the church by lay people.

Low comedy. See **comedy.**

Mansion. Scenic structure used in medieval drama to indicate the locale or scene of the action. Mansions were elaborate structures built on pageant wagons to present **mystery plays** outside the church.

Mask. A covering used to disguise or ornament the face; used by actors in Greek drama and revived in the later **commedia dell'arte** and court **masque** to heighten dramatic effect.

Masque (also *mask*). A short but elaborately staged court drama, often mythological and allegorical, principally acted and danced by masked courtiers. (Professional actors often performed the major speaking and singing roles.) Popular in England during the late sixteenth and early seventeenth centuries, masques were often commissioned to honor a particular person or occasion. Ben Jonson was the most important masque writer; the genre's most elaborate sets and costumes were designed by Jonson's occasional partner Inigo Jones. (See **antimasque.**)

Mekane. See *deus ex machina.*

Melodrama. A suspenseful play filled with situations that appeal to the audience's emotions. Justice triumphs in a happy ending; the good characters (completely virtuous) are rewarded, and the bad characters (thoroughly villainous) are punished.

Method acting. A naturalistic technique of acting developed by the Russian director Constantin Stanislavski and adapted for American actors by Lee Strasberg, among others. The Method actor identifies with the character he or she portrays and experiences the emotions called for by the play in an effort to render the character with emotional **verisimilitude.**

Middle Comedy. See **comedy.**

Mimesis. The Greek word for "imitation." Aristotle used the term to define the role of art as an imitation of an action.

Miracle play. A type of medieval sacred drama that depicts the lives of saints, focusing especially on the miracles performed by saints.

Mise-en-scène. The stage setting of a play, including the use of scenery, props, and stage movement.

Moira. Greek word for "fate."

Morality play. Didactic late medieval drama (flourishing in England c. 1400–1550) that uses **allegory** to dramatize some aspects of the Christian moral life. Abstract qualities or entities such as Virtue, Vice, Good Deeds, Knowledge, and Death are cast as characters who discuss with the **protagonist** issues related to salvation and the afterlife. *Everyman* is an example.

Motivation. The reasons for a character's actions in a drama. For drama to be effective, the audience must believe that a character's actions are justified and plausible given what they know about him or her.

Mouth of hell. A stage prop in medieval drama suggesting the entrance to hell. Often in the shape of an open-mouthed monster's head, the mouth of hell was positioned over a pit in the stage that belched smoke and fire and appeared to swallow up sinners.

Mystery play. A sacred medieval play dramatizing biblical events such as the creation, the fall of Adam and Eve, and Christ's birth and resurrection. The genre probably evolved from **liturgical drama;** mystery plays were often incorporated into larger **cycles** of plays.

Naturalism. Literary philosophy popularized during the nineteenth century that casts art's role as the scientifically accurate reflection of a "slice of life." Naturalism is aligned with the belief that each person is a product of heredity and environment, driven by internal and external forces beyond his or her control. August Strindberg's *Miss Julie,* with its focus on reality's sordidness and humankind's powerlessness, draws on naturalism.

Neoclassicism. A movement in sixteenth-century Italy and seventeenth-century France to revive and emulate classical attitudes toward art based on principles of order, harmony, unity, restrained wit, and **decorum.** The neoclassical movement in France gave rise to a corresponding movement in England during the late seventeenth and eighteenth centuries.

New Comedy. See **comedy.**

Ode. A dignified three-part song sung by the **chorus** in Greek drama. The parts are the **strophe,** the **antistrophe,** and the **epode.**

Old Comedy. See **comedy.**

Orchestra. Literally, the "dancing place"; the circular stage where the Greek chorus performed.

Pageant cart. A movable stage or wagon (often called a *pageant wagon*) on which a set was built for the performance of medieval drama. The term *pageant* can also refer to the spectacle itself.

Pallium. Long white cloak or mantle worn by Greek actors or Romans in Greek-based plays.

Pantomime. Silent acting using facial expression, body movement, and gesture to convey the plot and the characters' feelings.

Parodos. The often stately entrance song of the **chorus** in Greek drama. The term also refers to the aisles (plural, *paradoi*) on either side of the orchestra by which the chorus entered the Greek theater.

Pastoral drama. A dramatic form glorifying shepherds and rural life in an idealized natural setting, usually implying a more negative view of urban life.

Pathos. The quality of a drama that evokes pity.

Performance art. An art form that arose in the mid-twentieth century and often mixes media: music, video, film, opera, dance, and spoken text. It was originally defined in terms of artists using a live production for dramatic effect; Anna Deavere Smith's work is a good example. However, the definition has widened to include performances that cross dramatic "boundaries." Dancers Martha Clarke and Pina Bausch, musicians such as Laurie Anderson, and experimental directors such as Richard Foreman have been identified as performance artists.

Peripeteia. A reversal of fortune, for better or worse, for the **protagonist.** Used especially to describe the main character's fall in Greek tragedy.

Phallus. An appendage meant to suggest the penis, added to the front of blatantly comic male characters' costumes in some Greek comedy. Associated chiefly with the Greek **satyr play.**

Play. A literary genre whose plot is usually presented dramatically by actors portraying characters before an audience.

Play-within-the-play. A brief secondary drama presented to or by the characters of a play that reflects or comments on the larger work. An example is the Pyramus and Thisbe episode in Shakespeare's *A Midsummer Night's Dream.*

Plot. The events of a play or narrative; the sequence and relative importance a **dramatist** assigns to these events.

Anticlimax. An unexpectedly trivial or insignificant conclusion to a series of significant events; an unsatisfying resolution that often occurs in place of a conventional climax.

Catastrophe. The outcome or conclusion of a play, usually applied specifically to tragedy. (*Denouement* is a parallel term applied to both comedy and tragedy.)

Climax. The turning point in a drama's action, preceded by the rising action and followed by the falling action. Also known as *crisis.*

Complication. The part of the plot preceding the climax that establishes the entanglements to be untangled in the denouement; part of the rising action.

Conflict. The struggle between the **protagonist** and the **antagonist** that propels the rising action of the plot and is resolved in the denouement.

Denouement. The "unknotting" of the plot's complication; the resolution of a drama's action.

Double plot. A dramatic structure in which two related plots function simultaneously.

Exposition. The presentation of essential information, especially about events that have occurred prior to the first scene of a play. The exposition appears early in the play and initiates the rising action.

Falling action. The events of the plot following the climax and ending in the catastrophe or resolution.

Rising action. The events of the plot leading up to the climax.

Subplot. A secondary plot intertwined with the main plot, often reflecting or commenting on the main plot.

Underplot. Same as *subplot.*

Problem play. A drama that argues a point or presents a problem (usually a social problem). Ibsen was a notable writer of problem plays.

Prologos. In Greek drama, an introductory scene for actor or actors that precedes the entrance of the **chorus.** This **convention** has evolved into the modern dramatic introductory monologue or **prologue.**

Prologue. A preface or introduction preceding the play proper.

Proscaena. The space in front of the *scaena* in a Roman theater.

Proscenium arch. An arched structure over the front of the stage from which a curtain often hangs. The arch frames the action onstage and separates the audience from the action.

Proskenion. The playing space in front of the *skene,* or scene house, in Greek drama.

Protagonist. The main character in a drama. This character is usually the most interesting and sympathetic and is the person involved in the conflict driving the plot.

Protasis. Classical term for the introductory act or exposition of a drama.

Psychomachia. Psychological struggle; a war of souls.

Quem Quaeritis trope. A brief dramatized section of the medieval church's Easter liturgy. The oldest extant **trope** and the probable origin of **liturgical drama,** it enacts the visit of the three Marys to Christ's empty tomb (*quem quaeritis* means "Whom do you seek?" in Latin).

Realism. The literary philosophy holding that art should accurately reproduce an image of life. Avoiding the use of dramatic **conventions** such as **asides** and **soliloquies,** realism depicts ordinary people in ordinary situations. Ibsen's *A Doll House* is an example of realism in drama.

Recognition. See *anagnorisis.*

Repartee. Witty and pointed verbal exchanges usually found in the comedy of manners.

Repertory. A theater company or group of actors that presents a set of plays throughout a season. The term also refers to the set of plays itself.

Restoration comedy. A type of comedy of manners that developed in England in the late seventeenth century, often featuring **repartee** in the service of complex romantic plots. Oliver Goldsmith's *She Stoops to Conquer* is an example.

Revenge tragedy. Sensational tragedy popularized during the Elizabethan age that is notable for bloody plots involving such elements as murder, ghosts, insanity, and crimes of lust.

Reversal. See *peripeteia.*

Riposte. A quick or sharp reply, similar to **repartee.**

Rising action. See **plot.**

Ritual. Repeated formalized or ceremonial practices, many of which have their roots in primitive cultures. Certain theorists hold that primitive ritual evolved into drama.

Satire. A work that makes fun of a social institution or human foible, often in an intellectually sophisticated way, to persuade the audience to share the author's views. Molière's *Tartuffe* contains social satire.

Satyr play. A comic play performed after the tragic trilogy in Greek tragedy competitions. The satyr play provided **comic relief** and was usually a farcical, boisterous treatment of mythological material.

Scaena. The stage house in Roman drama; the facade of the *scaena* (called the *frons scaena*) was often elaborately ornamented.

Scenario. The plot outline around which professional actors of the **commedia dell'arte** improvised their plays. Most scenarios specified the action's sequence and the entrances of the main characters.

Scene. Division of an **act** in a drama. By traditional definition, a scene has no major shift in place or time frame, and it is performed by a fixed group of actors onstage (in French drama, if an actor enters or exits, the group is altered, and the scene, technically, should change). The term also refers to the physical surroundings or locale in which a play's **action** is set.

Scenery. The backdrop and set (furniture and so on) onstage that suggest to the audience the surroundings in which a play's **action** takes place.

Scenography. Painting of backdrops and hangings.

Senecan tragedy. Tragic drama modeled on plays written by Seneca. The genre usually has five acts and features a **chorus**; it is notable for its thematic concern with bloodshed, revenge, and unnatural crimes. (See **revenge tragedy**.)

Sentimental. Arousing tender emotions in excess of what the situation calls for.

Sentimental comedy. See **comedy**.

Setting. All details of time, location, and environment relating to a play.

Skene. The building or scene house in the Greek theater that probably began as a dressing room and eventually was incorporated into the action as part of the scenery.

Slapstick. See **comedy**.

Slice of life. See **naturalism**.

Social problem play. Another term for **problem play**.

Social realism. Drama that reflects the difficulties of modern life; drama with political content and aimed at reforming society.

Sock. A term derived from the Latin *soccus*, referring to a light slipper or sock worn by Roman comic actors.

Soliloquy. A speech in which an actor, usually alone onstage, utters his or her thoughts aloud, revealing personal feelings. Hamlet's "To be, or not to be" speech is an example.

Spectacle. In Aristotle's terms, the costumes and scenery in a drama—the elements that appeal to the eye.

Stage business. Minor physical action, including an actor's posture and facial expression, and the use of props,

all of which make up a particular interpretation of a character.

Stasimon (plural, *stasima*). In a Greek tragedy, a song sung by the **chorus** after it has taken its position. The chorus stands still and is not interrupted by dialogue during the stasimon.

Stichomythia. Dialogue in which two speakers engage in a verbal duel in alternating lines.

Stock character. A stereotypical character type whose behavior, qualities, or beliefs conform to familiar dramatic conventions, such as the clever servant or the **braggart soldier**. Also called *type character*.

Strophe. The first of the three parts of the verse **ode** sung by a Greek **chorus**. While singing the **strophe**, the chorus moves in a dancelike pattern from right to left. See also **antistrophe** and **epode**.

Subplot. See **plot**.

Subtext. A level of meaning implicit in or underlying the surface meaning of a text.

Surrealism. A literary movement flourishing in France during the early twentieth century that valued the unwilled expression of the unconscious (usually as revealed in dreams) over a rendering of "reality" structured by the conscious mind.

Suspense. The sense of tension aroused by an audience's uncertainty about the resolution of dramatic conflicts.

Suspension of disbelief. An audience's willingness to accept the world of the drama as reality during the course of a play.

Symbolism. A literary device in which an object, event, or action is used to suggest a meaning beyond its literal meaning. The lantern in *The Rising of the Moon* has a symbolic function.

Theater. The building in which a play is performed. Also used to refer to drama as an art form.

Theater in the round. The presentation of a play in an **arena theater**, where the stage is surrounded by the audience.

Theater of the absurd. A type of twentieth-century drama presenting the human condition as meaningless, absurd, and illogical. An example of the genre is Samuel Beckett's *Endgame*.

Theater of cruelty. A type of drama created by Antonin Artaud in the 1930s that uses shock techniques to expose the audience's primitive obsessions with cruelty and sexuality. The purpose was to overwhelm spectators' rational minds, leading them to understand and even participate in the cycle of cruelty and ritual purgation dramatized in the performance.

Theme. Main idea or general topic of a play, which is not always easy to determine. Some plays have several topics that develop simultaneously.

Three unities. Unity of time, action, and locale. Aristotle noted that a play's action usually occurs in one day or a little more and that the plot should reveal clearly ordered actions and incidents moving toward the plot's resolution. Later scholars and critics, especially those in the neoclassical tradition, interpreted Aristotle's ideas as rules and added a third: a play's action should occur in a single locale.

Thrust stage. A stage extending beyond the **proscenium arch,** usually surrounded on three sides by the audience.

Tiring house. From "attiring house," the backstage space in Elizabethan public theaters used for storage and as a dressing room. The term also refers to the changing space beneath the medieval pageant wagon.

Total theater. A concept of the theater as an experience synthesizing all the expressive arts, including music, dance, and lighting.

Tragedy. Serious drama in which a **protagonist,** traditionally of noble position, suffers a series of unhappy events culminating in a catastrophe such as death or spiritual breakdown. Shakespeare's *Hamlet,* which ends with the prince's death, is an example of Elizabethan tragedy.

Tragicomedy. A play that combines elements of tragedy and comedy. Chekhov's *The Cherry Orchard* is an example. Tragicomedies often include a serious plot in which the expected tragic catastrophe is replaced by a happy ending.

Trope. Interpolation into or expansion of an existing medieval liturgical text. These expansions, such as the *Quem Quaeritis* trope, gave rise to **liturgical drama.**

Type character. See **stock character.**

Underplot. See **plot.**

Unity. The sense that the events of a play and the actions of the characters follow one another naturally to form one complete action. Unity is present when characters' behavior seems **motivated** and the work is perceived to be a connected artistic whole. See also **three unities.**

Verfremdungseffekt. German term coined by Bertolt Brecht to mean "alienation." See **alienation effect.**

Verisimilitude. The degree to which a dramatic representation approximates an appearance of reality.

Well-made play. Drama that relies for effect on the suspense generated by its logical, cleverly constructed plot rather than on characterization. Plots often involve a withheld secret, a battle of wits between hero and villain, and a resolution in which the secret is revealed and the **protagonist** saved. The plays of Eugène Scribe (1791–1861) have defined the type.

Acknowledgments

(continued from p. iv)

TEXT CREDITS

Greek Drama

The Oedipus Rex of Sophocles: An English Version by Dudley Fitts and Robert Fitzgerald, copyright 1949 by Houghton Mifflin Harcourt Publishing Company, and renewed 1977 by Cornelia Fitts and Robert Fitzgerald. Reprinted by permission of Houghton Mifflin Harcourt Publishing Company. CAUTION: All rights, including professional, amateur, motion picture, recitation, lecturing, public reading, radio broadcasting, television and the rights of translation into foreign languages are strictly reserved. Inquiries on all rights should be addressed to Houghton Mifflin Harcourt Publishing Company, Royalties, Copyrights & Permissions, Orlando, 9400 South Park Center Loop, Orlando, FL 32819–8605.

"Poetics: Comedy and Epic and Tragedy" by Aristotle, from *Poetics*, translated by Gerald F. Else. Copyright © 1967. Reprinted by permission of The University of Michigan Press.

Excerpt (pages 432–435) from "The Structural Study of Myth" by Claude Lévi-Strauss in *Myth: A Symposium* in *The Journal of American Folklore*, Volume 68, No. 270, October-December 1955. Reprinted by permission of the American Folklore Society.

Lysistrata: An English Version from *Aristophanes: Four Comedies* by Dudley Fitts, copyright 1954 by Houghton Mifflin Harcourt Publishing Company and renewed 1982 by Cornelia Fitts, Daniel H. Fitts and Deborah W. Fitts. Reprinted by permission of Houghton Mifflin Harcourt Publishing Company. CAUTION: Professionals and amateurs are hereby warned that all titles included in this volume, being fully protected under the copyright laws of the United States of America, Canada, the British Empire and all other countries which are signatories to the Universal Copyright Convention and the International Copyright Union, are subject to royalty. All rights, including professional, amateur, motion picture, recitation, lecturing, public reading, radio broadcasting, television and the rights of translation into foreign languages are strictly reserved. Inquiries on professional rights should be addressed to Lucy Kroll Agency, 390 West End Avenue, New York, NY 10024. Inquiries on all other rights should be addressed to Houghton Mifflin Harcourt Publishing Company, Royalties, Copyrights & Permissions, Orlando, 9400 South Park Center Loop, Orlando, FL 32819-8605.

Roman Drama

Excerpt from *The Twin Menaechmi* (Act III) from *Six Plays of Plautus* by Plautus, translated by Lionel Casson. Translation copyright © 1963 by Lionel Casson. Reprinted by permission of Doubleday, a division of Random House, Inc.

Excerpt from *The Brothers* from *The Mother-In-Law* by Terence from *Comedies of Terence*, translated by Robert Graves. Reprinted by permission of Carcanet Press Limited on behalf of The Trustees of the Robert Graves Copyright Trust.

Excerpt from *Thyestes* by Seneca from *The Complete Roman Drama* by George E. Duckworth. Translated by Ella Isabel Harris. Copyright 1942 and renewed 1970 by Random House, Inc. Reprinted by permission of Random House, Inc.

Medieval Drama

Everyman from *Everyman and Medieval Miracle Plays* edited by A. C. Cawley (J. M. Dent, 1956) is reprinted by permission of Everyman's Library, an imprint of Alfred A. Knopf.

Renaissance Drama

Notes for *Hamlet* and *The Tempest* from *The Complete Works of Shakespeare*, 4th edition, edited by David Bevington, pp. 1060–1065 and 1526–1529. Copyright © 1992. Reprinted by permission of Pearson Education, Inc., Upper Saddle River, NJ.

"Hamlet and His Problems" from "Hamlet" in *Selected Essays* by T.S. Eliot, copyright 1950 by Houghton Mifflin Harcourt Publishing Company, renewed © 1978 by Esme Valerie Eliot. Reprinted by permission of Houghton Mifflin Harcourt Publishing Company and Faber and Faber Ltd.

"The Tempest." Excerpt from *Shakespeare: A Survey* by E. K. Chambers. Copyright © 1926. Reprinted by permission of Oxford University Press.

From *A Tempest* by Aimé Césaire, translated by Richard Miller. Copyright © 1969 by Aimé Césaire. Copyright English translation © 1985, 1992. Published by Theatre Communications Group. Used by permission of Theatre Communications Group.

Excerpt from *Gender, Race, Renaissance Drama* by Ania Loomba reprinted by permission of the author.

Excerpt from *Shakespeare After All* by Marjorie Garber, copyright © 2004 by Marjorie Garber. Used by permission of Pantheon Books, a division of Random House, Inc.

Late-Seventeenth- and Eighteenth-Century Drama

Tartuffe by Moliere, English translation copyright © 1963, 1962, 1961 and renewed 1991, 1990 and 1989 by Richard Wilbur, is reprinted by permission of Houghton Mifflin Harcourt Publishing Company. CAUTION: Professionals and amateurs are hereby warned that this translation, being fully protected under the copyright laws of the United States of America, the British Empire, including the Dominion of Canada, and all other countries which are signatories to the Universal Copyright Convention and the International Copyright Union, is subject to royalty. All rights, including professional, amateur, motion picture, recitation, lecturing, public reading, radio broadcasting, and television, are strictly reserved. Particular emphasis is laid on the question of readings, permission for which must be secured from the author's agent in writing. Inquiries on professional rights (except for amateur rights) should be addressed to Mr. Gilbert Parker, William Morris Agency, 1325 Avenue of the Americas, New York, NY 10019; inquiries on translation rights should be addressed to Houghton Mifflin Harcourt Publishing Company, Royalties, Copyrights & Permissions, Orlando, 9400 South Park Center Loop, Orlando, FL 32819-8605. The stock and amateur acting rights of *Tartuffe* are controlled exclusively by the Dramatists Play Service, Inc., 440 Park Avenue South, New York, NY. No amateur performance of the play may be given without obtaining in advance the written permission of the Dramatists Play Service, Inc., and paying the requisite fee.

Review of *Tartuffe* by Mel Gussow from *The New York Times*, September 9, 1991. Copyright © 1991 by The New York Times Company. Reprinted by permission.

The Love Suicides at Sonezaki by Chikamatsu Monzaemon. From *Major Plays of Chikamatsu*, translated by Donald Keene. Copyright © 1961, 1990 by Donald Keene. Reprinted by permission of Columbia University Press.

"The Development of Theater Buildings," excerpt from "The Social Environment of Tokugawa Kabuki" in *Studies in Kabuki: Its Acting, Music and Historical Context* by James R. Berandon, William P. Malm and Donald H. Shively. Copyright © 1978. Reprinted with the permission of the University of Hawaii Press.

Nineteenth-Century Drama to the Turn of the Century

A Doll House from *The Complete Major Prose Plays of Henrik Ibsen* by Henrik Ibsen, translated by Rolf Fjelde. Translation copyright © 1965, 1970, 1978, by Rolf Fjelde. Used by permission of Dutton Signet, a division of Penguin Group (USA) Inc.

"*A Doll's House*: Ibsen the Moralist" by Muriel C. Bradbrook from *Ibsen the Norwegian* by Muriel C. Bradbrook. Reprinted by permission of the author.

Miss Julie by August Strindberg, and excerpt from the Preface to *Miss Julie* from *Strindberg: Five Plays*, edited and translated by Harry G. Carlson.

Drama in the Early and Mid-Twentieth Century

Contemporary Drama

IMAGE CREDITS

Greek Drama

Roman Drama

Medieval Drama

Renaissance Drama

Late-Seventeenth- and Eighteenth-Century Drama

Nineteenth-Century Drama through the Turn of the Twentieth Century

Drama in the Early and Mid-Twentieth Century

Contemporary Drama